1980

TIME-SAVER
STANDARDS

A Handbook of Architectural Design

JOHN HANCOCK CALLENDER
Editor-in-Chief
Professor of Architecture, Pratt Institute

Fourth Edition

McGRAW-HILL·BOOK COMPANY

New York
San Francisco
Toronto
London
Sydney

TIME-SAVER STANDARDS

PREFACE TO THE FOURTH EDITION

Time-Saver Standards began in the pages of the *American Architect* in the middle 1930s. When that magazine was later merged with the *Architectural Record,* "Time-Saver Standards" was continued and soon became one of the most useful and popular features of the *Record.* In 1946 the TSS sheets which had been published up to that time were first issued in book form. In 1950 and again in 1954 the book was reissued with the addition of the pages which had been published in the *Record* since the previous edition.

This fourth edition of *Time-Saver Standards* has been completely revised and greatly expanded. Not only have the TSS sheets published in the *Architectural Record* since 1954 been included but also a great deal of material never previously published. Many obsolete pages from the earlier editions have been eliminated and most of the other pages have been revised and updated.

Time-Saver Standards is intended primarily to meet the needs of those who design buildings. It will also be found to be almost equally useful to draftsmen, contractors, superintendents, maintenance engineers, and students—to all, in fact, who design, construct, or maintain buildings.

The editor takes this opportunity to thank the scores of specialists, many of them recognized authorities in their fields, who have contributed their expertise to this edition of *Time-Saver Standards.*

John Hancock Callender

LIST OF CONTRIBUTORS

RONALD ALLWORK, AIA, Architect

JAMES ARKIN, AIA, Consultant, Architectural Woodwork Institute

LOUIS A. BELLO, Syska & Hennessy, Inc., Consulting Engineers

GLEN H. BEYER, Housing Research Center, Cornell University

WILLIAM BLACKWELL, Architectural Consultant

BYRON C. BLOOMFIELD, AIA, Executive Director, Modular Building Standards Association

E. J. BROWN, Research Associate in Mechanical Engineering, University of Illinois

JOHN HANCOCK CALLENDER, Professor of Architecture, Pratt Institute

WALTER E. CAMPBELL, FAIA, Campbell and Aldrich, Architects

WILLIAM J. CAVANAUGH, Bolt Beranek and Newman Inc., Consultants in Acoustics

L. T. CHANDLER, Architect, Edwards Company

ALONZO W. CLARK, AIA, Smith, Smith, Haines, Lundberg, and Waehler, Architects

RAY E. CUMRINE, AIA, Ketchum and Sharp, Architects

WILLIAM DEMAREST, Director, Plastics in Building, Manufacturing Chemists' Association, Inc.

ALBERT G. H. DIETZ, Professor, Department of Civil and Sanitary Engineering,
   Massachusetts Institute of Technology

HAROLD EDELMAN, AIA, Architect

DR. N. L. ENGELHARDT, JR., Engelhardt, Engelhardt and Leggett, Educational Consultants

ROBERT E. FAUCETT, Outdoor Lighting Department, General Electric Company

N. C. FERGUSON, Eastman Kodak Company

THOMAS P. GALBRAITH, Architect, Architectural and Engineering Branch, Division of Hospital and Medical
   Facilities, Public Health Service, U.S. Department of Health, Education and Welfare

BURDETT GREEN, Executive Vice President, Fine Hardwoods Association

ALFRED GREENBERG, P.E., Environmental Consultant

BERNARD F. GREENE, Lighting Consultant

NOYCE L. GRIFFIN, Electrical Engineer, Architectural and Engineering Branch, Division of Hospital and
   Medical Facilities, Public Health Service, U.S. Department of Health, Education and Welfare

VICTOR GRUEN, AIA, Architect

G. B. GUSRAE, P.E., Consulting Engineer

ARTHUR HOCKMAN, National Bureau of Standards, U.S. Department of Commerce

AUGUST HOENACK, Chief, Architectural and Engineering Branch, Division of Hospital and Medical Facilities,
   Public Health Service, U.S. Department of Health, Education and Welfare

SEYMOUR HOWARD, Professor of Architecture, Pratt Institute

O. B. IVES, Architect, Architectural and Engineering Branch, Division of Hospital and Medical Facilities,
   Public Health Service, U.S. Department of Health, Education and Welfare

PETER N. JENSEN, Architect, Architectural and Engineering Branch, Division of Hospital and Medical Facilities,
   Public Health Service, U.S. Department of Health, Education and Welfare

GEORGE R. JERUS, P.E., Meyer, Strong and Jones, Mechanical and Electrical Engineers

RUDARD A. JONES, AIA, Small Homes Council, University of Illinois

W. H. KAPPLE, AIA, Architectural Consultant

AARON N. KIFF, AIA, Kiff, Voss, and Franklin, Architects

ALEXANDER KIRA, Housing Research Center, Cornell University

S. KONZO, Professor of Mechanical Engineering, University of Illinois

WAYNE F. KOPPES, AIA, Architectural Consultant

WILLIAM J. LeMESSURIER, Professor, Department of Civil and Sanitary Engineering, Massachusetts Institute
   of Technology

F. M. LESCHER, AIA, Architectural Consultant

HENRY L. LOGAN, Vice President in charge of Research, Holophane Company, Inc.

HENDRIK P. MAAS, AIA, Architect

STANLEY McCANDLESS, Professor of Lighting, Yale University; Research and Development,
   Century Lighting, Inc.

CONTENTS

Preface to the Fourth Edition III
List of Contributors V

SECTION I: BASIC DATA

Graphic Symbols:
Materials 3
Piping 5
Heating, ventilating, and air conditioning 6
Plumbing 8
Electrical 10
Abbreviations:
For use on drawings 11
Dimensions of the Human Figure 14
Mathematics:
Properties of the circle 16
Circular sections 18
Areas 20
Surfaces and volumes 21
Trigonometric functions 22
Units of measurement 24
Useful Curves and Curved Surfaces:
Introduction 26
Parabola 27
Ellipse 29
Hyperbola 31
Catenary 32
Cycloid 35
Trochoid 36
Sine curve 37
Geometrical mean 37
Spirals 38
Surfaces and skew curves 39
Cylinders and prisms 42
Polygon patterns 43
Cones 44
Spheres 47
Polyhedra 51
Geodesic domes 53
Hyperbolic paraboloid 56
Ellipsoid 59
Elliptic paraboloid 60
Hyperboloids 61
Spherical trigonometry 64
Drawing Accurate Curves 65
Area-Perimeter Ratios 69
Modular Coordination 72
Solar Angles:
Calculations 79
Azimuth and altitude 82

SECTION II: STRUCTURAL DESIGN

Structural Forms—Wood:
Long span construction 87
Laminated wood 88
Lamella construction 94
Plywood beams 95

Structural Forms—Steel:
Rigid frames 96
Space structures 100
Space frames 101
Domes 103
Suspension structures 107
Structural Forms—Concrete, Thin Shell:
Curved in one direction 111
Curved in two directions 118
Folded plate 126
Design Loads:
Dead loads 127
Live loads 129
Structural Design:
Beam formulae 134
Structural Design—Wood:
Allowable stresses 136
Properties of sections 138
Decking 140
Ceiling joists 140
Floor joists 141
Rafters and roof joists 142
Beams 144
Columns 146
Trusses 147
Bolted connections 148
Plywood box beams 148
Stressed-skin panels 151
Wood Construction:
Light wood framing 154
Nailing 158
Threaded nails 160
Trussed rafters 164
Heavy timber 166
Structural Design—Steel:
Type of steel 168
Beams 168
Joists 172
Columns 177
Connection details 179
Lally columns 180
Plastic design 182
Welding 184
Structural Design—Concrete:
Materials 185
Design criteria 186
Beams 187
Columns 189
Details 190
Slabs 191
Joists—one way 191
Joists—two way 192
Lift slabs 194
Tilt-up 197
Prestressed 200
Floor Framing Systems 209
Structural Design—Masonry:
Materials and mortar mixes 214
Allowable stresses 215

Bond	216	Wood	324
Workmanship	217	Steel	336
Arches	217	Aluminum	346
Reinforced masonry	219	Sliding Glass Doors	354
Lintels, steel	223	Skylights:	
Lintels, reinforced masonry	224	Plastic	358
Lintels, reinforced brick	224	Metal frame	360
Lintels, reinforced tile	226	Glass block	363
Lintels, reinforced concrete	227	Curtain Walls:	

Masonry—Brick and Tile:
Modular sizes 228
Modular details 228
Modular estimating tables 230
Nonmodular quantities and courses 232
Pattern bonds 234
Cavity walls 235
Solid metal-tied walls 238
SCR brick 239
Surface treatments 242
Terra cotta 243
Ceramic veneer 243
Structural clay tile partitions 244
Structural clay facing tile partitions ... 246
Chemical-resistant tile and brick 249
Solar screens 251

Masonry—Concrete:
Types and sizes 253
Properties 254
Courses and quantities 256
Wall construction 258

Masonry Construction:
Thermal expansion 266
Flexible anchorage 269
Parapet walls 271
Cracking of masonry walls 273
Anchoring to masonry walls 276

SECTION III: BUILDING MATERIALS,
COMPONENTS, AND TECHNIQUES

Waterproofing:
Foundation drains 281
Permeability of concrete 285
Integral and membrane 286
Plastic and iron coatings 287
Vapor seals 288
Paved roofs 289
Walls and parapets 290
Termite Shields 291

Flashing:
Multistory masonry walls 295
Walls and parapets 297
Copings: drips and edge strips 298
Roof at walls 299
Spandrels and windows 300
Openings in frame walls 301
Gravel stops; door heads 302
Valleys 303
Vents 304
Chimneys 304
Aluminum gravel stops 306

Roofing:
Asphalt strip shingles 307
Copper 310

Roof Drainage:
Leader design 314
Gutters 315
Stock items 319

Windows:
General 320
Types and uses 321

Curtain Walls:
General 365
Structural design 366
Movement 367
Infiltration 370
Insulation 371
Condensation 374
Joints 376
Sealants 378
Panels 382
Specifications 384
Precast concrete 385

Architectural Metals:
Gages, coefficients, stresses 388
Finishes 390
Aluminum 391
Stainless steel 394
Copper, brass, and bronze 402
Porcelain enamel 403

Glass:
Types 409
Sizes 411
FHA requirements 412
Glazing 413
Structural glass veneer 416

Plastics:
Characteristics 418
Terminology 418
Applications 421
Design recommendations 423
Fire resistance requirements 424

Stone:
Characteristics 426
Classifications 427
Finishes 428
Checklist 429
Marble 432
Veneer 435
Interior 441

Fireproofing:
Materials and methods 444
Columns 446
Beams and girders 448
Floor and roof systems 451
Notes to table 459
Acoustical ceilings 461
Reinforced concrete 462
Partitions 464

Plaster:
Materials 465
Bases 466
Mixes and coats 467
Walls and partitions 470
Ceilings 471

Wallboards:
Gypsum board 476
Insulation board 483
Hardboard 488
Particle board 491
Plastic laminates 492
Plywood 493

Wood:
Grades and dimensions 502
Softwoods 504

Hardwoods 505
Cabinet work 520
Tile:
  Ceramic 529
  Metal and plastic 536
Flooring:
  Terrazzo 538
  Epoxy 542
  Wood 543
  Resilient 548
Finishes:
  Wall coverings 552
  Wall coatings 553
  Paints 554
  Cabinet work 558
Stairs:
  Tread and riser data 562
  Critical dimensions and clearances 564
  Unit planning data 566
  Steel 568
  Concrete 569
  Ramps and ladders 570
Fireplaces 572
Steel Doors and Frames 574
Hardware:
  Hand of doors 579
  Types of locks and latches 580
  Types of finishes 582
  Hinges 584
  Door closing devices 587
  Door holders and stops 590
  Door pulls, push plates, and kick plates 592
  Panic exit devices 593
  Door bolts 595
  Lock functions 596
  Lock dimensions 600
  Sliding doors 601
  Screen and storm doors 605

SECTION IV: ENVIRONMENTAL CONTROL

Acoustics:
  Introduction 609
  Definitions 610
  Criteria 614
  Sound absorption 616
  Sound isolation 625
  Auditoriums 636
  Sound reinforcing systems 641
  FHA requirements 644
Insulation:
  Introduction 649
  Definitions 649
  Theory 649
  Estimation of economies 650
  U factors for frame walls 653
  U factors for masonry walls 656
  U factors for frame ceilings 658
  U factors for flat roofs 658
  U factors for pitched roofs 661
  U factors for floors 662
  FHA requirements 662
  Concrete floor slabs 663
Floor slabs 665
Crawl Spaces 668
Condensation Control:
  Causes 671
  Design 671
  Details 675
  Vapor barriers—ceilings 677
  Vapor barriers—attics 678

Vapor barriers—roof ventilation 679
FHA requirements 680
Residential Heating and Air Conditioning:
  Furnaces 682
  Outlets 683
  Distribution systems 683
  Duct systems 685
  Summer air conditioning 688
Heating Systems for Houses:
  One-pipe steam systems 691
  One-pipe forced hot water systems 694
  Forced hot water systems 698
  Two-pipe forced hot water systems 700
  Hot water baseboard systems 703
  Hot water radiant systems 709
  Controls for hot water radiant systems 721
  Electric radiant systems 725
  Use of gypsum plaster with radiant heating .. 729
Gas Appliances 732
Heating, Ventilating, and Air Conditioning:
  Heating loads 739
  Cooling loads 743
  Solar loads 749
  Air distribution 756
  Refrigerating plant 767
  Heating plant 771
  Piping 776
  Controls 779
  Apartments 781
  Hotels and motels 782
  Office buildings 782
  Stores 783
  Eating places 785
  Places of assembly 786
  Schools 787
  Libraries and museums 788
  Hospitals 789
  Industrial buildings 791
  Laboratories 796
  Garages 799
Unit Heaters:
  Types 801
  Heat sources 801
  Boiler capacities 801
  Characteristics 802
  Locations 802
  Selection data 802
  Capacities 803
  Controls 804
  Fresh air connections 804
  Piping connections 804
  Louvers, grilles, and deflectors 806
Incinerators:
  Apartment buildings 807
  Municipal and industrial 809
Plumbing:
  Supply and distribution:
    Piping systems 812
    House tanks 814
    Multistory zoning 815
    Domestic hot water 818
    Special distribution systems 821
  Drainage systems:
    Sizing and ratings 825
    Cast-iron fittings 831
  Fixtures:
    Public facilities 840
    Industrial facilities 844
  Sewage disposal:
    Design 846
    Septic and siphon tanks 848
    Grease traps 849

Sludge pits 851
Distribution boxes 851
Leaching cesspools 851
Subsoil disposal beds 853
Sand filters 854
Daylighting 856
Lighting:
General 868
Glossary 873
Offices 875
Industrial 885
Schools 886
Hospitals 893
Churches and synagogues 894
Stores 897
Cinemas 904
Hotels 906
Residential 907
Other building types 912
Sports 912
Parking areas 914
Wiring:
Loads 915
Hospitals 919
Residential 923
Telephones:
Equipment 929
Sound Systems:
Sample specifications and definitions 930
Design considerations 931
Wiring symbols 932
Churches 933
Pipe Organs:
Churches 934
Fire Protection:
Fire alarm systems 937
Sprinkler systems 939
Elevators:
Passenger 941
Hospital 943
Freight 944
Hydraulic 946
Escalators 947

SECTION V: DESIGN ELEMENTS—RESIDENTIAL

Furniture:
General 951
Living room 951
Dining room 960
Bedroom 963
Kitchens:
Planning considerations 967
Critical dimensions 968
Storage 970
Plan types 973
Appliances 976
Cabinets 984
Laundries:
Planning considerations 988
Space requirements 988
Kitchen-laundry plans 991
Separate laundry room plans 992
Multi-use laundry rooms 994
Bathrooms:
Planning considerations 995
Dimensions at lavatory 998
Dimensions at bathtub and shower ... 999
Two-fixture plans 1000
Three-fixture plans 1001

Compartmented plans 1002
Fixtures 1003
Storage:
Planning considerations 1007
Bedroom closets for men 1009
Bedroom closets for women 1011
Bedroom closets for children 1013
Coat closets 1014
Miscellaneous closets 1015
Closet fixtures 1019
Home Workshops 1021
Darkrooms:
Design 1024
Small 1025
Advanced 1026
Community 1027
Housing for the Aged 1028
Apartments:
Building types 1032
Plan types 1033
FHA and PHA requirements—sites 1034
FHA and PHA requirements—exits 1037
Planning considerations 1038
Room count and minimum room sizes .. 1040
Minimum storage space 1041
Dormitories 1042
Hotels:
Planning considerations 1045
Types of guest rooms 1046
Bathrooms 1048
Plans 1049
Space allotments—general 1054
Space allotments—public areas 1056
Space allotments—concession and rental areas ... 1056
Space allotments—food and beverage services . 1058
Space allotments—general service areas 1060
Schedule of space allotments 1062
Motels:
General 1064
Site location 1064
Site plan 1068
Room groups and parking 1068
Space allotments 1071
Hotel Laundries:
Advantages and disadvantages 1075
Utility requirements 1076
Equipment requirements 1077

SECTION VI: DESIGN ELEMENTS—NON RESIDENTIAL

Shopping Centers 1081
Retail Stores:
Merchandise list 1090
Fixtures 1091
Store fronts 1095
Restaurants and Bars 1096
Motion Picture Theaters:
General requirements 1101
Projection booths 1104
Auditoriums:
Basic seating data 1107
Seating dimensions 1109
Offices:
Furniture 1111
Clearances 1113
Layout 1115
Schools:
Site planning 1116

Site selection 1117
Playgrounds 1117
Circulation 1121
Working heights 1123
Pupil capacity 1124
Lockers 1125
Classrooms 1128
Classroom facilities 1130
Multipurpose rooms 1132
Gymnasiums 1133
Auditoriums 1137
Libraries 1138
Cafeterias 1140
Science 1144
Fine arts 1146
Music 1147
Homemaking 1148
Shops 1149
Language laboratory 1150
Ventilation 1151
Libraries:
    School libraries 1152
    Bookstack data 1153
    Carrels 1155
Hospitals:
    Introduction and flow charts 1157
    Bedrooms 1158
    Nursing units 1161
    Surgical suite 1162
    Nursery 1166
    Pediatric department 1170
    Diagnostic x-ray suite 1173
    Teletherapy unit 1180
    Cobalt-60 1182
    Electroencephalographic suite 1185
    Laboratory 1187
    Physical therapy department 1188
    Occupational therapy department 1193
    Checklist for mental health center 1197
Design for the Handicapped 1198
Service Stations 1202
Truck Terminals:
    Docking facilities 1203
    Terminal plan 1205
Bus Terminals:
    General requirements 1207
    Loading docks and concourse 1209
Railroad Terminals:
    Details 1211
Hangar Doors:
    Balanced canopy doors 1213

Accordion and canopy doors 1214
    Sliding doors 1215
Firehouses:
    Design 1216
    Construction details 1217
Jails:
    Cell design 1218
    Cell construction 1219

SECTION VII: SITE PLANNING AND RECREATION

Site Planning 1223
Automobiles:
    Dimensions 1238
    Garages, residential 1239
    Garages, parking 1240
    Parking lots 1243
    Driveways 1245
Landscaping:
    Driveways 1248
    Gutters and curbs 1249
    Drainage 1250
    Walks and terraces 1251
    Steps 1253
    Furniture 1254
    Banks 1254
    Walls 1255
    Trees 1256
    Lighting 1256
    Pools 1257
    Fountains 1258
Recreation:
    Children 1260
    Adults 1263
    Tennis courts 1268
    Squash courts 1270
    Locker rooms 1272
    Bath houses 1274
    Public swimming pools 1276
    Diving pools 1282
    Residential swimming pools 1284
    Stadia: seating design 1287
    Stadia: exit design 1288
    Community buildings: planning 1291
    Community buildings: details 1292

Index 1293

SECTION I: BASIC DATA

Graphic Symbols:
    Materials 3
    Piping 5
    Heating, ventilating, and air conditioning 6
    Plumbing 8
    Electrical 10
Abbreviations:
    For use on drawings 11
Dimensions of the Human Figure 14
Mathematics:
    Properties of the circle 16
    Circular sections 18
    Areas 20
    Surfaces and volumes 21
    Trigonometric functions 22
    Units of measurement 24
Useful Curves and Curved Surfaces:
    Introduction 26
    Parabola 27
    Ellipse 29
    Hyperbola 31
    Catenary 32
    Cycloid 35
    Trochoid 36
    Sine curve 37
    Geometrical mean 37
    Spirals 38
    Surfaces and skew curves 39
    Cylinders and prisms 42
    Polygon patterns 43
    Cones 44
    Spheres 47
    Polyhedra 51
    Geodesic domes 53
    Hyperbolic paraboloid 56
    Ellipsoid 59
    Elliptic paraboloid 60
    Hyperboloids 61
    Spherical trigonometry 64
Drawing Accurate Curves 65
Area-Perimeter Ratios 69
Modular Coordination 72
Solar Angles:
    Calculations 79
    Azimuth and altitude 82

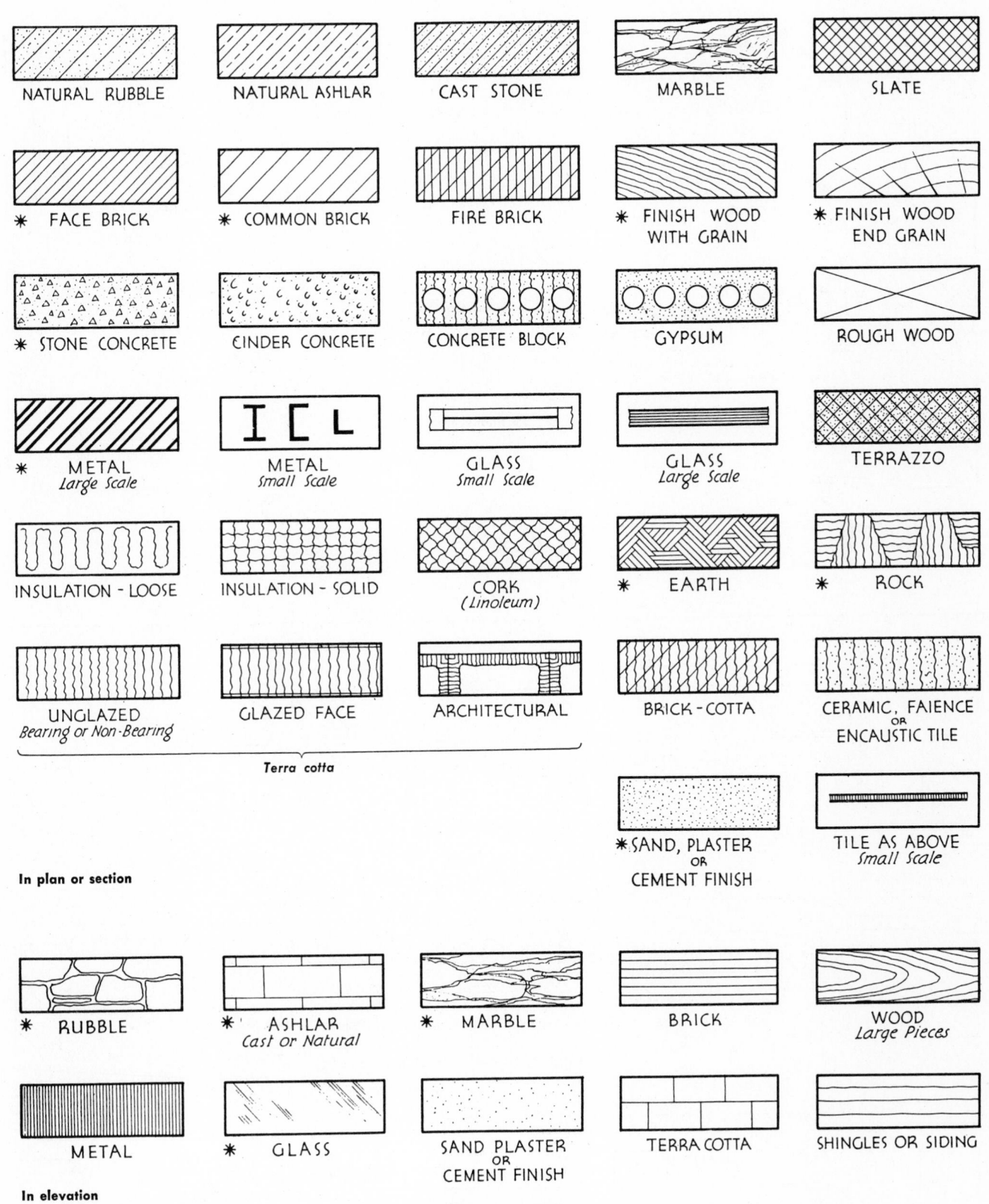

NATURAL RUBBLE

NATURAL ASHLAR

CAST STONE

MARBLE

SLATE

* FACE BRICK

* COMMON BRICK

FIRE BRICK

* FINISH WOOD WITH GRAIN

* FINISH WOOD END GRAIN

* STONE CONCRETE

CINDER CONCRETE

CONCRETE BLOCK

GYPSUM

ROUGH WOOD

* METAL *Large Scale*

METAL *Small Scale*

GLASS *Small Scale*

GLASS *Large Scale*

TERRAZZO

INSULATION - LOOSE

INSULATION - SOLID

CORK *(Linoleum)*

* EARTH

* ROCK

UNGLAZED *Bearing or Non-Bearing*

GLAZED FACE

ARCHITECTURAL

BRICK - COTTA

CERAMIC, FAIENCE OR ENCAUSTIC TILE

Terra cotta

*SAND, PLASTER OR CEMENT FINISH

TILE AS ABOVE *Small Scale*

In plan or section

* RUBBLE

* ASHLAR *Cast or Natural*

* MARBLE

BRICK

WOOD *Large Pieces*

METAL

* GLASS

SAND PLASTER OR CEMENT FINISH

TERRA COTTA

SHINGLES OR SIDING

In elevation

GRAPHIC SYMBOLS

Graphic symbols shown above are for use on drawings in plan or section and in elevation. Symbols marked with an asterisk are American Standards (ASA Y14.2–1957). All others are recommended symbols that should be incorporated in a legend on each drawing when applicable. Specific kinds of metal, stone, and the like should not be indicated since they are the province of the specification.

Walls

Face Brick / T.C. Tile / Plaster / Col. / Furred Pipe Space

Face Brick / Common Brick / T.C Furring / Plaster

Face Brick / Rubble / Wood furr'g / Plaster

Face Brick / Concrete / Air space / Plaster

Arch. T.C. / Common Brick / Furring / Plaster

Natural Ashlar / Common Brick / Furring / Plaster

Studs

MATERIALS

Cast Stone / Common Brick / Furring / Plaster

Plaster / Sheathing / Waterproof Paper / Air Space / Face Brick or Stone

Exterior Finish / Waterproof Paper / Sheathing / Plaster / Studs

Face Brick

8" Brick Plastered

Fire Brick on Brick

Terra Cotta (bearing or non-bearing)

Terra Cotta (Glazed)

Concrete Block

Gypsum Block

Solid Plaster

Metal

Glass

Office (wood or metal)

Stud / Insulation

Partitions

Plaster / Furring / Common Brick / Terra Cotta Brick

Masonry / Plaster / Structural Glass

Cement — Cinder Conc.

Marble

Tile

Terrazzo — Cinder Conc.

Natural Stone

Brick

Wood — Finish / Rough

Floors

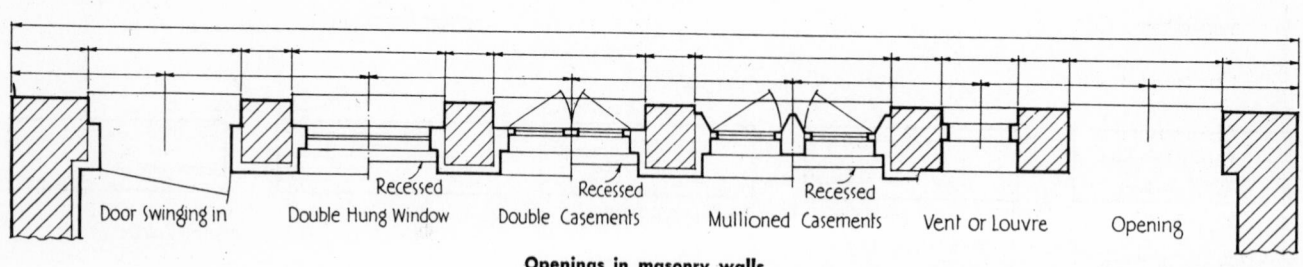

Masonry (furred) / Masonry (not furred) / Furring / Masonry / Not furred / Terra Cotta / Furred or Panelled / Terra Cotta / Furred or Panelled / Stud / Stud / Face of Stud / Brick Veneer

Walls

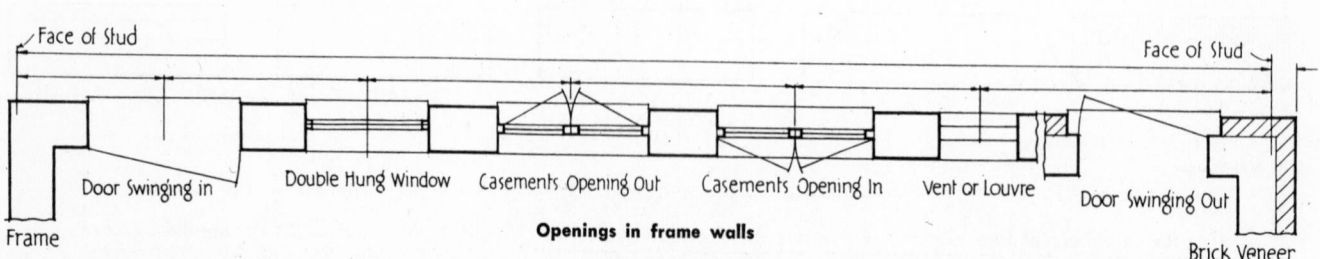

Door Swinging in / Double Hung Window / Recessed / Double Casements / Recessed / Mullioned Casements / Recessed / Vent or Louvre / Opening

Openings in masonry walls

Face of Stud / Frame / Door Swinging in / Double Hung Window / Casements Opening Out / Casements Opening In / Vent or Louvre / Door Swinging Out / Face of Stud / Brick Veneer

Openings in frame walls

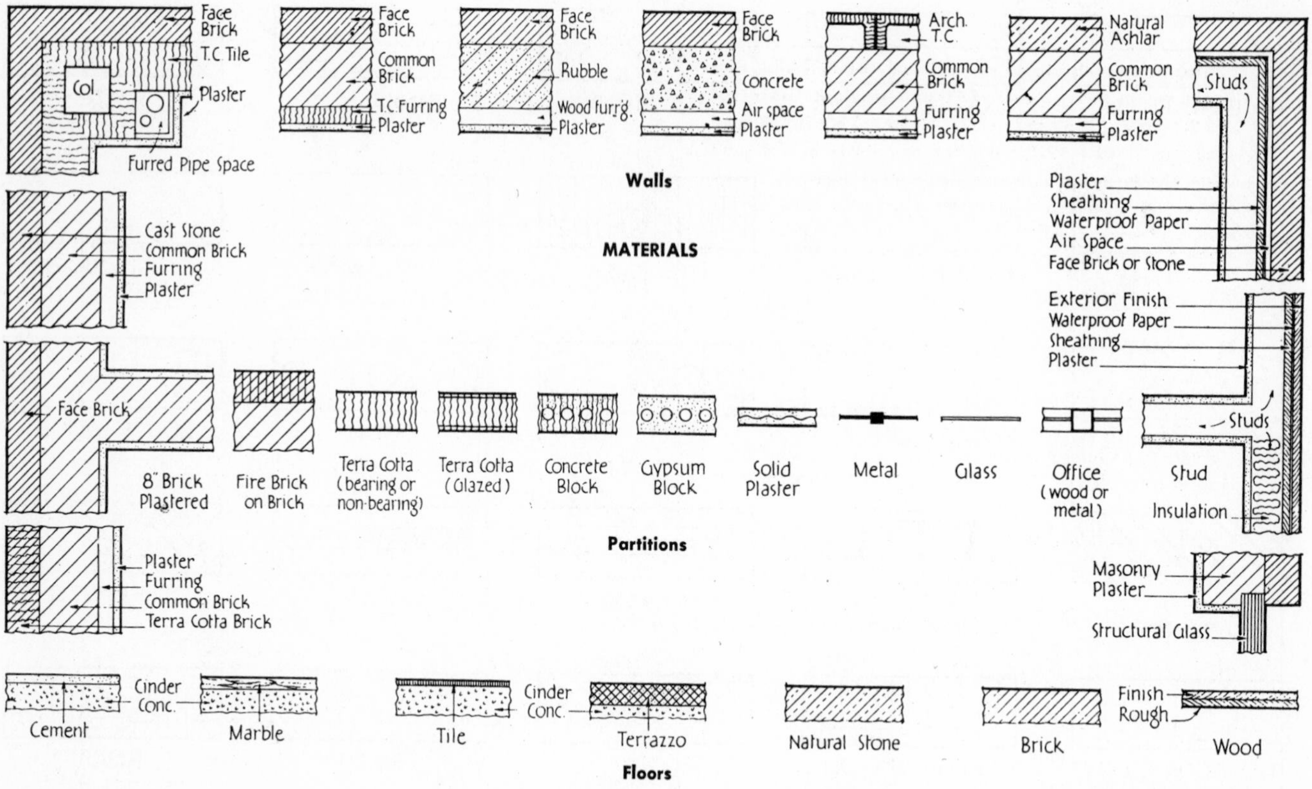

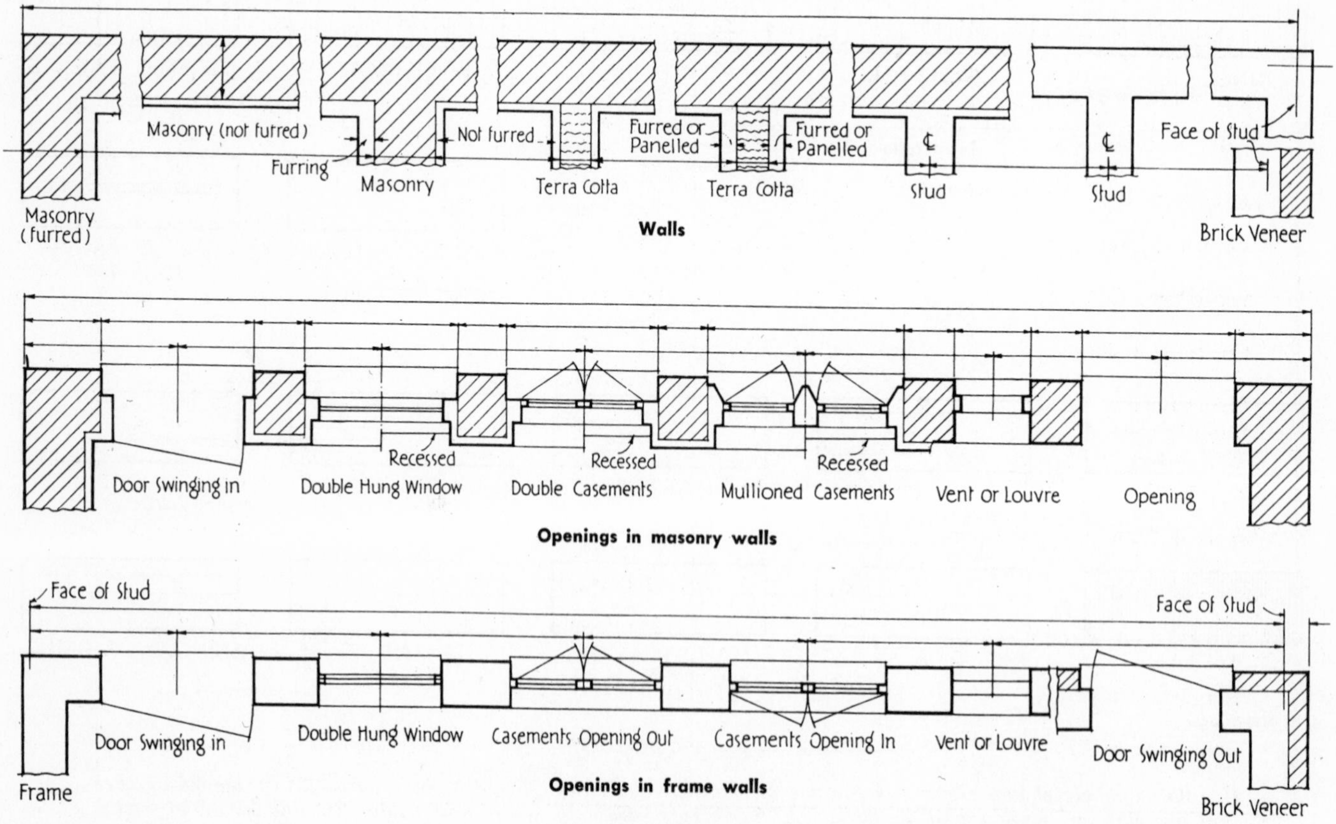

DIMENSIONS

Graphic symbols shown on this and the following four pages have been extracted from American Standards Z32.2.3–1949 (reaffirmed 1953), Z32.2.4–1949 (reaffirmed 1953), and Y32.4–1955, with the permission of the publisher, The American Society of Mechanical Engineers. Designations of the relevant publications are also given at the bottom of each page.

AIR CONDITIONING

Brine Return

Brine Supply

Circulating Chilled or Hot-Water Flow

Circulating Chilled or Hot-Water Return

Condenser Water Flow

Condenser Water Return

Drain

Humidification Line

Make-Up Water

Refrigerant Discharge

Refrigerant Liquid

Refrigerant Suction

HEATING

Air-Relief Line

Boiler Blow Off

Compressed Air

Condensate or Vacuum Pump Discharge

Feedwater Pump Discharge

Fuel-Oil Flow

Fuel-Oil Return

Fuel-Oil Tank Vent

High-Pressure Return

High-Pressure Steam

Hot-Water Heating Return

Hot-Water Heating Supply

Low-Pressure Return

Low-Pressure Steam

Make-Up Water

Medium-Pressure Return

Medium-Pressure Steam

PLUMBING

Acid Waste

Cold Water

Compressed Air

Drinking-Water Flow

Drinking-Water Return

Fire Line

Gas

Hot Water

Hot-Water Return

Soil, Waste or Leader (Above Grade)

Soil, Waste or Leader (Below Grade)

Vacuum Cleaning

Vent

PNEUMATIC TUBES

Tube Runs

SPRINKLERS

Branch and Head

Drain

Main Supplies

Air Eliminator		Access Door	
Anchor		Adjustable Blank Off	
Expansion Joint		Adjustable Plaque	
Hanger or Support			
Heat Exchanger		Automatic Dampers	
Heat Transfer Surface, Plan (Indicate type such as convector)		Canvas Connections	
Pump (Indicate type such as vacuum)		Deflecting Damper	
Strainer			
Tank (Designate type)		Direction of Flow	
Thermometer		Duct (1st figure, side shown; 2nd side not shown)	12 X 20
Thermostat		Duct Section (Exhaust or Return)	(E OR R 20x12)
Trap, Boiler Return		Duct Section (Supply)	(S 20 x 12)
Trap, Blast Thermostatic		Exhaust Inlet Ceiling (Indicate type)	CR 20 x 12 - 700 Cfm / CG 20 x 12 - 700 Cfm
Trap, Float		Exhaust Inlet Wall (Indicate type)	TR - 12X8 700Cfm
Trap, Float and Thermostatic		Fan and Motor with Belt Guard	
Trap, Thermostatic		Inclined Drop in Respect to Air Flow	
Unit Heater (Centrifugal fan), Plan		Inclined Rise in Respect to Air Flow	
Unit Heater (Propeller), Plan		Intake Louvers on Screen	
Unit Ventilator, Plan		Louver Opening	L 20x12 - 700 Cfm
Valve, Check		Supply Outlet Ceiling (Indicate type)	20" DIAM. 1000 Cfm
Valve, Diaphragm			
Valve, Gate		Supply Outlet Wall (Indicate type)	TR - 12x8 700 Cfm
Valve, Globe			
Valve, Lock and Shield		Vanes	
Valve, Motor Operated			
Valve, Reducing Pressure			
Valve, Relief (Either pressure or vacuum)			
Vent Point	VENT	Volume Damper	

From ASA Z32.2.4–1949 (reaffirmed 1953)

Capillary Tube	
Compressor	
Compressor, Enclosed, Crankcase, Rotary, Belted	
Compressor, Open Crankcase, Reciprocating, Belted	
Compressor, Open Crankcase, Reciprocating, Direct Drive	
Condenser, Air Cooled, Finned, Forced Air	
Condenser, Air Cooled, Finned, Static	
Condenser, Water Cooled, Concentric Tube in a Tube	
Condenser, Water Cooled, Shell and Coil	
Condenser, Water Cooled, Shell and Tube	
Condensing Unit, Air Cooled	
Condensing Unit, Water Cooled	
Cooling Tower	
Dryer	
Evaporative Condenser	
Evaporator, Circular, Ceiling Type, Finned	
Evaporator, Manifolded, Bare Tube, Gravity Air	
Evaporator, Manifolded, Finned, Forced Air	
Evaporator, Manifolded, Finned, Gravity Air	
Evaporator, Plate Coils, Headered or Manifold	
Filter, Line	
Filter & Strainer, Line	
Finned Type Cooling Unit, Natural Convection	
Forced Convection Cooling Unit	
Gauge	
High Side Float	
Immersion Cooling Unit	
Low Side Float	
Motor-Compressor, Enclosed Crankcase, Reciprocating, Direct Connected	

Motor-Compressor, Enclosed Crankcase, Rotary, Direct Connected	
Motor-Compressor, Sealed Crankcase, Reciprocating	
Motor-Compressor, Sealed Crankcase, Rotary	
Pressurestat	
Pressure Switch	
Pressure Switch With High Pressure Cut-Out	
Receiver, Horizontal	
Receiver, Vertical	
Scale Trap	
Spray Pond	
Thermal Bulb	
Thermostat (Remote bulb)	
Valve, Automatic Expansion	
Valve, Compressor Suction Pressure Limiting, Throttling Type (Compressor Side)	
Valve, Constant Pressure, Suction	
Valve, Evaporator Pressure Regulating, Snap Action	
Valve, Evaporator Pressure Regulating, Thermostatic Throttling Type	
Valve, Evaporator Pressure Regulating, Throttling Type (Evaporator side)	
Valve, Hand Expansion	
Valve, Magnetic Stop	
Valve, Snap Action	
Valve, Suction Vapor Regulating	
Valve, Thermo Suction	
Valve, Thermostatic Expansion	
Valve, Water	
Vibration Absorber, Line	

From ASA Z32.2.4–1949 (reaffirmed 1953)

GRAPHIC SYMBOLS—6
Plumbing

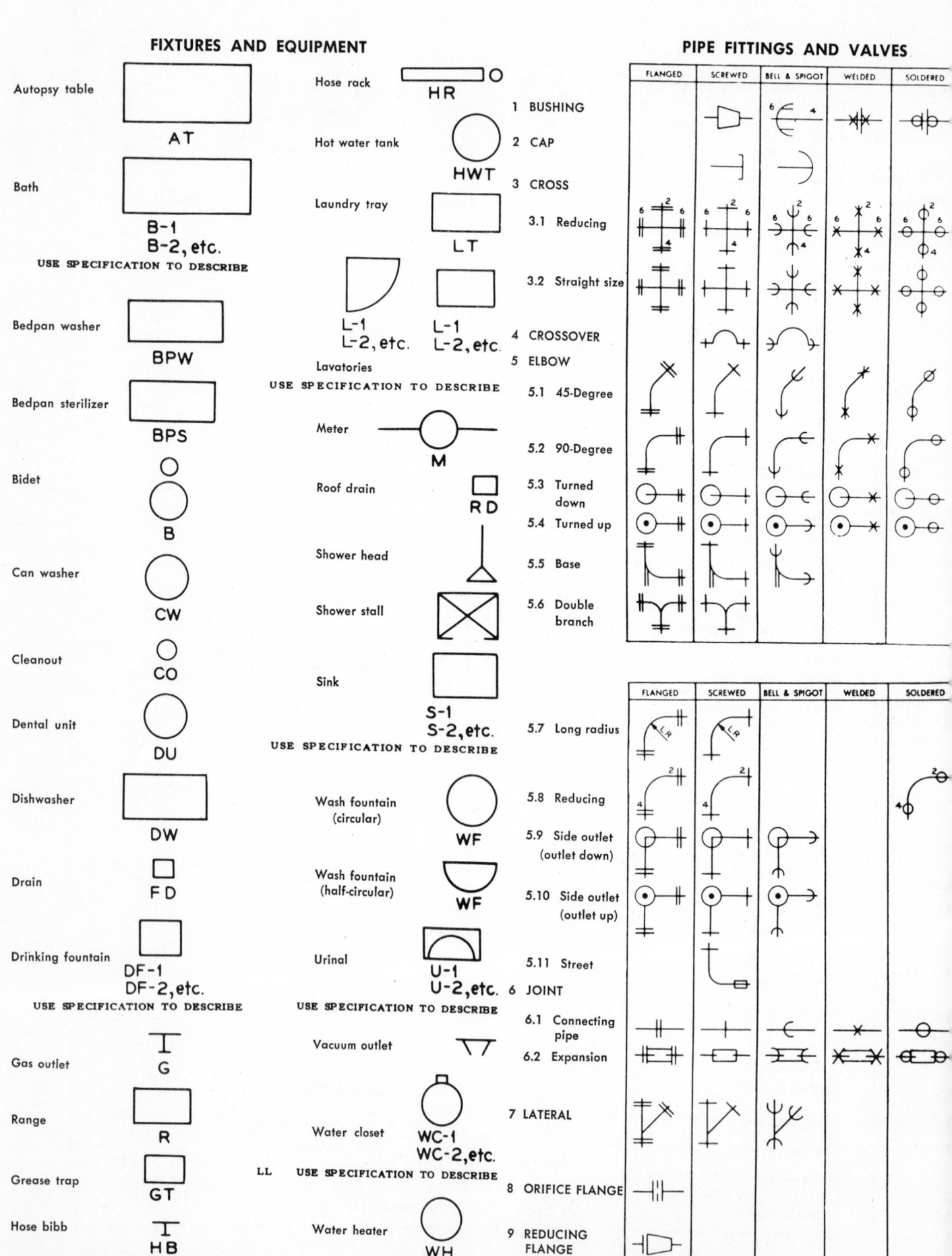

FIXTURES AND EQUIPMENT

Autopsy table — AT

Bath — B-1 B-2, etc.
USE SPECIFICATION TO DESCRIBE

Bedpan washer — BPW

Bedpan sterilizer — BPS

Bidet — B

Can washer — CW

Cleanout — CO

Dental unit — DU

Dishwasher — DW

Drain — FD

Drinking fountain — DF-1 DF-2, etc.
USE SPECIFICATION TO DESCRIBE

Gas outlet — G

Range — R

Grease trap — GT

Hose bibb — HB

Hose rack — HR

Hot water tank — HWT

Laundry tray — LT

Lavatories — L-1 L-2, etc.   L-1 L-2, etc.
USE SPECIFICATION TO DESCRIBE

Meter — M

Roof drain — RD

Shower head

Shower stall

Sink — S-1 S-2, etc.
USE SPECIFICATION TO DESCRIBE

Wash fountain (circular) — WF

Wash fountain (half-circular) — WF

Urinal — U-1 U-2, etc.
USE SPECIFICATION TO DESCRIBE

Vacuum outlet

Water closet — WC-1 WC-2, etc.
LL   USE SPECIFICATION TO DESCRIBE

Water heater — WH

PIPE FITTINGS AND VALVES

1 BUSHING
2 CAP
3 CROSS
3.1 Reducing
3.2 Straight size
4 CROSSOVER
5 ELBOW
5.1 45-Degree
5.2 90-Degree
5.3 Turned down
5.4 Turned up
5.5 Base
5.6 Double branch
5.7 Long radius
5.8 Reducing
5.9 Side outlet (outlet down)
5.10 Side outlet (outlet up)
5.11 Street
6 JOINT
6.1 Connecting pipe
6.2 Expansion
7 LATERAL
8 ORIFICE FLANGE
9 REDUCING FLANGE

FLANGED	SCREWED	BELL & SPIGOT	WELDED	SOLDERED

FLANGED	SCREWED	BELL & SPIGOT	WELDED	SOLDERED

PIPE FITTINGS AND VALVES

	FLANGED	SCREWED	BELL & SPIGOT	WELDED	SOLDERED
PLUGS					
10.1 Bull plug					
10.2 Pipe plug					
REDUCER					
11.1 Concentric					
11.2 Eccentric					
SLEEVE					
TEE					
3.1 Straight size					
3.2 (Outlet up)					
3.3 (Outlet down)					
3.4 Double sweep					
3.5 Reducing					
3.6 Single sweep					

	FLANGED	SCREWED	BELL & SPIGOT	WELDED	SOLDERED
4.7 Side outlet (outlet down)					
4.8 Side outlet (Outlet up)					
UNION					
ANGLE VALVE					
6.1 Check					
6.2 Gate (elevation)					
6.3 Gate (plan)					
6.4 Globe (elevation)					
6.5 Globe (plan)					
6.6 Hose angle	SAME AS	SYMBOL	23.1		
AUTOMATIC VALVE					
5.1 Bypass					

PIPE FITTINGS AND VALVES

	FLANGED	SCREWED	BELL & SPIGOT	WELDED	SOLDERED
16.2 Governor-operated					
16.3 Reducing					
17 CHECK VALVE					
17.1 Angle check	SAME AS	SYMBOL	15.1		
17.2 (Straight way)					
18 COCK					
19 DIAPHRAGM VALVE					
20 FLOAT VALVE					
21 GATE VALVE					
21.1 Gate					
21.2 Angle gate	SAME AS	SYMBOLS	15.2 & 15.3		
21.3 Hose gate	SAME AS	SYMBOL	23.2		

	FLANGED	SCREWED	BELL & SPIGOT	WELDED	SOLDERED
21.4 Motor-operated					
22 GLOBE VALVE					
22.1 Globe					
22.2 Angle globe	SAME AS	SYMBOLS	15.4 & 15.5		
22.3 Hose globe	SAME AS	SYMBOL	23.3		
22.4 Motor-operated					
23 HOSE VALVE					
23.1 Angle					
23.2 Gate					
23.3 Globe					
24 LOCKSHIELD VALVE					
25 QUICK-OPENING VALVE					
26 SAFETY VALVE					
27 STOP VALVE	SAME AS	SYMBOL	21.1		

Graphic symbols shown on this page have been extracted from American Standard Y32.9—1943, with the permission of the publisher, The American Institute of Electrical Engineers. These symbols have been made as simple as possible and are not intended to depict the structure of the electrical devices shown. The symbols should be drawn to a size commensurate with the particular drawing being made. Additional symbols, or those not yet commonly accepted, should be included in a legend.

ELECTRICAL SYMBOLS FOR ARCHITECTURAL PLANS

Description	Ceiling	Wall	Description	Symbol	Description	Symbol
GENERAL OUTLETS			**SWITCHES**		**PANELS, CIRCUITS, MISC.**	
Outlet	○	─○	Single Pole Switch	S	Generator	Ⓖ
Blanket Outlet	Ⓑ	─Ⓑ	Double Pole Switch	S_2	Motor	Ⓜ
Clock Outlet	Ⓒ	─Ⓒ	Three Way Switch	S_3	Instrument	Ⓘ
Drop Cord	Ⓓ		Four Way Switch	S_4	Transformer	Ⓣ
Electrical Outlet: use when plain circle may be confused with column or other symbols	Ⓔ	─Ⓔ	Automatic Door Switch	S_D	Controller	▷◁
			Electrolier Switch	S_E	Isolating Switch	▭⌐
Fan Outlet	Ⓕ	─Ⓕ	Key Operated Switch	S_K	**AUXILIARY or Low Voltage SYSTEMS**	
Junction Box	Ⓙ	─Ⓙ	Switch and Pilot Lamp	S_P	Push Button	◉
Lamp Holder	Ⓛ	─Ⓛ	Circuit Breaker	S_{CB}	Buzzer	◻
Lamp Holder with Pull Switch	Ⓛ_PS	─Ⓛ_PS	Weatherproof Circuit Breaker	S_{WCB}	Bell	◻◗
Pull Switch	Ⓢ	─Ⓢ	Momentary Contact Switch	S_{MC}	Annunciator	◇
Outlet for Vapor Discharge Lamp	Ⓥ	─Ⓥ	Remote Control Switch	S_{RC}	Telephone	◀
Exit Light Outlet	Ⓧ	─Ⓧ	Weatherproof Switch	S_{WP}	Interconnecting Telephone	◁
CONVENIENCE OUTLETS			**SPECIAL OUTLETS**		Telephone Switchboard	◁▷
Duplex Convenience Outlet	⊖		Any standard symbol, with a lower case subscript added, may be used for special indications. When so used, a legend on each drawing and description in specifications are strongly recommended	○ a,b,c etc. ⊖ a,b,c etc. S a,b,c etc.	Electric Door Opener	▢D
Convenience Outlet other than Duplex 1 = Single, 3 = Triplex, etc.	⊖ 1,3				Fire Alarm Bell	Ⓕ○
Weatherproof Conv. Outlet	⊖ WP				Fire Alarm Station	Ⓕ
Range Outlet	⊖ R		**PANELS, CIRCUITS, MISC.**		City Fire Alarm Station	⊠
Switch and Convenience Outlet	⊖─S		Lighting Panel	▬	Fire Alarm Central Station	▢FA
Radio and Convenience Outlet	⊖─▢R		Power Panel	▨	Automatic Fire Alarm Device	▢FS
Special Purpose Outlet (desc. in Spec.)	▲		*Branch Circuit — Ceiling or Wall	───	Watchman's Station	▢W
Floor Outlet	◉		*Branch Circuit — Floor	─ ─ ─	Watchman's Central Station	▢Ⓦ
			*without other designation indicates 2-wire circuit. For 3 wires, use For 4 wires	─⫫─ ─⫴─	Horn	▢H
			Feeders: use heavy lines and designate by number for quick reference	───	Nurse's Signal Plug	▢N
					Maid's Signal Plug	▢M
					Radio Outlet	▢R
					Signal Central Station	▢SC
			Underfloor Duct & Junction Box - Triple System: for double or single systems use two lines or one. Symbol also adaptable to Auxiliary or Low Voltage systems	≡▭≡	Interconnection Box	▭
					Battery	⫟⫟⫟⫟
					Auxiliary System Circuits: without other designation indicates 2-wire circuit. For others, use numbers, as: ── 12 - #18 W - ¾"C. or designate by number for quick reference	─ ─ ─ ─
					Special Auxiliary Outlets: subscripts refer to notes in plans, schedules or specifications	▢ a,b,c

Abbreviations on this and the following two pages have been selected from *American Standard Abbreviations for Use on Drawings* (ASA Z32.13–1950), sponsored by the American Institute of Electrical Engineers and the American Society of Mechanical Engineers, and published by the American Standards Association.

These abbreviations are for use on drawings only; for abbreviations in text see *American Standard Abbreviations for Scientific and Engineering Terms* (ASA Z10.1). Note that periods are used in abbreviations only when necessary to avoid misinterpretation. The standard abbreviations in common use for metals and chemicals are also accepted for use on drawings.

A

Actual	ACT.
Addendum	ADD.
Addition	ADD.
Adhesive	ADH
Aggregate	AGGR
Air condition	AIR COND
Alarm	ALM
Allowance	ALLOW.
Alternate	ALT
Alternating current	AC
Aluminum	AL
American Concrete Institute	ACI
American Gas Association	AGA
American Institute of Architects	AIA
American Institute of Electrical Engineers	AIEE
American Institute of Steel Construction	AISC
American Iron & Steel Institute	AISI
American Society of Civil Engineers	ASCE
American Society of Heating, Refrigerating & Air-Conditioning Engineers	ASHRAE
American Society of Mechanical Engineers	ASME
American Society for Testing Materials	ASTM
American Standards Association	ASA
American wire gage	AWG
Ampere	AMP
Apartment	APT.
Appendix	APPX
Approved	APPD
Approximate	APPROX
Arc weld	ARC/W
Artificial	ART.
Area	A
Asbestos	ASB
Asphalt	ASPH
Assistant	ASST
Association	ASSN
Automatic	AUTO
Avenue	AVE
Average	AVG

B

Barrel	BBL
Beam	BM
Bearing	BRG
Bell and spigot	B&S
Bench mark	BM
Bending moment	M
Between	BET.
Bill of material	B/M
Birmingham wire gage	BWG
Blower	BLO
Blueprint	BP
Board	BD
Boiler	BLR
Both sides	BS
Brass	BRS
Brinnell hardness	BH
British thermal units	BTU
Bronze	BRZ
Brown & Sharp	B&S
Building	BLDG
Building line	BL

C

Cabinet	CAB.
Calking	CLKG
Carload	CL
Cast iron	CI
Cast-iron pipe	CIP
Catalog	CAT.
Ceiling	CLG
Cement	CEM
Center	CTR
Centerline	CL
Center to center	C to C
Centigrade	C
Centimeter	CM
Ceramic	CER
Change order	CO
Circle	CIR
Circuit	CKT
Circular mil	CM
Circumference	CIRC
Cleanout	CO
Clear	CLR
Closet	CLO
Coated	CTD
Coefficient	COEF
Cold rolled	CR
Cold water	CW
Column	COL
Combination	COMB.
Common	COM
Company	CO
Composition	COMP
Compressor	COMPR
Concrete	CONC
Conduit	CND
Construction	CONST
Continue	CONT
Contractor	CONTR
Corporation	CORP
Corrugate	CORR
Countersink	CSK
Courses	C

D

Cross section	XSECT
Cubic centimeter	CC
Cubic feet per minute	CFM
Cubic foot	CU FT
Cubic inch	CU IN.
Cubic yard	CU YD
Dead load	DL
Decibel	DB
Decimal	DEC
Degree	(°) DEG
Delineation	DEL
Department	DEPT
Design	DSGN
Detail	DET
Dew point	DP
Diagonal	DIAG
Diagram	DIAG
Diameter	DIA
Dimension	DIM.
Direct current	DC
Ditto	DO.
Division	DIV
Double	DBL
Down	DN
Downspout	DS
Dozen	DOZ
Drain	DR
Drawing	DWG
Duplicate	DUP

E

East	E
Electric	ELEC
Elevation	EL
Enamel	ENAM
Engineer	ENGR
Engineering	ENGRG
Equal	EQ
Equipment	EQUIP.
Equivalent direct radiation	EDR
Estimate	EST
Excavate	EXC
Exhaust	EXH
Existing	EXIST.
Expanion (joint)	EXP
Exterior	EXT
Extra heavy	X HVY
Extra strong	X STR
Extrude	EXTR

F

Fabricate	FAB
Fahrenheit	F
Federal specifications	FS

Feet	(') FT	Inch	(") IN.	Membrane	MEMB
Feet board measure	FBM	Incinerator	INCIN	Memorandum	MEMO
				Metal	MET.
Figure	FIG.	Include	INCL	Meter (instrument or measure of	
Finish	FIN.	Incorporated	INC	length)	M
Fireproof	FPRF	Industrial	IND		
Fitting	FTG	Information	INFO	Mezzanine	MEZZ
Fixture	FIX.	Inside diameter	ID	Military	MIL
				Millimeter	MM
Flashing	FL	Insulate	INS	Minimum	MIN
Floor	FL	Intercommunication	INTERCOM	Minute	(') MIN
Floor drain	FD	Interior	INT		
Flooring	FLG	Iron	I	Miscellaneous	MISC
Fluorescent	FLUOR	Iron-pipe size	IPS	Mixture	MIX.
				Model	MOD
Foot	(') FT	**J**		Month	MO
Foot-candle	FC			Motor	MOT
Foot-lambert	FL	Joint	JT		
Foot-pounds	FT LB	Junction	JCT	Motor generator	MG
Footing	FTG	Junior	JR	Multiple	MULT
Foundation	FDN				
		K		**N**	
G					
		Kilogram	KG	National Bureau of Standards	NBS
Gage or Gauge	GA	Kilometer	KM	National Electric Code	NEC
Gallon	GAL	Kilowatt	KW	National Electrical Manufacturers	
Gallons per minute	GPM	Kilowatt hour	KWH	Association	NEMA
Galvanize	GALV	Kip (1,000 lb)	K	National Lumber Manufacturers	
Galvanized iron	GI	Knocked down	KD	Association	NLMA
		Knockout	KO		
Gas	G			Natural	NAT
Girder	G	**L**		Negative	NEG
Glass	GL			Nominal	NOM
Government	GOVT	Laboratory	LAB	North	N
Grade	GR	Laminate	LAM	Not to scale	NTS
Gypsum	GYP	Latitude	LAT	Number	NO.
		Lavatory	LAV		
H		Left	L	**O**	
Half-hard	½H	Left hand	LH	Obscure	OB
Half-round	½RD	Length	LG	Obsolete	OBS
Hard	H	Length over-all	LOA	Octagon	OCT
Hardware	HDW	License	LIC	Office	OFF.
Head	HD	Light	LT	On center	OC
Heater	HTR	Linear	LIN	Opening	OPNG
Heavy	HVY	Live load	LL	Opposite	OPP
Height	HGT	Logarithm	LOG.	Original	ORIG
Hexagon	HEX	Long	LG	Ounce	OZ
High point	H PT	Low pressure	LP	Outside diameter	OD
		Lumens per watt	LPW		
High pressure	HP			Over-all	OA
Highway	HWY	**M**		Overhead	OVHD
Horizontal	HOR				
Horsepower	HP	Main	MN	**P**	
Hospital	HOSP	Malleable iron	MI		
		Manhole	MH	Page	P
Hot water	HW	Manual	MAN.	Pair	PR
Hour	HR	Manufacturing	MFG	Panel	PNL
House	HSE			Paragraph	PAR.
Hydraulic	HYD	Mark	MK	Parallel	PAR.
		Material	MATL		
I		Material list	ML	Part	PT
		Maximum	MAX	Partition	PTN
Illuminating Engineering Society	IES	Mechanical	MECH	Passenger	PASS.
Illustrate	ILLUS			Patent	PAT.
Impregnate	IMPG	Medium	MED	Penny (nails, etc.)	d
				Perforate	PERF

Permanent	PERM	Rockwell hardness	RH	Telephone	TEL
Perpendicular	PERP	Roof	RF	Teletypewriter exchange	TWX
Phase	PH	Room	RM	Television	TV
Photograph	PHOTO	Round	RD	Temperature	TEMP
				Terra cotta	TC
Piece	PC	**S**			
Pint	PT			Terrazzo	TER
Plate	PL	Safety	SAF	That is	IE
Plumbing	PLMB	Sanitary	SAN	Thermostat	THERMO
Pneumatic	PNEU	Schedule	SCH	Thick	THK
		Second	(") SEC	Thousand	M
Point	PT	Section	SECT	Through	THRU
Pole	P			Tolerance	TOL
Polish	POL	Select	SEL	Tongue & groove	T&G
Porcelain	PORC	Separate	SEP	Total	TOT.
Positive	POS	Service	SERV	Transformer	TRANS
		Sewer	SEW.		
Post office	PO	Sheet	SH	Tubing	TUB.
Pound	LB			Typical	TYP
Pounds per cubic foot	PCF	Shipment	SHPT		
Pounds per square foot	PSF	Side	S	**U**	
Pounds per square inch	PSI	Siding	SDG		
		Similar	SIM	Ultimate	ULT
Prefabricated	PREFAB	Sketch	SK	Underwriters' Laboratories, Inc.	UL
Preferred	PFD			United States gage	USG
Private automatic exchange	PAX	Society of Automotive Engineers	SAE	Urinal	UR
Private branch exchange	PBX	Soil pipe	SP		
Project	PROJ	South	S	**V**	
		Speaker	SPKR		
Public address	PA	Special	SPL	Vacuum	VAC
Publication	PUB			Valve	V
		Specific gravity	SP GR	Vent pipe	VP
Q		Specification	SPEC	Ventilate	VENT.
		Square	SQ	Versus	VS
Quality	QUAL	Stainless steel	SST		
Quart	QT	Standard	STD	Vertical	VERT
Quarter	QTR			Vitreous	VIT
Quarter-hard	¼H	Steam	ST	Volt	V
Quarter-round	¼RD	Steel	STL	Volume	VOL
		Stock	STK		
R		Storage	STG	**W**	
		Storm water	ST W		
Radiator	RAD			Warehouse	WHSE
Radius	R	Street	ST	Watercloset	WC
Railroad	RR	Structural	STR	Water heater	WH
Received	RECD	Substitute	SUB	Watt	W
Receptacle	RECP	Superintendent	SUPT	Weather stripping	WS
		Supersede	SUPSD		
Reference	REF			Weatherproof	WP
Refractory	REFR	Supervise	SUPV	Week	WK
Refrigerate	REFR	Supply	SUP	Weight	WT
Register	REG	Surface	SUR	West	W
Reinforce	REINF	Switch	SW	Width	W
		Switchboard	SWBD		
Relative humidity	RH			With	W/
Remove	REM			Without	W/O
Repair	REP	Symmetrical	SYM	Wood	WD
Replace	REPL	Synthetic	SYN	Wrought iron	WI
Reproduce	REPRO	System	SYS		
				Y	
Required	REQD				
Requisition	REQ	**T**			
Return	RET.				
Revise	REV	Tangent	TAN.	Yard	YD
Right hand	RH	Tarpaulin	TARP	Year	YR
		Technical	TECH	Yield point	YP
Right of way	R/W	Tee	T	Yield strength	YS
Road	RD				

Dimensions of adults

The dimensions and clearances shown for the average adult (Fig. 2.) represent minimum requirements for use in planning building layouts and furnishings. If possible, clearances should be increased to allow comfortable accommodations for persons larger than average. The height of tabletops shown on the next page is 2 ft 5 in.; some authorities prefer 2 ft 6 in., or sometimes 2 ft 6½ in.

Since doorways and passageways must normally be dimensioned to permit the movement

of furniture, they should seldom be designed merely on the needs of the average adult. (See section of this book relating to furniture sizes.)

Dimensions of children

Children do not have the same physical proportions as adults, especially during their early years, and their heights vary greatly, but their space requirements can be approximated from the following table and from Fig. 1. (For heights of children's furniture and equipment, see section on "Schools.")

Average height of children

Age	Height, in.	Age	Height, in.
5	44	11	56
6	46	12	58
7	48	13	60
8	50	14	62
9	52	15	64
10	54	16	66

References: Ernest Irving Freese, The Geometry of the Human Figure, *American Architect* (July, 1934): William W. Caudill, *Space for Teaching,* Bulletin of Texas Agricultural and Mechanical College.

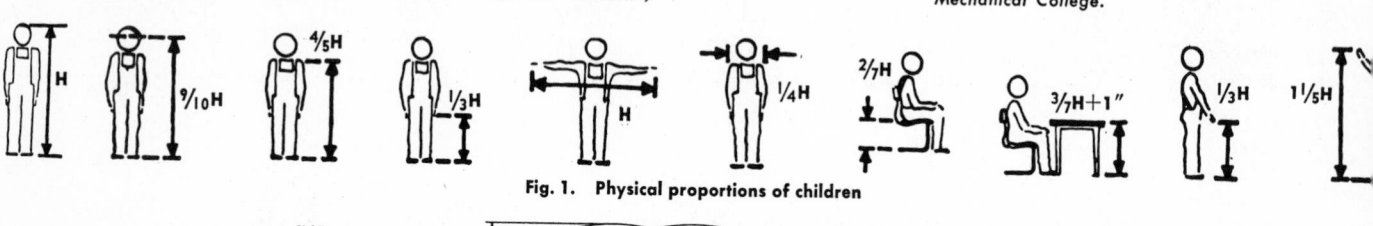

Fig. 1. Physical proportions of children

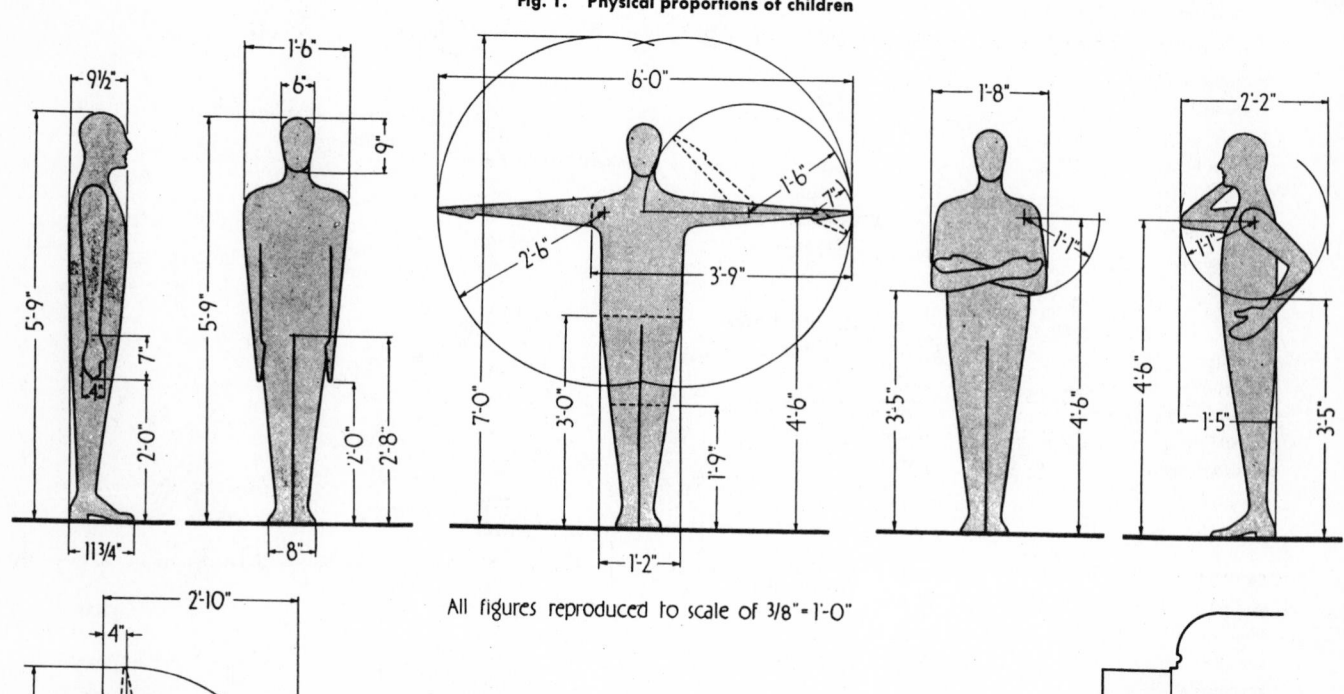

All figures reproduced to scale of 3/8" = 1'-0"

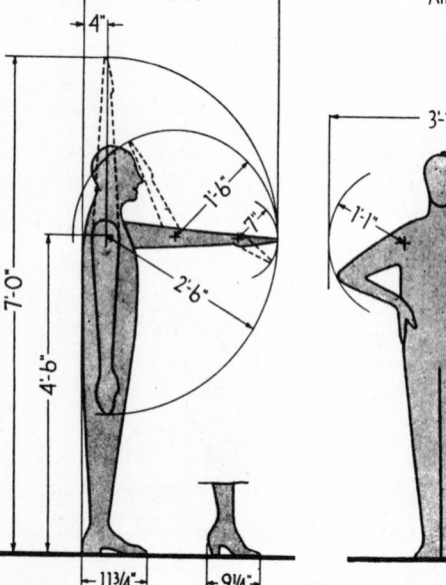
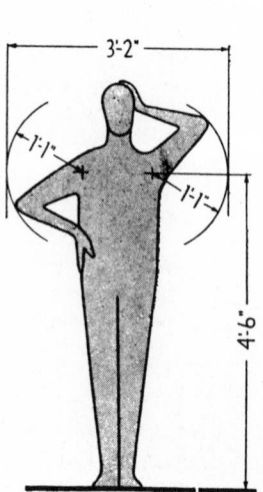
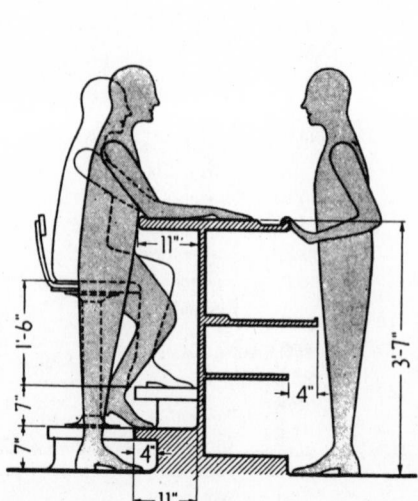
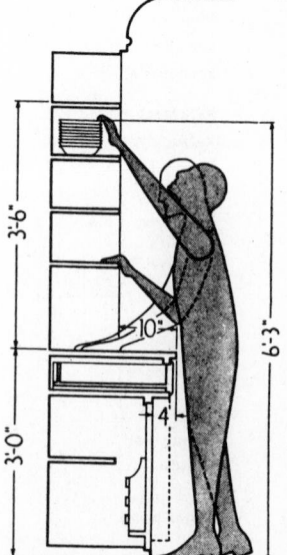

Fig. 2. Dimensions and clearances for adults

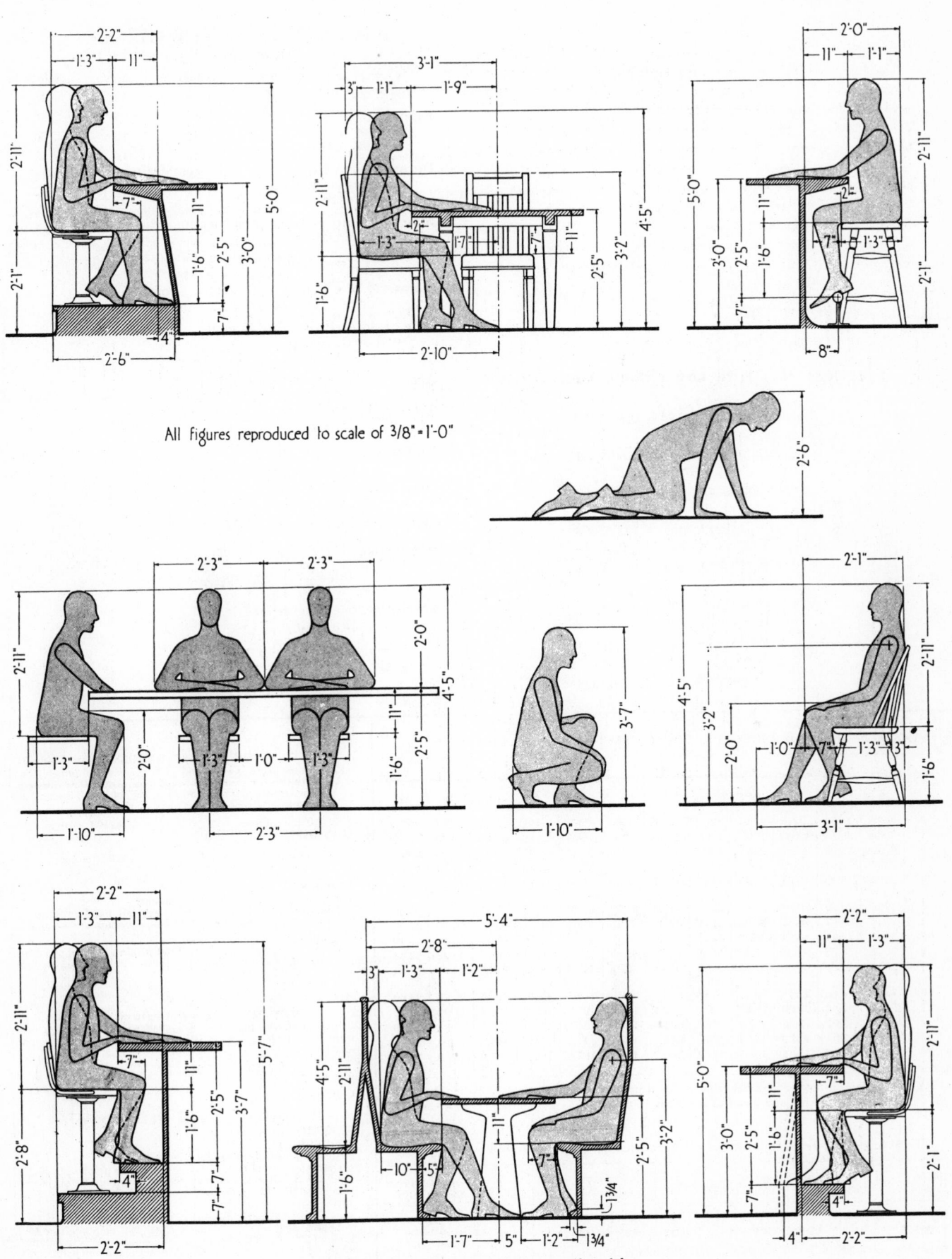

All figures reproduced to scale of 3/8" = 1'-0"

Fig. 2 (cont.) Dimensions and clearances for adults

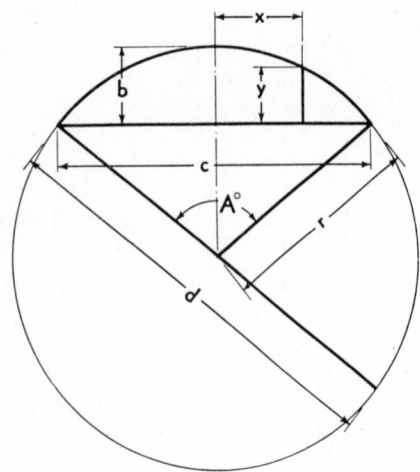

Functions of π with Logarithmic Equivalents

$\pi = 3.14159265,\ \log = 0.4971499$

$\dfrac{1}{\pi} = 0.3183099,\ \log = \overline{1}.5028501$

$\pi^2 = 9.8696044,\ \log = 0.9942997$

$\dfrac{1}{\pi^2} = 0.1013212,\ \log = \overline{1}.0057003$

$\sqrt{\pi} = 1.7724539,\ \log = 0.2485749$

$\sqrt{\dfrac{1}{\pi}} = 0.5641896,\ \log = \overline{1}.7514251$

$\dfrac{\pi}{180} = 0.0174533,\ \log = \overline{2}.2418774$

$\dfrac{180}{\pi} = 57.2957795,\ \log = 1.7581226$

PROPERTIES OF THE CIRCLE

Circumference = C
$= d\,\pi = d \times 3.1416$
$= 2\,\pi\,r = 2 \times r \times 3.1416$

Diameter = d
$= C \div 3.1416$
$= C \times 0.31831$

Diameter of Circle, having circumference equal to periphery of square
$= \text{side of square} \times 1.27324$

Side of Square, having periphery equal to circumference of circle
$= \dfrac{d\pi}{4} = d \times 0.7854$

Diameter of Circle, circumscribed about square
$= \text{side of square} \times 1.41421$

Side of Square, inscribed in circle
$= d \times 0.70711$

Arc, $a = \dfrac{\pi\,r\,A^\circ}{180} = 0.017453\ r\,A^\circ$

Angle, $A^\circ = \dfrac{180^\circ\,a}{\pi\,r} = 57.29578\,\dfrac{a}{r}$

Radius, $r = \dfrac{4\,b^2 + c^2}{8\,b}$

Diameter, $d = \dfrac{4\,b^2 + c^2}{4\,b}$

Chord, $c = 2\sqrt{2\,b\,r - b^2} = 2\,r\,\sin\dfrac{A^\circ}{2}$

Rise, Trigonometric Calculations
$b = \dfrac{c}{2}\tan\dfrac{A^\circ}{4} = 2\,r\,\sin^2\dfrac{A^\circ}{4}$

Rise, Algebraic Calculations
$b = r + y - \sqrt{r^2 - x^2}$
$b = r - \tfrac{1}{2}\sqrt{4\,r^2 - c^2}$
$x = \sqrt{r^2 - (r + y - b)^2}$
$y = b - r + \sqrt{r^2 - x^2}$

TABLE 1—AREAS OF CIRCLES IN SQUARE FEET—Diameter in Feet and Inches

Feet	Inches											
	0	1	2	3	4	5	6	7	8	9	10	11
0	.0000	.0055	.0218	.0491	.0873	.1364	.1963	.2673	.3491	.4418	.5454	.6600
1	.7854	.9218	1.069	1.227	1.396	1.576	1.767	1.969	2.182	2.405	2.640	2.885
2	3.142	3.409	3.687	3.976	4.276	4.587	4.909	5.241	5.585	5.940	6.305	6.681
3	7.069	7.467	7.876	8.296	8.727	9.168	9.621	10.08	10.56	11.04	11.54	12.05
4	12.57	13.10	13.64	14.19	14.75	15.32	15.90	16.50	17.10	17.72	18.35	18.99
5	19.63	20.29	20.97	21.65	22.34	23.04	23.76	24.48	25.22	25.97	26.73	27.49
6	28.27	29.07	29.87	30.68	31.50	32.34	33.18	34.04	34.91	35.78	36.67	37.57
7	38.48	39.41	40.34	41.28	42.24	43.20	44.18	45.17	46.16	47.17	48.19	49.22
8	50.27	51.32	52.38	53.46	54.54	55.64	56.75	57.86	58.99	60.13	61.28	62.44
9	63.62	64.80	66.00	67.20	68.42	69.64	70.88	72.13	73.39	74.66	75.94	77.24
10	78.54	79.85	81.18	82.52	83.86	85.22	86.59	87.97	89.36	90.76	92.18	93.60
11	95.03	96.48	97.93	99.40	100.9	102.4	103.9	105.4	106.9	108.4	110.0	111.5
12	113.1	114.7	116.3	117.9	119.5	121.1	122.7	124.4	126.0	127.7	129.4	131.0
13	132.7	134.4	136.2	137.9	139.6	141.4	143.1	144.9	146.7	148.5	150.3	152.1
14	.153.9	155.8	157.6	159.5	161.4	163.2	165.1	167.0	168.9	170.9	172.8	174.8

If given diameter is not found in this table, reduce diameter to feet and decimals of a foot by aid of the following auxiliary table, and then find area from Table 4.

TABLE 2—Conversion from Inches and Fractions of an Inch to Decimals of a Foot

Inches	1	2	3	4	5	6	7	8	9	10	11
Feet........	.0833	.1667	.2500	.3333	.4167	.5000	.5833	.6667	.7500	.8333	.9167

Inches......	⅛	¼	⅜	½	⅝	¾	⅞
Feet........	.0104	.0208	.0313	.0417	.0521	.0625	.0729

Example. 5 ft. 7⅜ in. = 5.0 + 0.5833 + 0.0313 = 5.6146 ft.

NOTE 1
HOW TO FIND CIRCUMFERENCES (from Table 3)
This table gives the product of π times any number D from 1 to 10; that is, it is a table of multiples of π. (D = diameter.) Moving the decimal point **one** place in column D is equivalent to moving it **one** place in the body of the table.

$$\text{Circumference} = \pi \times \text{diam.} = 3.141593 \times \text{diam.}$$
Conversely,
$$\text{Diameter} = \frac{1}{\pi} \times \text{circumf.} = 0.31831 \times \text{circumf.}$$

Examples:
Diameter given; Circumference sought:
Diameter = 3.57 feet. Find 3.5 in left hand column, read right to column 7 and find 11.22 feet = circumference.
Circumference given; Diameter sought:
Circumference = 20.17 feet. Find 20.17 in body of table, read left and find 6.4, note 20.17 is in column 2, which add = 6.4 + .02 = 6.42 = diameter.

NOTE 2
HOW TO FIND AREAS (from Table 4)
Moving the decimal point **one** place in column D is equivalent to moving it **two** places in the body of the table. (D = diameter.)

$$\text{Area of circle} = \frac{\pi}{4} \times (\text{diam.}^2) = 0.785398 \times (\text{diam.}^2)$$
Conversely,
$$\text{Diam.} = \sqrt{\frac{4}{\pi}} \times \sqrt{\text{area}} = 1.128379 \times \sqrt{\text{area}}$$

Examples:
Diameter given; Area sought:
Diameter = 12.3 feet. Move decimal one point right = 1.23. Find 1.2 in left column, read right to column 3, find area of 1.23 = 1.188. Move decimal **two points right** = 118.8 sq. ft. = area.
Area given; Diameter sought:
Area = 4927 sq. in. Move decimal two points left = 49.27. Find 49.27. Read left and find 7.9. Note 49.27 is in column 2, which add = 7.9 + .02 = 7.92. Move decimal one point right = 79.2 inches = diameter.

TABLE 3—CIRCUMFERENCES BY HUNDREDTHS. SEE NOTE 1

D	0	1	2	3	4	5	6	7	8	9
1.0	3.142	3.173	3.204	3.236	3.267	3.299	3.330	3.362	3.393	3.424
.1	3.456	3.487	3.519	3.550	3.581	3.613	3.644	3.676	3.707	3.738
.2	3.770	3.801	3.833	3.864	3.896	3.927	3.958	3.990	4.021	4.053
.3	4.084	4.115	4.147	4.178	4.210	4.241	4.273	4.304	4.335	4.367
.4	4.398	4.430	4.461	4.492	4.524	4.555	5.587	4.618	4.650	4.681
1.5	4.712	4.744	4.775	4.807	4.838	4.869	4.901	4.932	4.964	4.995
.6	5.027	5.058	5.089	5.121	5.152	5.184	5.215	5.246	5.278	5.309
.7	5.341	5.372	5.404	5.435	5.466	5.498	5.529	5.561	5.592	5.623
.8	5.655	5.686	5.718	5.749	5.781	5.812	5.843	5.875	5.906	5.938
.9	5.969	6.000	6.032	6.063	6.095	6.126	6.158	6.189	6.220	6.252
2.0	6.283	6.315	6.346	6.377	6.409	6.440	6.472	6.503	6.535	6.566
.1	6.597	6.629	6.600	6.692	6.723	6.754	6.786	6.817	6.849	6.880
.2	6.912	6.943	6.974	7.006	7.037	7.069	7.100	7.131	7.163	7.194
.3	7.226	7.257	7.288	7.320	7.351	7.383	7.414	7.446	7.477	7.508
.4	7.540	7.571	7.603	7.634	7.665	7.697	7.728	7.760	7.791	7.823
2.5	7.854	7.885	7.917	7.948	7.980	8.011	8.042	8.074	8.105	8.137
.6	8.168	8.200	8.231	8.262	8.294	8.325	8.357	8.388	8.419	8.451
.7	8.482	8.514	8.545	8.577	8.608	8.639	8.671	8.702	8.734	8.765
.8	8.796	8.828	8.859	8.891	8.922	8.954	8.985	9.016	9.048	9.079
.9	9.111	9.142	9.173	9.205	9.236	9.268	9.299	9.331	9.362	9.393
3.0	9.425	9.456	9.488	9.519	9.550	9.582	9.613	9.645	9.676	9.708
.1	9.739	9.770	9.802	9.833	9.865	9.896	9.927	9.959	9.990	10.022
.2	10.05	10.08	10.12	10.15	10.18	10.21	10.24	10.27	10.30	10.34
.3	10.37	10.40	10.43	10.46	14.49	10.52	10.56	10.59	10.62	10.65
.4	10.68	10.71	10.74	10.78	10.81	10.84	10.87	10.90	10.93	10.96
3.5	11.00	11.03	11.06	11.09	11.12	11.15	11.18	11.22	11.25	11.28
.6	11.31	11.34	11.37	11.40	11.44	11.47	11.50	11.53	11.56	11.59
.7	11.62	11.66	11.69	11.72	11.75	11.78	11.81	11.84	11.88	11.91
.8	11.94	11.97	12.00	12.03	12.06	12.10	12.13	12.16	12.19	12.22
.9	12.25	12.28	12.32	12.35	12.38	12.41	12.44	12.47	12.50	12.53
4.0	12.57	12.60	12.63	12.66	12.69	12.72	12.75	12.79	12.82	12.85
.1	12.88	12.91	12.94	12.97	13.01	13.04	13.07	13.10	13.13	13.16
.2	13.19	13.23	13.26	13.29	13.32	13.35	13.38	13.41	13.45	13.48
.3	13.51	13.54	13.57	13.60	13.63	13.67	13.70	13.73	13.76	13.79
.4	13.82	13.85	13.89	13.92	13.95	13.98	14.01	14.04	14.07	14.11
4.5	14.14	14.17	14.20	14.23	14.26	14.29	14.33	14.36	14.39	14.42
.6	14.45	14.48	14.51	14.44	14.58	14.61	14.64	14.67	14.70	14.73
.7	14.77	14.80	14.83	14.86	14.89	14.92	14.95	14.99	15.02	15.05
.8	15.08	15.11	15.14	15.17	15.21	15.24	15.27	15.30	15.33	15.36
.9	15.39	15.43	15.46	15.49	15.52	15.52	15.58	15.61	15.65	15.68
5.0	15.71	15.74	15.77	15.80	15.83	15.87	15.90	15.93	15.96	15.99
.1	16.02	16.05	16.08	16.12	16.15	16.18	16.21	16.24	16.27	16.30
.2	16.34	16.37	16.40	16.43	16.46	16.49	16.52	16.56	16.59	16.62
.3	16.65	16.68	16.71	16.74	16.78	16.81	16.84	16.87	16.90	16.93
.4	16.96	17.00	17.03	17.06	17.09	17.12	17.15	17.18	17.22	17.25
5.5	17.28	17.31	17.34	17.37	17.40	17.44	17.47	17.50	17.53	17.56
.6	17.59	17.62	17.66	17.69	17.72	17.75	17.78	17.81	17.84	17.88
.7	17.91	17.94	17.97	18.00	18.03	18.06	18.10	18.13	18.16	18.19
.8	18.22	18.25	18.28	18.32	18.35	18.38	18.41	18.44	18.47	18.50
.9	18.54	18.57	18.60	18.63	18.66	18.69	18.72	18.76	18.79	18.82
6.0	18.85	18.88	18.91	18.94	18.98	19.01	19.04	19.07	19.10	19.13
.1	19.16	19.20	19.23	19.26	19.29	19.32	19.35	19.38	19.42	19.45
.2	19.48	19.51	19.54	19.57	19.60	19.63	19.67	19.70	19.73	19.76
.3	19.79	19.82	19.85	19.89	19.92	19.95	19.98	20.01	20.04	20.07
.4	20.11	20.14	20.17	20.20	20.23	20.26	20.29	20.38	20.36	20.39
6.5	20.42	20.45	20.48	20.51	20.55	20.58	20.61	20.64	20.67	20.70
.6	20.73	20.77	20.80	20.83	20.86	20.89	20.92	20.95	20.99	21.02
.7	21.05	21.08	21.11	21.14	21.17	21.21	21.24	21.27	21.30	21.33
.8	21.36	21.39	21.43	21.46	21.49	21.52	21.55	21.58	21.61	21.65
.9	21.68	21.71	21.74	21.77	21.80	21.83	21.87	21.90	21.93	21.96
7.0	21.99	22.02	22.05	22.09	22.12	22.15	22.18	22.21	22.24	22.27
.1	22.31	22.34	22.37	22.40	22.43	22.46	22.49	22.53	22.56	22.59
.2	22.62	22.65	22.68	22.71	22.75	22.78	22.81	22.84	22.87	22.90
.3	22.93	22.97	23.00	23.03	23.06	23.09	23.12	23.15	23.18	23.22
.4	23.25	23.28	23.31	23.34	23.37	23.40	23.44	23.47	23.50	23.53
7.5	23.56	23.59	23.62	23.66	23.69	23.72	23.75	23.78	23.81	23.84
.6	23.88	23.91	23.94	23.97	24.00	24.03	24.06	24.10	24.13	24.16
.7	24.19	24.22	24.25	24.28	24.32	24.35	24.38	24.41	24.44	24.47
.8	24.50	24.54	24.57	24.60	24.63	24.66	24.69	24.72	24.76	24.79
.9	24.82	24.85	24.88	24.91	24.94	24.98	25.01	25.04	25.07	25.10
8.0	25.13	25.16	25.20	25.23	25.26	25.29	25.32	25.35	25.38	25.42
.1	25.45	25.48	25.51	24.54	25.57	25.60	25.64	25.67	25.70	25.73
.2	25.76	25.79	25.82	25.86	25.89	25.92	25.95	25.98	26.01	26.04
.3	26.08	26.11	26.14	26.17	26.20	26.23	26.26	26.30	26.33	26.36
.4	26.39	26.42	26.45	26.48	26.52	26.55	26.58	26.61	26.64	26.67
8.5	26.70	26.73	26.77	26.80	26.83	26.86	26.89	26.92	26.95	26.99
.6	27.02	27.05	27.08	27.11	27.14	27.17	27.21	27.24	27.27	27.30
.7	27.33	27.36	27.39	27.43	27.46	27.49	27.52	27.55	27.58	27.61
.8	27.65	27.68	27.71	27.74	27.77	27.80	27.83	27.87	27.90	27.93
.9	27.96	27.99	28.02	28.05	28.09	28.12	28.15	28.18	28.21	28.24
9.0	28.27	28.31	28.34	28.37	28.40	28.43	28.46	28.49	28.53	28.56
.1	28.59	28.62	28.65	28.68	28.71	28.75	28.78	28.81	28.84	28.87
.2	28.90	28.93	28.97	29.00	29.03	29.06	29.09	29.12	29.15	29.19
.3	29.22	29.25	29.28	29.31	29.34	29.37	29.41	29.44	29.47	29.50
.4	29.53	29.56	29.59	29.63	29.66	29.69	29.72	29.75	29.78	29.81
9.5	29.85	29.88	29.91	29.94	29.97	30.00	30.03	30.07	30.10	30.13
.6	30.16	30.19	30.22	30.25	30.28	30.32	30.35	30.38	30.41	30.44
.7	30.47	30.50	30.54	30.57	30.60	30.63	30.66	30.69	30.72	30.76
.8	30.79	30.82	30.85	30.88	30.91	30.94	30.98	31.01	31.04	31.07
.9	31.10	31.13	31.16	31.20	31.23	31.26	31.29	31.32	31.35	31.38

TABLE 4—AREAS BY HUNDREDTHS. SEE NOTE 2

D	0	1	2	3	4	5	6	7	8	9
1.0	0.785	0.801	0.817	0.833	0.849	0.866	0.882	0.899	0.916	0.933
.1	0.950	0.968	0.985	1.003	1.021	1.039	1.057	1.075	1.094	1.112
.2	1.131	1.150	1.169	1.188	1.208	1.227	1.247	1.267	1.287	1.307
.3	1.327	1.348	1.368	1.389	1.410	1.431	1.453	1.474	1.496	1.517
.4	1.539	1.561	1.584	1.606	1.629	1.651	1.674	1.697	1.720	1.744
1.5	1.767	1.791	1.815	1.839	1.863	1.887	1.911	1.936	1.961	1.986
.6	2.011	2.036	2.061	2.087	2.112	2.138	2.164	2.190	2.217	2.243
.7	2.270	2.297	2.324	2.351	2.378	2.405	2.433	2.461	2.488	2.516
.8	2.545	2.573	2.602	2.630	2.659	2.688	2.717	2.746	2.776	2.806
.9	2.835	2.865	2.895	2.926	2.956	2.986	3.017	3.048	3.079	3.110
2.0	3.142	3.173	3.205	3.237	3.269	3.301	3.333	3.365	3.398	3.431
.1	3.464	3.497	3.530	3.563	3.597	3.631	3.664	3.698	3.733	3.767
.2	3.801	3.836	3.871	3.906	3.941	3.976	4.011	4.047	4.083	4.119
.3	4.155	4.191	4.227	4.264	4.301	4.337	4.374	4.412	4.449	4.486
.4	4.524	4.562	4.600	4.638	4.676	4.714	4.753	4.792	4.831	4.870
2.5	4.909	4.948	4.988	5.027	5.067	5.107	5.147	5.187	5.228	5.269
.6	5.309	5.350	5.391	5.433	5.474	5.515	5.557	5.599	5.641	5.683
.7	5.726	5.768	5.811	5.853	5.896	5.940	5.983	6.026	6.070	6.114
.8	6.158	6.202	6.246	6.290	6.335	6.379	6.424	6.469	6.514	6.560
.9	6.605	6.651	6.697	6.743	6.789	6.835	6.881	6.928	6.975	7.022
3.0	7.069	7.116	7.163	7.211	7.258	7.306	7.354	7.402	7.451	7.499
.1	7.548	7.596	7.645	7.694	7.744	7.793	7.843	7.892	7.942	7.992
.2	8.042	8.093	8.143	8.194	8.245	8.296	8.347	8.398	8.450	8.501
.3	8.553	8.605	8.657	8.709	8.762	8.814	8.867	8.920	8.973	9.026
.4	9.079	9.133	9.186	9.240	9.294	9.348	9.402	9.457	9.511	9.566
3.5	9.621	9.676	9.731	9.787	9.842	9.898	9.954	10.01	10.07	10.12
.6	10.18	10.24	10.29	10.35	10.41	10.46	10.52	10.58	10.64	10.69
.7	10.75	10.81	10.87	10.93	10.99	11.04	11.10	11.16	11.22	11.28
.8	11.34	11.40	11.46	11.52	11.58	11.64	11.70	11.76	11.82	11.88
.9	11.95	12.01	12.07	12.13	12.19	12.25	12.32	12.38	12.44	12.50
4.0	12.57	12.63	12.69	12.76	12.82	12.88	12.95	13.01	13.07	13.14
.1	13.20	13.27	13.33	13.40	13.46	13.53	13.59	13.66	13.72	13.79
.2	13.85	13.92	13.99	14.05	14.12	14.19	14.25	14.32	14.39	14.45
.3	14.52	14.59	14.66	14.73	14.79	14.86	14.93	15.00	15.07	15.14
.4	15.21	15.27	15.34	15.41	15.48	15.55	15.62	15.69	15.76	15.83
4.5	15.90	15.98	16.05	16.12	16.19	16.26	16.33	16.40	16.47	16.55
.6	16.62	16.69	16.76	16.84	16.91	16.98	17.06	17.13	17.20	17.28
.7	17.35	17.42	17.50	17.57	17.65	17.72	17.80	17.87	17.95	18.02
.8	18.10	18.17	18.25	18.32	18.40	18.47	18.55	18.63	18.70	18.78
.9	18.86	18.93	19.01	19.09	19.17	19.24	19.32	19.40	19.48	19.56
5.0	19.63	19.71	19.79	19.87	19.95	20.03	20.11	20.19	20.27	20.35
.1	20.43	20.51	20.59	20.67	20.75	20.83	20.91	20.99	21.07	21.16
.2	21.24	21.32	21.40	21.48	21.57	21.65	21.73	21.81	21.90	21.98
.3	22.06	22.15	22.23	22.31	22.40	22.48	22.56	22.65	22.73	22.82
.4	22.90	22.99	23.07	23.16	23.24	23.33	23.41	23.50	23.59	23.67
5.5	23.76	23.84	23.93	24.02	24.11	24.19	24.28	24.37	24.45	24.54
.6	24.63	24.72	24.81	24.89	24.98	25.07	25.16	25.25	25.34	25.43
.7	25.52	25.61	25.70	25.79	25.88	25.97	26.06	26.15	26.24	26.33
.8	26.42	26.51	26.60	26.69	26.79	26.88	26.97	27.06	27.15	27.25
.9	27.34	27.43	27.53	27.62	27.71	27.81	27.90	27.99	28.09	28.18
6.0	28.27	28.37	28.46	28.56	28.65	28.75	28.84	28.94	29.03	29.13
.1	29.22	29.32	29.42	29.51	29.61	29.71	29.80	29.90	30.00	30.09
.2	30.19	30.29	30.39	30.48	30.58	30.68	30.78	30.88	30.97	31.07
.3	31.17	31.27	31.37	31.47	31.57	31.67	31.77	31.87	31.97	32.07
.4	32.17	32.27	32.37	32.47	32.57	32.67	32.78	32.88	32.98	33.08
6.5	33.18	33.29	33.39	33.49	33.59	33.70	33.80	33.90	34.00	34.11
.6	34.21	34.32	34.42	34.52	34.63	34.73	34.84	34.94	35.05	35.15
.7	35.26	35.36	35.47	35.57	35.68	35.78	35.89	36.00	36.10	36.21
.8	36.32	36.42	36.53	36.64	36.75	36.85	36.96	37.07	37.18	37.28
.9	37.39	37.50	37.61	37.72	37.83	37.94	38.05	38.16	38.26	38.37
7.0	38.48	38.59	38.70	38.82	38.93	39.04	39.15	39.26	39.37	39.48
.1	39.59	39.70	39.82	39.93	40.04	40.15	40.26	40.38	40.49	40.60
.2	40.72	40.83	40.94	41.06	41.17	41.28	41.40	41.51	41.62	41.74
.3	41.85	41.97	42.08	42.20	42.31	42.43	42.54	42.66	42.78	42.89
.4	43.01	43.12	43.24	43.36	43.47	43.59	43.71	43.83	43.94	44.06
7.5	44.18	44.30	44.41	44.53	44.65	44.77	44.89	45.01	45.13	45.25
.6	45.36	45.48	45.60	45.72	45.84	45.96	46.08	46.20	46.32	46.45
.7	46.57	46.69	46.81	46.93	47.05	47.17	47.29	47.42	47.54	47.66
.8	47.78	47.91	48.03	48.15	48.27	48.40	48.52	48.65	48.77	48.89
.9	49.02	49.14	49.27	49.39	49.51	49.64	49.76	49.89	50.01	50.14
8.0	50.27	50.39	50.52	50.64	50.77	50.90	51.02	51.15	51.28	51.40
.1	51.53	51.66	51.78	51.91	52.04	52.17	52.30	52.42	52.55	52.68
.2	52.81	52.94	53.07	53.20	53.33	53.46	53.59	53.72	53.85	53.98
.3	54.11	54.24	54.37	54.50	54.63	54.76	54.89	55.02	55.15	55.29
.4	55.42	55.55	55.68	55.81	55.95	56.08	56.21	56.35	56.48	56.61
8.5	56.75	56.88	57.01	57.15	57.28	57.41	57.55	57.68	57.82	57.95
.6	58.09	58.22	58.36	58.49	58.63	58.77	58.90	59.04	59.17	59.31
.7	59.45	59.58	59.72	59.86	59.99	60.13	60.27	60.41	60.55	60.68
.8	60.82	60.96	61.10	61.24	61.38	61.51	61.65	61.79	61.93	62.07
.9	62.21	62.35	62.49	62.63	62.77	62.91	63.05	63.19	63.33	63.48
9.0	63.62	63.76	63.90	64.04	64.18	64.33	64.47	64.61	64.75	64.90
.1	65.04	65.18	65.33	65.47	65.61	65.76	65.90	66.04	66.19	66.33
.2	66.48	66.62	66.77	66.91	67.06	67.20	67.35	67.49	67.64	67.78
.3	67.93	68.08	68.22	68.37	68.51	68.66	68.81	68.96	69.10	69.25
.4	69.40	69.55	69.69	69.84	69.99	70.14	70.29	70.44	70.58	70.73
9.5	70.88	71.03	71.18	71.33	71.48	71.63	71.78	71.93	72.08	72.23
.6	72.38	72.53	72.68	72.84	72.99	73.14	73.29	73.44	73.59	73.75
.7	73.90	74.05	74.20	74.36	74.51	74.66	74.82	74.97	75.12	75.28
.8	75.43	75.58	75.74	75.89	76.05	76.20	76.36	76.51	76.67	76.82
.9	76.98	77.13	77.29	77.44	77.60	77.76	77.91	78.07	78.23	78.38

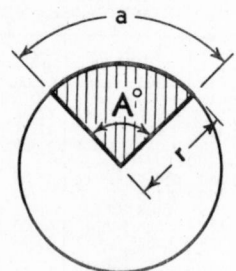

FIG. 1

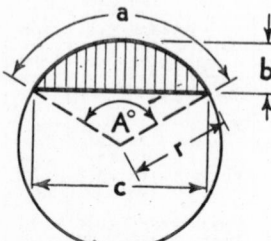

FIG. 2

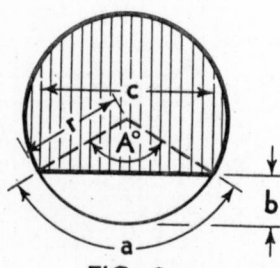

FIG. 3

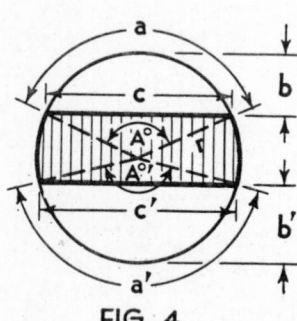

FIG. 4

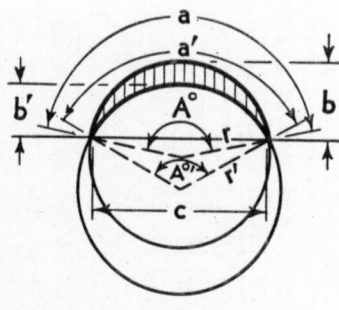

FIG. 5

Nomenclature—(From Serial No. 23)

$A°$ = Angle in degrees = $\dfrac{180° \, a}{\pi \, r}$

a = Arc = $0.017453 \, r \, A°$

b = Rise = $2 \, r \sin^2 \dfrac{A°}{4}$

c = Chord = $2 \, r \sin \dfrac{A°}{2}$

d = Diameter = $2 \, r = \dfrac{4 \, b^2 + c^2}{4 \, b}$

π = 3.1416

r = Radius = $\dfrac{d}{2} = \dfrac{4 \, b^2 + c^2}{8 \, b}$

S = Area = $\dfrac{\pi \, d^2}{4} = 0.7854 \, d^2$

AREA OF CIRCULAR SECTOR—Figure 1

Area = $\dfrac{a \, r}{2} = \dfrac{S \, A°}{360}$

AREA OF CIRCULAR SEGMENT—Figure 2
(Less than half circle)

Area = $\dfrac{a \, r - c \, (r - b)}{2} = \dfrac{S A°}{360} - \dfrac{c \, (r - b)}{2}$

AREA OF CIRCULAR SEGMENT—Figure 3
(Greater than half circle)

Area = $S - \left[\dfrac{a \, r - c \, (r - b)}{2} \right] = S - \left[\dfrac{S \, A°}{360} - \dfrac{c \, (r - b)}{2} \right]$

AREA OF CIRCULAR ZONE—Figure 4

Area = $S - \left[\dfrac{a \, r - c \, (r - b)}{2} + \dfrac{a^1 \, r - c^1 \, (r - b^1)}{2} \right]$

$= S - \left[\dfrac{S \, A°}{360} - \dfrac{c \, (r - b)}{2} + \dfrac{S A°^1}{360} - \dfrac{c^1 \, (r - b^1)}{2} \right]$

AREA OF CIRCULAR LUNE—Figure 5

Area = $\left[\dfrac{a \, r - c \, (r - b)}{2} \right] - \left[\dfrac{a^1 \, r^1 - c \, (r^1 - b^1)}{2} \right]$

$= \left[\dfrac{S A°}{360} - \dfrac{c \, (r - b)}{2} \right] - \left[\dfrac{S^1 A°^1}{360} - \dfrac{c \, (r^1 - b^1)}{2} \right]$

AREA OF CIRCULAR SEGMENT—From Table 1
(Using Rise and Chord)

Area = $c \times b \times$ coefficient.

Example: chord, c = 3.52; rise, b = 1.49

$\dfrac{b}{c} = \dfrac{1.49}{3.52} = 0.4233$

coefficient of 0.4233 = 0.7542

$3.52 \times 1.49 \times 0.7542 = 3.9556$ = area of segment

AREA OF CIRCULAR SEGMENT—From Table 2
(Using Rise and Diameter)

Area = $d^2 \times$ coefficient

Example: diameter, $d = 5\frac{3}{32}$; rise, $b = 2\frac{7}{16}$

$5\frac{3}{32} = 5.09375$; $2\frac{7}{16} = 2.4375$

$\dfrac{b}{d} = \dfrac{2.4375}{5.09375} = 0.478528$

Interpolation:

Coefficient for 0.479 = 0.371705
          0.478 = 0.370706
          .001   = 0.000999

.478528
.478000
.000528 $\times$ 528
                  0.000527

Coefficient   + 0.370706
for 0.478528 = 0.371233

$5.09375 \times 5.09375 \times 0.371233 = 9.6321$ = area of segment

AREAS OF CIRCULAR SEGMENTS

TABLE 1—FOR RATIOS OF RISE AND CHORD

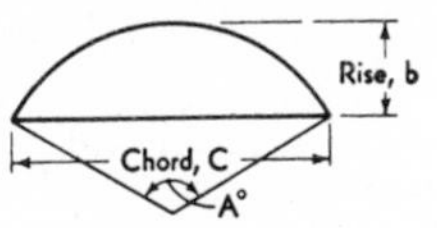

Rise, b · Chord, C · A°

Area = C x b x Coefficient

A°	Coefficient	b/C	A°	Coefficient	b/C	A°	Coefficient	b/C	A°	Coefficient	b/C
61	.6764	.1363	91	.6895	.2097	121	.7100	.2916	151	.7408	.3871
62	.6768	.1387	92	.6901	.2122	122	.7109	.2945	152	.7421	.3906
63	.6771	.1410	93	.6906	.2148	123	.7117	.2975	153	.7434	.3942
64	.6775	.1434	94	.6912	.2174	124	.7126	.3004	154	.7447	.3977
65	.6779	.1457	95	.6918	.2200	125	.7134	.3034	155	.7460	.4013
66	.6782	.1481	96	.6924	.2226	126	.7143	.3064	156	.7473	.4049
67	.6786	.1505	97	.6930	.2252	127	.7152	.3094	157	.7486	.4085
68	.6790	.1529	98	.6936	.2279	128	.7161	.3124	158	.7500	.4122
69	.6794	.1553	99	.6942	.2305	129	.7170	.3155	159	.7514	.4159
70	.6797	.1577	100	.6948	.2332	130	.7180	.3185	160	.7528	.4196
71	.6801	.1601	101	.6954	.2358	131	.7189	.3216	161	.7542	.4233
72	.6805	.1625	102	.6961	.2385	132	.7199	.3247	162	.7557	.4270
73	.6809	.1649	103	.6967	.2412	133	.7209	.3278	163	.7571	.4308
74	.6814	.1673	104	.6974	.2439	134	.7219	.3309	164	.7586	.4346
75	.6818	.1697	105	.6980	.2466	135	.7229	.3341	165	.7601	.4385
76	.6822	.1722	106	.6987	.2493	136	.7239	.3373	166	.7616	.4424
77	.6826	.1746	107	.6994	.2520	137	.7249	.3404	167	.7632	.4463
78	.6831	.1771	108	.7001	.2548	138	.7260	.3436	168	.7648	.4502
79	.6835	.1795	109	.7008	.2575	139	.7270	.3469	169	.7664	.4542
80	.6840	.1820	110	.7015	.2603	140	.7281	.3501	170	.7680	.4582
81	.6844	.1845	111	.7022	.2631	141	.7292	.3534	171	.7696	.4622
82	.6849	.1869	112	.7030	.2659	142	.7303	.3567	172	.7712	.4663
83	.6854	.1894	113	.7037	.2687	143	.7314	.3600	173	.7729	.4704
84	.6859	.1919	114	.7045	.2715	144	.7325	.3633	174	.7746	.4745
85	.6854	.1944	115	.7052	.2743	145	.7336	.3666	175	.7763	.4787
86	.6869	.1970	116	.7060	.2772	146	.7348	.3700	176	.7781	.4828
87	.6874	.1995	117	.7068	.2800	147	.7360	.3734	177	.7799	.4871
88	.6879	.2020	118	.7076	.2829	148	.7372	.3768	178	.7817	.4914
89	.6884	.2046	119	.7084	.2858	149	.7384	.3802	179	.7835	.4957
90	.6890	.2071	120	.7092	.2887	150	.7396	.3837	180	.7854	.5000

A°	Coefficient	b/C	A°	Coefficient	b/C	A°	Coefficient	b/C	A°	Coefficient	b/C
1	.6667	.0022	16	.6674	.0350	31	.6691	.0681	46	.6722	.1017
2	.6667	.0044	17	.6674	.0372	32	.6693	.0703	47	.6724	.1040
3	.6667	.0066	18	.6675	.0394	33	.6694	.0725	48	.6727	.1063
4	.6667	.0087	19	.6676	.0416	34	.6696	.0747	49	.6729	.1086
5	.6667	.0109	20	.6677	.0437	35	.6698	.0770	50	.6732	.1109
6	.6667	.0131				36	.6700	.0792			
7	.6668	.0153	21	.6678	.0459	37	.6702	.0814	51	.6734	.1131
8	.6668	.0175	22	.6679	.0481	38	.6704	.0837	52	.6737	.1154
9	.6669	.0197	23	.6680	.0504	39	.6706	.0859	53	.6740	.1177
10	.6670	.0218	24	.6681	.0526	40	.6708	.0882	54	.6743	.1200
			25	.6682	.0548				55	.6746	.1224
11	.6670	.0240	26	.6684	.0570	41	.6710	.0904	56	.6749	.1247
12	.6671	.0262	27	.6685	.0592	42	.6712	.0927	57	.6752	.1270
13	.6672	.0284	28	.6687	.0614	43	.6714	.0949	58	.6755	.1293
14	.6672	.0306	29	.6688	.0636	44	.6717	.0972	59	.6758	.1316
15	.6673	.0328	30	.6690	.0658	45	.6719	.0995	60	.6761	.1340

AREAS OF CIRCULAR SEGMENTS

TABLE II—FOR RATIOS OF RISE AND DIAMETER

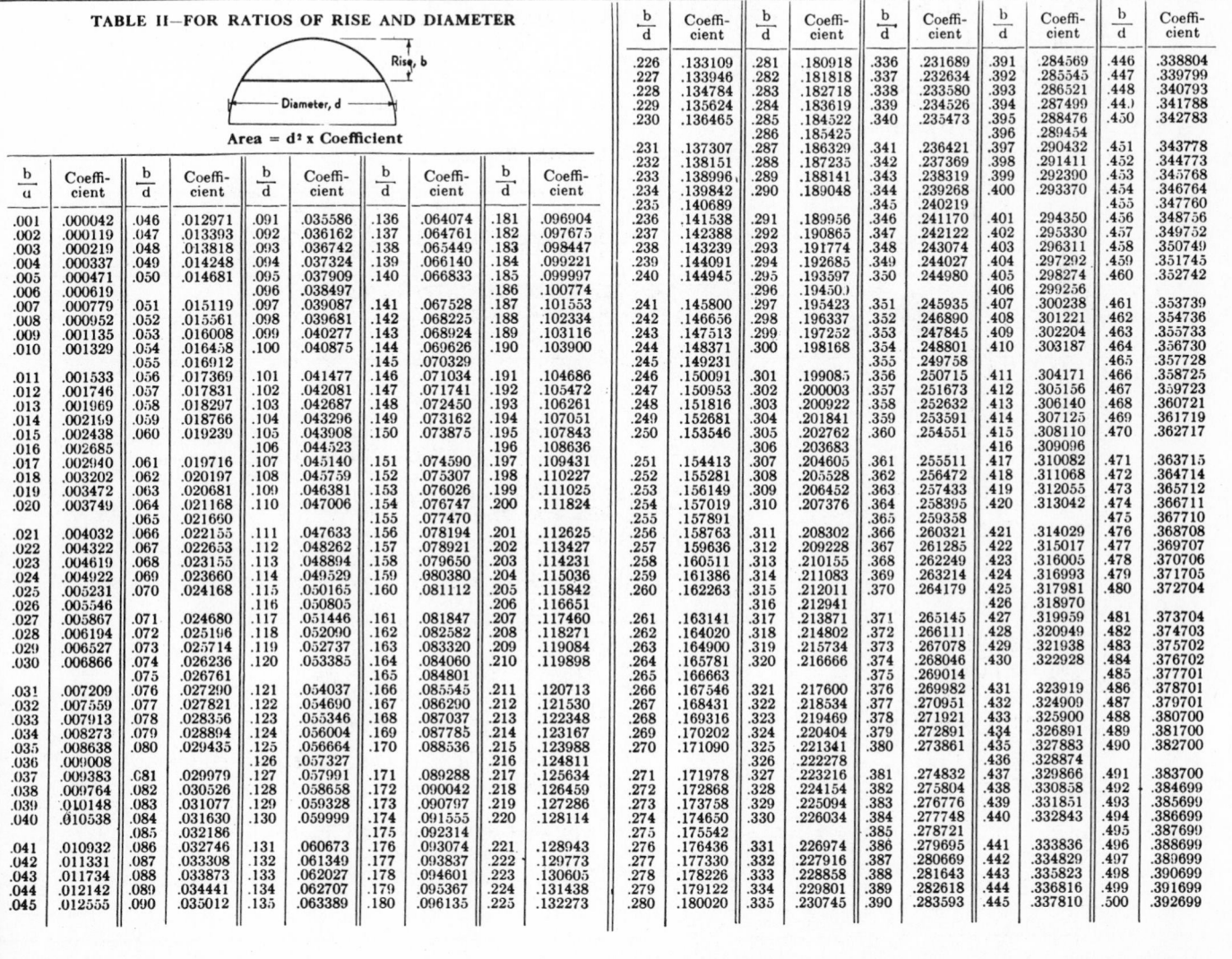

Rise, b · Diameter, d

Area = d² x Coefficient

b/d	Coefficient	b/d	Coefficient	b/d	Coefficient	b/d	Coefficient	b/d	Coefficient	b/d	Coefficient
.001	.000042	.046	.012971	.091	.035586	.136	.064074	.181	.096904	.226	.133109
.002	.000119	.047	.013393	.092	.036162	.137	.064761	.182	.097675	.227	.133946
.003	.000219	.048	.013818	.093	.036742	.138	.065449	.183	.098447	.228	.134784
.004	.000337	.049	.014248	.094	.037324	.139	.066140	.184	.099221	.229	.135624
.005	.000471	.050	.014681	.095	.037909	.140	.066833	.185	.099997	.230	.136465
.006	.000619			.096	.038497			.186	.100774		
.007	.000779	.051	.015119	.097	.039087	.141	.067528	.187	.101553	.231	.137307
.008	.000952	.052	.015561	.098	.039681	.142	.068225	.188	.102334	.232	.138151
.009	.001135	.053	.016008	.099	.040277	.143	.068924	.189	.103116	.233	.138996
.010	.001329	.054	.016458	.100	.040875	.144	.069626	.190	.103900	.234	.139842
		.055	.016912			.145	.070329			.235	.140689
.011	.001533	.056	.017369	.101	.041477	.146	.071034	.191	.104686	.236	.141538
.012	.001746	.057	.017831	.102	.042081	.147	.071741	.192	.105472	.237	.142388
.013	.001969	.058	.018297	.103	.042687	.148	.072450	.193	.106261	.238	.143239
.014	.002199	.059	.018766	.104	.043296	.149	.073162	.194	.107051	.239	.144091
.015	.002438	.060	.019239	.105	.043908	.150	.073875	.195	.107843	.240	.144945
.016	.002685			.106	.044523			.196	.108636		
.017	.002940	.061	.019716	.107	.045140	.151	.074590	.197	.109431	.241	.145800
.018	.003202	.062	.020197	.108	.045759	.152	.075307	.198	.110227	.242	.146656
.019	.003472	.063	.020681	.109	.046381	.153	.076026	.199	.111025	.243	.147513
.020	.003749	.064	.021168	.110	.047006	.154	.076747	.200	.111824	.244	.148371
		.065	.021660			.155	.077470			.245	.149231
.021	.004032	.066	.022155	.111	.047633	.156	.078194	.201	.112625	.246	.150091
.022	.004322	.067	.022653	.112	.048262	.157	.078921	.202	.113427	.247	.150953
.023	.004619	.068	.023155	.113	.048894	.158	.079650	.203	.114231	.248	.151816
.024	.004922	.069	.023660	.114	.049529	.159	.080380	.204	.115036	.249	.152681
.025	.005231	.070	.024168	.115	.050165	.160	.081112	.205	.115842	.250	.153546
.026	.005546			.116	.050805			.206	.116651		
.027	.005867	.071	.024680	.117	.051446	.161	.081847	.207	.117460	.251	.154413
.028	.006194	.072	.025196	.118	.052090	.162	.082582	.208	.118271	.252	.155281
.029	.006527	.073	.025714	.119	.052737	.163	.083320	.209	.119084	.253	.156149
.030	.006866	.074	.026236	.120	.053385	.164	.084060	.210	.119898	.254	.157019
		.075	.026761			.165	.084801			.255	.157891
.031	.007209	.076	.027290	.121	.054037	.166	.085545	.211	.120713	.256	.158763
.032	.007559	.077	.027821	.122	.054690	.167	.086290	.212	.121530	.257	.159636
.033	.007913	.078	.028356	.123	.055346	.168	.087037	.213	.122348	.258	.160511
.034	.008273	.079	.028894	.124	.056004	.169	.087785	.214	.123167	.259	.161386
.035	.008638	.080	.029435	.125	.056664	.170	.088536	.215	.123988	.260	.162263
.036	.009008			.126	.057327			.216	.124811		
.037	.009383	.081	.029979	.127	.057991	.171	.089288	.217	.125634	.261	.163141
.038	.009764	.082	.030526	.128	.058658	.172	.090042	.218	.126459	.262	.164020
.039	.010148	.083	.031077	.129	.059328	.173	.090797	.219	.127286	.263	.164900
.040	.010538	.084	.031630	.130	.059999	.174	.091555	.220	.128114	.264	.165781
		.085	.032186			.175	.092314			.265	.166663
.041	.010932	.086	.032746	.131	.060673	.176	.093074	.221	.128943	.266	.167546
.042	.011331	.087	.033308	.132	.061349	.177	.093837	.222	.129773	.267	.168431
.043	.011734	.088	.033873	.133	.062027	.178	.094601	.223	.130605	.268	.169316
.044	.012142	.089	.034441	.134	.062707	.179	.095367	.224	.131438	.269	.170202
.045	.012555	.090	.035012	.135	.063389	.180	.096135	.225	.132273	.270	.171090

b/d	Coefficient	b/d	Coefficient	b/d	Coefficient	b/d	Coefficient	b/d	Coefficient
.226	.133109	.281	.180918	.336	.231689	.391	.284569	.446	.338804
.227	.133946	.282	.181818	.337	.232634	.392	.285545	.447	.339799
.228	.134784	.283	.182718	.338	.233580	.393	.286521	.448	.340793
.229	.135624	.284	.183619	.339	.234526	.394	.287499	.449	.341788
.230	.136465	.285	.184522	.340	.235473	.395	.288476	.450	.342783
		.286	.185425			.396	.289454		
.231	.137307	.287	.186329	.341	.236421	.397	.290432	.451	.343778
.232	.138151	.288	.187235	.342	.237369	.398	.291411	.452	.344773
.233	.138996	.289	.188141	.343	.238319	.399	.292390	.453	.345768
.234	.139842	.290	.189048	.344	.239268	.400	.293370	.454	.346764
.235	.140689			.345	.240219			.455	.347760
.236	.141538	.291	.189956	.346	.241170	.401	.294350	.456	.348756
.237	.142388	.292	.190865	.347	.242122	.402	.295330	.457	.349752
.238	.143239	.293	.191774	.348	.243074	.403	.296311	.458	.350749
.239	.144091	.294	.192685	.349	.244027	.404	.297292	.459	.351745
.240	.144945	.295	.193597	.350	.244980	.405	.298274	.460	.352742
		.296	.19450(1)			.406	.299256		
.241	.145800	.297	.195423	.351	.245935	.407	.300238	.461	.353739
.242	.146656	.298	.196337	.352	.246890	.408	.301221	.462	.354736
.243	.147513	.299	.197252	.353	.247845	.409	.302204	.463	.355733
.244	.148371	.300	.198168	.354	.248801	.410	.303187	.464	.356730
.245	.149231			.355	.249758			.465	.357728
.246	.150091	.301	.199085	.356	.250715	.411	.304171	.466	.358725
.247	.150953	.302	.200003	.357	.251673	.412	.305156	.467	.359723
.248	.151816	.303	.200922	.358	.252632	.413	.306140	.468	.360721
.249	.152681	.304	.201841	.359	.253591	.414	.307125	.469	.361719
.250	.153546	.305	.202762	.360	.254551	.415	.308110	.470	.362717
		.306	.203683			.416	.309096		
.251	.154413	.307	.204605	.361	.255511	.417	.310082	.471	.363715
.252	.155281	.308	.205528	.362	.256472	.418	.311068	.472	.364714
.253	.156149	.309	.206452	.363	.257433	.419	.312055	.473	.365712
.254	.157019	.310	.207376	.364	.258395	.420	.313042	.474	.366711
.255	.157891			.365	.259358			.475	.367710
.256	.158763	.311	.208302	.366	.260321	.421	.314029	.476	.368708
.257	.159636	.312	.209228	.367	.261285	.422	.315017	.477	.369707
.258	.160511	.313	.210155	.368	.262249	.423	.316005	.478	.370706
.259	.161386	.314	.211083	.369	.263214	.424	.316993	.479	.371705
.260	.162263	.315	.212011	.370	.264179	.425	.317981	.480	.372704
		.316	.212941			.426	.318970		
.261	.163141	.317	.213871	.371	.265145	.427	.319959	.481	.373704
.262	.164020	.318	.214802	.372	.266111	.428	.320949	.482	.374703
.263	.164900	.319	.215734	.373	.267078	.429	.321938	.483	.375702
.264	.165781	.320	.216666	.374	.268046	.430	.322928	.484	.376702
.265	.166663			.375	.269014			.485	.377701
.266	.167546	.321	.217600	.376	.269982	.431	.323919	.486	.378701
.267	.168431	.322	.218534	.377	.270951	.432	.324909	.487	.379701
.268	.169316	.323	.219469	.378	.271921	.433	.325900	.488	.380700
.269	.170202	.324	.220404	.379	.272891	.434	.326891	.489	.381700
.270	.171090	.325	.221341	.380	.273861	.435	.327883	.490	.382700
		.326	.222278			.436	.328874		
.271	.171978	.327	.223216	.381	.274832	.437	.329866	.491	.383700
.272	.172868	.328	.224154	.382	.275804	.438	.330858	.492	.384699
.273	.173758	.329	.225094	.383	.276776	.439	.331851	.493	.385699
.274	.174650	.330	.226034	.384	.277748	.440	.332843	.494	.386699
.275	.175542			.385	.278721			.495	.387699
.276	.176436	.331	.226974	.386	.279695	.441	.333836	.496	.388699
.277	.177330	.332	.227916	.387	.280669	.442	.334829	.497	.389699
.278	.178226	.333	.228858	.388	.281643	.443	.335823	.498	.390699
.279	.179122	.334	.229801	.389	.282618	.444	.336816	.499	.391699
.280	.180020	.335	.230745	.390	.283593	.445	.337810	.500	.392699

FORM		METHOD OF FINDING AREAS
TRIANGLE		Base × ½ perpendicular height. $\sqrt{s(s-a)(s-b)(s-c)}$, s = ½ sum of the three sides a, b, c.
TRAPEZIUM		Sum of area of the two triangles
TRAPEZOID		½ sum of parallel sides × perpendicular height.
PARALLELOGRAM		Base × perpendicular height.
REG. POLYGON		½ sum of sides × inside radius.
CIRCLE		πr^2 = 0.78540 × diam^2. = 0.07958 × circumference^2
SECTOR OF A CIRCLE		$\dfrac{\pi r^2 A°}{360}$ = 0.0087266 $r^2 A°$, = arc × ½ radius
SEGMENT OF A CIRCLE		$\dfrac{r^2}{2}\left(\dfrac{\pi A°}{180} - \sin A°\right)$
CIRCLE of same area as a square		Diameter = side × 1.12838
SQUARE of same area as a circle		Side = diameter × 0.88623
ELLIPSE		Long diameter × short diameter × 0.78540
PARABOLA		Base × ⅔ perpendicular height.

IRREGULAR PLANE SURFACE

Divide any plane surface A, B, C, D, along a line a - b into an even number, n, of parallel and sufficiently small strips d, whose ordinates are h_1, h_2, h_3, h_4, h_5, ... h_{n-1}, h_n, h_{n+1}, and considering contours between three ordinates as parabolic curves, then for section A B C D,

$$\text{Area} = \frac{d}{3}\left[\, h_1 + h_{n+1} + 4\,(h_2 + h_4 + h_6 \cdots + h_n) + 2\,(h_3 + h_5 + h_7 \cdots + h_{n-1})\,\right]$$

or, approximately, Area = sum of ordinates × width d.

METHOD OF FINDING SURFACES AND VOLUMES OF SOLIDS

SHAPE	FORMULAE	SHAPE	FORMULAE
	S = lateral or convex surface V = volume		S = lateral or convex surface V = volume

Parallelopiped

S = perimeter, P, perp. to sides × lat. length l : Pl :
V = area of base, B, × perpendicular height, h : Bh.
V = area of section, A, perp. to sides, × lat. length l : Al.

Prism right, or oblique, regular or irregular

S = perimeter, P, perp. to sides × lat. length l : Pl :
V = area of base, B, × perpendicular height, h : Bh.
V = area of section, A, perp. to sides, × lat. length l : Al.

Cylinder, right or oblique, circular or elliptic etc.

S = perimeter of base, P, × perp. height, h : Ph. S_1 = perimeter, P_1, perp., × lat. length, l : $P_1 l$.
V = area of base, B, × perp. height, h : Bh. V = area of section, A, perp. to sides × lat. length l : Al.

Frustum of any prism or cylinder

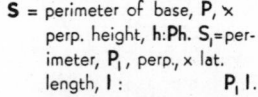

V = area of base, B, × perpendicular distance h, from base to centre of gravity of opposite face: Bh.
for cylinder, $\frac{1}{2} A \,(l_1 + l_2)$

Pyramid or Cone, right and regular

S = perimeter of base, P, × $\frac{1}{2}$ slant height l : $\frac{1}{2} Pl$.

V = area of base, B × $\frac{1}{3}$ perpendicular ht., h : $\frac{1}{3} Bh$.

Pyramid or Cone, right or oblique, regular or irregular

V = area of base, B, × $\frac{1}{3}$ perp. height, h : $\frac{1}{3} Bh$.
V = $\frac{1}{3}$ vol. of prism or cylinder of same base & perp. height.
V = $\frac{1}{2}$ vol. of hemisphere of same base and perp. height.

Frustum of pyramid or cone, right and regular, parallel ends

S = (sum of perimeter of base, P, and top, p) × $\frac{1}{2}$ slant height l : $\frac{1}{2} l\,(P + p)$.
V = (sum of areas of base, B, and top, b + sq. root of their products) × $\frac{1}{3}$ perp. height, h : $\frac{1}{3} h\,(B + b + \sqrt{Bb})$.

Frustum of any pyramid or cone, parallel ends

V = (sum of areas of base, B, and top, b, + sq. root of their products) × $\frac{1}{3}$ perpendicular height, h : $\frac{1}{3} h\,(B + b + \sqrt{Bb})$.

Wedge, parallelogram face

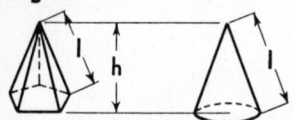

V = $\frac{1}{6}$ (sum of three edges, $a\,b\,a$, × perpendicular height, h, × perpendicular width, d) : $\frac{1}{6} d h\,(2a + b)$.

Sphere

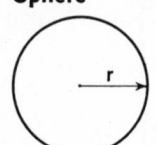

$S = 4\pi r^2 = \pi d^2 = 3.14159265\, d^2$.
$V = \frac{4}{3}\pi r^3 = \frac{1}{6}\pi d^3 = 0.52359878\, d^3$.

Spherical Sector

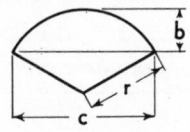

$S = \frac{1}{2}\pi r\,(4b + c)$.
$V = \frac{2}{3}\pi r^2 b$.

Spherical Segment

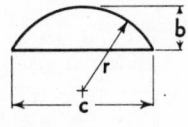

$S = 2\pi r b \doteq \frac{1}{4}\pi\,(4b^2 + c^2)$.
$V = \frac{1}{3}\pi b^2\,(3r - b) = \frac{1}{24}\pi b\,(3c^2 + 4b^2)$.

Spherical Zone

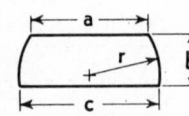

$S = 2\pi r b$.
$V = \frac{1}{24}\pi b\,(3a^2 + 3c^2 + 4b^2)$.

Circular Ring

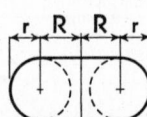

$S = 4\pi^2 R r$.
$V = 2\pi^2 R r^2$.

Ungula of right, regular cylinder
1. Base = segment, bab. 2. Base = half circle

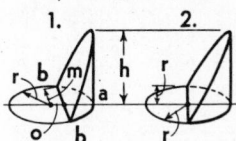

$S = (2rm - o × \text{arc, bab}) \dfrac{h}{r - o}$. $S = 2rh$.
$V = (\frac{2}{3}m^3 - o × \text{area, bab}) \dfrac{h}{r - o}$. $V = \frac{2}{3} r^2 h$.

1. Base = segment, cac. 2. Base = circle

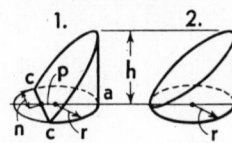

$S = (2rn + p × \text{arc, cac}) \dfrac{h}{r + p}$. $S = \pi r h$.
$V = (\frac{2}{3}n^3 + p × \text{area, cac}) \dfrac{h}{r + p}$. $V = \frac{1}{2} r^2 \pi h$.

Ellipsoid

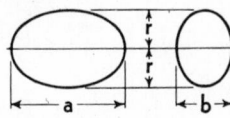

$V = \frac{1}{3}\pi r a b$.

Paraboloid

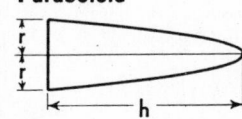

$V = \frac{1}{2}\pi r^2 h$.
Ratio of corresponding volume of a Cone, Paraboloid, Sphere & Cylinder of equal height: $\frac{1}{3}, \frac{1}{2}, \frac{2}{3}, 1$.

RIGHT-ANGLED TRIANGLES

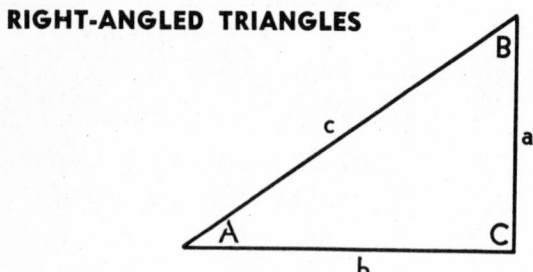

Given	Sought	Formulae
a, c	A, B, b	$\sin A = \dfrac{a}{c}$, $\quad \cos B = \dfrac{a}{c}$, $\quad b = \sqrt{c^2 - a^2}$
	Area	Area $= \dfrac{a}{2}\sqrt{c^2 - a^2}$
a, b	A, B, c	$\tan A = \dfrac{a}{b}$, $\quad \tan B = \dfrac{b}{a}$, $\quad c = \sqrt{a^2 + b^2}$
	Area	Area $= \dfrac{a\,b}{2}$
A, a	B, b, c	$B = 90°-A$, $\quad b = a \cot A$, $\quad c = \dfrac{a}{\sin A}$
	Area	Area $= \dfrac{a^2 \cot A}{2}$
A, b	B, a, c	$B = 90°-A$, $\quad a = b \tan A$, $\quad c = \dfrac{b}{\cos A}$
	Area	Area $= \dfrac{b^2 \tan A}{2}$
A, c	B, a, b	$B = 90°-A$, $\quad a = c \sin A$, $\quad b = c \cos A$
	Area	Area $= \dfrac{c^2 \sin A \cos A}{2}$ or $\dfrac{c^2 \sin 2A}{4}$

OBLIQUE-ANGLED TRIANGLES

$$S = \frac{a+b+c}{2}$$

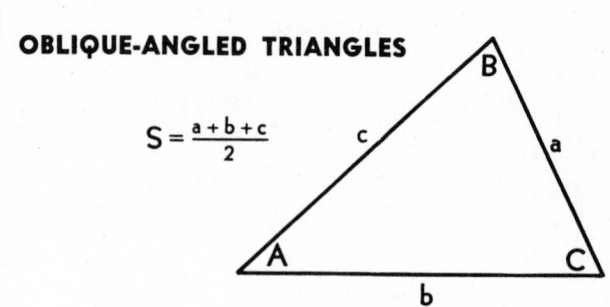

Given	Sought	Formulae
a, b, c	A	$\sin \tfrac{1}{2} A = \sqrt{\dfrac{(s-b)\,(s-c)}{b\,c}}$, $\cos \tfrac{1}{2} A = \sqrt{\dfrac{s(s-a)}{b\,c}}$, $\tan \tfrac{1}{2} A = \sqrt{\dfrac{(s-b)\,(s-c)}{s(s-a)}}$
	B	$\sin \tfrac{1}{2} B = \sqrt{\dfrac{(s-a)\,(s-c)}{a\,c}}$, $\cos \tfrac{1}{2} B = \sqrt{\dfrac{s(s-b)}{a\,c}}$, $\tan \tfrac{1}{2} B = \sqrt{\dfrac{(s-a)\,(s-c)}{s(s-b)}}$
	C	$\sin \tfrac{1}{2} C = \sqrt{\dfrac{(s-a)\,(s-b)}{a\,b}}$, $\cos \tfrac{1}{2} C = \sqrt{\dfrac{s(s-c)}{a\,b}}$, $\tan \tfrac{1}{2} C = \sqrt{\dfrac{(s-a)\,(s-b)}{s(s-c)}}$
	Area	Area $= \sqrt{s\,(s-a)\,(s-b)\,(s-c)}$
a, A, B	b, c	$b = \dfrac{a \sin B}{\sin A}$ $\quad c = \dfrac{a \sin C}{\sin A} = \dfrac{a \sin (A+B)}{\sin A}$
	Area	Area $= \tfrac{1}{2}\,a\,b \sin C = \dfrac{a^2 \sin B \sin C}{2 \sin A}$
a, b, A	B	$\sin B = \dfrac{b \sin A}{a}$
	c	$c = \dfrac{a \sin C}{\sin A} = \dfrac{b \sin C}{\sin B} = \sqrt{a^2 + b^2 - 2\,ab \cos C}$
	Area	Area $= \tfrac{1}{2}\,a\,b \sin C$
a, b, C	A	$\tan A = \dfrac{a \sin C}{b - a \cos C}$, $\quad \tan \tfrac{1}{2}(A-B) = \dfrac{a-b}{a+b} \cot \tfrac{1}{2} C$
	c	$c = \sqrt{a^2 + b^2 - 2\,ab \cos C} = \dfrac{a \sin C}{\sin A}$
	Area	Area $= \tfrac{1}{2}ab \sin C$

$a^2 = b^2 + c^2 - 2bc \cos A$, $\quad b^2 = a^2 + c^2 - 2\,ac \cos B$ $\quad c^2 = a^2 + b^2 - 2\,ab \cos C$

SINES

Degrees	0′	10′	20′	30′	40′	50′	60′	Cosines
0	0.00000	0.00291	0.00582	0.00873	0.01164	0.01454	0.01745	89
1	0.01745	0.02036	0.02327	0.02618	0.02908	0.03199	0.03490	88
2	0.03490	0.03781	0.04071	0.04362	0.04653	0.04943	0.05234	87
3	0.05234	0.05524	0.05814	0.06105	0.06395	0.06685	0.06976	86
4	0.06976	0.07266	0.07556	0.07846	0.08136	0.08426	0.08716	85
5	0.08716	0.09005	0.09295	0.09585	0.09874	0.10164	0.10453	84
6	0.10453	0.10742	0.11031	0.11320	0.11609	0.11898	0.12187	83
7	0.12187	0.12476	0.12764	0.13053	0.13341	0.13629	0.13917	82
8	0.13917	0.14205	0.14493	0.14781	0.15069	0.15356	0.15643	81
9	0.15643	0.15931	0.16218	0.16505	0.16792	0.17078	0.17365	80
10	0.17365	0.17651	0.17937	0.18224	0.18509	0.18795	0.19081	79
11	0.19081	0.19366	0.19652	0.19937	0.20222	0.20507	0.20791	78
12	0.20791	0.21076	0.21360	0.21644	0.21928	0.22212	0.22495	77
13	0.22495	0.22778	0.23062	0.23345	0.23627	0.23910	0.24192	76
14	0.24192	0.24474	0.24756	0.25038	0.25320	0.25601	0.25882	75
15	0.25882	0.26163	0.26443	0.26724	0.27004	0.27284	0.27564	74
16	0.27564	0.27843	0.28123	0.28402	0.28680	0.28959	0.29237	73
17	0.29237	0.29515	0.29793	0.30071	0.30348	0.30625	0.30902	72
18	0.30902	0.31178	0.31454	0.31730	0.32006	0.32282	0.32557	71
19	0.32557	0.32832	0.33106	0.33381	0.33655	0.33929	0.34202	70
20	0.34202	0.34475	0.34748	0.35021	0.35293	0.35565	0.35837	69
21	0.35837	0.36108	0.36379	0.36650	0.36921	0.37191	0.37461	68
22	0.37461	0.37730	0.37999	0.38268	0.38537	0.38805	0.39073	67
23	0.39073	0.39341	0.39608	0.39875	0.40142	0.40408	0.40674	66
24	0.40674	0.40939	0.41204	0.41469	0.41734	0.41998	0.42262	65
25	0.42262	0.42525	0.42788	0.43051	0.43313	0.43575	0.43837	64
26	0.43837	0.44098	0.44359	0.44620	0.44880	0.45140	0.45399	63
27	0.45399	0.45658	0.45917	0.46175	0.46433	0.46690	0.46947	62
28	0.46947	0.47204	0.47460	0.47716	0.47971	0.48226	0.48481	61
29	0.48481	0.48735	0.48989	0.49242	0.49495	0.49748	0.50000	60
30	0.50000	0.50252	0.50503	0.50754	0.51004	0.51254	0.51504	59
31	0.51504	0.51753	0.52002	0.52250	0.52498	0.52745	0.52992	58
32	0.52992	0.53238	0.53484	0.53730	0.53975	0.54220	0.54464	57
33	0.54464	0.54708	0.54951	0.55194	0.55436	0.55678	0.55919	56
34	0.55919	0.56160	0.56401	0.56641	0.56880	0.57119	0.57358	55
35	0.57358	0.57596	0.57833	0.58070	0.58307	0.58543	0.58779	54
36	0.58779	0.59014	0.59248	0.59482	0.59716	0.59949	0.60182	53
37	0.60182	0.60414	0.60645	0.60876	0.61107	0.61337	0.61566	52
38	0.61566	0.61795	0.62024	0.62251	0.62479	0.62706	0.62932	51
39	0.62932	0.63158	0.63383	0.63608	0.63832	0.64056	0.64279	50
40	0.64279	0.64501	0.64723	0.64945	0.65166	0.65386	0.65606	49
41	0.65606	0.65825	0.66044	0.66262	0.66480	0.66697	0.66913	48
42	0.66913	0.67129	0.67344	0.67559	0.67773	0.67987	0.68200	47
43	0.68200	0.68412	0.68624	0.68835	0.69046	0.69256	0.69466	46
44	0.69466	0.69675	0.69883	0.70091	0.70298	0.70505	0.70711	45
Sines	60′	50′	40′	30′	20′	10′	0′	Degrees

COSINES

COSINES

Degrees	0′	10′	20′	30′	40′	50′	60′	Sines
0	1.00000	1.00000	0.99998	0.99996	0.99993	0.99989	0.99985	89
1	0.99985	0.99979	0.99973	0.99966	0.99958	0.99949	0.99939	88
2	0.99939	0.99929	0.99917	0.99905	0.99892	0.99878	0.99863	87
3	0.99863	0.99847	0.99831	0.99813	0.99795	0.99776	0.99756	86
4	0.99756	0.99736	0.99714	0.99692	0.99668	0.99644	0.99619	85
5	0.99619	0.99594	0.99567	0.99540	0.99511	0.99482	0.99452	84
6	0.99452	0.99421	0.99390	0.99357	0.99324	0.99290	0.99255	83
7	0.99255	0.99219	0.99182	0.99144	0.99106	0.99067	0.99027	82
8	0.99027	0.98986	0.98944	0.98902	0.88858	0.98814	0.98769	81
9	0.98769	0.98723	0.98676	0.98629	0.98580	0.98531	0.98481	80
10	0.98481	0.98430	0.98378	0.98325	0.98272	0.98218	0.98163	79
11	0.98163	0.98107	0.98050	0.97992	0.97934	0.97875	0.97815	78
12	0.97815	0.97754	0.97692	0.97630	0.97566	0.97502	0.97437	77
13	0.97437	0.97371	0.97304	0.97237	0.97169	0.97100	0.97030	76
14	0.97030	0.96959	0.96887	0.96815	0.96742	0.96667	0.96593	75
15	0.96593	0.96517	0.96440	0.96363	0.96285	0.96206	0.96126	74
16	0.96126	0.96046	0.95964	0.95882	0.95799	0.95715	0.95630	73
17	0.95630	0.95545	0.95459	0.95372	0.95284	0.95195	0.95106	72
18	0.95106	0.95015	0.94924	0.94832	0.94740	0.94646	0.94552	71
19	0.94552	0.94457	0.94361	0.94264	0.94167	0.94068	0.93969	70
20	0.93969	0.93869	0.93769	0.93667	0.93565	0.93462	0.93358	69
21	0.93358	0.93253	0.93148	0.93042	0.92935	0.92827	0.92718	68
22	0.92718	0.92609	0.92499	0.92388	0.92276	0.92164	0.92050	67
23	0.92050	0.91936	0.91822	0.91706	0.91590	0.91472	0.91355	66
24	0.91355	0.91236	0.91116	0.90996	0.90875	0.90753	0.90631	65
25	0.90631	0.90507	0.90383	0.90259	0.90133	0.90007	0.89879	64
26	0.89879	0.89752	0.89623	0.89493	0.89363	0.89232	0.89101	63
27	0.89101	0.88968	0.88835	0.88701	0.88566	0.88431	0.88295	62
28	0.88295	0.88158	0.88020	0.87882	0.87743	0.87603	0.87462	61
29	0.87462	0.87321	0.87178	0.87036	0.86892	0.86748	0.86603	60
30	0.86603	0.86457	0.86310	0.86163	0.86015	0.85866	0.85717	59
31	0.85717	0.85567	0.85416	0.85264	0.85112	0.84959	0.84805	58
32	0.84805	0.84650	0.84495	0.84339	0.84182	0.84025	0.83867	57
33	0.83867	0.83708	0.83549	0.83389	0.83228	0.83066	0.82904	56
34	0.82904	0.82741	0.82577	0.82413	0.82248	0.82082	0.81915	55
35	0.81915	0.81748	0.81580	0.81412	0.81242	0.81072	0.80902	54
36	0.80902	0.80730	0.80558	0.80386	0.80212	0.80038	0.79864	53
37	0.79864	0.79688	0.79512	0.79335	0.79158	0.78980	0.78801	52
38	0.78801	0.78622	0.78442	0.78261	0.78079	0.77897	0.77715	51
39	0.77715	0.77531	0.77347	0.77162	0.76977	0.76791	0.76604	50
40	0.76604	0.76417	0.76229	0.76041	0.75851	0.75661	0.75471	49
41	0.75471	0.75280	0.75088	0.74896	0.74703	0.74509	0.74314	48
42	0.74314	0.74120	0.73924	0.73728	0.73531	0.73333	0.73135	47
43	0.73135	0.72937	0.72737	0.72537	0.72337	0.72136	0.71934	46
44	0.71934	0.71732	0.71529	0.71325	0.71121	0.70916	0.70711	45
Cosines	60′	50′	40′	30′	20′	10′	0′	Degrees

SINES

TANGENTS

Degrees	0′	10′	20′	30′	40′	50′	60′	Cotangents
0	0.00000	0 00291	0.00582	0.00873	0.01164	0.01455	0.01746	89
1	0.01746	0.02036	0.02328	0.02619	0.02910	0.03201	0.03492	88
2	0.03492	0.03783	0.04075	0.04366	0.04658	0.04949	0.05241	87
3	0.05241	0.05533	0.05824	0.06116	0.06408	0.06700	0.06993	86
4	0.06993	0.07285	0.07578	0.07870	0.08163	0.08456	0.08749	85
5	0.08749	0.09042	0.09335	0.09629	0.09923	0.10216	0.10510	84
6	0.10510	0.10805	0.11099	0.11394	0.11688	0.11983	0.12278	83
7	0.12278	0.12574	0.12869	0.13165	0.13461	0.13758	0.14054	82
8	0.14054	0.14351	0.14648	0.14945	0.15243	0.15540	0.15838	81
9	0.15838	0.16137	0.16435	0.16734	0.17033	0.17333	0.17633	80
10	0.17633	0.17933	0.18233	0.18534	0.18835	0.19136	0.19438	79
11	0.19438	0.19740	0.20042	0.20345	0.20648	0.20952	0.21256	78
12	0.21256	0.21560	0.21864	0.22169	0.22475	0.22781	0.23087	77
13	0.23087	0.23393	0.23700	0.24008	0.24316	0.24624	0.24933	76
14	0.24933	0.25242	0.25552	0.25862	0.26172	0.26483	0.26795	75
15	0.26795	0.27107	0.27419	0.27732	0.28046	0.28360	0.28675	74
16	0.28675	0.28990	0.29305	0.29621	0.29938	0.30255	0.30573	73
17	0.30573	0.30891	0.31210	0.31530	0.31850	0.32171	0.32492	72
18	0.32492	0.32814	0.33136	0.33460	0.33783	0.34108	0.34433	71
19	0.34433	0.34758	0.35085	0.35412	0.35740	0.36068	0.36397	70
20	0.36397	0.36727	0.37057	0.37388	0.37720	0.38053	0.38386	69
21	0.38386	0.38721	0.39055	0.39391	0.39727	0.40065	0.40403	68
22	0.40403	0.40741	0.41081	0.41421	0.41763	0.42105	0.42447	67
23	0.42447	0.42791	0.43136	0.43481	0.43828	0.44175	0.44523	66
24	0.44523	0.44872	0.45222	0.45573	0.45924	0.46277	0.46631	65
25	0.46631	0 46985	0.47341	0.47698	0.48055	0.48414	0.48773	64
26	0.48773	0.49134	0.49495	0.49858	0.50222	0.50587	0.50953	63
27	0.50953	0.51320	0.51688	0.52057	0.52427	0.52798	0.53171	62
28	0.53171	0.53545	0.53920	0.54296	0.54674	0.55051	0.55431	61
29	0.55431	0.55812	0.56194	0.56577	0.56962	0.57348	0.57735	60
30	0.57735	0.58124	0.58513	0.58905	0.59297	0.59691	0.60086	59
31	0.60086	0.60483	0.60881	0.61280	0.61681	0.62083	0.62487	58
32	0.62487	0.62892	0.63299	0.63707	0.64117	0.64528	0.64941	57
33	0.64941	0.65355	0.65771	0.66189	0.66608	0.67028	0.67451	56
34	0.67451	0.67875	0.68301	0.68728	0.69157	0.69588	0.70021	55
35	0.70021	0.70455	0.70891	0.71329	0.71769	0.72211	0.72654	54
36	0.72654	0.73100	0.73547	0.73996	0.74447	0.74900	0.75355	53
37	0.75355	0.75812	0.76272	0.76733	0.77196	0.77661	0.78129	52
38	0.78129	0.78598	0.79070	0.79544	0.80020	0.80498	0.80978	51
39	0.80978	0.81461	0.81946	0.82434	0.82923	0.83415	0.83910	50
40	0.83910	0.84407	0.84906	0.85408	0.85912	0.86419	0.86929	49
41	0.86929	0.87441	0.87955	0.88473	0.88992	0.89515	0.90040	48
42	0.90040	0.90569	0.91099	0.91633	0.92170	0.92709	0.93252	47
43	0.93252	0.93797	0.94345	0.94896	0.95451	0.96008	0,96569	46
44	0.96569	0.97133	0.97700	0.98270	0.98843	0.99420	1.00000	45
Tangents	60′	50′	40′	30′	20′	10′	0′	Degrees

COTANGENTS

COTANGENTS

Degrees	0′	10′	20′	30′	40′	50′	60′	Tangents
0	∞	343.77371	171.88540	114.58865	85.93979	68.75009	57.28996	89
1	57.28996	49.10388	42.96408	38.18846	34.36777	31.24158	28.63625	88
2	28.63625	26.43160	24.54176	22.90377	21.47040	20.20555	19.08114	87
3	19.08114	18.07498	17.16934	16.34986	15.60478	14.92442	14.30067	86
4	14.30067	13.72674	13.19688	12.70621	12.25051	11.82617	11.43005	85
5	11.43005	11.05943	10.71191	10.38540	10.07803	9.78817	9.51436	84
6	9.51436	9.25530	9.00983	8.77689	8.55555	8.34496	8.14435	83
7	8.14435	7.95302	7.77035	7.59575	7.42871	7.26873	7.11537	82
8	7.11537	6.96823	6.82694	6.69116	6.56055	6.43484	6.31375	81
9	6.31375	6.19703	6.08444	5.97576	5.87080	5.76937	5.67128	80
10	5.67128	5.57638	5.48451	5.39552	5.30928	5.22566	5.14455	79
11	5.14455	5.06584	4.98940	4.91516	4.84300	4.77286	4.70463	78
12	4.70463	4.63825	4.57363	4.51071	4.44942	4.38969	4.33148	77
13	4.33148	4.27471	4.21933	4.16530	4.11256	4.06107	4.01078	76
14	4.01078	3.96165	3.91364	3.86671	3.82083	3.77595	3.73205	75
15	3.73205	3.68909	3.64705	3.60588	3.56557	3.52609	3.48741	74
16	3.48741	3.44951	3.41236	3.37594	3.34023	3.30521	3.27085	73
17	3.27085	3.23714	3.20406	3.17159	3.13972	3.10842	3.07768	72
18	3.07768	3.04749	3.01783	2.98869	2.96004	2.93189	2.90421	71
19	2.90421	2.87700	2.85023	2.82391	2.79802	2.77254	2.74748	70
20	2.74748	2.72281	2.69853	2.67462	2.65109	2.62791	2.60509	69
21	2.60509	2.58261	2.56046	2.53865	2.51715	2.49597	2.47509	68
22	2.47509	2.45451	2.43422	2.41421	2.39449	2.37504	2.35585	67
23	2.35585	2.33693	2.31826	2.29984	2.28167	2.26374	2.24604	66
24	2.24604	2.22857	2.21132	2.19430	2.17749	2.16090	2.14451	65
25	2.14451	2.12832	2.11233	2.09654	2.08094	2.06553	2.05030	64
26	2.05030	2.03526	2.02039	2.00569	1.99116	1.97680	1.96261	63
27	1.96261	1.94858	1.93470	1.92098	1.90741	1.89400	1.88073	62
28	1.88073	1.86760	1.85462	1.84177	1.82907	1.81649	1.80405	61
29	1.80405	1.79174	1.77955	1.76749	1.75556	1.74375	1.73205	60
30	1.73205	1.72047	1.70901	1.69766	1.68643	1.67530	1.66428	59
31	1.66428	1.65337	1.64256	1.63185	1.62125	1.61074	1.60033	58
32	1.60033	1.59002	1.57981	1.56969	1.55966	1.54972	1.53987	57
33	1.53987	1.53010	1.52043	1.51084	1.50133	1.49190	1.48256	56
34	1.48256	1.47330	1.46411	1.45501	1.44598	1.43703	1.42815	55
35	1.42815	1.41934	1.41061	1.40195	1.39336	1.38484	1.37638	54
36	1.37638	1.36800	1.35968	1.35142	1.34323	1.33511	1.32704	53
37	1.32704	1.31904	1.31110	1.30323	1.29541	1.28764	1.27994	52
38	1.27994	1.27230	1.26471	1.25717	1.24969	1.24227	1.23490	51
39	1.23490	1.22758	1.22031	1.21310	1.20593	1.19882	1.19175	50
40	1.19175	1.18474	1.17777	1.17085	1.16398	1.15715	1.15037	49
41	1.15037	1.14363	1.13694	1.13029	1.12369	1.11713	1.11061	48
42	1.11061	1.10414	1.09770	1.09131	1.08496	1.07864	1.07237	47
43	1.07237	1.06613	1.05994	1.05378	1.04766	1.04158	1.03553	46
44	1.03553	1.02952	1.02355	1.01761	1.01170	1.00583	1.00000	45
Cotangents	60′	50′	40′	30′	20′	10′	0	Degrees

TANGENTS

SECANTS

Degrees	0′	10′	20′	30′	40′	50′	60′	Cosecants
0	1.00000	1.00000	1.00002	1.00004	1.00007	1.00011	1.00015	89
1	1.00015	1.00021	1.00027	1.00034	1.00042	1.00051	1.00061	88
2	1.00061	1.00072	1.00083	1.00095	1.00108	1.00122	1.00137	87
3	1.00137	1.00153	1.00169	1.00187	1.00205	1.00224	1.00244	86
4	1.00244	1.00265	1.00287	1.00309	1.00333	1.00357	1.00382	85
5	1.00382	1.00408	1.00435	1.00463	1.00491	1.00521	1.00551	84
6	1.00551	1.00582	1.00614	1.00647	1.00681	1.00715	1.00751	83
7	1.00751	1.00787	1.00825	1.00863	1 00902	1.00942	1.00983	82
8	1.00983	1.01024	1.01067	1.01111	1.01155	1.01200	1.01247	81
9	1.01247	1.01294	1.01342	1.01391	1.01440	1.01491	1.01543	80
10	1.01543	1.01595	1.01649	1.01703	1.01758	1.01815	1.01872	79
11	1.01872	1.01930	1.01989	1.02049	1.02110	1.02171	1.02234	78
12	1.02234	1.02298	1.02362	1.02428	1.02494	1.02562	1.02630	77
13	1.02630	1.02700	1.02770	1.02842	1.02914	1.02987	1.03061	76
14	1.03061	1.03137	1.03213	1.03290	1.03368	0.03447	1.03528	75
15	1.03528	1.03609	1.03691	1.03774	1.03858	1.03944	1.04030	74
16	1.04030	1.04117	1.04206	1.04295	1.04385	1.04477	1.04569	73
17	1.04569	1.04663	1.04757	1.04853	1.04950	1.05047	1.05146	72
18	1.05146	1.05246	1.05347	1.05449	1.05552	1.05657	1.05762	71
19	1.05762	1.05869	1.05976	1.06085	1.06195	1.06306	1.06418	70
20	1.06418	1.06531	1.06645	1.06761	1.06878	1.06995	1.07115	69
21	1.07115	1.07235	1.07356	1.07479	1.07602	1.07727	1.07853	68
22	1.07853	1.07981	1.08109	1.08239	1.08370	1.08503	1 08636	67
23	1.08636	1.08771	1.08907	1.09044	1.09183	1.09323	1.09464	66
24	1.09464	1.09606	1.09750	1.09895	1.10041	1.10189	1.10338	65
25	1.10338	1.10488	1.10640	1.10793	1.10947	1.11103	1.11260	64
26	1.11260	1.11419	1.11579	1.11740	1.11903	1.12067	1.12233	63
27	1.12233	1.12400	1.12568	1.12738	1.12910	1.13083	1.13257	62
28	1.13257	1.13433	1.13610	1.13789	1.13970	1.14152	1.14335	61
29	1.14335	1.14521	1.14707	1.14896	1.15085	1.15277	1.15470	60
30	1.15470	1.15665	1.15861	1.16059	1.16259	1.16460	1.16663	59
31	1.16663	1.16868	1.17075	1.17283	1.17493	1.17704	1.17918	58
32	1.17918	1.18133	1.18350	1.18569	1.18790	1.19012	1.19236	57
33	1.19236	1.19463	1.19691	1.19920	1.20152	1.20386	1.20622	56
34	1.20622	1.20859	1.21099	1.21341	1.21584	1.21830	1.22077	55
35	1.22077	1.22327	1.22579	1.22833	1.23089	1.23347	1.23607	54
36	1.23607	1.23869	1.24134	1.24400	1.24669	1.24940	1.25214	53
37	1.25214	1.25489	1.25767	1.26047	1.26330	1.26615	1.26902	52
38	1.26902	1.27191	1.27483	1.27778	1.28075	1.28374	1.28676	51
39	1.28676	1.28980	1.29287	1.29597	1.29909	1.30223	1.30541	50
40	1.30541	1.30861	1.31183	1.31509	1.31837	1.32168	1.32501	49
41	1.32501	1.32838	1.33177	1.33519	1.33864	1.34212	1.34563	48
42	1.34563	1.34917	1.35274	1.35634	1.35997	1.36363	1.36733	47
43	1.36733	1.37105	1.37481	1.37860	1.38242	1.38628	1.39016	46
44	1.39016	1.39409	1.39804	1.40203	1.40606	1.41012	1.41421	45
Secants	60′	50′	40′	30′	20′	10′	0′	Degrees

COSECANTS

COSECANTS

Degrees	0′	10′	20′	30′	40′	50′	60′	Secants
0	∞	343.77516	171.88831	114.59301	85.94561	68.75736	57.29869	89
1	57.29869	49.11406	42.97571	38.20155	34.38232	31.25758	28.65371	88
2	28.65371	26.45051	24.56212	22.92559	21.49368	20.23028	19.10732	87
3	19.10732	18.10262	17.19843	16.38041	15.63679	14.95788	14.33559	86
4	14.33559	13.76312	13.23472	12.74550	12.29125	11.86837	11.47371	85
5	11.47371	11.10455	10.75849	10.43343	10.12752	9.83912	9.56677	84
6	9.56677	9.30917	9.06515	8.83367	8.61379	8.40466	8.20551	83
7	8.20551	8.01565	7.83443	7.66130	7.49571	7.33719	7.18530	82
8	7.18530	7.03962	6.89979	6.76547	6.63633	6.51208	6.39245	81
9	6.39245	6.27719	6.16607	6.05886	5.95536	5.85539	5.75877	80
10	5.75877	5.66533	5.57493	5.48740	5.40263	5.32049	5.24084	79
11	5.24084	5.16359	5.08863	5.01585	4.94517	4.87649	4.80973	78
12	4.80973	4.74482	4.68167	4.62023	4.56041	4.50216	4.44541	77
13	4.44541	4.39012	4.33622	4.28366	4.23239	4.18238	4.13357	76
14	4.13357	4.08591	4.03938	3.99393	3.94952	3.90613	3.86370	75
15	3.86370	3.82223	3.78166	3.74198	3.70315	3.66515	3.62796	74
16	3.62796	3.59154	3.55587	3.52094	3.48671	3.45317	3.42030	73
17	3.02030	3.38808	3.35649	3.32551	3.29512	3.26531	3.23607	72
18	3.23607	3.20737	3.17920	3.15155	3.12440	3.09774	3.07155	71
19	3.07155	3.04584	3.02057	2.99574	2.97135	2.94737	2.92380	70
20	2.92380	2.90063	2.87785	2.85545	2.83342	2.81175	2.79043	69
21	2.79043	2.76945	2.74881	2.72850	2.70851	2.68884	2.66947	68
22	2.66947	2.65040	2.63162	2.61313	2.59491	2.57698	2.55930	67
23	2.55930	2.54190	2.52474	2.50784	2.49119	2.47477	2.45859	66
24	2.45859	2.44264	2.42692	2.41142	2.39614	2.38107	2.36620	65
25	2.36620	2.35154	2.33708	2.32282	2.30875	2.29487	2.28117	64
26	2.28117	2.26766	2.25432	2.24116	2.22817	2,21535	2.20269	63
27	2.20269	2.19019	2.17786	2.16568	2.15366	2.14178	2.13005	62
28	2.13005	2.11847	2.10704	2.09574	2.08458	2.07356	2.06267	61
29	2.06267	2.05191	2.04128	2.03077	2.02039	2.01014	2.00000	60
30	2.00000	1.98998	1.98008	1.97029	1.96062	1.95106	1.94160	59
31	1.94160	1.93226	1.92302	1.91388	1.90485	1.89591	1.88709	58
32	1.88708	1.87834	1.86970	1.86116	1.85271	1.84435	1.83608	57
33	1.83608	1.82790	1.81981	1.81180	1.80388	1.79604	1.78829	56
34	1.78829	1.78062	1.77303	1.76552	1.75808	1.75073	1.74345	55
35	1.74345	1.73624	1.72911	1.72205	1.71506	1.70815	1.70130	54
36	1.70130	1.69452	1.68782	1.68117	1.67460	1.66809	1.66164	53
37	1.66164	1.65526	1.64894	1.64268	1.63648	1.63035	1.62427	52
38	1.62427	1.61825	1.61229	1.60639	1.60054	1.59475	1.58902	51
39	1.58902	1.58333	1.57771	1.57213	1.56661	1.56114	1.55572	50
40	1.55572	1.55036	1.54504	1.53977	1.53455	1.52938	1.52425	49
41	1.52425	1.51918	1.51415	1.50916	1.50422	1.49933	1.49448	48
42	1.49448	1.48967	1.48491	1.48019	1.47551	1.47087	1.46628	47
43	1.46628	1.46173	1.45721	1.45274	1.44831	1.44391	1.43956	46
44	1.43956	1.43524	1.43096	1.42672	1.42251	1.41835	1.41421	45
Cosecants	60′	50′	40′	30′	20′	10′	0′	Degrees

SECANTS

Units of measurement

LINEAR MEASURE

Measures of Length

12 inches	= 1 foot
3 feet	= 1 yard
5½ yards = 16½ feet	= 1 rod, pole or perch
40 poles = 220 yards	= 1 furlong
8 furlongs = 1760 yards = 5280 feet	= 1 mile
3 miles	= 1 league
4 inches	= 1 hand
9 inches	= 1 span

Nautical Units

6080.20 feet	= 1 nautical mile
6 feet	= 1 fathom
120 fathoms	= 1 cable length
1 nautical mile per hr.	= 1 knot

Surveyor's or Gunter's Measure

7.92 inches	= 1 link
100 links = 66 ft. = 4 rods	= 1 chain
80 chains	= 1 mile
33⅓ inches	= 1 vara (Texas)

Length Equivalents

Centimeters	Inches	Feet	Yards	Meters	Chains	Kilometers	Miles
1	0.3937	0.03281	0.01094	0.01	0.0_34971	10^{-5}	0.0_56214
2.540	1	0.08333	0.02778	0.0254	0.001263	0.0_4254	0.0_41578
30.48	12	1	0.3333	0.3048	0.01515	0.0_33048	0.0_31894
91.44	36	3	1	0.9144	0.04545	0.0_39144	0.0_35682
100	39.37	3.281	1.0936	1	0.04971	0.001	0.0_36214
2012	792	66	22	20.12	1	0.02012	0.0125
100000	39370	3281	1093.6	1000	49.71	1	0.6214
160935	63360	5280	1760	1609	80	1.609	1

Subscripts after any figure, 0_3, 9_4, etc., mean that that figure is to be repeated the indicated number of times.

MEASURES OF AREA

144	square inches	= 1 square foot
9	square feet	= 1 square yard
30¼	square yards	= 1 square rod, pole or perch
160	square rods	
	= 10 square chains	
	= 43,560 sq. ft.	= 1 acre
	= 5645 sq. varas (Texas)	

640 acres = 1 square mile = 1 "section" of U. S. Govt. surveyed land

Area Equivalents

Square Meters	Square Inches	Square Feet	Square Yards	Square Rods	Square Chains	Roods	Acres	Square Miles or Sections
1	1550	10.76	1.196	0.0395	0.002471	0.0_39884	0.0_32471	0.0_63861
0.0_36452	1	0.006944	0.0_37716	0.0_42551	0.0_51594	0.0_66377	0.0_61594	0.0_92491
0.09290	144	1	0.1111	0.003673	0.0_32296	0.0_49184	0.0_42296	0.0_73587
0.8361	1296	9	1	0.03306	0.002066	0.0_38264	0.0002066	0.0_63228
25.29	39204	272.25	30.25	1	0.0625	0.02500	0.00625	0.0_59766
404.7	627264	4356	484	16	1	0.4	0.1	0.0001562
1012	1568160	10890	1210	40	2.5	1	0.25	0.0_33906
4047	6272640	43560	4840	160	10	4	1	0.001562
2589998	....	27878400	3097600	102400	6400	2560	640	1

(1 hectare = 100 ares = 10,000 centiares or square meters)

Subscripts after any figure 0_3, 9_4, etc., mean that that figure is to be repeated the indicated number of times.

VOLUMETRIC MEASURE

Measures of Volume

1728 cubic inches	= 1 cubic foot
27 cubic feet	= 1 cubic yard
1 cord of wood	= 128 cu. ft.
1 perch of masonry	= 16½ to 25 cu. ft.

Dry Measure

2 pints	= 1 quart
8 quarts	= 1 peck
4 pecks	= 1 bushel

1 std. bbl. for fruits and vegetables = 7056 cu. in. or 105 dry quarts, struck measure

Board Measure

1 board foot = $\begin{cases} 144 \text{ cu. in.} = \text{volume of board 1 ft. sq. and} \\ 1 \text{ in. thick.} \end{cases}$

No. of board feet in a log = $[¼(d-4)]^2L$, where d = diam. of log (usually taken inside the bark at small end), in., and L = length of log, ft. The 4 in. deducted is an allowance for slab. This rule is variously known as the Doyle, Conn. River, St. Croix, Thurber, Moore and Beeman, and the Scribner rule.

Liquid or Fluid Measure

4 gills	= 1 pint
2 pints	= 1 quart
4 quarts	= 1 gallon
7.4805 gallons	= 1 cubic foot

(There is no standard liquid barrel; by trade custom, 1 bbl. of petroleum oil, unrefined = 42 gal.)

Volume and Capacity Equivalents

Cubic inches	Cubic feet	Cubic yards	U. S. Apothecary liquid ounces	U. S. quarts Liquid	U. S. quarts Dry	U. S. gallons Liquid	U. S. gallons Dry	Bushels U.S.	Liters (l)
1	0.0_35787	0.0_42143	0.5541	0.01732	0.01488	0.0_24329	0.0_23720	0.0_34650	0.01639
1728	1	0.03704	957.5	29.92	25.71	7.481	6.429	0.8036	28.32
46656	27	1	25853	807.9	694.3	202.0	173.6	21.70	764.6
1.805	0.001044	0.0_43868	1	0.03125	0.02686	0.007813	0.006714	0.0_38392	0.02957
57.75	0.03342	0.001238	32	1	0.8594	0.25	0.2148	0.02686	0.9464
67.20	0.03889	0.001440	37.24	1.164	1	0.2909	0.25	0.03125	1.101
231	0.1337	0.004951	128	4	3.437	1	0.8594	0.1074	3.785
268.8	0.1556	0.005761	148.9	4.655	4	1.164	1	0.125	4.405
2150	1.244	0.04609	1192	37.24	32	9.309	8	1	35.24
61.02	0.03531	0.001308	33.81	1.057	0.9081	0.2642	0.2270	0.02838	1

Subscripts after any figure, 0_3, 9_4, etc., mean that that figure is to be repeated the indicated number of times.

MEASURES OF WEIGHT

Weights

(The grain is the same in all systems)

Avoirdupois Weight

16 drams = 437.5 grains	= 1 ounce
16 ounces = 7000 grains	= 1 pound
100 pounds	= 1 cental
2000 pounds	= 1 short ton
2240 pounds	= 1 long ton
1 std. lime bbl., small	= 180 lb. net
1 std. lime bbl., large	= 280 lb. net

Also (in Great Britain):

14 pounds	= 1 stone
2 stone = 28 lb.	= 1 quarter
4 quarters = 112 lb.	= 1 hundred-weight (cwt.)
20 hundredweight	= 1 long ton

Troy Weight

24 grains	= 1 pennyweight (dwt.)
20 pennyweights = 480 grains	= 1 ounce
12 ounces = 5760 grains	= 1 pound

1 Assay Ton = 29,167 milligrams, or as many milligrams as there are troy ounces in a ton of 2000 lb. avoirdupois. Consequently, the number of milligrams of precious metal yielded by an assay ton of ore gives directly the number of troy ounces that would be obtained from a ton of 2000 lb. avoirdupois.

Apothecaries' Weight

20 grains	= 1 scruple ℈
3 scruples = 60 grains	= 1 dram ʒ
8 drams	= 1 ounce ℥
12 ounces = 5760 grains	= 1 pound

Mass Equivalents

Kilograms	Grains	Ounces Troy and apoth.	Ounces Avoirdupois	Pounds Troy and apoth.	Pounds Avoirdupois	Tons Short	Tons Long	Tons Metric
1	15432	32.15	35.27	2.6792	2.205	0.0_21102	0.0_39842	0.001
0.0_46480	1	0.0_22083	0.0_22286	0.0_31736	0.0_31429	0.0_77143	0.0_76378	0.0_76480
0.03110	480	1	1.09714	0.08333	0.06857	0.0_43429	0.0_43061	0.0_43110
0.02835	437.5	0.9115	1	0.07595	0.0625	0.0_43125	0.0_42790	0.0_42835
0.3732	5760	12	13.17	1	0.8229	0.0_34114	0.0_53673	0.0_33732
0.4536	7000	14.58	16	1.215	1	0.0005	0.0_34464	0.0_34536
907.2	140_6	29167	320_3	2431	2000	1	0.8929	0.9072
1016	15680_4	32667	35840	2722	2240	1.12	1	1.016
1000	15432356	32151	35274	2679	2205	1.102	0.9842	1

Subscripts after any figure, 0_3, 9_4, etc., mean that that figure is to be repeated the indicated number of times.

DECIMAL OF AN INCH AND OF A FOOT

Fractions of Inch or Foot		Inch Equiv. to Foot Fractions	Fractions of Inch or Foot		Inch Equiv. to Foot Fractions	Fractions of Inch or Foot		Inch Equiv. to Foot Fractions	Fractions of Inch or Foot		Inch Equiv. to Foot Fractions
	.0052	1/16		.2552	3 1/16		.5052	6 1/16		.7552	9 1/16
	.0104	1/8		.2604	3 1/8		.5104	6 1/8		.7604	9 1/8
1/64	.015625	3/16	17/64	.265625	3 3/16	33/64	.515625	6 3/16	49/64	.765625	9 3/16
	.0208	1/4		.2708	3 1/4		.5208	6 1/4		.7708	9 1/4
	.0260	5/16		.2760	3 5/16		.5260	6 5/16		.7760	9 5/16
1/32	.03125	3/8	9/32	.28125	3 3/8	17/32	.53125	6 3/8	25/32	.78125	9 3/8
	.0365	7/16		.2865	3 7/16		.5365	6 7/16		.7865	9 7/16
	.0417	1/2		.2917	3 1/2		.5417	6 1/2		.7917	9 1/2
3/64	.046875	9/16	19/64	.296875	3 9/16	35/64	.546875	6 9/16	51/64	.796875	9 9/16
	.0521	5/8		.3021	3 5/8		.5521	6 5/8		.8021	9 5/8
	.0573	11/16		.3073	3 11/16		.5573	6 11/16		.8073	9 11/16
1/16	.0625	3/4	5/16	.3125	3 3/4	9/16	.5625	6 3/4	13/16	.8125	9 3/4
	.0677	13/16		.3177	3 13/16		.5677	6 13/16		.8177	9 13/16
	.0729	7/8		.3229	3 7/8		.5729	6 7/8		.8229	9 7/8
5/64	.078125	15/16	21/64	.328125	3 15/16	37/64	.578125	6 15/16	53/64	.828125	9 15/16
	.0833	1		.3333	4		.5833	7		.8333	10
	.0885	1 1/16		.3385	4 1/16		.5885	7 1/16		.8385	10 1/16
3/32	.09375	1 1/8	11/32	.34375	4 1/8	19/32	.59375	7 1/8	27/32	.84375	10 1/8
	.0990	1 3/16		.3490	4 3/16		.5990	7 3/16		.8490	10 3/16
	.1042	1 1/4		.3542	4 1/4		.6042	7 1/4		.8542	10 1/4
7/64	.109375	1 5/16	23/64	.359375	4 5/16	39/64	.609375	7 5/16	55/64	.859375	10 5/16
	.1146	1 3/8		.3646	4 3/8		.6146	7 3/8		.8646	10 3/8
	.1198	1 7/16		.3698	4 7/16		.6198	7 7/16		.8698	10 7/16
1/8	.1250	1 1/2	3/8	.3750	4 1/2	5/8	.6250	7 1/2	7/8	.8750	10 1/2
	.1302	1 9/16		.3802	4 9/16		.6302	7 9/16		.8802	10 9/16
	.1354	1 5/8		.3854	4 5/8		.6354	7 5/8		.8854	10 5/8
9/64	.140625	1 11/16	25/64	.390625	4 11/16	41/64	.640625	7 11/16	57/64	.890625	10 11/16
	.1458	1 3/4		.3958	4 3/4		.6458	7 3/4		.8958	10 3/4
	.1510	1 13/16		.4010	4 13/16		.6510	7 13/16		.9010	10 13/16
5/32	.15625	1 7/8	13/32	.40625	4 7/8	21/32	.65625	7 7/8	29/32	.90625	10 7/8
	.1615	1 15/16		.4115	4 15/16		.6615	7 15/16		.9115	10 15/16
	.1667	2		.4167	5		.6667	8		.9167	11
11/64	.171875	2 1/16	27/64	.421875	5 1/16	43/64	.671875	8 1/16	59/64	.921875	11 1/16
	.1771	2 1/8		.4271	5 1/8		.6771	8 1/8		.9271	11 1/8
	.1823	2 3/16		.4323	5 3/16		.6823	8 3/16		.9323	11 3/16
3/16	.1875	2 1/4	7/16	.4375	5 1/4	11/16	.6875	8 1/4	15/16	.9375	11 1/4
	.1927	2 5/16		.4427	5 5/16		.6927	8 5/16		.9427	11 5/16
	.1979	2 3/8		.4479	5 3/8		.6979	8 3/8		.9479	11 3/8
13/64	.203125	2 7/16	29/64	.453125	5 7/16	45/64	.703125	8 7/16	61/64	.953125	11 7/16
	.2083	2 1/2		.4583	5 1/2		.7083	8 1/2		.9583	11 1/2
	.2135	2 9/16		.4635	5 9/16		.7135	8 9/16		.9635	11 9/16
7/32	.21875	2 5/8	15/32	.46875	5 5/8	23/32	.71875	8 5/8	31/32	.96875	11 5/8
	.2240	2 11/16		.4740	5 11/16		.7240	8 11/16		.9740	11 11/16
	.2292	2 3/4		.4792	5 3/4		.7292	8 3/4		.9792	11 3/4
15/64	.234375	2 13/16	31/64	.484375	5 13/16	47/64	.734375	8 13/16	63/64	.984375	11 13/16
	.2396	2 7/8		.4896	5 7/8		.7396	8 7/8		.9896	11 7/8
	.2448	2 15/16		.4948	5 15/16		.7448	8 15/16		.9948	11 15/16
1/4	.2500	3	1/2	.5000	6	3/4	.7500	9	1	1.0000	12

METRIC CONVERSION FACTORS

METRIC TO AMERICAN

Millimeters ÷ 25.4 = inches
Centimeters × 0.3937 = inches
Meters × 39.27 = inches
Millimeters × 0.003281 = feet
Centimeters × 0.03281 = feet
Meters × 3.281 = feet
Meters × 1.094 = yards
Kilometers × 0.621 = miles
Kilometers × 3280.7 = feet
Square millimeters ÷ 645.1 = square inches
Square centimeters ÷ 6.451 = square inches
Square meters × 10.764 = square feet
Square kilometers × 247.1 = acres
Hectares × 2.471 = acres
Cubic centimeters ÷ 16.383 = cubic inches
Cubic meters × 35.315 = cubic feet
Cubic meters × 1.308 = cubic yards
Cubic meters × 264.2 = gallons
Liters × 61.022 = cubic inches
Liters × 0.2642 = gallons
Liters ÷ 28.316 = cubic feet
Hectoliters × 3.531 = cubic feet
Hectoliters × 2.84 = bushels
Hectoliters × 0.131 = cubic yards
Hectoliters × 26.42 = gallons
Kilograms × 2.2046 = pounds
Kilograms ÷ 1102.3 = tons

AMERICAN TO METRIC

Inches × 25.4 = millimeters
Inches × 2.54 = centimeters
Inches × 0.0254 = meters
Feet × 304.8 = millimeters
Feet × 30.48 = centimeters
Feet × 0.3048 = meters
Yards × 0.9143 = meters
Miles × 1.6093 = kilometers
Feet ÷ 3280.7 = kilometers
Square inches × 645.1 = square millimeters
Square inches × 6.451 = square centimeters
Square feet ÷ 10.764 = square inches
Acres ÷ 247.1 = square kilometers
Acres ÷ 2.471 = hectares
Cubic inches × 16.383 = cubic centimeters
Cubic feet ÷ 35.315 = cubic meters
Cubic yards ÷ 1.308 = cubic meters
Gallons (231 cu. in.) ÷ 264.2 = cubic meters
Cubic inches ÷ 61.022 = liters
Gallons × 3.78 = liters
Cubic feet × 28.316 = liters
Cubic feet ÷ 3.531 = hectoliters
Bushels ÷ 2.84 = hectoliters
Cubic yards ÷ 0.131 = hectoliters
Gallons ÷ 26.42 = hectoliters
Pounds ÷ 2.2046 = kilograms
Tons × 1102.3 = kilograms

METRIC MEASURES

Linear	Liquid and Dry	Weights
10 millimeters = 1 centimeter	10 milliliters = 1 centiliter	10 milligrams = 1 centigram
10 centimeters = 1 decimeter	10 centiliters = 1 deciliter	10 centigrams = 1 decigram
10 decimeters = 1 METER (m)	10 deciliters = 1 LITER (l)	10 decigrams = 1 GRAM (g)
10 meters = 1 decameter	10 liters = 1 decaliter	10 grams = 1 decagram
10 decameters = 1 hectometer	10 decaliters = 1 hectoliter	10 decagrams = 1 hectogram
10 hectometers = 1 kilometer	10 hectoliters = 1 kiloliter	10 hectograms = 1 kilogram

USEFUL CURVES AND CURVED SURFACES—1
Introduction

By SEYMOUR HOWARD, *Architect*
Associate Professor, Pratt Institute

The forms most suitable for the solution of many structural problems require facility in drawing and using curves. Many good designs have never been carried out because information has not been readily available on curve characteristics and methods for laying them out. These and subsequent sheets will provide such information, not only on the familiar curves, but also on curves used for geodesic lines on surfaces and for thin shells.

Simple, direct methods exist for drawing some curves. Most, however, require the setting of points by calculation or by geometrical construction. Great care must be taken in connecting the points to obtain a "fair" curve.

A fair curve is one in which there are no local undesired irregularities. The easiest way to judge fairness is to look along the curve as nearly as possible in the plane of the curve.

When a large number of similar curves must be drawn it is economical to use special machines.

Plastic or wooden templates are available in many types for joining points in a smooth curve. Sets of railroad curves are arcs of circles of varying radii and different arc lengths. Copenhagen ship curves are based on the most usual curves found in hull design. Small circle and ellipse templates are often an aid in drafting. Parabolic templates would be a great help for making structural analysis drawings. The usual French curves can be manipulated to join points by smooth curves, but they must be used carefully when they do not fit the curve exactly.

For drawing curves which do not lend themselves to simple mathematical analysis, the best method is to use wood splines or battens, held in position by lead weights called ducks.

It is not always necessary or desirable that a curve be one for which a simple equation can be written. The curves which determine the shape of a ship's hull, for example, are developed by eye on the basis of experiment and past experience.

Curves developed purely by drawing should be drawn on a material unaffected by changes in temperature or humidity, or the temperature and humidity should be kept constant in the drawing room. Marble slabs are sometimes used. If paper must be used, check points or grid lines can be marked for subsequent verification.

Such curves can be reproduced by measuring offsets from a baseline or preferably from the nearest gridline. Once a table of offsets has been made the curve can be redrawn easily at any time and at any scale.

Remarks on Curves Included

Each curve on the following sheets is accurately drawn, and its most characteristic relationships are shown. In architectural design and layout, direct geometrical methods of constructing the curve and finding tangents, etc. are the most useful and are shown where possible. For use in checking points and for engineering calculations the formulas may be more useful.

The *standard form* of the equation of a curve is one based on rectangular Cartesian coördinates in which the y ordinates are given as a function of the x intercepts. It is the form most often used in the building field.

The *parametric* equation is also based on rectangular coördinates but both the y ordinates and the x intercepts are expressed in terms of a third variable. (Such as $x = a \cos t$; $y = b \sin t$.)

The *polar equation* of a curve gives points as measured along a line from a central point or pole. The distance from the pole is expressed as a function of the angle between the base line and the line along which the distance is measured. Curves such as spirals are best given in this form.

In field layout the polar equation can be used to find points on a curve by chaining out from a centrally located transit, measuring off angles from a base line.

Tangents and normals to a curve at various points are necessary in order to work out neatly the intersections of straight lines or curves with the particular curve under consideration. The tangent and normal at any point on a curved structure such as an arch or a shell also give the directions along which forces should be resolved in order to analyze their effect on the structure most easily.

If the centers of curvature for all points on a curve are plotted, a new curve will be generated called the *evolute*, which is useful in visualizing the curvature of the curve. In engineering analysis the curvature of a deflection curve is the link by which deflection and bending moment (and therefore shear and loading) can be related.

From the evolute the original curve can be generated as indicated in Fig. 2.

Lengths of curves are given where convenient expressions exist. For practical drafting room use the length can be found most quickly by measuring along the curve with a strip of paper. By ticking off points as this is done the work can be done accurately and can be checked. For other purposes, such as determining lengths of cables for cutting, the exact formulas must be used, with allowance for stretch due to loading and temperature.

The *moment of inertia* of a curve

can be useful for long-barrel thin-shell structures in which the cross section of the shell (basically only a curved line) corresponds to the cross section of a beam.

The *areas* under certain curves and their centroids or centers of gravity are given and can be used for calculating the cubages and surfaces of parts of a building. They may also be useful in calculation of deflection (the moment-area method).

Conic Sections

Curves formed by the intersection of a plane with a right circular cone are all of the class called *conic sections*. The relationship between the plane, the cone and the conic section can be seen by the construction in Fig. 1.

A right circular cone is shown with vertex at V, cut by the plane of a conic. The plane is tangent at F to a sphere which lies wholly inside of the cone and which is tangent to the cone along a circle (like a latitude circle on the earth). The center of this tangent circle is at M; the center of the sphere is at C. The centerline of the cone lies on the line VNMC, in

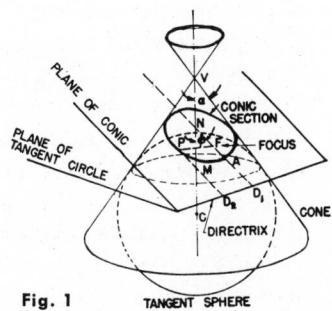

Fig. 1   TANGENT SPHERE

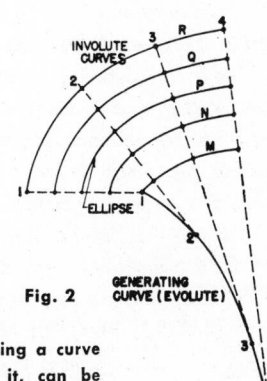

Fig. 2   GENERATING CURVE (EVOLUTE)

Right: The use of an evolute curve in generating a curve such as an ellipse, and curves parallel to it, can be visualized by imagining a flexible, elastic ruler starting at point 1 on curve R and lying along the evolute curve. As it springs away from the evolute, its straight portion would be 2-2, 3-3, 4-4, etc. In this sketch only curve P is a true ellipse; other curves are parallel

Left: Basic relationships of a conic section. See also Sheet 19

which N is the intersection of the centerline or axis of the conic section with the centerline of the cone.

In all conic sections (ellipse, parabola, hyperbola) the focus is the point of tangency between the plane of the conic and the tangent sphere; and the directrix is the line of intersection of the plane of the conic with the plane of the tangent circle.

If α is the angle which the axis of the cone makes with the side of the cone and ϕ is the angle which the

plane of the conic makes with the axis of the cone.

$$\frac{PF}{PD_2} = \frac{\cos \phi}{\cos \alpha}$$

This is called the eccentricity of the conic.

Note that the same shape of curve can be generated on cones of different slope (α) by varying the angle of the plane of the conic (ϕ). For the same shape of curve only $\dfrac{\cos \phi}{\cos \alpha}$ must have the same value.

PARABOLA

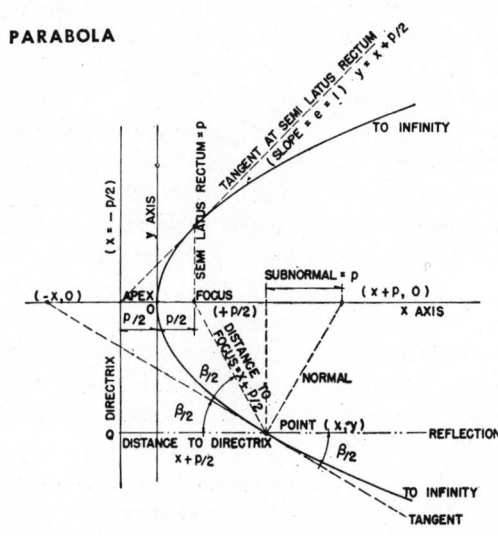

Definition:

$$\frac{\text{Distance from any point to focus}}{\text{Distance from point to directrix}} = \frac{PF}{PQ} = 1 = \text{eccentricity (e)}$$

Equation (standard form): $y^2 = 2px$

Note from characteristics of tangent, that a line from the focus (a ray of light, for example) to any point on the parabola will be reflected parallel to the axis of the parabola

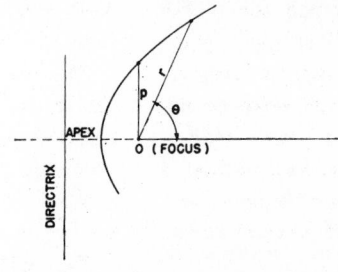

Equation (polar form, pole at focus): $r = \dfrac{p}{1 - \cos \phi}$

METHODS OF DRAWING A PARABOLA

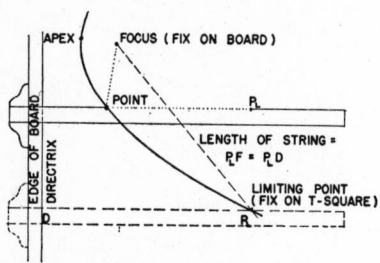

STRING METHOD

Above: attach a string (length equal to distance from limiting point on parabola to the focus) to the edge of the T-square and to the focus; hold string taut against T-square with a pencil and slide T-square.

Below: the parabola also can be constructed by knowing the heights of ordinates expressed as a ratio of the apex height (in this sketch 100.0). All parabolas have the same shape, differing only in scale. These relations hold true no matter what the ratio of height to width, provided the apex is included.

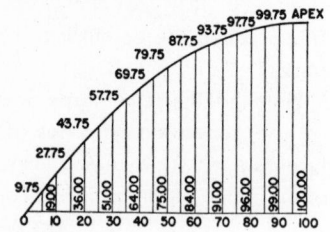

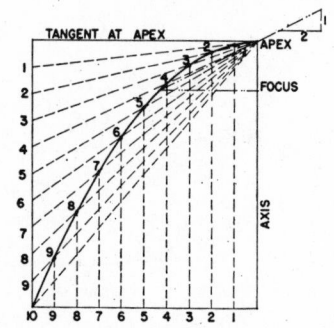

PARALLELOGRAM METHOD

To draw a parabola knowing apex, axis and one point: divide distance from point to axis in any number of equal parts; divide distance from point to the tangent through the apex into the same number of parts; draw lines parallel to the axis through points in the first line; draw lines from points in second line to apex; intersections of corresponding lines are points on the curve. To find focus, draw line through apex with slope = 1/2; from intersection with parabola drop perpendicular to axis

LENGTHS OF ARCS

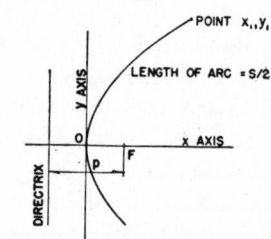

Length of arc from origin to point x_1, y_1

$$\frac{S}{2} = \frac{y_1}{2p} \sqrt{y_1^2 + p^2}$$

$$+ \frac{p}{2} \log_e \left[\frac{y_1 + \sqrt{y_1^2 + p^2}}{p} \right]$$

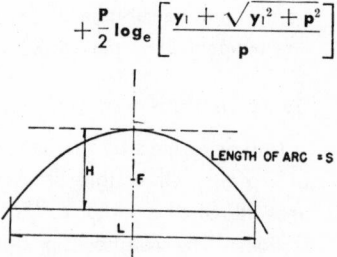

Length of parabola

Let $\frac{H}{L} = n$

Exact formula:

$$S = 2L \left\{ \sqrt{n^2 + \frac{1}{16}} + \frac{1}{16n} \left[\log_e \left(n + \sqrt{n^2 + \frac{1}{16}} \right) + \log_e 4 \right] \right\}$$

Approximate formula:

$$S = L \left(1 + \frac{8}{3} n^2 \right),$$ sufficiently accurate for construction purposes up to $n = 1/8$

CENTERS OF CURVATURE

Radius of curvature: $R = \dfrac{(p + 2x)^{3/2}}{\sqrt{p}}$

Equation of evolute: $y^2 = \dfrac{8}{27p}(x - p)^3$ (curve of centers of curvature)

To find center of curvature C_4 for a point P_4, draw a line through P_4 parallel to x axis; set off $P_4Q_4 = 2P_4F$ and draw perpendicular through Q_4; draw normal P_4N_4 to P_4 by setting off subnormal $M_4N_4 = p$, and extend to meet perpendicular from Q_4 at C_4.

Radius of curvature at apex,
$P_1C_1 = p$; $(P_1F = p/2 = FC_1)$
Center of curvature can also be found by same procedure as shown for ellipse and hyperbola: P_4N_4; N_4Q; QC_4 (see Evolute of Ellipse, Sheet 5).

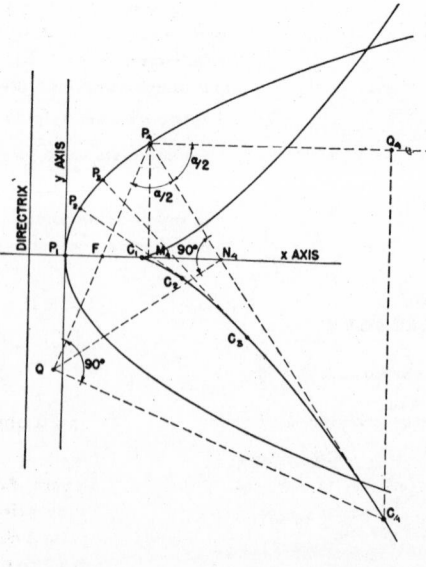

AREAS AND CENTROIDS

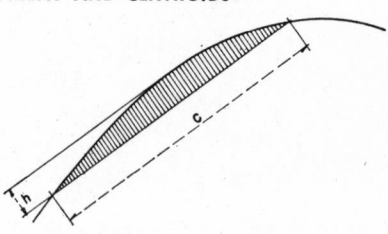

Area (A) of any segment = $\frac{2}{3}$ ch

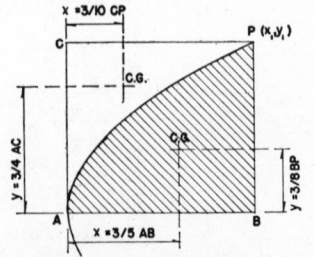

Area of half segment (APB) =
$\frac{2}{3}$ AB $\times$ BP
Area of spandrel (ACP) =
$\frac{1}{3}$ AC $\times$ CP

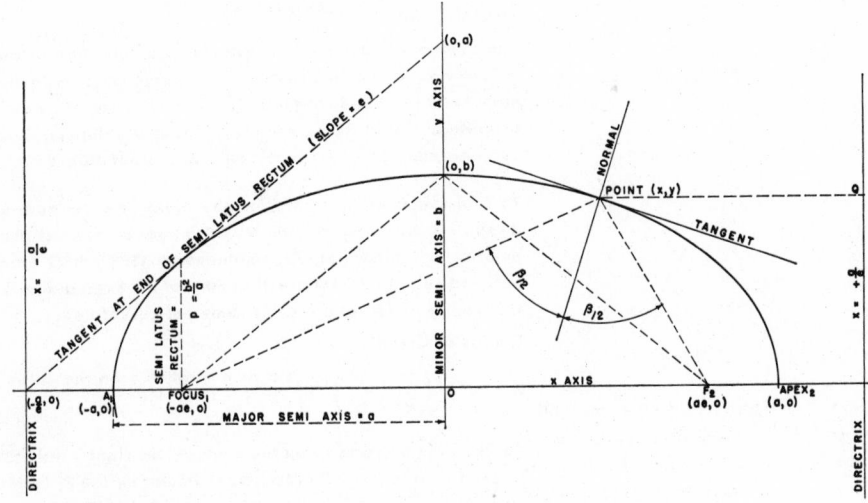

Note from characteristics of tangent (see diagram) that a line from a focus (a ray, for example) will be reflected by the ellipse and will pass through the other focus.

STANDARD FORM

$$\frac{x^2}{a^2} + \frac{y^2}{b^2} = 1$$ (b always less than a, except for circle when a = b)

Definition 1: $\dfrac{\text{Distance of Any Point to Focus}}{\text{Distance of Point to Directrix}} = \dfrac{PF}{PQ} = \text{Constant} = \text{Eccentricity (e)} = \sqrt{1 - \dfrac{b^2}{a^2}} = \text{Less Than 1}$

Definition II: Distance of Any Point to Focus$_1$ + Distance from Point to Focus$_2$ = PF$_1$ + PF$_2$ = Constant = 2a

See Sheet 20 for Conjugate Diameters, Sheet 34 for Parallelogram Method.

To Draw: (String Method) Find foci by swinging arc = a from end of minor semi axis; insert pins at foci and at end of minor semi axis; tie string around three pins; replace pin on minor axis by pencil; slide pencil against string, keeping string taut. The larger the ellipse, the better this method is (smallest practical size, major axis = 12 in.) It can easily be used for full size layout. For smaller ellipses, use method based on parametric equation.

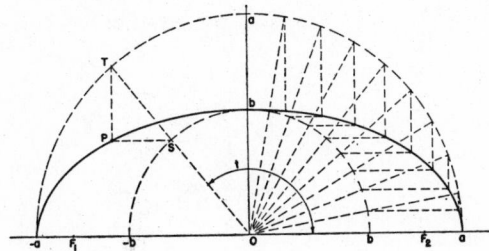

PARAMETRIC FORM

$$x = a \cos t$$
$$y = b \sin t$$

To Draw: Draw one circle with radius = a and one with radius = b, centers at O; from O draw any straight line, intersecting circle of radius b at S and circle of radius a at T; draw line through S parallel to x axis and a line through T parallel to y axis; the intersection of these lines is a point on the ellipse. Angle t is called the eccentric angle of point P (see Sheet 37).

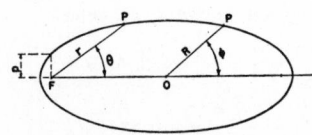

For the circle these equations become

$$r = R = a = b$$

POLAR FORM

Pole at focus: $r = \dfrac{P}{1 - e \cos \theta}$

Pole at intersection of axes:

$$R^2 = \frac{a^2 b^2}{a^2 \sin^2 \phi + b^2 \cos^2 \phi}$$

$$P = \frac{b^2}{a} \text{ (semi-latus rectum)}$$

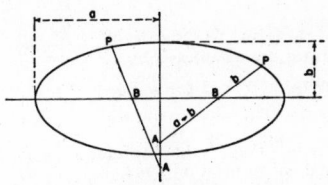

TRAMMEL METHOD

Make a stick (or piece of paper) of length PA = a; mark off PB = b, slide point A along minor axis and point B along major axis, point P will describe ellipse

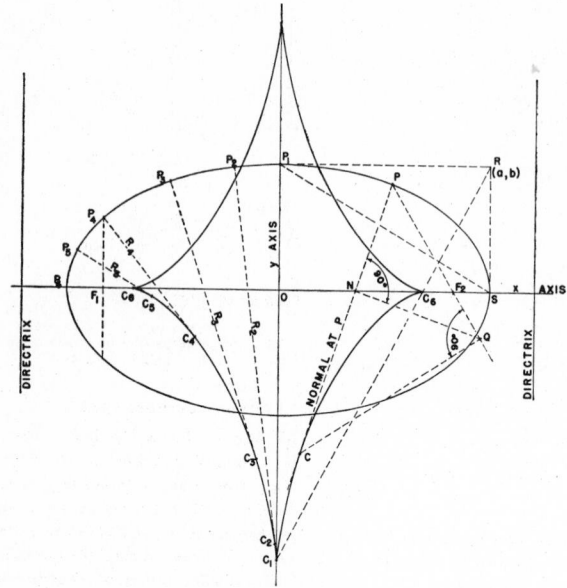

EVOLUTE OF ELLIPSE

The evolute can be used to visualize the curvature of the ellipse and to aid in constructing a curve parallel to the ellipse. (For example the intrados and extrados of an arch of uniform thickness whose centerline is an ellipse.) Such curves, called parallels to the ellipse, are not ellipses.

To find center of curvature for any point P: draw normal through P; from intersection N with major axis, erect perpendicular intersecting PF_2 extended at Q; from Q erect perpendicular to PQ intersecting normal PN extended at C. C is center of curvature, CP is radius of curvature.

Radius of Curvature

$$R = a^2 b^2 \left(\frac{x^2}{a^4} + \frac{y^2}{b^4} \right)^{3/2} \text{ for any point } x, y \text{ on the ellipse}$$

To find points C_1 and C_6 on the evolute (see right hand half of curve): from point R drop perpendicular to line P_1 S; this cuts major axis at C_6, minor axis extended at C_1.

$$\text{Radius } C_6 P_6 = \frac{b^2}{a} = p \qquad \text{Radius } C_1 P_1 = \frac{a^2}{b}$$

Equation of Evolute (Standard form)

$$a^{2/3} x^{2/3} + b^{2/3} y^{2/3} = (a^2 - b^2)^{2/3}$$

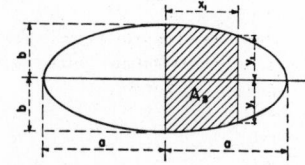

LENGTH OF ELLIPSE

Total Length

$$L = \pi \left[a+b \right] \left[1 + \tfrac{1}{4} \left(\frac{a-b}{a+b} \right)^2 + \frac{1}{64} \left(\frac{a-b}{a+b} \right)^4 + \frac{1}{256} \left(\frac{a-b}{a+b} \right)^6 + \cdots \right]$$

For lengths of arcs of ellipse, see the following publications: Smithsonian Mathematical Formulas and Tables of Elliptic Functions (Smithsonian Publ. No. 2672) Smithsonian Elliptic Functions Tables (Smithsonian Publication No. 3863).

AREAS

Total area bounded by ellipse $= A = \pi a b$

Area of segment bounded by ellipse, axis and line x $= x_1$ (as shaded) $A_s = x_1 y_1 + ab \arcsin \dfrac{x_1}{a}$

Note that these equations hold true for a circle, when $a = b = r$ and the eccentricity is zero.

ORDINATES of Quadrant of Circle. To find corresponding ordinates of quadrant of an ellipse, multiply each ordinate as figured for circle by the ratio $\frac{b}{a}$. This process is called a *dilatation*.

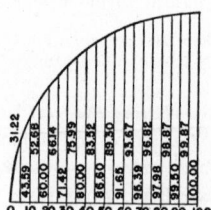

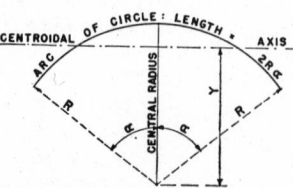

CENTROIDAL AXIS

For an arc of a circle the distance of the centroidal axis (normal to the central radius) from the center of the circle is:

$$Y = \frac{R \sin \alpha}{\alpha} \quad (\alpha \text{ in radians})$$

The "moment of inertia" of this arc about the centroid =

$$I = R^3 \left[\alpha + \tfrac{1}{2} \sin 2\alpha - \frac{2 \sin^2 \alpha}{\alpha} \right]$$

α in radians

Unfortunately there is no simple equation for finding the centroidal axis for an arc of an ellipse.

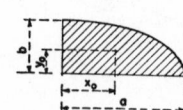

CENTROID

("Center of Gravity") of quadrant bounded by ellipse and two semi axes $\left(\text{Area} = \frac{\pi ab}{4} \right)$

$$x_o = \frac{4}{3\pi} a = 0.4244 a$$

$$y_o = \frac{4}{3\pi} b = 0.4244 b$$

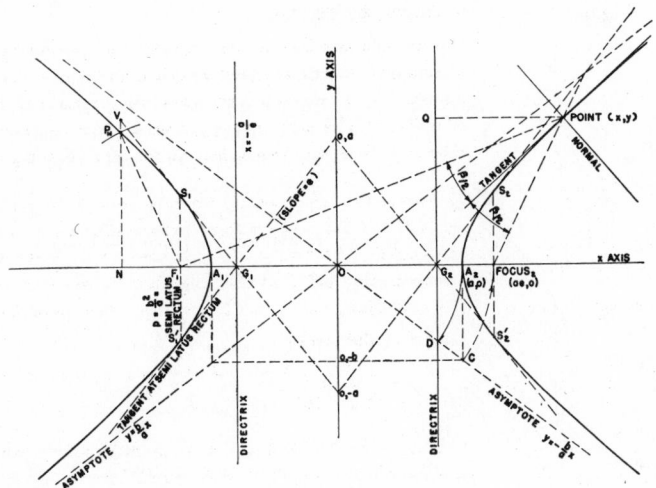

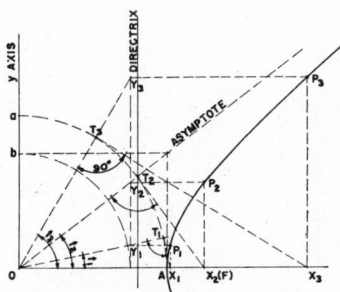

STANDARD FORM

$$\frac{x^2}{a^2} - \frac{y^2}{b^2} = 1 \quad \text{Asymptotes (tangents at infinity)} \begin{cases} \dfrac{x}{a} - \dfrac{y}{b} = 0 \\ \dfrac{x}{a} + \dfrac{y}{b} = 0 \end{cases}$$

Note that b may be greater than a; in that case the curve is flatter. When a = b, asymptotes are at right angles to each other (called a rectangular hyperbola).

Definition I: $\dfrac{\text{Distance of any Point to Focus}}{\text{Distance of Point to Directrix}} =$

$$\frac{PF}{PQ} = \text{Constant} = \text{Eccentricity (e)} = \sqrt{1 + \frac{b^2}{a}} = \text{Greater Than 1}$$

Definition II: Distance of Any Point to Focus$_1$ — Distance of Point to Focus$_2$ = PF_1 — PF_2 = Constant = $2a$

To Draw: Given a and b, draw asymptotes. Apex is at a or — a on x axis. Find directrix by swinging arc = Oa to intersect asymptote at D (see lower right quadrant). Find focus by swinging arc OC to intersect x axis at F (OC = $\sqrt{a^2 + b^2}$ = ae). Erect perpendicular through F. From points O, a and O, — a, draw lines through G_1 and G_2 and intersecting perpendiculars through F_1 and F_2 at S_1, S'_1, S_2, S'_2. To find any point on hyperbola (P_n, upper left quadrant), erect perpendicular at N to intersect $G_1 S_1$ at V. From F_1 swing an arc = NV to intersect NV at P_n. See also Sheet 33 for other methods.

PARAMETRIC FORM

$$x = a \sec t = \frac{a}{\cos t}$$

$$y = b \tan t$$
(only one quadrant shown)

To Draw: Draw circles with radii = a and = b, centers O. From O draw any line, intersecting circle of radius a at T. From T erect perpendicular (tangent to circle) intersecting x axis at X. From intersection of circle of radius b with x axis, erect perpendicular intersecting OT at Y. Through Y draw line parallel to x axis, which will intersect a line parallel to y axis drawn through X at P. P is a point on the hyperbola.

Note that tangent to circle of radius a at intersection with asymptote passes through focus.

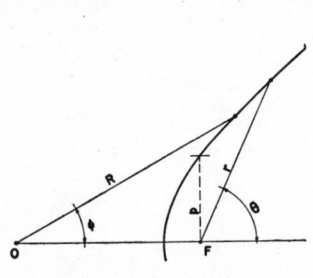

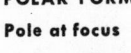

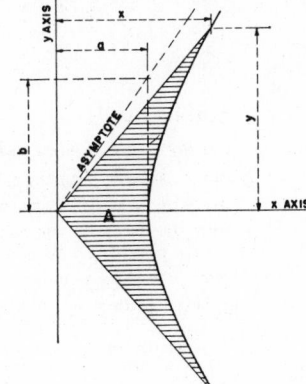

POLAR FORM

Pole at focus

$$r = \frac{P}{1 - e \cos \theta}$$

Pole at center O

$$R^2 = \frac{a^2 b^2}{b^2 \cos^2 \phi - a^2 \sin^2 \phi}$$

AREA

$$A = ab \log_e \left(\frac{x}{a} + \frac{y}{b} \right)$$

$$= ab \cosh^{-1} \frac{x}{a}$$

$$= ab \sinh^{-1} \frac{y}{b}$$

$$= ab \tanh^{-1} \frac{ay}{bx}$$

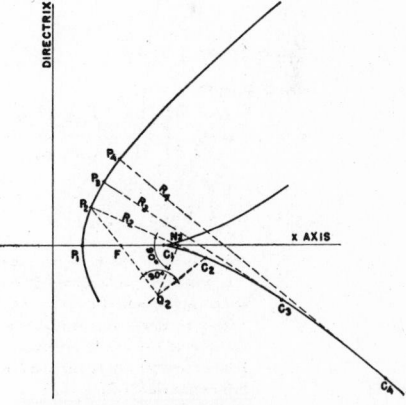

EVOLUTE OF HYPERBOLA

(For part of one quadrant)

Radius of Curvature

$$R = a^2 b^2 \left(\frac{x^2}{a^4} + \frac{y^2}{b^4} \right)^{3/2} \quad \text{For any point}$$

x, y on the hyperbola.

At apex (P_1), Radius $C_1 P_1 = \dfrac{b^2}{a} = p$

Equation of Evolute

Standard form: $a^{2/3} x^{2/3} + b^{2/3} y^{2/3} = (a^2 + b^2)^{2/3}$

Center of curvature of hyperbola can be found by same procedure as shown for ellipse.

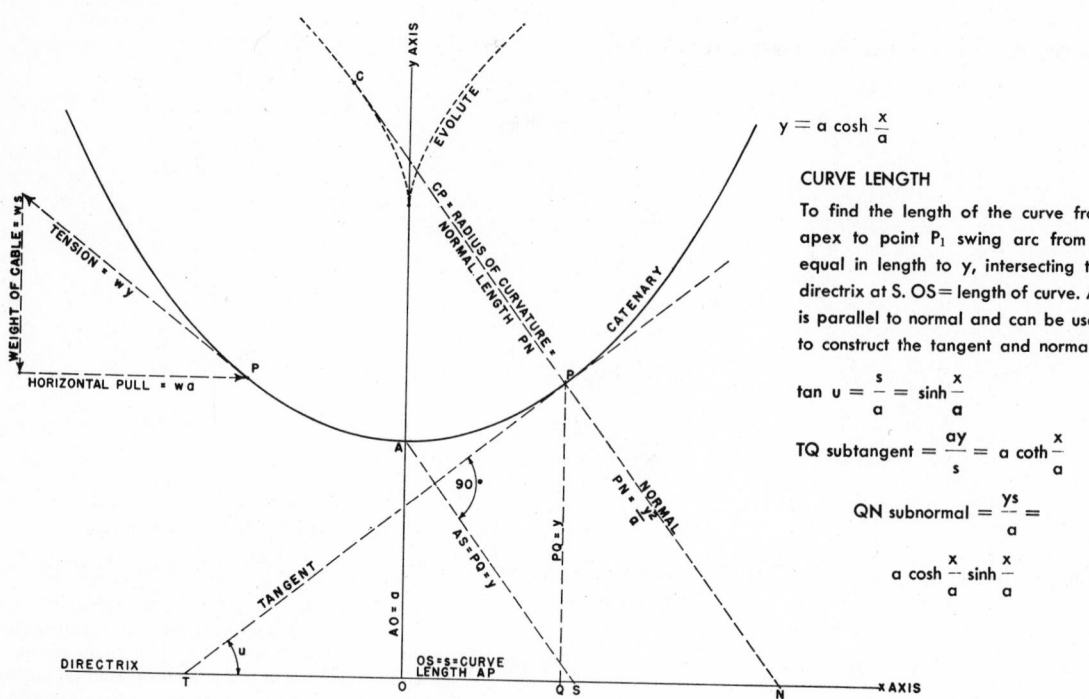

$$y = a \cosh \frac{x}{a}$$

CURVE LENGTH

To find the length of the curve from apex to point P_1 swing arc from A equal in length to y, intersecting the directrix at S. OS = length of curve. AS is parallel to normal and can be used to construct the tangent and normal.

$$\tan u = \frac{s}{a} = \sinh \frac{x}{a}$$

$$TQ \text{ subtangent} = \frac{ay}{s} = a \coth \frac{x}{a}$$

$$QN \text{ subnormal} = \frac{ys}{a} =$$

$$a \cosh \frac{x}{a} \sinh \frac{x}{a}$$

DEFINITION

The catenary is the curve described by a perfectly flexible cord of uniform weight, hanging freely between two supports. All catenaries have the same shape and differ only in scale (size). The measure of this scale is the parameter "a," which is the distance from the apex to the directrix.

The relationship between the tension at any point in the cable and the horizontal and vertical components is shown above. w = weight of cable per unit of length.

Upside down, the catenary is also the curve of the pressure line of an arch of uniform cross section, loaded only by its own weight. When the catenary is reversed, what is tension in the cable becomes compression in the arch.

METHODS OF DRAWING: THE CATENARY AS THE ROULETTE OF A PARABOLA

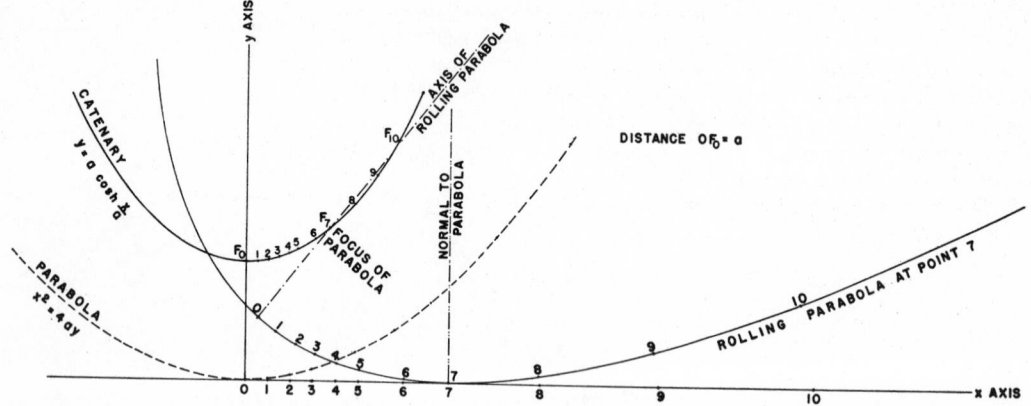

The catenary may be drawn by calculating points for the equation $y = a \cosh \frac{x}{a}$ and joining points, or it can be generated directly by rolling a parabola along the directrix. In either case the parameter "a," must be determined. As this is a trial and error procedure, the values of a in terms of SAG/SPAN ratios have been calculated and can be found directly from the graph on sheet 9. Having determined "a," the catenary can be drawn directly by first drawing a parabola with a parameter of 4a (2p in the notation on parabolas, Sheet 2–3), shown here as the parabola $x^2 = 4ay$. The parabola is then rolled along the x axis as shown above and its focus will describe the desired catenary.

This is known as a roulette curve (cycloids are the most well known roulettes). The only practical difficulty consists in preventing the rolling curve from slipping as it is rolled. The curve which is to be rolled (in this case the parabola) should be drawn on a piece of tracing paper. Make a hole in the paper at the point whose locus is sought (in this case the focus). Draw the curve (in this case the x axis) along which the curve is to be rolled on another piece of paper. Mark points along the length of the parabola and draw normal (and/or tangent) at each point. Mark points at the same distances measured along the straight line and draw normal at each point. Roll the parabola along the straight line, matching points and lining up normals (and/or tangents) at each point. Mark through the hole the corresponding point of the roulette (in this case the catenary).

PROBLEMS OF THE CATENARY FALL INTO THREE GENERAL CASES:

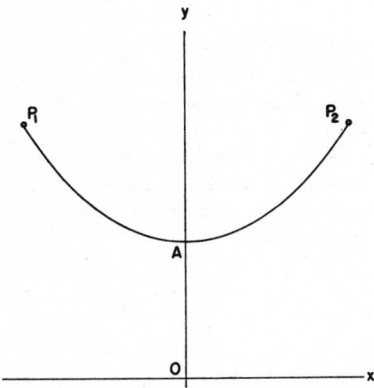

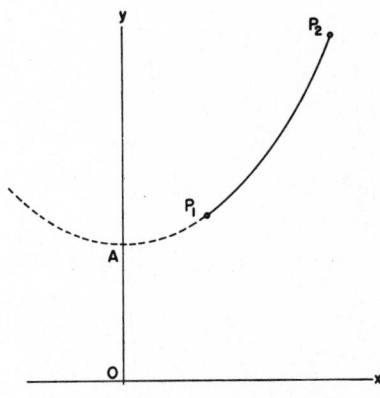

CASE 1: BOTH SUPPORTS AT SAME LEVEL

CASE II: SUPPORTS AT DIFFERENT LEVELS, LOW POINT IN BETWEEN

CASE III: SUPPORTS AT DIFFERENT LEVELS, NO LOW POINT BETWEEN

1. If locations of P_1, P_2 and A are known, the SAG/SPAN ratio can be calculated and the parameter "a" found from curve on sheet 9.

2. If only the locations of P_1 and P_2 are known, some additional information must be available. This may be:

a. The length of the curve between P_1 and P_2. With this it is possible to find "a" by trial and error graphically, remembering that the shape of the catenary is fixed and that the problem is one of scale. Over a catenary curve which has been accurately drawn,

establish points P_1 and P_2 to some scale. The angle between the line which joins them and the y or x axis will be fixed. Measure the distance from P_1 to P_2 along the curve to this same scale. If this distance is less than the given distance, the points P_1 and P_2 must be moved higher (keeping their relative positions the same). (If greater, the points must be slid down the curve.) The correct scale for the new position must be worked out, the length along the curve measured according to the new curve and so on. When the scale is correct, measure the distance from A to O

using this scale, and you will have the correct "a." This procedure can also be done algebraically, solving $S = a \sinh \frac{x}{a}$ by trial and error for each of the two distances P_1 A and P_2 A.

b. The tension in the cable and the weight per unit of length. Since $y = \dfrac{\text{tension}}{\text{unit weight}}$, the distance from P_1 or P_2 to the x axis can be found, and by adjusting the scale and drawing over an accurate curve, the apex A can be found and the parameter "a" calculated.

NOTES

TABLES OF HYPERBOLIC FUNCTIONS CAN BE FOUND:

1. "Smithsonian Mathematical Tables: Hyperbolic Functions," Pub. No. 1871, Gov. Printing Office, 1909, gives values to 5 decimal places
    for x = 0.0001 to x = 0.1000
    for x = 0.001 to x = 3.000
    and for x = 3.00 to x = 6.00

2. "Tables of Circular and Hyperbolic Sines and Cosines for Radian Arguments," published as a WPA project, New York, 1939, gives values to 9 decimal places
    for x = 0.0001 to x = 1.9999
    and for x = 2.0   to x = 10.00

CATENARY AS ROULETTE OF PARABOLA

The demonstration of the catenary as the roulette of a parabola was first made by James Clerk Maxwell, "Theory of Rolling Curves," Transactions Royal Soc. Edin., Vol. XVI, Part 5 (1849), republished in "Scientific Papers of James Clerk Maxwell," edited by W. D. Niven, Dover Pub., New York, 1952.

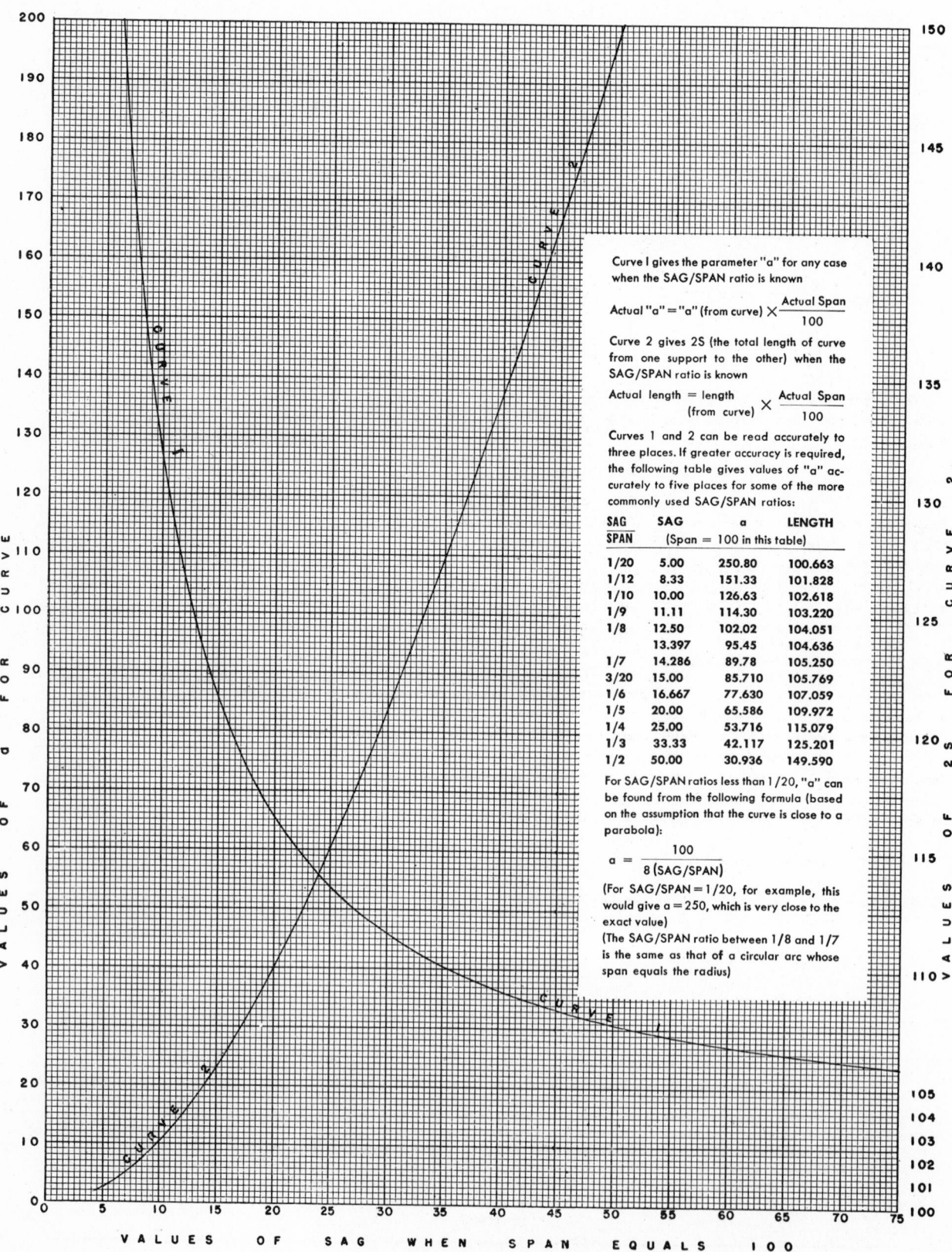

Curve I gives the parameter "a" for any case when the SAG/SPAN ratio is known

$$\text{Actual "a"} = \text{"a" (from curve)} \times \frac{\text{Actual Span}}{100}$$

Curve 2 gives 2S (the total length of curve from one support to the other) when the SAG/SPAN ratio is known

$$\begin{array}{c}\text{Actual length} \\ \text{(from curve)}\end{array} = \begin{array}{c}\text{length} \\ \end{array} \times \frac{\text{Actual Span}}{100}$$

Curves 1 and 2 can be read accurately to three places. If greater accuracy is required, the following table gives values of "a" accurately to five places for some of the more commonly used SAG/SPAN ratios:

SAG/SPAN	SAG (Span = 100 in this table)	a	LENGTH
1/20	5.00	250.80	100.663
1/12	8.33	151.33	101.828
1/10	10.00	126.63	102.618
1/9	11.11	114.30	103.220
1/8	12.50	102.02	104.051
	13.397	95.45	104.636
1/7	14.286	89.78	105.250
3/20	15.00	85.710	105.769
1/6	16.667	77.630	107.059
1/5	20.00	65.586	109.972
1/4	25.00	53.716	115.079
1/3	33.33	42.117	125.201
1/2	50.00	30.936	149.590

For SAG/SPAN ratios less than 1/20, "a" can be found from the following formula (based on the assumption that the curve is close to a parabola):

$$a = \frac{100}{8\,(\text{SAG/SPAN})}$$

(For SAG/SPAN = 1/20, for example, this would give a = 250, which is very close to the exact value)
(The SAG/SPAN ratio between 1/8 and 1/7 is the same as that of a circular arc whose span equals the radius)

VALUES OF SAG WHEN SPAN EQUALS 100

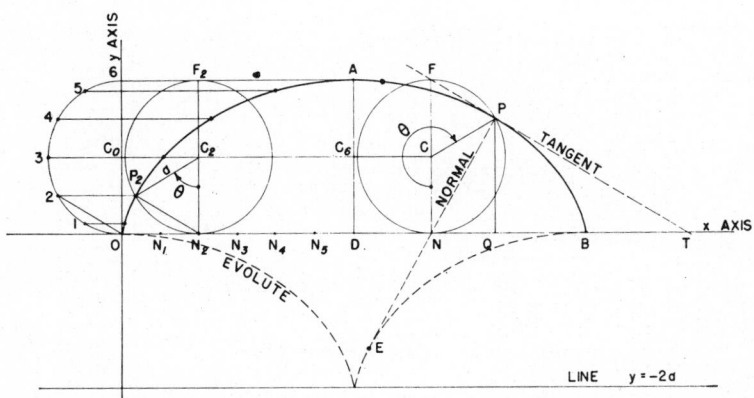

DEFINITION

The locus of a point P on the circumference of a circle which rolls along a straight line without slipping is called a cycloid. It has been used as a cross section of concrete shells.

PARAMETRIC EQUATION (most convenient):

$$x = a(\theta - \sin\theta)$$
$$y = a(1 - \cos\theta) \qquad (\theta \text{ in radians})$$

STANDARD FORM

$$x = a \arccos\left(\frac{a-y}{a}\right) - \sqrt{2ay - y^2}$$

METHODS OF DRAWING

1. Draw directly as a roulette (see definition, sheet 7) by rolling a circle of radius "a" along x axis. Take care that circle does not slip.

2. On y axis draw generating circle, radius = a, center at C_0 ($C_0O = a$). Divide half circumference into whole number of arcs (here 6). On x axis lay off the lengths of these arcs ON_1, N_1N_2, N_2N_3, etc., by measuring directly or by measuring $OD = \pi a$ and dividing into same number of parts. Draw a horizontal line through C and project points N_1, N_2, etc.

up to find successive positions of center of circle. At each center draw the radius vector, where θ is the corresponding multiple of

$$\frac{180°}{\text{number of arcs}} \quad (C_2P_2 = a, \ \theta_2 = 2 \times \frac{180}{6} = 60°$$

for example). P_2 also lies on a horizontal line through point 2 on the generating circle as shown in initial position.

3. Proceed as directed in method 2, as far as measuring arc lengths along x axis. Then through points 1, 2, 3, etc. on circle in initial

position, draw horizontal lines. Measure on each line the corresponding length of arc and the corresponding point on the cycloid will be found. (For example, to find P_2, measure 2, $P_2 = ON_2$.)

4. Proceed as directed in method 2, as far as measuring arc lengths along x axis. To find P_2 shown, describe arc of radius 0, 2 from center N_2 and intersect horizontal line drawn through 2. Note that P_2N_2 is the normal to point P_2 and is half the length of the radius of curvature at P_2.

TANGENT to any point P passes through F at top of generating circle in corresponding position. Subtangent $QT = a\dfrac{(1 - \cos\theta)^2}{\sin\theta}$

NORMAL to any point P passes through N at bottom of generating circle. Normal $PN = \sqrt{2ay}$. Subnormal $QN = a\sin\theta$.

LENGTH OF CURVE for one arch = 8a. Centroid of this length is $\dfrac{4a}{3}$ above x axis.

LENGTH OF AN ARC of curve $AP = 2 \times PF$ (length of arc $BP = 4a - 2\,PF$)

AREA UNDER ONE ARCH = $3\pi a^2$. Centroid of this area is $\dfrac{5a}{6}$ above x axis.

RADIUS OF CURVATURE = EP = twice length of normal $PN = 2\sqrt{2ay}$.

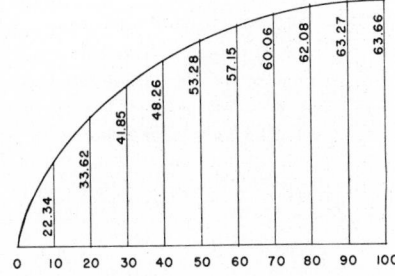

ORDINATES OF A CYCLOID expressed in terms of a half length of 100.

$$x = \frac{100}{\pi}(\theta - \sin\theta)$$

$$y = \frac{100}{\pi}(1 - \cos\theta)$$

$$\frac{100}{\pi} = 31.831$$

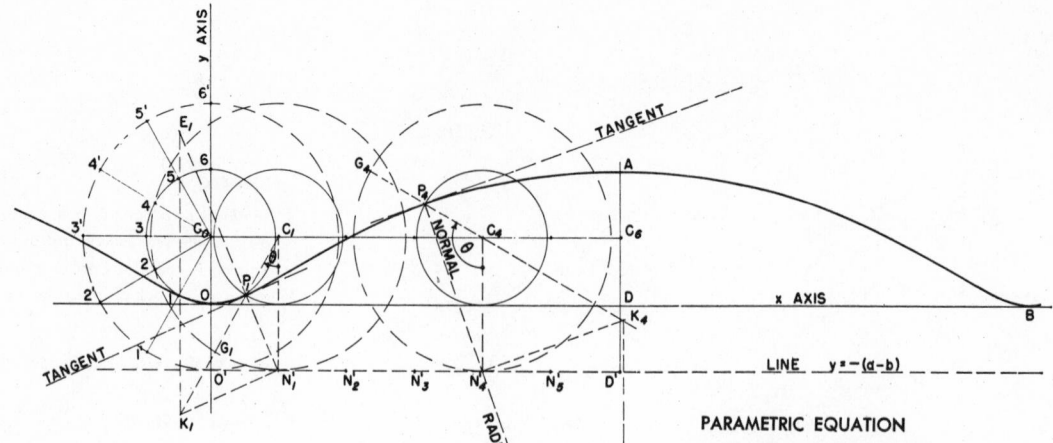

PARAMETRIC EQUATION

$x = a\theta - b \sin \theta$ (θ in radians)

$y = b (1 - \cos \theta)$

a is radius of rolling circle = CG

b is distance from center of circle to point = CP

NORMAL to any point P passes through N' at bottom of generating circle.

TANGENT is found as perpendicular to normal at P

RADIUS OF CURVATURE = PE. Point E is found as follows. Erect perpendicular to normal at N'. Extend radius line PC to intersect perpendicular at K. Draw vertical line through K to intersect PN' extended at E. E is center of curvature and PE is radius of curvature.

Equation:

$$PE = R = \frac{[a^2 - 2ab \cos \theta + b^2]^{3/2}}{2a^2 - ab(\cos \theta + 2) + b^2}$$

At point 0, $\theta = 0$ and

$$R = \frac{(a - b)^3}{2a^2 - 3ab + b^2}$$

At point A, $\theta = 180° = \pi$ and

$$R = \frac{(a + b)^3}{2a^2 - ab + b^2}$$

EVOLUTE for the prolate trochoid is in two parts, one on each side of the curve. The normal which makes the smallest angle with the x axis passes through the point of contraflexure and is asymptotic to each portion of the evolute.

DEFINITION

The locus of a point P on the radius of a circle which rolls along a straight line without slipping is called a trochoid. If P lies inside the circle it is a prolate trochoid shown here. If outside, a curtate trochoid. The curtate trochoid curve has little possibility of use in the building field. The prolate trochoid has potentialities as a section for corrugated concrete shells (see Structural Forms—Reinforced Concrete). It is also used (upside down from position shown) as the curve of ocean waves for ship analysis, with a height (DA) equal to 20 times length (OB) and a length equal to length of ship.

METHODS OF DRAWING

The same methods as described for drawing a cycloid may be used. Note that the distance OB on the x axis is equal to $2\pi a$ and the height AD = 2b. Lengths of arcs must be measured on the circumference of the outer circle, heights from the inner circle.

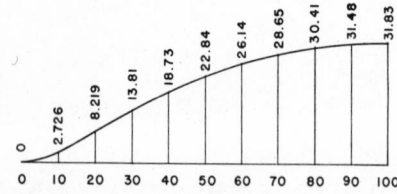

ORDINATES FOR A TROCHOID in which a = 2b, expressed in terms of a half-length of 100. This might be used as the cross-section of a shell roof.

$$x = \frac{50}{\pi} (2\theta - \sin \theta)$$

$$y = \frac{50}{\pi} (1 - \cos \theta)$$

$$\left[\frac{50}{\pi} = 15.915 \right]$$

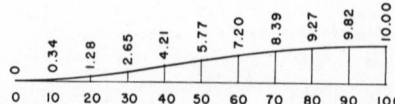

ORDINATES FOR A TROCHOID whose height is $\frac{1}{20}$ of its length, expressed in terms of a half-length of 100. This is the standard ocean wave, but upside down, i.e. the "0" ordinate is the crest, the "10" ordinate the hollow of the wave.

$$x = 5 \left(\frac{20}{\pi} \theta - \sin \theta \right) \qquad \left[\frac{20}{\pi} = 6.366 \right]$$

$$y = 5 (1 - \cos \theta)$$

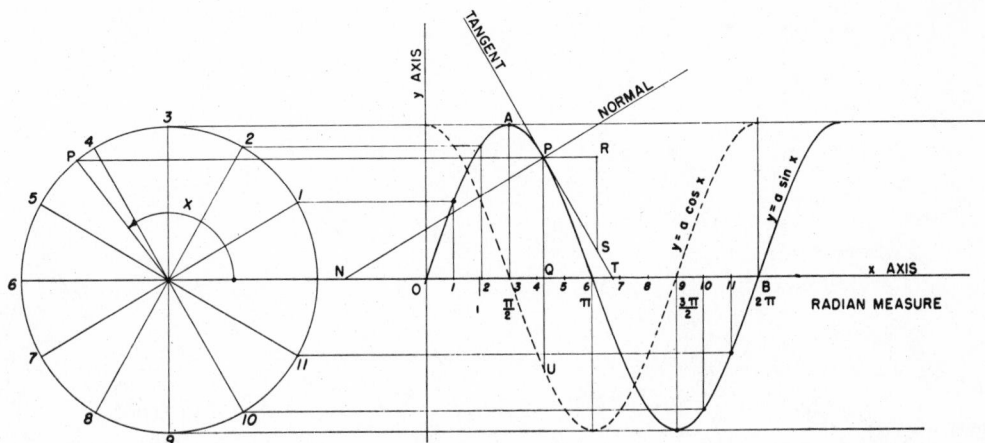

DEFINITION

The Sine Curve represents the vertical projection of a point P, moving with uniform velocity on the circumference of a circle, plotted against angular displacement. If a is the radius of the circle and b is the angular velocity of the point P on its circumference, and t is time; then $x = bt$ and $y = a \cos bt$. The amplitude $= a$ and the period $= 2\pi$ or $360° = OB$.

In building work this curve has been used as the centerline of the cross section of corrugated of parts (here 12). Lay off the distance OB on the x axis and divide into the same number of parts. Erect a perpendicular at each point of division of the x axis. Draw horizontal lines through the corresponding points on the circumference of the circle and the intersections will be points on the curve. Note that distance concrete shells (see Structural Forms—Reinforced Concrete). It is also the elevation of a so-called spiral (helical) stair. And it is the projection of geodesic lines on a cylinder, such as plan projections of lamella arches.

EQUATION

$y = a \sin x$

METHODS OF DRAWING

1. Draw the generating circle with radius a and divide circumference into a whole number

$\pi/2$ radians or $90°$ to the left. To draw the tangent at P, draw a horizontal line through P and measure $PR = 1$ radian. Draw a vertical line through P intersecting x axis at Q and

$OB = 2\pi$ radians and that $57°18' = $ one radian. To find the point at which $x = 1$ radian, divide OB into 2π or 6.283 parts and locate 1 on this scale.

2. Calculate and plot points using table of sines.

TANGENT

The slope of the tangent at any point $= a \cos x$. The curve $y = a \cos x$ has been drawn and has exactly the same shape but is displaced extend to intersect cosine curve at U. Draw a vertical line RS through R of length $RS = QU$. The line PS is tangent to the sine curve at P, and can be extended to cut x axis at T.

NORMAL is drawn as perpendicular to tangent.

AREA under one arch (from origin to π or $180°$) $= 2a$. Centroid of this area is $\dfrac{\pi a}{8}$ above x axis.

RADIUS OF CURVATURE $R = \dfrac{(1 + a^2 \cos^2 x)^{3/2}}{a \sin x}$. At apex A, $R = \dfrac{1}{a}$

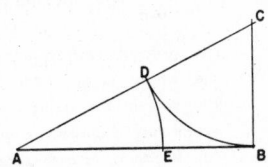

GOLDEN SECTION

Used by Greek artists and architects and often revived in theories of proportion. Basis of Modular of Le Corbusier, using 2 m 26 (or 7 ft 5 in.) or 1 m 13 (or 3 ft 8½ in.) as starting points for his two series. If a line AB is divided so that $\dfrac{AB}{AE} = \dfrac{AE}{EB}$ it is in golden section. Or if g is ratio such that $AE = gEB$,

$g^2 = g + 1$ or $g - \dfrac{1}{g} = 1$ and $g = \dfrac{\sqrt{5} + 1}{2} = 1.6180$

To find graphically, erect perpendicular $CB = \dfrac{AB}{2}$ and swing arc $CD = CB$. Then swing arc AD to cut AB at E.

The angle which the diagonal of a rectangle whose sides are in the ratio g:1 makes with the short side $=$ arc tan $1.618 = 58°\ 17'$.

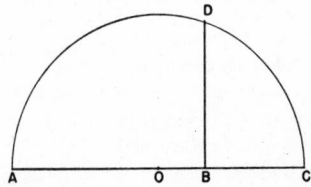

GEOMETRICAL MEAN

General case of which golden section is a particular case. To find distance BD which is geometrical mean or mean proportional between AB and BC, divide AC in half at O and with O as center and radius equal to $AO = OC$, draw semicircle. Draw perpendicular at B to intersect circle at D

Then $BD^2 = AB \times BC$ or $\dfrac{AB}{BD} = \dfrac{BD}{BC}$

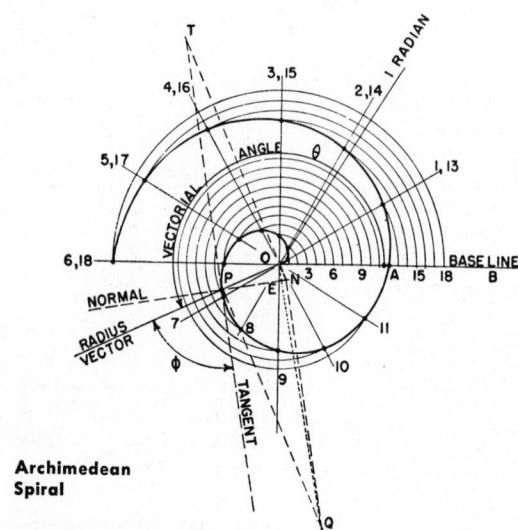

Archimedean Spiral

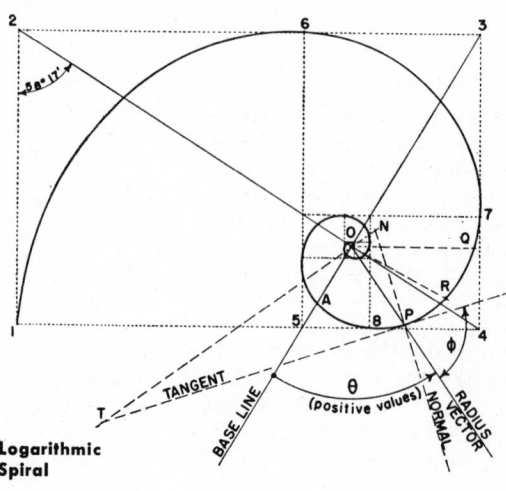

Logarithmic Spiral

ARCHIMEDEAN SPIRAL

The locus of a point P which moves with uniform linear velocity along a line OP as OP revolves with uniform angular velocity about O is called a Spiral of Archimedes.

EQUATION:

$r = a\theta$ (θ in radians)

METHOD OF DRAWING (only positive values of θ are shown)

Draw baseline OB. Measure off OA = $2\pi a$. Divide OA into whole number of parts (here 12). Through O draw radial lines at equal spaces corresponding to the same number of parts (here $\frac{360}{12} = 30°$ or $\frac{2\pi}{12} = \frac{\pi}{6}$ radians). With O as center, draw arcs of circles with radii = O1, O2, O3 etc. Where each radius intersects corresponding radial line is a point on the spiral. Note that successive values of r are in arithmetical progression. To measure a, draw radial line at 1 radian (57° 18'), where r = a.

NORMAL

Through O draw ON = a perpendicular to radius vector OP. PN is normal. TANGENT is drawn at right angles to normal at P. Note that the angle Φ between radius vector and tangent is the angle whose tangent = $\frac{r}{a}$ and that this angle is constantly increasing as θ increases.

RADIUS OF CURVATURE

Through N draw NQ parallel to tangent.

Through P draw PQ at right angles to radius vector. Line OQ cuts PN at E. E is center of curvature to spiral at P. Radius of curvature

$$R = \frac{(r^2 + a^2)^{\frac{3}{2}}}{r^2 + 2a^2}$$

LENGTH OF ARC = OP

$$\frac{a}{2}\left[\theta\sqrt{1 + \theta^2} + \log_e(\theta + \sqrt{1 + \theta^2}\,)\right]$$

LOGARITHMIC (EQUIANGULAR) SPIRAL

The curve that cuts the radius vector at a constant angle Φ is called an Equiangular Spiral. If successive values of the vectorial angle θ are in arithmetical progression, the corresponding values of the radius vector are in geometric progression.

EQUATION

$r = ae^{m\theta}$ or $\log_e \frac{r}{a} = m\theta$

$m = \cot an\ \Phi$ and $a = r = OA$ (when $\theta = 0°$)

METHODS OF DRAWING

In general, draw radial lines from pole O for equal increments of θ, calculate corresponding values of r and measure on each radial line. If r is calculated for large increments of θ and the points plotted, intermediate points can be found as follows: If OP and OQ are any two radii and if OR is a radius bisecting angle POQ, then OR is the mean proportional between OQ and OP (see sheet 12 for drawing method).

NORMAL

Through O draw ON = rm = r cot Φ perpendicular to radius vector OP. PN is normal. TANGENT is drawn at right angles to normal at P and intersects ON extended at T.

RADIUS OF CURVATURE

$R = PN = r\sqrt{1 + m^2} = r\ cosec\ \Phi$.

Center of curvature is at N. Evolute is an identical spiral whose axis is inclined $\left[\frac{\pi}{2} - \frac{\log_e m}{m}\right]$ to axis of given spiral.

LENGTH OF SPIRAL from O to p = r sec Φ = PT

AREA swept by radius (from r = O to r = OP) = $\frac{r^2}{4m}$ = ½ triangle OPT

The **golden section spiral** shown here is one whose radius vectors, separated by 90°, are in the golden section ratio. It is extensively discussed in theories of proportion. It can be drawn geometrically, without calculation. Here the rectangle 1234 is shown whose sides are in the golden section ratio. If a square (here 1265) is cut off, a similar rectangle (3456) is left, turned through 90°. This process can be continued indefinitely. Note the value of the diagonals in drawing the rectangles correctly. The diagonals cross at right angles at the pole O and are the axes of the equiangular spiral for which $\Phi = 73°$ (approx.). The corners of the squares (1, 6, 7, 8 etc.) are points on the spiral. The spiral crosses outside of the rectangle at these points.

ANALYTIC DESCRIPTION

Surfaces and skew curves can be described by a greater variety of analytical systems than curves which exist in only one plane. In architectural and related work we do not need all of these and will limit the descriptions to three types: 1. Triaxial Cartesian coordinates (a point is fixed by its projected distance on x, y and z axes); 2. Cylindrical coordinates (a point is fixed by a plane normal to a z axis and by its radius vector from a pole on this axis); and 3. Spherical coordinates (the familiar latitude and longitude or meridian lines). The purposes in analyzing a surface are:

a) to be able to recreate the surface;
b) to know its area and the volume enclosed;
c) to discover the stresses acting in the surface;
d) to discover the manner in which the surface will reflect light, heat, sound.

METHODS OF STUDY

Models are the best, and should be made as large as practicable. Wire and string can be used; sheet materials (cardboard, plastic) can be bent into the shape of developable surfaces, or can be cut to represent planes cutting the surface and put together like an egg-crate. Soft white pine can be carved in the solid and its surface studied. A solution of soap and glycerine* can be used to make minimal surfaces or membranes between wire boundary curves. From the models the surfaces can be transferred to paper, showing the traces of the surface as it is cut by a system of planes. Once drawn, the best method of construction in the field can be worked out. Usually a table of offsets should be prepared.

SKEW CURVE

A **skew curve** (also called a space curve or a twisted curve) is one which does not lie entirely in one plane. (See dwg.) The tangent line at any point defines the direction of the curve at that point. The normals to the tangent define the normal plane. The osculating

*Soap solution recommended: Dissolve 10 grams of dry sodium oleate in 500 grams of distilled water. Mix 15 cubic parts of this solution with 11 cubic parts of glycerine. Alternatively, buy a prepared solution.

plane makes a right angle with the normal plane, contains the tangent and is the plane in which the curve most closely lies at the given point. The curve will pass through the osculating plane at a regular or ordinary point. The principal normal is the intersection of the osculating and normal planes. The radius of curvature (R) is found on this principal normal. The ratio $\frac{1}{R}$ is called the first curvature. The third orthogonal line of reference at the point is called the binormal and its plane the rectifying plane. The angular rate of change of the binormal as a point moves along the curve is called the torsion or second curvature.

SURFACES

At any regular (i.e. not singular) point on a surface there will exist a **tangent plane**. If the surface is cut by any variable plane, the tangent to the curve of intersection at the given point will always lie in this tangent plane. For a cup-shaped region of a surface this tangent plane will be entirely on one side of the surface; for a saddle-shaped region it will cut the surface. (See dwg.)

At right angles to the tangent plane an infinity of normal planes can be drawn. Each of these cuts the surface in a curve called a normal section; each of these sections has a radius of curvature at the given point. One of these radii will have a minimum value R_1 and another a maximum R_2. The normal planes in which these two radii lie are called the **principal normal planes** and they are at right angles to each other. The tangents to the principal normal sections are called the **principal directions**. For a cup-shaped region of a surface the centers of both radii will lie on the same side of the surface, (See dwg.), and will have the same sign. Such a point is called an elliptic point and the curvature of the surface is called positive. For a saddle-shaped region the center of one radius will lie on one side, and the center of the other on the opposite side of the surface; and the radii will have opposite signs. Such a point is called a hyperbolic point and the curvature is called negative. Parabolic points also exist; at these the maximum radius of curvature is infinite.

On a surface can be traced a **line of curvature**, which lies along one of the principal directions of each of a sequence of points.

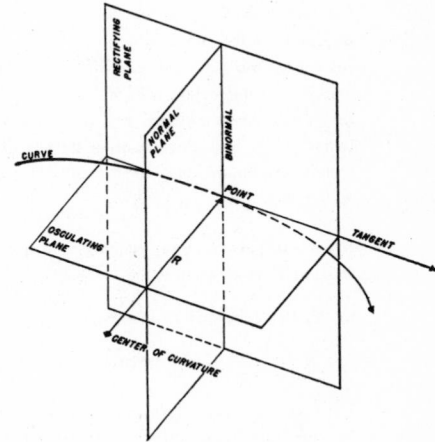

Skew Curve

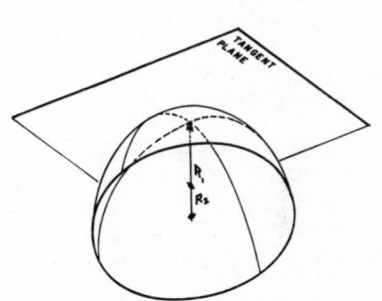

Surface of Positive Curvature

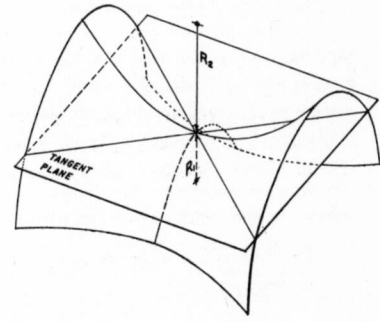

Surface of Negative Curvature

Through each point there will regularly be two such lines of curvature, which are at right angles to each other. On any surface of revolution the lines of curvature are the meridians (intersection with the surface of a plane containing the axis) and the circles of latitude. On any developable surface the rulings constitute one family of lines of curvature.

The **mean (or average) curvature** of a surface at a given point is the arithmetic mean of the two principal curvatures: $\frac{1}{2}\left(\frac{1}{R_1} + \frac{1}{R_2}\right)$. It is always zero for a minimal surface.

The **Gaussian curvature** (also called the total curvature) of a surface at a given point is the product of the two principal curvatures: $\frac{1}{R_1 R_2}$. It is positive at elliptic (cup-shaped) points, negative at hyperbolic (saddle-shaped) points, and zero at parabolic points. When a surface is bent, its Gaussian curvature does not change. This fact can be used to determine whether one surface can be formed or developed into another.

The **Dupin indicatrix** at a point is found by plotting, on the tangent plane, in the direction of every normal section, a distance from the point equal to the square root of the radius of curvature corresponding to that section. The indicatrix is always a conic section (including the degenerate conics). At an elliptic **point** (cup-shaped or synclastic region) the Dupin indicatrix is an ellipse. When both radii of curvature are equal, the ellipse becomes a circle and the point is called an **umbilic**. The umbilics are therefore singular points and have no principal directions. At a **hyperbolic point** the indicatrix is a hyperbola for all the radii of curvature on one side of the surface and the conjugate hyperbola for all the radii on the other side. The asymptotes of the hyperbolas give the **asymptotic directions**. The **asymptotic lines** consist of the family of curves which follow the asymptotic directions for every hyperbolic point and form a net over a negative surface. At a **parabolic point** one of the radii of curvature usually becomes infinite (and the corresponding curvature vanishes) and the Dupin indicatrix becomes a pair of straight lines.

On a surface on which some regions are negative, some positive, the locus of points separating the two regions traces a curve called the **parabolic curve** of the surface.

A **ruled surface** is generated by a straight line (called a generator of the surface) which moves continuously in some predetermined manner with respect to a curve or curves (called the directrix) and/or a point.

A **developable surface** is always a ruled surface, and the tangent plane to the surface at any point as the point moves along a given ruling lies in one plane throughout the length of the ruling. Cones and cylinders are typical. In general any surface generated by the tangents to a skew curve is a developable surface (called the tangential developable of the curve.) The Gaussian curvature of a developable surface is everywhere zero (as is that of a plane) and all its points are parabolic.

For all **other ruled surfaces** (which are not developable) the tangent plane at any point as the point moves along a given ruling turns through two right angles as it moves from infinity at one end to infinity at the other. The point at which the tangent has moved through only one right angle is called the **center point**. The locus of center points for the surface is called the **line of striction**.

Doubly ruled surfaces have two distinct families of rulings or straight lines on them. Only two such surfaces exist: the hyperbolic paraboloid and the hyperboloid of one sheet. The rulings are the asymptotic lines of the surfaces. The Gaussian curvature is everywhere negative and all the points are hyperbolic.

A **conoid** is generated by a straight line which, remaining parallel to a given plane, moves along a straight line (which is not parallel to the plane) and along some other geometrical figure. The hyperbolic paraboloid is thus a conoid as are the helicoids. The surface commonly referred to as a conoid in construction is Pluecker's conoid or cylindroid, generated by a straight line which moves along a straight line and an ellipse (or circle).

A **surface of revolution** is generated by rotating a curve about an axis. Typical are: the right circular cone and cylinder; the spheroids; the paraboloid of revolution; the hyperboloids of revolution, of one sheet and of two sheets; the unduloids (generated by rotating the roulette of any conic curve.) The two centers of curvature at any point on a surface of revolution are: 1) In the meridian plane, the center of curvature of the curve whose rotation generates the surface; and 2) The intersection with the axis of revolution of the line normal to the surface.

A **geodesic curve** is the shortest distance, measured on the surface, between two points on the surface. For any developable surface it can be found by drawing a straight line on the surface when developed out onto a plane and then bending the plane back onto the surface. Through any point on a surface there exists in general an infinite number of geodesic curves, going out from it in every direction and joining it to every other point on the surface. On a sphere all the geodesics are great circles. On a cylinder all the geodesics are helices (including meridian lines which are helices of infinite pitch and latitude circles which are helices of zero pitch). On a surface of revolution all the meridians are geodesics, but the other geodesics cannot be found so simply. The circles of latitude are generally not geodesics.

A **minimal surface** is the surface of smallest area among all the surfaces bounded by a given closed curve or curves. It is created automatically by the membrane formed when a wire model of the boundary curve(s) is dipped into a soap solution. Except for the plane, a minimal surface is saddle-shaped (anticlastic) at all points; all points are therefore hyperbolic. The Gaussian curvature is everywhere negative. The mean curvature vanishes for every point; i.e.

$$\frac{1}{2}\left(\frac{1}{R_1} + \frac{1}{R_2}\right) = 0.$$

In other words the least radii of curvature at any point are equal in magnitude and on opposite sides of the surface. The Dupin indicatrix for every point is an equilateral hyperbola and the asymptotic lines form an orthogonal net over the entire surface.

Reflection. Analysis of the reflective properties of surfaces can always be made by knowing the point source of energy (heat, light, sound) and the tangent plane at all points on the surface. Rays can be drawn to each point on the surface and the reflected ray found by the law: angle of reflection equals angle of incidence. It is more revealing to find the image of the source on the opposite side of the surface and then, using this as a center, to draw concentric circles or rays. In general a concave surface will concentrate rays, a convex surface will scatter them.

Structural. In general a curved surface will carry the external forces acting on it by direct stresses only, provided the supports can furnish the required vertical and horizontal reactions and provided the boundaries or edges are properly stiffened. Bending stresses may be set up near the boundaries, near the supports and at points of application of concentrated loads. Bending stresses may be set up where the curvature of the surface changes rapidly and especially at "knuckles" or sharp ridges. These bending stresses can be taken care of by thickening the shell or adding stiffening rings or ribs to the shell.

A surface of double curvature will be stiffer and deform less under load than one of single curvature, but generally it will be more expensive to calculate and to construct. While any imaginable three-dimensional surface can be drawn and built, whether it is susceptible of simple mathematical analysis or not, the description of a surface by relatively simple equations enables the engineer to make a more accurate estimate of the stresses to be expected. The mathematical surface should be taken at the centerline of the thickness of the shell or skin.

The usual procedure is first to analyze the so-called membrane stresses. These are all direct stresses and are found by analyzing a typical region of the surface on the assumption that it has no boundaries. The disturbances set up by the existence of boundaries are taken care of by separate calculations. So-called line loads are applied to the edges. The stresses set up by these are added to the membrane stresses and the net stress calculated. (This is similar to the methods of analyzing continuous frames.)

As in the case of all statically indeterminate structures, curved shells (or stressed skin constructions generally) must be drawn accurately and completely dimensioned before they can be calculated. It is essential that the preliminary guess of shape and dimension be made on the basis of the maximum amount of experience, since the loads to be carried may consist largely of the weight of the structure itself. Simple, rough calculation methods should be used in the early stages until the lightest, thinnest and stiffest combination is found. Then more detailed calculations can be made.

	SINGLE CURVATURE DEVELOPABLE	DOUBLE CURVATURE NOT DEVELOPABLE				
		Negative Curvature (Saddle-Shaped)				Positive Curvature (Cup-Shaped)
RULINGS	All Ruled Singly	Ruled Singly	Ruled Doubly (Only Two Exist)		Unruled	All Unruled
NAMES of Some Surfaces	Cones; Cylinders; Tangential Developables of Space Curves	Conoids; Right Circular Helicoid	Hyperbolic Paraboloid	Hyperboloid of One Sheet	Hyperboloid of Two Sheets; Elliptic Paraboloid; Catenoid; Pseudosphere; Inner Half of Torus; Parts of Unduloids; General Helicoid	Sphere; Spheroid; Ellipsoid; Outer Half of Torus; Parts of Unduloids
SURFACES OF REVOLUTION	Cone and Circular Cylinder Only	None	None	May Be	May Be	May Be
MINIMAL SURFACES Mean Curvature = 0 Gaussian Curvature Always Negative	None	May Be (Right Circular Helicoid, for example)	None	None	May Be. Usually Fall in This Group	None
MEAN CURVATURE $\frac{1}{2}\left(\frac{1}{R_1}+\frac{1}{R_2}\right)$	+	+, 0, −	+, 0, −	+, 0, −	+, 0, −	+. Sphere Is Only Surface (Without a Boundary) of Constant Positive Mean Curvature
GAUSSIAN CURVATURE $\frac{1}{R_1 R_2}$	0	−	−	−	−. A few Surfaces Such as Pseudosphere Exist With Constant Negative Curvature	+. Sphere Is Only Surface (Without a Boundary) Of Constant Positive Curvature

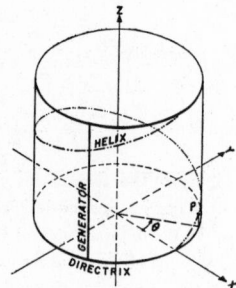

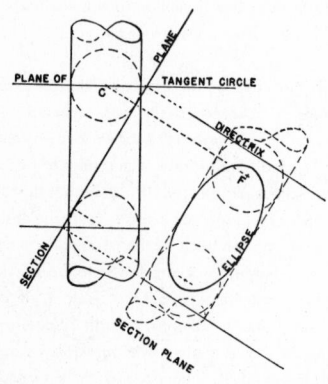

A cylinder is generated by a straight line element (the generator or generatrix) which moves along a plane curve (the directrix) parallel to an axis which is not in the plane of the curve. When the axis makes a right angle with the plane of the curve, the surface is called a right cylinder. For design purposes we can always arrange the cylinder to be right.

Any curve can be used for the directrix. If a conic is used, the cylinders are quadric surfaces and all sections are also conics. Only quadric cylinders are shown here, but other forms such as a catenary cylinder may be preferable for structural reasons.

The **right circular cylinder** is the surface
$$x^2 + y^2 = r^2; \; z = z$$
or, in cylindrical coordinates: $r = r, \; z = z$
$$x = r \cos \theta; \; y = r \sin \theta; \; z = z$$
[The elliptical cylinder, not shown, would have similar equations derived from those of the ellipse, (see sheet 4 on curves).]

The geodesics on the right circular cylinder are all circular helices and the most useful form of their equation is:
$$x = r \cos \theta; \; y = r \sin \theta; \; z = k \theta$$

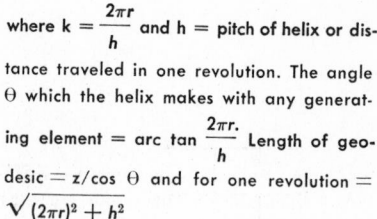

where $k = \dfrac{2\pi r}{h}$ and h = pitch of helix or distance traveled in one revolution. The angle Θ which the helix makes with any generating element = arc tan $\dfrac{2\pi r}{h}$. Length of geodesic = $z/\cos \Theta$ and for one revolution = $\sqrt{(2\pi r)^2 + h^2}$

The projection of the circular helix on the xz or yz planes (i.e. "side elevation") is always a sine curve (see sheet 12 on curves).

The lamellas or elements of a lamella roof (see Structural Forms—Wood) trace helices on the surface of a cylindrical roof. The drawing of the parabolic cylinder explains this.

Any **section of a circular cylinder** is an ellipse. The foci of the ellipse are the projections on the section plane of the centers of the spheres tangent to the cylinder and to the plane. They are also the points of tangency of these spheres and the section plane. The directrix of the ellipse is the intersection of the section plane with the plane of the circle of tangency of the sphere.

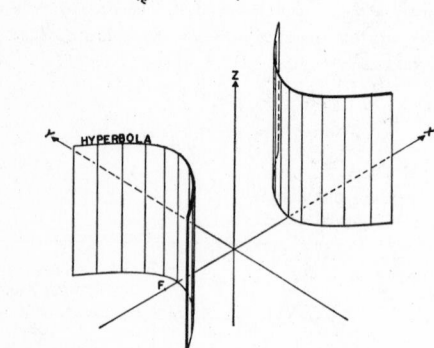

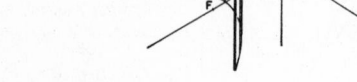

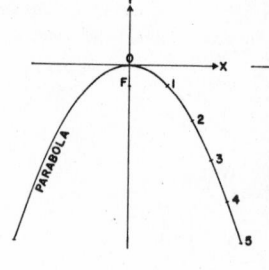

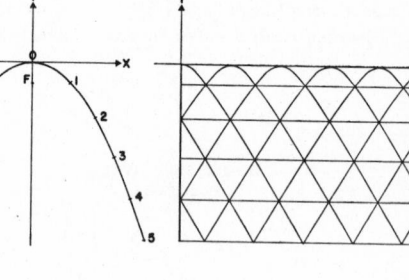

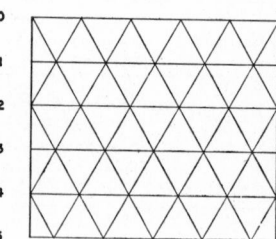

The **hyperbolic cylinder** is the surface
$$\frac{x^2}{a^2} - \frac{y^2}{b^2} = 1; \; z = z$$

All sections are conics and are most easily drawn by projecting a few points and using Pascal's method.

The **parabolic cylinder** (coordinates as shown) is the surface
$$x^2 = -2py; \; z = z$$
Sections are all conics and are drawn as

described for the hyperbolic cylinder.

The parabolic cylinder is shown in orthogonal projection with lines of equal arc length drawn on the surface. To find the geodesics, the developed surface is drawn showing these same lines. Then any system of straight lines drawn on this developed surface is a system of geodesics. They can then be projected back on the yz plane.

This method of drawing geodesics can be used for any developable surface. In the case of cylinders the geodesics are all helices or portions of helices. (See sheet 18 for possible regular patterns.)

Prisms or anti-prisms offer convenient approximations to cylinders or may be chosen for their own shape. Any regular polygon can be used for the two bases; for the anti-prisms the two bases are twisted so that the vertices of one are above the mid points of the sides of the other.

(For areas, surfaces and volumes of cylinders, prisms, and anti-prisms see Mathematics—Areas and Solids.)

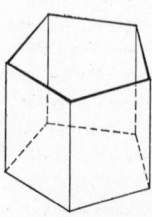

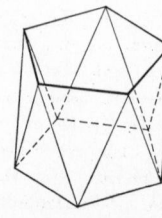

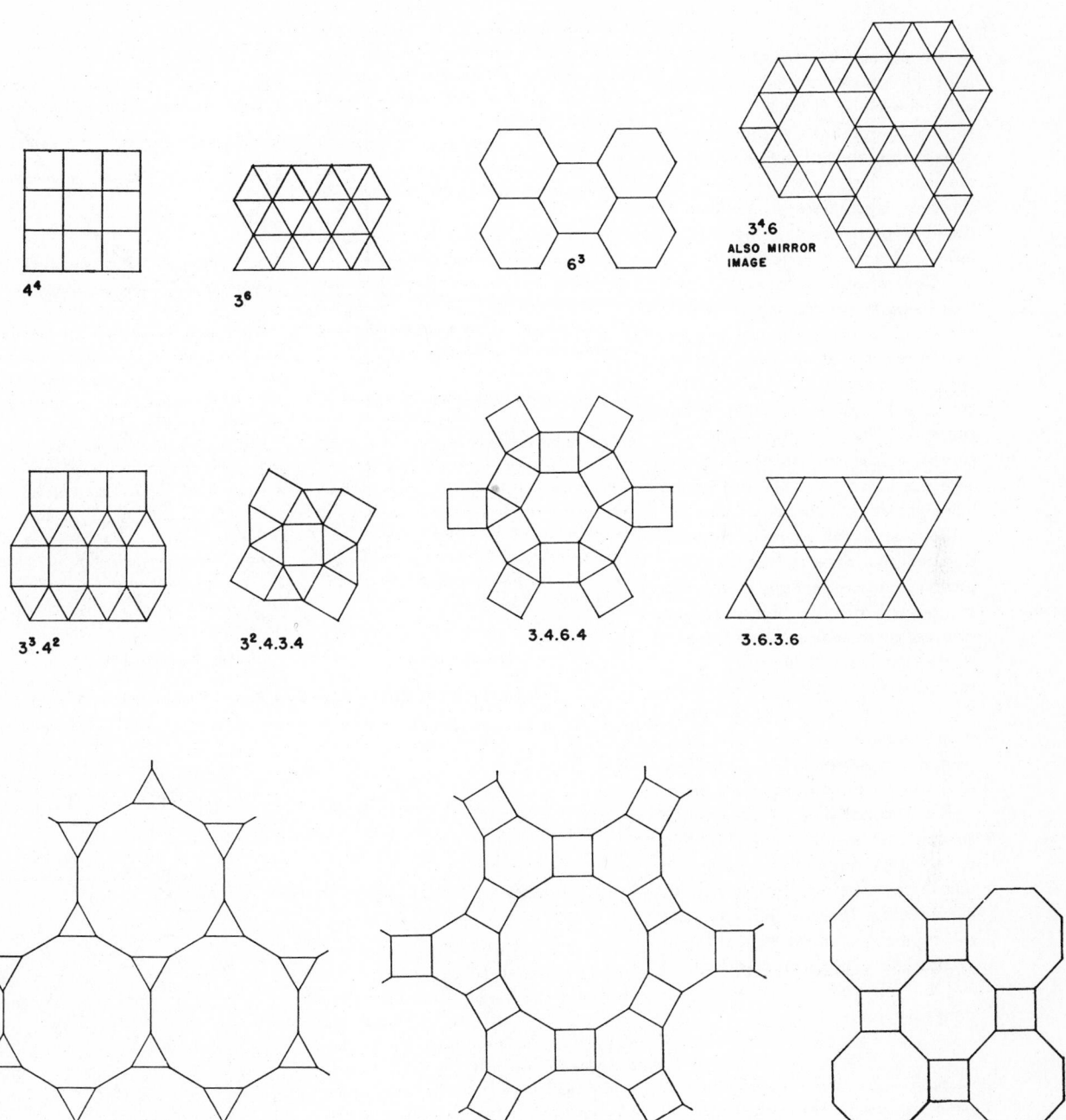

4^4

3^6

6^3

$3^4.6$
ALSO MIRROR
IMAGE

$3^3.4^2$

$3^2.4.3.4$

3.4.6.4

3.6.3.6

3.12^2

4.6.12

4.8^2

REGULAR AND SEMI-REGULAR PATTERNS

The division of a plane into regular polygons is often necessary for structural or decorative reasons. There are only three regular tessellations (patterns) in which all the polygons are identical. There are only eight semi-regular tessellations in which all the polygons are regular but not identical; all the sides are of equal length. One of the semi-regular tessellations has two forms which are mirror-images of each other. All vertices are congruent. The notation is based on the vertex figure of each tessellation. The polygons are listed by the number of sides as they are found in sequence around a vertex. These tessellations are related not only to the plane but to every surface which is developable and which can therefore be drawn without distortion on a plane. The sides of the polygons will, of course, all be geodesics. Not every tessellation can be used for every surface; it will be necessary to experiment to find which will fit and which will be most suited to the structural or esthetic purpose. Any polygon used structurally must be held rigid, either by division into triangles or by provision of a continuous membrane.

If every point on a plane curve is joined by a straight line to a point not in the plane of the curve, a cone is generated. Each straight line is called an element (or generator) of the cone; the curve is called the directrix. Since there is an infinity of possible plane curves, there is an infinity of possible cones. Every cone is a developable surface.

It helps in constructing a cone to know that every section of the surface is a curve of the same general type or degree as the directrix curve. All sections parallel to the plane of the directrix curve are curves which are parallel to the directrix curve (i.e. they are of the same shape, but larger or smaller.)

This fact is of value in drawing perspectives, since perspective projection consists essentially in drawing sections of a cone. Every second degree curve (conic section) drawn in perspective will therefore be a second degree curve. And every third degree curve will be some third degree curve; every transcendental curve (trig. functions, etc.) will be a transcendental curve.

The second degree or quadric cone is the one most used. Such a cone will be generated by using an ellipse, parabola or hyperbola as the directrix. These do not constitute different cones, in the way different cylinders are generated (see Sheet 17) but all generate cones of the general type:

$$\frac{x^2}{a^2} + \frac{y^2}{b^2} = \frac{z^2}{c^2}$$

Or, where $k = \tan \alpha = \dfrac{a}{c}$ and

$$l = \tan \beta = \frac{b}{c}$$

$$\frac{x^2}{k^2} + \frac{y^2}{l^2} = z^2$$

See drawing of the general elliptic cone on Sheet 20.

All sections of this cone parallel to a tangent plane of the cone are parabolas; all sections which cut only one nappe or sheet (surface on one side of the vertex) are ellipses,

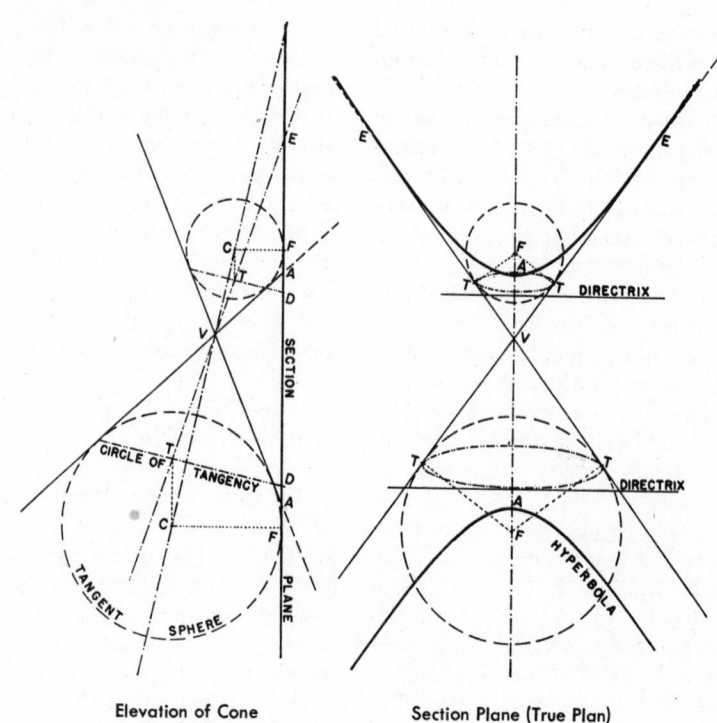

Elevation of Cone   Section Plane (True Plan)

Section of a Right Circular Cone By a Plane Which Cuts Both Nappes

(See also Sheet 20 for text)

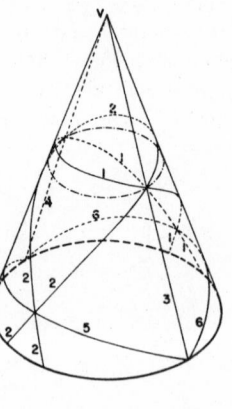
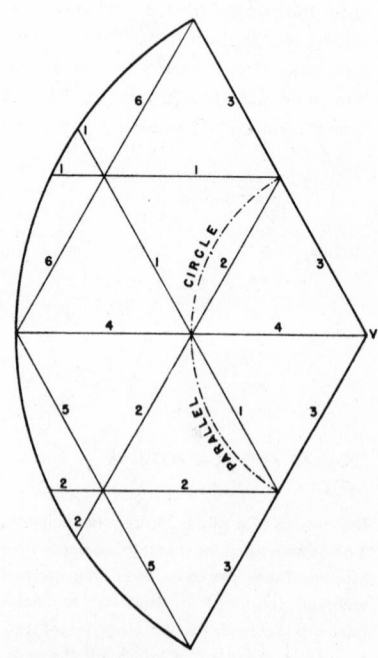

Isometric Projection of a Right Circular Cone and Its Development, Showing Geodesics

(See also Sheets 20, 21 for text)

the circle being a special case; and all sections which cut both nappes are hyperbolas.

It often happens that a pair of conjugate diameters of an ellipse are known, but not the major and minor axes. In the figure below (which shows the same ellipse as used for the generator of the general elliptic cone shown) the conjugate diameters Q_1CQ_2 and P_1CP_2 are known along the isometric axes. (Q_1CQ_2 and P_1CP_2 are defined as conjugate diameters if the tangents at Q_1 and Q_2 are parallel to P_1CP_2 and if the tangents at P_1 and P_2 are parallel to Q_1CQ_2.)

To find the major and minor axes, draw P_1A perpendicular to CQ_1. Make $P_1B_1 = P_1B_2 = CQ_1$. The line bisecting the angle B_1CB_2 is the major axis D_1CD_2. The minor axis is the line E_1CE_2 at right angles. Then find F, the midpoint of CB_2. Join P_1 to F, cutting CD at G and CE at H. The distance P_1G equals the semi-minor axis CE and P_1H equals the semi-major axis CD.

In the case of the isometric projection of a circle, the conjugate diameters are the 30 degree axes and the major and minor axes are along vertical and horizontal lines. Knowing P on the 30 degree axis, the line corresponding to PF can be drawn directly at 45 degrees.

The cone most often used, because it is the simplest, is the right circular cone, in which the directrix is a circle and the vertex is on the straight line which is perpendicular to the plane of the circle and which passes through the center of the circle. The equations of the right circular cone simplify from those of the elliptic cone to:

$$x^2 + y^2 = k^2z^2$$

and, in cylindrical coordinates:

$$r = kz$$

and in spherical coordinates, where ϕ is the co-latitude:

$$\phi = \text{constant} = \alpha.$$

The properties of the sections of the right circular cone are discussed on Sheet 2 of this series and also are the same as mentioned above under the general elliptic cone. In order to show clearly how the foci and directrices of the conic sections can be found geometrically, the diagram on Sheet 19 has been drawn showing a plane which cuts both nappes; the section is therefore an hyperbola. (The ellipses and parabolas are found in a similar fashion. See also the similar construction for the section of a cylinder, which gives an ellipse, on Sheet 17.)

Draw the two spheres which are tangent to the cone and to the section plane. Find the intersection of the plane of the circle of tangency with the section plane. This line is the directrix of the hyperbola. The point of tangency of the sphere with the section plane is the focus. It is also the projection of the center of the sphere. With the directrices and the foci established, follow one of the procedures of Sheet 6 for drawing the hyperbola.

Note that the traces of the sides of the cone as projected can be located by drawing on the elevation a line through the center of the sphere parallel to the section plane. The point T where this intersects the circle of tangency is a point on the trace. The line joining this point to the vertex is the edge desired. The point E is the intersection of this edge with the section plane.

The most useful way to draw a right circular cone so that it can be drawn in any projection, including perspective, is to utilize spheres which are tangent to the inside of the surface of the cone. The spheres are circles in any projection and the cone is always tangent.

To develop the surface of a right circular cone, draw an arc of a circle with the vertex as center and an element (straight line on the side) as radius. Measure off on this arc a length equal to circumference of the base circle. Join end points to vertex. (See drawing, Sheet 19.)

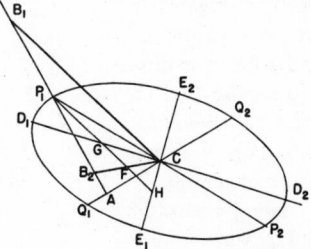

Conjugate Diameters of An Ellipse

General definition of Conjugate Diameters (true for all conic sections): A and B are conjugate diameters if both are lines through the center and if B bisects all the chords parallel to A, and if A bisects all the chords parallel to B.

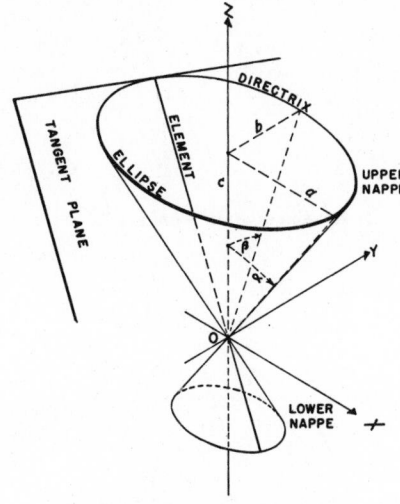

General Elliptic Cone (Isometric Projection)

(See also text on Sheet 19)

Geodesics can always be found by drawing straight lines on this developed surface when flat. One triangular net of geodesics which might be used structurally is shown. The development, of course, gives the true area of any portion of the surface.

The lines of curvature on a right circular cone are the straight elements (or meridians), lines 3 and 4 on the drawing on Sheet 19, and the parallel (or latitude) circles, only one of which is shown here as a dot-dash line.

Note that the parallel circles are not geodesics, although the elements are. The parallel circles show as arcs on the development.

The conical helix (not shown) is the space curve which lies on the surface of the right circular cone and which makes a constant angle with each parallel or latitude circle. Its plan projection is a logarithmic spiral (see Sheet 13). It is not a geodesic line.

To develop any arbitrary conical surface (see drawing): Given the plan and elevaton, divide the length of the directrix curve into any convenient number of parts by a series of points, here 16. Draw the straight line elements joining each of these points to the vertex. Starting with number one, find the true length of each element, by setting V'V as the true height of the vertex and V'1 as the true plan projection. The hypotenuse V.1 is the true length. For the development, from the vertex draw a line V1; then swing an arc of length V2 from V, and from 1 swing an arc of the true arc length 1.2; where these intersect is the developed position of 2. Continue in this way until all the elements are drawn. Then draw a smooth curve through all the numbered points. It will be noted that the accuracy of this method depends on the number of elements used, since the chord lengths are used as arc lengths in the development.

The elements are also lines of curvature; the other lines of curvature are found by drawing arcs on the development with the vertex as center. One such line is shown here as a dotted line. These can then be transferred to the plan and elevations or other projections. These lines of curvature are helpful when using rolls to bend a flat plate into a cone; the axes of the rollers can be inclined, and the lines of curvature which are at right angles to the elements must form closed curves.

Pyramids are surfaces generated by joining every point on a polygon to a point not in the plane of the polygon. They may be used to approximate cones or for their own sake.

For areas and volumes of pyramids and cones see Mathematics—Areas and Solids.

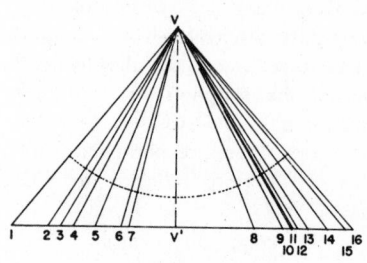

Elevation

True Lengths of Elements

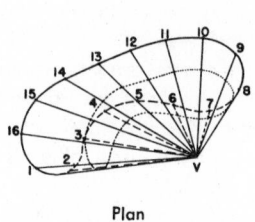

Plan

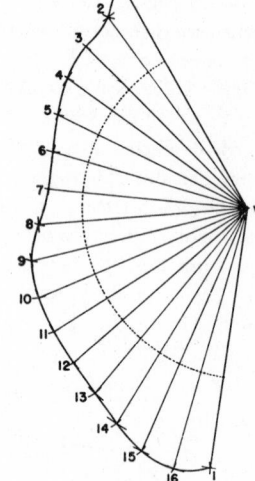

Development

Development of an Arbitrary Cone

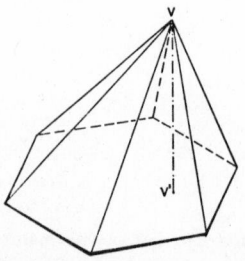

An Oblique Regular Hexagonal Pyramid

DEFINITION

Every point on the sphere is equidistant from a fixed point called the center. It is the only surface for which this is true. It is also the surface of revolution generated by the rotation of a circle about a diameter. Every section of a sphere is a circle. When the section plane contains the center, the circle is called a great circle or geodesic and has the same radius as the sphere; otherwise the section will be a "little circle" and may have any radius less than that of the sphere and more than zero. Longitude circles (or meridians) on the earth are all great circles; and latitude circles except the equator are little circles.

Every point on a sphere is an umbilical point; i.e. there is no principal direction and no line of curvature (see Sheets 14 and 15). Every geodesic line is a portion of a great circle. The mean curvature is everywhere constant and positive (equaling 1/R); the sphere is the only closed surface (without a boundary) for which this is true. The Gaussian curvature is also everywhere constant and positive (equaling 1/R²); and again it is the only closed surface for which this is true.

Of all closed surfaces the sphere contains the maximum possible volume for a given amount of surface.

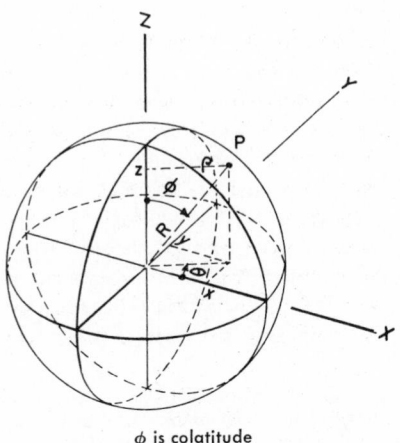

ϕ is colatitude

Equations:

In rectangular coordinates:

$$x^2 + y^2 + z^2 = R^2$$

In cylindrical coordinates:

$$z^2 = R^2 - \rho^2$$

[where $x = \rho \cos \Theta$
and $y = \rho \sin \Theta$]

In spherical coordinates:

$$r = R$$

[where $x = R \sin \phi \cos \Theta$
$y = R \sin \phi \sin \Theta$
$z = R \cos \phi$]

The area of the sphere = $4\pi\ R^2$ = lateral area of circumscribed cylinder.

The volume enclosed = $\frac{4}{3}\pi\ R^3 = \frac{2}{3}$ volume of circumscribed cylinder.

A lune (sometimes called a gore) is the surface between two great circles passing through the same pair of poles. A spherical wedge is the volume between the planes of these two great circles and the lune.

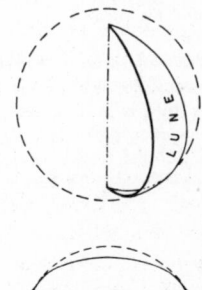

A zone is the surface between any two parallel section planes. The volume is called a segment and equals

$$\frac{1}{6}\pi h \left(3\rho_1{}^2 + 3\rho_2{}^2 + h^2\right)$$

where h = distance between two planes and ρ_1 and ρ_2 are radii of section circles.
Area = $hR2\pi$

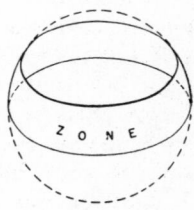

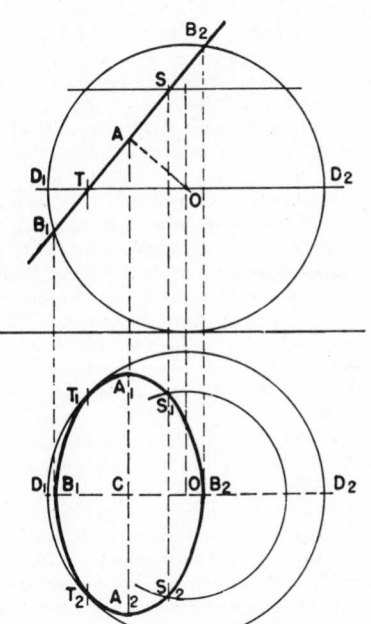

To draw the plan projection of the section of a sphere by any plane normal to the elevation, given the elevation: (Unless the section plane is parallel to that of the plane, the section will be projected as an ellipse.)

1. Draw AO normal to B_1B_2. Draw D_1OD_2 parallel to the plan.

2. Draw the plan below. Project B_1 and B_2 onto D_1OD_2 in the plan. The line joining B_1B_2 is the minor axis. Project A as a line normal to D_1OD_2 on the plan. This lies on the major axis and in plan $A_1C = CA_2 =$ true radius of the little circle, which can be measured as AB from the elevation.

3. With these two axes given, an ellipse can now be drawn by any of the methods shown on Sheet 4. T_1 and T_2 are the points of tangency of the ellipse with the plan. If desired, other points such as S_1 and S_2 can be found by drawing a line through S on the elevation parallel to the plan. The length of this line is the diameter of the little circle through S. Draw this circle on the plan and project S down to S_1 and S_2.

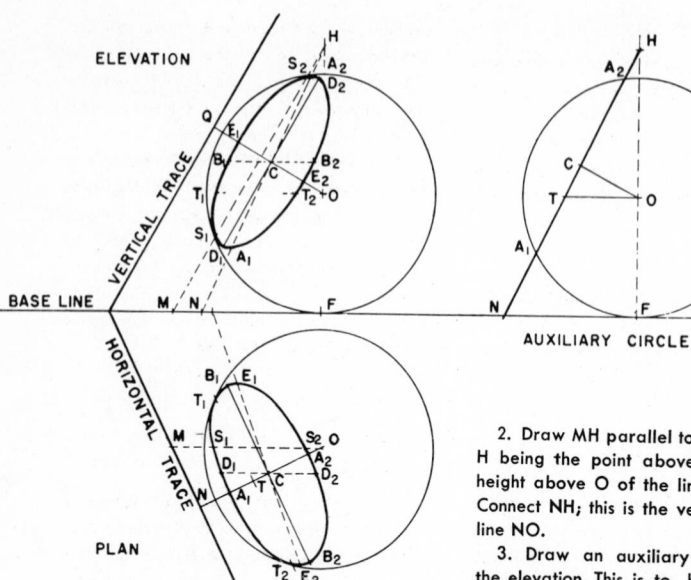

ELEVATION

AUXILIARY CIRCLE

PLAN

To draw the plan and elevation projections of the section of a sphere cut by any plane, given the horizontal and vertical traces of the plane on the plan and elevation. (The Base Line is the plane of the plan as seen in elevation and the plane of the elevation as seen in plan.)

1. On the plan, draw ON normal to the horizontal trace. This line represents a plane cutting the sphere in a great circle and cutting the section plane in a straight line. Draw OM parallel to the elevation plane. Project N and M up to the Base Line.

2. Draw MH parallel to the vertical trace, H being the point above O. H is the true height above O of the line NO in the plan. Connect NH; this is the vertical trace of the line NO.

3. Draw an auxiliary circle in line with the elevation. This is to be the true elevation of the plane through NO; the section plane appearing as the line NH. Set FH = FH and NF = true plan length = NO measured on the plan. Join NH: this cuts the circle at A_1 and A_2. Draw OC normal to A_1A_2. C is the center of the little circle which is the required section of the sphere, and is the center of the ellipses in plan and elevation which are the projections of this little circle.

4. Project C back onto NH on the elevation and the plan. The axes of the ellipse in plan lie along NO and a line through C parallel to the horizontal trace. The axes

of the ellipse in elevation lie along CQ, normal to the vertical trace and a line through C parallel to the vertical trace.

5. From the auxiliary circle, project A_1 and A_2 onto NH in elevation. These are points on the ellipse in elevation. Project them down to the plan; they are the ends of the minor axis of the ellipse in plan. Draw a line through C parallel to the horizontal trace and measure $CB_1 = CB_2$, equal to the diameter of the little circle, which can be measured from the auxiliary circle as A_1C. B_1 and B_2 are the ends of the major axis of the ellipse in plan. The ellipse can be completed by any convenient method (see Sheet 4). To verify the points of tangency T_1 and T_2, draw OT on the auxiliary circle. Transfer the distance OT onto the plan and draw T_1TT_2 parallel to the horizontal trace.

6. From the plan ellipse the elevation ellipse can be drawn. On the plan, draw a line through C parallel to the Base Line, cutting the plan ellipse at D_1 and D_2. This is the plan projection of the major axis of the ellipse in elevation. Draw a line through C in the elevation, parallel to the vertical trace and project D_1 and D_2 up onto it. These are the ends of the major axis. The length $CD_1 = CD_2$ (in elevation) $= CB_1 = CB_2$ (in plan) and is equal to the true diameter of the little circle. This is the plan projection of the minor axis of the ellipse in elevation. Project E_1 and E_2 up to the elevation; these are the ends of the minor axis. Draw the ellipse. The points of tangency S_1 and S_2 can be checked by projecting S_1 and S_2 on OM up from the plan to the elevation.

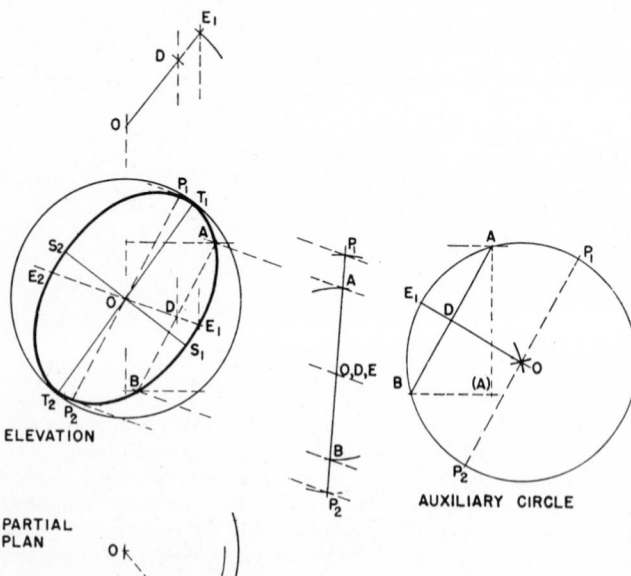

ELEVATION

PARTIAL PLAN

AUXILIARY CIRCLE

Given any two points, A and B, on the elevation of a sphere, to draw the projection of the geodesic (arc of great circle) through them. (This projection will be typically an ellipse.)

1. Draw the chord AB on the elevation. Join the center O to the midpoint D of the chord AB. Draw a line through O parallel to AB. These two lines through O lie on perpendicular diameters of the great circle and therefore lie on conjugate diameters of the ellipse.

2. Draw part of the plan below, showing the portions of the arcs of the little circles on which A and B lie. Project down A and B.

3. From the elevation project horizontal lines through A and B. On one of these lines measure B (A) equal to the true plan length AB. Erect a perpendicular on (A) to A. The hypotenuse of this right triangle is the true length of the chord AB. Draw the circle, of the same radius as the sphere, through A and B. Draw the diameter EDO normal to the chord AB and draw the diameter P_1OP_2 at right angles. (This auxiliary circle is the true plan or elevation of the great circle and gives the true angular length of the geodesic AEB.)

4. With proportional dividers or by measuring along oblique lines, as shown here, find the projected points P_1, P_2 and E on the elevation.

5. OP_1 and OE on the elevation are now conjugate semi-diameters of the ellipse. Use method of Sheet 20 to find the major axis T_1OT_2 and the minor axis S_1OS_2 and draw the ellipse. T_1 and T_2 are of course the points of tangency between the circle and the ellipse, the length of the major axis always being the diameter of the circle.

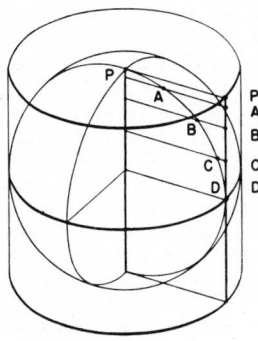

MAPPINGS OF THE SPHERE

Since the sphere cannot be developed onto a plane, many methods of studying it in various projections or mappings have been devised. The construction of spherical domes, particularly the newly developed "geodesic dome," is facilitated by understanding some of these.

A. Cylindrical projection

This is an "area-preserving" mapping of the sphere onto a cylinder. Each point on the sphere is projected onto the circumscribed cylinder along the normals to the cylinder. The area (zone) on the sphere cut off by any two parallel planes, normal to the axis of the cylinder, will be equal to the corresponding area cut off on the cylinder.

The great circles which have the axis of the cylinder as a diameter (i.e. longitude lines) become straight lines; the latitude circles are mapped as straight lines. All geodesics except the longitude lines and the equator are mapped as curves. The whole sphere is mapped onto a plane rectangular area, $2\pi R$ wide and $2R$ high.

B. Mercator's Projection

Like the cylindrical projection, this shows all meridian and latitude lines as straight lines, forming an orthogonal network. The longitude lines are equally spaced, proportionately to the degree of longitude; the latitude lines are spaced further and further apart as the latitude angle increases. On the map $x = R\Theta$; $y = R \log_e (\sec \psi + \tan \psi)$ where Θ is longitude and ψ latitude. This projection was developed for navigation: to map rhumb lines or loxodromes as straight lines. The rhumb line is a curve on the sphere which cuts all meridians at the same angle; it is the path taken by a ship whose course is fixed on a constant bearing with respect to true north. The whole sphere is mapped on a plane strip $2\pi R$ wide and of infinite height (although it is only the last fraction of a latitude degree which goes to infinity). Angles are preserved. The only geodesics which become straight lines are the longitude lines and the equator.

C. Stereographic projection

All points on the sphere are projected onto a plane which is tangent to the sphere, by rays from the pole which is diametrically opposite the point of tangency. All circles, geodesics and little circles, on the sphere are preserved as circles on the mapping. The arc of a geodesic is shown here as a dotted line. The radii of the projected circles are generally not the same as the circles on the sphere; the geodesics which pass through the pole are mapped as straight lines (which can be considered as circles whose radii are infinite). The angles between lines on the sphere are preserved on the mapping. Areas and distances are increasingly distorted as the mapping goes outward. However, the ratios of distances in any small area are approximately correct, and the stereographic projection can therefore be called a "conformal" mapping. The whole sphere is mapped onto the whole infinite plane once.

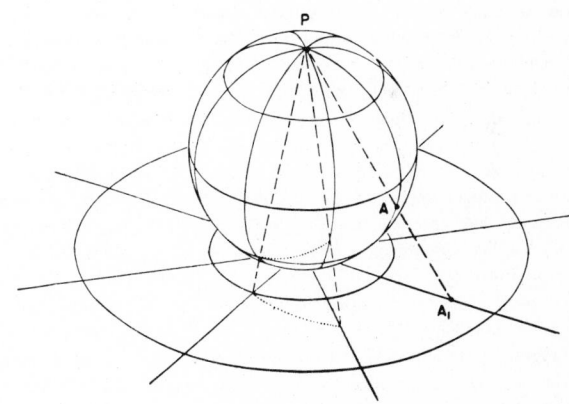

D. Central projection (sometimes called gnomonic projection)

If a sphere is projected from its center onto a tangent plane, all geodesics become straight lines. A geodesic is shown here as a dotted line. Such a projection is called a geodesic map, because all the geodesics on one surface, i.e. the sphere, are geodesics on the other, i.e. the plane. Angles are not preserved, nor are areas. The whole sphere is mapped twice onto the infinite plane; in other words each half of the sphere covers the plane once.

Both stereographic and central projections may be useful in studying geodesic domes. The plane of projection can be moved about at will to show different portions with a minimum of distortion.

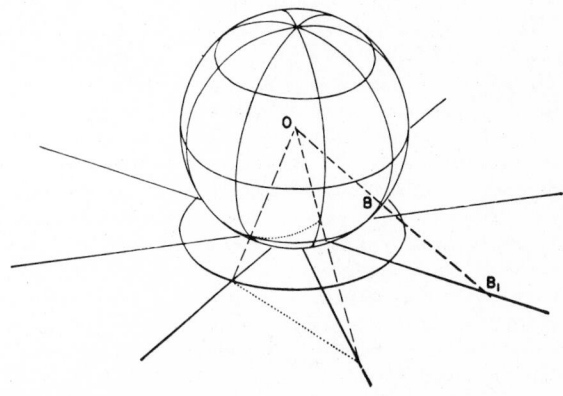

Since the sphere is curved in two directions and cannot be developed, many methods have been used to build domes of this shape. These may be grouped under the headings of radial domes and geodesic domes.

1. Radial Domes. This is the most commonly used method and is based on the image of latitude and longitude circles. Curved ribs are built along the longitude circles, radiating from the top, with or without transverse ribs on the latitude lines. The lune or gore spaces between the ribs are filled with thinner vaulting or paneling. If the lune (see Sheet 22) is thought of as the unit, this method is adaptable for prefabrication; domes have been built with a minimum of formwork by first erecting two diametrically opposite lunes, forming an arch against which the others can be constructed. The only difficulty is to join the many ribs which converge at the top; this is solved by introducing a compression ring. The ring may be closed or open.

If the radial dome is constructed as a triangulated network, with one side of each triangle lying on a latitude line, this system has the inconvenience of presenting ever diminishing triangles as the latitude circles become smaller toward the top. The lamella dome is built on this principle, with the latitude ribs replaced by a membrane or by simple struts.

Essentially similar is the method of building by zones (see Sheet 22), particularly adapted to small vaults. All the stones in one zone can be cut alike, but those in the next higher zone must be different. If the blocks follow along some kind of a helical line, as in an igloo, every block would have to be different to make an accurate sphere.

2. Geodesic Domes. The so-called spherical geodesic dome consists of a network of framing members which make a more or less uniform pattern over the whole surface, particularly the truncated icosahedron and the snub dodecahedron. (See drawings of polyhedra, Sheet 26.) It could be built with curved members which would lie along geodesic curves and thus be a portion of a true sphere, but is usually built as a polyhedron with straight members which form the chords of geodesic arcs. The perimeter of the dome at the bottom usually presents an irregular, ragged line.

If one attempts to cover a sphere with such a network, certain basic principles must be observed. Since the triangle is the simplest polygon and also the only one which is rigid in itself, the network will usually consist of triangles. These form larger configurations, depending on how many triangles meet at a point or vertex.

If six equilateral triangles meet on a plane surface, they form a regular hexagon. This is impossible on a sphere because the sum of the angles must be less than 360° around the vertex. On the sphere, therefore, all the members cannot be of the same length and the hexagons formed cannot be regular. Even if the pattern is made up of irregular hexagons, no matter how distorted, it is impossible to cover a complete sphere with them. A minimum of 12 pentagons must be introduced in order to satisfy Euler's formula.

Euler's formula states that, in any convex polyhedron, the number of faces (F), the number of vertices (V) and the number of edges (E) are related:

$$F + V - 2 = E$$

This formula can be used to check a dome which is not a complete sphere by considering the open bottom as a single face or non-plane polygon, the number of whose sides equals the number of members along the perimeter of the framework of the dome.

The basic possibilities and limitations of this type of framework are given by studying all the regular and semi-regular polyhedra and their duals, remembering that polygonal faces can be subdivided. Their number is quite limited.

There are only five regular polyhedra, all of whose edges are the same length and all of whose faces are regular, identical polygons. Called the Platonic polyhedra, they can have a sphere inscribed within them touching each face in its center, or have a sphere circumscribed about them, passing through every vertex. These points of tangency or vertices are the only regular systems of points which are equidistant from each other on the surface of a sphere.

There are the 13 semi-regular polyhedra, called Archimedean. All edges are the same length and every face is a regular polygon, but all the faces are not identical. The vertices are all congruent (identical) but not regular (the angles between pairs of edges are not all the same). These polyhedra can have a sphere circumscribed about them, passing through each vertex. Prisms and anti-prisms (see sheet 17 for drawings) also meet these conditions if the top and bottom polygons are regular and if the sides are squares in the case of the prisms and equilateral triangles in the case of the anti-prisms.

There are also the 13 duals of the Archimedean polyhedra. A polyhedron P_2 is the dual of polyhedron P_1 if the faces of P_2 correspond to the vertices of P_1. Thus, the octahedron is the dual of the cube, the icosahedron is the dual of the dodecahedron. The number of vertices and the number of faces are interchanged; the number of edges remains constant. The vertices of the Archimedean duals do not fall on a sphere, but a sphere tangent to every face at its center can be inscribed within each dual. Every face is identical but is not a regular polygon. Every vertex is regular but all vertices are not identical. (The duals of the prisms are called dipyramids, made of two pyramids placed base to base. The faces are all isosceles triangles. The duals of the antiprisms are called trapezohedra. The faces are kites, or quadrilaterals with adjacent pairs of sides of equal length.)

In order to keep strut lengths as short as possible and avoid buckling, and in order to provide complete triangulation for rigidity, the polygons forming the polyhedra can be subdivided into triangles, and all triangles can be further subdivided. If the members thus added are the same length as the others, the added vertex will not be on the sphere; if the added vertex is held on the sphere, the added members will have to be of a different length. Continuous membranes, plane or warped, may also be used to provide rigidity.

See Sheets 26 and 27 following for diagrams and schedules of the polyhedra. The index number lists the number of faces of the polygons meeting at a vertex (see sheet 18 for similar index numbering system). For the Archimedean duals the index number of the corresponding semi-regular polygon is used with the prefix V.

Drawings of the Polyhedra, shown in plan, with name of each and number of faces, vertices, and edges of each. (Cube not shown.)

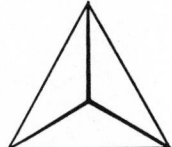

Tetrahedron
F	V	E
4	4	6

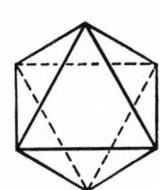

Octahedron
F	V	E
8	6	12

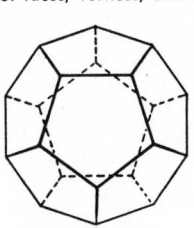

Dodecahedron
F	V	E
12	20	30

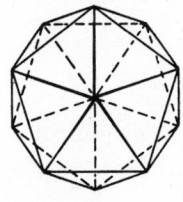

Icosahedron
F	V	E
20	12	30

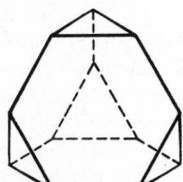

Truncated Tetrahedron
F_3	F_4	V	E
4	4	12	18

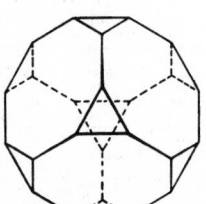

Truncated Cube
F_3	F_8	V	E
8	6	24	36

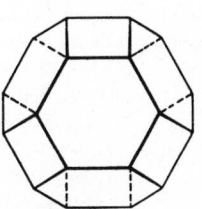

Truncated Octahedron
F_4	F_6	V	E
6	8	24	36

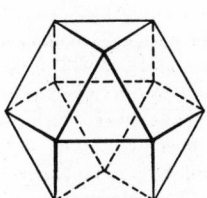

Cuboctahedron
F_3	F_4	V	E
8	6	12	24

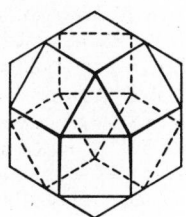

Rhombicuboctahedron
F_3	F_4	V	E
8	18	24	48

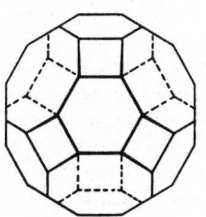

Truncated Cuboctahedron
F_4	F_6	F_8	V	E
12	8	6	48	72

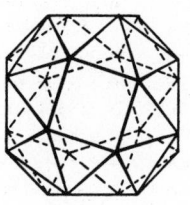

Snub Cube
F_3	F_4	V	E
32	6	24	60

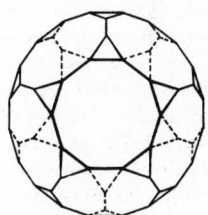

Truncated Dodecahedron
F_3	F_{10}	V	E
20	12	60	90

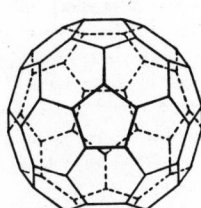

Truncated Icosahedron
F_5	F_6	V	E
12	20	60	90

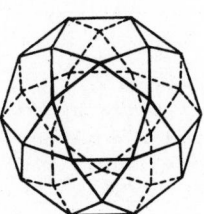

Icosidodecahedron
F_3	F_5	V	E
20	12	30	60

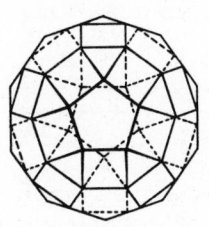

Rhombicosidodecahedron
F_3	F_4	F_5	V	E
20	30	12	60	120

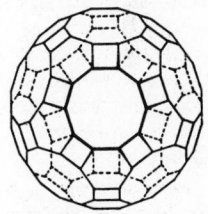

Truncated Icosidodecahedron
F_4	F_6	F_{10}	V	E
30	20	12	120	180

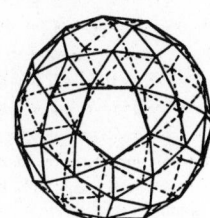

Snub Dodecahedron
F_3	F_5	V	E
80	12	60	150

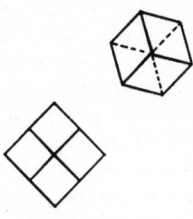

Plans

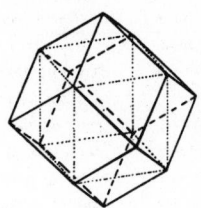
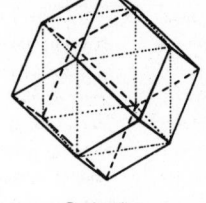

Rhombic Dodecahedron
F	V	E
12	14	24

Projection

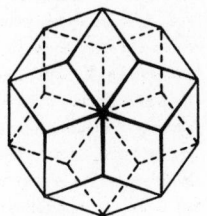

Rhombic Triacontahedron
F	V	I
30	32	60

Notes:
1. Only two of the Archimedean duals are shown. The rhombic dodecahedron is drawn in an oblique or axonometric projection, as well as in two plan views. Note it is a cube (shown in fine dotted line) with a square pyramid added to each face. The others can be drawn from the corresponding Archimedean polyhedron: (a) Draw plan with vertex in center; (b) Draw on plan the perpendicular bisector of each edge which meets at vertex; (c) Extend all bisectors until they intersect; they form irregular polygonal face of the dual.
2. For making models, polygons can be drawn on a flat sheet, with some edges of each polygon in common with adjacent polygons, making a continuous strip called a net.

INDEX NO.	DUALS OF SEMI-REGULAR POLYHEDRA	E/r	DIHEDRAL ANGLE	FACE ANGLES	R/r
V.3.6²	Triakis Tetrahedron	3.127 / 1.876	129° 32'	112° 53', 33° 33½'	1.2222
V.3.8²	Triakis Octahedron	2.083 / 1.219	147° 21'	117° 14', 31° 23'	1.0858
V.4.6²	Tetrakis Hexahedron	1.491	143° 8'	83° 37', 48° 11½'	1.1111
V.(3.4)²	Rhombic Dodecahedron (Octahedric Granatohedron)	1.118 / 1.225	120°	109° 28', 70° 32'	1.3333
V.3.4³	Trapezoidal Icositetrahedron	0.887 / 0.686	138° 7'	115° 16', 81° 34½'	1.1464
V.4.6.8	Hexakis Octahedron	1.070 / 0.878 / 0.656	155° 5'	87° 12', 55° 1½', 37° 46½'	1.0488
V.34.4	Pentagonal Icositetrahedron (Two Enantiomorphs)	0.727 / 0.513	136° 20'	114° 48¼', 80° 46'	1.1602
V.3.10²	Triakis Icosahedron	1.254 / 0.728	160° 36'	119° 3', 30° 28½'	1.0302
V.5.6²	Pentakis Dodecahedron	0.780 / 0.692	156° 43'	68° 36', 55° 42'	1.0425
V.(3.5)²	Rhombic Triacontahedron (Icosahedric Granatohedron)	0.727	144°	116° 34', 63° 26'	1.1056
V.3.4.5.4	Trapezoidal Hexecontahedron	0.584 / 0.379	154° 8'	118° 16', 86° 59', 67° 46'	1.0530
V.4.6.10	Hexakis Icosahedron	0.689 / 0.586 / 0.373	164° 54'	89° 0', 58° 14', 32° 46'	1.0174
V.345	Pentagonal Hexecontahedron (Two Enantiomorphs)	0.500 / 0.286	153° 10'	118° 8', 67° 28'	1.0574

INDEX NO.	REGULAR POLYHEDRA	e/R	DIHEDRAL ANGLE	Θ	R/r
3³	Tetrahedron	1.633	70° 32'	109° 28'	3.00
4³	Cube	1.155	90°	70° 32'	1.732
3⁴	Octahedron	1.414	109° 28'	90°	1.732
5³	Dodecahedron	0.714	116° 34'	41° 49'	1.258
3⁵	Icosahedron	1.051	138° 11'	63° 26'	1.258

INDEX NO.	SEMI-REGULAR POLYHEDRA	e/R	DIHEDRAL ANGLES — Faces	DIHEDRAL ANGLES — Angles	Θ
3.6²	Truncated Tetrahedron	0.853	6-6, 6-3	70° 32', 109° 28'	50° 28'
3.8²	Truncated Cube	0.562	8-8, 8-3	90°, 125° 16'	32° 39'
4.6²	Truncated Octahedron (Tetrakaidecahedron)	0.6325	6-4, 6-6	125° 16', 109° 28'	36° 52'
(3.4)²	Cuboctahedron	1.00		125° 16'	60°
3.4³	Rhombicuboctahedron	0.715	4-4, 3-4	135°, 144° 44'	41° 53'
4.6.8	Truncated Cuboctahedron	0.431	8-4, 8-6, 6-4	135° 16', 125° 16', 144° 44'	24° 55'
34.4	Snub Cube (Two Enantiomorphs)	0.744	4-3, 3-3	142° 59', 153° 14'	43° 40'
3.10²	Truncated Dodecahedron	0.337	10-10, 10-3	116° 34', 142° 37'	19° 24'
5.6²	Truncated Icosahedron	0.4035	6-6, 6-5	138° 11', 142° 37'	23° 17'
(3.5)²	Icosidodecahedron (Triacontagon)	0.618		142° 37'	36°
3.4.5.4	Rhombicosidodecahedron	0.448	5-4, 3-4	148° 17', 159° 6'	25° 52'
4.6.10	Truncated Icosidodecahedron	0.263	10-6, 10-6, 6-4	148° 17', 142° 37', 159° 6'	15° 6'
3¹.5	Snub Dodecahedron (Two Enantiomorphs)	0.464	5-3, 3-3	152° 56', 164° 10'	26° 50'

NOTES:

e = length of edge of regular and semi-regular polyhedra. θ = angle subtended by edge at center (for regular and semi-regular polyhedra). R = Radius of circumscribed sphere (regular + semi-regular polyhedra). r = radius of inscribed sphere (regular polyhedra and duals of semi-regular polyhedra). E = length of edges of duals of semi-regular polyhedra. R/r: This ratio, when given for the Archimedean duals, is the ratio of the radius of the circumscribed sphere of the corresponding Archimedean polyhedron to the radius of the sphere inscribed within the dual. Enantiomorph means form of opposite hand (in drawing, change broken lines to solid and solid lines to broken). There are only five possible ways of filling up three dimensional spaces with only one type of regular or Archimedean polyhedra and their duals = cubes; triangular prisms; hexagonal prisms; truncated octahedra; rhombic dodecahedra. There are three additional ways, using more than one type = tetrahedra + octahedra; tetrahedra + truncated tetrahedra; octahedra + cuboctahedra.

References: Cundy and Rollett, Mathematical Models (Oxford, 1951); Matila C. Ghyka, Esthetique des Proportions (Gallimard, 1927).

The most perfect development of the geodesic dome has been made by R. Buckminster Fuller. Combining the tetrahedron and the sphere, it is derived from his concept of "energetic geometry." Of all regular convex polyhedra the tetrahedron encloses the minimum of space with the maximum of surface, and is the stiffest form against external and tangential pressures. The sphere encloses the maximum of space with a minimum of surface and is the strongest form against internal or radial pressures.

In the Fuller dome a space-frame, built up of elongated tetrahedra, is given the overall shape of a sphere. The basic unit is rhombus or diamond shaped in plan, triangular in elevation.

The unit may be built of struts or, in the type being manufactured by the Kaiser Aluminum Co., of a bent sheet, stiffened by edge flanges and with one strut across the short axis.

The tetrahedral units are combined to form a complete framework by joining six units together. Assuming the diagonal members to be fastened already to the short axis and long axis members, a six-way fastener is required at the vertices of the short axes. As the units are combined to cover the whole sphere, there will be a minimum of 12 cases where five instead of six units come together. (See sheet 25 for explanation.)

The framework is dimensioned so that

TETRAHEDRON UNITS

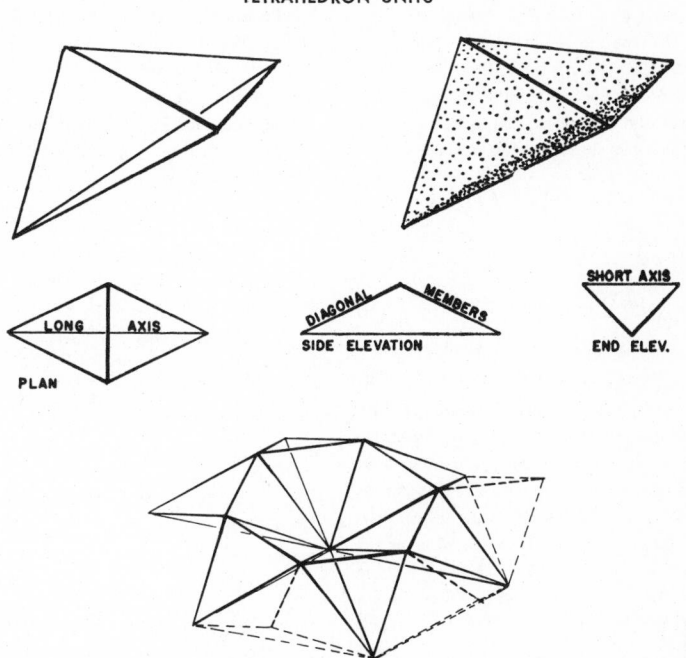

The structures designed according to the information in this article are covered by United States Patent No. 2,682,235 and Canadian Patent No. 512,422 granted to R. Buckminster Fuller. They include any building framework designed with an overall pattern of three-way great circle gridding.

all the long axis vertices of the tetrahedra lie on a sphere. The struts forming the long axes thus lie along chords of geodesic arcs. The other struts are placed to lie outside the surface of the sphere and are dimensioned to give the depth of

frame considered necessary for stiffness. (In the aluminum dome manufactured by Kaiser this depth is 12 in. and is used for their standard dome with a sphere radius of 80 ft. See Sheet 9 of Structural Forms—Steel.)

The method of subdividing the surface of the sphere to find the correct position of these long axis vertices is as follows:

1. Divide the surface of the sphere into 20 equilateral spherical triangles. Graphically this can most easily be done by starting with icosahedron (see Sheets 26 and 27) and joining the vertices by geodesic arcs instead of by straight lines. All the angles of the equilateral triangle are 72^0; the sides are 63^0 $26'$ $5.47''$ or 1.107147 radians. This is a spherical icosahedron and is the maximum number of equilateral triangles into which a sphere can be divided. Usually only five of these equilateral triangles would be used, making a dome that is one-quarter of a sphere, with a $\frac{rise}{span}$ ratio of about $\frac{1}{3}$. The method of division can be carried out

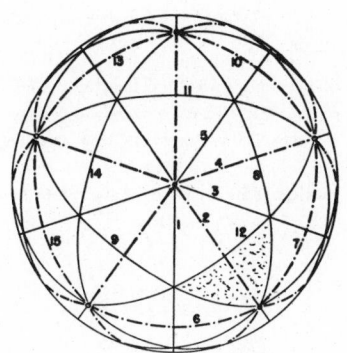

PLAN
Plan of opposite side is identical, but rotated through 36^0

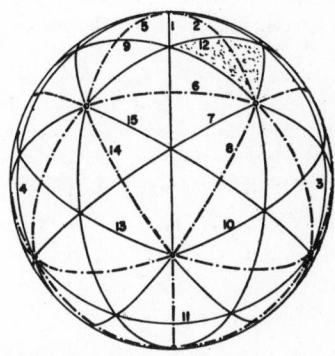

ELEVATION
Elevation from other side is identical, but turned upside down

Shaded area is typical spherical isosceles triangle, as analyzed on the following page and as shown on Sheet 9 of Structural Forms—Steel.

over the whole surface of a sphere, however, and will be described in this way.

2. Draw the medians of each of these triangles, dividing each side in half. This is the same as extending the sides of all triangles to form 15 complete great cir-

cles. These lines will be the only complete symmetrically spaced, great circles on the sphere, no matter how much further it is subdivided. (In the diagrams the icosahedral division is shown with a dot-dash line, the medians and other subdivisions with a full line.)

3. The medians divide each equilateral triangle into six identical spherical right triangles, with the angles 90°, 60° and 36.° On the complete sphere there are 6 x 20 or 120 of these right triangles.

4. Pair off the 120 right triangles into 60 isosceles triangles. The apex angle is 72°, the two base angles are each 60°.

The lengths of the two equal sides are 37° 22' 38.5" (0.652358 radians); the length of the base 41° 48' 37.1" (0.729727658 radians). The altitude is 31° 43' 2.7" (0.553574 radians) or half the side of the original equilateral triangle.

5. The 60 identical spherical isosceles triangles are further subdivided by using the base as the measuring line. The base is divided into any even number of equal arcs, called the "frequency" and referred to by the Greek letter nu ν. From each point of division a great circle arc is projected out at 90° to the base across the triangle until it intersects the other side. The simplest cases in order are:

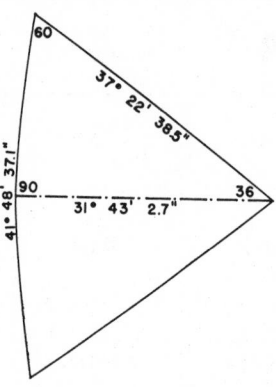

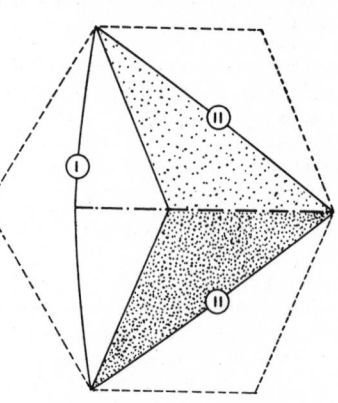

6. The minimum number of divisions or the smallest "frequency" is 2. For $\nu=2$, the only arc projected is the altitude of the isosceles triangle itself. The lengths of the long axes of the tetrahedra or diamonds (marked as I and II) are the lengths of the sides of the triangle. The dimensions are given on sheet 30. In the plan of the basic isosceles triangle we now have three "half" diamonds, the other halves being provided by the neighboring triangles (shown here dashed). The diagonal struts

and the short axis struts are above or outside of the sphere. There are a total

of 3/2 x 60 = 90 diamonds for a complete sphere.

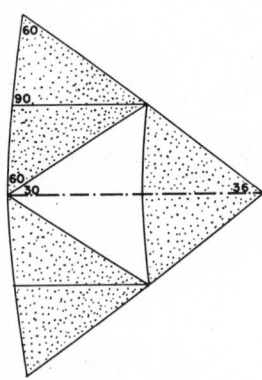

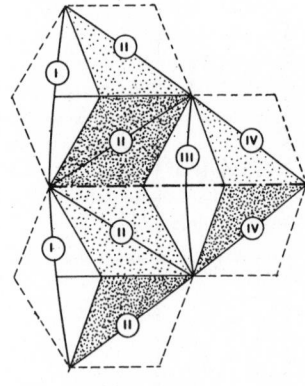

7. For a "frequency" of 4 ($\nu = 4$), the base is divided into four equal arcs. Three arcs at 90° to the base are projected into the triangle from the points of division; and two additional arcs are projected at 60° to the base from the second or center point of division. All calculations can be performed on the basis of the formulas for spherical right triangles (see Sheet 39 for the list of these formulas). These 60° lines divide the large isosceles triangle into four smaller, non-identical isosceles triangles of three sizes. The sides of

these triangles are the long axis diagonals of the tetrahedra or diamonds. They are marked I, II, III and IV and the lengths are tabulated on Sheet 30. We now have four types of diamond and a total of three

complete and six half diamonds within the plan of the basic isosceles triangle. Thus there are 6 x 60 = 360 diamonds in the complete sphere.

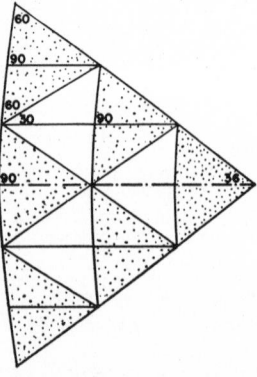

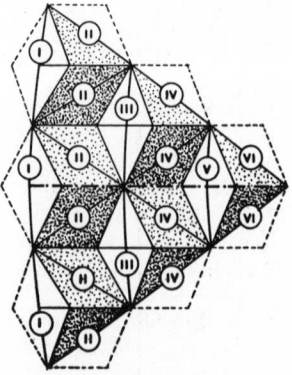

8. For a "frequency" of 6 (v = 6), the base is divided into six equal arcs. Five arcs at 90° to the base are projected into the triangle from the points of division; and two additional arcs are projected at 60° to the base from both the second and fourth points of division. These 60° lines divide the basic isosceles triangle into nine smaller isosceles triangles of five sizes. The sides of these triangles are the long axis diagonals of the tetrahedra or diamonds. They are marked I, II, III, IV, V and VI; the lengths are tabulated below.

We now have six types of diamonds and a total of nine complete and nine half diamonds in the plan of the basis isosceles

triangle. Thus there are 13½ x 60 = 810 diamonds on the complete sphere.

9. This procedure can be continued without limit. In every case:

a) The number of smaller isosceles triangles into which the basic isosceles triangle is divided is $\left(\dfrac{\nu}{2}\right)^2$.

b) The number of types of tetrahedra or diamonds is equal to the frequency number ν (number of divisions of the base.)

c) The number of tetrahedra or diamonds in one of the basic isosceles triangles is $\dfrac{3}{2}\left(\dfrac{\nu}{2}\right)^2$. Since there are 60 basic isosceles triangles, the number of tetrahedra to a complete sphere is $90\left(\dfrac{\nu}{2}\right)^2$.

The following table gives the lengths of the long axes of the tetrahedra for different frequencies. The lengths are measured as geodesic arcs along the surface of the sphere.

Frequency ν or number of divisions of base		**2**	**4**	**6**	**8**	**10**	**12**
Number of types of tetrahedra		2	4	6	8	10	12
Number of tetrahedra to complete sphere $90\left(\dfrac{\nu}{2}\right)^2$		**90**	**360**	**810**	**1440**	**2250**	**3240**
LENGTHS OF LONG AXIS DIAGONALS IN DEGREES AND RADIANS. To convert to linear measure, multiply length in radians by radius of sphere	**I**	41° 48′ 37.12″ 0.729728	20° 54′ 18.56″ 0.364864	13° 56′ 12.4″ 0.243243	10° 27′ 9.3″ 0.182432	8° 21′ 43.4″ 0.145946	6° 58′ 6.2″ 0.121621
	II	37° 22′ 38.5″ 0.652358	20° 15′ 8.4″ 0.353470	13° 44′ 11.4″ 0.239747	10° 22′ 1.4″ 0.180939	8° 19′ 4.8″ 0.145176	6° 56′ 34.2″ 0.121175
	III		19° 56′ 1″ 0.347908	13° 37′ 59.2″ 0.237943	10° 19′ 17.8″ 0.180146	8° 17′ 39.4″ 0.144762	6° 55′ 43.9″ 0.120932
	IV		17° 7′ 30.1″ 0.298888	12° 39′ 33.5″ 0.220947	9° 53′ 7″ 0.172531	8° 3′ 51.7″ 0.140750	6° 47′ 37.2″ 0.118572
	V			12° 51′ 22.8″ 0.224385	9° 58′ 0.5″ 0.173954	8° 6′ 17.4″ 0.141456	6° 48′ 59.6″ 0.118971
	VI			10° 58′ 53.6″ 0.191664	9° 3′ 23.8″ 0.158068	7° 36′ 18.5″ 0.132735	6° 30′ 57″ 0.113723
	VII				9° 27′ 51.9″ 0.165185	7° 49′ 23.5″ 0.136540	6° 38′ 40.3″ 0.115969
	VIII				8° 4′ 6.3″ 0.140820	7° 0′ 58″ 0.122454	6° 8′ 36.5″ 0.107224
	IX					7° 28′ 57.6″ 0.130597	6° 25′ 41.4″ 0.112193
	X					6° 22′ 25.5″ 0.111243	5° 42′ 54.6″ 0.099748
	XI						6° 11′ 11″ 0.107973
	XII						5° 15′ 59″ 0.091916

The hyperbolic paraboloid, a quadric surface, is shown here in isometric and orthogonal projection. It is a doubly curved surface and therefore not developable. However, since it is ruled surface, it can easily be formed or molded in a framework of straight members.
It can be generated in two ways:

1. A generating parabola (AOA in diagrams) is moved along another directrix parabola (BOB) in such a way that the successive positions of the plane of AOA are always parallel and the successive positions of the line AA are always parallel.

2. As a ruled surface: Given two straight lines (here 5'5' and 5 5) lying in a horizontal plane, two vertical planes containing these straight lines. Move one of these lines, say 5'5', called the generator, along the other (5 5), called the directrix, in such a way that its successive positions are always skew but always parallel to its initial position. Thus no plane can contain any two positions of the line 5'5'. These successive positions are the straight lines of one family, sometimes called a regulus. The other family is found by sliding the other straight line 5 5 along the line 5'5'.

The equation, with axes as shown:

$$\frac{x^2}{a} - \frac{y^2}{b^2} = \frac{z}{c}$$

(See below for the equations referred to the asymptotes as axes.)

All sections containing the z axis are parabolas. As such a section is rotated about the z axis, from one principal plane (the xz) to the other (the yz), the parabolas become wider and wider, but all with their centers of curvature above the xy plane, until at the sections containing 5 5 or 5'5', the parabola becomes a straight line; as rotation continues, the parabolas have their centers of curvature below the xy plane, and become narrower until the section plane reaches the yz plane. All sections parallel to any given plane containing the z axis are identical parabolas (or a straight line).

Every section parallel to the xy plane is a hyperbola. The lines 5'5' and 5 5 are the asymptotes of all of these hyperbolas. Every section above the xy plane will be a hyperbola with its axis parallel to the x axis; every section below the xy plane has its axis parallel to the y axis. The hyperbolas at the same distance above and below the xy plane (i.e. when z = +d or —d) are conjugate. On the xy plane the hyperbola becomes the pair of straight lines 5'5' and 5 5.

Every section which is not parallel to a plane containing the z axis is also a hyperbola (or a straight line). There are no elliptical or circular sections.

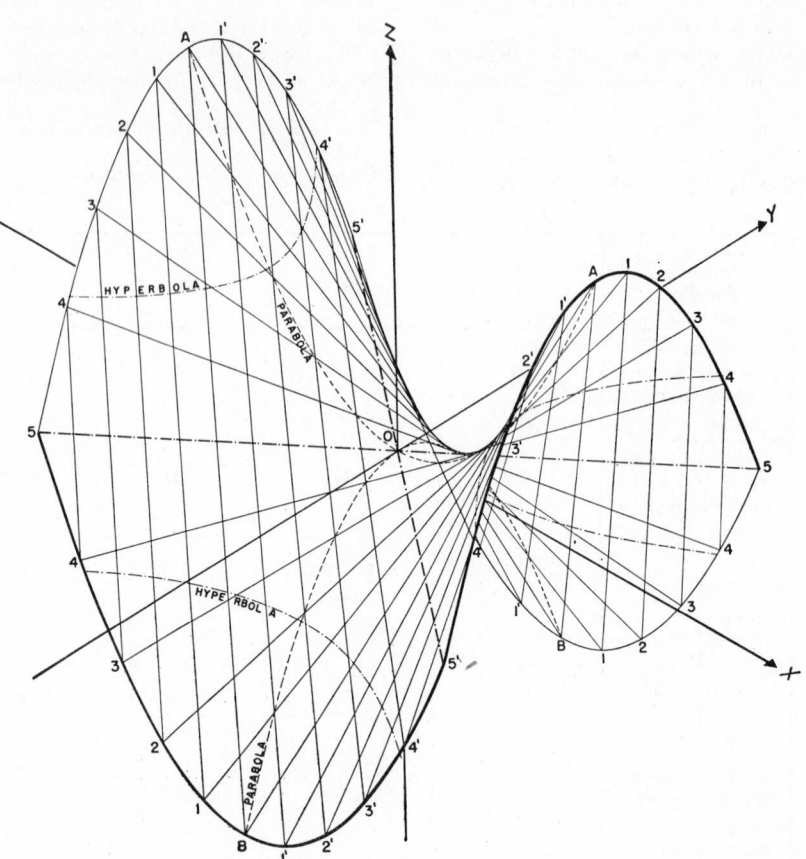

Isometric Projection

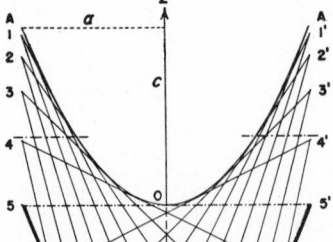

X Z-Plane

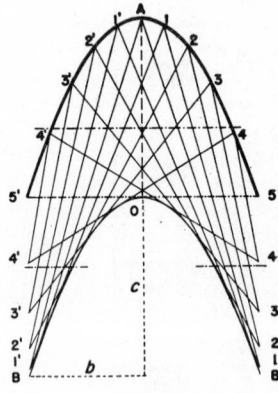

Y Z-Plane

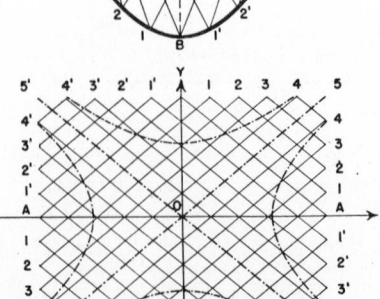

Plan

Every contour or visible edge in axonometric or orthogonal projection is a parabola.

A plane can be passed through any two straight lines of different families or reguli; no plane can be passed through two straight lines of the same family. Through any point on the surface pass only two straight lines, one from each family. The tangent plane at that point is defined by these two straight lines.

Note that the plan projection consists of two families of parallel lines, forming a network of identical rhombuses. When $a = b$, the rhombus becomes a square. Note also that, although the angle between two straight lines of different families is constant in plan, it varies on the surface. (Therefore the hyperbolic paraboloid cannot be a minimal surface, since two such straight lines are the asymptotic lines at the point. On a minimal surface asymptotic lines must meet everywhere at right angles.) The lines of curvature bisect the angles between the straight lines on the surface.

TO DRAW: Given the rectangular plan with the parabolas 5'A5, 5A5', 5'B5 and 5B5' as the sides, divide each side into the same number of spaces (here 10) and draw the diagonal straight lines connecting corresponding points. These are the plan projections of the straight line generators of the surface. See Sheet 31.

The numbered points can be used to construct the parabolas, in elevation, in isometric or other projection, following the method of Sheet 31. These points are equidistant from the xz or yz planes; they are not equidistant along the true length of the parabolas.

Draw the elevations (projections on the xz and yz planes) by establishing the height c of A above the xy plane and the equal height c of B below the xy plane. Join the corresponding points on the parabolas with straight lines. With the numbering system shown, for example, each point such as 2 is joined by two straight lines to the two nearest points also numbered 2, the point such as 2' is joined to the nearest points numbered 2'. These straight lines will generate the surface.

In elevation the straight lines are tangents to the contour parabola AOA; this parabola is identical to the parabola 5B5'. In axonometric projection (here an isometric) the contour is also always a parabola, which can be drawn from the straight line tangents.

Warped Parallelogram

Axonometric projection

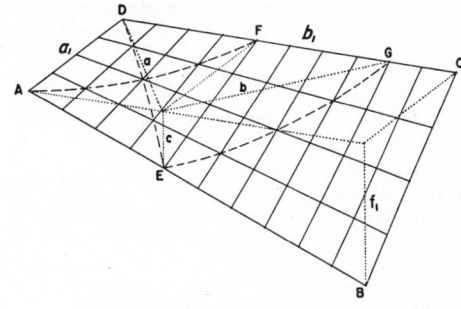

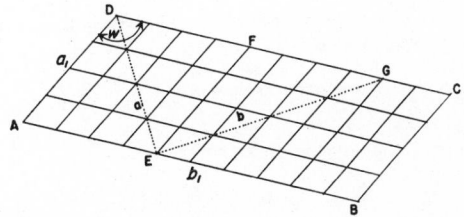

Plan

The hyperbolic paraboloid as a warped parallelogram. A surface which is a parallelogram in plan can be set so that three corners (here A, C and D) are all in one plane (here horizontal), and the fourth corner (B) is not in the plane (here lowered). Divide the sides into equal spaces and join the pairs of opposite sides by straight lines. The surface will be a portion of a hyperbolic paraboloid.

Comparing this with the diagrams on Sheet 31, the lines AD and DC correspond to the lines 05 and 05'. The parabola DE corresponds to the parabola OB. The parabolas AF and EG correspond to the parabola AOA as it slides down OB; and their tangents are horizontal at the intersections with DE.

In writing the equation, the edges AD (length a_1) and DC (length b_1) are usually taken as axes, with the angle w between them. The equation is

$$k \, x_1 y_1 \sin w = z \quad \text{Where } k = \frac{f}{a_1 b_1 \sin w}$$

Note that, since $c = \frac{a_1}{b_1} f_1$, $k = \frac{c}{a_1^2 \sin w}$

This therefore corresponds to the equation $x_1 y_1 = a_1^2 \frac{z}{c}$ (see below). The area of the plan projection of the parallelogram is $a_1 b_1 \sin w$.

When the edges of the parallelogram, corresponding to the principal asymptotes of the hyperbolic paraboloid, are taken as the axes, care must be used to compare the constants used in the two types of equation. The difference is basically the same as that between the equation of a hyperbola referred to its center line and that referred to its asymptotes. (When $z = c$, the section of the hyperbolic paraboloid is the hyperbola whose parameters are a and b.)

For the hyperbola, the two cases are:

1. The equilateral hyperbola (corresponding to rectangular hyperbolic paraboloid). In standard form, referred to x and y axes:

$$x^2 - y^2 = a^2 \text{ or } \frac{x^2}{a^2} - \frac{y^2}{a^2} = 1$$

Axes rotated through $45°$ to x_1 and y_1:

$$x_1 y_1 = a_1^2,$$

where

$$a_1 = \frac{a}{\sqrt{2}}$$

2. The general hyperbola. In standard form, referred to x and y axes:

$$\frac{x^2}{a^2} - \frac{y^2}{b^2} = 1$$

Axes changed from rectangular to oblique and rotated to x_1 and y_1

$$x_1 y_1 = a^2_1$$

where

$$a_1 = \sqrt{\frac{a^2 + b^2}{2}}$$

Or, if w = angle between x_1 and y_1,

$$x_1 y_1 \sin w = \frac{ab}{2}$$

All equations referred to the asymptotes as axes can be checked by the fact that the area of the parallelogram made by the x_1 and y_1, coordinates of any point on a hyperbola is constant. This is shown shaded on the diagrams.

The values of the functions of the angle w are:

$$\tan \frac{w}{2} = \frac{b}{a} \qquad \tan w = \frac{2ab}{a^2 - b^2}$$

$$\sin \frac{w}{2} = \frac{b}{\sqrt{a^2 + b^2}} \qquad \sin w = \frac{2ab}{a^2 + b^2}$$

$$\cos \frac{w}{2} = \frac{a}{\sqrt{a^2 + b^2}} \qquad \cos w = \frac{a^2 - b^2}{a^2 + b^2}$$

The drawing of hyperbolas may be simplified by using one of these two methods instead of those shown on Sheet 6.

1. Secant or chord method. Given the two asymptotes as shown and any point P_1 (which may be the apex). Draw any secant line through P_1, cutting the asymptotes at A and B. Measure BP_2 equal to AP_1. P_2 is a point on the hyperbola. This process can be continued, using more lines through P_1 or through P_2.

2. Parallelogram method. Given the apex A_1 and the apex A_2 and one point P. Draw the axis through A_1 A_2. Draw PN perpendicular to the axis. Draw PB parallel to the axes and of length A_2N. Divide PB into any number of equal spaces (here four); divide PN into the same number of equal spaces. From A_1, draw lines to the points on PN; from A_2, draw lines to the points on PB. The intersections of corresponding lines are points on the hyperbola. (This is basically the same method as that shown on Sheet 3 for drawing the parabola.)

Two Cases For Hyperbola

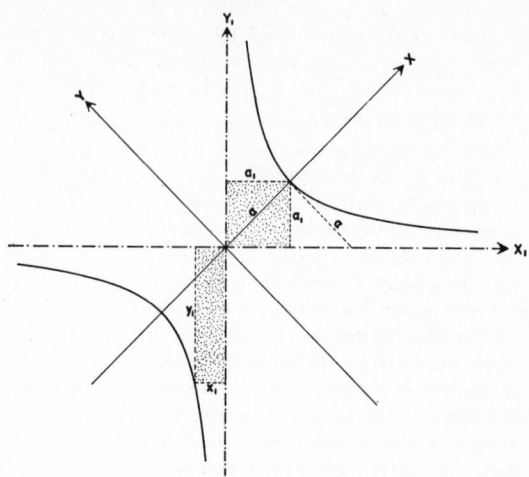

1

2

Drawing of Hyperbolas

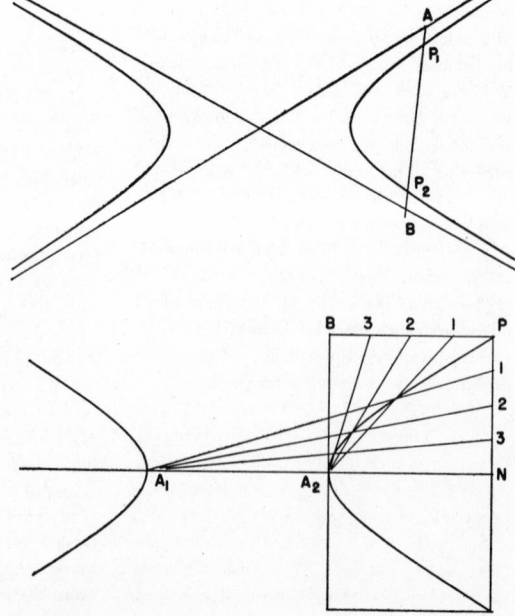

The ellipsoid, shown here in isometric projection, is one of the quadric surfaces and is generated by rotating a variable ellipse about an axis. It has three principal sections, shown here as the sections by the xy, xz and yz planes.

Its equation:

$$\frac{x^2}{a^2} + \frac{y^2}{b^2} + \frac{z^2}{c^2} = 1$$

where a = OA in the diagram,
   b = OB
   c = OC

Every section is an ellipse (or a circle; for the circular sections, see construction right). When b = a, the ellipsoid becomes the surface of revolution called an oblate spheroid (Dutch cheese shape); when b = c, it is a prolate spheroid (watermelon shape), also a surface of revolution. When a = b = c, it is, of course, a sphere. The volume is $\frac{4}{3}\pi$ a b c. There is no simple formula for the area.

To draw in projection, first draw the projections of the ellipses on the three principal planes. The axes will be conjugate diameters (see Sheet 20) and the ellipses can be constructed from them. Then, second, draw the ellipse which is the projected or contour edge of the ellipsoid; (a) find its points of tangency T_1 and T_2 with the ellipse on the xy plane by simply drawing any two parallel chords (see separate diagram below giving general method of finding points of tangency); (b) construct the auxiliary ellipse (one quarter of which is shown) which is the section of the ellipsoid by the vertical plane through the z axis normal to the plane of projection; draw a chord DD normal to the plane of projection, find M the midpoint, draw OM extended to V_1; this is the point on the contour ellipse corresponding to the vertical plane through the z axis; (c) project V_1 back onto the isometric projection and mark V_2 at the same distance on the opposite side of O; (d) V_1V_2 and T_1T_2 are conjugate diameters of the contour ellipse; use method of Sheet 20 or parallelogram method to complete ellipse; (e) check points of tangency between contour ellipse and ellipse of xz plane by drawing a chord parallel to the y axis, finding its midpoint and extending to cut the ellipse at the point of tangency; repeat procedure for ellipse of yz plane, using a chord parallel to x axis.

Parallelogram method of drawing ellipse. This is often easier than other methods, particularly in projections. Given two diameters D_1D_2 and D_3D_4, draw the surrounding parallelogram. Divide one of the sides into any number of equal spaces; divide the intersecting diameter into the same number of equal spaces. From D_2 draw rays through

the points on the diameter; from D_1 draw rays through the points on the side. The points of intersection of the rays lie on the ellipse. The same construction can be used with any two conjugate diameters. (This is basically the same construction as shown on Sheet 3 for the parabola; in the case of the parabola, D_2 is at infinity and the rays from it through the points on the chord D_3D_4 are all parallel).

To find the points of tangency between an ellipse and the tangents to it drawn from any external point: From P draw any two lines cutting the ellipse at A B C D. Draw CB and DA extended to meet at Q. Draw the diagonals of the quadrilateral ABCD, intersecting at R. Draw QR, cutting the ellipse at T_1 and T_2, which are the required points of tangency. When P is at infinity, AB and CD become parallel chords and the line QR bisects both of them.

Construction of Ellipsoid: Lamellas. Ellipsoids have been built as domes on the

lamella principle, using a radial distribution of points of intersection of the lamellas along latitude lines, similar to the lamella construction of a spherical dome. This means that every lamella in a half ellipse is different; there is no repetition along a given latitude line such as there is on a sphere.

Circular Sections. Another method, which might simplify construction, is based on the fact that on every ellipsoid there are two families of parallel circles which are sections of the ellipsoid. Looking at the isometric drawing of the ellipsoid, imagine the plane yz rotated about the mean axis. The minor semi-axis of the ellipse which is OC in the vertical position will increase continuously until the plane is coincident with the xy plane, when this semi-axis will become equal to OA. Somewhere between these two values, this semi-axis will have the value equal to OB and the section would therefore be a circle.

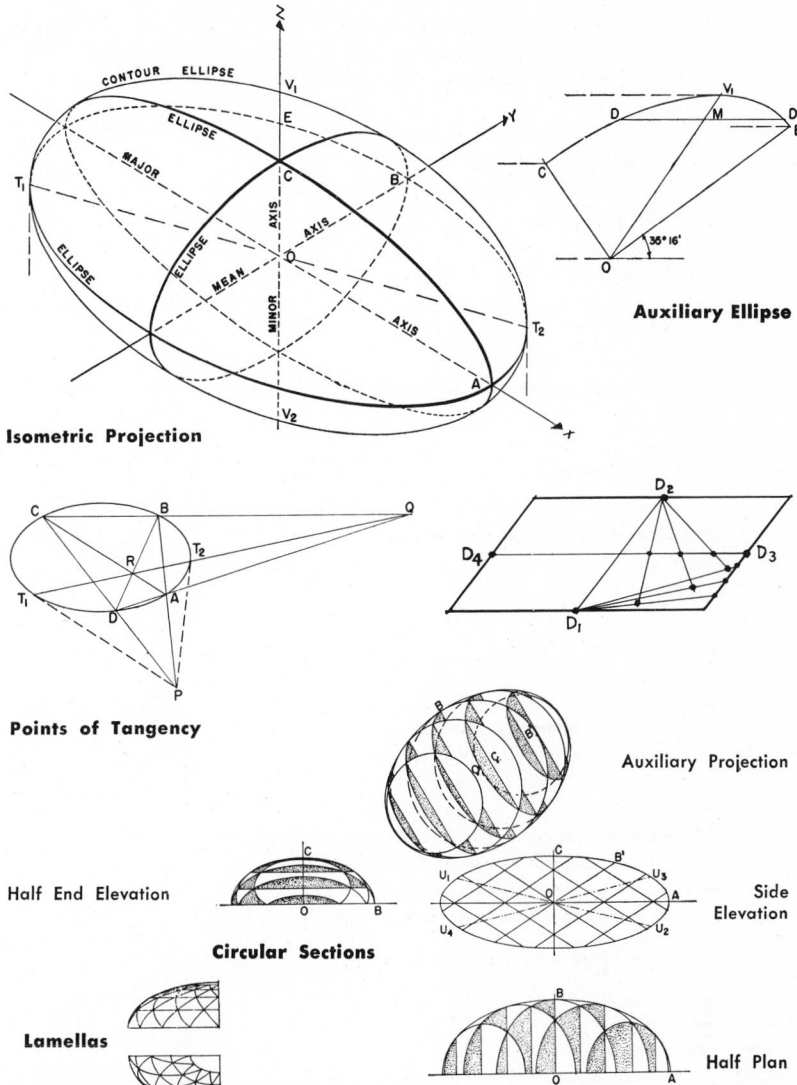

Isometric Projection

Auxiliary Ellipse

Points of Tangency

Auxiliary Projection

Half End Elevation

Circular Sections

Side Elevation

Lamellas

Half Plan

Given an ellipsoid, to find the two families of circles which are its sections.

Draw the side elevation of the ellipsoid, showing an ellipse with semi-axes OA and OC. Swing an arc OB of length equal to half the mean axis to intersect the ellipse at B'. All the circular sections of one family will be parallel to this radius vector; the other family will be symmetrical, making the same angle with the base on the opposite side of the minor axis.

On the side elevation the lines U_1OU_2

and U_3OU_4 are the conjugate diameters of the two principal circular sections (shown here as straight lines passing through O). Each bisects every chord of the family. The four points U are the umbilical points of the ellipsoid.

Lines of curvature on the ellipsoid are the traces of the intersection of the ellipsoid with the hyperboloids of one and two sheets which are confocal with the ellipsoid. At the umbilical points the curvature is the same for all normal sections. A drawing

can be found in Hilbert "Geometry and The Imagination," p. 189.

The principal sections of the ellipsoid are lines of curvature and are also the only closed geodesic curves on the ellipsoid. All other geodesics are not closed curves and are very difficult to work out in detail. Every geodesic passing through one umbilical point passes through the umbilical point diametrically opposite, but not symmetrically. One set of geodesic curves is shown in Hilbert on p. 223.

Elliptic Paraboloid

The elliptic paraboloid, shown here in isometric projection, is one of the quadric surfaces and is generated by rotating a variable parabola about an axis.

Its equation (with the axis as shown)

$$\frac{x^2}{a^2} + \frac{y^2}{b^2} = \frac{c-z}{c}$$

The sections of the surface by any plane parallel to the z axis is a parabola. The two principal sections are the xz and yz planes. All other sections are ellipses. The section by the xy plane is an ellipse with semi-major axis equal to the constant a (OA in the diagram) and semi-minor axis equal to constant b (OB in the diagram). This ellipse is drawn here as the bottom of the paraboloid, although the surface actually continues to infinity. When a equals b, it is a paraboloid of revolution, and its equation may also be written in cylindrical coordinates as:

$$\frac{r^2}{a^2} = \frac{c-z}{c}$$

Volume = ½ (area of base) (altitude)

To draw in projection, first draw the projections of the paraboloids on the xz and yz planes. These will also be parabolas in projection. Second, draw the projection of the ellipse on the xy plane. Third, on z axis, measure CW equal to OC. W is the vertex of an elliptic cone which is tangent to the paraboloid at every point around the ellipse in the xy plane. Fourth, draw tangents WT_1 and WT_2 to the ellipse (see method of finding exact points of tangency above), and draw T_1T_2. Fifth, find M the midpoint of T_1T_2, which will be on the vertical line OW, and find V the midpoint of MW. Sixth, with MV as vertical axis and T_1MT_2 as base, draw a parabola. This is the parabola which is the contour or visible edge of the paraboloid in projection. To check the point of tangency between the contour parabola and the parabola in the xz plane, draw a chord of the xz parabola

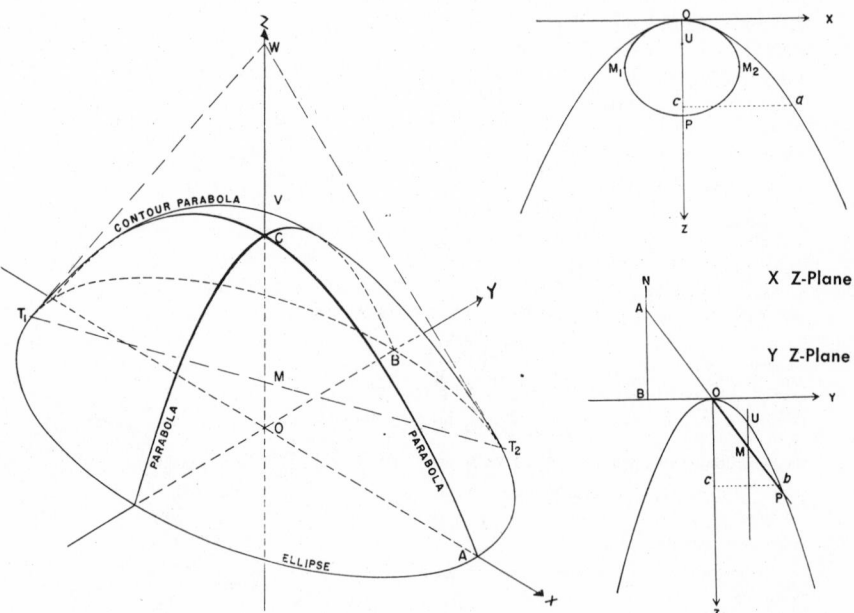

Isometric Projection

Circular Sections

X Z-Plane

Y Z-Plane

parallel to the y axis; find the midpoint of the chord and draw a line parallel to the z axis through it; the point where this line cuts the parabola is the required point of tangency. The point of tangency between the contour parabola and the parabola in the yz plane is found in the same way, using a chord parallel to the x axis.

All sections parallel to a plane containing the z axis are identical parabolas; i.e. they are all the same size. All sections normal to a plane containing the z axis are ellipses of the same proportions; i.e. the major axis is always equal to $\frac{a}{b}$ times the minor axis.

To find the circular sections: On every elliptic paraboloid there are two families of parallel circles which are sections of the surface (this is similar to the general ellipsoid, see sheet 34. Given the elliptic

paraboloid $\frac{x^2}{a^2} + \frac{y^2}{b^2} = \frac{z}{c}$, draw the

projections on the yz and xz planes as shown. Draw OB of length b along the y axis and draw BN at right angles at B. Swing an arc OA of length a to intersect BN at A. Draw AO extended to cut the parabola at P. OP is the trace of one of the circular sections. It is shown in projection, as an ellipse, on the xz plane.

The planes of all the other circular sections of this family will be parallel to OP. The other family is symmetrical on the opposite side of the z axis.

To find the umbilical point U, find M the midpoint of OP. Draw a line through M parallel to the z axis. This line is the conjugate diameter (i.e. passes through the mid-points) of all the chords parallel to OP. It cuts the parabola at U. Every elliptic paraboloid has only two umbilical points. In the case of the paraboloid of revolution, the two families of circular sections coincide (as parallels of "latitude") and the two umbilici coincide at the vertex O.

Another quadric surface, the hyperboloid of one sheet (or of one nappe) is shown here in isometric and orthogonal projections. It is one of the only two possible doubly ruled curved surfaces; the other is the hyperbolic paraboloid. It is easily constructed from straight members. It can be generated in several ways:

1. As a ruled surface: A straight line (such as 3'12) is moved so that it touches at all times three given, non-intersecting straight lines (such as 3'18, 4'19 and 5'20), no two of which are in the same plane and which are not all parallel to any one plane. The three given straight lines are all members of one family or regulus; the successive position of the line 3' 12 generate the other family (such as 4' 13, 5' 14, 6' 15, etc.).

2. By the rotation of a variable hyperbola about its conjugate axis (here the z axis), with its apex always in contact with an ellipse (the throat ellipse) which is in a plane normal to this axis. When the throat ellipse is a circle, the hyperbola does not vary and the surface is a hyperboloid of revolution of one sheet.

3. By the translation of a variable (but always similar) ellipse with its plane always normal to a straight line through its center (here the z axis) and with the extremities of its axes on two fixed hyperbolas (here the sections of the xz and yz planes) whose planes are perpendicular and whose conjugate axis is this straight line.

The equation (axes as shown): $\dfrac{x^2}{a^2} + \dfrac{y^2}{b^2} - \dfrac{z^2}{c^2} = 1$

(The equation of the asymptotic cone, shown here in section as a dotted line, is $\dfrac{x^2}{a^2} + \dfrac{y^2}{b^2} - \dfrac{z^2}{c^2} = 0$)

All sections containing the z axis are hyperbolas. The xz and yz hyperbolas are principal sections. All sections parallel to any given plane containing the z axis are hyperbolas whose asymptotes are the projections on this section plane of the parallel section of the asymptotic cone containing the z axis. Such vertical sections which cut the throat ellipse will have the axes of the hyperbolas in the xy plane; sections which do not, will have their axes parallel to the z axis. The vertical section which is tangent to the throat ellipse will consist of the pair of straight lines passing through the point of tangency. (The dotted lines shown on the xz and yz planes are projections of these.) Portions of the hyperboloid as cut off by two parallel planes, both parallel to the z axis, have been used for shell roofs, such as the Hippodrome at Madrid by Torroja.

All sections parallel to the xy plane are similar ellipses.

All other sections are conics, including circles, ellipses, parabolas and hyperbolas. Circular sections are shown on Sheet 38. The contour edge of the "inside" will be an ellipse, of the "outside" a hyperbola.

The nature of such curves can be determined for each case by a simple test (see diagram). Given a curve such as ACB. Draw the chord AB and the tangents AO and BO. Find the midpoint M of AB. Draw OM, cutting the curve at C. If C lies at the midpoint of OM (such as C_2) the curve is a parabola; if C is closer to M (such as C_1) it is an elipse; if closer to O (such as C_3) a hyperbola.

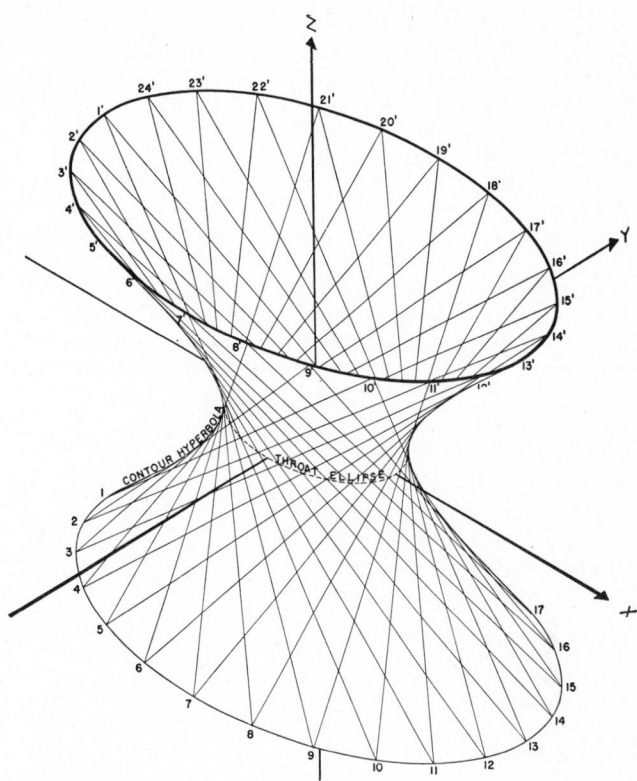

Isometric Projection

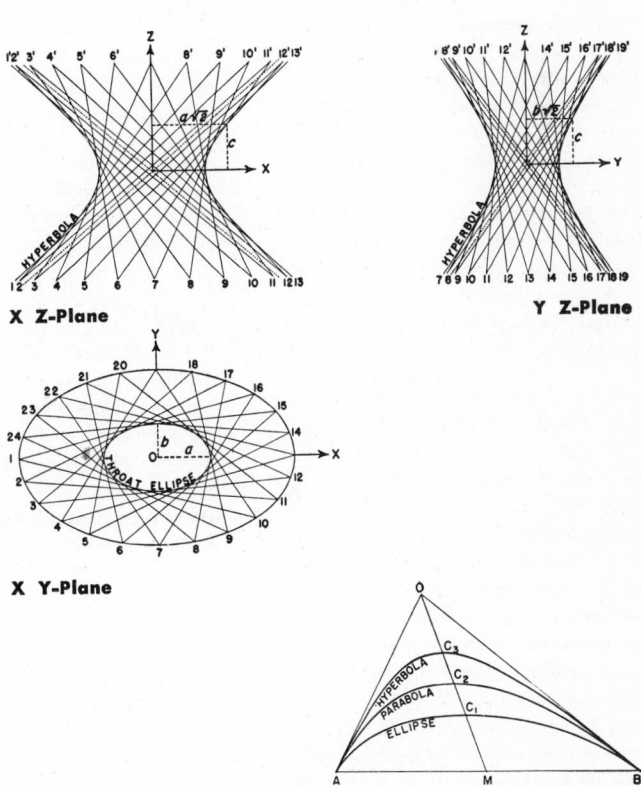

X Z-Plane

Y Z-Plane

X Y-Plane

Test Diagram

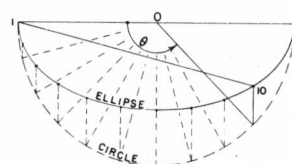

As in the case of the hyperbolic paraboloid, two straight lines, and only two, one from each family, pass through every point on the surface. These two define the tangent plane at that point.

The hyperboloid of one sheet is not a minimal surface. The minimal surface connecting two circular sections (corresponding to the top and bottom ellipses shown in drawing of the hyperboloid) is a catenoid; the edges which are hyperbolas for the hyperboloid are catenaries for the catenoid.

To Draw:

Given the two principal hyperbolas, draw them on the xz and yz planes. Draw the plan, showing the upper (and lower) and throat ellipses. In plan, from a point (such as 1') on the upper ellipse, draw the two tangents to the throat ellipse. These are the plan projections of the two straight lines, one from each family, passing through point 1'.

To find the angular distance (in plan) between this point 1' and the two points where the straight lines touch the lower

ellipse (here numbered 10 and 16) we use the eccentric angle of points on the ellipse. See diagram, where θ is the eccentric angle, in this case 135°. Dividing this into a convenient number of parts, here 9, we find the corresponding points on the ellipse whose eccentric angles all have a constant difference, (here 15°). It is then easy to draw the rulings on the surface, in elevation or projection.

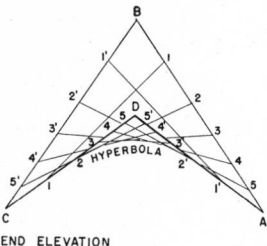

END ELEVATION

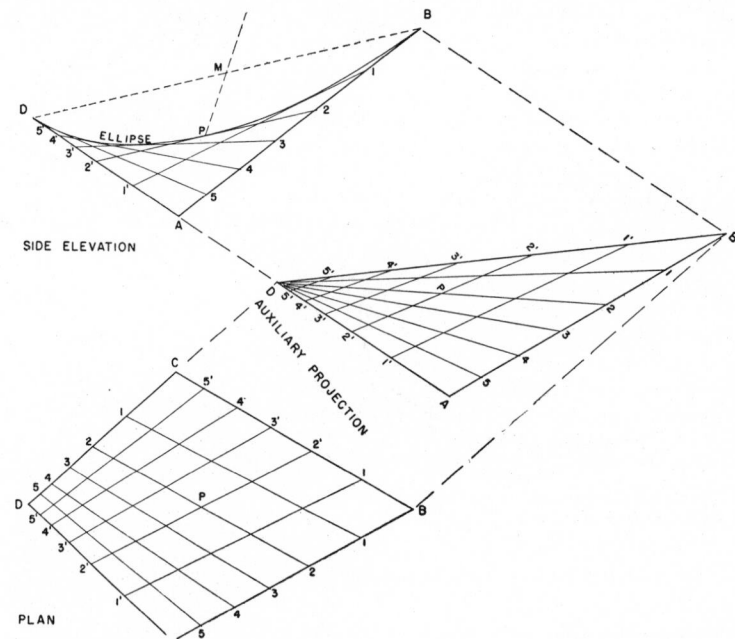

SIDE ELEVATION

AUXILIARY PROJECTION

PLAN

The hyperboloid of one sheet as a warped quadrilateral

Given the quadrilateral in space ABCD, shown in plan, side and end elevations, to draw a hyperboloid of one sheet passing through these four lines and one point P. P has been chosen here on the plane of symmetry passing through BD and the midpoint of AC and also on a line between this midpoint and the midpoint M of BD, closer to M.

Draw the auxiliary projection which makes DC appear as a point, locate P and draw DP extended to intersect AB at 2. Project this point 2 back onto side elevation and plan. Draw 2'P 2' symmetrically on the plan, project the points 2' back onto the side elevation and onto the auxiliary projection. (If this is done correctly, the line 2' P 2 on the side elevation will be found to be parallel to BD).

On the auxiliary projection we now have three skew lines (CD, 2'P 2' and AB) of one family (N') and line AD and CB of the other family (N). To find other lines of N family, draw rays through D on the auxiliary projection to intersect lines 2'2' and AB at various points. Project these points back onto the side elevation and plan. The rulings on the surface can now be drawn and the end elevation completed.

The contour edge DPB in elevation must here be an ellipse, while the contour in end elevation is a hyperbola. Note that if P were chosen as closer to the midpoint of AC than to M, the contour edge DPB of the

side elevation would become a hyperbola and the contour edge of the end variation would become an ellipse.

The warped quadrilateral as a hyperbolic paraboloid

If P is chosen at the midpoint between the midpoint of AC and M, the surface would be a hyperbolic paraboloid. This would be evident on the auxiliary projection, where all the lines of the N' family

(5'5, 4'4', etc.) would be found to be parallel (satisfying one condition for the hyperbolic paraboloid). Also the points in plan would be found to be evenly spaced along each side. In this case the Z axis of the hyperbolic paraboloid would be parallel to the line PM; the xy plane can be found from the rulings which would appear normal to the line PM in side elevation.

SUMMARY OF SYSTEMS OF DOUBLE RULINGS

Given, in Space;	Two Families of Rulings Will Generate;
Two Parabolas or three Straight lines, non-intersecting but parallel to one plane	a Hyperbolic Paraboloid
Two Circles or two Ellipses or one Hyperbola and one Ellipse or three general Straight Lines	a Hyperboloid of One Sheet
Two Hyperbolas or one Hyperbola and one Parabola or two Straight Lines, non-intersecting or a general Quadrilateral	a Hyperbolic Paraboloid or a Hyperboloid of One Sheet

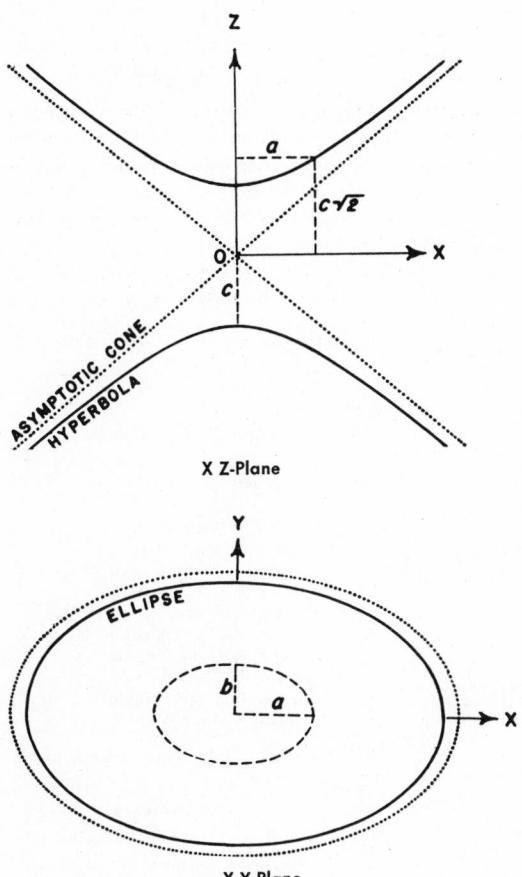

X Z-Plane

Y Z-Plane

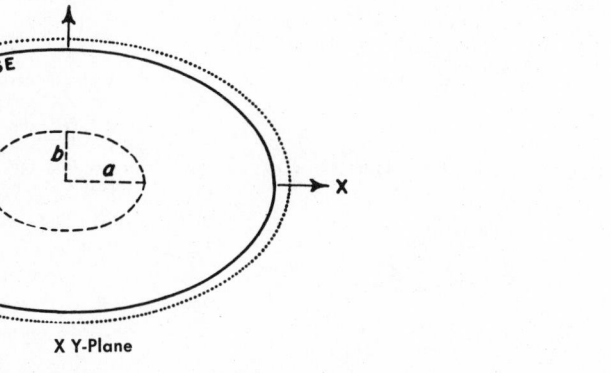

X Y-Plane

Hyperboloid of Two Sheets

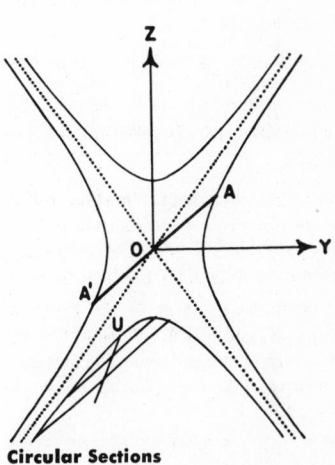

Circular Sections

One of the nine quadric surfaces, the hyperboloid of two sheets (or two nappes) is shown here in orthogonal projections. It consists of two cup-shaped surfaces facing each other across the xy plane, each extending into infinity on its own side. The curvature is always positive and there are no straight lines on the surface.

The equation: $\dfrac{z^2}{c^2} - \dfrac{x^2}{a^2} - \dfrac{y^2}{b^2} = 1$

All sections parallel to the xy plane are similar ellipses (except for the region between $z = c$ and $z = -c$). All sections parallel to any given plane containing the z axis are hyperbolas whose asymptotes are the projection on this section plane of the parallel section of the asymptotic cone containing the z axis. All other sections are also conics, in general of the

same type as corresponding sections of the asymptotic cone.

Circular Sections of the Elliptic Cone and of the Hyperboloids of One and Two Sheets

As for the ellipsoid and the elliptic paraboloid, there exist circular sections of these three surfaces. (See sheet 34 on the ellipsoid for more discussion.)

To find the circular sections, we make use of the hyperboloid of one sheet. The equations of the three surfaces are as given above in describing each type.

Draw the section by the yz plane, showing all three surfaces. The section of the asymptotic cone is drawn as a dotted line, the other two by solid lines. Note that the z axis is the axis of the cone and of the hyperboloid of two sheets, but is the con-

jugate axis of the hyperbola which is the section of the hyperboloid of one sheet.

From O swing an arc of length equal to a, intersecting the hyperboloid of one sheet at A and A'. This line is in the plane of a circular section of the hyperboloid of one sheet. All planes parallel to this will cut all three surfaces in circles. There is also a symmetrical system of planes making the same angle with the xy plane, but tilted from upper left to lower right.

There are no umbilics on the cone or the hyperboloid of one sheet.

To find the umbilics on the hyperboloid of two sheets, draw on the yz section any two chords parallel to the plane of circular sections (as shown), to find their midpoints, join them by a line which cuts the hyperbola at U. The other three umbilics are symmetrically arranged about O.

In order to calculate in detail any spherical dome or any astronomical information, such as sun angles and insolation, we must use the formulas of spherical trigonometry.

SPHERICAL TRIANGLE

In the diagram, ABC is a spherical triangle. The letters A, B, and C refer to the *angles* at the vertices (measured in degrees or radians). Angle A, for example, is the angle between the tangents to the sides b and c at the vertex. Angle A is also the dihedral angle between the plane containing the side b and the center O and the plane containing the side c and the center O. The letters a, b, and c refer to the three *sides* and are measured in degrees or radians. Each side is a portion or arc of a great circle, and its length is sometimes referred to as the central angle. The side b, for example, is the angle AOC. Both OA and OC are radii of the sphere.

Unlike plane triangles, the *sum of the angles* is not the same for all spherical triangles. It is always greater than 180° and less than 540°:

$$180° \text{ (or } \pi) < \Sigma (A + B + C) < 540° (3\pi)$$

The amount by which the sum of the angles exceeds 180° (or π) is called the *spherical excess:*

$$E = \Sigma (A + B + C) - 180° \text{ (or } \pi)$$

E can be used to find the area of a spherical triangle:

$$\frac{\text{Area of spherical triangle}}{\text{Area of sphere } [4\pi P^2]} = \frac{E°}{720°}$$
$$= \frac{E \text{ (in radians)}}{4\pi}$$

Thus,

Area of spherical triangle $= E_{\text{(radians)}} R^2$

A *steradian* is the solid angle subtended by the portion of a sphere whose area $= R^2$. (The area of a spherical polygon can be found in the same manner. If N is the number of sides of the polygon, the spherical excess

$$E° = \Sigma (A + B + C + D \ldots + X_N) \\ - (N-2) \ 180°$$

E° can be substituted in the formula given above for the spherical triangle.) The sum of the sides is always less than 360°:

$$\Sigma (a + b + c) < 360° \text{ (or } 2\pi)$$

The sides and the angles are related by the following formulas:

Law of cosines:

$\cos a = \cos b \cos c + \sin b \sin c \cos A$
$\cos b = \cos c \cos a + \sin c \sin a \cos B$
$\cos c = \cos a \cos b + \sin a \sin b \cos C$
$\cos A = - \cos B \cos C + \sin B \sin C \cos a$
$\cos B = - \cos A \cos C + \sin A \sin C \cos b$
$\cos C = - \cos A \cos B + \sin A \sin B \cos c$

Law of sines:

$$\frac{\sin A}{\sin a} = \frac{\sin B}{\sin b} = \frac{\sin C}{\sin c}$$

Haversine formula:

$\text{hav } a = \text{hav } (b - c) + \sin b \sin c \text{ hav } A$
$\text{hav } b = \text{hav } (a - c) + \sin a \sin c \text{ hav } B$
$\text{hav } c = \text{hav } (a - b) + \sin a \sin b \text{ hav } C$

The haversine of any angle θ is defined as

$$\text{hav } \theta = \frac{1 - \cos \theta}{2}$$

Haversine is an abbreviation for half versed sine.

Half-angle formula:

$$\tan \frac{A}{2} = \frac{f}{\sin (s - a)}$$

$$\tan \frac{B}{2} = \frac{f}{\sin (s - b)}$$

$$\tan \frac{C}{2} = \frac{f}{\sin (s - c)}$$

in which

$$s = \frac{a + b + c}{2}$$

and

$$f = \sqrt{\frac{\sin (s - a) \sin (s - b) \sin (s - c)}{\sin s}}$$

Half-side formula:

$$\tan \frac{a}{2} = F \cos (S - A)$$

$$\tan \frac{b}{2} = F \cos (S - B)$$

$$\tan \frac{c}{2} = F \cos (S - C)$$

in which

$$S = \frac{A + B + C}{2}$$

and

$$F = \sqrt{\frac{- \cos S}{\cos (S - A) \cos (S - B) \cos (S - C)}}$$

The significance of f and F in the half-angle and half-side formulas is found in the inscribed and circumscribed circles of the spherical triangle: the tangent of the radius of the inscribed circle $= f$; the tangent of the radius of the circumscribed circle $= F$. These radii are arcs of great circles and are measured from their respective centers, which are the poles of the corresponding circles. The inscribed and circumscribed circles are always little circles.

SPHERICAL RIGHT TRIANGLE

If one (or more) of the angles of a spherical triangle is a right angle, the triangle is a spherical right triangle. The diagram shows two spherical right triangles: ABC and $a_2 \ b_2 \ c_2$, with C equal to a right angle.

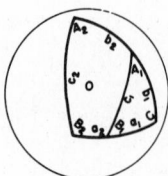

Spherical triangle

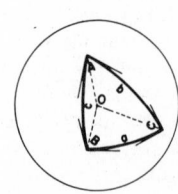

Spherical right triangle

The formulas can be simplified as follows:

$\sin \ a = \sin A \sin c$
$\sin \ b = \sin B \sin c$
$\sin \ a = \cot B \tan b$
$\sin \ b = \cot A \tan a$
$\cos \ c = \cos a \cos b$
$\cos \ c = \cot A \cot B$
$\cos A = \sin B \cos a$
$\cos B = \sin A \cos b$
$\cos A = \tan b \cot c$
$\cos B = \tan a \cot c$

If B is also a right angle, then b and c are both right angles and $A = a$. Conversely, if $b = c = 90°$, then $B = C = 90°$ and $A = a$; if $A = B = C = 90°$, then $a = b = c = 90°$, and conversely.

REFERENCES FOR COMPLETE SERIES

1. *Practical Geometry* by David Allen Low, Longmans Green, 1912.
2. *Mechanical Engineers' Handbook* by Lionel S. Marks — section "Mathematics" by E. V. Huntington (McGraw Hill, 1941).
3. *The Mathematics of Engineering* by Ralph E. Root (Bailliere, Tindall and Cox, 1927).
4. *Elements of the Differential and Integral Calculus* by Granville, Smith and Longley (Ginn 1941).
5. *Geometry and the Imagination* by D. Hilbert and S. Cohn-Vossen (Chelsea, 1952).
6. *Mathematical Models* by H. Martyn Cundy and A. R. Rollett (Oxford 1951).
7. *The Geometry of Repeating Design* by A. Day Bradley (Columbia, 1933).
8. *Elementary Crystallography* by M. J. Buerger (Wiley, 1956).
9. *Engineering Graphics* by John T. Rule and Earle F. Watts (McGraw-Hill, 1951).
10. *Technical Descriptive Geometry* by B. Leighton Williams (McGraw-Hill, 1957).
11. *What is Mathematics?* by Richard Courant and Herbert Robbins (Oxford, 1941).
12. *Solid Analytical Geometry and Determinants* by Arnold Dresden (Wiley, 1930).

By STERLING M. PALM, *Architect*

THE handling of curved and double curved surfaces has long been commonplace in the shipbuilding, automotive and airplane industries. Although such surfaces have not appeared so frequently in architectural design, they are becoming more and more apparent in contemporary design. It is not the intent of the present discussion to go into the method of such surface delineation, but a brief statement of the basic principle provides a good starting point.

A curved surface, to be a smooth surface, without humps or depressions, must be so formed that a section through the surface will be projected as a "smooth" regular curve in that plane. A curve to be "smooth" must be such that the rate of curvature, or radius, at any point does not change too rapidly with respect to the rate of curvature at any adjacent point. All conics meet this requirement and, in general, any curve that is pleasing to the eye will usually be found to be a "conic" of some type, or a combination of conics. Thus a review of the characteristics of the conics is essential to the study of surfaces.

The study of these curves also provides a valuable tool for the delineation of curves of any type and has a number of practical applications in architectural or engineering work.

A "conic" may be defined as any curve formed by the intersection of a plane with a right circular cone. Referring to Fig. 1, it is evident that an infinite variety of curves is possible, dependent on the slope of the sides of the cone, the slope of the cutting plane, and the relation between the cutting plane and the axis of the cone.

All of the conics described by planes *A* to *D* in Fig. 1 are familiar curves, susceptible of simple mathematical description and analysis.

Although the mathematics of the conics forms an interesting study, no space will be devoted to it here. We are primarily interested in an understanding of the conditions differentiating one curve from another, and in a practical application of the principles involved. Fortunately these principles are extremely simple and entirely general in nature. To anyone familiar with the procedure it should no longer be necessary to refer to a handbook to refresh one's memory as to the method of constructing a parabola or hyperbola; for these, together with an ellipse or even a circle, can all be constructed by the same simple process.

In the latter part of this discussion I will, for the benefit of those interested, develop a proof of the method about to be described. However, for those who just wish something for ready reference, it will only be necessary to follow the procedure outlined in Figs. 3 to 7 inclusive. Fig. 2 is introductory, but shows clearly the entire procedure necessary for the determination of any one point on the curve, developed to greater length in Fig. 3.

It can be shown that every conic or second-degree curve can be determined, given any one of the following five sets of conditions:

Case I. One point and two point-slopes (direction of tangent).

Case II. Three points and one point-slope.

Case III. Five points.

Case IV. Two points and a point-slope-curvature.

Case V. A point-slope and a point-slope-curvature.

Cases IV and V will not be discussed as their treatment would require more space than warranted. Fig. 5 illustrates the method of determining a sixth point on a conic given five points (Case III). In practice it generally will be found that one or two tangents are known, together with one or two points of tangency and with an additional point or points on the curve available, so that Cases I and II above will

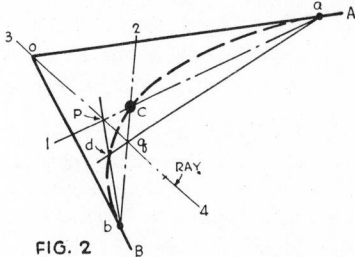

FIG. 2

be found to be those most generally useful. These cases are illustrated in Figs. 3 and 4.

Referring to Fig. 2, we have two tangents, *OA* and *OB*, with two points of tangency, *a* and *b*. Point *a* on the tangent *OA* and point *b* on the tangent *OB* constitute two point-slopes. These are, in themselves, insufficient to determine a curve. If, however, we are given an additional point, such as point *c*, it will be seen that we have the previously listed first set of conditions, namely, "one point and two point-slopes."

In order to find any other point on the curve the procedure is as follows: Draw a line through *a* and *c* prolonged to intersect *OB* at *1*, and a line through *b* and *c* prolonged to intersect *OA* at *2*. Now through *O* draw any line, *3–4*, known as a "ray," or in later reference, a "Pascal line." Designate as *p* the intersection of this ray with line *a–1* and as *q* the intersection of the ray with line *b–2*. Draw lines through *a* and *q* and through *b* and *p*. These lines extended will intersect in a point, *d*, which is the point sought lying on the curve. Additional points on the curve are found by repeating the above process, after which the points are connected with a smooth curve by means of a french curve, ship curve or spline.

Fig. 3 illustrates merely an expansion of the above principle so as to determine a number of points on the curve. Fig. 4 illustrates the application of the method by the second set of conditions, namely three points (*P*, *A* and *B*) and one point-slope (point of tangency *T* on the tangent *XY*).

It will at times be found necessary to draw a tangent to a given curve at a given point. Figs. 6 and 7 illustrate the application of the foregoing principle, in reverse, in determining such tangents.

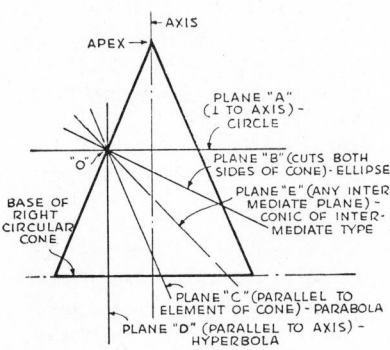

FIG. 1

DRAWING ACCURATE CURVES—2

Fig. 3. TO CONSTRUCT A SECOND-DEGREE CURVE THROUGH A CONTROL POINT D AND TANGENT TO LINES OA AND OB AT POINTS A AND B:

1. Draw line BE through D and line AF through D.
2. Divide DF into any number of spaces, e.g. four. This gives points G_1, G_2, and G_3.
3. Draw BG_1, BG_2, and BG_3.
4. Draw OG_1, OG_2, and OG_3, intersecting BE at H_1, H_2, and H_3.
5. From A, draw AH_1, AH_2, and AH_3, extended to intersect BG_1, BG_2, and BG_3, respectively, at points P_1, P_2, and P_3, which are points on required curve.
6. Additional points P_4, P_5, and P_6 are found likewise.
7. Curve fitted to these points is the required curve.

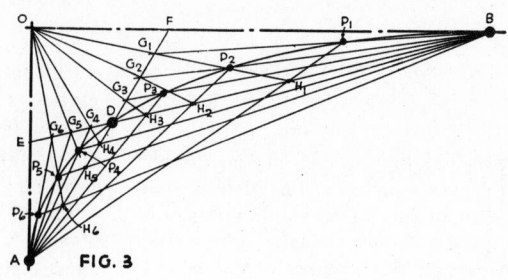
FIG. 3

Fig. 4. TO CONSTRUCT A SECOND-DEGREE CURVE TANGENT TO LINE XY AT POINT T; GIVEN THREE OTHER POINTS ON THE CURVE, P, A, AND B:

1. Draw lines BT and PA extended to intersect at point 1.
2. Draw lines PB and TA, intersecting at point 2.
3. Draw a line through points 1 and 2, extending to intersect tangent XY at point O.
4. Draw line OP, which will be tangent to the required curve.
5. Having two tangents, OT and OP, two points of tangency, T and P, and a control point, A or B (whichever is more convenient), proceed as in Fig. 3 to find additional points on the curve.

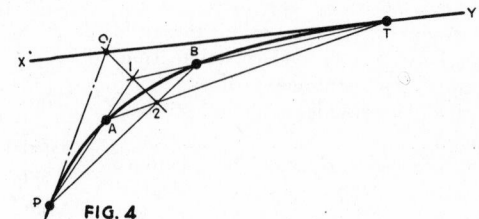
FIG. 4

Fig. 5. TO FIND A SIXTH POINT WHEN FIVE POINTS (1, 2, 3, 4, AND 5) ARE GIVEN:

1. Draw lines 1–3 and 2–4, calling intersection point o.
2. Draw lines 2–5 and 1–5.
3. Draw any "ray," AB, through point o, cutting line 2–5 at p and line 1–5 at q.
4. Draw lines through 3 and p and through 4 and q, intersecting at point 6, which will be an additional point on the curve.
5. Repeat procedure with different rays to find other points.

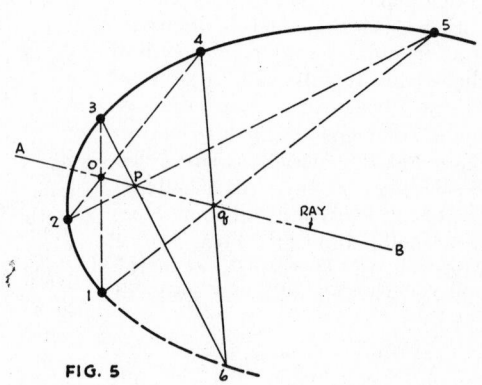
FIG. 5

Fig. 6. TO CONSTRUCT A TANGENT:

(Given, second-degree curve OB, tangent to CO and CB at points O and B, respectively; tangent to be constructed at any point, P.)

1. Select any two points, M and N, on curve OB.
2. Draw PN and BM, intersecting at point D.
3. Draw PS and BN extended to intersect PS at point E.
4. Draw a line through intersections D and E, extending it to intersect tangent BC at point R.
5. Draw a line through P and R, which will be required tangent.

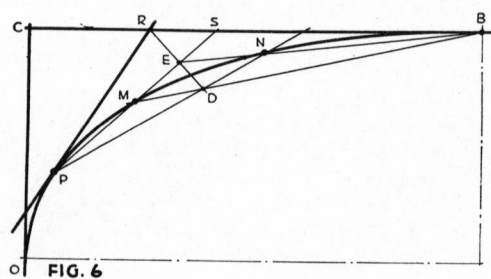
FIG. 6

Fig. 7. TO CONSTRUCT A TANGENT:

(Given, second-degree curve HJ; tangents to be constructed at any two points, P and T.)

1. Select any three points, A, B, and C, located conveniently between points P and T.
2. From P, draw lines PA, PB, and PC.
3. From point T, draw TA, TB, and TC.
4. Extend PA and TC to intersect at E.
5. Extend TB to intersect PE at G.
6. Call intersection of lines TA and PC, point D, and intersection of lines TA and PB, point F.
7. Draw lines DE and FG, extended to intersect at R.
8. Lines RP and RT are required tangents at points P and T.

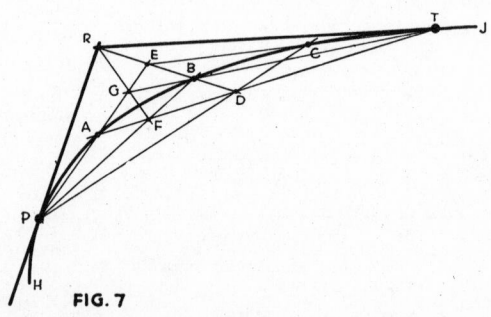
FIG. 7

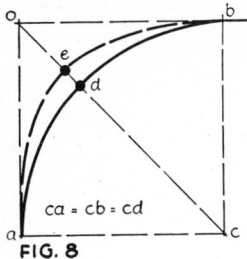

FIG. 8

$ca = cb = cd$

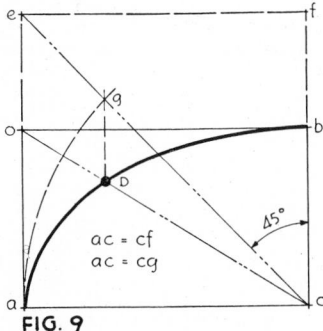

FIG. 9

$ac = cf$
$ac = cg$
45°

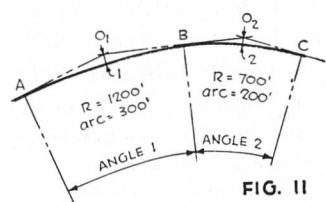

FIG. 11

$R = 1200'$
$arc = 300'$

$R = 700'$
$arc = 200'$

ANGLE 1   ANGLE 2

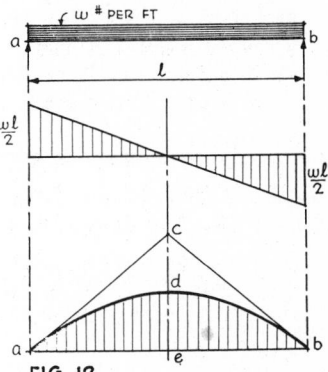

FIG. 12

$w\ \#\ PER\ FT$

l

$\frac{wl}{2}$ $\frac{wl}{2}$

Following the procedure previously outlined and using the conditions stated, it will be found that an accurate ellipse will result.

A parabola, hyperbola or other conic will be determined similarly when there is given, in addition to the point-slopes, a control point which is known to lie on the curve in question. Mathematically, the slope of the tangents can be determined once the equation of the parabola or hyperbola is known. In a great number of cases however the tangents will be given, so that it will be possible to construct these curves without recourse to mathematics.

PRACTICAL APPLICATIONS

There are many practical applications of the foregoing principles, among which might be included the following examples. In all, it should be noted that the process consists of determining two points of tangency on their respective tangents (*i.e.*, two point-slopes) together with a control point. Following this, the method outlined in Figs. 2 and 3 is followed to determine points along the curve.

Possibly one of the most useful applications consists of transforming a curve, carefully determined by freehand methods, into a definite geometric figure which can be duplicated, enlarged or otherwise utilized. Such a curve thus becomes definitely tied down. Fig. 10 might represent a profile, a section of a surface or possibly a roadway.

The usual method of duplicating this curve would be to determine, by trial, a series of radii describing sections of the curve, or possibly a system of offsets from a traverse line might be established. Both of these methods or others of a similar nature are tedious, inaccurate, and crude as compared to the simple and direct method of conics. This principle, as applied to the case at hand, would consist of splitting the curve up into convenient sections, such as *ab*, *bc* and *cd* of Fig. 10. Tangents would then be determined at points *a*, *b*,

Referring again to Fig. 2, it should be noted that the point *c*, which was selected somewhat at random in this case, is of particular importance, in that, with two point-slopes *oa* and *ob* given, the character of the curve will vary considerably depending on the location of the point *c*, known as the "control" or "shoulder" point. The extent to which the control or shoulder point influences the shape of the conic is illustrated in Fig. 8, in which, with two equal tangents, $ob = oa$, the control point *d* is so taken that $cd = cb = ca$. The resulting curve in this case will be, as expected, an arc of a circle.

If point *e* were to be used as a control point, the resulting curve would be a parabola or other conic, depending on the exact location of point *e*.

In Fig. 9, the control point *D* is determined by projecting down to diagonal *oc* from the intersection of circular arc *ag* with diagonal *ec*. With *D* as a control point, tangents *ob* and *oa* and points of tangency *b* and *a*, a quarter ellipse would be anticipated.

c and *d* and control points in each section, such as k_1, k_2, and k_3. The curve is now definitely tied down and can be reproduced exactly. Some points on the curve should be checked by the method described in Fig. 3, and if discrepancies appear it will undoubtedly be apparent that the freehand curve was not smooth at the point in question.

A similar application is illustrated in Fig. 11, which represents a street line consisting of two circular arcs *AB* and *BC* of radii such that the centers are inaccessible or off the drawing. The arc lengths being given, the central angles, *1* and *2*, can easily be determined and consequently the tangents for both sections can be plotted. The distances $O_1 1$ and $O_2 2$ may then be computed, being in each case equal to *R* times exsec of half the angle. We would then have established for each section the two tangents and control point, after which points on the curve would be determined as previously described.

Fig. 12 illustrates the application of the principle to the construction of a moment diagram, such as might be required for use in the design of a plate girder. The bending moment curve for the portion of a beam subject to uniform loading can be described as a portion of a parabola. Inasmuch as the shear diagram gives the slope of the parabola representing the moment diagram at any point along the span, the slope at the two supports *a* and *b* are each equal to

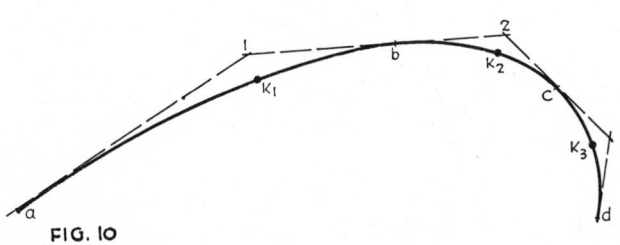

FIG. 10

one-half of *wl*. The ordinate *ce* is thus equal to *wl*² divided by 4, while the ordinate *de* is half of this or *wl*² divided by 8. With *w* and *l* given, it is necessary only to plot, at some convenient scale, the two tangents *ac* and *bc* and the ordinate *de* locating the control point *d*, after which additional points on the curve are determined, as before. This method will, in a great number of cases, be found considerably simpler than the usual method of determining points by figuring moments at various points along the span.

Always bearing in mind that the two tangents and a control point fix definitely the shape of the curve, the principle outlined can be put to use in solving problems such as the intersection of surfaces of all types, vaulting and vault ribs, graphs and diagrams, or in fact any problem involving curves or curved surfaces. The examples just given have all fallen under the previously cited Case I, involving two tangents and a control point. It will be found in practice that these conditions are usually present or can be established. Where this is not possible it will only then be necessary to fall back upon one of the other applications, Cases II and III as illustrated in Figs. 4 and 5 respectively.

BASIC THEORY

It will possibly be of interest to some readers to follow the development of the relationship upon which the foregoing is based. This relationship, known as the "Pascal Theorem," is diagrammed in Fig. 13, and may be stated as follows: "If the extremities of any hexagram inscribed in a conic are numbered in consecutive order 1 to 6 as shown in the sketch, the intersection of the opposite pairs of sides *1–3* and *2–4*, *4–6* and *1–5*, and intersection of the diagonals *2–5* and *3–6* will always lie in a straight line, known as a 'Pascal line'." Thus the intersections *o*, *p* and *q* lie on a "Pascal line" *ab*.

A "hexagram" may be briefly described as a six-pointed star, and in Fig. 13 is clearly visible as such when the sides *3–5* and *2–6* (dotted) are drawn. The term "hexagram" is, however, possible of much broader application: the figure need not be regular in shape, nor is the curve in which the hexagram is inscribed limited, except in one respect — it must be a conic.

In Fig. 14, the same relationship is again indicated, the nomenclature of Fig. 13 being retained; the hexagram in this case being irregular in form and inscribed in an ellipse. In both Figs. 13 and 14, lines *1–3* and *2–4* intersect at *o*, lines *1–5* and *4–6* intersect at *q* and lines *2–5* and *3–6* intersect at *p*. From the "Pascal theorem" above stated, points *o*, *p* and *q* will always lie in a straight line known as a Pascal line.

Earlier in this article we stated as Case III the condition that five points on a conic curve were sufficient to determine the curve, or stated otherwise: five points on a conic are sufficient to establish a sixth point, also on the conic. A comparison of Fig. 14 with Fig. 5 will show that the procedure outlined in Fig. 5 is derived directly from the relationship shown in Fig. 14, the only difference being that in Fig. 5, with five points given, the Pascal line passed through the point *o* at random determines the two other intersection points *p* and *q*, which immediately determine the location of the sixth point as shown.

It will be observed that as the position of the fifth point varies the sixth will also vary, but the ensuing curve will be the same. Referring again to Fig. 5 it will be noticed that if point *3* is moved, but always remains between points *2* and *4*, the intersection *o* will lie on the inside of the curve. If point *3* is moved, however, until it lies between points *1* and *2* the intersection of lines *2–4* and *1–3* will lie outside the curve. If now we assume that point *2* is rotated clockwise until it coincides with point *4*, and point *3* is rotated counterclockwise until it coincides with point *1*, indicating the combined points *2–4* and *1–3*, as in Fig. 15, it will be seen that the lines joining points *1* and *3* and points *2* and *4* must be tangents to the curve at the combined points *1–3* and *2–4* respectively. As before, the intersection of these two lines will be indicated as point *o*.

It was previously indicated that the fifth point was not restricted as to position as long as it remained on the conic. Assume point *5*, in Fig. 15, to be intermediate between the combined points *1–3* and *2–4*. With this arrangement we would now have established the first set of conditions mentioned earlier: "One point and two point-slopes."

Proceeding as in Fig. 5, we draw

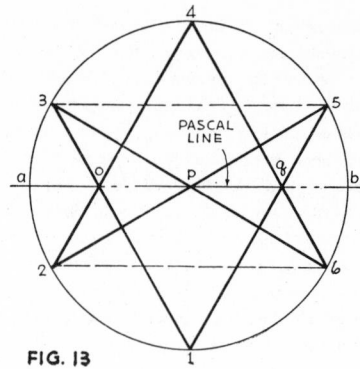

FIG. 13

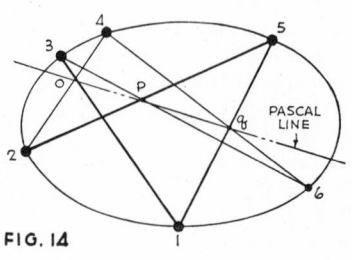

FIG. 14

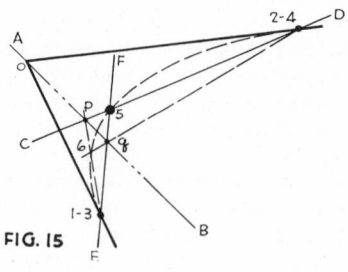

FIG. 15

lines *CD* through points *2* and *5* and *EF* through points *1* and *5*. If we then pass a Pascal line *AB* at random through point *A* and call the intersection of this line with line *CD* (or *2–5*) the point *p* as before, and also the intersection with line *EF* (or *1–5*) the point *q*, we will then have retained the same relationship of lines and points in both cases. Continuing as in Fig. 5, we will draw lines through points *3* and *p* and through *4* and *q* intersecting at point *6*, which is the point sought. If we now compare Fig. 15 with Fig. 2, it will be seen that the procedure is the same as previously outlined.

Also, since the procedure followed in Figs. 5 and 15 was identical it is apparent that the method is general as to Cases I and III. A study of Fig. 4 will show that the procedure in Case II is likewise similar.

By WILLIAM BLACKWELL

Geometry in architecture, sometimes boldly expressed and sometimes artfully concealed, is a part of the common core of knowledge and understanding which the architect uses to enclose space for human needs—one of his instruments, one of the tools, to be used in organizing and planning and decorating and integrating spaces so they can be built and understood and used. This study of some of the formal, basic series of geometric shapes which the architect uses, or may use, takes as its structure the unchanging relationship between the area and the perimeter of each shape.

Some shapes enclose an area with more or less perimeter than others, and this is a characteristic of the shape which can easily be expressed mathematically.

For example, the area enclosed by each unit of perimeter of a square is equal to the length of a side divided by four. The larger the square, the greater will be the area enclosed per unit of perimeter—the area/perimeter value. The same thing is true of a circle where the area enclosed per unit of circumference is equal to the diameter divided by four; and so the larger the circle, the greater will be the area/perimeter value. It is true also of any other shape that the larger it is the larger will be the area/perimeter value.

Because of this scale effect, because the area/perimeter value of all shapes changes with size in the same way, they have always the same relationship one to the other with respect to their area enclosure properties. For any given area then, the area/perimeter value of one shape can be expressed relative to the area/perimeter value of another shape.

Because a circle encloses a given area with less perimeter than any other closed shape, its area/perimeter value will always be greater —and so it is used here to express the relative area enclosure properties of other plane shapes. The area/perimeter value of a square, for instance, will always be 88.6 per cent of the area/perimeter value of a circle with the same area. This value is the area/perimeter factor, a comparison of the area enclosure properties of a square to those of a circle. Similar values can be found for other shapes, regular or irregular, by using the equation:

$$A_f = \frac{2\sqrt{\pi a}}{p} \times 100 \text{ or } \frac{354.5\sqrt{A}}{p}$$

Once the area/perimeter factor has been found for a shape, the process can be reversed and the area/perimeter factor used to find the actual area or perimeter of a shape if one or the other is known, providing a useful numerical relationship between the two similar to the 'k' and 'f' factors sometimes employed in handbooks to simplify calculations.

If the area is known, the perimeter can be found using the equation in this way:

$$p = \frac{2\sqrt{\pi A}}{A_f / 100} \text{ or } \frac{354.5\sqrt{A}}{A_f}$$

If the perimeter is known, the area can be found by the equation:

$$A = \frac{1}{4\pi}\left[\frac{A_f}{100} \times p\right]^2 \text{ or } .0796\left[\frac{A_f}{100} \times p\right]^2$$

For circles, squares or rectangles finding the area or perimeter isn't a very serious problem but in the case of many sided polygons, ellipses or irregular shapes, the area/perimeter factor can be useful.

The reciprocal of the area/perimeter factor can also be used to express the difference in the area enclosure properties of a shape and a circle. A square has a perimeter/area value of 1.128 (100/88.6) compared to a circle of 1, which is to say that a square has 12.8 per cent more perimeter than a circle with the same area.

It might be emphasized, too, that although the area/perimeter factor is independent of "the scale effect" and is an unchanging factor regardless of the size of the shape, it is nonetheless an expression of the relative area enclosure properties of shapes for a given area. A large square might have an actual area/perimeter value twice that of a small circle. The usefulness of the factor lies then only in comparing the area enclosure properties of shapes for a given area.

The chart below illustrates the relative area enclosure properties of four related series of geometric shapes. They are arranged from bottom to top according to their area/perimeter factors, from 0 to 100 per cent, and from left to right according to the number of sides in the shape, from one to infinity.

In outline form and starting with the square are also shown some rectangles of different proportion to illustrate the change that occurs in the area enclosure properties of rectangles as the length-to-width ratio changes.

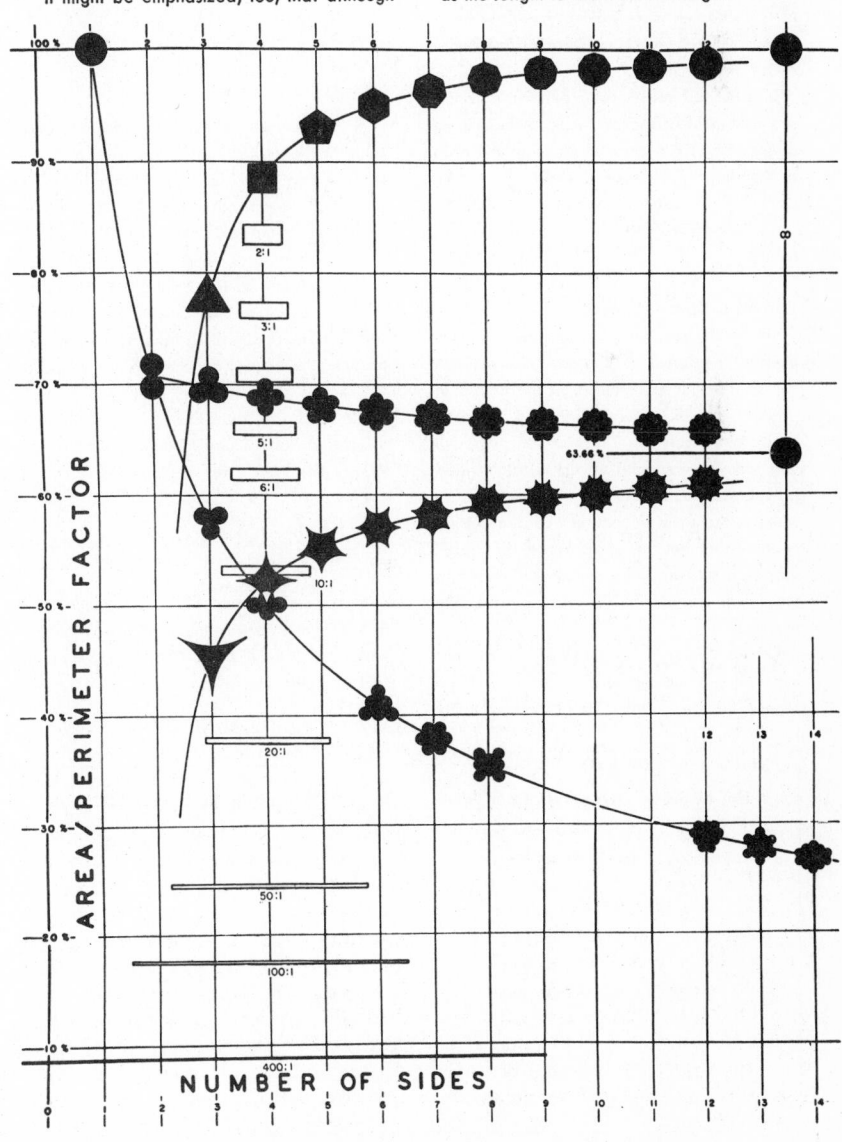

The shapes on the chart all have the same area, so the difference in apparent size, as between one shape and another, can be seen.

The Regular Polygons

First of the four series of shapes shown in black on the chart is the regular straight-sided polygon series—the triangle, square, pentagon, etc. It begins, theoretically, with a straight line. Having two sides, a perimeter equal to twice its length but zero area, a straight line has an area/perimeter factor of 0 per cent. The first solid equilateral shape is the equilateral triangle (77.7 per cent), then a square (88.6 per cent), the five-sided pentagon (93 per cent) and so on—gradually approaching a circle (100 per cent) as the number of sides increases to infinity. Area/perimeter factors for some of the polygons in this series are given in the table below. The latter shapes in this series are extremely compact, with polygons of 13 sides or more having area/perimeter factors within 1 per cent of the area/perimeter factor of a circle.

In a limited sense, area/perimeter factors are a kind of efficiency factor, reflecting the degree of proximity of a shape to the area enclosure properties of a circle—as for instance, when a circular structure is divided into a number of straight sides for ease of fabrication.

Concave-Convex Series:

Under the regular polygons are two complementary series of shapes, seldom used, but still familiar to architects as the shapes of brightly colored rose windows and vertically lined, fluted columns. These are the concave and convex aspects of the straight-sided polygons. Actually, which is which depends on whether the point of view is from the outside or the inside but the upper curve, the "rose" shapes, are taken to be the convex series and the lower curve, the "fluted" shapes, the concave.

Of the shapes in these two series, the most interesting is the three-sided concave shape formed by the interior arcs of three mutually

tangent circles. It might be called a "triarc." This shape has an area/perimeter factor of 45.2 per cent, the lowest of the regular geometric shapes. Although actually having the same area, it appears larger than any other shape on the chart. The circle and the "triarc" represent two extremes in area enclosure— the one with minimum and the other with maximum perimeter for a given area in a regular shape. Because of this difference (a 55 per cent difference in area/perimeter factors) and because of their opposite curvature, the two together form a very strong contrast in shape.

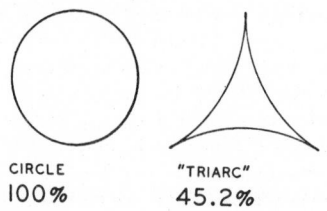

CIRCLE
100%

"TRIARC"
45.2%

As the number of arcs in the circumference of both the concave and convex shapes increases, they converge on what appears to be a circle. Theoretically, it is a circle with its circumference made up of a very large number of very small arcs. With the area of each shape the same as it is on the chart, the arcs in the circumference become smaller as more are added. Finally, they are no longer apparent—the shape appears to be a circle. The actual circumference, greatly enlarged, would appear to be a line of semi-circles, like a series of arches, turned outward for the convex shapes, inward for the concave:

OR

Because of the small arcs, the circumference is 1.57 times longer than the circumference would be without them. The area/perimeter factor of the shape then is 1:1.57 or 63.66 per cent.

The Area/Perimeter Factor For Any Number of Separate Identical Shapes:

Beginning with one circle at the upper left-hand corner of the chart is a curve showing the area/perimeter factor for various groups containing different numbers of circles. The groups shown were arrived at by starting with one, two or three circles at the center and proceeding outward, adding circles in the vacant pockets of each concentric ring. The same number of circles might, however, have been arranged in any other manner or even randomly placed and still have the same area/perimeter factor. Providing they all are of the same size, only the number of circles considered determines the area/perimeter factor.

The area/perimeter factor of any number of separate circles of the same size is equal to the area/perimeter factor of one circle (100 per cent) divided by the square root of the number of circles considered. And, it happens that this is true of other shapes: the area/perimeter factor of any number of separate, identical shapes taken as a whole is equal to the area/perimeter factor of one of the shapes divided by the square root of the number of shapes. One square has an area/perimeter factor of 88.6 per cent; nine squares, 29.5 per cent (88.6/3). A single leaf on a tree might have an area/perimeter factor of say 50 per cent, but if all the leaves are counted they would as a whole have an area/perimeter factor of very nearly zero.

The curve showing the area/perimeter factor for groups containing a different number of circles, then, illustrates what happens to the area/perimeter factor of any shape when it is divided into a number of separate identical shapes.

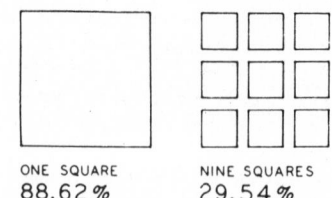

ONE SQUARE
88.62%

NINE SQUARES
29.54%

Instead of being arranged in their more compact form as they are on the chart, the same number of circles might have been arranged in a ring, adjacent to one another and equidistant from the center, as illustrated on the next page.

Lines between the centers (or the points of tangency) of adjacent circles form the regular straight-sided polygon series—the pentagon

REGULAR POLYGON SERIES:			
No. of Sides	Area/Perimeter Factor	No. of Sides	Area/Perimeter Factor
3	77.756%	20	99.587
4	88.623	24	99.714
5	92.995	25	99.736
6	95.231	27	99.774
8	97.368	30	99.817
9	97.931	32	99.839
10	98.330	36	99.872
12	98.846	40	99.897
15	99.264	45	99.920
16	99.354	48	99.929
18	99.490	50	99.934

in the illustration. The exterior perimeter of the whole form is the convex aspect of the polygon and the interior perimeter of the circles the concave. The circles themselves, the regular polygon and its concave and convex aspects make up the four series of shapes shown in black on the chart.

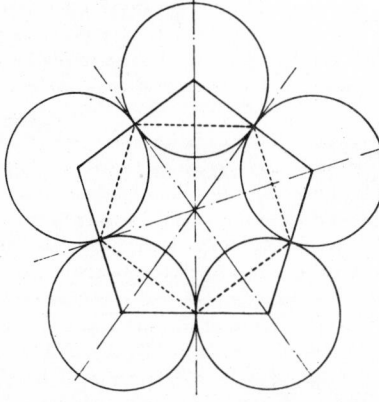

Rectangles:

In outline form, and starting with the square in the regular polygon series are some rectangles, the shapes most frequently used by architects because of the ease with which they accommodate most needs for enclosed space. The area/perimeter factor of a rectangle is determined simply by the length-to-width ratio, the proportion. A square (1:1) has the highest factor, 88.6 per cent, and the farther the rectangle deviates from the square in proportion, the lower will be its area/perimeter factor. As the length becomes very great with respect to the width, the "width" disappears, leaving a straight line with an area/perimeter factor of 0 per cent. It is possible then for a rectangle, depending on its proportion, to have any area/perimeter factor from 0 to 88.6 per cent.

The greatest difference in the area/perimeter factors of two closed shapes is, of course, 100 per cent—reached between a straight line and a circle and approached between a circle and a very long rectangle. There is one example of this contrast, used architecturally to a softer degree, in the chapel Saarinen designed for M.I.T. Here one enters the dimly-lighted, circular brick chapel through a lightly enclosed rectangular passageway. Between the high area/perimeter factor of the circle and the lower factor of the rectangular entry, there is a difference of about 25 per cent. Looking at the chart and the range of shapes normally used architecturally, this is a very considerable difference.

Room shapes, for instance, are normally nearly square in plan, with length-to-width ratios from 1:1 to about 1½:1; seldom greater than 2:1. The difference in the area/perimeter

factor of a square room and one with a relatively high length-to-width ratio of 2:1 is only about 5 per cent.

Building shapes, especially low buildings, cover virtually the whole range of rectangles, from squares to the mile-long production line enclosures of the Second World War. "L" and "T" and other arrangements are equivalent to relatively long rectangles. Because they have lower area/perimeter factors (more perimeter) they have also a higher degree of light and openness and flexibility in the arrangement and rearrangement of the internal spaces than the more compact shapes.

On the other hand, economy of exterior perimeter is an important consideration in almost every building, too, because of material and labor saving, maintenance costs, and reduction in heating and cooling loads. It is particularly important in multistory buildings where the outside wall surface is very large compared to the roof area. These buildings tend to have more compact shapes, with the perimeter reduced just to the point where if it were reduced further the spaces within would be adversely affected. To give one example, the glass-enclosed rectangles of Lever House have a length-to-width ratio of about 3:1 and an area/perimeter factor of 77.5 per cent. A square plan (88.6 per cent) might have been more economical in terms of the perimeter but would not have the same degree of light and openness and planning flexibility (and interest, too) that the rectangular shape has with some additional perimeter.

As a matter of interest, the "golden section" (1.62:1) has an area/perimeter factor of 86.12 per cent, 2½ per cent less than a square. The area/perimeter factor for other rectangles can be found by using the equation

$$A_f = \frac{\sqrt{\pi l/w}}{1 + l/w} \times 100$$

or taken directly from the curve below.

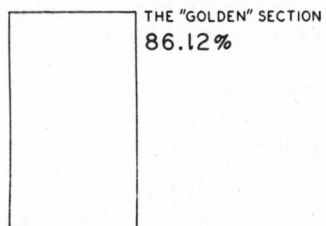

THE "GOLDEN" SECTION
86.12%

Ellipses:

On the same graph with the rectangle curve is another curve showing the area/perimeter factor for ellipses of different proportion. In the same manner as the rectangles, ellipses have lower and lower area/perimeter factors the further they deviate from a circle in proportion. It happens that for proportions less than about 5.75:1 ellipses have higher area/perimeter factors than rectangles of the same proportion but for proportions greater than 5.75:1 rectangles have the higher factors. With a length-to-width ratio of 5.75:1, both have an area/perimeter factor of 62.98 per cent.

When the major and minor axis of an ellipse are known, the area can be found using the equation, π ab. The circumference can then be found by taking the approximate area/perimeter factor from the curve and using the basic equation:

$$p = \frac{2\sqrt{\pi A}}{A_f/100}$$

This will be as accurate as the area/perimeter factor can be read from the curve, plotted from tabulated values of elliptic integrals.

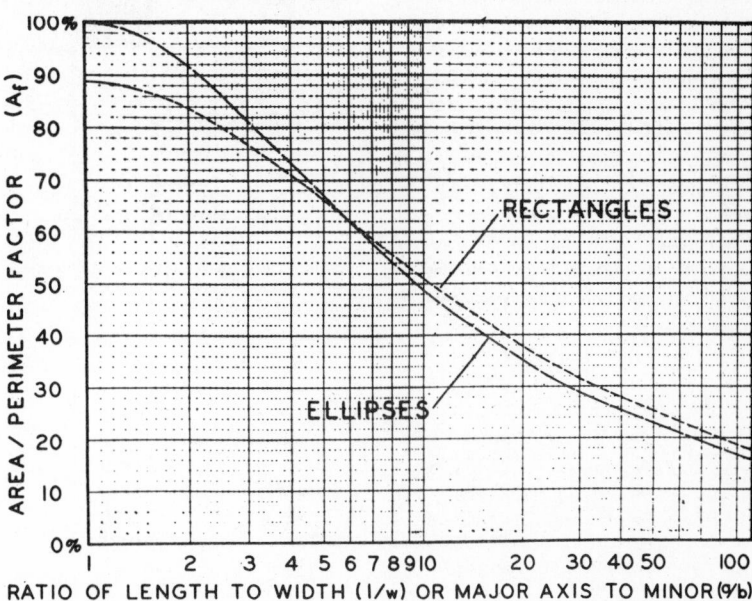

RATIO OF LENGTH TO WIDTH (l/w) OR MAJOR AXIS TO MINOR (9/b)

MODULAR COORDINATION—1

By BYRON C. BLOOMFIELD, *AIA*
Executive Director,
Modular Building Standards Association

Modular coordination is a method of sizing building components so that they will fit together without having to be cut in the field.[1] Conventional building practice is notoriously wasteful of both material and labor. Even the simplest building requires thousands of individual components (some of which are shown in Fig. 1). These manufactured products, which are completely unrelated in dimension, are assembled at the site, where they must be cut and fitted together by skilled workmen. Building components manufactured in modular sizes (Fig. 2), however, can be assembled without the necessity of field cutting, and thus permit great savings in materials and labor. Equally important are the savings that result from simplified practices in the drafting room, estimating office, and in the field.

Basic methods

The basis of the modular method is *joint-centerline to joint-centerline* dimensioning for all components, using multiples of the standard 4-in. module. The three drawings in Fig. 3 illustrate the principle of joining different modular materials. Material "A" represents a component produced in any multiple of 4 in., with sufficient manufacturing tolerance and joint clearance to permit installation without cutting. Material "B" represents another modularly dimensioned material or component. Different materials ordinarily have different joint thickness requirements, but for all modular materials one-half the minimum joint thickness at any edge provides sufficient clearance for installation. The third drawing in Fig. 3 illustrates the method of dimensioning modular materials or components to be joined. Material "A," for example, could be a door-frame assembly and material "B" a masonry wall, or material "A" could be a window assembly, material "B" a wood-frame wall, and material "C" a door unit. This method applies to all parts of a building and indicates the ease of assembly of modular materials.

[1] *The current reference is* American Standard Basis for the Coordination of Dimensions of Building Materials and Equipment *(ASA A62.1, revised 1957). Information on modular methods and assistance in their adoption can be obtained from the Modular Building Standards Association, 2029 K Street N.W., Washington 6, D.C.*

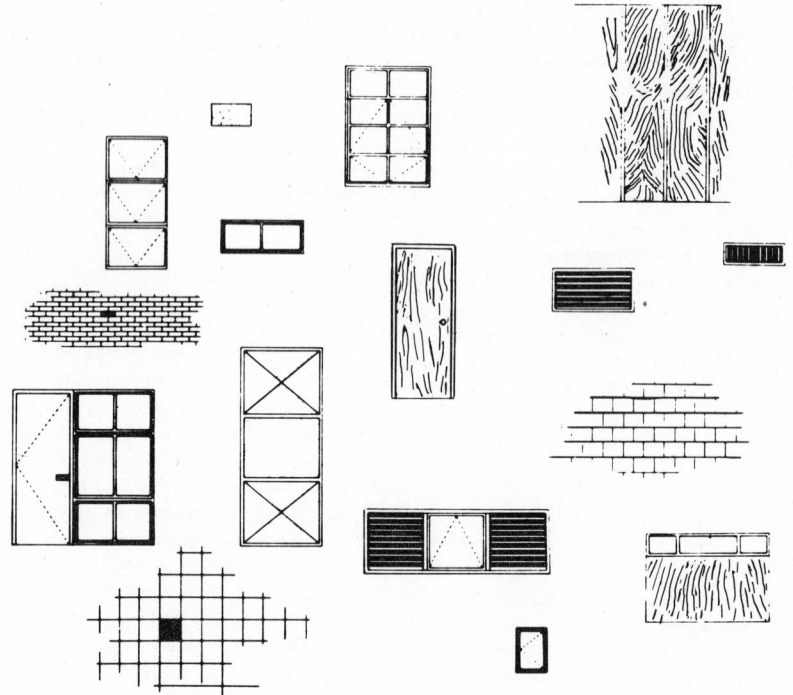

Fig. 1.   Conventional components of a specific building

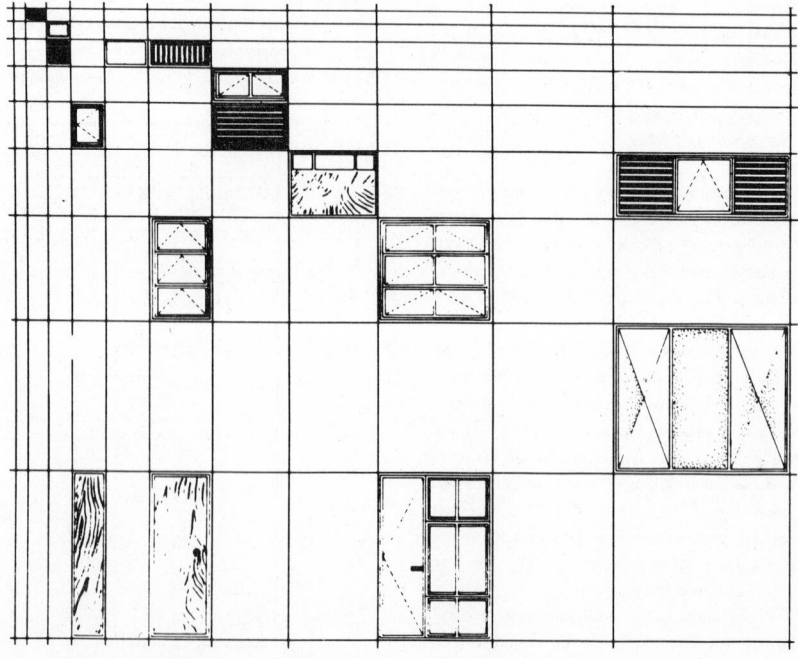

Fig. 2.   Coordinated range of components

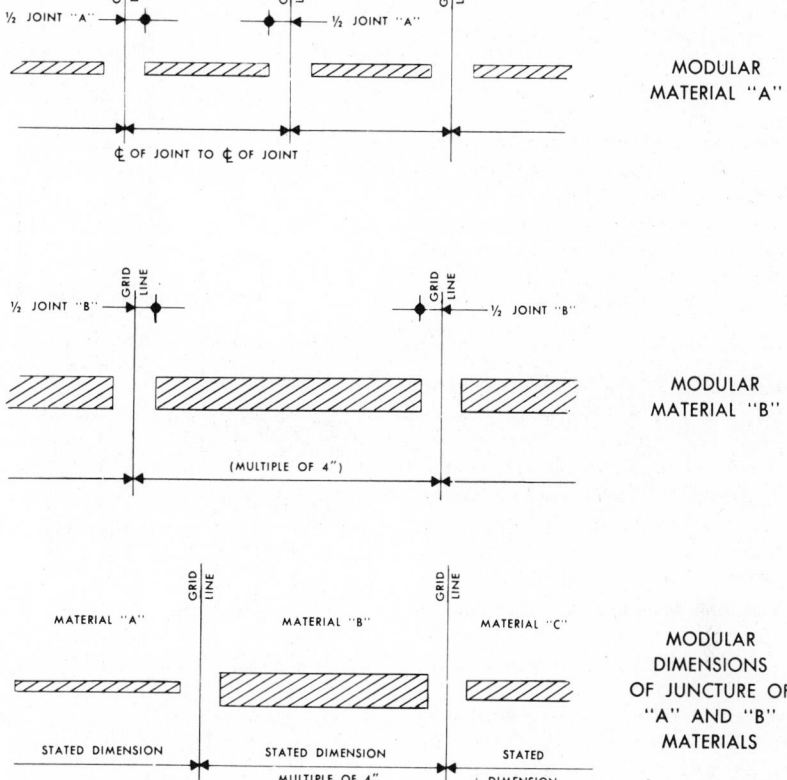

The joint-centerline to joint-centerline principle is summarized in Fig. 4, which also shows how the actual size of a modular component is determined. The application of this method to the sizing of a particular product is shown in Fig. 5. Note the undersizing of the material on all faces by the thickness of the half-joints.

The method of combining modular products, which was illustrated in principle in Fig. 3, is shown for a specific component—a door-frame assembly—in Fig. 6. Note that it is the outside dimensions of the frame that are important, not the size of the door itself.

Fig. 3. Modular jointing principle

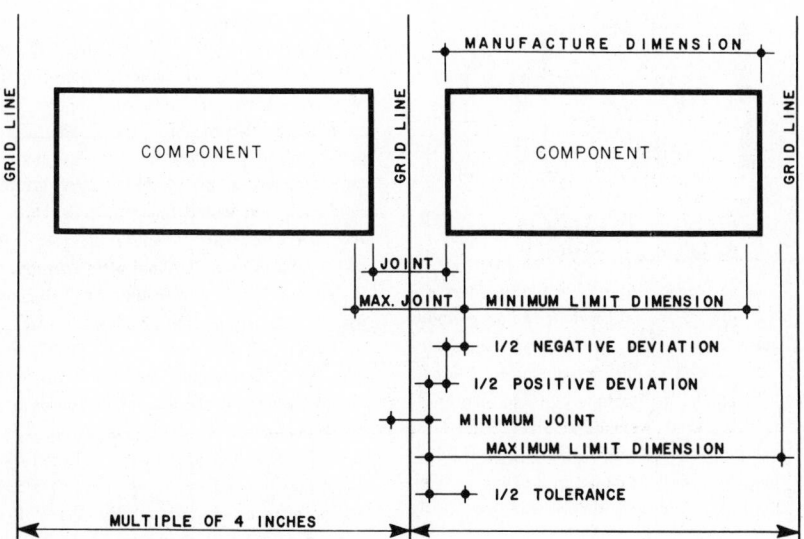

Fig. 4. Basis for sizing a component

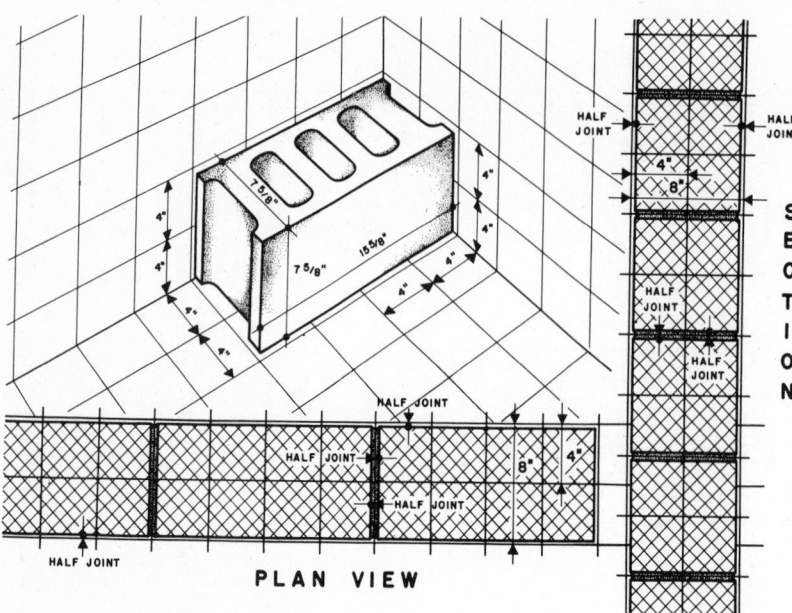

Fig. 5. Example of a modular unit

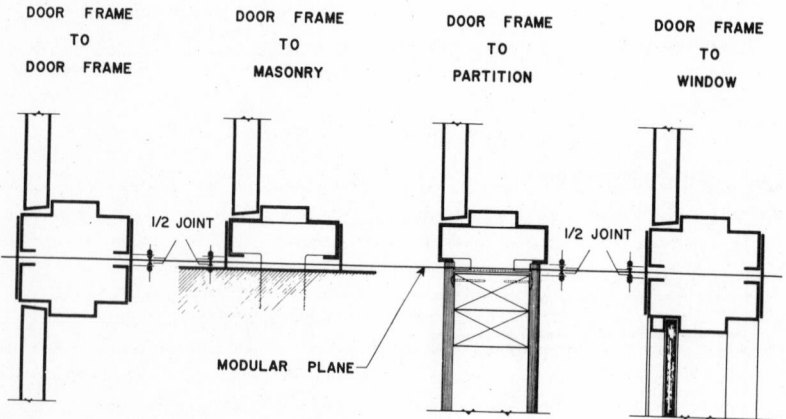

Fig. 6. Combining modular components

To be used for dimensions related to the location of grid lines exclusively.

To be used for dimensional reference to points other than grid lines. Use only when essential to the clarity of the drawing.

To be considered as occurring every 4", horizontally and vertically throughout the structure and to be shown on the plans where dimensional reference points are required.

Fig. 7. Modular drafting conventions

Modular drafting

If the advantages of modular coordination are to be realized, modular methods must be used by the architectural draftsman as well as the manufacturer. There is little gain in having building materials manufactured in modular sizes if modular methods are not used in the design of buildings. Fortunately, modular drafting conventions are few and simple and are easily put into practice. The three basic conventions are the grid, the arrowhead, and the dot (Fig. 7). The grids provide imaginary reference planes extending through the structure in a three-dimensional egg-crate fashion, 4 in. on center in all directions. When drafting, the architect actually draws *some* grid lines on large-scale drawings that provide key dimensional reference planes, such as the location of foundation lines, and door and window heads and jambs. (Some

large multiple of the 4-in. module may, if desired, be used as a planning grid and may, at the architect's discretion, be shown in plan.)

The arrowhead is used for all dimensions that originate or terminate on a 4-in. grid line. Dots are used for off-grid dimensions.

Two observations can be made: (1) If only dots were to be used on a drawing, it would not differ from any "premodular" architectural drawing; and (2) The fewer the number of dots and the greater the number of arrowheads, the greater the simplicity of the structure and the joining problems. Theoretically, if only arrowheads were used, the architect would enjoy the ultimate in drafting simplicity and the building would benefit from the ultimate in construction simplicity.

The use of basic drafting conventions throughout the dimensioning of all plans, elevations, and details obviates the need for most fractional dimensions on the drawings and the corresponding possibility of errors in the addition and subtraction of series of numbers involving such fractions. The drawings are simpler to make and simpler to use, resulting in savings all along the line: preliminaries, working drawings, details, checking, estimating, field layout, and supervision.

Modular masonry units

Let us consider, for example, the use of modular dimensioning in the assembly of *units* to comprise a building element in masonry construction. Figure 8 shows the relative positions of the masonry *units* to the grid lines in *plan* and *section*. The actual units would not, of course, appear in the final plan, nor would the grid lines. Notice that the arrowheads identify the locations of the grid planes. The final plan expression is shown in Fig. 9, and further illustrates the use of the drafting conventions.

The use of dots and arrows quickly reveals that the column centerlines are not on grid planes, although the distances between columns are indeed multiples of 4 in. Jointing conditions around the windows will be further defined as the architect develops his larger-scale window details. One of the chief virtues of this procedure is that it permits significant details to be worked out before their relationships are made final in working drawings.

From the preliminaries, it is possible to determine the critical jointing conditions. The room dimensions and wall thicknesses will determine the location of grid references. Starting with the intersection of the principal horizontal and vertical grids, the detail can then be rapidly worked out in

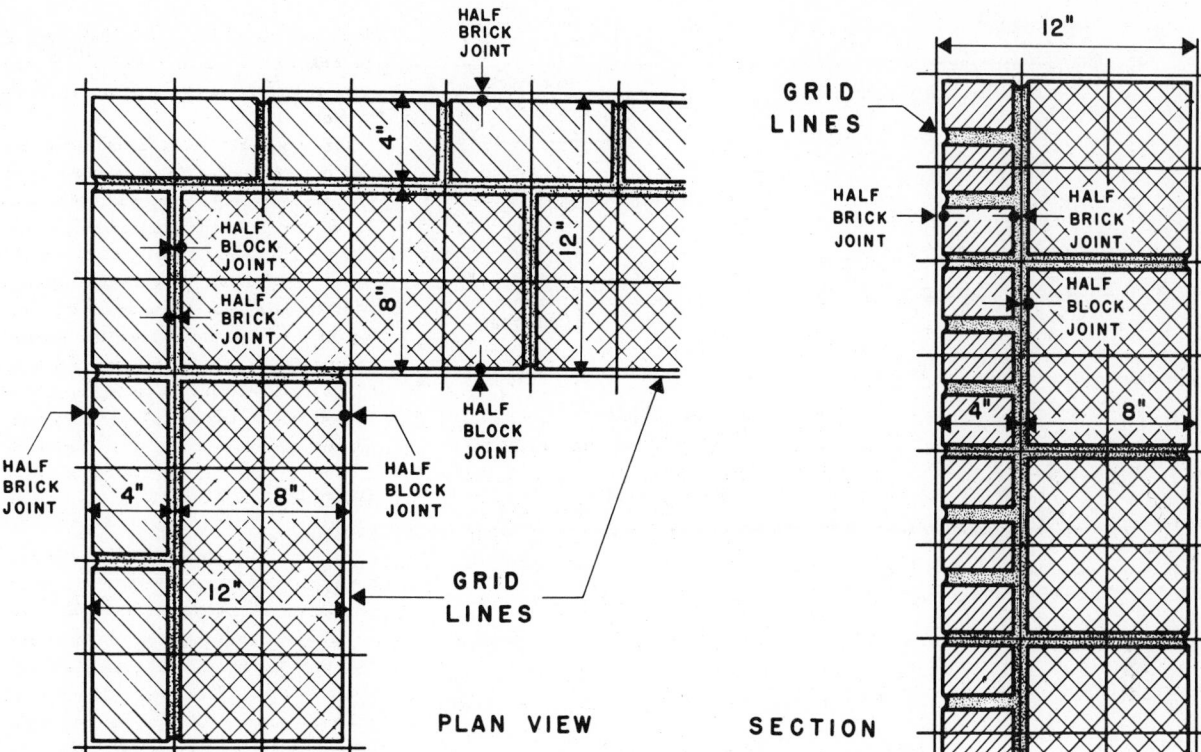

Fig. 8. Expression of modular grid in plan and section

freehand or drafted in final form. All that remains is to correlate plan and detail by simply showing on the plan the location of the same reference grid lines used in the large detail. The development of such a detail is shown in Fig. 10.

The application of dimensions to full cross sections is shown in Fig. 11. Note that many of the dimensions and dimensional refer-

ence points correspond to the elevation shown in Fig. 12. In both cases, the dimensional reference points identified by arrowheads can be easily located on the large-scale details and also serve as reference planes for structural drawings. Figure 13 shows the evolution of a large-scale detail from its relationship in cross section. To start the detail study, the intersection of the floor

grid plane and the principal foundation grid plane was marked off. From this point, it was then possible to relate, downward, the floor-slab thickness, insulation, gravel fill, and top of footing. From the outside foundation grid plane the foundation thickness and sill-width dimensions were then established. Although it is optional, the complete 4-in. grid, horizontally and ver-

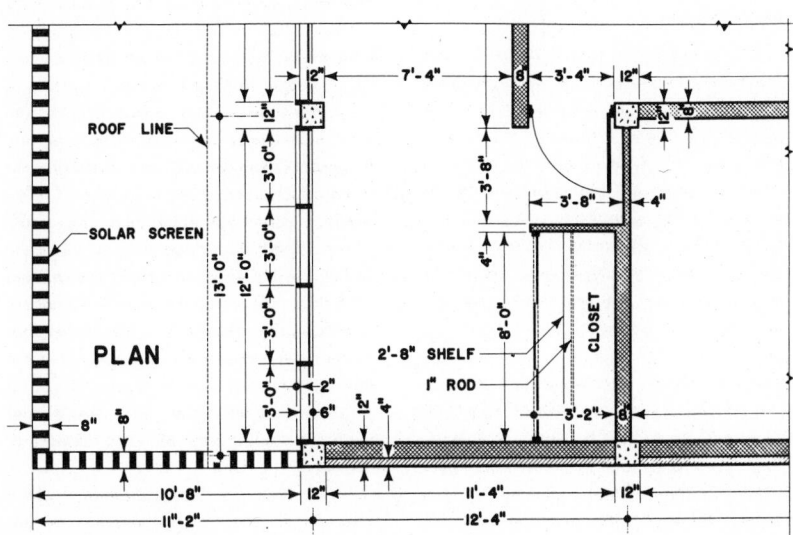

Fig. 9. Dimensioned masonry plan

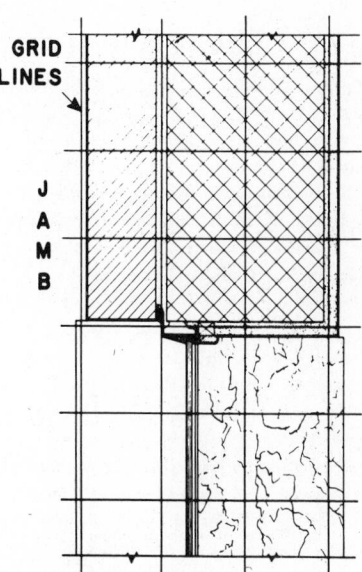

Fig. 10. Modular window detail

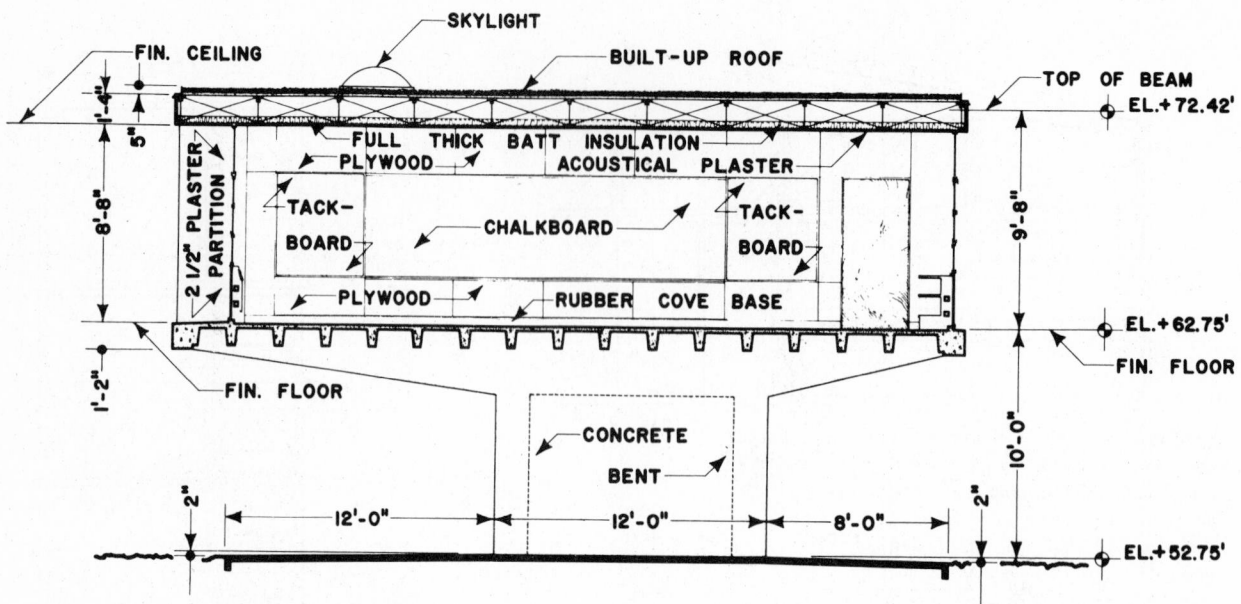

Fig. 11.   Cross section of a modular building

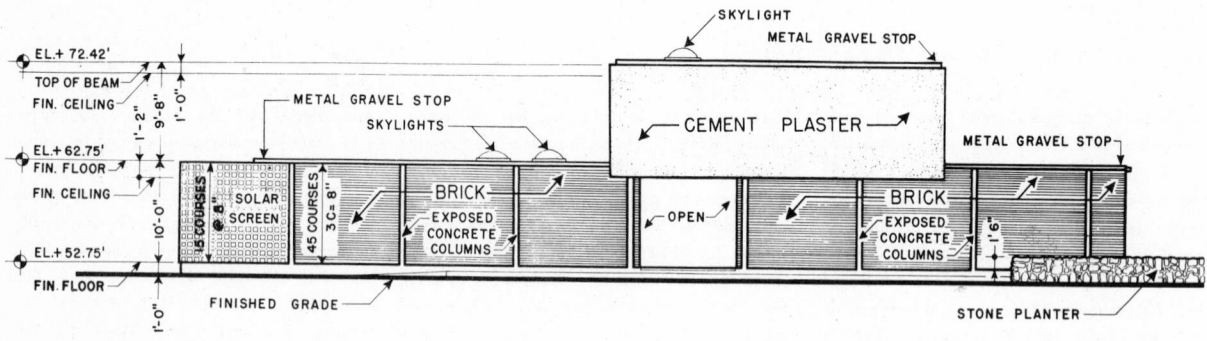

Fig. 12.   Exterior elevation of a modular building

tically, is shown on the working-drawing detail.

The brick-veneer construction shown in Fig. 14 is an example of the choices available in delineating modular construction. In general, typical wood-frame construction is most efficiently planned when the stud framing members are centered *between* grid lines. Then both the sheathing and the interior finish materials can be efficiently installed in multiples of 4 in. In masonry veneer, however, the 10-in. total wall thickness requires further consideration of the best location of grid lines. Either the studs or the masonry may be centered between grid lines. Construction efficiency would not necessarily be affected by either choice; the over-all masonry, gypsum board, and sheathing dimensions would still remain multiples of 4 in. However, the drawings themselves

are simplified by making the outside reference planes conform to the masonry placement and using centerline notations for all wood-frame interior partitions, as shown in Fig. 14.

Another decision that must be made by the architect is the method of construction. Notice that in detail A-A of Fig. 14 the *floor grid* does not coincide with an 8-in. increment of masonry. Door heads, window heads, and eave details must all be considered in establishing the first course of brick. Depending on these details, it might be better to provide an offset in the poured foundation to permit the alignment of the floor grid with a horizontal brick joint. Again, the detail is generated by establishing the principal grids and then determining the desired construction method.

Panelized construction usually results in

simpler dimensional relationships than other types of construction. Modular drafting is particularly appropriate for panelized construction because it permits easy and continuous checking for the most efficient use of standard production items.

For purposes of illustration and study, detail A-A of Fig. 15 includes the complete modular grid. Also, all sash-extrusion sizes have been shown, although under normal conditions the principal grids, plus a typical mullion size, would be adequate. From the plan and detail drawings, the structural engineer can easily establish the proper steel sizes, plan location, and elevations. (See also Fig. 16.)

In general, modular coordination is a dimensional reference system that encourages simplified construction details and takes advantage of the inherent dimensional

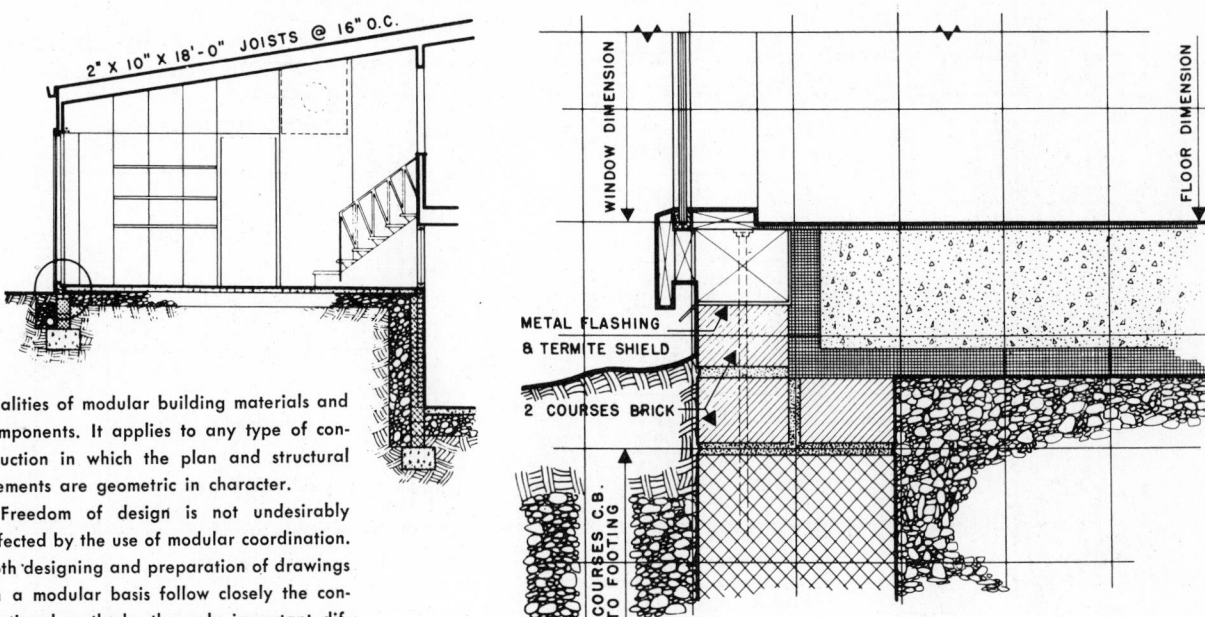

Fig. 13. Section and detail of frame building

qualities of modular building materials and components. It applies to any type of construction in which the plan and structural elements are geometric in character.

Freedom of design is not undesirably affected by the use of modular coordination. Both designing and preparation of drawings on a modular basis follow closely the conventional methods; the only important difference is the helpful discipline of a 4-in. grid. The small size of the grid and the

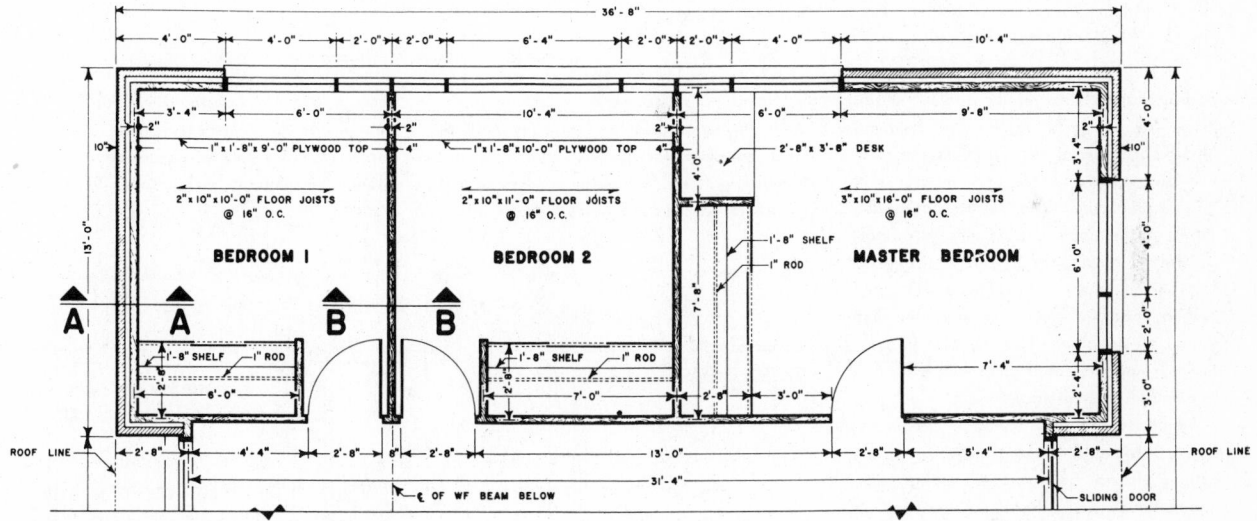

possibility of integrating nonmodular-sized items permit as infinite a variety of plan and elevation solutions as the more traditional practices.

Planning on a modular system can be divided into five steps:

1. Preliminary drawings
2. Selection of over-all dimensions
3. Identification of significant details
4. Development of modular details
5. Correlation of details on working drawings.

Preliminary plans are developed from the schematics prepared for presentation to the client and for cost estimates. The grid placement, discussed on the preceding

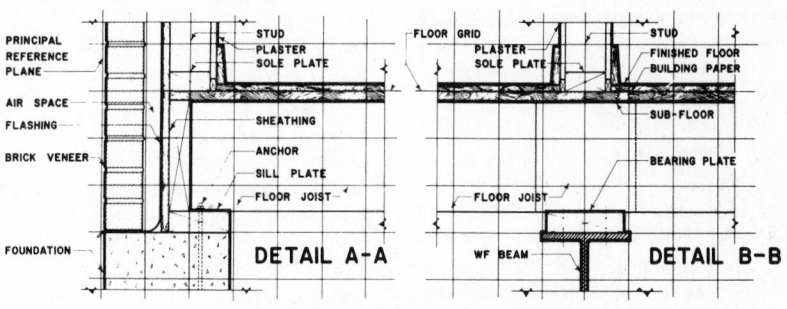

Fig. 14. Plan and details of brick-veneer construction

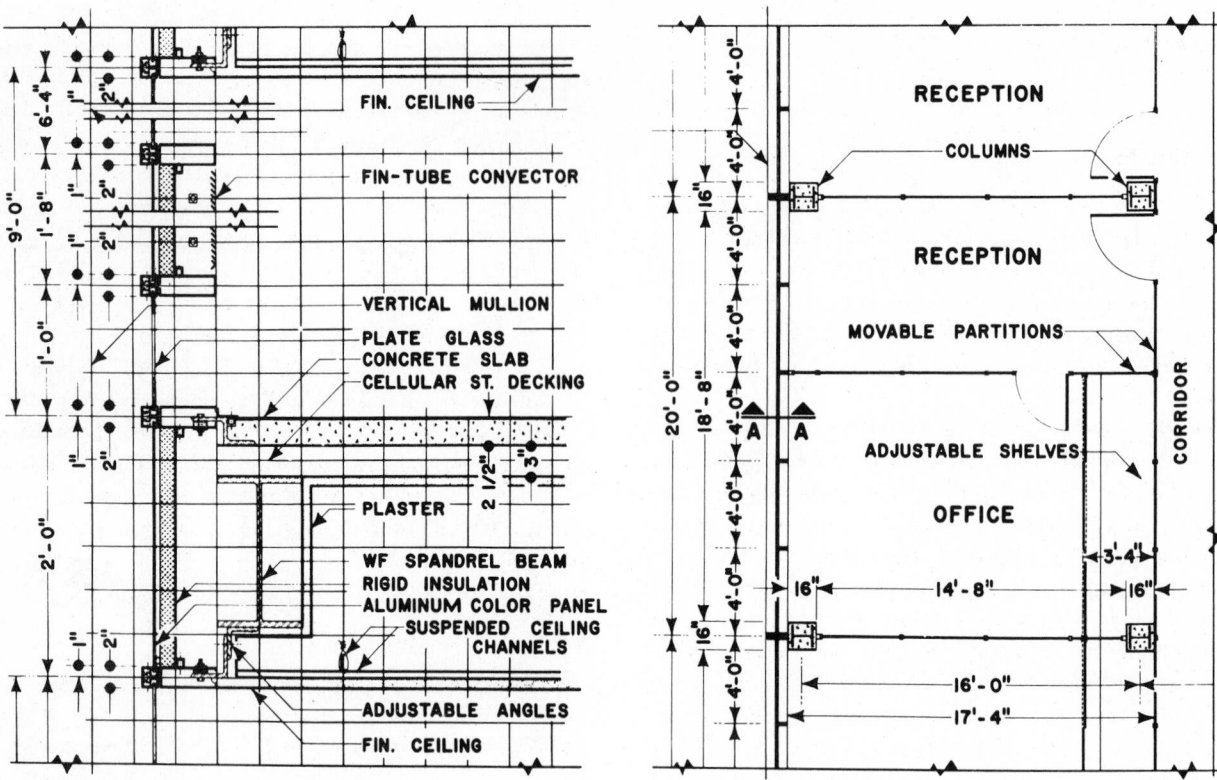

Fig. 15. Plan and detail of modular curtain wall

pages, should be carefully studied at this stage. The 4-in. grid may be used for these plans, but more often a large layout module using some multiple of 4 in., say 4 ft 8 in., is employed. Grid lines are not usually shown at the small scale of these drawings.

Over-all dimensions for the entire structure, wall lengths, opening widths and heights, partition locations, and the like should all be planned in multiples of 4 in. to ensure agreement of plans with grid, and to eliminate unnecessary details.

Significant details should be chosen for development into working drawings; duplications should be avoided. Similar sills, heads, jambs, and other details that fall on corresponding grid openings need only be shown once.

Modular details are then chosen from standards or catalogs, or if these do not satisfy the problem, are individually developed.

Correlation of details with working drawings is accomplished by the use of appropriate symbols to key the detail to plans and sections.

Modular architectural plans are most successful if the structural drawings are also modular. Simplified checking results when all shop drawings are submitted on the basis of modular drafting. These considerations are often included in the engineering contract and in the appropriate paragraphs

of the bidding documents. Most contractors in the United States have already built at least one modular project, and thus are familiar with the dimensioning system and its use in construction layouts. Some architects include notes on the dimensioning conventions on the first sheet of their drawings. Prepared notes can be purchased from the Stanpat Company, Whitestone 57, New York.

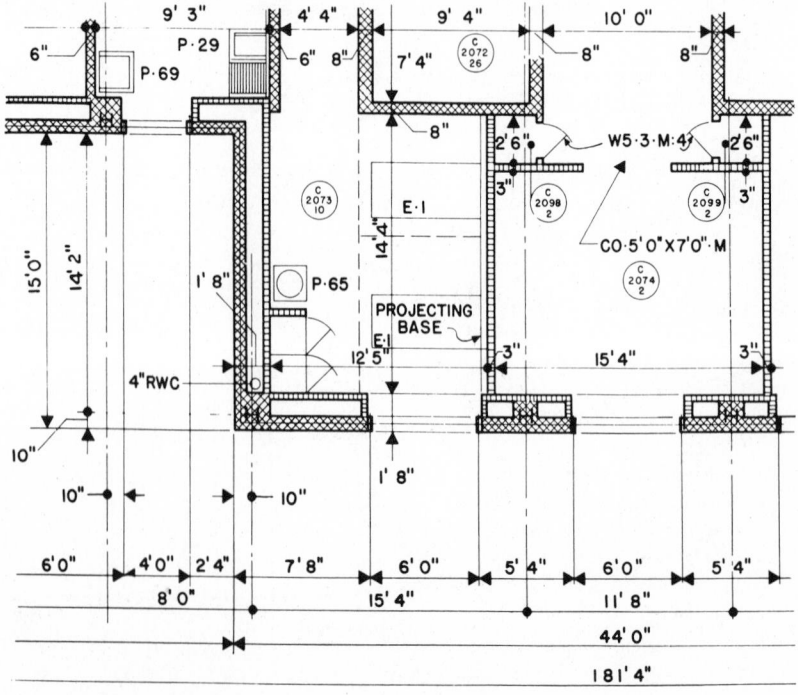

Fig. 16. Dimensioning of skeleton-frame construction

By HENDRIK P. MAAS, AIA

Short Cuts to Solar Angles

WITH the increasing use of larger glass areas and more emphasis generally on solar orientation, it is increasingly important for an architect to have in his files information on the sun's position as it varies from season to season and from hour to hour. Only with that information can he solve problems of sunlight and shade.

The purpose of this presentation is to simplify the architect's calculations. While the determination of the sun's position at any given time has involved the author in some fairly complicated exercises in navigational mathematics, the data here given should leave little for the reader to do, except, of course, to apply the data to his own design. This involves only some graphic projection of a routine nature. For the designer who demands hairline accuracy the necessary formulas are appended. But a navigator's accuracy could hardly ever be required for a building problem; the charts and tables on succeeding pages should eliminate the mathematics for all normal purposes of architects.

The scope of the data is for selected hours between sunrise and sunset, at each fifth parallel of latitude from 70° North to 70° South, for the critical dates of December 22, March 21, September 23, and June 22. These dates give, of course, the extreme and the mean conditions for sun angles. For the latitudes of the United States (see map), diagrams illustrating the sun's angles are given with the tables on pages 80 and 81. The diagrams are really horizontal projections of the sun's paths, as illustrated a bit more graphically in the sketch at the top of page 78. For other latitudes the data is given only in tables, page 82.

The diagrams and tables may be used directly for the latitudes given; for intermediate latitudes the answer is readily obtained by interpolation between the figures given, for the desired hour, for the nearest latitudes above and below.

Solar Angles Made Easy

The position of the sun with respect to any point on the earth's surface is defined by the angle of AZIMUTH and the angle of ALTITUDE. These angles, of course, are determined by the latitude, the date, and the hour.

LATITUDES IN THE UNITED STATES

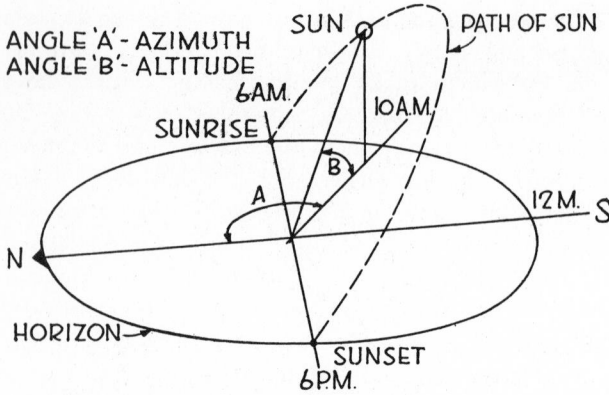

ANGLE 'A'- AZIMUTH
ANGLE 'B'- ALTITUDE

The AZIMUTH is simply the angle measured horizontally from the North meridian. For morning hours it is measured in an Easterly direction; for afternoon hours, Westerly.

The ALTITUDE is the angle, measured vertically, between the sun and the horizontal plane of the horizon. These angles are illustrated in the sketch above. It should be noted that the North meridian is the true North, not the magnetic North. The diagrams with the actual data, pages 80 and 81, represent the path of the sun for the given date and the given latitude, as shown in plan. The eliptical curve represents the horizontal projection of the path of the sun. The heavier lines are the horizontal projections of the angles of altitude for each line of azimuth shown. The angles of azimuth and altitude for various hours are tabulated below the diagrams. The earliest and latest hours are those of sunrise and sunset, to the nearest ten minutes.

The diagrams and tables may be applied to southern latitudes simply by transposing the summer and winter dates and the fall and spring dates.

How to Use the Tables

To illustrate the procedure for using the tables we will determine, graphically, the condition of sunlight on a simple one-room structure with a roof overhang, choosing, just for instance, the hour of 11 A.M. on June 22, and the latitude of 42° (New York City). We shall locate the line of the shadow cast by the roof overhang.

For the calculation, the plan of the structure is drawn in the normal manner. Next the North line is drawn on the sheet, just as in any plot plan. This North lines gives us the starting point for the graphic solution of the problem.

Now we refer to the diagrams and tables (page 81) to find azimuth and altitude angles for the given condition. Here comes the interpolation. Azimuth of 40°, 11 A.M., summer, is 138°. For 45°, same time, 145°30'. By simple interpolation, we get an azimuth

for 42° of 141°. In the same manner the altitude for 42° N, 11 A.M., summer, is found to be 67°30'.

Now, on the plan at any convenient point, we draw the line A-B, 141° East of the North position indicated on the plan.

Parallel to A-B, a ray line is drawn on the plan, through the point we are interested in, the point C' at the juncture of the wall and the roof. Now we project this point on line A-B and thus get a starting point for drawing an elevation (or as much of an elevation as is necessary) of the building on A-B. On this elevation the critical point we are locating is point C.

Next we add the altitude to the calculation, by drawing, through point C, a line at 67°30' from A-B. This line crosses A-B at point P, which gives us another projection point. Projecting this back to the plan we locate P_1 on the ray line R_4. At this point we have located the shadow line on the terrace — it will run along the terrace through P_1 parallel to the roof line.

We can continue, if we like, to get other shadow lines, until we can outline the shadow of the building all around, and even learn where the sun will strike the floor inside (through the window). To carry on, we project point P_1 down to a section below, to the terrace level at P_2. Now from C_2 to P_2 we get still another angle, which is measured and found to be 80°30'. This angle, it will be seen, has been found graphically; it is the direct elevation of the angle at which the sunlight at this particular time casts shadows around our particular building.

Using this new angle, 80°30', we can carry the projection process backwards from section to plan, and so outline the shadow of the building.

FORMULAS FOR DETERMINING AZIMUTH AND ALTITUDE

For those who may have a special need of knowing accurately the AZIMUTH and ALTITUDE for a particular date or hour not given in the tables the following formulas and information are given:

I $\sin h = \sin L \sin d + \cos L \cos d \cos t$

II $\sin Z = \sin t \cos d \sec h$

III $\cos t = -\tan L \tan d$ (when h = 0°)

IV $\cos Z = \sin d \sec L$ (when h = 0°)

V $\cos t = \dfrac{\sin h - \sin L \sin d}{\cos L \cos d}$
  in which:

L = latitude
d = declination; i.e., the angle between a line connecting the centers of the sun and earth and the plane of the equator.

t = time of day expressed in degrees. Since there are 24 hours and also 360 degrees in one revolution of the earth, 1 hour = 15°, 1 minute = 15′ and 1 second = 15″. This angle is always measured from the noon position of the sun, therefore noon = 0°, 10 A.M. = 30°, 4 P.M. = 60°, etc.

Z = AZIMUTH
h = ALTITUDE

Declination of the sun varies for each day of the year from approximately 23°27′ North to 23°27′ South. When the declination is North, it is considered plus (+), when South, minus (−). The precise declination as it varies for each year can be found in the American Nautical Almanac issued annually by the U. S. Naval Observatory, Washington, D. C., and may be purchased from the Superintendent of Documents, Washington 25, D.C. For convenience a table of declinations for each seventh day of the year, simplified to the nearest 5′ is included (below). Intermediate declinations may be interpolated with reasonable results. The reader is cautioned to remember that when the declination is South it carries a minus (−) sign in which case, in the above formulas, the sin and tan will have a negative value while the cos will have a plus value.

When h = 0°0′ it is the hour of sunrise or sunset.
Example: Find AZIMUTH and ALTITUDE of sun at 2 P.M., May 15, at Latitude 42° N.

L = 42°
d = +18°40′ (interpolated between +19°25′ and +17°40′ from Table of Declinations)
t = 30°

Computations by Slide Rule

From   I $\sin h = \sin 42° \sin 18°40′ + \cos 42° \cos 18°40′ \cos 30°$
$$= .670 \times .320 + .745 \times .950 \times .865$$
$$= .215 + .612 = .827$$
$$h = 56°$$

From II $\sin Z = \sin 30° \cos 18°40′ \sec 56°$
$$= .500 \times .950 \times 1.79$$
$$Z = 59° \text{ or } 121°$$

Since Z is measured from the North meridian, by inspection the proper answer is 121° to the West.

The hour of sunrise (or sunset) and its AZIMUTH may be found from III and IV.

Local sun time * may be found from V.

The noon ALTITUDE of the sun may be quickly found for any latitude and any declination by the following additional formulas.

a. $h = 90° - (L - d)$ when L is greater than d

b. $h = 90° - (d - L)$ when d is greater than L
   (L and d same name)

c. $h = 90° - (L + d)$
   (L and d contrary name)

---

* Sun time is the hour of day as determined by the position of the sun with relation to its noon meridian. Since standard time (clock time) is based on the sun time at the center of each hourly time zone, sun time may vary as much as ½ hour from standard time depending on the locality.

PLAN

SECTION

Declination of the Sun—to Nearest 5′

DATE	DECLINATION	DATE
June 22	+ 23°-30′	
15	+ 23°-15′	June 29
8	+ 22°-45′	July 6
1	+ 21°-55′	13
May 25	+ 20°-50′	20
18	+ 19°-25′	27
11	+ 17°-40′	Aug. 3
4	+ 15°-45′	10
Apr. 26	+ 13°-20′	18
19	+ 11°- 0′	25
12	+ 8°-30′	Sept. 1
5	+ 5°-55′	8
Mar. 28	+ 2°-50′	16
21	0°- 0′	23
14	− 2°-50′	Oct. 1
7	− 5°-35′	8
Feb. 28	− 8°-15′	15
21	− 10°-50′	22
14	− 13°-15′	29
7	− 15°-30′	Nov. 5
Jan. 31	− 17°-30′	12
24	− 19°-20′	19
17	− 20°-50′	26
10	− 22°- 0′	Dec. 3
3	− 22°-50′	10
Dec. 27	− 23°-20′	17
	− 23°-30′	22

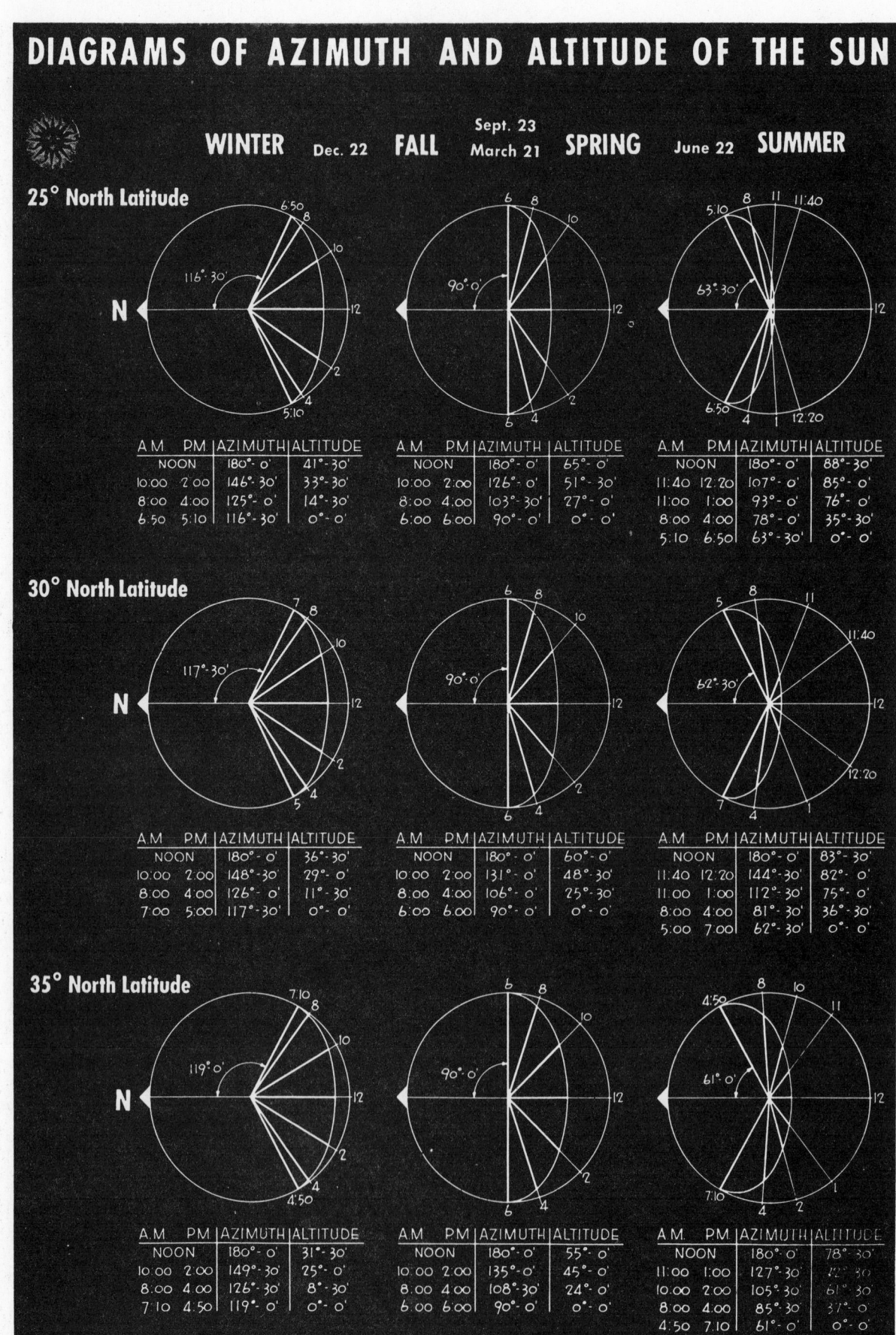

DIAGRAMS OF AZIMUTH AND ALTITUDE OF THE SUN

WINTER Dec. 22   **FALL** Sept. 23 March 21   **SPRING** June 22 **SUMMER**

25° North Latitude

A.M.	P.M.	AZIMUTH	ALTITUDE
NOON		180°-0'	41°-30'
10:00	2:00	146°-30'	33°-30'
8:00	4:00	125°-0'	14°-30'
6:50	5:10	116°-30'	0°-0'

A.M.	P.M.	AZIMUTH	ALTITUDE
NOON		180°-0'	65°-0'
10:00	2:00	126°-0'	51°-30'
8:00	4:00	103°-30'	27°-0'
6:00	6:00	90°-0'	0°-0'

A.M.	P.M.	AZIMUTH	ALTITUDE
NOON		180°-0'	88°-30'
11:40	12:20	107°-0'	85°-0'
11:00	1:00	93°-0'	76°-0'
8:00	4:00	78°-0'	35°-30'
5:10	6:50	63°-30'	0°-0'

30° North Latitude

A.M.	P.M.	AZIMUTH	ALTITUDE
NOON		180°-0'	36°-30'
10:00	2:00	148°-30'	29°-0'
8:00	4:00	126°-0'	11°-30'
7:00	5:00	117°-30'	0°-0'

A.M.	P.M.	AZIMUTH	ALTITUDE
NOON		180°-0'	60°-0'
10:00	2:00	131°-0'	48°-30'
8:00	4:00	106°-0'	25°-30'
6:00	6:00	90°-0'	0°-0'

A.M.	P.M.	AZIMUTH	ALTITUDE
NOON		180°-0'	83°-30'
11:40	12:20	144°-30'	82°-0'
11:00	1:00	112°-30'	75°-0'
8:00	4:00	81°-30'	36°-30'
5:00	7:00	62°-30'	0°-0'

35° North Latitude

A.M.	P.M.	AZIMUTH	ALTITUDE
NOON		180°-0'	31°-30'
10:00	2:00	149°-30'	25°-0'
8:00	4:00	126°-30'	8°-30'
7:10	4:50	119°-0'	0°-0'

A.M.	P.M.	AZIMUTH	ALTITUDE
NOON		180°-0'	55°-0'
10:00	2:00	135°-0'	45°-0'
8:00	4:00	108°-30'	24°-0'
6:00	6:00	90°-0'	0°-0'

A.M.	P.M.	AZIMUTH	ALTITUDE
NOON		180°-0'	78°-30'
11:00	1:00	127°-30'	72°-30'
10:00	2:00	105°-30'	61°-30'
8:00	4:00	85°-30'	37°-0'
4:50	7:10	61°-0'	0°-0'

DIAGRAMS OF AZIMUTH AND ALTITUDE OF THE SUN

WINTER Dec. 22   **FALL** Sept. 23 / March 21   **SPRING** June 22 **SUMMER**

40° North Latitude

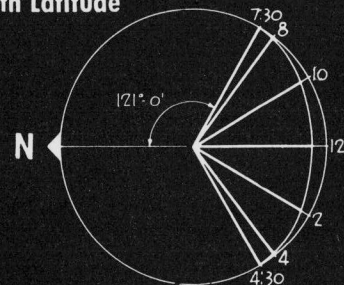
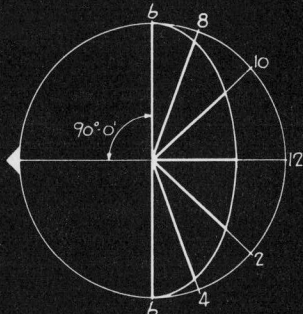
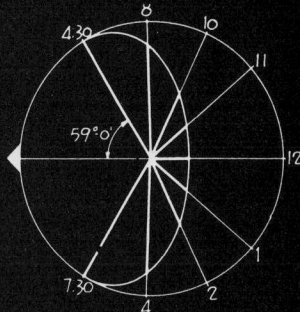

A.M.	P.M.	AZIMUTH	ALTITUDE
NOON		180°- 0'	26°- 30'
10:00	2:00	150°- 30'	20°- 30'
8:00	4:00	127°- 0'	5°- 30'
7:30	4:30	121°- 0'	0°- 0'

A.M.	P.M.	AZIMUTH	ALTITUDE
NOON		180°- 0'	50°- 0'
10:00	2:00	138°- 0'	41°- 30'
8:00	4:00	110°- 30'	22°- 30'
6:00	6:00	90°- 0'	0°- 0'

A.M.	P.M.	AZIMUTH	ALTITUDE
NOON		180°- 0'	73°- 30'
11:00	1:00	138°- 0'	69°- 0'
10:00	2:00	114°- 0'	60°- 0'
8:00	4:00	89°- 0'	37°- 30'
4:30	7:30	59°- 0'	0°- 0'

45° North Latitude

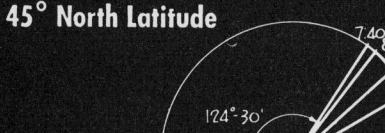
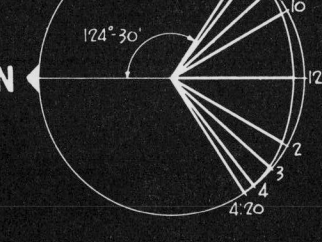
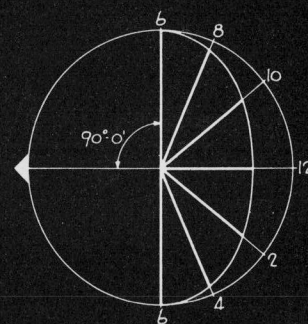
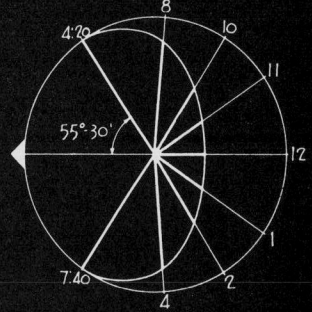

A.M.	P.M.	AZIMUTH	ALTITUDE
NOON		180°- 0'	21°- 30'
10:00	2:00	151°- 30'	16°- 0'
9:00	3:00	139°- 0'	10°- 0'
8:00	4:00	127°- 30'	2°- 30'
7:40	4:20	124°- 30'	0°- 0'

A.M.	P.M.	AZIMUTH	ALTITUDE
NOON		180°- 0'	45°- 0'
10:00	2:00	141°- 0'	38°- 0'
8:00	4:00	112°- 0'	20°- 30'
6:00	6:00	90°- 0'	0°- 0'

A.M.	P.M.	AZIMUTH	ALTITUDE
NOON		180°- 0'	68°- 30'
11:00	1:00	145°- 30'	65°- 30'
10:00	2:00	121°- 30'	57°- 30'
8:00	4:00	93°- 0'	37°- 30'
4:20	7:40	55°- 30'	0°- 0'

50° North Latitude

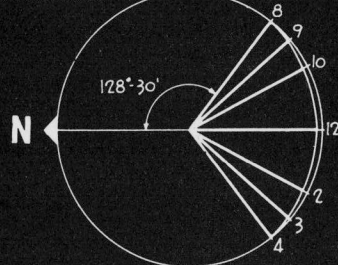
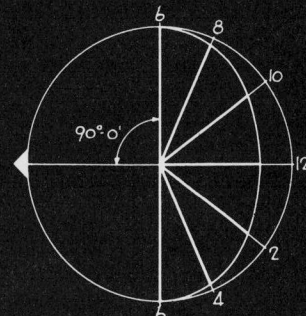
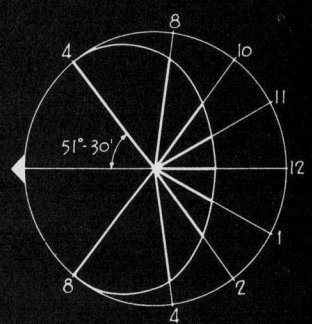

A.M.	P.M.	AZIMUTH	ALTITUDE
NOON		180°- 0'	16°- 30'
10:00	2:00	152°- 0'	12°- 0'
9:00	3:00	139°- 30'	6°- 30'
8:00	4:00	128°- 30'	0°- 0'

A.M.	P.M.	AZIMUTH	ALTITUDE
NOON		180°- 0'	40°- 0'
10:00	2:00	143°- 0'	34°- 0'
8:00	4:00	114°- 0'	18°- 30'
6:00	6:00	90°- 0'	0°- 0'

A.M.	P.M.	AZIMUTH	ALTITUDE
NOON		180°- 0'	63°- 30'
11:00	1:00	150°- 30'	61°- 0'
10:00	2:00	127°- 30'	54°- 30'
8:00	4:00	97°- 0'	37°- 0'
4:00	8:00	51°- 30'	0°- 0'

TABLE OF AZIMUTH AND ALTITUDE OF THE SUN
From Latitude 0° to 20° N. and 55° N. to 70° N.

		Dec. 22 WINTER		FALL	Sept. 23 Mar. 21	SPRING		June 22 SUMMER	
	A.M.–P.M.	Azi.	Alt.	A.M.–P.M.	Azi.	Alt.	A.M.–P.M.	Azi.	Alt.
0°	Noon	180°–0′	66°–30′	Noon	90°–0′	90°–0′	Noon	0°–0′	66°–30′
	10–2	131°–0′	52°–30′	10–2	90°–0′	60°–0′	10–2	49°–0′	52°–30′
	8–4	116°–30′	27°–30′	8–4	90°–0′	30°–0′	8–4	63°–30′	27°–30′
	6–6	113°–30′	0°–0′	6–6	90°–0′	0°–0′	6–6	66°–30′	0°–0′
5° N.	Noon	180°–0′	61°–30′	Noon	180°–0′	85°–0′	Noon	0°–0′	71°–30′
	10–2	135°–30′	49°–0′	10–2	98°–30′	59°–30′	10–2	54°–30′	55°–30′
	8–4	119°–0′	25°–0′	8–4	93°–0′	30°–0′	8–4	66°–0′	29°–30′
	6:10–5:50	114°–0′	0°–0′	6–6	90°–0′	0°–0′	5:50–6:10	66°–30′	0°–0′
10° N.	Noon	180°–0′	56°–30′	Noon	180°–0′	80°–0′	Noon	0°–0′	76°–30′
	10–2	139°–0′	45°–30′	11–1	123°–0′	72°–0′	11–1	45°–0′	70°–30′
	8–4	120°–30′	22°–30′	10–2	106°–30′	58°–30′	10–2	61°–0′	58°–30′
	6:20–5:40	114°–0′	0°–0′	8–4	95°–30′	29°–30′	8–4	68°–30′	31°–30′
				6–6	90°–0′	0°–0′	5:40–6:20	66°–0′	0°–0′
15° N.	Noon	180°–0′	51°–30′	Noon	180°–0′	75°–0′	Noon	0°–0′	81°–30′
	10–2	142°–0′	41°–30′	11–1	134°–0′	69°–0′	11–1	56°–30′	73°–30′
	8–4	122°–30′	20°–0′	10–2	114°–0′	57°–0′	10–2	68°–30′	60°–30′
	6:30–5:30	114°–30′	0°–0′	8–4	98°–30′	29°–0′	8–4	71°–30′	33°–0′
				6–6	90°–0′	0°–0′	5:30–6:30	65°–30′	0°–0′
20° N.	Noon	180°–0′	46°–30′	Noon	180°–0′	70°–0′	Noon	0°–0′	86°–30′
	10–2	144°–30′	37°–30′	11–1	142°–0′	65°–0′	11:40–12:20	52°–0′	84°–0′
	8–4	124°–0′	17°–0′	10–2	120°–30′	54°–30′	11–1	73°–0′	75°–30′
	6:40–5:20	115°–0′	0°–0′	8–4	101°–0′	28°–0′	8–4	74°–30′	34°–30′
				6–6	90°–0′	0°–0′	5:20–6:40	65°–0′	0°–0′
55° N.	Noon	180°–0′	11°–30′	Noon	180°–0′	35°–0′	Noon	180°–0′	58°–30′
	10–2	152°–30′	7°–30′	10–2	145°–0′	30°–0′	11–1	154°–30′	56°–30′
	9–3	139°–30′	3°–0′	8–4	115°–30′	16°–30′	10–2	132°–30′	51°–30′
	8:30–3:30	134°–30′	0°–0′	6–6	90°–0′	0°–0′	8–4	100°–30′	36°–0′
							3:30–8:30	45°–30′	0°–0′
60° N.	Noon	180°–0′	6°–30′	Noon	180°–0′	30°–0′	Noon	180°–0′	53°–30′
	11:20–12:40	171°–0′	6°–0′	10–2	146°–30′	29°–30′	10–2	137°–0′	48°–0′
	10–2	153°–0′	3°–0′	8–4	116°–30′	14°–30′	8–4	104°–0′	35°–0′
	9:10–2:50	143°–0′	0°–0′	6–6	90°–0′	0°–0′	6–6	77°–30′	20°–0′
							2:50–9:10	37°–0′	0°–0′
65° N.	Noon	180°–0′	1°–30′	Noon	180°–0′	25°–0′	Noon	180°–0′	48°–30′
	10:30–1:30	162°–0′	0°–0′	10–2	147°–30′	21°–30′	10–2	140°–0′	44°–0′
				8–4	117°–30′	12°–0′	8–4	107°–30′	33°–30′
				6–6	90°–0′	0°–0′	6–6	79°–30′	21°–0′
							1:30–10:30	14°–30′	0°–0′
70° N.	Sun does not rise from about Nov. 22nd to Jan. 21st			Noon	180°–0′	20°–0′	Noon	180°–0′	43°–30′
				10–2	148°–30′	17°–0′	10–2	143°–0′	40°–30′
				8–4	118°–30′	10°–0′	8–4	110°–30′	36°–0′
				6–6	90°–0′	0°–0′	6–6	81°–30′	22°–0′
							4–8	54°–30′	12°–30′
							Midnite	0°–0′	3°–30′

SECTION II: STRUCTURAL DESIGN

Structural Forms—Wood:
    Long span construction 87
    Laminated wood 88
    Lamella construction 94
    Plywood beams 95
Structural Forms—Steel:
    Rigid frames 96
    Space structures 100
    Space frames 101
    Domes 103
    Suspension structures 107
Structural Forms—Concrete, Thin Shell:
    Curved in one direction 111
    Curved in two directions 118
    Folded plate 126
Design Loads:
    Dead loads 127
    Live loads 129
Structural Design:
    Beam formulae 134
Structural Design—Wood:
    Allowable stresses 136
    Properties of sections 138
    Decking 140
    Ceiling joists 140
    Floor joists 141
    Rafters and roof joists 142
    Beams 144
    Columns 146
    Trusses 147
    Bolted connections 148
    Plywood box beams 148
    Stressed-skin panels 151
Wood Construction:
    Light wood framing 154
    Nailing 158
    Threaded nails 160
    Trussed rafters 164
    Heavy timber 166
Structural Design—Steel:
    Type of steel 168
    Beams 168
    Joists 172
    Columns 177
    Connection details 179
    Lally columns 180
    Plastic design 182
    Welding 184
Structural Design—Concrete:
    Materials 185
    Design criteria 186
    Beams 187
    Columns 189
    Details 190
    Slabs 191
    Joists—one way 191
    Joists—two way 192
    Lift slabs 194
    Tilt-up 197
    Prestressed 200
Floor Framing Systems 209

Structural Design—Masonry:
Materials and mortar mixes 214
Allowable stresses 215
Bond 216
Workmanship 217
Arches 217
Reinforced masonry 219
Lintels, steel 223
Lintels, reinforced masonry 224
Lintels, reinforced brick 224
Lintels, reinforced tile 226
Lintels, reinforced concrete 227
Masonry—Brick and Tile:
Modular sizes 228
Modular details 228
Modular estimating tables 230
Nonmodular quantities and courses 232
Pattern bonds 234
Cavity walls 235
Solid metal-tied walls 238
SCR brick 239
Surface treatments 242
Terra cotta 243
Ceramic veneer 243
Structural clay tile partitions 244
Structural clay facing tile partitions 246
Chemical-resistant tile and brick 249
Solar screens 251
Masonry—Concrete:
Types and sizes 253
Properties 254
Courses and quantities 256
Wall construction 258
Masonry Construction:
Thermal expansion 266
Flexible anchorage 269
Parapet walls 271
Cracking of masonry walls 273
Anchoring to masonry walls 276

By SEYMOUR HOWARD, *Architect*
Associate Professor, Pratt Institute

GENERAL CONSIDERATIONS OF WOOD AS STRUCTURAL MATERIAL:

CHARACTERISTIC	CONSEQUENCE
1. Not homogeneous (orthotropic) (long cylindrical cells parallel to one axis)	1. Allowable stresses vary for pure tension & compression, tension & compression (extreme fiber) in bending, compression across grain, and also for shape of cross section ("Form factor"); depend on direction of stress with respect to direction of grain
2. Natural defects (cross-grain, spiral & diagonal; knots)	2. Allowable stresses reduced to compensate. Theory of probability used in laminated sections permits higher stresses than for solid sections
3. Decay hazard in exposed conditions	3. Preservative treatments for permanent structures. Reduced allowable stresses for temporary structures
4. Swells or shrinks with changes in humidity	4. Wood dried to expected service conditions of humidity before fabrication & assembly; for glued laminated sections, all laminations held to a 5% range of moisture content (e.g. 6% to 10% incl.)
5. Although remaining elastic, under long-term loads, a permanent sag or deflection takes place	5. Use double calculated dead loads or normal E÷2 for figuring allowable deflection

Note: These characteristics are listed as important differences between wood and the idealized, perfectly homogeneous and perfectly elastic material used in the mathematical analysis of strength of materials.

FIRE SAFETY

As is well known, heavy timber (6 in. nom, 5 in. min actual in least dimension) and plank construction is much better fire risk than thin sections and boarding. This fact gives glued laminated arches and frames some advantage over wood trusses and lamella arches. It also explains usual spacing of 8 ft for arches and frames, with 2 in. planking. (Next step is usually 16 to 20 ft spacing with purlins.) Small width (2 in. nom) arch rafters, spaced 24 in. o.c., with 1 in. boarding, are usually limited to farm structures and small warehouses.

RECOMMENDED SPANS (Maxima in Parenthesis)

TYPE OF STRUCTURAL UNIT	SPAN	SPACING	TYPE OF STRUCTURAL UNIT	SPAN	SPACING
Joists	Up to 24 ft	16 to 24 in.			
Sawn Beams	Up to 30 (40) ft	4 to 20 ft			
Glued Laminated Beams	Up to 60 (100) ft	4 to 20 ft			
BOWSTRING TRUSS DEPTH/SPAN ≈ 1/7*	40 to 150 ft (250 ft)	16 to 20 ft	TRUSSED RAFTER	20 to 60 ft	24 in.
FINK TRUSS BEST FOR SLOPES OVER 25°	40 to 60 ft (90 ft)	12 to 20 ft	ARCH RAFTER OR ARCH RIB RISE/SPAN ≈ 0.45 (THREE-HINGED ARCH)	20 to 60 (80) ft	24 in.
BELGIAN TRUSS			TWO-HINGED ARCH RISE/SPAN - MIN 1/8 USUAL 1/6 TO 1/4	30 to 100 ft (175 ft)	2, 8 ft or 16 to 20 ft
PRATT TRUSS FOR SLOPES UNDER 25°					
PRATT TRUSS (FLAT) DEPTH/SPAN ≈ 1/8 † (WARREN & HOWE ALSO USED)	40 to 120 ft (120 ft)	12 to 20 ft	THREE-HINGED ARCH RISE/SPAN - 1/1 OR MORE	20 to 100 ft (200 ft)	2, 4 to 8 ft or 16 to 20 ft
CRESCENT TRUSS	40 to 80 ft (250 ft)	16 to 20 ft	THREE-HINGED ARCH RISE/SPAN - MIN 1/8 USUAL 1/6 TO 1/4	30 to 100 ft (175 ft)	8 ft or 16 to 20 ft
LAMELLA ARCH RISE/SPAN: MIN 1/8 USUAL 1/6 TO 1/4 MAX 1/1	40 to 120 ft (165 ft)	— —	THREE-HINGED RIGID FRAME		

Note: Glued laminated sections used in trusses for curved chords and heavily loaded straight chords and web members. Steel may be used for tension members. Glued laminated sections used for all arches and rigid frames, except that joist sections (2 by 8 to 2 by 12s) used for lamella arches.
Recommendations based on articles by Verne Ketchum (Chief Engineer, Timber Structures, Inc.) and Architectural Construction by Theodore Crane (Wiley, 1956), and other sources.
* Some authorities recommend 1/8 to 1/4 for depth/span ratio.
† Some authorities recommend 1/8 to 1/10.

GLUED LAMINATED WOOD—BASIC DATA

(USUAL)

TYPICAL SECTIONS

Note that grain of all laminations is parallel to length of member (in plywood, grain directions of adjacent plies are at right angles)

Outer plies can be chosen for high strength and/or appearance

Lower-grade wood can be used for inner plies

Wood throughout section can be inspected before fabrication, unlike solid timbers, which may contain hidden defects

Wood throughout section can be seasoned uniformly, reducing chances of large checks and shakes often found in solid timbers

For service conditions involving low moisture contents, inspection and seasoning permit higher design stresses than for solid timbers

KINDS OF WOOD

SPECIES	USE
Douglas fir	General
Southern yellow pine	General
White oak	Ships
Sitka spruce	Aircraft

1. Other species may be used for special purposes of appearance or service
2. Gluing of treated wood is very difficult, almost impossible with creosoted wood. Techniques are being developed, but it is best to treat wood after gluing.

KINDS OF GLUE

INTERIOR USE (normal moisture not more than 15% in service conditions)
Water-resistant adhesives:
1. Casein glue, mold resistant, Federal Specification MMM-A-125

EXTERIOR USE (outdoors, underwater or service conditions causing greater than 15% moisture content, as, for example, in some textile industries)
Waterproof adhesives:
1. Phenol-, Resorcinol-, and Melamine-type resin glues, room- and intermediate-temperature setting, Joint Military Specification MIL-A-397B
2. Phenol-, Resorcinol-, and Melamine-type resin glues, high-temperature setting, Joint Military Specification MIL-A-5534A

Notes: Chemists and manufacturers are still developing new adhesives; at present time water-resistant types are less expensive

END AND EDGE JOINTS IN LAMINATIONS

VERTICALLY LAMINATED BEAM

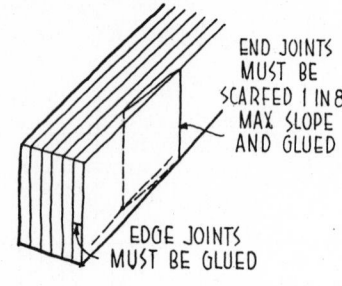

END JOINTS MUST BE SCARFED 1 IN 8 MAX SLOPE AND GLUED

EDGE JOINTS MUST BE GLUED

HORIZONTALLY LAMINATED SECTIONS

END JOINTS, SCARFED TYPE, SHOULD BE WELL SCATTERED IN ADJACENT LAMINATIONS

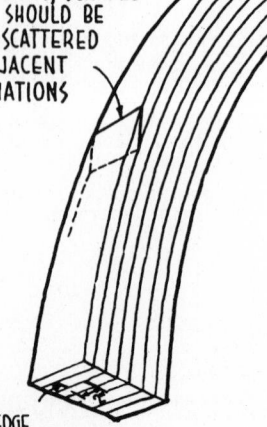

GLUED-EDGE JOINTS ARE GENERALLY REQUIRED ONLY FOR EXPOSED WORK. OUTSIDE LAMINATION IS FREQUENTLY EDGE-GLUED FOR APPEARANCE

EXTREME SECTION

proportions recommended for curved members to prevent elastic instability

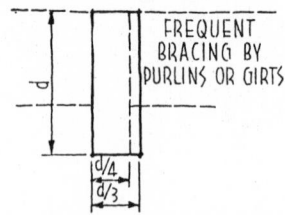

FREQUENT BRACING BY PURLINS OR GIRTS

RADII TO WHICH LAMINATIONS CAN BE BENT
(Dimensions in feet and inches)

Thickness	Douglas Fir, Southern Yellow Pine (F.P.L.)	Douglas Fir (T.S.)	Oak (F.P.L.)
1/4	2–7	2–1	1–6
5/16	3–5	3–1	2–0
3/8	4–3	4–0	2–6
7/16	5–3	—	3–0
1/2	6–2	6–0	3–7
5/8	8–2	7–8	4–10
3/4	10–5	9–4	6–1
13/16	11–5	—	6–7
1	14–5	—	8–9
1 3/16	—	15–10	—
1 1/4	18–11	—	11–8
1 1/2	23–7	20–10	14–8
1 5/8	—	23–0	—
1 3/4	26–11	—	18–1
2	33–4	—	21–4

Note: F.P.L. = Forest Products Laboratory recommendations; T.S. = Timber Structures, Inc. (who will fabricate to these radii).

METHODS OF VARYING
DEPTH OF SECTION

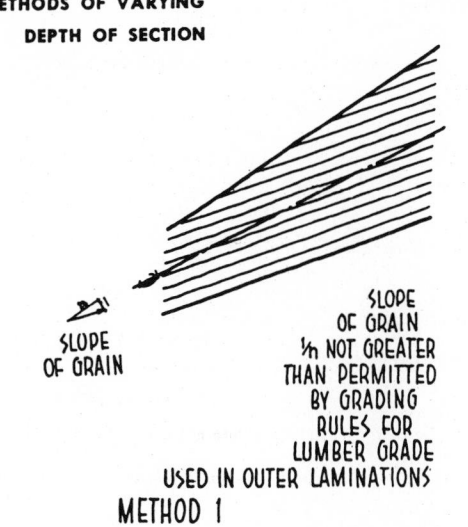

SLOPE
OF GRAIN

SLOPE
OF GRAIN
⅟n NOT GREATER
THAN PERMITTED
BY GRADING
RULES FOR
LUMBER GRADE
USED IN OUTER LAMINATIONS

METHOD 1

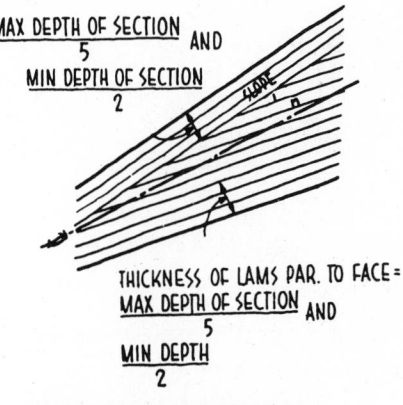

MAX DEPTH OF SECTION / 5 AND
MIN DEPTH OF SECTION / 2

THICKNESS OF LAMS PAR. TO FACE =
MAX DEPTH OF SECTION / 5 AND
MIN DEPTH / 2

SLOPE OF GRAIN ⅟n NOT GREATER THAN
SCARF SLOPE PERMITTED IN OUTER LAMS

METHOD 2

TYPICAL FASTENING DETAILS

Notes: • Special details should be developed for bases of frames and arches exposed to the weather to prevent water from lying around ends of members.
• Indoors as well as outdoors, ends of members should be painted two coats or otherwise treated to reduce tendency to check.
• When more than one bolt is used (except parallel to long axis of wood) slotted holes should be used in jointing metal plate to permit movement caused by swelling or shrinking.

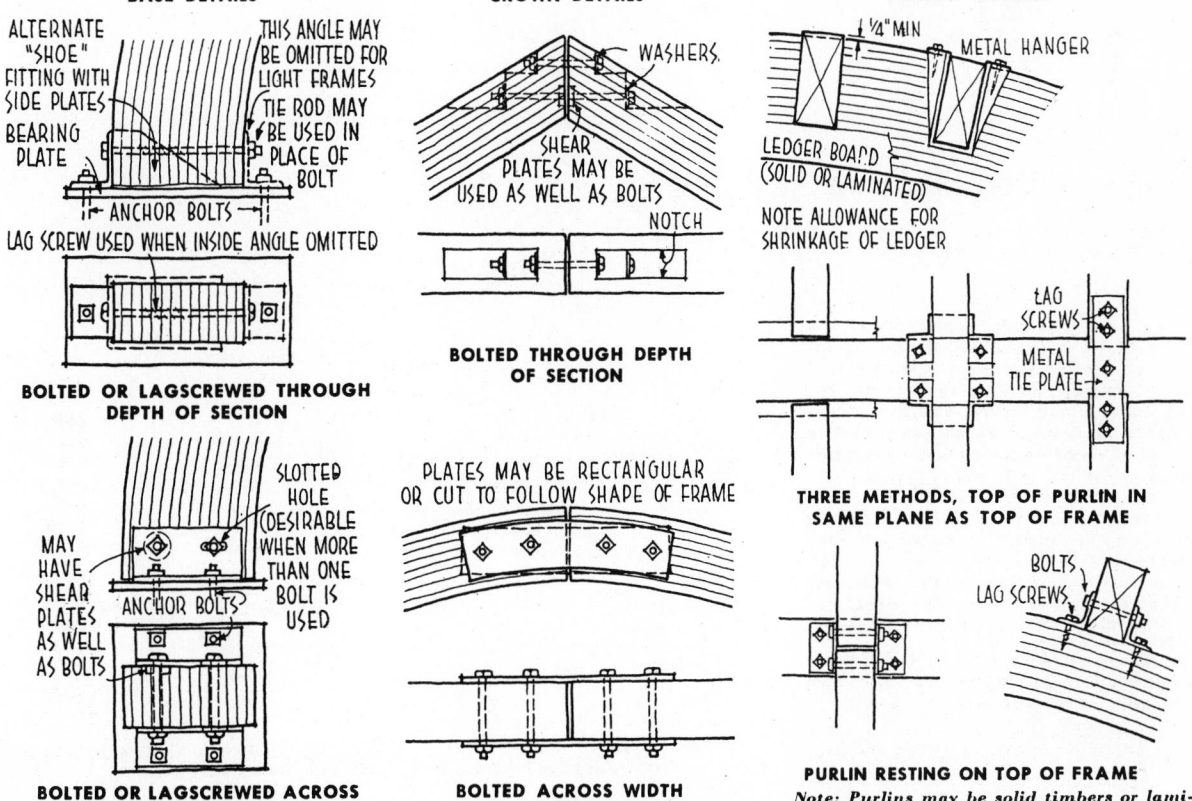

BASE DETAILS

ALTERNATE "SHOE" FITTING WITH SIDE PLATES
BEARING PLATE

THIS ANGLE MAY BE OMITTED FOR LIGHT FRAMES
TIE ROD MAY BE USED IN PLACE OF BOLT

ANCHOR BOLTS

LAG SCREW USED WHEN INSIDE ANGLE OMITTED

BOLTED OR LAGSCREWED THROUGH DEPTH OF SECTION

MAY HAVE SHEAR PLATES AS WELL AS BOLTS

SLOTTED HOLE (DESIRABLE WHEN MORE THAN ONE BOLT IS USED)

ANCHOR BOLTS

BOLTED OR LAGSCREWED ACROSS WIDTH OF SECTION

CROWN DETAILS

WASHERS.

SHEAR PLATES MAY BE USED AS WELL AS BOLTS

NOTCH

BOLTED THROUGH DEPTH OF SECTION

PLATES MAY BE RECTANGULAR OR CUT TO FOLLOW SHAPE OF FRAME

BOLTED ACROSS WIDTH OF SECTION

PURLIN DETAILS

1¼" MIN   METAL HANGER

LEDGER BOARD (SOLID OR LAMINATED)

NOTE ALLOWANCE FOR SHRINKAGE OF LEDGER

LAG SCREWS

METAL TIE PLATE

THREE METHODS, TOP OF PURLIN IN SAME PLANE AS TOP OF FRAME

BOLTS
LAG SCREWS

PURLIN RESTING ON TOP OF FRAME
Note: Purlins may be solid timbers or laminated.

SPECIAL CONSIDERATIONS FOR CURVED MEMBERS

**REDUCTION IN
ALLOWABLE STRESS**

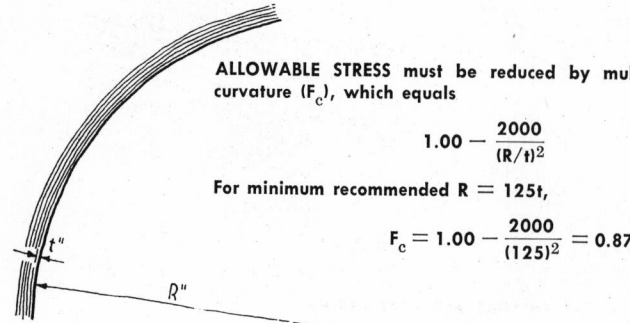

ALLOWABLE STRESS must be reduced by multiplying by factor of curvature (F_c), which equals

$$1.00 - \frac{2000}{(R/t)^2}$$

For minimum recommended $R = 125t$,

$$F_c = 1.00 - \frac{2000}{(125)^2} = 0.872$$

**RADIAL STRESS

CAUSED BY BEND-

ING OF CURVED

MEMBER**

NEGATIVE MOMENT creates compressive radial stress, stress should not exceed allowable compressive stress perpendicular to grain

MAXIMUM RADIAL STRESS OCCURS ON CENTERLINE PLANE

Magnitude $= \dfrac{3}{2}\dfrac{M}{Rbh}$

POSITIVE MOMENT creates tensile radial stress; stress should not exceed (soft woods) ⅓ allowable shear stress; (hardwoods) ⅜ allowable shear stress

FABRICATION CONSIDERATIONS

Transportation clearances

The gluing of laminated wood members is not adaptable to normal job site conditions. Minimum glue pressures are about 100 lbs/sq in. Clamping times, curing processes and temperatures must follow adhesive manufacturers' recommendations closely. Nailing instead of clamping for pressure is not permitted.

Therefore, laminated wood members are best produced in a factory under controlled conditions of humidity, temperature and cleanliness. The size of members is determined by transportation facilities, underpass clearances, state laws on trailer sizes, etc., between factory and job site. Field splices can be provided for large units.

In planning a building for laminated wood construction the architect should contact fabricators as soon as possible.

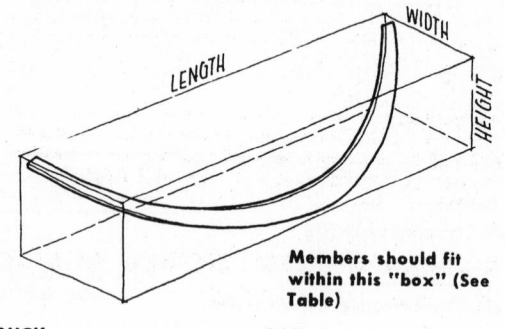

Members should fit within this "box" (See Table)

	TRUCK		RAIL		SHIP
	USUAL	MAX	USUAL	MAX	
Length	45'	80' (110' has been done)	50' (box car) 60' (gondola)	65' 120'	No limitations except size of ship and access to shipping piers by fabricator and by building contractor (site location)
Width	8'	8'	9'-8"	9'-8" 6'-8"	
Height	12'-6"	14'-0"	9'-8" (box) 12'-6"	14'-6"	

Note "Usual" dimensions require no permits; "maximum" dimensions require special truck permits or approved routings by railroad.

THREE-HINGED RIGID FRAMES

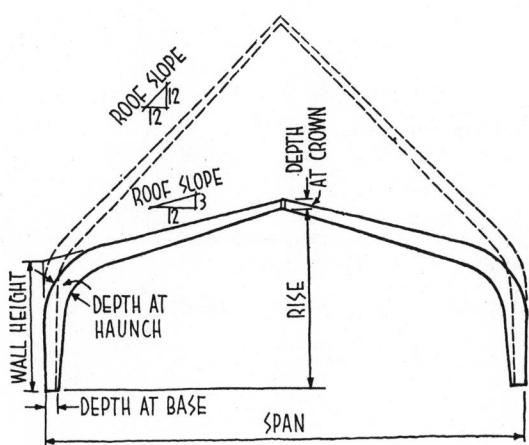

Note: Two-hinged rigid frames are impractical in wood. Fabrication and transportation usually require frame to be made in two parts. A crown connection to take the midspan moment of a two-hinged frame is impractical in wood.

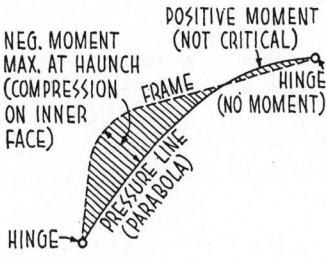

TYPICAL MOMENT CURVE

Three-Hinged Frame

Uniform loading across entire span (half span only shown)

Note differences between this curve and pressure line for two-hinged frame (Fig 2, Sheet 2, Rigid Frames in Steel)

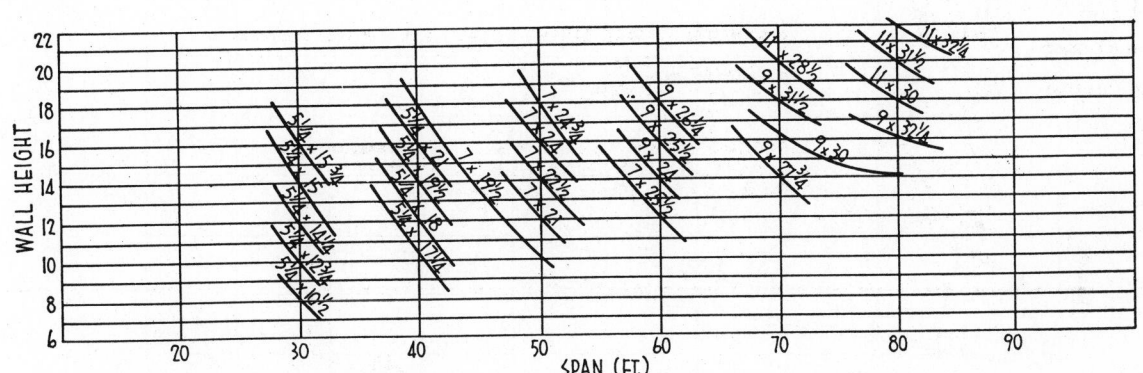

For vertical load of 1000 lbs/lin ft of span—no wind load (wind load may require heavier sections) and roof slope of 3 in 12 (steeper roof slopes require smaller sections down to about 85 per cent of depth for 12 in 12 slope)

Notes: Based on f = 2600; c = 2000 lbs/sq in.

For preliminary approximation of depth at base use: $0.4 \times$ (span in feet)$'' - 4''$

For depth at crown use: $0.1 \times$ (span in feet)$'' + 4''$

DIAGRAM OF FRAME SECTIONS AT HAUNCH (Width″ x Depth″)

(For Preliminary approximation only)

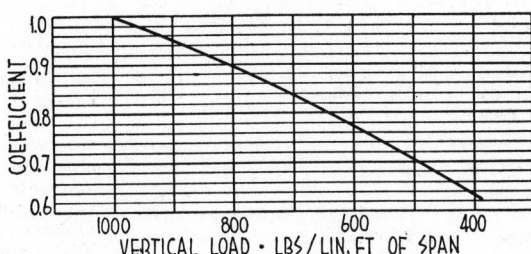

Multiply depth of section by coefficient for other loadings. (Width remains as shown on frame section diagram)

Width Given (b_1)	Width Wanted (b_2)	Multiply Depth By = $\sqrt{b_1/b_2}$
3¼ in.	5¼ in.	0.787
5¼ in.	3¼ in.	1.272
5¼ in.	7 in.	0.866
7 in.	5¼ in.	1.155
7 in.	9 in.	0.882
9 in.	7 in.	1.134
9 in.	11 in.	0.904
11 in.	9 in.	1.106

Effect of varying width of section on depth of section for constant section modulus

TWO-HINGED SEGMENTAL ARCH

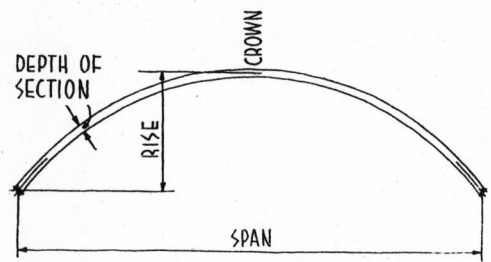

Three-hinged arch similar, with joint at crown

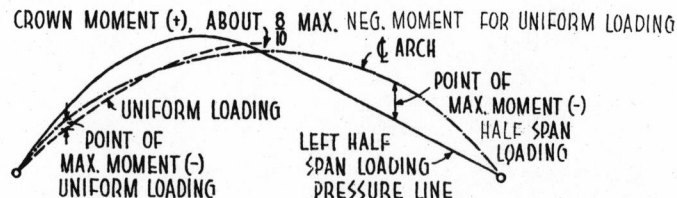

TYPICAL BENDING MOMENT CURVES FOR TWO-HINGED ARCH

Note: For a three-hinged arch, the pressure line for all loadings must pass through the centerline of the arch at the crown.

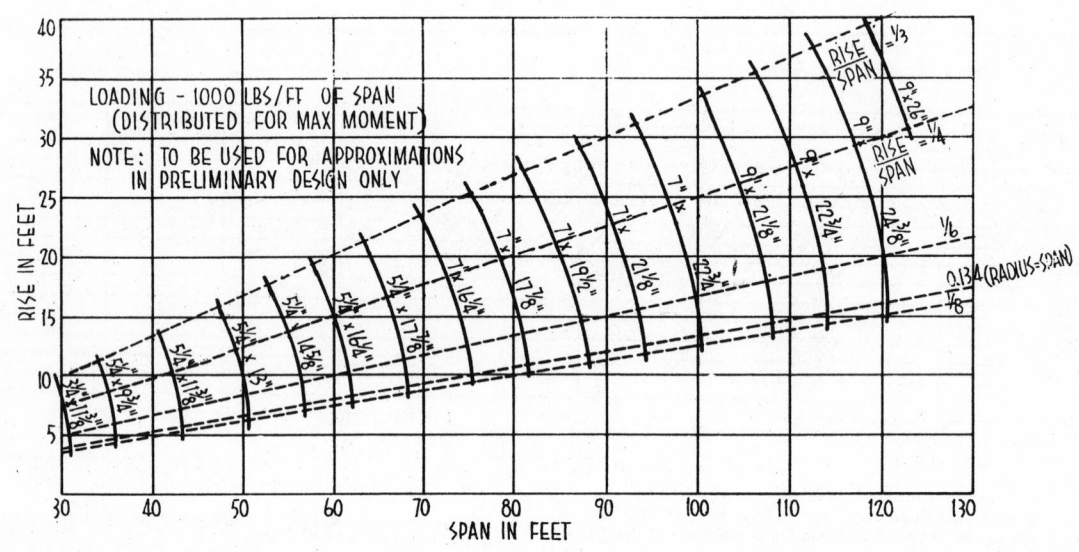

TYPICAL SECTIONS — TWO-HINGED CIRCULAR SEGMENTAL ARCHES

Based on f = 2600 lbs/sq in.; c = 2000 lbs/sq in.
For other loadings, multiply depth of section by coefficient from diagram
To vary width of section, multiply depth by coefficient from diagram
For preliminary approximations, use this diagram for three-hinged arches also

RADIUS =

$$\text{SPAN}\left[\frac{1}{8}\times\frac{\text{SPAN}}{\text{RISE}}+\frac{1}{2}\times\frac{\text{RISE}}{\text{SPAN}}\right]$$

FOR RISE/SPAN	SPAN X Coeff Below = Radius	NOTES
⅛	1.0625	
0.134	1.00	This ratio commonly used for stock arches
1/7	0.946	
⅙	0.833	This ratio commonly used for stock arches
1/5	0.725	
¼	0.625	
⅓	0.542	

TYPICAL BENDING MOMENT CURVES FOR UNIFORM LOADING, THREE-HINGED ARCHES

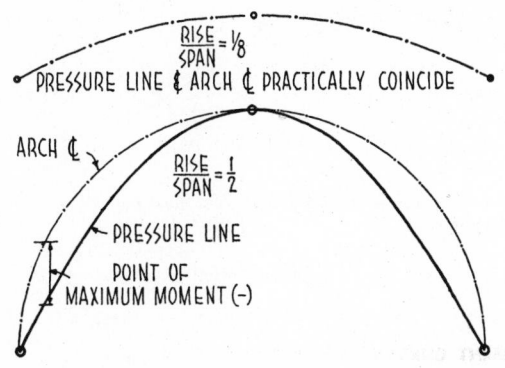

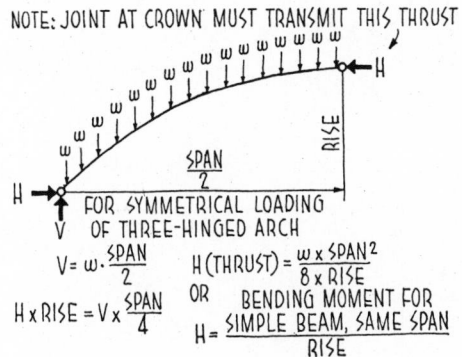

NOTE: JOINT AT CROWN MUST TRANSMIT THIS THRUST

FOR SYMMETRICAL LOADING OF THREE-HINGED ARCH

$$V = \omega \cdot \frac{SPAN}{2}$$

$$H\,(THRUST) = \frac{\omega \times SPAN^2}{8 \times RISE}$$

$$H \times RISE = V \times \frac{SPAN}{4}$$

OR

$$H = \frac{BENDING\ MOMENT\ FOR\ SIMPLE\ BEAM,\ SAME\ SPAN}{RISE}$$

te that as $\frac{rise}{span}$ ratio increases, the shape of the arch becomes more portant. In designing for high $\frac{rise}{span}$ ratios more care should be given make arch centerline correspond to actual pressure lines. Glued minated wood can be used easily for any shape of arch. (Constant ctions are usually cheaper than variable sections)

THRUST OF THREE-HINGED ARCH
This method can also be used safely for calculating the approximate thrusts of two-hinged arches, which are slightly less

LUED LAMINATED BEAMS & GIRDERS

ch and rigid frame shapes in wood may not be the most practical to use for long spans in ood. Glued laminated beams or plywood girders have their place particularly for one-story ildings extending many bays in two directions, for heavy loadings such as gantry cranes d for multi-story buildings:

ERENCES

Dietz, A. G. H. Engineering Laminates. n Wiley & Sons, New York (1949).

Fabrication and Design of Glued Lami- ed Wood Structural Members. Technical letin 1069, Forest Products Laboratory, . Department of Agriculture (1954).

National Design Specifications for ess-Grade Lumber and Its Fastenings. tional Lumber Manufacturers Associa- n, Washington, D.C. (1960).

Standard Specifications for Structural ed Laminated Douglas Fir (Coast Re- n) Lumber: Design and Fabrication. st Coast Lumbermen's Association, rtland, Ore. (1957).

Timber Design and Construction Hand- ok. Prepared by Timber Engineering mpany. F. W. Dodge Corporation, New rk (1956).

Additional information and data have en furnished by the following fabrica- s: McKeown Brothers Co., Chicago, Ill.; co. Laminated Products, Inc., St. Paul, nn.; Summerbell Roof Structures, Los geles, Calif.; Timber Structures, Inc., rtland, Ore.; Unit Structures, Inc., Pesh- o, Wis.

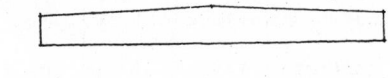

Top edge tapered for roof drainage

Double cantilever sections

Besides beams (and columns) of uniform section, tapered and cambered members are easily made. For calculating sections, use "allowable unit stresses for structural glued laminated lumber" in National Lumber Manufacturers Association's *National Design Specifications.* (See table below for most frequently used values for southern yellow pine and coast region Douglas fir.)

	For Dry Conditions of Use	For Wet Conditions of Use
"E"	1,800,000 lbs/in.²	1,600,000 lbs/in.²
Extreme Fiber (bending)	2200 lbs/in.²	1800 lbs/in.²
Horizontal Shear	165 lbs/in.² (D.F.)	145 lbs/in.² (D.F.)
	200 lbs/in.² (Y.P.)	175 lbs/in.² (Y.P.)

STANDARD LAMELLA ROOF CONSTRUCTION DATA

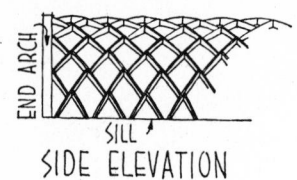

SIDE ELEVATION

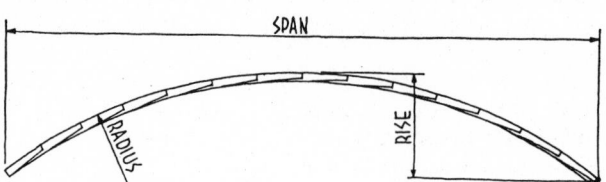

SECTION
Note that this is essentially a two-hinged arch; thrust must be taken by buttresses or tie rods

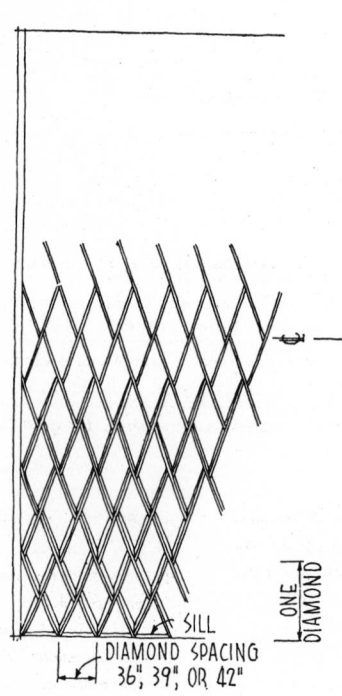

Edge support at ends of arch is essential: this may be an end arch, designed to take sidewise thrust (as shown), an end arch with rafters, or a broached lamella arch (with axis at right angles and diagonal ribs at intersection). Tie rods may be used parallel to centerline with lighter end arches. The centerline trace of lamellas (without offsets is a right circular helix, which is a geodesic on the cylindrical surface

DIAMOND SPACING 36", 39", OR 42"

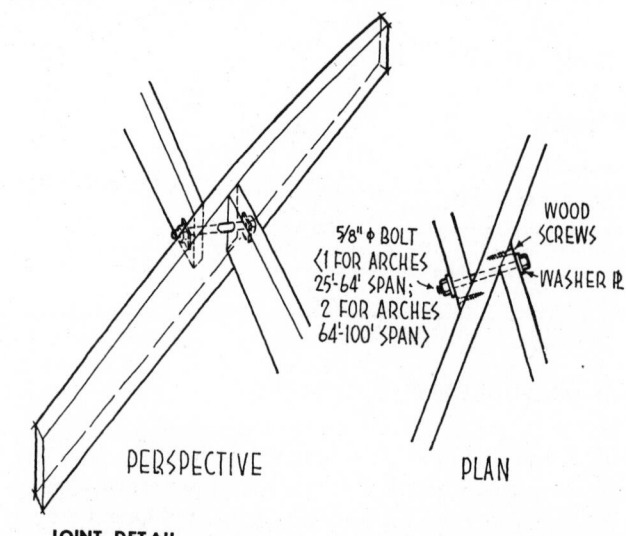

PERSPECTIVE   PLAN

JOINT DETAIL
Note shape of lamella. Curvature is obtained by cutting upper edge only. Bolt size is minimum, and nails can replace wood screws. Special cast or welded fittings are available to eliminate the offset at the joint, such as those of Theodor Ahlborn (U.S. Patent No. 1,975,384)

TYPICAL SILL DETAILS

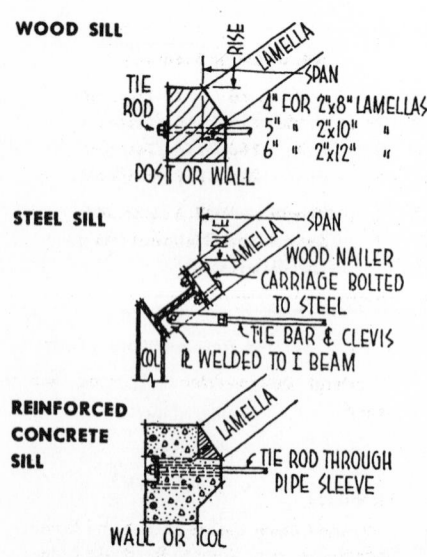

WOOD SILL

4" FOR 2"x8" LAMELLAS
5" " 2"x10" "
6" " 2"x12" "

STEEL SILL

REINFORCED CONCRETE SILL

Note: Sills must be designed for both vertical & horizontal (thrust) components of reaction

"STANDARD" LAMELLA ROOF CONSTRUCTION DATA

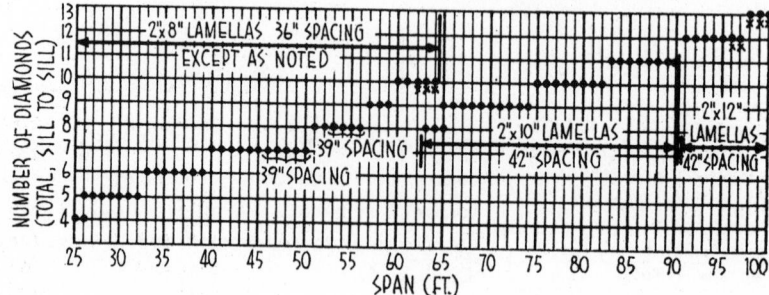

Rise = ⅙ span
Radius = 5/6 span } Except spans marked x, for which see table

Thrust = approx $(21.6 \times \text{span}' - 30)$ lbs per lin ft. Based on 20 lbs/sq ft live load

SPAN	RISE	RADIUS	SPAN	RISE	RADIUS
62 ft	10 ft— 8 in.	50 ft— 4 in.	97 ft	17 ft— 8 in.	75 ft— 5 in.
63 ft	10 ft—10 in.	51 ft— 3 in.	98 ft	17 ft—10 in.	76 ft— 3 in.
64 ft	11 ft— 8 in.	49 ft— 9 in.	99 ft	18 ft— 0 in.	77 ft— 1 in.
96 ft	16 ft—10 in.	76 ft—10 in.	100 ft	18 ft— 2 in.	77 ft—11 in.

Note: Information based on data furnished by Summerbell Roof Structures, Los Angeles 11, Calif.

BOX BEAMS—TYPICAL CONSTRUCTION DETAILS

From Douglas Fir Plywood Association, Fir Plywood Box Beam Handbook.

Tapered and cambered shapes can easily be made in plywood beams and girders. Stock plywood dimensions should be used if possible. Maximum span is about 120 ft; usual depth is about 1/8 to 1/12 span, minimum depth 1/22 span.

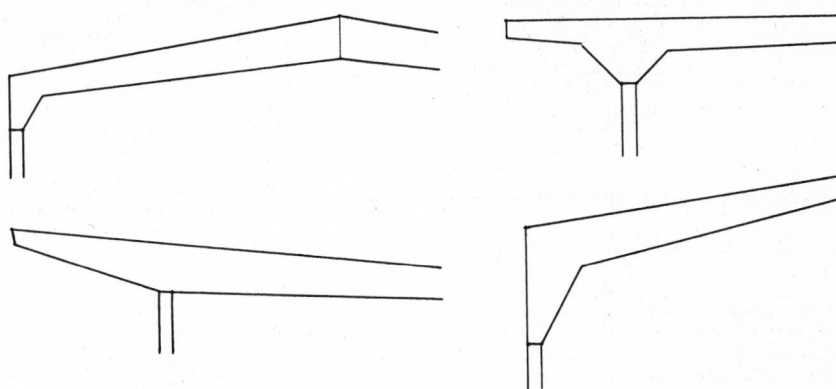

I Section

Limited by available plywood thickness to shorter spans

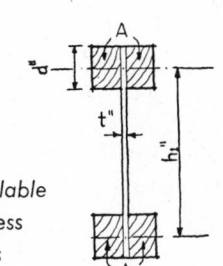

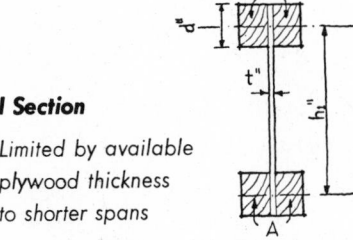

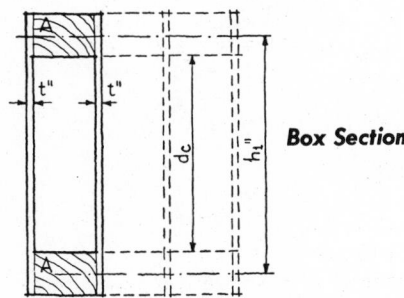

Box Section

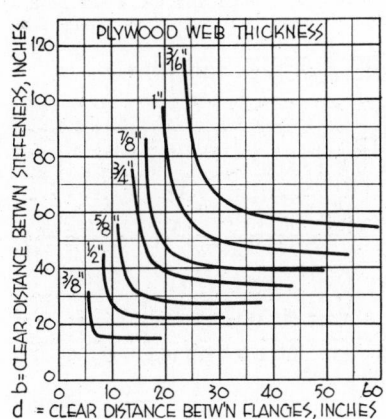

For approximate calculations, assume flanges take all the moment, web takes all shear.

$$\text{Area (of one flange)} = \frac{M}{\text{total depth} \times \text{allowable unit stress, compression } \parallel \text{ to grain}}$$

$$t'' \text{ (or } \Sigma t'') = \frac{5}{4} \times \frac{V}{\text{total depth} \times \text{allowable shear stress for grade of plywood}}$$

If nails are used without glue for fastening webs to flanges, the spacing of the nails in inches (p) can be determined from the equation

$$p = \frac{2rh_1}{V}$$

in which r is the allowable bearing value of nail in pounds, and h_1 is the vertical distance between nails in inches.

For nail-gluing, provide one nail for each 8–10 in. of glue joint. Spacing of nails should not exceed 6 in., even in region of minimum shear.

Typical Values

Allowable shear stress in plywood		Allowable nail loading	
Exterior DFPA–A–A	210 lbs./in.²	8d	78 lbs/nail
" " A–B; A–C	192 lbs./in.²	10d; 12d	94 lbs/nail
" " B–C; C–C		16d	107 lbs/nail
" B–B	180 lbs./in.²	20d	139 lbs/nail
Interior A–A; B–B; C–D	178 lbs./in.²	(Based on Nat'l. Lumber Mfrs.	
" A–B; A–D	163 lbs./in.²	Association "National Design	
" B–D	153 lbs./in.²	Specifications")	

Flanges may be solid or laminated wood. They may be nailed, nail-glued, or glued to plywood web (see sections above). Depth of flange d should be minimum 4t" for glued assembly, more for nailed, depending on the amount of nailing required. (For glues, see Sheet 2 of "Structural Forms—Wood.")

Upper flanges must be braced laterally; decking or joists can serve this purpose. Plywood splice plates are used at each joint in the web, but may be omitted if joints are scarfed. Joints should be staggered.

Spacing of stiffeners, as shown on the chart above, will prevent web buckling and develop full plywood shear strength. Spacing may be increased to 3b as shear stress decreases to ½ allowable. Additional stiffeners are required under point loads and at supports.

For data on plywood box beams, see "Structural Design—Wood: Plywood box beams."

References

Plywood Beam Design Factors, by David Countryman and Vernon D. Haskell, Report No. 58 (1952); *Technical Data on Plywood; Fir Plywood Box Beam Handbook* (1958). All published by Douglas Fir Plywood Association, Tacoma, Wash.

By SEYMOUR HOWARD, *Architect*
Associate Professor, Pratt Institute

Purpose of this section: To give the architect a description and analysis of the principal features of certain structural forms as they affect preliminary architectural design.

WARNING. In no case should shapes or sizes approximated from these diagrams and tables be used without a complete structural analysis based on the specific problem, even if the conditions of loading seem to be exactly the same as those on which these diagrams and tables are based. The reference material cited in each case can be used for the more complete analysis.

RIGID FRAMES IN STEEL

Shape of frame—structural considerations

For each condition of loading there exists a corresponding frame shape in which bending stresses can be eliminated. This shape is the *pressure line* and can be found from the string polygon for the given loading (Fig. 1).

A frame when built, however, is not subject to only a single condition of loading. The self-weight of the structure is constant, but the shape will be distorted by temperature changes, by axial strains, and may be deformed by foundation movement. And the imposed, live-loads, will vary with weather and with the use of the structure.

These variations in loading can be properly anticipated by choosing a shape which corresponds best to the loadings expected for most of the time and which corresponds safely to the loadings expected at any time. This form will require the least material and will usually not cause tensile stresses.

Shape of frame—architectural considerations

Although they are often the most satisfying aesthetically, the curved (or polygonal) forms, and the large height-to-span ratios required by purely structural considerations, are often wasteful of cubage and expensive to construct. (See Fig. 2, Sheet 2.)

Fig. 1 *Frame shapes to eliminate bending stresses for various loadings. The bending moment or funicular curve for a simply supported beam with the same loading gives the desired curve*

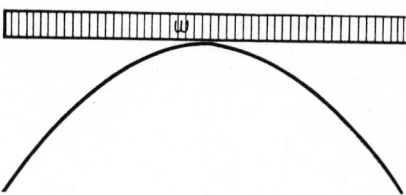

For exactly equal horizontal loading,
A Parabola

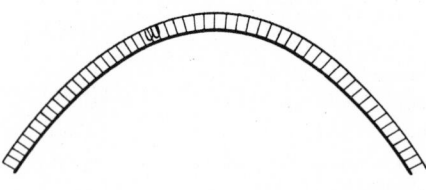

For the dead weight of a constant section,
A Catenary

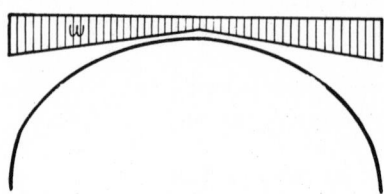

For increasing load toward the abutments,
A Third-Degree Parabola

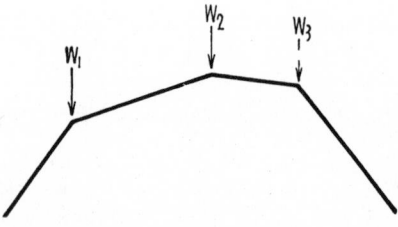

For point loads,
A Polygon

When architectural considerations necessitate rectangular shapes, bending moments are introduced and larger sections are required. The more the shape of the frame departs from the pressure line, the greater the bending stresses introduced. In fact, the bending moment at any point on the frame can be calculated from the distance between that point and the corresponding point on the pressure line (Figs. 3, 4).

Slight changes in the shape of the pressure line with all except heavy concentrated loads have little effect on the frame design. This is true even for typical arch design where, theoretically, it is possible to make the arch axis and the pressure line coincide (for any single load condition) for the full span.

If the axis and the pressure line do not coincide, additional material is required to resist the moments induced. However, this added material is not entirely wasted because it provides an additional safety factor against unusual unbalanced load conditions. It is for this reason that unbalanced loads are so critical in the case of curved arches and are relatively of little concern in the typical rigid frame.

Where dead weight of the frame is extreme or where loads are unusual, some economies can be effected by careful study of the pressure line location.

Since rectangular frames depart the most from the usual pressure line, the diagrams have been prepared for this type. Section depths chosen on the basis of the rectangular frame can be used for preliminary purposes for other shapes as well.

Fig. 2 *Frames following the shape of the pressure line may waste cubage*

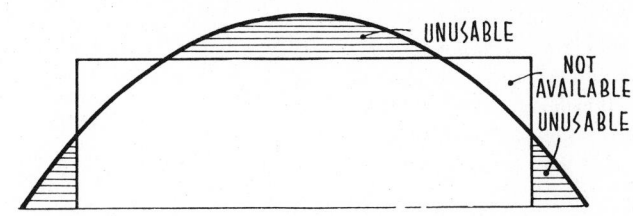

Fig. 3

FRAME, HINGED BASES

Bending moment varies in proportion to the distance from the frame to the pressure line

Fig. 4

FRAME, FIXED BASES

Depth of section has been used as the principal function because this is usually the major consideration in preliminary design.

In making the final calculations for a frame, it may be found economical to use one depth of section for the girder and another for the column portion. These variations will affect the distribution of moments in the frame as in Fig. 5 shown below.

Whether the column and girder sections are of the same depth or not, a frame in which rolled sections are used is less expensive to fabricate than a frame of variable section,

Fig. 5 *Effect of girder and column sizes on bending moments*

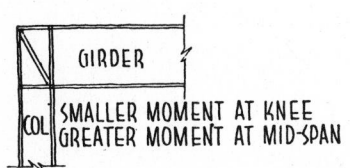

GIRDER
COL
SMALLER MOMENT AT KNEE
GREATER MOMENT AT MID-SPAN

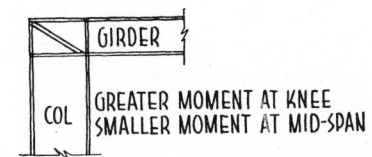

GIRDER
COL
GREATER MOMENT AT KNEE
SMALLER MOMENT AT MID-SPAN

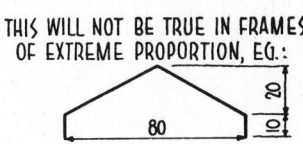

THIS WILL NOT BE TRUE IN FRAMES
OF EXTREME PROPORTION, E.G.:
80

though it will require more material. Variable depth section frames are therefore more often used for long span frames, which cannot be fabricated from rolled sections (Fig. 6).

Few frames are built without haunches at the knee and relatively few are built with horizontal girders. Therefore, the depths shown in Diagram 1 are somewhat larger than those normally used. Table A gives a comparison between a few "complete" designs (with normal knee haunches) and the recommendations of Diagram 1. (See Table A.)

Note: For exact calculations for a given frame, use "Single Span Rigid Frames In Steel," by John D. Griffiths, published by American Institute of Steel Construction, Inc., 101 Park Avenue, New York 17, N. Y. or standard texts on indeterminate structures.

Fig. 6

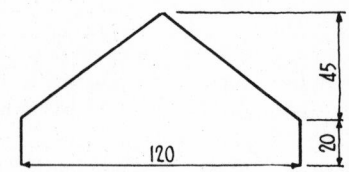

FRAME OF VARYING SECTION
GREATER HORIZONTAL THRUST
GREATER MOMENT AT KNEE
SMALLER MOMENT AT MID-SPAN

As the frame departs from a rectangular shape, moments are reduced. For a simple gable shape, the reduction will permit up to a maximum of about 20% reduction in depth of section for relatively extreme proportions as shown above right

Table A

Span, ft	Height, ft	Column, in.	Girder, in.	(See Diagram 1) Depth of Section, in.
40	12	14	12	17
60	16	18	16	22
80	16	24	24	27
100	16	30	27	32
120	16	36	30	38

Actual Conditions with haunched frames / Theoretical Conditions

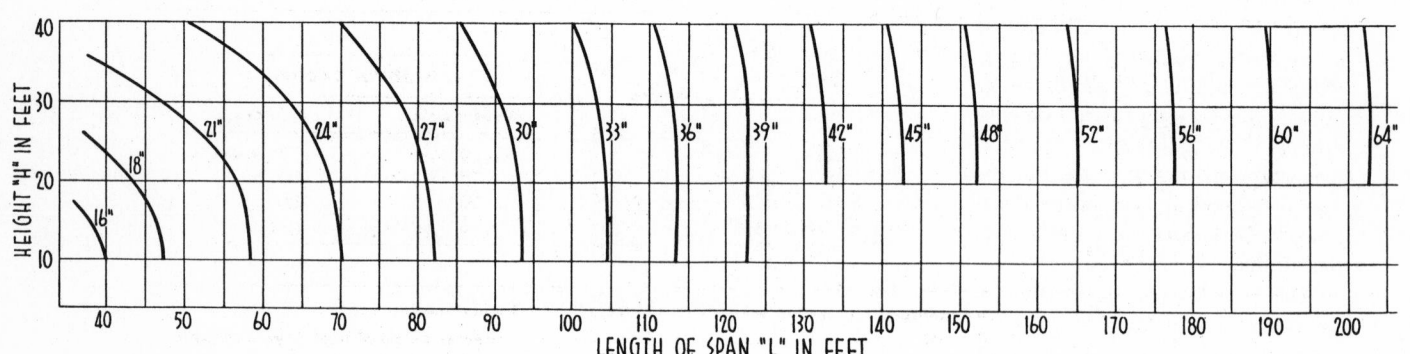

Diagram 1. Depth of section as function of length of span and height

Calculated for rectangular frames, spaced as shown in Diagram 2, and carrying total vertical load (including structure) of 50 lbs/sq ft and a horizontal load of 30 lbs/sq ft

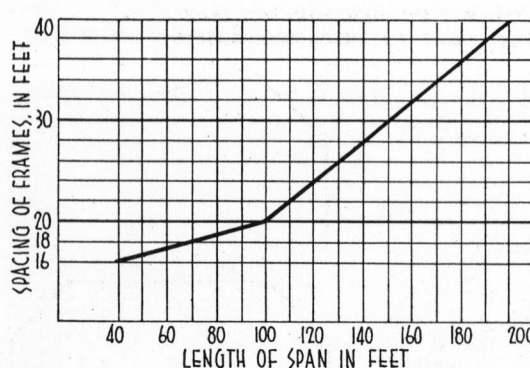

Diagram 2

Showing spacing of frames used to make calculations for Diagram 1

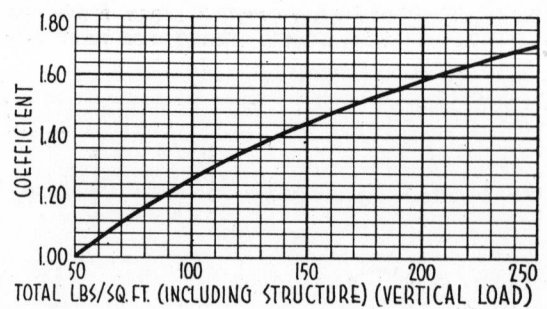

Diagram 3

Multiply depth of frame as found in Diagram 1 by coefficient corresponding to actual total load per sq ft

Fig. 7

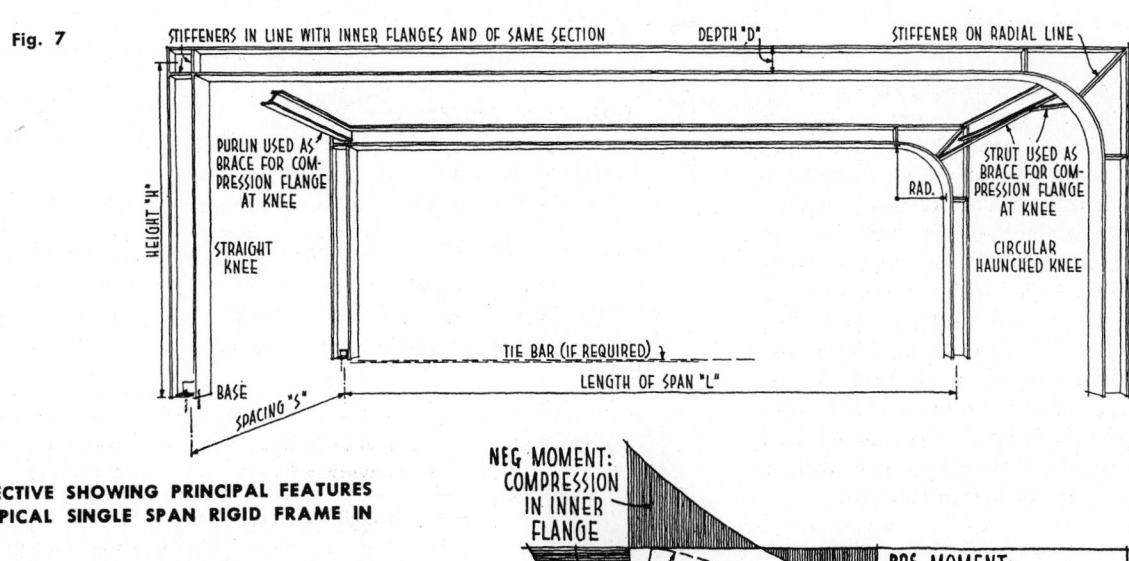

STIFFENERS IN LINE WITH INNER FLANGES AND OF SAME SECTION

DEPTH "D"

STIFFENER ON RADIAL LINE

PURLIN USED AS BRACE FOR COMPRESSION FLANGE AT KNEE

STRAIGHT KNEE

HEIGHT "H"

STRUT USED AS BRACE FOR COMPRESSION FLANGE AT KNEE

CIRCULAR HAUNCHED KNEE

RAD.

BASE

SPACING "S"

TIE BAR (IF REQUIRED)

LENGTH OF SPAN "L"

PERSPECTIVE SHOWING PRINCIPAL FEATURES OF TYPICAL SINGLE SPAN RIGID FRAME IN STEEL

Either straight knee or haunched knee (circular or polygonal) may be used. Frame can be made equally strong with either. Haunched knee increases thrust, increasing moment at knee and decreasing midspan moment

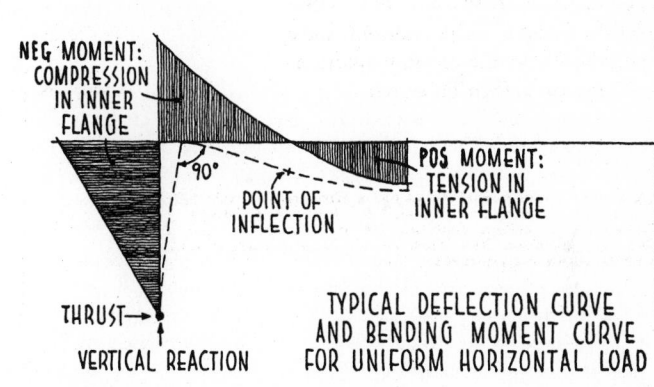

NEG MOMENT: COMPRESSION IN INNER FLANGE

POS MOMENT: TENSION IN INNER FLANGE

90°

POINT OF INFLECTION

THRUST

VERTICAL REACTION

TYPICAL DEFLECTION CURVE AND BENDING MOMENT CURVE FOR UNIFORM HORIZONTAL LOAD

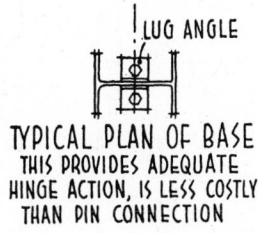

LUG ANGLE

TYPICAL PLAN OF BASE
THIS PROVIDES ADEQUATE HINGE ACTION, IS LESS COSTLY THAN PIN CONNECTION

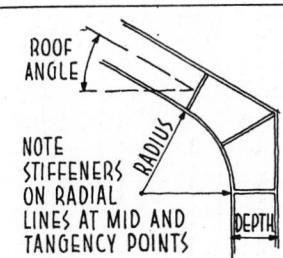

ROOF ANGLE

RADIUS

DEPTH

NOTE STIFFENERS ON RADIAL LINES AT MID AND TANGENCY POINTS

HAUNCH RADIUS	
Roof Angle	Radius
0°	3 x Depth
15°	2.5 x "
30°	2.0 x "
45°	1.75 x "

GENERAL CONSIDERATIONS

Advantages (compared with column & truss design)

Decrease in height (and cube) of building

Increase in clear headroom within building

Simpler maintenance

Clean appearance

Simpler erection

Disadvantages

Greater weight of steel may be required

Builder and fabricator may be unfamiliar with detailing and erection

Fig. 8 **OTHER TYPICAL ONE STORY RIGID FRAME SHAPES INCLUDE TYPES DESIGNED FOR MAXIMUM USABLE CUBAGE, FOR PARTICULAR ROOF COVERINGS AND FOR MONITOR LIGHTING**

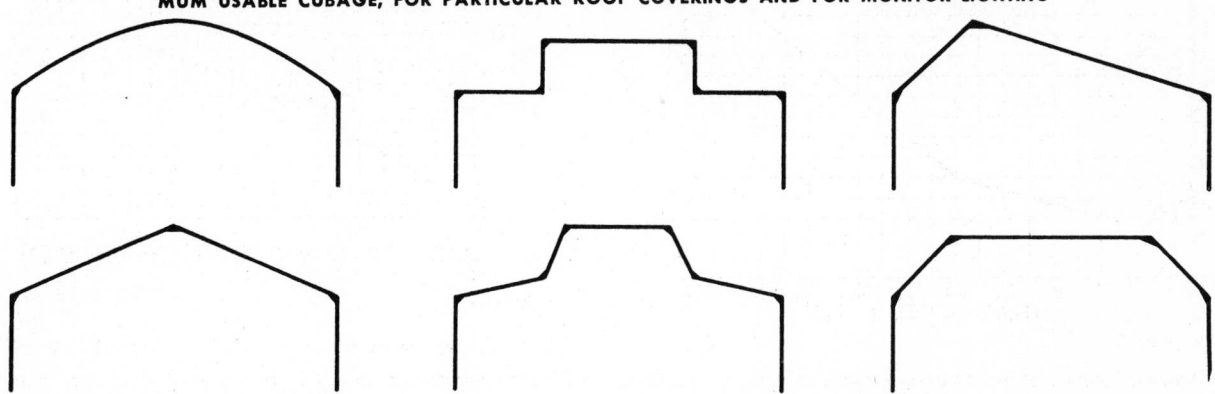

STRUCTURAL FORMS—STEEL—5
Space structures

By ROBERT E. RAPP, *Regional Engineer, American Institute of Steel Construction, Ir.c.*

Space structures are of three general types: simple monolithic grid, double layer grid (space frame), and co-planar systems (folded or curved structures).

Grid systems are illustrated in Fig. 9. It is apparent that the analysis and fabrication costs would be less for the rectangular or diagonal arrangements than for the other types shown. The diagonal system, commonly called "diagrid," is more rigid than the rectangular type and therefore is usually preferred. The advantages of grid construction as compared to beam and girder framing are: reduction (up to 50 per cent) in required structural depth, saving (up to 25 per cent) in the amount of steel required, simplification of fabrication due to repetition of members, and better resistance to earthquake and other horizontal forces.

Double layer grids (space frames) are used for longer spans where the monolithic grid becomes too cumbersome. These three-dimensional planar systems are designed in many geometric patterns and have many names. This subject is discussed in more detail on the following pages. A typical double layer grid is shown in Fig. 10.

Domes, vaults, and folded plates are examples of co-planar space grids. Domes of several types are illustrated and discussed further on in this section. Folded plate roofs are usually simple alternations of ridges and valleys spanning rectangular areas, but they may also be used with a circular plan to produce a dome-like structure (Fig. 11). Greater spans may be achieved with the folded plate spatial grid by the use of the rhombic or lattice truss (Fig. 12). Although lattice trusses are indeterminate, they make possible the spanning of long distances with relatively light members. Spans up to 300 ft are practical and economical with lattice structures.

Analysis. Even the simplest of the grid space systems are highly complex to analyze. The complexity may be greatly reduced by assuming that the joints are hinge-connected instead of rigid, and by ignoring the torsional forces; the results will err on the conservative side. Dr. Makowski's method (see reference below) permits the solution of rectangular or diagrid frames in a matter of minutes. If lightness of the structure is the prime factor in the design, however, more exact analysis must be employed. This analysis is highly redundant, especially with the co-planar or double layer systems. Where many complex designs are involved it would probably be advisable to use an electronic computer.

REFERENCES

Dr. Z. S. Makowski, An Analysis of Open Grid Frameworks, *Architectural Association Journal*, London, March, 1961.

Oliver A. Baer, Steel Frame Folded Plate Roof, *Journal of Structural Division Proceedings*, American Society of Civil Engineers, New York.

A bibliography on grid and space frames is available without charge from the American Institute of Steel Construction, Inc., 101 Park Ave., New York 17, N. Y.

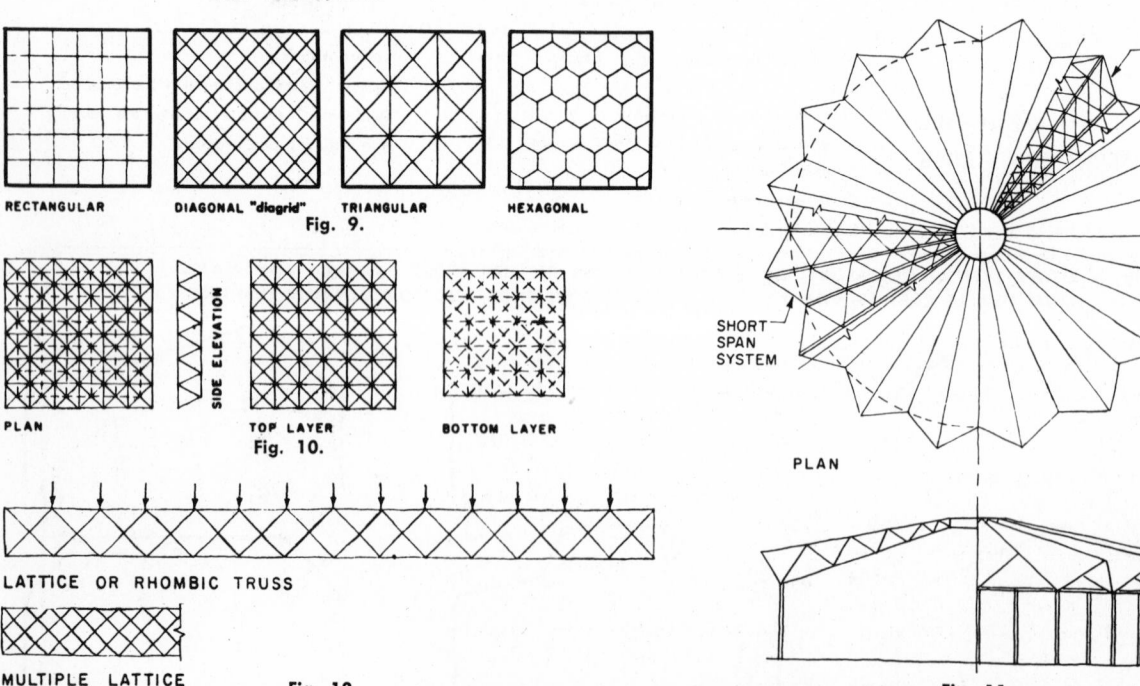

RECTANGULAR   DIAGONAL "diagrid"   TRIANGULAR   HEXAGONAL

Fig. 9.

PLAN   SIDE ELEVATION   TOP LAYER   BOTTOM LAYER

Fig. 10.

LATTICE OR RHOMBIC TRUSS

MULTIPLE LATTICE   Fig. 12.

LONG SPAN SYSTEM

SHORT SPAN SYSTEM

PLAN

Fig. 11.

By SEYMOUR HOWARD, *Architect*
Associate Professor, Pratt Institute

Known also as lattice structures or three-dimensional trusses, space frames may be most simply thought of as three-dimensional equivalents of the commonly used plane trusses. Some of their characteristics are described below.

Nature of members

As for a plane truss, roof or floor decking and other elements should be so arranged that all loads are transferred to the joints of the truss. In that way all members of the truss can act as two-force members. The members should theoretically have spherical (ball-and-socket) hinges at their ends—a most difficult condition to realize in practice. The construction of the joints, even with a certain amount of restraint, is a difficult and costly problem, and is, as a result, the principal basis for patents. It is also the chief reason why space frames are not more frequently used.

Materials

Space frames can be built of reinforced concrete or, more typically, of steel or aluminum. If the joint problem is solved, space frames are feasible even of wood. In order to simplify construction, engineers tend to use members of uniform size. If all the members are made of tubes of the same outside diameter, the wall thickness can be varied (although at considerable expense) to maintain uniform stresses in the material. Otherwise the majority of the members must be oversized for the most heavily loaded not to be overstressed.

Depth

The principal purpose of the depth of any structural assembly is to provide an adequate moment arm between the upper and lower edges. The depths of space frames therefore correspond fairly closely to those of plane trusses under similar loadings. A single prismatic frame with heavy loads would require a depth of from 1/6 to 1/12 of the span. A complete floor system, however, with the top and bottom chords forming a two- or three-way grid similar to a system of closely spaced joists, would permit a minimum depth of 1/20 to 1/24 of the span.

Methods of determining forces

Most plane trusses used in building construction are statically determinate, and the forces (bar stresses) found through statics equations or Maxwell-Cremona diagrams are reasonably accurate. For three-dimensional trusses, however, even though statically determinate, the forces found through

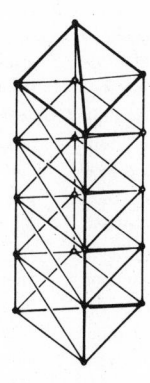
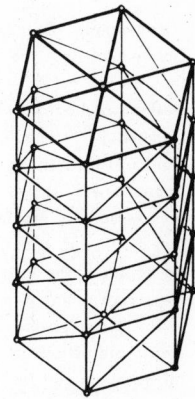

Triangular

Square

Hexagonal

Fig. 13. Space-frame towers

statics equations alone are often not sufficiently accurate for an economical design. Their configurations are such that one or more members at a particular joint would often be statically redundant for a given loading. The end conditions at the joints must also be taken into account. Solutions based on energy equations are more satisfactory, but are tedious. Model testing is probably the best, but is also the most costly method.

The basic geometrical unit in space frames is the tetrahedron, corresponding to the triangle in plane trusses.

The minimum number of members (m) necessary for a rigid truss, is related to the number of joints (j) by the following formula:

$$m = 3j - 6$$

Although the corresponding formula for plane trusses ($m = 2j - 3$) is seldom used, since the triangulation can usually be checked by eye, the formula for three-dimensional trusses should always be used as a check on the number of members. The hexagonal, parallel-plane space truss shown in Fig. 9, for example, would require at least three hexagons to satisfy the formula; the type S isometric space truss (Fig. 11) would require at least six squares in the upper plane.

This formula expresses a necessary condition for rigidity, but not a sufficient one. Some configurations meet this condition but still permit deformation. For such configurations additional checks such as the "zero-load test" should be made. (For an example, see *Theory of Structures* by S. Timoshenko and D. H. Young, McGraw-Hill, 1945.)

TYPES

The various types of space frames can be classified by the polyhedra from which they are built up.

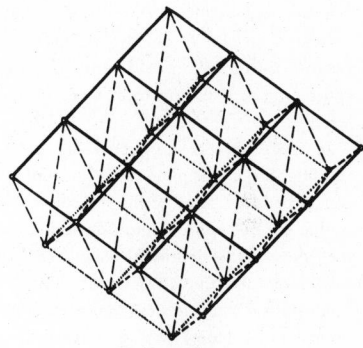

Triangular

Rectangular

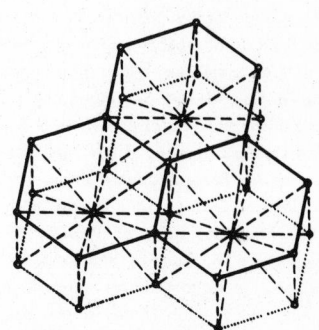

Hexagonal

Fig. 14. Space trusses for floors and roofs

For simple structures such as towers or isolated trusses, the space frame can be thought of as a single polyhedron. Any closed polyhedron whose faces are rigid (completely triangulated) must be itself rigid. Thus the triangular, square, and hexagonal towers shown in Fig. 13 can be completely hollow, provided the top and bottom planes are triangulated. Or they could be hollow if the tower were to be laid on its side as a single trussed girder.

The three towers are drawn in axonometric projection. All vertical and horizontal members can be the same length; only the diagonals on the sides and across the top and bottom of the square tower must be longer.

Other polyhedra (such as those shown on Sheets 26 and 27 of "Useful Curves and Curved Surfaces") would also be rigid space frames if all the faces were triangulated.

In searching for a space-frame pattern suitable for a complete floor or roof, we can investigate some of the lattices formed by the various space-filling polyhedra. (See the notes at the bottom of Sheet 27, "Useful Curves and Curved Surfaces.") We are interested in those lattices that give a level upper plane (floor) and a parallel lower plane (ceiling or floor). In Fig. 14, all members in the upper plane are drawn with full lines, all those in the bottom plane with dotted lines, and those in between with broken lines.

The *triangular prism*, used as the basic geometrical unit, gives two sets of plane trusses, which meet at an angle (here, 90 deg). All the trusses in one of the sets lie in parallel vertical planes; all those in the other set lie in inclined planes corresponding to the diagonal chords of the trusses in the first set.

The *cube* (or rectangular prism) also gives two sets of plane trusses. All the trusses in one of the sets lie in parallel vertical planes; all the trusses in the other set lie in parallel vertical planes at right angles to the first set. Note that diagonals are not generally provided in plan; thus, for rigidity, at least two complete edges of the floor system must be triangulated as shown. Floor or roof decking might be used to achieve this rigidity.

A system of trusses of this type was used for the Air Force Academy dining-hall roof (Skidmore, Owings, and Merrill, architects and engineers; stress analysis by J. Sbarounis and M. Gaus of that firm). In their design, the bottom chords were all in one plane, but the top chords sloped up from the roof edge to the center, giving a depth at the edge of 8 ft 6 in. and at the center of 11 ft 8 in. The clear span was 266 ft in both directions.

The *hexagonal prism* gives an upper and a lower plane of hexagons, connected vertically at each corner and diagonally from each upper corner to the diametrally opposite lower corner. Note the joint where the diagonals intersect. Three hexagonal prisms are needed for rigidity. (For an application of this system to a curved surface, see information on geodesic domes on Sheets 9 and 10 of "Structural Forms—Steel.")

Octahedra plus tetrahedra give what may well be called *isometric space frames*. These lattices, which can be generated by the regular rhombohedron (itself made up of one octahedron and two tetrahedra), permit all members to be the same length. They correspond to the crystallographer's "face-centered cubic." (See diagram in Fig. 15.)

If an isometric space lattice is cut by any plane containing the faces of the octahedra (and the tetrahedra), the result is what is labeled here a type T isometric space frame (so-called because of its triangular pattern on the plan).

If, on the other hand, the lattice is cut by any plane containing the central squares of the octahedra, the result is what is labeled here a type S isometric space frame (because of the squares that appear on the plan). This truss has the advantage of conforming easily to the plan of rectangular buildings. (It has been used, for example, in two experimental structures erected for Unistrut Corp., and also as a full story-height truss in the mechanical-equipment floor of the Texas Instrument Co.) Note that the formula for the number of members is not satisfied unless there are at least six squares in the upper plane and two in the lower, and also that triangulation is required in at least one plane for rigidity.

These two isometric space frames are drawn here only in plan, section, and elevation, because their axonometric projections would be confusing. They are most easily studied in model form; models can be readily made with round toothpicks and Duco cement.

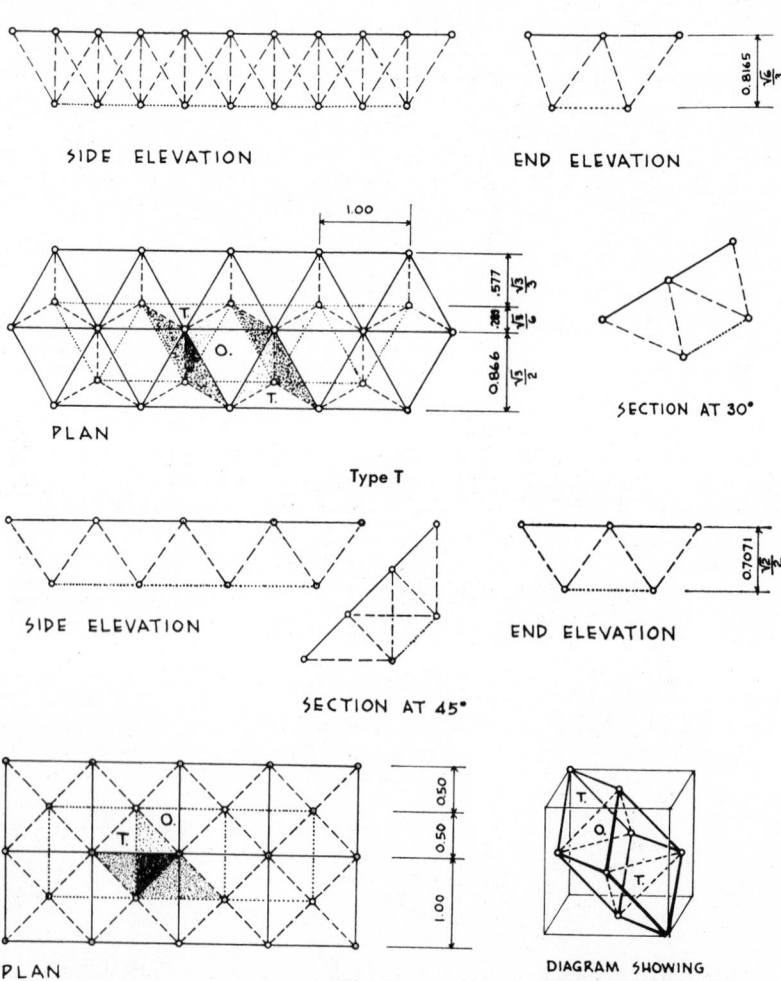

Fig. 15.   Two types of isometric space truss

Metal Domes

Metal domes are generally built on some variation of the radial principle (see "Useful Curves and Curved Surfaces," Sheet 25). The principal types are illustrated in Fig. 16 and 17.

One of the initial decisions to be made is whether the dome should be a portion of a true sphere or a polyhedron. Rolled steel sections are most commonly used, since the depths of section needed can easily be found in the standard sizes. As straight members they form a polyhedron. If the members are closely spaced, however, the visual effect will be that of a sphere, particularly if the roof decking can be curved. If curved members are desired, light trusses can be fabricated to the correct radii.

Lengths of members are typically in the range of 15 to 25 ft. This will determine the spacing of radial and parallel ribs.

The most usual ratio of rise to span (diameter) is in the range $\frac{1}{5}$ to $\frac{1}{8}$. Often the span is taken as equal to the radius, which gives a ratio of 0.134.

Schwedler System

The original Schwedler dome or cupola (first published in 1866) is shown here as the "basic type with diagonals." Such a polyhedron is statically determinate and is indeformable, since the entire surface is divided into triangles. As a three-dimensional framework it satisfies the

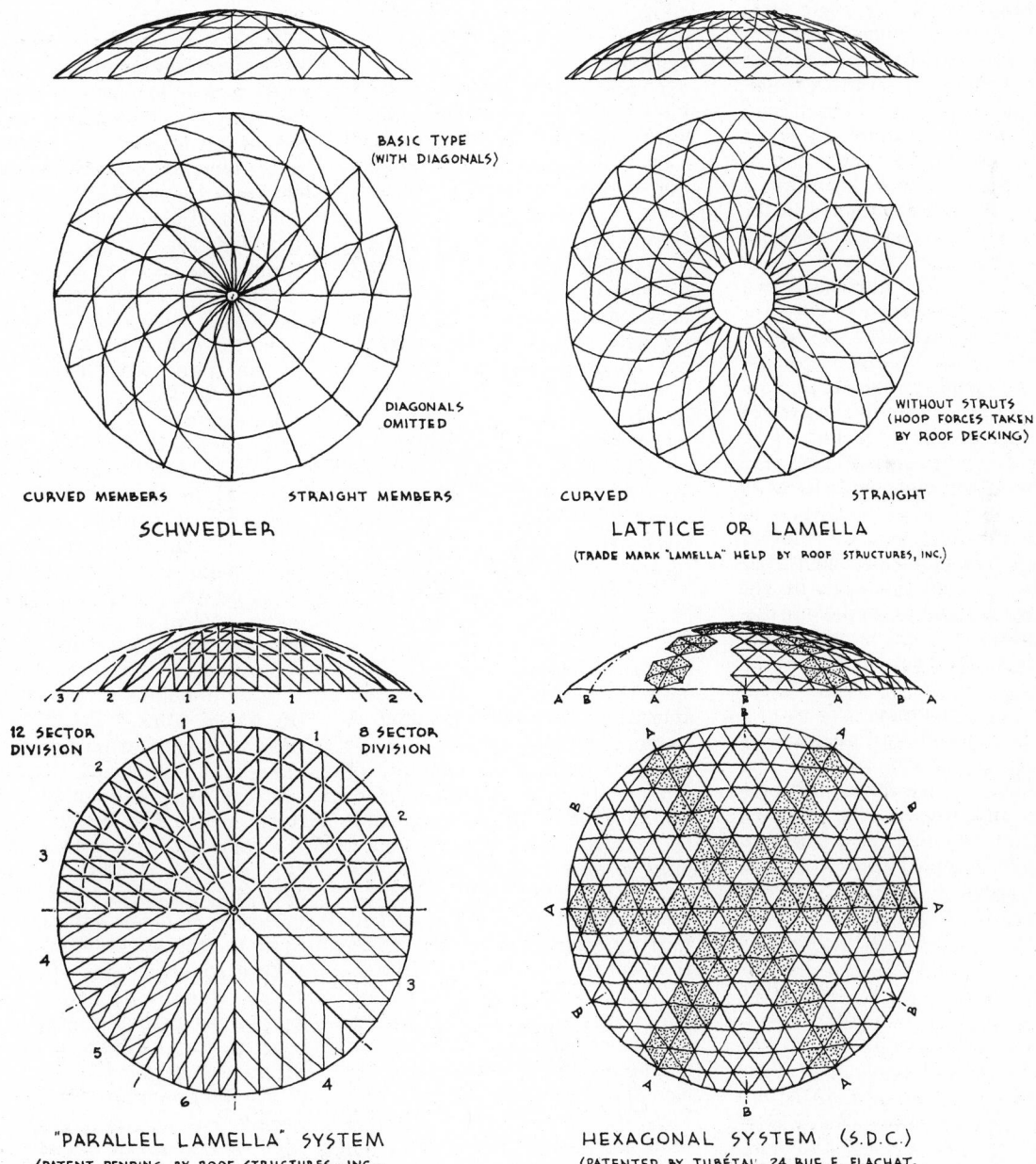

BASIC TYPE (WITH DIAGONALS)

DIAGONALS OMITTED

CURVED MEMBERS   STRAIGHT MEMBERS

SCHWEDLER

WITHOUT STRUTS (HOOP FORCES TAKEN BY ROOF DECKING)

CURVED   STRAIGHT

LATTICE OR LAMELLA
(TRADE MARK "LAMELLA" HELD BY ROOF STRUCTURES, INC.)

12 SECTOR DIVISION   8 SECTOR DIVISION

"PARALLEL LAMELLA" SYSTEM
(PATENT PENDING BY ROOF STRUCTURES, INC., 331 THORNTON AVE, WEBSTER GROVES 19, MO.)

HEXAGONAL SYSTEM (S.D.C.)
(PATENTED BY TUBÉTAL, 24 RUE E. FLACHAT, PARIS, 17ᵉ, FOR STÉPHANE DU CHÂTEAU)

Fig. 16   Types of steel domes

statical conditions for rigidity.

Recent investigations by Professor Paul Anderson of the University of Minnesota indicate that in practice the diagonals are not necessary. The simplest type, therefore, is a Schwedler dome with diagonals omitted, consisting of straight members which are the chords of meridian (longitude) and parallel (latitude) circles.

Lamella System

In the lattice or lamella system all of the intersections of members lie on radial lines but each meridian rib is replaced by a pair of diagonal ribs. These ribs together with the struts, which are chords of latitude circles, form a triangular, three-dimensional network which is rigid. The roof decking panels can be designed to replace the struts, a technique commonly used in the case of wood lamella domes with wood planking.

The *"Parallel Lamella"* System was developed to reduce the number of ribs at the top of the dome, where the close spacing makes assembly difficult and requires a reduction in the size of members if they are not to be grossly overdesigned for the forces acting on them. Although each sector is symmetrical about its own centerline, the visual effect is to emphasize one of the radial ribs at the edge of the sector, causing an apparent dissymmetry which is somewhat disturbing esthetically.

Hexagonal System

The hexagonal system was developed for a framework of steel tubes which are fitted into special joints of cast or pressed steel and welded. The tubes in turn can support roof panels of sheet steel, steel plus concrete, terra cotta blocks covered with concrete, and so forth. Because of the characteristics of the sphere and the hexagon (see "Useful Curves and Curved Surfaces," Sheets 25–27) all of the tubes cannot be of the same length, although the variation can be kept small. The typical length of one bar is about 6 ft. In the diagram the shaded hexa-

gons (along lines A) are all identical hexagonal pyramids; the six center bars of each must be slightly longer than the six edge bars. The lines B are axes of symmetry for the regions in between, where the lengths of bars tend to be shorter, but all the joints still lie on the surface of the sphere.

Thin Shells

Not illustrated, but occasionally used, are the ribless steel shells in which all forces are carried by the steel plating. The danger of buckling is the principal design problem. As a result the plating must be quite thick: for example, $5/8$-in. plate at 25.6 lb per sq ft of surface was needed for a 200-ft diameter hemisphere built according to the specifications of the American Petroleum Institute.

Forces

An approximate idea of the magnitude of forces involved can most easily be found by assuming the spherical structure to act as a membrane. The most heavily loaded member is of course the tension ring at the lower edge. If the sphere is brought down to the ground by means of inclined piers, buttresses or A-frames, a continuous footing can be used as the tension ring; or the thrust can be taken directly by the ground if the soil is suitable.

Geodesic Domes

This type of dome might be considered as derived from an effort to construct a spherical dome solely by means of elements of uniform length. (Its inventor, R. Buckminster Fuller, describes it as "a structure impervious not only to extreme differential between internal and external loads or impact forces—yet permitting omnidirectionally effective controlled penetrability.") But the sphere is a surface which cannot be divided by any arbitrary number of arcs of the same length. Therefore, the elements must be of different lengths, although the pattern is more or less uniform. For a complete study of this problem see

Sheet 25, "Useful Curves and Curved Surfaces."

One of the advantages of this type of dome is the simplicity of erection. One method is to fasten sections of the dome together like a skirt around a central mast. This portion is raised up enough so that another zone of sections can be fastened to the first portion, and so on. Or it can also be built like other domes, from the bottom up: the lowest zone erected on the piers, forming a complete circle; the next higher zone erected on the lowest, and so on. Since any complete zone is stable in itself, this procedure can be followed with a minimum of scaffolding.

Because the pattern of members or truss elements in the geodesic dome is an "overall" one, always related to the entire sphere, the perfect geodesic dome is the complete ball. As such it is ideally suited to withstand radial pressures and should prove of value in gas storage tanks and vehicles and stations for outer space. The depth of the space truss usually employed as the surface of the sphere gives it great stiffness and resistance to high winds.

When other than hemispherical or plane truncated segments are used, the edges are the main architectural problem. These lie along segments of five great circles and are sometimes supported by several piers, all at different heights. They can also be supported by arches, making only five points of support for the whole dome. These piers or edge arches must be designed to carry the thrust of the dome, and the drag and uplift due to wind loads. The connections of the dome to the piers are designed to permit a considerable amount of radial movement due to temperature changes (on the order of 3 in. for an aluminum dome with a sphere radius of 112 ft). If soil conditions are poor the piers must be held together by a tension ring of steel or prestressed concrete.

R. Buckminster Fuller, who received U.S. patents on his spherical geodesic dome in 1954, now has 100 licensees using

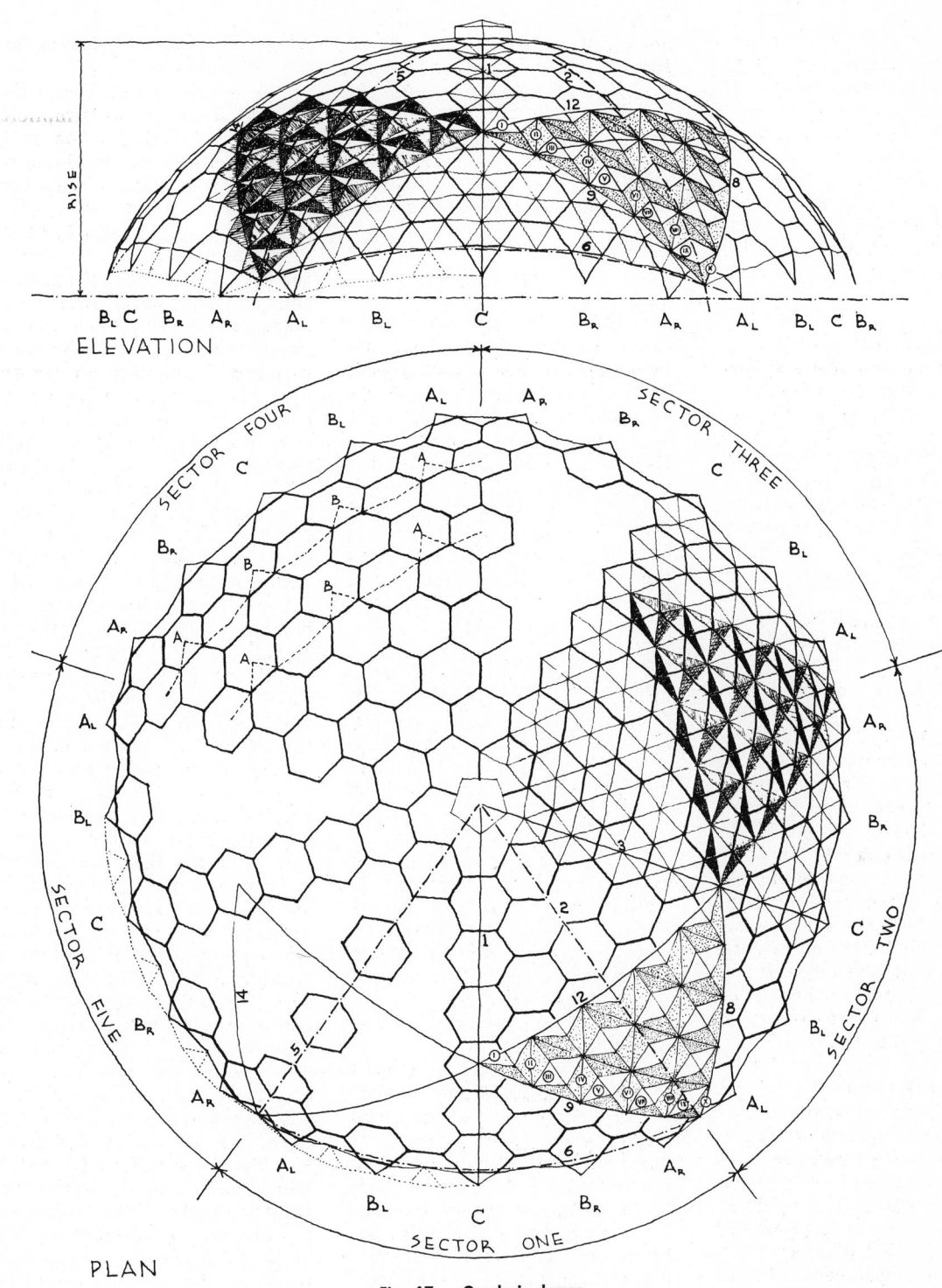

ELEVATION

PLAN

Fig. 17 Geodesic domes

some of his principles. Synergetics, Inc., 3013 Hillsboro St., Raleigh, North Carolina (James W. Fitzgibbon, Executive Vice-President) has designed some of the special domes such as:

1) Steel dome for the Union Tank Car Co., in Baton Rouge, La. Plan diameter 384 ft; rise 120 ft; frequency 36; 48-in. deep space truss; 2) Aluminum dome for the American Society of Metals, near Cleveland. Plan diameter 277 ft; rise 102 ft; frequency 24; 30-in. deep space truss; 3) Projected dome for Shoppersville in Montreal. Plan diameter 525 ft; rise 96 ft above tension ring; frequency 56; 72-in. deep space truss.

All of these are designed with a space truss using an octahedron as the basic unit instead of a tetrahedron. (See Fig. 19 for octahedron unit, and Sheet 28, "Useful Curves and Curved Surfaces," for tetrahedron unit.)

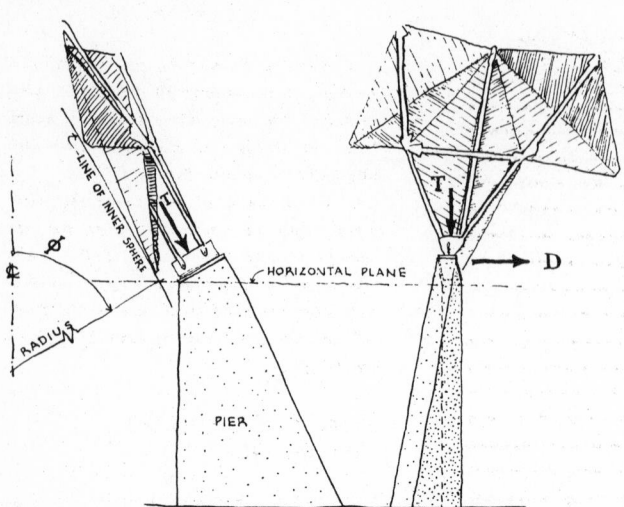

Fig. 18   Pier for geodesic dome (see Table 2)

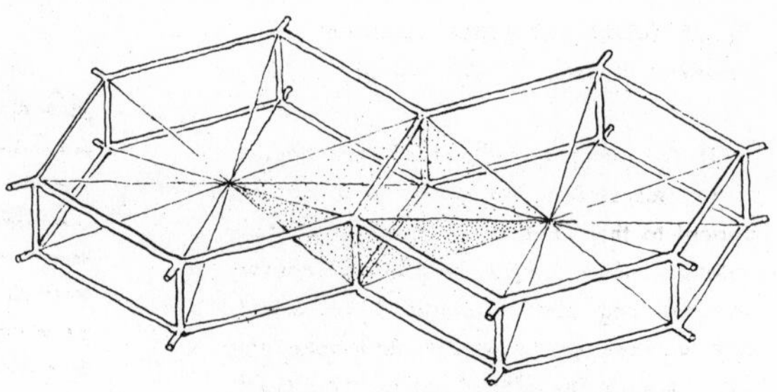

Fig. 19   Octahedron space truss

The Kaiser Aluminum and Chemical Sales Co., 919 North Michigan Ave., Chicago 11, Illinois, has designed aluminum domes based on Fuller's patents, and some of its own patents covering the system of stressed skin space truss using diamond shaped panels. Kaiser is currently marketing two basic series, each of three sizes of type A domes. (See Table 2.)

The plan and elevation shown in Fig. 17 are of Kaiser's type A-80-15.3 (approximately a quarter sphere). In plan the surface is divided into five identical sectors, corresponding to the five upper spherical triangles of the spherical icosahedron; they are joined by a pentagonal lantern at the top. Each sector is supported by five symmetrically arranged piers: C in the center (highest); B_L and A_L to the left, looking up at the dome; B_R and A_R to the right.

The geometry of the division of the dome surface is described in detail on Sheets 28–30, "Useful Curves and Curved Surfaces." A typical basic spherical triangle is shown in lines 8, 9 and 12 on both plan and elevation. The divisions are marked to correspond to those shown on Sheet 29; here the frequency (γ) is 10.

The panels and struts are drawn in detail in two other similar spherical triangles: between sectors two and three in plan and between sectors five and one in elevation.

Each unit consists of a sun-

burst-crease formed, diamond shaped panel of aluminum sheet (maximum length 140 in.) with the central cambered valley approximately a chord of a great circle on the inner sphere (radius 80 ft). Six of these panels meet at a point on the inner sphere. The flanged edges of the panels go out to meet the struts, which form a hexagonal pattern

with their vertices on the outer sphere (radius 81 ft). The creased valley and the four edges of the panel plus one strut comprise the six edges of the unit tetrahedron. (This has been patented by Kaiser Aluminum, Don L. Richter, inventor; other patents are pending.) Filler panels (as shown dotted in sectors five and one) can be hung from the lower edge to bring the dome down to a more uniform line.

In sector four, broken lines show the piers as they are required for the two small domes (A-80-11.5 and A-80-7.0), which can be built using the same panels but taking smaller portions of the same sphere.

Table 2.   Data on Kaiser domes

Dome Code No.	Type	Radius Inner Sphere (Add one foot for outer)	Plan Area × 10³ Sq. Ft.	Surface Area × 10³ Sq. Ft.	Volume × 10³ Cu. Ft.	Rise, Top of Lowest Pier to High Point of Inner Sphere	Frequency (γ)	Number of Piers Per Sector (5 Sectors Per Dome)	Pier Letter	Radius in Plan To Point on Inner Sphere Opposite Pier (See Figure 3)	$\emptyset°$ (See Figure 3)	Max. Downward Thrust T with Snow Load	Max. Uplift −T with 100 m.p.h. Wind	Max Drag D (Snow or Wind)
A - 80 - 15.3		21.9	603		46'-10¾"	10	5	A	72'-10"	65.6°	15.4 (30 lb. snow)	− 5.7	5.8
								B	71'- 6⅛"	63.4°	21.7	− 8.3	8.6
								C	70'-11¼"	62.5°	23.2	− 9.1	7.5
A - 80 - 11.5		14.5	230.7		31'- 9½"	10	4	A	63'-10⅛"	53.0°	21.0 (30 lb. snow)	− 8.8	10.4
								B	61'- 6⅝"	50.3°	28.2	−12.9	11.6
A - 80 - 7.0		8.1	87		18'- 5⅝"	10	3	A	51'- 1½"	39.7°	24.6 (20 lb. snow)	−15.2	12.6
								B	48'- 6¾"	37.4°	33.3	−22.7	10.3
A - 112 - 30.0		42.7	1180		64'- 5½"	14	7	A	101'- 4½"	64.9°	22.6 (40 lb. snow)	− 7.2	10.7
								B	99'-10"	62.1°	31.4	− 9.4	13.4
								C	98'- 7⅝"	61.8°	35.3	−11.1	13.5
								D	98'- 2"	61.3°	36.0	−11.4	12.7
A - 112 - 24.7		32.2	733		46'- 5⅜"	14	6	A	92'-10½"	56.1°	32.3 (40 lb. snow)	−11.0	15.2
								B	90'- 4⅜"	53.8°	42.2	−14.3	15.4
								C	88'- 9⅝"	52.5°	44.5	−15.2	13.3
A - 112 - 18.7		22.6	403		35'-10 "	14	5	A	82'- 1⅛"	47.2°	42.5 (40 lb. snow)	−15.1	18.0
								B	78'- 2⅜"	44.3°	56.7	−20.2	15.4
								C	76'-10¼"	43.4°	56.9	−20.4	10.0

Note: All of these domes except A-80-7.0 can safely withstand winds of 125 m.p.h.; uplift and snag loads on piers will be increased by about 55% over those given here for 100 m.p.h. wind.

By SEYMOUR HOWARD, *Architect*
Associate Professor, Pratt Institute

Of the various methods of spanning a space, suspension systems have a special appeal to the imagination because of their potential efficiency in the use of material and the long spans possible. Steel, aluminum, or fiber can be used to their maximum advantage in the form of cable or rope. All the loads can be carried in direct tension; there need be no reduction in the allowable stress to provide for the danger of buckling. The drawing of steel into wire form increases the proportional limit to stresses on the order of 160,000 psi (instead of 30,000 to 40,000 psi for structural steel) and the breaking stress to over 222,000 psi.[1] What economy of material and lightness this seems to promise!

Yet, apart from the familiar suspension bridge, very few permanent structures of this type have actually been built, because of the limitations of suspension systems.

MULTISTORY SYSTEMS: CABLES FOR VERTICAL SUPPORTS

One suspension system that crops up perennially in architectural projects is shown in Fig. 20. A series of floors are supported by tension cables that are fastened to an overhead truss.[2] The principal advantage

[1] *The modulus of elasticity, E, for a single wire (29 million psi) is not changed by wire-drawing, but the effective E when the wires are twisted into cable form goes down to 24 million psi for galvanized bridge strand and 20 million psi for the more flexible galvanized bridge rope. This reduction does not occur in the main cables of suspension bridges, which are spun in place with the wires parallel.*

[2] *Paul Chelazzi's "Suspen-Arch" system for multistory buildings is essentially the same, with the substitution of several "Suspen-Arches" at various levels instead of the single truss at the top.*

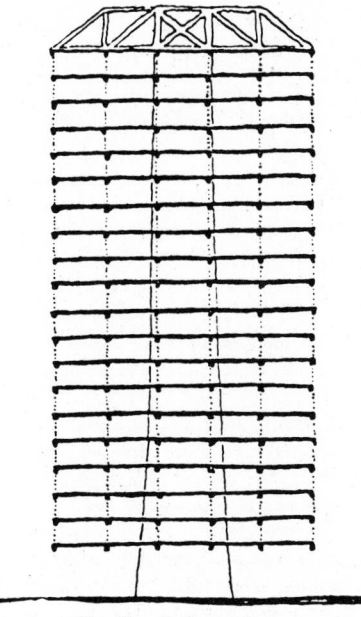

Fig. 20. Hanging floors

claimed for this type of construction is that the cross-sectional area of vertical elements is reduced to a minimum, and that, as a result, the plan provides maximum flexibility in floor layout.

Limitations

1. Although the area of the tension cables themselves is small, the addition of necessary fireproofing around them increases that area considerably.

2. The spacing of vertical supports is determined by the floor framing system. Therefore the limitations on the layout of offices are essentially the same as if the floor were supported by columns. Neither a column nor a hanger is a welcome obstruction in the middle of a room.

3. Considering the building as a whole, vertical loads must travel a path about three times as long to get to the ground as in normal columnar design.

4. Wind forces must be resisted entirely by the central compression shaft. With conventional columnar framing, on the other hand, the stiffness of all the columns can help resist horizontal forces.

5. The tendency of floors to swing horizontally can be eliminated by correct fastenings to the compression shaft. These fastenings must, however, permit relative vertical movement, because the central shaft will shorten under loading while the cables will lengthen.

SINGLE-STORY SYSTEMS: THE HANGING ROOF

If there is one general category for classifying the limitations of hanging roofs, it is *movement*. Under this broad heading can be grouped most of the problems that can be foreseen.

Nondestructive movements

1. *Changes in shape due to moving loads:* One of the advantages of tension structures is the simplicity with which one can visualize the shape of the tension elements under a load. A perfectly flexible cable or string will take a different shape for every variation in loading, according to the familiar "funicular curve" or "string polygon" (Fig. 21).

2. *Changes in shape due to unsymmetrical loading*, such as snow, over only a portion of the roof, are essentially the same as those due to moving loads. In both cases, the greater the ratio of live load to dead load, the greater the movement.

3. *Changes in shape due to wind loads:* On a roof surface, wind will act principally as an upward force (suction), unless the slope is more than about 30 deg. Some means of resisting this force must be provided: secondary tie-down cables curving upward, tie-down guy wires, or an excess of dead weight.

4. *Temperature changes* can be provided for by hinges that permit rotation as cable lengths change (Fig. 22). Particular care is

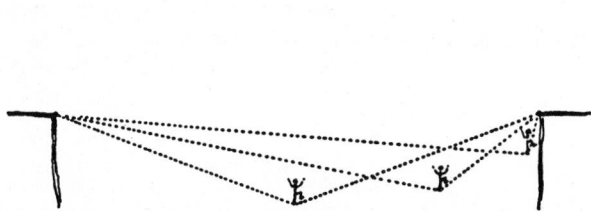

Fig. 21. Changing shapes

Fig. 22. Heat and cold

required with structures that are partly outdoors and partly indoors.

Potentially destructive movements

Vibration: Flapping, rippling, fluttering, and galloping are all forms of vibration and thus potentially destructive movements.

Every mass has its own natural period of vibration with its fundamental and higher modes. The period depends on the density of the mass, on its geometrical distribution or shape, and on the magnitude of the stresses set up by its own weight and other permanent forces acting on it. The most familiar example is a stretched wire, whose musical note depends on its material, length, and tension.

The number of half-waves formed by the vibrating wire is always a whole number; therefore one of the ways of controlling vibration is by irregular spacing of framing members, ties, and supports.

When an external pulsating force is applied to such a mass as a cable, it will be set in motion. This motion can be represented by an infinite number of superimposed modes of vibration. If one of these modes coincides with the natural frequency or fundamental mode of the mass, resonance will ensue. The amplitude or deflection will be increased, and the effect of the pulsating force may also be increased. This process could continue until the structure was destroyed.

The possible causes of vibration include wind, the most usual and the principal danger to suspended structures; and movement of vehicles and the operation of reciprocating and rotating machinery on the structure or on the ground nearby.

Wind: The flapping of simple suspended elements like a flag, a sail, or a canvas awning is very familiar, but how does the wind really act to cause a rhythmic force?

1. *Karman vortices:* If a steady wind blows against a cylinder or other obstruction, the wake takes the form of a vortex street (Fig. 23). The shedding of these vortices on the leeward side causes forces to act on the cylinder at right angles to the direction of the wind, first from one side

and then from the other. The frequency is

$$f = 0.22 \frac{V}{D}$$

in which V = velocity and D = diameter.[1]

2. *Dynamically unstable shapes:* The force of the wind on a prismatic shape is usually not in line with the direction of the wind. An analysis of its effect indicates that the force is divided into two components: drag and lift, parallel and perpendicular to the direction of the wind, as shown in Fig. 24. The magnitude of these components will vary with the angle of attack and with the section of the mass involved. Some shapes are unstable; if the wind blows at certain angles, the lift force will cause them to wobble. The dynamic stability of a given shape can be determined only by experiment. If suspension roof structures are to find more general use, experiments will have to be performed to determine the dynamic stability of various surfaces.

DAMPING

If a damping force can be provided to act in the opposite direction to that of the structure's motion when vibration starts, and if that force is proportional to the velocity of the structure (the faster it moves, the greater the damping force required), vibration can be prevented or greatly diminished. This method is often called viscous damping because a small plunger in a dashpot filled with viscous liquid will provide this type of resisting force. It is similar to the action of the cylinder of a door closer.

[1] *A Karman vortex about 39 ft long was the cause of the famous Tacoma Bridge collapse, which occurred under a steady 42-mph wind. The deck twisted about 45 deg from the horizontal in both directions until it broke. The deck was rebuilt with a box section instead of the original H section, thus increasing the resistance to torsion a hundredfold. The new section was made up of open trusses on the sides and an openwork deck, to prevent the formation of large eddies or significant pressure differences between the upper and lower surfaces.*

The curves in Fig. 25 show graphically the effect of damping. The abscissas measure the relationship:

$\frac{\omega}{\omega_n}$ or frequency of exciting force / natural frequency of structure

The ordinates measure the relationship:

$\frac{x_0}{x_{stat}}$ or amplitude of vibration due to exciting force / ampl. of deflection due to statical force of same magnitude

The curves plot the effect of various degrees of damping, from none (curve A) to perfect. In curve E, showing critical or perfect damping ($c/c_0 = 1.0$), the amplitude is always less than the statical deflection, indicating that the damping has no effect if the exciting force is applied very, very slowly, but has an ever-increasing effect as the frequency of the exciting force increases.

EXAMPLES OF SUSPENSION STRUCTURES

Apart from the suspension bridge, there is to date no generally accepted body of "good practice"; relatively few suspension-structure buildings have been built. The field is new; experiments and patents are many. Among the notable buildings, however, are the following:

Transportation Building, Chicago World's Fair, 1933. Steel masts and cables, flat roof, polygonal plan. Bennett, Burnham, Holabird, Architects.

French Pavilion, Zagreb, Yugoslavia, 1935. Single layer of cables, steel compression ring, 110-ft diam. Bernard Lafaille, Engineer.

North Carolina State Fair Pavilion, Raleigh, 1953. Concrete arches support single layer of cables in 300-ft roof of negative curvature (Fig. 29). William Dietrick, Architect; Mathew Nowicki, Consultant; Severud-Elstad-Krueger, Engineers.

Municipal Stadium, Montevideo, Uruguay, 1957. Single layer of cables, concrete compression ring, 308-ft diam. Mondina, Viera, Miller, Architects.

U.S. Pavilion, Brussels World's Fair, 1958. "Bicycle wheel" roof, double layer of cables,

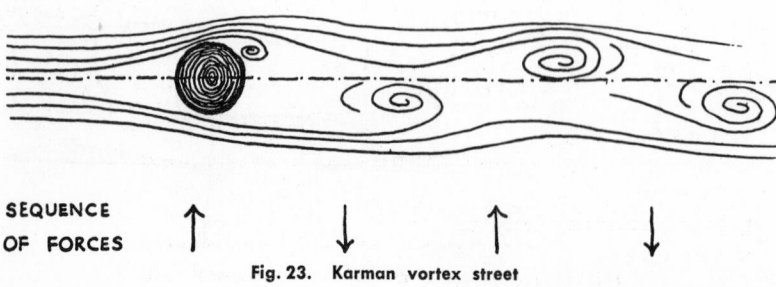

SEQUENCE OF FORCES

Fig. 23.   Karman vortex street

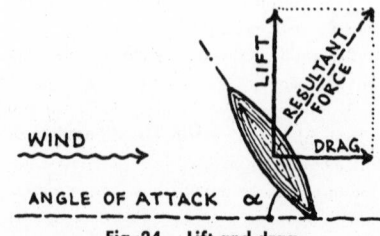

WIND

ANGLE OF ATTACK α

Fig. 24.   Lift and drag

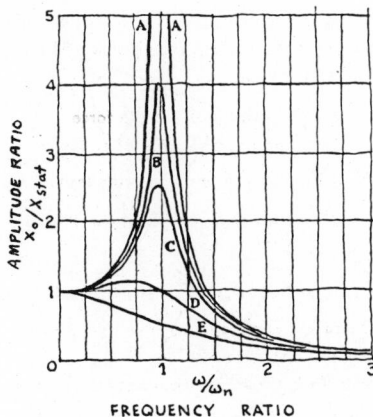

Fig. 25. Vibration with various degrees of damping

steel compression ring, 350-ft diam. Edward D. Stone, Architect.

French Pavilion, Brussels World's Fair, 1958. Steel masts and cables; roof is irregular in plan, 121 by 174 ft. Baucher, Blondel, Filippone, Architects; René Sarger, Engineer.

Hockey Rink, Yale University, 1958. Arched concrete ridge supports single layer of cables anchored to concrete side walls, lyre-shaped in plan. Eero Saarinen, Architect; Douglas Orr, Associated; Severud-Elstad-Krueger, Engineers.

Municipal Auditorium, Utica, N.Y., 1960. "Bicycle wheel" roof, double layer of cables, concrete compression ring, 240-ft diam (Fig. 26). Gehron & Seltzer, Architects; Frank Delle Cese, Associated; Lev Zetlin, Engineer.

A number of airplane hangars have been built since 1955 on the scheme shown in Fig. 22. The same principle was used with an elliptical plan for the Pan-American World Airways Passenger Terminal in New York; Tippetts-Abbot-McCarthy-Stratton, Architects; Ives, Turano, Gardner, Associated.

The first building employing the system shown in Fig. 20, scheduled for completion in 1962 in Antwerp, Belgium, for British Petroleum, Ltd., consists of twelve stories suspended from prestressed concrete roof trusses by laminated steel plate hangers. Stijnen, DeMeyer, and Reussens, Architects.

PRINCIPAL ELEMENTS OF SUSPENSION STRUCTURES

1. *Compression:* Provided by towers and masts.

2. *Tension:* Provided by main cables and hanger members.

3. *Stiffening:* For holding down against wind uplift, for preventing vibration and for maintaining shape under unsymmetrical loading. May be provided by trusses, diagonal tension stays, guy wires, secondary cables with upward curvature (these may

be prestressed), and the dead weight of the structure itself.

4. *Anchorage:* For vertical components, may be the ground (bedrock), the weight of concrete deadmen, or the dead weight of part of the structure (such as side walls). For horizontal components, may be bedrock, the resistance to sliding of concrete deadmen, or part of the structure (such as a floor, a deck, or a circumferential ring).

Principles of construction

The most promising principles for constructing roof surfaces are as follows:

1. Use two families of cables, one curved downward (concave) and the other curved upward (convex).

2. Prestress both families of cables, so that they will always be in tension and never go slack, no matter what the loading. Prestressed cables will require anchorages or edge supports able to withstand forces at least three times as great as nonprestressed cables. Force is being used instead of mass to prevent flutter, but a good deal of the avoided mass reappears in the anchorages.

If followed correctly for every part of a roof surface, these principles will ensure a "rigid" tensile membrane that can carry any load vibrations by corresponding variations in the tensile stresses in the surface. They may not by themselves *prevent* vibration, however; for this further study is required.

Some examples embodying these principles are shown in Figs. 26 to 30.

ROOFS OF NEGATIVE CURVATURE

If, as in the double dome or "bicycle wheel" roof (Fig. 26), every point is tied to two systems of cables with opposing curvature, two "surfaces" are needed. The negative or anticlastic surfaces offer another possibility. Their basic characteristics are shown in Figs. 27 to 30.

Figure 27 shows a straight-edged surface,

with the high points marked A and the low B. The framework necessary to support the surface is indicated in Fig. 28. The struts at A are necessary for the stability of the structure as a whole, the two points of support at B being insufficient unless they were built in as moment connections.

From the edges hang the principal cables, curved downward, which we can call family "a." Hanging under its own weight, each cable will describe a catenary curve. By themselves these cables would be very unstable, moving under the slightest applied load. A second set of cables is therefore laid over them to stabilize them and to resist uplift forces due to the wind. These cables are all curved upward; call them family "b." The points of intersection of the cables all lie on a surface of negative curvature.

In order to resist the considerable bending set up in the edge beams, structures have been built with the edges curved into arch form so as to resist the pull of the cables by compression alone. Figure 29 shows this design, which is familiar from the North Carolina State Fair Pavilion, and also from Frei Otto's work in Germany. Note that the edge arches need some vertical support from mullions to ensure the stability of the entire structure. In simple hanging roofs of this kind the "b" family of cables is only moderately prestressed, and flutter must be prevented by the addition of guy wires.

The next step is to provide so much prestress in the "b" cables, thus also prestressing the "a" cables (or vice versa), that the surface will be much more resistant to any changes in loading and will act like a rigid membrane. The difficulty is in prestressing the cables. One solution has been patented by René Sarger and used by him for the French Pavilion at the Brussels Fair and other structures. It consists of lowering the A-points by pulling down on the edge beam, as shown in Fig. 30.

Hyperbolic paraboloid roofs

It is important to distinguish the action

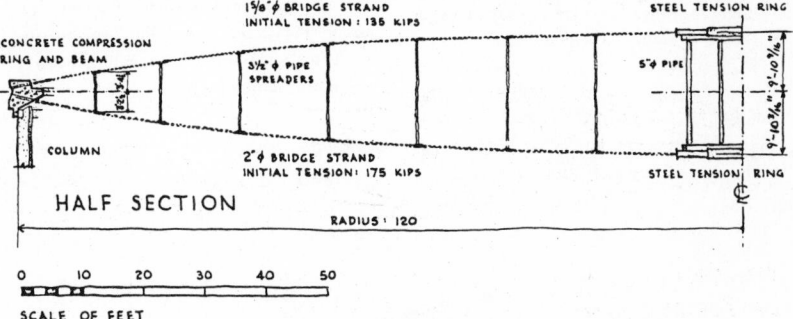

Fig. 26. Prestressed double dome ("bicycle wheel" roof)

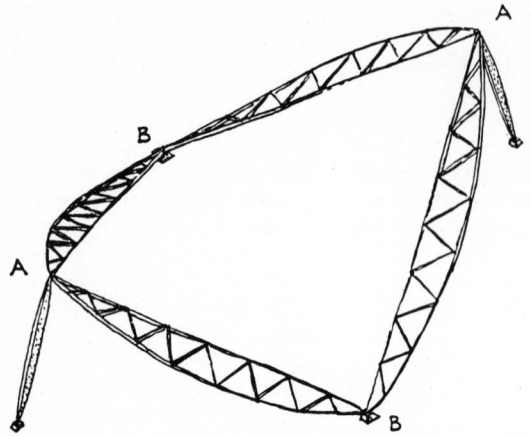

Fig. 27. Hanging roof, negative curvature

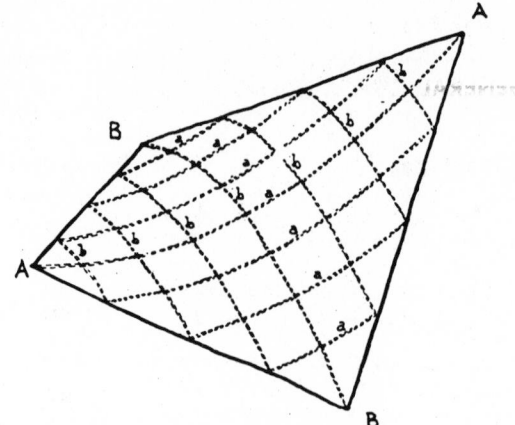

Fig. 28. Supporting framework

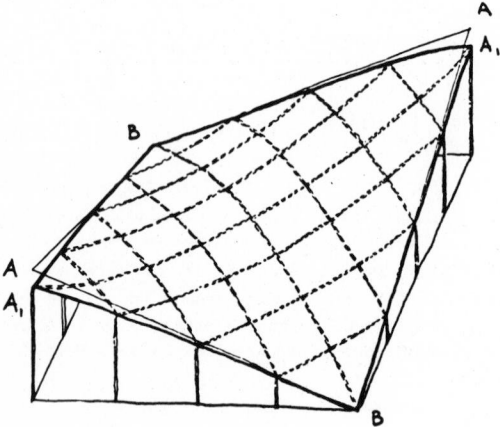

Fig. 29. Arched edges

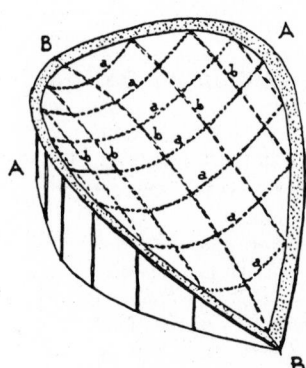

Fig. 30. Method of prestressing

of the various roof shapes that follow the hyperbolic paraboloid:

1. *The thin-shell surface*, acting as a membrane under uniform vertical loads. Tensile forces follow the lines corresponding to the "a" family and compression forces follow the "b" family. The magnitude of these membrane forces is the same at every point, and the compression and tensile forces cancel each other out at the edge. This leaves only a shearing force of the same magnitude, which the edge can support with a relatively slender column.

2. *The hanging roof, not prestressed:* Under uniform vertical loading no forces can be carried by the "b" family cables. The relatively large horizontal forces needed to support the ends of the cables of the "a" family require the edges to be designed as beams, supported at A and B. These horizontal forces will vary considerably with changes in snow and wind loads.

3. *The prestressed suspension roof:* In order to prestress both families of cables, horizontal reactive forces at least three times as large as usual must be permanently provided by the edges. However, for any variation in loading on the roof caused by snow or wind, the prestressed surface will now act similarly to the thin-shell roof, up to the point where the "compressive" force set up in the "b" family cancels out the initial tension.

Weights

Prestressed suspension roofs have been built as hyperbolic paraboloids and also as conoids (for instance, at the Brussels Fair) with remarkably light dead loads, on the order of 3 psf for cables and planking for spans of over 200 ft in both directions. These light loads were achieved, however, only by using very heavy edge beams and vertical supports, which brought the average weight up to about 40 psf.

References

Farquharson, F. B. Wind Forces on Structures: Structures Subject to Oscillation. ASCE Paper 1718.

Hartog, J. P. Den. *Mechanical Vibrations* (4th ed.). McGraw-Hill Book Co., Inc., New York (1956).

Otto, Dr. Ing. Frei. *Das Hangende Dach.* Bauwelt Verlag, Berlin (1954).

By SEYMOUR HOWARD, *Architect*
Associate Professor, Pratt Institute

GENERAL CONSIDERATIONS

Advantages

1. "No other structural system makes such an economical use of materials."[1]

2. Freedom of design shapes, both in plan and in section.

3. Ease of providing natural light over large areas.

4. Great capacity to carry unbalanced loads.

5. Fireproof.

6. Great reserve strength. Local damage, even at critical point, will not cause general collapse.

Special Problems

1. Formwork must be carefully designed. Minimum of four reuses of forms required for economy.

2. Construction problems unfamiliar to most contractors.

3. Design procedure unfamiliar to many engineers; complicated shapes involve lengthy calculations. "Design of large thin shell roofs is a major engineering problem."[1]

4. Insulation must be provided, preferably above shell and ribs.

5. Surface treatment of exposed concrete must be studied for architectural effect.

[1]From *Design of Cylindrical Concrete Shell Roofs*, Manual No. 31, American Society of Civil Engineers, N. Y., 1952.

A   SHELLS CURVED IN ONE DIRECTION

Transverse stiffeners are essential. They may be:
• Integral with the supports in the form of rigid frames (as shown)
• Arches, carried on columns or directly on the ground:
• Vertical diaphragms, carried on columns or continuing to ground. (Some designs have been built with ribless stiffeners.)

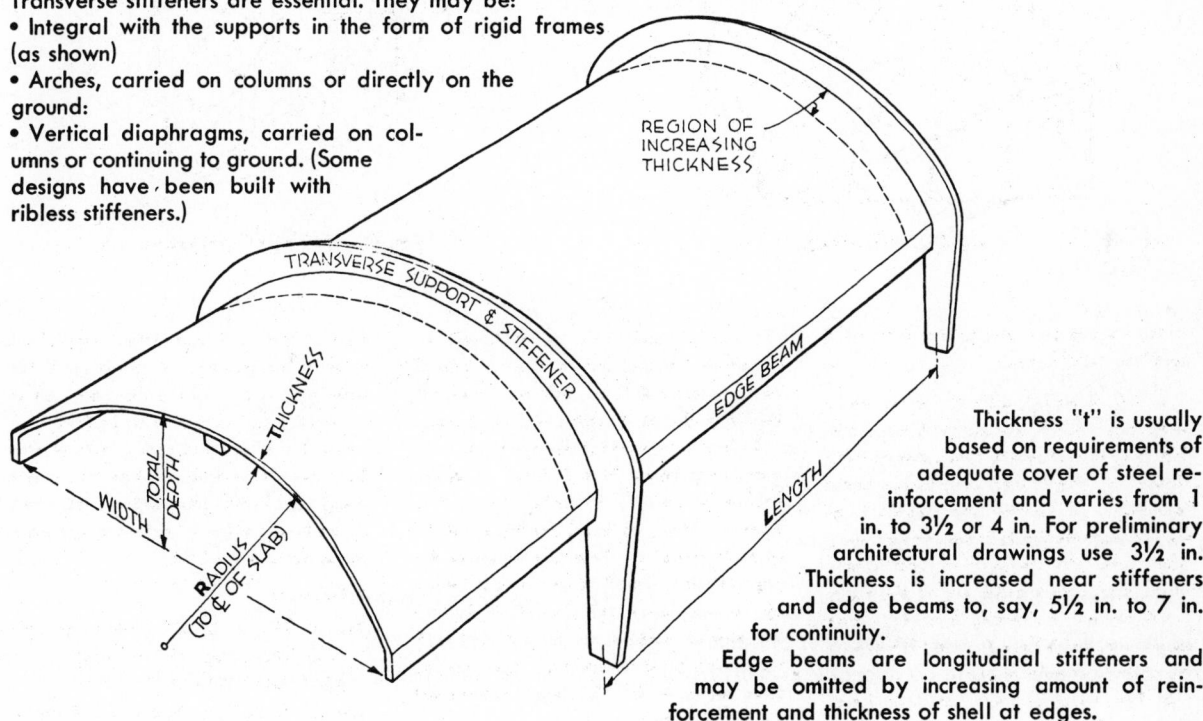

Thickness "t" is usually based on requirements of adequate cover of steel reinforcement and varies from 1 in. to 3½ or 4 in. For preliminary architectural drawings use 3½ in. Thickness is increased near stiffeners and edge beams to, say, 5½ in. to 7 in. for continuity.
Edge beams are longitudinal stiffeners and may be omitted by increasing amount of reinforcement and thickness of shell at edges.

Shells derive their strength from their ability to transfer loads by membrane stresses. These are direct stresses—compression, tension and shear—acting over the entire thickness of the shell at any point. There is no bending of an element of the shell such as exists in an element of a flat slab (except of minor magnitude caused by edge and end conditions). There is no need for continuous longitudinal support as for a masonry barrel vault incapable of supporting tensile stresses.

A(cont.) **SHELLS CURVED IN ONE DIRECTION**

Comparison of forces acting on unit elements of shell, slab and vault. Intermediate form between long barrel shell and flat slab is tee-beam and slab.

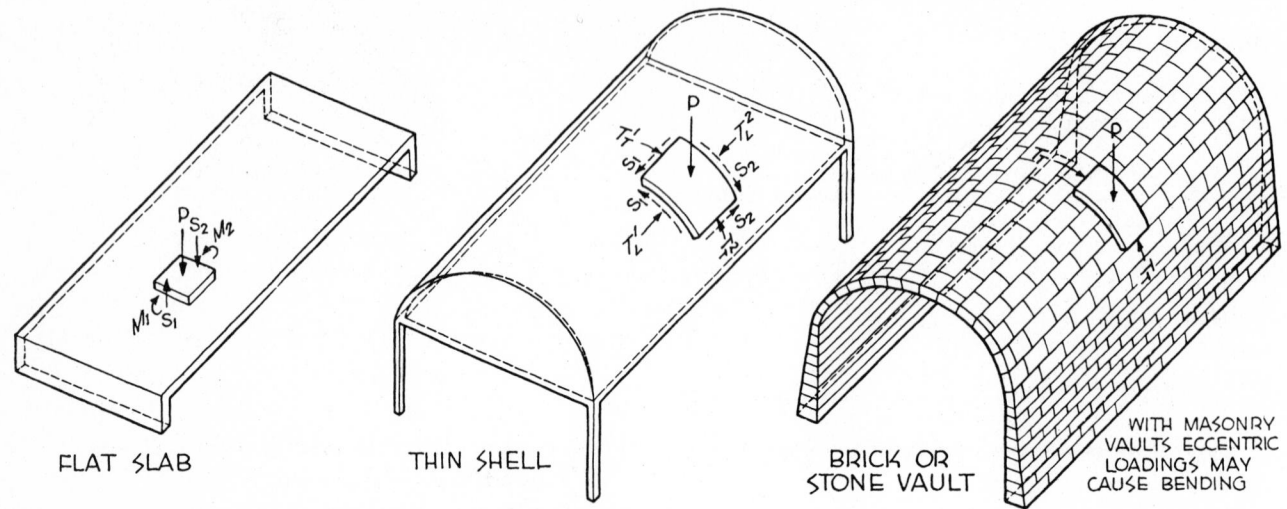

FLAT SLAB   THIN SHELL   BRICK OR STONE VAULT

WITH MASONRY VAULTS ECCENTRIC LOADINGS MAY CAUSE BENDING

A-1   **CENTER(S) OF CURVATURE BELOW SHELL**

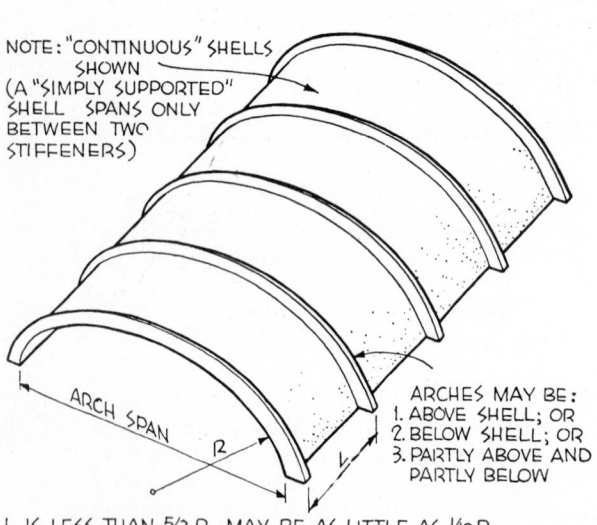

NOTE: "CONTINUOUS" SHELLS SHOWN (A "SIMPLY SUPPORTED" SHELL SPANS ONLY BETWEEN TWO STIFFENERS)

ARCH SPAN

ARCHES MAY BE:
1. ABOVE SHELL; OR
2. BELOW SHELL; OR
3. PARTLY ABOVE AND PARTLY BELOW

L IS LESS THAN 5/3 R, MAY BE AS LITTLE AS 1/10 R

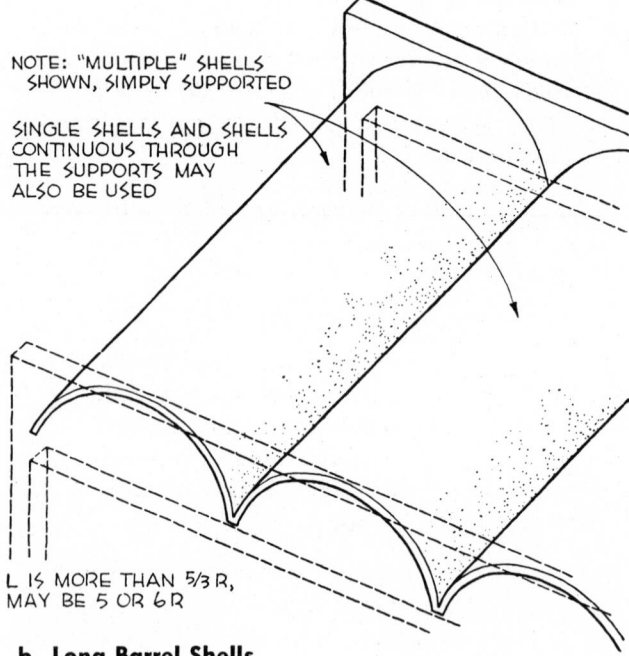

NOTE: "MULTIPLE" SHELLS SHOWN, SIMPLY SUPPORTED

SINGLE SHELLS AND SHELLS CONTINUOUS THROUGH THE SUPPORTS MAY ALSO BE USED

L IS MORE THAN 5/3 R, MAY BE 5 OR 6 R

a. Short Barrel Shells

Usually used for very wide spaces (i.e. Stiffening arch spans of over 150 ft, occasionally as short as 50 ft)

Max. arch span built—340 ft

Max. arch span possible—500 to 600 ft or more

Length of shell "L" usually 20 to 40 ft

Transverse forces govern (T_T above) for shell. Arch design is primary consideration. Depth at crown varies $\frac{1}{50}$ to $\frac{1}{100}$ of arch span. Usual provisions for thrust and vertical load must be carefully designed

b. Long Barrel Shells

Max. length of shell built—236 ft (Need for expansion joints limits length). Usual lengths 50 to 135 ft

Width of shell 30 to 50 ft

Depth of shell including edge beam (if used) usually about $\frac{1}{10}$ length

Longitudinal forces govern (T_L above)

Note: For calculating cylindrical short and long barrel shells, refer to "Design of Cylindrical Concrete Shell Roofs," Manual No. 31 American Society of Civil Engineers, N. Y., 1952

A-1(cont.)   CENTER(S) OF CURVATURE BELOW SHELL

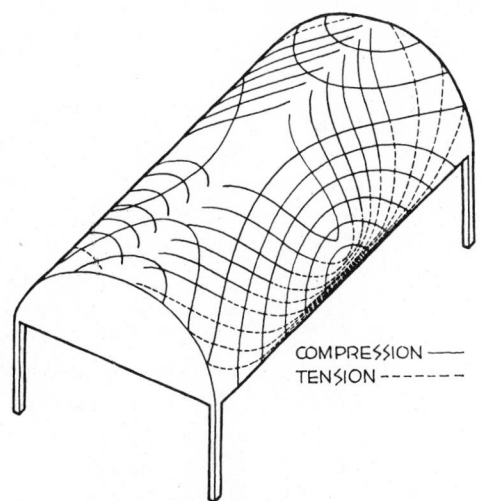

COMPRESSION ─────
TENSION ─ ─ ─ ─ ─

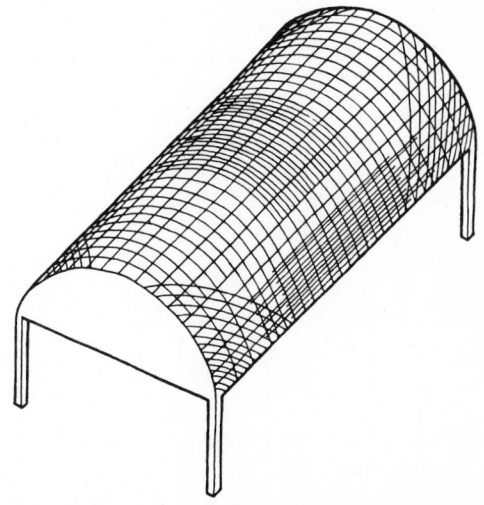

Typical stress trajectories in a simply supported, single long barrel shell

Note concentration of tensile forces at lower edge in center of shell lengths.

Horizontal component of these forces (in plan) causes lower edges of shell to move *inward* toward longitudinal Center Line. This is exactly the opposite of the movement of conventional masonry barrel vault or arch.

Typical arrangement of reinforcement in a simply supported, single long barrel shell

While it is desirable to place the reinforcement exactly along the lines of principal stress, this requires careful bending and placement. A rectilinear arrangement as shown above is easier to bend and place, although more steel will be required. Diagonal bars cannot be avoided at the lower edges of the shell near the supports.

For continuous and cantilevered shells, tensile stresses will exist at top of shell over the supports, and compressive stresses at lower edges

(See elevation diagram at bottom of page)

TRANSVERSE BARS AT TOP RESIST SOME MOMENT AND SHRINKAGE STRESSES

DIAGONAL BARS AT BOTTOM RESIST DIAGONAL TENSION

LONGITUDINAL BARS IN CENTER RESIST MAIN TENSILE FORCES BELOW NEUTRAL AXIS; REMAINDER FOR SHRINKAGE

Placement of bars in shell

Reinforcement may be in the form of bars or a combination of bars and mesh

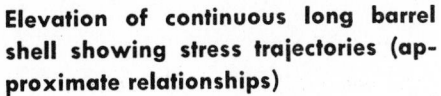

Section through transverse Center Line of multiple barrel shell

The tendency of the lower edges to move inward, as shown in broken line, must be resisted by adequate transverse tensile reinforcement

Elevation of continuous long barrel shell showing stress trajectories (approximate relationships)

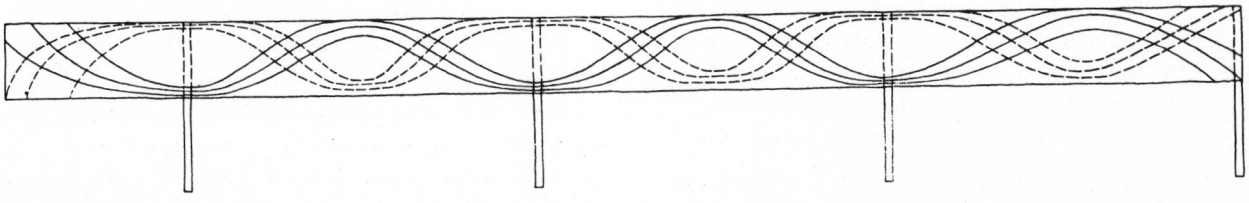

A-1(cont.)   CENTER(S) OF CURVATURE BELOW SHELL

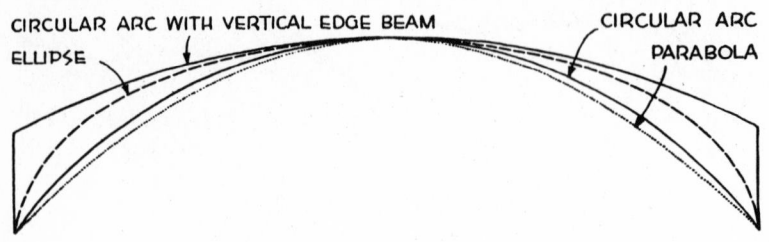

CIRCULAR ARC WITH VERTICAL EDGE BEAM

ELLIPSE

CIRCULAR ARC

PARABOLA

Some Typical Cross Section Curves

The parabola is as flat a curve as should be used. The vertical tangents at the bottom edges of the ellipse and of a shell with edge beams will reduce or eliminate edge moments. It is not practical to place concrete at angles steeper than 45° without top forms; therefore job economy favors flatter curves. This requirement would limit depth to width ratio to 1 to 5 with circular arc. Cycloid has been used because of vertical tangent at bottom edges, but requires a depth to width ratio of 1 to π or 0.318 to 1.

NOTE: For short barrels the curve is based on the arches and follows the pressure line for them, normally close to a parabola or catenary. The catenary would lie between the parabola and the circular segment.

Natural lighting can be provided by circular holes cut in shell, 3 ft-0 in. to 4 ft-0 in. diameter, or by glass prisms cast directly with the concrete

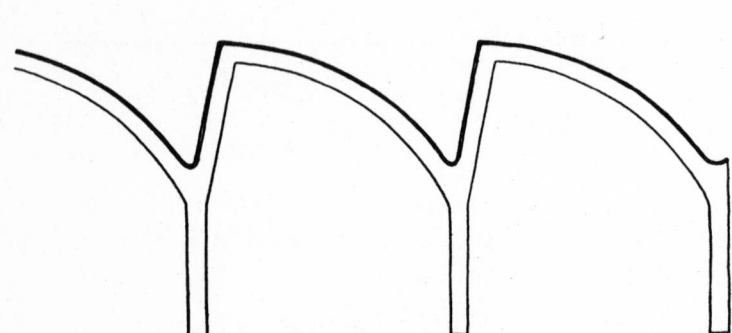

Typical "North Light" Shells

Note that, although these can be continuous, they cannot be multiple.

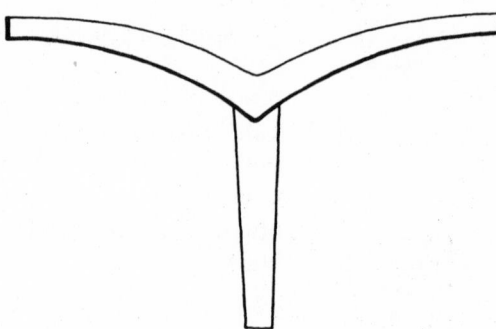

"Butterfly" Shell (Twin Cantilever)

Can be used as shown for train or bus platforms; also grouped in pairs with skylight between and occasional ties to eliminate need for wide, rigid footings.

A-1(cont.)   CENTER(S) OF CURVATURE BELOW SHELL

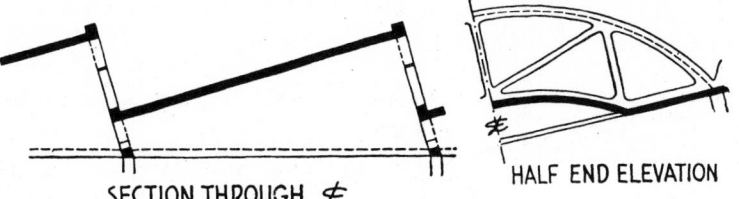

SECTION THROUGH ℄   HALF END ELEVATION

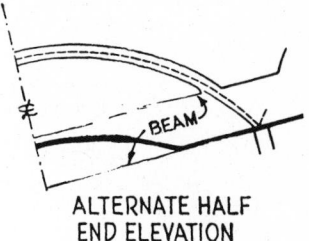

BEAM

ALTERNATE HALF
END ELEVATION

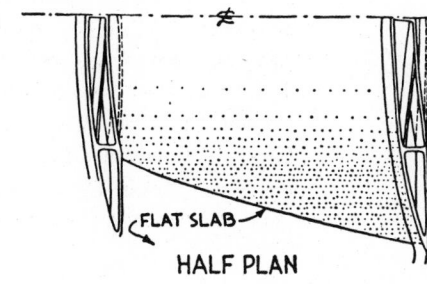

FLAT SLAB

HALF PLAN

Tilted Cylindrical Shell

NOTE that: Shell has same radius of curvature throughout its length; intersection of shell and flat slab traces part of an ellipse in plan.

Awkward flat areas between shells can only be eliminated by using another type of surface for the shell, such as cone (see below) or a conoid (see later sheet on B-3, shells curved in two directions); or by using another type of surface for the area between shells (such as an inverted shell).

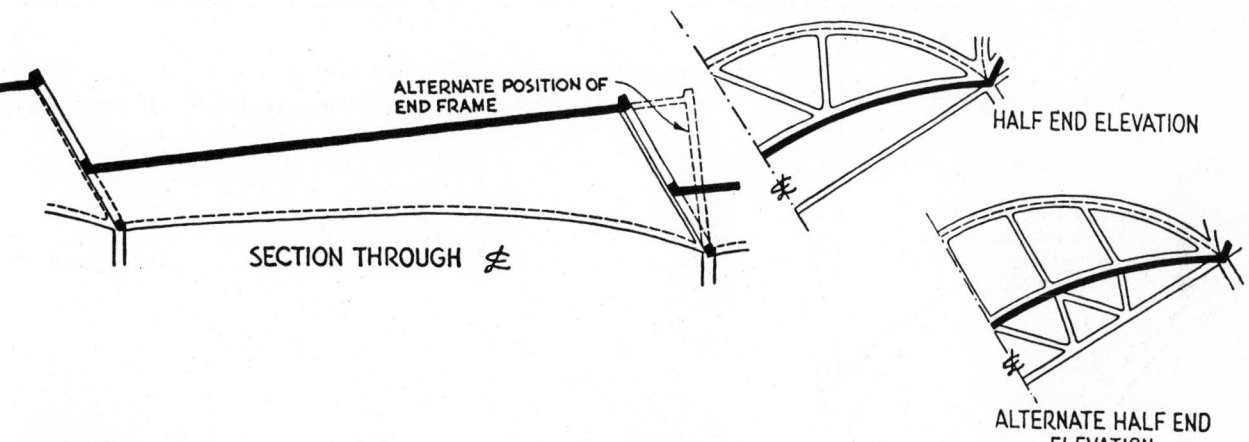

ALTERNATE POSITION OF
END FRAME

SECTION THROUGH ℄

HALF END ELEVATION

ALTERNATE HALF END
ELEVATION

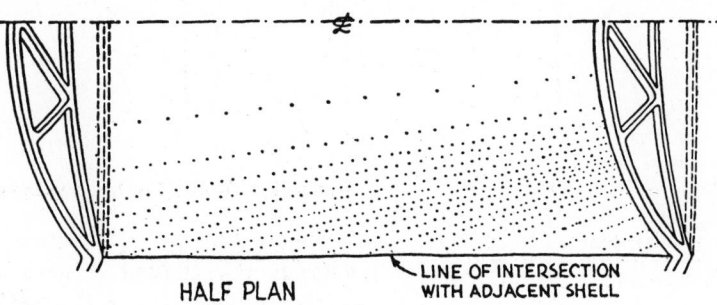

HALF PLAN

LINE OF INTERSECTION
WITH ADJACENT SHELL

Tilted Conical Shell

NOTE that: Shell has radius of curvature which varies uniformly throughout its length; intersection of adjacent shells traces part of a hyperbola in side elevation.

If cone is not tilted and if shorter radius is not used at outside curve of end elevation, large flat slab portions would have to be used between shells, similar to those formed between tilted cylinders (see above and also later sheet on A-2 Center of curvature above shell).

If end frame is placed in alternate position (see section), at right angles to side of cone instead of at right angles to center line of cone, the end elevation of frame would show ellipses instead of circles.

A-1(cont.)   CENTER(S) OF CURVATURE BELOW SHELL

For short barrel shells the arch and its abutments become the primary consideration. Some typical sections:

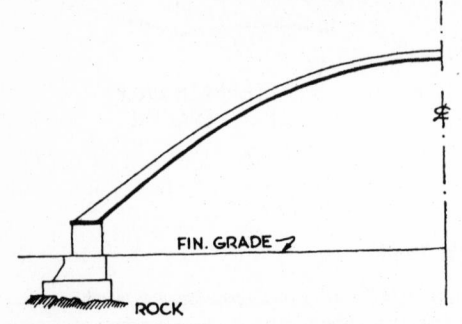

PEDESTAL AND VERTICAL BUTTRESS ON ROCK
ON POOR SOIL, USE TIE BARS

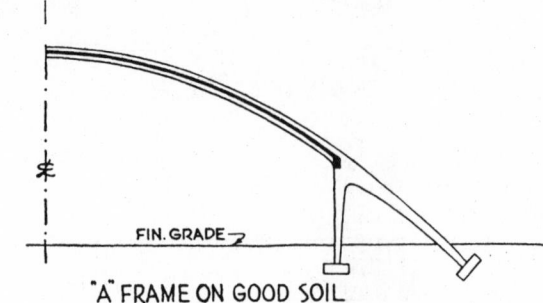

"A" FRAME ON GOOD SOIL

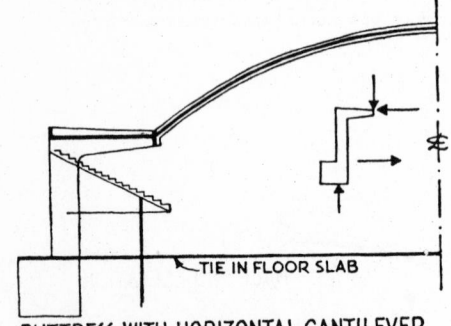

BUTTRESS WITH HORIZONTAL CANTILEVER

Horizontal component of arch thrust forms couple with tie, which is balanced by couple formed by vertical component of arch thrust and vertical reaction of foundation.

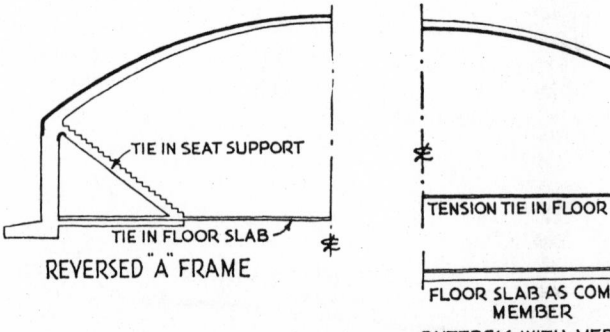

REVERSED "A" FRAME

BUTTRESS WITH VERTICAL CANTILEVER

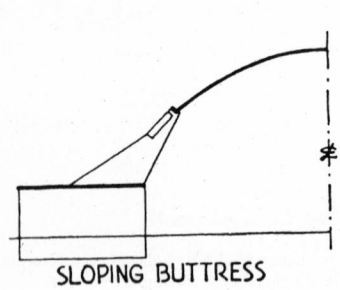

SLOPING BUTTRESS

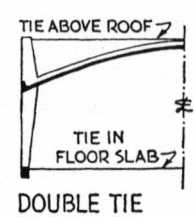

DOUBLE TIE

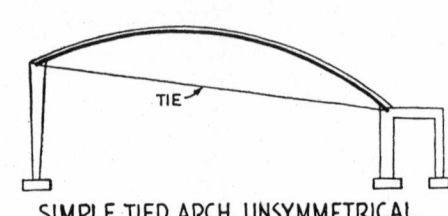

SIMPLE TIED ARCH, UNSYMMETRICAL

Transverse joints can be provided as shown in these three side elevations:

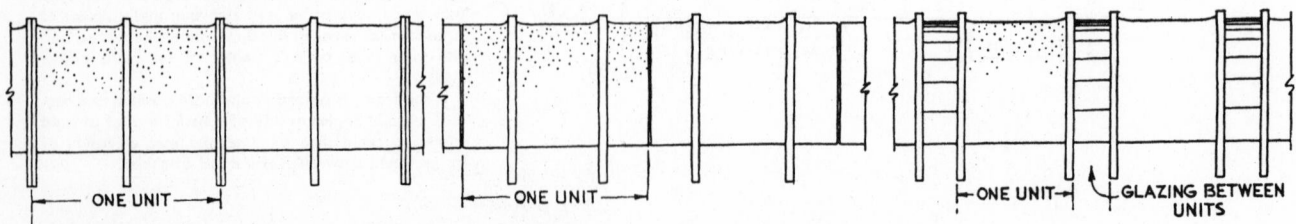

Joints are necessary for expansion, for construction convenience (limit of formwork) or to permit introduction of another element such as glazing.

A-2   CENTER(S) OF CURVATURE ABOVE SHELL

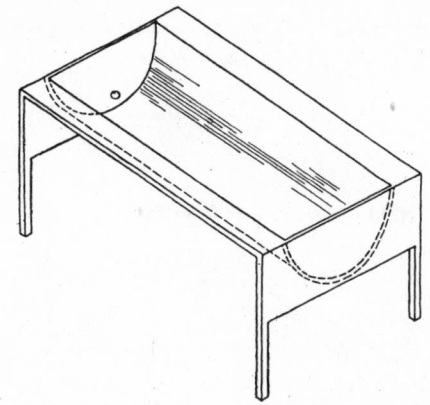

Inverted, concave shells are basically shapes best realized in tensile materials, such as wire or fiber rope, canvas, steel. The danger of buckling of the free edges of the shell requires stiffening or frequent bracing. Concave shells are therefore used chiefly as a supplement to convex shells, which have their centers of curvature below.

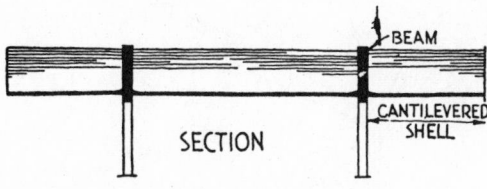

SECTION

BEAM

CANTILEVERED SHELL

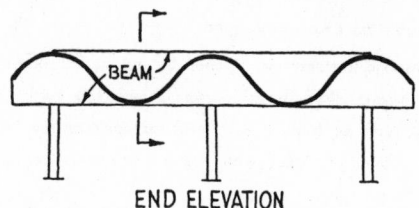

BEAM

END ELEVATION

Typical Flat Corrugated Shell

Between the supports the concave part of the shell will carry the main tensile reinforcement. In the cantilevered ends the concave part will provide the main compressive strength. The shape of the corrugations has little statical importance; segments of circles are shown, but others may be used including the sine curve.

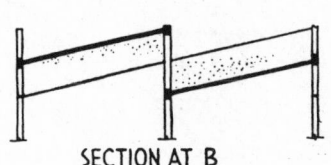

SECTION AT B

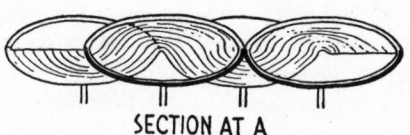

SECTION AT A

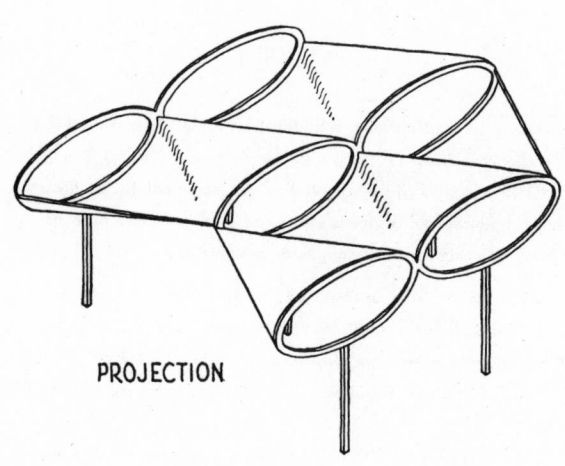

PROJECTION

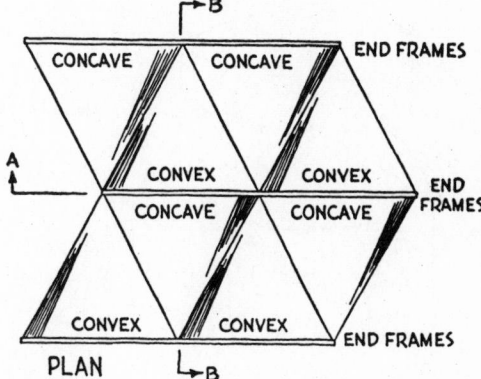

CONCAVE   CONCAVE   END FRAMES

A

CONVEX   CONVEX   END FRAMES

CONCAVE   CONCAVE

CONVEX   CONVEX   END FRAMES

PLAN

B

Inverted Shells Used to Fill Spaces Between Conical Shells

(Bracing members not shown in end frames, for clarity.) (This is c scheme of Architect Horacio Carminos and Engineer Antonio B. Aracibio of Argentina.)

B SHELLS CURVED IN TWO DIRECTIONS

These provide greater stiffness by their shape alone than shells curved in only one direction. Their surfaces are nondevelopable. They cannot be made by bending a flat sheet as can all surfaces curved in only one direction. The formwork, therefore, is usually more complicated and they have been used less frequently.

B-1 BOTH SETS OF CENTERS OF CURVATURE BELOW SHELL *(Synclastic or Dome Surfaces)*

General Case:

Surface generated by one curve ("a") sliding along another ("b") at right angles to it.

Curve "a" may vary as it slides; curve "b" may be of any shape, provided the center of curvature is always below. It is possible to vary curve "a" so that the surface will curve smoothly down to the flat plane (vertical edge frames would disappear).

Edge frames correspond to transverse stiffeners or end frames shown for shells curved in one direction. Edge frames may be: vertical diaphragm; rigid frame or truss, integral with supports or simply supported; stiffeners in edge of shell, with tension ties between points of support.

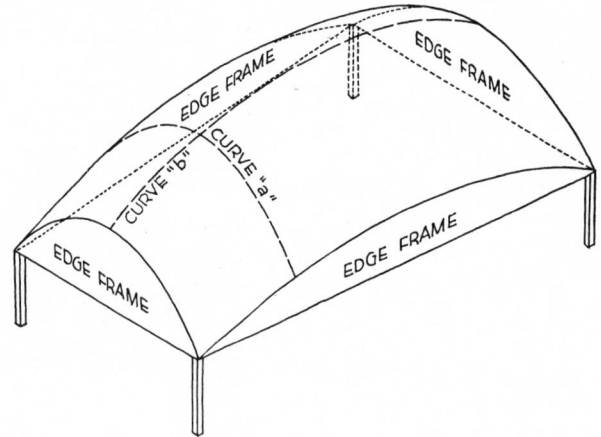

Extreme Cases:

Curve "b" of much greater radius than curve "a"

Rise may be 1/8 of length of span; width may be 1/10 of length of span; depth may be 1/10 of width of span; Max. length of span 500 ft or ▶ more. This shell approaches an arch of curved cross section. This type can be effectively combined with anticlastic shells of similar dimensions to form a corrugated surface (see B–3, Sheet 13).

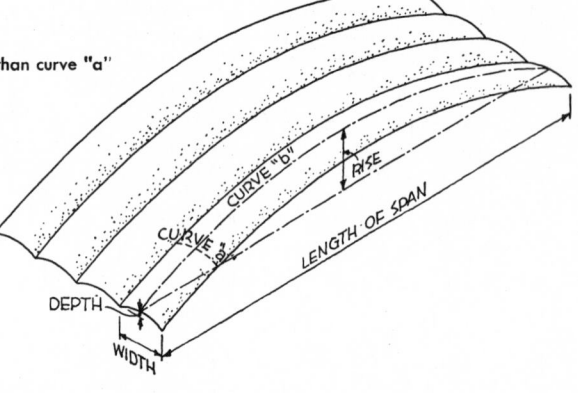

Curve "b" of same radius as curve "a"

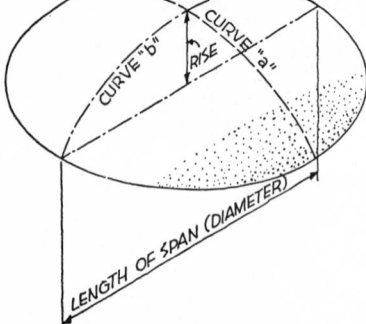

▲

Rise may be as low as ⅛ of length of span. Max. length of span built 156 ft; much greater possible. This type is most simply considered as a surface of revolution.

Thickness is based on same considerations as for shells curved in one direction (see Sheet 1). Danger of buckling starts with 2 5/8 in. thick- for 100-ft radius of curvature. For non spherical shells, thickness should be increased at points where radius of curvature decreases in comparison with radius of imaginary circumscribed sphere.

REFERENCES: As listed on Sheet 12 (see especially Eric C. Molke and J. E. Kalinka, Journal A.C.I., May–June 1938). See also International Association for Bridge and Structural Engineering, Zurich:

   Vol. 1 (1932); F. Dischinger: "Contribution to theory of wall-like girders"

   Vol. 4 (1936); F. Dischinger: "Shell construction in reinforced concrete"

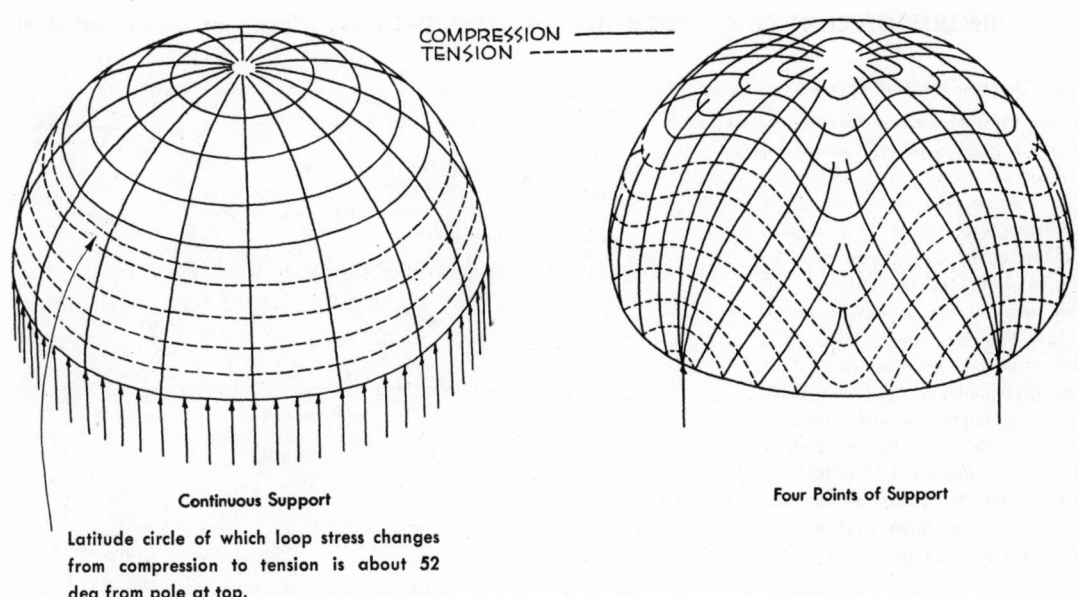

COMPRESSION ————
TENSION - - - - - -

Continuous Support

Four Points of Support

Latitude circle of which loop stress changes from compression to tension is about 52 deg from pole at top.

Stress Trajectories for uniformly loaded spherical domes

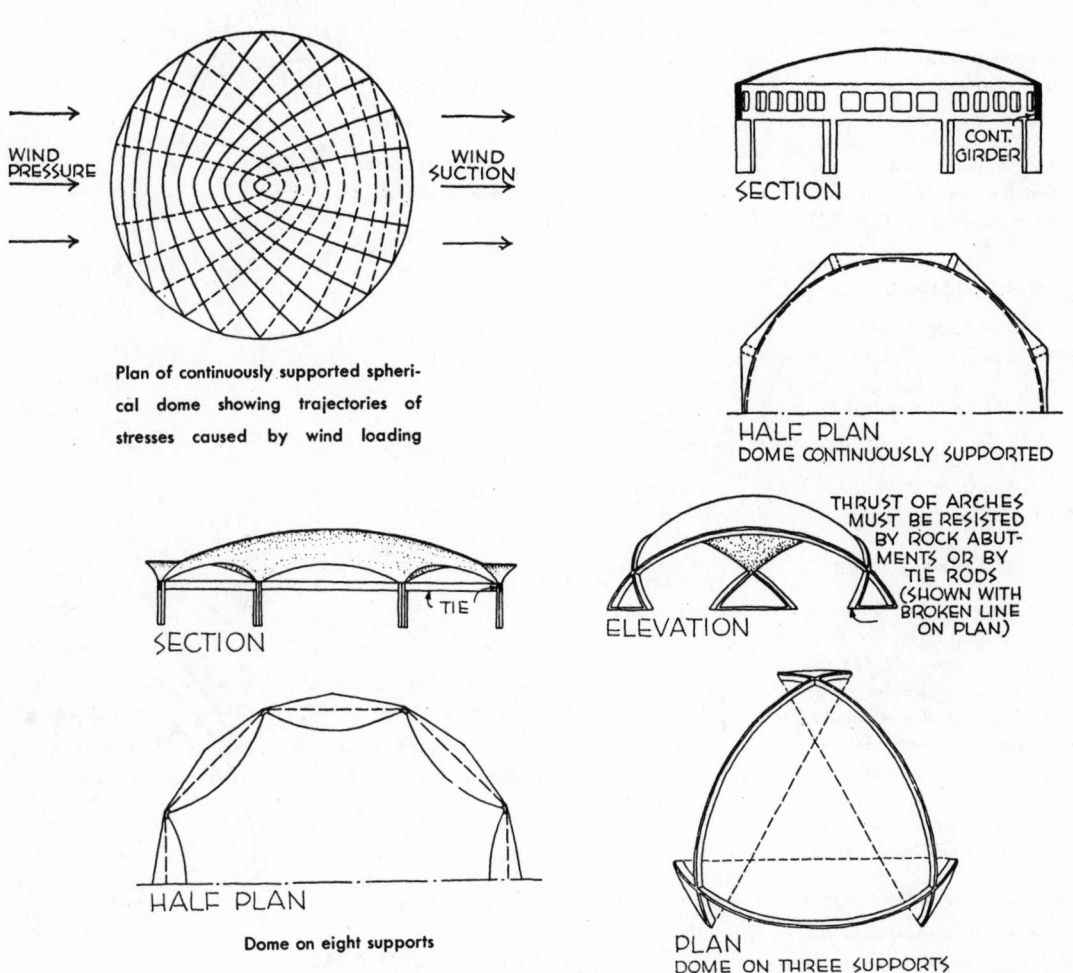

WIND PRESSURE

WIND SUCTION

Plan of continuously supported spherical dome showing trajectories of stresses caused by wind loading

SECTION

CONT. GIRDER

HALF PLAN
DOME CONTINUOUSLY SUPPORTED

SECTION

TIE

HALF PLAN

Dome on eight supports

ELEVATION

THRUST OF ARCHES MUST BE RESISTED BY ROCK ABUTMENTS OR BY TIE RODS (SHOWN WITH BROKEN LINE ON PLAN)

PLAN
DOME ON THREE SUPPORTS

Examples of various arrangements of supports

B-1 BOTH SETS OF CENTERS OF CURVATURE BELOW SHELL (synclastic or dome surfaces)

Membrane forces in spherical domes

If the thickness of a dome does not exceed 2 per cent of the radius of its sphere, the shell can be assumed to act as a membrane. In other words, only uniform tensile or compressive forces would act throughout the thickness of the dome; there could be no bending within the shell thickness. (If the shell were not continuously supported at its edges, however, some bending would probably occur in those regions.)

At any given point on the dome, specified by its colatitude or angular distance ϕ from the vertical axis, the meridian or vertical force (T_ϕ) and the hoop or horizontal force (T_θ) can be found from the diagrams and equations for a uniform dead load (weight w per unit area of dome surface), for a uniform snow load (weight w_s per unit area of plan projection), and for a uniform collar load such as an oculus (weight p per unit length of collar). These forces will have the dimensions of force per unit of length measured along the surface of the dome (that is, pounds per foot of latitude or meridian circle). To convert them to stress, divide by the thickness.

Example

Given $R = 150$ ft, thickness 4 in., and $w = 50$ psi; find the stresses at $\phi = 20$ deg. From Diagram A, we read: $T_\phi = 0.52$ Rw, and $T_\theta = 0.43$ Rw.

$$T_\phi = 0.52 \times 150 \times 50 = 3{,}900 \text{ lb per lin ft}$$

$$\text{meridian stress} = \frac{3{,}900}{12 \text{ in./ft} \times 4 \text{ in.}}$$

$$= 81.2 \text{ psi (compression)}$$

$$T_\theta = 0.43 \times 150 \times 50 = 3{,}225 \text{ lb per lin ft}$$

$$\text{hoop stress} = \frac{3{,}225}{12 \times 4}$$

$$= 67.2 \text{ psi (compression)}$$

Note from the diagrams that, for dead and snow loads, the hoop forces are compressive until quite far down (52 deg for dead load, 45 deg for snow); for collar loads, however, they are always tensile. The meridian forces are always compressive, except for an internal outward pressure or wind load (wind loads are usually not critical for a concrete dome, although they may be for a light metal frame dome).

Reactive forces in spherical domes

The lower edge of a dome must of course be supported. Unless the dome is a complete hemisphere, there will always be a horizontal component of the thrust at that

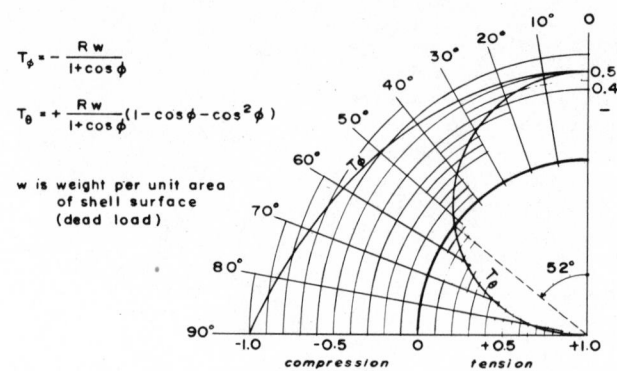

$$T_\phi = -\frac{Rw}{1+\cos\phi}$$

$$T_\theta = +\frac{Rw}{1+\cos\phi}(1-\cos\phi-\cos^2\phi)$$

w is weight per unit area
of shell surface
(dead load)

A. UNIFORM SHELL LOADING
multiply values by R·w

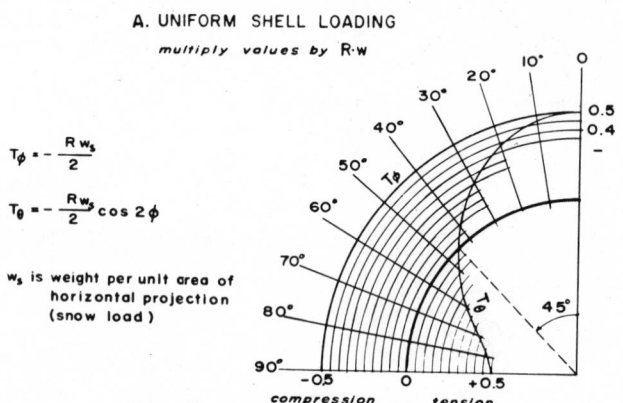

$$T_\phi = -\frac{Rw_s}{2}$$

$$T_\theta = -\frac{Rw_s}{2}\cos 2\phi$$

w_s is weight per unit area of
horizontal projection
(snow load)

B. UNIFORM VERTICAL LOADING
multiply values by R·w_s

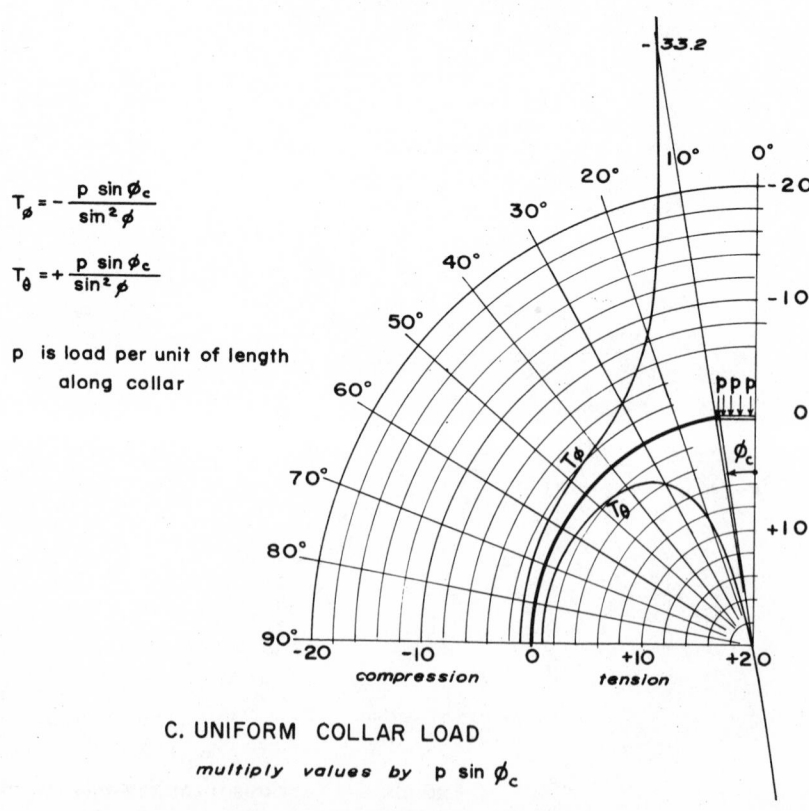

$$T_\phi = -\frac{p\sin\phi_c}{\sin^2\phi}$$

$$T_\theta = +\frac{p\sin\phi_c}{\sin^2\phi}$$

p is load per unit of length
along collar

C. UNIFORM COLLAR LOAD
multiply values by p sin φ_c

B-1(cont.)   BOTH SETS OF CENTERS OF CURVATURE BELOW SHELL

edge; this thrust is usually resisted by a tension ring. The magnitude of the total tension in the ring (usually the largest concentration of force in the structure) can be found by using the graph for coefficients, where ϕ_E is the colatitude of the lower edge. The vertical reaction at the lower edge is $T_{\phi_E} \sin \phi_E$; for convenience, the broken line in the graph gives values of $\sin \phi_E$.

Example

Given $R = 150$ ft, thickness 4 in., $w = 50$ psi, and $\phi_E = 35$ deg; find total tension in supporting ring and vertical reaction per foot of edge. From Diagram A, we read: $T_\phi = 0.55\ Rw$.

$T_\phi = 0.55 \times 150 \times 50 = 4,125$ lb per lin ft

From the graph for coefficients, we read: $T = 0.47\ RT_{\phi_E}$.

T = total tension in ring
$= 0.47 \times 150 \times 4,125 = 291,000$ lb

From the graph for coefficients, we read: $V = 0.57 T_{\phi_E}$.

$V = 0.57 \times 4,125$
$= 2,350$ lb per lin ft of edge

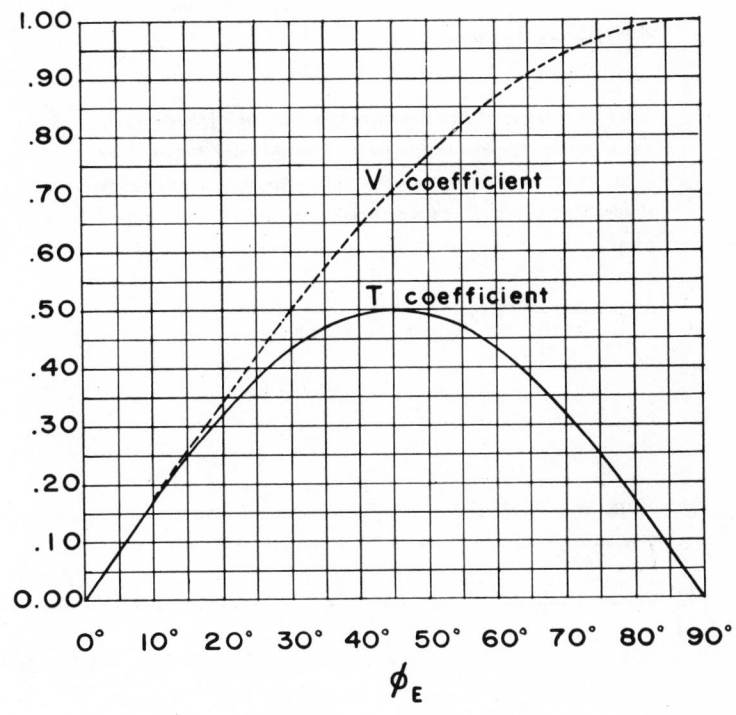

COEFFICIENTS FOR T AND V

$V = \text{coefficient} \times T_{\phi_E}$

$T = \text{coefficient} \times T_\phi \times R$

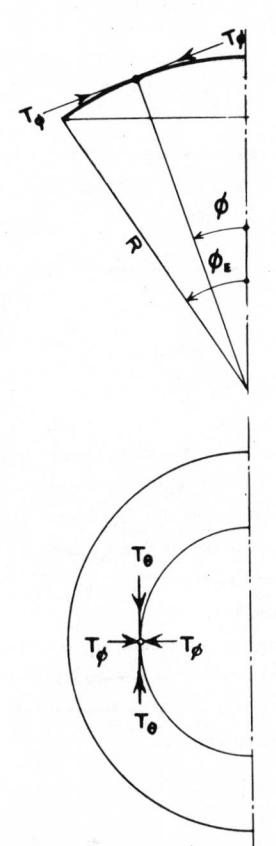

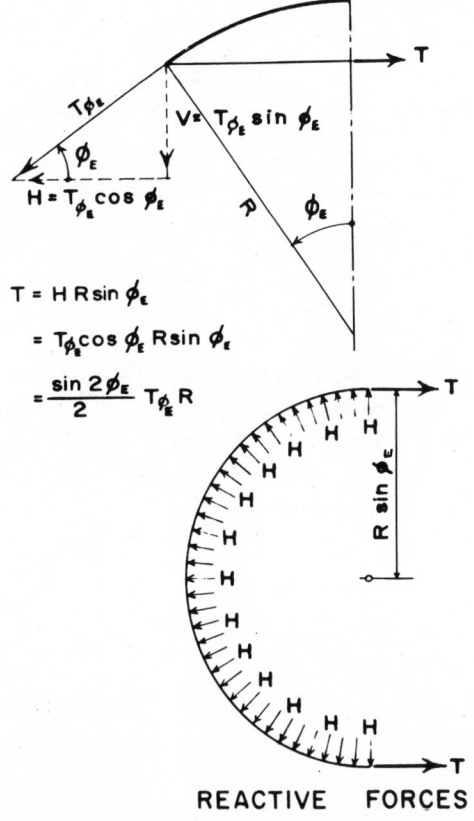

$T = H R \sin \phi_E$

$= T_\phi \cos \phi_E\ R \sin \phi_E$

$= \dfrac{\sin 2\phi_E}{2} T_{\phi_E} R$

MEMBRANE FORCES   **REACTIVE FORCES**

B-1(cont.)   BOTH SETS OF CENTERS OF CURVATURE BELOW SHELL

Polygonal Domes:

These are made up of short sections of cylindrical shells (curved in only one direction); the lines of intersection form stiffening frames. They approximate surfaces of revolution and at the same time provide simpler formwork and an easier transition to a non-circular ground plan.

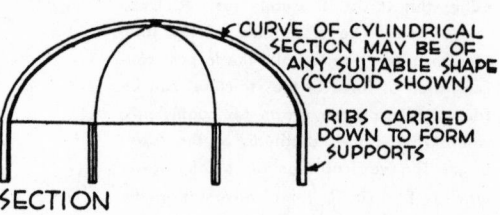

CURVE OF CYLINDRICAL SECTION MAY BE OF ANY SUITABLE SHAPE (CYCLOID SHOWN)

RIBS CARRIED DOWN TO FORM SUPPORTS

SECTION

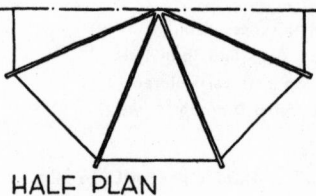

NOTE: With symmetrical loading, no bending moments are induced in the ribs at the intersection of adjacent shell sectors

HALF PLAN

B-2   BOTH SETS OF CENTERS OF CURVATURE ABOVE SHELL

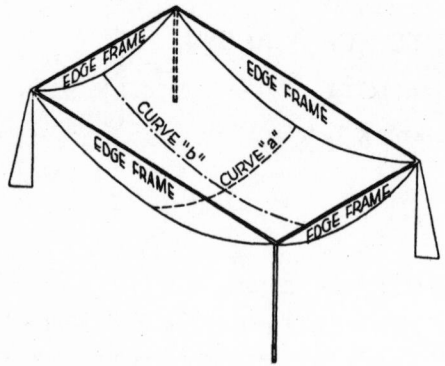

EDGE FRAME
EDGE FRAME
EDGE FRAME
EDGE FRAME
CURVE "b"
CURVE "a"

A shell of this type is exactly the opposite of type **B-1** and the surface generated in same way, except that the center(s) of curvature of both curve "a" and curve "b" lie above the shell.

This is essentially a tensile form of relatively limited use, except for the bottoms of tanks (reservoirs, silos, etc.)

REFERENCES:

See reference noted on sheet 2 ; this book contains extensive bibliography.

Hajnal-Konyi: "Shell Concrete Construction" in Architect's Year Book:2. London 1947.

Felix Candela: "Simple Concrete Shell Structures." Journal American Concrete Institute December 1951.

Charles S. Whitney: "Cost of Long Span Concrete Shell Roofs." Journal American Concrete Institute June 1950.

Eric C. Molke and J. E. Kalinka: "Principles of Concrete Shell Design." Journal A.C.I. May–June 1938.

February 1953. A.C.I. Journal has three articles on shell construction:

Anton Tedesko "Construction Aspects of Thin-Shell Structures."

Charles S. Whitney "Reinforced Concrete Thin Shell Structures."

Pier Luigi Nervi "Precast concrete offers new possibilities for design of shell structures."

International Association for Bridge and Structural Engineering, Zurich; many articles in their published "Mémoires."

Interviews with:

Robert Zaborowski, of Roberts and Schaefer Co.; Boyd G. Anderson and Edward Cohen, of Ammann and Whitney; John Hogan of the Portland Cement Association.

B-3 ONE SET OF CENTERS OF CURVATURE BELOW SHELL AND ONE SET OF CENTERS OF CURVATURE ABOVE SHELL

(Anticlastic or saddle shaped surfaces)

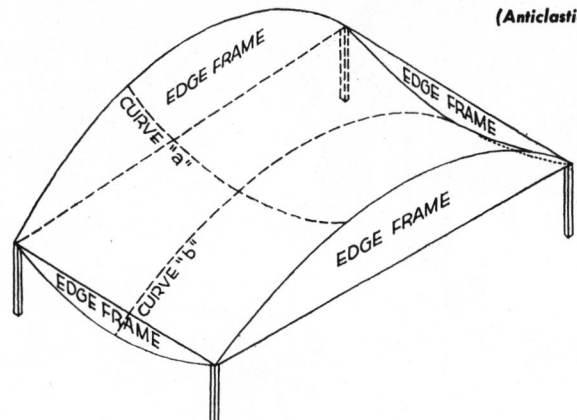

General Case

The difference between this type and B-1 & B-2 is that the centers of curvature of curve "a" are on the opposite side of the shell from the centers of curvature of curve "b"

This type of shell derives greater stiffness from its shape alone than any other type. In practice this form is used as either a hyperbolic paraboloid or as a conoid. (Hyperboloids of one sheet also have been used)

B-3-a HYPERBOLIC PARABOLOIDS

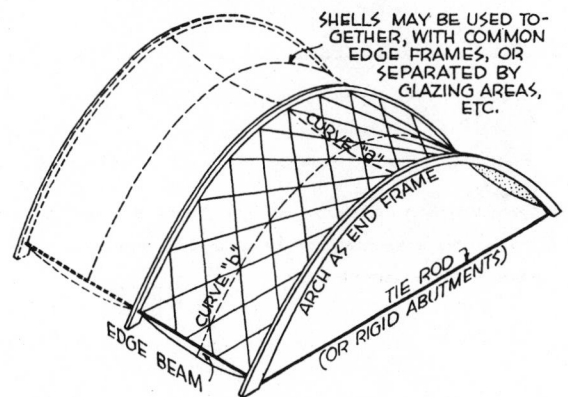

In a true hyperbolic paraboloid surface, both curves "a" and "b" are parabolas, while the traces of horizontal planes intersecting the surface are hyperbolas. The surface is generated by connecting successive points on the two arches by straight lines, which lie in parallel planes. The fact that the warped surface is created from straight lines makes formwork relatively simple. The arches can be built first and straight beams hung on them to support the form boarding. (See section of this book on "Useful Curves and Curved Surfaces")

STRAIGHT EDGED FORM

If one corner of a rectangle in plan is raised above the other three and straight lines lying in parallel planes are drawn connecting each pair of opposite sides, a hyperbolic paraboloid surface will be generated.

Corner 3 is higher than 1, 2 & 4; edges 1–2 and 3–4 are divided into equal spaces and the points are connected; similarly edges 1–4 and 2–3.

Corner 3 might also be located below instead of above the other three

Example of anticlastic and synclastic shells used together to form continuous corrugated surface

A shell of this type has been built of 330 ft span, 40 ft rise, spacing of corrugations (crest to crest) 32 ft, depth of corrugation 7 ft, shell thickness 2⅜ in., with corrugations stiffened by diaphragms. (Marignane Airport, Marseilles, 1952; Nicolas Esquillan, Engineer)

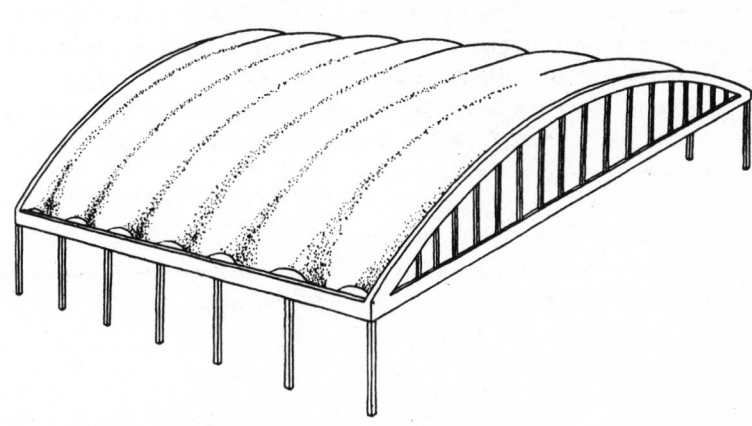

B-3-a(cont.) HYPERBOLIC PARABOLOIDS

Combinations of straight edged form

NOTE: In addition to edge stiffeners, beams or thickenings of the slab are required along lines of gables or abrupt changes (knuckles) in the surface of the shell

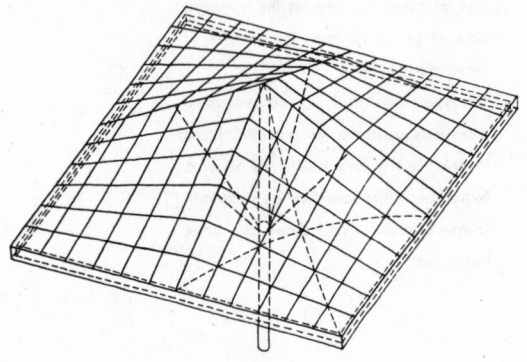

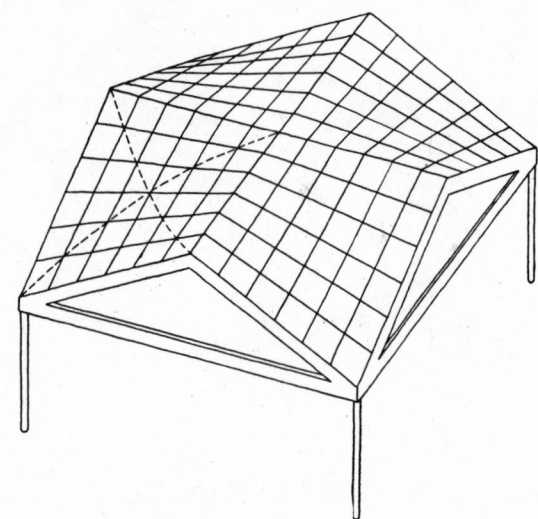

The Umbrella Form

Made by combining four hyperbolic paraboloid surfaces, each one having three low corners and one high corner. Diagonal struts may be required from column to ridges to take eccentric loading. This type would require column to be cantilevered up from wide footing if used alone. Stability can be achieved more easily by using minimum of four

The Four Gable Form

Made by combining four hyperbolic-paraboloid surfaces, each one having three high corners and one low corner.

This type can stand alone or be combined: (downspouts can be provided in the columns)

 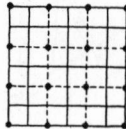

B-3-b CONOIDS

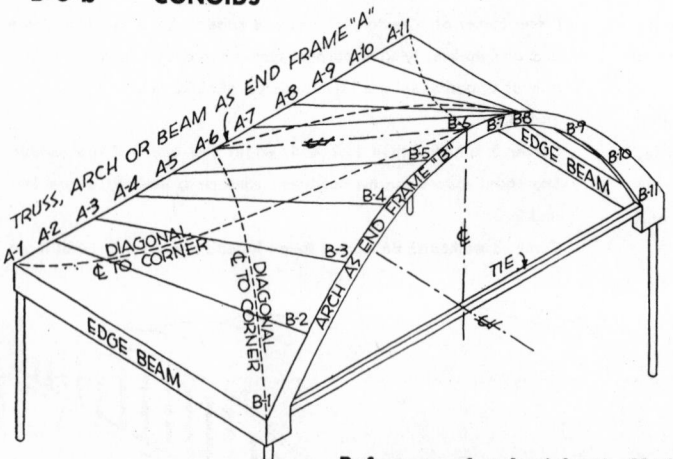

Surface generated by straight lines connecting corresponding points on opposite sides. Points are found by passing vertical planes parallel to vertical center line plane through both sides. Sides "A" and "B" may both be curved (of different curvatures), or one side may be straight and one curved (as shown).

Lines A-1 to B-1, A-2 to B-2, A-3 to B-3, etc., are all straight and all lie in planes parallel to center line plane through A-6 and B-6

References for Anticlastic Shells

Most Important: International Association for Bridge & Structural Engineering, Zurich—Vol. 4, pp. 1–112 F. Aimond: "Étude Statique De Voiles Minces En Paraboloide Hyperbolique Travaillant Sans Flexion"
• Ditto—Vol. 2, pp. 167–179. M. Fauconnier "Essai De Rupture D'une Voute Mince Conoïde En Beton Armé"
• Ditto—Vol. 3, pp. 295–332. B. Laffaille—"Memoire Sur L'Étude Générale Des Surfaces Gauches Minces"
• American Concrete Institute Journal, March 1953—F. Candela "Skew Shells Make Unusual House Roof."

B-3-b(cont.) **CONOIDS**

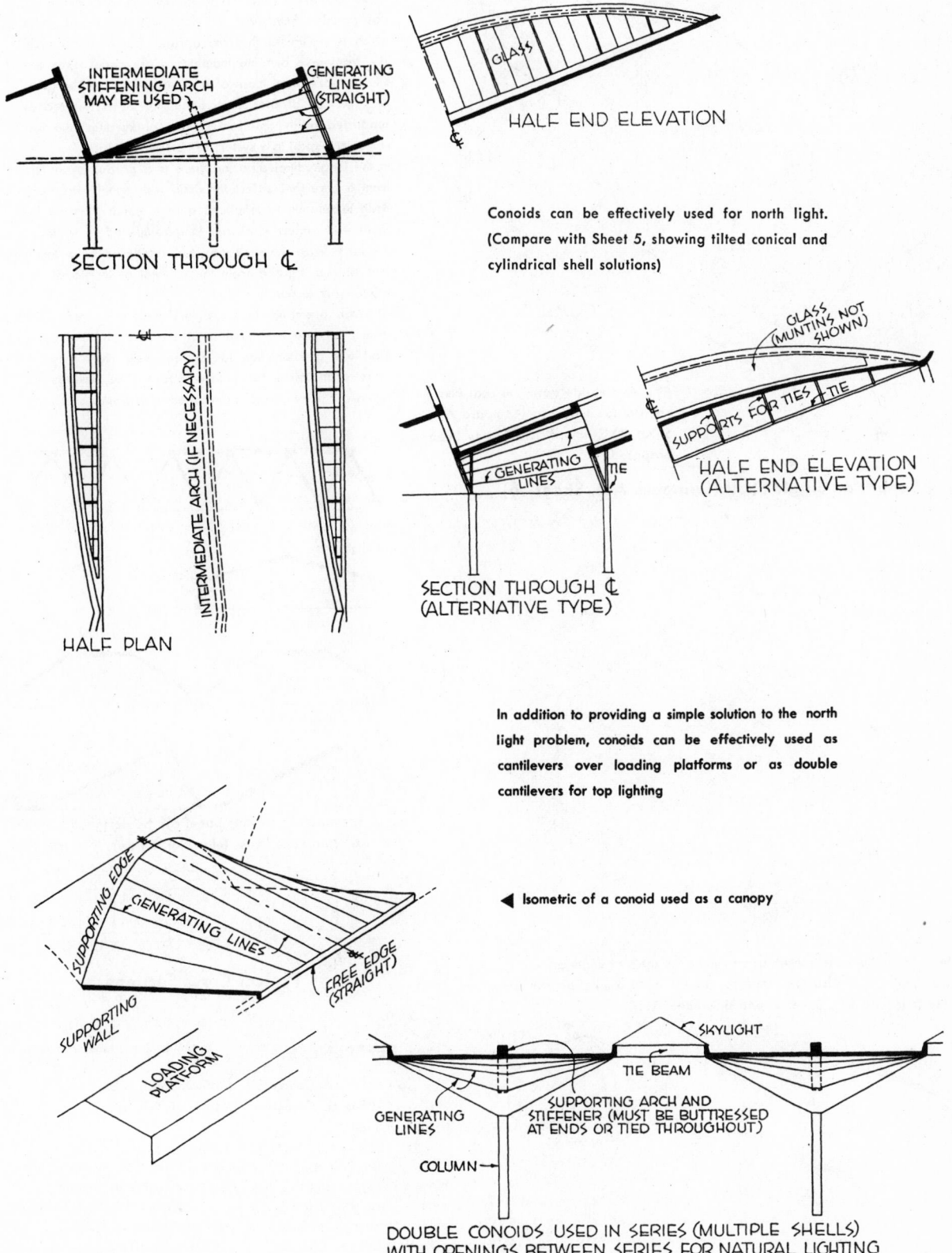

INTERMEDIATE STIFFENING ARCH MAY BE USED

GENERATING LINES (STRAIGHT)

SECTION THROUGH ₵

GLASS

HALF END ELEVATION

Conoids can be effectively used for north light. (Compare with Sheet 5, showing tilted conical and cylindrical shell solutions)

INTERMEDIATE ARCH (IF NECESSARY)

HALF PLAN

GENERATING LINES

TIE

SECTION THROUGH ₵ (ALTERNATIVE TYPE)

GLASS (MUNTINS NOT SHOWN)

SUPPORTS FOR TIES

TIE

HALF END ELEVATION (ALTERNATIVE TYPE)

In addition to providing a simple solution to the north light problem, conoids can be effectively used as cantilevers over loading platforms or as double cantilevers for top lighting

SUPPORTING EDGE

GENERATING LINES

FREE EDGE (STRAIGHT)

SUPPORTING WALL

LOADING PLATFORM

◀ Isometric of a conoid used as a canopy

SKYLIGHT

TIE BEAM

SUPPORTING ARCH AND STIFFENER (MUST BE BUTTRESSED AT ENDS OR TIED THROUGHOUT)

GENERATING LINES

COLUMN →

DOUBLE CONOIDS USED IN SERIES (MULTIPLE SHELLS) WITH OPENINGS BETWEEN SERIES FOR NATURAL LIGHTING

C   PRISMATIC SHELLS (also called folded-plate, hipped-plate, or tilted-slab construction)

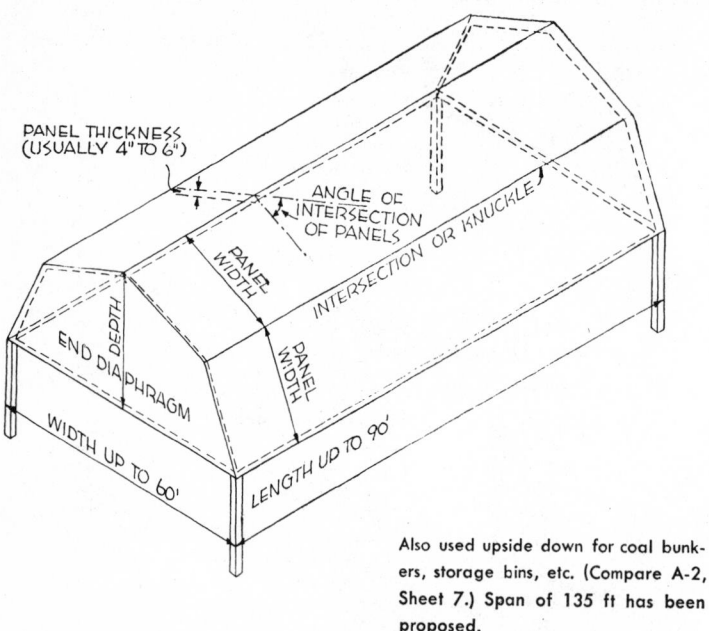

PANEL THICKNESS (USUALLY 4" TO 6")
ANGLE OF INTERSECTION OF PANELS
INTERSECTION OR KNUCKLE
PANEL WIDTH
END DEPTH
END DIAPHRAGM
PANEL WIDTH
WIDTH UP TO 60'
LENGTH UP TO 90'

Also used upside down for coal bunkers, storage bins, etc. (Compare A-2, Sheet 7.) Span of 135 ft has been proposed.

These are approximations to the curved shells made by flat panels. They bear a relationship to curved shells which is similar to that of a rigid frame to an arch. The transverse bending moments in the panel slabs are much greater than those of a curved shell, and the thickness must be greater. Each panel can be considered as supported at the intersection lines or knuckles and becomes one span in a system of continuous beams.

In the longitudinal direction there is a gradual transition from a pure shell effect for shells with panels which are wide in relation to length to a pure bending effect for shells with panels which are long compared to width. In the latter case the shell may be considered as a beam and stresses figured from the moment of inertia of the whole cross section.

Although prismatic shells are rarely used for very long spans, because the thickness of concrete and the dead load are greater than for curved shells, they may be more economical for shorter spans. The savings on formwork may offset the cost of additional concrete.

Simply Supported Single Shell (Compare A-1, Sheet 6)

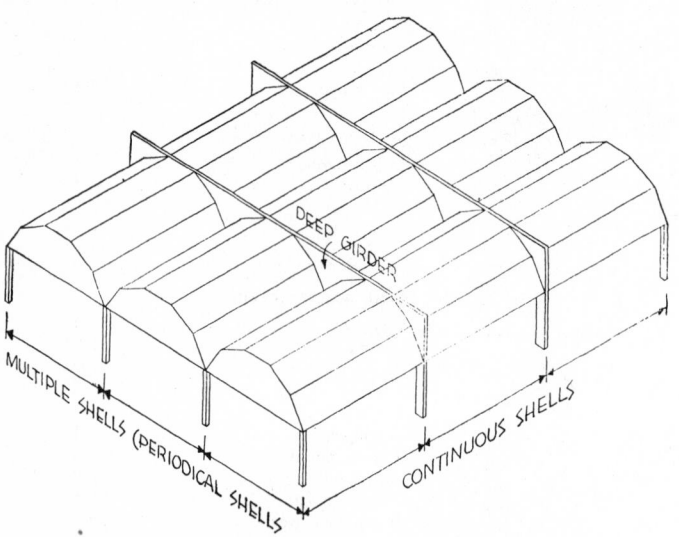

DEEP GIRDER
MULTIPLE SHELLS (PERIODICAL SHELLS)
CONTINUOUS SHELLS

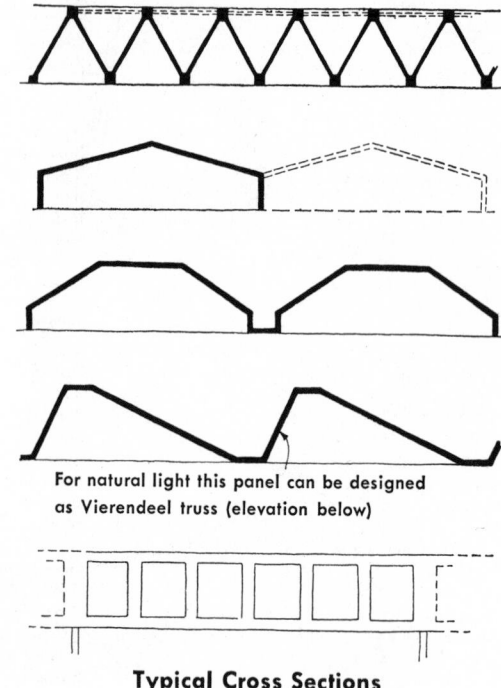

For natural light this panel can be designed as Vierendeel truss (elevation below)

Typical Cross Sections

In addition to prismatic shells which approximate the shells of single curvature, prismatic shells can also be used to approximate shells of double curvature (compare B-1, Sheet 8, and B-2, Sheet 12):

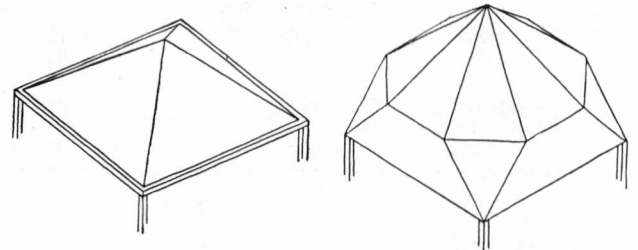

Innumerable crystalline shapes are possible. They may be used as shown or upside down.

REFERENCES:

American Concrete Institute Journal, Feb., 1953. H. Craemer: "Design of Prismatic Shells"

Ditto—Jan., 1947. G. Winter and M. Pei "Hipped Plate Construction."

Also Articles in Publications of Int'l Ass'n For Bridge & Structural Engineering

Weights of miscellaneous materials

	Weight, lb per cu ft			Weight, lb per cu ft			Weight, lb per cu ft
Metals, alloys, ores			**Timber, seasoned (Cont.)**			**Minerals (Cont.)**	
Aluminum; cast-hammered	165		Chestnut	30		Slag (Cont.)	
bronze	481		Cypress	32		machine	96
Antimony	416		Ebony	76		sand	52
Brass, cast-rolled	526		Fir; Douglas	34		Sandstone, bluestone	147
Bronze, 7.9 to 14% Sn	552		eastern	26		Shale, slate	172
Chromium	428		Elm, rock	44		Soapstone, talc	169
Copper; cast-rolled	556		Hemlock, eastern	28			
ore, pyrites	262		Hickory	51		**Stone, quarried, piled**	
Gold; cast-hammered	1205		Locust	48		Basalt, granite, gneiss	96
bars, stacked	1133		Maple; hard	42		Limestone, marble, quartz	95
coin in bags	1084		soft	34		Sandstone	82
Iron; cast, pig	450		Oak; red	44		Shale	92
wrought	480		white	46		Greenstone, hornblende	107
steel	489		Pine; Norway	32			
spiegel-eisen	468		ponderosa	28		**Bituminous substances**	
ferro-silicon	437		white	25		Asphaltum	81
ore, hematite	325		yellow, long-leaf	41		Coal; anthracite	97
ore, hematite, in bank	160–180		yellow, short-leaf	35		bituminous	84
ore, hematite, loose	130–160		Poplar	30		lignite	78
ore, limonite	237		Redwood, California	28		peat, turf, dry	47
ore, magnetite	315		Spruce, white, black	28		charcoal, pine	23
slag	172		Walnut; black	38		charcoal, oak	33
Lead	710		white (butternut)	27		coke	75
ore, galena	465					Graphite	135
Magnesium	109		**Various liquids**			Paraffine	56
Manganese	456		Alcohol, 100%			Petroleum; crude	55
Mercury	848		Acids; muriatic 40%	75		refined	50
Molybdenum	562		nitric 91%	94		benzine	46
Nickel	545		sulphuric 87%	112		gasoline	42
monel metal	556		Lye, soda, 66%			Pitch	69
Platinum, cast-hammered	1330		Oils; vegetable	58		Tar, bituminous	75
Silver, cast-hammered	656		mineral, lubricants	57			
bars, stacked	590		Water; 4° C, max. density	62.428		**Coal and coke, piled**	
coin in bags	590		100° C	59.830		Coal; anthracite	47–58
Tin; cast-hammered	459		ice	57.2		bituminous, lignite	40–54
babbit metal	443		snow, fresh fallen	8		peat, turf	20–26
ore, cassiterite	418		sea water	64		charcoal	10–14
Tungsten	1180					coke	23–32
Vanadium	350		**Minerals**				
Zinc; cast-rolled	449		Asbestos	153		**Earth, etc., excavated**	
ore, blende	253		Barytes	281		Clay; dry	63
			Basalt	184		damp, plastic	110
Various solids			Bauxite	159		Clay and gravel, dry	100
Carbon, amorphous, graphitic	129		Borax	109		Earth; dry, loose	76
Cement, portland, loose	90		Chalk	137		dry, packed	95
Cinders, dry, in bulk	45		Clay, marl	137		moist, loose	78
Cork	15		Dolomite	181		moist, packed	96
Fats	58		Feldspar, orthoclase	159		mud, flowing	108
Glass; common, plate	160		Gneiss, serpentine	159		mud, packed	115
crystal	184		Granite, syenite	175		Riprap; limestone	80–85
flint	220		Gravel, dry	104		sandstone	90
Phosphorus; white	114		Greenstone, trap	187		shale	105
Porcelain, china	150		Gypsum; alabaster	159		Sand, gravel, dry; loose	90–105
Resins, Rosin, Amber	67		loose	70		packed	100–120
Rubber, caoutchouc	58		Hornblende	187		wet	118–120
Sand; clean and dry	90		Lime, hydrated; loose	32			
river, dry	106		compacted	45		**Excavations in water**	
Silicon	155		Limestone, marble	165		Sand or gravel	60
Sulphur, amorphous	128		Magnesite	187		with clay	65
Wax	60		Phosphate rock, apatite	200		Clay	80
			Porphyry	172		River mud	90
Timber, seasoned			Pumice, natural	40		Soil	70
(Moisture content 12%)			Quartz, flint	165		Stone riprap	65
Ash, white	41		Slag; bank	70			
Cedar, white, red	22		bank screenings	108			

MINIMUM DESIGN LOADS

The following data on minimum design loads have been adapted from *American* *Standard Building Code Requirements for Minimum Design Loads in Buildings and Other Structures (ASA A58.1–1955),* sponsored by the National Bureau of Standards.

Dead loads—weights of building materials and constructions

Weights of masonry include mortar but not plaster. For plaster, add 5 psf for each face plastered. Average values are given. In some cases there is a considerable range of weight for the same construction.

	Load, psf		Load, psf		Load, psf
Walls		**Partitions (Cont.)**		**Roof and wall coverings (Cont.)**	
Clay brick; 4-in., high-absorption	34	Gypsum block; 2-in.	9½	Copper or tin	1
4-in., medium-absorption	39	3-in.	10½	Corrugated asbestos-cement roofing	4
4-in., low-absorption	46	4-in.	12½	Corrugated iron	2
8-in., high-absorption	69	5-in.	14	Fiberboard, ½-in.	¾
8-in., medium-absorption	79	6-in.	18½	Gypsum sheathing, ½-in.	2
8-in., low-absorption	89	Solid plaster; 2-in.	20	Skylight, metal frame, ⅜-in. wire glass	8
12½-in., high-absorption	100	4-in.	32	Slate; ³⁄₁₆-in.	7
12½-in., medium-absorption	115	Hollow plaster, 4-in.	22	¼-in.	10
12½-in., low-absorption	130	Concrete block; 4-in., heavy-aggregate	30	Wood sheathing, per inch of thickness	3
17-in., high-absorption	134	4-in., light-aggregate	20	Wood shingles	3
17-in., medium-absorption	155	6-in., heavy-aggregate	42		
17-in., low-absorption	173	6-in., light-aggregate	28		
22-in., high-absorption	168	8-in., heavy-aggregate	54		Load lb per cu ft
22-in., medium-absorption	194	8-in., light-aggregate	34		
22-in., low-absorption	216	12-in., heavy-aggregate	85	**Materials**	
Sand-lime brick; 4-in.	38	12-in., light-aggregate	55	Cast-stone masonry (cement, stone, sand)	144
8-in.	74	Wood studs, 2x4-in.; unplastered	4	Cinder fill	57
12½-in.	105	plastered one side	12	Concrete, plain; cinder	108
17-in.	138	plastered two sides	20	expanded-slag aggregate	100
22-in.	173			haydite (burned-clay aggregate)	90
Concrete brick; 4-in., heavy-aggregate	46	**Glass-block masonry**		slag	132
4-in., light-aggregate	33	4-in. glass-block walls and partitions	18	stone (including gravel)	144
8-in., heavy-aggregate	89			vermiculite and perlite aggregate, nonloadbearing	25–50
8-in., light-aggregate	68	**Split furring tile**		other light aggregate, load-bearing	70–105
12½-in., heavy-aggregate	130	1½-in.	8		
12½-in., light-aggregate	98	2-in.	8½	Concrete, reinforced; cinder	111
17-in., heavy-aggregate	174			slag	138
17-in., light-aggregate	130	**Concrete slabs per inch of thickness**		stone (including gravel)	150
22-in., heavy-aggregate	216	Reinforced; stone	12½	Masonry, ashlar; granite	165
22-in., light-aggregate	160	cinder	9¼	crystalline limestone	165
Brick, 4-in.; with 4-in. loadbearing structural clay-tile backing	60	lightweight	9	oolitic limestone	135
with 8-in. loadbearing structural clay-tile backing	75	Plain; stone	12	marble	173
Brick, 8-in., with 4-in. loadbearing structural clay-tile backing	102	cinder	9	sandstone	144
Structural clay tile; 8-in. load-bearing	42	lightweight	8½	Masonry, brick; hard (low-absorption)	130
12-in. loadbearing	58	**Ceilings**		medium (medium-absorption)	115
Concrete block; 8-in., heavy-aggregate	55	Plaster on tile or concrete	5	soft (high-absorption)	100
8-in., light-aggregate	37	Plaster on wood lath	8	Masonry, rubble; granite	153
12-in., heavy-aggregate	85	Suspended metal lath and gypsum plaster	10	crystalline limestone	147
12-in., light-aggregate	55	Suspended metal lath and cement plaster	15	oolitic limestone	138
Furring tile, 2-in., one side of masonry wall, add to above figures	12			marble	156
		Roof and wall coverings		sandstone	137
Partitions		Asphalt shingles	2	Terra cotta, architectural; voids filled	120
Clay tile; 3-in.	17	Cement-asbestos shingles	4	voids unfilled	72
4-in.	18	Cement tile	16	Timber, seasoned; commercial white ash	41
6-in.	28	Clay tile (for mortar add 10 lb.)		commercial red and white oak	45
8-in.	34	2-in. book tile	12	Douglas fir, coast region	34
10-in.	40	3-in. book tile	20	southern cypress	32
Facing tile; 2-in.	15	Roman	12	southern yellow pine	39
4-in.	25	Spanish	19	redwood	28
6-in.	38	Ludowici	10	red, white, and Sitka spruce	28
		Composition; three-ply ready roofing	1		
		four-ply felt and gravel	5½		
		five-ply felt and gravel	6		

Dead loads—weights of building materials and constructions (cont.)

Depth, in. (rib depth + slab thickness)	Width of rib, in.					Add for tapered ends
	4	5	6	7	8	
	Weight, psf					

Ribbed Slabs

12-in. clay-tile fillers:

	4	5	6	7	8	
4 plus 2	49	51	52	54		
6 plus 2	60	63	65	67		
8 plus 2½	79	82	85	87		
10 plus 3	96	100	103	106		
12 plus 3	108	112	116	120		

20-in. metal fillers:

	4	5	6	7	8	
6 plus 2	41	43	45	47		4
8 plus 2½	51	54	57	60		5
10 plus 3	63	67	70	74		5
12 plus 3	69	74	78	82	86	5
14 plus 3	75	81	82	87	91	5

30-in. metal fillers:

	4	5	6	7	8	
6 plus 2½	41	43	45	47		3
8 plus 2½	45	48	50	54		4
10 plus 3	56	59	61	65		4
12 plus 3		63	67	70	73	4
14 plus 3		69	72	76	80	4

2-way clay-tile fillers (12 x 12):

	4	5	6
4 plus 2	61	62	64
6 plus 2	87	89	90
8 plus 2½	100	103	107
10 plus 3	121	126	131
12 plus 3	136	141	146

2-way metal fillers (16 x 16):

	4	5	6
4 plus 2	44	47	50
6 plus 2	55	60	63
8 plus 2½	72	78	83
10 plus 3	91	96	103
12 plus 3	103	111	118
14 plus 3	116	125	133

2-way metal fillers (20 x 20):

	4	5	6
4 plus 2	42	44	46
6 plus 2	50	54	58
8 plus 2½	66	71	76
10 plus 3	83	88	94
12 plus 3	93	100	107
14 plus 3	105	113	120

	Finish floor to top slab, in.	Load, psf
Floor Finish and Fill		
Double ⅞-in. wood on sleepers, light-concrete fill	4	19
Double ⅞-in. wood on sleepers, stone-concrete fill	4	28
Single ⅞-in. wood on sleepers, light-concrete fill	4	23
Single ⅞-in. wood on sleepers, stone-concrete fill	4	40
3-in. wood block on mastic, no fill	3	10
⅞-in. wood block on stone-concrete fill	4	40
1-in. cement finish on stone-concrete fill	4	48
1-in. terrazzo on stone-concrete fill	4	48
Clay tile on stone-concrete fill	4	48
Marble and mortar on stone-concrete fill	4	50
Linoleum on stone-concrete fill	4	46
Linoleum on light-concrete fill	4	27

	Thickness, in.	Load, psf
Floor Finish		
1½-in. asphalt mastic flooring	1½	18
3-in. wood block on ½-in. mortar base	3½	16
Solid flat tile on 1-in. mortar base	2	23
2-in. asphalt block, ½-in. mortar	2½	30
1-in. terrazzo, 2-in. stone concrete	3	38
Waterproofing		
Five-ply membrane	½	5
Five-ply membrane, mortar, stone concrete	5	55
2-in. split tile, 3-in. stone concrete	5	45
Floor Fill		
Cinder concrete, per inch		9
Lightweight concrete, per inch		7
Sand, per inch		8
Stone concrete, per inch		12

Joist size, in.	12-in. spacing, psf	16-in. spacing, psf
Wood-Joist Floors (No Plaster), Double Wood Floor		
2x 6	6	5
2x 8	6	6
2x10	7	6
2x12	8	7
3x 6	7	6
3x 8	8	7
3x10	9	8
3x12	11	9
3x14	12	10

LIVE LOADS

Floor loads: Floors should be designed to support safely the uniformly distributed live loads prescribed in Table 1 or the concentrated load in pounds given in Table 2, whichever produces the greater stresses. Unless otherwise specified, the indicated concentration is assumed to occupy an area of 2½ ft square, so located as to produce the maximum stress conditions in the structural members.

Roof trusses: Any panel point of the lower chord of roof trusses or any point of other primary structural members supporting roofs over garage, manufacturing, and storage floors should be capable of carrying safely a suspended concentrated load of not less than 2,000 lb.

Elevators: All moving elevator loads should be increased 100 per cent for impact. The structural supports should be designed within the limits of deflection prescribed by the *American Standard Safety Code for Elevators, Dumbwaiters, and Esca-*

Table 1.   Minimum uniformly distributed live loads

Occupancy or Use	Live Load lb per sq ft	Occupancy or Use	Live Load lb per sq ft
Apartments (*see* Residential)		Residential:	
Armories and drill rooms	150	Multifamily houses:	
Assembly halls and other places of assembly:		Private apartments	40
Fixed seats	60	Public rooms	100
Movable seats	100	Corridors	60
Balcony (exterior)	100	Dwellings:	
Bowling alleys, poolrooms, and similar		First floor	40
recreational areas	75	Second floor and habitable attics	30
Corridors:		Uninhabitable attics	20
First floor	100	Hotels:	
Other floors, same as occupancy served		Guest rooms	40
except as indicated		Public rooms	100
Dance halls	100	Corridors serving public rooms	100
Dining rooms and restaurants	100	Public corridors	60
Dwellings (*see* Residential)		Private corridors	40
Garages (passenger cars)	100	Reviewing stands and bleachers*	100
Floors shall be designed to carry 150		Schools:	
percent of the maximum wheel load		Classrooms	40
anywhere on the floor.		Corridors	100
Grandstands (*see* Reviewing stands)		Sidewalks, vehicular driveways, and yards,	
Gymnasiums, main floors and balconies	100	subject to trucking	250
Hospitals:		Skating rinks	100
Operating rooms	60	Stairs, fire escapes, and exitways	100
Private rooms	40	Storage warehouse, light	125
Wards	40	Storage warehouse, heavy	250
Hotels (*see* Residential)		Stores:	
Libraries:		Retail:	
Reading rooms	60	First-floor, rooms	100
Stack rooms	150	Upper floors	75
Manufacturing	125	Wholesale	125
Marquees	75	Theaters:	
Office buildings:		Aisles, corridors, and lobbies	100
Offices	80	Orchestra floors	60
Lobbies	100	Balconies	60
Penal institutions:		Stage floors	150
Cell blocks	40	Yards and terraces, pedestrians	100
Corridors	100		

For detailed recommendations, see American Standard, Places of Outdoor Assembly (Grandstands and Tents) *(ASA Z20.3).*

Table 2.   Concentrated loads

Location	Load, lb
Elevator machine-room grating (on area of 4 sq in.)	300
Finish light floor plate construction (on area of 1 sq in.)	200
Garages, passenger cars (see Table 1)	
Office floors	2,000
Scuttles, skylight ribs, and accessible ceilings	200
Sidewalks	8,000
Stair treads (on center of tread)	300

produces the greater stresses. The unit load recommended is a minimum. It is intended to provide for loads incidental to construction and repair, for sleet loads and minor snow loads, and to ensure reasonable stiffness in the roof. In preparing a local code, the snow records of the nearest U.S. Weather Bureau station or, if Weather Bureau records are not available, the snow-load map shown in Fig. 1 should be consulted and the indicated unit snow load for the locality, if larger, substituted for the minimum. Accordingly, the local code should permit any excess over 20 psf to be reduced for each degree of pitch over 20 deg by $S/40 − \frac{1}{2}$, in which S is the total snow load in pounds per square foot.

Promenade roofs: Roofs used for incidental promenade purposes shall be designed for a minimum live load of 60 psf; and 100 psf if used for roof-garden or assembly purposes.

WIND LOADS

Exterior walls

Every exterior wall should be designed to withstand the pressures (either inward or outward) specified in Table 3.

Roofs

Outward pressures: The roofs of all buildings or other structures should be designed to withstand pressures, acting outward normal to the surface, equal to 1¼ times those specified for the corresponding height zone in which the roof is located. The height is considered as the mean height of the roof structure above the average level of the ground adjacent to the building or other structure, and the pressure is assumed to act on the entire roof area.

Inward pressures: Roofs or sections of roofs with slopes greater than 30 deg should be designed to withstand pressures, acting inward normal to the surface, equal to those specified for the height zone in

lators (ASA A17.1), and *American Standard Inspection of Elevators (Inspectors' Manual)* (ASA A17.2).

Heavy machinery: For the purpose of design, the weight of heavy machinery and moving loads should be increased not less than 25 per cent for impact, unless otherwise specified.

Craneways: All craneways should be designed to resist a horizontal transverse force equal to 25 per cent of the crane capacity plus the weight of the trolley applied one-half at the top of each runway rail for impact; and a horizontal longitudinal force equal to 12½ per cent of the total of the maximum wheel loads applied at the top of each rail.

Reduction in floor live loads

Live loads 100 psf or less: For live loads of 100 psf or less, the design live load on any member supporting 150 sq ft or more may be reduced at the rate of 0.08 per cent per sq ft of area supported by the member, except that no reduction should be made for areas to be occupied as places of public assembly. The reduction should exceed neither R as determined by the following formula, nor 60 per cent:

$$R = 100 \times \frac{D+L}{4.33L}$$

in which

R = reduction in per cent
D = dead load per square foot of area supported by the member
L = design live load per square foot of area supported by the member

Live loads exceeding 100 psf: No reduction should be made for live loads exceeding 100 psf, except for design live loads on columns, which may be reduced 20 per cent.

Roof live loads: No reduction should be applied to the roof live load.

Roof loads

Flat, pitched, or curved roofs: Ordinary roofs—flat, pitched, or curved—should be designed for a load of not less than 20 psf of horizontal projection in addition to the dead load, and in addition to either the wind or the earthquake load, whichever

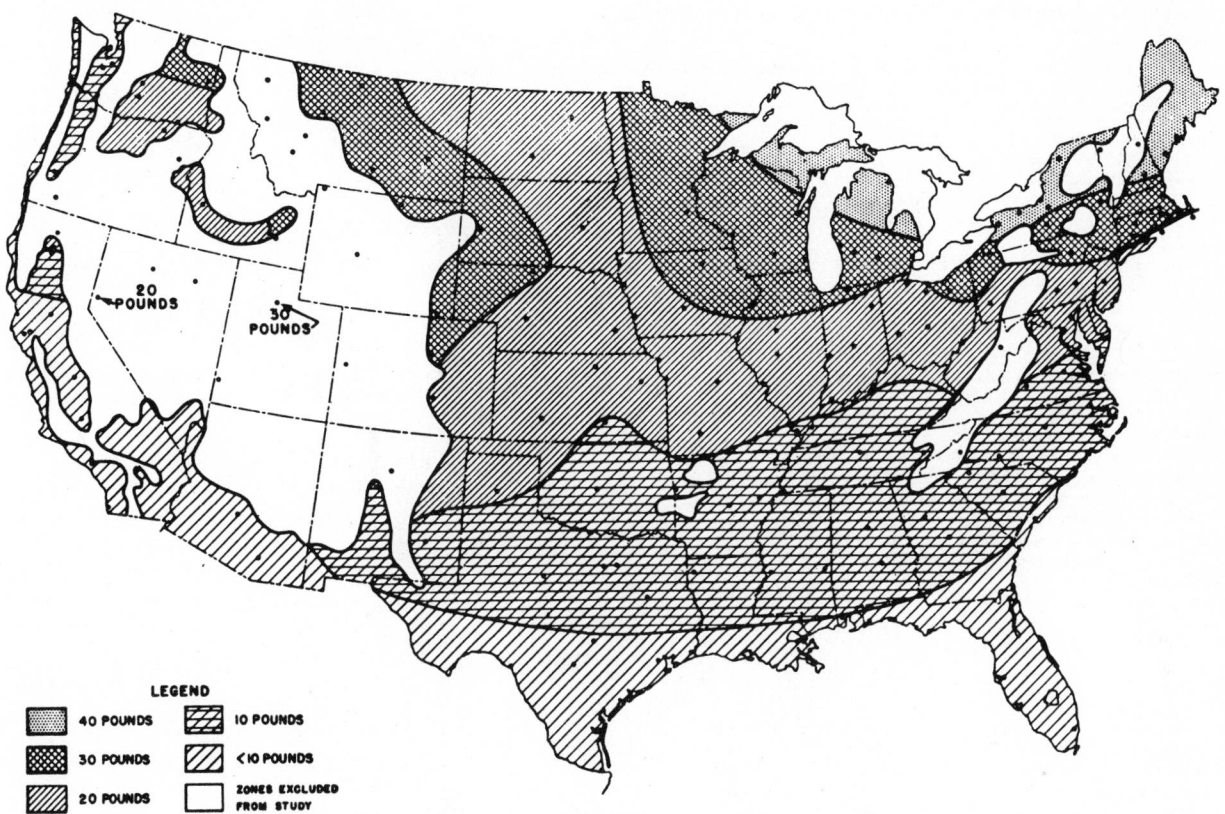

LEGEND

▨ 40 POUNDS	▨ 10 POUNDS		
▨ 30 POUNDS	▨ <10 POUNDS		
▨ 20 POUNDS	☐ ZONES EXCLUDED FROM STUDY		

Fig. 1. Estimated weight in pounds per square foot of seasonal snowpack equaled or exceeded one year in ten

Table 3. Design wind pressures in pounds per square foot of wall for various height zones

To use this table, select the wind-pressure column that is headed by a value corresponding to the minimum permissible resultant wind pressure indicated for the particular locality in Fig. 2. The figures given are recommended as minimum requirements; they do not provide for tornadoes.

Height Zone Above Ground (ft.)	Minimum Allowable Resultant Wind Pressure, as shown on Map																				
	20			25			30			35			40			45			50		
	inward	outward	total	inward	outward	total	inward	outward	total	inward	outward	total	inward	outward	total	inward	outward	total	inward	outward	total
Less than 30	9	6	15	12	8	20	15	10	25	15	10	25	18	12	30	22	13	35	25	15	40
30 to 49	12	8	20	15	10	25	18	12	30	22	13	35	25	15	40	28	17	45	31	19	50
50 to 99	15	10	25	18	12	30	25	15	40	28	17	45	31	19	50	34	21	55	37	23	60
100 to 499	18	12	30	25	15	40	28	17	45	34	21	55	37	23	60	43	27	70	46	29	75
500 to 1199	22	13	35	28	17	45	34	21	55	37	23	60	43	27	70	49	31	80	55	35	90
1200 & over	25	15	40	31	19	50	37	23	60	43	27	70	49	31	80	55	35	90	62	38	100

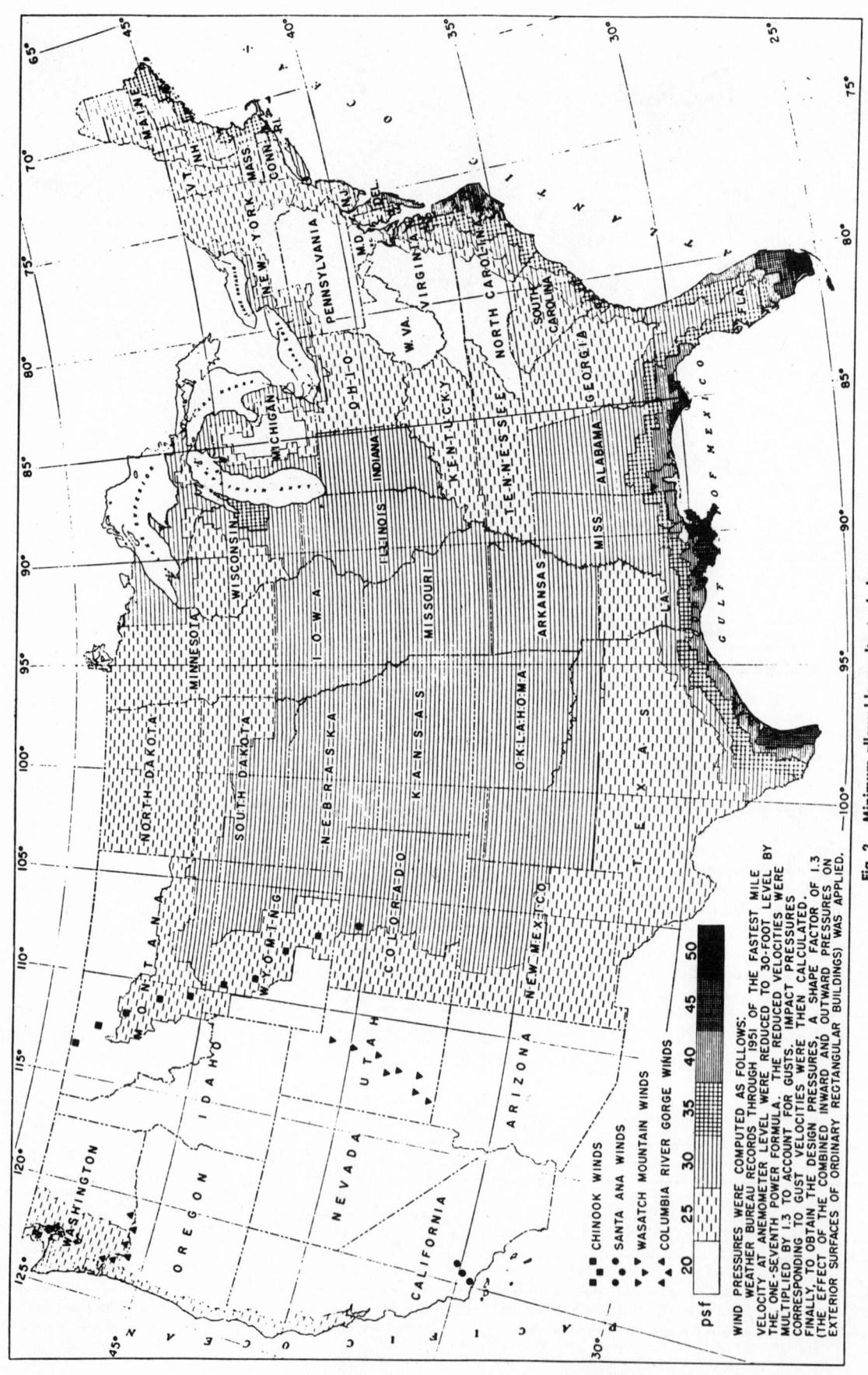

WIND PRESSURES WERE COMPUTED AS FOLLOWS: WIND
VELOCITY AT ANEMOMETER LEVEL WERE REDUCED TO 30-FOOT LEVEL BY
THE ONE-SEVENTH POWER FORMULA. THE REDUCED VELOCITIES WERE
MULTIPLIED BY 1.3 TO ACCOUNT FOR GUSTS. IMPACT PRESSURES
CORRESPONDING TO GUST VELOCITIES WERE THEN CALCULATED.
FINALLY, TO OBTAIN THE DESIGN PRESSURES, A SHAPE FACTOR OF 1.3
(THE EFFECT OF THE COMBINED INWARD AND OUTWARD PRESSURES ON
EXTERIOR SURFACES OF ORDINARY RECTANGULAR BUILDINGS) WAS APPLIED.

Fig. 2. Minimum allowable resultant wind pressures

Live loads for storage warehouses

Material	Pounds per Cubic Foot of Space	Height of Pile, Feet	Pounds per Square Foot of Floor
Produce, Grain, Fruit, Etc.			
Grain, in bulk			
Barley and Corn..............	37	8	296
Oats..........................	26	8	208
Rye and Wheat................	48	8	384
Fruit and Vegetables, in bulk			
Apples, Pears, etc............	38	8	304
Potatoes, Turnips, etc........	44	8	352
Miscellaneous Produce, packed			
Beans, in bags...............	40	8	320
Corn, in bags................	31	8	248
Cornmeal, in barrels..........	37	6½	240
Oats, in bags................	26	9	234
Rice, in bags................	58	5	290
Wheat, in bags...............	39	8	312
Wheat Flour, in barrels.......	40	7	280
Hay, in bales, not compressed.......	14	9	126
Hay, in bales, compressed....	24	9	216
Straw, in bales, compressed.........	19	9	171
Groceries			
Miscellaneous Articles, packed			
Butter, Lard, etc., in barrels.........	32	6	192
Canned Goods, Preserves, etc., in cases	58	6	348
Cheese........................	30	8	240
Coffee, green, in bags.........	39	8	312
Coffee, roasted, in bags......	33	8	264
Dates and Figs, in cases, average....	65	5	325
Meat, Beef, Pork, etc., in barrels....	37	5	185
Molasses, in barrels..........	48	5	240
Salt, finely ground, in sacks..	60	5	300
Soap Powder, in cases........	38	8	288
Starch, in barrels............	25	7	175
Sugar, in barrels.............	43	5	215
Tea, in chests................	25	8	200
Wines, Liquors, etc., in barrels......	48	5	240
Dry Goods, Cotton, Wool, Etc.			
Cotton, in bales, compressed, average...	25	9	225
" unbleached goods, in bales.....	24	9	216
" tickings and duck, in bales.....	35	8	280
" printed goods, in bales.........	19	9	171
" printed goods, in cases........	31	8	248
" quilts and flannels, in cases....	16	9	144
" yarn, in cases..........	25	8	200
Hemp, in bales, compressed......	22	8	176
" Manila, in bales, compressed...	26	9	234
" Sisal, in bales, compressed......	24	9	216
" Tow, in bales, compressed......	29	9	261
" Burlaps, in bales, compressed...	43	6	258
Jute, in bales, compressed...........	41	6	246
Linen, bleached goods, in cases.......	35	7	245
" damask goods, in cases........	50	5	250
Wool, in bales, not compressed.......	13	9	117
" in bales, compressed........	48	5	240
" dress goods, flannels, in cases..	18	9	162
" worsted goods, in cases........	27	9	243
Rags, in bales, compressed...........	19	9	171
Excelsior, in bales, compressed........	19	9	171

Material	Pounds per Cubic Foot of Space	Height of Pile, Feet	Pounds per Square Foot of Floor
Drugs, Oils, Paints, Etc.			
Chemicals:			
Acids, Muriatic and Nitric, in carboys	45	1⅔	75
" Sulphuric, in carboys........	60	1⅔	100
Ammonia, in carboys..........	30	1⅔	50
Alum, Pearl Alum, in barrels.......	33	7	231
Bleaching Powder, in hogsheads....	31	3⅓	103
Copper Sulphate, Blue Vitriol, in bbls.	45	5	225
Soda, Caustic Soda, in iron drums....	88	3⅓	294
Soda, Soda Ash, in hogsheads......	62	2¾	170
Soda Crystals, Sal Soda, in barrels..	30	5	150
Soda Nitrate, Niter, in barrels......	45	5	225
Soda Silicate, in barrels...........	53	5	265
Zinc Sulphate, White Vitriol, in barrels	40	5	200
Oils, Fats, Resins, etc.:			
Glycerine, in cases............	52	6	312
Oils, Animal, Lard, etc., in barrels....	34	6	204
" Vegetable, Linseed, in barrels..	36	6	216
" Mineral, Lubricants, in barrels..	35	6	210
" Petroleum, Kerosene, in barrels..	33	6	198
" Naphtha, Gasolene, in barrels..	28	6	168
Rosin, in barrels.............	48	6	288
Shellac Gum, in boxes.........	38	6	228
Tallow, in barrels............	37	6	222
Dye Stuffs, Paints, etc.:			
Indigo, in boxes..............	43	6	258
Logwood Extract, in boxes.........	70	4½	315
Sumac, in boxes..............	39	5	195
Red Lead, Litharge, dry, in barrels..	132	3¾	495
White Lead, dry, in barrels.......	86	4¾	409
White Lead, paste, in cans.......	174	3½	609
Building Materials			
Cement, Natural, in barrels.......	59	6	354
" Portland, in barrels........	73	6	438
Lime, Quick Lime, ground, in barrels..	50	5	250
Plaster of Paris, ground in barrels......	53	5	265
Sheet Metal and Wire			
Sheet Tin, in boxes.................	278	1½	417
Wire, insulated copper, in coils........	63	5	315
" galvanized iron, in coils..........	74	4½	333
" magnet wire, on spools.........	75	6	450
Miscellaneous			
Chinaware, Glassware, in crates........	40	8	320
" in casks.........	14	9	126
Glass, in boxes....................	60	6	360
Hardware, door and sash checks, in cases	46	6	276
" hinges, in cases.........	64	6	384
" locks, in cases..........	31	6	186
" screws, in boxes.........	101	4	404
Hides, raw, not compressed, in bales....	13	10	130
" raw, compressed, in bales.......	23	10	230
Leather, in bales.................	16	10	160
Paper, calendered paper.............	50	6	300
" newspaper, manila, strawboards..	35	6	210
" writing paper...............	64	6	384
Rope in Coils.....................	42	6	252

which the roof is located, and applied to the windward slope only.

Eaves and cornices: Overhanging eaves and cornices should be designed to withstand outward pressures equal to twice those specified in Table 3.

Anchorage: Adequate anchorage of the roof to walls and columns, and of walls and columns to the foundations, should be provided to resist overturning, uplift, and sliding.

Chimneys, tanks, and towers

Chimneys, tanks, and solid towers should be designed to withstand the pressures specified in Table 3, multiplied by the following factors:

Horizontal cross section	Factor
Square or rectangular	1.00
Hexagonal or octagonal	0.80
Round or elliptical	0.60

Overturning and sliding

Overturning: The overturning moment due to the wind load should not exceed 66⅔ per cent of stability of the building or other structure due to the dead load only, unless the building or other structure is anchored to resist the excess overturning moment without exceeding the allowable stresses for the materials used. The axis of rotation for computing the overturning moment and the moment of stability should be taken as the intersection of the outside wall line on the leeward side and the plane representing the average elevation of the bottoms of the footings. The weight of earth superimposed over footings may be used in computing the moment of stability due to dead load.

Sliding: If the total resisting force due to friction is insufficient to prevent sliding, the building or other structure should be anchored to withstand the excess sliding force without exceeding the allowable stresses for the materials used. Anchors provided to resist overturning moment may also be considered as providing resistance to sliding.

Stresses during erection

Provision should be made for wind stress during erection of the building or other structure.

STRUCTURAL DESIGN—1
Beam formulae

NOMENCLATURE W = Load in lbs., L = Length in ft., R = Reaction in lbs., V = Shear in lbs., M = Bending moment in ft. lbs., D = Deflection in feet, a = Spacing, b = Spacing, x = Distance, E = Modulus of elasticity, I = Moment of inertia, < = Less than, > = Greater than.

DIAGRAMS	REACTIONS = R SHEAR = V	BENDING MOMENT = M	DEFLECTION = D

CASE 1. - Beam Supported Both Ends - Continuous Load, Uniformly Distributed.

$$R = R_1 = V\,(\text{max.}) = \frac{W}{2}$$

At x:
$$V = \frac{W}{2} - \frac{Wx}{L}$$

At center:
$$M\,(\text{max.}) = \frac{WL}{8}$$

At x:
$$M = \frac{Wx}{2L}(L-x)$$

At center:
$$D\,(\text{max.}) = \frac{5}{384}\frac{WL^3}{EI}$$

At x:
$$D = \frac{Wx}{24\,EIL}\left(L^3 - 2Lx^2 + x^3\right)$$

CASE 2. - Beam Supported Both Ends - Concentrated Load at Any Point.

$$R = \frac{Wb}{L}$$
$$R_1 = \frac{Wa}{L}$$

V (max.) = R when a < b and R_1 when a > b

At x:
$$V = \frac{Wb}{L}$$

At point of load:
$$M\,(\text{max.}) = \frac{Wab}{L}$$

At x: when x < a
$$M = \frac{Wbx}{L}$$

At x: when $x = \sqrt{a(a+2b)\div 3}$ and a > b
$$D\,(\text{max.}) = Wab\,(a+2b)\sqrt{3a(a+2b)} \div 27\,EIL$$

At x: when x < a
$$D = \frac{Wbx}{6\,EIL}\left[2L(L-x) - b^2 - (L-x)^2\right]$$

At x: when x > a
$$D = \frac{Wa(L-x)}{6\,EIL}\left[2Lb - b^2 - (L-x)^2\right]$$

CASE 3. - Beam Supported Both Ends - Two Unequal Concentrated Loads, Unequally Distributed.

$$R = \frac{1}{L}\left[W.(L-a) + W_1 b\right]$$
$$R_1 = \frac{1}{L}\left[Wa + W_1(L-b)\right]$$

V (max.) = Maximum Reaction

At x: when x > a and < (L-b)
$$V = R - W$$

At point of load W:
$$M = \frac{a}{L}\left[W(L-a) + W_1 b\right]$$

At point of load W_1:
$$M_1 = \frac{b}{L}\left[Wa + W_1(L-b)\right]$$

At x: when x > a or < (L-b)
$$M = W\frac{a}{L}(L-x) + W_1\frac{bx}{L}$$

CASE 4. - Beam Supported Both Ends - Three Unequal Concentrated Loads, Unequally Distributed.

$$R = \frac{Wb + W_1 b_1 + W_2 b_2}{L}$$
$$R_1 = \frac{Wa + W_1 a_1 + W_2 a_2}{L}$$

V (max.) = Maximum Reaction

At x: when x > a and < a_1
$$V = R - W$$

At x: when x > a_1 and < a_2
$$V = R - W - W_1$$

At x: when x = a
$$M = Ra$$

At x: when x = a_1
$$M_1 = Ra_1 - W(a_1 - a)$$

At x: when x = a_2
$$M_2 = Ra_2 - W(a_2 - a) - W_1(a_2 - a_1)$$

M (max.) = M when W = R or > R

M (max.) = M_1 when $\begin{cases} W_1 + W = R \text{ or} > R \\ W_1 + W_2 = R_1 \text{ or} > R_1 \end{cases}$

M (max.) = M_2 when $W_2 = R_1$ or > R_1

CASE 5. - Beam Fixed Both Ends - Continuous Load, Uniformly Distributed.

$$R = R_1 = V\,(\text{max.}) = \frac{W}{2}$$

At x:
$$V = \frac{W}{2} - \frac{Wx}{L}$$

At center:
$$M\,(\text{max.}) = \frac{WL}{24}$$

At supports:
$$M_1\,(\text{max.}) = \frac{WL}{12}$$

At x:
$$M = \frac{W}{2L}\left(-\frac{L^2}{6} + Lx - x^2\right)$$

At center:
$$D\,(\text{max.}) = \frac{1}{384}\frac{WL^3}{EI}$$

At x:
$$D = \frac{Wx^2}{24\,EIL}\left(L^2 - 2Lx + x^2\right)$$

CASE 6. - Beam Fixed Both Ends - Concentrated Load at Any Point.

$$R = W\left(\frac{b^2(3a+b)}{L^3}\right)$$
$$R_1 = W\left(\frac{a^2(3b+a)}{L^3}\right)$$

V (max.) = R when a < b
= R_1 when a > b

At x: when x < a
$$V = R$$

At support R:
$$M_1 \left(\begin{matrix}\text{max. neg. mom.}\\ \text{when } b > a\end{matrix}\right) = -W\frac{ab^2}{L^2}$$

At support R_1:
$$M_2 \left(\begin{matrix}\text{max. neg. mom.}\\ \text{when } a > b\end{matrix}\right) = -W\frac{a^2 b}{L^2}$$

At point of load:
$$M\,(\text{max.}) = Ra + M_1 = Ra - W\frac{ab^2}{L^2}$$

At x:
$$M = Rx - W\frac{ab^2}{L^2}$$

At x: when $x = \frac{2aL}{3a+b}$ and a > b
$$D\,(\text{max.}) = \frac{2W\,a^3 b^2}{3\,EI\,(3a+b)^2}$$

when x < a
$$D = \frac{W\,b^2 x^2}{6\,EIL^3}\left(3aL - 3ax - bx\right)$$

NOMENCLATURE W=Load in lbs., L=Length in ft., R=Reaction in lbs., V=Shear in lbs., M=Bending moment in ft. lbs., D=Deflection in feet, a=Spacing, b=Spacing, x=Distance, E=Modulus of elasticity, I=Moment of inertia, <=Less than, >=Greater than.

DIAGRAMS	REACTIONS=R SHEAR=V	BENDING MOMENT=M	DEFLECTION = D

CASE 7. - Beam Fixed at One End (Cantilever) - Continuous Load, Uniformly Distributed.

$R_1 = V \text{ (max.)} = W$

At x: $V = \dfrac{Wx}{L}$

At fixed end: $M \text{ (max.)} = \dfrac{WL}{2}$

At x: $M = \dfrac{Wx^2}{2L}$

At free end: $D \text{ (max.)} = \dfrac{WL^3}{8EI}$

At x: $D = \dfrac{W}{24EIL}\left(x^4 - 4L^3x + 3L^4\right)$

CASE 8. - Beam Fixed at One End (Cantilever) - Concentrated Load at Any Point.

$R_1 = V \text{ (max.)} = W$

At x: when $x > a$
$V = W$

At x: when $x < a$
$V = 0$

At fixed end: $M \text{ (max.)} = Wb$

At x: when $x > a$
$M = W(x-a)$

At free end: $D \text{ (max.)} = \dfrac{WL^3}{6EI}\left[2 - \dfrac{3a}{L} + \left(\dfrac{a}{L}\right)^3\right]$

At point of load: $D = \dfrac{W}{3EI}(L-a)^3$

At x: when $x > a$
$D = \dfrac{W}{6EI}\left(\begin{array}{l}-3aL^2 + 2L^3 + x^3 - \\ 3ax^2 - 3L^2x + 6aLx\end{array}\right)$

CASE 9. - Beam Fixed at One End, Supported at Other - Concentrated Load at Any Point.

$R = W\left(\dfrac{3b^2L - b^3}{2L^3}\right)$

$R_1 = W\left(\dfrac{3aL^2 - a^3}{2L^3}\right)$

At x: when $x < a$
$V = R$

At x: when $x > a$
$V = R - W$

At point of load: $M \text{ (max.)} = Wa\left(\dfrac{3b^2L - b^3}{2L^3}\right)$

At fixed end: $M_1 \text{ (max.)} = WL\left(\dfrac{3b^2L - b^3}{2L^3}\right) - W(L-a)$

At x: when $x < a$
$M = Wx\left(\dfrac{3b^2L - b^3}{2L^3}\right)$

At x: when $x > a$
$M = Wx\left(\dfrac{3b^2L - b^3}{2L^3}\right) - W(x-a)$

At x: when $x = a = .414L$
$D \text{ (max.)} = .0098\dfrac{WL^3}{EI}$

At x: when $x < a$
$D = \dfrac{1}{6EI}\left[\begin{array}{l}3RL^2x - Rx^3 - \\ 3W(L-a)^2 x\end{array}\right]$

At x: when $x > a$
$D = \dfrac{1}{6EI}\left[\begin{array}{l}R_1(2L^3 - 3L^2x + x^3) - \\ 3Wa(L-x)^2\end{array}\right]$

CASE 10. - Beam Fixed at One End, Supported at Other - Continuous Load, Uniformly Distributed.

$R = \dfrac{3}{8}W$

$R_1 = V \text{ (max.)} = \dfrac{5}{8}W$

At x: $V = \dfrac{3}{8}W - \dfrac{Wx}{L}$

At x: when $x = \dfrac{3}{8}L$
$M \text{ (max.)} = \dfrac{9}{128}WL$

At fixed end: $M_1 \text{ (max.)} = \dfrac{1}{8}WL$

At x: $M = \dfrac{Wx}{L}\left(\dfrac{3}{8}L - \dfrac{1}{2}x\right)$

At x: when $x = .4215L$
$D \text{ (max.)} = .0054\dfrac{WL^3}{EI}$

At x: $D = \dfrac{Wx}{48EIL}\left[-3Lx^2 + 2x^3 + L^3\right]$

CASE 11. - Beam Overhanging Both Supports, Unsymmetrically Placed - Continuous Load, Uniformly Distributed.

$\dfrac{W}{a+L+b} = w = $ load per unit of length
$R = w\left[(a+L)^2 - b^2\right] \div 2L$
$R_1 = w\left[(b+L)^2 - a^2\right] \div 2L$
$V \text{ (max.)} = wa$ or $R - wa$
At x: when $x < a$ $V = w(a-x)$
At x_1: when $x_1 < L$ $V = R - w(a + x_1)$
At x_2: when $x_2 < b$ $V = w(b - x_2)$

At x_1: when $x_1 = \dfrac{R}{w} - a$
$M \text{ (max.)} = R\left(\dfrac{R}{2w} - a\right)$
At R:
$M_1 = \frac{1}{2}wa^2$
At R_1:
$M_1 = \frac{1}{2}wb^2$
At x: when $x < a$ $M = \frac{1}{2}w(a-x)^2$
At x_1: when $x_1 < L$ $M = \frac{1}{2}w(a+x_1)^2 - Rx_1$
At x_2: when $x_2 < b$ $M = \frac{1}{2}w(b - x_2)^2$

CASE 12. - Beam Overhanging Both Supports, Symmetrically Placed - Two Equal Concentrated Loads at Ends.

$R = R_1 = V \text{ (max.)} = \dfrac{W}{2}$

At x: when $x < a$
$V = \dfrac{W}{2}$

At x_1: when $x_1 < L$
$M \text{ (max.)} = \dfrac{Wa}{2}$

At x: when $x < a$
$M = \dfrac{W}{2}(a-x)$

At free ends: $D = \dfrac{Wa^2(3L + 2a)}{12EI}$

At center: $D = \dfrac{WaL^2}{16EI}$

By JOHN G. MASCIONI, P.E. *Associate Professor of Structural Design, School of Architecture, Pratt Institute*

The allowable unit stresses indicated in Table 1 apply to sawn lumber used under continuously dry conditions. Values are taken from the *National Design Specification for Stress-grade Lumber and Its Fastenings*, National Lumber Manufacturers Association (1960). For short-term loading, the allowable stresses should be increased as follows: 15 per cent for two months' duration (as for snow loads), 25 per cent for seven days' duration, 33⅓ per cent for wind or earthquake, and 100 per cent for impact. If a member is to be fully stressed to the maximum allowable stress for many years, either continuously or cumulatively, use stresses 90 per cent of those indicated in the table.

For lumber whose moisture content is at or above the fiber saturation point, the following adjustments should be made: the allowable unit stresses in compression parallel to the grain, c, should be reduced one-tenth; the allowable unit stresses in compression perpendicular to the grain, $c_\perp$, should be reduced one-third; and the values for modulus of elasticity, E, should be reduced one-eleventh.

Lumber classifications

Beams and stringers: Lumber of rectangular cross section, 5 in. or more in thickness and 8 in. or more in width, graded according to its strength in bending when loaded on the narrow face.

Joists and planks: Lumber of rectangular cross section, 2 to 4 in. in thickness and 4 in. or more in width, graded according to its strength in bending when loaded either on the narrow face as a joist or on the wide face as a plank.

Posts and timbers: Lumber of square or approximately square cross section, 5 by 5 in. or larger, graded primarily for use as posts or columns carrying longitudinal loads, but also suitable for miscellaneous uses in which strength in bending is not especially important.

Wood decking

Plank or laminated decks may be used in residential or industrial buildings for floors and roofs. In residential construction, where loads are light, deflection and appearance usually govern design. Since the modulus of elasticity of a species of wood remains the same for all stress grades, however, deflection does not affect grade selection. Growth characteristics are most conspicuous in the low-cost grades and may be used to provide a rustic effect. The high-priced stress grades, in which growth characteristics are negligible, are more suitable for high standards of appearance.

An important consideration in determining the stiffness and deflection of a deck is the arrangement of deck pieces that span supports. There are three basic span types.

Table 1. Allowable unit stresses for stress-grade lumber

f = *extreme fiber stress in bending*; t = *tensile stress parallel to grain*; H = *horizontal shearing stress*; $c_\perp$ = *compressive stress perpendicular to grain*; c = *compressive stress parallel to grain*; E = *modulus of elasticity*; SR = *stress rated*; KD = *kiln dried*.

Species	Use	Grade	Allowable unit stresses, psi				
			f and t	H	c $\perp$	c	E, psi
Cedar, western red	Decking	Select dex	900		240		1,100,000
		Commercial dex	700		240		
Douglas fir, coast region	Light framing	Dense select structural	2,050	120	455	1,500	1,760,000
		Select structural	1,900	120	415	1,400	
		1500 f industrial	1,500	120	390	1,200	
		1200 f industrial	1,200	95	390	1,000	
	Joist and planks	Dense select structural	2,050	120	455	1,650	
		Select structural	1,900	120	415	1,500	
		Dense construction	1,750	120	455	1,400	
		Construction	1,500	120	390	1,200	
		Standard	1,200	95	390	1,000	
	Beams and stringers	Dense select structural	2,050	120	455	1,500	
		Select structural	1,900	120	415	1,400	
		Dense construction	1,750	120	455	1,200	
		Construction	1,500	120	390	1,000	
	Posts and timbers	Dense select structural	1,900	120	455	1,650	
		Select structural	1,750	120	415	1,500	
		Dense construction	1,500	120	455	1,400	
		Construction	1,200	120	390	1,200	
	Decking	Select dex	1,500		390		
		Commercial dex	1,200		390		
Douglas fir	Joist and planks	Dense select structural	2,050	120	455	1,650	1,760,000
		Select structural	1,900	120	415	1,500	
		Dense structural	1,750	120	455	1,400	
		Structural	1,500	120	390	1,200	
		Standard structural	1,200	95	390	1,000	
	Posts and timbers	Dense select structural	1,900	120	455	1,650	
		Select structural	1,750	120	415	1,500	
		Dense structural	1,500	120	455	1,400	
		Structural	1,200	120	390	1,200	
Hemlock, eastern	Joist and planks	Select structural	1,300	85	360	850	1,210,000
		Prime structural	1,200	60	360	775	
		Common structural	1,100	60	360	650	
		Utility structural	950	60	360	600	
	Beams and stringers	Select structural	1,300	85	360	850	
	Posts and timbers	Select structural			360	850	

Table 1 (cont.). Allowable unit stresses for stress-grade lumber

Species	Use	Grade	f and t	H	c ⊥	c	E, psi
			Allowable unit stresses, psi				
Hemlock, west coast	Light framing	Select structural	1,600	100	365	1,100	1,540,000
		1500 f industrial	1,500	100	365	1,000	
		1200 f industrial	1,200	80	365	900	
	Joist and planks	Select structural	1,600	100	365	1,200	
		Construction	1,500	100	365	1,100	
		Standard	1,200	80	365	1,000	
	Beams and stringers	Construction	1,500	100	365	1,000	
	Posts and timbers	Construction	1,200	100	365	1,100	
	Decking	Select dex	1,300		365		
		Commercial dex	1,000		365		
Larch	Joist and planks	Dense select structural	2,050	120	455	1,650	1,760,000
		Select structural	1,900	120	390	1,500	1,760,000
		Dense structural	1,750	120	455	1,400	1,760,000
		Structural	1,500	120	390	1,200	1,760,000
		Standard structural	1,200	95	390	1,000	1,760,000
	Posts and timbers	Dense select structural	1,900	120	455	1,650	1,760,000
		Select structural	1,750	120	390	1,500	1,760,000
		Dense structural	1,500	120	455	1,400	1,760,000
		Structural	1,200	120	390	1,200	1,760,000
Pine, Norway	Joist and planks	Prime structural	1,200	75	360	900	1,320,000
		Common structural	1,100	75	360	775	1,320,000
		Utility structural	950	75	360	650	1,320,000
Pine, southern	2 in. thick	Dense structural 86 KD	3,000	165	455	2,250	1,760,000
		Dense structural 72 KD	2,500	150	455	1,950	
		Dense structural 65 KD	2,250	135	455	1,800	
		Dense structural 58 KD	2,050	120	455	1,650	
		No. 1 dense KD	2,050	135	455	1,750	
		No. 1 KD	1,750	135	390	1,500	
		No. 2 Dense KD	1,750	120	455	1,300	
		No. 2 KD	1,500	120	390	1,100	
		Dense structural 86	2,900	150	455	2,200	
		Dense structural 72	2,350	135	455	1,800	
		Dense structural 65	2,050	120	455	1,600	
		Dense structural 58	1,750	105	455	1,450	
		No. 1 dense	1,750	120	455	1,550	
		No. 1	1,500	120	390	1,350	
		No. 2 dense	1,400	105	455	1,050	
		No. 2	1,200	105	390	900	
	3 and 4 in. thick	Dense structural 86	2,900	150	455	2,200	
		Dense structural 72	2,350	135	455	1,800	
		Dense structural 65	2,050	120	455	1,600	
		Dense structural 58	1,750	105	455	1,450	
		No. 1 dense SR	1,750	120	455	1,750	
		No. 1 SR	1,500	120	390	1,500	
		No. 2 dense SR	1,400	105	455	1,050	
		No. 2 SR	1,200	105	390	900	
	5 in. thick or up	Dense structural 86	2,400	150	455	1,800	
		Dense structural 72	2,000	135	455	1,550	
		Dense structural 65	1,800	120	455	1,400	
		Dense structural 58	1,600	105	455	1,300	
		No. 1 dense SR	1,600	120	455	1,500	
		No. 1 SR	1,400	120	390	1,300	
		No. 2 dense SR	1,400	105	455	1,050	
		No. 2 SR	1,200	105	390	900	
Redwood	Joist and planks } Beams and stringers { Posts and timbers	Dense structural	1,700	110	320	1,450	1,320,000
		Heart structural	1,300	95	320	1,100	
		Dense structural			320	1,450	
		Heart structural			320	1,100	
Spruce, eastern	Joist and planks	1450 f structural grade	1,450	110	300	1,050	1,320,000
		1300 f structural grade	1,300	95	300	975	
		1200 f structural grade	1,200	95	300	900	

Table 2. Properties of sections (S4S)—sawn lumber

The first part of this table lists sizes when used as joists or beams; the second part lists sizes when used as planks. Each part is arranged in the order of ascending section modulus.

Nominal size, in. (bxh)	Surfaced size, in. (bxh)	Area, in.² $A = bh$	Section modulus, in.³ $S = \dfrac{bh^2}{6}$	Moment of inertia, in.⁴ $I = \dfrac{bh^3}{12}$	Weight, lb per lineal ft (Unseasoned at 38 lb per cu ft)	Board feet per lin ft of piece
			Joists and beams			
2x 4	1⅝x 3⅝	5.89	3.56	6.45	1.55	0.67
3x 4	2⅝x 3⅝	9.52	5.75	10.42	2.51	1.00
4x 4	3⅝x 3⅝	13.14	7.94	14.39	3.47	1.33
2x 6	1⅝x 5½	8.94	8.19	22.55	2.36	1.00
3x 6	2⅝x 5½	14.44	13.24	36.41	3.82	1.50
2x 8	1⅝x 7½	12.19	15.23	57.13	3.22	1.33
4x 6	3⅝x 5½	19.94	18.28	50.27	5.26	2.00
2x10	1⅝x 9½	15.44	24.44	116.10	4.07	1.67
3x 8	2⅝x 7½	19.69	24.61	92.29	5.20	2.00
6x 6	5½x 5½	30.25	27.73	76.26	7.98	3.00
4x 8	3⅝x 7½	27.19	33.98	127.44	7.17	2.67
2x12	1⅝x11½	18.69	35.82	205.95	4.93	2.00
3x10	2⅝x 9½	24.94	39.48	187.55	6.58	2.50
2x14	1⅝x13½	21.94	49.36	333.18	5.79	2.33
6x 8	5½x 7½	41.25	51.56	193.36	10.9	4.00
4x10	3⅝x 9½	34.44	54.53	259.00	9.09	3.33
3x12	2⅝x11½	30.19	57.86	332.69	7.97	3.00
8x 8	7½x 7½	56.25	70.31	263.67	14.8	5.33
3x14	2⅝x13½	35.44	79.73	538.21	9.35	3.50
4x12	3⅝x11½	41.69	79.90	459.43	11.0	4.00
6x10	5½x 9½	52.25	82.73	392.96	13.8	5.00
3x16	2⅝x15½	40.69	105.11	814.60	10.7	4.00
4x14	3⅝x13½	48.94	110.11	743.24	12.9	4.67
8x10	7½x 9½	71.25	112.81	535.86	18.8	6.67
6x12	5½x11½	63.25	121.23	697.07	16.7	6.00
10x10	9½x 9½	90.25	142.90	678.76	23.8	8.33
4x16	3⅝x15½	56.19	145.15	1,124.92	14.8	5.33
8x12	7½x11½	86.25	165.31	950.55	22.8	8.00
6x14	5½x13½	74.25	167.06	1,127.67	19.6	7.00
10x12	9½x11½	109.25	209.40	1,204.03	28.8	10.0
6x16	5½x15½	85.25	220.23	1,706.78	22.5	8.0
8x14	7½x13½	101.25	227.81	1,537.73	26.7	9.33
12x12	11½x11½	132.25	253.48	1,457.51	34.9	12.0
6x18	5½x17½	96.25	280.73	2,456.38	25.4	9.0
10x14	9½x13½	128.25	288.56	1,947.80	33.8	11.67
8x16	7½x15½	116.25	300.31	2,327.42	30.7	10.67
6x20	5½x19½	107.25	348.56	3,398.48	28.3	10.0
12x14	11½x13½	155.25	349.31	2,357.86	41.0	14.0
10x16	9½x15½	147.25	380.40	2,948.07	38.9	13.33
8x18	7½x17½	131.25	382.81	3,349.61	34.6	12.00
8x20	7½x19½	146.25	475.3	4,634	38.6	13.3
10x18	9½x17½	166.2	484.9	4,243	43.9	15.0
10x20	9½x19½	185.2	602.1	5,870	48.9	16.7
12x20	11½x19½	224.2	728.8	7,106	59.2	20.0
12x22	11½x21½	247.2	886.0	9,524	65.2	22.0
12x24	11½x23½	270.2	1,058	12,437	71.3	24.0
12x26	11½x25½	293.2	1,246	15,890	77.4	26.0
12x28	11½x27½	316.2	1,500	19,930	83.4	28.0
12x30	11½x29½	339.2	1,668	24,603	89.5	30.0
14x28	13½x27½	371.2	1,701	23,396	98.0	32.7
14x30	13½x29½	398.2	1,958	28,881	105.0	35.0
16x30	15½x29½	457.2	2,248	33,160	121.0	40
			Planks			
4x 2	3⅝x 1⅝	5.9	1.60	1.30	1.55	0.67
6x 2	5½x 1⅝	8.9	2.42	2.01	2.36	1.00
8x 2	7½x 1⅝	12.2	3.30	2.68	3.22	1.33
4x 3	3⅝x 2⅝	9.5	4.16	5.46	2.51	1.00
12x 2	11½x 1⅝	18.7	5.06	4.11	4.93	2.00
6x 3	5½x 2⅝	14.4	6.46	8.48	3.82	1.50
6x 4	5½x 3⅝	19.9	12.32	22.33	5.26	2.00
12x 3	11½x 2⅝	30.2	13.21	17.33	7.97	3.00

Table 3. Properties of sections—structural glued laminated lumber

From Douglas Fir Use Book, *West Coast Lumbermen's Association (1958). Structural glued laminated lumber is any member comprising an assembly of wood laminations in which the grain of all laminations is approximately parallel longitudinally and in which the laminations are bonded with adhesives. The laminations may vary as to species, number, size, shape, and thickness, provided they meet the requirements for density, allowable unit stresses, and the like. This table gives properties of sections of structural glued laminated lumber based on 1⅝-in. laminations. Data are arranged in the order of ascending section modulus.*

Net Finished Size* b × h (in)	Number of 1⅝" Laminations*	Area of Section (Sq In)	Section Modulus $S=\frac{bh^2}{6}$	Moment of Inertia $I=\frac{bh^3}{12}$	Weight in Lb per Lineal Ft at 12% Moisture Content	Total Board Feet Required Per Lineal Foot of Piece
2¼ x 6½	4	14.6	15.8	51.5	3.45	2.00
3¼ x 6½	4	21.1	22.9	74.4	4.98	2.67
2¼ x 8⅛	5	18.3	24.8	101.	4.31	2.50
4¼ x 6½	4	27.6	29.9	97.3	6.52	3.33
5 x 6½	4	32.5	35.2	114.	7.67	4.00
2¼ x 9¾	6	21.9	35.7	174.	5.18	3.00
3¼ x 8⅛	5	26.4	35.8	145.	6.23	3.33
5¼ x 6½	4	34.1	37.0	120.	8.05	4.00
4¼ x 8⅛	5	34.5	46.8	190.	8.15	4.17
2¼ x 11⅜	7	25.6	48.5	276.	6.04	3.50
3¼ x 9¾	6	31.7	51.5	251.	7.48	4.00
5 x 8⅛	5	40.6	55.0	223.	9.59	5.00
5¼ x 8⅛	5	42.7	57.8	235.	10.1	5.00
4¼ x 9¾	6	41.4	67.3	328.	9.78	5.00
3¼ x 11⅜	7	37.0	70.1	399.	8.72	4.67
7 x 8⅛	5	56.9	77.0	313.	13.4	6.67
5 x 9¾	6	48.8	79.2	386.	11.5	6.00
5¼ x 9¾	6	51.2	83.2	406.	12.1	6.00
3¼ x 13	8	42.3	91.6	595.	9.97	5.33
4¼ x 11⅜	7	48.3	91.7	521.	11.4	5.83
5 x 11⅜	7	56.9	108.	613.	13.4	7.00
7 x 9¾	6	68.3	111.	541.	16.1	8.00
5¼ x 11⅜	7	59.7	113.	644.	14.1	7.00
3¼ x 14⅝	9	47.5	116.	847.	11.2	6.00
4¼ x 13	8	55.3	120.	778.	13.0	6.67
5 x 13	8	65.0	141.	915.	15.3	8.00
3¼ x 16¼	10	52.8	143.	1,162.	12.5	6.67
9 x 9¾	6	87.8	143.	695.	20.7	10.00
5¼ x 13	8	68.3	148.	961.	16.1	8.00
7 x 11⅜	7	79.6	151.	859.	18.8	9.33
4¼ x 14⅝	9	62.2	152.	1,108.	14.7	7.50
5 x 14⅝	9	73.1	178.	1,303.	17.3	9.00
4¼ x 16¼	10	69.1	187.	1,520.	16.3	8.33
5¼ x 14⅝	9	76.8	187.	1,369.	18.1	9.00
9 x 11⅜	7	102.	194.	1,104.	24.2	11.67
9 x 13	8	91.0	197.	1,282.	21.5	10.67
5 x 16¼	10	81.3	220.	1,788.	19.2	10.00
4¼ x 17⅞	11	76.0	226.	2,023.	17.9	9.17
5¼ x 16¼	10	85.3	231.	1,877.	20.1	10.00
11 x 11⅜	7	125.	237.	1,349.	29.5	14.00
7 x 14⅝	9	102.	250.	1,825.	24.2	12.00
9 x 13	8	117.	254.	1,648.	27.6	13.33
5 x 17⅞	11	89.4	266.	2,380.	21.1	11.00
4¼ x 19½	12	82.9	269.	2,626.	19.6	10.00
5¼ x 17⅞	11	93.8	280.	2,499.	22.2	11.00
7 x 16¼	10	114.	308.	2,503.	26.8	13.33
11 x 13	8	143.	310.	2,014.	33.8	16.00
4¼ x 21⅛	13	89.8	316.	3,339.	21.2	10.83
5 x 19½	12	97.5	317.	3,090.	23.0	12.00
9 x 14⅝	9	132.	321.	2,346.	31.1	15.00
5¼ x 19½	12	102.	333.	3,244.	24.2	12.00
12½ x 13	8	163.	352.	2,289.	38.4	18.67
5 x 21⅛	13	106.	372.	3,928.	24.9	13.00
7 x 17⅞	11	125.	373.	3,332.	29.5	14.67
5¼ x 21⅛	13	111.	390.	4,124.	26.2	13.00
11 x 14⅝	9	161.	392.	2,867.	38.0	18.00
9 x 16¼	10	146.	396.	3,218.	34.5	16.67
5 x 22¾	14	114.	431.	4,906.	26.9	14.00
7 x 19½	12	137.	444.	4,325.	32.2	16.00
12½ x 14⅝	9	183.	446.	3,258.	43.1	21.00
5¼ x 22¾	14	119.	453.	5,151.	28.2	14.00
9 x 17⅞	11	161.	479.	4,284.	38.0	18.33
11 x 16¼	10	179.	484.	3,933.	42.2	20.00
5 x 24⅜	15	122.	495.	6,034.	28.8	15.00
14½ x 14⅝	9	212.	517.	3,780.	50.1	24.00
5¼ x 24⅜	15	128.	520.	6,336.	30.2	15.00
7 x 21⅛	13	148.	521.	5,499.	34.9	17.33
12½ x 16¼	10	203.	550.	4,470.	47.9	23.33
5 x 26	16	130.	563.	7,323.	30.7	16.00
9 x 19½	12	176.	570.	5,561.	41.4	20.00
11 x 17⅞	11	197.	586.	5,235.	46.4	22.00
5¼ x 26	16	137.	592.	7,690.	32.2	16.00
7 x 22¾	14	159.	604.	6,868.	37.6	18.67
14½ x 16¼	10	236.	638.	5,185.	55.6	26.67
12½ x 17⅞	11	223.	666.	5,949.	52.7	25.67
9 x 21⅛	13	190.	669.	7,071.	44.9	21.67
7 x 24⅜	15	171.	693.	8,448.	40.3	20.00
11 x 19½	12	215.	697.	6,797.	50.6	24.00
14½ x 17⅞	11	259.	772.	6,901.	61.2	29.33
9 x 22¾	14	205.	776.	8,831.	48.3	23.33
7 x 26	16	182.	789.	10,250.	43.0	21.33
12½ x 19½	12	244.	792.	7,724.	57.5	28.00
11 x 21⅛	13	232.	818.	8,642.	54.8	26.00
7 x 27⅝	17	193.	890.	12,300.	45.6	22.67
9 x 24⅜	15	219.	891.	10,860.	51.8	25.00
14½ x 19½	12	283.	919.	8,960.	66.7	32.00
12½ x 21⅛	13	264.	930.	9,820.	62.3	30.33
11 x 22¾	14	250.	949.	10,790.	59.1	28.00
7 x 29¼	18	205.	998.	14,600.	48.3	24.00
9 x 26	16	234.	1,014.	13,180.	55.2	26.67
12½ x 22¾	14	284.	1,078.	12,270.	67.1	32.67
14½ x 21⅛	13	306.	1,078.	11,390.	72.3	34.67
11 x 24⅜	15	268.	1,089.	13,280.	63.3	30.00
7 x 30⅞	19	216.	1,112.	17,170.	51.0	25.33
9 x 27⅝	17	249.	1,145.	15,810.	58.7	28.33
7 x 32½	20	228.	1,232.	20,030.	53.7	26.67
12½ x 24⅜	15	305.	1,238.	15,090.	71.9	35.00
11 x 26	16	286.	1,239.	16,110.	67.5	32.00
14½ x 22¾	14	330.	1,251.	14,230.	77.9	37.33
9 x 29¼	18	263.	1,283.	18,770.	62.1	30.00
7 x 34⅛	21	239.	1,359.	23,180.	56.4	28.00
11 x 27⅝	17	304.	1,399.	19,320.	71.7	34.00
12½ x 26	16	325.	1,408.	18,310.	76.7	37.33
9 x 30⅞	19	278.	1,430.	22,070.	65.6	31.67
14½ x 24⅜	15	353.	1,436.	17,500.	83.4	40.00
7 x 35¾	22	250.	1,491.	26,650.	59.1	29.33
11 x 29¼	18	322.	1,569.	22,940.	75.9	36.00
9 x 32½	20	293.	1,584.	25,750.	69.0	33.33
12½ x 27⅝	17	345.	1,590.	21,960.	81.5	39.67
14½ x 26	16	377.	1,634.	21,240.	89.0	42.67
9 x 34⅛	21	307.	1,747.	29,800.	72.5	35.00
11 x 30⅞	19	340.	1,748.	26,980.	80.2	38.00
12½ x 29¼	18	366.	1,782.	26,070.	86.3	42.00
14½ x 27⅝	17	401.	1,844.	25,470.	94.5	45.33
9 x 35¾	22	322.	1,917.	34,270.	75.9	36.67
11 x 32½	20	358.	1,936.	31,470.	84.4	40.00
12½ x 30⅞	19	386.	1,986.	30,660.	91.1	44.33
14½ x 29¼	18	424.	2,068.	30,240.	100.	48.00
9 x 37⅜	23	336.	2,095.	39,160.	79.4	38.33
11 x 34⅛	21	375.	2,135.	36,430.	88.6	42.00
12½ x 32½	20	406.	2,201.	35,760.	95.9	46.67
9 x 39	24	351.	2,282.	44,490.	82.8	40.00
14½ x 30⅞	19	448.	2,304.	35,560.	106.	50.67
11 x 35¾	22	393.	2,343.	41,880.	92.8	44.00
12½ x 34⅛	21	427.	2,426.	41,390.	101.	49.00
9 x 40⅝	25	366.	2,476.	50,290.	86.3	41.67
14½ x 32½	20	471.	2,553.	41,480.	111.	53.33
11 x 37⅜	23	411.	2,561.	47,860.	97.0	46.00
12½ x 35¾	22	447.	2,663.	47,590.	105.	51.33
9 x 42¼	26	380.	2,678.	56,560.	89.7	43.33
11 x 39	24	429.	2,789.	54,380.	101.	48.00
14½ x 34⅛	21	495.	2,814.	48,020.	117.	56.00
9 x 43⅞	27	395.	2,888.	63,350.	93.2	45.00
12½ x 37⅜	23	467.	2,910.	54,380.	110.	53.67
11 x 40⅝	25	447.	3,026.	61,460.	105.	50.00
14½ x 35¾	22	518.	3,089.	55,210.	122.	58.67
9 x 45½	28	410.	3,105.	70,650.	96.6	46.67
12½ x 39	24	488.	3,169.	61,790.	115.	56.00
11 x 42¼	26	465.	3,273.	69,130.	110.	52.00
14½ x 37⅜	23	542.	3,376.	63,090.	128.	61.33
12½ x 40⅝	25	508.	3,438.	69,840.	120.	58.33
11 x 43⅞	27	483.	3,529.	77,420.	114.	54.00
14½ x 39	24	566.	3,676.	71,680.	133.	64.00
12½ x 42¼	26	528.	3,719.	78,560.	125.	60.67
11 x 45½	28	501.	3,795.	86,350.	118.	56.00
14½ x 40⅝	25	589.	3,988.	81,020.	139.	66.67
12½ x 43⅞	27	548.	4,010.	87,980.	129.	63.00
11 x 47⅛	29	518.	4,071.	95,930.	122.	58.00
12½ x 45½	28	569.	4,313.	98,120.	134.	65.33
14½ x 42¼	26	613.	4,314.	91,130.	145.	69.33
11 x 48¾	30	536.	4,357.	106,200.	127.	60.00
12½ x 47⅛	29	589.	4,627.	109,010.	139.	67.67
11 x 50⅜	31	554.	4,652.	117,180.	131.	62.00
14½ x 43⅞	27	636.	4,652.	102,060.	150.	72.00
12½ x 48¾	30	609.	4,951.	120,680.	144.	70.00
14½ x 45½	28	660.	5,003.	113,820.	156.	74.67
12½ x 50⅜	31	630.	5,287.	133,160.	149.	72.33
14½ x 47⅛	29	683.	5,367.	126,460.	161.	77.33
14½ x 48¾	30	707.	5,743.	139,990.	167.	80.00
14½ x 50⅜	31	730.	6,133.	154,470.	172.	82.67

* With structural glued laminated lumber, many additional sizes may be obtained. Greatest economy will result from the use of standard widths and depths that are multiples of standard board and dimension lumber thicknesses.

The first is the simple span, in which deck pieces of uniform length bear on two supports. This span type produces the maximum deflection. The second is the fully continuous span, in which deck pieces bear on at least three supports. This span type requires great lengths but reduces deflection to less than half that of the simple span. The third is the partially continuous span, in which

at least half the deck pieces extend over one support. There are many methods of developing the latter type, but the use of random-length pieces is the method most frequently used for multiple spans—it is the most economical and reduces the deflection of the simple span by 30 per cent. Although any degree of continuity would have a similar effect on the reduction of bending

moments, allowable loads are conservatively based on $M = wl^2/8$, which corresponds to the moment for a simple span.

Joists and beams

Table 10 indicates the total uniformly distributed loads that joists and beams may support at various span lengths. Values are based on sizes of S4S (surfaced four sides)

Table 4. Total allowable loads for wood decking

The total allowable loads, including the weight of the deck, apply to seasoned lumber used under normal loading conditions.

$E = 1,760,000$ psi and $f = 1,200$ psi. *For other stresses or moduli of elasticity, allowable loads can be determined by direct proportion. Values for deflection are based on random-length decking using the formula*

$$\Delta = \frac{wl^4}{100EI}$$

Span length, ft	Nominal thickness of deck, in.											
	2			3			4			6		
	Deflection		Bending	Deflection		Bending	Deflection		Bending	Deflection		Bending
	$\Delta=1/180$	$\Delta=1/240$	$f=1,200$	$\Delta=1/180$	$\Delta=1/240$	$f=1,200$	$\Delta=1/180$	$\Delta=1/240$	$f=1,200$	$\Delta=1/180$	$\Delta=1/240$	$f=1,200$
	Load, psi											
6	135	102	117	569	427	306						
7	85	64	86	358	268	225						
8	57	43	66	240	180	172	631	474	328			
9	40	30	52	168	126	136	444	333	259			
10	29	22	42	122	92	110	323	242	210			
11	22	17	35	92	69	91	244	182	174	849	637	400
12	17	13	29	72	53	77	188	141	146	654	491	336
13	13	10	25	56	42	65	147	111	124	514	385	286
14				44	34	56	119	89	107	411	309	247
15				37	27	49	96	73	93	335	251	215
16				30	22	43	79	60	82	276	207	189
17				25	18	38	66	50	73	230	173	167
18							56	42	65	194	146	149
19							47	35	58	165	124	134
20							40	30	53	141	106	121

Table 5. Maximum spans for ceiling joists

$E = 1,760,000$ psi and $f = 1,200$ psi. *Design assumptions for deflection and bending are as follows: live load—none; dead load—weight of joist, weight of ceiling at 10 psf.*

Nominal size, in.	Spacing, center to center, in.	Deflection		Bending
		$\Delta=1/240$	$\Delta=1/360$	$f=1,200$
		Span length, ft–in.		
2x 4	12	13– 0	11– 4	15– 8
	16	11–11	10– 5	13–10
	24	10– 6	9– 2	11– 6
2x 6	12	19– 3	16–10	23– 0
	16	17–10	15– 7	20– 5
	24	15–10	13–10	17– 1
2x 8	12	25– 8	22– 5	28– 0
	16	23–10	20–10	27– 2
	24	21– 3	18– 7	22–11
2x10	12	28– 0	27–10	28– 0
	16	28– 0	25–11	28– 0
	24	26– 7	23– 3	28– 0
2x12	12	28– 0	28– 0	28– 0
	16	28– 0	28– 0	28– 0
	24	28– 0	27–10	28– 0

Table 6. Maximum spans for attic-floor joists

$E = 1,760,000$ psi and $f = 1,200$ psi. *Design assumptions for deflection and bending are as follows: live load—20 psf; dead load—weight of joist, weight of floor at 2.5 psf, and weight of ceiling at 10 psf.*

Nominal size, in.	Spacing, center to center, in.	Deflection		Bending
		$\Delta=1/240$	$\Delta=1/360$	$f=1,200$
		Span length, ft–in.		
2x 4	12	9– 1	7–11	9– 2
	16	8– 3	7– 3	8– 0
	24	7– 3	6– 4	6– 7
2x 6	12	13– 8	11–11	13– 9
	16	12– 6	10–11	12– 0
	24	10–11	9– 7	9–10
2x 8	12	18– 5	16– 1	18– 6
	16	16–11	14– 9	16– 2
	24	14–10	13– 0	13– 4
2x10	12	23– 2	20– 3	23– 1
	16	21– 3	18– 7	20– 4
	24	18– 9	16– 4	16–10
2x12	12	27–10	24– 4	27– 8
	16	25– 7	22– 4	24– 5
	24	22– 7	19– 9	20– 3

Table 7. Maximum spans for floor joists

This table is based on the following conditions:

Deflection: Span lengths are based on a limiting deflection equal to 1/360 of the span using a modulus of elasticity of E = 1,760,000 psi. For other moduli of elasticity, multiply the span lengths given below by E/1,760,000. Assumed dead loads are weight of joist, weight of floor at 5 psf.

Bending: Assumed dead loads are weight of joist, weight of floor at 5 psf, and weight of ceiling at 10 psf. If ceiling is not used, the live-load capacity is 10 psf greater.

Nominal size, in.	Spacing, center to center, in.	Deflection $\Delta = 1/360$	Bending $f = 1,200$	Bending $f = 1,500$	Deflection $\Delta = 1/360$	Bending $f = 1,200$	Bending $f = 1,500$
		Live load, 30 psi			Live load, 40 psi		
		Span length, ft–in.			Span length, ft–in.		
2x 6	12	11– 8	11– 8	13– 3	10– 9	10– 8	11–11
	16	10– 8	10– 4	11– 7	9–10	9– 4	10– 5
	24	9– 4	8– 5	9– 6	8– 7	7– 8	8– 6
2x 8	12	15– 9	15– 9	17– 8	14– 7	14– 6	16– 2
	16	14– 5	13– 8	15– 5	13– 4	12– 8	14– 1
	24	12– 8	11– 4	12– 8	11– 8	10– 4	11– 7
2x10	12	19– 9	19–10	22– 2	18– 4	18– 2	20– 4
	16	18– 2	17– 4	19– 5	16–10	15–11	17– 9
	24	16– 0	14– 4	16– 0	14– 9	13– 1	14– 8
2x12	12	23– 9	27– 9	26– 8	22– 1	21–10	24– 5
	16	21–10	24– 4	23– 4	20– 3	19– 2	21– 5
	24	19– 3	20– 3	19– 4	17–10	15– 9	17– 8
3x 6	12	13– 6	14–11	16– 8	12– 6	13– 5	15– 0
	16	12– 4	13– 1	14– 7	11– 5	11– 9	13– 1
	24	10–10	10– 9	12– 1	10– 0	9– 8	10– 9
3x 8	12	18– 2	19– 8	22– 0	16–10	18– 1	20– 3
	16	16– 8	17– 3	19– 4	15– 6	15–10	17– 9
	24	14– 9	14– 3	16– 0	13– 7	13– 1	14– 7
3x10	12	22– 9	24– 7	27– 6	21– 2	22– 8	25– 4
	16	20–11	21– 8	24– 2	19– 5	19–11	22– 3
	24	18– 7	18– 0	20– 1	17– 2	16– 6	18– 5
3x12	12	27– 3	29– 5		25– 5	27– 1	30– 0
	16	25– 2	26– 0	29– 0	23– 5	23–11	26– 8
	24	22– 4	21– 8	24– 3	20– 8	19–10	22– 2
		Live load, 50 psi			Live load, 100 psi		
2x 6	12	10– 1	9–10	11– 0	8– 2	7– 6	8– 4
	16	9– 2	8– 7	9– 7	7– 5	6– 6	7– 3
	24	8– 1	7– 0	7–10	6– 6	5– 4	5–11
2x 8	12	13– 8	13– 4	14–11	11– 1	10– 2	11– 4
	16	12– 6	11– 8	13– 0	10– 2	8–10	9–11
	24	10–11	9– 7	10– 8	8–10	7– 3	8– 1
2x10	12	17– 3	16–10	18–10	14– 1	12–10	14– 4
	16	15– 9	14– 8	16– 5	12–10	11– 2	12– 6
	24	13–10	12– 1	13– 6	11– 3	9– 2	10– 3
2x12	12	20– 9	20– 3	22– 8	17– 0	15– 5	17– 3
	16	19– 0	17– 9	19–10	15– 6	13– 6	15– 1
	24	16– 9	14– 7	16– 4	13– 7	11– 1	12– 4
3x 6	12	11– 9	12– 5	13–10	9– 7	9– 5	10– 7
	16	10– 9	10–10	12– 1	8– 9	8– 3	9– 2
	24	9– 5	8–11	9–11	7– 8	6– 9	7– 6
3x 8	12	15–10	16– 9	18– 9	13– 0	12–10	14– 4
	16	14– 6	14– 8	16– 5	11–10	11– 2	12– 6
	24	12– 9	12– 1	13– 6	10– 5	9– 2	10– 3
3x10	12	19–11	21– 0	23– 6	16– 4	16– 1	18– 0
	16	18– 4	18– 5	20– 7	14–11	14– 1	15– 9
	24	16– 2	15– 2	17– 0	13– 1	11– 7	12–11
3x12	12	24– 0	25– 2	28– 2	19– 9	19– 5	21– 8
	16	22– 0	22– 2	24– 9	18– 1	17– 0	19– 0
	24	19– 5	18– 4	20– 6	15–10	13–11	15– 7

lumber, and for normal conditions of loading. Although the table is not comprehensive, it includes the most commonly used sections for each span length. Total loads, which include the weight of the beam, are given for both a stress condition, W, and deflection, W_Δ. The total allowable load, W, is limited by either the maximum allowable fiber stress in bending, f, or the allowable shearing stress, H. Values in the table are based on 1,500 psi for f and 120 psi for H. The total allowable load limited by deflection, W_Δ, is based on a modulus of elasticity of E = 1,760,000 psi and a maximum deflection of 1/360 of the span.

Table 8. Maximum spans for rafters and roof joists (light roofing)

This table is based on the following conditions:
Deflection: Span lengths are based on a limiting deflection equal to 1/360 of the span using a modulus of elasticity of E = 1,760,000 psi. For other moduli of elasticity, multiply the span lengths given below by E/1,760,000. Assumed dead loads are weight of joist, weight of sheathing at 2.5 psf, and weight of light roofing at 2.5 psf.

Bending: Assumed dead loads are weight of joist, weight of sheathing at 2.5 psf, and weight of light roofing at 2.5 psf.

Nominal size, in.	Spacing, center to center, in.	Deflection Δ = 1/360	Bending f = 1,200	Bending f = 1,500	Deflection Δ = 1/360	Bending f = 1,200	Bending f = 1,500
		Live load, 20 psi			Live load, 30 psi		
		Span length, ft–in.			Span length, ft–in.		
2x 6	12	12–11	15– 6	17– 4	11– 8	13– 3	14–10
	16	11–10	13– 7	15– 2	10– 8	11– 7	12–11
	24	10– 5	11– 2	12– 6	9– 4	9– 6	10– 8
2x 8	12	17– 5	20– 9	23– 3	15– 9	17–10	20– 0
	16	16– 0	18– 3	20– 5	14– 5	15– 8	17– 6
	24	14– 1	15– 2	16–11	12– 8	12–11	14– 5
2x10	12	21–10	25–11	28– 0	19– 9	22– 4	25– 0
	16	20– 1	22–11	25– 7	18– 2	19– 8	22– 0
	24	17– 9	19– 0	21– 3	16– 0	16– 3	18– 2
2x12	12	26– 2	28– 0	28– 0	23– 9	26– 9	28– 0
	16	24– 2	27– 5	28– 0	21–10	23– 7	26– 5
	24	21– 5	22–10	25– 6	19– 3	19– 7	21–10
3x 6	12	14–11	19– 2	21– 5	13– 6	16– 6	18– 6
	16	13– 8	16–11	18–11	12– 4	14– 6	16– 3
	24	12– 1	14– 0	15– 8	10–10	12– 0	13– 5
3x 8	12	20– 0	25– 6	28– 7	18– 2	22– 2	24– 9
	16	18– 5	22– 8	25– 4	16– 8	19– 6	21–10
	24	16– 4	18–11	21– 1	14– 9	16– 2	18– 1
3x10	12	24–11	31– 7	32– 0	22– 9	27– 7	30–10
	16	23– 1	28– 2	31– 6	20–11	24– 5	27– 3
	24	20– 6	23– 8	26– 5	18– 7	20– 4	22– 8
3x12	12	29– 9	32– 0	32– 0	27– 3	32– 0	32– 0
	16	27– 7	32– 0	32– 0	25– 2	29– 2	32– 0
	24	24– 8	28– 3	31– 7	22– 4	24– 4	27– 3
		Live load, 40 psi			Live load, 50 psi		
2x 6	12	10– 9	11– 9	13– 2	10– 1	10– 8	11–11
	16	9–10	10– 3	11– 6	9– 2	9– 4	10– 5
	24	8– 7	8– 5	9– 5	8– 1	7– 8	8– 6
2x 8	12	14– 7	15–11	17– 9	13– 8	14– 6	16– 2
	16	13– 4	13–11	15– 6	12– 6	12– 8	14– 1
	24	11– 8	11– 5	12– 9	10–11	10– 4	11– 7
2x10	12	18– 4	20– 0	22– 4	17– 3	18– 2	20– 4
	16	16–10	17– 6	19– 7	15– 9	15–11	17– 9
	24	14– 9	14– 5	16– 1	13–10	13– 1	14– 8
2x12	12	22– 1	23–11	26– 9	20– 9	21–10	24– 5
	16	20– 3	21– 0	23– 6	19– 0	19– 2	21– 5
	24	17–10	17– 4	19– 5	16– 9	15– 9	17– 8
3x 6	12	12– 6	14– 9	16– 6	11– 9	13– 5	15– 0
	16	11– 5	12–11	14– 5	10– 9	11– 9	13– 1
	24	10– 0	10– 8	11–11	9– 5	9– 8	10– 9
3x 8	12	16–10	19–10	22– 2	15–10	18– 1	20– 3
	16	15– 6	17– 5	19– 5	14– 6	15–10	17– 9
	24	13– 7	14– 5	16– 1	12– 9	13– 1	14– 7
3x10	12	21– 2	24– 9	27– 8	19–11	22– 8	25– 4
	16	19– 5	21–10	24– 5	18– 4	19–11	22– 3
	24	17– 2	18– 1	20– 3	16– 2	16– 6	18– 5
3x12	12	25– 5	29– 7	32– 0	24– 0	27– 1	30– 4
	16	23– 5	26– 1	29– 3	22– 0	23–11	26– 8
	24	20– 8	21– 9	24– 4	19– 5	19–10	22– 2

For conditions that differ from those assumed in the table, allowable loads limited by deflection, W_Δ, may be found by direct proportion. For example, if a species of wood with a modulus of elasticity of 1,540,000 psi is to be used, the total load limited by deflection can be determined by multiplying by the factor 1.54/1.76, or 0.88. If the limiting deflection is to be 1/300 of the span, the allowable load for deflection would be W_Δ multiplied by the factor 360/300, or 1.2.

Conversion of the total allowable load, W, for different stresses is more complicated because W is limited by two stresses,

Table 9. Maximum spans for rafters and roof joists (heavy roofing)

This table is based on the following conditions:
Deflection: *Span lengths are based on a limiting deflection equal to 1/360 of the span using a modulus of elasticity of E = 1,760,000 psi. For other moduli of elasticity, multiply the span lengths given below by E/1,760,000. Assumed dead loads are weight of joist, weight of sheathing at 2.5 psf, and weight of heavy roofing at 8 psf.*
Bending: *Assumed dead loads are weight of joist, weight of sheathing at 2.5 psf, and weight of heavy roofing at 8 psf.*

Nominal size, in.	Spacing, center to center, in.	Deflection Δ = 1/360	Bending f = 1,200	Bending f = 1,500	Deflection Δ = 1/360	Bending f = 1,200	Bending f = 1,500
		Live load, 20 psi			Live load, 30 psi		
		Span length, ft–in.			Span length, ft–in.		
2x 6	12	12– 2	14– 1	15– 9	11– 1	12– 4	13–10
	16	11– 1	12– 4	13–10	10– 2	10–10	12– 1
	24	9– 9	10– 2	11– 4	8–11	8–10	9–11
2x 8	12	16– 5	19– 0	21– 3	15– 1	16– 8	18– 8
	16	15– 0	16– 8	18– 8	13– 9	14– 7	16– 4
	24	13– 3	13– 9	15– 5	12– 1	12– 0	13– 5
2x10	12	20– 7	23– 9	26– 7	18–11	20–11	23– 5
	16	18–11	20–11	23– 5	17– 4	18– 4	20– 6
	24	16– 8	17– 4	19– 5	15– 3	15– 2	16–11
2x12	12	24– 9	28– 0	28– 0	22– 9	25– 1	28– 0
	16	22– 9	25– 1	28– 0	20–11	22– 1	24– 8
	24	20– 1	20–10	23– 4	18– 5	18– 3	20– 5
3x 6	12	14– 0	17– 7	19– 8	12–11	15– 6	17– 3
	16	12–11	15– 5	17– 3	11–10	13– 7	15– 2
	24	11– 4	12– 9	14– 4	10– 5	11– 2	12– 6
3x 8	12	18–11	23– 6	26– 3	17– 5	20– 9	23– 2
	16	17– 5	20– 9	23– 2	16– 0	18– 3	20– 5
	24	15– 5	17– 3	19– 3	14– 1	15– 1	16–11
3x10	12	23– 8	29– 2	32– 0	21–10	25–11	28–11
	16	21–10	25–11	28–11	20– 1	22–10	25– 7
	24	19– 4	21– 7	24– 2	17– 9	19– 0	21– 3
3x12	12	28– 3	32– 0	32– 0	26– 2	30–11	32– 0
	16	26– 2	30–11	32– 0	24– 1	27– 4	30– 7
	24	23– 3	25–11	29– 0	21– 4	22–10	25– 6
		Live load, 40 psi			Live load, 50 psi		
2x 6	12	10– 4	11– 2	12– 5	9– 9	10– 3	11– 5
	16	9– 5	9– 8	10–10	8–11	8–11	9–11
	24	8– 3	8– 0	8–11	7–10	7– 3	8– 2
2x 8	12	14– 1	15– 1	16–10	13– 3	13–10	15– 6
	16	12–10	13– 2	14– 9	12– 1	12– 1	13– 6
	24	11– 3	10–10	12– 1	10– 7	9–11	11– 1
2x10	12	17– 8	18–11	21– 2	16– 9	17– 5	19– 5
	16	16– 2	16– 7	18– 6	15– 4	15– 2	17– 0
	24	14– 3	13– 8	15– 3	13– 5	12– 6	14– 0
2x12	12	21– 4	22– 9	25– 5	20– 2	20–11	23– 5
	16	19– 6	19–11	22– 3	18– 5	18– 4	20– 6
	24	17– 2	16– 5	18– 5	16– 3	15– 1	16–10
3x 6	12	12– 1	14– 0	15– 7	11– 5	12–10	14– 4
	16	11– 0	12– 3	13– 8	10– 5	11– 3	12– 6
	24	9– 8	10– 1	11– 3	9– 2	9– 3	10– 4
3x 8	12	16– 3	18–10	21– 0	15– 5	17– 4	19– 4
	16	14–11	16– 6	18– 5	14– 1	15– 2	16–11
	24	13– 2	13– 7	15– 3	12– 5	12– 6	14– 0
3x10	12	20– 6	23– 6	26– 4	19– 5	21– 8	24– 3
	16	18– 9	20– 8	23– 2	17– 9	19– 1	21– 4
	24	16– 7	17– 2	19– 2	15– 8	15– 9	17– 7
3x12	12	24– 7	28– 2	31– 5	23– 4	26– 0	29– 1
	16	22– 7	24–10	27– 9	21– 5	22–11	25– 7
	24	20– 0	20– 7	23– 1	18–11	18–11	21– 2

f and *H*. When *W* is converted for a different bending stress, *f*, the shearing stress, *H*, should be checked. However, if the stress adjustment is due to the duration of loading, the same adjustment will apply to both stresses so that the total load *W* may be determined by direct proportion.

Columns

Table 11 indicates the maximum allowable axial loads for simple solid columns at various unsupported lengths. Load values are for net finished sizes of S4S (surfaced four sides) lumber, seasoned, and for the normal duration of loading. The allowable load, P, for any section is equal to its area multiplied by an allowable stress limited either by the grade of wood (short column) or by buckling (long column). The allowable stress in a short column is based on c, the allowable unit stress in compression parallel to the grain, and is dependent upon the stress-grade lumber used. For long columns, the allowable stress, P/A, depends on the column formula and is a function of the modulus of elasticity, E, and the slenderness ratio (unsupported length divided by the column face). Values of P are equal to the area of each column section times the smaller of these two allowable stresses. In the table, $E = 1,760,000$ psi and $c = 1,200$ psi. For other values of E and c, the allowable unit stresses can be found by direct proportion. The column capacity, P, can then be determined by multiplying the adjusted allowable stress by the area of the section.

Design notations and formulas are as follows:

$A =$ area, sq in.

$l =$ unsupported length, in.

$d =$ net dimension of column face under consideration, in.

$E =$ modulus of elasticity, psi

$c =$ allowable unit stress in compression parallel to grain, psi

$P/A =$ allowable unit stress in compression parallel to grain for buckling, psi

$P =$ maximum allowable axial load, lb

For rectangular and square columns:

$$P/A = \frac{0.30E}{(l/d)^2}$$

$$P = Ac \text{ (short columns)}$$

$$P = AP/A \text{ (long columns)}$$

Values are based on $c = 1,200$ psi and $E = 1,760,000$ psi.

Table 10. Total uniformly distributed loads for joists and beams

$W_\Delta = $ *total uniformly distributed load in pounds for deflection of 1/360 of the span;* $W = $ *total uniformly distributed load in pounds for allowable* bending stress f or allowable shearing stress H. All values are based on the following allowable stresses: $f = 1,500$ psi; $H = 120$ psi; and $E = 1,760,000$ psi.

Nominal size, in.	Span length, ft											
	8		9		10		11		12		13	
	W_Δ	W	W_Δ	W	W_Δ	W	W_Δ	W	W_Δ	W	W_Δ	W
2x 8	2,330	1,910	1,840	1,690	1,490	1,520	1,230	1,390	1,030	1,270	881	1,170
2x10	4,730	3,060	3,740	2,720	3,030	2,450	2,500	2,200	2,100	2,040	1,790	1,880
3x 8	3,760	3,080	2,970	2,730	2,410	2,460	1,990	2,240	1,670	2,050	1,420	1,890
4x 8	5,190	4,250	4,100	3,780	3,320	3,400	2,750	3,090	2,310	2,830	1,970	2,610
2x12	8,390	3,930	6,630	3,800	5,370	3,580	4,440	3,260	3,730	2,980	3,180	2,760
3x10	7,640	4,930	6,040	4,390	4,890	3,950	4,040	3,590	3,400	3,290	2,890	3,040
2x14	13,600	4,880	10,700	4,680	8,690	4,530	7,180	4,410	6,030	4,110	5,140	3,800
4x10	10,600	6,820	8,340	6,060	6,750	5,450	5,580	4,960	4,690	4,540	4,000	4,190
3x12	13,600	6,350	10,700	6,140	8,670	5,790	7,170	5,260	6,020	4,820	5,130	4,450
3x14	21,900	7,890	17,300	7,560	14,000	7,320	11,600	7,130	9,740	6,640	8,300	6,130
4x12	18,700	8,770	14,800	8,470	12,000	7,990	9,900	7,260	8,320	6,660	7,090	6,150
6x10	16,000	10,300	12,600	9,190	10,200	8,270	8,470	7,520	7,120	6,890	6,060	6,360
3x16	33,200	9,610	26,200	9,130	21,200	8,780	17,600	8,510	14,700	8,300	12,600	8,090
4x14	30,300	10,900	23,900	10,400	19,400	10,100	16,000	9,840	13,500	9,180	11,500	8,470
6x12	28,400	13,300	22,400	12,900	18,200	12,100	15,000	11,000	12,600	10,100	10,800	9,330
4x16	45,800	13,300	36,200	12,600	29,300	12,100	24,200	11,700	20,400	11,500	17,400	11,200
8x12	38,700	18,100	30,600	17,500	24,800	16,500	20,500	15,000	17,200	13,800	14,700	12,700
6x14	45,900	16,500	36,300	15,800	29,400	15,300	24,300	14,900	20,400	13,900	17,400	12,900
6x16	69,500	20,100	54,900	19,100	44,500	18,400	36,800	17,800	30,900	17,400	26,300	16,900
8x14	62,600	22,500	49,500	21,600	40,100	20,900	33,100	20,400	27,000	19,000	23,700	17,500
	14		15		16		17		18		19	
2x12	2,740	2,560	2,390	2,390	2,100	2,240	1,860	2,110	1,660	1,990	1,490	1,890
3x10	2,490	2,820	2,170	2,630	1,910	2,470	1,690	2,320	1,510	2,190	1,350	2,080
2x14	4,430	3,530	3,860	3,290	3,390	3,090	3,010	2,900	2,680	2,740	2,410	2,600
4x10	3,450	3,890	3,000	3,640	2,640	3,410	2,340	3,210	2,080	3,030	1,870	2,870
3x12	4,430	4,130	3,860	3,860	3,390	3,610	3,000	3,400	2,680	3,210	2,400	3,040
3x14	7,160	5,700	6,240	5,320	5,480	4,980	4,860	4,690	4,330	4,430	3,890	4,200
4x12	6,110	5,710	5,320	5,330	4,680	4,990	4,140	4,700	3,700	4,440	3,320	4,210
6x10	5,230	5,910	4,550	5,510	4,000	5,170	3,550	4,870	3,160	4,600	2,840	4,350
3x16	10,800	7,510	9,440	7,010	8,300	6,570	7,350	6,180	6,560	5,840	5,580	5,530
4x14	9,890	7,870	8,610	7,340	7,570	6,880	6,710	6,480	5,980	6,120	5,370	5,800
6x12	9,270	8,660	8,080	8,080	7,100	7,580	6,290	7,130	5,610	6,730	5,030	6,380
4x16	15,000	10,400	13,000	9,680	11,500	9,070	10,100	8,540	9,050	8,060	8,130	7,640
8x12	12,600	11,800	11,000	11,000	9,680	10,300	8,580	9,720	7,650	9,180	6,870	8,700
6x14	15,000	11,900	13,100	11,100	11,500	10,400	10,200	9,830	9,080	9,280	8,150	8,790
6x16	22,700	15,700	19,800	14,700	17,400	13,800	15,400	13,000	13,700	12,200	12,300	11,600
8x14	20,500	16,300	17,800	15,200	15,700	14,200	13,900	13,400	12,400	12,700	11,100	12,000
6x18	32,700	19,500	28,500	18,700	25,000	17,500	22,000	16,500	19,800	15,600	17,700	14,800
10x14	25,900	20,600	22,600	19,200	19,800	18,000	17,600	17,000	15,700	16,000	14,100	15,200
8x16	31,000	21,500	27,000	20,000	23,700	21,900	21,000	17,700	18,700	16,700	16,800	15,800
6x20	45,200	22,300	39,400	21,900	34,600	21,500	30,700	20,500	27,400	19,400	24,500	18,300
10x16	39,200	27,200	34,200	25,400	30,000	23,800	26,600	22,400	23,700	21,100	21,300	20,000
8x18	44,600	26,500	38,800	25,500	34,100	23,900	30,200	22,500	27,000	21,300	24,200	20,100
8x20	61,600	30,500	53,700	29,900	47,200	29,400	41,800	28,000	37,300	26,400	33,500	25,000
10x18	56,400	33,600	49,200	32,300	43,200	30,300	38,300	28,500	34,100	26,900	30,600	25,500
8x22	82,600	34,700	72,000	33,900	63,300	33,200	56,000	32,700	50,000	32,100	44,900	30,400

Table 10 (cont.). Total uniformly distributed loads for joists and beams

Nominal size, in.	20 W_Δ	20 W	21 W_Δ	21 W	22 W_Δ	22 W	23 W_Δ	23 W	24 W_Δ	24 W	25 W_Δ	25 W
3x12	2,170	2,890	1,970	2,750	1,790	2,630	1,640	2,510	1,510	2,410		
3x14	3,510	3,990	3,180	3,800	2,900	3,620	2,650	3,470	2,440	3,220	2,250	3,190
4x12	2,990	3,990	2,720	3,800	2,470	3,630	2,260	3,470	2,080	3,330		
3x16	5,310	5,250	4,820	5,000	4,390	4,780	4,020	4,570	3,690	4,380	3,400	4,200
4x14	4,850	5,500	4,390	5,240	4,000	5,010	3,660	4,790	3,360	4,590	3,100	4,400
6x12	4,540	6,060	4,120	5,770	3,760	5,510	3,440	5,270	3,160	5,050		
4x16	7,330	7,260	6,650	6,910	6,060	6,600	5,540	6,310	5,090	6,050	4,690	5,810
8x12	6,200	8,260	5,620	7,870	5,120	7,510	4,690	7,190	4,300	6,890		
6x14	7,350	8,350	6,670	7,960	6,070	7,590	5,560	7,260	5,100	6,960	4,700	6,680
6x16	11,100	11,000	10,100	10,500	9,190	10,000	8,410	9,580	7,730	9,180	7,120	8,810
8x14	10,000	11,400	9,090	10,800	8,280	10,400	7,580	9,900	6,960	9,490	6,420	9,110
6x18	16,000	14,000	14,500	13,400	13,200	12,800	12,100	12,200	11,100	11,700	10,200	11,200
10x14	12,700	14,400	11,500	13,700	10,500	13,100	9,600	12,500	8,820	12,000	8,130	11,500
8x16	15,200	15,000	13,800	14,300	12,500	13,600	11,500	13,100	10,500	12,500	9,710	12,000
6x20	22,200	17,400	20,100	16,600	18,300	15,800	16,800	15,200	15,400	14,500	14,200	13,900
10x16	19,200	19,000	17,400	18,100	15,900	17,300	14,500	16,500	13,300	15,900	12,300	15,200
8x18	21,800	19,100	19,800	18,200	18,000	17,400	16,500	16,600	15,200	16,000	14,000	15,300
8x20	30,200	23,800	27,400	22,600	25,000	21,600	22,800	20,700	21,000	19,800	19,300	19,000
10x18	27,700	24,200	25,100	23,100	22,900	22,000	20,900	21,100	19,200	20,200	17,700	19,400
8x22	40,500	28,900	36,700	27,500	33,500	26,300	30,600	25,100	28,100	24,100	25,900	23,100
10x20	38,300	30,100	34,700	28,700	31,600	27,400	28,900	26,200	26,600	25,100	24,500	24,100
8x24	52,900	34,500	48,000	32,900	43,700	31,400	40,000	30,000	36,700	28,800	33,800	27,600
12x20	46,300	36,400	42,000	34,700	38,300	33,100	35,000	31,700	32,200	30,400	29,600	29,200
10x22	51,300	36,600	46,500	34,900	42,400	33,300	38,800	31,800	35,600	30,500	32,800	29,300
10x24	67,000	43,700	60,700	41,600	55,300	39,700	50,600	38,000	46,500	36,400	42,900	35,000
12x22	62,100	44,300	56,300	42,200	51,300	40,300	46,900	38,500	43,100	36,900	39,700	35,400
14x22	72,900	52,000	66,100	49,500	60,200	47,300	55,100	45,200	50,600	43,300	46,600	41,600
12x24	81,100	52,900	73,500	50,400	67,000	48,100	61,300	46,000	56,300	44,100	51,900	42,300
14x24	95,200	62,100	86,300	59,200	78,700	56,500	72,000	54,000	66,100	51,800	60,900	49,700
12x26	104,000	59,600	93,900	59,600	85,600	56,700	78,300	54,200	71,900	51,900	66,300	49,900

Nominal size, in.	26 W_Δ	26 W	27 W_Δ	27 W	28 W_Δ	28 W	29 W_Δ	29 W	30 W_Δ	30 W	32 W_Δ	32 W
6x16	6,580	8,470	6,110	8,150	5,680	7,870	5,290	7,590				
8x14	5,930	8,760	5,500	8,440	5,110	8,130	4,770	7,850				
6x18	9,470	10,800	8,790	10,400	8,170	10,000	7,610	9,680	7,120	9,360	6,250	8,770
8x16	8,980	11,500	8,330	11,100	7,740	10,700	7,210	10,400	6,740	10,000	5,930	9,380
6x20	13,100	13,400	12,200	12,900	11,300	12,400	10,500	12,000	9,850	11,600	8,650	10,900
10x16	11,400	14,600	10,500	14,100	9,810	13,600	9,140	13,100	8,540	12,700	7,510	11,900
8x18	12,900	14,700	12,000	14,200	11,100	13,700	10,400	13,200	9,700	12,800	8,530	12,000
8x20	17,900	18,300	16,000	17,600	15,400	17,000	14,400	16,400	13,400	15,800	11,800	14,900
10x18	16,400	18,600	15,200	18,000	14,100	17,300	13,200	16,700	12,300	16,200	10,800	15,200
8x22	24,000	22,000	22,200	21,400	20,700	20,600	19,300	19,900	18,000	19,300	15,800	18,100
12x18	19,800	22,600	18,400	21,700	17,100	21,000	15,900	20,200	14,900	19,600	13,100	18,300
10x20	22,600	23,200	21,000	22,300	19,500	21,500	18,200	20,800	17,000	20,100	14,900	18,800
8x24	31,300	26,500	29,000	25,600	27,000	24,700	25,100	23,800	23,500	23,000	20,700	21,600
12x20	27,400	28,000	25,400	27,000	23,600	26,000	22,000	25,100	20,600	24,300	18,100	22,800
10x22	30,300	28,100	28,100	27,100	26,200	26,100	24,400	25,200	22,800	24,400	20,000	22,900
10x24	39,600	33,600	36,800	32,400	34,200	31,200	31,900	30,200	29,800	29,100	26,200	27,300
12x22	36,700	34,100	34,100	32,800	31,700	31,600	29,500	30,500	27,600	29,500	24,200	27,700
12x24	48,000	40,700	44,500	39,200	41,400	37,800	38,600	36,500	36,000	35,300	31,700	33,100
14x24	56,300	47,800	52,200	46,000	48,600	44,400	45,300	42,800	42,300	41,400	37,200	38,800
12x26	61,300	47,900	56,800	46,200	52,900	44,500	49,300	43,000	46,000	41,500	40,500	38,900
12x28	76,900	55,700	71,300	53,700	66,300	51,800	61,800	50,000	57,700	48,300	50,700	45,300
12x30	94,900	64,200	88,000	61,800	81,800	59,600	76,300	57,500	71,300	55,600	62,600	52,100
14x28	90,200	65,400	83,700	63,000	77,800	60,800	72,500	58,700	67,800	56,700	59,600	53,000
14x30	111,000	75,300	103,000	72,500	96,100	69,900	89,500	67,500	83,700	65,300	73,500	61,200
16x30	128,000	86,500	119,000	83,300	110,000	80,300	103,000	77,500	96,100	74,900	84,400	70,300

Data useful in the design of trusses are given on this and the following page. For laminated wood arches and lamella construction, see "Structural Forms—Wood"; for trussed rafters, see "Wood Construction."

The formula for beams notched at bearing points is

$$V = \frac{2bd^2H}{3h}$$

in which

V = maximum end reaction
H = maximum permitted horizontal shear stress
b = breadth of joist
d = height of joist above notch
h = total depth of joist

The formula for compression on surfaces inclined to the grain is

$$n = \frac{cq}{c \sin^2 \Theta + q \cos^2 \Theta}$$

in which

n = allowable unit stress on inclined surface
c = unit stress in compression parallel to grain
q = unit stress in compression perpendicular to grain
Θ = angle in degrees between direction of load and direction of grain

For each individual member of a spaced column, l/d should not exceed 80, and $(l_2 d)$ 1.25 should not exceed 50. For condition "a," the connector is within $l/20$ from the column end. The formula is

$$P/A = \frac{0.75E}{(l/d)^2}$$

For condition "b," the connector is from $l/20$ to $l/10$ from the column end. The formula is

$$P/A = \frac{0.90E}{(l/d)^2}$$

Bolted connections

The following data on bolted connections

have been derived from *National Design Specification for Stress-grade Lumber and Its Fastenings*, National Lumber Manufacturers Association (1960).

Service conditions: Tabulated loads as adjusted for condition of lumber apply to bolted joints used under continuously dry

Table 11. Maximum allowable axial loads for columns

$P/A = $ *allowable unit stress in compression parallel to grain for buckling, psi;*
$P = $ *maximum allowable axial load, lb.*

Nominal size, in.	Area, sq in.	Unsupported length, ft												
		8		9		10		11		12		13		14	
		P/A	P	P/A	P	P/A	P	P/A	P	P/A	P	P/A	P	P/A	P
4x 4	13.14	752	9,890	595	7,820	482	6,330	398	5,230	335	4,400	286	3,750	246	3,230
4x 6	19.94	752	15,000	595	11,900	482	9,610	398	7,940	335	6,670	286	5,680	246	4,900
4x 8	27.19	752	20,500	595	16,200	482	13,100	398	10,800	335	9,100	286	7,750	246	6,680
4x10	34.44	752	25,900	595	20,500	482	16,600	398	13,700	335	11,500	286	9,820	246	8,470
4x12	41.69	752	31,400	595	24,800	482	20,100	398	16,600	335	13,900	286	11,900	246	10,200
4x14	48.94	752	36,800	595	29,100	482	23,600	398	19,500	335	16,400	286	14,000	246	12,000
4x16	56.19	752	42,300	595	33,400	482	27,100	398	22,400	335	18,800	286	16,000	246	13,800
6x 6	30.25	1,723	36,300	1,374	36,300	1,111	33,600	917	27,700	806	23,300	655	19,900	568	17,100
6x 8	41.25	1,723	49,500	1,374	49,500	1,111	45,800	917	37,800	806	31,800	655	27,100	568	23,300
6x10	52.25	1,723	62,700	1,374	62,700	1,111	58,000	917	47,900	806	40,200	655	34,300	568	29,600
6x12	63.25	1,723	75,900	1,374	75,900	1,111	70,200	917	58,000	806	48,700	655	41,500	568	35,800
6x14	74.25	1,723	89,100	1,374	89,100	1,111	82,400	917	68,100	806	57,200	655	48,700	568	42,000
6x16	85.25	1,723	102,000	1,374	102,000	1,111	94,600	917	78,100	806	65,700	655	56,000	568	48,200
6x18	96.25	1,723	116,000	1,374	116,000	1,111	107,000	917	88,200	806	74,100	655	63,200	568	54,500
8x 8	56.25	3,223	67,500	2,546	67,500	2,063	67,500	1,704	67,500	1,432	67,500	1,221	67,500	1,052	59,200
8x10	71.25	3,223	85,500	2,546	85,500	2,063	85,500	1,704	85,500	1,432	85,500	1,221	85,500	1,052	75,000
8x12	86.25	3,223	104,000	2,546	104,000	2,063	104,000	1,704	104,000	1,432	104,000	1,221	104,000	1,052	90,800
8x14	101.25	3,223	122,000	2,546	122,000	2,063	122,000	1,704	122,000	1,432	122,000	1,221	122,000	1,052	107,000
8x16	116.25	3,223	140,000	2,546	140,000	2,063	140,000	1,704	140,000	1,432	140,000	1,221	140,000	1,052	122,000
8x18	131.25	3,223	158,000	2,546	158,000	2,063	158,000	1,704	158,000	1,432	158,000	1,221	158,000	1,052	138,000
10x10	90.25			4,062	108,000	3,325	108,000	2,733	108,000	2,286	108,000	1,963	108,000	1,685	108,000
10x12	109.25			4,062	131,000	3,325	131,000	2,733	131,000	2,286	131,000	1,963	131,000	1,685	131,000
10x14	128.25			4,062	154,000	3,325	154,000	2,733	154,000	2,286	154,000	1,963	154,000	1,685	154,000
10x16	147.25			4,062	177,000	3,325	177,000	2,733	177,000	2,286	177,000	1,963	177,000	1,685	177,000
10x18	166.25			4,062	200,000	3,325	200,000	2,733	200,000	2,286	200,000	1,963	200,000	1,685	200,000
10x20	185.25			4,062	222,000	3,325	220,000	2,733	220,000	2,286	220,000	1,963	220,000	1,685	220,000
12x12	132.25									3,378	159,000	2,854	159,000	2,477	159,000
12x14	155.25									3,378	186,000	2,854	186,000	2,477	186,000
12x16	178.25									3,378	214,000	2,854	214,000	2,477	214,000
12x18	201.25									3,378	242,000	2,854	242,000	2,477	242,000
12x20	224.25									3,378	269,000	2,854	269,000	2,477	269,000

Nominal size, in.	Area, sq in.	15		16		18		20		22		24		26	
		P/A	P	P/A	P	P/A	P	P/A	P	P/A	P	P/A	P	P/A	P
6x 6	30.25	494	14,900	433	13,100	342	10,400	278	8,390	229	6,930				
6x 8	41.25	494	20,300	433	17,900	342	14,100	278	11,400	229	9,450				
6x10	52.25	494	25,800	433	22,600	342	17,900	278	14,500	229	12,000				
6x12	63.25	494	31,200	433	27,400	342	21,700	278	17,500	229	14,500				
6x14	74.25	494	36,600	433	32,200	342	25,400	278	20,600	229	17,000				
6x16	85.25	494	42,000	433	36,900	342	29,200	278	23,600	229	19,500				
6x18	96.25	494	47,400	433	41,700	342	32,900	278	26,700	229	22,100				
8x 8	56.25	917	51,600	806	45,300	637	35,800	516	29,000	426	24,000	358	20,100	305	17,200
8x10	71.25	917	65,300	806	57,400	637	45,400	516	36,700	426	30,400	358	25,500	305	21,700
8x12	86.25	917	79,100	806	69,500	637	54,900	516	44,500	426	36,800	358	30,900	305	26,300
8x14	101.25	917	92,800	806	81,600	637	64,500	516	52,200	426	43,100	358	36,300	305	30,900
8x16	116.25	917	107,000	806	93,700	637	74,000	516	59,900	426	49,500	358	41,600	305	35,500
8x18	131.25	917	120,000	806	106,000	637	83,600	516	67,700	426	55,900	358	47,000	305	40,000
10x10	90.25	1,478	108,000	1,294	108,000	1,025	92,200	825	74,700	683	61,700	575	51,800	491	44,200
10x12	109.25	1,478	131,000	1,294	131,000	1,025	112,000	825	90,400	683	74,700	575	62,800	491	53,500
10x14	128.25	1,478	154,000	1,294	154,000	1,025	131,000	825	106,000	683	87,700	575	73,700	491	62,800
10x16	147.25	1,478	177,000	1,294	177,000	1,025	150,000	825	122,000	683	101,000	575	84,600	491	72,100
10x18	166.25	1,478	200,000	1,294	200,000	1,025	170,000	825	138,000	683	114,000	575	95,500	491	81,400
10x20	185.25	1,478	220,000	1,294	220,000	1,025	189,000	825	153,000	683	127,000	575	106,000	491	90,700
12x12	132.25	2,142	159,000	1,893	159,000	1,494	159,000	1,209	159,000	998	133,000	845	111,000	719	94,900
12x14	155.25	2,142	186,000	1,893	186,000	1,494	186,000	1,209	186,000	998	156,000	845	131,000	719	111,000
12x16	178.25	2,142	214,000	1,893	214,000	1,494	214,000	1,209	214,000	998	179,000	845	150,000	719	128,000
12x18	201.25	2,142	242,000	1,893	242,000	1,494	242,000	1,209	242,000	998	202,000	845	169,000	719	144,000
12x20	224.25	2,142	269,000	1,893	269,000	1,494	269,000	1,209	269,000	998	225,000	845	189,000	719	161,000
14x14	182.25			2,619	219,000	2,063	219,000	1,667	219,000	1,374	219,000	1,164	195,000	990	180,000
16x16	240.25			3,433	288,000	2,733	288,000	2,197	288,000	1,827	288,000	1,526	288,000	1,307	288,000

FINK   BELGIAN   PRATT

TRIANGULAR ROOF TRUSSES

SCISSORS   CAMB. FINK

CAMBERED TRUSSES

BOWSTRING TRUSS

DOUBLE WARREN   FLAT TOP PRATT   SINGLE WARREN

FLAT ROOF TRUSSES

 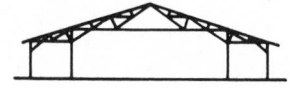

SAWTOOTH   SHED   FACTORY

FACTORY ROOF TRUSSES

Typical wood trusses

$$V = \frac{2bd^2H}{3h} \quad \text{in which.}$$

V = Maximum end reaction
H = Maximum permitted horizontal shear stress
b = Breadth of joist
d = Height of joist above notch
h = Total depth of joist

Beams notched at bearing points

conditions (as in most covered structures) and for normal loading.

Materials for side members: Tabulated bolt loads are for side members of wood. The bearing thrust on side plates is assumed to be parallel to the fibers. If wood splice plates are used, the allowable load perpendicular to the grain should not exceed the

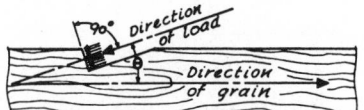

$$n = \frac{cq}{c \sin^2 \theta + q \cos^2 \theta} \quad \text{in which:}$$

n = Allowable unit stress on inclined surface
c = unit stress (compression) parallel to grain
q = unit stress (compression) perpendicular to grain
θ = angle in degrees between direction of load and direction of grain

Compression on surfaces inclined to grain

load parallel to the grain for any given size and quality of timbers. If steel plates are used for side members, the tabulated loads parallel to the grain should be increased by 25 per cent; however, no increase should be made for loads perpendicular to the

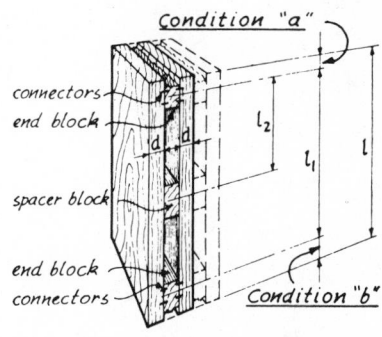

For each individual member:
$\frac{l}{d}$ should not exceed 80
nor should $\frac{l_2}{d} \times 1.25$ exceed 50

Condition "a" = connector within $\frac{l}{20}$ from column end
$$P/A = \frac{0.75E}{(l/d)^2}$$
Condition "b" = connector from $\frac{l}{20}$ to $\frac{l}{10}$ from column end
$$P/A = \frac{0.90E}{(l/d)^2}$$

Spaced column

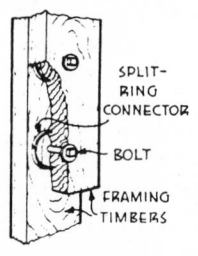

SPLITTING-RING CONNECTOR
BOLT
FRAMING TIMBERS

EXAMPLE OF USE

SPLIT
RINGS

TOOTHED.

WITH HUB   WITHOUT HUB
CLAW PLATES

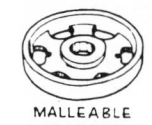 

MALLEABLE FLANGED   PRESSED STEEL FLANGED
SHEAR PLATES

FLAT

SINGLE CURVED

SPIKE GRIDS

DOUBLE CURVED

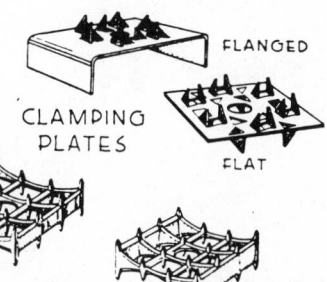

FLANGED
CLAMPING PLATES
FLAT

Connectors

Bolted connections

grain. Steel plates should be of ample strength.

Dimensions of side members: Tabulated loads apply if side members of wood are each one-half the thickness of the main member. If the side members are thicker than one-half the thickness of the main member, no increase in tabulated loads is permissible. If the side members are less than one-half the thickness of the main member, the tabulated loads indicated for a main member that is twice the thickness of the thinnest side member used shall apply. For example, with 2-in. side members and a 10-in. center member, the tabulated loads for a 4-in. center member should be used.

Number of members in joint: Tabulated loads are for a joint consisting of three members (double shear). The length of the bolt (*l*) is measured in the main member (that is, in the thickness of the piece). If a joint consists of two members (single shear) of equal thickness, one-half the tabulated load for a piece twice the thickness of the thinner member should be used.

Plywood box beams

The following data on plywood box beams have been derived from the *Fir Plywood Box Beam Handbook,* Douglas Fir Plywood Association (1958).

Plywood box beams consist of an assembly of simple wood elements fastened together in a manner that develops the capacity of its components. Shear resistance is furnished by two or more plywood webs, and moment capacity is developed by wood flanges, usually of a 2-in. nominal thickness. Stiffeners are placed at intervals to prevent buckling of the plywood webs. Both flanges are axially stressed, and although the allowable stress in tension is greater than

Table 12. Allowable loads on bolted connections

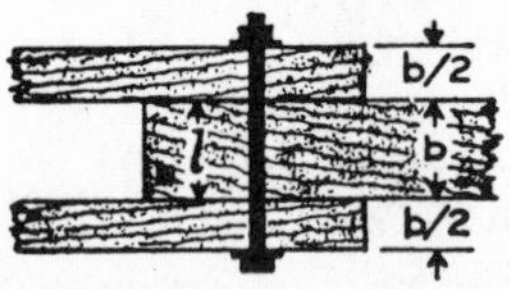

Length of bolt in main member	Diameter of bolt	l/d	Projected area of bolt	CEDAR, WESTERN RED		CYPRESS, SOUTHERN		DOUGLAS FIR, COAST REGION AND DOUGLAS FIR		PINE, NORTHERN (Eastern White), PONDEROSA, SUGAR, AND IDAHO WHITE		PINE, SOUTHERN		REDWOOD	
				Parallel to grain	Perpendicular to grain	Parallel to grain	Perpendicular to grain	Parallel to grain	Perpendicular to grain	Parallel to grain	Perpendicular to grain	Parallel to grain	Perpendicular to grain	Parallel to grain	Perpendicular to grain
l	d		$A = l \times d$	P	Q	P	Q	P	Q	P	Q	P	Q	P	Q
Inches	*Inches*		*Sq. in.*												
1⅝	½	3.3	.8125	680	300	1,010	450	1,010	480	710	380	1,010	480	940	380
	⅝	2.6	1.0156	850	340	1,290	510	1,290	540	890	420	1,290	540	1,200	420
	¾	2.2	1.2188	1,010	380	1,550	570	1,550	600	1,070	470	1,550	600	1,450	470
	⅞	1.9	1.4219	1,190	420	1,810	620	1,810	670	1,250	520	1,810	670	1,690	520
	1	1.6	1.625	1,360	450	2,070	680	2,070	730	1,430	570	2,070	730	1,930	570
2	½	4.0	1.00	840	370	1,180	550	1,180	590	860	460	1,180	590	1,100	460
	⅝	3.2	1.25	1,050	420	1,560	630	1,560	670	1,100	520	1,560	670	1,460	520
	¾	2.7	1.50	1,250	470	1,910	700	1,910	740	1,320	580	1,910	740	1,780	580
	⅞	2.3	1.75	1,470	510	2,230	770	2,230	820	1,540	640	2,230	820	2,080	640
	1	2.0	2.00	1,670	560	2,550	840	2,550	890	1,760	700	2,550	890	2,380	700
2⅝	½	5.3	1.3125	1,010	490	1,280	730	1,280	780	980	610	1,280	780	1,180	610
	⅝	4.2	1.6406	1,360	550	1,890	820	1,890	880	1,390	690	1,890	880	1,760	690
	¾	3.5	1.9688	1,650	610	2,430	920	2,430	980	1,720	760	2,430	980	2,250	760
	⅞	3.0	2.2969	1,920	670	2,900	1,010	2,900	1,080	2,020	840	2,900	1,080	2,700	840
	1	2.6	2.625	2,190	730	3,340	1,100	3,340	1,170	2,310	920	3,340	1,170	3,110	920
3	½	6.0	1.50	1,070	550	1,290	830	1,290	890	1,000	690	1,290	890	1,200	690
	⅝	4.8	1.875	1,510	630	1,980	940	1,980	1,000	1,490	780	1,980	1,000	1,850	780
	¾	4.0	2.25	1,870	700	2,660	1,050	2,660	1,120	1,930	870	2,660	1,120	2,470	870
	⅞	3.4	2.625	2,190	770	3,250	1,150	3,250	1,230	2,300	960	3,250	1,230	3,020	960
	1	3.0	3.00	2,510	840	3,790	1,260	3,790	1,340	2,640	1,050	3,790	1,340	3,530	1,050
3⅝	½	7.3	1.8125	1,070	670	1,290	950	1,290	1,020	1,000	830	1,290	1,020	1,200	830
	⅝	5.8	2.2656	1,660	760	2,010	1,140	2,010	1,210	1,560	950	2,010	1,210	1,860	950
	¾	4.8	2.7188	2,190	840	2,860	1,270	2,860	1,350	2,170	1,050	2,860	1,350	2,680	1,050
	⅞	4.1	3.1719	2,630	930	3,680	1,390	3,680	1,490	2,700	1,160	3,680	1,490	3,450	1,160
	1	3.6	3.625	3,030	1,010	4,430	1,520	4,430	1,620	3,160	1,270	4,430	1,620	4.120	1,270
4	½	8.0	2.00	1,070	710	1,290	980	1,290	1,040	1,000	890	1,290	1,040	1,200	890
	⅝	6.4	2.50	1,670	840	2,010	1,250	2,010	1,330	1,560	1,050	2,010	1,330	1,870	1,050
	¾	5.3	3.00	2,330	930	2,890	1,400	2,890	1,490	2,230	1,160	2,890	1,490	2,690	1,160
	⅞	4.6	3.50	2,850	1,020	3,830	1,540	3,830	1,640	2,860	1,280	3,830	1,640	3,570	1,280
	1	4.0	4.00	3,330	1,120	4,720	1,680	4,720	1,790	3,430	1,400	4,720	1,790	4,400	1,400
4½	½	9.0	2.25	1,070	720	1,290	960	1,290	1,020	1,000	900	1,290	1,020	1,200	900
	⅝	7.2	2.8125	1,670	940	2,010	1,350	2,010	1,440	1,560	1,170	2,010	1,440	1,870	1,170
	¾	6.0	3.375	2,420	1,050	2,890	1,570	2,890	1,680	2,250	1,310	2,890	1,680	2,690	1,310
	⅞	5.1	3.9375	3,110	1,150	3,920	1,730	3,920	1,840	3,010	1,440	3,920	1,840	3,670	1,440
	1	4.5	4.50	3,670	1,260	4,980	1,890	4,980	2,010	3,710	1,570	4,980	2,010	4,660	1,570
	1⅛	4.0	5.0625	4,210	1,370	5,980	2,050	5,980	2,190	4,340	1,710	5,980	2,190	5,560	1,710
5½	⅝	8.8	3.4375	1,670	1,020	2,010	1,360	2,010	1,450	1,560	1,270	2,010	1,450	1,870	1,270
	¾	7.3	4.125	2,420	1,270	2,890	1,820	2,899	1,940	2,250	1,590	2,890	1,940	2,690	1,590
	⅞	6.3	4.8125	3,310	1,410	3,940	2,100	3,940	2,250	3,060	1,760	3,940	2,250	3,670	1,760
	1	5.5	5.50	4,180	1,540	5,120	2,300	5,120	2,460	3,970	1,920	5,120	2,460	4,770	1,920
	1⅛	4.9	6.1875	4,960	1,670	6.440	2,510	6,440	2,680	4,870	2,090	6,440	2,680	6,000	2,090
7½	⅝	12.0	4.6875	1,670	960	2,010	1,220	2,010	1,300	1,570	1,200	2,010	1,300	1,870	1,200
	¾	10.0	5.625	2,420	1,330	2,890	1,760	2,890	1,880	2,250	1,660	2,890	1,880	2,690	1,660
	⅞	8.6	6.5625	3,310	1,740	3,940	2,340	3,940	2,500	3,060	2,180	3,940	2,500	3,670	2,180
	1	7.5	7.50	4,290	2,070	5,140	2,940	5,140	3,130	4,000	2,590	5,140	3,130	4,790	2,590
	1⅛	6.7	8.4375	5,450	2,280	6,500	3,370	6,500	3,610	5,090	2,850	6,500	3,610	6,050	2,850
9½	¾	12.7	7.125	2,420	1,260	2,890	1,580	2,890	1,690	2,250	1,570	2,890	1,690	2,690	1,570
	⅞	10.9	8.3125	3,310	1,670	3,940	2,190	3,940	2,350	3,060	2,080	3,940	2,350	3,670	2,080
	1	9.5	9.50	4,290	2,140	5,140	2,860	5,140	3,050	4,000	2,680	5,140	3,050	4,790	2,680
	1⅛	8.4	10.6875	5,450	2,680	6,500	3,630	6,500	3,830	5,090	3,350	6,500	3,830	6,050	3,350
	1¼	7.6	11.875	6,780	3,060	8,040	4,310	8,040	4,590	6,260	3,820	8,040	4,590	7,480	3,820
11½	1	11.5	11.50	4,290	2,060	5,140	2,680	5,140	2,850	4,000	2,580	5,140	2,850	4,790	2,580
	1⅛	10.2	12.9375	5,450	2,600	6,500	3,440	6,500	3,660	5,090	3,260	6,500	3,660	6,050	3,260
	1¼	9.2	14.375	6,780	3,160	8,040	4,210	8,040	4,490	6,260	3,950	8,040	4,490	7,480	3,950

the allowable stress in compression parallel to the grain, the flanges are usually made the same size. Plywood box beams are light in weight and are readily adaptable to the design of tapered, arched, or curved forms.

The construction method used in the fabrication of box beams is of vital importance. Gluing is considered the most satisfactory method, although nailing and bolting, either alone or with gluing, have also been used. For maximum efficiency and reliability, plywood box beams should be shop fabricated. Such important factors as the moisture content of the lumber, the air temperature, and the spread of the glue are extremely difficult to control outside the shop.

The critical structural requirement in the design of box beams is usually shear. Two types of shearing stresses are involved: horizontal and rolling. Horizontal shearing stresses may be controlled by providing an adequate web area. Rolling shear stresses, however, depend on the contact area of the flange and thus usually require inner webs (as illustrated by types C-1 and C-2 of the box-beam sections).

Table 13 lists the general characteristics of typical plywood box beams and the loads that can be supported at various spans. Other load capacities can be obtained by varying the thickness of the plywood web and the size of the lumber flanges. The design of beams is based on seasoned lumber and normal loading conditions. The allow

able stress in compression parallel to the grain is 2,000 psi; the modulus of elasticity is 1,800,000 psi. The deflection values are based on a limiting deflection of 1/240 of the span length. Values for different limiting deflections may be found by direct proportion.

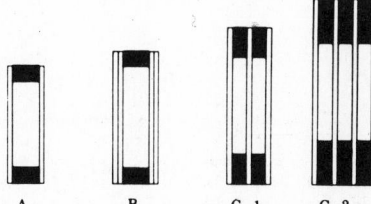

A   B   C 1   C 2

Table 13. Allowable loads for plywood box beams

Beam description	Type	Surfaced dimensions, in. (width by depth)	Weight, lb per lin ft	Design function	20	24	28	32	36	40	44	52	60	70	80
					Load, lb per lin ft										
20-in. nominal depth 5/8-in. plywood web Two 2x6-in. flanges	A	4⅜ x19⅝	14.1	Bending	690	318	352	269	213	172	143				
				Shear	380	317	271	238	211	190	173				
				Deflection	1,000	611	400	278	197	145	110				
	B	5⅝ x19⅝	18.6	Bending	830	576	424	324	256	208	172				
				Shear	746	623	534	467	415	374	340				
	C–1	5 x19⅝	16.4	Bending	757	525	387	296	234	190	157				
				Shear	564	470	403	353	314	283	257				
24-in. nominal depth ¾-in. plywood web Five 2x4-in. flanges	A	9⁵⁄₁₆x23½	23	Bending	1,690	1,170	863	660	522	423	350	250	188		
				Shear	616	513	440	385	342	308	280	237	205		
				Deflection	2,220	1,450	983	698	508	382	293	183	121		
	C–2	10¹³⁄₁₆x23½	28	Bending	1,840	1,280	938	718	568	460	380	272	204		
				Shear	1,200	998	854	748	655	598	544	460	399		
30-in. nominal depth 1-in. plywood web Four 2x6-in. flanges	A	8¼ x29½	32	Bending	2,460	1,710	1,260	960	760	615	508	364	273		
				Shear	993	827	709	620	551	497	451	382	331		
				Deflection	3,890	2,560	1,770	1,260	920	694	535	337	224		
	C–1	9¼ x29½	37	Bending	2,610	1,810	1,330	1,020	805	652	539	371	290		
				Shear	1,460	1,220	1,050	915	814	733	665	563	489		
	C–2	10¼ x29½	41	Bending	2,780	1,930	1,420	1,080	857	694	573	410	308		
				Shear	1,930	1,610	1,380	1,210	1,070	965	878	743	644		
36-in. nominal depth 1-in. plywood web Five 2x8-in. flanges	A	9¹³⁄₁₆x35½	46	Bending	4,680	3,250	2,390	1,830	1,450	1,170	968	693	520	382	293
				Shear	1,180	979	839	735	653	588	534	452	392	336	294
				Deflection	6,820	4,720	3,370	2,470	1,850	1,420	1,110	709	478	312	212
	B	11⁵⁄₁₆x35½	55	Bending	5,150	3,500	2,630	2,010	1,590	1,290	1,060	761	572	420	322
				Shear	2,040	1,700	1,460	1,280	1,130	1,020	928	785	680	583	510
	C–2	11¹³⁄₁₆x35½	58	Bending	5,200	3,610	2,660	2,030	1,610	1,300	1,080	769	578	425	325
				Shear	2,320	1,930	1,650	1,450	1,290	1,160	1,050	891	778	663	579
42-in. nominal depth 1-in. plywood web Five 2x8-in. flanges	A	9¹³⁄₁₆x41½	50	Bending		4,100	3,100	2,300	1,820	1,480	1,220	872	655	482	369
				Shear		1,180	1,010	882	783	705	642	542	470	403	353
				Deflection		6,040	4,410	3,300	2,510	1,950	1,540	1,000	682	446	320
	B&C-2	11¹³⁄₁₆x41½	63	Bending		4,530	3,330	2,540	2,020	1,630	1,350	966	725	533	408
				Shear		2,240	1,920	1,680	1,490	1,340	1,220	1,030	894	765	670
48-in. nominal depth 1⅛-in. plywood web Six 2x10-in. flanges	A	11⅝ x47½	71	Bending			5,040	3,860	3,050	2,470	2,040	1,460	1,100	806	707
				Shear			1,280	1,120	991	892	811	686	595	510	465
				Deflection			7,250	5,540	4,290	3,390	2,700	1,790	1,240	822	632
	B&C-2	13⅞ x47½	89	Bending			5,620	4,300	3,400	2,750	2,280	1,630	1,220	900	745
				Shear			2,510	2,200	1,950	1,750	1,600	1,350	1,170	1,000	735
	C1	12¾ x47½	80	Bending			5,340	4,090	3,240	2,620	2,160	1,550	1,160	854	737
				Shear			1,890	1,660	1,470	1,320	1,200	1,020	883	757	688

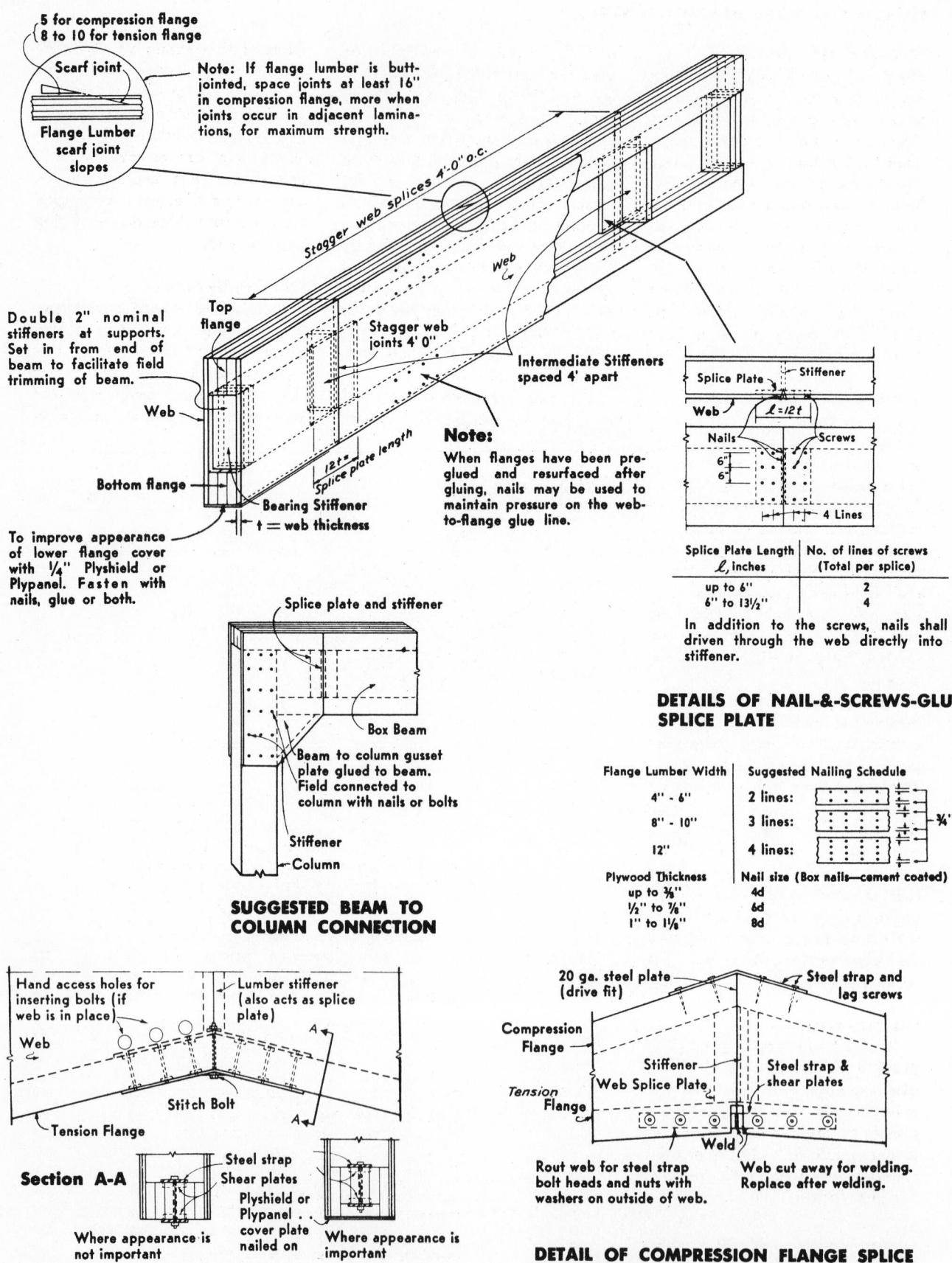

5 for compression flange
8 to 10 for tension flange

Scarf joint

Flange Lumber scarf joint slopes

Note: If flange lumber is butt-jointed, space joints at least 16" in compression flange, more when joints occur in adjacent laminations, for maximum strength.

Stagger web splices 4'-0" o.c.

Web

Top flange

Stagger web joints 4' 0"

Intermediate Stiffeners spaced 4' apart

Double 2" nominal stiffeners at supports. Set in from end of beam to facilitate field trimming of beam.

Web

Bottom flange

Bearing Stiffener

$12t =$ Splice plate length

$t =$ web thickness

Note:
When flanges have been preglued and resurfaced after gluing, nails may be used to maintain pressure on the web-to-flange glue line.

To improve appearance of lower flange cover with ¼" Plyshield or Plypanel. Fasten with nails, glue or both.

Splice Plate — Stiffener

Web — $\ell = 12t$

Nails — Screws

6"
6"

4 Lines

Splice Plate Length ℓ, inches	No. of lines of screws (Total per splice)
up to 6"	2
6" to 13½"	4

In addition to the screws, nails shall be driven through the web directly into the stiffener.

DETAILS OF NAIL-&-SCREWS-GLUED SPLICE PLATE

Splice plate and stiffener

Box Beam

Beam to column gusset plate glued to beam. Field connected to column with nails or bolts

Stiffener

Column

Flange Lumber Width	Suggested Nailing Schedule
4" - 6"	2 lines:
8" - 10"	3 lines:
12"	4 lines:

¾"

Plywood Thickness	Nail size (Box nails—cement coated)
up to ⅜"	4d
½" to ⅞"	6d
1" to 1⅛"	8d

SUGGESTED BEAM TO COLUMN CONNECTION

Hand access holes for inserting bolts (if web is in place)

Lumber stiffener (also acts as splice plate)

Web

A

Stitch Bolt

A

Tension Flange

20 ga. steel plate (drive fit)

Steel strap and lag screws

Compression Flange

Stiffener

Web Splice Plate

Tension Flange

Steel strap & shear plates

Weld

Section A-A

Steel strap

Shear plates

Plyshield or Plypanel . . cover plate nailed on

Where appearance is not important

Where appearance is important

Rout web for steel strap bolt heads and nuts with washers on outside of web.

Web cut away for welding. Replace after welding.

BOLTED TENSION FLANGE SPLICE

DETAIL OF COMPRESSION FLANGE SPLICE & FIELD-WELDED TENSION FLANGE SPLICE

By WILLIAM J. LeMESSURIER and ALBERT G. H. DIETZ*

Stressed-Skin Panels

The drawings on this and the following pages present cross sections of stressed-skin plywood panels for floors and roofs of houses. A panel consists of a bottom face of ¼-in. 3-ply plywood, four joists and two headers, and a top face of ⅜-in. 5-ply or ¾-in. 5-ply plywood. All panels use standard 4-ft-wide plywood with the face grain parallel to the joists. The lengths of the panels are variable, the maximum safe length being given in each case as a function of loading.

Structural Characteristics

In its structural action a stressed-skin panel is similar to a wide-flange steel beam. The top face carries compressive stress and the bottom face tension. Due to the tendency of the top and bottom faces to slip horizontally with relation to one another, important shearing stresses exist between the plywood and the joists and also within the joists. The only practical way to transmit this shear is by a glued joint between plywood and joists.

The top face of the panel has additional stresses resulting from slab action since it must carry local loads between joists. When the top face serves as a floor with only an asphalt tile, linoleum or carpet covering, it must be ¾ in. thick to carry local loads up to 250 lb without excessive deflection. For roof construction not intended for use as a deck and for floors where a finish hardwood floor is laid over the plywood, a ⅜-in.-thick top cover is satisfactory.

Gluing Technique

To obtain satisfactory glued joints pressure must be applied along the glue line. The best technique, obtainable only in a shop, is to use presses to apply a pressure of 150 lb per square inch of contact area uniformly along the entire glue line. For those panels with narrow joists

* *Assistant Professor and Professor, respectively, in the Department of Civil and Sanitary Engineering, Course in Building Engineering and Construction, Massachusetts Institute of Technology.*

of $\frac{25}{32}$ in. this method must be used. An alternative method is to use nails to provide pressure. To provide proper pressure 6d common nails at 2 in. on center must be used for ¼-in. plywood, at 3 in. on center for ⅜-in. plywood and for ¾-in. plywood 8d common nails at 5 in. on center are required. Sufficient pressure will be achieved by nailing when a uniform squeeze-out of the wet glue along the juncture of plywood and joist or header is visible. This nail-gluing method is satisfactory for all panels with joists 1⅝ in. wide.

The glue employed is extremely important. For panels which are not exposed to weather or high relative humidities, casein and urea resin glues will provide satisfactory bonds. For panels exposed to moisture, a highly moisture-resistant adhesive such as resorcinol formaldehyde or, with heated presses, phenol formaldehyde resins and melamine formaldehyde resins may be employed.

Framing Details

There are no unusual requirements in framing details for plywood panels. In general these panels may replace ordinary joist construction. The only unusual problem is the joint between panels. In floors with-

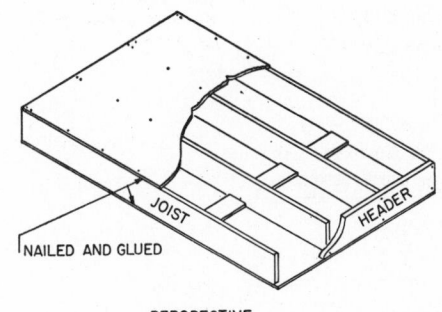

PERSPECTIVE

NAILED AND GLUED

JOIST   HEADER

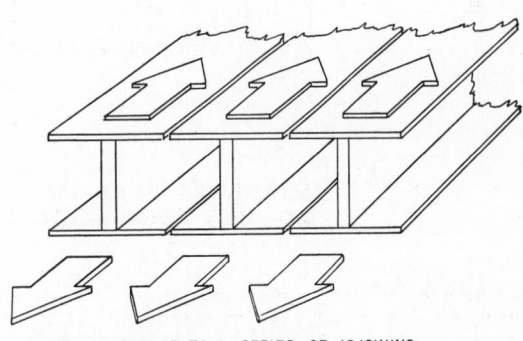

ACTION IS SIMILAR TO A SERIES OF ADJOINING BUILT-UP WOODEN I BEAMS

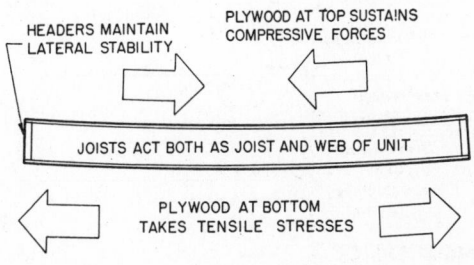

HEADERS MAINTAIN LATERAL STABILITY

PLYWOOD AT TOP SUSTAINS COMPRESSIVE FORCES

JOISTS ACT BOTH AS JOIST AND WEB OF UNIT

PLYWOOD AT BOTTOM TAKES TENSILE STRESSES

out finish wood a spline joint should be provided to prevent uneven deflections. In other cases panels may be simply butted together.

For panels longer than 16 ft, the plywood faces must be spliced, since plywood is not obtainable in longer sheets. These splices should be located at a point not more than one quarter of the span from the ends of the panel for joist depths of 6 in. or less and not more than one third of the panel length from the end for joist depths greater than 6 in. The splice may be made with a strip of plywood 10 in. wide of the same thickness as the plywood joined, and glued under pressure.

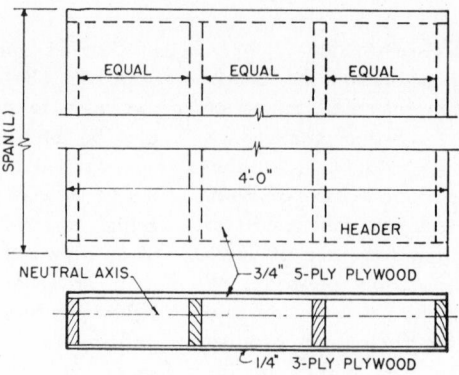

PLAN AND SECTION OF TYPICAL PANEL

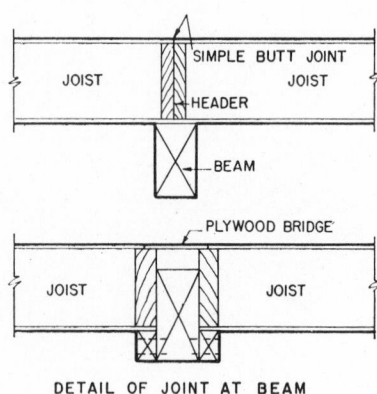

DETAIL OF JOINT AT BEAM

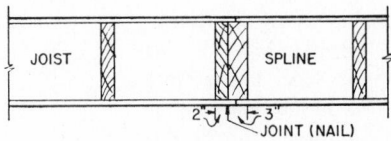

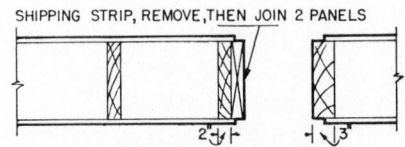

Nominal thicknesses shown above

SPLINE DETAIL
(METHOD OF JOINING TWO ADJACENT PANELS)

Design Specifications:

Exterior Douglas Fir Plywood Grade A-B
Top panel: ¾-in. 5-ply plywood
Bottom panel: ¼-in. 3-ply plywood
No. 2 Structural Douglas Fir Joists

Design Data:

250 lb point load *or*
40 psf distributed load
10 psf dead load
Maximum deflection:
  1/300 for full load
  1/360 for live load

Note: *Type designations: FH stands for a floor panel with a heavy (thick) top layer; the first number is the joist thickness in inches; the second number or pair of numbers is the joist depth in inches (nominal dimensions). For example, FH212 is a heavy floor panel having joists 2 in. thick and 12 in. deep.*

FLOOR PANELS (HEAVY)

JOIST DEPTH—SPAN TABLE

Floor Panels for Use with Composition or Cork Flooring or Carpeting (Without Finished Wood Floor)

Type	Joist	Maximum Span Limited by		I in ^{4}/ft of width	Glue type
		Deflection	Stress		
FH14	$^{25}/_{32}''$ x 3⅝''	....	7' 2''	25.0	Pressure
FH16	$^{25}/_{32}''$ x 5⅝''	....	11' 4''	59.4	Pressure
FH24	1⅝'' x 3⅝''	11' 9''	14' 0''	29.0	Nail
FH26	1⅝'' x 5⅝''	16' 0''	18' 6''	72.5	Nail
FH28	1⅝'' x 7½''	19' 10''	22' 8''	136.8	Nail
FH210	1⅝'' x 9½''	23' 8''	27' 0''	235.6	Nail
FH212	1⅝'' x 11½''	27' 8''	31' 2''	372.0	Nail

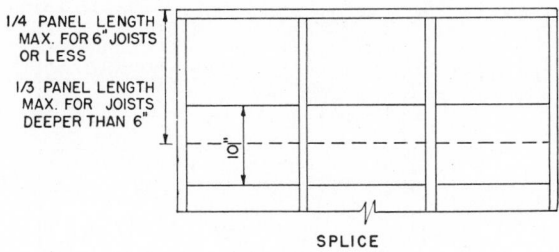

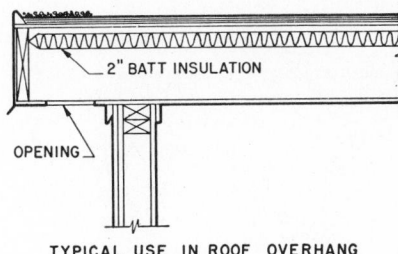

1/4 PANEL LENGTH MAX. FOR 6" JOISTS OR LESS

1/3 PANEL LENGTH MAX. FOR JOISTS DEEPER THAN 6"

10"

SPLICE

2" BATT INSULATION

OPENING

TYPICAL USE IN ROOF OVERHANG

FLOOR PANELS (LIGHT)

JOIST DEPTH — SPAN TABLE
Floor Panels for Use with ⅞-in. Finished Wood Floor

Type	Joist	Maximum Span Limited by		I in ⁴/ft of width	Glue type
		Deflection	Stress		
FL14	25/32″ x 3⅝″	....	9′ 5″	18.06	Pressure
FL16	25/32″ x 5⅝″	....	13′ 4″	44.4	Pressure
FL24	1⅝″ x 3⅝″	10′ 7″	12′ 6″	21.0	Nail
FL26	1⅝″ x 5⅝″	14′ 6″	16′ 5″	55.0	Nail
FL28	1⅝″ x 7½″	18′ 4″	20′ 2″	107.2	Nail
FL210	1⅝″ x 9½″	22′ 2″	23′ 9″	189.5	Nail
FL212	1⅝″ x 11½″	25′ 11″	27′ 7″	305.0	Nail

Design Specifications:

Exterior Douglas Fir Plywood Grade A-B
Top panel: ⅜-in. 5-ply plywood
Bottom panel: ¼-in. 3-ply plywood
No. 2 Structural Douglas Fir Joists

Design Data:

250 lb point load *or*
40 psf distributed load
10 psf dead load
Maximum deflection:
   I/300 for full load
   I/360 for live load

Note: Type designations: R stands for roof panel; FL stands for a floor panel with a light (thin) top layer. The first number is the joist thickness in inches; the second number or pair of numbers is the joist depth in inches. For example, R210 is a roof joist 2 in. thick and 10 in. deep. FL14 is a light floor panel having joists 1 in. thick and 4 in. deep (all nominal dimensions).

Design Specifications:

Exterior Douglas Fir Plywood Grade A-B
Top panel: ⅜-in. 5-ply plywood
Bottom panel: ¼-in. 3-ply plywood
No. 2 Structural Douglas Fir Joists

Design Data:

20, 30, 40 psf distributed load
15 psf dead load
Maximum deflection:
   I/240 for full load

ROOF PANELS

ROOF JOIST — SPAN TABLE

Roof Panels for Use with Insulation, Tar and Gravel or Shingles

Type	Joist	Maximum Span Limited by						I in ⁴/ft of width	Glue type
		Defl.	Stress	Defl.	Stress	Defl.	Stress		
		Live Load 20 psf		Live Load 30 psf		Live Load 40 psf			
R14	25/32″ x 3⅝″	12′ 3″	13′ 1″	....	10′ 2″	......	8′ 4″	18.06	Pressure
R16	25/32″ x 5⅝″	16′ 7″	18′ 0″	....	14′ 10″	......	12′ 2″	44.4	Pressure
R24	1⅝″ x 3⅝″	12′ 10″	14′ 10″	11′ 10″	13′ 1″	11′ 1″	11′ 11″	21.0	Nail
R26	1⅝″ x 5⅝″	17′ 10″	19′ 8″	16′ 4″	17′ 5″	15′ 4″	15′ 8″	55.0	Nail
R28	1⅝″ x 7½″	22′ 3″	23′ 11″	20′ 5″	21′ 2″	19′ 1″	19′ 2″	107.2	Nail
R210	1⅝″ x 9½″	26′ 11″	28′ 5″	24′ 7″	25′ 2″	......	22′ 10″	189.5	Nail
R212	1⅝″ x 11½″	31′ 5″	32′ 10″	28′ 11″	29′ 2″	......	26′ 5″	305.0	Nail

Data on this and the following three pages from Manual for House Framing, National Lumber Manufacturers Association

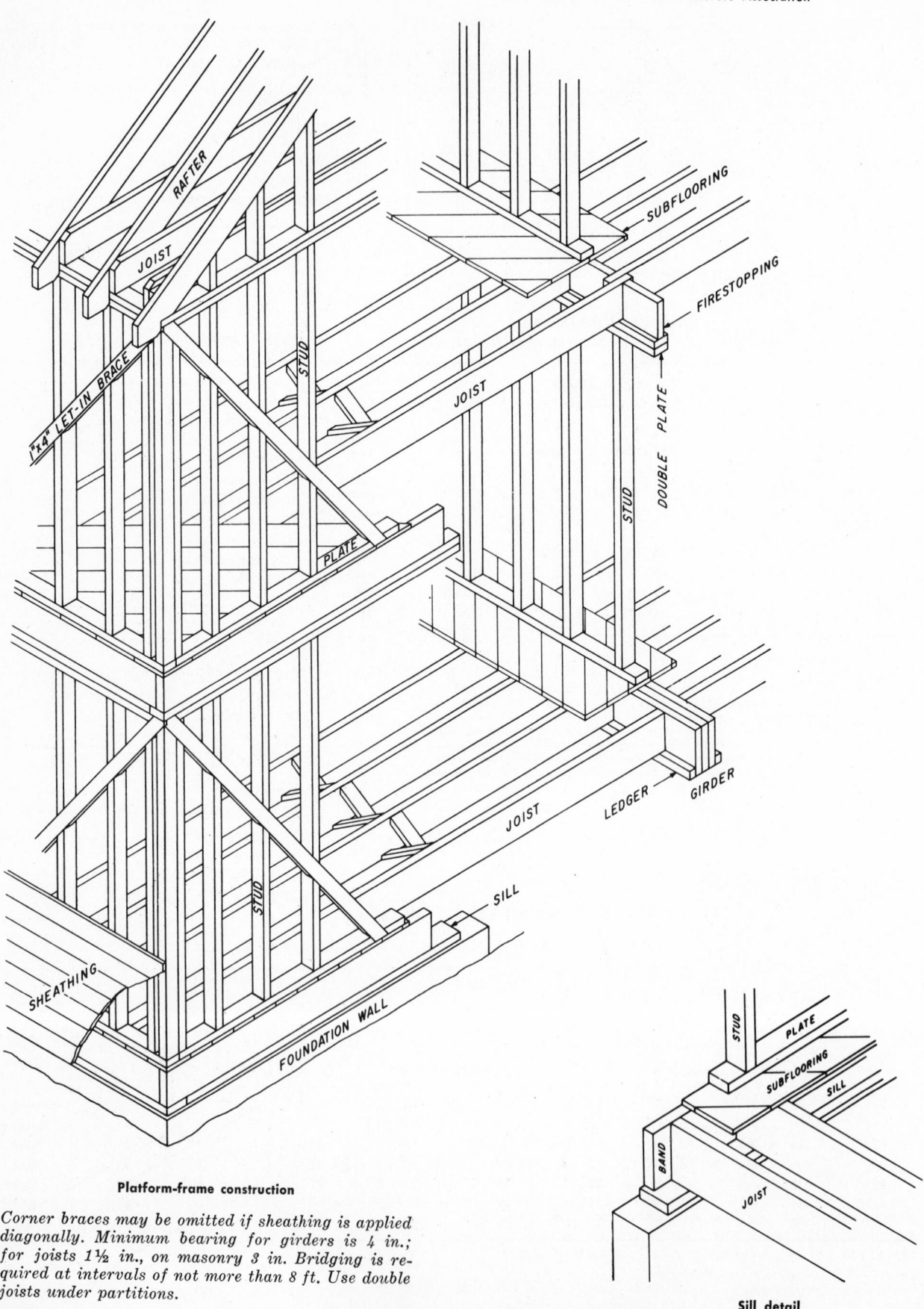

RAFTER

JOIST

SUBFLOORING

FIRESTOPPING

1"x4" LET-IN BRACE

STUD

JOIST

DOUBLE PLATE

STUD

PLATE

JOIST

LEDGER

GIRDER

STUD

SILL

SHEATHING

FOUNDATION WALL

Platform-frame construction

Corner braces may be omitted if sheathing is applied diagonally. Minimum bearing for girders is 4 in.; for joists 1½ in., on masonry 3 in. Bridging is required at intervals of not more than 8 ft. Use double joists under partitions.

STUD

PLATE

SUBFLOORING

SILL

BAND

JOIST

Sill detail

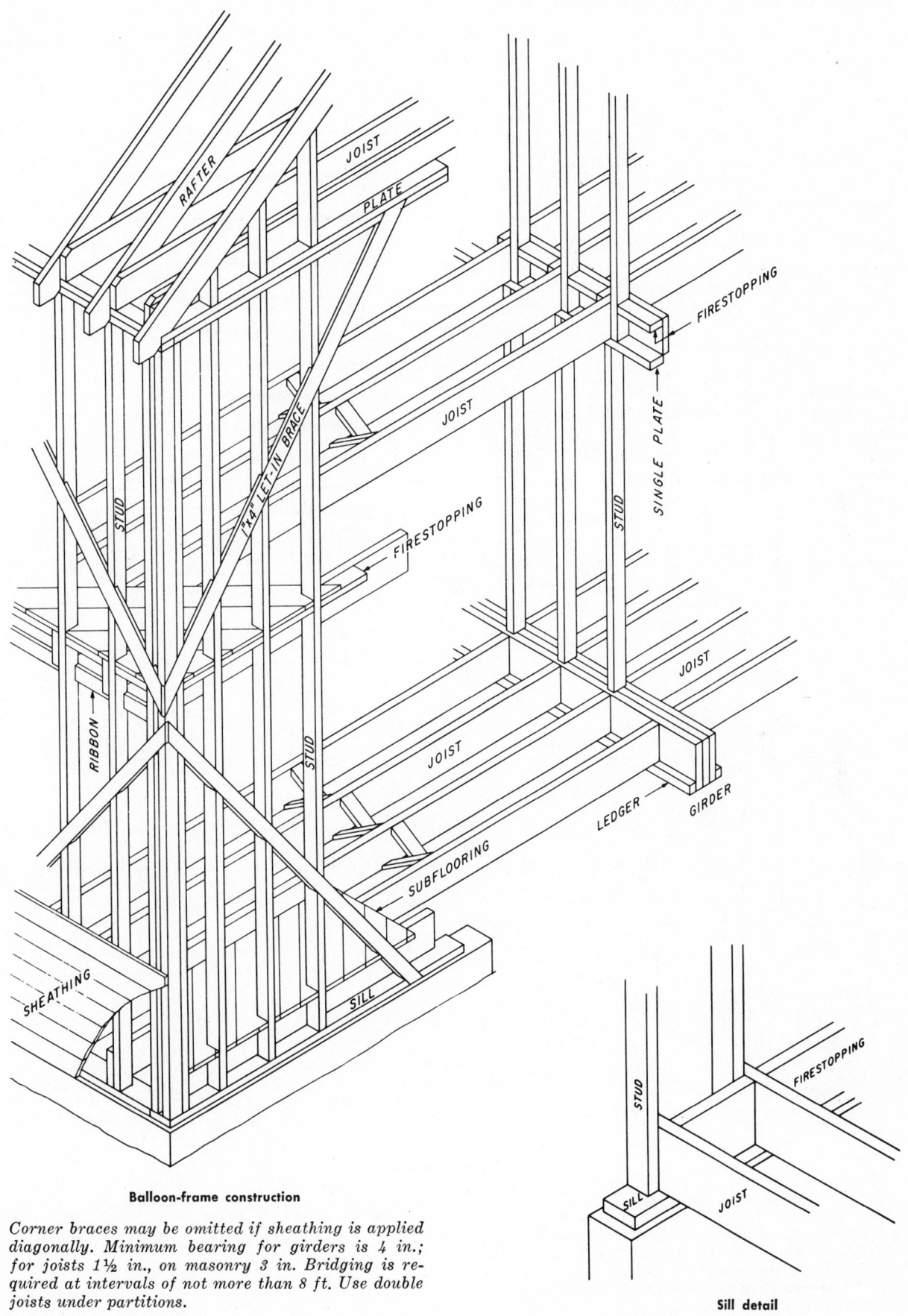

Balloon-frame construction

Corner braces may be omitted if sheathing is applied diagonally. Minimum bearing for girders is 4 in.; for joists 1½ in., on masonry 3 in. Bridging is required at intervals of not more than 8 ft. Use double joists under partitions.

Sill detail

WOOD CONSTRUCTION—3
Light wood framing

RECOMMENDED NAILING SCHEDULE USING COMMON NAILS

Joist to sill or girder, toe nail................. 3-8d
Bridging to joist, toe nail each end........... 2-8d
Ledger strip........................... 3-16d
                                    at each joist
1″ x 6″ subfloor or less to each joist, face nail.. 2-8d
Over 1″ x 6″ subfloor to each joist, face nail... 3-8d
2″ subfloor to joist or girder, blind and face nail. 2-16d
Sole plate to joist or blocking, face nail....... 16d @ 16″ oc
Top plate to stud, end nail................... 2-16d
Stud to sole plate, toe nail................. 4-8d
Doubled studs, face nail.................... 16d @ 24″ oc
Doubled top plates, face nail................ 16d @ 16″ oc
Top plates, laps and intersections, face nail.... 2-16d
Continuous header, two pieces............... 16d @ 16″ oc
                                    along each edge
Ceiling joists to plate, toe nail.............. 3-8d
Continuous header to stud, toe nail........... 4-8d
Ceiling joists, laps over partitions, face nail.... 3-16d
Ceiling joists to parallel rafters, face nail...... 3-16d
Rafter to plate, toe nail.................... 3-8d
1-inch brace to each stud and plate, face nail... 2-8d
1″ x 8″ sheathing or less to each bearing,
    face nail 2-8d
Over 1″ x 8″ sheathing to each bearing, face nail 3-8d
Built-up corner studs..................... 16d @ 24″ oc
Built-up girders and beams................. 20d @ 32″ oc
                                    along each edge

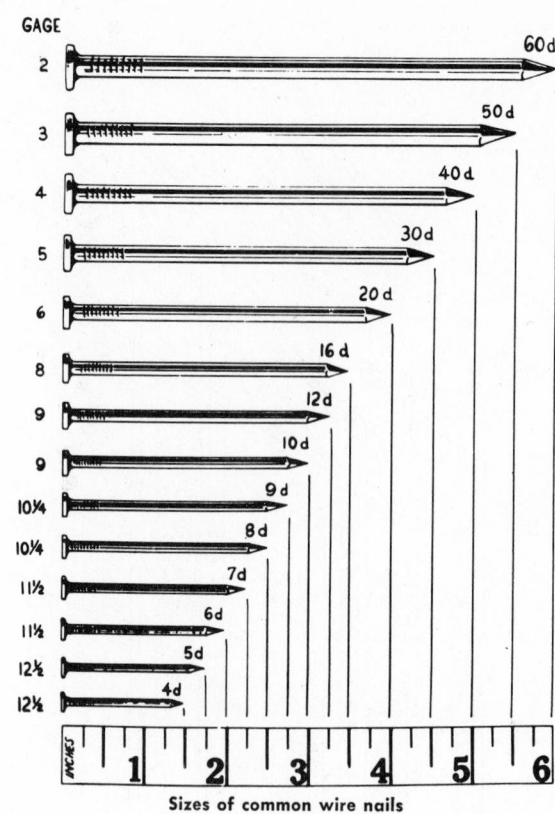

GAGE

Sizes of common wire nails

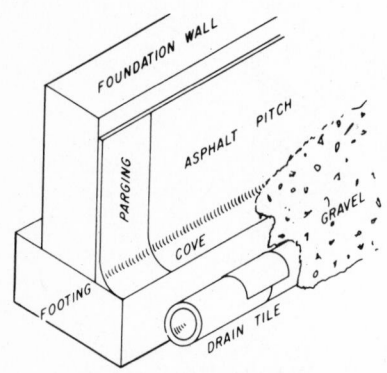

Foundation wall and footing

Footing depth is usually made equal to the foundation wall thickness, and footing width twice the wall thickness.

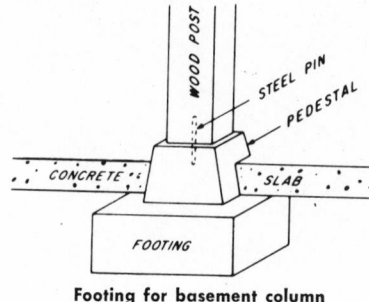

Footing for basement column

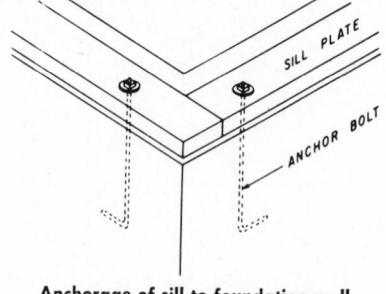

Anchorage of sill to foundation wall

Anchor bolts, ½ in. in diameter, should be spaced not more than 8 ft apart, and embedded at least 6 in. in concrete or 15 in. in masonry.

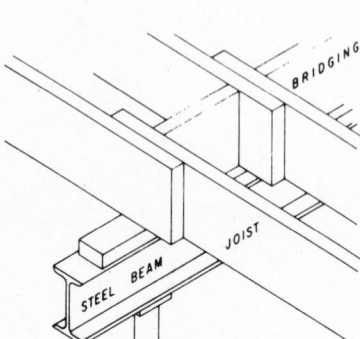

Joists on steel girder

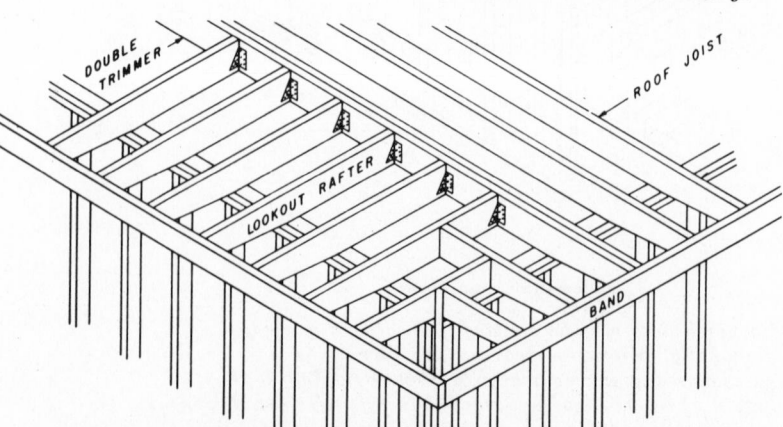

Corner detail of overhanging flat roof

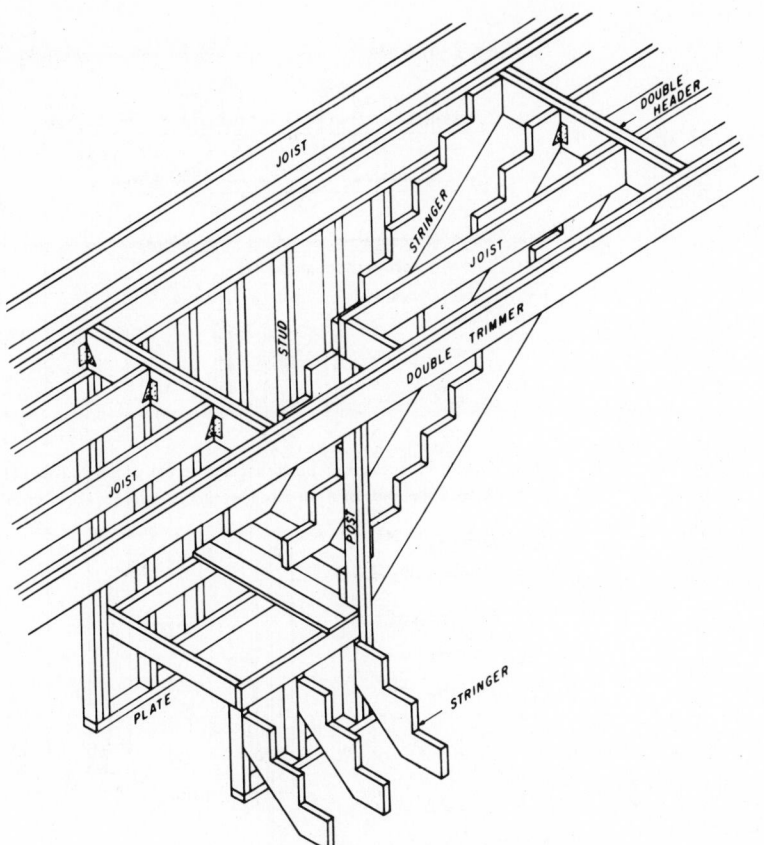

Framing for stairway with landing

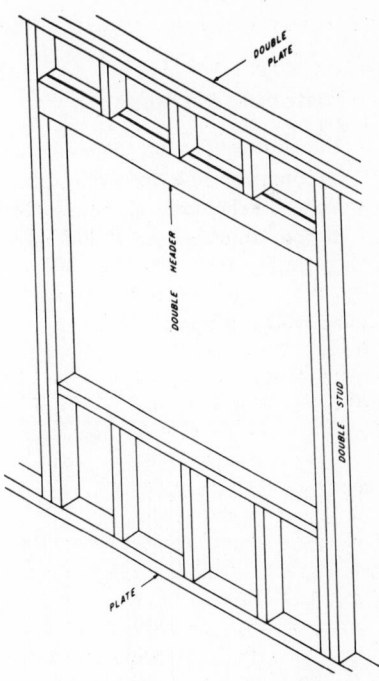

Framing around exterior wall opening

For openings over 6 ft wide, use triple studs, with the header bearing on two studs at each side.

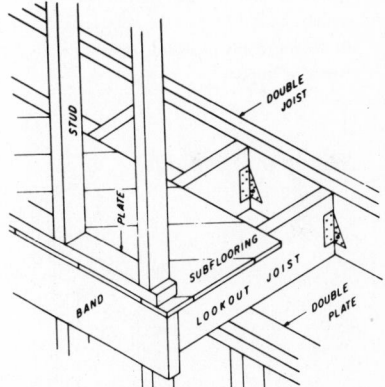

Overhanging second floor with joists parallel to wall below

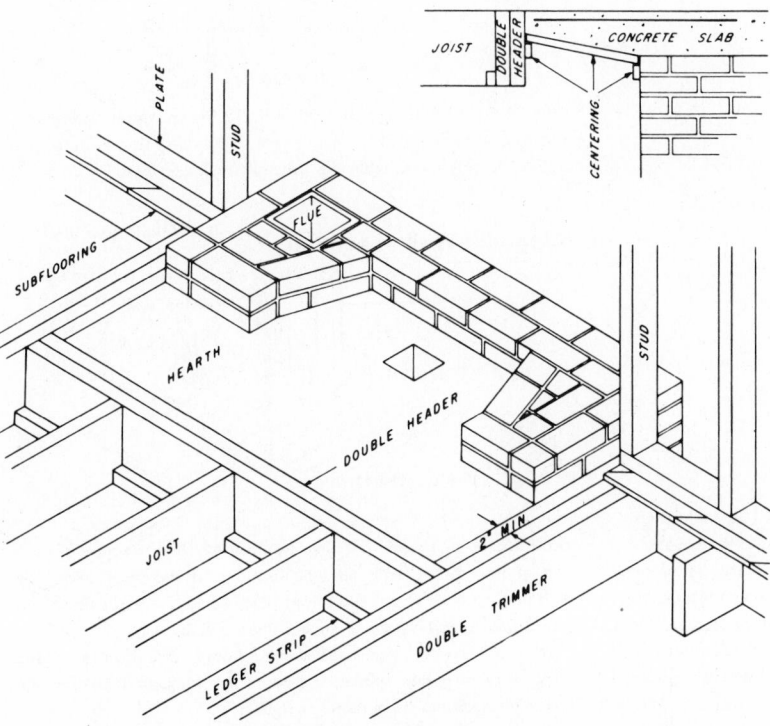

Floor framing around fireplace

Wood framing must be kept 2 in. clear of all fireplace and chimney masonry.

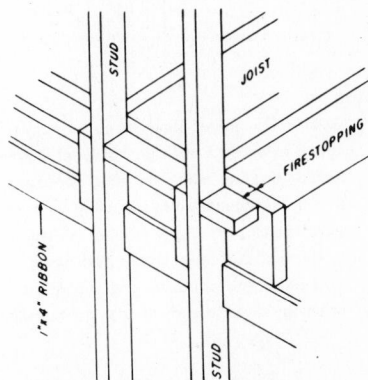

Second-floor framing at exterior wall—balloon-frame construction

WOOD CONSTRUCTION—5
Nailing

Fastening Methods

The illustrations of common nailing practices shown on this and the following page have been taken from "Techniques of House Nailing," a publication of the Housing and Home Finance Agency (HHFA)

Door Openings

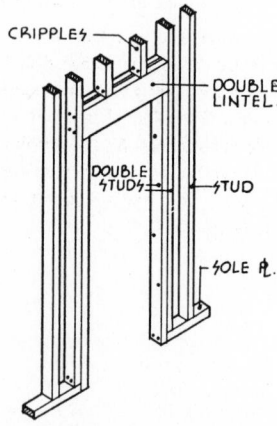

Cripples toenailed to each part of lintel with one 10d nail. Studs nailed to ends of each part of lintel with two 10d nails; double studs nailed together with 10d nails spaced 16 in. apart and staggered as shown. Studs alongside opening nailed into end of sole plate with two 10d nails

Window Openings

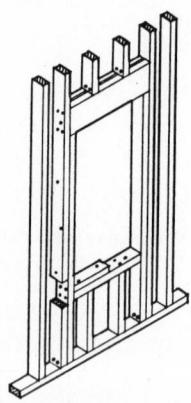

Cripples toenailed to each part of lintel with one 10d nail. Studs nailed to ends of each part of lintel with two 10d nails; double studs nailed together with 10d nails, spaced 16 in. apart, staggered as shown, and toenailed to sole plate with four 10d nails, two from each side. Lower part of sill member nailed to end of each stud below it with two 10d nails. Upper part of sill member nailed to lower with 10d nails, spaced 8 in., and staggered as shown. Studs alongside opening nailed to ends of each part of sill member with two 10d nails

Nailing Symbols

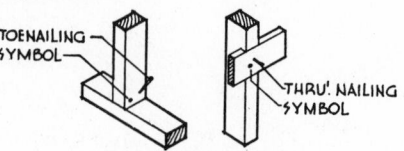

Open circles can represent toenailing in drawings, for extra clarity; closed circles, direct or through nailing

Top Plate

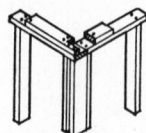

Lower part of plate nailed to each stud and corner post with two 16d nails, two near the ends of each piece; others staggered 16 in. apart

Corner Post

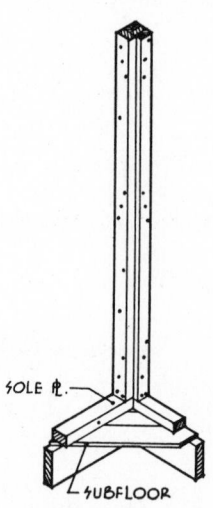

Studs nailed together with 10d nails 12 in. on center, staggered, and to each filler block with three 10d nails. Corner post toenailed to sole plate with two 8d nails on each face.

Diagonal Wall Sheathing

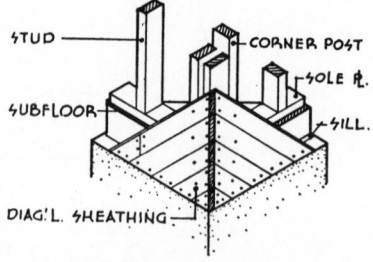

Use 8d nails for boards 8 in. and less in width. Use two nails at each end of board; two nails through each board into studs and three nails through each board into corner post assembly. For wider boards, an additional nail is used at each of these points.

Joints in adjacent lengths of sheathing boards should be separated by at least two stud spaces. If boards are tongued and grooved, end joints need not be made over studs

Plywood Sheathing

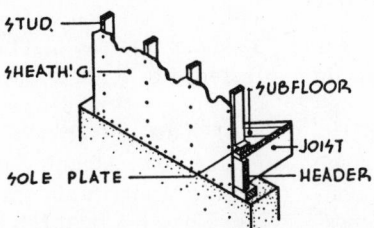

Sheathing less than ½ in. thick is nailed with 6d nails spaced 5 in. apart along edges; 10 in. apart on intermediate framing members. Plywood ½ in., or more, thick and fiberboard wall sheathings are nailed with 8d nails and require the same spacing. Nails for fiberboards should be rust resistant.

Bevel Siding and Drop Siding

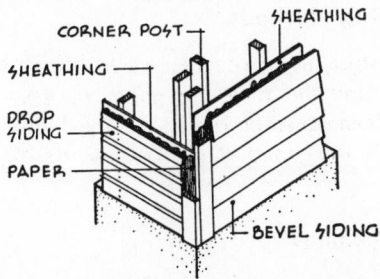

Are face-nailed to each stud; bevel siding with two 8d rust resistant casing nails driven through overlap of siding, then sheathing into each stud; drop siding with two 9d casing nails, one near top of flat surface and the other at bottom. When siding is applied in jig, corner boards are placed and nailed after tip-up. A poor practice is to allow siding to start and end at corners, then cover with corner boards. The spaces between corner boards and siding are likely to rot when water settles in these spaces

Special Fastening Device Applications Are Shown Below

Metal Grip Applications

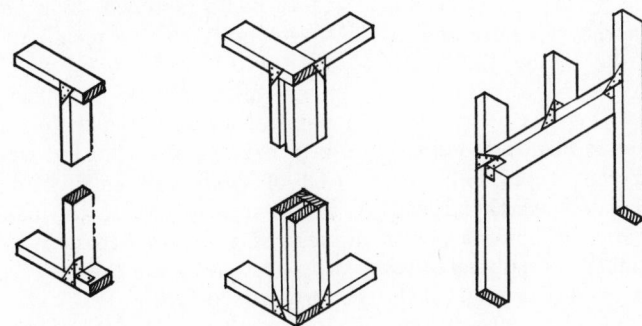

Hurricane Brace Applications

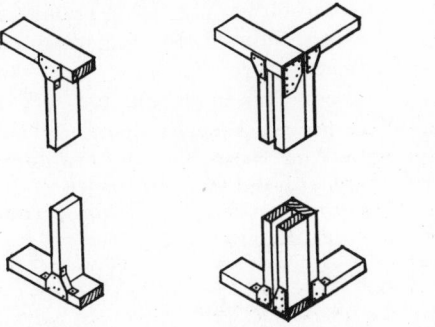

By HOWARD P. VERMILYA, AIA

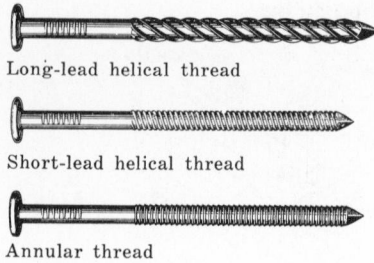

Long-lead helical thread

Short-lead helical thread

Annular thread

Nails are the oldest type of metal fastening device for wood joints. They are easily applied and inexpensive. Developments during the last 25 years made possible the mass production of properly designed threaded nails which have retained these qualities and considerably increased their effectiveness as fasteners.

Basic types

The *helically threaded nail* with medium lead angle (approximately 60° from a plane perpendicular to the nail axis) turns like a screw during hammer driving and forms a thread in the wood similar to that of the nail. The *annularly threaded nail*, with rings perpendicular to its shank, when driven forces the wood fibers over the thread crests and into the space between the thread shoulders so as to greatly resist withdrawal.

Variations

Not only may the heads and points be of the many types now available with common wire nails, but the pattern of the thread may be varied to adapt it most effectively to the specific problem. In common with plain-shank wire nails, the wire size, metal composition and finish of threaded nails may be varied. Heat treating and tempering can provide added strength and stiffness.

Uses

The threaded nail has demonstrated its merit in a number of applications. The *gypsum wallboard nail*, the heat-treated *hardwood flooring nail*, the *plywood*

sheathing nail and the *roofing nail* are only a few of those that are recognized as doing a superior job.

A further contribution is the application of threaded nails to *nailed trussed rafters*. The superiority in double shear and the stiffness of the high-carbon steel, heat-treated and hardened, helically threaded nail make it possible to build an all-nailed trussed rafter practically as stiff and equally as strong as a nail-glued one, with only two and one-half times as many nails and without the attendant problems of gluing either in the plant or in the field.

The development of threaded nails and the recognition of their advantages by users are the result to a great extent of the comprehensive research program sponsored over the last decade by the Independent Nail and Packing Company at the Virginia Polytechnic Institute's Wood Research Laboratory under the direction of Professor E. George Stern.

Advantages of threaded nails

1. When green or partially seasoned lumber is used, the threaded nail retains its holding power as the lumber is subjected to changes in moisture content or temperature. The plain-shank common wire nail, however, may lose up to four-fifths of its initial holding power, in as little as six weeks' time.

2. The threaded nail is not likely to loosen or pop as a result of creep induced by moisture or temperature changes in the wood. This same quality serves to prevent squeaky floors, caused by the loose flooring rubbing against the nail or itself.

3. V.P.I. research demonstrated that hardened-steel threaded nails may be slimmer than standard plain-shank nails when substituted for them. These thinner and stiffer nails may be driven faster with less danger of bending and less likelihood of split-

ting. This is particularly advantageous where nails must be closely spaced as in the joints of all-nailed trussed rafters.

4. When plywood diaphragms are fastened to their frames, shorter but thicker threaded nails can be used more effectively than the longer plain-shank nails, and permit easier and faster driving. (The 1½ by 0.135 in. bright threaded nail has 2.8 times the holding power of an 8d, 2½ by 0.129 in. common wire nail and 1.1 times the delayed lateral strength.)

5. The increased holding power of the threaded point end of the nail makes it possible to nail from one side only when nailing joints in single, double and multiple shear. This permits easier and faster nailing. Further, by providing clearance (a plain shank section) between the head of the nail and the threaded portion equal to the thickness of the piece to be fastened, it is possible to pull the two members together. A ⅛ in. to ¼ in. plain shank pilot can be used for the point of a threaded nail to facilitate driving into harder woods. All of these refinements in design serve to add to the usefulness of the threaded nail.

Strength factors

Both the allowable lateral strength and the withdrawal resistance of threaded nails are determined by the diameter, the configuration and slope of the thread, the composition and temper of the metal wire. Further variables are the amount of penetration and the specific gravity and moisture content of the wood into which the nails are to be driven.

Annularly threaded nails are specially resistant to *axial withdrawal* and provide maximum service as fasteners of sheet materials to plywood or softwood.

Helically threaded nails are particularly *effective in hardwoods* and in providing *resistance* to bending.

1 2 3 4 5 6 7 8 9 10 11 12 13 14 15 16 17 18 19 20 21 22 23 24 25 26

1, 2. Annular thread and spiral thread "common nails": for framing and general use.

3, 4. Annular thread and spiral thread sinkers: for sub-floors, boarding in, etc.

5. Flooring nails; hardened steel, spiral thread (prevent squeaking).

6. Underlay floor nails (prevent squeaking; eliminate bumps in linoleum, tile, carpeting).

7. Parquet floor nails.

8. Shear-resistant, spiral threaded nails: for fastening plywood diaphragms, gusset plates, etc.

9. Dry wall nails (designed to eliminate "popping and loosening").

10. Asbestos board nails; heat-treated and tempered.

11. Acoustic tile nails (can be driven without marring tile).

12. Rachet nails: for use with nailable channels.

13. Interior hardboard nails; hardened steel, small head, annular thread.

14, 15, 16. Wallboard nails.

17. Wood shingle face nails (eliminate tendency of shingles or shakes to curl).

18, 19, 20. Asbestos shingle nails; type "F" thread, annular or screw thread.

21, 22. Roofing nails with neoprene washers; annular thread and spiral thread: for application of corrugated or sheet metal material.

23, 24. Roofing nails for asphalt shingles; spiral or annular threads; or smooth.

25, 26. Roofing and siding nails: for fastening wood, asphalt or asbestos shingles and siding to plywood sheathing; roofing (25), siding (26).

27, 28. Built-up roofing nails; annular thread for wood and plywood (28); spiral thread for gypsum decking (27).

29. Concrete stub nail, hardened: for fastening plywood and metal fixtures to concrete.

30. Masonry nails: for fastening mudsills and partition plates to concrete.

31. Masonry nails: for fastening materials to brick, concrete, etc.

32. Exterior hardboard nails (eliminate predrilling).

33. Trussed rafter nails.

34. Roof decking nails: for applying insulating roof decking.

35. Pole-type construction nails.

36. Purlin nails.

37. Gutter spikes.

Drawings from Independent Mail and Packaging Co.

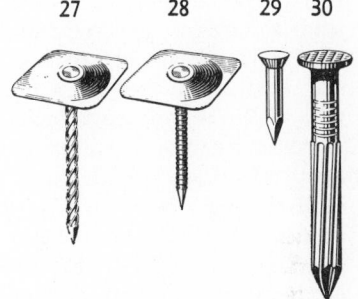

27 28 29 30

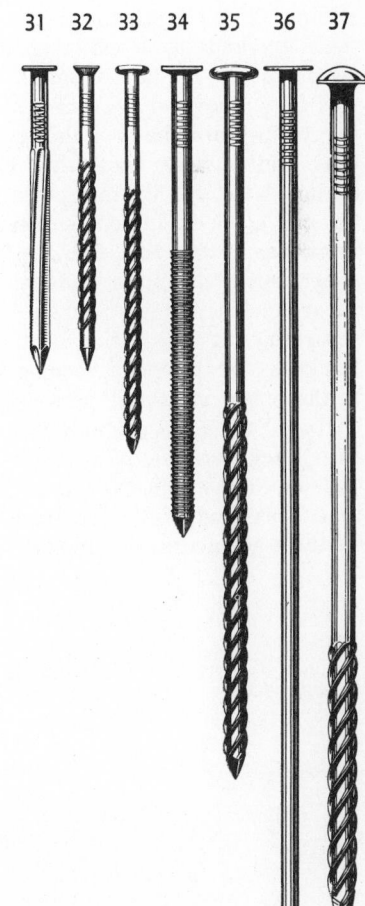

31 32 33 34 35 36 37

Lateral strength

The deformation of the nailed joint, loaded laterally, is the primary consideration in establishing an allowable lateral load. The common wire nail has about the same resistance as the low-carbon-steel helically threaded nail when driven into side-grain lumber. The high-carbon-steel, hardened, helically threaded nail, because of its greater stiffness and increased withdrawal resistance, even under lateral load conditions, can use the design value normally credited to the common wire plain-shank nail which is one gauge heavier.

Professor Stern states as a result of his work with threaded nails at Virginia Polytechnic Institute's Wood Research Laboratory that a helically threaded, hardened nail loaded in double shear can transmit twice the design load attributed to that nail in single shear, in a joint consisting of two nominal 1-in. side members and one nominal 2-in. center member. The *Douglas Fir Use Book*, however, in commenting upon plain-shank nails says that limited tests show that at design level of holding power, the nail capacity in double shear is at least twice that for single shear, but at ultimate loads, the shear efficiency is less and varies according to the ratio of the thickness of the side members to the center member. It, as well as the *National Design Specification for Stress-Grade Lumber and its Fastenings*, recommends that when a nail fully penetrates all three members, the allowable load be increased over that for single shear by one-third when each side member is not less than about one-third the thickness of the center member, increased by two-thirds when each side member is equal in thickness to the center member. This refers to plain-shank nails whereas Professor Stern's recommendation referred specifically to high-carbon-steel, hardened, helically threaded nails.

Tests of full-size trussed rafter assemblies carried out at Wood Research Laboratory of Virginia Polytechnic Institute, with joints having multiple nails in double shear using the design values ascribed to these threaded nails by Professor Stern (namely twice that of nails in single shear), have withstood loads of from five-and-one-half to seven times the design load before failure. In all cases the failure had been in the wood members of the assembly rather than in the joints, with joint deformation held to a negligible amount.

Withdrawal strength

Nails loaded in direct withdrawal from side-grain lumber are not so efficient in strength as when loaded laterally. Withdrawal resistance of nails is materially affected by the specific gravity of the wood, varying with the density even within species. The significant loss in holding power concurrent with wood seasoning and the numerous uncertainties in joints of this type have resulted in the practice of ascribing a factor of safety of six in determining allowable loads for plain-shank nails. Professor Stern, as a result of the higher and longer lasting holding power observed in his research with threaded nails, recommends that this factor of safety be reduced to two when applied to the ultimate test load for a properly threaded nail loaded in axial withdrawal. Consequently, withdrawal design values for such threaded nails of the same diameter or gauge can be at least three times that for plain-shank nails.

Other design factors

When more than one nail is used in the same joint the total allowable load in withdrawal or lateral resistance is the sum of the allowable loads for the individual nails. This applies provided the edge and end distances, and spacings parallel and perpendicular to the grain are sufficient to develop the full strength of the nails without splitting the member. Spacing of threaded nails should be as follows (same as for plain-shank nails): not less than five Diameters from the edge of the member, 15 D-20 D from the end, and not less than five D against and 15 D-20 D with the grain.

To further reduce the hazard of splitting, plain-shank and threaded nails may be driven into prebored holes of approximately 70 per cent of the shank or thread-root diameter in width, and 70 per cent of the depth or penetration.

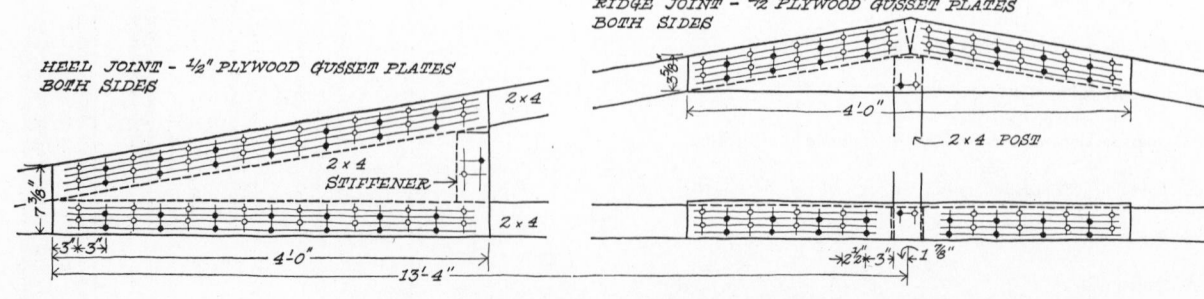

Design of an all-nailed, king-post trussed rafter, 26-ft 8-in. span

Safe lateral load-carrying capacity (shear resistance) and withdrawal resistance

(Common Wire Nails and Threaded Nails in Douglas Fir and Southern Pine)

Penny-weight	Length, Inches	Common Wire Nail — Diameter, Inches	Common Wire Nail — Count per Pound	Hardened Threaded Nail — Diameter, Inches	Hardened Threaded Nail — Count per Pound	Lateral (Single Shear) Common Wire Nail, Douglas Fir & Southern Pine	Lateral Hardened Helically Threaded Nail* (a)	Lateral Hardened Helically Threaded Nail* (b)	Side-Grain Common Wire Dense Coast-Type Dougl. Fir	Side-Grain Common Wire Dense Coast-Type Dougl. Fir	Side-Grain Common Wire S.P.	Side-Grain Hardened DF (c)	(c')	(d)	(d')	Side-Grain Hardened S.P. (e)	(e')	(f)	End-Grain Common Wire Nail	End-Grain Hardened S.P. (g-e)	(g-e')	(g-f)
6d	2	0.113	181	0.105	190	63	69	93	29	33	42	67	81	78	93	97	116	…	Plain-Shank Nails NOT to be Loaded in Withdrawal from End-Grain of Wood	81	97	…
8d	2½	0.131	106	0.120	117	78	82	106	34	39	48	77	92	89	106	111	133	187		92	111	156
10d	3	0.148	69	0.135	78	94	94	188	38	44	55	87	104	100	120	124	149	206		104	124	172
12d	3¼	0.148	63	0.135	73	94	94	188	38	44	55	87	104	100	120	124	149	206		104	124	172
16d	3½	0.162	49	0.148	57	107	107	212	42	48	60	95	114	109	131	136	164	…		114	136	…
20d	4	0.192	31	0.177	36	139	139	262	49	57	71	114	136	131	157	163	196	256		136	163	213
30d	4½	0.207	24	0.177	31	154	139	262	53	61	76	114	136	131	157	163	196	256		136	163	213
40d	5	0.225	18	0.177	27	176	139	262	58	67	83	114	136	131	157	163	196	256		136	163	213
50d	5½	0.244	14	0.177	23	202	139	262	63	72	90	114	136	131	157	163	196	256		136	163	213
60d	6	0.263	11	0.177	18	223	139	262	68	78	97	114	136	131	157	163	196	256		136	163	213
Shear Resistant Spiral Threaded Nail†	1½	….	…	0.135	158	…	94	188	…	…	…	87	104	100	120	124	149	206		104	124	172
	2½	….	…	0.135	101	…	94	188	…	…	…	87	104	100	120	124	149	206		104	124	172

Based on page 65 of "National Design Specification for Stress-Grade Lumber and its Fastenings" (1960 edition), subject to adjustments (see Section 203A, etc.).

Limitations: Design values for lateral load-carrying capacity of common wire nails based on two-thirds shank penetration and those of hardened helically threaded Screw-Tite® nails based on one-half shank penetration of shortest nail of given diameter.

Selection of Design Values of Threaded Nails: Column (b) is based on derivation procedures generally accepted for common wire nails and indicates the extreme conservatism of the design values shown in Column (a). Columns (f) and (g-f) take into consideration the fact that the test values for delayed withdrawal resistance of properly threaded nails are similar to the immediate test values. This fact eliminates the need for a factor of safety of six for immediate ultimate withdrawal resistance which is customarily applied to common wire nails. A factor of safety of two is fully adequate. Again, these design values indicate the conservatism of the design values presented in Columns (c), (d), (e), and (g-e).

(a) Design values for one-gauge larger common wire nail.
(b) One-sixth of test value (page 26 of V.P.I. Wood Research Laboratory Bulletin No. 3).
(c) 1150x3x0.186 D (acc. to FPL).   (d) 1150x3x0.214 D.   (e) 1150x3x0.267 D.
(c') 1380x3x0.186 D (acc. to NDS).   (d') 1380x3x0.214 D.   (e') 1380x3x0.267 D.
Three times design value for plain-shank nail of same wire diameter.
(f) One-half of test value (page 26 of V.P.I. Wood Research Laboratory Bulletin No. 3).
(g) Five-sixths of design value for side-grain penetration (Timber News, Vol. 59, No. 2138, pp. 490-492, December, 1950).

Table prepared by Professor E. George Stern, Virginia Polytechnic Institute Wood Research Laboratory. Threaded nail values based on products of the Independent Nail & Packing Company, Bridgewater, Mass.

* tests based on use of Screw-Tite® nails made by Independent Nail & Packing Company
† tests based on use of Hi-Load® nails (For plywood diaphragms and gusset plates) made by same company

The designs shown on this and the following page are from *Typical Designs of Timber Structures*, 3rd ed., Timber Engineering Company, Washington, D.C. (1955), and are intended for guidance only. All designs are based on live load plus dead load on roof of 35 psf, dead load on ceiling of 10 psf, and a spacing of 2 ft. Bowstring design is based on stresses of $c = 1,200$ psi and $f = 1,450$ psi; for all other designs $C = 900$ psi and $f = 900$ psi; in all cases $E = 1,600,000$ psi. All designs provide a ½ to ¾-in. camber in the lower chord.

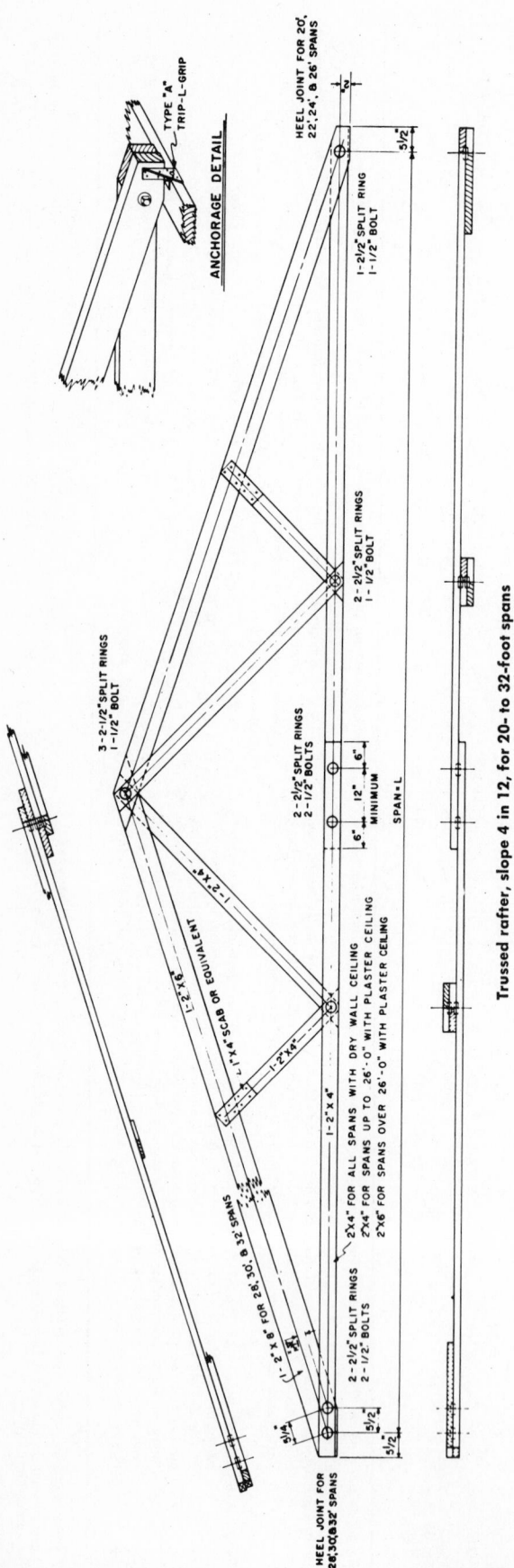

Trussed rafter, slope 4 in 12, for 20- to 32-foot spans

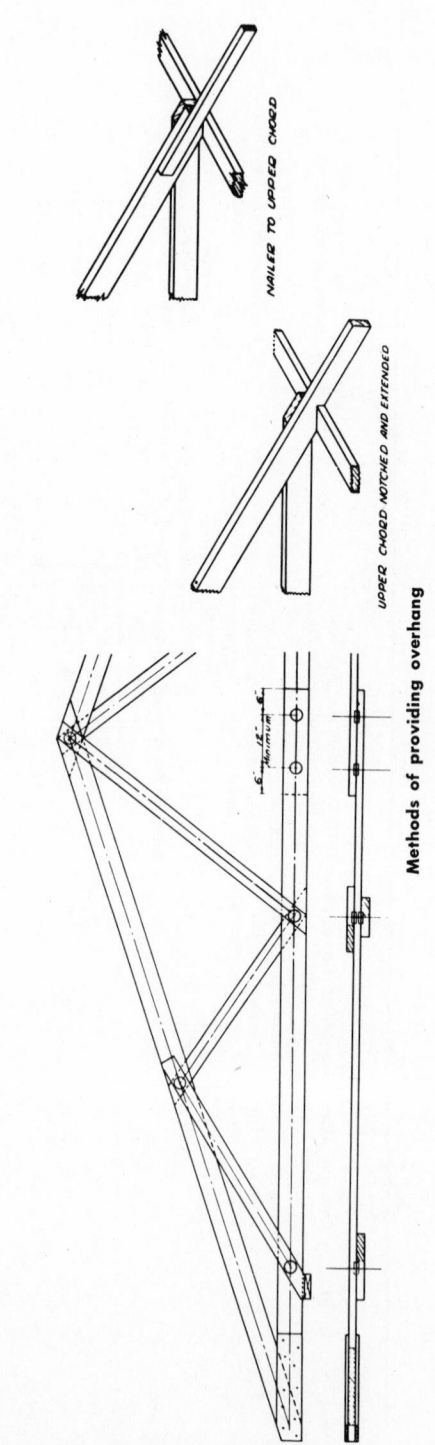

Methods of providing overhang

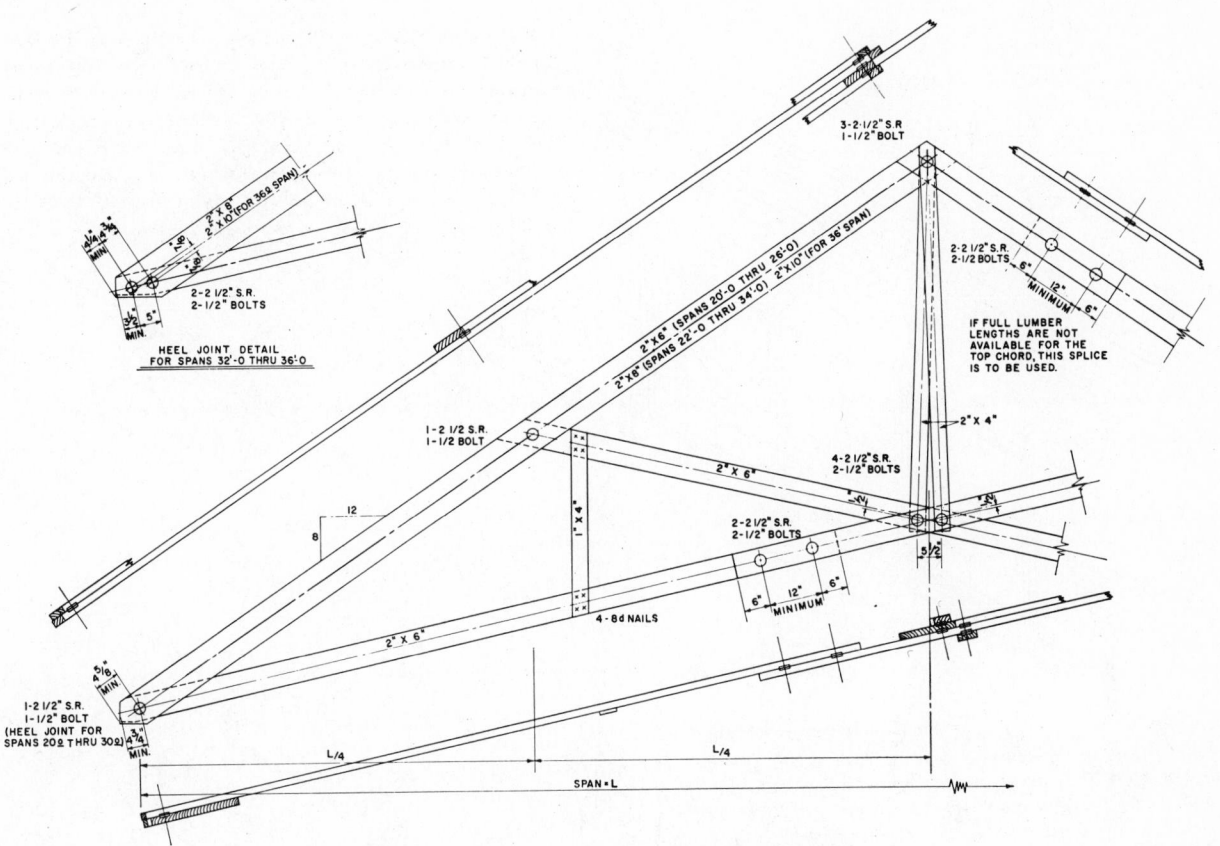

Scissors trussed rafter, slope 8 in 12, for 20- to 36-ft spans

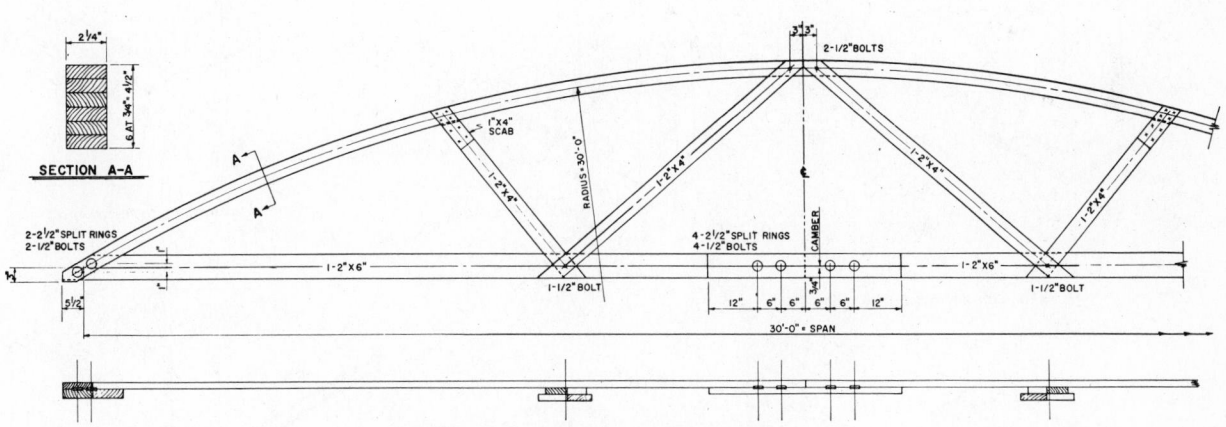

Bowstring trussed rafter, rise 4 ft, for 30-ft span

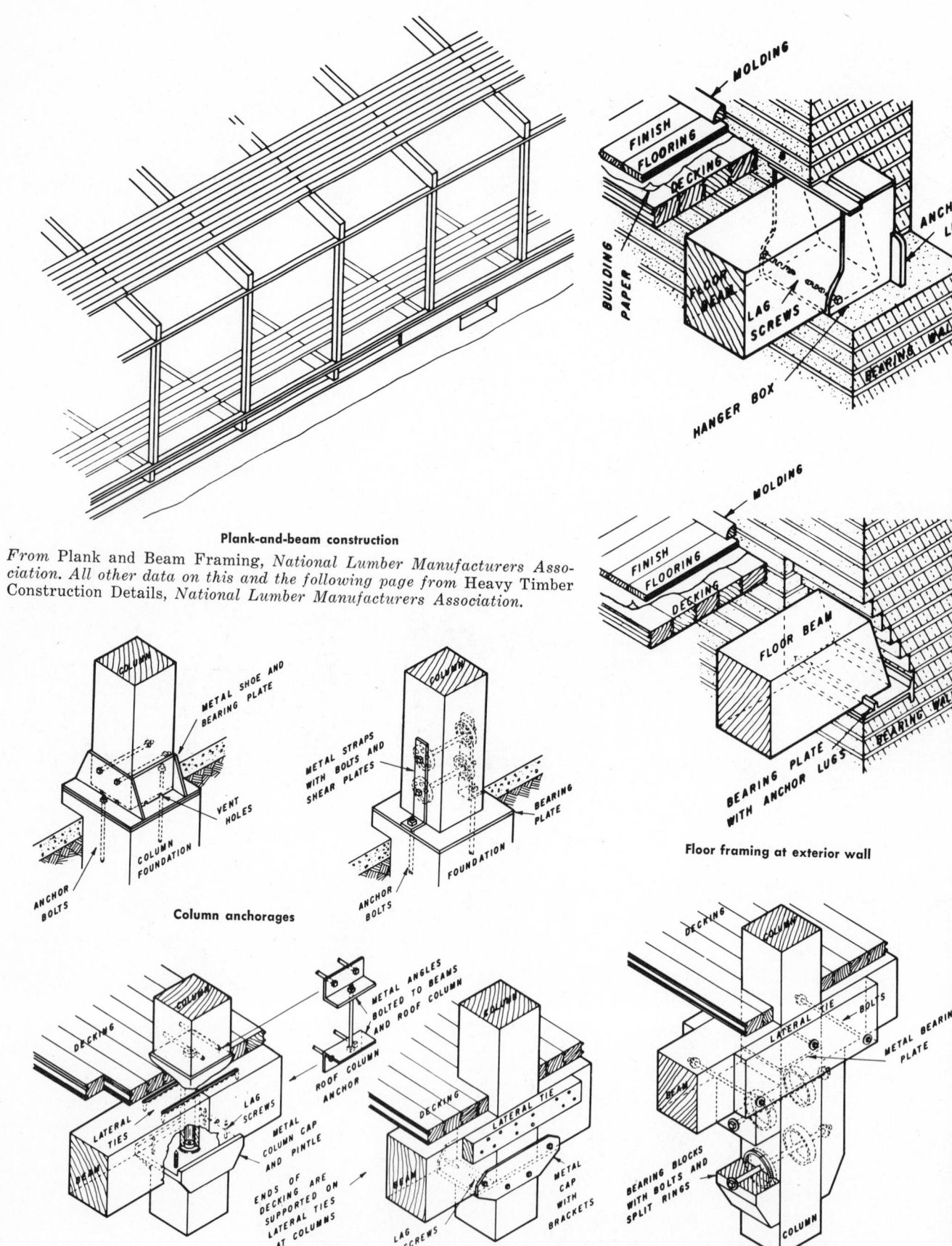

Plank-and-beam construction

From Plank and Beam Framing, *National Lumber Manufacturers Association. All other data on this and the following page from* Heavy Timber Construction Details, *National Lumber Manufacturers Association.*

Column anchorages

Floor framing at exterior wall

Floor, beam, and column framing

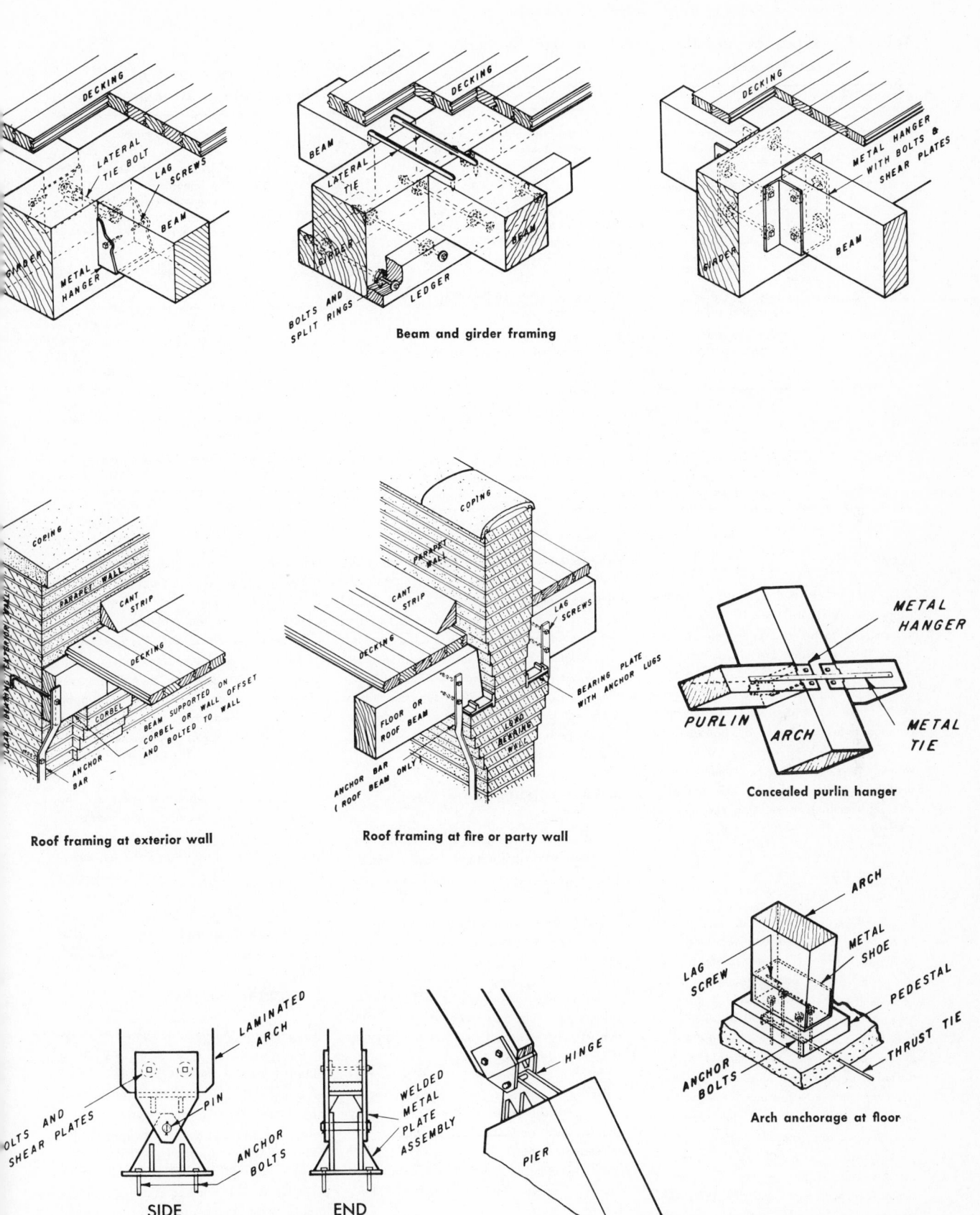

Beam and girder framing

Roof framing at exterior wall

Roof framing at fire or party wall

Concealed purlin hanger

TYPICAL HINGE CONNECTION

SIDE

END

Arch anchorage to exterior pier

Arch anchorage at floor

STRUCTURAL DESIGN—STEEL—1
Types of steel; beams

By JOHN G. MASCIONI, *P.E.*
Associate Professor of Structural Design, School of Architecture, Pratt Institute

Table 1. Types of structural steel for use in building construction

ASTM designation	Primary use in construction
Carbon steel	
A7	Formerly most common type for construction of buildings and bridges
A373	Construction of welded bridges
A36	For use in buildings and bridges where A7 or A373 was formerly used; weldability similar to A373; yield strength greater than A7 and A373; has generally replaced A7 and A373
High-strength low-alloy steel	
A440	Riveted or bolted structures where weight saving is important; corrosion resistance twice that of carbon steel
A441	Welded structures where weight saving is important; excellent impact resistance; corrosion resistance twice that of carbon steel
A242	For exceptionally high corrosion resistance—4 to 6 times that of carbon steel
Heat-treated alloy steel	
None	Very high strength; for use where high strength and weight saving are important; can be welded; corrosion resistance 4 times that of carbon steel

Table 2. Proprietary names of high-strength structural steels

ASTM designation or other	Proprietary names
A440	Armco High Strength #4-R or -S; AW Dynalloy (modified); Yoloy M; USS Man-Ten; Republic Type M; Hi-Man 440; N-A-X High Manganese; Medium Manganese; IH 50; Structural High Strength R
A441	USS Tri-Ten; Republic Type Mang-Vanadium; Tri-Steel; Manganese-Vanadium
A242	Armco High Strength #1; AW Dynalloy or Alten; Lukens' Manganese-Vanadium; Yoloy E; Maxeloy; USS Cor-Ten; Republic Type 50; Jalten; Hi-Steel or Tri-Steel; N-A-X High-Tensile or N-A-X Finegrain; Manganese-Vanadium or Mayari-R; Kaisaloy #1; Phoenix 50
Heat-treated alloy steel	Sheffield Super Strength 100; T-1 or T-1 Type A; Jalloy S; N-A-Xtra 100

BEAMS

The design of steel beams must satisfy many conditions. In practice, however, the determining factor is usually the bending stress. The applicable formula in beam design is $S = M/f_b$, in which S is the section modulus in in.^{3}, M is the bending moment in lb-in., and f_b is the allowable bending stress in pounds per square inch. Wide flange (WF) sections, which are formed to develop the maximum section modulus per unit weight, are the most efficient members in resisting the bending moment.

TABULAR DATA

Data from the AISC safe-load tables[1] have been condensed and rearranged in Table 4 to provide an immediate solution for symmetrically loaded beams for spans ranging from 9 to 40 ft. Table 4 gives W the total allowable uniformly distributed load in kips (1,000 lb) including the weight of the beam itself, which should be deducted to find the net load that the beam will carry. It is assumed that the beams are simply supported and that their compression flanges are laterally supported. The working stress is 24,000 psi for compact sections and 22,000 psi for non-compact sections, in accordance with the 1963 AISC specifications for A36 steel. No non-compact sections have been included in Table

[1] *Manual of Steel Construction (6th ed.). American Institute of Steel Construction, New York (1963).*

4. Tabulated loads will develop live-load deflections that will not exceed 1/360 of the span length when the ratio of live load to dead load is approximately 1.0. For the solution of unsymmetrically loaded beams, section moduli of the various sections are given. As an aid in detailing, the widths of flanges are also shown. Although the table does not provide a complete list of beams that may be used for each span, this will rarely be a consideration.

SPECIAL CONDITIONS

Table 4 is applicable only on the assumptions described above. Special conditions that restrict the use of the table are as follows:

1. Combined axial and bending stresses: An example of combined axial and bending stresses is a canopy beam supported by an inclined cable.

2. Unsymmetrical bending: Unsymmetrical bending indicates bending about both axes as in the case of roof purlins framing into sloping beams.

3. Web crippling: Web crippling is the presence of a high concentration of stress in the web caused by the application of a concentrated load, such as a column or an inadequate length of bearing at the support. This condition may not prohibit the use of a beam if the web is properly reinforced or stiffened.

4. Torsion stresses: Torsion stresses are developed by eccentric loading. A common example is that of a spandrel beam supporting a wall whose center of gravity is off the centerline of the beam. This prob-

lem usually is not serious, however, because very often the indeterminate effect of this type of loading is compensated for by a reduction in the working stress.

5. Impact and vibration: The loads given in Table 4 are assumed to be static and gradually applied. Beams that develop dynamic loads, such as beams that support elevators or escalators, must be designed with a reduced stress as specified by the governing code to resist impact and vibration.

6. Laterally unsupported beams: The working stress for a beam whose compression flange (the top in a simply supported beam) is laterally unsupported is determined by its cross-sectional properties and the span length. This condition does not necessarily require a reduction in the working stress. (The procedure to be followed in this case is outlined in the AISC Manual.)

CONVERSION FACTORS

1. Stresses: The loads indicated in Table 4 are for ASTM Type A36 steel. If a different type of steel (A220, A440, A441) is used, different allowable stresses are applicable. The allowable loads for these steels can be obtained by multiplying the tabulated values by the conversion factors listed in the AISC Manual.

2. Loads: Fig. 1 indicates the equivalent tabular loads to be used for concentrated loads. For example, a beam supporting 3 concentrated loads of 10 kips at the quarter points is equivalent to a load of 4 P or a total uniformly distributed load of 40 kips.

Table 3. Strength and cost comparison of structural steels for buildings

ASTM designation*	Product	Thickness, in.	Minimum yield, psi	Allowable working stress (tensile), psi‡	Cost difference from A36 steel, dollars per ton§	Strength-to-cost coefficients relative to A36 steel‖		
						Tension members and beam	Short columns (L/r=50)	Long columns (L/r=120)
Carbon steel								
A36	Shapes & Plates	All	36,000	22,000		1.00	1.00	1.00
A7	Shapes	All	33,000	20,000	−1.00	0.92	0.92	1.01
	Plates	¾ & under			−1.00	0.92	0.91	0.99
		over ¾ to 4			−7.00	0.96	0.97	1.11
A373	Shapes	All	32,000	20,000	+2.00 to +6.00	0.88 avg	0.88	0.97 avg
	Plates	½ & under				0.90	0.90	1.00
		over ½ to ¾			+4.00	0.87	0.88	0.97
		over ¾ to 1			−2.00	0.92	0.93	1.02
		over 1 to 1½			+11.00	0.83	0.83	0.92
		over 1½ to 4			−2.00	0.92	0.92	1.01
High-strength, low-alloy steel								
A440	Shapes	¾ & under	50,000	30,000		1.12	1.08	0.82
		over ¾ to 1½	46,000	28,000	+24.00	1.05	1.01	0.82
		over 1½ to 4	42,000	25,000		0.94	0.94	0.82
	Plates	¾ & under	50,000	30,000	+23.00	1.12	1.09	0.83
		over ¾ to 1½	46,000	28,000	+17.00	1.10	1.08	0.88
		over 1½ to 4	42,000	25,000	+13.00	1.03	1.04	0.91
A441	Shapes	¾ & under	50,000	30,000		0.98	0.95	0.72
		over ¾ to 1½	46,000	28,000	+44.00	0.91	0.89	0.72
		over 1½ to 4	42,000	25,000		0.81	0.82	0.72
	Plates	¾ & under	50,000	30,000	+43.50	0.96	0.94	0.72
		over ¾ to 1½	46,000	28,000	+37.50	0.95	0.94	0.76
		over 1½ to 4	42,000	25,000	+24.50	0.95	0.97	0.84
A242	Shapes	¾ & under	50,000	30,000		0.89	0.91	0.69
		over ¾ to 1½	46,000	28,000	+50.00	0.88	0.85	0.69
		over 1½ to 4	42,000	25,000		0.78	0.79	0.69
	Plates	¾ & under	50,000	30,000	+50.00	0.94	0.91	0.69
		over ¾ to 1½	46,000	28,000	+44.00	0.92	0.90	0.73
		over 1½ to 4	42,000	25,000	+31.00	0.91	0.93	0.81
Heat-treated alloy steel								
None	Plates	1 & under	100,000†	60,000	+135.00	1.25	1.07	0.46
		over 1 to 2½	100,000	60,000	+182.00	1.05	0.90	0.39
		over 2½ to 6	90,000	54,000	+182.00	1.13	0.89	0.43

Consult steel producers for recommendations on preheating and electrode welding.

† Quenched and tempered steels do not always show a yield point. Reference here is to the 0.2 per cent offset yield strength.

‡ Allowable working stress is based on approximately 60 per cent of minimum yield strength.

§ Based on costs as of June 1, 1961.

‖ Strength-to-cost coefficients are determined from base prices,

and specification and quality extras only, at the mill. These are subject to change.

A value greater than 1.00 indicates the material has a strength-to-cost coefficient (working stress, kips per sq in., over cost in dollars per ton) better than A36 steel.

High-strength steels may offer economy through reduction in dead weight, or simplified fabrication, in addition to a good strength-to-cost coefficient for the material only.

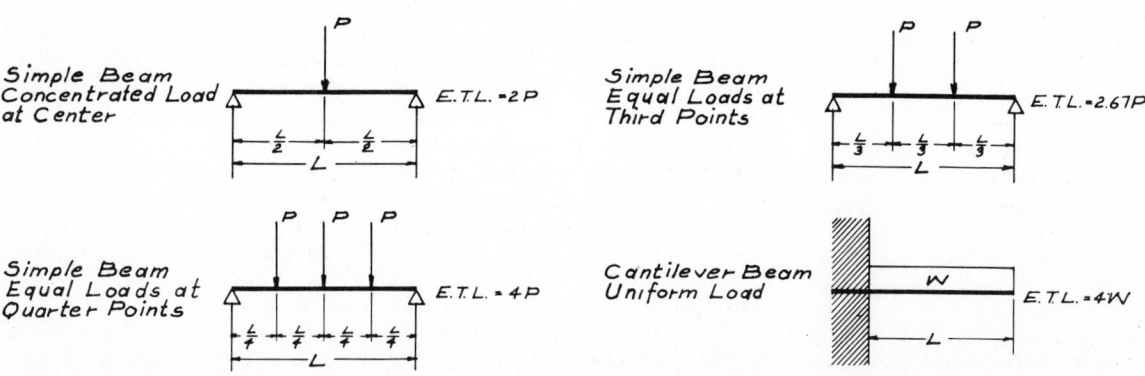

Fig. 1. Equivalent tabular load factors

Table 4. Allowable uniformly distributed loads in kips for beams laterally supported for ASTM Type A36 steel ($F_y = 36$ ksi)

Beam designation	Section modulus, in.³	Flange width, in.	9	10	11	12	13	14	15	16	17	18	19	20	21	22	23	24
8 B 13	9.9	4	17.6	15.8	14.4	13.2	12.2	11.3	10.5	9.9	9.3							
8 B 15	11.8	4	21.0	18.9	17.2	15.7	14.5	13.5	12.6	11.8	11.1							
8 WF 17	14.1	5¼	25.1	22.6	20.5	18.8	17.4	16.1	15.0	14.1	13.3							
8 I 18.4	14.2	4	25.2	22.7	20.7	18.9	17.5	16.2	15.1	14.2	13.4							
8 WF 20	17.0	5¼	30.2	27.2	24.7	22.7	20.9	19.4	18.1	17.0	16.0							
8 I 23	16.0	4⅛	28.4	25.6	23.3	21.3	19.7	18.3	17.1	16.0	15.0							
8 WF 24	20.8	6½	37.0	33.3	30.3	27.7	25.6	23.8	22.2	20.8	19.6							
8 WF 28	24.3	6½	43.2	38.9	35.3	32.4	29.9	27.9	25.9	24.3	22.9							
10 B 15	13.8	4	24.5	22.1	20.1	18.4	17.0	15.8	14.7	13.8	13.0	12.3	11.6	11.0	10.5			
10 B 17	16.2	4	28.8	25.9	23.6	21.6	19.9	18.5	17.3	16.2	15.2	14.4	13.6	13.0	12.3			
10 B 19	18.8	4	33.4	30.1	27.3	25.1	23.1	21.8	20.1	18.8	17.7	16.7	15.8	15.0	14.3			
10 WF 21	21.5	5¾	38	34	31	29	26	25	23	22	20	19	18	17	16			
10 WF 25	26.4	5¾	47	42	38	35	32	30	28	26	25	23	22	21	20			
10 I 25.4	24.4	4⅝	43	39	35	32	30	28	26	24	23	22	20	19	18			
10 WF 29	30.8	5¾	55	49	45	41	38	35	33	31	29	27	26	25	23			
10 I 35	29.2	5	52	47	42	39	36	33	31	29	27	26	25	23	22			
10 WF 39	42.2	8	75	68	61	56	52	48	45	42	40	38	36	34	32			
10 WF 45	49.1	8	87	79	71	65	60	56	52	49	46	44	41	39	37	36		
12 B 19	21.4	4	38	34	31	28	26	24	23	21	20	19	18	17	16	15.6	14.9	14.3
12 B 22	25.3	4	45	40	37	31	29	27	25	24	22	21	20	19	18	17.6	16.9	16.2
12 WF 27	34.1	6½	61	55	50	45	42	39	36	34	32	30	29	27	26	25	24	23
12 WF 31	39.4	6½	70	63	57	53	48	45	42	39	37	35	33	32	30	29	27	26
12 I 31.8	36.0	5	64	58	52	48	44	41	38	36	34	32	30	29	27	26	25	24
12 WF 36	45.9	6⅝	82	73	67	61	56	52	49	46	43	41	39	37	35	33	32	31
12 WF 40	51.9	8	92	83	75	69	64	59	55	52	49	46	44	42	40	38	36	35
12 WF 45	58.2	8	103	93	85	78	72	67	62	58	55	52	49	47	44	42	40	39
12 WF 50	64.7	8⅛	115	104	94	86	80	74	69	65	61	58	54	52	49	47	45	43
12 WF 53	70.7	10	121	113	103	94	87	81	75	71	67	63	60	57	54	51	49	47
14 B 22	28.8	5	51	46	42	38	35	33	31	29	27	26	24	23	22	21	20	19
14 B 26	34.9	5	62	56	51	46	43	40	37	35	33	31	29	28	26	25	24	23
14 WF 30	41.8	6¾	74	67	61	56	51	48	45	42	39	37	35	33	32	30	29	28
14 WF 34	48.5	6¾	86	78	71	65	60	55	52	49	46	43	41	39	37	35	34	32
14 WF 38	54.6	6¾	97	87	79	73	67	62	58	55	51	49	46	44	42	40	38	36
14 WF 43	62.7	8	111	100	91	84	77	72	67	63	59	56	53	50	48	46	44	42
14 WF 48	70.2	8	125	112	102	94	86	80	75	70	66	62	59	56	53	51	49	47
14 WF 53	77.8	8	138	124	113	104	96	89	83	78	73	69	66	62	59	57	54	52
14 WF 61	92.2	10	152	148	134	123	113	105	98	92	87	82	78	74	70	67	64	61
16 B 26	38.1	5½	68	61	55	51	47	43	41	38	36	34	32	30	29	28	26	25
16 B 31	47.0	5½	83	75	68	63	58	54	50	47	44	42	40	38	36	34	33	31
16 WF 36	56.3	7	100	90	82	75	69	64	60	56	53	50	47	45	43	41	39	38
16 WF 40	64.4	7	114	103	94	86	79	74	69	64	61	57	54	52	49	47	45	43
16 WF 45	72.4	7	129	116	105	97	89	83	77	72	68	64	61	58	55	53	50	48
16 WF 50	80.7	7⅛	143	129	117	108	99	92	86	81	76	72	68	65	61	59	56	54
16 WF 58	94.1	8½	167	151	137	125	116	108	100	94	89	84	79	75	72	68	65	63
16 WF 64	104.2	8½	185	167	152	139	128	119	111	104	98	93	88	83	79	76	72	69
18 WF 45	78.9	7½	140	126	115	105	97	90	84	79	74	70	66	63	60	57	55	53
18 WF 50	89.0	7½	158	142	129	119	110	102	95	89	84	79	75	71	68	65	62	59
18 WF 55	98.2	7½	175	157	143	131	121	112	105	98	92	87	83	79	75	71	68	65
21 WF 55	109.7	8¼	195	176	160	146	135	125	117	110	103	98	92	88	84	80	76	73
21 WF 62	126.4	8¼	225	202	184	169	156	144	135	126	119	112	106	101	96	92	88	84

Table 4. (cont.) Allowable uniformly distributed loads in kips for beams laterally supported for ASTM Type A36 steel ($F_y = 36$ ksi)

Beam designation	Section modulus, in.³	Flange width, in.	25	26	27	28	29	30	31	32	33	34	35	36	40	44	50	60
14 B 22	28.8	5	18.4	17.7	17.1	16.5	15.9	15.4										
14 B 26	34.9	5	22.3	21.5	20.7	19.9	19.3	18.6										
14 WF 30	41.8	6¾	27	26	25	24	23	22										
14 WF 38	54.6	6¾	35	34	32	31	30	29										
14 WF 53	77.8	8	50	48	46	44	43	41										
14 WF 74	112.3	10⅛	72	69	67	64	62	60										
14 WF 84	130.9	12	84	81	78	75	72	70										
16 B 26	38.1	5½	24.4	23.4	22.6	21.8	21.0	20.3	19.7	19.1	18.5	17.9						
16 B 31	47.0	5½	30.1	28.9	27.9	26.9	25.9	25.1	24.3	23.5	22.8	22.1						
16 WF 36	56.3	7	36	35	33	32	31	30	29	28	27	26						
16 WF 40	64.4	7	41	40	38	37	36	34	33	32	31	30						
16 WF 45	72.4	7	46	45	43	41	40	39	37	36	35	34						
16 WF 50	80.7	7⅛	52	50	48	46	45	43	42	40	39	38						
16 WF 58	94.1	8½	60	58	56	54	52	50	49	47	46	44						
16 WF 64	104.2	8½	67	64	62	60	57	56	54	52	51	49						
16 WF 71	115.9	8½	74	71	69	66	64	62	60	58	56	55						
16 WF 78	127.8	8⅝	82	79	76	73	71	68	66	64	62	60						
16 WF 88	151.3	11½	97	93	90	86	83	81	78	76	73	71						
16 WF 96	166.1	11½	106	102	98	95	92	89	86	83	81	78						
18 WF 45	78.9	7½	50	49	47	45	44	42	41	39	38	37	36	35				
18 WF 50	89.0	7½	57	55	53	51	49	47	46	45	43	42	41	40				
18 WF 55	98.2	7½	63	60	58	56	54	52	51	49	48	46	45	44				
18 WF 60	107.8	7½	69	66	64	62	59	57	56	54	52	51	49	48				
18 WF 64	117.0	8¾	75	72	69	67	65	62	60	59	57	55	53	52				
18 WF 70	128.2	8¾	82	79	76	73	71	68	66	64	62	60	59	57				
18 WF 77	141.7	8¾	91	87	84	81	78	76	73	71	69	67	65	63				
18 WF 85	156.1	8⅞	100	96	93	89	86	83	81	78	76	73	71	69				
18 WF 96	184.4	11¾	118	113	109	105	102	98	95	92	89	87	84	82				
21 WF 55	109.7	8¼	70	68	65	63	61	59	57	55	53	52	50	49	44			
21 WF 62	126.4	8¼	81	78	75	72	70	67	65	63	61	59	58	56	51			
21 WF 68	139.9	8¼	90	86	83	80	77	75	72	70	68	66	64	62	56			
21 WF 73	150.7	8¼	96	93	89	86	83	80	78	75	73	71	69	67	60			
21 WF 82	168.0	9	108	103	100	96	93	90	87	84	81	79	77	75	67			
24 WF 68	153.1	9	98	94	91	87	84	82	79	77	74	72	70	68	61	56	49	
24 WF 76	175.4	9	112	108	104	100	97	94	91	88	85	83	80	78	70	64	56	
24 WF 84	196.3	9	126	121	116	112	108	105	101	98	95	92	90	87	79	71	63	
24 WF 94	220.9	9	141	136	131	126	122	118	114	110	107	104	101	98	88	80	71	
24 WF 100	248.9	12	159	153	147	142	137	133	128	124	121	117	114	111	100	91	80	
24 WF 110	274.4	12	176	169	163	157	151	146	142	137	133	129	125	122	110	100	88	
24 WF 120	299.1	12⅛	191	184	177	171	165	160	154	150	145	141	137	133	120	109	96	
27 WF 84	211.7	10	135	130	125	121	117	113	109	106	103	100	97	94	85	77	68	
27 WF 94	242.8	10	155	149	144	139	134	129	125	121	118	114	111	108	97	88	78	
27 WF 102	266.3	10	170	164	158	152	147	142	137	133	129	125	122	118	107	97	85	
27 WF 114	299.2	10⅛	191	184	177	171	165	160	154	150	145	141	137	133	120	109	96	
27 WF 145	402.9	14	258	248	239	230	222	215	208	201	195	190	184	179	161	147	129	
30 WF 99	269.1	10½				154	148	144	139	135	130	127	123	120	108	98	86	72
30 WF 108	299.2	10½				171	165	160	154	150	144	141	136	133	120	109	96	80
30 WF 116	327.9	10½				187	180	175	169	164	158	154	149	146	131	119	105	87
30 WF 124	354.6	10½				203	196	189	183	177	172	167	162	158	142	129	113	95
33 WF 118	358.3	11½				205	197	191	184	179	173	169	163	159	143	130	115	96
33 WF 130	404.8	11½				231	223	216	209	202	196	190	185	180	162	147	130	108
33 WF 141	446.8	11½				255	247	238	230	223	216	210	205	199	179	162	143	119
36 WF 135	438.6	12				251	243	234	226	219	212	206	201	195	175	159	140	117
36 WF 150	502.9	12				287	279	268	259	251	244	237	230	224	201	183	161	134

Table 5. Standard load table for open web steel joists, J-series,* 8 to 14 in. (based on allowable stress of 22,000 psi)

Adopted by the Steel Joist Institute, 1961 and by the American Institute of Steel Construction, 1963.
The following table gives the TOTAL safe uniformly distributed load-carrying capacities, in pounds per linear foot, of J-series open web steel joists. The weight of dead loads, including the joists, must in all cases be deducted to determine the live load-carrying capacities of the joists. Loads above the heavy lines are governed by shear.

Joist Designation	8J2	10J2	10J3	10J4	12J2	12J3	12J4	12J5	12J6	14J3	14J4	14J5	14J6	14J7
Depth in Inches	8	10	10	10	12	12	12	12	12	14	14	14	14	14
Resisting Moment In Inch Pounds	56,000	70,000	89,000	111,000	85,000	108,000	135,000	161,000	196,000	127,000	159,000	190,000	230,000	276,000
Max. End Reaction In Pounds	1900	2000	2200	2400	2200	2300	2500	2700	3000	2400	2800	3100	3400	3700
Approx. Joist Wgt. Pounds Per Foot	4.2	4.2	4.8	6.0	4.5	5.1	6.0	7.0	8.1	5.2	6.4	7.3	8.4	9.7
Span In Feet														
8	475													
9	422													
10	373	400	440	480										
11	309	364	400	436										
12	259	324	367	400	367	383	417	450	500					
13	221	276	338	369	335	354	385	415	462					
14	190	238	303	343	289	329	357	386	429	343	400	443	486	529
15	166	207	264	320	252	307	333	360	400	320	373	413	453	493
16	146	182	232	289	221	281	313	338	375	300	350	388	425	463
17		161	205	256	196	249	294	318	353	282	329	365	400	435
18		144	183	228	175	222	278	300	333	261	311	344	378	411
19		129	164	205	157	199	249	284	316	235	294	326	358	389
20		117	148	185	142	180	225	268	300	212	265	310	340	370
21					128	163	204	243	286	192	240	287	324	352
22					117	149	186	222	270	175	219	262	309	336
23					107	136	170	203	247	160	200	239	290	322
24					98	125	156	186	227	147	184	220	266	308
25										135	170	203	245	294
26										125	157	187	227	272
27										116	145	174	210	252
28										108	135	162	196	235

* Open web high strength steel joists, H-series, are made in the same sizes as the J-series, but are based on an allowable stress of 30,000 psi.

Load tables are applicable for concentrated top chord loadings (such as are developed in bulb-tee roof construction) when the sum of the equal concentrated top chord loadings does not exceed the allowable uniform loading for the joist type and span and the loads are placed at spacings not exceeding 33 in. along the top chord.

Table 5 (cont.)   Standard load table for open web steel joists, J-series,* depths 16 to 24 in. (based on allowable stress of 22,000 psi)

Joist Designation	16J4	16J5	16J6	16J7	16J8	18J5	18J6	18J7	18J8	20J5	20J6	20J7	20J8	22J6	22J7	22J8	24J6	24J7	24J8
Depth In Inches	16	16	16	16	16	18	18	18	18	20	20	20	20	22	22	22	24	24	24
Resisting Moment In Inch Pounds	173,000	216,000	258,000	310,000	359,000	243,000	293,000	352,000	406,000	265,000	316,000	382,000	455,000	335,000	420,000	493,000	367,000	460,000	540,000
Max. End Reaction In Pounds	3000	3300	3600	4000	4300	3500	3900	4200	4500	3800	4100	4300	4600	4200	4500	4800	4400	4700	5000
Approx. Joist Wgt Pounds Per Foot	6.6	7.6	8.5	10.1	11.3	7.9	9.0	10.2	11.3	8.1	9.2	10.6	11.9	9.6	10.5	11.9	9.9	11.1	12.4
Span In Feet																			
16	375	413	450	500	538			467	500				460						
17	353	388	424	471	506			442	474				438						
18	333	367	400	444	478	389	433	420	450		410	430	418		409	436			
19	316	347	379	421	453	368	411	400	429	380	390	410	400	382	391	417		392	417
20	288	330	360	400	430	350	390	382	409	362	373	391	383	365	375	400	367	376	400
21	262	314	343	381	410	333	371	365	391	345	357	374	368	350	360	384	352	362	385
22	238	298	327	364	391	318	355	350	375	330	342	358	354	336	346	369	338	348	370
23	218	272	313	348	374	304	339	336	360	307	328	344	341	323	333	356	326	336	357
24	200	250	299	333	358	281	325	323	346	283	312	331	329	306	321	343	312	324	345
25	185	230	275	320	344	259	312	311	333	261	289	319	317	285	310	331	291	313	333
26	171	213	254	306	331	240	289	299	321	242	269	307	307	266	300	320	272	303	323
27	158	198	236	283	319	222	268	279	310	225	250	297	297	248	290	310	255	294	313
28	147	184	219	264	305	207	249	261	300	210	234	283	288	232	273	300	239	282	303
29	137	171	205	246	285	193	232	244	282	196	219	265	279	218	257	291	225	265	294
30	128	160	191	230	266	180	217	229	264	184	206	249	262	205	242	282	212	250	286
31	120	150	179	215	249	169	203	215	249	173	193	234	248	193	229	268	200	237	278
32	113	141	168	202	234	158	191	203	234	162	182	220	234	182	216	254	189	224	263
33						149	179	192	221	153	172	208	222	172	205	240	179	212	249
34						140	169	181	209	144	163	197	210	163	194	228	169	202	237
35						132	159			136	154	186	199	155	184	216	161	192	225
36						125	151			129	146	176	190	147	175	205	153	182	214
37										122	139	167		140	167	196	146	174	204
38										116	132	159		133	159	186	139	166	195
39										110				127	151	178	132	158	186
40														121	145	170	126	151	178
41														115			121	145	170
42																	116	139	163
43																	111		
44																	106		
45																			
46																			
47																			
48																			

See notes on opposite page.

Table 6. Standard load table for open web steel joists, longspan or LA-series,* depths 18 to 28 in. based on allowable stress of 22,000 psi.

Adopted by the American Institute of Steel Construction, and the Steel Joist Institute, 1961.

The following table gives the TOTAL safe uniformly distributed load-carrying capacities in pounds per linear foot of span. The weight of dead loads, including weight of joists, must in all cases be deducted to determine the live load-carrying capacities which must be reduced for concentrated loads. Approximate weights per linear foot of joists include accessories.

When holes are required in top or bottom chords, the above carrying capacities must be reduced in proportion to reduction of chord areas. The top chords are considered as being stayed laterally by floor slab or roof deck.

This load table applies to joists with either parallel chords or standard pitched top chords. When top chords are pitched, the carrying capacities are determined by the nominal depth of the joists at center of the span. Standard pitch is ⅛ in. per ft. If pitch exceeds this standard, the load table does not apply.

Loads below heavy stepped line are governed by maximum end reaction. Loads printed in lightface type are to be used for roof construction only.

The weight of dead loads, including weight of joists, must in all cases be deducted to determine the live load carrying capacities which must be reduced for concentrated loads. Approximate weights per linear foot of joists include accessories.

When holes are required in top or bottom chords, the above carrying capacities must be reduced in proportion to reduction of chord areas.

The top chords are considered as being stayed laterally by floor slab or roof deck.

CLEAR OPENING OR NET SPAN IN FEET

Joist Description	Approx. Wt. in Lbs. per Linear Ft.	Depth in Inches	Maximum End Reaction Lbs.	25	26	27	28	29	30	31	32	33	34	35	36
18LA02	13	18	4,031	314	295	278	263	248	235	222	211	200	190	181	172
18LA03	14	18	4,549	354	334	315	297	281	266	252	239	227	216	205	196
18LA04	16	18	5,493	428	402	378	355	335	316	299	283	268	255	241	228
18LA05	17	18	5,970	465	438	413	390	369	349	331	314	298	283	270	257
18LA06	19	18	7,135	556	522	490	462	435	411	388	368	348	330	312	295
18LA07	21	18	7,648	596	574	540	508	479	453	428	406	385	364	344	326
18LA08	23	18	8,334	649	625	602	581	547	516	487	461	436	414	393	373
18LA09	25	18	8,611	671	646	623	601	581	562	530	502	475	450	428	406
18LA10	27	18	9,217	718	691	666	643	621	601	582	550	520	493	468	444
18LA11	29	18	9,539	743	715	690	665	643	622	602	584	567	550	523	497
18LA12	31	18	10,216	796	766	739	713	689	666	645	625	607	589	573	544

Joist Description	Approx. Wt. in Lbs. per Linear Ft.	Depth in Inches	Maximum End Reaction Lbs.	25	26	27	28	29	30	31	32	33	34	35	36	37	38	39	40
20LA03	14	20	4,703	366	347	328	311	295	280	266	253	241	230	219	209	200	191	183	175
20LA04	16	20	5,776	450	424	400	377	357	338	320	304	288	274	261	249	237	226	216	207
20LA05	17	20	6,177	481	455	431	408	387	368	349	332	316	301	287	274	262	251	240	230
20LA06	19	20	7,349	573	551	520	491	464	439	416	395	375	356	339	323	308	294	281	269
20LA07	21	20	7,887	615	591	570	539	510	483	458	435	413	393	374	357	340	325	311	297
20LA08	23	20	8,525	664	639	616	595	575	556	526	498	473	449	427	406	387	369	352	337
20LA09	25	20	9,063	706	680	655	632	611	591	572	542	515	489	465	442	422	402	384	367
20LA10	27	20	9,552	744	716	690	666	644	623	603	585	567	538	511	486	463	441	421	402
20LA11	29	20	10,129	789	760	732	707	683	661	640	620	602	584	568	541	515	492	470	449
20LA12	31	20	10,692	833	802	773	746	721	697	675	655	635	617	600	583	568	541	516	493
20LA13	36	20	11,587	903	869	838	808	781	756	732	709	688	669	650	632	615	599	584	570

Joist Description	Approx. Wt. in Lbs. per Linear Ft.	Depth in Inches	Maximum End Reaction Lbs.	33	34	35	36	37	38	39	40	41	42	43	44	45	46	47	48
24LA04	16	24	5,333	317	303	289	277	265	254	243	233	224	215	207	199	191	184	177	17
24LA05	17	24	5,693	338	324	311	298	286	274	264	253	244	235	226	218	210	202	195	18
24LA06	19	24	6,942	412	394	376	360	344	330	316	303	291	280	269	259	249	240	231	22
24LA07	21	24	7,606	452	432	413	395	379	363	348	334	321	308	296	285	275	265	255	24
24LA08	23	24	8,892	528	504	481	459	439	420	402	385	369	354	340	327	314	302	291	28
24LA09	25	24	9,668	574	548	523	499	477	457	437	419	402	386	370	356	342	329	317	30
24LA10	27	24	10,199	606	588	572	556	531	508	485	465	445	427	409	393	378	363	350	33
24LA11	29	24	10,791	641	623	605	589	573	558	535	512	491	472	453	435	419	403	388	37
24LA12	31	24	11,595	689	669	650	632	616	600	585	570	546	524	503	483	464	446	429	41
24LA13	36	24	12,753	758	736	715	696	677	660	643	627	612	598	584	571	549	528	507	48
24LA14	38	24	13,290	790	767	745	725	706	687	670	654	638	623	609	595	582	570	546	52

Joist Description	Approx. Wt. in Lbs. per Linear Ft.	Depth in Inches	Maximum End Reaction Lbs.	41	42	43	44	45	46	47	48	49	50	51	52	53	54	55	56
28LA06	19	28	6,530	313	302	291	281	271	262	253	244	236	228	221	214	207	201	194	18
28LA07	21	28	7,156	343	331	319	308	298	288	278	269	260	251	243	236	228	221	215	20
28LA08	23	28	8,390	403	388	373	359	346	334	322	311	300	290	281	272	263	254	246	23
28LA09	25	28	9,126	438	422	406	391	377	364	351	339	327	316	306	296	286	277	269	26
28LA10	27	28	10,239	491	472	454	437	421	406	391	377	364	351	340	328	317	307	297	28
28LA11	29	28	11,147	535	515	496	478	461	445	429	414	400	387	374	362	350	339	329	31
28LA12	31	28	12,180	585	571	558	537	517	498	480	463	447	432	417	403	390	377	365	35
28LA13	36	28	13,539	650	635	620	606	593	580	568	548	529	511	494	477	462	447	432	41
28LA14	38	28	14,302	687	670	655	640	626	613	600	588	576	565	545	526	509	491	473	45
28LA15	43	28	14,776	709	693	677	662	647	633	620	607	595	583	572	561	551	531	512	49

* High strength longspan, or LH-series joists are made in the same sizes as LA-series joists but are based on an allowable stress of 30,000 psi.

Table 6 (cont.) Standard load table open web steel joists, longspan or LA-series,* depths 32 to 48 in. (based on allowable stress of 22,000 psi)

See notes on opposite page.

CLEAR OPENING OR NET SPAN IN FEET

Joist Description	Approx. Wt. in Lbs. per Linear Ft.	Depth in Inches	Maximum End Reaction Lbs.	49	50	51	52	53	54	55	56	57	58	59	60	61	62	63	64
32LA07	21	32	6,800	274	266	258	250	243	236	229	223	217	211	205	199	194	189	184	179
32LA08	23	32	8,003	322	312	302	293	284	275	267	259	252	245	238	231	225	218	212	207
32LA09	25	32	8,705	351	340	329	319	309	300	291	282	274	266	259	252	245	238	232	225
32LA10	27	32	9,796	394	382	369	358	346	336	326	316	306	297	289	280	272	265	258	250
32LA11	29	32	10,637	428	415	402	390	378	367	356	346	336	326	317	308	300	291	284	276
32LA12	31	32	12,034	485	469	454	439	426	413	400	388	376	365	355	345	335	326	317	308
32LA13	36	32	14,043	565	554	537	520	504	488	473	459	445	432	420	408	396	385	375	365
32LA14	38	32	15,061	606	595	583	572	561	543	526	510	495	480	465	452	439	426	414	403
32LA15	43	32	15,878	639	627	615	603	592	581	570	560	551	532	514	498	482	466	452	438
32LA16	48	32	17,314	697	683	670	657	645	633	622	611	600	590	580	571	562	553	535	519

Joist Description	Wt.	Depth	End Reaction	57	58	59	60	61	62	63	64	65	66	67	68	69	70	71	72
36LA08	23	36	7,685	267	259	252	246	239	233	227	221	216	210	205	200	195	190	186	182
36LA09	25	36	8,359	290	282	275	267	260	254	247	241	235	229	223	218	213	207	203	198
36LA10	27	36	9,437	327	318	309	301	293	285	277	270	263	256	250	244	238	232	226	221
36LA11	29	36	10,215	354	345	336	327	318	310	302	295	287	280	273	267	260	254	248	242
36LA12	31	36	11,596	402	391	380	370	360	350	341	332	324	315	307	300	292	285	278	271
36AL13	36	36	13,709	475	462	450	437	426	414	403	393	383	373	364	355	346	337	329	321
36LA14	38	36	15,398	534	519	504	490	476	463	450	438	427	415	405	394	384	375	365	356
36AL15	43	36	16,744	581	571	561	552	537	522	509	495	482	467	453	440	428	416	404	393
36LA16	48	36	18,396	638	627	617	606	597	587	578	569	560	546	532	518	505	493	479	466
36LA17	54	36	19,598	680	668	657	646	636	625	616	606	597	588	579	571	563	555	541	528

Joist Description	Wt.	Depth	End Reaction	65	66	67	68	69	70	71	72	73	74	75	76	77	78	79	80
40LA09	25	40	8,061	246	240	234	229	224	218	214	209	204	200	195	191	187	183	179	175
40LA10	27	40	9,131	278	271	265	258	252	246	241	235	230	225	220	215	210	205	201	197
40LA11	29	40	9,851	300	293	286	280	273	267	261	255	250	244	239	234	229	224	219	214
40LA12	31	40	11,224	342	334	325	318	310	303	296	289	283	276	270	264	258	253	247	242
40LA13	36	40	13,269	404	394	385	376	367	358	350	342	334	327	319	312	306	299	293	286
40LA14	38	40	14,948	455	444	433	422	412	402	392	383	374	365	357	349	341	333	326	319
40LA15	43	40	16,801	512	499	487	475	464	453	442	432	422	412	403	394	385	375	366	357
40LA16	48	40	18,977	578	569	561	553	539	527	514	502	491	479	468	458	448	438	428	419
40LA17	54	40	20,338	619	610	601	592	584	576	568	560	552	540	527	516	504	493	482	472
40LA18	61	40	22,010	670	660	651	641	632	623	614	606	598	590	582	574	567	560	553	540

Joist Description	Wt.	Depth	End Reaction	73	74	75	76	77	78	79	80	81	82	83	84	85	86	87	88
44LA10	27	44	8,864	241	235	230	226	221	216	212	207	203	199	195	191	187	184	180	177
44LA11	29	44	9,528	259	253	248	243	238	233	229	224	220	215	210	205	201	197	192	188
44LA12	31	44	10,896	296	289	283	277	271	266	260	255	250	245	240	235	230	226	222	217
44LA13	36	44	12,880	350	342	335	328	321	314	308	302	295	290	284	278	273	267	262	257
44LA14	38	44	14,555	395	386	378	370	361	354	346	339	332	325	318	312	305	299	293	287
44LA15	43	44	16,342	444	434	425	416	407	398	390	382	374	366	359	352	345	338	331	325
44LA16	48	44	19,024	516	505	494	484	473	463	453	444	435	426	417	409	401	393	385	378
44LA17	54	44	21,040	571	564	556	544	533	521	510	500	489	479	470	460	451	442	434	425
44LA18	61	44	22,872	621	613	605	597	589	582	574	567	560	553	542	531	520	509	499	489
44LA19	68	44	24,621	668	659	651	642	634	626	618	610	603	596	589	582	575	568	562	555

Joist Description	Wt.	Depth	End Reaction	81	82	83	84	85	86	87	88	89	90	91	92	93	94	95	96
48LA11	29	48	9,234	226	222	217	212	208	203	199	195	191	187	183	179	176	172	169	166
48LA12	31	48	10,601	260	255	250	245	240	236	231	227	223	219	215	211	207	203	199	195
48LA13	36	48	12,350	307	301	295	290	284	279	274	269	264	259	254	250	245	240	236	231
48LA14	38	48	14,204	348	341	334	328	321	315	309	303	297	292	286	281	276	271	266	261
48LA15	43	48	15,930	390	383	375	368	361	354	347	341	335	328	322	317	311	305	300	295
48LA16	48	48	18,550	454	445	437	428	420	412	404	397	389	382	375	368	362	355	349	343
48LA17	54	48	20,875	511	501	491	482	473	464	455	446	438	430	422	415	407	400	393	386
48LA18	61	48	23,735	581	574	567	561	550	539	528	518	508	498	489	480	471	462	454	445
48LA19	68	48	25,460	624	616	609	601	594	588	581	574	568	562	555	545	535	525	515	506

Table 7. Short-span bridging

Joist span, ft	Maximum spacing
to 14	1 row at center of span
14–21	2 rows at ⅓ points of span, symmetrical about center
21–32	3 rows at ¼ points of span
32–40	4 rows at 1/5 points of span

Table 8. Long-span bridging

Joist type, suffix	Maximum spacing (on centers), ft
02–08	10
09–16	12
17–17	16

Table 9. Fire resistance ratings

Hours	Top slab	Ceiling
¾	1-in. tongue and groove on 2 × 2-in. wood strips attached to joists	¾-in. sanded gypsum plaster on metal or wire lath
1–1½	2-in. reinforced concrete or 2-in. precast reinforced gypsum tile	¾-in. portland cement sand plaster or ¾-in. sanded gypsum plaster
2	2¼-in. reinforced concrete or 2-in. reinforced gypsum tile with ¼-in. mortar finish	¾-in. sanded gypsum plaster
2½	2-in. reinforced concrete or 2-in. reinforced gypsum tile with ¼-in. mortar finish	1-in. neat gypsum plaster or ¾-in. gypsum-vermiculite plaster
2½	2½-in. reinforced concrete	⅞-in. sanded gypsum plaster
3	2½-in. reinforced concrete or 2-in. reinforced gypsum tile with ½-in. mortar finish	1-in. neat gypsum plaster or ¾-in. gypsum-vermiculite plaster
3*	2-in. concrete floor slab on metal lath or 2¾-in. reinforced portland cement concrete plank	1-in. gypsum-vermiculite plaster on metal lath
4	2½-in. reinforced concrete or 2-in. reinforced gypsum slabs with 2-in. mortar finish	1-in. gypsum-vermiculite plaster on metal lath

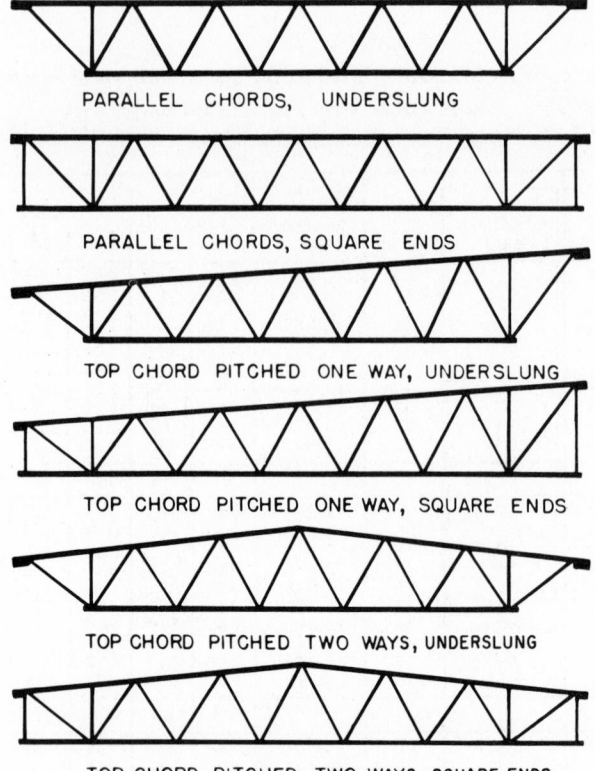

Fig. 2.   Types of long-span joists

PARALLEL CHORDS, UNDERSLUNG

PARALLEL CHORDS, SQUARE ENDS

TOP CHORD PITCHED ONE WAY, UNDERSLUNG

TOP CHORD PITCHED ONE WAY, SQUARE ENDS

TOP CHORD PITCHED TWO WAYS, UNDERSLUNG

TOP CHORD PITCHED TWO WAYS, SQUARE ENDS

Warren web systems are shown, although other web systems may also be used, depending on the manufacturer.

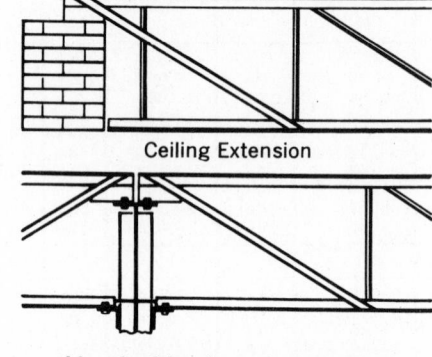

Ceiling Extension

LA series joists for roof construction on structural steel columns

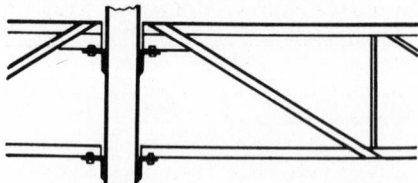

LA series joists for floor construction on structural steel columns

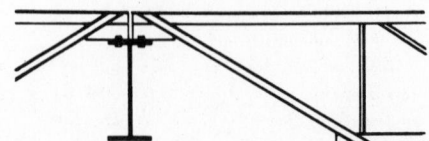

Fig. 3.   End connections for open-web joists

Span

The clear span of steel joists should not exceed 24 times their depth. In floor construction, spans greater than 32 ft should not exceed 20 times the depth of the joist.

Bearing

The depth of the bearing portion of underslung joists is 2½ in. for J-series and 5 in. for LA-series joists.

Minimum length of the bearing for J-series joists is 2½ in. on steel and 4 in. on other materials; for LA-series, 4 in. on steel and 6 in. on other materials.

Bearing areas on supports other than steel should be so proportioned that the unit pressure does not exceed 250 psi.

Deflection

The deflection due to the design live load should not exceed 1/360 of the span.

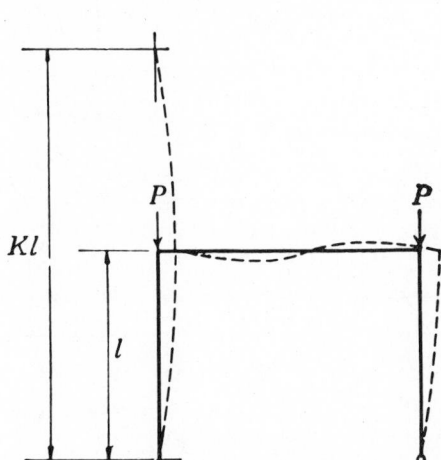

Fig. 4. Effective column length compared to actual unbraced length

	(a)	(b)	(c)	(d)	(e)	(f)
Buckled shape of column is shown by dashed line	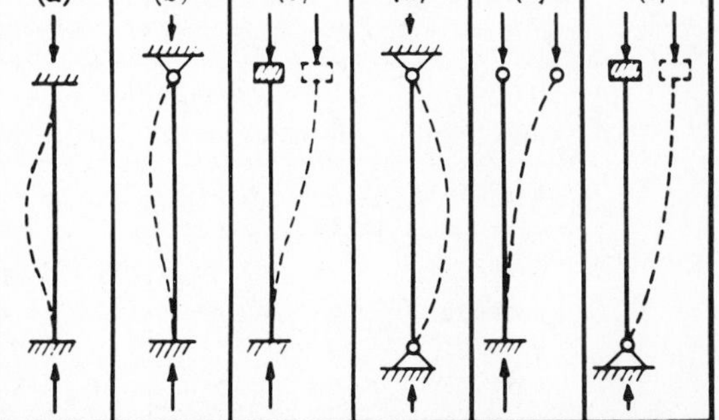					
Theoretical K value	0.5	0.7	1.0	1.0	2.0	2.0
Recommended design value when ideal conditions are approximated	0.65	0.80	1.2	1.0	2.10	2.0
End condition code	Rotation fixed and translation fixed					
	Rotation free and translation fixed					
	Rotation fixed and translation free					
	Rotation free and translation free					

Fig. 5. K-values for various end conditions

COLUMNS

General notes

The allowable load tables which follow are for axially loaded members having the effective unsupported length indicated at the top of the table. The effective length KL is the actual unbraced length, in fact, multiplied by the effective length factor K which is dependent upon the restraint at the ends of the unbraced length and the means available to resist lateral movements. The values and notes shown here have been extracted from the *AISC Manual of Steel Construction*, 6th ed., 1963. For a complete range of values and a comprehensive discussion of the new design approach to steel columns, the Manual should be consulted.

Figure 5, which appears in the Manual, in the Commentary on the AISC Specification, affords a guide to the solution of the K factor. Interpolation between the idealized cases presented is a matter of engineering judgment.

The loads in the tables have been computed in accordance with the provisions of the AISC Specification for columns using ASTM Type A36 steel ($F_y = 36$ ksi). For columns using ASTM A242, A440, and A441 steel (F_y ranges from 42 to 50 ksi) see AISC Manual, 6th ed.

The loads in the tables are tabulated for main members. All values to the left of the heavy line are for Kl/r ratios equal to or less than 120. Values for Kl/r greater than 120 are shown to the right of the

heavy line. Values are omitted when Kl/r exceeds 200. The radius of gyration r is taken about the Y-Y (minor) axis.

Slenderness ratio—Kl/r

One of the most important changes in column design introduced in the sixth edition of the AISC Manual concerns slenderness ratio. The following discussion is taken from the Commentary on AISC Specification.

Considerable attention has been given in the technical literature to the subject of "effective" column length (as contrasted with actual unbraced length) as a factor in estimating column strength.

Two conditions opposite in their effect upon column strength under axial loading must be considered. If enough axial load is applied to the columns in a frame dependent entirely upon its own bending stiffness for stability against sidesway, i.e., uninhibited lateral movement as shown in Fig. 4, the "effective" length of these columns will exceed their actual length. On the other hand, if the same frame were braced in such a way that lateral movement of the tops of the columns with respect to their bases (translation or sidesway) were prevented, the effective length would be less than the actual length, due to the restraint (resistance to joint rotation) provided by the horizontal member. The ratio K, effective column length to actual unbraced length, may be greater or less than 1.0.

The theoretical K-values for six idealized conditions in which joint rotation and translation are either fully realized or nonexistent are tabulated in Fig. 5. Also shown are suggested design values recommended by the Column Research Council for use when these conditions are approximated in actual design. In general, these suggested values are slightly higher than their theoretical equivalents, since joint fixity is seldom fully realized.

If the column base in case (f) of Fig. 5 were truly pinned, K would actually exceed 2.0 for a frame such as that pictured in Fig. 4 because the flexibility of the horizontal member would prevent realization of full fixity at the top of the column. On the other hand, it has been shown that the restraining influence of foundations, even where these footings are designed only for vertical load, can be very substantial in the case of flat-ended column base details with ordinary anchorage. For this condition a design K value of 1.5 would generally be conservative in case (f).

While ordinarily the existence of masonry walls provides enough lateral support for tier building frames to prevent sidesway, the increasing use of light curtain wall construction and wide column spacing, for high-rise structures not provided with a positive system of diagonal bracing, can create a situation where only the bending stiffness of the frame itself provides this support.

Table 10. Columns—allowable concentric loads in kips

The loads given in this table are for main members using ASTM Type A36 steel ($F_y = 36$ ksi). Values on right of heavy line are for Kl/r ratios over 120 but not exceeding 200.

Column designation	Depth, in.	Width, in.	6	8	9	10	11	12	14	16	18	20	22	24	26	28
			Effective length in feet KL with respect to least radius of gyration													
6 WF 20	6¼	6	109	101	96	91	85	80	67	54	42	34	28	24		
6 WF 25	6⅜	6	137	126	120	114	107	100	85	69	55	44	36	31		
8 WF 24	7⅞	6½	133	123	118	113	107	101	88	73	59	47	39	33	28	
8 WF 28	8 1/16	6½	155	144	138	132	125	118	103	86	69	56	46	39	33	
8 WF 31	8	8	178	169	164	159	154	148	136	123	110	95	79	66	57	49
8 WF 35	8⅛	8	201	191	186	180	174	168	155	141	125	109	91	76	65	56
8 WF 40	8¼	8⅛	230	219	213	206	200	193	177	161	144	125	105	88	75	65
8 WF 48	8½	8⅛	277	264	257	249	241	233	219	197	176	154	131	110	94	81
8 WF 58	8⅜	8¼	335	319	311	302	293	283	262	239	215	189	161	135	115	100
8 WF 67	9	8¼	387	370	360	350	339	328	304	279	251	221	190	159	136	117
10 WF 33	9¾	8	189	179	173	167	161	155	142	127	112	95	78	66	56	48
10 WF 39	10	8	224	212	206	199	193	185	170	153	135	116	96	81	69	60
10 WF 45	10⅛	8	258	245	238	231	223	215	197	178	158	136	113	95	81	70
10 WF 49	10	10	289	279	273	268	262	256	242	228	213	197	180	161	142	123
10 WF 54	10⅛	10	319	308	302	296	289	282	268	253	236	218	200	180	159	138
10 WF 60	10¼	10⅛	355	343	336	329	322	314	299	281	263	244	223	201	178	154
10 WF 66	10⅜	10⅛	390	377	370	362	354	346	329	310	290	269	246	222	197	171
10 WF 72	10½	10⅛	426	411	404	395	387	378	359	339	317	294	270	244	216	188
10 WF 77	10⅝	10¼	456	440	432	424	414	405	385	363	340	316	290	262	233	203
10 WF 89	10⅞	10¼	527	510	500	490	480	469	447	422	396	368	339	307	274	240
10 WF 100	11⅛	10⅜	593	573	563	552	541	529	503	476	447	416	383	349	312	273
10 WF 112	11⅜	10⅜	663	642	631	618	606	592	564	534	502	468	432	394	353	310
12 WF 40	12	8	229	217	210	203	196	188	172	154	135	115	95	80	68	59
12 WF 45	12	8	257	244	236	228	220	212	193	174	152	129	107	90	76	66
12 WF 50	12¼	8⅛	286	271	263	255	246	236	216	195	171	146	121	102	87	75
12 WF 53	12	10	312	301	295	288	282	275	260	244	227	209	189	169	147	127
12 WF 58	12¼	10	342	330	323	316	309	302	286	269	250	231	210	188	165	142
12 WF 65	12⅛	12	389	379	373	367	361	355	341	326	311	295	277	259	240	220
12 WF 72	12¼	12	431	420	413	407	400	393	378	362	345	327	308	288	268	245
12 WF 79	12⅜	12⅛	473	461	454	447	439	432	415	398	380	360	339	317	295	271
12 WF 85	12½	12⅛	509	496	489	481	473	465	448	429	410	389	367	343	319	293
12 WF 106	12⅞	12¼	636	620	611	602	592	582	561	538	514	489	462	433	404	372
12 WF 133	13⅜	12⅜	799	779	768	757	745	733	707	679	649	618	585	550	514	476
12 WF 190	14⅜	12⅝	1143	1116	1101	1085	1069	1052	1017	979	938	895	850	803	753	701
14 WF 43	13⅝	8	245	231	224	216	208	200	181	162	140	117	97	81	69	60
14 WF 48	13⅞	8	273	259	251	242	233	224	204	182	159	133	110	93	79	68
14 WF 53	14	8	302	286	277	268	258	248	226	202	177	149	123	103	88	76
14 WF 61	13⅞	10	359	345	338	331	323	315	297	279	259	237	215	191	165	142
14 WF 68	14	10	400	385	377	369	360	351	332	311	289	266	241	214	186	160
14 WF 74	14¼	10⅛	435	420	411	402	393	383	363	340	317	291	264	236	205	177
14 WF 78	14	12	467	454	447	440	433	425	409	391	372	352	331	309	286	262
14 WF 84	14⅛	12	503	490	482	475	467	458	441	422	402	381	359	335	310	284
14 WF 95	14⅛	14½	577	565	559	552	546	539	524	508	492	474	456	436	416	395
14 WF 111	14⅜	14⅝	674	661	653	646	638	630	613	595	576	555	534	511	488	463
14 WF 142	14¾	15½	867	851	843	834	825	815	795	774	751	728	703	676	649	621
14 WF 184	15⅜	15⅝	1121	1101	1090	1079	1068	1056	1031	1004	975	946	914	881	847	811
14 WF 246	16¼	16	1501	1475	1461	1447	1432	1416	1383	1349	1312	1273	1232	1189	1145	1098
14 WF 320	16¾	16¾	1954	1921	1903	1885	1866	1846	1804	1759	1712	1662	1610	1556	1499	1439

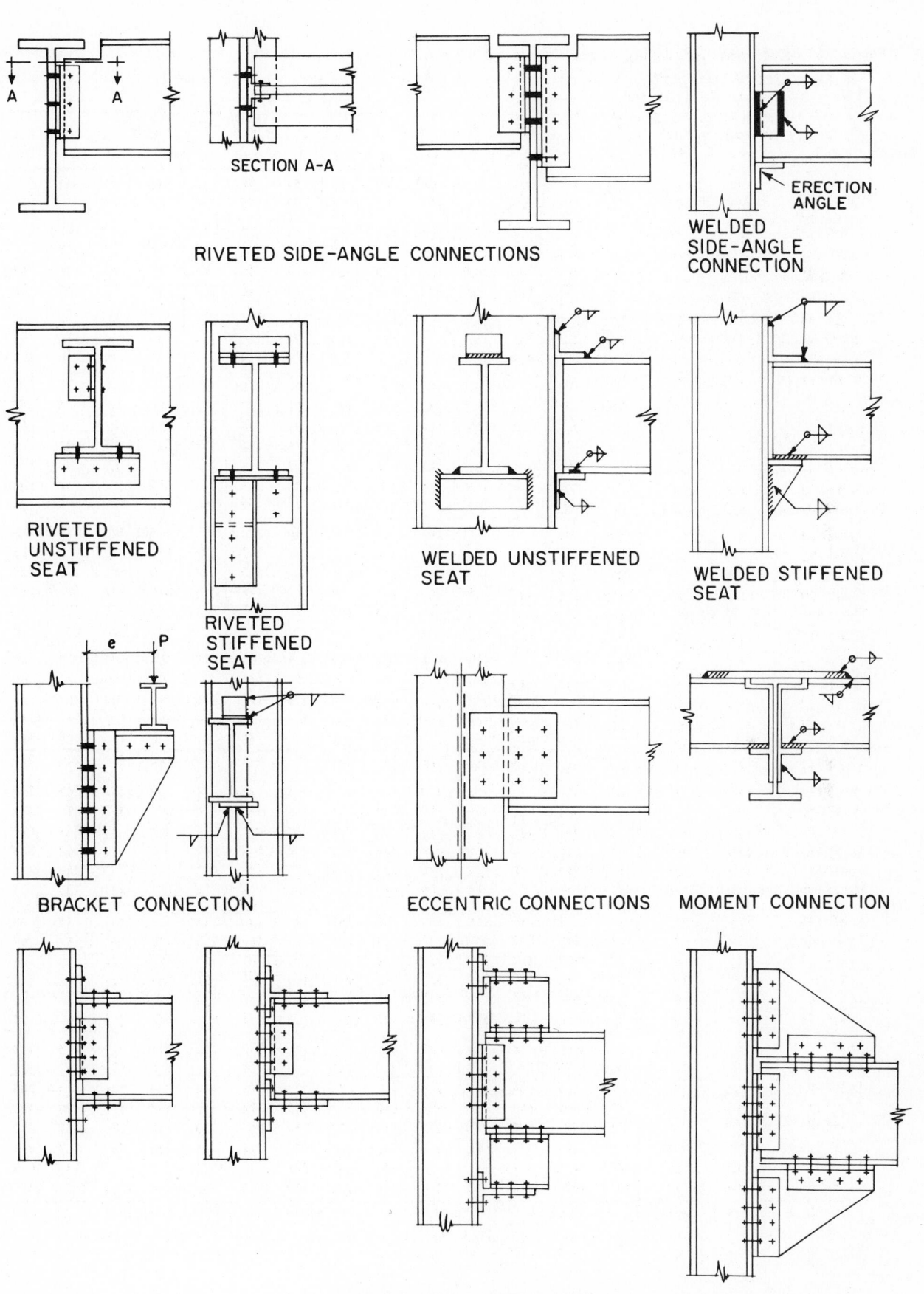

RIVETED SIDE-ANGLE CONNECTIONS

SECTION A-A

WELDED SIDE-ANGLE CONNECTION

ERECTION ANGLE

RIVETED UNSTIFFENED SEAT

RIVETED STIFFENED SEAT

WELDED UNSTIFFENED SEAT

WELDED STIFFENED SEAT

BRACKET CONNECTION

ECCENTRIC CONNECTIONS

MOMENT CONNECTION

WIND MOMENT CONNECTION

Fig. 6 Connection details

Lally columns

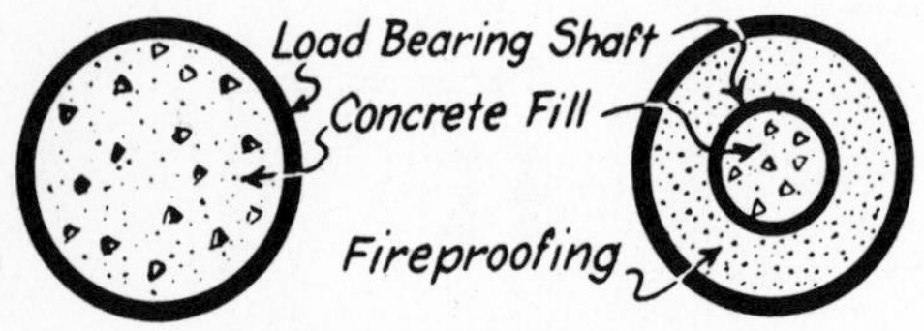
Load Bearing Shaft
Concrete Fill
Fireproofing

STANDARD AND FIREPROOF LALLY COLUMNS

Fireproofing is furnished in the specified thickness required for any fire rating by local building codes. To ensure that new steel pipe of the proper thickness is furnished, always specify the weight in pounds per foot of every column as given in the tables (for example, "SHW 8⅝ in. × 81 lb").

ECCENTRIC LOADING

The safe concentric loads in Tables 11-15 apply only to Lally columns and are based on all loads being applied axially. The strength of Lally columns under eccentric loading is determined as follows: For each 10,000-in.-lb bending moment due to eccentrically applied loads, add the factor *f* given in the tables to the sum of all vertical loads in kips.

ECCENTRIC LOAD MOMENTS

The following illustrations indicate the method of determining equivalent direct loads for each 10,000-in.-lb bending moment with the use of the factor *f* given in the last column of the tables for safe concentric loads.

LALLY EQUIDEPTH CONSTRUCTION

Lally columns are furnished with Lally shear heads for use in flat plate concrete floors to secure flat ceilings with maximum usable floor space, light, and ventilation in fireproof construction. Shear heads consist of channels, small structural beams, or reinforced steel plates, covered by U.S. patent. Columns and connections are pre-

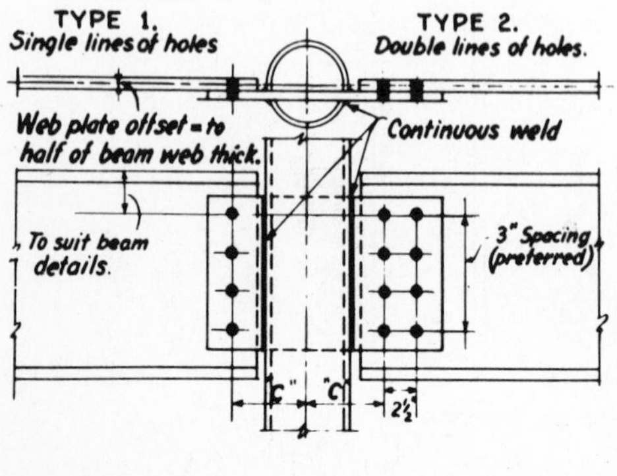
TYPE 1.
Single lines of holes
TYPE 2.
Double lines of holes.
Web plate offset = to half of beam web thick.
Continuous weld
To suit beam details.
3" Spacing (preferred)
"C"
"C"
2½

Table 11. Safe concentric loads in kips for standard heavyweight columns

Size of col. in.	Wt. per ft. lbs.	Area of steel sq. in.	Area of conc. sq. in.	Unbraced length of column in feet: 6	8	10	12	14	16	18	19	20	25	30	35	40	f Kips
3½	15	2.23	7.39	45	40	33	26			STANDARD HEAVY WEIGHT							15.3
4	20	2.68	9.89	58	53	47	39	30									13.4
4½	24	3.17	12.73	72	67	61	54	45	35			SHW					12.0
5	29	3.69	15.96	87	82	76	69	61	51	41							10.8
5½	36	4.30	20.01	105	101	95	88	80	71	60	55	50					9.6
6⅝	49	5.58	28.89	144	140	134	128	120	110	100	94	88	60				8.2
7⅝	64	6.92	38.74	186	181	176	170	162	153	143	138	132	99	70			7.2
8⅝	81	8.40	50.03	232	228	223	217	209	200	191	185	180	148	111	82		6.3
9⅝	100	9.97	62.79	283	279	274	268	260	252	243	238	232	201	161	126	94	5.7
10¾	123	11.91	78.86	347	343	338	332	325	316	307	302	297	266	228	183	144	5.1
12¾	169	14.58	113.10	457	452	448	443	436	427	419	414	409	379	343	300	250	4.4
14	193	16.06	137.88	529	525	520	515	509	500	492	487	482	454	419	378	330	4.1
16	245	18.47	182.65	654	651	646	641	634	627	619	615	610	582	549	510	464	3.6
18	304	20.76	233.71	791	787	782	777	770	764	755	750	746	718	685	644	599	3.4
20	370	23.12	281.36	920	916	913	908	901	895	888	883	879	855	824	791	747	2.9

Table 12. Safe concentric loads in kips for extra heavyweight columns

Size of col. in.	Wt. per ft. lbs.	Area of steel sq. in.	Area of conc. sq. in.	Unbraced length of column in feet: 6	8	10	12	14	16	18	19	20	25	30	35	40	f Kips
4	21	3.68	8.89	72	65	57	48	37	29		EXTRA HEAVY WEIGHT						13.5
4½	27	4.41	11.50	89	83	76	66	55	44	35			XHW				11.9
5½	39	6.11	18.19	131	126	119	110	100	88	75	68	62					9.6
6⅝	56	8.41	26.07	185	180	173	165	155	143	130	123	116	79				8.1
8⅝	91	12.76	45.66	297	292	285	277	268	258	245	239	232	192	145	108		6.2
10¾	133	16.10	74.66	409	404	398	391	383	374	363	357	350	315	272	220	173	5.0
12¾	178	19.24	108.44	527	523	517	511	503	495	484	480	474	440	400	352	297	4.3

Table 13. Safe concentric loads in kips for double extra heavyweight columns.

Size of col. in.	Wt. per ft. lbs.	Area of steel sq. in.	Area of conc. sq. in.	Unbraced length of column in feet: 6	8	10	12	14	16	18	19	20	22	24	26	30	f Kips
4	29	6.72	5.86	112	101	88	71	55	42	DOUBLE EXTRA HEAVY WEIGHT							14.5
4½	35	8.10	7.80	142	130	117	102	83	66	51			XXHW				12.8
5½	52	11.34	12.90	205	196	185	170	154	134	112	102	93	77				10.1
6⅝	72	15.64	18.86	290	281	270	257	240	221	199	188	175	150	128	109		8.5
8⅝	110	21.30	37.12	423	416	406	395	381	366	349	339	329	307	283	258	204	6.3

Table 14. Safe concentric loads in kips for reinforced shell columns

These columns can be reinforced with angles or other structural shapes.

SIZE OF COL. IN.	REIN-FORCE MENT SIZE	WT. PER FT. LBS.	AREA OF STEEL SQ.IN.	AREA OF CONC. SQ.IN.	UNBRACED LENGTH OF COLUMN IN FEET												f Kips
					6	8	10	12	14	16	20	25	30	35	40	45	
3½	5½" ■	18	3.48	6.14	63	57	49	40	30	23							13.1
4	5½" ■	22	3.93	8.64	76	71	64	55	45	36							11.4
4½	6½" ■	27	4.67	11.43	94	89	83	75	65	54	36						9.9
5	6½" ■	31	5.19	14.46	106	102	96	89	80	71	50						8.8
5½	6½" ■	43	5.80	18.57	128	123	118	110	102	92	69	45					8.3
6⅝	6-⅝" ■	56	7.93	26.54	179	175	169	162	154	145	122	89	62				6.8
7⅝	7-¾" ■	73	10.86	35.36	246	241	236	229	221	212	189	154	115	85			5.7
8⅝	8-¾" ■	90	12.90	45.53	300	296	291	285	276	268	247	213	173	133	101		5.1
9⅝	9-¾" ■	109	15.03	57.73	360	355	351	344	337	329	308	276	237	192	151	117	4.5
10¾	9-⅞" ■	136	18.80	71.97	450	446	441	435	428	419	400	368	330	284	233	188	4.0
12¾	10-1" ■	184	24.58	103.10	609	605	600	594	587	579	561	533	496	453	405	347	3.3

(table also marked: REINFORCED SHELL / RHW)

✳ NOTE: *RHW Columns can be Reinforced with Angles or other Structural Shapes.*

Table 15. Safe concentric loads in kips for rectangular columns

SIZE OF COLUMN INCHES	WT PER FT. LBS.	AREA OF STEEL SQ.IN.	AREA OF CONC. SQ.IN.	UNBRACED LENGTH OF COLUMN IN FEET												f-Kips A-A	f-Kips B-B
				6	8	10	12	13	14	16	18	20	22	24	28	A-A	B-B
3×3×¼	16	2.75	6.25	51	45	37	28	24								13.4	13.4
3×6×¼	29	4.25	13.75	86	77	66	51	45	39							12.2	7.5
3½×3½×¼	20	3.25	9.00	65	60	53	44	39	35	27						11.4	11.4
4×4×¼	26	3.75	12.25	81	76	69	61	57	52	42	34					10.0	10.0
4×6×¼	36	4.75	19.25	109	102	94	84	79	73	59	48	38				9.5	7.2
4×8×¼	46	5.75	26.25	137	130	120	107	100	93	76	62	50				9.2	5.7
5×5×¼	37	4.75	20.25	113	109	103	96	92	88	79	68	57	48	40		8.1	8.1
6×6×¼	50	5.75	30.25	150	146	141	134	131	127	118	108	97	85	74	54	6.8	6.8

(table also marked: SQUARE AND RECTANGULAR)

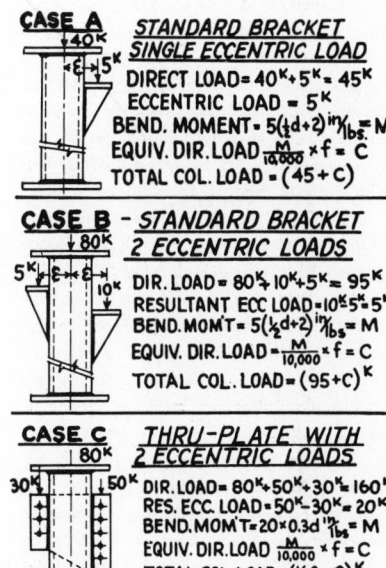

CASE A — STANDARD BRACKET SINGLE ECCENTRIC LOAD
DIRECT LOAD = $40^K + 5^K = 45^K$
ECCENTRIC LOAD = 5^K
BEND. MOMENT = $5(\tfrac{1}{2}d + 2)^{in} lbs = M$
EQUIV. DIR. LOAD $\frac{M}{10,000} \times f = C$
TOTAL COL. LOAD = $(45 + C)$

CASE B — STANDARD BRACKET 2 ECCENTRIC LOADS
DIR. LOAD = $80^K + 10^K + 5^K = 95^K$
RESULTANT ECC LOAD = $10^K - 5^K = 5^K$
BEND. MOM'T = $5(\tfrac{1}{2}d + 2)^{in} lbs = M$
EQUIV. DIR. LOAD = $\frac{M}{10,000} \times f = C$
TOTAL COL. LOAD = $(95 + C)^K$

CASE C — THRU-PLATE WITH 2 ECCENTRIC LOADS
DIR. LOAD = $80^K + 50^K + 30^K = 160^K$
RES. ECC. LOAD = $50^K - 30^K = 20^K$
BEND. MOM'T = $20 \times 0.3d^{in} lbs = M$
EQUIV. DIR. LOAD $\frac{M}{10,000} \times f = C$
TOTAL COL. LOAD = $(160 + C)^K$

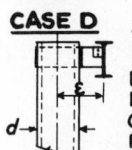

CASE D — THRU-PLATE WITH LOAD AT RIGHT ANGLES
DETERMINE MOMENT IN INCH POUNDS WITH ECCENTRICITY "e" AND TRANSFORM INTO EQUIVALENT DIR. LOAD BY APPLYING FACTOR "f". THRU-PLATE WELDED TO BOTH SIDES OF COLUMN.

fabricated and delivered to the job ready for construction. Typical channel heads are shown in the accompanying drawings. When a reinforced concrete spandrel beam is provided to support the column band load and to resist the torsion incident to negative restraint of the floor band, the outer arms of the shear head can be omitted on exterior columns. (For design and structural details see *Lally Handbook, 1958.*) Lally equidepth construction is restricted to use with Lally columns.

CONTINUITY IN STEEL STRUCTURES

With rare exceptions, the conventional steel building has been designed with simple, flexible connections. This practice has endured despite the fact that the notable advantages of continuity have long been established. Depth of sections and weight of members, for example, are invariably reduced in continuous structures and thus permit savings in material cost. The argument against their employment is that the required rigid connections entail an additional fabricating expense that more than nullifies savings in weight of members and is therefore not economically justifiable. This resistance has gradually lessened in recent years as a result of economical and successful use of continuous steel structures. The development of plastic design in steel and the widespread acceptance of welding are two factors that will increase the use of continuous structures.

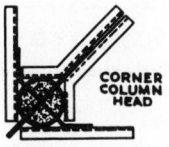

CORNER COLUMN HEAD

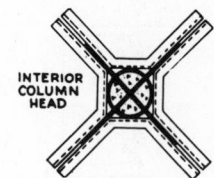

INTERIOR COLUMN HEAD

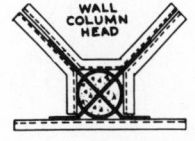

WALL COLUMN HEAD

PLASTIC THEORY

The limitations of the elastic, straight-line relationship between stress and strain have long been recognized. The design of riveted connections, for example, assumes inelastic behavior. The 1963 AISC specification permits beams and girders which are continuous over supports or are rigidly framed to columns to be proportioned for $9/10$ of the negative moments produced by gravity loading, which are maximum at points of support. (This does not apply to loading on cantilever beams.)

The plastic theory has been formulated to take into account realistically the unique characteristic of steel—ductility. The stress-strain relationship of steel (Fig. 7) is composed of an elastic (proportional) range OA and an inelastic range AD. It is in the transition AC from the elastic to inelastic deformations that the important phenomenon of plastic yielding takes place. Figure 8, in which strains are plotted to an expanded scale, illustrates this stage. The significant feature of this stage is that on reaching the yield stress, F_y (36,000 psi minimum), strains in the order of 15 times the strain at yield e_y are produced with

virtually no change in stress. Within the elastic range, stresses are directly proportional to strains, which, in turn, are proportional to their distance from the neutral axis. As a result of yielding, however, virtually all fibers, independent of their distance from the neutral axis, may undergo strains that permit development of yield stress. This stage is known as plastication, from which is derived the term plastic moment (Mp), indicating the moment required for its full development. Figure 9 represents the stress and strain patterns at initial yield, at intermediate point (taken arbitrarily as $3e_y$), and at complete yielding.

Two practical effects result from plastic yielding. The first effect is the increase in the true moment capacity of a section within the limits of yield stress. For the typical rolled steel section this increase is obtained by the utilization at yield stress of the web as well as the entire flange. The ratio between plastic moment and elastic moment at yield stress, Mp/My, is known as the shape factor (u). For most shapes, u is equal to approximately 1.12, which indicates an increase in load capacity of 12 per cent beyond initial yield.

The second and more significant effect

concerns the relative rotations that take place during yielding. The curve shown in Fig. 8 is also representative of the idealized relationship between the applied moment (stress) and the angle of rotation (strain). At yield, when the plastic moment is reached at a critical section, the moment is maintained at approximately constant value, while the section rotates in a manner simulating a hinge. This hinge action at the critical section permits a "redistribution" of larger moments to other portions of the structure.

The principles of the plastic theory can be simply illustrated in the behavior of a uniformly loaded beam with fixed ends (Fig. 10). Figure 11 shows the moments at elastic yield (phase 1) and at ultimate load (phase 2). Figures 12 and 13 indicate the rotations and moments corresponding to those loading conditions. At phase 1, the ends of the beam have reached the elastic limit, at which point they enter into the yield stage and begin hinge action. The moments at this point based on elastic analysis are WI/12 at the ends and WI/24 at the center of the span. As loading is increased (phase 1–2), the "hinged" ends permit the beam to act as if simply sup-

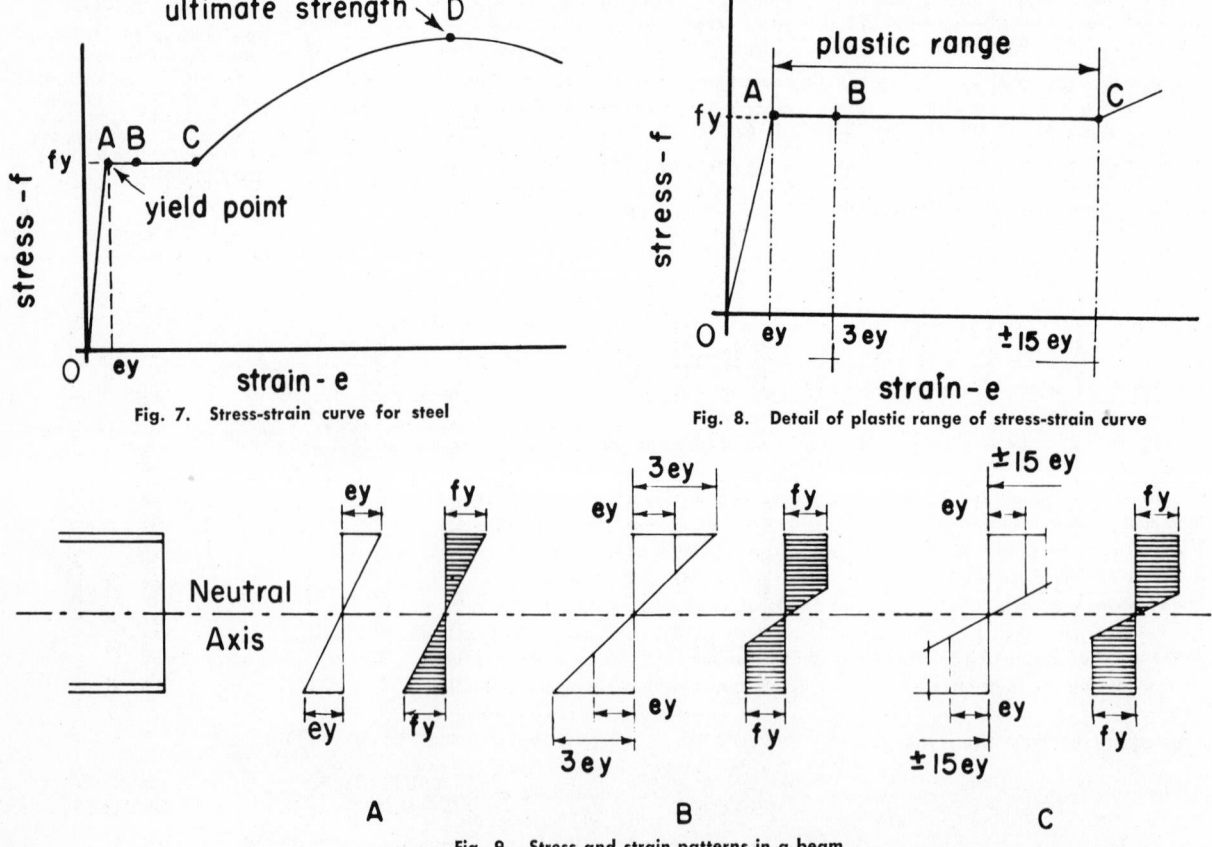

Fig. 7. Stress-strain curve for steel

Fig. 8. Detail of plastic range of stress-strain curve

Fig. 9. Stress and strain patterns in a beam

ported and to utilize the available capacity of the less stressed center portion of the beam. The shaded portion of the moment diagram in Fig. 11 represents the additional load-carrying capacity determined by the plastic theory.

Although the design is based on ultimate capacity utilizing the plastic range of yield, the structure at working loads is almost always stressed well within the elastic limit. Deflections are larger than those obtained by an elastic design but are smaller than those of simply supported members. Special consideration should be given to non-static loading, except for buildings, where loads are basically static.

The importance of the plastic theory extends beyond the practical value of producing more economical structures. Based on the ultimate capacity of a structure, it provides a clearer account of the method of collapse and a more rational design procedure. Safety (load) factors are, consequently, more consistent than in the elastic theory. Moreover, the complex analysis of indeterminate structures is simplified by avoiding approximations and assumptions that require redesign and reanalysis. Since this design method is new and relatively unfamiliar to the professional field, a standard reference is indispensable. In 1959, the AISC published an excellent manual, *Plastic Design in Steel*, which fully illustrates analysis and design procedures.

WELDING

After a long period of trial and research, welding has become fully accepted as a means of joining structural members in buildings. It has the inherent advantage of fusing the metals to be joined, thereby simplifying connections and fabricating operations. In addition, it provides greater opportunities in architectural and structural design—particularly for rigid, continuous structures. Considering the extensive use of welding in other industries, such as ship building, we can hardly consider it an innovation. These industries have been largely responsible for the progress in welding equipment and the training of supervisory and working personnel. Fabricators have now acquired the necessary organization and experience to ensure reliable and economic work.

The fusion welding process most generally used in structural steel work employs an electric arc (Fig. 15). In this process, energy in the form of heat is supplied by establishing an arc between the base or parent metal (the parts to be joined) and a metal electrode. As the arc is formed, tremendous heat is concentrated at the point of welding. Instantly, the materials are at melting-point temperature. The parent metal melts in a small pool and additional metal supplied by the electrode is transferred through the arc and deposited in the pool. As the electrode continues along the joint, the molten metal left behind solidifies to form the weld. Most welding is done with coated electrodes. The function of the coating is to form a gaseous shield, which protects the arc and molten metal from contact with the air. Oxides and nitrides resulting from contact with the air tend to produce brittle welds. The coating also forms a slag-flux shield, which floats above the molten metal, protecting it from the atmosphere. The slag is easily removed after the weld has cooled.

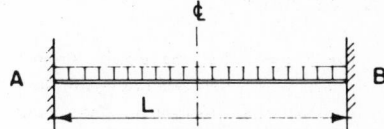

Fig. 10. Uniformly loaded beam with fixed ends

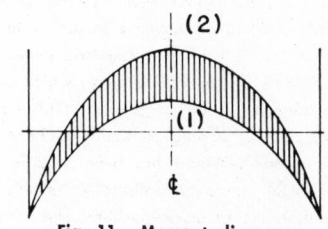

Fig. 11. Moment diagram
1 — at elastic yield, 2 — at ultimate load; true also for Fig. 12–13.

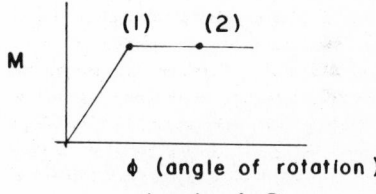

Fig. 12. Rotation at ends of beam

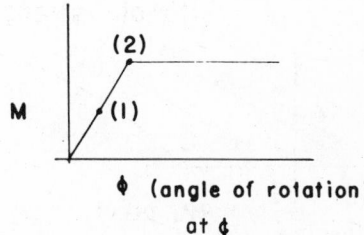

Fig. 13. Rotation at center of beam

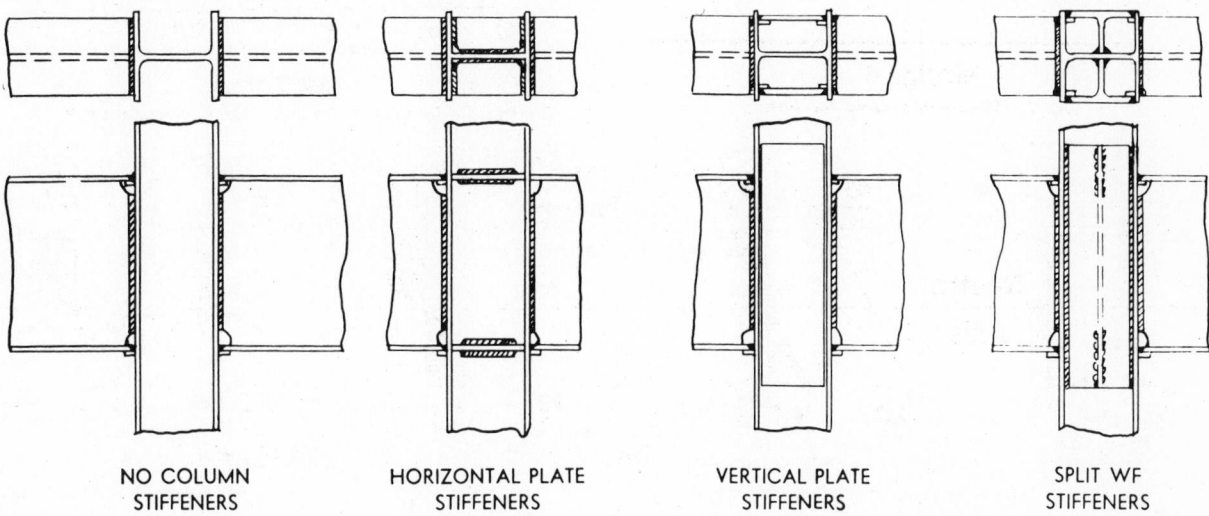

NO COLUMN STIFFENERS   HORIZONTAL PLATE STIFFENERS   VERTICAL PLATE STIFFENERS   SPLIT WF STIFFENERS

Fig. 14. Welded column and beam connections

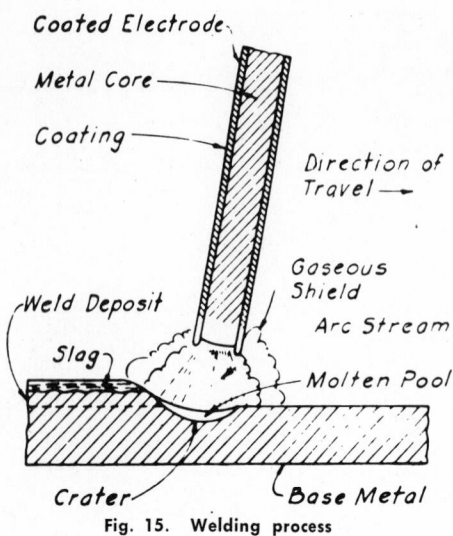

Fig. 15. Welding process

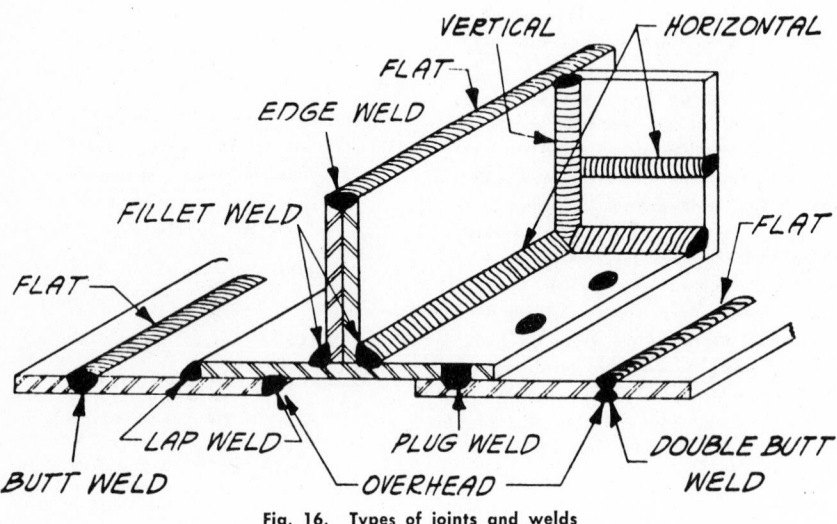

Fig. 16. Types of joints and welds

CLASSIFICATION OF WELDS

Types

1. *Fillet* weld is of approximately triangular cross section joining two surfaces approximately at right angles to each other. The size of the fillet weld is determined by the length of leg. The allowable stress may be computed on the basis of 600 pounds per linear inch per $\frac{1}{16}$ in. of leg size. For welds made with an E60 or E70 electrode and for welding A7, A373, and A36 steel. For welding A36, A440, A441, and weldable A242 steel, an E70 electrode should be used and the allowable stress may be computed on the basis of 700 pounds per linear inch per $\frac{1}{16}$ in. of leg size. The fillet weld is the most common type of weld used in structural work.

2. Groove weld is made by depositing filler metal in a groove between two members to be joined. The standard types of grooves are square, V, bevel-U, and J. With the exception of the square groove, all grooves may be either single or double.

3. *Plug* or *slot* weld is made in a circular hole (plug) or elongated hole (slot) in one member of a lap joint, joining that member to the portion of the surface of the other member that is exposed through the hole.

Positions

There are four positions in welding. In order of economy, they are the flat, horizontal, vertical and overhead positions. Overhead welds, which are the most difficult, should be avoided whenever possible.

Joints

The three most common joints used in structural work are the butt, T, and lap joints. Other types are the edge and corner joints. Fillet welds are applicable to T, lap, and corner joints; groove welds are applicable to all joints with the exception of lap joints.

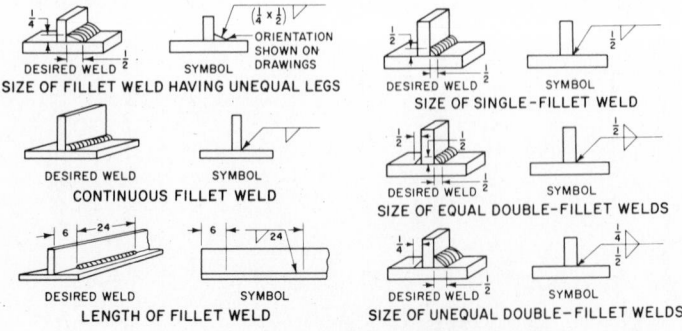

Fig. 17. Welding symbols—examples of use

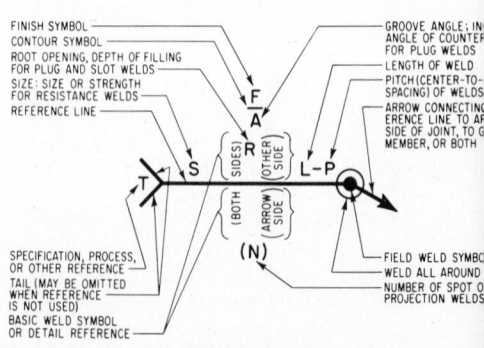

Fig. 18. Standard welding symbols

by JOHN G. MASCIONI, P.E., Associate Professor, School of Architecture, Pratt Institute

All the data contained in this section are intended exclusively for use in preliminary study and design. They provide a quick means of obtaining realistic sizes of members in a structure, and can also serve in comparing different framing schemes and column layouts. The design tables are based on the working stress method in accordance with the current American Concrete Institute Building Code Requirements for Reinforced Concrete (ACI 318). The final design should be prepared by a structural engineer. Should the designer wish to undertake the final design, appropriate references and codes should be consulted. The final design may vary from that given by the tables because of revisions in the ACI Code and differences between the ACI Code and local building code requirements. In many cases additional economy may be achieved in the final design by use of ultimate strength procedures.

PLAIN CONCRETE

Concrete is a mixture composed of a paste binding together an inert filler, or aggregate. The paste is formed by the chemical reaction between cement and water. The usual proportions (by volume) range from 22 per cent paste (15 per cent water and 7 per cent cement) and 78 per cent aggregate for a lean, stiff mixture, to 34 per cent paste (20 per cent water and 14 per cent cement) and 66 per cent aggregate for a rich, workable mixture. Compressive strength, in addition to being the most important quality of concrete, is indicative of its other properties. Tensile and shearing strength, modulus of elasticity, durability, and impermeability are all directly related to compressive strength. Shown in Table 1 are the ACI Code allowable unit stresses based on f_c', the specified ultimate compressive strength of concrete at 28 days.

Proportioning

The paste or cementing medium is the fundamental basis of strength development of concrete. The inherent strength of the paste is a function of the ratio of its two components expressed in gallons of water per sack of cement (known as the "water-cement" ratio). The manner in which this ratio influences the compressive strength of concrete is illustrated in Fig. 1. Type I cement is normal portland cement and Type III is high-early-strength cement. In a concrete mixture, the maximum amount of aggregate should be used to produce an economical mix with low shrinkage. The amount of aggregate used depends on its effect on the workability or consistency of a mix. The limiting amount, then, is the maximum amount that can be used and still attain full compaction of the concrete. Consistency is determined by "slump" tests, which measure the number of inches a mass of concrete will settle after the slump cone has been removed from the concrete. Table 2 indicates the recommended slumps for various types of construction.

Lightweight aggregates

Lightweight aggregates for structural concrete are now used extensively, and are a practical necessity for tall, reinforced concrete structures. These aggregates, generally produced by artificial means, are obtained by expanding, calcinating, or

Table 1. Allowable stresses in concrete

Description		For any strength of concrete in accordance with Section 502	For strength of concrete shown below			
			$f_c' =$ 2,500 psi	$f_c' =$ 3,000 psi	$f_c' =$ 4,000 psi	$f_c' =$ 5,000 psi
Modulus of elasticity ratio; n		$\dfrac{29,000,000}{w^{1.5}\,33\sqrt{f_c'}}$				
For concrete weighing 145 lb per cu ft (see Section 1102)	n		10	9	8	7
Flexure: f_c						
Extreme fiber stress in compression	f_c	$0.45f_c'$	1,125	1,350	1,800	2,250
Extreme fiber stress in tension in plain concrete footings and walls	f_c	$1.6\sqrt{f_c'}$	80	88	102	113
Shear: v (as a measure of diagonal tension at a distance d from the face of the support)						
Beams with no web reinforcement†	v_c	$1.1\sqrt{f_c'}$	55*	60*	70†	78*
Joists with no web reinforcement	v_c	$1.2\sqrt{f_c'}$	61	66	77	86
Members with vertical or inclined web reinforcement or properly combined bent bars and vertical stirrups	v	$5\sqrt{f_c'}$	250	274	316	354
Slabs and footings (peripheral shear, Section 1207)*	v_c	$2\sqrt{f_c'}$	100*	110*	126*	141*
Bearing: f_c						
On full area		$0.25f_c'$	625	750	1,000	1,250
On one-third area or less†		$0.375f_c'$	938	1,125	1,500	1,875

For shear values for lightweight aggregate concrete see Section 1208.

†*This increase shall be permitted only when the least distance between the edges of the loaded and unloaded areas is a minimum of one-fourth of the parallel side dimension of the loaded area. The allowable bearing stress on a reasonably concentric area greater than one-third but less than the full area shall be interpolated between the values given.*

Table 2. Recommended slumps for various types of construction*

Type of construction	Slump, in.	
	Maximum	Minimum
Reinforced foundation walls and footings	5	2
Plain footings, caissons, and substructure walls	4	1
Slabs, beams, and reinforced walls	6	3
Building columns	6	3
Pavements	3	2
Heavy mass construction	3	1

If high-frequency vibrators are used, the values given should be reduced about one third.

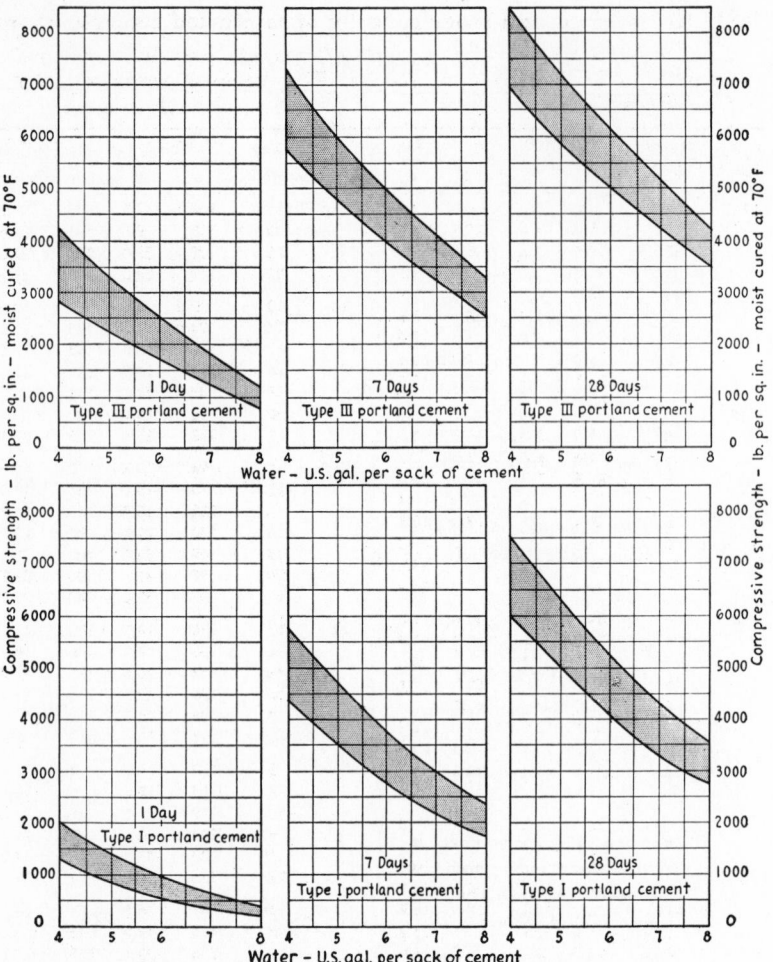

Fig. 1. Relation of compressive strength to water-cement ratio

From Design and Control of Concrete Mixes, *Portland Cement Association.*

Table 3. ACI design coefficients for moment and shear

This table is applicable only under the following conditions: the larger of two adjacent spans must not exceed 20 per cent of the shorter span; loads must be uniformly distributed; the unit live load must not exceed three times the unit dead load. w = unit uniform load. l' = span in feet.

Moment or shear	Design coefficient
Positive moment at end spans	
If discontinuous end is unrestrained	$wl'^2/11$
If discontinuous end is integral with the support	$wl'^2/14$
Positive moment at interior spans	$wl'^2/16$
Negative moment at exterior face of first interior support	
Two spans	$wl'^2/9$
More than two spans	$wl'^2/10$
Negative moment at other faces of interior supports	$wl'^2/11$
Negative moment at face of all supports for (a) slabs with spans not exceeding 10 ft, and (b) beams and girders where ratio of sum of column stiffnesses to beam stiffness exceeds eight at each end of the span	$wl'^2/12$
Negative moment at interior faces of exterior supports for members built integrally with their supports	
If the support is a spandrel beam or girder	$wl'^2/24$
If the support is a column	$wl'^2/16$
Shear in end members at first interior support	$wl'/2$
Shear at all other supports	$wl'/2$

sintering materials such as blast-furnace slag, shale, slate, and clay. The unit weight of lightweight-aggregate concrete ranges from 90 to 115 lb per cu ft as compared with 145 to 150 lb per cu ft for normal concrete. Most of the properties of concrete using lightweight aggregate are comparable to those of concrete of the same compressive strength using normal-weight gravel or crushed stone. Flexural and bond strength are approximately equal, and the water-cement ratio is still the governing factor in strength development. Lightweight-aggregate concrete, however, generally has a lower shear or diagonal tension strength, lower modulus of elasticity, and greater shrinkage.

Curing

The purpose of curing is to influence the rate of the chemical reaction between cement and water. Curing is an important consideration in structural concrete, particularly in precast and prestressed work requiring high-early-strength development. Availability of water and control of temperature are the main requirements for curing. Ponding, sprinkling, and saturating the aggregate prior to its use are three of the methods used to ensure adequate moisture for continued hydration. Minimum temperatures for the air surrounding normal concrete are 70°F for the first three days after placement or 50°F for five days. For high-early-strength concrete the requirements are 70°F for two days or 50°F for three days. If the amount of time available to develop the necessary strength is limited, the temperature should be increased. In one method, saturated steam employing temperatures in the range of 140 to 165°F is used. Insulation, which retains the heat liberated from the reaction between cement and water, will also contribute to rapid strength development.

Table 4. Weight and dimensions of standard deformed bars

Bar No.	Diam, in.	Area, sq in.	Weight, lb per lin ft
2	0.250	0.05	0.167
3	0.375	0.11	0.376
4	0.500	0.20	0.668
5	0.625	0.31	1.043
6	0.750	0.44	1.502
7	0.875	0.60	2.044
8	1.000	0.79	2.670
9	1.128	1.00	3.400
10	1.270	1.27	4.303
11	1.410	1.56	5.313

Design procedure

Since a monolithic reinforced concrete structure is inherently rigid, it produces an indeterminate system. The relative size of members, span lengths, and the effect of alternate loading all influence the magnitude of the design moments and shears and theoretically require an elastic analysis. The interaction of so many variables renders loading tables of limited value. Through the use of the ACI design coefficients (Table 3), however, design moments and shears can be determined empirically with minimum effort and time. Preliminary members can then be selected from the tables giving capacities of various balanced sections. It is important to note that these coefficients apply only when the ratios between adjacent spans and between the uniformly distributed live and dead loads are within the required limits.

Moment and shear

Based on two qualities of concrete, $f_c' = 2,500$ psi and 3,000 psi, Table 5 gives the flexural capacity of a balanced section, M_c, in foot-kips, and the concrete shear capacity, V_c, in kips, for rectangular sections. Flexural capacities greater than those indicated in the table are possible if (1) compressive reinforcement is added or (2) the design bending moment is positive (as in a simple span) and the slab forms a flange to develop a T-section. Since the amount of reinforcement required for both conditions is high, the values given for M_c can be regarded as the desirable maximum bending moment for each section.

The design of reinforced concrete beams with web reinforcement consisting of vertical stirrups or inclined bars is a normal procedure. The shear capacity of the concrete alone, V_c, should not be considered, then, as a limiting value for a section. The values for V_c are included only to indicate the point at which web reinforcement would be required. Shears twice the magnitude of V_c can usually be developed with little difficulty.

Comprehensive tables that directly relate allowable loads to beam sizes for various spans are impractical for continuous reinforced concrete structures. The bending moment, which usually determines the allowable load, varies with the type of support, number of spans, and ratio of adjacent span lengths in addition to the span length. With the use of the ACI coefficients given in Table 3, however, the design moment can be readily determined. Once the design moment has been determined, either by the use of the ACI coefficients or by elastic analysis, the appropriate section can be selected from Table 5.

Table 5. Moment and shear capacity of reinforced concrete beams

$f_c' = $ ultimate compression strength of concrete, psi; $M_c = $ flexural capacity of balanced section, ft-kips; $V_c = $ concrete shear capacity for rectangular section, kips.

Depth, in.	Width, in.	$f_c' = 2,500$		$f_c' = 3,000$		Depth, in.	Width, in.	$f_c' = 2,500$		$f_c' = 3,000$	
		M_c	V_c	M_c	V_c			M_c	V_c	M_c	V_c
10	8	8.3	3.5	10.3	3.8	22	16	104	17.6	125	19.2
	10	10.4	4.4	12.5	4.8		18	118	19.8	141	21.6
	12	12.5	5.3	15.1	5.8		20	130	22.0	158	24.0
	14	14.8	6.2	17.7	6.7		22	144	24.2	173	26.4
	16	16.7	7.0	20.0	7.7	24	10	79.0	9.7	95.0	10.6
	18	18.8	7.9	22.6	8.6		12	94.8	14.5	113	15.8
	20	20.9	8.8	25.1	9.6		14	110	16.9	132	18.5
	22	22.9	9.7	27.4	10.6		16	126	19.3	151	21.1
	24	25.1	10.6	30.2	11.5		18	148	21.8	171	23.8
12	8	13.1	4.4	15.8	4.8		20	158	24.2	190	26.4
	10	16.3	5.5	19.6	6.0		22	173	26.6	209	29.1
	12	19.6	6.6	23.6	7.2	26	10	94.2	13.2	113	14.4
	14	22.9	7.7	27.5	8.4		12	113	15.8	136	17.3
	16	26.2	8.8	31.4	9.6		14	132	18.5	158	20.2
	18	29.4	9.9	35.3	10.8		16	150	21.2	181	23.0
	20	32.7	11.0	39.2	12.0		18	169	23.8	203	25.9
	22	35.8	12.1	43.0	13.2		20	188	26.4	226	28.8
	24	39.2	13.2	47.0	14.4		22	207	29.0	249	31.7
14	8	18.8	5.3	22.6	5.8	28	10	110	14.3	133	15.6
	10	23.5	6.6	28.3	7.2		12	133	17.2	160	18.7
	12	28.2	7.9	34.0	8.6		14	154	20.0	186	21.8
	14	33.0	9.2	39.3	10.1		16	176	22.8	213	25.0
	16	37.7	10.6	45.2	11.5		18	198	25.8	239	28.1
	18	42.3	11.9	50.8	13.0		20	221	28.6	266	31.2
	20	47.1	13.2	56.5	14.4	30	10	128	15.4	154	16.8
	22	51.6	14.5	62.2	15.8		12	154	18.5	185	20.2
	24	56.5	15.8	67.9	17.3		14	179	21.6	216	23.5
16	8	25.7	6.2	30.8	6.7		16	204	24.6	247	26.9
	10	31.9	7.7	38.4	8.4		18	230	27.7	278	30.3
	12	38.4	9.2	46.2	10.1		20	256	30.8	308	33.6
	14	44.7	10.8	53.8	11.8	32	10	147	16.5	177	18.0
	16	51.2	12.3	61.5	13.4		12	176	19.8	212	21.6
	18	57.5	13.9	69.1	15.1		14	206	23.1	248	25.2
	20	64.0	15.4	76.8	16.8		16	236	26.4	282	28.8
	22	70.3	16.9	84.5	18.5		18	265	29.7	318	32.4
	24	76.1	18.5	92.4	20.2		20	294	33.0	354	36.0
18	10	41.7	8.8	50.3	9.6	34	10	167	17.6	202	19.2
	12	50.2	10.5	60.4	11.5		12	200	21.1	242	23.0
	14	58.5	12.3	70.2	13.4		14	234	24.6	282	26.9
	16	67.0	14.1	80.3	15.3		16	268	28.2	322	30.7
	18	75.2	15.8	90.2	17.3		18	301	31.7	363	34.6
	20	83.4	17.6	101	19.2		20	334	35.2	403	38.4
	22	91.9	19.3	110	21.1	36	12	228	22.4	274	24.5
	24	100	21.2	121	23.0		14	264	26.2	318	28.6
20	10	52.9	9.9	63.8	10.8		16	301	29.9	363	32.6
	12	63.5	11.9	76.4	13.0		18	340	33.6	409	36.7
	14	74.0	13.9	89.7	15.1		20	377	37.4	453	40.8
	16	84.7	15.8	102	17.3	38	12	254	23.8	305	25.9
	18	95.2	17.8	114	19.4		14	296	27.7	356	30.2
	20	106	19.8	128	21.6		16	339	31.7	407	34.6
22	10	65.4	11.0	78.6	12.0		18	381	35.6	458	38.9
	12	78.4	13.2	94.4	14.4		20	424	39.6	509	43.2
	14	91.5	15.4	110	16.8						

Design notations and formulas

$b = $ width of section

$d = $ effective depth (total depth less 2 in.)

$f_c' = $ ultimate compressive strength of concrete

$f_c = $ allowable compressive strength in extreme fiber $= 0.45 f_c'$

$f_s = $ stress in tensile reinforcement $= 20,000$ psi

$j = 0.866$ (value for stresses used)

$k = 0.403$ (value for stresses used)

$v = $ unit shearing stress $= 1.1\sqrt{f_c'}$

$\quad = 55$ psi for 2,500 psi concrete

$\quad = 60$ psi for 3,000 psi concrete

(a) $$K = \frac{1}{2} f_c j k$$

For 2,500-psi concrete:

$$K = \frac{1}{2} \times 1,125 \times 0.866 \times 0.403 = 196$$

For 3,000-psi concrete:

$$K = \frac{1}{2} \times 1,350 \times 0.866 \times 0.403 = 236$$

(b) $$M_c = \frac{Kbd^2}{12,000} \text{ in foot-kips}$$

(c) $$V_c = \frac{vbd}{1,000} \text{ in kips}$$

Table 6. Total uniformly distributed loads for beams with balanced reinforcement

Depth, in.	Width, in.	Span length, ft													
		9	10	11	12	13	14	15	16	17	18	19	20	21	22
		Load, kips per lin ft													
10	8	1.24	1.00	0.83	0.69	0.59									
	10	1.54	1.25	1.03	0.88	0.74	0.64								
12	8	1.92	1.56	1.29	1.08	0.92	0.80	0.69							
	10	2.42	1.96	1.62	1.36	1.16	1.00	0.87	0.76						
14	8	2.78	2.25	1.85	1.56	1.33	1.15	1.00	0.88	0.78	0.69				
	10	3.47	2.81	2.32	1.95	1.66	1.43	1.25	1.10	0.97	0.87	0.77	0.70	0.63	
	12	4.17	3.38	2.79	2.35	2.00	1.72	1.50	1.32	1.17	1.04	0.94	0.84	0.76	0.70
16	8	3.77	3.06	2.53	2.12	1.81	1.56	1.36	1.19	1.05	0.95	0.85	0.76	0.69	0.63
	10	4.74	3.83	3.17	2.66	2.26	1.95	1.70	1.49	1.32	1.18	1.06	0.96	0.87	0.79
	12	5.68	4.61	3.82	3.21	2.73	2.35	2.05	1.80	1.59	1.42	1.27	1.15	1.04	0.95

Depth, in.	Width, in.	14	16	18	20	22	24	26	28	30	32	34	36	38	40
18	8	2.05	1.56	1.24	1.00	0.83	0.69								
	10	2.56	1.96	1.55	1.25	1.04	0.87	0.74							
	12	3.07	2.35	1.85	1.50	1.24	1.04	0.89	0.77						
20	8	2.59	1.98	1.56	1.23	1.04	0.88	0.75	0.65						
	10	3.24	2.48	1.96	1.57	1.31	1.10	0.94	0.81	0.70					
	12	3.89	2.98	2.35	1.90	1.57	1.32	1.13	0.97	0.84					
22	8	3.19	2.45	1.93	1.56	1.29	1.08	0.92	0.80	0.69					
	10	4.00	3.07	2.42	1.96	1.62	1.36	1.16	1.00	0.87	0.77				
	12	4.79	3.67	2.90	2.36	1.94	1.63	1.39	1.19	1.04	0.91	0.81			
24	10	4.83	3.70	2.92	2.37	1.95	1.64	1.40	1.20	1.05	0.92	0.82			
	12	5.79	4.45	3.51	2.84	2.34	1.97	1.68	1.44	1.26	1.10	0.98			
	14	6.76	5.16	4.09	3.32	2.73	2.29	1.96	1.68	1.47	1.29	1.15	1.02		
26	10		4.42	3.49	2.83	2.33	1.96	1.67	1.44	1.25	1.10	0.97	0.87		
	12		5.30	4.20	3.40	2.81	2.35	2.01	1.73	1.50	1.32	1.16	1.04		
	14		6.17	4.89	3.96	3.25	2.74	2.34	2.01	1.75	1.54	1.36	1.22	1.09	
28	10		5.16	4.07	3.31	2.73	2.29	1.95	1.67	1.47	1.28	1.15	1.02	0.92	
	12		6.21	4.89	3.98	3.28	2.75	2.35	2.02	1.76	1.55	1.37	1.22	1.10	
	14		7.22	5.71	4.62	3.82	3.21	2.73	2.34	2.06	1.79	1.61	1.42	1.29	
30	12			5.68	4.61	3.81	3.19	2.72	2.34	2.05	1.79	1.60	1.42	1.28	
	14			6.73	5.36	4.44	3.73	3.18	2.74	2.39	2.10	1.86	1.66	1.49	1.34
	16			7.58	6.16	5.08	4.27	3.64	3.14	2.73	2.39	2.13	1.89	1.70	1.53
32	12				5.31	4.38	3.70	3.14	2.71	2.35	2.07	1.83	1.64	1.47	1.32
	14				6.18	5.11	4.29	3.66	3.15	2.74	2.41	2.14	1.91	1.71	1.54
	16				7.05	5.83	4.90	4.17	3.59	3.13	2.74	2.43	2.17	1.95	1.76
34	12				6.02	4.97	4.18	3.56	3.07	2.68	2.35	2.08	1.86	1.67	1.50
	14				7.03	5.82	4.88	4.16	3.59	3.13	2.74	2.43	2.17	1.95	1.75
	16				8.02	6.63	5.57	4.74	4.09	3.56	3.14	2.78	2.47	2.23	2.00
36	14					6.55	5.51	4.69	4.04	3.52	3.09	2.75	2.45	2.20	1.96
	16					7.46	6.28	5.36	4.62	4.03	3.53	3.13	2.79	2.51	2.26
	18					8.42	7.08	6.04	5.21	4.53	3.98	3.53	3.15	2.83	2.55
38	14					7.34	6.17	5.25	4.53	3.94	3.46	3.07	2.74	2.46	2.21
	16					8.40	7.06	6.01	5.18	4.52	3.96	3.52	3.14	2.82	2.54
	18					9.45	7.92	6.76	5.84	5.07	4.46	3.95	3.52	3.17	2.85

Table 7. Total safe axial load for tied columns

Column size, in.		$f_s = 16,000$					$f_s = 20,000$
		f_c'					f_c'
		2,000	2,500	3,000	3,750	5,000	5,000
		Load, kips					
10	12	104	115	126	142	169	185
	14	122	135	148	167	198	216
	16	140	154	168	190	226	246
	18	157	173	189	214	254	277
	20	174	192	210	237	282	307
12	12	126	139	152	171	204	222
	14	146	162	177	199	237	259
	16	157	184	202	228	271	296
	18	189	208	228	257	305	332
	20	209	231	253	285	339	370
	22	230	254	277	313	373	407
	24	251	277	303	341	406	443
14	14	171	188	206	232	276	301
	16	196	216	236	266	317	345
	18	220	242	265	299	356	388
	20	244	269	294	332	395	431
	22	269	297	324	366	435	474
	24	293	323	353	398	474	517
16	16	223	246	269	304	361	394
	18	251	277	303	341	406	443
	20	279	308	337	370	452	493
	22	307	338	370	418	497	542
	24	335	370	404	456	543	592
18	18	283	312	341	385	458	499
	20	314	346	378	427	508	554
	22	346	381	417	470	559	609
	24	377	415	454	513	610	665
	26	408	451	493	556	661	721
20	20	349	385	421	475	565	615
	22	383	423	463	522	621	678
	24	419	462	505	570	678	739
	26	453	500	547	617	734	801
	28	489	539	589	665	791	860
22	22	422	466	509	575	684	746
	24	460	508	555	626	745	813
	26	499	550	602	679	808	881
	28	537	592	648	731	869	948
	30	572	630	688	775	932	1,017
24	24	502	554	606	684	813	887
	26	544	600	656	740	881	961
	28	586	646	707	798	949	1,035
	30	628	693	758	855	1,017	1,118
	32	670	744	808	912	1,085	1,183
26	26	589	650	711	802	954	1,041
28	28	683	754	824	930	1,107	1,208
30	30	785	866	947	1,069	1,271	1,386
32	32	893	985	1,077	1,215	1,476	1,577
34	34	1,008	1,112	1,216	1,372	1,642	1,780

Table 8. Total safe axial load for square spiral columns

Column size, in.	$f_s = 16,000$				$f_s = 20,000$
	f_c'				f_c'
	2,500	3,000	3,750	5,000	5,000
	Load, kips				
14	232	254	287	343	373
15	277	302	340	403	440
16	294	335	378	450	491
17	338	394	443	524	574
18	382	418	472	564	614
19	403	493	554	655	718
20	450	519	587	699	762
21	473	547	621	745	808
22	522	626	707	844	918
23	573	656	745	894	969
24	599	738	835	997	1,084
25	652	771	876	1,052	1,139
26	704	855	969	1,159	1,259
27	734	891	1,014	1,219	1,319
28	790	978	1,110	1,331	1,443
29	822	1,016	1,158	1,395	1,507
30	880	1,056	1,208	1,461	1,574
31	939	1,147	1,310	1,580	1,705
32	975	1,190	1,363	1,651	1,776
33	1,037	1,284	1,467	1,774	1,911

Table 9. Total safe axial load for round spiral columns

Column diam, in.	$f_s = 16,000$				$f_s = 20,000$
	f_c'				f_c'
	2,500	3,000	3,750	5,000	5,000
	Load, kips				
14	209	226	252	295	325
15	249	269	299	349	386
16	263	286	320	376	413
17	303	328	367	430	473
18	343	372	415	486	536
19	359	391	439	519	569
20	402	437	490	579	635
21	420	459	517	615	671
22	464	507	571	678	749
23	509	555	625	742	810
24	529	580	657	784	852
25	576	631	714	852	926
26	623	682	772	921	1,003
28	695	765	869	1,042	1,130
30	772	851	970	1,169	1,263
32	851	942	1,077	1,204	1,404
34	959	1,062	1,215	1,471	1,584
36	1,044	1,161	1,331	1,619	1,738
38	1,154	1,290	1,481	1,800	1,931
40	1,284	1,422	1,634	1,987	2,131

Allowable loads

Table 6 lists the total uniformly distributed allowable load in kips (1,000 lb) per lineal foot given one set of stresses, $f_s = 20,000$ psi and $f_c = 1,350$ psi, and one condition of end restraint, end span free on one end and continuous on the other. In accordance with the ACI design coefficients, the design moment for the assumed end condition is equal to $wl^2/10$. By equating M_c, the resisting moment of a balanced section as given in Table 5, to the design moment and rearranging terms, we obtain $w = 10 \, M_c/l^2$. Since Table 6 contains a limited number of beams, alternate sections that have the same M_c may be selected from Table 5.

Axial loads

Design data on safe axial loads (Tables 7, 8, and 9) are in accordance with the ACI Code. Capacities are based on the maximum number of bars that can be accommodated in a column section. The formula for tied columns is

$$P = (0.18 f_c' A_g + 0.8 \, f_s A_s) \div 1,000$$

The formula for square and round spiral columns is

$$P = (0.225 f_c' A_g + f_s A_s) \div 1,000$$

in which

P = total allowable axial load, kips
f_c' = ultimate compressive strength of concrete
A_g = gross area of column
f_s = allowable stress in vertical reinforcement
A_s = effective cross-sectional area of reinforcement in compression

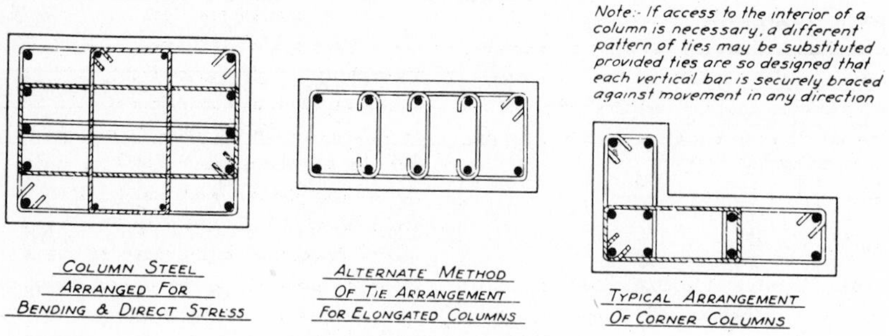

Note: If access to the interior of a column is necessary, a different pattern of ties may be substituted provided ties are so designed that each vertical bar is securely braced against movement in any direction
Column Steel Arranged For Bending & Direct Stress
Alternate Method Of Tie Arrangement For Elongated Columns
Typical Arrangement Of Corner Columns

Typical special-purpose columns

Lower bar
Upper bar
Section A'-A'
A'
A'
Slope 1 to 6 maximum
4 Spaces @ 3"

Typical tied column

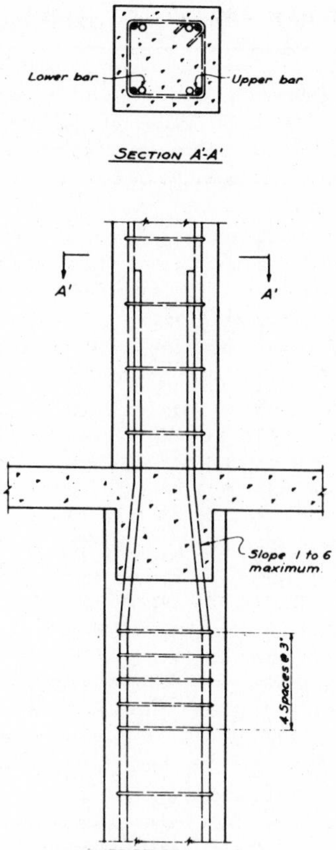

Welded Anchor Bolts.
A
A

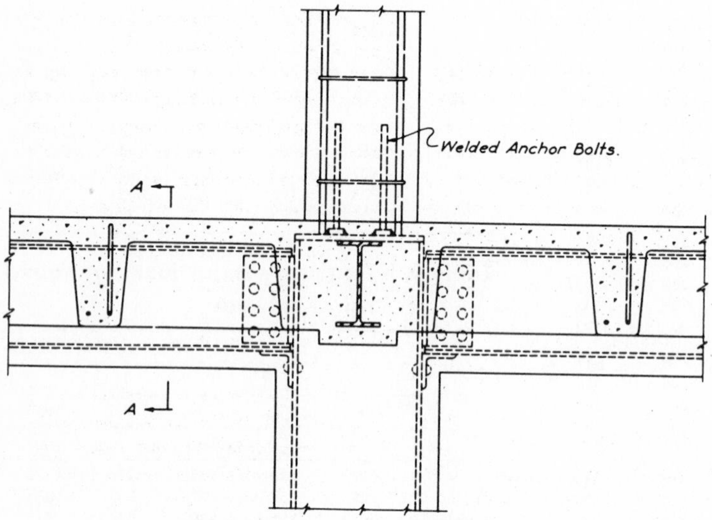

Steel construction to floor; concrete above

Fig. 2. Typical details of reinforced concrete beams, girders, and columns

From Manual of Standard Practice for Detailing Reinforced Concrete Structures, *ACI 315, American Concrete Institute.*

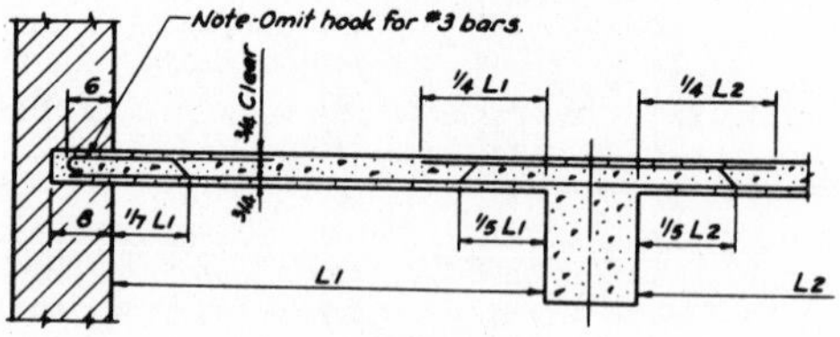

Note-Omit hook for #3 bars.
6
3/4 Clear
3/4
8
1/7 L1
1/4 L1
1/5 L1
1/4 L2
1/5 L2
L1
L2

Slab detail

Section A-A

1/7 L1 Where Specified
1-0 Min.
2 For Beams
3 For Girders
1/4 Greater L
1/4 Greater L
Top Bars
2
6
Beams
Girders
8
12
1/7 L1
2 Clear
1 Clear
Embed 17d
1/5 L1
1/4 L2
L1
L2
This may be increased to 1/5 L1 to maintain 1-0 minimum above.
#3 Stirrup Spacer
1½ Clear
D
W
Section

Beam and girder detail

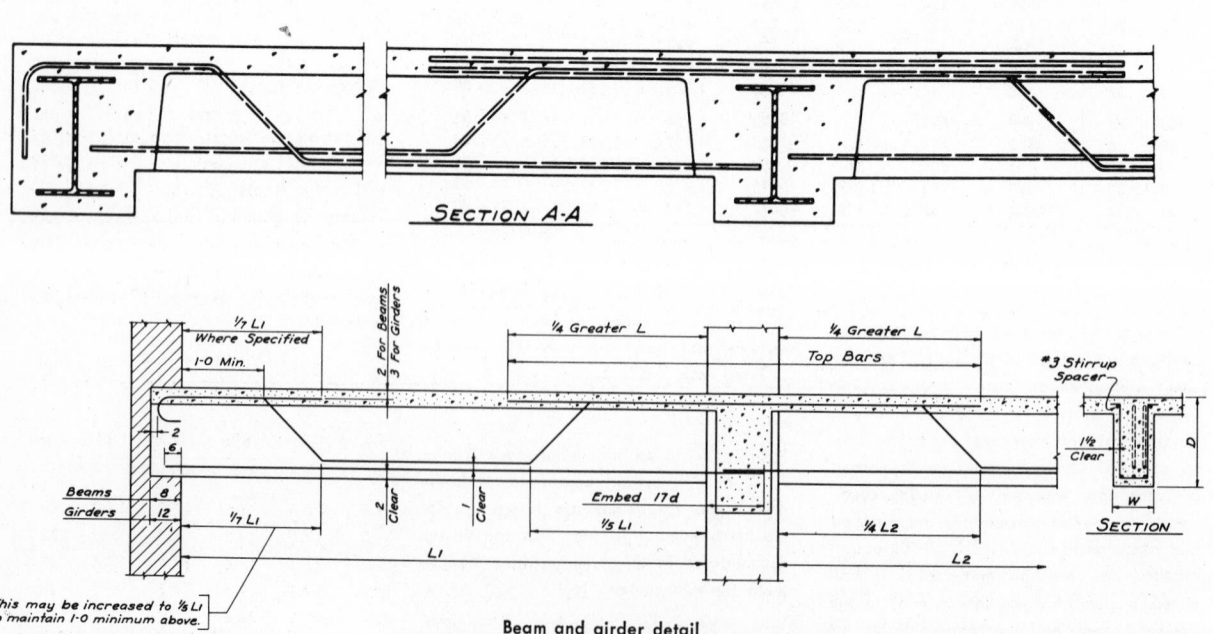

FLAT SLABS AND TWO-WAY SLABS

Flat slabs and two-way slabs are highly indeterminate systems in which the floor slab is reinforced in two or more directions. For each system, the ACI Code stipulates a minimum thickness of slab and provides an empirical method of analysis giving the flexural and shear requirements. Table 10 indicates the maximum dimensions these slabs may take in accordance with this requirement. Although the thickness of slab may be adequate to fulfill design requirements, the purpose of the table is only to establish the upper limit of the dimensions for each thickness of slab. For the maximum spans shown, the thickness of flat slabs must be at least $L/40$ for slabs with drop panels and $L/36$ for slabs without drop panels. L is equal to the length of the longest side of the panel. The ratio of length to width must not exceed 1.33 and adjacent spans must not vary by more than 20 per cent for panels designed by the empirical method. The thickness of two-way slabs must be at least equal to the perimeter of the panel divided by 180. For each thickness of two-way slabs, Table 10 gives the maximum sum of length plus width of panel from which any combination of the two sides can be made. Also included are dimensions for a square

panel and for a rectangular panel in which 0.8 has been taken arbitrarily as the ratio of the short to long side. A ratio of 0.5 between the short and the long side is the practical limit to which two-way action will take place.

ONE-WAY SOLID SLABS

Resisting moment

For various qualities of concrete, Table 11 gives the flexural resisting capacity, M_c, in foot-kips, of one-way solid slabs. Once the design moment has been determined, either from the ACI design coefficients (Table 3) or from an elastic analysis, the appropriate thickness of slab can be selected directly from Table 11. Values correspond to those of a balanced rectangular section 12 in. wide. For values greater than those indicated, compressive reinforcement would have to be added to already heavily reinforced sections. The effective depth, d, used in all cases is equal to the thickness of the slab minus 1 in. The 1 in. represents a clearance of ¾ in. plus one half the diameter of a No. 4 bar, which is the assumed reinforcement. The use of larger bars will not significantly change the given values.

Safe superimposed loads

Table 12 lists the safe superimposed load

in pounds per square foot for various spans, given one set of stresses, $f_s = 20,000$ psi and $f_c = 1,350$ psi, and one condition of end restraint, end span free on one end and continuous on the other. In accordance with the ACI design coefficients, the design moment for the assumed end condition is equal to $wl^2/10$. By equating M_c, the resisting moment of a balanced section as given in Table 11, to the design moment and rearranging terms, we have $w = 10M_c/l^2$.

For different conditions of end restraint or different concrete stresses, values may be modified by proportion. Often the values given greatly exceed the weight of slab that already has been deducted in computing w', the superimposed load. Since the ACI coefficients are based on a maximum ratio of live load to dead load, the superimposed load must consist of sufficient dead load to fulfill this requirement.

Design notations and formulas

b = width (12 in.)
d = effective depth
f_c = allowable stress in flexural compression
j = 0.866 (value for stresses used)
k = 0.403 (value for stresses used)
w = total allowable distributed load
w' = allowable superimposed load

(a)
$$K = \frac{1}{2}f_c jk$$
$$= \frac{1}{2} \times 1,350 \times 0.87 \times 0.40 = 236$$

(b)
$$M_c = \frac{Kbd^2}{12,000}$$

(c)
$$w = \frac{10M_c}{l^2}$$

(d)
$$w' = w - \text{weight of slab}$$

CONCRETE JOISTS

Concrete joist construction consists of narrow ribs or joists and a top slab of concrete, the whole of which is formed by creating longitudinal void spaces by means of permanent or removable forms of steel or removable forms of wood. Joist widths vary from 4 in. to 7 or 8 in. Standard

Table 10. Maximum dimensions of flat slabs and two-way slabs

| Slab thickness, in. | Flat slab | | Two-way slab | | |
	Without drop panel, Span L, ft–in.	With drop panel, Span L, ft–in.	Sum of two sides, L + W ft–in.	Square Panel, L (each side), ft–in.	Rectangular panel (W/L = 0.8), LxW, ft–in.
5	15–0	16–8	37–6	18–9	20–10x16–8
5½	16–6	18–4	41–3	20–7	22–11x18–4
6	18–0	20–0	45–0	22–6	25–0 x20–0
6½	19–6	21–8	48–9	24–4	27–1 x21–8
7	21–0	23–4	52–6	26–3	29–2 x23–4
7½	22–6	25–0	56–3	28–1	31–3 x25–0
8	24–0	26–8	60–0	30–0	33–4 x26–8
8½	25–6	28–4	63–9	31–10	35–5 x28–4
9	27–0	30–0	67–6	33–9	37–6 x30–0
10	30–0	33–4	75–0	37–6	41–8 x33–4

Table 11. Resisting moment of one-way solid slabs

| f_c' | f_c | Slab thickness, in. | | | | | | | | | | | | | | |
		4	4½	5	5½	6	6½	7	7½	8	8½	9	9½	10	11	12
		Resisting moment, ft-kips														
2,000	900	1.41	1.92	2.51	3.2	3.9	4.7	5.7	6.6	7.7	8.8	10.0	11.3	12.7	15.7	19.0
2,500	1,125	1.76	2.40	3.14	4.0	4.9	5.9	7.1	8.3	9.6	11.0	12.5	14.2	15.9	19.6	23.7
3,000	1,350	2.12	2.89	3.78	4.8	5.9	7.1	8.5	10.0	11.6	13.3	15.1	17.1	19.1	23.6	28.6
3,750	1,700	2.68	3.65	4.77	6.0	7.5	9.0	10.7	12.6	14.6	16.8	19.1	21.5	24.1	29.8	36.1
5,000	2,250	3.54	4.81	6.29	8.0	9.8	11.9	14.1	16.6	19.3	22.1	25.2	28.4	31.8	39.3	47.6

forms for the void spaces are usually 20 or 30 in. wide and have a depth of 6, 8, 10, 12, or 14 in. The top slab is usually 2, 2½, or 3 in. thick, but not less than 1/12 of the clear distance between ribs. Temperature reinforcement in the concrete top slab over forms and in a direction normal to the span of the joists may consist of either bars or welded wire fabric. For floor construction, distributing ribs with at least one No. 4 bar top and bottom are required. One rib near the center is required for spans from 20 to 30 ft and two near the third points for spans over 30 ft. The capacity of the joists can be increased by the use of tapered end forms, which are available for both 20 and 30-in.-wide forms. The recommended maximum span for joist floor construction is 24 times the total depth of the construction. For roofs, or where time-sagging is not important, the ratio of span to depth may exceed 24.

Safe superimposed loads

The data in Table 13 have been derived from comprehensive tables prepared by the Concrete Reinforcing Steel Institute. These tables give the safe superimposed loads for various combinations of joist width, depth of form and slab, end condition, and reinforcement. Table 13 is mainly illustrative: it indicates the upper limits of the capacity of one-way joists for one set of conditions. Designs conform to the ACI Code for end spans for which the design moment is equal to $wl^2/10$. A joist width of 5 in. is held constant throughout. Increasing or decreasing the joist width to 4 or 6 in. would have a corresponding effect on the loads given. Since the loads given require heavy reinforcement, including trussed bars and comprehensive reinforcement, Table 13 should not be considered representative of economical designs. The loads given would also frequently require the use of tapered

ends, as shown in Fig. 4. The stresses employed are as follows:

$$f_c' = 3,000 \text{ psi}$$
$$f_c = 1,350 \text{ psi}$$
$$f_s = 20,000 \text{ psi}$$

TWO-WAY DOME SLABS

The two-way dome slab has rows of joists at right angles to each other, with domes omitted around the columns to form drop panels. The columns must be of sufficient size to keep the diagonal tension within the allowable values or a flaring cap must be provided. Shallower domes are sometimes used around the drop panel to provide space for heavy top bars. Joists in each direction are divided into two bands or strips, one over the columns and extending the width of the drop panel, designed to provide reinforcement for the column strip, and the other filling in be-

Table 12. Safe superimposed loads for one-way solid slabs

Span, ft–in.	Slab thickness, in.															
	4	4½	5	5½	6	6½	7	7½	8	8½	9	9½	10	11	12
	Load, psf															
7–0	383	534													
8–0	281	395	528	681											
9–0	212	301	404	523	653										
10–0	162	233	315	411	515	629									
10–6	143	206	281	367	462	565	686								
11–0	125	183	249	328	412	506	614	732							
11–6	111	163	224	294	372	458	557	654	780						
12–0	97	144	199	264	335	412	502	601	705	819					
12–6	86	129	179	239	303	375	457	548	644	748	857				
13–0	75	115	160	215	274	339	415	498	587	681	782	891			
13–6	66	102	145	195	249	309	379	456	537	625	718	821	925		
14–0		91	130	176	226	281	345	417	492	573	658	754	850	1,063	
14–6		81	117	159	206	257	317	382	453	528	606	696	785	983	1,210
15–0		72	105	144	187	234	289	350	416	486	560	641	723	913	1,120
15–6			94	131	171	215	266	323	384	449	517	594	671	846	1,040
16–0			84	118	155	196	244	297	353	414	477	549	621	785	970
16–6			76	107	142	180	224	273	326	382	443	510	578	731	900
17–0			68	97	129	165	206	252	302	356	410	473	536	679	841
17–6				88	117	151	190	233	279	329	381	440	499	635	785
18–0				79	106	138	174	215	258	305	354	409	465	590	733
18–6				71	97	127	160	198	239	283	329	381	433	553	686
19–0					88	115	147	183	221	263	305	355	414	517	643
19–6					80	105	135	169	205	245	284	331	378	484	602
20–0					72	96	124	156	190	227	265	308	353	454	556
20–6						87	114	144	176	211	247	287	330	424	531
21–0						80	105	132	163	196	229	268	308	397	498
21–6						73	96	123	151	182	214	251	288	374	470
22–0							88	113	139	169	199	235	270	350	442
22–6							79	104	129	157	186	219	252	329	416
23–0								95	119	146	175	204	237	310	392
23–6								87	110	135	161	191	221	290	369
24–0								80	101	125	149	178	207	272	347

tween consecutive column strips and designed to provide reinforcement for the middle strip. A second set of similar strips of joists runs at right angles to the first. If shears exceed the relatively low allowable values, flat, welded stirrups are added, usually just for the length of a single dome.

The panels listed in Table 15 are in multiples of 3 ft so that the joists space out exactly. Spans of 21, 30, and 33 ft have a joist on the column center; spans of 24, 27, 36, and 39 ft have a row of domes on the column center, arranged to provide the proper size of drop panel. Narrower domes are available to fill out column spacings that are not multiples of 3 ft. Since suppliers vary considerably in standards, the designer should obtain detailed information on the types of domes most readily available at any given locality.

Although values have been given only for square panels, it is possible to estimate values for a rectangular panel by using the long side for one set of joists and the short side for the other. The ACI Code limits the ratio of the long to short side to 1.33. Because of the considerable width of domes and the two-way nature of the slab, the designer should sketch the spacings for a typical panel and correlate them with the column spacings as a part of the early planning.

Table 15 is based on one set of stresses: $f_c' = 3,000$ psi and $f_s = 20,000$ psi. The allowable load represents the safe superimposed load including all live and dead loads except the weight of the structural

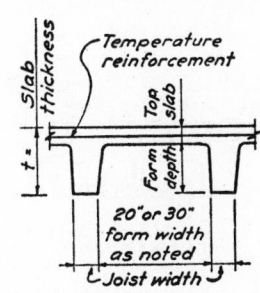

Fig. 3. Typical section, concrete joists

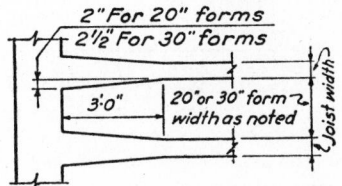

Fig. 4. Plan showing tapered ends

Table 13. Safe superimposed loads for one-way concrete joists

20-in.-wide forms—5-in. joists at 25 in. o.c.

Joist form depth + topping, in.	Span length, ft														
	12	13	14	15	16	17	18	19	20	21	22	23	24	25	26
	Load, psf														
6 + 2	304	277	246	214	189	167	150								
6 + 2½	322	293	260	226	199	176	157	142							
6 + 3		309	274	237	208	184	164	147	131						
8 + 2			322	281	248	221	199	179	163	149	137	126			
8 + 2½			337	293	259	230	207	187	169	154	141	130			
8 + 3				304	268	238	213	192	174	158	144	133			
10 + 2					308	275	247	225	204	187	172	159	147	137	127
10 + 2½					318	285	255	231	210	192	177	163	151	139	129
10 + 3					328	292	262	237	215	196	180	166	152	141	130
	22	23	24	25	26	27	28	29	30	31	32	33	34	35	36
12 + 2	206	189	175	162	152	141	131	124	116	109	103	98			
12 + 2½	209	193	178	165	154	143	134	125	117	109	103	98			
12 + 3	214	197	182	168	156	145	136	126	118	110	103	97			
14 + 2	240	223	207	192	179	167	156	147	137	129	122	115	108	102	97
14 + 2½	244	225	208	193	179	167	156	147	137	129	122	115	108	102	97
14 + 3	247	228	211	196	182	169	158	148	138	129	122	115	108	102	97

30-in.-wide forms—5-in. joists at 35 in. o.c.

Joist form depth + topping, in.	Span length, ft														
	12	13	14	15	16	17	18	19	20	21	22	23	24	25	26
	Load, psf														
6 + 2½	222	201	177	153	134	117	103	93							
6 + 3	232	210	185	158	138	121	106	94	83						
8 + 2½	286	260	231	200	175	155	138	124	111	100	91	83			
8 + 3	298	272	240	207	181	160	142	127	114	102	92	84			
10 + 2½				249	218	194	173	156	141	128	117	107	99	90	83
10 + 3				255	224	198	177	159	144	130	118	108	99	90	83
	22	23	24	25	26	27	28	29	30	31	32	33	34	35	36
12 + 2½	141	130	119	110	101	93	87	81	75	70	65	61			
12 + 3	142	130	119	110	101	93	87	80	73	68	62	58			
14 + 2½	166	152	140	129	119	111	103	95	90	84	78	73	68	64	59
14 + 3	166	153	141	130	119	111	103	95	88	82	77	71	66	61	57

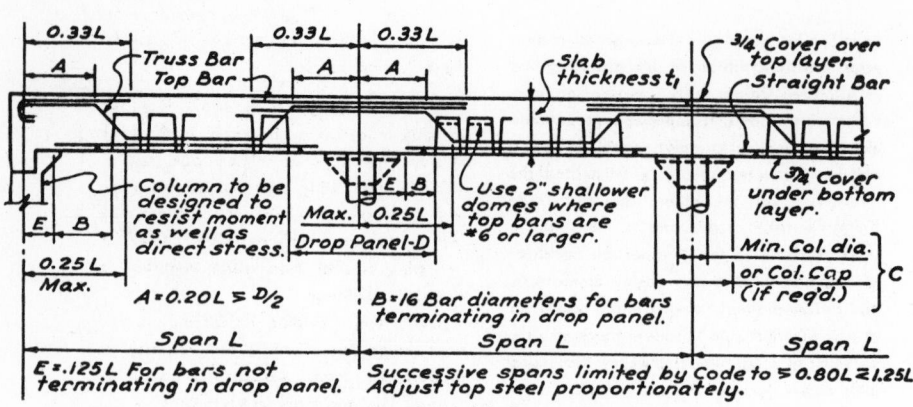

Fig. 5. Two-way dome slab floor construction

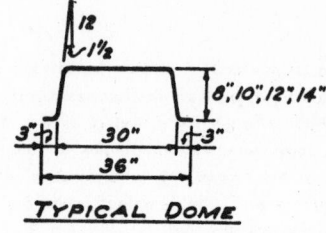

Fig. 6. Section through typical dom

Table 15. Two-way dome floor slabs—square panels

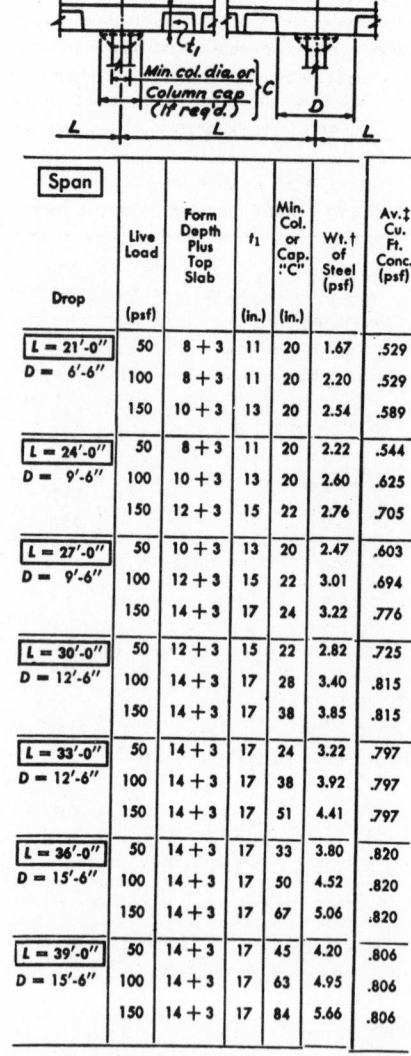

Span / Drop	Live Load (psf)	Form Depth Plus Top Slab	t_1 (in.)	Min. Col. or Cap. "C" (in.)	Wt.† of Steel (psf)	Av.‡ Cu. Ft. Conc. (psf)
L = 21'-0"	50	8 + 3	11	20	1.67	.529
D = 6'-6"	100	8 + 3	11	20	2.20	.529
	150	10 + 3	13	20	2.54	.589
L = 24'-0"	50	8 + 3	11	20	2.22	.544
D = 9'-6"	100	10 + 3	13	20	2.60	.625
	150	12 + 3	15	22	2.76	.705
L = 27'-0"	50	10 + 3	13	20	2.47	.603
D = 9'-6"	100	12 + 3	15	22	3.01	.694
	150	14 + 3	17	24	3.22	.776
L = 30'-0"	50	12 + 3	15	22	2.82	.725
D = 12'-6"	100	14 + 3	17	28	3.40	.815
	150	14 + 3	17	38	3.85	.815
L = 33'-0"	50	14 + 3	17	24	3.22	.797
D = 12'-6"	100	14 + 3	17	38	3.92	.797
	150	14 + 3	17	51	4.41	.797
L = 36'-0"	50	14 + 3	17	33	3.80	.820
D = 15'-6"	100	14 + 3	17	50	4.52	.820
	150	14 + 3	17	67	5.06	.820
L = 39'-0"	50	14 + 3	17	45	4.20	.806
D = 15'-6"	100	14 + 3	17	63	4.95	.806
	150	14 + 3	17	84	5.66	.806

concrete. The structure must have at least three consecutive panels in a row in each direction to satisfy the ACI Code values for moments. If the building is narrower, a special analysis must be made. The lengths of successive spans must not differ by more than 20 per cent of the longer span. Concrete quantities given per square foot of floor area include all structural concrete in slab and drop panel. The weight of main steel is the average weight in pounds per square foot of all longitudinal straight and truss bars. Tables 14 and 15 and Figs. 3–6 are from *CRSI Design Handbook*, 2d ed., Concrete Reinforcing Steel Institute (1957).

LIFT-SLAB CONSTRUCTION

Lift-slab construction is a method of erecting a building in accordance with the following sequence of operations:

1. Erect the columns for the building and secure their lowermost ends to the foundation.

2. Pour the first slab around these columns.

3. Apply a layer of bond-preventing material to the top of this slab.

4. Cast one, two, or more concrete slabs directly on top of the first slab, with each slab separated only by a layer of bond-preventing material.

5. Attach the lifting equipment to the columns and the slab to be lifted.

6. Lift the top slab to a predetermined elevation on the columns.

7. To prevent sidesway, maintain a sliding and guided relationship between the collars and the columns while the slab is being lifted.

8. Temporarily or permanently secure the lifted slab to the columns.

9. Connect the lifting equipment to the next lower slab or slabs to be lifted (if two or more are to be lifted together).

10. Repeat each step and extend the columns (if necessary) until all the slabs are brought to their final grades.

Lift slab is primarily a method of erection rather than design. Basically the design conforms to accepted engineering practices and codes used for formed-in-place construction. The major design difference is in the method of supporting the slabs on the columns. In lift slab, steel collars are placed around the columns for each slab connection before the concrete is placed. They become an integral part of the slab and are designed for attachment of the lifting equipment as well as to support the loads at each column. After the slabs are lifted into place, the collars are attached to the columns by welding, bolting, or pinning.

The use of lift slab will depend largely on the advantages that may occur in items affected by the operation during construction, such as forming, handling materials,

† Weight of steel per sq ft is the average weight in pounds per sq ft of all longitudinal straight, truss, and top bars in the slab not including stirrups or welded wire fabric.

‡ Average cu ft of concrete per sq ft of floor includes ribs, top slabs and drop panels but not column caps.

Adapted from CRSI Design Handbook, *2d ed., Concrete Reinforcing Steel Institute (1957).*

Table 14. Dome data

Depth (in.)	Volume (cf per dome)	Weight of displaced concrete (lb per dome)	With 3" top slab	
			Equiv. slab thickness (in.)	Weight (psf)
8	3.9	580	5.8	73
10	4.8	720	6.6	83
12	5.7	850	7.4	93
14	6.5	970	8.3	104

speed of erection, ceiling treatment, insurance rates, and weather protection. Installation of structural materials and a large percentage of electrical and mechanical work are accomplished at ground level, where labor operations and safety are the most efficient.

No slab should be lifted until the concrete has reached a compressive strength of at least 2,700 psi as determined by standard cylinder test, and is at least 14 days old.

Vertical construction joints, where necessary, should be located at or near the midpoints of spans of slabs, beams, and walls. All continuous reinforcing should be carried through the joints.

Variable slab elevations within small areas should be avoided, although recesses for corridors and other areas create no special problems. Such recesses can be built up with cement grout, waste forms, or other forming materials for casting the next slab above. Slabs are sometimes cast directly into shallow recesses if the resulting offset in the ceiling above falls within a wall or other unobjectionable location. If each level of a split elevation covers a reasonably large area, the slabs can be divided into sections for placing and lifting.

During the preparation of a layout, efforts should be made to locate large slab openings outside of column strips and as near the center of bays as possible, or at the edge of slabs. The most desirable loca-

tions for stairwells, elevators, or other features requiring large openings are at the ends of a building or outside the slab line.

Simplicity and uniformity of building layout are the basic criteria for obtaining the maximum potential economy from lift slab.

Structural systems

Lift slab is generally used in flat-plate construction with spans ranging from 14 to 26 ft. The method is readily adaptable to almost any flat-plate project. Coffered and voided slabs are lifted for heavy loads and long spans. Inverted beams are often used for long-span roof construction. Beams or drop panels can be formed in recesses below the ground or first-floor level for one-story roof construction or for the first elevated slab in multistory buildings. Uniform and simple column arrangements are desirable and will contribute to over-all economy.

Columns can be of any type of structural steel or concrete, and can be round, square, or nearly square, in shape. Minimum sizes are desirable because the cost of slab-to-column connections increases for large columns.

Cost criteria

Lift slab generally does not change the quantities of materials required in similar types of slab systems and columns used for formed-in-place construction. The cost of the lifting operation is controlled primarily

by labor and time, and may be affected by the following items:

1. *Spans:* Lifting cost generally decreases as span lengths increase because the area of slab lifted at each column increases.
2. *Height:* Lifting cost increases slightly with increases in heights of buildings. The cost can be reasonably controlled, however, by lifting two or more slabs together in multistory buildings.
3. *Welding:* Welding at column connections should be limited to that required to support the loads. Excessive welding increases time and labor unnecessarily.

Prestressing

Prestressing is frequently used in lift-slab construction and can contribute to over-all economy. Prestressing permits longer spans and reduces slab thickness, thus resulting in lower lifting costs and fewer materials. It is possible with a prestressed slab to reach virtually zero deflection for a given loading condition. This is achieved by properly placing the prestressing tendons in the slab to balance the deflections produced by the given loads.

Both normal-weight and lightweight concrete have been used in prestressed lift-slab construction. The concrete strength used is usually 4,000 psi at 28 days; the stressing takes place when the strength reaches 3,500 psi.

In general, there will be little cost ad-

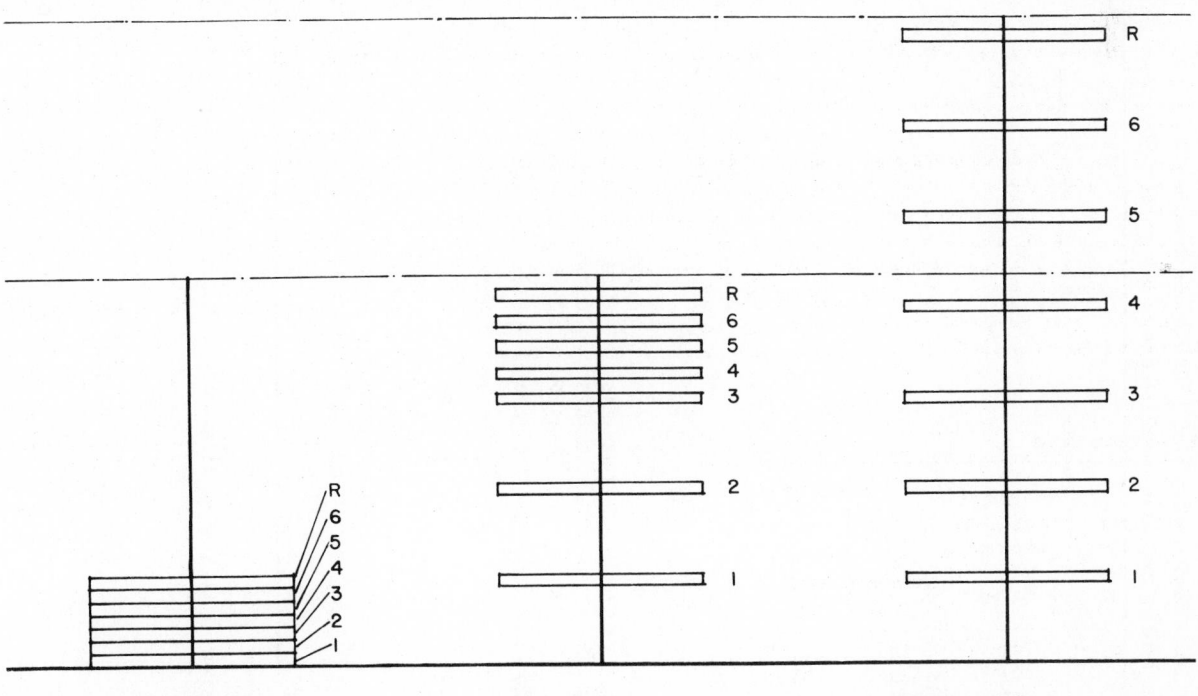

INITIAL POSITION   FIRST LIFT   FINAL LIFT
Fig. 7. Lifting procedure

Table 16. Cost analysis of lift-slab construction

Courtesy of Lift Slab Research and Development Corporation, San Antonio, Texas, January 1960.

Bay sizes, ft	Superimposed load, psf	Thickness,* in.	Volume, cu ft per sq ft of area	Mild reinforcing, psf		Cost per lifted sq ft								
						Mild reinforcing†		Concrete‡		Total cost		Steel collars	Lifting and welding	
				Reg. wt.	Lt. wt.	Reg. wt.	Lt. wt.	Reg. wt.	Lt. wt.	Reg. wt.	Lt. wt.		1–4 stories	5–8 stories
Solid slab														
15x15	50	5½	0.458	2.62	2.09	$0.29	$0.23	$0.25	$0.31	$0.54	$0.54	$0.156	$0.34	$0.42
20x20	30	7	0.583	4.08	3.15	0.41	0.32	0.32	0.40	0.73	0.72	0.07	0.32	0.40
	50	7	0.583	4.24	3.38	0.42	0.34	0.32	0.40	0.73	0.72	0.10	0.33	0.41
	75	8	0.667	5.10	4.15	0.51	0.42	0.37	0.46	0.88	0.88	0.10	0.34	0.42
	125	9	0.750	6.04	5.11	0.60	0.51	0.42	0.51	1.02	1.02	0.12	0.35	0.43
25x25	30	9	0.750	4.83	3.58	0.48	0.36	0.42	0.51	0.90	0.87	0.08	0.30	0.38
	50	9	0.750	6.00	4.80	0.60	0.48	0.42	0.51	1.02	0.99	0.11	0.31	0.39
	75	10	0.833	5.98	4.75	0.60	0.48	0.46	0.57	1.06	1.05	0.11	0.32	0.40
	125	11	0.917	7.05	5.85	0.71	0.59	0.51	0.63	1.22	1.22	0.16	0.33	0.41
Waffle slab														
25x25	30	2½ + 8 (5.75)	0.479	3.27	2.70	0.33	0.27	0.27	0.33	0.60	0.60	0.06	0.28	0.36
	50	3 + 12 (8.16)	0.680	3.57	2.85	0.36	0.28	0.38	0.47	0.74	0.75	0.09	0.29	0.37
	75	2½ + 10 (6.75)	0.562	4.09	3.45	0.41	0.35	0.31	0.58	0.72	0.73	0.09	0.30	0.38
	125	2½ + 12 (7.75)	0.645	4.84	4.17	0.48	0.42	0.36	0.44	0.84	0.86	0.12	0.32	0.40
25x30	50	3 + 12 (9.14)	0.762	4.00	3.20	0.44	0.35	0.42	0.52	0.86	0.87	0.10	0.28	0.36
25x35	50	3 + 12 (9.33)	0.778	4.50	3.60	0.50	0.40	0.43	0.53	0.93	0.93	0.10	0.27	0.35
30x30	30	2½ + 12 (8.25)	0.687	4.17	3.20	0.42	0.32	0.38	0.47	0.80	0.79	0.08	0.26	0.34
	50	3 + 12 (8.80)	0.733	4.80	3.84	0.48	0.38	0.41	0.50	0.89	0.88	0.09	0.27	0.35
	75	2½ + 12 (8.40)	0.700	5.55	4.50	0.56	0.45	0.39	0.48	0.95	0.93	0.11	0.28	0.36
	125	2½ + 12 (8.60)	0.716	7.09	6.03	0.71	0.60	0.40	0.49	1.11	1.09	0.10	0.29	0.37
30x40	50	3 + 14 (10.8)	0.910	6.05	4.85	0.61	0.49	0.51	0.62	1.12	1.11	0.08	0.25	0.32
40x40	50	3 + 14 (11.2)	0.930	8.00	6.40	0.80	0.64	0.52	0.64	1.32	1.28	0.10	0.31	0.37

* Figures in parentheses indicate equivalent slab.
† Mild reinforcing at $200.00 per ton.
‡ Regular-weight concrete at $15.00 per cu yd in place (no finish); lightweight concrete at $18.50 per cu yd in place (no finish).

vantage in prestressing slabs with spans less than 22 to 24 ft long for average loads and less than 18 to 20 ft long for heavy loads. Prestressing tendons will cost about 60 cents per sq ft in place for conditions similar to those outlined in the cost analysis (Table 16).

The prestressing usually employs some type of unbonded tendon with a buttonhead type of end anchorage. The size of the tendon should be small enough to permit curvature to the proper cable profile.

Limitations

1. Lift slab is limited to flat systems, except where beams or drop panels are feasible (as indicated above), or where horizontal offsets are used at the edges of successive slabs, thus permitting spandrel beams.

2. A cantilever system is desirable, but not essential. Slab edges should extend at least far enough beyond columns to permit one row of reinforcing bars to pass between the columns and the edge of the slab.

3. Close, irregular spacing of building or column lines and frequent large openings in slabs may require structural systems not appropriate for lifting.

4. Short spans averaging less than 12 ft usually are not economically feasible for lifting.

5. Lifting economy is usually limited to a minimum total slab area of 5,000 to 10,000 sq ft for a single project unless

lifting can be accomplished at a time when equipment is available in the immediate area.

Other uses

Lift-slab equipment is adaptable to steel structures. It is frequently used for lifting steel roofs of existing structures to new elevations when expansion is required. The equipment is also used for lifting powerplant generators, bridges, and the superstructure of offshore oil-drilling barges.

TILT-UP CONSTRUCTION

Tilt-up construction is a special form of precast construction in which the elements, usually walls, are cast in a horizontal position on the site, tilted to the vertical position, set in place, and made an integral part of the completed structure. The principal advantages of this method are economy and reduced construction time.

The most common wall thickness is 6 in., nominal or actual, because this dimension generally meets structural requirements and permits average-size panels to be erected without extreme care. The use of the nominal dimension results in an appreciable saving because 2 by 6-in. dressed lumber can be used for the edge forms.

There are a great many different ways of designing, detailing, and erecting such structures. It will be advantageous for the designer to consult with contractors before the design and construction details are

definitely established. The designer should at least consider the personnel and equipment available in the area. Even small changes in design or construction procedure may save much time and money as well as provide a better structure.

Most buildings constructed by the tilt-up method are one story in height, although some are as high as eight stories. The multistory buildings have generally been constructed by tilting the walls for one story, placing the floor above, and then repeating the process. In some instances, walls two stories in height have been cast and tilted as a unit. Various schemes using tilted platforms have been tried, but by far the most common method is to cast the wall panels on the concrete floor (using the floor as the bottom form) and then tilt them into position. In the past, improved hand equipment was used for tilting, but now most of the work is done with various types and capacities of power equipment, some of which can handle loads of up to 50 tons.

Design

Wall panels must be designed to withstand stresses both in the completed structure and during erection. The general design of the building will determine whether the walls are loadbearing or nonloadbearing with a continuous footing or supported on the column footings only. Once the walls are in position, the design requirements differ little if any from those

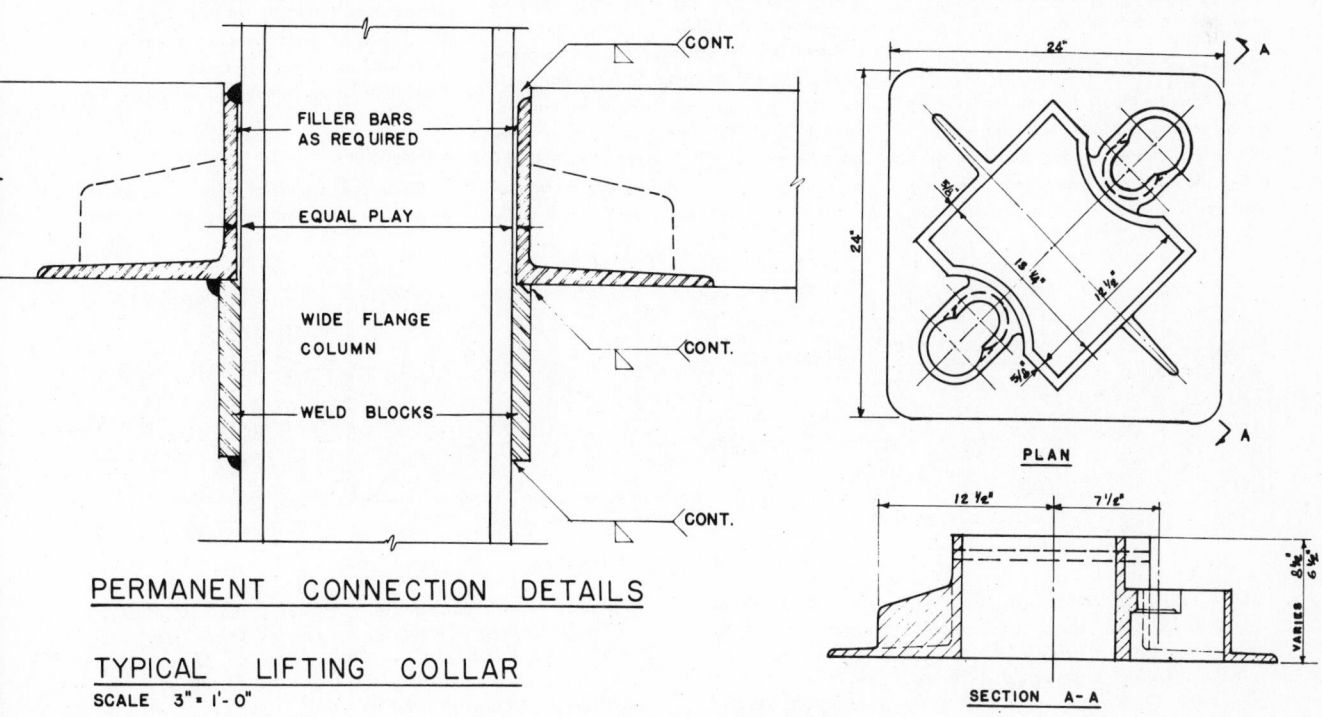

PERMANENT CONNECTION DETAILS

TYPICAL LIFTING COLLAR

SCALE 3" = 1'-0"

PLAN

SECTION A-A

Fig. 8. Connection details of lifting collars·

of conventionally built reinforced concrete walls; the only difference is in details.

Tilting a wall panel creates stresses not encountered in conventional, cast-in-place construction, and with some tilt-up arrangements an exact analysis may be complicated. The method of attaching the lifting equipment must be known in order to determine the stresses. If the attachment is to a stiff channel, or angle bolted to the top edge of the panel, then that panel will be designed as a simply supported slab. Openings present a special design problem. A general rule of thumb that is satisfactory for ordinary conditions, however, is to consider the weight of the panel as distributed over the total area including openings. The steel that would normally extend through the openings is concentrated at the sides of the openings, both horizontally and vertically. Strongbacks are advantageous where openings in the panel appreciably reduce its strength at critical sections.

Wall reinforcement is similar to that of conventional reinforced concrete walls except that special provision must be made for the stresses caused by lifting. The reinforcement may consist of bars or welded wire fabric or a combination of the two. Since lifting stresses occur only during tilting, higher unit stresses may be allowed for lifting than for other design purposes. As with reinforced concrete construction, a large number of small bars gives better crack control than the same weight of larger bars. The small bars cost slightly more per pound, however, and require a little more time to place.

Construction details

The concrete floor slab generally serves as the casting platform, although occasionally a stationary wooden platform or a tilting platform has been used. The ideal platform is a level, smoothly troweled con-

crete slab. Pipes or other utilities to be extended upward through the floor slab may be stopped below the floor surface and their openings temporarily closed. It should be remembered that any imperfections in the surface of the casting platform will show on the wall panel.

Many different wall finishes may be obtained economically when the wall is cast in the horizontal position. Some of these are the following: smooth float, swirled float, hand-troweled, brushed or broomed, patterned, colored, and ground. Regardless of the method employed, all panels and all parts of each panel should have a uniform finish.

Many variations of float finishes may be obtained in exactly the same manner as on floors and sidewalks. A fairly smooth float finish collects less dirt than a rough finish. Troweling provides a smooth surface but increases the possibility of surface crazing and magnifies inequalities in finishing. In harsh climates, the most severely exposed portions of the surface may gradually lose their smoothness and thus the entire surface will not retain a uniform appearance.

A pleasing finish may be produced by drawing a brush or broom over the trowel finish. This method tends to minimize any irregularities in the surface and removes laitance, which may cause surface crazing. Applying the brush marks in the vertical rather than the horizontal direction of the panel reduces the collection of dirt and increases the washing effect of rain on walls. Therefore, any horizontal brushing should be very light.

Color may be obtained by adding a colored concrete topping before the base concrete hardens. Panels may be painted, but it must be remembered that once painted they must be repainted periodically to retain a good appearance. A ground finish may be applied to wall panels while

they are in the horizontal position. The same methods are used as in finishing terrazzo floors. Patterns may be made by cutting the surface with a center bead.

Wall joints

Various materials and methods have been used in forming the horizontal joint between the wall panel and its supporting member. The most common material is portland cement mortar, but premolded joint filler has also been used, either alone or in combination with mortar.

The simplest method of using mortar is to spread a layer of it on the foundation and tilt the wall onto the mortar bed. This method produces a strong, watertight joint. The main objection to the use of mortar is that it may squeeze out unevenly and permit little opportunity for adjusting the level of the wall. With some details of columns and roofs, however, a small variation is not important. A refinement of this method is to place carefully leveled pads or blocks on the foundation in order to hold the panel at the proper level until the mortar sets.

Normally rain will not penetrate very far into a vertical joint or crack even though it may be relatively wide. If, under severe conditions, rain does penetrate into the crack and runs down, no damage will be done if it drains outside the building at the bottom of the joint. Trouble may develop, however, if water accumulating at the bottom of the vertical joint drains into the building. To reduce this possibility, the top of the floor should be an inch or so above the horizontal joint. Experience has shown that with such an offset, panels can be tilted into place without difficulty (see Fig. 9).

Column joints

There are probably more variations in column details than in any other feature

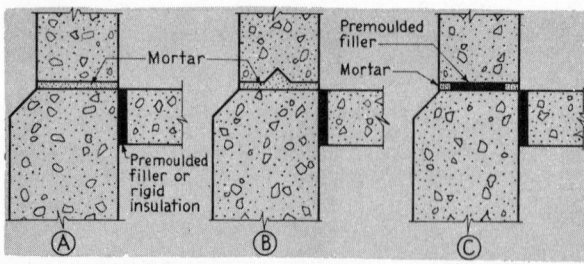
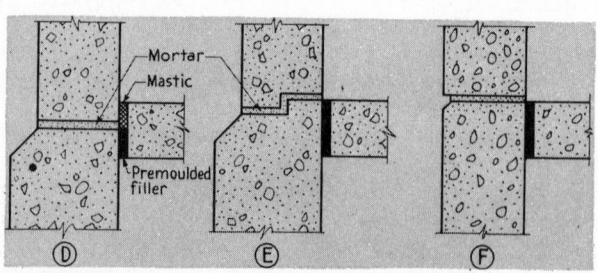

Fig. 9. Wall joints at foundation

From Tilt-up Construction, *Portland Cement Association. Shown above are typical joints subject to many variations. Sketches A and C show the simplest and most commonly used wall joints. The offset from the floor level in sketch D and the offset in the wall in sketch E reduce the possibility of leakage.*

However, if the foundation or lower wall is sloped or offset slightly (as shown in the sketches) so that there is no horizontal surface to catch the water, there is little possibility of leakage. Certainly the possibility of leakage at this point is no greater than with any unit masonry wall.

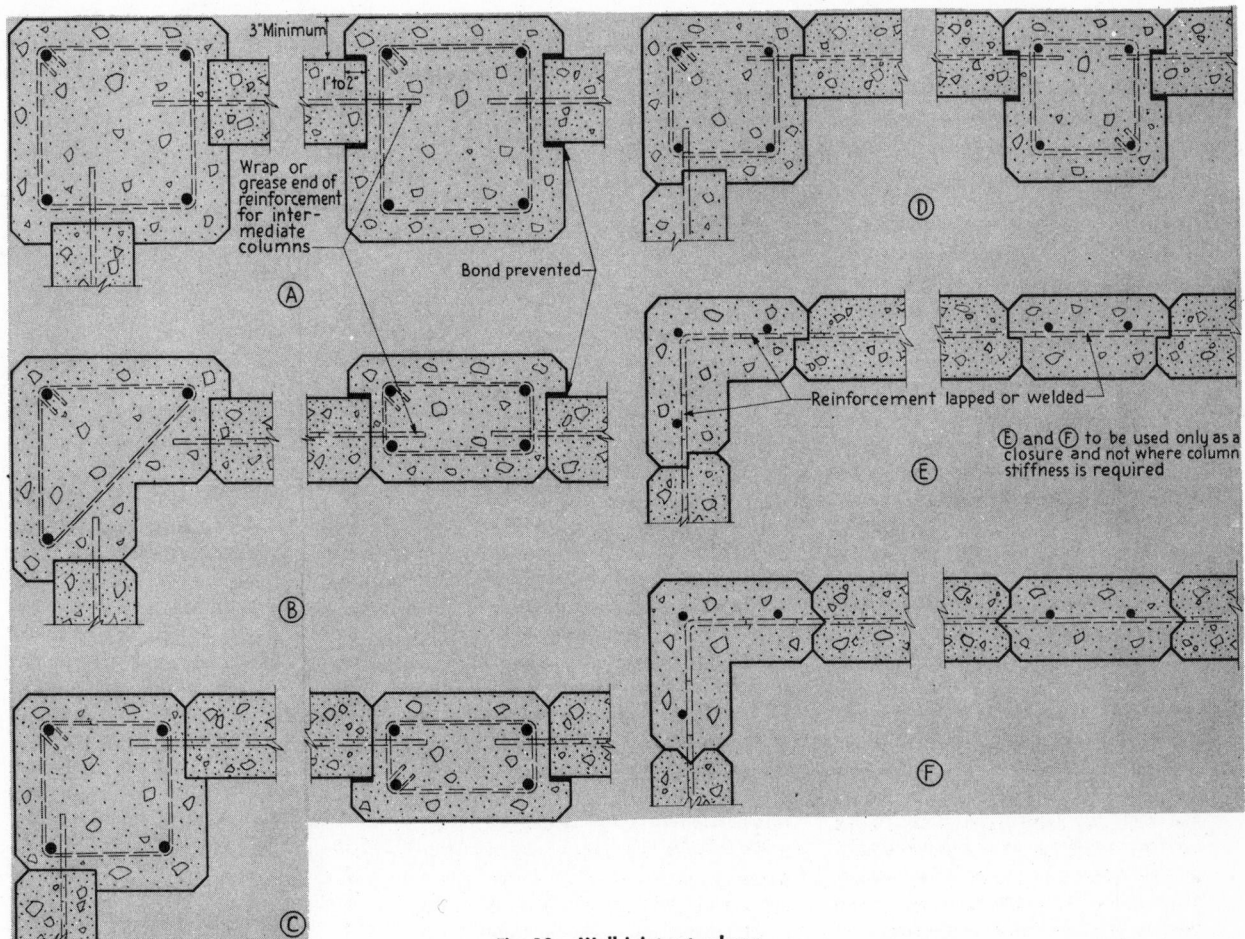

3"Minimum

1" to 2"

Wrap or grease end of reinforcement for intermediate columns

Bond prevented

Reinforcement lapped or welded

Ⓔ and Ⓕ to be used only as a closure and not where column stiffness is required

Ⓐ Ⓑ Ⓒ Ⓓ Ⓔ Ⓕ

Fig. 10. Wall joints at column

From Tilt-up Construction, *Portland Cement Association. Sketches A to D show typical joints for use where movement at the joints is desired. They can also be used for rigid joints by lapping the reinforcement and omitting the bond-prevention material.*

Even where movement is desired at intermediate columns, the corner columns are bonded to the wall panels. V-joints should be used wherever the face of the wall is flush with the column.

of tilt-up construction. Columns may be placed either after or before the panels are tilted. Both methods have advantages. On most jobs, however, the columns are cast after the panels are in place. This method permits the use of simple and economical details, particularly where the column overlaps the wall panel on both faces. Casting the column first has the advantage of greatly simplifying the temporary bracing of panels.

For large buildings in parts of the country where it is not necessary to design for earthquake forces, nearly all column connections are designed to allow relative movement between adjacent wall panels. Thus the panels can expand and contract, owing to moisture and temperature changes, without developing stresses that would tend to crack the walls. A survey of buildings constructed by the tilt-up method has shown that there is movement in the majority of

joints between panels and columns and that cracks in the panels are extremely rare.

If the columns are cast after the walls are in place, they may overlap the panels on one or both sides. This overlap hides any irregularities in the panel edges and variations in the planes of adjacent panels. Even though the space between the panels may vary because of inaccuracies in panel dimensions or setting, the overlap permits uniform column widths and repeated use of the column form without adjustments. The possibility of leakage is also reduced by overlap.

It is sometimes desirable to have the column flush with the panels on one or both sides of the wall. In such cases, a V-joint or other definite rustication should be used between the wall panel and the column. This rustication will (1) hide and protect the crack that will form at this point, (2) permit caulking if necessary, (3) provide a

straight, true joint, (4) prevent smearing of panels with leakage from concrete cast in the column, and (5) break the wall surface so that variations in the planes of adjacent panels will be inconspicuous (see Fig. 10).

Insulation

As in other types of construction, the heat-insulation value of tilt-up walls may be increased by the use of furring, blanket insulation, or rigid insulation and plaster in the usual manner after the wall has been erected. The heat-insulation value may also be increased by using lightweight concrete and, of course, by increasing the thickness. Other methods are to cast the panel on rigid insulating board that bonds to the panel, to use lightweight-aggregate concrete for the interior face of the panel, or to construct the wall as a sandwich panel.

Part of the wall thickness (on the inside

face) may be made of concrete having a high insulating value, such as that made with aggregates of very light weight. The thickness of the insulating concrete will depend on the insulation desired. From 1 to 6 in. has been used in panels with a total thickness of 6 to 8 in., although about 2 in. of insulating concrete will usually provide sufficient insulation.

Sandwich-type panels are made by placing a layer of concrete, a layer of insulation, and then a layer of concrete, the last two layers being placed before the first one has hardened. Reinforcement is placed in both layers of concrete and the two layers are fastened together by ties. The insulating material should bond to, but not be adversely affected by, the fresh concrete.

PRESTRESSED CONCRETE CONSTRUCTION

The main purpose of prestressing is to induce desirable strains and stresses in a structure and its components. Since the tensile strength of concrete is negligible compared to its compressive strength, prestressing is necessary to counteract any significant tensile stress. Prestressing is normally accomplished by stretching high-tensile steel and then transferring the stress to the concrete by either bond or end anchorages. In a fully prestressed concrete member the entire section is in compression and therefore, is fully utilized. In contrast, a reinforced concrete member subjected to flexure utilizes less than half its concrete. This constitutes the basic difference between the two materials or systems of construction. They also differ in the use of steel. In a reinforced concrete member the steel acts with the concrete and is consequently limited by the cracking of the concrete. In a prestressed concrete member, however, the

steel acts upon but independently of the concrete. A prestressed concrete member can thus be considered as a plain concrete member subjected to two types of forces: an internal prestressing force and external loads.

Design principles

If the magnitude and location of the prestressing are controlled, compressive stresses are introduced which will counteract the anticipated tensile stresses due to external loads. The effects of these two forces are considered separately in Figs. 11a and 12a and superimposed in Fig. 13a to show the final condition. Figure 11a indicates a simple rectangular beam subjected to a prestressing force, F, applied with an eccentricity, e. This condition represents the first working stage. Because of the eccentric application of the prestressing force, the beam is subjected to a moment, Fe, as well as to a direct load. The stress pattern produced by the prestressing force is shown in Fig. 11b and is equal to the algebraic sum of the uniform axial stresses, F/A, and the flexural stresses due to the eccentricity, Fey/I, as shown in Fig. 11c and d. At the end of the first working stage, the prestressing steel and the concrete develop maximum stresses. The controlling factors in the concrete (Fig. 11b) are the maximum allowable compressive stress in the bottom fiber and little or no tensile stress in the extreme top fiber. At this stage the beam has an upward deflection or camber. In the absence of the expected superimposed loads, the camber may remain and its effects should be considered.

Shown in Fig. 12a is the beam subjected to external loads, with the corresponding stress pattern indicated in Fig. 12b. The anticipated tensile stresses that are counteracted by the prestress are shown dotted.

Both the prestressing force and the external loads are shown in Fig. 13a in what is the second or working-load stage. The stress pattern at this final stage is shown in Fig. 13b and is equal to the algebraic sum of the stresses produced by the two forces. The controlling factors in the concrete are now the maximum allowable compressive stress in the top fiber and little or no tension in the bottom fiber. This is the opposite of the critical condition of the first stage. Since tension is a controlling factor in both stages, some design procedures permit limited tension in the concrete provided that the total tensile force is small and that cracking of the concrete is prevented. Nonprestressed reinforcement is often added in such cases.

The principles outlined in the above example have a wide range of applications and modifications. Slabs, shells, composite construction, and continuous beams can all benefit from prestressing. Curved or bent prestressing steel is more effective than straight steel and is usually used unless practical considerations dictate against it. Flanged shapes such as the symmetrical and unsymmetrical I- and T-sections are the most efficient and commonly used sections for prestressed concrete. Finally, it should be emphasized that the success with which prestressing counteracts stresses resulting from external loads makes it an extremely versatile structural technique.

Materials and stresses

Although many materials can be used to supply prestress, high-tensile steel is used almost universally in prestressed concrete. Prestressing steel (also called "tendons") comes in the form of wires, strands, or bars. The type of prestressing steel selected will depend on the method of prestressing, the type of anchorage, and the magnitude of

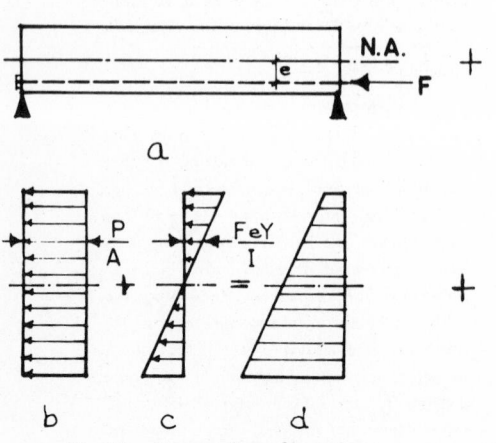

Fig. 11. Stress pattern due to prestressing

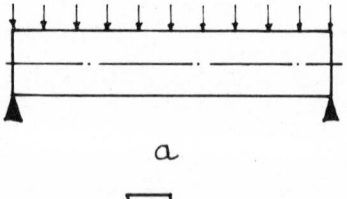
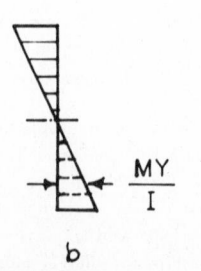

Fig. 12. Stress pattern due to superimposed loads

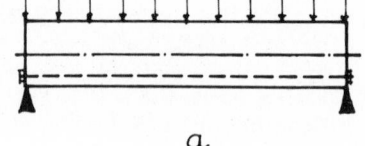
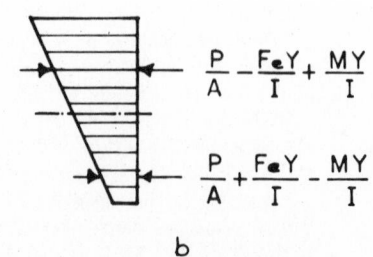

Fig. 13. Stress pattern at working loads

the force to be applied. Specific characteristics of the steel vary with the many manufacturing processes. The normal range of ultimate strength is 200,000 to 330,000 psi for wires, 200,000 to 270,000 psi for strands, and 140,000 to 170,000 psi for bars. Allowable stresses in the steel at the first working stage are about 85 per cent of the yield strength, or from 60 to 80 per cent of the ultimate strength.

To fully exploit prestressing, high-strength concrete is required. If early hardening of the concrete is desirable, as in a precasting factory, high-early-strength cement is used. Special curing procedures, such as steam curing, are extremely important in attaining high strength at an accelerated rate. The quality of concrete usually ranges from 5,000 to 8,000-psi ultimate strength at 28 days. The allowable flexural compressive stress at the working-load stage is usually 45 per cent of the ultimate strength. At the first stage, where there is less likelihood of overloading, the usual allowable stress is from 40 to 60 per cent of the ultimate 28-day strength.

Prestressing methods

The two basic methods of prestressing concrete are pretensioning and posttensioning. As their names imply, the difference between them depends on whether the concrete has hardened before or after the steel is stretched. In the pretensioning method, steel is stretched in the lower part of an empty form and anchored to bulkheads. Concrete is then poured into the forms and becomes firmly bonded to the elongated steel. After the concrete has attained the required strength, the steel is cut free from the anchorages. As the steel attempts to shorten and return to its original length, it compresses the beam by transferring the prestressing force by bond to the concrete.

In the posttensioning method, the steel is stretched after the concrete has attained its design strength. To achieve this result, bond between the steel and the concrete must be prevented, either by greasing the steel or by threading the steel through conduits that have been formed in the concrete. After the tendons are in place, they are stretched against the ends of the member. Final transfer of prestress from steel to concrete can be achieved either by mechanical devices at the end anchorages or by placing grout in the conduits and developing bond.

The pretensioning method is particularly suitable for mass production of members. Casting beds hundreds of feet long permit one pouring operation and the cutting of individual members to the desired length.

In addition, this method eliminates expensive anchorage accessories and conduits. If the location of a prestressing plant or the size of elements makes transportation costs excessive, the posttensioning method is recommended. Posttensioning is also recommended for cast-in-place concrete and continuous construction requiring curved or bent tendons.

Comparison with reinforced concrete

1. In prestressed concrete, the concrete is two to three times as strong, and the steel three to four times as strong, as that used in reinforced concrete.

2. By precompressing the concrete, the entire section is effective, whereas in reinforced concrete only the portion above the neutral axis is effective.

3. Diagonal tension, which governs the shear capacity, is reduced in prestressed concrete because the entire section is in compression.

4. The higher quality and more efficient performance of materials in prestressed concrete produce smaller sections and permit longer spans and the support of heavier loads. A prestressed concrete member usually has about 0.70 to 0.80 the depth of a reinforced concrete member.

5. In prestressed concrete, stresses developed in the first, or prestressing, stage are often at their design maximum, in which case the member is actually pretested for working loads.

6. Both types of construction have economic advantages. The use of fewer materials, even at a higher unit cost, recommends prestressed concrete; however, additional accessories and more expensive labor are required. Formwork is much more complicated and expensive in prestressed concrete than in reinforced concrete. Indeed, the extent to which formwork can be reused will frequently determine the economic feasibility of prestressed concrete.

Continuity

The theoretical reasons why continuity is economical in reinforced concrete also apply to prestressed concrete. In addition, continuity in prestressed concrete has two specific advantages: first, expensive end anchorages over intermediate supports are eliminated; and second, the same prestressing tendon can be used for both positive and negative moments by bending the tendon in accordance with the tensile requirements. Peaks of maximum negative moment, which are characteristic of continuity, are usually designed by varying the concrete section and the amount of prestressing steel (see Fig. 14).

Continuous prestressed beams can be

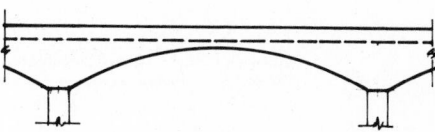

a. STRAIGHT TENDONS IN CURVED BEAMS

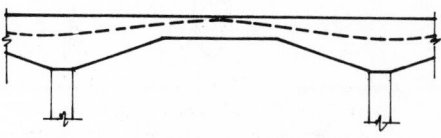

b. CURVED TENDONS IN HAUNCHED OR CURVED BEAMS
Fig. 14.   Fully continuous beams

either fully continuous or partially continuous. For full continuity all the tendons are prestressed in place and are generally continuous from one end to the other. Tendons may be encased in concrete during pouring, threaded through preformed holes, or placed outside the web. Either bonded or unbonded tendons may be used. For partial continuity each span is first precast as a simple beam and prestressed for erection tresses. After the simple elements have been erected in place, additional elements, sometimes nonprestressed, are inserted to provide continuity over the supports (see Fig. 15).

Continuity in prestressed concrete, however, has certain inherent disadvantages. Secondary stresses due to prestressing, creep and shrinkage, temperature change, and settlements of supports must be controlled. The frictional loss in continuous tendons, particularly where there are many reversed curves, must be evaluated. The

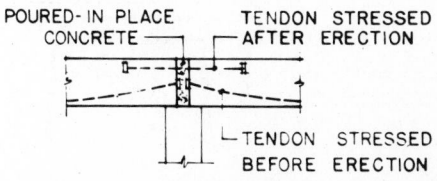

a. SHORT TENDONS STRESSED OVER SUPPORTS

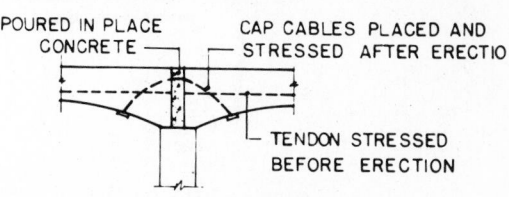

b. CAP CABLES OVER SUPPORTS
Fig. 15.   Partially continuous beams

Data on this and the following page from Precast Concrete Institute

14" DOUBLE TEE

Span in feet	48	51	54
lbs/sq. ft.	47	37	27

14" DOUBLE TEE with 2" COMPOSITE POUR

Span in feet	26	36	46
lbs/sq. ft.	200	103	41

18" DOUBLE TEE

Span in feet	22	55	64
lbs/sq. ft.	63	60	29

18" DOUBLE TEE with 2" COMPOSITE POUR

Span in feet	34	44	56
lbs/sq. ft.	200	112	39

14" CHANNEL

Span in feet	28	56	63
lbs/sq. ft.	47	47	27

14" CHANNEL with 2" COMPOSITE POUR

Span in feet	33	43	53
lbs/sq. ft.	200	100	45

18" CHANNEL

Span in feet	59	63	67
lbs/sq. ft.	60	43	26

18" CHANNEL with 2" COMPOSITE POUR

Span in feet	23	44	65
lbs/sq. ft.	210	154	25

Prestressed concrete roof and floor sections

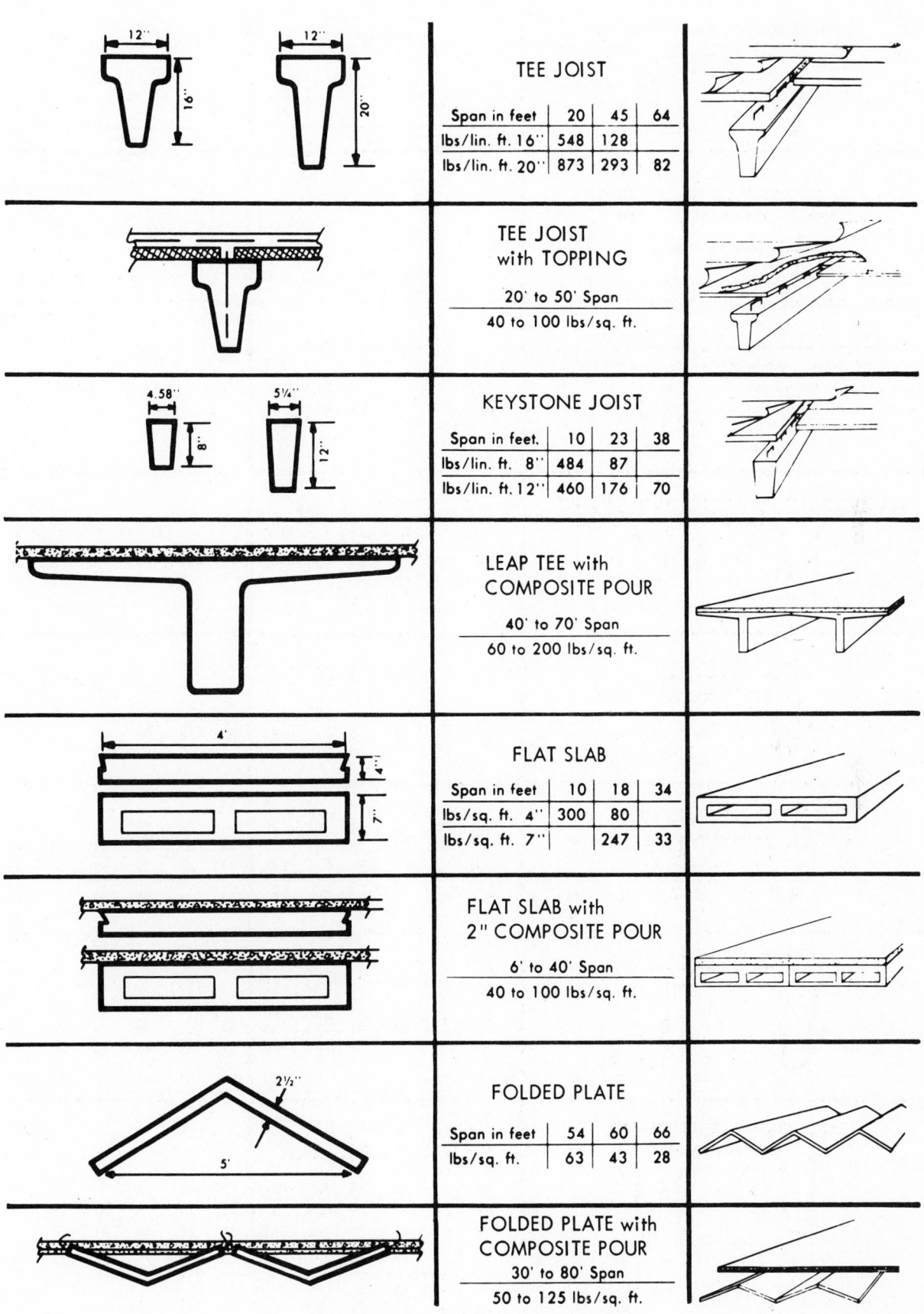

TEE JOIST

Span in feet	20	45	64
lbs/lin. ft. 16"	548	128	
lbs/lin. ft. 20"	873	293	82

TEE JOIST with TOPPING

20' to 50' Span

40 to 100 lbs/sq. ft.

KEYSTONE JOIST

Span in feet.	10	23	38
lbs/lin. ft. 8"	484	87	
lbs/lin. ft. 12"	460	176	70

LEAP TEE with COMPOSITE POUR

40' to 70' Span

60 to 200 lbs/sq. ft.

FLAT SLAB

Span in feet	10	18	34
lbs/sq. ft. 4"	300	80	
lbs/sq. ft. 7"		247	33

FLAT SLAB with 2" COMPOSITE POUR

6' to 40' Span

40 to 100 lbs/sq. ft.

FOLDED PLATE

Span in feet	54	60	66
lbs/sq. ft.	63	43	28

FOLDED PLATE with COMPOSITE POUR

30' to 80' Span

50 to 125 lbs/sq. ft.

Prestressed concrete roof and floor sections (cont.)

Data on this and the following page from Leap Associates, Lakeland, Florida

Table 17. Physical properties of T-sections

Section, depth by width	Area, sq in.	I (moment of inertia), in.⁴	Weight, lb per lin ft	Weight, psf
24 in. x 6 ft	384	20,870	400	66
30 in. x 6 ft	436	39,112	455	76
36 in. x 6 ft	489	65,085	509	85
36 in. x 8 ft	533	70,126	555	69
30 in. x 6 ft (with 2-in. topping)	580	51,394	605	101

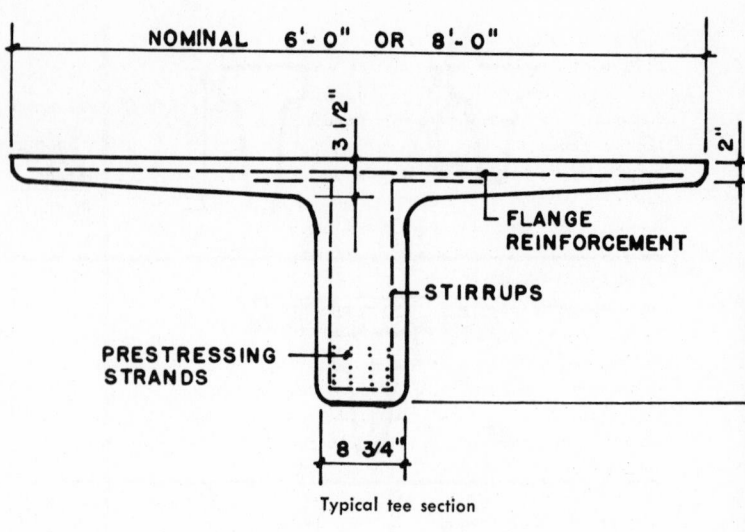

Typical tee section

(Labels: NOMINAL 6'-0" OR 8'-0"; 3 1/2"; 2"; FLANGE REINFORCEMENT; STIRRUPS; PRESTRESSING STRANDS; 8 3/4")

possibility of a reversal of moments due to heavy live loads may prevent the economical design of a continuous prestressed concrete beam. The shortening of long continuous beams under prestress may produce excessive lateral forces and moments in the columns if they are rigidly connected to the beams.

Table 18. Safe superimposed loads for Tee sections

Topping is required for floor loads.

Load, psf (Span length, ft)

24 in. x 6 ft

No. of 7/16-in. strands	44	46	48	50	52	54	56	58	60	62	64	66	68	70	72	74	76	78	80	82
8	81	68	52	48	40	33	26													
12				91	79	69	60	53	45	37	30	26								
16							88	78	69	59	52	46	40	34	29					
20										86	75	67	60	53	46	40	34	29	26	
24												88	79	70	62	55	49	43	37	32

30 in. x 6 ft

No. of 7/16-in. strands	60	62	64	66	68	70	72	74	76	78	80	82	84	86	88	90	92	94	96	98
12	70	62	54	45	38	32	26													
16			84	75	66	58	51	44	37	31	26									
20					82	73	65	57	50	44	38	32	27							
24							86	78	70	63	56	49	44	38	33	27				
28									87	78	71	63	57	51	46	41	36	31	27	
32												80	73	66	59	53	48	42	38	

36 in. x 6 ft

No. of 7/16-in. strands	76	78	80	82	84	86	88	90	92	94	96	98	100	102	104	106	108	110	112	114
16	56	48	42	36	31	26														
20	84	72	68	60	53	47	41	35	30	26										
24			80	72	64	57	51	45	40	35	30	26								
28					81	75	67	61	55	49	44	39	34	29						
32							84	77	70	64	57	52	47	41	36	32	28			
36									86	78	71	65	59	54	48	44	39	34	30	
40											85	78	71	65	59	54	49	44	40	

36 in. x 8 ft

No. of 7/16-in. strands	76	78	80	82	84	86	88	90	92	94	96	98	100	102	104	106	108	110	112	114
16	42	37	32	27																
20	62	56	50	44	39	34	29	26												
24	80	73	66	59	53	48	43	38	34	30	26									
28			84	76	70	63	57	52	46	41	37	32	28							
32					85	77	71	65	59	53	48	43	39	34	30	27				
36							84	77	71	64	59	54	50	45	41	36	33	29	26	
40									83	77	71	65	60	54	49	45	41	37	33	29

30 in. x 6 ft (with 2-in. topping)

No. of 7/16-in. strands	40	42	44	46	48	50	52	54	56	58	60	62	64	66	68	70	72	74	76	78
12	200	196	174	155	138	123	107	91	76	63	51	40								
16					200	187	164	143	125	109	94	80	68	57	47	38				
20							188	171	155	141	132	116	101	88	76	65	56	46	38	
24													103	94	85	78	71	64	58	52

Although prestressing has a wide variety of applications, it is most efficient when used in the manufacture of prefabricated elements. The development of standard sections similar to those used in the steel industry is most important for the manufacturing process. The tables on the following pages provide a reasonable basis for standardization, and should prove useful in preliminary study and design. Sections and data refer to elements produced by Leap Associates (Lakeland, Florida), but similar standard sections produced by other manufacturers are commercially available throughout the country. Ultimately, the selection of a prestressed concrete element will depend on the structural and mechanical requirements, the number of units, and the specific conditions of the geographical area.

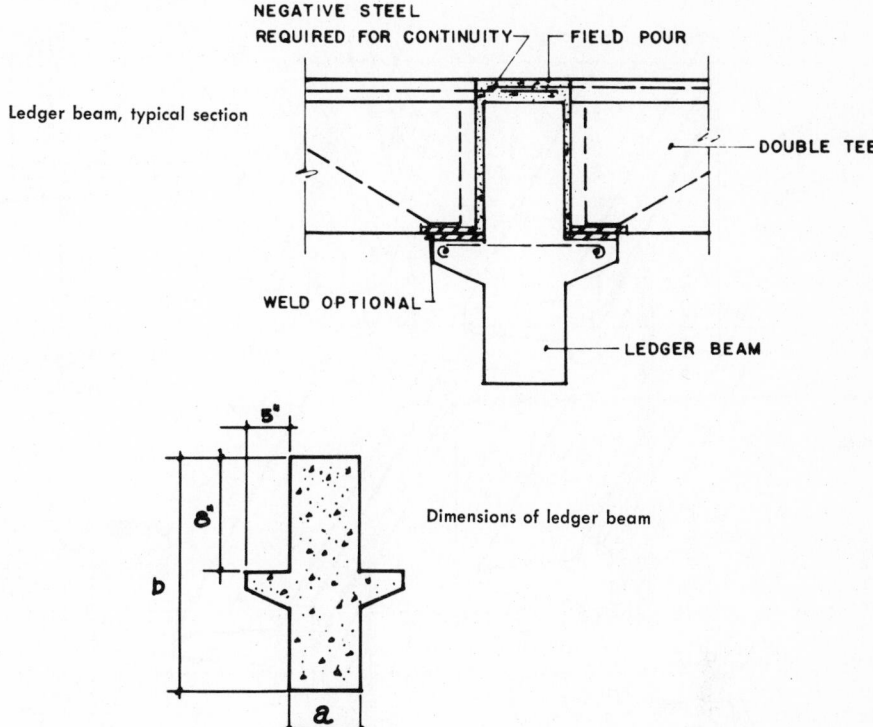

Ledger beam, typical section

Dimensions of ledger beam

Table 19. Safe superimposed loads for beams

Size of beam		Span length, ft				
Width, ft	Depth, in.	20	30	40	50	60
		Load, lb per lin ft				
5¾	20	1,387	529			
	24	2,009	792	367		
	28	2,797	1,130	546		
	32	3,745	1,538	765	408	
	36	4,836	2,009	1,020	562	314
7½	20	1,817	700	310		
	24	2,632	1,045	490		
	28	3,660	1,485	724	371	
	32	4,882	2,011	1,006	541	
	36	6,290	2,619	1,334	739	417
9¼	20	2,247	871	390		
	24	3,259	1,300	614		
	28	4,523	1,840	901	466	
	32	6,019	2,483	1,246	673	363
	36	7,740	3,227	1,647	916	520
11	20	2,676	1,042	470		
	24	3,938	1,577	751	368	
	28	5,386	2,195	1,079	562	
	32	7,158	2,957	1,487	807	438
	36	9,186	3,833	1,960	1,093	622
12¾	20	3,108	1,214	551		
	24	4,560	1,829	874	431	
	28	6,248	2,550	1,256	657	332
	32	8,295	3,430	1,728	939	512
	36	10,637	4,442	2,273	1,270	724
14½	20	3,538	1,384	631		
	24	5,142	2,064	986	488	
	28	7,115	2,907	1,434	753	383
	32	9,435	3,904	1,969	1,073	587
	36	12,131	5,070	2,597	1,454	832

STRUCTURAL DESIGN—CONCRETE—22
Prestressed

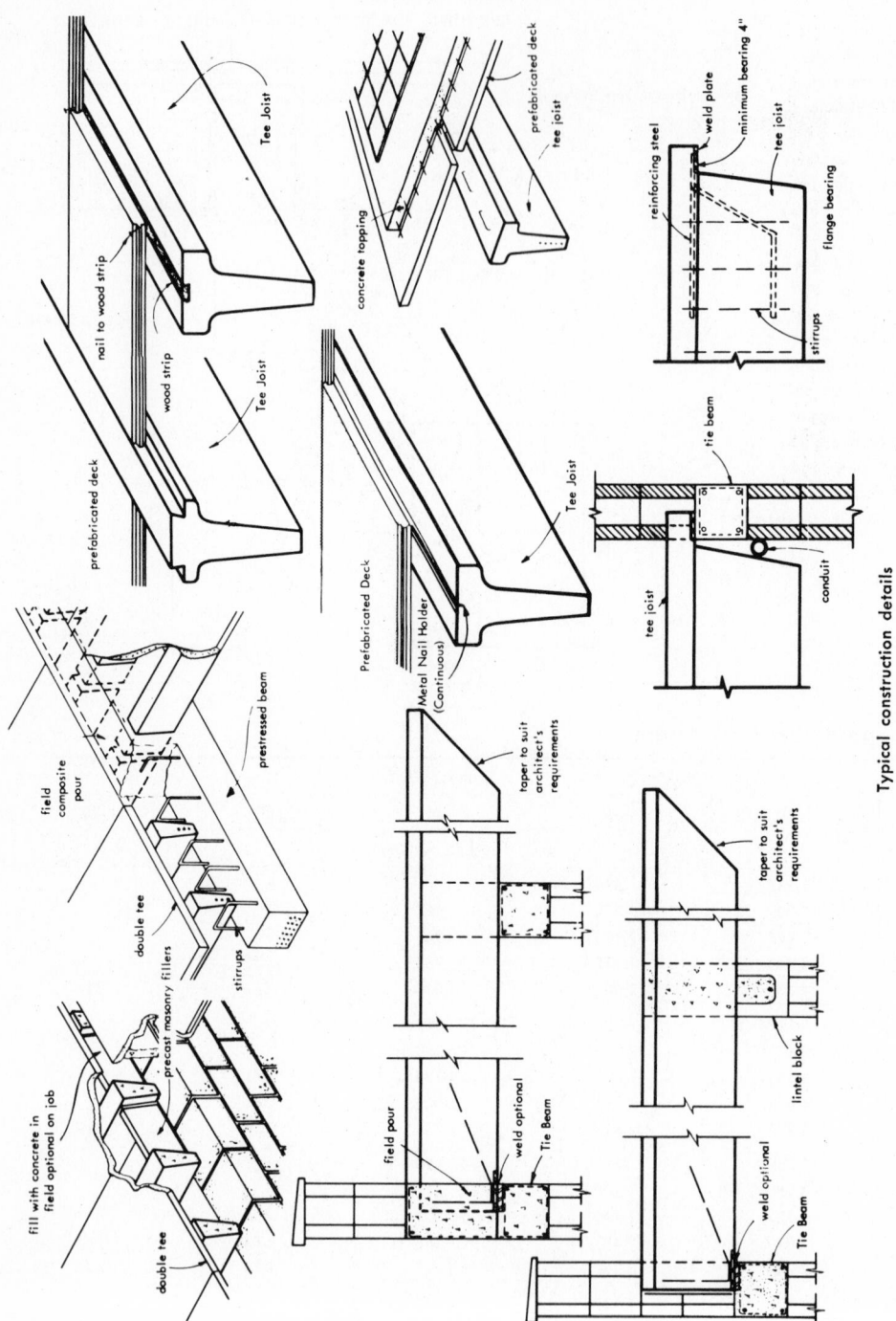

Typical construction details

206

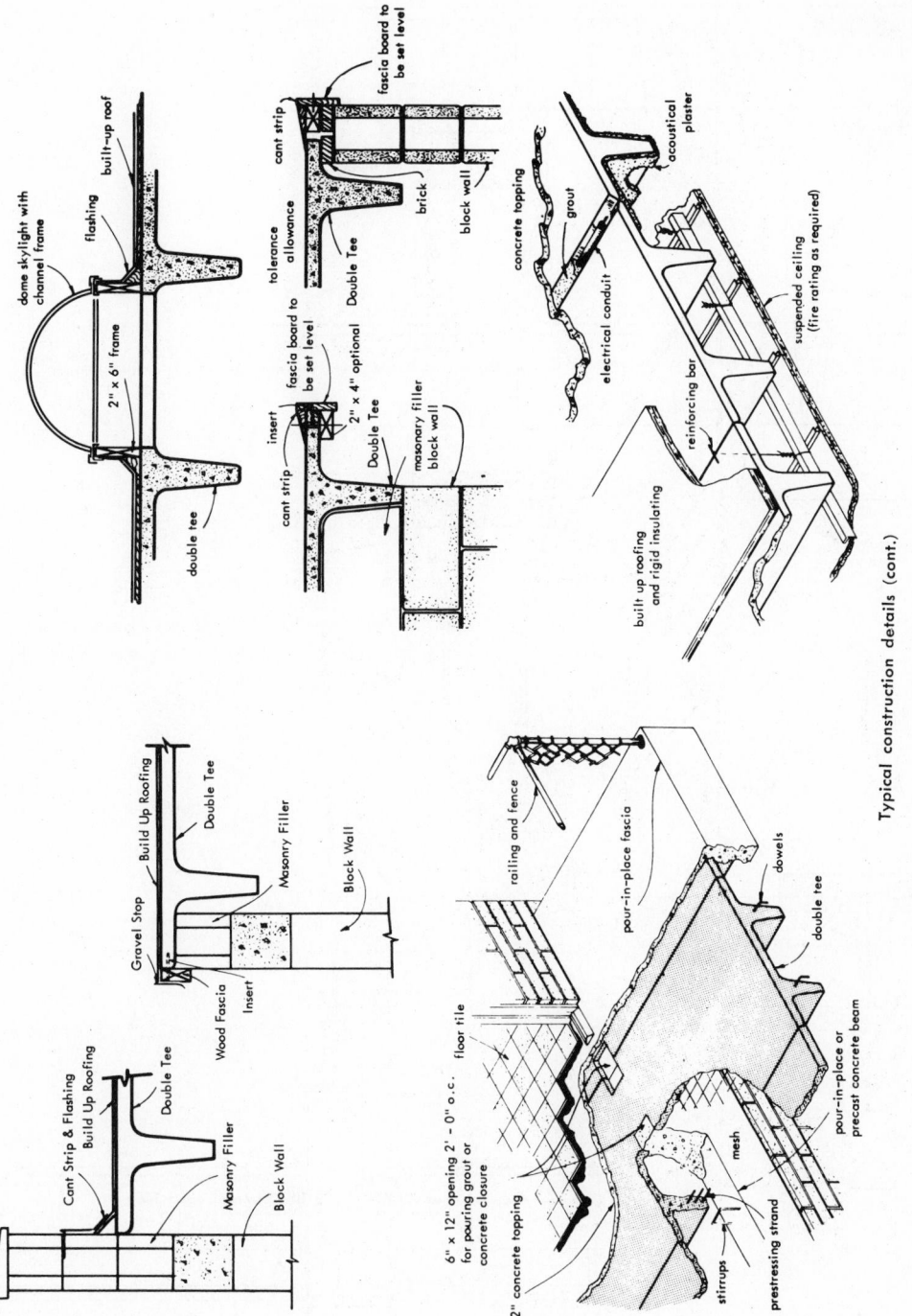

built-up roof

flashing

dome skylight with channel frame

2" x 6" frame

double tee

fascia board to be set level

cant strip

tolerance allowance

brick

Double Tee

black wall

insert

fascia board to be set level

cant strip

2" x 4" optional

Double Tee

masonry filler block wall

concrete topping

grout

electrical conduit

acoustical plaster

reinforcing bar

suspended ceiling (fire rating as required)

built up roofing and rigid insulating

Typical construction details (cont.)

Build Up Roofing

Double Tee

Gravel Stop

Masonry Filler

Block Wall

Wood Fascia

Insert

Cant Strip & Flashing

Build Up Roofing

Double Tee

Masonry Filler

Block Wall

railing and fence

pour-in-place fascia

dowels

double tee

floor tile

6" x 12" opening 2' - 0" o.c. for pouring grout or concrete closure

2" concrete topping

mesh

pour-in-place or precast concrete beam

stirrups

prestressing strand

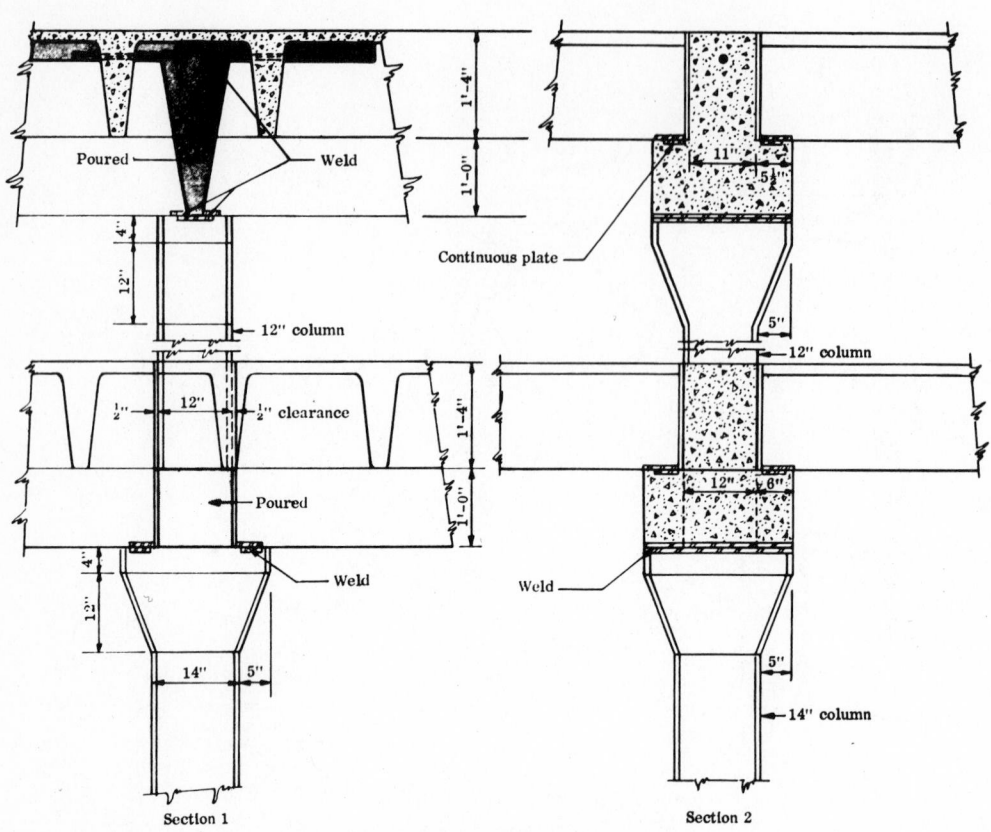

Section 1

Section 2

Multistory buildings

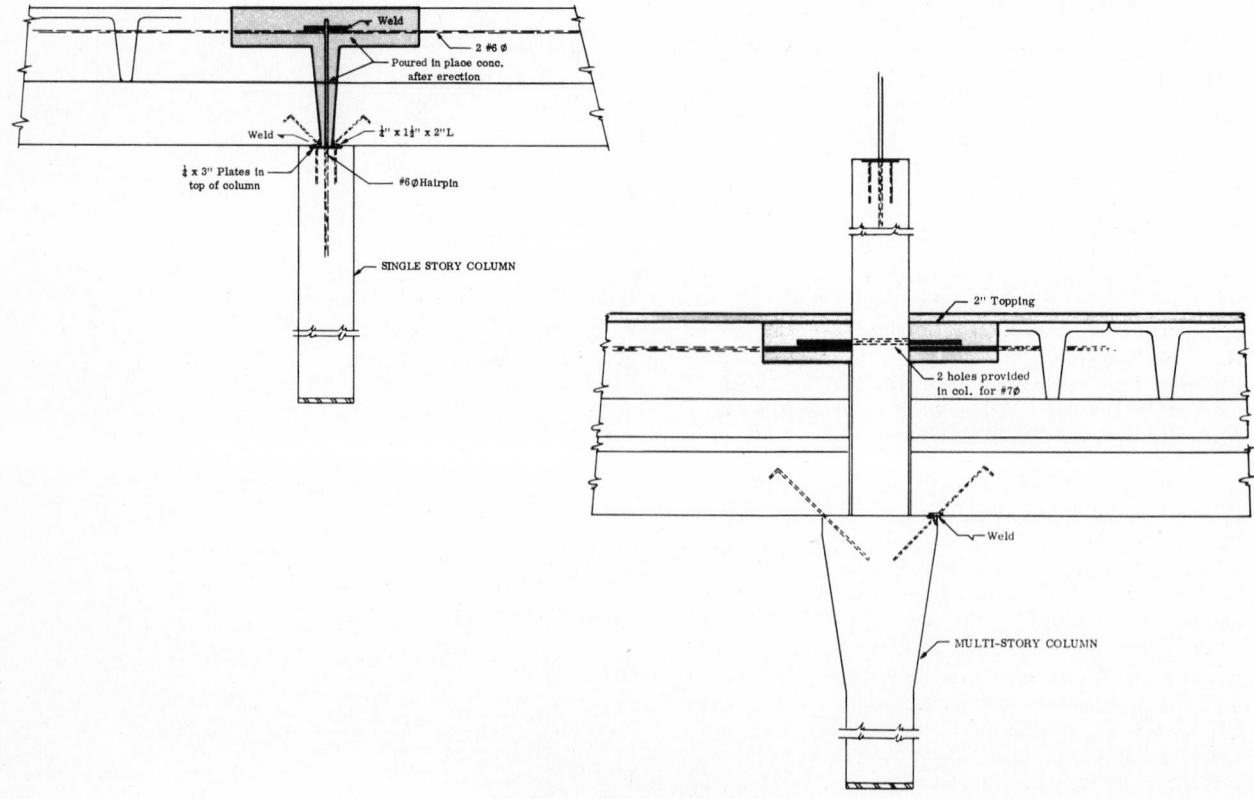

Building beams and connections

by JOHN G. MASCIONI, P.E., Associate Professor, School of Architecture, Pratt Institute

Basic floor framing schemes are illustrated and described on the following pages. For comparison, typical designs have been developed for each scheme. Four bay sizes, 20 by 20 ft, 20 by 24 ft, 20 by 28 ft, and 20 by 32 ft, have been investigated to note the relative effect of span length on the depth of construction. In general, the average area of the four bays, 520 sq ft, may be considered larger than the economical size bay for wood construction and solid concrete floor systems; approximately economical for the ribbed concrete floor sys-

tems; and smaller than the economical bay for steel and prestressed concrete floor systems. Design is based upon a total superimposed load of 60 lb per sq ft. All dead loads with the exception of the structural floor should be deducted to arrive at the effective live load. As the key plan shows, equal spans are assumed on the sides of the bay investigated. Beams, therefore, are designed to support loads from adjacent bays. Design of the spandrel beam, which depends on all the various construction and architectural re-

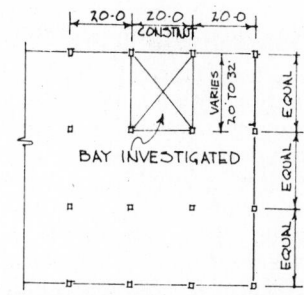

quirements, has been omitted. Reinforced concrete design is based upon 3000 psi (f_c') concrete. The allowable stress in steel for both steel framing and reinforced concrete is 20,000 psi.

Wood joists

A wood-framed structural floor used primarily for residences and one-story buildings. Deflection limits its application for long spans. It is used frequently with wood or masonry wall bearing construction. Design of joists is based upon an $E = 1,650,000$ psi and $f = 1200$ psi. Supporting the joists are plywood box beams with reinforced plywood webs for the heavy shear loads. An adaptation of this system is the stressed skin panel in which the strength and stiffness are increased considerably by glue-nailing plywood to the top and bottom of the wood joists.

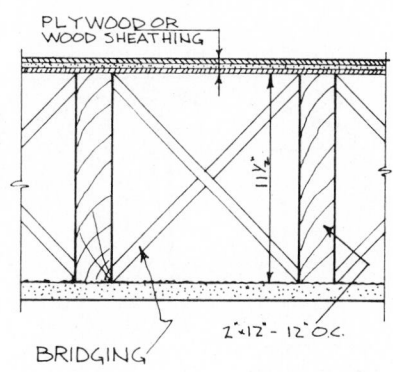

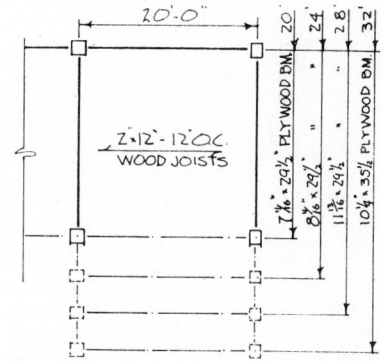

Wood plank and beam

The depth of floor construction is considered the thickness of the decking which is usually a nominal thickness of 2 in., 3 in., or 4 in. Decking can be either planking laid flat or laminated lumber laid on edge and side nailed. The underside of the decking is usually left exposed. Minimum depth of construction, an important advantage, produces large deflections and limits the application of this system primarily to roofs. Random length planking in which only one end bears on a support is the most economical. Design is based upon an $E = 1,760,000$ psi for wood purlins and 1,800,000 for glue-laminated girders. In smaller buildings a post could be placed under the purlins thereby eliminating the girder.

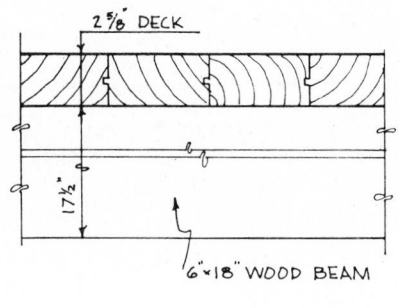

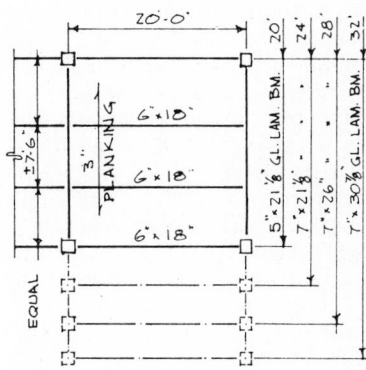

Open-web steel joists

This floor system is widely used and is very economical for light occupancy loads. In addition to the poured concrete slab shown here, it is employed with wide variety of decking and planking commercially available. Open webs facilitate the installation of pipes, ducts, and conduits. Joists tested by the Steel Joist Institute are standardized in depth up to 48 in. for spans up to 96 ft for roofs. The span of joists should not exceed 24 times the depth.

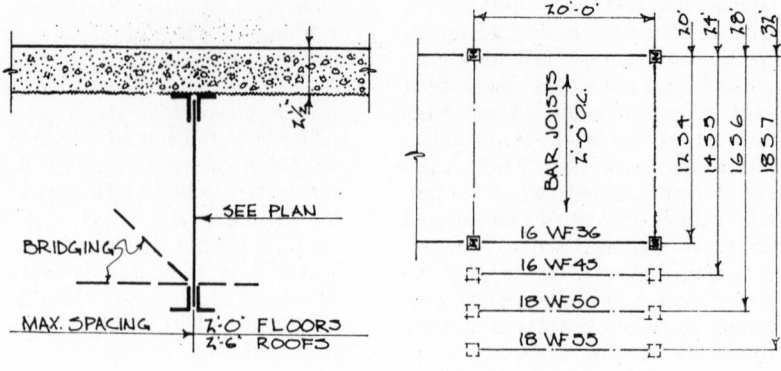

Steel purlins and concrete slab

This system is one of the oldest fire-resistant floor systems. Beams should be spaced at approximately 8 ft to permit the use of welded wire fabric. Light weight concrete is used to reduce the dead load of the slab. For its principal application, office buildings, fill is required for the installation of utilities. A modification of this system consists of using lighter sections, such as Junior beams, at closer spacing so that standard plywood forms may be clipped to flanges and easily removed after the slab has hardened.

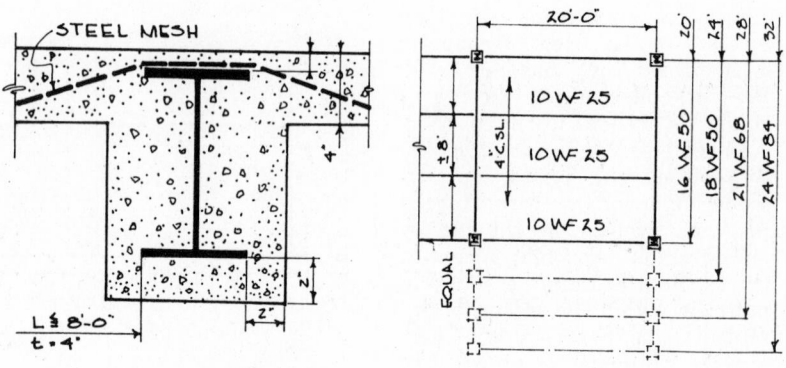

Cellular metal decking

The principal advantage of this floor system is the flexibility provided by the cells for the installation of utilities and for the location of electrical and telephone outlets. Other important advantages are light weight and fast erection. It is widely used to advantage in office buildings. Available in various depths for both short spans and long spans. Light weight concrete is not structural but serves as fill and finish and for fire protection of the top. In addition to the unit shown here, there are other similar products commercially available. For non-fireproof roofs, decking may be left exposed and the concrete fill omitted.

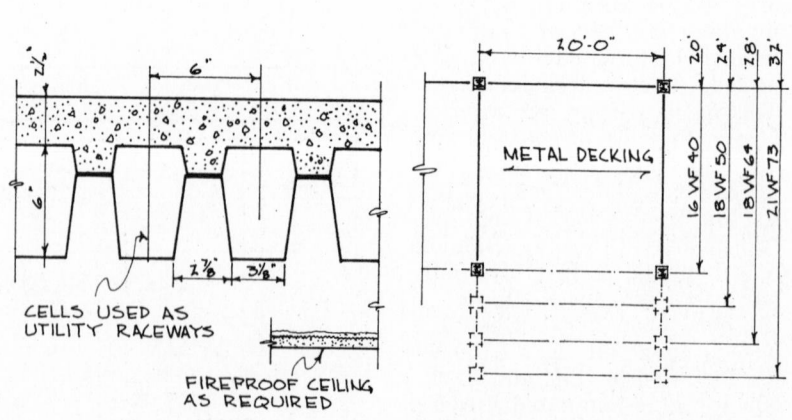

Composite metal decking

This floor system features an extremely efficient use of structural materials. The metal deck serves as positive steel reinforcement and as a form for the structural concrete slab. Like cellular metal decking, principal advantages of this system are light weight and fast erection. Decking may be either corrugated or of the rib type. On long spans temporary shoring may be required. Connections to the supporting steel are made by welding. Utilities are embedded in the concrete slab and do not affect the strength of the slab.

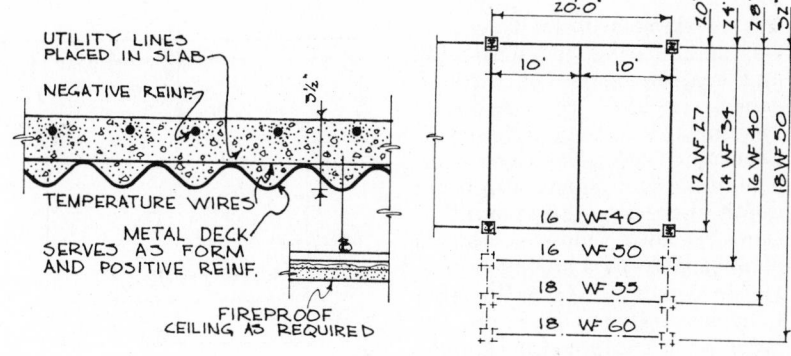

Long-span concrete plank

This floor system may be used with reinforced concrete and masonry structures as well as with steel frames. The cores may serve as the passage of utility lines and can also be utilized for warm air heating systems. The slab used in this design employs prestressing only to control deflections that would be developed by the small depths of slab. The smooth undersurface of the slab may be caulked and painted directly. Other products commercially available use concrete block, clay tile and may be either partially or fully prestressed.

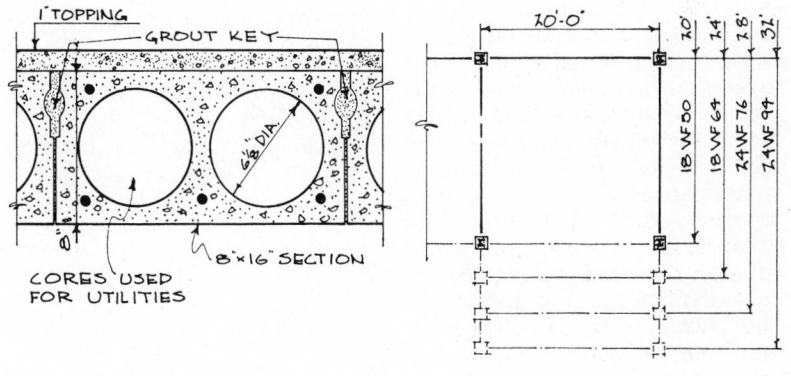

One-way solid slab

The conventional one-way solid slab with beams and girders is usually limited to smaller bays than those considered here. It is effective for supporting heavy and concentrated loads. Because of its dead weight, this floor system is most suitable for spans less than 16 ft. The principal disadvantages of this system are the depth of construction and the formwork required for the beams and girders.

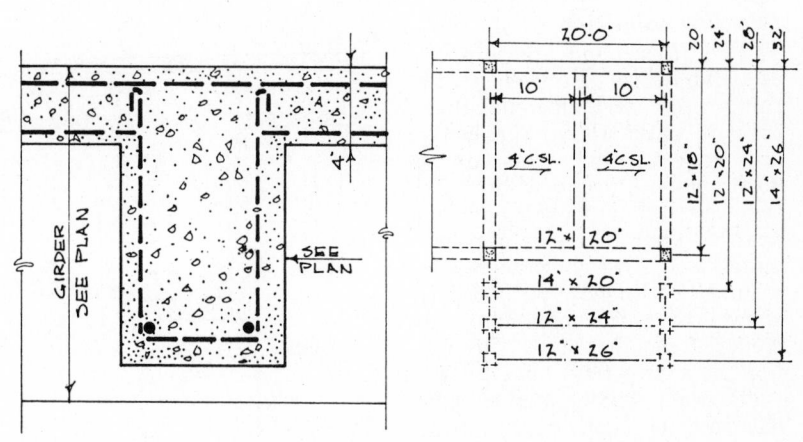

Slab band

This system is basically a one-way solid slab system with wide and shallow beams, called slab bands. It has been used for apartment buildings by Fred N. Severud, Consulting Engineer. The desirable reduction in beam depth increases the amount of reinforcement; however, this is compensated by a saving in slab reinforcement due to the slab haunches. Slab bands do not have to be centered on columns and exterior and interior columns may be placed independently of each other.

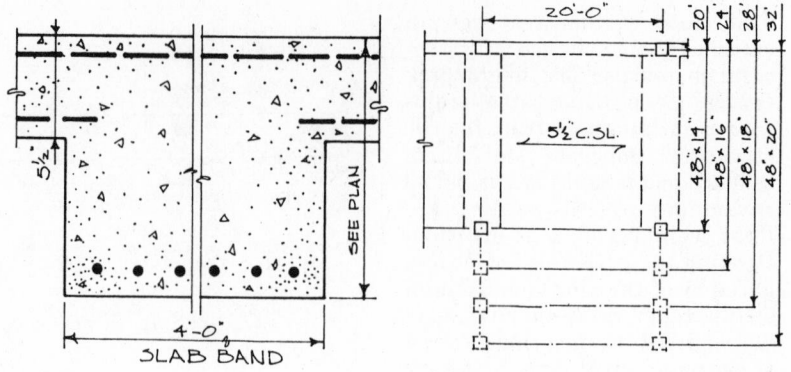

One-way concrete joist

The elimination of concrete that provides little or no moment resistance reduces the dead weight and permits this floor system to support light loads for fairly long spans. Re-usable metal or plastic pans are used for this purpose. Shear and moment capacity may be increased by the use of tapered forms at supports. Other methods of reducing the dead weight are the use of filler block and the placing of paper tubes in the slab. Both of the latter methods have the advantage of providing a flat under-surface that may be easily treated.

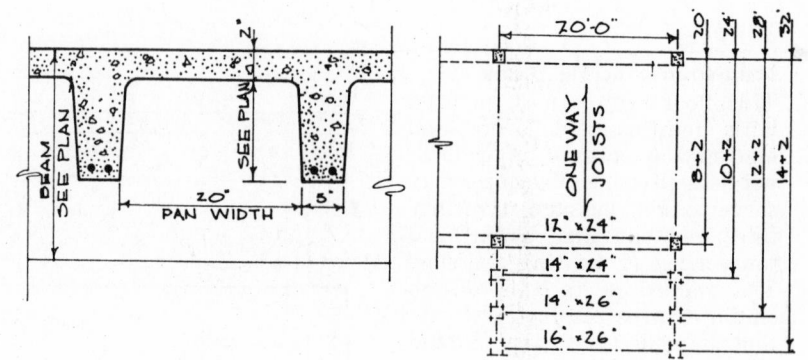

Two-way solid slab

The reinforcement and support of a slab in two directions makes this system very efficient structurally, particularly for heavy and concentrated loads, up to 30-ft spans. A practical limit for two way action is a ratio of long span to short span of approximately 1.7. All two-way systems should be used with fairly square bays for maximum efficiency. A modification of this system is a two-way joist or rib system in which unnecessary concrete is replaced by dome pans or filler blocks.

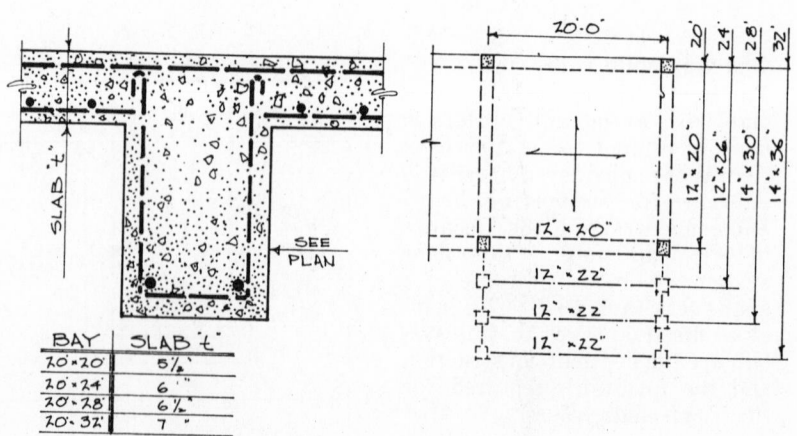

BAY	SLAB t
20 × 20	5½"
20 × 24	6"
20 × 28	6½"
20 × 32	7"

Flat plate

Flat plate is a special type of flat slab construction in which column capitals and drop panels, as well as beams, are eliminated. It is used primarily for relatively light loads and modest spans. Shear at the columns is often the governing factor but may be controlled by special shearhead reinforcement. The increased amount of reinforcement due to shallow depth is usually offset by advantages of the flat plate system. These include minimum depth of construction, and simple and economical formwork which increases the speed of construction. Flat plate also permits flexibility in the location of columns.

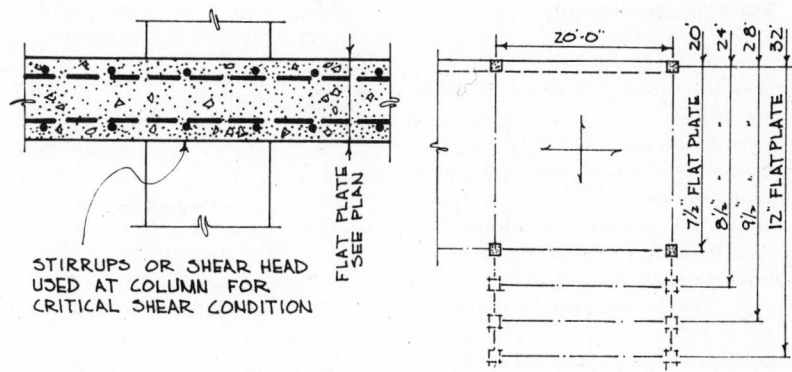

STIRRUPS OR SHEAR HEAD USED AT COLUMN FOR CRITICAL SHEAR CONDITION

Waffle slab

A waffle slab is a solid flat plate with dome forms placed in the slab to produce ribs or joists in two directions. The elimination of the dead weight of concrete not needed to resist moment increases the spans for which this system may be used. For the critical moments and shears that occur at the columns a solid area of concrete is required approximately equal to one third the span in each direction. Filler blocks, instead of dome forms, may also be used to replace concrete.

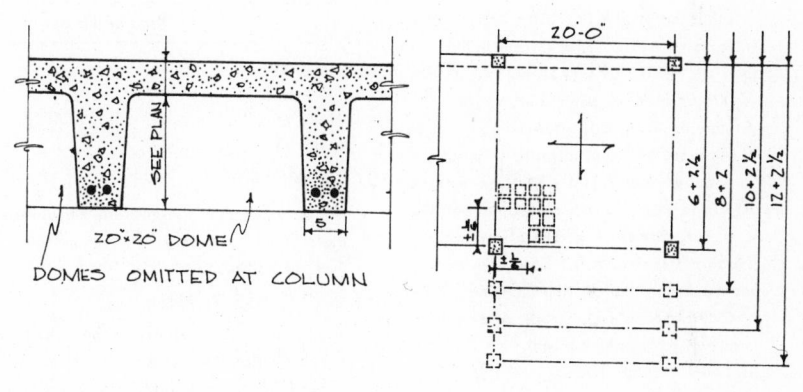

DOMES OMITTED AT COLUMN

Prestressed concrete

The use of manufactured precast and prestressed concrete elements permits a wide variety of framing solutions. In addition to the double tee shown here, prestressed channels, joists, tee's and planks could be used. The feasibility of using prestressed elements will often depend upon the accessibility of a manufacturing plant. Prestressed concrete elements are used to advantage with large spans and with all types of construction. Prestressing may also be used effectively to increase the spans and capacity of cast-in-place concrete systems.

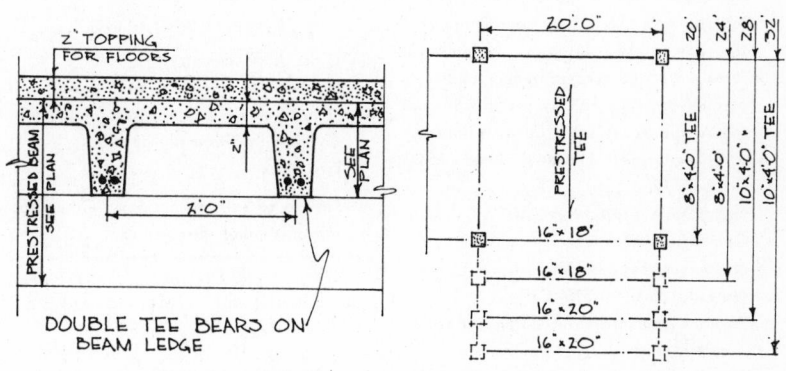

DOUBLE TEE BEARS ON BEAM LEDGE

ASA CODE REQUIREMENTS

American Standard Building Code Requirements for Masonry (ASA A41.1–1953), prepared under the sponsorship of the National Bureau of Standards, is a complete code of minimum requirements for masonry construction and is recommended for adoption by local building code authorities. This code, hereafter referred to as the ASA Code, is summarized on this and the following two pages. Specifications cited are those of the American Society for Testing and Materials (ASTM), American Standards Association (ASA), Structural Clay Products Institute (SCPI), and American Concrete Institute (ACI).

Materials should conform to the following standards of quality:

Brick; clay or shale: ASTM C62 (ASA A98.1), Grade SW for use in contact with earth where subject to freezing, Grade MW or SW for other exterior use. (Note by SCPI: Grade NW may be used in all other cases. Facing brick should conform to ASTM C216, Grade MW.)
  Sand-lime: ASTM C73 (ASA A78.1), Grade SW or MW, as prescribed above.
  Concrete: ASTM C55 (ASA A75.1), Grade A where exposed to weather or soil.
Tile; loadbearing: ASTM C34 (ASA A74.1), Grade LBX where exposed to weather or soil, Grade LB or LBX elsewhere.
  Nonloadbearing: ASTM C56 (ASA A76.1).
Concrete block; hollow, loadbearing: ASTM C90 (ASA A79.1), Grade A where exposed to weather or soil.
  Hollow, nonloadbearing: ASTM C129 (ASA A80.1).
  Solid, loadbearing: ASTM C145 (ASA A81.1), Grade A where exposed to weather or soil.
Cast stone: ACI 704.
Gypsum tile and block: ASTM C52.
Note: Glazed and unglazed structural facing tile are covered by specifications of the Facing Tile Institute. Architectural terra cotta and ceramic veneer and their erection are covered by specifications of the Architectural Terra Cotta Institute.
Mortar materials; hydrated lime: ASTM C207, Type S.
  Hydraulic hydrated lime: ASTM C141.
  Quicklime: ASTM C5.
  Masonry cement: ASTM C91.
  Natural cement: ASTM C10.
  Portland cement: ASTM C150, Type I, II, or III.
  Air-entraining portland cement: ASTM C175, Type IA, IIA, or IIIA.
  Portland blast-furnace cement: ASTM C205, Type IS or ISA.
  Gypsum: ASTM C22 (ASA A49.1).

Aggregate: ASTM C144.
Mortar; ASTM C270: For types and proportions, see Table 1. Masonry should be laid in mortar of the types specified in Table 2. Mortar should be mixed with the max- imum amount of water that it is possible to use and still produce a workable mix. (One of the most common defects of mortar is oversanding.)
Grout: Type M, S, or N mortar, to which

Table 1. Mortar types (ASTM C270–59T)

Mortar type	Minimum average compressive strength of three 2-in. cubes at 28 days, psi	Parts by volume			
		Portland cement	Masonry cement	Hydrated lime or lime putty	Aggregate measured in damp, loose condition
M (A–1)	2,500	1	1 (Type II)		Not less than 2¼ and not more than 3 times the sum of the volumes of the cements and lime used.
		1		¼	
S (A–2)	1,800	½	1 (Type II)		
		1		Over ¼ to ½	
N (B)	750		1 (Type II)		
		1		Over ½ to 1¼	
O (C)	350		1 (Type I or II)		
		1		Over 1¼ to 2½	
K (D)	75	1		Over 2½ to 4	

Table 2. Types of mortar required for various kinds of masonry

Kind of masonry	Types of mortar required
Foundations:	
Footings	M or S
Walls of solid units	M, S, or N
Walls of hollow units	M or S
Hollow walls	M or S
Masonry other than foundation masonry:	
Piers of solid masonry	M, S, or N
Piers of hollow units	M or S
Walls of solid masonry	M, S, N, or O
Walls of solid masonry, other than parapet walls or rubble stone walls, not less than 12 in. thick nor more than 35 ft. in height, supported laterally at intervals not exceeding 12 times the wall thickness	M, S, N, O, or K
Walls of hollow units; loadbearing or exterior, and hollow walls 12 in. or more in thickness	M, S, or N
Hollow walls, less than 12 in. in thickness where assumed design wind pressure:*	
(a) exceeds 20 psf	M or S
(b) does not exceed 20 psf	M, S, or N
Glass-block masonry	M, S, or N
Nonbearing partitions of fireproofing composed of structural clay tile or concrete masonry units	M, S, N, O, or gypsum
Gypsum partition tile or block	Gypsum
Fire brick	Refractory air-setting mortar
Linings of existing masonry, either above or below grade	M or S
Masonry other than above	M, S, or N

For design wind pressures, consult American Standard Building Code Requirements for Minimum Design Loads in Buildings and Other Structures *(ASA A58.1).*

sufficient water should be added to produce a pouring consistency.

Gypsum mortar: Proportions by weight are 1 part gypsum to not more than 3 parts aggregate.

Lateral support: The ratio of the unsupported height or length of a wall to its thickness should not exceed 20 for bearing walls of solid masonry laid in Type M, S, N, or O mortar, nor 12 if laid in Type K mortar, and should not exceed 18 for hollow walls or wall of hollow units regardless of the type of mortar used. To compute the ratio for cavity walls, the thickness should be taken as the sum of the thicknesses of the inner and outer wythes. The distance between lateral supports of nonbearing partitions should not exceed 36 times the actual thickness of the partition including plaster.

Lateral support, measured horizontally, may be obtained from cross walls, piers, or buttresses; and measured vertically, from floors and roofs. Where floor or roof joists

Table 3. Allowable compressive stresses in masonry

Construction; grade of unit	Allowable compressive stresses on gross cross-sectional area (except as noted), psi				
	Type M mortar	Type S mortar	Type N mortar	Type O mortar	Type K mortar
Solid masonry of brick and other solid units of clay or shale; sand-lime or concrete brick:					
8,000 psi or more	400	350	300	200	100
4,500 to 8,000 psi	250	225	200	150	100
2,500 to 4,500 psi	175	160	140	110	75
1,500 to 2,500 psi	125	115	100	75	50
Grouted solid masonry of brick and other solid units of clay or shale; sand-lime or concrete brick:					
4,500 psi or more	350	275	200		
2,500 to 4,500 psi	275	215	155		
1,500 to 2,500 psi	225	175	125		
Solid masonry of solid concrete masonry units:					
Grade A	175	160	140	100	
Grade B	125	115	100	75	
Masonry of hollow units	85	75	70		
Piers of hollow units, cellular spaces filled	105	95	90		
Hollow walls (cavity or masonry bonded)*					
Solid units:					
Grade A or 2,500 psi or more	140	130	110		
Grade B or 1,500 to 2,500 psi	100	90	80		
Hollow units	70	60	55		
Stone ashlar masonry:					
Granite	800	720	640	500	
Limestone or marble	500	450	400	325	
Sandstone or cast stone	400	360	320	250	
Rubble stone, coursed, rough, or random	140	120	100	80	

* On gross cross-sectional area of wall minus area of cavity between wythes (leaves). The allowable compressive stresses for cavity walls are based upon the assumption that the floor loads bear upon only one of the two wythes. When hollow walls are loaded concentrically, the allowable stresses may be increased by 25 per cent.

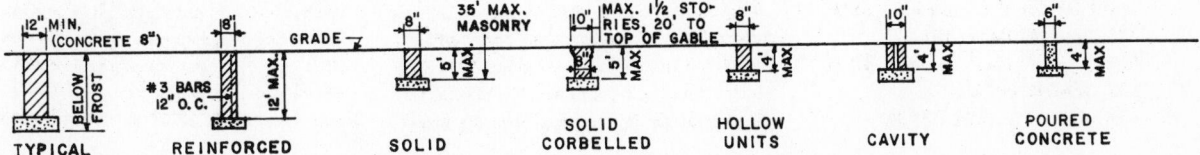

Fig. 1. Minimum thicknesses of masonry bearing walls

Rubble stone should be 4 in. thicker than shown above, but not less than 10 in. in any case. Poured concrete may be 2 in. thinner than shown above, but not less than 8 in. except where 6-in. walls are permitted. Non-bearing walls may be 4 in. thinner than shown above, but not less than 8 in., except where 6-in. walls are permitted.

Fig. 2. Minimum thicknesses of masonry foundation walls

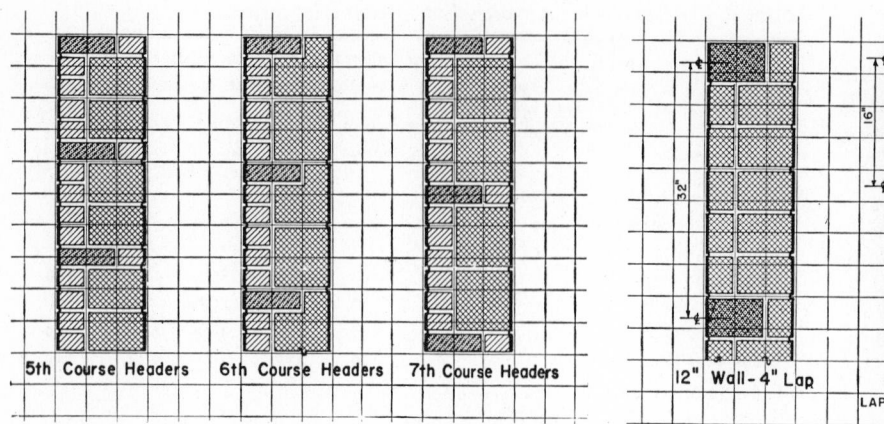

Fig. 3. Bonding of solid masonry walls

Fig. 4. Bonding walls of hollow units

are parallel to the wall, metal anchors spaced not less than 6 ft apart horizontally, should engage at least three joists, which should be solidly bridged at these points.

For isolated piers, the ratio of unsupported height to the smallest dimension should not exceed 10; if built of hollow units, the ratio should not exceed 4, unless the cellular spaces are filled solidly with concrete or with Type M or S mortar.

Allowable stresses should not exceed those shown in Table 3.

Minimum thicknesses of bearing walls and foundations are shown in Figs. 1 and 2, respectively.

BOND

Masonry walls more than one unit thick must be bonded transversely by means of either overlapping masonry units or metal ties.

Masonry bonders

In walls of solid masonry, bonders (also known as headers) should make up not less than 4 per cent of the wall area. Bonders should extend not less than 4 in. into the backing and should be spaced not more than 24 in. apart horizontally or vertically (Fig. 3).

In ashlar masonry, bondstones should be uniformly distributed and should constitute not less than 10 per cent of the area of the wall. In rubble masonry, bondstones should be spaced not more than 3 ft vertically or

horizontally; if the wall is more than 24 in. thick, bondstones should be provided for each 6 sq ft of wall surface on each side.

In walls of hollow masonry more than one unit in thickness, bonders lapping at least 4 in. over the unit below should occur at vertical intervals of not more than 34 in., or bonders that are at least 50 per cent greater in thickness than the units below shall be used at vertical intervals not exceeding 17 in. (Fig. 4).

Metal ties

Metal ties must be used for the bonding of cavity walls and may be used for the bonding of solid walls. Ties should be 3/16-in.-diam steel rods or other material of equivalent stiffness, with ends bent at a 90-deg angle to form hooks not less than 2 in. long. For walls built of hollow masonry units, ties of rectangular shape should be used. Metal ties should be made of, or coated with, corrosion-resistant metal, and should be embedded in the horizontal joints of the masonry. There must be not less than one metal tie for each 4½ sq ft of wall area. Ties in alternate courses should be staggered and the vertical distance between courses should not exceed 18 in.; the horizontal distance between ties should not exceed 36 in. (Fig. 5).

Cavity walls

Cavity walls must be bonded with metal ties, as described above. Additional bonding ties should be provided at all openings,

spaced not more than 3 ft apart around the perimeter and within 12 in. of the opening. The cavity must be kept clear of mortar droppings and be properly flashed and drained at the bottom.

Grouted masonry

Masonry units in outer wythes should be laid with full head and bed joints of Type M or S mortar. Interior joints should be filled with grout, and longitudinal joints should be not less than ¾ in. wide. Each grout pour should be stopped 1½ in. below the top of the masonry units and properly stirred. Headers should not be used (metal ties are required).

Chases and recesses

Chases and recesses should be not deeper than one-third the wall thickness, nor longer than 4 ft. horizontally, and should have at least 8 in. of masonry at the back and sides. The total area of chases and recesses should not exceed one-fourth the wall area. In residential buildings not over two stories high, vertical chases 4 in. deep and not over 4 sq ft in area are permitted in 8-in. walls; lintels should be used above chases or recesses more than 12 in. wide.

Corbeling

Projection of a masonry unit should not exceed one-half its vertical dimensions; projection of brick should not exceed 1 in. per course. Total projection should not exceed one-half the wall thickness.

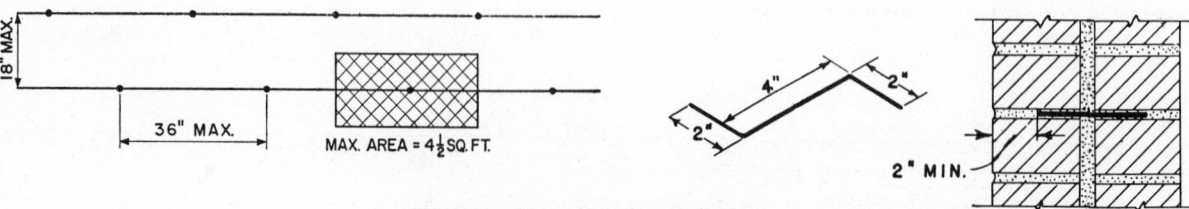

Fig. 5. Location and spacing of metal ties

WORKMANSHIP

High-absorption brick must be thoroughly wetted before laying; sprinkling is not sufficient. However, brick should be surface dry when laid. All bed and head joints should be completely filled. The mortar bed should be thick and uniform, and furrowed only lightly, if at all; it should be spread over only a few brick at a time. Mortar should be applied to the ends of brick and to the entire side of header brick before they are laid: "slushing" the head joints will not completely fill all the voids. Holes caused by the removal of nails or line pins should be plugged immediately. Proper tooling of exterior joints reduces water penetration of the wall; concave joints are best for this purpose. Additional insurance against leakage may be obtained by parging or back-plastering with mortar the face of the backup before the facing is laid. Solid metal-tied walls are recommended by SCPI for superior resistance to water penetration, especially for 8-in. walls.

ARCHES

Data and illustrations on this and the following page have been derived from *Technical Notes on Brick and Tile Construction,* published by the Structural Clay Products Institute.

An arch is a form of construction in which a number of units span an opening by transferring vertical loads laterally to adjacent units and thus to the supports. It is essentially a beam curved in the plane of the loads. Any section in an arch, therefore, may be subjected to moment and shear, as in an ordinary beam. In addition it is subjected to thrust from components of vertical loads in the direction of the arch axis.

In a fixed arch, as all masonry arches are, three conditions must be maintained to ensure pure arch action:

1. The length of the span must remain constant.

2. The elevation of the ends must remain unchanged.

3. The inclination of the skewback must be fixed.

If any of these conditions is violated by sliding, settlement, or rotation of the abutments, critical stresses, for which the arch was not designed, may develop. Such stresses may result in failure of the arch.

STRUCTURAL DESIGN

All theories for the design of masonry arches are in fact methods of verification. Dimensions of the arch are first assumed, based on common practice or an empirical

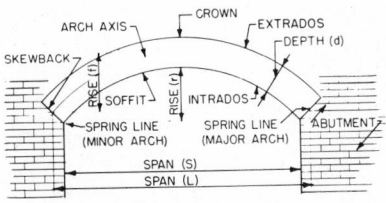

Fig. 6. Arch terminology

formula, and the assumed arch is then tested by one or more of the theories.

There are two classes of theories of the stability of a masonry arch: line of thrust and the elastic deformation. The line-of-thrust theories consider the stability of the arch ring as depending upon the friction and the reactions between the several arch sections or voussoirs. The elastic theories consider the arch as a curved beam whose stability depends upon internal stresses.

In general, the line-of-thrust theories are most applicable to symmetrical masonry arches loaded uniformly over the entire span or subjected to symmetrically placed concentrated loads. For such arches, the line of resistance, which is the line connecting the points of application of the resultant forces transmitted to each voussoir, is required to fall within the middle third of the arch section so that neither the intrados nor extrados of the arch will be in tension.

For arches subjected to nonsymmetrical loading, which may develop tensile stresses in the arch, the elastic theories provide a more accurate method of analysis than the line-of-thrust theories.

Line-of-thrust analysis

One of the oldest line-of-thrust theories is based upon the hypothesis of least crown thrust. This hypothesis can be applied to the

analysis of an arch by static methods, provided the external forces acting upon the arch are known and the point of application and direction of the crown thrust are assumed.

It is customary to assume the direction of the crown thrust as horizontal and its point of application at the upper extremity of the middle third of the section; that is, two-thirds the arch depth from the intrados.

With the above assumptions, the forces acting on each section of the arch may be determined by analytical and graphic methods. The first step in such an analysis is to determine the joint of rupture. This is that joint for which the tendency of the arch to open at the extrados is the greatest and which, therefore, requires the greatest crown thrust applied at the upper extremity of the middle third to prevent the joint from opening. At this joint the line of resistance of the arch will fall on the lower extremity of the middle third of the section.

For segmental arches of short spans (not exceeding 6 ft) and of low rise-to-span ratios (not exceeding 0.15), the joint of rupture may be assumed to be the skewback of the arch. Based on this assumption and the hypothesis of least crown thrust, the magnitude of the crown thrust and the magnitude and direction of the reaction at the skewback may be determined graphically (Fig. 7).

In this analysis, since the arch is symmetrical and uniformly loaded over the entire span, one-half the arch is considered. Figure 7a shows the external forces acting upon the arch section. For equilibrium, the lines of action of these three forces $W/2$, H, and R must intersect at one point, as shown in Fig. 7b. Since H is assumed to act horizontally, this determines the direction of

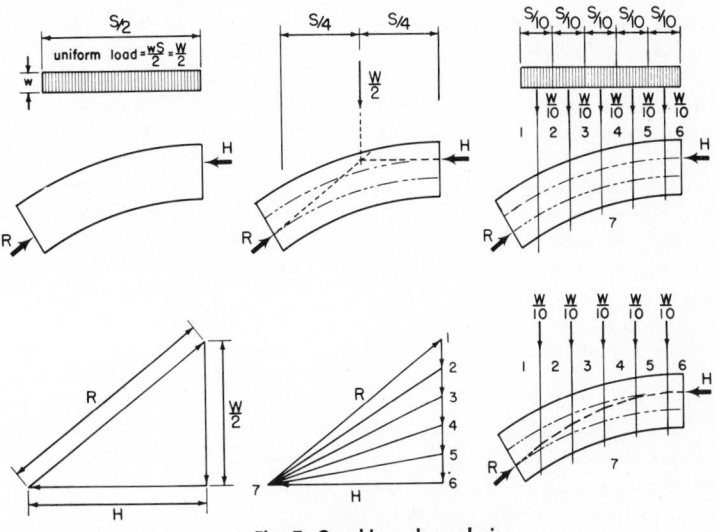

Fig. 7. Graphic arch analysis

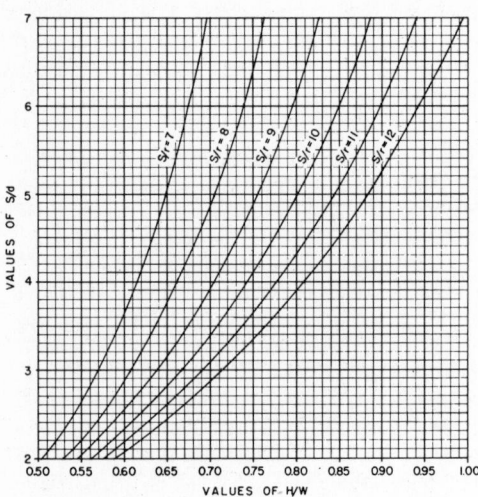

Fig. 8. Thrust coefficients for segmental arches

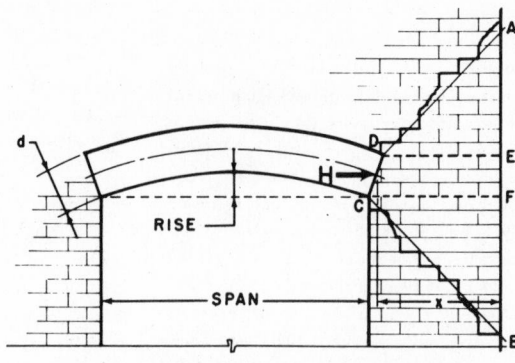

Fig. 9. Calculating resistance to horizontal thrust

force R. Its magnitude may be obtained by constructing a force diagram (Fig. 7d).

The next step in the graphic analysis is to divide the arch into voussoirs and to transform the uniform load into the equivalent concentrated loads, acting on each voussoir or section (Fig. 2c). Starting at any convenient point (in this example, the point between the reaction and the first load segment past the skewback), we place numbers between each pair of forces (Fig. 2c). Now each force is identified by a number; for example, the reaction is 7–1 and the first vertical load is 1–2.

The side of the force diagram representing W/2 is divided into the same number of equivalent loads as was done in Fig. 7c. The numbers previously used for identification are placed in the manner shown to identify the forces in the force diagram. Thus, 7–1 is the skewback reaction, 6–7 the horizontal thrust, and so on. From the intersection of H and R (7–1 and 6–7), a line is drawn to each intermediate point on the leg representing W/2. (See Fig. 7e.)

The equilibrium polygon may now be drawn in the following manner: Extend the line of the reaction until it intersects the line of action of 1–2. Through this point draw a line parallel to the line 7–2, of Fig. 7e, until it intersects the line of action of 2–3. Through this point draw a line parallel to 7–3 of Fig. 7e. Complete the equilibrium polygon in this manner. (See Fig. 7f.)

If the polygon lies completely within the middle third, the arch is stable.

Elastic deformation analysis

Many methods of elastic analysis suitable for arches have been developed; in most instances, however, the application is complicated and time-consuming. *Frames and Arches* by Valerian Leontovich (McGraw

Hill Book Co., 1959) provides equations for the design of parabolic arches of both constant and variable cross section which substantially simplify this type of analysis.

MINOR ARCH DESIGN

There are three methods of failure of unreinforced masonry arches: by rotation of one section of the arch about the edge of a joint, by the sliding of one section of the arch on another or on the skewback, and by crushing of the masonry.

Rotation: The assumption that the equilibrium polygon lies entirely within the middle third of the arch section, precludes the rotation of one section of the arch about the edge of a joint or the development of tensile stresses in either the intrados or extrados.

Sliding: The coefficient of friction between the units composing a brick or tile masonry arch is at least 0.50, without considering the additional resistance to sliding resulting from bond between mortar and the masonry units. This coefficient corresponds to an angle of friction of approximately 27 deg. If the angle that the line of resistance of the arch makes with the normal to the joint between arch sections is less than the angle of friction, the arch is stable against sliding. This first angle can be determined graphically.

For minor segmental arches, the angle between the line of resistance and the normal to the joint is greatest at the skewback.

For segmental arches with radial joints, the angle γ between the skewback and the vertical is

$$\gamma = \tan^{-1} \frac{4rS}{S^2 - 4r^2}$$

or in terms of the radius of curvature

$$\gamma = \sin^{-1} \frac{S}{2R}$$

in which

S = span
r = rise
R = radius of curvature

Figure 8 is a graphic representation of thrust coefficients, H/W, for segmental arches subjected to uniform load over the entire span. Once the thrust coefficient is determined for a particular arch, the horizontal thrust H may be determined as the product of the thrust coefficient and the total load W. To determine the proper thrust coefficient, one must first determine the characteristics of the arch, S/r and S/d, in which d = the depth of the arch and S, r, and d are all expressed in the same units.

Once the horizontal thrust has been determined, the maximum compressive stress in the masonry is determined by the following formula:

$$f_m = \frac{2H}{bd}$$

in which

f_m = maximum compressive stress in the arch, psi
H = horizontal thrust, lb
b = breadth of the arch, in.
d = depth of the arch, in.

Thrust resistance

Resistance to horizontal thrust, developed by the arch, is provided by the adjacent mass of masonry. In areas where limited masonry is available, such as corners and openings, it may be necessary to check the resistance of the wall to the horizontal thrusts. Figure 9 illustrates how such resistance may be calculated.

It is assumed that the thrust of the arch attempts to move a volume of masonry enclosed by the boundary lines ABCD. For calculating purposes the area CDEF is equivalent in resistance. It can be seen that the thrust is acting against two planes of resistance, CF and DE. The resistance to arch thrust is determined by the following formula:

$$H_r = v_m n x t$$

H_r = resisting thrust, lb
v_m = allowable shearing stress in masonry wall, psi
n = number of resisting shear planes
x = distance from the center of skew-back to end of wall, in.
t = wall thickness, in.

The minimum distance from a corner or opening at which an arch may be located is easily determined by writing the formula to solve for x, substituting actual arch thrust for resisting thrust:

$$x = \frac{H}{v_m n t}$$

For brick with mortar Type M or S, v_m = 50; with mortar Type N, v_m = 35.

REINFORCED MASONRY

Reinforced masonry utilizes steel in combination with masonry to produce greatly increased resistance to tensile, shear, and compressive forces. The basic principle is the same as that of reinforced concrete, and the method of design and the terminology employed are very similar to those used in reinforced concrete design.

Design and construction of reinforced masonry are governed by local codes and by the *American Standard Building Code*

Requirements for Reinforced Masonry (ASA A41.2-1960). The principal provisions of the latter code, excluding those which are the same as in the ASA Code for Masonry (A41.1), are summarized below.

Reinforcement should conform to the following standards of quality: Deformed reinforcing bars—ASTM A305; billet-steel bars—ASTM A15 (ASA A50.1); rail-steel bars—ASTM A16 (ASA A50.2); welded steel fabric—ASTM A185 (ASA G45.1); steel for bridges and buildings—ASTM A7 (ASA G24.1).

Aggregate for masonry grout: ASTM C404, coarse aggregate No. 8.

Mortar proportions by volume: 1 part portland cement, ¼ to ½ part hydrated lime or lime putty, and fine aggregate consisting of 2¼ to 3 times the sum of the separate volumes of the cement and lime. (These proportions correspond to mortar Type S, ASTM C270.)

Grout proportions by volume: Type MG (mortar grout)—1 part portland cement, ¼ part hydrated lime or lime putty, and fine aggregate consisting of 2¼ to 3 times the sum of the separate volumes of the cement and lime (mortar Type M, ASTM C270), to which sufficient water should be added to cause the mixture to flow readily. Stir at frequent intervals to prevent separation of materials. Type PG (pea gravel grout)—1 part portland cement, ¼ part hydrated lime or lime putty, 2¼ to 3 parts

fine aggregate, and 1 to 2 parts coarse aggregate; the sum of the volumes of the fine and coarse aggregates should not exceed 4 times the sum of the volumes of the cement and lime.

Allowable stresses

Compressive strength of masonry (f_m') should be determined preferably by test of a masonry prism, following the procedure described in ASA A41.2. In the absence of a test, compressive strength of masonry should be as shown in Table 4. Allowable stresses in reinforcement (longitudinal f_s and web f_v) should not exceed those shown in Table 5. Allowable stresses in reinforced masonry (f_m) should not exceed those shown in Table 6.

Reinforced grouted masonry

Masonry units should be laid in full head and bed joints, with no mortar fins projecting into spaces to be filled with grout. Metal ties should be used to bond the two outer wythes of the wall to each other. Longitudinal joints to receive grout should be not less than ¾ in. wide. If the longitudinal joint (core) is less than 2 in. wide, the maximum height of grout pour should be 12 in. If the longitudinal joint is 2 in. or more in width, the maximum height of grout pour should not exceed 48 times the joint width for MG grout or 64 times the joint width for PG grout, but not to exceed a height of 12 ft. (Fig. 13). Grout pour should be stopped 1½ in. below the top of masonry units. In walls built of hollow masonry units, minimum dimensions of continuous vertical cores should be 2 by 3 in. and the maximum height of grout pour should be 4 ft. (Fig. 12).

Reinforcement should be completely embedded in grout. The minimum distance

Table 4. Compressive strength of masonry

Values shown are for gross area of solid masonry units, net area of hollow masonry units.

Compressive strength of the units, psi	Assumed compressive strength of masonry (f_m'), psi
1,000 to 1,500	900 to 1,150
1,501 to 2,500	1,151 to 1,550
2,501 to 4,000	1,551 to 2,000
4,001 to 6,000	2,001 to 2,400
6,001 to 8,000	2,401 to 2,700
8,001 to 10,000	2,701 to 2,900
10,001 to 12,000	2,901 to 3,000
Over 12,000	3,000

Table 5. Allowable stresses in reinforcement (f_s or f_v)

Condition	Grade of steel	Stress, psi
Tensile	Structural (bars and shapes)	18,000
	Intermediate and hard*	20,000
Compressive (column verticals)	Intermediate	16,000
	Hard*	20,000

* Billet, rail, or axle steel.

Table 6. Allowable stresses in masonry

Description	Symbol	Allowable stress
Compressive:*		
Axial: Walls (h/t = 10 or less)	f_m	0.20 f_m'
(h/t = 25)	f_m	0.15 f_m'
Flexural	f_m	0.33 f_m'
Shear: Beams with no web reinforcement	v_m	50 psi†
Beams with web reinforcement	v	150 psi
Bond: Plain bars	u	80 psi
Deformed bars (ASTM A305)	u	160 psi
Bearing	f_m	0.25 f_m'
Modulus of elasticity	E_m	1,000 f_m'
Modulus of rigidity	E_v	400 f_m'

*For allowable stress on columns, see Section 9.4 of ASA A41.2.
† See Section 8.7.1 (c) of ASA A41.2.

between parallel bars is one diameter. The minimum coverage of bars is 3 in. at the bottom of footings, 2 in. in vertical members exposed to weather or soil, 1½ in. in columns and on bottoms and sides of girders and beams, ¾ in. in walls not exposed to weather or soil, and one diameter but not less than ¾ in. above all horizontal bars not exposed to weather or soil.

Minimum joint thickness: The thickness of grout or mortar between masonry units and reinforcement bars should be not less than ¼ in., except that ¼-in.-diam bars may be placed in ½-in. horizontal joints.

Columns

Columns should be not less than 12 in. in either dimension, and the unsupported height should not exceed 20 times the smallest dimension. The ratio of area of the vertical reinforcement to gross area of column section should be not less than 0.005 nor more than 0.04. Reinforcement should consist of at least 4 bars of not less than ½-in. diam. Ties should be not less than ¼-in. diam, spaced not more than

16 bar diameters, 48 tie diameters, smallest dimension of column, or 16 in.

Walls

Bearing walls should be not less than 6 in. thick, and the unsupported height should not exceed 25 times the thickness. Nonbearing walls may have an unsupported height of 30 times the thickness. The area of steel reinforcement should be not less than 0.002 times the cross-sectional area of the wall; maximum spacing of reinforcement should not exceed 6 times the wall thickness, or 48 in. Horizontal reinforcement should be provided in the top of footings, at the bottom and top of wall openings, at the floor and roof levels, and at the top of parapet walls. In addition there should be not less than one ½-in. diam bar around all window and door openings and extending at least 24 in. beyond the corners of the openings (Fig. 14).

Details of reinforced masonry construction, illustrated on this and the following two pages, are from *Technical Notes on Brick and Tile Construction*, published by

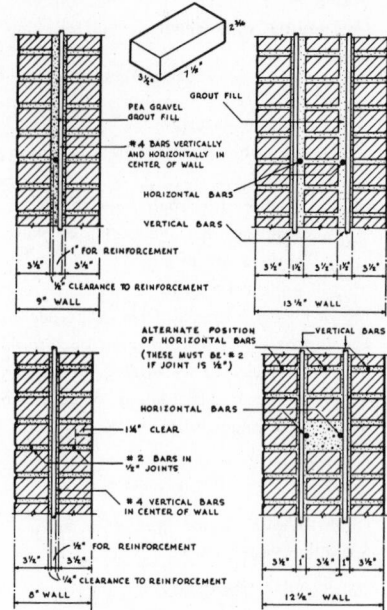

Fig. 10. Typical wall sections using modular brick

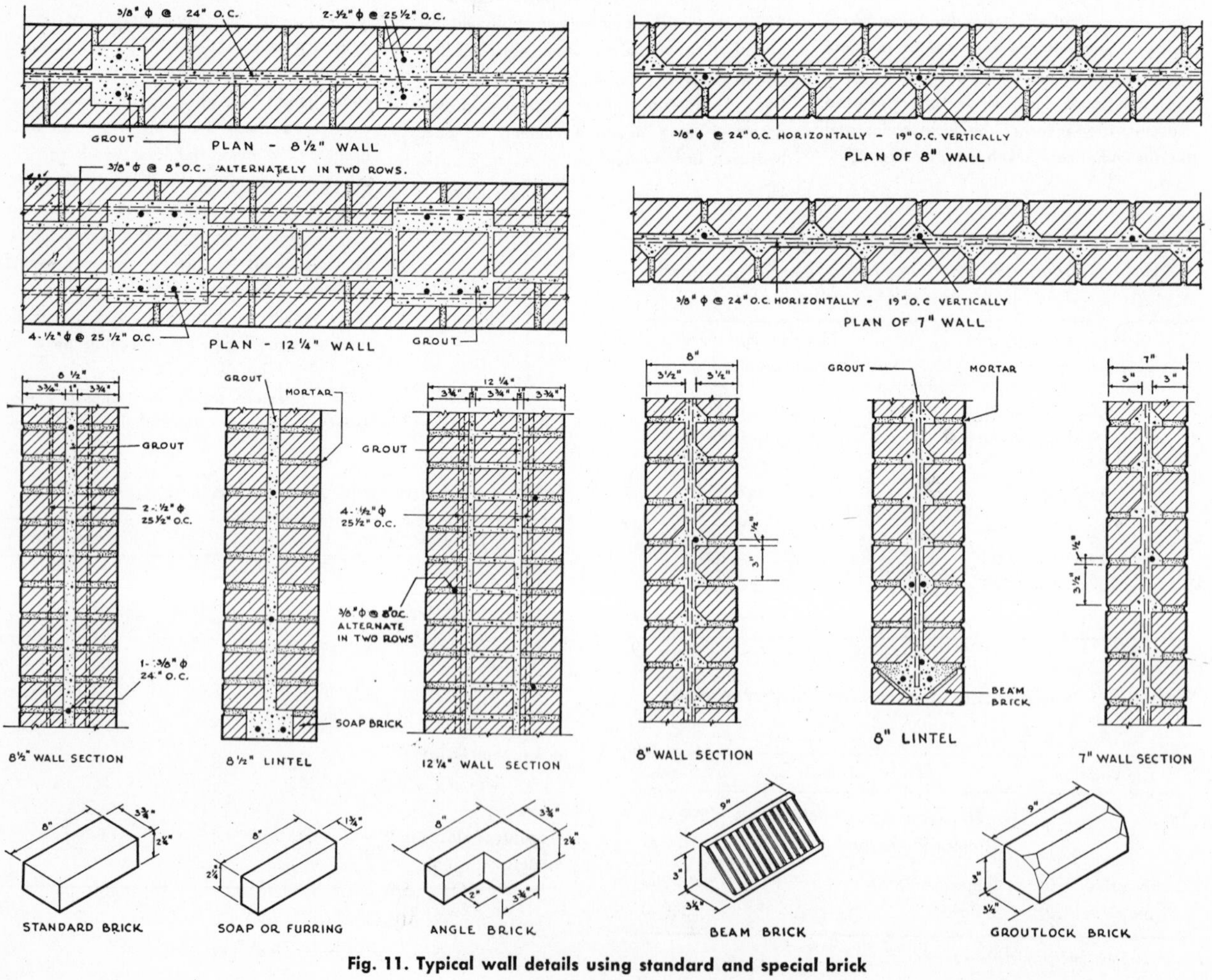

Fig. 11. Typical wall details using standard and special brick

the Structural Clay Products Institute. Reinforced masonry walls of modular brick are shown in Fig. 10. In some areas special "shaped" brick are available for use in reinforced masonry construction; several of these are illustrated in Fig. 11.

Reinforced masonry is well suited to the resistance of lateral forces and is widely used in the seismic areas of the Pacific coast. It is also well adapted to the construction of blast-resistant structures. Reinforced masonry may be used as curtain walls in framed structures. If such walls are tied rigidly to the frame they can be designed to resist all or most of the lateral forces acting on the building.

Reinforced masonry is most often used for vertical elements such as walls and columns. Since no formwork is required, the cost is competitive with that of rein-

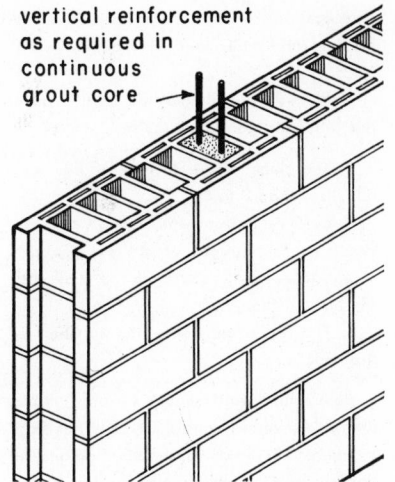

Fig. 12. Reinforced structural facing tile

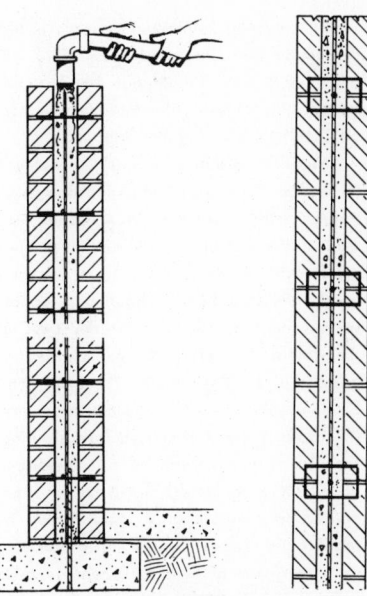

Fig. 13. "High-lift" reinforced masonry; section and plan

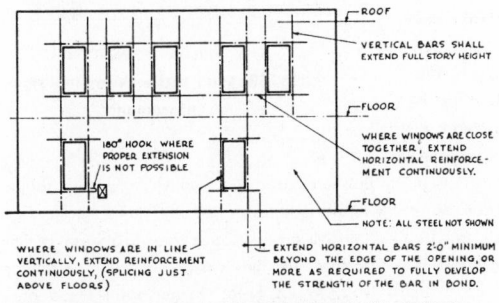

WALL ELEVATION SHOWING REINFORCEMENT AROUND OPENINGS

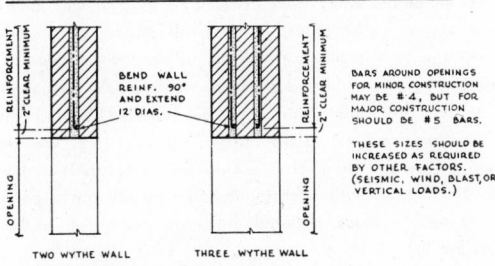

SECTIONS AT EDGE OF OPENINGS

Fig. 14. Typical reinforcement around wall openings

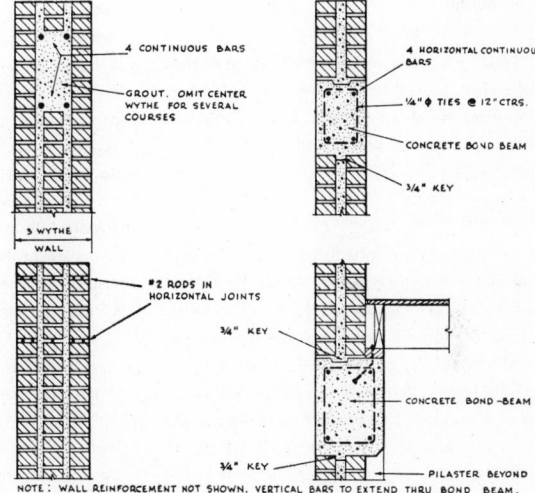

Fig. 15. Sections through typical bond beams

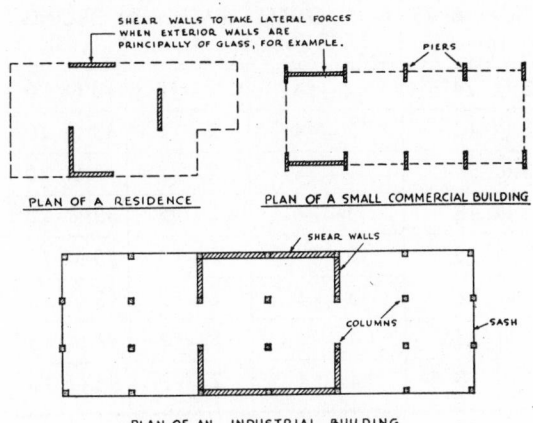

Fig. 16. Reinforced masonry shear walls

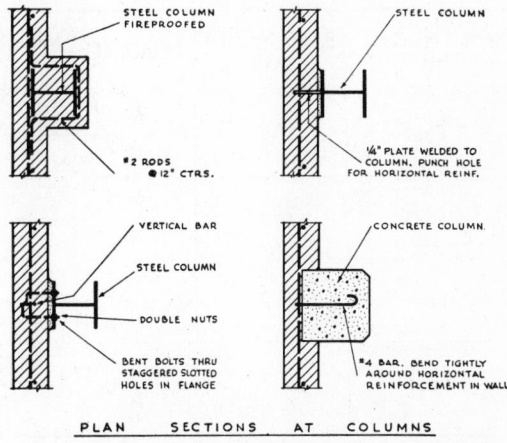

PLAN   SECTIONS   AT   COLUMNS

Fig. 17. Attachment of reinforced masonry curtain walls to structural columns

forced concrete. Reinforced masonry is also frequently used for bond beams (Fig. 15) and for lintels. Continuous bond beams at each floor level are recommended for all buildings with loadbearing walls.

"High-lift" grouting (Fig. 13), developed in the San Francisco area, has now been approved by local and ASA Codes. The wall may be built as shown, with a minimum cavity width of 2 in., to a maximum height of 12 ft before grouting. Cleanout spaces must be provided at the base of the wall so that the cavity can be cleaned daily during construction. The wall must be allowed to cure for at least three days (five days in wet weather) before grouting. The first grout should be a cement-sand slurry (1 part cement to 2 parts sand) poured to a depth of 2 in., followed by regular PG grout poured at a constant rate: maximum of 1 ft in 10 minutes, minimum of 1 ft in 20 minutes; after each 3 ft of pour, wait 30 to 60 minutes. Intermittent vibration is necessary during all stages of grouting.

Data and illustrations on this and the following pages have been derived from *Technical Notes on Brick and Tile Construction*, published by the Structural Clay Products Institute.

Retaining walls

Reinforced masonry is frequently used for minor retaining walls, especially in locations where appearance is important. Table 7 may be used for the design of retaining walls not over 6 ft in height. (Walls higher than 6 ft should be designed by an engineer.) Because a retaining wall —even a low one—can be subjected to a wide variety of loading conditions, two

classifications of walls are listed: "M" or medium-duty walls, and "H" or heavy-duty walls.

Medium-duty walls may be used if all of the following conditions exist:

1. The slope of the surface of the backfill is less than 3 to 1.
2. Surcharge from wheel loads, or bearing from foundations of structures above, is no closer to the back of the wall than 1½ times its height.
3. The soil is not dense and can be well drained.

Heavy-duty walls should be used if any one of the above conditions does not exist.

Figure 18 shows construction details for the low, reinforced masonry retaining walls covered in Table 7. Alternate foundations are shown, but no matter which foundation is used, the dimensions must not be less than those shown, since sufficient mass is needed to overcome a sliding tendency resulting from the horizontal forces. The location of the stem on the footing is determined by the minimum dimension *x*. In heavy-duty walls, because of the greater loading, the eccentricity of the resultant forces acting on the base must be controlled. Therefore, the stem must not be placed as far out on the footing as it is in medium-duty walls.

Materials and workmanship should be in accordance with the ASA Code as described on previous pages. Type PG grout is recommended for retaining walls.

When backfilling is undertaken, it is important that earth be placed in front of the foundation and well tamped *before* replacing the earth behind the wall. The depth to the frost line or adequate bearing will determine the distance below the

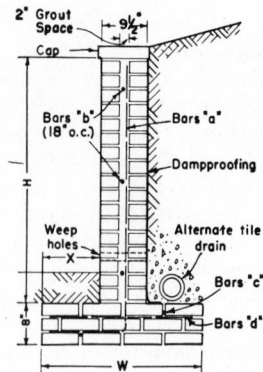

WALL SECTION

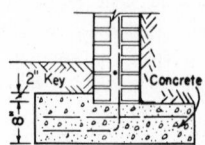

ALTERNATE FOUNDATION
Fig. 18. Wall section showing steel placement

finished grade to which the foundation should extend.

Provision for adequate drainage is important in the design of any retaining wall. Weep holes, larger than those normally used in building construction, should be placed at intervals above the finished grade in the front of the wall. Instead of, or in addition to, weep holes, a continuous drain may be installed behind the wall at the base of the stem (Fig. 18). The drain pipe should be perforated or laid with open joints and covered with a pervious material, such as gravel or broken stone.

Table 7. Steel required for low, reinforced masonry retaining walls

WALL HEIGHT (H)	BASE WIDTH (W)	LOADING	MIN. DISTANCE (x)	VERTICAL BARS (a)	HORIZONTAL BARS (b)	BASE REINFORCING (c)	(d)
3 Feet	1'-9"	M	4"	#3 @ 24"	2—#4	2—#2	#3 @ 20"
		H	6"	#3 @ 15"	2—#4	2—#2	#3 @ 20"
4 Feet	2'-5"	M	7"	#3 @ 24"	3—#4	2—#2	#3 @ 20"
		H	9"	#4 @ 18"	3—#4	2—#2	#3 @ 20"
5 Feet	3'-0"	M	10"	#3 @ 15"	3—#4	2—#3	#3 @ 15"
		H	12"	#4 @ 12"*	3—#4	2—#3	#3 @ 15"
6 Feet	3'-7"	M	13"	#4 @ 15"	4—#4	2—#3	#4 @ 15"
		H	16"	#4 @ 8"*	4—#4	2—#3	#4 @ 15"

Design factors for the use of the table are as follows: Allowable stress in steel, f_s, is 20,000 psi; allowable compression in masonry, f_m, is 650 psi; allowable soil bearing is 2,000 psf.

 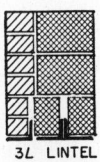 

2L LINTEL 8" WALL   3L LINTEL 12" WALL   I BEAM & PLATE 12" WALL   CHANNELS & LS 16" WALL

Fig. 19. Typical steel lintels

TERRA COTTA LINTEL

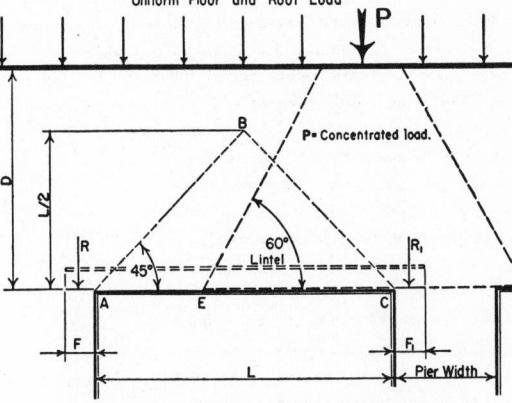

Fig. 20. Computing loads on a lintel

The back of the wall should be damp-proofed in the following manner: a ½-in. parge coat should be troweled onto the wall, beveled at the top, and coved out at the base. After at least seven days and when the surface has dried, the parge coat should be covered with a dampproofing consisting of one coat of creosote oil and two coats of coal-tar pitch, heated to flow freely but not above 350° F.

Backfill placed directly behind the wall should be of broken stone or gravel if the soil is too dense to provide rapid drainage.

LINTELS STEEL

A lintel is a horizontal member or beam placed over a wall opening to carry the superimposed weight above. Lintels may be of structural steel, reinforced masonry, or reinforced concrete. Masonry arches, widely used in the past, are rarely employed today.

Structural steel shapes are the most commonly used type of lintel. Steel angles are the simplest shapes and are suitable for spanning openings of moderate width and where the superimposed loads are not excessive. Wide openings or heavy loads may require steel channels, I-beams, or combinations of these with angles or plates (Fig. 19). The outstanding leg of the angle or plate should be at least 3½ in. to support a nominal 4-in. wythe of masonry. The specifications of the American Institute of Steel Construction require that the minimum thickness of such exterior members, if partially exposed to the weather, be $\frac{5}{16}$ in. for one- and two-story structures, and $\frac{7}{16}$ in. for stuctures over two stories in height. Table 8 gives allowable uniform loads on steel angles used as lintels. (For wide-flange sections, see load tables in "Structural Design—Steel: Beams.")

Load calculations: Determination of the load to be supported by the lintel is illustrated in Fig. 20. The weight of the masonry above the opening can be safely assumed as the weight of a triangular section whose height is one-half of the clear span of the opening. In other words, the lintel supports a triangle of masonry (ABC) in which the sides form a 45-deg angle with the base. Corbelling action of

the masonry above the top of the opening may be counted upon to support the weight of the masonry outside the triangle.

To the dead load of the wall must be added the uniform dead and live loads of floors and roofs that frame into the wall above the opening and below the apex of the 45-deg triangle. Any such load above the apex may be neglected. In Fig. 20, D is greater than L/2, so the floor load may be ignored. If, however, D were less than L/2, the uniform dead and live loads of the floor would be added to the uniform dead load of the triangular section of the wall (ABC).

Concentrated loads from beams, girders, or trusses framing into the wall above the opening must also be considered. Such

loads may be distributed over a wall length equal to the base of a triangle whose apex is at the point of load application and whose sides form an angle of 60 deg with the horizontal. In Fig. 20, the portion of the concentrated load P carried by the lintel would be distributed over the length EC.

Bearing area: In order to determine the over-all length of a steel lintel, the required bearing area must be determined. The stress in the masonry supporting each end of the lintel must not exceed the allowable unit stress for the type of masonry used. (See Table 3, Allowable compressive stresses in masonry.)

Deflection: Structural cracks in the masonry above the lintel are usually caused

Table 8.   Allowable uniformly distributed loads on steel angle lintels

Data from Steel Construction Manual *of the American Institute of Steel Construction. Loads shown below will result in deflections not exceeding 1/360 of the span.*

Angle size,* in.	Weight, lb per ft	Span length, ft									
		2	3	4	5	6	7	8	9	10	12
		Load, kips									
3½x3½x$\frac{5}{16}$	7.2	6.5	4.4	3.3	2.6	2.2	1.9	1.6			
4 x3½x$\frac{5}{16}$	7.7	8.7	5.8	4.3	3.5	2.9	2.5	2.2	1.9		
5 x3½x$\frac{5}{16}$	8.7	12.7	8.4	6.3	5.1	4.2	3.6	3.2	2.8	2.5	
5 x3½x$\frac{3}{8}$	10.4	15.3	10.2	7.7	6.1	5.1	4.4	3.8	3.4	3.1	
5 x3½x½	13.6	20.0	13.3	10.0	8.0	6.7	5.7	5.0	4.4	4.0	
		4	5	6	7	8	9	10	12	14	16
6x4x$\frac{3}{8}$	12.3	11.0	8.8	7.3	6.3	5.5	4.9	4.4	3.7		
7x4x$\frac{3}{8}$	13.6	14.7	11.7	9.8	8.4	7.3	6.5	5.9	4.9	4.2	
7x4x$\frac{7}{16}$	15.8	17.0	13.6	11.3	9.7	8.5	7.6	6.8	5.7	4.9	
8x4x$\frac{7}{16}$	17.2	22.0	17.6	14.7	12.6	11.0	9.8	8.8	7.3	6.3	5.5
8x4x½	19.6	25.0	20.0	16.7	14.3	12.5	11.1	10.0	8.3	7.1	6.2
8x4x$\frac{5}{8}$	24.2	30.0	24.0	20.0	17.5	15.3	13.6	12.3	10.2	8.8	7.7
9x4x½	21.3	31.0	25.0	21.0	17.7	15.5	13.8	12.4	10.3	9.0	7.8
9x4x$\frac{9}{16}$	23.8	35.0	28.0	23.0	19.8	17.3	15.4	13.8	11.5	9.9	8.7
9x4x$\frac{5}{8}$	26.3	38.0	31.0	26.0	22.0	19.1	17.0	15.3	12.8	10.9	9.6
9x4x$\frac{3}{4}$	31.2	45.0	36.0	30.0	26.0	23.0	20.0	18.1	15.1	13.0	11.3
9x4x$\frac{7}{8}$	36.1	52.0	42.0	35.0	30.0	26.0	23.0	21.0	17.4	14.9	13.1
9x4x1	40.8	59.0	47.0	39.0	33.0	29.0	26.0	23.0	19.6	16.8	14.7

* Dimensions given are vertical leg by horizontal leg by thickness.

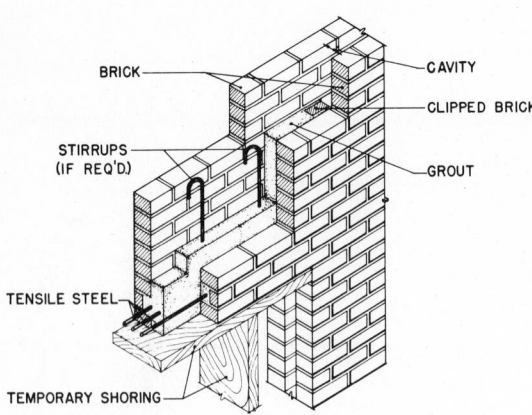

Fig. 21. Reinforced brick lintel in cavity wall

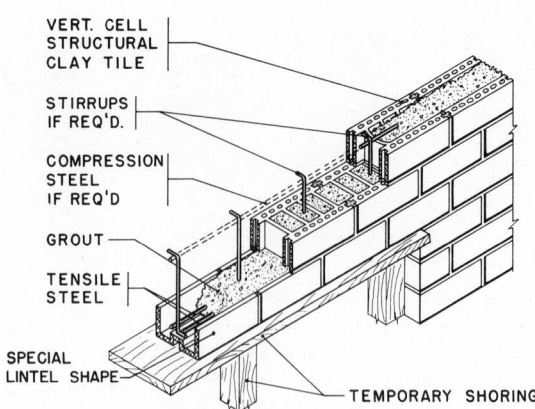

Fig. 22. Reinforced tile lintel in tile wall

by excessive deflection of the lintel. To avoid such cracks, deflection of the lintel should be limited to $1/360$ of the span.

Fireproofing: Code requirements for the fireproofing of lintels should be carefully checked and provided for in the design.

Flashing: The design of a steel lintel is not complete until provision has been made for adequate flashing. It is always good insurance to provide weep holes in the facing at the lowest point of the flashing so that any accumulated moisture can easily escape.

REINFORCED MASONRY LINTELS

Reinforced masonry lintels offer certain advantages over structural steel lintels: savings obtained by a reduction in the amount of steel used and by the elimination of painting, and additional safety through built-in fireproofing.

Reinforced brick and tile lintels are simply special applications of reinforced masonry, described on previous pages, and should be designed in accordance with the ASA Code for Reinforced Masonry (A41.2).

Materials

All standard clay masonry units—solid and hollow, brick and tile, glazed and unglazed—are adaptable to reinforced masonry design. In addition, special soffit shapes are often available for lintel design. Mortar must be of portland cement, lime, and sand, conforming to ASTM Specification C270, Type M or S. The use of masonry cements in mortar for reinforced masonry is not allowed. Grout may be Type MG, which is generally used on jobs requiring a small amount of reinforced masonry, or Type PG, which is more economical for large jobs.

Load

Determination of the load to be supported by the lintel is the same as that described on the previous page for steel lintels.

Design

Reinforced masonry lintels are usually designed as simple beams. In short or deep lintels, there is little likelihood of cracking due to deflection or end rotation. In relatively long, shallow, or heavily loaded lintels, there is a possibility of cracking, and in such cases it may be advisable to use top, or negative, steel. For such steel to be effective it must be continuous with column steel or must extend into the wall beyond the jamb. Often the easiest solution is to provide a continuous bond beam around the building.

Shear: The maximum allowable shear in lintels with no web reinforcement is 50 psi. If the shearing stress is above 50 psi, but less than 150 psi, stirrups are required. Shearing stress in a lintel must never exceed 150 psi.

Bond: The perimeter of tension steel must be sufficient to ensure that bond stress does not exceed the allowable. Tension steel should extend a minimum of 4 in. beyond the face of the supports. Special anchorage may be accomplished by hooking the bars.

Positioning of steel: There must be at least a ¼-in. clearance between steel reinforcement and adjacent masonry, except that ¼-in. bars may be placed in ½-in. mortar joints and No. 6 gage wire or smaller may be placed in ⅜-in. mortar joints.

Parallel bars for main reinforcing should have a clearance of one diameter between bars.

Tabular data

Tables 9 to 17 give resisting moments and shears for various brick and tile lintel sections. The tables have been compiled for modular units with ½-in. mortar joints, as indicated in the figures accompanying

the tables. The tables, therefore, are conservative for lintels of slightly larger dimensions. Other assumptions, under which the tabulated values have been compiled, are given in Fig. 23. For masonry having an ultimate compressive strength, f_m', less than 2,000 psi, these tables are not valid. For masonry of greater compressive strength, the tables are conservative.

Resisting moments tabulated in the tables are those determined by masonry or by reinforcing steel, whichever governs design. Where resisting moments are governed by the steel, values are in bold face type.

Tabulated are two values of resisting shears, one as diagonal tension in the masonry, V_m, and another as bond on the tensile steel, V_o. For lintels in which no stirrups are provided, the smaller resisting shear governs. V_m is based upon an allowable working stress in diagonal tension of 50 psi. The allowable working stress for shear as diagonal tension, when web reinforcement is provided, is 150 psi. Accordingly, resisting shears could have values 3 times as great as those indicated in column V_m, if stirrups are provided. A glance at the table will indicate that, before such high shearing stresses are reached, bond may govern design. In Tables 9 and 10, bond governs all shear values and, therefore, values of V_m are not given.

For brick laid 3 courses to 8 in. vertically, the effective depth may be expressed in courses (for example, $2c = 2$ courses) for purposes of selecting values from the tables. Through the use of this method, it becomes unnecessary to calculate the effective depth in inches in order to use the tables. The effective depths listed in the tables have been rounded off to the nearest 0.1 in.

The effective depth d, in Tables 9 and 10, is based upon a ¼-in. reinforcement centered within mortar joints. In Tables 11

DESIGN ASSUMPTIONS

$f'_m = 2000$ psi.

$f_s = 20,000$ psi.

$v = 50$ psi. (no stirrups)

$v = 150$ psi. (stirrups)

$u = 80$ psi. (plain bars)

$u = 160$ psi. (deformed bars)

$n = 15$

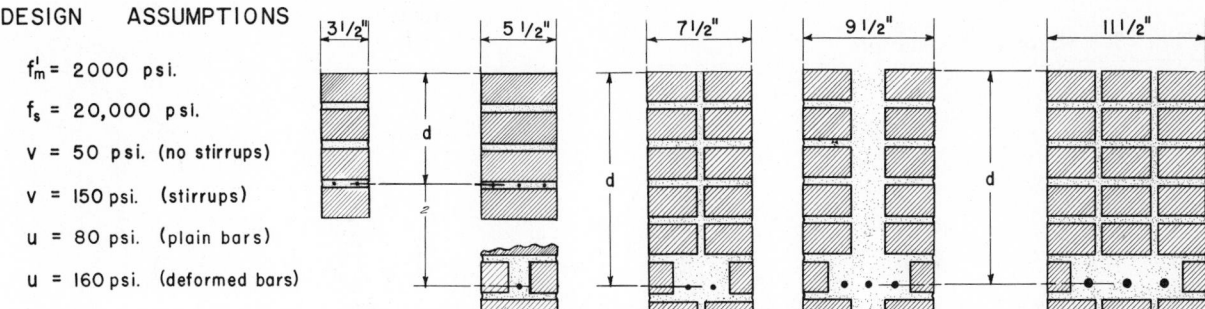

Fig. 23. Typical sections, reinforced brick lintels

Table 9. Nominal 4-in. lintels

Reinforcing in bed joint.

Depth	d = 5.1" (2c)		d = 7.8" (3c)		d = 10.5" (4c)	
Reinf.	M	V_o	M	V_o	M	V_o
1—#2	390	220	605	455	820	620
2—#2	750	430	1180	890	1600	1210

Table 10. Nominal 6-in. lintels

Reinforcing in bed joint.

Depth	d = 5.1" (2c)		d = 7.8" (3c)		d = 10.5" (4c)		d = 13.1" (5c)		d = 15.8" (6c)	
Reinf.	M	V_o	M	V_o	M	V_o	M	V_o	M	V_o
2—#2	780	440	1200	905	1630	1230	2060	1550	2490	1400
3—#2	1140	645	1770	1340	2410	1820	3040	2290	3670	2080

Table 11. Nominal 6-in. lintels

Reinforcing in grout space.

Depth	d = 4.6" (2c)			d = 7.3" (3c)			d = 10.0" (4c)			d = 12.6" (5c)			d = 15.3" (6c)			d = 18.0 (7c)		
Reinf.	M	V_m	V_o	M	V_m	V_o	M	V_m	V_o	M	V_m	V_o	M	V_m	V_o	M	V_m	V_o
1—#3	770	*	790	1230	*	1260	1700	*	1730	2170	*	2230	2640	*	2720	3120	*	3200
1—#4	1060	*	1010	2160	*	1630	3000	*	2260	3840	*	2890	4700	*	3550	5530	*	4180
1—#5	1190	1060	1210	2600	1730	1970	4400	2410	2750	5810	3090	3540	7120	3800	4330	8410	4480	5120

Table 12. Nominal 8-in. lintels

Depth	d = 4.6" (2c)			d = 7.3" (3c)			d = 10.0" (4c)			d = 12.6" (5c)			d = 15.3" (6c)			d = 18.0" (7c)		
Reinf.	M	V_m	V_o	M	V_m	V_o	M	V_m	V_o	M	V_m	V_o	M	V_m	V_o	M	V_m	V_o
2—#3	1380	1540	1550	2420	2480	2500	3350	3420	3440	4280	4380	4400	5220	5340	5360	6160	6300	6340
3—#3	1570	1500	2260	3360	2430	3660	4930	3360	5070	6310	4310	6490	7690	5250	7920	9100	6210	9360
2—#4	1630	1470	1970	3530	2380	3200	5890	3310	4450	7560	4250	5700	9230	5190	6960	10900	6140	8240
2—#5	1800	1410	2350	4000	2300	3860	6820	3210	5380	10170	4140	6930	13970	5070	8500	16600	6010	10100
2—#6	1910	1350	2720	4350	2230	4480	7510	3120	6290	11300	4040	8110	15600	4950	9950	20500	5880	11800

Table 13. Nominal 10-in. lintels

Depth	d = 7.3" (3c)			d = 10.0" (4c)			d = 12.5" (5c)			d = 15.3" (6c)			d = 18.0" (7c)			d = 20.6" (8c)		
Reinf.	M	V_m	V_o	M	V_m	V_o	M	V_m	V_o	M	V_m	V_o	M	V_m	V_o	M	V_m	V_o
2—#3	2450	*	2510	3380	*	3470	4310	*	4430	5260	*	5400	6200	*	6370	7150	*	7350
3—#3	3600	3110	3710	4980	4300	5120	6380	5510	6560	7780	6720	8020	9190	7930	9440	10600	9150	10900
2—#4	4130	3060	3230	5950	4240	4480	7630	5440	5760	9320	6640	7020	11000	7850	8300	12700	9060	9580
3—#4	4630	2990	4750	7960	4160	6610	11200	5340	8480	13700	6530	10400	16300	7730	12300	18800	8930	14200
2—#5	4720	2950	3900	7980	4120	5460	11500	5300	7010	14100	6490	8590	16700	7680	10200	19300	8890	11800
2—#6	5170	2870	4540	8850	4020	6380	13300	5180	8220	18300	6350	10100	23300	7540	12000	26900	8730	13900
3—#5	5320	2880	5710	9110	4030	8000	13700	5190	10300	18800	6360	12600	24600	7540	15000	28500	8720	17300
2—#7	5530	2780	5150	9600	3910	7250	14500	5060	9380	20200	6220	11500	26500	7400	13700	33400	8560	15900
3—#6	5750	2790	6660	9980	3910	9310	15100	5060	12000	21000	6210	14800	27500	7380	17600	34800	8550	20400

Table 14. Nominal 12-in. lintels

Depth	d = 10.0" (4c)			d = 12.6" (5c)			d = 15.3" (6c)			d = 18.0" (7c)			d = 20.6" (8c)			d = 23.3" (9c)		
Reinf.	M	V_m	V_o	M	V_m	V_o	M	V_m	V_o	M	V_m	V_o	M	V_m	V_o	M	V_m	V_o
2—#4	5990	*	4530	7680	*	5810	9380	*	7070	11100	*	8370	12800	*	9650	14500	*	10900
3—#4	8840	5080	6670	11300	6520	8540	13800	7970	10400	16400	9420	12400	18900	10900	14300	21500	12400	16200
2—#5	9060	5040	5500	11600	6480	7070	14200	7920	8660	16800	9370	10200	19500	10800	11800	22100	12300	13400
4—#4	9800	5010	8750	14800	6430	11200	18200	7870	13800	21600	9310	16300	25000	10800	18800	28300	12200	21400
2—#6	10100	4920	6450	15000	6330	8300	19800	7770	10200	23500	9210	12100	27100	10600	14000	30800	12100	15900
3—#5	10400	4940	8080	15500	6350	10400	21000	7780	12800	24900	9220	15100	28700	10700	17500	32600	12100	19800
2—#7	11000	4800	7340	16500	6190	9470	23000	7610	11600	30100	9030	13800	36400	10500	16000	41400	11900	18200
4—#5	11300	4850	10600	17000	6250	13600	23500	7670	16800	30700	9090	19900	37800	10500	23000	43000	12000	26100
3—#6	11400	4800	9440	17200	6200	12200	23800	7600	14900	31200	9020	17700	39400	10400	20500	45500	11900	23400
4—#6	12400	4710	12300	18800	6090	16000	26100	7480	19600	34300	8880	23300	43400	10300	27000	53200	11700	30700
3—#7	12400	4670	10700	18800	6040	13900	26200	7430	17100	34500	8840	20300	43500	10300	23500	53300	11700	26800
4—#7	13300	4590	14000	20300	5940	18200	28400	7310	22400	37500	8690	26600	47600	10100	30900	58600	11500	35100

Table 15. Nominal 4-in. lintels

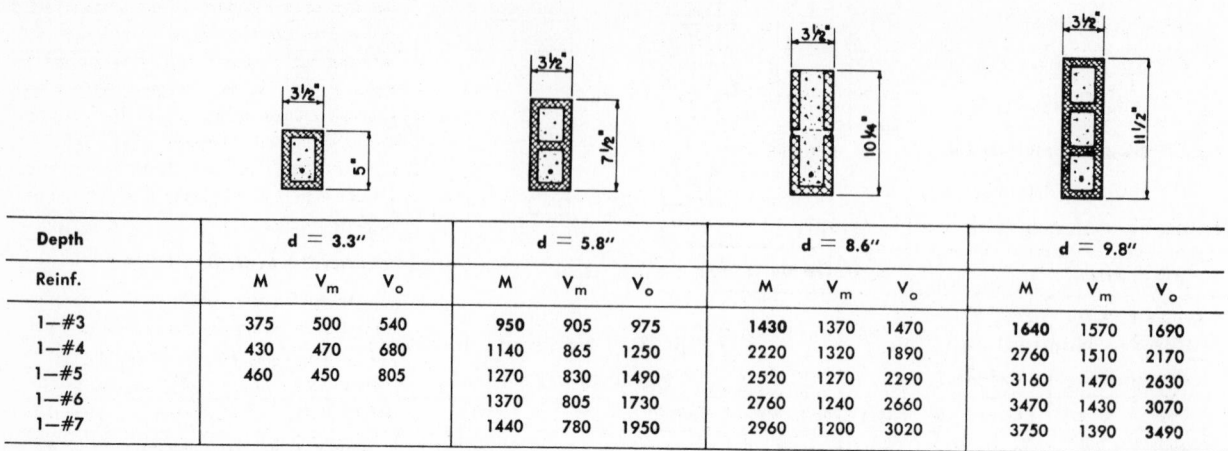

Depth	d = 3.3″			d = 5.8″			d = 8.6″			d = 9.8″		
Reinf.	M	V_m	V_o	M	V_m	V_o	M	V_m	V_o	M	V_m	V_o
1—#3	375	500	540	950	905	975	1430	1370	1470	1640	1570	1690
1—#4	430	470	680	1140	865	1250	2220	1320	1890	2760	1510	2170
1—#5	460	450	805	1270	830	1490	2520	1270	2290	3160	1470	2630
1—#6				1370	805	1730	2760	1240	2660	3470	1430	3070
1—#7				1440	780	1950	2960	1200	3020	3750	1390	3490

Table 16. Nominal 6-in. lintels

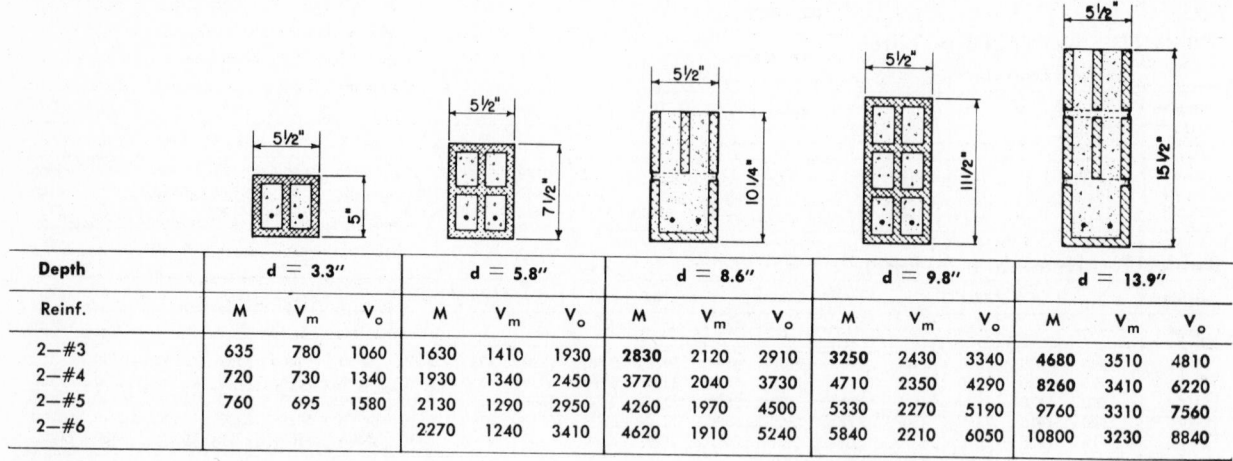

Depth	d = 3.3″			d = 5.8″			d = 8.6″			d = 9.8″			d = 13.9″		
Reinf.	M	V_m	V_o	M	V_m	V_o	M	V_m	V_o	M	V_m	V_o	M	V_m	V_o
2—#3	635	780	1060	1630	1410	1930	**2830**	2120	2910	**3250**	2430	3340	**4680**	3510	4810
2—#4	720	730	1340	1930	1340	2450	3770	2040	3730	4710	2350	4290	**8260**	3410	6220
2—#5	760	695	1580	2130	1290	2950	4260	1970	4500	5330	2270	5190	9760	3310	7560
2—#6				2270	1240	3410	4620	1910	5240	5840	2210	6050	10800	3230	8840

Table 17. Nominal 8-in. lintels

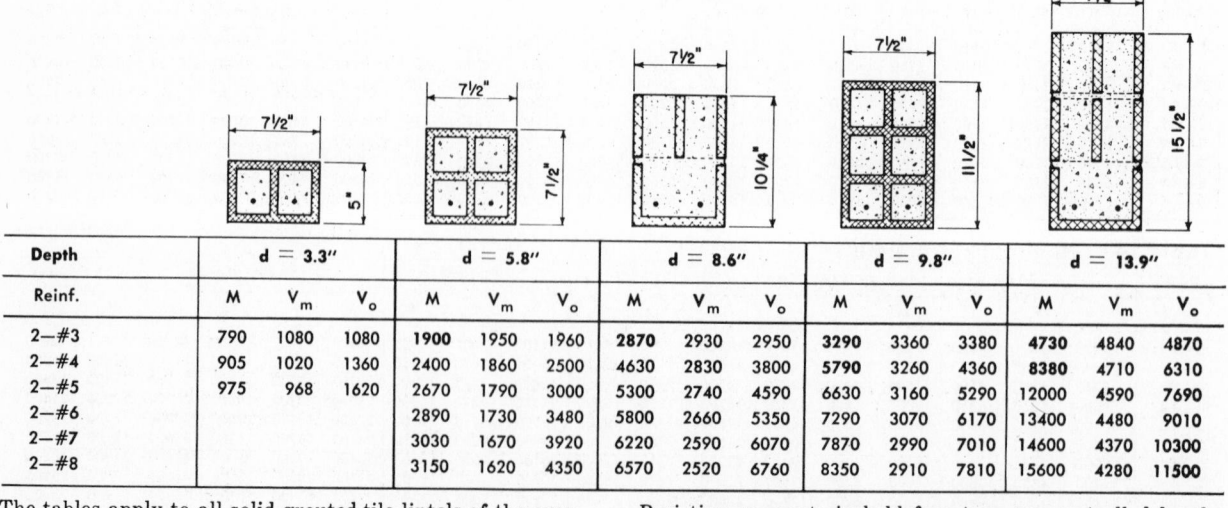

Depth	d = 3.3″			d = 5.8″			d = 8.6″			d = 9.8″			d = 13.9″		
Reinf.	M	V_m	V_o	M	V_m	V_o	M	V_m	V_o	M	V_m	V_o	M	V_m	V_o
2—#3	790	1080	1080	**1900**	1950	1960	**2870**	2930	2950	**3290**	3360	3380	**4730**	4840	4870
2—#4	905	1020	1360	2400	1860	2500	4630	2830	3800	5790	3260	4360	**8380**	4710	6310
2—#5	975	968	1620	2670	1790	3000	5300	2740	4590	6630	3160	5290	12000	4590	7690
2—#6				2890	1730	3480	5800	2660	5350	7290	3070	6170	13400	4480	9010
2—#7				3030	1670	3920	6220	2590	6070	7870	2990	7010	14600	4370	10300
2—#8				3150	1620	4350	6570	2520	6760	8350	2910	7810	15600	4280	11500

The tables apply to all solid grouted tile lintels of the overall dimensions shown.

Resisting moments are given in foot-pounds.

Resisting moments in bold face type are controlled by the steel; others are controlled by the masonry.

Resisting shears are given in pounds.

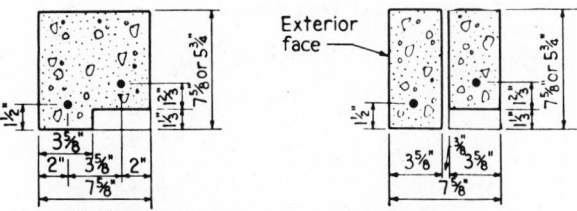

Fig. 24. One-piece lintel (see Table 18) and split lintel (see Table 19)

Table 18. Lintels with wall load only

| Size of lintel | | Clear span of lintel ft. | Bottom reinforcement | |
Height in.	Width in.		No. bars	Size of bars
5¾	7⅝	Up to 7	2	⅜-in. round deformed
5¾	7⅝	7 to 8	2	⅝-in. round deformed
7⅝	7⅝	Up to 8	2	⅜-in. round deformed
7⅝	7⅝	8 to 9	2	½-in. round deformed
7⅝	7⅝	9 to 10	2	⅝-in. round deformed

Table 19. Split lintels with wall load only

| Size of lintel | | Clear span of lintel ft. | Bottom reinforcement | |
Height in.	Width in.		No. bars	Size of bars
5¾	3⅝	Up to 7	1	⅜-in. round deformed
5¾	3⅝	7 to 8	1	⅝-in. round deformed
7⅝	3⅝	Up to 8	1	⅜-in. round deformed
7⅝	3⅝	8 to 9	1	½-in. round deformed
7⅝	3⅝	9 to 10	1	⅝-in. round deformed

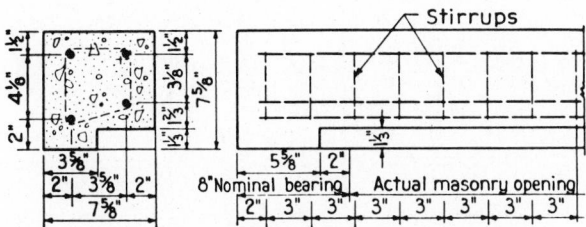

Fig. 25. One-piece lintel with stirrups (see Table 20)

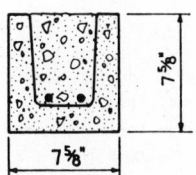

Fig. 26. Lintel block

through 14, the effective depths are based upon reinforcement placed in grout with a ½-in. clearance between the steel and the top of the adjacent unit immediately below. True effective depth, therefore, varies with the bar diameter. This variation, however, is small in the range of bar sizes chosen for these tables. The effective depths shown are listed primarily to aid the designer when using units that are not laid 3 courses to 8 in. vertically (such as roman brick or oversize brick).

REINFORCED CONCRETE LINTELS

The tables and illustrations shown on this page are from *Concrete Masonry Handbook*, published by the Portland Cement Association.

Design data

Design data for one-piece and split (two-piece) lintels, supporting wall loads only, are shown in Fig. 24 and Tables 18 and 19. Data for lintels that support both wall and floor loads are shown in Fig. 25 and Table 20. All designs are based on concrete having an ultimate strength of 2,000 psi.

Split lintels should never be used to support combined wall and floor loads, because it is difficult to design the inner section for the same deflection as the outer section, which carries wall loads only. Differences in deflection of the two sections would probably result in cracking of the masonry wall. Split lintels are light in weight and easy to handle. The air space between the sections provides some insulation.

Reinforced concrete lintels should have a minimum bearing area of at least 8 in. at each end. Larger bearing areas are required for lintels that have long spans or carry heavy loads. All but short simple lintels act as reinforced concrete beams and should be designed by an engineer.

In locations where it is desirable that lintels have a surface texture matching that of the concrete masonry wall, special cast-in-place or precast lintels can be made by using channel-shaped lintel block (Fig. 26).

Table 20. Lintels with wall and floor loads

Floor load is assumed to be 85 psf with 20-ft span.

| Size of lintel | | Clear span of lintel ft. | Reinforcement | | Web reinforcement No. 6 gage wire stirrups. Spacings from end of lintel—both ends the same |
Height in.	Width in.		Top	Bottom	
7⅝	7⅝	3	None	2—½-in. round	No stirrups required
7⅝	7⅝	4	None	2—¾-in. round	3 stirrups, Sp.: 2, 3, 3 in.
7⅝	7⅝	5	2—⅜-in. round	2—⅞-in. round	5 stirrups, Sp.: 2, 3, 3, 3 in.
7⅝	7⅝	6	2—½-in. round	2—⅞-in. round	6 stirrups, Sp.: 2, 3, 3, 3, 3, 3 in.
7⅝	7⅝	7	2— 1-in. round	2— 1-in. round	9 stirrups, Sp.: 2, 2, 3, 3, 3, 3, 3, 3, 3 in.

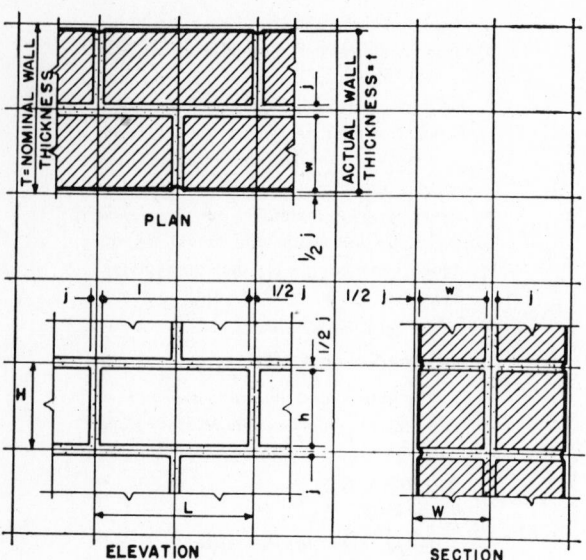

Fig. 1. Modular masonry dimensions

Capital letters signify nominal dimensions. Lower-case letters signify standard or specified dimensions. Thickness of standard mortar joint is indicated by "j." Actual unit dimensions may vary from standard or specified dimensions by not more than the permissible tolerances for variations of dimensions.

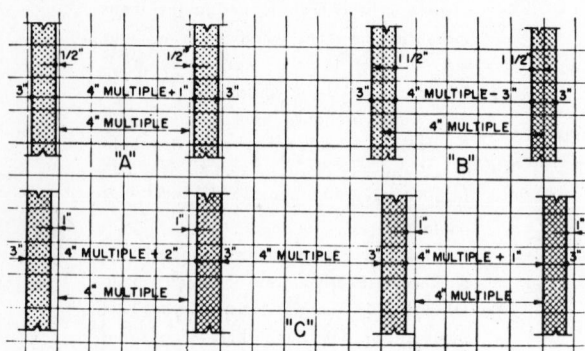

Fig. 2. Grid locations of masonry walls

Table 1. Nominal modular sizes of brick (in inches)

Thickness	Face Dimension in Wall	
	Height	Length
4	2	12
4	$2\frac{2}{3}$	8 or 12
4	4	8 or 12
4	$5\frac{1}{3}$	8 or 12

Table 2. Nominal modular sizes of structural clay load-bearing backup tile (in inches)

Thickness	Face Dimension in Wall	
	Height	Length
4	$5\frac{1}{3}$	12
4	8	8 or 12
4	$10\frac{2}{3}$	12
6	$5\frac{1}{3}$	12
6	8	12 [1]
6	$10\frac{2}{3}$	12
8	$5\frac{1}{3}$	12 [1]
8	8	8 or 12 [1]
8	$10\frac{2}{3}$	12

[1] Includes stretcher and header units.

Data and illustrations on this and the following three pages have been derived from *Technical Notes on Brick and Tile Construction*, published by the Structural Clay Products Institute.

UNIT DIMENSIONS

Modular clay masonry units are designated by nominal dimensions, equal to the standard or actual dimension plus the thickness of the mortar joint with which the unit is designed to be laid, as illustrated in Fig. 1. For example, a modular unit whose nominal length is 12 in. would actually be 11½ in. if the unit were designed to be laid with a ½-in. mortar joint, or 11⅝ in. if designed for a ⅜-in. joint.

The standard mortar joint thicknesses for modular clay masonry units are ¼ in. for glazed brick and tile, ⅜ in. or ½ in. for facing brick and unglazed facing tile, and ½ in. for building brick and structural tile.

Sizes of brick: Table 1 lists the sizes of modular brick currently available. However, since few manufacturers produce *all* the sizes listed, the purchaser should ascertain the sizes available in any locality before proceeding with the design.

Sizes of structural clay tile: Modular or nominal sizes of structural clay tile are given in Tables 2, 3, and 4. Only the dimensions of the full-size stretcher units are shown. Half lengths and half heights, as well as corner and jamb units, are available in most series for bonding. Here also, few if any manufacturers will produce *all* of the sizes listed.

Sizes of partition tile: No modular standards have as yet been established for sizes of partition tile by the American Standards Association.

MODULAR DETAILS (see section on *Modular coordination*)

Modular details show the relation of the building parts to the 4-in. grid, and thus their relation to one another. This rela-

Table 3. Nominal modular sizes of structural clay load-bearing wall tile (in inches)

Thickness	Face Dimension in Wall	
	Height	Length
4	5⅓	12
4	8	8 or 12
4	12	12 [1]
6	5⅓	12
6	12	12 [1]
8	5⅓	12
8	8	8, 12 or 16
8	12	12 [1]
10	5⅓	12
10	8	12
10	12	12 [1]
12	12	12 [1]

[1] Partition tile.

Table 4. Nominal modular sizes of structural clay facing tile (in inches)

Thickness	Face Dimension in Wall	
	Height	Length
2, 4, 6 and 8	4	8 and 12
2, 4, 6 and 8	5⅓	8 and 12
2, 4, 6 and 8	8	12 and 16 [1]

[1] 16-in. lengths in 2 and 4 in. thicknesses only.

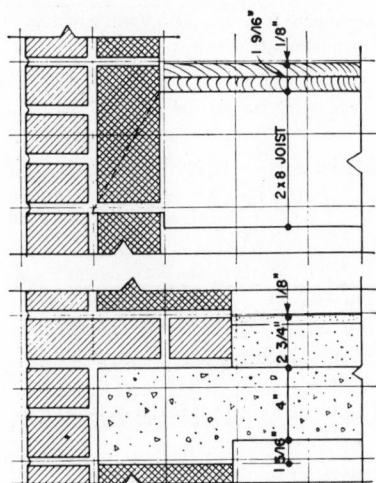

Fig. 3. Modular masonry walls with two types of floor construction

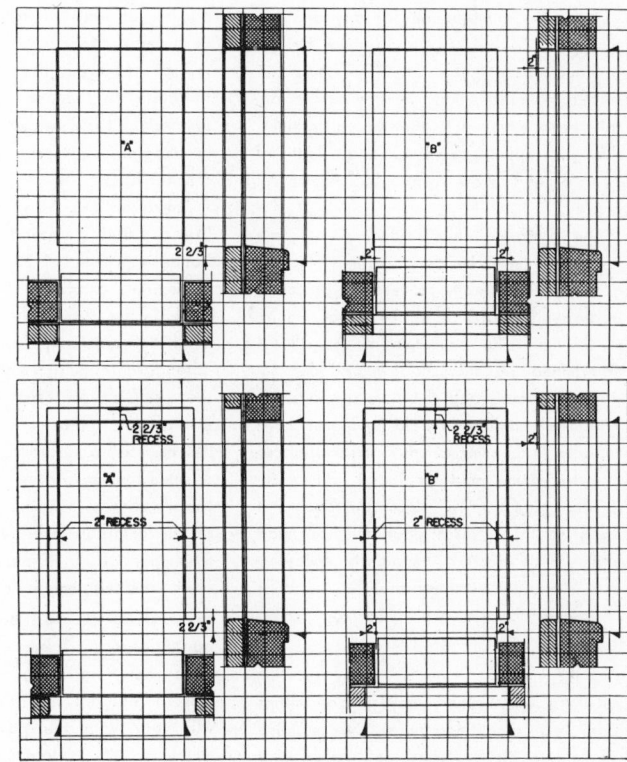

Fig. 4. Grid position of openings

tionship is shown by reference dimensions to grid lines on the large-scale details. In order to correlate building layouts with details, layout dimensions must maintain the grid positions of the modular details. For this reason, the selection of grid locations of critical parts of the structure, such as walls and floors, is one of the first steps to be taken in the development of a modular design.

Grid locations of masonry walls: Alternate grid locations for walls are shown in Fig. 2. Symmetrical grid positions for walls (either centered between or on grid lines) have certain fundamental advantages. In details "A" and "B," the difference between grid dimensions and actual dimensions is a single constant. In detail "C," however, there are three alternate values for this difference and they must be identified on the plans.

Grid location of floors: The surface of finished floors bearing on masonry walls should be placed ⅛ in. below the grid line in order to maintain a constant relation between the floor masonry openings for exterior doors. Figure 3 illustrates modular details of two types of floor construction and their relationship to the grid and the exterior masonry wall.

Grid position of openings: Opening details involve the coordination of many products, such as modular masonry (both facing and backup), windows, doors, glass block, and trim. Because of the interchangeability provided by coordination, the jamb, head, and sill details are each referenced to the standard grid, permitting them to be drawn as separate modular

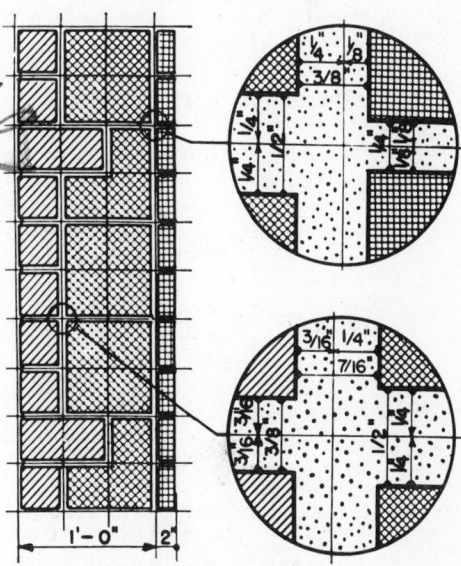

Fig. 5. Coordination of modular masonry products

Exterior facing brick are shown with ⅜-in. joints, backed up with structural clay tile with ½-in. joints. Inside facing of glazed-tile soaps is laid with ¼-in. joints.

details. The combination for any one job may then be selected and shown by the architect. Since it is essential for their correct combination that these separate details be referenced to the same grid lines, the grid opening is used and identified by the half-arrow symbol as shown in Fig. 4.

The conformation of openings at jamb and head may be flush or may include a recess. The depth of recesses at jambs is always 2 in., and, at the head, 1⅓ in. or 2⅔ in. The conformation at sills is determined by the window or door installation detail and the type of sill used. Windows and doors should be placed horizontally in a symmetrical grid position so that the same modular detail will apply to each jamb. This placement does not apply to the vertical position since head and sill details are essentially different.

It is usually essential that the head of an opening coincide with a horizontal mortar joint.

Taking off masonry material quantities is greatly simplified under the modular system. No matter what the mortar joint thickness, the number of modular units of any given size required per square foot of wall will be the same. Under the non-modular system, the number of brick required per square foot varies with the joint thickness. Under the modular system there are only three standard joint thicknesses: ¼ in. for glazed brick and tile, ⅜ in. or ½ in. for facing brick and unglazed facing tile, and ½ in. for building brick and structural tile.

ESTIMATING METHODS

Multiply the net wall areas (gross areas less the areas of all openings) by the number of brick or tile required per square foot. The tables that follow contain the

number of units of various sizes required per square foot and the cubic feet of mortar required for joints of different thickness. To the net quantity of masonry units should be added an allowance for breakage: 2 per cent for tile and 5 per cent for brick.

The quantities shown in Table 5 are for brick laid in running bond. For other bonds in which full headers are used, the correction factors in Table 7 must be added. The 2⅔ by 4 by 8-in. size of brick is commonly referred to as the "Standard Modular" size. In Table 6, only the two sizes of brick that are used for backup are shown. Here also, the quantities must be adjusted for the proper bond selected, using Table 7. The correction factors shown in Table 7 must be *added* to the facing-brick quantities and *deducted* from the backup. If backup tile are to be used, the equivalent quantities of brick to be deducted must be converted to tile quantities, using Table 8.

As shown in Table 9, the quantity of mortar required for any one size of tile will vary with the position of the cells when the tile is laid in the wall. A tile laid with its cells in a horizontal position will require more mortar than one laid with its cells in a vertical position.

Select- and standard-quality ceramic-glaze and salt-glaze facing tile (Table 10) are designed for use with ¼-in. mortar joints; smooth, unglazed facing tile is designed for use with either ¼-in. or ⅜-in. mortar joints.

The sizes of clay flue linings shown in Table 11 are those adopted by the American Standards Association. These dimensions are *nominal* outside dimensions; the *actual* outside dimensions are ½ in. less in both directions. The standard lengths are always 24 in.

Three types of mortar are shown in Table 12 and may be described as follows:

Type A: Proportions by volume are 1 part portland cement, ¼ part hydrated lime or lime putty, and 3 parts sand. Type A is a high-strength mortar suitable for general use and recommended specifically for masonry below grade and in contact with earth, and for reinforced brick masonry. (Type A corresponds to ASTM Type M.)

Type B: Proportions by volume are 1 part portland cement, 1 part hydrated lime or lime putty, and 6 parts sand. Type B is a medium-strength mortar suitable for general use in exposed masonry above grade. (Type B corresponds to ASTM Type N.)

Type C: Proportions by volume are 1 part portland cement, 2 parts hydrated lime or lime putty, and 9 parts sand. Type C is a low-strength mortar suitable for nonloadbearing walls. It may also be used for loadbearing construction where the masonry will not be subjected to freezing and thawing in the presence of excessive moisture, and to compressive stresses exceeding 100 psi. (Type C corresponds to ASTM Type O.)

In Table 12, cement is figured on the basis of one 94-lb bag per cu ft. Hydrated lime is figured at 40 lb per cu ft and 50 lb to the bag. Sand is based on average conditions, in which 1 cu ft of loose, damp sand, as normally used in construction, contains approximately 80 lb of dry sand. This table assumes the use of hydrated lime in its dry form. If lime putty is used, 25 lb of pulverized quicklime, 28.5 lb of lump quicklime, or 43.5 lb of hydrated lime are required to produce 1 cu ft of lime putty.

Example: Estimate the quantity of standard modular brick and mortar required in 800 sq ft of a 12-in. solid brick wall with 4 in. of facing brick laid with ⅜-in. joints and 8 in. of backup brick laid with ½-in. joints. The wall will be laid in common bond with continuous full headers

Table 5. Four-inch brick facing walls in running bond

Quantities shown are for walls with full bed and head joints.

NOMINAL SIZE OF BRICK*	NUMBER OF BRICK PER SQ FT OF WALL..	CU FT OF MORTAR PER SQ FT OF WALL**		CU FT OF MORTAR PER 1000 BRICK**	
		3/8"JOINT	1/2" JOINT	3/8"JOINT	1/2"JOINT
2 2/3 x 4 x 8	6.75	0.0608	0.0765	8.90	11.30
2 2/3 x 4 x 12	4.50	0.0535	0.071	11.90	15.80
2 x 4 x 12	6.00	0.0676	0.09	1130	15.00
4 x 4 x 8	4.50	0.0432	0.0575	960	12.80
4 x 4 x 12	3.00	0.039	0.052	1300	17.30

*Actual size plus thickness of one joint
**10% added for waste

Table 6. Eight- and twelve-inch brick backup walls in running bond

Quantities shown are for walls with full bed, head, and collar joints.

NOMINAL SIZE OF BRICK*	8" WALL			12"WALL		
	NUMBER OF BRICK	CU FT OF MORTAR**		NUMBER OF BRICK	CU FT OF MORTAR**	
		3/8"JOINT	1/2"JOINT		3/8"JOINT	1/2"JOINT
2 2/3 x 4 x 8	13.50	01544	01988	2025	0.2489	0.3211
4 x 4 x 8	9.00	0.1210	0.1610	13.50	0.1984	0.2641

* Actual size plus thickness of one joint
**10% added for waste
Mortar for interior vertical joints (parging or plastering) per 100 sq ft of joint.
3.13 cu ft. ——— 3/8" joint.
3.65 cu ft. ——— 7/16" joint.
4.17 cu ft. ——— 1/2" joint.

Data and illustrations on this and the following pages have been derived from *Technical Notes on Brick and Tile Construction*, published by the Structural Clay Products Institute.

Table 7. Correction factors for 4-in. wall quantities

Correction factors should be applied to 4-in. wall quantities in Table 1 for estimating the required number of facing brick in various bonds.

TYPE OF BOND	CORRECTION FACTOR
Common, with full header every 5th course....	20.0% or 1/5
Common, with full header every 6th course....	16.7% or 1/6
Common, with full header every 7th course....	14.3% or 1/7
English, alternate courses full headers....	50.0% or 1/2
English or Dutch, with full headers every 6th course and blind headers in intermediate courses....	16.7% or 1/6
Flemish, with alternate stretchers and full headers every course..	33.3% or 1/3
Flemish, with stretchers and full headers every 6th course, intermediate courses with blind headers....	5.6% or 1/18
Flemish cross, alternate courses with stretchers and headers....	16.7% or 1/6
Double header and stretcher every 6th course....	8.3% or 1/12
Double header and stretcher every 5th course....	10.0% or 1/10

Table 8. Brick and tile equivalents

NOMINAL SIZE OF TILE	EQUIVALENT BRICK UNITS	
	2 2/3 x 4 x 8	4 x 4 x 8
4 x 4 x 12	2.25	1.50
4 x 5 1/3 x 12	3.00	2.00
4 x 8 x 12	4.50	3.00
8 x 4 x 12	4.50	3.00
8 x 5 1/3 x 12	6.00	4.00
8 x 8 x 12	9.00	6.00
12 x 12 x 12	20.25	13.50
4 x 12 x 12	6.75	4.50

Table 9. Structural clay tile walls

NOMINAL SIZE OF TILE*	POSITION OF CELLS WHEN LAID	BED JOINT	TILE PER SQ. FT. OF WALL	CU. FT. OF MORTAR**			
				SQ. FT. OF WALL		1000 UNITS	
				3/8"JOINT	1/2"JOINT	3/8"JOINT	1/2"JOINT
4x4x12	Horizontal	Full	3.00	0.0344	0.0443	11.5	14.8
4x4x12	Vertical		3.00	0.0243	0.0315	8.1	10.5
4x51/3x12	Horizontal	Full	2.25	0.0267	0.0344	11.9	15.3
4x51/3x12	Vertical		2.25	0.0211	0.0273	9.4	12.1
4x8x12	Horizontal	Full	1.50	0.01897	0.0245	12.7	16.4
4x8x12	Vertical		1.50	0.0179	0.0231	11.9	15.4
4x12x12	Horizontal	Full	1.00	0.0149	0.0199	14.9	19.9
4x12x12	Vertical		1.00	0.0168	0.0222	16.8	22.2
8x4x12	Horizontal	Full	3.00	0.0688	0.0901	22.9	30.0
8x4x12	Horizontal	Divided	3.00	0.0505	0.0672	16.8	22.4
8x4x12	Vertical		3.00	0.0254	0.0333	8.5	11.1
8x51/3x12	Horizontal	Full	2.25	0.0525	0.0688	23.3	30.6
8x51/3x12	Horizontal	Divided	2.25	0.0388	0.0516	17.2	22.9
8x51/3x12	Vertical		2.25	0.0222	0.0292	9.9	13.0
8x8x12	Horizontal	Full	1.50	0.0362	0.0474	24.1	31.6
8x8x12	Horizontal	Divided	1.50	0.0271	0.0356	18.0	24.0
8x8x12	Vertical		1.50	0.0189	0.0258	12.6	17.2
12x12x12	Horizontal	Full	1.00	0.0367	0.0485	36.7	48.5
12x12x12	Vertical		1.00	0.0168	0.0223	16.8	22.3

*Actual size plus thickness of one joint.
**10% added to side construction and 20% to end construction tile for waste.

Table 10. Four-inch structural clay facing-tile walls in running bond

Quantities shown are for walls with full bed joints and, for series 4S, full head joints.

NOMINAL FACE SIZE OF TILE*	NUMBER OF TILE PER SQ.FT. OF WALL AREA	CU. FT. OF MORTAR**			
		PER. SQ. FT. OF WALL		PER. 1000 UNITS	
		1/4"JOINT	3/8"JOINT	1/4"JOINT	3/8"JOINT
4S 2 2/3 x 8	6.75	0.042	0.0608	6.2	8.9
4D 5 1/3 x 8	3.375	0.0206	0.0297	6.1	8.8
6T 5 1/3 x 12	2.25	0.0193	0.0267	8.5	11.9
8W 8 x 16	1.125	0.0131	0.019	11.6	16.9

*Actual size plus thickness of one joint.
**10% added for waste.

Table 11. Freestanding chimneys of various sizes

Brick and mortar quantities are listed per foot of height of freestanding chimneys.

SIZE OF FLUE LINING*	ONE WYTHE OF BRICK			TWO WYTHES OF BRICK		
	BRICK	CU.FT. OF MORTAR**		BRICK	CU.FT. OF MORTAR**	
		3/8"JOINT	1/2"JOINT		3/8"JOINT	1/2"JOINT
4 x 8	22.5	0.29	0.344	63.0	0.86	1.01
4 x 12	27.0	0.362	0.427	72.0	1.00	1.18
4 x 16	31.5	0.433	0.509	85.5	1.19	1.39
8 x 8	27.0	0.362	0.427	72.0	1.00	1.18
8 x 12	31.5	0.433	0.509	85.5	1.19	1.39
8 x 16	36.0	0.504	0.591	90.0	1.29	1.51
12 x 12	36.0	0.504	0.591	90.0	1.29	1.51
12 x 16	40.5	0.573	0.671	99.0	1.43	1.67
16 x 16	45.0	0.645	0.753	108.0	1.57	1.83
16 x 20	49.5	0.716	0.834	117.0	1.71	1.99
20 x 20	54.0	0.787	0.916	126.0	1.85	2.16
20 x 24	58.5	0.857	0.997	135.0	1.99	2.32
24 x 24	67.5	0.967	1.13	148.5	2.18	2.53

*Nominal outside dimensions.
**Mortar quantities include slushing between brick and liner, also the vertical collar joint in case of two wythes.

The three types of mortar shown in the table below are generally known as cement mortar, cement-lime mortar, and lime mortar, respectively, reading from top to bottom. These correspond with mortar Types A, B, and C, respectively, except that Type A mortar has 1/4 part lime instead of the 0.15 part permitted in cement mortar. These three mortars also correspond generally with Types A-1, B, and C, respectively, as described in *American Standard Building Code Requirements for Masonry* (ASA Code), and to mortars M, N, and O, respectively, of ASTM Specification C270.

Table 12. Quantities of cement, lime, and sand required per cubic foot of mortar

TYPE A MORTAR					
BY WEIGHT — LB.			BY VOLUME — CU.FT.		
CEMENT	HYDRATED LIME	SAND	CEMENT	HYDRATED LIME	SAND
28.2	3	73.6	0.3	.075	0.92

TYPE B MORTAR					
BY WEIGHT — LB.			BY VOLUME — CU.FT.		
CEMENT	HYDRATED LIME	SAND	CEMENT	HYDRATED LIME	SAND
15.28	6.5	78.4	0.163	0.163	0.983

TYPE C MORTAR					
BY WEIGHT — LB.			BY VOLUME — CU.FT.		
CEMENT	HYDRATED LIME	SAND	CEMENT	HYDRATED LIME	SAND
10.34	8.75	79.2	0.11	0.22	0.99

Nonmodular, quantities and courses

QUANTITIES OF MATERIALS
per 100 sq. ft. Brick Wall

Based on standard brick (2¼" x 3¾" x 8") with joints completely filled. No allowance for waste. Hydrated lime assumed.

WALL, Thickness	8" Solid			12"			12¼"		
JOINT, Thickness	⅜"	½"	⅝"	⅜"	½"	⅝"	⅜"	½"	⅝"
BRICK, Number	1310	1232	1161	1965	1848	1742	1965	1848	1742
MORTAR, Cu. Ft.	15.5	18.6	21.3	23.3	27.8	31.9	25.3	29.9	34.0
MIX 1-0.15-3 Cement, Bags	4.80	5.75	6.60	7.20	8.60	9.88	7.83	9.26	10.52
MIX 1-0.15-3 Lime, Lbs.	29	35	40	44	52	60	47	56	64
MIX 1-0.15-3 Sand, Cu. Yd.	0.54	0.64	0.74	0.80	0.96	1.10	0.87	1.03	1.17
MIX 1-1-6 Cement, Bags	2.55	3.07	3.51	3.84	4.58	5.26	4.17	4.93	5.60
MIX 1-1-6 Lime, Lbs.	102	123	141	154	184	210	167	197	224
MIX 1-1-6 Sand, Cu. Yd.	0.57	0.68	0.78	0.86	1.02	1.17	0.93	1.10	1.25
MIX 1-2-9 Cement, Bags	1.72	2.06	2.36	2.58	3.08	3.53	2.80	3.31	3.76
MIX 1-2-9 Lime, Lbs.	138	165	189	207	246	283	224	265	301
MIX 1-2-9 Sand, Cu. Yd.	0.57	0.69	0.79	0.86	1.03	1.18	0.93	1.10	1.26

¼" JOINT + 2¼" Brick = 2½" COURSE

DIMENSIONS

No. of Courses	Ft.–In.	No. of Courses	Ft.–In.	No. of Courses	Ft.–In.
1	2½	51	10- 7½	101	21- 0½
2	5	52	10-10	102	21- 3
3	7½	53	11- 0½	103	21- 5½
4	10	54	11- 3	104	21- 8
5	1- 0½	55	11- 5½	105	21-10½
6	1- 3	56	11- 8	106	22- 1
7	1- 5½	57	11-10½	107	22- 3½
8	1- 8	58	12- 1	108	22- 6
9	1-10½	59	12- 3½	109	22- 8½
10	2- 1	60	12- 6	110	22-11
11	2- 3½	61	12- 8½	111	23- 1½
12	2- 6	62	12-11	112	23- 4
13	2- 8½	63	13- 1½	113	23- 6½
14	2-11	64	13- 4	114	23- 9
15	3- 1½	65	13- 6½	115	23-11½
16	3- 4	66	13- 9	116	24- 2
17	3- 6½	67	13-11½	117	24- 4½
18	3- 9	68	14- 2	118	24- 7
19	3-11½	69	14- 4½	119	24- 9½
20	4- 2	70	14- 7	120	25- 0
21	4- 4½	71	14- 9½	121	25- 2½
22	4- 7	72	15- 0	122	25- 5
23	4- 9½	73	15- 2½	123	25- 7½
24	5- 0	74	15- 5	124	25-10
25	5- 2½	75	15- 7½	125	26- 0½
26	5- 5	76	15-10	126	26- 3
27	5- 7½	77	16- 0½	127	26- 5½
28	5-10	78	16- 3	128	26- 8
29	6- 0½	79	16- 5½	129	26-10½
30	6- 3	80	16- 8	130	27- 1
31	6- 5½	81	16-10½	131	27- 3½
32	6- 8	82	17- 1	132	27- 6
33	6-10½	83	17- 3½	133	27- 8½
34	7- 1	84	17- 6	134	27-11
35	7- 3½	85	17- 8½	135	28- 1½
36	7- 6	86	17-11	136	28- 4
37	7- 8½	87	18- 1½	137	28- 6½
38	7-11	88	18- 4	138	28- 9
39	8- 1½	89	18- 6½	139	28-11½
40	8- 4	90	18- 9	140	29- 2
41	8- 6½	91	18-11½	141	29- 4½
42	8- 9	92	19- 2	142	29- 7
43	8-11½	93	19- 4½	143	29- 9½
44	9- 2	94	19- 7	144	30- 0
45	9- 4½	95	19- 9½	145	30- 2½
46	9- 7	96	20- 0	146	30- 5
47	9- 9½	97	20- 2½	147	30- 7½
48	10- 0	98	20- 5	148	30-10
49	10- 2½	99	20- 7½	149	31- 0½
50	10- 5	100	20-10	150	31- 3

SCALES

¾" = 1'-0": 4, 8, 12, 16, 20, 24, 28, 32, 36, 40, 44

½": 4, 8, 12, 16, 20, 24, 28, 32, 36, 40, 44, 48, 52, 56, 60, 64, 68

¼": 4, 8, 12, 16, 20, 24, 28, 32, 36, 40, 44, 48, 52, 56, 60, 64, 68, 72, 76, 80, 84, 88, 92, 96, 100, 104, 108, 112, 116, 120, 124, 128, 132, 136, 140

⅜" JOINT + 2¼" Brick = 2⅝" COURSE

DIMENSIONS

No. of Courses	Ft.–In.	No. of Courses	Ft.–In.	No. of Courses	Ft.–In.
1	2⅝	51	11- 1⅞	101	22- 1⅛
2	5¼	52	11- 4½	102	22- 3¾
3	7⅞	53	11- 7⅛	103	22- 6⅜
4	10½	54	11- 9¾	104	22- 9
5	1- 1⅛	55	12- 0⅜	105	22-11⅝
6	1- 3¾	56	12- 3	106	23- 2¼
7	1- 6⅜	57	12- 5⅝	107	23- 4⅞
8	1- 9	58	12- 8¼	108	23- 7½
9	1-11⅝	59	12-10⅞	109	23-10⅛
10	2- 2¼	60	13- 1½	110	24- 0¾
11	2- 4⅞	61	13- 4⅛	111	24- 3⅜
12	2- 7½	62	13- 6¾	112	24- 6
13	2-10⅛	63	13- 9⅜	113	24- 8⅝
14	3- 0¾	64	14- 0	114	24-11¼
15	3- 3⅜	65	14- 2⅝	115	25- 1⅞
16	3- 6	66	14- 5¼	116	25- 4½
17	3- 8⅝	67	14- 7⅞	117	25- 7⅛
18	3-11¼	68	14-10½	118	25- 9¾
19	4- 1⅞	69	15- 1⅛	119	26- 0⅜
20	4- 4½	70	15- 3¾	120	26- 3
21	4- 7⅛	71	15- 6⅜	121	26- 5⅝
22	4- 9¾	72	15- 9	122	26- 8¼
23	5- 0⅜	73	15-11⅝	123	26-10⅞
24	5- 3	74	16- 2¼	124	27- 1½
25	5- 5⅝	75	16- 4⅞	125	27- 4⅛
26	5- 8¼	76	16- 7½	126	27- 6¾
27	5-10⅞	77	16-10⅛	127	27- 9⅜
28	6- 1½	78	17- 0¾	128	28- 0
29	6- 4⅛	79	17- 3⅜	129	28- 2⅝
30	6- 6¾	80	17- 6	130	28- 5¼
31	6- 9⅜	81	17- 8⅝	131	28- 7⅞
32	7- 0	82	17-11¼	132	28-10½
33	7- 2⅝	83	18- 1⅞	133	29- 1⅛
34	7- 5¼	84	18- 4½	134	29- 3¾
35	7- 7⅞	85	18- 7⅛	135	29- 6⅜
36	7-10½	86	18- 9¾	136	29- 9
37	8- 1⅛	87	19- 0⅜	137	29-11⅝
38	8- 3¾	88	19- 3	138	30- 2¼
39	8- 6⅜	89	19- 5⅝	139	30- 4⅞
40	8- 9	90	19- 8¼	140	30- 7½
41	8-11⅝	91	19-10⅞	141	30-10⅛
42	9- 2¼	92	20- 1½	142	31- 0¾
43	9- 4⅞	93	20- 4⅛	143	31- 3⅜
44	9- 7½	94	20- 6¾	144	31- 6
45	9-10⅛	95	20- 9⅜	145	31- 8⅝
46	10- 0¾	96	21- 0	146	31-11¼
47	10- 3⅜	97	21- 2⅝	147	32- 1⅞
48	10- 6	98	21- 5¼	148	32- 4½
49	10- 8⅝	99	21- 7⅞	149	32- 7⅛
50	10-11¼	100	21-10½	150	32- 9¾

SCALES

¼": 4, 8, 12, 16, 20, 24, 28, 32, 36, 40, 44, 48, 52, 56, 60, 64, 68, 72, 76, 80, 84, 88, 92, 96, 100, 104, 108, 112, 116, 120, 124, 128, 132

½": 4, 8, 12, 16, 20, 24, 28, 32, 36, 40, 44, 48, 52, 56, 60, 64

¾" = 1'-0": 4, 8, 12, 16, 20, 24, 28, 32, 36, 40, 44

½" JOINT + 2¼" Brick = 2¾" COURSE

SCALES

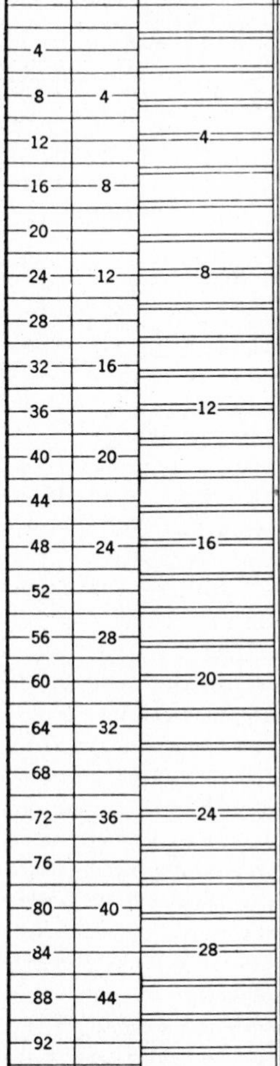

¼"
½"
¾"=1'-0"
4 8 12 16 20 24 28 32 36 40 44 48 52 56 60 64 68 72 76 80 84 88 92 96 100 104 108 112 116 120 124 128
4 8 12 16 20 24 28 32 36 40 44 48 52 56 60 64
4 8 12 16 20 24 28 32 36 40

DIMENSIONS

No. of Courses	Ft.-In.	No. of Courses	Ft.-In.	No. of Courses	Ft.-In.
1	2¾	51	11- 8¼	101	23- 1¾
2	5½	52	11-11	102	23- 4½
3	8¼	53	12- 1¾	103	23- 7¼
4	11	54	12- 4½	104	23-10
5	1- 1¾	55	12- 7¼	105	24- 0¾
6	1- 4½	56	12-10	106	24- 3½
7	1- 7¼	57	13- 0¾	107	24- 6¼
8	1-10	58	13- 3½	108.	24- 9
9	2- 0¾	59	13- 6¼	109	24-11¾
10	2- 3½	60	13- 9	110	25- 2½
11	2- 6¼	61	13-11¾	111	25- 5¼
12	2- 9	62	14- 2½	112	25- 8
13	2-11¾	63	14- 5¼	113	25-10¾
14	3- 2½	64	14- 8	114	26- 1½
15	3- 5¼	65	14-10¾	115	26- 4¼
16	3- 8	66	15- 1½	116	26- 7
17	3-10¾	67	15- 4¼	117	26- 9¾
18	4- 1½	68	15- 7	118	27- 0½
19	4- 4¼	69	15- 9¾	119	27- 3¼
20	4- 7	70	16- 0½	120	27- 6
21	4- 9¾	71	16- 3¼	121	27- 8¾
22	5- 0½	72	16- 6	122	27-11½
23	5- 3¼	73	16- 8¾	123	28- 2¼
24	5- 6	74	16-11½	124	28- 5
25	5- 8¾	75	17- 2¼	125	28- 7¾
26	5-11½	76	17- 5	126	28-10½
27	6- 2¼	77	17- 7¾	127	29- 1¼
28	6- 5	78	17-10½	128	29- 4
29	6- 7¾	79	18- 1¼	129	29- 6¾
30	6-10½	80	18- 4	130	29- 9½
31	7- 1¼	81	18- 6¾	131	30- 0¼
32	7- 4	82	18- 9½	132	30- 3
33	7- 6¾	83	19- 0¼	133	30- 5¾
34	7- 9½	84	19- 3	134	30- 8½
35	8- 0¼	85	19- 5¾	135	30-11¼
36	8- 3	86	19- 8½	136	31- 2
37	8- 5¾	87	19-11¼	137	31- 4¾
38	8- 8½	88	20- 2	138	31- 7½
39	8-11¼	89	20- 4¾	139	31-10¼
40	9- 2	90	20- 7½	140	32- 1
41	9- 4¾	91	20-10¼	141	32- 3¾
42	9- 7½	92	21- 1	142	32- 6½
43	9-10¼	93	21- 3¾	143	32- 9¼
44	10- 1	94	21- 6½	144	33- 0
45	10- 3¾	95	21- 9¼	145	33- 2¾
46	10- 6½	96	22- 0	146	33- 5½
47	10- 9¼	97	22- 2¾	147	33- 8¼
48	11- 0	98	22- 5½	148	33-11
49	11- 2¾	99	22- 8¼	149	34- 1¾
50	11- 5½	100	22-11	150	34- 4½

QUANTITIES - BRICK and MORTAR
per 100 sq. ft. Wall Area

Based on standard brick (2¼" x 3¾" x 8) with ½" joints, completely filled. No allowance for waste

Type of Wall	2" Veneer	4" Veneer
	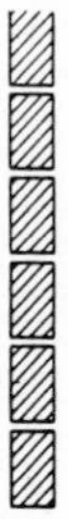	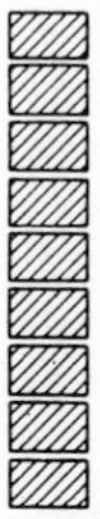
BRICK, Number	399	616
MORTAR, Cu. Ft.	3.2	7.2

Type of Wall	8" Solid	12" Solid
		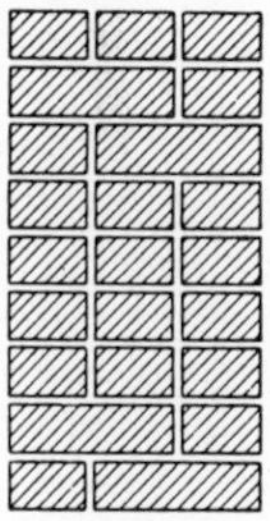
BRICK, Number	1232	1848
MORTAR, Cu. Ft.	18.6	27.8

⅝" JOINT + 2¼" Brick = 2⅞" COURSE

DIMENSIONS

No. of Courses	Ft.-In.	No. of Courses	Ft.-In.	No. of Courses	Ft.-In.
1	2⅞	51	12- 2⅝	101	24- 2⅜
2	5¾	52	12- 5½	102	24- 5¼
3	8⅝	53	12- 8⅜	103	24- 8⅛
4	11½	54	12-11¼	104	24-11
5	1- 2⅜	55	13- 2⅛	105	25- 1⅞
6	1- 5¼	56	13- 5	106	25- 4¾
7	1- 8⅛	57	13- 7⅞	107	25- 7⅝
8	1-11	58	13-10¾	108	25-10½
9	2- 1⅞	59	14- 1⅝	109	26- 1⅜
10	2- 4¾	60	14- 4½	110	26- 4¼
11	2- 7⅝	61	14- 7⅜	111	26- 7⅛
12	2-10½	62	14-10¼	112	26-10
13	3- 1⅜	63	15- 1⅛	113	27- 0⅞
14	3- 4¼	64	15- 4	114	27- 3¾
15	3- 7⅛	65	15- 6⅞	115	27- 6⅝
16	3-10	66	15- 9¾	116	27- 9½
17	4- 0⅞	67	16- 0⅝	117	28- 0⅜
18	4- 3¾	68	16- 3½	118	28- 3¼
19	4- 6⅝	69	16- 6⅜	119	28- 6⅛
20	4- 9½	70	16- 9¼	120	28- 9
21	5- 0⅜	71	17- 0⅛	121	28-11⅞
22	5- 3¼	72	17- 3	122	29- 2¾
23	5- 6⅛	73	17- 5⅞	123	29- 5⅝
24	5- 9	74	17- 8¾	124	29- 8½
25	5-11⅞	75	17-11⅝	125	29-11⅜
26	6- 2¾	76	18- 2½	126	30- 2¼
27	6- 5⅝	77	18- 5⅜	127	30- 5⅛
28	6- 8½	78	18- 8¼	128	30- 8
29	6-11⅜	79	18-11⅛	129	30-10⅞
30	7- 2¼	80	19- 2	130	31- 1¾
31	7- 5⅛	81	19- 4⅞	131	31- 4⅝
32	7- 8	82	19- 7¾	132	31- 7½
33	7-10⅞	83	19-10⅝	133	31-10⅜
34	8- 1¾	84	20- 1½	134	32- 1¼
35	8- 4⅝	85	20- 4⅜	135	32- 4⅛
36	8- 7½	86	20- 7¼	136	32- 7
37	8-10⅜	87	20-10⅛	137	32- 9⅞
38	9- 1¼	88	21- 1	138	33- 0¾
39	9- 4⅛	89	21- 3⅞	139	33- 3⅝
40	9- 7	90	21- 6¾	140	33- 6½
41	9- 9⅞	91	21- 9⅝	141	33- 9⅜
42	10- 0¾	92	22- 0½	142	34- 0¼
43	10- 3⅝	93	22- 3⅜	143	34- 3⅛
44	10- 6½	94	22- 6¼	144	34- 6
45	10- 9⅜	95	22- 9⅛	145	34- 8⅞
46	11- 0¼	96	23- 0	146	34-11¾
47	11- 3⅛	97	23- 2⅞	147	35- 2⅝
48	11- 6	98	23- 5¾	148	35- 5½
49	11- 8⅞	99	23- 8⅝	149	35- 8⅜
50	11-11¾	100	23-11½	150	35-11¼

SCALES

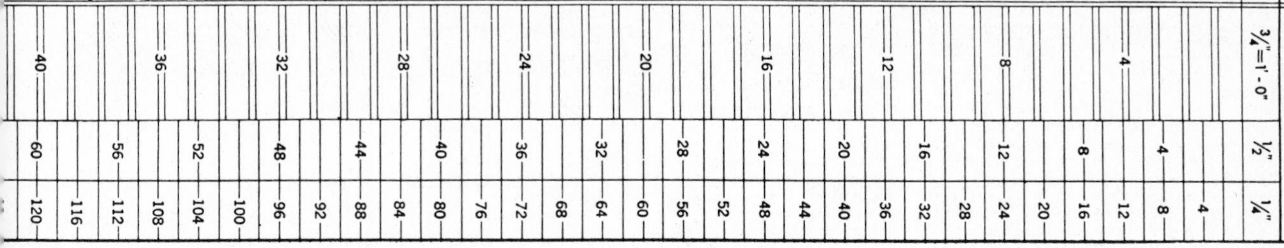

¾"=1'-0"
½"
¼"
4 8 12 16 20 24 28 32 36 40
4 8 12 16 20 24 28 32 36 40 44 48 52 56 60
4 8 12 16 20 24 28 32 36 40 44 48 52 56 60 64 68 72 76 80 84 88 92 96 100 104 108 112 116 120

Fig. 6. Running bond

Fig 7. Common bond with headers every sixth course

Fig. 8. Common bond with Flemish headers every sixth course

every seventh course and with Type B mortar.

Facing brick

Table 5—800 × 6.75	5,400
Table 7—Add $\frac{1}{7}$ × 5,400	771
	6,171
Add 5% for breakage	309
Total number facing brick	6,480

Backup brick

Table 6—800 × 13.5	10,800
Table 7—Deduct $\frac{1}{7}$ × 5,400	771
	10,029
Add 5% for breakage	501
Total number of backup brick	10,530

Mortar

Table 5, for $\frac{3}{8}$-in. joints in facing

800 × 0.0608	48.64 cu ft

Table 6, for $\frac{1}{2}$-in. joints in backup

800 × 0.1988	159.04 cu ft

Table 6, for $\frac{7}{16}$-in. collar joint and $\frac{1}{2}$-in. collar joint

8 × (3.65 + 4.17)	62.56 cu ft
Total mortar required	270.24 cu ft

Table 12—271 cu ft of Type B mortar requires:

Cement	271 × 0.163 =	44.17 cu ft
Hydrated lime	271 × 0.163 =	44.17 cu ft
Sand	271 × 0.983 =	266.00 cu ft

TYPE OF BOND

The five pattern bonds in most common use today are running bond, common or American bond, Flemish bond, English bond, and English cross or Dutch bond.

Variations of these basic bonds include double-stretcher Flemish, garden wall, stack or block, and others too numerous to mention here. (For a more detailed discussion, see *Bonds and Mortars in the Wall of Brick*, Structural Clay Products Institute.)

Running bond is the simplest of the basic pattern bonds and consists entirely of stretchers. Since there are no headers, metal ties must be used for structural bond. Running bond is used largely in cavity-wall construction and in brick-veneered walls. Figure 6 shows conventional running bond with vertical joints centered on the stretchers above and below. With Roman brick, nominally 12 in. long, the vertical joints often occur at the third points of the units above and below. This arrangement is commonly known as "one-third bond."

Common or American bond is a variation of running bond with a complete course of full-length headers at regular intervals—the interval depending upon the size of the units and the bonding requirements. These headers provide structural bonding as well as a definite pattern on the wall surface. Header courses usually occur at every fifth, sixth, or seventh course. Figure 7 shows common bond with headers at every sixth course. A "three-quarter" brick must start each header course at the corner and a three-quarter brick closer must be used in the face of the wall in which the end of the starter brick appears. Common bond may be varied by using a Flemish header course (Fig. 8) instead of continuous headers.

Flemish bond (Fig. 9) consists of alternate stretchers and headers, with the headers centered on the stretchers above and below. Headers used outside the structural bonding courses may be "blind headers" or half brick. Two methods are used for starting the corners of Flemish bond work. Shown on the left is the "Dutch corner," in which a three-quarter brick is used to start each course. On the right is the "English corner," in which a 2-in. or quarter-brick closer is used.

English bond (Fig. 10) has alternate courses of headers and stretchers. The headers are centered on the stretchers and the joints between stretchers. The vertical joints between stretchers in all courses line up vertically. Blind headers of half brick may be used in courses that are not required to be structural bonding courses.

English cross or Dutch bond is a variation of English bond and differs only in the lack of alignment of the vertical joints between the stretchers in alternate courses. These joints center on the stretchers themselves in the courses above and below. Either an English or a Dutch corner may be used to start English or Dutch bond.

Block or stack bond is a pure pattern bond; all vertical joints are aligned and there is no overlapping of the units in the face of the wall. Metal ties are usually employed to provide structural bond between the facing and the backup. Stack bond is also used extensively in facing-tile work, with structural bond provided by the use of extra-wide stretcher units or metal ties. Curved walls, where radial stretcher brick are not available, are usu-

DUTCH CORNER   ENGLISH CORNER
Fig. 9. Flemish bond

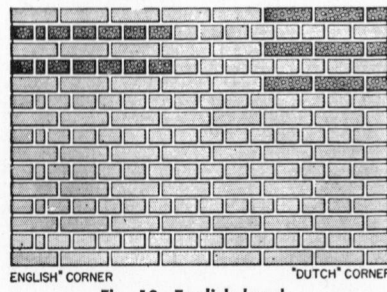

ENGLISH" CORNER   "DUTCH" CORNER
Fig. 10. English bond

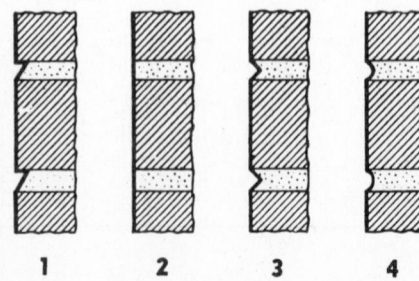

1   2   3   4
Fig. 11. Joint treatments

ally built entirely of headers, which may be laid in running bond but are more frequently laid in stack bond.

TYPE OF JOINT

Joints are of great importance in the appearance of the wall. Four types of exposed joints are shown in Fig. 11: (1) Weathered, (2) Flush, (3) V, and (4) Concave. All are superior in weather resistance to struck joints (not illustrated), which may, however, be used for interior work. Tooled joints (3 and 4), which compress and spread the mortar after it has partially set, result in the best weathering properties. The color of the joints is also extremely important for the over-all appearance of the wall; if other than natural color is desired, mortar color should be specified.

CAVITY WALLS

The cavity wall consists of two tiers or wythes of masonry separated by a continuous air space not less than 2 in. wide. It may be composed of brick or structural clay tile or a combination of both. Metal ties are used to connect the two wythes (Fig. 12). The exterior or facing wythe is always a nominal 4-in. thickness, whereas the interior wythe may be 4, 6, or 8 in., depending on the requirements of the structure, such as the height of the wall and the loads to be carried. Nominal over-all thicknesses of cavity walls, therefore, may be 10, 12, or 14 in., if the air space is maintained at a nominal 2 in.

The advantages of the cavity walls are its resistance to rain penetration which results from the complete separation of the inner and outer surfaces, and its thermal insulation provided by the cavity between the wythes, either as an air space or filled with suitable insulating material. Although these advantages are of major importance in many structures and amply

justify the use of cavity walls, the flexibility of the metal tie, which permits some differential movement between the inner and outer wythes of the masonry, may often be of equal significance in contributing to satisfactory performance.

PROPERTIES OF WALLS

Strength: Tests of all-brick and brick-and-tile cavity walls, conducted at the National Bureau of Standards (BMS Report No. 23, 24, and 136), showed that the strength of cavity walls subjected to compressive, transverse, concentrated, racking, and impact loads is similar to that of solid walls containing the same amount of masonry; that is, a 10-in. cavity wall is generally equal in strength to an 8-in. solid wall.

Heat transmission: Cavity walls have 25 per cent greater insulating value than solid walls of the same materials (BMS 136). In many areas, notably the Southwest, the insulation provided by cavity walls against heat loss or heat gain is adequate for the occupancy requirements of the structure, and, in those climates where the major problem is to reduce heat gain during the summer months, masonry cavity walls have been found to be most effective, because of their heat storage capacity.

Ventilation of the cavity by means of weep holes, as recommended on the following pages, does not materially affect the insulating value of the cavity (BMS 136).

Furring increases the resistance to heat flow but tends to reduce the economy of cavity-wall construction which is obtained by applying the plaster directly to the masonry, or, as is frequently desired, by leaving the masonry exposed. If additional insulation is required, it should be installed in the cavity. Tests have shown

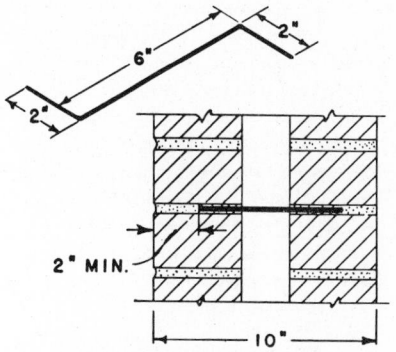

Fig. 12. Location of metal tie

that only under the most extreme conditions is a vapor barrier required.

Fire resistance: Fire tests conducted at the National Bureau of Standards (BMS 92) indicate that the fire resistance of brick-and-tile cavity walls might be expected to be between 4 and 5 hr (Table 13).

Moisture resistance: Moisture penetration tests conducted at the National Bureau of Standards (BMS 82) indicate that cavity walls constructed with average or commercial workmanship can be considered moisture-resistant and will remain dry even under severe exposure.

Sound resistance: Since the resistance to sound transmission of homogeneous walls is a factor of the weight per unit of the wall, the sound-transmission loss of cavity walls may be expected to be equivalent to that of solid walls of the same weight per square foot; that is, on the order of 50 to 55 db.

DESIGN REQUIREMENTS

Provisions of the ASA Code covering the design of cavity walls can be found in "Structural Design—Masonry." All the model codes (Basic, Uniform, National, and Southern) contain substantially the same provisions.

Table 13. Properties of brick-and-tile cavity walls

Wall Thickness, in.		Materials		Allowable Distance between Lateral Supports, Ft.	Fire Resistant Rating, hr.		Transmittance "U"			
							Uninsulated		Insulated [1]	
Gross	Net	Ext. Wythe	Int. Wythe		Unplastered	⅝" Sand Plastered	Unplastered	⅝" Sand Plastered	Plastered or Unplastered	
10	8	4" brick	4" brick	13'-4"	5	6	.33	.32	.13	
10	8	4" brick	4" str. tile	12'-0"	3	4	.30	.29	.12	
10	8	4" str. tile	4" str. tile	12'-0"	2	3	.25	.24	.11	
12	10	4" brick	6" brick	16'-8"	6	7	.29	.28	.12	
12	10	4" brick	6" str. tile	15'-0"	4	5	.27	.26	.11	
12	10	4" str. tile	6" str. tile	15'-0"	2	3	.23	.22	.10	
14	12	4" brick	8" brick	20'-0"	10	11	.25	.24	.11	
14	12	4" brick	8" str. tile	18'-0"	5	6	.23	.22	.11	
14	12	4" str. tile	8" str. tile	18'-0"	3	4	.21	.20	.10	

Mortar: Transverse-load tests indicate that maximum lateral strength can be obtained with Type S mortar, which should therefore be used for cavity walls if lateral strength is an important design factor.

Allowable stresses: Recommended allowable working stresses for cavity walls are given in Table 14. Compressive stresses are from the ASA Code; tension and shearing stresses are from the Uniform Code of the International Building Officials Conference (1955).

Bond: The ASA Code provides that metal ties be spaced not more than 36 in. apart horizontally and 18 in. vertically. Since 18 in. is not a modular dimension, 16 in. is the usual spacing. The Structural Clay Products Institute, however, recommends a vertical spacing of 24 in. The crimp often seen in the center of the metal ties, intended to act as a drip, is not recommended; tests have shown that it provides little moisture protection and materially weakens the compressive strength of the tie.

Draining the cavity

Since resistance to rain penetration is the most important single feature of the cavity wall, the minimum 2-in. cavity width should be maintained. An air space of less than 2 in. is difficult to keep free of mortar "bridging" or "droppings."

The proper draining of the cavity depends a great deal on the ease with which moisture is permitted to escape at the bottom. Drainage is provided by weep holes placed in the exterior wythe at the bottom of the cavity. To prevent infiltration of moisture, the bottom of the cavity should be at least 6 in. above finished grade (Fig. 13).

In curtain and panel wall construction, the weep holes over lintels or spandrel-beam supports should be spaced 32 in. (4 brick lengths) apart. Spacing of weep holes at the foundation support should be 2 ft on centers.

Open weep holes at lintels and spandrels may contribute to wall staining and, during high winds, may reduce the re-

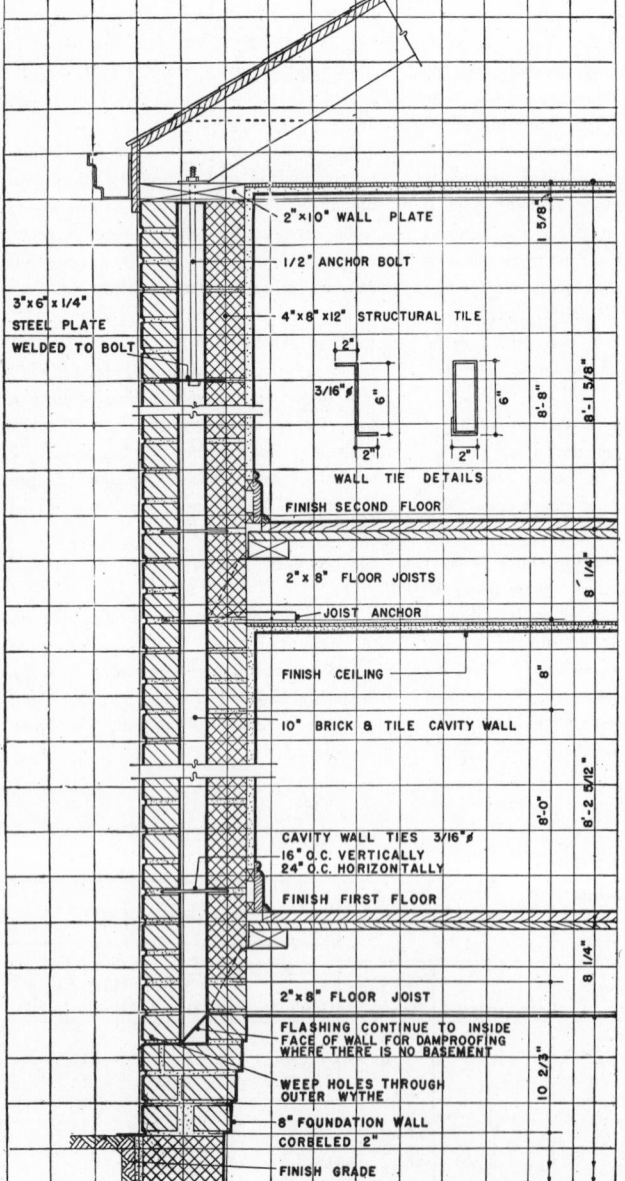

Fig. 13. Typical cavity-wall section—residential construction

Table 14. Allowable working stresses in cavity and metal-tied walls

	Solid Units		Hollow Units
	2500 psi plus	1500 to 2500 psi	
Compressive,[1] Mortar type:			
M(A-1)	140	100	70
S(A-2)	130	90	60
N(B)	110	80	55
Tension in Flexure or Shear,[2] Mortar type:			
M(A-1)	12	12	12
S(A-2)	10	10	10
N(B)	10	10	10

[1] On gross cross-sectional area of wall minus area of cavity between wythes (leaves). The allowable compressive stresses for cavity walls are based upon the assumption that the floor loads bear upon but one of the two wythes. When cavity or metal tied walls are loaded concentrically, the allowable stresses may be increased by 25 per cent.

[2] Net area.

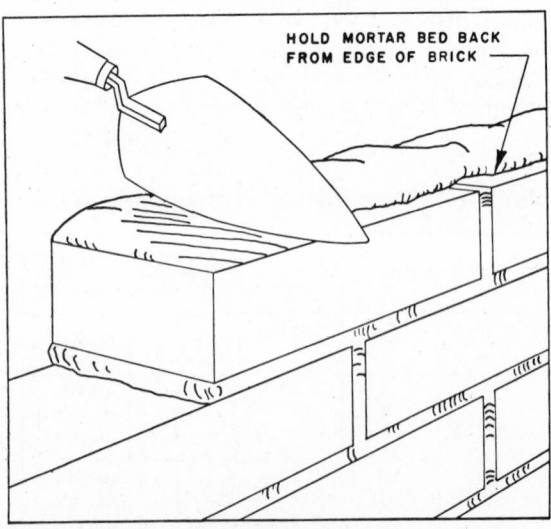

Fig. 14. Beveled bed joint to prevent mortar from protruding into cavity

sistance of the wall to heat flow. It is therefore recommended that "wicks" be placed in weep holes. The wicks should be made of glass fiber or similar inorganic material. If the weep holes are formed by omitting the mortar from whole vertical joints, a piece of ½-in. glass fiber insulation can be placed in such joints.

Weep holes are not effective in draining the cavity if they become plugged with mortar droppings as the wall is constructed. A skilled mason, however, can easily keep the cavity clean and free of mortar droppings. The simplest method consists of beveling the cavity edge of the mortar bed (Fig. 14). When the mortar is spread in this way, very little if any mortar will be squeezed out of the bed joints into the cavity where the units are laid.

Immediately following the setting of the masonry unit, the mason should spread any mortar that protrudes into the cavity

over the back of the unit, using the flat of his trowel. This prevents the mortar from falling to the bottom of the cavity and clogging the weep holes, and also provides a relatively smooth interior surface that aids in placing insulation if it is used.

Another method commonly used to keep the cavity clean consists of a wood strip to which two lengths of wire are attached. This strip, which may be 4 to 6 ft long, is placed on the first tier of metal ties. The mason then builds up the two wythes to the level of the next row of ties and, before proceeding with the wall, lifts out the wood strip, bringing with it any accumulated droppings.

Insulation

Insulation for cavity walls must not hamper the cavity's function as a barrier to moisture penetration by permitting moisture to be transmitted across the cavity.

Cavity-wall insulation may consist of a loose fill or of a rigid material. Loose-fill insulation must be such that its thermal efficiency will not be significantly impaired by the presence of moisture; it must be capable of sustaining its own weight in cavity heights of 25 ft without settlement; and it must be capable of being poured in lifts of not less than 4 ft. Two types of water-repellent granular insulation (one of glass fiber, the other of vermiculite) have been developed specifically for this purpose and have been extensively tested by the Structural Clay Products Institute. Recommended thermal coefficients for each type of insulation are given in Table 15. Rigid board insulation (foamed glass, foamed plastic, or glass fiber) may be installed in cavity walls. It should be placed against the inner wythe, leaving an air space at least 1 in. wide between the insulation and the outer wythe.

Vapor barrier

In most instances a vapor barrier is not required in cavity-wall construction. Recent

Table 15. Recommended thermal coefficients

INSULATION	VERMICULITE		GLASS FIBER	
WALL TYPE	R	$U = \dfrac{1}{R}$	R	$U = \dfrac{1}{R}$
Brick and brick, exposed	7.15	0.140	8.77	0.114
Brick and tile, exposed	7.85	0.127	9.47	0.106
Brick and tile, plastered*	7.99	0.125	9.61	0.104
Tile and tile, exposed	8.55	0.117	10.17	0.098
Tile and tile, plastered*	8.69	0.115	10.31	0.097

* ¾-in. sand-gypsum plaster.

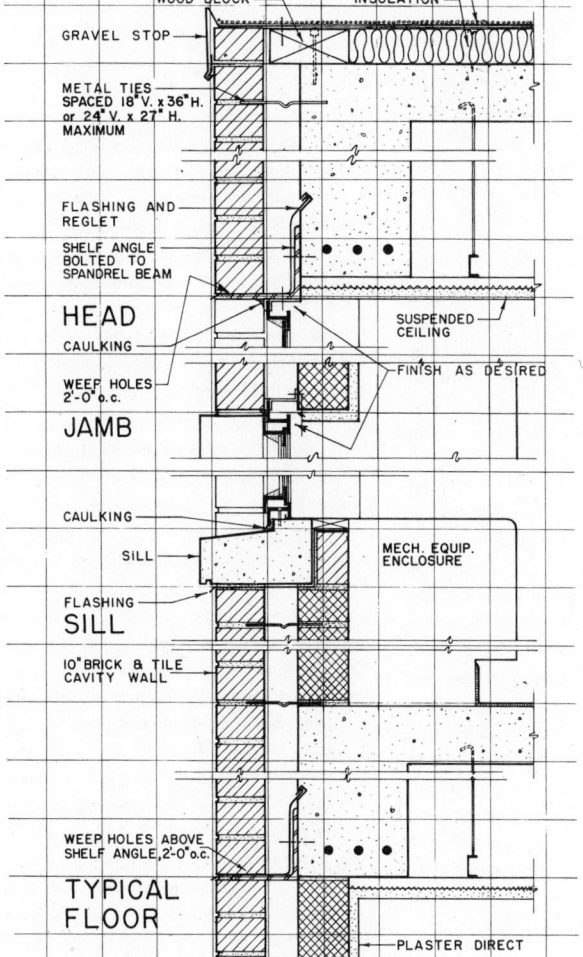

Fig. 15. Typical wall section—cavity curtain wall

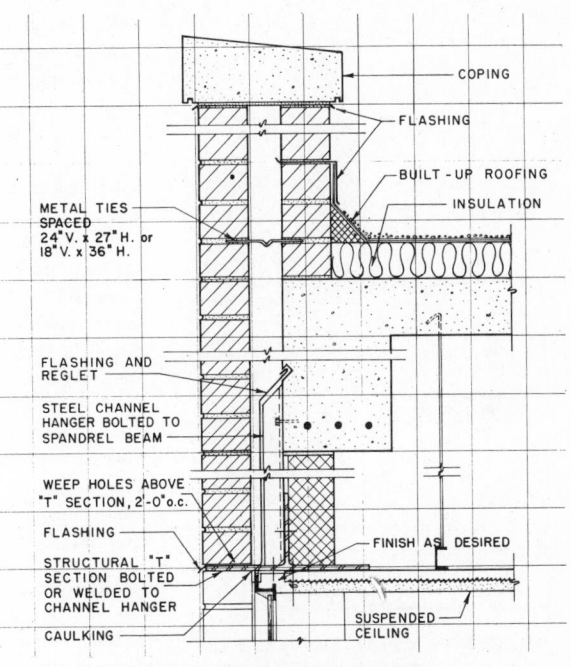

Fig. 16. Alternate parapet detail

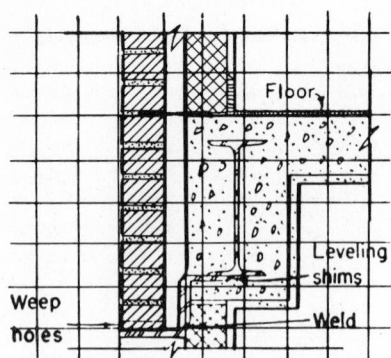

Fig. 17. Alternate spandrel detail—curtain wall

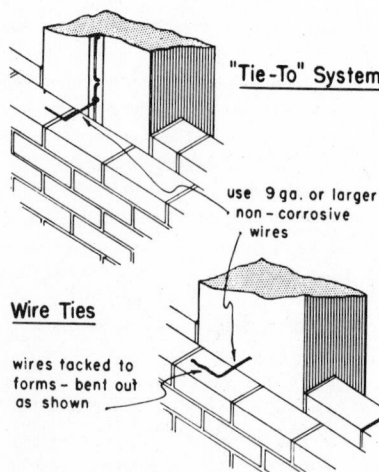

Fig. 18. Methods of anchoring outer wythe to column

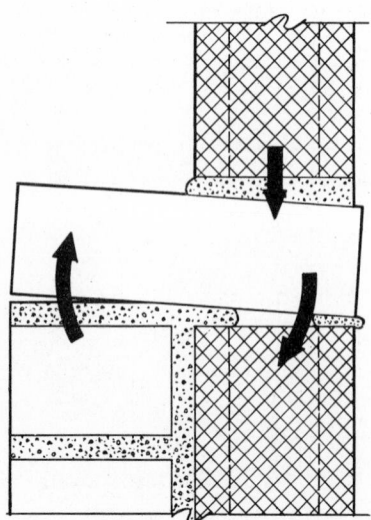

Fig. 19. Effect of heavy backup on brick header

tests have shown that a vapor barrier is required only if the permeabilities exceed 3 perms, if the vapor-pressure gradient exceeds 1 in. of mercury, or if the duration of the extreme conditions exceeds 30 days (as in a cold-storage warehouse). If a vapor barrier is required, it should consist of a brush coat of vapor-resistant asphalt emulsion, applied to the outer face of the inner wythe, which must be built up several courses ahead of the outer wythe for this purpose.

Curtain walls

As shown in the details on this and the previous page (Figs. 15, 16, 17), the inner wythe of masonry rests on the individual floor levels and is laid to the face of the columns. The outer wythe rests on shelf angles and is tied to the structure by means of metal anchors or ties, which are fastened to the inner wythe of masonry and to the framing members themselves. Two methods of anchoring the outer wythe are shown in Fig. 18.

For most panel wall construction a 10-in. cavity wall will be adequate. Where the distance between lateral supports is abnormally long, however, building regulations may require a thicker wall section. In such instances, the use of a 6- or 8-in. backup wythe is recommended. Table 13 shows the maximum allowable distance between lateral supports required by the ASA Code.

Flashing

Continuous flashing should be installed at the bottom of the cavity and over all wall openings not protected by projecting hoods or eaves. Flashing may consist of sheet metal, bituminous membrane material, or a combination of both. Weep holes should be provided just above all flashings. An excessive number of weep holes should be avoided, particularly in high buildings, since the pressure in the cavity, resulting from air entering the openings during high wind velocity, may cause infiltration of moisture. Where the outer wythe is supported on spandrel beams in panel wall construction, galvanized shelf angles, flashed where end joints abut, may be used to provide both structural support and cavity flashing in one member, thus eliminating the need for continuous strip flashing. In lieu of galvanized angles, flashing may be installed over the top face of steel shelf angles.

SOLID METAL-TIED WALLS

Solid metal-tied walls are similar to cavity walls, except that the space between the wythes is reduced to ½ in. and is filled solidly with mortar by parging the inner or backup wythe as the wall is built. The ASA Code provides that metal ties for solid walls conform to the requirements for cavity-wall ties.

Weather resistance

Many masonry walls, as now constructed, consist of an exterior wythe of brick backed up with structural clay tile or concrete masonry units bonded to the facing with brick headers. Experience has indicated that, particularly in the case of 8-in. walls where the brick header is continuous through the full thickness of the wall, extreme care must be exercised in construction in order to obtain a wall that will resist the penetration of heavy rains accompanied by high (50 mph or more) winds.

Among the many factors that make 8-in. masonry-bonded walls vulnerable to rain penetration are the following:

1. The difficulty encountered by the mason in obtaining full mortar joints between brick headers. This problem applies to all types of masonry backup.

2. The practical difficulty of bonding brick and large, relatively heavy, backup units without impairing the bond between brick headers and mortar during construction (Fig. 19). If the backup is laid ahead of the facing, as is done when the mason works on the outside of the wall, brick headers can be placed over the backup as the facing brick reach the proper height. Immediately following the laying of the header course, a heavy backup unit can be set on the back of the brick headers. With many types of concrete-block backup, the brick header is supported on the backup unit only by two thin (approximately 1 in.) strips of mortar. If a backup unit is set on the brick header before the mortar under the header has had time to stiffen, the header brick will settle unevenly and a crack may develop in the mortar joint below the header course in the face of the wall.

3. Perhaps most important are the differences in the thermal- and moisture-expansion coefficients of facing and backup. These differences are greatest in brick and concrete-block walls. In such construction, movement of the concrete-block backup, caused by shrinkage as the wall dries out, creates an eccentric load on the brick headers that tends to rupture the bond between headers and mortar at the external wall face.

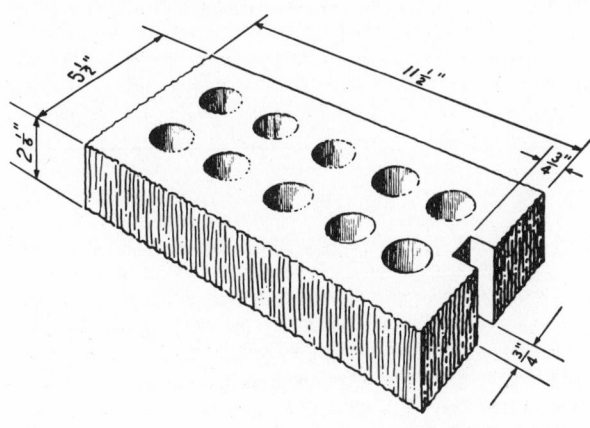

*Reg US Pat Off , Pat Pend , SCPRF.

Fig. 20. SCR brick*

Table 16. Structural properties of SCR brick wall construction

Mortar		Ultimate Compressive Load * lb. per lin. ft.	Ultimate Transverse Load ** lb. per sq. ft.	Ultimate Racking Load * lb. per ft.	Ultimate Impact Load * ft.
Type	Compressive Strength 28 days psi				
M (1:¼:3)	4590	.....	87.0	.....	.....
S (1:1½:4½)	2745	.....	86.5	.....	.....
N (1:1:6)	1695	100,420	68.5	8140	1.58***

*Average of three tests.
**Average of five tests for each mortar type. Span 7' 6".
***Maximum height of drop 60-lb. sack of sand.
NOTE: Except for the specimens used in the racking tests which were 8 ft. wide, all specimens were 4 ft. wide and 8 ft. high. Average weight of wall was 55.9 lb. per sq. ft. Mortars are portland cement, lime, sand by volume.

Properties of walls

Although few tests have been reported on solid metal-tied walls, it is reasonable to assume that the strength of such walls would be at least equivalent to the strength of cavity walls built of similar materials. Moreover, it is probable that the transverse and racking strengths of metal-tied solid walls would be substantially greater than the strengths of similar cavity walls, because of the effect of the collar joint in bonding the facing to the backup.

Other properties of solid metal-tied walls, such as heat transmission, fire resistance, and sound transmission, may be assumed to be the same as for masonry-bonded solid walls constructed of similar materials.

SCR BRICK

The "SCR brick" is a modular unit whose nominal dimensions are 2⅔ by 6 by 12 in. (Fig. 20). Designed to be laid with ½-in. joints, its actual dimensions are 2¹⁄₁₆ by 5½ by 11½ in. The unit is vertically cored by means of ten holes, each 1⅜ in. in diameter. Since the volume of coring is less than 25 per cent, it is classified as a solid masonry unit.

A jamb slot is formed in each brick to facilitate the installation of windows.

The SCR brick is a "through-the-wall" unit, requiring no backup units to build a nominal 6-in. wall. The face size is that of standard "Norman" brick. SCR brick are designed to be laid in common (half) bond with full bed and head mortar joints of ½-in. thickness. Vertically, the brick are laid up three courses to 8 in. of wall height. A total of 450 units are required per 100 sq ft of wall area. Approximately 15.5 cu ft of mortar will be required to lay 100 sq ft of wall when using full ½-in.-thick bed and head joints. This quantity includes an allowance for mortar entering the cores and also provides for 10 per cent waste. On the same basis of figuring, 1,000 SCR brick will require 34¼ cu ft of mortar.

Code acceptance: All nationally recognized building codes permit the use of exterior loadbearing 6-in. masonry walls for one-story, single-family dwellings where the wall height does not exceed 9 ft to the eaves or 15 ft to the peak of the gables.

Mason productivity: A bricklayer can easily lay 450 SCR brick per day, or a total of 100 sq ft of wall area. Actual productivity figures of 500 to 600 units or more per 8-hr day have been reported on jobs located in various parts of the country. These higher figures represent from 110 to more than 130 sq ft of wall area built in one day by one mason.

Wall construction: The SCR brick is designed for use with furring on which the interior finish and insulation can be applied. The size of furring recommended is 2 by 2 in., which will provide a "cavity" large enough to (1) provide a positive barrier to moisture penetration, (2) permit easy installation of electrical facilities, and (3) permit the use of blanket insulation.

Tests have shown that anchoring 2 by 2-in. furring strips at the bottom, mid-height, and top will be adequate. Only two furring anchors will be required on the side walls, since the strips can be nailed to the top wall plate. The type of furring clip recommended is illustrated in Fig. 21. The clip holds the furring at least ¼ in. out from the face of the wall. Thus air can circulate behind the strips and any moisture that might be present can easily drain down the back face of the wall and out through weep holes in the bottom course. Typical construction details of SCR brick walls are shown in Figs. 23 to 26.

Wall layout: SCR brick is most economical if the dimensions of the building, and as many of the masonry opening widths as possible, are kept in multiples of 12 in.

Strength: Specimens of masonry walls built with SCR brick have been tested in accordance with *ASTM Standard Methods of Conducting Strength Tests of Panels for Building Construction* (E-72). Three panels each were tested for compression, impact, and racking. All of these panels were constructed with Type N mortar (1:1:6). The average results of these tests are shown in Table 16.

Because of the thinness of the wall, it was thought that the most critical test for this type of construction would be the transverse-strength test. Thirty-three panels constructed with three types of mortar (eleven specimens of each) were tested

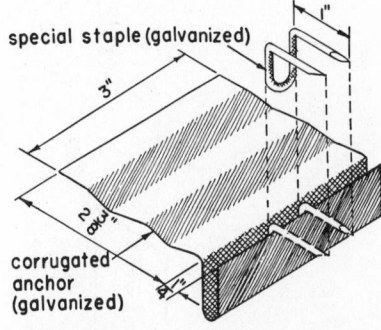

Fig. 21. Recommended type of furring clip

Alternate version has galvanized "wrap-around" strap instead of staple.

for transverse strength. The mean transverse strength of all thirty-three specimens was 81.81 psf. The results of these tests (see Table 16) indicate that there is no significant difference between the walls built with either Type M or Type S mortar, but that the transverse strength of walls built with Type N mortar is about 20 per cent less. In general, the results of the strength tests indicate that the SCR

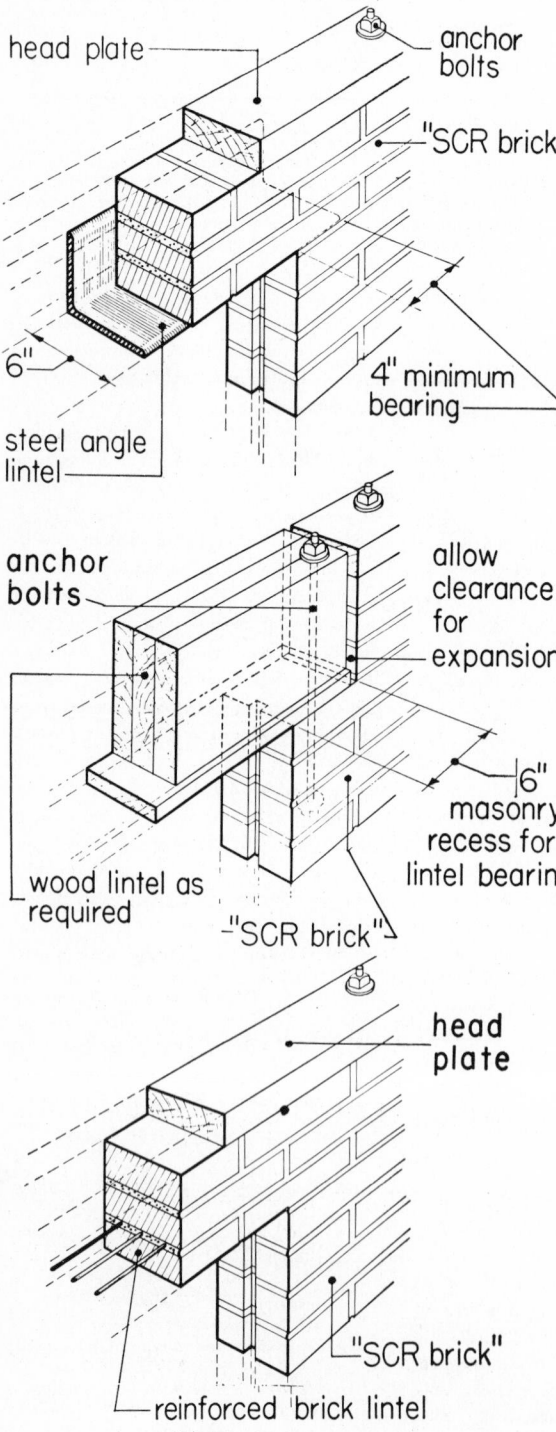

Fig. 22. Lintel construction

Table 17. Heat-transmission coefficients for SCR brick walls

Heat-transmission coefficients for SCR brick walls with various interior finishes and insulations are corrected for 15-mph wind velocity.

Type of interior finish and insulation (2x2-in. furring)	U factor
1-in. roll insulation, ½-in. insulating board lath, ½-in. vermiculite plaster	0.12
1-in. roll insulation, ⅜-in. gypsum board (dry wall)	0.16
1-in. roll insulation, metal lath, ¾-in. gypsum plaster	0.16
⅜-in. gypsum lath with aluminum foil, ½-in. vermiculite plaster	0.23
½-in. insulating board lath, ½-in. vermiculite plaster	0.23
½-in. gypsum board (dry wall) with aluminum foil	0.26
⅜-in. gypsum lath, ½-in. vermiculite plaster	0.33
Metal lath, ¾-in. gypsum plaster	0.40

Table 18. Maximum allowable bending moment and shear for reinforced SCR brick lintels[1]

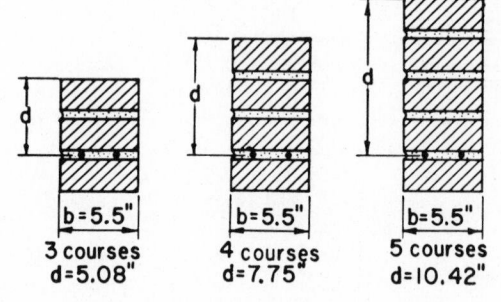

d in.	Wt. of Lintel lb./ft.	No. and Size of Bars	Area of Steel sq. in.	Maximum Moment ft.-lb.	Maximum Shear Without Stirrups lb.	Maximum Shear With Stirrups lb.
5.08	35	2-¼ "	0.10	740	560 [2]	560 [2]
		3-¼ "	0.15	1115	840 [2]	840 [2]
		2-⅜ "	0.22	1303 [3]	1225	1620 [2]
		3-⅜ "	0.33	1476 [3]	1225	2350 [2]
		4-⅜ "	0.44	1600 [3]	1225	3100 [2]
7.75	46	2-¼ "	0.10	1130	880 [2]	880 [2]
		3-¼ "	0.15	1695	1280 [2]	1280 [2]
		2-⅜ "	0.22	2480	1850	2510 [2]
		3-⅜ "	0.33	3015 [3]	1850	3700 [2]
		4-⅜ "	0.44	3296 [3]	1850	4800 [2]
10.42	60	2-¼ "	0.10	1520	1180 [2]	1180 [2]
		3-¼ "	0.15	2280	1720 [2]	1720 [2]
		2-⅜ "	0.22	3330	2500	3460 [2]
		3-⅜ "	0.33	5000	2500	5100 [2]
		4-⅜ "	0.44	5429 [3]	2500	6700 [2]

[1] Based on the use of Type M (A-1) mortar (1:¼:3) and the following allowable stresses:

f'_m = 2000 psi f_s = 20,000 psi
f_m = 660 psi   v = 50 psi (150 psi with stirrups)
u (plain bars) = 80 psi   u (deformed bars) = 160 psi

[2] Limited by bond.

[3] Limited by compression in masonry.

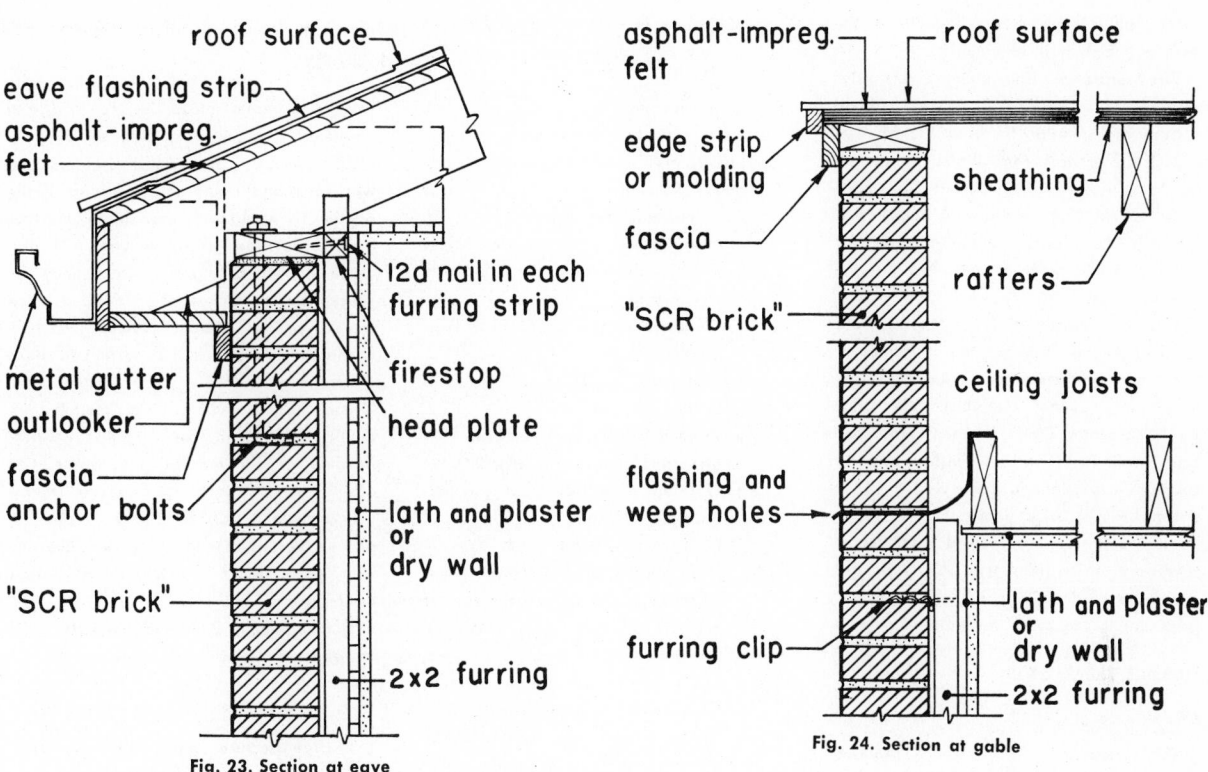

Fig. 23. Section at eave

Fig. 24. Section at gable

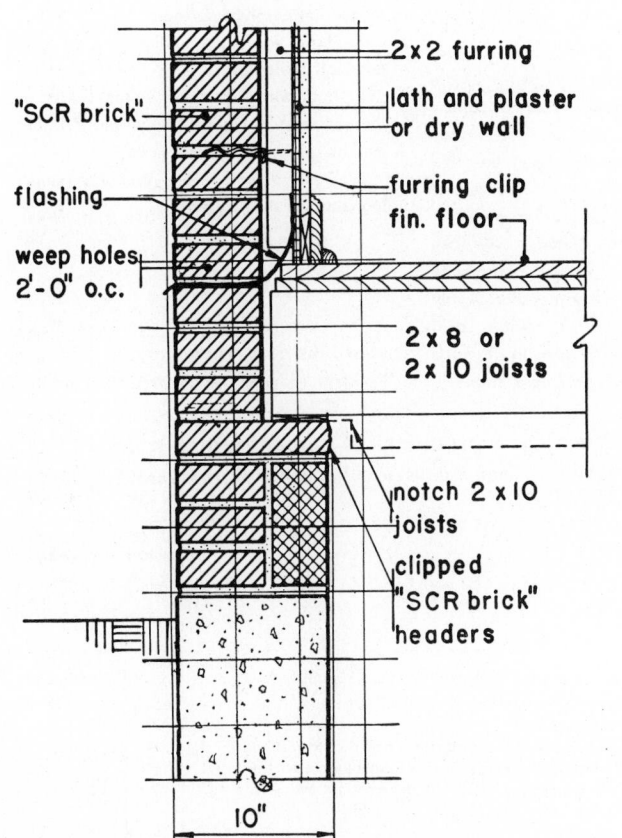

Fig. 25. Section at sill—basement or crawl space

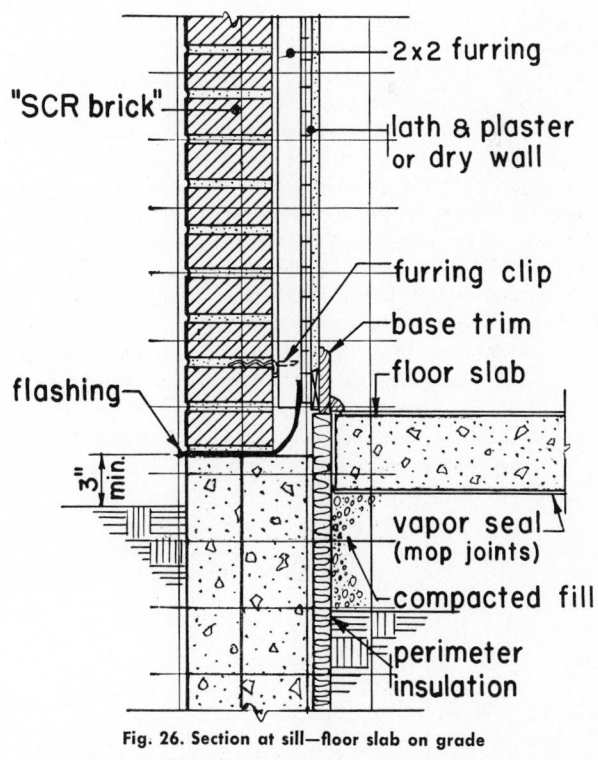

Fig. 26. Section at sill—floor slab on grade

CONSTRUCTION DETAILS OF SCR BRICK WALLS

Scale: 1 in. = 1 ft

brick wall is more than adequate for the use for which it is intended.

Fire resistance: The ultimate fire-resistance period of an SCR brick wall, without furring and interior finish, is 2½ hr.

Moisture penetration: Water permeability tests performed on furred SCR brick walls reveal that, even with poor workmanship, no moisture penetrates to the interior finish material or even to the furring strips.

Heat transmission: Based on the ASHRAE Guide figure of 0.44 for the resistance of 4 in. of high-density brick, the resistance R of the nominal 6-in.-thick SCR brick would average 0.60. U values for SCR brick walls with various finishes and insulations are given in Table 17.

Lintels: SCR brick lintels (Fig. 22) may be of wood, steel, reinforced concrete, or reinforced brick masonry. The structural properties of three sizes of reinforced SCR brick lintels are given in Table 18.

SURFACE TREATMENTS

Efflorescence

The formation of efflorescence requires (1) water-soluble salts in the masonry, (2) water in contact with these salts for sufficient time to dissolve them, and (3) a construction that permits the solution to migrate to the surface of the masonry where the salts are deposited upon evaporation of the water. Obviously, if masonry could be constructed which contained no water-soluble salts or if no water penetrated the masonry, efflorescence would not occur. In masonry exposed to the weather, however, neither of these conditions can be met completely. Consequently, the practical way to eliminate efflorescence is to reduce all contributing factors to a minimum. The following procedures are recommended as a means to that end.

1. Reduce the amount of soluble salts in the masonry materials by:
   a. Specifying that all wall facing and trim materials pass a "wick test" for efflorescence (ASTM C67).
   b. Testing mortar for efflorescence; if necessary add calcium stearate (0.2 per cent by weight of combined cement and lime).
2. Prevent contact between facing and backup by use of cavity-wall construction or flashing.
3. Keep moisture out of wall by use of:
   a. Hard-burned brick or tile facing.
   b. Cavity-wall or solid metal-tied wall construction.
   c. Good workmanship (all joints thoroughly filled).
   d. Protection of the tops of walls during construction.
   e. Projecting sills and copings, with drip slots underneath (Fig. 27).
   f. Flashing, especially at all intersections of wall and roof, under all horizontal elements such as copings and sills, and just above finished grade, to prevent rise of moisture by capillarity from the foundation.
   g. Caulking, carefully applied, around all door and window frames.
   h. Vapor barrier and ventilation to prevent condensation within walls.

Cleaning

New buildings: Many buildings have been irreparably damaged by improper cleaning. Commonest causes of such damage are (1) failure to saturate masonry before application of cleaning agent, (2) use of too strong acid solution, and (3) failure to protect windows and trim. It is recommended that any cleaning agent be tried first on a sample wall (minimum area of 20 sq ft) and left for at least a week.

To clean *unglazed masonry surfaces*, remove large particles with a putty knife and saturate the surface with water. Apply a 10 per cent solution of muriatic acid (not more than 1 part acid to 9 parts water) to an area of not more than 15 to 20 sq ft. Then wash the surface with clear water.

To clean *glazed surfaces*, scrub with soap and water only. Use no acid and no metal scrapers on glazed surfaces.

Efflorescence can usually be removed with soap and water and a stiff scrubbing brush. If necessary, use dilute muriatic acid, as described above. A type of efflorescence known as "green stain" may be caused by the action of muriatic acid on some types of masonry. Since this type cannot be foreseen it is important to make a preliminary test on a sample wall. Green stain is difficult to remove: try oxalic acid (2 lb per 5 gal of water) brushed or sprayed on and washed off after several hours; if necessary follow with sodium hydroxide ("Drano"—one 12-oz can per qt of water) applied liberally with paint brush and hosed off after three days.

Old buildings: Cleaning methods listed in order of frequency of use are as follows:

1. *High-pressure steam*—best for relatively impervious facing materials.
2. *Sand blasting*—used mostly on porous materials such as limestone, sandstone, and unglazed brick; cannot be used on glazed or polished surfaces.
3. *Hand washing*—expensive; used only on small buildings.
4. *High-pressure cold water*—good if there is ample water supply and suitable method of disposing of waste.
5. *Chemical and steam*—used for removing coatings such as paint.

Stains

The removal of stains, such as those caused by rust, smoke, copper, oil, and the like, requires special treatment appro-

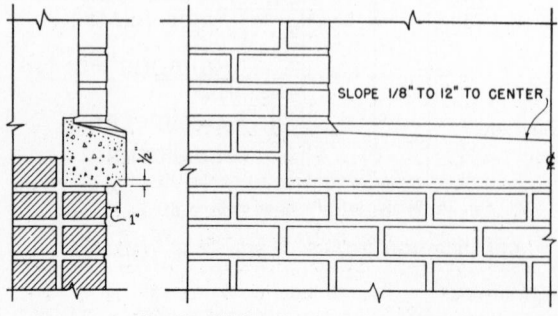

SLOPE 1/8" TO 12" TO CENTER

Fig. 27. Sill detail to prevent wash

Table 19. Ingredients of cement-water paints

Values given below comply with Federal Specification TT–P–21.

Ingredient	Type 1 Class A		Type 2 Class A	
	Max.	Min.	Max.	Min.
Portland cement	—	65	—	80
Hydrated lime	25	—	10	—
Carbonates (calculated as carbon dioxide CO_2)	3	—	3	—
Water repellents (calcium or aluminum stearate)	1	0.5	1	0.5
Hygroscopic salts (calcium or sodium chloride)	5	3	5	3
Titanium dioxide (TiO_2), Zinc sulfide (ZnS) or mixture	5	3	5	3

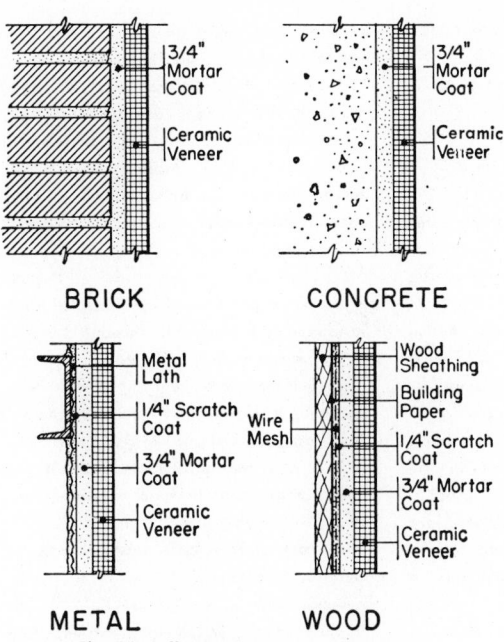

BRICK — 3/4" Mortar Coat, Ceramic Veneer

CONCRETE — 3/4" Mortar Coat, Ceramic Veneer

METAL — Metal Lath, 1/4" Scratch Coat, 3/4" Mortar Coat, Ceramic Veneer

WOOD — Wood Sheathing, Building Paper, Wire Mesh, 1/4" Scratch Coat, 3/4" Mortar Coat, Ceramic Veneer

Fig. 28. Adhesion-type ceramic veneer

This veneer is adaptable to both new and remodeling work and, as illustrated here, for attachment to various types of backings.

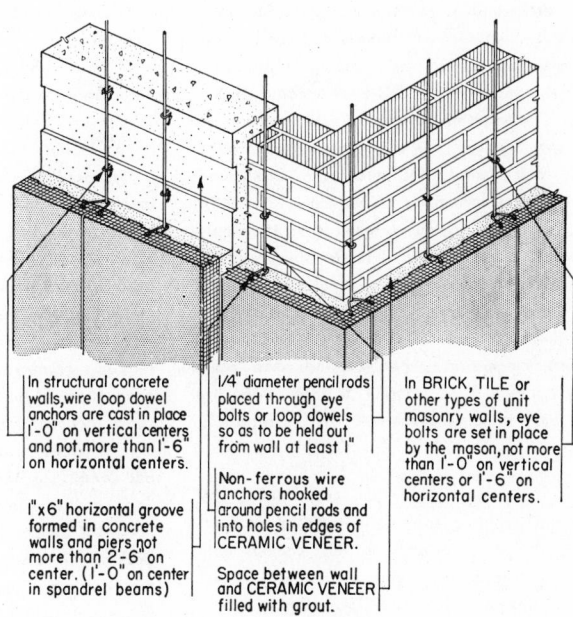

In structural concrete walls, wire loop dowel anchors are cast in place 1'-0" on vertical centers and not more than 1'-6" on horizontal centers.

1"x6" horizontal groove formed in concrete walls and piers not more than 2'-6" on center. (1'-0" on center in spandrel beams)

1/4" diameter pencil rods placed through eye bolts or loop dowels so as to be held out from wall at least 1".

Non-ferrous wire anchors hooked around pencil rods and into holes in edges of CERAMIC VENEER.

Space between wall and CERAMIC VENEER filled with grout.

In BRICK, TILE or other types of unit masonry walls, eye bolts are set in place by the mason, not more than 1'-0" on vertical centers or 1'-6" on horizontal centers.

Fig. 29. Anchored-type ceramic veneer

The ceramic-veneer slabs may be set with the ribs or scoring in a horizontal position or, as shown here, in a vertical position.

priate to the type of stain. (See *Technical Notes on Brick and Tile Construction*, Vol. 8, No. 12, Structural Clay Products Institute.)

Painting

Paints are applied to masonry walls for decorative effect and as a barrier to rain penetration. They must not, however, prevent the wall from "breathing," that is, prevent moisture within the wall from escaping by evaporation from the surface. *Cement-water paints* are superior to organic paints in this respect, and are also more durable when exposed to weathering. (See National Bureau of Standards publications BMS 95 and 110, and American Concrete Institute publication 616.49.) Federal Specification TT-P-21, covering two types of cement-water paint, is given in Table 19. Class B is the same as Class A with the addition of 20 to 40 per cent by weight of white silica (No. 100 to No. 20 sieve). Cement-water paint should be applied to a uniformly damp but not dripping surface, by means of a stiff scrubbing brush, and kept damp for at least 24 hours; the second coat should then be applied and kept damp for at least 48 hours. Organic paints suitable for use on masonry walls are *resin-emulsion paints*, *synthetic-rubber paints*, and *oil-base paints*. The first two may be applied to either damp or dry walls; new masonry should be allowed to age at least three weeks

before painting. Oil-base paints, however, should never be applied to a damp wall, and should not be applied to new masonry until it has aged at least six to twelve months. For all organic paints, a prime coat of cement-water paint is recommended to seal pores and cracks in mortar joints.

Waterproofing

Colorless waterproofers are solutions or emulsions of water-repellent substances such as waxes, oils, resins, and, recently, silicones, in an organic solvent. They are applied by brush or spray to a wall that is surface dry. The silicone type appears to be the most effective. *Bituminous compounds* in the form of asphalt or coal tar are applied hot with a brush or mop, and in the form of asphalt emulsions are applied cold with a trowel. They are used principally below grade or where appearance is not important.

TERRA COTTA

Modern architectural terra cotta is both machine-extruded and hand-made (molded or pressed). The machine-made product, shaped by extruding the plastic clay through dies, is often referred to as "ceramic veneer." Both hand-made and machine-extruded terra cotta or ceramic veneer are available in an almost unlimited range of colors. Both are custom products

and thus provide the architect with complete freedom in design.

CERAMIC VENEER

Ceramic veneer is used extensively on large plain areas of modern buildings. The present discussion will be confined to the installation of adhesion- and anchored-type ceramic veneer.

Adhesion type

Adhesion-type ceramic veneer (Fig. 28) is commonly called "thin ceramic veneer," since the maximum over-all thickness of the slab is 1⅛ in. The maximum face area of individual slabs does not exceed 540 sq in. The maximum over-all face dimensions, therefore, are about 18 by 30 in. or 20 by 27 in. This type of ceramic veneer requires no metal anchorage, but is held in place by the adhesion of the mortar to the ceramic-veneer body and the backing wall. The over-all thickness from the face of the ceramic veneer to the face of the backing wall will be only 1¾ to 2 in.

Extensive shear tests on adhesion-type ceramic-veneer wall panels indicate that the shearing strengths developed by such a method of anchorage are much greater than those required by building codes.

The mortar recommended for adhesion-type ceramic veneer consists of 1 part portland cement, ½ part high calcium lime putty, and 4 parts sand, by volume. To this mixture may be added ammonium stearate, or the equivalent, in the proportions recommended by the manufacturer.

The ceramic veneer should conform to specifications of the Architectural Terra Cotta Institute for quality of finish and physical properties of the units. The units should be so dimensioned that they may be set with uniform joints approximately ¼ in. in width. The face lengths and widths should not vary by more than $\frac{1}{16}$ in. from the dimensions called for on the setting drawings, and the faces of the units should not vary from a true plane by more than an average of $\frac{1}{16}$ in. per sq ft.

Erection

1. Dampen wall; if recommended by manufacturer, soak units in water for 1 hr.
2. Apply brush coat of cement and water to back of unit and to wall.
3. Apply mortar to back of unit and to wall.
4. Set unit, plumb and level, tap to remove air pockets; use wood wedges in joints.

5. Tool or rake face joints ½ in. deep and point.
6. Wash with clean water and soap, if necessary; use no acid.

Anchored type

Anchored-type ceramic veneer (Fig. 29) is recommended if the architect desires a large-scale slab. Ribs or scoring are provided on the backs of such units, and the over-all slab thicknesses range from 2 to approximately 2½ in. Depending on the slab thickness, a total of 3 to 4½ in. is required from rough wall to finished veneer surface to provide adequate grout space between the veneer and the backing. Anchor holes are provided in the bed edges of the slabs for the installation of the anchors, which, in turn, are fastened to pencil rods anchored to the backing or inserted in dovetail slots in the backing. Once the anchors are in place, the units are bonded to the wall by a reinforced grout core, keyed into the horizontal groove in the rough masonry

backing. The ribs on the back of the panel are keyed into the grout.

The cement grout used with anchored-type ceramic veneer consists of 1 part portland cement, 1 part sand, and 5 parts graded pea gravel passed through a ¼-in. sieve. Sufficient water is added to cause the mixture to flow readily.

Erection

1. When pencil rods are used, insert ¼-in. diam rods vertically through loops of dowel anchors in rough wall.
2. Set ceramic-veneer unit with wood wedges in joints. Insert wire anchors in top edge, and tie to vertical rods.
3. When one horizontal course is complete, pour grout in space between backs of units and rough wall.
4. Point joints and wash surface, as described above.

Acid cleaning or the use of abrasives is not recommended for ceramic-glazed surfaces, nor should metal cleaning tools be used. If hard lumps of mortar must

Table 20. Average weights of clay tile partitions*

	Nominal thickness, in.					
	2	3	4	6	8	12
Weight, psf	15	16	17	24	32	46

* No plaster finishes are included.

Table 21. Maximum heights of clay tile partitions

Cells may be vertical or horizontal.

	Nominal thickness, in.						
	2	3	4	6	8	10	12
Maximum unsupported height, ft	9*	12	15	20	25	30	36

* Maximum unsupported horizontal length is 6 ft.

Table 22. Ultimate fire resistance of structural clay tile partitions

Data given below are for partitions laid in portland cement-lime mortar.

Description of Partition	Thickness (in.)	Minimum per cent solid (in. units)	No Plaster A hr. min.	No Plaster B hr. min.	Plaster on unexposed side A hr. min.	Plaster on unexposed side B hr. min.	Plaster on fire exposed side A hr. min.	Plaster on fire exposed side B hr. min.	Plaster on both sides A hr. min.	Plaster on both sides B hr. min.
One cell in wall thickness	3	50	0 10	0 20	0 20	0 20	0 30	0 45	0 45	1 0
	4	40	10	20	20	25	30	45	45	1 0
	4	50	15	25	25	30	45	1 0	1 0	1 15
	6	30	15	20	25	35	45	1 0	1 15	1 30
	6	40	20	25	30	40	1 0	1 05	1 15	1 30
Two cells in wall thickness	4	50	25	30	35	45	1 0	1 15	1 15	1 30
	4	60	30	35	40	1 0	1 15	1 30	1 30	2 0
	6	45	45	1 0	1 0	1 15	1 15	1 30	1 30	2 0
One cell in wall thickness plus double shells	4	45	20	0 25	0 30	0 35	0 45	1 0	1 15	1 30
One cell in wall thickness, cells filled [1]	4	40	1 15	1 15	1 30	1 30	1 45	1 45	2 30	2 30
	6	30	2 0	2 0	2 30	2 30	2 30	2 30	3 30	3 30

Notes: [1] Cells filled with broken tile, crushed stone, slag, cinders, or sand, mixed with mortar.

Ratings in column A are for dense hard-burned clay or shale tile.
Ratings in column B are for medium-burned clay tile. All shale tile are classified under A.
Not less than ⅝-in. thickness of 1:3 sanded gypsum plaster is required to develop the above ratings for plastered partitions.

be removed, sharpened wood paddles are recommended.

STRUCTURAL CLAY TILE PARTITIONS

Unit dimensions

Structural clay partition tile have 12 by 12-in. faces and thicknesses of 2, 3, 4, 6, 8, 10, and 12 in. In nonmodular tile, these are the actual dimensions. In modular tile, the actual dimensions are smaller by the thickness of one joint, usually ½ in. All units have three cells in width. Units up to and including 6 in. in thickness have one cell; units thicker than 6 in. are two cells deep.

Physical properties

The following physical properties of struc-

tural clay tile partitions are covered in the tables: weight, Table 20; stability (maximum heights), Table 21; fire resistance, Table 22 (National Bureau of Standards tests, reported in BMS 92); and sound resistance, Table 23 (National Bureau of Standards tests, reported in BMS 17 and supplements).

Plaster adhesion

For many years, scored surfaces were considered necessary to obtain a strong bond between plaster and tile. Extensive tests at the National Bureau of Standards and other laboratories have indicated that ample bond strength is developed between plaster and tile surfaces that are smooth, combed, or roughened (wire cut).

Construction

Nonbearing partitions, where suspended ceilings do not occur, should extend from the top of the structural floor to the bottom surface of the floor construction above and should be wedged with small pieces of tile. The top joint should then be filled with mortar.

Partitions should be bonded at intersections and properly anchored to door bucks and adjoining masonry walls. Partitions that abut intersecting walls should be anchored with metal ties or clips at least ⅞ in. wide and of not less than No. 16 gage galvanized iron, at vertical intervals of not more than 4 ft.

Multiple-unit nonbearing tile partitions should be bonded at vertical intervals not

Table 23. Sound-transmission loss in decibels

Material in Test Panel	Weight psf.	Average Reduction Factors
12″ Hollow Tile—two different types of units, plaster both sides, brown and white finish.	65	48.6
12″ Hollow Tile—two different types of units, plaster both sides, brown and white finish.	66	50.0
8″ Hollow Tile—plaster both sides, brown and smooth white finish.	48	49.8
6″ Hollow Tile—plaster both sides, brown coat and smooth white finish.	39	47.1
6″ Hollow Tile—plaster both sides, brown coat and smooth white finish.	37	45.7
4″ Hollow Tile—plaster both sides, brown coat and smooth white finish.	29	44.0
4″ Hollow Tile—plaster both sides, brown coat and smooth white finish.	29	43.5
3″ Hollow Tile—plaster both sides, brown coat and smooth white finish.	28	44.4
8″ Hollow Tile (Heath cubes)—plaster both sides, brown coat and smooth white finish.	55	51.0
4″ Hollow Tile—wood furring, paper, metal lath and plaster both sides.	34	57.5
4″ Hollow Tile (on pads)—wood furring, paper, metal lath and plaster both sides.	34	58.3
8″ Hollow Tile—2 units, 1¾″ apart, filled with Flax-li-num and ½″ Flax-li-num pads at top, bottom and sides of one wythe.	50	59.2

Table 24. Ultimate fire resistance of structural facing-tile partitions

Nominal Wall Thickness in.	Description	Ultimate Fire Resistance
6	Glazed or unglazed facing tile cored not in excess of 25 per cent, 2 units in wall thickness.	3 hr.
6	2-in. glazed or unglazed facing tile cored not in excess of 25 per cent and 4-in. structural tile cored not in excess of 40 per cent, plastered on unglazed side with ¾-in. gypsum sand plaster (1:3 by volume).	3 hr.
4	Glazed or unglazed facing tile cored not in excess of 25 per cent, plastered on unglazed side with ¾-in. gypsum sand plaster (1:3 by volume).	2 hr.
4	Glazed or unglazed facing tile cored not in excess of 30 per cent, plastered on unglazed side with ¾-in. vermiculite plaster.	2 hr.
4	Glazed or unglazed facing tile meeting requirements of ASTM Specifications for Structural Clay Load-Bearing Wall Tile, C34, except that the shells of solid shell horizontal cell units shall be not less than ¾-in. thick, plastered on unglazed side with ¾-in. gypsum sand plaster (1:3 by volume).	1 hr.

Note: All plastered partitions plastered on unexposed side.

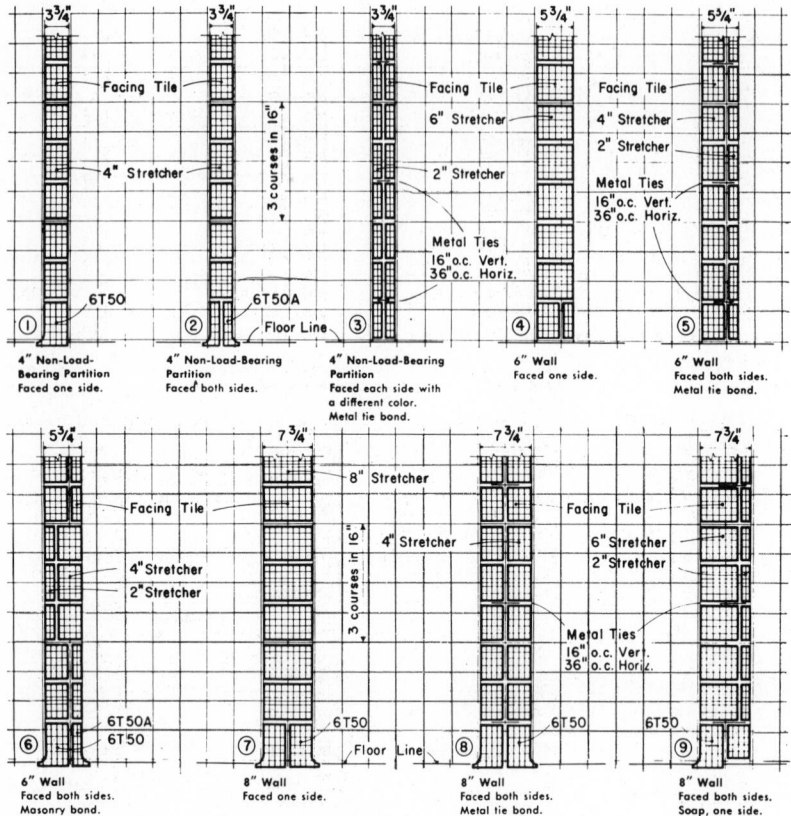

Fig. 30. Wall sections

exceeding 34 in. by lapping one unit at least 3¾ in. over the unit below; by lapping with units at least 50 per cent greater in thickness than the units below at vertical intervals not exceeding 17 in.; or by galvanized corrugated metal ties at least ⅞ in. wide and not lighter than No. 22 gage, or other approved ties. At least one tie should be used for each 2 sq ft of wall area with ties spaced not farther apart than 24 in. either vertically or horizontally.

In plastered construction, wood or steel channel door bucks should be approximately 1½ in. wider than the thickness of the tile to act as grounds for the plaster.

STRUCTURAL CLAY FACING TILE PARTITIONS

Fire-resistance ratings of five structural clay facing-tile partitions are given in Table 24, and are based on standard fire tests performed at Ohio State University.

Other properties of seventeen walls using structural clay facing tile, alone or in combination with other materials, are given in Table 25. Wall sections are shown in Fig. 30.

Allowable load has been computed from the unit working stresses prescribed in the *American Standard Building Code Requirements for Masonry*. Allowable loads are computed on the net area and the following working stresses: Type M (A-1) mortar, 85 psi; Type S (A-2) mortar, 75 psi; Type N (B) mortar, 70 psi.

Material quantity: Mortar quantities shown are for tile laid with ¼-in. joints. If ⅜-in. joints are used, mortar quantities should be increased by 40 per cent.

Lateral-support requirements conform to the ASA Code, which generally permits a 100 per cent increase in required spacing of supports for nonloadbearing partitions as compared to loadbearing partitions. Lateral support may be obtained horizontally from across walls or piers and vertically from floors or roofs.

Wall weights are taken from *American Standard Building Code Requirements for Minimum Design Loads for Buildings and Other Structures* (ASA A58.1). For plastered walls, add 5 psf for ⅝-in. gypsum plaster.

Sound resistance: Sound-transmission losses are based on test results, where available. In other cases, they have been computed in accordance with National Bureau of Standards Research Paper No. 48.

Modular design: All structural clay facing tile manufactured by members of the Facing Tile Institute are designed for modular coordination. All wall sections on the following three pages are drawn on the standard 4 by 4-in. modular grid.

Stack bond

In addition to the conventional half, third, and quarter bonds, structural clay facing tile is often laid in stack bond (block or plumb bond), in which all

Table 25.   Properties of wall sections

WALL NUMBER		1	2	3	4	5	6	7	8	9
Allowable Load (lbs./linear ft.)	Type M Mortar (85 psi) S (75 psi) N (70 psi)	— — —	— — —	— — —	5,870 5,180 4,830	5,870 5,180 4,830	5,870 5,180 4,830	7,900 6,980 6,510	7,900 6,980 6,510	7,900 6,980 6,510
Material Quantity (per 100 sq. ft.)	Mortar (cu. ft.) 25% waste added Units (F. T.) 2% " " (F. T.) 2% " " Metal Ties 2% " "	2.19 230 — —	2.19 230 — —	2.19[1] 460 — 25.5	3.36 230 — —	3.36[1] 230 230 25.5	3.36[1] 230 230 —	4.53 230 — —	4.53[1] 230 460 25.5	4.53[1] 230 230 25.5
"U" Value (BTU/sq. ft./hr./°F.)	Unplastered Partition	.40	.40	.39	.35	.34	.34	.31	.30	.30
Lateral Support Spacing Required (ft.)	Non-Load-Bearing Load-Bearing	12 —	12 —	12 —	18 9	18 9	18 9	24 12	24 12	24 12
Wall Weight (lbs./sq. ft.)	Unplastered	30	30	33	41	47	47	50	60	58
Sound Resistance (db.)	Unplastered	45	45	46	47	48	48	49	50	50

[1] If collar joint is filled, add 2.6 cu. ft. per 100 sq. ft. of wall.

joints, vertical as well as horizontal, are aligned. The units may be placed with their long axes in either a horizontal or a vertical direction, and are referred to on this page as "stretcher stack bond" and "soldier stack bond," respectively.

Unit

If structural clay facing tile is laid in stack bond, it is particularly important that the size of units be within extremely close tolerances, since the continuous joints accentuate any variation in size between adjacent units. In order to ensure minimum variation of face dimensions, it is recommended that the units be specified as "Select Quality, Gaged" or "Select Quality, Ground Edge." Permissible tolerances for this grade are plus or minus $\frac{1}{16}$ in.; the maximum difference between the largest and smallest unit in one lot is $\frac{3}{32}$ in. Standard face dimensions are 5, 7¾, 11¹¹⁄₁₆, and 15¾ in. All three of the most common series of structural facing tile (4D—nominal face size 5⅓ by 8 in.; 6T—5⅓ by 12 in.; 8W—8 by 16 in.) are readily adaptable for use in stack bond. No special shapes are needed, although standard shapes may sometimes be used in unconventional positions.

Bonding

Figure 31 shows seven typical wall sections in which structural clay facing tile is used in stack bond, both soldier and stretcher. As may be seen, structural bonding of stretcher stack bond walls is similar to conventional methods. Although most of the sections shown indicate masonry bond between the various wythes of the wall, bonding by means of noncorrosive metal ties is equally suitable. Structural bonding of soldier stack bond walls, shown

in Fig. 31, is typical and the designer may find other methods that are better suited to a specific job.

Maximum heights and lengths

When structural facing tile or any other masonry units are laid in stack bond, they do not have the interlocking quality of half bond. This does not materially weaken the wall laterally, since it rarely relies

upon horizontal stability in this manner. In addition, with the exception of walls composed entirely of through-the-wall units, a form of half bond will usually exist, because the various wythes will seldom have coinciding head joints. Where additional strength is required, it is recommended that steel reinforcement be used in accordance with accepted design procedures.

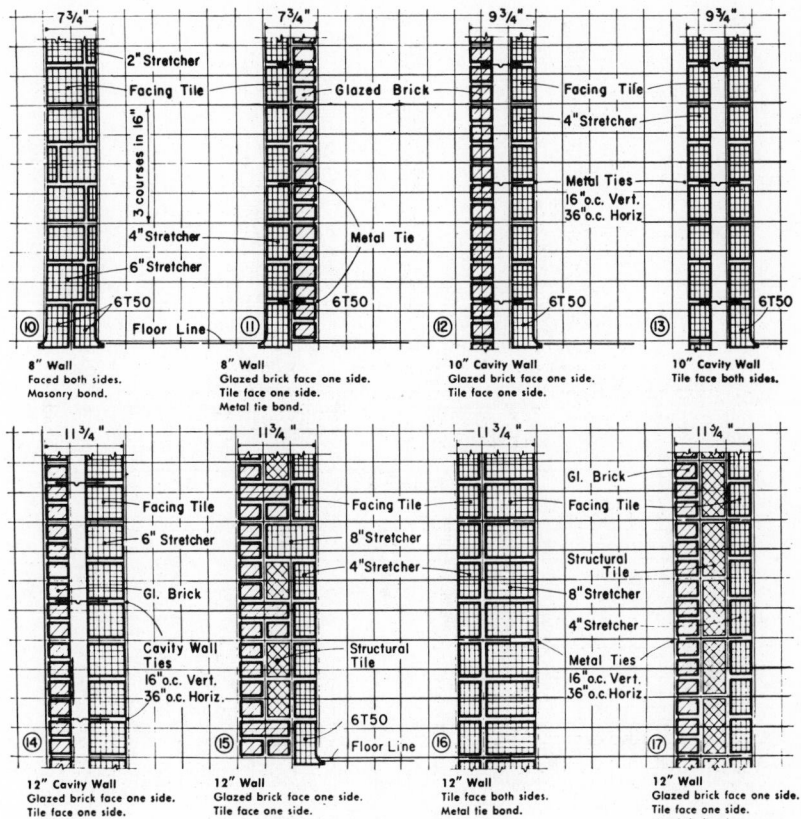

Fig. 30 (cont.) Wall sections

Table 25 (cont.)   Properties of wall sections

WALL NUMBER		10	11	12	13	14	15	16	17
Allowable Load (lbs./linear ft.)	Type M Mortar (85 psi)	7,900	7,900	6,300[3]	6,300[3]	7,970[3]	12,000	12,000	12,000
	S (75 psi)	6,980	6,980	5,400[3]	5,400[3]	6,840[3]	10,580	10,580	10,580
	N (70 psi)	6,510	6,510	4,950[3]	4,950[3]	6,270[3]	9,860	9,860	9,860
Material Quantity (per 100 sq. ft.)	Mortar (cu. ft.) 25% waste added	4.53[1]	9.57	6.97	4.38	8.14	14.33	9.32	16.59
	Units (F. T.) 2% " "	230[4]	230	230	460	230	192/38	230[2]	230
	(S. T.) 2% " "	—	—	—	—	—	115	—	153
	(Brick) 5% " "	—	709	709	—	709	945	—	709
	Metal Ties 2% " "	—	25.5	25.5	25.5	25.5	—	25.5	25.5
"U" Value (BTU/sq. ft./hr./°F.)	Unplastered Partition	.30	—	—	—	—	—	—	—
	Exterior Wall	—	.41	.30	.25	.23	.31	.30	.31
	2" Insulation	—	—	.08	.08	.08	—	—	—
Lateral Support Spacing Required (ft.)	Non-Load-Bearing	24	24	24	24	30	36	36	36
	Load-Bearing	12	12	12	12	15	18	18	18
Wall Weight (lbs./sq. ft.)	Unplastered	58	67	67	60	79	90	80	89
Sound Resistance (db.)	Unplastered	50	52	54	52	58	58	57	57

[1] If collar joint is filled, add 2.6 cu. ft. per 100 sq. ft. of wall.
[2] 230 each of 4" and 8" stretchers.
[3] Eccentrically loaded. For concentric loading increase allowable load 25%.
[4] 230 each of 2" and 6" stretchers.

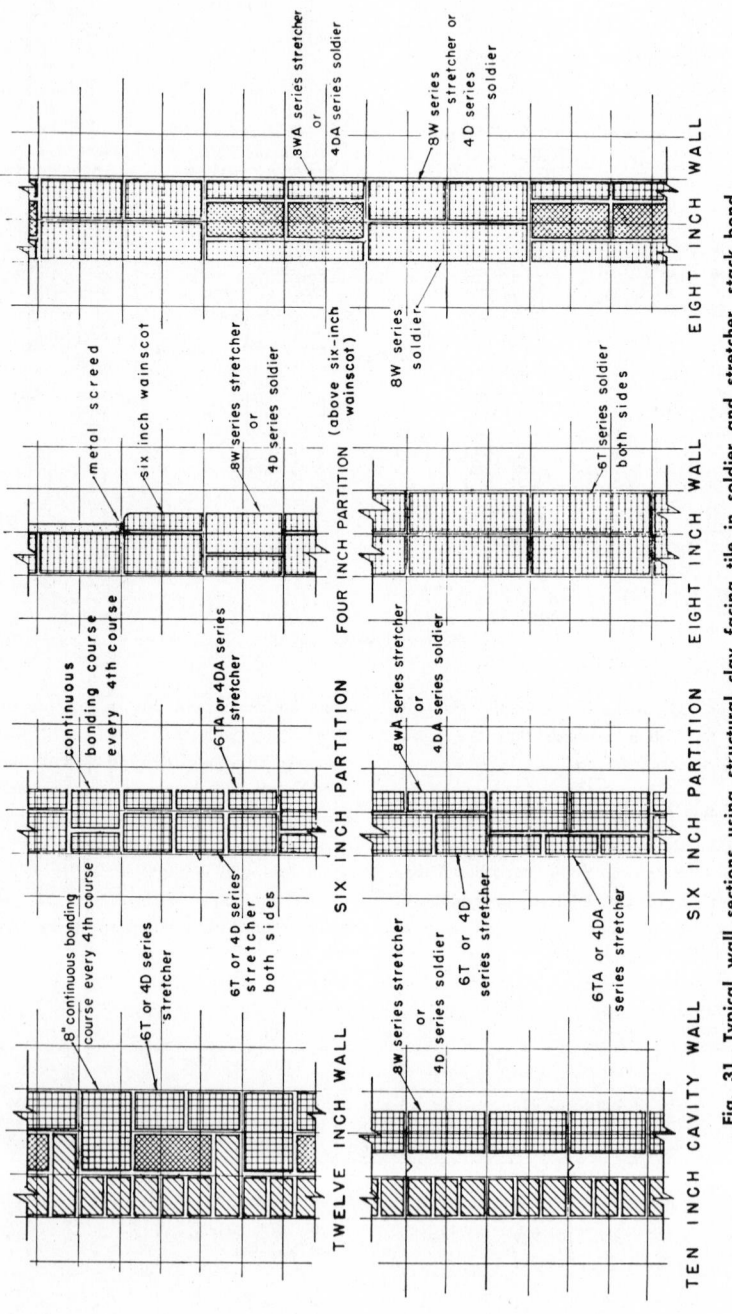

Fig. 31. Typical wall sections using structural clay facing tile in soldier and stretcher stack bond

Stretcher units may be horizontally or vertically cored, depending on the manufacturer.

Presented through the courtesy of Structural Clay Products Institute*

Chemical-resistant clay masonry is used extensively in many industries for floors, vats and tanks, where conventional materials would deteriorate when subjected to acids, alkalis, petroleum products, vegetable oils, fats, etc.

Chemical-resistant or "acid-proof" brick and tile will withstand mild alkalis and all acids except hydrofluoric.

"Carbon" brick may be necessary for strong alkalis and for hydrofluoric acid and its salts.

MASONRY UNITS

Acid-proof brick or tile must be structurally strong and free of laminations. There should be no pores, and the surface texture should be sufficiently roughened to insure a strong bond with the joints.

Size. The brick and tile range in thickness from approximately 1 to 4½ in.; in width from 1¾ to 6 in.; and in length from 7½ to 12 in.

JOINTS

The life of a chemical-resistant installation depends greatly on the proper jointing material. For example, there are few chemicals which do not attack regular portland cement mortars. Although the bricks or tile may not be affected by acids or alkalis, the joints may be attacked, causing disintegration of the joints, and eventual loosening of the masonry units.

In Table 26 on the following page are the types of chemicals to which the masonry might be exposed and the most common joint treatments recommended. Joints should be as narrow as possible to minimize exposed joint area and to reduce the amount of jointing material required. Instructions and limitations of any material, as recommended or noted by the manufacturers, should be observed explicitly.

* Information in these sheets originally appeared in "Technical Notes on Brick and Tile Construction," November 1953.

MORTARS

Type 1—Waterproofed Portland Cement.

Application. Can be used in joints of masonry floors, vats or tanks subjected to excessive moisture or liquids which do not attack portland cement.

Resistant To: Lactic acid (milk or milk products), petroleum and vegetable oils, molasses, etc.

Preparation: Cement is available with waterproofing medium already in it, or the mortar can be made waterproof by addition of the correct amount of integral admixture. Also there are surface treatments which will make the joints more impervious to moisture.

Type 2—Special Admixtures for Portland Cement.

Application: Often used in dairies, breweries, etc., where the solutions do not appreciably attack portland cement mortar, and where there is little abrasion.

Resistant To: Very mild acid solutions and some other chemicals.

Preparation: Admixtures can be added on the job in either powder or liquid form.

Type 3—Sodium Silicate Cements.

Application: Used for acid-resistant mortar setting beds and joints of brick or tile-lined chemical structures—vats, tanks etc.

Resistant To: Hot and cold acids of all strengths except hydrofluoric, and temperatures as high as 1800 F.

Not Resistant To: Alkaline solutions; may be soluble in water. Impractical for ordinary floors. Should not be applied directly to setting beds of portland cement (attacked by alkalis), unless it is coated with asphalt first.

Preparation: Such cements should be quick-setting and self-hardening. They are usually prepared by mixing the sodium silicate binder with

a dry powder or filler.

Type 4—Synthetic Resin Cements.

Application: Excellent for setting beds and joints of masonry lined apparatus, as well as for floors and walls in chemical plants, pulp mills, oil refineries, food and beverage packing plants, dairies and breweries.

Resistant To: Acids (except nitric and chromic), water, steam, oils, fats, and weak alkalis. Highly resistant to abrasion and washing action, thermal shock and temperatures up to 300 F. The cements are quick-setting and self-hardening. When used with units laid in a bed of portland cement mortars, the open joints should be washed with dilute hydrochloric acid to neutralize the alkalinity of portland cement.

Preparation: Resin solution mixed with dry powder, and applied cold.

Type 5—Sulfur Base Cements.

Application: Used primarily for joints of masonry lined chemical apparatus, floors, tanks, etc., subjected to severe deterioration due to acids.

Resistant To: All acids.

Not Resistant To: Weak alkalis and oils. Limited to temperatures less than 200 F.

Preparation: Available in powder or brick form and must be heated to molten state and poured into joints while hot. As the joint cools and hardens, it is tooled to smooth finish.

Type 6—Bituminous Mortars, Asphaltic Mixtures and Emulsions.

Application: Used as membranes, setting beds, grouting, and poured joints for certain types of chemical-resistant masonry installations.

Resistant To: Acids and certain alkalis.

Not Resistant To: Oils, fats, greases, and some organic solvents.

Preparation: Applied either hot or cold. Contain fillers such as portland cement, sand, asbestos, gypsum etc.

Chemical-resistant tile and brick

Table 26.   Recommended joint treatments

	Type of Chemical	Action on Regular Portland Cement Joints	Suggested Type of Joint or Joint Treatment
ACIDS	Acetic	yes	2, 3, 4, 5, 6
	Acid Waters	yes	2, 3, 4, 5, 6
	Carbolic	yes	2, 3, 4
	Carbonic	yes	2, 3, 4, 5, 6
	Humic	Conditional	2, 3, 4, 5, 6
	Hydrochloric	yes	3, 4, 5, 6
	Hydrofluoric (1)	yes	Attacks brick or tile
	Lactic	yes	1, 2, 3, 4, 5
	Muriatic	yes	3, 4, 5, 6
	Nitric	yes	3, 5, 6
	Oxalic	Conditional	2, 3, 4, 5, 6
	Phosphoric	yes	2, 3, 4, 5, 6
	Sulphuric	yes	2, 3, 4, 5, 6
	Sulphurous	yes	2, 3, 4, 5, 6
	Tannic	yes	2, 3, 4, 5, 6
SALTS AND ALKALIES	Carbonates of: Ammonia Potassium Sodium	Conditional	2, 4, 6
	Chlorides of: Calcium Potassium Sodium Strontium	Conditional	2, 3, 4, 5, 6
	Chlorides of: Ammonia Copper Iron Magnesium Mercury Zinc	yes	2, 3, 4, 5, 6
	Fluorides	Conditional	2, 4, 5
	Hydroxides of: Ammonia Potassium Sodium	yes	2, 6
	Nitrates of: Ammonia Calcium Potassium Sodium	Conditional	2, 3, 5, 6
	Potassium Permanganate	no	2, 3
	Silicates	no	2, 4, 6
	Sulphates of: Ammonia	yes	2, 3, 4, 5
	Sulphates of: Aluminum Calcium Cobalt Copper Iron Manganese Nickel Potassium Sodium Zinc	yes	2, 3, 4, 5, 6
PETROLEUM OILS	Heavy oils below 30° Baume	no	1, 2, 3, 4
	Light oils above 30° Baume	Penetration	1, 2, 3, 4
	Benzine Gasoline Kerosene Naptha	Penetration	1, 2, 3, 4

	Type of Chemical	Action on Regular Portland Cement Joints	Suggested Type of Joint or Joint Treatment
COAL TAR DISTILLATES	Alizarin Anthracene Benzol Carbozol Cumol Xylol	no	2, 3
	Paraffin Pitch Toluol	no	2, 3, 4
	Carbolineum Creosote Cresol Lysol Phenol	yes	2, 3
VEGETABLE OILS	Cotton seed	yes	1, 2, 3, 4
	Rosin	no	1, 2, 3, 4
	Almond Castor China-wood Cocoanut Linseed Olive Peanut Poppy seed Rape seed Soy-bean Tung Walnut	Conditional	1, 2, 3, 4
	Turpentine	Penetration	1, 2, 3, 4
FATS AND FATTY ACIDS (animal)	Fish oil Foot oil	Conditional	1, 2, 3, 4
	Lard and lard oil Tallow and tallow oil	Conditional	2, 3, 4
MISCELLANEOUS	Alcohol	no	2, 3, 4
	Ammonium hydroxide	Conditional	2, 3, 6
	Baking soda	Conditional	2, 3, 4, 6
	Beer	Conditional	3, 4, 6
	Bleaching powder	Conditional	2, 3, 4, 5
	Borax, Boric acid	Conditional	2, 3, 4, 5, 6
	Brine (salt)	yes	2, 3, 4, 5, 6
	Buttermilk	Conditional	1, 2, 3, 4, 5, 6
	Charged water	Conditional	2, 3, 4, 5, 6
	Caustic soda	yes	2, 6
	Cider	yes	3, 4, 5, 6
	Cinders	yes	2, 3, 4, 5, 6
	Coal	Conditional	2, 3, 4, 5, 6
	Corn syrup	yes	1, 2, 3, 4, 5, 6
	Electrolyte	yes	2, 3, 4, 5, 6
	Formalin	yes	2, 3, 4
	Fruit juices	Conditional	2, 3, 4, 5, 6
	Glucose	Conditional	2, 3, 4, 5, 6
	Glycerine	no	2, 5, 6
	Honey	no	2, 3, 4, 5, 6
	Lye	yes	2, 6
	Milk	Conditional	1, 2, 3, 4, 5, 6
	Molasses	Conditional	1, 2, 3, 4, 5, 6
	Niter	Conditional	2, 3, 4, 5, 6
	Sal Ammoniac	yes	2, 3, 4, 5, 6
	Sal Soda	Conditional	2, 3, 4, 5, 6
	Saltpeter	Conditional	2, 3, 4, 5, 6
	Sauerkraut	Conditional	3, 4, 5, 6
	Silage	yes	2, 3, 4, 5
	Tanning liquor	Conditional	2, 3, 4, 5, 6
	Vinegar	yes	2, 3, 4, 5, 6
	Washing soda	Conditional	2, 3, 4, 5, 6
	Whey	yes	1, 2, 3, 4, 5, 6
	Wine	Conditional	3, 6
	Wood pulp	Conditional	2, 3, 4, 6
	Sugars	Conditional	1, 2, 3, 4, 5, 6
	Sulphite liquor	Conditional	2, 3, 4, 6

(1) Special carbon resinous or carbon sulphur cements are recommended for use with hydrofluoric acid and its corrosive salts.

By HOWARD P. VERMILYA, AIA

Much has been written about masonry solar screens as shading devices and about how they may be most effective in reducing the sun's heat,* especially for air-conditioned buildings, but little information has been given on their structural aspects.

From their very nature, screen walls are rarely, if ever, load-bearing and while they may be of a variety of materials, those using hollow clay or concrete masonry units are more generally used.

Structural stability is attained by providing the screen wall with lateral support at proper intervals and by avoiding excessive compressive loads. Lateral support may be obtained by cross walls, piers, buttresses or columns when the limiting distance between lateral supports is measured horizontally, or by floors and roofs when the limiting distance is measured vertically (ASA Building Code Requirements for Masonry). The distance between these supports may be computed by the use of the following formulas derived by the Structural Clay Products Institute. (For complete derivation, refer to the Institute's *Technical Notes on Brick and Tile Construction*, Vol. 8 No. 3.)

(1) for restrained ends

$$L = 6.33 \times t \sqrt{\frac{A_b}{w \times k}}$$

*See section on "Heating, Ventilating, and Air Conditioning: Sun Angles, and Solar Loads." See also the book *Solar Control and Shading Devices* by Olgyay and Olgyay, Princeton University Press.

(2) for simply supported ends

$$L = 5.17 \times t \sqrt{\frac{A_b}{w \times k}}$$

Where:

L = allowable distance between lateral supports in feet

t = actual wall thickness in inches

A_b = ratio of actual bed joint length in a horizontal longitudinal plane to the total wall length.

(A_b = 1 for stack, running or common bond, and 0.5 for split bond patterns where each unit is lapped ⅓ over the lower unit.)

w = design wind pressure in pounds per square foot as taken from wind pressure map and wind pressure tables for height zones above ground.

Conditions Involved in Formulas

1. If the solar screen is supported by building it into a reinforced concrete structure, the end condition is fixed to a degree justifying the 1/12th moment coefficient used in Formula 1, while if the screen is supported on a steel shelf angle a ⅛th moment coefficient is indicated as in Formula 2.

Provisions should be made to anchor clay masonry solar screens to the building frame to prevent them from being sucked off their supports. The coefficient of static friction of

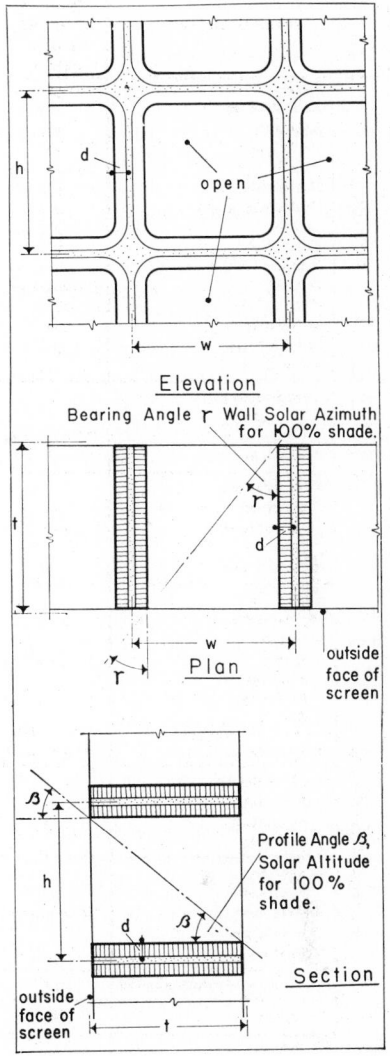

Elevation

Bearing Angle r Wall Solar Azimuth for 100% shade.

Plan

outside face of screen

Profile Angle β, Solar Altitude for 100% shade.

Section

outside face of screen

Table 27.

Rectangular Sizes				Structural Data		Shading Data		Units	Estimating Data			
Nominal Modular Dimensions in inches*			Specified Dimension in inches			100% Shading			Mortar			
									Cu. ft. per sq. ft. of Wall Area		Cu. ft. per 1000 Units	
h Face Height	w Face Width	t Length in Wall Thickness	d Shell Thickness	k Ratio of Solid Wall Area to Total Wall Area	Approximate Weight per sq. ft. of Wall Area in lb.	Profile Angle B	Bearing Angle r	No. per sq. ft. of Wall	½" joints	⅜" joints	½" joints	⅜" joints
4	8	6	⅝	.56	40	23°	49°	4.5	.092	.069	20.3	15.2
4	8	8	⅝	.56	54	17°	40°	4.5	.125	.094	27.8	20.8
4	8	12	⅝	.56	80	12°	29°	4.5	.193	.145	42.5	31.9
8	8	6	⅝	.39	30	49°	49°	2.25	.061	.046	27.1	20.3
8	8	8	⅝	.39	40	40°	40°	2.25	.828	.622	36.8	27.6
8	8	12	⅝	.39	60	29°	29°	2.25	.127	.095	56.5	42.4
8	12	6	¾	.375	30	48°	62°	1.5	.051	.382	34.5	26.9
8	12	8	¾	.375	40	39°	54°	1.5	.700	.525	46.6	35.0
8	12	12	¾	.375	60	28°	28°	1.5	.108	.081	72.0	54.0
12	12	6	⅞	.34	25	61°	61°	1.0	.042	.032	42.0	31.5
12	12	8	⅞	.34	33	53°	53°	1.0	.057	.043	57.2	43.0
12	12	12	⅞	.34	50	41°	41°	1.0	.880	.66	88.2	66.1

*Manufactured dimensions are ⅜ in. to ½ in. smaller than the nominal modular dimensions shown, depending on the manufacturer.

masonry on concrete, 0.70, and masonry on steel, 0.30, is not always sufficient to prevent horizontal movement of lightweight walls. Strap anchors can be employed to resist this movement.

Clay masonry screens which butt against or pass vertical members of concrete should be anchored in slots built into the concrete. Anchors, made of not less than 16-gage galvanized iron, should be at least ⅞-in. wide and spaced not more than 18 in. on center vertically.

2. Mortars for clay masonry units should conform to ASTM standard specifications, "Mortars for Unit Masonry" C 270. Types M or S shall be used when the distance between lateral supports exceeds 0.7 of the maximum permitted by Formula 1 or 2; when the distance is 0.7 or less, Type N mortar may be used. Mortar bed joints should be completely filled.

3. For structural considerations, units in split bond should not lap over the units below less than one third of their horizontal projection area.

4. L, the distance between lateral supports, may be measured either horizontally between walls or columns or vertically between floor slabs or beams when stack, running or common bond is used, but only vertically when split bond is used. (A revision of *Technical Notes on Brick and Tile Construction*, Vol. 8, No. 3 is contemplated soon, to provide a formula to take care of rotary shear or torsion in the bed joints when a screen wall using split bond is supported horizontally.)

Example:

Location: Dallas, Texas, 5th Floor.

Material: 8-by-8-by-8-in. hollow clay units in stack bond.

Frame or supports: reinforced concrete.

Mortar: Type S.

Wind Pressure: Map* shows 25 psf for Dallas. Table 29 shows 30 psf for wind at 54 ft (5 stories) from ground.

k: Table 27 shows 0.39 for 8-by-8-by-8-in. unit having shell thickness of ⅝ in. with ⅜-in. mortar joints.

A_b: 1 for stack bond

t: 7.5-in. actual thickness

$$L = 6.33 \times 7.5 \sqrt{\frac{1}{30 \times .39}}$$

$$L = 13.9 \text{ Feet}$$

If solar screen had been laid in type N mortar, allowable distance between supports could not exceed 0.7 of 13.9 ft or 9 ft 9 in.

*See section on "Design Loads."

Table 28. Physical properties of clay masonry solar screen units

Raw Materials:
Units shall be made of surface clay, shale, fire clay or mixtures thereof.

Finish:
Exposed ends shall be uncored and reasonably free from cracks, chips, surface roughness and other defects detracting from the appearance of the wall when viewed from a distance of 20 ft.

Water Absorption:
Maximum per cent by 1 hr. boiling;
Where the weathering index is more than 100

Average of 5 units....................... 9%
Individual units.........................11%
Where the weathering index is less than 100

Average of 5 tests......................16%
Individual units.........................19%

Dimensional Variation:
Maximum variation plus or minus from specified dimension in width, w; height, h; or length, t.................. 3%
The shell thickness, d, shall be not less than 1/16 in. under nor more than ¼ in. over the specified dimension given in Table 27.

Table 29. Wind pressures for various height zones above ground

Height Zone (ft.)	Wind-pressure-map areas * (lb. per sq. ft.)						
	20	25	30	35	40	45	50
Less than 30....	15	20	25	25	30	35	40
30 to 49.......	20	25	30	35	40	45	50
50 to 99.......	25	30	40	45	50	55	60
100 to 499......	30	40	45	55	60	70	75
500 to 1199....	35	45	55	60	70	80	90
1200 and over..	40	50	60	70	80	90	100

Tables from: *Technical Notes on Brick and Tile Construction*, Structural Clay Products Institute

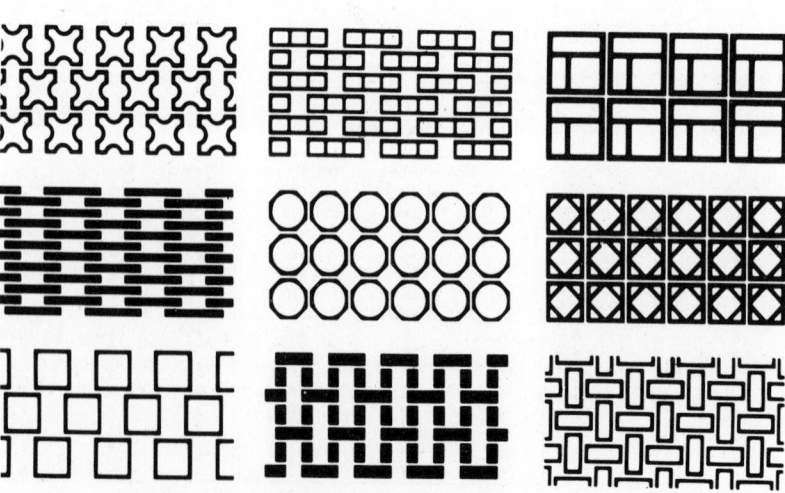

Fig. 32. Pattern variations in brick, tile and terra cotta screens

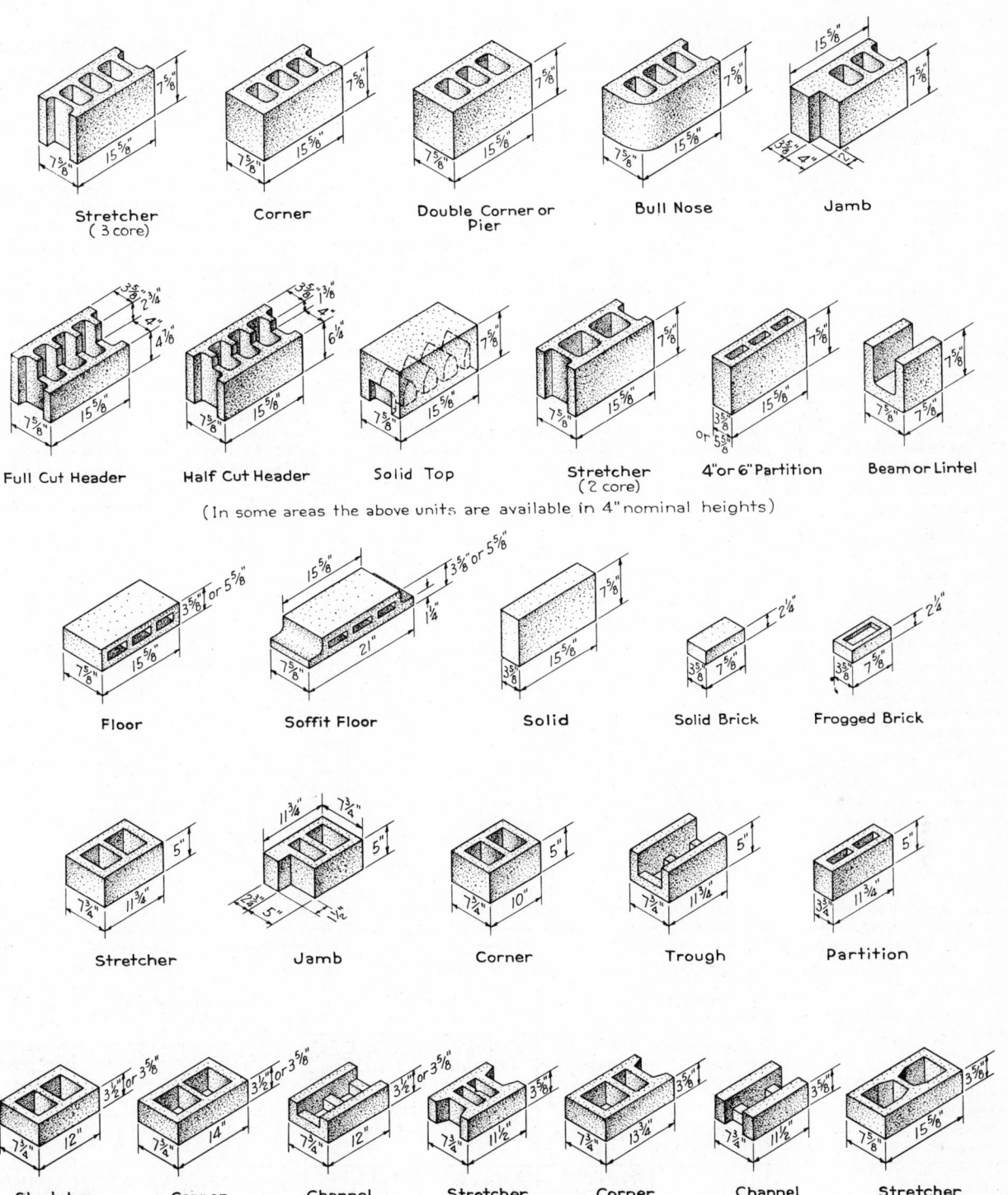

Stretcher (3 core)   **Corner**   **Double Corner or Pier**   **Bull Nose**   **Jamb**

Full Cut Header   **Half Cut Header**   **Solid Top**   **Stretcher** (2 core)   **4"or 6"Partition**   **Beam or Lintel**

(In some areas the above units are available in 4"nominal heights)

Floor   **Soffit Floor**   **Solid**   **Solid Brick**   **Frogged Brick**

Stretcher   **Jamb**   **Corner**   **Trough**   **Partition**

Stretcher   **Corner**   **Channel**   **Stretcher**   **Corner**   **Channel**   **Stretcher** (Modular)

Fig. 1. Typical shapes and sizes of concrete masonry units

Dimensions shown are actual unit sizes. A 7⅝ by 7⅝ by 15⅝-in. unit is commonly known as an 8 by 8 by 16-in. concrete block. Half-length units are usually available for most of the units shown above. See concrete products manufacturer for shapes and sizes of units locally available.

Data and illustrations on this and the following pages have been derived from *Concrete Masonry Handbook*, Portland Cement Association (1951).

Concrete masonry building units are divided into five categories:

1. Hollow loadbearing concrete block
2. Solid loadbearing concrete block
3. Hollow nonloadbearing concrete block
4. Concrete building tile
5. Concrete brick.

HEAVYWEIGHT AND LIGHTWEIGHT UNITS

The five types of units listed above are regularly made with either heavyweight or lightweight aggregates and are known as heavyweight and lightweight units respectively. A hollow loadbearing concrete block of 8 by 8 by 16-in. nominal size will weigh from approximately 40 to 50 lb when made with heavyweight aggregate, and from 25 to 35 lb when made with lightweight aggregate. Heavyweight units are made with such aggregates as sand, gravel, crushed stone, and air-cooled slag. Lightweight units are made with coal cinders, expanded shale, clay, or slag, and natural lightweight materials such as volcanic cinders, pumice, and scoria. Heavyweight and lightweight units are used for all types of masonry construction. The choice of heavyweight or lightweight units generally depends on their availability and the requirements of the structure under consideration.

Table 1. Summary of physical requirements for various types of concrete masonry units

Specification, serial designation, and latest revised date	Minimum face-shell thickness, in.	Compressive strength, minimum, psi, average gross area		Water absorption, maximum, lb. per cu.ft. of concrete, average of 5 units	Moisture content, maximum, per cent of total absorption, average of 5 units
		Average of 5 units	Individual unit		
Hollow load-bearing concrete masonry units ASTM C90, 1952	1¼ or over: Grade A[a,c] Grade B[b,c] Under 1¼ and over ¾	1000 700 1000	800 600 800	15 — 15	40 40 40
Hollow non-load-bearing concrete masonry units ASTM C129, 1952	Not less than ½	350	300	—	40
Solid load-bearing concrete masonry units ASTM C145, 1952[d] Grade A Grade B	— —	1800 1200	1600 1000	15 15	40 40
Concrete units; masonry, hollow Federal SS-C-621, 1935				Average of 3 units	Average of 3 units
Load-bearing units	1¼ or more ¾ to 1¼	700 1000	600 800	16 16	40 40
Non-load-bearing units	Not less than ¾	350	—	—	40

	Compressive strength, minimum, psi, average gross area (brick flatwise)		Modulus of rupture, minimum, psi, (brick flatwise)		Water absorption, maximum		Moisture content, maximum, per cent of total absorption
	Average of 5 brick	Individual	Average of 5 brick	Individual			
Concrete building brick ASTM C55, 1952 Grade A[e] Grade B[f]	2500 1500	2000 1250	— —	— —	15 lb. per cu. ft. —		40 40
Brick; concrete Federal SS-B-663, 1932					Average of 5 brick	Individual	
H—Hard	—	—	600+	400	7 oz.	9.5 oz.	30
M—Medium	—	—	450–600	300	8 oz.	10 oz.	30
S—Soft	—	—	300–450	200	no limit	no limit	30

[a] For use in exterior walls below grade and for unprotected exterior walls above grade that may be exposed to frost action.

[b] For general use above grade in walls not subjected to frost action or where protected from the weather with two coats of portland cement paint or other satisfactory waterproofing treatment approved by the purchaser.

[c] Regardless of the grade of unit used, protective coatings such as portland cement paint may be desirable on exterior walls for waterproofing purposes. In this connection purchasers should be guided by local experience and the manufacturer's recommendations.

[d] Units with 75 per cent or more net area. The classification is based on strength.

[e] Brick intended for use where exposed to temperature below freezing in the presence of moisture.

[f] Brick intended for use as back-up or interior masonry.

Table 2. Standard for concrete masonry units of Underwriters' Laboratories, Inc.

Type of aggregate	Minimum face shell and web thicknesses*					
	Class D-2 retardants**		Class C-3 retardants**		Class B-4 retardants**	
	Face shell minimum in.	Web minimum in.	Face shell minimum in.	Web minimum in.	Face shell minimum in.	Web minimum in.
Natural, by-product, and processed, except those listed below	1¼	1	1½	1	2⅛	1½
Burned clay or shale	1⅛	1	1⅜	1		
Expanded slag	1⅛	1	1⅜	1	1⅝	1
Pumice					1¼	1

*The minimum face shell for the largest core hole at the thinnest point. This may be the average of the two face shells in the same core. The end and internal webs in each core hole to be measured at the thinnest point.

**Class D-2 includes units classified as at least 2-hour, but less than 3-hour retardants. Class C-3 includes units classified as at least 3-hour, but less than 4-hour retardants. Class B-4 includes units classified as at least 4-hour, but less than 8-hour retardants.

SOLID AND HOLLOW UNITS

A solid concrete block is defined in the American Society for Testing and Materials specifications as a unit in which the core area is not more than 25 per cent of the gross cross-sectional area.

A hollow concrete block is a unit having a core area greater than 25 per cent of its gross cross-sectional area. Generally, the core area of hollow units is from 40 to 50 per cent of the gross area.

SIZES AND SHAPES

Concrete building units are made in sizes and shapes to fit different construction needs. They include stretcher, corner, double corner or pier, jamb, header, bull nose, partition, and concrete floor units. All are made in both full- and half-length units. Various sizes and shapes are illustrated in Fig. 1.

Concrete unit sizes are usually referred to by their nominal dimensions. Thus, a unit measuring 7⅝ in. wide, 7⅝ in. high, and 15⅝ in. long is known as an 8 by 8 by 16-in. unit. When it is laid in a wall with ⅜-in. mortar joints, this unit will occupy a space exactly 16 in. long and 8 in. high. This is in accordance with the modular coordination of design based on a 4-in. module.

Architects are urged to determine in advance the sizes of units that are available for the proposed construction.

SPECIFICATIONS AND CODES

Concrete masonry units are made to comply with the requirements of local building codes, Federal Specifications, or the applicable specifications of the American Society for Testing Materials or other specifying agencies. A summary of some of these specifications, covering requirements such as compressive strength, absorption and moisture content, is given in Table 1.

Structural properties: Masonry walls built of hollow or solid concrete units are covered by the ASA Code, which is summarized in the section on "Structural Design—Masonry." The maximum allowable compressive stress on walls built of hollow units is 70 psi with Type N mortar and 85 psi with Type M mortar.

Insulation value: U values for walls of concrete masonry of various types are given in the section on "Insulation." The insulating value of lightweight units is generally 35 to 40 per cent greater than that of heavyweight units. The cells of hollow units may be filled with insulation, which should be the special water-repellent type previously mentioned in the section on cavity walls. The use of this type of insulation cuts the U value of the wall approximately in half.

Fire resistance: Concrete masonry is highly fire-resistant; the lightweight units are somewhat more efficient in this respect than the heavyweight units. Fire-resistance ratings of concrete masonry walls of various thicknesses are given in the section on "Fireproofing." Requirements for minimum face-shell and web thicknesses for various fire-retardant classifications are given in Table 2. This table is taken from *Standard for Concrete Masonry Units,* Underwriters' Laboratories, Inc. (1953), which contains additional requirements such as the design and dimensions of the units, type of aggregates, cement-aggregate proportions, curing methods, and strength.

Acoustical properties: Exposed concrete masonry walls will absorb from 18 to 68 per cent of the sound waves striking them. The variation depends on the surface texture, not on the type of aggregate used. Paint applied to any acoustically absorbent material tends to close the pores and reduce its value for sound control. Spray painting reduces the value less than brush painting, and water-base paints less than oil-base paints.

Concrete masonry, like any other masonry, is an effective sound isolation material. Where sound isolation is desirable, a transmission loss of 40 db or more is usually required. Table 3 lists the many types of lightweight concrete masonry walls meeting this requirement.

DESIGN OF CONCRETE MASONRY WALLS

Modular design is recommended (see section on "Modular Coordination"). For economy in construction, walls should be laid out to make maximum use of full- and half-length units (see Tables 5–7). This minimizes cutting and fitting units on the job—operations that slow up construction. All dimensions such as over-all length and height of wall, width and height of door and window openings, and wall areas between doors, windows, and corners should be planned to use full- and half-sized units that are commonly carried in stock (see Fig. 2). Full advantage of modular design for concrete masonry requires that window and door frames be of

Table 3. Reduction factors in sound transmission through walls of hollow concrete masonry

Walls of hollow concrete masonry	Weight per sq.ft. of wall area, lb.	Average reduction factor, decibels
3″ Cinder, ⅝″ plaster on both sides[a]	32.2	45.1
4″ Cinder, ⅝″ plaster on both sides[a]	35.8	45.6
4″ Cinder, 1″ plaster[b]	32.3	47.0
8″ Expanded slag, 1″ plaster[b]	56.0	52.6
4″ Celocrete, ½″ plaster on both sides[c]	30.0	42.6
8″ Celocrete, unplastered[c]	28.6	43.7
8″ Celocrete, ½″ plaster on both sides[c]	40.0	52.9
Cavity wall, two 4″ Celocrete, ½″ plaster on one inner face[c]	45.0	57.1
3″ Haydite, unplastered[c]	—	36.0
3″ Haydite, 1″ plaster[c]	—	42.0
4″ Haydite, unplastered[c]	—	37.0
4″ Haydite, 1″ plaster[c]	—	43.0
6″ Haydite, unplastered[c]	—	44.8
6″ Haydite, 1″ plaster[c]	—	48.5
8″ Haydite, unplastered[c]	—	47.8
8″ Haydite, 1″ plaster[c]	—	50.5
12″ Haydite, unplastered[c]	—	52.0
12″ Haydite, 1″ plaster[c]	—	54.0
4″ Pumice, ½″ plaster on both sides[d]	25.3	37.4
4″ Pumice, ½″ plaster on one side only	20.4	34.6
4″ Waylite, ½″ plaster on both sides[c]	31.0	50.0
8″ Waylite, ½″ plaster on both sides[c]	47.0	53.0
3″ Waylite, 2 coats cement paint each side[c]	16.75	44.1
4″ Waylite, unpainted[c]	16.5	33.2
4″ Waylite, 2 coats cement paint each side[c]	16.5	46.7
6″ Waylite, unpainted[c]	21.0	39.7
6″ Waylite, 2 coats cement paint each side[c]	21.0	52.2
Cavity wall, two 3″ Waylite, ⅜″ plaster on one unexposed face[c]	17.0	56.1

[a]National Bureau of Standards Report BMS17
[b]Data reported in *Acoustics and Architecture* by Paul E. Sabine
[c]Tests conducted at Riverbank Laboratories
[d]National Bureau of Standards Supplement to Report BMS17

Table 4. Nominal length of concrete masonry walls by stretchers

Actual length of wall is measured from outside edge to outside edge of units and is equal to the nominal length minus ⅜″ (one mortar joint.)

No. of stretchers	Nominal length of concrete masonry walls	
	Units 15⅝″ long and half units 7⅝″ long with ⅜″ thick head joints.	Units 11⅝″ long and half units 5⅝″ long with ⅜″ thick head joints.
1	1′ 4″	1′ 0″
1½	2′ 0″	1′ 6″
2	2′ 8″	2′ 0″
2½	3′ 4″	2′ 6″
3	4′ 0″	3′ 0″
3½	4′ 8″	3′ 6″
4	5′ 4″	4′ 0″
4½	6′ 0″	4′ 6″
5	6′ 8″	5′ 0″
5½	7′ 4″	5′ 6″
6	8′ 0″	6′ 0″
6½	8′ 8″	6′ 6″
7	9′ 4″	7′ 0″
7½	10′ 0″	7′ 6″
8	10′ 8″	8′ 0″
8½	11′ 4″	8′ 6″
9	12′ 0″	9′ 0″
9½	12′ 8″	9′ 6″
10	13′ 4″	10′ 0″
10½	14′ 0″	10′ 6″
11	14′ 8″	11′ 0″
11½	15′ 4″	11′ 6″
12	16′ 0″	12′ 0″
12½	16′ 8″	12′ 6″
13	17′ 4″	13′ 0″
13½	18′ 0″	13′ 6″
14	18′ 8″	14′ 0″
14½	19′ 4″	14′ 6″
15	20′ 0″	15′ 0″
20	26′ 8″	20′ 0″

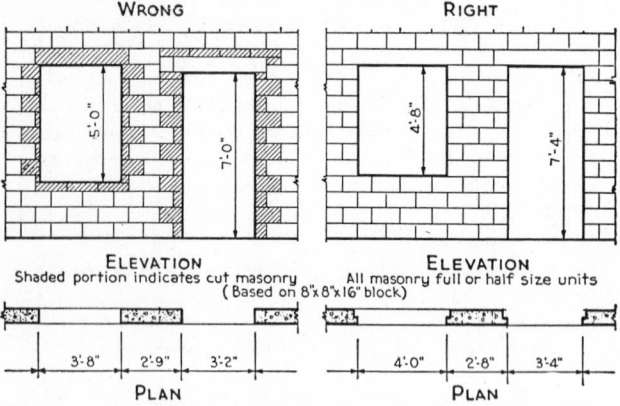

WRONG — ELEVATION
Shaded portion indicates cut masonry
(Based on 8″x8″x16″ block)
5′-0″ · 7′-0″
PLAN — 3′-8″ · 2′-9″ · 3′-2″

RIGHT — ELEVATION
All masonry full or half size units
4′-8″ · 7′-4″
PLAN — 4′-0″ · 2′-8″ · 3′-4″

Fig. 2. Examples of wrong and right planning of concrete masonry wall openings

modular dimensions that fit modular full- and half-size units. All horizontal dimensions will then be in multiples of nominal half-length units, and all vertical dimensions will be multiples of nominal full-height units. Thus, with the nominal 8 by 8 by 16-in. block, both horizontal and vertical dimen-

sions should be designed to be in multiples of 8 in.

Structural design is normally governed by local building codes on allowable stresses, heights, thicknesses, lateral support, and mortar types. For the provisions of the ASA Code, see "Structural Design—Masonry."

DRY UNITS ESSENTIAL

When delivered to the job, concrete masonry units should be dry enough to comply with the specified limitation for moisture content. They should be maintained in this dry condition by stockpiling them on planks or other supports free from contact with the ground and by covering them with roofing paper or tarpaulin for protection against wetting. Moreover, if work is stopped at any time, the top of the wall should be covered with tarpaulins or boards to prevent rain or snow from entering the cores of the block. Concrete masonry units should never be wetted immediately before and during laying in the wall, a practice customary with some masonry materials. These precautions to lay only dry units will minimize shrinkage in the finished wall.

Sometimes it may be advisable to dry block below the moisture content given in most specifications, particularly if exposed concrete masonry walls are to be used in buildings where relatively high tem-peratures and low humidities are likely to occur over extended periods of time, as during the winter heating season. Experience has shown that damp concrete masonry units can be artificially dried to the air-dry condition that they will attain in service. This can be done by blowing heated air through the cores and the spaces between the units that are stacked to facilitate drying.

FOOTINGS

Footings for masonry walls should be of sufficient width and thickness to carry the expected loads in accordance with local building code requirements. Footings should be placed on firm, undisturbed soil of adequate loadbearing capacity and below frost penetration. In areas where there are no applicable local building codes, it is general practice to make footings for small buildings twice as wide as the thickness of the walls that will bear on them. The thickness of such footings is made equal to one-half their width (Fig. 3).

SUBSURFACE DRAINAGE

Unless the groundwater level in wet seasons is well below the footing or the basement floor, the placing of a line of drain tile along the outer side of footings is recommended. The tile line should have a fall of at least ½ in. in 12 ft and should drain to a suitable outlet. Pieces of roofing felt placed over the joints prevent sediment from entering the tile during backfilling. The tile line should be covered to a depth of 12 in. with a permeable fill of coarse gravel or crushed stone ranging from 1 to 1½ in. in size. The balance of the trench can then be filled with earth from the excavation after the first floor is in place.

Table 5. Nominal height of concrete masonry walls by courses

For concrete masonry units 7⅝" and 3⅝" in height laid with ⅜" mortar joints. Height is measured from center to center of mortar joints.

No. of courses	Nominal height of concrete masonry walls	
	Units 7⅝" high and ⅜" thick bed joint	Units 3⅝" high and ⅜" thick bed joint
1	8"	4"
2	1' 4"	8"
3	2' 0"	1' 0"
4	2' 8"	1' 4"
5	3' 4"	1' 8"
6	4' 0"	2' 0"
7	4' 8"	2' 4"
8	5' 4"	2' 8"
9	6' 0"	3' 0"
10	6' 8"	3' 4"
15	10' 0"	5' 0"
20	13' 4"	6' 8"
25	16' 8"	8' 4"
30	20' 0"	10' 0"
35	23' 4"	11' 8"
40	26' 8"	13' 4"
45	30' 0"	15' 0"
50	33' 4"	16' 8"

Table 6. Weights and quantities of materials for concrete masonry walls

Actual unit sizes (width x height x length) in.	Nominal wall thickness in.	For 100 sq.ft. of wall				For 100 concrete units
		Number of units	Average weight of finished wall		Mortar*** cu.ft.	Mortar*** cu.ft.
			Heavyweight aggregate lb.*	Lightweight aggregate lb.**		
3⅝x3⅝x15⅝	4	225	3050	2150	13.5	6.0
5⅝x3⅝x15⅝	6	225	4550	3050	13.5	6.0
7⅝x3⅝x15⅝	8	225	5700	3700	13.5	6.0
3⅝x7⅝x15⅝	4	112.5	2850	2050	8.5	7.5
5⅝x7⅝x15⅝	6	112.5	4350	2950	8.5	7.5
7⅝x7⅝x15⅝	8	112.5	5500	3600	8.5	7.5
11⅝x7⅝x15⅝	12	112.5	7950	4900	8.5	7.5

Table based on ⅜-in. mortar joints.
*Actual weight within ±7% of average weight.
**Actual weight within ±17% of average weight.
***With face-shell mortar bedding. Mortar quantities include 10% allowance for waste.
Actual weight of 100 sq.ft. of wall can be computed by formula $W(N)+150(M)$ where:

W = actual weight of a single unit
N = number of units for 100 sq.ft. of wall
M = cu.ft. of mortar for 100 sq.ft. of wall

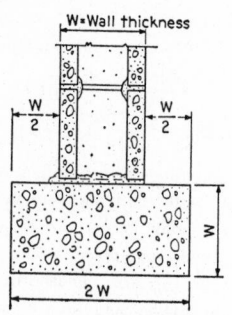

Fig. 3. Recommended footing dimensions for small buildings

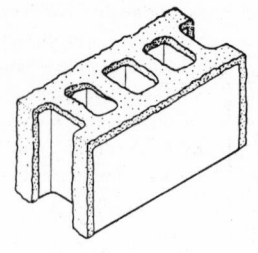

Full mortar bedding

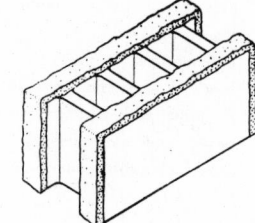

Face-shell mortar bedding

Fig. 4. Examples of full bedding and face-shell mortar bedding

LAYING CONCRETE MASONRY

Two types of mortar bedding are common with concrete masonry—full mortar bedding and face-shell bedding (Fig. 4). In the full mortar bedding, the webs as well as the face shells are covered and bedded in mortar. It is used in laying the first or starting course of block on a footing or foundation wall. It is also commonly used in building concrete masonry columns, piers, and pilasters that are intended to carry heavy loads. For all other concrete masonry work it is usual practice to use face-shell bedding.

Type M mortar should be used for isolated piers and for walls subject to extremely heavy loads, violent winds, earthquakes, or severe frost action. Elsewhere Type N mortar may be used.

The mortar squeezed from the joints is struck off flush with the wall surface as each unit is laid. When the mortar has stiffened somewhat, it is firmly compacted

with a jointing tool. This compaction is important since mortar, when hardening, has a tendency to shrink slightly and thus may pull away from the edges of the block. Pressing the mortar against the units with a jointing tool after the mortar has stiffened restores intimate contact between the mortar and the masonry unit and helps to make a weathertight joint. It may be necessary to add mortar, particularly to the vertical joints, to ensure that they are well filled. Concave or V-shaped joints ⅜ in. thick are recommended.

For weathertightness, walls should be properly flashed and all sills and other projecting members should be provided with drips. Weathertightness of the wall may be further improved by the application of paint or stucco, as discussed later in this section.

For more detailed information on laying concrete masonry see *Recommended Practices for Laying Concrete Block*, published by the Portland Cement Association.

BASEMENT WALLS

Special care should be taken in building basement walls to ensure that they will remain dry and weathertight. The earth side of concrete masonry basement walls should always be given two ¼-in.-thick coats of plaster. Either portland cement plaster (1:2½ mix by volume) or the mortar used in laying up the block should be used for this purpose (see Fig. 5). In hot, dry weather, the wall surface should be very lightly dampened with a fog spray of water prior to application of the first coat. The first coat of plaster is roughened after it has partly hardened to provide bond for the second coat. It is allowed to harden at least 24 hours before the second coat is applied. The first coat is lightly dampened just before the second coat is put on. The second coat is kept slightly damp for at least 48 hours after application.

In very wet soils the plastered surfaces

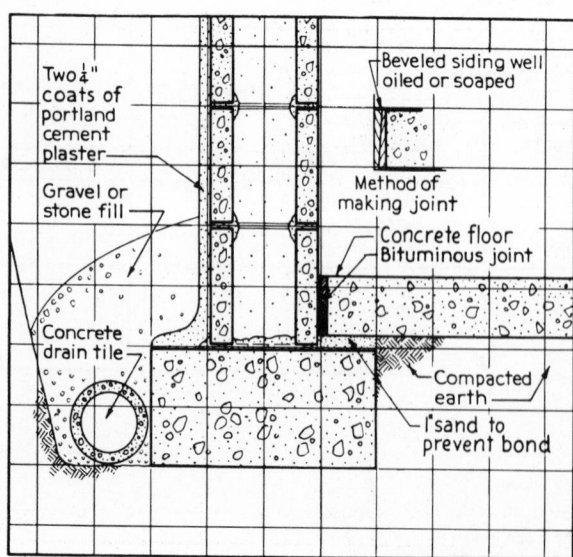

Fig. 5. Footing for 8-in. basement wall

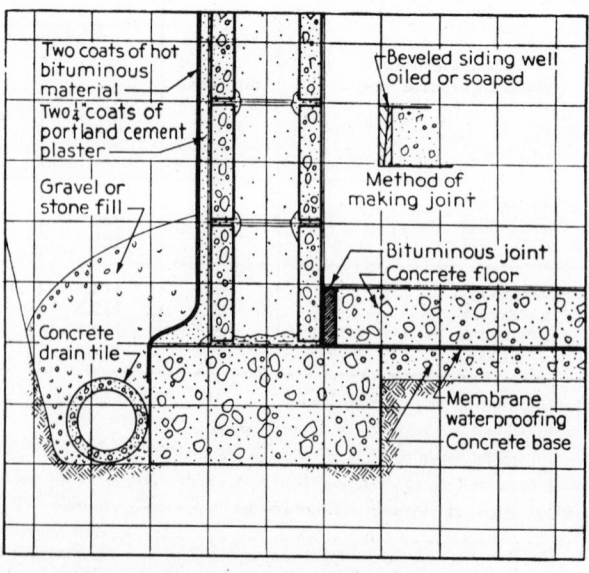

Fig. 6. Footing for 8-in. basement wall (very wet soil)

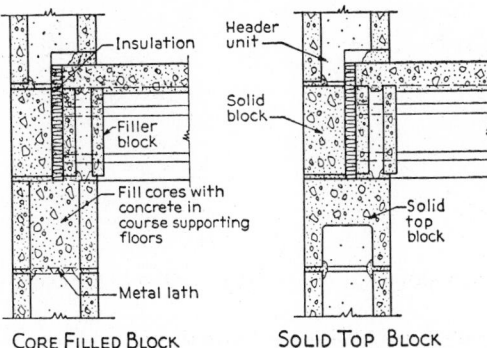

CORE FILLED BLOCK   SOLID TOP BLOCK

Fig. 7. Methods of constructing courses supporting floors

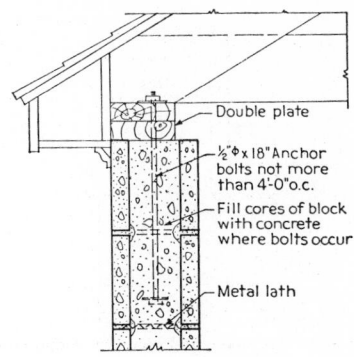

**Fig. 8. Method of fastening wood plate
to top of wall**

below grade are often given two continuous coatings of bituminous material brushed on over a suitable priming coat (Coal-Tar Pitch ASTM D450 Type B and Creosote Primer ASTM D43; or Asphalt ASTM D449 Type B and Asphalt Primer D41). The second coat is applied with brush strokes at right angles to those of the first coat. The plaster must be dry when primer is applied to it and the primer coat must be dry when the bituminous material is applied (see Fig. 6).

No filling against concrete masonry basement walls should be permitted until the first floor is in place.

Interior bearing walls should rest on their own footings and should be isolated from floor slabs, as shown in Fig 9.

For more detailed information on basement construction see *Recommended Practices for Building Waterproof Basements of Concrete*, published by the Portland Cement Association.

SUPPORT OF FLOOR AND ROOF LOADS

Masonry courses that support floor beams or floor slabs should be of solid masonry. This helps to distribute the loads over the wall and provides a barrier against termites. Such courses can be constructed by filling the cores of hollow block with concrete or mortar (Fig. 10) or by using solid masonry units without cores. For filling cores a 1:2½:2½ concrete mix with all coarse aggregate passing a ½-in. screen is recommended. When local regulations permit, the cores may be filled with mortar similar to that used in laying the wall. Strips of expanded metal lath, laid in the bed joint below, support the concrete or mortar filling in the cores. Cores should be completely filled. Some regulations require at least 4 in. of solid masonry for courses supporting floors or roofs. Solid top block with the top 4 in. solid are made to meet such requirements (see Fig. 7).

ATTACHING PLATES

Plates are fastened to the wall by anchor bolts about 18 in. long, ½ in. in diameter and spaced not more than 4 ft apart. The bolts are placed in the cores of the top two courses (Fig. 8). The cores are then filled with concrete or mortar, pieces of metal lath having been placed at the base of the cores to support the concrete mixture. After the concrete has hardened around the anchor bolts the plates are attached.

MEETING AND INTERSECTING WALLS

Bearing walls

Intersecting concrete-block bearing walls should not be tied together in a masonry bond, except at the corners. Instead, one wall should terminate at the face of the other wall with a control joint at that point. For lateral support, bearing walls

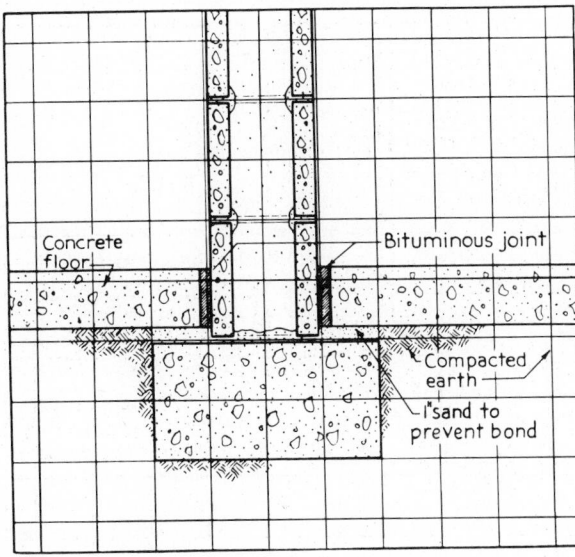

Fig. 9. Footing for 8-in. interior basement bearing wall

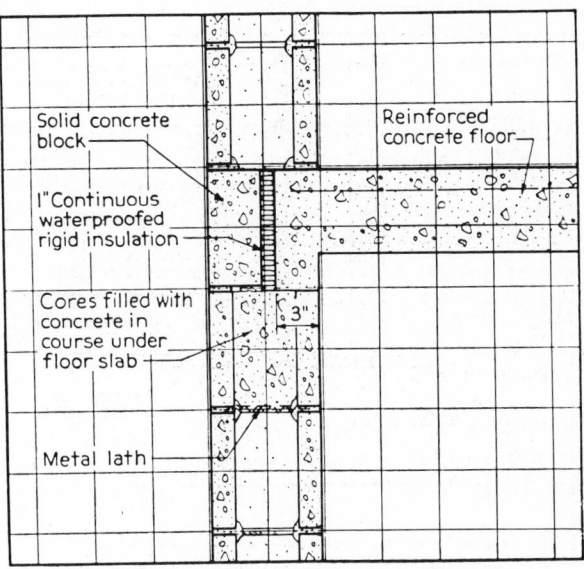

Fig. 10. Framing of wall and concrete slab floor

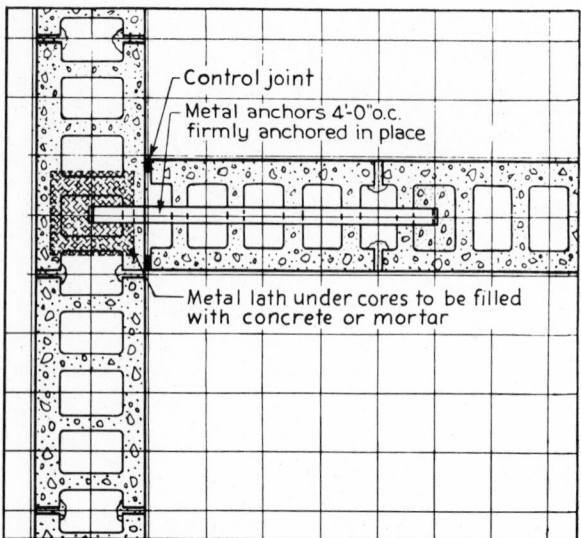

Fig. 11. Bonding intersecting bearing walls

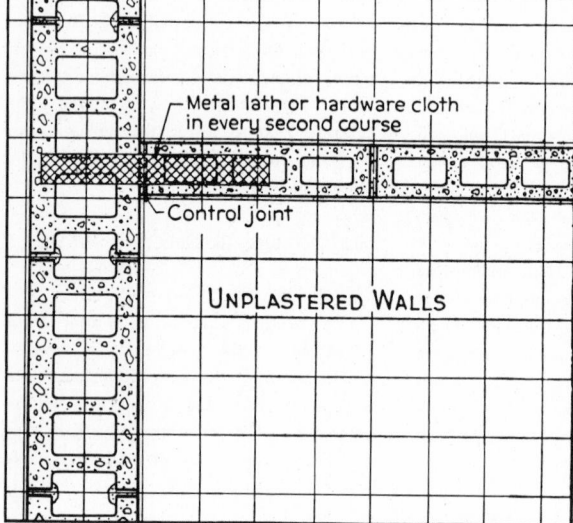

Fig. 12. Intersection of bearing and nonbearing walls

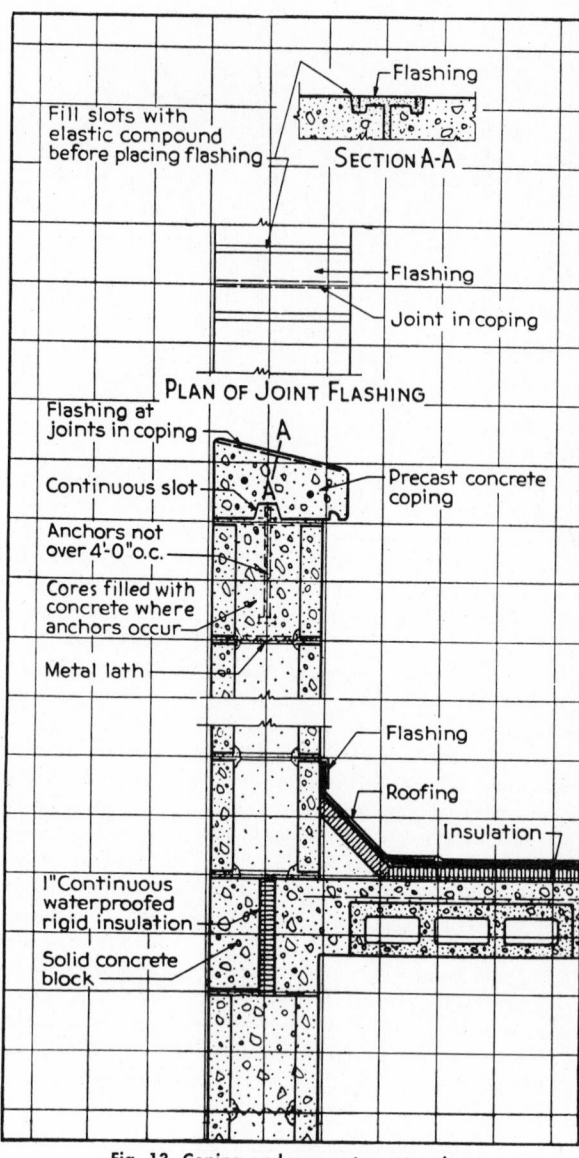

Fig. 13. Coping and parapet construction

are tied together with a metal tiebar ¼ in. thick, 1¼ in. wide, and 28 in. long, with 2-in. right-angle bends on each end. The bends at the ends of the tiebars are embedded in cores filled with mortar or concrete. Pieces of metal lath placed under the cores support the concrete or mortar filling (see Fig. 11).

If the control joint at the intersection of the two bearing walls is to be exposed to view or subjected to weathering, the mortar should be raked out to a depth of ¾ in. and sealed with a calking compound.

Nonbearing walls

For tying nonbearing block walls to other walls, strips of metal lath or ¼-in. mesh

galvanized hardware cloth are placed across the joint between the two walls (see Fig. 12). The metal strips are placed in alternate courses in the wall. When one wall is constructed first, the metal strips are built into the wall and later embedded in the mortar joint of the second wall.

Where the two walls meet, the vertical mortar joint is raked out to a depth of ¾ in. if it is to be exposed to view in the finished building, and calking compound is packed into the recess.

PARAPET WALLS

The construction of parapet walls and the method of anchoring copings are shown in Fig. 13.

WALL ANCHORAGE

Lateral support for concrete masonry walls is commonly provided by the floors and roof. Cast-in-place concrete floor or roof slabs bearing on masonry walls are considered to provide sufficient anchorage.

When wood joists or wood beams bear on masonry walls, the ends of the joists or beams are securely anchored to the walls at maximum intervals of 6 ft in one- and two-family dwellings and a maximum of 4 ft in other buildings. Metal anchors at least 16 in. long having a minimum cross section of ¼ by 1¼ in. are fastened securely to the ends of the joists or beams and are provided with split and upset ends

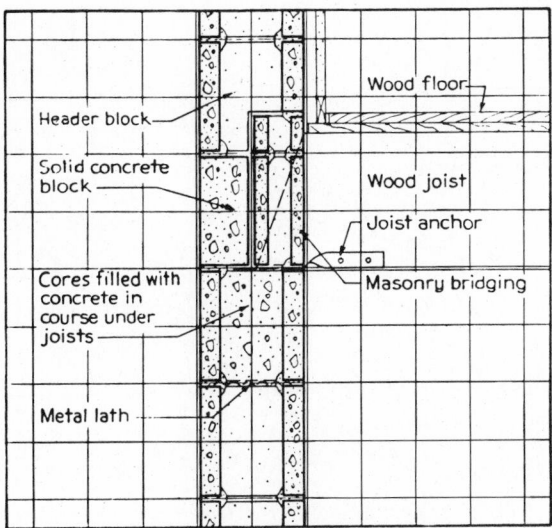

Fig. 14. Framing of wall and wood joist floor
(joists built into wall)

Header block
Solid concrete block
Cores filled with concrete in course under joists
Metal lath
Wood floor
Wood joist
Joist anchor
Masonry bridging

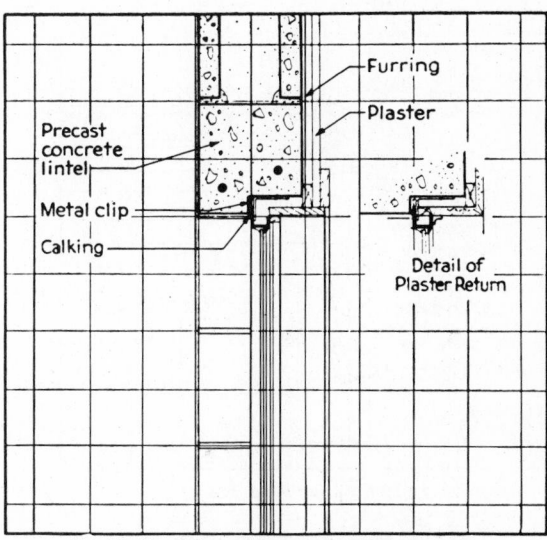

Fig. 15. Head for architectural projected window

Furring
Plaster
Precast concrete lintel
Metal clip
Calking
Detail of Plaster Return

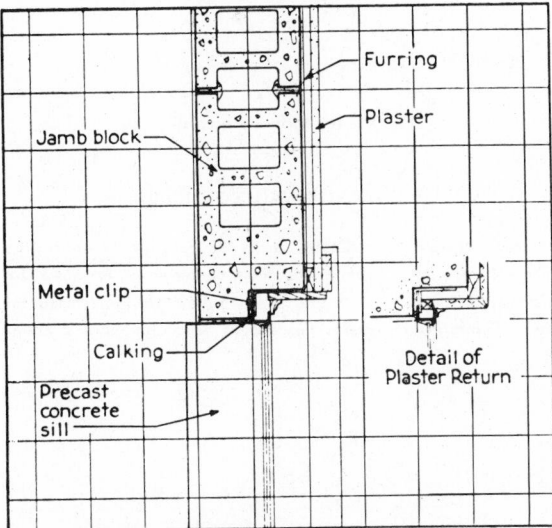

Fig. 16. Jamb for architectural projected window

Furring
Plaster
Jamb block
Metal clip
Calking
Precast concrete sill
Detail of Plaster Return

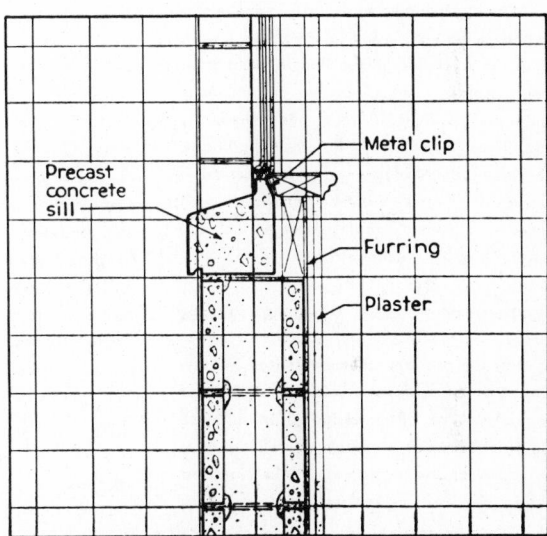

Fig. 17. Sill for architectural projected window

Metal clip
Precast concrete sill
Furring
Plaster

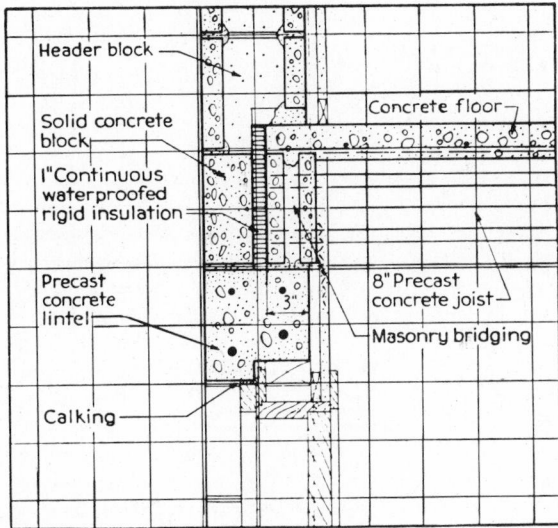

Fig. 18. Head for wood door

Header block
Solid concrete block
1" Continuous waterproofed rigid insulation
Precast concrete lintel
Calking
Concrete floor
8" Precast concrete joist
Masonry bridging
3"

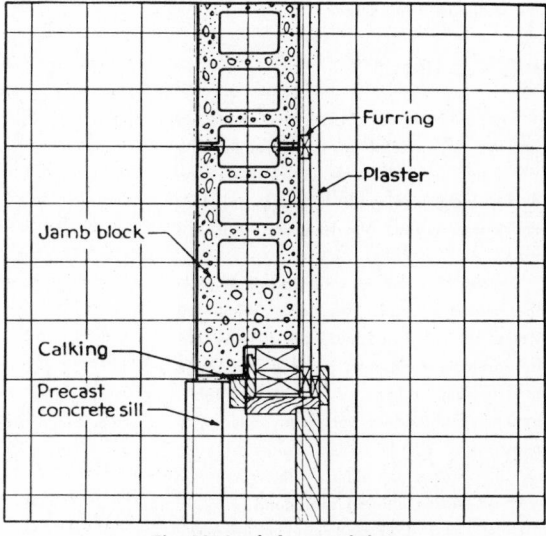

Fig. 19. Jamb for wood door

Furring
Plaster
Jamb block
Calking
Precast concrete sill

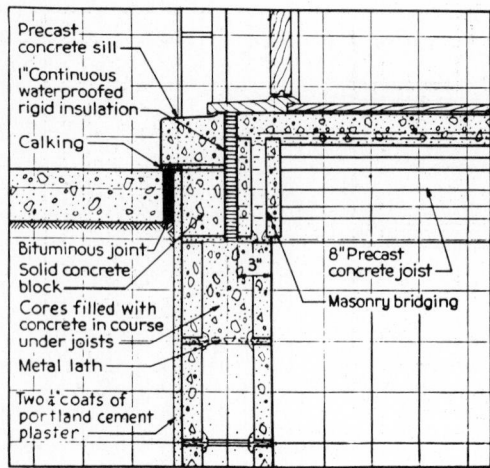

Fig. 20. Sill for wood door

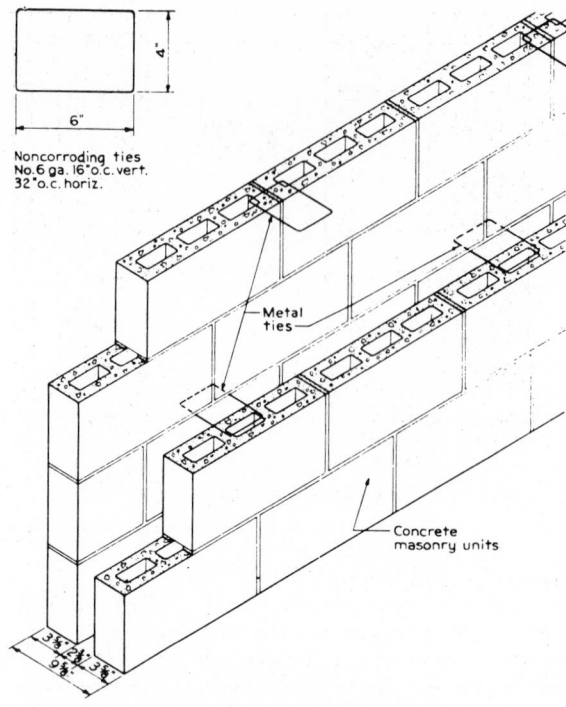

Fig. 21. Ten-inch cavity wall

or other approved means for building into masonry (see Fig. 14).

When masonry walls are parallel to wood joists or wood beams, the walls must be anchored to the floor or roof joists with metal anchors spaced at maximum intervals of 8 ft in one- and two-family dwellings and 6 ft in other buildings. Such anchors should engage at least three joists or beams and be provided with upset or T-ends that develop the full strength of the anchor strap.

SETTING DOOR AND WINDOW FRAMES

Jamb block are commonly used in laying up the sides of window and door openings. The offset design of these block and of precast concrete lintels permits window or door frames to be inserted after the walls have been laid up (Figs. 15–20). This method is preferred over the method of setting and bracing the frames in position on the wall and then building the walls up around them.

SILLS AND LINTELS

Figure 17 shows a precast concrete sill for use with metal window frames. The sill is sloped to drain water away quickly. A drip ledge causes the water to fall free and not run down the face and stain the wall.

Precast sills are usually installed after the masonry walls are laid. When installed as the wall is laid up, they should be protected against possible breakage or staining during construction. Joints under sills should be completely filled with mortar and tightly tooled. Joints at ends of sills should be filled with mortar or with an elastic calking compound.

Lintels over door and window openings

carry either the wall load or both the wall and floor loads as the design of the structure may require. Reinforced concrete lintels, one-piece or two-piece, precast, or poured in place, are suitable for use. (See "Structural Design—Masonry: Reinforced Concrete Lintels.")

CAVITY-WALL CONSTRUCTION

Cavity walls of concrete masonry are similar to those described previously except that when hollow units are used the metal ties should be rectangular in shape (Fig. 21).

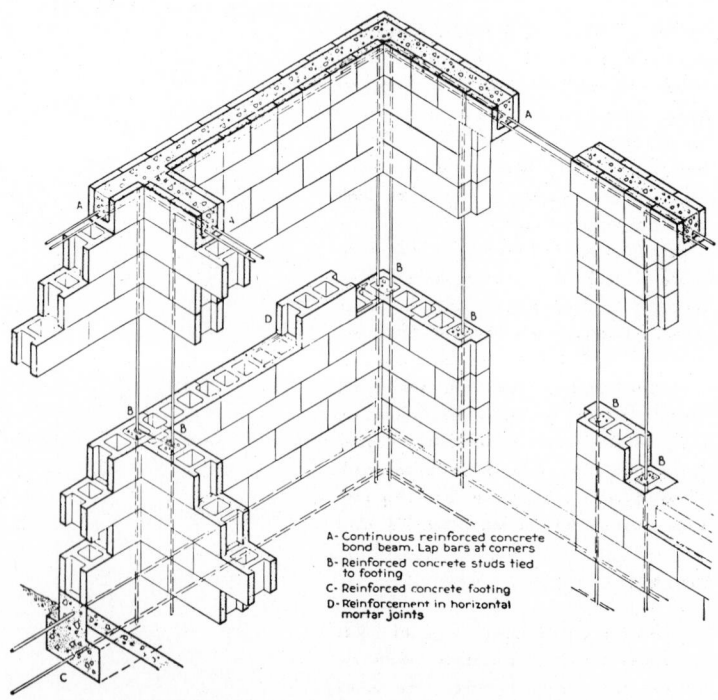

A- Continuous reinforced concrete bond beam. Lap bars at corners
B- Reinforced concrete studs tied to footing
C- Reinforced concrete footing
D- Reinforcement in horizontal mortar joints

Fig. 22. Methods of reinforcing concrete masonry walls

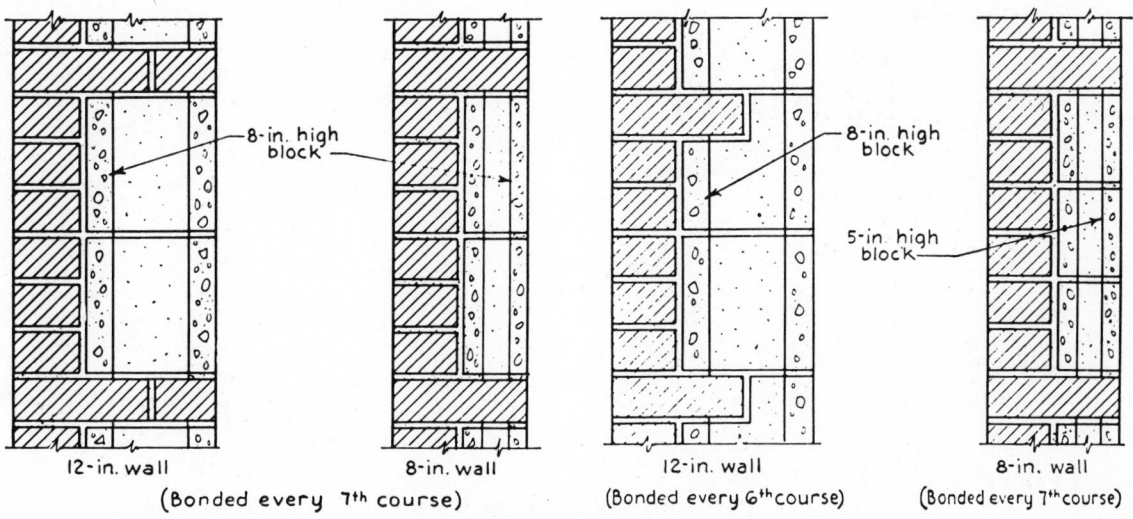

Fig. 23. Examples of concrete masonry used as back up for brick

12-in. wall (Bonded every 7th course) · 8-in. wall (Bonded every 7th course) · 12-in. wall (Bonded every 6th course) · 8-in. wall (Bonded every 7th course)

REINFORCED MASONRY WALLS

For conditions of unusual stress, such as earthquakes, hurricanes, unstable soil, excessive vibration, or very heavy loads, concrete masonry walls may be reinforced horizontally by continuous bond beams at each story height and vertically by studs at corners and openings and at regular intervals between (see Fig. 22). The concrete studs are tied in with the bond beams. Size and spacing of all reinforcement is usually governed by local codes.

CONCRETE MASONRY AS A BACKUP MATERIAL

Concrete block are becoming widely accepted as backup for various facing materials such as brick, cut stone, and cast stone. Virtually any masonry facing material can be used with concrete block, and when securely bonded the two materials will act together in developing high wall strength and stability.

Furring strips can usually be nailed directly to the block or mortar joints without requiring nailing plugs, clips, or other means of attachment. Special hardened nails are available for this purpose.

In building 8-in. and 12-in. walls with brick facing and concrete masonry backup, every seventh course of brick is a header course. The 12-in. walls can also be bonded every sixth brick course by using concrete masonry header units (see Fig. 23).

CONTROL JOINTS

Increasing use is being made of joints to control cracking in masonry walls resulting from unusual stresses. The joints are built into the walls in such locations

and in such a manner as to permit slight wall movement without cracking the masonry.

The spacing and location of these joints will depend upon a number of factors: the length of the wall, architectural details, and especially the experience records on the need for control joints in the particular locality where the structure is to be built. Control joints should be placed at junctions of bearing as well as nonbearing walls, at junctions of walls and columns (Fig. 24), at pilasters, and in walls weakened by chases and openings. In long walls, joints are ordinarily spaced at approximately 20-ft intervals, again depending on local experience.

Control joints should be of the built-in type with a ⅜-in. vertical joint running the full height of the wall. After the mortar has stiffened the mason rakes out the joint to a depth of ¾ in. This recess is later filled with a knife-grade elastic calking compound.

It may be advisable to paint the joint with a prime coat before calking. This will extend the life of the calking compound by preventing the porous masonry surfaces from absorbing the oils from the compound. The calking compound manufacturer's recommendations for joint primer should be followed.

Various methods of constructing control joints are detailed in Figs. 25–27.

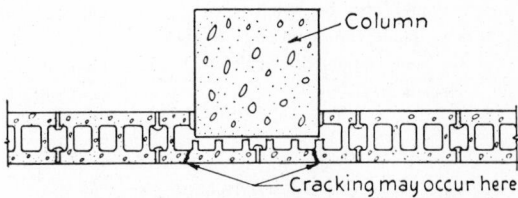

Notching of units in order to preserve masonry pattern across face of column may result in cracks, as indicated, due to column restraints
WRONG

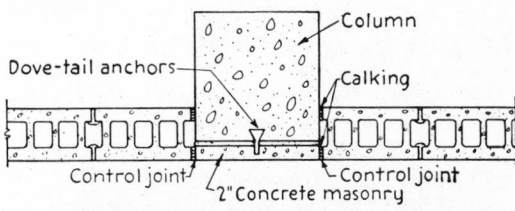

Stresses in walls due to column restraints are minimized by control joints
RIGHT

Fig. 24. Wrong and right methods of constructing concrete masonry walls around columns

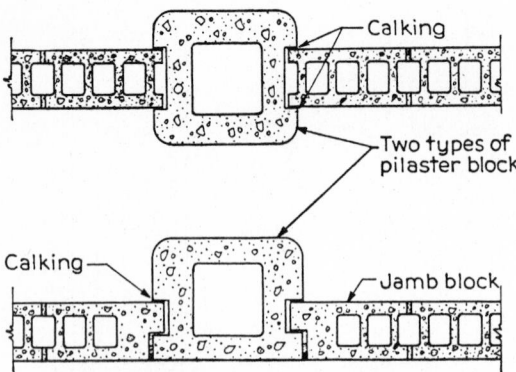

Fig. 25. Pilaster block with control joints
For control joint details see Fig. 27.

CONCRETE MASONRY WALL FINISHES

Sample panels

Regardless of which finish is selected, sample panel walls should be constructed on all important jobs as a means of conveying to block producers, masons, and building contractors the grade of materials, quality of workmanship, and precise appearance desired in the finished walls. Such panels are much more effective than written words or photographs in defining and specifying the quality of work required.

Panels should be about 40 in. long, at least four courses high; and constructed of block of the same type, size, and surface texture as will be used in the finished wall. The units also should be laid in the same pattern with the same kind of joints as will be required in the finished work. If finished walls are to be painted, panels should also be painted.

Panels should be kept for reference until the construction is completed in a satisfactory manner.

Wall patterns and surface treatments

Architects have worked out many interesting variations in treatment of course heights and joints. The units may be laid in regular courses of the same height, or in courses of two or more different heights, or several sizes of units may be laid up in a prearranged ashlar pattern.

In some wall treatments all the joints are accentuated by deep tooling; in others only the horizontal joints are accentuated. In the latter treatment the vertical joints after tooling are refilled with mortar and then rubbed flush after the mortar has partially hardened to give it a texture similar to that of the concrete masonry units. In this treatment the tooled horizontal joints stand out in strong relief.

Another variation in finish is obtained by extruded joints. An excess of mortar is used. Some of the mortar is squeezed out or extruded as the block are set and pressed into place. This mortar is not trimmed off but is left to harden in its extruded form. This treatment is best

suited to dry climates since the extruded joints may not be entirely weathertight.

Slump block are used to achieve special and unusual architectural effects. Slump block are made with a concrete mixture of such consistency that they sag or slump when removed from the molds, with the result that the irregularly faced units vary considerably in height, surface texture, and general appearance.

Split-block afford another variation in wall finish. They are made by splitting a hardened concrete unit lengthwise. The units are laid in the wall with the fractured faces exposed, producing a wall of rugged appearance.

Painted walls

Portland cement paint when properly applied to concrete masonry walls serves two practical purposes: (1) It provides attractive finishes, and (2) It helps to make masonry surfaces weathertight.

Portland cement paint is sold in powdered form in a variety of colors and is mixed with water before applying. It should meet the requirements of the Federal Specification for Paint, Serial Designation TT-P-21, Type II, Class A or Class B. Class A paint is used where the surface texture of the masonry wall is to be preserved. Class B paint contains a filler that gives the paint more body and is used to fill open porous surfaces.

Tests[1] conducted on various types of paints on masonry walls have found that portland cement base paints are highly effective as weatherproofing and have a high durability rating.

Portland cement paint should be applied to surfaces that are clean and free from oil, oil paint, dirt, or any substance that will prevent proper adhesion. Cracks or

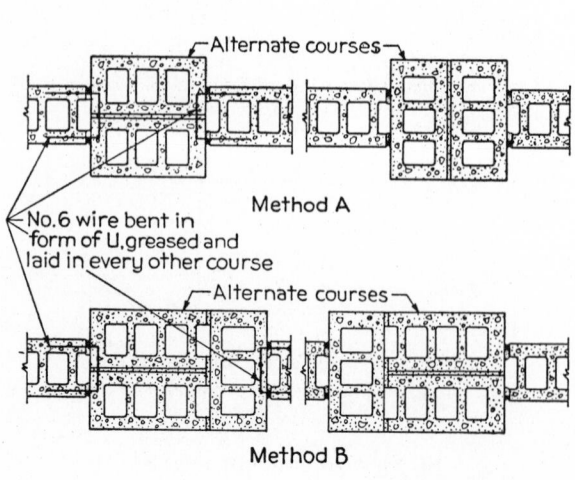

Fig. 26. Pilasters with control joints—methods A and B

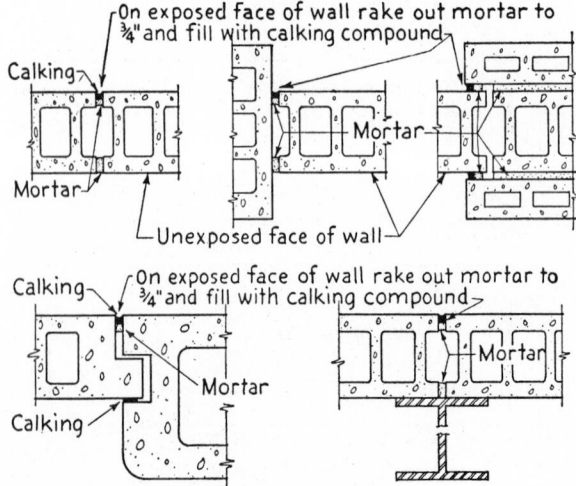

Fig. 27. Details of control joints

other wall imperfections should be cleaned of loose particles, dampened, filled with a stiff portland cement grout, and allowed to cure before painting.

The surface should be lightly dampened but not soaked with water before painting is begun so that the wall will not absorb mixing water needed for proper hardening of the cement paint. A garden pressure-sprayer with a fine fog spray nozzle is recommended for this purpose. The surface should be uniformly damp but not wet when painted.

Portland cement base paint should be prepared by mixing with water in the manner and to the consistency recommended in the instructions furnished by the manufacturer. Frequent stirring is necessary to keep the paint powder in suspension. A shallow pan 4 to 6 in. deep and 12 in. or more wide provides a good container. In such a pan the paint can be stirred easily and quickly. When the pan is filled to a depth of only 2 or 3 in. the paint can be stirred by the painter as he refills his brush.

Brushes with stiff fiber bristles not over 2 in. long, such as scrub and fender brushes, should be used to scrub the paint into surface pores. Brushes should be designed to protect the hands from unnecessary contact with the paint.

The first coat, when scrubbed into the surface, will eliminate any small pinholes through which water otherwise might enter the wall. Mortar joints around each block should be painted first.

When the first coat has hardened sufficiently, usually not sooner than 12 hours, the second coat should be applied after first dampening the surface. After the painting has been started it should be continued to some natural stopping point,

such as corners, doors, or belt courses. Frequent stirring of the paint is essential.

Paint should not be applied to frosty surfaces, nor should painting be attempted if the temperature is likely to drop below 40°F during the following 12 hours.

Properly applied and cured, portland cement paint bonds to and becomes a part of the concrete masonry wall, sealing the mortar joints and block surfaces.

High winds, excessive heat, and strong sunshine will dry cement paint quickly and render it ineffective as a weathertight coating unless it is properly moist cured. Improperly cured portland cement base paints may chalk or dust. The first coat should, therefore, be kept in a slightly damp condition for at least 12 hours and the finish coat for 48 hours. Keeping the paint moist with a fine fog spray should start as soon as the paint is hard enough to resist damage.

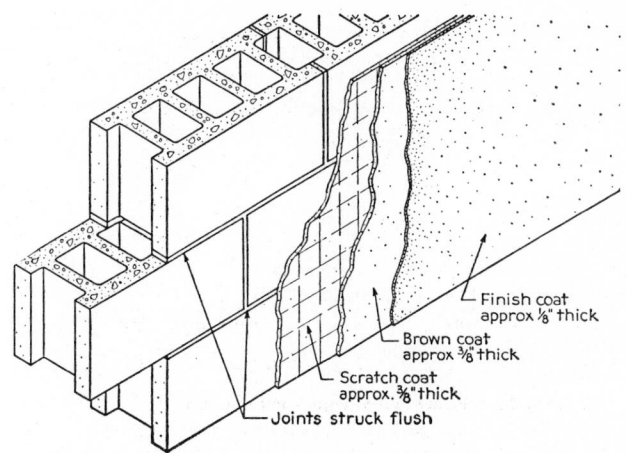

Fig. 28. Application of portland cement stucco to concrete masonry walls

Similar construction is used for portland cement plaster.

Stuccoed or plastered walls

Concrete masonry walls provide good bond for portland cement stucco and plaster finishes (Fig. 28). For details on the application of portland cement stucco and portland cement plaster to walls of concrete masonry, see the specifications of the American Standards Association (ASA A42.2 and A42.3) and the *Plasterer's Manual*, published by the Portland Cement Association.

[1] *Cyrus C. Fishburn and Douglas E. Parsons,* Tests of Cement-Water Paints and Other Waterproofings for Unit-Masonry Walls *(BMS 95), National Bureau of Standards; Clara Stentel,* Paints for Exterior Masonry Walls *(BMS 110), National Bureau of Standards; R. E. Copeland and C. C. Carlson,* Tests of the Resistance to Rain Penetration of Walls Built of Masonry and Concrete, *American Concrete Institute Proceedings, Vol. 36, p. 169.*

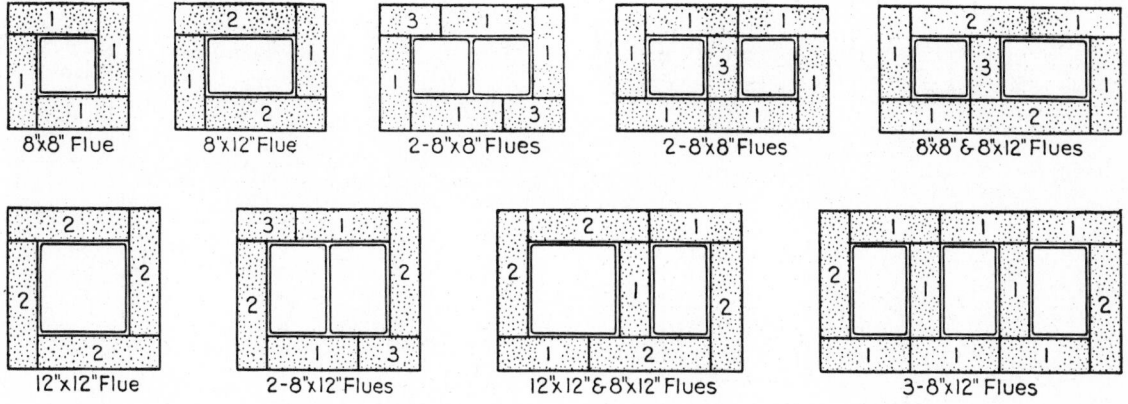

Fig. 29. Concrete masonry chimneys—block layouts

Data on this and the following page were obtained from reports of the British Building Research Station, from other publications, and from current engineering practice. Material was prepared by Jule Robert von Sternberg, Architect.

THERMAL EXPANSION

Two types of temperature variation induce movement in a structure (Fig. 1). The first of these is the slow, seasonal change from winter to summer; the second, relatively rapid fluctuations which take effect within a few hours. Design of almost any large building involves consideration of both. In small buildings, the rapid fluctuations are more likely to cause damage.

Fortunately, concrete and medium steel have similar coefficients of expansion (Table 1). Where buffers must be provided between stressed materials, expansion joints, properly protected against wear and weather, usually suffice.

EXPANSION JOINTS

Where a large building—or one of its parts—is restrained from moving by the pressure of an adjoining building, or other mass, provision must be made to take up the thrust. Expansion joints (Fig. 2), therefore, normally occur between new and old buildings and also between a wing of a building over 150 ft long and the main body of the structure.

Movement also takes place between parts of the same structure exposed to different temperatures. Ordinarily, roofs become much hotter, and expand more than walls, especially shaded walls. To prevent damage, roofs are frequently ringed with expansion joints. In addition, the roof structure, particularly if it is rigid, may be large enough to require a transecting expansion joint—one which passes through the roof, walls, and sometimes lower floors. Such transecting expansion joints vary in size and design with the size and construction of the building and the location of the joint.

In monolithic reinforced concrete buildings, expansion joints should completely divide the structure, cutting roof, walls, and floors. Joints are sometimes provided 100 ft on centers. The usual practice is to space them every 200 ft. With the use of longitudinal reinforcing, buildings up to 300 ft in length have been successfully constructed without expansion joints.

Steel-framed buildings: Practice varies in the steel-framed building with curtain walls. Although expansion joints that completely divide the buildings are also used in this type, 200 to 250 ft on centers, many successful slab-roofed buildings have been constructed with expansion joints in roofs and top-floor walls only, stopping at the top floor line. The expanding roof slab moves faster and farther than do the walls. Flexibility of the top-floor steel columns is relied upon to yield to the thrust set up by the roof slab, completely absorbing it and preventing its transmission to lower stories. Movement of masonry in lower floors is taken up in individual joints, and is further restrained by the steel framing.

Solid masonry buildings: Freestanding solid masonry buildings usually require joints about 100 ft on centers. With an average winter-summer temperature differential of about 100°F, a masonry wall will expand about 0.4 in. in every 100 ft of length. Expansion joints at 100-ft intervals must be approximately ½ in. wide, and are easily concealed in the average mortar joint.

PROVISIONS AT GRADE

Provision must be made for the building equipped with transecting expansion joints to slip on its foundation. In solid masonry buildings, the mortar joint between the concrete foundation and the masonry wall provides a satisfactory slipping surface. Monolithic buildings, however, require slip joints between the walls and foundation to permit movement of the superstructure. Since the foundation is buried in the ground, and thus has little temperature differential to influence it, it is not affected by temperature fluctuations of the air.

SPECIAL BUILDING TYPES

Structures in which unusually low summer temperatures are maintained, as in breweries and cold-storage warehouses, must allow for much greater expansion than other building types.

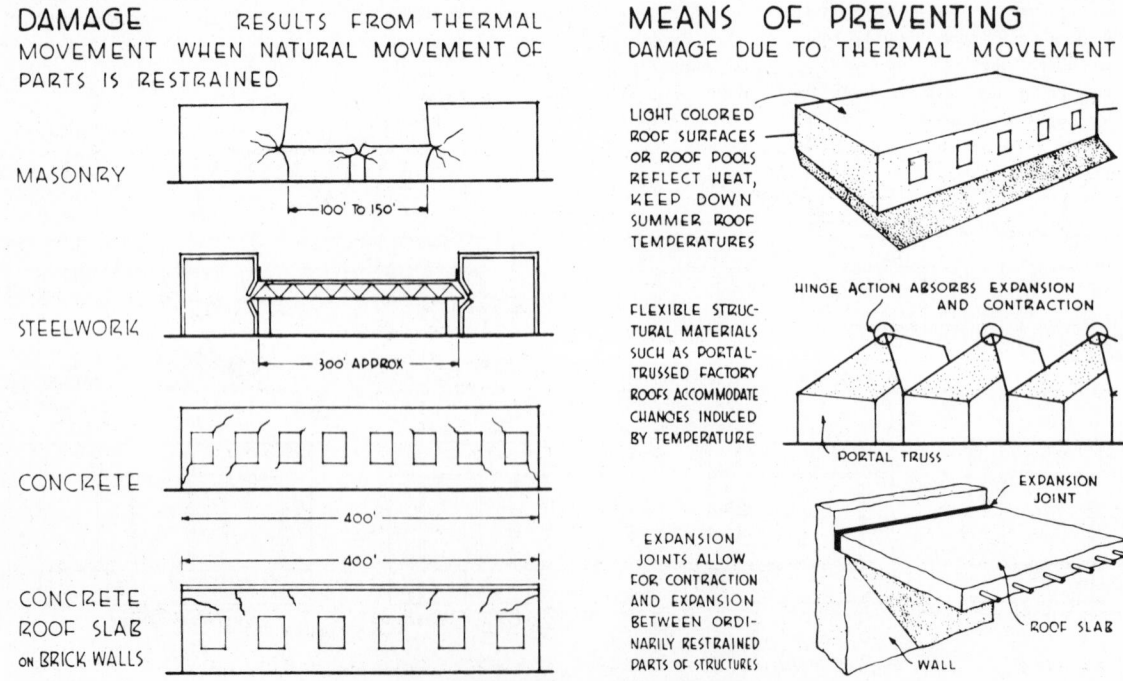

DAMAGE RESULTS FROM THERMAL MOVEMENT WHEN NATURAL MOVEMENT OF PARTS IS RESTRAINED

MASONRY — 100' TO 150'

STEELWORK — 300' APPROX

CONCRETE — 400'

CONCRETE ROOF SLAB ON BRICK WALLS — 400'

MEANS OF PREVENTING DAMAGE DUE TO THERMAL MOVEMENT

LIGHT COLORED ROOF SURFACES OR ROOF POOLS REFLECT HEAT, KEEP DOWN SUMMER ROOF TEMPERATURES

FLEXIBLE STRUCTURAL MATERIALS SUCH AS PORTAL-TRUSSED FACTORY ROOFS ACCOMMODATE CHANGES INDUCED BY TEMPERATURE

HINGE ACTION ABSORBS EXPANSION AND CONTRACTION

PORTAL TRUSS

EXPANSION JOINTS ALLOW FOR CONTRACTION AND EXPANSION BETWEEN ORDINARILY RESTRAINED PARTS OF STRUCTURES

EXPANSION JOINT

ROOF SLAB

WALL

Fig. 1. **Damage due to thermal movement**

Table 1. Coefficients of linear expansion (in inches per degree Fahrenheit)

METALS, ALLOYS	
aluminum, wrought	.0000128
brass	.0000104
bronze	.0000101
copper	.0000093
gray cast iron	.0000059
steel, hard	.0000073
steel, medium	.0000067
steel, soft	.0000061
STONE, MASONRY	
ashlar masonry	.0000035
brick masonry	.0000031
cement, Portland	.0000059
concrete	.0000079
concrete masonry	.0000067
granite	.0000047
limestone	.0000044
marble	.0000056
plaster	.0000092
rubble masonry	.0000035
sandstone	.0000061
slate	.0000058
TIMBER, parallel to fiber	
fir	.0000021
maple	.0000036
oak	.0000027
pine	.0000030
TIMBER, transverse	
fir	.000032
maple	.000027
oak	.000030
pine	.000019

EXPANSION JOINTS ARE NEEDED:

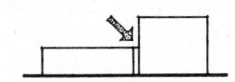

1. WHERE A LONG LOW STRUCTURE ABUTS A RIGID MASS.

3. WHEN A NEW BUILDING ADJOINS AN EXISTING BUILDING

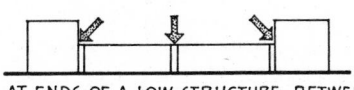

2. AT ENDS OF A LOW STRUCTURE BETWEEN TWO HEAVY MASSES AND AT APPROPRIATE INTERVALS – USUALLY EVERY 150 FEET

4. IN FREE STANDING BUILDINGS, THROUGH EXPANSION JOINTS ARE REQUIRED AT INTERVALS OF APPROXIMATELY 200 FT.

5. WHEN INTERIOR AND EXTERIOR TEMPERATURE DIFFERENTIALS ARE EXCESSIVE, AS IN A COLD STORAGE BUILDING.

FUNCTIONS:

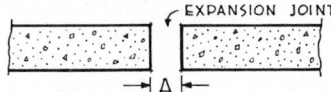

MUST PROVIDE FOR MAXIMUM THERMAL-INDUCED MOVEMENT LIKELY TO BE ENCOUNTERED. [WIDTH OF JOINT "A" = SPAN (INCHES) X 100 (AVERAGE WINTER-SUMMER TEMP. DIFF.) X 𝑛 (COEFFICIENT OF EXPANSION OF THE MATERIAL)]

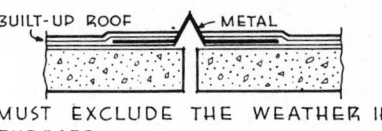

MUST EXCLUDE THE WEATHER IF EXPOSED

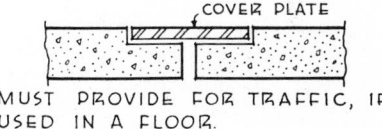

MUST PROVIDE FOR TRAFFIC, IF USED IN A FLOOR.

MUST BE CONCEALED IF IT IMPAIRS APPEARANCE

TYPICAL EXPANSION JOINTS:

NOTE: DRAWINGS NOT TO SCALE

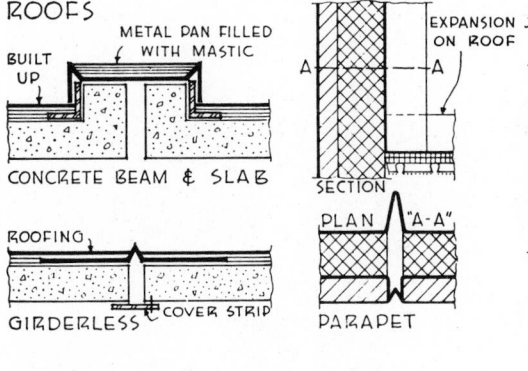

ROOFS

CONCRETE BEAM & SLAB

GIRDERLESS

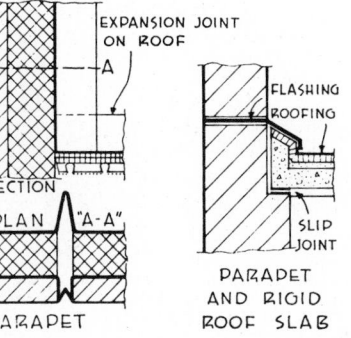

PARAPET

PARAPET AND RIGID ROOF SLAB

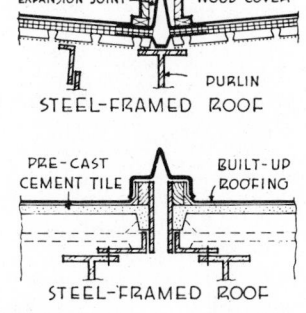

STEEL-FRAMED ROOF

STEEL-FRAMED ROOF

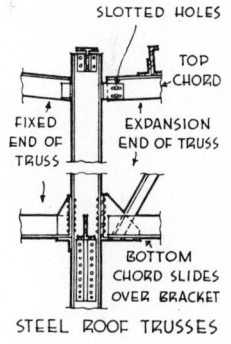

STEEL ROOF TRUSSES

WALLS

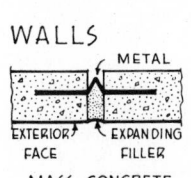

MASS CONCRETE

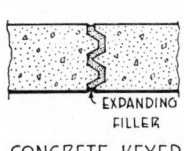

CONCRETE, KEYED

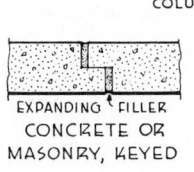

CONCRETE OR MASONRY, KEYED

STEEL AND MASONRY, KEYED

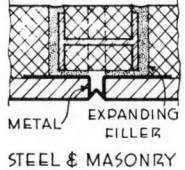

STEEL & MASONRY

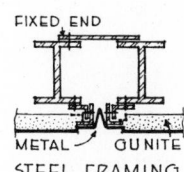

STEEL FRAMING

FLOORS

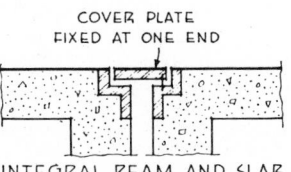

FLAT SLAB

INTEGRAL BEAM AND SLAB

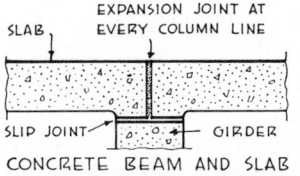

CONCRETE BEAM AND SLAB

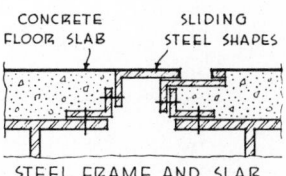

STEEL FRAME AND SLAB

Fig. 2. Typical expansion joints and their functions

MASONRY CONSTRUCTION—3
Thermal expansion

Data and illustrations on this and the following two pages have been derived from *Technical Notes on Brick and Tile Construction,* published by the Structural Clay Products Institute.

Recent investigations have shown that thermal expansion and contraction contribute to the cracking of masonry walls and that former recommendations for the location and spacing of expansion joints should be revised.

There are several reasons why greater provision must be made for thermal movement now than was required several decades ago:

1. *Thin walls:* Codes now permit the use of thinner masonry walls, especially for nonloadbearing curtain walls. Temperature variations are greater in thin walls because of reduced heat storage capacity.

2. *Insulation:* Increased use of insulation on the inside of masonry walls results in greater temperature variations in the masonry.

3. *Composite walls:* Increased use of walls faced with brick and backed up with hollow units (tile or concrete) that have different coefficients of expansion results in differential thermal movement.

4. *Sills and lintels:* Sills and lintels also produce differential movement, which, in the case of metal window and door frames and lintels, can be relatively large.

5. *Parapets and foundations:* There is often a substantial temperature difference between parapets and building walls and between building walls and foundation, particularly in heated buildings, which results in differential movements of these elements.

Masonry failures resulting from thermal movement may be classified under two headings: cumulative expansion and differential expansion.

1. *Cumulative expansion:* In the absence of restraint, a brick wall 100 ft long may be expected to expand ⅜ in. owing to a temperature increase of 100°F. When the wall contracts, however, its tensile strength is not sufficient to overcome frictional resistance, and thus one or more cracks will appear. The same cumulative expansion causes failure of walls at offsets where the masonry at right angles to the long wall is placed in bending and shear by the thermal expansion of the long wall.

2. *Differential expansion:* The effect of differential movements of different materials in a composite masonry wall may be sufficient to cause cracking of one of the wall elements, generally the one having the lowest coefficient of expansion. Differential movement between masonry and metal that may be built into it is much greater than the movement between masonry materials, and numerous examples may be found of masonry cracking caused by expansion of metal members.

COEFFICIENTS OF EXPANSION

Table 2 gives average coefficients of expansion of masonry materials and of steel and aluminum, the metals most commonly used in conjunction with masonry.

RECOMMENDATIONS

Offsets and junctions: In general, expansion joints should be located at offsets, provided the wall expanding into the offset is 50 ft or more in length, and at junctions of walls in L-, T-, or U-shaped buildings. Figure 3 shows such locations and Fig. 4 shows details of typical expansion joints.

Long walls: Recommended spacing of expansion joints in long walls is given in Table 3. Such joints should be approximately ¾ in. thick and, where two or more expansion joints are required, it is suggested that the distance from the corner to the nearest expansion joint not exceed one-half the distances given in Table 3. Figure 5 shows details of typical expansion joints in long walls.

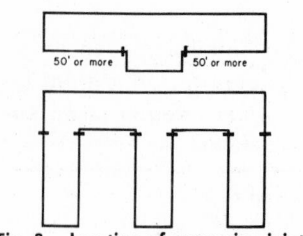
Fig. 3. Location of expansion joints

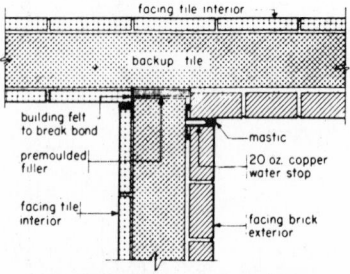
EXPANSION JOINT AT WALL OFFSET

EXPANSION JOINT AT JUNCTURE OF INTERSECTING WALLS
Fig. 4. Expansion joints in walls

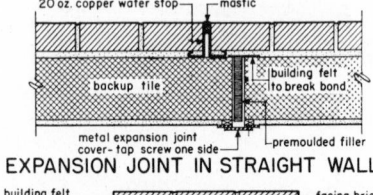
EXPANSION JOINT IN STRAIGHT WALL

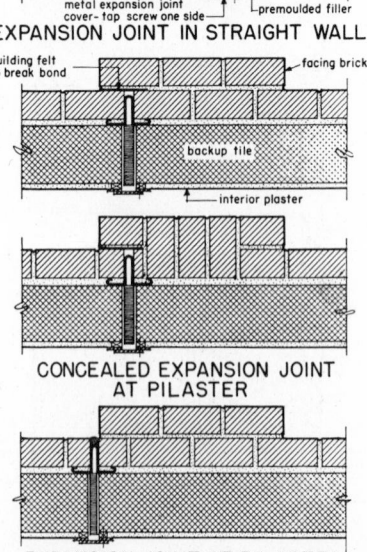
CONCEALED EXPANSION JOINT AT PILASTER

EXPANSION JOINT AT PILASTER
Fig. 5. Expansion joints in straight walls

Table 2. Thermal expansion

Materials	Average Coefficients of Thermal Expansion in millionths (.000001) per degree F.	Thermal Expansion, inches per 100 feet for 100° F. temperature increase (to closest 1/16 inch)	
Clay or shale brick masonry	3.6	.43	(7/16)
Fire clay brick masonry	2.5	.30	(5/16)
Structural clay tile masonry	3.3	.40	(3/8)
Dense concrete block masonry	5.0	.60	(5/8)
Light concrete block masonry	3.0	.36	(3/8)
Building stone	4.5	.54	(9/16)
Reinforced concrete	5.5	.66	(11/16)
Structural steel	6.0	.72	(3/4)
Aluminum	12.8	1.54	(1 9/16)

Table 3. Recommended spacing of expansion joints

Outside Temperature Ranges F.*	Maximum Length of Wall, ft.			
	Unheated or Insulated		Heated not Insulated	
	Solid	Openings†	Solid	Openings†
100 and over	200	100	250	125
Less than 100	250	125	300	150

*The range from the lowest average temperature to the highest.
†Openings 20 per cent more of wall area.

Masonry walls in skeleton-frame construction are especially susceptible to cracking caused by thermal and other kinds of movement. In addition to thermal movement within the wall itself (discussed on the previous page), there may be differential movement between the wall and the building frame. Perhaps even more important is the fact that skeleton frames are more flexible than masonry walls and undergo greater deflection due to floor loads and to wind and other lateral forces.

A solution to this problem is the use of flexible ties between the masonry walls and the columns and spandrel beams of the building frame. Recommended details of such flexible anchorages are shown on this and the following page.

If the building is not too high, the exterior walls can be erected completely independent of the columns and beams for vertical support. The walls then carry their own dead weight to the foundation, and thus reduce the size and cost of the frame. The skeleton frame provides the wall with lateral support and carries all other vertical loads. The wall is tied to the frame by flexible anchors that take tension and compression, but no shear, and thus permit differential longitudinal and vertical movements between the frame and the wall (Figs. 6–9). A schematic diagram for such a structural system is shown in Fig. 6.

Metal ties should be No. 6 gage galvanized steel or other noncorrosive metal of equal strength. To avoid buckling of the ties, the distance between the inside face of the wall and the anchor seat should not exceed 3 in., and preferably not more than ¾ in. The size and spacing of ties is based on tensile and compressive loads induced by wind suction and pressure on the wall. Table 4 shows the maximum spacing of No. 6 gage ties on spandrel beams for three wind pressures, based on the maximum distance between lateral supports for several wall types. If lateral support is provided only by columns, the spacing of ties should be the same as shown in Table 4.

Steel or concrete columns, beams, and spandrels should not be surrounded with masonry unless absolutely necessary. It is especially important that masonry not be placed in contact with columns. Physical

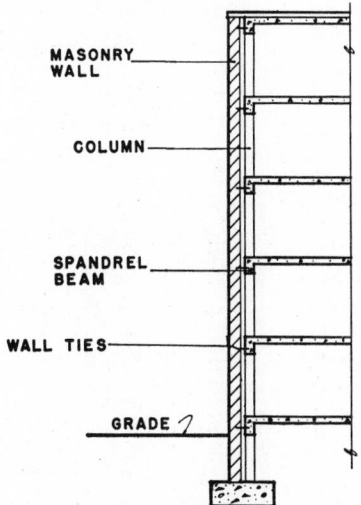

Fig. 6. Masonry wall braced but not supported by building frame

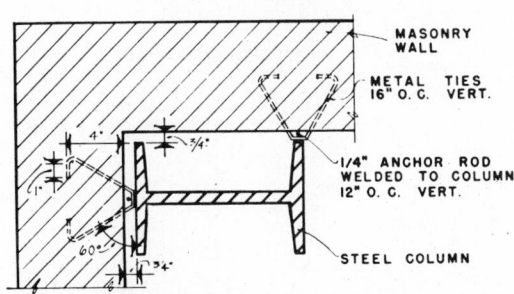

PLAN OF WALL ANCHORAGE TO STEEL COLUMN

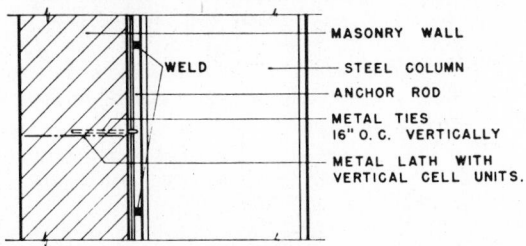

ELEVATION OF WALL ANCHORAGE TO STEEL COLUMN

Fig. 7. Wall anchorage to steel column

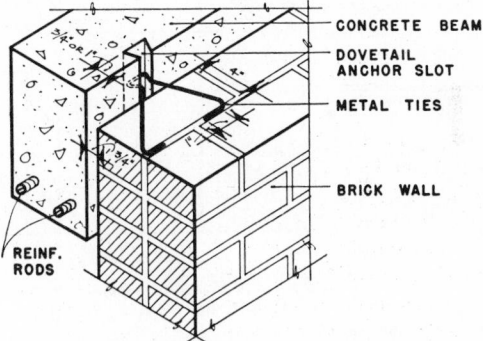

WALL ANCHORAGE TO CONCRETE BEAM

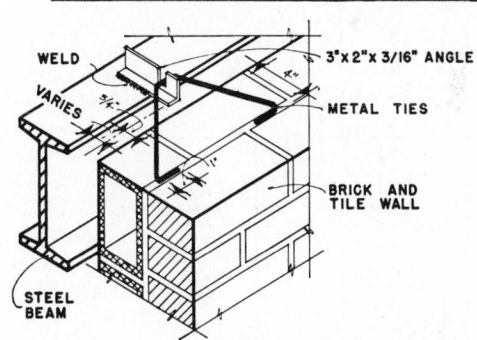

WALL ANCHORAGE TO STEEL BEAM

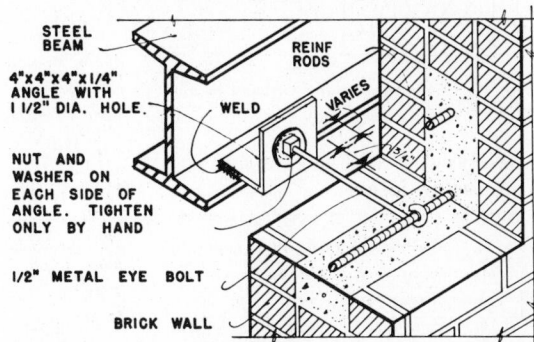

ALTERNATE WALL ANCHORAGE TO STEEL BEAM

Fig. 8. Typical beam-wall anchorage

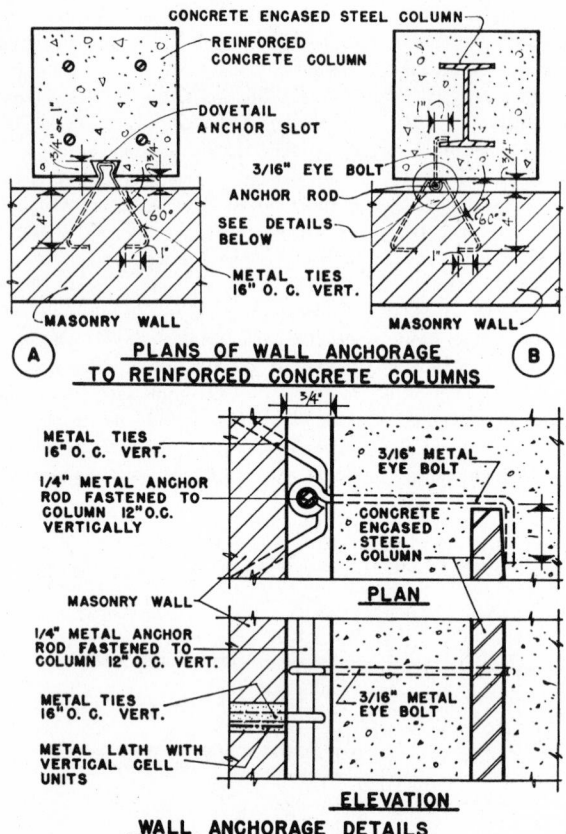

PLANS OF WALL ANCHORAGE TO REINFORCED CONCRETE COLUMNS

WALL ANCHORAGE DETAILS

Fig. 9. Wall anchorage details

Table 4. Spacing of wall ties

Wall Type	Maximum Distance Between Lateral Supports for Walls	Maximum Spacing of No. 6 Gage Tie Anchors at Lateral Supports		
		40 psf	30 psf	20 psf
6″ tile	10'-0″	1'-6″	2'-0″	2'-0″
6″ brick or 8″ tile	12'-0″	1'-3″	1'-8″	2'-0″
8″ brick	13'-4″	1'-3″	1'-6″	2'-0″
12″ tile	18'-0″	1'-0″	1'-6″	1'-8″
12″ brick	20'-0″	0'-8″	1'-0″	1'-6″

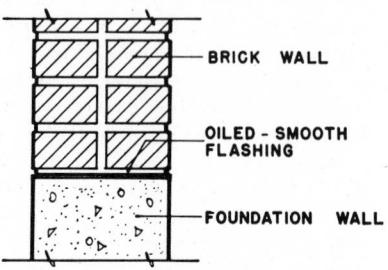

Fig. 11. Prevention of bond at foundation

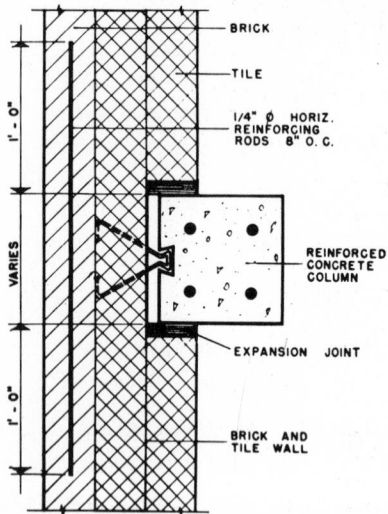

Fig. 10. Column partially encased in masonry wall

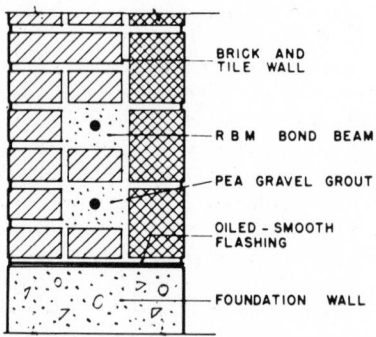

Fig. 12. Reinforcement of wall at foundation

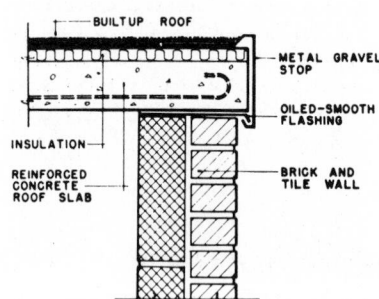

Fig. 13. Prevention of bond between masonry wall and roof slab

contact between the edges of decks or floor slabs and the inside face of masonry walls should be prevented. If steel columns are fire-protected by masonry or other material, the fireproofing should not be in contact with the masonry wall.

If it is considered necessary to encase columns, the encasement should not exceed 4 in. in a 12-in. wall (Fig. 10). Columns should not be encased in an 8-in. wall.

To prevent cracks resulting from differential movement between the foundation and the wall, the detail shown in Fig. 11 will break the bond between the two and permit each to move independently. This detail may be used in structures for which it is not necessary to anchor the walls to the foundation. In general, such anchorage is unnecessary for skeleton-frame structures in which the enclosing walls may be anchored to the frame.

Additional resistance to cracking resulting from any forces that may be transmitted to the wall by friction may be obtained by incorporating a reinforced "bond beam" in the base of the wall (Fig. 12).

A somewhat similar condition occurs where masonry bearing walls support a concrete floor or roof slab. Investigations have shown that such slabs as a rule not only shrink horizontally but also curl upward at the corners. If the walls are tied rigidly to the slab, cracking of the masonry is almost certain to result. This condition is most severe in roof slabs, and in such cases it is recommended that parapets be eliminated and that positive means be provided to break the bond between wall and slab. A suggested detail for this condition is shown in Fig. 13. The natural struggle between the inside and outside portions of

a wall becomes most intense at the juncture of roof and parapet wall. This struggle may continue until there is, literally, an explosion. Indeed, cracked or broken parapet walls, particularly at roof corners, are quite common.

Every wall of any thickness is strained by the differences in exposure and temperature between inside and outside. The outer surface, or outer layer, gets wet and then is heated by the sun, or, more to the point, it is subject to freezing temperature while the inner layer is heated. Thus the outside layer wants to contract, the inner one to expand. Sooner or later each goes its own way and an explosion follows, leaving a break in the wall.

This problem is especially important in the design of parapets. For here differences in exposure and temperature reach the extreme, above the point where the outside wall gets any heat at all from inside. Heat in the top story rises to the underside of the roof slab, causing it to expand. Insulation on top will free the slab from the influence of the cold outside, and the slab will stretch comfortably. But the parapet wall, exposed to the cold, will shrink from each free end, toward the center. (The free end refers only to the top of the wall; the bottom is fixed at the roof line.) At the corner, the pull is along each wall. The roof slab is pushing the bottom corner of the parapet wall outward; the top of each wall is being pulled inward. Thus the corner cracks often take the pattern shown in Fig. 14.

Masonry wall cracks at or near the junction of parapet and roof line are perhaps the most difficult of all types of masonry cracking to eliminate. This difficulty is due to the severe exposures to which the parapet is subjected, to its relatively light weight, to movements between parapet and building walls, and perhaps to other factors often hard to identify.

There is no single solution of the problem of cracking of parapet walls. Many methods have been tried by different designers with varying success. Figure 15 shows a reinforced parapet wall construction recommended by the Structural Clay Products Institute to minimize vertical cracking. Figure 16 shows standard details used in the office of Fred N. Severud, Consulting Engineer. These details, despite the

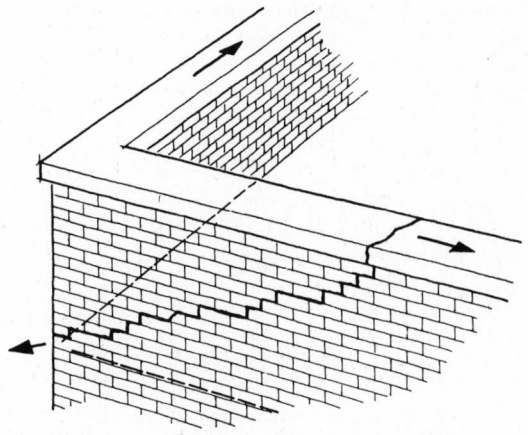

Fig. 14.   Typical corner crack on parapet walls

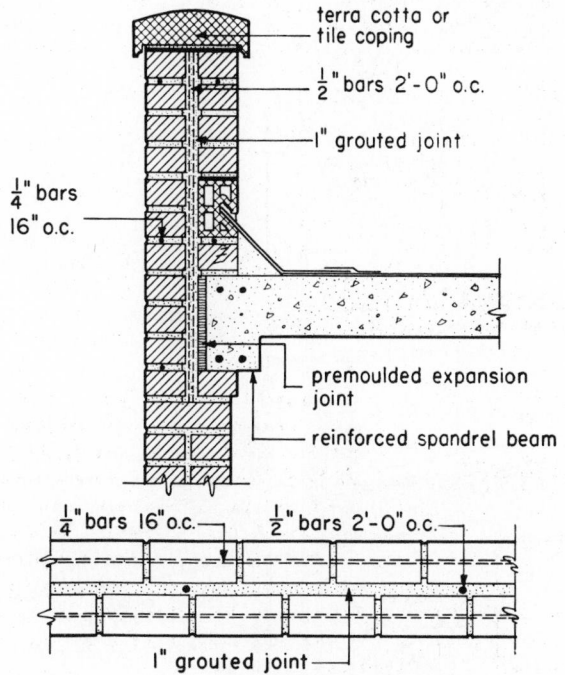

terra cotta or tile coping

$\frac{1}{2}$" bars 2'-0" o.c.

1" grouted joint

$\frac{1}{4}$" bars 16" o.c.

premoulded expansion joint

reinforced spandrel beam

$\frac{1}{4}$" bars 16" o.c. $\frac{1}{2}$" bars 2'-0" o.c.

1" grouted joint

Fig. 15.   Reinforced parapet wall

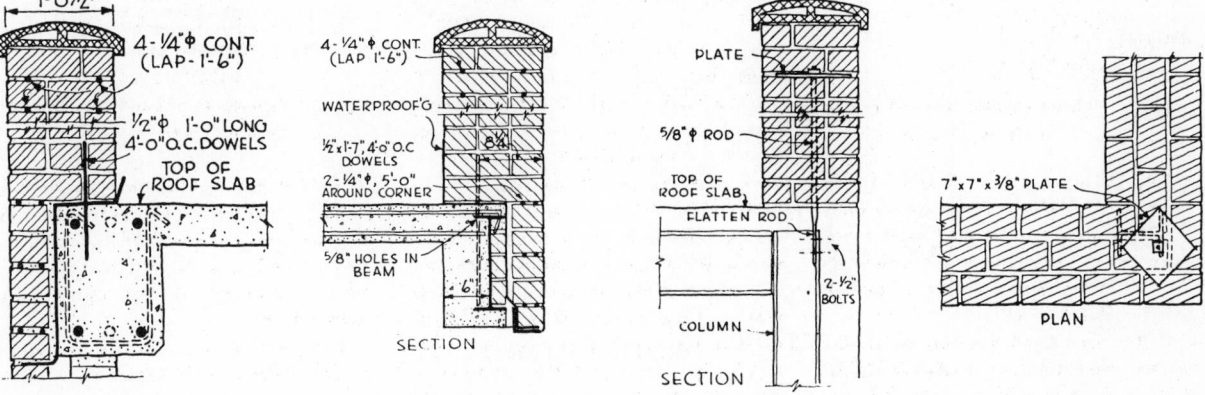

Fig. 16.   Standard details for parapet wall

similarity of the horizontal reinforcing, differ significantly: the SCPI design provides flexibility between the wall and the spandrel beam, whereas the Severud designs anchor the two firmly together. An entirely different approach is shown in Fig. 17, in which a concrete fence is substituted for the parapet wall. Concrete struts, poured with the spandrel beams, act as fence posts; precast concrete planks are set in slots in the posts.

The only sure way to prevent the cracking of parapet walls is to eliminate the parapet entirely. SCPI and many other authorities in this field recommend the elimination of parapets wherever possible. Figure 18 shows a standard detail of the New York City Housing Authority for a pipe railing instead of a parapet. See also the eave detail shown in Fig. 13.

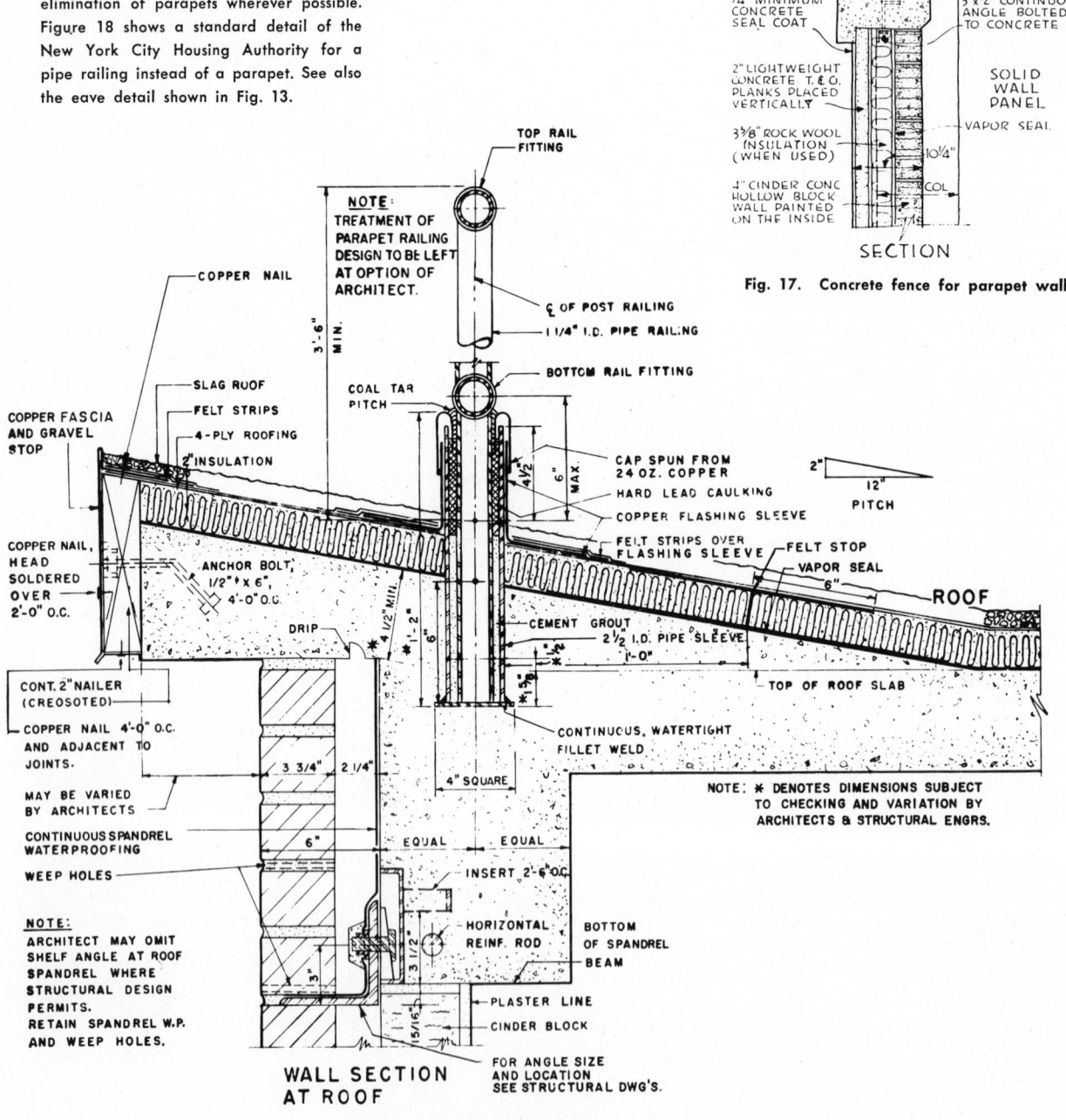

Fig. 17. Concrete fence for parapet wall

Fig. 18. Pipe railing for parapet wall

By ELWYN E. SEELYE, *Seelye, Stevenson, Value and Knecht, Consulting Engineers*

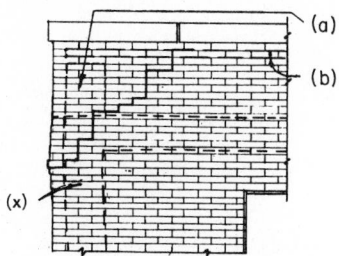

CAUSE: Parapet corner crack resulting from temperature expansion and contraction of parapet in relation to slab and walls below. (x) Elastic distortion of columns and spandrel beams.

PREVENTION: (a) Raise corner column stubs above roof; (b) Install horizontal reinforcing rods in joints of brickwork or (c) Omit a masonry parapet wall.

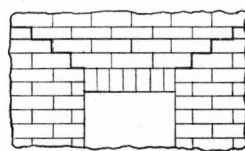

CAUSE: Lacks lintel or rowlock arch supports.

PREVENTION: Provide lintel or rowlock arch. (Flat masonry arches should not exceed 5 ft without lintel.)

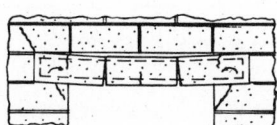

CAUSE: Deflection of a shallow lintel due to load, transfers stress to inelastic masonry over opening.

PREVENTION: (a) Use stiffer lintel; (b) Predeflect lintel by loading material on it prior to building wall above; (c) Mastic joints in vicinity of bearing.

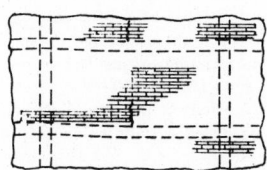

CAUSE: Deflection of spandrel beams carrying exterior masonry wall. Deflection of interior beams carrying masonry partition.

PREVENTION: (a) Use stiffer beams; (b) Prestress by loading material on beam prior to building wall.

CAUSE: Random vertical cracks in face brick.

PREVENTION: (a) Do not permit use of mortar set accelerators; (b) Perforated face brick may be cause of this weakness.

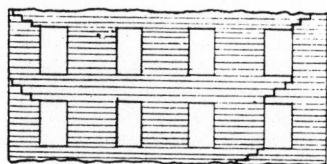

CAUSE: Cracks at wall openings a result of relief at weakest section, of longitudinal stress from shrinkage, or settlement.

PREVENTION: (a) For shrinkage control see (below); (b) Design adequate foundations.

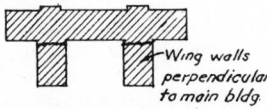

Wing walls perpendicular to main bldg.

PLAN OF BUILDING

CAUSE: Shrinkage in cinder block back-up increases tendency of masonry keyed to it to crack, (see above example) and causes tendency of perpendicular wings to crack off. In block walls having no face brick, there is an increased tendency for the walls to crack from shrinkage.

PREVENTION: (a) Thorough curing of blocks (blocks should be at least 3 weeks old) and steam curing of blocks; (b) More expansion joints; (c) Specify lean mortar and avoid using mortar set accelerators; (d) Reinforce walls with horizontal rods placed in joints, at zones of weakness.

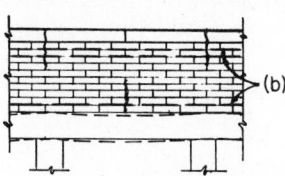

CAUSE: Parapet wall cracks at points of maximum positive and negative moment due to flexibility of spandrel beams; plus temperature expansion and contraction of parapet wall.

PREVENTION: (a) Use stiffer spandrels or predeflect them; (b) Install horizontal reinforcing rods in joints of brickwork.

CAUSE: Cracks due to settlement of new building in relation to old.

PREVENTION: (a) Joint separating wall of new building from old; (b) Reduce the design unit load on the footings of the new building adjoining the old.

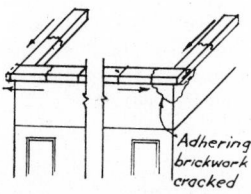

Adhering brickwork cracked

CAUSE: Shoved coping stones result from temperature expansion and contraction acting on parapet. Long coping stones, with thin non-compressible joints do not allow elastic adjustments.

PREVENTION: Use a watertight, elastic joint material. For example, pack occasional joint with oakum covered with caulking compound.

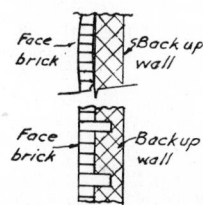

Face brick — *Back-up wall*

Face brick — *Back-up wall*

CAUSE: Bulging face brick resulting from inadequate headers or broken headers plus frost.

PREVENTION: Provide the standard amount of headers and/or galvanized anchors and keys.

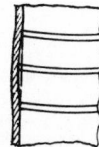

CAUSE: Very dangerous situation. The thrust may be due to thermal expansion of contents in buildings; to foundation settlement, or to buckling from heavy loads without adequate ties being furnished by floor system.

PREVENTION: (a) Use wall anchors and straps to connect floor system with walls; (b) Use tie rods for granular storage or cold storage; provide adequate foundations.

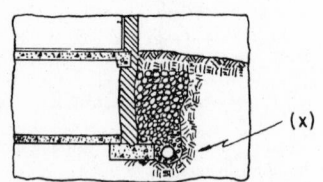

CAUSE: Very dangerous bulging basement wall resulting from inadequate section to act as retaining wall. Lack of drainage of base of wall causes build-up of hydrostatic pressure.

PREVENTION: Use adequate thickness to resist earth and frost thrusts (x). Provide for draining when ground does not drain away from wall naturally.

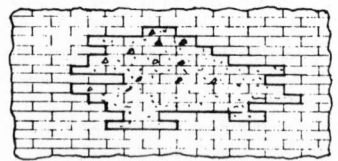

CAUSE: Surface shelled off because of under burned (salmon) brick.

PREVENTION: Specify that brick is to conform to an A.S.T.M. designation and send sample to lab. for civil testing. (Refer to Data Book for Engineers Vol. II) Elwyn E. Seelye, John Wiley And Sons, Inc., New York, 1951.

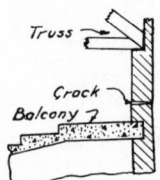

CAUSE: Top of wall overturned from roof truss expansion.

PREVENTION: Adequate structural design.

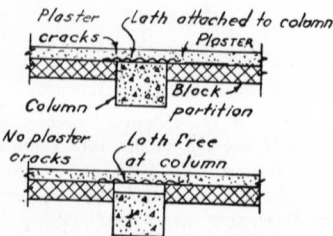

CAUSE: Short Lap. Not enough length of stretch for lath over each joint between column and masonry.

PREVENTION: Leave lath unattached to column and extend at least 8 in. beyond column and staple to partition.

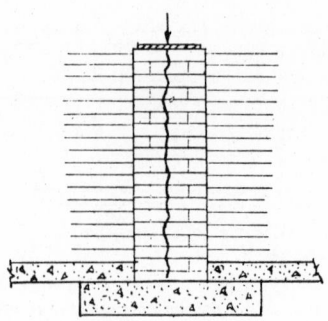

CAUSE: Danger signal of overloaded masonry pilaster or pier is appearance of vertical cracks. Also an indication of corroding of imbedded steel column.

PREVENTION: (a) Provide adequate section to reduce unit stress to within safe limits; (b) Parge column with cement or paint with bitumastic paint.

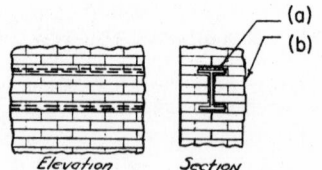

CAUSE: Rusting and resulting expansion of wall steel and lintels embedded in exterior masonry.

PREVENTION: Specify parging with ½ in. cement mortar, all steel embedded in exterior masonry.

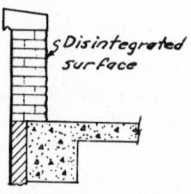

CAUSE: Disintegration of interior surface of parapet wall.

PREVENTION: (a) Use face brick on interior surfaces; (b) Do not waterproof inside surface with bitumen, so that surface is permitted to breathe.

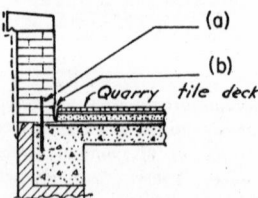

CAUSE: Parapet wall shoved on account of the expansion of deck.

PREVENTION: (a) Dowels between wall and spandrel beam; (b) Expansion joint.

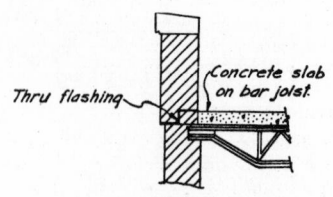

CAUSE: Expansion of concrete slab on bar joists thru flashing.

PREVENTION: (a) Provide lugs on top of joist; (b) Provide dowels; (c) Raise column stubs up into parapet.

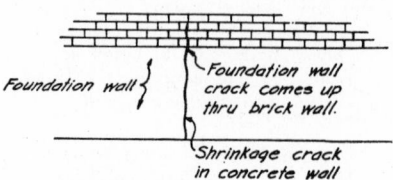

CAUSE: Shrinkage in concrete.

PREVENTION: (a) Provide adequate belt steel reinforcement; (b) Pour concrete wall in short alternate sections to take up initial set.

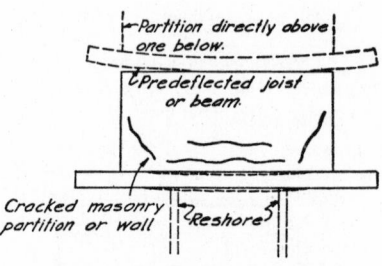

CAUSE: (a) Deflection of supporting double joist or shallow steel beam; (b) Leaving in reshores while building partition.

PREVENTION: Predeflect supporting beam by loading with partition material equal to the weight of partition before building same. Do not leave in reshores when partition is built. Where similar condition occurs above, predeflect supporting beam or joist before building partition up to same, or do not build partition up tight to beam or joist until deflection of beam or joist has taken place.

Note: Variations of this would be constructing offset exterior walls on flexible beams.

For the prevention of cracks in masonry walls, it is recommended that the following requirements, where applicable, be added to standard masonry specifications.

WORKMANSHIP

1. Predeflection of Shallow Beams, Spandrels or Slabs Carrying Walls or Partitions:

Where called for on the structural plans, the material for partitions or walls shall be assembled adjacent to the structural member in order to predeflect same before the partition or wall is built.

2. Elastic Joints in Stone Masonry at Bearing Adjacent to Long Shallow Lintels and at Points of Maximum Positive and Negative Moments of Spandrel Beams:

Add a clause to standard stone masonry specification to provide for plastic mortar joints in these areas.

3. Under Cold Weather Protection add:

Accelerating or anti-freeze admixtures will not be permitted.

4. Reinforcing Steel:

Where called for on the structural plans, reinforcing rods and dowels shall be laid in the joints of the masonry work. The requirements for reinforcing steel as set forth in the "Structural Concrete" section of the specification, shall apply equally to this section.

5. Expansion Joints:

Expansion joints shall be provided in the masonry work where shown and in accordance with the details on the plans.

Note—Suggestions for locations and types of expansion joints:

(a) Provide expansion joint where the walls of a perpendicular wing join the main building, and where large units of a connected group of buildings join each other. How elaborate the joint should be will depend on whether the building is a monumental, utility or temporary structure.

(b) Provide expansion joint where the walls of a new addition connect to an old building. This can be a two-strip copper water-stop, allowing for vertical movement, or a mastic joint, depending on the probable life of the old building.

(c) Provide expansion joint where large area-way walls, retaining walls, and similar masonry structures abut and are perpendicular to the building wall. A mastic joint will usually suffice.

(d) Coping stones should be provided with a joint every 20 or 30 ft to be made ½ in. wide and caulked with oakum and covered with caulking compound.

(e) Provide expansion joints in quarry tile roofs and exterior quarry tile decks.

Joints of premolded asphalt, cork or metal should be called for about every 20 ft in both directions and at the junction of the deck with the parapet walls and other vertical surfaces.

6. Headers and/or Anchors:

(See Data Book for Civil Engineers—Volume 11, Specifications & Costs, Elwyn E. Seelye, John Wiley and Sons, Inc., New York 1951)

7. Parging of Embedded Structural Steel:

Steel members, embedded in exterior masonry, shall be "buttered" with not less than ½ inch of setting mortar on all surfaces that are not indicated to be fireproofed with concrete.

MATERIAL

1. Face Brick:

Face brick shall conform to the Standard Specification of the A.S.T.M. C 216, latest edition.

Note—The type of face brick selected should be one with a reasonably porous surface in order to obtain good bond with the mortar. For common brick and sand lime brick specifications, refer Page 3-09, Data Book for Civil Engineers—Volume II.

2. Mortar for Concrete Block Back-up Walls:

Specify concrete block back-up walls to be laid in lime-cement mortar, not Portland cement mortar. The lime cement mortar should be weak to permit wall to take up volumetric changes locally rather than in large cracks. A mortar such as 1 part cement, 1 part putty and 12 parts sand by volume is suggested.

GENERAL DESIGN NOTES

The following notes on general design are offered to assist in preventing cracks in masonry:

1. Lintels:

Provide lintels for flat masonry arches exceeding 5 feet in clear span.

2. Footings:

When designing the footings for an addition to an existing building, it is good practice to reduce the relative settlement by using smaller unit loadings on the design of the new footings than were used on the old.

3. Parapet Walls:

When a masonry parapet wall is to be used, design the corner columns and exterior columns to extend above the roof level one or two feet to prevent shoving of the parapet corners and the cracking of the parapet wall. As an extra precaution also provide ¼ in. rods in every other horizontal brick joint from the line of the top floor window heads to the top of the parapet wall. These rods should extend back from corners 20 ft on each side. Rods should also be inserted in the parapet wall at locations where they will take the tension in the masonry over the points of maximum positive and negative moment in the supporting spandrel beam. Where there is possibility of thrust from expansion of a roof covering, such as quarry tile, provide vertical dowels between parapet wall and spandrel beam.

4. Exterior Concrete Block Walls:

In exterior concrete block walls having no face brick, the decided tendency for the walls to crack from shrinkage at the zones of weakness should be counteracted by placing ¼ in. rods in the horizontal joints at the corners of the building from ground level to top of parapet, and extending back 20 ft on each side. Also, continuous rods should be placed around the perimeter of the building at the level of the window heads and sills.

5. Ashlar Steps:

Lay ashlar steps on mortar pads ½ in. clear of concrete supporting member. Provide plastic or premolded expansion joints at intervals of not more than 20 ft in each direction. The water that will come through can be drained off into the subgrade if the space below is unexcavated. Where space under steps is occupied, a membrane waterproofing must be provided.

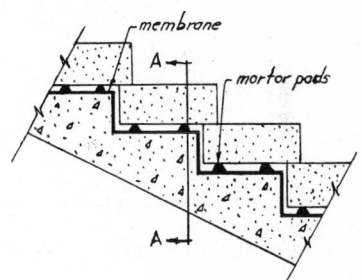

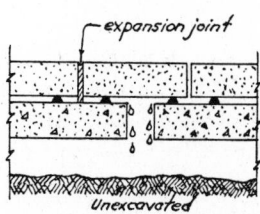

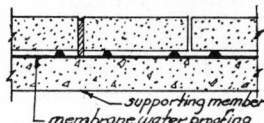

Data and illustrations on this and the following page have been derived from *Technical Notes on Brick and Tile Construction*, published by the Structural Clay Products Institute.

ATTACHING WOOD TRIM

The most common method of anchoring such items as baseboards, chair rails, and picture moldings to masonry walls is by the use of wood nailing blocks placed in vertical mortar joints by the mason as he builds the wall. These blocks should be of seasoned soft wood and creosoted to prevent shrinkage or rot. They should never be placed in horizontal mortar joints.

Metal nailing or "wall" plugs (Fig. 19) provide better construction. They are made of galvanized metal, either with or without a wood or fiberboard insert. Like the wood nailing blocks, the metal wall plugs are built into the joints as the masonry is erected. Their exact location is not a serious problem when used to fasten baseboards or chair rails, but it may be difficult to predetermine their location for fixtures, cabinets, shelving, and the like.

Attaching fixtures and cabinets: Several methods of attaching fixtures, cabinets, shelving, and trim are shown in Fig. 20. The methods illustrated in Fig. 20a, b, and d can be used only with structural clay tile walls and are installed after the

walls are built and the exact location of the fixture is determined.

Figure 20c illustrates a method of fastening that can be used with either brick or tile construction, by building the wood plug in as the wall is built, or by driving it into a hole drilled into the masonry after it has been erected.

Fig. 20e and f show two methods that may be used with either brick or tile construction. Usually, the expansion shields or fiber plugs are placed in holes drilled in the mortal joints. As required, such holes may be drilled through the face shells of tile, or into the mortar joints with hard steel or carbide tipped drills. In some cases where softer tile are used, as in plastered partitions, small holes may be made by the use of an ordinary 1/8-in. punch and hammer.

A relatively new method of attaching to solid masonry walls employs a power-actuated tool that, in effect, "rams" or drives an anchor or pin into the masonry instantaneously. There are suitable pins for almost any type of anchorage desired. Three typical pins are illustrated in Fig. 21.

Furring applications: Although there are many examples of brick, structural clay tile, and composite brick and tile walls with plaster finish applied directly to the interior masonry surface, furring on 8-in. walls is recommended, particularly in northern areas and for residential construction.

Furring may be of wood, metal, or hollow tile, depending upon the type of construction and the local building requirements.

Several typical methods of attaching wood furring are shown in Fig. 22. The wood furring strips are either 1x2 in. or 2x2 in. and are applied vertically to the wall at intervals usually 16 in. on center. The wood strips may be attached by nailing into wood nailing blocks or metal wall plugs as shown in Fig. 22c, or directly into the mortar joints by the use of case-hardened "cut" nails or special spiral-threaded masonry nails as shown in Fig. 22d. Special anchor nails fastened to the masonry wall with an adhesive cement is a recent development for installing furring and is illustrated in Fig. 22a. Such fastenings are easily and quickly installed without drilling, plugging, or nailing. Brick-size porous clay nailing blocks are available in some areas. Since such blocks are completely inert, there is no danger of nail disintegration from chemical reaction. The use of such blocks is illustrated in Fig. 22b.

Metal furring strips consist of standard light steel channels fastened by either tie wires built into the mortar joint or by special clips designed for this purpose.

Tile furring may be either attached or free-standing. Hollow or cored structural clay units for use as attached furring may be 2, 3, or 4 in. in nominal thickness. The

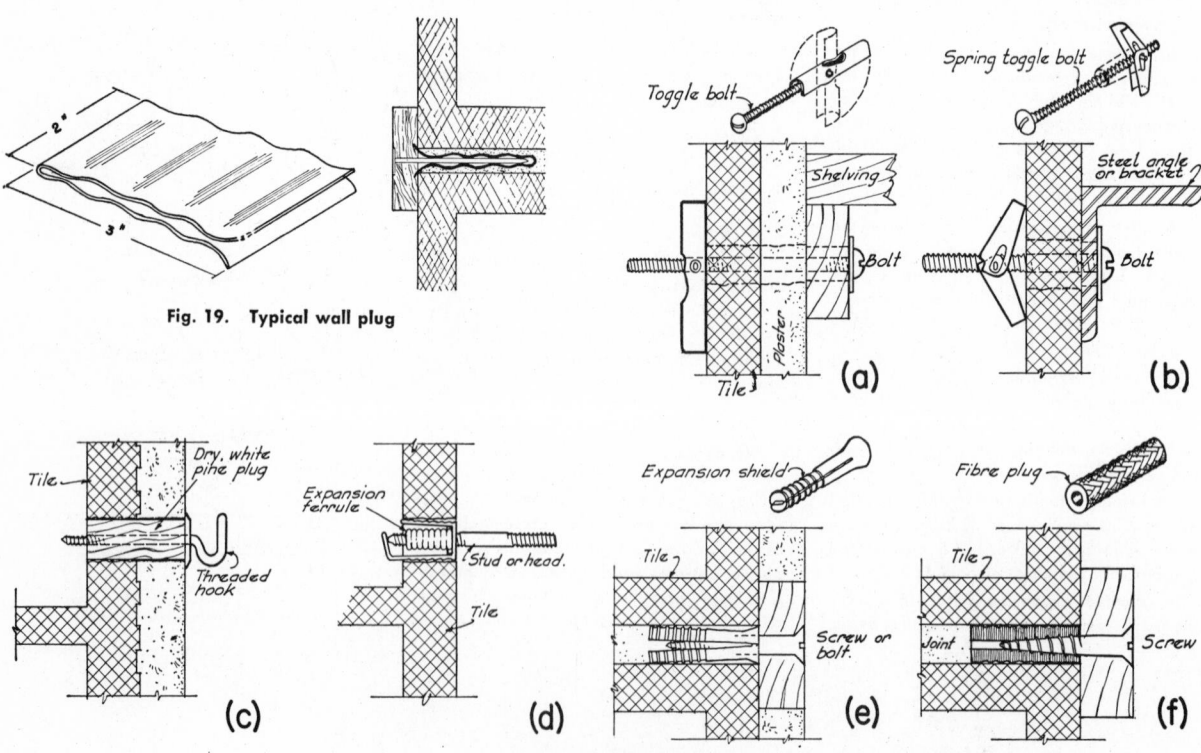

Fig. 19. Typical wall plug

Fig. 20. Wall plugs

2-in. thickness is available either as a solid-back unit or as "split" furring. The split units should always be applied directly to the wall without mortar on the back of the ribs, thus providing an uninterrupted air space. Since the solid-back furring tile have one or more air cells through their thicknesses, the space between the units and the wall may be filled with mortar, if desired for greater rigidity or where exterior wall parging is specified. Figure 23 illustrates a typical method of applying split furring tile.

Several different methods of attaching tile furring to masonry walls may be used. Table 5 gives the proper spacing of anchors or ties for attached furring, together with height and length limitations of the furring itself.

Nailing: Drive 10d nails into the mortar joints of the main wall and clinch the heads of the nails down into the cells of the tile or over the ends of the split tile as shown in Fig. 23.

Wire ties: Heavy wire ties, not less than No. 11 gage, may be built into the mortar joints of the wall as the masonry is erected, and bent down into the cells of the furring tile as they are erected.

Corrugated or crimped metal ties should be at least 7/8 in. wide and not lighter than No. 22 gage.

Wire mesh should be at least 4 in. wide strips of 1/2-in. mesh, No. 20 gage galvanized wire fabric. These ties should extend at least 3 in. into the masonry wall and to within 1/2 in. of the face of the furring.

Anchors: Tile furring is attached to concrete by the use of dovetail anchors inserted into metal slots embedded in the concrete. These anchors should be at least 7/8 in. wide and not lighter than No. 16 gage.

Grout or adhesives: When solid-back hollow units are used they may often be applied directly to the structural wall without metal anchors or ties by utilizing the high adhesive bond obtained by filling the back space with cement grout. Or a waterproof adhesive may be used.

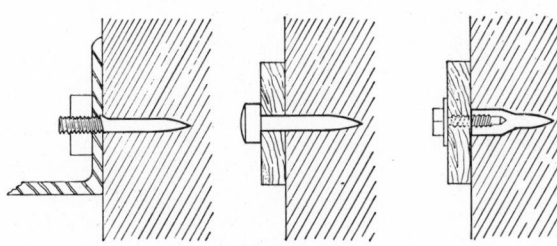

Fig. 21.   Pins

Table 5.   Height and length limitations for attached furring tile and spacing of metal ties and anchors

Type and Thickness of Furring	Maximum Allowable Spacing of Ties		
	No Ties Required	24" Vertical 24" Horizontal	16" Vertical 24" Horizontal
2-in. Split	—	Up to 14 ft.	14 to 35 ft.
2-in. Hollow	9 ft.[1]	9 to 14 ft.	14 to 35 ft.
3-in. Hollow	12 ft.	12 to 18 ft.	18 to 35 ft.
4-in. Hollow	15 ft.	15 to 22 ft.	22 to 35 ft.

[1] Not over 6 ft. in length.

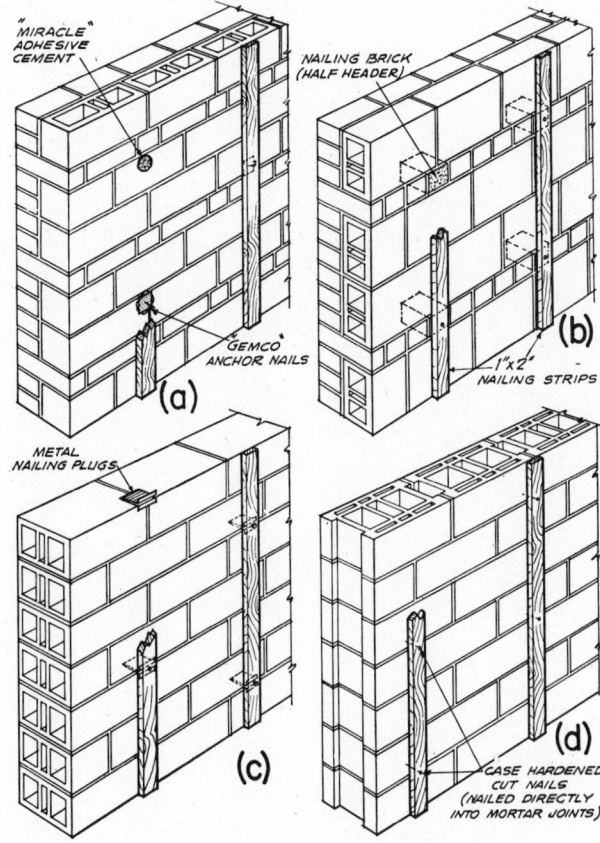

Fig. 22.   Methods of attaching wood furring

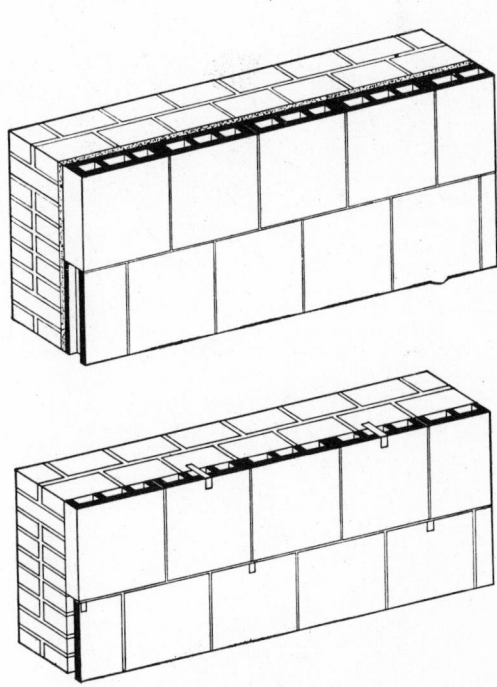

Fig. 23.   Nailing

SECTION III: BUILDING MATERIALS, COMPONENTS, AND TECHNIQUES

Waterproofing:
    Foundation drains 281
    Permeability of concrete 285
    Integral and membrane 286
    Plastic and iron coatings 287
    Vapor seals 288
    Paved roofs 289
    Walls and parapets 290
Termite Shields 291
Flashing:
    Multistory masonry walls 295
    Walls and parapets 297
    Copings: drips and edge strips 298
    Roof at walls 299
    Spandrels and windows 300
    Openings in frame walls 301
    Gravel stops; door heads 302
    Valleys 303
    Vents 304
    Chimneys 304
    Aluminum gravel stops 306
Roofing:
    Asphalt strip shingles 307
    Copper 310
Roof Drainage:
    Leader design 314
    Gutters 315
    Stock items 319
Windows:
    General 320
    Types and uses 321
    Wood 324
    Steel 336
    Aluminum 346
Sliding Glass Doors 354
Skylights:
    Plastic 358
    Metal frame 360
    Glass block 363
Curtain Walls:
    General 365
    Structural design 366
    Movement 367
    Infiltration 370
    Insulation 371
    Condensation 374
    Joints 376
    Sealants 378
    Panels 382
    Specifications 384
    Precast concrete 385
Architectural Metals:
    Gages, coefficients, stresses 388
    Finishes 390
    Aluminum 391
    Stainless steel 394
    Copper, brass, and bronze 402
    Porcelain enamel 403
Glass:
    Types 409
    Sizes 411
    FHA requirements 412
    Glazing 413
    Structural glass veneer 416
Plastics:
    Characteristics 418
    Terminology 418
    Applications 421
    Design recommendations 423
    Fire resistance requirements 424

Stone:

    Characteristics 426

    Classifications 427

    Finishes 428

    Checklist 429

    Marble 432

    Veneer 435

    Interior 441

Fireproofing:

    Materials and methods 444

    Columns 446

    Beams and girders 448

    Floor and roof systems 451

    Notes to table 459

    Acoustical ceilings 461

    Reinforced concrete 462

    Partitions 464

Plaster:

    Materials 465

    Bases 466

    Mixes and coats 467

    Walls and partitions 470

    Ceilings 471

Wallboards:

    Gypsum board 476

    Insulation board 483

    Hardboard 488

    Particle board 491

    Plastic laminates 492

    Plywood 493

Wood:

    Grades and dimensions 502

    Softwoods 504

    Hardwoods 505

    Cabinet work 520

Tile:

    Ceramic 529

    Metal and plastic 536

Flooring:

    Terrazzo 538

    Epoxy 542

    Wood 543

    Resilient 548

Finishes:

    Wall coverings 552

    Wall coatings 553

    Paints 554

    Cabinet work 558

Stairs:

    Tread and riser data 562

    Critical dimensions and clearances 564

    Unit planning data 566

    Steel 568

    Concrete 569

    Ramps and ladders 570

Fireplaces 572

Steel Doors and Frames 574

Hardware:

    Hand of doors 579

    Types of locks and latches 580

    Types of finishes 582

    Hinges 584

    Door closing devices 587

    Door holders and stops 590

    Door pulls, push plates, and kick plates 592

    Panic exit devices 593

    Door bolts 595

    Lock functions 596

    Lock dimensions 600

    Sliding doors 601

    Screen and storm doors 605

By PHILIP P. PAGE, JR., *Supervising Engineer, Seelye, Stevenson, Value and Knecht*

An understanding of the problems involved in foundation drain design can best be had by studying the nature of groundwater. Groundwater is water in the pores of the soil, and as such it follows the laws of hydraulics. Its origin is rainwater, which seeps through the soil until it is stopped by some impervious layer. This layer may be at a very great depth. The top of this water in the soil is called the groundwater level. The water flows through the soil until it emerges aboveground in a body of water. The friction between the soil and the water flowing through it is overcome by building up a higher groundwater level away from the point of emergence. Therefore, the following points can be made about groundwater:

1. The groundwater level varies seasonally with the amount of rainfall.
2. The groundwater level follows the general contour of the land, but is closer to the surface in low ground and farther from the surface in high ground.
3. The direction of groundwater flow is always in the direction of the lower groundwater level.

Hydrostatic Head

Groundwater, following the laws of hydraulics, always produces a hydrostatic head or water pressure which at any point is equal to the depth of that point below groundwater level times the unit weight of water, 62.4 psf. The effect of this pressure upon a building is illustrated at right. The earth pressure is reduced (from 240 to 100 psf) because of the buoyant effect of the water on the soil particles, but the total pressure is greatly increased.

Purpose of Foundation Drains

Foundation drains lower the groundwater, thus preventing building up of a hydrostatic head against the walls or floor of a building with resultant leakage or structural damage. A drainage system should consist of footing drains of sufficient size and an adequate outfall or method of water disposal. The enlarged detail at right shows the basic elements of a foundation drain.

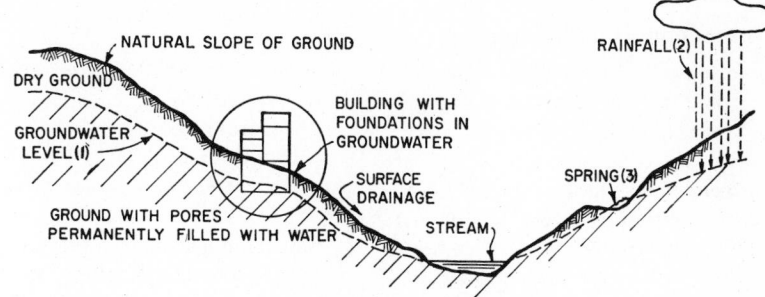

BASIC FACTORS AFFECTING GROUNDWATER LEVEL

(1) Groundwater level tends to follow ground contour—deeper on hills, shallower in valleys. (2) Rainfall percolates through ground to recharge groundwater. Groundwater level varies with amount of rainfall. (3) Springs occur where local ground depressions place ground level below groundwater level.

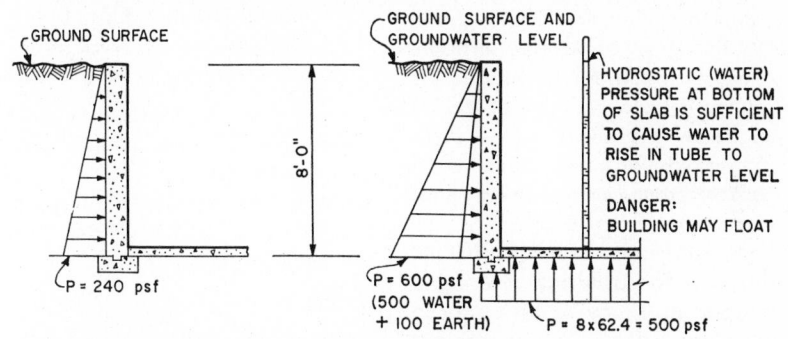

EFFECT OF HYDROSTATIC PRESSURE ON A BUILDING

Note: Waterproofing is not sufficient in itself to protect walls against groundwater unless they can take heavy earth and water loads

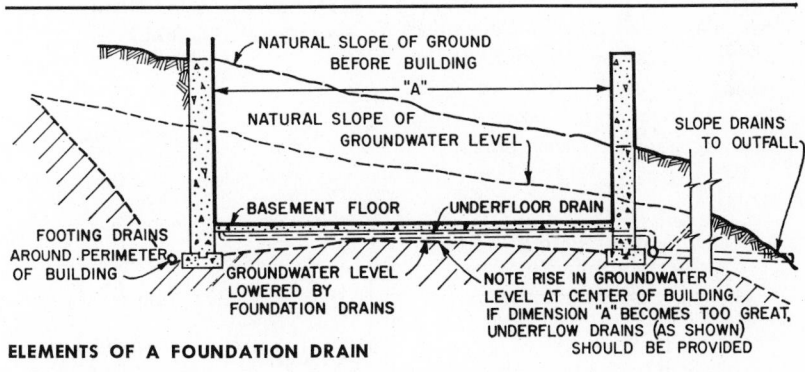

ELEMENTS OF A FOUNDATION DRAIN

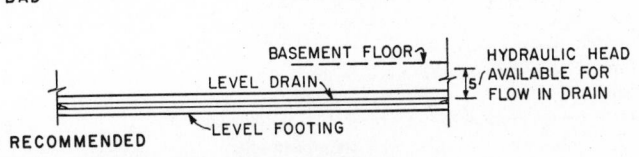

RELATIONSHIP OF FOOTING ELEVATION TO DRAIN

Estimation of Infiltration

The amount of infiltration varies according to the type of soil and height of groundwater above footings. Clays have such a small flow of groundwater that nominal 4-in. drains are satisfactory for all but the largest installations. Silts have more flow. Sands and gravels can have such a heavy flow that pumping tests are required to determine the flow quantity.

Location of Drains

Drains are placed around the periphery of a building far enough below floor level to develop sufficient hydraulic head for drainage. The footing is always placed at least 4 in. below the invert of the drain (bottom of the inside diameter) to prevent groundwater flowing under the footing from washing out soil fines, with resultant settlement of the structure. For buildings covering a large area it may be necessary to place underfloor drains to prevent the building up of head in the center.

Selection of Size of Drain

Once the infiltration has been established and the plan of the drains laid out, the size of pipe and elevation of invert must be established. The nomograph at right can be used. The selection of the proper drain then requires an economic study.

Example

Given: Inflow of 100 gpm, established by a pumping test during excavation

Length of drain—350 ft

Friction factor for pipes—$n = 0.015$

Find: Underdrainage design required to keep cellar dry

Solution: Assume a 6-in. pipe. From nomograph, required slope for a 6-in. pipe and 100 gpm discharge is 0.0024. Hydraulic drop is 350 x 0.0024 = 0.84 ft. Bottom of drain should be, therefore, 0.84 + 0.5 (thickness of floor slab) = 1.34 ft below surface of floor.

To adjust for $n = 0.019$, multiply inflow by 0.019/0.015 and then use nomograph.

To adjust for $n = 0.013$, multiply inflow by 0.013/0.015 and then use nomograph.

Example

Inflow of 100 gpm

Friction factor—$n = 0.019$

Solution

$100 \times 0.019/0.015 = 126$

Taking line from 126 on Discharge bar through 6-in. Drain Diam. gives Slope of 0.0040

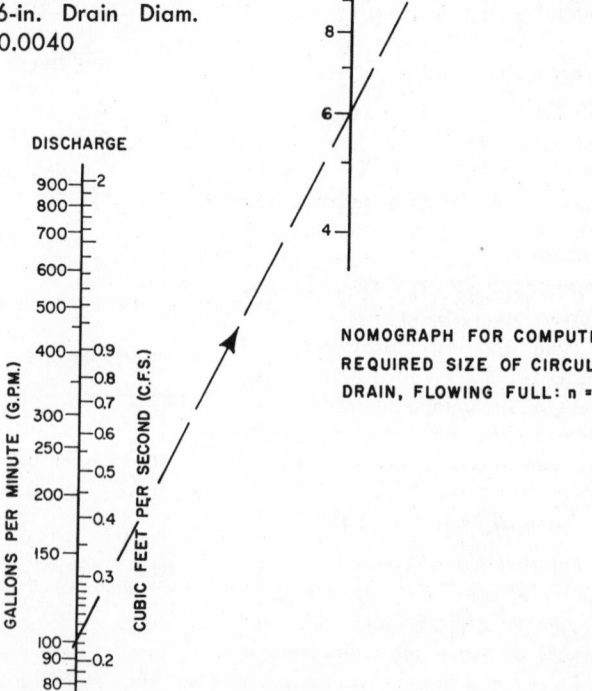

NOMOGRAPH FOR COMPUTING REQUIRED SIZE OF CIRCULAR DRAIN, FLOWING FULL: n = 0.015

Note: Nomograph prepared with assistance of J. L. Staunton and Paul Kluger, both of Seelye Stevenson Value & Knecht

PLAN

ON SOME BUILDINGS UNDERFLOOR DRAINS MAY BE REQUIRED TO PREVENT WATER FROM RISING UNDER FLOOR

NATURAL SLOPE OF GROUND

FOOTING

FOUNDATION DRAIN

FOUNDATION DRAIN

PITCH OUTFALL PIPE WITH CLOSED JOINTS

Note: If gravity outflow is not practical or possible, a sump has to be used with a pump to draw out groundwater

Type of Drain

To permit the entry of water but prevent the entry of soil a reverse filter surrounds the foundation drain. This reverse filter consists of coarse gravel next to the pipe followed by layers of coarse and then fine sand. Porous or perforated pipe is preferable to open joint pipe. The table below shows the basic characteristics of the main types of pipe used. The pipe generally is laid level, without slope, to avoid the problem of sloping footing bottoms, as shown on Sheet 1. A footing seal of impervious material should be provided to prevent the flow of water under the footing. Perforated clay pipe which has holes only on the bottom should be laid on a gravel bed over the clay seal.

Outfall

Disposal of the water collected in the drains must be given careful thought. Too often drawings simply indicate an arrow to an outfall or a dry well. The outfall must be capable of taking the discharge without becoming surcharged. Generally the connection to sanitary sewers is prohibited by law and certainly is not to be encouraged. Dry wells should not be specified, for obvious reasons, when they would be below the water table. This would be like pulling a cork out of the hole in the bottom of a rowboat to let the water out. Dry wells are satisfactory, though, when they will stay above the water table and when the soil is permeable enough to dissipate the inflow.

Good outfalls consist of storm sewers or other drainage devices located at a lower elevation than that of the footings. Sometimes such an outfall is impossible to reach and it becomes necessary or more economical to collect the water in a sump and to pump out to surface drainage.

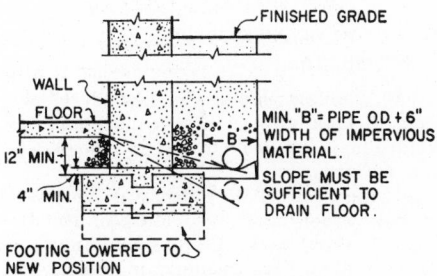

Slope is increased as pipe diameter is decreased, as can be seen in nomograph on Sheet 2. When drain is lowered to increase slope, footing must be lowered to stay below level of drain and thus prevent silt from being washed away from under footing. Selection of drain size usually depends on cost differential between small pipe, and therefore more excavation for lowering of footings, and more costly large pipe but less digging.

Basic characteristics of drain pipes

Type	n	Advantages	Disadvantages
Porous concrete	0.015	Freedom from silting, erosion and corrosion; easily laid; resists surcharge load	Most expensive
Perforated concrete	0.015	Same as porous	Expensive
Perforated metal	0.019	Freedom from silting; resists surcharge load	Possible corrosion; high n value
Open joint concrete	0.015	Strong; resists surcharge load	Joints may permit entry of silt, which clogs line; harder to lay; backfill must be laid with more care
Open joint clay	0.019	Least expensive; resists corrosion	Joints may silt up; high n value; more easily broken by careless backfill or surcharge
Vitrified clay	0.013	Low n value; best for runs to outfall; resists corrosion and erosion	Least effective entry of water

POROUS CONCRETE TO PERMIT INFILTRATION OF WATER

CONCRETE LOCKING JOINT

HOLES TO PERMIT INFILTRATION OF WATER

JOINT

HOLES ON BOTTOM 1/3 OF PIPES

COUPLING

HOLES IN BOTTOM FOR WATER

TAR PAPER ON TOP TO PREVENT ENTRY OF SILT

OPEN JOINT TO ALLOW ENTRY OF WATER

TAR PAPER ON TOP TO PREVENT ENTRY OF SILT

OPEN JOINT TO ALLOW ENTRY OF WATER

BELL & SPIGOT JOINT

SOMETIMES HOLES ARE PROVIDED ON BOTTOM FOR INFLOW

From data supplied by R. W. SEXTON

PROTECTION OF UNDERGROUND
CONSTRUCTION

The problem should be considered from three angles, 1. The causes and conditions, 2. Preventive measures, and 3. Cures.

In times past little effort was made to waterproof buildings. Most of the important public or private buildings were built on high ground for natural drainage, if possible. The cellars of houses were expected to leak after exceptionally heavy rainstorms. Waterproofing first became vitally important when the tall building, with deep basement containing mechanical equipment, entered the field of construction. Today, the economy of the times makes it imperative to plan buildings in which all available space is put to practical use. Basements of houses, which in times past would have been used only for storage, are now planned to contain livable rooms. It is not feasible to put permanent interior finishes into such rooms unless the surrounding walls and the floors are built to exclude water, moisture, and dampness.

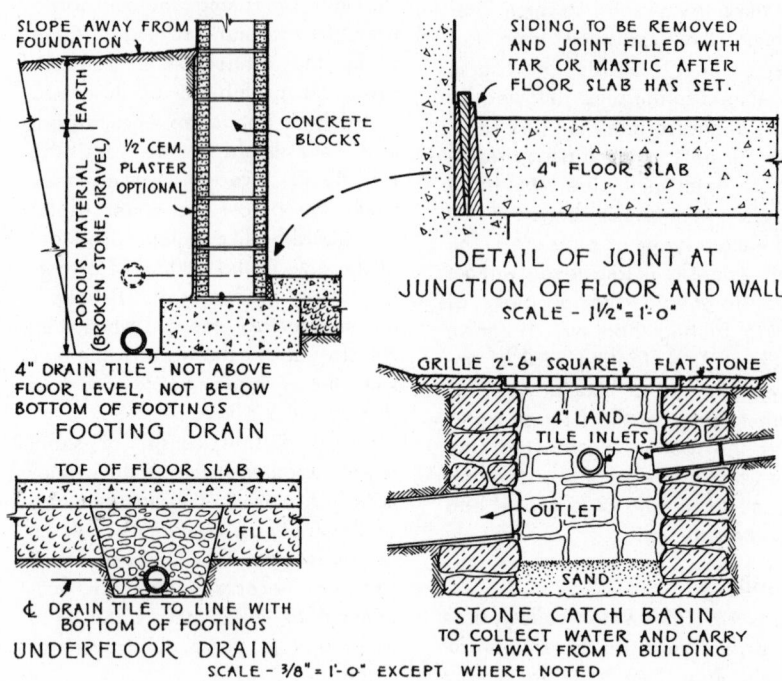

SLOPE AWAY FROM FOUNDATION
½" CEM. PLASTER OPTIONAL
POROUS MATERIAL (BROKEN STONE, GRAVEL)
EARTH
CONCRETE BLOCKS
4" DRAIN TILE – NOT ABOVE FLOOR LEVEL, NOT BELOW BOTTOM OF FOOTINGS
FOOTING DRAIN

SIDING, TO BE REMOVED AND JOINT FILLED WITH TAR OR MASTIC AFTER FLOOR SLAB HAS SET.
4" FLOOR SLAB
DETAIL OF JOINT AT JUNCTION OF FLOOR AND WALL
SCALE – 1½" = 1'-0"

TOP OF FLOOR SLAB
FILL
℄ DRAIN TILE TO LINE WITH BOTTOM OF FOOTINGS
UNDERFLOOR DRAIN
SCALE – ⅜" = 1'-0" EXCEPT WHERE NOTED

GRILLE 2'-6" SQUARE
FLAT STONE
4" LAND TILE INLETS
OUTLET
SAND
STONE CATCH BASIN
TO COLLECT WATER AND CARRY IT AWAY FROM A BUILDING

CAUSES AND CONDITIONS: LOCATION,
SOIL, WATER TABLE

The foundations of the simplest building go below frost line, and water conditions of some kind are almost sure to be encountered. A large portion of the earth's surface consists of bedrock and soil underlaid with water. The water flows through the materials themselves, if they are porous, and through the open spaces between the different geological substances. The water table is the name given to the surface of this ground water. The height of the water table varies somewhat with the amount of rainfall, and with the type of substance of which the ground is made, but it generally follows the contour of the ground, coming nearer the surface in the valleys than on the ridges. Irregularities of distribution of soft and hard materials often cause the level of the water to rise and drop perceptively within a comparatively small area.

Above the level of the water table the soil contains surface water. This is sometimes called capillary water because it lies in minute pores so close to one another that capillary action takes place. The rate at which this water is transmitted through the ground depends upon the size of the pores of the various substances of which the ground is made. The pores of clay are usually filled with water even though the underground water level is many feet below. As oil will

rise in a lampwick, surface water will come to the surface by capillary action from a considerable depth. Capillary water cannot be drained out of the soil by any system of drainage.

Occasionally a building site will prove to have definite upward water pressure, similar to a true artesian well. On sites which are near rivers subject to floods, or on low marshy land, steady or intermittent heads of water will often be encountered. Because of marked variation in the properties of soil and rock within short distances and at different depths, it is always well to investigate underground conditions by means of test pits or borings. The porosity of the soil, besides being related to the possibility of infiltration of water, also has a bearing on the amount of weight foundations will support. It is not unusual to find soil with high bearing power underlaid with material with less resistance to weight.

PREVENTIVE MEASURES

Since prevention may be cheaper than cure, every effort should be made to keep water away from foundations where it can be harmful. In large buildings with deep foundations this may not be possible. In rare cases, where a plentiful source of power is

near at hand, it may be more economical to pump water out of basements than to build walls strong enough to resist its entry. In a majority of cases, however, it is possible to drain water away from basements, especially when buildings are placed on land higher than their immediate surroundings. When it is known that the site of a building is going to be wet, every effort should be made, at the very outset of the job, to correct the condition. Catch basins, with or without drainage lines, may be installed around the perimeter of the proposed location to collect the water and carry it away to lower ground. Basements in which water 2 or 3 ft. deep has collected during the excavation period, are sometimes made entirely dry by installation of such drains. When drains cannot be installed, sump pumps placed in pits below the basement floor, operated electrically or hydraulically, may serve the same purpose. They are useful on rocky ground where blasting out trenches would be difficult and expensive.

Footing drains are the best means of attracting and collecting water that is present in the immediate vicinity of foundations. They consist of lines of drain tile placed around the outside or the inside of foundation walls, connected to some suitable outlet.

IMPERMEABILITY OF CONCRETE

Poured concrete, if well made, can be practically watertight. The impermeability will depend largely upon the care with which it is mixed and placed. All the aggregates should be of low absorption value, and the cement should adhere to each particle. The materials should be carefully selected, the proportions accurately calculated, and the workmanship rigorously supervised. To produce the dense, yet plastic and workable mix that is desirable, there should not be over 6 gals. of water per bag of cement. The mixture should be tamped with rods or agitated by electric vibrators to secure proper density. The hydration of the cement—that is, combining the cement and the water —takes time. Strength is gained and porosity is reduced during the period of hardening or curing. These changes take place rapidly during the first few days, more slowly thereafter. Most concrete should be kept wet for at least 7 days. Fabric coverings, straw, or other coatings are used to retain the water. The tendency of concrete to dry rapidly is usually noticeable in the hot, dry days of summer. The accompanying chart shows, for three different mixes of concrete, the relation of curing time to permeability.

Though concrete may not permit the passage of water through it, moisture may creep in. Even if the pores are very minute and compacted they may connect with one another. They may act as capillary tubes, drawing in and filling themselves with water. This action may cause the wall to be damp.

CRACKS AND JOINTS IN MASONRY

All types of masonry walls are subject to cracking due to settlement or to shrinkage caused by temperature changes. Even the well-proportioned concrete wall will crack unless there are a sufficient number of expansion joints. Brick, stone, and concrete block walls, besides being made of porous materials, have a large number of joints. Particularly when such walls are built in water-logged soil, great care should be exercised to keep the joints, which are the weakest link in the barrier against the entry of water, as tight as possible. All forms of construction seams are critical spots from the standpoint of waterproofing. The junction between the floor slab and the walls, generally known as the "floor line," is particularly vulnerable. A concrete slab may shrink as it sets, pull away from the surrounding walls and leave an opening for water. It is sometimes advisable to purposely make an open joint and later fill it

RECOMMENDED CONCRETE MIXTURES FOR FOUNDATION WALLS AND BASEMENTS

KIND OF WORK	STRENGTH IN LBS/ SQ. IN. AT 28 DAYS	GALLONS OF WATER FOR EACH ONE-SACK BATCH IF SAND IS:			TRIAL MIXTURE FOR FIRST BATCH			MAX. SIZE OF AGGREGATE, INCHES
		DAMP	WET	VERY WET	CEMENT	SAND	PEBBLES	
ORDINARY RESIDENTIAL FOUNDATIONS	2000	6¼	5½	4¾	1	2¾	4	1½
WATERTIGHT FOUNDATIONS FOR POORLY DRAINED SOIL	3000	5½	5	4¼	1	2¼	3	1½

EFFECT OF CURING TIME ON PERMEABILITY
FOR CONCRETES MADE WITH VARYING AMOUNTS OF WATER

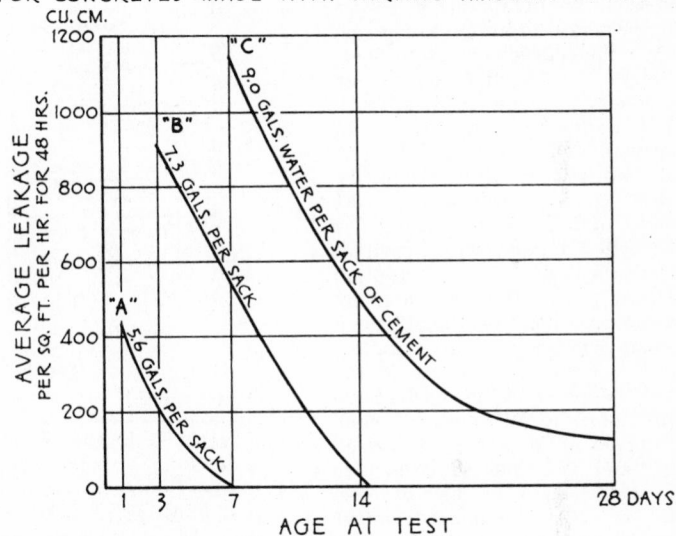

MIX "A" BECAME WATERTIGHT IN 7 DAYS.
MIX "B" BECAME WATERTIGHT IN 14 DAYS (BUT WAS FAR FROM IT IN 7 DAYS).
MIX "C" WAS NOT WATERTIGHT AFTER 4 WEEK CURE.
THESE DATA FROM PORTLAND CEMENT ASSOCIATION.

with impervious material. Pieces of bevelled siding, greased so that they will come out easily, may be set in place before the slab is poured. When the slab has set, the boards are removed, and a rich mixture of concrete, or bituminous waterproofing placed in the crack.

HYDROSTATIC PRESSURE

When measurable water pressure is encountered, precautions to keep it out of basements become engineering problems. A permanent 1 ft. head of water above the bottom of a slab will exert an upward pressure of 62½ lb. per sq. ft. on the slab. When the head is 10 ft. the pressure will become 625 lb. per sq. ft. The slab must be designed and reinforced to resist the pressure to which it is subjected. Sometimes thickening and reinforcing the floor slab will hold the water out.

Water pressure around the foundations of many large buildings is severe, and there is frequently no way to relieve it either by drainage or by pumping. When a concrete wall or slab is made thicker, the impermeability of the material is not proportionally increased, but the additional weight offers greater resistance to the pressure of the water.

Sometimes the pressure of the water will be greater than the normal dead load on the floor. In such cases buildings may be designed to carry the upward force of the water to the points of load concentration above. There are cases where it may be more economical to thicken the upper floors to obtain weight rather than thickening the lowest slab which is subjected to the direct force of the water. This is because every foot of depth added to the lowest slab (if the floor heights are kept constant) will increase the hydrostatic head, and the only gain would be the difference between tne weight of the concrete and the weight of the water. The construction of some basements under high pressure is similar to the construction of tanks, except that they are built to resist pressure from without rather than from within. Study of the soil conditions and distribution of horizontal and vertical reactions must be studied.

INTEGRAL WATERPROOFING

The method consists of putting a compound, designed to increase impermeability, into the concrete mix. Experience has shown that few, if any, compounds are able to give the concrete a degree of perfection greater than would be obtainable if it were possible perfectly to grade, proportion and place the ingredients of the concrete itself. One kind of compound, which comes in powdered form, is designed to improve the workability of the concrete, thus reducing the number of interstices which might be formed if the mixture was not rich enough or of the proper consistency. Another type contains water-repellent admixtures which reduce absorption and retard penetration of water by capillary attraction. Tests have shown that some compounds have an injurious effect on the strength of the concrete. More desirable results have been obtained by the use of compounds made of inert materials such as clay, sand, and lime, which help to fill the voids, than by use of compounds in which chemical changes create water-repellent action.

MEMBRANE WATERPROOFING

The membrane method is the oldest form of waterproofing and until recently was the one in most common use. It consists of the application of alternate layers of bituminous material—such as asphalt, coal tar, or pitch—and fabric, like felt, burlap or canvas. The bituminous substance is heated and mopped on to the surface to be protected and on to the alternate layers of fabric. The materials used should be elastic and cohesive as well as waterproof, because they are subjected to strains which will tend to make them crack, and to dryness which will decrease their flexibility. A well applied membrane seals the pores of a wall against penetration of moisture, and obstructs the flow of any water.

Membranes should never be put on the inside of a foundation wall if it is possible to put them on the outside. Effective installations provide for continuous barrier of protection. Where a wall meets a floor, the membrane is

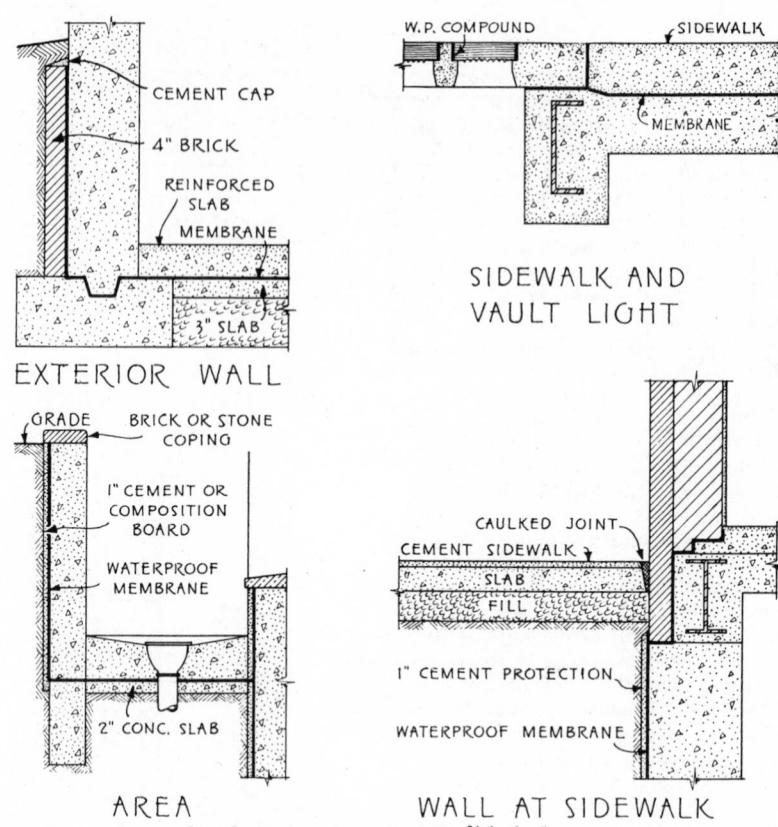

EXTERIOR WALL

SIDEWALK AND VAULT LIGHT

AREA

WALL AT SIDEWALK

SCALE OF THESE DRAWINGS 3/8"=1'-0"

HEAD OF WATER	COAL TAR AND FELT	COMMERCIAL ASPHALT AND FELT	SPECIAL FELT AND COMPOUNDS	THICKNESS OF ASPHALT MASTIC
0 FEET	2	2	1	1/4 INCH
1	3	3	2	5/8
2	4	4	3	5/8
6	5	5	4	3/4
8	6	6	5	3/4
10	7	7	6	3/4
15	8	8	7	3/4
20	9	9	8	3/4

NUMBER OF PLIES OF WATERPROOFING MATERIAL REQUIRED FOR VARYING HEADS OF WATER.

THESE DATA FROM "MODERN METHODS OF WATERPROOFING" BY M. H. LEWIS

usually run through a keyed footing. A similar key is used at the intersection of an interior partition with an exterior wall.

The protection of the membrane is very important. On the outside, if it is in direct contact with earth, it is subject to upheaval by frost, puncture by roots of trees, deterioration by acids in the soil. Several methods of protection are employed, all of which consist of placing another material between the membrane and the earth. A thin wall of brick or concrete is often built. Composition board may also be

used. Some boards available are manufactured to resist termites, dry rot, fungus, and other cellulose destroying agencies. They are also insoluble, and have insulating value. Their low conductivity will protect the bitumen in the membrane from the heat of the sun during the period of application. Such boards are embedded in the outer layer of fabric when it is given its final mopping. Blows with a wooden mallet insure overall contact of the board and the underlying surface. Bitumen is then mopped on the outside, to protect the board and the joints.

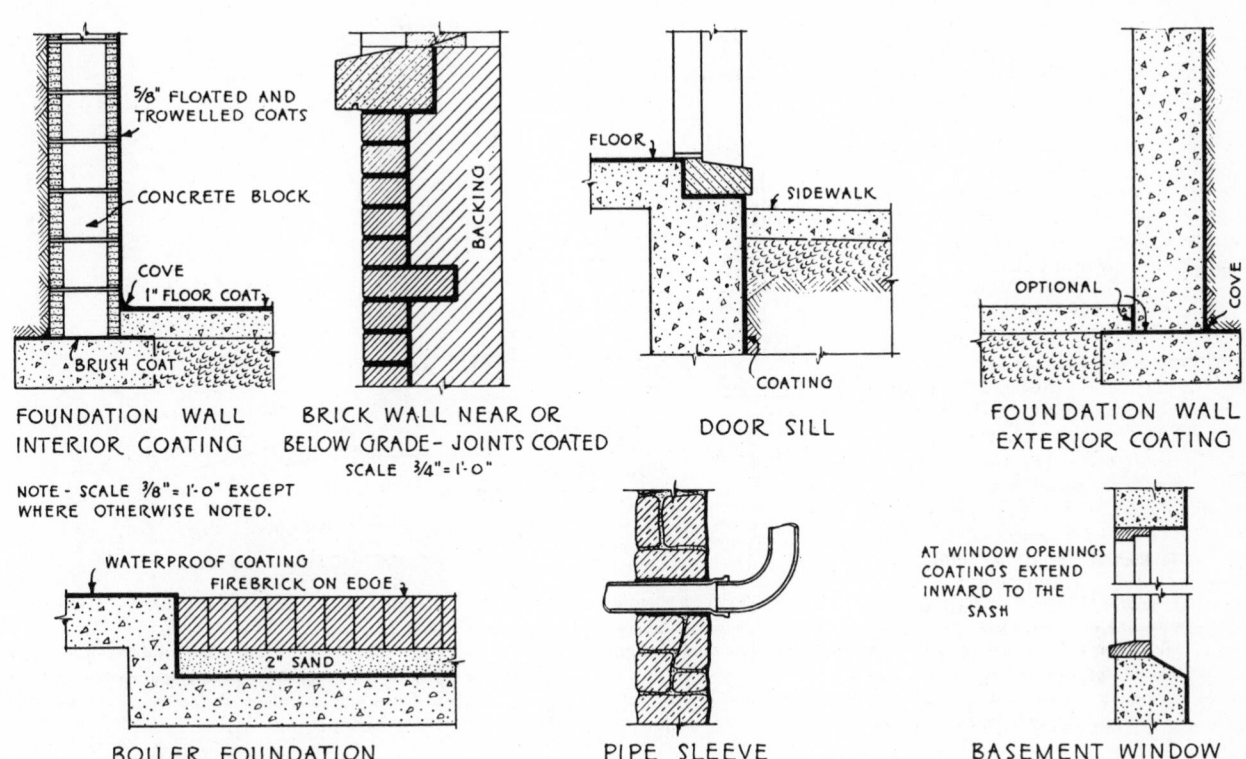

5/8" FLOATED AND TROWELLED COATS

CONCRETE BLOCK

COVE
1" FLOOR COAT

BRUSH COAT

FOUNDATION WALL
INTERIOR COATING

BACKING

BRICK WALL NEAR OR
BELOW GRADE- JOINTS COATED
SCALE 3/4"= 1'-0"

NOTE- SCALE 3/8"= 1'-0" EXCEPT
WHERE OTHERWISE NOTED.

FLOOR

SIDEWALK

COATING

DOOR SILL

OPTIONAL

COVE

FOUNDATION WALL
EXTERIOR COATING

WATERPROOF COATING
FIREBRICK ON EDGE
2" SAND

BOILER FOUNDATION
SCALE 3/4"= 1'-0"

PIPE SLEEVE

AT WINDOW OPENINGS
COATINGS EXTEND
INWARD TO THE
SASH

BASEMENT WINDOW

CEMENT-BASE WATERPROOF COATINGS

There are several compounds available today, which, when applied to either the interior or the exterior surface of any type of basement wall, or to the upper surface of a floor slab, will render the wall or floor waterproof by sealing the pores. Most of these materials achieve and retain their hold on the surface by the bonding of Portland Cement. The basic ingredient of most of the compounds is cement, but some are sold in paste, powder, or liquid form to be mixed with cement by the consumer. These materials should not be confused with cement-base paints. The coatings have a hard wearing surface, and have been known to resist a hydrostatic head of 190 ft.

One type of coating contains ingredients of an organic nature, another type has a mineral base, being composed principally of iron.

A mineral type of compound which is commonly known as iron coating, takes advantage of the fact that iron, when it oxidizes, will expand to several times its original volume. Properly prepared iron will retain its ability to expand even when mixed with sand, cement, and water. In so doing, it fills the voids left by the water when it evaporates, leaving the surface to which it has been applied sheathed with dense iron-cement that will withstand considerable pressure.

Before application of either type of coating is made, any hydrostatic pressure which exists should be relieved, either by pumping or by drainage. Holes made for this purpose may later be filled and finished. Sometimes a steel drum is placed below the level of the floor and the water is pumped out of it. When the waterproofing of the space has been completed, the drum itself is left in place and given a coating, and the floor is built over it.

Smooth surfaces which are to receive plaster coatings must first be roughened with cold chisels, bush hammers, or sandblasting so that a satisfactory bond will be secured. They should then be cleaned with scrubbing brushes, and rinsed until all traces of alien matter have disappeared. While the surface is wet, plaster coatings should then be floated on with a trowel. If two coats are to be applied, the second coat should go on while the initial set of the first coat is taking place. Coatings on inside walls are usually ½ or ⅝ in. thick, on floors 1 in. thick. Walls and floors should be done, insofar as possible, in one operation. The coatings will not absorb water, after the water with which they are made has evaporated.

Iron undercoats are put on with a brush. Enough time should elapse between two coats to allow for complete oxidation of the iron. The first coats are made of iron compound mixed with water, the final coat is iron mixed with water, cement, and sand, and it may be put on either with a brush or with a trowel. Since iron coatings are not suitable wearing surfaces, when they are used on floors they must be covered with 1 in. topping of cement.

It is generally preferable to use cement-base coating on the inside of buildings. If walls are subject to freezing temperatures, they may be furred and the coating put on the furring. Being rigid, plaster coats are subject to cracking. They should never cover expansion joints. Coatings on the inside are accessible for easy and economical repair, and they may be applied to various parts of the building as it goes up without interfering with the normal progress of the work.

NECESSITY FOR SUPERVISION

Too much emphasis cannot be placed on the necessity of consulting men who have made a special study of waterproofing. The success of any job will depend on the skill and experience of the men who supervise and do the work.

Vapor seals

By ELWYN E. SEELYE, Seelye, Stevenson, Value and Knecht, Consulting Engineers, New York City

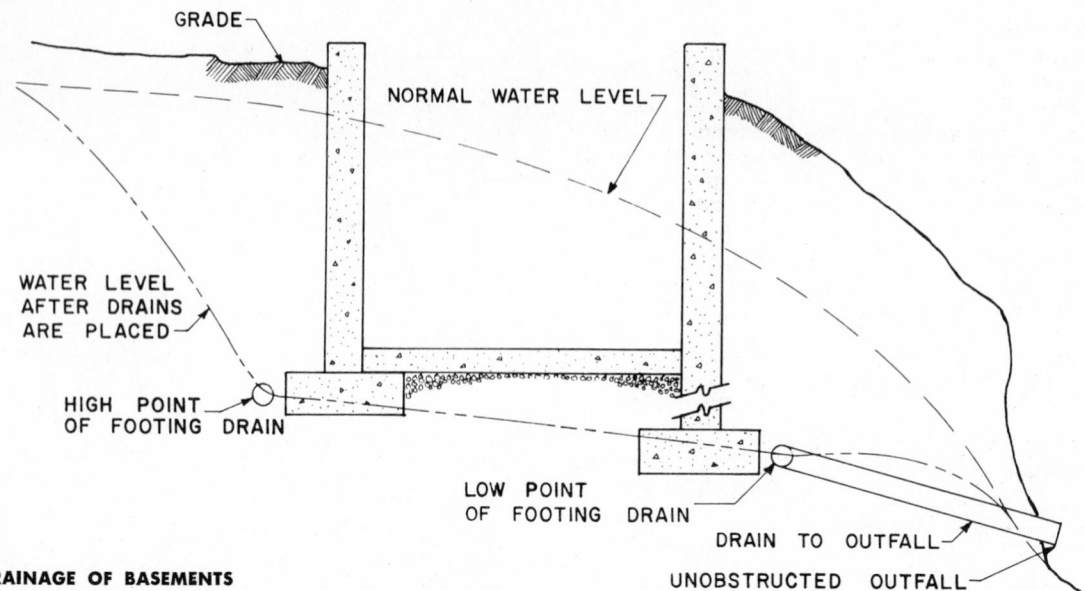

1. DRAINAGE OF BASEMENTS

Basement drainage must be taken care of by gravity drainage, assuming that extremely high ground water is not safely below the lowest basement. In general it consists of a system of footing drains and/or sub-floor drains.

Footing drains should be low enough to keep the water from coming up on the concrete floor on the inside, but not so low as to cause the possibility of loss of material under the footings due to drainage action.

Locate invert low enough: a. To drain underside of floor; b. To give satisfactory slope from high point. Lower footing bottom, if required, to keep drains above bottom of footing to avoid loss of material from under footing.

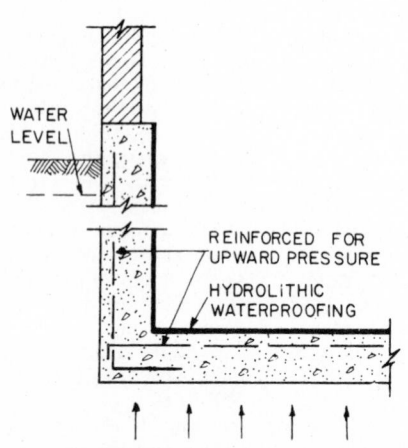

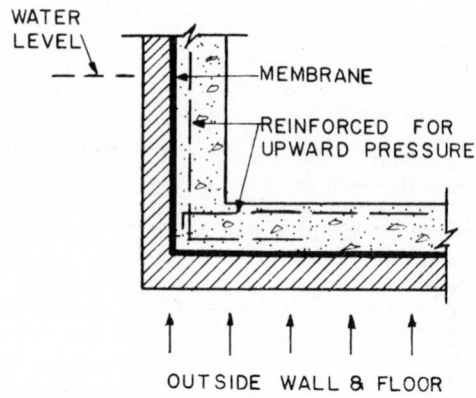

2. REINFORCED CONCRETE MAT OR RAFT

Reinforced concrete mats or rafts are reinforced concrete floor slabs or walls designed to resist the head of water expected. They are usually waterproofed.

In some cases expensive waterproofing may be omitted if construction joints are properly caulked and if a slight amount of seepage can be taken care of by floor gutters and sub-drain.

a) Hydrolithic methods consist of the application of coats of cement plaster containing iron filings or a similar type of waterproof plaster to the inside surfaces of the floors and walls.

b) Membrane Waterproofing—As it must be installed on the outside of walls and under floors, a membrane may be subject to a leak which will be neither accessible nor easy to locate. This membrane also has the disadvantage that secondary walls or floors must be provided for its application.

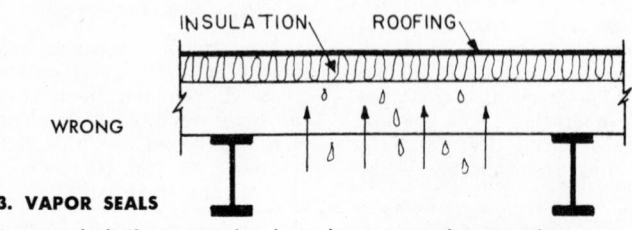

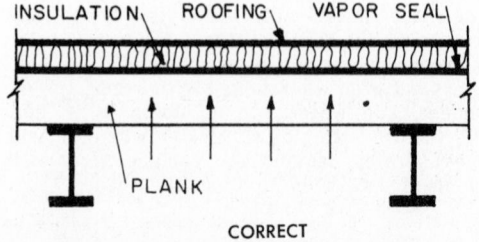

3. VAPOR SEALS

A great deal of attention has been drawn to condensation due to water vapor hitting a cold surface.

3. Vapor Seals

Even such a brief description as this must start with certain principles, as follows:

By Dalton's Law, in the case of two adjoining rooms, one containing a high degree of humidity and the other a low degree of humidity, the humidities will tend to equalize themselves through the partition, if it is not waterproofed or vapor sealed. This, naturally, applies to a top story room and the outside air. If the vapor seal for the roof is applied underneath the insulation the moist air coming up against the vapor seal will find a relatively warm surface and will not tend to condense. If the vapor seal is placed on top of the insulation the moist air coming up against the roof fabric will tend to condense and come back into the insulation as free water, with unsatisfactory results.

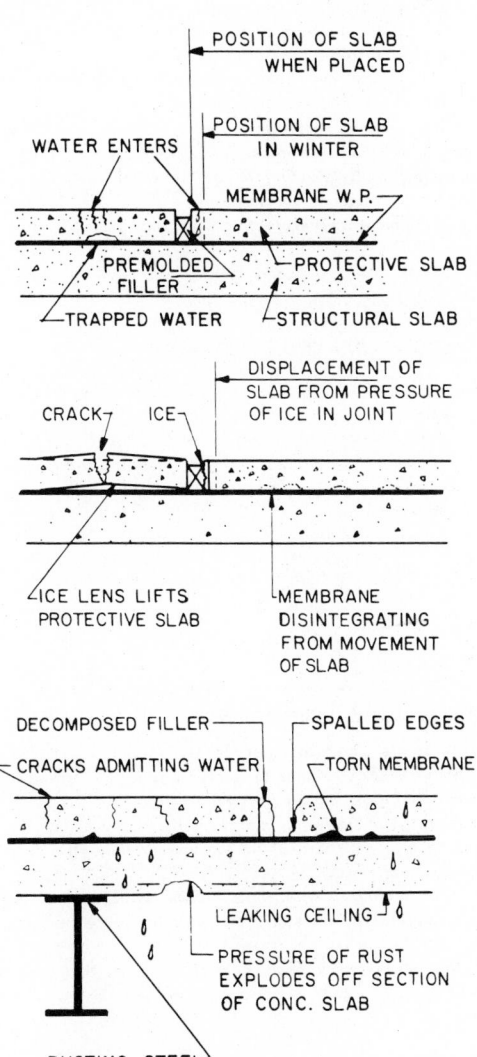

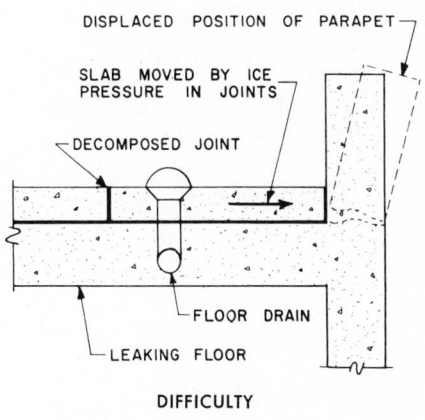

DIFFICULTY

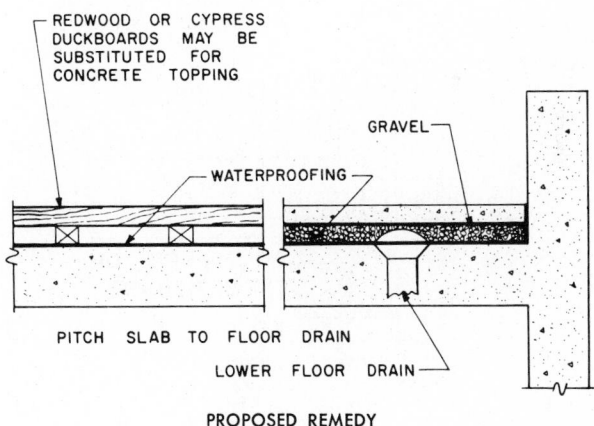

PROPOSED REMEDY

4. WATERPROOFING PAVED AREAS OVER UTILITY SPACES

The membrane is to be preferred for structures where the seepage is downward, such as sidewalk vault ceilings. The danger here is that the membrane which lies between the finished surface and the main supporting slab will trap water and cause the protective slab to freeze and heave, perhaps breaking the membrane.

To avoid this, drains must be installed at the membrane level and gravel or porous fill should be placed on top of the finished membrane before the finish surface is placed.

5. CORRECTION OF LEAKY WALLS

Driving rains may come through walls, even if flashings are correctly inserted. Leaky walls may be waterproofed by paraffin or colorless coating similar to silicone.

The most difficult type of leak to control seems to be one where the water comes down in or on the inside face of the wall and reaches the floor where it spreads out on the floor staining the ceiling or wall below.

Attempts to meet this with a spandrel flashing have not been entirely successful because of:
a) Failure to provide weep holes in the wall to assist in draining the water out. b) Failure to provide an adequate continuous watertight gutter clear of mortar droppings to catch water coming down the inside face of the wall.

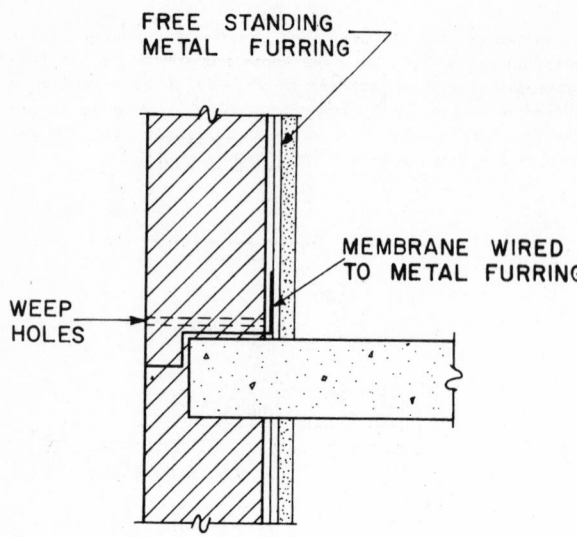

WEEP HOLES

FREE STANDING METAL FURRING

MEMBRANE WIRED TO METAL FURRING

6. WALL WATERPROOFING

Regarding the question of waterproofing walls, a checkup on the situation at this time leads us to conclude that the following are the best thoughts for obtaining waterproof walls:

a) Thorough workmanship in laying the brick, full beds, no voids, etc.
b) Lime cement mortar, that is, 1-1-6.
c) Reasonably porous face brick for bond.
d) Parging back of face brick with mortar.
e) Continuous spandrel flashing at floors.
f) An independent furring.
g) Coating back of wall with hot asphalt emulsion applied with a spray or troweled.
h) Drips on all overhanging edges.
i) Sills projecting beyond the jambs, not ending flush at jambs.
j) Pointing of face with "weathered" or "concave" joints.
k) Lintel flashings turned up at ends.
l) Preformed bituminous waterproofing units may be built into the wall.
m) Pretest—hosing water between furring and wall may be required as a test.

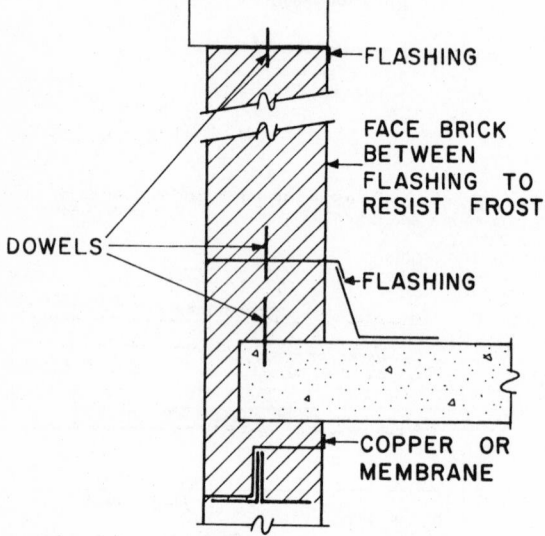

FLASHING

FACE BRICK BETWEEN FLASHING TO RESIST FROST

DOWELS

FLASHING

COPPER OR MEMBRANE

7. PARAPET WALL WATERPROOFING

Suggestions to obtain waterproof parapet walls:

a) A through wall cap flashing to seal off and lead down the water in the upper part of the parapet.
b) Shear anchorage of dowels or masonry offsets to prevent creeping, particularly under corners, of the parapet wall relative to the main wall—a common defect.
c) Avoidance of sealing in the water in the parapet wall with a bituminous coating. It will cause the wall to freeze and scale off brick.
d) Use of face brick or a hard burned brick in the rear of parapet walls.

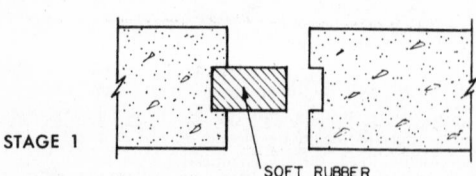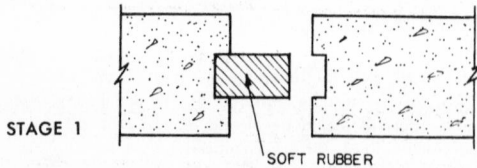

STAGE 1

SOFT RUBBER

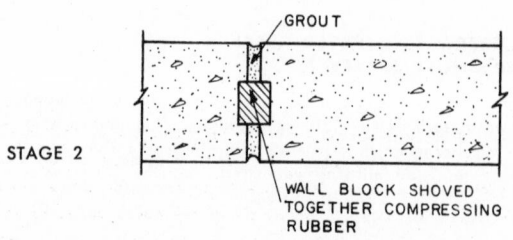

GROUT

STAGE 2

WALL BLOCK SHOVED TOGETHER COMPRESSING RUBBER

8. PRECAST MASONRY UNITS

Problems in connection with precast masonry units include:

The exposed concrete should be waterproofed with integral waterproofing to avoid wet diaper appearance after a rainstorm.

Horizontal joints should be tongue-and-grooved in such a way as to throw out the water coming down the surface.

Vertical joints must depend upon mastic or cement and as there are considerable volumetric changes due to temperature and shrinkage, reliance must be had on an elastic mastic to caulk the joints. Perhaps vertical joints might be set up with compressed live or foam rubber between them.

Prepared by Copper Development Association, Inc.

Termites require damp, rotting wood, and will carry in moisture and fungi to rot sound wood so they can feed on it. This requires a constant source of moisture, usually obtained from the soil. Entrance to unprotected structures is gained through cracks in concrete or masonry foundations or walls, through the wood portion of the house frame, or by building tunnel-like structures called shelter tubes over foundation posts and walls.

Properly installed shields will not only prevent termites from invading the wooden portion of the structure but will also act as an effective moisture barrier.

Termite shields may be of either one of two forms: the barrier, or the deflector (Figures 3a and 3b), or a combination of the two (Figure 3c).

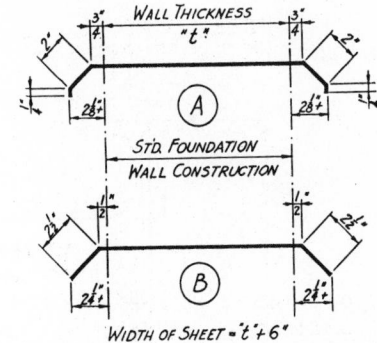

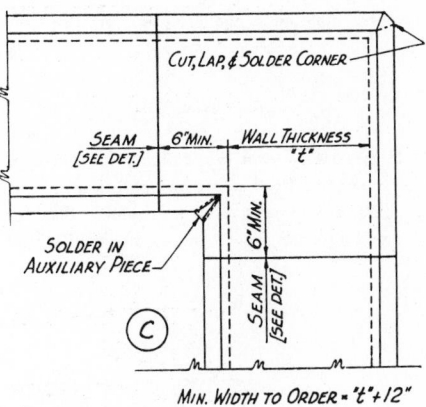

Drawings above and below show details for using cold rolled copper sheet

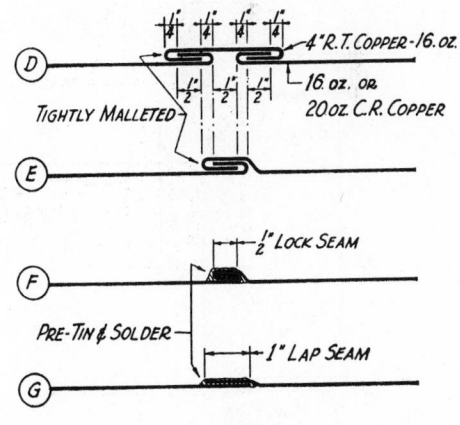

FIGURE 1

ESTIMATING TABLE
For Straight Runs

WALL THICKNESS	WIDTH OF SHEETS
8 in.	14 in.
10 in.	16 in.
12 in.	18 in.
16 in.	22 in.

BARRIER SHIELD In installations where inspection of the shield is impossible, a barrier type is required. It is designed so that termites building up over the stone or concrete foundations are blocked from entry into the woodwork of the house above by the projection of the shield. Two basic barrier type shields are shown in A and B of *Figure 1*.

The A type with a vertical turn-down edge is preferable, but the B type is also satisfactory and under some conditions easier to apply. The sharp edge of the metal, either vertical or at 45°, provides a 180° angle around which the termites are unable to construct a shelter tube. (A shelter tube is a tunnel-like structure

built by termites over foundation walls and posts through which they can bring fungi and moisture to dry wood.) Some shield designs have a rolled edge, but they are not recommended because shelter tubes might be built around the roll.

At corners, as in standard types of through-wall flashing, it is better to use a specially formed piece as in C than to have a diagonal seam across the corner. Four types of cross seams are shown at D, E, F, and G. Types D and E should be tightly malleted. When the soldered types (F or G) are used, the edge of the sheets should be pre-tinned to ensure a solid joint. Any loose joint provides access for termites to enter the structure.

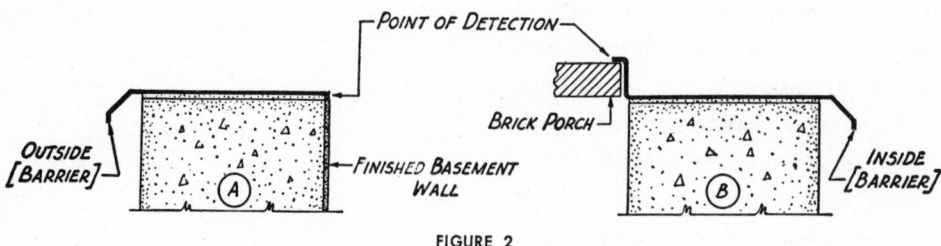

FIGURE 2

DEFLECTOR SHIELD This shield, illustrated in *Figure 3b*, does not in itself provide an impossible barrier to the termites. It is employed only in areas accessible for periodic inspections, such as the interior wall of a basement recreation room, or on the outside of a brick porch.

Termites building a shelter tube from the ground moisture to house woodwork are forced to move out around the shield as indicated at the "point of detection" *(Figure 2)*. The shelter tube, exposed at this point, can be easily broken off and the termites that have gained access to the building are cut off from their essential moisture. This simple procedure, repeated several times, apparently discourages the tube-building termites.

VENTILATION Termites in a building isolated by shields generally make a strong effort to restore contact with ground moisture. If a shallow, unexcavated area is available they have been known to connect a joist to the ground by means of a shelter tube. Proper ventilation however, should defeat such attempts. Under moist conditions, lengthy shelter tubes can be formed, but under dry conditions the tubes have the consistency of sand and tend to crumble and collapse.

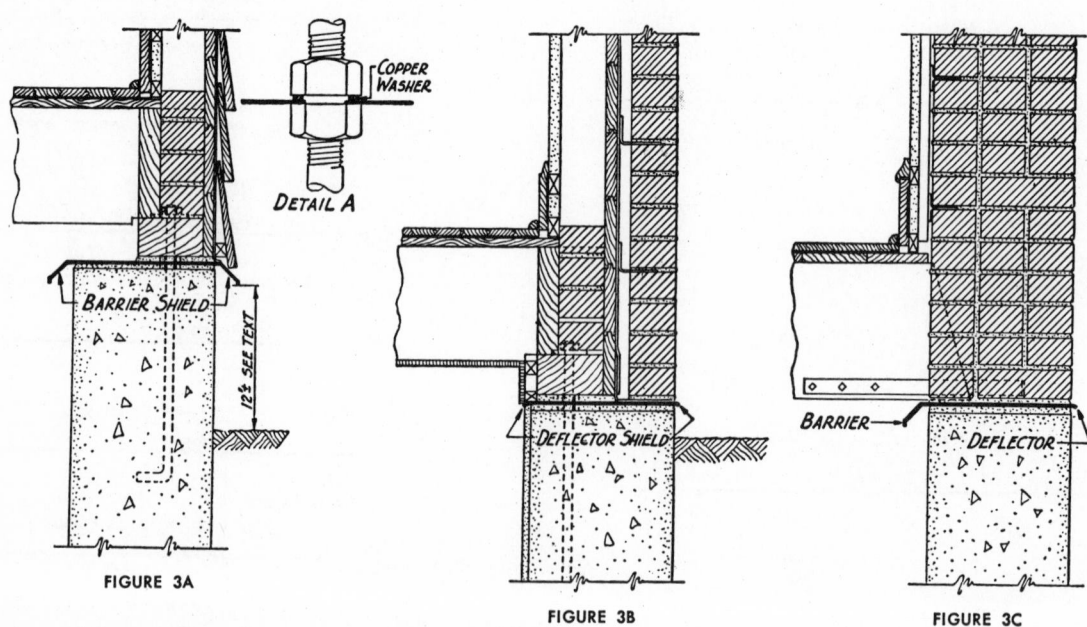

FIGURE 3A

FIGURE 3B

FIGURE 3C

TYPICAL FOUNDATION WALLS *Figure 3a* shows the foundation wall installation of a shield for a frame house. Here a barrier type is necessary. With veneer construction, as shown in *Figure 3b*, a deflector shield is generally satisfactory. Similarly, a deflector shield generally is used in solid masonry construction, *Figure 3c*, although in this illustration the interior has been assumed to be inaccessible for periodic inspection; therefore, a barrier shield is shown installed on the inside.

In the southern part of the United States the shield should be from 12 to 18 in. above ground level; in the northern part, from 9 to 15 in. is usually sufficient. The degree of local infestation also must be considered in determining proper clearance.

When there is objection to the line of shielding shown on the outside of the house it often can be camouflaged with shrubbery, or a modification of a true barrier type can be employed. This design, of course, will demand periodic inspections to discover if any termite shelter tubes have been built and care should be taken that shrubbery does not provide a by-pass of the shield.

Detail A *(Fig. 3a)* shows how an anchor-bolt pentrating the shield is made termite-proof. Instead of the washer as shown, special nuts with grooves may be used. In either case, the two should be drawn so tightly that termites can't squeeze through.

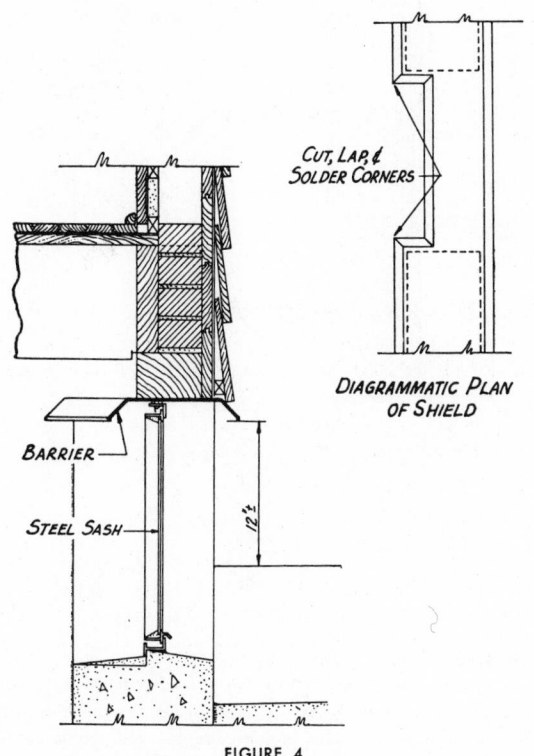

CUT, LAP, &
SOLDER CORNERS

DIAGRAMMATIC PLAN
OF SHIELD

BARRIER

STEEL SASH

12½

FIGURE 4

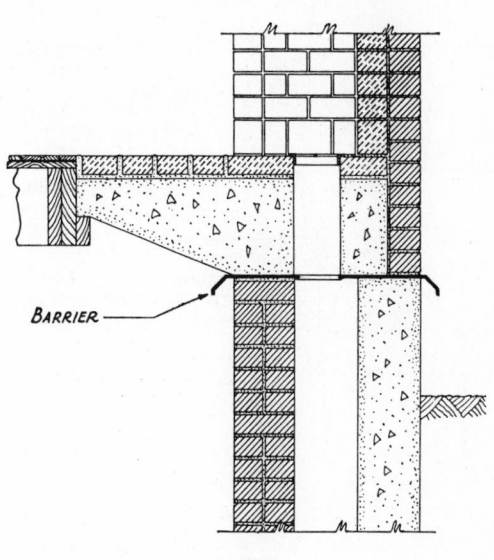

BARRIER

FIGURE 5

TYPICAL CELLAR WINDOW *Figure 4* shows a detail of shielding construction at a typical cellar window. As the window itself is below the level of the shield, to secure complete protection the window should be a metal one. When the window is above the ground level, a shield beneath the window will give ample protection.

FIREPLACE *Figure 5* shows a fireplace protected by a barrier shield over the foundation wall. The ash-dump is above the shield and the ash-flue below. Utmost caution should be exercised in the installation of the termite shield under the fireplace. The seal should be tight and permanent. Termites can squeeze through the narrowest of crevices.

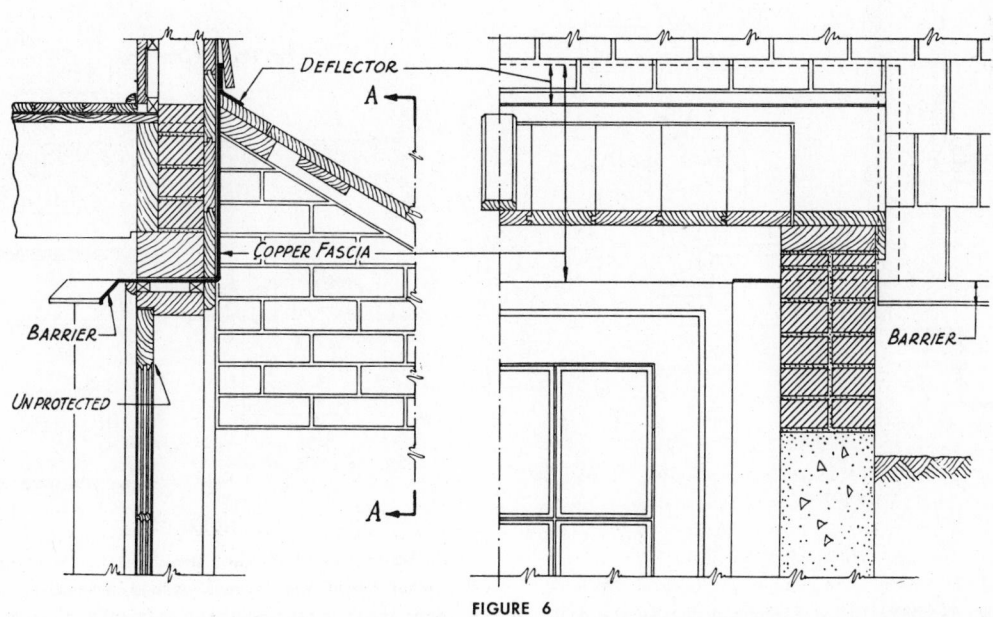

DEFLECTOR

A

COPPER FASCIA

BARRIER

BARRIER

UNPROTECTED

A

FIGURE 6

CELLAR HATCHWAY *Figure 6* shows a typical cellar hatchway installation. Note that this application combines barrier with partial deflector type shields, because where the shield extends vertically it is conceivable that shelter tubes might be built around it. The combination of shields, plus inspection, will ensure protection of the building. In this example the door shown is of wood construction and it is located beneath the protection of the shield. To be termite-proof the door [unless treated] should be metal.

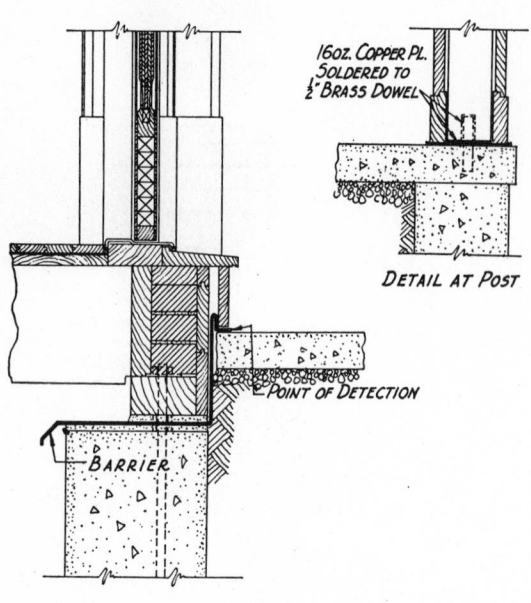

FIGURE 7

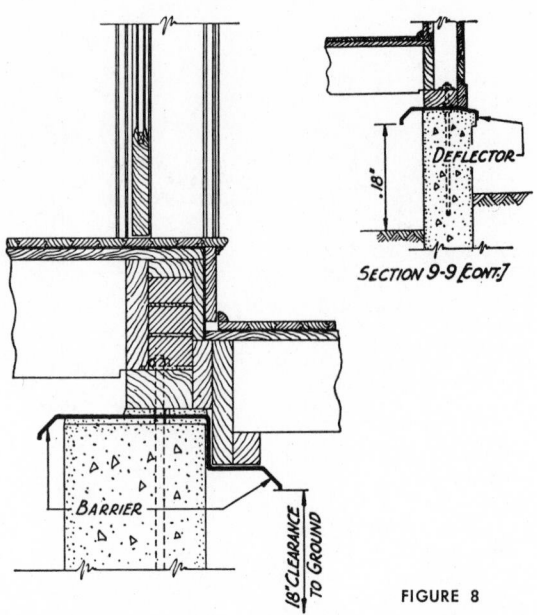

FIGURE 8

DOOR SILL *Figure 7* shows another combination shield applied under a door sill adjoining a concrete (or brick) porch. A deflector type is used on the outside because of ease of inspection, while the inner one is a true barrier type. Note that the shield is bent up behind the kickboard to form a water stop. The detail at the upper right illustrates a deflector shield inserted under a wood post resting on a concrete (or brick) porch.

PORCHES *Figure 8* shows shielding applied at a house wall adjoining a porch of wood construction. A barrier shield is necessary throughout, particularly as the area under the porch is rarely easy to inspect. This area should also be well ventilated. The detail at the upper right shows a shield at the outside of the porch. When exposed, a deflector shield can be employed as illustrated, otherwise a barrier type should be used.

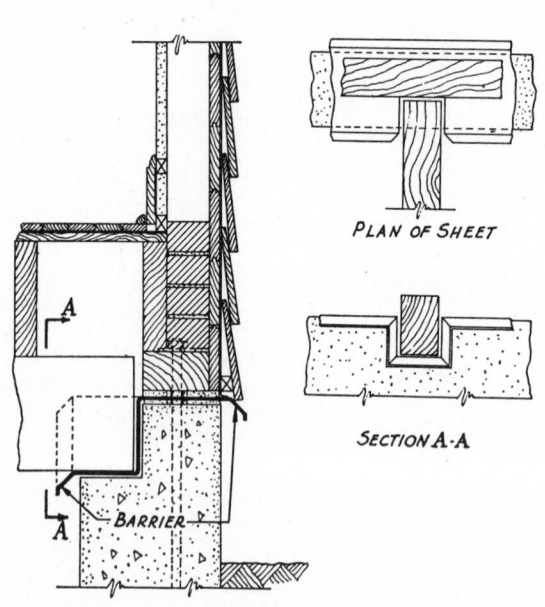

FIGURE 9

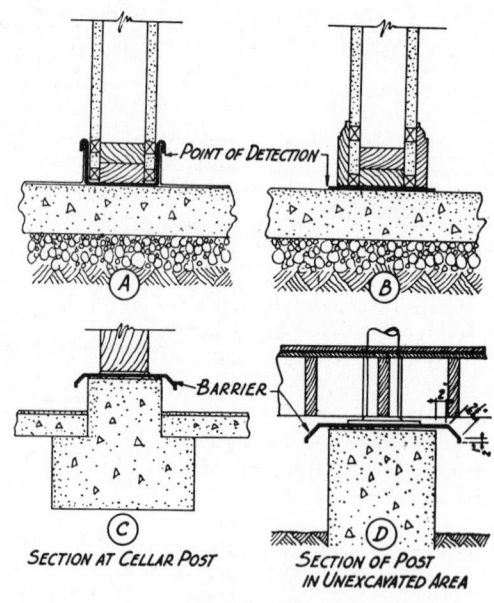

FIGURE 10

CELLAR BEAM POCKETS *Figure 9* shows a barrier shield installed at a cellar beam pocket. In this application the shield must be cut, fitted and soldered to meet the dimensional specifications of the beam, thickness of wall, etc. If a bolt is inserted through the termite shield, extreme care must be taken to assure an absolutely tight joint.

PARTITIONS *Figure 10* shows shield details for cellar partitions and other miscellaneous areas. A and B illustrate methods of deflector shield installations between a cellar floor and a cellar partition. Similar applications can be made between a partition and a cellar side wall. Inspection for shelter tubes should be made regularly.

The barrier shield shown in detail C protects the cellar post. Detail D is self-explanatory.

Information on this page was collected and prepared by Ronald Allwork from publications of the British Building Research Station, and the Copper Development Association, and the National Association of Sheet Metal Contractors.

MOISTURE PENETRATION

Moisture penetrates masonry walls because of (1) the porous nature of the wall material or (2) the opening up of joints as a result of expansion and contraction. The depth to which moisture penetrates cannot be precisely determined; it averages about 4½ in. but under severe conditions may be as much as 9 in. (These figures do not apply to walls subject to continuous or prolonged wetting.) The diagrams at the right show possible courses of penetration for typical walls. Note that the points of final penetration (designated by the circles) often occur immediately after the water has encountered a change of material in its downward course.

Parapet walls are exposed to weather on both sides and on top. Because few forms of construction will withstand such exposure, particularly penetration from the top, the coping is of first importance.

Copings provide greater protection for walls if they are (1) made of a material of low permeability and good frost resistance, (2) given an overhang and provided with a drip, (3) designed to shed water in the direction of the roof, and (4) provided with saddleback (or similar) joints.

DESIGN OF WALL FLASHINGS

1. Consider the effective life of a flashing material in relation to the life of the wall.
2. Bear in mind the corrosion factor of the flashing material due to (a) local atmospheric conditions and (b) contact with wall materials.
3. Investigate the suitability of the flashing material from the standpoint of (a) tensile strength to withstand perforation, (b) flexibility to conform to the mortar bed, and (c) resistance to squeezing out because of the weight of the wall.
4. Study the location of flashings to provide for the diversion of water to the exterior surface of the wall at its vulnerable points.
5. Provide for the stability of the masonry above through-wall flashings by the use of dowels, keying, steps, or other means.

TYPES OF FLASHINGS

Sheet metal, metal-and-paper, and fabric (or membrane) flashings are available either as basic sheet materials, from which flashings are job-fabricated, or as preformed flashings. Most preformed flashings are patented types offered under various trade names. Fabric flashings are also available with integral reinforcing, and both metal and fabric types can be obtained in special shapes (or with other special provisions) for maintaining an effective masonry bond.

COPPER FLASHING

Temper: Cold-rolled (cornice-temper) copper should be used for all flashings, whether exposed or concealed. Because of its greater strength, cold-rolled copper is better able to resist the thermal and other stresses to which flashings may be subjected than is soft (roofing-temper) copper.

Weight: Where flashings are fully exposed and subject to severe stresses, as in copings and gravel stops, use 20-oz copper. Through-wall flashings partly exposed should be 16-oz; under stone belt-courses and sills, 20-oz. Fully concealed through-wall flashings may be 10 oz. Spandrel flashing may be a 6-oz sheet, or a membrane consisting of 3-oz copper on reinforced kraft paper. This membrane is also suitable for flashing around door and window openings. With slate or tile roofs, open valley flashings should be 20 oz and closed valley flashings 24 oz. For all other flashings, use 16 oz. (For the thicknesses of copper sheets of various weights, see "Architectural Metals," Sheet 1.)

Expansion: Continuous runs of any type of flashing must be provided with expansion joints spaced not more than 30 ft apart. A loose-locked joint filled with elastic cement or white lead is generally used for this purpose.

Fastenings: All nails and screws used with copper flashing must be copper or copper alloy. Flashings more than 12 in. wide should be secured by 2-in. cleats of 16-oz copper spaced 12 in. on centers.

Lead-coated copper may be used for flashings adjacent to light-colored stone or white-painted wood which might be stained by the weathering of bare copper.

Other metals, such as galvanized or aluminum-clad steel, aluminum, stainless steel, and monel, may also be used for flashing. Installation details are generally similar to those shown here for copper flashing.

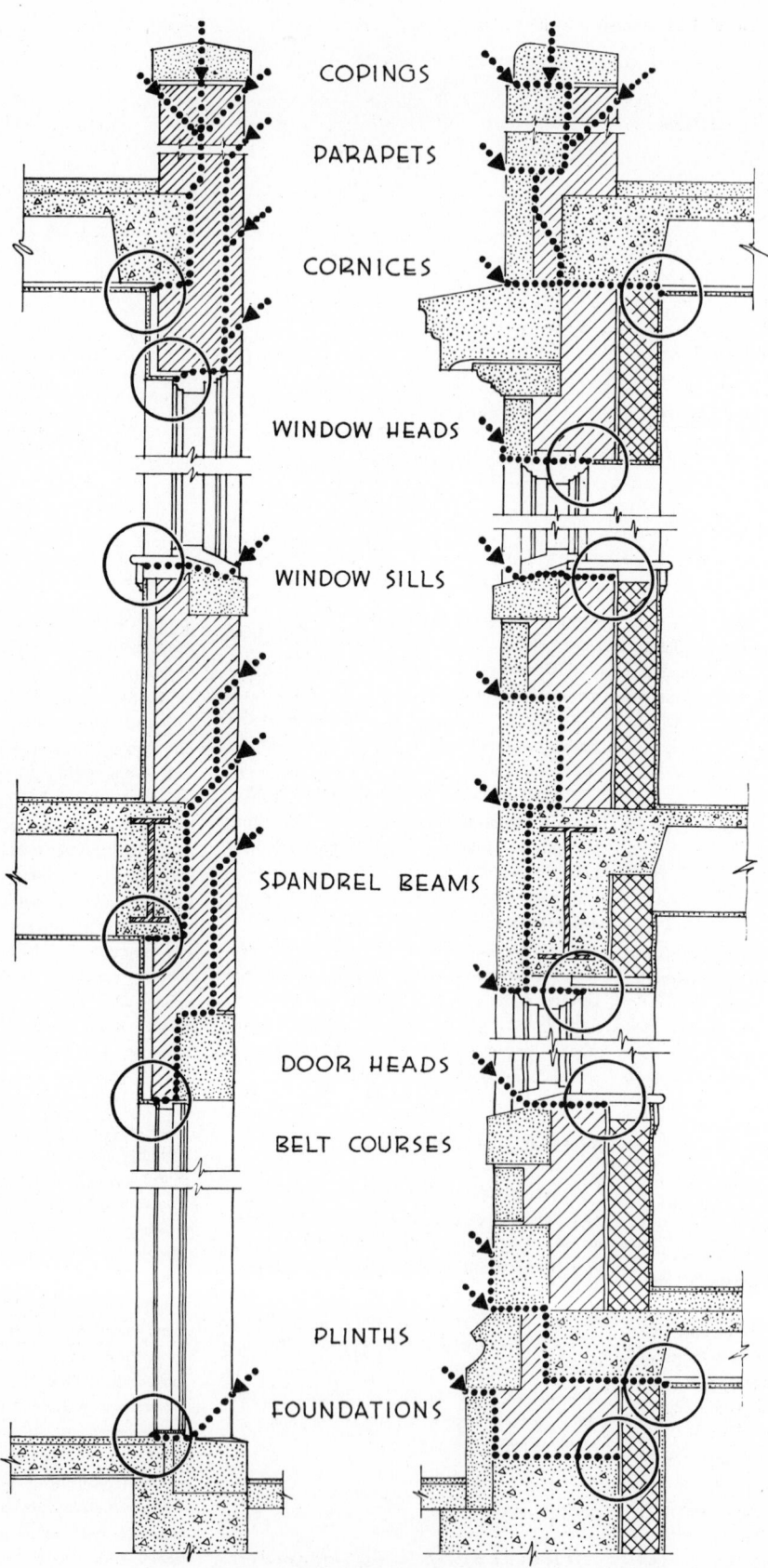

COPINGS

PARAPETS

CORNICES

WINDOW HEADS

WINDOW SILLS

SPANDREL BEAMS

DOOR HEADS

BELT COURSES

PLINTHS

FOUNDATIONS

Moisture penetration of multistory masonry walls

Data from Modern Applications of Sheet Copper in Building Construction, Copper Development Association, Inc.

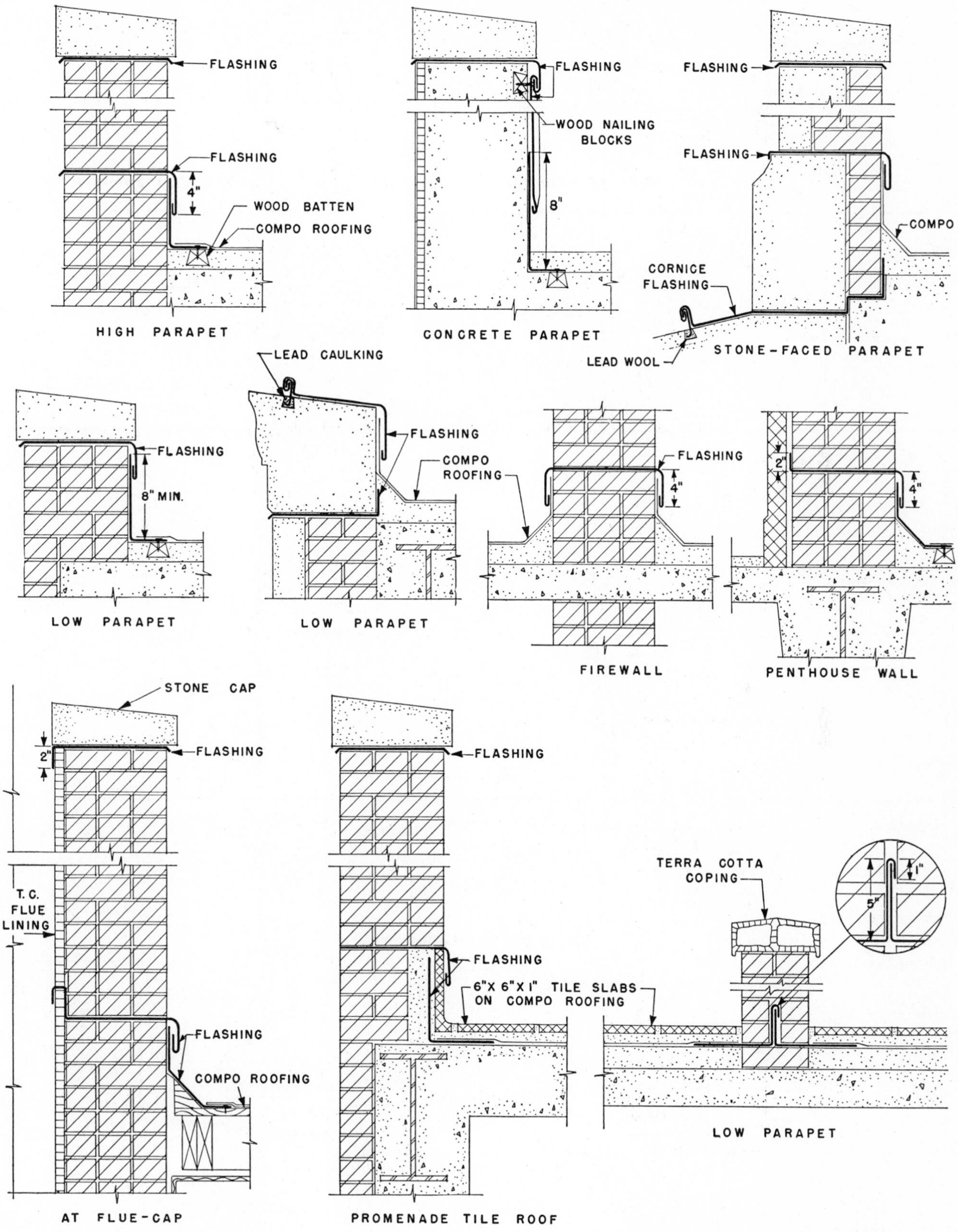

FLASHING

FLASHING

4"

WOOD BATTEN

COMPO ROOFING

HIGH PARAPET

FLASHING

WOOD NAILING BLOCKS

8"

CONCRETE PARAPET

FLASHING

FLASHING

COMPO

CORNICE FLASHING

LEAD WOOL

STONE-FACED PARAPET

LEAD CAULKING

FLASHING

8" MIN.

LOW PARAPET

FLASHING

COMPO ROOFING

LOW PARAPET

FLASHING

4"

FIREWALL

2"

4"

PENTHOUSE WALL

STONE CAP

FLASHING

2"

T. C. FLUE LINING

FLASHING

COMPO ROOFING

AT FLUE-CAP

FLASHING

FLASHING

6"X 6"X I" TILE SLABS ON COMPO ROOFING

PROMENADE TILE ROOF

TERRA COTTA COPING

1"

5"

LOW PARAPET

Flashing for walls and parapets

FLASHING—4
Copings: drips and edge strips

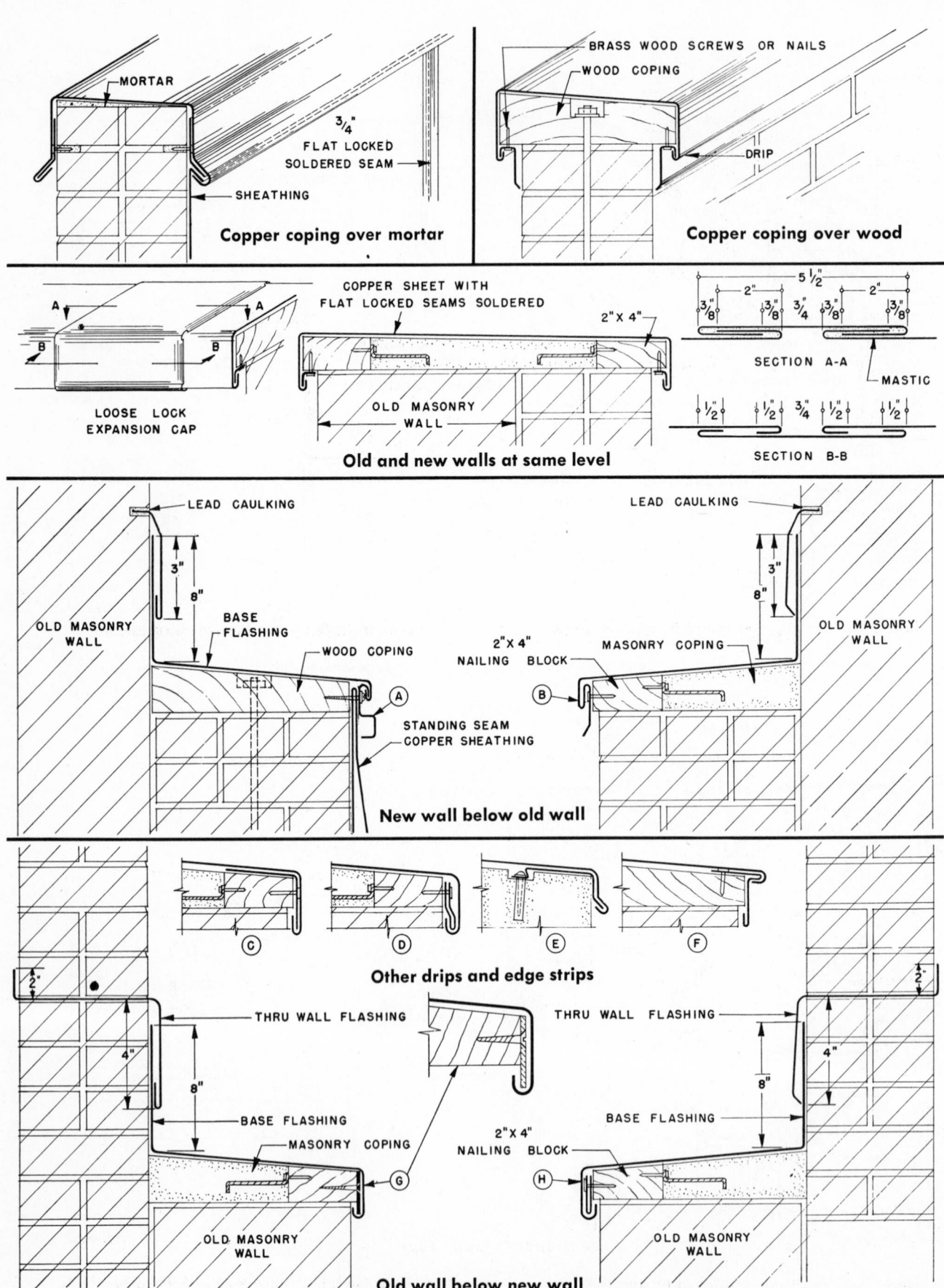

MORTAR

3/4" FLAT LOCKED SOLDERED SEAM

SHEATHING

Copper coping over mortar

BRASS WOOD SCREWS OR NAILS

WOOD COPING

DRIP

Copper coping over wood

LOOSE LOCK EXPANSION CAP

A B

COPPER SHEET WITH FLAT LOCKED SEAMS SOLDERED

2" X 4"

OLD MASONRY WALL

Old and new walls at same level

5 1/2"
2"   2"
3/8" 3/8" 3/4" 3/8" 3/8"

SECTION A-A

MASTIC

1/2" 1/2" 3/4" 1/2" 1/2"

SECTION B-B

LEAD CAULKING

LEAD CAULKING

OLD MASONRY WALL

3"
8"

BASE FLASHING

WOOD COPING

2"X 4" NAILING BLOCK

MASONRY COPING

3"
8"

OLD MASONRY WALL

A

B

STANDING SEAM COPPER SHEATHING

New wall below old wall

C   D   E   F

Other drips and edge strips

2"

THRU WALL FLASHING

THRU WALL FLASHING

2"

4"
8"

BASE FLASHING

MASONRY COPING

2"X 4" NAILING BLOCK

BASE FLASHING

4"
8"

G

H

OLD MASONRY WALL

OLD MASONRY WALL

Old wall below new wall

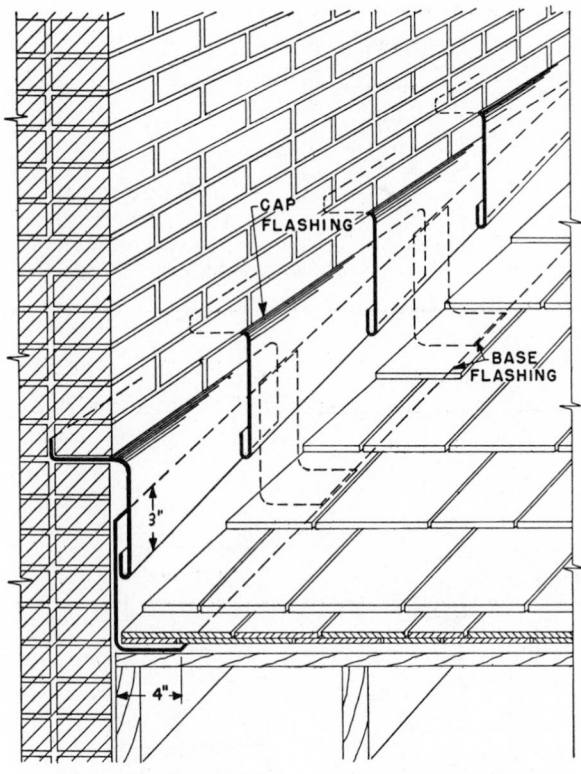

Side wall flashing, shingle roof against brick

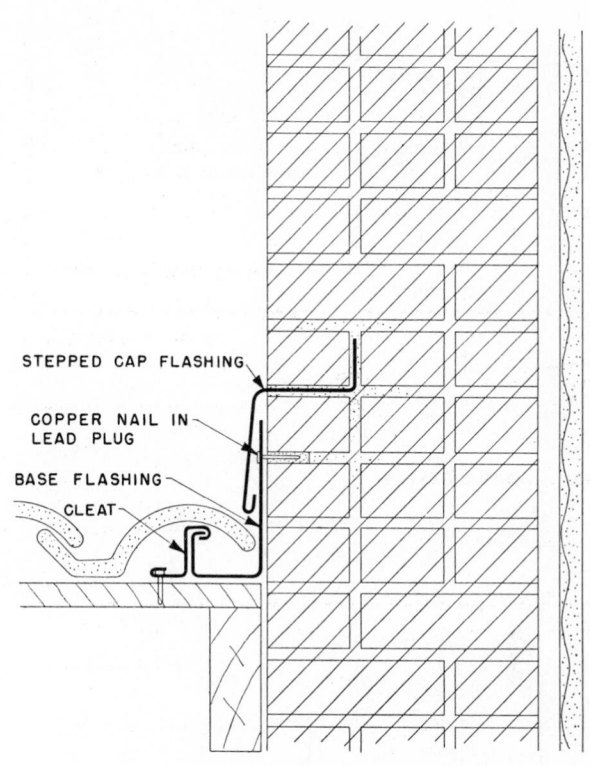

Side wall flashing, tile roof against brick

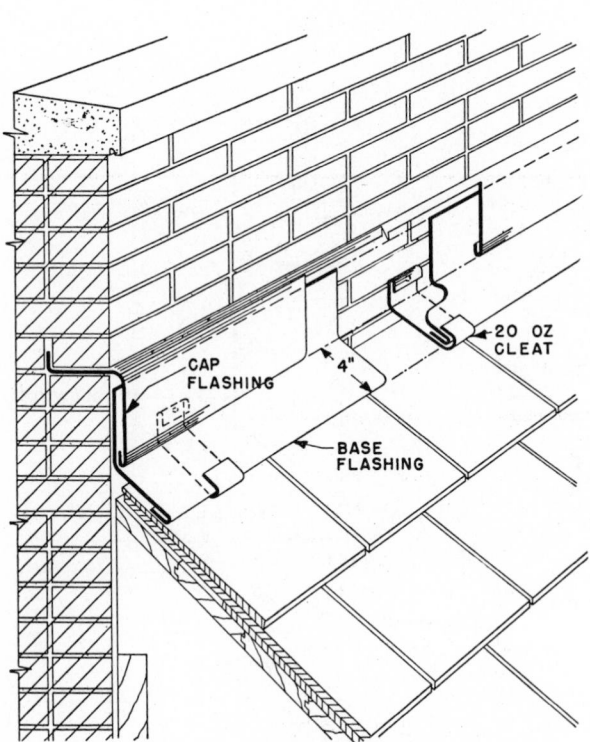

Head wall flashing, shingle roof against brick

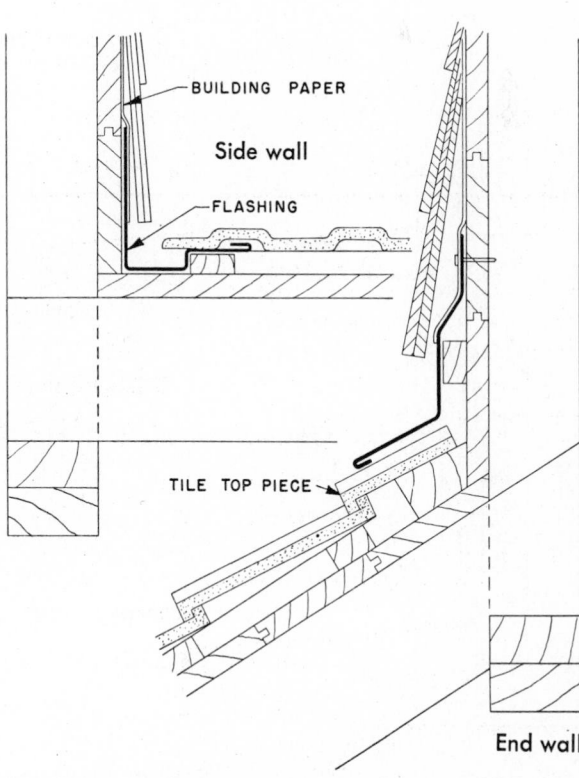

Head wall flashing, tile roof against frame

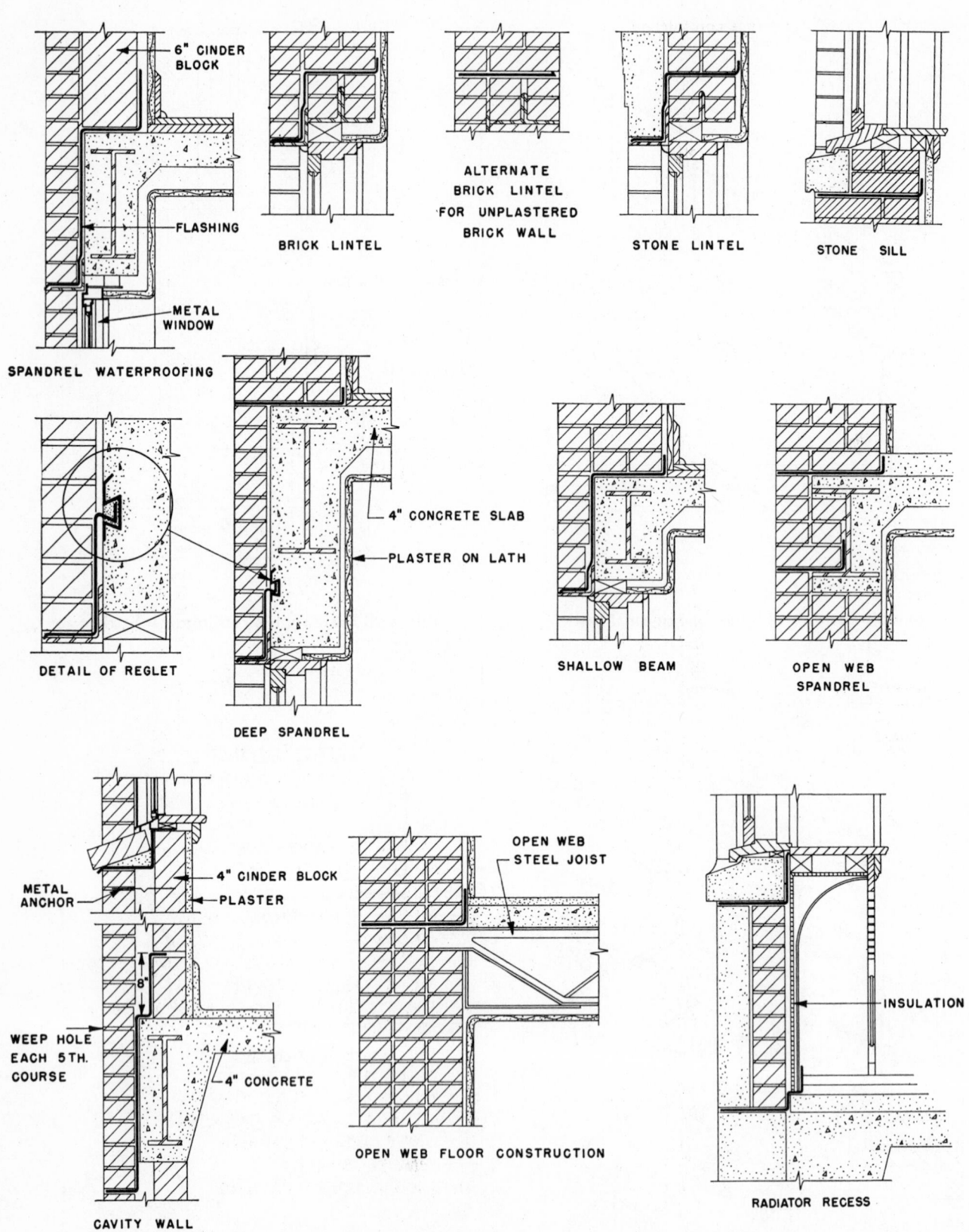

6" CINDER BLOCK

FLASHING

METAL WINDOW

SPANDREL WATERPROOFING

BRICK LINTEL

ALTERNATE BRICK LINTEL FOR UNPLASTERED BRICK WALL

STONE LINTEL

STONE SILL

DETAIL OF REGLET

4" CONCRETE SLAB

PLASTER ON LATH

DEEP SPANDREL

SHALLOW BEAM

OPEN WEB SPANDREL

METAL ANCHOR

4" CINDER BLOCK

PLASTER

8"

WEEP HOLE EACH 5TH. COURSE

4" CONCRETE

CAVITY WALL CONSTRUCTION

OPEN WEB STEEL JOIST

OPEN WEB FLOOR CONSTRUCTION

INSULATION

RADIATOR RECESS

Flashing for spandrels and windows

Wood-frame construction

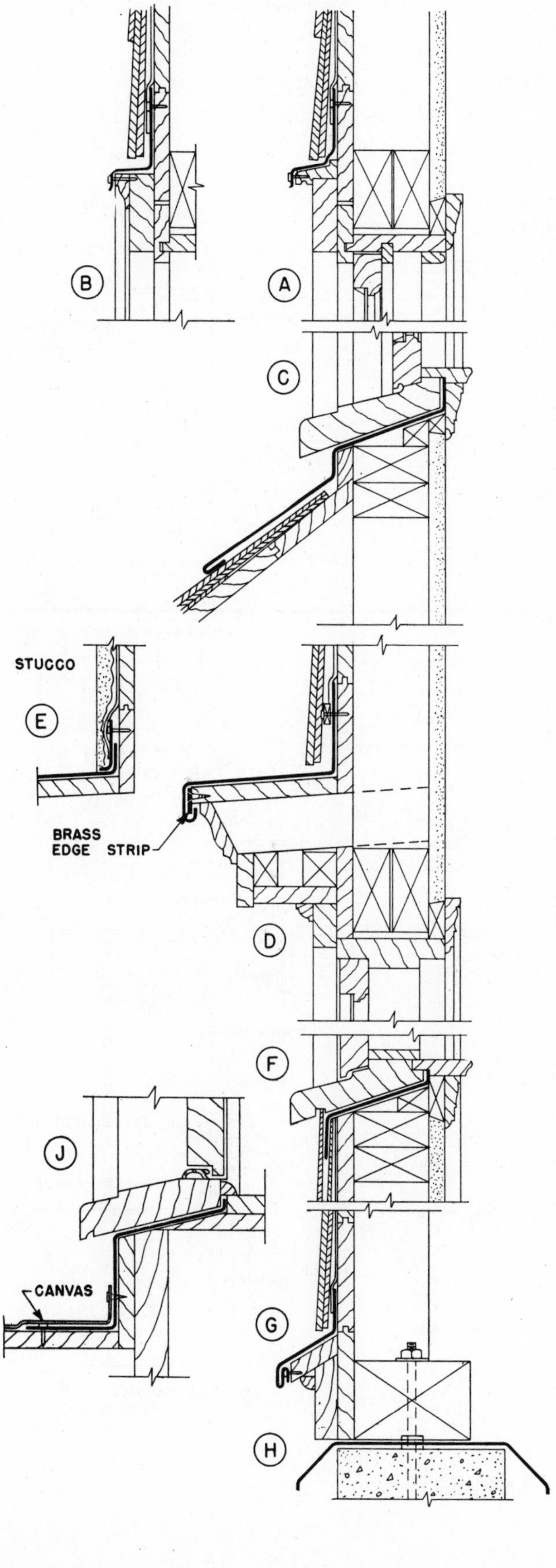

Brick veneer on wood frame

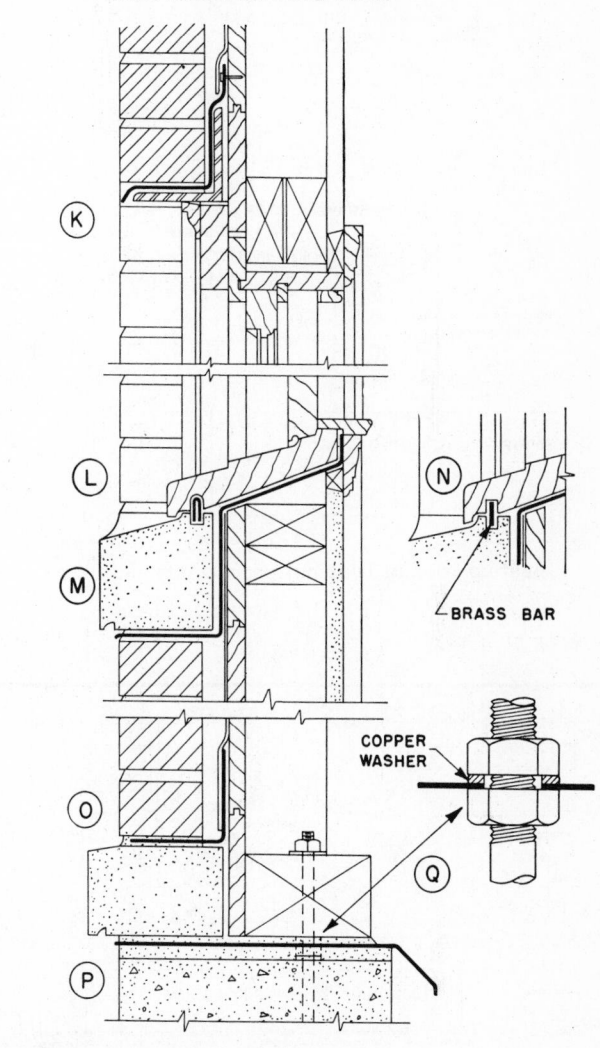

STUCCO

BRASS
EDGE STRIP

CANVAS

BRASS BAR

COPPER
WASHER

A — CASING FLASHING - DRIP CAP
B — CASING FLASHING - MOLDING
C — DORMER SILL FLASHING
D — WINDOW HEAD CORNICE - SHINGLES
E — WINDOW HEAD CORNICE - STUCCO
F — CASEMENT WINDOW SILL FLASHING - HIDDEN
G — WATER TABLE FLASHING
H — TERMITE SHIELD ON FOUNDATION WALL
J — DOOR SILL ABOVE CANVAS DECK
K — WINDOW HEAD FLASHING
L — WATER BAR - COPPER
M — WINDOW SILL FLASHING
N — ALTERNATE WATER BAR - BRASS
O — WATER TABLE FLASHING
P — TERMITE SHIELD
Q — ANCHOR BOLT FLASHING

Flashing for window and sill

FLASHING—8
Gravel stops; door heads

Gravel stops

GRAVEL STOP
NAILING STRIP
INSERT
4"
EDGE
STRIP

Built-up roofing (sloping) on concrete slab

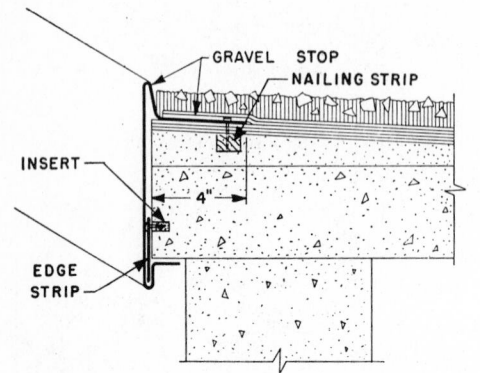

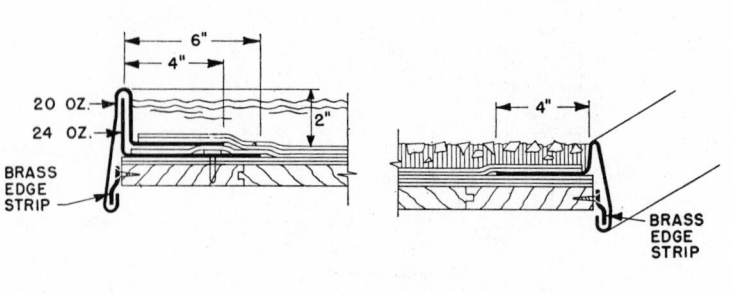

6"
4"
20 OZ.
24 OZ.
2"
BRASS
EDGE
STRIP

Dam for roof panel

4"
BRASS
EDGE
STRIP

Built-up roofing (level) on wood

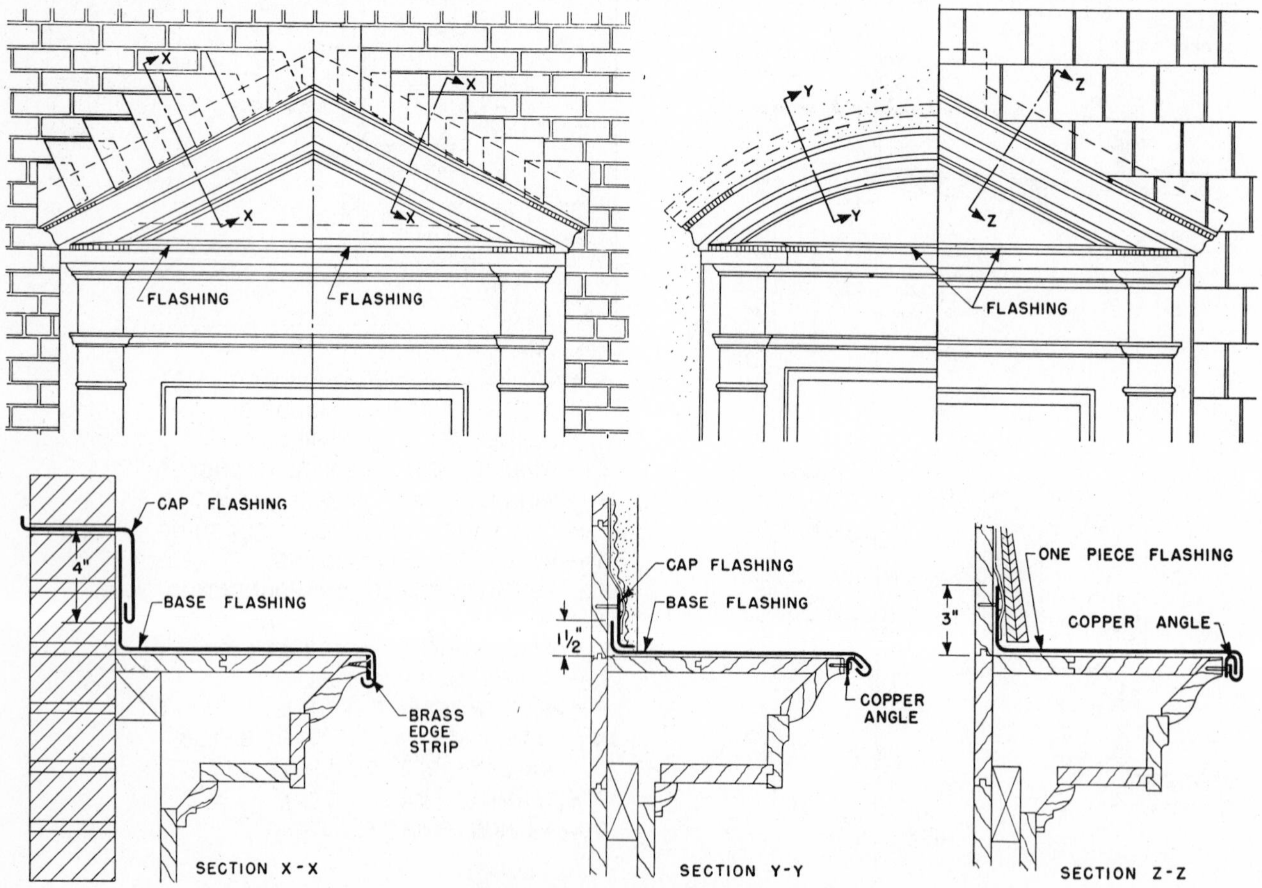

X
X
X
X
FLASHING
FLASHING
Y
Y
Z
Z
FLASHING
CAP FLASHING
4"
BASE FLASHING
BRASS
EDGE
STRIP
SECTION X-X
CAP FLASHING
BASE FLASHING
1½"
COPPER
ANGLE
SECTION Y-Y
ONE PIECE FLASHING
3"
COPPER ANGLE
SECTION Z-Z

Flashing for doorheads

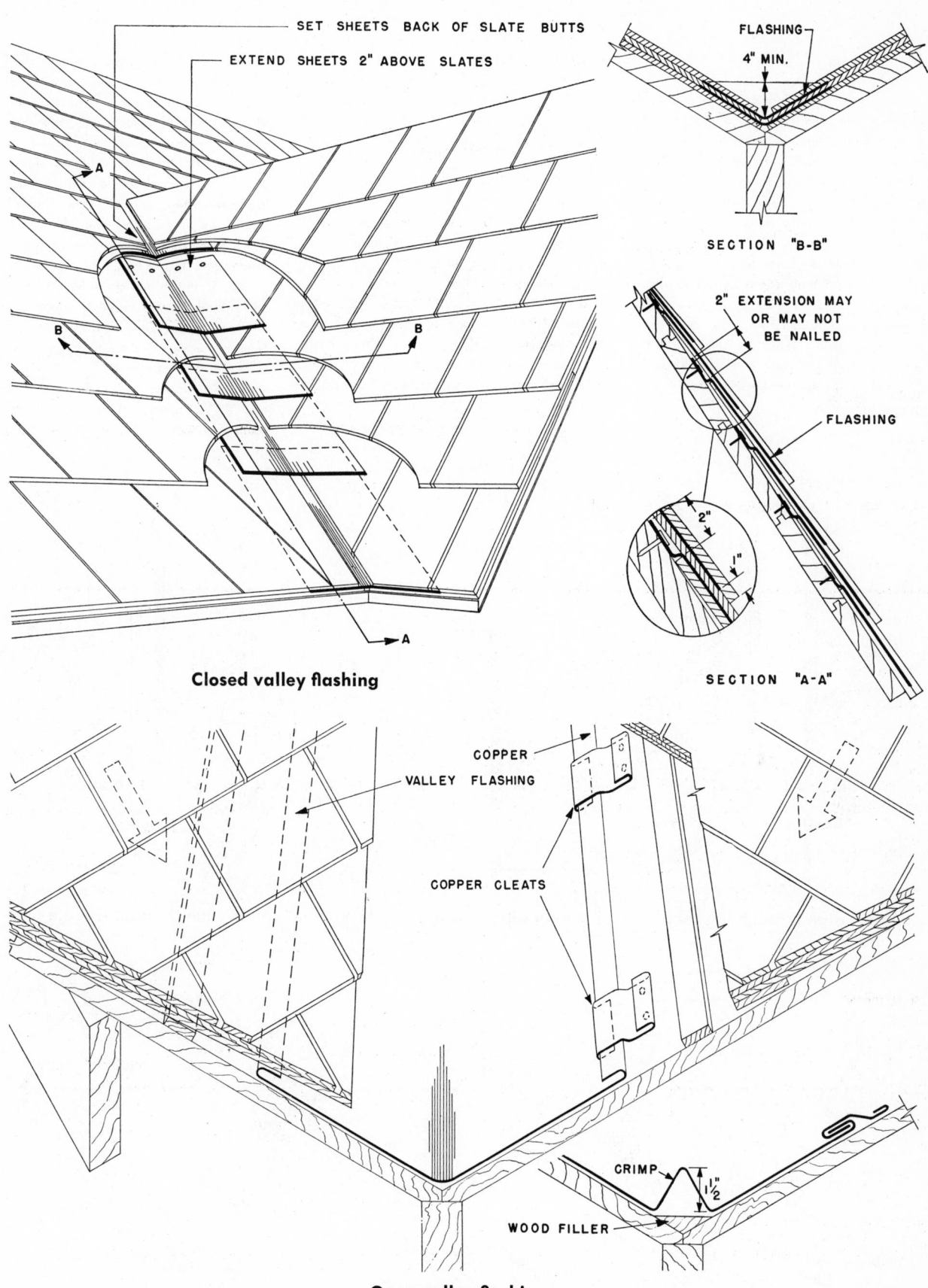

SET SHEETS BACK OF SLATE BUTTS

EXTEND SHEETS 2" ABOVE SLATES

A

B B

A

Closed valley flashing

FLASHING

4" MIN.

SECTION "B-B"

2" EXTENSION MAY OR MAY NOT BE NAILED

FLASHING

2"

1"

SECTION "A-A"

COPPER

VALLEY FLASHING

COPPER CLEATS

CRIMP

1½"

WOOD FILLER

Open valley flashing

When two roof slopes deliver unequal amounts of water to a valley, the larger amount may force the smaller amount to back up and overflow the top of the flashing. To prevent this backup, a 1½-in. crimp is formed in the copper at the bottom of the valley, as shown in the detail.

VENT FLASHING

In tile roofs, flashing of a vent pipe is essentially the same as for a shingle roof. For built-up roofing, horizontal flashing should extend on the roof 6 in. in all directions. It must be placed on several layers of felt and covered with at least two layers.

On shingle or slate roofs, the lower edge of the base flashing has to overlap the shingles at least 4 in., whereas the sides and top normally extend 6 in. and are placed under the shingles. The edges of the flashing to the side are folded over ½ in. to prevent water from driving under the shingles. If the flashing is 12 in. or more in width, the lower edge should be turned back on itself ½ in. to stiffen the metal.

CHIMNEY FLASHING

On shingle, slate, or flat tile roofs, the base flashing extends out on the shingles 4 to 6 in. at the bottom, with the edge turned back on itself ½ in. for stiffness. Flashing is also carried up the chimney so that the cap flashing will lap at least 4 in. over it.

The lowest shingle flashing on each side folds around the corner of the chimney and is soldered to the base flashing. Separate shingle flashings, which serve as base flashings up the sides, are inserted with each course of shingles, and are hooked over the top edge of the shingles. Each shingle flashing should lap the one below at least 3 in., and the roofing should lap over the metal 4 in. at the sides.

Base and shingle flashings are cap-flashed as shown. Along the lower side, where cap flashing is horizontal, it is continuous, but up the sides it is made of separate pieces, stepped as required by the slope of the roof. The separate sheets should have side laps of at least 3 in. and should lap the base flashings everywhere at least 4 in. Cap flashings should be inserted as the chimney is constructed, carried all the way through to the inside, and turned up 1 in. against the flue linings. If this is not possible, the mason can leave sand courses at joints where the flashings will come. The sand courses are easily removed, after which the flashings are inserted to a depth of at least 2 in. into the brickwork and secured by lead plugs 1 in. wide and 8 in. apart. Joints are finished with roofing cement.

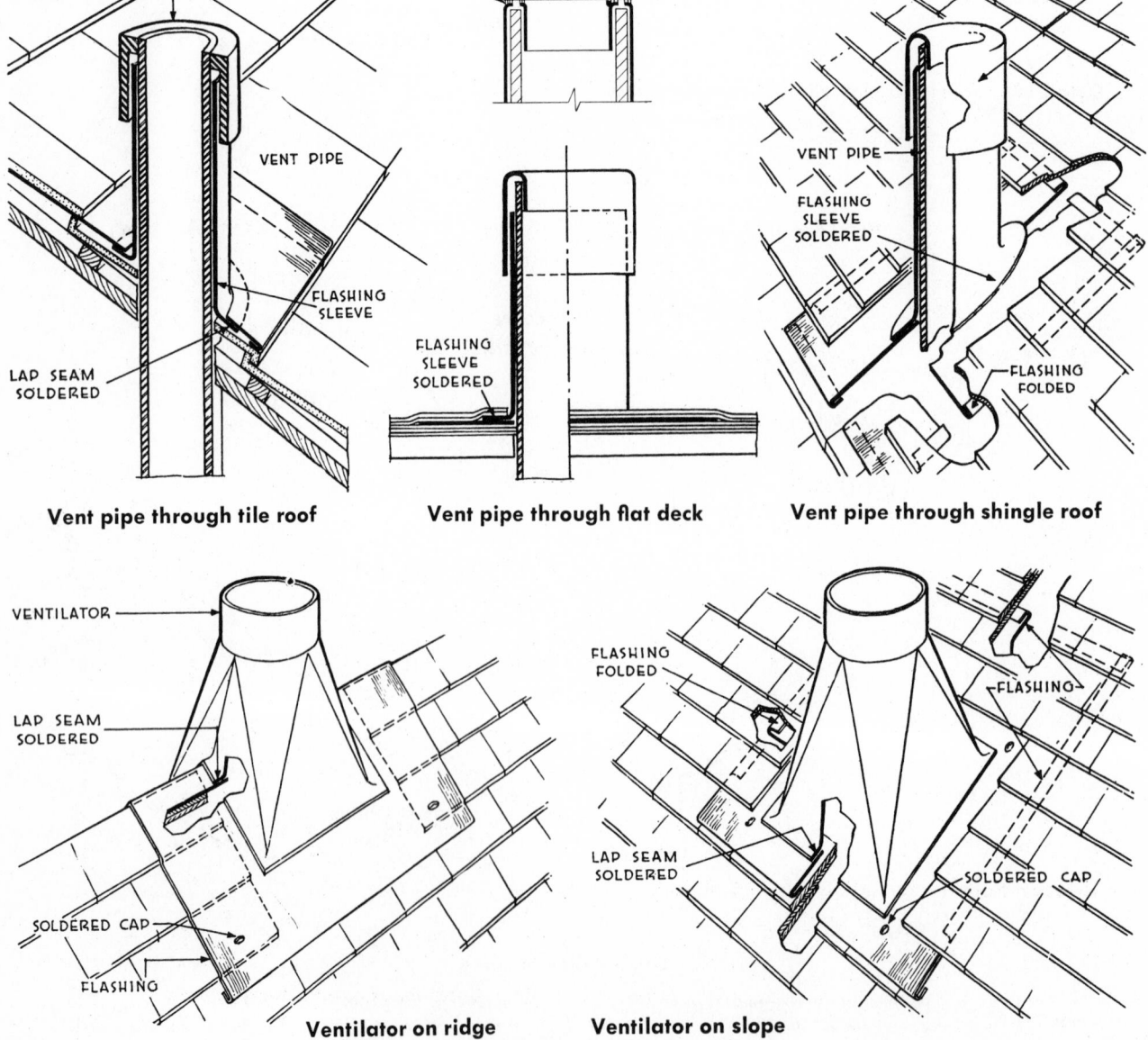

Vent pipe through tile roof

Vent pipe through flat deck

Vent pipe through shingle roof

Ventilator on ridge

Ventilator on slope

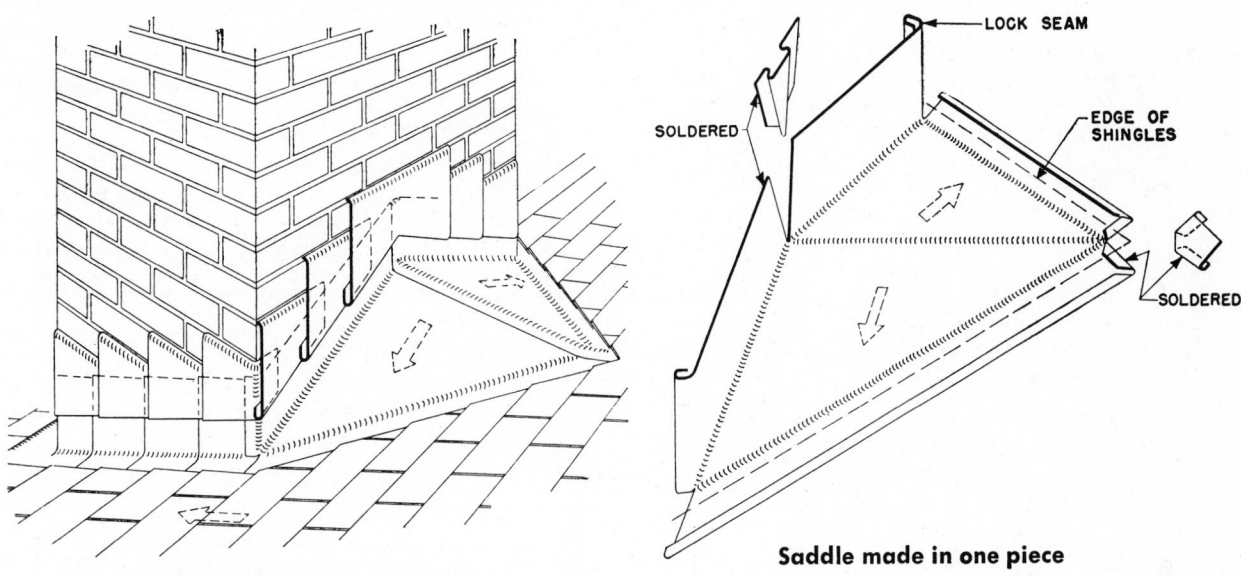

Detail of saddle or cricket (stepped cap flashing)

LOCK SEAM

SOLDERED

EDGE OF SHINGLES

SOLDERED

Saddle made in one piece

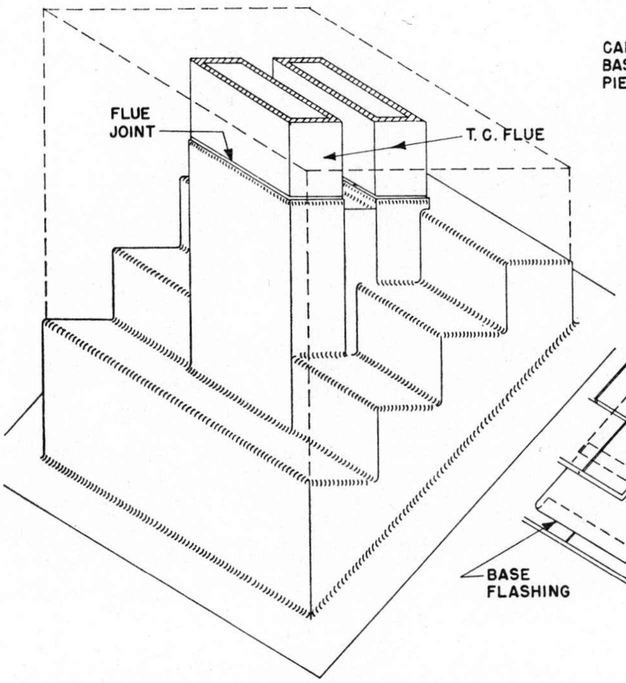

ALTERNATE

CAP AND BASE ONE PIECE

LOCK SEAM

FLUE JOINT

T. C. FLUE

CAP FLASHING

LOCK SEAM

BASE FLASHING

4"

SOLDERED LAP SEAM

Through-flashing extending into T. C. flues

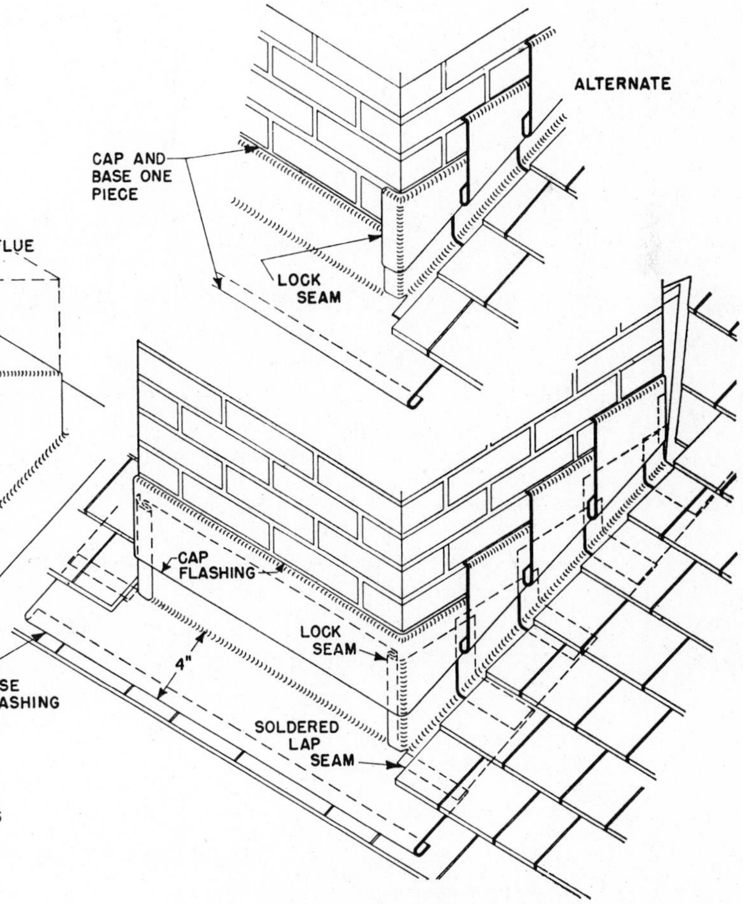

Continuous cap flashing at base

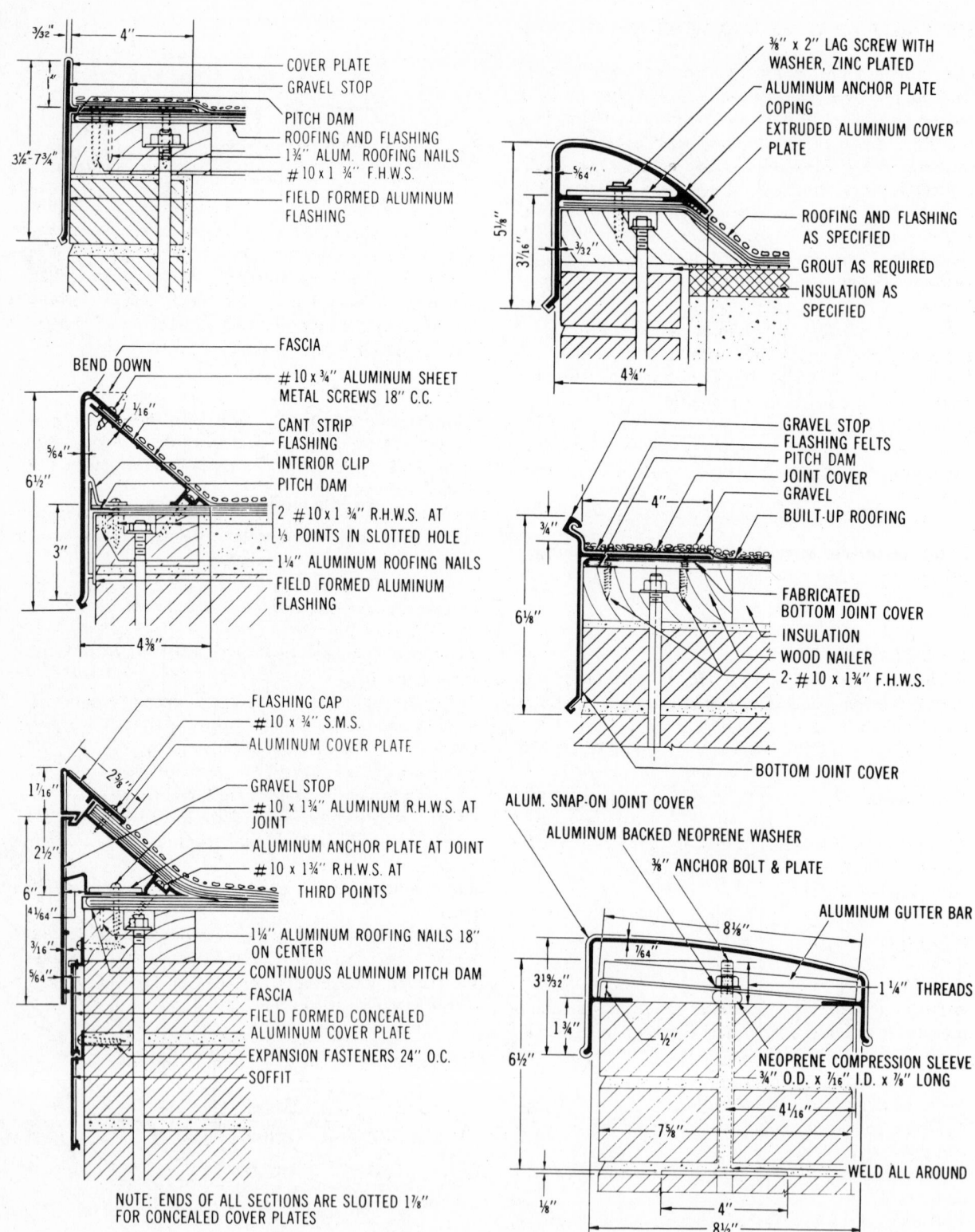

Gravel stops and copings

Extruded aluminum copings, gravel stops, and fascias are available as proprietary products from several manufacturers. Those shown here (courtesy of Reynolds Metals Company) are typical, but many other *designs are available. All types include provision for expansion, waterproof joint covers (usually concealed), and all necessary clips and accessories.*

By HOWARD P. VERMILYA, AIA

RESISTANCE TO WIND AND WIND-DRIVEN RAIN

New materials and methods of application offer solutions to former difficulties with asphalt shingle roofs caused by high winds and low-sloped roofs. High winds could lift tabs and permit wind-driven water to penetrate the roof. If winds were strong enough, they could rip off the tabs. Previously the industry-recommended minimum roof slope for asphalt shingles was 4 in 12, because lower roof slopes were susceptible to wind-driven rain penetration. Now, however, the industry recommends the use of asphalt shingles for slopes as low as 2 in 12.

This was made possible through the technique of cementing the shingle tabs with a quick-setting adhesive as they are laid. More recently new products have been introduced to achieve the same result and these include:
1. A factory-applied self-sealing adhesive which is activated after application by pressure and/or solar heat.
2. Interlocking tabs (square butt strip shingle).
3. Increased size and weight, resulting in increased stiffness and triple coverage.

APPLICATION

1. The standard 210-lb, 12-by-36-in. square butt strip shingle providing double coverage at exposure of 5 in. is applied as follows:

ROOF PITCH	UNDERLAYMENT
a. 7 or more in 12	none
b. 4 thru 6 in 12	single layer
c. 2 thru 3 in 12	double layer*

2. The heavy 300 lb, 15-by-36-in. square butt strip shingle providing triple coverage at exposure of 5 in. is applied as follows:

ROOF PITCH	UNDERLAYMENT
a. 4 or more in 12	none
b. 3 in 12	single layer
c. 2 in 12	double layer

● Single layer of No. 15 asphalt saturated felt underlayment is applied with a 2-in. headlap and a 6-in. endlap.
● Double layer of underlayment is applied with a 19-in. headlap and a 6-in. endlap.
● Starter course of shingles shall be doubled and project about ⅜ to ½ in.
● Eaves flashing (Where design temperature is 25 F or colder):
1. Provide double layer of underlayment extending back from eaves to a line 24 in. inside the inner face of exterior wall, and
2. Where roof slope is less than 4 in 12, seal lap of double underlay with continous layer of asphalt cement.

* Cement tabs of strip shingles, use self-sealing strip shingle, or use lock tab type shingle.

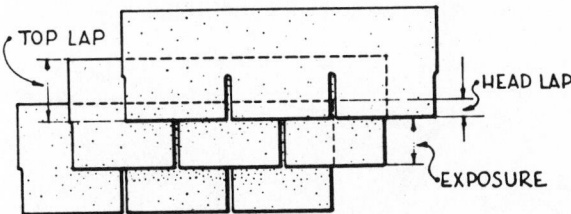

Fig. 1 TERMS relating to lapping of shingles

● Roofing nails should be corrosion resistant with deformed shanks made from 11 or 12 gauge wire with at least a ⅜-in. head. The nail should penetrate the roof deck at least 1 in. At least four and preferably six nails should be used in each strip. Special fasteners may be used if recommended.

TERMINOLOGY
Weight Approximate shipping weight per square.
Square of roofing Amount of roofing which, when applied at the usual exposure, will cover 100 sq ft of roof surface.
End or Side Lap Shortest distance in inches by which horizontally adjacent roofing elements overlap each other.
Headlap Distance from the lower edge of an overlapping shingle to the upper edge of the one in the second course below.
Exposure Distance between exposed edges of overlapping shingles.
Coverage Number of layers of shingle covering a given area, usually double or triple for strip shingles. Cutouts less than ¾ in. are ignored.
Saturated Felts Used for underlayment. No. 15 weighing approximately 15 lb is recommended.
Plastic Asphalt Cement Usually used as part of a flashing assembly where roof meets a wall, chimney or other vertical surface.
Lap Cement Usually used where one sheet overlaps another.
Quick-Setting Adhesive Cement Adhesive of either brush, trowel or gun consistency, is usually used for sealing tabs of strip shingles or for sealing laps of roll roofing.

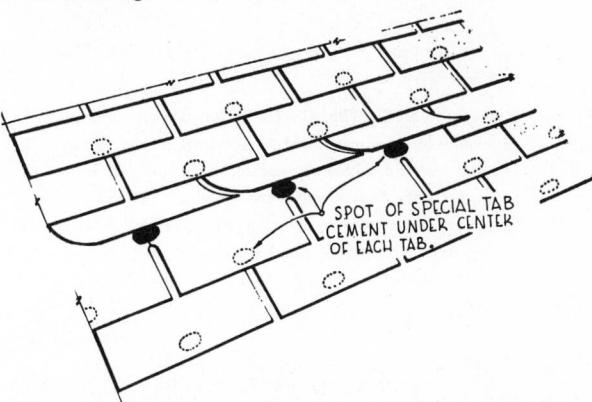

Fig. 2 CEMENTING of shingle tabs is used for low-slope roofs and for roofs in windy areas

GENERAL APPLICATION PROCEDURES

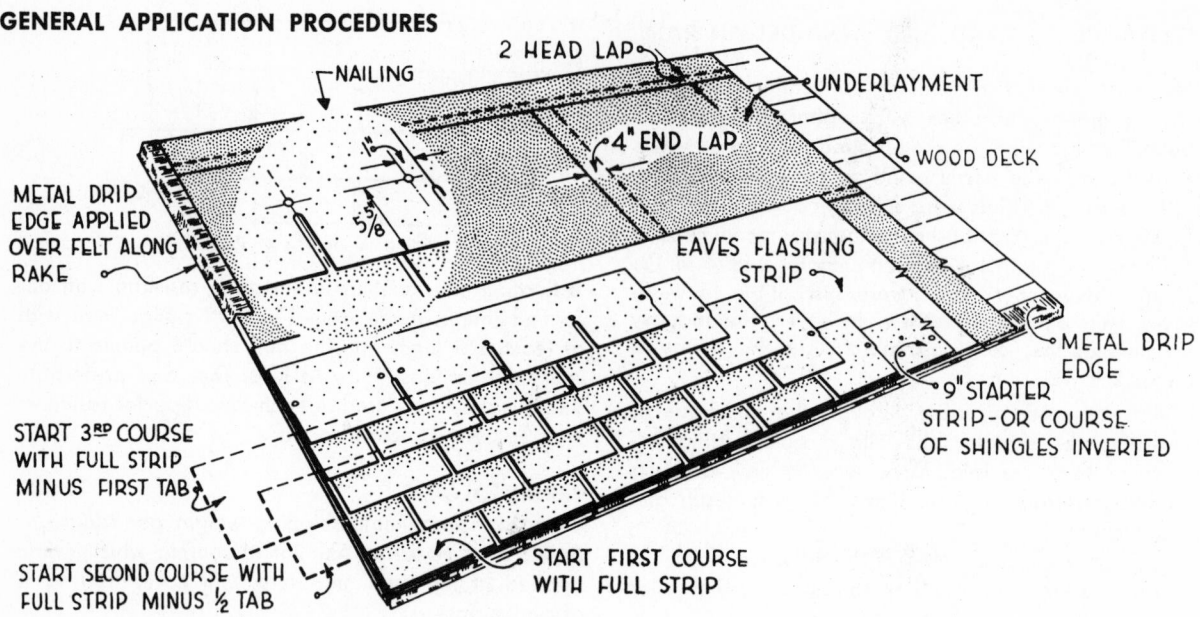

Fig. 3 PROCEDURE FOR APPLYING square-butt asphalt shingles

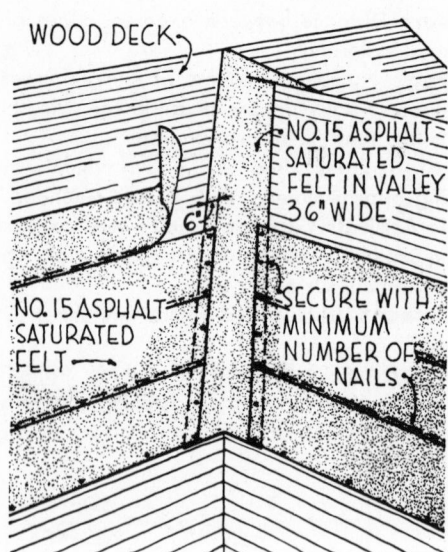

Fig. 4 DECK PREPARATION for a valley. Saturated felt underlayment is centered in the valley and secured with only enough nails to hold it in place until the shingles are applied. The courses of felt underlay are cut to overlap the valley strip by not less than 6 in. The eave flashing strip is then applied.

All drawings are from the publication, *Manufacture, Selection and Application of Asphalt Roofing and Siding Products*, August 1959, by J. L. Strahan, Technical Director, Asphalt Roofing Industry Bureau, New York City

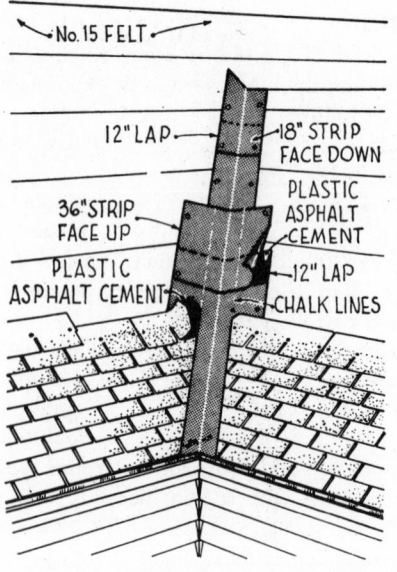

Fig. 5 VALLEY FLASHINGS are made from mineral surfaced asphalt roll roofing. An 18-in.-wide layer of mineral surfaced roll roofing is centered in the valley, surfaced side down, and the lower edge is cut to conform to and be flush with the eave flashing strip. When necessary to splice the material, the ends of the upper segments overlap the lower segments and are secured with plastic asphalt cement as shown. Only enough nails are used in rows 1 in. in from each edge to hold the strip smoothly in place. The upper corner of each end shingle is clipped as shown to prevent water from penetrating between the courses. The roofing material is cemented to the valley lining.

LOW SLOPE APPLICATION

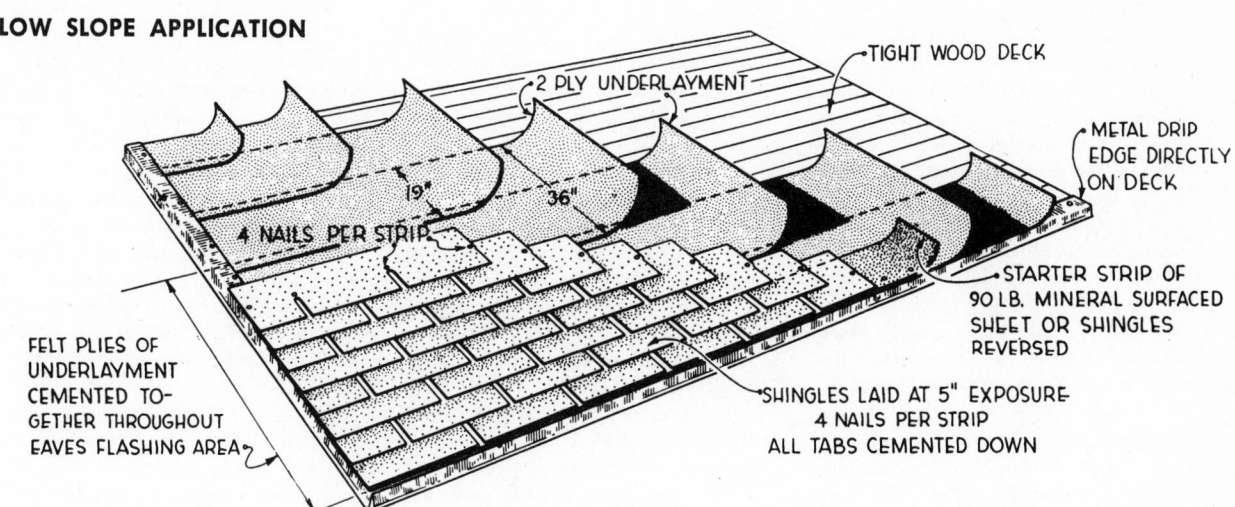

Fig. 6 SQUARE-TAB STRIP SHINGLES are recommended for use on decks having a slope lower than 4 in 12 but not less than 2 in 12 when special application methods are used to compensate for the slower water run-off resulting from the lower roof slope. These application methods involve: (a) double underlayment; (b) a special cemented eaves flashing strip; (c) use of quick-setting cement to fasten shingle tabs.

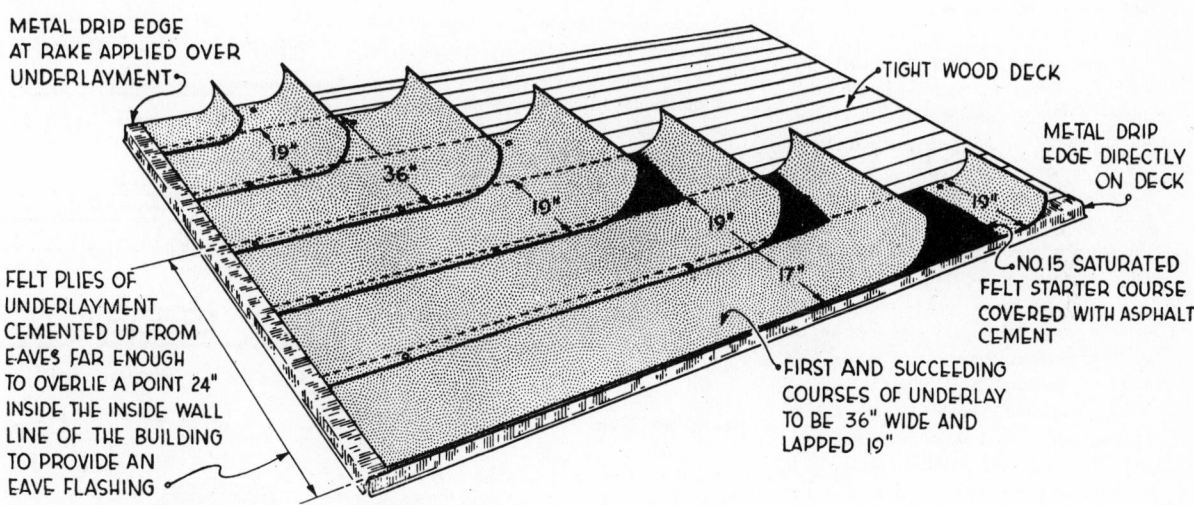

Fig. 7 FELT UNDERLAY application on a low slope deck.

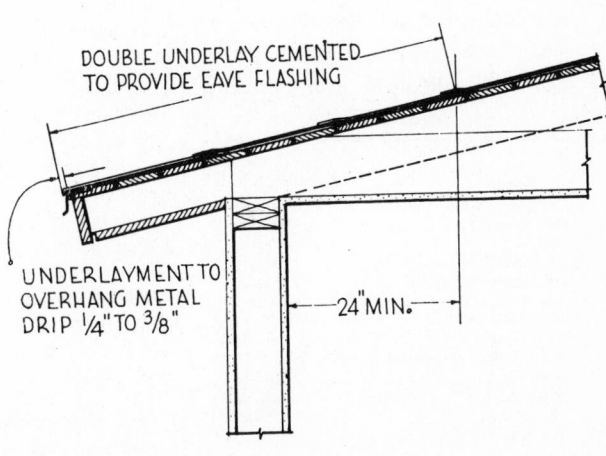

Fig. 8 EAVE FLASHING. The felt underlay that extends from the eave up the roof far enough to overlie a point 24 in. from the inside wall line of the building is treated as follows: A continuous layer of plastic asphalt cement is applied to the surface of the underlay starter course before the first full course is applied, and also to the 19-in. underlying portion of each succeeding course which lies within the eaves flashing area, before placing the next course. Fig. 6 shows how the shingles are applied over the underlayment. The exposure is 5 in. and four nails are required.

Copper

Data and illustrations from Modern Applications of Sheet Copper in Building Construction, Copper Development Association, Inc.

Copper is one of the oldest of roofing materials. Although more expensive initially than some other roofing materials, copper is extremely durable and, if properly installed, is practically maintenance-free. Weathering of copper produces a blue-green patina which protects the surface from further corrosion. Copper is highly ductile and readily conforms to the contours of domes and other curved and irregular shapes. Copper roofs, like those of other metals (except lead), are light in weight (see Table 1), and thus require less structural framing than is necessary with heavier roofing materials. The three standard types of metal roofing—batten seam, standing seam, and flat seam—are described on the following pages.

Copper is produced in two standard grades of hardness or temper: "soft" (roofing temper) and "cold-rolled" (cornice temper). In general, cold-rolled copper is recommended for all sheet metal work in building construction, except standing- and batten-seam roofing, and for caps and through-wall flashings. The thickness of copper sheet is denoted by the weight in ounces per square foot of sheet; for equivalent thicknesses in inches, see section on "Metals."

Common types of seams in sheet metal work are shown in Figs. 9–13. Of these, probably the commonest is the lock seam. All fastenings for sheet copper must be of copper or copper alloy. All copper sheets more than 12 in. wide should be secured in such a manner as to permit free movement. The standard technique for this purpose is the cleat, shown in Fig. 14.

Surfaces on which copper roofing is to be laid must be smooth and free of all small projections, such as nailheads, and must be absolutely dry. Wood sheathing, after being laid, should be allowed to weather for several days, protected from rain. Well-seasoned shiplap sheathing is recommended. For maximum durability, use kiln-dried, pressure-treated sheathing. Concrete decks should be smoothed by a wash of neat cement or by heavy coats of asphalt paint; in the latter case the asphalt must be covered by rosin-sized or similar building paper before copper is applied.

Table 1. Weights of roofing materials

Material	Approx. Weight of 100 Sq. Ft. Laid
Clay Shingle Tile	1000 – 2000 lbs.
Clay Spanish Tile	800 – 1500 "
Slate	600 – 1600 "
Hard Lead Sheet (about ⅛")	600 – 800 "
Felt and Gravel (Slag 100 lbs. less)	550 – 650 "
Asbestos Shingles	265 – 650 "
Asphalt Shingles	130 – 325 "
Wood Shingles	200 – 300 "
22 g. Galv. Iron (Corrugated)	175 "
16-oz. Copper	116 – 145 "
26 g. Galv. Iron (Standing Seam)	100 – 125 "
Tinned Steel	65 – 100 "
Aluminum	35 – 60 "

Some provision, such as wood battens or nailing inserts, must be made for receiving the nails that fasten the cleats. Various nailing concretes are available. Cinder concrete is injurious to copper and should be covered with a heavy coating of asphalt paint.

A layer of roofing felt covered by a layer of smooth (such as rosin-sized) building paper should be placed under all copper roofing, valleys, and gutter linings. The National Board of Fire Underwriters recommends an asphalt-saturated asbestos felt weighing about 14 lb per 100 sq ft.

Copper need not be painted for protection. It may be painted, if desired, for decoration or to prevent the staining of adjacent materials. In either case, or where the appearance of lead is desired, lead-coated copper may be used to advantage.

BATTEN SEAM

Batten (or ribbed) seam roofing (Fig. 15) may be used on slopes of 3 in. or more to the foot, although in localities where ice and snow collect on the roof it should not be used on a slope as low as 3 in 12. Battens should preferably be of cypress, well seasoned and straight, and impregnated against rot. Nail-, screw-, or boltheads must be countersunk. For the ultimate in durability, battens of heavy copper may be used. Battens are usually spaced 20 to 30 in. apart, the exact spacing being adjusted to fit the stock widths of copper sheets, which are available in multiples of 2 in. From the mechanical standpoint, narrow spacing (24 in. or less) is recommended. With the type of batten shown in Fig. 16, the width of the sheets will be 3 in. greater than the center-to-center spacing of the battens. Standard sheet length is 96 in.

STANDING SEAM

Standing seam roofing (Figs. 17–21) is the simplest and most economical form of metal roofing. It is applicable to the same building types and the same roof pitches as batten seam roofing. Standing seams are usually made 1 in. high, which results in a spacing between seams of 3¼ in. less than the sheet width. Spacing of seams is a matter of architectural scale, but for economy, stock sheet widths should be used. Recommended maximum sheet size is 20 by 96 in., resulting in a seam spacing of 16¾ in. For most conditions, 16-oz sheets should be used; for seam spacings greater than 20 in., 20-oz sheets. For economy, small houses may be roofed with 10-oz copper in 16-in. widths, formed into seams ¾ in. high, spaced 13¾ in. apart.

FLAT SEAM

Flat seam roofing is used mostly on flat roofs and decks but also on the curved

and warped surfaces of spires, domes, and cupolas, where the small size of the sheets is an advantage in fitting them to the curved surface. Sheets of 20-oz copper, not larger than 16 by 20 in., with ¾-in. seams flat-locked and soldered, are recommended. On domes and steeples where there is no possibility of water collecting on the roof, seams may be left unsoldered and filled with white lead. Sheets are held down by 2-in. copper cleats, two on each of two adjacent sides; the other two sides are held by the edges of the adjacent sheets already cleated. Since soldered flat seams, unlike batten or standing seams, do not provide for expansion, expansion joints must be installed at approximately 37-ft intervals in each direction, as illustrated in Fig. 22.

Flat seam roofing may also be used to line the bottom of planting areas in roof gardens or elsewhere. A detail is shown in Fig. 23.

OTHER METALS

The installation details shown here for copper roofing also apply, with minor variations, to other metals used for roofing, such as galvanized steel, terneplate, aluminum, stainless steel, and monel.

Fig. 9. Lap seam, soldered

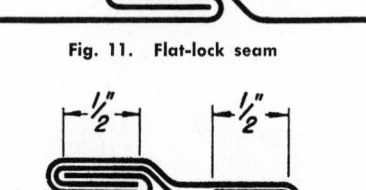

Fig. 10. Common lock, or hook, seam

Fig. 11. Flat-lock seam

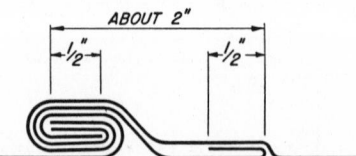

Fig. 12. Flat-lock seam with cleat

Fig. 13. Double-lock seam with cleat

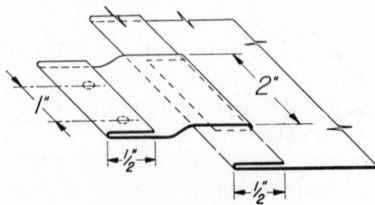

Fig. 14. Cleat

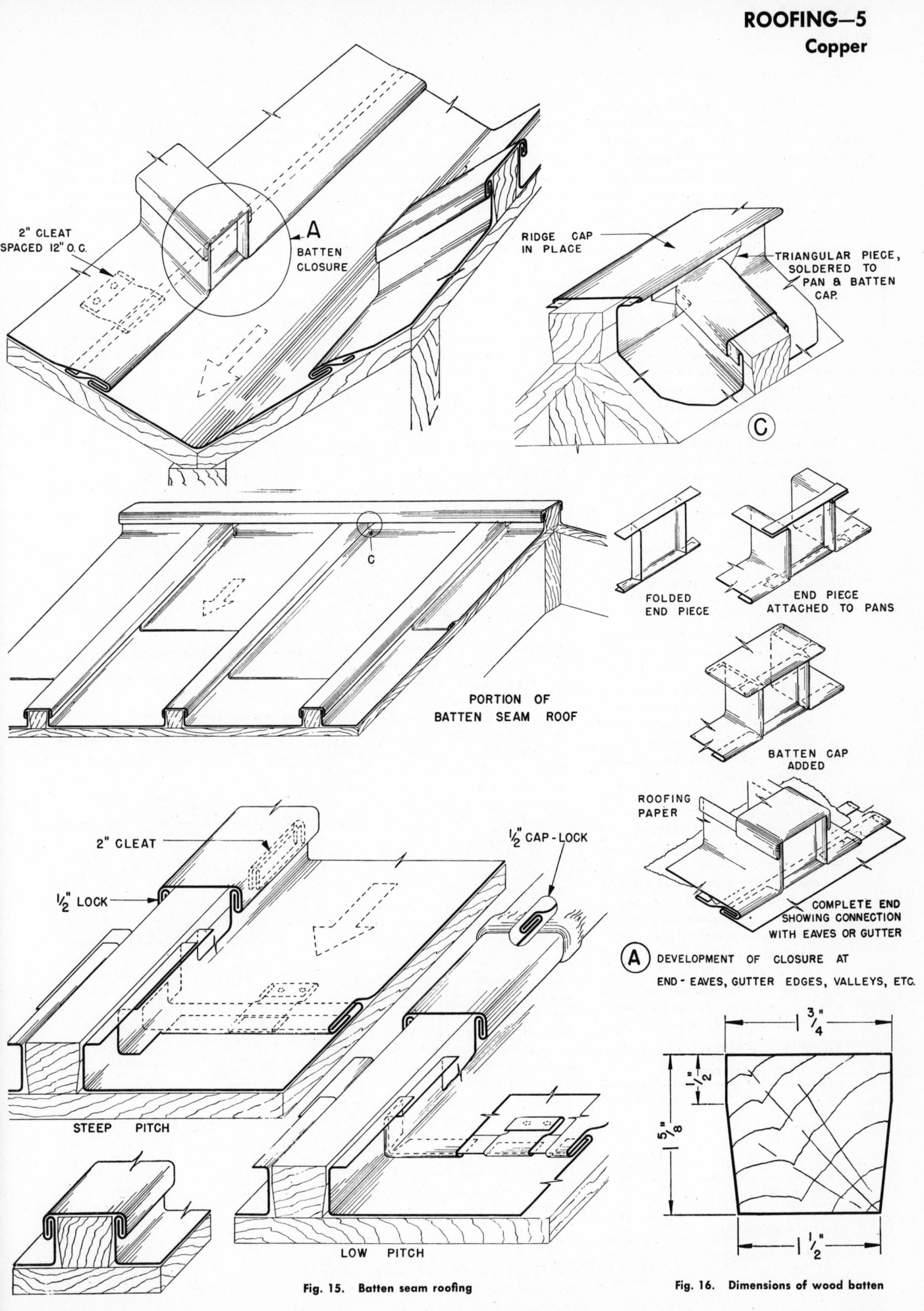

2" CLEAT
SPACED 12" O.C.

A
BATTEN CLOSURE

RIDGE CAP IN PLACE

TRIANGULAR PIECE, SOLDERED TO PAN & BATTEN CAP.

C

PORTION OF BATTEN SEAM ROOF

FOLDED END PIECE

END PIECE ATTACHED TO PANS

BATTEN CAP ADDED

ROOFING PAPER

COMPLETE END SHOWING CONNECTION WITH EAVES OR GUTTER

A DEVELOPMENT OF CLOSURE AT END - EAVES, GUTTER EDGES, VALLEYS, ETC.

2" CLEAT

1/2" LOCK

1/2" CAP - LOCK

STEEP PITCH

LOW PITCH

3/4"

1/2"

5/8"

1/2"

Fig. 15. Batten seam roofing

Fig. 16. Dimensions of wood batten

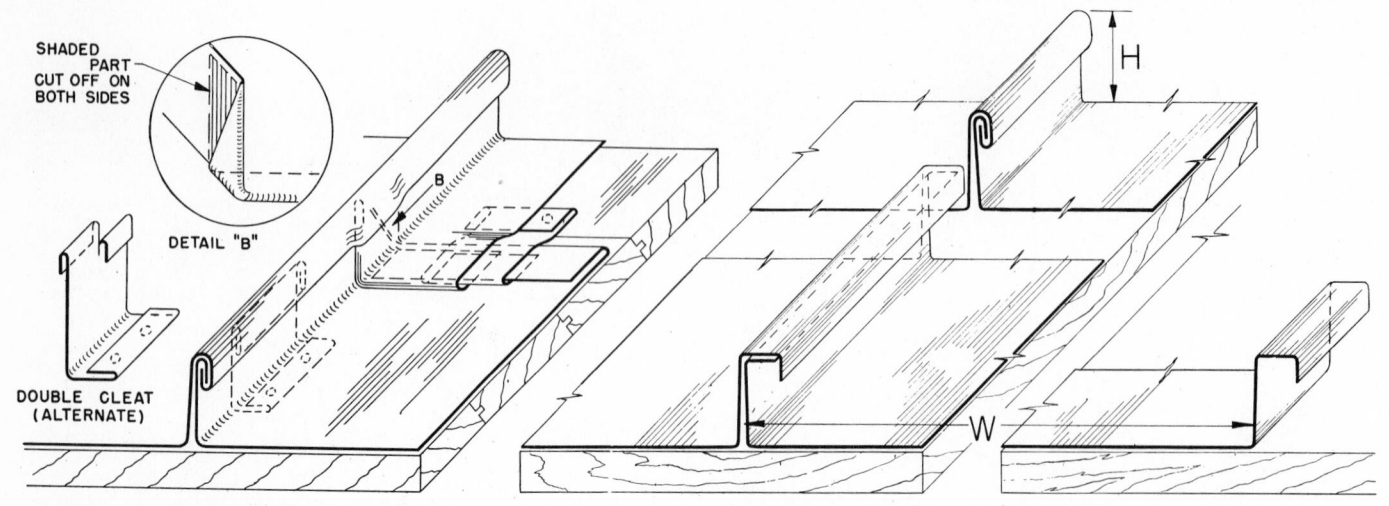

SHADED
PART
CUT OFF ON
BOTH SIDES

DETAIL "B"

B

H

DOUBLE CLEAT
(ALTERNATE)

W

Fig. 17. Standing seam roofing—formed in place

Fig. 18. Standing seam roofing—preformed pans

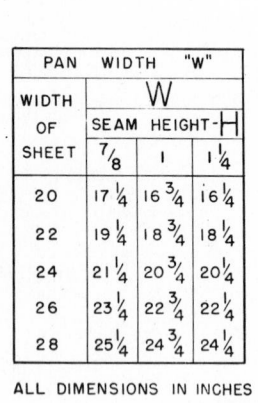

PAN	WIDTH	"W"	
WIDTH OF SHEET	SEAM HEIGHT—H		
	$7/8$	1	$1\frac{1}{4}$
20	$17\frac{1}{4}$	$16\frac{3}{4}$	$16\frac{1}{4}$
22	$19\frac{1}{4}$	$18\frac{3}{4}$	$18\frac{1}{4}$
24	$21\frac{1}{4}$	$20\frac{3}{4}$	$20\frac{1}{4}$
26	$23\frac{1}{4}$	$22\frac{3}{4}$	$22\frac{1}{4}$
28	$25\frac{1}{4}$	$24\frac{3}{4}$	$24\frac{1}{4}$

ALL DIMENSIONS IN INCHES

CAP FLASHING
3" MINIMUM

BASE FLASHING
8" MINIMUM

LOCK SEAM

2" CLEAT

STANDING SEAM

Fig. 19. Intersection of roof and wall

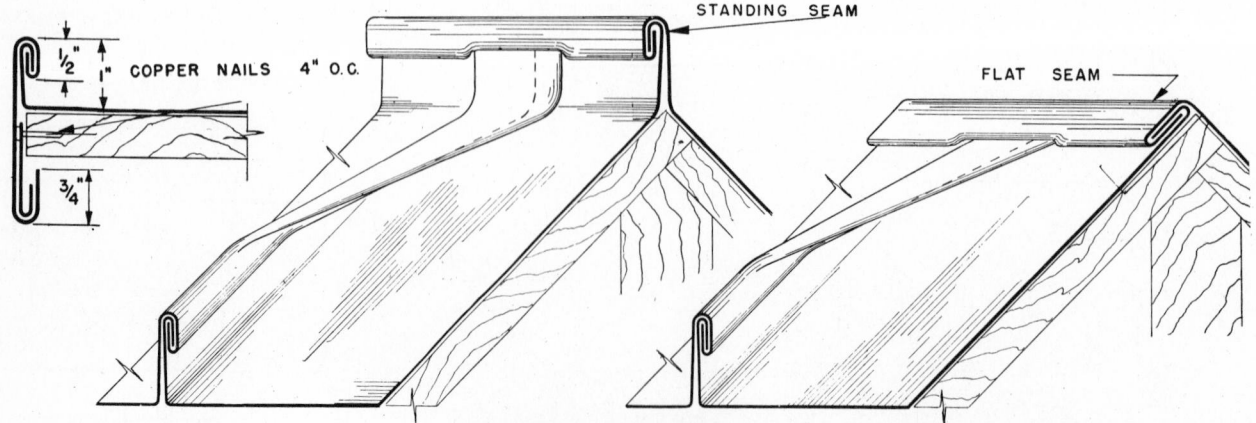

STANDING SEAM

$\frac{1}{2}$"

1" COPPER NAILS 4" O.C.

$\frac{3}{4}$"

FLAT SEAM

Fig. 20. Gable and ridge details

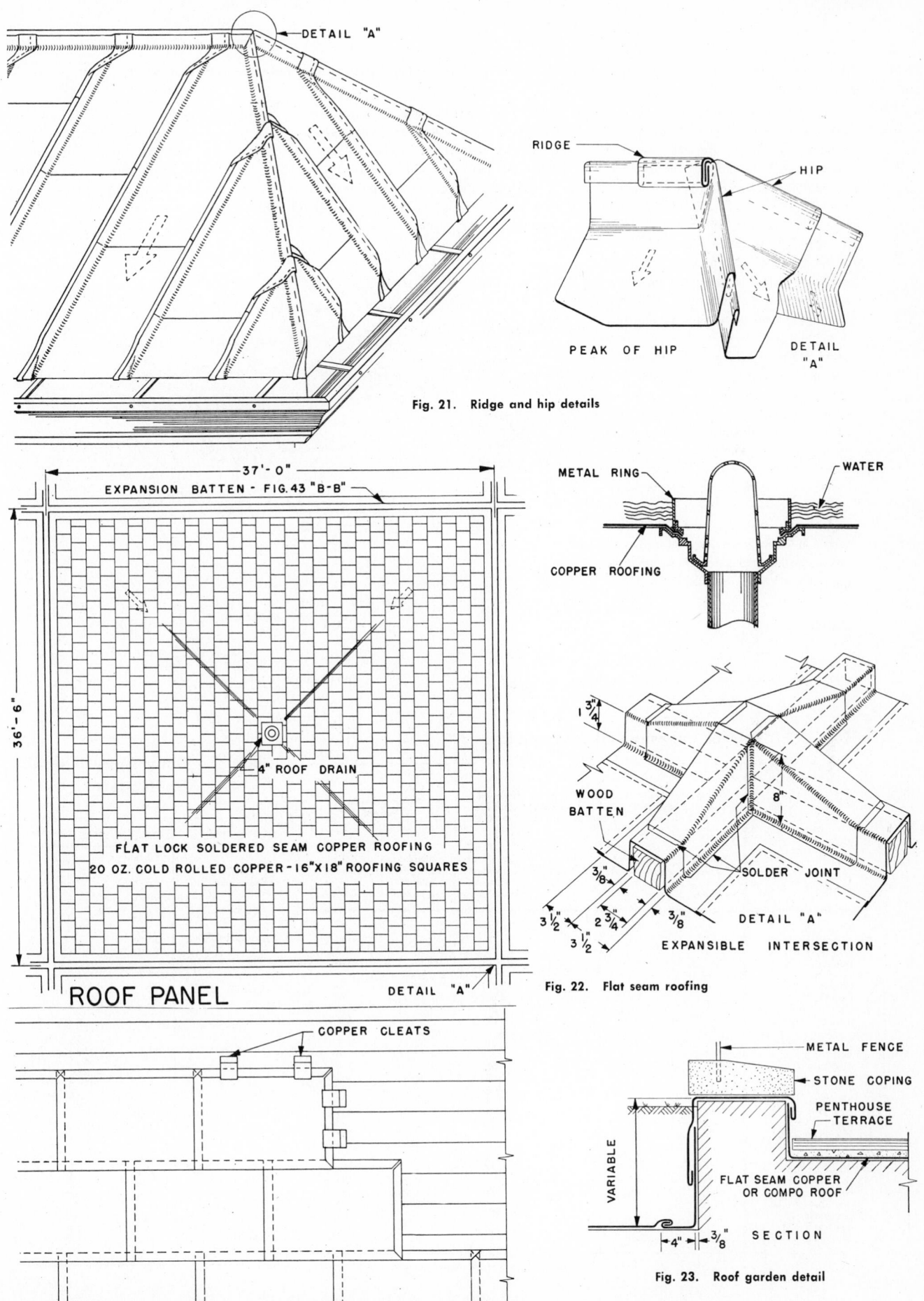

DETAIL "A"

RIDGE

HIP

PEAK OF HIP

DETAIL "A"

Fig. 21. Ridge and hip details

37'-0"

EXPANSION BATTEN - FIG. 43 "B-B"

36'-6"

4" ROOF DRAIN

FLAT LOCK SOLDERED SEAM COPPER ROOFING
20 OZ. COLD ROLLED COPPER-16"X18" ROOFING SQUARES

ROOF PANEL

DETAIL "A"

COPPER CLEATS

METAL RING

WATER

COPPER ROOFING

1 3/4"

WOOD BATTEN

8"

3/8"

3 1/2"

2 3/4"

3/8"

3 1/2"

SOLDER JOINT

DETAIL "A"

EXPANSIBLE INTERSECTION

Fig. 22. Flat seam roofing

METAL FENCE

STONE COPING

PENTHOUSE TERRACE

VARIABLE

FLAT SEAM COPPER OR COMPO ROOF

4"

3/8"

SECTION

Fig. 23. Roof garden detail

Data and illustrations from Modern Applications of Sheet Copper in Building Construction, Copper Development Association, Inc.

The design of a roof drainage system depends on the amount of water to be handled, which in turn depends on the intensity and duration of the rainfall in the particular locality. Table 1 shows the rainfall intensity for 23 cities for which the U.S. Weather Bureau has recorded this type of data since about 1896.

The type of structure for which the drainage system is being designed should be considered. In residential construction, for example, no great harm usually results if gutters overflow in a storm once in five years. On the other hand, the drainage system of a monumental building, with built-in gutters, parapets, or other details which would cause an overflow to have serious consequences, should be designed for maximum (most severe) conditions.

The roof area used in computations should be the actual area and not the horizontal projection or plan of the roof. Rain seldom falls vertically, and the maximum condition exists when the rain strikes perpendicularly to the plane of the roof, making the total roof area effective.

LEADERS

Leaders should be no smaller than 4 in. round or rectangular (except for small porch roofs) and should be spaced not more than 75 ft apart. They are best located near the corners of the building so that the gutter water will not have to flow far beyond a sharp turn. After the locations have been determined, the roof area tributary to each leader should be computed. By reference to Tables 1 and 2, the proper size can then be selected for each leader. The cross-sectional area of a leader should remain constant throughout its length, and long drops should have leader heads every 40 ft to prevent a vacuum.

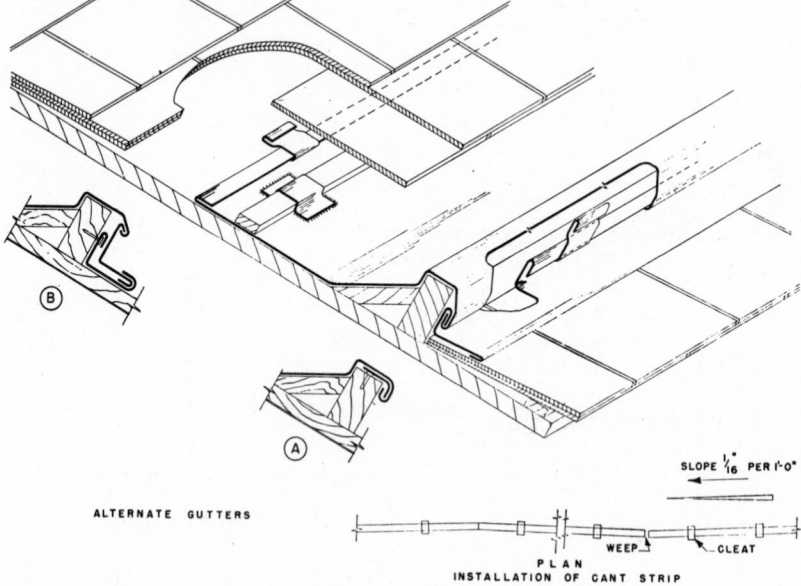

ALTERNATE GUTTERS

SLOPE 1/16" PER 1'-0"

WEEP CLEAT

PLAN
INSTALLATION OF CANT STRIP

Fig. 1. Pole gutter

Table 1. Rainfall intensity and drainage factors

	A Storms which should be exceeded only once in 5 years		B Storms which should be exceeded only once in 10 years		C Maximum record Storms	
	Intensity in Ins./Hr. lasting 5 minutes	Sq. Ft. of actual roof drained per Sq. In. of Leader area	Intensity in Ins./Hr. lasting 5 minutes	Sq. Ft. of actual roof drained per Sq. In. of Leader area	Intensity in Ins./Hr. lasting 5 minutes	Sq. Ft. of actual roof drained per Sq. In. of Leader area
Albany, N. Y.	6	200	7	175	7	175
Atlanta, Ga.	7	175	7	175	11	110
Boston, Mass.	5	240	6	200	7	175
Buffalo, N. Y.	5	240	5	240	10	120
Chicago, Ill.	6	200	7	175	8	150
Detroit, Mich.	6	200	6	200	10	120
Duluth, Minn.	5	240	6	200	7	175
Kansas City, Mo.	7	175	8	150	10	120
Knoxville, Tenn.	5	240	6	200	7	175
Louisville, Ky.	6	200	7	175	9	130
Memphis, Tenn.	5	240	6	200	9	130
Montgomery, Ala.	7	175	7	175	8	150
New Orleans, La.	7	175	7	175	9	130
New York City, N. Y.	6	200	8	150	9	130
Norfolk, Va.	6	200	7	175	8	150
Philadelphia, Pa.	6	200	7	175	8	150
Pittsburgh, Pa.	6	200	6	200	9	130
St. Louis, Mo.	6	200	8	150	8	150
St. Paul, Minn.	6	200	6	200	8	150
San Francisco, Cal.	2	600	2	600	4	300
Savannah, Ga.	6	200	7	175	9	130
Seattle, Wash.	3*	400	3*	400	3.5*	370
Washington, D. C.	6	200	7	175	10	120

* From local records

Table 2. Dimensions of standard leaders

Type	Area in Sq. In.	Nominal Leader Sizes
Plain Round	7.07	3″
	12.57	4″
	19.63	5″
	28.27	6″
Corrugated Round	5.94	3″
	11.04	4″
	17.72	5″
	25.97	6″
Polygon Octagonal	6.36	3″
	11.30	4″
	17.65	5″
	25.40	6″
Square Corrugated	3.80	1¾″ x 2¼″ (2″)
	7.73	2⅜″ x 3¼″ (3″)
	11.70	2¾″ x 4¼″ (4″)
	18.75	3¾″ x 5″ (5″)
Plain Rectangular	3.94	1¾″ x 2¼″
	6.00	2″ x 3″
	8.00	2″ x 4″
	12.00	3″ x 4″
	20.00	4″ x 5″
	24.00	4″ x 6″
S.P.S. Pipe	7.38	3″
	12.72	4″
	20.00	5″
	28.88	6″
Cast Iron Pipe	7.07	3″
	12.57	4″
	19.64	5″
	28.27	6″

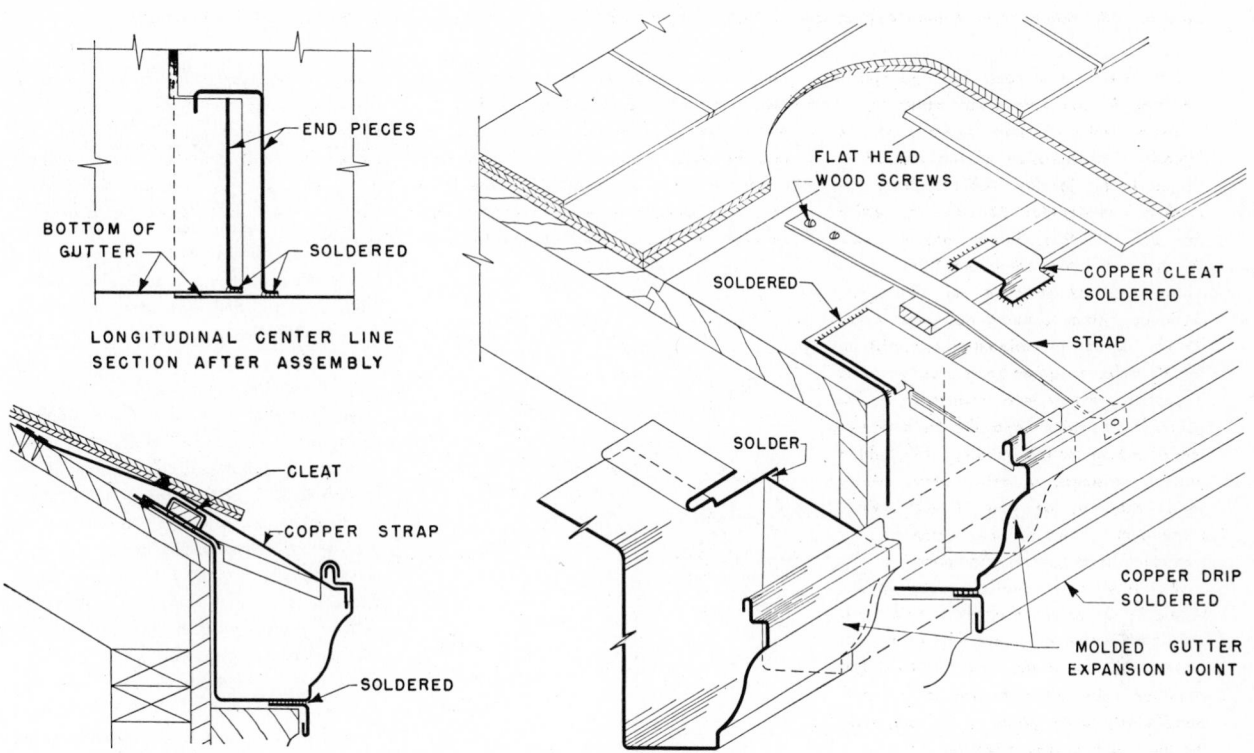

Fig. 2. Molded gutter

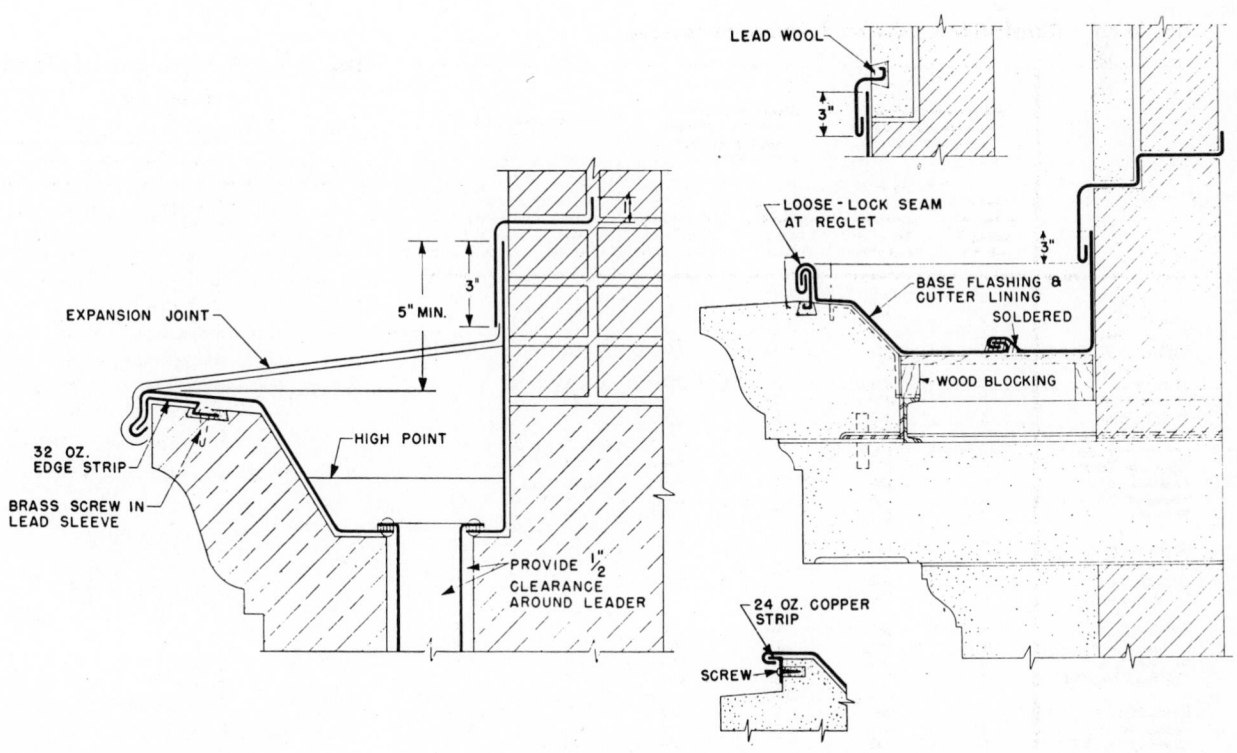

Fig. 3. Stone cornice and built-in gutter

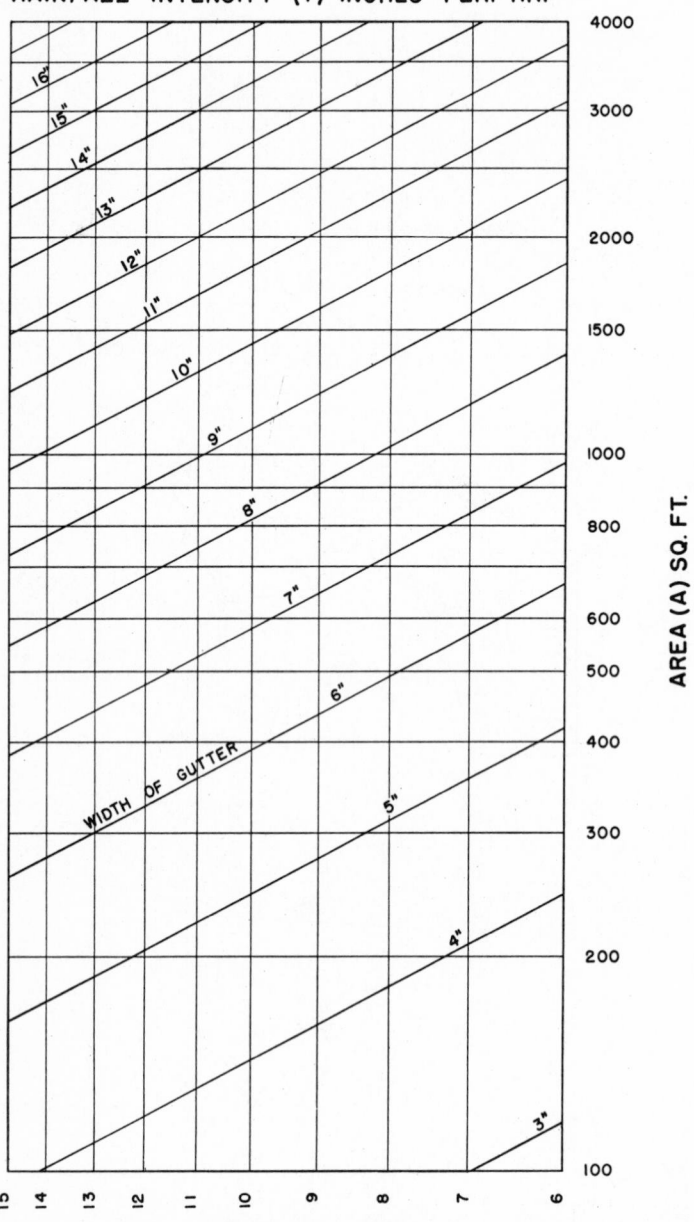

RAINFALL INTENSITY (I) INCHES PER. HR.

Fig. 4.   Width of semicircular gutters

Table 3.   Maximum distances between leaders of built-in copper gutters (with expansion joints midway between)

Width of Gutter Bottom in Inches	Side Angles of 45° and 60°				Side Angles of 60° and 90°			
	Weight of Sheet				Weight of Sheet			
	16 oz.	20 oz.	24 oz.	32 oz.	16 oz.	20 oz.	24 oz.	32 oz.
	Distance Between Downspouts in Feet							
8	30	35	45	—	35	45	55	—
12	20	30	40	65	25	35	45	80
16	—	25	30	55	—	30	40	70
20	—	20	25	50	—	25	35	60
24	—	—	25	45	—	—	30	55

GUTTERS

The size of gutters depends on the slope of the roof, the proportions of the gutter, and the number, size, and spacing of the outlets. The depth of a gutter should be not less than half nor more than three-fourths of its width; gutter sizes are therefore usually expressed in width only. Half-round gutters are economical and highly efficient; they are commonly used as eaves troughs and less often as built-in gutters. Other common types of gutter are the pole gutter (Fig. 1), molded gutter (Fig. 2), and the built-in gutter (Fig. 3).

In residential work, a minimum slope of $\frac{1}{16}$ in. per ft is required. Gutter size is determined as follows: if the spacing of the leaders is 20 ft or less, the gutter size can be the same as the leader size (but not less than 4 in.); if the spacing of the leaders is more than 20 ft, add 1 in. to the leader diameter for every additional 30 ft on peaked roofs or 40 ft on flat roofs. In practice, 4-in. gutters are rarely used because they are difficult to solder and thus increase the labor cost.

For built-in gutters in large buildings the following formulas, and Figs. 4 and 6 which were derived from them, are recommended. These formulas were developed empirically from tests conducted by the National Bureau of Standards in Washington, D.C.

For semicircular gutters:
$$W = 1.3 \, Q^{2/5}$$

For rectangular gutters:
$$W = 0.481 \, m^{-4/7} \, I^{3/28} \, Q^{5/14}$$

in which,

W = width of gutter, ft
m = depth/width
I = length of gutter, ft
Q = total gutter inflow, cu ft per sec

These formulas are for level gutters. Where the slope exceeds 2 per cent, the gutter should be narrowed and deepened.

Gutter cross sections must be such as to prevent an expansive thrust of ice from splitting the seams. The top should be

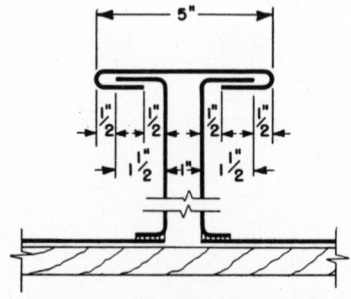

Fig. 5.   Expansion joint

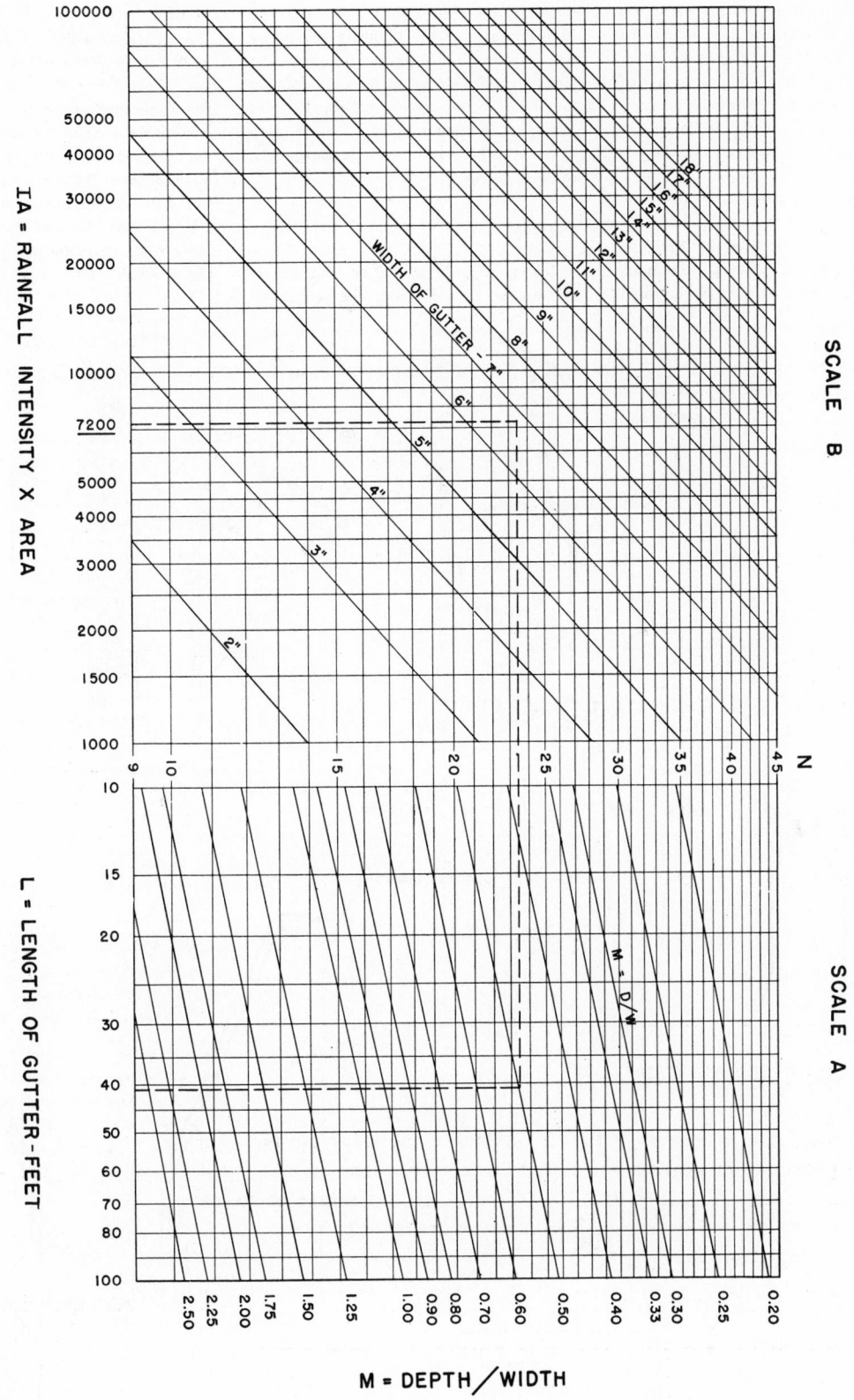

Fig. 6.   Width of rectangular gutters

Enter at bottom of Chart A at proper value for L. Follow vertical line to intersection with oblique line for proper value of M. Proceed left into Chart B to intersection with vertical line for proper value of IA. Nearest oblique line above intersection gives the width of the gutter.

wider than the bottom, and the depth less than the bottom width. A slope of 60 deg from the horizontal is recommended for at least one side of the gutter. Gutters and the linings of built-in gutters must be unrestrained except at the outlet. Maximum distances between outlets are shown in Table 3.

EXPANSION

Gutters of all types must be designed with provision for longitudinal expansion. The standard expansion joint is illustrated in principle in Fig. 5. In practice it necessarily varies with the shape of the gutter and may be fairly complex. The expansion joint is usually placed at the high point of the slope of the gutter, midway between outlets. It is often treated as the meeting of the closed ends of two separate gutters, as shown in Fig. 2.

OUTLETS

Outlets (Fig. 7) should be elliptical or rectangular in plan, with the longer dimension in the direction of gutter flow. The longer dimension should be the same as the gutter width and the shorter dimension about two-thirds of the gutter width. For larger gutters the width of the outlet may be the same as the width of the gutter and the length of the outlet about half again as long. The outlet should be tapered to the size of the leader within a length of 1½ to 2 times the diameter of the leader, but not less than the maximum dimension of the outlet.

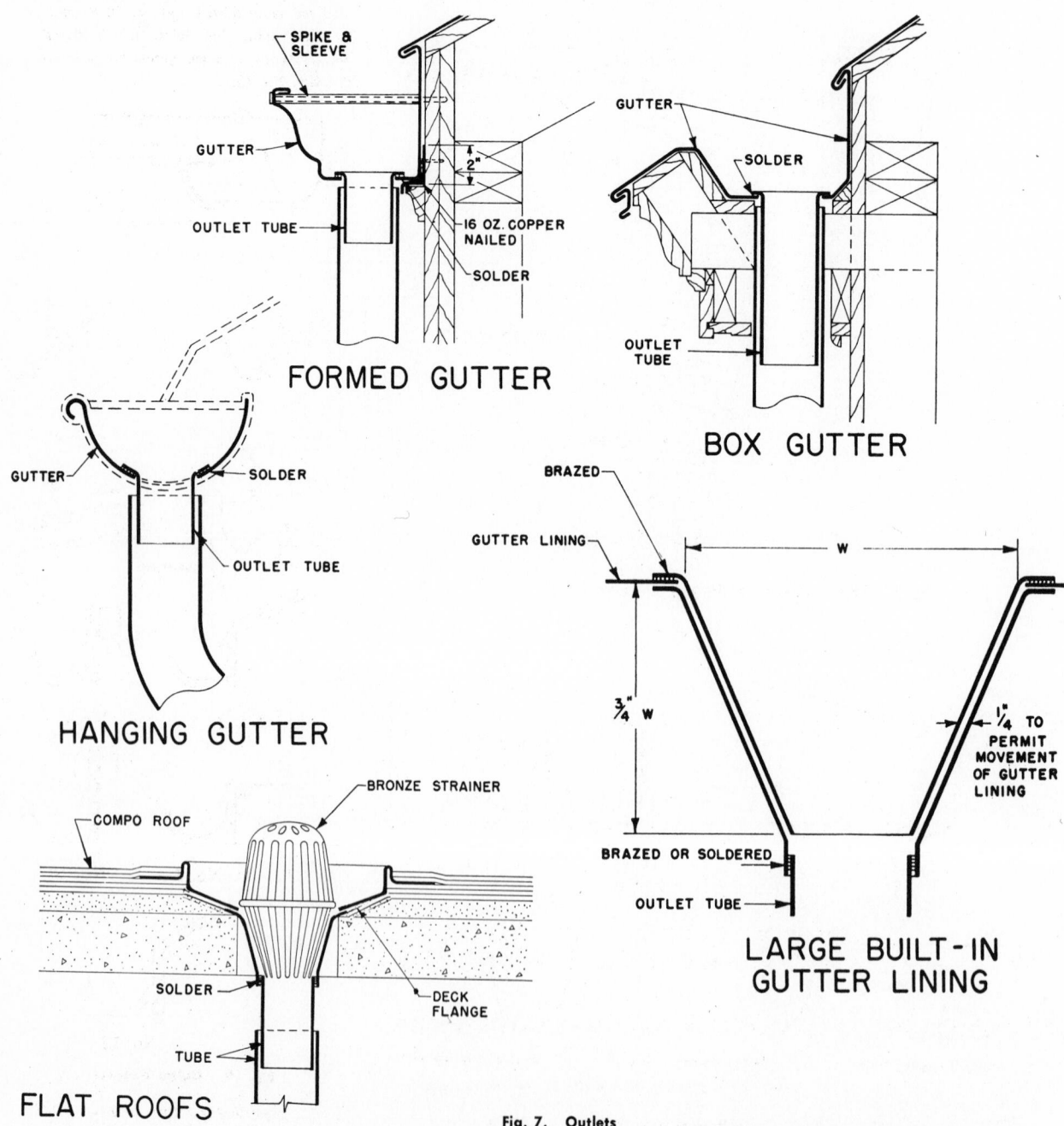

Fig. 7. Outlets

The outlet should be soldered to the gutter but not to the leader; it should extend about 6 in. into the leader. There should be enough space between the outlet and the leader to prevent the formation of a vacuum.

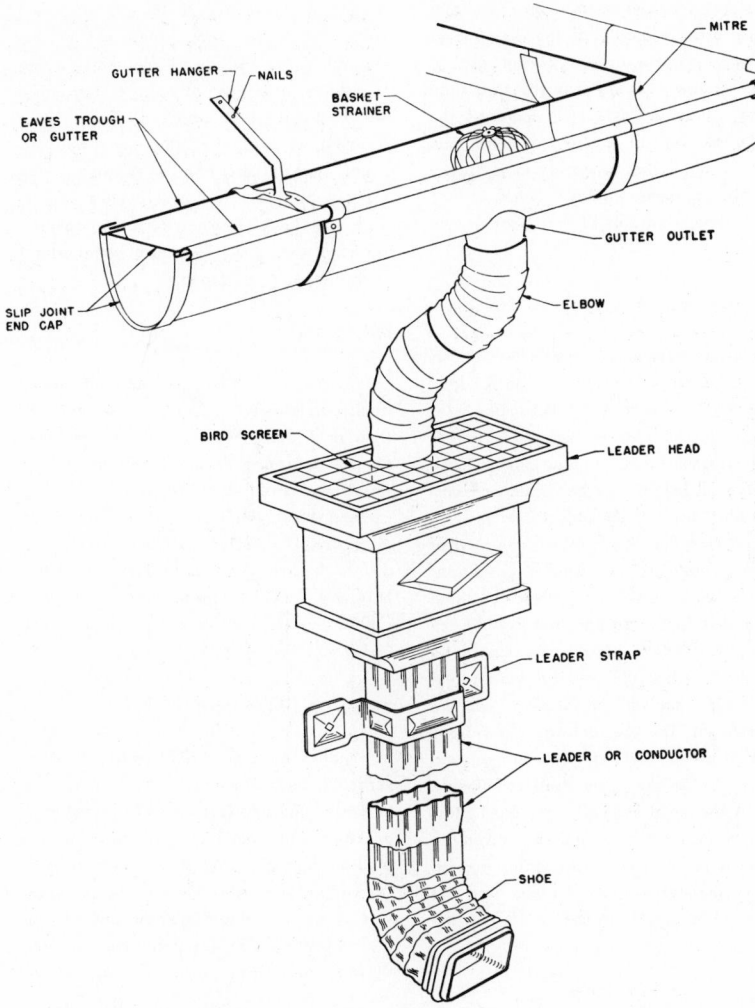

Fig. 8. Factory-made roof drainage products

FACTORY-MADE ROOFING PRODUCTS

In Fig. 8 are shown the various parts of gutters, leaders, and accessories made and stocked by manufacturers and distributors throughout the country. Molded gutters, including the half-round type, are made in several designs, two of which are shown in Fig. 9. The most commonly used is the 16-oz single-bead half-round eaves trough. Standard length is 10 ft, available with either lap-joint or slip-joint ends. Slip joints provide for expansion and contraction in long runs of gutter; they are used for every third length, or 30 ft apart; the intervening lap joints are soldered. Several types of stock gutter hangers are shown in Fig. 10.

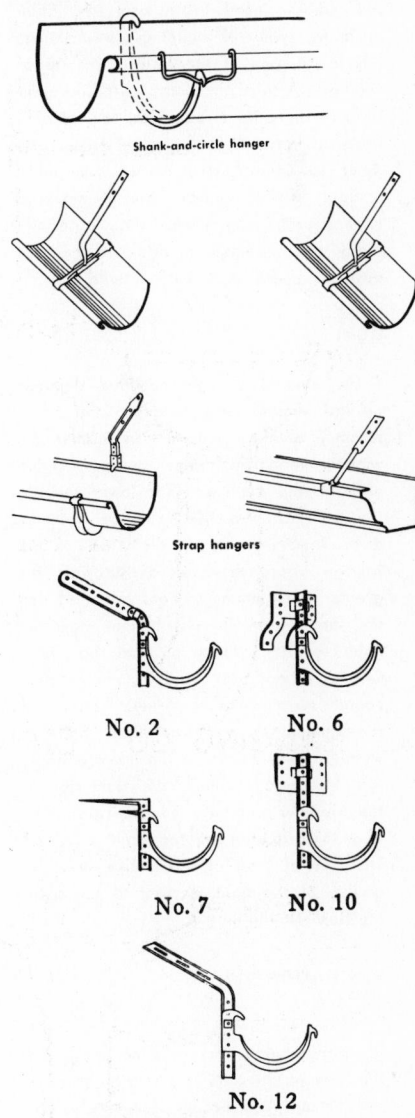

Fig. 10. Gutter hangers

Number 12 has bronze circle for double-bead gutters; other circles are for single-bead gutters.

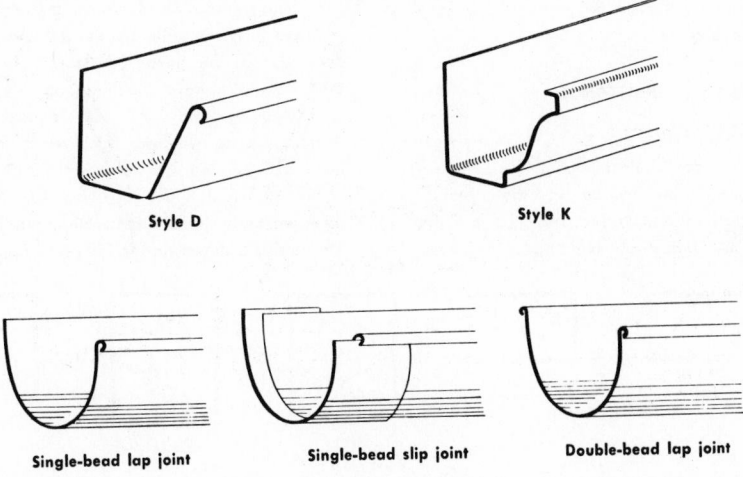

Style D

Style K

Single-bead lap joint

Single-bead slip joint

Double-bead lap joint

Half-round type

Fig. 9. Molded gutters

WINDOWS—1
General

By JOHN HANCOCK CALLENDER, *Professor of Architecture, Pratt Institute*

Traditionally, the window was considered an "opening" in the wall, and many building codes and building professionals still use that term. With the increasing use of glass, however, windows now often form the entire wall, and thus the traditional distinction between wall and window is no longer valid. Most metal window manufacturers now offer complete curtain wall systems (see "Curtain Walls").

Windows, or window walls, perform several distinct functions. The most important of these is normally the admission of *light,* both from a practical standpoint and for its psychological and aesthetic effect on the interior space. A second function of windows is *ventilation.* Although the rapid increase in the use of air conditioning has reduced the need for natural ventilation in many types of buildings, nevertheless this is still one of the major purposes of windows. A third function of windows is to permit *vision,* in or out. This, too, is both practical and psychological. Fourth, windows sometimes serve as an *emergency escape.* Finally, windows are *elements of architectural composition* and, especially today, are extremely important in the total aesthetic effect created by a building.

LIGHT

The amount of light admitted depends on the number, size, location, and transparency of the windows. The higher the window head, the deeper the penetration of light into the room. The lower the sill, the less shadow on the floor near the window. The more nearly the area of the window approaches that of the wall, the greater the amount of light admitted and the more even its distribution. Reflected light from the ground or from roof decks will enter adjacent windows; if the horizontal surfaces have a high reflectivity, the amount of reflected light admitted through the windows, at an upward angle, will be considerable. The orientation of the windows will have an important effect upon the quality of the light admitted. The type of glass used will also affect the quality of the light, as well as the quantity (see "Daylighting").

VENTILATION

Where windows are used for ventilation, the requirements vary with the season and the climate. In cold weather the principal requirement is freedom from drafts. This is usually achieved by the use of a window (such as the hopper type) that will deflect the entering air upward. In hot dry summer weather, on the other hand, it is often desirable to admit as much breeze as possible. Here windows with 100 per cent opening are preferable. If the direction of the wind can be predicted, the use of larger windows on the leeward side than on the windward side will increase the velocity of the air passing through the room. In hot rainy climates, it is highly desirable to have windows (such as the awning type) that can be left open in the rain.

VISION

The vision function of glass in windows works both ways, permitting one to look out as well as to look in. For many uses "looking out" has disadvantages in that it may be distracting or unpleasant. In such cases the sill height may be raised or translucent glass used. If the object is to prevent someone from looking in, the same devices may be employed or curtains or shades may be used to ensure privacy. Where looking out is a pleasure that can be indulged, large clear glass areas should be used with as few divisions as possible located where they will not interfere with the lines of sight. The use of large glass areas not only permits the view to be enjoyed but also makes the room itself seem more spacious. In the design of large fixed glass areas, consideration should be given to the problems of solar heat gain, accessibility of the outside for cleaning, and the danger of injury from failure to see the glass.

ESCAPE

Windows used for emergency escape must be easy to open, have reasonably low sills, and openings large enough to go through without difficulty. Screens and storm sash must be easily and quickly removable.

WEATHER RESISTANCE

Windows must be sufficiently weatherproof for their intended use. There is a considerable range in the degree of weathertightness that may be acceptable; some industrial buildings, for example, may tolerate a degree of air (or even water) infiltration that would not be acceptable in a residence. Weatherstripping is usually necessary if a high degree of weathertightness is required. Some types of windows are inherently more weatherproof than others; the double-hung window is probably the best in this respect and the jalousie the worst; out-opening windows are generally more weathertight than in-opening windows.

MATERIALS

Windows are commonly made of wood, steel, and aluminum; less often of stainless steel or bronze. Wood windows are inexpensive and provide good insulation, but shrink and swell with changes in moisture content. Steel windows have strength and dimensional stability. Aluminum windows do not require painting. All metal windows, however, provide poor insulation and are subject to condensation on their inner surfaces.

TYPES OF OPERATION

Window vents may slide horizontally or vertically (double-hung); they may be hinged at the side (casement), top (awning), or bottom (hopper); or they may be pivoted horizontally (industrial) or vertically. Combinations of two or even three of these vent types in a single window are not uncommon. Shown on this page are standard symbols used on elevation drawings to indicate the type of vent operation.

Out-opening windows must be screened on the inside—an arrangement that puts the screen where it can easily be kept clean, but necessitates the use of through- or under-screen operators. Pivoted windows are almost impossible to screen. In-opening windows interfere with shades and draperies and may be hazardous to people in the room. Windows opening out on a terrace or walkway are also a hazard. Some types of windows, such as double-hung and jalousie, are difficult to clean.

The principal types of windows, with notes on their characteristics and appropriate uses, are shown on the following pages.

 (a)   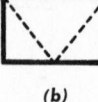 (b)    (c)    (d)    (e)

Fig. 1. Standard symbols for ventilator operation (windows viewed from the outside)

(a) Hinged at top open out; (b) Hinged at bottom open in; (c) Hinged at left; (d) Hinged at right; (e) Pivoted—vertically or horizontally.

SPECIAL WINDOW TYPES

For use in prisons and mental institutions, special windows have been developed which offer differing degrees of detention and appearance of detention. Many types are available in steel and a few in reinforced aluminum. A similar type of window, called a "security window," is used in warehouses and many other types of buildings to prevent forcible entry.

For use in air-conditioned buildings, a special type of vertically pivoted window has been developed which can be opened only by key for cleaning.

"Classroom windows" consist of a large fixed glass area with two or more small awning or hopper vents at the bottom. They are intended for use in one-story schools where ventilation is supplied mechanically. Special "escape windows" have also been developed for use in this type of school.

"Fire windows" required by building codes and insurance inspection agencies are usually designed to meet the requirements of the National Fire Protection Association Standards (NFPA No. 80) and must bear the seal of the Underwriter's Laboratory Inc. They are permitted in walls of Class E (moderate) and Class F (light) exposure and may be of hollow metal or solid sections. Glass areas are limited to 720 sq in. and must not exceed 54 in. in height and 48 in. in width for Class E; and are limited to 2,916 sq in. and must not exceed 54 in. in height or width for Class F. Sash must be glazed with ¼-in. fire-resistant wire glass. Reference should be made to the standard for more detailed requirements regarding the design and installation of window units.

Because of their large scale, "church windows" have traditionally required special treatment, and several firms specialize in this and other types of custom work. These specialists make to order windows of any material.

ACCESSORIES

The following accessories are generally available from window manufacturers: anchors, clips, fins, subframes, metal sills, mullions, mullion covers, casings and other trim, window cleaning anchors, glazing beads, special hardware for pole or chain operation, mechanical operators (manual or power), screens, and storm sash.

Wood windows are usually sold glazed and are installed by carpenters. Metal windows are usually unglazed and are installed by the manufacturer or a special subcontractor.

SHADES AND SHADING DEVICES

Window frames should provide, when necessary, means for attaching roller-type shades. In designing interior window surrounds, attachments and clearances for other shading devices such as venetian blinds, vertical blinds, or curtains and draperies should be considered. The orientation of the window may necessitate exterior shading, particularly if air conditioning is contemplated. The more nearly the window faces the west the more significant and the more difficult shading becomes. Shading-type insect screening, roof overhangs, horizontal or vertical louvers, and open lattice-like screens of wood, metal, or masonry have been used effectively when properly designed for the particular application. Heat-absorbing or tinted glass may also be used to reduce the solar heat load (see "Glass").

REFERENCES

The following publications of the Building Research Institute contain much useful information: *Windows and Glass in the Exterior of Buildings,* (1957), *Workshop on Windows,* (1959), *Selection of Windows,* Technical Reprint 5.

WINDOW TYPES

Double-hung

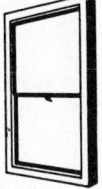

Available in wood, steel, aluminum, and kalamein, in a wide variety of weights and sizes. Single-hung, triple-hung, and combination with hopper vent also available. Counterweights or spring balances used for larger sizes, spiral balances for smaller. Maximum opening 50 per cent. Hard to clean. Some residential types have sash removable for cleaning. Double-hung windows are used for all types of buildings except industrial.

Wood, steel, aluminum, bronze. Made in a variety of weights for uses varying from residential to monumental. Maximum opening 100 per cent. Screens and storm sash must be on inside and under-screen operators provided. Maximum width of ventilator about 2 ft. Extension hinges permit cleaning of outside surface. Used mostly in residential buildings.

Casement

Reversible

Available in wood and steel. Similar to double-hung in appearance, but may be tilted for better control of ventilation, or reversed for cleaning. Maximum opening 50 per cent. Used for residential and industrial buildings.

Wood, steel, aluminum. Construction similar to residential casements or industrial windows. Used wherever inexpensive utilitarian windows are required.

Basement and utility

Austral

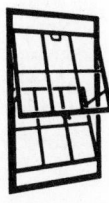

Wood and steel. When closed, similar to double-hung in appearance. Upper and lower sash counterbalanced on arms pivoted to frame; upper and lower sash operate simultaneously. Maximum opening 50 per cent. Good ventilation. Difficult to screen, shade or curtain. Used in schools, hospitals and other institutional buildings.

Wood, aluminum. Maximum opening 50 per cent. Sash usually removable for cleaning. Large sash sizes are practical. Used mostly in residential buildings.

Horizontally sliding

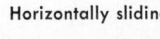
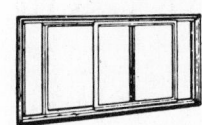

Projected

Available in steel and aluminum. Ventilators operate by either projecting out at bottom as top slides down or in at top as bottom slides up ("hopper vent"). Can be left open in rain. Inside screens required with through-screen operators. Used for commercial, institutional, and public buildings.

Available in steel and aluminum. Inexpensive windows for use in industrial and utilitarian buildings. Often used continuously horizontally and vertically to form entire walls. Mechanical operators available. Screens impractical.

Horizontally pivoted

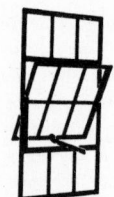

Combination

Steel, aluminum. Combination of casement and projected ventilators. Used for commercial, institutional, and public buildings.

Steel, aluminum. Similar to above in construction and use, but the projected ventilators give better control of ventilation, permit screening, and may be left open in the rain. Mechanical operators are available.

Commercial projected

Awning

Wood, steel, aluminum. Ventilators operate in unison by manual control or by concealed mechanical operators. Maximum opening 100 per cent. Can be left open in rain. Heavy type in steel or aluminum used for industrial and institutional buildings. Lighter type in wood or aluminum used for residential buildings. Awning windows with shallow ventilators are sometimes called "louver windows." Types with ventilators 6 in. or less in height may be used for light security or detention purposes.

Steel, aluminum. Made of the same "industrial" sections used for the previous two types, but are better made and more weathertight. Often used in office portions of industrial buildings and in many types of commercial and institutional buildings.

Architectural projected

Steel only. Heavy construction top-hung windows for mechanical operation only. Available in heights of 3, 4, 5, and 6 ft and lengths in multiples of 2 ft. Typically used in monitors of industrial buildings, hence, often called "monitor windows."

Continuous

Jalousie

Aluminum only. A louver window in which the ventilators are strips of glass 3 or 4 in. high which are held in metal frames only at the sides. Louvers are operated simultaneously by crank and mechanical operator concealed in frame. Maximum opening 100 per cent. Screens and storm sash are installed on inside. Louvers when open do not project beyond building line. Used mostly on residential buildings.

Steel. For use in commercial and other types of buildings to prevent forcible entry. Muntins form continuous grille in window frame; ventilator and frame superimposed on inner surface of grille. Ventilators usually project in. For greater protection, a type is available having maximum grille openings of 88 sq in.

Security

Vertically pivoted

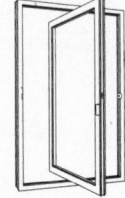

Aluminum, stainless steel. Opens by key for cleaning only, not for ventilation. Large sizes are practical. For use in high-class air-conditioned commercial or public buildings.

Steel. Similar to security windows except that the purpose is to prevent forcible exit from the building; often called "guard windows." Made of heavy steel sections. For use in prisons and psychiatric hospitals.

Detention

Table 1. Characteristics of various types of windows

From "Selection of Windows," Technical Reprint No. 5, Building Research Institute.

X indicates characteristics	double hung	double hung (reversed)	casement (out)	casement (in)	awning, canopy	pivoted (vertical)	pivoted (horizontal)	top hinged (out)	bottom hinged (in)	fixed sash	jalousie	monitor, continuous	projected	horizontal sliding
ADVANTAGES														
not apt to sag	x	x			x	x	x	x	x	x		x		x
screen & storm sash easy to install	x	x		x	x			x						x
provides 100% vent opening			x	x	x	x	x	x	x		x	x		
easy to wash with proper hardware		x		x		x	x		x					
will deflect drafts			x	x	x	x	x		x		x	x		
offers rain protection while partly open					x		x	x	x		x	x	x	
diverts inflowing air upward					x		x		x		x	x	x	
odd sizes economically available											x			x
large sizes practical										x				x
DISADVANTAGES														
only 50% of area openable	x	x												x
does not protect from rain when open	x	x	x			x								x
inconvenient operation when over an obstruction	x	x					x	x						x
presents a hazard if vent low and close to walkways			x		x	x	x	x				x	x	
requires weather stripping	x	x	x	x		x	x	x	x					x
horizontal members obstruct view	x	x			x		x				x	x	x	
vertical members obstruct view			x	x										x
will sag if not structurally strong			x	x										
glass soils quickly when vent open					x		x	x	x		x	x	x	
inflowing air cannot be diverted downward	x	x	x		x	x		x	x		x		x	x
excessive air leakage											x			
hard to wash											x			
interferes with furniture drapes, blinds, etc.				x		x	x		x					
screens—storm windows difficult to provide						x	x							x
sash has to be removed for washing	x							x		x		x		x

By HOWARD P. VERMILYA, AIA

Although wood windows are still made to custom designs—as double-hung units for institutional buildings and as fixed and operating sash in custom residential work (Figs. 2–5)—the vast majority of wood windows produced today are of stock design and manufactured as separate sash and frames or more often as complete window units.

Under the auspices of the National Woodwork Manufacturers Association (NWMA) and the U.S. Department of Commerce, the following Commercial Standards have been established for the production of wood windows:

CS163-59—*Pondersosa Pine Windows, Sash, and Screens:* This standard covers 1⅜-in.-thick check-rail windows and casement and cellar sash; 1⅛-in.-thick plain-rail windows and storm and cellar sash and screens; and ¾-in.-thick screens. Standard sizes are listed for each (Tables 2–5, Figs. 6 and 7).

CS190-59—*Standard Stock Double-Hung Wood Window Units:* This standard provides minimum requirements for double-hung wood window units including assembly of the component parts, window frames, 1⅜-in. double-hung check-rail windows (sash), balancing, weatherstripping, 1⅛-in. storm sash, and ¾-in. and 1⅛-in. window screens. Weatherstripping should limit air infiltration to not more than 0.75 cfm per lin ft of sash-crack perimeter when submitted to wind pressure equivalent to 25 mph.

CS193-53—*Standard Stock Ponderosa Pine Insulating-Glass Windows and Sash:* This standard provides minimum requirements for 1⅜-in.-thick windows and sash to accommodate ½-in.-thick insulating glass, and for 2¼-in.-thick stationary sash to accommodate 1-in.-thick insulating glass (Tables 6 and 7, Figs. 8 and 9, respectively). Sizes of glass are also specified.

CS204-59—*Standard Stock Wood Awning Window Units and Projected Awning and Stationary Sash Units:* This standard provides minimum requirements for material, construction, grading, and tolerances for frames, sash, operating mechanism, weatherstripping, storm sash, screens, and assembly of component parts into a wood awning unit of projected awning and stationary sash unit. Operative sash should be weatherstripped to prevent air infiltration in excess of 0.5 cfm per lin ft of sash-crack perimeter when subjected to wind pressure equivalent to 25 mph.

CS205-59—*Standard Stock Wood Casement Window Units:* This standard provides minimum requirements for material, construction, assembly, grading, and tolerances of units. Essential construction requirements cover casement frames, sash, oper-

ating mechanism, weatherstripping, storm sash, screens, and assembly of component parts into a wood casement unit. Sizes are not specified. Weatherstripping should limit air infiltration to not more than 0.5 cfm ft of sash perimeter when subjected to wind pressure equivalent to 25 mph.

CS208-57—*Standard Stock Exterior Wood Windows and Door Frames:* This standard provides minimum specifications for standard stock exterior window and casement and cellar sash frames and exterior door frames. Data include construction, grading, and tolerances.

STANDARD OPENING SIZES

The opening sizes for windows, sash, and screens given in the tables are normally employed in structures of modular design, and were designed to meet the basic requirements of *American Standard Basis for the Coordination of Dimensions of Building Materials and Equipment* (ASA A62.1), sponsored by American Institute of Architects and the Producers' Council (see "Modular Coordination").

The sizes of dimensions for coordination, although based on a 4-in. module or increment, are not necessarily multiples of 4 in. As shown in the illustrations, the standards for double-hung windows meet the requirements for coordination by being built to widths that are multiples of 4 in. and heights that are multiples of 4 in., plus 2 in.

It can be observed from Fig. 10 that the grid opening is a multiple of 4 in. both in width and in height. To meet the requirements for coordination it is essential that the window and its frame be confined within a certain number of 4-in. increments as indicated by the dotted grid lines. The standard window opening in all cases is 4 in. less in width and 6 in. less in height than the grid opening.

PRESERVATIVE TREATMENT

Water-repellent wood preservative treatment of all wood parts after machining is required by all these standards. The preservative as well as the method of treatment must conform to NWMA Standards, which require a 3-minute dip in open tank or application by vacuum process.

WOOD SPECIES

Ponderosa pine is almost universally used for stock window units using shop grades. The wood should be dried to a moisture content of 6 to 12 per cent and should be free from defects. Light-brown

stain and light-red kiln burn are not considered defects. Frames may have plugs if the plugs are hidden by stops; finger jointing is allowed except in the sill and wide outside casings. Other species of wood may also be used (see Table 8).

WEATHERSTRIPPING, STORM SASH, SCREENS

Weatherstripping may be factory applied or installed at the site. It reduces air infiltration anywhere from 50 to 85 per cent, depending upon how well the window and frame are fitted and upon the quality of the weatherstripping. *Storm sash* also serve to reduce air leakage, in addition to reducing heat loss through the glass. Storm sash are available for all standard-size window openings. Sash or windows designed for ½-in. or 1-in.-thick insulating glass are available in many sizes (see Tables 6 and 7). *Screens* also may be obtained in stock sizes (in either half- or full-size) to fit standard double-hung window openings (Table 9). Other types of screens—stationary, hinged, sliding or roll—are usually coordinated to modular-sized openings.

HARDWARE

Stock window units usually come with all hardware applied and ready to set in place. If sash and frames are assembled at the job, hardware is usually field applied, using the type recommended by the manufacturer.

WOOD WINDOW TYPES

In addition to the double-hung, casement, and awning windows, for which standards have been established, other types of window units are generally available. These include the *sliding window* with one sliding and one fixed sash, two sliding sash, or two sliding and one fixed (center) sash, and with two sliding sash under a picture or fixed sash. Sizes have not been standardized but range from approximately 2 ft to 4 ft 6 in. in height and sometimes higher, and from 3 ft to 5 or 6 ft in width for the two sash openings. Sash are usually removable for cleaning. Some are available with double glazing; others are available with combination self-storing storm sash and sash screens. The *picture window* has received much recent development. It is incorporated in a single frame, usually as the center element, with double-hung, awning, or casement windows. It has been developed as a bow window unit with or without operating

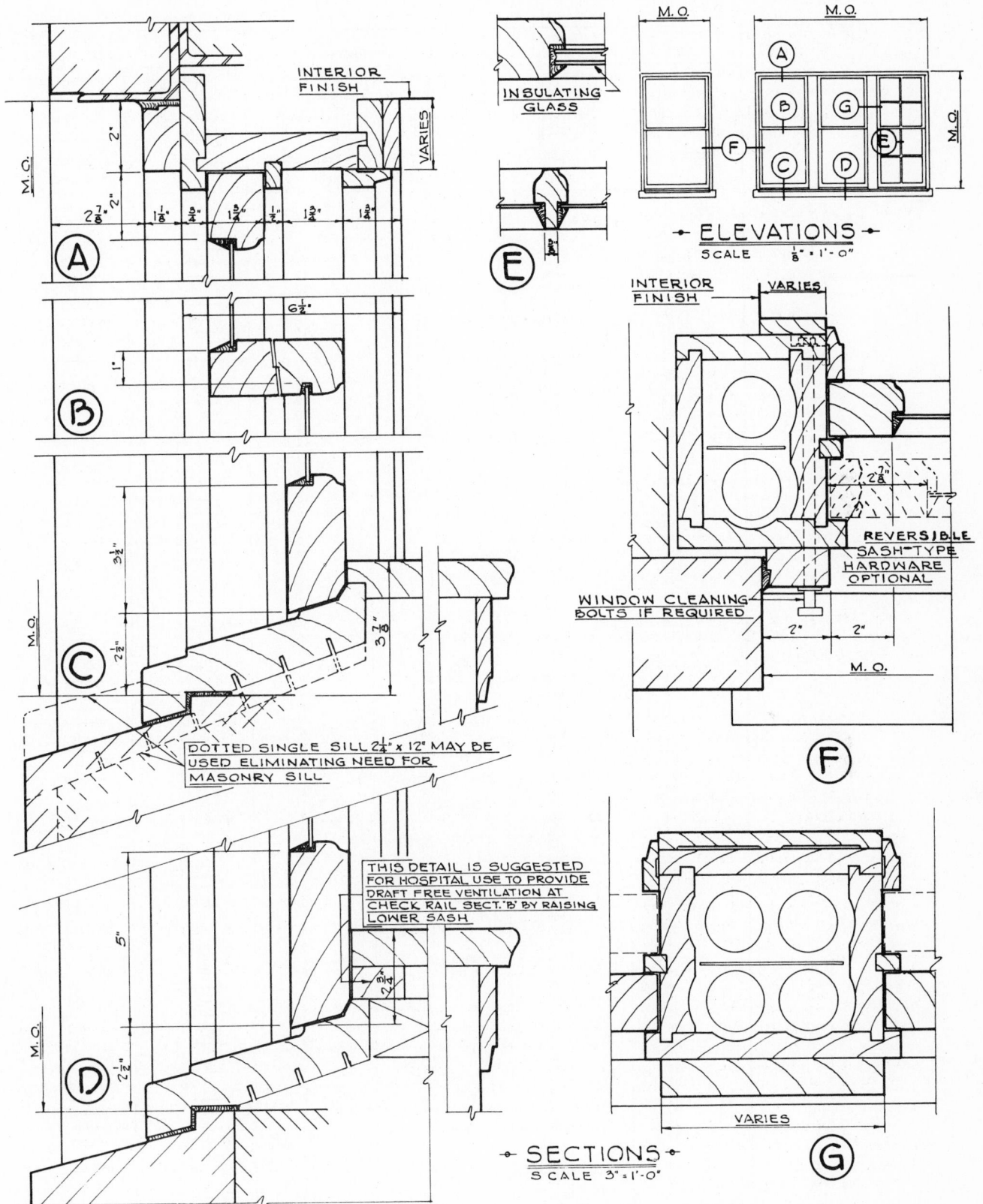

INTERIOR FINISH

VARIES

M.O.

2"

$2\frac{7}{8}$" 2" $1\frac{1}{8}$" $\frac{3}{4}$" $1\frac{3}{4}$" $1\frac{1}{2}$" $1\frac{3}{4}$" $1\frac{3}{4}$"

A

$6\frac{1}{2}$"

1"

B

$3\frac{1}{2}$"

$2\frac{1}{2}$"

$3\frac{7}{8}$"

M.O.

C

DOTTED SINGLE SILL $2\frac{1}{4}$" x 12" MAY BE USED ELIMINATING NEED FOR MASONRY SILL

5"

$2\frac{3}{4}$"

$2\frac{1}{2}$"

M.O.

D

THIS DETAIL IS SUGGESTED FOR HOSPITAL USE TO PROVIDE DRAFT FREE VENTILATION AT CHECK RAIL SECT. 'B' BY RAISING LOWER SASH

INSULATING GLASS

$\frac{3}{4}$"

E

M.O. M.O.

A

B G

F

C D E

M.O.

ELEVATIONS
SCALE $\frac{1}{8}$" = 1'-0"

INTERIOR FINISH

VARIES

$2\frac{7}{8}$"

REVERSIBLE SASH-TYPE HARDWARE OPTIONAL

WINDOW CLEANING BOLTS IF REQUIRED

2" 2"

M.O.

F

VARIES

G

SECTIONS
SCALE 3" = 1'-0"

Fig. 2. Typical double-hung window for institutional type building

Courtesy American Woodwork Institute, James Arkin, AIA, Consultant

Table 2. Check-rail windows, 1⅜ in. thick

The windows on this page are made ⅛ in. narrower and 1/16 in. shorter than window opening sizes listed. Dimensions for wood parts such as stiles, muntins, etc. are face measurements.

Window opening sizes in feet and inches (width x height)	2 Lt	4 Lt high	Top 2, 3, 4 Lt w	Top 4, 6, 8 Lt	12 Lt	8, 16 Lt
1–8 x 3–2	16 x 16	16 x 7¾	(Top 2 Lt w) 7⅞ x 16	(Top 4 Lt) 7⅞ x 8		(8 Lt) 8 x 8
3–6	18	8¾	18	9		9
3–10	20	9¾	20	10		10
4–2	22	10¾	22	11		11
4–6	24	11¾	24	12		12
4–10	26	12¾	26	13		13
5–2	28	13¾	28	14		14
5–6	30	14¾	30	15		
5–10	32	15¾	32	16		
2–0 x 2–6	20 x 12	20 x 5¾	(Top 3 Lt w) 6½ x 12	(Top 6 Lt) 6½ x 6		
2–10	14	6¾	14	7		
3–2	16	7¾	16	8	6 21/32 x 8	10 x 8
3–6	18	8¾	18	9	9	9
3–10	20	9¾	20	10	10	10
4–2	22	10¾	22	11	11	11
4–6	24	11¾	24	12	12	12
4–10	26	12¾	26	13	13	13
5–2	28	13¾	28	14	14	14
5–6	30	14¾	30	15	15	15
5–10	32	15¾	32	16		16
2–4 x 2–6	24 x 12	24 x 5¾	7 27/32 x 12	7 27/32 x 6		
2–10	14	6¾	14	7	8 x 7	
3–2	16	7¾	16	8	8	
3–6	18	8¾	18	9	9	
3–10	20	9¾	20	10	10	
4–2	22	10¾	22	11	11	
4–6	24	11¾	24	12	12	12 x 12
4–10	26	12¾	26	13	13	
5–2	28	13¾	28	14	14	14
5–6	30	14¾	30	15	15	
5–10	32	15¾	32	16		16
2–8 x 2–10	28 x 14	28 x 6¾	9 5/32 x 14	9 5/32 x 7	9 11/32 x 7	
3–2	16	7¾	16	8	8	
3–6	18	8¾	18	9	9	
3–10	20	9¾	20	10	10	
4–2	22	10¾	22	11	11	
4–6	24	11¾	24	12	12	
4–10	26	12¾	26	13	13	
5–2	28	13¾	28	14	14	
5–6	30	14¾	30	15	15	
5–10	32	15¾	32	16	16	14 x 16
3–0 x 2–10	32 x 14	32 x 6¾	(Top 4 Lt w) 7 13/16 x 14	(Top 8 Lt) 7 13/16 x 7	10 21/32 x 7	(16 Lt)
3–2	16	7¾	16	8	8	7 13/16 x 8
3–6	18	8¾	18	9	9	9
3–10	20	9¾	20	10	10	10
4–2	22	10¾	22	11	11	11
4–6	24	11¾	24	12	12	12
4–10	26	12¾	26	13	13	13
5–2	28	13¾	28	14	14	14
5–6	30	14¾	30	15	15	
5–10	32	15¾	32	16	16	
3–4 x 2–10	36 x 14	36 x 6¾	8 13/16 x 14	8 13/16 x 7		
3–2	16	7¾	16	8		8 13/16 x 8
3–6	18	8¾	18	9		9
3–10	20	9¾	20	10		10
4–2	22	10¾	22	11		11
4–6	24	11¾	24	12	12 x 12	12
4–10	26	12¾	26	13		13
5–2	28	13¾	28	14	14	14
5–6	30	14¾	30	15		15
5–10	32	15¾	32	16	16	16
3–8 x 3–6	40 x 18	40 x 8¾	9 13/16 x 18	9 13/16 x 9		
3–10	20	9¾	20	10		
4–2	22	10¾	22	11		
4–6	24	11¾	24	12		
4–10	26	12¾	26	13		
5–2	28	13¾	28	14		9 13/16 x 14
5–6	30	14¾	30	15		15
5–10	32	15¾	32	16		16

Stiles			1 29/32″	St. 1 29/32″	St. 1 21/32″	St. 1 29/32″
Top Rail			1 29/32″	T.R. 1 29/32″	T.R. 1 21/32″	T.R. 1 21/32″
Bottom Rail			3″	B.R. 3″	B.R. 2 ¾″	B.R. 2 ¾″
Vertical Bar			3/16″	V.B. 3/16″	V.B. 3/16″	V.B. 3/16″
Horizontal Bar			7/16″	Mun. 3/16″	Mun. 3/16″	Mun. 3/16″
Check Rail			1 3/32″	C.R. 1 3/32″	C.R. 1 3/32″	C.R. 1 3/32″

Other standard types are 4, 6, 15, 18, 20, and 24 light and cottage windows.

sash of the awning, casement, or projected type. Heights range from about 3 ft 6 in. to 6 ft 8 in., and widths from about 6 to 12 ft. Other popular combinations with the picture window are one or more operating sash (awning or sliding) above or below the fixed sash. Another recent development is the *window wall* constructed of stacked, projected, and fixed window units. Some of these units may be reversed as hopper units to open in, or even used as casements when placed on their sides. They are available with either double glass or storm sash, and with screens.

INSTALLATION

The NWMA recommends that sash be installed after the plaster is thoroughly dry, at the same time that trim is applied to the inside of the building. Openings can be closed during construction with plastic film.

Courtesy of Architectural Woodwork Institute

SPECIFICATIONS

Wood

All wood for window sash and exposed portions of frames should be clear and all wood dried to moisture content as follows:

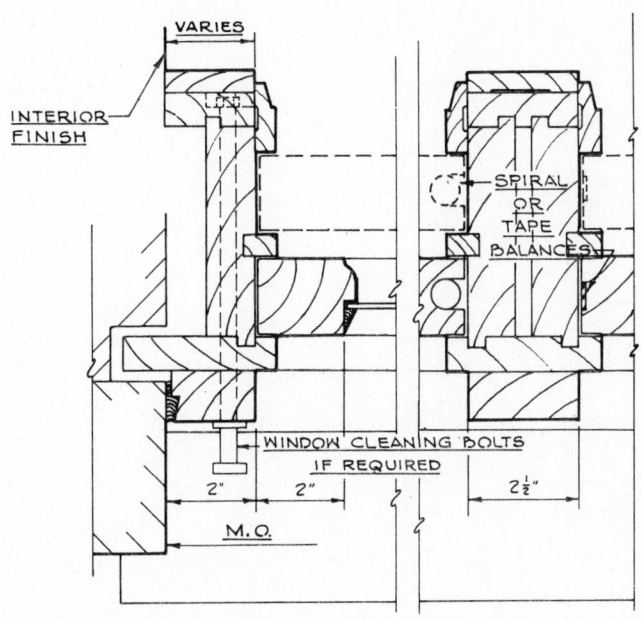

Fig. 3. Double-hung window with spring balances

Courtesy American Woodwork Institute, James Arkin, AIA, Consultant

	United States		Canada	
	Dry Southwestern states	All other states	Alberta, Manitoba Ontario, Quebec Saskatchewan	East & west coast provinces, incl. Newfoundland
Average for entire quantity	9%	12%	12%	13%
Range permitted in individual pieces	7–12%	9–14%	10–15%	11–15%

All edges of woodwork should be eased to increase strength, reduce slivers, and improve paintability.

Redwood (Clear Heart) is desirable where natural or stained finished wood is used.

For frames that are to be painted, the following woods are listed in approximate order of their ability to stay in place and their adaptability: redwood, African mahogany, northern white pine, Idaho pine, sugar pine, vertical grain fir, ponderosa pine, Sitka spruce, and southern yellow pine.

The following woods are adaptable to sash manufacture: African mahogany, sugar pine, Idaho pine, northern white pine, ponderosa pine, redwood, vertical grain fir, and Sitka spruce.

Sash

In general, all institutional sash should be at least 1¾ in. thick. Insulating glass, ½ in. thick, can be used with 1¾-in. sash; however, 2¼-in. sash are recommended because insulating glass becomes too heavy for 1¾-in. sash in most sizes. For ¾- and 1-in. insulating glass, 2¼-in. sash are mandatory.

Nails

All weather-exposed nails that cannot be set should be monel. All other nails, sash pins, or fasteners on the exterior should be hot-dipped galvanized or nonstaining metal.

Glazing

It is recommended that all glazing be done with a proven glazing compound, knife consistency, chocolate brown or gray color. All glass should be bedded with the same material (Fig. 11). At bottom of fixed glass in frame or sash, back bed and pin every 8-in. with ⅞-in. pure zinc greenhouse points. No bottom outside bead or compound is necessary on fixed sash. Where possible, glazing should be done at the factory.

Caulking

All caulking material should be of Thiokol-base type.

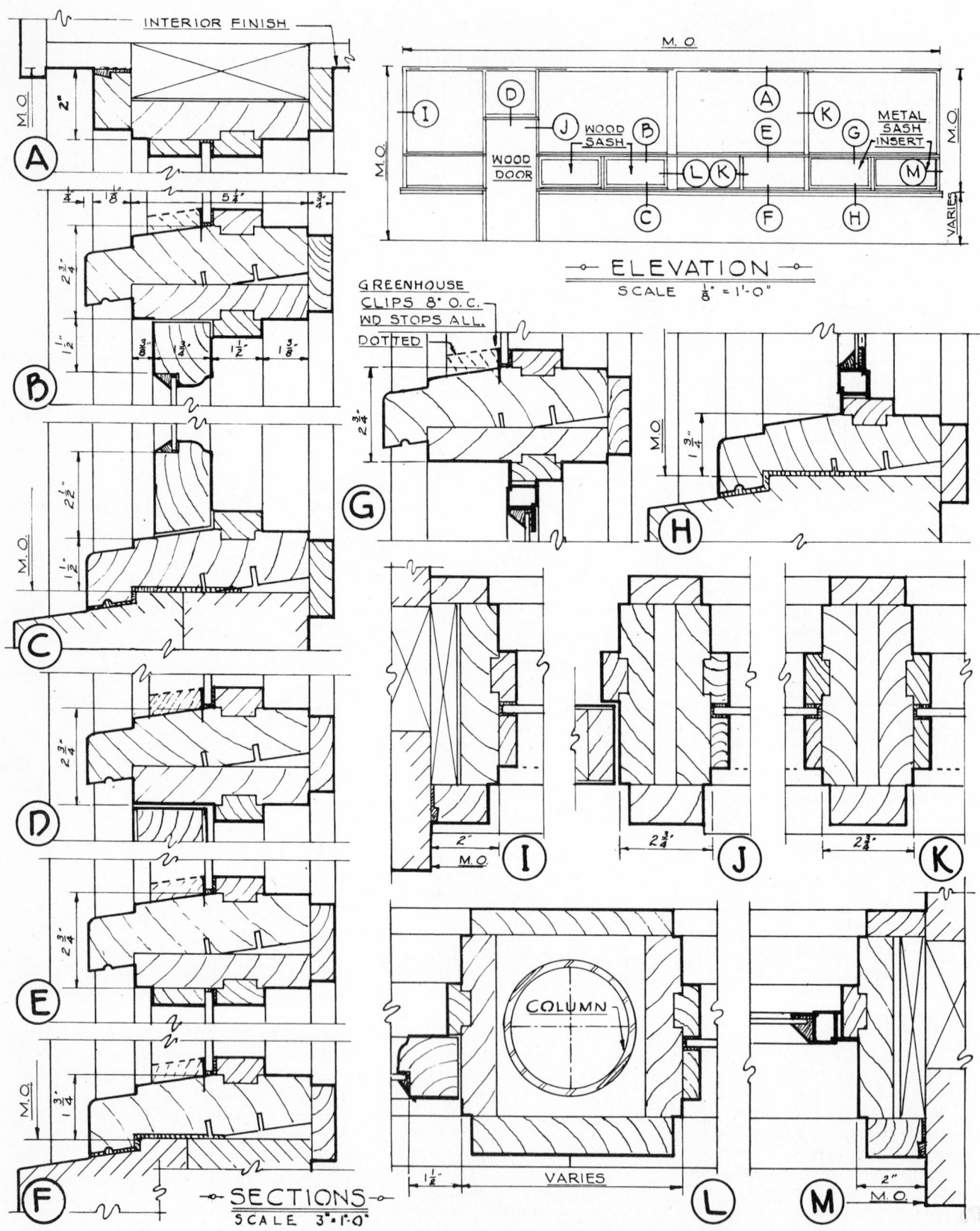

Fig. 4. Typical details, awning sash with fixed glass

Courtesy American Woodwork Institute, James Arkin, *AIA, Consultant*

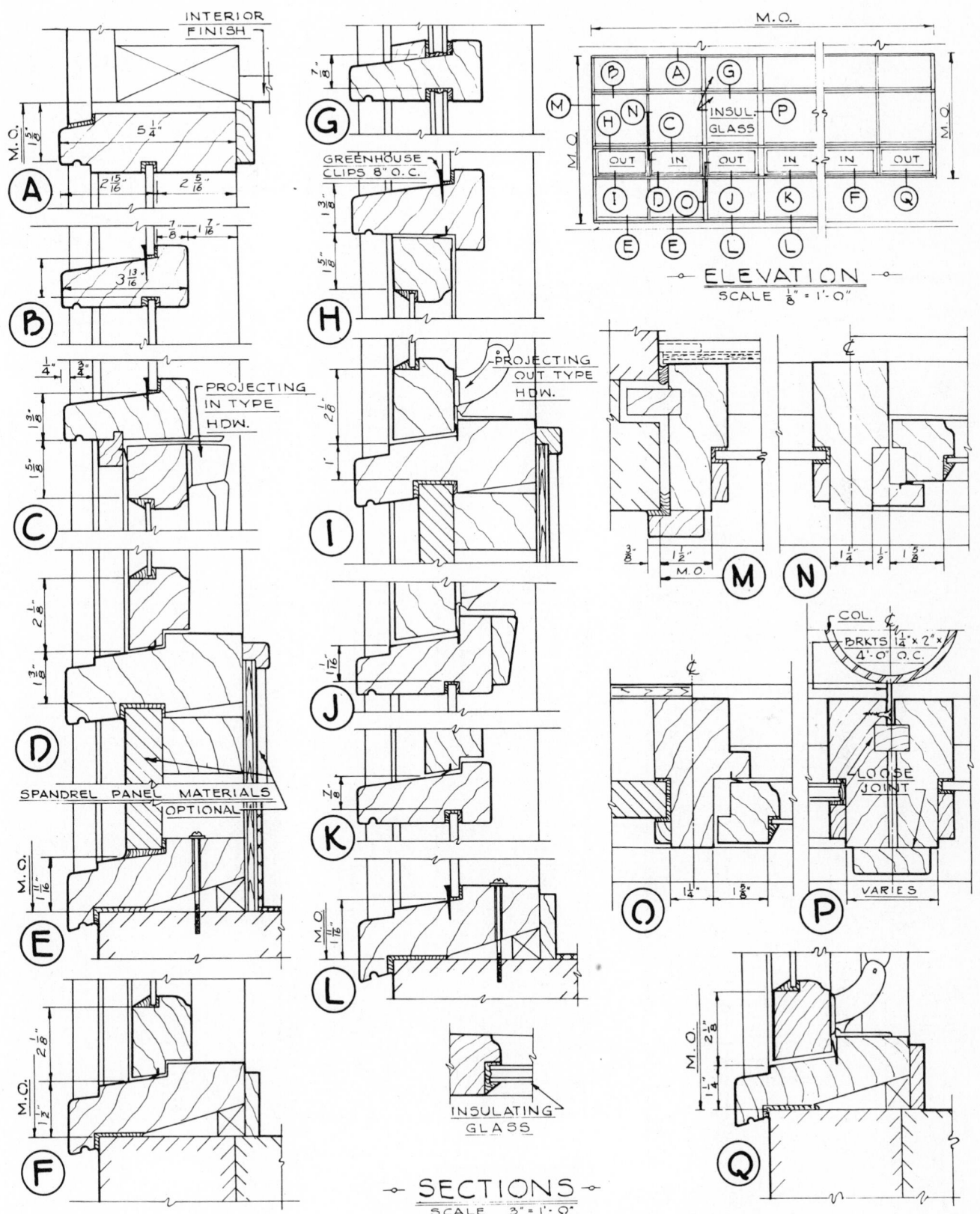

Fig. 5. Window-wall details

Courtesy American Woodwork Institute, James Arkin, *AIA, Consultant*

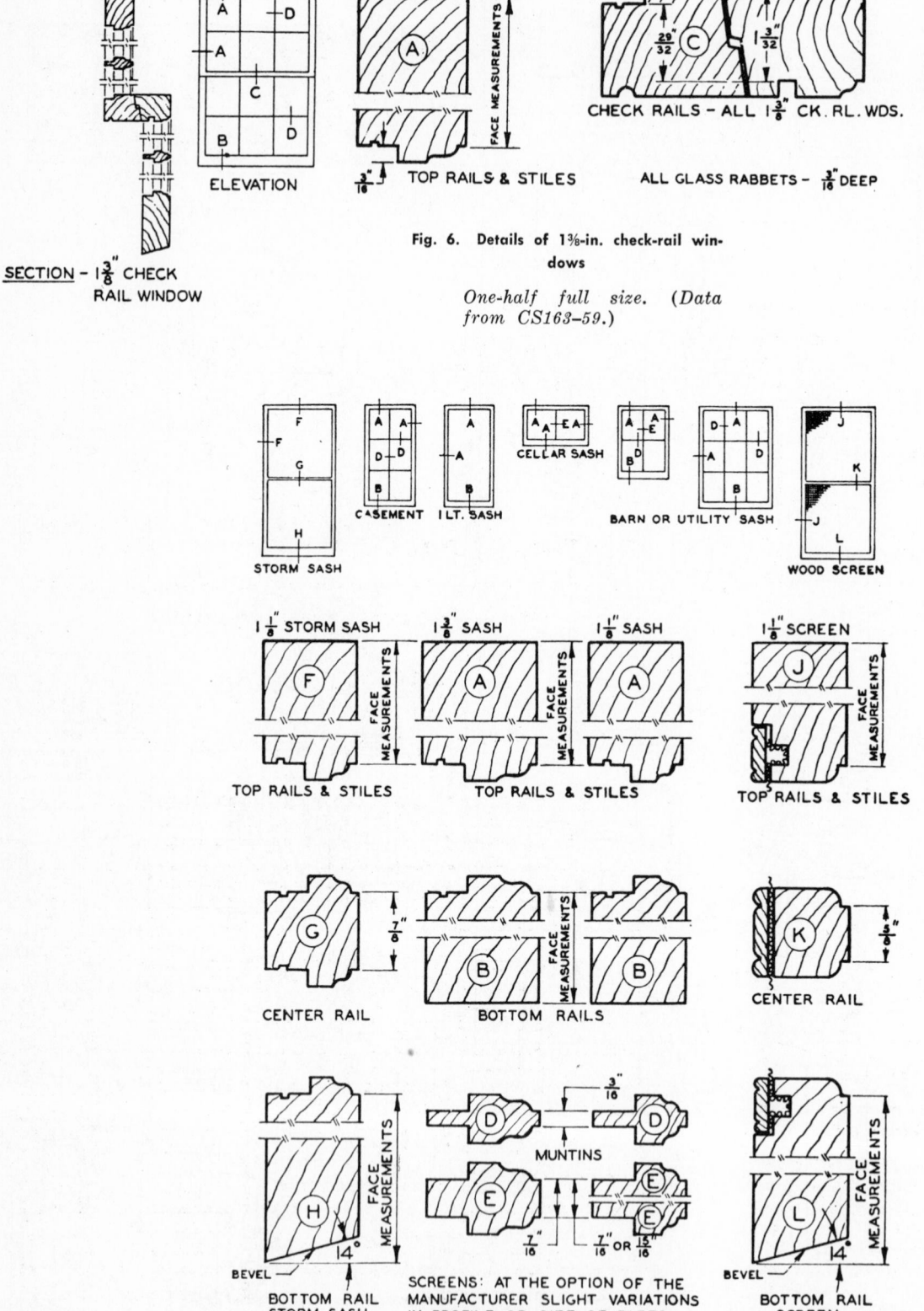

SECTION – $1\frac{3}{8}$" CHECK RAIL WINDOW

ELEVATION

$1\frac{3}{8}$" CK. RL. WDS.

TOP RAILS & STILES

CHECK RAILS – ALL $1\frac{3}{8}$" CK. RL. WDS.

ALL GLASS RABBETS – $\frac{3}{16}$" DEEP

$\frac{3}{16}$"

14° BEVEL

BOTTOM RAILS

FACE MEASUREMENTS

Fig. 6. Details of 1⅜-in. check-rail windows

One-half full size. (Data from CS163–59.)

STORM SASH

CASEMENT 1 LT. SASH

CELLAR SASH

BARN OR UTILITY SASH

WOOD SCREEN

$1\frac{1}{8}$" STORM SASH

$1\frac{3}{8}$" SASH

$1\frac{1}{8}$" SASH

$1\frac{1}{8}$" SCREEN

TOP RAILS & STILES

TOP RAILS & STILES

TOP RAILS & STILES

CENTER RAIL

BOTTOM RAILS

CENTER RAIL

$\frac{7}{8}$"

$\frac{9}{16}$"

FACE MEASUREMENTS

BEVEL 14°

BOTTOM RAIL STORM SASH

MUNTINS

$\frac{3}{16}$"

$\frac{7}{16}$"

$\frac{7}{16}$" OR $\frac{15}{16}$"

SCREENS: AT THE OPTION OF THE MANUFACTURER SLIGHT VARIATIONS IN PROFILE OR SIZE OF PARTS ARE PERMISSIBLE

BEVEL 14°

BOTTOM RAIL SCREEN

Fig. 7. Details of storm sash, single sash, and screens

One-half full size. (Data from CS163–59.)

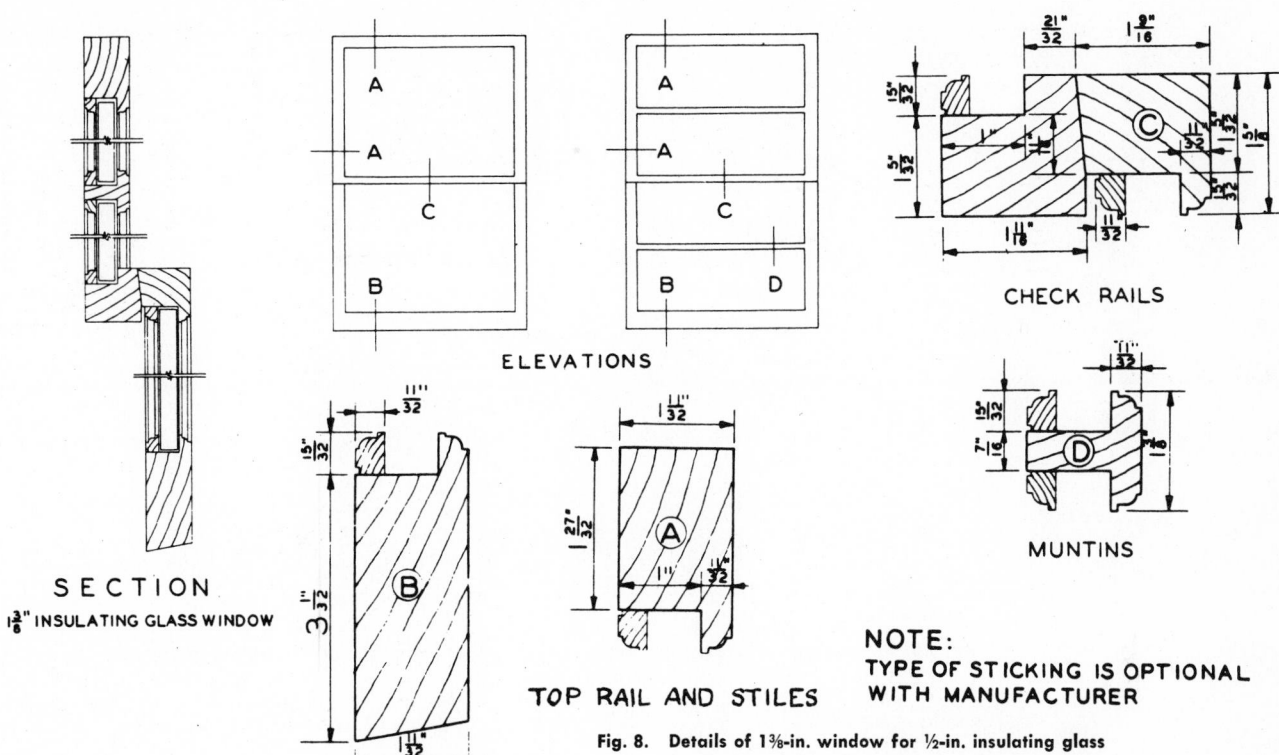

SECTION
1⅜" INSULATING GLASS WINDOW

ELEVATIONS

CHECK RAILS

MUNTINS

BOTTOM RAIL

TOP RAIL AND STILES

NOTE:
TYPE OF STICKING IS OPTIONAL WITH MANUFACTURER

Fig. 8. Details of 1⅜-in. window for ½-in. insulating glass

One-half full size. (Data from CS193–53.)

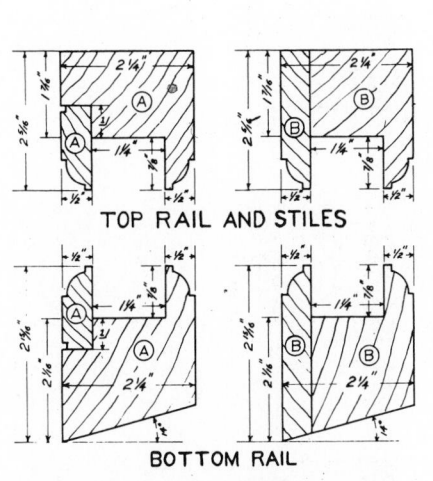

TOP RAIL AND STILES

BOTTOM RAIL

Fig. 9. Details of 2¼-in. stationary sash for 1-in. insulating glass

One-half full size. Stationary sash may be made in accordance with either of the above details at the option of the manufacturer. Depth of the rabbet is optional, but must not be less than ½ in. (Data from CS193–53.)

Fig. 10. Relation of window to grid opening in brick wall

Data from CS163–59.

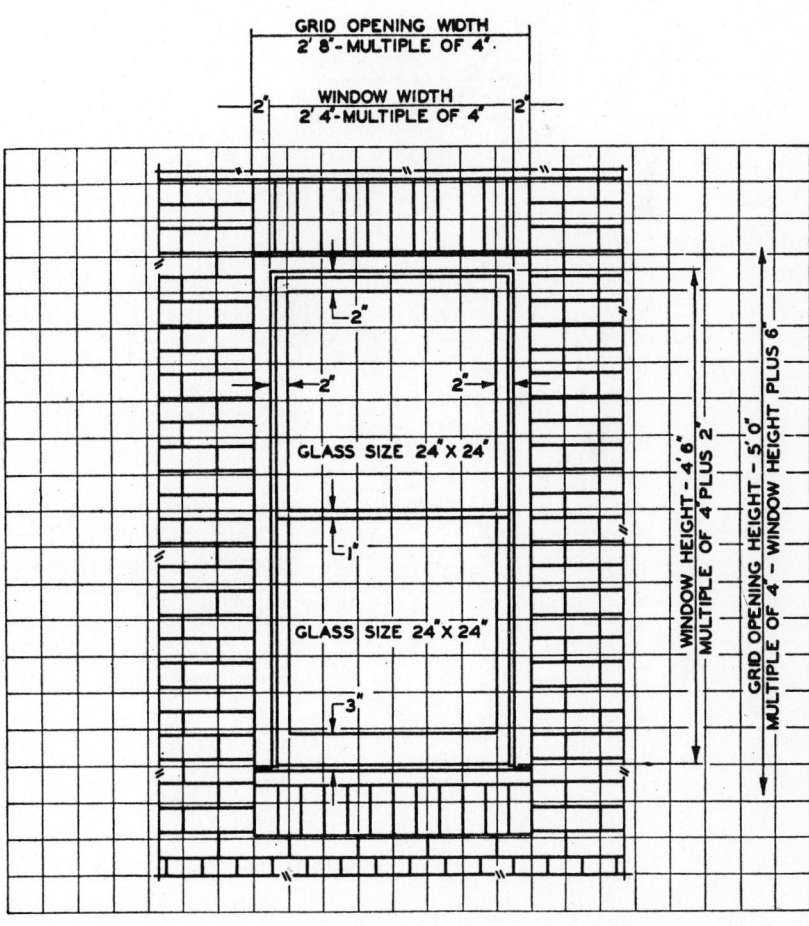

GRID OPENING WIDTH
2' 8"-MULTIPLE OF 4'
WINDOW WIDTH
2' 4'-MULTIPLE OF 4'

GLASS SIZE 24"X 24"

GLASS SIZE 24"X 24"

WINDOW HEIGHT - 4' 6"
MULTIPLE OF 4' PLUS 2"

GRID OPENING HEIGHT - 5' 0"
MULTIPLE OF 4' - WINDOW HEIGHT PLUS 6"

Table 3. Standard sizes of casement sash, 1⅜ in. thick

Sash are made ⅛ in. narrower and 1/32 in. shorter than the opening sizes listed. (Data from CS163–59.)

Prefit face measurements (in.)

Stiles	$1\frac{21}{32}$	Vertical bar	$\frac{3}{16}$
Top rail	$1\frac{29}{32}$	Muntin	$\frac{3}{16}$
Bottom rail	3		

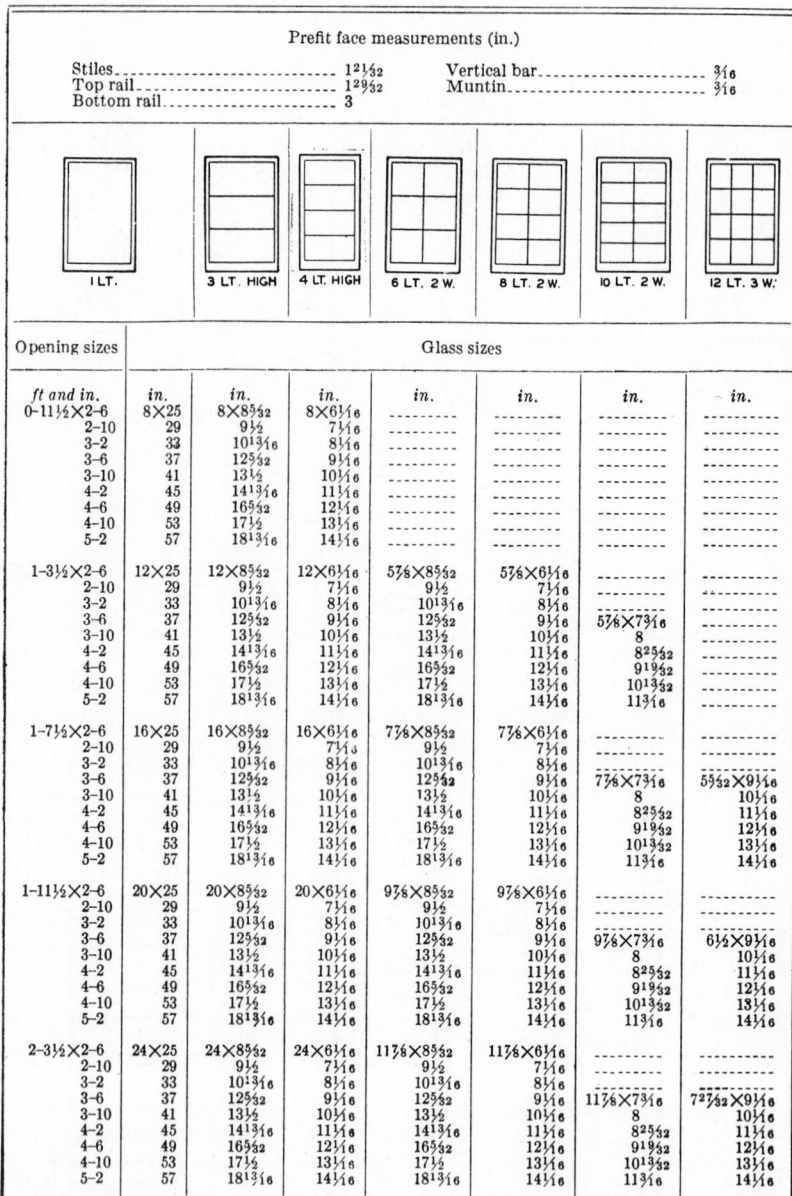

Opening sizes	Glass sizes						
	1 LT.	3 LT. HIGH	4 LT. HIGH	6 LT. 2 W.	8 LT. 2 W.	10 LT. 2 W.	12 LT. 3 W.
ft and in.	*in.*	*in.*	*in.*	*in.*	*in.*	*in.*	*in.*
0-11½×2-6	8×25	$8\times8\frac{5}{32}$	$8\times6\frac{1}{16}$	---------	---------	---------	---------
2-10	29	$9\frac{1}{2}$	$7\frac{1}{16}$				
3-2	33	$10\frac{13}{16}$	$8\frac{1}{16}$				
3-6	37	$12\frac{5}{32}$	$9\frac{1}{16}$				
3-10	41	$13\frac{1}{2}$	$10\frac{1}{16}$				
4-2	45	$14\frac{13}{16}$	$11\frac{1}{16}$				
4-6	49	$16\frac{5}{32}$	$12\frac{1}{16}$				
4-10	53	$17\frac{1}{2}$	$13\frac{1}{16}$				
5-2	57	$18\frac{13}{16}$	$14\frac{1}{16}$				
1-3½×2-6	12×25	$12\times8\frac{5}{32}$	$12\times6\frac{1}{16}$	$5\frac{7}{8}\times8\frac{5}{32}$	$5\frac{7}{8}\times6\frac{1}{16}$	---------	---------
2-10	29	$9\frac{1}{2}$	$7\frac{1}{16}$	$9\frac{1}{2}$	$7\frac{1}{16}$		
3-2	33	$10\frac{13}{16}$	$8\frac{1}{16}$	$10\frac{13}{16}$	$8\frac{1}{16}$		
3-6	37	$12\frac{5}{32}$	$9\frac{1}{16}$	$12\frac{5}{32}$	$9\frac{1}{16}$	$5\frac{7}{8}\times7\frac{3}{16}$	
3-10	41	$13\frac{1}{2}$	$10\frac{1}{16}$	$13\frac{1}{2}$	$10\frac{1}{16}$	8	
4-2	45	$14\frac{13}{16}$	$11\frac{1}{16}$	$14\frac{13}{16}$	$11\frac{1}{16}$	$8\frac{25}{32}$	
4-6	49	$16\frac{5}{32}$	$12\frac{1}{16}$	$16\frac{5}{32}$	$12\frac{1}{16}$	$9\frac{19}{32}$	
4-10	53	$17\frac{1}{2}$	$13\frac{1}{16}$	$17\frac{1}{2}$	$13\frac{1}{16}$	$10\frac{13}{32}$	
5-2	57	$18\frac{13}{16}$	$14\frac{1}{16}$	$18\frac{13}{16}$	$14\frac{1}{16}$	$11\frac{3}{16}$	
1-7½×2-6	16×25	$16\times8\frac{5}{32}$	$16\times6\frac{1}{16}$	$7\frac{7}{8}\times8\frac{5}{32}$	$7\frac{7}{8}\times6\frac{1}{16}$	---------	---------
2-10	29	$9\frac{1}{2}$	$7\frac{1}{16}$	$9\frac{1}{2}$	$7\frac{1}{16}$		
3-2	33	$10\frac{13}{16}$	$8\frac{1}{16}$	$10\frac{13}{16}$	$8\frac{1}{16}$		
3-6	37	$12\frac{5}{32}$	$9\frac{1}{16}$	$12\frac{5}{32}$	$9\frac{1}{16}$	$7\frac{7}{8}\times7\frac{3}{16}$	$5\frac{5}{32}\times9\frac{1}{16}$
3-10	41	$13\frac{1}{2}$	$10\frac{1}{16}$	$13\frac{1}{2}$	$10\frac{1}{16}$	8	$10\frac{1}{16}$
4-2	45	$14\frac{13}{16}$	$11\frac{1}{16}$	$14\frac{13}{16}$	$11\frac{1}{16}$	$8\frac{25}{32}$	$11\frac{1}{16}$
4-6	49	$16\frac{5}{32}$	$12\frac{1}{16}$	$16\frac{5}{32}$	$12\frac{1}{16}$	$9\frac{19}{32}$	$12\frac{1}{16}$
4-10	53	$17\frac{1}{2}$	$13\frac{1}{16}$	$17\frac{1}{2}$	$13\frac{1}{16}$	$10\frac{13}{32}$	$13\frac{1}{16}$
5-2	57	$18\frac{13}{16}$	$14\frac{1}{16}$	$18\frac{13}{16}$	$14\frac{1}{16}$	$11\frac{3}{16}$	$14\frac{1}{16}$
1-11½×2-6	20×25	$20\times8\frac{5}{32}$	$20\times6\frac{1}{16}$	$9\frac{7}{8}\times8\frac{5}{32}$	$9\frac{7}{8}\times6\frac{1}{16}$	---------	---------
2-10	29	$9\frac{1}{2}$	$7\frac{1}{16}$	$9\frac{1}{2}$	$7\frac{1}{16}$		
3-2	33	$10\frac{13}{16}$	$8\frac{1}{16}$	$10\frac{13}{16}$	$8\frac{1}{16}$		
3-6	37	$12\frac{5}{32}$	$9\frac{1}{16}$	$12\frac{5}{32}$	$9\frac{1}{16}$	$9\frac{7}{8}\times7\frac{3}{16}$	$6\frac{1}{2}\times9\frac{1}{16}$
3-10	41	$13\frac{1}{2}$	$10\frac{1}{16}$	$13\frac{1}{2}$	$10\frac{1}{16}$	8	$10\frac{1}{16}$
4-2	45	$14\frac{13}{16}$	$11\frac{1}{16}$	$14\frac{13}{16}$	$11\frac{1}{16}$	$8\frac{25}{32}$	$11\frac{1}{16}$
4-6	49	$16\frac{5}{32}$	$12\frac{1}{16}$	$16\frac{5}{32}$	$12\frac{1}{16}$	$9\frac{19}{32}$	$12\frac{1}{16}$
4-10	53	$17\frac{1}{2}$	$13\frac{1}{16}$	$17\frac{1}{2}$	$13\frac{1}{16}$	$10\frac{13}{32}$	$13\frac{1}{16}$
5-2	57	$18\frac{13}{16}$	$14\frac{1}{16}$	$18\frac{13}{16}$	$14\frac{1}{16}$	$11\frac{3}{16}$	$14\frac{1}{16}$
2-3½×2-6	24×25	$24\times8\frac{5}{32}$	$24\times6\frac{1}{16}$	$11\frac{7}{8}\times8\frac{5}{32}$	$11\frac{7}{8}\times6\frac{1}{16}$	---------	---------
2-10	29	$9\frac{1}{2}$	$7\frac{1}{16}$	$9\frac{1}{2}$	$7\frac{1}{16}$		
3-2	33	$10\frac{13}{16}$	$8\frac{1}{16}$	$10\frac{13}{16}$	$8\frac{1}{16}$		
3-6	37	$12\frac{5}{32}$	$9\frac{1}{16}$	$12\frac{5}{32}$	$9\frac{1}{16}$	$11\frac{7}{8}\times7\frac{3}{16}$	$7\frac{27}{32}\times9\frac{1}{16}$
3-10	41	$13\frac{1}{2}$	$10\frac{1}{16}$	$13\frac{1}{2}$	$10\frac{1}{16}$	8	$10\frac{1}{16}$
4-2	45	$14\frac{13}{16}$	$11\frac{1}{16}$	$14\frac{13}{16}$	$11\frac{1}{16}$	$8\frac{25}{32}$	$11\frac{1}{16}$
4-6	49	$16\frac{5}{32}$	$12\frac{1}{16}$	$16\frac{5}{32}$	$12\frac{1}{16}$	$9\frac{19}{32}$	$12\frac{1}{16}$
4-10	53	$17\frac{1}{2}$	$13\frac{1}{16}$	$17\frac{1}{2}$	$13\frac{1}{16}$	$10\frac{13}{32}$	$13\frac{1}{16}$
5-2	57	$18\frac{13}{16}$	$14\frac{1}{16}$	$18\frac{13}{16}$	$14\frac{1}{16}$	$11\frac{3}{16}$	$14\frac{1}{16}$

¹ Certain modifications in size may be necessary for modular coordination, depending upon the type and design of frame used.

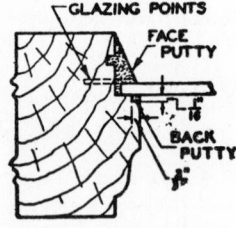

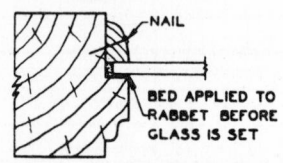

Fig. 11. Glazing details in 1⅜-in. sash

One-half full size. (Data from CS163–59.)

Table 4. Standard sizes of picture sash, $1\frac{3}{8}$ in. thick

Sash are made $\frac{1}{8}$ in. narrower and $\frac{1}{32}$ in. shorter than the opening sizes listed. (Data from CS163–59.)

Prefit face measurements (in.)

Stiles	$1\frac{29}{32}$	Bottom rail	$2\frac{3}{4}$
Top rail	$1\frac{21}{32}$	Bars and muntins	$\frac{7}{16}$

Opening sizes	Glass sizes			
	 4 HORIZ. LTS.	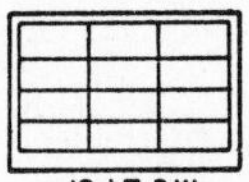 12 LT. 3 W.	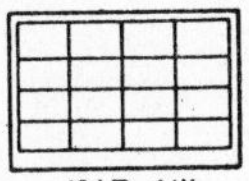 16 LT. 4 W.	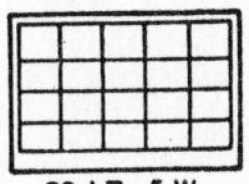 20 LT 5 W.
ft and in.	*in.*	*in.*	*in.*	*in.*
4-4×4-6	48×12	$15\frac{21}{32}$×12	$11\frac{5}{8}$×12	----------
5-2	14	14	14	----------
5-0×4-6	56×12	----------	$13\frac{5}{8}$×12	$10\frac{13}{16}$×12
5-2	14	----------	14	14
5-8×4-6	------	----------	$15\frac{5}{8}$×12	$12\frac{13}{32}$×12
5-2	------	----------	14	14

Table 5. Standard sizes of cellar sash, $1\frac{3}{8}$ and $1\frac{1}{8}$ in. thick

Sash are made $\frac{1}{8}$ in. narrower and $\frac{1}{8}$ in. shorter than the opening sizes listed. (Data from CS163–59.)

	Prefit face measurements (in.)			
Stiles	$1\frac{21}{32}$		$1\frac{21}{32}$	
Top rail	$1\frac{29}{32}$		$1\frac{29}{32}$	
Bottom rail	$1\frac{29}{32}$		$1\frac{29}{32}$	
Vertical bar	$\frac{7}{16}$		$\frac{3}{16}$	
	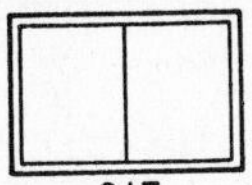 2 LT.		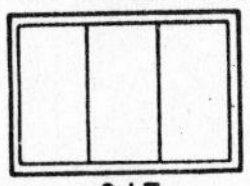 3 LT.	
Opening sizes	Glass sizes		Opening sizes	Glass sizes
ft and in.	*in.*		*ft and in.*	*in.*
1-8×1-4	8×12		2-0×1-0	$6\frac{21}{32}$×8
2-0×1-4	10×12		2-4×1-4	8×12
1-8	16		1-8	16
2-0	20			
			2-8×1-0	$9\frac{11}{32}$×8
2-4×1-4	12×12		1-4	12
1-8	16		1-8	16
2-0	20		2-0	20
2-8×1-4	14×12		3-0×1-4	$10\frac{21}{32}$×12
1-8	16		1-8	16
2-0	20		2-0	20
			3-4×1-4	12×12
			1-8	16
			2-0	20
			2-4	24

Treatment

Water-repellent pentachlorophenol preservative treatment: It is recommended strongly that exterior windows, frames and outside finish of all species of wood be treated with nonswelling water-repellent paintable preservative according to the 3-minute immersion process as defined by the NWMA. Such treatment to be carried out after final machining. Brush coating of emergency cuts made after dipping is recommended. A certificate or stamp should be furnished to certify this treatment.

Finishing

Natural, weathered effects: Redwood (Clear Heart, vertical grain preferred) may be used without further finishing when a natural appearance is desired. In such instances, a longer 5-minute dip in preservative is recommended.

Weathered effects may be speeded by using bleaching oil or shingle stain after preservative treatment, or a mixture of both.

Clear finishes: Natural wood color cannot be maintained indefinitely without further protection with products such as clear P.A.R. (Slight color additives to these finishes may be desirable.)

Stained finishes: Very durable stains are possible when comprised of boiled linseed oil, drier, and concentrated stain.

Painted finishes: Painting should be done no sooner than 72 hours after preservative treatment. Standard good practice painting procedures should be followed.

Awning and Hopper-type Windows

Hardware: Dalmo "C" Series or Whitco 100 AW or 200 AW or approved equal operators are recommended for all $1\frac{3}{4}$-in. sash.

Fasteners should be similar to Dalmo H-45 or H-30. Two fasteners should be used on all sash over 3 ft wide. Near the seacoast, operators and fasteners should be bronze.

Weatherstripping: Weatherstripping is recommended on all projecting type windows and where possible should be installed at the factory. Only the best quality high-tension spring bronze should be used.

Double-hung Windows

Hardware:

1. Pulley-type Frames—Pulleys should be installed at the factory and should be closed faced with bronze face plate. Wheels are to be sized to center weights in the pockets. They should have steel axles, oilite wood bushing and wheels for

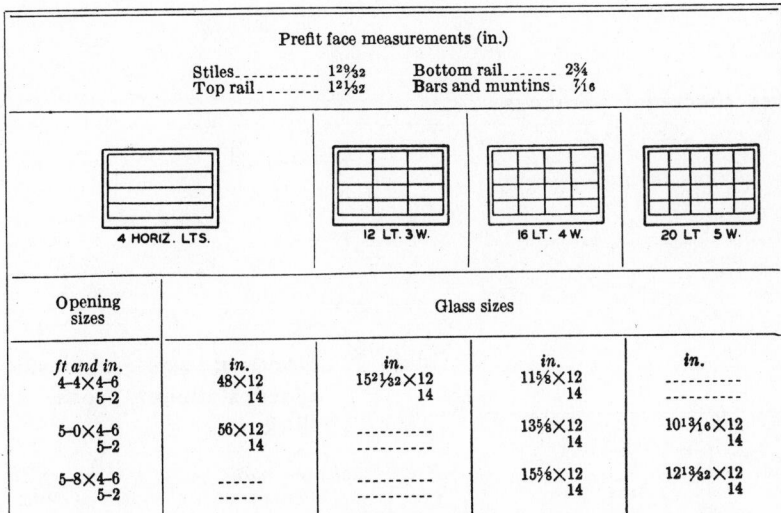

chain and be similar to those made by the Cleveland Lock Works or Stanley #7008½ or 7004½. Chain should be copper plated over galvanized steel, usually size #30. Pendulum strips should be provided of sheet galvanized iron. Weight pockets are to be conveniently located and pulley arrangements designed to use practical size of iron or lead weight and result in smooth operation.

2. Sash Balance Type—Where narrow mullions are desired, Unique Sash Balances or Caldwell or Pullman tape types are recommended.

Weatherstripping: This is optional but recommended. If weatherstripping is not applied at the factory it should be installed after the plaster is dry and the priming coats of paint have been applied.

Workmanship

Workmanship shall be of the highest quality. All joints shall be well made and tight and caulked where necessary. Nailing and other specifications not specifically mentioned above should be as under U.S. Commercial Standards CS190-59 and CS204-59.

Table 6. Standard sizes of insulating-glass check-rail windows, 1⅜ in. thick

Windows are made ⅛ in. narrower and ⅟₁₆ in. shorter than the sash opening sizes listed. (Data from CS193-53.)

Prefit face measurements (in.)

Stiles	1 27/32	Check rails	1 5/32
Top rail	1 27/32	Muntins	7/16
Bottom rail	3 1/32		

Sash opening sizes	TWO-LIGHT WINDOWS		FOUR-LIGHT WINDOWS	
	Glass sizes	Glass opening sizes	Glass sizes	Glass opening sizes
ft. and in.	in.	in.	in.	in.
2-0 x 4-6	20 x 24	20 3/16 x 24 3/16	20 x 11 11/16	20 3/16 x 11 7/8
5-2	28	28 3/16	13 11/16	13 7/8
2-4 x 3-2	24 x 16	24 3/16 x 16 3/16	------------	----------------
4-6	24	24 3/16	24 x 11 11/16	24 3/16 x 11 7/8
5-2	28	28 3/16	13 11/16	13 7/8
2-8 x 3-2	28 x 16	28 3/16 x 16 3/16	------------	----------------
4-6	24	24 3/16	28 x 11 11/16	28 3/16 x 11 7/8
5-2	28	28 3/16	13 11/16	13 7/8
3-0 x 3-2	32 x 16	32 3/16 x 16 3/16	------------	----------------
4-6	24	24 3/16	32 x 11 11/16	32 3/16 x 11 7/8
5-2	28	28 3/16	13 11/16	13 7/8
3-4 x 4-6	36 x 24	36 3/16 x 24 3/16	36 x 11 11/16	36 3/16 x 11 7/8
5-2	28	28 3/16	13 11/16	13 7/8

Table 7. Standard sizes of insulating-glass stationary sash, 2¼ in. thick

Prefit sash are made ⅛ in. less in width than the sash opening sizes listed. (Data from CS193-53.)

Prefit face measurements (in.)

Stiles	1 7/16
Top rail	1 7/16
Bottom rail	2 1/16

Sash opening sizes	Glass sizes	Glass opening sizes
ft. and in.	in.	in.
4-4 x 4-6	48 1/2 x 50	49 x 50 1/2
5-2	.58	58 1/2
5-0 x 4-6	56 1/2 x 50	57 x 50 1/2
5-2	58 1/8	58 1/2
5-8 x 4-6	64 1/2 x 50	65 x 50 1/2
5-2	58	58 1/2
6-4 x 4-6	72 1/2 x 50	73 x 50 1/2
5-2	58	58 1/2
7-0 x 4-6	80 1/2 x 50	81 x 50 1/2
5-2	58	58 1/2
8-4 x 4-6	96 1/2 x 50	97 x 50 1/2
5-2	58	58 1/2

Table 8.   Grade recommendations for window frames and sash

Data from Architectural Woodwork Institute

Verify the availability of any one of these woods or others in your area.

SOFTWOOD LUMBER

SPECIES	FRAMES	SASH	JURISDICTION Publishers of Grading Rules
Northern White Pine Eastern Spruce	No. 1 Common or D Select	No. 1 Common and Better	Northeastern Lumber Mfrs. Association
Tidewater Red Cypress	Clear Heart Faces, All Heart Sill	Clear Heart or Clear	Southern Cypress Mfrs. Association
Southern Pine	B and Better or C Finish Grade	Quality as specified	Southern Pine Inspection Bureau
Northern White Pine Norway Pine Eastern Spruce Western White Spruce	B and Better Select or C Select	Usual shop grades	Northern Pine Manufacturers Association
California Redwood	Clear All Heart or A Grade (if wood preservative is specified)	Clear All Heart or A Grade (if wood preservative is specified)	California Redwood Association
White Fir	No. 1 and No. 2 Clear C Select	Usual shop grades	Western Pine Assocation, including U.S.A., Alberta and Saskatchewan
Larch	C Select	Usual shop grades	
Douglas Fir (Inland Type)	C Select	Usual shop grades	
Ponderosa Pine	B and Better or C Select	Usual shop grades	
Sugar (Genuine) White Pine	No. 1 and 2 Clear or C Select	Usual shop grades	
Idaho (Genuine) White Pine	Supreme-Choice	Usual shop grades	
Engelmann Spruce	D and Better Select	Usual shop grades	
Lodgepole Pine	D and Better Select	Quality as specified	
Eastern Hemlock Tamarack Northern White Cedar	D and Better Finish, or No. 1 Boards	D and Better Finish	Northern Hemlock and Hardwood Mfrs. Association
Northern White Pine Norway Pine Eastern Spruce	B and Better Select or C Select	Usual shop grades	
West Coast Hemlock	B and Better	Quality as specified	West Coast Lumbermen's Association, including U.S.A., and British Columbia
Western Red Cedar	B and Better	Quality specified	
Sitka Spruce	B and Better	Quality specified	
Douglas Fir (Coast Region)	B and Better	Quality specified	

HARDWOOD LUMBER

The choice of hardwoods for exteriors should be governed by the architectural effects desired, by the cost and availability of the wood and the natural properties which make the wood best adapted to the intended use. For window frames and sash two such properties are essential. The wood must take and hold paint or other finishes well, and it must stay put when placed in use.

USE	KINDS OF HARDWOOD	GRADE OR QUALITY
Window Frames Sash	Poplar, Birch, Ash, Cherry, Hard Maple, White Oak and Red Oak	Clear, or natural markings as indicated by design

Table 9.   Dimensions of storm sash and screens

Data from CS163-59

Storm Sash		Screens	
St.	$1\frac{29}{32}''$	St.	$1\frac{27}{32}''$
T.R.	$1\frac{29}{32}''$	T.R.	$1\frac{27}{32}''$
B.R.	$4\frac{1}{16}''$	B.R.	$3''$
C.R.	$\frac{7}{8}''$	C.R.	$\frac{5}{8}''$

Storm Sash and Screens are made ⅛" narrower and 1" longer than window opening sizes.

Available for all modular-sized window or sash openings.

By HOWARD P. VERMILYA, AIA

Steel windows are made in a wide variety of type and grade combinations of ventilator openings. The sizes and types have been largely standardized through the efforts of the Steel Window Institute. Except for residential casements, all standard types are sized in accordance with the principles of modular coordination described in American Standards Association ASA A62. Within the range of standard sizes established, those designated as warehouse types are available for immediate delivery; other sizes are available on order from the factory.

WINDOW TYPES

The classification of window types is based generally on the grade for a common or probable use, often with several weights and design types for each grade. The types listed in the Steel Window Institute's *Recommended Standards for Steel Windows* (1964) are as follows:

Residential
  Casement
  Basement
  Utility
  Ranch
  Picture
Commercial, industrial, institutional
  Projected
  Casement
  Combination
  Classroom
  Guard
  Psychiatric
  Awning
  Architectural projected
  Commercial projected
  Horizontally pivoted
  Security
  Continuous

Types other than those listed above are manufactured but have not been standardized as to size or specification. Among these are: *double-hung* (heavy) for commercial and institutional buildings, *vertically pivoted* (stainless steel) for high-class air-conditioned buildings, and *escape* windows (intermediate) for educational buildings.

Grades of steel windows are determined by the weight of the combined outside frame and ventilator members in pounds per linear foot or by the depth and thickness of the individual sections. Standards establish maximum vent sizes and infiltration requirements and other items pertinent to the particular type of window. Screens are supplied for most types, with provision for window operation where necessary. Storm sash are available from some manufacturers. Insulating glass up to ½ in. thick can be installed in most types. All glazing is done at the site by the glazing contractor.

Shop finish comprises cleaning in a hot alkali solution, rinsing, bonderizing, rinsing, and dipping or spraying on a coat of paint, then preferably baking for at least 30 min at a temperature not less than 300°F. Double-hung windows must be electrogalvanized or tight-coat hot-galvanized before forming. The weight of the galvanized coating should conform to Class B2, ASTM A386-55.

One manufacturer has developed an alternate finish consisting of a bonderizing treatment, followed by an epoxy-resin-type primer baked on, over which an alkydamine-type enamel is baked on as a finish coat. This coating complies with Federal Specifications TT-E-489b and TT-R-266a.

Residential windows

Casement, picture, and *ranch* windows should have frames and ventilators made of hot-rolled structural steel sections having a minimum depth of 1 in. and a minimum weight of 2 lb per lin ft. At a wind velocity of 25 mph, the maximum infiltration permitted is 1 cu ft per lin ft of ventilator perimeter. *Basement* and *utility* windows should have frames and ventilators of hot-rolled steel sections having a minimum depth of 1 in. and a minimum weight of 1.7 lb per lin ft.

Maximum casement ventilator size is 1 ft 11¼ in. in width by 4 ft 1⅜ in. in height. Two types of casement operation are standard: *roto* (crank-operated, under screen) and *simplex* (manually operated, with friction hinges). In the latter case screens are provided with a sliding wicket to give access to the window. Muntins may be omitted if desired (some manufacturers only). Typical installation details of residential casement windows are shown in Fig. 12.

Casement, basement, and utility windows have been standardized in size, as shown in Fig. 13. Picture windows have not been standardized, but they are usually available in the standard casement heights of 3 ft 2⅜ in., 4 ft 2⅝ in., and 5 ft 3 in. Ranch windows also have not been standardized as to size, but most manufacturers base their designs on a fixed glass size of 24 in. by 36 in. This results in window widths of approximately 3 ft 1 in., 6 ft 2 in., and 9 ft 3 in., and heights of 2 ft 1 in., 4 ft 2 in., and 6 ft 3 in. For more precise information on ranch and picture windows, consult manufacturers' catalogs.

Double-hung windows (light) are made from cold-formed strip steel that has been

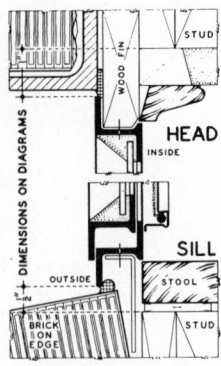

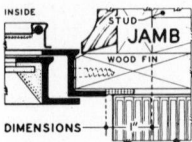

Fig. 12. Residential casement window in brick-veneer construction—scale 3 in. = 1 ft.

Courtesy Hope's.

galvanized before forming. The minimum depth of the frame is 3¾ in.; the minimum thickness of the sill is 0.060 in., of all other members of the frame and ventilators, 0.048 in. Parting strips may be extruded aluminum, and muntins may be hot-rolled steel tees, ungalvanized. Maximum width is 4 ft; maximum height is 7 ft 1½ in. or, with sill ventilator, 8 ft 1½ in. At a wind velocity of 25 mph, maximum infiltration is 1 cu ft per lin ft of ventilator perimeter and maximum glass thickness is ¼ in. Screens are installed on the outside and may be top-hinged or sliding. Standard sizes are shown in Fig. 14 and typical details in Fig. 15.

Intermediate windows

Intermediate windows are made of heavier and better constructed sections than those used for residential windows. They are made in a number of window types and are intended for a wide range of uses. *Projected, casement,* and *combination* windows are long-established types and are widely used in the better class of commercial and institutional buildings. *Classroom* windows are a more recent development, intended primarily for use in school buildings but well suited to many other applications. They consist of a large, fixed glass area for light and view, with one or more small projected ventilators at the bottom for controlled ventilation. The four window types mentioned above have been standardized as to size (Figs. 16–19). Other intermediate types that have not been standardized will be noted later.

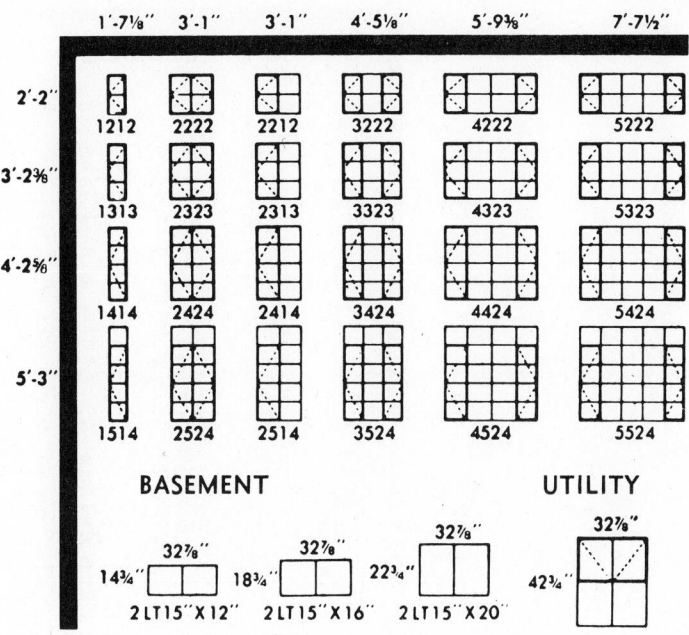

BASEMENT   **UTILITY**

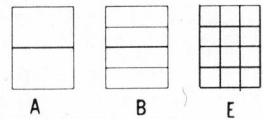

Fig. 13. Residential casement windows: types and sizes

Eastern sizes shown apply to all states except California, Oregon, Washington, Idaho, Nevada, Utah, and Arizona. For western sizes consult manufacturers' catalogs. All sizes shown are warehouse types. Dimensions are over-all out-to-out measurements. Single ventilators may swing from right or left. Fixed types furnished for all sizes shown. (From "Recommended Standards for Steel Windows," Steel Window Institute, 1964.)

DOUBLE HUNG · LIGHT TYPE

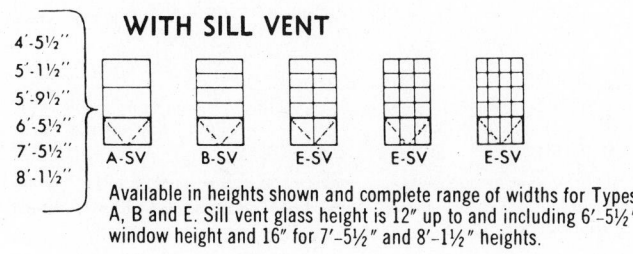

A   B   E

widths: 1'-8" 2'-0" 2'-4" 2'-8" 3'-0" 3'-4" 3'-8" 4'-0"
heights: 3'-1½" 3'-9½" 4'-5½" 5'-1½" 5'-9½" 6'-5½" 7'-1½"

"A" Type in 2'-5½" height and "B" Types in 3'-1½", 3'-9½", 4'-5½" and 5'-1½" heights are also available in widths of 4'-4", 4'-8" and 5'-0".

WITH SILL VENT

4'-5½"
5'-1½"
5'-9½"
6'-5½"
7'-5½"
8'-1½"

A-SV   B-SV   E-SV   E-SV   E-SV

Available in heights shown and complete range of widths for Types A, B and E. Sill vent glass height is 12" up to and including 6'-5½" window height and 16" for 7'-5½" and 8'-1½" heights.

NOTE: The accompanying types and sizes of double-hung windows represents the entire list of standard types available from the leading manufacturers of this type window. All dimensions shown are window dimensions.

TYPE E Vertical Muntins
1'-8" and 2'-0" widths—one vertical muntin
2'-4" and 3'-0" widths—two vertical muntins
3'-4" and 4'-0" widths—three vertical muntins

EXAMPLES OF WINDOW CODING:
Type, E, 2'-4" x 4'-5½" = E2445
Type B, 3'-0" x 5'-9½" = B3059

TYPE E COLONIAL

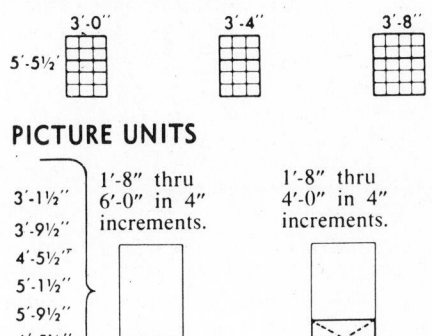

3'-0"   3'-4"   3'-8"

5'-5½"

PICTURE UNITS

3'-1½"
3'-9½"
4'-5½"
5'-1½"
5'-9½"
6'-5½"
7'-5½"
8'-1½"

1'-8" thru 6'-0" in 4" increments.

1'-8" thru 4'-0" in 4" increments.

F STANDARD   F-SV WITH SILL VENT

Fig. 14. Residential double-hung windows: types and sizes

From "Recommended Standards for Steel Windows," Steel Window Institute, 1964.

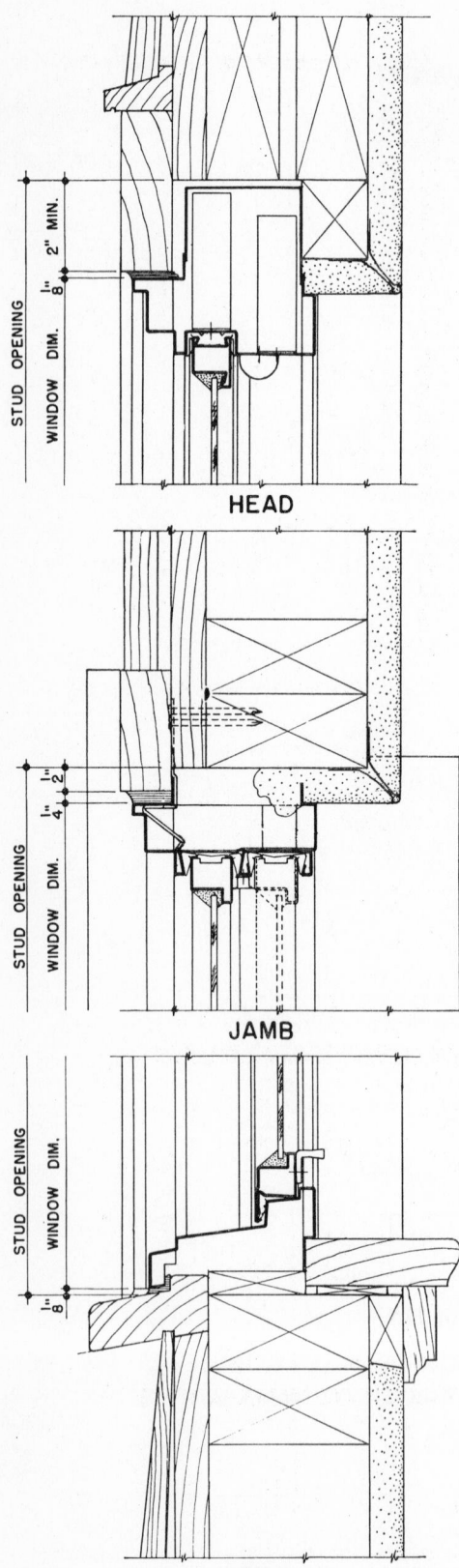

HEAD

JAMB

SILL

Fig. 15. Residential double-hung window in wood-frame construction—scale: 3 in. = 1 ft

Courtesy Truscon.

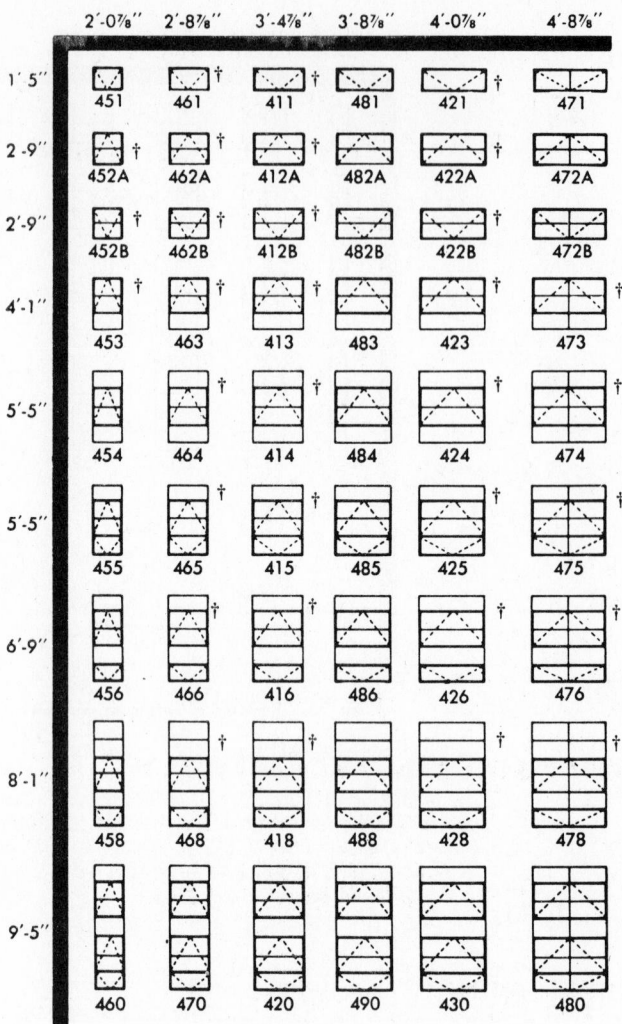

(Swing of vents only as indicated)

Fig. 16. Intermediate * projected windows: types and sizes

*Architectural projected windows are available in the same types and sizes including warehouse types, shown above. To specify architectural projected windows, change the first digit of the code number from 4 to 2 (251, 261, etc.). Fixed or stationary units may be supplied for all types shown. *For heavy intermediate, add the suffix "H"; for heavy custom, add the suffix "HC." (From "Recommended Standards for Steel Windows," Steel Window Institute, 1964.)*

The symbol † indicates warehouse types and sizes.

Intermediate windows are manufactured from hot-rolled structural steel, in three weights or grades, standard, heavy, and heavy custom. Minimum weights and dimensions of the members and maximum sizes of the vents for each grade are shown in Table 10. At a wind velocity of 25 mph, maximum infiltration permitted is 1 cu ft per lin ft of ventilator perimeter.

Casement ventilators that exceed 5 ft 6 in. in height should have three hinges and a two-point-connected locking device. Projected ventilators whose top edges are more than 6 ft 6 in. above the floor should be provided with hardware designed for pole or chain operation.

A typical installation detail of an intermediate projected window is shown in Fig. 20, and various glazing details for intermediate windows are given in Fig. 21.

Guard windows are designed for use in jails and correctional institutions. They are available in standard sizes and in three types of construction that provide "minimum," "moderate," or "maximum" detention. The basic design employs fixed main

Table 10. Specification for intermediate windows

Data from Recommended Standards for Steel Windows, *Steel Window Institute, 1962.*

	Standard intermediate	Heavy intermediate	Heavy custom
Minimum combined weight of frame and vent members, lb per lin ft	3.0	3.5	4.2
Minimum depth (front to back) of frame and vent members, in.	1¼	1⁵⁄₁₆	1½
Maximum vent size			
Casement:			
Width, ft–in.	2–3	2–6	3–0
Height, ft–in.	5–6	6–0	8–0
Area, sq ft			24
Projected			
Width, ft–in.	4–8	5–0	6–0
Height, ft–in.	2–8	3–0	4–0
Area, sq ft			20

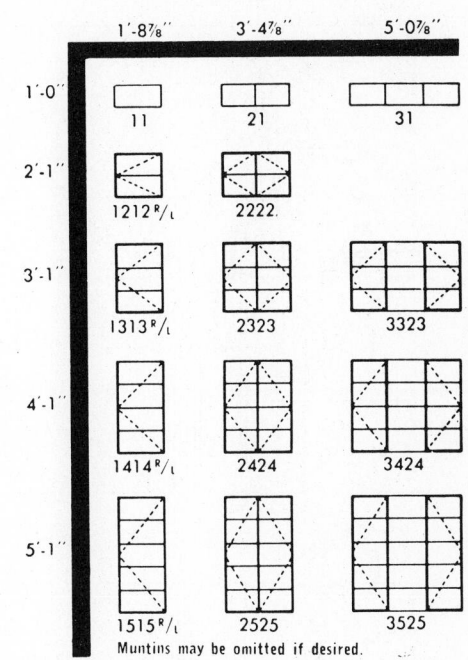

Muntins may be omitted if desired.

Fig. 17. Intermediate * casement windows: types and sizes

(From "Recommended Standards for Steel Windows," Steel Window Institute, 1964.)

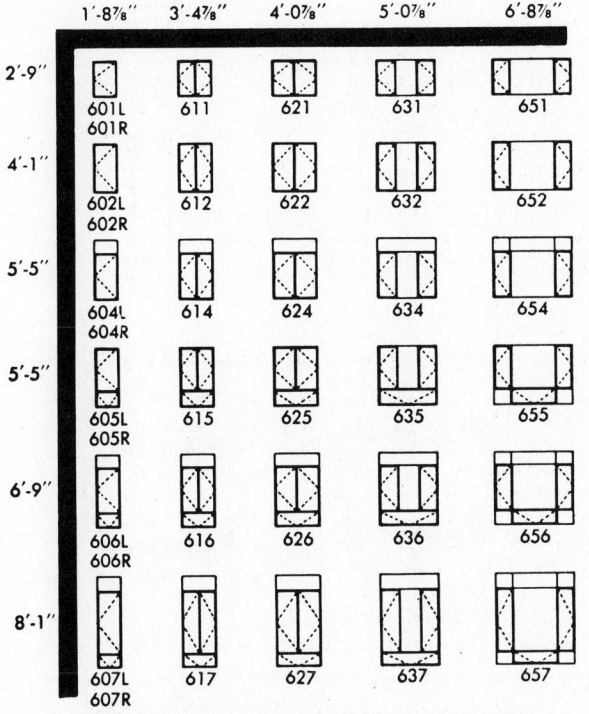

Muntins may be added if based on 20" or 24" bar centers for width and 16" bar centers for height. Sill vents may be omitted in favor of fixed light at sill.

FIXED or STATIONARY UNITS may be supplied for all types shown.
(*) For HEAVY INTERMEDIATE, add the suffix "H"
For HEAVY CUSTOM, add the suffix "HC"

Fig. 18. Intermediate * combination windows: types and sizes

(From "Recommended Standards for Steel Windows," Steel Window Institute, 1964.)

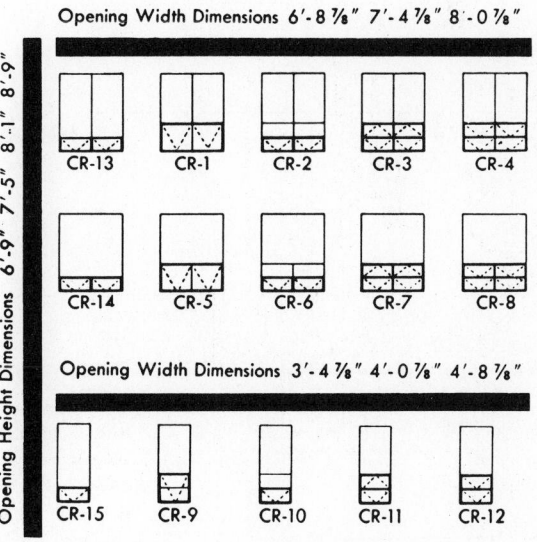

Fig. 19. Intermediate * classroom windows: types and sizes

(From "Recommended Standards for Steel Windows," Steel Window Institute, 1964.)

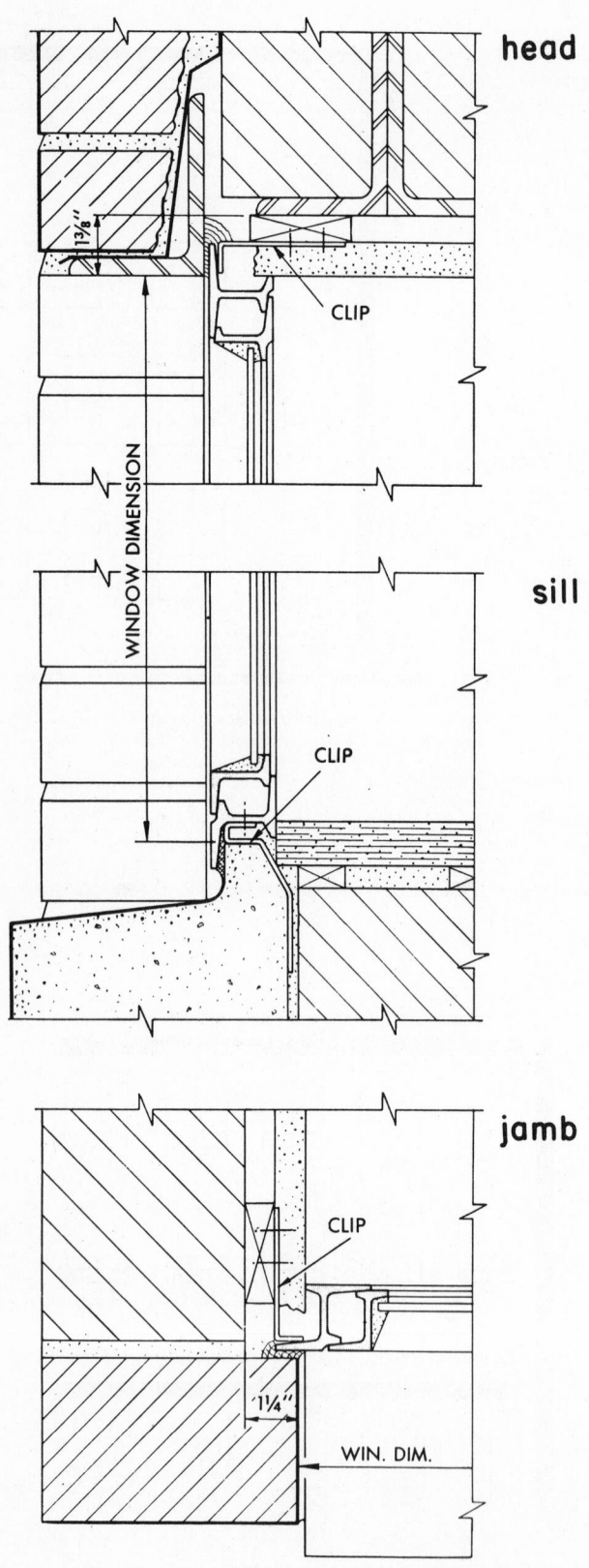

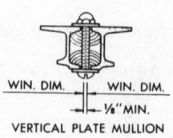
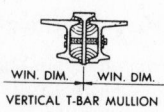

Equal-leg frames, available from most manufacturers, may be used to form narrow mullions, as shown in the two small details. (Courtesy Ceco.)

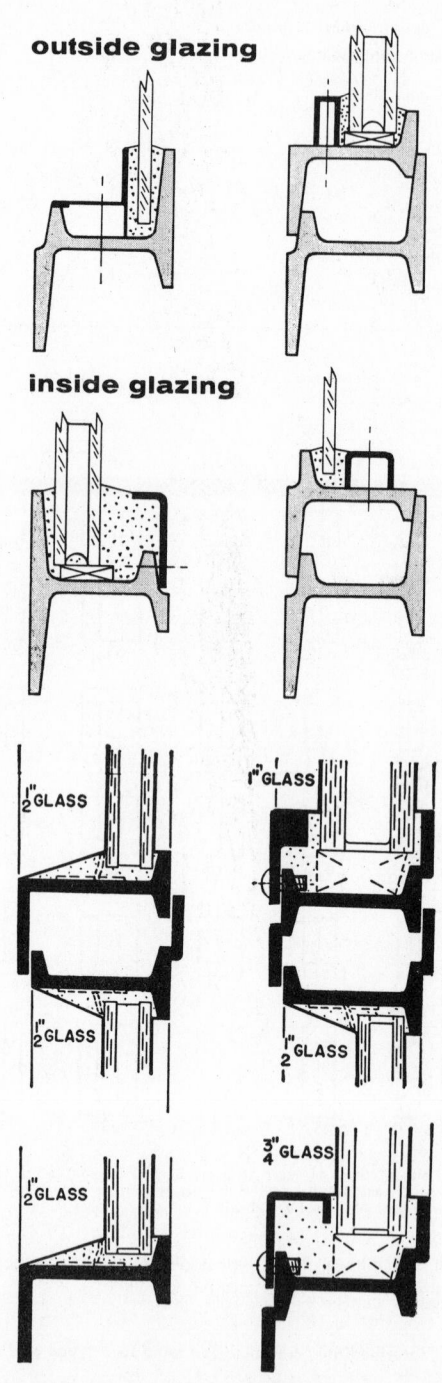

Fig. 20. Intermediate projected window in masonry construction—scale: 3 in. = 1 ft

Fig. 21. Glazing details for intermediate windows: glazing clips and various thicknesses of insulating glass—one-half full size

Courtesy, left, Ceco; right, Bayley.

frames with restricted glass openings and superimposed ventilators attached to the inside or outside of the grille (see manufacturers' catalogs).

Psychiatric windows are designed for use in mental institutions. Heavy intermediate sections and construction are used in conjunction with restricted glass openings and ventilator heights and with special hardware and screens. Ventilators may open in or out (see manufacturers' catalogs).

Awning windows provide a series of ventilators projecting outward and operating in unison. They are made of heavy intermediate materials and construction. Although sizes have not been standardized in the industry, awning windows are made in a wide range of sizes up to 16 ft in height or 20 ft in width. Size is usually limited to about 100 sq ft by the number of ventilators that can be opened by one operator. Some manufacturers provide awning windows with narrow, louver-type ventilators that can be used for detention purposes.

Architectural projected windows

Architectural projected windows occupy a middle place between intermediate projected and commercial projected windows. They are widely used in the less expensive types of commercial and institutional buildings. They are made from hot-rolled steel sections with a minimum depth of 1⅜ in. (1¼ in. if corners are welded and ground) and a minimum thickness of ⅛ in. Maximum vent size is 5 ft 0 in. wide by 2 ft 8 in. high, with a vertical muntin in vents over 4 ft wide. There are no requirements as to infiltration. Architectural projected windows are made in the same types and sizes as intermediate projected windows, shown in Fig. 16. Vents shown to project out may be made to project in, provided that all vents in the same unit do so. Outside glazing is standard, but inside glazing is available on order from some manufacturers. Typical installation details are shown in Fig. 22.

Commercial projected windows

Often referred to as "industrial windows" or "factory sash," commercial projected windows are used not only in industrial buildings but also in many types of commercial buildings. The projected type has now largely replaced the *horizontally pivoted* type, which, however, is still obtainable on order from most manufacturers. Sizes are the same for both types and are shown in Fig. 23. Commercial projected, like architectural projected, windows are made from hot-rolled steel sections with a minimum depth of 1⅜ in. (1¼ in. if corners are welded) and a minimum thickness

of ⅛ in. Maximum vent size is 5 ft 0 in. wide by 2 ft 8 in. high, with vertical muntins as shown. Again, there are no requirements as to infiltration. All sash are designed for inside glazing. Screens are available except for the pivoted type. Windows bearing underwriters' labels (Class E, moderate fire exposure) are available from some manufacturers, subject to the established limitations of size, installation, and glazing. Typical details of commercial projected windows are given in Figs. 24 and 25.

Security

Security windows are similar to commercial projected except that the frame and muntins form a continuous fixed grille on which the ventilator is superimposed. Ventilators open in. Security windows are used in warehouses, stores, factories, and other buildings, to prevent forcible entry. Standard sizes are shown in Fig. 26.

Continuous

Continuous windows are used in monitor or sawtooth roofs in factories and similar buildings. The 1964 SWI "Standards" classifies continuous windows as a specialty and

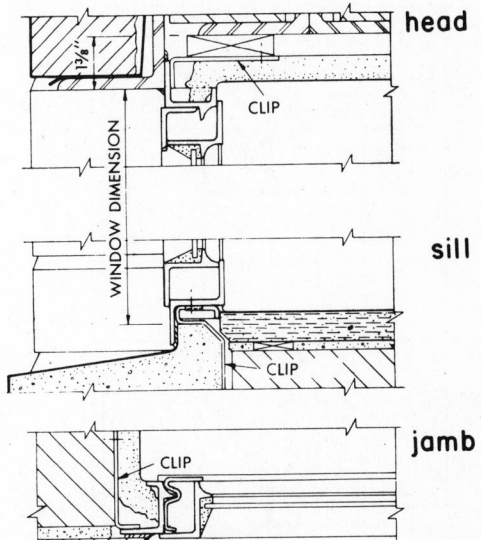

Fig. 22. Architectural projected windows in masonry construction—scale: 3 in. = 1 ft

Courtesy Ceco.

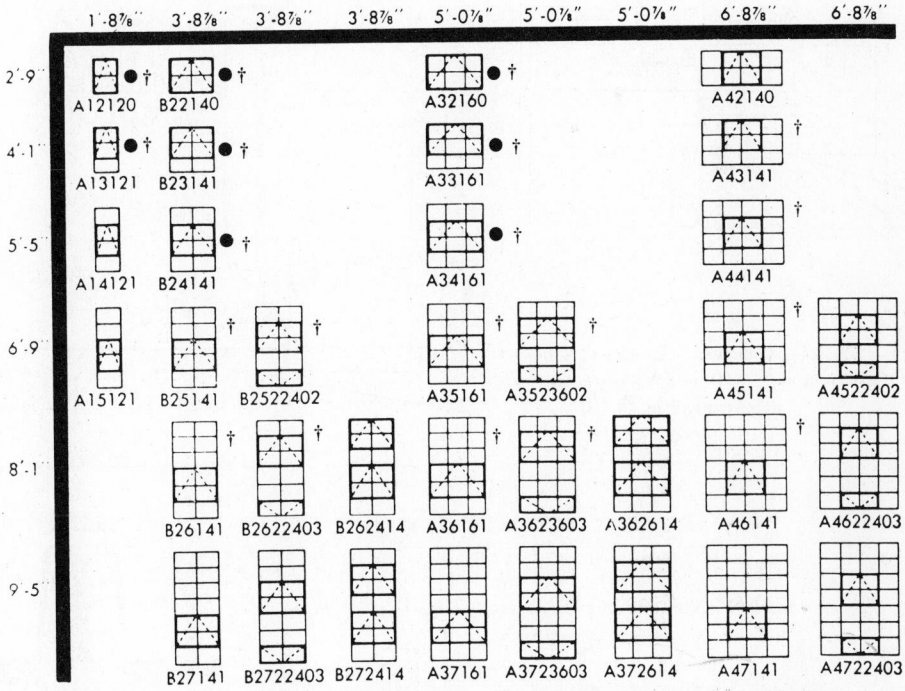

Fixed (non-ventilating) units available for all above types. ● Also made as warehouse types with vents project in.

Fig. 23. Commercial projected windows: types and sizes

Horizontally pivoted windows are available on special order in the various sizes and ventilating sash arrangements indicated for commercial projected windows. Consult individual manufacturer's catalog for availability. (From "Recommended Standards for Steel Windows," Steel Window Institute, 1964.)

The symbol † indicates warehouse types and sizes.

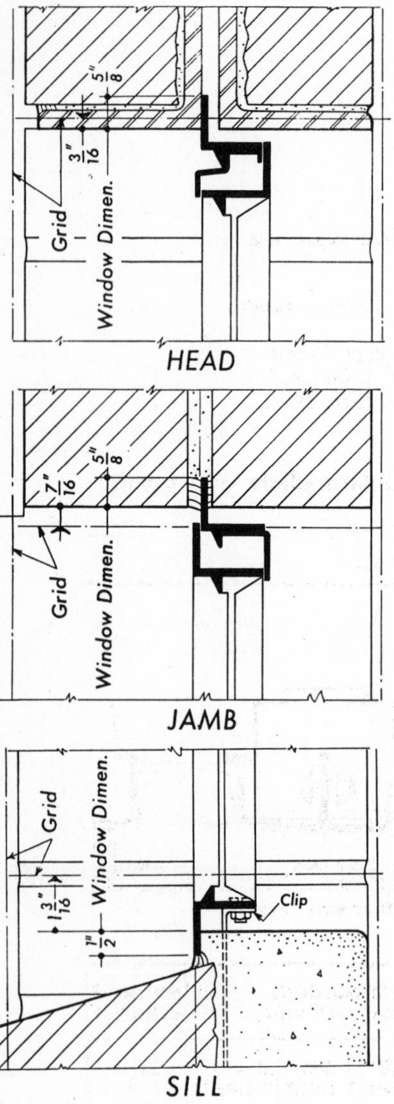

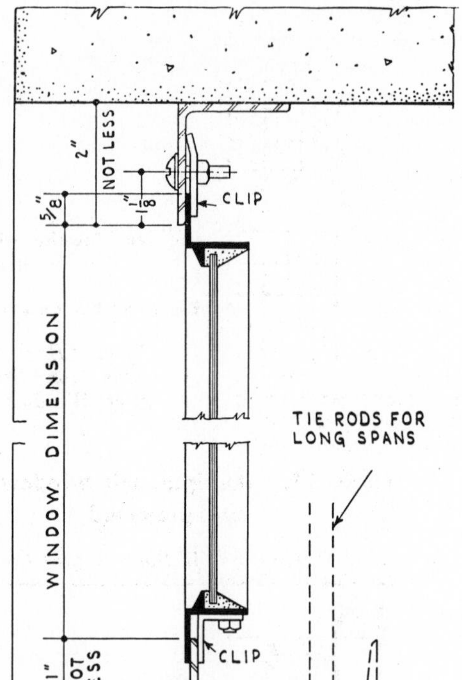

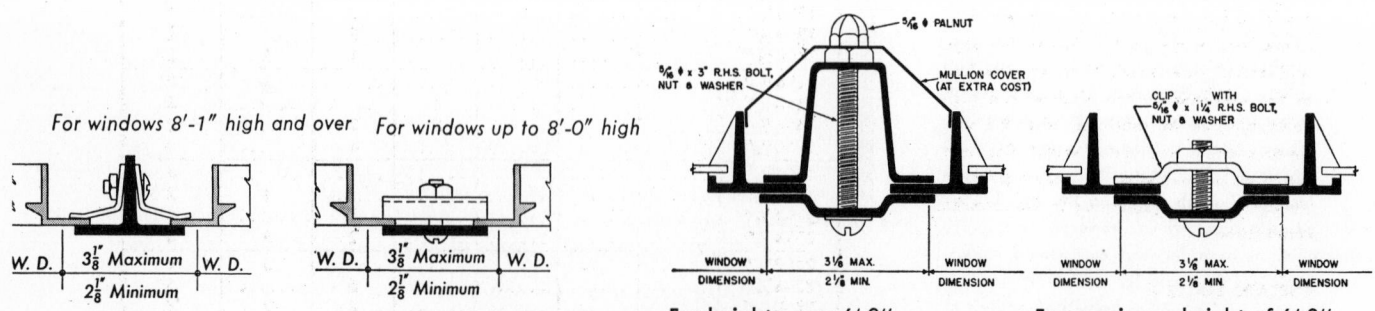

HEAD

JAMB

SILL

Grid

Window Dimen.

$\frac{5}{8}$"

$\frac{3}{16}$"

$\frac{7}{16}$"

$\frac{5}{8}$"

$1\frac{3}{16}$"

$\frac{1}{2}$"

Clip

Fig. 24. Commercial projected windows in masonry (left) and concrete construction—scale: 3 in. = 1 ft

Courtesy Lupton.

WINDOW DIMENSION

CLIP

NOT LESS

2"

$\frac{5}{8}$"

$\frac{1}{8}$"

TIE RODS FOR LONG SPANS

CLIP

1" NOT LESS

NOT LESS 2"

$\frac{1}{8}$"

$\frac{7}{16}$" HOLES NOT OVER 20" ℄ TO ℄ BY STEEL CONTR.

TYPICAL HORIZONTAL MULLION

CLIP

$\frac{1}{2}$"

gives neither specifications nor sizes. The following information from the 1960 SWI "Standards" will serve to give a general idea of the sizes and construction of these windows. The principal members should be made of hot-rolled steel sections having the following minimum weights in pound per linear foot: top rail, 1.6; bottom rail, 3.0; end rails, 1.2. Window units are manufactured in heights of 3, 4, 5, and 6 ft and in even-foot lengths, with vertical muntins on 2-ft centers. The outswinging ventilator units must overlap, by about 2 ft, stationary storm panels at each end. The 3-ft high windows open to a maximum horizontal distance of 22 in.; the larger sizes open to 30 in.

Multiple units

Multiple units for large openings are formed by the use of standard mullions of various shapes, depending upon the height of the windows (Fig. 25). Mullions are 3⅛ in. wide, but in most cases the space between window units can be reduced to 2⅛ in. by compressing the detail. The sizes of openings formed by the use of multiple units of intermediate and commercial projected windows are shown in Tables 11 and 12, respectively. Since commercial projected windows are often used continuously past columns, Table 12 also gives suggested selections of multiple units for various column spacings.

MECHANICAL OPERATORS

Manual or motor-driven mechanical operators are used for opening and closing groups of windows. Standard types are as follows: The *lever-arm* operator (manual only) provides rapid opening for short runs of pivoted or projected ventilators. The *rack-and-pinion* operator (manual or motor) acts more slowly but can control longer runs. It is also suitable for short runs of continuous windows. *Tension* operators (motor only) are designed for opening and closing continuous windows. Screw-type op-

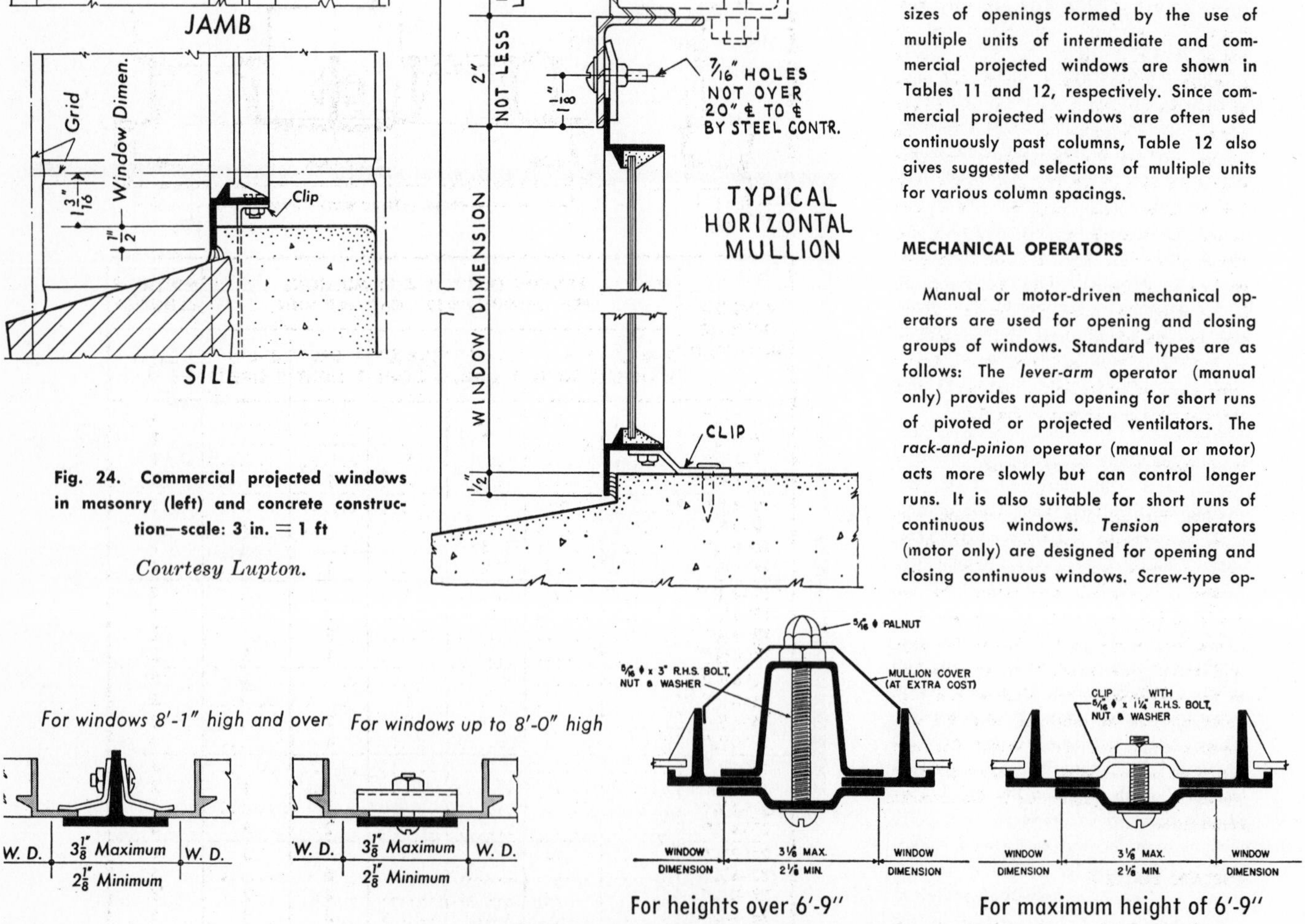

For windows 8'-1" high and over

For windows up to 8'-0" high

W. D.   3⅛" Maximum   W. D.
        2⅛" Minimum

W. D.   3⅛" Maximum   W. D.
        2⅛" Minimum

$\frac{5}{16}$" ∅ PALNUT

$\frac{5}{16}$" ∅ x 3" R.H.S. BOLT, NUT & WASHER

MULLION COVER (AT EXTRA COST)

CLIP WITH $\frac{5}{16}$" ∅ x 1¼" R.H.S. BOLT, NUT & WASHER

WINDOW DIMENSION   3⅛ MAX. 2⅛ MIN.   WINDOW DIMENSION

WINDOW DIMENSION   3⅛ MAX. 2⅛ MIN.   WINDOW DIMENSION

For heights over 6'-9"

For maximum height of 6'-9"

Fig. 25. Typical mullions for commercial projected windows—scale: 3 in. = 1 ft

Courtesy Lupton, above; Bogert and Carlough, below.

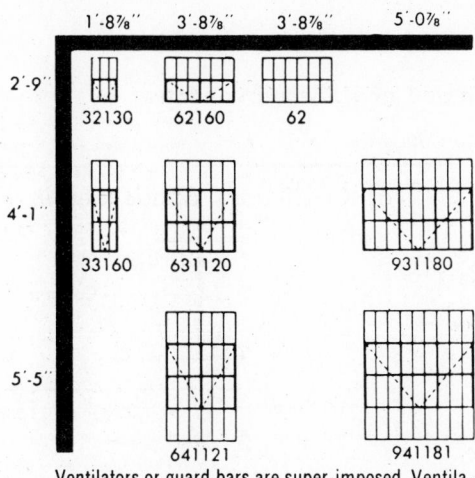

Fig. 26. Security windows: types and sizes

All items shown are warehouse types.

From "Recommended Standards for Steel Windows," Steel Window Institute, 1964.

Ventilators or guard bars are super-imposed. Ventilators open in behind fixed unit muntins as shown.

Table 11. Multiple unit windows: intermediate and architectural projected

Courtesy William Bayley Company.

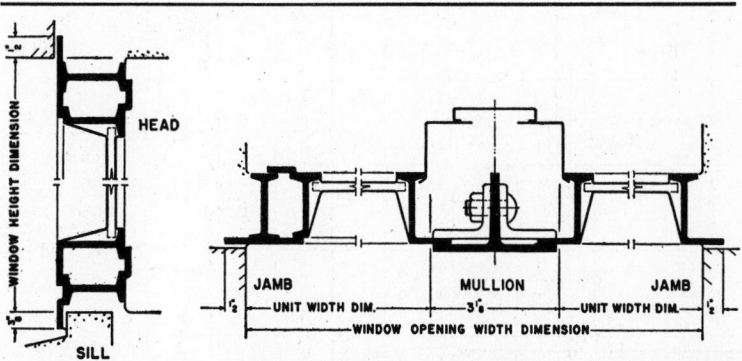

erators (manual only) are designed for group control of pivoted or projected ventilators in vertical arrangement, as in power houses, auditoriums, and similar structures. Recommended lengths of runs of windows controlled from a single power station are indicated in Table 13. The power unit for the tension-type operator should be located at the end of the run. For all other operators, the power unit should be located approximately at the center of the run. If power must be located at the end of the run, reduce lengths shown in the table by one-third. Manual power may be applied by chain and sprocket or by solid shaft with gear and crank. Lever-arm and rack-and-pinion operators and chain control are shown in Fig. 27.

FINS, SUBFRAMES, SURROUNDS

Metal fins or clips for anchoring windows to adjacent construction are available for most window types. Metal subframes or surrounds and metal trim are available for some types of windows. Subframes are made of No. 12 or 14 gage cold-formed steel sheet; they are installed as the wall is built; the windows can then be installed in the subframes after the wall construction is complete. Wood fins and surrounds are available for some residential windows, to aid installation in wood-frame construction.

CURTAIN WALLS

Complete curtain wall systems are offered by most steel window manufacturers (see "Curtain Walls").

WINDOW OPENING DIMENSION	NUMBER OF UNITS AND MULLIONS PER OPENING AND LIGHTS PER UNIT						MULLIONS REQUIRED
	2'-0⅞" 1 LIGHT	2'-8⅞" 1 LIGHT	3'-4⅞" 1 LIGHT	3'-8⅞" 1 LIGHT	4'-0⅞" 1 LIGHT	4'-8⅞" 2 LIGHTS	3⅛"
5'-8⅞"	......	2	......	......	......	......	1
7'-0⅞"	......	......	2	......	......	......	1
7'-8⅞"	......	......	......	2	......	......	1
8'-4⅞"	......	......	......	......	2	......	1
9'-4⅞"	......	2	1	......	......	......	2
9'-8⅞"	......	......	......	......	......	2	1
10'-8⅞"	......	......	3	......	......	......	2
11'-4⅞"	......	......	2	......	1	......	2
11'-8⅞"	......	......	......	3	......	......	2
12'-8⅞"	......	......	......	......	3	......	2
13'-4⅞"	......	......	......	......	2	1	2
14'-0⅞"	......	......	......	......	1	2	2
14'-8⅞"	......	......	......	......	......	3	2
15'-8⅞"	......	......	......	4	......	......	3
16'-4⅞"	......	......	......	2	2	......	3
17'-0⅞"	......	......	......	......	4	......	3
18'-0⅞"	......	......	5	......	......	......	4
19'-8⅞"	......	......	......	......	......	4	3
21'-4⅞"	......	......	......	......	5	......	4
23'-4⅞"	......	......	......	......	2	3	4
24'-8⅞"	......	......	......	......	......	5	4
25'-8⅞"	......	......	......	......	6	......	5
27'-0⅞"	......	......	......	......	4	2	5
28'-4⅞"	......	......	......	......	2	4	5
29'-8⅞"	......	......	......	......	......	6	5
30'-8⅞"	......	......	......	......	6	1	6
32'-0⅞"	......	......	......	......	4	3	6

Table 12. Multiple unit windows: commercial projected and pivoted windows

Courtesy Michael Flynn Manufacturing Company.

For Steel or Masonry Openings

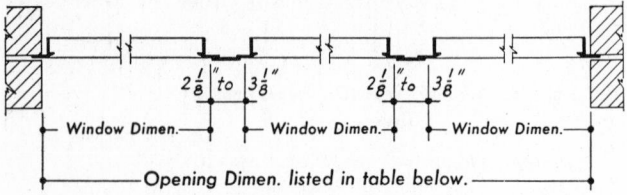

2⅛" to 3⅛"   2⅛" to 3⅛"

← Window Dimen. →← Window Dimen. →← Window Dimen. →

← Opening Dimen. listed in table below. →

For Continuous Bands Set in Front of Columns

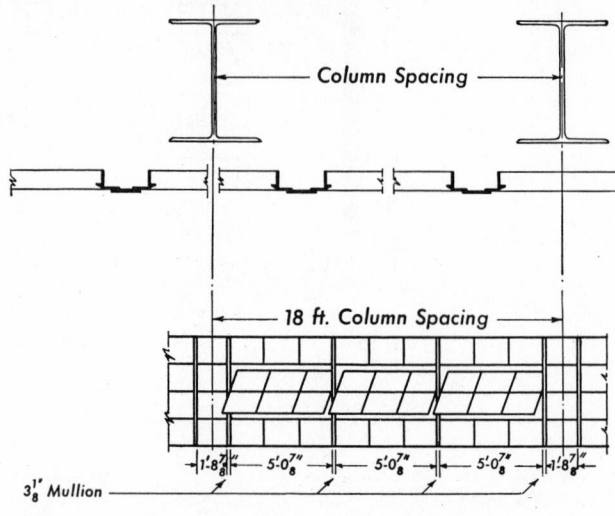

Column Spacing

18 ft. Column Spacing

3⅛" Mullion — 1'-8⅞" | 5'-0⅞" | 5'-0⅞" | 5'-0⅞" | 1'-8⅞"

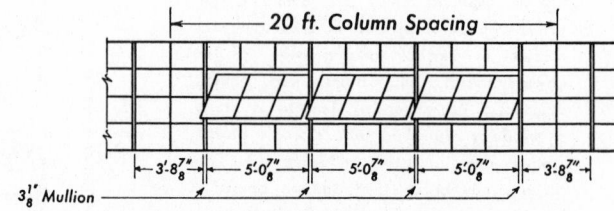

20 ft. Column Spacing

3⅛" Mullion — 3'-8⅞" | 5'-0⅞" | 5'-0⅞" | 5'-0⅞" | 3'-8⅞"

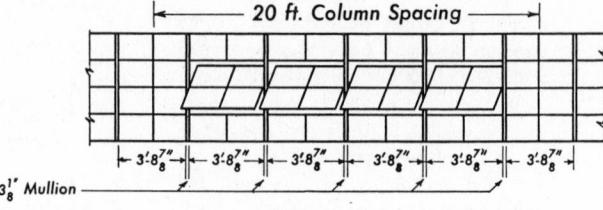

20 ft. Column Spacing

3⅛" Mullion — 3'-8⅞" | 3'-8⅞" | 3'-8⅞" | 3'-8⅞" | 3'-8⅞" | 3'-8⅞"

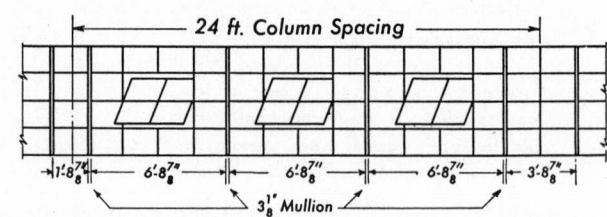

24 ft. Column Spacing

1'-8⅞" | 6'-8⅞" | 6'-8⅞" | 6'-8⅞" | 3'-8⅞"   3⅛" Mullion

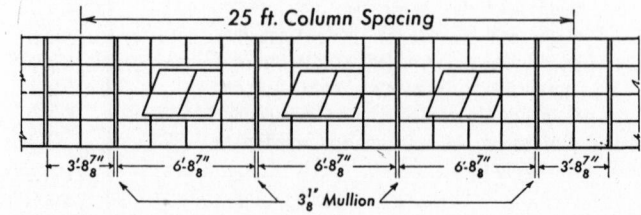

25 ft. Column Spacing

3'-8⅞" | 6'-8⅞" | 6'-8⅞" | 6'-8⅞" | 3'-8⅞"   3⅛" Mullion

Combinations of units that can be arranged symmetrically

WIDTH OF OPENING		DESIGN			
2⅛" MULLIONS	3⅛" MULLIONS	QUANTITY AND SIZE OF UNITS	UNITS WIDE	LIGHTS WIDE	QUANT. MULLS.
7'-7⅞"	7'-8⅞"	2@ 3'-8⅞"	2	4	1
8'-10⅞"	9'-0⅞"	2@ 1'-8⅞" 1@ 5'-0⅞"	3	5	2
9'-6⅞"	9'-8⅞"	1@ 1'-8⅞" 2@ 3'-8⅞"	3	5	2
10'-3⅞"	10'-4⅞"	2@ 5'-0⅞"	2	6	1
11'-6⅞"	11'-8⅞"	3@ 3'-8⅞"	3	6	2
12'-2⅞"	12'-4⅞"	1@ 1'-8⅞" 2@ 5'-0⅞"	3	7	2
12'-10⅞"	13'-0⅞"	2@ 3'-8⅞" 1@ 5'-0⅞"	3	7	2
13'-7⅞"	13'-8⅞"	2@ 6'-8⅞"	2	8	1
14'-2⅞"	14'-4⅞"	1@ 3'-8⅞" 2@ 5'-0⅞"	3	8	2
14'-6⅞"	14'-8⅞"	2@ 3'-8⅞" 1@ 6'-8⅞"	3	8	2
15'-5⅞"	15'-8⅞"	4@ 3'-8⅞"	4	8	3
15'-6⅞"	"	3@ 5'-0⅞"	3	9	2
17'-2⅞"	17'-4⅞"	2@ 5'-0⅞" 1@ 6'-8⅞"	3	10	2
17'-6⅞"	17'-8⅞"	1@ 3'-8⅞" 2@ 6'-8⅞"	3	10	2
18'-1⅞"	18'-4⅞"	2@ 3'-8⅞" 2@ 5'-0⅞"	4	10	3
18'-10⅞"	19'-0⅞"	1@ 5'-0⅞" 2@ 6'-8⅞"	3	11	2
19'-4⅞"	19'-8⅞"	5@ 3'-8⅞"	5	10	4
20'-6⅞"	20'-8⅞"	3@ 6'-8⅞"	3	12	2
20'-8⅞"	21'-0⅞"	4@ 3'-8⅞" 1@ 5'-0⅞"	5	11	4
20'-9⅞"	"	4@ 5'-0⅞"	4	12	3
21'-5⅞"	21'-8⅞"	2@ 3'-8⅞" 2@ 6'-8⅞"	4	12	3
22'-0⅞"	22'-4⅞"	3@ 3'-8⅞" 2@ 5'-0⅞"	5	12	4
23'-3⅞"	23'-8⅞"	6@ 3'-8⅞"	6	12	5
24'-1⅞"	24'-4⅞"	2@ 5'-0⅞" 2@ 6'-8⅞"	4	14	3
24'-8⅞"	25'-0⅞"	1@ 3'-8⅞" 4@ 5'-0⅞"	5	14	4
25'-4⅞"	25'-8⅞"	3@ 3'-8⅞" 2@ 6'-8⅞"	5	14	4
25'-2⅞"	"	1@ 1'-8⅞" 6@ 3'-8⅞"	7	13	6
26'-0⅞"	26'-4⅞"	5@ 5'-0⅞"	5	15	4
27'-2⅞"	27'-8⅞"	7@ 3'-8⅞"	7	14	6
27'-5⅞"	"	4@ 6'-8⅞"	4	16	3
27'-8⅞"	28'-0⅞"	1@ 6'-8⅞" 4@ 5'-0⅞"	5	16	4
28'-6⅞"	29'-0⅞"	6@ 3'-8⅞" 1@ 5'-0⅞"	7	15	6
29'-4⅞"	29'-8⅞"	1@ 1'-8⅞" 4@ 6'-8⅞"	5	17	4
31'-1⅞"	31'-8⅞"	8@ 3'-8⅞"	8	16	7
31'-4⅞"	"	1@ 3'-8⅞" 4@ 6'-8⅞"	5	18	4
31'-3⅞"	"	6@ 5'-0⅞"	6	18	5
32'-8⅞"	33'-0⅞"	1@ 5'-0⅞" 4@ 6'-8⅞"	5	19	4
33'-0⅞"	33'-8⅞"	1@ 1'-8⅞" 8@ 3'-8⅞"	9	17	8
33'-2⅞"	"	1@ 1'-8⅞" 6@ 5'-0⅞"	7	19	6

Variations—Variations from widths shown above may be made by varying the mullion dimension between 2⅛" and 3⅛".

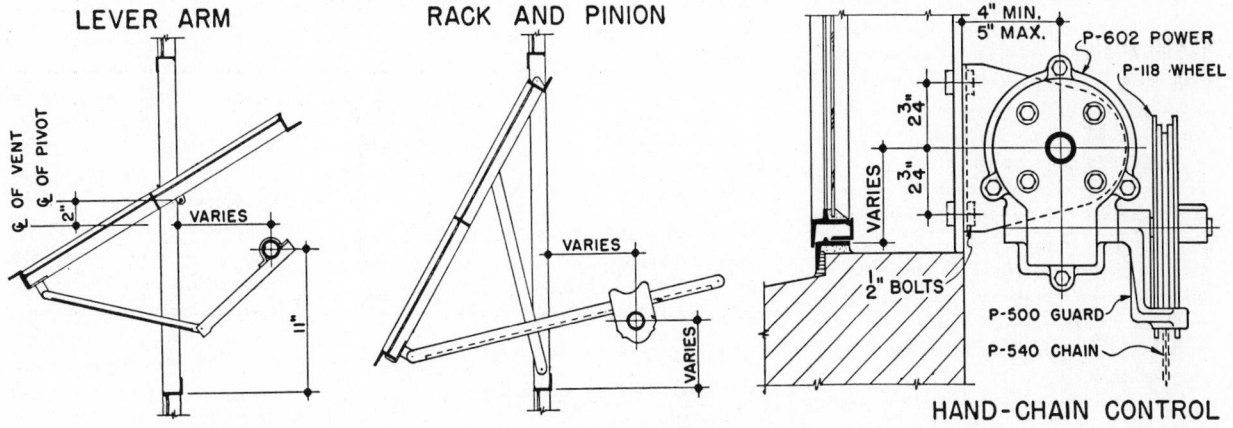

Fig. 27.   Mechanical operators—scale: left and center, ¾ in. = 1 ft; right, 1½ in. = 1 ft

Courtesy Truscon.

CHECK LIST FOR SPECIFYING STEEL WINDOWS

(Courtesy of Federal Windows Manufacturing Company, Inc.)

SAFETY: Are there windows in passageways that should swing out to clear pedestrian traffic? Are there any on lot lines which should swing in? Does Code require underwriters' labels or similar construction?

HAZARD: Is some special arrangement of ventilators or operating hardware necessary for self-closing in fire or automatic opening in explosion?

CLEANING: Will ventilator arrangement permit washing from inside building? Should there be provision for outside cleaning?

MATERIAL: Have you adequately identified the quality of window required by weight, depth and industry classification?

FINISH: Is standard bonderizing and prime coat of paint required; or galvanizing before shop painting? Is first field coat specified to be applied promptly after windows are received on the job and before glazing?

GLAZING: Is glazing to be outside with glazing compound, inside with glazing beads or outside with glazing beads?

HARDWARE: Is hardware to be polished bronze, solid bronze unpolished, white bronze, die cast lacquered or iron? Is hardware within reach from floor or should windows be operated by pole or other special arrangement? How many poles are required?

SUBFRAMES: What gage of metal is wanted? Are joints to be welded and ground smooth?

TRIM: Is trim such as closures, column covers, stools or other miscellaneous material to be furnished by window manufacturer?

SCREENS: Are insect screens required, and if so, for which windows? Are screens to have wickets for access to locking handles or be flat with hardware operating through or under the screen?

SHADES: Is preparation for mounting shades required? If dark shades are used, is special head and jamb framing required? Who furnishes shade brackets?

ERECTION: Have you specified that windows are to be installed by the manufacturer or an approved responsible company specializing in this kind of work?

CAULKING: Is bedding in mastic specified under "Windows" and caulking under "Masonry"? Is a particular kind of compound required?

Table 13.   Maximum lengths of run for mechanical operators

From "Recommended Standards for Steel Windows," Steel Window Institute, 1964.

LIMITS IN LENGTHS of RUNS (lineal feet)	LEVER ARM				RACK and PINION				
	dust shield		oil enclosed		dust shield		oil enclosed		
	chain	rod	chain	rod	chain	rod	chain	rod	elect.
PROJECTED	—	—	—	—	100	90	140	120	200
PIVOTED	100	80	150	120	160	140	200	180	240

CONTINUOUS TOP HUNG	TENSION TYPE					RACK and PINION				
	vert.	sloped 30° from vert.				vert.	sloped 30° from vert.			
	6'0"	3'0"	4'0"	5'0"	6'0"	6'0"	3'0"	4'0"	5'0"	6'0"
Manual	200	160	140	120	100	150	120	100	80	60
Electric	300	240	210	180	150					

WINDOWS—27
Aluminum

By HOWARD P. VERMILYA, AIA

In recent years aluminum has become one of the foremost materials for window construction. Many manufacturers of aluminum windows were originally, and still are, producers of steel windows. With some types (double-hung, combination, classroom, pivoted, and projected), it is possible to procure windows for the same-sized openings in either steel or aluminum, although the largest sizes of aluminum may not be available from all sources. On the other hand, aluminum casements are available in the same sizes but offer a wider range than do the intermediate steel-casement sizes.

Practically all shapes or sections are made from aluminum alloys designed for extruding. The most widely used alloy is 6063-T5, which has an ultimate tensile strength of 27,000 psi. Some use is also made of alloy 6063-T6, with a tensile strength of 35,000 psi, particularly where a thinner section or a harder surface is desired. The *Aluminum Window Specifications* of the Architetural Aluminum Manufacturers Association requires a minimum tensile strength of 22,000 psi. Alloy 3003 or 5050 sheet may be used for cold-formed work, mullion covers, trim, and screens.

WINDOW TYPES

Aluminum window types, as established by the Architectural Aluminum Manufacturers Association, and for which specifications with performance standards and use grades have been formulated, are as follows:

Double-hung
  Residential (DH-A1)
  Commercial (DH-A2)
  Monumental (DH-A3)
Casement
  Residential (C-A1)
  Commercial (C-A2)
  Monumental (C-A3)
Projected
  Residential (P-A1)
  Commercial (P-A2)
Awning
  Residential (A-A1)
  Commercial (A-A2)
Horizontal sliding (double and single)
  Residential (HS-A1)
  Commercial (HS-A2)
Jalousie
  Residential (J-A1)
Vertical sliding
  Residential (VS-A1)

Additional types of windows manufactured in aluminum are as follows:

Reversible (vertically pivoted)
Industrial (horizontally pivoted)
Folding
Classroom
Emergency-exit
Detention (security)
Corridor
Ribbon (glass-block installations).

The *Specifications* of the Architectural Aluminum Manufacturers Association sets certain minimum requirements for all aluminum windows. These refer to:

1. Alloys, their composition and strength.
2. Minimum section thickness of 0.062 in. except as noted.
3. Fasteners, hardware, and anchors—aluminum, nonmagnetic stainless steel or other noncorrosive material compatible with aluminum. Concealed fasteners may be coated steel if hidden when window is open. Plated or coated hardware must be insulated from aluminum. Steel anchors may be used if insulated from aluminum.
4. Joints are either mechanical or welded. Both provide satisfactory joints if well designed and well fabricated. Casement and projected windows are usually welded.
5. Weatherstrip material (plastic, woven, or metallic) must be compatible with aluminum.
6. Aluminum-to-aluminum contact between hardware parts or window members that move against one another is not permitted.
7. All windows except sliding and jalousie windows are to be assembled at the factory.
8. Standard glazing practice is to design for ⅛-in. glass except for jalousies. Other glass thicknesses may be used when specified. Compound or glazing beads compatible with aluminum may be used, depending on the manufacturer's design and practice. Glazing compound should meet Federal Specification TT-G-00410 for aluminum windows and not require paint protection.
9. Finishes may be any of the following when offered by manufacturers.
   a. Mill finish—natural finish after cleaning.
   b. Satin finish produced by etching in caustic, belt polishing, or rubbing with emery cloth or steel wool.
   c. Bright finish produced by buffing.

d. Anodized finish—an electrolytic finish—provides a thicker oxide coating than is naturally produced on aluminum. It may be specified for any of the first three finishes.
10. Protective coatings are used to protect the window from:
    a. Construction abuses—preferred coating is clear water-white methacrylate-type lacquer resistant to mortar and plaster.
    b. Steel or wood subframes—protect with alkali-resistant bituminous paint or zinc-chromatic primer in the case of steel and with wood preservative in the case of wood.

The *Specifications* of the Architectural Aluminum Manufacturers Association also gives the particular requirements of each window design and use type. It includes references to materials, construction, and hardware and gives performance requirements relating to horizontal, vertical, and uniform load tests and to air infiltration tests. Ventilator torsion tests are required for monumental casements and commercial and monumental projected windows. Hardware load tests are required for commercial and monumental casements, residential projected, awning, and jalousie windows. Water-resistance tests are required for awning type, Class II sliding windows, and jalousie windows. These tests are similar in method as applied to the various grades of windows but have differing applied loads and limits for determining performance. Residential-type windows are subject to less severe conditions of use and therefore are not required to comply with the more rigorous tests given to the commercial or monumental types.

The results of these tests are of value to architects in judging the relative merits of windows of various grades and of various manufacturers within grades. The air infiltration and water resistance test results are useful in evaluating different types of windows.

Hurricane specifications require certain tests in addition to those required of all window types. Air infiltration tests are the same. Water-resistance tests are the same as those required of awning, horizontal sliding, and jalousie windows. Physical load tests require a uniform load of 40 psf on the entire outside area (equal to a 127-mph wind) to be followed by a load of 20 psf on the interior surface, each applied for a period of 10 seconds, without glass breakage or permanent damage causing the window to be inoperable.

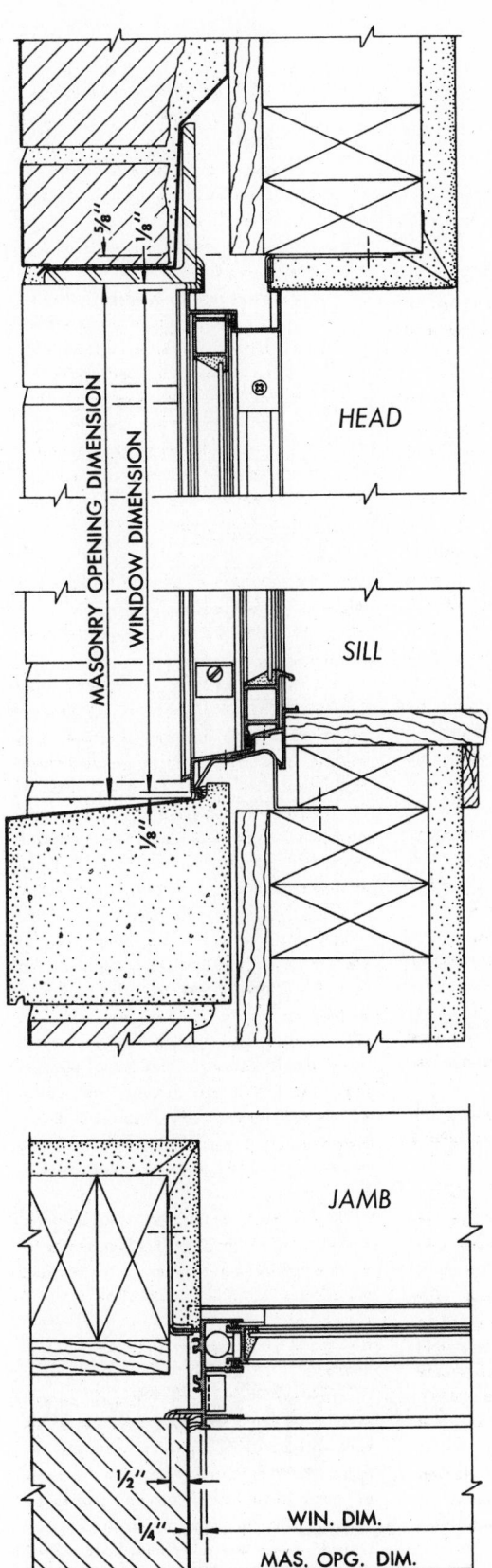

HEAD

SILL

MASONRY OPENING DIMENSION

WINDOW DIMENSION

5/8"

1/8"

1/8"

JAMB

1/2"

1/4"

WIN. DIM.

MAS. OPG. DIM.

Double-hung, residential windows—brick veneer

Courtesy Ceco

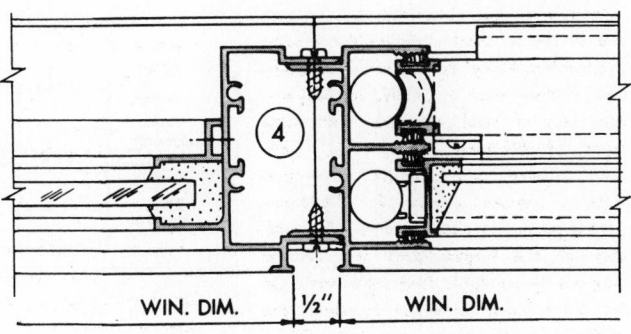

4

WIN. DIM.

1/2"

WIN. DIM.

Residential picture window combined with double hung

Courtesy Ceco

Details *Scale 3" = 1'—0"*

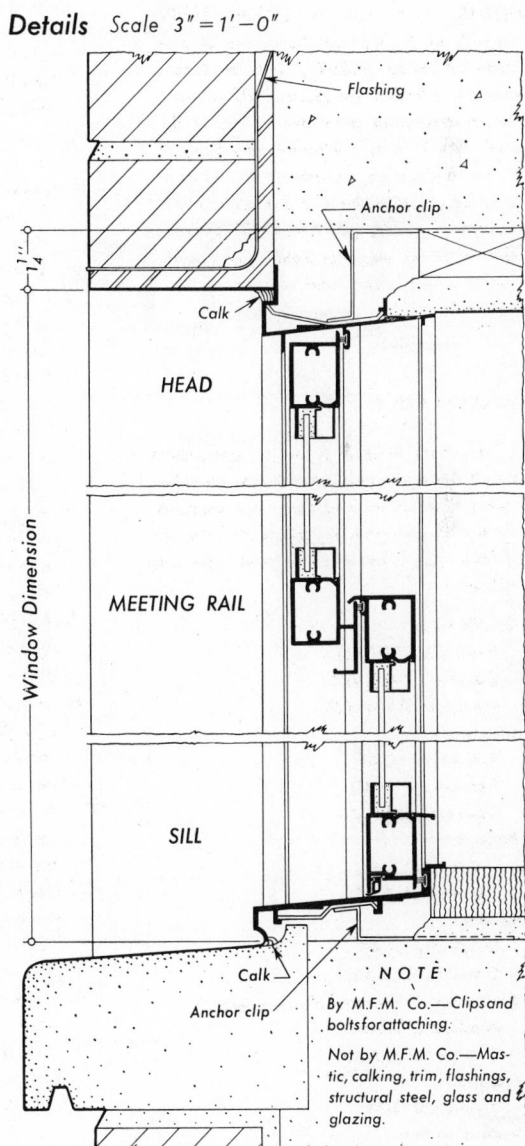

Flashing

Anchor clip

Calk

HEAD

1 1/4"

Window Dimension

MEETING RAIL

SILL

Calk

Anchor clip

NOTE

By M.F.M. Co.—Clips and bolts for attaching.

Not by M.F.M. Co.—Mastic, calking, trim, flashings, structural steel, glass and glazing.

Double-hung monumental window

Courtesy Lupton

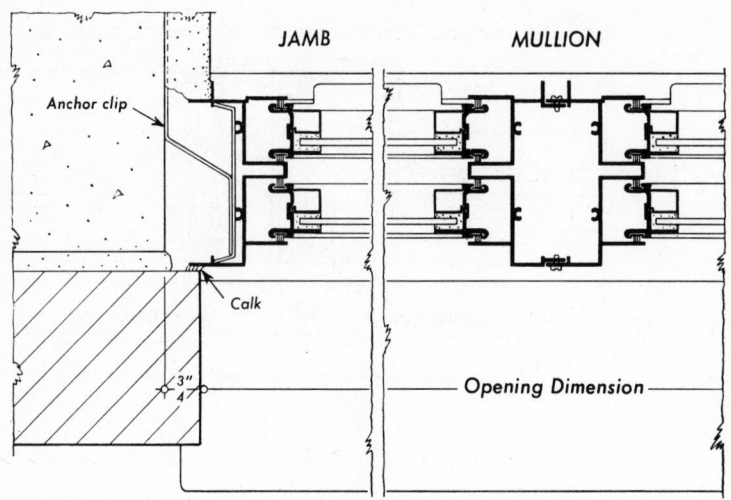

Double-hung monumental window

Courtesy Lupton

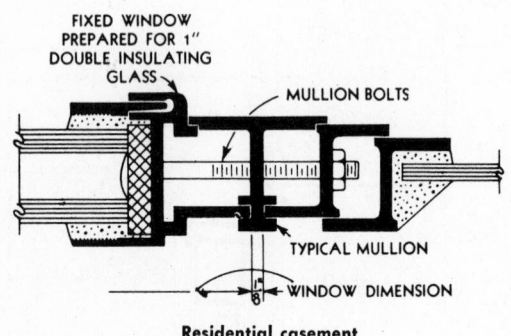

Residential casement

Courtesy Lemco

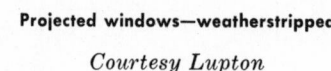

Projected windows—weatherstripped

Courtesy Lupton

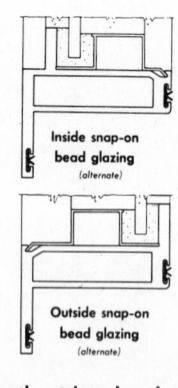

Weatherstripped projected windows

Courtesy Lupton

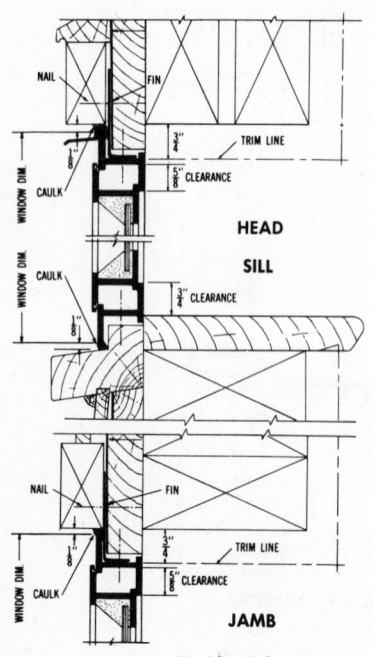

Residential casement

Courtesy Reynolds

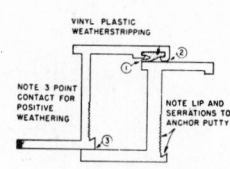

Residential casement

Courtesy Truscon

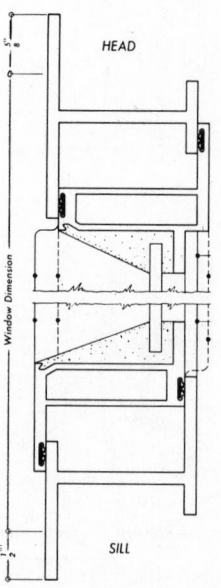

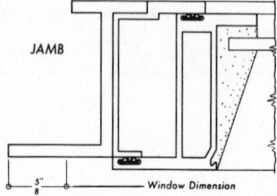

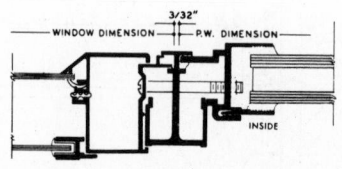

Residential awning window

Combination ventilating window—1-in. insulating glass. (Courtesy Lemco)

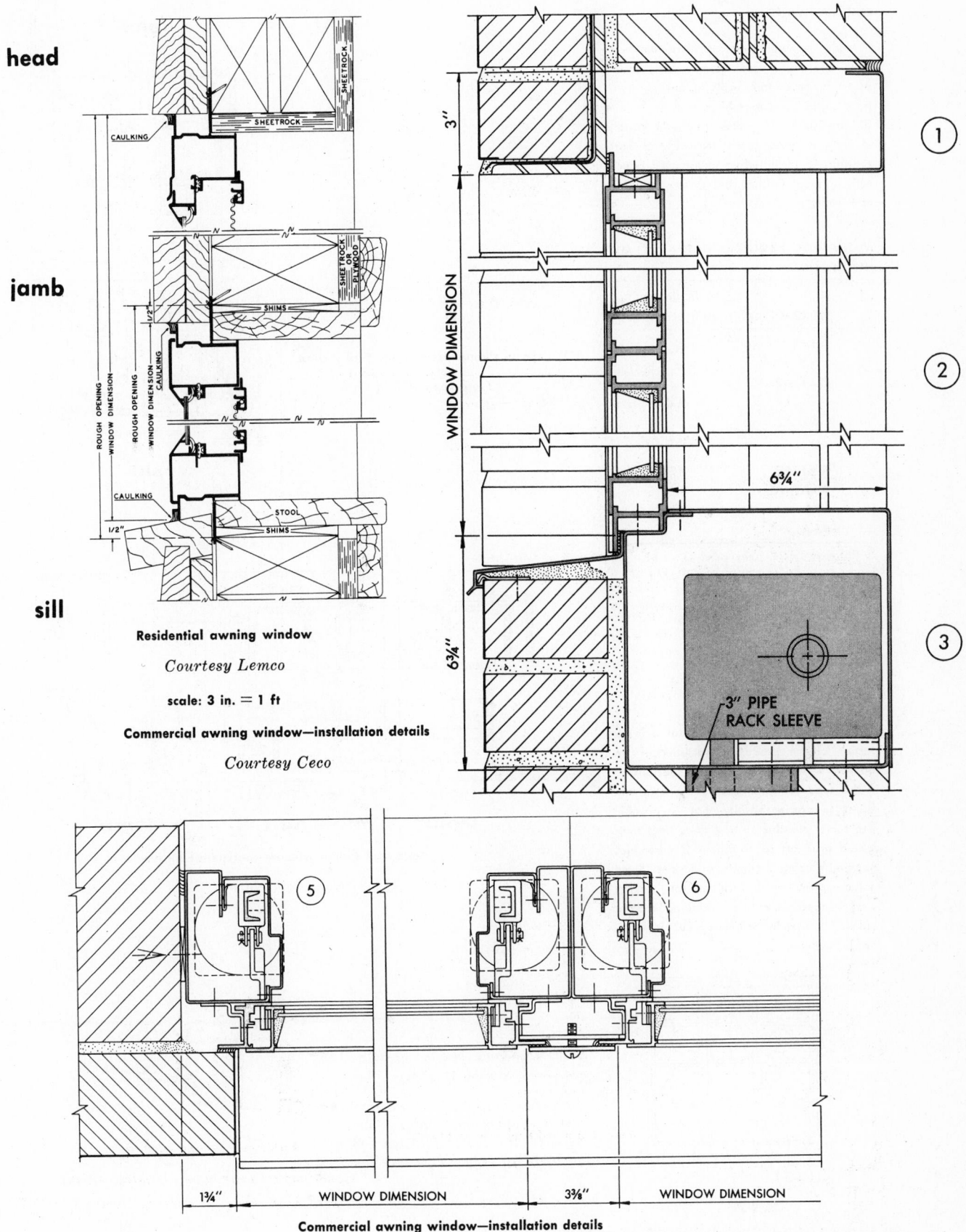

head

jamb

sill

Residential awning window

Courtesy Lemco

scale: 3 in. = 1 ft

Commercial awning window—installation details

Courtesy Ceco

3" PIPE
RACK SLEEVE

1¾"   WINDOW DIMENSION   3⅜"   WINDOW DIMENSION

Commercial awning window—installation details

Courtesy Ceco

(See next page for key elevation.)

CURTAIN WALLS

Many manufacturers of aluminum windows offer their products assembled or for assembly as curtain walls in one- or two-story sections or assemblies, and in various widths. These assemblies include a variety of mullion types, both vertical and horizontal, and insulated or uninsulated panels with optional finishes and cores (see "Curtain Walls").

Minimum requirements for air infiltration

Window Type	Air Infiltration,* cu ft per lin ft
DH-A1	¾
A2, A3	½
C-A1, A2, A3	1 †
	½ ‡
P-A1, A2	1 †
	½ ‡
A-A1, A2	1 §
HS-A1, A2	¾
J-A1	1½ §
VS-A1	¾

*Static air pressure of 1.56 psf equal to wind pressure at velocity of 25 mph. Sash closed and locked.
† For nonweatherstripped windows.
‡ For weatherstripped windows.
§ Cu ft per sq ft of ventilated area (not lin ft of ventilator perimeter).

SPECIAL TYPES

Custom-made windows represent a large portion of the production facilities of the industry with some companies specializing in this type of work. Church windows represent the great variety that is possible with some manufacturers. Others limit their custom products to variations in openings, muntins, glazing methods, and sizes. Some manufacturers have facilities for making windows and assemblies including curtain walls of bronze or stainless steel, in addition to aluminum.

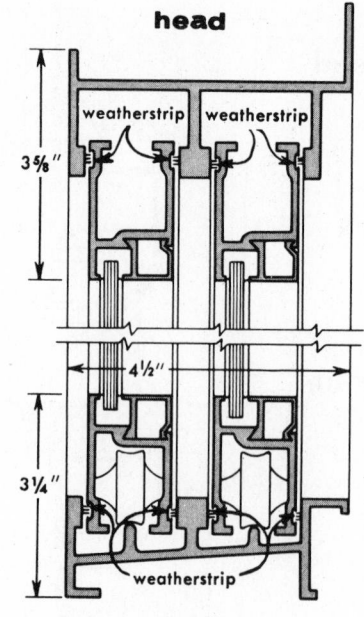

head

sill

Horizontal sliding window—vertical section

Courtesy Albro

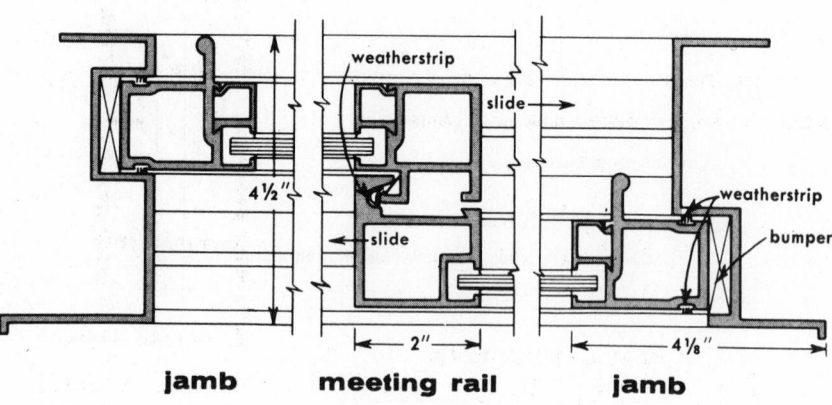

jamb   **meeting rail**   **jamb**

Horizontal sliding window—horizontal section

Courtesy Albro

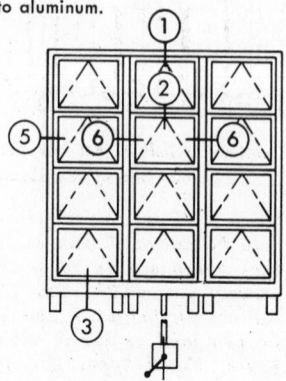

Key elevation for commercial awning window

Courtesy Ceco

Jalousie operator location up to and including 17 louvers

Jalousies over 63 in. high are dual operated. Obscure glass may be used in the lower louvers for privacy. (Courtesy Truscon.)

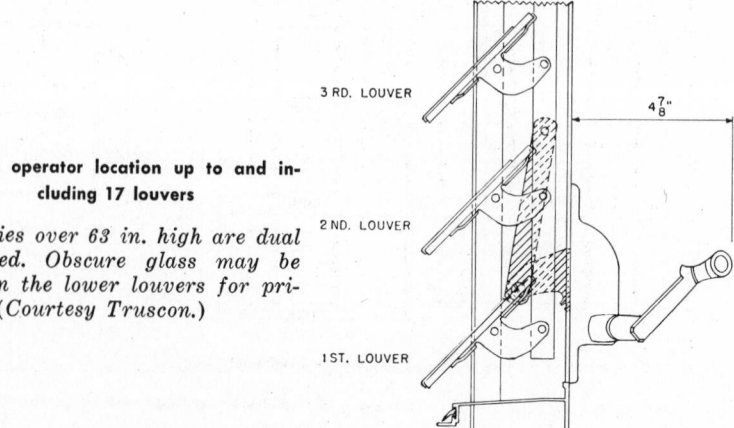

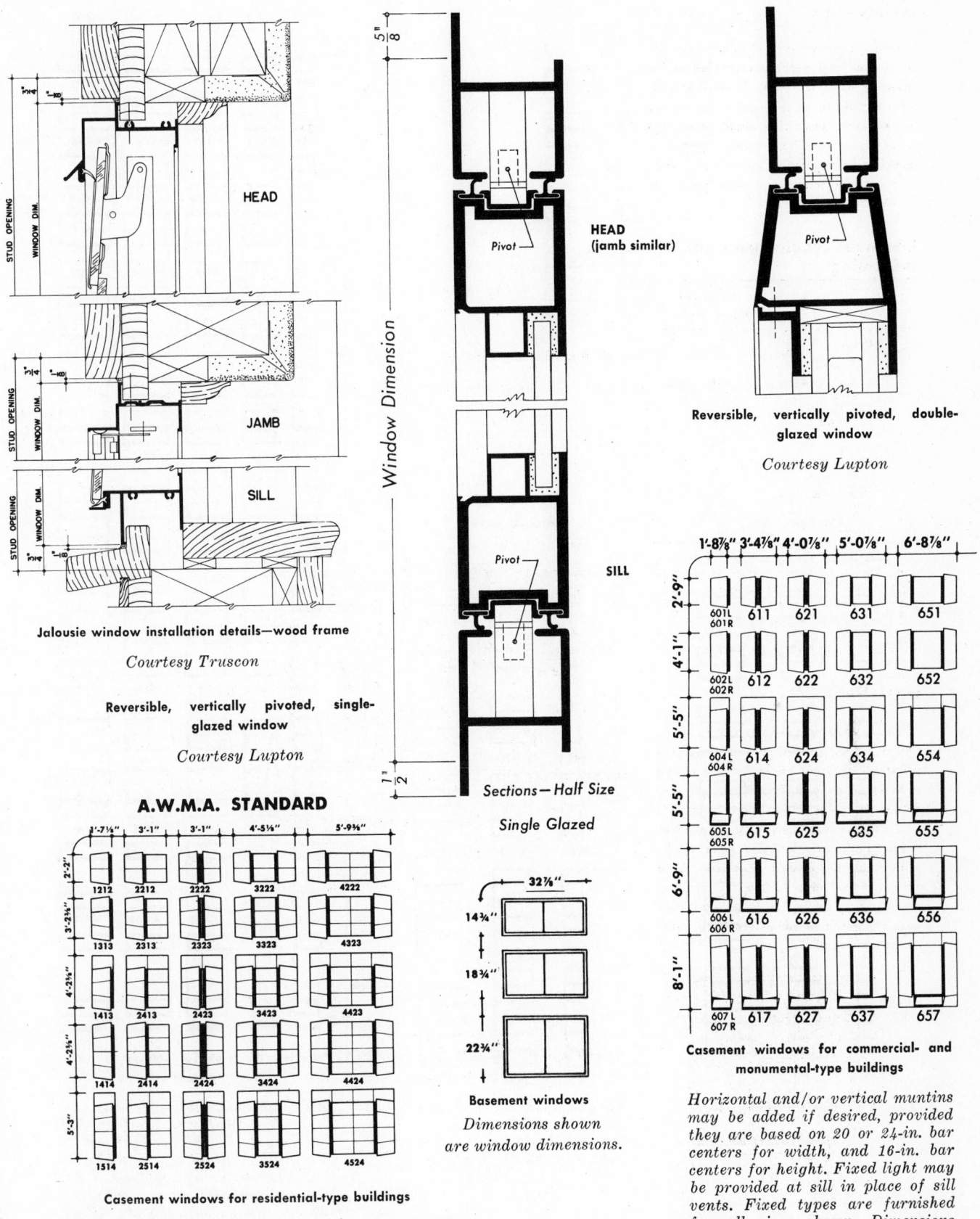

HEAD

JAMB

SILL

Jalousie window installation details—wood frame

Courtesy Truscon

Reversible, vertically pivoted, single-glazed window

Courtesy Lupton

A.W.M.A. STANDARD

Casement windows for residential-type buildings

Units with single ventilator may be hinged either right or left. Fixed types are furnished for all sizes shown. Dimensions shown are window dimensions.

HEAD (jamb similar)

Pivot

Pivot

SILL

Window Dimension

Sections—Half Size

Single Glazed

Basement windows

Dimensions shown are window dimensions.

Reversible, vertically pivoted, double-glazed window

Courtesy Lupton

Casement windows for commercial- and monumental-type buildings

Horizontal and/or vertical muntins may be added if desired, provided they are based on 20 or 24-in. bar centers for width, and 16-in. bar centers for height. Fixed light may be provided at sill in place of sill vents. Fixed types are furnished for all sizes shown. Dimensions shown are window opening dimensions.

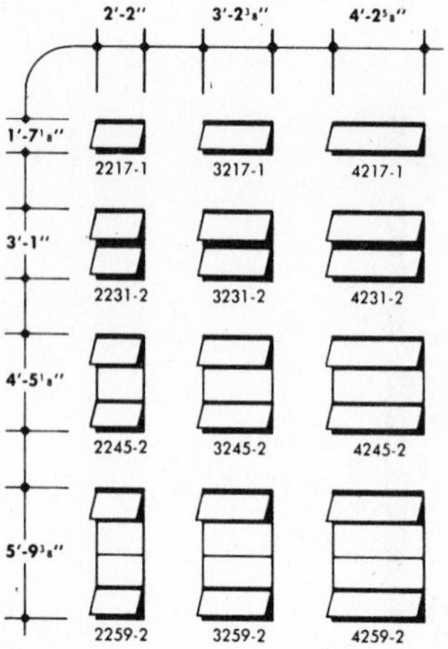

2'-2"
3'-2⅜"
4'-2⅝"
1'-7⅛"
3'-1"
4'-5⅛"
5'-9⅜"
2217-1
3217-1
4217-1
2231-2
3231-2
4231-2
2245-2
3245-2
4245-2
2259-2
3259-2
4259-2

Projected windows for residential-type buildings

Dimensions shown are window dimensions.

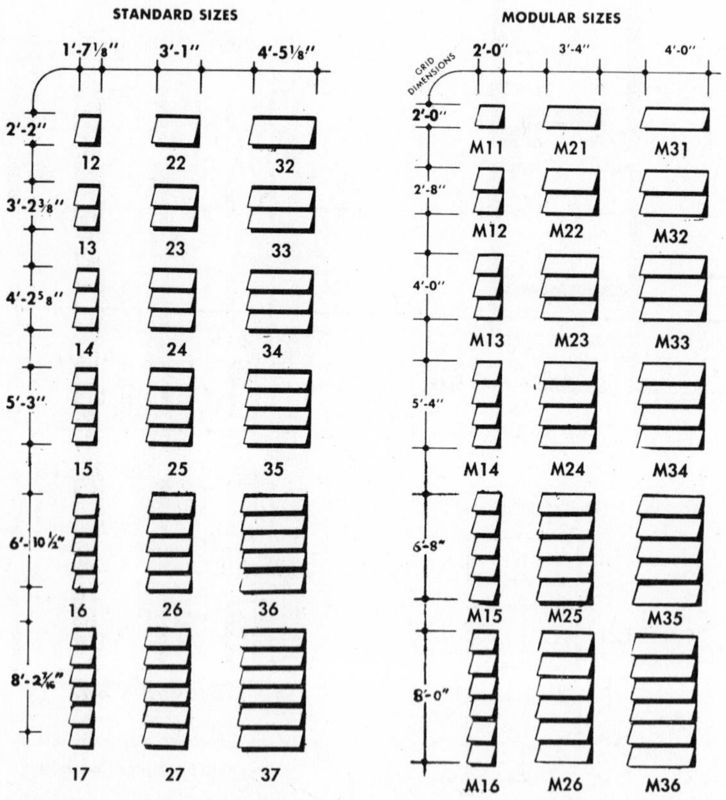

STANDARD SIZES
1'-7⅛"
3'-1"
4'-5⅛"
2'-2"
3'-2⅜"
4'-2⅝"
5'-3"
6'-10½"
8'-2⁷⁄₁₆"
12
22
32
13
23
33
14
24
34
15
25
35
16
26
36
17
27
37
MODULAR SIZES
GRID DIMENSIONS
2'-0"
3'-4"
4'-0"
2'-0"
2'-8"
4'-0"
5'-4"
6'-8"
8'-0"
M11
M21
M31
M12
M22
M32
M13
M23
M33
M14
M24
M34
M15
M25
M35
M16
M26
M36

Awning windows for commercial-, residential-, and monumental-type buildings

All dimensions are out-to-out of sash frame.

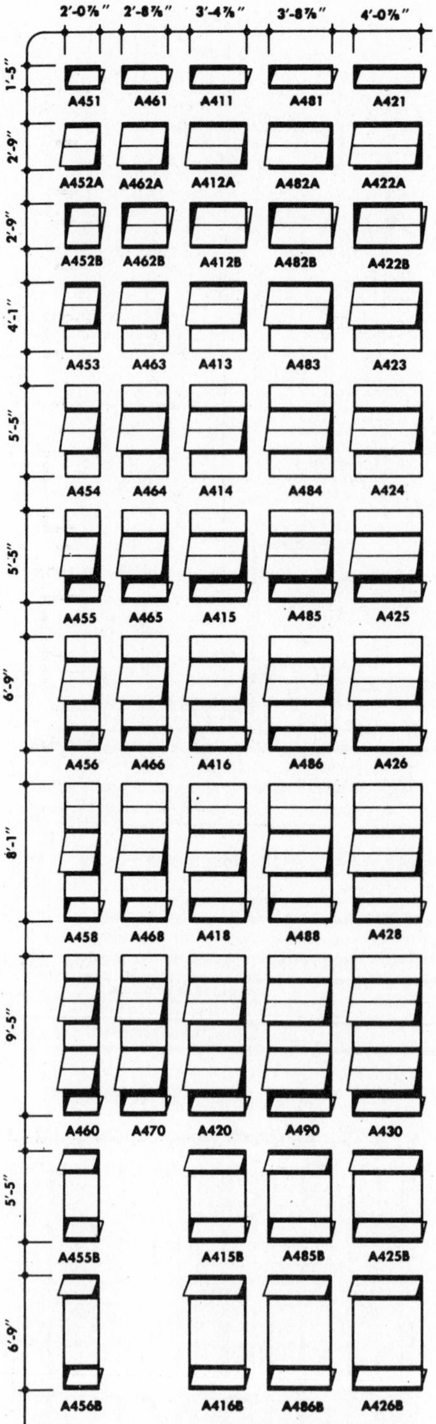

2'-0⅞"
2'-8⅞"
3'-4⅞"
3'-8⅞"
4'-0⅞"
1'-5"
2'-9"
2'-9"
4'-1"
5'-5"
5'-5"
6'-9"
8'-1"
9'-5"
5'-5"
6'-9"
A451
A461
A411
A481
A421
A452A
A462A
A412A
A482A
A422A
A452B
A462B
A412B
A482B
A422B
A453
A463
A413
A483
A423
A454
A464
A414
A484
A424
A455
A465
A415
A485
A425
A456
A466
A416
A486
A426
A458
A468
A418
A488
A428
A460
A470
A420
A490
A430
A455B
A415B
A485B
A425B
A456B
A416B
A486B
A426B

Projected windows for commercial- and monumental-type buildings

All vents shown to project out may be made to project in provided that all vents in the same unit project in. Vertical muntins may be added to 200 and 400 series windows if desired, provided they are based on 20- or 24-in. bar centers. Fixed types are furnished for all types shown. Dimensions shown are window opening dimensions.

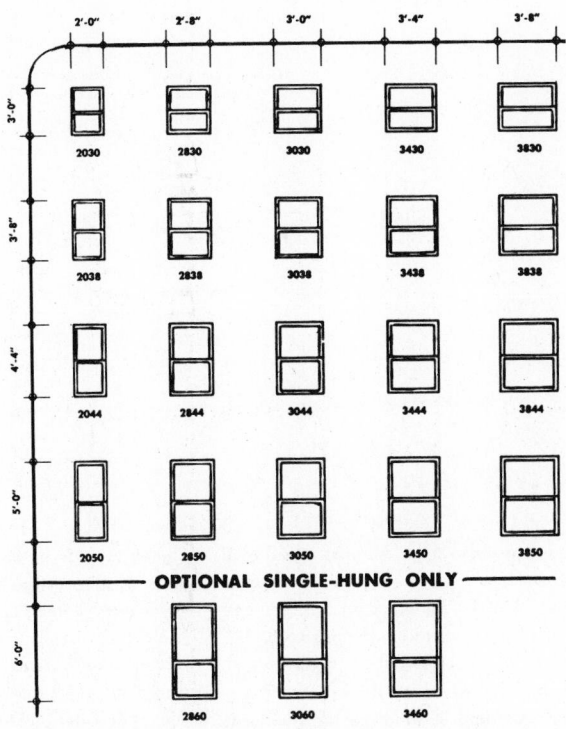

Double-hung (single-hung) windows for residential-type buildings

Dimensions shown are maximum dimensions for that portion of the frame that fits into the rough opening.

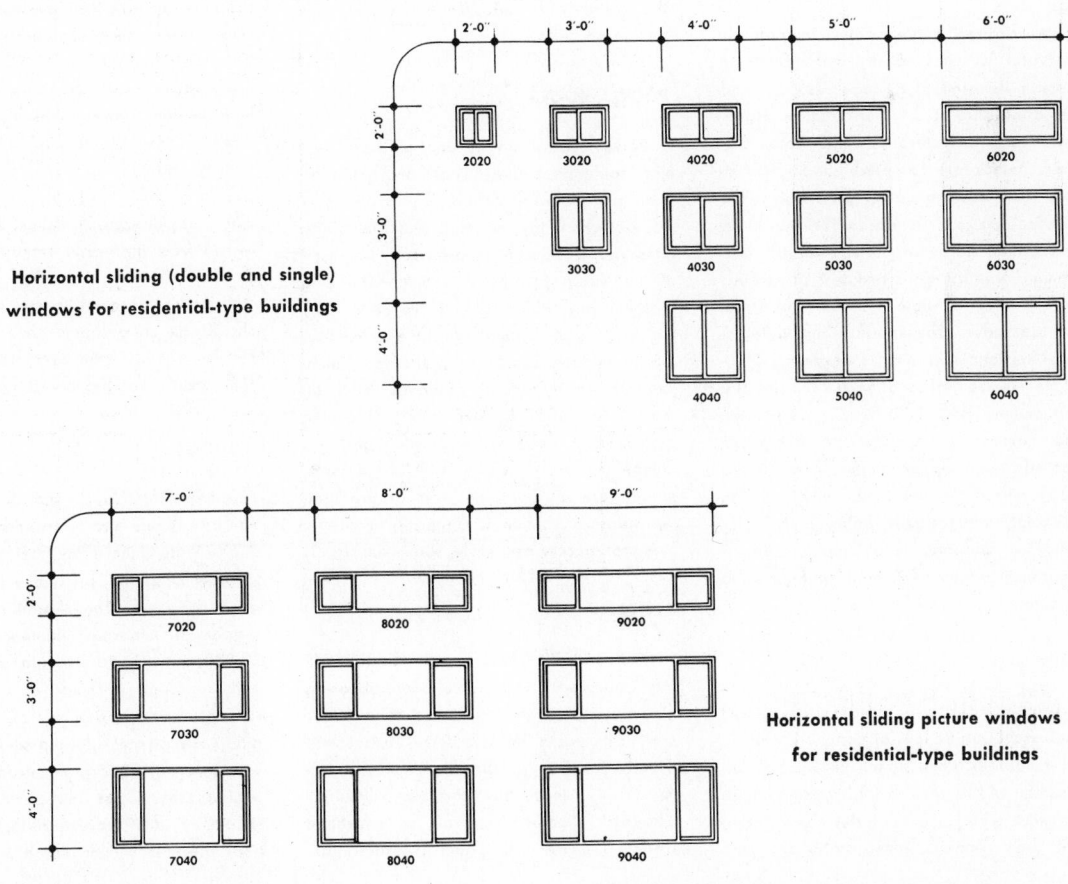

Horizontal sliding (double and single) windows for residential-type buildings

Horizontal sliding picture windows for residential-type buildings

By HOWARD P. VERMILYA, AIA

Sliding glass doors are usually framed with aluminum extrusions, although a few companies produce them in steel and wood. The industry originally developed in California but has spread throughout the country in recent years. Consequently, a greater emphasis has been placed on the weathering qualities of the doors to meet the more severe requirements of colder climates. Originally used only in houses, they are now found in apartments, hotels, institutions, and commercial buildings.

Standardization has become increasingly important as the industry has sought to improve its product through research and the establishment of performance standards. The Architectural Aluminum Manufacturers Association has established specifications for aluminum sliding glass doors. The specifications set standards for materials, finish, and hardware and establish performance requirements and test procedures pertaining to strength, weather resistance, and operation. The specifications differentiate between two grades of doors: SGD-A1 for residential and limited commercial applications and SGD-A2 for residential and commercial applications where increased size and/or better performance are required. In addition, either of the foregoing designations followed by "H" indicates conformance to the section of the specifications pertaining to high wind loading.

DOOR SIZE

Sizes of doors are based on panel unit sizes and combinations of panels. The nominal height of stock panels is 6 ft 10 in.; nominal widths are 3, 4, 5, and 6 ft. The stock types of doors include two, three, and four panels, some stationary and others movable (Fig. 1). For the most part, only one track is used, but some custom multiple sliding door installations use three or four tracks. Heights of 8, 10, and 12 ft are produced in custom sizes. Sizes are limited in height by the frame section used and in width by the standard sizes of double insulating glass (33 and 45-in. widths in ⅝-in thickness, and 33, 45, and 57-in. widths in 1-in. thickness, all 76¾ in. high). For single glazing, the size is limited by the thickness of the glass and the design wind load for the locality (see section on "Glass").

POCKET DOORS

Pocket doors are available from several companies. These doors are generally used on interior installations but also may be designed for exterior wall locations. Obscure translucent glass may be used where visual privacy is desired. The wall pocket into which the doors slide may be built wide enough to take one, two, or three door panels using the same number of tracks. Pockets may be built on both sides, each to take one half of the panels used in the opening. Although these openings are usually special designs, panels are of the same sizes as are used for standard openings. Generally available types of pocket doors are shown in Fig. 1.

DESIGN

Most manufacturers supply bottom-rolling doors with adjustable sealed-bearing sheaves on either aluminum or stainless-steel sill tracks. Stainless-steel tracks are usually inserted in the aluminum sill; alternatively, they may cap the aluminum sill track. Some types roll on overhead tracks. The movable panel is usually designed to slide inside the stationary panel. It is good practice to avoid aluminum-to-aluminum contact of moving parts. Such contact is usually prevented by using a silicone-treated woven wool pile weather-stripping, which provides protection against air and water infiltration. Neoprene and vinyl are also used as weatherstripping. Sliding panels are designed for removal in the unlocked position. Sills for interior installations are usually horizontal and recessed flush with the finished floor. Sills for exterior wall locations usually slope or step down and contain provisions for drainage of possible condensation. Screens, using either glass fiber or aluminum mesh in aluminum frames, slide on rollers on a track in the sill, usually outside the stationary panel. Although screens are a standard item they must be ordered specially if desired. Latches that can be locked from the inside are usually supplied as standard equipment, but cylinder locks may be obtained on special order. Latches should be so designed that they will not be damaged if the panel is closed while the latch is in the locked position.

SECTIONS

Sections of frame and sliding or stationary panels are extrusions, usually of 6063-T5 aluminum alloy having an ultimate strength of 27,000 psi and a yield strength of 21,000 psi. The AAMA specifications require a minimum ultimate strength of 22,000 psi, a yield strength of 16,000 psi, and a section thickness of 0.062 in. The sections may be tubular- or H-shaped or other open types. Tubular-shaped sections are generally considered stronger but any section that passes the performance tests should be satisfactory. Strength and deflection data for sections used by the manu-

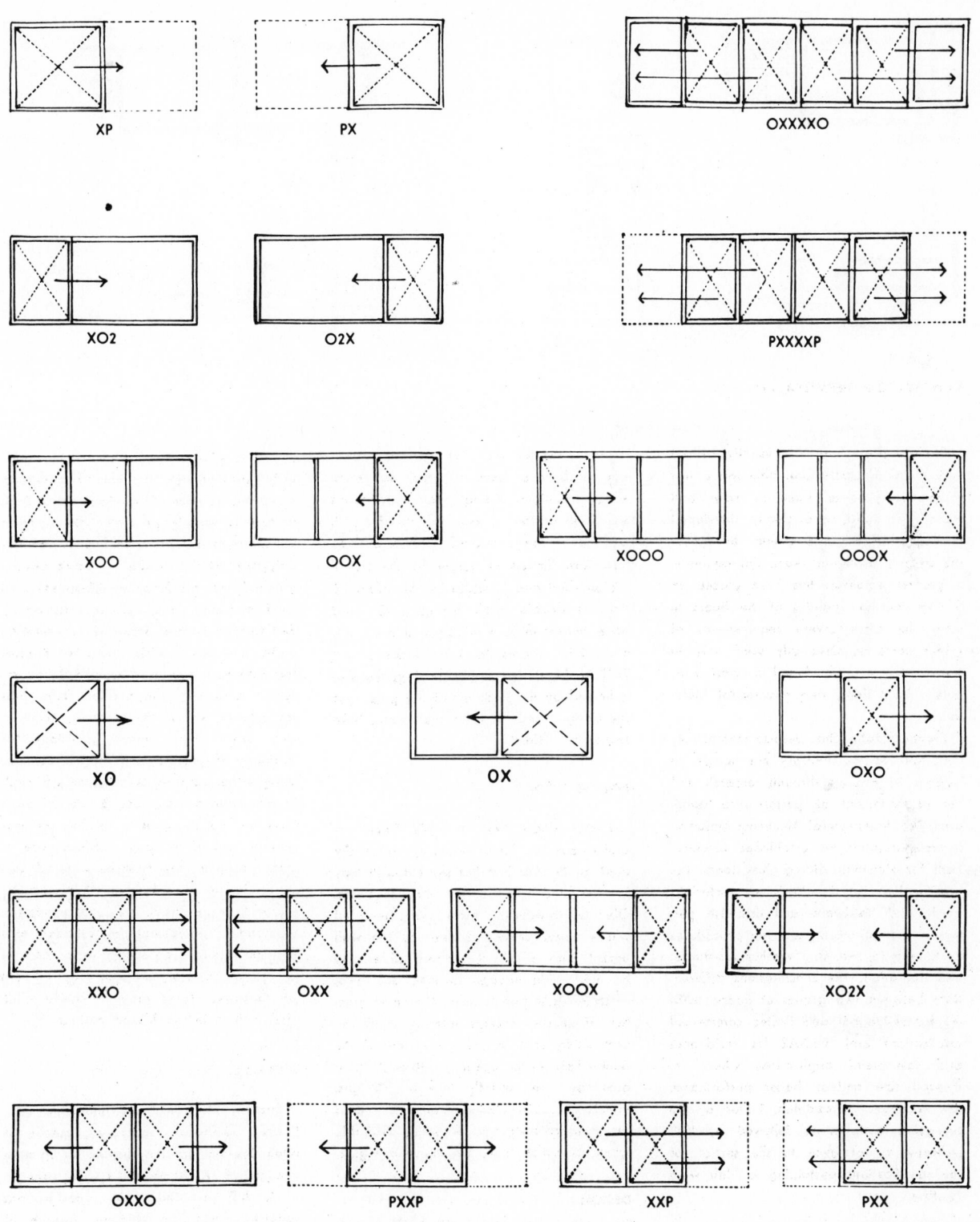

Fig. 1. Sliding glass door types

The standard height of all doors is 6 ft 10 in. Key: X designates sliding panel; O designates stationary panel; and P designates pocket. The nomenclature for stock door sizes, with immediate delivery by most manufacturers, is as follows: OX and XO doors have stock widths of 6, 8, 10, and 12 ft; OXO, XOO, and OOX doors have stock widths of 9, 12, and 15 ft; and OXXO doors have stock widths of 12 and 16 ft. Included in the standard dimensions are both steel and aluminum frames. Custom doors are furnished to meet individual requirements. All types illustrated are viewed "outside looking in." (Courtesy Architectural Aluminum Manufacturers Association.)

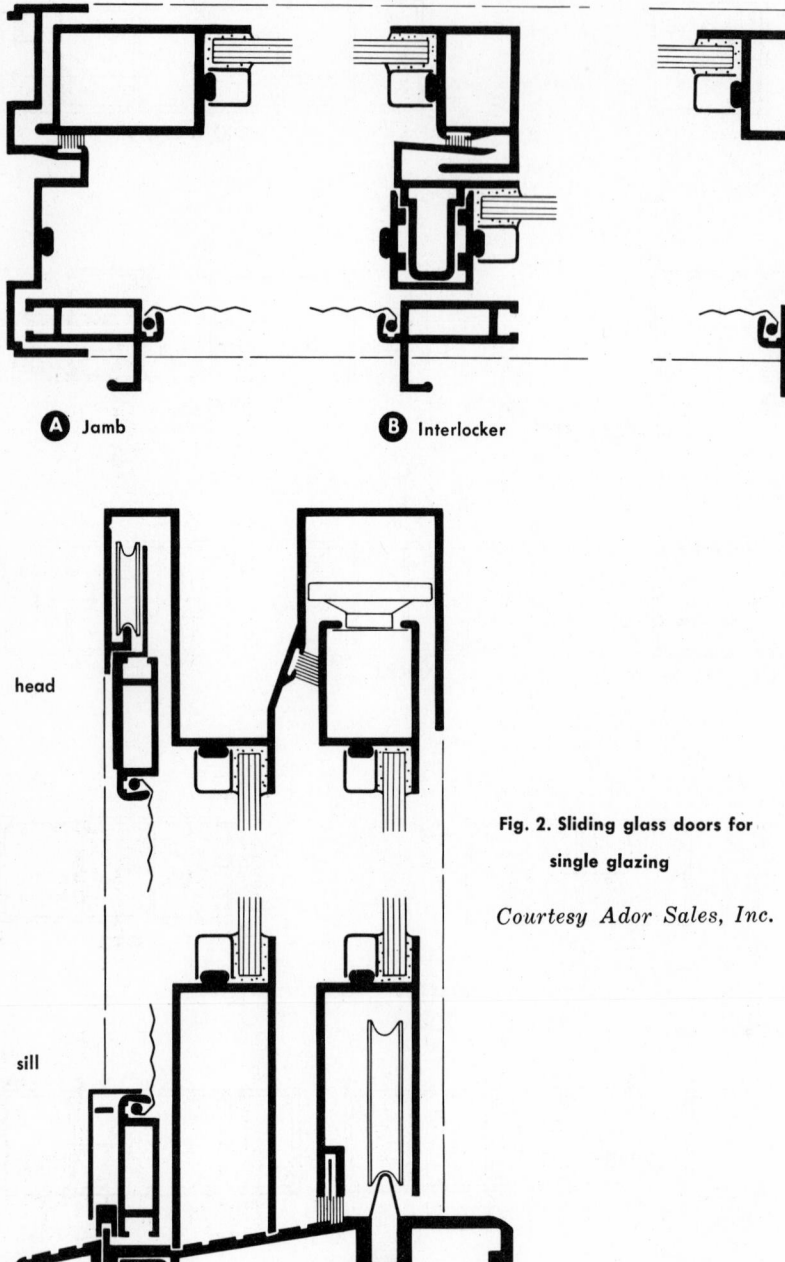

Ⓐ Jamb   Ⓑ Interlocker   Ⓗ Meeting stile

head

sill

Fig. 2. Sliding glass doors for single glazing

Courtesy Ador Sales, Inc.

facturer should be available upon application. The strength and weather resistance of the section determine the major differences between the various grades of doors. Connections of panels and frames at corners should be rigid and designed to permit complete weatherstripping. Connections are usually mechanical to permit KD shipment and local assembly, but some manufacturers use welded connections. Connectors should be noncorrosive and are usually aluminum or stainless steel. Muntins are available from some manufacturers.

Condensation on the aluminum frames is a serious problem in cold climates. To combat this, one manufacturer has eliminated the through-conductivity of the metal by inserting less conductive material between the inner and outer parts of sections for both panels and frames.

FINISH

The AAMA specifications require that all sliding doors and frames have a protective coating. The minimum coating is a clear lacquer, intended principally for pro-

tection during construction. The better classes of doors usually have an anodized finish of either 0.00025 or 0.0004-in. thickness or heavier, protected by a coating of methacrylate lacquer.

One manufacturer offers an epoxy coating in a range of colors. This coating has been subjected to weatherometer and salt-spray tests and is reported to be durable and impact- and chip-resistant.

GLAZING

Sliding doors are usually glazed by the installer, although some companies offer preglazed sash. The panels may be obtained for either single or double glazing; some manufacturers provide interchangeable glazing beads to permit the use of either type of glass. Formed vinyl glazing strips or channels are generally used, rather than glazing compounds. The aluminum glazing bead, if used, may be of the snap-on type or may be screwed in place. Construction details of doors for single glazing are shown in Fig. 2 and 3.

WEATHER RESISTANCE

Manufacturers can generally furnish data on the rate of air and water infiltration under various wind conditions and rates of rainfall. These figures should be obtained when comparing various classes of doors made by several manufacturers. Air infiltration for class A-1 should not exceed 1 cfm per sq ft of frame area with a wind of 25 mph. For class A-2, infiltration should not exceed 0.50 cfm. For class H, no water should penetrate beyond the threshold under conditions simulating a 2-in. rainfall and a 45-mph wind for a period of 15 min.

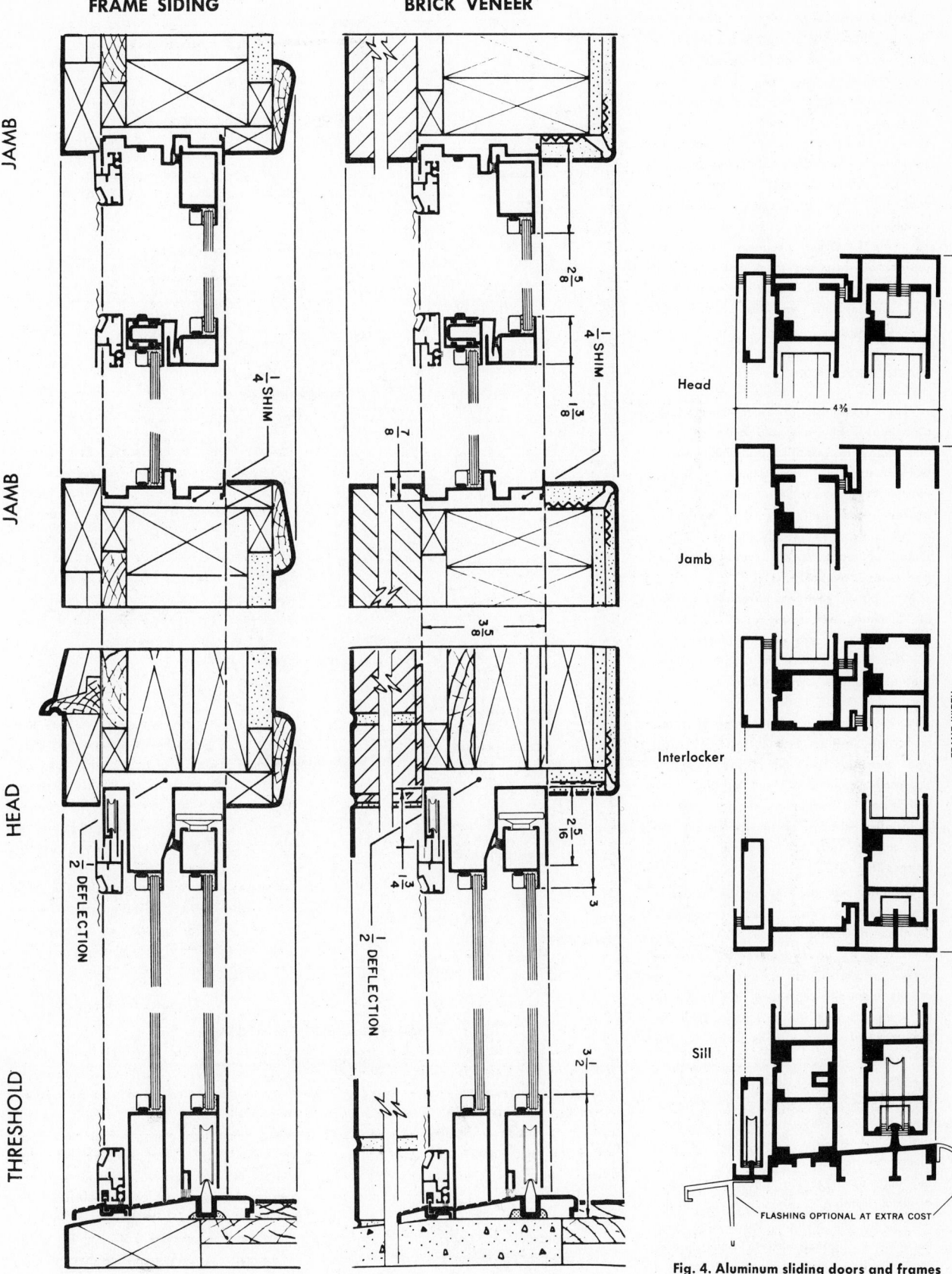

FRAME SIDING **BRICK VENEER**

JAMB

JAMB

HEAD

THRESHOLD

Head

Jamb

Interlocker

Sill

Fig. 3. Sliding glass doors for single glazing

Courtesy Ador Sales, Inc.

Fig. 4. Aluminum sliding doors and frames for insulating glass

Courtesy Miller Sliding Glass Door Co., Inc.

By HOWARD P. VERMILYA, AIA, and JOHN HANCOCK CALLENDER, *Professor of Architecture, Pratt Institute*

Skylights serve primarily to admit light through the roofs of buildings. They may also supply ventilation or access to the roof, and they may serve as fire or explosion vents. Skylights make possible an even distribution of natural light in enclosed spaces of any size, without the structural complexities of clerestories or monitors. Since skylights are part of the roof, they must of course be absolutely weatherproof, which is not always easy to achieve. Other problems of skylight design, all resulting from their overhead location, are sunlight and sun heat, shading, condensation, and the hazard from glass breakage.

PLASTIC SKYLIGHTS

Plastic skylights are now the most widely used type. They are sold as a complete unit ready to install and, being light in weight, they are very simple to install. Plastic skylights eliminate the hazard from broken glass and, since they have few or no joints, they greatly reduce the likelihood of leaks. A wide variety of sizes and types is available.

Most plastic skylights have frames made of aluminum extrusions (usually 6063-T5) that fit over a curb and are fastened to it. The frame, which is usually in two pieces, forms a condensation gutter on the inside and a drip on the outside (Fig. 1). Some types provide integral frame, curb, and flashing (Fig. 2). Insulated curbs and aluminum well liners are available on some models. A "self-flashing" type which has no frame and requires no curb is installed directly on the roof deck, and the roofing felts are mopped over the flanges (Fig. 3).

Skylights may provide for ventilation in any of several ways: fixed or operable louvers or ventilating fans in the sidewalls (Fig. 4), or devices for opening the skylight itself. Opening mechanisms are usually manually controlled, but they may be equipped with fusible links so that the skylight will open automatically in the event of fire.

Other common skylight accessories include plastic diffusing panels, plastic eggcrate grilles, operable aluminum louvers, and roller shades; these items are all placed at or near the plane of the ceiling (Fig. 5). If ceiling diffusers are used, artificial lighting is often installed in the well below the skylight. The skylight thus becomes a lighting fixture and ensures that all light, natural and artificial, will come from the same source.

Plastic skylights may consist of a single thickness of plastic, or two sheets with sealed edges and an air space between,

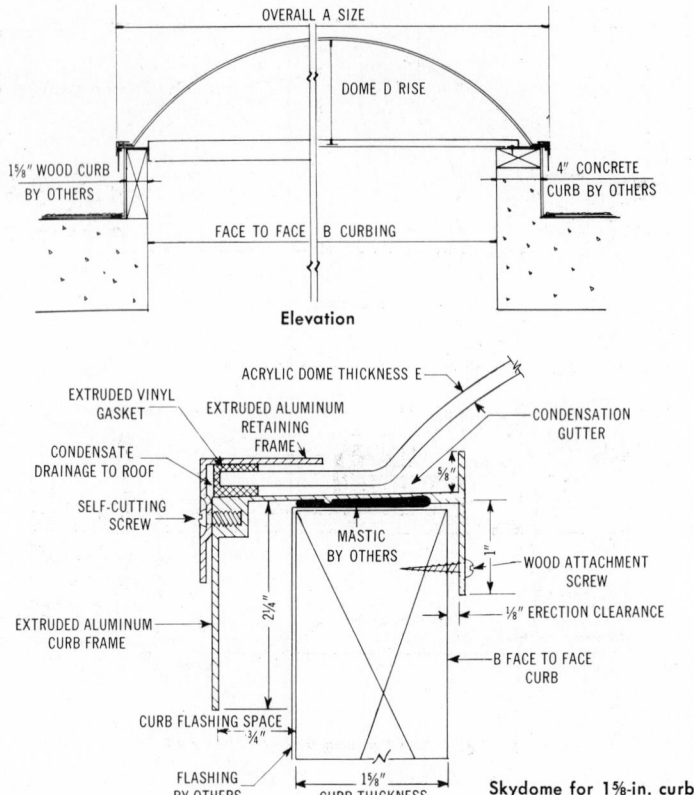

Elevation

Skydome for 1⅝-in. curb

Skydome for 4-in. curb

Fig. 1. Typical plastic dome skylight

Courtesy Wasco.

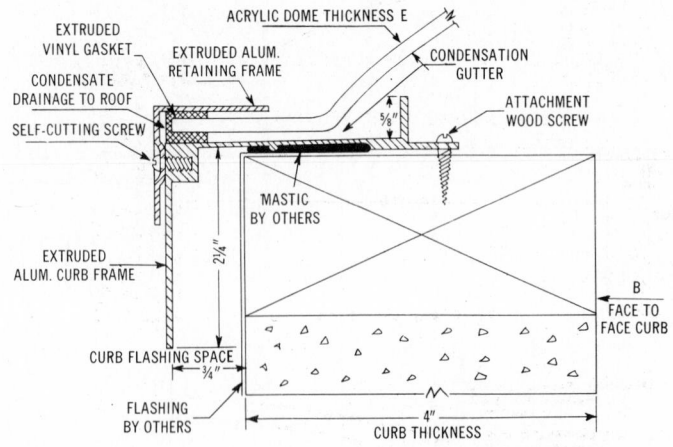

Fig. 2. Extruded frame, double dome skydome

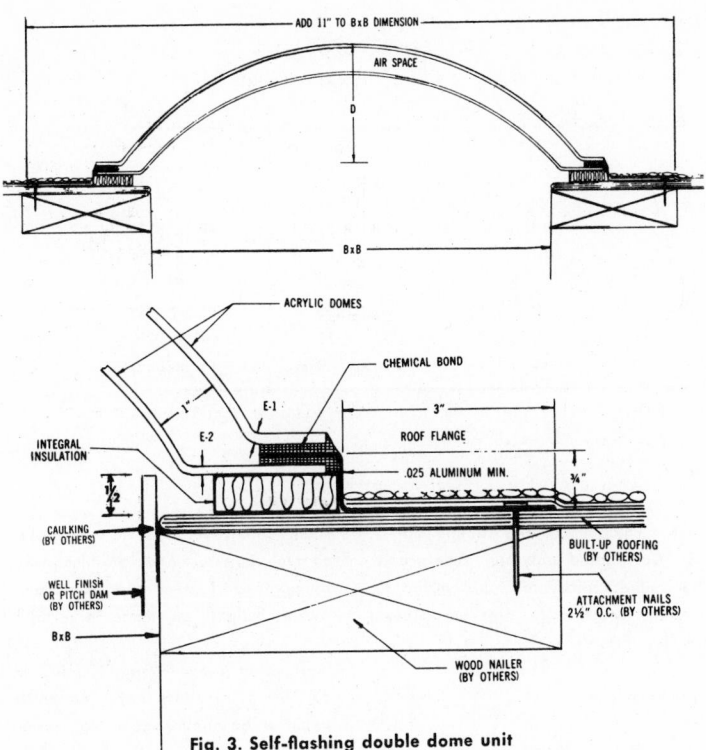

Fig. 3. Self-flashing double dome unit

or even three sheets with two air spaces. Double and triple "glazing" greatly improves the thermal characteristics of skylights and reduces or eliminates condensation; it also improves light diffusion (Figs. 2, 3, and 7).

The translucent plastic is usually an acrylic or a glass fiber reinforced polyester. Acrylic plastics may be transparent or translucent and are characteristically used in the domed form. They are available in various degrees of light transmission, diffusion, and heat gain; one manufacturer offers as many as eight types. Polyester sheets are translucent only, and may be white or colored. They are characteristically used in either flat or corrugated sheets.

Skylights that are circular, square, or nearly square in plan are generally domed acrylic plastic. Long, rectangular skylights are usually corrugated polyester, slightly arched (Fig. 6). Completely flat panels are available in the form of polyester-faced sandwich panels with aluminum eggcrate cores and frames. Both the corrugated and the sandwich-type polyester skylights are available in the curbless or "low silhouette" model as well as in the models for installation over a curb (Fig. 7).

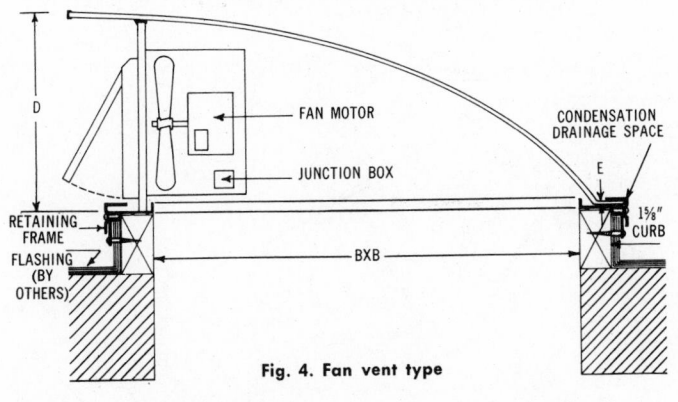

Fig. 4. Fan vent type

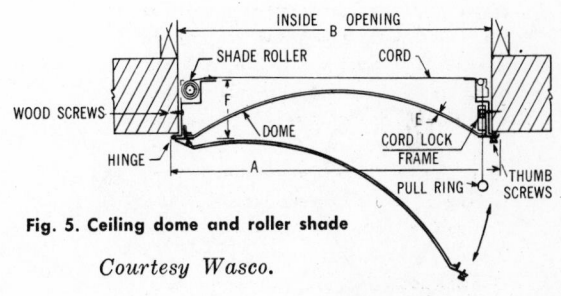

Fig. 5. Ceiling dome and roller shade

Courtesy Wasco.

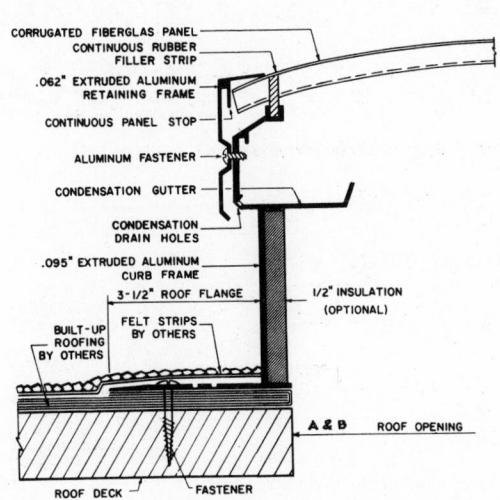

Fig. 6. Corrugated-plastic, integral-curb skylight

Courtesy Vanco.

Fig. 7. Sandwich panel, aluminum-grid-core skylight

Courtesy Kalwall.

OPENING DIMENSION

PANEL DIMENSION

Table 1. Types and sizes of skylights

The thickness of the plastic and the height of the dome vary with the size of the skylights. The thickness varies from ⅛ to ¼ in., the dome height from 1½ to 25 in.

Type	Inside curb measurement, in.		
	Small	Medium	Large
Square dome on 1⅝-in. curb	14¼x14¼	37 x 37	99½x 92½
Rectangular dome on 1⅝-in. curb	14¼x22¼	37 x 75	93¼x113¼
Round dome inside curb—diameter	24	43	91
Corrugated rectangular, inside frame*	23½x39½	35½x109½	71½x144½
Plastic-faced aluminum grid 1⁹⁄₁₆ in. thick	22¼x22¼	37 x 37	44½x 92½
Plastic-faced aluminum grid 2¾ in. thick	44½x92½	44½x140½	44½x236½

* *Supports are required under panel laps if the width dimension between frames exceeds 47½ in.*

Sizes of skylights are not uniform, although there is some similarity within the industry. Table 1 indicates the range of types and sizes available.

Corrugated polyester sheets may be used without frames to form economical skylights in roofs built of corrugated metal or asbestos cement. The corrugated plastic matches the corrugations of the roofing and is installed at the same time and by the same techniques as the roofing sheets (Fig. 8). Corrugated polyester sheets may also be nailed directly to wood purlins to form entire roofs over porches, patios, and the like (Fig. 9).

METAL SKYLIGHTS

Metal skylights are usually custom made of aluminum extrusions or galvanized steel. Other metals such as copper, lead-coated copper, monel, stainless steel, and aluminum-clad steel are sometimes used. Metal skylights are made in certain standard shapes or styles (Fig. 10). Although most often used in single units, skylights can be designed to cover an entire roof, as in a baseball cage or a museum. Besides light they can provide various types of ventilation as well as access to the roof.

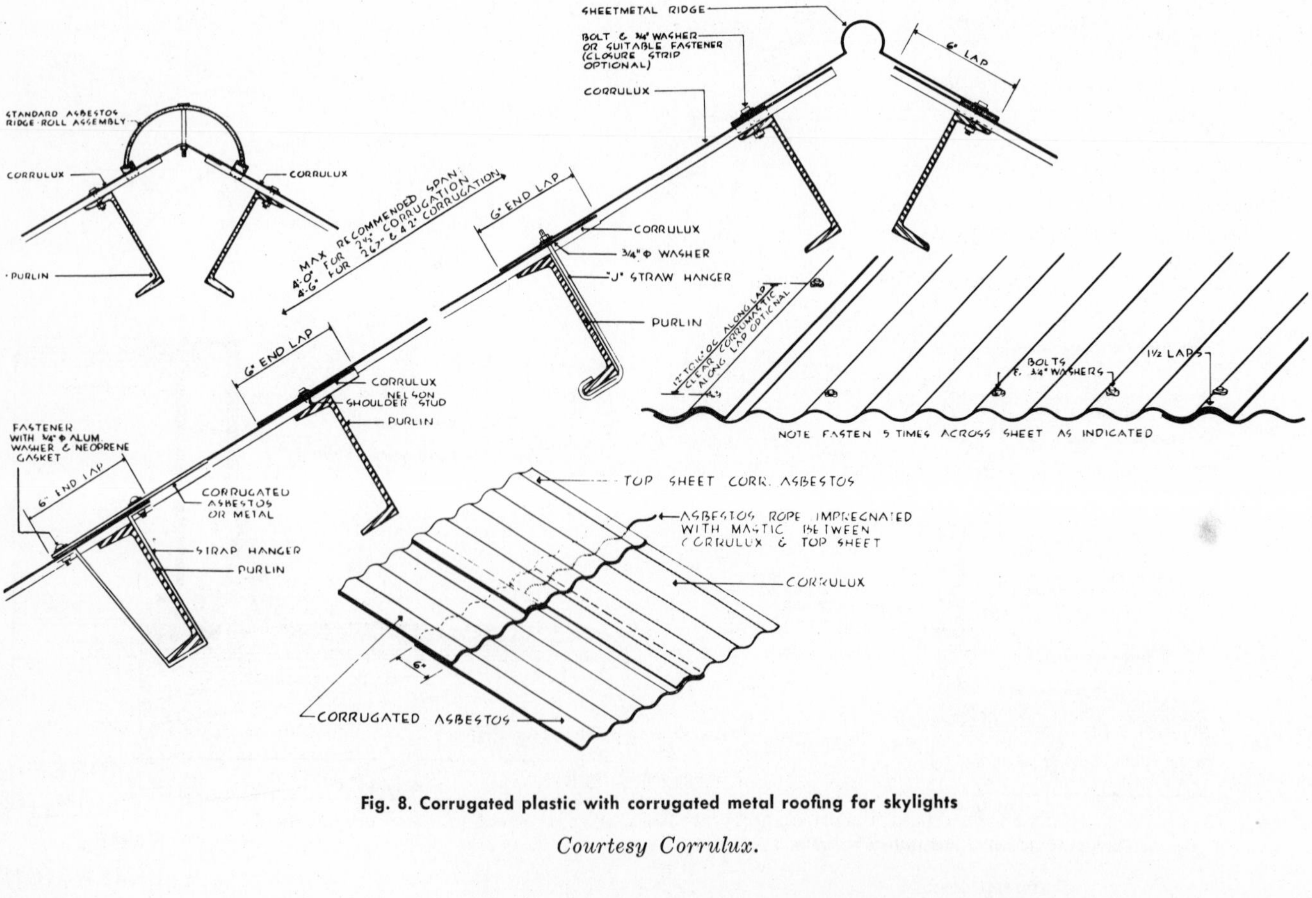

Fig. 8. Corrugated plastic with corrugated metal roofing for skylights

Courtesy Corrulux.

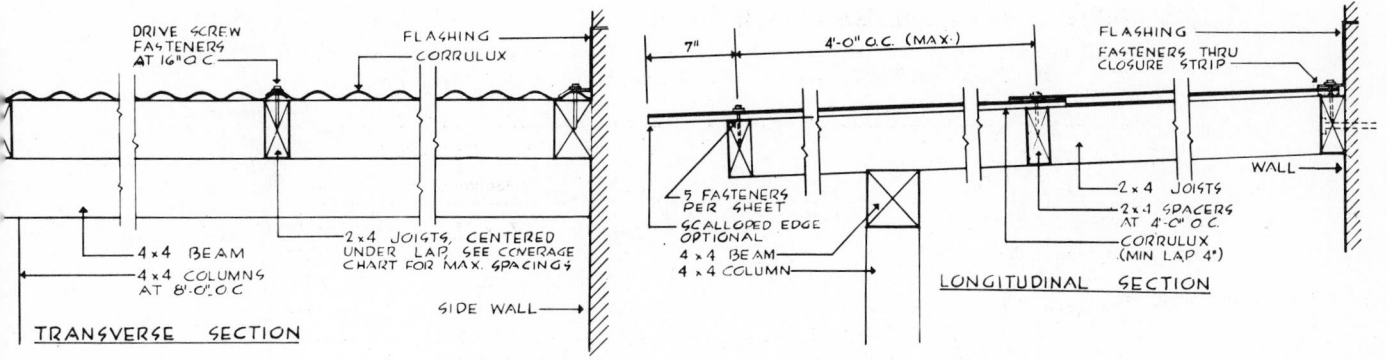

Fig. 9. Corrugated plastic on wood purlins for skylights

Courtesy Corrulux.

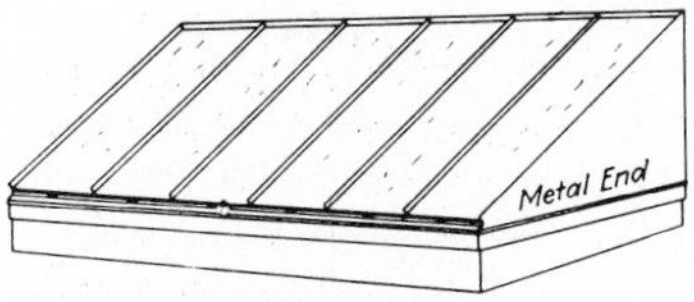

Single-pitch skylight

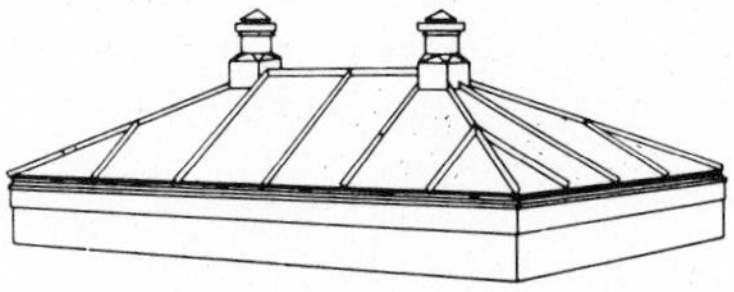

Hipped skylight with tubular ventilators

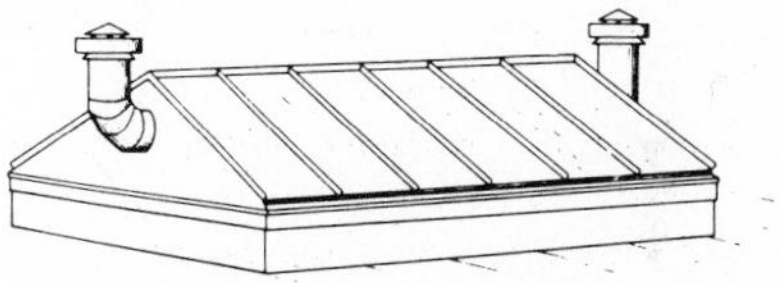

Double-pitch skylight with tubular ventilators at ends

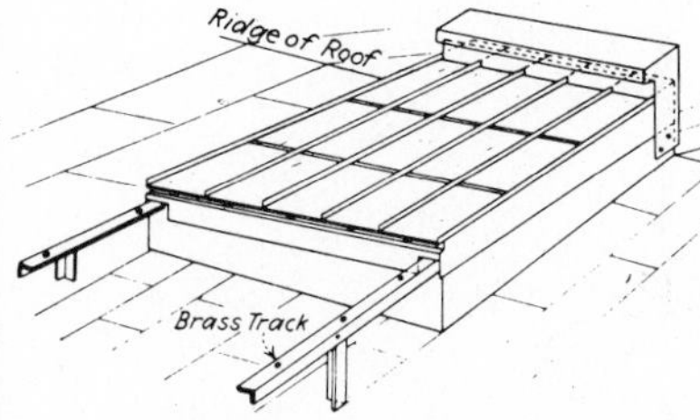

Theater stage skylight of the rolling type; may also be double pitch or hipped

Stationary or movable louvers under hipped skylight

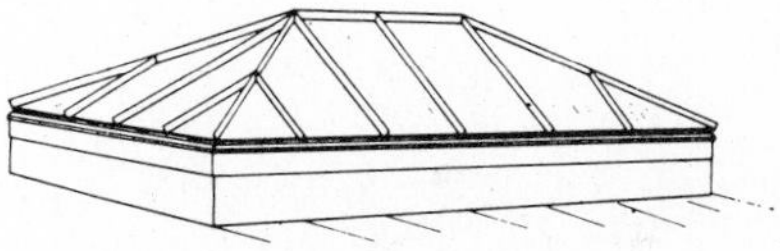

Plain hipped skylight

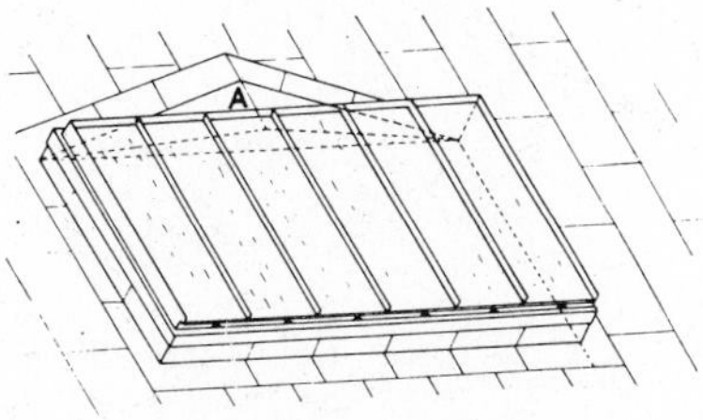

Double-pitch skylight

Flat skylight on pitched roof; may be hinged to serve as scuttle

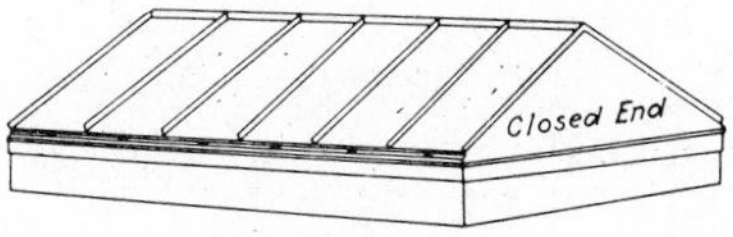

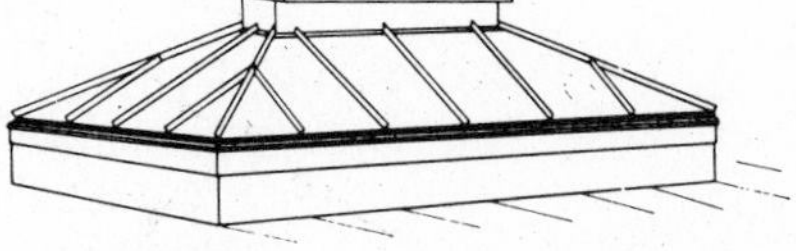

Hipped skylight with ridge ventilator

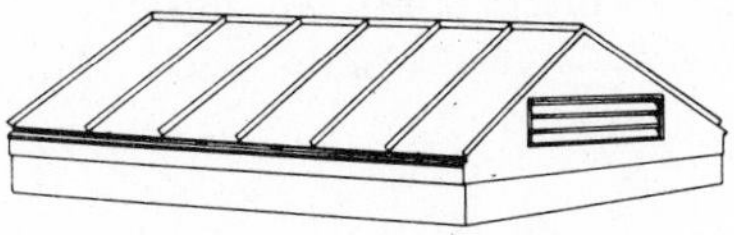

Double-pitch skylight with stationary or movable louvers at ends

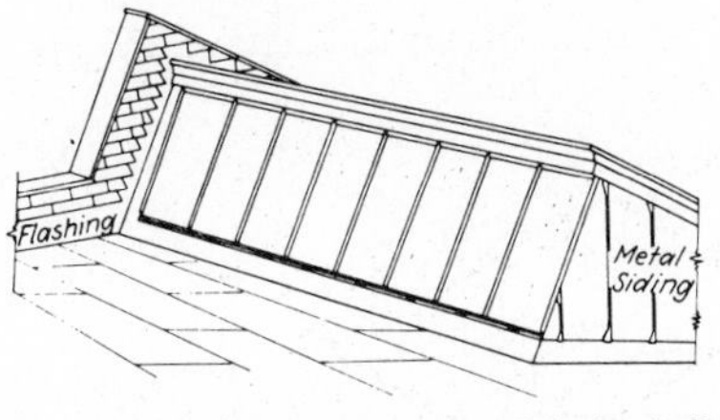

Partial view of sawtooth or north-light skylight

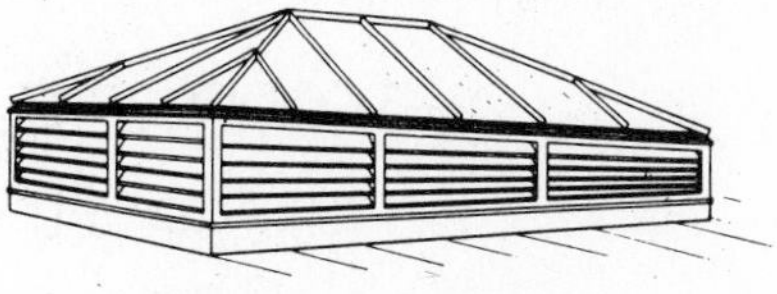

Stationary or movable sash under hipped skylight

Fig. 10. Sheet metal skylights

From Standard Practice in Sheet Metal Work, *Sheet Metal Contractors National Association, Inc. (1956).*

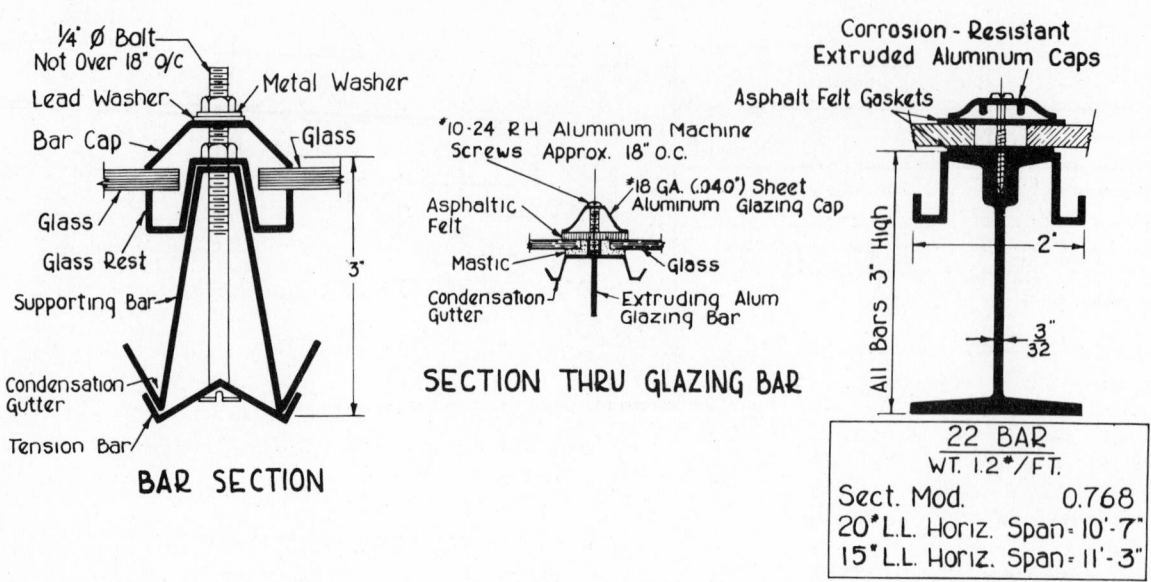

¼" Ø Bolt
Not Over 18" O/c
Metal Washer
Lead Washer
Bar Cap
Glass
Glass
Glass Rest
Supporting Bar
Condensation Gutter
Tension Bar
3"

BAR SECTION

#10-24 RH Aluminum Machine Screws Approx. 18" O.C.
#18 GA. (.040") Sheet Aluminum Glazing Cap
Asphaltic Felt
Mastic
Glass
Condensation Gutter
Extruding Alum Glazing Bar

SECTION THRU GLAZING BAR

Corrosion - Resistant Extruded Aluminum Caps
Asphalt Felt Gaskets
All Bars 3" High
2"
3"/32

22 BAR
WT. 1.2#/FT.
Sect. Mod.   0.768
20# L.L. Horiz. Span = 10'-7"
15# L.L. Horiz. Span = 11'-3"

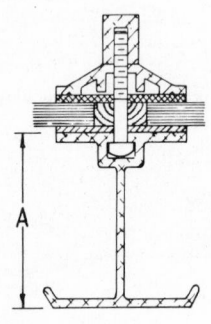

A

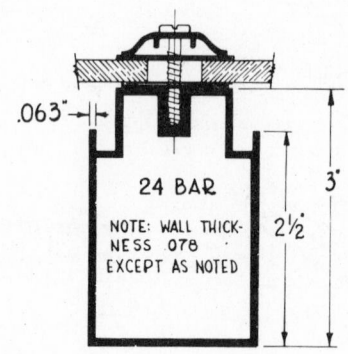

.063"
24 BAR
NOTE: WALL THICK-
NESS .078
EXCEPT AS NOTED
3"
2½"

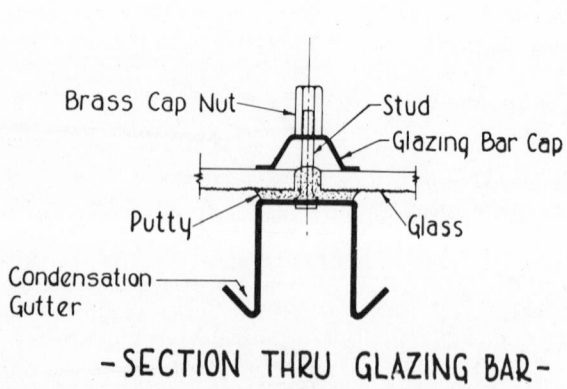

Brass Cap Nut
Stud
Glazing Bar Cap
Putty
Glass
Condensation Gutter

-SECTION THRU GLAZING BAR-
STANDARD PUTTY CONSTRUCTION

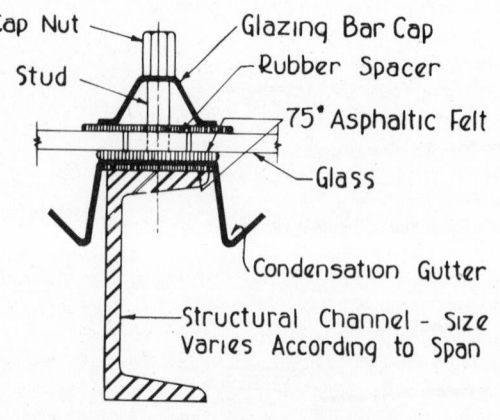

Cap Nut
Stud
Glazing Bar Cap
Rubber Spacer
75# Asphaltic Felt
Glass
Condensation Gutter
Structural Channel - Size Varies According to Span

SECTION THRU GLAZING BAR

Fig. 11. Glazing bar sections

From Standard Practice in Sheet Metal Work, *Sheet Metal Contractors National Association, Inc. (1956).*

The essential element in the metal skylight is the "sash bar" or "glazing bar" (Fig. 11), many of which are patented. Most designs include condensation gutters with weep holes for drainage. Details have been developed which eliminate putty and the maintenance problem it presents; some designs use direct metal-to-glass contact, others use felt, cork, or other composition as gaskets or cushions. Standard designs are usually based on a glass width of 24 in.

The glass used in skylights is generally ¼-in. wired glass in ribbed, hammered, or rough patterns with the smooth face out, and is limited in size to 24 in. in width and 48 in. in length. Other types of glass such as sheet, plate, tempered, safety, heat-absorbent, or glare-reducing may be used, as may various types of plastic sheets. Double glazing with two separate sheets of glass with an air space between may be incorporated in the design, or sealed double glass may be used.

In addition to the standard types shown in Fig. 10, two others should be noted. One is the curbless, depressed-head skylight used on pitched roofs (Fig. 12). The other is the automatic stage ventilator, which is required by law in many cities (Fig. 13).

Metal skylights need not be limited to the standard types. Possibilities in custom-designed skylights are limited only by the imagination of the architect. An example of imaginative design is shown in Fig. 14.

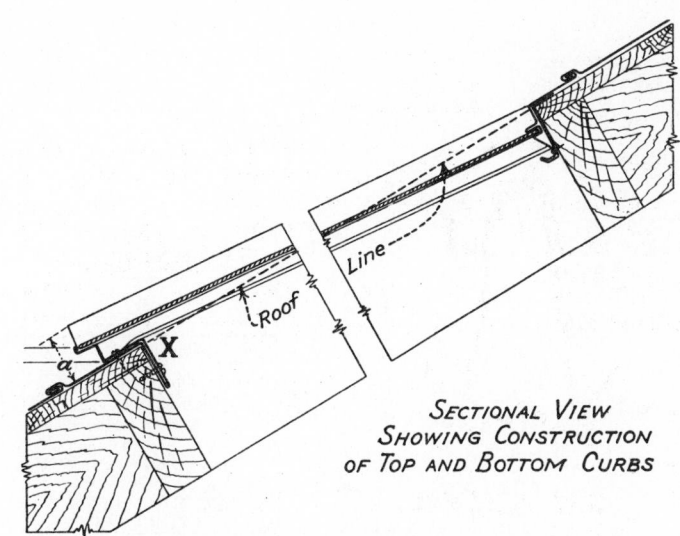

SECTIONAL VIEW SHOWING CONSTRUCTION OF TOP AND BOTTOM CURBS

Fig. 12. Curbless flat skylight on pitched roof

From Standard Practice in Sheet Metal Work, *Sheet Metal Contractors National Association, Inc. (1956).*

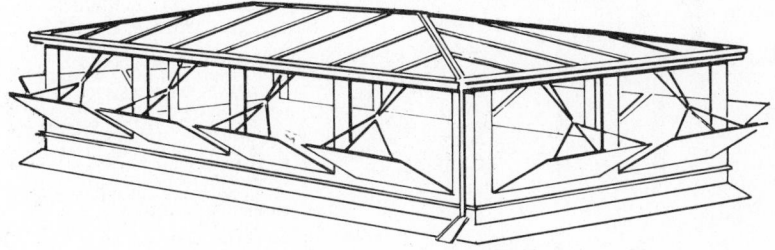

Fig. 13. Automatic stage ventilators

Courtesy Vanco.

FIRE PROTECTION

To provide against emergencies resulting from fires, the glass in the skylight should be plain glass not thicker than ⅛ in. so that it may be pierced easily. This type of skylight is used over theater stages to provide venting for a fire on the stage in order to prevent its spread to the auditorium (Fig. 13). It is also used at the top of required exit stair enclosures and vent shafts. Where thin glass is required, screens (removable to permit cleaning) are commonly provided above the glass as protection against flying brands and below as protection against falling glass. Plastic skylights with fusible links operating opening mechanisms have been developed to serve as automatic vents, but are not as easily pierced from the outside as is thin glass.

When skylights are used primarily for light or light and ventilation the *National Building Code* (1955) of the National Board of Fire Underwriters requires that they have sashes and frames of noncom-bustible material and be glazed with wire glass, approved glass block, or an approved plastic that does not present a fragmentation hazard. (Wood frames may be used by special permission in foundries and where acid fumes are present.) Where combustible plastic is used the Code establishes the following requirements for skylights:

1. They shall have curbs at least 4 in. high.
2. They shall not exceed 100 sq ft in area and the total area shall not exceed 20 per cent of the floor area.
3. They shall be separated by at least 5 ft.
4. They shall be not closer than 20 ft to a wall in which the openings are required to be protected. (This figure does not apply to dwellings or buildings constructed of frame or unprotected noncombustible construction.)
5. They shall be screened from flying brands where they are likely to land on the plastic.

GLASS-BLOCK SKYLIGHTS

Glass block may also be used in skylights. They offer the advantages of excellent light diffusion and good thermal insulation. The blocks may be preassembled in aluminum or concrete grids, or they may be installed individually in job-built grids of reinforced concrete (Figs. 15 and 16). In the latter case the concrete may be poured directly around the blocks to seal them as well as support them, or they may be installed in waterproof mastic so that a unit can be easily replaced if damaged. One type of block is specially designed to exclude summer sunlight striking at a high angle, but to admit winter sun that strikes at a low angle, and to admit north light at all times. These units must be installed with correct orientation. All glass-block skylights must be installed with a minimum pitch of ¼ in. per ft for drainage.

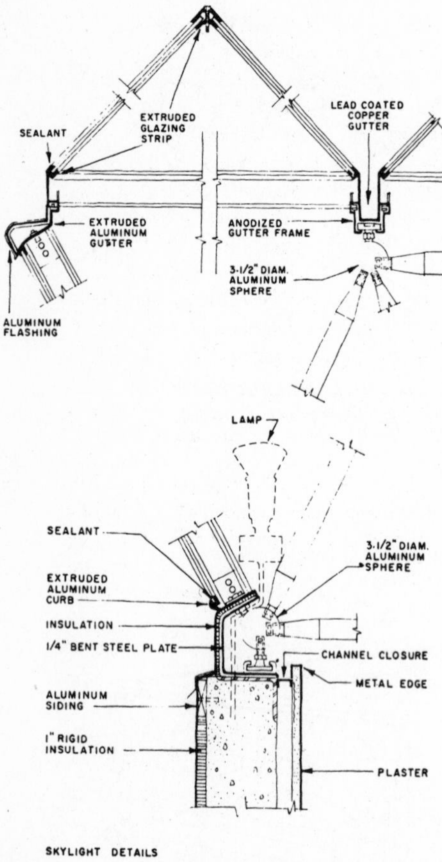

SEALANT
EXTRUDED GLAZING STRIP
LEAD COATED COPPER GUTTER
EXTRUDED ALUMINUM GUTTER
ANODIZED GUTTER FRAME
3-1/2" DIAM. ALUMINUM SPHERE
ALUMINUM FLASHING
LAMP
SEALANT
EXTRUDED ALUMINUM CURB
INSULATION
1/4" BENT STEEL PLATE
3-1/2" DIAM. ALUMINUM SPHERE
CHANNEL CLOSURE
METAL EDGE
ALUMINUM SIDING
1" RIGID INSULATION
PLASTER
SKYLIGHT DETAILS

Fig. 14. Space-frame skylight

A space frame of bright aluminum rods and spheres supports a gutter system of extruded aluminum sections which in turn holds the ¼-in. wire glass in such a fashion that movement is possible without leakage. Reynolds Building, Detroit; Yamasaki, Architect.

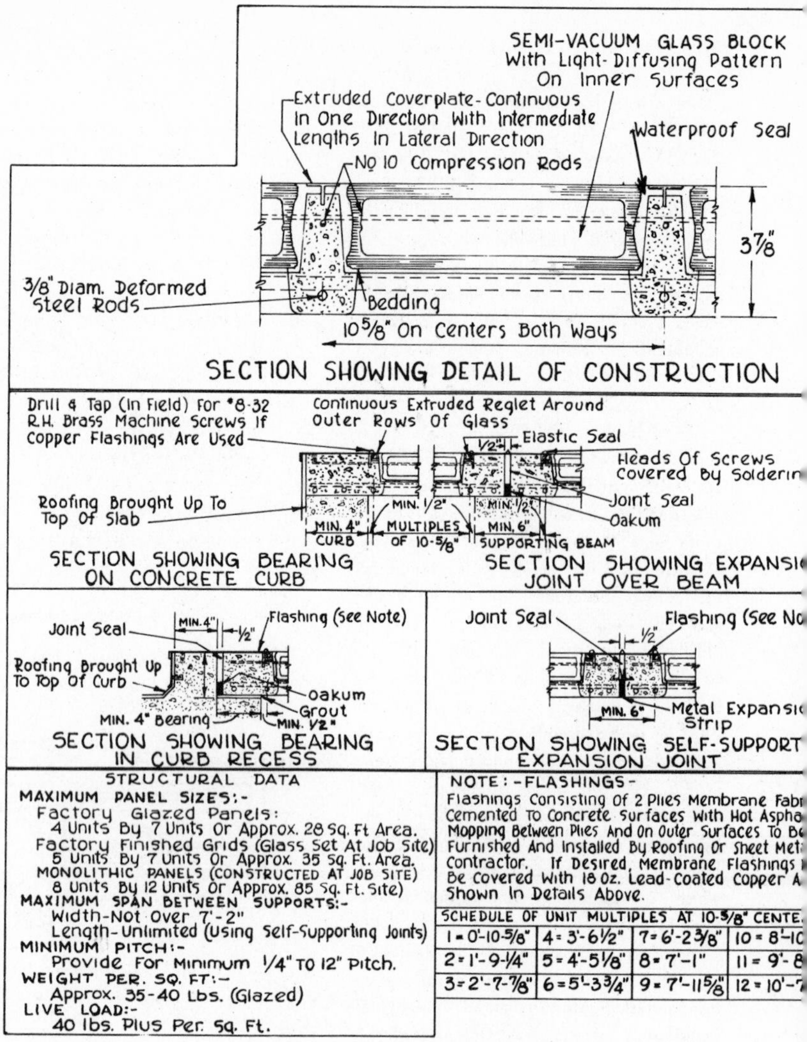

SEMI-VACUUM GLASS BLOCK With Light-Diffusing Pattern On Inner Surfaces
Extruded Coverplate-Continuous In One Direction With Intermediate Lengths In Lateral Direction
Waterproof Seal
No 10 Compression Rods
3⅞"
3/8" Diam. Deformed Steel Rods
Bedding
10⅝" On Centers Both Ways
SECTION SHOWING DETAIL OF CONSTRUCTION
Drill & Tap (In Field) For #8-32 R.H. Brass Machine Screws If Copper Flashings Are Used
Continuous Extruded Reglet Around Outer Rows Of Glass
Elastic Seal
Heads Of Screws Covered By Solderin
Roofing Brought Up To Top Of Slab
MIN. 1/2"
MIN. 1/2"
Joint Seal
Oakum
MIN. 4" CURB
MULTIPLES OF 10-5/8"
MIN. 6" SUPPORTING BEAM
SECTION SHOWING BEARING ON CONCRETE CURB
SECTION SHOWING EXPANSI JOINT OVER BEAM
Joint Seal
MIN. 4"
1/2"
Flashing (See Note)
Roofing Brought Up To Top Of Curb
Oakum
Grout
MIN. 4" Bearing
MIN. 1/2"
SECTION SHOWING BEARING IN CURB RECESS
Joint Seal
1/2"
Flashing (See No
MIN. 6"
Metal Expansi Strip
SECTION SHOWING SELF-SUPPORT EXPANSION JOINT
STRUCTURAL DATA
MAXIMUM PANEL SIZES:-
Factory Glazed Panels:
4 Units By 7 Units Or Approx. 28 Sq. Ft Area.
Factory Finished Grids (Glass Set At Job Site)
5 Units By 7 Units Or Approx. 35 Sq. Ft. Area.
MONOLITHIC PANELS (CONSTRUCTED AT JOB SITE)
8 Units By 12 Units Or Approx. 85 Sq. Ft. Site)
MAXIMUM SPAN BETWEEN SUPPORTS:-
Width-Not Over 7'-2"
Length-Unlimited (Using Self-Supporting Joints)
MINIMUM PITCH:-
Provide For Minimum 1/4" To 12" Pitch.
WEIGHT PER. SQ. FT:-
Approx. 35-40 Lbs. (Glazed)
LIVE LOAD:-
40 lbs. Plus Per. Sq. Ft.
NOTE:-FLASHINGS-
Flashings Consisting Of 2 Plies Membrane Fabr Cemented To Concrete Surfaces With Hot Aspha Mopping Between Plies And On Outer Surfaces To B Furnished And Installed By Roofing Or Sheet Met Contractor. If Desired, Membrane Flashings Be Covered With 18 Oz. Lead-Coated Copper A Shown In Details Above.
SCHEDULE OF UNIT MULTIPLES AT 10-5/8" CENTE
1 = 0'-10-5/8" | 4 = 3'-6½" | 7 = 6'-2⅜" | 10 = 8'-10
2 = 1'-9-1/4" | 5 = 4'-5⅛" | 8 = 7'-1" | 11 = 9'-8
3 = 2'-7-7/8" | 6 = 5'-3¾" | 9 = 7'-11⅝" | 12 = 10'-7

Fig. 16. Glass block in concrete grid

From Standard Practice in Sheet Metal Work, *Sheet Metal Contractors National Association, Inc. (1956).*

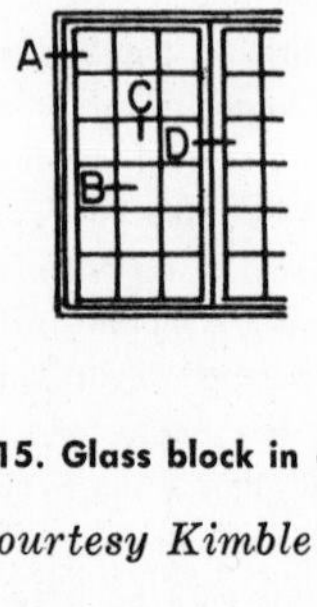

A
B
C
D

Fig. 15. Glass block in aluminum grid

Courtesy Kimble Glass Co.

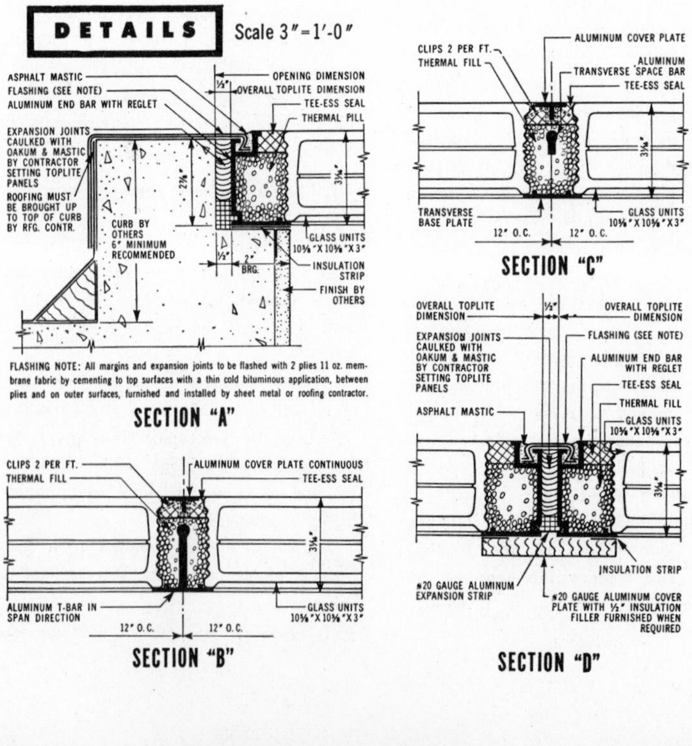

DETAILS
Scale 3" = 1'-0"
ASPHALT MASTIC
FLASHING (SEE NOTE)
ALUMINUM END BAR WITH REGLET
OPENING DIMENSION
OVERALL TOPLITE DIMENSION
TEE-ESS SEAL
THERMAL FILL
EXPANSION JOINTS CAULKED WITH OAKUM & MASTIC BY CONTRACTOR SETTING TOPLITE PANELS
ROOFING MUST BE BROUGHT UP TO TOP OF CURB BY RFG. CONTR.
CURB BY OTHERS 6" MINIMUM RECOMMENDED
GLASS UNITS 10⅝"X10⅝"X3"
INSULATION STRIP
FINISH BY OTHERS
FLASHING NOTE: All margins and expansion joints to be flashed with 2 plies 11 oz. membrane fabric by cementing to top surfaces with a thin cold bituminous application, between plies and on outer surfaces, furnished and installed by sheet metal or roofing contractor.
SECTION "A"
CLIPS 2 PER FT.
THERMAL FILL
ALUMINUM COVER PLATE CONTINUOUS
TEE-ESS SEAL
ALUMINUM T-BAR IN SPAN DIRECTION
GLASS UNITS 10⅝"X10⅝"X3"
12" O.C.
12" O.C.
SECTION "B"
CLIPS 2 PER FT.
THERMAL FILL
ALUMINUM COVER PLATE
ALUMINUM TRANSVERSE SPACE BAR
TEE-ESS SEAL
TRANSVERSE BASE PLATE
GLASS UNITS 10⅝"X10⅝"X3"
12" O.C.
12" O.C.
SECTION "C"
OVERALL TOPLITE DIMENSION
OVERALL TOPLITE DIMENSION
EXPANSION JOINTS CAULKED WITH OAKUM & MASTIC BY CONTRACTOR SETTING TOPLITE PANELS
FLASHING (SEE NOTE)
ALUMINUM END BAR WITH REGLET
ASPHALT MASTIC
TEE-ESS SEAL
THERMAL FILL
GLASS UNITS 10⅝"X10⅝"X3"
INSULATION STRIP
#20 GAUGE ALUMINUM EXPANSION STRIP
#20 GAUGE ALUMINUM COVER PLATE WITH ½" INSULATION FILLER FURNISHED WHEN REQUIRED
SECTION "D"

By WAYNE F. KOPPES, *Architectural Consultant*

Metal and glass, like all other construction materials, impose their own disciplines upon the designer. Their performance is governed by fundamental laws of physics, and a properly designed metal curtain wall necessarily reflects a proper regard for these laws. Since these materials react in their own ways to the ever-present forces of nature—heat, light, air, gravity, and sound—a clear understanding of the effects of these forces is a basic essential in contemporary wall design.

Moreover, the use of factory-assembled components requires greater precision and coordination than the older, on-site construction methods. Thus a review of the design principles dictated both by the nature of the materials and by the techniques associated with their fabrication and assembly becomes a necessary prerequisite to good metal curtain wall design.

DEFINITION

The *Metal Curtain Wall Manual*, published by the National Association of Architectural Metal Manufacturers, defines a metal curtain wall as "an exterior building wall which carries no floor or roof loads, and which may consist principally of metal or of a combination of metal, glass, and other surfacing materials supported in a metal framework."

It is important to note that the determining distinction in this widely accepted definition is the material used in the supporting framework, rather than that used for surfacing the wall. Many materials, such as glass, masonry, or plastic, may be used for the "infilling" panels, which may cover a large part of the wall surface, but if these materials are carried in a metal framework to provide a nonbearing wall system, the term "metal curtain wall construction" properly applies. It is obviously not necessary, therefore, that the design include metallic panels in order to qualify under this definition.

TYPES

Variations in metal curtain wall construction are almost infinite, and it is impossible to pigeonhole the many types in certain clearly defined categories. Early research, both in the Princeton studies[1]

[1] *J. H. Callender et al.* Curtain Walls of Stainless Steel. *School of Architecture, Princeton University, Princeton (1955).*

and by the Building Research Institute,[2] proposed three bases of classification: (1) Visual characteristics, (2) Method of support, and (3) Method of assembly. Although this system of classification is perfectly valid, it may prove to be rather unwieldy for general usage. It seems preferable to use a simpler, though technically less accurate, system and to consider metal curtain walls under three broad classifications that reflect both the general architectural character and the relative cost of the wall construction, as well as its typical usage. These type classifications are widely accepted, and in order (generally) of decreasing cost they are:

1. *Custom type:* Walls designed for one project, using parts and details specially made for this purpose. Such walls may be used on buildings of any height but are generally typical of multistory buildings. Included in this category are the highly publicized (and often expensive) walls that serve as design pace-setters.

[2] *Charles R. Koehler, ed.* Architectural Metal Curtain Wall Workshop—Conference. *Report of Five Workshops, Building Research Institute, Washington (1956).*

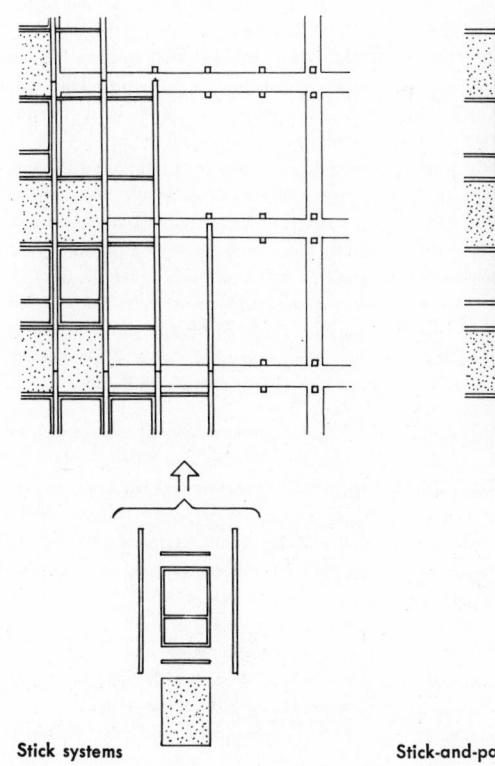

Stick systems

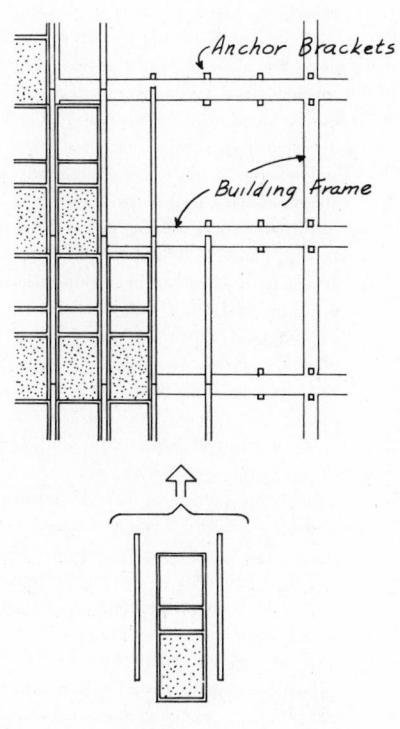

Anchor Brackets

Building Frame

Stick-and-panel systems

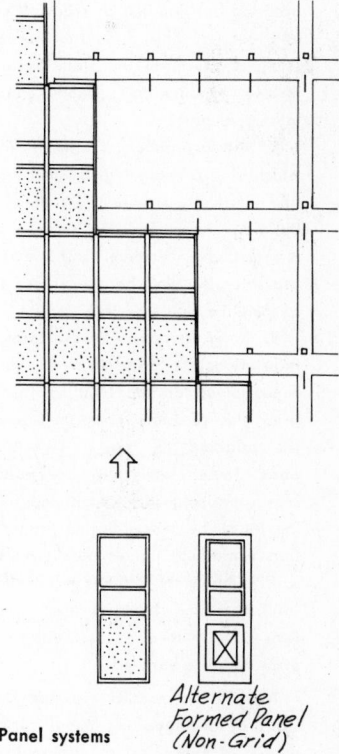

Panel systems

Alternate Formed Panel (Non-Grid) Type

Fig. 1. Types of metal curtain wall construction

CURTAIN WALLS—2
General

2. *Commercial type:* Walls made up principally of parts and details standardized by the manufacturer and assembled either in the manufacturer's stock patterns or in accordance with the architect's design. Such types are offered by many manufacturers and are typically used on one- and two-story buildings, although many multistory buildings have used such systems too. Often they offer advantages in both proven performance and the lower costs attributable to quantity production.

3. *Industrial type:* Walls in which ribbed, fluted, or otherwise preformed metal sheets in stock sizes are used, along with standard metal sash, as the principal components. This type of metal curtain wall has a long history of satisfactory performance and, in its insulated form, is widely used in buildings outside the industrial field.

Still other distinctions as to types of metal curtain wall construction are common in the trade and deserve explanation. These are based on technical considerations of fabrication and installation and also include three categories (Fig. 1):

1. *Stick systems:* Wall systems that are generally shipped "knocked down," to be assembled in place, piece by piece, on the building frame. Mullion members, rail sections, sash, and panels are generally prefitted but handled as separate elements, and consequently they are installed consecutively to form the wall. Such systems involve handling the greatest number of individual parts.

2. *Stick-and-panel systems:* Walls in which the primary "grid" members (usually vertical) are first installed on the building frame and the subassemblies of intermediate members, sash, and panels are later installed between these members to form the wall assembly.

3. *Panel systems:* Walls consisting of full-story-height preassembled units which, when joined on the building frame, comprise the complete enclosure system with the addition of few if any additional parts. These panels may be metal stampings containing sash or glazing frames, or they may be assemblies of framing members containing panels, sash, and/or other wall components, sometimes complete with insulation and interior finish. These systems usually involve the smallest number of parts to be handled.

There is no conflict between these two ways of distinguishing metal curtain wall types; in fact a clear designation often involves the use of both. Thus a custom- or commercial-type wall may be designed

as a stick system, a stick-and-panel system, or a panel system.

MATERIALS

By definition, metal is the principal structural material in these walls, although it is frequently not the most conspicuous material. Sometimes a large portion of the wall area is sheathed with metal, but more often the apparent quantity of metal is only the minimum required to provide necessary support and stiffness for the nonmetallic infilling materials.

The metals used include carbon steel, aluminum, stainless steel, and bronze. Carbon steel, the least expensive of these, has generally been used only in industrial and commercial walls, and always, of course, it requires a protective coating, which may or may not be decorative, to prevent corrosion. Aluminum has undoubtedly been used more extensively, in all types of curtain walls, than any other metal. By far its most common use, in custom and commercial walls, is in the form of extruded shapes for mullion members and rail and sash sections, but it is also often used in the form of sheet or plate for column covers, fascias, soffits, and panels. Stainless steel, being a more costly metal, has been used to a lesser extent and generally only in custom walls. With increased knowledge of its capabilities and efficient use, however, it is becoming more competitive in cost and its use is increasing. Because of the expense involved in producing extruded shapes in stainless steel, this metal is typically used either in sheet form or in sections that are brake-formed or roll-formed from sheet or strip material. Bronze has been the least commonly used of all the architectural metals in metal curtain wall work, but its use also appears to be on the increase. Like aluminum, it may be easily extruded or cast, or it may be used in the form of sheet or plate.

Many types of glass are used in metal curtain wall construction. Both clear and tinted plate glass are used for transparent glazing, and the opaque colored "structural" types of sheet glass are widely used as panel materials in custom and commercial walls. Many outstanding buildings have walls almost entirely of glass, with a minimum of exposed metal framing.

Numerous other materials are also used as infilling panels. Porcelain-enameled metal, either carbon steel or aluminum, is probably the most popular material, used as the exterior facing of hollow insulated panel and sandwich-panel constructions.

Several types of masonry materials—marble, stone, tile, and brick—are also used in panel areas. Ceramic tile facings, applied either to precast concrete slabs or to rigid, nonmetallic sheet materials, are popular in many areas. Additionally, plastic materials have been used as panel facings, although their use has, in the past, been comparatively limited.

STRUCTURAL CAPACITY

Since metal curtain walls are essentially envelopes attached to the building frame and do not support the floors or roof, the principal loads imposed on them are wind loads. These not only vary in maximum intensity in different parts of the country, but in any given location they also vary with the height above the ground. Both the location and the height of the building should therefore be determining factors in considering the design wind loads to be used.

The National Association of Architectural Metal Manufacturers (NAAMM) recommends in principle that the determination of wind loads to be used in the design of metal curtain walls follow the procedure specified in *American Standard Minimum Design Loads in Buildings and other Structures* (ASA A58.1). Instead of using in every instance the full unit loads therein specified, however, the NAAMM distinguishes between buildings with and without substantial interior partitions.

To determine the wind load in any specific case, reference is first made to the map showing minimum allowable resultant wind pressures in all parts of the country (see section on "Design Loads," Fig. 2). This map indicates the resultant pressures at a height of 30 ft above the ground. The actual design pressure is then selected from the table of design wind pressures (see "Design Loads," Table 3) in accordance with the following provisions:

1. For buildings having substantial and continuous interior partitions (that is, where the opening of windows or the blowout of glass or panels in one exterior wall will not result in the rapid increase of pressure differentials on the opposite exterior wall), the exterior walls shall be designed to withstand both the *inward pressure* acting inward and the *outward pressure* acting outward, the two pressures being *applied separately.*

2. For loft buildings and other buildings having open floor areas without substantial and continuous interior partitions, the exterior walls shall be designed to with-

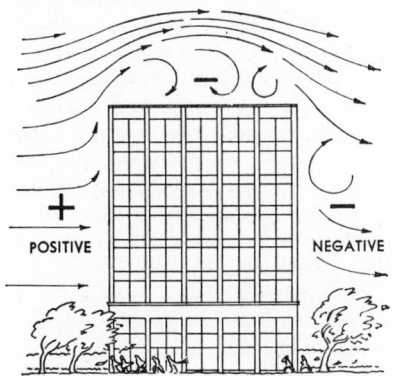

Fig. 2. Wind suction and pressure

POSITIVE   NEGATIVE

stand the *total* design pressure listed, acting *either inward or outward*.

It must be remembered that winds produce suction as well as pressure on the face of a building (Fig. 2) and that all walls should be securely anchored to prevent their being pulled off the building frame in high winds, as well as to enable them to resist without damage the positive wind forces acting inward against the building. In hurricanes, far more glass is blown *out* of buildings than into them.

A basic consideration in detailing the design of the wall is the unit stress to be allowed in the metal itself. If ferrous metals are used, these allowable stresses are readily obtainable from standard handbooks. Allowable stresses for nonferrous metals are not as clearly stipulated, partly because of the larger variety of alloys available, each with different properties, and also because of the apparent reluctance of some suppliers to define minimum properties. The NAAMM *Metal Curtain Wall Manual*, however, has established a general guide for determining reasonable unit stresses to be used for bending in all cases, although some of these values are tentative and have not received official sanction. (For table of maximum allowable unit stresses in bending, see "Architectural Metals.")

In walls where panels of glass, metal, or other materials are set within surrounding metal frames, these panels must invariably transmit the wind loads to the frame through a relatively soft sealing material. The wall frame, in turn, carries the loads to the frame of the building through the wall connections at the points of anchorage. Consequently, the sealing material must have sufficient compressive strength, extensibility, and recovery ability to serve its function under countless cycles of loading, and anchor connections must

be adequate to resist similar but far greater and highly concentrated loading effects. The problem is compounded, of course, by the concurrent movements in expansion and contraction due to temperature changes and by the necessity of maintaining an effective over-all seal against penetration by water or air under these combined effects.

Structural capacity implies both strength and stiffness. The elements of the wall may have ample strength to carry without damage the loads imposed on them yet lack the stiffness needed to prevent excessive bending when the loads are applied. Thus, under heavy wind loads the wall, although adequately strong, may bow or bulge conspicuously, frightening the building occupants. Improperly designed framing members could, without exceeding their safe strength, deflect enough to permit glass to break or even blow out. In some cases, then, the flexibility of the glass itself may be the limiting factor in determining required stiffness.

Permissible deflection-span ratios have generally been established on rather arbitrary bases. A deflection of $^1/_{360}$ of the span, or 1 in. in 30 ft, has long been the accepted reasonable maximum where plaster surfaces are involved. Approximately twice this amount, or $^1/_{175}$ of the span, is recommended as the "psychological" limit beyond which the average observer may feel insecure. In this connection, the NAAMM *Metal Curtain Wall Manual* specification stipulates that "The deflection of any metal framing member, in a direction *normal* to the plane of the wall, shall not exceed $^1/_{175}$ of the clear span of the member or ¾ in., whichever is least, except that when a plastered surface is affected this deflection shall not be more than $^1/_{360}$ of the span." Formulas for calculating the deflection of uniformly loaded simple and fixed beams are given in Fig. 7 and illustrated as applied to vertical members loaded horizontally.

The permissible deflection of framing members due to vertical dead loads (such as panels and glass) is of course limited also, but here the actual *distance* the member deflects is usually more critical than the deflection-span ratio. The NAAMM specification requires that "the deflection of any member, in a direction *parallel* to the wall plane, when the member carries its full design load, shall not exceed 75 per cent of the design clearance dimension between that member and the panel, sash, or glass immediately below it." It is important also, of course, that

members carrying panels or glass sealed in glazing pockets should be sufficiently stiff to maintain the recommended minimum edge "bite" on such panels or glass at all points.

From the standpoint of structural efficiency, considerably greater deflections might be permissible within safe stress limits, particularly under intermittent loading such as that produced by wind forces. So long as the stresses are well below the yield point, some designers may feel justified in accepting greater deflections because of the economic advantages to be gained. Other designers may feel that even smaller limits than these specifications permit should be designated, but it must be recognized that such restrictions might make heavier and more expensive sections necessary.

Some of the more monumental curtain wall buildings, especially those with all fixed glass and complete air conditioning, include permanently installed window-washing equipment operated from mobile cranes on the rooftop. In such installations mullion members must usually be designed to serve as guide rails for the mechanically operated cleaning platforms. This loading may be a critical design factor, requiring careful analysis based on loading data obtained from the manufacturer of the cleaning equipment.

Another important aspect of structural design is the selection of the proper metal to be used for fasteners. Obviously they must be noncorrosive, but the corroding effects of weather alone are not the only ones to be considered. The corrosion of dissimilar metals by electrolysis is even more critical and, in fact, generally determines the selection.

PROVISION FOR MOVEMENT

Adequate provision for movement is one of the most important considerations in metal curtain wall design. Movements are continually taking place within the various components themselves, these parts are moving in relation to one another, and the whole wall is moving in relation to the building frame. The entire structure, in fact, is actually, though microscopically, alive and active. To consider it otherwise, as a static assembly, is to ignore the facts.

The chief causes of movement are:

Thermal expansion and contraction
Wind loads
Gravity forces
Loads and vibrations affecting the building frame.

If some components of the wall are of absorptive materials, the effects of moisture should also be considered.

The effects of expansion and contraction induced by temperature changes are especially significant in metal curtain wall construction. In comparison with older types of construction, these walls involve the use of materials that have (1) much higher expansion coefficients, (2) relatively larger units, and (3) smaller heat capacities. These factors acting in concert obviously magnify the problems of movement.

Temperatures inside modern buildings are controlled within a narrow range the year around; the fluctuation in outdoor temperature and the resulting through-wall temperature differentials dictate the requirements of the wall design. The actual metal (surface) temperature may vary daily, in winter, as much as 100°F in most parts of the country and 150°F in some northern areas. If the metal surface is dark-colored and nonreflective, these variations may be even higher.

Whatever may be the cause of movement in the wall, the problem of providing for it reduces essentially to the problem of joint design, because it is in the joints that movement is typically absorbed. Experienced designers all agree that the proper detailing of joints is usually the most difficult and important part of metal curtain wall design. If the wall units are large factory assemblies, shipped and erected as complete wall sections, their expansion and contraction under temperature changes are accommodated at the joints *between* these units, rather than at joints within the unit. Since the "working" joints are thus reduced to only those between units, it is often argued that the units should be made as large as possible in order to minimize the number and total length of these joints. It should be remembered, however, that the amount of thermal movement in any component is proportional to its size, and as the number of joints is decreased, the amount of movement to be accommodated in each increases. Beyond a certain point, then, the maintenance of weathertightness obviously becomes much more difficult.

Naturally, the effects of thermal movement are more conspicuous in the larger panels and longer sections. Metal-faced panels, however constructed, deform to some degree with changes in ambient temperature. Laminated panels, being essentially bimetallic plates, tend to bulge inward on cold, cloudy days and outward when heated by the sun. Hollow panels

and unstiffened sheets, when restricted at their edges, tend to bow or "oil-can" in an unpredictable fashion. Therefore, all panels must be framed with ample edge clearance in order to permit movement in the plane of the wall.

Lengthwise expansion in long metal members such as mullions must of course be accommodated at the end joints between sections, and provision must be made for both vertical and horizontal movement in the plane of the wall. These movements may be absorbed by (1) relative displacement (slipping) of the joining parts, (2) deformation (bending) of the member, (3) increase in internal stresses, or (4) a combination of these effects. To avoid permanent deformation, any build-up in stress must of course be kept below the yield point of the metal, and in framing members it should not be sufficient to cause noticeable bending.

If movement is entirely restrained, thermal forces may build up sufficient stresses within the member to cause buckling or even failure. In some cases such deformation is a calculated design feature, but when deformation must be avoided, either the necessary displacement must be accommodated or the member must be designed with enough strength and stiffness to resist the imposed stresses. Loads on mullion members resulting from temperature changes, for example, can be severe if the members are rigidly anchored top and bottom. This condition is often found in single-story construction. The most critical situation occurs on hot summer days when long aluminum mullions tend to expand far more than the building frame to which they are anchored.

In wall designs employing mullion framing members (grid designs), it is customary to provide for horizontal movement at each mullion. Four common ways of accomplishing this are illustrated in Fig. 3. In the split mullion system (A), the two channel-shaped halves of the mullion are not rigidly joined but are permitted to move relative to each other; in the bellows mullion (B), the projecting mullion jambs are sufficiently flexible to permit the mullion width to vary as the panels expand and contract; in the batten mullion (C), inner and outer cap sections clamp the edges of adjacent panels but are not directly connected to them; and in the structural gasket system (D), the elastic gasket provides a flexible link between the panel and mullion.

Of course, whether the design of the wall is one of the widely popular grid types or some other, the details must still allow for movement. A second type, for

example, employs heavy-gage stamped metal panels directly joined at their edges and concealing or eliminating the supporting framework (Fig. 4). When formed metal units of this kind are used, they are typically designed with deep corrugated flanges rigidly connected along their inner edges, as shown in the detail. Thermal forces can thus be accommodated by a combination of stress and deformation in these flexible flanges.

In multistory buildings, movement in a vertical direction is typically accommodated in the wall design at each floor level. When the wall components are two stories in height (the usual maximum), the provision is made at two-story intervals instead, but of course correspondingly greater movement must be provided for. When mullions are a design feature, their sections are spliced with some form of telescoping slip joint (Fig. 5). Instead of using an inside sleeve as shown, the designer may offset the upper end of the lower member by swaging to accomplish the same purpose.

Anchorage details, too, may be very significant in determining the effect of stresses in the vertical framing members. The deflection of a member under wind loading may be limited by providing some degree of fixity, rather than a simple pin joint, at its ends. A mullion is a vertical beam, and when simply supported its maximum deflection under uniform loading is five times that caused by the same loading if the ends are rigidly fixed. Complete rigidity in end connections is seldom practical, and most end conditions are likely to be nearer a pin-joint condition than a fixed condition, but in some instances added rigidity can be supplied to advantage (Fig. 6).

Movement at anchorage points is often permitted, theoretically at least, by the use of slotted holes. The true functional value of this device as typically used, however, is often questionable. The bolts are usually drawn up so tightly that the value of the slot is eliminated by friction, if not by subsequent corrosion. Frequently this type of connection resists movement until high stresses accumulate, and then it may suddenly release with a cracking sound. If slotted holes are to ensure the displacement intended, either shoulder bolts or sleeves should be used, as shown in Fig. 7, with Bellville or molded nylon washers to provide light but positive pressure and to prevent rattling. Without such devices, a common procedure is to "recommend" that the nut be drawn tight, then backed off one-half or three-quarters of a turn. But without constant supervision there is no

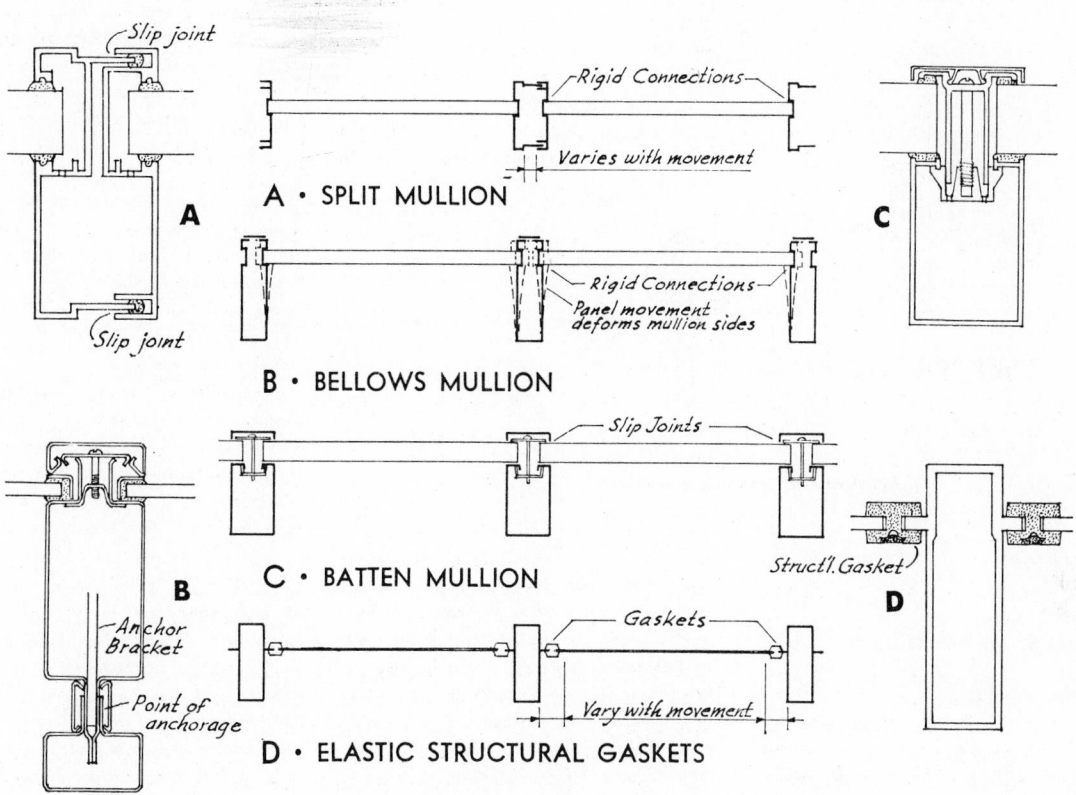

A · SPLIT MULLION

B · BELLOWS MULLION

C · BATTEN MULLION

D · ELASTIC STRUCTURAL GASKETS

Fig. 3. Methods of providing for movement

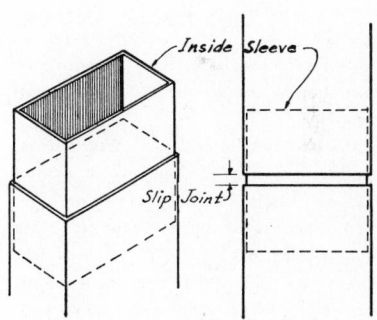

Fig. 5. Typical joint in vertical mullion

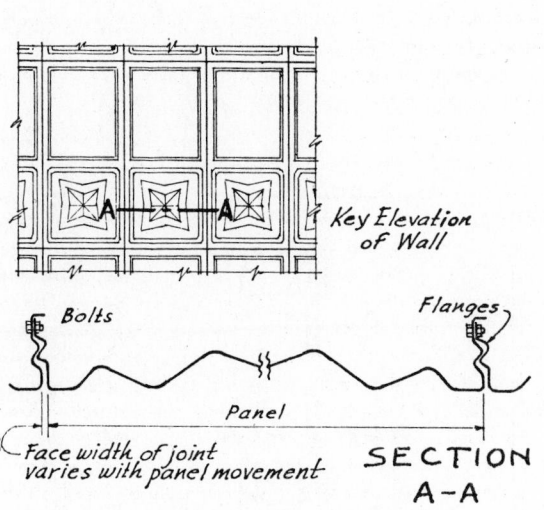

Fig. 4. Joints between stamped metal panels

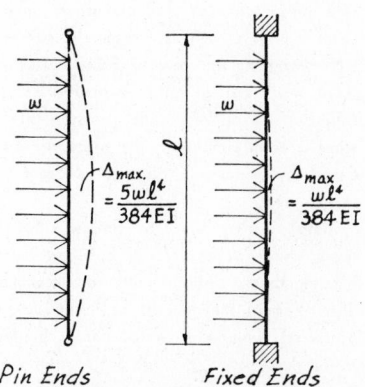

Fig. 6. Deflection of vertical beams

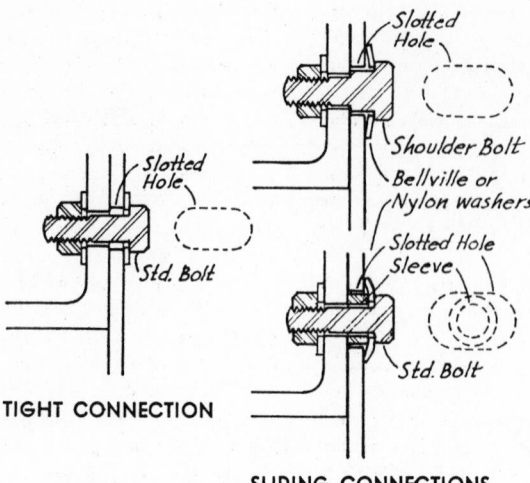

TIGHT CONNECTION

SLIDING CONNECTIONS

Fig. 7. Bolted anchorage connections

insurance that such instructions will be followed.

WATER AND AIR INFILTRATION

Ideally, a wall would permit no water to penetrate its exterior surface from outside but at the same time would permit any moisture within the wall to escape through this same surface to the atmosphere. Needless to say, this ideal function is rarely if ever realized, since we do not yet have a surfacing material with the requisite characteristic of one-way permeability.

The NAAMM *Metal Curtain Wall Manual* specification, after defining water infiltration as "the appearance of water other than condensation on the room-side face of any part of the wall," requires that "no water infiltration shall occur when the wall is tested under the positive wind load specified . . . (by the designer as a basis for structural design). . . ." The nature and severity of the tests employed in verifying watertightness vary somewhat with the quality of wall concerned. In all cases the test wall is completely covered with water at the rate of 2.5 gal per sq ft of wall per hr and is simultaneously subjected to either static pressure or a wind stream, simulating the pressures produced by winds at velocities of from 25 to 125 mph.

Metal walls typically contain "weak spots," such as butt joints between framing members, sliding joints to accommodate thermal movements, or inadequately protected weepholes, which permit limited water penetration through their outer surfaces. Consequently it is usually impossible and often undesirable to eliminate all vul-

nerability to leakage through the outer skin, and good design usually requires the incorporation of a secondary defense against water penetration through the wall. By such means it should always be possible to prevent leakage through the outer surface from causing damage within the wall construction or passing through the wall to the interior of the building.

One way of accomplishing this "secondary defense" on buildings of only a few stories is to so detail the wall that any small amount of water penetrating the joints and seals will be collected, either directly or indirectly, inside hollow mullion sections that serve as downspouts. The sketches in Fig. 8 indicate diagrammatically how this is accomplished. On high-rise buildings, though, the advisability of using this type of drainage system is questionable, because the quantity of water

accumulated in long runs of mullions may be excessive, and it is difficult to provide drainage from the mullions at intermediate levels. The preferred practice in tall buildings, therefore, is to drain the horizontal members themselves directly to the outdoors by means of baffled weepholes (Fig. 9).

Any interior drainage system within the wall should be intended to function only under extreme conditions and should not be considered as the primary defense against leakage. The proper detailing of joints and their sealing should always be the chief deterrent to water penetration under normal conditions.

Weepholes are usually essential design features of metal curtain wall construction, serving to drain away condensate on cold interior surfaces and moisture from leaks within the wall. But if they are not carefully designed, they may also be points of weakness in the defense against water penetration. In heavy storms the pressure of high winds on the wall face often forces rain water to flow *upward* on the wall, thus entering openings in soffit areas which would not be subject to penetration under normal rainfall conditions. It is imperative, therefore, that they be either so located that penetration by wind-driven rain is impossible or so backed up by baffles that no damage will result from such penetration.

The phenomenon of surface wetting— that property of water which causes it to adhere to a surface—is of special significance in metal-wall constructions. The provision of positive-drip profiles at the outer edges of soffit areas is therefore of even greater importance than in masonry construction, where more absorptive materials are used (Fig. 10).

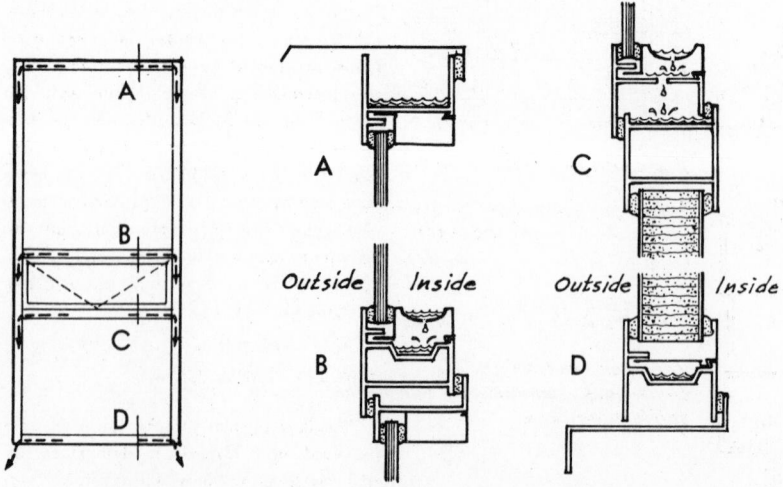

Fig. 8. Diagram of drainage sytem in a preassambled unit

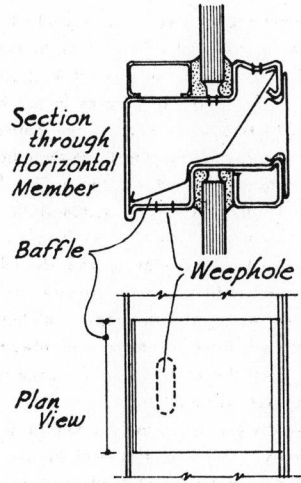

Fig. 9. Drainage by means of weepholes

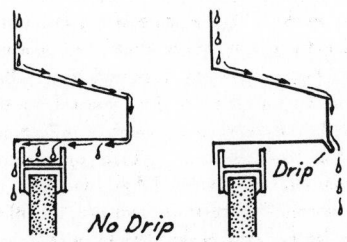

Fig. 10. Why drips are needed on horizontal members

Capillary action is another characteristic of water to be recognized in the detailing of a metal wall. Because of it, water may travel surprising distances between adjacent surfaces, even in defiance of gravity and without abnormal pressure. This may be a source of leakage, particularly in "dry" or uncaulked joints, and the capillary effect is greatly aggravated,

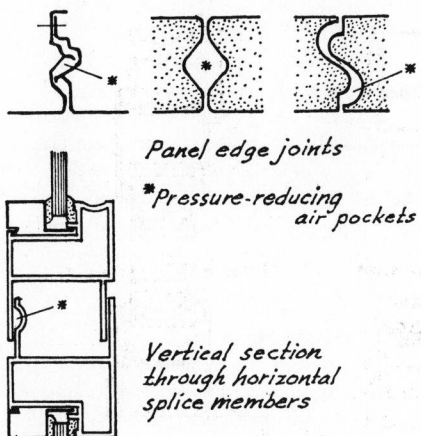

Fig. 11. Typical capillary breaks in joints

of course, by wind pressure. To discourage water infiltration by capillarity, it is often advisable to provide "capillary breaks" in detailing vulnerable joints. This is done by deforming or grooving the contacting surfaces in such a way as to form interrupting gaps in the narrow space between them, instead of permitting the parts to be in close contact for the full depth of the joint (Fig. 11).

The infiltration of air is much less likely than water infiltration to have a damaging effect on the building interior. To some degree air infiltration may be desirable, but the amount must be controlled within permissible limits to avoid drafts and maintain comfort. Up to a point, such infiltration as may occur through the wall tends to vary with wind velocity, but with higher wind velocities this relationship no longer holds.

Control of air infiltration through the typical metal wall depends chiefly on two factors: the tightness of joint seals and the presence of operable sash. With proper design of the former and tight weatherstripping of the latter it will seldom be significant.

When preformed elastomeric or plastic gaskets are used to seal sliding joints between wall parts, it is usually advisable to provide a double seal as insurance against excess infiltration of either water or air. When these materials are used as periphery seals around panels or glass, it is particularly important that no gaps be permitted at their corner joints. Unless continuity is provided by vulcanizing or heat-sealing, the abutting strips must be carefully and tightly fitted at corners, and positive contact must be permanently maintained under constant compression.

Operable sash of the hinged or projected types should also have at least two continuous contacting surfaces in the depth of the sash, with ample weathering overlaps and should be provided with double weatherstripping, and all weatherstripping should be readily accessible for replacement when worn or deteriorated. Sliding sash must have continuous tight and effective weathering on all edges and at meeting rails. Sash hardware, too, must be adequately strong and rigid to lock windows tightly shut, assuring a good seal all around.

THERMAL TRANSMISSION

The flow of heat through the wall, both outward and inward, is determined by the resistance to thermal transmission provided by the materials composing the wall assembly. Heat is very readily conducted

through metals, much less readily through glass, and very slowly through light, porous, insulating materials and across confined air spaces. Typically, the thermal values advertised for walls are those of certain components of the wall rather than of the complete assembly, though it is the latter that is of chief significance, of course. The over-all U value (Btu per hour per square foot per degree of temperature difference between air on the outside and inside surfaces) is the result of the complex interrelationship of the transmission values of the individual component materials. It is difficult to calculate theoretically and can be determined accurately only by actual testing of the whole assembly. To date, only a few manufacturers have undertaken such testing, because most consumers will accept poor thermal performance in preference to better insulating value at a slightly higher cost. This situation is changing, however, as operating costs are receiving more attention and as a few manufacturers are finding ways of upgrading thermal performance.

The fact that over-all thermal values are generally inferior to those of some of the principal components is due chiefly to the presence of metal parts extending through the wall and serving as heat conductors. Even in moderate climates, therefore, it is important that the amount of such through-metal be minimized, and in cold climates it is mandatory. As illustrated in Fig. 12, metallic parts extending through the wall, even in the form of fasteners, provide paths of heat flow which not only contribute to heat loss but may also cause moisture to condense either within the wall or on its interior face.

For many years the principal concern in wall design was to reduce the heat *loss* from the building in cold weather, to save fuel. This is still a vital consideration, but now we demand summer comfort in our buildings too. The values of air conditioning are well established, and the necessity of preventing heat *gain* from solar effects has become an even more important consideration in many parts of the country than preventing heat loss in the winter. Even in the northern states, summer air conditioning is generally required. Since the cost of cooling is always much greater, per Btu, than the cost of heating, efficient air conditioning requires *better* insulation than equally efficient heating.

The location of the wall insulation in respect to the structural frame of the building is an important consideration. In the interests of economy it is better to locate the insulation *outside* the building frame, as shown in Fig. 13, for two

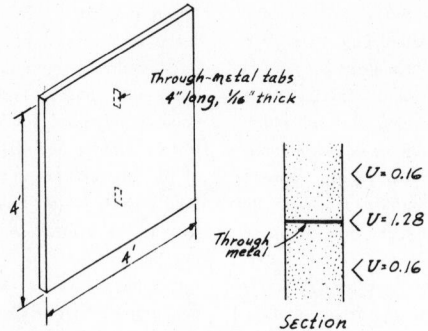

Fig. 12. Effect of through-metal conductivity

Theoretical calculations indicate that if an insulated panel 16 sq ft in area contains through metal of only ½ sq in. cross-sectional area (normal to the direction of heat flow), its insulating value is reduced approximately as follows:

	U value	Increase, per cent
With no through metal	0.16	—
	0.20	—
With through-steel tabs	0.19	19
	0.23	15
With through-aluminum tabs	0.30	87
	0.33	65

reasons: (1) The uninsulated floor edges and spandrel beams act as heat-exchange fins, contributing to heat loss and resulting in cold floors near the perimeter of the building, and (2) The exterior structural framing, when insulated, remains at relatively constant temperature, and its thermal movements are minimized. Since any such movements are necessarily cumulative (no expansion joints being provided in the frame), they can be the cause of major sealing problems and high maintenance costs, particularly in tall buildings. When design requirements dictate that structural framing elements be exposed outside the curtain wall, an insulative covering of these members may be advisable.

In typical custom and commercial metal curtain walls the proportion of transparent glazed area is large, varying between 50 and 80 per cent of the total wall area. Since glass has a relatively poor over-all insulating value as compared with most wall panes, both the proportion and the type of glass used largely determine the over-all thermal value of the wall. Therefore a reduction of heat flow through the glazed areas is highly significant in improving this value. Regular ¼-in. plate glass has a thermal conductivity (U value) of about 1.13, whereas factory-sealed insulating glass, with a U value of 0.55, transmits only about half as much heat (except for solar radiation). Thus the use of insulating glass has a major effect on

the thermal value of the wall, especially if the glass area is large (Table 1 and Fig. 14). Admittedly the initial cost of insulating glass is higher, but usually the cost difference is reclaimed in lower installation and operating expenses for heating and cooling within a few years, and substantial savings result thereafter.

Invariably, as insulation of the wall is increased, by whatever means, the costs of heating and air conditioning are lowered. There are usually limits, however, beyond which the addition of more insulation is not economically justified, when the interest on the capital investment exceeds the return in savings. This limit varies with local conditions and costs. It cannot be determined by any rule of thumb but always deserves careful attention in wall designs that involve long-term costs.

The proportional value of insulation in the solid or opaque areas of the wall varies with the extent of the transparent glazed area, as well as with the type of glass used. This value increases as the

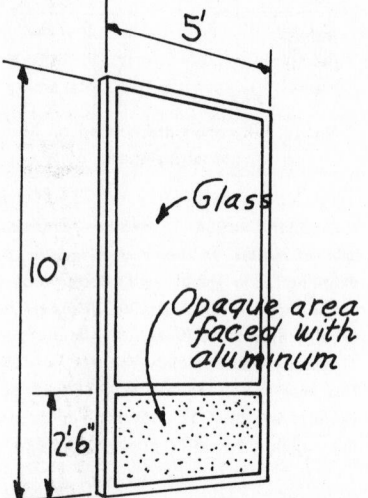

Fig. 14. Panel proportions (see Table 1)

glazed area is reduced, and as Fig. 14 illustrates, it has greater significance when insulating glass is used than when the glazing is of a single thickness. Regardless of the proportion of glazed to solid-wall area, however, each unit of heat transfer eliminated represents the same amount of saving, and the time required to amortize the cost of insulation by such saving remains the same.

The value of panel insulation is particularly significant where spandrel panels occur adjacent to heating elements. Here, high local temperatures exist during the heating season, with a high indoor-outdoor temperature differential. One of the func-

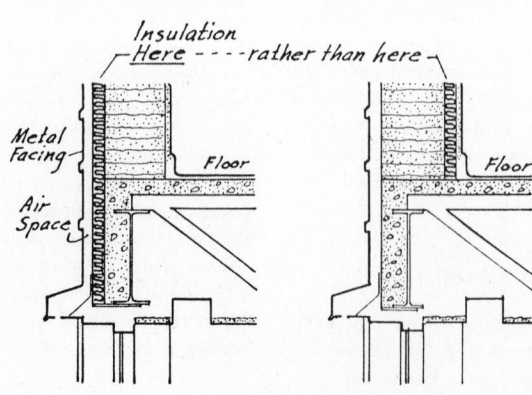

Fig. 13. Location of wall insulation

Table 1. Calculated thermal values

Allowance has been made for conduction of aluminum frame.

Opaque area	U value of opaque area	Over-all U value of 5x10-ft unit	
		With single-plate glass (U=1.13)	With insulating glass (U=0.55)
2-in. paper honeycomb	0.27	1.09	0.70
2-in. glass fiber	0.12	1.06	0.65
2-in. glass fiber plus 8-in. lightweight concrete block	0.09	1.05	0.65

tions of such panels (shown in Fig. 15) is to confine this heat within the building. Obviously, then, high insulating value is an essential requirement here, regardless of its effect on the over-all thermal value of the wall.

From a purely functional standpoint, the logical location for wall insulation would be outside the metal wall framework itself, but this is inconsistent with design concepts to date. In grid designs, the pattern of the framing elements is the dominant design feature, and insulated panels are not placed outside these elements but between them. It follows that the metal elements themselves are not insulated but instead serve as conductive paths by which heat readily penetrates the wall. This not only raises the over-all *U* value of the wall, as was previously pointed out, but may also result in the formation of condensation on the inside surfaces of the metal in cold weather.

The extent of this effect depends a great deal on the details of the mullion design. As illustrated in Fig. 16, the proportion

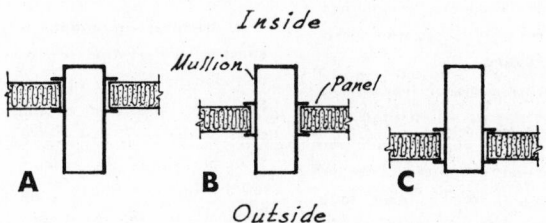

Fig. 16. Location of mullion in relation to plane of wall

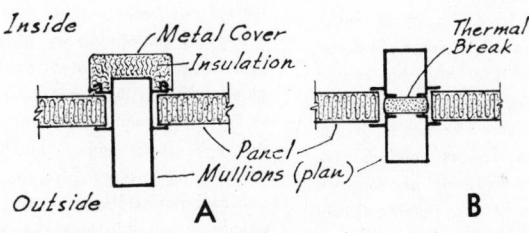

Fig. 17. Methods of preventing heat flow through mullions

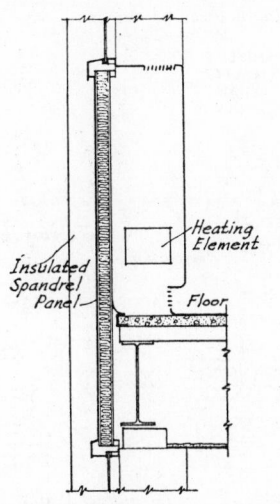

Fig. 15. Insulated panel adjacent to heating element

of the member exposed to inside air is highly significant, because of the warming effect on the member. When a large proportion of it is exposed to the outside temperature, as in Sketch A, the inside warming effect will be small. This is the worst condition for interior condensation, and, unfortunately, the most popular design concept. Sketch B illustrates a compromise arrangement that will perform satisfactorily in all but the most severe climates. Sketch C is the best arrangement, as far as the effect of "fin heat loss" is concerned. Most of the metal surface is inside the building, and the relatively small area exposed to the cold is normally not large enough to lower the temperature of the inner face to the point where condensation will occur.

If deep outside exposure of the framing members is necessary for the desired design effect, there are ways of minimizing heat loss and condensation problems, even in cold climates. One way to prevent condensation is to provide, by peripheral heating, an interior warm-air curtain of sufficient intensity to overcome the natural low surface temperature of the member; another method is to reduce the moisture content of the interior air, thus lowering its dewpoint. Actually to reduce the heat flow through the member, though, one of the methods illustrated in Fig. 17 should be considered. Probably the more economical way is to cover the interior exposed surface of the member with added insulation, as shown in Sketch A. Another is to provide a "thermal break" in the member itself by incorporating a nonmetallic spacer between its outside and inside parts, as shown in Sketch B. To perform its function properly, such an insulating spacer must be adequately thick; thin "barriers" are of very little value.

WATER VAPOR AND CONDENSATION

The presence of condensed moisture on the inner face of a wall is always annoying, and if it collects within the wall itself it may cause serious damage. With present-day knowledge of water-vapor movement and behavior, condensation within buildings and in the shell construction itself can be avoided if proper attention is given to the matter in the planning stage, but it may be both difficult and expensive to correct poor design if trouble develops in an occupied building. When moisture appears on the inner surface of a wall it is usually an indication of improper design, ill-advised use of materials, or unforeseen moisture-producing operations within the building.

A brief review of some of the elementary principles of physics will suggest how condensation in and on building walls can be prevented. Water evaporates into the atmosphere, changing from a liquid to a gas and becoming invisible water vapor. The amount of vapor the air can contain depends on the air temperature; the warmer the air, the more water it can hold. Thus, if warm moisture-laden air is cooled, it releases its excess vapor, which again takes the form of water. Such reduction in temperature may be caused by the air coming in contact with a cooler surface, in which case the water is deposited on this surface as condensation. Everyone has observed this phenomenon on the outside of a glass containing a cold drink or on dew-laden grass in the cool of a summer evening. Appropriately enough, the temperature of the air at which its contained moisture begins to condense is known as its "dew point."

In designing for moisture control, it is essential to recall certain important facts concerning the nature of water vapor:

1. Vapor in the air results in pressure, just as with any other gas. As the amount increases, in absolute terms of "grains of water per pound of dry air," the greater becomes the "vapor pressure." Cold air has a lower vapor pressure than equally saturated warm air, and as the relative humidity increases, these differences in vapor pressure between cold and warm air also increase.

2. The movement of water vapor is largely determined by differences in vapor pressure, much as air movement (wind) is caused by differences in atmospheric pressure. Like the air in a toy balloon, it is always seeking to escape from high-pressure areas, such as a heated building, to areas of lower pressure, such as the colder out-of-doors.

3. Water vapor's movement may be independent of that of the air containing it, and it is even independent of gravity. Just as with heat, however, the transfer of vapor may be affected by a moving air stream, especially if the air is moving toward an area of lower vapor pressure. Thus ventilation, even by natural forces, is an important deterrent to condensation.

4. Water vapor can penetrate microscopic openings through which even air cannot pass.

5. Water vapor condenses on surfaces that impede its normal flow and are colder than the dew point of the air containing it.

It becomes apparent, then, that the effect of water vapor on a wall construction depends chiefly upon two factors: (1) The vapor pressures existing on the two sides of the wall, and (2) The permeability characteristics of the wall's component materials. The first factor is generally predetermined by the conditions of use and location of the building, but the second imposes on the designer not only the necessity of selecting the proper materials but also the importance of using them in their proper relationships.

Building materials vary widely in vapor permeance, as indicated in Table 2. In general terms, those having a permeance of less than unity are considered to be *relatively* good vapor barriers. Metals, even in foil thickness, are for all practical purposes perfect barriers, and it is principally this fact that makes proper moisture control so important in the design of metal curtain wall construction.

Moisture within nonresidential buildings may come from a variety of sources (Table 3). In new buildings most of it may have been introduced in large amounts with wet materials of construction. In older buildings, moisture is constantly being released in many ways—by industrial processes, by washing of floors, by plant life, by human respiration and perspiration, and often, during the heating season at least, by artificial means of humidification. Within the wall itself, moisture may also result from external leakage through weepholes or through exterior joints in the wall construction.

The condensation of moisture from such sources will usually occur on the room-side face of the wall only in cold weather, and even then it will be negligible if the heating system is designed to sweep these surfaces with sufficient warm air to keep their temperatures above the dew point of the impinging air. If the heating system is not so designed, the condensation on single glazed and cold metal surfaces on cold

days may be troublesome, but since it can be seen and removed, it is seldom dangerous. Far more critical is the occurrence of condensation hidden within the wall itself. Here the undetected collection of moisture may deteriorate organic materials, impair the value of insulation, and cause corrosion of metallic parts by galvanic action, if not by rusting.

The significance of these facts leads to four important rules governing the design of the wall:

1. Provide a vapor barrier on or near the warm side of the wall.

2. Provide sufficient insulation to keep critical surfaces warmer than the dew-point temperature of the indoor air. (A critical surface is one that tends to impede the flow of water vapor).

3. Provide for vapor release on the cold side of the wall.

4. Avoid using a tight vapor barrier on both sides of the wall. This creates a vapor trap in which condensation can accumulate.

The logic of these principles is illustrated in Fig. 18. As indicated, some vapor will pass through even the best barrier materials, at their joints or seams, and moisture is likely to enter the wall also by leakage from the outside. Therefore, in an ideal wall the outer skin will have a permeance rating at least five times that of the inner skin. With metal walls this ideal situation is often impossible—in fact the reverse may be true. Either both skins are of metal (a perfect vapor barrier), or the outer skin is of metal and the inner skin is of some relatively permeable material. In both cases, ventilation within the wall is a necessity, regardless of whether or not insulation is provided for in the space (Fig. 19). Condensation is almost certain to occur on the inner side of the

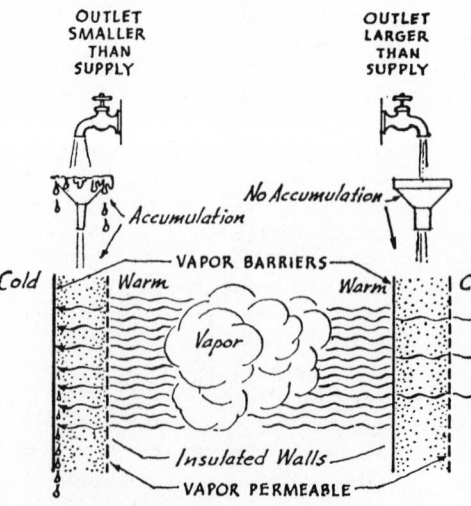

Fig. 18. Vapor barriers and vapor releases

Table 2. Approximate permeability characteristics of building materials

Material	Permeance (perms)	Permeability (perm-inches)
Aluminum foil, 0.0006", on paper	0.02	
Aluminum foil, 0.004"	0.00	
Polyethylene film, 0.001"	0.67	
0.004"	0.17	
0.008"	0.08	
Cellular glass		0.00
Foamed polystyrene		1.0 - 2.0
Asphalt-coated paper, glossy, 10#/sq.	0.35	
Laminated Kraft building paper, 7.5#/sq.	0.42	
Oilcloth	0.96	
Paint:		
2 coats asphalt paint on plywood	0.43	
2 coats aluminum paint on plywood	1.29	
3 coats exterior paint on wood	0.3 - 1.0	
¼" DF plywood, exterior type	0.72	
interior type	1.86	
Vegetable fiber insulating board, uncoated	20.0 - 50.0	
Glass fiber insulating board	50.0 - 90.0	
Plaster, ¾" on metal lath	15.0	
½" on gypsum lath	20.0	
Gypsum wall board, ⅜"	50.0	
Concrete, 1-2-4 mix		3.2
4" Brick wall	0.8 - 1.1	
Still air		120.0

Table 3. Sources of indoor moisture (in approximate amounts of water)

OCCUPANTS	Avg. of 2¼ lb. per person, per 8-hr. day in sedentary occupations
PLANT LIFE	About 1¾ lb. per plant, in 24 hours
WASHING FLOORS	3 lb. per 100 s.f. per washing
CONSTRUCTION	Stone Concrete— 2 lb./s.f. of 4" slab Gypsum Concrete— 5.4 lb./s.f. of 2" roof slab Gypsum Plaster— 1.6 lb./s.f. of 1" plaster } must eventually be evaporated Heating Salamander — 1.3 gal. of water per gallon of oil burned

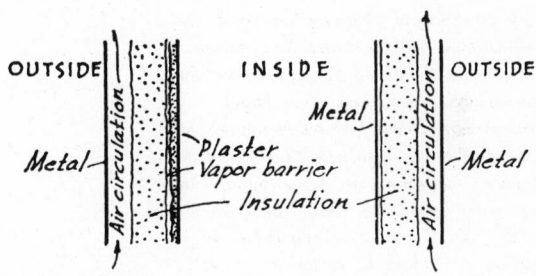

Fig. 19. Ventilation of metal curtain wall panels

outer metal skin if the construction is reasonably tight, and this must be prevented, or at least the moisture must be evaporated, by permitting air to circulate behind it. In addition, a means should be provided for draining any excess moisture that may accumulate at the bottom of this vent space.

In metal-clad walls of the industrial type (Fig. 20), these principles may govern the design of a large portion of the total wall area and are of special importance, of course, when it is a question of housing industrial processes requiring high humidities. In commercial and custom walls proper moisture control can usually be provided only in the panel areas. It is important there, whether the panels be simply facings over masonry backup or a composite, insulated assembly comprising the complete wall. In the former case, as illustrated in Fig. 21, the insulation should preferably be placed outside the masonry, and a well-ventilated and drained space should always be provided behind the facing.

It has sometimes been recommended that the edges of composite panels be completely sealed with a film impermeable to vapor. This is logical only if (1) the air within the panel is dehumidified before the edge seal is applied, and (2) it can be guaranteed that the hermetic seal will remain perfect during the life of the building. Some means of fulfilling these requirements may eventually be developed, as it has been for insulating glass. Otherwise, the sealing of panel edges against the passage of vapor is ill advised and results in a vapor trap. With the bellows action that occurs in a sealed hollow panel

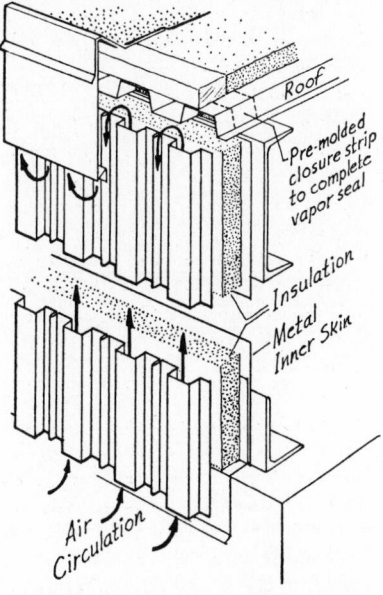

Fig. 20. Ventilation of industrial-type curtain wall

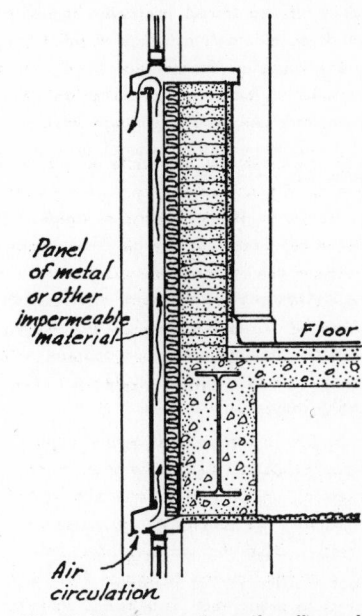

Fig. 21. Ventilation of metal wall panel with masonry backup

because of fluctuating air temperatures and volume, vapor is sucked in through any microscopic opening in the seal as the panel cools and is likely to condense at the low point of the temperature cycle. Over a period of time the panel becomes a reservoir of water, and trouble follows.

In composite panel assemblies, whether they be the laminated- or hollow-pan type, ventilation is usually essential. The only exception is laminated construction employing a core material of closed-cell structure, which in itself is a good vapor barrier.

Instead of being sealed, the edges of most panel constructions should be highly permeable to vapor and deliberately ventilated. The ventilation must of course be provided in such a way as to prevent the entrance of rain or snow, but this is a common feature of good panel designs. With some types of laminated panels it may be advisable to apply protective tape around the edges to prevent damage in transit and handling, but such tape should either be removed or be deliberately punctured, in areas to be protected from the weather, before the panels are installed.

JOINTS

The successful functioning of any metal curtain wall depends largely upon the design of the joints between the component parts. Proper detailing of the joints is the most critical, and often the most difficult, part of the whole wall design. As discussed previously, relative movement of the wall components is a prime factor affecting the entire design concept, and it is chiefly in the detailing of the joints that this movement must be accommodated. Consequently an analysis of the functions and characteristics of joints is essential to an intelligent approach to the joint problem.

Wall assemblies in general include two broad categories of joints:

1. *Closed joints,* which are intended to effect a tight seal against the entrance of weather at all times
2. *Operable joints,* such as those surrounding a ventilator sash, which may on occasion be deliberately opened but when closed are intended to provide a weathertight contact of the joined parts.

Since it is the closed joints which present most of the problems in metal curtain wall design, the discussion will be concerned primarily with that category.

The typical closed-joint assembly is composed of three basic elements:

1. The *joint shape,* or the conformation of the joining parts

2. The *joint seal,* or the material or technique used to make the assembly weathertight
3. The *fasteners,* upon which the structural integrity of the assembly depends.

It should be recognized, however, that some joints, notably the accordion-flange type of mating joint, are designed to function without the necessity of adding a sealing material.

Criteria of good design require that any closed joint perform certain functions and have certain characteristics. It should:

1. Give durable protection from the infiltration of air and moisture
2. Provide structural and thermal insulation values comparable to those of the adjacent wall areas
3. Have few parts and ample dimensional tolerances
4. Facilitate installation and replacement of the wall components.

Durable protection

The most important function of the joint assembly is to exclude water, dust, and air from the building interior, but it must also protect the wall construction itself and insure its durability. If the joining components themselves are invulnerable to moisture, the penetration of water into the joint between them may not be harmful, provided electrolytic action is prevented and prompt drainage to the exterior is effected. If water contained in a joint should freeze, however, either movement or stress, or both, result, and these must be accommodated without damage to the wall.

The sealing material is typically the most critical element of the joint assembly affecting durability. Good, long-lived seals are more expensive than short-lived sealing material, and there is often a temptation to "economize" on this detail, with concern only for initial cost and little thought for later maintenance expense. Particularly on large buildings sealing material that will require maintenance should be avoided at all costs. The charges for such work are likely to be far greater than the original cost of using even the best and most durable (but commensurately expensive) material; thus, to select a sealing material on the basis of initial cost alone is a false economy.

Structural value

Joints between wall components must have sufficient strength to transmit forces from either joined part to the other. These forces, imposed principally by the wind or by temperature changes, may subject the

joint assembly to any of the usual structural forces of shear, tension, compression, or flexure. The nature and intensity of the forces will of course vary with the position and function of the joint.

When members are rigidly and continuously joined, as by welding, the functions of sealing and fastening are performed simultaneously by the joining technique and the strength of the assembly is determined by the "seal" itself. Typically, however, the joint seal is provided by a nonrigid material which contributes only partially, if at all, to the strength of the assembly. In most cases, therefore, it is the joint shape and the fasteners which must provide the essential structural value.

Thermal insulation

In general, joint details have relatively little effect on the over-all thermal insulation value of the wall, but poor joint design may result in objectionable cold spots on the building interior. As previously noted, the use of through-metal in the joint assembly should always be avoided but is particularly dangerous in cold climates. Fasteners are the most frequent offenders in this respect, but a poor choice of joint shape may be even more critical in reducing thermal insulation value.

Number of parts

The simplest design that will meet all the critical requirements is usually the best. The number of loose parts, such as battens, gaskets, and splines, should be as small as possible, and no more fasteners should be used than are necessary to provide adequate strength and stiffness. It is always desirable to keep to a minimum the number of types of joints used and to employ the same joint shape, sealing method, and fastening device as widely as possible throughout the installation. Uniformity in these respects not only permits lower manufacturing and erection costs but also provides for greater interchangeability of similar parts.

Dimensional tolerances

Costs of manufacture and installation are greatly affected also by the degree of precision required. If these costs are to be kept within reasonable limits, the necessity of close dimensional tolerances should be avoided. Metal curtain wall construction usually involves the marriage of factory-made units to a field-constructed frame, thus relating two widely differing concepts of precision. This should be recognized in the design of joints. Factory tolerances may readily be held to a few thousandths of an inch, but field construction tolerances

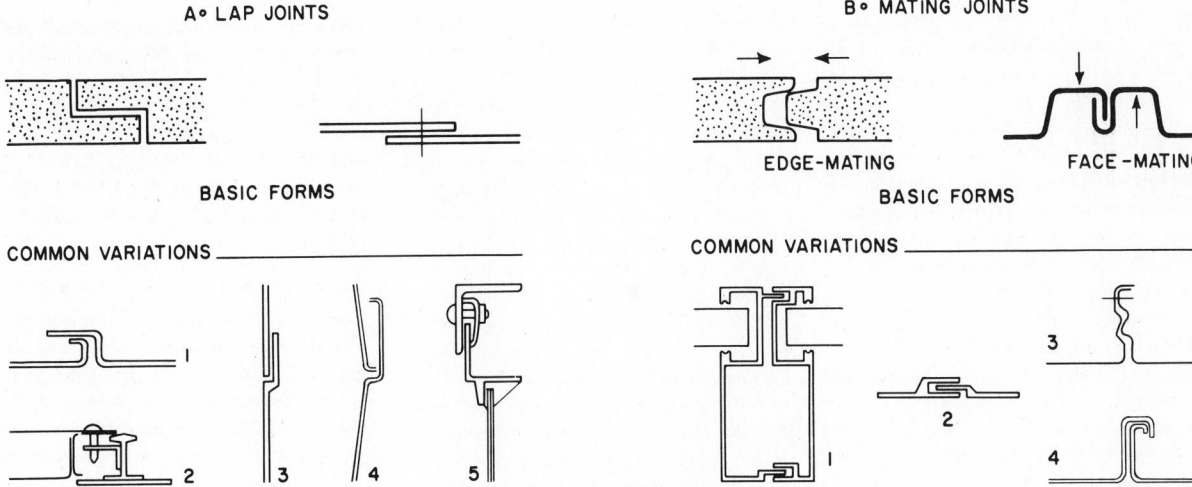

Fig. 22. Integral-type joints

are measured in major fractions of an inch. Since field conditions necessarily govern installation, designs based on "machine-fit" assemblies and tolerances are unrealistic. Unless ample allowance is made for dimensional variations, particularly in the joint shape, expensive field adjustments are likely to result.

Facility of installation and replacement

Alignment of parts should be largely automatic, and the necessity of tedious positioning or force-fitting should always be avoided. Wherever possible, the joining and anchoring methods should be such that the wall can be installed with few and simple tools and without exterior scaffolding. A joint shape may require that components be installed in some definite order or that the last panel installed be of a special type; preferably, however, the design should permit wide latitude in the order of assembly.

It is advantageous, too, if the joint assembly can be designed to allow for removal of any panel or unit for replacement without the necessity of disturbing

a number of adjacent units. Such facility is a feature which metal curtain walls can offer as an advantage over masonry construction, where replacement of wall units, if required, is usually a major operation.

Joint shapes

The term "joint shape," as used in this discussion, refers to the physical form of those parts, other than the sealing material and fasteners, which make up the joint assembly. It includes the edge profiles of the joining parts, as well as the forms of added parts such as cover strips or inserts, which may be required to complete the assembly. Joint shapes are of two basic types:

1. The *integral type*, in which the edges of the joining parts themselves constitute the joint assembly

2. The *accessory type*, in which extra pieces are required to complete the assembly.

The *integral type* (Fig. 22) has two principal forms:

1. *Lap joints,* in which the joining edges lap each other, either in full or partial thickness.

2. *Mating joints,* in which the edges of the joining members are formed in complementary "male and female" profiles. These joints may be assembled either edgewise (edge-mating), restricting relative movement of the parts normal to their faces, or facewise (face-mating), preventing relative movement parallel to their faces.

A third type of integral joint, comparatively rare in metal wall construction, is the *butt joint.* If certain new sealing techniques still under development should prove to be practical, this type of joint may be more commonly used in the future.

The accessory type (Fig. 23) includes three common forms:

1. *Batten joints,* in which the joint opening is covered, on one or both faces, with a nonstructural cover strip or batten. Battens, in this terminology, are distinguished from splines by the fact that they are applied (and can be removed) from the *face*

A∘ BATTEN JOINTS

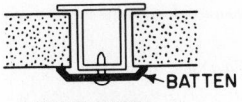

BASIC FORM

COMMON VARIATIONS _____

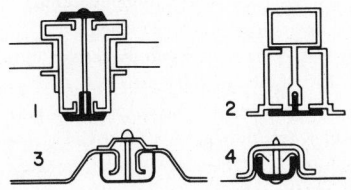

B∘ SPLINE JOINTS

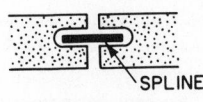

BASIC FORM

COMMON VARIATIONS _____

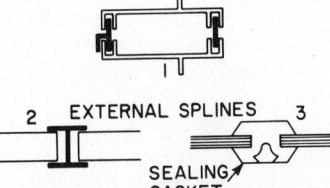

C∘ FRAME & STOP JOINTS

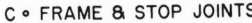

COMMON VARIATIONS _____

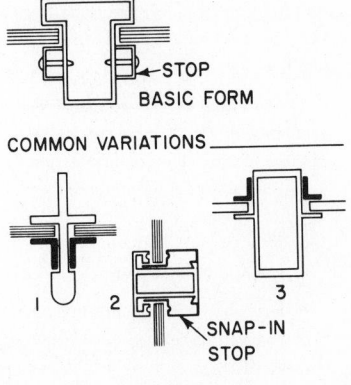

Fig. 23. Accessory-type joints

of the joint. They may be attached to a backup frame, to intermittent clips, or to another batten on the opposite face of the wall.

2. *Spline joints,* in which an accessory piece bridges the joint gap, either by fitting into grooves in opposite panel edges (interior splines) or by providing back-to-back grooves in the spline itself to receive the edges of the joining parts (exterior splines). Splines are always applied in the *edges* of the joining members; hence, they must either be installed before the members are finally positioned or be inserted lengthwise between the members after they are in position.

3. *Frame-and-stop joints,* in which members are installed within a surrounding frame, usually structural, by means of the attachment to the frame of retaining "stop moulds."

To a limited extent the joint shape itself affects the over-all performance of the total joint assembly, but it is seldom, if ever, the sole factor that determines satisfactory performance. Good joint design necessitates an appropriate combination of the complementary advantages offered by each of the three joint elements—shape, seal, and fasteners—working together. The good qualities of any one of these are never adequate to offset deficiencies in the others. The best joint shape will produce a poor assembly if the seal or fasteners fail, and the best seal can be of little value in a poorly designed shape. Even when both the shape and seal are excellent, the assembly may fail because of poor fastenings.

SEALING MATERIALS

Many types of material are used for sealing the variety of joints in metal curtain wall construction, and these differ not only in physical form but also in functional characteristics. All of them, however, have a common purpose and should therefore meet the same performance criteria. Regardless of the type used, the joint seal should possess these essential qualities:

1. The ability to maintain watertight contact with the joining parts, regardless of dimensional changes in the joint size
2. Durability and integrity under all weather effects
3. Ease of handling and application
4. Long-range economy.

It must be remembered that the need to accommodate ever-present movement is the source of most problems in the design of metal curtain wall joints. Generally it is the seal which is most critically affected by dimensional changes in the joint. It is relatively easy to design the joint shape and fasteners to permit movement, but it is far more difficult to insure that the sealing material will perform similarly over a long period, at the same time maintaining a completely tight closure.

It is essential, of course, that the seal withstand the differentials of temperature and vapor pressure existing between the two faces of the wall. Vapor pressure especially may be a very real load, particularly in cold weather, and the seal must usually be sufficiently impermeable to prevent the entrance of damaging moisture into the construction from the interior as well as the exterior of the building.

In general, joint seals may be considered to be of two basic types: rigid and nonrigid. Except for welding and soldering, however, where the molten metal may be thought of as the sealing material, the rigid type currently has very limited application in the field assembly of wall components. And since joint rigidity eliminates differential movement of the joining parts, the rigid joint is not germane to this discussion. In the consideration of appropriate materials, therefore, attention will be confined to the far more common nonrigid type of joint seal.

For nonrigid seals in *closed* joints, the usual materials employed are:

1. Bulk compounds
2. Preformed shapes (gaskets) of plastic, elastomeric, or felt materials.

For sealing *operable* joints, the customary materials are:

3. Preformed shapes (gaskets) of plastic or elastomeric materials
4. Formed thin metallic strips
5. Pile weather seals.

Being primarily concerned here with the problem of sealing closed joints, most of the discussion will concern the first and second types of materials.

The terms used to designate these two forms imply differences both in application and performance characteristics, but in some cases the same basic material may be used in either form. Bulk compounds are applied in or to the joint by a gun or knife *after* the joining parts are brought together. The preformed shapes, which vary from a puttylike to a rubberlike consistency, are used as gaskets, and they are necessarily applied to one or both of the joining edges or placed in the joint *before* it is assembled. The two types differ also in the way in which the sealing function is performed. Bulk compounds depend essentially upon their *adhesion and cohesion* under all conditions of stress. Some of the preformed shapes, the non-resilient types in particular, also have adhesive qualities, but in general their effectiveness in sealing depends on being held *constantly under compression* by the joining parts.

Bulk compounds

Generically this type of sealing material is the oldest, dating back many centuries, and in all forms it is still often identified by the layman, without reservation, simply as "caulking." As used here, however, the term includes not only the conventional oil-base caulking and glazing compounds but also the recently developed synthetic rubber and plastic compounds of various types, which have superior properties for typical uses in metal wall construction. Reference to Table 4 will reveal that the characteristics of these compounds vary widely.

Since the bulk materials depend for their sealing action upon adhesion and cohesion, to accommodate joint movement they must also have high extensibility. To insure adhesion it is always of the utmost importance, regardless of the type of material being used, that the surface to which it is applied be absolutely clean. In all cases, too, the durability of the seal is dependent on the *retention* of its elastic properties under the action of sun and rain over a period of many years. If the material can be shielded from direct exposure to the elements, its useful life will be greatly extended.

Conventional oil-base compounds have definite limitations which are apparent from a study of the table. As compared with the other types listed, their adhesion is inferior, and elongation after ten years' service is much less. Consequently, on some of the earlier large metal wall installations they were found unsatisfactory after only brief service. The unsuitability of these compounds for typical large installations should not necessarily eliminate them, though, from consideration in all cases. Where joint movement is small and the seal is protected from exposure to the sun, and especially where periodic maintenance is not an expensive item, the oil-base materials may be appropriate because of their low cost and easy handling.

Nonskinning compounds generally have as their basic ingredients either polybutenes or a blend of polybutenes and polyisobutylenes (butyls), with fibrous inert materials added. They have better adhesion and cohesion than the oil-base compounds

Table 4. Comparative data on bulk sealing compounds

	Oil-base caulking and glazing compounds	Nonskinning compounds	Two-part rubber-base compounds	One-part elastic compounds	
				Solvent-release type	Curing type
Chief ingredients	Vegetable oils, hydrocarbon oils, synthetic drying oils, asbestos fibers, and other inert ingredients	Polybutenes or blends of polybutenes and polyisobutylenes (butyls) with asbestos fibers or other inert ingredients	Polysulfide liquid polymers (as supplied by Thiokol Corp.) combined with pigments and resins	Butyls, acrylics, neoprenes, nitriles, vinyls, or hypalons, with pigments and inert fillers and a volatile liquid vehicle	Polysulfides, silicones, or polyurethanes, combined with pigments and inert fillers and containing a curing agent
Packaged forms	Drums, pails, cans, and cartridges	Drums, pails, cans, and cartridges	Pint, quart, and gallon cans (base and accelerator separate)	Pails, cans, and cartridges	Cartridges, tightly sealed
Per cent solids	Caulking: 75–95 Glazing: 95–100	Caulking: 85–95 Glazing: 95–100	95–100	80–90	95–100
Colors available	Wide variety	Generally gray, tan, and aluminum	Black, gray, tan, aluminum	Wide variety	Black, white, and gray; polysulfides also aluminum
Normal storage life	1 year or more	1 year or more	6–9 months at temperatures under 90°F	Generally 1 year or more	Polysulfides, 90 days or more at 77 ± °F; 6 months or more at 35°F; silicones, 3 months or more at 90°F, longer at lower temps.
Curing requirements	Caulking: skins overnight at 75°F, becomes firm to stiff in 1–5 years Glazing: becomes firm in 1–6 weeks at 75°F, stiff to hard in 5 years	Caulking: nondrying; remains "self-healing" indefinitely Glazing: becomes firm in 1–6 months, very little change thereafter	Dependent on temperature and humidity; initial cure in 6 days at 40°F, 10–15 hr at 70°F, 1½–6 hr at 100°F; final cure requires 3–8 times as long	Cure by release of volatile liquid vehicle; tack-free time, 2–10 hr; initial cure, 70°F, 18–36 hr; firm cure, 2–6 weeks	Cure by reaction with moisture or oxygen in atmosphere; tack-free time: polysulfides, 2–6 days, silicones, 1 hr or less; initial cure: polysulfides 4–12 days, silicones, 1–2 days; firm cure: polysulfides, 2–6 weeks, silicones, 4–7 days
Temperature range, deg F for application in service (intermittent)	40–100 −40–200	0–100 −60–200 Caulking: −60–200 Glazing: −40–175	50–80 −60–250	Generally 50–100 Generally −20–200	(silicones, 0–120) (silicones, −80–350)
Elongation, per cent at break, 75°F, 24-hr cure at rupture, weathered seal max. usable as effective seal	(Do not return to original dimension after elongation) Caulking 25–200, 0–125, 10 Glazing 25±, 0–25, 2	Caulking 200–600, 100–350, 100 Glazing 25–50, 10–20, 5–10	200–600 100–350 100	100–600 25–300 25–100	200–1,000 100–350 75–100
Adhesion	Poor to fair	Fair to good	Good to excellent	Fair to excellent	Fair to excellent
Effect of weathering	Hardening of surface, gradual loss of plasticity	Caulking: nondrying, remains permanently tacky but becomes slightly stiffer Glazing: surface crusts, bulk firms but remains tacky	Hardness increases with age; loss of adhesion may occur as hardness reaches 80–90 Shore A durometer	Hardness of all types increases somewhat with age Probable maximum hardness: butyls: 40–50 Shore A acrylics: 55–60 Shore A	Probable maximum hardness: 30 ± 5 Shore A
Life expectancy	5–10 years	Caulking: 15–20 years Glazing: 10–15 years	20 years (estimated)	Unknown; 15–20 years probable	15–20 years probable
Average cost $ per gal ¢ per lin ft, ¼-in. bead (material only)	2–3 ½–¾	3–5 ¾–1¼	20±5 5±1	5–15 1¼–4	20–35 5–9
Chief limitations	Caulking should be used only where expected elongation is not more than 10%; glazing where not more than 2%	Nondrying; should be used only in concealed locations because of tendency to pick up dirt	Requires accurately controlled premixing and careful application; accelerator may be toxic; smears hard to remove	Relatively long curing time; some types deficient in adhesion to glass and metal, requiring a special surface conditioner or primer Shrinkage of 10–16%; below 75°F cartridges of acrylic compounds must be heated	Careful handling and storage required, to prevent premature curing

and permanently retain these qualities. They do not dry out or cure with age but do become somewhat stiffer, and, being essentially or wholly solvent-free, they are subject to little, if any, shrinkage. Their chief disadvantages are that they have poor recovery properties, being subject to flow under pressure because of lack of resiliency and compressive strength, and that they remain permanently tacky, often causing dirt to collect on their exposed surfaces. Because of these characteristics their use is usually limited to that of bedding compounds in protected locations.

Two-part rubber-base compounds also have superior qualities of adhesion and elasticity and cure to a tough rubbery consistency with lasting resilience. As a class, these compounds far surpass conventional caulking for typical metal curtain wall requirements. It must be recognized, though, that not all of these "Thiokol" sealants have equal merit. Some are properly compounded, others are not. It is a mistake, in fact, to refer to any of these materials as Thiokols, since this name identifies not a material but the company which supplies the polysulfide liquid polymer used as the base ingredient in their manufacture.

The initial cost of these two-part compounds, both for the material itself and for its installation, is comparatively high. They are also more difficult to handle than other types of bulk compounds, and care and experience are essential to good results. As the name implies, they are supplied in two packages, one containing the liquid polymer, fillers, and additives combined in a viscous paste; the other containing the curing agent, usually a paste-like suspension of lead dioxide in a small quantity of plasticizer. Proper and thorough mixing of the ingredients by the applicator is critical, and the work life of the mixed compound depends largely on the ambient temperature. If frozen, the compound can be stored for some time, then thawed and used, but at room temperature the curing process begins to interfere with workability in from 3 to 6 hours. In some cases mixing is done on the job just prior to use; other applicators prefer to do the mixing at the shop, preparing a day's supply in advance, storing it at low temperature in polyethylene cartridges, and then delivering it in a cold box to the construction site. In some areas suppliers furnish the compound to applicators premixed and frozen.

One-part elastic compounds have been on the market for only a short time but are the result of extensive research and testing in development, and they give promise of significant advantages. There are already several types of such compounds, and undoubtedly more are on the way. Two different approaches have been employed in providing these one-package products: either a volatile vehicle is used, as in the case of compounds having a butyl or acrylic base, or a curing agent is incorporated, as with the polysulfide and silicone compounds. In the latter case curing begins on exposure to air or moisture, and packaging in airtight containers is of course mandatory.

Most of these one-part compounds are alleged to provide physical properties and sealing characteristics similar to those of the two-part compounds but without the necessity of on-the-job mixing with consequent savings in labor costs. The storage life of some types is rather limited, but others may be stored for a year or more before using. In no case is freezing required to preserve the compound until ready for use, as is necessary with the two-part compounds after mixing. Generally, these one-part products "set up" slowly, require more time for curing, and remain relatively soft, though the silicone compounds are said to cure quite rapidly, usually forming a "firm rubber" overnight. Some of them require the application of a special primer or "surface conditioner" to obtain satisfactory adhesion to metal and glass. The silicone compounds, it should be noted, have the unique properties of being applicable in any working temperature and performing over an extremely wide range of temperatures. Although they are the most expensive type, they have proved quite satisfactory in many test applications.

Preformed shapes

A wide variety of materials are produced in the form of ribbons, beads, channels, and numerous other shapes for use as gaskets in sealing closed joints. Broadly classified, all such materials may be considered under two headings: resilient and nonresilient. The more common types in both categories are listed and compared in Table 5.

The most commonly used *nonresilient shapes* are made from mastic materials quite similar to those sold in bulk form as nonskinning bulk compounds. These mastic "tape sealers" include two general types which use either polybutenes or butyls as the base material and are identified in the table as the "nonvulcanized" and "partially vulcanized" types respectively. As will be noted, the two have many properties in common but differ in certain significant respects. The nonvulcan-

ized polybutene tapes have been widely used for many years and have found appropriate applications in many fields; the partially vulcanized butyl tapes are newer and possess superior qualities of adhesion and cohesion, but they are also more expensive.

Another and quite different type of nonresilient material, long used as gasketing in joints, is impregnated wool felt. This is supplied in rolls of tape of various widths and thicknesses and coated on one side with pressure-sensitive adhesive. Its applications in metal curtain wall work have been relatively few, being limited generally to mechanically fastened joints in protected locations. It has been used for years, however, in industrial applications where durable resistance to abrasion and vibration are essential requirements for gasketing between positively connected surfaces.

Currently, most *resilient shapes* are being produced either in vinyl (polyvinyl chloride) or neoprene, although in recent years butyl rubbers also have entered the field. This type of seal was used as weatherstripping for doors and windows long before the advent of contemporary metal wall construction, but the unique requirements of the latter have led to the development of many new specifically appropriate products.

The resilient gaskets typically depend on flexibility and elasticity, rather than adhesion, for their sealing action, although several types are being offered which incorporate adhesive properties. Their effectiveness for specific purposes is largely determined by the appropriateness of the compound and shape used, and their proper functioning depends to a great extent also on meticulous design. As contrasted with the bulk materials, which are suitable for an infinite variety of applications, the resilient shapes are generally designed on a custom basis for specific applications, with performance characteristics "built in" to suit requirements. In spite of this, the materials are generally competitive in the over-all cost of installation.

It is important to recognize the difference between the plastic material, vinyl, and the elastic materials, neoprene and butyl, in respect to the effects of heat and cold. Vinyl, being a thermoplastic material, is more affected by temperature changes, tending to become stiffer at low temperatures and more susceptible to plastic flow at elevated temperatures. On the other hand, being heat-sealable, vinyl shapes are customarily supplied in continuous coils and can be cut to length and

Table 5. Comparative data on preformed sealing materials

	Nonresilient types			Resilient types		
	Elastomeric		Impregnated wool felt	Vinyl	Neoprene	Butyl
	Nonvulcanized	Partially vulcanized				
Description	Liquid polybutene blended with asbestos fibers and other inert materials, some types with asphalt; may be reinforced with various materials	Butyl rubber (polyisobutylene) with carbon black and other inert filler materials	Wool felt, impregnated with nonhardening anticorrosive chromate or similar compound	Vinyl-chloride polymers	Polychloroprene	Isobuytylene-isoprene copolymers
Gasket forms available	Beads and tapes, either plain or reinforced		Cut tapes, adhesive coated 1 side	Extrusions of any desired shape and size; also available in sponge, either sheet or extruded		
Colors available	Black, white, gray, and green; others on special order	Black only	Natural brown only	Large variety of colors	Black recommended, but others available	Many colors available
Physical properties						
specific gravity	—	0.9±	0.75	1.2–2.6	1.2–2.8	1.2–2.8
tensile strength, psi	Very low, unless reinforced	10–25	225–325	1,400–3,500	400–4,000	800–2,500
elongation, per cent	Very high, unless reinforced	Up to 300	Small	250–350	250–500	200–800
recovery from compression	Negligible	Poor	Poor to fair	Poor to fair	Very good	Good
Resistance properties						
sunlight	Good	Excellent	Good, except fading	Good	Excellent	Good
ozone	Good	—	Excellent	Good	Excellent	Good
oil	—	—	—	Excellent	Good	Poor
Temperature range recommended for use, deg F	−40–200	−40–250	Not affected below ignition temperature of wool	−20–150	−40–225	−30–300
Method of joining corners	Self-adhering		Joining not feasible	Heat sealing	Vulcanizing	
Average cost						
typical extrusion, $ per lb	—	—	—	0.75–1.00	0.60–1.05	0.35–0.90
⅛x½ in. tape, ¢ per lin ft	1½–5	12–15	3–5	—	—	—
¼ in. solid bead, ¢ per lin ft	—	—	—	2	2	1½
Chief limitations	Non-skin-forming, permanently tacky, exposed surfaces collect dirt; compressive confinement required for effective sealing		Limited sealing ability; splices and intersections not sealable	Adverse effects of high and low temperatures	Inferior color retention, except black; not field-sealable	Color retention only fair, poor resistance to oil; not field-sealable

readily "welded" at abutting corners with a hot blade. The sealing of joints in elastomeric materials must be done by vulcanizing, using special equipment—a process which is not feasible at the job site. When resilient gaskets alone are used to seal joints around panels or glass, the joining of the gasket strips at corners is critical in preventing leakage. Careful fitting to provide positive compression of the abutting pieces may accomplish this, but to achieve complete continuity, heat-sealing or vulcanizing is always preferable.

PANELS

A great variety of materials is used in the panel areas of metal curtain wall construction. Where fire-resistant construction in these areas is required by local building codes, masonry backup is usually employed, and in such cases the panels are essentially decorative in nature and may or may not include thermal insulation. When such requirements do not govern, the panels may constitute the complete wall construction, providing within one thin, preassembled unit the exterior facing, the interior finish, and the intermediate insulation.

The numerous common panel types may be considered under four principal categories:

1. *Solid sheets:* Uninsulated panels made from such materials as heavy-gage metal, structural glass, or thin slabs of marble or other stone and typically employed as facings over masonry backup. With such panels, insulation is often provided separately.

2. *Hollow metal pans:* Panels formed by flanging metal sheets into shallow pans, attached back-to-back to form hollow panels which usually contain insulation. They may be used either as facing panels over masonry or more often to provide the complete wall construction.

3. *Laminated ("sandwich") assemblies:* Composite constructions having thin dense surfaces adhesively bonded onto both sides of a low-density core material. In most cases good thermal insulating qualities are provided by using a lightweight porous material as the core, and such "sandwiches" may either comprise the complete wall or be used simply as facing panels. Thin, noninsulating sandwich panels are often used to ensure flatness of the facing panels.

4. *Precast concrete units:* Panels made of reinforced concrete, either in solid form or with a core of insulating material, and with various integral or applied surface finishes.

Most panel constructions may be readily classified as one of these four principal and distinct types, although some constructions combine the characterisitcs of two or more types and others belong to none of these classifications. A closer look at these four varieties (particularly the second and third), however, will provide a fairly comprehensive explanation of the common panel constructions and the important considerations relative to their design and use.

Solid sheet panels

Most facing panels of this type are of either glass or metal. Two types of "structural" glass are appropriate for this use:

1. *Colored structural glass,* which is made by the continuous batch method sometimes used in the manufacture of plate glass but with metal oxides incorporated in the mix to produce a variety of opaque colors. It is available in polished, rough, and "suede" or "twill" finishes and in thicknesses ranging from ¼ to 1¼ in.

2. *Ceramic colored glass,* which is made by fusing color onto the back of ¼-in. plate glass. A large variety of colors is available, and both polished and textured finishes are standard, with a number of special finishes and custom colors obtainable on special order.

The colored structural glass should be "heat-strengthened" (tempered) for exterior use, especially in the darker colors; the ceramic colored glass is heat-strengthened in its process of manufacture and is intended specifically for exterior uses. Because heat-strengthened glass cannot be cut in the field, it is essential that sizes be accurately predetermined and that any required notching or drilling be completely detailed for factory fabrication.

Metal sheet panels may be constructed in several ways. They may be:

1. Thin plate material, with smooth or polished finish

2. Sheet metal press-formed into sculptural designs

3. Corrugated or ribbed metal sheets, produced by roll- or brake-forming

4. Assemblies of interlocking extruded shapes

5. Single castings or assemblies of castings.

The chief problem with the first type of panel is to achieve a sufficiently flat surface to avoid the appearance of waviness or "oil-canning." Since the visual effect of waviness is a function of light reflection, it is proportional to the degree of polish used on the surface. Waviness is seldom

objectionable on nonreflective dark matte surfaces. It is impractical to require "optical flatness" on panel surfaces because this is virtually impossible to accomplish, and a requirement of "visual flatness" is not definitive. Flatness criteria based on the *slope* of the surface, as suggested in the Princeton studies of stainless-steel curtain walls, seem the most logical and are recommended in the NAAMM *Metal Curtain Wall Manual* specification.

Hollow metal pans (mechanically assembled)

This is probably the most common type of panel construction in custom and commercial walls. Typically these panels consist of an outer pan of porcelain-enameled steel, usually 16 gage, and an inner pan of galvanized iron, often prime-painted. Occasionally the outer pan does not have a flat surface but may be fluted or otherwise deformed. The two pans are flanged in a variety of conformations and are connected by mechanical means at their edges to form a hollow box containing lightweight inorganic insulation. Many manufacturers also offer a variation of this construction in which the outer pan, especially in panels of large area, is partially filled with a cementitious material to improve its rigidity and flatness.

Most frequently the insulation used is of the flexible blanket type, but rigid cellular glass is also employed. When blanket insulation is used, it must of course be permanently positioned within the panel, either by adhesive attachment to the inner pan or by the use of noncorrosive spacers. If its thickness is less than the full panel depth, the resulting air space should be between the insulation and the *outer* panel face, and a natural circulation of air should occur in this space to minimize the collection of moisture due to condensation.

For best results, manufacturers generally recommend that, when the outer pan is not reinforced by a backup filler, the face area of these panels should be limited to 16 sq ft, or 24 sq ft when cementitious fill is used. These limitations are imposed both by considerations of flatness and by the fact that typical production equipment cannot accommodate widths greater than 52 in. The over-all thickness of the panels usually ranges from 1¼ to 2½ in.

A number of typical variations of edge shapes and details are illustrated in Fig. 24.

Laminated (sandwich) assemblies

This type includes by far the greatest variety of constructions, since a large num-

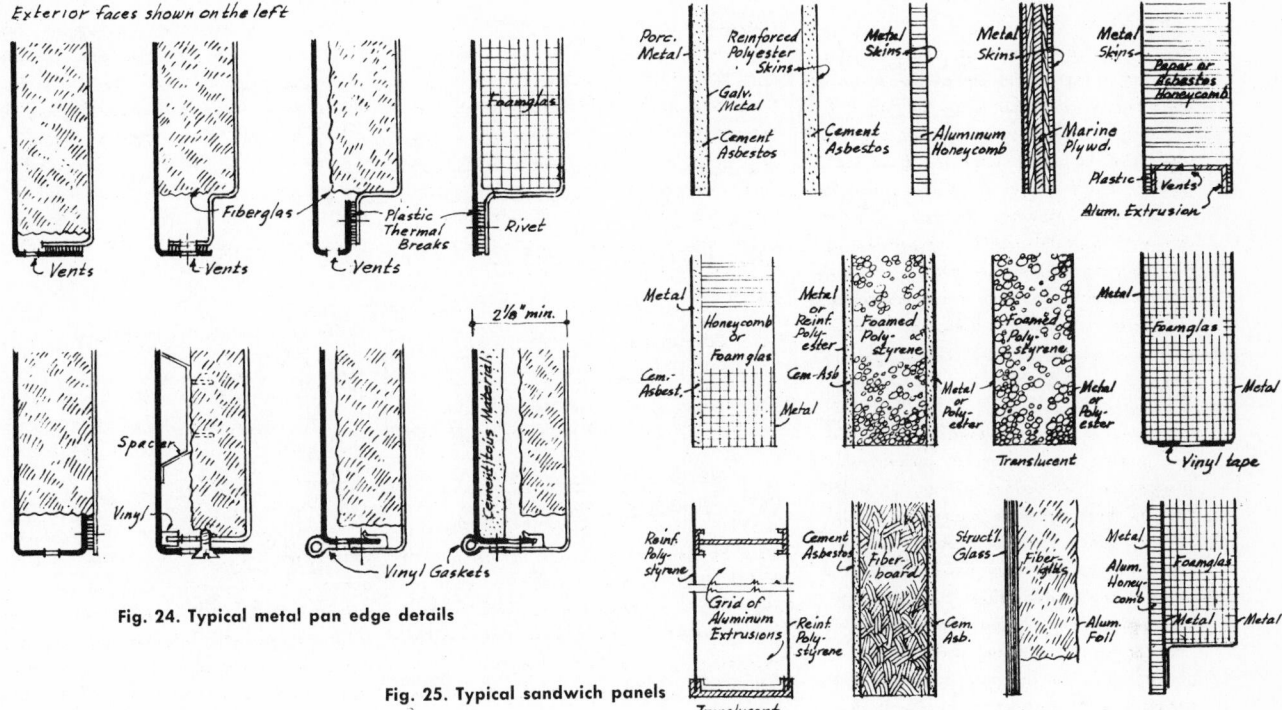

Fig. 24. Typical metal pan edge details

Fig. 25. Typical sandwich panels

ber of both skin and core materials can be assembled in innumerable combinations. Among the materials most commonly used are the following:

Core materials

Insulating (low density):
Kraft paper honeycomb (impregnated)
Foamed glass
Foamed polystyrene
Asbestos paper honeycomb
Aluminum honeycomb
Aluminum "eggcrate"
Fiberboard
Low-density cementitious materials

Noninsulating (high density):
Cement-asbestos board
Plywood

Skin materials

Porcelainized steel
Aluminum: anodized, polished, porcelain-ized; smooth or textured
Stainless steel: polished or colored, smooth or textured
Ceramic tile (on sheet backing)
Polyester, reinforced with glass fiber
Cement asbestos
Glass
Marble

It is common practice with the light-gage metals, and sometimes with the poly-ester facings, to use a composite skin, con-sisting of the thin facing material laminated to a thicker, rigid backup sheet of non-metallic material such as cement-asbestos

board or hardboard, to provide the re-quired stiffness, flatness, and resistance to indentation. By this means, metals of al-most foil thinness have been successfully used, both in smooth and textured finishes, as the outer skin material.

All these sandwich constructions depend entirely on adhesive bonding, usually under heat and high pressure, for their structural integrity, and they are generally charac-terized by more-than-adequate strength and stiffness. In the absence of mechanical fast-enings, thorough testing is essential to in-sure against eventual failure of the assem-bly by delamination, and testing procedures for this purpose have become pretty well standardized over a period of years (ASTM D-1037). With the help of present-day adhesives and improved manufacturing techniques, these laminated constructions have found wide acceptance, not only in exterior building panels but in many other building applications as well, and when made by reputable manufacturers have proved wholly satisfactory.

Some of the denser noninsulating lami-nates, such as metal-faced plywood, ce-ment-asbestos board and hardboard, and also cement-asbestos-faced fiberboard, are available in large-size standard sheets which can be cut to desired dimensions. With these exceptions, low-density-core as-semblies are apt to be produced only on order, to meet specific requirements of size, finish, thermal insulating value, and the like.

Representative details of some of the more common types of laminated assem-blies are shown in Fig. 25.

Edge sealing and venting of panels

With most types of metal-faced com-posite panels, ventilation of the panel in-terior is an important consideration, and it becomes particularly important when the insulation used is capable of absorbing moisture. As discussed in connection with "Water Vapor and Condensation," the attempt to hermetically seal the panel edges can rarely be justified and is even more rarely accomplished with success. In-stead of being sealed, the edges of most composite-panel constructions, whether of the hollow-pan or laminated type, should be highly permeable to water vapor and deliberately ventilated.

If proper venting is to result, the manner in which the periphery sealing of the panels is accomplished within the support-ing framework also deserves careful at-tention. It does little good to provide vents in the edge of the panel itself if their function is impeded by the use of imper-meable sealing materials around the panel. Instead of using a solid-setting bed of compound or full-depth gaskets at these locations, seals should ideally be placed only at the outer and inner panel faces (Fig. 26), leaving the space adjacent to the weepholes clear for venting and drain-age.

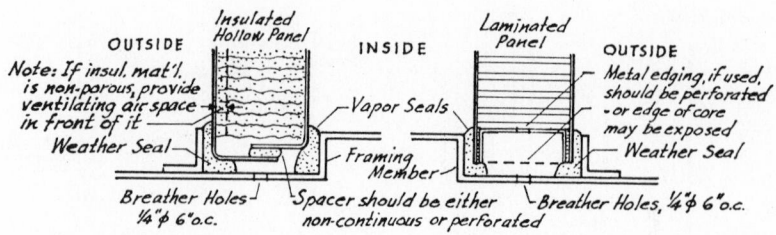

DETAILS OF VENTING BOTTOM EDGES OF COMPOSITE PANELS

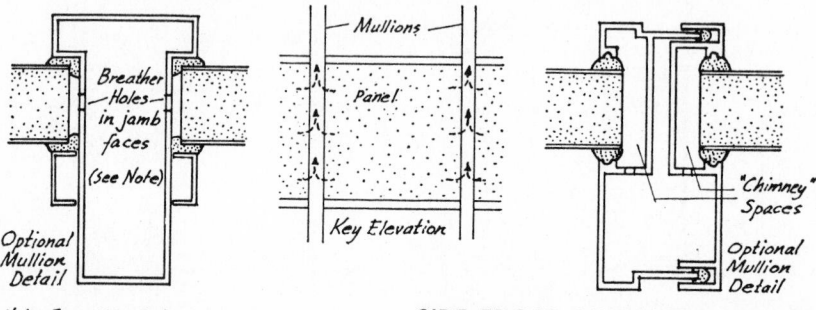

Note: If mullion is to serve as downspout, breather holes must be protected by baffles.

SIDE EDGES OF PANELS MAY BE
VENTED INTO HOLLOW MULLIONS

Fig. 26. Methods of venting interiors of panels

Precast units

Panels of precast concrete are occasionally used in the spandrel areas of metal curtain walls, although such units are more typically used as a complete wall enclosure. They will be discussed later in this section.

SPECIFICATIONS

To a large extent, the achievement of satisfactory results with a metal curtain wall design depends on the quality of the architect's specifications. In fact, in many respects the specifications may be more important than the drawings. Manufacturers often prefer to develop their own details, even for custom walls, but complete and explicit specifications are always essential if the architect's requirements are to be correctly interpreted.

The *Metal Curtain Wall Manual* published by the National Association of Architectural Metal Manufacturers is the most complete guide to the preparation of specifications yet published, with references to accepted standards for most of the essential component materials. This work is the result of impartial and objective collaboration by technical experts in many fields, and it is accompanied by a comprehensive commentary text explaining the reasons for, and the significance of, many of the specification clauses themselves. The discussion presented here will treat only the more important general principles to be observed in specifying metal curtain wall construction; for detailed information on the subject the NAAMM *Manual* should be consulted.

To begin with, it is generally advisable to list "Metal Curtain Walls" as a separate section of the architectural specifications, even for small jobs. This is preferable to specifying the metal work under one section, the glass under another, and other parts and materials under still different headings. If a good job is to be expected, the entire wall—fabrication, erection, caulking, and glazing—must be the responsibility of a single contractor; otherwise there may be endless buck-passing, with the owner usually "holding the bag." Thus a separate section in the specifications is obviously most important.

Regardless of the size of the job and whether the preference is for a streamlined version or for the conventional form, metal curtain wall specifications, like those for other trades, can usually be classified under the major topics of "General," "Scope of the Work," "Over-all Performance Standards," and "Materials and Workmanship," with the latter perhaps subdivided into "fabrication" and "erection." A brief discussion of some of the important provisions under each of these headings will serve to indicate the essential features of a good specification.

Under the heading of "General," of course, should be explained the significance of the "general conditions" and probably also the meaning of abbreviations used throughout. Here also should be listed the architectural drawings that apply, and information should be given as to the nature of shop drawings and samples required. It is important, too, to clarify what qualifications are required of the contractor and what will be his responsibilities. If mock-ups of any kind are expected, they must be specified and completely described. As for the guarantee, it is generally considered reasonable to stipulate that the work be guaranteed free from defects in materials and workmanship for a period of two years following its acceptance by the owner.

The "Scope of the Work" should be defined with the utmost care and should clearly identify both the "work included" and the "work not included," since there can be no doubt about either if the estimator is to prepare an accurate bid. As an aid to insuring complete coverage, the NAAMM *Manual* includes a check list of 62 items representing most of the "typical components and accessories."

Under "Over-all Performance Standards" should be clearly stated the various design criteria to be observed. In some cases the architect may furnish complete wall details, expecting them to be religiously followed, and thereby he assumes most of the responsibility for compliance with code requirements as well as for satisfactory performance of the wall. Often, however, the architect may choose to leave many of the decisions on details to the experienced judgment of the fabricator-contractor, and this is an advisable procedure. In any case, if the contractor is to be held responsible for guaranteeing satisfactory performance of the wall, he must be advised of the criteria governing the design, so that he may be guided accordingly.

The principal performance characteristics to be defined here, in addition to conformity with local codes, are (1) provision for thermal movement, (2) structural strength and stiffness, (3) water infiltration, and (4) air infiltration. In respect to the latter two NAAMM has developed recommended standards, as well as the testing procedures to verify them. In specifying performance testing, however, the *Manual* cautions that "most test procedures involve extra costs, and tests should therefore be specified only when the additional time and expense are justified. Many of the commercial types of metal curtain wall not only have undergone rigorous testing in the course of their development, but also have to their credit a history of satisfactory performance. With unproven designs, on the other hand, tests may not only be warranted but necessary."

As supplementary information in this connection, the NAAMM *Manual* contains a listing of nineteen agencies in the United States and Canada prepared to make various types of tests on walls and their components.

The section on "Materials" is often the largest subdivision of the curtain wall specifications because in it must be clearly defined all the various materials comprising the wall. In the case of industrial or commercial walls, proprietary wall components such as industrial sheets, windows, subassemblies, or perhaps standard wall units will probably be included; for custom walls, the various metals, glass, insulation, sealing materials, etc., will be scheduled and specified. In any case, of course, these materials must be completely identified. It is not sufficient, for example, simply to call for a "weatherproof and durable finish" on aluminum, or "a neoprene gasket"; such terms are subject to a wide range of interpretation, depending upon the integrity of the bidder, and they open the gate for cut-rate competition. Finishes and quality of materials can make a big

difference in the cost of a metal curtain wall, and if a good job is to be expected, pains must be taken to spell out exactly what is required.

In defining many of the materials involved, reference to standards already developed by such bodies as ASTM, ASA, PEI, and NAAMM will be found very helpful, and this is a practice to be recommended. It is essential, however, that the specification writer be acquainted with the standards to which he refers and certain that they apply to the specific material in question.

Specifications governing "Workmanship" may be made all-inclusive, covering general requirements as well as those applying specifically to procedures of fabrication and erection. On all but the smaller jobs, however, the treatment of this subject under three headings rather than one will probably contribute to general clarification. Under the "general" category in this case would be included those topics which relate to both shop and field work, such as the types of fasteners to be used, the protection of metals against galvanic action and other corrosive influences, and the use of sealing materials. Under a second subdivision, "fabrication," might be specified those requirements relating specifically to procedures of shop manufacturing. These would include provisions for trial shop assembly of units, their fitting, marking disassembly, and packing; the degree of precision and fit required in jointing; procedures to be followed in welding and soldering; precautions to be observed in the handling of stainless steel; shop painting of carbon steel; and so forth. A third subsection on "erection" would specify procedures to be used at the building site. In this connection, it is important to clarify the contractor's responsibility to examine the building frame prior to installing the wall and to report any conditions which would "prevent the proper execution of his work or endanger its permanency" (NAAMM *Manual*). The erection of the wall should not be allowed to proceed until such conditions have been corrected. Other conditions affecting field erection procedures often require clarification too, such as the proper scheduling of contiguous metal work and masonry, the postponement of building certain parts of the wall enclosure in order to permit bringing materials into the building, the provision for suitable storage of wall components at the site, and the establishment of bench marks. Definition of the dimensional tolerances to be permitted in the erection of the

wall is a matter of great importance, too. In addition to dealing with such procedural matters, the subsection on "erection" should contain specifications governing such trade practices as field welding, field painting of steel, and installation of insulation and glazing, stipulating any specific precautions to be observed. And finally, but by no means least, the responsibilities for protecting the work during erection, and for its final cleaning, should be defined.

Although writing a good specification is of prime importance, the architect's responsibility does not end here. Like any law, this contract document is only as effective as its enforcement, and just as with laws, honest and rigid enforcement is usually rewarded with respect. Respect for a good architectural specification is evidenced in better workmanship, both in the factory and in the field. Well-written specifications, designating specific materials and definite performance requirements instead of dealing in vague generalities, will result in more accurate and reliable bidding and are an invaluable aid to competent and effective field supervision.

PRECAST CONCRETE CURTAIN WALLS

Precast concrete, as previously noted, may be used as a panel material in metal-framed curtain wall construction, but it is more often used as a complete curtain wall system in which the concrete panels are attached directly to the building frame. Of the several types that have been developed, the most successful, as well as the most technologically advanced, is the concrete sandwich panel. Typical details of this type of construction are shown in Fig. 27.

Notable advantages of the precast concrete curtain wall are fire resistance, economy, large-size units, and a wide variety of finishes. Unlike metal curtain walls, which must rely upon masonry backup to meet code requirements for fire resistance, the concrete sandwich panel is integrally fire resistant and 2-hr ratings have been obtained in several cities. In the economical "broomed" finish (a striated texture), concrete sandwich panels can compete in cost with brick and block construction and the industrial type of metal curtain walls. Panels may be obtained in sizes up to 10 by 30 ft; the large sizes and the absence of mullions or other accessory parts result in far fewer pieces to handle and fewer joints to seal than in any other curtain wall system. In addition to the broomed finish, which is also available in white cement, concrete sandwich panels are obtainable in a wide variety of colors and textures provided by exposed aggregate. The colored aggregate may be rough or smooth, or it may be ground and polished like terrazzo. Or panels may be faced with ceramic tile that is monolithically bonded to the panel by being placed face down in the mold before the panel is poured.

Typical panels are 5 in. thick with a 1½-in.-thick core of rigid insulation which may be foamed glass, foamed plastic, or glass fiberboard. The U value is 0.14 Btu. Panels over 8 by 20 ft in size must be 6 in. thick. The 5-in. panels weigh 45 psf and the 6-in. panels 57½ psf. Reinforcing is 6 by 6 in. No. 8, or 4 by 4 in. No. 10, welded wire mesh, placed 1 in. back from each face of the panel; shear ties are 13 gage expanded metal 1½ in. diamond mesh bent into channel shape and placed around the perimeter of the panel and 2 ft on centers in the panel in the direction of the span.

TYPICAL WALL PANEL

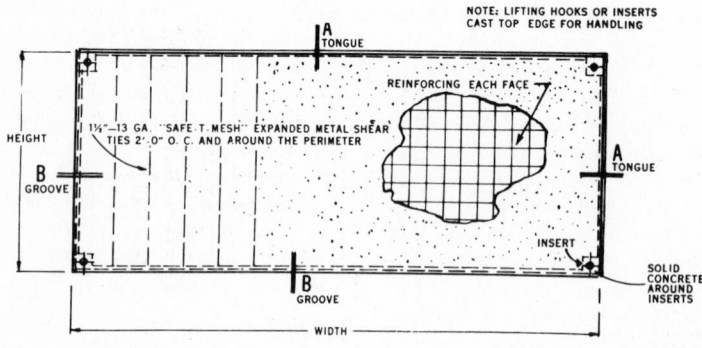

TYPICAL HORIZONTAL JOINT

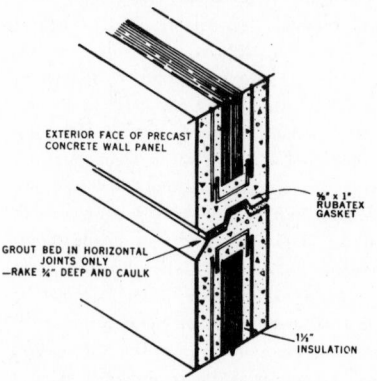

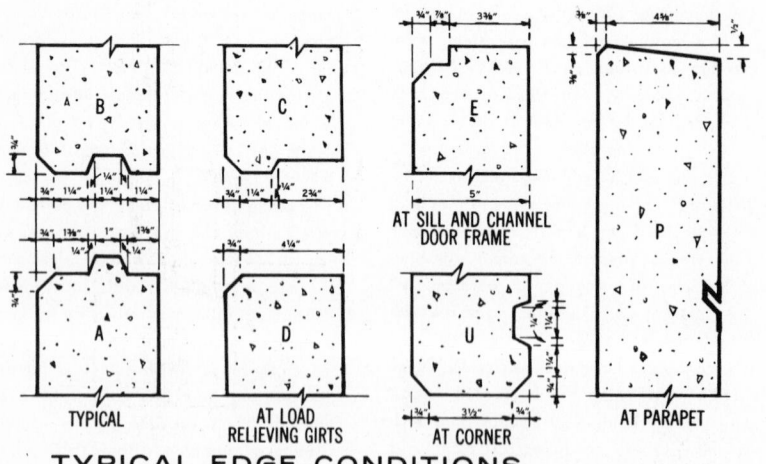

TYPICAL EDGE CONDITIONS

FOUNDATION DETAILS

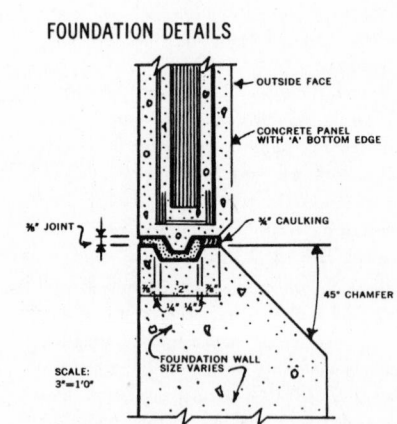

Fig. 27. Typical construction details

Courtesy Marietta Concrete Division, American Marietta Company.

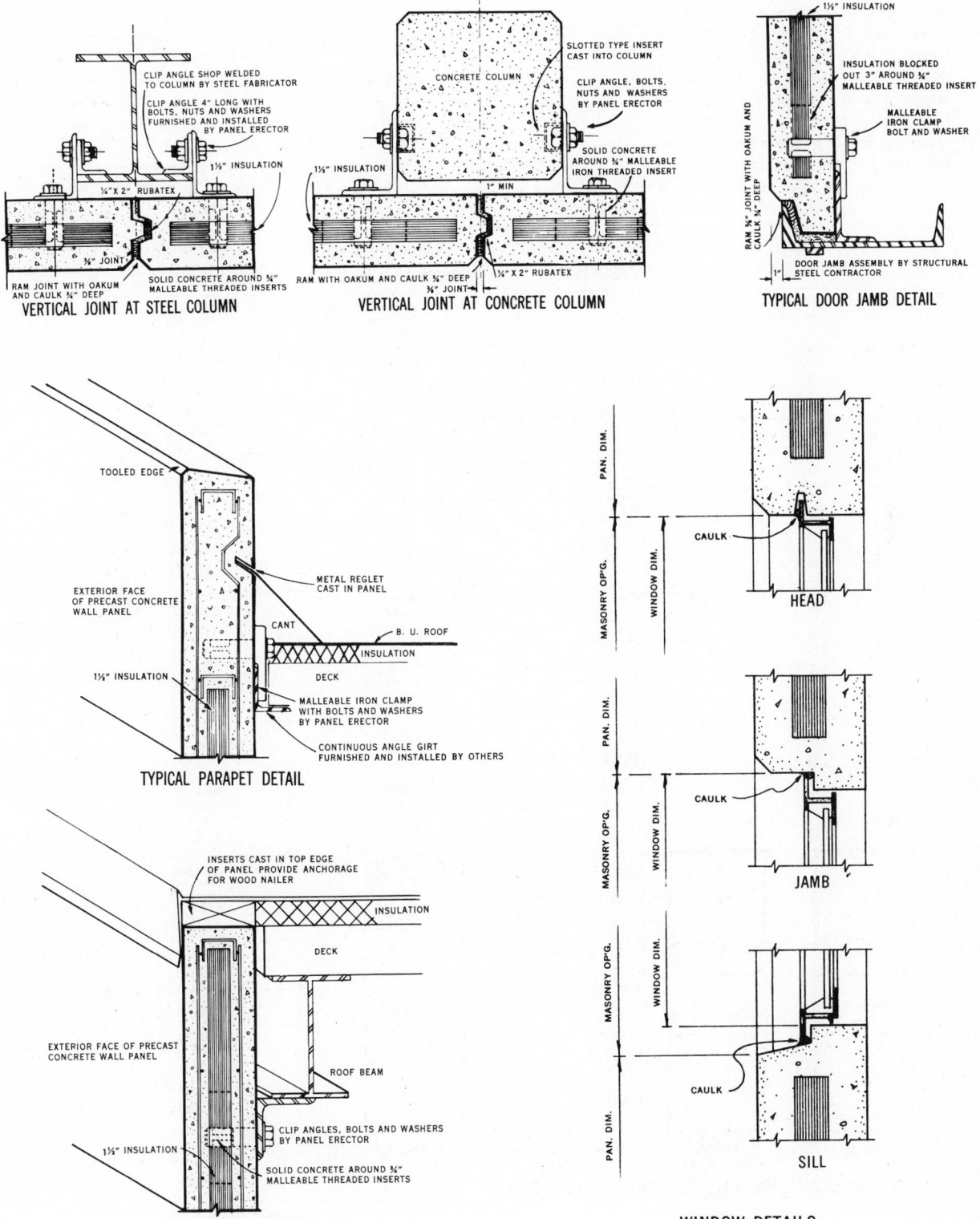

VERTICAL JOINT AT STEEL COLUMN

CLIP ANGLE SHOP WELDED TO COLUMN BY STEEL FABRICATOR

CLIP ANGLE 4" LONG WITH BOLTS, NUTS AND WASHERS FURNISHED AND INSTALLED BY PANEL ERECTOR

1½" INSULATION

¼" X 2" RUBATEX

¾" JOINT

RAM JOINT WITH OAKUM AND CAULK ¾" DEEP

SOLID CONCRETE AROUND ¾" MALLEABLE THREADED INSERTS

VERTICAL JOINT AT CONCRETE COLUMN

SLOTTED TYPE INSERT CAST INTO COLUMN

CONCRETE COLUMN

CLIP ANGLE, BOLTS, NUTS AND WASHERS BY PANEL ERECTOR

1½" INSULATION

SOLID CONCRETE AROUND ¾" MALLEABLE IRON THREADED INSERT

1" MIN

RAM WITH OAKUM AND CAULK ¾" DEEP

¾" JOINT

¼" X 2" RUBATEX

TYPICAL DOOR JAMB DETAIL

1½" INSULATION

INSULATION BLOCKED OUT 3" AROUND ¾" MALLEABLE THREADED INSERT

MALLEABLE IRON CLAMP BOLT AND WASHER

RAM ¾" JOINT WITH OAKUM AND CAULK ¾" DEEP

DOOR JAMB ASSEMBLY BY STRUCTURAL STEEL CONTRACTOR

1"

TYPICAL PARAPET DETAIL

TOOLED EDGE

EXTERIOR FACE OF PRECAST CONCRETE WALL PANEL

METAL REGLET CAST IN PANEL

CANT

B. U. ROOF

INSULATION

DECK

1½" INSULATION

MALLEABLE IRON CLAMP WITH BOLTS AND WASHERS BY PANEL ERECTOR

CONTINUOUS ANGLE GIRT FURNISHED AND INSTALLED BY OTHERS

TYPICAL EAVE DETAIL

INSERTS CAST IN TOP EDGE OF PANEL PROVIDE ANCHORAGE FOR WOOD NAILER

INSULATION

DECK

EXTERIOR FACE OF PRECAST CONCRETE WALL PANEL

ROOF BEAM

CLIP ANGLES, BOLTS AND WASHERS BY PANEL ERECTOR

1½" INSULATION

SOLID CONCRETE AROUND ¾" MALLEABLE THREADED INSERTS

WINDOW DETAILS

HEAD

PAN. DIM.

MASONRY OP'G.

WINDOW DIM.

CAULK

JAMB

PAN. DIM.

MASONRY OP'G.

WINDOW DIM.

CAULK

SILL

MASONRY OP'G.

WINDOW DIM.

CAULK

PAN. DIM.

Fig. 27. (cont.) Typical construction details

By WAYNE F. KOPPES, Architectural Consultant

Table 1. Thickness equivalents of sheet metal gages

These data are provided primarily for reference purposes, rather than to facilitate the use of gage numbers in specifying metal thicknesses. The lack of consistency between the various gage systems frequently leads to confusion and errors, but these dangers can be avoided if thickness is specified in decimal inches instead. (Courtesy National Association of Architectural Metal Manufacturers.)

Thickness in Inches

Gage Number	Manufacturers' Standard Gage — Uncoated Steel Sheets and light Plates	U. S. Standard Gage — Stainless Steel Sheet and Strip	Browne & Sharpe Gage — Non-Ferrous Sheets and Wire
0		.3125	.3249
1		.28125	.2893
2		.26563	.2576
3	.2391	.250	.2294
4	.2242	.23438	.2043
5	.2092	.21875	.1819
6	.1943	.20313	.1620
7	.1793	.1875	.1443
8	.1644	.17188	.1285
9	.1495	.15625	.1144
10	.1345	.14063	.1019
11	.1196	.125	.0907
12	.1046	.10938	.0808
13	.0897	.09375	.0720
14	.0747	.07813	.0641
15	.0673	.07031	.0571
16	.0598	.0625	.0508
17	.0538	.05625	.0453
18	.0478	.050	.0403
19	.0418	.04375	.0359
20	.0359	.0375	.0320
21	.0329	.03438	.0285
22	.0299	.03125	.0253
23	.0269	.02813	.0226
24	.0239	.025	.0201
25	.0209	.02188	.0179
26	.0179	.01875	.0159
27	.0164	.01719	.0142
28	.0149	.01563	.0126
29	.0135	.01406	.0113
30	.0120	.0125	.0100

Table 2. Thickness of copper sheet and strip

Courtesy Copper Development Association, Inc.

WEIGHT Ounces per Sq. Ft.	THEORETICAL THICKNESS in Inches	MINIMUM THICKNESS in Inches at any point	LOT WEIGHT TOLERANCES Based on Case or Crate Weight normally approximately 500 lbs Minimum	Maximum
32	.0431	.0405	95%	105%
24	.0323	.0300	95%	105%
20	.0270	.0245	95%	105%
18	.0243	.0225	95%	105%
16*	.0216	.0190	97%	103%
14*	.0189	.0160	97%	103%
10	.0135	.0120	95%	105%

Applicable to sheet and strip furnished flat up to 36" wide, inclusive, and up to 120" long, inclusive.
Thickness calculated for a unit weight of 0.322 pounds per cubic inch.
* *14- and 16-ounce strip copper is commonly stamped with the ounce weight.*

Table 3. Maximum allowable unit stresses in bending

		Typical structural members subject to dead loads or combined dead and live loads	Members subject only to stresses produced by wind forces (⅓ increase)*
Extreme fiber stress on net section:		psi	psi
Carbon steel, hot rolled structural grade		20,000	26,670
Carbon steel, cold formed sheet, Grade C		18,000	24,000
Carbon steel, cold formed sheet, Grade B		16,500	22,000
Carbon steel, cold formed sheet, Grade A		13,500	18,000
Stainless steel alloys	General formula: $\dfrac{\text{yield stress**}}{1.65}$		
	Examples: Type 302 annealed:	24,240	32,320
	Type 302 ¼ hard:	45,450	60,600
Aluminum alloys	General: $\dfrac{1}{2.4}$ x average of guaranteed yield and ultimate stresses**		
	Examples: Alloy 6063-T5:	7,920	10,560
	Alloy 6063-T6:	11,875	15,830
Bronze alloys	General: $\dfrac{\text{ultimate stress}}{3}$ or $\dfrac{\text{yield stress}}{1.5}$, whichever is less**		
	Example: Architectural Bronze:	13,335	16,000

*Allowable stress not to exceed ⅔ of yield stress in any case.
Members subject to combined wind and other loads may be designed for unit stresses ½ greater than those allowed for combined dead and live loads, *provided* the section thus required is no smaller than that required for the combination of dead load, live load and impact (if any).

**Tentative, pending official industry recommendation.

Table 4. Thermal expansion of building materials

Material	Inches per Inch per Degree F (x 10⁻⁶)	Inches in Ten Feet for a Temperature Rise of 100°F	150°F
Wood: perpendicular to grain	1.9 to 3.2	.023 to .039	.034 to .058
parallel to grain	2.1 to 3.6	.025 to .043	.038 to .065
Brick masonry	3.1	.037	.056
Limestone masonry	3.5	.042	.063
Cellular glass	4.0	.048	.072
Plate glass	5.1	.061	.092
Stainless steel, Type 430	5.8	.070	.104
Concrete	6.5	.078	.117
Structural steel	6.7	.080	.121
Plaster	9.2	.110	.166
Copper	9.3	.112	.167
Stainless steel, Type 302	9.6	.115	.173
Bronze	10.1	.121	.182
Brass	10.4	.125	.187
Aluminum	12.9	.155	.232
Lead	15.9	.190	.286
Zinc, rolled	17.3	.208	.311
Plastics: Phenolics	8.5 to 25	.102 to .300	.153 to .450
Glass-reinforced polyesters	10 to 14	.120 to .168	.180 to .252
Acrylics	60	.720	1.080

ELECTROLYTIC CORROSION

Data courtesy of Copper Development Association, Inc.

When dissimilar metals are in contact in the presence of an electrolyte, such as water containing very small amounts of acid, they set up a galvanic action that results in the deterioration of one of them. The following is a list of the more common commercial metals according to what is known as the electrochemical series:

1. Aluminum
2. Zinc
3. Steel
4. Iron
5. Nickel
6. Tin
7. Lead
8. Copper
9. Stainless steel

When any two metals in this list are in contact, with an electrolyte present, the one with the lower number is corroded. The galvanic action increases as the metals are farther apart in the electrochemical series.

Insulation between dissimilar metals will prevent galvanic action. Recommended insulators, in order of preference, are asbestos, lead, heavy tinning of ferrous metal, good-quality moisture-proof building paper or felt, and a heavy coat of asphalt paint.

Table 5. Schedule of fastener metals

Metallic fasteners joining metal parts shall be made of the metals listed in the following table, at the intersection of the column and line headed by the respective metals to be joined.

		(Listing in order of decreasing nobility)			
METALS JOINED	Stainless Steel	Bronze	Brass	Carbon Steel	Aluminum
Aluminum	Stainless Steel	Bronze	Brass	Stainless Steel	Aluminum or St. Steel
Carbon Steel	Stainless Steel	Bronze	Brass	Metallic-coated Carb. Steel	
Brass	St. Steel or Brass	Bronze or Brass	Brass		
Bronze	St. Steel or Bronze	Bronze or Brass		In addition to the fastener metals shown, metallic-coated carbon steel may be used in all cases, in locations not exposed to dampness or moisture.	
Stainless Steel	Stainless Steel				

Alloys used for stainless steel and aluminum fasteners shall be as follows:

Fastener Metal	Types or Alloys
Stainless steel:	
where exposed to weather	300 series
protected or interior locations	300 or 400 series
Aluminum:	
screws and bolts	2024
rivets	1100, 6053 or 6061

ARCHITECTURAL METALS—3
Finishes

By WAYNE F. KOPPES, *Architectural Consultant*

The cost of protective finishes naturally varies with their service values. The over-all significance of even the greater cost differential is small, and the use of the cheapest type may easily result in the greatest total expense if used inappropriately. All finishes should be required to match in appearance the samples previously approved by the architect.

MECHANICAL FINISHES

The mechanical finishes on architectural metals are, in general, those produced by polishing, buffing, and rubbing. They vary somewhat from one metal to another, and each industry has its own terminology. In addition to the numerous standard mechanical finishes, the producers of all the architectural metals offer many special proprietary finishes, which should be specified by name or number and name of the producer. The costs of various mechanical finishes differ significantly, and an inappropriate choice may involve needless expense. In the interests of economy, therefore, the architect should investigate comparative costs before making his selection.

Standard finishes of aluminum are defined in "Standard Mechanical Finishes for Architectural Aluminum" published by the National Association of Architectural Metal Manufacturers. Standard finishes of stainless steel are defined in *Steel Products Manual, Stainless and Heat-Resisting Steels* published by the American Iron and Steel Institute. Standard finishes of copper and copper alloys are defined in the "Terminology" of the "Standards Manual" published by the Copper Development Association, Inc.

CHEMICAL AND ELECTROCHEMICAL FINISHES

Chemical and electrochemical finishes are currently used more with aluminum than with other architectural metals. The so-called caustic etch finish is relatively inexpensive, being obtained by treating the work in a solution that is basically caustic soda or equivalent. This process removes the natural oxide surface film from the metal, but this film reforms upon exposure to the atmosphere. When caustic etch is to be the final finish, the etched surfaces should be coated with a clear organic coat-

ing for protection during handling and erection. The organic coating should have a minimum thickness of 0.5 mil. An etch is often used before anodizing, particularly when dealing with large flat areas, where the control of color matching is important.

The anodized finishes are oxide coatings obtained by immersing the work in an electrolytic bath, using an electrolyte such as sulphuric or other acid. The metal is made the anode in this process, and the surface is converted into essentially aluminum oxide which is an integral part of the metal.

The architect is cautioned that there is a wide range of quality in anodizing work, and some of the competitive commercial work in this field is of doubtful value. In specifying anodized finishes the critical characteristics to be insisted upon are coating thickness, density, and seal of coating.

The NAAMM *Standard Chemical, Electrochemical and Applied Finishes for Architectural Aluminum* lists two grades of anodizing, both approved for exterior use. Type NA-1A provides the thinner coating, and is intended for work that will be regularly maintained, such as store fronts, doors, and entrance trim. No thinner coating than this should be used. Type NA-2A provides a thicker coating and should be specified for all items subject to maximum abrasion (such as push bars) and for areas not likely to receive regular maintenance care.

Color is produced in anodic coatings either by the nature of the alloy itself or by impregnating the oxide coating with suitable dyes or pigments. The silicon alloys (4000 series), for example, produce various shades of gray when anodized. Whether the colors are inherent or are added by absorption, the pores of the anodic coating are subsequently sealed to produce a stain-resistant and durable surface.

Because of the nature of the finishing process, minor shade variations can be expected from one colored element to another, particularly between sheet and extrusions. This inherent characteristic of the finish need be no problem if properly anticipated in the design.

Color anodizing is still largely custom work, with each producer using his own proprietary process. Consequently, few industry standards have been established

for this type of work. In specifying it, the architect should follow the recommendations of the manufacturer or supplier whose process is to be used.

APPLIED FINISHES

The term "applied finishes" refers to those finishes involving the use of some added material as a surface film or coating, as opposed to converting the surface of the metal itself into an integral coating. These applied finishes are usually decorative as well as protective in nature, and may be either inorganic, such as porcelain enamel, or organic, as with synthetic films, air-dried or baked enamels, and lacquer coatings.

Porcelain enamel can be applied to any of the architectural metals, but in store fronts and entrance work it is most commonly used on aluminum, enameling iron (or steel), or stainless steel. The aluminum alloys generally used as a base are 3003 (sheet), 6061 (sheet or extrusions), and 43 (castings). Certain aluminum alloys, however, are not suitable for porcelain enameling; when in doubt consult an aluminum manufacturer. When porcelain enamel is scheduled as a finish, both the color and finish (gloss or semigloss) should be indicated.

The Porcelain Enamel Institute, Inc. has long been active in promoting high-quality standards in architectural porcelain enamel work of all kinds, and has formulated standards and specifications for such work which are generally observed throughout the industry. PEI has also established various standard test methods for determining resistance to acid, abrasion, and weather, impact strength, gloss, reflectivity, and other properties. Copies of all these specifications and standards are available to the architect upon request from PEI.

Organic coatings are now being applied to most of the architectural metals. These include a variety of materials from field-applied enamels to baked-on enamels and lacquers of good durability, and represent a wide range of cost, mechanical properties, and weathering characteristics. These coatings are generally proprietary products not covered by industry standards, and should therefore be specified explicitly by name and manufacturer.

Guide for the selection of aluminum alloys

Typical Applications	Alloy	Comments

SHEET AND PLATE

Panels, fascias, column covers, louvers, sunshades, ductwork, gutters, flashing

General purpose non-heat-treatable alloys:

3003 — Economical for sheets having fair mechanical properties and excellent formability. Should not be specified for anodizing, as yellowish cast results.

5052 — Slightly better mechanical properties and higher cost than Alloy 3003. Good workability and excellent resistance to corrosion, even in salt air exposures. Excellent weldability. Assumes yellowish cast with anodic coatings thicker than .0005", but thinner coatings can provide fair match with anodized 6063 extrusions.

Non-heat-treatable alloys suitable for anodizing:

1100 — Low strength alloy, appropriate for applications requiring high degree of formability. Finishes well, but subject to structural streaking in large flat areas.

1135 — Somewhat higher purity than Alloy 1100, and sometimes recommended as having superior finishing qualities. Mechanical properties similar to Alloy 1100.

5005 — Commonly used for low-cost all-purpose sheets having good formability and finishing characteristics. Slightly better mechanical properties than Alloy 1100. Good anodized appearance match with 6063 extrusions, but structural streaking may sometimes occur in large flat areas.

5050 — Stronger than Alloy 5005. Excellent weldability and corrosion resistance. One of the better finishing alloys, having a comparatively clear white appearance after etching.

Clad sheets providing good anodized appearance match with 6063 extrusions:

No. 31 / No. 32 — Often referred to an "anodizing sheets" or "Alumiliting sheets." Excellent finishing characteristics; mechanical properties similar to those of Alloys 1135 and 1100 respectively. Being clad products, they should not be specified where belt sanding or grinding is required.

Proprietary alloys designed for high-quality applications where excellent anodized appearance is critical:

Alcoa: Anoclad sheet, Types 5, 10, 20, 30, and 40, for "Alcoa Architectural Color Finishes."

Kaiser: Nos. 10 and 10A Architectural Sheets for natural anodizing; Nos. 20, 30 & 40 Architectural Sheets for gray color anodizing; Nos. 32, 33, 52, 55, 57, 61 and 86 Architectural Sheets for Kalcolor anodizing.

Olin: Anodizing quality sheets 1100, 3003 and 5005 for natural anodizing; Sheets No. 10, 20, 30 and 40 for special finishes.

Reynolds: RF-10 sheet for natural anodizing; RF-10, RF-15, RF-20, RF-30 and RF-40 sheets for color anodizing.

Heat-treatable alloys:

6061 — Most economical and versatile of the heat-treatable alloys. Used chiefly for roll-formed structural shapes or high strength extrusions. Should not be specified where anodized appearance match with 6063 extrusions is desired.

Roofing and siding

Alclad 3004 — Used for standard corrugated, ribbed and V-beam industrial roofing and siding sheets.

Porcelain Enameling

3003 / 6061 — See above for characteristics.

Proprietary sheets developed especially for this use:

Alcoa: Alcoa Nos. 1 and 3 Porcelain Enamel Sheets.

Kaiser: Nos. 300 and 600 sheet and plate.

Olin: Porcelain Enamel Sheets Nos. 1 and 2.

Reynolds: Porcelain Enamel Sheet.

EXTRUSIONS

Mullions, Sash, Fascias, Copings, Thresholds, Handrails, Trim etc.

6063 — Most commonly used extrusion alloy. Good anodized appearance match with 1100, 5005, Nos. 31 and 32, and proprietary natural anodizing sheets.

6061 — Used for extrusions requiring high strength.

6062 — High strength alloy which extrudes more easily than 6061, but retains comparable strength.

Proprietary alloys designed for high quality applications where excellent anodized appearance is critical:

Alcoa: Anoclad Extrusion, Types 5, 10, 20, 30 & 40, for Architectural Color Finish match with Anoclad sheet types of the same numbers.

Kaiser: No. 10 Architectural Extrusions for anodized appearance match with Nos. 10 & 10A Architectural Sheets; Nos. 20, 30 & 40 Architectural Extrusions for anodized appearance match with Architectural Sheets of same numbers; Nos. 51, 61, 63 Architectural Extrusions for Kalcolor anodizing.

Olin: Anodizing Quality Extrusions Nos. 10, 20, 30 & 40 for special color requirements.

Reynolds: RF-10, RF-15, RF-20 and RF-30 for anodized appearance match with sheet types of same numbers; RF-40 for dark gray color when clear anodized.

Guide for the selection of aluminum alloys (cont.)

Typical Applications	Alloy	Comments
Porcelain Enameling	6061	See above for characteristics.
		Proprietary alloys developed especially for this use:
	Alcoa:	No. 1 Porcelain Enameling Extruded Shapes.
	Olin:	Porcelain Enamel Quality Extrusions.
	Reynolds:	6061-F (Porcelain Enamel Quality).

CASTINGS

	Alloy	Comments
Decorative panels	43	For ornamental castings in which strength is relatively unimportant. Castings turn gray after anodizing.
panels	214	Stronger than Alloy 43; produces best anodized appearance match with 6063 extrusions.
Hardware items	356	High strength casting alloy; turns gray after anodizing.

FASTENERS

Alloy	Typical Applications	
1100	Low strength rivets, washers.	
2024	Bolt, nuts, screws.	
5056 } 6061 }	Nails	All fasteners except nails may be plain or anodized.
6053	Medium strength rivets.	
6061	High strength rivets, nuts, washers.	

Table 6. Standard mechanical finishes for architectural aluminum

With tentative NAAMM designations (pending recommended designations by the Aluminum Association).

Alcoa	Kaiser	Olin	Reynolds	Tentative NAAMM Designation	Definition of Finish
as fab	NF	NF	XX0X	NA-0	As fabricated.
no symbol	M1	M1	no symbol	NA-1	Polished with aluminum oxide compound. Grits to be coarser than 320; final polishing with a 320 grit, using peripheral wheel speed about 6,000 ft/min.
A1	M2	M2	XX2X	NA-2	Polished with aluminum oxide compound. Grits to be coarser than 320; final polishing with a 320 grit, using peripheral wheel speed of about 6,000 ft/min. Polishing followed by buffing, using aluminum oxide buffing compound and peripheral wheel speed of about 7,000 ft/min.
A2	no symbol	no symbol	no symbol	NA-22	A buffed finish with no prepolish, generally applied with a muslin or cotton buffing wheel and aluminum oxide buffing compound with a peripheral wheel speed of about 6,000 ft/min.
E	M3	M3	XX3X	NA-3	Coarse satin finish producing a surface with parallel scratch lines. Grit used to be a 120 to 140 aluminum oxide type; peripheral wheel speed about 6,000 ft/min.
D	M4	M4	XX5X	NA-4	Medium satin finish producing a surface with parallel scratch lines. Grit used to be a 140 to 180 aluminum oxide type; peripheral wheel speed of about 6,000 ft/min.
C1	M5	M5	XX5X	NA-5	Fine satin finish producing a surface with parallel scratch lines. Grit used to be a 180 to 220 aluminum oxide type; peripheral wheel speed of about 6,000 ft/min.
C2	M6	M6	no symbol	NA-6	Hand-rubbed finish, using stainless steel wool lubricated with neutral soap solution. Final rubbing with #0 steel wool.
K	M7	M7	no symbol	NA-7	Wire wheel brush finish, using stainless steel wire brush. Wire diameter 0.0095", peripheral wheel speed 6,000 ft/min.
C3	M8	M8	no symbol	NA-8	Vonnegut wheel finish, using #220 aluminum oxide type abrasive, flat type wheel for flat surfaces, shredded type for uneven surfaces.
G4	M9	M9	XX4X	NA-9	Coarse sand blast finish, using 16 to 20 mesh silica sand if darkening is not a problem; otherwise aluminum oxide type abrasive. Air pressure 30 to 90 lb (depending on gage of material); gun distance 1 ft from work at an angle of 60 to 90 deg.
G3	M10	M10	XX4X	NA-10	Medium sand blast finish, using 40 to 50 mesh silica sand if darkening is not a problem; otherwise aluminum oxide type abrasive. Air pressure 30 to 90 lb (depending on gage of material); gun distance 1 ft from work at an angle of 60 to 90 deg.
G2	M11	M11	XX4X	NA-11	Fine sand blast finish, using 100 to 200 mesh silica sand if darkening is not a problem, otherwise aluminum oxide type abrasive. Air pressure 30 to 90 lb (depending on gage of material), gun distance 1 ft from work at an angle of 60 to 90 deg.
no symbol	M12	M12	no symbol	NA-12	Shot blast finish, varying in texture with the size of shot and amount of air pressure used.
AIR5	no symbol	no symbol	XX7X	NA-13	Buffed and chemically brightened finish.
N	no symbol	no symbol	no symbol	NA-14	A uniform, matte surface created by loose sand, gravel, and steel balls used in an agitating process. Suited for castings and flat sheet.

Proprietary Designations [1]

[1] *Data concerning proprietary finish designations were not available from other suppliers at the time of publication (February, 1962).*

Table 7. Standard chemical, electrochemical, and applied finishes for architectural aluminum

With tentative NAAMM designations (pending recommended designations by the Aluminum Association).

Proprietary Designations[1]				Tentative NAAMM Designation	Definition
Alcoa	Kaiser	Olin	Reynolds		
R1	C1	C1	XX6X	NA-CE	Caustic etch, using solution of sodium hydroxide or sodium hydroxide and sodium fluoride. Degree of etch to be controlled by time, temperature and strength of solution.
R5	no symbol	no symbol	XX1X	NA-CB*	Chemically brightened finish, highly lustrous and bright.
204	A1	A1	no symbol	NA-1A	Clear anodized finish having a minimum coating thickness of .0004″ and minimum coating weight of 17 mg. per square inch.
214	A2	A2	no symbol	NA-2A	Clear anodized finish having a minimum coating thickness of .0008″ and minimum coating weight of 35 mg. per square inch.
no symbol	API	API	no symbol	NA-L	Clear, water-white methacrylate lacquer applied over a suitably cleaned surface to a minimum thickness of .5 mil.

Combined Finishes

To designate combination finishes, the designation consists simply of a combination of the symbols identifying the various component finishes. As an example, the NAAMM designation of the equivalent of Alcoa's 215-R1 would be NA-CE2A or Alcoa's 204-A1-R1 would be NA2-CE-1A.

---

*This is a chemical treatment that is very seldom used with architectural finishes. It is non standard with NAAMM members.

Table 8. Color matching of anodized aluminum alloys

Alloys having similar preparatory and anodizing treatment.

Form:	Sheet and Plate					Extrusions		Castings
				Anodizing Sheet				
Alloy:	1100	3003	5005	No. 31	No. 32	6062	6063	214
Match with Alloy:								
1100	Good	Poor	Good	Good	Good	Fair	Good	Fair
3003	Poor	Good	Poor	Poor	Poor	Poor	Poor	Poor
5005	Good	Poor	Good	Good	Good	Fair	Good	Fair
No. 31	Good	Poor	Good	Good	Good	Fair	Good	Fair
No. 32	Good	Poor	Good	Good	Good	Fair	Good	Fair
6062	Fair	Poor	Fair	Fair	Fair	Good	Fair	Fair
6063	Good	Poor	Good	Good	Good	Fair	Good	Fair

Note: It is important to recognize that perfect color match is not always obtainable, even with items of the same alloy. Matches indicated as "Good" in the above table, even though the best obtainable, should not necessarily be assumed to be consistently excellent.

ARCHITECTURAL METALS—7
Stainless steel

By WAYNE F. KOPPES, *Architectural Consultant*

"Stainless steel" is a generic name for a large family of steel alloys, offering the combined qualities of high strength, superlative corrosion resistance, great durability and low maintenance costs. These alloys have distinct differences in properties as well as in cost. Consequently, the choice of the proper alloy for the application in mind becomes a matter of primary importance, if unnecessary costs are to be avoided.

TYPES OF STAINLESS STEEL

The American Iron and Steel Institute has established standard numerical designations for thirty-nine different stainless alloys in four series; the 200 series, the 300, the 400, and the 500 series. However, the architect is usually concerned with only four types; those alloys designated as Types 202, 302, 316, and 430. Of these, Type 302 is by far the most generally useful and most commonly used.

Type 202

Type 202 is one of the newer alloys, designed to conserve the use of nickel. It has higher strength values than other architectural alloys, and equally excellent corrosion resistance. These characteristics, coupled with favorable price, make it attractive for many architectural applications, both interior and exterior.

Type 302

Type 302 is the popular "18-8" (18% chromium, 8% nickel) alloy, and the general purpose stainless most frequently used for outdoor applications on buildings. It possesses high strength, excellent wearing qualities, and is amply corrosion-resistant for normal exposures.

Type 316

Type 316 is a modification of Type 302, very highly resistant to corrosion, and more expensive. It is recommended for applications exposed to salt water atmosphere or damaging industrial fumes, and its uses architecturally are not very common.

Type 430

Type 430 is one of the straight chromium alloys (no nickel), and is used primarily for interior architectural trim and builders' hardware. It is a little less corrosion-resistant than the other three types, and is the least expensive of the four. It has been used successfully on exteriors of buildings where regular maintenance of the surface by washing can be provided.

AVAILABLE WIDTHS, LENGTHS AND THICKNESSES

Stainless steel is available from the mill either in coil stock or in cut sheets. Any width less than 24 in. is termed "strip"; widths of 24 in. and greater are termed "sheet." The cost of strip widths is slightly less per square foot than that of sheet widths. Both sheet and strip come in a wide range of cut lengths or in coils. Sheets are available in thicknesses from 0.005 to 0.109 in., while strip comes in thicknesses from 0.0015 to 0.090 in.

GAGES AND WEIGHTS

Before gages and weights can be considered properly, it must be remembered that all architectural metals are not measured by the same standards. Stainless steel, for example, is measured by the United States Standard Gage, while aluminum is measured by the Brown & Sharpe Gage, and thicknesses differ as shown in the Comparative Gage Table (Table 1).

In specifying thickness, it should be remembered that standard industry tolerance allows thickness variations ranging from 8 per cent for 11 gage to as high as 22 per cent for 32 gage, and that the weights of specified sheets may vary accordingly. Since all metals are purchased by the pound, not by the square foot, sheets of 18 gage stainless, for example, might vary as much as 20 per cent (—10 per cent to +10 per cent) in their cost per square foot, although the price per pound is constant.

FINISHES

The No. 2 finishes, because of their relative economy, are quite satisfactory for many exterior uses, and should be considered whenever close-up appearance is not critical, as on building walls above the lower stories. There is one limitation, however, which should be recognized. Wherever welding is required on the finished surface and must be made invisible, or where other fabrication marks may require removal, the No. 2 finishes are not appropriate. The grinding and polishing necessary to remove weld beads or other defects would necessarily be objectionably conspicuous. In these cases a polished finish (such as No. 3 or No. 4) on the parent metal is usually mandatory, so that remedial polishing may be "blended in," wholly concealing weld locations or defects.

The polished finish most commonly used architecturally is the No. 4 finish, though it is scarcely distinguishable from the cheaper No. 3 finish. For the whole facade of a building either one of these finishes is extravagant, and would be generally undesirable because of high reflectivity. These finishes have the remarkable property of reflecting any light source, regardless of its shape, as a brilliant line. This line will always appear at right angles to the "grain" of the polish, and in sheets longer than 48 in. this grain necessarily parallels the length of the sheet. The direction of the reflection lines on the face of the building will consequently be determined by the position of the sheets with respect to the direction of the polish. Thus, positioning is particularly important when polished finishes are selected.

FABRICATION METHODS

Stainless steel requires no unique fabrication methods or equipment. With the exception of extruding (which is possible, but expensive) it is amenable to all the usual fabricating processes: brake forming, roll forming, pressing and bending. The cost of rolls and dies is high, regardless of the metal being formed, and these processes are economical only in large scale production of repetitive shapes. Therefore, in typical building applications brake forming usually proves to be the most economical fabrication method.

All the stainless steels can be readily welded or soldered. Soldering, however, should be used only as a means of filling or sealing a joint; it should not be subjected to stresses or loading.

TEXTURE

A large variety of decorative surface textures are available in stainless sheets. These are produced in relief by roll forming with matched rolls, with pattern impressions ranging in depth from 0.005 to 1.5 in., and in widths from 0.125 to 8 in. Designs thus produced are of two general types: over-all and unidirectional

The use of textures is often desirable for both practical and aesthetic reasons. Most textures contribute significantly to the stiffness of the sheet, permitting the use of thinner metal, and at the same time the relief patterns diffuse reflections and reduce "oil-canning" effects.

ECONOMICAL DESIGN WITH STAINLESS

Designers contemplating the efficient use of stainless steel should give full attention to the unique properties of the material.

Obviously, the economical use of stainless steel depends basically on using the least thickness necessary. The high strength, stiffness, and durability of the material makes this feasible. One method of comparing necessary thicknesses would be on the basis of equal indentation resistance.

With any sheet metal it is a highly questionable objective to attempt to achieve perfect glass-like polished flatness in large areas. Such flatness may logically be expected only with heavy rigid materials, and to attempt to accomplish it with thin metal sheets is usually expensive and only rarely successful, by any of the presently used techniques. The effect of "oil-canning" inevitably results if the surface is polished, even when plate thicknesses are used.

There appears to be a choice, then, of two alternatives; either to accept some waviness in large flat areas as a natural characteristic of the material, or to eliminate the cause of this appearance (reflectivity of light) by breaking up the surface with patterns or texture in relief. The latter course is currently the usual preference.

In summary, these are the important clues to the economical use of stainless steel:

1. Choose the appropriate type for the use and exposure intended.

2. Use the minimum necessary thickness; details should be engineered to take full advantage of the superior strength and stiffness of stainless steel.

3. Avoid the use of large flat surfaces, especially with polished finishes.

4. Use textured sheets wherever possible, to increase stiffness and minimize the appearance of waviness.

5. Whenever convenient, use widths under 36 in. and cut lengths between 60 and 120 in.

6. Don't waste money on unnecessary finishes, especially in locations inaccessible to close inspection.

Table 9. Standard mechanical finishes for architectural stainless steel

As established by the American Iron and Steel Institute.

Finish Designation	Definition
Unpolished Finishes:	
No. 1	A rough dull surface produced by hot rolling to the specified thickness, followed by annealing and descaling.
No. 2D *(for widths under 24", referred to as "No. 1 Strip Finish")*	A dull cold rolled finish produced by cold rolling to the specified thickness, followed by annealing and descaling. May also be accomplished by a final light roll pass on dull rolls.
No. 2B *(for widths under 24", referred to as "No. 2 Strip Finish")*	A bright cold rolled finish commonly produced in the same way as No. 2D finish, except that the annealed and descaled sheet receives a final light cold roll pass on polished rolls. This is a general purpose cold rolled finish, and is more readily polished than the No. 1 or No. 2D finishes.
Polished Finishes:	
No. 3	An intermediate polished surface obtained by finishing with a 100 grit abrasive. Generally used where a semi-finished polished surface is required for subsequent finishing operations following fabrication.
No. 4	A general purpose bright polished surface obtained by finishing with a 120-150 mesh abrasive, following initial grinding with coarser abrasives.
No. 6	A soft satin finish having lower reflectivity than No. 4 finish. It is produced by Tampico brushing the No. 4 finish in a medium of abrasive and oil.
No. 7	A highly reflective finish produced by buffing a surface which has first been finely ground with abrasive of approximately 240-280 mesh.
No. 8	The most reflective finish commonly produced. It is obtained by polishing with successively finer abrasives, finishing with 320-400 mesh, then buffing extensively with a very fine buffing compound.

Presented through the Courtesy of the Committee of Stainless Steel Producers, American Iron and Steel Institute

Use of Stainless Steel In Design

Its characteristics put stainless steel into a separate category of sheet metal work; properties are sufficiently different from other architectural metals to influence design techniques.

Briefly, stainless steel is stronger, stiffer, harder, and has a higher melting temperature than any of the nonferrous metals. It is more weather-resistant than galvanized steel. Stainless is most often left unpainted and uncoated. It costs more per pound than many of the other metals.

All these factors affect the way stainless steel is employed in architectural designs. Here are some of the results:

• Thin sheets and strip are most used.

• Rigid members are produced by forming, not by using thick sections.

• Most joints are welded, screwed or seamed.

• Stainless often covers and protects other materials.

Use of Chromium or Chromium-Nickel

There has been a vast increase in use of Type 430, 17 per cent chromium stainless. Before, Type 302, 18–8 chromium-nickel stainless had been employed almost universally because of its easy fabrication and general availability. Although Type 430 was used in the automotive field and was recommended to architects for interior work, it had gained relatively little recognition in the building fields.

Today, great military and industrial demands for nickel have forced architects and designers to become familiar with the qualities of Type 430. Its corrosion resistance, slightly less than that of Type 302, has been studied carefully. Conclusions are that, while some extra precautions may be entailed, Type 430 stainless steel can be used for practically all kinds of architectural metal work.

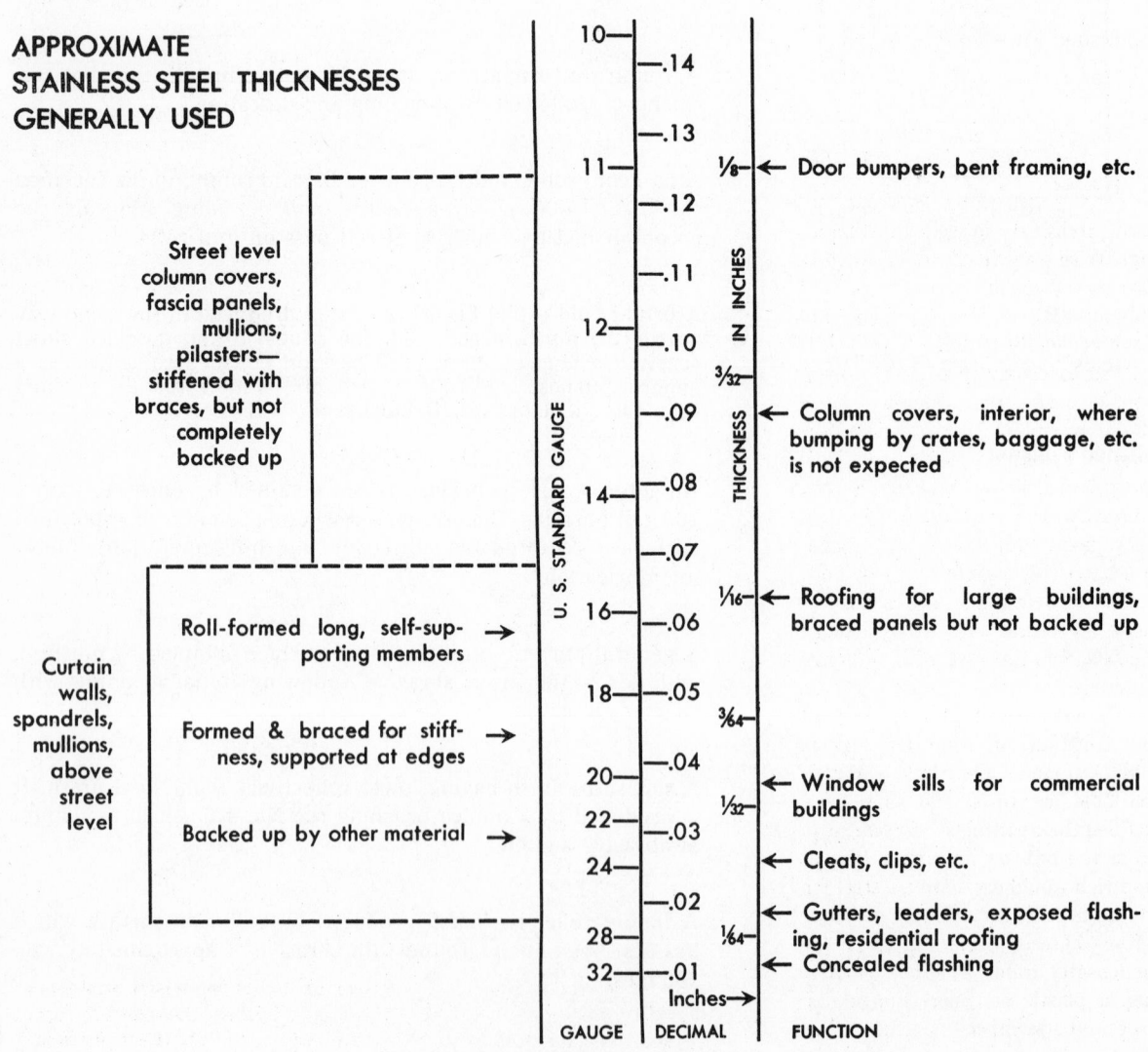

APPROXIMATE STAINLESS STEEL THICKNESSES GENERALLY USED

Street level column covers, fascia panels, mullions, pilasters—stiffened with braces, but not completely backed up

Curtain walls, spandrels, mullions, above street level

Roll-formed long, self-supporting members →

Formed & braced for stiffness, supported at edges →

Backed up by other material →

U. S. STANDARD GAUGE

THICKNESS IN INCHES

Door bumpers, bent framing, etc.

Column covers, interior, where bumping by crates, baggage, etc. is not expected

Roofing for large buildings, braced panels but not backed up

Window sills for commercial buildings

Cleats, clips, etc.

Gutters, leaders, exposed flashing, residential roofing

Concealed flashing

GAUGE | DECIMAL | FUNCTION

Stainless Exteriors

Stainless steel does not absorb moisture. It weathers well. It is light for its strength, and it stays strong through fire-test temperatures.

Stainless steel is used in exterior walls for different purposes:

1. Stock, roll-formed sections suitable for walls, roofs or decks are available in stainless. They have been

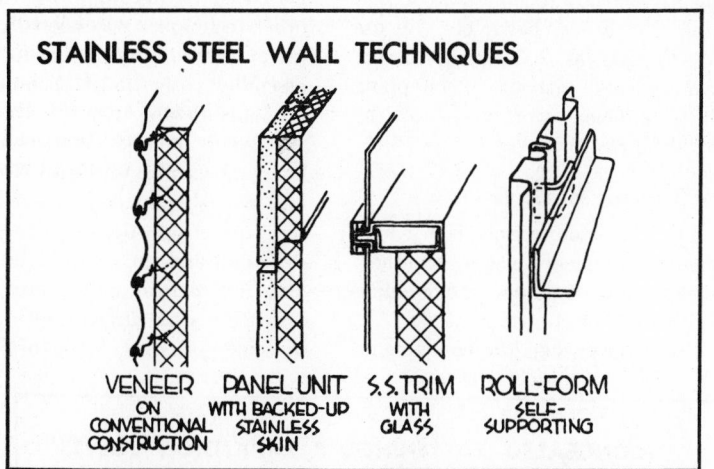

STAINLESS STEEL WALL TECHNIQUES

VENEER ON CONVENTIONAL CONSTRUCTION — PANEL UNIT WITH BACKED-UP STAINLESS SKIN — S.S. TRIM WITH GLASS — ROLL-FORM SELF-SUPPORTING

used extensively for industrial buildings. With some insulation they have also served on office structures, but only (to date) in structures not subject to code fire-testing.

2. As external veneer over conventional construction, stainless steel plays many roles. It has been used as stamped spandrels, formed mullions, trim, fascia strips, bulkheads, etc., exposed to the weather. Advantages are gained in appearance and design, in economy of maintenance, but not usually in weight or space-saving because structural and fire-resistance requirements are met with ordinary materials.

3. Sandwich units that embody all wall functions in composite panels have been made. They have met conventional fire tests, and they have justified their existence economically. From the outside inward, a typical sandwich would use stainless steel for appearance and imperviousness, some porous material or an air space for condensate drain, a vapor barrier, then a plastic or concrete insulator structural member. Because the stainless skin is not expected to resist

wind loads, extremely thin-gage metal can be specified and corresponding economies are gained. Stainless doesn't need extra material for a "corrosion allowance."

4. Buildings made from glass windows and glass spandrels require trim of another material. The easy cleaning quality of glass, which prompts this type of exterior, points to stainless steel as another easily cleaned material for exterior work made of metal.

Use of Bent Shapes to Prevent "Oilcanning"

The problem of avoiding a wavy surface arises whenever a highly finished material is involved. Although used in thin sections, stainless is often formed into finished members that are designed to look massive and solid. As stainless is almost invariably found at a focal, eye-catching spot in the design, imperfections are seldom overlooked.

Wavy, "oilcan" appearance may result when a thin, flat surface is distorted by fasteners, welding (thermal strains), or very minor inaccuracies in fabrication. There are many things to do to prevent it.

First, break large flat areas into panels or strips. Second, bend the stainless pieces to form relatively rigid shapes — at least along one axis. Third, keep fasteners off the flat surfaces; put them beyond stiffening bends or returns.

Finally, if any of these general rules must be violated, there will probably be no ill effects if considerably thicker metal or embossed, textured stainless stock is used.

It might also be added that a large area of bright metal, like the side of a stainless-steel covered skyscraper, might best have walls with many angled facets or curves to prevent development of a single concentrated glare from reflected sunlight.

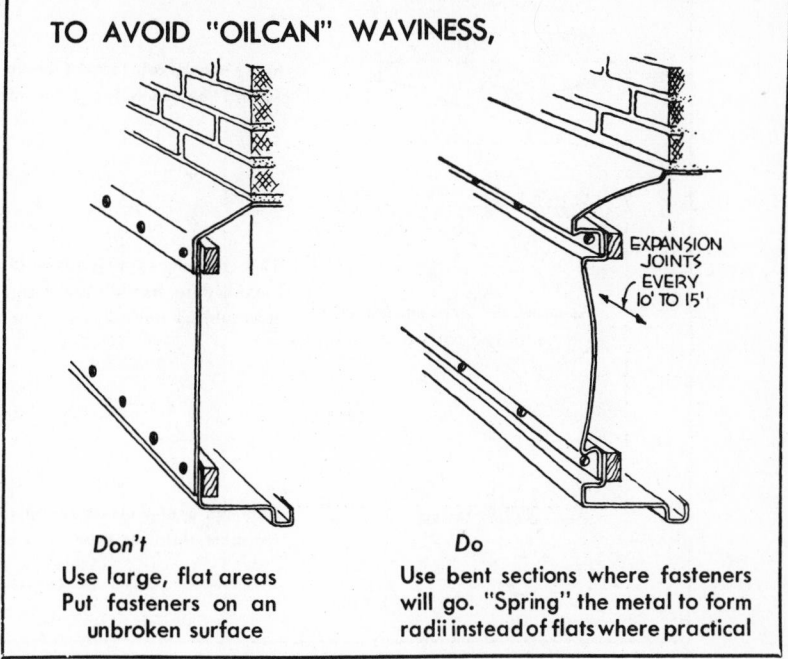

TO AVOID "OILCAN" WAVINESS,

EXPANSION JOINTS EVERY 10' TO 15'

Don't
Use large, flat areas
Put fasteners on an unbroken surface

Do
Use bent sections where fasteners will go. "Spring" the metal to form radii instead of flats where practical

Stainless Steel Ceilings

Flat stainless sheets are used occasionally as ceilings for high rooms, such as lobbies. Perforated stainless ceilings are employed for acoustical reasons. Sometimes the space above such ceilings is a ventilating plenum chamber. Also, sanitary considerations dictate the use of stainless steel walls and ceilings in many kitchens and food-handling areas.

In all these, the important design feature is the expansion joint. Any large metal area must have freedom to expand and contract with thermal changes otherwise it buckles or wrinkles. It becomes almost impossible to stiffen such areas adequately for good appearance. Any frame or angle rigidly attached to stainless sheets should also be stainless steel because differential expansion of two metals causes warping.

JOIN STAINLESS PIECES WITH:

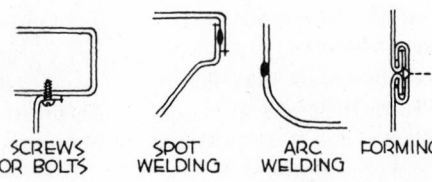

SCREWS OR BOLTS   SPOT WELDING   ARC WELDING   FORMING

It should be noted that most joints have two other functions in addition to their expansion function: they add stiffness at the edges; they frequently embody schemes for concealing screw heads, bolts, etc. Choose an arrangement that satisfies design requirements without overstepping the economical work-range of the metal fabricator.

Fastening Methods

There are four principle ways of putting stainless pieces together: screws, spot welding, arc welding and seamed or clipped joints.

Use screws when the components must be taken apart occasionally. It may sometimes be wise to specify screwed fastenings in case the fabricators and installers should be inexperienced or unequipped to handle other techniques. Occasionally sheet metal screws reduce fabrication and assembly costs to the point where economy dictates their use. However, jobs involving large numbers of similar parts usually warrant extra tooling, more shop-made joints and fewer screwdriver operations on the site.

Screws and nuts should be stainless. If dissimilar metals are joined, insulate faying surfaces with a coat of sealer of some kind to prevent

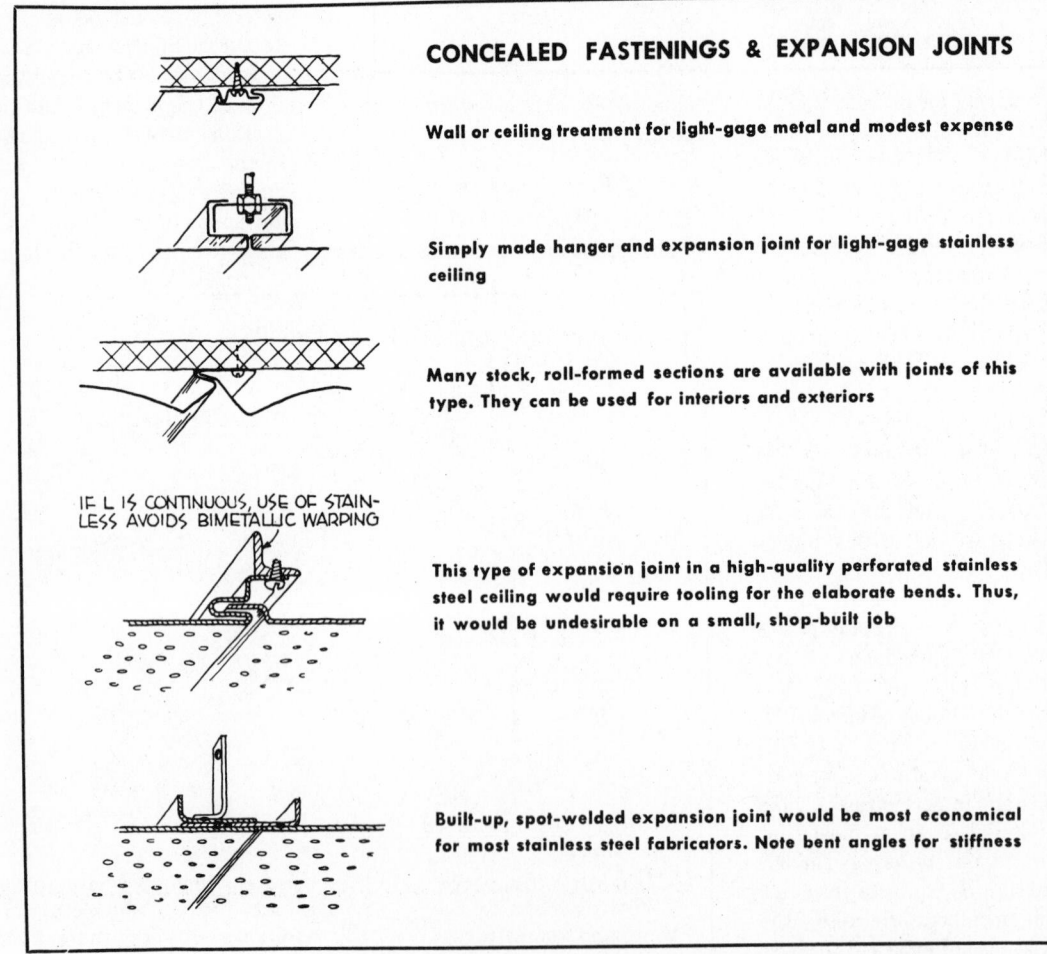

CONCEALED FASTENINGS & EXPANSION JOINTS

Wall or ceiling treatment for light-gage metal and modest expense

Simply made hanger and expansion joint for light-gage stainless ceiling

Many stock, roll-formed sections are available with joints of this type. They can be used for interiors and exteriors

IF L IS CONTINUOUS, USE OF STAINLESS AVOIDS BIMETALLIC WARPING

This type of expansion joint in a high-quality perforated stainless steel ceiling would require tooling for the elaborate bends. Thus, it would be undesirable on a small, shop-built job

Built-up, spot-welded expansion joint would be most economical for most stainless steel fabricators. Note bent angles for stiffness

electrolytic action. On exterior work, use stainless steel fasteners even in concealed locations as a precaution against unsightly rust streaks.

Spot welding offers a very inexpensive way to "stitch" thin metal sheets together. It is normally a shop operation. It has all the advantages and disadvantages of being a permanent joint.

There has to be enough room on both sides of a spot welded joint so that the electrodes can be brought to bear during welding. It is not economical to make specially-shaped electrodes except for a high-production job.

Marks left at the welds can be polished off if necessary. It is possible to make this job easier by using a flatter, larger electrode on the side of the joint that must look good.

Arc welding with butt joints is a standard method of fabricating sanitary food-handling equipment of stainless steel. The weld head can be ground down and polished until it blends with adjacent metal.

Architects can use this technique to obtain longer or larger pieces than stock sheets or fabricator's equipment can normally supply. Several sections may be welded together into a continuous unit. Welding and polishing can be performed on the site, but a better, easier job is possible using shop equipment.

Possibilities of seamed, clipped, cleated and snap-into-place joints are almost infinite. They are used in stainless steel in the same places and for the same reasons that sheet-metal workers have always employed them on other materials. Many special proprietary fasteners are made of stainless.

Lap-seam joints used in stainless roofing and flashing are often soldered for a watertight seal. This practice has long proved satisfactory and economical. However, solder by itself does not have enough strength to serve as a joint between stainless members; some mechanical lock is therefore required in addition.

Wall Ties and Masonry Anchors of Stainless Steel

Masonry anchors are nominally protected from the weather. Yet seepage and frost-broken mortar can expose them to corrosive conditions. Failures have been recorded. In many older buildings, masonry has had to be removed because rusted tie bars created hazards from falling stone, brick or terra cotta.

To specify a corrosion resisting material like 17 per cent chromium, Type 430 stainless steel for masonry ties and anchors may often be a soundly justified precaution.

Roofing, Drainage, Flashing

For roofing, gutters, leaders and all kinds of flashing, the same designs are used with stainless as with any other metal. Lighter weight sections are permitted by stainless steel's greater strength. For this reason it is often practicable to work with larger pieces and longer lengths.

Stainless Mesh and Grids Need No Paint

Bars, rods, wire mesh, expanded metal and formed plates serve the designer by imparting a feeling of light, airy tracery to his work. These elements, in stainless, need be no heavier nor thicker than design requirements indicate, and allowances for rusting are unnecessary. Since corrosion resistant stainless steel needs no protective coating of any kind, maintenance costs on such hard-to-paint surfaces are cut considerably.

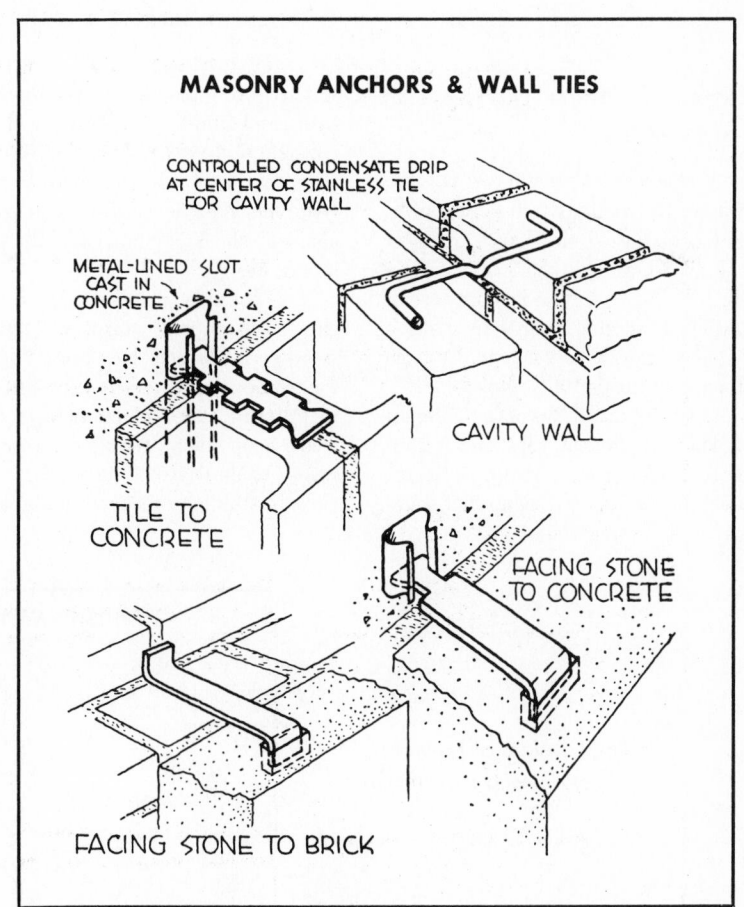

MASONRY ANCHORS & WALL TIES

CONTROLLED CONDENSATE DRIP AT CENTER OF STAINLESS TIE FOR CAVITY WALL

METAL-LINED SLOT CAST IN CONCRETE

CAVITY WALL

TILE TO CONCRETE

FACING STONE TO CONCRETE

FACING STONE TO BRICK

Effects of Weather on Exterior Surfaces

Like glass, stainless steel, when it gets dirty, shows the dirt, but its smooth surface is easy to clean. Designs should both include precautions against accumulation of unsightly dirt, and take advantage of natural rain washing in most climates. When relatively clean water, uncontaminated by rusty iron drippings, flows over stainless steel it does not increase maintenance requirements, but may aid appearance.

Rusty dirt-ladened water should be diverted before it reaches important visible areas. Internal drains like the one sketched here will help assure cleanliness.

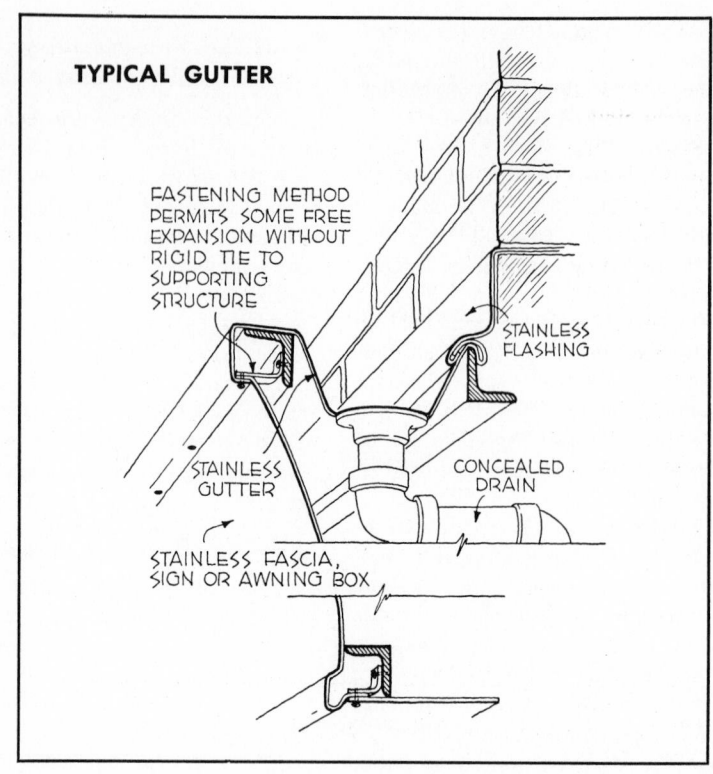

TYPICAL GUTTER

FASTENING METHOD PERMITS SOME FREE EXPANSION WITHOUT RIGID TIE TO SUPPORTING STRUCTURE

STAINLESS FLASHING

STAINLESS GUTTER

CONCEALED DRAIN

STAINLESS FASCIA, SIGN OR AWNING BOX

Display Window Glass Framing

Architectural metal work has many antecedents in carpentry. These historical ties have too tight a hold when solid bars of stainless steel (as big as 1 by 5 in.) are assembled like wooden boards to make a window sash. This has actually been done, and incidentally, looks fine.

Adopting traditions of the cabinetmaker but working out the details more economically, many designers assemble brake-bent sections of stainless steel to build simple, rectangular sash and mullions. More resilient construction results from the use of sheet metal. This has an advantage in that the glass is cradled somewhat against shock, vibration, thermal strain, etc.

It is possible, if desired, to retain the conventional spirit of milled woodwork (which has been copied for some time in the non-ferrous metal trim), and yet employ an efficient, economical, functional component. Modern stock store-front sections in stainless steel are available in many designs. Cross sections range from simple rectangles to beaded moulding shapes. Units are designed for convenience of installation and glass setting as well as for resilient support.

Future design developments may be anticipated: using stainless steel for its mechanical properties, without regard for historic customs, designers will certainly evolve some improved components. Greatest advantages may grow out of designs that require more work of a mass-production nature in factories and less hand work at site.

Internal designs of type at right vary among manufacturers

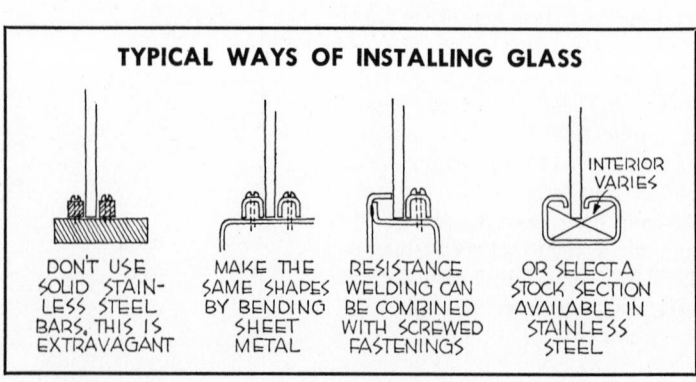

TYPICAL WAYS OF INSTALLING GLASS

DON'T USE SOLID STAINLESS STEEL BARS, THIS IS EXTRAVAGANT

MAKE THE SAME SHAPES BY BENDING SHEET METAL

RESISTANCE WELDING CAN BE COMBINED WITH SCREWED FASTENINGS

INTERIOR VARIES

OR SELECT A STOCK SECTION AVAILABLE IN STAINLESS STEEL

Formed Tubing

It would be uneconomical to specify solid stainless steel members for railings, struts, built-in furniture and the like. Parts of this kind, designed to look solid, are usually made from stainless tubing shaped into the desired cross section. Suppliers of stainless steel architectural tubing have tools for producing a tremendous variety of special-purpose cross-sectional shapes.

Joining methods that can be used with this tubing include spot welding, fusion welds (ground smooth and polished), nuts and bolts, sheet metal screws, etc.

TYPICAL TREATMENT FOR LIGHTWEIGHT RAILING

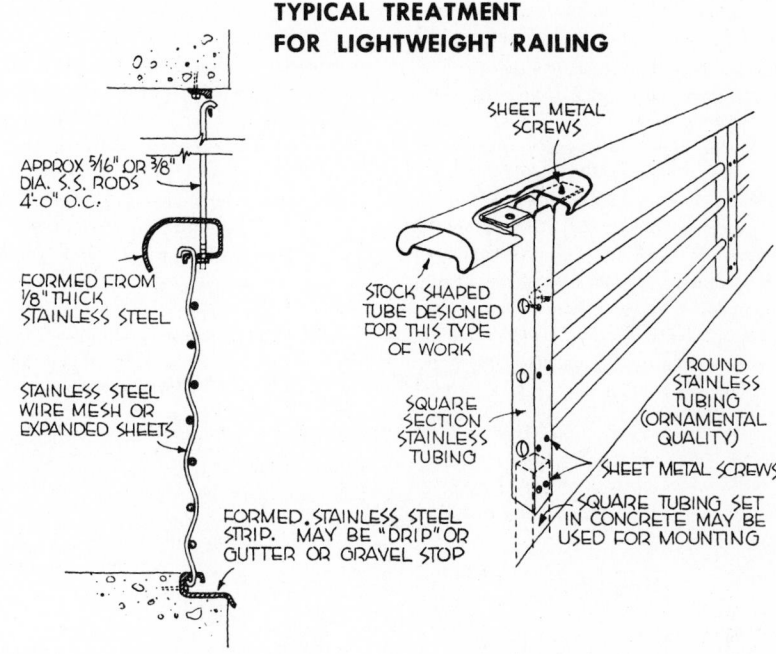

APPROX 5/16" OR 3/8" DIA. S.S. RODS 4'-0" O.C.

FORMED FROM 1/8" THICK STAINLESS STEEL

STAINLESS STEEL WIRE MESH OR EXPANDED SHEETS

FORMED STAINLESS STEEL STRIP. MAY BE "DRIP" OR GUTTER OR GRAVEL STOP

SHEET METAL SCREWS

STOCK SHAPED TUBE DESIGNED FOR THIS TYPE OF WORK

SQUARE SECTION STAINLESS TUBING

ROUND STAINLESS TUBING (ORNAMENTAL QUALITY)

SHEET METAL SCREWS

SQUARE TUBING SET IN CONCRETE MAY BE USED FOR MOUNTING

TYPICAL COLUMN COVER WITHOUT VISIBLE FASTENERS

BRACKETS WELDED TO STEEL

NOTCHED CLIP BOLTED AND TACK WELDED TO BRACKET

ALLOW CLEARANCE FOR SETTING

STRUCT. COLUMN AND FIREPROF.

NOTCHED CLIPS ARE ALIGNED AND TACK WELDED. THEN COVER HALVES ARE HUNG IN PLACE. FLOOR & CEILING FINISHED AFTERWARD

ZEE-SECTION HOOP STIFFENER

SPOT WELD

STAINLESS COLUMN COVER

NOTCHED CLIP

SECTION A-A

KEY SLOT

STUD WELDED OR BRAZED TO OTHER HALF

SECTION B-B

Column Covers With Invisible Fasteners

Structural columns that encroach on pedestrian traffic are frequently given stainless steel sheathings. At building entrances or set-back storefronts, in lobbies and in public rooms, the stainless cover can give a neat appearance, and eliminate painting or other periodic refinishing problems.

Sometimes column covers show exposed screw heads; sometimes screws are concealed by snap-in moulding strips. Jobs are also frequently designed with a hairline joint, with no visible indication of how it is secured.

Most of the concealed fasteners for such members are variations of a wedging or "keyhole" slot. If the sheathing consists of several separate panels, the accessible panels may first be screwed or bolted to a suitable framework. However, the pieces that "go on last" are treated differently. During installation they are lifted slightly, then lowered into place over hooks or studs of some kind. Finish plastering of ceiling and floor occurs after this operation. Because of this, the stainless cover cannot be removed without destroying enough plaster to free it.

By JOHN HANCOCK CALLENDER, *Professor of Architecture, Pratt Institute*

Data on this page from the Copper Development Association, Inc. and the illustrations are by courtesy of American Brass Company.

Copper and its alloys were the first metals used by man. Many bronze artifacts exist today which were made more than 5,000 years ago, proving the remarkable durability of this metal.

The Copper Development Association, Inc. lists a total of 178 standard coppers and copper alloys; 53 of these are shown in the accompanying table. Copper and its alloys are classified in nine groups: coppers, brasses, leaded brasses, tin brasses, phosphor bronzes, silicon bronzes, nickel silvers, cupro nickels, and beryllium copper.

Fortunately for the architect only a few of these alloys are generally used in building construction. They are the following: 110 electrolytic tough-pitch copper, 220 commercial bronze (10 per cent zinc), 230 red brass (15 per cent zinc), 260 cartridge brass (30 per cent zinc), 280 Muntz metal (40 per cent zinc), 385 architectural bronze (3 per cent lead and 40 per cent zinc), and occasionally 655 high silicon bronze and 745 and 754 nickel silver. In color these metals range from copper through the reddish tones to yellow to the white of nickel silver.

Not all alloys are available in all forms. It is therefore necessary for the architect to know which alloys are good color matches. The most widely used combination of color-matching alloys is architectural bronze for extrusions, Muntz metal for sheets and fastenings, red brass for drawn shapes such as tubes and bars, and statuary bronze (a close relative of architectural bronze) for cast ornament. The original bronze color may be retained by the application of clear lacquer, or the metals may be allowed to weather naturally to a dark brown with some greenish tones, or the dark brown color may be imparted at the outset by rubbing with oil, the so-called "statuary bronze" finish.

The Seagram Building in New York, an outstanding example of the use of bronze in building, has spandrels of Muntz metal and extruded mullions of architectural bronze, both finished in dark brown statuary bronze.

Cartridge brass is the familiar yellow brass used mostly indoors for hardware, lighting fixtures, candlesticks, andirons, railings, and the like.

Nickel silver contains no silver; its white color results from the presence of nickel (10–18 per cent) and zinc (25–17 per cent). Ten per cent nickel (745) produces a warm white with a slight yellowish tint. Fifteen per cent or more of nickel gives a silvery white color.

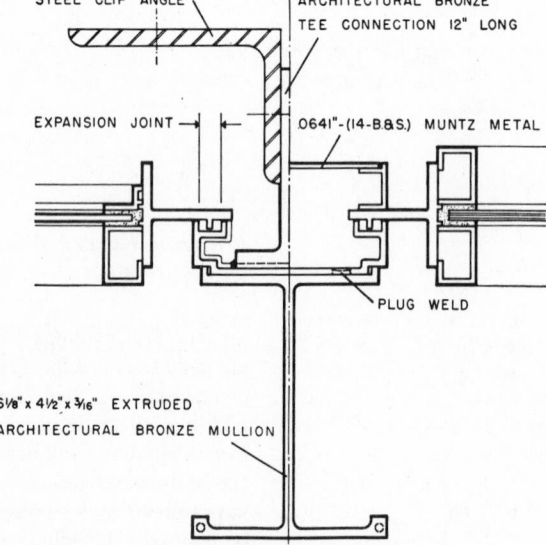

Fig. 1. Section through mullion, Seagram Building

Table 10. Standard copper and copper alloy numbers and previously accepted trade names

COPPER NUMBER	PREVIOUSLY ACCEPTED TRADE NAME
102	Oxygen-Free Copper
110	Electrolytic Tough-Pitch Copper
122	Phosphorus Deoxidized High Residual Phos. Copper

COPPER ALLOY NUMBER	PREVIOUSLY ACCEPTED TRADE NAME
210	Gilding, 95%
220	Commercial Bronze, 90%
226	Jewelry Bronze, 87½%
230	Red Brass, 85%
240	Low Brass, 80%
260	Cartridge Brass, 70%
268	Yellow Brass, 66% (Sheet)
270	Yellow Brass, 65% (Rod and Wire)
280	Muntz Metal, 60%
314	Leaded Commercial Bronze
330	Low Leaded Brass (Tube)
332	High Leaded Brass (Tube)
335	Low Leaded Brass
340	Medium Leaded Brass, 64½%
342	High Leaded Brass, 64½%
353	High Leaded Brass, 62%
356	Extra High Leaded Brass
360	Free-Cutting Brass
365	Leaded Muntz Metal, Uninhibited
366	Leaded Muntz Metal, Arsenical
367	Leaded Muntz Metal, Antimonial

COPPER ALLOY NUMBER	PREVIOUSLY ACCEPTED TRADE NAME
368	Leaded Muntz Metal, Phosphorized
370	Free-Cutting Muntz Metal
377	Forging Brass
385	Architectural Bronze
443	Admiralty, Arsenical
444	Admiralty, Antimonial
445	Admiralty, Phosphorized
464	Naval Brass
465	Naval Brass, Arsenical
466	Naval Brass, Antimonial
467	Naval Brass, Phosphorized
485	Naval Brass, High Leaded
502	Phosphor Bronze E
510	Phosphor Bronze A
521	Phosphor Bronze C
524	Phosphor Bronze D
544	Phosphor Bronze B-2
614	Aluminum Bronze D
651	Low Silicon Bronze B
655	High Silicon Bronze A
675	Manganese Bronze A
687	Aluminum Brass, Arsenical
706	Copper Nickel, 10%
715	Copper Nickel, 30%
745	Nickel Silver 65-10 (Sheet)
752	Nickel Silver 65-18
754	Nickel Silver 65-15
757	Nickel Silver 65-12
770	Nickel Silver 55-18

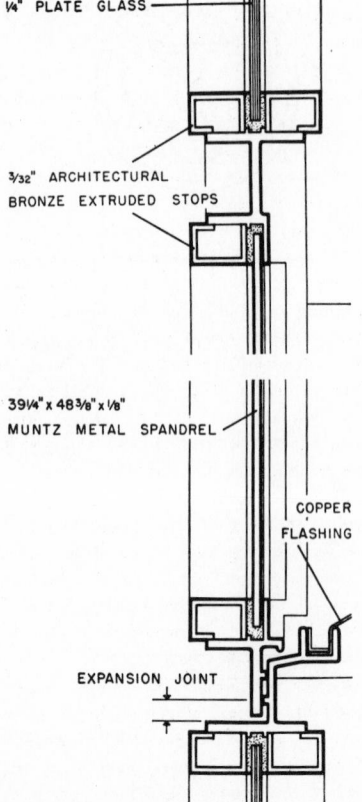

Fig. 2. Section through spandrel, Seagram Building

By HOWARD P. VERMILYA, AIA

Porcelain enamel fused to metal provides a surface that has the hardness of glass. It has a wide variety of uses in construction, particularly in appliances and equipment. As a wall material, porcelain enamel on steel or aluminum is used in panel constructions.

The character of its impervious, inorganic, vitreous surface makes porcelain enamel suitable for use wherever cleanability, ease of maintenance, freedom from reaction to chemicals, durability, and resistance to heat, abrasion, and corrosion are necessary or desirable. It is commonly used for shower, toilet, and lavatory partitions. As an interior wall material, it is used in sheet form or as tile in laboratories, kitchens, hospitals, and other service areas. Matching enameled moldings are available.

As an exterior wall material, porcelain enamel has been used as a veneer over masonry and recently as surfacing for curtain walls. Here the possibilities of color (almost unlimited), design and surface molding, corrugations, embossing, textures, and patterns are more fully exploited. A recent decorative device is the use of porcelain-enameled expanded-metal grids as divider screens, louvers, and in similar applications.

The metal base (steel, aluminum, cast iron, stainless steel, or copper) to which the porcelain enamel is fused is generally fully fabricated prior to finishing to ensure the effectiveness of the finish. This requires complete forming, with joints and lugs welded and holes drilled. Enameling iron, a special low-carbon steel, is usually employed, although other steels may be used when firing temperatures are in the lower ranges. Aluminum alloys 1100, 3003, and 6061 are recommended for sheet and 6062 and 6063 for extrusions. The basic material of the coating is frit, a special glass in granular form. Frit, water, clay, color pigments, and electrolytes are ground in a porcelain-lined ball mill, producing a thick, creamy, fluid substance called "slip." The metal surfaces are then sprayed, flow- or dip-coated with slip, after which they are passed through enameling furnaces at high temperatures designed to fuse the coating to the metal. The back as well as the face of the metal is coated to ensure equal firing and panel flatness. Temperatures in the furnace may range from as low as 850°F for aluminum to as high as 1850°F for stainless steel.

Physical properties: The relative importance of various properties in a given situation may determine the composition of the porcelain enamel, as well as the type of base metal used. There are acid- or alkali-resistant types of enamel. A standard Porcelain Enamel Institute test classifies enamels into AA, A, and B

groups, depending upon their degree of acid resistance. C and D enamels are called non-acid resistant. Acid-resistant grades are recommended where severe weathering is likely to occur, particularly in contaminated atmospheres.

In general, porcelain enamel will withstand temperatures within 300°F of its firing temperature without damage. Most types will withstand attack by boiling water for long periods—days and weeks—but continued exposure to hot water at temperatures above 165°F will cause some porcelain to fail. One special type will withstand longtime exposure to temperatures above 2,000°F. Other properties which may or may not be present are resistance to abrasion, impact, and torsion or bending.

Finishes may be modified to suit the end use. They may be satin, mat, semimat, and metallic, as well as glossy. Full mat is used for chalk boards, semimat and satin for decorative purposes, and glossy where minimum friction, ease of cleaning, highest reflectance, and greatest sheen are desired.

The mixing of two or three frits for ground coats and the use of a nickel dip in the pretreatment of steel have resulted in more consistent production. Use of the newer titania-opacified cover-coat frits has led to a reduction in the over-all thickness. Mechanical damage has been reduced by these two developments. Frits with lower required firing temperatures permit the use of lighter gage, nonpremium grades of steel without deformation. The use of aluminum and stainless steel permits cutting, punching, and drilling after enameling without the danger of corroding the underlying metal.

Several companies manufacture porcelain enamel panels for application to interior

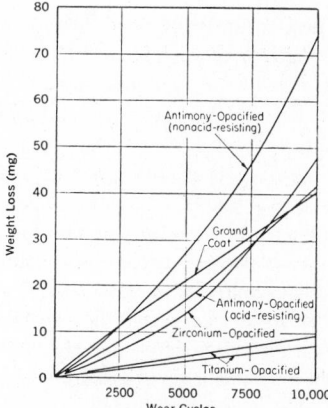

Fig. 3. **Abrasion resistance of standard enamels tested in Tabor abrasor**

Courtesy Porcelain Enamel Institute.

or exterior walls or partitions by laminating the enameled metal sheet to a backing of tempered hardboard or asbestos-cement board in order to prevent waviness in the metal. The backed panel may then be laminated to a low-density core material to form a sandwich panel, or it may be fastened to a metal frame to form a curtain wall panel. Partition panels are faced on both sides of the core with porcelain enamel sheets. The hardboard or asbestos-cement backing is from ⅛ in. to ¼ in. thick. Widths of panels range from 24 in. up to 48 in., and lengths from 6 to 12 ft. The interior panels are adhesively applied, usually to a solid backing of plaster, wallboard, or plywood; in the case of masonry, the panels are attached by adhesive to wood or metal furring. Joints are caulked where moisture seepage is anticipated. Sheets may be cut with power tools. Moldings at edges of panels may be either aluminum, stainless steel, or porcelain enamel.

Table 11. Physical characteristics of porcelain enamel

Courtesy Porcelain Enamel Institute.

Hardness (Moh)	5–6
Abrasion resistance (PEI), %[a]	30–85 residual specular gloss
Abrasion resistance (Tabor), g.[b]	0.0078 for best types
Torsion resistance (rev. PEI), inch[c]	0.016, 40–50°
	0.009, 85–140°
Acid resistance	Highly resistant enamels available
Alkali	Not resistant to hot alkali solution
Solvents, organic	Resistant to all
Temperature, ° F.	700–1100[d]
Ultraviolet light	Not affected
Diffuse reflectance	As desired up to + 80%[e]
Total reflectance	As desired up to + 85%[f]
Weathering	Acid-resistant grades not affected

[a] By same test, good plate glass retains 50% specular gloss.
[b] 16,000 cycles with 1000-gram load and CS17F wheel.
[c] Right-angle shaped specimens 12 inches long, and having ³/₁₆-inch radius at right-angle bend, twisted until failure at radius of bend.
[d] Higher temperatures are resisted by special types of enamels.
[e] For normal application weights. Higher values have been obtained in special circumstances. Normal commercial diffuse reflectances on appliances average about 78%.
[f] As total reflectance is related to diffuse reflectance, [e] applies here also.

By HAROLD EDELMAN, AIA

Proper designing and fabrication are extremely important in producing satisfactory finished panels. To develop in the panel the strength required to withstand the repeated fusing operations, attention must be given to many factors, such as proper gage of metal, size and shape of piece, correct method of forming, rigidity, holes for hanging, etc. Close cooperation between the designer and those responsible for the fabricating, enameling and assembly of the parts is necessary to avoid processing difficulties.

In general, a designer should keep in mind the following points:

1. Make all designing of products a cooperative job between designer and enameler.

2. Select sheet metal of the proper gage and working properties.

3. Keep shapes as simple as possible.

4. Keep sizes proportionate. Avoid long, narrow shapes.

5. Avoid unsymmetrical embosses and offsets.

6. Use flanges for strengthening where necessary. A 1-in. depth is standard size; less is usually not recommended.

7. Weld flanges at corners.

8. Avoid cutouts in flanges.

9. Avoid cutouts in body of parts wherever possible.

10. Provide holes for hanging during firing. Such holes should be spaced to give uniform weight distribution.

11. Keep double thickness of metal to a minimum.

12. Avoid large angle reinforcements welded to back of parts.

Architect's Drawings and Shop Drawings

Architect's drawings should show overall sizes, panel back-up materials (if any), wall construction, type of furring (if any), required colors (from manufacturer's standard color numbers) and required profiles of special shapes, sign letters, etc. Drawings should not be over-dimensioned or over-detailed as this may limit work to bids of one manufacturer or force him to make special shapes or connections when his standard details may, to all intents and purposes, be the same. If the joints are an important feature of the design, the panel sizes and rough details should be established with a manufacturer during the early stages of the work. Otherwise these sizes may be left to be shown on the shop drawings. Drawings and specifications should clearly call out whether such items as electric signs, flashings and furring are to be provided by the porcelain enamel contractor.

All manufacturers will provide the architect with thorough and careful shop drawings as well as samples of edge details, clips, connections, colors, etc. whenever these are required.

TYPES OF FORMED EDGES

ATTACHMENT OF FLAT SHEETS — | **Usually used on interiors under dry conditions**

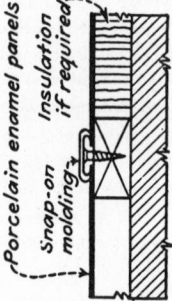

Porcelain enamel panels — Insulation if required — Snap-on molding

SNAP ON MOLDING — made in many types and metals — may be caulked underneath, and used on all four sides or on two sides with a different edge condition on the other two sides

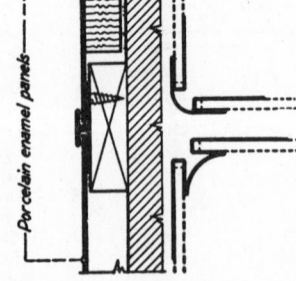

Porcelain enamel panels

ROLLED MOLDINGS — may be stainless steel or stainless steel clad — allow proper expansion and contraction of the panels

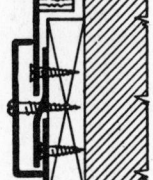

BATTEN — can be used on exterior work with flashing along the horizontal joints. Batten may be porcelain enamel

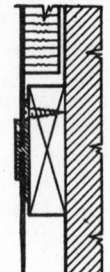

EXTRUDED MOLDING — many varieties — panels are assembled progressively

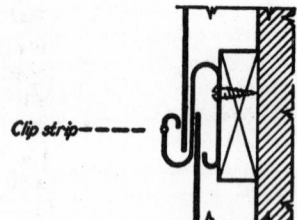

Clip strip

CLIP STRIP — made of stainless steel — ends of panels are overlapped — holes in middle leg of strip allow introduction of a screwdriver

EXTRUDED MOLDING — the inside or "gripping member" is applied to the wall first, and the sheets attached with the "holding member." Moldings are aluminum

ATTACHMENT OF FLAT SHEETS   (*Continued*)

WELDED LUG — an interlocking system which is the same as lug and pan system used for flanged panels. Joints may be made very fine

VEE CLAMP — a rigid installation with grooved edges is cemented to the panel. A continuous square strip at the top of the lower panel is nailed to the studding or blocking, and the next panel dropped in place

ATTACHMENT OF SHEETS WITH FORMED EDGES

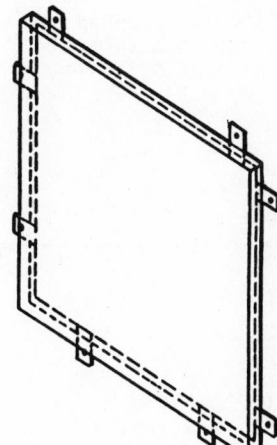

LUG AND PAN — an interlocking system of panels is also used for flat sheets. There are many variations of this basic system

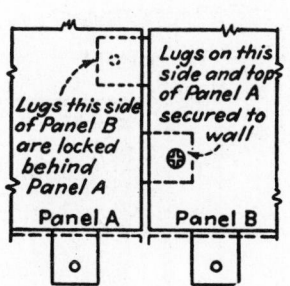

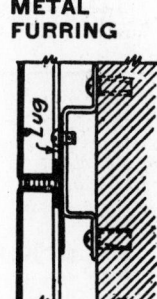

METAL FURRING

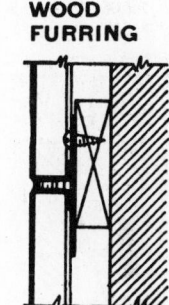

WOOD FURRING

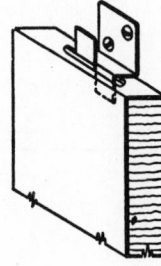

LOCK CLIP — the clips hold the top of one panel and the bottom of the panel above by passing through a slot in the flange. The clips are secured after the lower panel is set

HANGING HOOK — the hook holds the top of one panel and the bottom of the panel above, by passing through a slot in the flange

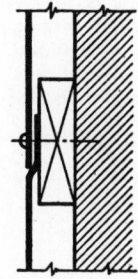

LAP JOINT — for interior work with exposed fastenings. Two adjacent edges are formed, two are flat

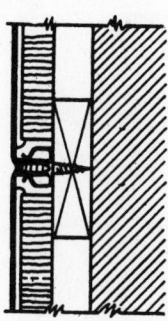

SPRING STEEL CLAMP — may be used for exterior work with caulking or interior work with dry, tight joints

ATTACHMENT OF SHEETS WITH FORMED EDGES (*Continued*)

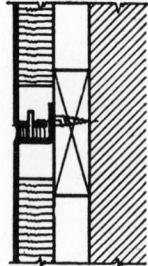

PINS AND HOLES — pins are welded to the top flange of the lower panel and fit through holes in the bottom flange of the upper panel. Top of panel acts as flashing, but an additional strip of metal is required for flashing behind vertical joints. Sides have straight flanges

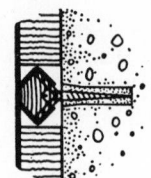

ANGLE CLAMP — a continuous steel angle is set horizontally in the top joint of the lower panel and the bottom of the upper panel fitted over it

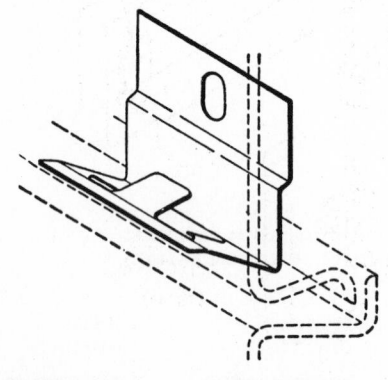

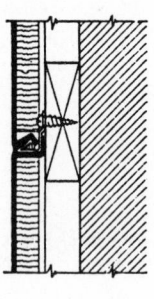

SPRING CLIP — bottom clips are applied first, the panel is placed and top clips are applied

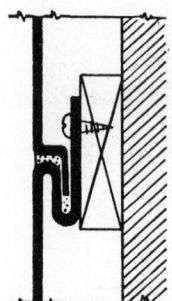

INTERLOCKING EDGE — must be assembled from bottom up. Two adjacent edges are male, two female

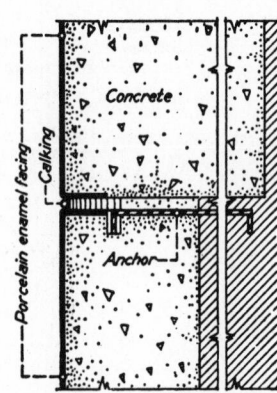

MASONRY BACKED PANELS

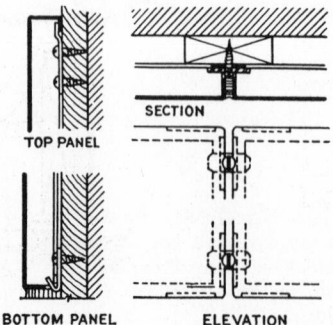

SLOT AND CLIP — bottom row of panels is attached with simple hook that fits through slots in the flanges. Clip is fastened after one panel is in place, and the adjoining panel is slipped into place

Courtesy Architectural Division, Porcelain Enamel Institute

PORCELAIN ENAMEL VENEER

Veneer-type porcelain enamel is used frequently for exterior and interior walls, exterior trim and special details. Typical usages in the form of detailed drawings are shown on the following two pages.

Sizes

The average size porcelain enamel on steel panel is 10 to 12 sq ft, with a recommended maximum size of 15 to 16 sq ft. Where large-size panels are required, special provisions may be required to avoid waviness.

Attachment

In general, the attachment device is screwed to furring previously fastened to the wall surface. Furring may be chemically protected wood, painted or galvanized metal set behind vertical or horizontal joints. Sometimes panels are fastened directly to the wall surface, but this is not recommended for remodeling or irregular surfaced structures because of alignment problems.

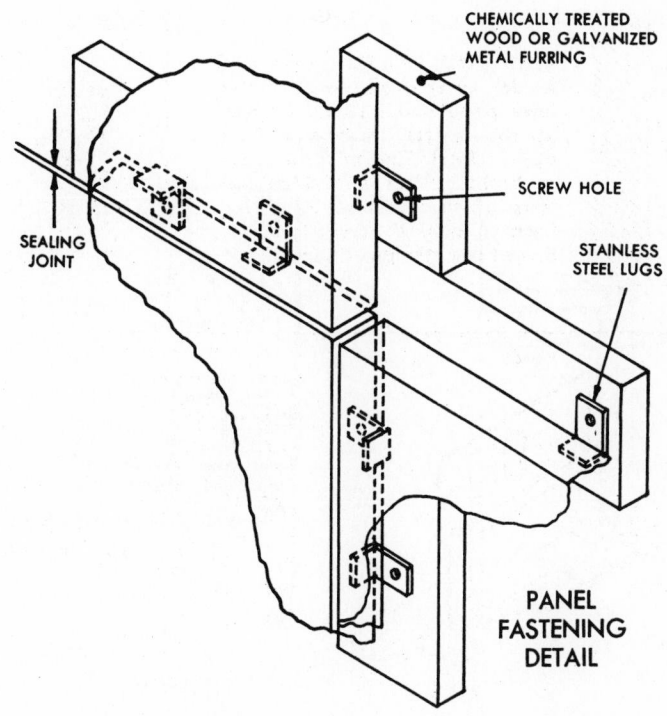

PANEL FASTENING DETAIL

EXTERIOR WALL SECTIONS

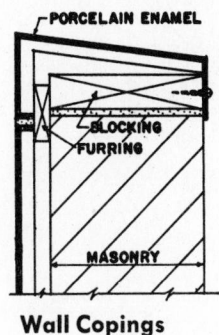
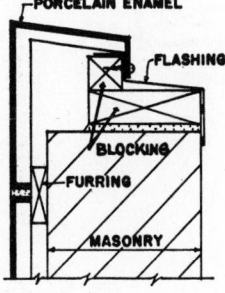
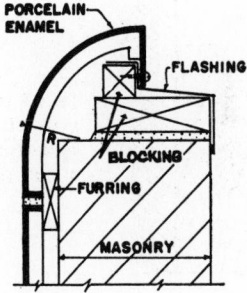

Wall Copings

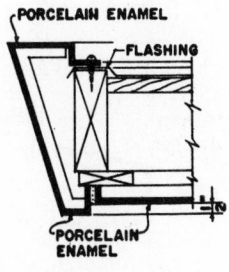
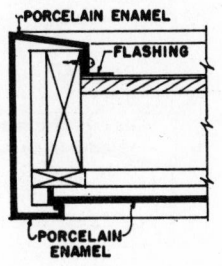
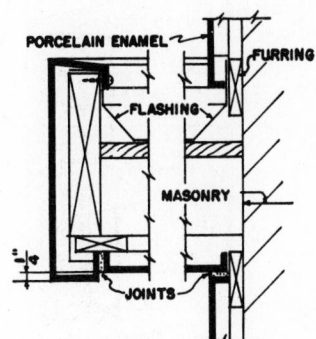

Canopy Fascias

ARCHITECTURAL METALS—21
Porcelain enamel

Back-up

Veneer installations normally are installed without back-up. However, unusually large panels, desire for exacting flatness etc., sometimes necessitates use of angle stiffeners, laminated backing or filler materials.

Panels often are sound deadened to some extent by asphaltic compounds. In some cases plywood is bonded to backs of panels.

EXTERIOR WALL CORNERS AND RETURNS

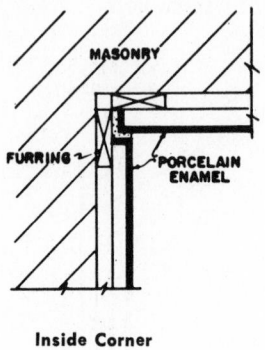

Inside Corner

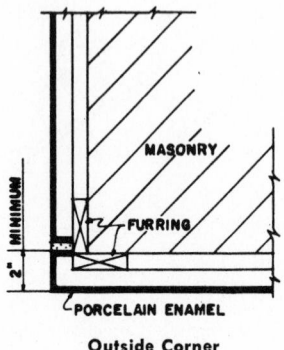

Outside Corner

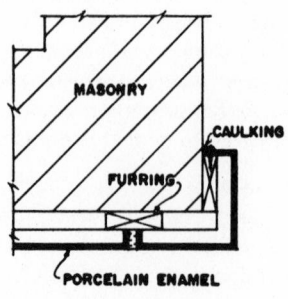

End Return—Square Corner

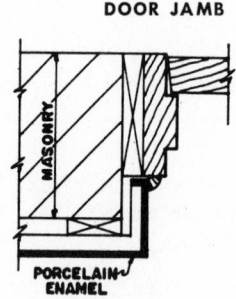

DOOR JAMB

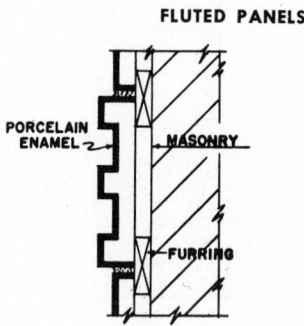

FLUTED PANELS

WINDOW TRIM

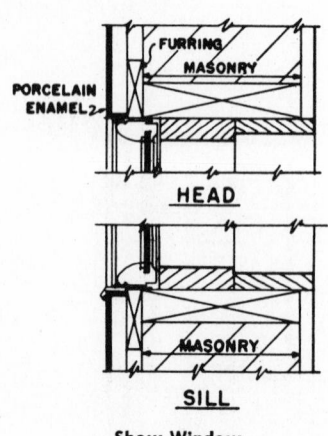

HEAD

SILL

Show Window

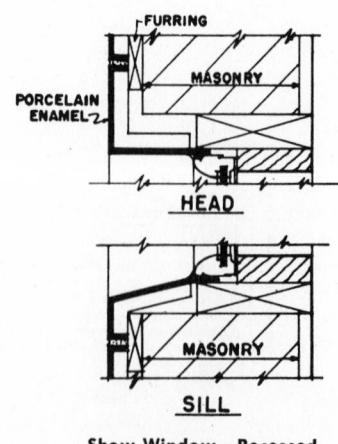

HEAD

SILL

Show Window—Recessed

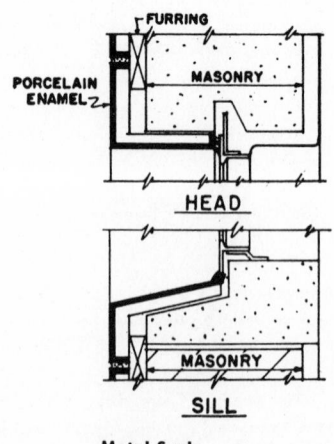

HEAD

SILL

Metal Sash

By WAYNE F. KOPPES, *Architectural Consultant*

TYPES OF GLASS USED IN BUILDING

Sheet

Clear sheet glass includes two types: Window glass—two thicknesses, Single Strength (SS), nominally $\frac{3}{32}$ in. and Double strength (DS), nominally $\frac{1}{8}$ in. Heavy sheet—three thicknesses, $\frac{3}{16}$, $\frac{7}{32}$, and $\frac{1}{4}$ in.; sizes up to 76x120 in.

Sheet glass is made in three quality grades, window glass being available in all three, but heavy sheet usually only in the latter two:

AA—best quality obtainable; sometimes labeled "premium"

A —highest standard grade for commercial purposes

B —contains more small defects than "A" quality, but suitable for general glazing purposes.

All sheet glass is drawn, either flat or vertically, is *not* mechanically polished, and contains slight wave distortions more detectable in large sheets than in small ones. These distortions, or "draws" run in one direction, and for best appearance, should be placed horizontally when glazing. To insure this, the *width dimension should always be stated first*, in listing sizes.

Plate

Polished plate glass includes several types:

Regular plate—two thicknesses, $\frac{1}{8}$ and $\frac{1}{4}$ in. and three quality grades: "silvering" and "mirror glazing," not always available, and rarely used for glazing purposes, "glazing," for all normal glazing.

Heavy plate—thicknesses of $\frac{5}{16}$, $\frac{3}{8}$, $\frac{1}{2}$, $\frac{5}{8}$, $\frac{3}{4}$, 1, and $1\frac{1}{4}$ in. Usually available in glazing quality only.

Rough plate glass is plate glass before polishing. It is essentially a transparent glass, but its rough crepe-like surface texture makes it translucent with relatively high obscurity. Available in thicknesses from $\frac{9}{32}$ through $1\frac{3}{8}$ in., its principal uses are in building interiors, but it may be used on exteriors as well, where obscurity is desired. As it may be directional in appearance, the width dimension should be stated first in listing sizes.

Wire

Wire glass may be polished, clear sheet, corrugated, figured or processed: thicknesses: polished, $\frac{1}{4}$ in. only; corrugated, $\frac{3}{8}$ in. only; other types, $\frac{1}{4}$ and $\frac{3}{8}$ in.

Two types of wire mesh are available; the hexagonal "netting" mesh, twist-joined, and the nearly square "diamond" welded mesh. The latter type is more precisely geometric in appearance and a little more expensive.

Rules of the National Board of Fire Underwriters limit the size of wire glass used in openings exposed to fire hazard; the unsupported area shall not exceed 48 in. in either dimension, or 720 sq in. (5 sq ft).

Corrugated

Corrugated glass is $\frac{3}{8}$ in. thick, with corrugations $2\frac{1}{2}$ in. on center. It is made with either deep corrugations, giving 1 in. over-all thickness, or with flat corrugations and an over-all thickness of only $\frac{1}{2}$ in. Typically, one side of the glass is smooth, the other textured, and it is available with wire reinforcement if desired. For convenience in cutting, the use of widths in multiples of $2\frac{1}{2}$ in. is advisable, but other widths can be obtained by grinding. Fifty in. is usually the maximum width available.

Rolled figured

Rolled figured glass (also referred to as "pattern" or "textured") is a rolled flat glass having a pattern or texture impressed on one or both sides in the process of rolling. It is commonly available in thicknesses of $\frac{1}{8}$, $\frac{7}{32}$, $\frac{1}{4}$, and $\frac{3}{8}$ in. Numerous designs are offered, including flutes, ribs, grids, and a variety of other patterns, all of which provide translucency with more or less obscurity. If the pattern is directional, the width dimension should be stated first, in listing sizes.

Processed

Processed glass, as defined in Federal Specification DD-G-451a, is any "glass whose surface has been altered by etching, sandblasting, chipping, grinding, etc. Either one or both surfaces may be so treated." Surfaces of some of these types may be a little difficult to clean.

Heat absorbing and glare reducing

Because of aesthetic considerations of color, as well as the practical advisability of controlling solar heat and glare in large glass areas, glass manufacturers have introduced a variety of tinted glasses, designed to have distinct advantages, both aesthetically and functionally, over clear glass. These products differ significantly in performance characteristics, however, and there is often confusion in distinguishing between them.

Both heat absorption and glare reduction are accomplished by incorporating mineral admixtures in the glass, resulting in some degree of tinting. Any such tinting reduces transmittance of both visual light and radiant energy, as well as changing the appearance. Consequently any tinted glass, by comparison with clear glass, may properly be termed "heat absorbing." Federal Specification DD-G-451a stipulates, however, that to qualify as heat absorbing *in terms of that standard*, a $\frac{1}{4}$ in. thick glass shall have light transmittance of *not less than 65 per cent* and radiant energy transmittance of *not more than 50 per cent*,

and corresponding limits are specified for other thicknesses as well.

Tinted glasses may, in general, be considered in three categories: those designed primarily for heat absorption, those designed primarily for glare reduction, and those designed for both functions.

A listing of some representative proprietary and nonproprietary types of glass, with their transmittance values, is given in Table 1.

Heat-absorbing glass, as defined in Federal Specification DD-G-451a, may be obtained in thicknesses of $\frac{1}{8}$ and $\frac{1}{4}$ in., in both polished plate and patterns. Tinted glare-reducing glass is available in both sheet and polished plate, in most of the standard thicknesses of those types.

Insulating

Insulating glass refers to those preassembled units which are edge-sealed in the factory by a process of fusion, as opposed to "double glazing units" which may also be factory assembled but are not permanently sealed. There are two types of these sealed units:

Glass edge type—two sheets of SS or DS window glass fused together at their edges, enclosing a nominal $\frac{3}{16}$ in. air space. Over-all nominal thicknesses, $\frac{3}{8}$ and $\frac{1}{2}$ in.

Metal edge type—two sheets of $\frac{1}{8}$, $\frac{3}{16}$ or $\frac{1}{4}$ in. glass, enclosing a $\frac{1}{4}$ or $\frac{1}{2}$ in. air space and hermetically sealed at their edges with a permanent metal-to-glass bond. Nominal over-all thicknesses from $\frac{17}{32}$ to $1\frac{1}{16}$ in. Available in various combinations of glass. Clear plate may be combined with heat-absorbing, glare-reducing, tempered or patterned glass, but the glasses used in combination should differ in thickness by not more than $\frac{1}{16}$ in.

Both types are available in a large number of standard sizes. Special sizes, within established maximums, are also available on order, but generally involve somewhat higher cost and longer delivery time. A listing of maximum sizes and standard dimensional tolerances is included in Table 2.

Laminated

Laminated "safety glass" consists of two pieces of glass with a sheet of transparent vinyl plastic sandwiched between. An adhesive applied with heat and pressure cements the layers into one unit. The elasticity of the plastic cushions any blow against the glass and the cracked glass is held firmly in place. Multiple laminations to a total thickness of 1 in. or more produce "bulletproof glass."

A type of glare-reducing glass is made by using a tinted vinyl sheet between clear glass faces. Colored and patterned plastics sandwiched between sheets of clear glass are also used for decorative pur-

Table 1. Transmittance values of heat-absorbing and glare-reducing glass

Type of Glass	Nominal Thickness	Nominal Transmittance, %*	
		Visual	Heat Energy
Clear polished plate	¼"	88-89	77-80
" " "	¾"	82-83	59-63
Franklin Plate: Blue-green	¼"	75	45
" " Gray**	"	6	36
" " "	"	57	66
" " Rose	"	39	61
" " Tan	"	33	51
L-O-F Heat Absorbing Plate	¼"	75	46
" Parallel-O-Grey	"	44	47
Mississippi Coolite	⅛"	45	22
" " hammered**	"	60	28
" " "	¼"	36	14
" " " **	"	50	20
PPG Solex Plate	¼"	75	45
" Solargray Plate	"	42	45
Clear sheet (DS)	⅛"	90	85
AWG Lustragray Sheet	¼"	52	63
Pennvernon Graylite "56"	⁷⁄₃₂"	56	71
" " "31"	⅛"	31	59
" " "14"	⁷⁄₃₂"	14	45

*Representative values, variable within manufacturer's tolerances
**Also available with other intermediate combinations of values

Table 2. Insulating glass—maximum sizes and dimensional tolerances

	Nominal Glass Thickness	Maximum Area* Square Feet	Dimensional Tolerances	
			Overall Thickness	Size
Glass edge units:	SS or DS	Approx. 12	± ¹⁄₃₂"	under 48", ± ¹⁄₁₆"
Metal edge units:	⅛"	" 15	± ¹⁄₃₂"	over 48", + ⅛", — ¹⁄₁₆"
	³⁄₁₆"	Approx. 22	± ¹⁄₃₂"	+ ⅛", — ¹⁄₁₆"
	¼" (plate)	67 to 70	± ¹⁄₃₂"	+ ³⁄₁₆", — ¹⁄₁₆"
	¼"h.a. + ¼"pl.	50	± ¹⁄₃₂"	+ ³⁄₁₆", — ¹⁄₁₆"

*Size limits vary slightly between manufacturers and should be verified.

poses and as a means of serious artistic expression somewhat akin to stained glass.

Tempered

When glass is reheated to just below its melting point and then cooled suddenly, it becomes three to five times stronger against both impact and thermal stresses. When tempered glass is broken it disintegrates into small pieces which do not usually present a serious hazard. Since tempered glass can not be cut or drilled on the site, the exact size required and any special conditions must be specified when ordering.

Ceramic colored

Colored ceramic glass is a heat-strengthened product designed primarily for exterior use. It is made by fusing opaque color onto the back side of ¼-in. plate glass. A large variety of colors is available. Both polished and textured finishes are standard, but a number of special finishes and custom colors may be obtained on order. As with any tempered or heat-strengthened glass, it cannot be drilled or cut after firing. Consequently the *exact size and all fabrication details must be accurately specified* when ordering. Thickness and cut size tolerances are within the limits specified for flat glass in Federal Specifications DD-G-451a. Flatness tolerance requires that when the glass is vertically supported and measured within a ¾-in. edge margin, the warp or bow along any edge shall not exceed ¹⁄₁₆ in. in any 12 in. or total more than ⅛ in. in 36 in., ¼ in. in 60 in., or ½ in. in 84 in.

Colored "structural"

Colored "structural" glass is made by the noncontinuous pot or batch method sometimes used in making plate glass, with metal oxides incorporated in the mix to produce a variety of opaque colors. It is available in polished, rough and "suede" or "twill" finishes and in thicknesses from ¼ to 1¼ in. For exterior applications the dark heat-absorbing colors should be "heat-strengthened" by tempering to provide resistance to damage by thermal stresses. Under this treatment perfect flatness cannot be maintained, and slight warping normally results. For established tolerances in flatness, the manufacturer should be consulted. Tolerances in thickness and cut size are as defined in Federal Specification DD-G-451a for flat glass.

INDUSTRY STANDARD

Federal Specification DD-G-451a has long been accepted as the industry standard. This specification establishes quality standards and dimensional tolerances (see Table 3) for most types of glass. Many manufacturers regularly produce to lower tolerances than those in the Federal Specification.

SIZES

Maximum glass size depends upon thickness and the design wind load and should not exceed the areas shown in Table 4. As stated earlier, maximum sizes and dimensional tolerances of insulating glass are given in Table 2. Glass clearances and setting dimensions are specified in Table 5.

Table 3. Dimensional tolerances for flat glass

Data from Federal Specification DD-G-451a.

Nominal thickness, inches:	$\frac{1}{4}$	$\frac{3}{8}$	$\frac{1}{2}$	$\frac{5}{8}$	$\frac{3}{4}$	1
Tolerances, inches ±:						
Thickness	$\frac{1}{32}$	$\frac{1}{16}$	$\frac{1}{16}$	$\frac{3}{32}$	$\frac{1}{8}$	$\frac{1}{8}$
Cut size	$\frac{1}{16}$	$\frac{3}{32}$	$\frac{1}{8}$	$\frac{5}{32}$	$\frac{3}{16}$	$\frac{1}{4}$

Table 4. Maximum sizes of various glass thicknesses for glazing vertical windows supported on four sides

These sizes are based on practical experience, and are entirely safe.

Wind Velocity (mph)	Glass Thickness:	Square Feet of Area									
		SS	DS	$\frac{1}{8}''$	$\frac{3}{16}''$	$\frac{1}{4}''$	$\frac{5}{16}''$	$\frac{3}{8}''$	$\frac{1}{2}''$	$\frac{5}{8}''$ to 1"	$1\frac{1}{4}''$
30		(35)*	(64.5)	(72)	162	288	244**				
40		(17.5)	(32.2)	(36)	81	144	255	248**			
55		11.6	(21.5)	(24)	54	96	150	216			
65		8.7	(16.1)	(18)	41	72	112	162	244**		
80		5.8	10.8	12	27	48	75	108	192		
100		3.5	6.4	7	16	29	45	65	115		
120		2.5	4.6	5	11	20	32	46	82	85**	81**

*SS, DS and $\frac{1}{8}''$ glass, because of flexibility, should never be used in areas exceeding 12 square feet. Areas in parentheses are theoretical values exceeding this practical maximum.

**Maximum size available.

SOURCE: "Glazing Manual," Flat Glass Jobbers Association, 1958.

Table 5. Clearance and setting dimensions for glass

Minimum face clearance: $\frac{1}{16}''$ for all flat glass $\frac{1}{8}''$ or less in thickness
$\frac{1}{8}''$ for patterned glass of $\frac{1}{8}''$ thickness and for all flat glass over $\frac{1}{8}''$ in thickness

Minimum edge clearance: $\frac{1}{8}''$ for all glass $\frac{3}{16}''$ or less in thickness and for $\frac{1}{2}''$ insulating glass
$\frac{1}{4}''$ for all glass over $\frac{3}{16}''$ in thickness and for 1" insulating glass

Minimum edge "bite": $\frac{1}{4}''$ for glass $\frac{1}{8}''$ or less in thickness
$\frac{3}{8}''$ for $\frac{3}{16}''$ glass, $\frac{7}{32}''$ glass and $\frac{1}{2}''$ insulating glass
$\frac{1}{2}''$ for all glass $\frac{1}{4}''$ or more in thickness, and for 1" insulating glass

NEW FHA REQUIREMENTS FOR GLASS *

Increasing use of large areas of glass in residential construction, including high-rise apartments, has prompted the FHA to revise its Minimum Property Standards pertaining to glass.

Principal modifications to the standards involve maximum permissible glass areas for various thicknesses based on three wind zones (see map). These specified areas are based on safety considering wind pressure alone. Impact and operational uses were not considered in the calculations.

Another portion of the revised glass standards requires some form of safety glass in all exterior doors where glass areas are large and visual barriers are nonexistent or ineffectual. At present the standards limit this requirement only to the door glass itself, and not to glass in fixed windows.

The safety glass must be either tempered glass, laminated glass or wired glass. Tempered and laminated glass must be permanently labeled in the lower corner where it will be visible when installed.

Maximum areas of panes of glass in windows and doors, including storm windows and doors, must not exceed the values listed in Table 6. Applicable wind zones may be determined by reference to the map. Insulating glass may exceed by not more than 50 per cent the tabular values for single glass of the same thickness.

Glass used in doors is subject to the following additional requirements:

1. For "single strength" glass the short dimension must not exceed 15 in.

2. For exterior doors, including sliding doors, where glass panes larger than 6 sq ft in area are less than 18 in. from the floor, the glass must be at least $\frac{7}{32}$ in. thick, and horizontal muntins or bars must be provided on the exterior and interior at a height of not more than 36 in. above the floor, or "safety glass" must be used.

3. For shower doors and enclosures of either stall or tub type, "safety glass" must be used.

"Safety glass" as required above may be any of the following:

1. *Fully tempered glass:* When tested by fracturing, no individual piece can exceed 0.15 oz. Minimum thickness is $\frac{3}{16}$ in. Maximum size may exceed the values shown in the table by not more than 50 per cent.

2. *Laminated glass* must conform with

impact tests Nos. 9 and 12 of ASA Z26.1. Minimum thickness is ¼ in. and maximum size is 60 per cent of the values listed in the table.

3. *Wire glass* must conform with impact test No. 11 of ASA Z26.1. Minimum thickness is ¼ in. and maximum area is 50 per cent of values shown in Table 6.

Table 6. Maximum glass area in square feet [1, 2, 3]

Wind Zone	Nominal Glass Thickness (inches)									
	S.S.	1/8	D.S.	3/16	13/64	7/32	1/4	5/16	3/8	1/2
Low 60–80 mph	10.7	16.1	19.5	40.0	48.0	60.0	75.0	90.0	120.0	160.0
Medium 80–90 mph	7.3	11.0	13.2	27.0	32.0	41.0	51.0	62.0	79.0	113.0
High 90–120 mph	4.8	7.2	8.7	18.0	21.0	27.0	34.0	41.0	52.0	73.0

1. Areas in table apply to regular plate or sheet glass only, and do not apply to special types of glass.

2. Areas apply only when glass is not more than 30 ft above grade. Above 30 ft reduce maximum glass areas as follows:

> For 31 to 40 ft reduce area to 93 per cent of table
> For 41 to 60 ft reduce area to 86 per cent of table
> For 61 to 100 ft reduce area to 71 per cent of table
> For 101 to 150 ft reduce area to 63 per cent of table
> For 151 to 200 ft reduce area to 58 per cent of table
> For 201 to 300 ft reduce area to 52 per cent of table

3. Areas are calculated on a length to width ratio of 1 to 2 or less. Maximum glass areas may be increased in accordance with the following:

> From 1-2 to 1-3 ratio—add 20 per cent to area in table
> From 1-3 to 1-4 ratio—add 50 per cent to area in table
> From 1-4 to 1-5 ratio—add 100 per cent to area in table

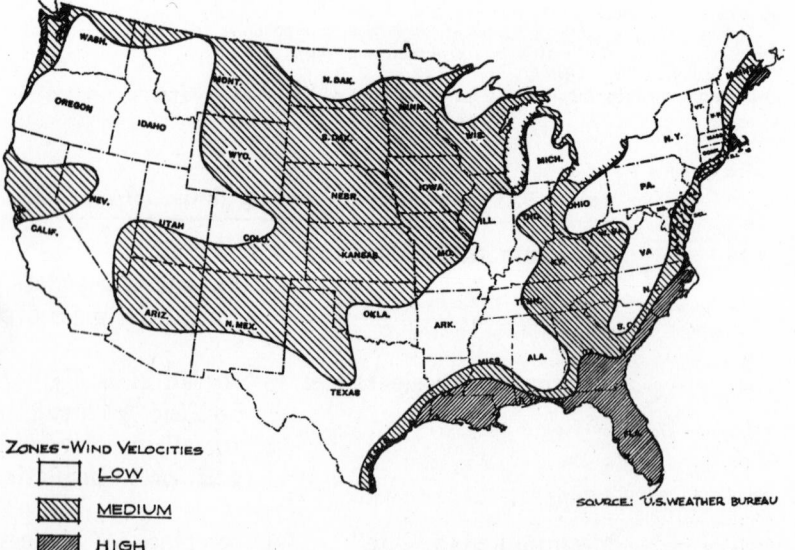

ZONES-WIND VELOCITIES
- LOW
- MEDIUM
- HIGH

SOURCE: U.S. WEATHER BUREAU

---

* *Interim Revision No. 13a to Minimum Property Standards, Federal Housing Administration. Effective April 1, 1963.*

STORAGE OF GLASS ON THE SITE

Glass delivered to the site should be stored in a safe dry location and not unpacked until needed for installation. Although glass is an impervious and weatherproof material, it may be permanently stained if stored under adverse moisture conditions.

GLAZING MATERIALS

Wood Sash Putty

Wood sash putty is generally a mixture of pigment and linseed oil. Application of a suitable primer, such as priming paints or boiled linseed oil, to wood sash before applying putty is a necessary practice. Putty should not be painted until it is thoroughly set. All putty should be painted for proper protection.

Metal Sash Putty

Metal sash putty differs from wood sash putty in that it is formulated to adhere to a nonporous surface. It is used for the glazing of aluminum or steel sash, either inside or outside. Metal sash putty should be painted within two weeks after application, but should be thoroughly set and hard before painting commences.

Elastic Glazing Compound

These compounds differ from wood and metal sash putties both in composition and performance. They are used for either inside or outside glazing, and should surface dry but remain slightly soft and plastic underneath for considerable periods of time. This soft or plastic condition is desirable where windows or doors are subject to twisting or vibration. The glazing compound does not have to be painted but may be, if desired. Certain compounds are available in a range of colors.

Polybutene Tape

This material is a nondrying mastic which is available in extruded ribbon shapes of varying widths and thicknesses. The tape remains plastic or resilient over extremely long periods of time. It possesses great adhesion qualities. It should not be used as a substitute or replacement for spacers. This tape must be pressure applied for proper adhesion.

Polysulfide Elastomer Sealing Compound

This material is a two-part synthetic rubber based on a polysulfide polymer. Its consistency after mixing is similar to a caulking compound. The mixed compound is applied by either caulking gun or spatula. It is well suited to many applications in modern curtain wall construction. Good

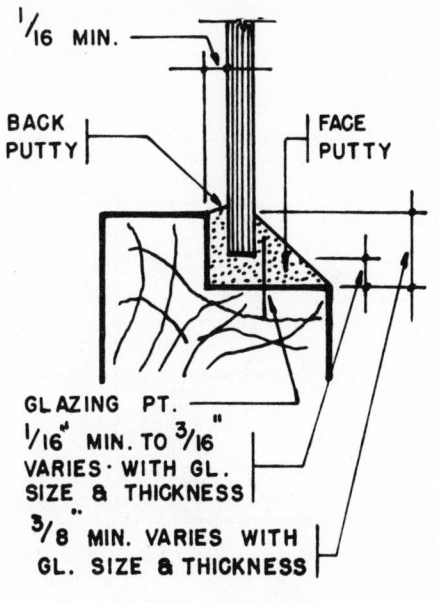

Fig. 1. Wood sash, face glazing

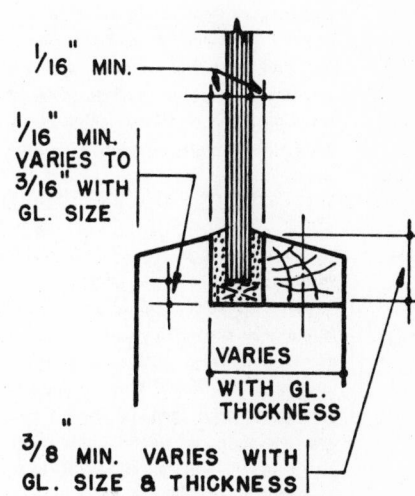

Fig. 2. Wood sash with glazing bead

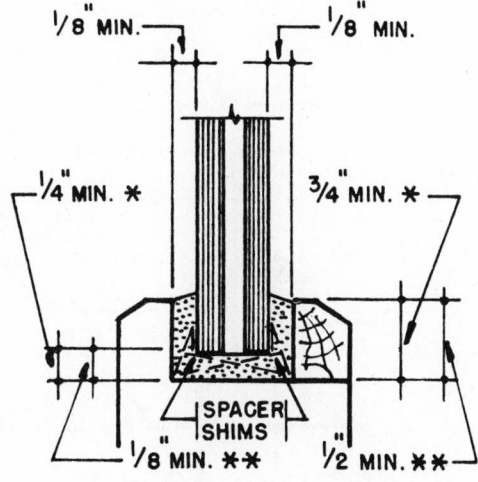

✱ UNITS USING 3/16" & 1/4" GLASS

✱✱ UNITS USING 1/8" GLASS

Fig. 3. Wood sash with glazing bead, insulating glass

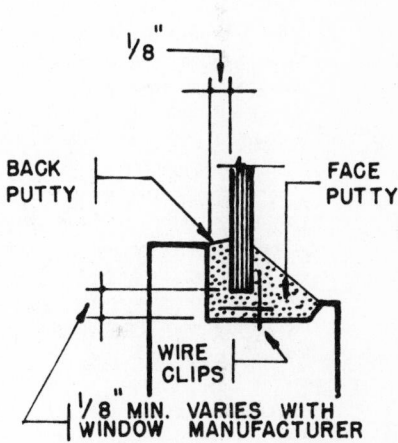

Fig. 4. Metal sash, face glazing

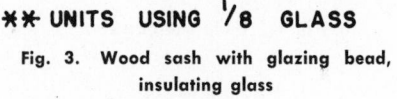
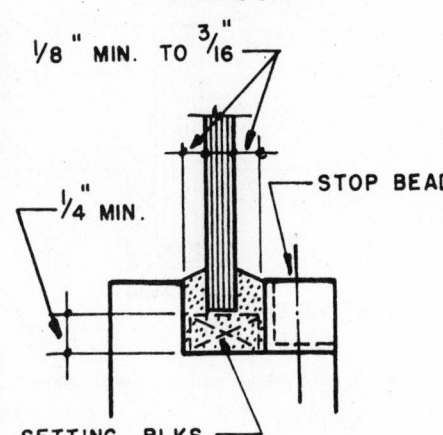

Fig. 5. Metal sash and bead, heat-absorbing or glare-reducing glass

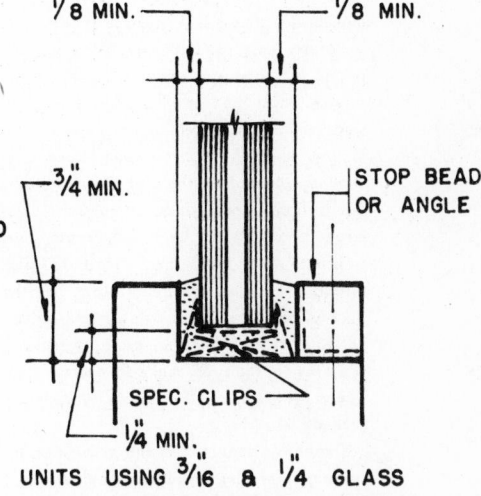

UNITS USING 3/16" & 1/4" GLASS

Fig. 6. Metal sash and bead, insulating glass

performance requires that the sealing surfaces be extremely clean. Excess and spilled material must be removed and surfaces cleaned during the working time of the material as it is almost impossible to remove with solvents when set.

Compression Material: Neoprene: Vinyl: Rubber

This material is extruded or molded in various shapes; channel, angle, etc. It may be used as a continuous gasket or intermittently as spacer shims. The varying thicknesses and cross sections are dependent upon the particular type of glazing or glazing material combinations. To establish and maintain a weathertight joint, the gasket must be compressed not less than 15 per cent, assuming no flow or adhesion (see also data on sealing materials in "Curtain Walls").

SASH PREPARATION

Remove all rivet, screw, bolt, or nail heads, welding fillets and other projections from specified clearances in glazing rabbet.

Seal all sash corners and fabrication intersections to make sash weathertight. Weep rabbet outdoors at sill.

Prime paint all sealing surfaces of wood sash and of carbon steel sash. Use appropriate solvents to remove greases, lacquers, and other organic protective finishes from sealing surfaces of aluminum sash. All sealing surfaces must be clean, dry, and dust free before glazing begins.

GLAZING PRACTICE

Glazing should not be done at a temperature below 40°F. At such temperatures condensation is very likely to cause a film of moisture, which may be invisible, to be deposited on the sealing surfaces. Trapped moisture is almost sure to cause seal failure.

Before the glass is placed, bedding compound or tape and setting blocks, if required, must be installed in the rabbet. Care should be taken to center the glass in the opening and between stops. The *Glazing Manual* of the Flat Glass Jobbers Association recommends: "Maintain centered position and sealer thickness, and transmit wind loads from glass to sash through the use of setting blocks at the sill and centering shims indoors and out on all four sides *whenever glass dimensions are larger than 50 united inches*" (i.e., when the sum of the length and width exceeds 50 inches).

Generally neoprene is the recommended material for both purposes, and it is readily available in a number of bar, ribbon and channel shapes designed for the

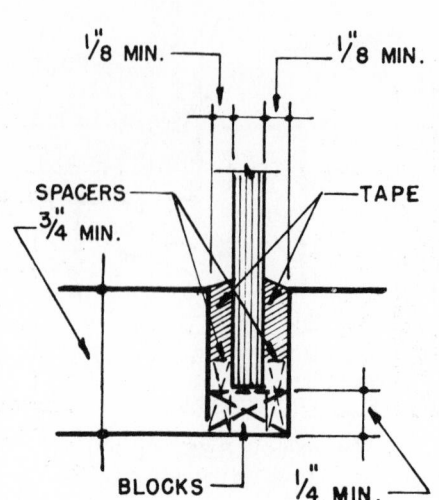

Fig. 7.   Tape seal

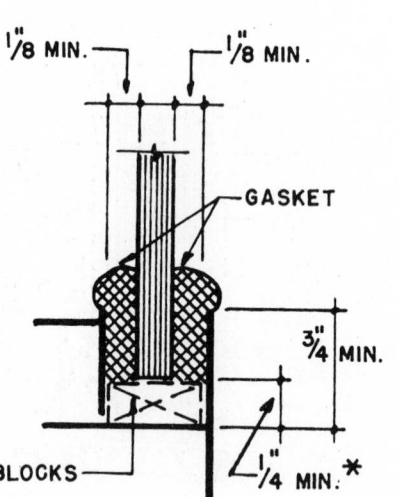

✶ ⁵⁄₁₆" MIN.   FOR ALUMINUM

Fig. 8.   Neoprene gasket

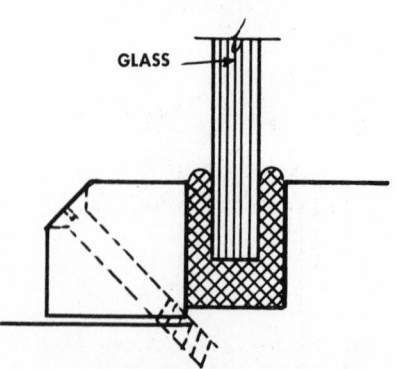

Fig. 9.   Neoprene gasket, compression bead

Fig. 12.   Multiple seal—polysulfide and glazing compound

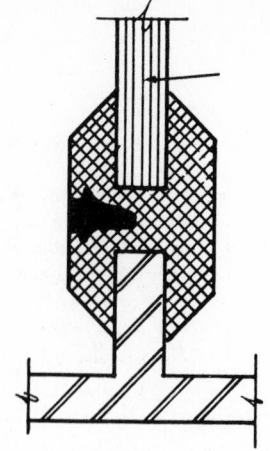

Fig. 10.   Neoprene structural gasket, with "zipper"

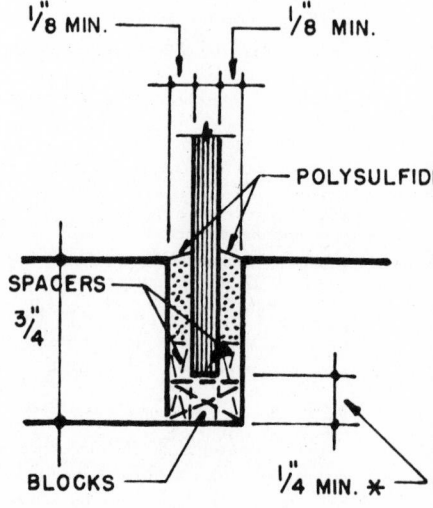

⁵⁄₁₆" MIN.   FOR ALUMINUM

Fig. 11.   Polysulfide seal

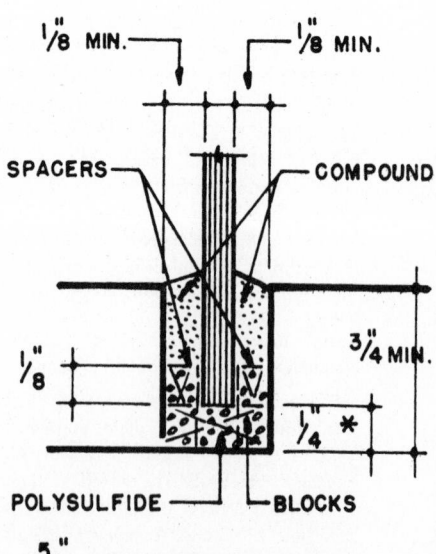

✶ ⁵⁄₁₆" MIN.   FOR ALUMINUM

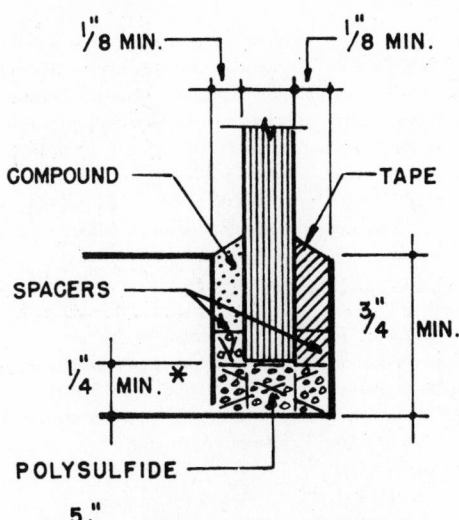

Fig. 13. Multiple seal—polysulfide, tape, and compound

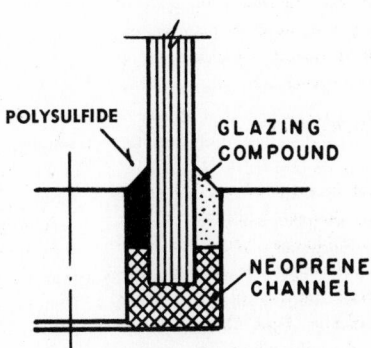

Fig. 14. Multiple seal—polysulfide, neo-preme, and compound

purpose. Eighty-durometer stock is recommended for the rectangular setting blocks, 50-durometer stock for channel-shaped blocks and shim strips.

The glass should be firmly and evenly pressed against the bedding compound or tape. If glazing beads or stops are not used the glass must be secured by means of glazing points or metal clips, which should be noncorrosive. Care should be taken to ensure that neither clips nor beads exert an unequal pressure against the glass.

For heat-absorbing and glare-reducing glass, it is advisable to provide larger glazing clearances and to limit excessive edge cover which produces "cold edge" effects and may result in cracking because the shielded edge remains cold after the exposed area of the glass has been warmed by sunshine.

Clean-cut edges are required to avoid edge stress concentration and the resulting breakage which may be expected to begin where edge flaws occur. For this reason, "nipping" the edge of a light of heat-absorbing glass must be avoided.

For insulating glass, use full bed of glazing compound in edge clearance on bottom of sash, enough at sides and top to make weathertight seal. It is most important that the metal channel at the perimeter of each unit be covered by at least ⅛ in. of compound in order to insure a lasting seal.

Note: Much of the data in this section has been taken, with permission, from the *Metal Curtain Wall Manual*, 1960, published by the National Association of Architectural Metal Manufacturers, and the *Glazing Manual*, 1958, published by the Flat Glass Jobbers Association.

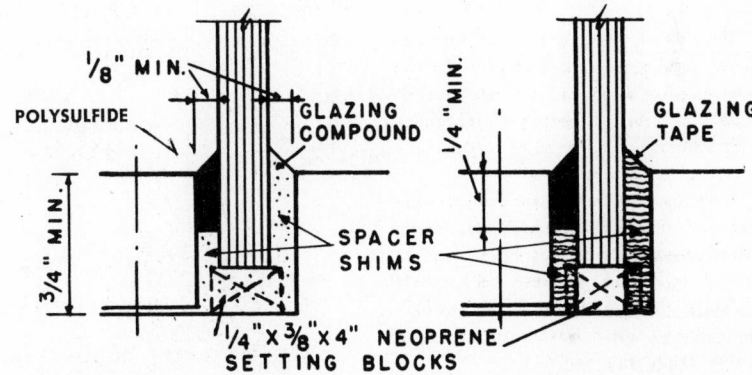

Fig. 15. Multiple seal—polysulfide and compound

Fig. 16. Multiple seal—polysulfide and tape

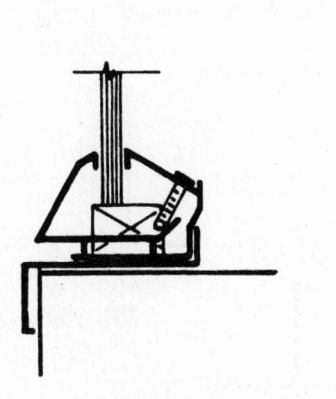

Fig. 17. Store front glazing—metal to glass

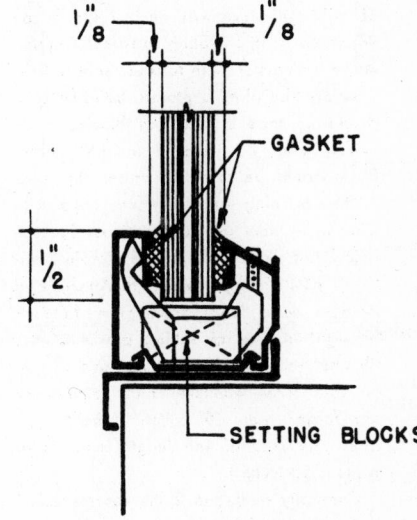

Fig. 18. Store front glazing—with gasket

Structural glass veneer

By HOWARD P. VERMILYA, AIA

Structural glass is made by the same process as plate glass but with metallic oxides blended into the batch to give it opacity and color. Since it is impervious to grease, grime, moisture, chemicals and pencil marks; will not absorb odors; and is easily cleaned, it is obvious that it would find its use in kitchens, toilets and hospital operating rooms. Its large size (77x130 in. maximum stock) permits its use in many cases without intermediate joints. Aside from its strictly functional qualities, its color and texture, which may be highly polished, smooth suede, or rough, justify its use for purely decorative purposes on either interior or exterior walls and partitions, and for built-in fixtures such as counters and shelves.

As a wall surfacing unit, applied with either mastic adhesives of high tensile strength to a solid backing material (not wood) or with mechanical fasteners, angles or brackets, it is usually used in the $\frac{11}{32}$ in. or $\frac{7}{16}$ in. thicknesses although it is available also in ¾ in. As a partition or freestanding material (polished both sides) it is available in ⅞ in. and 1¼ in. thicknesses.

Cutting, grinding edges, and drilling of structural glass are factory processes so that sizes within the maximum production limitations are largely dictated by design criteria. It may be tempered or semitempered for extra strength; this is strongly recommended for the darker colors when

used on exteriors. On exteriors where expansion and contraction of differing materials must be considered, sizes are limited, above 15 ft from sidewalk level, to 6 sq ft, and below that to 10 sq ft, with a maximum length of 4 ft.

While usually used as flat-, square- or rectangular-shaped plates, structural glass may be bent to order to conform to a curved wall, or it may be cut in circular or free-form shapes. It may be sand carved for decoration or for use as a sign. The joints may be emphasized or minimized by the width and color of the pointing compound, using either a matching or complementary scheme.

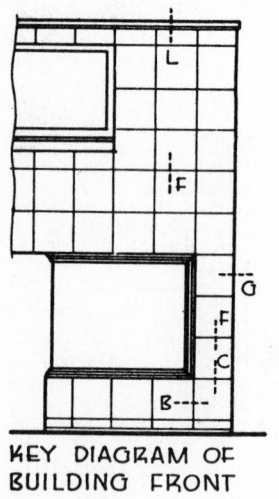

KEY DIAGRAM OF
BUILDING FRONT

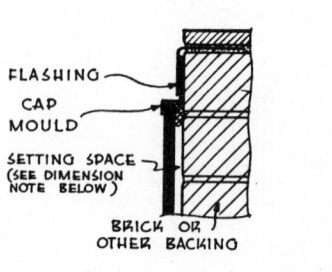

FLASHING
CAP MOULD
SETTING SPACE
(SEE DIMENSION NOTE BELOW)
BRICK OR OTHER BACKING

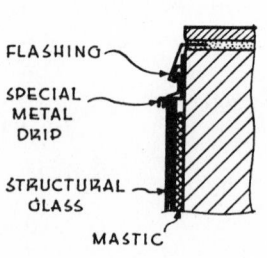

FLASHING
SPECIAL METAL DRIP
STRUCTURAL GLASS
MASTIC

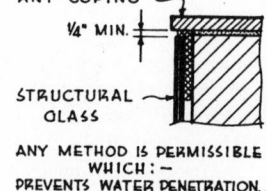

ANY COPING
¼" MIN.
STRUCTURAL GLASS

ANY METHOD IS PERMISSIBLE WHICH:—PREVENTS WATER PENETRATION, HELPS SECURE THE STRUCTURAL GLASS AND PERMITS EXPANSION.

DETAILS AT "L"
COPINGS

SCALE OF ALL DETAILS APPROXIMATELY 1½"=1'-0"

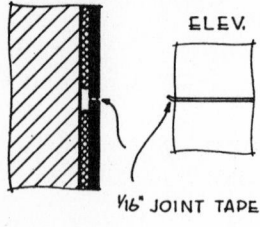

ELEV.
1/16" JOINT TAPE

DETAIL AT "C"

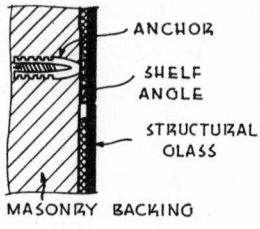

ANCHOR
SHELF ANGLE
STRUCTURAL GLASS
MASONRY BACKING

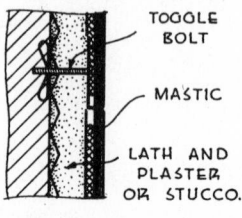

TOGGLE BOLT
MASTIC
LATH AND PLASTER OR STUCCO.

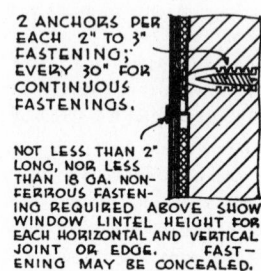

2 ANCHORS PER EACH 2" TO 3" FASTENING; EVERY 30" FOR CONTINUOUS FASTENINGS.

NOT LESS THAN 2" LONG, NOR LESS THAN 18 GA. NON-FERROUS FASTENING REQUIRED ABOVE SHOW WINDOW LINTEL HEIGHT FOR EACH HORIZONTAL AND VERTICAL JOINT OR EDGE. FASTENING MAY BE CONCEALED.

ALTERNATE DETAILS AT "F"
HORIZONTAL JOINTS

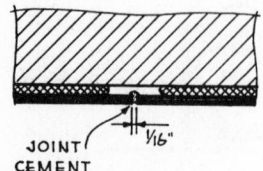

JOINT CEMENT
1/16"

DETAIL AT "B"
VERTICAL JOINTS

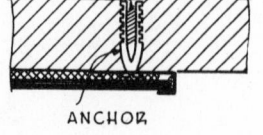

ANCHOR

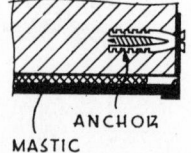

ANCHOR
MASTIC

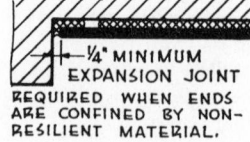

¼" MINIMUM EXPANSION JOINT REQUIRED WHEN ENDS ARE CONFINED BY NON-RESILIENT MATERIAL.

DETAILS AT "G"
TERMINATIONS

USEFUL DIMENSIONS	STRUCTURAL GLASS THICKNESSES OF $\frac{11}{32}$", $\frac{7}{16}$" AND ¾" REQUIRE ¾", ⅞" AND 1⅛" RESPECTIVELY FROM FINISH FACE TO ROUGH.

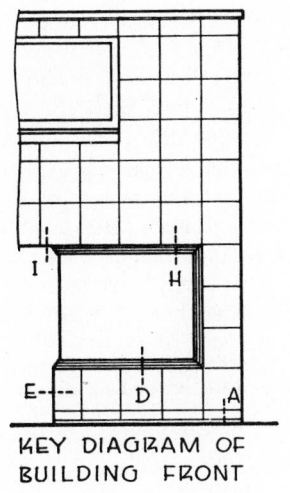

KEY DIAGRAM OF
BUILDING FRONT

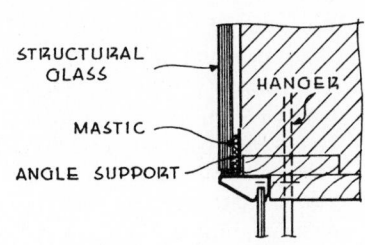

STRUCTURAL GLASS

MASTIC

ANGLE SUPPORT

HANGER

DETAIL AT "H"

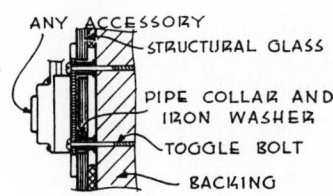

ANY ACCESSORY

STRUCTURAL GLASS

PIPE COLLAR AND
IRON WASHER

TOGGLE BOLT

BACKING

SIGNS OR
ACCESSORIES

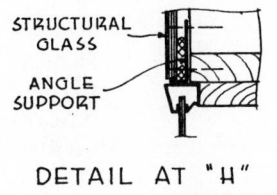

STRUCTURAL
GLASS

ANGLE
SUPPORT

DETAIL AT "H"
SHOW WINDOW HEADS

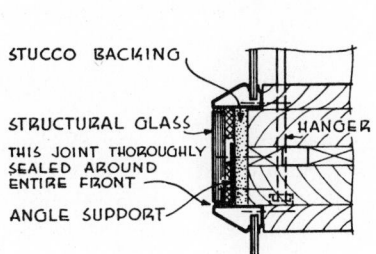

STUCCO BACKING

STRUCTURAL GLASS

THIS JOINT THOROUGHLY
SEALED AROUND
ENTIRE FRONT

ANGLE SUPPORT

HANGER

DETAIL AT MULLION

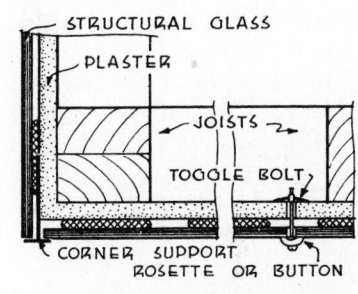

STRUCTURAL GLASS

PLASTER

JOISTS

TOGGLE BOLT

CORNER SUPPORT

ROSETTE OR BUTTON

DETAIL AT "I"
VESTIBULE CEILING

SCALE OF ALL DETAILS APPROXIMATELY 1½" = 1'-0"

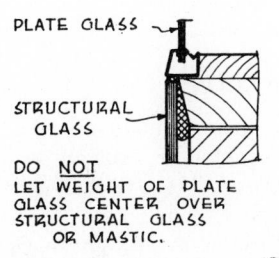

PLATE GLASS

STRUCTURAL
GLASS

DO NOT
LET WEIGHT OF PLATE
GLASS CENTER OVER
STRUCTURAL GLASS
OR MASTIC.

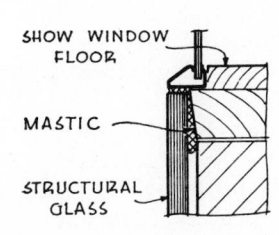

SHOW WINDOW
FLOOR

MASTIC

STRUCTURAL
GLASS

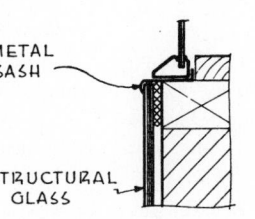

METAL
SASH

STRUCTURAL
GLASS

DETAILS AT "D"
SHOW WINDOW SILLS

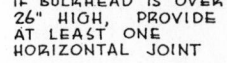

20"
26"
20"

IF BULKHEAD IS OVER
26" HIGH, PROVIDE
AT LEAST ONE
HORIZONTAL JOINT

ELEVATION AT "E"

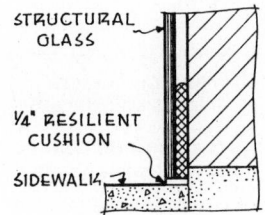

STRUCTURAL
GLASS

¼" RESILIENT
CUSHION

SIDEWALK

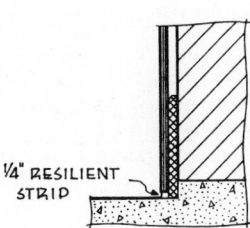

¼" RESILIENT
STRIP

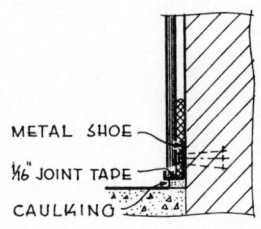

METAL SHOE

1/16" JOINT TAPE

CAULKING

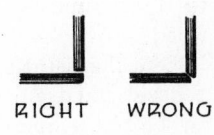

RIGHT   WRONG

MITRES ARE PERMITTED
ONLY FOR VERY
WIDE (ALMOST 180°)
ANGLES

DETAILS "A" AT SIDEWALK LEVEL

PLASTICS—1
Characteristics

By WILLIAM DEMAREST, *Director, Plastics in Building, Manufacturing Chemists' Association, Inc.*

CHARACTERISTICS

Although our laboratories are synthesizing more and more materials that do not occur in nature, this is not a random process and the plastics—so far, the greatest group devised by man—constitute a recognizable class of materials, analogous to the woods or the metals.

Chemists describe this group as organic "polymers" and can explain why similarities in the structure of plastics' molecules give rise to many similarities in engineering properties. Fairly safe generalizations can be made about the physical characteristics of these materials, just as with metals and other materials. Further, it is useful to recognize the basic division among plastics, which is reflected in their engineering properties. Not unlike the distinctions between "non-ferrous" and "ferrous," or "hardwoods" and "softwoods," the two major divisions into one of which all the plastics must fall are:

The Thermoplastics, which become soft when exposed to sufficient heat and harden when cooled, no matter how often the process is repeated. Although some need more heat than others, softening with heat is their distinguishing characteristic, very much like the behavior of candle wax.

The Thermosets, which are set into permanent shape when heated during forming. Reheating will not soften them (any more than it would the white of an egg), and the only change that can be brought about by increasing heat is actual chemical decomposition—analogous to the charring and burning of wood.

Ten characteristics of plastics in general have an important bearing on building applications. They are exhibited in varying degree, often being especially marked in one or the other of the two basic subclasses—thermoplastic and thermosetting plastics.

1. *Excellent electrical-insulating properties,* in terms both of resistivity and dielectric strength. There are also other good electrical properties which are important in specific applications that are of more significance in electrical engineering than in building.

2. *Good corrosion resistance.* At least one plastic material can be found to resist practically any corrosive condition found in building. Many instances can be cited—in industrial piping, for example—where plastics have far out-performed costlier metals, such as copper or stainless steel, under corrosive conditions.

3. *Creep.* Some plastics, especially the thermosets, are essentially elastic within certain limits of stress: deformation in proportion to the load applied which disappears quickly when the load is released. Others, especially the thermoplastics, exhibit plastic behavior: they flow, or "creep," when stressed, depending not only on the load, but also on the rate at which it is applied and its duration, and increasing with increases in temperature. This characteristic is comparable to that of steel or other metals when stressed, perhaps at high temperatures, beyond the elastic limit. When the load is removed, the material may eventually recover part of the deformation, or all of it.

4. *Low tensile strength* is generally characteristic of unreinforced plastics, although in laminated or reinforced form, plastics can compare quite favorably with metals.

5. *Low modulus of elasticity* is also characteristic, but glass-fiber-reinforced thermosetting plastics offer roughly the same range of stiffness as wood or concrete.

6. *Low maximum service temperatures.* In contrast with a number of structural building materials in common use, plastics in general are best used at temperatures below the wood-char point of 380-400 deg F. This is only an approximate statement, due to the varied conditions of actual use and to differing combinations of temperature-affected properties that may be relevant: tensile strength, creep, chemical stability, and the like.

7. *High thermal coefficient of expansion.* Plastics typically expand, per unit of temperature increase, several times as much as metals. Thermoplastics, as a group, have a higher coefficient than thermosets.

8. *Flammability.* In the sense that they can be destroyed by fire, plastics can be grouped with all other organic materials. However, a number of them—including certain thermoplastics—will extinguish themselves once the igniting flame has been removed.

9. *Low thermal conductivity.* Typical "k-value" for the plastics in common use is about 1.5, or slightly higher than wood. As low-density foams, plastics provide some of the most efficient thermal insulators available for building; a 2 lb per cu ft polystyrene foam, for example, might offer a "k" of 0.25.

10. *Light weight,* per unit volume. Unmodified with fillers, reinforcements, or other additives, the more common of these materials range from a specific gravity of just under 0.9 (polypropylene) to roughly 1.5 polyvinyl chloride, PVC. Strength-to-weight ratios thus compare favorably with those of other materials.

TERMINOLOGY

A certain amount of chemical-industry terminology cannot be avoided in discussing plastics. A few of the following terms are included because their meanings in this context are somewhat more precise than in common parlance.

COLD FLOW:
Creep occurring at room temperature.

COPOLYMER:
A substance consisting of long-chain molecules formed from two or more different monomers.

CREEP:
The change in dimension of a plastic under load over a period of time. Does not include the initial instantaneous elastic deformation.

CROSS-LINKING:
The chemical union of polymer molecules to form a three-dimensional network. Cross-linked polymers are usually infusible thermosets.

Tensile strength of plastics is comparable to wood and concrete, but increases to the range of metal alloys when reinforced or laminated with other materials or when drawn into fine filaments. Although plastics are inherently low in stiffness, when reinforced they range higher even than wood and concrete. Forming into structural shapes also increases stiffness. Thermal conductivity is about as low as wood, making plastics excellent insulators. Although most plastics are damaged above about 200 deg F, many do not support their own combustion or burn with difficulty

Note: Charts are reproduced from "Physical and Engineering Properties of Plastics" by Albert G. H. Dietz, a paper delivered at the 1954 conference on plastics held by the Building Research Institute and published in the conference report "Plastics in Building."

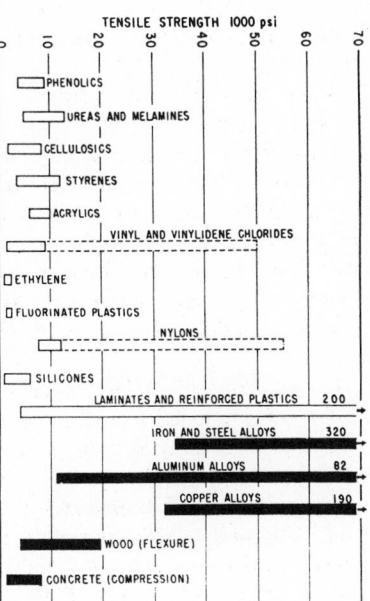

Fig. 1. Tensile Strength of Plastics and Other Materials at 1000 psi

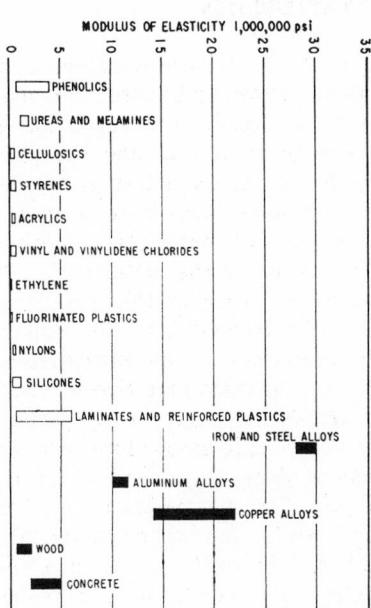

Fig. 2. Modulus of Elasticity of Plastics and Various Other Materials at 1,000,000 psi

CURE:
Changing physical properties of a material by chemical reaction—usually to a harder or more permanent form.

DEFLECTION TEMPERATURE:
Degrees Fahrenheit at which a plastic material under fixed stress distorts as temperature increases, according to standard ASTM test procedure. (D 648-56).

DEGRADATION:
Molecular change to the polymer, usually from exposure to light, fire, or heat, becoming apparent as charring, discoloration, clouding of transparent plastics, embrittlement, or other loss of original properties.

DISPERSION:
A liquid with finely-divided insoluble particles scattered uniformly throughout. Called a "colloid" if particles are fine enough. "Dispersion" and "suspension" contrast with a "solution."

ELASTOMER:
A material which at room temperature can be stretched repeatedly to at least twice its original length and, upon release of the stress, will return instantly and with force to its approximate original length.

EXOTHERMIC:
Adjective indicating a chemical reaction that gives off heat.

FILM:
Sheeting of nominal thickness not greater than 10 mils.

FLASH:
Extra plastic attached to a molding along the parting line. It must be removed before the piece can be considered finished.

HIGH-PRESSURE LAMINATES:
Laminates molded and cured at pressures not lower than 1000 psi, (commonly 1200-2000 psi).

INHIBITOR:
A substance that slows down chemical reaction—often used to prolong "shelf" or storage life.

LATEX:
A suspension in water of fine particles of rubber, (which today includes synthetic rubber).

LINEAR:
Adjective to describe a long-chain molecule with a minimum of side-chains or branches.

LOW-PRESSURE LAMINATES:
In general, laminates molded and cured in the range of pressures from 400 psi down to and including

pressures obtained by the mere contact of the plies.

MONOFILAMENT:
A continuous thread made up of only one filament.

MONOMER:
A substance constituted of a simple molecule, of relatively low molecular weight, that is capable of reacting with like molecules to form long-molecular-chain "polymers" (or, with both like and unlike molecules, to form "copolymers").

ORGANIC:
Adjective to distinguish those compounds, like plant and animal matter, which contain the very prevalent carbon atom. "Inorganic" compounds are those that do not contain carbon.

PLASTICIZER:
Materials added to a plastic to improve flexibility or to facilitate compounding.

POLYMER:
A substance consisting of long-chain molecules formed by the union of many small molecules that are alike. (See "monomer.")

POLYMERIZATION:
The process by which polymers and copolymers are formed.

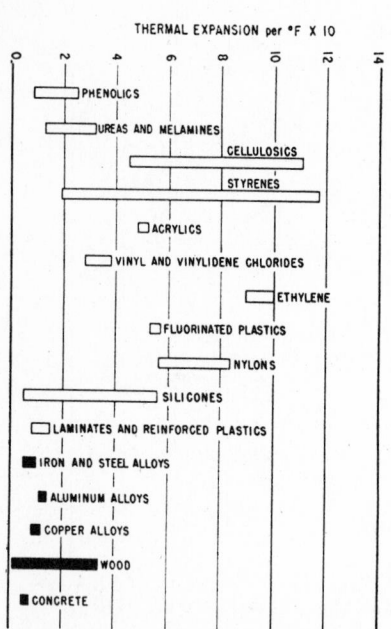

Fig. 3. Thermal Expansion of Plastics and Various Other Materials

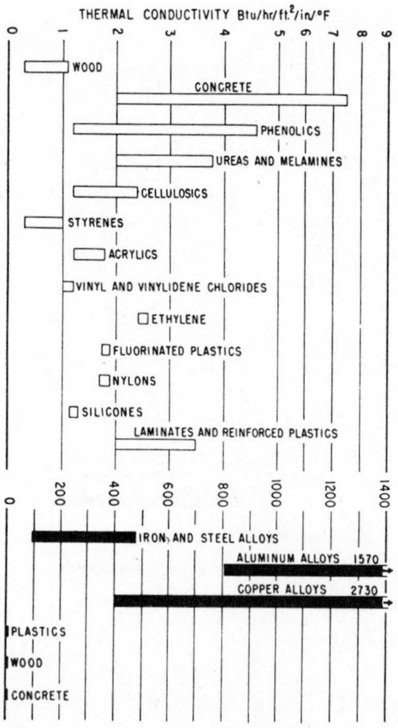

Fig. 4. Thermal Conductivity of Plastics and Other Materials

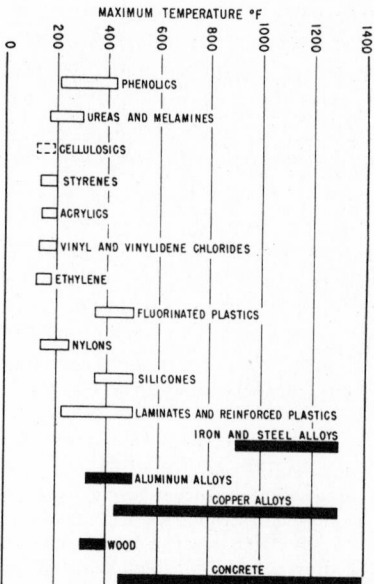

Fig. 5. Approximate Temperature Limits for Plastics Compared with Other Materials

POSTFORMING:
Bending phenolic laminates or certain other thermosetting sheet materials into simple (substantially permanent) shapes by heat and pressure after initial cure.

RESIN (SYNTHETIC):
Polymeric synthetic products having some of the characteristics of natural resins. Some serve as base ingredients of plastics; others are important ingredients of finishes, adhesives, etc.

RESORCINOL:
Generic noun for a group of synthetic polymers, much like the phenolics, that are chiefly used as heat and water resistant adhesive.

ROVING:
A form of fibrous glass in which spun strands are woven into a tubular rope.

SUSPENSION:
A liquid with small, solid particles dispersed more or less uniformly throughout.

THERMOPLASTIC:
Term identifying that category of plastics which soften whenever heated sufficiently.

THERMOSET AND THERMOSETTING:
Terms identifying the other category of plastics, which undergo a chemical change and harden permanently when heated (in contradistinction to the thermoplastics).

THIXOTROPIC:
Said of materials that are gel-like at rest, but fluid when agitated (desirable in paints).

VACUUM FORMING:
Method of sheet forming in which the plastic sheet is clamped in a stationary frame, heated and drawn down by a vacuum into a mold.

VINYL:
Alone, this word has a precise meaning to chemists. But as used in building, it is a vague term for certain polymers or copolymers. It is safe to assume that "vinyl" means, in connection with latex paints, "polyvinyl acetate" or—anywhere else in building—"polyvinyl chloride" (PVC), or a preponderantly-PVC copolymer.

PRINCIPAL TYPES OF PLASTICS
Thermoplastics
ABS PLASTICS:
Compounds of acrylonitrile, buta-

diene, and styrene. Important characteristics are toughness, chemical resistance, and non-brittleness at low temperatures.

ACETATE:
See "Cellulosics."

ACRYLICS:
Popularly known trade names are "Lucite" or "Plexiglas"; chemical name, "polymethyl methacrylate." These materials combine the transparency of glass with plastics' shatterproof quality. Their weathering performance has been better than other common plastics and is being constantly improved.

BUTYRATE:
See "Cellulosics."

CELLULOSICS:
(Primarily cellulose acetate or butyrate.) Also transparent, "acetate" is well known as photographic safety-film. These plastics are amazingly tough—one common use is tool handles.

FLUOROCARBONS:
A group of extremely inert plastics. As resins, dispersions, oils, greases, and waxes, they have high thermal stability and excellent resist-

nce to chemical attack.

METHYL MECHACRYLATE:
See "Acrylics."

NYLON:
Molded-nylon products have qualities as spectacular as those of the longer known nylon fabrics. They are tough, have a low frictional coefficient, and they resist mechanical wear better than many metals. Nylon's high softening temperature is exemplified by its replacement of brass for mixing-valves in automatic washers.

POLYCARBONATE:
A new polymer offering outstanding impact strength, dimensional stability under varying humidity or temperature, and heat resistance.

POLYETHYLENE:
Waxy and chemically inert, flexible even at low termperatures, this material is one of the best known plastics. It is a water barrier and retards the passage of water vapor. The plain, colorless substance is short lived in sunlight, but carbon-black-pigmented polyethylene has a good weathering record. (A new, "linear" polyethylene with properties more desirable for certain applications, is now available.)

POLYPROPYLENE:
A thermoplastic material composed of polymers of propylene. The lightest of all commercial plastics, its properties are roughly comparable with those of linear polyethylene.

POLYSTYRENE:
Non-water-absorbent, it is found in colorful, but brittle, wall tiles. Copolymers of styrene with rubber can be very tough. Polystyrene is one of several plastics used in electric-lighting diffusers. In foamed form, it has become an important thermal insulation.

PVC (POLYVINYL CHLORIDE):
The resin itself is rigid; plasticizers add flexibility to excellent resistance to wear and abuse.

SARAN:
A cousin of PVC, chemically as well as in its properties. Unlike PVC,

which must be "stabilized" against degradation under ultraviolet light, Saran performs well outdoors without special formulation.

Thermosets

ALKYDS:
These appear chiefly as molded electrical parts. They are also important constituents of certain paints.

EPOXY:
Relatively new and still quite expensive, epoxy is already used in building because of its remarkable adhesive qualities and chemical resistance.

MELAMINE AND UREA:
Hard, durable, and dimensionally stable, these quite similar plastics are resistant to chemicals, electrical potential, and heat. This last property makes lower-priced urea useful for incandescent-light diffusion. With a wider color range, melamine is well known to the public in the form of molded dishes and laminates, such as counter tops.

PHENOLIC:
Familiar for years as Bakelite in the old, black telephone handsets, it is strong, durable, and both electrical- and heat-resistant. This low-cost "workhorse" plastic is limited to dark colors.

POLYESTER:
Appears in film form under trade names such as "Mylar" and "Videne." It has been known longer as the plastic most commonly used in large glass-fiber-reinforced translucent panels that are strong, rigid, and impact-resistant. Polyesters' resistance to abrasion can be poor, as can its ultraviolet-light resistance, but properties vary widely with differences in formulation.

SILICONES:
Being semi-inorganic substances, silicones might not be classified strictly as "plastics." In building, they are applied to masonry to improve its water-repellance and weatherability.

URETHANE, properly called polyurethane:
Newly developed thermosetting polymer, appearing as flexible and rigid

foams and coatings, also as adhesives and as elastomers.

APPLICATIONS
Solid finish surfacing*

FLOOR COVERING
Plastics typically employed—PVC; vinyl-asbestos.
Preferred because—Permanent color; chemical and wear resistance.
Remarks—Share some problems of all resilient floorings, such as shrinkage, selection of proper adhesives and indentation.

COUNTERTOPS
Plastics typically employed—Melamine on phenolic laminate; PVC or polyester laminated to hardboard or other substrate.
Preferred because—Ease of cleaning, no maintenance, withstand abuse and variety of colorful designs.
Remarks—Best heat resistance offered by decorative melamine-surfaced laminates; some are cigarette proof. But the others are more adaptable to complex shapes.

INTERIOR WALL SURFACING
Plastics typically employed—Polystyrene tile or boards; PVC, either in sheets (often fabric-backed) or impregnated in fabric; polyester, often factory- or field-applied to masonry.
Preferred because—Variety of colorful designs; easy maintenance; withstand abuse; do-it-yourself application of wall tiles.
Remarks—PVC provides top-quality wall coverings for such hard-use installations as hotels and institutions. Field-applied polyesters' uses include sanitary locations such as dairies and bakeries.

EXTERIOR WALL SURFACING
Plastics typically employed—Polyester (reinforced with glass fibers); acrylic, (often similarly reinforced); PVC.
Preferred because—Integral color; large-area units possible, with fewer joints than brick, shingles, etc.; lightweight; relatively easy to clean.
Remarks—None of these building materials have been in use long enough to establish weatherability comparisons; acrylics have stood

up thus far for more than 20 years. Architectural possibilities offered by added feature of translucency only beginning to be explored. These are organic materials and will burn.

GLAZING

Plastics typically employed—(see also translucent exterior wall surfacing, above), Acrylic; polyester; PVC; polyethylene.

Preferred because—Shatterproof; conducts only ¼ as fast as glass; because readily formed, offers self-flashing shapes such as single-unit skylights.

Remarks—Optically, not as good as the best glass, but decorative possibilities unlimited. Polyethylene uses temporary only, as during construction.

Water and vapor barriers

MEMBRANES, FLASHING, TAPES

Plastics typically employed—Polyethylene; PVC; Saran.

Preferred because—Flexible; sealable, thus offering waterproof sheeting of any size. Sufficient elasticity can be formulated to accommodate building's movements, also to seal around penetrating nails, pipes, etc.

Remarks—Plastic foams employed as thermal insulation often double as vapor barriers; so can plastic films applied to sheets such as plywood. With flashing and tapes, it must be kept in mind that some plastics are formulated only for placement within the construction, not for exposure to ultra-violet and weather.

WEATHERSTRIPPING, WATERSTOPS

Plastics typically employed—PVC; polyurethane.

Preferred because—Can be formulated for elasticity approaching that of synthetic rubbers, which are also common in these applications. No corrosion; no staining. Thermoplastics, such as PVC, readily joined at mitered corners by "welding," or thermal-pressure-joinery.

Remarks—Such flexible materials, in extruded form, offer ideal waterstop-expansion-joint between adjacent pours of concrete slab or wall. Another class of synthetics somewhat related to plastics are also important in building as water-barriers: "elastomers" (i.e. rubbery ma-

terials) such as neoprene gaskets and sheeting, polysulfide and butadiene sealants, silicone polymers, synthetic-rubber roof coatings, and the like.

Thermal insulation

Plastics typically employed—Polystyrene, polyurethane (foams).

Preferred because—Insulating properties not reduced by wetting; density readily controlled; special properties possible: adhesiveness, vapor barrier, some structural strength, decorative translucence.

Remarks—Where desirable to fill voids, may be foamed-in-place. Although these foams burn when held in a flame, they usually are self-extinguishing.

Structural elements

Plastics typically employed—Polyester or epoxy, reinforced with glass fibers; rigid PVC.

Preferred because—Make possible high strength-to-weight ratios.

Remarks—Plastics have been used in sandwich panels for faces, adhesives and cores. Phenolic impregnated kraft honeycomb is probably the most used core material. More recently polystyrene and polyurethane foams have come into use. So far plastics have been little used structurally for load-bearing panels sandwich.

Finish hardware

Plastics typically employed—Almost all the thermoplastics listed here and most of the thermosets.

Preferred because—Good decorative characteristics; minimal maintenance; inexpensive even when intricately shaped. Certain properties often determine specific applications; for instance, nylon's superb wear-resistance has introduced it into door hardware.

Remarks—Plastic or plastic-coated insect screening popular because non-corroding. Plastic drawers now as commonplace as plastic chairs. Plastics safer than glass or ceramic for knobs and handles, towel bars, etc.

Electrical components

Plastics typically employed—All.

Preferred because—Superior electrical properties, especially under adverse conditions such as pro-

longed dampness, vibration, etc. Translucency the basis for widespread use as electric-light diffusers, including "luminous ceilings."

Remarks—First major commercial area for plastics (in the 1920's) was electrical applications; this continues to broaden with the increase of electrical and electronic complexity in buildings.

Plumbing

Plastics typically employed—For fixtures and fittings, reinforced polyester, rigid PVC, ABS; for piping, polyethylene, PVC, and various butadiene blends akin to ABS.

Preferred because—No corrosion. Easy to handle, to assemble. Fewer joints; easy maintenance.

Remarks—At present only higher-priced plastic pipes will handle hot liquids under pressure; therefore plastic pipe is generally limited to industrial uses. But lower-priced plastics to do this are just around the corner and may revolutionize residential plumbing.

Miscellaneous construction aids

Translucent polyethylene film provides an ideal temporary enclosure for wintertime construction. The same material is widely used as an inexpensive tarpaulin to protect equipment or materials stored on site. A top-quality, very durable tarpaulin is PVC-coated nylon fabric. Plastic chairs to support reinforcing rods in concrete make good use of the non-corrosive properties of plastics. Various plastic coatings for concrete forms produce smoother concrete, prolong the life of the forms, and make their removal easier. Strippable plastic coatings are used to protect plumbing fixtures and finished metal surfaces during construction.

The synthetic resins upon which most paints are based today are closely identified with the plastics discussed here; so, too, are a number of adhesives and binders that are important in building: phenolic adhesives for exterior-grade plywood, phenolic binders for glass-fiber insulating batts and boards, urea particle-board binders, resorcinol or epoxy adhesives, and similar materials.

DESIGNING FOR PLASTICS
Thermal coefficient

Thermal expansion and contraction of plastics is typically high; the coefficient is five or more times that of metals. This calls for special care in detailing, keeping in mind movement in the major axis or plane of the component. Thus means should be devised for avoiding or disguising distortion of large sheets. In the same general connection, an important advantage of plastics for use in building is their capability of being formed fairly readily to resist stress concentrations, whether arising from thermal movement or other causes.

Durability

Weathering of plastics outdoors and the general durability of plastics when not exposed to the weather, are questions uppermost in the minds of designers and specifiers. Unfortunately, the plastics industry has not yet succeeded in developing accelerated laboratory tests that reliably predict the weathering performance of materials over periods of 20 years and more.

The record of actual exposures, of course, grows longer and more complete all the while. There are acrylics that have stood up well under outdoor exposures exceeding 20 years. A few other plastics can point to exterior installations 15 years or more old, with negligible deterioration. With new formulations constantly appearing, the designer can only cautiously weigh the variables. The more easily replaceable components —glazing, for example—might not have to prove themselves by decades of actual exposure-history if replacement costs were counterbalanced by other factors: low initial installed cost, good appearance, resistance to damage, ease of maintenance.

Aside from weather-erosion and deterioration under ultra-violet light, the general durability of plastics in typical building applications has been very good. PVC for example provides perhaps the best resilient flooring from the viewpoint of standing up under neglect. According to accelerated tests, nylon outwears bronze mechanically. Many plastics offer impact resistance that makes them more durable than alternative materials for the same application. (The success of plastic and plastic-coated luggage illustrates this.) Sometimes the properties which provide durability in plastics also enhance their attributes for safety. For example, the use of plastics in shower doors and room dividers is appropriate since it is almost impossible to fall through them. Even if broken they are a negligible hazard.

Corrosion and stain resistance

Another aspect of plastics' durability which can be all-important to the designer is that they are not subject to chemical corrosion or to electrolytic action. This generalization must be modified, however, by pointing out that some plastic materials are selectively attacked by certain classes of solvents—mostly chemicals that are not likely to be found outside laboratory or industrial buildings. (Where a plastic is to be put to a new use, the designer would be wise to check the possibilities against a listing of the degree to which a number of chemicals will attack it. Such tabulations are available from the producer of the basic material.) This absence of ordinary corrosion means absence of staining as well as increased durability.

Fire behavior

Being organic materials, all plastics can be destroyed by fire. Although some plastics burn of themselves, many are self-extinguishing when the flame igniting them has been removed. Among these flammable plastics, there is a great range of the degree of ease of ignition. Another organic material, wood, perhaps exemplifies the average burning characteristics of plastics and is easily kept in mind by the designer. Where actual fire hazards may be present, specific properties of the material must be considered. Thermoplastics, for instance, will soften —perhaps melt—before a fire even reaches them. Partly depending on the softening temperature, this may be bad or good: Underwriters' Laboratories approves those plastics for ceiling light-diffusion that can be relied upon in case of fire to fall out of position soon enough so as not to interfere with effectiveness of sprinklers placed above the suspended ceiling.

Most building codes do not take ease of ignition into account, but the designer should do so wherever he believes that this could bear on fire safety. Codes do emphasize two characteristics of materials, both of which presuppose an out-of-control blaze already going: One is fire retardation, and this is something only for heavy constructions of brick, concrete, etc.—not for organic materials. The other is the rate at which flame may spread across the surface of a flammable material. Especially in spaces used by the public, this can become a fire- and panic-hazard and should be kept in mind, building code or no. According to the various standard tests used for measuring this characteristic, the flammable plastics present a wide range of surface-flame-travel. Some will hardly spread flame at all; others will do so faster than woods.

Deformation under load

"Creep" is a property of most materials, but, with traditional materials of construction, it is reasonable to assume elastic behavior within certain limits of stress. However, many plastics, especially the thermoplastics, exhibit time-dependent plastic behavior: flow, or creep, of the material under load, so deformation depends not only on the load, but also on the rate at which it is applied and on its duration. Further, this phenomenon is greater at elevated temperatures. In the case of many plastics, these relationships are of major significance and must be taken into account; otherwise, failures may occur. Appropriate stress levels and factors of safety must be employed. For materials exhibiting no sharply defined yield points or elastic limits, the working stresses are likely to depend upon the degree of creep that can be tolerated.

Fire resistance requirements

From the *Code Manual* (Feb. 1959) of the New York State Building Code Commission

With the great influx of plastics into building construction, there has been some doubt in the past as to how these new materials should be treated in connection with building codes. To help alleviate this situation, *A Model Chapter on Plastics for Inclusion in a Building Code* was drafted in 1956 by The Society of the Plastics Industry in cooperation with The Manufacturing Chemists' Association, Inc. In 1959 the New York State Building Code Commission included a new section in the revised edition of their *Code Manual* on "Plastic Materials," patterned after the aforementioned *Chapter on Plastics,* and relevant to a performance type building code. The basic material has been rearranged and tabulated, and put into an easy-to-use form. As such, it should prove useful to the designer in selecting the proper plastics to meet fire-resistance requirements.

General

An acceptable plastic material is one which is suitable functionally for the purpose for which it is to be used, which has a flame-spread rating of not more than 225 [This is the flame spread rating given by the Underwriters' Laboratories tunnel test], and which in burning will not give off excessive amounts of smoke or objectionable gases.

Classification

Class A—Plastic materials, reinforced or unreinforced, which are self-extinguishing or which stop burning when removed from the igniting flame.

Class B—Plastic materials which are not self-extinguishing and are reinforced with 20 per cent or more, by weight, of glass fiber or other noncombustible material.

Class C—Plastic materials which are not self-extinguishing and are reinforced with less than 20 per cent but not less than 10 per cent, by weight, of glass fiber or other noncombustible material.

Class D—Plastic materials other than Class A, B, or C.

Structural Requirements

Plastic materials, assemblies, connections, fastenings and the structural members to which they are attached shall conform to the general structural requirements of the [governing code]. Provisions shall be made for expansion and contraction.

Interior Finish and Trim

Plastic materials for interior finish and trim shall conform to the requirements of the [governing code].

Glaze of Openings

Plastic materials may be used for glazing doors and sash and light transmitting panels in exterior walls which are not required to have a fire-resistance rating. For limitations, see Table A.

Roof Panels

In roofs which are not required to have a fire-resistance rating and in roofs where sprinkler protection is provided, panels of plastic materials may be used, except that such plastic roof panels shall not be used directly over assembly spaces, or directly over areas [used for the following: institutional buildings such as homes for ill and infirm; hospitals and clinics; jails, prisons and mental institutions; and similar building types] or over areas in which flammable or explosive materials are made, stored, or handled. For limitations see Table B.

Table A. Glazing of doors, sash, and light-transmitting wall panels

Classification of plastic	Type of building [2]	Building distance separation	Maximum aggregate area, per cent of exterior wall area	Maximum panel area in sq ft	Maximum panel size		Minimum distance between panels	
					Horizontal length in feet	Height in feet	Horizontally in feet	Vertically in feet
A or B..........	2, 3 or 4	10 to 20	10	100	25	12	4	8 [1]
A or B..........	2, 3 or 4	20 to 30	15	150	50	12	3	6 [1]
A or B..........	2, 3 or 4	30 or more	30	300	100	12	2	4
A or B..........	5	30 or more	30	300	100	12	4	8 [1]
C or D..........	2, 3, 4 or 5	30 or more	15	150	100	12	4	8 [1]

1. *Four feet for panels not more than 6 feet in horizontal length.*
2. *Type 2, noncombustible; Type 3, heavy timber; Type 4, ordinary; Type 5, wood frame.*

Table B. Roof panels

Classification of plastic	Minimum slope of roof panel	Maximum aggregate area, per cent of roof covered	Maximum panel area in sq ft	Minimum distance between panels	
				Along slope of roof in feet	Horizontally in feet
A........................	4 on 12	33⅓	300	10	8
B........................	4 on 12	25	300	10	8
C or D..................	4 on 12	15	100	10	8

Skylights

Plastic materials may be used in skylights except those directly over assembly spaces, over spaces [used for institutional buildings, such as homes for ill and infirm; hospitals and clinics; jails, prisons and mental institutions; and similar building types] or over areas in which flammable or explosive materials are manufactured, stored, or handled. Material used in skylights over exits or shafts shall be Class A. Such skylights shall be mounted on a noncombustible curb at least 12 in. high above the roof in the following building types: apartments, hotels, motels, etc.; business; mercantile; industrial; storage; assembly; dormitories; and similar types. The curb should be 6 in. high above the roof of one- or two-family dwellings. For limitations, see Table C.

Exterior Wall Facing

Plastic material may be used for facing exterior walls provided it is attached to a noncombustible backing. For limitations, see Table D.

Luminous Ceilings or Light Diffusing Panels

Plastic materials may be used in luminous ceilings or in light-diffusing panels in buildings of low hazard occupancy, and in buildings of moderate or high hazard occupancy equipped with a sprinkler system. Where used in exits or over assembly space in any building; in buildings of mercantile and dormitory occupancies or over hazardous areas in which highly flammable or explosive materials are manufactured, stored or handled, the plastic material shall be class A and have a heat distortion temperature of at least 225 F. Plastic luminous ceilings or plastic light diffusing materials, in mounted or recessed fixtures, in other rooms and spaces, and having an area exceeding 30 per cent of the area of the room shall conform to the flame spread requirements for interior finishes or be of class A material which will distort and fall from its mounting at an ambient temperature at least 200 F below its ignition temperature. Individual sheets of such material shall not exceed 75 sq ft in area between supports. Luminous ceilings below sprinkler heads shall be of material which will distort and fall from its mounting at a temperature at least 15 degrees lower than the operating temperature of the sprinklers.

Partitions

Class A and B plastic materials may be used for partitions wherever partitions of wood or other combustible materials are permitted, providing the surfaces conform to the applicable code requirements for interior finishes.

Note: *the Code Manual can be used as a guide by architects and engineers in interpreting the New York State Building Construction Code. It is not law, but purely advisory.*

Table C.   Skylights

Classification of plastic	Minimum slope [1] of skylight	Maximum aggregate area, per cent of room covered	Maximum skylight area in sq ft	Maximum dimension along slope of roof in feet	Minimum distance between skylights or to exterior wall of building in feet
A............................	3 on 12	33⅓	300	10	5
B............................	3 on 12	25	300	10	5
C & D........................	4 on 12	15	100	8	5

[1] *Rise of dome-shaped skylights at least 10 per cent of maximum span of 5 inches, whichever is greater.*

Table D.   Exterior wall facing

Classification of plastic	Maximum height above grade		Maximum panel area [1]		Minimum distance between panels	
	Within fire limits	Outside fire limits, feet	Within fire limits, sq ft	Outside fire limits, sq ft	Vertically in feet	Horizontally in feet
A............................	1 story	35	150	225	6	3
B............................	1 story	35	150	225	6	3
C............................	1 story	35	50	75	6	3
D............................	Not permitted					

No dimension of any panel shall exceed 15 feet.

Data from International Cut Stone Contractors and Quarrymen's Association.

Characteristics of Various Building Stones

Limestone

Oolitic — a calcite-cemented calcareous stone formed of shells and shell fragments, practically non-crystalline in character. It is found in massive deposits, located almost entirely in Lawrence, Monroe and Owen Counties, Indiana, and in Alabama, Kansas and Texas. This limestone is characteristically a freestone, without cleavage planes, possessing a uniformity of composition, texture and structure. It possesses a high internal elasticity, adapting itself without damage to extreme temperature changes.

Dolomitic — a limestone rich in magnesium carbonate, frequently somewhat crystalline in character. It is found in ledge formations in a wide variety of color tones and textures. Generally speaking, its crushing and tensile strengths are greater than the oolitic limestones, and its appearance shows greater variety in texture.

Crystalline — a limestone which is predominantly composed of calcium carbonate crystals, though not of the re-crystallized nature characteristic of marble. It is high in crushing and tensile strength, very low in absorption, and usually shows only slight variations from a uniform light gray color and smooth texture.

Sandstone

A sedimentary rock consisting usually of quartz cemented with silica, iron oxide or calcium carbonate. Sandstone is durable, has a very high crushing and tensile strength, and a wide range of colors and textures.

Quartzite

A compact granular rock composed of quartz crystals, usually so firmly cemented as to make the mass homogeneous and as hard as many granites. The stone is generally quarried in stratified layers, the surfaces of which are unusually smooth. Its crushing and tensile strengths are extremely high. The color range is wide.

Rubble (ledge stone), Flagging

A natural cleft stone, which may be limestone, sandstone or quartzite, particularly adaptable as a veneer. Since a large number of stones can be classified as rubble, there is also a wide variety of colors and textures. This stone is broken to standard widths and in random lengths from 6 in. to whatever the various quarries supply.

Chesapeake-Hue (Maryland quartzite) split face, random ashlar

Indiana Limestone (oolitic) shot sawed finish

Indiana Limestone (oolitic) split face

Penn-Kress Stone (Pennsylvania quartzite) split face veneer

Colorado Red Sandstone (quartzite sandstone) split face

Sunset Stone (Wisconsin limestone) split face, random ashlar

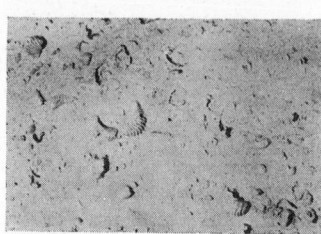
Cordova Shell Limestone (Texas oolitic) smooth machine finish veneer

Tennquartz (Tennessee Stone quartzite) strip rubble veneer, random lengths

Carthage Stone (Missouri crystalline limestone) split face, random lengths, coursed

Winona Travertine Stone (Minnesota dolomitic limestone) split face, random ashlar

Classifications of Building Stone

Cut Stone

This includes all stone cut or machined to a given size, dimension or shape, and produced in accordance with working or shop drawings which have been developed from the architect's structural drawings.

Ashlar Facing

Strictly speaking, any exposed stone facing made from broken or cut stone, set at random or in uniform courses, is an ashlar facing. In this sense, cut stone may be set as an ashlar facing, or the word ashlar may apply to various forms of facing with stone which is not measured and cut, according to shop drawing specifications, but is set at the discretion of the stone mason on the job. Ashlar facing may be of several surface finishes, viz:

Split Face. (Sawed Bed) This is customarily furnished in unit heights, generally speaking 4 in. on the beds, and is delivered to the job in strips or lengths from 18 in. to 4 ft. Usually split face is sawed on the beds and is split either by hand or with machine so that the surface face of the stone exhibits the natural quarry texture.

Strip Rubble. Strip rubble, generally speaking, comes from a ledge quarry. The beds of the stone, while uniformly straight, are of the natural cleft as the stone is removed from the ledge, and then split by machine to approximately 4 in. widths.

Sawed Face. This is a plain stone, the surface of which is the natural sawed finish. Like split face, it is furnished in unit heights, 4 in. on the bed and in lengths of 2 ft to 5 ft.

Rock (Pitch) Face. This is similar to split face, except that the face of the stone is pitched to a given line and plane, producing a bold appearance rather than the comparatively flush face obtained in split face. It occasions additional labor and necessarily an increased cost over split face.

Flagstone

Sawed — So furnished it is sawed from dimension blocks of limestone or sandstone, usually in 2 in. thicknesses. Monotones of buff or gray or variegated are obtainable in this type.

Ledgestone — The majority of flagstones come from ledge quarries and are furnished in thicknesses from ½ in. to 2 in. Such flagging comes in various colors: tan, brown, gray, red, blue, white, green, pink, buff, purple, yellow, orange and combinations of these. Most quarries furnish it either in random, irregular sizes, or broken to definite or pre-determined dimensions.

Color and Pattern in Building Stone

Color

Building stone is available today in very wide variety of colors. It is true, of course, that some of the startling "decorator" hues which have become common for interior decoration will not be found in natural stone. The basic colors themselves are there, but always reduced in intensity. There are reds and greens, blues, yellows, grays, and various mixtures, either as solid colors, or as variegated combinations.

Some stones, like the limestones, gain effectiveness through the quality of the material, even though the color be monotone. Others, such as the strip rubble stones, frequently offer a wide range of hues which are normal to the stone as it comes from the quarry.

PATTERN can be established by variations in size, setting methods, color, finish

Surface Finishes of Cut Stone

Surface finishing of cut stone is frequently an important factor in its final quality as set in a job. Variations in texture which result from different finishes, increase greatly the working palette of the architect, since the original wide range of stones is made broader still by a consideration of the choice of finishes.

Not all stones, of course, take every finish. And where a finish is applicable, it should be analyzed for cost, particularly if hand labor is required.

More detailed information than can be provided here may be obtained from any of the Stone Association members which will be listed in the March issue.

Smooth Planer Finish

This is the finish left on the stone as it comes from the planer, with such tool marks as may exist being carefully removed from the finished surface of the stone. It is the finish most generally specified.

Carbo-Finish

This is a very smooth finish produced by the use of a carborundum machine instead of a planer.

Rubbed Finish

This requires the rubbing of the stone with an abrasive, after the stone has been planed. Today, with carboloy tipped planer tools, this operation is generally unnecessary, since the planer tool takes the stone down to a finish comparable to a rubbed finish. Rubbing stone adds to the cost.

Sawed Finish, Sand-Sawed

This is the finish which is left as the stone comes from the gang-saw. As such, it provides a moderately smooth, granular surface, varying in texture with the type of stone.

Sawed Finish, Chat-Sawed

Finish is produced by sawing with coarse chat under the sawing blade, resulting in an interesting, rough surface texture.

Sawed Finish, Shot-Sawed

Finish is similar to chat-sawed, except that chilled steel shot is used under the blades. The finished surface is heavily ribbed with irregular, roughly parallel grooves.

Tooled Finishes

Since tooled finishes are usually costly, they seldom are used in modern construction. It is recommended that an Association member be consulted before specifying these finishes.

Hand Finishes

There is also a wide variety of hand finishes applicable to cut stone. These are usually expensive and should be considered only when cost is not an important factor. Information about such finishes as bush hammer, crandal, pick point, stripping, etc., is available from any of the Association members.

Planer Finish

Rubbed Finish

Sand Sawed Finish

Chat Sawed Finish

Shot Finish

Tooled Finish

Checklist of principal building stones

State	Name	Crushing strength, psi	Wt., pcf	Texture	Color
				Sandstone	
Ark.	Cherry Blend	—	—	Medium	Brown, gray, cream, buff, pink
	Multi-ledge	—	—	—	Brown, pink, gray, variegated
	Rainbow Ledge	13,400	159	Medium	Brown, tan, yellow, pink, white, gray
	Harmony Ledge	13,667	159	Fine	Pink, brown, gray
Ariz.	Canyon	13,600	—	Coarse	Pink, buff, tan
	Dunbar	—	—	—	"Grand Canyon colors"
	Kaibab Arizona	13,600	—	Medium	Buff, pink, tan, red, yellow, variegated
Ind.	Sienna	4,000	150	Fine	Red, pink, brown, tan, yellow, cream, buff
Kans.	Bandera	8,446	—	—	Gray, buff
Mass.	Brownstone	4,500	155	Fine	Brown
Mo.	Clear Creek	—	—	Fine	Buff, gold, brown
Nev.	Kaibab Neva	18,069	—	Medium	Red, white, brown, yellow, purple
	Yasu	17,000	158	Medium	White, yellow, pink, purple, red, brown
N.Y.	Bluestone	12,500	160	Fine	Blue, gray, buff, lilac, green, tan
	Lenroc	27,500	165	Fine	Blue, gray, brown, rust, tan
	Mountain Hue	—	—	—	Blue green, gray, lilac, buff
Ohio	Berea, Amherst, Cleveland	8,500	140	—	Gray, buff, variegated
	Briar Hill Golden Tone	5,000	150	Fine	Gray, buff, brown, pink, tan
	Pearl	—	—	Fine	Gray, buff, brown, pink
Pa.	Delaware	3,800	180	Medium	Brown, gray, russet, tan, rose
	Penn-Kress	—	—	—	Gray, green, purple
Utah	Bear Valley Green	—	—	Medium	Green
				Nugget sandstone	
Utah	Sandy	—	—	Fine	Buff, gray, red, purple
				Quartzitic sandstone	
Ala.	Oneonta	5,228	160	Fine	Pink, buff, gray, brown
Colo.	Berthoud Pink, B. Variegated	6,000	159	Fine	Pink, orchid, variegated
	Colorado Pink, C. Rose, C. Red	—	162	—	Pink, rose, red, buff, cream, gray, variegated
	Loveland Buff	—	150	Medium	Buff, white, gray, brown stripes
	Lyons Redstone	—	155	Medium	Red, pink, rose, white stripes, brown, blue
N.Y.	Adirondack Hue	37,400	157	Fine	Pink, buff, gray
Utah	New Park Mining	14,400	154	Fine	Buff to red
				Quartzite	
Ga.	Pine Log	7,000	160	Coarse	Ivory, tan, red, gray, brown, buff
Md.	Chesapeake-hue	20,400	170	—	Gray, blue, brown, beige, cream, green, rust
Pa.	Allegheny	—	—	Fine	Blue, green, red, lilac, gray
Tenn.	Crab Orchard	19,060	162	Fine	Pink, buff, tan, blue, gray
	Tennessee Variegated	20,850	162	—	Pink, tan, buff, gray, variegated
	Tennquartz	26,833	162	—	Pink, tan, buff, gray, variegated
Utah	Turquoise	7,000	150	Coarse	Turquoise, green
				Oolitic limestone	
Ala.	Rockrange, Rockwood	4,553	145	Fine	Buff, gray, white
	Veined Gray	4,553	145	Fine	Gray with darker stripes
Ind.	Indiana Limestone	{ 2,500 10,000 }	{ 135 180 }	Fine	Buff, gray, variegated

Checklist of principal building stones (cont.)

State	Name	Crushing strength, psi	Wt., pcf	Texture	Color
	Victor Huro	17,500	185	Fine	Buff
	Victor Rouge, V. Travertine	5,500	175	Coarse	Rouge, buff
Kans.	Junction City, Silverdale	4,706	130	Fine	Buff
Tex.	Cordova Cream, Liberty Hill Cream	2,070 / 2,300	124	Fine	Cream
	Cordova Shell, Liberty Hill Shell	1,070 / 2,005	119	Shelly	Light golden

Dolomitic limestone

State	Name	Crushing strength, psi	Wt., pcf	Texture	Color
Calif.	Santa Maria	21,700	—	—	White, cream, rust
Ind.	Laurelstone	20,000+	—	—	Buff, brown, gray
Minn.	Kasota Cream, K. Pink	15,000	157	Fine	Cream, pink
	Mankato Buff, M. Cream, M. Gray	13,500 / 15,000	157	—	Buff, cream, gray
	Plum Valley	—	—	—	Pink, tan
	Winona Travertine	17,000	158	Travertine	Yellow, white, buff, pink, gray
Mo.	Ste. Genevieve	—	155	—	Cream
Wis.	Conco Lannon	22,200	—	Fine	Ivory, gray, buff
	Fond du Lac	—	180	Fine	White, gray, blue, rose, tan
	Halquist Lannon	31,936	—	—	White, cream, buff, rust, blue
	Lannon	35,000	170	Fine	Blue, gray, rust
	Quality Lannon	—	—	Fine	Blue, green, gray, lilac, buff
	Sunset	16,078	159	Fine	Variegated

Silicified limestone and chert

State	Name	Crushing strength, psi	Wt., pcf	Texture	Color
Calif.	Flagstone, Mossback, Oatmeal, Ornamental, Plaster Rock, Specimen, Waterwash	—	—	Medium / Coarse	White, gray, buff, variegated

Crystalline limestone

State	Name	Crushing strength, psi	Wt., pcf	Texture	Color
Mo.	Carthage	20,000	167	—	Light gray

Marble (see section on Marble)

State	Name	Crushing strength, psi	Wt., pcf	Texture	Color
Ga.	Crystal White, Etowah Pink, Creole, Cherokee, Pale Pink, Golden Vein, Variegated	10,356 / 13,590	155	—	White with gray, black, or gold veins; pink; pink with gray or black veins
Tenn.	Tennessee Marble	14,000 / 18,000	170	Fine	Pink, gray, brown
Vermont	Emerald White, Emerald Green, Sunset Blue	—	169	Fine	White with green veins, green with white clouds, blue-gray with white clouds

Agate

State	Name	Crushing strength, psi	Wt., pcf	Texture	Color
Utah	Desert Onyx	16,710	150	Fine	White, pale peach

Mica schist

State	Name	Crushing strength, psi	Wt., pcf	Texture	Color
Pa.	Pennsylvania Mica	2,000 / 4,000	160	—	Gray, gold, brown

Granite

State	Name	Crushing strength, psi	Wt., pcf	Texture	Color
Conn.	Mt. Coral Pink	—	—	—	Wide variations in color and texture
Ga.	Blue Diamond, Keershaw Pink, Congaree	25,180	165	Fine to coarse	Gray or pink with dark specks
	Salisbury	—	—	—	Orange pink

Checklist of principal building stones (cont.)

State	Name	Crushing strength, psi	Wt., pcf	Texture	Color
Maine	Deer Island, Sherwood Pink	—	—	Medium	Gray, pink
	Moose-a-Bec Pink	—	—	—	Pink-brown
	North Jay	—	—	Fine	White, light gray
	Swenson Pink	—	—	Medium	Pink with black waves
Mass.	Chelmsford Bullfinch, C. Gray, C. White	—	—	Fine	Buff, gray, white
	Extra Dark Quincy	—	—	—	Occasional small black spots
	Milford Buff, M. Pink	—	—	Medium	Brown or pink with dark spots
	Plymouth, Weymouth	—	—	—	Soft grays and greens, buff, tan, yellow, brown, purple
	Rockport Gray	—	—	—	Medium gray
Minn.	Cold Spring Agate	—	—	Medium	Brownish red
	Cold Spring Diamond Pink	—	—	Medium	Gray buff with black spots
	Cold Spring Rainbow	—	—	Fine	Pink and black
	Crystal Gray	—	—	Coarse	Dark gray to purple
	Diamond Gray	—	—	Medium	Light gray
	Opalescent	—	—	Coarse	Dark green-gray with brown and black spots
	Oxford Gray	—	—	Fine	Dark gray
	Rockville	—	—	Coarse	Light to medium gray
	Ruby Red	—	—	Fine	Brownish red
Mo.	Mission Red	—	—	—	Occasional thin dark veins
N.H.	Bears Den Quarry	—	—	Medium	Green-gray and brown variegated
	Conway Green	—	—	Coarse	Dark green-gray with black spots
	Conway Pink	—	—	Coarse	Pink with gray and black spots
	Mason	—	—	Medium	Dark to greenish gray
	Souhegan White	—	—	—	Uniform texture
	Swenson Buff Antique, S. Gray	—	—	Fine	Light to medium brown, gray
N.Y.	Westchester	34,500	166	Fine	Dark to medium gray with pink specks
N.C.	Balfour Pink	34,700	165	Medium	Pink, pale to reddish
	Carolina White	51,900	165	Medium	Light gray with small flecks
	Mount Airy	29,233	165	Medium	White, light gray
	Rowan Pink	34,700	165	Medium	Gray white to pale pink
Pa.	French Creek Black	40,000	190	Fine	Black
S.Dak.	Cold Spring Carnelian	—	—	Fine	Brownish red
	Imperial Mahogany	—	—	—	Some waves and veining
Tex.	Texas Pink	—	—	Coarse	Pink
Wis.	Cold Spring Bright Red	—	—	Fine	Bright red
	Cold Spring Veined Ebony	—	—	Medium	Black (bronze)

Argillite

State	Name	Crushing strength, psi	Wt., pcf	Texture	Color
N.J.	Princeton	11,600	150	Fine	Dark brown, blue, purple, gray, buff

Slate

State	Name	Crushing strength, psi	Wt., pcf	Texture	Color
N.Y.	Yorkmont	—	—	—	Green, gray, black, purple, red
Pa.	Pennsylvania Black	—	—	—	Blue-black
Vt.	Vermont Slate	—	—	—	Red, green, purple, gray, mottled
Va.	Buckingham	—	—	—	Blue-black

Soapstone

State	Name	Crushing strength, psi	Wt., pcf	Texture	Color
Va.	Albarene	—	—	—	Dark green

Data from International Cut Stone Contractors and Quarrymen's Association, Granite Association, and various manufacturers.

By ARTHUR HOCKMAN, *National Bureau of Standards, U.S. Department of Commerce*

PHYSICAL PROPERTIES OF 113 DOMESTIC MARBLES

Marble has always been regarded as an attractive and durable building material. In recent years the use of thin marble in the form of panels, slabs, and through-the-wall units in curtain wall structures has become more prevalent. For this reason, the National Bureau of Standards has compiled pertinent data regarding some of its physical properties.

The following sheets give the results of tests for abrasive hardness, absorption and specific gravity for 113 samples of domestic marbles originally obtained from 25 quarries located in nine states.

Geologically, marble is defined as a metamorphic, recrystallized limestone composed predominantly of crystalline grains of calcite or dolomite or both, having interlocking or mosaic structure. Commercially, marble is any crystalline rock capable of taking a high polish and composed predominantly of one or more of the following minerals: calcite, dolomite or serpentine. About 85 per cent of the samples were in the class of marble as defined from the geological standpoint, while the remaining 15 per cent were classed as commercial marbles.

MARBLE CLASSIFICATION

The marble samples have been classed by the producers into four groups—A, B, C or D. The groups are defined by the Marble Institute of America [1] in their Marble Engineering Handbook (1960) as follows:

GROUP A—"Sound marbles and stones with uniform and favorable working qualities." qualities. They may have occasional natural faults. A limited

GROUP B—"Marbles and stones similar in character to those in Group A, but with somewhat less favorable working

amount of waxing [1] and sticking may be necessary."

GROUP C—"Marbles and stones of uncertain variation in working qualities. Geological flaws, voids, veins and lines of separation are common. Standard shop practice is to repair these variations of nature by sticking, waxing and filling. These techniques have recently been greatly improved by the use of new adhesives. Rodding,[2] liners,[3] and other forms of reinforcement may be freely employed when necessary."

GROUP D—"Marbles and stones similar to Group C, subject to the same methods of finishing and manufacture, but with a larger proportion of natural faults. These have also a maximum variation in working qualities. This group comprises many of the highly colored marbles prized for their decorative qualities."

Marbles that are used for monumental, structural or veneer purposes and are to be exposed to the weather are generally selected from Group A. Marbles in Groups B, C, and D are usually selected for their color and decorative effects. Occasionally carefully selected marbles from these groups are used on surfaces exposed to the weather.

[1] Waxing, sticking and filling are methods used in the marble trade to repair and improve the appearance of marbles containing natural flaws, voids, veins, etc. Materials such as wax, shellac, coloring and marble dust are used for this purpose.

[2] Rodding is a method of reinforcing a slab of marble by cementing stainless steel or aluminum rods to the back of the slab.

[3] Liner is a thin slab of marble that is cemented to the back of the original slab in order to reinforce it.

DESCRIPTION OF SAMPLES

Most of the domestic samples were in the form of hand specimens 3- by 5-in., ranging in thickness from 1/4 in. to 7/8 in. With the small size and number of samples available for the tests, the test results should not be interpreted to represent the entire marble deposit available from each respective source.

The physical properties of marble as determined by laboratory test are given in Table 1. Tests also show that the flexural strength of marble is reduced by aging. To compensate for the aging effect, the ultimate flexural strength of marble is considered to be half of its actual tested strength. To calculate allowable stress in the design of transversely loaded marble walls, multiply one half the ultimate failure stress by 40 per cent. This produces a total safety factor of 5, which the Marble Institute recommends for contemporary curtain wall and veneer design. Where marble is used for stair treads, lintels, or otherwise as a loadbearing material, a safety factor of 10 is recommended. The actual strength of the marble being used should be determined, and this value should be used for the final design.

TEST PROCEDURES

ASTM Standard Test C241–51, *Abrasion Resistance of Stone Subjected to Foot Traffic.*

ASTM Standard Test C97–47, *Absorption and Bulk Specific Gravity of Natural Building Stone.*

ASTM Standard Test C97–47, *Bulk Specific Gravity.*

Table 1. Physical properties of marble *

PROPERTY	DIRECTION OF LOAD TO BEDDING PLANE	HIGHEST VALUE OBTAINED	LOWEST VALUE OBTAINED	AVERAGE VALUE OBTAINED
Compressive Strength (psi)	Parallel	15,331	6,012	10,223
	Perpendicular	16,750	7,537	10,974
Transverse Strength (psi) (Mod. of Rupture or Flexural Strength)	Parallel	2,580	1,095	1,930
	Perpendicular	2,709	1,092	1,927
Shear Strength (psi)	Parallel	4,812	1,683	3,358
	Perpendicular	4,331	2,351	3,204
Modulus of Elasticity (Millions psi)	Parallel	13.00	1.97	8.35
	Perpendicular	14.85	4.33	9.56
Density (lbs./cu. ft.) (Weight)		172.4	163.0	168.0
Absorption (%) (48 hour soak)		.61	.07	.17
Thermal Conductivity (k) (BTU/in/hr/sq.ft./°F)		15.65	10.45	13.58
Moisture Transmission (Perm inches)		4.46	.32	1.72
Coefficient of Thermal Expansion (in/in/°F)		.000012	.000004	.000007
Creep Deflection (inches) (after 24 hours)		.00033	.00000	.00008

* *Test procedures available from Marble Institute of America, Inc. on request.*

SOURCE, DESCRIPTION AND PROPERTIES OF DOMESTIC MARBLES

NO.	SOURCE	DESCRIPTION [1]	ABRASIVE HARDNESS (H_a value) [3]	ABSORPT'N (48 hr) %	BULK [4] SPECIFIC GRAVITY	GROUP [5]
1	ALABAMA	[2] IVORY CREAM, TRANSLUCENT, very few green markings	14	.11	2.71	B
2		WHITE AND CREAM, TRANSLUCENT, bold prominent markings	14	.14	2.70	A
3		WHITE, TRANSLUCENT, well-distributed prominent markings	13	.13	2.70	A
4		CREAM, TRANSLUCENT, uniform clouded markings	9	.14	2.70	A
5		CREAM, TRANSLUCENT, some veining or clouding	11	.14	2.70	A
6		IVORY-CREAM, TRANSLUCENT, occasional traces of color	10	.14	2.70	A
7		WHITE, green veining predominating	20	.11	2.71	B
8		WHITE AND CREAM, very bold and prominent markings	18	.10	2.71	B
9		WHITE, prominent light clouds	16	.08	2.71	A
10		WHITE, light clouds	11	.09	2.71	A
11	ARKANSAS	DARK GRAY, light gray spottings	38	.14	2.69	B
12		GRAY WITH BROWN TONE, and white spots	18	.34	2.68	B
13		RED, WHITE AND GOLD spots, red veining	17	.19	2.65	C
14		ROSE, white and yellow spots	13	.23	2.67	C
15		GRAY WITH BROWN TONE, golden spots and veins	26	.27	2.68	B
16		DARK BROWN, abundance of small white spots	13	.43	2.66	C
17		DARK BROWN, abundance of small white spots	24	.22	2.68	C
18	COLORADO	LIGHT BROWN TO CREAM, some light rose (travertine)	13	1.10	2.47	C
19		LIGHT BROWN TO RED (travertine)	20	.75	2.52	C
20		CREAM, light brown to red veining (travertine)	18	1.58	2.46	C
21	GEORGIA	WHITE, profusion of blue-black veining	17	.09	2.71	A
22		GRAY, dark gray, wavy veins	16	.11	2.71	A
23		WHITE, gray veins and clouding	16	.12	2.71	A
24		WHITE, few gray veins and clouds	16	.10	2.71	A
25		ROSE TO LIGHT PINK, dark green and gray veining	13	.08	2.71	A
26	MARYLAND	DARK GREEN, mottled veins and markings (serpentine)	55	1.03	2.66	C
27		LIGHT GREEN, mottled veins and markings (serpentine)	43	1.56	2.63	C
28	MISSOURI	LIGHT GRAY, distinct darker gray veining	16	.59	2.64	A
29		LIGHT GRAY, gray veins resembling clouds	19	.83	2.64	A
30		GRAY, without any distinct veining	17	.86	2.63	A
31		ROSE, gray fossil markings	16	.14	2.69	C
32		LIGHT ROSE, numerous light and dark fossils	15	.16	2.68	C
33		GRAY, dark gray veinings, light brown markings	15	.63	2.64	C
34		LIGHT TO DARK GRAY, light brown veining	17	.36	2.68	C
35		GRAY, yellow or golden veins, fossil markings	20	.18	2.68	C
36		LIGHT GRAY AND GOLD, yellow veins	18	.40	2.67	C
37		LIGHT TO MEDIUM GRAY, many light and dark fossils	17	.30	2.67	C
38		MEDIUM BROWN, light and dark veining	19	.43	2.68	C
39		LIGHT TO MEDIUM GRAY, fine pencil-like markings	17	.46	2.64	A
40	N. CAROLINA	GRAY, blue-black wavy veining	19	.07	2.72	A
41	TENNESSEE	DARK PINK, dark veins	24	.07	2.70	A
42		GRAY, SLIGHT TINT OF RED, blue veinings	22	.07	2.70	A
43		DARK BROWN, white spots	25	.07	2.70	A
44		BROWNISH RED, with white veinings and markings	31	.06	2.71	A
45		VARIEGATED RED AND GRAY, white veinings	28	.07	2.71	C
46		GRAYISH PINK, blue veining and white spots	25	.07	2.71	A
47		GRAYISH RED, small blue veinings	23	.08	2.70	A
48		BLACK, occasional white markings	38	.15	2.72	B
49		DARK BROWN, white and red spots	27	.07	2.71	A
50		DARK BROWN, pinkish-gray spots	26	.05	2.70	A
51		REDDISH BROWN, white spots	22	.07	2.70	A
52		BROWNISH RED, variegated with white markings	44	.06	2.71	C
53		DEEP BROWNISH RED, mixed with gray markings, white spots	37	.02	2.71	C
54		BROWNISH RED, variegated with white markings	39	.01	2.71	C
55		BROWNISH RED, mixed with gray and white markings	27	.05	2.71	C

[1] The various descriptions of the samples were supplied by the respective producers.
[2] Capitalized portion of the description signifies the background color of the marble.
[3] The H_a value is an expression of wear resistance and is the reciprocal, multiplied by 10, of the volume of material abraded in a 5 min tests, using the National Bureau of Standards Abrasion Machine. The higher the H_a value, the more resistant to abrasion is the material.
[4] The weight per cubic foot can be determined by multiplying the bulk specific gravity by 62.4.
[5] As defined in the text.

SOURCE, DESCRIPTION AND PROPERTIES OF DOMESTIC MARBLES (cont.)

NO.	SOURCE	DESCRIPTION [1]	ABRASIVE HARDNESS (H_a value) [3]	ABSORPT'N (48 hr) %	BULK [4] SPECIFIC GRAVITY	GROUP [5]
56	TENNESSEE	[2] GRAYISH PINK, mottled with white, pink, red and black	27	.05	2.71	A
57		BROWN, dark brown veinings, white spots	21	.09	2.70	A
58		DEEP BROWNISH PINK, fine dark veining	26	.04	2.71	A
59		DEEP RICH RED, small blue veining	22	.05	2.70	A
60		DARK TO MEDIUM GRAYISH RED, white spots	25	.07	2.70	A
61		VARIEGATED GRAYISH PINK TO RED, blue veinings	23	.08	2.70	A
62		LIGHT TO DARK PINK, small blue veinings	25	.06	2.70	A
63		MEDIUM TO LIGHT PINK, blue veinings	23	.05	2.70	A
64		GRAYISH PINK TO RED, dark veins, some fossils	22	.07	2.70	A
65		LIGHT PINK, dark colored veining	24	.09	2.70	A
66		GRAYISH RED, white spots	23	.01	2.70	A
67		GRAYISH LIGHT RED, white spots	27	.05	2.71	A
68		GRAYISH RED, white spots, red veining	28	.06	2.70	A
69		LIGHT PINK, blue veining	25	.06	2.70	A
70		GRAY, SLIGHT TINGE OF PINK, small blue veining	22	.07	2.70	A
71		GRAYISH PINK, darker veins	23	.08	2.70	A
72		GRAYISH PINK, small blue veining	24	.07	2.70	A
73		CREAM, yellowish brown veins, some fossils	21	.09	2.70	A
74		GRAYISH PINK, blue veining	21	.10	2.70	A
75		PINK AND GRAY, white clouds, veins, fossils	26	.05	2.70	C
76		PINK AND GRAY, reddish veining, some fossils	28	.11	2.69	C
77		DEEP RED TO PINK AND GRAY, dark veins	22	.06	2.70	A
78		GRAY WITH SLIGHT PINK, blue veinings	22	.10	2.70	A
79		GRAY, very close dark veinings	23	.09	2.70	A
80		LIGHT GRAY, few dark veinings	20	.11	2.69	A
81		PEARL, some blue-black veinings, clouds	23	.10	2.69	A
82		LIGHT AND GRAYISH PINK, dark veins, shell markings	21	.06	2.70	A
83		GRAY, scattering of white spots	28	.06	2.70	A
84		LIGHT CREAM, irregular gold veining	25	.58	2.65	C
85		DEEP ROSE, dark brown spots, white and gray markings	29	.02	2.71	C
86		LIGHT TO DARK ROSE, irregular blue veining	27	.07	2.71	C
87		LIGHT BROWN, white and gray fossils	28	.05	2.70	A
88	VERMONT	WHITE, gray clouds	13	.12	2.70	A
89		GRAY, darker gray veining	10	.14	2.70	A
90		WHITE, gray clouds	10	.12	2.70	A
91		WHITE, gray green clouds	11	.15	2.70	A
92		LIGHT GRAY, dark gray clouds	13	.11	2.70	A
93		NEARLY BLACK, gray flecks	24	.14	2.70	A
94		DARK GREEN, white veins (serpentine)	77	.18	2.72	C
95		MAHOGANY RED, white spots	34	.16	2.81	C
96		WHITE, faint flecks	8	.20	2.70	A
97		WHITE, faint green clouds	7	.20	2.70	A
98		WHITE, light green markings	8	.19	2.70	A
99		WHITE, light green clouds	9	.19	2.70	A
100		WHITE, CREAM, light green veining	10	.20	2.70	A
101		WHITE, light green veining	8	.17	2.70	A
102		CREAM, faint green veining	12	.17	2.71	A
103		WHITE, narrow green stripes	11	.21	2.70	A
104		WHITE, wide green bands	11	.17	2.70	A
105		WHITE, light green mottle	9	.16	2.71	A
106		LIGHT GREEN, occasional tan markings	9	.16	2.72	A
107		LIGHT GRAY, dark green veining	9	.19	2.72	A
108		GREEN, white clouds	10	.21	2.71	A
109		WHITE, heavy green clouds	9	.18	2.71	A
110		WHITE, abundant green clouds	8	.17	2.71	A
111		GRAY, darker gray clouds	9	.15	2.70	A
112		WHITE, gray veining	11	.15	2.70	A
113	VIRGINIA	BLACK, SLIGHT GREENISH CAST, occasional white or gray veins	53	.07	2.86	A

[1] The various descriptions of the samples were supplied by the respective producers.
[2] Capitalized portion of the description signifies the background color of the marble.
[3] The H_a value is an expression of wear resistance and is the reciprocal, multiplied by 10, of the volume of material abraded in a 5 min tests, using the National Bureau of Standards Abrasion Machine. The higher the H_a value, the more resistant to abrasion is the material.
[4] The weight per cubic foot can be determined by multiplying the bulk specific gravity by 62.4.
[5] As defined in the text.

STONE—10
Veneer

Stone veneer is attached to the building structure by means of metal anchors and supports, such as those illustrated in Fig. 1. Marble veneers are usually 2 in. or less in thickness; other stone veneers are generally 3 or 4 in. thick. Typical details for the attachment of marble veneer are shown in Fig. 2, and for limestone veneer in Figs. 3 and 4. Stone veneer used in curtain wall construction is shown in Figs. 5 and 6. Details of more conventional applications are given in Figs. 7 and 8.

RESIDENTIAL

Stones commonly used in residential work are available in several patterns, as illustrated in Fig. 9. Veneer thickness averages 3½ to 4 in. Joint widths vary from ½ in. for sawed-bed ashlar to a maximum of 3 in. for rubble and mosaic. Joints may be flush or raked ⅜ in. deep. In many types of stones sawed-bed ashlar is available with modular vertical dimensions, the height of the larger stones being multiples of the height of the smallest stone plus the

width of one joint. The term "2, 3, or 4 rise" refers to this type of masonry, the numbers indicating the number of heights. In laying this type of masonry, the following rules should be observed for the most pleasing appearance: no vertical joint should extend above the top of the highest stones; stones of the same height should not be laid end to end; no horizontal joint should exceed the length of two stones. The method of attaching stone veneer to wood-frame or masonry walls is shown in Fig. 10.

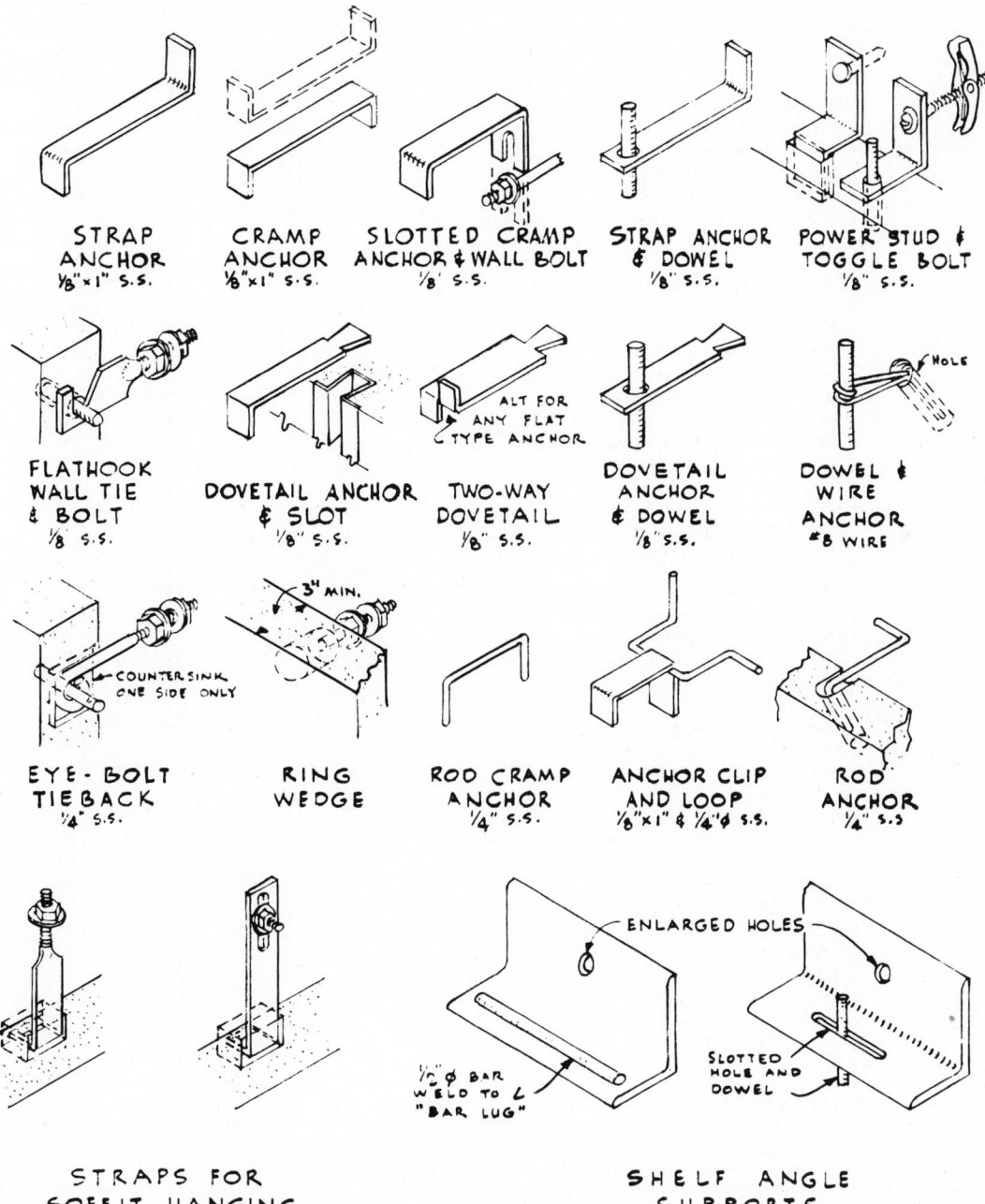

STRAP ANCHOR ⅛"x1" S.S.   CRAMP ANCHOR ⅛"x1" S.S.   SLOTTED CRAMP ANCHOR & WALL BOLT ⅛" S.S.   STRAP ANCHOR & DOWEL ⅛" S.S.   POWER STUD & TOGGLE BOLT ⅛" S.S.

FLATHOOK WALL TIE & BOLT ⅛" S.S.   DOVETAIL ANCHOR & SLOT ⅛" S.S.   TWO-WAY DOVETAIL ⅛" S.S.   DOVETAIL ANCHOR & DOWEL ⅛" S.S.   DOWEL & WIRE ANCHOR #8 WIRE

EYE-BOLT TIEBACK ¼" S.S.   RING WEDGE   ROD CRAMP ANCHOR ¼" S.S.   ANCHOR CLIP AND LOOP ⅛"x1" & ¼"φ S.S.   ROD ANCHOR ¼" S.S.

STRAPS FOR SOFFIT HANGING   SHELF ANGLE SUPPORTS

Fig. 1.   Anchors and supports for stone veneer

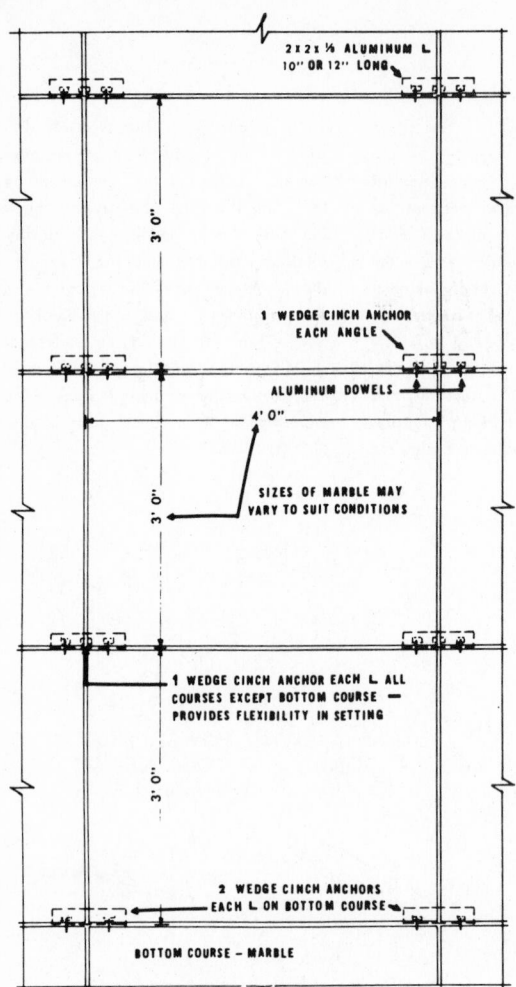

2 X 2 X ⅛ ALUMINUM L
10" OR 12" LONG

3' 0"

1 WEDGE CINCH ANCHOR
EACH ANGLE

ALUMINUM DOWELS

4' 0"

3' 0"

SIZES OF MARBLE MAY
VARY TO SUIT CONDITIONS

1 WEDGE CINCH ANCHOR EACH L ALL
COURSES EXCEPT BOTTOM COURSE —
PROVIDES FLEXIBILITY IN SETTING

3' 0"

2 WEDGE CINCH ANCHORS
EACH L ON BOTTOM COURSE

BOTTOM COURSE — MARBLE

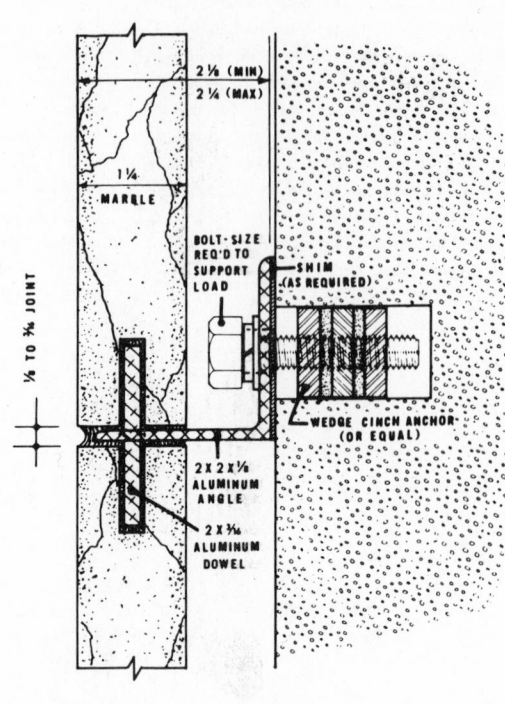

2 ⅛ (MIN)
2 ¼ (MAX)

1 ¼
MARBLE

BOLT-SIZE
REQ'D TO
SUPPORT
LOAD

SHIM
(AS REQUIRED)

½ TO ¾ JOINT

WEDGE CINCH ANCHOR
(OR EQUAL)

2 X 2 X ⅛
ALUMINUM
ANGLE

2 X ¾₆
ALUMINUM
DOWEL

Fig. 2.   Anchorage and support for thin marble veneer

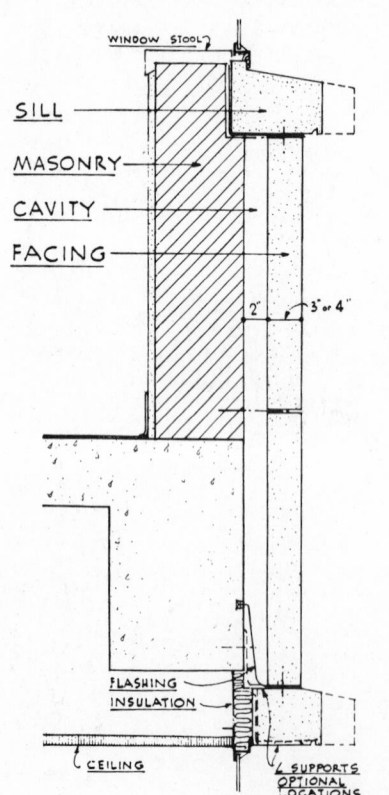

WINDOW STOOL

SILL

MASONRY

CAVITY

FACING

2"   3' or 4"

FLASHING
INSULATION

CEILING

SUPPORTS
OPTIONAL
LOCATIONS

Fig. 3.   Limestone spandrel with masonry
backup

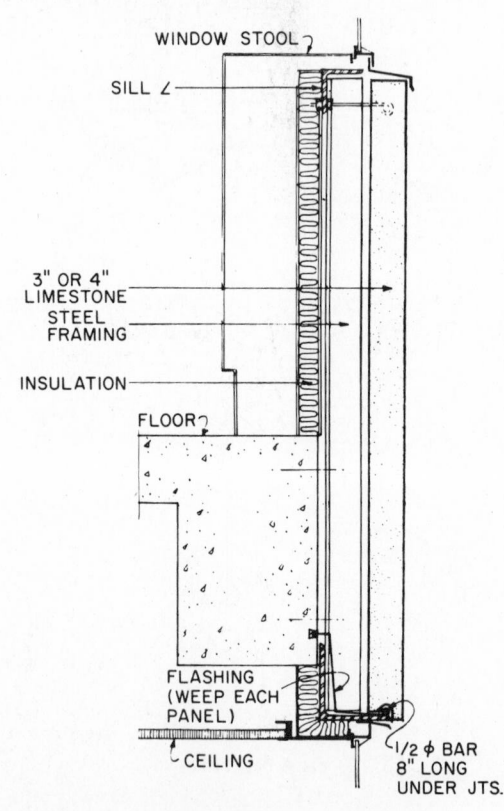

WINDOW STOOL

SILL L

3" OR 4"
LIMESTONE
STEEL
FRAMING

INSULATION

FLOOR

FLASHING
(WEEP EACH
PANEL)

CEILING

½ φ BAR
8" LONG
UNDER JTS.

Fig. 4.   Limestone spandrel on insulated
metal frame

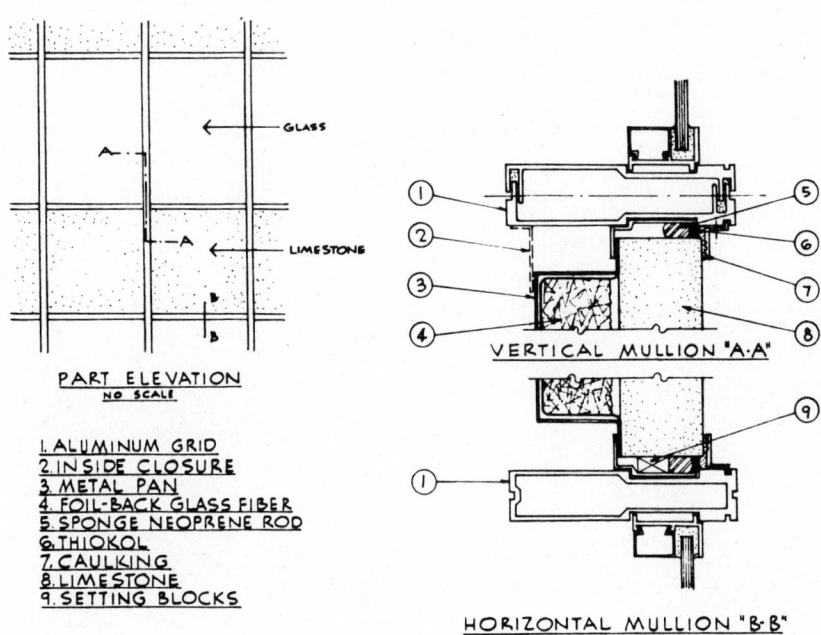

PART ELEVATION
NO SCALE

1. ALUMINUM GRID
2. INSIDE CLOSURE
3. METAL PAN
4. FOIL-BACK GLASS FIBER
5. SPONGE NEOPRENE ROD
6. THIOKOL
7. CAULKING
8. LIMESTONE
9. SETTING BLOCKS

VERTICAL MULLION "A·A"

HORIZONTAL MULLION "B-B"

Fig. 5.   Limestone insulated curtain wall panel
Thickness 3⅞ in., weight 26 psf, *U* value 0.14

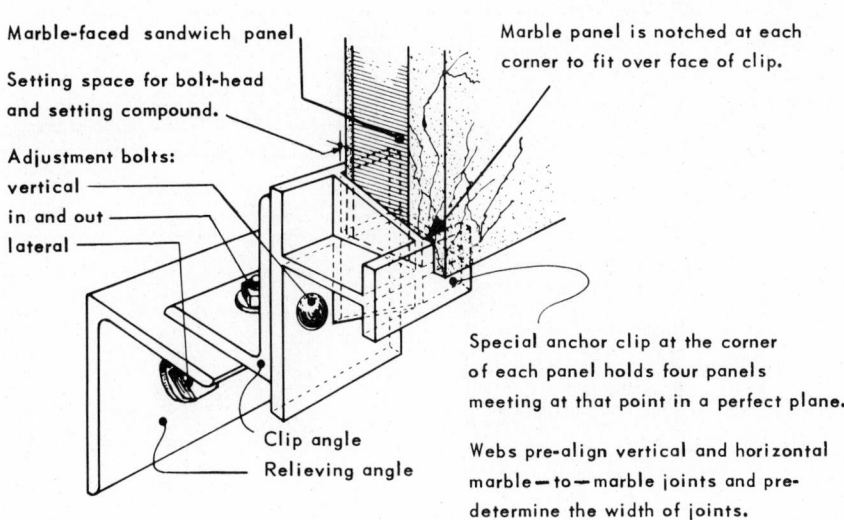

Marble-faced sandwich panel

Setting space for bolt-head and setting compound.

Adjustment bolts:
vertical
in and out
lateral

Clip angle
Relieving angle

Marble panel is notched at each corner to fit over face of clip.

Special anchor clip at the corner of each panel holds four panels meeting at that point in a perfect plane.

Webs pre-align vertical and horizontal marble—to—marble joints and pre-determine the width of joints.

Fig. 6.   Marble insulated curtain wall panel

COPINGS
AND
PARAPETS

SOFFITS FOR WINDOWS, ETC.
(JAMBS AND EXTERIOR ANGLES SIMILAR)
FOR METHODS OF ANCHORING SEE REVERSE

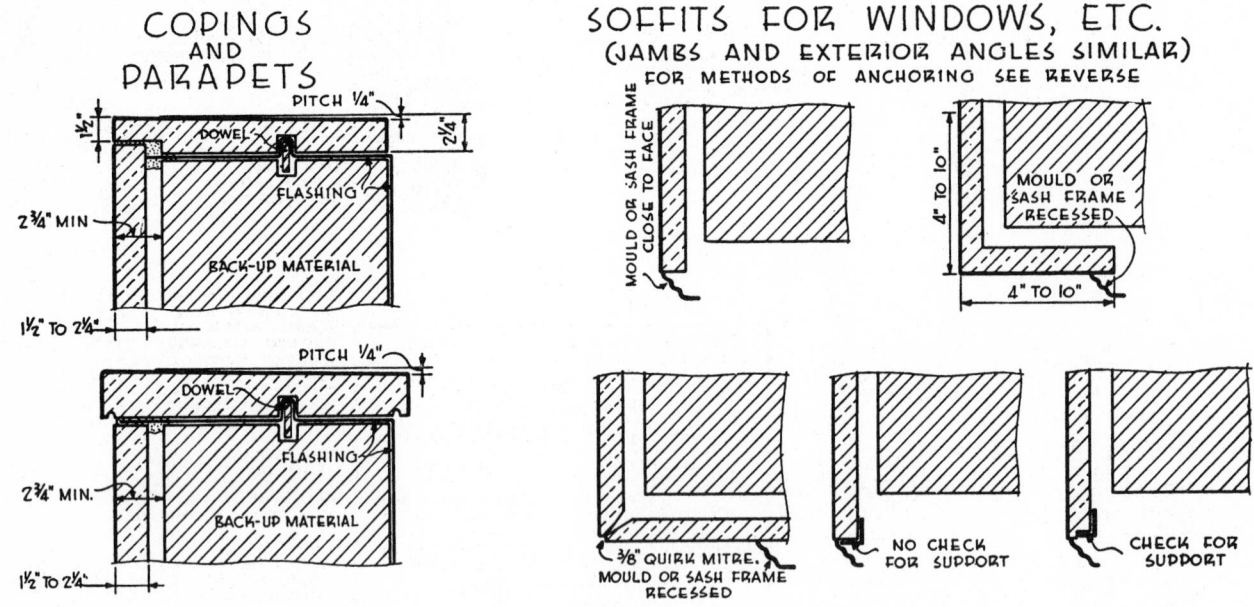

HARD OR CRYSTALLINE STONES
SUCH AS GRANITE

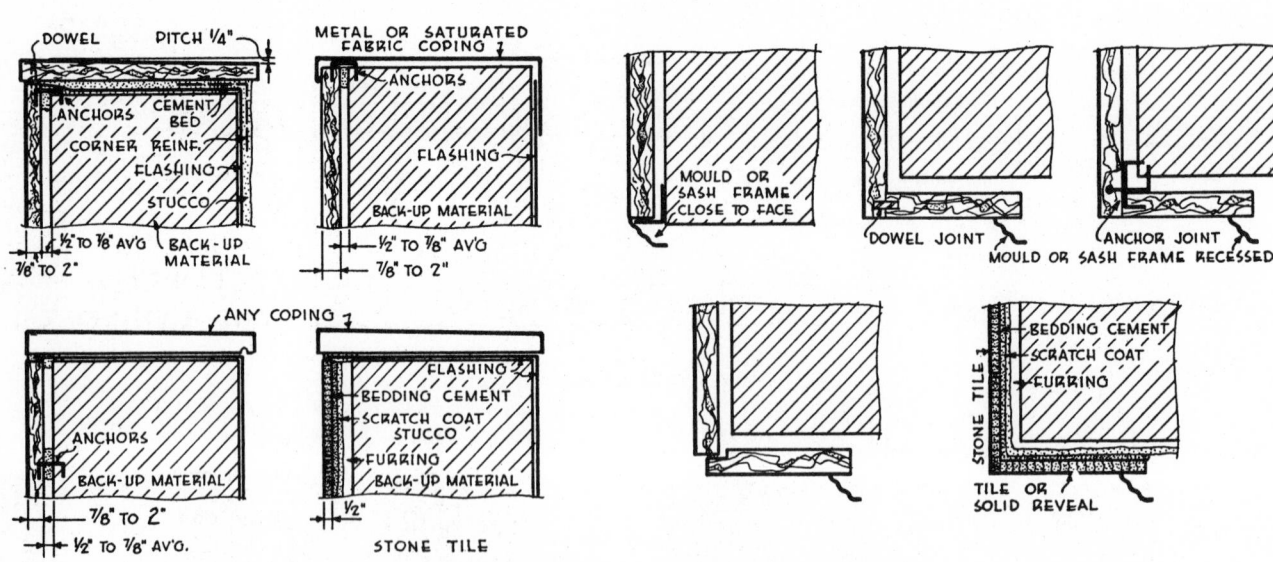

RELATIVELY SOFT STONES
SUCH AS MARBLES, SOAPSTONES, ETC.
SCALE OF ALL DRAWINGS 1" = 1'-0"

Fig. 7.   Details of stone veneer construction—copings and window reveals

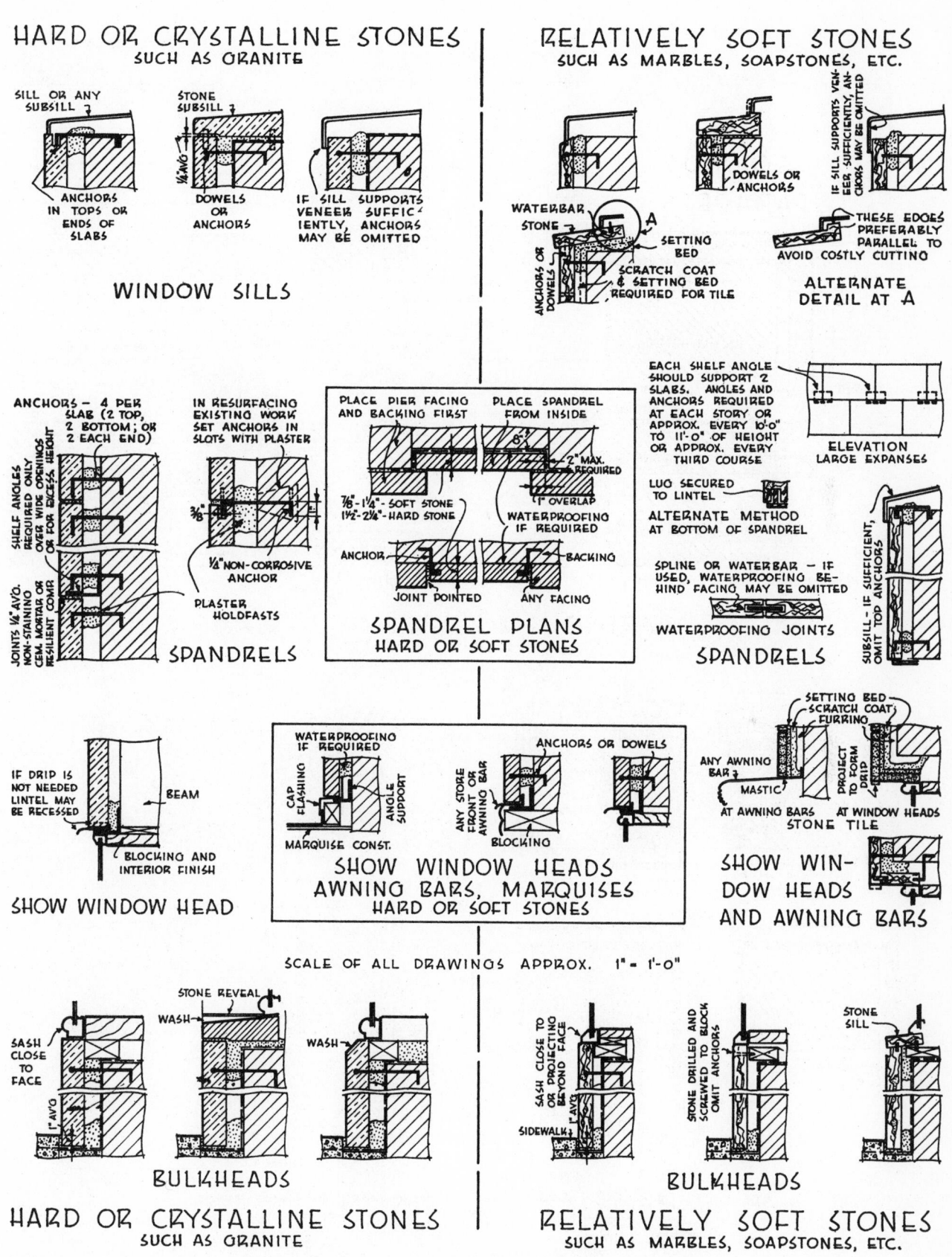

HARD OR CRYSTALLINE STONES
SUCH AS GRANITE

RELATIVELY SOFT STONES
SUCH AS MARBLES, SOAPSTONES, ETC.

SILL OR ANY SUBSILL

STONE SUBSILL

ANCHORS IN TOPS OR ENDS OF SLABS

DOWELS OR ANCHORS

IF SILL SUPPORTS VENEER SUFFICIENTLY, ANCHORS MAY BE OMITTED

WINDOW SILLS

DOWELS OR ANCHORS

IF SILL SUPPORTS VENEER SUFFICIENTLY, ANCHORS MAY BE OMITTED

WATERBAR
STONE
SETTING BED
SCRATCH COAT & SETTING BED REQUIRED FOR TILE
ANCHORS OR DOWELS

THESE EDGES PREFERABLY PARALLEL TO AVOID COSTLY CUTTING

ALTERNATE DETAIL AT A

ANCHORS - 4 PER SLAB (2 TOP, 2 BOTTOM; OR 2 EACH END)

SHELF ANGLES REQUIRED ONLY OVER WIDE OPENINGS OR FOR EXCESS HEIGHT

JOINTS ½" AVG. NON-STAINING CEM. MORTAR OR RESILIENT COMP.

IN RESURFACING EXISTING WORK SET ANCHORS IN SLOTS WITH PLASTER

¼" NON-CORROSIVE ANCHOR

PLASTER HOLDFASTS

SPANDRELS

EACH SHELF ANGLE SHOULD SUPPORT 2 SLABS. ANGLES AND ANCHORS REQUIRED AT EACH STORY OR APPROX. EVERY 10'-0" TO 11'-0" OF HEIGHT OR APPROX. EVERY THIRD COURSE

ELEVATION LARGE EXPANSES

LUG SECURED TO LINTEL

ALTERNATE METHOD AT BOTTOM OF SPANDREL

SPLINE OR WATERBAR - IF USED, WATERPROOFING BEHIND FACING MAY BE OMITTED

WATERPROOFING JOINTS

SUBSILL - IF SUFFICIENT, OMIT TOP ANCHORS

SPANDRELS

PLACE PIER FACING AND BACKING FIRST

PLACE SPANDREL FROM INSIDE

2" MAX. REQUIRED

⅞"-1¼"- SOFT STONE
1½"-2¼"- HARD STONE

1" OVERLAP

WATERPROOFING IF REQUIRED

ANCHOR

BACKING

JOINT POINTED

ANY FACING

SPANDREL PLANS
HARD OR SOFT STONES

IF DRIP IS NOT NEEDED LINTEL MAY BE RECESSED

BEAM

BLOCKING AND INTERIOR FINISH

SHOW WINDOW HEAD

WATERPROOFING IF REQUIRED

CAP FLASHING

ANGLE SUPPORT

MARQUISE CONST.

ANCHORS OR DOWELS

ANY STORE FRONT OR AWNING BAR

BLOCKING

SHOW WINDOW HEADS
AWNING BARS, MARQUISES
HARD OR SOFT STONES

SETTING BED
SCRATCH COAT
FURRING

ANY AWNING BAR

MASTIC

AT AWNING BARS

PROJECT TO FORM DRIP

AT WINDOW HEADS
STONE TILE

SHOW WINDOW HEADS AND AWNING BARS

SCALE OF ALL DRAWINGS APPROX. 1" = 1'-0"

STONE REVEAL

WASH

SASH CLOSE TO FACE

WASH

1" AVG.

BULKHEADS

SASH CLOSE TO OR PROJECTING BEYOND FACE

SIDEWALK

STONE DRILLED AND SCREWED TO BLOCK OMIT ANCHORS

STONE SILL

BULKHEADS

HARD OR CRYSTALLINE STONES
SUCH AS GRANITE

RELATIVELY SOFT STONES
SUCH AS MARBLES, SOAPSTONES, ETC.

Fig. 8.   Details of stone veneer construction—window sills, spandrels, and bulkheads

a. Coursed ashlar

b. Coursed ashlar

c. Random ashlar, sawed bed

d. Random ashlar, sawed bed, 3-rise

e. Random ashlar, hand cut

f. Random ashlar, hand cut

g. Random rubble

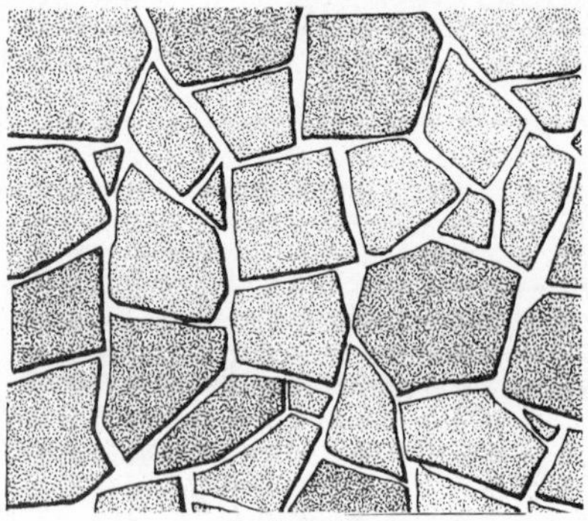

h. Mosaic

Fig. 9. Stone veneer patterns

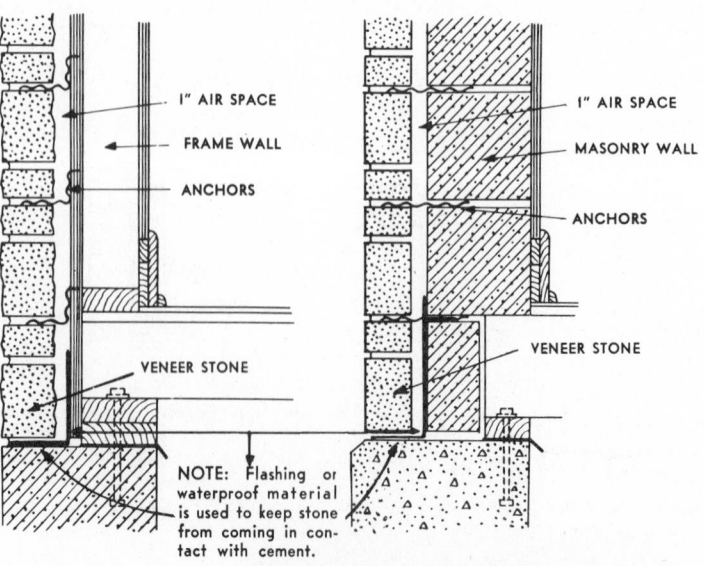

1" AIR SPACE

FRAME WALL

ANCHORS

1" AIR SPACE

MASONRY WALL

ANCHORS

VENEER STONE

VENEER STONE

NOTE: Flashing or waterproof material is used to keep stone from coming in contact with cement.

Fig. 10. Anchorage of stone veneer to wood-frame wall and to masonry wall

By HOWARD P. VERMILYA, AIA

The primary interior stones are the various marbles and slate. Exterior stones are also often used for dramatic effects as interior wall materials in residential and commercial structures and in churches. The smooth-surfaced marbles are more likely to be found as wall or flooring material in monumental or institutional buildings and in commercial buildings such as banks and quality office buildings. Slate and other flagging have their major interior use as a flooring material in residential, ecclesiastical, and institutional buildings.

MARBLE

Interior marble

Interior marble is usually ⅞ in. thick when used in large slabs as standing marble or as tile on floors. Wall tile ½ in. thick is now furnished in modular sizes 8 by 8 in., 8 by 12 in., or 12 by 12 in. Standard (⅞-in.) floor tile sizes are 8 by 16 in., 12 by 12 in., and 10 by 20 in. Wall tile may be used on floors where traffic is not heavy, as in residences. Toilet stall partitions of marble are usually ⅞ in. thick, but the stiles should be 1¼ in. thick. Standard window stools and lavatory tops are ⅞ in. thick. Stair risers are ⅞ in. thick and treads 1¼ in. thick unless heavy traffic is anticipated. Some manufacturers provide for antislip inserts in stair treads. Thicker slabs (1½ in. and 2 in.) are used for counters. Standard thicknesses of marble are ⅞, 1¼, 1½, and 2 in.

Standing interior marble (Fig. 11) is set by spotting with plaster of Paris and using concealed corrosion-resistant wire anchors secured to the wall backing. Joints, usually ¹⁄₁₆ in. wide, should be fully buttered with plaster of Paris as each slab is set. When standing marble is set in wet locations or in unheated places subject to moisture or condensation, however, spotting should consist of portland cement plus a shrinkage-reducing accelerator.

The optimum setting space, that is, the distance from rough wall backing to the finish face of the marble, is 1½ in.; where liners are required the setting space should be 2½ in. External angles are usually butt joints. The use of quirk mitre joints (not recommended on base courses) should be specially noted in the specifications as they are not standard practice.

Standing interior marble

If the optimum setting space is not available, plasticized synthetic resin-based, nonstaining, moisture-resistant bonding cements or dry-set mortars may be used. Thin marble tile is usually set with bonding cements or dry-set mortars similar to those used on

ceramic tile. Elastic, nonstaining, pointing and caulking mastics are also used instead of plaster of Paris or portland cement, particularly with thin marble tile. Joints should be ⅛ to ³⁄₁₆ in. thick.

Floor marble

For floor marble, the concrete base or cinder fill above the slab floor should be within 2½ in. of the finish floor line (Fig. 12a). The cement bed should be mixed quite dry and the marble tamped until fully bedded to the proper level of the floor. The marble tile is then removed and the back parged with wet cement or the bed sprinkled with water and cement and back of tile wet. Fully buttering edges of tile as it is laid is also an approved method. Joints are ¹⁄₁₆ in. They should be grouted with neat cement later if not buttered when laid.

The standard specifications of the Marble Institute of America approve several methods for the installation of marble flooring. Method No. 1 calls for a sand or tar paper cleavage bed between the rough floor slab and the setting bed. Method No. 2 employs a minimum ⅛-in. dry-set portland cement mortar setting bed (Fig. 12b). Method No. 3 for thin (½-in.) marble tile, specifies a setting bed of portland cement permitting a minimum 1¼-in. distance from the rough concrete slab to the finish floor (Fig. 12c). Method No. 4, for thin marble tile, calls for a ⅛-in.-thick dry-set portland cement mortar setting bed as in Method No. 2 above (Fig. 12d).

Finishes

Finishes for interior marble are as follows:

1. Natural finish, produced by sawing with sand.
2. Sand-rubbed or wet sand finish, a smooth surface produced on a cast-iron rubbing bed with sand and water. Used for treads and floors, sometimes after floors have been set.
3. Grit finish, a smooth, dull finish between sand and hone, produced by grits. On floors the finish is produced by surfacing after setting.
4. Hone or egg shell finish, a dull gloss surface giving relatively little reflection, produced by hand or machine. Used on floors and standing marble.
5. Polish finish, a gloss surface that will reflect light and emphasize color and markings, produced by a buffer with putty powder applied to a honed surface. It is generally used for standing marble.

As noted on a previous page, marbles are classified in four groups (A, B, C, and

D) according to the characteristics and working qualities in finishing.

Manufactured granite or marble

Manufactured granite or marble is a masonry material used for either exterior or interior facing. Granite or marble aggregates in a wide variety of colors are formed by special bonding agents to produce slabs of great density and strength and low absorption. The slabs are usually formed in 1½ or 2¼-in. thicknesses for use in a manner similar to standing marble, but they may be formed in deeper sections to include reinforcing as lintels or for other structural purposes. They are often finished with a high polish. Erection is similar to other building stone surfacing units.

SLATE

Slate is used for roofing, exterior and interior wall panels, flooring, and other uses such as window sills, stair treads and risers, toilet stall partitions, and blackboards. The slate may be split to provide a natural cleft surface, or it may be sawed, planed, semirubbed, sand rubbed, or honed and polished. Edges may be sheared, smooth sawed, sand rubbed, or honed. The honed finish is rarely used on floors or treads. Exposed edges are usually sand rubbed. Colors, which vary with the quarry, are slate gray, blue-black, green, mottled green and purple, purple and red.

Interior slate flooring nominally ½ in. thick varies from ½ to ⅝ in. in actual thickness; 1-in. flooring varies from ⅞ to 1⅛ in. The ½-in. thickness is generally used unless exceptionally heavy traffic is anticipated. The slate is manufactured in a wide variety of standard sizes—from a nominal 6 by 6 in. up to 18 by 24 in.—many of which permit the development of patterns using one, two, or three sizes. Slate is also widely used in precut random rectangular patterns, as well as in quarry run irregular flagging. Some manufacturers provide slate sawn to a uniform thickness of ⅜ in. and cut to standard size for use as tile. Slate is laid similarly to floor marble over a concrete base in a portland cement mortar setting bed with joints ½ in. or more in width.

FLAGSTONE

Flagstone is the generic name for any stone used for paving an area to be walked on. Any hard stone that splits easily into large, relatively thin slabs may be used for this purpose. In addition to slate, many varieties of sandstones, quartzite, and limestone are commonly used as flagging, depending upon local availability and preferences. In the Middle Atlantic States the word flagstone has long meant only bluestone, a hard sandstone quarried in New York and Pennsylvania. Any stone used for flagging must be smooth enough for comfortable walking, but not so smooth as to be slippery when wet. For indoor use, smoother finishes and narrower joints are usually specified. Common flagstone patterns are shown in Fig. 13 and installation details are shown in Fig. 14.

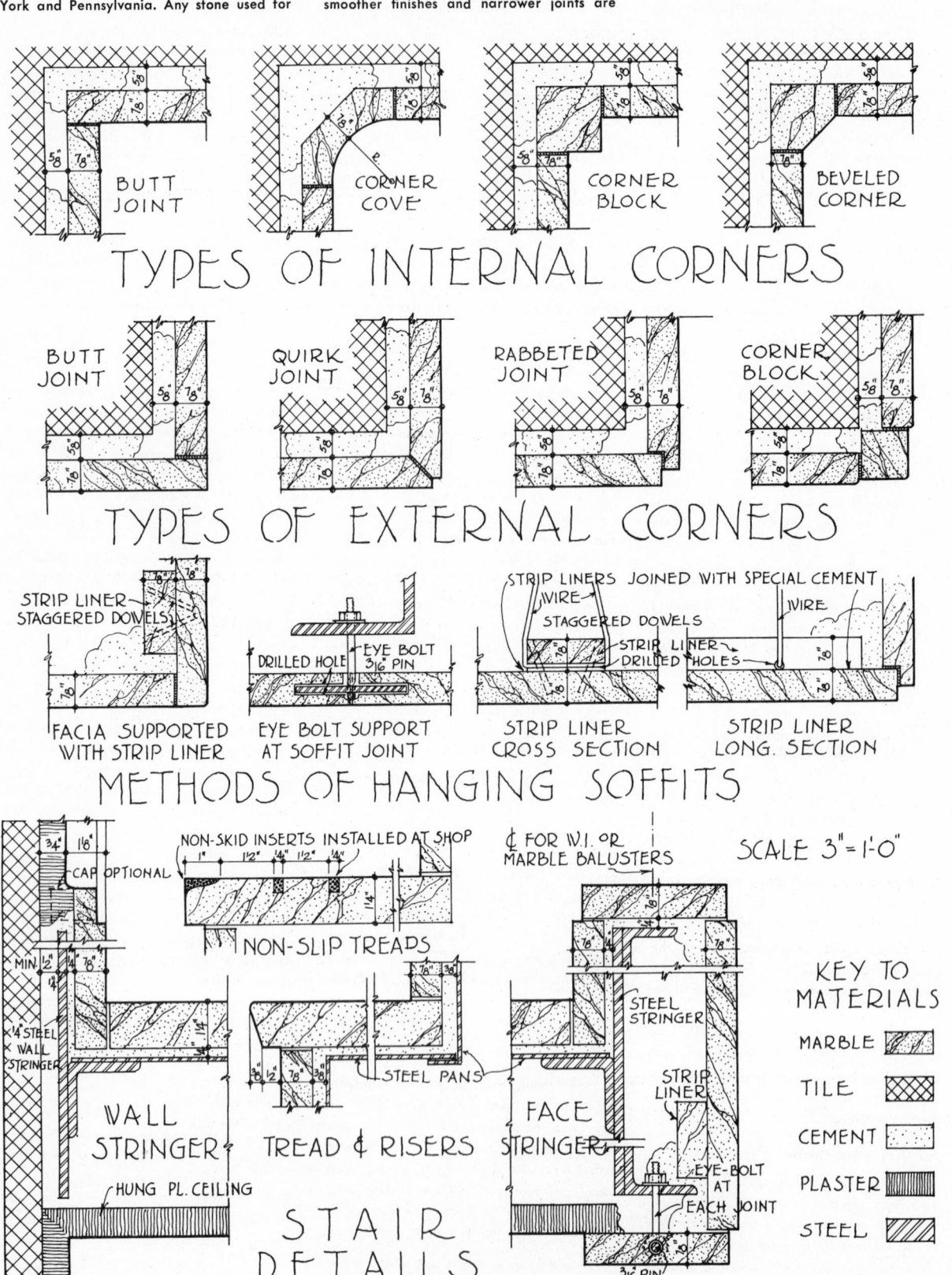

Fig. 11. Interior marble details

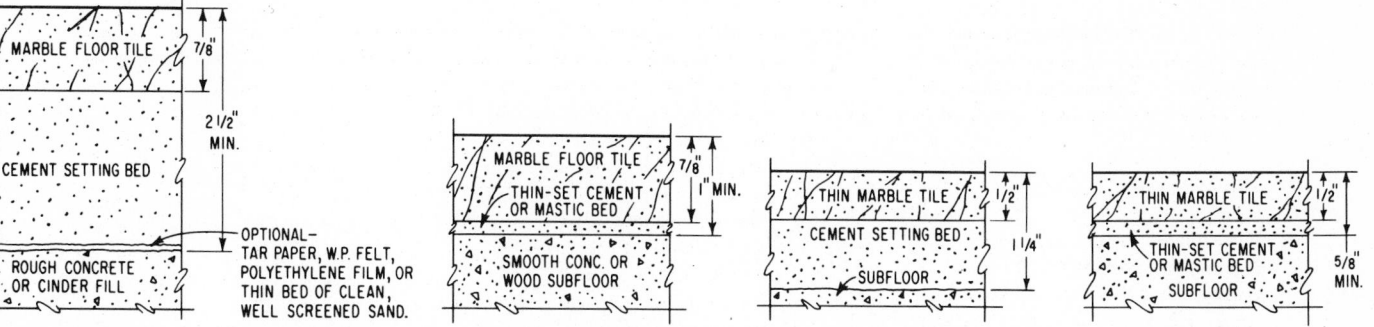

a. Standard floor tile, preferred method b. Standard floor tile, thin-set method c. Thin marble tile, preferred method d. Thin marble tile, thin-set method

Fig. 12. Marble floor setting methods

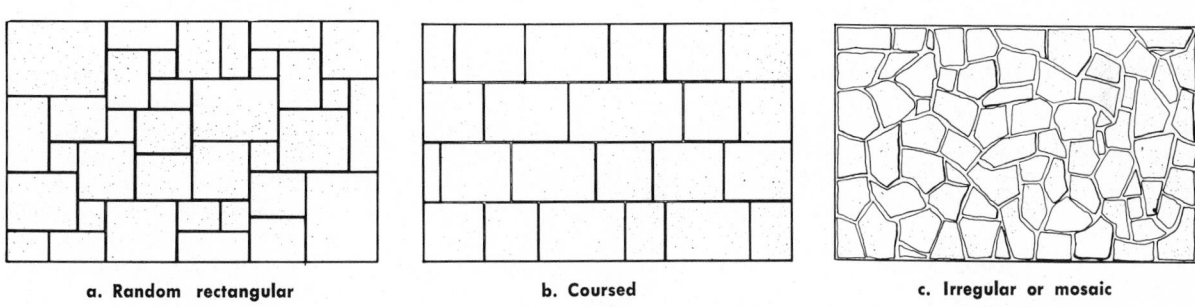

a. Random rectangular   b. Coursed   c. Irregular or mosaic

Fig. 13. Flagging patterns

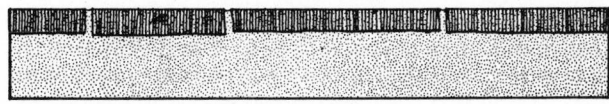

a. On sand bed

Flagging 1 to 1½ in.
Sand bed 4 in.

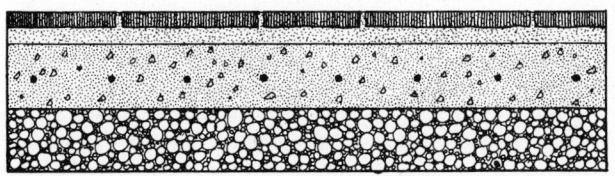

b. On concrete slab on grade

Flagging ¾ to 1 in.
Setting bed 1 to 1½ in.
Reinforced concrete slab 4 in.
Gravel or cinders 4 in.

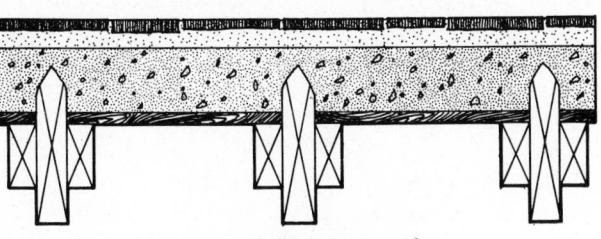

c. On wood joist construction

Flagging ¾ to 1 in.
Setting bed 1 to 1½ in.
Reinforced concrete slab 4 in.
Wood subfloor ¾ in.

Fig. 14. Flagstone setting methods

FIREPROOFING—1
Materials and methods

By HOWARD P. VERMILYA, AIA

BUILDING CODE REQUIREMENTS

Modern building codes specify minimum fire-resistance requirements based on studies by fire protection engineers. The degree of fire hazard in each type and size of construction and for each class of occupancy is evaluated, and the degree of fire resistance required for each building component is determined. The degree of fire resistance required for any structural component is expressed in terms of its ability to withstand fire exposure in accordance with the requirements of the standard time-temperature fire test of the American Society for Testing and Materials.

The ASTM Standard fire test specification (E 119-58) is the universally accepted standard for classifying the duration and intensity of fires and for measuring the degree of fire resistance provided by building materials and constructions. The fire-resistance rating is expressed as the time, in hours, that the assembly is able to withstand exposure to the standard fire (Fig. 1) before the first critical point in its behavior is reached. These tests indicate the length of time that structural members,

such as columns and beams, maintain their strength and rigidity, and that floors, roofs, walls, and partitions remain intact and prevent the spread of fire and the passage of flame, hot gases, and excessive heat. Actual tests of building assemblies form the basis of the fire-resistance rating and are now generally accepted by all nationally recognized model building codes that use this performance requirement in determining the degree of fire resistance for each construction and occupancy.

CONSTRUCTION MATERIALS

Construction materials must provide the following characteristics or properties in order to qualify as safe, dependable fireproofing:

1. They must not burn or support combustion.
2. They must prevent the rapid and excessive flow of heat for a definite period of time.
3. They must be sufficiently standardized and controlled to ensure consistent, dependable protection.

Gypsum

Gypsum, a mineral with unusual fire-resistant qualities, slowly releases water of crystallization in quantities up to one-half its volume when subjected to high temperatures. Until this water has been completely released and the gypsum has been dehydrated, the side away from the fire remains at approximately 212°F. Gypsum plaster, machine or manually applied to metal or gypsum lath, is very satisfactory fireproofing material. It may be combined with lightweight aggregates, wood fiber, or sand. Poured or precast gypsum slabs may be used with cellular steel floors, steel deck, or other floor or roof systems. Gypsum wallboard, in the form of lath or finish material, and gypsum tile are used as components of fire-resistant constructions.

Vermiculite and perlite

Vermiculite and perlite are lightweight aggregates possessing high thermal insulation qualities. They are used both in gypsum and cement plaster and in concrete. The weight of these aggregates is one-tenth that of sand. They are also used as ingredients in acoustical plaster with excellent fire-resistant as well as acoustical and insulating properties. Acoustical plaster usually consists of a colloidal clay or gypsum binder, vermiculite or perlite aggregate, mineral fibers, and a foaming agent added to create porosity. The plaster may be machine-applied directly to the underside of light-gage steel floors or roof decks, columns or beams, or to gypsum or metal lath.

Mineral fiber

Mineral fiber, combined with a mineral binder, air, and water, forms a very efficient fireproofing material. Applied with a special spray gun, the material will bond directly to steel, metal lath, and to most other clean rigid surfaces such as gypsum lath and concrete. In some constructions an adhesive is applied to the surface, and then the mineral fiber is sprayed on while the adhesive is still tacky, to increase the bond to the backing material. Mineral fiber has excellent fire-resistant qualities as well as acoustical qualities when applied to the underside of floors and roofs and also to steel structural members, such as columns, beams, girders, and trusses. Mineral fiber acoustical tile has also demonstrated its fire-resistant qualities when densely packed and faced with a finish coating.

Portland cement

Portland cement concrete continues to be useful as a fireproofing material. When subjected to high temperatures, it releases water in a manner similar to gypsum, although to a lesser degree. The selection

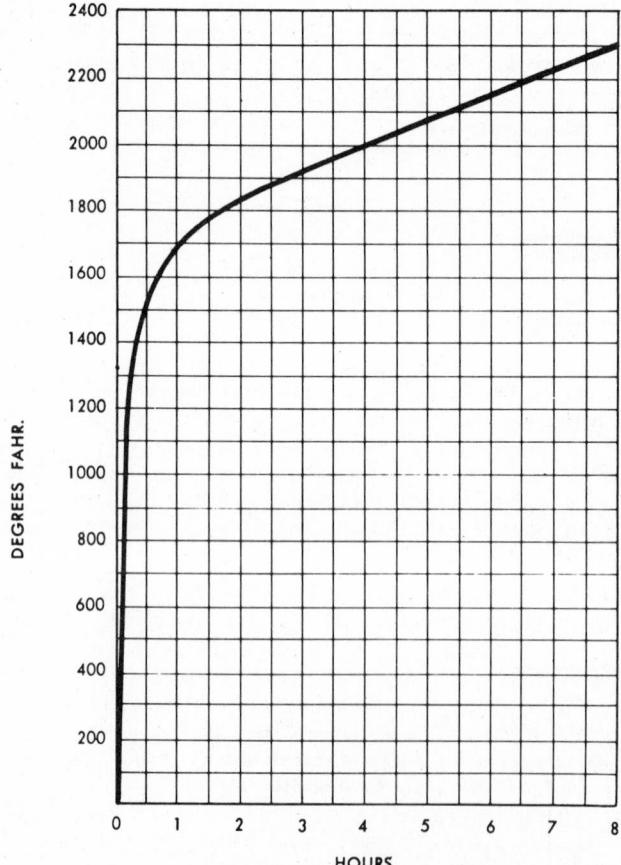

Fig. 1. ASTM time-temperature curve

In the standard fire test, air temperature rises to 1000°F in only 5 minutes, reaches 1,700°F at 1 hour, and 2,000°F at 4 hours.

of aggregate is critical to the fire resistance of concrete. Aggregate containing 60 per cent or more of quartz, chert, or granite is not as fire-resistant as limestone or trap rock and therefore the concrete must be increased in thickness to obtain a comparable fire rating. The use of light aggregates instead of stone greatly improves the fire resistance of concrete. Concrete is now used largely for fire protection in reinforced concrete, over steel floor and roof decks, and for steel columns (where it also provides protection from abrasion due to traffic). Portland cement plaster is also used for fire protection. Mixing it with lightweight aggregates and mineral fiber greatly improves its fire resistance. It is preferred to gypsum plaster if there is exposure to the weather or high humidity.

Masonry

Masonry (brick, clay tile, concrete or cinder blocks, gypsum tile) is mainly used for walls and partitions, for protection to spandrels, and as backup for curtain walls. Its weight and thickness have caused it to be less used than formerly in steel-framed buildings.

LIGHTWEIGHT CONSTRUCTION

Lightweight fire-resistant construction is a development of recent years. Concrete, steel-cellular, or composite-form floors and roofs, steel and precast concrete joists, junior beams, and corresponding wall elements have to a great extent replaced earlier heavier construction. Combinations of these elements with lightweight plaster and concrete, insulation, and sprayed-on or membrane fireproofing have made possible this lighter fire-resistant construction. The new performance codes using the ASTM fire ratings, instead of the old specification codes requiring a thickness of a specified number of inches, have aided this development.

The reduction in weight of the fireproofing alone has been significant. Lighter beams, girders, columns, and footings, or wider spacings with more free space, have been obtained. The American Institute of Steel Construction reports that if lightweight plaster or sprayed acoustical ceiling were suspended under a 24 by 24-ft floor bay designed for a 50-psf live load, the elimination of individual concrete fireproofing encasement of the supporting floor beams could reduce the dead load of that bay by more than 35 psf or 10½ tons. The Institute reports also that the use of a cellular or composite-form floor with thin topping could eliminate another 8 tons, a total saving of 18½ tons for a single bay.

MEMBRANE FIREPROOFING

Membrane fireproofing of floors and roofs consists of a thin, lightweight, fire-resistant ceiling interposed between the fire source and the incombustible floor or roof to be protected. The membrane may be directly attached to the lower surfaces of the framing members, or furred or suspended below them, and extends from wall to wall. Ducts, piping, wiring, and other mechanical equipment may be housed in the space between the floor or roof and the finished, fireproofing membrane ceiling below. Ceilings of vermiculite-, perlite-, or sand-gypsum plaster on metal or gypsum lath have served as membranes. All three aggregates are satisfactory for ratings up to and including 2 hr; the lightweight aggregates must be used for greater exposures. Most building code and fire insurance authorities recognize the equivalence of perlite and vermiculite aggregates for fire-resistance ratings. Thus their use is generally interchangeable. Gypsum lath used is ⅜ in. thick perforated. It is attached to furring channels with special clips; for greater fire resistance, 14 gage wire is inserted between lath and clip. For 4-hr resistance, 20 gage galvanized 1-in. hexagonal wire mesh is wire-tied beneath the gypsum lath. Tested fire-resistance ratings have been established for suspended ceilings pierced for ducts and electric outlets. These tested ratings show that the openings have little effect on the fire resistance if their total area is not greater proportionally than 100 sq in. per 100 sq ft of ceiling, or if the openings are protected. Acoustical plaster and sprayed mineral fiber on metal or gypsum lath, and mineral fiber acoustical tiles on suspension systems as membranes, have also received excellent fire ratings. Membrane fireproofing has made unnecessary the individual fireproofing of beams and girders supporting the incombustible floor or roof above and at the same time gives valuable protection to the hidden equipment, thus reducing fire losses significantly.

CONTACT FIREPROOFING

Contact fireproofing is applied directly to the surface of the structural component to be protected. In floor and roof systems, acoustical plaster or sprayed mineral fiber (usually proprietary products) is machine-applied directly to the underside of cellular or composite-form steel floors. With contact fireproofing, all supporting beams and girders must also be protected. This may be done by encasing them with lath or by spraying the plaster or fiber directly on the beam, maintaining a uniform thick-ness over exposed surfaces of flanges and web. In addition to their fireproofing characteristics these materials provide excellent sound absorption and thermal insulation.

"DOUBLE HUNG" CEILINGS

Costs can often be reduced with "double hung" ceilings by selecting the right combination that will also perform necessary functions like sound conditioning, fireproofing, thermal insulation, and air distribution. The price of these features installed separately can be more than the cost of two ceilings.

The first ceiling is placed below the floor and structural steel. It consists of a combination fireproofing, sound-absorbing, and thermal-insulating material like sprayed fiber applied to metal lath. A second ceiling of perforated metal acoustic pans is suspended below the air-conditioning ducts and other utilities. The use of a combination fireproofing and sound-absorbing material eliminates the need for the usual mineral wool batts behind the metal pans. The air-conditioning ducts open directly into the plenum chamber formed by the two ceilings, and the whole perforated pan system acts as a giant air diffuser.

ACOUSTICAL TILE CEILINGS

The use of acoustical tile ceilings as fire protection to incombustible and combustible floor and roof decks is a relatively recent development. Fire-resistant tile (Federal Specification SS-A-118b, Class A), 12 by 12 in. or larger, ⅝ or ¾ in. thick, in fissured or perforated patterns, are used in a special steel suspension system. Fire-resistance ratings of up to 4 hr can be attained by the use of this system below unprotected steel beams or joists supporting an incombustible floor deck. Ratings of up to 1½ hr can be achieved for wood floors supported on wood joists.

REFERENCES

Fire-resistance Ratings. National Board of Fire Underwriters (April 1959).

Fire-resistant Construction in Modern Steel-framed Buildings. American Institute of Steel Construction, Inc. (1959).

Lathing and Plastering Assemblies. National Bureau for Lathing and Plastering, Inc.

Membrane Fireproofing. Gypsum Association.

Metal Lath Membrane Fireproofing for Steel Buildings. Technical Bulletin No. 3, Metal Lath Manufacturers Association.

National Building Code. National Board of Fire Underwriters (1955).

Vermiculite Fire-resistance Ratings. Vermiculite Institute (Revised, October 1960).

Table 1. Fire-resistance ratings of various assemblies

Superscript numbers refer to notes at the end of this table. *This table is from* Fire-resistant Construction in Modern Steel-framed Buildings, *published by American Institute of Steel Construction (1959).*

Columns

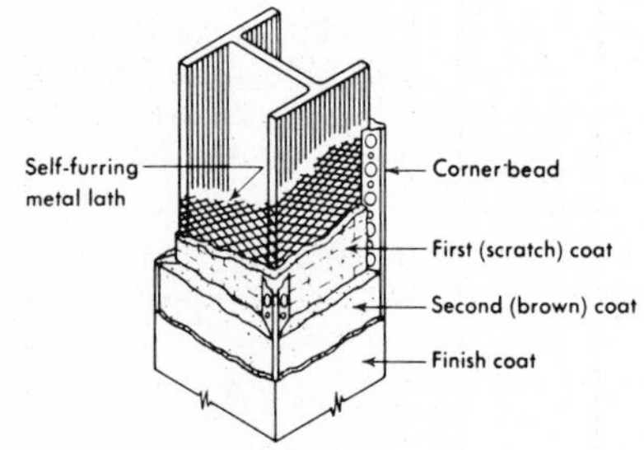

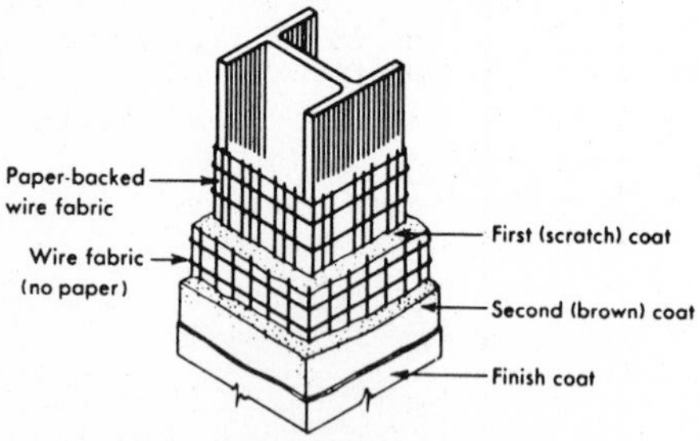

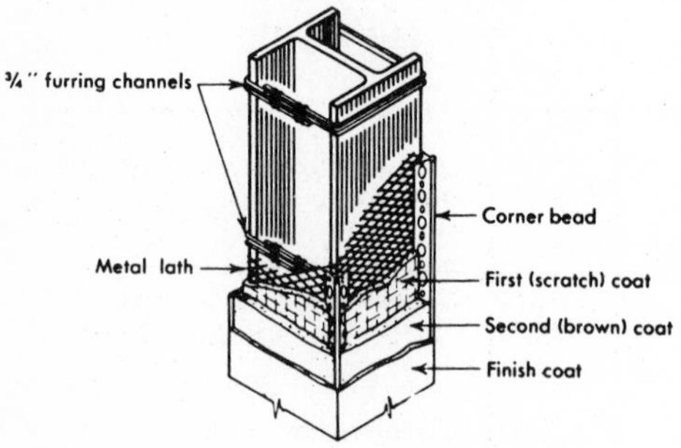

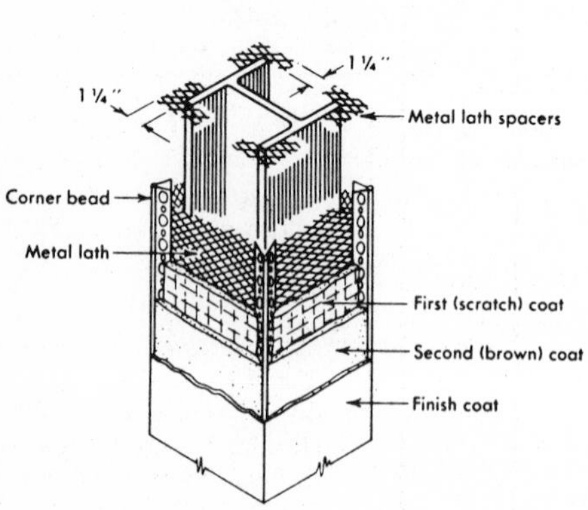

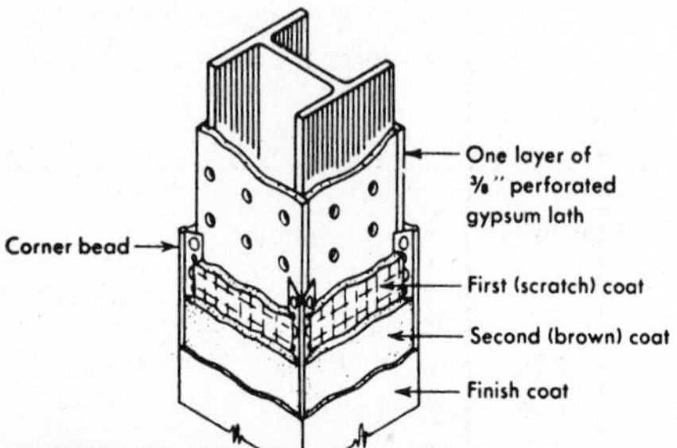

No.	Description	Rating (Hours)	Authority [1]
1	1¾" vermiculite- or perlite-gypsum plaster [2] on self-furring metal lath. [3]	4	Underwriters' Lab., Inc. Ret. 3187-4 (Design 6-4 hr.) Ret. 2851-6 (Design 9-4 hr.)
2	1⅜" vermiculite- or perlite-gypsum plaster [2] on self-furring metal lath. [3]	3	Underwriters' Lab., Inc. Ret. 3187-7 (Design 6-3 hr.) Ret. 2851-5 (Design 8-3 hr.)
3	1" perlite-gypsum plaster [2] on self-furring metal lath. [3]	2	Underwriters' Lab., Inc. Ret. 3187-5 (Design 2-2 hr.)
4	2" vermiculite-portland cement plaster [4] on paper-backed wire fabric, [5] with an additional layer of wire fabric (no paper) [6] over scratch coat.	4	Underwriters' Lab., Inc. Ret. 3653-3 (Design 10-4 hr.)
5	Same as No. 4 above, except: 2⅛" perlite-portland cement plaster. [7]	4	Underwriters' Lab., Inc. Ret. 3329-2 (Design 8-4 hr.)
6	1½" perlite-gypsum plaster [2] on metal lath [8] spaced from column flanges by ¾" steel furring channels. No back fill plaster required between metal lath and column flanges.	4	Underwriters' Lab., Inc. Ret. 3187-6 (Design 7-4 hr.)
7	Same as No. 6 above, except: ¾" sand-gypsum plaster [9] **or** 1" portland cement plaster [10] on metal lath. [11]	1	Nat'l Bureau of Standards BMS 92—Table 40
8	1½" vermiculite- or perlite-gypsum plaster [2] on metal lath. [8] Lath spaced 1¼" from column flanges. Space behind lath on flange faces filled with plaster.	4	Underwriters' Lab., Inc. Ret. 2851-2 (Design 1-4 hr.) Ret. 3187-3 (Design 2-4 hr.)
9	Same as No. 8 above, except: 1" vermiculite- or perlite-gypsum plaster. [2]	3	Underwriters' Lab., Inc. Ret. 2851-1 (Design 1-3 hr.) Ret. 3187-1 (Design 3-3 hr.)
10	Same as No. 8 above, except: 1½" vermiculite-gypsum plaster [2] with **no** plaster fill behind lath.	3	Underwriters' Lab., Inc. Ret. 3422-2 (Design 9-3 hr.)
11	Same as No. 8 above, except: 1" perlite-gypsum plaster [2] with **no** plaster fill behind lath.	2	Underwriters' Lab., Inc. Ret. 3187-2 (Design 1-2 hr.)
12	1⅜" perlite-gypsum plaster [2] **or** 2" sand-gypsum plaster [12] on one (1) layer of ⅜" perforated gypsum lath.	3	Nat'l Bureau of Standards Test 321 and Test 344
13	1" perlite-gypsum plaster [2] **or** 1⅜" sand-gypsum plaster [12] on one (1) layer of ⅜" perforated gypsum lath.	2	Nat'l Bureau of Standards BMS 135—Test 275 Test 351
14	½" sand-gypsum plaster [13] on one (1) layer of ⅜" perforated gypsum lath.	1	Nat'l Bureau of Standards BMS 135—Test 273

Table 1. (Cont.) Fire-resistance ratings of various assemblies

Superscript numbers refer to notes at the end of this table. Asterisks identify tests conducted 5 hours or more without reaching critical limits. This table is from Fire-resistant Construction in Modern Steel-framed Buildings, *published by American Institute of Steel Construction (1959).*

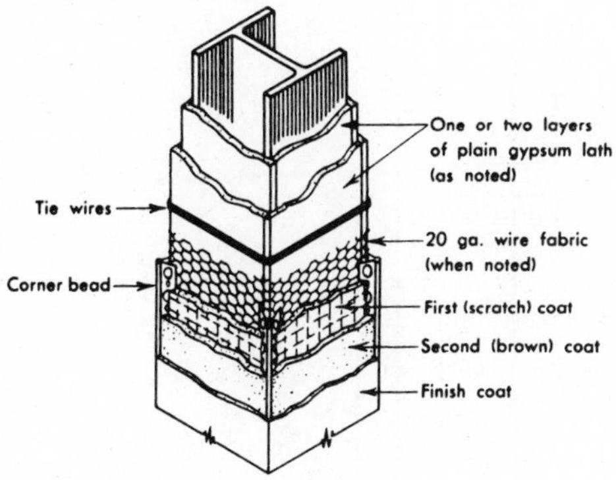

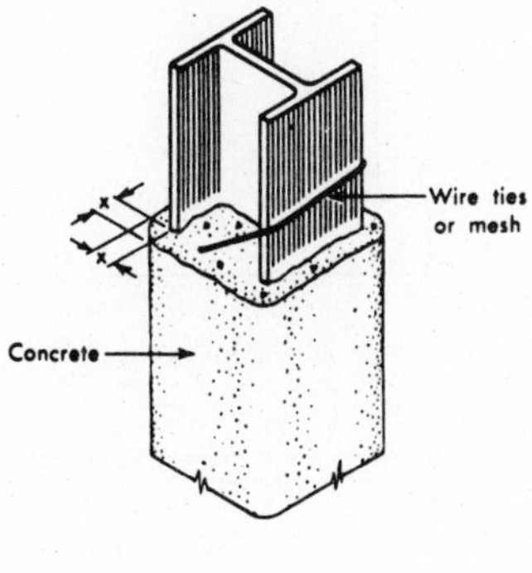

One or two layers of plain gypsum lath (as noted)
Tie wires
Corner bead
20 ga. wire fabric (when noted)
First (scratch) coat
Second (brown) coat
Finish coat

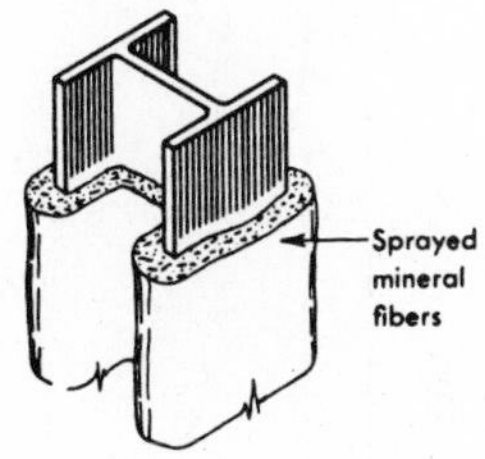

No.	Description		Rating (Hours)	Authority [1]
15	1½″ perlite- or vermiculite-gypsum plaster [2] on two (2) layers of ½″ thick plain gypsum lath wrapped with one (1) layer of 20 ga. wire mesh fabric, 1″ mesh (poultry netting).		4	Nat'l Bureau of Standards BMS 135—Tests 278, 279, 280, 294
16	2⅛″ (⅝″ scratch coat and 1½″ brown coat) perlite-gypsum plaster [14] on one (1) layer of ½″ thick plain gypsum lath. 17 ga. wire mesh fabric, 1″ mesh (poultry netting) over scratch coat; **no** fabric over lath.		4	Underwriters' Lab., Inc. Ret. 3329-1 (Design 4-4 hr.)
17	1½″ (¾″ scratch coat and ¾″ brown coat) perlite-gypsum plaster [2] on one (1) layer of ½″ thick plain gypsum lath. One (1) layer of 20 ga. wire mesh fabric, 1″ mesh (poultry netting) over scratch coat; **no** fabric over lath.		3	Nat'l Bureau of Standards BMS 135—Test 277
18	Same as No. 15 above, except: 1″ perlite-gypsum plaster.[2]		3	Nat'l Bureau of Standards BMS 135—Test 276
19	1⅜″ perlite-gypsum plaster [2] on two (2) layers of ½″ thick plain gypsum lath; no fabric over scratch coat or lath.		3	Nat'l Bureau of Standards BMS 135—Tests 289, 293
20	2½″ sprayed mineral fibers [15] applied directly to column coated with special adhesive.		4*	Underwriters' Lab., Inc. Ret. 3749-4 (Design 11-5 hr.)
21	2″ sprayed mineral fibers [15] applied directly to column coated with special adhesive.		3	Underwriters' Lab., Inc. Ret. 3705-2 (Design 7-3 hr.)
22	1½″ sprayed mineral fibers [15] applied directly to column coated with special adhesive.		2	Underwriters' Lab., Inc. Ret. 3705-3 (Design 4-2 hr.)
23	Concrete encasement: Grade "A" concrete.[16]	$x = 2″$ $x = 1½″$ $x = 1″$	4, 3 2 1	Nat'l Bureau of Standards** BMS 92—Table 39 TP 184
24	Concrete encasement: Grade "B" concrete.[17]	$x = 2½″$ $x = 2″$ $x = 1½″$	4 3 2, 1	**Listed ratings are **not** tested ratings, but are based on the results of standard tests described in these references.[19]
25	Concrete encasement: Grade "C" concrete.[18]	$x = 3″$ $x = 2½″$ $x = 2″$ $x = 1½″$	4 3 2 1	
26	Gypsum concrete encasement; 4″ x 4″ wire mesh reinforcement wrapped around column.	$x = 2″$	4[20]	Nat'l Bureau of Standards Research Paper No. RP563
27	Brick; 3¾″ thick; reentrant spaces filled with brick and mortar. No plaster.		4*	Nat'l Bureau of Standards BMS 92—Table 40
28	Same as No. 27 above, except: 2¼″ thick.		1	

Table 1 (Cont.) Fire-resistance ratings of various assemblies

Superscript numbers refer to notes at the end of this table. Asterisks identify tests conducted 5 hours or more without reaching critical limits. This table is from Fire-resistant Construction in Modern Steel-framed Buildings, *published by American Institute of Steel Construction (1959).*

No.	Description	Rating (Hours)	Authority [1]
29	2″ gypsum block, solid, plus ½″ sand-gypsum plaster.[9] Cramps at horizontal joints. Mortar on flange only at horizontal joints. No fill. Minimum area of solid material to be 105 sq. inches.	4	
30	Same as No. 29 above, except: 3″ gypsum block, hollow, plus ½″ sand-gypsum plaster.[9] Minimum area of solid material to be 120 sq. inches.	4*	
31	Same as No. 29 above, except: No plaster. Minimum area of solid material to be 85 sq. inches.	2	
32	Same as No. 30 above, except: No plaster. Minimum area of solid material to be 95 sq. inches.	2	
33	2″, 3″ or 4″ hollow clay or shale tile; reentrant spaces filled with concrete. Wire mesh in horizontal joints; Mortar between tile and column flanges. No plaster. Minimum area of solid material to be 225 sq. inches.	4	Nat'l Bureau of Standards BMS 92—Table 40
34	4″ hollow clay tile in two 2″ layers; Mortar between tile and column flanges. Wire mesh in horizontal joints. Reentrant spaces filled with tile and mortar. No plaster. Minimum area of solid material to be 250 sq. inches.	4	
35	Same as No. 33 above, except: Minimum area of solid material to be 180 sq. inches.	3	
36	Same as No. 33 above, except: Minimum area of solid material to be 110 sq. inches.	2	
37	Same as No. 33 above, except: Reentrant spaces not filled. Minimum area of solid material to be 70 sq. inches.	1	
38	3″ cinder block, hollow. Reentrant spaces filled with block and mortar. No plaster. Minimum area of solid material to be 240 sq. inches.	4 [21]	

Fill (when noted)

Masonry units

Plaster (when noted)

Beams, girders, and trusses: individually fireproofed

No.	Description	Rating (Hours)	Authority [1]
39	1½″ vermiculite- or perlite-gypsum plaster [2] on self-furring metal lath.[3]	4* [22]	Underwriters' Lab., Inc. Ret. 2689-5 (Design 19-4 hr.) Ret. 3413-4 (Design 8-4 hr.) Ret. 4197-1
40	1⅛″ vermiculite-gypsum plaster [2] on flat expanded metal lath [8] furred from flanges by ¾″ furring channels.	4	Underwriters' Lab., Inc. Ret. 3372-3 (Design 16-4 hr.)
41	1¼″ perlite-gypsum plaster [2] on flat expanded metal lath.[8]	3	Underwriters' Lab., Inc. Ret. 4197-1

(See drawing, top of next page.)

Table 1 (Cont.). Fire-resistance ratings of various assemblies

Superscript numbers refer to notes at the end of this table. Asterisks identify tests conducted 5 hours or more without reaching critical limits. This table is from Fire-resistant Construction in Modern Steel-framed Buildings, *published by American Institute of Steel Construction (1959).*

No.	Description	Rating (Hours)	Authority [1]
42	1″ vermiculite-gypsum plaster [2] on flat expanded metal lath.[8]	$2\frac{1}{2}$ [23]	Underwriters' Lab., Inc. Ret. 3413-10 (Design 3-2 hr.)
43	Same as No. 42 above, except: $\frac{7}{8}$″ vermiculite-gypsum plaster.[2]	2	Underwriters' Lab., Inc. Ret. 3413-9 (Design 7-3 hr.)
44	2″ vermiculite or perlite acoustic plaster [15] on self-furring metal lath,[3] or flat expanded metal lath.[8]	4	Underwriters' Lab., Inc. Ret. 3413-7 (Design 10-4 hr.) Ret. 3983-1
45	$1\frac{3}{4}$″ perlite acoustic plaster [15] on flat expanded metal lath.[8]	3	Underwriters' Lab., Inc. Ret. 3413-11 (Design 7-2 hr.)
46	Sprayed mineral fibers,[15] $1\frac{1}{4}$″ thick on sides of beam, $1\frac{1}{2}$″ thick below beam on ribbed metal lath.[24] No adhesive.	4*	Underwriters' Lab., Inc. Ret. 3705-3 (Design 20-4 hr.)
47	$1\frac{7}{8}$″ sprayed mineral fibers [15] applied directly to beam coated with special adhesive.	4	Underwriters' Lab., Inc. Ret. 2923-4
48	$1\frac{7}{16}$″ sprayed mineral fibers [15] applied directly to beam coated with special adhesive.	3	Underwriters' Lab. of Canada Ret. 193-2 (Design C9-3 hr.)
49	$1\frac{1}{8}$″ sprayed mineral fibers [15] applied directly to beam coated with special adhesive.	2	Underwriters' Lab. of Canada Ret. 193-3
50	Concrete encasement: Use same ratings and constructions designated for column protections in Fire Resistance Ratings Nos. 23, 24 and 25 listed on page 28.	4,3,2,1	Estimated ratings based on column tests.

Beams, girders, and trusses: fire-protected by a membrane ceiling

No.	Description	Rating (Hours)	Authority [1]
51	1″ vermiculite-gypsum plaster.[26] $x = 0$″	4	Nat'l Bureau of Standards BMS 92—Table 43
52	$\frac{7}{8}$″ perlite-gypsum plaster.[2] $x = 2\frac{3}{4}$″ Note: Ceiling pierced with duct openings (70 sq. inches in each 100 sq. feet of ceiling area) and electrical outlets (one in each 90 sq. feet of ceiling area). Duct openings protected with fusible link dampers.	4	Underwriters' Lab., Inc. Ret. 3724-1 (Design 8-3 hr.)
53	$\frac{3}{4}$″ perlite-gypsum plaster.[2] $x = 3\frac{1}{2}$″ Note: Ceiling pierced same as No. 52 above, except duct openings 113 sq. inches in each 100 sq. feet of ceiling area.	4	Underwriters' Lab., Inc. Ret. 3574-6 (Design 11-3 hr.)
54	$\frac{5}{8}$″ vermiculite-gypsum plaster [2] base plus $\frac{1}{2}$″ finish vermiculite acoustic plaster.[15] (Total thickness $1\frac{1}{8}$″ over face of lath.) $x = 2\frac{1}{2}$″	4	Underwriters' Lab., Inc. Ret. 2773-5 (Design 4-4 hr.)

Note: Superior numbers refer to notes on page 40.

Asterisks (*) identify tests conducted 5 hours or more without reaching critical limits.

Table 1 (Cont.) Fire-resistance ratings of various assemblies

Superscript numbers refer to notes at the end of this table. Asterisks identify tests conducted 5 hours or more without reaching critical limits. This table is from Fire-resistant Construction in Modern Steel-framed Buildings, *published by American Institute of Steel Construction (1959).*

No.	Description	Rating (Hours)	Authority [1]
55	$\frac{7}{8}$" vermiculite-gypsum plaster.[2] $x = 3\frac{1}{2}$" Note: Ceiling pierced same as No. 52 above, except duct openings 85 sq. inches in each 100 sq. feet of ceiling area.	3	Underwriters' Lab., Inc. Ret. 2689 (Design 1-3 hr.)
56	$\frac{3}{4}$" vermiculite-gypsum plaster.[26] $x = 0$"	3	
57	1" neat wood-fibered gypsum plaster. $x = 0$"	3	
58	$1\frac{1}{8}$" sand-gypsum plaster.[27] $x = 0$"	3	
59	$1\frac{1}{2}$" sand-gypsum plaster.[28] $x = 0$"	$2\frac{1}{2}$	
60	1" sprayed asbestos fibers.[15] $x = 0$"	$2\frac{1}{2}$	Nat'l Bureau of Standards BMS 92—Tables 43 and 44 TRBM 44—Tables 18 and 22
61	$\frac{3}{4}$" sand-gypsum plaster.[12] $x = 0$"	2	
62	1" sand-portland cement plaster.[29] $x = 0$"	2	
63	$\frac{3}{4}$" sprayed asbestos fibers.[15] $x = 0$"	2	
64	$\frac{3}{4}$" sand-portland cement plaster with asbestos fibers added.[30] $x = 0$"	$1\frac{1}{2}$	
65	$\frac{5}{8}$" sprayed asbestos fibers.[15] $x = 0$"	$1\frac{1}{2}$	
66	$\frac{1}{2}$" perlite-gypsum plaster,[2] reinforced with 1" hexagonal wire mesh stretched under lath. $x = \frac{3}{4}$"	4*	Nat'l Bureau of Standards BMS 141—Test 312
67	$\frac{5}{8}$" perlite-gypsum plaster,[2] reinforced with No. 14 ga. wires secured below lath on the diagonal, corner to corner of lath. $x = \frac{3}{4}$"	4	Nat'l Bureau of Standards BMS 141—Test 313
68	$\frac{1}{2}$" perlite-gypsum plaster,[2] reinforced with No. 14 ga. wires secured below lath on the diagonal, corner to corner of lath. $x = \frac{3}{4}$"	$2\frac{1}{2}$	Nat'l Bureau of Standards BMS 141—Test 318
69	$\frac{5}{8}$" sand-gypsum plaster,[12] reinforced with No. 14 ga. wires secured below lath on the diagonal, corner to corner of lath. $x = \frac{3}{4}$"	$1\frac{1}{2}$	Nat'l Bureau of Standards Test 345
70	1" perlite-gypsum plaster,[2] no reinforcement. $x = \frac{3}{4}$"	$1\frac{1}{2}$	Nat'l Bureau of Standards BMS 141—Test 295
71	$\frac{1}{2}$" perlite-gypsum plaster,[2] no reinforcement. $x = \frac{3}{4}$"	1	Nat'l Bureau of Standards BMS 141—Tests 317, 319
72	$\frac{3}{4}$" mineral fiber acoustic tile suspended from runners and T-shaped clipped splines.[38]	4*	Underwriters' Lab., Inc. Ret. 4177-2 (Design 21-4 hr.)

(See drawing, bottom of preceding page.)

Floor construction of required fire resistance

Membrane ceiling (pierced as noted)

$\frac{3}{8}$" perforated gypsum lath

x = minimum clearance from underside of bottom flange to back of metal lath.

Floor construction of required fire resistance

Suspension system with main runners and T-clip splines

1" mineral fiber acoustic tiles with coated faces

Table 1 (Cont.)   Fire-resistance ratings of various assemblies

Superscript numbers refer to notes at the end of this table.
Asterisks identify tests conducted 5 hours or more without
reaching critical limits. This table is from Fire-resistant

Construction in Modern Steel-framed Buildings, *published*
by American Institute of Steel Construction (1959).

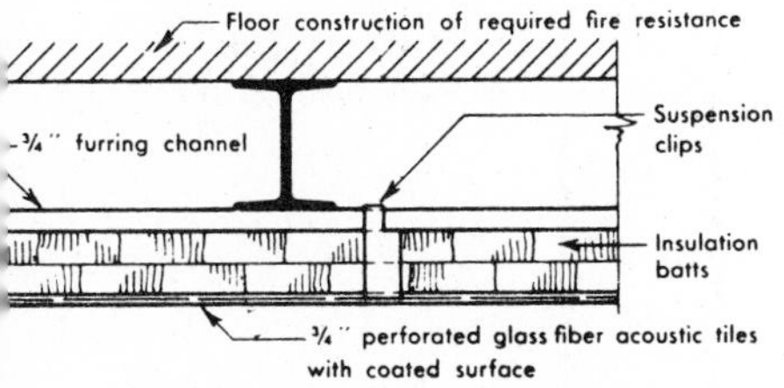

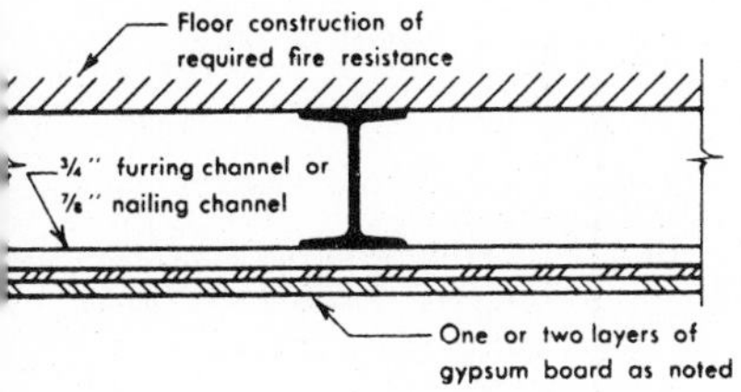

	No.	Description	Rating (Hours)	Authority [1]
	73	4" of mineral wool insulating batts (2 layers, 2" thick each), plus 3/4" perforated glass fiber acoustic tile clipped to furring channels.	2	Underwriters' Lab., Inc. Ret. 3583-1 (Design 1-2 hr.)
	74	1/2" gypsum wallboard, nailed 6" o.c. into nailing channels, over 5/8" gypsum coreboard. Joints of wallboard staggered from coreboard joints.	1½	Underwriters' Lab., Inc. Ret. 1319-26 (Design 2-1½ hr.)
	75	One layer 5/8" gypsum wallboard or coreboard nailed into nailing channels, or screwed into furring channels.	1	Underwriters' Lab., Inc. Ret. 2717-16 (Design 2-1 hr.) Ret. 1319-14 (Design 5-1 hr.) Ret. 3501-18 (Design 8-1 hr.)

Floor and roof systems: light-gage steel systems—membrane fireproofed

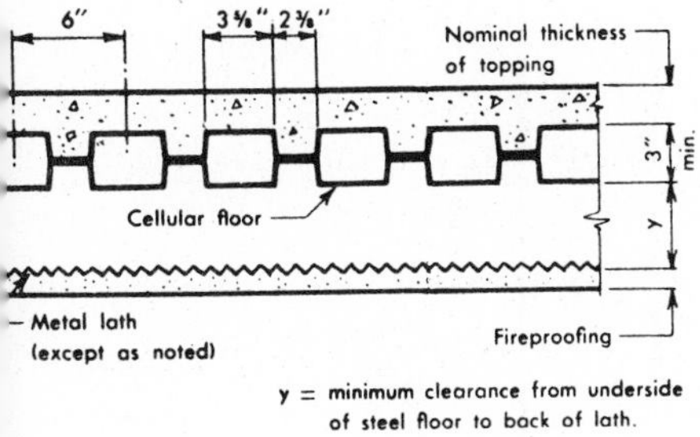

	No.	Description	Rating (Hours)	Authority [1]
	76	Topping: 2" sand-gravel concrete. Fireproofing: 1" vermiculite-gypsum plaster [26] on metal lath. $y = 2"$	4	Nat'l Bureau of Standards BMS 92—Table 45
	77	Topping: 2" perlite-concrete. Fireproofing: 1" perlite-gypsum plaster on metal lath. $y = 3"$	4	Underwriters' Lab., Inc. Ret. 2993 (Design 3-4 hr.)
	78	Topping: 2" sand-gravel concrete. Fireproofing: 1" neat fibered gypsum plaster [2] on metal lath.[8] $y = 9"$	4	Nat'l Bureau of Standards BMS 92—Table 45
	79	Topping: 2½" sand-gravel concrete. Fireproofing: 5/8" vermiculite-gypsum plaster [2] base plus 1/2" finish vermiculite acoustic plaster.[15] (Total thickness 1⅛" over face of metal lath). $y = 7¼"$	4	Underwriters' Lab., Inc. Ret. 2773-5 (Design 4-4 hr.)
	80	Topping: 2½" sand-gravel concrete. Fireproofing: 3/4" perlite-gypsum plaster [2] base plus 1/2" acoustic plaster.[15] (Total thickness 1¼" over face of metal lath). $y = 7¼"$	4*	Nat'l Bureau of Standards Test 338
	81	Topping: 3¼" sand-gravel concrete. Fireproofing: 1" perlite-gypsum plaster [2] on metal lath [24] tied directly to underside of floor. $y = 0"$	4*	Underwriters' Lab., Inc. Ret. 3789-1 (Design 15-5 hr.)
	82	Topping: 2" sand-gravel concrete. Fireproofing: 7/8" vermiculite-gypsum plaster [2] on metal lath.[8] $y = 15⅜"$	3	Underwriters' Lab., Inc. Ret. 2689 (Design 1-3 hr.)
		Note: Ceilings pierced with duct openings (85 sq. inches in each 100 sq. feet of ceiling area) and electrical outlets (one in each 90 sq. feet of ceiling area). Duct openings protected with fusible link dampers.		

Table 1 (Cont.) Fire-resistance ratings of various assemblies

Superscript numbers refer to notes at the end of this table.
Asterisks identify tests conducted 5 hours or more without
reaching critical limits. This table is from Fire-resistant

Construction in Modern Steel-framed Buildings, *published*
by American Institute of Steel Construction (1959).

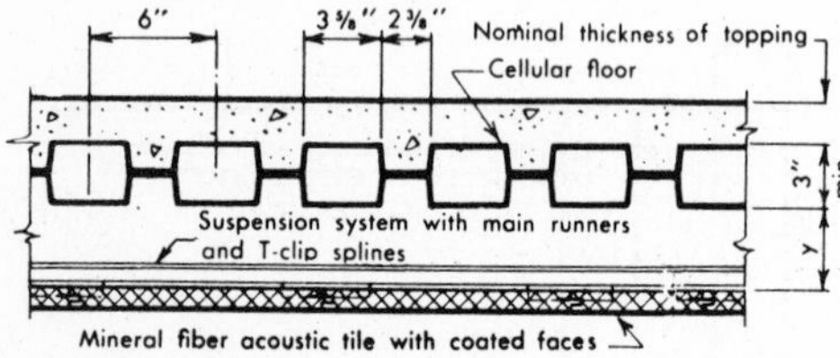

No.	Description	Rating (Hours)	Authority [1]
83	Topping: 2″ sand-gravel concrete. Fireproofing: ¾″ perlite-gypsum plaster [2] on metal lath.[8] $y = 15\frac{1}{2}″$ Note: Ceilings pierced same as No. 82 above, except duct openings 113 sq. inches in each 100 sq. feet of ceiling area.	3	Underwriters' Lab., Inc. Ret. 3574-6 (Design 11-3 hr.)
84	Topping: 2″ sand-gravel concrete. Fireproofing: 1″ neat fibered gypsum plaster on metal lath. $y = 2″$	3	Nat'l Bureau of Standards BMS 92—Table 45
85	Topping: 2½″ sand-gravel concrete. Fireproofing: ½″ perlite-gypsum plaster [2] on ⅜″ perforated gypsum lath. $y = 7\frac{1}{4}″$	3	Nat'l Bureau of Standards Test 337
86	Topping: 2″ sand-gravel concrete. Fireproofing: 1″ sprayed mineral fibers [15] on metal lath [24] coated with special adhesive. $y = 4\frac{1}{4}″$	3	Underwriters' Lab., Inc. Ret. 2923-1 (Design 2-3 hr.)
87	Topping: 2½″ sand-gravel concrete. Fireproofing: ¾″ mineral fiber acoustic tiles, tongued and grooved, on T-spline suspension system. $y = 10\frac{7}{8}″$	4	Underwriters' Lab., Inc. Ret. 4177-2 (Design 21-4 hr.)
88	Topping: 2″ cinder-concrete. Fireproofing: ⅞″ vermiculite-gypsum plaster [2] on metal lath.[8] $y = 2\frac{1}{2}″$	4	Underwriters' Lab., Inc. Ret. 2689 (Design 1-4 hr.)
89	Topping: 2″ sand-gravel concrete. Fireproofing: ⅞″ perlite-gypsum plaster [2] on metal lath.[8] $y = 15\frac{1}{2}″$ Note: Ceilings pierced with duct openings (70 sq. inches in each 100 sq. feet of ceiling area) and electrical outlets (one in each 90 sq. feet of ceiling area). Duct openings protected by fusible link dampers.	4	Underwriters' Lab., Inc. Ret. 3355 (Design 5-4 hr.)
90	Same as No. 89 above, except: $y = 14\frac{3}{4}″$	3	Underwriters' Lab., Inc. Ret. 3724-1 (Design 8-3 hr.)
91	Topping: 2″ sand-gravel concrete. Fireproofing: 1⅛″ sprayed mineral fibers [15] applied to metal lath [24] coated with special adhesive. $y = 4\frac{1}{2}″$ Note: Minimum depth of cellular floor to be 4½″.	3	Underwriters' Lab., Inc. Ret. 3372-1 (Design 4-3 hr.)

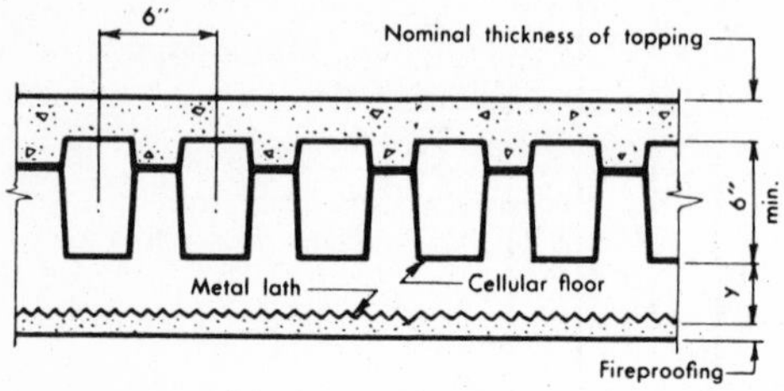

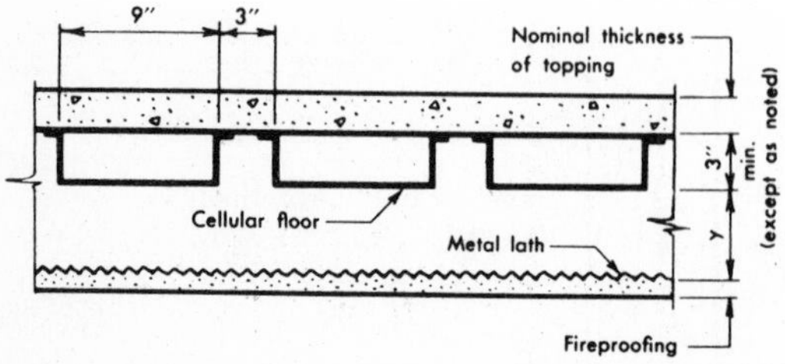

Figure (row 87):
6″   3⅛″ 2⅜″
Nominal thickness of topping
Cellular floor
3″ min.
Suspension system with main runners and T-clip splines
Mineral fiber acoustic tile with coated faces

Figure (row 88):
6″
Nominal thickness of topping
6″ min.
Metal lath — Cellular floor
Fireproofing
y = minimum clearance from underside of steel floor to back of lath.

Figure (row 89–91):
9″   3″
Nominal thickness of topping
3″ min. (except as noted)
Cellular floor
Metal lath
Fireproofing
y = minimum clearance from underside of steel floor to back of lath.

Table 1. (Cont.) Fire-resistance ratings of various assemblies

Superscript numbers refer to notes at the end of this table. Asterisks identify tests conducted 5 hours or more without reaching critical limits. This table is from Fire-resistant Construction in Modern Steel-framed Buildings, *published by American Institute of Steel Construction (1959).*

Temperature rod — Nominal thickness of slab — Composite-form floor — Metal lath — Fireproofing — y = minimum clearance from underside of steel floor to back of lath.

Nominal thickness of topping — Poured topping — Rigid topping — Roof deck — Metal lath — Fireproofing — y = minimum clearance from underside of steel floor to back of lath.

No.	Description	Rating (Hours)	Authority [1]
92	Slab: 4½" sand-gravel concrete. Fireproofing: 1" vermiculite-gypsum plaster [2] on metal lath. [8] y = 14½"	4	Underwriters' Lab., Inc. Ret. 3413-1 (Design 7-4 hr.)
93	Topping: 2" sand-gravel concrete. Fireproofing: 15/16" perlite-gypsum plaster [2] on metal lath. [8] y = 15½" Note: Ceilings pierced with duct openings (113 sq. inches in each 100 sq. feet of ceiling area) and electrical outlets (one in each 90 sq. feet of ceiling area). Duct openings protected with fusible link dampers.	4	Underwriters' Lab., Inc. Ret. 3574 (Design 12-4 hr.)
94	Topping: 2" precast vermiculite concrete. [32] Fireproofing: 1" vermiculite-gypsum plaster [2] on metal lath. [8] y = 10¾"	4	Nat'l Bureau of Standards TR 10235-2 Test No. 60
95	Topping: 1" thick insulation board [37] of shredded wood bonded with portland cement, over layer of 15 lbs. asphalt saturated asbestos-felt cemented to deck as a seal sheet. Fireproofing: 1" vermiculite-gypsum plaster [2] on metal lath. [8] y = 10¾"	3	
96	Topping: 1" thick insulation board [37] of felted glass fiber, covered on underside with impregnated paper vapor seal. Fireproofing: 1" vermiculite-gypsum plaster [2] on metal lath. [8] y = 10¾"	2	

Floor and roof systems: light-gage steel systems—contact fireproofed

Nominal thickness of topping — Cellular floor — Nominal thickness of fireproofing

No.	Description	Rating (Hours)	Authority [1]
97	Topping: 2½" sand-gravel concrete. Fireproofing: ½" sprayed mineral fibers. [15] No adhesive.	4	Underwriters' Lab., Inc. Ret. 3705-3 (Design 20-4 hr.)
98	Topping: 2½" sand-gravel concrete. Fireproofing: 11/16" vermiculite acoustic plaster. [15]	4	Underwriters' Lab., Inc. Ret. 2689-5 (Design 19-4 hr.)
99	Topping: 2½" sand-gravel concrete. Fireproofing: ½" vermiculite acoustic plaster. [15]	2½ [23]	Underwriters' Lab., Inc. Ret. 2689-3 (Design 2-2 hr.)

Table 1 (Cont.)   Fire-resistance ratings of various assemblies

Superscript numbers refer to notes at the end of this table. Asterisks identify tests conducted 5 hours or more without reaching critical limits. This table is from Fire-resistant Construction in Modern Steel-framed Buildings, *published by American Institute of Steel Construction (1959).*

	No.	Description	Rating (Hours)	Authority [1]
	100	Same as No. 98 above, except: 24" wide air cell added to construction, with ¾" thick aluminum foil faced fiber glass insulation board [31] plus 1⅛" vermiculite acoustic plaster [15] under air cell.	4	Underwriters' Lab., Inc. Ret. 2689-5 (Design 19-4 hr.)
	101	Topping: 2½" sand-gravel concrete. Fireproofing: 1½" sprayed mineral fibers. [15] Special adhesive pre-applied to underside of steel floor.	4*	Underwriters' Lab., Inc. Ret. 3431-2 (Design 17-5 hr.)
	102	Topping: 2½" sand-gravel concrete. Fireproofing: ¾" sprayed mineral fibers [15] or 1⁷⁄₁₆" vermiculite acoustic plaster. [15] Sprayed fibers require special adhesive pre-applied to underside of steel floor.	3	Underwriters' Lab., Inc. Ret. 2689-4 (Design 12-3 hr.) Ret. 3749-3 (Design 14-3, 15-3 hr.)
	103	Topping: 2½" sand-gravel concrete. Fireproofing: ½" sprayed mineral fibers. [15] Special adhesive pre-applied to underside of steel floor. (Tested on cellular units only).	2	Underwriters' Lab. of Canada Ret. 193-3
	104	Slab: 4½" sand-limestone concrete. Fireproofing: ½" vermiculite acoustic plaster. [15]	4	Underwriters' Lab., Inc. Ret. 3413-7 (Design 10-4 hr.)
	105	Slab: 4½" sand-limestone concrete. Fireproofing: ⅞" sprayed mineral fibers. [15] Special adhesive pre-applied to underside of steel floor.	4	Underwriters' Lab., Inc. Ret. 3372-2 (Design 9-4 hr.)
	106	Slab: 4½" expanded slag concrete. Fireproofing: ⅜" perlite-gypsum plaster [2] on metal lath [8] attached directly to floor. Sufficient plaster pushed through lath to fill corrugations in the floor units.	4	Underwriters' Lab., Inc. Ret. 3413-4 (Design 8-4 hr.)
	107	Same as No. 106 above, except: Electrical raceways and junction boxes built into floor slab. Plaster thickness below junction boxes to be 1". Not more than one junction box per 90 sq. feet of floor area.	3	Underwriters' Lab., Inc. Ret. 3413-4 (Design 5-3 hr.)

Table 1 (Cont.) Fire-resistance ratings of various assemblies

Superscript numbers refer to notes at the end of this table. Asterisks identify tests conducted 5 hours or more without reaching critical limits. This table is from Fire-resistant Construction in Modern Steel-framed Buildings, *published by American Institute of Steel Construction (1959).*

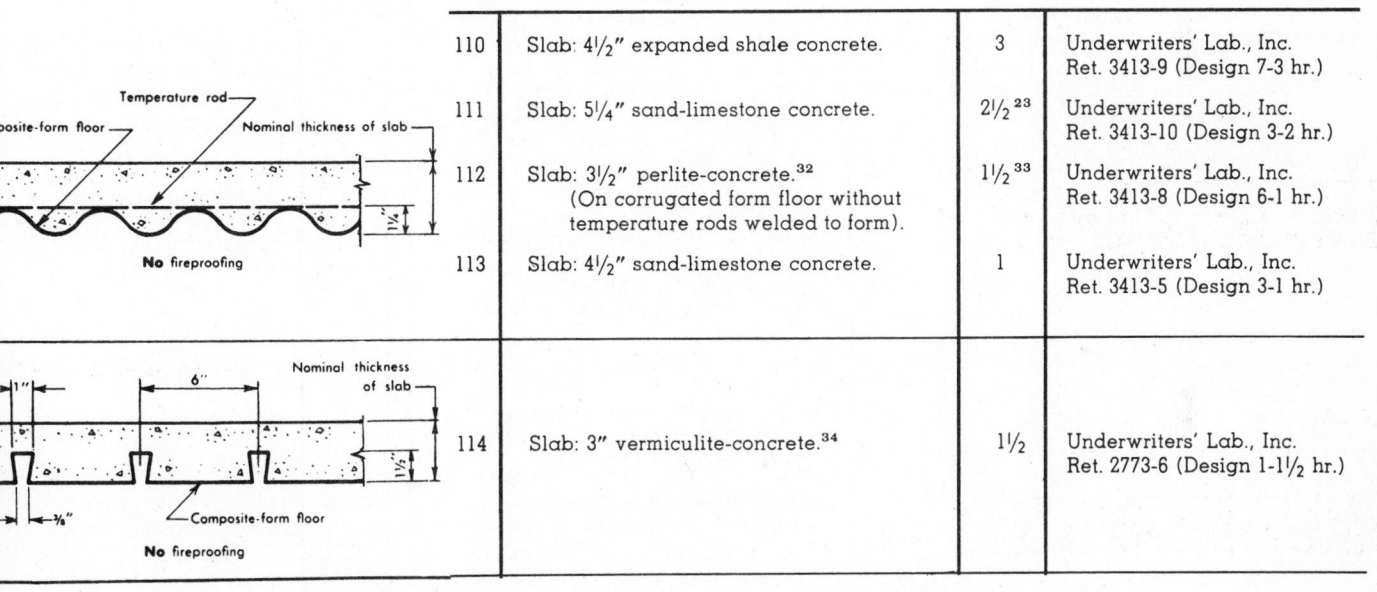

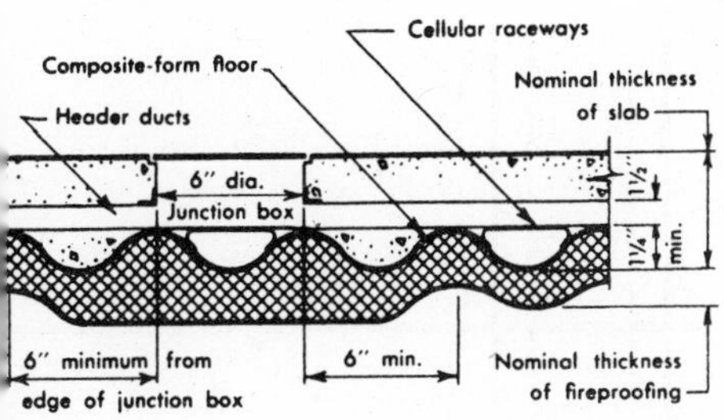

	No.	Description	Rating (Hours)	Authority [1]
	108	Slab: 4½″ expanded shale concrete with header ducts and junction boxes built in. Header ducts rest on steel floor. (Duct size 6¼″ wide by 1½″ deep, spaced 9½″ apart). Fireproofing: ¾″ perlite acoustic plaster [15] following contour of form, except 2″ thick under junction boxes.	4	Underwriters' Lab., Inc. Ret. 3983-1
	109	Same as No. 108 above, except: Fireproofing: **None** except 1″ perlite acoustic plaster [15] under cellular raceways, ⅞″ under header ducts, 2″ under junction boxes.	2½ [23]	Underwriters' Lab., Inc. Ret. 3413-11 (Design 7-2 hr.)

Floor and roof systems: light-gage steel systems—not fireproofed

	No.	Description	Rating (Hours)	Authority
	110	Slab: 4½″ expanded shale concrete.	3	Underwriters' Lab., Inc. Ret. 3413-9 (Design 7-3 hr.)
	111	Slab: 5¼″ sand-limestone concrete.	2½ [23]	Underwriters' Lab., Inc. Ret. 3413-10 (Design 3-2 hr.)
	112	Slab: 3½″ perlite-concrete.[32] (On corrugated form floor without temperature rods welded to form).	1½ [33]	Underwriters' Lab., Inc. Ret. 3413-8 (Design 6-1 hr.)
	113	Slab: 4½″ sand-limestone concrete.	1	Underwriters' Lab., Inc. Ret. 3413-5 (Design 3-1 hr.)
	114	Slab: 3″ vermiculite-concrete.[34]	1½	Underwriters' Lab., Inc. Ret. 2773-6 (Design 1-1½ hr.)

Floor and roof systems: precast concrete cellular systems—not fireproofed

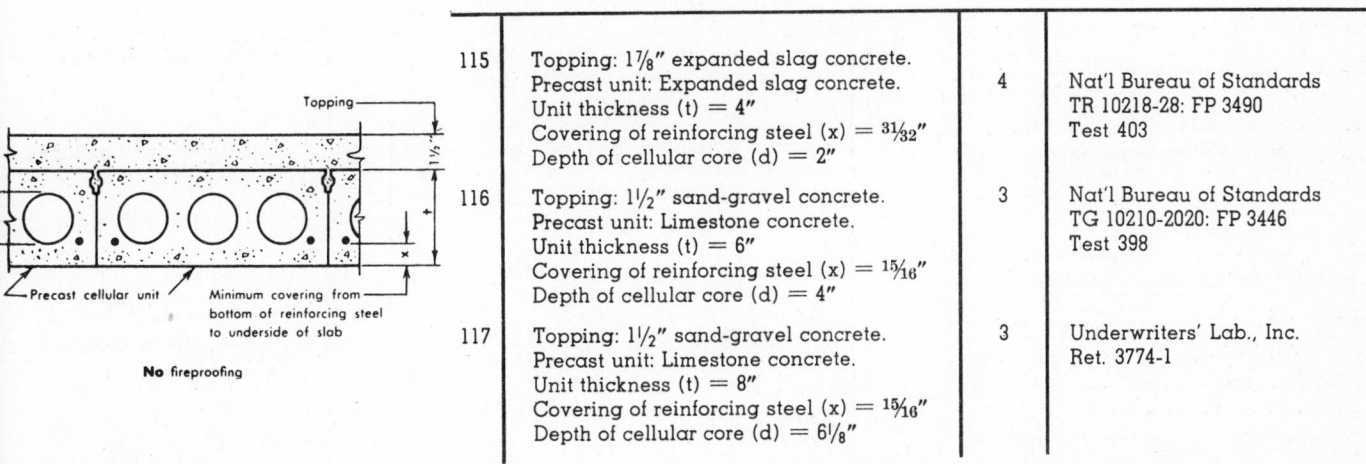

	No.	Description	Rating (Hours)	Authority
	115	Topping: 1⅞″ expanded slag concrete. Precast unit: Expanded slag concrete. Unit thickness (t) = 4″ Covering of reinforcing steel (x) = ³¹⁄₃₂″ Depth of cellular core (d) = 2″	4	Nat'l Bureau of Standards TR 10218-28: FP 3490 Test 403
	116	Topping: 1½″ sand-gravel concrete. Precast unit: Limestone concrete. Unit thickness (t) = 6″ Covering of reinforcing steel (x) = ¹⁵⁄₁₆″ Depth of cellular core (d) = 4″	3	Nat'l Bureau of Standards TG 10210-2020: FP 3446 Test 398
	117	Topping: 1½″ sand-gravel concrete. Precast unit: Limestone concrete. Unit thickness (t) = 8″ Covering of reinforcing steel (x) = ¹⁵⁄₁₆″ Depth of cellular core (d) = 6⅛″	3	Underwriters' Lab., Inc. Ret. 3774-1

Table 1 (Cont.) Fire-resistance ratings of various assemblies

Superscript numbers refer to notes at the end of this table. Asterisks identify tests conducted 5 hours or more without reaching critical limits. This table is from Fire-resistant Construction in Modern Steel-framed Buildings, published by American Institute of Steel Construction (1959).

Floor and roof systems: joist and slab systems (open-web or solid-web steel joists)—membrane fireproofed

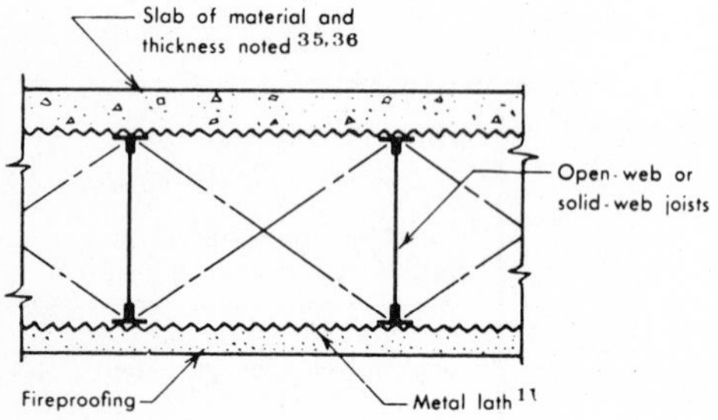

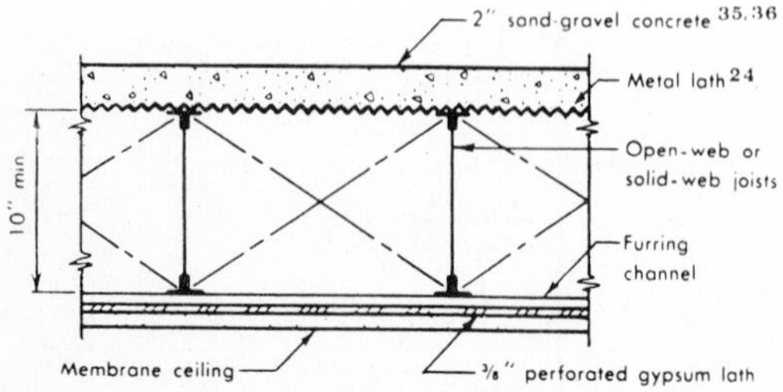

No.	Description	Rating (Hours)	Authority [1]
118	Slab: 2½" sand-gravel concrete (**or** 2" gypsum tile covered with ½" mortar). Ceiling: 1" vermiculite-gypsum plaster.[26]	4	Nat'l Bureau of Standards BMS 92—Table 43
119	Slab: 2½" sand-gravel concrete (**or** 2" gypsum tile covered with ½" mortar). Ceiling: ¾" vermiculite-gypsum plaster [26] **or** 1" neat wood-fibered gypsum plaster.	3	
120	Slab: 2½" perlite-concrete.[32] Ceiling: ¾" perlite-gypsum plaster.[2]	3	Underwriters' Lab., Inc. Ret. 3454-2 (Design 6-3 hr.)
121	Slab: 2" sand-gravel concrete (**or** 2" gypsum tile covered with ¼" mortar). Ceiling: ¾" vermiculite-gypsum plaster [26] **or** 1" neat wood-fibered gypsum plaster.	2½	Nat'l Bureau of Standards BMS 92—Table 43 TRBM 44—Table 18
122	Slab: 2½" sand-gravel concrete. Ceiling: 1" sprayed asbestos fibers.[15]	2½	
123	Slab: 2¼" sand-gravel concrete (**or** 2" gypsum tile covered with ¼" mortar). Ceiling: ¾" sand-gypsum plaster.[26]	2	
124	Slab: 2½" sand-gravel concrete. Ceiling: ¾" sprayed asbestos fibers.[15]	2	
125	Slab: 2" sand-gravel concrete (**or** 2" gypsum tile, no top mortar). Ceiling: ¾" sand-gypsum plaster,[26] **or** ¾" sand-portland cement plaster with asbestos fibers.[30]	1½	
126	Slab: 2" sand-gravel concrete. Ceiling: ⅝" sprayed asbestos fibers.[15]	1½	
127	Ceiling: 1" perlite-gypsum plaster,[2] reinforced with 1" hexagonal wire mesh stretched under lath.	4	Nat'l Bureau of Standards BMS 141—Test 311
128	Ceiling: ½" perlite-gypsum plaster,[2] reinforced with 1" hexagonal wire mesh stretched under lath.	3	Nat'l Bureau of Standards BMS 141—Test 312
129	Ceiling: ⅝" perlite-gypsum plaster,[2] reinforced with No. 14 ga. galvanized wires secured below lath on the diagonal.	3	Nat'l Bureau of Standards BMS 141—Test 313
130	Ceiling: Same as No. 129 above, except: ½" thickness of plaster.	2½	Nat'l Bureau of Standards BMS 141—Test 318
131	Ceiling: Same as No. 129 above, except: ⅝" sand-gypsum plaster.[28]	1½	Nat'l Bureau of Standards Test 345
132	Ceiling: 1" perlite-gypsum plaster,[2] no reinforcement.	1½	Nat'l Bureau of Standards BMS 141—Test 295
133	Ceiling: ½" perlite-gypsum plaster,[2] no reinforcement.	1	Nat'l Bureau of Standards BMS 141—Tests 317, 319

Slab of material and thickness noted [35,36]

Open-web or solid-web joists

Fireproofing

Metal lath [11]

2" sand-gravel concrete [35,36]

Metal lath [24]

Open-web or solid-web joists

Furring channel

10" min

Membrane ceiling

⅜" perforated gypsum lath

Table 1 (Cont.)   Fire-resistance ratings of various assemblies

Superscript numbers refer to notes at the end of this table. Asterisks identify tests conducted 5 hours or more without reaching critical limits. This table is from Fire-resistant Construction in Modern Steel-framed Buildings, *published by American Institute of Steel Construction (1959).*

	No.	Description	Rating (Hours)	Authority [1]
	134	Ceiling: ¾" sand-gypsum plaster.[26]	1	Nat'l Bureau of Standards TRBM 44—Table 18
	135	Roof: Composition roof plank,[37] 2" thick tongued and grooved joints covered with 6" wide strips of felt and hot mopping asphalt. Screws to joists 10" o.c., holes filled with perlite-gypsum plaster.[2] Roof covering of 4-ply asphalt-saturated felt and hot mopping asphalt. Ceiling: ¾" perlite-gypsum plaster.[2]	2	Underwriters' Lab., Inc. Ret. 3472-5 (Design 4-2 hr.)
	136	Ceiling: 1" mineral fiber acoustic tiles, tongued and grooved, on T-spline suspension system.[38]	2½ [23]	Underwriters' Lab., Inc. Ret. 4177-1 (Design 6-2 hr.)
	137	Ceiling: 4" of mineral wool insulating batts (2 layers of 2" thickness each) plus ¾" perforated glass fiber acoustic tile clipped to furring channels.	2	Underwriters' Lab., Inc. Ret. 3583-1 (Design 1-2 hr.)
	138	Ceiling: ½" gypsum wallboard nailed 6" o.c. into nailing channels, over ⅝" gypsum coreboard. Joints of wallboard staggered from coreboard joints.	1½	Underwriters' Lab., Inc. Ret. 1319-26 (Design 2-1½ hr.)
	139	Ceiling: One layer ⅝" gypsum wallboard or coreboard nailed into nailing channels, or screwed into furring channels.	1	Underwriters' Lab., Inc. Ret. 2717-16 (Design 2-1 hr.) Ret. 1319-14 (Design 5-1 hr.) Ret. 3501-18 (Design 8-1 hr.)

Table 1 (Cont.)   Fire-resistance ratings of various assemblies

Superscript numbers refer to notes at the end of this table. Asterisks identify tests conducted 5 hours or more without reaching critical limits. This table is from Fire-resistant Construction in Modern Steel-framed Buildings, *published by American Institute of Steel Construction (1959).*

Floor and roof systems: reinforced concrete slabs—not fireproofed

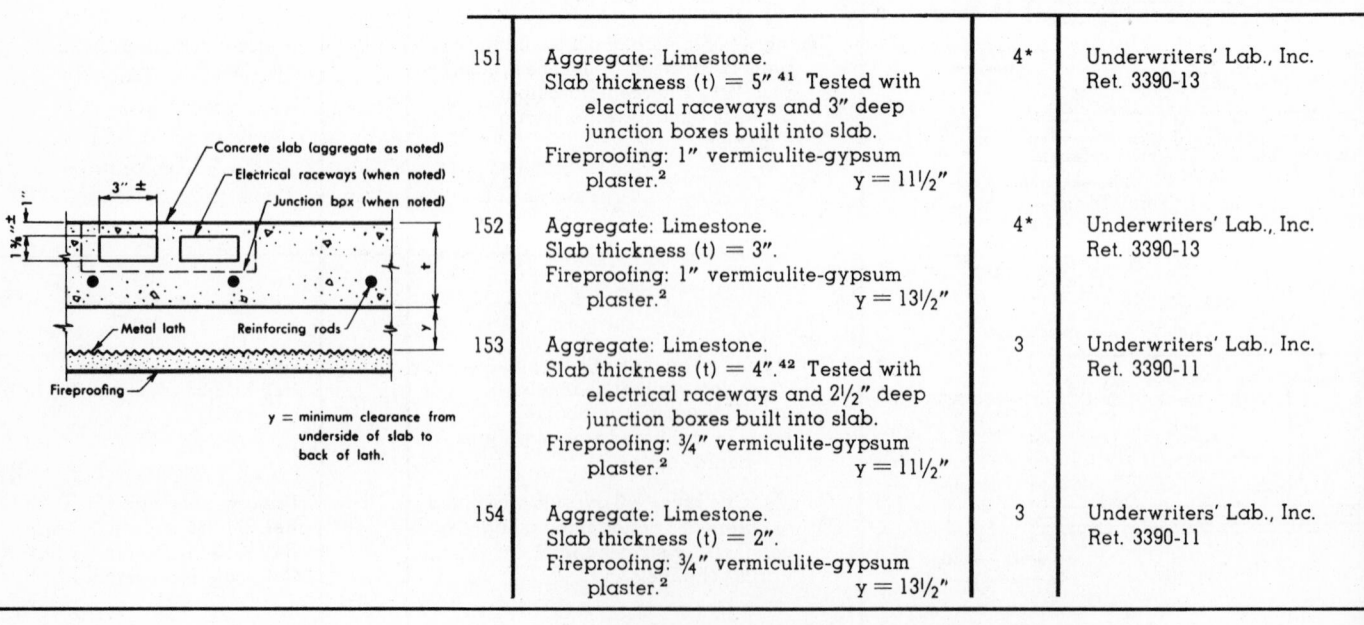

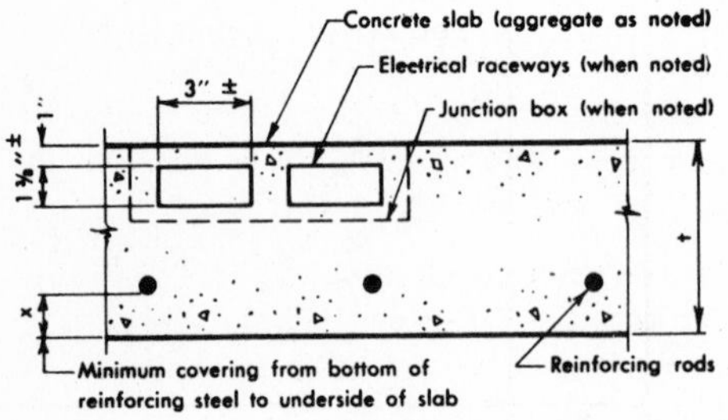

No.	Description	Rating (Hours)	Authority [1]
140	Aggregate: Expanded slag. Slab thickness (t) = 4½". x = ¾"	4	Underwriters' Lab., Inc. Ret. 3390-7
141	Aggregate: Air-cooled slag. Slab thickness (t) = 6". x = 1"	4	Underwriters' Lab., Inc. Ret. 3390-12
142	Aggregate: Traprock, calcareous gravel, or crushed limestone. Slab thickness (t) = 6". x = 1"	3	Underwriters' Lab., Inc. Ret. 3390 Ret. 3390-5 Ret. 3390-10
143	Aggregate: Siliceous sand and gravel. Slab thickness (t) = 8". x = 1½"	3 [39]	Nat'l Bureau of Standards Test 38A
144	Aggregate: Crushed limestone. Slab thickness (t) = 6". Tested with electrical raceways and 2½" deep junction boxes built into slab. x = 1"	3	Underwriters' Lab., Inc. Ret. 3390-17
145	Aggregate: Air-cooled slag. Slab thickness (t) = 4¾". x = ¾"	2½	Underwriters' Lab., Inc. Ret. 3390-15
146	Aggregate: Calcareous gravel or crushed limestone. Slab thickness (t) = 4¾". x = 1"	2	Underwriters' Lab., Inc. Ret. 3390-3 Ret. 3390-4
147	Aggregate: Traprock. Slab thickness (t) = 4¾". x = ¾"	2	Underwriters' Lab., Inc. Ret. 3390-9
148	Aggregate: Siliceous sand and gravel. Slab thickness (t) = 6". x = 1"	2 [40]	
149	Aggregate: Siliceous sand and gravel. Slab thickness (t) = 5" or 6". x = ¾"	1½	Nat'l Bureau of Standards TRBM 44—Table 19
150	Aggregate: Siliceous sand and gravel. Slab thickness (t) = 4". x = ¾"	1	

Floor and roof systems: reinforced concrete slabs—membrane fireproofed

No.	Description	Rating (Hours)	Authority [1]
151	Aggregate: Limestone. Slab thickness (t) = 5" [41] Tested with electrical raceways and 3" deep junction boxes built into slab. Fireproofing: 1" vermiculite-gypsum plaster.[2] y = 11½"	4*	Underwriters' Lab., Inc. Ret. 3390-13
152	Aggregate: Limestone. Slab thickness (t) = 3". Fireproofing: 1" vermiculite-gypsum plaster.[2] y = 13½"	4*	Underwriters' Lab., Inc. Ret. 3390-13
153	Aggregate: Limestone. Slab thickness (t) = 4" [42] Tested with electrical raceways and 2½" deep junction boxes built into slab. Fireproofing: ¾" vermiculite-gypsum plaster.[2] y = 11½"	3	Underwriters' Lab., Inc. Ret. 3390-11
154	Aggregate: Limestone. Slab thickness (t) = 2". Fireproofing: ¾" vermiculite-gypsum plaster.[2] y = 13½"	3	Underwriters' Lab., Inc. Ret. 3390-11

Notes to Table 1: Fire-resistance ratings of various assemblies

1. Listed for each test conducted at Underwriters' Laboratories, Inc. is the Underwriters' Retardant Number which identifies both the test and its sponsor. Following each Retardant Number is the corresponding "Column" or "Floor, Roof and Ceiling" Design Number by which the test is identified in Underwriters' Building Materials List.
   National Bureau of Standards tests are identified by either a test number or the number of the publication in which the test result is reported.

2. Scratch Coat: 2 to 3 cu. ft. aggregate to 100 lbs. fibered gypsum.
   Brown Coat: Same.
   (Tested plaster mixes may have been 2, 2½ or 3 cu. ft. per 100 lbs. National Bureau of Standards tests indicate that this variation in ratio of vermiculite or perlite has a negligible effect on fire resistance.)

3. 3.4 lbs. per sq. yd. ⅜" diamond mesh expanded self-furring metal lath, to fur lath ¼" from steel.

4. Scratch Coat: 4 cu. ft. aggregate to 94 lbs. of portland cement and 5 oz. of air-entraining agent.
   Brown Coat: Same.

5. Paperbacked wire fabric. No. 16 ga. wire in 2" o.c. squares, with alternate squares divided by a vertical wire into 1" spaces, with 0.010 inches thick absorptive paper backing.

6. Wire fabric. No. 16 ga. wire spaced 2" o.c.

7. Scratch Coat: 3½ cu. ft. aggregate to 94 lbs. of portland cement, 8 oz. of air-entraining agent and 1 lb. of calcium aluminate cement.
   Brown Coat: Same.

8. 3.4 lbs. per sq. yd. No. 24 ga. ⅜" diamond mesh flat expanded metal lath.

9. Scratch Coat: 3 lbs. aggregate to 1 lb. fibered gypsum.
   Brown Coat: Same.

10. Scratch Coat: 2½ lbs. dry sand to 1 lb. portland cement.
    Brown Coat: Same.

11. Metal lath of appropriate weight for the spacing of supports. Expanded metal, woven wire or paper-backed.

12. Scratch Coat: 2 lbs. aggregate to 1 lb. fibered gypsum.
    Brown Coat: 3 lbs. aggregate to 1 lb. fibered gypsum.

13. Scratch Coat: 2½ lbs. aggregate to 1 lb. fibered gypsum.
    Brown Coat: Same.

14. Scratch Coat: 3½ cu. ft. aggregate to 100 lbs. unfibered gypsum.
    Brown Coat: 4 cu. ft. aggregate to 100 lbs. unfibered gypsum.

15. Sprayed mineral fiber and acoustic plaster fireproofing materials may vary with each manufacturer. Thickness listed is minimum, and tested fire rating for products of each manufacturer should be verified. The need for adhesive should be checked in each case.

16. Grade A Concrete is concrete in which at least 60% of the coarse aggregate consists of pumice, limestone, calcareous gravel, trap rock, blast furnace slag, or burned clay or shale.

17. Grade B Concrete is concrete in which at least 60% of the course aggregate consists of granite, sandstone, cinders, or mixture of any of these aggregates with aggregates for Grade A Concrete.

18. Grade C Concrete is any concrete not classed as Grade A or Grade B. (Siliceous gravels such as quartz and chert are included in this group.)

19. Ratings given in BMS 92 are based on "x" dimensions (outside protection) of 2, 3 and 4 inches, for four classes of concrete aggregate. These ratings vary from 1¾ hours to 14 hours. Because these tested ratings are of limited practical value to the designer, most building code officials have adopted modified rating schedules interpolated from actual test data. Ratings No. 23, 24, and 25 in this appendix are the ratings adopted by the Uniform Building Code. Other model codes such as National Building Code and Southern Building Code have similar but different schedules. In general the ratings shown are more conservative than those of other model codes, except that the Southern Building Code requires heavier protections when concrete fireproofing contains siliceous aggregate having a total of more than 60% quartz, chert or flint.

20. Tested with covering of ½" sand-gypsum plaster, for which the rating was 6 hours.

21. Tested with covering of ⅜" sand-gypsum plaster, for which the rating was 7 hours.

Notes to Table 1: Fire-resistance ratings of various assemblies

22. Retardant 2689-5 rates the vermiculite-gypsum protection at 5 hours. Tests in Retardants 3413-4 and 4197-1 were stopped at 4 hours, before test limits were reached.

23. Rated at 2 hours by Underwriters' Laboratories, Inc., although test results indicate 2½-hour rating.

24. 3.4 lbs. per sq. yd. 24 ga. metal rib lath.

25. In tested constructions beams projected below ceiling line by varying distances, but for convenience the following rule from NBFU "Fire Resistance Ratings" is applied:

    "Ratings given are applicable where there is no combustible material or construction in the enclosed ceiling space. Ceiling to be at such a level that the beams, girders or trusses to be considered as protected by the ceiling, will not extend below the level of the ceiling more than 6 inches (as illustrated), unless otherwise specified. This depth at any point to be considered as the average depth on the two sides. Ratings are for protection only from fire beneath the ceiling."

26. Scratch Coat: 1 lb. aggregate to 2 lbs. fibered gypsum.
    Brown Coat: 1 lb. aggregate to 3 lbs. fibered gypsum.

27. 1 lb. aggregate to 1 lb. fibered gypsum.

28. 2 lbs. aggregate to 1 lb. fibered gypsum.

29. Scratch Coat: 2 lbs. aggregate to 1 lb. portland cement (with 10 lbs. hydrated lime added per bag of cement.)
    Brown Coat: 2½ lbs. aggregate to 1 lb. portland cement (hydrated lime added same as Scratch Coat.)

30. 3 lbs. asbestos fiber and 15 lbs. hydrated lime per 100 lbs. portland cement.

31. Insulation Board: ¾" aluminum foil faced fiber glass weighing 0.5 lbs. per sq. ft., ash content 91% by weight.

32. 6 cu. ft. aggregate to 94 lbs. portland cement.

33. Rated at 1-hour by Underwriters' Laboratories, Inc., although test results indicate 1½-hour rating.

34. 4 cu. ft. of aggregate to 94 lbs. of portland cement.

35. Specified minimum thickness of slab refers to thickness above joists. In tested constructions the thickness between joists was greater due to sagging of the metal lath form. If rigid forms prevent the sagging the slab thickness should be ¼" greater. Concrete plank may be substituted for the poured concrete slab if joints are thoroughly grouted and the plank is ¼" thicker than the specified slab thickness.

36. Wood nailers may be placed in top slabs provided they are separated from the top of the steel joist by the following minimum thickness of concrete or gypsum:

1½-hour Fire-Resistant Construction —	1 inch
2 -hour Fire-Resistant Construction —	1⅛ inch
2½-hour Fire-Resistant Construction —	1⅜ inch
3 -hour Fire-Resistant Construction —	1⅝ inch
4 -hour Fire-Resistant Construction —	1⅝ inch

37. Proprietary roof plank.

38. Tested construction included open-web joists. Main runner support clips were wrapped around lower chord of joist.

39. Retardant 3390-6 lists a 6" thick siliceous gravel slab with 1" covering as achieving a 3-hour rating. This discrepancy may be due to differences in quality of the siliceous aggregate.

40. Retardant 3390-8 lists a 4¾" siliceous gravel slab with 1" covering as achieving a 2-hour rating. This discrepancy may be due to differences in the quality of the siliceous aggregate.

41. Portions of slab not containing electrical raceways and junction boxes may consist of a 3" slab.

42. Portions of slab not containing electrical raceways and junction boxes may consist of a 2" slab.

Table 2. Fire resistance of acoustical tile ceilings

All acoustical tiles meet Federal Specification SS-A-118b, Class A. Data furnished by Armstrong Cork Company.

Item No.	Authority	Fire-resistance rating, hr	Description
1	Underwriters' Laboratories Series R-4177-5 Des. 31 R-4177-6 Des. 21	4	12x12x¾-in. tongue-and-groove and kerf acoustical tile; proprietary suspension system employing concealed clips; runners attached to 1½-in. carrying channels 4 ft o.c.
2	R-4177-7 Des. 13 (Beam 3 hr) R-4177-8 Des. 21	2	24x48-in. or 24x24x⅝-in. acoustical tile; proprietary suspension system employing exposed grid for lay-in units
3	R-4177-3 Des. 8 R-4337-1 Des. 16 R-4355-1 Des. 19	2	12x12x⅝-in. tongue-and-groove and kerf acoustical tile; suspension system using concealed zee bars 12-in. o.c. attached to bar joists
4	R-4177-11 Des. 8	1½ (combustible)	24x48x⅝-in. acoustical tile; proprietary suspension system—exposed grid for lay-in units—hung from 3x8-in. wood joists supporting double wood floor
5	R-4177-4 Des. 9	1 (combustible)	12x12x⅝-in. acoustical tile with tongue-and-groove and kerf on concealed zee bar suspension system attached directly by clips to 2x10-in. wood joists supporting double wood floor

Item 1 drawing: WIRES SUSPENDED FROM STRUCTURAL FLOOR OR ROOF; 1½" CHANNEL APPROX. 4'-0" O.C.; GALVANIZED CLIP; ARMSTRONG TDR MAIN RUNNER 12" O.C.; ¾" ARMSTRONG ACOUSTICAL FIRE GUARD

Item 2 drawing: SECTION OF MAIN RUNNER AND CROSS TEE; WIRES SUSPENDED FROM STRUCTURAL FLOOR OR ROOF; HANGER SPLICE CLIP; MAIN RUNNER 4'-0" O.C. CROSS TEE; ⅝" ARMSTRONG ACOUSTICAL FIRE GUARD

Item 3 drawing: OPEN-WEB BAR JOIST; WIRE CLIP; #25 GA. STEEL ZEE RUNNER 12" O.C.; ⅝" ARMSTRONG ACOUSTICAL FIRE GUARD

See drawing for item 2

Item 5 drawing: JOIST; CLIP; RUNNER; ACOUSTICAL TILE

Table 3. Fire resistance of vermiculite plaster ceiling on wood joist floors or roofs
Data from Vermiculite Institute.

Type	Description	Fire-resistance rating, hr	Authority	Item No.
Metal lath ceiling	¾-in. vermiculite plaster	1¾	National Bureau of Standards	1
Gypsum lath ceiling	½-in. vermiculite plaster on ⅜-in. plain gypsum lath; 20 gage, 1-in. wire mesh nailed to joists through lath	1½	Vermiculite Institute	2
	½-in. vermiculite plaster on ⅜-in. perforated gypsum lath	1		

Table 4. Fire-resistance ratings of reinforced concrete construction
Data from National Building Code, *National Board of Fire Underwriters (1955).*

Type	Description of construction	Rating, hr	Authority
Beams, girders, and trusses	1½-in.* concrete; coarse aggregate: air-cooled slag, expanded slag, crushed limestone, calcareous gravel, siliceous gravel, or traprock	4	Underwriters' Laboratory, Inc.
	1-in.* concrete	1	Estimated National Building Code, NBFU
Columns	1½-in.* concrete; coarse aggregate: limestone, calcareous gravel, traprock, or blast-furnace slag, 12 in. or larger round or square columns	4	National Bureau of Standards, No. 272, 1925
	2½-in.* concrete; coarse aggregate: granite, sandstone, or siliceous gravel; 16 in. or larger round or square column	4	
Slab floor or ceiling	4½-in. slab: expanded slag aggregate—¾-in. protection to steel reinforcement	4	Underwriters' Laboratory, Inc. R–3390
	6-in. slab with traprock, calcareous gravel, or siliceous gravel aggregate—1-in. protection to steel reinforcement	3	
	4¾-in. slab with traprock or siliceous gravel aggregate—¾-in. protection to steel reinforcement	2	
	4¾-in. slab with calcareous gravel or crushed limestone aggregate—1-in. protection to steel reinforcement	2	
	3-in. slab with limestone aggregate—¾-in. protection to steel reinforcement.	1	

* Thickness of concrete over steel reinforcement.

Table 5. Fire-resistance ratings of concrete and masonry walls and partitions

Estimated ratings given below are from National Building Code, *National Board of Fire Underwriters (1955).**

Type	Details of construction	Minimum equivalent thickness,† in., for ratings of:			
		4 hr	3 hr	2 hr	1 hr
Concrete masonry units‡	Coarse aggregate, expanded slag, or pumice	4.7	4.0	3.2	2.1
	Coarse aggregate, expanded clay, or shale	5.7	4.8	3.8	2.6
	Coarse aggregate, limestone, cinders, or unexpanded slag	5.9	5.0	4.0	2.7
	Coarse aggregate, calcareous gravel	6.2	5.3	4.2	2.8
	Coarse aggregate, siliceous gravel	6.7	5.7	4.5	3.0

Type	Details of construction	Minimum thickness,§ in., for ratings of:			
		4 hr	3 hr	2 hr	1 hr
Plain concrete	Solid walls	7.5	6.5	5.5	4#
Reinforced concrete	Solid walls, unplastered:				
	Group 1 aggregates,‖ ¾ in. maximum size	6.5	6	5	3.5
	Group 2 aggregates,‖ ¾ in. maximum size	7.5	6.5	5.5	4#
	Solid walls plastered each side with ¾-in. portland cement stucco or portland cement or gypsum plaster:				
	Group 1 aggregates,‖ ¾ in. maximum size	5	4	3#	3#
	Group 2 aggregates,‖ ¾ in. maximum size	6	5	4	3#
Stone masonry	Solid walls	12	12	12	8

Authority—Tests of the Fire Resistance and Strength of Walls of Concrete Masonry Units, *Portland Cement Association (January 1934).*

† *Equivalent thickness is the average thickness of the solid material in the wall, which equals the volume of the wall unit less the volume of the core spaces divided by the area of the face of the unit. Thickness of plaster or brick facings may be added to determine equivalent thickness. Where noncombustible members frame into wall, the thickness of solid material between end of member and opposite side of wall or other noncombustible members will not be less than 93 per cent of thickness shown in table.*

‡ *If there are members framed in the wall, they are noncombustible.*

§ *Thickness does not include plaster where plaster is specified.* Authority—Tests of the Fire Resistance and Thermal Properties of Solid Concrete Slabs and their Significance *by Carl A. Menzel,* ASTM Proceedings, *Vol. 43 (1943).*

Nonbearing.

‖ *Aggregates are defined as follows:*

Group 1: Blast-furnace slag, limestone, calcareous gravel, traprock, burnt clay or shale, cinders containing more than 25 per cent of combustible material and not more than 5 per cent of volatile material, and other materials meeting the requirements of these specifications and containing not more than 30 per cent quartz, chert, flint, and similar materials.

Group 2: Granite, quartzite, siliceous gravel, sandstone, gneiss, cinders containing more than 25 per cent, but not more than 40 per cent of combustible material and not more than 5 per cent of volatile material and other materials meeting the requirements of these specifications, and containing more than 30 per cent of quartz, chert, flint, and similar materials.

Table 6. Fire-resistance ratings of various partitions

Construction	Description	Fire-resistance rating, hr	Authority	Item No.
	Solid plaster partitions			
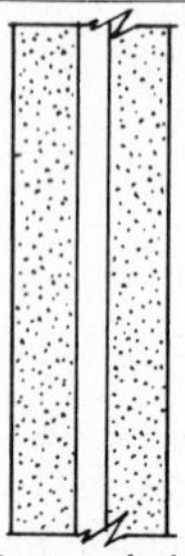 Gypsum lath	1 in. of vermiculite plaster applied to each face of ½-in.-thick long-length plain gypsum lath, no studs, over-all thickness of partition 2½ in.	2	National Bureau of Standards	1
	¾ in. of vermiculite plaster applied to each face of ½-in.-thick long-length plain gypsum lath, no studs, over-all thickness of partition 2 in.	1	Vermiculite Institute	2
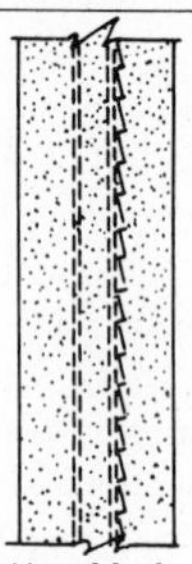 Metal lath	Vermiculite plaster applied on metal lath fastened to incombustible studs spaced 16 in. o.c., over-all thickness of partition 2½ in.	2	National Bureau of Standards	3
	Vermiculite plaster applied on metal lath fastened to incombustible studs spaced 16 in. o.c., over-all thickness of partition 2-in.	1	Vermiculite Institute	4
	Solid masonry unit			
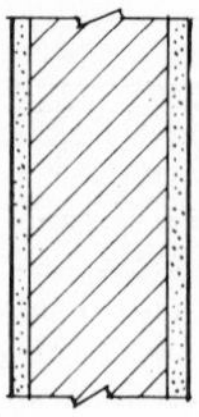	7⅝-in. brick, faced each side with ⅝-in. gypsum sand (1:3) plaster, over-all thickness 8⅞.	4	NBFU*	5
	3⅝-in. brick, faced each side with ⅝-in. gypsum sand (1:3) plaster, over-all thickness 4⅞ in.	2	NBFU*	6
	3-in. gypsum block, faced each side with ½-in. gypsum sand (1:3) plaster, over-all thickness 4 in.	3	NBFU*	7
	3⅝-in. concrete block, faced each side with ½-in. gypsum sand (1:3) plaster, over-all thickness 4⅝ in.	2	NBFU*	8
	4-in. clay tile, faced each side with ⅝-in. gypsum sand (1:3) plaster, over-all thickness 5¼ in.	1	NBFU*	9
	Steel stud (hollow)			
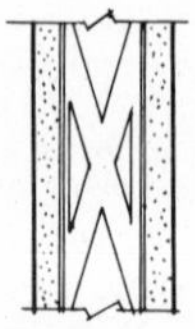	Metal stud 2½ in., 16 in. o.c., faced each side with ¾-in. gypsum sand (1:2) plaster on metal lath, over-all thickness 4 in.	1	NBFU*	10
	Metal stud 2½ in., 16 in. o.c., faced each side with ⅞-in. gypsum sand (1:2) plaster on gypsum lath ⅜ in., over-all thickness 4¼ in.	1	NBFU*	11
	Wood stud partitions			
Metal lath on both sides of studs	¾-in. vermiculite plaster	1	Underwriters' Laboratories, Inc. Ret. 2773—8/31/44.	12
Gypsum lath on both sides of studs	½-in. vermiculite plaster on ⅜-in. perforated lath (Bearing) (Nonbearing)	1¼ 1½	National Bureau of Standards	13

* *NBFU rating from* Fire-resistance Ratings, *National Board of Fire Underwriters (April 1959).*

By HOWARD P. VERMILYA, AIA

Plaster as a finish material for exterior and interior walls and ceilings dates back to the ancient Egyptians. Its greatest practical advantage is that it can provide a continuous surface without joints. It is also useful for concealing rough construction and the spaces for piping and wiring. Because it is completely inorganic, plaster is fireproof, rot proof, and vermin proof. As its name implies, it has no characteristic form—it can be flat or curved, smooth or rough, textured or molded, hard or soft. It can be integrally colored and serve as the finish surface, or it may form a base for the application of other finish materials such as paint, paper, textiles, tile, marble, plastic, and plywood. Plaster can be mixed and applied by hand or by machine.

PLASTERING MATERIALS

Plaster is composed of a mixture of cementitious materials, aggregates, and water. Admixtures are sometimes added, preferably at the mill, to retard or accelerate the setting. Of the three cementitious materials used in plaster, *lime*, the oldest, is now used primarily for the finish coats, and as a plasticizer in the base and finish coats with other cementitious materials; *portland cement* is used primarily for service applications where strength and resistance to moisture are paramount considerations; *calcined gypsum* is now the most widely used material for basecoat and finish plaster.

Standard specifications for various plastering materials are listed in Table 1.

Gypsum

Gypsum is commercially available in four forms for basecoat work.

1. Neat plaster contains no aggregate but may or may not contain fibers.

2. Ready-mix plaster contains aggregate mixed in by the manufacturer and requires only the addition of water to be ready for use.

3. Wood-fiber plaster contains no less than 0.75 per cent by weight of non-staining wood fibers. Sand, if used, may be added at the site.

4. Bond plaster is designed to be used for direct application to properly prepared monolithic concrete surfaces.

Gypsum is commercially available in the following five forms for finish coat work.

1. Ready-mix finish plasters are proprietary products designed for use over gypsum basecoats. They may or may not include fine aggregates and are available for various finishes. They may be painted as soon as they have set.

2. Acoustical plasters are proprietary products designed for sound absorption.

3. Gaging plasters are combined with lime putty. They are designed for slow, normal, or quick set or for strength.

4. Molding plaster is used for molding or casting.

5. Keene's cement, which is calcined at higher temperatures, is used to produce high-density plaster. It is usually mixed with lime to increase the plasticity.

Gypsum plasters are designed for application over metal lath, fiberboard lath, gypsum lath, and gypsum tile. The set is controlled by the use of admixtures by the manufacturer. Gypsum plasters, other than Keene's cement, should not be retempered.

Lime

Lime, used in building, is classified as either finishing lime or mason's lime; the former is usually used in plaster base and finish coats. These are further classified as quicklime or hydrated lime. Finishing or mason's hydrated limes are available as normal (Type N) or special (Type S) hydrated limes. Quicklime requires slaking for use as lime putty, a slow and time-consuming process, whereas Type N hydrated lime requires soaking 12 to 16 hours (overnight) and Type S hydrated lime may be mixed with water to develop its plasticity almost instantly. In addition Type S is apt to provide greater plasticity since the unhydrated oxides are limited to 8 per cent whereas there is no limit to them for Type N. Mill-fibered hydrated lime is available.

Lime basecoats are mixed using lime putty (a stiff paste resulting from slaking quicklime or soaking hydrated lime in water), sand, and water. Gaging plaster, which may be gypsum gaging plaster, Keene's cement, or portland cement, is often added to produce early strength and counteract possible shrinkage in setting.

Lime finish coats are made from the same ingredients as basecoats except that finer sand is used as aggregate.

Portland cement

Portland cement plaster is usually made from Type I or II portland cement or from types IA or IIA air-entrained portland cement; Type II is more resistant to sulphate attack and freezing damage. For interior plastering, portland cement is usually mixed with an aggregate, either sand or lightweight, and lime putty or dry hydrated lime (Type S). Portland cement with or without aggregate is used for base and finish coats on masonry, roughened monolithic concrete, and metal lath. It is not recommended for use over wood, fiberboard, or gypsum laths or over gypsum tile or basecoats. It is used where resistance to humidity, wetting and drying, and freezing and thawing are desired, in addition to strength. It is available in ready-mix form, with color added if desired.

Aggregates

Aggregates are used in plaster to provide dimensional stability and bulk. Since they are less expensive than the cementitious material, there is a possibility that

Table 1. Standard specifications for plastering materials

Materials	Specifications	
	ASTM	Federal
Gypsum plasters		
Neat plaster	C 28	SS–P–402 (Type N)
Ready-mixed	C 28	—
Wood-fibered	C 28	SS–P–402 (Type W)
Bond plaster	C 28	—
Acoustical plaster	—	SS–A–111
Gaging plaster	C 28	SS–P–402 (Type G)
Keene's cement	C 61	SS–C–00161
Lime (structural)		
Quicklime	C 5	SS–Q–351
Finishing hydrate		
Normal (Type N)	C 6	—
Special (Type S)	C 206	SS–L–351
Mason's hydrate	C 207	SS–L–351
Portland cement		
Regular (Types I–V)	C 150	SS–C–192b
Air-entraining (Types IA, IIA, IIIA)	C 175	SS–C–192b
Aggregates: sand, vermiculite, perlite	C 35	—
Metal lath	—	QQ–B–101C*
Gypsum lath	C 37	SS–L–0030

* See also *Simplified Practice Recommendation R3-57, U.S. Dept. of Commerce.*

lime and gypsum plasters may be mixed with more aggregate than they can properly bond. Strength of plaster basecoats is related to proportion of aggregate, and cracking is related to strength. The lightweight aggregates serve to reduce the over-all weight of the plaster, from 104 to 120 lb per cu ft for sanded plaster to 50 to 55 lb per cu ft for vermiculite or perlite plaster. They increase the sound absorption and fire resistance and lower the heat transmission values. Aggregates also serve to provide color and texture. They should be inert, clean, graded in size from coarse to fine and sharp and rough rather than round and smooth in shape.

Sand should be clean and washed if necessary. The variation in chemical composition of sand from local sources has caused manufacturers of gypsum plasters to vary the admixtures in some localities in order to offset the influence of the sand on setting times. American Society for Testing Materials standards are used for sieve analysis (Table 2) and for determining the amount of inorganic impurities and water-soluble chemicals in sand (ASTM C-40).

Vermiculite, a micaceous material, when expanded by heat treatment becomes a lightweight aggregate weighing from 7.5 to 10 lb per cu ft. It is manufactured in five types according to size. Type III is used in plastering and when combined with gypsum or special binder produces acoustical, insulating, or fire-resistant plaster. It is used in basecoats; when used in finish coats as fines or as acoustical plaster it should be applied only over vermiculite basecoats. It has a tannish color.

Perlite, an inert siliceous volcanic rock, when expanded by heat treatment becomes a lightweight aggregate weighing from 7.5 to 15 lb per cu ft. It is similar to vermiculite in function but has a grayish white color. It is used quite generally in gypsum ready-mix plaster as an aggregate.

Pumice is similar in structure to perlite but its weight, 28 to 32 lb per cu ft, limits its use to areas where it is produced.

Wood fiber, added to neat gypsum plaster preferably at time of manufacture, improves the working qualities and produces the strongest of commonly used basecoats. ASTM C 28 specifies not less than 0.75 per cent wood fiber by weight.

Hair, sisal, manila, or glass fiber may be added to gypsum plaster scratch coats and should be added to lime and lime–portland cement scratch and brown coats for all bases, and to portland cement scratch coats over metal lath. Fiber is sometimes added to hydrated lime at the mill.

Water should be potable. Water containing salt or lime will accelerate and

water containing organic or vegetable material will retard the set of plaster. Too much water decreases the strength of plaster and also its density.

Admixtures are added to the cementitious material to control the time of setting. Retarders usually serve to lower the strength. They are better added by the manufacturer.

Acoustical plasters are usually proprietary products, some being applied over basecoats and others being sprayed directly onto the structure, including steel decks, beams and girders, and columns. Since they are softer than other plasters their use is generally confined to ceilings and to walls above door head height.

Table 2. Sieve analysis of aggregates for gypsum plaster (ASTM C35)

Percentage retained on each sieve

Sieve size	Perlite by volume Max	Perlite by volume Min	Vermiculite by volume Max	Vermiculite by volume Min	Sand by weight Max	Sand by weight Min
No. 4	0	—	0	—	0	—
No. 8	5	0	10	0	5	0
No. 16	60	10	75	40	30	5
No. 30	95	45	95	65	65	30
No. 50	98	75	98	75	95	65
No. 100	100	88	100	90	100	90

PLASTER BASES

Plaster bases for the most part consist of lath or masonry. Lath is used where it is necessary to span open spaces between vertical or horizontal structural members. It is also used over masonry walls to provide a key, or where the wall has been dampproofed with a bituminous coating. Spacing of supports for various types of lath is given in Table 3.

Wood lath has been almost completely replaced by metal or gypsum lath.

Metal lath is made from cold-rolled sheets of mild low-carbon steel with 0.25 per cent copper added. All metal lath, unless galvanized, is coated with a rust-inhibitive paint. It is the most versatile plaster base, being used for interiors and exteriors, and where curved forms are used. Diamond mesh lath is produced by expanding sheet steel, and sheet lath is produced by punching it.

Diamond mesh metal lath is suitable for all types of plastering. It is available in 2.5 and 3.4 lb per sq yd weights painted, and in 3.4 lb galvanized. The standard

Table 3. Types, weights, and spacing, center to center, of supports of various types of laths

From "Recommended Specifications for Lathing, Furring, and Plastering," Contracting Plasterers' and Lathers' International Association, 1960.

Type of Lath	Minimum Weight of Lath, lb. per sq. yd	Vertical Supports Metal — Wood	Vertical Supports Metal — Solid Partitions	Vertical Supports Metal — Others	Horizontal Supports — Wood or Concrete	Horizontal Supports — Metal
Diamond Mesh (Flat expanded) metal lath	2.5	16	16	12	0	0
	3.4	16	16	16	16	13½
Flat rib expanded metal lath	2.75	16	16	16	16	12
	3.4	19	16	24	19	19
3/8 Rib expanded metal lath[2]	3.4	24	..	24	24	24
	4.0	24	..	24	24	24
Sheet metal lath[2]	4.5	24	..	24	24	24
Wire Lath	2.48	16	16	16	13½	13½
V-stiffened wire	3.3	24	24	24	19	19
Wire Fabric	[3]	16	0	16	16	16
Wood lath, Fiber Insulation lath, ⅜-inch Gypsum Lath		16	0	16	16	16

[1] Lath may be used on any spacings, center to center, up to the maximum shown for each type and weight.

[2] These spacings are based on a narrow bearing surface for the lath—when supports with relatively wide bearing surfaces are used, these spacings may be increased accordingly, and still insure satisfactory work.

[3] Paper-backed wire fabric, No. 16 gage wire, 2 by 2" mesh with stiffener.

sheet sizes are 24 or 27 in. wide by 96 in. long, although they are available in longer lengths for use in solid partitions. Self-furring diamond lath in the same sizes is available for use over masonry walls and ceilings and old surfaces, and for wrapping around steel columns. Paper-backed diamond mesh lath is used for machine application.

Rib lath has V-shaped ribs to provide the stiffness necessary for widely spaced supports. For plastering it comes in two forms: (1) flat ribbed lath with ⅛-in. ribs, weighing 2.75 and 3.4 lb per sq yd, and (2) ⅜-in. ribbed lath weighing 3.4 or 4.0 lb per sq yd. Ribbed lath sheet sizes are the same as for diamond mesh.

Sheet lath comes in 4.5 lb per sq yd and heavier sheets.

Wire lath is made of No. 19 U.S. gage wire with 2½ meshes per inch coated with zinc or rust-inhibitive paint. V-stiffened wire lath is made from No. 20 U.S. gage wire with No. 24 U.S. gage V-rib stiffeners spaced not more than 8 in. apart.

Paper-backed wire fabric consists of No. 16 U.S. gage zinc-coated wire spaced not to exceed 2x2 in. with stiffening ribs spaced not to exceed 5 in. o.c. with absorptive paper backing attached with No. 17 U.S. gage stitch wire 2 in. o.c.

Metal lath accessories are composed of such items as metal grounds, corner beads, screeds, expansion joints, picture molds, casing beads, studs, tracks, clips, runners, channels, base and chair rails, and access panel frames. There are several varieties of each to choose from and most are proprietary, being related to a particular assembly.

Gypsum lath has a core of gypsum plaster between two layers of absorbent paper. It may be plain, perforated with ¾-in. holes on 4-in. centers, or insulating lath, backed with aluminum foil to provide a vapor barrier and reflective insulation. It is available in ⅜ and ½ in. thicknesses and in sheets 16 or 24 in. wide and 48 in. long. Longer lengths may be specified for use in special systems such as solid partitions.

Fiberboard insulation lath (Federal Specification LLL-F-321b) may be single or multiple ply board in ½ in., ¾ in., and multiples of ½ in. thicknesses, in widths of 16, 18, or 24 in. and 48-in. lengths.

Foamed plastic is also used as a plaster base, as noted below.

MIXING AND APPLICATION

Plaster formulas

The selection of the plaster ingredients is concerned with the choosing of the cementitious material and aggregate whose properties when combined provide the kind of finish desired and are compatible with

the plaster backing and mixing method used. (See American Standard, ASA 42.1-1955 for recommended specifications for gypsum plastering.) The properties of gypsum basecoat and finish plasters are given in Tables 4 and 5.

Water when mixed with the cementitious material forms a paste which coats the aggregate particles and when it dries bonds them together. Only enough water should be added to provide plasticity or workability, since greater amounts reduce the strength and density of the plaster. The amount, shape, and size of aggregates, especially where there is an excess of fines, affect the plasticity and strength since more cement is required to coat the particles.

Tables 6 and 7 give the recommended mixes and maximum amounts of aggregate for basecoats over various backings and finish coats, without reference to the amount of water to be used. These tables refer to job-mixed plaster, hand applied, and not to ready-mixed materials and machine mixed or applied plasters. Measurement equivalents are shown in Table 8.

Plaster thickness cannot be overemphasized as a factor in the strength of plaster. Recommended minimum thicknesses should be heeded. Rigidity, stiffness, deflection, and cracking are all related to the thickness of plaster.

The number of coats in which plaster is applied may vary from one to two to three—more for solid partitions. The usual practice is to use two or three coats, depending on the plaster or base used. When two-coat work is used, the scratch and brown coats are applied without an inter-

val to permit the scratch coat to set. The Contracting Plasterers' and Lathers' International Association in its recommended Specification for Lathing Furring and Plastering (October, 1960) states as follows: "Plastering with gypsum, Keene's cement, lime, portland cement, or portland cement—lime plaster shall consist of not less than three coats, scratch, brown, and finish, when applied over metal lath, wire lath, or wire fabric, and shall consist of not less than two coats when applied over wood lath, gypsum lath, or fibre insulation lath, or unit masonry and shall consist of a bond coat and finish coat when applied direct to concrete."

Basecoats, in addition to the cementitious material and aggregate, should contain hair or fiber either as "mill fibered" (added by the manufacturer) or added as mixed. Basecoats of lime or portland cement plaster, individually or in combination, should not be applied directly to fiber insulation lath or gypsum lath or gypsum tile, nor should portland cement plaster be applied directly to wood lath. Both scratch and brown coats should be scratched to provide a mechanical key. Cracking is related to strength of basecoats. This in turn is related to thickness and proportion and type of aggregate used in basecoats.

Finish coats generally use one of three finishing methods: troweling, floating, or spraying. Trowel finishes are used to create a flat smooth surface usually for further decoration by painting or papering. The use of not less than ½ cu ft fine silica sand or perlite to each 100 lb of gaging plaster or Keene's cement increases

Table 4. Properties of gypsum job-mixed basecoat plasters

Property	Sand		Perlite		Vermiculite		Wood Fibered to Sand	
	1:2	1:3	1:2	1:3	1:2	1:3	1:0	1:1
Compressive Strength Pounds per sq. in.	775-1050	525-700	600-800	450-600	400-525	250-325	1750-2350	
Tensile Strength Pounds per sq. in.	150-200	100-150	165-170	90-150	130-160	70-100	280-400	240-250
Modulus of Elasticity Pounds per sq. in. x 10⁶	1.0	1.15-1.20	0.21-0.33			0.028	0.65-0.75	
Density In-Place Pounds per cu. ft.	104-120	104-120	50-56	41-45	50-55	42-45	79-82	
Coefficient of Linear Expansion inches/inch/degree F x 10⁻⁶	6.50	6.75	7.35	7.30	8.35	8.60	9.30	
Thermal Conductivity BTU/sq. ft./hour/°F/ inch thickness	5.51	5.60	1.64	1.31	1.74	1.42	3.15	

Source: Gypsum Association.

Table 5. Properties of gypsum finish coat plasters

| Materials | Ready-mix finish plaster | Gypsum gaging-lime putty plasters | | Keene's cement | | Acoustical plaster | Ready-mix colored plaster |
		Regular	High strength	Medium	Hard		
Mix (dry weight)	Neat	1:2	1:1	2:1	4:1	Neat	Neat
Compressive strength, psi	—	2,000–3,000 avg 1,200 min	5,000 min	4,000–5,000 avg 2,500 min		Low	—
Hardness, kg*	55	56	108	50	70	Soft	Hard
Setting time, minutes	—	20–40	20–40	20–360		—	—
Workability	Fair	Very good	Good	Fair	Poor	Poor	Poor
Remarks	May be painted as soon as set, no alkali reaction with paint		Requires less water than standard gaging plaster	Can be retempered, less susceptible to moisture than regular calcined gypsum		Good sound absorption	Float finish

* Kilograms required to force a 10-mm ball 0.01 in. into plaster face.

Table 6. Maximum aggregate proportions for job-mixed basecoat plasters over various backings

| Proportion Units | Gypsum | Lime | | Lime-Portland Cement | | Portland Cement |
| | | *Types of Plaster* | | | | |
		Dry Mix	Putty Mix	Dry Mix	Putty Mix	
1 Part Cementitious Material =	100 lbs. gypsum	100 lbs. hydrated finishing lime (Type "S")	1 cu. ft. lime putty (Type "N")	100 lbs. hydrated finishing lime (Type "S") + 94 lbs. Portland Cement	Cu. ft. lime putty (Type "N") to 94 lb. Bags of Portland Cement	94 lbs. Portland Cement
1 Part Aggregate =	100 lbs. sand or 1 cu. ft. perlite or vermiculite	100 lbs. sand	100 lbs. sand	100 lbs. sand	100 lbs. sand	100 lbs. sand or 1 cu. ft. perlite or vermiculite
Plaster Bases	*Two Coat Work*					
Gypsum lath	1:2.5					
Gypsum partition tile	1:3 or 1 wood fibered plaster: 1 sand	1:7.5	1:3.5	1:7.5	2:1:9	
High suction masonry						
Medium suction masonry						
Low suction masonry						
Concrete ceilings	Bond plaster					
	Three Coat Work					
Gypsum lath	1:2, 1:3 or Both 1:2.5	1:6.75, 1:9	1:3, 1:4	1:7.5, 1:9	1:1:6, 2:1:7	Both 1:3 to 1:5°
Metal Lath						
Gypsum partition tile	Both 1:3, or Both 1 wood fibered plaster: 1 sand					Both 1:3 to 1:5°
High suction masonry						
Medium suction masonry						
Low suction masonry						
Concrete walls and columns	Sc.-Bond plaster, Br.-1:3					

*Up to 10% by weight of dry hydrated lime or up to 25% by volume of lime putty may be added for each part of portland cement as a plasticizer.

NOTE: Hair or fiber may be added to gypsum plaster scratch coats and should be added as follows (lbs. fiber per cu. yd. mortar): Lime: Scratch, 6, Brown, 3.4; Lime-portland cement: Scratch, 6, Brown, 3; Portland cement: Scratch, 4 to 5.

Table 7.   Standard proportions for job-mixed finish coat plasters

TROWEL FINISHES

1. LIME PUTTY   : GYPSUM GAUGING PLASTER

   (a) 3   :   1 by volume

   Equivalents

   200 lbs. dry hydrate : 100 lbs. gauging plaster
   5 cu. ft. putty   : 100 lbs. gauging plaster
   40 gal. putty   : 100 lbs. gauging plaster

   †(b) 4   :   1 by volume

   Equivalents

   300 lbs. dry hydrate : 100 lbs. gauging plaster
   7.5 cu. ft. putty   : 100 lbs. gauging plaster
   60 gal. putty   : 100 lbs. gauging plaster

   † Specifications of the Finishing Lime Association of Ohio.

2. LIME PUTTY   : KEENE'S CEMENT

   (a) MEDIUM-HARD FINISH
       50 lbs. dry hydrate : 100 lbs.

   Equivalents

   not more than 100 lbs. putty   : 100 lbs. Keene's Cement
   not more than 1¼ cu. ft. putty : 100 lbs. Keene's Cement
   not more than 9 gal. putty   : 100 lbs. Keene's Cement

   (b) HARD FINISH
       25 lbs. dry hydrate : 100 lbs.

   Equivalents

   not more than 50 lbs. putty   : 100 lbs. Keene's Cement
   not more than ⅝ cu. ft. putty : 100 lbs. Keene's Cement
   not more than 4¾ gal. putty   : 100 lbs. Keene's Cement

3. LIME PUTTY   :   PORTLAND CEMENT

   200 lbs. dry hydrate : 94 lbs. (bag)

   Equivalents

   5 cu. ft. putty   : 94 lbs.

4. PORTLAND CEMENT   :   SAND*

   94 lbs. (1 bag)   : 300 lbs. **

   * Finish may be troweled or floated.

   ** Lime may be added as a plasticizer in amounts up to 10% by weight of portland cement if dry hydrate or 25% by volume of portland cement if putty.

5. GYPSUM GAUGING
   OR NEAT PLASTER   :   VERMICULITE FINES
   100 lbs.   :   1 cu. ft.

FLOAT FINISHES

1. — LIME PUTTY : KEENE'S CEMENT : SAND
     2   :   1½   : 4½ by volume

2. — LIME PUTTY :
     GYPSUM GAUGING PLASTER   :   SAND
   1 dry hydrate :   1½   : 2.3 by weight

3. — LIME PUTTY : PORTLAND CEMENT : SAND
   2 dry hydrate :   1   : 2.5 by weight

4. — LIME PUTTY   :   SAND
     1   :   3 by volume

5. — GYPSUM NEAT PLASTER   :   SAND
     1   :   2   by weight

NOTE 1. Lime finishes may be applied over lime, gypsum & portland cement basecoats, other finishes should be applied only to basecoats containing the same cementitious material.

NOTE 2. A gypsum-vermiculite fines finish should be applied only to gypsum-vermiculite basecoats.

NOTE 3. Lime equivalents based on Type "N" hydrated lime.

Walls and partitions

Table 8. Measurement equivalents

Gypsum	1 bag = 100 lb
	1 cu ft = 60 lb
Portland cement	1 bag = 94 lb = 1 cu ft
Hydrated lime	1 bag = 50 lb
Lime putty	1 cu ft = 40 lb of dry material plus water
Sand	1 cu ft = 100 lb = 7 No. 2 shovelsful
Perlite	1 cu ft = 7.5–15 lb
Vermiculite	1 cu ft = 6–10 lb
Water	1 cu ft = 62.5 lb = 7.48 gal

the factor of safety in preventing cracking in trowel finishes. Varying degrees of hardness can be obtained by care in the troweling. Float finishes are used where a surface texture is wanted. The texture will vary with the type of aggregate used and the type of float (wood, carpet, sponge, etc.). Float finishes tend to show less cracking than trowel finishes. These plasters are used with float finishes: gypsum-sand, lime-Keene's cement-sand, gypsum–lightweight aggregate fines, colored plaster, and portland cement–sand. Spray finishes, being machine applied, provide great latitude in texture, depending on the techniques and machines. It is usually desirable to work from a previously agreed upon sample developed with the application contractor. Acoustical plaster finishes may be sprayed on or hand troweled, usually in two coats, to a thickness of ½ in.

PLASTERING SYSTEMS AND ASSEMBLIES

Walls and partitions are based upon three basic systems. The factors affecting the selection of the system are cost, fire resistance, weight, thickness or space occupied, sound transmission or absorption, and concealment of equipment (see Table 9).

Hollow walls may be bearing or non-bearing and are framed with wood or metal studs, the latter often involving a proprietary system. The thickness is determined by the load, the stiffness, the sound resistance, and the need for concealment of equipment. Wood studs are 2 by 4s or 2 by 6s and may be doubled or staggered for increased concealment or sound resistance. Metal studs may be prefabricated in 1⅝ to 6-in. widths (Fig. 1) or site fabricated from ¾ to 2-in. channels (Fig. 2). With channels, spacers or stiffeners are usually employed but may be omitted to improve the sound quality of the wall. Most metal-stud hollow systems use floor and ceiling runners, although some use clips. The lath is applied with nails, clips, wire, or staples. When resilient clips are used they serve to reduce the sound transmission.

Solid plaster partitions are economical, highly fire resistant, and occupy a minimum of space. However, they have limitations in height and length and offer very little space for concealment of electrical and mechanical equipment. They may be constructed (1) with metal or gypsum lath stretched vertically between floor and ceiling runners as studless partitions (Figs. 3 and 4) or (2) with vertical channel studs extending from floor to ceiling runners, to which lath is applied, as solid stud partitions (Fig. 5): These assemblies are embedded in plaster. Solid partitions are limited to a minimum thickness of 2 in. by the American Standard Specifications for Gypsum Plastering (ASA A42.1). The Contracting Plasterers' and Lathers' International Association in its specifications limit the height of studless gypsum lath solid partitions to 12 ft and metal lath solid partitions to 9 ft 6 in. Solid stud partitions may be built to a height of 24 ft at a thickness of 3¼ in.; lengths, however, are limited when the height is over 10 ft.

Solid plaster partitions are braced temporarily on one side until after the scratch coat of plaster has been applied to the other side and has set, then the bracing is removed to permit the application of the scratch or back up and brown coats to the previously braced side. After the latter sets, the brown coat is applied over the first scratch coat. Finish coats can then be applied to either side.

Masonry walls are customarily furred on the inside because of the likelihood of moisture penetration through the masonry. The inside surface of cavity walls may be plastered directly. The furred space provides some insulation and a place for the concealment of electrical and mechanical equipment. Furring may be of wood (1 by 2 in. or 2 by 2 in.) or metal (¾-in. channels) and is normally applied vertically. Insulation may be placed between the furring strips.

Foamed plastic (expanded polystyrene) slabs applied to the inside of exposed walls with ¼ in. of masonry cement mortar provide furring, insulation, vapor barrier, and lath, all in one operation. Manufacturer's application directions should be followed carefully. Material is available in thicknesses of 1 to 4 in. in multiples of ½ in. and in widths of 12, 16, or 24 in. and lengths of 8 and 9 ft.

Masonry partitions of concrete block, common brick (medium hard), medium hard structural clay tile, and many types of stone provide the best masonry bases for direct plastering. High suction units such as soft common brick, soft or porous structural tile, gypsum tile, and lightweight concrete block require more care, as they have a tendency to withdraw the mixing water from the plaster at excessive rates. The denser masonry units such as hard burned brick, glazed tile, and some stone, having low suction rates, present problems of bonding. All can be used as bases for either gypsum or portland cement plasters with the exception of gypsum tile, which requires gypsum plaster. Bonding can be improved with high suction units by dampening the base surface before plastering, and spray curing after applying basecoats, and with low suction units by using those materials which provide an adequate key for a mechanical bond. The joints should be struck flush and the surfaces clean. Self-furring metal lath may be applied directly to these surfaces, if necessary.

Table 9. Comparative analysis of partition systems for initial selection of partition type

Partition type*	Weight, lb per lin ft for 8' ht			Floor area occupied, sq ft per lin ft			Fire-resistance rating, hr			Sound transmission loss, db			Cost index		
	High	Low	Avg	High	Low	Avg	High	Low	Avg	High	Low	Avg	High	Low	Avg
Unit masonry	337	169	232	0.97	0.25	0.53	7.0*	0.5	2.92	58	37	44	1 sample L.W. conc. 142		
Solid plaster	203	70	135	0.25	0.13	0.19	2.5	0.42	1.19	47	33	38.7	126	100	113
Metal studs	214	65	130	0.83	0.21	0.42	2.5	0.5	1.33	55	30	44.9	137	114	125
Wood studs	160	77	122	0.61	0.22	0.45	2.0	0.42	0.89	55	33	43.1	135	110	120

All partitions plastered both sides.

Monolithic concrete, to be an adequate base for plaster, must also be clean and provide a mechanical key for an effective bond. Three approaches have been taken towards the providing of a positive key: (1) prior treatment of the forms, by using rough boards or by treating boards with ammonia to raise the grain, or by lining forms with materials or devices that deform the surface so as to provide a mechanical bond, (2) treatment of the concrete surfaces by stripping forms early to permit wire brushing or scratching, or by applying a retarder to the forms so that the slower setting surface of concrete can be brushed more easily, or by repeated etching of the surface with muriatic acid, and (3) coating the concrete surface with bond plaster consisting of a rich low-consistency cement and sand mixture as a dash coat (not considered as a base coat), or by application of bonding agents, which are usually proprietary water-based emulsions sprayed on to provide a built-up base equivalent to scratch and brown coats, to which the finish coat of plaster may be applied.

Ceilings

Contact ceilings have the lath or plaster applied directly to the under side of the floor or floor framing. For direct application of plaster to monolithic concrete ceilings see above. Special fireproofing and acoustical plasters (proprietary mixes) are also sprayed directly to the underside of

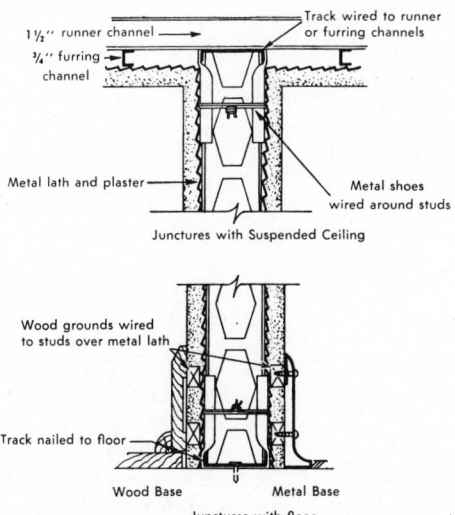

Fig. 1. Hollow partition—prefabricated metal stud

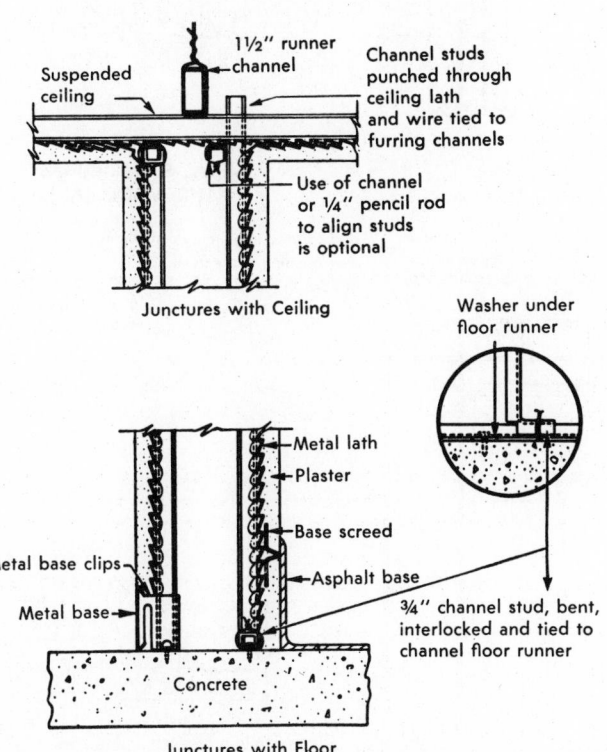

Fig. 2. Hollow partition—channel studs

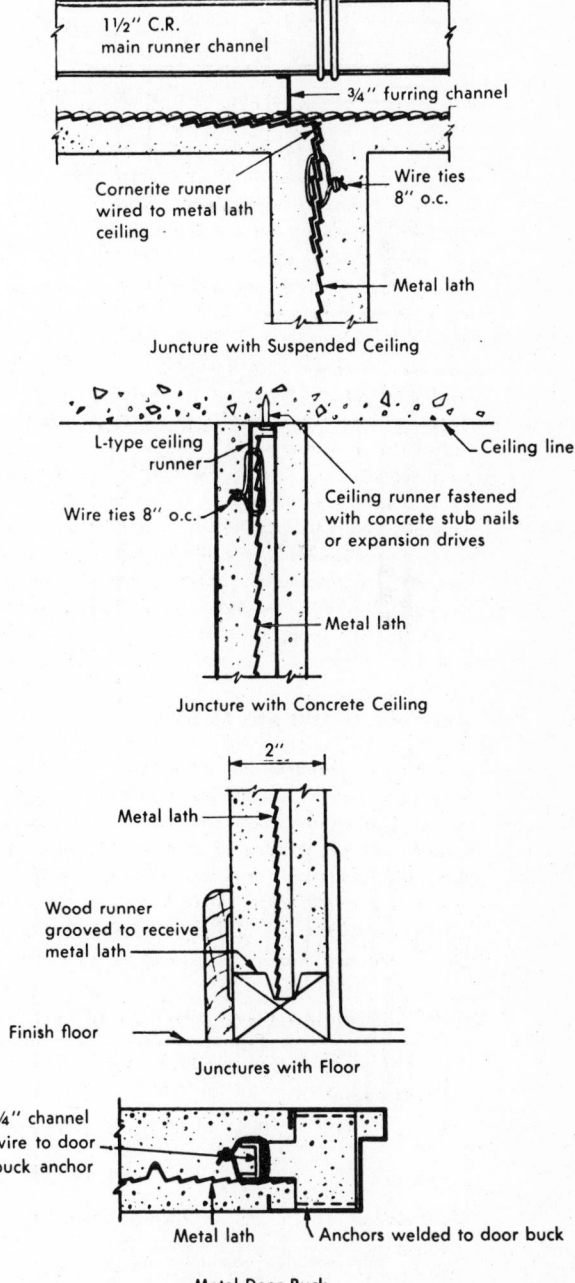

Fig. 3. Solid partition—studless—metal lath

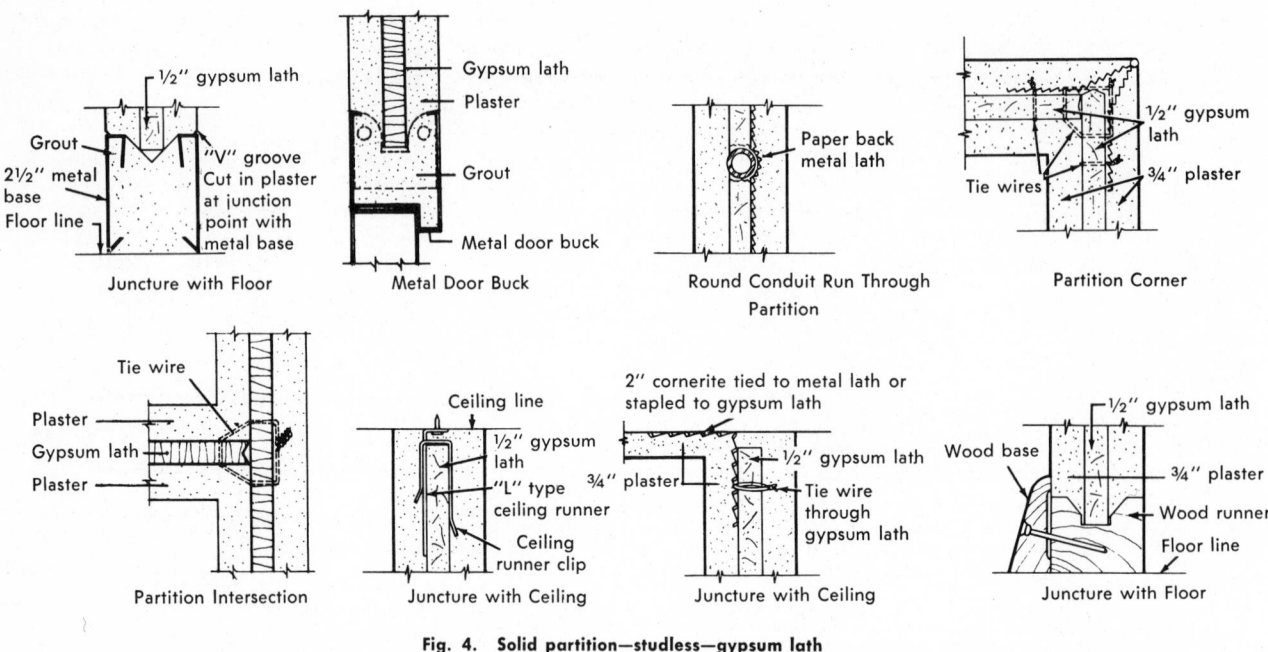

Fig. 4. Solid partition—studless—gypsum lath

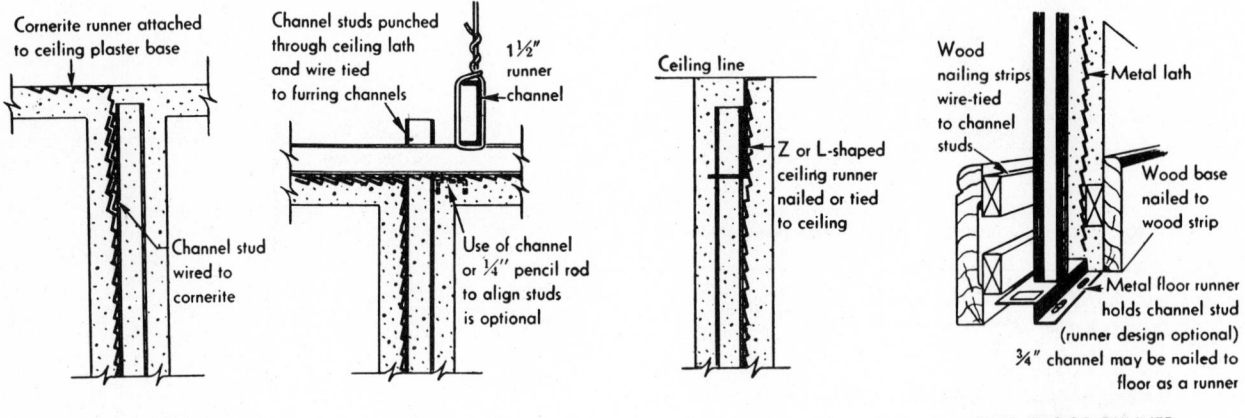

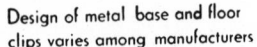

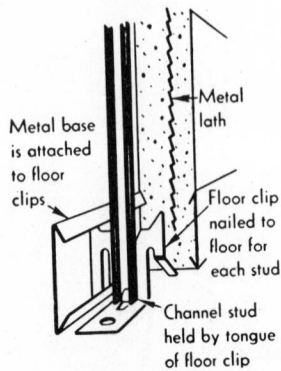

Fig. 5. Solid partition—channel studs

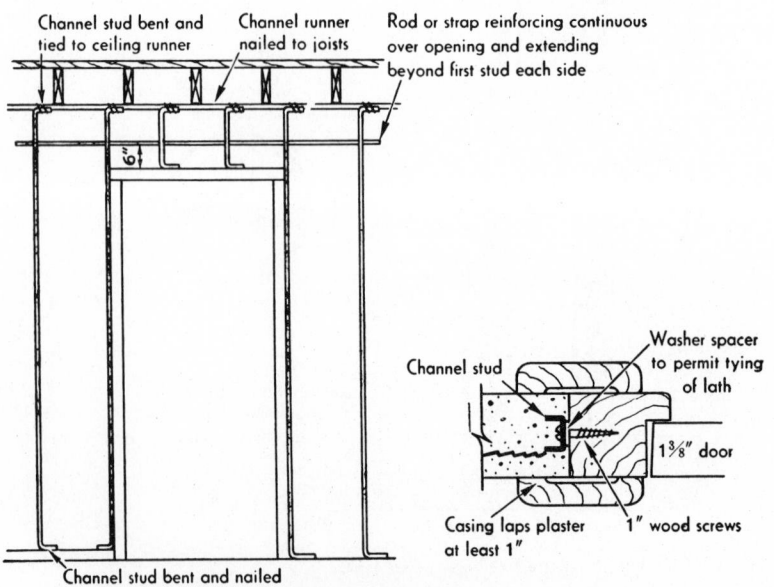

steel decks and their supports. Where the floor framing consists of wood, light-gage steel or reinforced concrete joists, it is customary where spacing permits (24 in. or under) to apply lath directly to the underside of the floor framing (Fig. 6). The type of fastener and its spacing must be adequate to support the lath and plaster. Cellular steel decks with punched flaps permit contact fastening of lath with wire ties.

Furred ceilings are used where the spacing of framing members is too great to permit direct application of lath, or where it is necessary to level or straighten the ceiling, or where improved sound conditions are desired. The furring may consist of wood strips, steel channels, round rods, clips, or other devices to provide a frame to which the lath may be applied. Because of the greater concentration of loads, fasteners need more consideration. Direct pull on fasteners in wood and nailable steel joists should be avoided (Fig. 7).

Suspended plaster ceilings, in which the ceiling framing is hung below the floor or roof system, usually are used to conceal lighting or mechanical equipment and often to permit formed ceilings of varying shapes. These frames consist of main runners and cross runners hung from the structure above with wire, rods, or flat hangers. The lath is fastened with wire or clips to the runners (see Fig. 8 and Tables 10–12).

Less cracking will usually be experienced when the joint between ceilings and walls uses unrestrained rather than restrained perimeter construction (Fig. 9 and Table 13). Control joints are recommended for large ceiling areas (60 ft or more in length).

Stucco (exterior plaster) is applied directly to masonry and can be applied to frame structures by either of two methods. One, known as the "open-frame method," consists of stucco applied to metal reinforcement that is attached directly to the structural frame. The second, known as "sheathed construction," differs from the first only in that sheathing and waterproof paper are interposed between the structural members and the metal reinforcement. If the frame is sufficiently rigid, open-frame construction is generally considered to have greater crack resistance than sheathed construction. This is especially true if back plastering is used. Metal reinforcement should in all cases be furred out sufficiently from the studs or sheathing to provide for complete embedment in the stucco. In open-frame construction that is not back plastered, paper-backed wire mesh is often used. As an alternate, 18 gage horizontal wires are stretched across the face of the studs at 6-in. intervals to support waterproof building paper, which is attached to the studs before the metal reinforcement is applied. American Standard Specifications for portland cement stucco (ASA A42.2-1946) recommends 12-in. stud spacing for either of these alternate constructions, but 16-in. spacing is more generally used. For light steel framing, ASA A42.2 recommends maximum stud spacings as follows: for open-frame back-plastered construction, 32 in., provided rigid across furring is applied at 16-in. intervals; sheathed frame, 24 in.; open-frame not back plastered, 16 in.

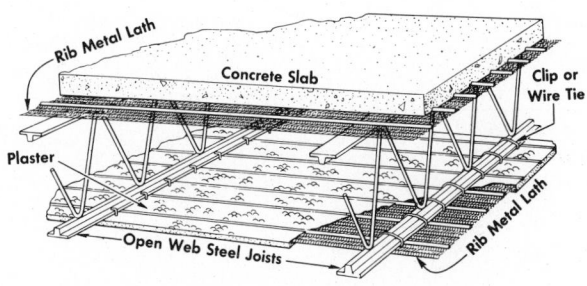

Fig. 6.   Contact ceiling—steel joist

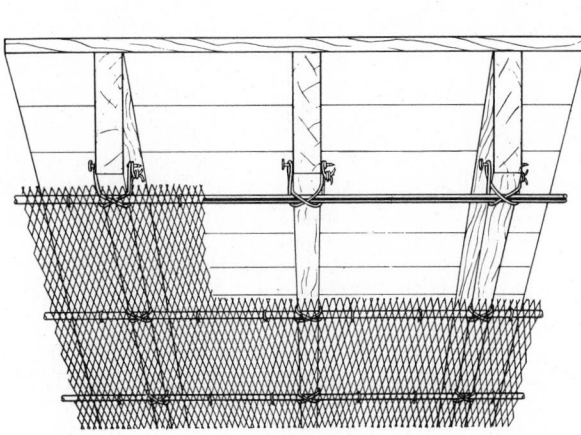

Fig. 7.   Furred ceiling—wood joists

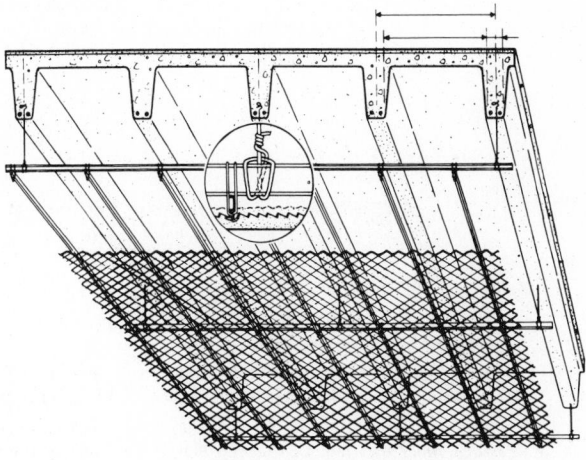

Fig. 8.   Suspended ceiling—concrete joists

Table 10. Hangers for suspended ceilings

Maximum ceiling area supported, sq ft	Minimum size of hangers
12.5	9 gage wire
16	8 gage wire
18	3/16-in. diameter, mild steel rod*
20	7/32-in. diameter, mild steel rod*
22.5	1/4-in. diameter, mild steel rod*
25.0	1x3/16 in. mild steel flat†

*It is highly recommended that all rod hangers be protected with a zinc or cadmium coating.

†It is highly recommended that all flat hangers be protected with a zinc or cadmium coating or with a rust-inhibitive paint.

Table 11. Spans and spacings of main runners*

Minimum sizes and maximum spans and spacings for main runners. From "American Standard Specifications for Gypsum Plastering and Interior Lathing and Furring," ASA A42.1 and A42.4, 1955

Minimum size and type	Maximum span between hangers or supports, ft	Maximum center-to-center spacing of runners, ft
3/4 in.–0.3 lb per ft, cold or hot rolled channel	2	3
1 1/2 in.–0.475 lb per ft, cold rolled channel	3	4
1 1/2 in.–0.475 lb per ft, cold rolled channel	3.5	3.5
1 1/2 in.–0.475 lb per ft, cold rolled channel	4	3
1 1/2 in.–1.12 lb per ft, hot rolled channel	4	5
2 in.–1.26 lb per ft, hot rolled channel	5	5
1 1/2x1 1/2x3/16 angle	5	5

*These spans are based on webs of channels being erected vertically. Other sections of hot or cold rolled members of equivalent beam strength may be substituted for those specified.

Table 12. Spans and spacings of cross furring*

Minimum sizes and maximum spans and spacings for cross furring. From "American Specifications for Gypsum Plastering and Interior Lathing and Furring," ASA A42.1 and A42.4, 1955.

Minimum size and type	Maximum span between runners or supports, ft	Maximum center-to-center spacing of cross furring members, in.
1/4 in. diameter pencil rods	2	12
3/8 in. diameter pencil rods	2	19
3/8 in. diameter pencil rods	2.5	12
3/4 in.–0.3 lb per ft, cold or hot rolled channel	3	24
	3.5	19
	4	16
1 in.–0.410 lb per ft, hot rolled channel	4	24
	4.5	19
	5	12

*These spans are based on webs of channels being erected vertically. Other sections of hot or cold rolled members of equivalent beam strength may be substituted for those specified.

REFERENCES

Diehl, John R., AIA., Manual of Lathing and Plastering. National Bureau for Lathing and Plastering (1960).

Lathing and Plastering Assemblies. National Bureau for Lathing and Plastering.

Recommended Specifications for Lathing, Furring and Plastering. Contracting Plasterers' and Lathers' International Association. (1960)

Plasterer's Manual. Portland Cement Association.

Manual of Gypsum Lathing and Plastering. Gypsum Association. (1956).

Performance of Lath and Plaster, Research Report and Recommendations. Gypsum Association.

U.S. Department of Commerce, National Bureau of Standards, Building Material and Structures Reports:

Suitability of Fiber Insulating Lath as a Plaster Base. BMS 3. (1938).

Effect of Aging on the Soundness of Regularly Hydrated Dolomitic Lime Putties. BMS 127. (1952).

Plasticity and Water Retentivity of Hydrated Limes for Structural Purposes. BMS 146 (1956).

Specifications for Lime and its Uses in Plastering, Stucco, Unit Masonry and Concrete. National Lime Association. (1945).

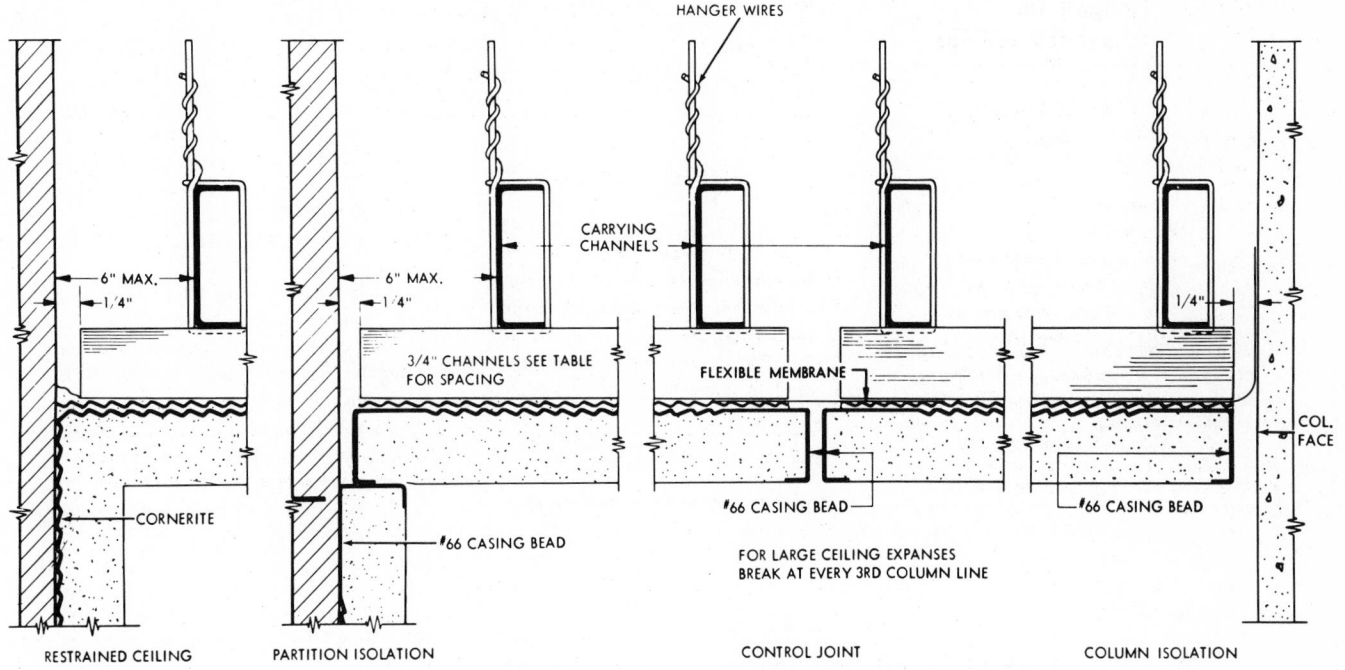

Fig. 9. Restrained and unrestrained ceilings and control joints

Table 13. Relative performance of lath and plaster systems with respect to crack resistance. Source: Gypsum Association

G = gypsum lath—3-coat plastering
G2 = gypsum lath—2-coat plastering
M = metal lath—3-coat plastering
WF = neat wood fiber scratch and gypsum sanded brown*
S = sanded plaster: 1:2†; 1:3‡

P = perlited plaster: 1:2¶
V = vermiculited plaster: 1:2¶
F = sand float finish*
T = smooth trowel finish*

PERFORMANCE	RESTRAINED CONSTRUCTION			UNRESTRAINED CEILING CONSTRUCTION		
	LATH BASE	PLASTER BASECOAT	FINISH COAT	LATH BASE	PLASTER BASECOAT	FINISH COAT
EXCELLENT	G or M	WF	F	G or M	WF	F
	G or M	S	F	G	S or P	F
				G or M	WF	T
				G	S	T
				M	S	F
GOOD	G or M	WF	T	G2	S or P	F
	G	P	F	G	V	F
	G	S	T	M	P	F
	G2	S	F	G2 or M	S	T
	G	V	F	G	P or V	T
	G2 or M	P	F	M	V	F
	G2 or M	S	T			
	G	P	T			
ACCEPTABLE	G2 or M	V	F	G2	V	F
	G	V	T	G2 or M	P	T
	G2 or M	P	T			
NOT RECOMMENDED	G2 or M	V	T	G2 or M	V	T

* All proportioning of basecoat and finish coat plaster as recommended in ASA 42.1, 1955.
† Scratch.

‡ Brown, 1:2½ for 2-coat work over gypsum lath.
¶ Scratch and brown.

WALLBOARDS—1
Gypsum board

By HOWARD P. VERMILYA, AIA

Unless otherwise noted, the data in this section are from the Gypsum Association and the manual of the Gypsum Drywall Contractors International.

Gypsum wallboard consists of a core of processed gypsum rock (hydrous calcium sulphate) sandwiched between two sheets of heavy, tough paper. Its use for interior wall and ceiling surfaces has grown—particularly in residential construction—largely because of the improved workmanship made possible by manufacturers' research programs and the increased number of trained applicators. Good workmanship provides a smooth-surfaced wallboard in which joints and nailheads are invisible.

Some manufacturers introduce other materials into the gypsum core to enhance its qualities. Vermiculite or perlite and glass or mineral fiber are added to increase fire resistance, glass fiber alone to increase strength and flexibility, and hydrated wood fiber to increase strength and reduce weight. Other fibers are similarly used.

The solid gypsum core is nonflammable and noncombustible. The board is durable and crack resistant and will withstand normal wall abuse. It is nonwarping and dimensionally stable. The erection in large sheets is dry; water is used only in the treatment of joints. The surface provides an excellent base for paint, textures, and wallpaper. It may be used in dry locations, and with special precautions in wet locations (over tub-showers and in shower stalls), as a base for various types of tile. It should not be used, however, in areas where it will be exposed directly to water or high-moisture conditions. It is also used on ceilings as a base for acoustical tile. Gypsum wallboard used in conjunction with radiant heating systems should not be subjected to temperatures in excess of 125°F.

Standard specifications for gypsum wallboard materials and application are as follows:

Material
Gypsum wallboard—ASTM C36
Gypsum backing board—ASTM C442
Methods of testing—ASTM C26
Definitions—ASTM C11
Annular-ring nails (GWB-54)—ASTM C380

Application
Gypsum wallboard finishes—ASA A97.1

TYPES OF GYPSUM WALLBOARD

Regular gypsum wallboard is made in three thicknesses: ¼ in., used as resurfacing material over other solid surfaces; ⅜ in., as covering for framing members, either wall or ceiling, spaced not over 16 in. on centers; and ½ in., for framing members spaced not over 24 in. on centers. Because of its greater stiffness, the ½-in. thickness is often used on 16-in. spacing in better construction. Not all manufacturers make the ¼-in. board; a few manufacturers make a ⅝-in. board. Sheet sizes are shown in Table 1.

Fire-rated (Type X) wallboard has a gypsum core specially compounded with fibers and lightweight aggregates to increase its fire resistance. It is furnished in ⅝-in. thicknesses, which give a rating of 1 hr, and ½-in. thicknesses, which give a rating of 45 min, on wood- or steel-frame partitions and ceilings. Some manufacturers have received ratings of 2 hr when two layers of their ⅝-in., Type X, fire-rated boards have been applied to walls and 1½ hr when they have been applied to ceilings. Fire-resistance ratings for Type X and regular board are shown in Table 2.

Backer-board, as its name implies, is intended for use as a backing material. It is produced with the regular gypsum core in ⅜-in. and ½-in. thicknesses, and with the fire-rated core in ⅝-in. thicknesses. It is generally made in 2 by 8-ft sheets with a gray paper on each side which will not take finishes. Wider and longer sheets are available from some manufacturers. It is used primarily as a backing material for adhesive application of acoustical tile on ceilings and for double-layer wall and ceiling applications. It is also used in ½-in. and 1-in. thicknesses for partition framing. In the 1-in. thickness it is called coreboard.

Insulating foil-back wallboard is made by most manufacturers in both ⅜-in. and ½-in. thicknesses, and by some in the ⅝-in. thickness for either regular or fire-rated cores. Backer-board also comes foil-backed. The aluminum foil, when faced with an air space of at least ¾ in., acts as reflective insulation. It serves also as an effective vapor barrier. It should not be used, however, as a backing material for ceramic, metal, or plastic tile. Thermal conductivities of plain and foil-backed gypsum board are given in Table 3.

Decorative gypsum wallboard is made in a number of prefinished forms, in both ⅜-in. and ½-in. thicknesses and in 16, 32, or 48-in. widths usually 8 ft long. Most manufacturers make "wood grained" fin-

Table 1. Types and sizes

Thickness, in.	Edge	Width, ft	Length, ft	Approximate weight, lb per 1,000 sq ft	Recommended support spacing, in., o.c.	Joint treatment	Decoration
⅝	Tapered	4	6, 7, 8, 9, 10, 12, 14	2,800	16 or 24	Tape and cement	Paint or wallpaper
½	Tapered	4	6, 7, 8, 9, 10, 12, 14	2,100	16 or 24	Tape and cement	Paint or wallpaper
⅜	Tapered or square	4	6, 7, 8, 9, 10, 12, 14	1,550	16	Tape and cement	Paint or wallpaper
⅜	Beveled	4	6, 7, 8, 9, 10, 12	1,550	16	No treatment required	Paint
¼	Square	4	8 & 10	1,100	16	Tape and cement, or batten strips	Paint or wallpaper

The above materials are available with insulating foil back in sizes given, at slight additional costs. Also available in ⅜-in. thicknesses are predecorated wood grain boards.

Table 2. Fire-resistance ratings

Material	Floor-ceiling construction	Loadbearing wood-stud partitions †
⅝-in. Type X gypsum wallboard *	1 hr	1 hr
½-in. Type X gypsum wallboard *	45 min	45 min
2 layers ⅜-in. regular gypsum wallboard		1 hr
½-in. regular gypsum wallboard		40 min
⅜-in. regular gypsum wallboard		25 min

*Type X (special fire retardant) designates gypsum wallboard, complying with the requirements of ASTM C36-60, that provides at least: (1) 1-hr fire-retardant ratings for ⅝-in. thick or (2) ¾-hr fire-retardant ratings for ½-in.-thick gypsum wallboard applied in single-layer-nailed application on each face of loadbearing wood framing members when tested in accordance with the requirements of Methods of Fire Test of Building Constructions and Materials (ASTM Designation E119).

† Fire-resistance ratings per Underwriters' Laboratory, Chicago, Illinois, and the National Bureau of Standards.

Table 3. Thermal conductivity values

Material	Conductance "C"	Resistance "R"
⅜" Gypsum wallboard	3.73	0.27
½" Gypsum wallboard	2.76	0.36
⅝" Gypsum wallboard	2.42	0.41
Air spaces		
*Bounded by ordinary materials (horizontal or vertical)	1.10	0.91
*One air space faced with aluminum foil:		
Heat flow upward or horizontally	0.46	2.17
Heat flow downward	0.15	6.51

* ¾" or more in width.

NOTE: Foil back gypsum wallboard is an efficient vapor barrier—less than 0.50 perms.

ishes that are photographic reproductions on paper of such woods as knotty pine, walnut, cherry, mahogany, in light and dark shades and in colors, some showing grooves to simulate random-width planks. The sheets, or planks as they are sometimes called, come with square, round, or beveled edges, which may be left open or covered with battens. They are applied vertically. A more recent development is vinyl-surfaced gypsum board, a durable, low-maintenance finish material, available in a range of colors.

EDGES

Gypsum wallboard is manufactured as a continuous strip usually 4 ft wide; the front is faced with a cream- or straw-colored, calendered sheet wrapped around the sides and overlapped by a gray sheet on the back. These paper-bound side edges are formed as square, beveled, round, V-shaped, or tongue-and-groove and are tapered or recessed. The strip is lopped or sheared off in desired lengths, leaving an open, unbound end. The tapered edge is designed to provide a smooth, very strong joint between sheets when the joint is taped and cemented.

ACCESSORIES

Tape, usually of perforated paper, approximately 2 to 2¼ in. wide is used to reinforce cemented joints. Metal-backed tape, with a 1⅛ to 1¼ in. electrogalvanized steel strip backing plain tape, is used similarly and also to prevent ridging or beading of the joint treatment and in lieu of back-blocking where joints occur between framing members. Joint cement is supplied as bedding cement for the first application in bedding the tape in the joint, and finish (topping) cement is supplied for the two finishing coats and for spotting dimpled nailheads. All nails in the face sheet of wallboard should be dimpled by hitting them with a crown-headed tool to sink the head below the surface of the board without breaking the paper. Finish cement is sanded to provide a flush smooth surface. Adhesives used with gypsum wallboard are of two types: one is used for application of the wallboard to wood framing, which permits a reduction in the number of nails, and the other is used for laminating boards in two-ply or double-layer installations. Manufacturers often recommend their joint cement for the latter application. Metal trim is available for corner reinforcement at outside angles of walls, beams, pilasters, or uncased openings (Fig. 1); metal casings for use at door openings and where wallboard abuts metal windows (Fig. 2). Metal trim provides a bead or straight edge for smooth application of joint cement. A system of metal corner channels has been developed to hold the board at wall-to-ceiling and wall-to-wall corners, eliminating nailing, blocking, and joint treatment at these intersections. In addition many accessories have been specially designed for various systems of assembling partitions and ceilings that use gypsum wallboard.

ERECTION

Horizontal versus vertical application of board: In the horizontal application, the long edges of the board are perpendicular to the studs or joists; in the vertical application the long edges of the board are parallel to the framing members of either walls or ceilings. Horizontal application is recommended for three reasons: (1) The board is stronger and stiffer in the long direction because the fibers in the paper faces also run in that direction; (2) There

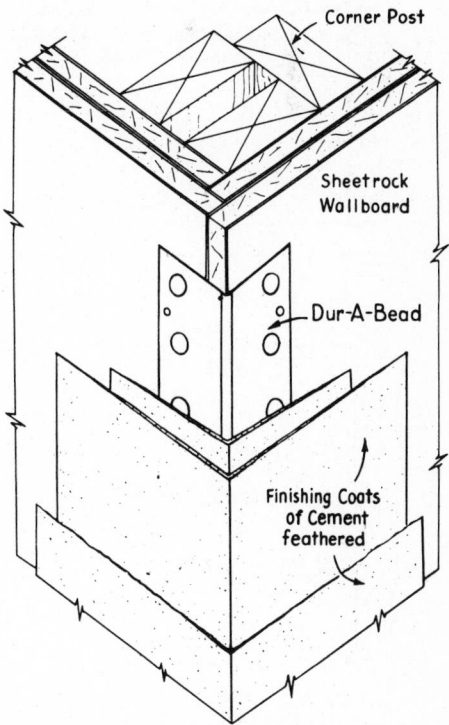

Fig. 1. Metal corner reinforcement

Courtesy U.S. Gypsum

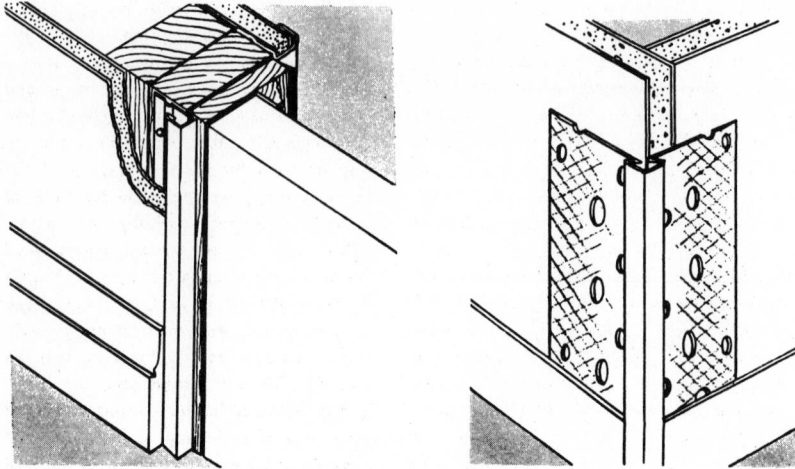

Fig. 2. Metal edging and corner strips

Courtesy Flintkote

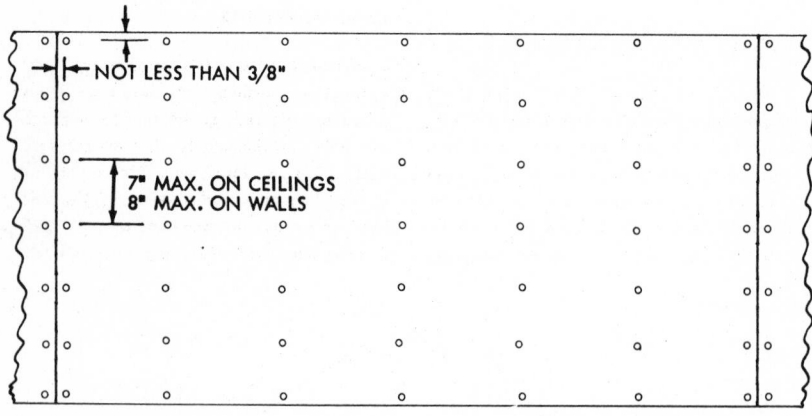

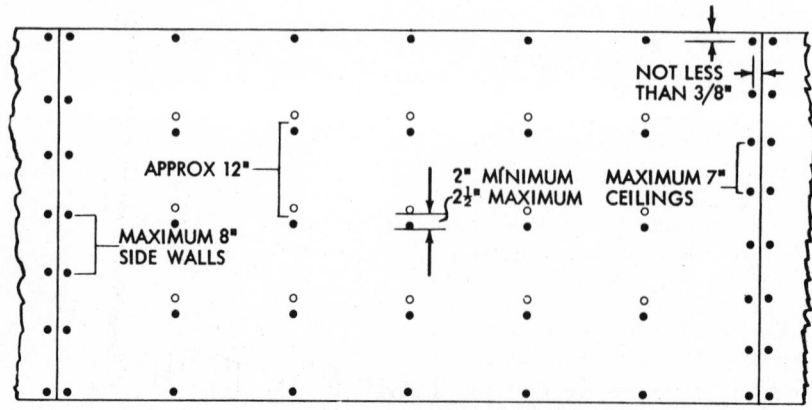

In the lower figure the solid dots represent the first nailing and the open circles the second nailing. (From ASA A97.1-1958.)

will usually be an appreciable reduction in the amount of joint work; and (3) Imperfections in the joint treatment are less apparent.

Lengths: The longest lengths possible should be used to avoid unnecessary joints. It is desirable to order the board from a carefully made layout.

Nailing

During the past few years research on nailing has determined that use of the right nails can greatly enhance the quality of a job. Length is particularly significant. The action of wood, shrinking or swelling with changes in moisture conditions, tends to cause the nail to pop by forcing it out or to dimple by pulling it in. The shorter the nail, the less this effect is. Annular-ring nails, because of their greater holding power, can be shorter than regular smooth-shank nails. The nailhead should be slightly concave, with thin edges. A short, pointed nail will drive straighter than one with a long, tapered point. All these factors and others relating to the nail shank and its diameter have been considered in the recommendations for nailing. Nail lengths recommended vary with the thickness of the board as follows:

⅜-in.-thick wallboard:

    1⅛" or 1¼" GWB-54 annular-ringed nail complying with ASTM C380

    1¼", 0.098 diameter smooth bright-finish nail with head conforming to ASTM C380

    1¼", 13 gage acid-etched phosphate-coated, "cupped" head.

½-in.-thick wallboard:

    1¼", GWB-54 annular-ringed nail complying with ASTM C380

    1⅜", 0.098 diameter smooth bright-finish nail with head conforming to ASTM C380

    1⅜", 13 gage acid-etched phosphate-coated, "cupped" head.

⅝-in.-thick wallboard:

    1⅜", GWB-54 annular-ringed nail complying with ASTM C380

    1½", 0.098 diameter smooth bright-finish nail with head conforming to ASTM C380

    1½", 13 gage acid-etched phosphate-coated, "cupped" head.

Double nailing is a recent development designed to ensure firm nailing of the board to the framing (see Fig. 3 for the spacing of nails for single and double nailing). In either case nailing should begin at the center and proceed out toward the ends.

Other methods of fastening

Adhesives, usually of the reclaimed-rubber latex type applied with caulking gun

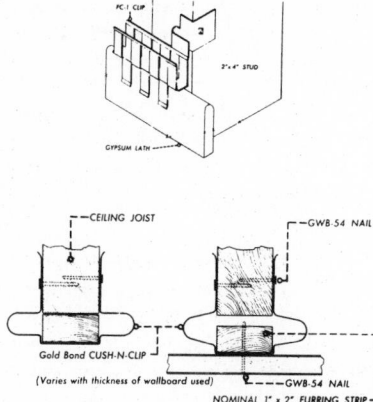

Fig. 4. Resilient clips

Courtesy National Gypsum

to the faces of framing members, are used to reduce the amount of nailing in the *adhesive nail-on method.* Nails are spaced 16 in. on centers on side walls and 12 in. on ceilings with this method which provides a saving in nails and in labor in driving and spotting nails and which reduces the hazard of nail-popping. *Staples* are used for fastening the first layer in two-ply applications. The accepted spacing is that used in single-layer applications. Staples with 1-in. legs with divergent points are used with ⅜-in. board and 1⅛-in. legs with ½-in. board. The crown of the staple should not cut the paper. Screws are recommended as fasteners by some manufacturers for special systems and where fire resistance is important in ceilings. To reduce transmission of impact sounds, *clips* are used, some with spring-like resilient connections, as ceiling joist and wall fasteners (Fig. 4). Clips, with or without the resilient feature, are also used for first-layer application to steel or wood studs. *Floating interior angles* are designed to minimize the stresses which may occur at interior corners of walls or walls and ceilings. The nails are omitted at the corners, the first row being placed about 7 in. away from the corner on each surface. The corner joint is treated as usual. This method, quite generally used, permits movement at the corner without cracking, since the angle is free (see Fig. 5). *Application sequence:* Wallboard is applied to the ceiling first, with the board inserted well into the corners so that ends and edges are concealed by the wallboard on the side walls. The upper wallboard is then applied with its long edge tight against the ceiling boards. The lower board on the side walls is applied last. Boards on opposite sides of partitions should not be joined on the same framing member.

BATH AND SHOWER AREAS

Bath and shower areas finished with ceramic, plastic, or metal tile, or plastic-finished panels, over gypsum wallboard: Framing members should permit the inside lip of the tub, receptor, or shower pan to line up with the face of the gypsum wallboard. This may require furring behind the fixture. Foil-backed gypsum board should not be used. A metal-angled spacer strip or beveled-wood furring should be installed to hold the lower edge of the wallboard ¼ in. above the upper rim of the fixture. This edge of the wallboard should be paper-covered (see Fig. 6). All joints should be taped, and both joints and nails should be covered with two coats of joint cement. A surface sealer that is compatible with the adhesive or dry-set mortar should be applied to waterproof the face of the gypsum wallboard. This may be a coat of the adhesive to be used, but it should not be shellac. The edges of all openings in the wallboard for pipe and accessories should be waterproofed and caulked. The joint between the fixture and the tile or plastic panel should be filled with tub-caulk.

TWO-PLY GYPSUM WALLBOARD

Two-ply gypsum wallboard applications are recommended where increased strength, durability, fire resistance, and sound insulation are desired. Various methods of application are recommended by manufacturers of wallboard. Two methods are in general use: one uses adhesive between

the first and second plys, and the other duplicates the nailing process for single-layer application so far as spacing is concerned but uses longer nails for the second ply, to give at least 1⅛ in. penetration into the framing. In either method backer-board may be used for the first layer, and the two layers may be applied in the same or opposite directions, vertically or horizontally. Joints in the exposed layers need not occur over framing members but should be offset at least 10 in. from those of the backing board. Any combination of wallboard thickness from ⅜ to ⅝ in. may be used for first and second plys, but ⅜ in. is more general for both layers. The face layer may also be any of the decorated boards. For adhesive application of the face ply, the inner board is nailed with spacing as for single-layer application. The adhesive (usually joint cement) is applied to the back of the face ply with a combed spreader, after which the face ply is placed against the inner board and nailed temporarily or held in place with shoring. After the adhesive has dried the nails may be removed, countersunk, or dimpled. The joints are treated in the usual manner.

JOINT TREATMENTS

Machine-treated joints provide the most satisfactory method of treating joints where experienced, qualified operators are available. Machines mix the cement and pump it to the applicator. The applicator applies the tape and cement to the flat joint or corner in one operation. Hand finishers filled from the pump are available

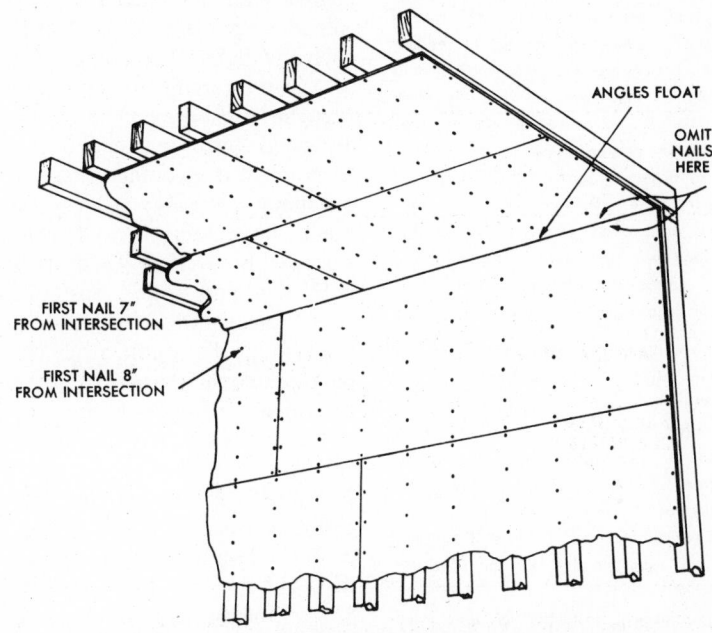

Fig. 5. "Floating angle" at intersection of wall and ceiling

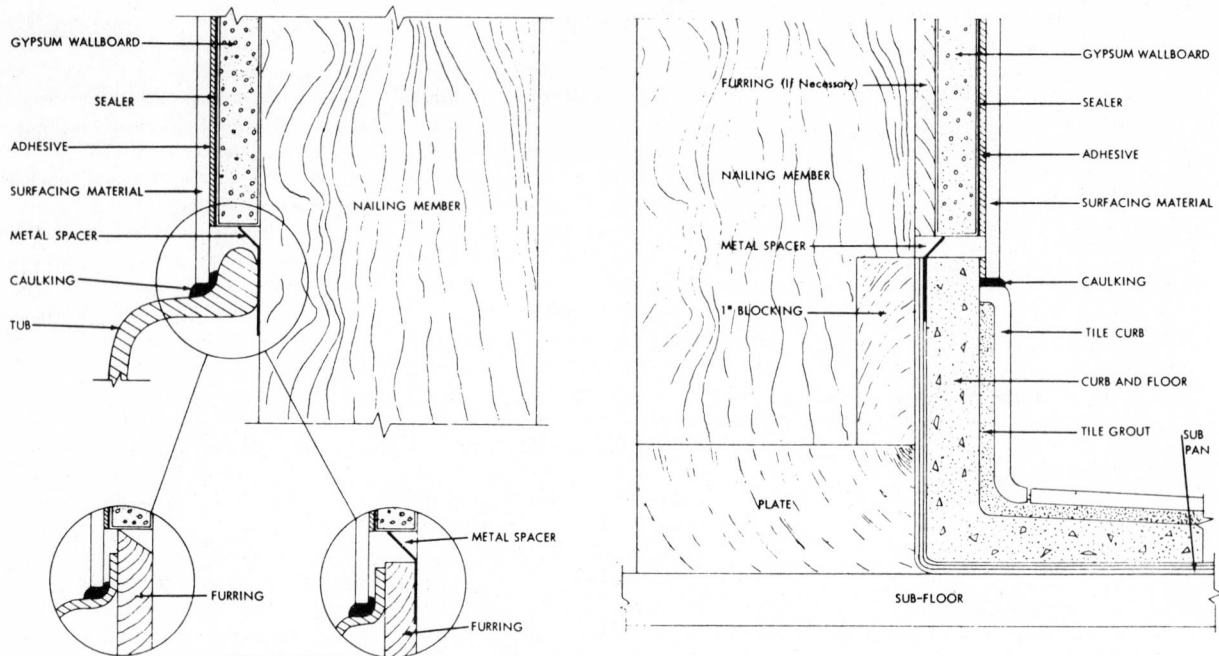

Fig. 6. Detail at bathtub and shower receptor

From ASA A 97.1-1958

in the following sizes: 7 in. wide for the first coat, 10 in. wide for the second coat and 11 in. wide for the finish coat.

DECORATION

Plain gypsum wallboard may be painted, textured, or covered with paper or other types of wall coverings, such as vinyl sheeting, plastic panels, and tile. Where the difference in suction or porosity of the surface of the board and the treated nails and joints is significant, as when oil paints are to be used, a primer sealer should be applied. The latter should also be used with wallpaper to permit its later removal for redecoration. Sealers are also recommended for rooms where high humidity conditions are anticipated. The following primer sealers are recommended for these types of decoration:

1. Casein and resin-emulsion paints: dry sealer or pigmented primer sealer
2. Most latex acrylic resins and rubber-base paints: first coat acts as primer sealer
3. Oil or oleo-resinous paint or lacquer: pigmented primer sealer, a latex-base paint, or a lime-locking, cold water primer
4. Texture paints: pigmented primer sealer, if recommended by manufacturer as needed
5. Wallpaper: latex-base paint, wall primer, varnish, or varnish size.

PARTITION SYSTEMS

"Systems" in the context of this article means a method of application of wallboard to, or to form, a wall or ceiling other than the conventional single or double layer method. This may involve the use of specially fabricated and designed metal or wood components, and may comprise the entire wall, partition or ceiling. Some of these systems are patented, but for the most part they have been designed by manufacturers to encourage the extended use of their products. In many cases manufacturers have secured ratings for their systems by having them tested for both fire and sound resistance. To secure acceptance of these ratings, they must be duplicated in detail, particularly with regard to the type and spacing of fastenings.

The systems may be classified as follows:

1. Steel framed walls and suspended ceilings
2. Solid laminated partitions (studless)
3. Laminated gypsum strip or stud partitions

4. Wall and ceiling furring systems
5. Column fireproofing

It is possible here to indicate only the types of systems available. Manufacturers' literature must be used for specific information.

1. Steel Framed Systems

At least four manufacturers have developed specially designed *steel studs* varying in width from 1⅝ in. minimum up to 6 in., to provide incombustible partition assemblies suitable for commercial or other types of occupancies.

The systems use metal floor and ceiling runners with, in some cases, spacers between studs. Metal baseboard also is available. All provide openings in studs for electrical wiring, and some for pipes. Spacing of the studs may be 16 in. o.c. or 24 in. o.c. depending on the thickness of the wallboard ⅜ in., ½ in. or ⅝ in.

Wall height limitations range from 9 ft for the narrower widths of studs to 16 ft for the larger sizes. Wall lengths are unlimited when they extend from floor to ceiling but may be

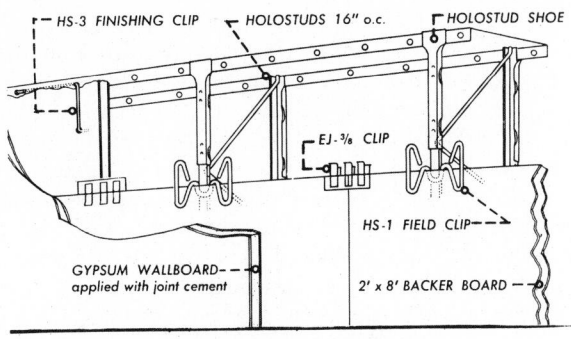

Fig. 7.   Steel stud system

Courtesy National Gypsum

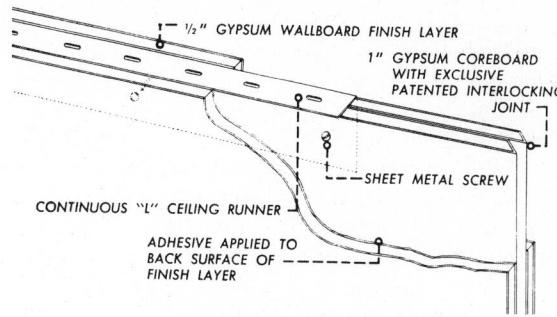

Fig. 8.   Solid laminated system

Courtesy U.S. Gypsum

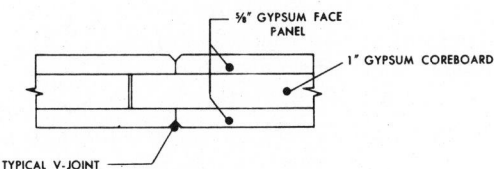

Fig. 9.   Demountable solid laminated system

Courtesy U.S. Gypsum

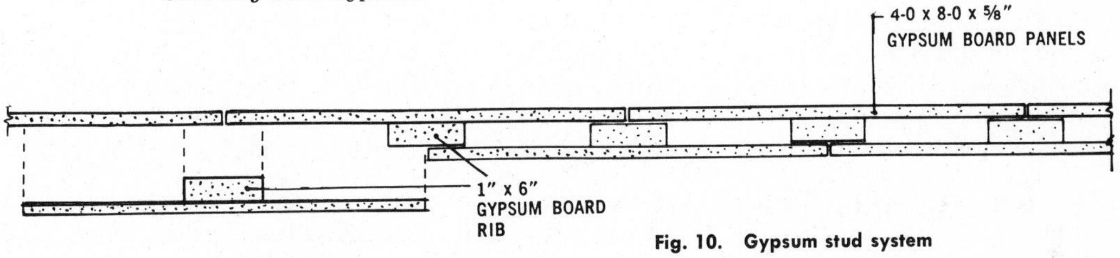

Fig. 10.   Gypsum stud system

Courtesy Pabco

limited to approximately 14 ft between intersecting walls when the partitions do not extend to the ceiling.

These studs are designed for attachment of the wallboard by either nails, screws or clips. The systems involving nail or screw application may use single or double laminated layers of gypsum board, but the clip applied studs require double layers.

The clips may be of the resilient type for reduced sound transmission. Fire resistances of from 45 minutes to two hours may be achieved depending on the thickness and number of layers of wallboard. Average sound transmission loss ratings in decibels will range in general from 36 to 46. One system using resilient clips effects an airborne sound reduction averaging 52 decibels.

2. Solid Laminated Systems

In solid laminated gypsum board partitions, the core may be either factory-laminated ½-in. backing board in 2 layers, or a 1 in. thick gypsum board, both types having gray paper surfaces. This core is then faced on each side with either ½ in. or ⅝ in. board laminated to the core in the field to make the overall thickness of the partition 2 in. or 2¼ in.

Some systems are movable. One of them uses sheets 24-in. wide, laminated in 3 layers with the core board center offset to provide a tongue and groove. Core board 1-in. thick is faced both sides with ⅝-in. fire rated board.

With the solid-type partitions, the face sheets have beveled edges. Joints of the face board, which

should be offset from those of the core board, are taped and treated with joint cement when 48 in. face boards are used. Either metal or wood runners are used at floor and at ceiling to secure the partitions in place. Wood or metal door bucks and frames for borrowed light may be inserted in the partition. Wiring is usually inserted in chases cut into the core board or in spaces between them. This may be conduit in some localities, but others will permit flexible cable. 1½ in. deep outlet boxes may be used. Heights for the 2 in. partition are limited to a maximum of 12 ft and for the 2¼ in. partition to 14 ft for partitions up to 12 ft long. When partitions are in excess of this length, the height should be reduced. 10-ft high partitions may be used for any length.

One manufacturer has developed a double laminated solid partition system which consists essentially of 2-1½ in. or 1⅝ in. solid sections separated by an air space. Each section consists of 1-in. core board applied vertically to which a single face layer of ½-in. or ⅝-in. wallboard, also vertically applied, is laminated. The space between may be used for piping, ductwork, or electrical wiring. To achieve a 46 decibel rating the space between the double laminated sections should be at least 1⅛ in. wide.

3. Gypsum Stud Partitions

These are probably the most varied in design and in application techniques of the various systems. Strips of gypsum board, usually backing board or core board, varying from 3 in. to 8 in. in width are laminated in the field to provide thicknesses of from ¾ in. to 1⅝ in.

One system uses a 3-in. wide, ⅝-in. thick strip between two 6 in.-wide, ½-in. thick strips to provide a groove for a spline of gypsum board where the laminated panels meet, to provide a movable system.

Another system has been developed to use only ⅜-in. board for strips and face layers.

Most systems apply the strips with adhesive cement to the rear side of the gypsum board sheets either to one side only or to both sides before erection so that when both sides of the partition are laminated in place, the wallboard is separated by these gypsum strips, usually placed 24 in. on center. Some systems use 24-in. wide boards and others 48-in. wide board applied vertically.

The vertical gypsum strips are usually made 1 ft shorter than partition height to allow a 6 in. or less space at top and bottom for wiring. Both metal and wood runners are used, the systems of some companies being adaptable to either. Overall thicknesses vary from 2 in. to 4½ in., the latter using staggered 1-in. gypsum strip studs.

4. Furring Systems

Furring made of ⅜-in. thick gypsum board and either 4- or 8-in. wide is used by one system as a base for face sheets ½-in. thick. The 4-in. wide strips are used at all interior and exterior corners while the 8-in. wide strips are used where edges butt and along the long center line of the sheet. The furring strips are nailed to the framing. Laminating adhesive is applied to the furring strip and the dry face sheet is fastened with nails and screws along the edges and the center of the board to these strips. Joints are later covered with joint treatment.

Metal furring channels for use on masonry walls and ceilings have been designed by another manufacturer. They are 2¾ in. wide with 1⅜ in. legs. The width permits the adjacent edges of two sheets to be fastened with self-tapping sheet metal screws. These furring channels are spaced 24-in. o.c. to receive ½ or ⅝ in. board.

5. Column fireproofing

Structural steel columns may be made fire resistant by the application of layers of ½ in. gypsum wallboard cemented by adhesive to the flanges of the column. Succeeding layers are cemented, and next to the last is wire-tied around the column. Two layers of ½ in. board so applied rates one hr, three layers—1½ hr and four layers—2½ hr.

Table 4. Gypsum board and other partitions

	Thickness, Overall, in.	Fire Resistance hrs	Sound Transmission loss, db	Weight per sq ft, lb
Steel Stud; sgl. layer each side ⅝ in. (Type X)* board	4⅞	1	39	6.5
Steel Stud; two layers each side ⅝ in. (Type X)* board	6⅛	2	46	11.0
Steel Stud; metal lath, ¾ in. sand aggregate plaster ea. side	5⅛	1	40	19.0
Solid Gypsum Board; 1 in. core, ½ in. (Type X)* board each side	2⅛	2	41	8.5
Solid Gypsum Board; 1 in. core, ⅝ in. (Type X)* board ea. side	2¼	2	36	9.7
Double, solid laminated; 1½ in. gypsum board faces, 1⅛ in. space	4¼	2	46	12.5
Gypsum Stud, 1 in. thick; ⅝ in. (Type X)* board each side	2¼	1		7.2
Gypsum Stud, 1 in. thick; two layers ⅝ in. (Type X)* board ea. side	3½	2		13.4
Gypsum Stud, 1 in. thick staggered; two layers ⅝ in. (Type X)* board each side	4½	3		13.4
Wood Stud (2 x 4); ½ in. board each side	4⅝	40 min.		5.9
Wood Stud (2 x 4); ⅝ in. (Type X)* board each side	4⅞	1		7.2
Wood Stud (2 x 4); two layers ⅝ in. (Type X)* board ea. side	6⅛	2		12.9
Solid Plaster Partition; gypsum lath, sand aggregate plaster	2	1	37	16.8
Solid Plaster Partition; gypsum lath; perlite aggregate plaster	2	1½	37	10.9
Solid Plaster Partition; metal lath, sand aggregate plaster	2	1	39	18.0
Solid Plaster Partition; metal lath, vermiculite aggregate plaster	2	1	34	8.8
Gypsum Block; ½ in. sand plaster each side	5	3	43	21.0
Gypsum Block; ½ in. lightweight plaster each side	5	2		15.0
Clay Tile, ⅝ in. sand plaster each side	5¼	1	41	29.0
Concrete Block, ½ in. sand plaster each side	4⅝	2	37	25.0
Brick, ⅝ in. sand plaster each side	4⅞	2	48	52.0

* Type "X" gypsum board is fire-rated, incorporating additives to increase fire resistance

By HOWARD P. VERMILYA, AIA

Insulation board, sometimes called "fiberboard" or "rigid insulation," is a generic term used to describe wood or vegetable fibers that have been compressed or felted to form rigid boards. The term is not generally used for boards made of inorganic fibers such as glass, asbestos, or mineral wool. The first wood-fiber insulating board was developed by the Insulite Company in 1914 and the first vegetable-fiber board, using bagasse or sugarcane fibers, was produced by the Celotex Corporation in 1920.

USES

Originally designed as an insulator, insulation board now has many uses:

1. Exterior sheathing
2. Interior wall and ceiling finish (building board)
3. Acoustical tile
4. Roof insulation
5. Roof deck
6. Form board (for gypsum or concrete decks)
7. Shingle backer strips
8. Exterior siding
9. Plaster lath
10. Floor underlayment
11. Panels (sandwich)

In order to meet the requirements of all the above, various modifications have been made in the basic product. Insulation board may be obtained which has been specially treated, integrally or by impregnation, to improve its resistance to moisture, rot, termites, and fire. For certain uses, densities have been increased to improve structural properties, particularly for sheathing and form board. Layers of board have been laminated to increase insulation and structural properties. These laminated boards are also used as cores for sandwich panels faced with other materials. A wide variety of decorative surfaces have been developed. Acoustical properties have been improved by drilling holes in the exposed face.

STANDARDS

Insulation board is manufactured to uniform industry standards established by the Insulation Board Institute and to comply with the following national standards:

1. Federal Specification LLL-F-321
2. Federal Specification SS-A-118b (acoustical tile)
3. Commercial Standard CS42-49
4. American Society for Testing and Materials: ASTM-C-208

The physical properties covered by these standards include density, thermal conductivity, transverse load without rupture, deflection at breaking load, tensile strength, water absorption, linear expansion, and decay and rot resistance. The standards are also concerned with the surface finishes for interior boards, plank, and tile, and provide test procedures for determining their compliance with flame-resistance standards.

Standard types and sizes of insulation board are given in Table 5. Types of fasteners used for the installation of insulation board are listed in Table 6.

EXTERIOR SHEATHING

Exterior sheathing is used to replace wood boards on walls and roofs and thereby reduce air infiltration and provide additional insulation. Sheathing boards are generally 4 by 8 or 4 by 9 ft, $\frac{25}{32}$ in. thick, and are impregnated, integrally treated, or coated with asphalt. These boards, when properly nailed to the frame, 3 in. on center at edges and 6 in. on center on intermediate studs, stiffen it so as to eliminate the need for corner bracing (Fig. 11). For horizontal application, sheathing boards 2 by 8 ft with V-joints along the long edges, are also available in this thickness, although they do not provide equivalent bracing (Fig. 12). A more recent development is a high-density, asphalt-treated board, 4 by 8 ft or 4 by 9 ft by ½ in. thick. This board has increased nail-holding power, which not only provides the required stiffness to permit omission of corner bracing but also permits the board to be used as a nailing base, with screw-type or annular-ring nails (Fig. 13), for the

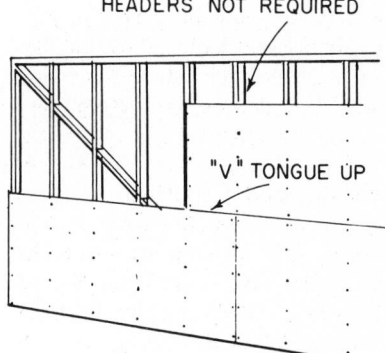

Fig. 12. Insulation board sheathing, 2 by 8 ft, applied horizontally

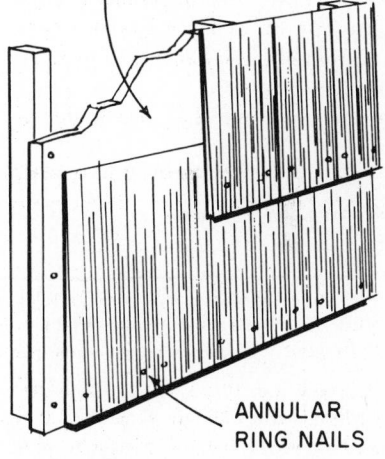

Fig. 13. Application of shingles to high-density insulation board sheathing

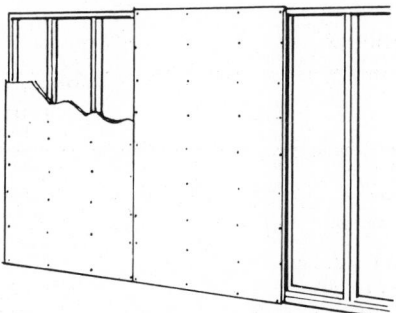

Fig. 11. Insulation board sheathing, 4 by 8 or 4 by 9 ft, applied vertically

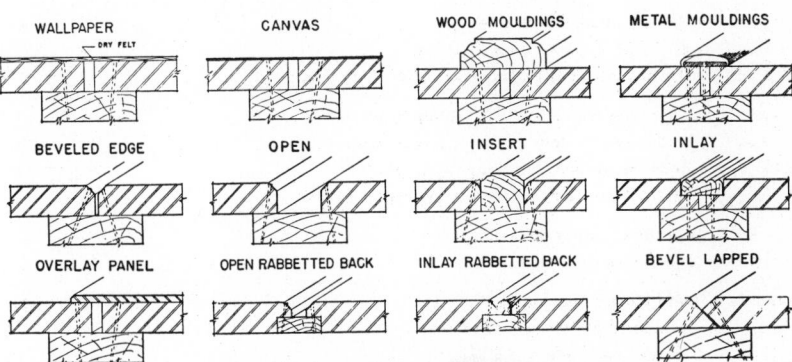

Fig. 14. Joint treatments for building board

Table 5. Standard sizes and thicknesses of structural insulation board products *

Courtesy Insulation Board Institute

Product	Thickness *	Sizes *	Edges	Major uses
Building board	½"	4'x6' 4'x7' 4'x8' 4'x9' 4'x10' 4'x12'	Square	General purpose structural insulating board; decorative interior finish; base for plastic paints, wall coverings and other interior decorative finishes
Insulating roof deck	Nominal C value 1½" 0.24 2" 0.18 3" 0.12	2'x8'	Fabricated long edges; short edges interlocking or square	Three-in-one product, roof deck, insulation, and interior finish for flat, pitched or shed-type open-beamed-ceiling roof construction
Roof insulation	Nominal C value ½" 0.72 1" 0.36 1½" 0.24 2" 0.19 2½" 0.15 3" 0.12	23"x47" 24"x48"	Varies	For roof insulation under built-up roofing on flat roofs and under certain types of roofing on pitched roofs. Floor insulation for masonry floors. Protection course for membrane waterproofing
Tile, plain or perforated	½"	12"x12" 12"x24" 16"x16" 16"x32"	Fabricated edges	Decorative, insulating wall and ceiling panels. Frequently used in conjunction with building board and/or plank
Plank	½"	8"x8' 8"x10' 12"x8' 12"x10' 16"x8' 16"x10'	Fabricated long edges	Decorative, insulating wall and ceiling finish. Frequently used in conjunction with building board and/or tileboard
Sheathing, regular density	½" or 25/32"	4'x8' 4'x9' 4'x10' 4'x12'	Square	Wall sheathing under brick veneer, siding, shingles, or stucco
	½" or 25/32"	2'x8'	Long edges fabricated; short edges sq.	
Sheathing, high-density	½"	4'x8' 4'x9'	Square	High-density product designed for use without supplementary corner bracing
Sheathing, nail-base	½"	4'x8' 4'x9'	Square	High-density product designed for use in frame construction to permit the direct attachment of exterior siding materials such as wood and asbestos shingles. The super strength of this material also eliminates the need for supplementary corner bracing
Shingle backer	5/16" or 3/8"	11¾"x48" 13½"x48" 15"x48" 15½"x48"	Square	Undercoursing for wood or asbestos-cement shingles applied over insulation board sheathing
Insulating form board	1" or 1½"	24", 32" and 48" widths; 4' to 12' in length	Square	Designed for use as a permanent form for reinforced gypsum or lightweight aggregate concrete poured-in-place roof construction

* For additional thicknesses and sizes, consult manufacturer.

direct application of asbestos or wood shingles. Sheathing paper may be omitted over asphalt-treated boards.

BUILDING BOARD

Building board is used as an interior finish material for walls and ceilings. It is usually manufactured ½ in. thick, although some manufacturers supply it in ⅜, ⅝, 1, 1⅜, and 1⅞-in. thicknesses. Others laminate ½-in. boards to achieve greater thicknesses. In the ⅜-in. thickness it is usually called

utility board. All manufacturers make it in 4 by 8-ft sheets and some supply it also in sheets up to 14 ft in length and 8 ft in width. The ½-in. board is intended for use over studs 16 in. on center and it should be supported on all edges. It is available with various predecorated finishes, plain or wood-grain, or primed for later painting. Various joint treatments are shown in Fig. 14. Plank in 8, 12, 16, and 24-in. widths, 8 and 10 ft long, is supplied predecorated for finishing walls. Ceiling tile, 12 by 12, 12 by 24, 16 by 16, and 16 by

32 in., is also made with various surface finishes for application to solid backing or to furring strips. Both the plank and tile have tongue and groove (T and G) or other edges which permit concealed fastening at the joints (Fig. 15). They may also be applied with adhesives.

ACOUSTICAL TILE

Acoustical tile made from insulation board may be obtained prefinished with a standard, coated finish or with a flame-re-

Table 6. Fasteners most commonly used for structural insulation board products

Courtesy Insulation Board Institute

Product	Application	Thickness, in.	Size and type of fastener
Building board	Framing 16 in. o.c.; fasteners 3 in. o.c. on edges and 6 in. o.c. on intermediate framing and ⅜ in. from edges	½	1½-in. 4d common nail 1½-in. galv. roofing nail 1½ in. 4d finishing nail
Insulating roof deck	Framing not less than 3 in. nom. width; spacing of framing members not less than 16 times thickness of deck; applied across roof beams with nails spaced approx. 4½ in. o.c. on each roof beam; 8 in. o.c. at all edges, ridges, eaves, and openings	1½ 2 3	3-in. 10d galv. or bright nail 3½-in. 16d galv. or bright nail 4½-in. 30d galv. or bright nail
Roof insulation	Wood decks—nail 12 in. o.c. (no vapor barrier)	½, 1, 1½, 2 2½, 3	Large headed galv. roofing nail with minimum ⁷⁄₁₆-in. head with sufficient length to penetrate the roof deck at least ¾ in.
Tile, plain or perforated	Nail or staple at three corners and 8 in. o.c. along framing members; 16 in. tile on 8 in. o.c. framing; 12 in. tile on 12 in. o.c. framing	½	3d brad 3d finishing 3d box ½ or ⁹⁄₁₆-in.-long staples
Plank	Planks applied at right angles to framing; nailed through nailing flange at each support; planks applied parallel to framing; space nails 6 in. apart	½	3d brad 3d finishing 3d box
Sheathing	4x8-ft and 4x9-ft board applied vertically; framing 16 in. o.c.; nailed or stapled 3 in. o.c. on edges and 6 in. o.c. on intermediate framing; 2x8-ft board applied horizontally with nails or staples spaced 4 in. o.c. at vertical edges and 8-in. o.c. at intermediate supports	½ ²⁵⁄₃₂	1½-in. galv. roofing nail 1¾-in. galv. roofing nail 1⅛-in. galv. staple, 16 gage with ⁷⁄₁₆-in. crown 1¾-in. galv. roofing nail 2-in. galv. roofing nail 8d common nail 1½-in. galv. staple, 16 gage with ⁷⁄₁₆-in. crown
Shingle backer	Applied over insulation board sheathing. Backer nailed with a 7d galv. box nail at each stud with ½-in. sheathing and 8d galv. box nails at each stud with ²⁵⁄₃₂-in. sheathing	⁵⁄₁₆ and ⅜	7d galv. box 8d galv. box
	Use 2-in. galv. annular-grooved nail for wood shingles		2-in. galv. annular-grooved

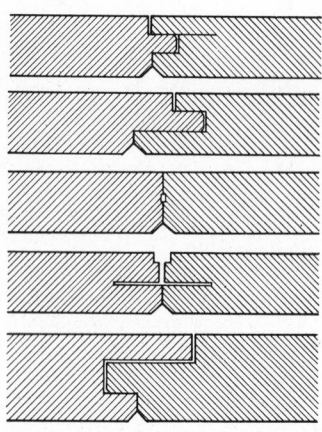

Fig. 15.   Joint treatments for ceiling tile

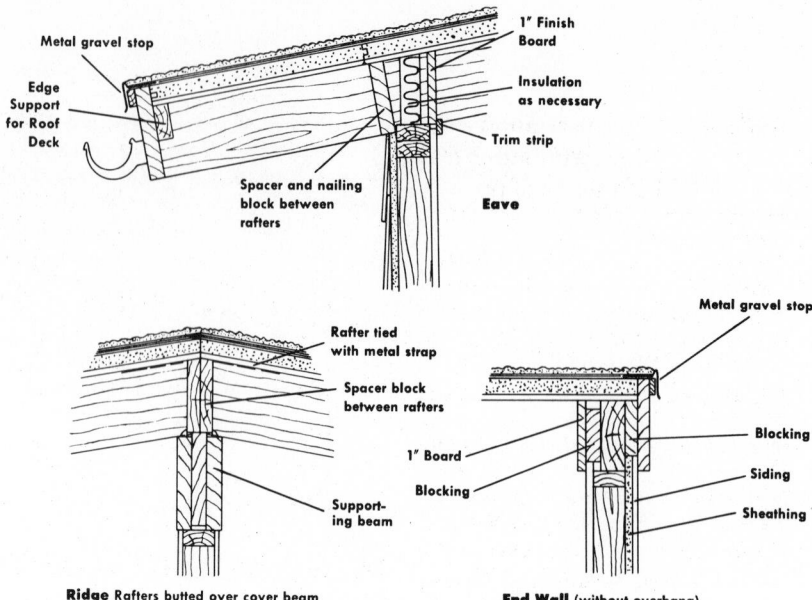

Ridge Rafters butted over cover beam   **End Wall** (without overhang)

Fig. 16.   Details of insulating roof deck

sistant surface treatment. Under Federal Specification SS-A-118b, these finishes are Class D and Class C, respectively. In addition, the surface may be textured, fissured, striated, or have drilled holes in regular or random patterns. The drilled types are commonly called "perforated," although the holes do not penetrate the entire thickness of the board. Acoustical tile is produced in ½, ¾, and 1-in. thicknesses, and sizes range in multiples of 12 in., from 12 by 12 up to 24 by 48 in. The edges are generally designed for concealed fastening by nails or staples, some are designed for use with suspension systems, and all types are suitable for adhesive application. The finishes are designed to clean easily and to permit repainting with nonbridging paints.

ROOF INSULATION

Roof insulation, usually of the same density as the building board, is applied over any type of roof decking as a base for built-up roofing. It is supplied plain, or coated or impregnated with asphalt, in thicknesses ranging from ½ up to 3 in. in increments of ½ in. Sheet size is 24 by 48 in. (Simplified Practice Recommendation R 257-55). Edges may be square, T and G, or shiplap. The insulation is usually laid on a mopped-on vapor barrier. Edge and cant strips are provided by several manu-

facturers. The weight ranges from 0.72 psf for ½-in. board to 4.79 psf for 3-in. board, and the thermal conductivity (C factor) ranges from 0.72 to 0.12.

ROOF DECK

Insulating roof deck is a laminated board in thicknesses of 1½, 2, and 3 in., 2 ft wide by 8 ft long. It is designed for use in exposed-beam construction, in which the underside of the roof deck forms the finished ceiling. Roof deck can be applied to flat or sloping roofs and provides (1) a structural roof deck, (2) insulation, and (3) a prefinished ceiling. Details of the construction are shown in Fig. 16. The bottom layer of board is usually plain insulation building board; the upper layers may be plain or asphalt-impregnated. Some manufacturers also provide an acoustical treatment to the ceiling with surface treatments complying with Federal Specification SS-A-

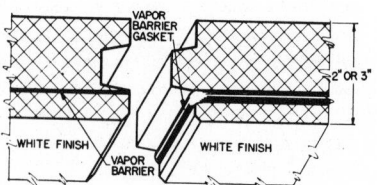

Fig. 17.   Insulating roof deck with vapor barrier

118b Class C (slow-burning) and Class D. For use in climates where the average daily January temperature may fall below 40°F, a board is available which has a vapor barrier applied between the bottom two layers in the 2 and 3-in. thicknesses (Fig. 17). The long edges have T and G joints, and special gasket-type inserts are available for boards incorporating vapor barriers. The short edges which must occur over framing members may be interlocking or square. The end joints, which should be

Table 7.   Insulating roof deck

Information shown is for board size of 2 by 8 ft

Thickness, in.	Maximum framing c. to c., in.	Weight, psf	U value (inc. roofing)
1½	24	2.3	0.19
2	32	3.1	0.15
3	48	4.5	0.11

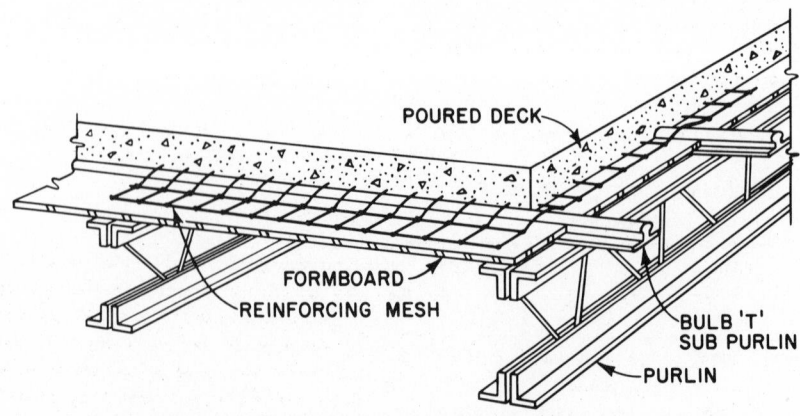

Fig. 18.   Insulating form board between subpurlins

Table 8. *U* value of roofs with 1-in. form board and built-up roofing

Deck thickness, in.	Gypsum	Vermiculite concrete 1:4	Perlite concrete 1:4
2	0.20	0.18	0.16
3	0.18	0.15	0.13

staggered, are caulked to prevent passage of water vapor. All open edges and surfaces must be protected from exposure. Minimum rafter thickness should be 3 in. to provide proper bearing. Rafter spacing is shown in Table 7. Built-up or selvedge-edge roll roofing may be applied in the normal way. Rigid shingles should be applied to furring strips. Asphalt shingles may be applied directly to the 2 and 3-in.-thick roof decks with galvanized or aluminum 1½-in. annular-ring nails, as recommended by the roofing manufacturer. Some manufacturers may recommend that self-sealing tab shingles be used or that tabs be cemented down. This would seem a wise precaution in windy areas.

FORM BOARD

Insulating form board in standard thicknesses of 1 in., widths of 24, 32, or 48 in., and lengths up to 12 ft, is used as a permanent form below poured roof decks such as gypsum or lightweight concrete. Thicknesses of ¾ and 1½ in. are also available. Form board is usually precut to fit between roof subpurlins (Fig. 18). Spacing of subpurlins is generally 32⅝ in. for gypsum decks and 24⅝ in. for lightweight concrete. End joints may be T and G to avoid the need for additional supports. Long edges are square. The board is treated to resist mildew and termites, and the bottom surface is either unfinished or primed for later painting, since it may be water-stained during the pouring of the roof deck. *U* values of form board roofs are given in Table 8.

Acoustical form board, with the lower surface drilled for acoustical absorption, is

Table 9. Shingle backer boards

Shingle backer width, in.	Shingle	Shingle exposure, in.
11¾	12-in. asbestos cement	10½
13½	16-in. wood	12
15	16-in. wood	13½
15½	18-in. wood	12–14

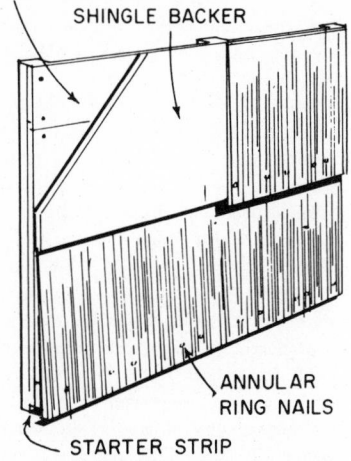

Fig. 19. Application of shingle backer board

made in the same sizes as regular form board and also in tiles 12 by 24 and 24 by 24 in. High-density board, sometimes asphalt impregnated in the upper laminations, provides strength, whereas low-density material in lower laminations provides the sound absorption.

SHINGLE BACKER BOARD

Shingle backer board (Fig. 19) is manufactured in 5⁄16 and ⅜-in. thicknesses and 48-in. lengths. The width varies from 11¾ to 15½ in., depending upon the size of shingle with which it is to be used. The uses and functions of backer board are similar to those of the under course of wood shingles in double coursing, using similar exposures. It provides insulation and a heavier shadow line with less nailing.

EXTERIOR SIDING

Some manufacturers make a high-density, water-resistant board suitable for use as exterior siding. It is available in nominal ½ or ⅝-in. thicknesses in plain or V-grooved sheets 4 by 8 up to 8 by 14 ft. As lap siding, it comes in 12-in. widths for a 10¾-in. exposure, and in 8 to 16-ft lengths.

INSULATING LATH

Insulating lath is used as the base for plaster (see section on "Plaster").

FLOORS

Insulating fiberboard is used in 4 by 4 or 4 by 8-ft sheets under wood subflooring as insulation and to reduce the transmission of airborne and impact sound. It is also used as underlayment on concrete or wood floors for wall-to-wall carpeting, resilient tile at least 3⁄16 in. thick, or wood tile. When laid over concrete, an asphalt-impregnated or integrally treated board should be used,

cemented to the slab with hot-asphalt or cold-asphalt mastic. When recommended by the manufacturer of the underlayment, an adhesive may also be used.

PANELS

Sandwich panels with cores of laminated fiberboard and faces of asbestos-cement board or hardboard are available and have been used as exterior walls and as partitions and roof decks. Asbestos-cement-faced panels are available in 11⁄16, 1⅛, 1⁹⁄16, and 2-in. thicknesses, 4-ft widths, and up to 12-ft lengths. The thicker panels are recommended for roof decks. The 4 by 8-ft panels, supported at all four edges, will carry 50 and 62.5 lbs per sq ft, respectively, for the 1⁹⁄16 and 2-in. thicknesses. Curtain wall and partition systems have been developed by the manufacturers (Fig. 20). Hardboard-faced panels are available in thicknesses of ⅝, 1⁹⁄16, and 1⅝ in., widths of 2 or 4 ft, and lengths of 8, 9, or 10 ft. The hardboard may be surfaced with a vinyl finish simulating wood grain. Long edges are grooved for splines.

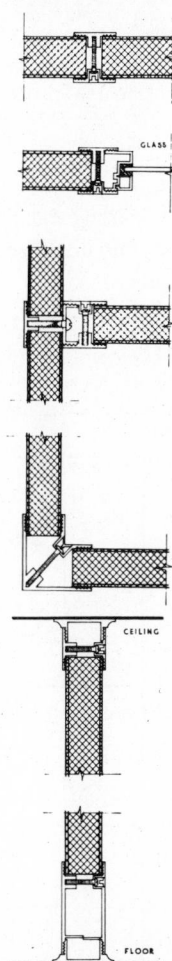

Fig. 20. Movable partition system utilizing sandwich panels and aluminum framing

By HOWARD P. VERMILYA, AIA

Hardboard is a versatile fiberboard manufactured from wood or other ligno-cellulosic fibers, refined or partly refined, and felted under pressure into a panel having a density range of approximately 50 to 80 lb per cu ft. Manufacturing is done under carefully controlled optimum conditions of consolidating pressure, heat, and moisture so that the fibers have a natural ligneous bond. Other materials may be added during manufacture to improve certain qualities. Hardboard is manufactured to industry standards established by the American Hardboard Association (Table 10) and Federal Specification LLL-H-35.

TYPES

Hardboards are of two types, standard (Type 1) and tempered or treated (Type 2).

Type 1: Standard hardboard is substantially as it comes from the press, except for drying and trimming to size.

Type 2: Tempered or treated hardboard is specially processed to improve the properties of stiffness, strength, and water resistance. Tempering is the process of adding a drying material in manufacture, such as drying oil blends of oxidizing resin, which are stabilized by baking or other heating.

CLASSES

Standard hardboards are divided into two classes primarily on the basis of strength. Type 2 hardboard is not divided into classes.

Type 1, Class 1: This is a standard hardboard of intermediate strength with a density range of 60 to 75 lb per cu ft.

Type 1, Class 2: This is a standard hardboard of moderate strength, less than Class 1, with a density range of 50 to 60 lb per cu ft.

Surface: Two surfaces are usually provided but not by all companies. Most board is produced as screen-back smooth-one-side (SIS). Screen-back results from the impression of a wet or damp mat when the board is pressed and dried in the hotpress. Smooth-two-sides (S2S) board is available from some manufacturers. It is made by using smooth hot platens to form both sides of the board.

USES

Type 1, Class 1 hardboard is suitable for applications where moderate water resistance and good strength are needed, such as in drawer bottoms and cabinet work; Class 2 is used where water resistance and strength are not critical, such as in wall and ceiling panels. Floor underlayment is made by some companies as Class 1 and by others as Class 2. Type 2 hardboard is more generally suitable for applications where higher strength, harder surfaces, and superior water resistance are required—such as wearing surfaces, storage bins, and exterior use. (Not all tempered hardboard is suitable for exterior use. Check manufacturers' recommendations.)

SPECIAL HARDBOARDS

Manufacturers produce a wide variety of special types designed for convenience of application, decorative effects, and particular engineering requirements.

Tile pattern is a Type 2 hardboard with

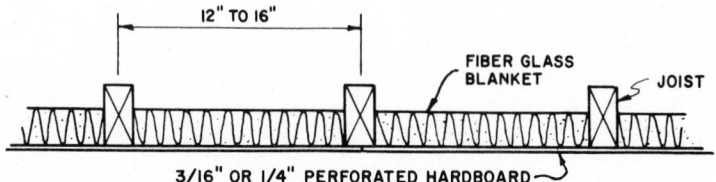

Fig. 21.   Perforated hardboard used as an acoustical ceiling

Table 10.   Physical properties of hardboard

Courtesy American Hardboard Association

CLASSIFICATION		SURFACE	NOMINAL THICKNESS	THICKNESS TOLERANCE	MODULUS OF RUPTURE MINIMUM	TENSILE *STRENGTH ‖MINIMUM‖		WATER RESISTANCE WATER ABSORP. MAX.	SWELLING MAX.
			INCH	INCH	PSI	PSI	PSI	%	%
TYPE 1 STANDARD	Class 1	S1S	1/12	0.070-0.090				43	30
			1/10	0.090-0.110				25	22
			1/8	0.115-0.155				20	16
			3/16	0.170-0.205	5000	2500	100	18	14
			1/4	0.225-0.265				16	12
			5/16	0.290-0.335				14	10
		S2S	1/10	0.090-0.110				30	25
			1/8	0.115-0.155				25	18
			3/16	0.170-0.205	5000	2500	100	25	18
			1/4	0.225-0.265				18	14
			3/8	0.350-0.400				12	10
	Class 2	S1S	3/16	0.170.0.205				25	15
			1/4	0.225-0.265	3000	1500	50	25	15
			3/8	0.350-0.400				25	15
		S2S	1/8	0.115-0.155				30	25
			3/16	0.170-0.205				27	25
			7/32	0.205-0.250	3000	1500	50	27	25
			1/4	0.225-0.265				27	25
TYPE 2 TEMPERED OR TREATED		S1S	1/8	0.115-0.155				15	11
			3/16	0.170-0.205				12	10
			1/4	0.225-0.265	7000	3500	150	10	8
			5/16	0.290-0.335				8	8
		S2S	1/8	0.115-0.155				15	15
			3/16	0.170-0.205	7000	3500	150	15	12
			1/4	0.225-0.265				12	12

* NOTE: ‖ PARALLEL TO SURFACE;   ⊥ PERPENDICULAR TO SURFACE

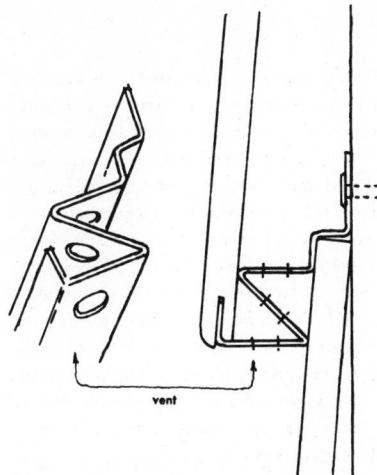

Fig. 22. Hardboard siding attached by means of aluminum strip

scored grooves that usually form 4-in. squares on one face.

Embossed patterns on Type 1 or 2 board pressed into one face may simulate leather, wood grain, a basket-weave effect, a fluted effect, and so on.

Striated patterns, similar to combed wood, are applied by pressing to or machining one surface of Type 2 board.

Perforated hardboard is a Type 1 or 2 hardboard, plain or decorated, which has punched or drilled holes spaced 1 in. on center or, on special order, ½ in. on center. The diameter of the holes is 3/16 in. on 1/8-in. board and 9/32 in. on 1/4-in. board. These boards are used as decoration and also, with specially designed hangers, to provide flexible and decorative wall mounting and storage facilities. When backed with a 1 or 2-in.-thick glass-fiber blanket of ¾ lb per cu ft density, the perforated board has a noise-reduction coefficient ranging from 0.60 to 0.75, depending upon the thickness of the blanket and the spacing of the holes (Fig. 21).

Underlayment is a standard-type board, 0.215 in. thick, and planed or sanded on one side used as a panel to which linoleum, asphalt tile, and similar resilient flooring materials may be bonded. It is usually used over wood-board subfloors or to bring finish floors level where different materials are used in the same area. Sizes are 4 by 4 and 4 by 3 ft.

Decorative printed or prefinished board is factory-coated Type 1 or 2 board. Simulated wood-grain finishes and solid colors,

on plain or tile board, are the most common forms of decoration. High-heat-baked, modified melamine finish is available from many manufacturers. Commercial Standard CS176 (*Prefinished Hardboard Wall Panels*) contains standards for the board and finishes. Preprimed boards are usually those designed for exterior use. Panels 16 in. wide may be grooved with shiplap edges for blind nailing or for application with clips. Tiles 16 by 16 in. are also available.

Plastic laminate cores: This board has a high perpendicular tensile strength and a smooth-sanded-or-planed surface, of uniform thickness, and is used for the application of high-pressure plastic laminates.

Concrete form hardboard: This board is usually a ¼-in.-thick Type 2 hardboard and is used as a liner in concrete forms and is capable of many reuses.

Siding: Hardboards manufactured specially for this purpose are usually sold in strips 10 in. or wider and up to 16 ft long for application as lap siding. Heavier shadow lines are provided either by integral strips applied to the siding or by separate metal strips designed to hide the nailing (Fig. 22).

Panel siding, with panels 4 ft wide up to 16 ft long, may be plain or have a surface pattern and have square or shiplap edges. Many manufacturers preprime their exterior siding.

Doors: Hardboard is extensively used for the faces of hollow-core flush doors.

Sheet sizes: The standard sheet width is 4 ft. Lengths vary in multiples of 1 ft up to 10 ft and in multiples of 2 ft up to 16 ft. Each manufacturer has his own range of lengths, and these vary for each board type, with 4 by 8 ft being the most universal. Planks are usually 16 in. wide in lengths of 7 and 8 ft.

APPLICATION

Workability: Hardboard may be cut, drilled, routed, shaped, or fastened with the usual carpenter's tools but power tools can do an even better job. Carbide-tipped saw blades are recommended. Twist high-speed drills perform better than auger bits; for routing and shaping, high-speed equipment with high-speed steel bits should be used.

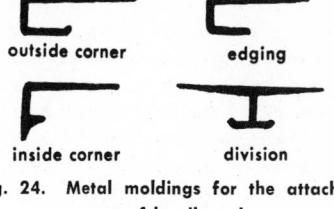

Fig. 24. Metal moldings for the attachment of hardboard

Nailing (see Table 11): Drive nails perpendicular to panel surface, nailing center of panel first and edges last. Nails should penetrate 1 in. into backing material on interior applications and 1½ in. on exterior applications. Space 8 in. on center on intermediate supports and 4 in. at edges. Edge clearance should be ¼ to 3/8 in. minimum. Do not toenail or nail into the edge.

Screws: Predrill holes and countersink for flathead screws that are long enough to penetrate 1 in. into supports. Sheet metal screws and bolts also hold well.

Staples: Divergent chisel-point staples (7/8 in.) driven with a power stapler or air gun may be used.

Clips designed for the particular application are often shipped by the manufacturer with decorated board to permit concealment of the fasteners and alignment of the joints.

Adhesives, for interior applications only, may be waterproof tile or linoleum adhesive, or contact cement. When attaching to a solid surface, apply adhesive with a notched trowel over the entire surface. Contact cement should be applied to both surfaces and may be used to apply board directly to wood framing.

Bending: The minimum radii of bends depend upon the thickness of the board, the density, the side exposed, and the method of bending. A ¾-in. radius is possible when using some 1/10-in. boards, but a radius of 7 to 12 in. is more common (see manufacturers' literature for recommendations for their board). Cold dry bends are made only over permanently supported framework. Cold moist bends can be made around a pattern and allowed to dry, using the soaking or wetting method to make the board more pliable.

Conditioning: The moisture content of

Round U-Joint	V-Joint	Division Strip	Bull Nose Wood Insert	Snap-On Metal Molding	Batten Nailing Pattern

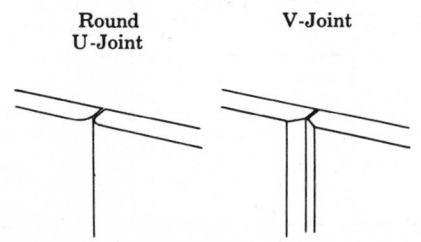
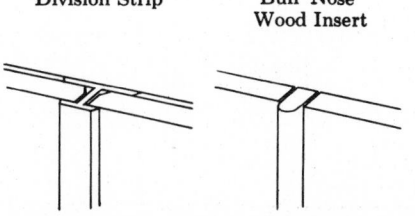
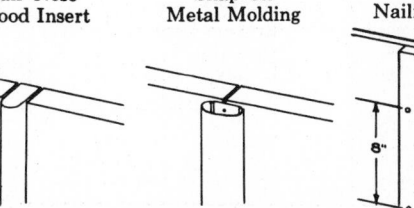

Fig. 23. Hardboard joint treatments

hardboard varies with humidity conditions, as do other cellulose products. Conditioning, by allowing the board to adapt to prevailing humidities or, in the case of exterior applications, by wetting the back side of the board and letting it stand for 24 hours before application, is recommended.

Backing: Over open framing 16 in. on center, use a ³⁄₁₆, ¼, or ⁵⁄₁₆-in. thickness; thinner boards should be applied over solid backing of wood, plywood, gypsum board, or plaster. Masonry exterior walls should be dampproofed and furred before applying hardboard; a vapor barrier is also desirable.

Joint treatments: Many joint treatments are possible using the square-edge boards (Fig. 23). Do not butt joints tightly; allow some space between panels—at least ¹⁄₁₆ in. for exterior panels. Manufacturers provide machined tongue-and-groove and shiplap joints for panel and plank edges, or metal moldings may be used, either plain or decorated to match the hardboard (Fig. 24).

Perforated board: To receive the hangers designed for use with perforated board, space them away from solid backing at least ¼ in. for ⅛-in. board and ½ in. for ¼-in. board.

Finishing: Every type of finish suitable for wood can be used with hardboard. These include oil and rubber-base paints, lacquer, enamels, penetrating sealers (for floors and work surfaces), stains, water-emulsion paints, varnish, shellac, and wax, when applied in accordance with manufacturers' recommendations. Finishes may be applied with brush, roller, or spray. Primers are recommended for most finishes, especially oil and enamel paints. Most latex paints are good sealers. Enamel undercoaters and alkyd-base primers and sealers are usually satisfactory. Clear filler-sealers, not varnish, resin, or penetrating-type, may be used as primers. Varnish should be applied over a sealer only.

Table 11. Application of hardboard

Courtesy Georgia-Pacific Plywood Company

Application	Type of hardboard	Maximum open framing, in.	Thickness, in.	Nail spacing		Fastening methods: any of the following for these hardboard applications
				Intermediate supports, in.	Around edges, in.	
Interior walls and ceilings	Standard, tempered	Solid backing, 16	⅛ ³⁄₁₆ ¼	8 8 8	4 4 4	Nails: 1¼" casing 1½" casing 1¼" finishing 1½" finishing 1¼" countersunk 1¼" box 1¼" 18 gage brads
	Factory-finished hardboard					
	Perforated hardboard (leave ⅜" or more open space between hardboard and wall)	16 16 16	⅛ ³⁄₁₆ ¼	8 8 8	4 4 4	Adhesives: The following waterproof adhesives may be used when applied according to manufacturers' recommendations: linoleum cement tileboard cement contact cement
Underlayment (floor)	Underlayment hardboard		0.215	6	4	Nails: 1¼" drive screws (flat head) 1¼" ring-grooved
Finish flooring	Tempered hardboard		¼	12	6	Nails: 1¼" coated casing
Protected exteriors	Standard or tempered hardboard	16	¼	6	4	Nails: 1¾" box, siding, or sinker
Panel siding	(With or without sheathing)					Nails:
	Tempered hardboard, grooved or ungrooved	16	⅜	8	4	2¼" galvanized siding 2¼" galvanized box
Lap siding	(With or without sheathing)					Nails: galvanized siding galvanized box 2" where wood, plywood, or no sheathing is used 2½" over all other types of sheathing
	Tempered hardboard, 12" or 16" wide	16	⅜	16 along bottom edge into studs		

By HOWARD P. VERMILYA, AIA

Particle board (or flake board) is a relatively new product. It is dry-formed of particles of wood bonded together with synthetic resin or other binder. The wood particles are manufactured from clean wood, classified for size, dried to a controlled moisture content, mat-formed, compressed to uniform density, and cured under heat and pressure. Some manufacturers make what they call a three-ply board with outer layers made of finely cut flakes to provide smooth hard surfaces, and an inner layer made of more coarsely cut material.

Particle board has the following characteristics: uniformity of thickness and density, freedom from knots and defects, no grain, no warp, dimensional stability, an excellent glue-bond surface, high nail- and screw-holding ability, resistance to indentation, and ease of workability with standard woodworking tools.

The principal use of particle board is as core stock for high-pressure plastic laminates and for hardwood veneers. As core stock it is used by manufacturers of furniture, cabinets, counter tops, wall paneling, partitions, and doors of all types.

Particle board is also used with clear or stained finishes or, when the surface is filled with wood-paste filler (factory-applied in some cases), painted for paneling, shelving, and doors. Unfinished board is used as an underlayment for resilient flooring materials, wood blocks, and wall-to-wall carpeting, over wood subflooring.

Most particle board is limited to interior use, but one company provides a ¾-in.-thick board made with a phenolic binder which is recommended for exterior use on walls and soffits and particularly for signs. Particle board is superior to the usual soft woods in screw-holding power, using either wood or sheet metal screws. It is also a satisfactory base for fastening with screw-type nails, coated nails, staples, and corrugated fasteners. It is easily machined and can be drilled, routed, grooved, dovetailed, rabbeted, tenoned, and doweled. Edge

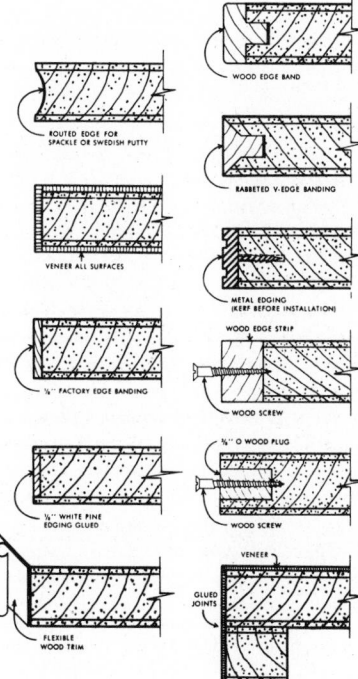

Fig. 25. Edge treatments

banding may be done with high-pressure laminates, metal or wood moldings, or wood veneers, or the edges may be filled for staining, lacquering, or painting (Fig. 25). Raw edges should not be exposed to moisture, wear, or abrasion. Joints may be treated in the same manner as with hardboard or plywood, or flush joints may be used, since the board is dimensionally stable.

Particle board is produced in several densities, ranging from 30 to 60 lb per cu ft. Thicknesses vary from ⅜ to 2 in., in increments of ⅛ in. Most thicknesses do not exceed 1 or 1⅛ in. Widths vary from 24 to 72 in. and lengths up to 16 ft. For building use, sizes usually are 2 by 4, 4 by 4, or 4 by 8 ft, and thicknesses are ⅜ or ¾ in.

The National Particleboard Association has established industry standards for the physical properties of the board when used as an underlayment (see Table 12).

Table 12. Physical properties of ¾-in. particle board underlayment

Properties indicated below have been tested in accordance with ASTM D-1037.

Property	Average	Minimum
Density, lb per cu ft	40	38
Modulus of rupture, psi	1,600	1,450
Modulus of elasticity, psi	250,000	200,000
Internal bond strength, psi	70	60
Water absorption, per cent	15	
Thickness swelling, per cent	10	
Hardness	500	450

Particle board is widely used for cabinet and closet doors (Figs. 26 and 27). It may also be used for movable partitions with wood or metal framing members (Fig. 28).

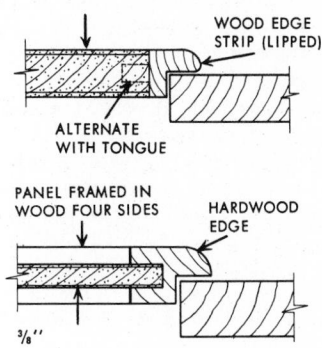

Fig. 26. Cabinet door edges

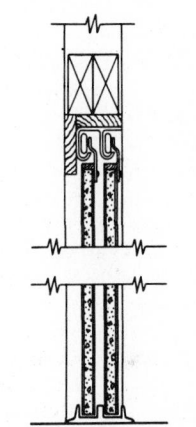

Fig. 27. Sliding closet doors

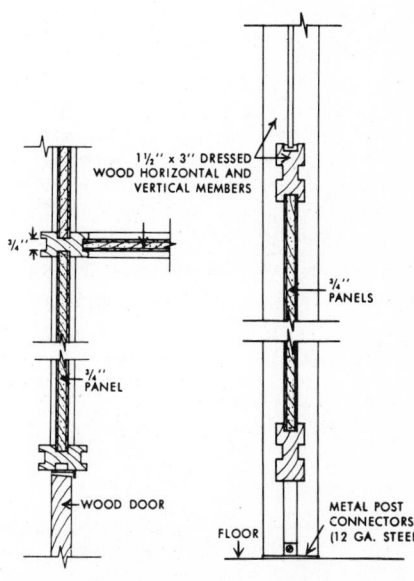

Fig. 28. Movable partitions

By HOWARD P. VERMILYA, AIA

DECORATIVE HIGH-PRESSURE PLASTIC LAMINATES

The typical plastic laminate sheet consists of a core of multiple layers of kraft paper impregnated with phenolic resins, to the face side of which is applied first a pattern sheet and then a transparent overlay both impregnated with melamine resin, and to the back of which is applied a plain melamine-impregnated sheet. The complete assembly of thermosetting resins is then cured under heat and pressure to produce the finished sheet which is usually $\frac{1}{16}$ in. thick.

Plastic laminate is a hard, durable surfacing material which is resistant to moisture, heat, and most chemicals. It is extensively used for the tops of tables, desks, bars, and counters, and for kitchen and bathroom cabinets, shower and tub enclosures, wall paneling (Fig. 29)[1] and doors.

Under the standard of the National Electric Manufacturers Association, NEMA LP2-1957, plastic laminate is produced in four types. These types and their properties are shown in Table 13. Types 1 and 2 are similar except for resistance to cigarette burns. Type 3 is not required to be as stain-resistant as the other types, but must postform without blistering, cracking, or delaminating (Fig. 30). All types are subjected to the same tests for resistance of the surface to boiling water and high temperature, and for color fastness and appearance.

General-purpose sheet (Type 1) is made in a wide variety of sizes: widths of 24, 30, 36, 48, and 60 in. and lengths of 5, 6, 8, 10, and 12 ft. A great variety of colors and patterns is available in two standard finishes, satin or gloss. Some patterns are original and others simulate textiles, leather, marble, or wood. Custom design service is available from one manufacturer.

Application. Plastic laminates can be applied with adhesives to various surfaces such as plywood, particle board, gypsum board, metal, concrete, plaster, honeycomb core, or foamed plastic core. When plastic laminate is applied to a board or core material, a backing sheet of the same material should be applied to the other face in order to produce balanced con-

[1] All figures courtesy of General Electric and Westinghouse.

Table 13. Types and properties of plastic laminates

Type	Thickness, in.	Resistance to cigarette burns, sec	Moisture absorption— max gain, per cent	Wear resistance, cycles	
				Class 1	Class 2
General purpose	$\frac{1}{16}$	110	6	400	200
Cigarette-proof	$\frac{1}{16}$	600	6	400	200
Postforming	1/20	75	12	400	200
Hardboard-core	$\frac{5}{32}$–$\frac{5}{16}$	110	25	250	

struction. A plastic laminate sheet backed by $\frac{1}{8}$-in. hardboard or plywood can be applied to eggcrate cores having voids up to 4 sq in. Close-grained plywoods should be used to avoid telegraphing the grain pattern through the plastic sheet. In 1/10-in. thickness, plastic laminate sheets can be applied directly to concrete and masonry, using a mastic type of adhesive. In any application the type of adhesive depends upon the surface to which the plastic is being applied; only those recommended by the manufacturer for the purpose should be used. Shop application is recommended, whenever possible.

Various edge and joint treatments are possible (Figs. 31 and 32). Postforming permits the elimination of joints (Fig. 30) wherever a curve with a minimum radius of $\frac{3}{4}$ in. is acceptable. Metal moldings surfaced with material to match the sheet are widely used. Wood moldings are often used, especially with the simulated wood pattern sheets.

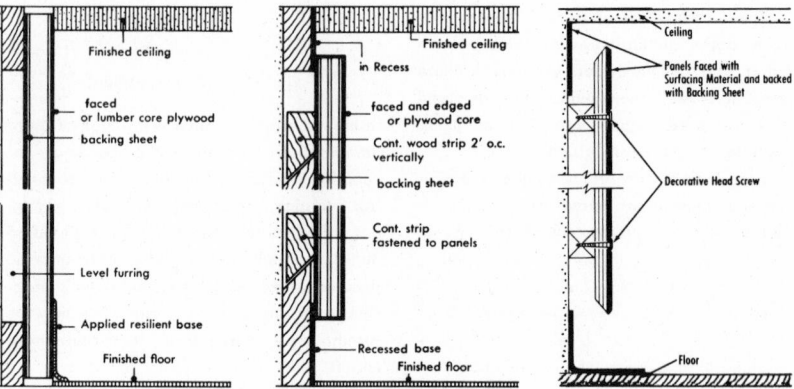

Fig. 29. Application to walls

Detail at right recommended for uneven walls; lighting may be concealed at top and bottom, if desired.

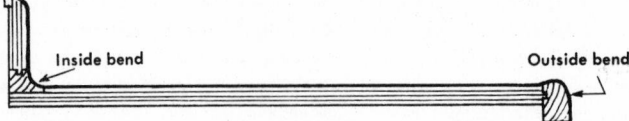

Fig. 30. One-piece postformed countertop, available in lengths up to 12 ft

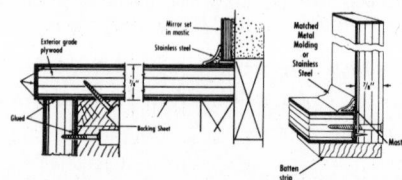

Fig. 31. Countertop details

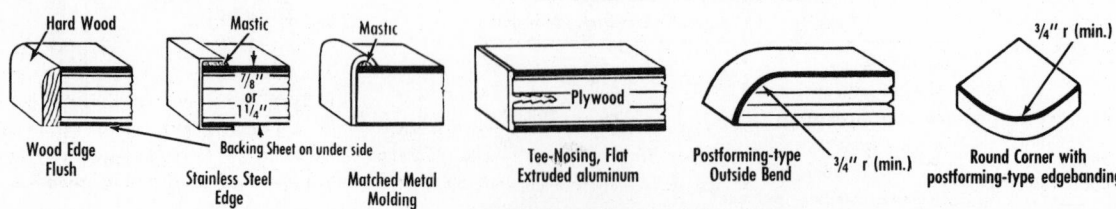

Fig. 32. Edge treatments

By HOWARD P. VERMILYA, *AIA*

Plywood is made of an odd number of layers or plies of thin wood (veneer) bonded together in such a way that the direction of the grain of adjacent plies is at right angles. The outside plies are called faces (or face and back), and the center ply (or plies) is called the core. In the case of five or more ply construction, the inner plies that are bonded directly and at right angles to the faces are called crossbands. Faces and crossbands are usually

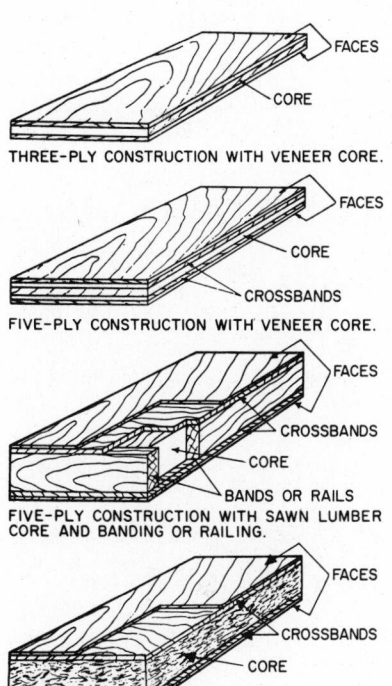

THREE-PLY CONSTRUCTION WITH VENEER CORE.

FIVE-PLY CONSTRUCTION WITH VENEER CORE.

FIVE-PLY CONSTRUCTION WITH SAWN LUMBER CORE AND BANDING OR RAILING.

FIVE-PLY CONSTRUCTION WITH PARTICLE-BOARD CORE.

Fig. 33. Typical plywood constructions

Courtesy of Hardwood Plywood Institute

veneer, while the core may be of veneer, lumber, or other material (see Fig. 33).

The principal advantages of plywood as compared with solid wood are (1) equalization of the strength along the length and across the width of the panel; (2) equalization and reduction of dimensional changes due to moisture; (3) greater resistance to checking, splitting, and warping; (4) reduction in construction labor, weight, and thickness resulting from the availability of wood in wallboard form. The greater the number of plies for a given total thickness, the more nearly equal are the strength and shrinkage properties along and across the panel and the greater is the resistance to splitting. Resistance to warping or twisting is the result of *balanced construction*, which means that the plies are arranged in matching pairs on either side of the core; this is why plywood always consists of an odd number of plies.

Plywood, like other forms of wood, is divided into softwood and hardwood, which are defined as the wood from coniferous and broad-leafed trees, respectively. This division has resulted in two separate plywood industries, each with its own standards and trade associations. In general, the softwood plywood industry is located on the West Coast; its principal product is rotary-cut Douglas fir, and its end use is predominantly structural. The hardwood plywood industry is located generally in the South and Middle West; its products include a wide variety of species and cuts, and their end use is principally for furniture, wall paneling, and doors.

SOFTWOOD

Practically all softwood plywood is manufactured from softwood species growing in the northwestern section of the United States and Western Canada. Softwood plywood is covered by the following Commercial Standards of the U.S. Department of Commerce:

CS45-60: Douglas fir (coast region) plywood, including western larch
CS122-60: Western softwood plywood, including cedar (Alaska, Port Orford, and western red), California redwood, Sitka spruce, Engelmann spruce, western larch, western hemlock, fir (noble, silver, grand, and white), and other softwoods such as the western pines, lauan, Douglas fir from coast or inland regions.
CS157-56: Pine plywood, including ponderosa, sugar, and Idaho white pine.

The major uses for softwood plywood, particularly Douglas fir, are structural. Its use as a finishing material is increasing, especially where structural and finish functions are combined. Manufacturing emphasis is being placed upon factory finishing techniques to make it more attractive as a finish material.

Structurally, plywood is employed where its large sheet size may function advantageously to brace the structure and to reduce the labor of installation. Among such uses are as sheathing on walls and roofs, as subfloors, as panel faces, and as concrete forms. It is also used as an underlayment for resilient flooring and wall-to-wall carpeting, and as a backing for ceramic and other tiles on floors and walls. It is employed extensively in cabinetwork and as shelving.

The *grade-trademark* program of the American Plywood Association, sponsors of the Commercial Standards for Douglas fir and western softwood plywood, involving as it does a continuing factory inspection and laboratory testing program, has

Table 14.   Types, grades, uses, and sizes of Douglas fir plywood

Grade	Description and uses	Face	Back	Inner plies	Width, ft	Length, ft	Thickness, in.
Exterior types							
A-A	Use where the appearance of both sides is important. Fences, carports, signs, boats, etc.	A	A	C	4	8	¼ ⅜ ½ ⅝ ¾ 1
A-B	For uses similar to EXT. A-A requiring one appearance surface, opposite side solid and smooth.	A	B	C	4	8	¼ ⅜ ½ ⅝ ¾ 1
A-C	Use where the appearance of only one side is important. Siding, soffits, fences, structural uses, etc.	A	C	C	4	8	¼ ⅜ ½ ⅝ ¾ 1
B-B Plyform	Concrete form grade, high re-use. Edge-sealed with distinctive red sealer. Mill-oiled unless otherwise specified.	B	B	C	4	8	⅝ ¾
B-C	An outdoor utility panel. For farm and work buildings, containers, etc.	B	C	C	4	8	¼ ⅜ ½ ⅝ ¾ 1
C-C Plugged	Use as a base for tile, linoleum, carpeting, where unusual moisture conditions exist.	C Plugged	C	C	4	8	¼ ⅜ ½ ⅝ ¾ 1
C-C	Unsanded grade with waterproof bond for sheathing, rough construction, farm buildings, etc.	C	C	C	4	8	5⁄16 ⅜ ½ ⅝ ¾
Interior types							
A-A	For interior applications where both sides will be viewed. Built-ins, toys, furniture, etc.	A	A	D	3 4	8	¼ ⅜ ½ ⅝ ¾
A-B	For use similar to INT. A-A requiring one appearance surface, opposite side solid and smooth.	A	B	D	3 4	8	¼ ⅜ ½ ⅝ ¾
A-D	Interior use where appearance of only one side is important. Paneling, built-ins, etc.	A	D	D	3 4	8	¼ ⅜ ½ ⅝ ¾
B-B Plyform	Re-usable concrete form plywood. Glue moisture-resistant, not waterproof. Green sealed edges, mill-oiled unless otherwise specified.	B	B	C	4	8	¾ 1
B-B	Utility panel. Use where two smooth sides are required.	B	B	D	4	8	¼ ⅜ ½ ⅝ ¾ 1
B-D	Utility panel. Use where one smooth side is required. Backing, sides of built-ins, etc.	B	D	D	4	8	¼ ⅜ ½ ⅝ ¾ 1
Under-layment	Underlayment or base for tile, linoleum, carpeting.	C Plugged	D	C or D Ply next to face C or better	4	8	¼ ⅜ ½ ⅝ ¾ 1
C-D Plyscord	Unsanded structural grade panel for sheathing, sub-flooring, limited exposure crates, containers and pallets.	C	D	D	4	8	5⁄16 ⅜ ½ ⅝ ¾
Plyscord exterior glue C-D	Same as Plyscord above, but with waterproof glue. Not a substitute for Exterior-type plywood.	C	D	D	4	8	5⁄16 ⅜ ½ ⅝ ¾
2-4-1	Combination subfloor and underlayment. Base for tile, linoleum, carpeting and wood strip flooring. Available with square edges or tongue and grooved sides (or sides and ends). Available with waterproof glue for added durability.	C Plugged	D	C or D If face veneer thickness is less than ⅛″, veneer next to face C or better.	4	8	7 ply 1⅛ only

Table 15. Special products, Douglas fir plywood

Kind	Description	Uses	Width	Length, ft	Thickness, in.
Special surface patterns					
Texture one-eleven (exterior)	Exterior type only, with parallel grooves ¼" deep, ⅜" wide. Unsanded, shiplapped edges. Grooves 2" or 4" o.c.	Siding, gable ends, patio fences, interior paneling or where textured accents are desired.	4'	8 10	⅝
Brushed, embossed and striated (exterior) (interior)	Grain of panel face accented to give depth and dimension. Both Exterior and Interior types.	Textured paneling, built-ins, counter facings, displays. For outdoor applications use Exterior type only.	4'	8	⁵⁄₁₆ ⅜
Overlaid panels					
Medium-density overlaid plywood (exterior)	Exterior-type only, with a smooth, hard, fused-resin fiber overlay. Overlaid one or both sides.	Especially surfaced for painting. Exterior siding, soffits. Kitchen cabinets, signs, etc.	12" 16" 24" 48"	8	⅜ ½ ⅝ ¾
High-density overlaid plywood (exterior)	Exterior-type only, with a hard translucent resin fiber overlay. Slight grain pattern. Abrasion resistant. Painting not required.	Concrete form work, signs, cabinets. Industrial uses.	4'	8	⅜ ½ ⅝ ¾
Plyron® (exterior) (interior)	Hardboard faced one or both sides. Available in Interior or Exterior types.	Concrete forms, counter tops, shelving, cabinet doors and built-ins.	4'	8	½ ⅝ ¾
Special items					
Natural finish N-N (interior)	Cabinet quality. Both sides select, all heartwood veneer. Special jointed core construction.	Furniture having a natural finish. Cabinet doors, built-ins, etc.	4'	8	¾
Natural finish N-A (interior)	Same as N-N except one side is A-faced for economy. Special jointed core construction.	Furniture having a natural finish. Cabinet doors, built-ins, etc.	4'	8	¾
Natural finish N-D (interior)	Has one side select, all heartwood veneer.	Wall paneling.	4'	8	¼
Marine exterior	Exterior-type panels. Special solid core construction for marine use. Available also in overlay grades.	Boat hulls, cabins and other marine application.	4'	8	¼ ⁵⁄₁₆ ⅜ ½ ⅝ ¾

Table 16. Minimum bending radii, Douglas fir plywood

Panel thickness, in.	Across grain	Parallel to grain
¼	15″	24″
⅜	36″	54″
½	6′	8′
⅝	8′	10′
¾	10′	12′

Average values for areas of clear, straight grain.
These minimum radii apply to areas of clear straight grain, carefully bent. When there is no assurance that such conditions will be met, it is suggested that these values be increased up to twice for design purposes.

been a major factor in the broadened use of plywood.

Softwood plywood is manufactured in two *types* and six *grades*. Type is determined by the glue bond and grade by the quality of the veneers used.

Exterior-type plywood is manufactured with a completely waterproof glue, and no veneer used is less than Grade C. The glue bond is stronger and more durable than the wood itself. It must withstand several cycles of cold soaking, baking, and boiling and a fire test.

Interior-type plywood is made with a highly water-resistant glue, which must withstand three cycles of cold soaking and drying. Mold-resistant and heat-resistant glues are used for sheathing, underlayment, and concrete form grades. Inner plies and backs of interior-type plywood may be of Grade D veneer.

Grade of veneers refers to their appearance quality and the allowable defects permitted. There are six grades, each designated by a letter:

N: Special-order "natural finish" veneer. Select, all heartwood. Free of open defects. Called A-1 in western softwood plywood.

A: Best standard veneer. Smooth and paintable. May be more than one piece, well jointed. Neatly made repairs permitted.

B: Solid-surface veneer. Circular repair plugs and tight knots permitted.

C: Minimum veneer permitted in exterior type. Knotholes to 1 in., splits, plugs, and other repairs permitted.

C: Plugged. Improved C veneer.

D: Used only in interior type for inner plys and backs where specified.

Number of plies varies with panel thickness. Panels ⅜ in. or less in thickness have a minimum of three plies, ½ through ¾ in. thickness a minimum of five plies, and thicker panels a minimum of seven plies.

In interior-type Douglas fir plywood, inner plies may be of other species of western softwoods except in grades B-B (concrete form) and C-D (sheathing), which must be of Douglas fir or western larch throughout.

In western softwood plywood, the species are classified by CS122 into three groups according to their relative stiffness:

Group 1: Western hemlock, noble fir, silver fir, grand fir, California red fir, Sitka spruce, Port Orford cedar, lauan and Douglas fir (interior North)
Group 2: White fir, redwood, Alaska cedar, red alder, Douglas fir (interior South)
Group 3: Engelmann spruce, western red cedar, western poplar, ponderosa pine, and white pines

Inner plies of western softwood plywood of a given species may be of any species in group 1, group 2, or group 3, except that inner plies of exterior-type B-B (con-

crete form) and C-C (sheathing) and interior-type C-D (sheathing) must be from the same group as the faces or from a lower-numbered group. Douglas fir from the coast region may be used for the inner plies of any panel.

Overlaid plywood is exterior-type plywood, to one or both sides of which is laminated under heat and pressure a resin-impregnated cellulose fiber facing sheet. *High-density* facing sheet contains 40 per cent or more of phenolic or melamine thermosetting resin and is at least 0.009 in. thick. It is normally a translucent sheet through which the grain of the wood can be partially seen; colors are also available. It does not require painting, but takes paint well, if desired. *Medium-density* sheet contains 20 per cent or more resin and is at least 0.012 in. thick. It is impervious to water but not to vapor, and provides an excellent base for paint.

Marine plywood is a special grade of exterior-type Douglas fir plywood containing all A or B veneers, as specified; core gaps and edge splits are limited. It is also available overlaid.

Types, grades, uses, and sizes of Douglas fir plywood are shown in Tables 14 and 15. Minimum bending radii are given in Table 16.[1] Data on the principal structural uses of plywood are given in Tables 17 and 18.

The structural use of plywood is approved by the Federal Housing Administration, by all the model building codes, and by most local codes. Tests at the U.S. Forest Products Laboratory have shown that the rigidity of a stud wall sheathed with ¼-in. plywood (applied vertically with 6d nails 5 in. on center along the edges and 10 in. elsewhere) is twice that of a wall with diagonal wood sheathing. When the plywood is glued as well as nailed to the studs, the rigidity of the wall is 3.7 times greater than that of a diagonally sheathed wall.

The recently developed "2.4.1" panel is a combination structural floor deck and underlayment. Its thickness of 1⅛ in. (seven plies) makes it possible to space the floor beams 4 ft apart; tongue-and-groove joints along the long edges eliminate the need for edge supports (Fig. 34). Resilient flooring may be installed directly on the upper surface of the panel, and the lower surface may be exposed as a beamed ceiling.

Structural components—prefabricated nailed-glued assemblies of wood and plywood—are now available from a number of licensed fabricators. These components include box beams for spans up to 100 ft; light roof trusses for spans up to 40 ft;

[1] All tables courtesy of American Plywood Association.

Table 17. Allowable shelf loads, Douglas fir plywood

Span, in. (C to C)	Single Spans Maximum loads, lbs/sq ft (thickness of plywood)					Multiple Spans Maximum loads, lbs/sq ft (thickness of plywood)				
	⅜″	½″	⅝″	¾″	1″	⅜″	½″	⅝″	¾″	1″
12	150	300				300				
16	75	100	200	300		150	200	300		
20	40	75	100	200	300	75	150	200	300	
24	20	40	75	100	150	50	100	150	200	300
32			30	40	100	20	40	75	100	200
40				20	50		20	40	50	100
48					30			20	30	75
60					20					40

Table 18. Structural application data
Recommendations of American Plywood Association

Wall sheathing and siding (Douglas fir, Western larch and Group 1, 2 and 3 Western Softwood Plywoods)

Application	Recommended thickness, in.	Maximum Spacing of supports, in. (C. to C.)	Nail size and type	Nail spacing, in.	
				Panel edges	Intermediate
Sheathing	5/16	16 (a)	6d common	6	12
	3/8–1/2	24	6d common	6	12
	5/8	24	8d common	6	12
Panel Siding	3/8	16 (c)	6d box or casing (b)	6	12
	1/2 or thicker	24	8d box or casing (b)	6	12
Lap Siding or Bevel Siding	3/8		6d box or casing (b)	One nail per stud along bottom edge and 4 in. at vertical joint	8 in. vertical spacing on intermediate studs
	1/2 or thicker		8d box or casing (b)		

(a) *Apply with face grain perpendicular to supports for maximum strength and stiffness.*
(b) *Use non-corrosive (hot-dipped galvanized or aluminum) nails.*
(c) *Applies to panel siding with no sheathing; with sheathing ⅜-in. panel siding can be used over supports spaced 24 in. o.c.*

Roof sheathing (Plywood continuous over 2 or more spans; grain of face plys across supports)

Plywod thickness, in.	Maximum spacing of supports, in. (C. to C.) (Total roof load, Pounds Per Square Foot)				Nail size and type	Nail spacing, in.	
	20	30	40	50		Panel edges (when over framing)	Intermediate
Douglas fir, Western larch and Group 1 (C-C and C-D sheathing grades only) Western softwood plywoods							
5/16 rough	20 (a)	20	20	19	6d Common	6	12
3/8 rough	24 (a)	24	24	23	6d Common	6	12
1/2 rough (b)	32 (a)	32	30	29	6d Common	6	12
5/8 rough (b)	42 (a)	42	39	36	8d Common	6	12
3/4 (b)	48 (a)	47	42	39	8d Common	6	12
13/16 rough (b)	60 (a)	53	48	45	8d Common	6	12
Group 2 Western softwood plywood							
3/4 rough	16 (a)	16	16	16	6d Common	6	12
3/8 rough	20 (a)	20	20	20	6d Common	6	12
1/2 rough (c)	26 (a)	26	26	25	6d Common	6	12
5/8 rough (c)	35 (a)	35	34	31	8d Common	6	12
3/4 (c)	40 (a)	40	37	34	8d Common	6	12

(a) *These spans shall not be exceeded for any load condition.*
(b) *Provide blocking, tongue and grooving or other suitable edge support, such as Plyclips, when span exceeds 28" for ½", 32" for ⅝", 36" for ¾", 40" for 13/16".*
(c) *Provide blocking, tongue and grooving or other suitable edge support, such as Plyclips, when span exceeds 24" for ½", 28" for ⅝", and 32" for ¾".*

Subfloors and underlayment (Plywood continuous over 2 or more spans; grain of face plys across supports)

Application	Plywood	Minimum recommended thickness, in.	Maximum spacing of supports, in. (c. to c.)	Nail size and type	Nail spacing, in.	
					Panel edges	Intermediate
Subflooring	Douglas fir, Western larch, WSP Group 1	1/2 (a)	16	6d common	6	10
		5/8 (a)	20	8d common	6	10
		3/4 (a)	24	8d common	6	10
		2.4.1 (1⅛)	48	8d deformed shank or 10d common	6	6
Subflooring	Group 2 WSP	5/8 (b)	16	8d common	6	10
		3/4 (b)	24	8d common	6	10
Underlayment		3/8 and thicker		6d Ring shank set 3/8 in.	6	8 each way

(a) *Blocking installed at edges unless underlayment, tongue and grooved edges, or 25/32-in. wood strip flooring is used. If wood strips are perpendicular to supports, ½ in. can be used on 24 in. spans.*
(b) *Blocking installed at edges unless underlayment, tongue and grooved edges, or 25/32-in. wood strip flooring is used. If wood strips are perpendicular to supports, ⅝ in. can be used on 24 in. spans.*

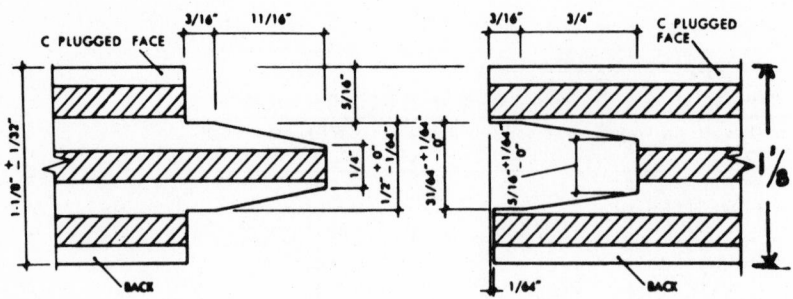

Fig. 34. Tongue-and-groove edge joint of "2.4.1" floor panels, approximately full-size

Courtesy of American Plywood Association

rigid frames, stressed skin and sandwich panels for walls, floors, and flat or folded plate roofs; and curved panels for vaulted roofs. These structural components were designed and tested by the American Plywood Association and are fabricated under the close supervision of the Association to ensure quality control.

As a *finish material*, softwood plywood is used, either stained or painted, as paneling on exterior and interior walls and ceilings and as doors and shelves in closets and cabinets. To improve its suitability for use as a finish material, Douglas fir plywood is available with several special surface textures: striated, brushed, embossed, and grooved. The last is known as "Texture One-Eleven" and consists of parallel grooves approximately ⅜ in. wide by ¼ in. deep on 2- or 4-in. spacings, cut into unsanded plywood ⅝ in. thick. Rabbeted edges are provided to permit concealed joints (Fig. 35).

Prefinished softwood plywood is a recent development. In addition to the conventional finishes, some manufacturers laminate clear or grained vinyl film to the face of the plywood. A unique finish is produced by heating the surface of the plywood to about 650°F, which causes the wood's natural resin (lignin) to flow; a penetrating additive is then added, and the board is pressure-rolled to produce a smooth glossy finish.

Special face veneers for natural finish are available in western softwood plywood: rift grain fir or redwood, knotty white pine or red cedar, Philippine mahogany (lauan) in ribbon or figured grain, and rotary-cut spruce, redwood, and aromatic cedar.

Pine plywood grading standards are generally similar to those of Douglas fir and western softwood plywood. It is used as an exterior or interior finish material wherever the qualities of pine are desired for either a natural or a painted finish. Pine plywood is extensively used as core stock for hardwood plywood and for plastic laminate panels; it is also used for furniture.

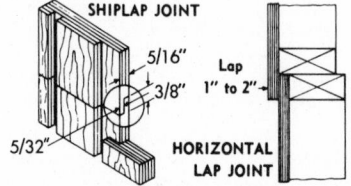

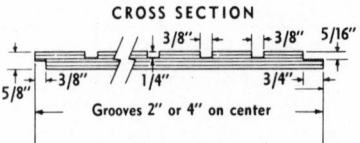

Fig. 35. Details of "Texture One-Eleven" siding, one-half full size

Courtesy of American Plywood Association

Concrete Forms

Recommended forming grades are: interior plyform, exterior plyform, and high-density overlaid plywood. Support spacings for various thicknesses of plyform panels under the conditions noted on the chart, are shown in Fig. 36. The allowable stress of .2,000 psi is based on the allowable stress bending (dry) of 1,875 psi, which has been reduced one fifth for the effect of wetting and increased one third for short-time loading. Added consideration has been given to moisture considerations by reducing the stiffness value 20 per cent. When the face grain is parallel with the supports, use the following proportions of the load values shown on the chart: for ½-in. thickness, 40 per cent; for ⅝-in. thickness, 51 per cent; for ¾-in. thickness, 73 per cent. On single spans, stiffness is only half that shown on the chart. For deflection limitation of 1/360 of span, increase load values by ratio of 360 to 270. Stresses, but not deflection values, can be increased 16 per cent for Exterior A-A grade and by 7 per cent for Exterior A-B grade, which are sometimes used in concrete forming. High-density overlaid panels may also be increased for stress and stiffness because the surfaces are relatively impervious to water.

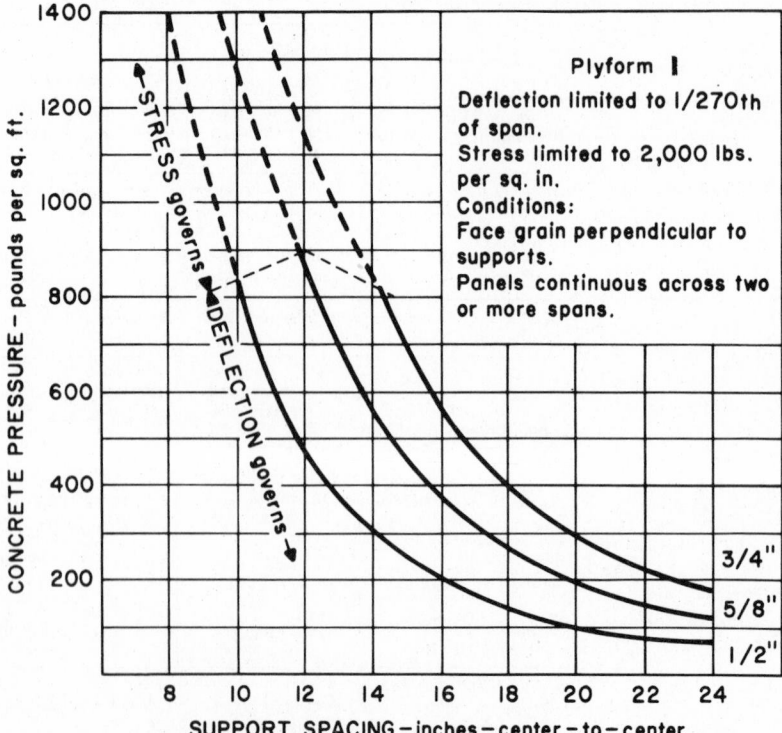

Fig. 36. Allowable support spacing for concrete forms

Courtesy of American Plywood Association

HARDWOOD

Hardwoods of more than 200 species from all parts of the world are used in making hardwood plywood. Those most commonly used and generally available in stock are listed in Table 19.

Most hardwood plywood manufactured in the United States conforms to Commercial Standard CS35–61. It is made in four types, six grades, and three core constructions.

Types

Technical: Fully waterproof bond. The construction is designed to provide approximately equal strength in both directions. Maximum veneer thickness: high density, 1/12 in.; medium density, 1/10 in.; low density, 1/8 in. Core must be all hardwood veneer. Bond must withstand boiling test and be unaffected by microorganisms.

Type I (Ext.): Fully waterproof bond. Maximum veneer thickness: high density, 1/8 in.; medium density, 3/16 in.; low density, 1/4 in. Bond must withstand boiling test and be unaffected by microorganisms.

Type II (Int.): Water-resistant bond. Bond must withstand ten cycles of cold-soaking test.

Type III (Int.): Moisture-resistant bond. Bond must withstand two cycles of cold-soaking test.

Grades

Premium (1): Veneers must be matched.
Good (1): For natural finish—sharp contrasts in color or pattern not permitted.
Sound (2): For smooth paint finish—minor defects filled.
Utility (3): Defects permitted, but less than in Grade 4.
Backing (4): Defects permitted—species at option of manufacturer.
Specialty (SP): Custom-made panels, such as architectural plywood, with special veneer selection and/or grain matching; also curved, molded, impregnated, or overlaid panels.

Core constructions

All-veneer plywood usually has three or five plies, but may have more. Except in Technical type, inner plies may be either hardwood (Grades 2 or 3) or softwood (Grades B or C); if face veneer is less than 1/16 in. thick, a softwood veneer immediately below it must be Grade B.

Lumber-core plywood is usually five-ply construction, with the grain of the core parallel to that of the face. It is used principally for furniture and cabinetwork because it can be doweled, splined, dovetailed, and butt-hinged. Low-density, even-grained hardwoods or softwoods with moderate shrinkage characteristics are suitable for lumber cores; poplar and basswood are most often used. The maximum width of the core strips varies with the density of the species: high density, 2½ in.; medium density, 3 in.; low density, 4 in. Mixing of species is not permitted. Grades of lumber core are as follows:

1. Clear—with full-length strips; no patches or plugs
2. Sound—with full-length strips
3. Regular—strips of random length, tight end joints
4. Clear edge—regular core with full-length edge strips 1½ in. or more wide
5. Banded—regular core banded on one or more edges, as specified
6. Mitered bands—or other special banding, as specified

Composite panels are those having cores of other than veneer or lumber. Cores may be solid (particle board, foamed plastic, mineral composition) or hollow (wood or fiberboard eggcrate, plastic-impregnated paper honeycomb, sections of paper cylinders). Solid-core panels are usually five-ply; hollow-core panels are often seven-ply. Both types are usually banded with wood on all edges. These core constructions are used principally in the manufacture of doors.

Sizes

Sizes generally available in stock (in inches) are as follows:

Widths—24, 30, 36, 42, 48.
Lengths—48, 60, 72, 84, 96.
Thicknesses—three ply, 1/8, 3/16, 1/4; five ply, 5/16, 3/8, 1/2, 5/8; seven ply, 5/8, 3/4; nine ply, 3/4; lumber core five ply, 3/4.

Lengths of 10 and 12 are available from many sources, and still longer and wider panels are available on special order. The smaller sizes are more economical. Some mills cut panels to size on large orders.

Tolerances in length and width are plus or minus 1/32 in.; in square, plus or minus 1/16 in.; in thickness, plus 0, minus 1/32 in.

Sanding

Type of sanding and number of surfaces to be sanded must be specified.

1. No sanding—tape not removed.
2. Rough sanding.
3. Regular sanding—surface clean and free of tape; may show sander streaks.
4. Polish sanding—clean and smooth.

Note: In no case is mill-sanded plywood to be considered as ready for painter's finish.

Special plywoods

Cigarette-proof. Plywood intended for use as table or bar tops may be made resistant to cigarette burns by the inclusion of a sheet of aluminum foil just below the face veneer.

Fire-retarded. Plywood, veneers, and lumber cores may be treated with chemicals which make them resistant to decay, termites, and fire. Where appearance is important, the face veneer may be left untreated.

Metal-faced. Plywood may be faced on one or both sides with sheet metal for increased strength, abrasion resistance, or fire resistance. Its principal use is for truck bodies.

Plastic-faced. Plywood may be faced with plastic sheets of various types, for improved resistance to wear or checking, or as a type of prefinished panel.

Table 19. Hardwood plywood species generally available

Species	Density	Cut		Species	Density	Cut	
Ash, white	H	R	S	Mahogany, African	M	R	S
Avodire	M	–	S	Mahogany, Honduras	M	–	S
Bay	M	R	–	Maple, sugar, black	H	R	S
Beech	H	R	S	Maple, silver, red	M	R	S
Birch	H	R	S	Oak, white, red	H	R	S
Cativo	L	R	–	Paldao	M	–	S
Cherry, black	M	R	S	Poplar	L	R	S
Elm, rock	H	R	S	Rosewood	H	–	S
Elm, white	M	R	S	Sapele	M	–	S
Gum	M	R	S	Sycamore	M	R	S
Lauan	M	R	S	Teak	H	–	S
Limba	M	R	S	Tupelo	M	R	–
Madrone	M	R	S	Walnut, American	M	R	S

NOTE: H—high density, specific gravity 0.56 and higher
M—medium density, specific gravity 0.41 to 0.55
L—low density, specific gravity 0.40 and lower
R—rotary-cut veneer
S—sliced veneer

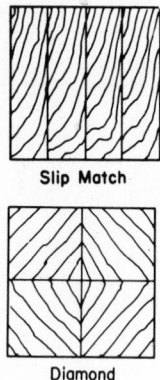
Slip Match

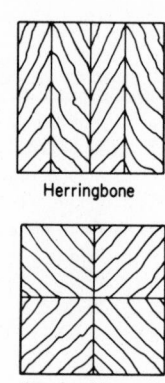
Herringbone

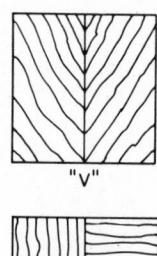
"V"

Book Match

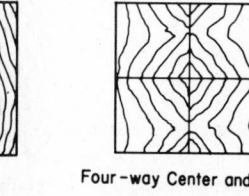
Four-way Center and Butt

Diamond

Reverse Diamond

Checkerboard

Box

Reverse Box

Fig. 37. Veneer matching patterns *Courtesy of U.S. Plywood*

Counterfronts. Plywood panels having the grain of the face veneer running the short way of the panel are available; their principal use is for store fixtures.

Prefinished. Prefinished wall paneling is available in a wide variety of species and finishes; it is usually ¼ in. thick, 16 to 48 in. wide, and 7 to 12 ft long. Fastenings may be concealed. Finishes include wax stains, lacquers, synthetic resins, and plastics. Prefinished flooring squares are also generally available.

Architectural plywood is custom made from veneer selected by the architect in the flitch. Veneers are sequence-matched in the pattern specified (Fig. 36); shop drawings are furnished and the panels are numbered. Architectural plywood is usually ¾-in. lumber core; face veneers are 1/20 to 1/28 in. and crossbands 1/10 to $\frac{1}{16}$ in. thick. Typical installation details are shown in Fig. 37. Architectural plywood is also furnished in ¼ or ⅜-in. thickness; in this case it should be applied over a backing of $\frac{5}{16}$-in. plywood installed horizontally. Panels should be sealed or back-primed before installation.

Ordering plywood

Specify the following: number of pieces, width, length, thickness, number of plies, core construction, grade of face, grade of back, type, sanding, special requirements.

All dimensions should be given in inches. "Width" means across the grain and "length" means parallel to the grain of the face veneer, regardless of the shape of the panel.

REFERENCES

Truax, Dr. T. R.: *Hardwood Plywood Manual,* Hardwood Plywood Institute (1962).
Quality Standards of the Architectural Woodwork Industry, Architectural Woodwork Institute (1962).

Panel joints

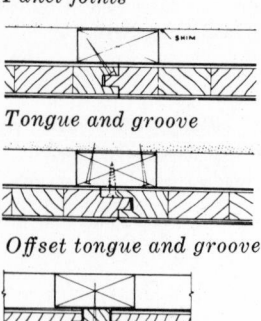

Tongue and groove

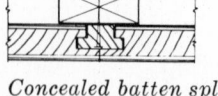

Offset tongue and groove

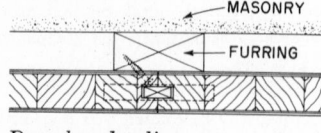

Concealed batten spline

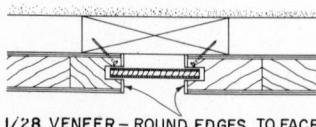

Dowel and spline

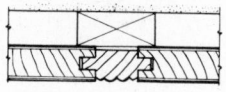

1/28 VENEER – ROUND EDGES TO FACE

Exposed spline

Decorative batten

Fig. 38. Lumber core plywood wall paneling

Panel joints

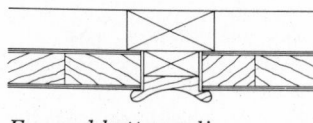

Exposed batten spline

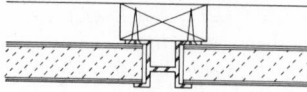

Extruded metal molding

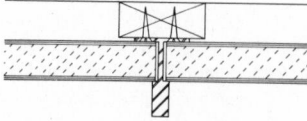

Extruded metal molding

Corners

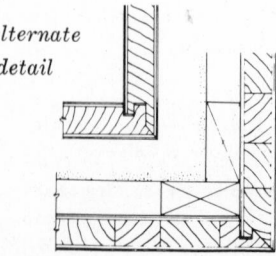

Alternate detail

Outside corner

Corners

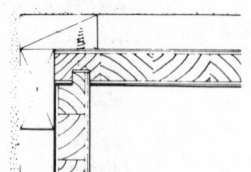

Inside corner

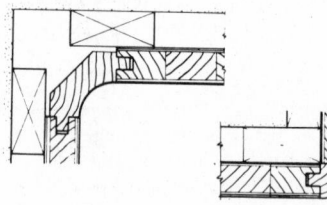

Hardwood corners

Cabinetwork

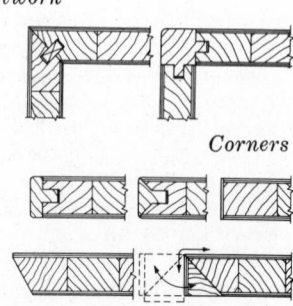

Corners

Edge treatments

Courtesy of Architectural Woodwork Institute and U.S. Plywood

By FREDERICK F. WANGAARD, *Associate Professor of Forest Products, Yale University*

INTERIOR FINISHES *

Plywood is adapted to a wide variety of finishing treatments including natural, stained, blonde, enameled, or painted finishes, or it may be covered with wallpaper. The most distinctive effects are, of course, obtainable only with finishes that permit the natural beauty of wood to be revealed.

Modern finishing treatments for plywood emphasize (1) the natural effect of the grain, color, and figure of the wood obtained through clear finishes or (2) the light effects which may be achieved without losing the distinctive characteristics of texture, grain, and figure by subduing the normal grain contrast of the wood with pigmented sealers. Prior to finishing, all nails should be countersunk and the holes filled with wood putty of matching color. The panel is then lightly sanded with 2/0 sandpaper and wiped clean.

Recommended finishing schedules vary with the species, but are illustrated by the following examples:
1. **Walnut:** Light natural finish. A coat of clear brushing lacquer is first applied. This coat should be steel wooled after drying (3–4 hours) and a second lacquer coat applied. This second coat is also rubbed with steel wool when dry and then rubbed with a good paste wax. A full finish, involving a third coat of lacquer, may be desired on trim or doors where heavy wear is anticipated.
2. **Rift white oak:** Blonde finish. Following preliminary sanding, a white pigmented resin sealer, which has been thinned 10–20 per cent with turpentine or mineral spirits, is brushed on the plywood. After setting for 3–5 minutes, it is rubbed into the pores of the wood, wiped clean, and allowed to dry for 24 hours. The surface is then lightly sanded with 2/0 sandpaper and finished with two coats of lacquer and wax as described for walnut.

Finishing recommendations for

* See also "Finishes."

other hardwood species vary in certain details from the relatively simple treatments described here and are available through plywood dealers. It is advisable, in any case, to sample any prescribed finishing treatment on scrap pieces of plywood before starting the job.

Light stain-glaze finishes which subdue the normal grain contrast of the species are very popular and effective finishing treatments for Douglas fir plywood. Steps in the treatment include (1) Application of interior white undercoat paint thinned with turpentine in the ratio 1 part undercoat to 1 part thinner. Within 10–20 minutes excess undercoat is wiped off with a cloth following the grain to attain the desired show-through of grain. When the surface is dry, it is lightly sanded with fine sandpaper. (2) A coat of thinned white shellac or clear resin sealer, the surface is again lightly sanded when dry. (3) Application of a color coat which may be a tinted interior undercoat, thinned enamel, color in oil, or a light stain. Only a thin color coat is applied and wiped or dry-brushed to the desired appearance. The surface is again sanded lightly when dry. (4) A final coat of flat varnish is then applied, and after drying, it is buffed with 3/0 steel wool.

Variations of the foregoing method include substitution of a white pigmented sealer (applied as described for blonde white oak) for steps 1 and 2. Another possibility is the elimination of step 1 (the white undercoat), otherwise following the procedure outlined.

A simple one-step finishing treatment for Douglas fir consists of a coat of stain wax, which is applied with a cloth or brush. This is wiped down after a few minutes to the desired shade.

The basic procedure for obtaining a **"bleached"** or **blonde finish** with Douglas fir consists of the application of thinned white undercoat which is wiped down following the grain to the desired tone before it becomes

tacky. After drying, the surface is lightly sanded and finished with a coat of clear shellac, flat varnish, or clear lacquer.

The only maintenance normally required for finishes of the types previously described is an occasional application of wax.

Highest quality enameled walls without visible joints are obtained by the following treatment of Douglas fir or gum plywood. For this type of finish, panels should be butted together closely and all nail holes, hammer marks, and joints filled with Swedish putty. The wood is next primed with thinned flat white oil paint followed by the application of inexpensive unbleached muslin (tobacco cloth grade). The muslin is applied similarly to wallpaper using ordinary wallpaper paste, which has been strained to remove lumps. After drying, a coat of glue size is brushed on. Any conventional enamel finishing system may be employed satisfactorily over this base. This type of treatment is especially desirable in kitchens and bathrooms.

Conventional wall and woodwork **paint finishes** are, of course, used successfully on plywood walls and built-ins. When water thinned paints are used, the plywood should first be sealed with a clear resin sealer, shellac, or a flat white paint to prevent raised grain.

Wallpapered walls require the close butting of plywood panels, which are commonly of Douglas fir, but may include some of the more economical hardwoods such as gum. Joints should be filled with Swedish putty and the surface primed with a thin flat white paint. The surface is next coated with wheat flour paste to which gelatin glue size has been added. Next is applied a layer of ¾-pound deadening or lining felt, which is treated with the same paste and size. After butting the felt neatly at the joints, and rolling it smooth, wallpaper may be hung in the usual manner, using ordinary wheat flour paste.

WOOD—1
Grades and dimensions

By JOHN HANCOCK CALLENDER, *Professor of Architecture, Pratt Institute*, and HOWARD P. VERMILYA, *AIA*

Wood is extensively used as an interior and exterior finishing material. Both hardwoods and softwoods are used in solid form as well as in plywood.

Dimensional stability

All wood shrinks and swells with changes in moisture content. The art of designing in wood is to know the extent and direction of the movement and the measures that can be taken to minimize it. Some species of wood are more dimensionally stable than others. Table 1 classifies the principal species according to this characteristic. While the difference between the woods in the first and last groups is significant, the difference between adjacent groups may be hardly discernible in actual use.

It is important that wood have the appropriate moisture content when purchased, and that it be protected from moisture before and after installation. Moisture content is appropriate when it corresponds to the average atmospheric conditions to which the wood will be exposed, indoors or out (Table 2). Kiln drying is essential for interior wood finish. Kiln-dried wood should not be brought to the job until the building is fully enclosed and the plaster thoroughly dry.

The dimensional stability of wood may be improved by treating it with a water-repellent preservative, to reduce its absorption of moisture. Water-repellent preservatives which conform to the standard of the National Woodwork Manufacturers Association (NWMA-M-2-55) or Federal Specification TT-W-572 contain a water-repellent ingredient and a chlorinated phenol preservative in a volatile petroleum vehicle. The preferred method of treat-

ment is by pressure or by dipping for 3 min, but a brush application is better than no treatment at all. If treated wood is cut, the exposed surface should be promptly re-treated. This provides protection during transit and on the job and eliminates the need for back priming. This treatment is most effective on softwoods, those generally used for exterior finish.

Coatings on the surface of the wood also reduce dimensional changes. While no coating is entirely moistureproof, a standard three-coat application of paint, varnish, or enamel will greatly lower the amount of moisture reaching the wood and penetrating into it.

The way a board is sawed from the log has an important effect on its stability. Quarter-sawed or edge-grain (vertical-grain) lumber shrinks and swells less and cups and twists less than plain-sawed and flat-grain lumber.

Table 1. Dimensional stability of various woods

Data supplied by Architectural Woodwork Institute

Hardwoods				
Group I (most stable)	Group II		Group III	Group IV (least stable)
White ash	Red alder	Rock elm	Beech	Cottonwood
Butternut	Black ash	Soft elm	Red gum	Sap gum
Cherry	Blue ash	Hard maple	Magnolia	Sycamore
Chestnut	Basswood	Soft maple		Tupelo
Poplar	Birch	Red oak		
Walnut	Hackberry	White oak		
Willow				

Softwoods		
Group I	Group II	Group III
Cedar, Alaska	Cedar, Port Orford	Douglas fir (coast and inland types)
Cedar, eastern red	Cypress, southern	Hemlock, western
Cedar, western red	Douglas fir (Rocky Mountain type)	Larch, western
Cedar, northern white	Fir, balsam	Pine, longleaf
Pine, northern white	Fir, white	Pine, Norway
Pine, sugar	Hemlock, eastern	Pine, shortleaf
Redwood	Pine, ponderosa	Pine, Idaho
	Spruce, Engelmann	Spruce, Sitka

Table 2. Recommended moisture content for woodwork at time of installation—in percentage of oven-dry weight

Data supplied by Architectural Woodwork Institute

Service condition	Quantity	Southwestern states	Southern coastal states	Remainder of the United States	Alberta, Saskatchewan, and Manitoba	Ontario and Quebec	East and west coast provinces, including Newfoundland
Interior wood finish	Average	6	11	7	6	7	10
	Range permitted in individual pieces	4–9	8–13	5–10	4–9	5–9	8–12
Exterior trim	Average	9	12	12	12	12	13
	Range permitted in individual pieces	7–12	9–14	9–14	10–15	10–15	11–15

Table 3. Lumber grades for architectural woodwork

Data from Quality Standards of the Architectural Woodworking Industry

Species or Groups of Species. Plain Sawn, except as noted below.	PREMIUM GRADE						CUSTOM GRADE						ECONOMY GRADE					
	① Min. Exposed Surface in Sq. In Sample Pc. in ( )	② % of Sapwood	③ Knots No.	Size	④ Checks No.	Size	① Min. Exposed Surface in Sq. In Sample Pc. in ( )	② % of Sapwood	③ Knots No.	Size	④ Checks No.	Size	① Min. Exposed Surface in Sq. In Sample Pc. in ( )	② % of Sapwood	③ Knots No.	Size	④ Checks No.	Size
"Natural" (Containing Heartwood & Sapwood) Ash, Birch, Gum, ⑤ Hard Maple, Poplar.	630 (5¼" x 120")	No Limit	0	0	1	.025" x 3"	486 (4½" x 108")	No Limit	0	0	2	.025" x 5"	336 (3½" x 96")	No Limit	1	½"	3	.04" x 6"
Select Red Birch, Select Red Gum, Select Brown Ash.	567 (5¼" x 108")	0	0	0	1	.025" x 3"	432 (4½" x 96")	5	0	0	2	.025" x 5"	294 (3½" x 84")	20	1	½"	3	.04" x 6"
Select White Birch, ⑤ Select White Maple, Select White Ash.	567 (5¼" x 108")	100	0	0	1	.025" x 3"	432 (4½" x 96")	95	0	0	2	.025" x 5"	294 (3½" x 84")	80	1	½"	3	.04" x 6"
Red Oak, White Oak, Mahogany, Teak.	630 (5¼" x 120")	0	0	0	2	.025" x 3"	486 (4½" x 108")	0	0	0	3	.025" x 5"	336 (3½" x 96")	10	2	½"	4	.04" x 6"
Rift or Quarter Sawn Red or White Oak.	384 (4" x 96")	0	0	0	2	.025" x 3"	189 (2¼" x 84")	0	0	¼"	2	.025" x 5"	108 (1½" x 72")	20	2	½"	4	.04" x 6"
⑥ Walnut, Cherry Butternut.	384 (4" x 96")	10	0	0	2	.025" x 3"	189 (2¼" x 84")	25	1	¼"	3	.025" x 5"	108 (1½" x 72")	No Limit	2	⅝"	4	.04" x 6"
"All Heart" (No Sapwood) Redwood, and Western Red Cedar.	1044 (7½" x 144")	0	0	0	2	.03" x 5"	693 (5¼" x 132")	0	0	0	3	.04" x 6"	540 (4½" x 120")	0	0	0	4	.04" x 7"
"Natural" Redwood and Western Red Cedar. Pine - Ponderosa, Sugar, Northern White. ⑦ Cypress, Fir, Spruce.	1044 (7½" x 144")	No Limit	0	0	2	.03" x 5"	693 (5¼" x 132")	No Limit	1	⅝"	3	.04" x 6"	540 (4½" x 120")	No Limit	2	1"	4	.04" x 7"
Pine - Southern Yellow	660 (5½" x 120")	No Limit	0	0	2	.03" x 5"	486 (4½" x 108")	No Limit	1	⅝"	3	.04" x 6"	336 (3½" x 96")	No Limit	2	1"	4	.04" x 7"

(A.) The total number of defects in a single member, including sapwood or heartwood when either is a defect, shall never exceed 75% of the total number of the several kinds of defects shown as allowable in the above table. The number of defects so computed shall be the nearest whole number. (75% of 1 = 1; 75% of 2 = 2; 75% of 3 = 2; and so on)

① This is the minimum number of square inches of exposed surface of any member in which any defect is allowed. Any member containing less square inches of exposed area shall be free of all defects. Note that sapwood is a defect **only** when and **only** to the extent it is restricted in this table. Test 100-G-6 allows edge gluing of hardwood wider than 7¼".

② This is the ratio of total exposed area of sapwood in a member divided by the total exposed surface of the member.

③ This is the number and size (maximum dimension) of round, tight knots that are allowed in a member of the minimum size given. Members containing less square inches of exposed area shall be free of knots.

④ This is the number and size of checks that are allowed in a member of the minimum size given. Members containing less square inches of exposed area shall be free of checks.

⑤ Mineral stain in Hard Maple is limited as follows: Premium Grade, none allowed; Custom Grade, none allowed in 75% of all members; Economy Grade, no limit.

⑥ Note that sapwood in these three species is permitted in varying proportions in all grades. If objectionable, it can be eliminated by sapstaining or toning. Clear Walnut is not normally available longer than 10'-0".

⑦ All Heart Tidewater Red Cypress is in extremely short supply.

Architectural woodwork

Architectural woodwork includes *millwork*, consisting of trim and paneling, and *cabinetwork*, consisting of cabinets and other built-in furniture. Since the distinction between these two classifications is no longer precise, architects preparing specifications are advised to include all such work, regardless of the degree of mill or site fabrication, in a single section called "architectural woodwork."

The *Quality Standards of the Architectural Woodwork Industry* cover the following categories of work:

Standing and running trim—casings, stops, stools, cornices, fascias, soffits, and board or plywood wall covering

Casework—cabinets, counters, enclosures

Panelwork—stiles and rails with flush or raised panels

Closet shelving

Miscellaneous ornamental items—mantels, columns, pediments, grilles, church items, etc.

Stairwork

Exterior frames, sash, screens, blinds, and shutters

Doors

Grades. It has long been traditional for architects to specify for millwork and cabinetwork lumber grades A or B Select for natural finish and C Select for paint finish (or Clear, Select, and Sound, respectively, for certain hardwoods). However, the Architectural Woodwork Institute recommends that lumber grades *not* be used for architectural woodwork, since even the highest grades permit defects, which makes them unacceptable for this type of work. The AWI has therefore established its own grades of Premium, Custom, and Economy, which are used not only for lumber (Table 3) and plywood, but also for details of construction and workmanship.

Not included in the standard lumber grades or in the AWI grades are the special forms of several species which are selected for certain abnormal features. Examples are knotty pine, wormy chestnut, pecky cypress, and wattled walnut.

In some species there is little difference in appearance between heartwood and sapwood, while in others the difference in color is marked. Where this contrast is not considered aesthetically desirable, the sapwood can be stained to match the heartwood as part of the finishing operation.

Only redwood and western red cedar are available in all-heartwood grades. For other species, if all-heartwood is required, it must be cut from the regular grade, which may seriously limit the maximum sizes that can be provided.

Dimensions of milled lumber vary slightly in different areas of the country, as shown in Table 4. Lengths are in 2-ft increments beginning with 6 or 8 ft. The usual maximum length is 16 ft, but some softwoods are available in 18- and 20-ft lengths. Actual length should be assumed to be 2 in. less than nominal length, to allow for end checking and shrinkage resulting from seasoning or kiln drying. For custom molding, it should be noted that the maximum capacity of most molding machines is 4 by 11½ in.

Exterior trim, as well as siding, is usually of softwood. Important considerations are resistance to decay and paint-holding characteristics. Redwood, cypress, and western red cedar are notably resistant to decay and are therefore sometimes called the "durable woods." Other species should be treated with a preservative. In paint-holding ability, the three durable woods, along with all the other cedars, constitute Group

Table 4. Dimensions of milled lumber, in.

Data supplied by Architectural Woodwork Institute

Thickness		Width	
Rough	Finished	Rough	Finished
1	11/16–25/32	2	1⅝
1¼	1 1/16–1⅛	3	2⅝
1½	1 5/16–1⅜	4	3½–3⅝
2	1⅝–1¾	5	4½–4⅝
2½	2⅛–2¼	6	5½–5⅝
3	2⅝–2¾	7	6½
3½	3⅛–3¼	8	7¼–7½
4	3½–3¾	9	8¼–8½
		10	9¼–9½
		11	10¼–10½
		12	11¼–11½
		14	13
		16	15

1 (best) in the Forest Product Laboratory's classification. Ponderosa pine, of which much stock millwork is made, is in Group 3. Douglas fir and southern yellow pine are in Group 4 (poorest). Fastenings for exterior trim should be of noncorroding metal, such as galvanized steel, aluminum, or stainless steel; note that cement-coated nails are not rustproof.

American softwoods

The principal softwoods used in finishing work are listed below, along with a brief summary of their characteristics pertinent to this use.

Cedar, Alaska (*Chamaecyparis nootkatensis*). Pacific Coast. Heartwood and sapwood clear yellow. Texture fine and uniform; works and finishes well. Decay resistant. Very low shrinkage.

Cedar, incense (*Libocedrus decurrens*). Pacific Coast. Reddish-brown with some contrasting cream-colored sapwood. Distinctive knots range from medium to large in size. Flourishes of grain.

Cedar, inland red. Northwest. Color varies from dark reddish-brown to light yellow; generally, this is the darkest of the cedars. Interesting grain flourishes; medium and larger knots.

Cedar, Port-Orford (*Chamaecyparis lawsoniana*). Pacific Coast. Heartwood light yellow to pale brown. Fine and uniform texture with straight grain. Moderately light, strong, and shock resistant. Shrinks moderately with little warping. Heartwood very decay resistant.

Cedar, western red (*Thuja plicata*). Northwest. Heartwood reddish-brown and highly resistant to decay. Light, soft, easily worked; very low shrinkage. Holds paint well. Available in all-heartwood grade.

Cedar, white (*Chamaecyparis occidentalis* and *C. thyoides*). North and East Coast. Heartwood light reddish-brown; sapwood lighter, sometimes nearly white. Texture fine and uniform. Light, soft, brittle, splits easily. Low shrinkage. Heartwood resistant to decay.

Cypress, southern (*Taxodium distichum*). Southeast. Heartwood varies from light yellowish-brown to dark brownish-red, brown, or chocolate. Sometimes contains decay pockets known as pecks. Shrinkage moderate. Highly resistant to decay. Holds paint well.

Douglas fir (*Pseudotsuga taxifolia*). Northwest. Orange-red in color with narrow, light-colored sap ring. Grain is distinct. Strong, hard, heavy. Knots are of medium size and blend with the color of the wood. Does not hold paint well.

Fir, balsam (*Abies balsamea*). Northeast and north. Nearly white, with little figure. Light in weight, soft, low in strength.

Fir, white (*Abies concolor* and *A. grandis*). West. White with reddish tinge. Interesting grain patern. Light, soft, straight-grained, uniform texture, easily worked. The whitest commercial softwood.

Hemlock, eastern (*Tsuga canadensis*). North and northeast. Heartwood is pale brown with reddish hue, coarse and uneven in texture. Knots characteristically small. Moderately light in weight and low in strength.

Hemlock, western (*Tsuga heterophylla*). Northwest. Heartwood and sapwood are almost white with a purplish tinge. Fine and uniform texture; straight grain. Many small tight black knots. Moderately light and strong with high shrinkage.

Larch, western (*Larix occidentalis*). Northwest. Heartwood mostly reddish with small amount of straw-colored sapwood. Interesting grain pattern. Little contrast between knot and wood color; knots usually small. Does not hold paint well.

Pine, Idaho, or *western white* (*Pinus monticola*). Northwest. Color varies from light to pale reddish-brown. Unusually straight and even grain. Characteristic red knots are neat, small to medium in size. High shrinkage.

Pine, lodgepole (*Pinus contorta*). West. Deep straw to creamy white in color with satiny sheen. Knots range in size from small to medium and are neat in appearance. Light in weight, low in strength.

Pine, northern white (*Pinus strobus*). North and northeast. Heartwood ranges from cream to light brown, often with a reddish tinge. Very uniform texture and straight grain. Easily worked; takes glue and paint well. Very low shrinkage.

Pine, ponderosa (*Pinus ponderosa*). West. Creamy white to deep straw color. Gentle grain configuration. Knots are generally smooth, small to large in size. Uniform texture; easy to work.

Pine, red, or *Norway* (*Pinus resinosa*). North. Heartwood pale red to reddish-brown; sapwood nearly white with yellowish tinge. Generally straight grain, coarse and uneven in texture, and somewhat resinous. High shrinkage.

Pine, southern yellow, including *longleaf* (*Pinus palustris*), *shortleaf* (*P. echinata*), *loblolly* or *North Carolina* (*P. taeda*). Southeast. Heartwood reddish-brown, sapwood yellowish-white. Longleaf pine is heavy, strong, and hard, but the less dense types are used for finishing lumber because they work more easily and hold finishes better. North Carolina pine is lighter and softer.

Pine, sugar (*Pinus lambertiana*). West. Soft-toned creamy white, darkens to pale brown, sometimes tinged with pink. Grain often shows light brown flecks. Knots medium to large, red in color. Low shrinkage. Unusually wide boards available.

Redwood (*Sequoia sempervirens*). Pacific Coast. Heartwood light cherry to dark mahogany color; narrow sapwood almost white. Straight-grained, easily worked, holds paint well, shrinks very little. Highly resistant to decay. Unusually wide boards obtainable. Available in all-heartwood grade.

Spruce, eastern (*Picea rubra, P. glauca, P. mariana*). North and northeast. Heartwood ranges from cream to light brown, often with a reddish tinge. Uniform texture, straight grain, easily worked, moderate shrinkage.

Spruce, Engelmann (*Picea engelmannii*). West. One of the whitest of western woods, its grain is nearly invisible from a short distance away. Characterized by neat array of small knots.

Spruce, Sitka (*Picea sitchensis*). Pacific Coast. Heartwood light pinkish-brown, sapwood creamy white. Fine uniform texture with straight grain. High shrinkage. Light but strong for its weight.

REFERENCES

Wood Handbook, Forest Products Laboratory, U.S. Department of Agriculture.

Quality Standards of the Architectural Woodworking Industry, Architectural Woodwork Institute, James Arkin, AIA, Consultant, Chicago (1961). Also other publications of the Institute.

Publications of the following trade associations:

- California Redwood Association, San Francisco, Calif.
- National Hardwood Lumber Association, Chicago, Ill.
- Southern Pine Association, New Orleans, La.
- West Coast Lumbermen's Association, Portland, Ore.
- Western Pine Association, Portland, Ore.

By BURDETT GREEN, *Executive Vice President, Fine Hardwoods Association,* and JAMES ARKIN, *AIA, Consultant, Architectural Woodwork Institute*

BIRCH, DOMESTIC AND CANADIAN

There are two species of commercial importance that are often marketed together, as listed below. They are so similar that it is not necessary to specify them. However, one should specify either "Natural Birch," "Selected White Birch" or "Selected Red Birch." Natural Birch combines both sapwood and heartwood. Selected White Birch includes only sapwood, and Selected Red Birch only heartwood.

BIRCH, SWEET (*Betula lenta*) — Black Birch, Cherry Birch
Source: Mainly from Adirondack and eastern Appalachian areas, although also as far south as northern part of Gulf States
Color: Brown tinged with red; thin, light brown or yellow sapwood
Pattern: Grain distinct but not prominent
Characteristics: Heavy; very strong and hard; close-grained
Uses: All cabinetwork where strength and hardness is desired
Availability: Abundant as both veneer (rotary, sliced) and lumber
Price Range: Medium

BIRCH, YELLOW (*Betula alleghaniensis,* formerly *Betula lutea*) — Gray Birch, Silver Birch, Swamp Birch
Source: Canada, Lakes states, New England south to North Carolina
Color: Cream, light brown tinged with red; thin, nearly white sapwood
Pattern: Plain and often curly or wavy
Characteristics: Heavy; strong; hard; close-grained; even texture
Uses: Interiors; furniture; doors; store fixtures; accessories; etc.
Availability: Veneer (both rotary and sliced) and lumber abundant. As veneers, sapwood of rotary birch is sold as "selected white" and heartwood as "selected red." Greater volume produced is "natural birch," and contains a normal combination of color tones
Price Range: Medium

MAPLE

The three species of maple described below are grown in widely separated areas and vary greatly in physical properties.

MAPLE, HARD (*Acer saccharum*) — Birds Eye Maple, Northern Maple, Rock Maple, Sugar Maple
Source: Lakes states, Appalachians, Northwest U. S., Canada
Color: Cream to light reddish-brown heartwood; thin white sapwood tinged slightly with reddish-brown
Pattern: Usually straight-grained; sometimes found highly figured with *curly, blistered, quilted, birds eye* or *burl grain,* scattered over entire tree or in irregular stripes and patches
Characteristics: Heavy; hard; strong; close-grained; tough; stiff; uniform texture. Excellent resistance to abrasion and indentation
Uses: Interiors; furniture; fixtures; flooring; decorative inlays
Availability: *Plain maple* veneer (quartered, sliced, half-round, rotary) plentiful. *Figured maple* (including birds eye, butts, etc.) veneer (quartered, sliced, half-round, rotary) rare
Price Range: *Plain maple* — medium. *Figured maple* — costly

MAPLE, SOFT (*Acer saccharinum*) — Silver Maple
Same general characteristics as hard maple, but not nearly so hard or strong. Usually shows considerable dark (mineral) streaks.
Availability: Plentiful as both veneer and lumber
Price Range: Medium to inexpensive

MAPLE, OREGON (*Acer macrophyllum*) — Big Leaf Maple
A true maple, but not so hard or strong as silver maple.
Source: Pacific Coast and Southern Canada
Availability: As both lumber and veneer, locally. As figured veneers (blistered, burl, etc.), rare
Price Range: Inexpensive for plain types. Moderate to costly for quilted and burls

Birch, Natural, rotary (1 piece)

Birch, Selected White, rotary (1 piece)

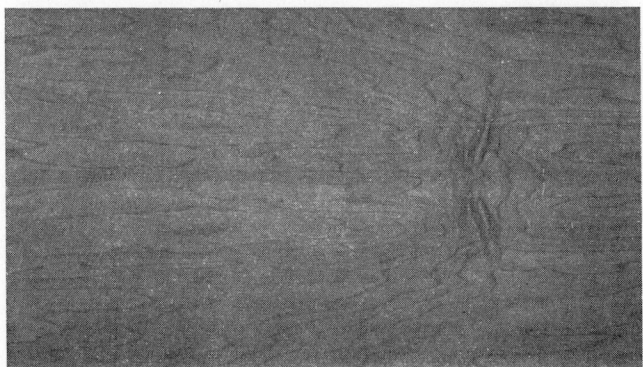
Maple, plain rotary (2 pieces, book-matched)

Maple, birds eye (1 piece)

MAHOGANY

An often misused name, applied to many woods not of the mahogany family. The three authentic commercial species of mahogany are *Swietenia mahogani*, *Swietenia macrophylla* and *Khaya ivorensis*. (All true mahoganies are the *Meliaceae* family, *genera Swietenia* or *Khaya*.) Their descriptions follow:

MAHOGANY, AFRICAN (*Khaya ivorensis*)

Source: Africa (Ivory Coast, Gold Coast, French Cameroon, Cape Lopez, Nigeria)

Color: Light pink to reddish-brown and tannish brown

Pattern: Although pores are distributed, this wood produces a very distinct, pleasing grain. The most lavishly figured mahogany offered in plain stripe, broken stripe, mottle, fiddleback, fine crotches and faux swirl

Characteristics: Available in great lengths and widths; milder textured with slightly larger pores than other mahogany species; relatively hard; works well; highly lustrous; polishes well; durable

Uses: Interiors, furniture; accessories and art objects; etc.

Availability: Veneer (quartered, sliced, half-round, rotary) abundant. Lumber abundant

Price Range: Medium; costly for highly figured veneers

Mahogany, African, swirl (1 piece)

MAHOGANY, CUBAN (*Swietenia mahogani*)

One of the finest of the several mahogany species. However, the exportation of this species from Cuba is no longer permitted

Source: Cuba, also throughout the West Indies

Color: Light red; yellowish-tan when cut; darkens rapidly to deep rich golden brown or brown-red; exceptionally fine color

Pattern: Highly figured, mottled, fiddle-back crotches, also plain stripes

Characteristics: Heavier and harder than the other mahoganies; wears exceptionally well; extremely durable; close-grained; takes excellent finish; has good strength and bending properties; ideal wood for turning and carving

Uses: Fine cabinetry

Availability: Haiti, Puerto Rico, and the Dominican Republic

Mahogany, African, quartered ribbon-striped (1 piece)

MAHOGANY, TROPICAL AMERICAN, including PERUVIAN and BRAZILIAN MAHOGANY (*Swietenia macrophylla*). (Brazilian Mahogany marketed as Amazon Mahogany)

Source: Mexico, Brazil, Peru and Central America (especially Honduras)

Color: Varies from a light reddish or yellowish-brown to a rich, dark red, depending upon country of origin and situation. Most supplies tend to be yellowish-tan, changing on brief exposure to rich, golden brown

Pattern: A considerable variety of figures, similar to African mahogany except crotches are not readily available. Straighter grain generally. Location influences appearance also

Characteristics: Lighter and softer than Cuban; mostly straight-grained but even when interlocked is exceptionally stable; more mellow texture than Cuban (West Indian); extremely good strength properties; works well; stains and finishes well; durable and decay-resistant. Central America produces more figured logs for fancy veneers

Uses: Paneling; furniture; fine joinery; exterior uses

Availability: Central American veneer (quartered, sliced, half-round) abundant. Lumber plentiful. Brazilian and Peruvian plentiful

Price Range: Inexpensive to medium

Mahogany, Tropical American, plain flat cut (1 piece)

Mahogany, Tropical American, figured flat cut (1 piece)

OAK, AMERICAN

Includes several species from the Red Oak and White Oak groups. Except for source and color, Red Oak and White Oak, the two leading American species, are very similar. Characteristics they have in common are:

Pattern: Quartered oak has a striking "flake" pattern caused by extremely large and wide rays that reflect light. Plain flat-sliced or sawn oak has an attractive figure of stripes and leafy grain caused by the distinct layers of springwood and summerwood and the large pores, especially concentrated in the springwood. Rift-cut (half-round) oak has a fine pin stripe. Rotary-cut oak has a distinct watery figure with great contrast

Characteristics: A heavy, ring-porous hardwood with larger, more prominent pores in the springwood than summerwood; very strong and very hard; stiff and heavy; durable under exposure; great wear-resistance; holds nails and screws well. Red and white oak look very similar when finished, and because of its large pores, oak takes a great variety of fine filled or textured finishes

Uses: Flooring (both solid and plywood tiles); furniture; paneling; general construction; display and store fixtures; handles

Availability: Veneer (quartered, sliced, half-round, rotary) plentiful. Lumber available

Price Range: Medium

OAK, RED (*Quercus borealis*)

Source: Throughout the eastern United States; especially in the Appalachians, Ohio, Kentucky

Color: Slightly redder tinge than white oak (though hard for an untrained eye to tell), and more uniform in color

Pattern: Flake figure less prominent than white oak

Characteristics: Slightly coarser grain, with large, rounded, open pores. Easier to finish than white oak, though both are excellent

Uses: All the same purposes as White Oak

OAK, WHITE (*Quercus alba*)

Source: Entire eastern United States, especially produced in the Central States and down through the Appalachian region

Color: From light brown with a grayish tinge in the heartwood to shades of ochre in the sapwood

Pattern: More pronounced and longer rays than red oak, and more frequently rift-sawn for the comb-grain, pin-striped figure than red oak. Occasionally crotches, swirls and burls

Characteristics: Pores are angular and very numerous and filled with a glistening substance called tyloses, which makes this wood especially suitable where water-resistance is required. Tannic acid in the wood protects it from fungi and insects. Closer grained than red oak

Uses: Nearly all common uses of hardwoods, and especially popular where strength and durability are required. Also for watertight or water-resistant purposes

OAK, ENGLISH BROWN will be treated in a later issue.

CHERRY, BLACK (*Prunus serotina*) — Rum Cherry, Wild Black Cherry

Source: Maine to Dakotas and Appalachians; production largely Pennsylvania to West Virginia

Color: Light reddish-brown

Pattern: Straight-grained; satiny; some figured. Small gum pockets are normal markings

Characteristics: Light; strong; rather hard; fine-grained

Uses: Woodwork; fine furniture

Availability: Veneer (quartered, sliced, half-round) plentiful. Very fine figured cherry available for architectural use. Lumber plentiful

Price range: Medium

Oak, White, plain flat cut (1 piece)

Oak, White, rift cut (2 pieces, book-matched)

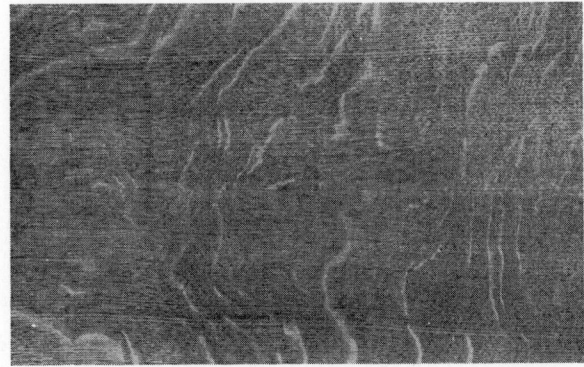

Oak, White, quartered (2 pieces, book-matched)

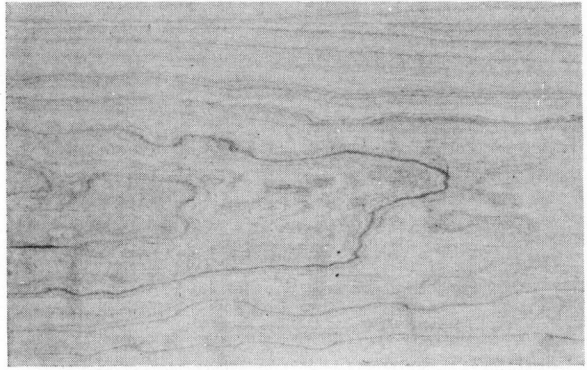

Cherry, plain sliced (1 piece)

WALNUT, AMERICAN (*Juglans nigra*)

Better than 95 per cent of all walnut used in the United States comes from one genus, *Juglans nigra*, formerly referred to as American Black Walnut. The wood itself is not black but a light to chocolate brown, sometimes slightly purplish brown. In specifying plywood or veneers, it is not enough simply to indicate "Walnut," or even "American Walnut," because this one species is available in more different figure or grain types than any other wood.

Source: Grows throughout the United States and Southern Canada, but its commercial range is confined largely to some fifteen Central States

Color: Light gray-brown to dark purplish brown

Pattern: Plain to highly figured. Produces a greater variety of figure types than any other hardwood (approached only by mahogany): longwood (flat-cut; half-round; quarters, both plain and figured), crotches, swirls, stumpwood and occasionally burls. Four of the most readily available types are described below:

Plain Flat Cut—Comes in reasonably good widths, from 8 to 18 in., and occasionally in "half-round" to even wider stocks. Flitches (or individual stock) usually contain from 1200 to 1800 sq ft. In lengths, 9 to 10 ft predominate; however, fine architectural logs may be had up to 12 or 14 ft and occasionally to 16 ft long

Figured Flat Cut—Leafy grain character caused by annual growth rings is the same as in "plain flat cut," but, in addition, one or more types of "cross figures," "roll figure" or "mottle" appear, usually distributed more or less evenly over the face. Uniformity over large areas should not be expected, because the figure varies even within one log

Quartered Plain—The growth rings on the sides of flat cut walnut produce a quartered effect. By cutting out the leafy heart (flat) grain, pure quarters result. Certain large logs are often quarter-cut to give the entire sheet a stripe. Quarters, which come from only one-quarter of the log, are therefore much narrower in width, ranging from 5 to 10 in., mostly 5 to 8 in. However, panels of any width may be obtained by matching in either of two ways: book matching or slip matching

Quartered Figured—As explained above, a small percentage of the logs that may be quartered have "cross figure." When book-matched, they produce a "fiddle-back" effect. Other types of cross figure may be had by specifying "slightly figured quarters" or "highly figured quarters"

Characteristics: Moderately heavy; very strong for its weight, exceptionally stable. Even "plain" types are often characterized by dapples (pin knots, which are really not knots) and slight variations in color. When chosen for this informal character, the wood is described as "Enchanted Walnut"

Uses: Architectural woodwork; furniture

Availability: Veneer abundant. Lumber plentiful

Price Range: Medium to costly for highly figured types

WALNUT, CLARO (*Juglans hindsii*)—California Walnut

There is considerable confusion as to the exact species of *Juglans* that produces fast-growing Claro Walnut. Some authorities claim it comes from *Juglans regia*. (Photograph on Sheet 5.)

Source: California and southern Oregon, east of Coast Range

Color: Tannish brown with dark brown

Pattern: Wavy grain; prominent light stripes

Characteristics: Moderately heavy; hard; rather open-grained

Uses: Highly decorative areas of fine furniture and paneled interiors

Availability: Quartered veneers rare. Lumber not available

Price Range: Medium to costly

Walnut, American, plain flat cut (1 piece)

Walnut, American, figured flat cut (1 piece)

Walnut, American, quartered sliced (2 piece· book-matched)

Walnut, American, quartered figured (2 pieces, book-matched)

WALNUT, EUROPEAN (*Juglans regia*)

Although walnut grows rather widely (though sparsely) over most of the world, only a small amount is imported, and it is mainly from Europe. The European walnuts are all from the same genus, *Juglans regia*, or Royal Walnut. Each type normally takes the name of the country of origin. The most important are:

WALNUT, CIRCASSIAN

Source: Europe
Color: Tawny
Pattern: Variegated streaks of black or dark brown (these pigment streaks passing across the growth rings are typical of Circassian Walnut). Occasionally crotches and swirls
Characteristics: Not so strong or hard as American Walnut, but otherwise about the same properties
Uses: Woodwork; highly decorative furniture
Availability: Veneer rare. Lumber scarce
Price Range: Expensive

WALNUT, ENGLISH OR FRENCH

Source: England and France
Color: Soft and quite gray-brown; lighter in color than American Walnut
Pattern: Fine, smooth grain; less prominent growth lines than Circassian Walnut
Characteristics: Very much like Circassian
Uses: Same as Circassian
Availability: Scarce
Price Range: Expensive

WALNUT, PERSIAN

Persian Walnut is the wood of European-Asiatic trees. It is grown in many countries and marketed as English, Italian, Turkish, Bulgarian, Spanish, Austrian and Russian Walnut, according to locale or source

BUTTERNUT (*Juglans cinerea*)—White Walnut

A true walnut.

Source: North Central States and Southern Canada
Color: Pale brown
Pattern: Satiny wood with leafy grain
Characteristics: Soft to medium textured, with occasional dark spots or streaks
Uses: Interior finish of houses; furniture
Availability: Veneer (sliced) and lumber somewhat more than "rare"
Price Range: Medium

ORIENTALWOOD (*Endiandra Palmerstoni*)—Australian Laurel, Australian Walnut, Oriental Walnut; formerly "Queensland Walnut"

Although this wood was introduced into America in the late 1920's as "Oriental Walnut," it is not related to the walnut family (see botanical names).

Source: Australia
Color: Pinkish-gray to brown
Pattern: Somewhat like plain quartered Claro Walnut but with dark stripes and even broader ones
Characteristics: Medium weight; turns and polishes well; firm to hard
Uses: Furniture; cabinetry
Availability: Veneer (quartered) scarce
Price Range: Costly

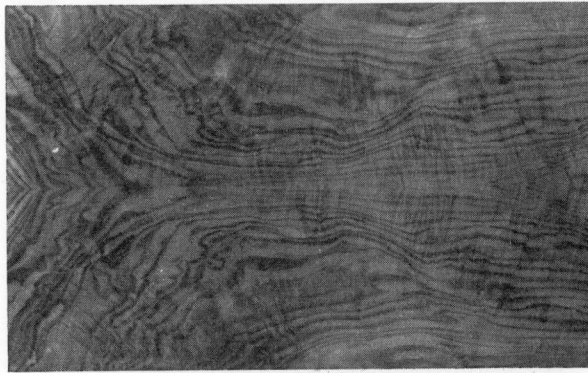

Walnut, Claro, flat cut (2 pieces, book-matched)

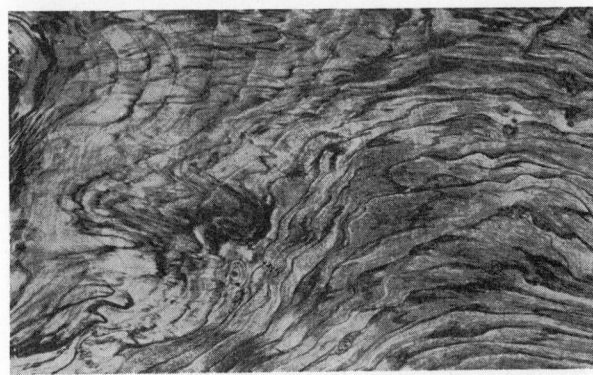

Walnut, Circassian (one piece)

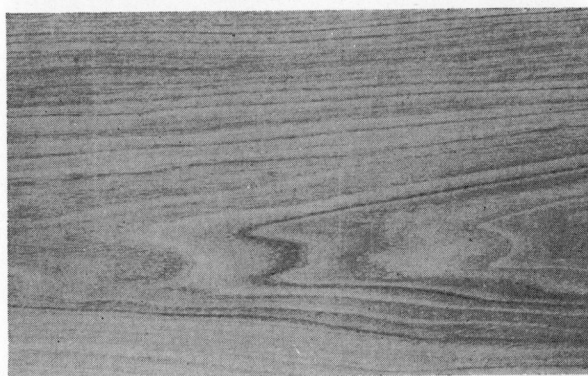

Butternut, plain flat cut (1 piece)

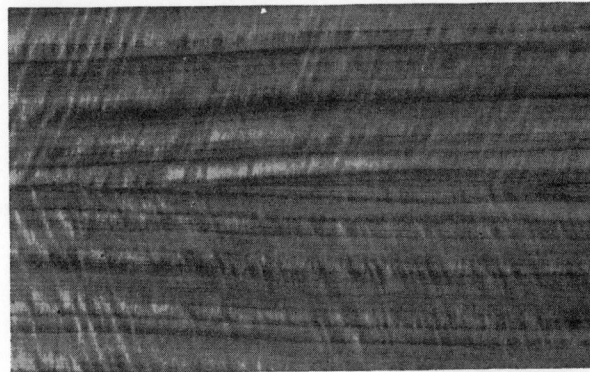

Orientalwood (2 pieces, book-matched)

ASH, AMERICAN

There are many American species of ash, but the three major commercial ones are, in order of importance:

ASH, BLACK (*Fraxinus nigra*)—Brown Ash, Hoop Ash, Swamp Ash
Source: Principally the Lakes States
Color: Warm brown heartwood with a thin white or light brown sapwood
Pattern: Clusters of eyes occasionally scattered over plain wood
Characteristics: Extremely stable; heavy; rather soft; tough
Uses: Veneer for faces of decorative plywood; lumber for solid plank wall panels and for chairs, especially bent frames
Availability: Veneers (largely rotary, rarely burls) rare to plentiful
Price Range: Medium

ASH, GREEN (*Fraxinus pennsylvanica lanceolsta*)—Swamp Ash, Water Ash; lumber sold as White Ash
Source: Principally South Atlantic States and Mississippi Valley
Color: Cream to very light brown heartwood with thick, lighter colored sapwood
Pattern: Both flat-cut and quartered; moderately open grain
Characteristics: Heavy; hard; strong; medium-grained; tough
Uses: Interiors; furniture
Availability: Largely for commercial veneers
Price Range: Medium

ASH, WHITE (*Fraxinus americana*)
Source: Principally Lakes States, also New England and Central States
Color: Cream to very light brown heartwood with thick, lighter colored sapwood
Pattern: Both flat-cut and quartered; moderately open grain
Characteristics: Heavy; hard; strong; medium-grained; tough
Uses: Interiors; furniture
Availability: Veneer (quartered, sliced, half-round, rotary) plentiful, (butts and figured sliced), rare. Lumber plentiful
Price Range: Medium

ASH, JAPANESE (*Fraxinus sieboldiana*)—Damo, Tamo
Source: Japan
Color: Brownish-tan through gray to almost white
Pattern: Plain to highly varied with swirls, fiddle-back mottle and a "peanut shell" figure. Extreme grain character
Characteristics: Bends easily; lighter weight than American and European Ash; glues well; finishes well; strong for its weight
Uses: Decorative interiors and furniture; inlays and overlays
Availability: Veneer (half-round) scarce
Price Range: Costly

AVODIRE (*Turraeanthus africana*)—Apaya
Source: African Gold Coast, Ivory Coast (Liberia, Cameroons)
Color: White to creamy gold
Pattern: Largely figured with a mottle; crotches and swirls
Characteristics: Medium texture; firm, clean grain; usually wavy or irregularly interlocked; lustrous; moderately hard; weighs about the same as African Mahogany
Uses: Architectural panels; furniture; fixtures
Availability: Veneer (quartered, sliced, half-round) plentiful, also crotches and swirls. Lumber available
Price Range: Moderate

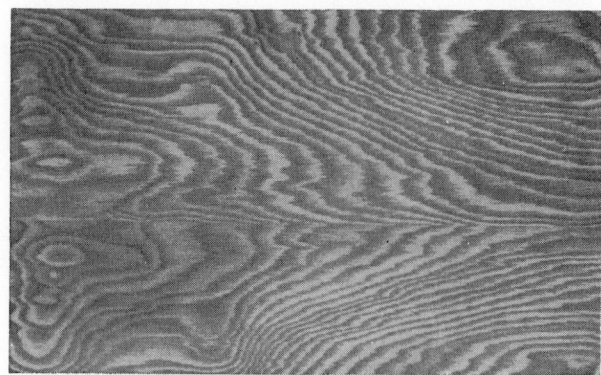

Ash, Brown (2 pieces, book-matched)

Ash, White (2 pieces, book-matched)

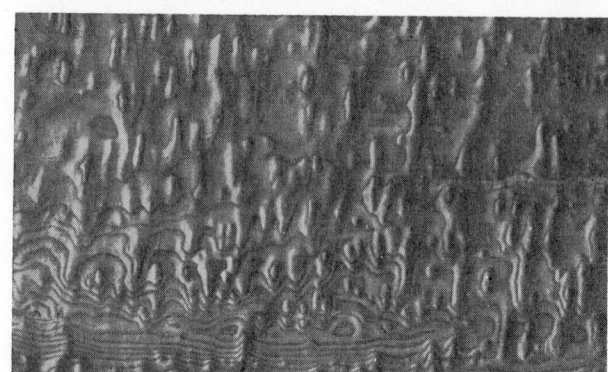

Ash, Japanese (1 piece)

Avodire, rope figure (2 pieces, book-matched)

BUBINGA (*Guibourtia demeusii*)—African Rosewood, Akume, Kewazinga

Source: West Africa

Color: Red with streaks or lines of ornamental dark purple

Pattern: From a rather plain stripe to a heavy mottle which occurs in the quarter-cut wood. Occasionally cut sliced and half-round

Characteristics: Very hard. While described as having a close grain, it has conspicuous and fairly large pores. Capable of being worked into fine cabinetry

Uses: General cabinetry

Availability: Plentiful in the form of veneers. Largely produced as longwood, but occasionally as crotches and swirls

Price Range: Medium to costly

Bubinga, quartered (2 pieces, book-matched)

CEDAR, AROMATIC RED (*Juniperus virginiana*)—Eastern Red Cedar, Juniper, Pencil Cedar, Red Cedar, Southern Red Cedar, Tennessee Red Cedar

Although Cedar is not one of the hardwoods, since it is a coniferous or needle-bearing tree rather than a "broad-leaf," which generally depicts hardwoods, this species is commonly produced by the hardwood industry. It is a very fine-textured wood which is used extensively along with hardwoods by the cedar chest industry and also for lining interiors of closets and cabinetry to be used for storage.

Source: Occurs over most of the eastern two-thirds of United States. Largest production in Southeastern and South Central States

Color: Light red with streaks of light sapwood

Pattern: Knotty, with other natural characteristics always present

Characteristics: Although brittle, it is regarded as a fine wood to work

Uses: Cedar storage chests; linings of closets and chests; small articles of woodenware

Availability: Veneer (sawn or sliced) plentiful; lumber plentiful, both in rather small sizes

Price Range: Medium

Cedar, Aromatic Red (3 pieces, unmatched)

ELM, AMERICAN (*Ulmus americana*)—Soft Elm, Water Elm, White Elm

Although there are several varieties of Elm that vary but slightly in character, the two commonly available types are Northern Brown Elm and Southern Elm.

Source: United States, east of the Rockies

Color: Light brownish

Pattern: Conspicuous growth pattern, like Ash

Characteristics: Heavy; hard; strong; tough; difficult to split; coarse-grained; bends exceedingly well

Uses: Widely used as veneers for containers; some for furniture. Although for years the most widely used wood for berry baskets and other containers, less of it is used for that purpose today and more of it is cut into veneers and lumber for both architectural plywood and fine furniture

Availability: Veneer (quartered, sliced, rotary) plentiful. Lumber available

Price Range: Medium

Elm, Northern Brown, flat cut (2 pieces, book-matched)

ELM, CARPATHIAN BURL (*Ulmus campestris*)—English Elm

Although not pictured here, it is a type of true Elm described as Carpathian Elm Burl and was rather widely used in the furniture and fixture trade during the 1920's. Although an especially highly figured burl, it is usually quite defective and is rarely used today.

Elm, American, quartered (3 pieces, book-matched)

GUMWOOD (*Liquidambar styraciflua*)

For years Gumwood has been one of the most widely used hardwoods in the furniture and woodworking industries. For many years it was extensively used for interior trim and woodwork, especially in areas to be painted. In certain sections of the country it was commonly finished natural. Today Sap Gum is most frequently used in a lumber form for the structural parts of furniture carrying plywood surfaces of other woods. Sap Gum, too, is widely used for the inner plies of "bonded" or plywood construction. Heartwood and sapwood are sold separately as Red Gum and Sap Gum.

GUM, RED (*Heartwood*) —Hazelwood, Southern Gum, Sweet Gum

Source: Wide range in the United States, but commercial production largely from lower Mississippi Valley
Color: Reddish-brown
Pattern: Dark streaks
Characteristics: Moderately heavy; hard; straight; close-grained; not exceedingly strong. Often selected for its attractive figure
Uses: Outside and inside finish of houses; cabinetry
Availability: Veneer (sliced, rotary) plentiful. Lumber available
Price Range: Medium

GUM, SAP (*Sapwood*)

Source: Same as Red Gum
Color: Pinkish-white, often blued by sap stains
Pattern: Plain but not strong; usually watery
Characteristics: Same as Red Gum except not as durable
Uses: Plywood (interiors) and lumber for furniture; architectural woodwork for paint; most widely used species for veneers in the United States
Availability: Veneer (rotary) abundant. Lumber abundant
Price Range: Inexpensive

HAREWOOD, ENGLISH GRAY (*Acer pseudoplatanus*)—Sycamore

The name "Sycamore" is normally applied to this species in its country of origin, England. As noted by its botanical name, *Acer*, it is a true maple, and it is a great deal like our Northern Hard Maple. *Pseudoplatanus* further indicates that it is a false *platanus*, which is the botanical name of plane-tree or sycamore.

Source: England
Color: Natural white. Called English white before dyeing. Usually dyed silver gray
Pattern: Both plain and figured
Characteristics: Same as Maple
Uses: Marquetry; inlay; paneling
Availability: Veneer (quartered, sliced) scarce. Lumber available
Price Range: Costly

IREME (*Terminalia ivorensis*)—African Teak, Black Afara, Emeri, Framerie, Idigbo, Iroko

In the European trade this is a very valuable timber of a light grayish-brown color. The grain is firm and hard and the wood machines well. It has been used for many years in England and France, and limited quantities have been brought into the United States.

Source: Africa, Gold Coast
Color: Pale yellow to light brown
Pattern: Faint ribbon stripe with intermediate grain and noticeable rays
Uses: Panels and cabinetwork
Availability: Plentiful as veneers
Price Range: Moderate

Gum, Red, figured (2 pieces, book-matched)

Gum, Sapwood (1 piece)

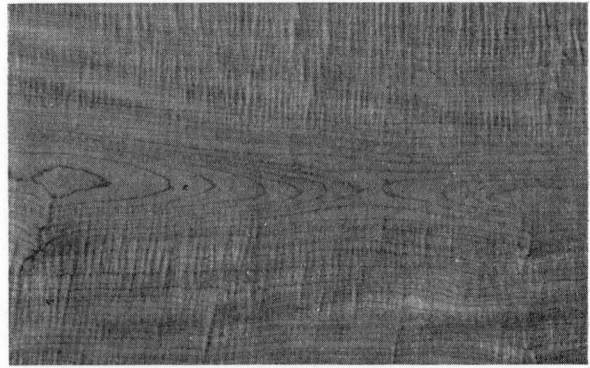

Harewood, English Gray, figured (1 piece)

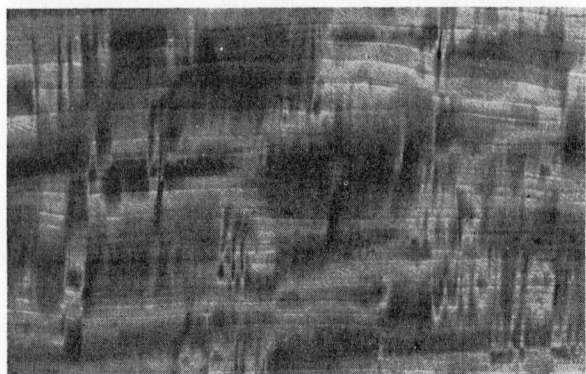

Ireme, mottled (1 piece)

LAUAN or PHILIPPINE HARDWOODS

The Philippine Islands are the source of a great variety of hardwoods only a few of which are imported into the United States. The greatest volume comes from a group sold commercially as "Philippine Mahogany," although it is not related to the true mahoganies. Several fine hardwoods from the Philippine Islands and that part of the world are known and marketed under their own names, such as Narra, Almon, Bella-Rosa, Sonora and Paldao. Those classified and sold as Philippine Mahogany are quite varied in color and texture. They include the softer species of *Shorea*, which are light-colored to reddish-brown in color, and the species of *Parashorea* and *Pentacme*. This group is divided into two classes, as follows: (1) Red Lauan *(Shorea negrosensis)*, Tanquile *(Shorea polysperma)* and Tiaong *(Shorea spp.)*; (2) Almon *(Shorea almon)*, White Lauan *(Pentacme contorta)*, Bagtikan *(Parashorea picata)* and Mayapis *(Shorea squamata)*. In general, these woods, as compared with the Tropical American and African Mahoganies, are more coarse-grained and stringy. They require a greater amount of sanding to produce a finishing surface and are much less stable under atmospheric (moisture) changes. Pictured here are the less common type of Red Lauan showing butterfly pattern and the run-of-mine type of Lauan that is reaching this country today, which has a mild ribbon stripe and is nearly all quartered.

LAUAN, RED *(Shorea negrosensis)*

Also called "Philippine Mahogany." Sold as Philippine Hardwoods.

Source: Philippine Islands
Color: Red to brown
Pattern: Ribbon stripe; interlocking grain
Characteristics: Coarse texture; large pores
Uses: Furniture; doors; cabinetry
Availability: Veneer (quartered, sliced, rotary) abundant. Lumber available
Price Range: Medium to inexpensive

LAUAN, WHITE *(Pentacome contorta)*

Same as above but for color.

NARRA *(Pterocarpus indicus, Pterocarpus echinatus)*—Angsena, Sena

Although this wood is another one of the Philippine Hardwoods, it has properties distinctly superior to those described above.

Source: Dutch East Indies, Philippines
Color: Rose to deep red. Some are golden yellow
Pattern: Distinct grain character; some ripple
Characteristics: Heavy and hard; not strong; durable
Uses: High-grade furniture; interior finish of ships and vehicles
Availability: Veneer (quartered) rare
Price Range: Costly

MAKORI *(Mimusops heckelii)*—African "Cherry," Baku, Cherry "Mahogany," Makore

Source: African Gold Coast, Nigeria
Color: Pinkish-brown to blood red or red-brown
Pattern: Somewhat similar to a close-grained Mahogany, but with dark red growth lines and smaller pores, as found in Cherry. Some logs are straight-grained and show figure like African Mahogany stripes; others have a striking, checkered figure sometimes streaked with darker color
Characteristics: Finer textured than true mahoganies, and denser, harder and heavier; tough; stiff; large sizes; strong; gummy and lustrous; glues well; works fairly easily
Uses: Furniture and cabinetry
Availability: Veneer (quartered, sliced) plentiful
Price Range: Medium

Lauan, Red, flat cut (2 pieces, book-matched)

Lauan, White (2 pieces, slip-matched)

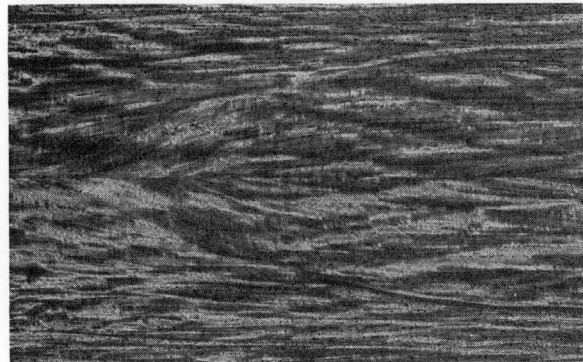

Narra, semi-figured (2 pieces, book-matched)

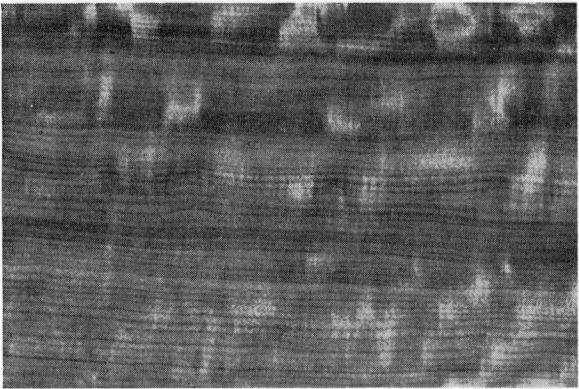

Makori, quartered, mottled (1 piece)

LACEWOOD (*Cardwellia sublimis*)—Australian Silky Oak, Queensland Silky Oak, Selano, Silky Oak.

Source: Queensland, Australia

Color: Light pink with silvery sheen

Pattern: Small flaky grain due to large rays

Characteristics: Very attractive over-all pattern when used on small areas

Uses: Often as borders and limited, highly figured areas of fine furniture

Availability: Veneer (quartered) scarce

Price Range: Costly

LAUREL, EAST INDIAN (*Terminalia tomentosa*)—East Indian Walnut
This species is closely related to Ireme (note botanical name). However, the Laurel principally imported into this country is a very important wood growing throughout India and Burma. It varies widely in color from a yellowish-brown through all stages to a rich, warm brown with dark streaks, handsomely marked, and many types of figure. Another type of Laurel produced in the United States, which is an entirely different species known as California Laurel or Oregon Myrtle, is usually produced in burl or clustered figure. This should not be confused with the Laurel from the Far East (*Terminalia*).

Source: India and Burma

Color: Gray or brown with black lines

Pattern: Striped; occasional block-mottle or fiddleback figure; indistinct rays

Characteristics: Coarse-grained; hard and brittle; pores not numerous

Uses: Fine cabinetry

Availability: Veneer (quartered) scarce. Lumber scarce

Price Range: Costly

LIMBA (*Terminalia superba*) — "Korina," Afara, Frake, Offram
Another *Terminalia* which has been widely publicized under the trade-name of "Korina." In recent years this species has become one of the most popular naturally blond woods brought into this country. It has an especial appeal for architectural use in view of the fact that it is available in large sizes, as is Mahogany, and as both veneers (plywood) and lumber.

Source: West Africa

Color: Pale yellow to light brown

Pattern: Rays fine and irregular; pores scarce, but large enough to give an interesting grain character

Characteristics: Medium texture and hardness; a naturally blond wood of good working properties

Uses: Architectural paneling and woodwork; contemporary furniture

Availability: Veneer (quartered, sliced) plentiful. Lumber available

Price Range: Medium

MYRTLE (*Umbellularia californica*)—Acacia Burl, Baytree, California Laurel, Oregon Myrtle, Pepperwood (at times called Acacia but no relation)

Source: West Coast of United States, especially Southern Oregon and Northern California

Color: Golden-brown and yellowish-green. Wide range from light to dark

Pattern: Mixture of plain wood, mottle, cluster, blistered, stump and burl figure with a scattering of dark purple blotches

Characteristics: Hard, strong pores the size and distribution of Walnut; a magnificent, highly figured veneer

Uses: Decorative panels for architectural interiors, store fixtures and furniture; novelties; many fine turnings, trays and carvings

Availability: Veneers (half-round), lengths usually under 5 ft although up to 8 ft, rare to scarce. Lumber scarce

Price Range: Costly

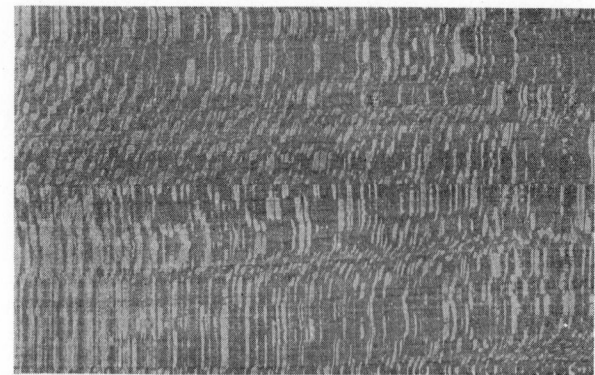

Lacewood, quartered (one piece)

Laurel, East Indian, quartered (2 pieces, book-matched)

Limba ("Korina"), quartered (one piece)

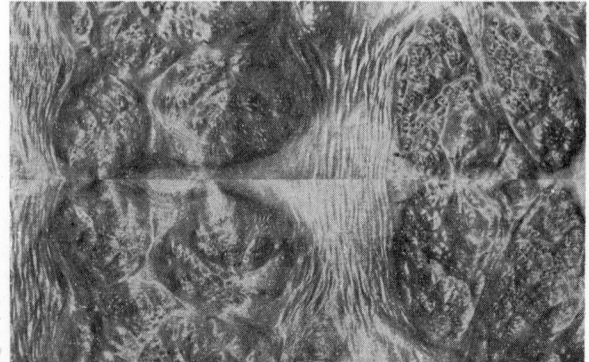

Myrtle Cluster, rotary (2 pieces, book-matched)

OAK, ENGLISH BROWN (*Quercus robur, L. Q.; Quercus sessiliflora, Salisb.*)—European Oak, Pollard Oak

Source: England

Color: Light tan to deep brown

Pattern: Black spots, sometimes creating an effect much like tortoise shell

Characteristics: Noticeable figure and grain character; especially pronounced flakes due to the medullary rays showing on the quartered surface

Uses: Architectural woodwork; some fine furniture

Availability: Veneer (quartered, sliced) scarce. Lumber scarce

Price Range: Costly

Oak, English Brown, sliced (2 pieces, book-matched)

PALDAO (*Dracontomelum dao*)—Dao

Source: Philippines, Indo-China and East Indies

Color: Gray to reddish brown

Pattern: Varied grain effects usually with irregular stripes, some occasionally very dark; occasional crotch or swirl

Characteristics: Pores are large, partially plugged; fairly hard; an exotic appearing wood

Uses: Architectural woodwork and furniture

Availability: Veneer (quartered, half-round) plentiful. Lumber available

Price Range: Medium

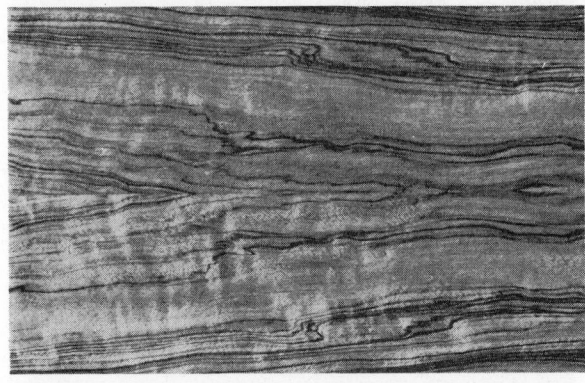

Paldao, quartered (2 pieces, book-matched)

PRIMA VERA (*Cybistax Donnell-smithii*)—Durango, Palo Blanco, San Juan (sometimes misnamed "White Mahogany")

Source: From Central Mexico, south through Guatemala and Honduras into Salvador (other species of *Tabebuia* found in northern South America)

Color: Yellow-white to yellow-brown

Pattern: Straight grain. Although often plain, it usually shows large mottle or diagonal block figure

Characteristics: Odorless and tasteless; medium to coarse textured; straight to somewhat striped grained; moderately light in weight

Uses: A fine, general-use cabinetwood

Availability: Veneer (quartered, sliced) scarce. Lumber available

Price Range: Costly

SATINWOOD

There are several somewhat similar woods imported under this name. The two most important are:

Prima Vera, quartered (2 pieces, book-matched)

SATINWOOD, CEYLON (*Chloroxylon swietenia, D.C.*)—East Indian Satinwood

Source: Ceylon and southern India

Color: Pale gold

Pattern: Ripples, straight stripes; bee's wing mottled

Characteristics: Hard; dense; interlocking grain; inclined to check

Uses: Furniture

Availability: Veneer (quartered, sliced, half-round) rare. Lumber rare

Price Range: Costly

SATINWOOD, WEST INDIAN (*Zanthoxylum flavum, Vahl.*)—San Domingan Satinwood

Source: Puerto Rico, British Honduras

Color: Creamy golden yellow

Pattern: Wavy grain

Characteristics: Fine grained; hard and quite heavy; works well with most tools

Uses: Furniture; marquetry; inlaying; turnery

Availability: Veneer (sliced) scarce. Lumber available

Price Range: Costly

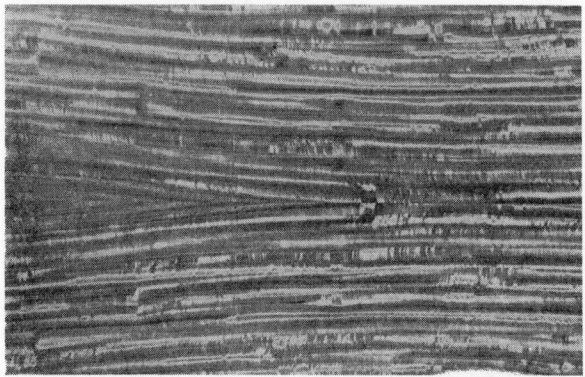

Satinwood, Ceylon, figured quartered (2 pieces, book-matched)

SAPELE (*Entandrophragma cylindricum*)—Aboudikrou, Sipo, Tiama

Source: African Ivory Coast, Nigeria

Color: Dark red-brown

Pattern: Stripe and bee's wing

Characteristics: Considerable variation in grain; light portions of stripes lustrous; works fairly well with hand and machine tools; tough; harder and heavier than African Mahogany

Uses: Veneers for furniture; cabinetwork; interior decoration

Availability: Veneer (quartered) plentiful. Lumber available

Price Range: Medium

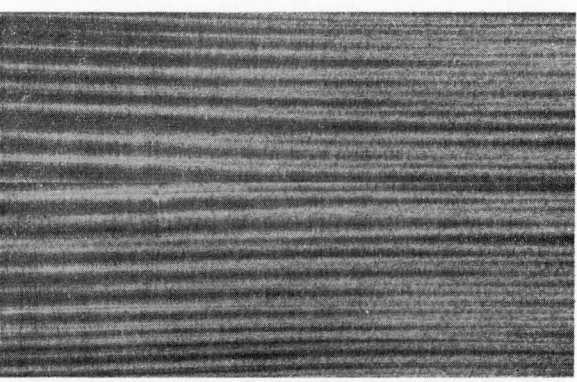
Sapele, quartered (2 pieces, book-matched)

TEAK (*Tectona grandis*)—Burma Teak, Rangoon Teak

Source: Burma, Java, East India, French Indo-China

Color: Tawny yellow to dark brown, often with lighter streaks, not black as many think

Pattern: A great deal like Walnut, sometimes mottled and fiddle-back

Characteristics: Strong; tough; oily. Like Walnut, except for oiliness, and is one of the finest cabinetwoods

Uses: Paneling; furniture; floors; ship decking

Availability: Veneer (quartered, sliced) plentiful. Lumber available

Price Range: Costly

Teak, flat cut, semi-figured (one piece)

TIGERWOOD (*Lovoa klaineana*)—Congowood (often misnamed African "Walnut," Benin Walnut and Nigerian Golden "Walnut")

Source: West Africa

Color: Gray-brown to gold with black streaks

Pattern: Pronounced ribbon stripe

Characteristics: Easily worked; transverse grain shows irregularly sized, scattered pores

Uses: Furniture; paneling

Availability: Veneer (quartered) plentiful. Lumber available

Price Range: Medium

Tigerwood, quartered (4 pieces, book-matched)

YEW

Two species of genuine Yew are available:

YEW, AMERICAN (*Taxus spp.*)—Florida, Pacific or Western Yew

Source: Pacific Coast and Southwestern Canada

Color: Reddish-brown

Pattern: Close-grained; often highly grain figured

Characteristics: Heavy; hard; available in very small sizes

Uses: Veneers—decorative areas of fine furniture

Availability: Rare as both veneers and lumber

Price Range: Costly

YEW, ENGLISH (*Taxus, baccata*)

Source: England

Color: Pale red, somewhat like Cherrywood or Pencil Cedar

Pattern: Smooth, lustrous grain. Wild grain gives much character

Characteristics: Strong; elastic

Availability: In small sizes, individual pieces often being only 4 to 6 in. wide and 2 to 6 ft long

Price Range: Costly

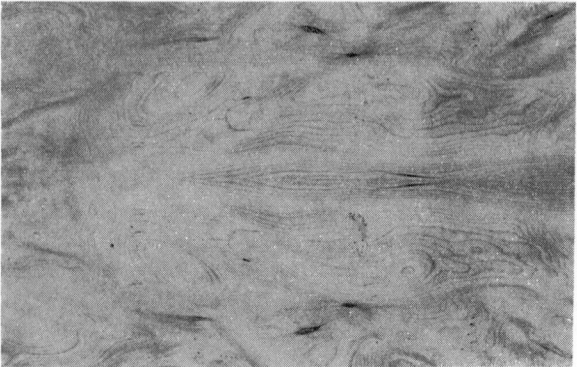
Yew, sliced (2 pieces, book-matched)

To conclude this series of better than fifty of the most interesting fine hardwoods that are both suitable and available for architectural interiors and fine furnishings, we present twelve fine hardwoods from Almon to Zebrawood, with a wide range of color and character. Actually, there are 99,000 different hardwoods in the world, of which some 200 are made available by the hardwood industry to American and Canadian specifiers and users. Of that 200, many are available for but limited use, due to quantity, size, cost, etc. In this Time-Saver Standards series we have presented "those most likely to succeed" along with the old reliables which are again being presented as "something new" when finished imaginatively.

ALMON (*Shorea almon*)

This wood is not to be confused with almond (*Prunus communis*), which is one of the rare nut woods.

Source: Philippine Islands
Color: Light cream or straw
Pattern: Quartered or rotary figure
Characteristics: Light; works well although stringy; finishes well; coarse-textured; cross-grained; moderately hard
Availability: Veneer (quartered, rotary) plentiful. Lumber available
Uses: Occasionally for cabinetry
Price Range: Inexpensive

CAPOMO (*Brosium Alicastrum*) — Breadnut, Capone, Laredo Ogechi, Ojoche, Ramon

Source: Central America
Color: Yellowish sapwood; reddish heartwood
Pattern: Cross ripple, lustrous. May be had in plain as well as figured types (such as is pictured here)
Characteristics: Hard
Uses: Furniture
Availability: Veneer (quartered) plentiful
Price Range: Medium

CHEN CHEN (*Antiaris africana*) — Ako, Quen Quen

Source: African Gold Coast to Cameroons
Color: White to yellow gray
Pattern: Stripe
Characteristics: Soft; works well; light in weight
Uses: Furniture; wall paneling
Availability: Not much Chen Chen lumber is used in America, nor is it widely used as veneers. However, it is available in good sizes and in clear grades of the prominent lustrous stripes
Price Range: Low to medium

CHERRY, BLACK (*Prunus serotina*) — Rum Cherry, Wild Black Cherry

Although this species has been reviewed previously (Sheet 3), only plain sliced cherry of the type used in considerable volume by the furniture industry was pictured. The photograph of figured sliced Cherry shown here illustrates the architectural type or those types which, as a result of the current popularity of Cherry for transitional and modern furniture, make available at below value prices unusually attractive forms of a well-known cabinetwood.

Source: Maine to Dakotas and Appalachians; production largely Pennsylvania to West Virginia
Color: Light reddish-brown
Pattern: Straight-grained; satiny; some figured. Small gum pockets are normal markings
Characteristics: Light; strong; rather hard; fine-grained
Uses: Fine furniture, woodwork and engraver's blocks
Availability: Veneer (quartered, sliced, half-round) plentiful. Lumber plentiful
Price Range: Medium

Almon, quartered (2 pieces, book-matched)

Capomo, figured (3 pieces, book-matched)

Chen Chen, sliced (2 pieces, book-matched)

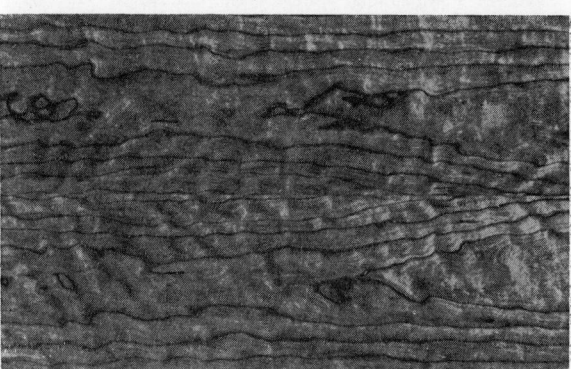

Cherry, figured (2 pieces, book-matched)

EBONY

Three types have come into the American market:

EBONY, BLACK (*Diospyros tomentosa*; also *Diospyros ebenum* and *Diospyros assimilis*)
Source: Northern India, Himalaya
Color: Black
Pattern: Rays very fine, joined at right angles by similar fine light-colored bars, forming a minute pattern
Characteristics: Exceedingly minute pores somewhat scarce; hard; dense and of great weight
Uses: Inlays and marquetry; handles
Availability: Scarce as veneer or lumber
Price Range: High

EBONY, GABOON (*Diospyros dendo*) — Black Ebony, Calabar, Gabun, Lagos
Source: Africa
Color: Very deep black
Pattern: Very indistinct grain
Characteristics: Hard
Uses: Turnery; inlaid work; fancy goods
Availability: Rare
Price Range: Costly

EBONY, MACASSAR (*Diospyros melanoxylon*) — Marblewood
Source: East Indies
Color: Dark brown to black; large proportion of logs streaked with yellow or yellowish-brown
Pattern: Rays fine and very indistinct; grain markings largely from brown streaks on black background
Characteristics: Dense, close grain
Uses: Ornamental work, such as brush backs and handles
Availability: Veneer (quartered, sliced) scarce. Lumber rare
Price Range: Costly

HACKBERRY (*Celtis occidentalis*) — Sugarberry
Source: New England to Virginia and west through Iowa, Missouri and Kansas
Color: Yellowish
Pattern: Rather distinct; fine sparkle from small rays when quartered
Characteristics: Heavy; moderately hard; not strong; coarse-grained
Uses: Furniture
Availability: Veneer (quartered, slices, half-round, rotary) plentiful. Lumber available
Price Range: Inexpensive to medium

KOA (*Acacia Koa*)
Source: Hawaii
Color: Golden brown with dark streaks
Pattern: Brown streaks, lustrous sheen. Occasionally develops a perfect fiddleback figure or other cross figure
Characteristics: Walnut-like texture, but not as hard
Uses: Fine furniture
Availability: Veneer (quartered, sliced) scarce. Lumber available
Price Range: Costly

REDWOOD, BURL (*Sequoia sempervirens*) — Big Tree
Source: California — northern coastal region
Color: Pink to deep red heartwood
Pattern: Clusters of eyes (burls)
Characteristics: Soft; light; close-grained; heartwood exceptionally durable; easily worked; except somewhat splintery
Uses: Decorative areas of cabinetry
Availability: Veneer (half-round) scarce. Lumber abundant
Price Range: Costly as burl veneers

Ebony, Macassar (4 pieces, book-matched)

Hackberry, rotary (one piece)

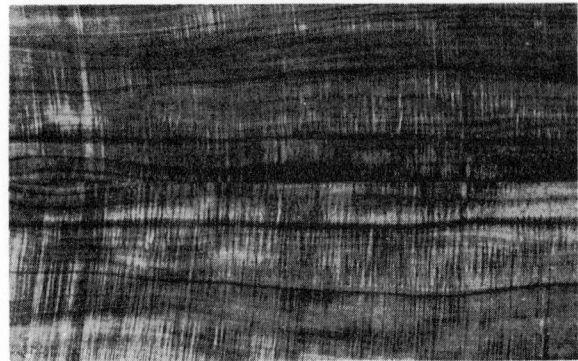
Koa, figured (2 pieces, book-matched)

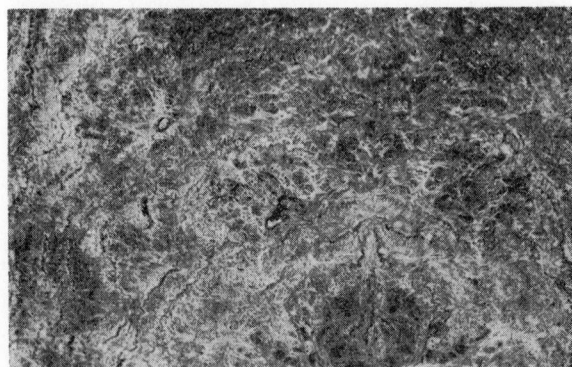
Redwood, burl (2 pieces, book-matched)

ROSEWOOD

Many woods are produced under the name of "Rosewood" in various parts of the world. The more important are these:

ROSEWOOD, BRAZILIAN (*Dalbergia nigra*) — Jacaranda, Rio Rosewood, Bahia Rosewood

Source: Brazil

Color: Various shades of dark brown — chocolate to violet; conspicuous black streaks

Pattern: Streaks of dark brown or black pigment lines

Characteristics: Rather large pores exceedingly irregular both in size and position

Uses: Limited use for walls and furniture

Availability: Veneer (quartered, sliced, half-round, rotary) scarce. Lumber available

Price Range: Costly

Rosewood, Brazilian (one piece)

ROSEWOOD, EAST INDIAN (*Dalbergia latifolia*) — Bombay Rosewood, Blackwood locally, Malobar

Source: Southern India and Ceylon

Color: Dark purple to ebony; streaks of red or yellow

Pattern: Small to medium pores in wavy lines; exceedingly fine rays; occasionally crotches and swirls

Characteristics: Stands up exceptionally well under all conditions; texture is close, firm and hard; requires rather a sharp tool to secure a smooth surface; very moderate shrinkage

Uses: Patternmaking (locally); fine furniture

Availability: Veneer (quartered, sliced, half-round) scarce

Price Range: Costly

Rosewood, East Indian, quartered (2 pieces, book-matched)

ROSEWOOD, MADAGASCAR (*Dalbergia Greveana*) — Madagascar Pilisander, French Rosewood

Source: Madagascar

Color: Dark to light rose-pink

Pattern: Pronounced lines of darker red shades

Characteristics: Very hard

Uses: Limited use for walls and furniture

Availability: Veneer scarce

Price Range: Costly

ROSEWOOD, MEXICAN (probably *Dalbergia Stevensonii*. However, there are about fifteen different species of Rosewood [*Dalbergia*] that produce good quality timber out of 250 species of trees and shrubs in this group)

Yellowpoplar, sliced (2 pieces, book-matched)

YELLOWPOPLAR (*Liriodendron tulipifera*) — Tuliptree, Whitewood

Source: New England to Michigan, Appalachians to Gulf

Color: Canary color, sometimes with slightly greenish cast and occasionally with rather dark streaks

Pattern: Even texture; straight grain

Characteristics: Light to medium weight; strong; soft; easily worked

Uses: As veneers, widely used for cross-banding and backs of plywood. As lumber, interior finish or fixtures (usually to be painted)

Availability: Veneer (quartered, sliced, half-round, rotary, occasionally burls) abundant. Lumber available

Price Range: Inexpensive

ZEBRAWOOD (*Microberlinia brazzavillanensia* or *Brachy-stegia*) — Zebrano, Zingana

Source: African Cameroon, Gaboon, West Africa

Color: Straw, dark brown; exceptionally pronounced fine stripes

Pattern: Striped; dark brown stripes; lustrous surface

Characteristics: Heavy; hard; with somewhat coarse texture

Uses: As veneer, inlays

Availability: Veneer (quartered) rare to available

Price Range: Costly

Zebrawood, quartered (one piece)

PURPOSE

Information on this sheet can be used as a general guide in the selection of wood, character of workmanship and types of joints for the detailing and specification of cabinet work. Drawings show only typical conditions and therefore cover a wide range of applications. They are intended to indicate principles of good joining rather than solutions to specific problems.

SELECTION OF WOOD

For painted surfaces wood must be fine grained, free from knots, sap or pitch and easy to work, with a surface that will not raise. Eastern white pine is ideal. Due to its scarcity, other woods are usually employed. Whitewood, redwood, and California, Idaho and Ponderosa pine are satisfactory materials. Basswood, poplar, sugar pine and gum are less satisfactory. The pines are often knotty but are used for paneling. Birch is harder and is adaptable to more expensive work containing carvings and mouldings.

For natural finishes woods with a decorative grain, as oak, walnut, mahogany and numerous imported woods, are most adaptable. These can be stained, oiled, varnished or waxed. So can gum, redwood, and white, Idaho or Ponderosa pine.

Seasoning is a requisite for cabinet work. All woods should be thoroughly kiln-dried and cabinet work should never be installed until all moisture within the building has been dissipated and plaster is bone-dry.

WORKMANSHIP

Differences between various classes of woodwork lie entirely in the workmanship; that is, in the character of the joining and finish. Types may be divided as follows:

Carpentry is least expensive, being done entirely on the job by more or less skilled mechanics.

Millwork is to some extent prefabricated. Mouldings, certain types of joints, and all exposed surfaces are run through machines and may or may not be assembled and machine-sanded before delivery, depending on the grade of work. Work must usually be scraped and sanded on the job. Joints are almost always assembled with finishing nails or screws and are of simplest type, avoiding undercuts, etc., requiring multiple machining or expensive workmanship.

Cabinet Work ("Joinery"), the most expensive class of architectural woodwork, is almost always shop-assembled, scraped and sanded. Joints must be absolutely accurate, depend principally on glue for strength, and consequently require expert craftsmen and expensive machinery. Work should be hand sanded after installation.

Furniture. A distinct class of work not usually related to architectural construction. Some methods, types of joints, etc., are adaptable to cabinet work.

All four classes overlap to some extent. Millwork and cabinet work are particularly considered here. In these classes, joints should be inconspicuous, of a type to control or eliminate shrinkage, and should conceal end wood unless part of the design. Surfaces and profiles should be clean cut and free from defects. Means of installation should be concealed.

CHARACTERISTICS OF JOINTS

Joints may be divided into four general types: *Butted, Shiplapped, Tongued-and-grooved,* and *Mitered.* Used in their simple basic form, none is satisfactory for cabinet work except the tongued-and-grooved type in certain instances. However, when variously combined or when reinforced with gluing and dowels or splines, satisfactory joints can be developed.

Butt joint. A simple but weak joint that opens easily and may show end wood when used at angles. Strength and range of use is greatly increased by use of the *mortise and tenon* and *dowels* and even more when a *straight spline* is included. Use of a glued *butterfly spline* with a butt joint produces an extremely strong joint. These variations are widely used to produce large flush surfaces of solid wood or backing for veneers.

Shiplap joint. Stronger than a butt joint but subject to opening from shrinkage. Rarely used in a simple form in cabinet work except for door rebates. It is often moulded to conceal shrinkage in quirks or combined as a *miter and shoulder* for corners. Another variation is the *shoulder joint.*

Tongue-and-groove joint. A strong joint, widely used for re-entrant angles. Effect of wood shrinkage is concealed when

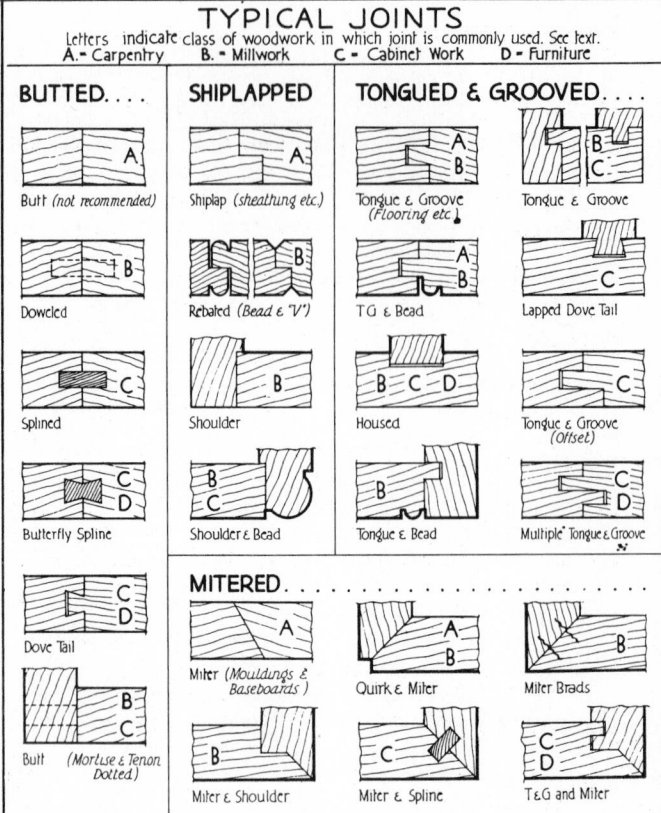

TYPICAL JOINTS

Letters indicate class of woodwork in which joint is commonly used. See text.
A.- Carpentry   B.- Millwork   C.- Cabinet Work   D.- Furniture

BUTTED....
- Butt (not recommended) — A
- Dowelled — B
- Splined — C
- Butterfly Spline — C D
- Dove Tail — C D
- Butt (Mortise & Tenon Dotted) — B C

SHIPLAPPED
- Shiplap (sheathing etc.) — A
- Rebated (Bead & 'V') — B
- Shoulder — B
- Shoulder & Bead — B C D

TONGUED & GROOVED....
- Tongue & Groove (Flooring etc.) — A B
- T G & Bead — A B
- Housed — B C D
- Tongue & Bead — B C D
- Tongue & Groove — B C
- Lapped Dove Tail — C
- Tongue & Groove (Offset) — C
- Multiple Tongue & Groove — C D

MITERED.........
- Miter (Mouldings & Baseboards) — A
- Miter & Shoulder — B
- Quirk & Miter — A B
- Miter & Spline — C
- Miter Brads — A B
- T & G and Miter — C D

the joint is beaded or otherwise moulded. In expensive cabinet work glued *dovetail* and *multiple tongue-and-groove* are used.

Miter joints are weak and difficult to fit if used alone. Joints with *miter brads* are sufficiently strong for short lengths. Joints made in combination with other forms, as a *tongue-and-groove miter,* are tight and sturdy.

USE OF JOINTS

Use of certain types of joints depends to a large degree upon the type of work and workmanship involved. The following notes indicate use of joints in various categories, but cannot be regarded as an inclusive check list.

For panels, shelving, etc. or wherever the end of one piece butts against the face of another; *housed joint,* with or without cover mould, or some type of *tongue-and-groove* joint. Omit glue to avoid splitting due to swelling or shrinkage.

For joining stiles and rails: *mortise and tenon,* glued in better work. Dowels may be used or hardwood wedges may be driven and glued into ends of tenons in high grade work.

For re-entrant corners: *shoulder joints* for inexpensive work. *Tongue-and-groove* is sturdier. Both should be glued, are often screwed together and may be glued to a rough frame.

For external corners: simple *miter* and *quirk and miter* both lack strength. *Miter brads* are practical only for short lengths. *Miter and shoulder* glued and face-screwed or nailed is satisfactory (generally "millwork"). *Miter and spline* is preferable. In high grade work exterior corners are reinforced by gluing to a corner post or short lengths of blocking.

Glued joints: when screws, nails, etc., can not be used, or when fine work is to be veneered, strength of the joint depends on accuracy of milling and total glue surface. Glue surface may be tremendously increased by using multiple or offset tongues and grooves, by forming miter cuts into waves, multiple shoulders, tongues and grooves, etc. Such work is cabinet work. If done by a reliable cabinet maker, a guarantee should be obtained and joint detail and composition of glue left to him.

Mouldings should be applied in continuous lengths if possible. Use simple miter for necessary joints, cope re-entrant angles unless excessively undercut, miter external corners.

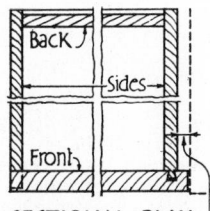

SECTIONAL PLAN

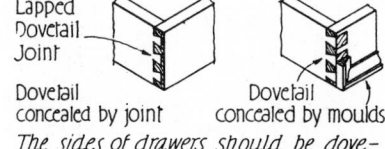

Lapped Dovetail Joint

Dovetail concealed by joint

Dovetail concealed by moulds

The sides of drawers should be dovetailed to fronts. Usual methods shown

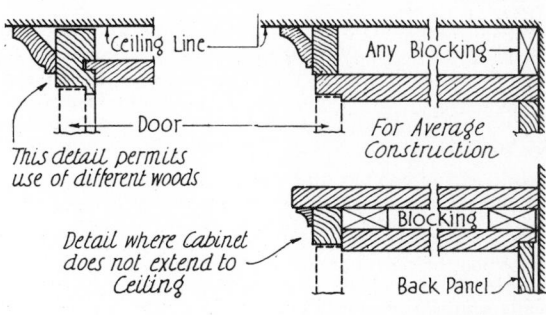

Ceiling Line — Any Blocking

This detail permits use of different woods

For Average Construction

Blocking

Detail where Cabinet does not extend to Ceiling

Back Panel

CORNICE

When any type of patented drawer slide is used, consult man'f's catalogue for this dimension. The lapped front conceals slide

Dust-Panels & top face of drawer Runners should be flush

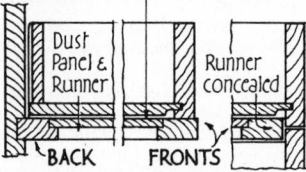

Dust Panel & Runner — Runner concealed

BACK **FRONTS**

Bottom rabeted to front and sides; secured to front only.

Runners & Guides preferably hardwood; Panels either veneer or solid

DRAWERS

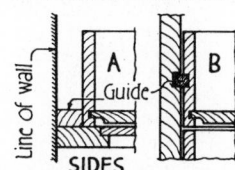

1. Bottomless — For towels, etc.
2. Flush Lattice Bottom — Permits air circulation for linens, etc.

Line of wall

A | B

Guide

SIDES

A Guide at side of drawer, fastened to Drawer Runner
B Guide (Hardwood) rabeted into side of Drawer.

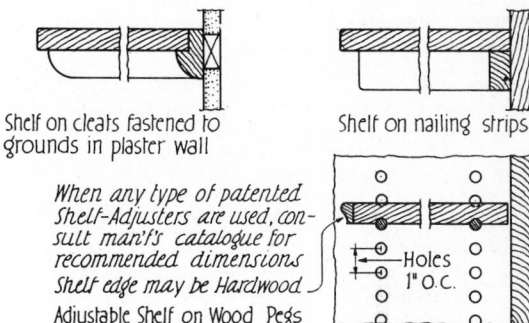

Shelf on cleats fastened to grounds in plaster wall

Shelf on nailing strips

When any type of patented Shelf-Adjusters are used, consult man'f's catalogue for recommended dimensions
Shelf edge may be Hardwood

Holes 1" O.C.

Adjustable Shelf on Wood Pegs

SHELVES

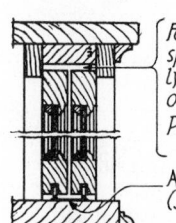

For Sliding Doors this space should be slightly greater than depth of wheel grooves to permit the removal of doors

Any suitable type track (See man'f's catalogue)

SLIDING DOORS
(Removable)

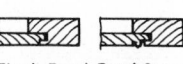

Flush Front Panel Doors

Felt Backing
Plate Glass Mirror
Removable Mouldings

DOOR WITH MIRROR

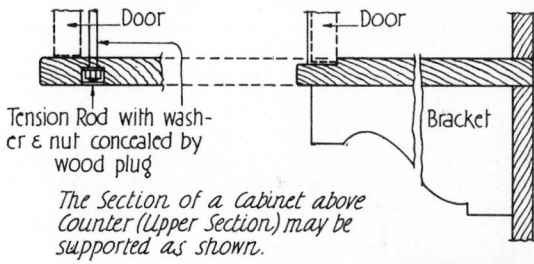

Door

Door

Tension Rod with washer & nut concealed by wood plug

Bracket

The Section of a Cabinet above Counter (Upper Section) may be supported as shown.

SUPPORTS

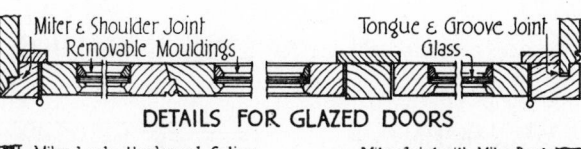

Miter & Shoulder Joint
Removable Mouldings

Tongue & Groove Joint
Glass

DETAILS FOR GLAZED DOORS

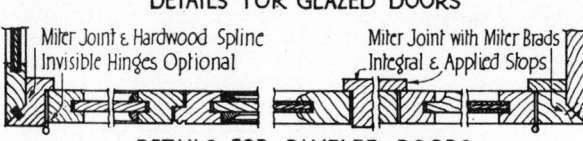

Miter Joint & Hardwood Spline
Invisible Hinges Optional

Miter Joint with Miter Brads
Integral & Applied Stops

DETAILS FOR PANELED DOORS
(Panels may be either plain or ply-wood)

DOORS

1. With drawer below
2. With moulding
3. With Backboard
4. Backboard with Cove Corner

Ground

Door
Drawer

1 **2** **3** **4**

COUNTERS

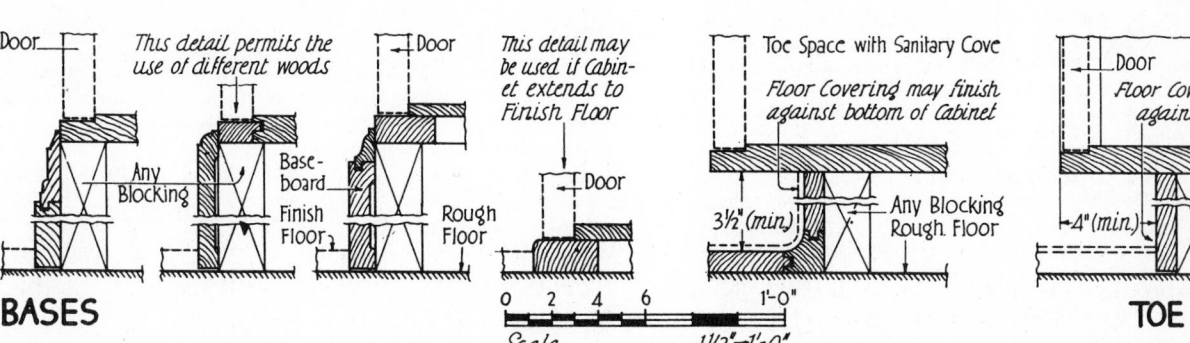

Door

This detail permits the use of different woods

Door

This detail may be used if Cabinet extends to Finish Floor

Any Blocking

Base-board
Finish Floor

Rough Floor

Door

Toe Space with Sanitary Cove

Floor Covering may finish against bottom of Cabinet

3½" (min.)

Any Blocking
Rough Floor

BASES

0 2 4 6   1'-0"
Scale
1½" = 1'-0"

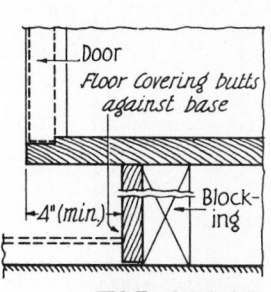

Door

Floor Covering butts against base

4" (min.)

Block-ing

TOE SPACE

PURPOSE

Information on this sheet outlines methods of assembly and installation of common cabinet work. Solutions of typical problems are presented without attempting to detail specific cabinets.

ASSEMBLY

High grade cabinet and veneered work is assembled as far as possible at the shop. Joints are glued and blocked, and sometimes secured with finishing nails or screws. Carpentry and millwork are generally put together with finishing nails if of soft wood, or with screws if of hardwood. Hardwood should be drilled to prevent splitting before using nails or screws, and heads should be countersunk and concealed by cover moulds, moulding quirks, or putty, plastic wood or other filler, colored to match the finish. No nails, screws or joints should be visible unless they are intentionally incorporated in design.

Shrinkage and warping effects can be largely eliminated by proper detailing and construction. *Wide flat surfaces* (solid or veneered) should be made up of several narrow strips glued and doweled, splined, or dovetailed together. Cleats may also be screwed or keyed to backs of wide surfaces. *Joints in corners, sheathing, etc.* should be concealed within quirks of moulds (as in moulded tongue-and-groove) or return faces (shoulder joints). *Panels* should be rigidly secured on one side only, and are often left entirely loose. Housed joints, not glued, permit panels to expand and contract without splitting.

Large moulded surfaces (such as cornices or mantels) should always be shop-assembled and delivered with scribe-moulds (see "Scribing" below) loosely tacked to assembled units.

INSTALLATION

All grades of woodwork should be preservative treated or back painted before erection, preferably before delivery to the job. Satisfactory priming coats are aluminum paint or white lead in linseed oil, thinned with turpentine or mineral spirits.

Preparation. On frame walls plaster may be limited to one or two coats, may be recessed between studs or may be omitted. In the latter case, building paper should be used between woodwork and studs. On masonry, plaster may consist of one or two coats or may be omitted. Masonry surfaces, particularly exterior walls, should be waterproofed or woodwork should be protected by a layer of waterproof paper and should always be furred out. When finish of the interior of cabinets is plaster, either plain or canvas covered, the final coat of plaster is applied after erection of cabinet.

Grounds of soft wood for attaching cabinet work must be accurately located, are secured directly to framing members or furring, and must be concealed.

Blocking of rough lumber should be erected for supporting raised floors and large or heavy cabinet work, if it can be concealed. Blocking must be accurately placed and secured with nails.

Shimming. Minor irregularities in blocking, furring, or placement of studs may be corrected by using shims (wedge shaped pieces of wood, often shingles) to bring completed work to plumb and level lines. Shimming should be concealed.

Scribing is the practice of fitting edges of cabinet work accurately to all irregularities of finish plaster, masonry or other abutting surfaces. Wood mouldings, panel frames or cabinet returns to be scribed should be provided with a beveled edge.

Prefabricated woodwork is generally delivered knocked down for assembly on the job and is erected similarly to custom made work. Consult manufacturers' data.

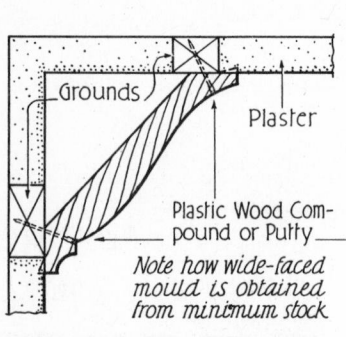

Note how wide-faced mould is obtained from minimum stock

NAILING TO GROUNDS

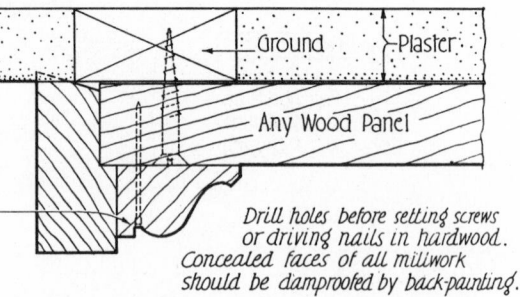

Drill holes before setting screws or driving nails in hardwood. Concealed faces of all millwork should be dampproofed by back-painting.

CONCEALING ATTACHMENT OF HARDWOODS

NAILING IN QUIRKS

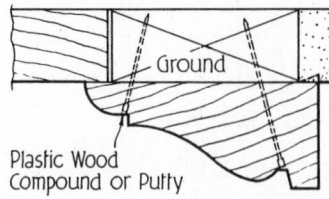

Nail to stiles or rails; avoiding panel

NAILING PANEL MOULD

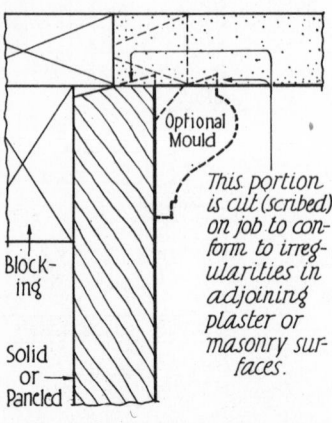

This portion is cut (scribed) on job to conform to irregularities in adjoining plaster or masonry surfaces

SCRIBING AGAINST PLASTER OR MASONRY

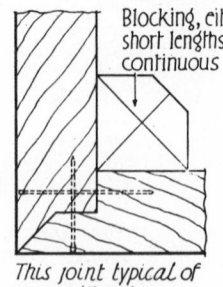

Blocking, either short lengths or continuous

This joint typical of millwork

Nailing & gluing a mortise and shoulder provides a strong, reasonably permanent joint

GLUING AND BLOCKING

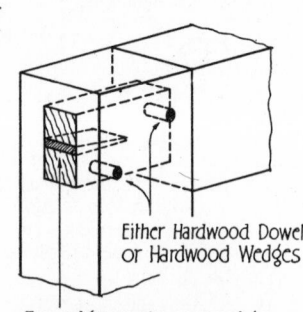

Either Hardwood Dowels or Hardwood Wedges

For wedges, make saw-cut in tenon before assembling. Holes for dowels may be offset to draw joint tight.

SECURING MORTISE & TENON

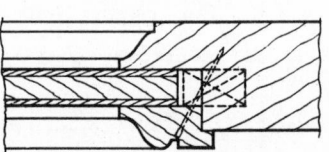 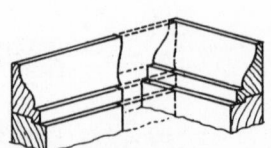

Cope by hand on job unless excessively undercut; if so, use miter. Flat members may be butted or Tongued-and-Grooved

COPING MOULDINGS RE-ENTRANT ANGLE

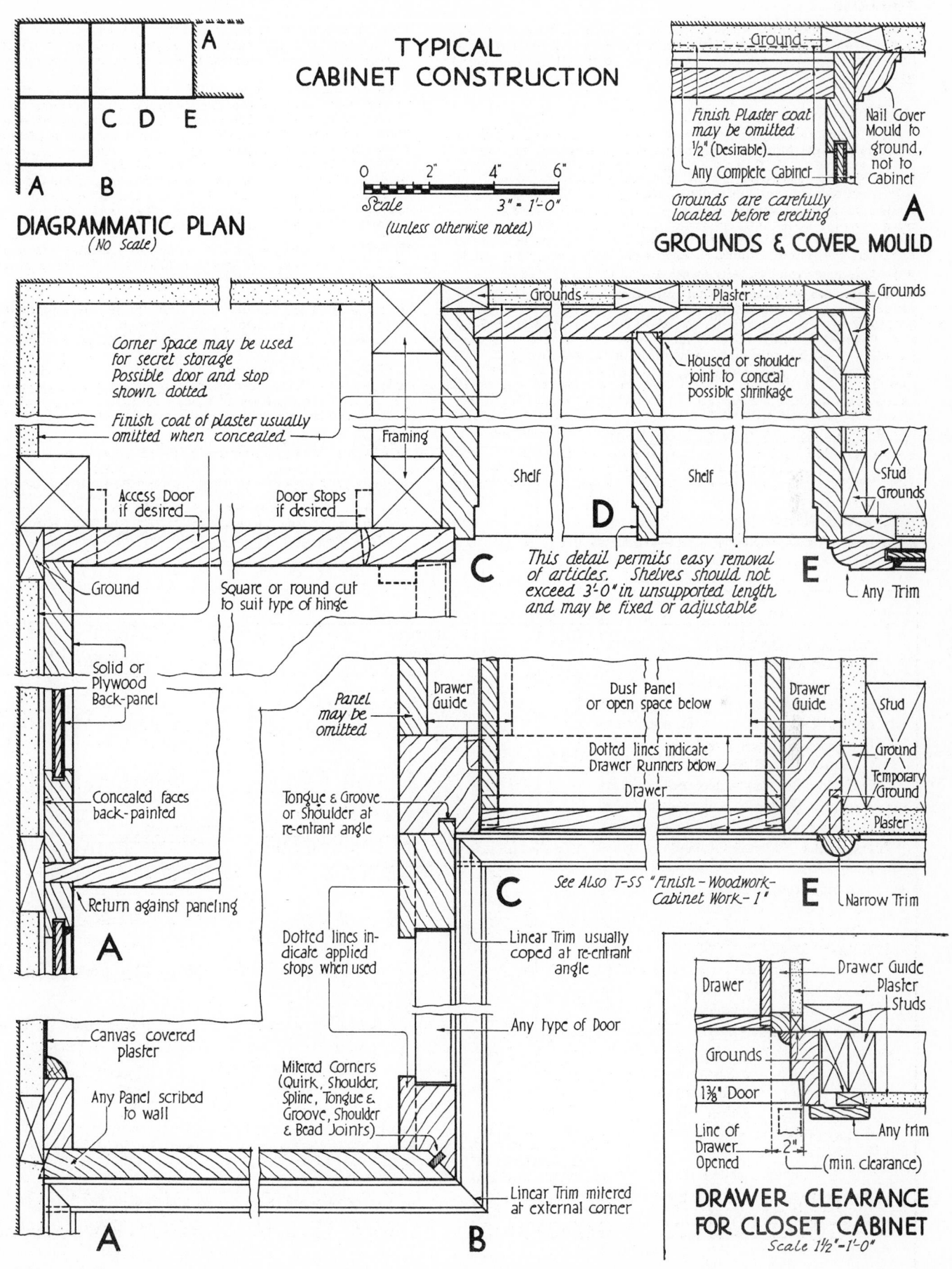

DIAGRAMMATIC PLAN
(No Scale)

TYPICAL
CABINET CONSTRUCTION

Scale 3" = 1'-0"
(unless otherwise noted)

Grounds are carefully
located before erecting

GROUNDS & COVER MOULD

Finish Plaster coat may be omitted ½" (Desirable)

Any Complete Cabinet

Nail Cover Mould to ground, not to Cabinet

Corner Space may be used for secret storage Possible door and stop shown dotted

Finish coat of plaster usually omitted when concealed

Framing

Access Door if desired

Door Stops if desired

Square or round cut to suit type of hinge

Ground

Housed or shoulder joint to conceal possible shrinkage

Shelf

Shelf

Stud Grounds

Any Trim

This detail permits easy removal of articles. Shelves should not exceed 3'-0" in unsupported length and may be fixed or adjustable

Solid or Plywood Back-panel

Concealed faces back-painted

Return against paneling

Panel may be omitted

Tongue & Groove or Shoulder at re-entrant angle

Drawer Guide

Dust Panel or open space below

Drawer Guide

Stud

Dotted lines indicate Drawer Runners below

Ground
Temporary Ground

Drawer

Plaster

See Also T-SS "Finish-Woodwork-Cabinet Work-1"

Narrow Trim

Dotted lines indicate applied stops when used

Linear Trim usually coped at re-entrant angle

Any type of Door

Canvas covered plaster

Any Panel scribed to wall

Mitered Corners (Quirk, Shoulder, Spline, Tongue & Groove, Shoulder & Bead Joints)

Linear Trim mitered at external corner

Drawer

Drawer Guide
Plaster
Studs

Grounds

1⅜" Door

Line of Drawer Opened

Any trim

2" (min. clearance)

DRAWER CLEARANCE
FOR CLOSET CABINET
Scale 1½"-1'-0"

Based on information from Nuroco Woodwork, New Rochelle, N.Y.

THE amount of woodwork and cabinet-work used in contemporary building, particularly residences, has increased by such leaps and bounds that it often constitutes one of the largest dollar outlays in a new house. A knowledge of standard modern woodworking practices, therefore, should not only stimulate design, but should be a means of exploiting valuable technical economies and eliciting fair and comparable estimates from woodworking contractors.

WOODWORK TRENDS

Four principal factors account for the great increase in residential woodwork. They are: (1) greater use of glass (accompanied by a more widespread use of jalousies, blinds and louvers); (2) the open-closed plan (when achieved by means of light, flexible walls of rolling, sliding or folding doors or wood panels); (3) built-in furniture and storage; and (4) a swing towards more natural interior finishes and greater texturing of interior surfaces.

Some traditional woodwork forms are undergoing change — trim is being simplified and emboldened in scale. The fussy classic mantel is being replaced by simpler wood frames that are more in scale with clean-lined contemporary furniture. Stair rails, balusters and newels are being given more unconventional expression. Some old forms have almost disappeared — false ceiling beams, the awesome front doorway and porchwork with its columnar dignity.

Woodwork trim, in other words, is going to work. The hackneyed melange of moldings which used to surround doors and windows indiscriminately is being replaced by moldings with more architectural effectiveness. Doorways "on ax" may be given bold-scale trim for emphasis; secondary doors, simply functional hairline moldings for impact- and wear-resistance. As in all phases of design, there is less orthodoxy than ever before.

The technique of woodwork manufacture has been changed only by the more common use of plywoods and

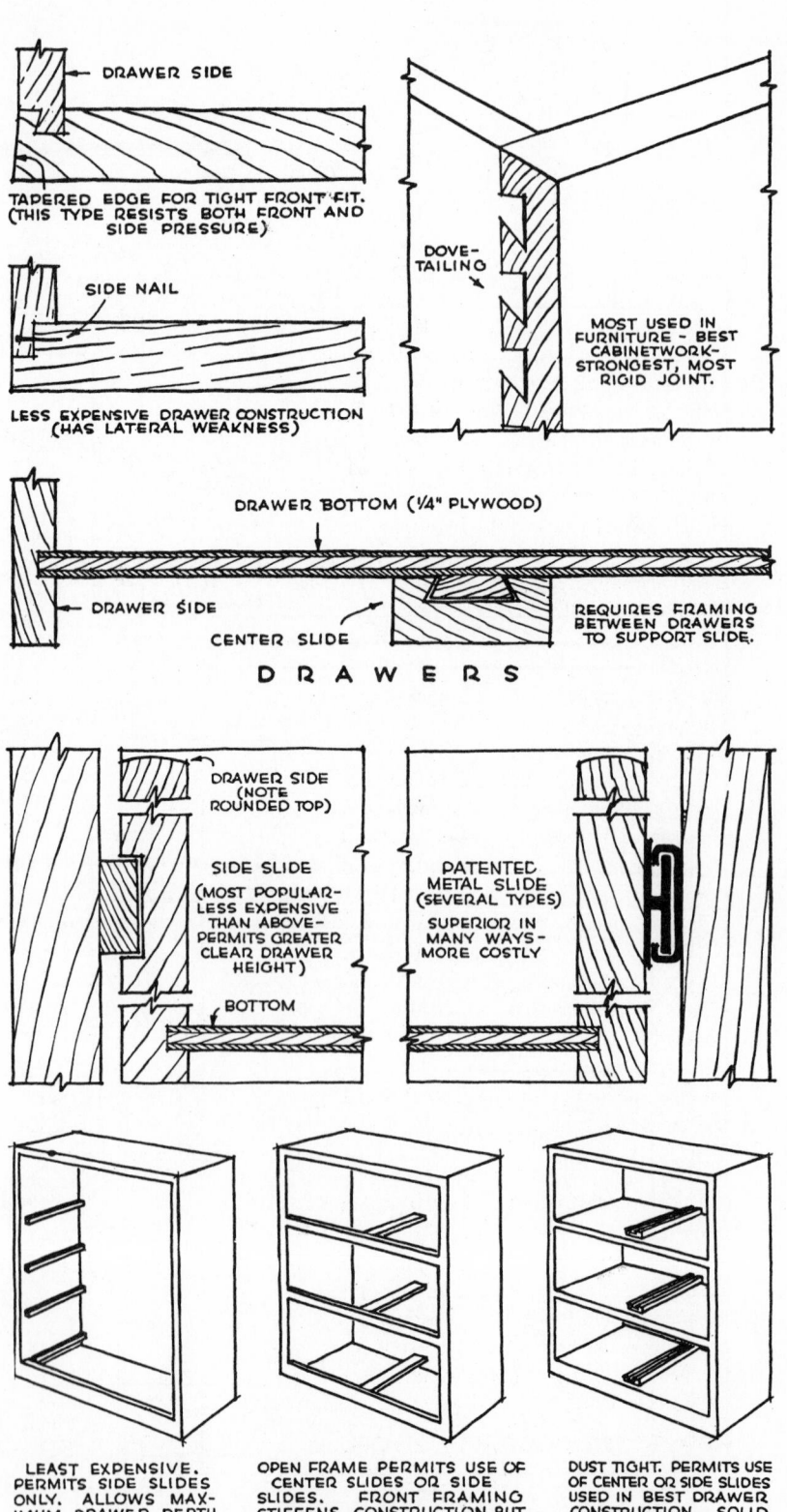

TAPERED EDGE FOR TIGHT FRONT FIT. (THIS TYPE RESISTS BOTH FRONT AND SIDE PRESSURE)

← DRAWER SIDE

SIDE NAIL

LESS EXPENSIVE DRAWER CONSTRUCTION (HAS LATERAL WEAKNESS)

DOVE-TAILING

MOST USED IN FURNITURE - BEST CABINETWORK- STRONGEST, MOST RIGID JOINT.

DRAWER BOTTOM (¼" PLYWOOD)

← DRAWER SIDE

CENTER SLIDE

REQUIRES FRAMING BETWEEN DRAWERS TO SUPPORT SLIDE.

D R A W E R S

DRAWER SIDE (NOTE ROUNDED TOP)

SIDE SLIDE (MOST POPULAR- LESS EXPENSIVE THAN ABOVE- PERMITS GREATER CLEAR DRAWER HEIGHT)

BOTTOM

PATENTED METAL SLIDE (SEVERAL TYPES)

SUPERIOR IN MANY WAYS- MORE COSTLY

LEAST EXPENSIVE. PERMITS SIDE SLIDES ONLY. ALLOWS MAXIMUM DRAWER DEPTH.

OPEN FRAME PERMITS USE OF CENTER SLIDES OR SIDE SLIDES. FRONT FRAMING STIFFENS CONSTRUCTION BUT REDUCES DRAWER HEIGHT, CREATES AN EDGE WHICH MAY SNAG DRAWER CONTENTS.

DUST TIGHT. PERMITS USE OF CENTER OR SIDE SLIDES USED IN BEST DRAWER CONSTRUCTION. SOLID SHELF PREVENTS SNAGGING OF DRAWER CONTENTS.

C H E S T S

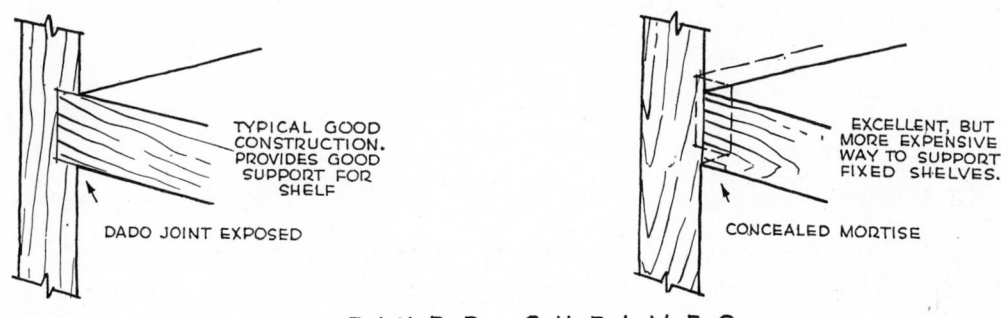

TYPICAL GOOD CONSTRUCTION. PROVIDES GOOD SUPPORT FOR SHELF

DADO JOINT EXPOSED

EXCELLENT, BUT MORE EXPENSIVE WAY TO SUPPORT FIXED SHELVES.

CONCEALED MORTISE

FIXED SHELVES

veneers. Although new methods of gluing and joining seem to offer promise of producing cheaper, stronger assemblies, there are many difficulties still to be overcome before they achieve fullest use. It is practically impossible, for example, to glue end-butt joints sufficiently strong to meet the requirements of ordinary service. End-to-side-grain joints are also difficult to glue properly. For these and other reasons, the traditional glued wood joinings (dowel, mortise and tenon, dado, tongue and rabbet, slip or lock corner, dovetail, blocked and tongue and groove) remain standard practice.

Some chemical applications are extending the usefulness of woodwork. Treatments to improve the rot and termite-resistance of wood and to control warping, shrinking, and swelling will not discolor the wood and will permit the use of natural finishes. Densifying processes that greatly increase the hardness of wood offer the possibility of endowing soft woods with the hardness of oak. The same process permits through-coloring of the treated lumber.

Plywoods with machine or chemically made textures are being increasingly used in cabinetwork. Striations, embossings, exaggerated grainings are examples. The use of such improvisations will undoubtedly increase to offset the shortage of hardwoods, and to meet the growing demand for more arresting surfaces.

HOW TO TELL GOOD WOODWORK
Surface

The surface should be free of all disfiguring defects such as raised grain, stains, evidences of poor and uneven

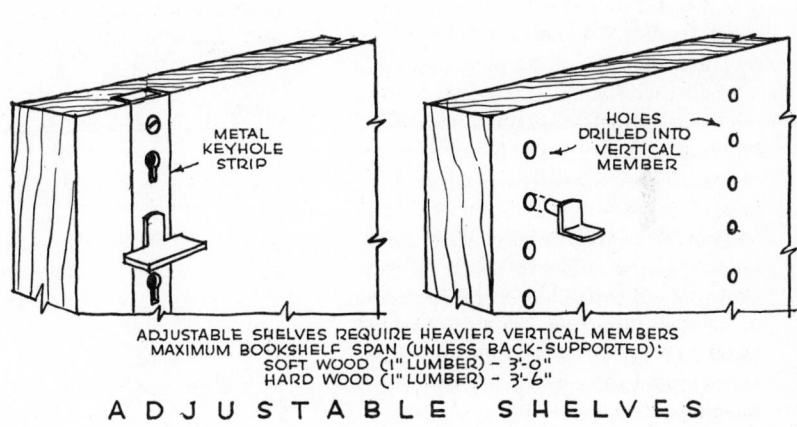

METAL KEYHOLE STRIP

HOLES DRILLED INTO VERTICAL MEMBER

ADJUSTABLE SHELVES REQUIRE HEAVIER VERTICAL MEMBERS
MAXIMUM BOOKSHELF SPAN (UNLESS BACK-SUPPORTED):
SOFT WOOD (1" LUMBER) - 3'-0"
HARD WOOD (1" LUMBER) - 3'-6"

ADJUSTABLE SHELVES

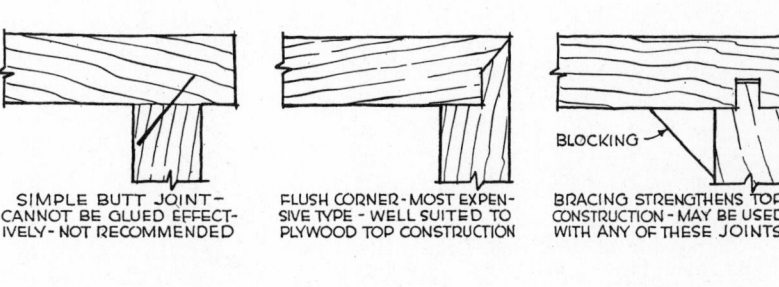

SIMPLE BUTT JOINT - CANNOT BE GLUED EFFECTIVELY - NOT RECOMMENDED

FLUSH CORNER - MOST EXPENSIVE TYPE - WELL SUITED TO PLYWOOD TOP CONSTRUCTION

BLOCKING

BRACING STRENGTHENS TOP CONSTRUCTION - MAY BE USED WITH ANY OF THESE JOINTS

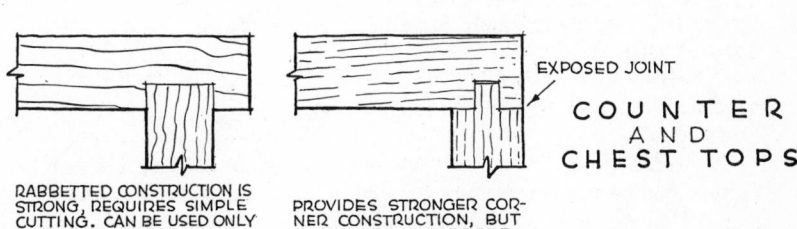

RABBETTED CONSTRUCTION IS STRONG, REQUIRES SIMPLE CUTTING. CAN BE USED ONLY WITH PROJECTING TOP

PROVIDES STRONGER CORNER CONSTRUCTION, BUT TOP EDGE IS EXPOSED

EXPOSED JOINT

COUNTER AND CHEST TOPS

planing, sanding, tool marks, gouges, scratches, dirt. Moldings should have clean edges, arrises and profiles. They should be crisp. There should be no chatter marks, caused by too rapid cutting, or any splintered edges. At the miters, profiles should match perfectly — evidence of perfect cutting.

If the material is to receive a natural finish, the color and graining should be uniform (or correctable with staining).

Joints

All joints should be cleanly matched, tight. Verticals should be plumb.

Look for signs of warping, splitting, checking, shrinking. If plywood is used in the construction, examine treatment of panel edges. If edges are face-veneered, check appearance and application of veneer.

Poor woodwork betrays itself in its joints. Low-cost joints often replace correct (and costlier) connections. Good woodwork has dado cuts in vertical pieces to support horizontal members, rabbetted construction to stiffen vertical members joined at right angles. Large mitered moldings should be doweled or secured by means of metal or wood splines. Blocking should be used to stiffen larger pieces and to secure tops to dressers, wardrobes and similar pieces.

Working Parts

Cheap construction of working parts, such as drawers and doors, makes for quick obsolescence. Drawer fronts should be dovetailed to sides, or secured by some other interlocking joint. Drawer backs and bottoms should be let into the sides. Drawer bottoms should be sufficiently strong to support the drawer contents without sagging. Drawer sides should be of hardwood to resist wear, unless drawer is supported on side runners. Drawer should fit snugly, not bind, snag, or rattle.

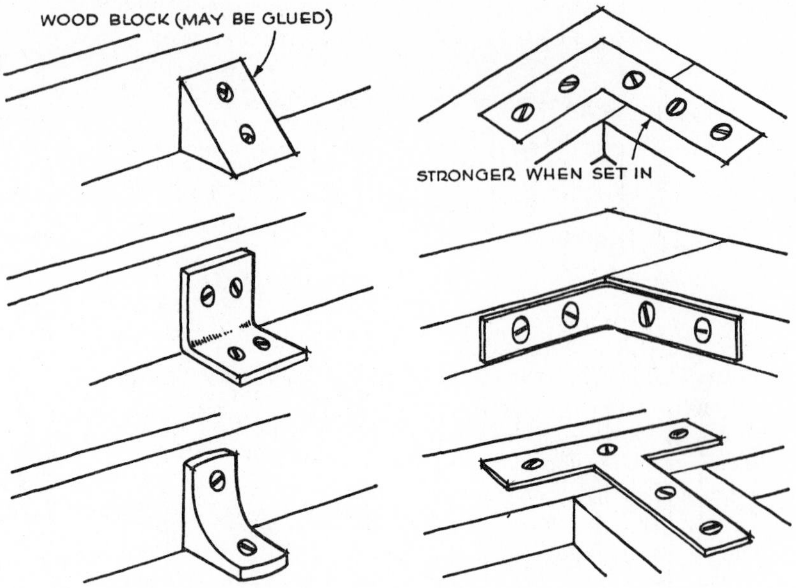

WOOD BLOCK (MAY BE GLUED)

STRONGER WHEN SET IN

B R A C I N G

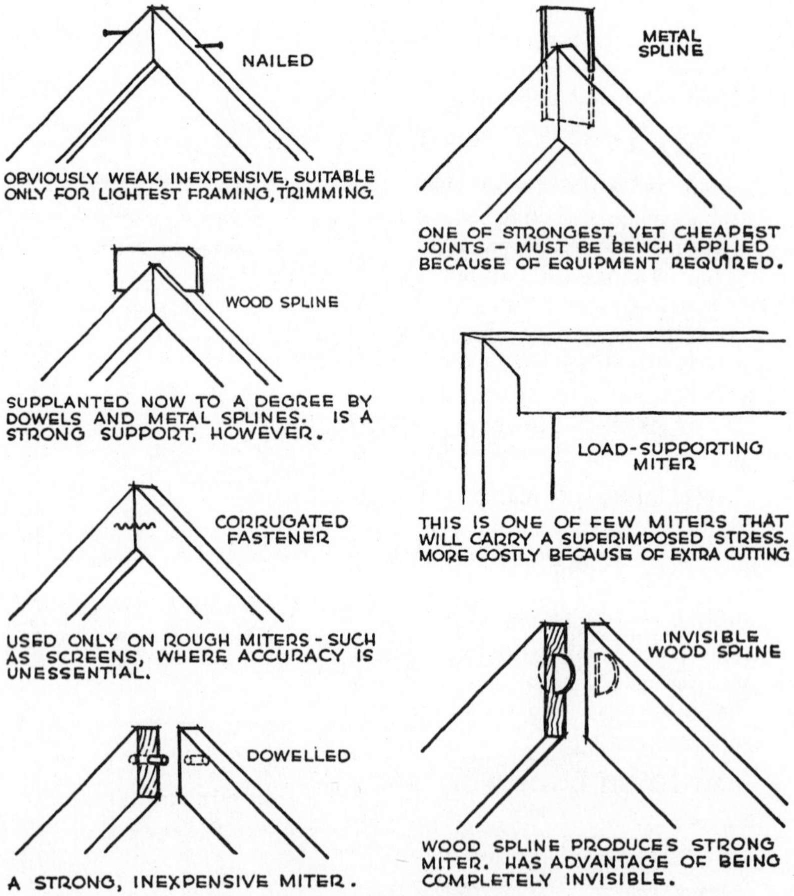

NAILED
OBVIOUSLY WEAK, INEXPENSIVE, SUITABLE ONLY FOR LIGHTEST FRAMING, TRIMMING.

METAL SPLINE
ONE OF STRONGEST, YET CHEAPEST JOINTS — MUST BE BENCH APPLIED BECAUSE OF EQUIPMENT REQUIRED.

WOOD SPLINE
SUPPLANTED NOW TO A DEGREE BY DOWELS AND METAL SPLINES. IS A STRONG SUPPORT, HOWEVER.

LOAD-SUPPORTING MITER
THIS IS ONE OF FEW MITERS THAT WILL CARRY A SUPERIMPOSED STRESS. MORE COSTLY BECAUSE OF EXTRA CUTTING.

CORRUGATED FASTENER
USED ONLY ON ROUGH MITERS — SUCH AS SCREENS, WHERE ACCURACY IS UNESSENTIAL.

INVISIBLE WOOD SPLINE

DOWELLED
A STRONG, INEXPENSIVE MITER.

WOOD SPLINE PRODUCES STRONG MITER. HAS ADVANTAGE OF BEING COMPLETELY INVISIBLE.

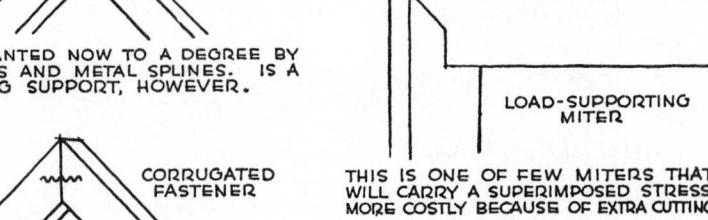

M I T E R S

PANELING

THE FRAME

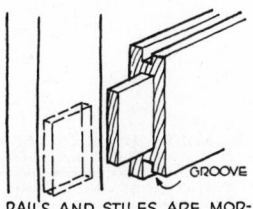

THE FRAME MUST BE RIGID. PANELS FLOAT FREE, THEIR EDGES HELD IN GROOVES IN THE FRAME.

RAILS AND STILES ARE MORTISED. GROOVES RECEIVE SPLINES OR PANEL EDGES. GROOVE

PANEL TYPES

SOLID STICKING PANEL - MAY BE USED IN EITHER SOLID OR PLYWOOD PANELS. USUAL PANEL CONSTRUCTION.

PANELS MAY ALSO BE SECURED BY MEANS OF APPLIED MOLDINGS, NAILED INTO WOOD SPLINES SLIPPED INTO GROOVES OF STILES AND RAILS. (IT COSTS LESS TO CUT GROOVES AND INSERT SPLINES THAN TO MAKE COMPLEX PROFILE WITH SPLINES INTEGRAL IN THE STILES).

LEAST EXPENSIVE METHOD - USED WHERE BACK OF PANEL IS NOT EXPOSED.

TRUE PANELING
(IN WHICH PANEL IS SET FREE IN A FRAME)

THE PANEL

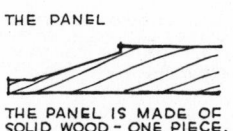

THE PANEL IS MADE OF SOLID WOOD - ONE PIECE,

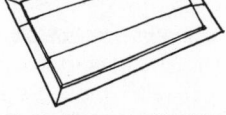

OR OF SEVERAL MATCHED PIECES GLUED TOGETHER,

OR OF PLYWOOD,

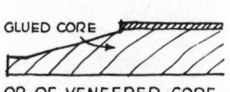

GLUED CORE

OR OF VENEERED CORE.

THE ADVANTAGE OF PLYWOOD PANELS IS THAT THEY PERMIT PERFECT MATCHING OF COLOR AND GRAIN IN ALL PANELS. PLYWOOD, TOO, EXPANDS AND CONTRACTS LESS THAN SOLID WOODS. DISADVANTAGE IS THAT PLYWOOD PANELS ARE DIFFICULT TO BEVEL. WHERE BEVELING IS REQUIRED, HERE ARE SOLUTIONS:

PLYWOOD
SOLID

USES SOLID WOOD FOR BEVEL; CALLS FOR CAREFUL MATCHING OF PLYWOOD IF PANEL IS TO BE NATURALLY FINISHED.

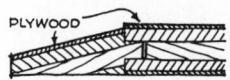

PLYWOOD

USES STRIPS FROM SAME PLYWOOD PANEL TO ACHIEVE PERFECT MATCH. SUPERIOR TO ABOVE; MAY BE COSTLIER.

WARDROBE AND CABINET DOORS

I. PLYWOOD FLUSH DOORS

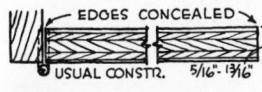

EDGES CONCEALED
USUAL CONSTR. 5/16"-13/16"

LEAST EXPENSIVE FLUSH DOOR. SELECT FOR UNIFORMITY OF GRAIN, PATTERN (IF NATURALLY FINISHED), GOOD CRUMBLE-FREE CORE. FOR METHODS OF TREATING EXPOSED PLYWOOD EDGES SEE "PLYWOOD EDGE TRIMMING".

EDGE EXPOSED

CAN BE USED ONLY AT CORNERS. - PRODUCES SIMPLE MODERN EFFECT.

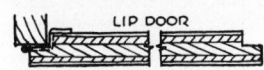

LIP DOOR

PRODUCES RAISED PANEL EFFECT. ESPECIALLY STRIKING WHEN MANY LIKE-SIZED PANELS ARE USED.

II. PANEL DOORS

USUAL CONSTRUCTION - USED WITH SOLID OR PLYWOOD PANELS.

BACK NAILING STRIP

BACK STRIP IS USED MAINLY TO SECURE GLASS PANELS. MAY ALSO BE USED TO SECURE WOOD PANELS IN SAME DOOR.

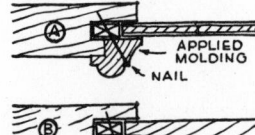

Ⓐ
APPLIED MOLDING
NAIL
Ⓑ
NAIL

APPLIED MOLDINGS ARE USED WHERE SHAPE OF MOLDING MAKES CUTTING IT FROM STILE WASTEFUL Ⓐ, OR WHERE PROFILE OF MOLDING PRECLUDES USE OF COPING AT CORNERS Ⓑ, OR WHERE MORE THAN ONE MOLDING DESIGN MAY BE USED IN A DOOR.

WARDROBES AND CABINETS

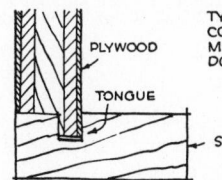

PLYWOOD
TONGUE
SOLID MEMBER

TYPICAL GOOD OUTSIDE CORNER CONSTRUCTION WHERE SOLID MEMBER FORMS WARDROBE DOOR FRAME.

GOOD OUTSIDE CORNER CONSTRUCTION WHERE NATURAL FINISH CONTINUES AROUND CORNER. RECOMMENDED WHERE BOTH MEMBERS ARE PLYWOOD. COSTLIER.

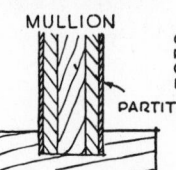

MULLION
PARTITION

GOOD MULLION CONSTRUCTION FOR WARDROBES AND OTHER CABINETS. PARTITION OF 3/4" PLYWOOD IS LET INTO MULLION.

PLYWOOD EDGE TRIMMING

MOST COMMON SOLUTION - REQUIRES EXPENSIVE CUTTING, GLUING. CORNERS ARE WEAK. GOOD WHEN ALL SIDES ARE EXPOSED.

WEAK HERE

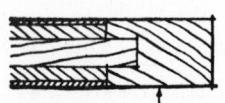

PROVIDES STRONG EDGE FOR HINGES, ABRASIVE WEAR, OR MOLDED WORK. INTRODUCES DIFFERENT WOOD GRAIN AND TEXTURE.

THIS PIECE MAY BE MOLDED

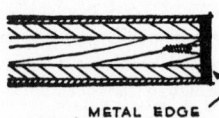

PROVIDES STRONG, WEAR-RESISTANT EDGE FOR WORK TOPS AND TABLES. TYPE SHOWN IS FLEXIBLE - CAN BE BENT TO FOLLOW MOST CURVES. FOR GOOD SEAL STRIP, SHOULD BE CEMENTED AND SCREWED TO THE TOP. USED MOSTLY FOR SERVICE TOPS.

METAL EDGE

TOP LIP HOLDS DOWN TOP VENEER - MAKES STRONGER, MORE DURABLE EDGE. WILL NOT BEND READILY.

METAL

UNTRIMMED EDGES

THIS CORNER TENDS TO BE WEAK. RECEDING EDGE HELPS CONCEAL EXPOSED EDGES OF PLIES.

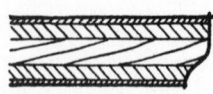

STRONGER AT TOP. CURVED EDGE HELPS CONCEAL EDGES OF PLIES.

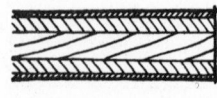

IF SURFACE IS TO BE PAINTED NO EDGE FINISH IS NECESSARY.

TABLE LEGS, APRONS
METHODS OF ATTACHING TOPS TO LEGS

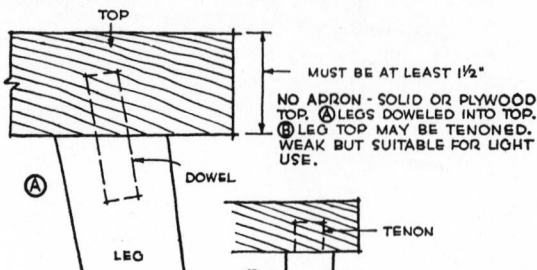

TOP

MUST BE AT LEAST 1½"

NO APRON - SOLID OR PLYWOOD TOP. Ⓐ LEGS DOWELED INTO TOP. Ⓑ LEG TOP MAY BE TENONED. WEAK BUT SUITABLE FOR LIGHT USE.

Ⓐ
DOWEL
LEG
TENON
Ⓑ

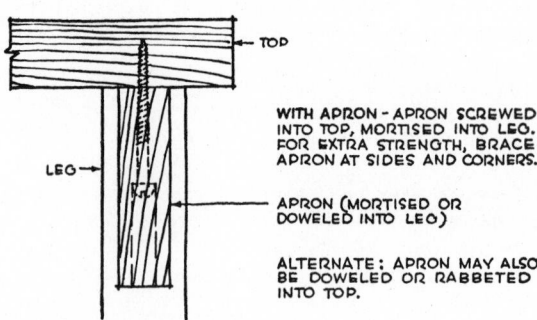

TOP
LEG

WITH APRON - APRON SCREWED INTO TOP, MORTISED INTO LEG. FOR EXTRA STRENGTH, BRACE APRON AT SIDES AND CORNERS.

APRON (MORTISED OR DOWELED INTO LEG)

ALTERNATE: APRON MAY ALSO BE DOWELED OR RABBETED INTO TOP.

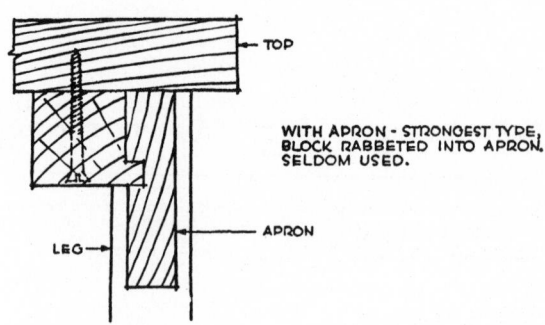

TOP

WITH APRON - STRONGEST TYPE, BLOCK RABBETED INTO APRON. SELDOM USED.

LEG
APRON

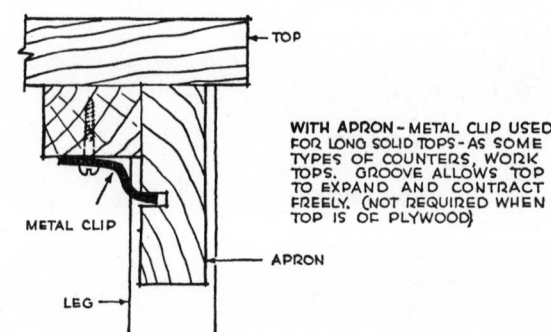

TOP

WITH APRON - METAL CLIP USED FOR LONG SOLID TOPS - AS SOME TYPES OF COUNTERS, WORK TOPS. GROOVE ALLOWS TOP TO EXPAND AND CONTRACT FREELY. (NOT REQUIRED WHEN TOP IS OF PLYWOOD)

METAL CLIP
APRON
LEG

By HOWARD P. VERMILYA, *AIA*

A tile is a relatively small, nonstructural, surfacing unit which is thin in relation to its width and length. Tiles may be made of various materials (such as stone, cement, plastic, metal, fiberboard, glass, rubber, asphalt, and cork), but clay is by far the most common, so much so that the Federal Trade Commission has ruled that the word "tile" when unmodified refers to a baked clay or ceramic product.

Ceramic tile

Ceramic tile, one of man's oldest building materials, has unique functional and decorative properties. Its imperviousness and its smooth surface have caused it to be widely used in hospitals, kitchens, bathrooms, swimming pools, dairies, bakeries, and the like—wherever the utmost in sanitation and easy maintenance is required. Other physical properties of tile, such as its hardness, durability, and fire resistance, may also be important functionally. As a decorative material, ceramic tile offers an almost unlimited choice of colors and patterns which do not fade, and it is practically indestructible. The decorative use of tile was carried to a very high point in medieval Islamic architecture ranging from Persia to Spain. It is also widely used in contemporary architecture.

Ceramic tile is made from clay, or a mixture of clay and other materials which is called the body of the tile. The tile may or may not have a glazed face and it is fired at a temperature above red heat, sufficiently high to result in specific physical properties and characteristics.

Standards are in general use throughout the industry. The principal standards pertaining to the manufacture and installation of ceramic tile are as follows:

- ASTM C242 *Standard Definitions of Terms Relating to Ceramic Whitewares and Related Products*
- SPR R61, Clay Tiles for Floors and Walls. Department of Commerce, Simplified Practice Recommendation
- Federal Specification SS-T-308b, 1959, Tile, Floor, Wall, and Trim Units, Ceramic
- ASA A108.1, *Glazed Ceramic Wall Tile Installed in Portland Cement Mortar*
- ASA A108.2, *Ceramic Mosaic Tile Installed in Portland Cement Mortar*
- ASA A108.3, *Quarry Tile and Pavers Installed in Portland Cement Mortar*
- ASA A108.5, *Installation of Ceramic Tile with Dry-set Portland Cement Mortar*
- ASA A118.1, *Specifications for Dry-set Portland Cement Mortar*
- CS181, *Water-resistant Organic Adhesives for Installation of Clay Tile.* Department of Commerce, Commercial Standard
- Code for Use of Flammable Anesthetics. NFPA Bulletin no. 56, chap. 25, article 252, May, 1960. National Fire Protection Association

Manufacturing processes: Two processes are in general use:

Dust-pressed process, in which the clays are ground to dust and mixed with a minimum of water, shaped in steel dies, and then fired

Plastic process, in which the clays are made plastic by mixing with water, shaped by extrusion or in molds, and then fired

Both processes are used to produce glazed or unglazed tile of various sizes, densities, and degrees of water absorption.

Grades are established by SPR R61 for ceramic mosaic, quarry tile, and glazed tile (except faience), as follows:

Standard grade (blue label): within specified limits as to dimension, warpage, blemishes, and other defects; 5 per cent seconds permitted

Seconds (yellow label): permits many but not all the defects prohibited in the standard grade.

Master-grade certificates covering an entire shipment will be issued if requested before shipment is made.

Sizes are shown in Table 1.

Classes: Ceramic tile is broadly classified as unglazed or glazed.

Unglazed tile is a hard, dense tile of homogeneous composition. Its colors and characteristics are determined by the materials used in the body, the method of manufacture, and the thermal treatment. It is used primarily for floors and walks.

Glazed tile has an impervious face of ceramic materials fused onto the body of the tile, which may be of any type. The glazed surface may be clear, white, or colored. Standard glazes may be *bright* (glossy), *semimatte* (less glossy), *matte* (dull), or *crystalline* (mottled and textured; good resistance to abrasion). Glazed tile is used principally for walls; crystalline glazed tile may be used for light-duty floors.

Bodies: Tile bodies are classified by ASTM C242 as to their degree of water absorption as follows:

Table 1. Sizes of ceramic tile, in.

Ceramic mosaic		*Wall tile*		*Quarry tile*	
		Square			
⅜x⅜#	A	1⅜x1⅜#	D	2¾x2¾x½	G
½x½#	C	2 1/16x2 1/16#	E	4x4x½	H
¾x¾	A	3x3#	D	6x6x½	G
15/16x15/16	B	4¼x4¼	E	6x6x¾	I
1 1/16x1 1/16	C	6x6	D	9x9x¾	J
1 9/16x1 9/16	A				
1 15/16x1 15/16	B				
2 3/16x2 3/16	C				
		Oblong (rectangular)			
1 9/16x¾	A	6x3#	D	6x2¾x½	G
1 15/16x15/16	B	6x4¼#	DE	8x4x½	H
2 3/16x1 1/16	C	8½x4¼#	E	8x4x¾	
		6x9#	D	8x3⅞x¾#	
				8x3¾x¾#	
Hexagonal				8x2⅜x¾#	
1 in.				8x2¼x¾	
				9x6x¾	IJ

NOTES: Paver tiles are usually 6 x 6, but may be smaller.

Sizes shown include all of the standard sizes of SPR R61 and some nonstandard sizes (indicated by #) which are generally available. Not all companies produce all the sizes shown, and some produce other sizes than those shown.

The capital letter following a size indicates that it is coordinated in dimension with the other sizes followed by the same letter.

Tile thicknesses are as follows: ceramic mosaic, ¼; wall tile, 5/16, ⅜#; paver tile, ½#; quarry tile, ½, ¾.

Tile joint widths are as follows: 2 3/16 square or smaller, 1/32 to 7/64, usually 1/16; over 2 3/16 to 4¼ square, 1/16 to ¼, usually ⅛; 6 x 6 and larger, ¼ to ¾; quarry, ⅜ to ¾; faience, all sizes, ⅛ to ½.

Shapes available other than square and oblong include diagonal half-tiles, pentagons, hexagons, octagons, equilateral triangles, diamonds, dots, and half-hexagons.

Impervious: 0.5 per cent or less
Vitreous: 0.5 to 3 per cent
Semivitreous: 3 to 7 per cent
Nonvitreous: over 7 per cent

Types of tile

Porcelain: a ceramic mosaic or paver generally made by the dust-pressed process, with a composition that is dense, fine-grained, and smooth, and has a sharply formed face. Colors are usually clear and luminous; they may have a granular blend

Natural clay tile: a tile, made by either the dust-pressed method or the plastic method from clays that produce a dense body, with a distinctive, slightly textured appearance

Ceramic mosaic: tile made by either the dust-pressed or plastic process, usually ¼ to ⅜ in. thick, and having a facial area of less than 6 sq in. It is usually mounted on sheets of paper, approximately 1 by 2 ft in size, to facilitate setting. Ceramic mosaic may be of either porcelain or natural clay composition and comes plain or with an abrasive mixture throughout. It may be unglazed or glazed

Pavers: unglazed porcelain or natural clay tile formed by the dust-pressed process, with a composition similar to that of ceramic mosaics but relatively thicker and having a facial area of 6 or more sq in

Quarry tile: unglazed tile, usually having 6 or more sq in. of surface area, made by the plastic extrusion process from natural clay or shales

Faience tile: glazed or unglazed tile, generally made by the plastic process, showing characteristic variations in the face, edges, and glaze that give a hand-crafted, nonmechanical effect

Faience mosaic: faience tile less than 6 sq in. in facial area. It is ⁵⁄₁₆ to ⅜ in. thick and is usually mounted

Glazed interior-wall tile: a glazed tile

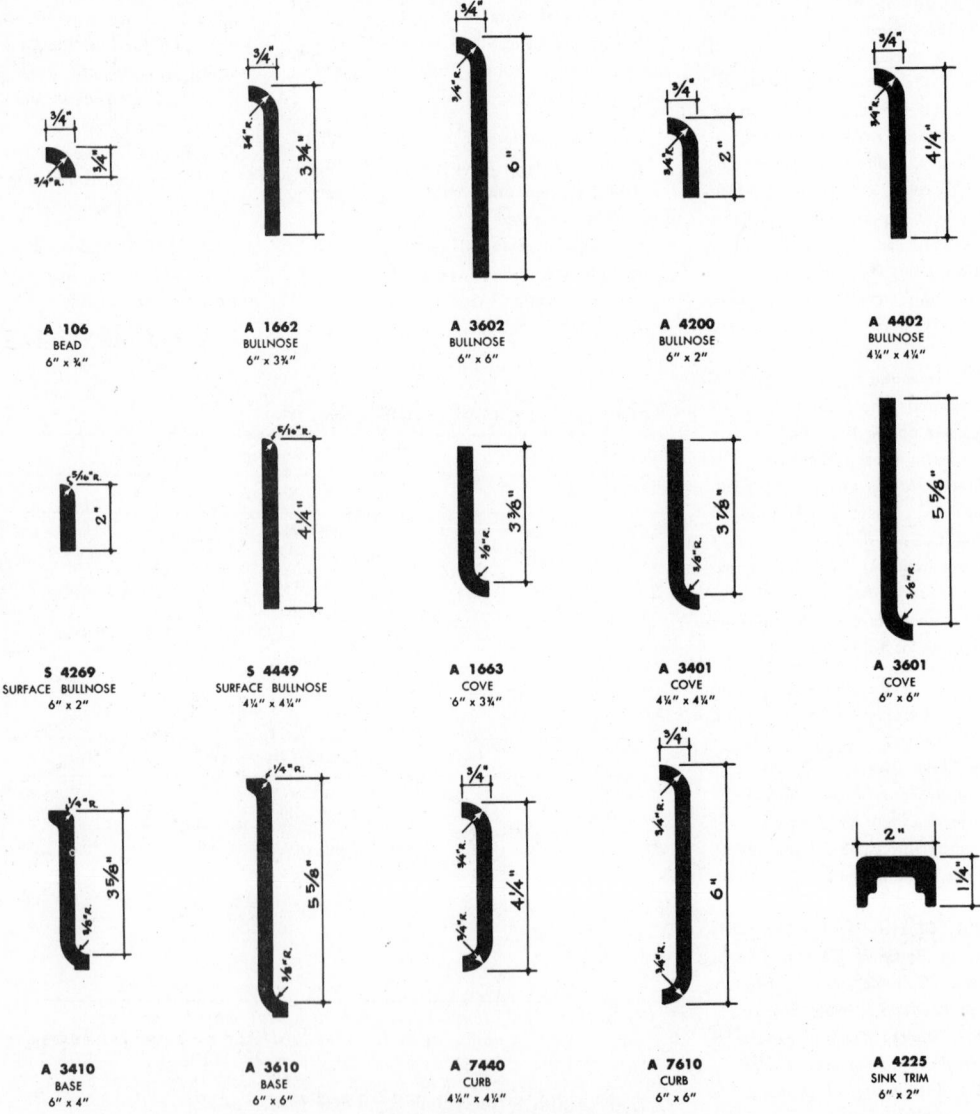

Fig. 1. Standard trim shapes and sizes

"A" numbers designate units for setting in conventional mortar bed. "C" numbers designate ceramic mosaic trim, conventional type. "S" numbers designate "surface type" units, including ceramic mosaic, for use with dry-set mortar or adhesive. (From Simplified Practice Recommendation 61-61.)

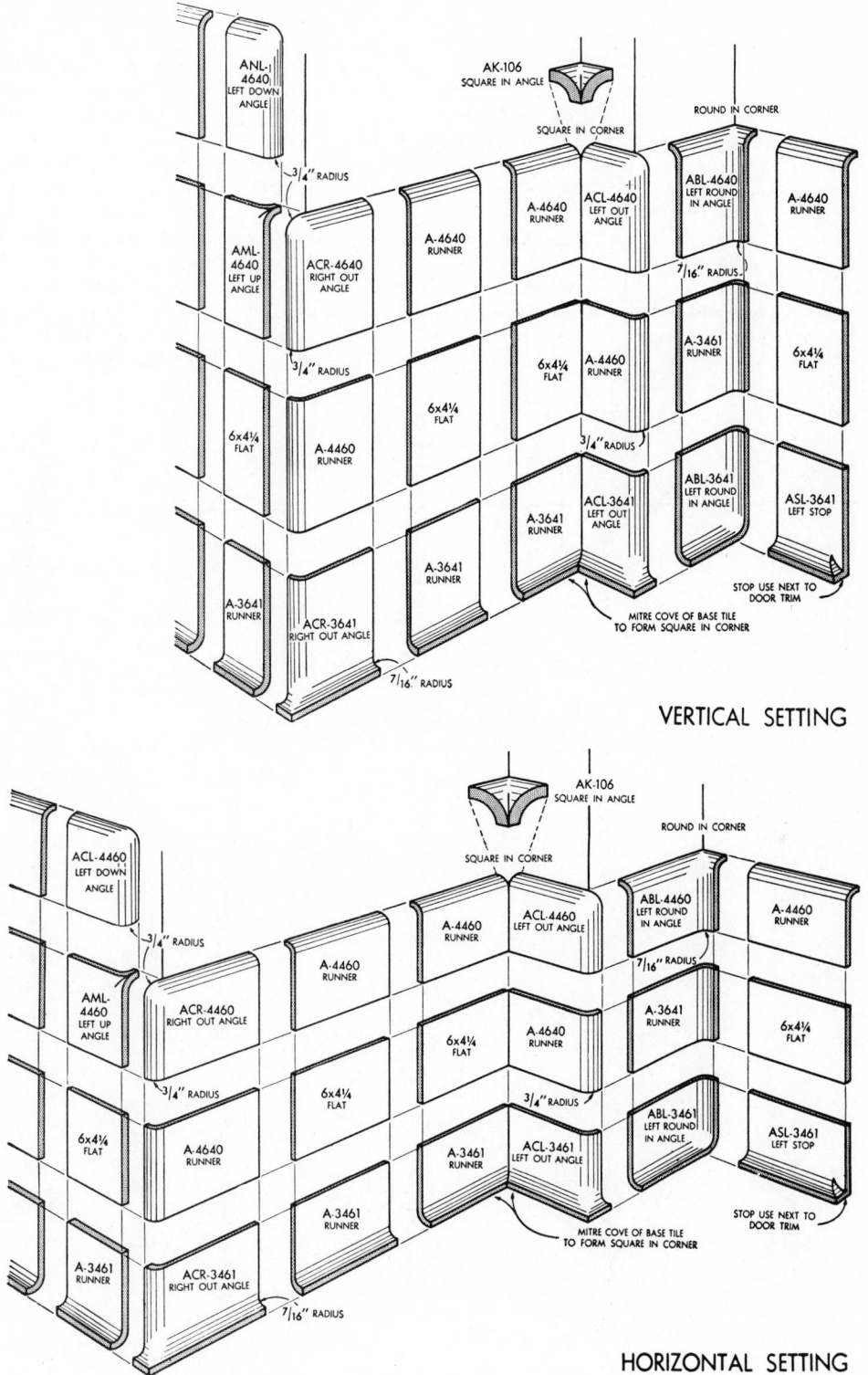

Fig. 2.   Standard trim shapes and designations

6 by 4¼ in. wall tile set in conventional mortar bed. (Courtesy American-Olean Tile Company.)

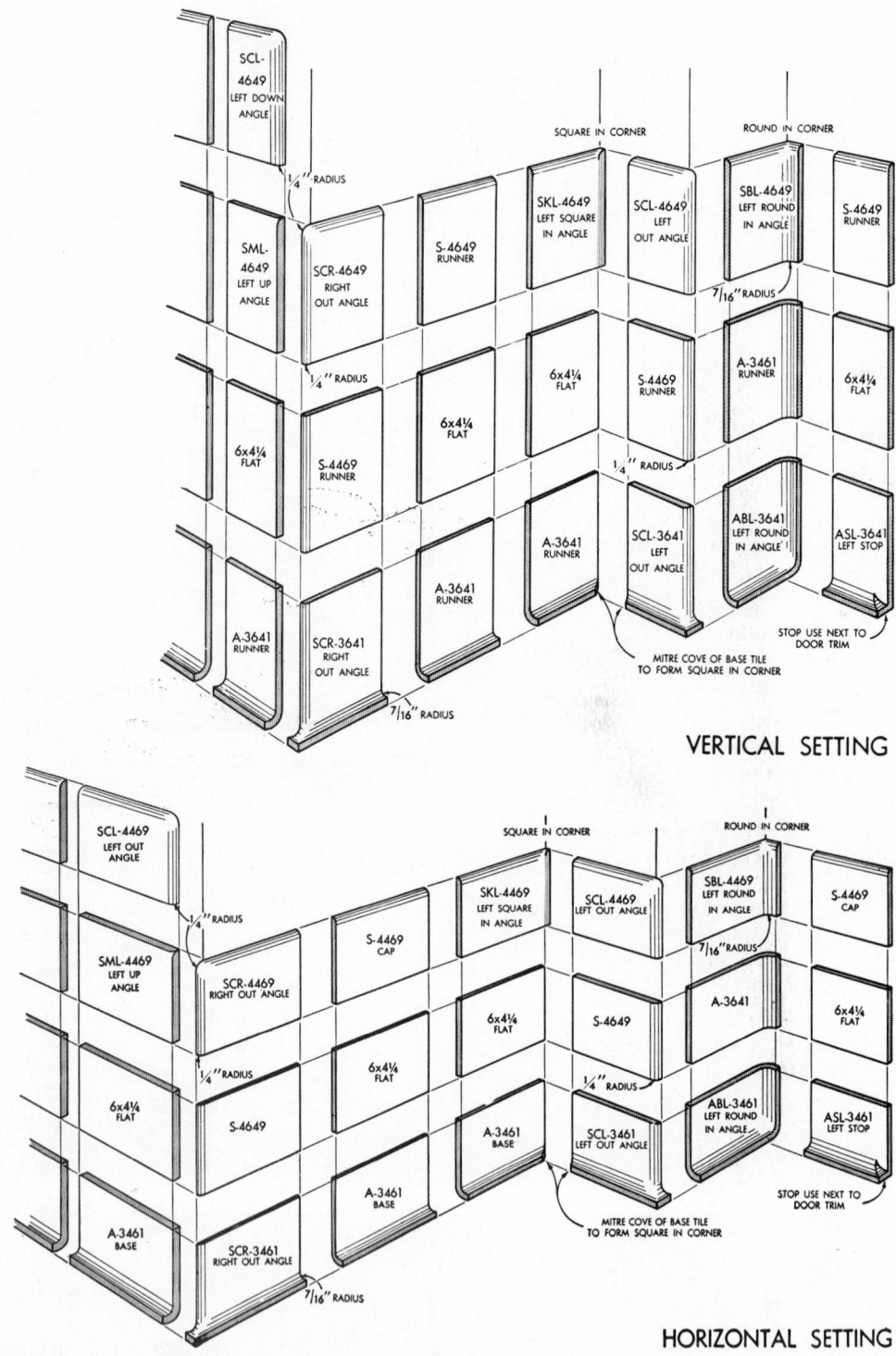

Fig. 3. Standard trim shapes and designations

6 by 4¼ in. wall tile set in dry-set mortar or adhesive. (Courtesy American-Olean Tile Company.)

with a body, usually nonvitreous, suitable for general interior use but not designed to withstand excessive impact or freezing and thawing conditions

Special-purpose tile: a tile, either glazed or unglazed, made to meet the requirements of particular uses. Some examples of special-purpose tile are:

Nonslip tile: produced by the addition of abrasive substances such as silicon carbide or other gritty particles to the body of unglazed or to the glaze of glazed tiles to be used for flooring

Frostproof tile: glazed or unglazed tile made on an impervious or vitreous body for use on exterior areas subject to freezing and also for interior surfaces of refrigerators and freezers

Acid-, alkali-, and stain-resistant tile: used principally for floors and counter tops in food processing and chemical plants, laboratories, and the like. Special grout must be used. Stain-resistant tile has been developed for use in chemically treated swimming pools

Ship or galley tile: a special quarry tile having an indented face pattern for nonslip effect

Packing-house tile: similar to quarry tile but thicker

Conductive tile: used to prevent static electrical discharge where such discharge might cause an explosion, as in a hospital operating room, munitions plant, laboratory, etc. Conductive tile, usually ceramic mosaic, has an impervious, unglazed body into which have been introduced certain iron oxides or acetylene black to provide moderate electrical conductivity for personnel and equipment in contact with the floor. The NFPA Standard requires an electrical resistance not greater than 500,000 ohms nor less than 25,000 ohms, with no single tile having a greater resistance than 2½ million ohms. Warranty to that effect will be furnished by the manufacturer if requested before shipment. Conduc-

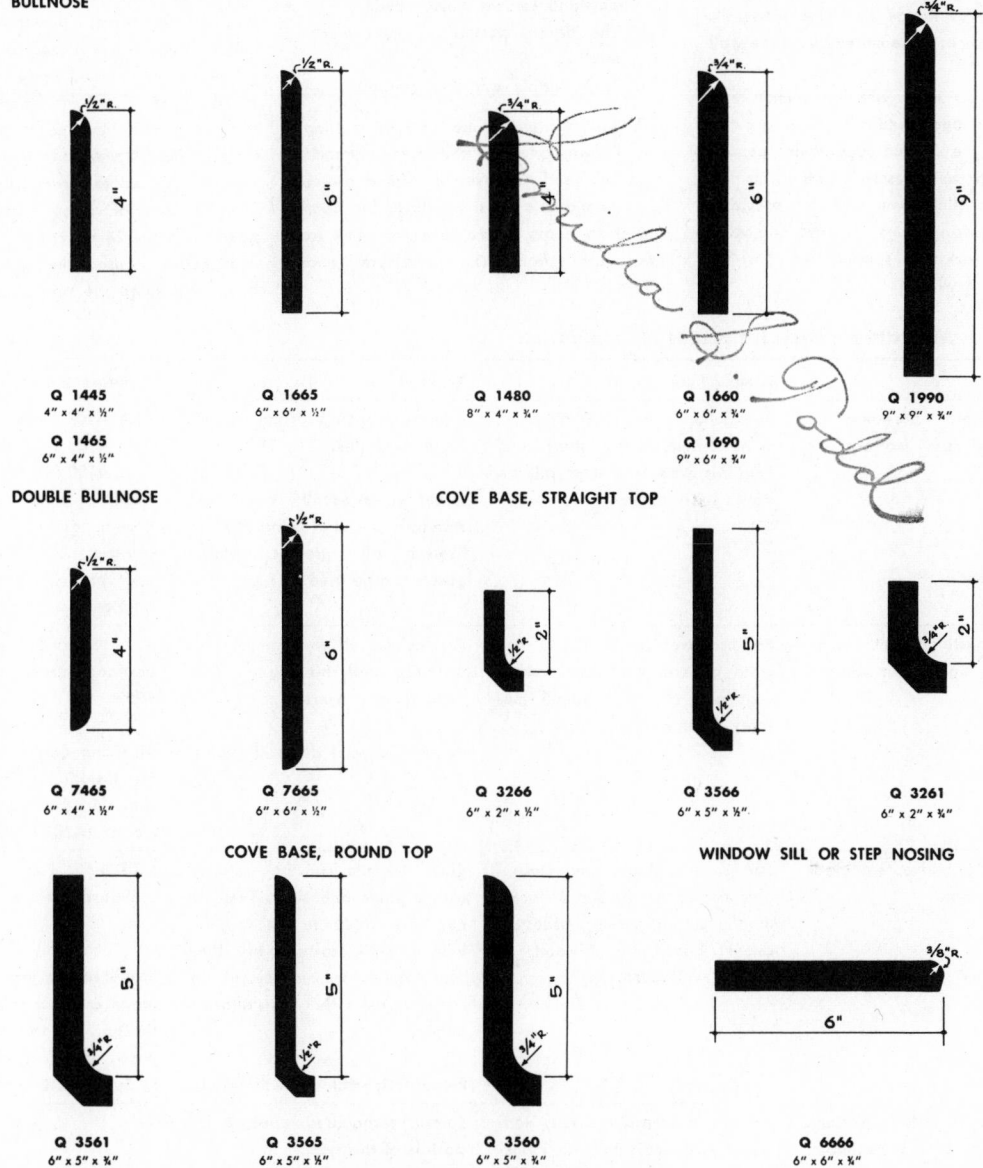

Fig. 4. Quarry tile trim shapes and sizes

"Q" numbers designate quarry tile trim. (From SPR 61-61.)

tive tile must be set in a special conductive cement bed or adhesive

Trim units: These are variously shaped ceramic units such as caps, bases, coves, bullnoses, corners, etc., which are necessary for edging a tile field or making a transition betwen intersecting planes. Trim is made to match flat tile in color and texture and to coordinate with it in dimension. It is made for both thick-bed and thin-set applications.

Accessories: Bathroom accessories such as the soap dish, paper holder, tumbler holder, towel bars, grab bars, hooks, and shelf brackets are made to match face-tile colors and textures. The units are glazed over ceramic or china bases and may be either flush or flange type; the latter fits over and conceals the cut edges of the wall tile.

Edges: Two types are in common use: the *square* edge, used with flush grouted joints, and the *cushion* edge, which permits the joints to be recessed slightly from the face of the tile. Some tiles are provided with *self-spacing* lugs on two adjacent edges to facilitate spacing the tile for uniform joint widths.

Mounted tile: Ceramic mosaic is usually furnished mounted on sheets of paper approximately 1½ to 2 sq ft in area. Until recently the paper mounting was always on the face of the tile and was soaked off after the tile had been permanently installed. Rear-mounted tile, using a perforated paper which permits adequate bonding of the tile to the setting bed, is now available. This enables the tile setter to see what he is doing and to exercise closer control over joint widths, levels, and patterns.

Installation: There are three accepted methods for installing ceramic tile (Table 2):

1. The conventional method using a portland cement mortar bed.
2. The dry-set portland cement mortar method.
3. The organic adhesive method.

The *conventional mortar-bed method,* also known as the "thick-bed method," should be used wherever the utmost protection is needed against moisture, for floors subject to heavy traffic, and for most exterior applications. The procedure is as follows:

1. Waterproof membrane should be applied over unstable surfaces such as wood subfloors or wood or steel wall framing; also over gypsum plaster, gypsum block, or gypsum wallboard.

2. Self-furring or self-supported metal reinforcing in middle of setting bed—mandatory when waterproof membrane is used.

3. Expansion joints not over 16 ft on center in both directions. Should cut entirely through setting bed. Mandatory in exterior tile work, desirable with large wood surfaces.

4. For floors and decks, mortar setting bed should be ¾ to 1¼ in. thick, consisting of 1 part (vol) portland cement, 5 to 6 parts sand, and 1/10 part hydrated lime type S. Waterproof cement or admixtures may be used. For walls and ceilings the mortar setting bed should be ¼ to ¾ in. thick, consisting of 1 part (vol) portland cement, 4 to 5 parts sand, and ½ part hydrated type S lime. On walls mortar setting bed may be applied to scratch, or scratch and leveling, coats of cement plaster after they have dried for 24 hours or if the *one-float-coat method* is used, the setting bed is applied directly to the reinforcing mesh.

Table 2.   Mortars for installation of ceramic tile

Mortar type	Areas of use	Remarks	Standard specifications
1. Conventional portland cement and sand mortar	For general use over masonry, wood frame, metal studs, etc. Requires wire lath over all unstable substructures.	Requires soaking of all non-vitreous, wall tile. — Grouting is usually done with standard portland cement grout; however, all presently available grouts can be used.	ASA A108.1-1958 A108.2-1958 A108.3-1958 American Standard Specifications for glazed ceramic wall tile, ceramic mosaic tile, quarry tile and pavers installed in portland cement mortar.
2. Dry-set portland cement mortar—with or without sand	For use over cinder block, concrete, gypsum wallboard, scratch coat and all other sound masonry surfaces.	Permits use of dry non-vitreous, wall tile, and thin (1/16 in. minimum) mortar layers. — Requires special dry-wall grouts.	ASA Specification for dry-set portland cement mortar A118.1-1959. — American Standard Specification for installation of ceramic tile with dry-set portland cement mortar. A108.5-1960
3. Organic adhesive, wall type and floor type	For use over all flat and reasonably smooth nondusting surfaces; usually cement plaster, asbestos-cement board, fir plywood, or gypsum wallboard.	Only dry tile can be installed with organic adhesives. They do not have indefinite life of portland cement mortars, but they can take more movement of substructure without installation damage. — Requires special dry-wall grouts.	CS-181-52 Federal Commercial Standard for ceramic tile adhesives. — Standard specification for installation of ceramic tile with water resistant organic adhesives (Proposed as an American Standard to Sectional Committee A108).
4. Acid-alkali resistant mortars. Various types are available. They are generally thin setting (mortar layer ¼ in. or less).	For use in corrosive areas, generally with quarry tile in industrial installation.	Special techniques required for mortars of this type. — Grouting is usually done with same material used for mortar.	

Table 3. Grouts for ceramic tile joints

Grout type	Use	Remarks	Colors
1. Portland cement conventional types	For grouting vitreous and wet non-vitreous tiles, usually in conventional portland cement and sand installations.	Used neat for most narrow ($\frac{1}{16}$ in.) wide grout joints, and with sand for quarry tile grout joints. Many proprietary formulations improve texture and shrinkage characteristcis.	White or gray; can be colored with inert pigment.
2. Dry-wall portland cement types	For grouting ceramic tile installations with dry-set portland cement or organic adhesives.	This type will not lose water to absorptive surfaces it contacts, as will conventional portland cement types.	White or gray; can be colored with inert pigments.
3. Organic types	For grouting all kinds of tile where impermeable, nonstaining surface is desired.	Relatively new category of tile grout, being pioneered by Tile Council of America. Resistant to acid and alkali attack.	White. Can be colored.
4. Flexible grouts	For grouting floors where some flexibility is desired.	Two-part grouts to be mixed on job.	Dark gray and black.
5. Acid-alkali resistant grout	For use in corrosive areas, generally with quarry tile in industrial installations.	Special technique required for most grouts of this type.	White, red, gray and black.
6. Tub caulks	For caulking between tub lip and tile walls.	Available in tubes from any hardware or building supplier.	White
7. Expansion joint fillers	For filling expansion and contraction joints.	Mostly two parts—to be mixed at job site.	Black, gray and aluminum.

5. While the setting bed is still plastic, trowel or dust on a $\frac{1}{32}$- to $\frac{1}{16}$-in. thickness of neat cement paste (float method) or apply to back of tile (buttering method), and set tile firmly on bed. Soak glazed wall tile before setting. Joint width is determined by strings, pegs, spacers, or other methods.

6. Beat tile into mortar bed. Cut through setting bed horizontally or vertically every 17 to 24 in.

7. Grout, clean, and prevent too rapid drying—damp-curing for three days is recommended. All recognized types of grout (portland cement, commercial-waterproof, flexible, and nonstaining) may be used (Table 3).

The *dry-set portland cement mortar method* uses a relatively new type of mortar developed by the Tile Council of America and produced under license by manufacturers. In the dry-set mortar, inorganic admixtures have been incorporated with the portland cement to increase water retentivity and the bonding action of the cement. This process makes it unnecessary to soak absorptive tile or damp-cure the setting bed; damp-curing of dry-set grout is recommended, however, particularly on floors, exteriors, and in wet locations.

The dry-set mortar method may be used in wet locations, showers, tub-shower recesses, etc., directly over portland cement plaster, concrete, concrete masonry, structural clay tile or brick, and in dry locations over ½-in. or ⅝-in. gypsum wallboard, when properly installed with taped and treated joints. Dry-set mortar over a compatible primer sealer has been used over gypsum wallboard in recessed tub-showers and in shower compartments. A water-proof cleavage membrane and a reinforced portland cement mortar setting bed ¾ to 1¼ in. thick should be used over wood floors to receive tile. Dry-set mortar may be used neat or mixed with fine sand according to the thickness of the bed and the type of tile used. The ratio of sand to cement used should follow the manufacturer's directions.

The procedure is as follows:

1. Float mortar over backing, using flat side of trowel, to a minimum thickness of $\frac{1}{16}$ in. for walls and ceilings, ⅛ in. for floors.

2. Comb mortar with notched trowel within 10 min of applying tile.

3. Soaking porous tile is unnecessary but may be done if desired or if conventional portland cement grout is to be used.

4. Press tile into bed, tap and beat into place. Ribbed-back tile may require application of mortar to back of tile to obtain full contact. If mounted tile is used, soak off paper, using as little water as possible, before initial set.

5. Grout and clean. Damp-cure for at least three days if conventional portland cement or dry-set mortar is used for grouting.

In the *Organic Adhesive Method*, the adhesive used should comply with Commercial Standard CS181-52, which requires container labels to provide instructions regarding storage, handling on job, tools to be used, effective solvents, and warnings of improper applications, conditions, and locations, including toxicity and flammability. Use only the type of adhesive recommended by the manufacturer for the particular function and conditions. The adhesive method can be used in dry areas directly over such backing materials as waterproof plywood, asbestos-cement board, hardboard, metal, gypsum board, and other materials. When the backing is properly waterproofed it may be used in wet locations. In either location the adhesive manufacturer's directions with reference to appropriate backing materials should be carefully followed.

The procedure is as follows:

1. Apply underlayment recommended by manufacturer, if surface needs leveling. This applies particularly to remodeling work over existing tile, terrazzo, or concrete floors, or other irregular surfaces.

2. Apply primer sealing coat to backing material or underlayment when recommended by manufacturer.

3. Set tile using either the float or the buttering method. The float method is usually recommended for ceramic mosaics, glazed tile, and faience mosaics; the buttering method, or combination float and buttering method, for pavers, quarry tile, and faience tile. The *float method* consists of spreading adhesive over the backing surface with a special trowel, notched as recommended by manufacturer, and pressing tile into it. The *buttering method* reverses the former procedure by applying the adhesive directly to the back of the tile in a thin layer and then pressing the tile onto the backing material.

4. Carefully remove all adhesive from face of tile, using only solvents recommended by adhesive manufacturer.

5. Grout may be portland cement mortar, in which case porous tile should be soaked, dry-set grout, commercial waterproof grout, flexible grout, or nonstaining grout.

A *conductive-tile mortar bed* may be the conventional portland cement mortar bed (1¼ in. thick), or a dry-set portland cement mortar or organic-adhesive setting bed, with additives to make it electrically conductive. These are usually proprietary products and the manufacturer's instructions should be carefully observed. The grout need not be conductive.

Acid- and alkali-resistant mortar beds and grouts are also generally proprietary products. They are usually of the thin-set type, mortar or adhesive. They are used principally in industrial and laboratory applications, usually with quarry tile. Manufacturer's directions should be followed strictly.

A two-component epoxy-resin setting bed and grout has been developed by the Tile Council of America and designated AAR-II. After mixing, it is troweled over the subsurface to a minimum thickness of ⅛ in., and the tile is installed in the usual manner. Grouting is normally done the following day, and the floor may be put into service the day after, although the resin does not attain its full strength for 28 days. Excess resin may be cleaned off the face of the tile and off tools with water.

Metal tile

Tile made of metal is available for wall and ceiling finish. It is made of several dif-

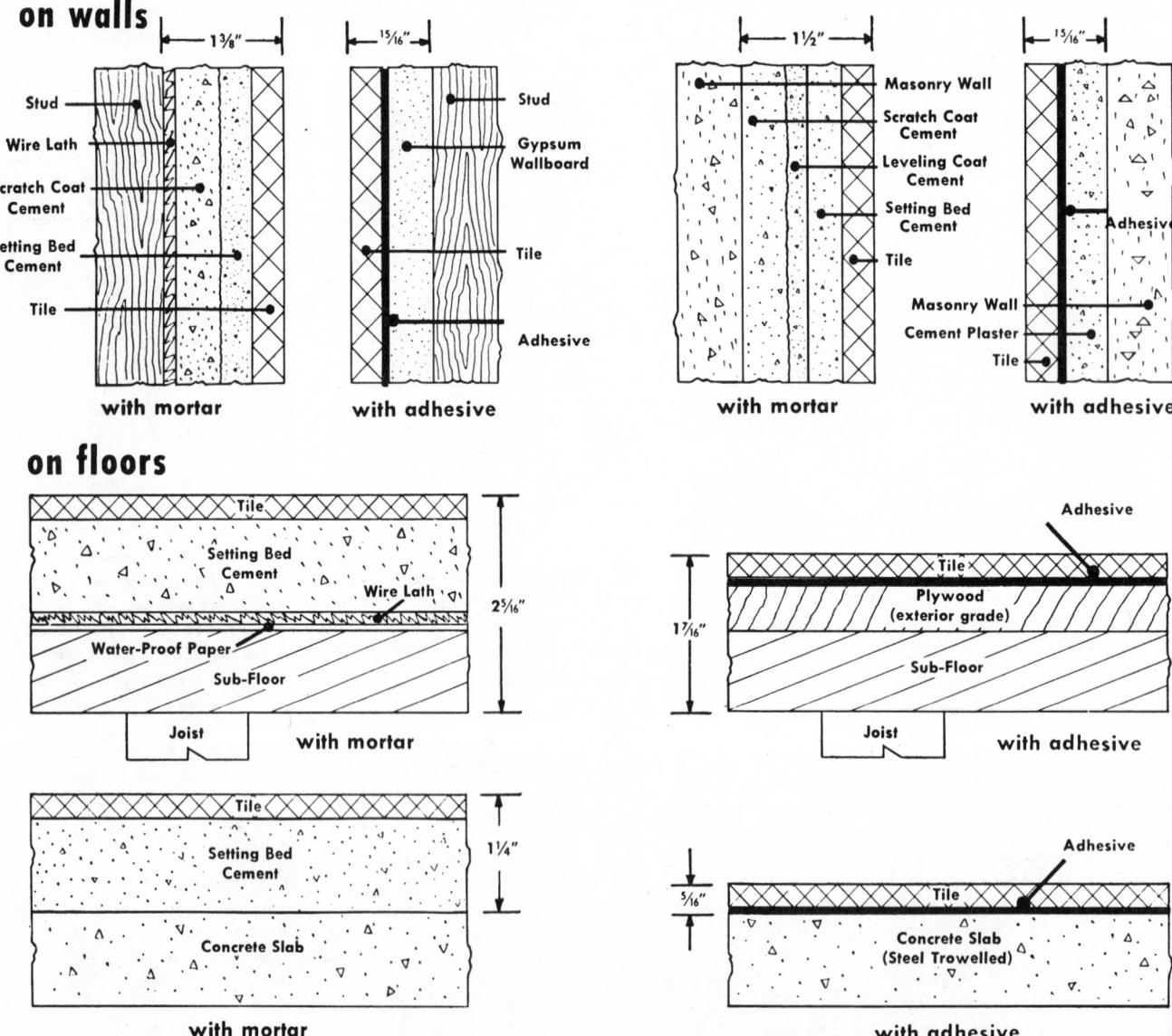

Fig. 5.   Typical details of tile installations on walls and floors—One-half full size

Courtesy Minnesota Mining and Manufacturing Company.

ferent metals, which may have various finishes. The principal advantages of metal as compared with ceramic tile are its light weight (1 lb per sq ft in place) and its thinness (⅛ to 3/32 in., including the adhesive). In other respects it has many of the desirable characteristics of ceramic tile, being smooth and impervious, which makes it sanitary and easy to clean, hard and durable, heat-resistant, and decorative.

Base metal: Tile may be formed from strip steel, aluminum, copper, brass, or stainless steel. Steel, 0.015 in. thick, is zinc-plated, bonderized, and spray-coated with zinc chromate before finishing. Aluminum is usually alloy 3003 half-hard; it is 0.020 in. thick for resin-enamel finish and 0.025 in. thick for porcelain enamel. Copper, brass, and stainless steel are 0.015 in. thick.

Finishes: The finish may be a clear or colored resin enamel, baked on at a temperature in excess of 300°F, or a porcelain enamel of either the low-temperature (on aluminum) or high-temperature type. The latter is very similar to the glaze on ceramic tile and has approximately the same characteristics. Exposed metals are usually given a brushed or satin finish. Brass, copper, and aluminum are protected from oxidation by a clear resin-enamel baked-on coating. Stainless steel needs no protection. Exposed metals may be had with a "hammered" pattern, if desired.

Sizes: Flat tile is available in three sizes: 4¼ by 4¼, 4¼ by 8½, and 8½ by 8½ in.

Trim: Three types of trim are available (Fig. 7): (1) Flat-cap, using the standard tile depth; (2) Bullnose-cap, showing a slightly bulbous projection to give an illusion of greater thickness to the tile; (3) Extended-depth, providing a rounded return at the top to give an even greater appearance of depth than the bullnose-cap. Each system employs related coves or bases, corners, and angles to provide a complete wall installation. The resin-enamel tile may be bent around corners, but the porcelain-enamel tile requires special corner shapes.

Installation: Metal tile is affixed to the backing material by the float method, using mastic. Brown-coat plaster or the various wallboards make excellent bases. Porous materials need sealing with primers. Two types of mastic are used:

1. *Oil-type mastic* with white lead or with titanium pigment, which must be applied with a notched trowel over two coats of orange shellac. The tile may be applied immediately to the mastic, which may also serve as grout between the tiles.

2. *Resinous-type mastic,* which may be applied without the use of a sealer but does require waiting before application of tile and does require the use of a grouting

compound. Also, a special cleaner is required to remove excess mastic from the face of the tile.

Plastic tile

Plastic tile is made by the injection molding process from a polystyrene molding compound to which fillers and pigments have been added. Its manufacture and installation are controlled by an industry standard, U.S. Department of Commerce Commercial Standard CS168-50 *Polystyrene Plastic Wall Tiles and Adhesives for Their Application.* This standard establishes requirements for thickness, size, heat resistance, color fastness, opacity, and defects not permitted. Minimum thickness is 0.062 in., and the lip must extend at least 0.033 in. beyond the back of the tile.

Plastic tile is as thin as metal tile and even lighter in weight (¾ lb per sq ft in place). It has an unlimited range of colors, plain or mottled, and the pattern extends through the thickness of the tile. It is available in various surface finishes: glossy, matte, striated, scored, or other textured finish. It is moisture-resistant and nonabsorptive, hence sanitary and easily cleaned but it is not as hard as metal or ceramic tile and it can be scratched. Plastic tile should not be used outdoors nor should it be subjected to continued direct radiation from sun lamps or germicidal lights. It is combustible but not hazardous, since it does not ignite easily and it burns slowly. It is adversely affected by certain chemicals, such as paste waxes and spray insecticides.

Sizes range from 1 in. sq to 12 in. sq, with the 4¼-in. size being the most generally used. The edges of the tile are rounded or cushioned to give an appearance of depth. Projections have been molded to the back of the tile by some manufacturers to minimize the concaving of the tile in the larger sizes. Spacer-type edges are provided by some manufacturers to facilitate spacing and alignment. Secondary ribs parallel to the edges have been molded in by some manufacturers to improve water resistance; mastic trapped in these grooves prevents moisture from entering the cavity behind the tile.

Installation: Plastic tile may be applied to walls or ceilings that are smooth, straight, dry, and structurally sound or rigid. The surface may be plaster, gypsum board, plywood, hardboard, fiberboard, asbestos-cement board, or concrete. Walls subject to moisture penetration or condensation should be furred-out and resurfaced. In wet locations, such as shower recesses, it may be desirable to prime the wall first. The adhesive manufacturer's directions should be followed carefully. Towel bars and other bath accessories should be fastened to the structural wall and not to the tile.

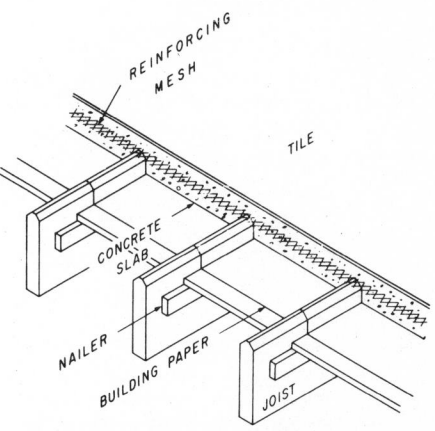

Fig. 6. Detail of thick-bed tile floor over wood joists

This detail is used to keep tile floor at same level as other finish floors. (Courtesy National Lumber Manufacturers Association.)

The mastic is applied with a notched trowel. Removal of a tile should show at least 75 per cent coverage of the tile with adhesive. Follow the manufacturer's directions as to rate of spread and thickness, as adhesives vary with reference to speed of drying, thickness required, and open times. Tile is usually set about ⅛ in. away from adjacent tile and then slid into place, allowing a small space at least 0.005 in. between tile. The mastic squeezed between the tile is then pointed or smoothed out to provide a grouted joint. Grout may be added if necessary. The tile may be set in place close to the adjacent tile if an ungrouted (clean joint) is desired. Tile never should be butted together tightly; room for expansion should be allowed, particularly when it is installed at a temperature below 70°F.

Special shapes of tile are available for caps, cove bases, and corners. Tile should either be cut with a guillotine-type cutter or sawed; snips or scissors should not be used. No attempt should be made to clean the tile until the mastic has set; then a special cleaner should be used with a soft cloth.

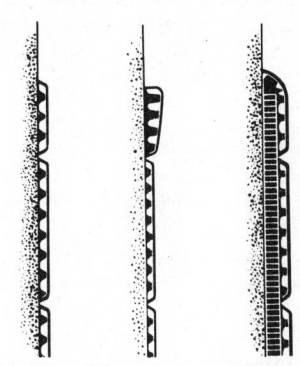

Fig. 7. Metal tile—sections through three types of caps: Flat, Bullnose, Extended depth

Courtesy Vikon Tile Corporation.

By HOWARD P. VERMILYA, AIA, and JOHN HANCOCK CALLENDER, Professor of Architecture, Pratt Institute

Terrazzo is a type of marble mosaic that utilizes a portland cement matrix. It is an extremely durable surface of great beauty and variety, made possible by the wide choice of colors and sizes of the marble chips, the design of the divider strips, and the possibility of using metal or mosaic inserts. Although its principal use is for interior and exterior floors, terrazzo, cast in place or precast, is also used for bases, wainscots, partitions, shower receptors, stairs, and many other items. As precast tile, usually made with large chips or broken marble, it is used on both floors and walls.

Marble is vulnerable to attack by acids and strong alkalies. Therefore terrazzo, being essentially a marble product, should *not* be used where it may come in contact with acids or strong alkali concentrations.

Terrazzo topping

The following types of terrazzo topping are included in "Specifications and Technical Data," issued by the National Terrazzo and Mosaic Association, Inc., in 1961:

1. *Standard.* Composed of No. 1 and No. 2 (and sometimes No. 3) marble chips (see Table 1); minimum thickness, ⅝ in.; uses 1¼-in.-deep divider strips.

2. *Venetian.* Composed of No. 1 through No. 8 marble chips; minimum thickness, 1 in.; uses 1½-in.-deep divider strips.

3. *Berliner* (Palladiana). Composed of broken marble ranging in size from 4 to 140 sq. in., with joints of standard terrazzo ranging in width from ½ to 5 in.; minimum thickness, 1 in.

4. *Rustic* (Washed). A standard or venetian topping which is washed or broomed before it has set and is later treated with acid; may or may not be ground; used principally outdoors.

5. *Conductive.* Same as standard type but includes acetylene carbon black in matrix and underbed to make it electrically conductive; used principally in hospital operating rooms.

6. *Abrasive.* Same as standard or venetian but includes abrasive aggregates in the matrix; used to prevent slipping in shower receptors, around swimming pools, and outdoors.

The last three types are discussed in more detail below.

Colors of terrazzo floors are those of the marbles used, and they may be mixed as desired. The National Terrazzo and Mosaic Association maintains a catalog of color plates which may be referred to by architects in specifying colors. The marble chips constitute at least 70 per cent of the terrazzo surface. The cement matrix may be white or gray cement, or it may be colored, using pigments which are non-fading and not affected by alkali.

The mix should be in the proportion of 200 lb of aggregate (marble chips) to 94 lb (1 bag) of portland cement (Type 1, ASTM C150), with not more than 5½ gal of water.

Installation. Once it is in place, the topping is rolled and then hand-troweled to an even surface exposing the top of the divider strips. After curing (minimum six days), the surface is machine-rubbed, while covered with water, using No. 24

grit or finer abrasive stones and followed with No. 80 grit or finer stones. Then a neat-cement grout is applied to the cleaned surface to fill the surface voids. Not less than 72 hours later, all surplus grout should be removed by regrinding in water, using No. 80 grit or finer abrasive stones. After cleaning, a terrazzo sealer should be applied and the floor buffed.

Abrasive terrazzo floors fall into three different types:

1. *Normal:* Abrasive aggregate sprinkled over topping before rolling (¼–½ lb abrasive aggregate per sq ft).

2. *Quarter-inch:* Standard terrazzo topping placed to within ¼ in. of finished floor level; abrasive mix containing 10–40 per cent abrasive to total aggregate (standard ratio of aggregate to cement being maintained) is placed immediately to bring to finished level.

Table 1.   Marble chip sizes (adopted by National Terrazzo and Mosaic Association)

Chip size number	Passes through screen Inches	Retained on screen Inches
0	⅛	1/16
1	¼	⅛
2	⅜	¼
3	½	⅜
4	⅝	½
5	¾	⅝
6	⅞	¾
7	1	⅞
8	1⅛	1

3. *Abrasive mixed throughout:* Abrasive mix to consist of 10–40 per cent abrasive to total aggregate. This type, which is placed in the same manner as standard terrazzo topping, is used only for very heavy-duty floors.

The surface in all types should show at least 70 per cent aggregate, marble and abrasive.

Conductive terrazzo floors require careful workmanship to meet the requirements of the National Fire Protection Association (Bulletin 56), which call for an electrical resistance of less than 1 million ohms and greater than 25,000 ohms. To prevent the development of static electricity, acetylene carbon black is mixed into the terrazzo topping and the underbed, a total minimum thickness of 1¾ in. Three pounds (dry weight) of acetylene black is added to the underbed mix and 2 lb is added to the topping for each 94 lb (1 bag) of cement; only 5 gal of water is used per bag of cement. The acetylene black is introduced as a thin paste mixed with a 1½ per cent solution of isopropyl alcohol, using ¾ gal for each pound. Machine mixing of this paste into the entire batch for a minimum of 1 min and a maximum of 3 min is required to obtain uniform dispersion. Excess mixing destroys the function of the acetylene black. Galvanized-iron reinforcing mesh (not grounded) is used in the underbed to provide uniform conductivity. Heavy-top nonconductive plastic divider strips on galvanized steel bottoms with suitable anchorage are used to divide the floor into 2- by 2-ft squares. Floors are cured for a minimum of fourteen days, then ground and grouted, and 2 lb of acetylene black per 94 lb of cement are added to the grout. Finishing should be done not earlier than seven days later. The floor is then cleaned, re-ground, and sealed. Sealers and cleaners should not leave a film which may destroy conductivity of the floor. Acids must not be used to clean terrazzo floors.

Rustic finish, usually used only on outdoor terrazzo, is achieved by washing the surface before it has set with water under pressure or with a stiff broom, to a depth of approximately $\frac{1}{16}$ in., taking care not to disturb the marble chips. After curing, the surface is saturated with water and then washed with a 10 per cent solution of muriatic acid, after which it is thoroughly cleaned with water. Surface is usually not ground, although it may be lightly ground when laid as a patio floor or swimming pool deck.

Underbeds

Underbed thicknesses vary with the type of construction. It is conventional to express this thickness in terms of the over-all thickness of the underbed and the terrazzo topping, ⅝ in. for standard or 1 in. for venetian.

1. *Bonded terrazzo,* where the underbed is bonded with a neat-cement coating to the structural slab; minimum thickness, 1¾ in. (outdoors, 2 in.) (Fig. 1).

2. *Sand-cushion terrazzo,* where the underbed is laid with reinforcing mesh over a waterproof-membrane-covered sand bed ¼ in. thick; minimum total thickness, 3 in. (Fig. 2).

3. *Terrazzo over wood,* where the underbed is laid with reinforcing mesh over a waterproof membrane laid on a tight wood deck; minimum thickness, 2 in. (Fig. 3).

Underbed used in the above types of construction is a mixture of one part portland cement (Type I) to four parts of sand. Reinforcing mesh is 2 by 2-in., galvanized, welded wire mesh. Waterproof membrane is 5-lb, asphalt-saturated roofing felt.

4. *Monolithic terrazzo,* where the topping is placed directly on a fresh, structural concrete slab, which must be at least 4 in. thick and reinforced. If the slab is on grade, as is usually the case, it should be poured over a waterproof and vapor-proof membrane laid on a thoroughly compacted drainage bed of broken stone or gravel. Topping should be installed preferably not later than 24 hours, and in no case more than 6 days, after the structural slab is poured.

The sand-cushion method offers the best assurance of a sound floor without cracks due to vibration or movement of the structure. The same principle of isolating the terrazzo from a substrate in which movement can be expected is used over wood construction. Monolithic terrazzo was developed to provide an attractive and durable floor finish at low initial cost, primarily for residences.

Divider strips

Divider strips are used to control and localize any shrinkage or flexure cracks. (If terrazzo is properly installed, shrinkage cracks will not occur.) The strips fulfill an important decorative purpose by creating scale and pattern and permitting changes of color to be made with ease and accuracy. They also serve, during installation of the topping, as grounds for establishing the level of the finished surface. Finally, they facilitate repair or replacement of damaged sections of topping.

The strips should be carried through the border to the wall or to the edge of the terrazzo. They should be placed over beams, girders, columns, and bearing walls, around stair openings, and wherever there is likely to be a change of stress in the floor. Expansion-type strips with neoprene cores should be placed not more than 30 ft apart in corridors and other places where considerable movement can be anticipated. In monolithic terrazzo, which is usually installed before the partitions, strips should be located under the partitions wherever there are significant changes of area, and they should be used to divide large areas into panels. Panel sizes vary from 16 to 50 in., depending upon the size of the floor area. Small panels are preferable but more expensive. Outdoor panels should not exceed 3 ft; conductive panels should not exceed 2 ft.

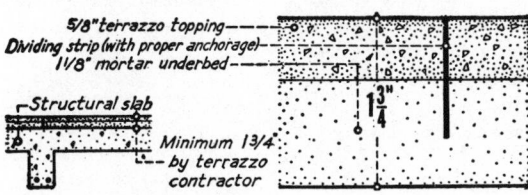

Fig. 1. Bonded terrazzo

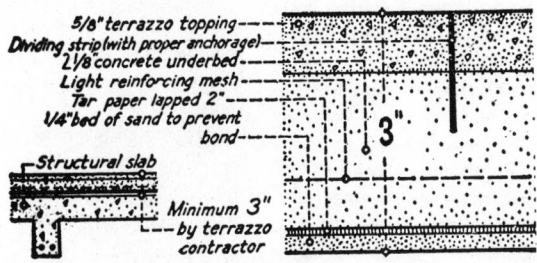

Fig. 2. Sand-cushion terrazzo

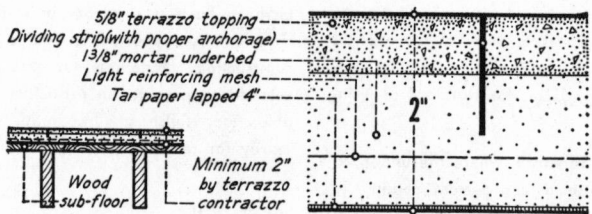

Fig. 3. Terrazzo on wood construction

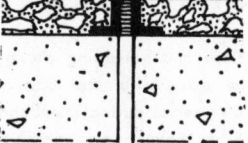

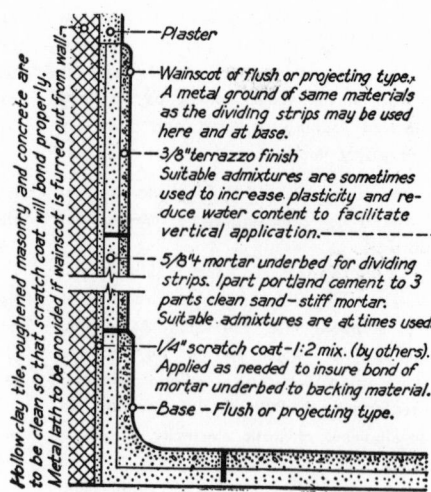

Fig. 6. Terrazzo wainscot

(Note) All figures courtesy of National Terrazzo and Mosaic Association.

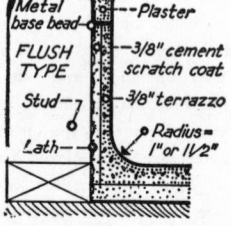

Fig. 4. Monolithic terrazzo with expansion-type divider strip

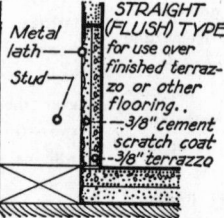

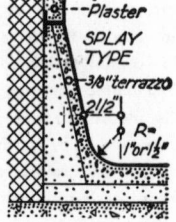

Fig. 5. Terrazzo bases

Fig. 7. Solid partition

Divider strips are made from half-hard brass, white alloy zinc (99 per cent zinc), or plastic (acetate butyrate) in a number of colors. Zinc strips should not be used outdoors. Thickness ranges from 18 gage (minimum) to ¼ in. or more. Strips ⅛ in. and thicker are of the heavy-top type, with a thin bottom member. These are usually fabricated to the architect's design in shops specializing in this work. Strips for standard terrazzo are 1¼ in. deep; for Venetian terrazzo they are 1½ in. deep. They are installed in the underbed while it is semiplastic, before the topping is placed. Strips for monolithic terrazzo are T- or L-shaped and ⅝ in. deep. They are fastened to the green underbed by cement nails or are set in grout. Expansion-type strips (Fig. 4) should be used over control or expansion joints in the structural slab.

Bases

Terrazzo bases are usually installed integrally with the floor. They may be flush, projected, or splayed, and the intersection with the floor may be a right angle or cove (Fig. 5). The bases are capped with a metal bead. Divider strips should align with those of the floor; the usual practice is to continue every other floor divider through the base. A precast terrazzo base is sometimes used, especially with other flooring materials.

Wainscots and partitions

Terrazzo wainscots and partitions consist of ⅜ in. topping and ⅝ in. underbed, applied to masonry or to a cement-plaster scratch coat on metal lath (Fig. 6). Solid partitions should be formed with ¾-in. furring channels 12 in. on center; a cement-plaster scratch coat is applied to both sides of the metal lath, to receive terrazzo underbed and topping (Fig. 7). Underbed for wainscots and partitions consists of a 1 to 3 mix of portland cement and sand. Divider strips should be spaced not more than 30 in. apart.

Stairs

Terrazzo is often used as a finish for stairs. Treads and risers may be poured in place or precast, and they may be installed over a concrete or steel base (Fig. 8). Topping for poured-in-place treads and risers should be ⅝ in. and the over-all thickness not less than 1½ in. for treads and 1 in. for risers. Strings may have ⅜ in. topping and ⅝ in. underbed. On steel stairs the underbed must be reinforced and anchored to the steel; NTMA recommends an over-all thickness of 2 in. for treads and 1½ in. for risers. However, risers are usually omitted here.

Shower receptors

The detail of a cast-in-place shower receptor is shown in Fig. 9. Precast types are also available.

Precast terrazzo

Precast terrazzo, also known as artificial marble, is used for floor and wall tile, bases, stair treads and risers, window stools, door saddles, shower receptors, counter tops and various specialty items. The mix is usually 2½ parts aggregate (marble chips) to 1 part cement, by weight.

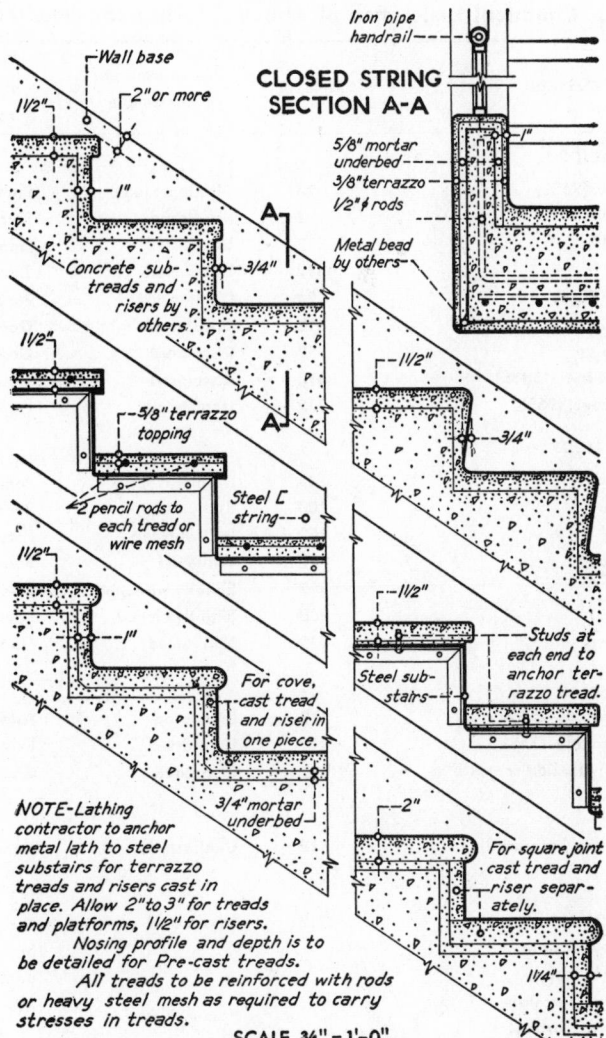

CLOSED STRING
SECTION A-A

Wall base
1½"
2" or more
1"
Concrete sub-
treads and
risers by
others.
¾"
5/8" terrazzo
topping
2 pencil rods to
each tread or
wire mesh
1½"
1"
For cove,
cast tread
and riser in
one piece.
¾" mortar
underbed

Iron pipe
handrail
5/8" mortar
underbed
3/8" terrazzo
½"ø rods
Metal bead
by others
1"
1½"
¾"
Steel C
string
1½"
Steel sub-
stairs
Studs at
each end to
anchor ter-
razzo tread.
2"
For square joint
cast tread and
riser separ-
ately.
1¼"

NOTE—Lathing
contractor to anchor
metal lath to steel
substairs for terrazzo
treads and risers cast in
place. Allow 2" to 3" for treads
and platforms, 1½" for risers.
    Nosing profile and depth is to
be detailed for Pre-cast treads.
    All treads to be reinforced with rods
or heavy steel mesh as required to carry
stresses in treads.

SCALE ¾" = 1'-0"

Fig. 8. Terrazzo stair details. Top: poured in place on concrete, two nosing designs. Center: on steel; left, poured in place; right, precast. Bottom: precast on concrete; left, tread and riser one piece; right, tread and riser two pieces.

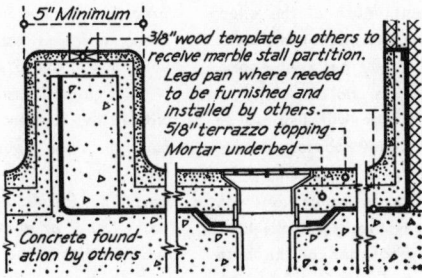

5" Minimum
3/8" wood template by others to
receive marble stall partition.
Lead pan where needed
to be furnished and
installed by others.
5/8" terrazzo topping
Mortar underbed
Concrete found-
ation by others

Fig. 9. Terrazzo shower receptor (poured in place)

It is cast by a compression and vibration process in watertight metal molds.

Thin-set terrazzo

Several types of thin-set terrazzo have been developed in recent years. Their principal advantage is the elimination of the underbed (1 to 2 in. thick). This not only reduces the dead load on the structure but also, in many cases, eliminates the need for depressing the structural slab where terrazzo meets another flooring material. Another important advantage is reduction in installation time from the ten days or more required for conventional terrazzo to as little as two days for some thin-set types. Most thin-set systems are proprietary; strict compliance with the manufacturer's instructions is necessary. Skilled workmanship is as important in thin-set as in conventional terrazzo installation.

The principal types of thin-set terrazzo are:

1. *Bonding agent.* An organic adhesive (polysulfide, neoprene, vinyl, or epoxy) is applied to the structural slab before the topping is poured. The topping is standard portland cement type, 5/8 in. thick, installed and finished in the conventional way. Divider strips are required; they are set in adhesive.

2. *Admixtures.* The addition of acrylic or vinyl emulsions to the standard topping mix results in a notable increase in the tensile and flexural strength of the terrazzo. Thickness of the topping may be reduced in some cases to as little as ¼ in. The use of a bonding agent is advisable. Divider strips are not required but are recommended for locations where stresses can be anticipated; they are set in adhesive. Over substrates subject to movement, glass-fabric reinforcement may be bedded in the adhesive.

3. *Plastic matrix.* In this type of terrazzo a plastic (epoxy or neoprene) replaces portland cement as the matrix. The cured topping has an extremely high tensile strength and can be as thin as the size of the marble chips will permit. In practice, epoxy terrazzo is usually ⅛ to 3/8 in. thick, and neoprene terrazzo is 3/8 to 5/8 in. thick. Divider strips are not required but are recommended for locations subject to stress. Since the epoxy has a limited "pot life," the strips may be used to mark off areas that can be completed within the time limit. Divider strips must be metal and are set in epoxy adhesive. A liquid primer is usually required; it is applied 2 to 3 hours before the installation of the terrazzo mix.

FLOORING—5
Epoxy

By GERALD R. WEISSMAN, *Director, Coatings Department, Foster D. Snell, Inc., Consulting Chemists*

Epoxy toppings for industrial floors

The outstanding advantage of epoxy toppings for concrete floors in industrial and laboratory buildings is their high degree of resistance to chemical attack from acids, alkalies, and solvents. The general range of this resistance is indicated in the accompanying table. The destructive effect of any chemical is determined by three things: concentration, temperature, and duration of exposure. The conditions occurring in a given plant are virtually impossible to duplicate in laboratory tests; therefore, whenever possible, it is prudent to subject samples to conditions similar to those which will be encountered in the building being designed. Usually, this can be done by putting various samples in one of the owner's present buildings.

Epoxy floor toppings develop ultimate compressive strengths of 10,000 to 15,000 psi. In abrasion resistance they are superior to average concrete floors, but not as resistant as the highest-quality concrete topping. In comparison with other industrial floor toppings epoxies are thin (⅛ to ¹⁄₁₆ in.), light in weight, jointless, and quick-curing. They can usually be put into service within 1 to 3 days, and they attain their maximum strength within 1 week. Where appearance is a factor, the glossy finish and wide choice of colors in epoxy is an advantage in its favor.

The principal ingredients in an epoxy floor are (1) silica sand, or some material with a high silicate content, or materials like glass cloth or crushed stone, which are inert to most chemical attack; (2) epoxy resin, which in its fully concentrated form also is inert to many chemicals. These ingredients are analogous in function to aggregate and cement in a concrete floor. Epoxy resin is the binder which holds the mass together and bonds it to the base slab. Aggregate adds impact strength and brings the coefficient of thermal expansion of the epoxy closer to that of the concrete to which it is bonded.

In addition, a curing agent and a flexibilizer also are used. The curing agent converts the liquid epoxy resin to a solid. Numerous agents are available, but to withstand industrial floor usage, only one type is normally suitable—an aliphatic amine curing agent that produces the best combination of temperature, chemical, and mechanical properties.

The flexibilizer improves crack and impact resistance. Thus, when stresses are set up by differences in thermal expansion between the epoxy and the concrete base, for example, during steam cleaning, the epoxy will not crack. The amount of flexibilizer used is critical: too little leaves

Table 1. Chemical resistance of epoxy flooring composition*

Material	Time, hr	Appearance of test sample	Evaluation of chemical resistance
MINERAL ACIDS			
Sulfuric-conc. (96%)	24	Disintegrated	Poor
Sulfuric—50%	312	Discolored	Fair-Good
Sulfuric—20%	312	Unaffected	Good
Sulfuric—10%	312	Unaffected	Good
Nitric-conc. (78%)	24	Disintegrated	Poor
Nitric—40%	312	Discolored slightly	Good
Nitric—20%	312	Discolored	Good
Hydrochloric-conc. (38%)	312	Discolored	Good
Phosphoric-conc. (86%)	312	Unaffected	Good
ORGANIC ACIDS			
Acetic, glacial (99.5%)	48	Disintegrated	Poor
Acetic—50%	100	Badly etched	Poor
Acetic—20%	150	Badly etched	Poor
Acetic—10%	312	Whitened	Fair-Good
Acetic—5%	312	Slightly whitened	Good
Lactic (100%)	200	Slightly etched	Poor-Fair
Oleic (100%)	312	Unaffected	Good
BASES			
Sodium hydroxide—50%	312	Discolored	Fair-Poor
Sodium hydroxide—25%	312	Unaffected	Excellent
Ammonium hydroxide conc. (57%)	312	Discolored	Good
SALTS			
Sodium bisulfite (saturated)	312	Unaffected	Good
SOLVENTS			
Mineral spirits, Xylol, Benzene, Ethyl acetate, Methyl ethyl ketone, Methyl cellosolve acetate, Butyl cellosolve, carbitol	312	Unaffected	Excellent (except for benzene which is rated as good)

Note: Samples listed were tested at room temperature. Compressive strength before exposure was 14,500 psi.

the floor brittle; too much reduces the floor's strength.

The maximum amount of aggregate that can be used without seriously impairing the properties of the topping is four times the combined weight of the epoxy resin and the curing agent. Much of the effectiveness of an epoxy floor depends on the way it is installed. A 100 per cent epoxy, correctly formulated, is not in itself a guarantee that the floor will live up to expectations. As in many phases of construction, workmanship is important.

An important factor in connection with adhesion of the epoxy topping to the base slab is adequate preparation of the base slab. Despite epoxy's fame for great adhesion, good bond will not occur unless the base slab surface is clean, dry, and roughened. Slab preparation is done either

by sand blasting or chemical etching. Workmen must do every inch of the floor carefully since only one defective spot is sufficient to cause trouble.

A properly prepared slab will permit the epoxy to achieve a bond strength greater than the internal strength of concrete, which is assurance that the bond will not fail under stress.

One other installation procedure is critical: the temperature. To achieve proper cure, the floor should be applied when the temperature is 70 to 80°F. Epoxies should never be installed if the temperature is below 60°F or above 105°F. At the lower temperature curing will not occur for an excessively long time, and at the higher temperature curing will occur so fast that it might be impossible to install the topping properly.

By HOWARD P. VERMILYA, AIA

Hardwoods commonly used as flooring are oak (white and red), hard (sugar) maple, birch, beech, and pecan. Walnut, teak, and other fine hardwoods are occasionally used. Softwoods used are generally the denser species such as Douglas fir and southern yellow pine. Redwood and western red cedar, although quite soft, are used for porch floors and outdoor decks because of their resistance to decay. All species are available in both quarter-sawed (vertical or edge-grain) and plain-sawed (flat-grain). Vertical-grain flooring wears better, especially in the softwoods, and has less tendency to cup and warp. End-grain wood blocks of southern yellow pine, upland oak, or hard maple are used for heavy-duty industrial flooring. The physical properties of the principal woods used for flooring are given in Table 2. Standard sizes of strip flooring are shown in Tables 3–5.

Oak, both red and white, is used principally as strip flooring, but also as plank, parquet, and block flooring. It is the most widely used of all species, especially for residential purposes. It is available in two grades of quarter-sawed and five grades of plain-sawed strip, either square-edged or tongued-and-grooved and end-matched. Red and white oak are graded separately in grades above No. 2 common, but color within the species is not considered. Both are light in color, white oak having a brownish tinge and red oak a pinkish cast. Oak strip flooring is covered by Commercial Standard CS56-60 of the U.S. Department of Commerce. Standard grades are as follows:

Quarter-sawed or plain-sawed:

Clear: The face shall be practically clear, admitting an average of ⅜ in. of bright sap. Bundles are to be 2 ft and up; average length, 4¼ ft.

Select: The face may contain sap, small streaks, pin worm holes, burls, slight imperfections in working, and small tight knots which do not average more than one to every 3 ft. Bundles are to be 2 ft and up; average length, 3¾ ft.

Plain-sawed only:

No. 1 common: This shall be of such nature as will lay a good residential floor and may contain varying wood characteristics such as flags, heavy streaks and checks, worm holes, knots, and minor imperfections in working. Bundles are to be 2 ft and up; average length, 3 ft.

No. 2 common: This may contain sound natural variations of the forest product and manufacturing imperfections. The purpose of this grade is to furnish an economical

floor suitable for homes or general utility use, or where character marks and contrasting appearance are desired. Bundles are to be 1¼ ft and up; average length, 2½ ft.

1¼ ft shorts: Pieces may range from 9 to 18 in. long, but they must average 15 in. There are two grade classifications: No. 1 (common and better), and No. 2 (common).

Prefinished oak flooring is available in the following grades (red and white oak are separated in each grade):

Prime: The face shall be selected for appearance after finishing, but sapwood and the natural variations of color are permitted. The minimum average length is 4 ft; bundles are to be 2 ft and longer.

Standard and better: A combination of prime and standard to contain the full product of the board except that no pieces are to be lower than standard grade. The minimum average length is 3½ ft; bundles are to be 1¼ ft and longer.

Standard: This will contain sound wood characteristics which are even and smooth after filling and finishing and will lay a sound floor without cutting. The minimum average length is 3 ft; bundles are to be 1¼ ft and longer.

Tavern: This shall be of such nature as will make and lay a serviceable floor without cutting, but shall purposely contain typical wood characteristics which are to be properly filled and finished. The minimum average length is 2½ ft; bundles are to be 1¼ ft and longer.

Hard maple, beech, and birch are available in four standard grades which do not consider color variation and in three special grades selected for color. Maple is the species most used for gymnasium floors

and is also widely used for industrial flooring. It is available in several heavy-duty thicknesses (Table 4). Grades (as listed in the Maple Flooring Manufacturers' *Specifications Manual*) are as follows:

First grade: 25/32 in. and thicker, its face shall be practically free of all defects, but the varying natural color of the wood shall not be considered a defect. Standard lengths in all widths in this grade shall be in 2-ft bundles and longer as the stock will produce. Not over 30 per cent of the total footage shall be in bundles under 4 ft.

Second grade: 25/32 in. and thicker, it admits of tight, sound knots and slight imperfections in dressing, but must lay without waste. Standard lengths in all widths in this grade shall be in 2-ft bundles and longer as the stock will produce. Not over 45 per cent of the total footage shall be in bundles under 4 ft.

Third grade: 25/32 in. and thicker, it must be of such character as will lay and give a good serviceable floor. Standard lengths in all widths of this grade shall be in 1¼-ft bundles and longer as the stock will produce. Not over 65 per cent of the total footage shall be in bundles under 4 ft.

Fourth grade: 25/32 in. and thicker, it may contain defects of all character, but must lay a serviceable floor, with some cutting. Standard lengths in all widths shall be in 1¼-ft bundles and longer as the stock will produce.

Special grades:

Selected first-grade light northern hard maple: This grade is carefully selected for uniformity of light color. The color tones in individual strips will vary somewhat,

Table 2. Physical properties of woods used for flooring

Species	Specific gravity*	Hardness†	
		End	Side
Beech, American	0.64	1590	1300
Birch, yellow	0.62	1480	1260
Pecan	0.66	1930	1820
Hickory, shagbark	0.72	—	—
Maple, sugar	0.63	1840	1450
Oak:			
Northern red	0.63	1580	1290
Southern red	0.59	1020	1060
White	0.68	1520	1360
Douglas fir, coast type	0.48	900	710
Pine, southern yellow shortleaf	0.51	750	690

* Moisture content, 12%.
† Load required to embed 0.044-in. steel ball to one-half its diameter.
SOURCE: Wood Handbook, Forest Products Laboratory, U.S. Department of Agriculture, 1955.

but after laying, this grade provides a luxurious "light"-appearing floor.

Selected first-grade amber northern hard maple: This grade is carefully selected for uniformity of amber color. The color tones in individual strips will vary somewhat, but after laying, this grade provides a luxurious "amber"-appearing floor.

Selected first-grade red: This grade is produced from all-red faced northern beech or birch and is selected especially for color. The color is a rich, warm tint peculiar to these woods.

Lengths are the same as for standard first grade.

Pecan is available in three standard grades and three special grades selected for color. Pecan, a species of hickory, is denser than the other hardwoods used for flooring. It is sometimes mixed with true hickory, an even denser wood, as strip flooring for industrial use. Grades are as follows:

First grade: It shall be practically free of defects, but the varying natural color of the wood shall not be considered a defect. Bundles shall be 2 ft and longer; not over 25 per cent of the footage shall be 2 and 3 ft.

First-grade red: This is the same as first grade except that the face shall be all heartwood.

First-grade white: This is the same as first grade except that the face shall be all bright sapwood.

Second grade: This will admit of tight, sound knots or their equivalent, pin worm holes, streaks, light stains, and slight imperfections in working. It shall be of such nature as to lay a sound floor without cutting. Bundles shall be 1¼ ft and longer; the proportion of 1¼- to 3-ft bundles shall not exceed 40 per cent of the footage.

Second-grade red: This is the same as second grade except that the face shall be all heartwood.

Third grade: This must be of such character as will give and lay a good, serviceable floor. Bundles shall be 1¼ ft and longer; the proportion of 1¼- to 3-ft bundles shall not exceed 60 per cent of the footage.

Prefinished beech and pecan is furnished in one grade only:

Tavern and better: A combination of prime, standard and tavern containing the full product of the board except that no pieces are to be lower than tavern grade. The minimum average length is 3 ft, bundles are 1¼ ft and longer.

Douglas fir is graded B or better, C, and D in vertical grain and C or better, D, and E in flat grain or mixed grain.

The vertical-grain grades are widely used

Table 3. Hardwood strip flooring sizes, counts, and weights

SOURCE: *Specification Manual of the National Oak Flooring Manufacturers' Association*

"Nominal" is the size designation used by the *trade*, but it is not always the actual size. Sometimes the actual thickness of hardwood flooring is 1/32-inch less than the so-called nominal size. "Actual" is the mill size for thickness and face width, excluding tongue width. "Counted" size determines the board feet in a shipment. Pieces less than 1 inch in thickness are considered to be 1 inch.

OAK

NOMINAL	ACTUAL	Counted	Weights M Ft.
TONGUED AND GROOVED-END MATCHED			
25⁄32 x 3¼ in.	25⁄32 x 3¼ in.	1 x 4 in.	2300 lbs.
25⁄32 x 2¼ in.	25⁄32 x 2¼ in.	1 x 3 in.	2100 lbs.
25⁄32 x 2 in.	25⁄32 x 2 in.	1 x 2¾ in.	2000 lbs.
25⁄32 x 1½ in.	25⁄32 x 1½ in.	1 x 2¼ in.	1900 lbs.
3⁄8 x 2 in.	11⁄32 x 2 in.	1 x 2½ in.	1000 lbs.
3⁄8 x 1½ in.	11⁄32 x 1½ in.	1 x 2 in.	1000 lbs.
½ x 2 in.	15⁄32 x 2 in.	1 x 2½ in.	1350 lbs.
½ x 1½ in.	15⁄32 x 1½ in.	1 x 2 in.	1300 lbs.
SQUARE EDGE			
5⁄16 x 2 in.	5⁄16 x 2 in.	face count	1200 lbs.
5⁄16 x 1½ in.	5⁄16 x 1½ in.	face count	1200 lbs.

BEECH, BIRCH, HARD MAPLE AND PECAN

NOMINAL	ACTUAL	Counted	Weights M Ft.
TONGUED AND GROOVED-END MATCHED			
25⁄32 x 3¼ in.	25⁄32 x 3¼ in.	1 x 4 in.	2300 lbs.
25⁄32 x 2¼ in.	25⁄32 x 2¼ in.	1 x 3 in.	2100 lbs.
25⁄32 x 2 in.	25⁄32 x 2 in.	1 x 2¾ in.	2000 lbs.
25⁄32 x 1½ in.	25⁄32 x 1½ in.	1 x 2¼ in.	1900 lbs.
3⁄8 x 2 in.	11⁄32 x 2 in.	1 x 2½ in.	1000 lbs.
3⁄8 x 1½ in.	11⁄32 x 1½ in.	1 x 2 in.	1000 lbs.
½ x 2 in.	15⁄32 x 2 in.	1 x 2½ in.	1350 lbs.
½ x 1½ in.	15⁄32 x 1½ in.	1 x 2 in.	1300 lbs.
SPECIAL THICKNESSES (T and G, End Matched)			
17⁄16 x 3¼ in.	33⁄32 x 3¼ in.	5/4 x 4 in.	2400 lbs.
17⁄16 x 2¼ in.	33⁄32 x 2¼ in.	5/4 x 3 in.	2250 lbs.
17⁄16 x 2 in.	33⁄32 x 2 in.	5/4 x 2¾ in.	2250 lbs.
JOINTED FLOORING—i.e., SQUARE EDGE			
25⁄32 x 2½ in.	25⁄32 x 2½ in.	1 x 3¼ in.	2250 lbs.
25⁄32 x 3¼ in.	25⁄32 x 3¼ in.	1 x 4 in.	2400 lbs.
25⁄32 x 3½ in.	25⁄32 x 3½ in.	1 x 4¼ in.	2500 lbs.
17⁄16 x 2½ in.	33⁄32 x 2½ in.	5/4 x 3¼ in.	2500 lbs.
17⁄16 x 3½ in.	33⁄32 x 3½ in.	5/4 x 4¼ in.	2600 lbs.

NOTE: Oak, Beech, Birch, Hard Maple and Pecan Flooring are bundled by averaging the lengths. A bundle may include pieces from 6 in. under to 6 in. over the nominal length of the bundle. No piece shorter than 9 in. admitted.

The percentages under 4 ft. referred to in the grading rules on this page apply on total footage in any one shipment of the item.

¾-in. allowance shall be added to the face length when measuring the length of each piece.

Flooring shall not be considered of standard grade unless the lumber from which the flooring is manufactured has been properly kiln-dried.

Table 4. Maple strip flooring sizes in inches

From the Specification Manual of the Maple Flooring Manufacturers' Association

Tongued-and-grooved flooring				
Thickness	Widths			
3⁄8	1½	2	2¼	
½	1½	2	2¼	
5⁄8	1½	2	2¼	
25⁄32	1½	2	2¼	3¼
33⁄32	1½	2	2¼	3¼
41⁄32			2¼	3¼
53⁄32			2¼	3¼

* *Jointed flooring (square-edge): all thicknesses in 2½ and 3¼ in. widths; also special widths 2¼, 3⅜, and 3½ in.*

Table 5. Softwood strip flooring sizes

Thickness, in.		Widths, in.	
Nominal	Dressed minimum	Nominal	Dressed minimum
3/8	5/16	2	1½
½	7/16	3	2⅜
5/8	9/16	4	3¼
1	25/32	5	4¼
1¼	1 1/16	6	5 3/16
1½	1 5/16		

Table 6. Nailing schedule for hardwood flooring
SOURCE: *Specification Manual of NOFMA*

Tongued and Grooved Flooring Must Always Be Blind-Nailed, Square-Edge Flooring Face-Nailed.

Size Flooring	Type and Size of Nails	Spacing
(Tongued & Grooved) 25/32 x 3¼	7d or 8d screw type or cut steel nail*	10-12 in. apart
(Tongued & Grooved) 25/32 x 2¼	Same as above	Same as above
(Tongued & Grooved) 25/32 x 1½	Same as above	Same as above
(Tongued & Grooved) ½ x 2, ½ x 1½	5d screw type or cut steel or wire nail	10 in. apart
Following flooring must be laid on wood sub-floor:		
(Tongued & Grooved) ⅜ x 2, ⅜ x 1½	4d bright casing nail — wire, cut or screw nail	8 in. apart
(Square-Edge) 5/16 x 2, 5/16 x 1½	1-in. 15 gauge fully barbed flooring brad, preferably cement coated	2 nails every 7 in.

*If steel wire flooring nail is used, it should be 8d, preferably cement coated. Newly developed machine-driven barbed fasteners of the size recommended by the manufacturer are acceptable.

in institutional and industrial buildings where a serviceable floor, under conditions of moderate wear, is desired. The flat-grain grades are used where little wear is expected and are also used as underlayment for other floor coverings.

Southern yellow pine is graded similarly to Douglas fir, and as strip flooring has similar uses. It is available in thicknesses of 2, 2½, 3, 4, and 5 in. for use as factory flooring. It is also used as *end-grain-block* flooring in industrial and other heavy traffic areas, often creosoted or otherwise treated with preservatives.

Grading rules are administered by the following agencies:

Oak, pecan, maple, beech, and birch—National Oak Flooring Manufacturers Association, Memphis, Tennessee.

Maple, beech, and birch—Maple Flooring Manufacturers Association, Chicago, Ilinois.

Douglas fir—West Coast Bureau of Lumber Grades and Inspection, Portland, Oregon.

Southern yellow pine—Southern Pine Inspection Bureau, New Orleans, Louisiana.

INSTALLATION

Strip flooring is usually applied over a subfloor, although in thicknesses of 1 in. nominal or greater, it may be applied directly at right angles to the floor framing or to screeds (sleepers) over concrete floors. When so applied, the spacing of the supports should not exceed 16 in. on center for 1-in. flooring.

Subfloors are usually 1-in. wood boards, preferably square edge and not over 6 in. wide, spaced ¼ in. apart (1½ in. over screeds). At least two 8d or 10d nails should be used at each bearing. Good practice recommends that subflooring be laid diagonally over joists or screeds to provide bracing and to permit the finish flooring to be laid in either direction, parallel or perpendicular to the framing. Subfloors may also be plywood, which should be installed with the grain of the face plies perpendicular to the framing. The maximum spacing of framing members is 16 in. for ½-in.-thick five-ply C-D structural interior grade Douglas fir plywood; 20 in. for ⅝ in., and 24 in. for ¾ in. If strip flooring is laid at right angles to the framing members, the spacing for ½- and ⅝-in. plywood may be 24 in. Western softwood plywood should be ⅛ in. thicker than Douglas fir for similar spans.

Over concrete slabs on grade, wood floors must be protected against moisture and dampness. Good practice calls for the installation of a moisture barrier above or below the slab. For installation on top of the slab, which is preferred, an asphalt primer should first be applied to the concrete, followed by a 2-mil or heavier polyethylene film laid in cold asphalt mastic, or a two-ply asphalt-felt membrane laid in hot asphalt. For installation under the slab a 4- or 6-mil polyethylene should be used with the seams taped. In any case the moisture barrier should be carried up the sides of the foundation to the finished floor level.

Screeds or sleepers should be pressure-treated with a preservative other than creosote, which may bleed through the nail holes and stain the finish floor. For standard double-floor construction, screeds should be spaced 16 in. on center; if the subfloor is to be omitted, screeds must be spaced not more than 12 in. on center. For the mastic-bedded method of installation, which is now generally used, sleepers should be 2 by 4 in. in random lengths from 24 to 36 in. They are laid flat in asphalt mastic, spaced 16 in. on center, with joints staggered and space between the butts for air circulation. Mastic, if used over the entire surface of the floor, should be 3/32 in. thick; if used in "rivers" under the screeds only, it should be ¼ in. thick. For FHA single-floor installations, the 2 by 4-in. screeds should be from 18 to 30 in. long, laid 12 in. on center, with joints staggered and ends lapped 4 in. or more.

The older and more expensive method of installing screeds by anchoring them mechanically to the slab is still used, especially in large installations (Figs. 11, 12). For this method, screeds are usually 2 by 2 or 2 by 3 in. in long lengths, securely attached to the slab by means of power-driven anchors, and wedged or shimmed level. Chair anchor inserts are less often used today because they interfere with concrete-finishing machines. Beveled screeds set in the slab or held in place by fill are not recommended because they can not be shimmed and they do not stay in place well.

Good *nailing* (Table 6) is essential if loose or squeaky floors are to be avoided. Nailing is done through the tongue at an angle of approximately 45 deg (Fig. 10); a nail set should be used to drive the nail home. The screw-type nail, because of its greater holding power, is largely replacing the traditional cut nail. Finish strip flooring is usualy laid parallel to the longest dimension of the room. Short lengths are used in closets and other inconspicuous places. Since strip flooring is kiln-dried, care must be taken to protect it from moisture at time of delivery and before laying, if cupping or buckling is to be avoided. Plastering should have been completed and allowed to dry before flooring is delivered to the job. Space for expansion should be allowed at all edges of the room. This space, usually 1 in. wide, is easily covered by base and shoe moldings, which are nailed to the wall and not to the flooring (Fig. 13).

Plank flooring is laid the same as strip flooring with blind-edge nailing spaced similarly. In addition, it is fastened to the subfloor with at least two screws at each end and others along the length of the piece arranged to provide adequate holding and an attractive pattern. All screws are countersunk and covered with a glued-in-place walnut plug. Planks should not be driven tightly together.

Block and parquet flooring may be nailed or laid in mastic on a wood subfloor; over a concrete base, the mastic method must be used. Nailing is done through the tongues, as in strip flooring application. The mastic, either cold or hot, in which the flooring is embedded is usually applied over asphalt felt (30 lb) on wood subfloors and over a dampproofing membrane on concrete floors (Figs. 13, 14). In either case the manufacturer's recom-

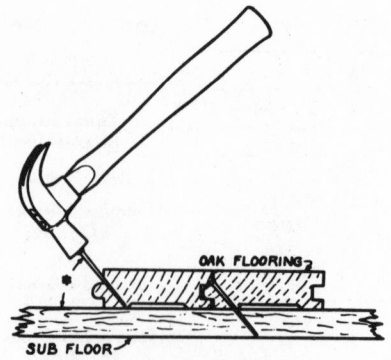

**40 to 50° dependent upon the type of nail used.*

Fig. 10. Blind nailing tongued-and-grooved strip flooring

From Commercial Standard CS56-60

mendations, since they vary somewhat based upon experience with the flooring, should be followed.

Block flooring (sometimes called wood "squares" or "tiles" to distinguish it from end-grain blocks used for industrial flooring) is produced in walnut, teak, and cherry, as well as the usual domestic hardwoods. Squares are usually 9 by 9 or 12 by 12 in., tongued and grooved, ⅜ to ¾ in. thick, unfinished or prefinished. There are two major types, unit-blocks and laminated blocks. In unit-blocks, each composed

of several small strips of flooring, the two tongue edges are at right angles to each other. In laminated blocks, made of three or five plies bonded with moisture-resistant glue, the tongues are on opposed sides. Allowance for expansion must be made with unit-blocks (see Fig. 13) but is unnecessary with laminated ones. Both kinds may be laid in square or diagonal patterns. Shapes other than square (rectangular, herringbone, end-to-end) are available in unit-blocks.

Institutional and industrial floors often present special problems, which have resulted in the development of many proprietary systems. Gymnasium and armory floors cover large unbroken areas, and must be resilient, smooth but not slippery, and easy to maintain. Industrial floors may also be very large in area, and they are often subjected to heavy, wheeled traffic and severe impact. Floors of this type are usually installed over concrete slabs on grade. They may be floated in mastic directly on the slab or installed on screeds anchored to the slab. Metal-channel screeds with interlocking metal clips for attaching the flooring are often used instead of wood screeds and nailing. Mastic-floated construction is used not only for blocks (squares), as previously mentioned, but also for end-grain blocks, herringbone parquet (Fig. 14), and steel-splined flooring (Fig. 15). The latter is 5/4-in. strip floor-

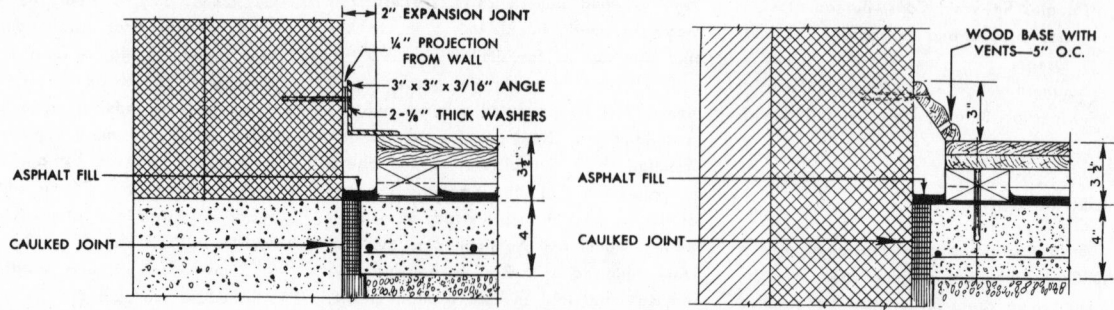

Fig. 11. Strip flooring on screeds on concrete slab with ventilating base in wood or metal

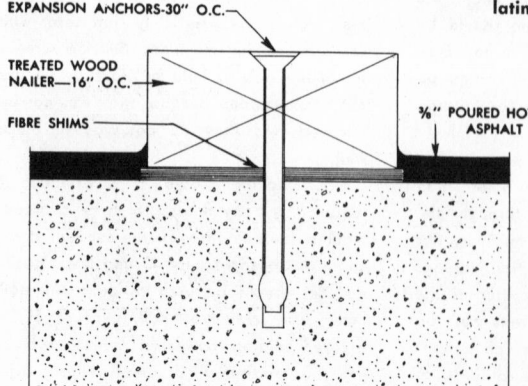

Fig. 12. Detail of wood screed anchored to concrete slab

Courtesy Wood Flooring Institute

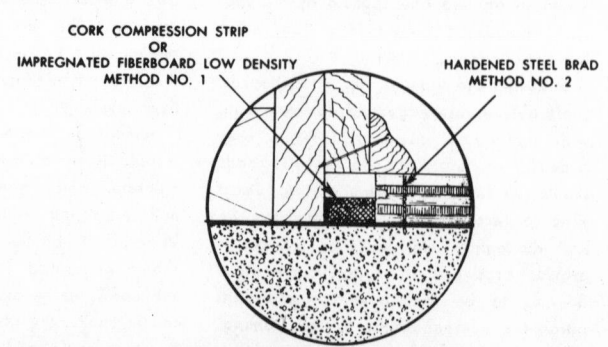

Fig. 13. Block flooring in mastic on concrete slab. Two methods of securing blocks at perimeter

Courtesy Wood Flooring Institute

ing in 12-in. lengths, with interlocking steel splines across the ends. The mastic-floated method is also used for bedding the subfloor in "mastic-nailed" construction. In this method, the pieces of subflooring, 5/4 by 4 in. and 18 in. long, are laid in mastic ½ in. apart, with end joints staggered. The spaces between the pieces are later filled with mastic and the surface is covered with mastic before the finish floor is nailed in place (Fig. 16).

The *resilience* of mastic-floated floors can be improved by the use of an underlayer of ½-in. corkboard, installed in mastic, over which the flooring is installed, also in mastic (Fig. 16). Extra resilience for floors on screeds can be provided by the use of cork or rubber pads under the screeds at each anchor.

Ventilation of the spaces between the screeds is important and, for large floor areas, mechanical ventilation is often used, especially if the floor is below grade or subject to adverse moisture conditions. The Wood Flooring Institute recommends that for floors up to 80 ft wide a ventilation trench 6½ by 15 in. be provided underneath and at right angles to the screeds; for floors more than 80 ft wide, two such trenches should be provided.

Adequate space for *expansion* must be provided on all sides of all wood flooring. The minimum space for all types except laminated block is 1 in. per 100 linear ft of flooring. In large floor areas on screeds the minimum edge space should be 1½ in. and preferably 2 in., in order to help ventilate the underfloor space; the base should be drilled or otherwise adapted to permit the circulation of air past it (Fig. 11). The edge pieces of \mastic-floated floors must be held in place by resilient filler, steel springs, or similar devices (Figs. 13, 14).

FINISHING

Unfinished wood floors require sanding before *finishing*. This is usually done with electric sanding machines. The first traverse, using No. 2 sandpaper, may be made across the grain or at a 45 deg angle (except for maple flooring, which should only be sanded with the grain); succeeding traverses should be made with the grain, using No. ½, then No. 0, and successively finer paper, depending upon the number of sandings desired. The first two sandings usually employ a drum sander and the final a rotary-disk sander. Hand sanding is done or edgers or scrapers used near walls, in corners and closets, and around pipes. The final sanding or hand buffing should not be done until immediately before finishing is to start, to prevent the grain of the unprotected wood from rising.

Open-grain flooring such as oak requires a filler; paste types have proved very satisfactory. Stain, if used, should be applied before the filler. An oil stain is advisable. Often it is combined with the filler as a pigmented filler. Three types of finish are employed most extensively: floor seal, varnish, or shellac, and occasionally lacquer. Floor seal penetrates the wood and wears with it. Worn spots can be retouched without the complete refinishing required by other types of finish. Floors are usually finally finished with paste wax, which provides a sheen and protection to the finish. Water-base waxes or the self-finishing liquid waxes are not recommended, as they have a tendency after frequent use to raise the grain and roughen the floor.

The Maple Flooring Manufacturers' Association offers a list of finish materials which are recommended for use with general-purpose maple flooring and for use with special flooring such as that in gymnasiums.

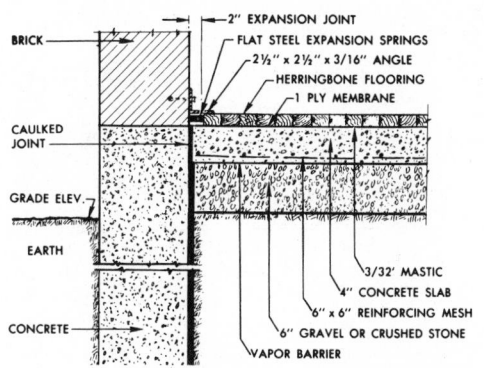
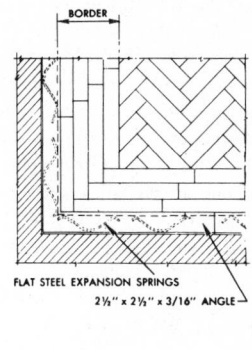

Fig. 14. Herringbone flooring in mastic on concrete slab; steel springs secure the edge pieces

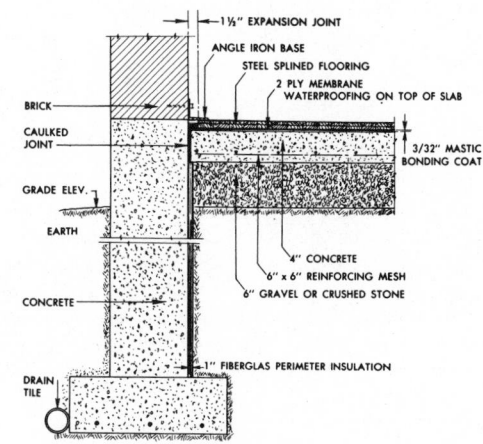

Fig. 15. Steel-splined flooring in mastic on concrete slab

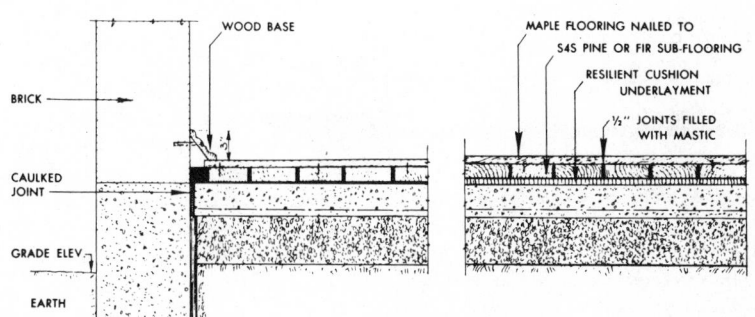

Fig. 16. Mastic-nailed flooring on concrete slab with and without resilient cushion underlayment

Courtesy Wood Flooring Institute

By HOWARD P. VERMILYA, AIA

Resilient flooring materials are produced in sheet or tile form in thicknesses ranging from $\frac{1}{16}$ to $\frac{3}{16}$ in. They are made of various compositions of resins, plasticizers, fibers, pigments, and fillers, formed under heat and pressure. Smooth-surface resilient flooring materials include asphalt tile, vinyl-asbestos tile, vinyl tile or sheet (backed or homogeneous), rubber tile or sheet, and cork tile (plain or vinyl-covered). Essential data on all types of resilient flooring are summarized in Table 7; additional data on each type will be found in the following text. Federal specifications and industry standards are listed in Table 8.

Asphalt tile. Composed through full thickness of asphaltic or resinous binder with asbestos or other fibers, fillers, and pigments, pressure-formed while hot. Sizes 12 by 12 and 18 by 24 in. available from some manufacturers. Classified by color as follows:

Group A—solid, dark colors
Group B—dark background colors
Group C—medium to light background colors
Group D—light background colors, including white

Group A is the lowest and Group D the highest in cost. Asphalt tile is the lowest in first cost and the least resilient of all types. Recommended for commercial, light industrial, and residential use. Not recommended for shower, toilet, or laundry rooms, for display windows, or for exterior use. Softens under heat. Not grease-resistant. *Grease-resistant* asphalt tile is available in two types:

Class 1—edible oil-resistant
Class 2—mineral oil-resistant

Slip-resistant type is also available; it is similar in all other respects to regular aphalt tile.

Vinyl-asbestos tile

Composed through full thickness of vinyl resins, plasticizers, pigments, fillers, and asbestos fibers, formed under pressure while hot. Sizes 12 by 12 and 18 by 24 in. available from some manufacturers. Excellent grease, alkali, and abrasion resistance; easy maintenance, poor resilience, moderate cost. In $\frac{1}{8}$-in. gage, recommended for severe commercial use; in thinner gages for residential use. Not recommended for toilets, showers, laundries, show windows, or sun rooms. Slip-resistant, heat-resistant, and conductive types are available.

Vinyl (-backed) sheet and tile

Wearing layer composed of vinyl resin, plasticizers, pigments, and fillers, overlaid on a backing of asphalt-saturated felt or an alkali-resistant material. Excellent grease, alkali, and abrasion resistance; fair resilience. Alkali-resistant sheet is also available in thicknesses of 0.070 and 0.090 in.

Vinyl (homogeneous) sheet and tile

Composed through full thickness of vinyl resin, plasticizers, pigments, and fillers, formed under pressure while hot. Sheet is available in widths of 27, 36, 45, and 54 in. in the three gages shown in Table 7. Tile is also available in $\frac{3}{16}$-in. thickness and in special sizes up to 36 by 36 in. and special shapes such as diamonds, hexagons, and octagons. Excellent resilience and resistance to indentation; excellent grease, alkali, and abrasion resistance; high cost. Conductive type is available.

Rubber sheet and tile

Composed through full thickness of natural, synthetic, or reclaimed rubber, or a combination of these, with reinforcing fibers, pigments, and fillers, vulcanized and molded under pressure. Also available in $\frac{1}{4}$-in. thickness. Tile also available in 12 by 12- and 18 by 36-in. sizes. Excellent resilience and resistance to indentation; good resistance to grease, alkali, and abrasion. Also available with cellular backing for extra comfort and quietness under foot.

Linoleum sheet and tile

Wearing layer composed of oxidized linseed oil or other oleo-resinous binder, ground cork, wood flour, mineral fillers, and pigments, pressed on a backing of burlap or asphalt-saturated felt; tile may be unbacked. Linoleum tile is also available in 12 by 12-in. size. Tile may be considerably denser than sheet, with better resistance to indentation but less resilience; can be used on suspended floors only. Excellent grease resistance, good resistance to abrasion, easy maintenance, poor alkali resistance. Heavy gage with burlap backing recommended for severe commercial uses; lighter gages for residential use. Conductive type available in heavy gage.

Cork tile

Composed through full thickness of compressed granulated cork bonded with a heat-processed resinous binder. Surface may be unfinished or finished with wax, lacquer, or resin. Thicknesses of ¼ and ½ in. are available on special order. In addition to the standard 9 by 9 in., the following sizes are available: 6 by 6, 6 by 12, 12 by 12, 12 by 24, and 36 by 36 in. Edges may be beveled or square. Excellent resilience—most comfortable and quiet of all resilient floors. Not recommended for heavy traffic locations.

Vinyl-faced cork tile

Wearing layer of clear vinyl sheet fused by heat and pressure to regular cork tile. It is available in the same sizes as regular cork tile and in thicknesses of ⅛ and 3/16 in., with square or beveled edges. Approximate installed cost is $1.75 to $1.85 per sq ft. It may be used on suspended or on-grade floors, but not below grade. Its thermal conductivity (k) is 0.7 btu. Maximum static load without permanent

indentation varies with the manufacturer from 75 to 150 psi. On the scale used in Table 7, it is judged to be very good in comfort, warmth, quietness, alkali resistance, and ease of maintenance, and to be excellent in grease resistance. Recommended for commercial use, moderate to heavy traffic.

Accessories

Borders, feature strips, inserts (standard and custom designs), bases, and edging strips are available from most manufacturers. Stair treads with integral nosings are available, made of heavy-gage rubber or homogeneous vinyl sheet, in colors and patterns to match flooring.

Selection of resilient flooring

Selection should be based upon consideration of the following factors, in the order given:

1. Moisture conditions, subfloor and surface
2. Functional qualities desired
3. Cost factors, initial and long-range
4. Visual or aesthetic considerations

Subfloor moisture causes some types of resilient flooring and some types of adhesives to deteriorate. It has therefore

become customary to classify flooring materials as to their suitability for use above grade, on grade, or below grade (Fig. 17). These classifications are the same whether the flooring is applied directly to a concrete slab or to a wood subfloor on screeds. An inadequately ventilated crawl space has the same effect as a floor on grade.

Excessive surface moisture, such as that to be expected around the equipment in laundries and lavatories, may affect adversely the adhesive, the backing, or the underlayment. Materials recommended for on-grade installation will generally give satisfactory service under surface moisture conditions if they are installed with a waterproof adhesive. Sheet material, having fewer seams than tile, is recommended for such conditions.

The performance requirements of the flooring should be the designer's next consideration. These include such factors as resilience, ease of maintenance, and durability. Resilience has two aspects: comfort under foot and quietness, the absorption of impact noises. Durability includes not only resistance to abrasion (traffic) but also to grease, alkalies, and chemicals, and to indentation. Other factors, such as warmth to the touch, slipperiness, light reflectivity, fire resistance, or electrical con-

Table 7.   Summary of data on resilient flooring materials

SOURCE: *Installation and Maintenance of Resilient Smooth-surface Flooring*, Building Research Institute, 1958.

TYPE OF FLOORING	ASPHALT		SEMI-FLEXIBLE ASBESTOS	VINYL				FLEXIBLE HOMO-GENEOUS	RUBBER		LINOLEUM		CORK ‡
				BACKED TYPES									
				REGULAR		ALKALI RESISTANT							
	REGULAR	GREASE-PROOF		SHEET	TILE	SHEET	TILE †	TILE	SHEET	TILE	SHEET	TILE	TILE
FORM AVAILABLE	TILE	TILE	TILE										
DIMENSIONS*													
Size or Width, Inches	9 x 9	9 x 9	9 x 9	72	9 x 9	45, 72	9 x 9	9 x 9	36	9 x 9	72	9 x 9	9 x 9
Thickness, Inches	0.125	0.125	0 0625	0 0625	0 0625	0.0625	0 0625	0 080	0 080	0.080	0 070	0 065	0 09375
	0.1875	0.1875	0 080	0 070		0 080	0 080	0 09375	0 125	0.125	0 090	0 090	0 125
			0 09375					0 125	0 1875	0.1875	0.125	0 125	0 1875
			0 125										0 3125
COST													
Approximate Installed Cost Per Square Foot in Cents For Thickness Indicated	0.125″ $.20– 45	0.125″ $.25– 50	0.0625″ $.25– 35	0 0625″ $ 30– 40	0.0625″ $ 30– 40	0 0625″ $ 50– 60	0 0625″ $ 50– 60	0 080″ $ 55– 80	0.080″ $ 45– 55	0.080″ $ 45– 55	0 070″ $ 25– 35	0.065″ $ .25– 35	0 09375″ $ 35– 45
	0 1875″ $.25–.50	0 1875″ $.30– 55	0 125″ $.40– 60	0 070″ $ 45– 50		0 080″ $ 55– 70	0.080″ $ 55– 70	0 09375″ $ 70–1 30	0 125″ $ 55– 70	0.125″ $ 55– 70	0 090″ $ 30– 45	0 090″ $ 30– 45	0 125″ $ 45– 55
								0 125″ $ 75–2 00	0.1875″ $ 70– 90	0 1875″ $ 70– 90	0 125″ $ 40– 60	0 125″ $ 50– 70	0 1875″ $ 55– 65
													0 3125″ $ 75– 90
USE LEVEL**													
Suspended	Yes	Yes	Yes	Yes	Yes	Yes	Yes	Yes	Yes	Yes	Yes	Yes	Yes
On Grade	Yes	Yes	Yes	No	Yes	Yes	Yes	Yes	Yes	Yes	No	No	Yes
Below Grade	Yes	Yes	Yes	No	No	Yes	Yes	Yes	Yes	Yes	No	No	No
PHYSICAL CHARACTERISTICS													
Thermal Conductivity Btu/Hr./Sq. Ft./°F/In.	3.1	3.1	3.1	1.4	1.4	1.2–3.3	1.2–3 3	5.3	5.3	5.3	1.5	1.5	0.5
Relative Maximum Static Load Without Permanent Indentation Expressed in Lbs./Sq. In.	25 (Fair)	25 (Fair)	25 (Fair)	75 (Good)	75 (Good)	75 (Good)	75 (Good)	200 (Excellent)	200 (Excellent)	200 (Excellent)	75 (Good)	75 (Good)	75 (Good)
Under Foot Comfort	Fair	Fair	Good	Good	Good	Good	Good	Excellent	Excellent	Excellent	Good	Good	Excellent
Apparent Warmth to Touch	Fair	Fair	Good	Good	Good	Good	Good	Good	Excellent	Excellent	Good	Good	Excellent
Quietness (Noise Level)	Fair	Fair	Good	Good	Good	Good	Good	Very Good	Very Good	Very Good	Good	Good	Excellent
Surface Alkali Resistance	Excellent	Excellent	Excellent	Excellent	Excellent	Excellent	Excellent	Excellent	Good	Good	Fair	Fair	Fair
Grease Resistance	Poor	Very Good	Excellent	Excellent	Excellent	Excellent	Excellent	Excellent	Good	Good	Excellent	Excellent	Fair
Ease of Maintenance	Fair	Good	Good	Very Good	Very Good	Very Good	Very Good	Very Good	Good	Good	Very Good	Very Good	Fair
Slipperiness	Varies with finish and waxing, normally all are slip-resistant when dry.												
Impact Resistance	All are resistant to shattering, splitting, cracking or other damage under normal impact conditions.												
Light Reflectivity	Varies from almost zero to 65% depending on color, surface texture and finish—consult manufacturer.												
Durability	All show excellent durability under use conditions for which they are individually suitable when installed and maintained as recommended by manufacturer.												

*Nominal commercial dimensions only are shown—other sizes, shapes, thicknesses and widths vary with manufacturer.
**When installed in accordance with the specific precautions and recommendations of the manufacturer.

†Also available in sheet; see text.
‡For data on vinyl-faced cork tile; see text.

ductivity, must sometimes be considered. Where sanitation is of primary importance, sheet material should be used in preference to tile. Besides having fewer joints generally, it can be coved up at the walls to eliminate the joint at the base. The seams of vinyl flooring can be heat-fused to form a jointless floor.

Installed costs range from $0.20 per sq ft to over $2.00. Cost varies not only with the type of material but also with the complexity of the design and the use of such accessories as feature strips and inserts. The shape of the floor area to be covered also affects the cost. Where long-range costs are an important consideration, special attention should be given to maintenance characteristics, resistance to wear, and ease of repair or replacement.

The appearance of the finished floor is affected by its resistance to indentation and by its dimensional stability, color fastness, and light reflectivity, in addition to the color and pattern selected by the designer. Permanent indentation not only impairs the use and maintenance of the floor but also has a disastrous effect on appearance. Indentation caused by static loads such as furniture can generally be prevented by attention to the limits of the material (Table 7) and the use of protective devices. Impact loads are less predictable, but they may also cause permanent indentation. The stiletto heels worn today can produce impact loads well in excess of 2,000 psi and can leave permanent indentations in all types of resilient flooring except rubber and homogeneous vinyl.

Lack of dimensional stability may result in buckling or in the opening of seams or joints. Exposure to direct sunlight sometimes causes shrinking or fading of flooring materials. Neutral colors have the best resistance to fading; pastel colors, especially yellows and pinks, are the poorest. Cork may become lighter after prolonged exposure to sunlight. Sheet materials resist shrinkage better than tiles.

Light reflectivity of the flooring is sometimes an important functional factor, and it also has an important effect upon the appearance of the floor. Glossy finishes have less total reflectivity than matte finishes and therefore appear somewhat darker, but they produce specular reflections which may be very bright when viewed directly. High-gloss finishes tend to show up minor irregularities in the subfloor; extra care is therefore necessary in the preparation of the subfloor; extra maintenance is also required. Light reflectivity values are generally available from the manufacturers for each color and pattern of each type of flooring.

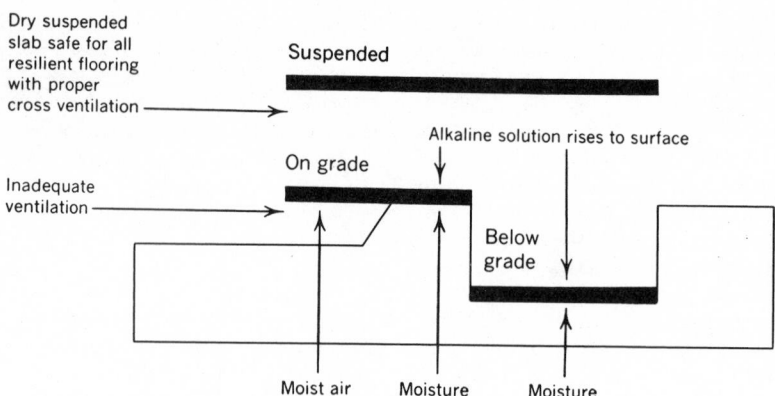

Fig. 17. Location of floors with respect to grade

Courtesy Armstrong Cork Company

The selection of color and pattern may be safely left to last because there is now such a wide choice of these in every type of flooring. Having determined the type of flooring from considerations of use, function, and cost, the designer can usually achieve, with the colors and patterns available in that type, the aesthetic effect he wants.

Installation

Resilient floors over concrete require careful selection of resilient materials and the adhesives used and, since resilient floors reflect the condition of the surface on which they are laid, care in finishing the subfloor. Many of the problems can be eliminated or minimized by protective measures taken as the slab is being laid and by proper curing of the concrete. For slabs on or below grade, membranes of vapor-resisting materials such as polyethylene film 0.004 or 0.006 in. thick, butyl rubber sheet, or 55-lb asphalt roofing felt under the slabs serve to prevent transmission of moisture from the ground. Adequate curing time, sometimes several months, is necessary to permit slabs to dry sufficiently to assure bonding of adhesives even on suspended slabs. Tests should be made to determine the moisture conditions within the slab and the adhesive to be used. Excess moisture may cause mold growth in flooring containing oleo-resinous binders or cellulosic fibers. Alkaline salts from concrete in solution can destroy the bond and leave salt deposits in cracks in the tile. Curing, hardening, and parting compounds as well as oil, grease, and paint on old floors, all prevent bonding of adhesives to concrete. Lightweight concrete in densities of from 20 to 90 lb per

cu ft should receive a 1-in. topping of standard concrete. If the density of light aggregate concrete exceeds 90 lb per cu ft and the surface is well-troweled so as to be smooth and even, it may be used as the subfloor. Only floorings which are alkali-resistant should be used over light aggregate floors, since the latter have much slower drying times, particularly when they are on grade, than floors of regular concrete. Cracks, minor holes, and crevices should be filled with a crack filler.

Underlayments of the latex, asphalt, or polyvinyl acetate type are used over rough, uneven, or worn concrete subfloors. These mastic underlayments contain resin binders in the mix and may be safely applied in thin layers or feathered out at the edges. Latex underlayments are troweled on to a maximum thickness of ⅛ in.; greater thicknesses require additional costs. They should not be used with solvent-type asphalt adhesives. Asphalt-type underlayments may be applied in greater thicknesses, approximately ½ in., with a minimum of ⅜ in., except for small areas which may be feathered. The asphalt type also should not be used with solvent-type adhesives or with certain types of chemical-set waterproof cements. Emulsion-type adhesive may be used with either underlayment. (NOTE: Since some manufacturers are prone to conceal their formulations, the reactions of underlayments and adhesives and their use should be checked with suppliers. Whenever possible it is advisable to specify flooring, adhesive, and underlayment from the same manufacturer.) Polyvinyl acetate resins mixed with portland cement as an additive provide the plastic qualities which permit its use as a thin underlayment, ranging from $\frac{1}{16}$ in. thick to featheredge, when applied over a prime coat of polyvinyl acetate concrete bonding compound.

Resilient materials over wood floors do not require board types of underlayment when applied over well-laid double floors using tongued-and-grooved face boards not over 3 in. wide, or over single layers of plywood ⅞ in. thick, where all edges are supported, or over 1⅛ in. 2-4-1 T and G Douglas fir plywood combination subfloor and underlayment. Square-edged board floors should be covered with 25/32-in. T and G wood flooring 3 in. or less in width, or with ½-in.-thick plywood (C-D plugged interior- or C-C plugged exterior-grade Douglas fir or western softwood plywood) underlayment. Underlayment-grade plywood, ¼ or preferably ⅜ in. thick, may be used over single tongued-and-grooved floors of narrow boards 3 in. or less in width, over double floors of tongued-and-grooved boards 4 in. or wider, or over ½- or ⅝-in. plywood subfloors supported on all edges and with the face-ply grain perpendicular to the floor framing, which should not be spaced more than 16 in. on center. Exterior-grade plywood should be used where surface moisture may be anticipated, as in bathrooms. Hardboard (not tempered) may also be used in lieu of ¼-in. plywood. Particle board is not recognized now as an acceptable underlayment in the specifications of resilient flooring associations. However, the National Particleboard Association recently established an underlayment performance standard for wood particle board which has been accepted by the Federal Housing Administration for use under resilient flooring materials.

Wood floors should be sanded, particularly if strip flooring is used. Nails should be set and all cracks should be filled. Latex underlayment is recommended where wood floors are uneven or cupped. The installation specifications of the Asphalt and Vinyl Asbestos Tile Institute provide that a 15-lb fully saturated asphalt-felt membrane be pasted down over wood-strip subfloors, subject to the tile manufacturers' recommendations. Lining felt should be omitted where latex underlayment is used and may be omitted where plywood is used. Wood subfloors not covered by felt or underlayment should be sealed with a prime coat of shellac or other sealer to prevent moisture absorption.

Adhesives are a most important factor in the life of a resilient floor. They also affect the ease of application and later removal, should that be desired. They vary widely in cost. Disregarding cost, the

Table 8. Federal specifications and industry standards

Federal specifications	
Tile, floor, asphalt	SS–T–306b
Tile, floor, asphalt, grease-resistant	SS–T–307
Tile, floor, vinyl-asbestos	Interim L–T–00345(COM–NBS)
Tile, floor, flame-retardant	MIL–T–18830 Navy Bureau of Ships
Flooring, vinyl plastic (homogeneous); type 1: Tile	Interim L–F–00450(COM–NBS)
Floor covering, rubber, sheet	ZZ–F–461a
Tile, floor, rubber	ZZ–T–301a
Linoleum, battleship	LLL–L–351b
Linoleum, plain, jaspe, and marbleized	LLL–L–367
Floor covering (linoleum), felt-backed	LLL–F–471
Tile, floor, cork:	Interim LLL–T–00431a(c)M–NBS
Class 1. Wax, lacquer, or resin finish	
Class 2. Clear-plastic-film finish	
Paste, linoleum	OP–106
Asphalt, emulsion-type	Interim SS–A–00138
Asphalt, cut-back type	Interim SS–A–128
Adhesive, linoleum and plastic tile	MIL–C–21016C
Simplified practice recommendation,	
U.S. Department of Commerce	
Asphalt tile	R225–56

Standard specifications, for materials only, are available from: Rubber and Vinyl Flooring Council of the Rubber Manufacturers Association, and Asphalt and Vinyl-Asbestos Tile Institute; both are in New York. Installation specifications are not standard but are issued by the various manufacturers for their own products. Manufacturers' specifications should be scrupulously observed, particularly as to type and condition of the subfloor and type of adhesive to be used.

selection of an adhesive is based upon: the type of resilient flooring to be used, the type of subfloor, the location of the subfloor with reference to moisture, the type of underlayment used, and the probability of surface moisture. In general, it is advisable to use the adhesives recommended by the manufacturer of the resilient flooring. The following is a list of the major types of adhesives:

Paste (linoleum)—water-soluble: an all-purpose adhesive for above-grade installations for lining felt, backed sheet materials, and tile other than asphalt and vinyl-asbestos.

Cement—waterproof-latex type: for concrete surfaces on or below grade for backed sheet materials and all tile permitted in these locations except asphalt and vinyl-asbestos. Alkali- and moisture-resistant.

Primer—solvent type: sealer for concrete surfaces before application of adhesives for asphalt and vinyl-asbestos tile. Should not be used over latex or asphalt-type underlayments.

Cut-back asphalt: on concrete surfaces at all grades and on lining felt over wood surfaces for asphalt and vinyl-asbestos tile—resists alkaline moisture—should not be used over latex or asphalt-type underlayment.

Emulsion-type—clay and asphalt base: all-purpose adhesive for asphalt and vinyl-asbestos tile at all grades. May be used over latex and asphalt-type underlayments. Resists alkali and moisture.

Brushing cement—asphalt and rubber-base: all types of subfloors—eliminates need for lining felt—used for vinyl-asbestos tile and asphalt tile—may be used over latex and asphalt-type underlayments.

Chemical-set waterproof—latex and powder: used for on- or below-grade concrete for rubber or vinyl tile—resists surface moisture.

Cement—resin-base: used on or above grade for cork or vinyl-cork and above grade for linoleum or vinyl sheet or tile where surface moisture is anticipated.

By HOWARD P. VERMILYA, AIA

VINYL

Vinyl wall coverings are tough, flexible materials, supplied in rolls, which can be applied by standard paper-hanging techniques to a variety of wall surfaces. They provide a durable, cleanable, stain-resistant wall finish especially suitable for institutional and commercial use where hard wear is anticipated. The material is supplied in widths of 24, 48, 50, and 54 in., and in lengths ranging from 6 to 35 yd. The wider rolls have the advantage of requiring fewer seams. A very wide range of colors and textures is available, many of them simulating other materials such as leather, fabric, straw, wood, and the like.

Vinyl wall coverings are made of pigmented vinyl resins and plasticizers which are applied to a backing material and covered by a clear vinyl surfacing sheet which is fused to the base sheet by heat and pressure. The backing is usually a tightly woven preshrunk cotton fabric, but other materials including nonwoven types may be used. Vinyl coverings designed for use on upholstery often have a knit or other type of stretchable backing which generally makes them unsuitable for use on walls.

recommended for use in areas where it replaces paint to eliminate maintainance; the medium-weight material, for areas where there is average traffic, such as offices, reception rooms, hospital wards, and dining rooms; and the heavyweight material, for such areas as corridors, schoolrooms, gymnasiums, and service areas where there is heavy traffic and hard wear, even that involving movable equipment.

Tests of vinyl wall coverings are usually in accordance with methods specified in Federal Specification CCC-T-191(b) involving weight of backing, coating, and thickness, and other factors such as tensile and tear strength, shrinkage, resistance to ultraviolet light, cold, heat, wear, and staining; also accelerated aging, adhesion, and cracking. Flame spread rate is determined by NFPA 255 or ASTM E84-61 based on the Underwriters' Laboratories, Inc., tunnel test; rating is affected by the adhesive used as well as by the wall surface to which it is applied. Most vinyl wall coverings can achieve a flame spread rate of 10 (the usual required rating) when applied with special adhesives to a noncombustible wall surface such as plaster.

Application. A vinyl wall covering may be applied to any smooth, rigid surface

their own adhesives and caution against the use of wheat or starch pastes. Joints should be butted and not lapped, as vinyl wall covering will not adhere to itself, and should not be made in or at corners formed by intersecting walls. The heavy materials are more difficult and costly to apply than the lighter ones.

Another type of vinyl wall covering is supplied in *sheets*, usually 23 by 95 in. and approximately 15 sq ft in area. The manufacturer of this product uses textured fabrics, ferns, leaves, and butterflies as elements in design. These are inserted between a layer of clear vinyl, which provides the durable surface, and a base layer of colored vinyl, behind which is a layer of aluminum foil which acts as a vapor barrier. This assembly is laminated to a paper backing. The sheets are designed for both edge and end butting, so they may be used with any ceiling height. They are applied by standard paper-hanging techniques.

FLEXIBLE WOOD VENEER

Very thin (0.012 in. or less) veneer is bonded to a backing material to make a wall covering similar to wallpaper. The veneer is treated to make it flexible so that it can be bent around corners parallel to the grain. It is provided as strips in widths up to 24 in. and in lengths up to 12 ft, depending on the woods selected and the matching pattern desired. It is installed like wallpaper.

One manufacturer supplies flexible wood veneer in rolls 27½ in. wide, in three lengths—40, 27, and 13 ft—and also in 25 by 25-in. squares. The veneer has a moisture-resistant finish, and the backing is paper. Other manufacturers supply the material bonded to a woven cotton fabric, with the veneer unfinished for finishing on the job in the same manner as wall paneling. "Architectural" grades of matched veneers are available, as well as random grades, in many species of wood.

The finished appearance is no better than the surface to which it is applied. Since the veneer is comparatively thin, a smooth surface is essential. Its flexibility makes it especially adaptable to curved walls or surfaces. When applied to an incombustible wall, it is permitted by building codes in many locations where untreated solid wood or plywood is not allowed.

Cotton preshrunk woven fabric backing

Types and weights most often used

Osnaburg	(2.35)*	38x28 threads/in.	3.6 oz/sq yd
Sheeting	(2.40)*	56x56 threads/in.	3.7 oz/sq yd
Drill	(1.85)*	68x40 threads/in.	4.9 oz/sq yd
Broken twill	(1.06)*	76x52 threads/in.	8.6 oz/sq yd

* *lineal yards per pound in greige, 58–60 in. wide.*

The weight of the wall covering has an appreciable bearing upon the wear resistance. The following tabulation classifies vinyl coverings as light, medium, or heavy by weight.

such as plaster, asbestos—cement board, gypsum wallboard, or plywood, and to smooth-faced concrete or terra cotta blocks. Where the surface is porous, a primer is usually recommended. Previously painted

Weight, oz/sq yd

Classification	Backing	Vinyl coating	Total	Range
Light weight	3.7	9.3	13.0	12–16
Medium weight	4.8	13.8	18.6	14–20
Heavy weight	8.6	15.4	24.0	20–26

Another classification gives as standard a wall covering weighing 9.5 oz per sq yd, and as heavy duty, one weighing 17.5 oz per sq yd. The lightweight material is

surfaces require special care, particularly if water-sensitive paints have been used. Glass and metal surfaces require special adhesives. Most manufacturers advise using

By HOWARD P. VERMILYA, AIA, and *JOHN HANCOCK CALLENDER, Professor of Architecture, Pratt Institute*

COLD—GLAZED

Field-applied cold-glazed wall coatings are characterized by a hard, glossy surface which resembles a ceramic glaze, which has led to their sometimes being referred to as "vitreous surfacings." They are well suited for use in industrial, commercial, and institutional buildings where a tough, sanitary, and easily cleaned surface is desired, at a cost less than that of ceramic tile. These glazed finishes have the advantage of being jointless; they are resistant to abrasion and impact and are not affected by most chemicals. They are available in a wide range of colors, including mottled and flecked patterns of two or more colors.

Cold-glazed coatings are usually spray-applied, but some types may be applied by brush or roller. Thicknesses vary from 5 to 70 mils, or from the thickness of a standard three-coat paint film to about $\frac{1}{16}$ in. Glazed coatings may be applied to almost any clean, dry, stable surface such as masonry, concrete, plaster, gypsum board, or asbestos—cement board. Porous surfaces, such as cinder blocks, usually require the prior application of a primer-filler. Masonry joints should be tooled, since the coating will not conceal them. These finishes are used mostly on interior walls and ceilings, but some types are suitable for use on exterior surfaces. All are proprietary products, and the manufacturer's directions should be carefully followed; experienced and skilled applicators are essential.

Cold-glazed coatings vary widely in composition, application techniques, and physical properties; there are no industry standards. The coatings may be classified on the basis of their composition into two general groups—cement-plastic and all-plastic. The former consists of products composed of portland cement and plastic in varying proportions, ranging from a basically cement product with organic additives to a basically plastic product with cement filler. Portland cement is, of course, inorganic and incombustible; it produces a hard surface of known durability which is waterproof but not vaporproof; it must be moist-cured. Plastics are organic and therefore combustible, to a greater or lesser degree;

being relatively new, their durability is not positively known; they are quick-drying, waterproof, and in most cases vaporproof. A vaporproof finish is highly desirable for an interior wall or ceiling, but is generally undesirable for an exterior surfacing. If a vapor barrier is used on the exterior surface of a wall, provision should be made for ventilating the interior of the wall.

Cement type. This is the oldest of the glazed finishes, having been used, mostly in Europe, for some 40 years. It is composed of white portland cement, finely ground silica sand, mineral oxide pigments, and organic hardeners and sealers. The glaze is said to be produced by crystallization of the cement molecules and therefore to be integral with the base coat. This type requires multiple-stage application and moist curing; including the latter, the complete process consists of six or seven applications. It is incombustible and vaporporous. Scraffito designs are feasible in this type.

PLASTIC

Plastic-cement type. This more recently developed type consists of a plastic emulsion base with portland cement added as a filler. It is somewhat less expensive than the cement type since it is only a two- or three-stage operation and moist curing is not required. Hardness and glaze are supplied by the all-plastic sealer coat. Depending upon the relative proportions of plastic and portland cement, this type may be combustible or incombustible and permeable or impermeable to vapor.

All-plastic type. Plastic coatings are also fairly new. They are usually applied in two coats and are therefore likely to be thinner than other types of glazed finish, although still considerably thicker than the usual three-coat paint film. The principal plastics used as field-applied coatings are epoxy, polyester, urethane, vinyl, and hypalon. Of these the first three are most nearly comparable with the cold-glazed finishes. They produce surfaces which are glossy and easily cleaned; they are very hard and tough, with good resistance to

abrasion and impact and to most chemicals. Epoxy, polyester, and urethane are thermosetting; they are cured by means of a heat-generating catalyst which is added just prior to application. These two-part materials have a very limited pot life and require experience and skill in their application. They are impervious to vapor. The materials are combustible; but when applied to an incombustible surface in the small thicknesses usually employed, they present no serious hazard. They will withstand heat up to 300 or even 400°F.

Vinyl and hypalon are in a somewhat different category. They do not produce a hard, glossy surface, but rather a resilient, tough, flexible surface with a satin finish. *Vinyl* is the "cocoon" material used to protect the Navy's "mothball fleet" after World War II. It is completely waterproof and weatherproof and may be used on interior or exterior surfaces including roofs and swimming pools. It can be applied in thicknesses ranging from 5 to 40 mils or more; for ordinary interior applications a thickness of 10 mils is recommended; for heavy-duty interiors and all exteriors, 20 to 25 mils; for roofs, 30 to 35 mils. Vinyl is a thermoplastic and will soften at temperatures above 170°F. Permeability to vapor varies with the thickness, but is sufficiently low to classify the material as a vapor barrier. It is combustible (slow-burning) and in the heavier thicknesses can be considered a hazard because of the heavy black smoke given off.

Hypalon is Du Pont's trade name for their recently developed synthetic rubber coating intended primarily for exterior use. Being a true rubber, it is waterproof and highly elastic (300 per cent elongation), but it differs from other rubbers in that it is very durable when exposed to the weather. Unlike its cousin neoprene, it can be obtained in white or light colors as well as dark. In addition to a primer, two coats are required and three are recommended. Neoprene, being less expensive, is sometimes used for the undercoats. Hypalon is used mostly for roofs but is occasionally used on exterior walls.

By RAY E. CUMRINE, AIA, Ketchum & Sharp, Architects

Specifications of paints for various surfaces and conditions

Specification of paints has become much more complicated as new materials have been developed through modern paint technology for practically every surface and service condition. Below is a check list of the principal paint types and their applications.

CHECK LIST

EXTERIOR SURFACE	PRIMER	FINISH
Concrete and Concrete Block	1. Polyvinyl Acetate 2. Acrylic 3. Styrene-butadiene 4. Cement	1. Polyvinyl Acetate or Styrene-butadiene 2. Acrylic 3. Styrene-butadiene 4. Cement
Brick, Cement Asbestos	1. Polyvinyl Acetate 2. Acrylic 3. Styrene-butadiene	1. Polyvinyl Acetate or Styrene-butadiene 2. Acrylic 3. Styrene-butadiene
Aluminum	1. Zinc Chromate	1. Linseed Oil
Galvanized Metal	1. Zinc Dust and Zinc Oxide, Zinc Chromate or Aluminum 2. Vinyl-alkyd wash	1. Linseed Oil or Alkyd 2. Vinyl-alkyd
Iron and Steel	1. Red Lead, Blue Lead or Zinc Chromate	1. Linseed Oil or Alkyd
	Chemical-Resistant	
	1. Neoprene 2. Wash Primer and Zinc Chromate Vinyl Resin 3. Phenolic Resin 4. Epoxy 5. Vinyl-alkyd wash	1. Neoprene 2. Vinyl Resin 3. Phenolic Resin 4. Epoxy 5. Vinyl-alkyd
Hot Metal (To 500°)	1. Zinc Dust or Aluminum	1. Aluminum
Metal Under Water	1. Phenolic Type Zinc Chromate 2. Neoprene	1. Phenolic Type Zinc Chromate 2. Neoprene
Wood	1. Linseed Oil 2. Alkyd 3. Acrylic	1. Linseed Oil 2. Alkyd 3. Acrylic
Plaster (Stucco)	1. Polyvinyl Acetate 2. Acrylic 3. Styrene-butadiene	1. Polyvinyl Acetate or Styrene-butadiene 2. Acrylic 3. Styrene-butadiene

INTERIOR SURFACE	PRIMER	FINISH
Concrete and Concrete Block	1. Linseed Oil 2. Cement 3. Chlorinated Rubber 4. Styrene-butadiene 5. Acrylic 6. Epoxy or Acrylic 7. Polyester 8. Polyvinyl Acetate 9. Alkyd	1. Linseed Oil 2. Cement 3. Chlorinated Rubber 4. Styrene-butadiene 5. Acrylic 6. Epoxy 7. Polyester 8. Polyvinyl Acetate, Styrene-butadiene or Alkyd 9. Alkyd
Brick, Cement Asbestos	1. Polyvinyl Acetate 2. Alkyd 3. Styrene-butadiene	1. Polyvinyl Acetate or Alkyd 2. Alkyd 3. Styrene-butadiene
Aluminum	1. Zinc Chromate	1. Alkyd
Galvanized Metal	1. Zinc Dust and Zinc Oxide, Zinc Chromate or Aluminum	1. Linseed Oil or Alkyd
Iron and Steel	1. Red Lead, Blue Lead or Zinc Chromate	1. Linseed Oil or Alkyd
Wood	1. Linseed Oil 2. Alkyd	1. Linseed Oil 2. Alkyd
Plaster	1. Alkyd or Polyvinyl Acetate 2. Polyvinyl Acetate or Styrene-butadiene 3. Acrylic	1. Alkyd 2. Styrene-butadiene 3. Acrylic

INTERIOR AND EXTERIOR

Paint is a medium which imparts to a surface, in addition to decor, both durability and protection against deteriorating elements to a degree that depends upon the ingredients in the solution and the type of surface. In this summary the qualities of the general categories of paints and finishes are presented with an eye toward their most practical applications to particular types of surfaces: interior masonry, interior wood trim, exterior masonry, exterior wood, floors and metal surfaces. No attempt has been made to include special waterproofing coatings, as these are a study in themselves.

With the exception of the most recently developed acrylic finishes, practically all conventional paints and accessory materials required for architectural uses are adequately covered by Federal Specifications, which are available from the U. S. Government Printing Office. These specifications provide criteria for the selection of paints and can be employed as a basis of quality and performance.

Definitions

Vehicles are the liquid portions of pigmented paints. They serve as "carriers" for the pigments. The vehicle usually contains *both* volatile and non-volatile components. The volatile, or solvent, component, such as mineral spirits or water, serves two major purposes: (1) it facilitates application of the paint, and (2) by its evaporation it contributes to the drying of the paint film. The non-volatile component, referred to as the "binder," remains as an integral part of the paint film to bind the pigment particles together. Durability of the paint and adhesion of the film to the surface are largely functions of the binder. Typical binders or non-volatile vehicles include drying oils (linseed, tung), alkyd and phenolic resins and acrylic and vinyl resin emulsions (latexes).

Pigments include natural and synthetic, organic and inorganic types. For example, titanium dioxide is a synthetic inorganic pigment, while toluidine red and yellow are synthetic organic pigments. Pigments are employed to impart color and hiding power, as well as to protect the organic vehicle binder from the damaging rays of the sun. Hiding power, or the ability of the paint to obscure underlying color, varies with the different types of pigments. Dark pigments are more effective than light pigments. Of the commonly used white pigments, titanium dioxide is the most effective, while white lead is the least effective. Fading and color change result partly from instability of the pigmentation. Blue and green pigments generally are most susceptible to fading outdoors, with even some variation among these.

Clear coatings include varnishes, unpigmented lacquers, shellacs, clear sealers, wax polishes and water-repellent coatings. In general, they do not have the same protection against sunlight as pigmented coatings.

Varnish is a homogeneous solution of resin, drying oil, drier and solvent. Varnish dries by evaporation of the solvent followed by oxidation and polymerization of the drying oils and resins. It is commonly used as the vehicle in pigmented paints and enamels of the quick-drying, smooth-leveling types.

Lacquer is any type of organic coating that dries rapidly and solely by evaporation of the solvent. Typical solvents are acetates, alcohols and ketones. Although lacquers were generally based on nitrocellulose, manufacturers currently use vinyl resins, plasticizers and reacted drying oils to improve adhesion and elasticity.

Shellac is a solution of refined lac resin in denatured alcohol. It dries by evaporation of the alcohol. The resin is generally furnished in orange and bleached grades. Shellac comes in various "cuts," which indicate the amount of resin in pounds added to 1 gal of solvent: 4-, 4.5- and 5-lb cuts cover the range of light, medium and heavy grades used. Shellac can be used to seal knots in wood prior to painting.

Emulsion paints generally employ synthetic emulsion resins today and are water-thinned.

Interior: Masonry, Plaster, Wallboard

New interior surfaces of plaster, wallboard and masonry should be coated first with a primer-sealer and then with finish coats. Alkyd-type primer-sealers are used more extensively today than conventional oil types, especially under alkyd paints, although they can be used under finishes of any base. The new acrylic primer-sealers, which can be used under any type finish, are finding wider use because of their ease of application, resistance to alkalinity and rapid drying time. Common finishes are listed below:

Acrylic resin emulsion paint	Excellent durability
	Excellent washability immediately upon drying
	Excellent resistance to moisture
	Excellent hiding power in colors, fair in white
Latex paint	Good durability, except on hot surfaces
	Excellent washability, contingent upon chemical curing, which varies from 30 to 90 days
	Excellent hiding power in white, fair in colors
Alkyd flat enamel	Good durability
	Good resistance to moisture and washing
	Excellent hiding power and appearance
Oil flat paint	Good durability
	Fair resistance to moisture and washing
	Good hiding power and appearance
Casein and alkyd resin emulsion paints	Still used, but to a much lesser extent because of poor resistance to moisture and washing

Prepared with the assistance of Benjamin J. Harris, Maintenance Coatings Co., Inc. and John C. Moore, National Paint, Varnish and Lacquer Association, Inc.

Exterior: Wood

Pigmented paints for exterior wood surfaces are generally of the ready-mixed, linseed-oil-vehicle type. The pigments, apart from extenders, usually consist of white lead, titanium dioxide and zinc oxide. When combined in the proper proportions, they provide the optimum in hiding power, durability and repainting characteristics. Especially recommended for areas where industrial fumes are present are the high-quality titanium dioxide paints without lead pigments. They are white initially and stay white even in heavy fume areas where other white paints containing lead turn to gray, yellow and brown. Although three-coat painting of exterior wood has been conventional, it is now possible to apply two coats if properly executed. Regardless of the number of coats, the total thickness should be about the same. For two coats the primer should be applied at about 450 sq ft per gal and the finish coat at 550. For three coats the primer should be applied at 550 sq ft per gal and the succeeding finish coats at about 650.

Exterior oil paint	Zinc oxide hardens film and prevents mildew growth
	Chalking-type titanium imparts self-cleaning and good repainting characteristics
	Very slow drying
Oil trim enamel	Retains gloss well
	Good resistance to fading
	Very slow drying
Spar varnish	Excellent for doors, handrails, thresholds, etc., where maximum outdoor durability is desired
Stain	Good shingle stains, in various shades of red, brown and green, permit "breathing"

Floors: Wood

Wood floor finishes are usually formulated with a varnish vehicle for weatherability and effective penetration into the wood. Two coats are usually applied.

Oil-base enamel	Good wear resistance
	Good moisture resistance
	Recommended for softwood porches, steps and floors, both inside and outside
Varnish	Penetrating varnish is an effective sealer and leaves a thin but durable coating
Shellac	Seals wood and leaves a hard-gloss finish
Polishing-type wax	Protects a clear-finished surface and improves its appearance
Wax emulsion	Practical for an inexpensive, no-buffing floor treatment

Exterior: Masonry

For concrete, plaster, stucco, asbestos-cement siding, concrete masonry, brick and cinder block the exterior finishes listed below are used. Washability is not important in exterior paints. Many are formulated to "chalk" gradually, thus becoming self-cleaning.

Acrylic resin emulsion paint	Excellent durability
	Excellent alkali resistance
	Excellent color retention
	Fast drying
Latex (styrene/ butadiene) paint	Excellent alkali resistance
	Good durability
	Color retention not so good as the acrylics
	Overnight drying
Polyvinyl acetate (p.v.a.) emulsion paint	Excellent alkali resistance
	Good durability
	Color retention not so good as the acrylics
	Overnight drying
Cement base paint	Suitable for coarse, rough surfaces. Smooth or glazed surfaces must be specially treated for roughening
	Excellent alkali resistance
	Good durability against moisture
	Overnight drying
Exterior oil paint	Good durability when applied to old masonry
	Vulnerable to attack by alkali

Floors: Concrete

Coatings on concrete floors do not vary much in appearance, at least not to an important degree. Their most important effects are the qualities they impart to the floor. Vehicles are usually selected on the basis of hardness and toughness, but they should not be so hard that they will be brittle and chip off when bumped. In addition to pigmentation to produce color and hiding power, inert pigments are sometimes added to contribute to the over-all wear and foot traffic resistance of the finish.

Epon resin base enamel	Excellent abrasion resistance
	Excellent alkali resistance
	Excellent adhesion
	Excellent resistance to grease and oil
Chlorinated rubber paint	Excellent wear resistance
	Excellent alkali resistance
	Excellent for damp floors
Varnish-base paint	Good wear resistance
	Good moisture resistance
	Excellent for dry, aged floors

Interior: Wood Trim

Interior wood trim can be painted with enamel or with a flat finish to be consistent with flat finishes on interior walls. Of course, semi-gloss and full-gloss finishes are still applied too. Pigmented paints for interior wood surfaces are generally formulated with quick-drying vehicles, such as varnish, alkyd resin or a mixture of varnish with linseed oil. New wood must have a prime coat before application of the finish coat. Three coats of pigmented paint are usually applied. However, two coats are often satisfactory. For estimating purposes, a coverage of approximately 400 to 500 sq ft per gal may be assumed. If treated with reasonable care, a good paint job on interior woodwork will last many years before repainting is required.

Alkyd flat enamel	Excellent leveling properties
	Excellent washability
	Excellent mar resistance
	Good durability
	Overnight drying
Acrylic resin emulsion paint	Excellent washability within 1 hr after application
	Very good durability
	Very good mar resistance
	Good leveling properties
	Fast drying
Oil flat paint	Good leveling properties
	Fair washability
	Fair durability
	Fair mar resistance
	Slow drying
Latex paint	Excellent washability, contingent upon chemical curing, which takes from 30 to 90 days
	Good durability after curing
	Good leveling properties
	Good mar resistance
Alkyd semi-gloss paint	Very good washability
Alkyd or oil-base full-gloss paint	Good hiding power
Varnish	Good, clear finish for trim
Stain	Frequently used in clear finish systems to intensify or modify the original color of the wood

Metal Surfaces

Before being finished with the desired type of protective and/or decorative coating, a metal surface must be properly cleaned and primed with a rust-inhibiting primer. The surface should be free of rust, scale, grease, oil, wax or other contaminant that will impair the adhesion of the primer. The function of the primer is to seal the surface to which it is applied, to inhibit corrosion of the metal surface, and to ensure good adhesion of the finish coat. Most of the finish paints described before for masonry and wood surfaces provide satisfactory finishes. Of the emulsion paints, the acrylics are best for primed hot radiator surfaces. In addition, a whole series of new paints has been developed, incorporating the resins of vinyl, epon, neoprene, phenolic, furane, etc., which resist acids and alkalies. This quality makes them particularly valuable for chemical plants, breweries, dairies, etc. Primers useful for metal surfaces are listed below, classified by pigment and vehicle, both of which are important. Regardless of which primer is used, the primed surface should be finish-coated in a reasonable length of time after application, because the primers are not intended to be weather-resistant.

Red lead pigment	Excellent for ferrous metalwork which cannot be cleaned of all rust
	Best for exterior use
	Most commonly used with oil vehicle
Zinc chromate pigment	Excellent for ferrous metalwork which is clean, bright, rust-free
	Most commonly used with alkyd resin vehicle
Zinc dust pigment	Good for all metal surfaces
	Excellent rust-inhibitive action
	Good for galvanized surfaces
Iron oxide pigment	Most commonly used to provide thick coating over thin zinc chromate coating
	Sometimes combined with zinc chromate to provide color
	Little rust-inhibitive action
Alkyd vehicle	Most commonly used with zinc pigments, but can be used with others
	Quick drying
Oil-base vehicle	Oil (about 25%) often added to other primers to get under old rust and so hold paint film better
	Slow drying
Phenolic vehicle	Good for metals which will be exposed to dampness or water immersion
	Quick drying
Vinyl vehicle (wash coat)	Excellent for non-ferrous metals, such as aluminum, copper, brass, etc. A thin, tightly adherent film is obtained over which any type paint can be applied
	Most commonly used with zinc chromate pigment
	Quick drying

Specifications recommended by the National Association of Store Fixture Manufacturers

TERMINOLOGY FOR FINISHING

Woods

1. *Fine textured woods*—Woods such as maple, beech, birch, gum, basswood, yellow poplar and sycamore, having small pores.

2. *Coarse textured woods*—Woods such as oak, walnut, Honduras mahogany, African mahogany, Philippine mahogany, ash, and elm having large, visible, open pores.

Stains

1. *Oil stain*—A transparent solution of a dye powder soluble in aromatic hydrocarbons. Normally dry to recoat in 2-4 hours. Need sealers over them which do not dissolve the stain and create bleeding. Shellac is normally used.

2. *Water stain*—A transparent solution of water soluble dye powders. Causes raised grain in most woods and requires long air drying before recoating.

3. *N.G.R. (non-grain-raising stain)*—A transparent solution of water stain powders, in solvents other than water, which does not swell the wood fibers and create raised grain.

4. *Pigmented wiping stain*—A thin oleo-resinous varnish with added specially ground color pigments, either earth or chemical. Must be kept agitated or settling occurs. Dries in 4 hours or more at moderate room temperature.

5. *Washcoat*—A thin solution of a sealer. A lacquer washcoat is normally a 4-6 per cent solids solution of a lacquer sealer. A shellac washcoat is normally the equivalent of a ½ lb cut of shellac. (See definition.) Primary purposes of the washcoats are: (1) to stiffen raised grain fibers and allow clean sanding, (2) to form a sealing layer between stain and succeeding color coats of finish, and (3) to allow cleaner, easier filler wiping.

This material was prepared by GLENN P. BRUNEAU of the Department of Wood Technology, University of Michigan, and appeared in "Specifications for the Manufacture of Store Fixtures," a publication prepared under the supervision of Dr. STEPHEN B. PRESTON and under the direction of the Specifications Committee of the National Association of Store Fixture Manufacturers.

6. *Lacquer sealer*—A quick drying lacquer, so formulated as to provide quick dry, good holdout of succeeding coats, and containing sanding agents such as zinc stearate to allow dry sanding of sealer. Requires constant stirring to avoid separation of ingredients. Usually contains 15-20 per cent solids at spray consistency. One full wet coat (see the definition) deposits approximately 1 mil of dry film thickness.

Lacquers

1. *Water-white lacquer*—A transparent lacquer having no apparent color, normally used over light colored surfaces. Usually contains approximately 1 mil of dry film thickness.

2. *Clear lacquer*—A transparent lacquer, unpigmented, but having some natural color, usually a light amber. Normally used over surfaces where slight darkening by topcoats is allowable. Usually contains approximately 20 per cent solids at spray consistency. One full wet coat deposits approximately 1 mil of dry film thickness.

3. *Flat lacquer*—A clear or water-white lacquer to which clear pigments have been added to diffuse light reflection from the surface of the dried film and simulate a rubbed surface. Usually contains approximately 20 per cent solids at spray consistency. One full wet coat deposits approximately 1 mil of dry film thickness.

4. *Hot lacquer*—A lacquer formulate for spraying at elevated temperatures, usually 160 F. Normally contains 30 per cent or greater solids content. Produces in two sprayed coats the equivalent of three coats of normal cold sprayed lacquer. Normally produces 1½ mils or greater dry film thickness in one sprayed coat.

5. *Lacquer enamel*—A clear lacquer to which has been added coloring pigments, bulking pigments and others. Forms an opaque film. Requires constant agitation to prevent color changes due to settling out of pigments. Usually contains 35 per cent or greater solids content at spray consistency. One full wet coat deposits approximately 2 mils or greater dry film thickness.

Other Finishing Materials

1. *Full wet coat*—A coat of finishing material applied in such manner as to exhibit an all over wet appearance (as contrasted to a dry or sandy spray). Usually considered to be near the maximum amount that can be applied on a vertical surface without sags or runs.

2. *Cut (of shellac)*—Number of pounds of resin added to each gallon of solvent. Liquid shellac is often supplied as a "4-lb cut." Equal parts of a "4-lb cut" of shellac and alcohol produce the accepted equivalent of a "2-lb cut." One part of a "4-lb cut" of shellac to seven parts of alcohol produces the accepted equivalent of a "½-lb cut".

3. *Uniforming*—Application of colored finishing materials to wood surfaces, finished or unfinished, to minimize variations in color or intensity of color. Usually performed where different woods are used in the same construction or to even up the color of all units in a group. Major use is on transparent and toned finishes.

4. *Lacquer undercoater*—A heavily pigmented lacquer enamel. Formulated to provide filling sealing and coloring. Can normally be sanded without lubricant. Air dries in 1 hour or more.

5. *Toner*—A thin lacquer enamel containing specially ground chemical and earth pigments. Thin applications have high hiding power. Dries rapidly, in 15 minutes or longer.

6. *Paste wood filler*—A mixture of oleo-resinous varnish, coloring pigments, bulking pigments (silex, others) and other ingredients. Usually reduced for application with VM&P naphtha at following rates: For walnut, Honduras mahogany and similar woods, 8-10 lb filler/gallon reducer. For oak, Philippine mahogany, ash and similar woods, 10-12 lb filler/gallon VM&P naphtha. Primary purpose is to fill and color vessels or pores of the wood and provide a level surface for succeeding coats. Formulated to air dry in 4 hours or more.

7. *Orange peel*—Roughness of a sprayed surface, resembling the surface of an orange peel, caused by lack of flow of sprayed finish droplets.

FINISH PROCEDURES
FOR EXPOSED
HARDWOOD SURFACES

1. Natural finish for exposed hardwood surfaces:

A. *Natural finish for coarse textured woods*

(1) Apply washcoat of lacquer sealer. Dry and sand lightly with 6/0 opencoat abrasive paper.

(2) Apply paste wood filler over all open grained wood. Filler should be allowed to "flash off" until a flat or dull appearance is noted. At this point, surfaces are padded by machine or by hand, with downward pressure across the grain, pushing excess filler into the pores. This initial padding is followed with a clean wipe across the grain to remove excess filler. After this operation, lightly wipe parallel to the grain with a clean cloth to remove all cross wipe marks. Excess filler in corners, carving or similar depressions should be brushed out or picked out cleanly. Dry filler thoroughly before sealing.

(3) Apply full wet coat of lacquer sealer. Dry.

(4) Sand out all roughness with 6/0 opencoat abrasive paper. Dust off thoroughly with air jet.

(5) Apply full wet coat water white lacquer. Dry.

(6) Scuff with 6/0 opencoat abrasive paper to remove any roughness present. Dust off with air jet.

*(7) Apply second full wet coat water white lacquer. Dry.

B. *Natural finish for fine textured woods*

(1) Follow exact procedure for "Natural finish for coarse textured woods," 1.A., except for elimination of steps (1) and (3). (Eliminate initial washcoating and filling operations.)

2. Stained finish for exposed hardwood surfaces:

A. *Stained finish for coarse textured woods*

*In any finish schedule, if hot lacquers (at 30-35 per cent solids) are used as the topcoats, two hot sprayed coats shall be considered sufficient to replace three coats of normal cold spray lacquer (20 per cent solids)

(1) Apply one coat of stain (water, N.G.R., oil or pigmented wiping stain).

(a) If water stain is used: Dry thoroughly after staining and apply even washcoat of lacquer sealer (4-6 per cent solids). Scuffs sand when dry with 6/0 abrasive paper to remove raised fibers.

(b) If N.G.R. stain is used: Dry thoroughly, apply even washcoat of lacquer sealer (4-6 per cent solids). Scuff lightly when dry with 6/0 opencoat abrasive paper.

(c) If oil stain is used: Dry thoroughly according to manufacturer's directions. Apply even washcoat of white shellac (½-lb cut). Dry completely and scuff sand lightly with 6/0 opencoat abrasive paper.

(d) If pigmented wiping stain is used: Wipe evenly and cleanly, removing accumulations in crevices, inside corners, etc. by dry brush or wiping. Dry according to manufacturer's directions and follow with a washcoat of lacquer sealer (4-6 per cent solids). Sand washcoat lightly with 6/0 opencoat. Avoid cutting through stain.

(2) Apply paste wood filler (following procedure shown under 1.A. step (2). Dry thoroughly.

(3) Apply one full wet coat lacquer sealer (15-20 per cent solids). Dry thoroughly.

(4) Sand sealer to remove all roughness and dust off with air jet.

(5) Apply one full wet coat clear lacquer (water white may be specified but is not essential for dark stained finishes). Dry completely.

(6) Apply second full wet coat clear lacquer (or water white if specified). Dry completely

B. *Stained finish for fine textured woods*

(1) Follow exact procedure under 2.A. except eliminate the filling operation, step (2).

3. Bleached finish for exposed hardwood surfaces:

A. *Bleach all exposed surfaces.* For bleaches requiring a neutralizing wash, neutralize according to manufacturer's directions. Since any free

alkali left on the bleached surface may have a serious effect on subsequence coats, each bleached surface should be tested for alkalinity, after neutralizing, as follows:

(1) A test solution containing the following ingredients should be formulated:

    1 part phenolpthalein
    50 parts ethyl alcohol
    50 parts water

(2) Several drops of this test solution should be placed at different points on the neutralized surface. If the spots turn red or pink, even momentarily, the surface is still alkaline.

(3) If the above test indicates alkalinity, the surface should be reneutralized with a 5-15 per cent solution of acetic acid and then sponged with clear water to remove bleaching residues.

Certain bleaches do not require a neutralizer. If not, eliminate neutralizing wash. All bleached surfaces should be dried thoroughly before recoating.

B. *Sand bleach surfaces* to remove all roughness with 6/0 abrasive paper. Any sandthrough of bleached surface to unbleached wood should be spot bleached to uniform surface color.

C. At this point, staining is to be done according to specification.

4. Toner finish for exposed hardwood surfaces:

A. *Toner finish for coarse textured woods*

(1) Spray uniform coat of toner over all surfaces. Avoid excessive buildup of coating at overlaps of spray pattern to avoid streaks. Natural pattern of the wood should not be obscured by toner application. Dry completely.

(2) Apply water white lacquer washcoat evenly over all exposed surfaces. Dry completely. Scuff sand lightly to remove roughness with 6/0 opencoat abrasive paper. Dust off thoroughly with air jet.

(3) Apply paste wood filler of correct color and consistency and complete schedule outlined under 1.A. starting with step (2), the filling operation.

4. Toner finish for exposed hardwood surfaces (continued):

B. *Finish for fine-textured woods*

(1) Toner finish—plain*

(a) Apply toner. Spray one light coat parallel to the grain of the wood, followed immediately by a second coat to even up coloration. The amount of toner sprayed should create a uniform color without closing the pores of the wood.

(b) Spray water-white lacquer washcoat and dry.

(c) Sand lightly with 6/0 opencoat abrasive paper. Dust off with air jet. Avoid cutting through to bare wood. Sandthrough to wood should require touch-up with toner and washcoat reapplication.

(d) Apply lacquer sealer and dry.

(e) Sand with 6/0 opencoat abrasive. Dust with air jet.

(f) Spray water-white lacquer topcoat and dry.

(g) Spray second topcoat water-white lacquer and dry.

(2) Toner-glaze finish.*

(a) Spray toner parallel to grain to uniform coloration. Dry thoroughly.

(b) Spray lacquer washcoat.

(c) Sand lightly with 8/0 opencoat abrasive paper, parallel to grain, and dust off with air jet.

(d) Apply glaze in thin coat over all toned surface. Wipe in circular pattern to deposit glaze evenly in small pores. Follow by wiping with a clean soft cloth parallel to the grain. A uniform color should be maintained overall. Deposits of glaze in corners and similar places should be removed.

(e) Spray lacquer sealer and dry.

(f) Sand sealer with 6/0 opencoat abrasive and dust with air jet.

(g) Spray topcoat of water-white lacquer and dry.

(h) Spray second topcoat of water-white lacquer and dry.

5. Opaque or pigmented finish for exposed hardwood surfaces:

A. *Opaque finish for coarse textured woods*

(1) Apply paste wood filler according to directions for filling under 1.A.(2).

(2) Dry thoroughly.

(3) Apply full wet coat of approved undercoating lacquer enamel. This undercoat shall be an appreciably different color from the finish coat to assure against skips in the spray pattern, and of a proper ground color with relation to the aforesaid finish coat. Dry.

(4) Sand all undercoated surfaces with 5/0 opencoat abrasive paper or finer, to complete removal of all roughness.

(5) Apply full wet coat of lacquer enamel. Dry thoroughly and scuff sand with 6/0 opencoat abrasive paper to remove accumulated roughness. Dust off completely with air jet.

(6) Apply second coat of lacquer enamel. Dry completely.

B. *Opaque finish for fine textured woods*

(1) Follow exact procedure outlined for coarse textured woods (5.A.) but eliminate step (1), the filling operation.

6. Finishing exposed particle board:

A. *Natural finish*

(1) Follow procedure under 1.B.

B. *Stained finish*

(1) Follow procedure under 2.B.

C. *Opaque or pigmented finish*

(1) Follow procedure under 5.B.

7. Opaque or pigmented finish for exposed paper-overlaid particle board:

Follow exact procedure outlined under 5.B., except eliminate second lacquer enamel topcoat.

8. Finishes for exposed fiberboard:

A. Natural—Follow procedure outlined under 1.B. (water-white lacquer shall not be mandatory).

B. Opaque or pigmented finish—Follow procedure under 5.B. eliminating second lacquer enamel topcoat.

RUBBING AND POLISHING

For each wood material used, and each finishing schedule used, the rubbing and polishing method should be selected by the architect from the following systems. He should specify which areas (tops, sides, etc.) will be rubbed and/or polished.

1. No rubbing or polishing:
Unexposed interior areas, drawer sides and interiors, shelving, and similar parts should not require any rubbing or polishing, other than removal by fine abrasive paper of any roughness created by the finishing process used.

2. Steel wool—Dull satin:
A. 3/0 steel wool should be used parallel to the grain of the wood, to remove roughness and create an all-over dull satin sheen in those areas specified by the designer.

(or) B. 4/0 steel wool should be used, parallel to the grain of the wood, to remove roughness and create an all-over dull satin sheen in those areas specified by the architect. 4/0 steel wool will create a slightly higher luster than 3/0 steel wool.

3. Dull satin:
A. Machine or hand sand, with 320 grit silicon carbide abrasive paper, using a non-blooming lubricant. All rubbing should be done parallel to the grain of the wood. Follow with an even rub in long continuous strokes with 4/0 steel wool. All lubricant and rubbing slush must be removed. Surface shall be clean and dry before waxing.

(or) B. Repeat procedure in (A) above, except use 360 grit silicon carbide abrasive paper in place of 4/0 steel wool.

4. Period satin:
A. Machine or hand sand with 320 or 360 grit silicon carbide abrasive paper, using a non-blooming lubricant, until all orange peel and other irregularities in surface film are removed. Follow this by hand rubbing with 3-F pumice using a soft felt pad, in long continuous strokes. All residual pumice and rubbing slush shall be removed. Dry completely before waxing.

(or) B. Repeat procedure outlined in (A) above, but substitute 500 grit silicon carbide abrasive paper for the

---

*In either schedule for fine textured woods, if the toner is one having a high lacquer binder content, washcoating may be eliminated. Light sanding with 8/0 opencoat abrasive paper should be used to smooth toned surfaces before proceeding. Any sandthrough of toned surface should require reapplication of toner to match surrounding area and resanding with 8/0 abrasive paper

3-F pumice. Rub in long continuous strokes parallel to the grain of the wood. Clean up thoroughly, dry and wax.

5. High sheen satin:

A. Sand, by machine or hand, with 360 grit silicon carbide abrasive paper, using a non-blooming lubricant, to remove all surface film irregularities. Follow with 4-F pumice by machine or hand, with soft felt rubbing pads. If a higher sheen is desired, small amounts of rotten-stone shall be added to the 4-F pumice.

6. High luster:

A. Sand surface, parallel to the grain, by machine or hand, with 320 or 360 grit silicon carbide abrasive paper, using a non-blooming lubricant. Follow with a final sanding with 400 grit silicon carbide abrasive paper to create an all-over fine scratch pattern. Irregularities in flat surfaces missed by these two operations should be rubbed by hand with soft felt pad, using 4-F pumice. Clean the surface so that no abrasive particles or pumice remain. Apply rubbing compound and buff with rotary buffer to all-over even sheen. Clean up excess compound and then polish lightly with rotary buffer and clean lambs wool pad. Care should be exercised in both the compounding and polishing operations to prevent burning or softening of finish by frictional heat.

FINISH FOR UNEXPOSED AREAS

1. Unexposed drawer surfaces:

A. Apply one coat of lacquer sealer on all inside surfaces of drawers and outside surfaces of drawer sides and back. Skips, in corners or elsewhere, shall not be allowed. When dry, hand sand with 6/0 opencoat abrasive paper to remove roughness. Dust thoroughly with air jet.

2. Accessible interior parts *(shelves, partitions, etc.)*:

A. Apply one coat lacquer sealer. Dry.

B. Remove any roughness by scuff sanding with 6/0 open coat abrasive paper.

UNIFORMING OF COLOR

1. Used where noticeable color differences exist on a unit, or between units in the same group.

2. Uniforming color should be applied without obvious lap marks or streaks, and shall not obscure the grain of the wood.

3. Wherever possible uniforming should be done on the last sealer coat, followed by a protective topcoat.

4. Uniforming colors should be formulated to give excellent adhesion to the surface on which they are applied.

5. Uniforming colors should have fade resistance equal to that of the entire finish system used.

6. Application of uniforming color on the final topcoat, instead of the sealer, should not create a surface roughness or sheen different from that of the topcoat.

FIELD PAINTING

1. Large panels and other items which cannot be satisfactorily finish painted in the shop may be painted in the field when specified by the architect.

A. All such items should be factory primed in a manner appropriate to the selected finish coat.

B. Finish painting in the field should conform to the appropriate preceding paragraphs presented in this article and the previous one (August).

WORKMANSHIP; PREPARATION
Workmanship Specifications

1. All workmanship shall be the very best with all materials evenly and smoothly applied. Runs, sags, bubbles, brush marks, heavy orangepeel, and other detrimental surface effects shall not be allowed. All finishing shall be performed under expert supervision.

2. Unless otherwise specified herein, all materials shall be applied in strict accordance with printed directions of the finishing-material manufacturer.

3. No finish shall be applied over a preceding coat unless the preceding coat is completely dry.

4. Doors and other components that are free to warp shall be given a sufficient number of coats of finishing material on opposite side and edges

to equalize moisture gain or loss and thus minimize warpage.

5. Holes for locks and catch strike plates shall be touched up to match adjoining surfaces.

Preparation for Finishing

1. Before any finish is applied, all wood surfaces shall be thoroughly sanded, by machine or hand sanding.

A. All sanding shall be done parallel to the grain of the wood.

B. A succession of grit sizes shall be used, each removing in turn all the coarser grooves created by the preceding grit.

2. For all exterior or exposed surfaces, a final grit size of 4/0 or finer shall be used.

3. Sandthrough at edges, corners or other areas of veneered surfaces shall not be allowed, except for opaque finishes.

4. Veneered panels having excessive bleedthrough of adhesive due to hot- or cold-press gluing shall be admitted for opaque finishes.

5. No cross-grain sanding marks shall be admissible for any finish system on veneered or solid wood members.

7. For surfaces to be water stained, the 4/0 sanding shall be followed by an application of glue sizing (one part, by volume, hot animal glue to 10 parts water at approximately 140 F) applied lightly and evenly over all sanded surfaces. The sized surfaces shall be thoroughly dried and then lightly sanded with 5/0 opencoat abrasive paper, by machine or hand, to remove all raised grain created by sizing. Water staining can then proceed with a minimum of raised grain.

8. All knife-edge corners shall be carefully eased with 4/0 abrasive paper.

9. All wood surfaces shall be kept free of dust, dirt, oil, adhesives, or other substances which would interfere with normal finishing procedure.

10. On surfaces to receive opaque finishes, dents, cuts, nail holes and similar damage shall be filled, dried completely and then sanded flush with 4/0 abrasive paper. The filling material selected shall be one giving excellent adhesion to uncoated wood surfaces.

PURPOSE

Data in this section make possible the quick solution of any stair problem ordinarily encountered in architectural practice. These data include a chart of proportional treads and risers and tabular material giving handrail heights, headroom, and stair gradients for stairs with risers from 5 to 9 inches.

Material in this section has been adapted from data originally developed by Ernest Irving Freese.

PROPORTIONAL TREAD AND RISER DIAGRAM

It has been found that dimensions of stair treads and risers are proportional to one another and can be plotted on a hyperbola, reproduced here in the form of a working chart. Rules for its use are given in the caption. No formulae are required to produce results desired, for dimensions are accurate to the nearest ⅛ in., a tolerance that is not ordinarily excessive in building practice. For mathematical accuracy, however, the following formulae can be solved to determine correct proportions of either tread or risers when one or the other is fixed.

T = Tread. R = Riser.

When T is fixed:
$$R = 9 - \sqrt{1/7\ (T-8)\ (T-2)}$$

When R is fixed:
$$T = 5 + \sqrt{1/7\ (9-R)^2 + 9}$$

In all cases the width of tread is exclusive of a nosing.

Use of this diagram makes unnecessary any adherence to former "rules" for proportioning of tread and riser. Both usual rules for stair layout are violated in the diagram. These are, "the sum of tread and riser shall not exceed 17½ in." and, "the product of tread and riser shall not exceed 75."

However, the average of the risers shown, 7 in., is proportional to a tread of 11 in., a combination that produces a stair which is comfortable to use and generally economical of floor space. At the lower extreme, a riser of 5 in. produces a tread of 16 in. which approximates the proportions of a brick step with a tread equal to two stretchers and a rise equal to two courses.

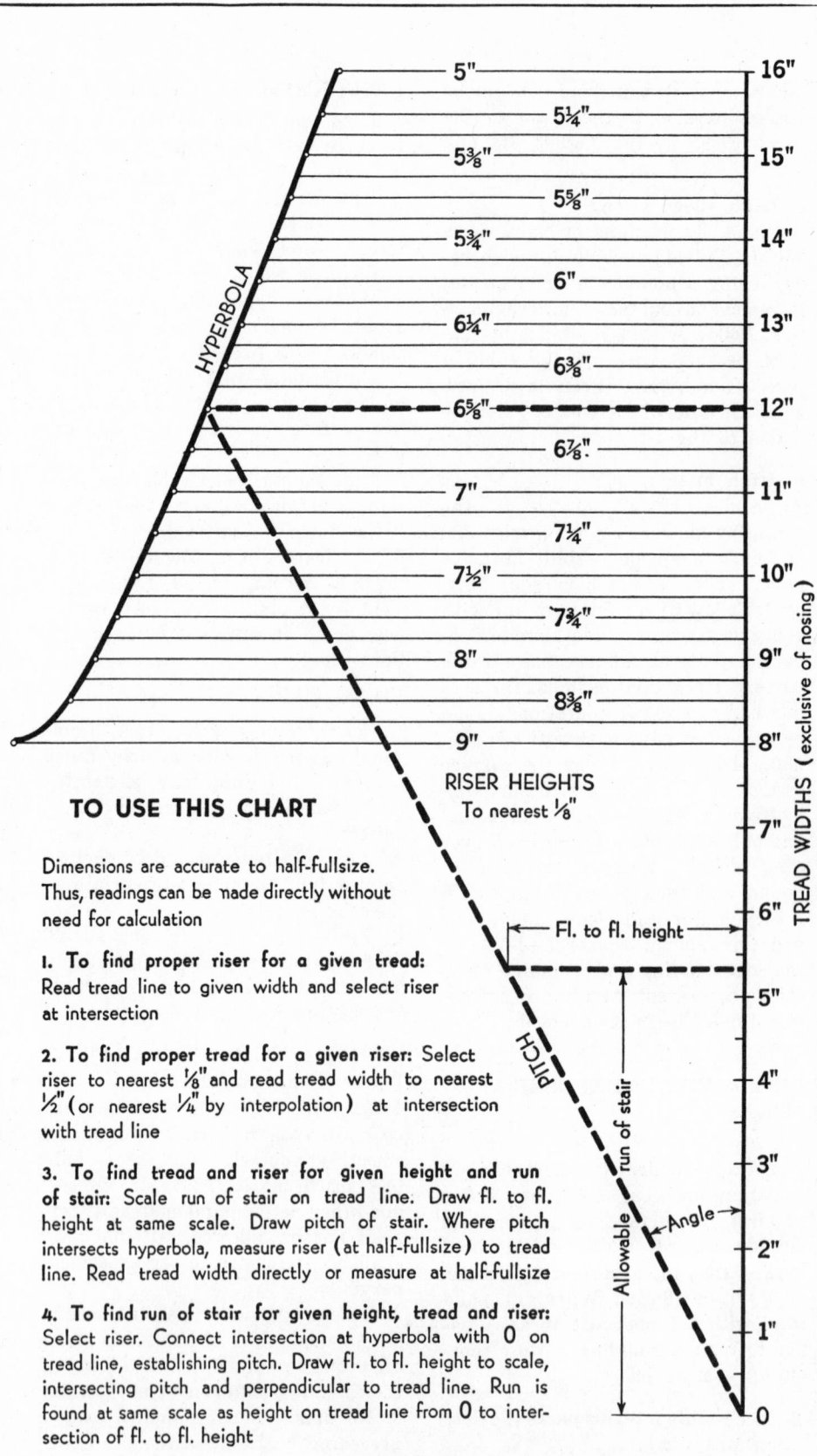

TO USE THIS CHART

Dimensions are accurate to half-fullsize. Thus, readings can be made directly without need for calculation

1. To find proper riser for a given tread: Read tread line to given width and select riser at intersection

2. To find proper tread for a given riser: Select riser to nearest ⅛" and read tread width to nearest ½" (or nearest ¼" by interpolation) at intersection with tread line

3. To find tread and riser for given height and run of stair: Scale run of stair on tread line. Draw fl. to fl. height at same scale. Draw pitch of stair. Where pitch intersects hyperbola, measure riser (at half-fullsize) to tread line. Read tread width directly or measure at half-fullsize

4. To find run of stair for given height, tread and riser: Select riser. Connect intersection at hyperbola with 0 on tread line, establishing pitch. Draw fl. to fl. height to scale, intersecting pitch and perpendicular to tread line. Run is found at same scale as height on tread line from 0 to intersection of fl. to fl. height

PROPORTIONAL TREAD AND RISER DIAGRAM
All Dimensions are at ½ Full Size

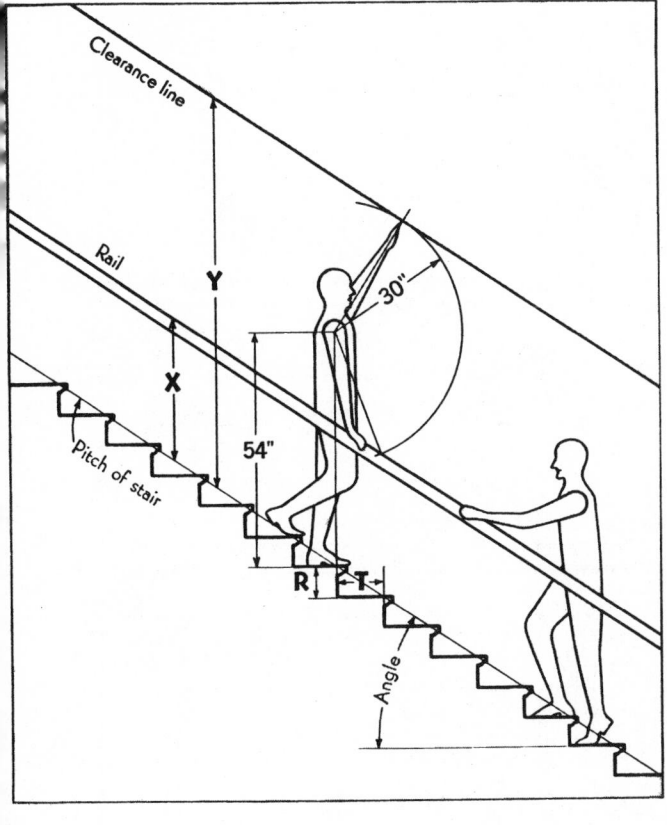

STAIRWAY LAYOUTS

Comfortable stairways cannot be designed except in relation to dimensions of the average human figure. As applied to stairways these dimensions and the equivalent of the average comfortable walking stride of about 24 in. fix the gradient of stairways, the proportional relation of treads and risers, the height of the handrail and the minimum necessary headroom.

The accompanying diagram indicates the influence of human figure dimensions and suggests the desirability of varying ceiling clearances and handrail heights according to variations in stair gradients. These variations are included in the table as related to dimensions of treads and risers developed from the Proportional Tread and Riser Diagram.

For the sake of practical classification a stairway can be defined as follows:

"A stepped footway having a gradient not less than 5:16 pitch, or 31¼ per cent, or an angle of 17 degrees and 21 minutes; and not greater than 9:8 pitch or 112½ per cent, or an angle of 48 degrees and 22 minutes."

Below these limits, footways become ramps; above them step-ladders. Both types of footways are subject to rules similar to those applicable to stairway design.

All building codes have strict specifications for stairs which are required exits. The model code of the National Board of Fire Underwriters and the New York City code both require that treads and risers be proportioned by the formula $T \times R = 70$ to 75, with risers not over 7¾ in. high and treads not less than 9½ in. wide, exclusive of nosings. Minimum stair width for most uses is 44 in., based on two 22-in. lanes of traffic. Handrails are required on both sides and may project a maximum of 3½ in. into the required width. Winders and open risers are prohibited. The maximum vertical rise permitted between landings is 12 ft; in places of assembly it is 8 ft. Stairs must be designed for a live load of 100 psf.

In single-family houses FHA will permit stairs as steep as 8¼-in. rise and 9-in. tread, but for main stairs FHA recommends a gradient between 30 and 35 deg. For exterior stairs risers should not exceed 6 in. and treads should not be less than 12 in.; the maximum rise permitted between landings is 5 ft, and handrails are required.

For garden steps see section on "Landscaping."

DIMENSIONS FOR STAIRWAYS

Step dimensions		Gradient designations		Headroom * Y in inches	Handrail height X in inches	NOTES
Riser R in inches	Tread T in inches	Per cent grade	Angle in degrees, minutes			
5	16	31.25	17 - 21	85		1. 7" by 11" is the proportion by which all steps are laid out
5¼	15½	33.87	18 - 43		33½	
5½	14¾	37.28	20 - 27	86		2. Risers from 5" to 6½" are suitable for exterior and "grand" interior stairs
5¾	14	41.07	22 - 20			
6	13½	44.44	23 - 58	87		3. Risers from 6⅝" to 7⅝" are most comfortable and most suitable for interior stairs
6¼	13	48.07	25 - 40		33	
6½	12¼	53.06	27 - 57	88		4. Risers for cellar and attic stairs may be up to 9" high
6¾	11¾	57.44	29 - 52			
7	11	63.63	32 - 28	89		5. Width - minimum for single-file travel, 30"
7¼	10½	69.04	34 - 37	90		
7½	10	75	36 - 52	91		6. Width - minimum for comfort, 36"
7¾	9½	81.57	39 - 12	93		
8	9	88.88	41 - 38	94	33½	7. Width - desirable (for furniture passage etc.), 42"
8¼	8½	97.05	44 - 9	96		
8½	8¼	103.02	45 - 51	97		8. Consult local building codes on all stair problems
8¾	8⅛	107.07	46 - 57	98	34	
9	8	112.5	48 - 22	99		

* Minimum for head clearance only can be safely taken as 84 in. for all gradients.

Critical dimensions and clearances

STAIR TABLE

Dimensions indicated on the accompanying diagram and listed in the table determine the vertical and horizontal areas and headroom clearances for stair systems with tread and riser proportions shown. They can be used directly in developing sketches or working drawings and eliminate the need for experimental stair plans or sections. All dimensions refer to face of treads without nosing.

Tabular data refer only to minimum conditions for straight run stairs. All figures may be adjusted according to requirements of design or stair use. For similar dimensional information controlling other types of stairways, see the following pages.

Widths of stairways may vary with these requirements. For passage of furniture minimum clear widths should be selected from the other table on this sheet.

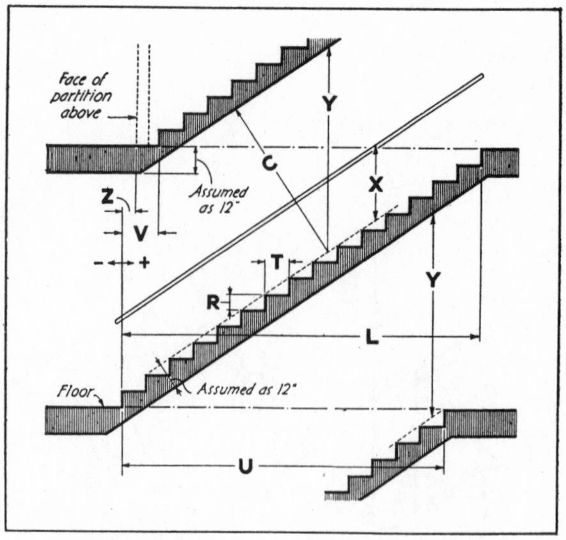

STAIR TABLE.... Dimensions in feet and inches

Floor to Floor Height		No. of Risers	Riser R	Tread T	Total Run L	Min. Headroom Y	Handrail X	Clearance C	Partition Above Z*	First Riser Below - U	First Riser Above - V*
8'-0"	†	11	8.73"	8¾"	6'-10½"	8'- 2"	2'-10"	5'- 8"	– 1'-10"	8'- 6"	– 1'- 7"
	†	12	8.00	9	8- 3	7-10	2- 9½	5-10½	– 1- 8½	9- 7½	– 1- 4
		13	**7.38**	**10¼**	**10- 3**	**7- 7**	**2- 9**	**6- 2**	**–1- 8½**	**11- 6**	**– 1- 1½**
		14	**6.86**	**11½**	**12- 5½**	**7- 4**	**2- 9**	**6- 4**	**–1- 7**	**13- 5½**	**– 9½**
	Δ	15	6.40	12½	14- 7	7- 3	2- 9	6- 7½	– 1- 6½	15- 5½	– 7½
	Δ	16	6.00	13½	16-10½	7- 3	2- 9	6- 7½	– 1- 9	17- 6	– 8
8'-6"	†	12	8.50	8½	7- 9½	8- 1	2- 9½	5- 8½	– 1- 3½	8-10	–11
	†	13	7.85	9¼	9- 3	7- 9	2- 9½	5-10½	– 1- 1	9-10	– 7½
		14	**7.29**	**10½**	**11- 4½**	**7- 6**	**2- 9**	**6- 2**	**–10½**	**12- 9**	**– 4**
		15	**6.80**	**11½**	**13- 8½**	**7- 4**	**2- 9**	**6- 4**	**–10½**	**13-10**	**– 1½**
	Δ	16	6.38	12½	15- 7½	7- 3	2- 9	6- 5½	– 7	15- 5½	+ 3½
	Δ	17	6.00	13½	18- 0	7- 3	2- 9	6- 7	– 7	17- 8	+ 5
9'-0"	†	12	9.00	8	7- 4	8- 3	2-10	5- 6	–11	8- 1	– 8
	†	13	8.31	8½	8- 6	8- 0	2- 9½	5- 9	– 9	8-11½	– 5
		14	**7.71**	**9½**	**10- 3½**	**7- 9**	**2- 9½**	**6- 0**	**– 6**	**10- 5**	**– ½**
		15	**7.20**	**10½**	**12- 3**	**7- 6**	**2- 9**	**6- 2½**	**– 3**	**11-10**	**+ 4½**
		16	**6.75**	**11¼**	**14- 8¼**	**7- 4**	**2- 9**	**6- 4**	**+ 2**	**13-11**	**+ 1- 0**
	Δ	17	6.35	12½	16- 8	7- 3	2- 9	6- 5½	+ 5	15- 5½	+ 1- 4
	Δ	18	6.00	13½	19- 1½	7- 3	2- 9	6- 7½	+ 6	17- 8	+ 1- 6
9'-6"	†	13	8.77	8	8- 0	8- 2	2-10	5- 5½	– 3½	8- 2	– ½
	†	14	8.14	9	9- 9	7-10	2- 9½	5- 9½	± 0	9- 5½	+ 5
		15	**7.60**	**9¾**	**11- 4½**	**7- 7**	**2- 9**	**5-11½**	**+ 4½**	**10- 7**	**+10½**
		16	**7.13**	**10¾**	**13- 5¼**	**7- 5**	**2- 9**	**6- 2**	**+ 9½**	**12- 2**	**+ 1- 5½**
		17	**6.71**	**11¾**	**15- 8**	**7- 4**	**2- 9**	**6- 4**	**+1- 1½**	**13-11½**	**+ 1-11**
	Δ	18	6.33	12½	17- 8½	7- 3	2- 9	6- 5½	+1- 5½	15- 7	+ 2- 4
	Δ	19	6.00	13½	20- 3	7- 3	2- 9	6- 8	+1- 8	17- 9	+ 2- 7½
10'-0"	†	14	8.57	8½	9- 2½	8- 1	2- 9½	5- 8½	+ 2	8- 8	+ 6
	†	15	8.00	9	10- 6	7-10	2- 9½	5-10½	+ 6½	9- 7	+11
		16	**7.50**	**10**	**12- 6**	**7- 7**	**2- 9**	**6- 1**	**+1- 1**	**10-11½**	**+1- 6½**
		17	**7.06**	**11**	**14- 8**	**7- 5**	**2- 9**	**6- 2½**	**+1- 7½**	**12- 5½**	**+2- 2½**
		18	**6.67**	**12**	**17- 0**	**7- 4**	**2- 9**	**6- 5**	**+2- 0**	**14- 3½**	**+2- 9**
	Δ	19	6.32	12½	18- 9	7- 3	2- 9	6- 6	+2- 5	15- 8	+ 3- 2½
	Δ	20	6.00	13½	21- 4½	7- 3	2- 9	6- 7½	+2-10	17- 9	+ 3- 8½
10'-6"	†	14	9.00	8	8- 8	8- 3	2-10	5- 5½	+ 6	8- 0	+ 9
	†	15	8.40	8½	9-11	8- 1	2- 9½	5- 8½	+ 9½	8-10	+ 1- 1
		16	7.88	9¼	11- 6¾	7- 9	2- 9½	5-10½	+ 1- 3½	9-10	+ 1- 8½
		17	**7.41**	**10**	**13- 4**	**7- 7**	**2- 9**	**6- 1**	**+1- 9½**	**11- 0**	**+ 2- 3½**
		18	**7.00**	**11**	**15- 7**	**7- 5**	**2- 9**	**6- 2½**	**+2- 5**	**12- 7½**	**+ 3- 0½**
		19	**6.63**	**12**	**18- 0**	**7- 4**	**2- 9**	**6- 4½**	**+2-11**	**14- 4**	**+ 3- 8½**
	Δ	20	6.30	12½	19- 9½	7- 3	2- 9	6- 6	+3- 5½	15- 7	+ 4- 3½
	Δ	21	6.00	13½	22- 6	7- 3	2- 9	6- 7½	+4- 0	17- 9	+ 5- 0
11'-0"	†	15	8.80	8	9- 4	8- 2	2-10	5- 6	+1- 0½	8- 1	+ 1- 2½
	†	16	8.25	8¾	10-11¼	8- 0	2- 9½	5-10	+1- 5	9- 2½	+ 1- 9
		17	**7.76**	**9½**	**12- 8**	**7- 9**	**2- 9½**	**6- 0**	**+2- 0**	**10- 3½**	**+2- 4½**
		18	**7.33**	**10¼**	**14- 6¼**	**7- 6**	**2- 9**	**6- 1½**	**+2- 7½**	**11- 4½**	**+3- 1½**
		19	**6.95**	**11**	**16- 6**	**7- 5**	**2- 9**	**6- 3**	**+3- 3**	**12- 8**	**+3- 9**
		20	**6.60**	**12**	**19- 0**	**7- 4**	**2- 9**	**6- 5**	**+3-10½**	**14- 5½**	**+4- 7½**
	Δ	21	6.29	12½	20-10	7- 3	2- 9	6- 6	+4- 5	15- 8	+ 5- 3
	Δ	22	6.00	13½	23- 7½	7- 3	2- 9	6- 7½	+5- 1	17- 8	+ 6- 0

Notes: Figures in bold face indicate stairs recommended for most interiors.

† Indicates stairs allowable only for attics and cellars but not recommended.

Δ Indicates stairs for exterior or monumental use.

* Dimensions given plus or minus; i.e. behind or in front of first riser (see diagram above).

CLEARANCES FOR FURNITURE PASSAGE

The information on this page supplements that contained in the Stair Table on the previous page. Width is not always a critical factor of stairway design but is important when the layout involves one or more turns with straight runs. Typical layouts for such stairways include the Long L, Double L, Wide U, Wide L, and Narrow U. (See the following pages for layouts and tabular data on these types.)

Stairways used solely as circulation from floor to floor can be 2'-0" wide for comfortable passage of one individual or 3'-6" for two, side-by-side. When furniture must be taken up and down, minimum clear widths of straight runs and landings must be carefully selected or corners will constitute obstructions in many instances.

Recommended minimum clear widths as shown in the table are not necessarily the width of stairs, either rough or wall-to-wall. Projections of newels, handrails or baseboards can obstruct passage of furniture and must be taken into account when determining actual stair widths.

Headroom is also a controlling factor of design. With minimum headroom conditions shown in the Stair Table, clear widths for furniture passage must be greater in most cases than may be necessary if headroom is unlimited or equal at least to the ceiling height. This is particularly important at the first riser and at turns, where the under rake of the first stair limits the vertical clearance of the stairway below. Therefore, if stairs must be comparatively narrow and if furniture must be transported over them, headroom, or vertical clearance, must be increased accordingly.

Landing widths may be increased to provide greater turning space for maneuvering furniture. If this is done, minimum clear widths can be proportionately decreased. However, this expedient is not effective unless hallways at either end of the stairway are at least equal to the landing width. Narrow hallways often offer as great an obstruction to furniture maneuvering as low headroom, narrow runs or cramped turns.

Open-well stairways give more opportunity to maneuver furniture, since even very bulky but light pieces may often be lifted over rails or newels. In general, a closed-string stair should be wider than an open-string type for the same degree of convenience.

Tabular data on this page reflect safe *average* clearances for transportation of items listed. Dimensions of furniture are subject to wide variations. Consequently, the minimum clear widths recommended here are susceptible to adjustment in certain instances.

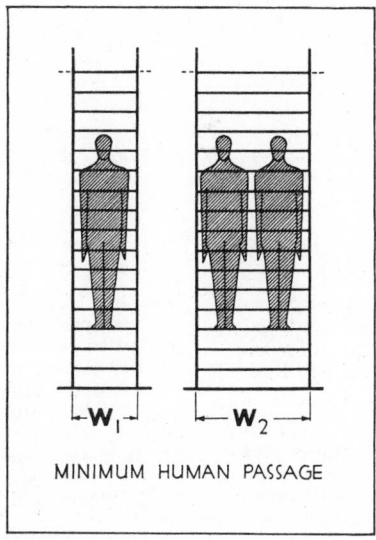

MINIMUM HUMAN PASSAGE

MINIMUM STAIR WIDTHS

Above: Stairs designed for comfortable human passage only may be relatively narrow. W_1 may be 2'-0" but 2'-6" is better. W_2 should be at least 3'-6".
Right: Furniture passage demands greater width. If stair landing is increased or headroom unlimited, W_F may be decreased. See table below.

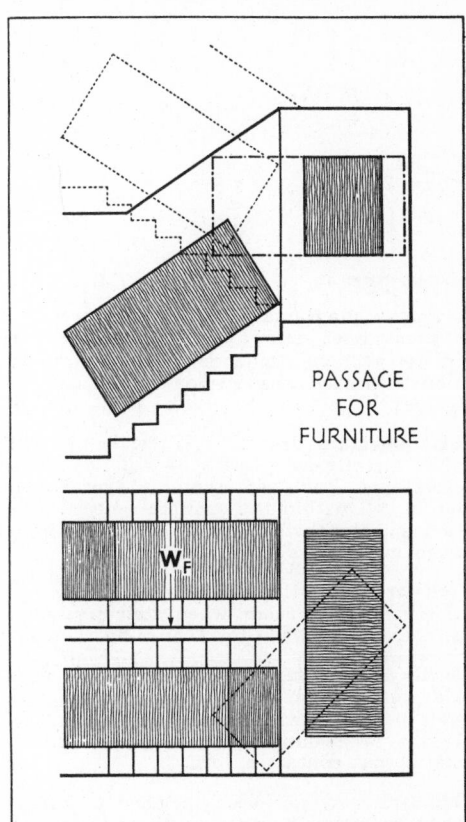

PASSAGE FOR FURNITURE

RECOMMENDED MINIMUM CLEAR WIDTHS OF STAIRS (W_F)*
for furniture movement

| Furniture | | Min. Headroom ▲ | | Unlimited Headroom | | |
| Article | Size | Wide U Type | Narrow U Type | Wide and Narrow U | Narrow U only ● | |
					Stair	Landing
Double Bed Box Spring	4'-6"x 6'-6"x 8"	3'- 2"	3'- 2"	2'- 3"		
Dressing Table	1'-10"x 4'-0"x 2'-6"	2'- 5"	2'- 5"	2'- 5"		
Bureau	2'-0"x 4'-0"x 3'-0"	2'- 8"	2'- 8"	2'- 8"		
Chiffonier	1'-8"x 3'-4"x 4'-8"	2'- 6"	2'- 6"	2'- 6"		
Chest of Drawers	1'-9"x 3'-4"x 4'-8"	2'- 7"	2'- 7"	2'- 7"		
Divan - Club	3'-6"x 7'-2"x 2'-9"	4'- 8"	4'- 8"	3'- 4"	3'-0"	3'-8"
Divan - Average	3'-0"x 6'-8"x 2'-6"	4'- 4"	4'- 4"	2'-11"		
Piano - Concert Grand	9'-0"x 5'-4"x 1'-8"	4'- 8"	4'- 8"	3'- 2" ■	3'-0" ■	3'-4" ■
Piano - Music Room Grand	7'-3"x 5'-2"x 1'-6"	3'-10"	3'-10"	3'- 0"		
Piano - Drawing Room Grand	6'-9"x 5'-0"x 1'-4"	3'- 6"	3'- 6"	2'-10"		
Piano - Baby Grand	5'-8"x 4'-10"x 1'-2"	3'- 0"	3'- 0"	2'- 8"		
Piano - Standard Upright	2'-2"x 5'-10"x 4'-6"	4'- 0"	3'- 9"	3'- 3"	3'-0"	3'-6"
Highboy - Large	2'-0"x 3'-6"x 7'-6"	4'- 4"	4'- 4"	2'-10"		
Highboy - Average	1'-8"x 3'-4"x 6'-0"	3'- 6"	3'- 6"	2'- 6"		
Secretary - Large	1'-10"x 3'-8"x 7'-2"	4'- 0"	4'- 0"	2'-10"		
Secretary - Average	1'-10"x 3'-0"x 6'-10"	3'-10"	3'-10"	2'- 6"		
Sideboard	1'-9"x 5'-0"x 3'-2"	2'- 6"	2'- 6"	2'- 6"		
Buffet	2'-1"x 3'-3"x 6'-6"	4'- 0"	4'- 0"	2'-10"		
Dresser	1'-9"x 6'-0"x 5'-6"	4'- 4"	3'- 6"	3'- 4"	3'-0"	3'-8"
Table (6 People)	3'-6"x 5'-0"x 2'-6"	3'- 2"	3'- 2"	3'- 2"	3'-0"	3'-4"
Table (8 People)	3'-6"x 7'-0"x 2'-6"	4'- 8"	4'- 4"	3'- 2"	3'-0"	3-4
Table (10 People) Rd.	6'-4" Diam.	4'- 8"	4'- 8"	3'- 0"		
Desk - Slope Top	2'-6"x 3'-8"x 3'-4"	3'- 3"	3'- 2"	3'- 2"	3'-0"	3'-4"
Desk - Flat Top	3'-0"x 5'-6"x 2'-6"	3'- 2"	3'- 0"	3'- 0"		
Desk - Executive's	3'-2"x 6'-0"x 2'-6"	4'- 2"	4'- 2"	3'- 1"	3'-0"	3'-2"
Trunk - Wardrobe	1'-11"x 2'-6"x 3'-7"	2'- 5"	2'- 5"	2'- 5"		

Notes : **✱** Clear width between faces of rails, newels etc. or between rail or newel and finish wall.
▲ Headroom limited to minimum for comfortable human passage (see "Stair Table" and text).
● Narrow stairs and wide landings.
■ Absolute minimum not recommended (see text).

PURPOSE

The six diagrams on this sheet represent unit plans for types of non-winder stairways which are most frequently encountered in the average residential planning problem. Tabular information with each was developed from data contained in the Stair Table.

Unit plans are drawn to ⅛" scale and therefore can be supplied directly as a check of stair layouts to sketch plans and elevations. Each represents an average condition with a stair pitch well within the comfort zone. The basis is a 9'-6" floor-to-floor height with 16 risers each 7.13" in height. Width is 3'-0" from wall to wall.

Tabular data with each unit plan indicates dimensional variations which occur when stairways of substantially similar pitches are planned for floor-to-floor heights from 8 to 11 feet.

Width is the only critical dimension missing from this unit plan information. This varies with requirements of design and stair use and should be selected from data on previous page. Width is a dimension controlling critical clearances on all stairs that contain a turn.

Winders have not been included in these unit plans because they represent a stair condition generally regarded as unde-

sirable. However, use of winders is sometimes necessary due to cramped space. In such instances, winders should be adjusted to replace landings so that the narrow portions of tread at the inside of the turn are at least equal to ¾" T. When this is done, dimensions of L_1 and L_2 are decreased by approximately ½T, the exact figure depending upon the width selected. The practice of adding a winder-riser to bisect the landing diagonally from the corner of a newel is to be avoided in all cases for it produces a dangerously narrow step in a particularly undesirable place.

APPLICATION OF UNIT PLANS

Diagrammatic data can be used on sketches as a graphic check as noted. Tabular data can be applied to either sketches or working drawings to eliminate the necessity of developing experimental stairway sections to determine run, proportional rise, horizontal and vertical areas and location of under-rake minimum headroom.

Dimensional data have been confined to a single pitch for all floor-to-floor heights. The pitch indicated is that most generally desirable for human comfort. Data for other pitches listed as tread and riser proportions in the Stair Table can be substituted for values of L_1, L_2, and M. and M.

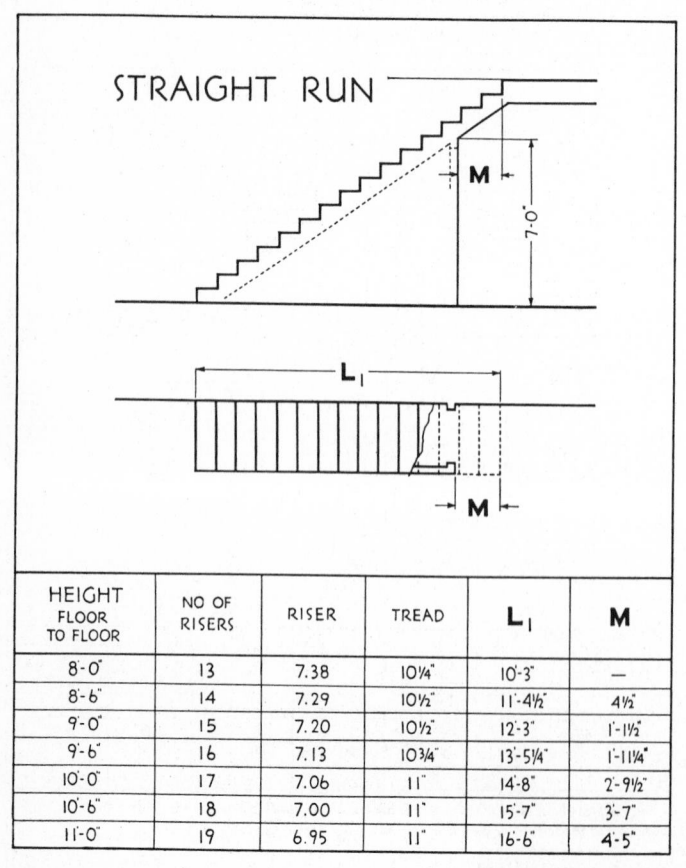

STRAIGHT RUN

HEIGHT FLOOR TO FLOOR	NO OF RISERS	RISER	TREAD	L_1	M
8'-0"	13	7.38	10¼"	10'-3"	—
8'-6"	14	7.29	10½"	11'-4½"	4½"
9'-0"	15	7.20	10½"	12'-3"	1'-1½"
9'-6"	16	7.13	10¾"	13'-5¼"	1'-11¼"
10'-0"	17	7.06	11"	14'-8"	2'-9½"
10'-6"	18	7.00	11"	15'-7"	3'-7"
11'-0"	19	6.95	11"	16'-6"	4'-5"

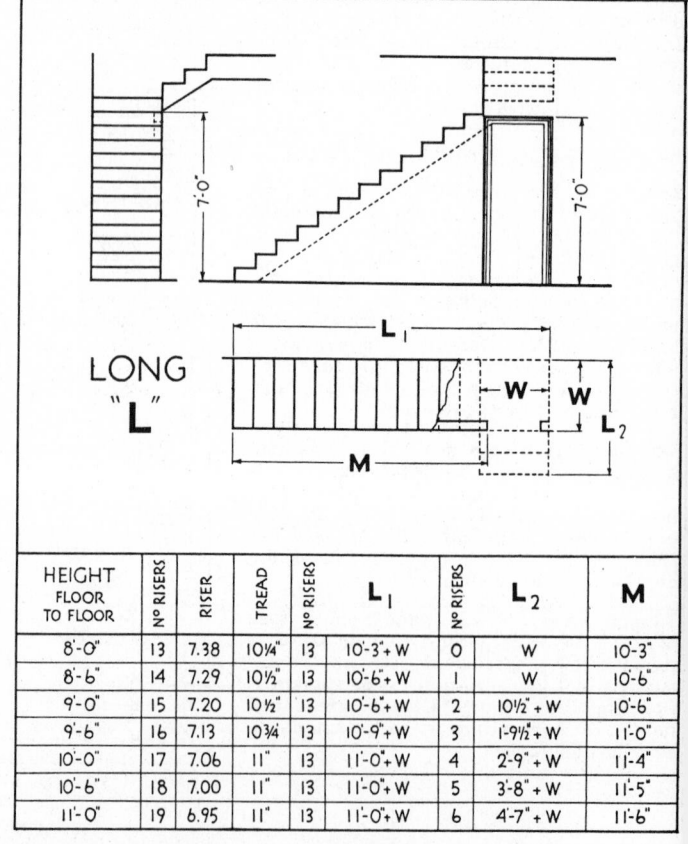

LONG "L"

HEIGHT FLOOR TO FLOOR	N° RISERS	RISER	TREAD	N° RISERS	L_1	N° RISERS	L_2	M
8'-0"	13	7.38	10¼"	13	10'-3"+W	0	W	10'-3"
8'-6"	14	7.29	10½"	13	10'-6"+W	1	W	10'-6"
9'-0"	15	7.20	10½"	13	10'-6"+W	2	10½"+W	10'-6"
9'-6"	16	7.13	10¾	13	10'-9"+W	3	1'-9½"+W	11'-0"
10'-0"	17	7.06	11"	13	11'-0"+W	4	2'-9"+W	11'-4"
10'-6"	18	7.00	11"	13	11'-0"+W	5	3'-8"+W	11'-5"
11'-0"	19	6.95	11"	13	11'-0"+W	6	4'-7"+W	11'-6"

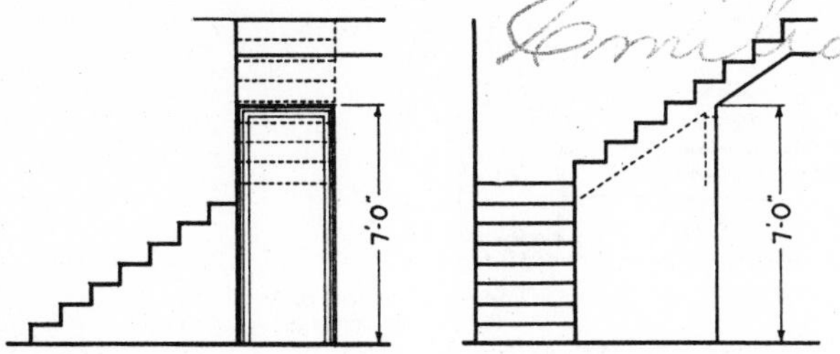

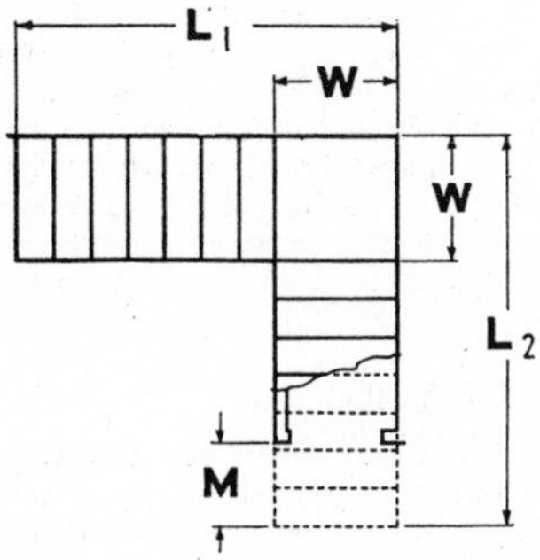

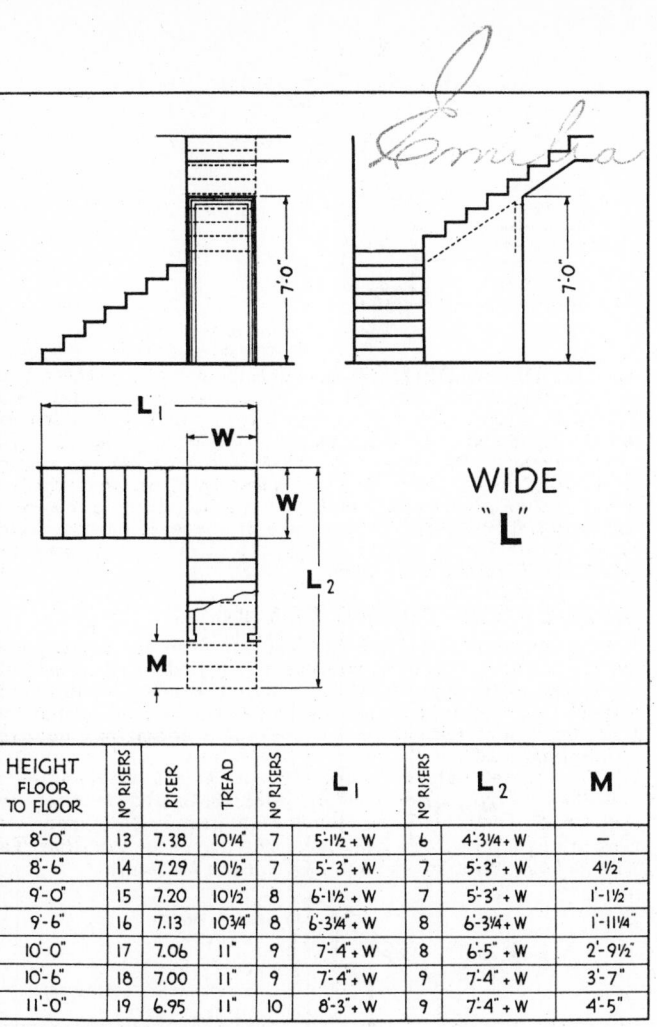

WIDE "L"

HEIGHT FLOOR TO FLOOR	Nº RISERS	RISER	TREAD	Nº RISERS	L1	Nº RISERS	L2	M
8'-0"	13	7.38	10¼"	7	5'-1½"+W	6	4'-3¼+W	–
8'-6"	14	7.29	10½"	7	5'-3"+W	7	5'-3"+W	4½"
9'-0"	15	7.20	10½"	8	6'-1½"+W	7	5'-3"+W	1'-1½"
9'-6"	16	7.13	10¾"	8	6'-3¼"+W	8	6'-3¼+W	1'-11¼"
10'-0"	17	7.06	11"	9	7'-4"+W	8	6'-5"+W	2'-9½"
10'-6"	18	7.00	11"	9	7'-4"+W	9	7'-4"+W	3'-7"
11'-0"	19	6.95	11"	10	8'-3"+W	9	7'-4"+W	4'-5"

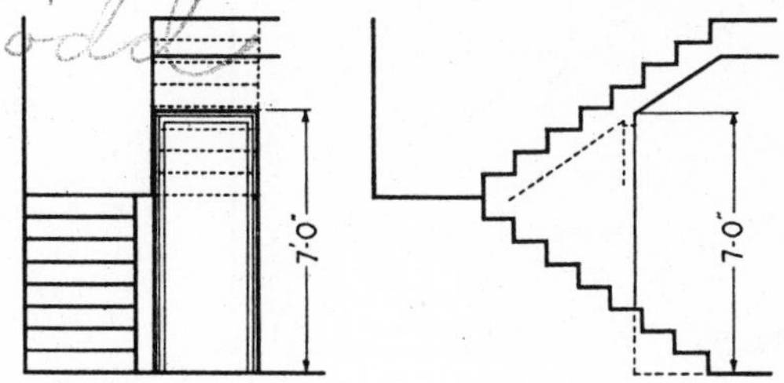

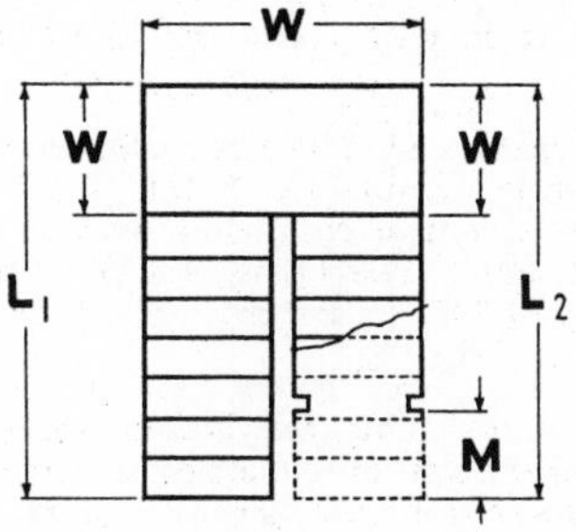

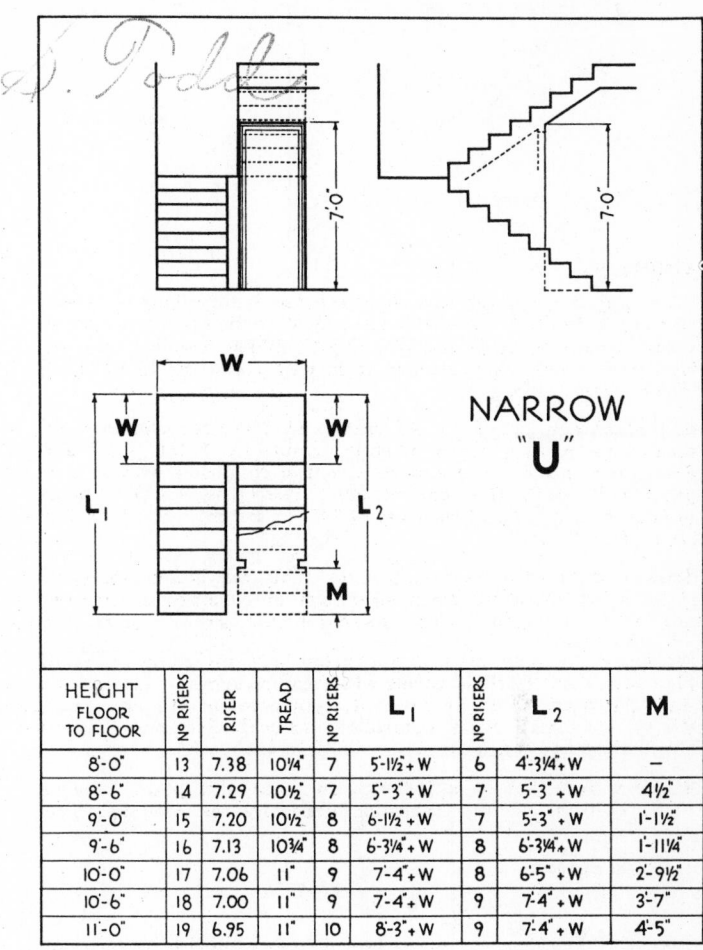

NARROW "U"

HEIGHT FLOOR TO FLOOR	Nº RISERS	RISER	TREAD	Nº RISERS	L1	Nº RISERS	L2	M
8'-0"	13	7.38	10¼"	7	5'-1½"+W	6	4'-3¼"+W	–
8'-6"	14	7.29	10½"	7	5'-3"+W	7	5'-3"+W	4½"
9'-0"	15	7.20	10½"	8	6'-1½"+W	7	5'-3"+W	1'-1½"
9'-6"	16	7.13	10¾"	8	6'-3¼"+W	8	6'-3¼"+W	1'-11¼"
10'-0"	17	7.06	11"	9	7'-4"+W	8	6'-5"+W	2'-9½"
10'-6"	18	7.00	11"	9	7'-4"+W	9	7'-4"+W	3'-7"
11'-0"	19	6.95	11"	10	8'-3"+W	9	7'-4"+W	4'-5"

DOUBLE "L"

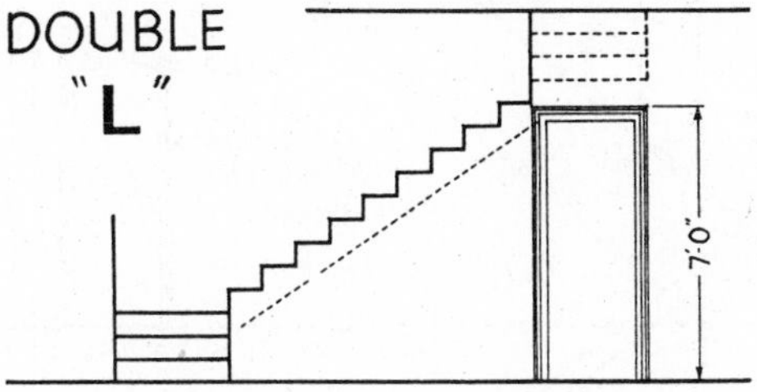

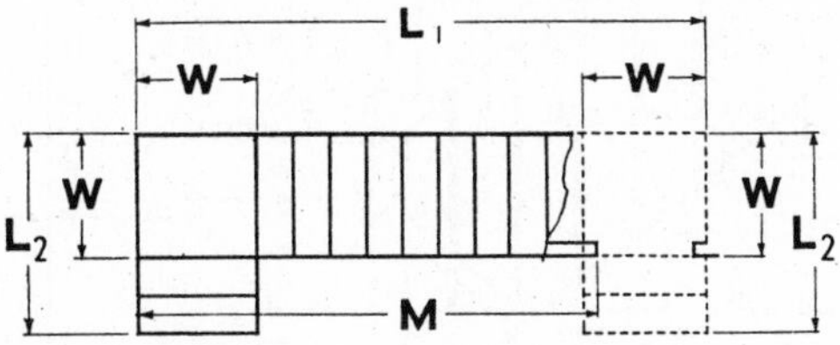

HEIGHT FLOOR TO FLOOR	Nº RISERS	RISER	TREAD	Nº RISERS	L1	Nº RISERS	L2	M
8'-0"	13	7.38	10¼"	13	10'-3"+2W	0	W	10'-3"+W
8'-6"	14	7.29	10½"	12	9'-7½"+2W	1	W	9'-7½"+W
9'-0"	15	7.20	10½"	11	8'-9"+2W	2	10½"+W	8'-9"+W
9'-6"	16	7.13	10¾"	10	8'-0¾"+2W	3	1'-9½"+W	8'-3¾"+W
10'-0"	17	7.06	11"	9	7'-4"+2W	4	2'-9"+W	7'-8"+W
10'-6"	18	7.00	11"	8	6'-5"+2W	5	3'-8"+W	6'-10"+W
11'-0"	19	6.95	11"	7	5'-6"+2W	6	4'-7"+W	6'-0"+W

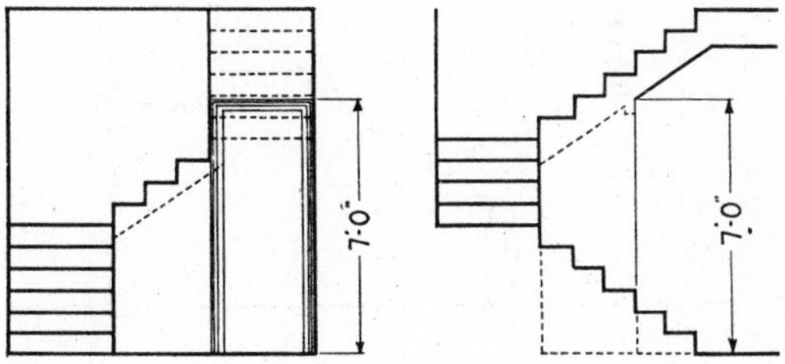

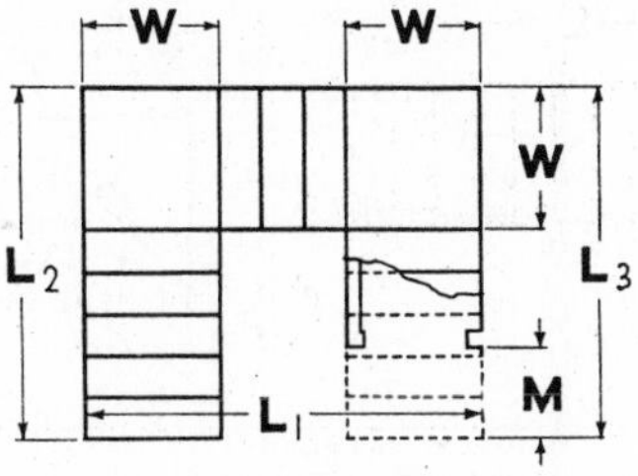

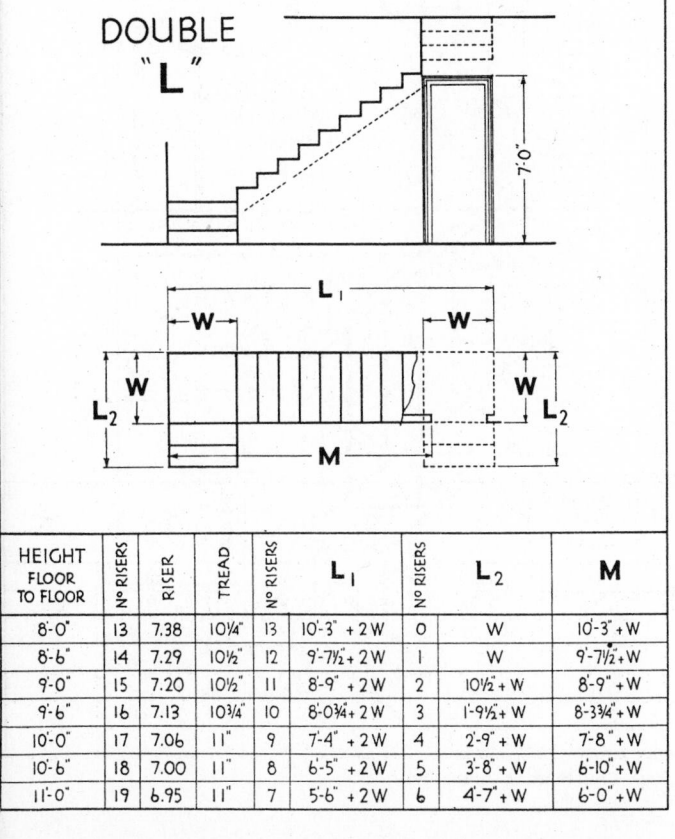

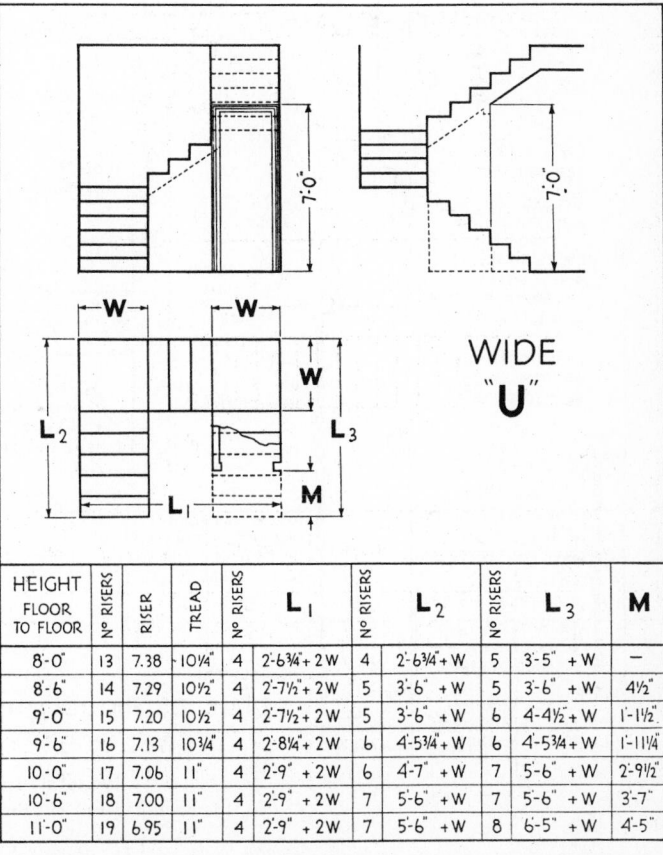

WIDE "U"

HEIGHT FLOOR TO FLOOR	Nº RISERS	RISER	TREAD	Nº RISERS	L1	Nº RISERS	L2	Nº RISERS	L3	M
8'-0"	13	7.38	10¼"	4	2'-6¾"+2W	4	2'-6¾"+W	5	3'-5"+W	–
8'-6"	14	7.29	10½"	4	2'-7½"+2W	5	3'-6"+W	5	3'-6"+W	4½"
9'-0"	15	7.20	10½"	4	2'-7½"+2W	5	3'-6"+W	6	4'-4½"+W	1'-1½"
9'-6"	16	7.13	10¾"	4	2'-8¼"+2W	6	4'-5¾"+W	6	4'-5¾+W	1'-11¼"
10-0"	17	7.06	11"	4	2'-9"+2W	6	4'-7"+W	7	5'-6"+W	2'-9½"
10'-6"	18	7.00	11"	4	2'-9"+2W	7	5'-6"+W	7	5'-6"+W	3'-7"
11'-0"	19	6.95	11"	4	2'-9"+2W	7	5'-6"+W	8	6'-5"+W	4'-5"

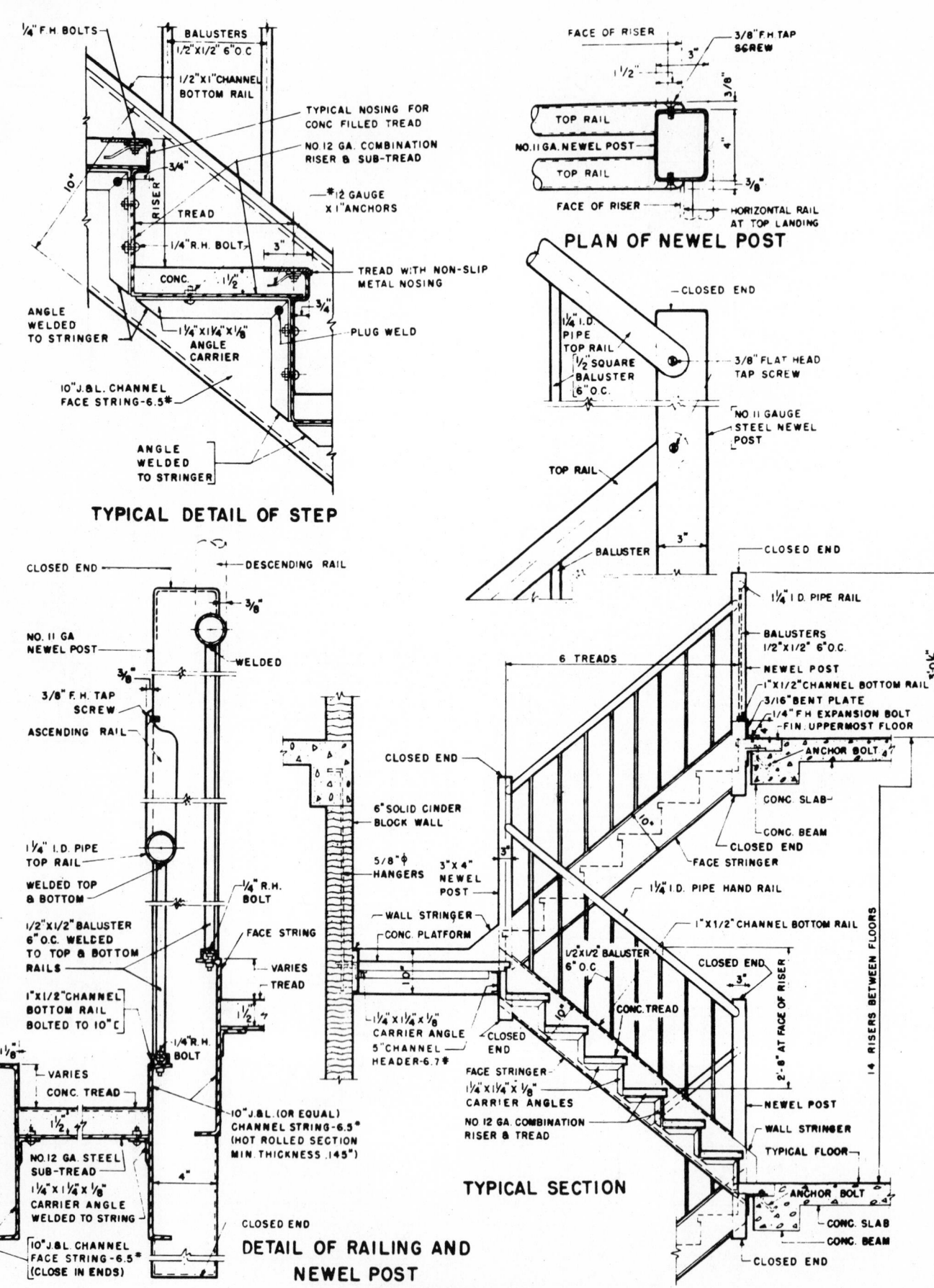

TYPICAL DETAIL OF STEP

PLAN OF NEWEL POST

DETAIL OF RAILING AND NEWEL POST

TYPICAL SECTION

Typical steel stair construction
(standard detail of the New York City Housing Authority)

Scale: section ⅜ in. = 1 ft; details 1½ in. = 1 ft.

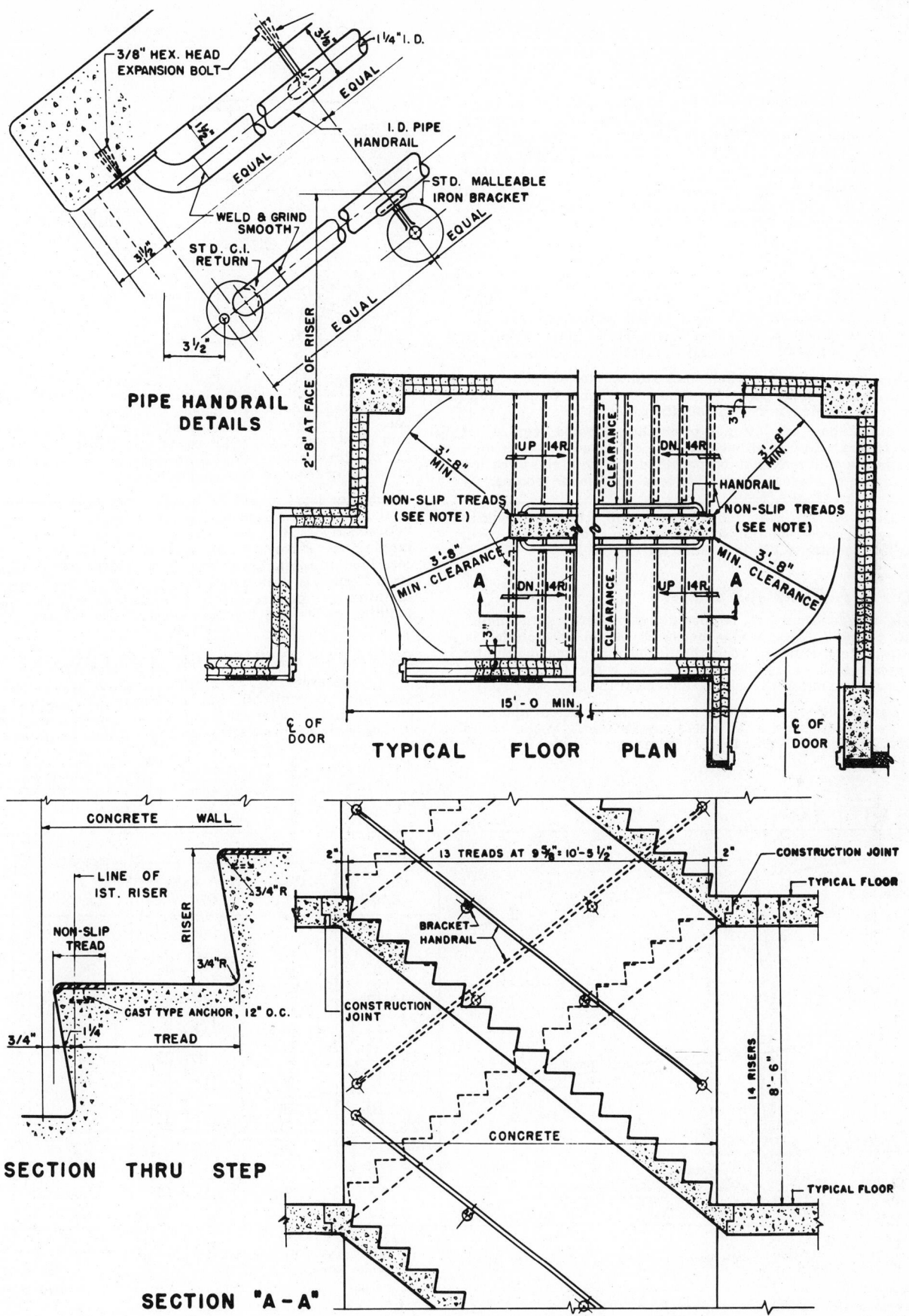

PIPE HANDRAIL DETAILS

- 3/8" HEX. HEAD EXPANSION BOLT
- 3/8"
- 1¼" I. D.
- EQUAL
- I. D. PIPE HANDRAIL
- STD. MALLEABLE IRON BRACKET
- EQUAL
- WELD & GRIND SMOOTH
- STD. C.I. RETURN
- 3½"
- 3½"
- 2'-8" AT FACE OF RISER
- EQUAL

TYPICAL FLOOR PLAN

- 3'-8" MIN.
- UP 14R
- CLEARANCE
- 3"
- DN. 14R
- 3'-8" MIN.
- HANDRAIL
- NON-SLIP TREADS (SEE NOTE)
- NON-SLIP TREADS (SEE NOTE)
- 3'-8" MIN. CLEARANCE
- A
- DN. 14R
- CLEARANCE
- UP 14R
- A
- 3'-8" MIN. CLEARANCE
- 3"
- ₵ OF DOOR
- 15'-0 MIN.
- ₵ OF DOOR

SECTION THRU STEP

- CONCRETE WALL
- LINE OF IST. RISER
- NON-SLIP TREAD
- RISER
- 3/4"R
- 3/4"R
- CAST TYPE ANCHOR, 12" O.C.
- 3/4"
- 1¼
- TREAD

SECTION "A-A"

- 13 TREADS AT 9⅝" = 10'-5½"
- 2"
- 2"
- CONSTRUCTION JOINT
- TYPICAL FLOOR
- BRACKET HANDRAIL
- CONSTRUCTION JOINT
- 14 RISERS
- 8'-6"
- CONCRETE
- TYPICAL FLOOR

Typical reinforced concrete scissors stair
(standard detail of New York City Housing Authority)

Scale: plan and section ¼ in. = 1 ft; details 1½ in. = 1 ft.

PURPOSE

Design of ladders and pedestrian ramps is more directly influenced by conditions of location and use than by theory. Exact formulae have not been developed. However, data on this sheet give such information as has been found to be practical. Tabular material has been adapted from data formulated by Ernest Irving Freese, from the New York City Building Code and from recommendations of the Workmen's Compensation Service Bureau.

DEFINITIONS

Ramps as considered here are inclined pedestrian passages without vertical risers and of a lower pitch than stairs. In general, they are easier to ascend or descend than stairs.

Ladders have a greater pitch than stairs. No ladder is comfortable, though some may be easier to climb than others. They can be divided into two classifications:

(1) Stepladders are lower in pitch than 75° and require flat treads. Risers may be either "open" or "closed" (see below). Handrails may or may not be provided. In this classification belong most fire escapes and ladders for boiler rooms, fly galleries, attics, decks, etc.

(2) Rung ladders are pitched more steeply than 75°, require extremely narrow treads or round rungs to provide knee-room and do not require additional handrails.

LAYOUTS AND REQUIREMENTS

Ramps steeper than 10% require non-slip surfaces and handrails. If possible, these safety measures should be included in all ramps. Most building codes limit the pitch, the maximum being about 2:12 or 16 2/3%. See Table I for recommended pitches, widths, handrail heights and clearances.

Stepladders require handrails on both sides when not confined between walls or when risers are "closed." When risers are "open," treads or the ladder frame may serve as hand-

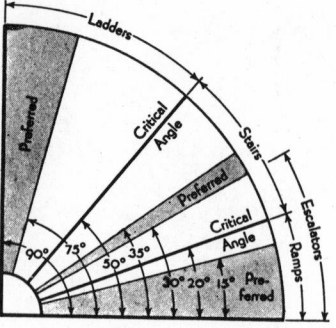

Diagram shows recommend[...] tions of the Workmen's Co[m]pensation Service Bureau f[or] pitch of ramps, stairs and la[d]ders. Pitches close to "critic[al] angles" should be avoide[d] wherever possible as these a[re] uncomfortable and unsafe[.]

holds. However, handrails should be provided wherever po[s]sible. Stepladders are normally "single-file" footways. Bein[g] used only where limitations of space will not permit installa[tion] of stairs they should be as narrow as possible. See Tabl[e] II for dimensions and clearances. In all cases consult loca[l] building codes and fire regulations.

Rung ladders should have round rungs if possible to provid[e] a maximum of knee-room. Rungs need not be evenly space[d] between floors, but irregular spaces should occur at the lowe[r] landing for safety. Rung spacing and clearances may be de[-]termined graphically as shown in Table III or taken directl[y] from Table III, Columns 4 and 5. Ladders necessary for prope[r] maintenance or fire safety of buildings are specified in mos[t] building codes and fire regulations.

PREFABRICATED STAIRS AND LADDERS

Various types of counterbalanced disappearing stairs ar[e] available, as well as iron pit-ladders, fire-escape equipmen[t] etc. Manufacturers' reference data should be consulted fo[r] necessary tolerances, structural requirements and recommende[d] installation practices.

TABLE I - RAMPS - 0° to 20° Pitch

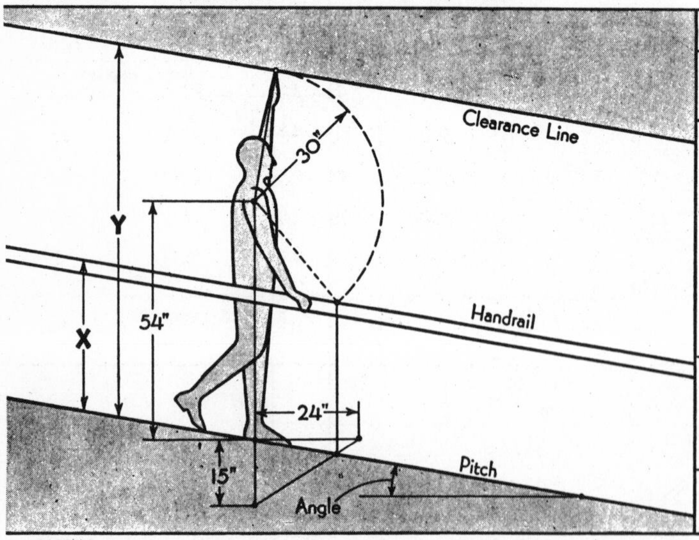

	GRADIENT			HANDRAIL HEIGHT	CLEARANCE
Pitch (ratio)	Grade (%)	Angle (deg. - min.)	X (inches)	Y (inches)	
½ : 12	4⅙	2 – 23	35		
½ : 10	5	2 – 52	35		
1 : 12	8⅓	4 – 46	34½		
1 : 10	10	5 – 43	34½	84	
1 : 8 } 1½ : 12	12½	7 – 7	34		
1½ : 10	15	8 – 23	34		
2 : 12	16⅔	9 – 28	34		
2 : 10	20	11 – 19	34		
2½ : 12	20⅚	11 – 46	33½		
2½ : 10 } 3 : 12	25	14 – 2	33½	85	
3½ : 12	29⅙	16 – 16	33½		
3 : 10	30	16 – 42	33½		

NOTES:

Overhead clearances and handrail heights may be determined graphically from the diagram

Maximum pitch:
- (1) Values below the dotted line ······ are prohibited by the New York City Building Code for theatre aisles, except for runs not exceeding 10' - 0" which may be pitched a maximum of 1:8
- (2) Values below the dash line — — — are prohibited by most other building codes

(3) All values above the solid line ——— are approved by the Workmen's Compensation Service Bureau

Minimum width:
- (1) For single file traffic = 30"
- (2) For furniture passage = 36" } determined by Ernest Irving Freese
- (3) Preferred single file min. = 42"
- (4) For theatre aisles = 36", increasing 1½" every 5' - 0" of run (N.Y.C. Bldg. Code)

TABLE II - STEPLADDERS - 50° to 75°

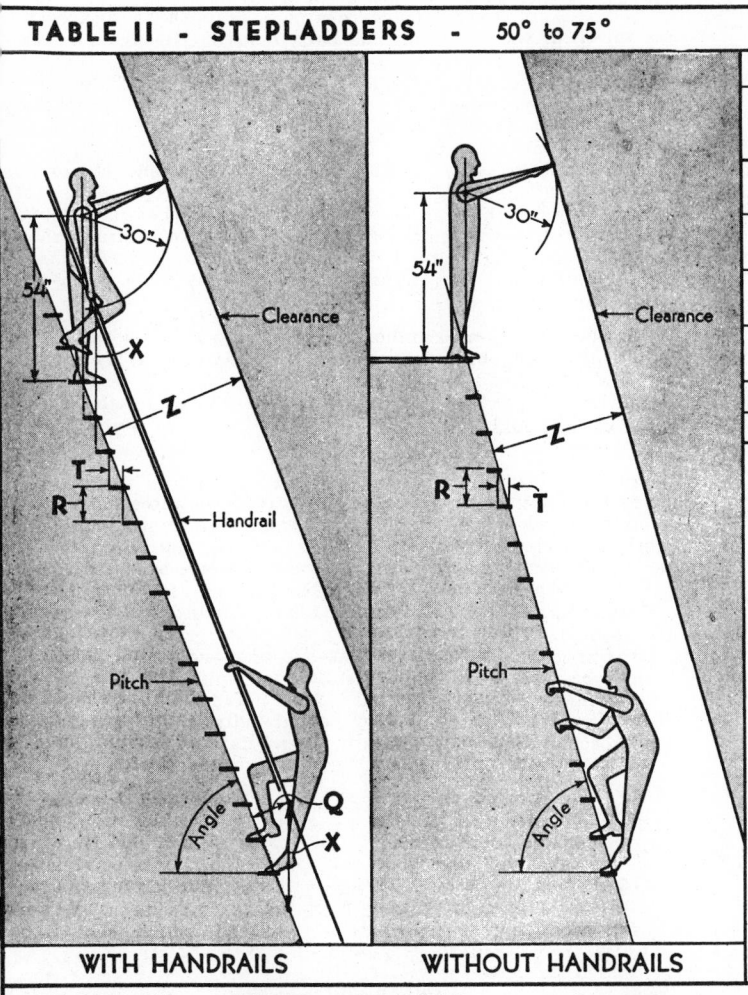

WITH HANDRAILS	WITHOUT HANDRAILS

STEP DIMENSIONS		GRADIENT		CLEAR-ANCE Z (inches)	HANDRAIL HEIGHT X (inches)
Riser R (inches)	Tread T (inches)	Grade (%)	Angle (deg. - min.)		
9⅜	7½	125	51 – 21	64	
9¾	7	139.28	54 – 19	62	34½
10⅛	6½	155.75	57 – 18	59	
10½	6	175	60 – 16	57	35
10⅞	5½	197.72	63 – 10	54	
11¼	5	225	66 – 2	52	35½
11⅝	4½	258.66	68 – 50	50	
12	4	300	71 – 34	47	36
12⅜	3½	353.21	74 – 12	45	36½
12¾	3	425	76 – 46	42	37

NOTES:

Clearance and handrail height may be determined graphically if desired

Handrails are required on both sides of stepladders if risers are not left "open" or if not confined between side walls

Maximum and minimum widths:
    With handrails: 21" to 24"
    Without handrails: variable
    Between sidewalls: 24" minimum

For fire escapes, etc., consult building codes and fire regulations

FORMULAE:

$$\text{Tread} = T = 20 - \tfrac{4}{3}R$$
$$\text{Riser} = R = 15 - \tfrac{3}{4}T$$

Perpendicular distance, pitch line to handrail =
$$Q = X \div \sqrt{\left(\tfrac{R}{T}\right)^2 + 1}$$

TABLE III - RUNG LADDERS - 75° to 90°

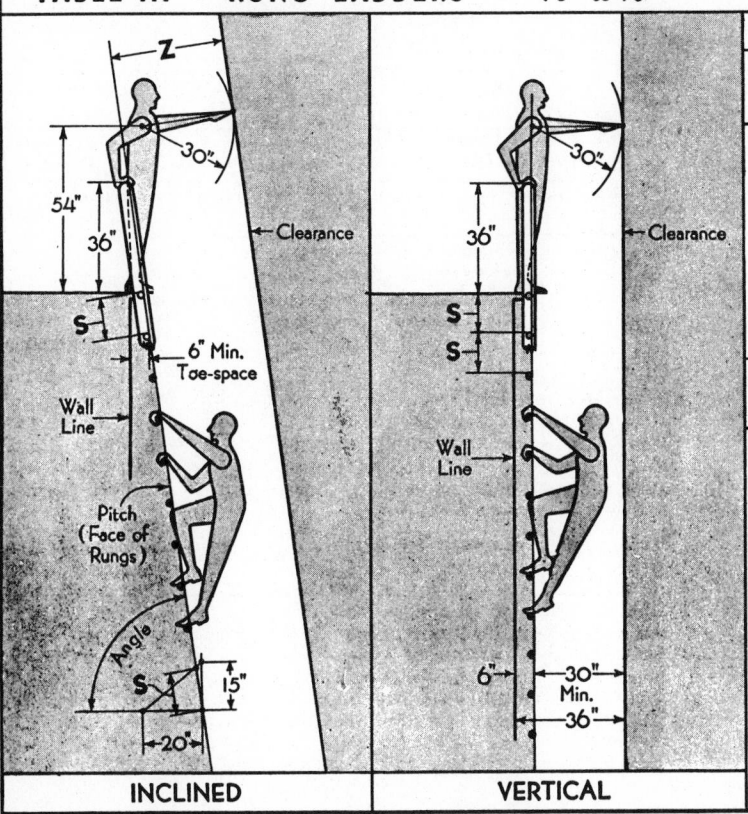

INCLINED	VERTICAL

GRADIENT			RUNG SPACING S (inches)	CLEAR-ANCE Z (inches)
Pitch (ratio)	Grade (%)	Angle (deg. - min.)		
12 : 2½	480	78 – 14	13¼	41
12 : 2	600	80 – 33	13½	39
12 : 1½	800	82 – 53	13¾	37
12 : 1	1200	85 – 14	14¼	35
12 : ½	2400	87 – 37	14½	32
Vertical		90 – 0	15 maximum 12 minimum	30

NOTES:

Clearances and handrail heights may be determined graphically if desired. Ladder frame should extend 3'-0" above platform

Widths:
    Minimum = 15"
    Desirable = 18"
    Minimum between sidewalls = 24"

PURPOSE

Correct proportions and mandatory requirements for the design of interior fireplaces, smoke chambers and fireplace flues are indicated on this sheet.

GENERAL

Dimensions of correctly designed fireplaces are proportional within certain limits, the basis for proper proportions being the width of the fireplace opening. The accompanying table includes simple formulae for various widths. When followed within the limits indicated, adequate draft is assured, thus eliminating the smoke nuisance always present in poorly designed fireplaces.

CONSTRUCTION DETAILS

Fireplace. Design practice common to some localities has produced fireplaces with proportions other than those recommended on this sheet. Much variation, however, from the proportions indicated here will tend to interfere with proper draft. These dimensions are also recommended for the construction of fireplaces designed to throw a maximum of heat into the room. For fireplaces larger than 84 inches similar proportions should obtain. However, such fireplaces usually require metal hoods to lower the effective height (H). The same result may be obtained by raising the back hearth. Lowering the back hearth from 2" to 4" will aid in keeping ashes within the back-hearth area. Effective height of the fireplace (H) is always height of clear opening.

The reflecting wall at the back should always be built as a plane surface sloping up into the lower edge of the throat and terminating slightly above the level of the lintel. When the back is built in a vertical curve, air currents are deflected under the lintel, thus causing smoke to roll past the throat and into the room.

Throat. This should extend the full width of the fireplace opening. Limiting dimensions for throats are given in the table on the next page. Unless a metal throat (see below) or masonry arch is used, iron or steel is usually required to support masonry lintels. Maximum thickness of masonry at the lintel in front of the opening ranges from 4 to 6 inches depending on the material used.

Smoke Shelf (also called "wind shelf"). This element is required in all fireplaces to prevent downdraft in the chimney from destroying the updraft and thus blowing smoke into the room. In all cases, parging on the smoke shelf is recommended as indicated in the detail. When this is done the normal downdraft tends to circle up, to mingle with hot gases and aid updraft through the chimney flue. Otherwise, a pocket may be formed within the smoke chamber which may produce uneven, turbulent downdraft currents and consequently, a smoky fireplace.

A smoke chamber is an essential part of fireplace construction. It provides space for the smoke to mix with cold chimney air before the flue is sufficiently heated to carry heated gases up the chimney through normal convection. Actual construction will vary with the type of throat and the size of the fireplace. In all cases, however, the smoke chamber should be constructed with a 60° slope from throat to chimney flue as indicated in the accompanying drawings, and should have a smooth interior surface so as not to impede drafts.

Flues. The proper size of flue has an important bearing on efficient operation of the fireplace. When possible, round flues are preferable to square or oblong flues; and a flue lining is recommended for use with fireplaces of all types and sizes. Unlined flues are usually rough. Deposits of inflammable creosote distilled from fireplace fuels tend to form on rough surfaces, producing a constant fire hazard which should be avoided. Effective areas of flues, particularly the rectangular type, are always less than the actual cross-sectional inside area. Sizes of square and round flue linings and of unlined flues are shown in the accompanying table of recommended flue dimensions.

Clay flue lining should conform to ASTM Specification C315–56. Square and rectangular flue linings are normally designated by their outside dimensions, round flue linings by their inside diameters. Flue linings are also available in modular sizes for use with modular masonry, in conformance with ASA A62.4 *Sizes of Clay Flue Lining.* Dimensions and effective areas of modular flue linings are shown in Table 1. Nonmodular sizes are shown in Tables 2 and 3. All tables are courtesy of the Clay Flue Lining Institute.

Ash dumps and pits. The ash dump should be fitted with a hinged cast-iron cover. It is common practice to locate the ash dump in the center of the back hearth. However, in certain cases where sub-construction makes it possible, the ash dump may be conveniently located on either side of the back hearth. The passage from ash dump to pit should be lined with at least an 8½" x 8½" flue tile if the pit is to serve more than one fireplace, or if it is not possible to construct a straight passage. Any bend in the ash passage should not be less than 60° to avoid the possibility of clogging. Floors of ash pits should be parged with mortar or otherwise sloped to a cast-iron cleanout door for convenience in removing ashes. The bottom of a cleanout door should be at least 8" above the cellar floor to permit use of an ash receptacle when the pit is being cleaned.

Wood framing members must be kept at least 2" away from all fireplace or chimney masonry. In addition, it is recommended that wood mantels and trim be kept 8" back from the fireplace opening at the sides and 12" clear above the opening, although custom or local ordinances often permit much less clearance.

Prefabricated fireplace equipment. All dimensions and details of construction shown on this sheet may be subject to some adjustment to conform to installation requirements of prefabricated metal dampers, throats, smoke chamber linings, ash dumps and cleanout doors. Each of these units is manufactured in a number of types. No common standard of dimensions has been established and manufacturers' data should be consulted in all cases prior to a selection for specific use.

Heating systems for fireplaces are also manufactured in a variety of types and sizes. Installation requirements of these units are also subject to variations noted and proportional dimensions given here should be carefully adjusted to their use in accordance with manufacturers' data.

Table 1. Square and rectangular clay flue linings—modular sizes

Minimum net inside area, sq in.	Nominal dimensions, in.*	Outside dimensions, in.	Minimum wall thickness, in.	Approx. maximum outside corner radius, in.
15	4x 8	3.5x 7.5	0.5	1
20	4x12	3.5x11.5	0.625	1
35	8x 8	7.5x 7.5	0.625	2
57	8x12	7.5x11.5	0.75	2
87	12x12	11.5x11.5	0.875	3
120	12x16	11.5x15.5	1.	3
162	16x16	15.5x15.5	1.125	4
208	16x20	15.5x19.5	1.25	4
262	20x20	19.5x19.5	1.375	5
320	20x24	19.5x23.5	1.5	5
385	24x24	23.5x23.5	1.625	6

* *Cross section of flue lining shall fit within rectangle of dimension corresponding to nominal size.*

Table 2. Square and rectangular clay flue linings—nonmodular sizes

Minimum net inside area, in.	Outside width of short side, in.	Outside width of long side, in.	Wall thickness, in.
22	4½	8½	⅝
36	4½	13	¾
51	8½	8½	¾
79	8½	13	⅞
108	8½	17¾	1
125	13	13	⅞
168	13	17¾	1
232	17¾	17¾	1¼
279	20	20	1⅜
338	20	24	1½
420	24	24	1⅝

Table 3. Round clay flue linings

Minimum net inside area, sq in.	Inside diameter, in.	Thickness, in.
26	6	⅝
47	8	¾
75	10	⅞
108	12	1
171	15	1⅛
240	18	1¼
330	21	1⅝
433	24	1¾
551	27	2
683	30	2⅛
990	36	2½

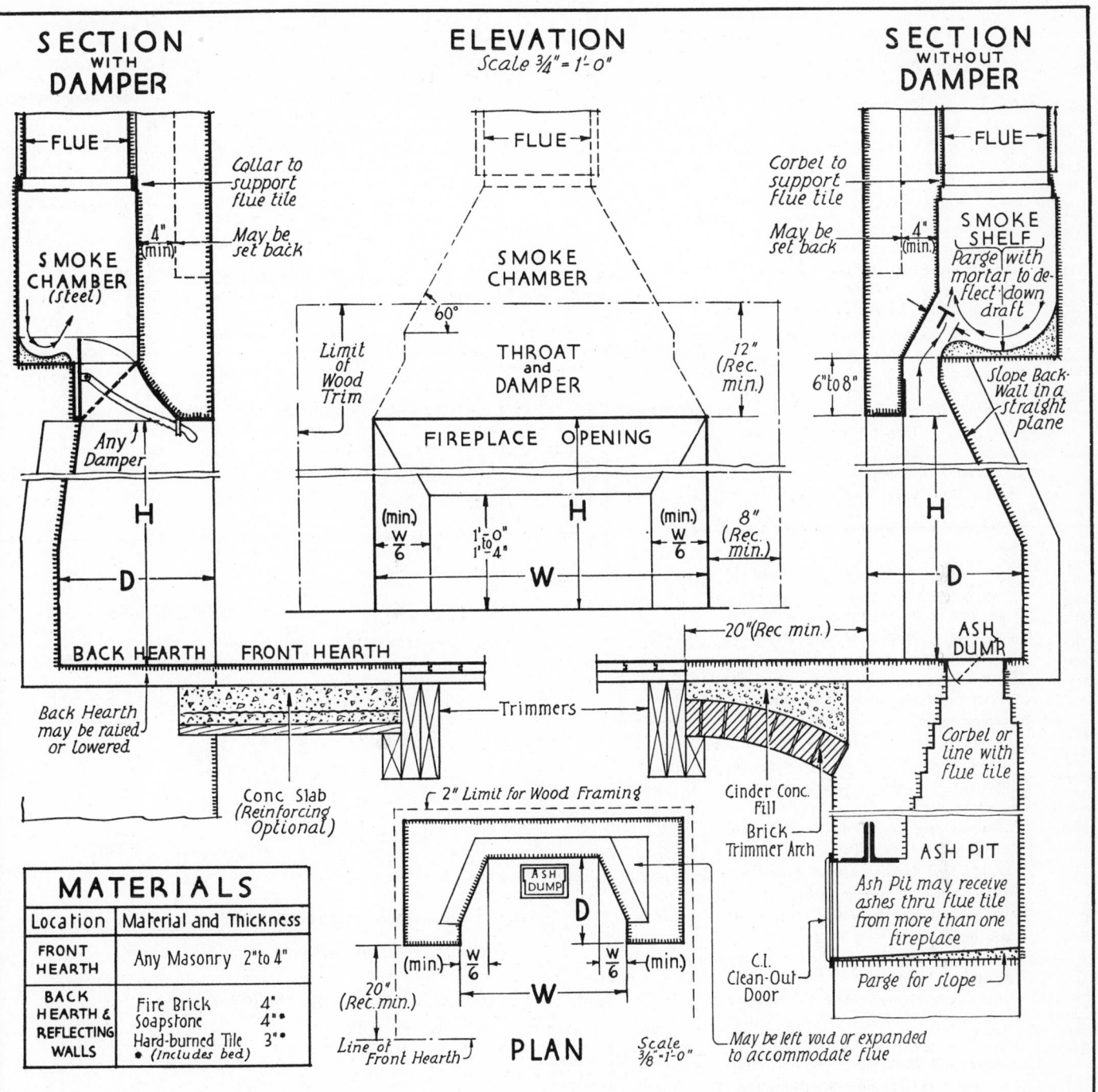

SECTION WITH DAMPER — ELEVATION (Scale ¾" = 1'-0") — SECTION WITHOUT DAMPER

MATERIALS

Location	Material and Thickness
FRONT HEARTH	Any Masonry 2" to 4"
BACK HEARTH & REFLECTING WALLS	Fire Brick 4" / Soapstone 4"* / Hard-burned Tile 3"* *(Includes bed)

FIREPLACE DIMENSIONS (In Inches)

W	24 to 84
H	$\frac{2}{3}$ to $\frac{3}{4}$ W
D	$\frac{1}{2}$ to $\frac{2}{3}$ H {16 to 24 (Rec) for Coal / 18 to 24 (Rec) for Wood}
FLUE (Effective Area)	$\frac{1}{8}$ WH for unlined flue / $\frac{1}{10}$ WH for rectangular lining / $\frac{1}{12}$ WH for circular lining
T (Area)	$\frac{5}{4}$ to $\frac{3}{2}$ FLUE AREA
T (Width)	3" minimum to 4½" maximum

RECOMMENDED FLUE SIZES (In Inches)

FIREPLACE WIDTH W	RECTANGULAR FLUES			EQUIVALENT ROUND	
	Nominal or Outside Dimension	Inside Dimension	Effective Area	Inside Diameter	Effective Area
24	8½ X 8½	7¼ X 7¼	41 ▢"	8	50.3 ▢"
30 to 34	8½ X 13	7 X 11½	70 ▢"	10	78.54 ▢"
36 to 44	13 X 13	11¼ X 11¼	99 ▢"	12	113.0 ▢"
46 to 56	13 X 18	11¼ X 6¼	156 ▢"	15	176.7 ▢"
58 to 68	18 X 18	15¾ X 5¾	195 ▢"	18	254.4 ▢"
70 to 84	20 X 24	17 X 21	278 ▢"	22	380.13 ▢"

Standard nomenclature for steel doors and frames, as proposed by the Steel Door Institute, is shown in Figs. 1 and 2, respectively.

Steel doors and frames should conform to one of the following commercial standards, published by the U.S. Department of Commerce:

CS242-62:   Standard Stock Commercial 1¾-inch Thick Steel Doors and Frames

CS211-57:   Flush-type Interior Steel Doors and Frames

The principal provisions of CS242 are as follows:

Standard opening sizes are shown in Table 1. Doors are sized to fit these openings with ⅛ in. clearance at head and jambs and a maximum of ¾ in. at the sill.

Minimum steel thicknesses are shown in Table 2.

Flush doors may be of hollow steel construction or of composite metal face construction. In the latter type, the face sheets must be bonded to the core with waterproof adhesive and welded to perimeter channels on all four edges.

Frames may be of the knocked-down type or welded. In either case they must be rigid and present a neat appearance when erected. Frames must be provided with not less than three wall anchors per jamb and an anchor to the floor at each jamb. Anchors should be at least 18 gage (0.0449 in.) steel.

Doors and frames should be prepared to receive locks, strikes, and hinges. Mounting and location of locks should be in accordance with ASA Specification for (Metal) Door and Frame Preparation for Door Locks and Flush Bolts, A115. Lock and latch sets should conform to Federal Specification FF-H-106 (Hardware, Builders', Locks and Door Trim), Series 86 (Mortise locks), Series 90 (Mortise unit type locks), Series 140 (Mortise integral type locks), or Series 161 (Bored or cylindrical locks). Center line of strike should be located $40\frac{5}{16}$ in. above the finished floor. Provision should be made for three regular weight hinges, 4½ by 4½ in.

Interior steel doors (CS211) are of lighter construction and are not more than 3 ft wide. Standard opening sizes are shown in Table 3 and minimum steel thicknesses in Table 4.

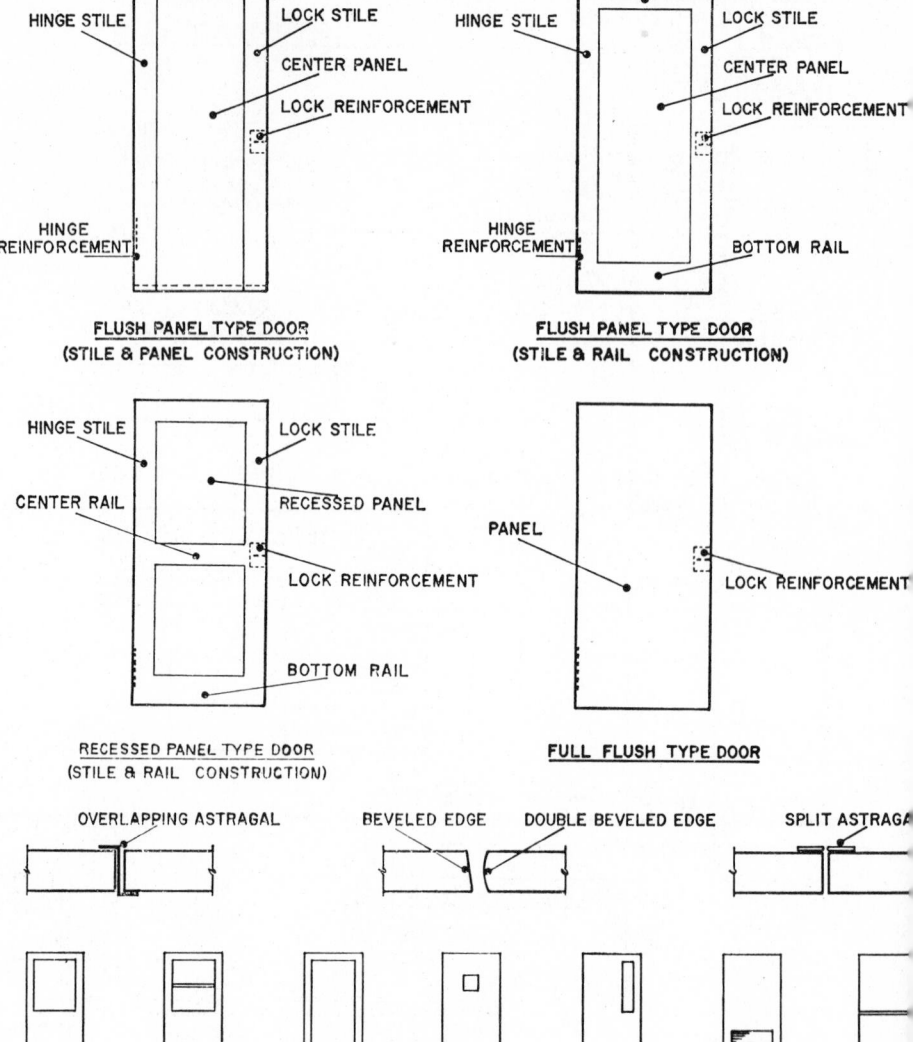

Fig. 1.   Nomenclature for steel doors

Courtesy Steel Door Institute

Table 1.   Standard opening sizes (CS242-62)

WIDTH & HEIGHT	WIDTH & HEIGHT	WIDTH & HEIGHT
2'0" x 6'8"	2'0" x 7'0"	2'0" x 7'2"
2'4" x 6'8"	2'4" x 7'0"	2'4" x 7'2"
2'6" x 6'8"	2'6" x 7'0"	
2'8" x 6'8"	2'8" x 7'0"	2'8" x 7'2"
3'0" x 6'8"	3'0" x 7'0"	3'0" x 7'2"
3'4" x 6'8"	3'4" x 7'0"	3'4" x 7'2"
3'6" x 6'8"	3'6" x 7'0"	
3'8" x 6'8"	3'8" x 7'0"	3'8" x 7'2"
4'0" x 6'8"	4'0" x 7'0"	4'0" x 7'2"

[1] Sizes shown are for single doors only, for pairs of doors use twice the width indicated.

Table 2.   Thickness of steel for component parts (CS242-62)

	Minimum gage of sheet metal	
	Gage No.	Equivalent Gage thickness
Door Frames	16	0.0598
Reinforcements for surface applied hardware	16	.0598
Doors—hollow steel construction . . . . Panels and stiles	18	.0478
Reinforcements for surface applied hardware	16	.0598
Doors—composite construction		
Perimeter channel	18	.0478
Surface sheets	22	.0299
Lock and strike reinforcements	16	.0598
Hinge reinforcements	[3]10	.1345
Flush bolt reinforcements	16	.0598
Glass moldings	20	.0359
Glass muntins	22	.0299

Table 3.   Standard opening sizes (CS211-57)

1⅜-in.-thick doors	1¾-in.-thick doors
2'0'' x 6'8''	2'6'' x 6'8''
2'4'' x 6'8''	2'8'' x 6'8''
2'6'' x 6'8''	3'0'' x 6'8''
2'8'' x 6'8''	
3'0'' x 6'8''	2'6'' x 7'0''
	2'8'' x 7'0''
	3'0'' x 7'0''

Table 4.   Thickness of steel for component parts (CS211-57)

Item	Gage	Equivalent thickness
	No.	*Inch*
Frames, 1⅜ in. thick	18	0. 0478
Frames, 1¾ in. thick	16	. 0598
Stiles for doors	20	. 0359
Panels for doors	20	. 0359
Lock and strike reinforcements	16	. 0598
Hinge reinforcements	11	. 1196
Closer reinforcements	14	. 0747

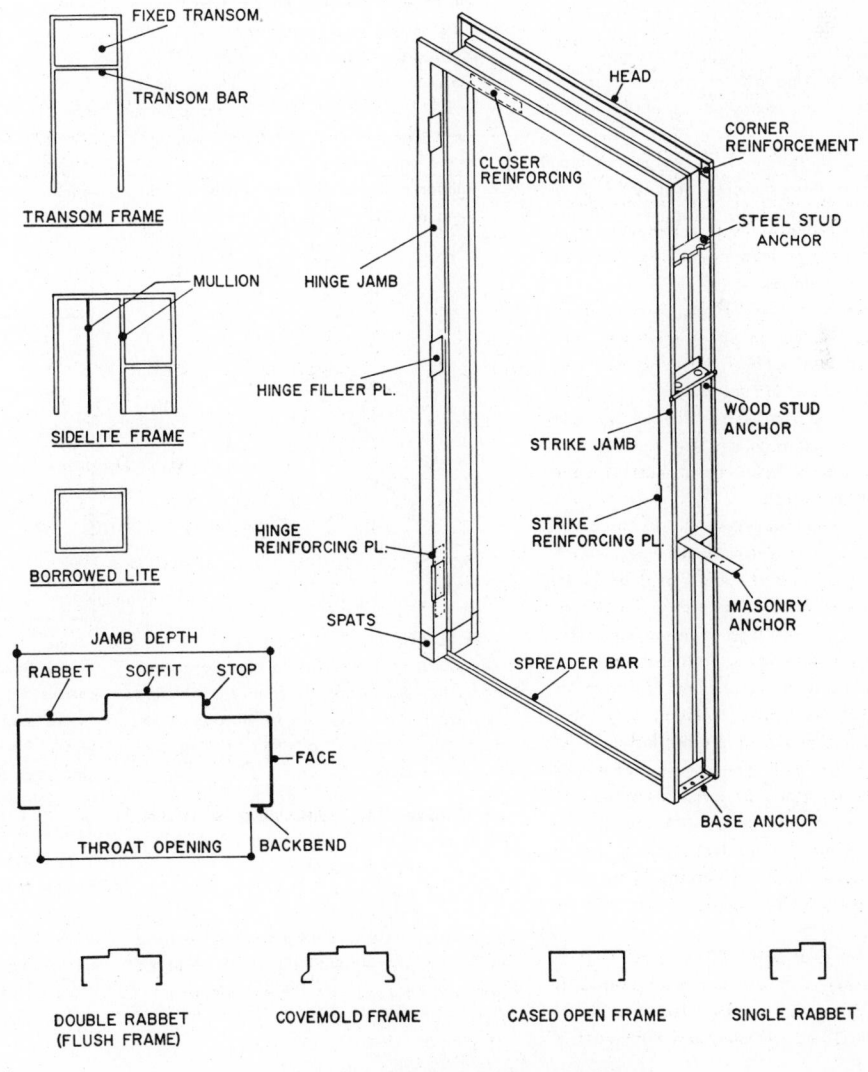

Fig. 2.   Nomenclature for steel door frames

Courtesy Steel Door Institute

PLASTER CRACKING

The control of chip cracking of plaster at steel door frames requires simple attention to a few details in design and specifications. If the door frame is free to twist upon impact or the trim returns are free to vibrate, the movement of the frame will loosen small pieces of finish coat and base coat plaster, and unsightly spalling will result.

The following comments and sketches illustrate the improper elements as well as the suggested recommendations, which are the result of field inspection of good and bad installations together with laboratory and field experiments.

The basic considerations are relatively simple:

1. The frame must be securely anchored in place.
2. The partition must enter the frame so that the two work as a unit. This includes both the structural elements of the partition, the plaster base and the plaster.
3. Vibration of the frame, especially the trim returns, must be dampened.
4. The steel door frame must be sufficiently wide to allow full plaster grounds.

Ear cracking off the corners of a door frame is not controlled as easily as chip cracking. The cause of ear cracking is difficult to isolate. It occurs in reinforced concrete walls, masonry walls and lath and plaster constructions. Apparently impact alone is not the cause since cracking will occur over the openings prior to installation of the doors.

The continuity of the wall or partition is broken by the opening and the weakest plane of the construction is at the opening. Ear cracking can be minimized by attention to the construction at the head of framed opening; the following details are important:

Masonry

1. Workmanship — Masonry units should be laid up with proper bond, full mortar bed and end joints.
2. Lintels should be used over all openings and not supported by the head of the steel door frame. The lintels should extend out from the door jamb sufficiently to eliminate a weak vertical joint adjacent to the face of the door jamb.
3. Reinforce the base coat plaster at the corner of door frame by using self-furring metal lath, 12 in. by 18 in., diagonally at the corner. The dimple of the self-furring metal lath holds the mesh out into the face of the base coat plaster, where the reinforcement is needed.

Studs (Steel or Wood)

1. Gypsum Lath in 16 in. by 96 in. sheets should be used over door frames to eliminate butt joints over or closely adjacent to the door frame.
2. Reinforce the base coat plaster by stapling a 12 by 18-in. piece of self-furring metal lath diagonally over the corners of the door frame. The self-furring metal lath will hold the mesh out at the face of the base coat plaster where the reinforcing is effective. Conventional diamond mesh lath flat against the lath is ineffective.

PLASTER GROUNDS

Masonry Partitions — Plaster grounds on all masonry partitions are ⅝ in.

Metal Lath — Plaster grounds are ⅝ in. from the face of the metal lath. Diamond mesh metal lath and plaster totals ¾ in.

Gypsum Lath — Plaster grounds are ½ in. from face of lath; plaster and lath = ⅞ in.

Note: Because gypsum is rigid and can be held away from structural members by attachment shoes, wire ties, etc., the overall thickness of the gypsum and plaster over *steel studs* must be detailed as 1 *in.*

PARTITION THICKNESS

Masonry	Partition
3 in.	4¼ in.
4 in.	5¼ in.
6 in.	7¼ in.
8 in.	9¼ in.

Steel Studs	Dia. Mesh Lath and Plaster	Gypsum Lath or ⅜ in. Rib-lath and Plaster
2½ in.	4 in.	4½ in.
3¼ in.	4¾ in.	5¼ in.
4 in.	5½ in.	6 in.
6 in.	7½ in.	8 in.

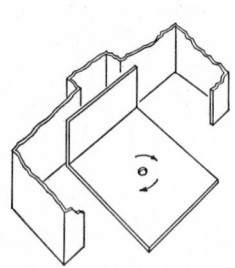

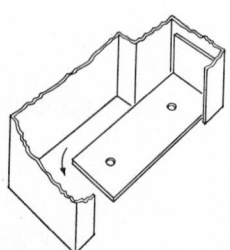

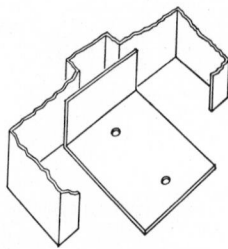

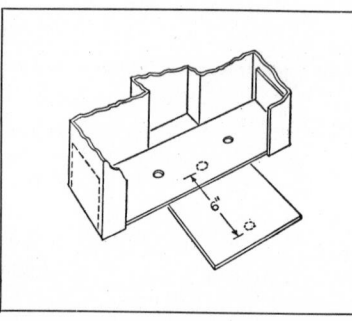

BASE PLATES

Very Poor (Top left) Single pin allows door frame to pivot on impact. Trim returns acting as plaster stops are free to vibrate on impact. All contribute to chip cracking and plaster spalling

Poor (Above) The double pin resists twisting of frame; since it is only attached to the jamb face it leaves trim returns free to vibrate on impact

Very Poor (left) Double pin holds the base plate from pivoting but the frame is anchored at one edge and twists. The end trim return is free to vibrate on impact

Good Base plate anchored to both trim returns with double pins resists twisting of frame and dampens vibration of trim returns. Powder actuated drives require clearance for the gun; T-shaped base plate may be required

ANCHORAGES

Very Poor Concrete nails have short penetration and cause spalling making a very insecure attachment

Very Good Ackerman, rawl or plastic screw anchors provide secure attachment

Very Good Powder actuated drives provide secure anchorage

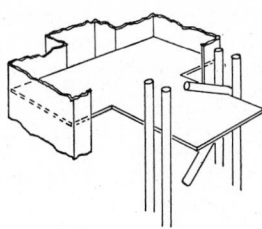

Very Poor Wire tying a stud strut to a loose masonry anchor makes an insecure attachment. The stud is outside the frame and will not resist twisting. The anchor doesn't prevent vibration of the trim returns

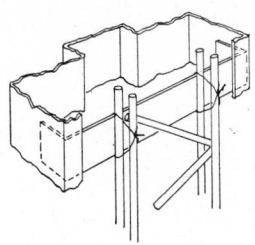

Poor Strap insert ties the trim returns together and dampens the vibration, but saddle tying the strut to the flat strap does not prevent the frame from sliding on impact

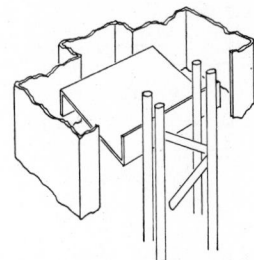

Very Poor The Z-shaped clip provides poor anchorage for the strut and fails to tie the trim returns together

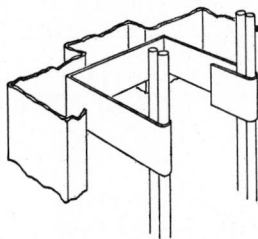

Very Poor Wrap around strap allows frame to shift on impact, and the trim returns are free to vibrate

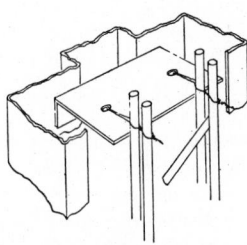

Poor Short insert clip provides good secure anchorage as notched and tied to the stud strut; however trim returns are again free to vibrate

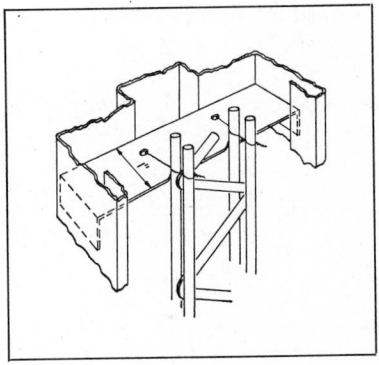

Very Good Jamb anchor insert is welded to the trim returns, dampening any vibration from impact. Notched clip holds the stud strut which is securely anchored by saddle tying.

The clip allows the strut to be set into the frame, reducing the turning moment on impact.

For large openings and heavy doors this frame can be grouted, embedding the strut in the mortar column.

The 180° return on the trim allows both lath and plaster to be let into the frame.

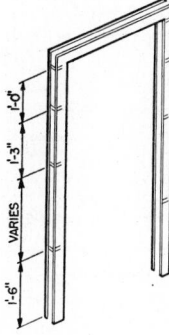

Good Minimum of four insert anchor clips spaced as dimensioned. For larger frames and heavier doors, use additional insert anchors and grout

CROSS-SECTION

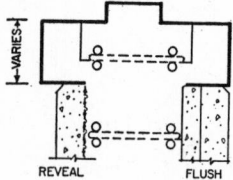

Very Poor Wide flange return acting as a plaster stop prevents the partition and frame from acting as a unit

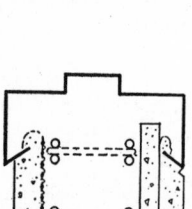

Poor While the plaster mortar keys slightly into the frame, the mass is limited and plaster can be chipped off

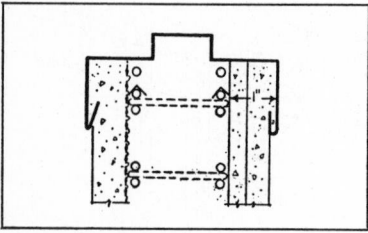

Good Lath and plaster entering the frame provides mass, strength and rigidity to the construction of the frame

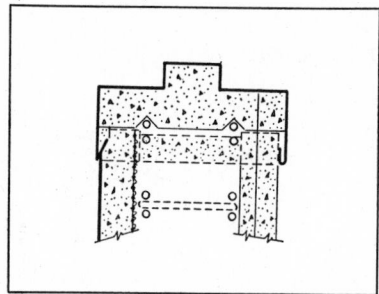

Very Good Grouting the frame and embedding the stud strut in the mortar is necessary for opening exceeding 3 ft–0 in. Grout must be raked out (dashed lines) to recess lath and base coat plaster into the frame

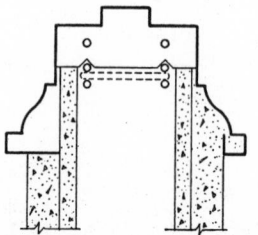

Special attention must be given to dampening vibration of long trim returns. The stud strut should be set well into the frame to resist the twisting action, and lath and plaster must enter and have sufficient mass to grout the returns

HEADER

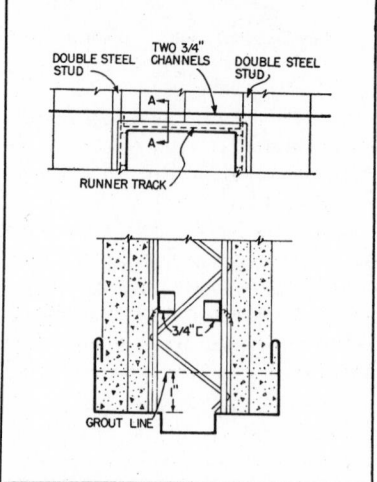

Good ¾ in. angles, saddle tied to the stud chords with the lath and plaster entering the frame stiffen the stud struts

Very Good Identical to above, but the head grouted, embedding the ends of the studs. Lath and base coat plaster should meet the grout (see dashed line)

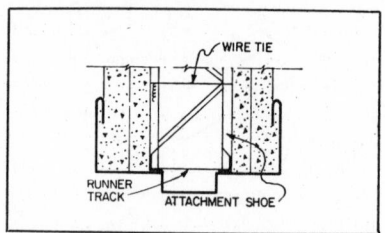

Good The runner track as a header, turned up and wire tied to the stud strut. Attachment shoe holds studs in place

---

DETAILS FOR OPEN WEB STEEL STUD PARTITION

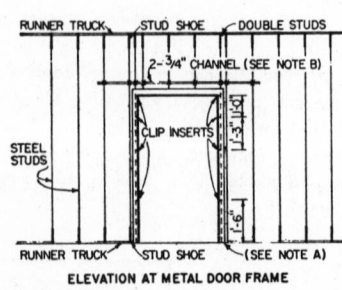

ELEVATION AT METAL DOOR FRAME

A. Base plate of the door frame to be welded to the trim returns and must be double-pinned to resist twisting

B. Channels should be wire tired to stud chords on each inside face

Cross-Section for Doors under 3 ft.

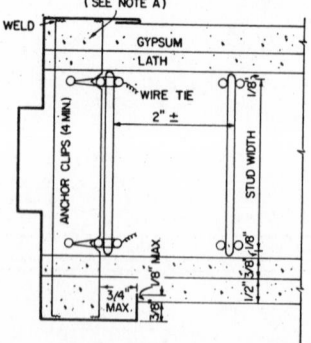

A. Gypsum lath and base coat plaster should carry into door frame as shown

Head

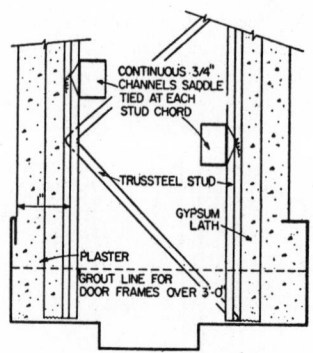

By SEYMOUR HOWARD, *Architect   Associate Professor, Pratt Institute*

The following data on hardware have been prepared in cooperation with the American Society of Architectural Hardware Consultants.

Conventions for the hand of hardware must be determined accurately so that there is no misunderstanding between specification writer, dealer, and manufacturer.

Hardware in general is of three main types: universal, reversible, and handed.

1. *Universal* can be used in any position (example, door stop).

2. *Reversible* can have the "hand" changed by revolving from left to right or by turning upside down or by reversing some part of the mechanism (example, many types of locks and latches).

3. *Handed* (not reversible) can be used only on doors of the hand for which the hardware is designed (example, most bevel or rabbeted front locks and latches, loose-joint butt hinges).

Although the hardware item specified may be reversible, or even universal, it is safe practice to state the hand completely, in accordance with the conventions shown here.

For all doors (except casements and doors with cremone bolts) the hand is determined from the outside. The outside is the side from which security is necessary. In a series of connecting rooms (as for a hotel suite) the outside will be the side of each successive door as you come to it proceeding from the entrance in. For two rooms of equal importance with a passage between, the outside is the passage side.

Strictly speaking, the door itself is only right or left hand; the locks and latches may be reverse bevel. It is best, however, to include the term reverse bevel and to specify in accordance with the conventions shown here. The specification writer can thus prevent any confusion over which side is the outside, particularly important when "split finishes" are desired. This method also places the responsibility for the correct choice on the hardware dealer or manufacturer.

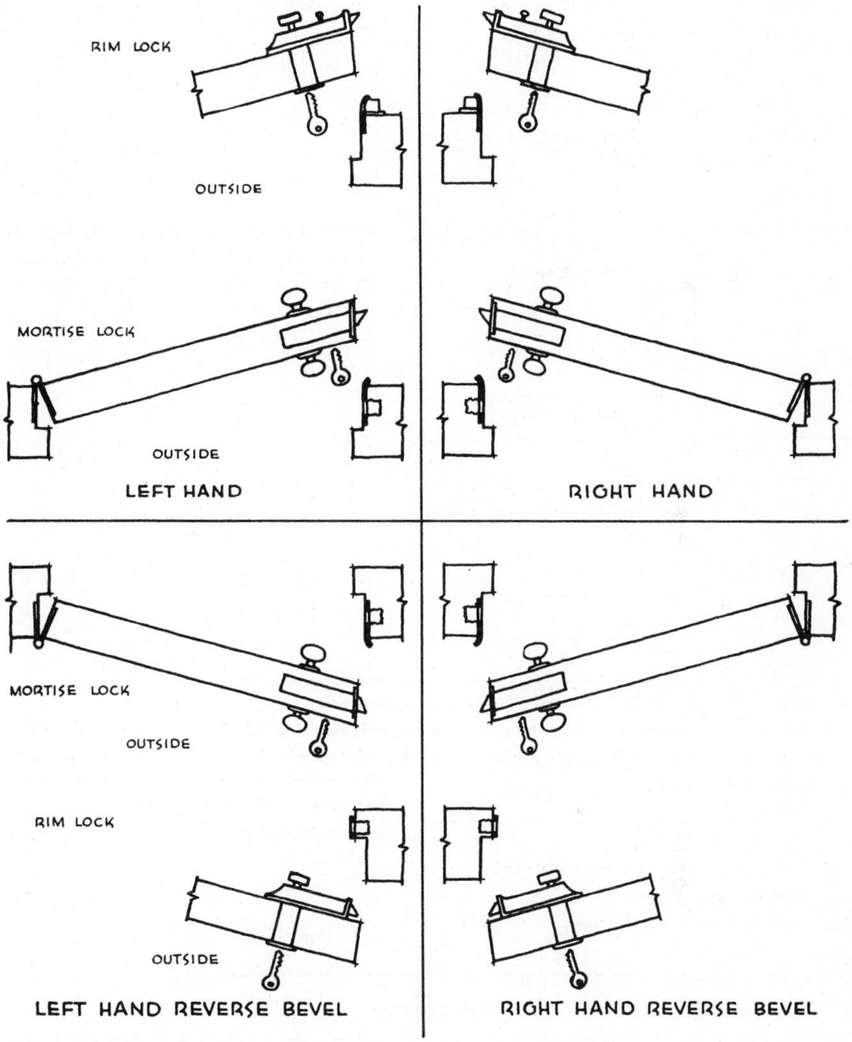

RIM LOCK

OUTSIDE

MORTISE LOCK

OUTSIDE

LEFT HAND   **RIGHT HAND**

MORTISE LOCK

OUTSIDE

RIM LOCK

OUTSIDE

LEFT HAND REVERSE BEVEL   **RIGHT HAND REVERSE BEVEL**

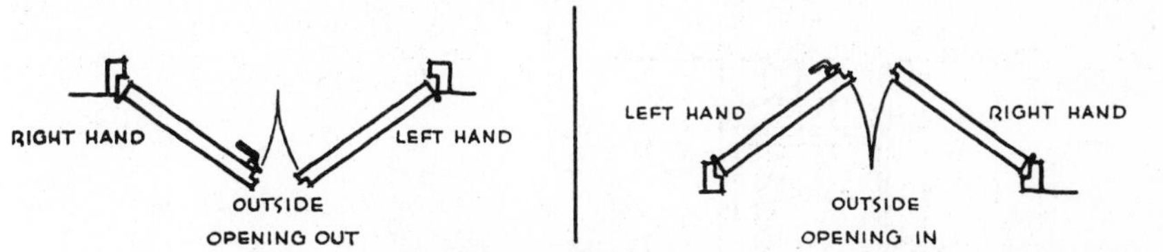

RIGHT HAND   LEFT HAND

OUTSIDE
OPENING OUT

LEFT HAND   RIGHT HAND

OUTSIDE
OPENING IN

CASEMENT WINDOWS – SPECIFY WHETHER IN- OR OUT- OPENING
ALSO APPLIES TO CREMONE BOLTS

Note: These conventions are exactly opposite to those followed by the Steel Window Institute

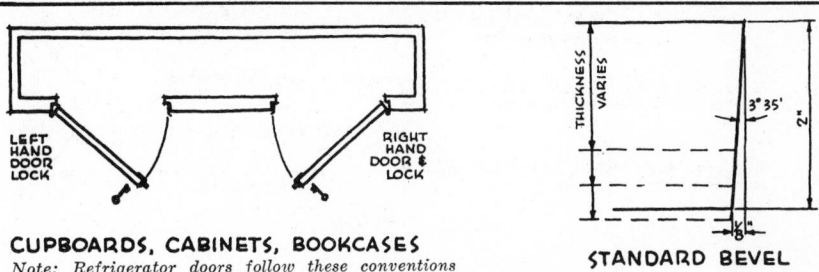

LEFT HAND DOOR LOCK   RIGHT HAND DOOR & LOCK

CUPBOARDS, CABINETS, BOOKCASES
Note: Refrigerator doors follow these conventions

THICKNESS VARIES

3° 35'

2"

⅛"

STANDARD BEVEL

THUMB LATCH

Oldest type; simple to install; difficult to adjust; may be padlocked. Made generally. Often used instead of outside knob for period front doors.

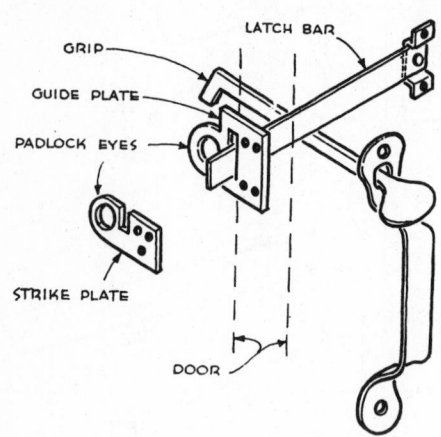

- GRIP
- LATCH BAR
- GUIDE PLATE
- PADLOCK EYES
- STRIKE PLATE
- DOOR

RIM LOCKS & LATCHES

Case and strike both mounted on face of door and trim without mortising; colonial design.

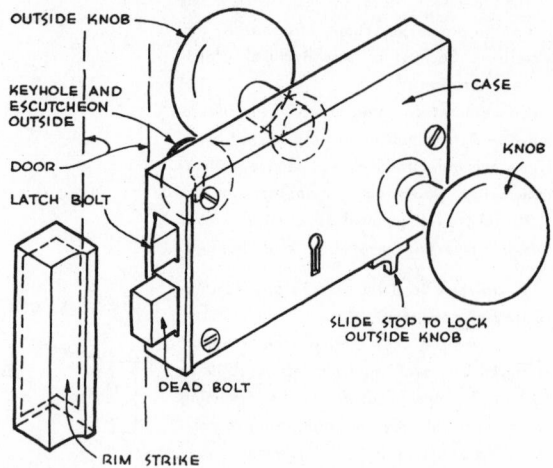

- OUTSIDE KNOB
- KEYHOLE AND ESCUTCHEON OUTSIDE
- DOOR
- LATCH BOLT
- CASE
- KNOB
- SLIDE STOP TO LOCK OUTSIDE KNOB
- DEAD BOLT
- RIM STRIKE

OTHER TYPES, SUCH AS RIM NIGHT LATCHES, OFTEN USED IN REMODELING WORK.

MORTISE LOCKS & LATCHES

Developed historically from rim types; large mortise makes for lengthy installation in wood doors; hollow metal doors easily fabricated to template to receive case, cylinder and spindle. Size of case and accessibility of mechanism make economically possible the maximum number and variety of key and latch functions. Made generally.

TYPICAL LOCK SET

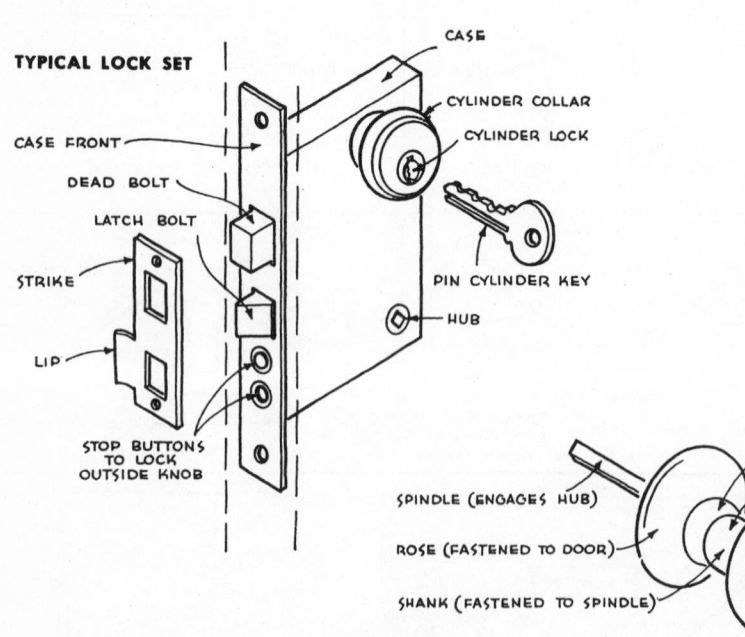

- CASE FRONT
- DEAD BOLT
- LATCH BOLT
- STRIKE
- LIP
- STOP BUTTONS TO LOCK OUTSIDE KNOB
- CASE
- CYLINDER COLLAR
- CYLINDER LOCK
- PIN CYLINDER KEY
- HUB

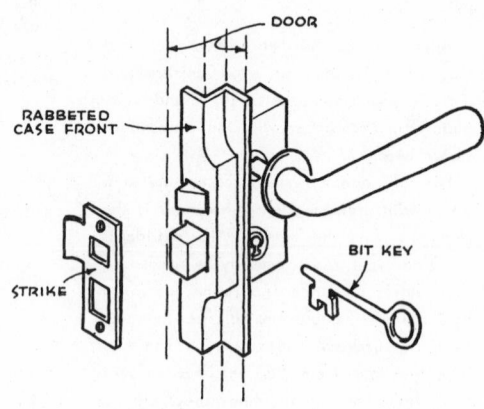

- DOOR
- RABBETED CASE FRONT
- STRIKE
- BIT KEY

TYPICAL LOCK SET WITH RABBETED FRONT & LEVER HANDLE FOR DOUBLE, NARROW STILE DOORS

- ROSE THIMBLE
- SHANK OF KNOB
- KNOB
- SPINDLE (ENGAGES HUB)
- ROSE (FASTENED TO DOOR)
- SHANK (FASTENED TO SPINDLE)

TYPICAL KNOB

580

UNIT LOCKS

Complete factory assembly eliminates much adjustment on job. Unit slid into notch cut on job (wood) or prepared at shop (metal doors). Dead bolt may be omitted to make simple latch set to match. Lock-set also made without dead bolt but with button in inside knob to prevent outside knob from turning (for bathroom, bedroom, etc.); made by relatively few manufacturers.

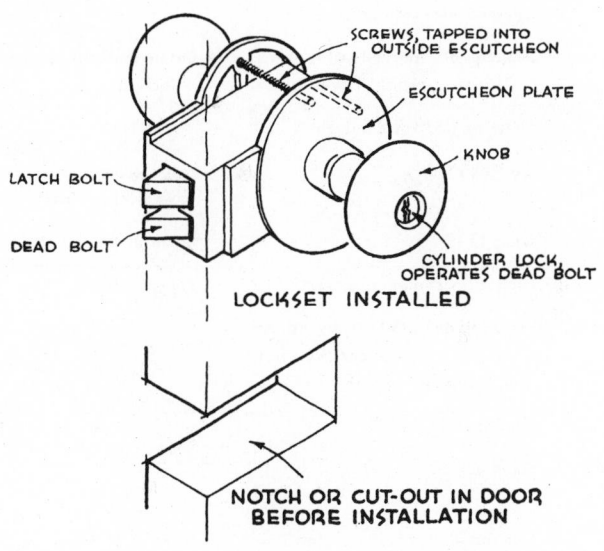

SCREWS, TAPPED INTO OUTSIDE ESCUTCHEON

ESCUTCHEON PLATE

KNOB

LATCH BOLT

DEAD BOLT

CYLINDER LOCK, OPERATES DEAD BOLT

LOCKSET INSTALLED

NOTCH OR CUT-OUT IN DOOR BEFORE INSTALLATION

BACKSETS & PROJECTIONS

NORMAL KNOBS

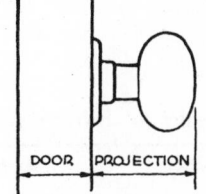

DOOR PROJECTION

KNOB PROJECTION USUALLY 2⅛" TO 2½"

KNOB DIAMETER USUALLY 1¾" TO 2¼"

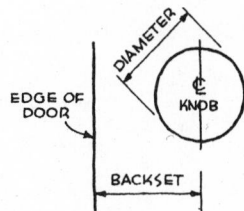

EDGE OF DOOR

DIAMETER

C KNOB

BACKSET

BACKSETS NORMALLY BETWEEN 2⅜" AND 2¾"

NARROW BACKSETS AVAILABLE AS SHORT AS 1" FOR NARROW STILE DOORS, FRENCH DOORS, ETC. LEVER HANDLES USUAL WITH THESE

EXTRA LONG BACKSETS (5", 7", 10" AND UP TO HALF WIDTH OF DOOR) AVAILABLE FOR CYLINDRICAL LOCK SETS.

LEVER HANDLES

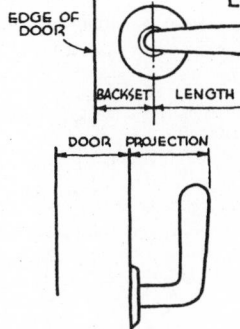

EDGE OF DOOR

BACKSET LENGTH

DOOR PROJECTION

LENGTH OF HANDLE VARIES FROM 2" TO 4"

PROJECTION OF LEVER HANDLES VARIES FROM 1⅛" TO 3" OR MORE (2"± MOST USUAL)

NOTE – LEVER HANDLES REQUIRE AUXILIARY SPRING IN MECHANISM TO RETURN HANDLE TO HORIZONTAL POSITION

BORE-IN LOCKS & LATCHES (TUBULAR & CYLINDRICAL TYPES)

Simple to install in wood doors; only two holes to bore and shallow mortise for case front; metal doors also can be easily fabricated to receive these types.

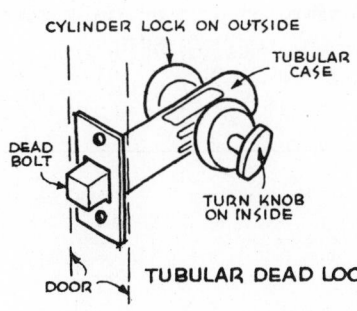

CYLINDER LOCK ON OUTSIDE

TUBULAR CASE

DEAD BOLT

TURN KNOB ON INSIDE

DOOR

TUBULAR DEAD LOCK

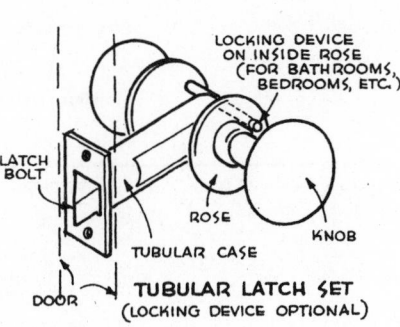

LOCKING DEVICE ON INSIDE ROSE (FOR BATHROOMS, BEDROOMS, ETC.)

LATCH BOLT

ROSE

KNOB

TUBULAR CASE

DOOR

TUBULAR LATCH SET
(LOCKING DEVICE OPTIONAL)

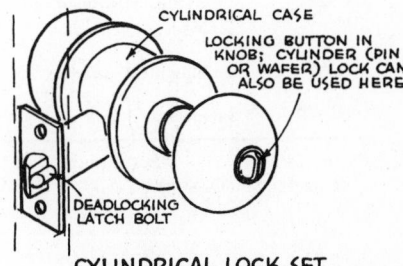

CYLINDRICAL CASE

LOCKING BUTTON IN KNOB; CYLINDER (PIN OR WAFER) LOCK CAN ALSO BE USED HERE

DEADLOCKING LATCH BOLT

CYLINDRICAL LOCK SET
ALSO AVAILABLE AS SIMPLE LATCH SET
AVAILABLE WITH LONG (5", 7", 10" ETC.) BACKSET

SEPARATE TUBULAR LOCK SETS AND LATCH SETS MADE BY MANY MANUFACTURERS.

THIS TYPE MADE TO DATE ONLY BY A FEW MANUFACTURERS.

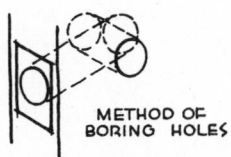

METHOD OF BORING HOLES

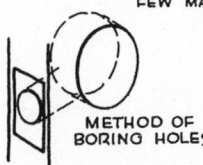

METHOD OF BORING HOLES

Standard finishes for builders' hardware

Symbol	General description	Metal applied to	How produced	Notes
USP	Primed for painting		Cleaned, one-coat paint	
US1B	Bright japanned	Usually iron, steel	Dipped or sprayed with black "Japan" varnish, baked on	Often used on cast-iron lock cases
US1D	Dead black	Same as US1B	Same as US1B without gloss	
US2C	Cadmium-plated	Same as US1B	Electroplated	Not recommended for wearing surfaces
US2G	Zinc, electroplated	Same as US1B	Same as US2C	Same as US2C
US2H	Zinc, hot-dipped	Same as US1B	Dipped in molten zinc bath	Same as US2C
*US3	Bright brass	Iron, steel, wrought and cast brass	Produced on solid brass by various polishing operations; on iron and steel by plating	
*US4	Dull brass	Same as US3	Same as US3	
*US10	Dull bronze	Iron, steel, wrought and cast bronze	Same as US3	
*US14	Nickel-plated	Iron, steel, wrought and cast brass or bronze	Electroplated directly to brass or bronze. Iron and steel: first copper-plated, then nickel-plated	Polished surfaces
*US26	Chromium-plated		Brass and bronze: first nickel-, then chromium-plated. Iron and steel: first copper-, then nickel-, then chromium-plated	Polished surfaces
*US26D	Chromium-plated, dull		Same as US26	
*US27	Satin aluminum, lacquered		Wrought, cast, or forged aluminum	Dull surface with sprayed clear lacquer
*US28	Satin aluminum, anodized		Wrought or forged aluminum	Anodic film on scoured surface
*US32	Stainless steel, polished		Stainless steel	
*US32D	Stainless steel, dull		Stainless steel	

Samples of these US standard finishes may be purchased from National Builders' Hardware Association, 515 Madison Avenue, New York 22, N.Y.

FINISHES

The finish of the metal must be carefully distinguished from the base metal. Some finishes can be obtained by electroplating on a different metal; indeed, for some finishes (such as chromium) this is the only method. A magnet can be used to detect iron or steel base metal beneath the plating.

DURABILITY

The durability of the finish is greater on unplated metals, when the finishing process is applied directly to the base metal. Nonferrous base metals and stainless steels finished in natural color are the most durable. Improvements in chromium plating make this a long-lasting finish.

BASE METAL

The base metal may be either wrought (fabricated) from thin sheet material or cast. Cast designs are heavier, more durable, and more expensive.

STANDARD FINISHES

In the table on the previous page, US numbers for finishes are not consecutive. The missing numbers were formerly in the list, but represent finishes that are no longer commonly used, such as gold, silver, and antique copper. If such finishes or any other special finishes are desired, the manufacturer should be consulted and time allowed for special work.

Many manufacturers do not use the US standard numbers for their finishes. However, they include an index of finishes in their catalogs showing their own numbers and the corresponding US number.

Practically all metals used are alloys of two or more elements, and each manufacturer may vary the chemical analyses of his alloys. Brass is essentially an alloy of copper and zinc. Technically, bronze is a copper-tin alloy; commercially, however, the term includes not only copper-tin alloys but also certain copper-zinc alloys having a typical bronze color. White bronze refers to a large number of copper-nickel-zinc alloys in which the copper predominates. Monel-metal, a nickel-copper alloy in which the nickel is 67 per cent, is well known for its great durability and corrosion resistance.

Aluminum is widely used as a hardware metal, with various alloys being employed to produce cast, wrought, extruded, or forged members. Exposed surfaces are usually given an anodic treatment which produces a surface film that preserves the original color.

Stainless steel is increasingly employed despite its relatively high cost. No surface treatment other than polishing or scouring is needed, nor is maintenance required to preserve this finish. Hardware in this metal is usually produced from sheets or extrusions, although some casting has been achieved. Its strength, durability, and resistance to corrosion make it highly desirable for heavy-duty use.

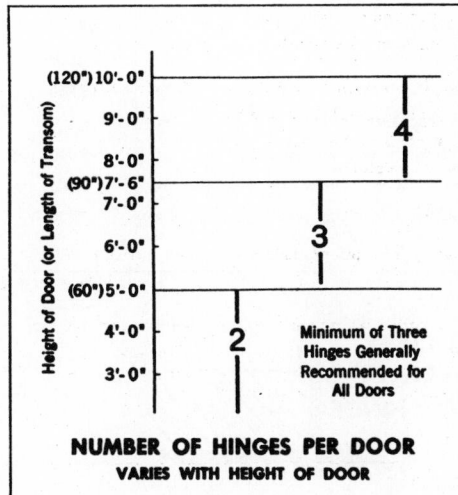

NUMBER OF HINGES PER DOOR
VARIES WITH HEIGHT OF DOOR

HOW TO SPECIFY HINGES

Number (in Pairs) – Either Ball or Oilite Bearings (if Required) – Type of Tips – Type of Screws – Type of Hinge – Metal – Height – Width (Required Only for Full Mortise Hinges) – Weight (Regular or Heavy) – Finish

TEMPLATE HINGES are Made to Standard, Templates or Patterns (Usually in Accordance with Government Standards) to Insure Exact Matching of Hinge and its Screw Holes with Metal Doors and Metal Jambs Fabricated by Other Manufacturers

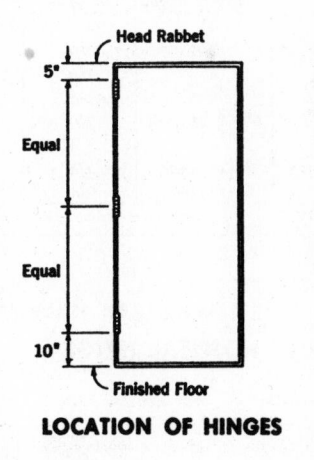

LOCATION OF HINGES

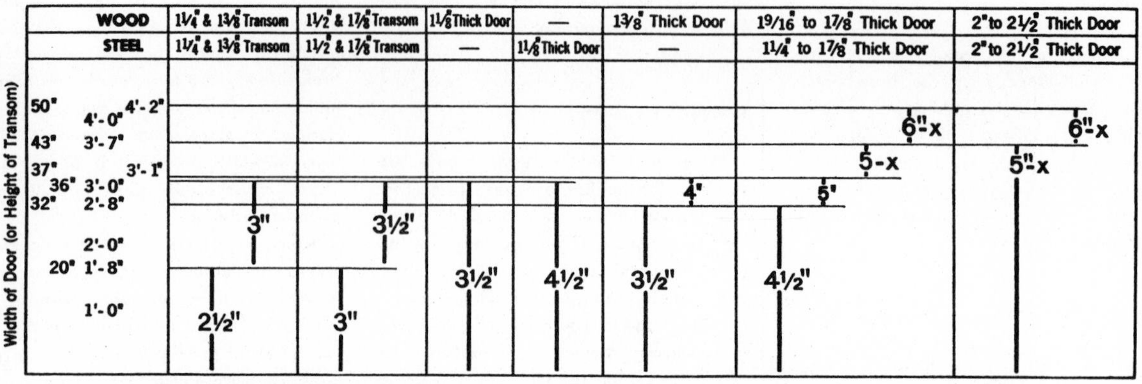
WOOD
1¼" & 1⅜" Transom
1½" & 1⅞" Transom
1⅛" Thick Door
—
1⅜" Thick Door
19/16" to 1⅞" Thick Door
2" to 2½" Thick Door
STEEL
1¼" & 1⅜" Transom
1½" & 1⅞" Transom
—
1⅛" Thick Door
—
1¼" to 1⅞" Thick Door
2" to 2½" Thick Door
Width of Door (or Height of Transom)
50"
4'-0"
4'-2"
43"
3'-7"
37"
3'-1"
36"
3'-0"
32"
2'-8"
2'-0"
20"
1'-8"
1'-0"
3"
3½"
2½"
3"
3½"
4½"
3½"
4"
4½"
5"
5-x
6"-x
5"-x
6"-x

HEIGHT (LENGTH) OF EACH HINGE - Varies with Width, Thickness and Material - (Note: - x Means Extra Heavy)

FOR HIGH FREQUENCY DOORS, USE EXTRA-HEAVY HINGES

Note: Doors of Wrought Bronze, Since They Weigh About 50% More Than Steel, Always Require Extra-Heavy Hinges

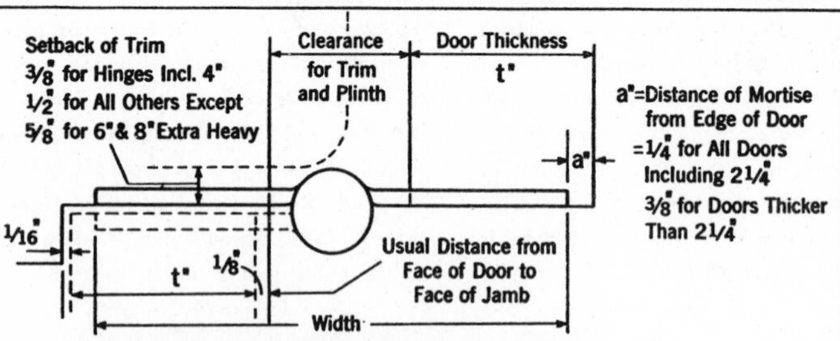
Setback of Trim
⅜" for Hinges Incl. 4"
½" for All Others Except
⅝" for 6" & 8" Extra Heavy
Clearance
for Trim and Plinth
Door Thickness
t"
a"=Distance of Mortise from Edge of Door
=¼" for All Doors Including 2¼"
⅜" for Doors Thicker Than 2¼"
a"
1/16"
t"
⅛"
Usual Distance from Face of Door to Face of Jamb
Width

WIDTH OF FULL MORTISE BUTT HINGE

Width = 2t" − 2a" + Clearance + ⅛"
= Usually = 2t" + Clearance − ⅜"
Conversely: Clearance = Hinge Width − 2t" + ⅜"

CLEARANCES WITH OTHER TYPES OF HINGES

Length of Hinge	Half Surface	Full Surface (Kalamein & Angle Iron Doors)	Full Surface (Tubular Steel Doors)	Half Mortise
3"	1"			
3½"	1¼"			
4"	1¼"			
4½"	1⅜"	1¾"		1¾"
4½" Extra Heavy	1⅞"	1⅞"	⅞"	1⅞"
5"	1⅞"	1⅞"		1⅞"
5" Extra Heavy	1⅞"	1⅞"	⅞"	1⅞"
6" Extra Heavy	2⅛"	2⅛"	⅞"	2⅛"

FREQUENCY OF OPERATION OF DOORS

HIGH FREQUENCY	DAILY	ANNUALLY
Large Department Store Entrance	5,000	1,500,000
Large Office Building Entrance	4,000	1,200,000
Theater Entrance	1,000	450,000
Schoolhouse Entrance	1,250	225,000
Schoolhouse Toilet Door	1,250	225,000
Store or Bank Entrance	500	150,000
Office Building Toilet Door	400	118,000
LOW FREQUENCY		
Schoolhouse Corridor Door	80	15,000
Office Building Corridor Door	75	22,000
Store Toilet Door	60	18,000
Dwelling House Entrance	40	15,000
Dwelling House Toilet Door	25	9,000
Dwelling House Corridor Door	10	3,600
Dwelling House Closet Door	6	2,200

SWING CLEAR HALF MORTISE HOSPITAL HINGE

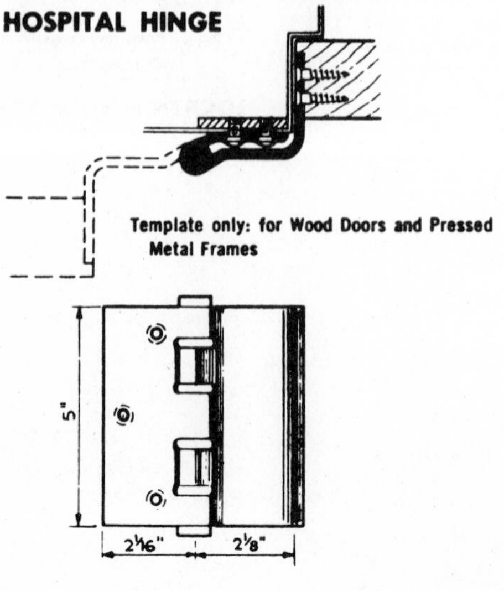
Template only: for Wood Doors and Pressed Metal Frames
5"
2 1/16"
2⅛"

SWING CLEAR FULL SURFACE HOSPITAL HINGE

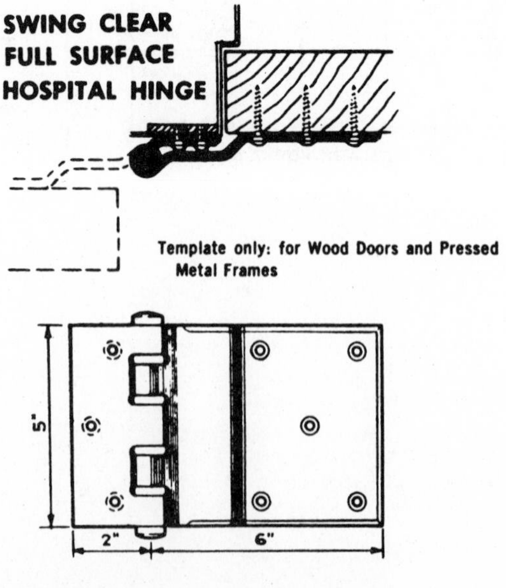
Template only: for Wood Doors and Pressed Metal Frames
5"
2"
6"

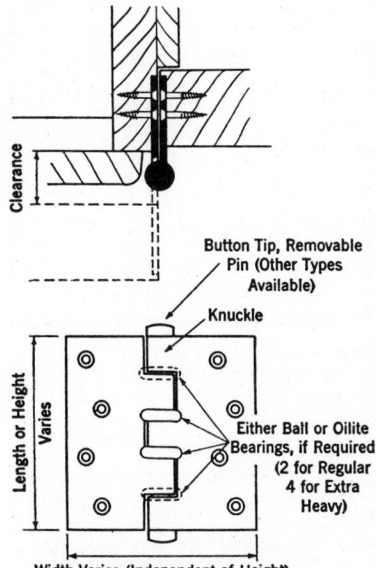

Width Varies (Independent of Height)
Non-Template Shown, also Made Template

FULL MORTISE BUTT HINGE

Non-Template: for Wood Doors and Wood Jambs (All Wood Screws)

Template: for Wood Doors and Pressed Metal Jambs (Order 1/2 Machine Screws); or for Hollow Metal Doors and Pressed Metal Jambs (Order All Machine Screws)

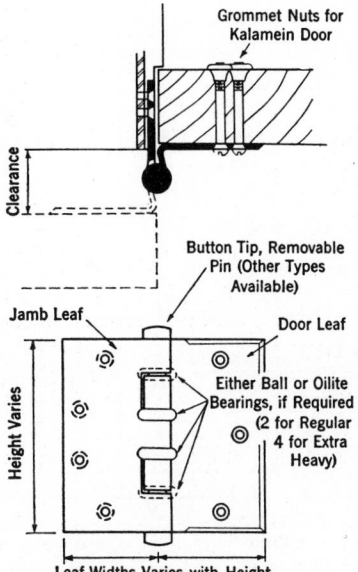

Leaf Widths Varies with Height
Template Shown, also Made Non-Template

HALF SURFACE BUTT HINGE

Non-Template: for Wood Doors and Jambs (All Wood Screws); or for Kalamein Doors and Kalamein Jambs (Order 1/2 Machine Screws with Grommet Nuts)

Template: for Kalamein Doors and Pressed Metal Jambs (Order All Machine Screws, 1/2 with Grommet Nuts)

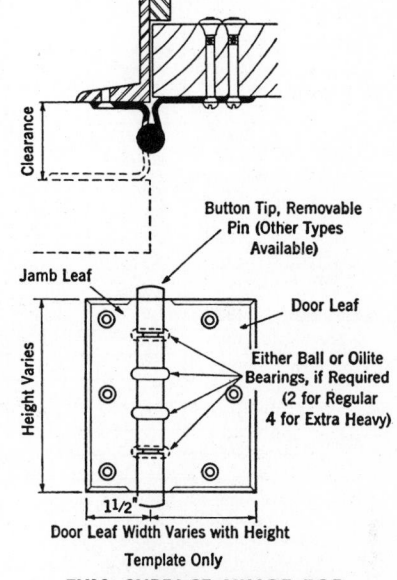

Door Leaf Width Varies with Height
Template Only

FULL SURFACE HINGE FOR KALAMEIN DOOR
(CHANNEL IRON FRAME)

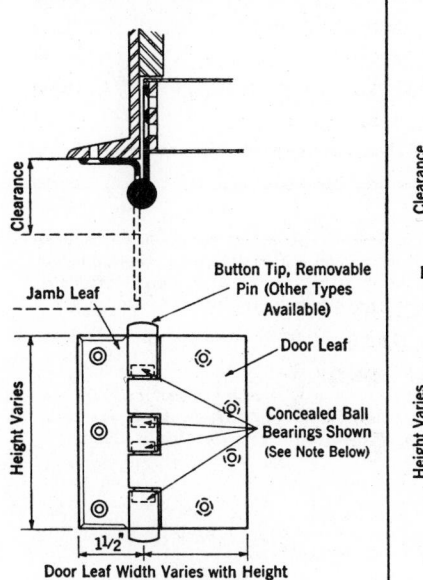

Door Leaf Width Varies with Height
Template Shown

HALF MORTISE BUTT HINGE

Template: for Hollow Metal Doors and Channel Iron Frames (Order All Machine Screws)

Note: Half Mortise Hinge is also Available with Other Types of Bearings (Plain, Ball or Oilite).
Full Mortise, Half Surface and Full Surface Hinges are also Available with Concealed Ball Bearings

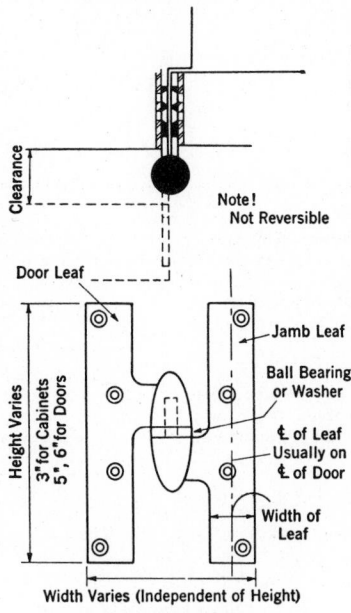

Width Varies (Independent of Height)
Right Hand Hinge Shown

OLIVE KNUCKLE (PAUMELLE) HINGE

Type of Loose Joint Hinge, Therefore Handed. Knuckle Alone Visible when Door Closed.
Made Template and Non-Template (See Notes Under Full Mortise Butt Hinge)
Note: for Clearances, See Manufacturers Catalogs

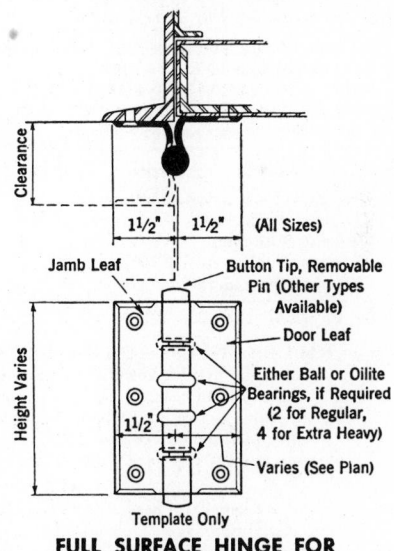

Template Only

FULL SURFACE HINGE FOR ANGLE IRON DOOR
(CHANNEL IRON FRAME)

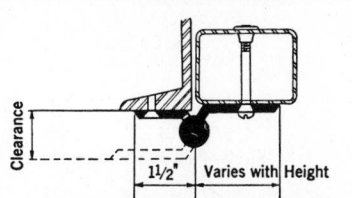

FULL SURFACE HINGE FOR TUBULAR STEEL DOOR

(Elevation as Shown for Hinge for Angle Iron Door)

HINGE SIZES AVAILABLE

SIZE OF HINGE (LENGTH OR HEIGHT)	THICKNESS OF METAL — NON-TEMPLATE AND TEMPLATE WROUGHT METAL (GOV. STNDS CS 22-40 & CS 9-33)	THICKNESS OF METAL — NON-TEMPLATE CAST METAL (GOV. STND CS 22-40)	THICKNESS OF METAL — TEMPLATE CAST METAL (GOV. STND CS 9-33)	DIA. OF KNUCKLE (USUAL)	FULL MORTISE, NON-TEMPLATE	FULL MORTISE, TEMPLATE	HALF SURFACE, TEMPLATE	FULL SURFACE, TEMPLATE (KAL. DOORS)	FULL SURFACE, TEMPLATE (ANGLE IRON DOORS)	FULL SURFACE, TEMPLATE (TUBULAR STEEL DOORS)	HALF MORTISE, TEMPLATE	HALF SURFACE, NON-TEMPLATE	OLIVE KNUCKLE TEMPLATE AND NON-TEMPLATE
2"	.083"	Specified			X	X						X	
2½"	.089"	by Weight			X	X						X	
3"	.092"	Only; for	.156"	.515"	X	X	X					X	X
3½"	.123"	Approxi-	.156"	.632"	X	X	X					X	
4	.130"	mations,	.172"	.632"	X	X	X					X	
4" Extra Heavy	.170"	Use Next	.250"			X							
4½"	.134"	Column	.187"	.695"	X	X	X	X	X		X	X	
4½" Extra Heavy	.180"		.250"	.831"	X	X	X	X	X	X	X		
5"	.146"		.203"	.731"	X	X	X	X	X		X	X	X
5" Extra Heavy	.190"		.281"	.831"	X	X	X	X	X	X	X		
6"	.160"			.784"	X	X							X
6" Extra Heavy	.203"		.312"	.906"	X	X	X	X	X	X	X		X
8" Extra Heavy	.203"			.971"	X	X							

Note: Above sizes are based on height (same as length) of hinge. Full mortise butt hinges are usually made of same width as their height (e.g.: 4½ by 4½ in., 6 by 6 in.), but are available in other widths. When clearance for trim (see Hinges, Sheet 7) make these widths unsuitable (e.g.: trim very narrow or omitted, or very wide plinth or trim), specify width desired, to nearest larger ½ in. dimension, and manufacturer will be able to furnish. Half surface, full surface and half mortise hinge widths are not variable.

METALS AND FINISHES USED

Recommended For Interior Doors:

Wrought steel, highly polished & heavily plated
Wrought steel, polished & plated
Wrought steel, planished & plated
Wrought steel, primed for painting
Cast iron (sometimes malleable iron)

Recommended For Exterior and Interior Doors:

Wrought or cast brass or bronze
Wrought or cast white bronze
Wrought aluminum
Wrought stainless steel
Wrought monel metal

NOTES

Note: All wrought steel hinges may have plain, ball or oilite bearings
Very accurately made; heavy copper plating before finish plating
Finish plating directly on polished steel
Finish plating directly on cold rolled steel
Inner edges of leaves cut back for paint clearance around knuckles
Free graphite in iron helps lubricate bearing

Should have either ball or oilite bearings; also stainless steel pin
Ditto
Ditto
May have either ball or oilite bearings; also stainless steel pin
Ditto

BALL BEARINGS and OILITE BEARINGS are regularly permanently fitted to knuckles to prevent accidental detachment and loss. Ball bearings are of hardened carbon steel; may be of stainless steel. Oilite is a powder metallurgy product: an alloy of 85 per cent copper, 10 per cent tin, 5 per cent graphite (typical composition), of porous or sponge-like structure, containing lubricating oil within its pores. Depending on manufacturer, bearings may be either externally visible or concealed within knuckles (see drawings of hinge types).

PINS are usually of hardened carbon steel; may be of stainless steel. "Removable" pins should be designed to be non-rising. "Non-removable" pins may be held by set screw in barrel to permit removal; or they may be "fast" pins, riveted, driven in, spun or welded at both ends. Fast pins make hanging of door more difficult. Types of tips available:

BUTTON

Standard with All Manufacturers;

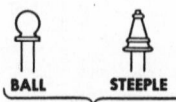

BALL   **STEEPLE**

Available to Order Except on Prime Coated Hinges

Leaf

HOSPITAL TIP ("FAST" PIN)

Available from All Manufacturers as Alternate to Ball or Button Tips; Used in Hospitals and Other Institutions for Added Safety and Cleanliness

For "Removable" Pins (or "Non-Removable" with Set Screw)

SPRING HINGES

Simplest closing device. Energy stored in spring closes door. No closing speed control unless additional device is used, such as surface type door check without spring.

DOUBLE ACTING SPRING BUTT HINGES

Note: Also available with button tip

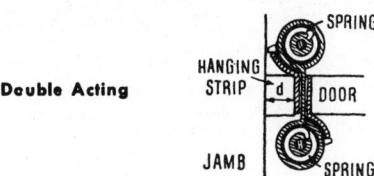

Double Acting

With hanging strip

Also available with clamp flanges and bolts for kalamein doors.

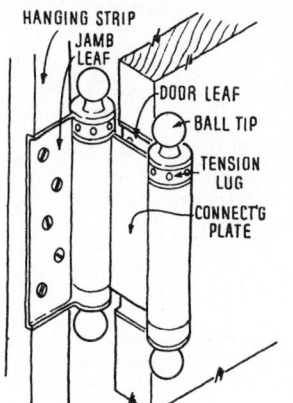

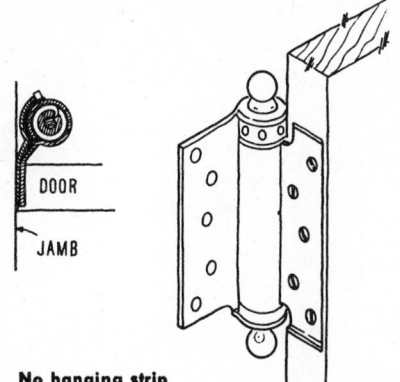

No hanging strip

SINGLE ACTING SPRING BUTT HINGES

Note: Also available with button tip

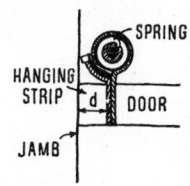
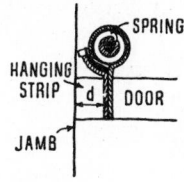

With hanging strip

(If jamb face is in line with door face, this type can be used without additional hanging strip).
Also available as half surface hinge for kalamein doors with pressed steel jambs (4, 6, and 7 in. sizes)

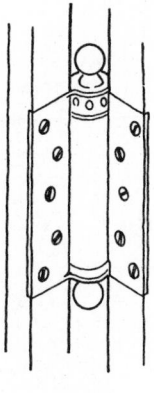

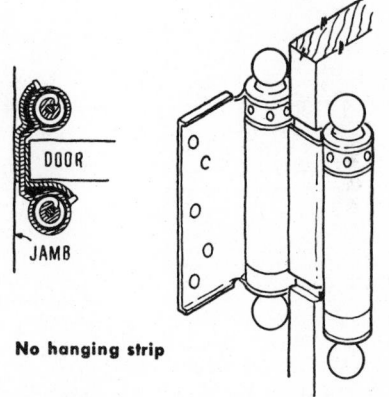

No hanging strip

SIZES OF SPRING BUTT HINGES	Size	Min Door Thickness	Max Door Thickness Wood	Max Door Thickness Metal	Max Door Width	Max Door Weight	Depth (d) Hanging Strip (if required)	General Rules
Note: Check all information and details for exact cases carefully with mfr.'s catalogs.	3″	¾″	1″	⅞″	2′–2″	30 lb.	½″	1. Use largest size hinge that thickness of hardwood and kalamein doors will permit
	4	⅞ (1)	1¼	1⅛	2–4	42	⅝	2. Use min door thickness only for light wood doors
Variations in door thickness for hinges of different mfrs. shown in parentheses.	5	1⅛ (1)	1½	1⅜	2–6	56	⅝	3. Use three hinges for doors that are extra heavy or frequently used. Place third hinge down ⅓ distance between upper and lower hinges.
	6	1¼ (1⅛)	1¾	1½	2–8	72	¾	
	7	1⅜ (1¼)	2	1¾	2–9	90	⅞	
* For hanging strip only.	8	1½	2¼	2	2–10	110	1	
	10	1¾	2½	2⅛	3–0	150	1⅛	
	12*	2¼	3	2⅝	3–2	190	1¼	

SPRING PIVOT HINGES

Double Acting

SIMPLE TOP PIVOT

TOP PIVOT SOCKET

SPRING-ACTUATED PLUNGER TOP PIVOT

NOTE: TOP PIVOTS MAY BE USED WITH ANY CENTER-PIVOTED DOOR

SCREW (WALKING BEAM) TOP PIVOT

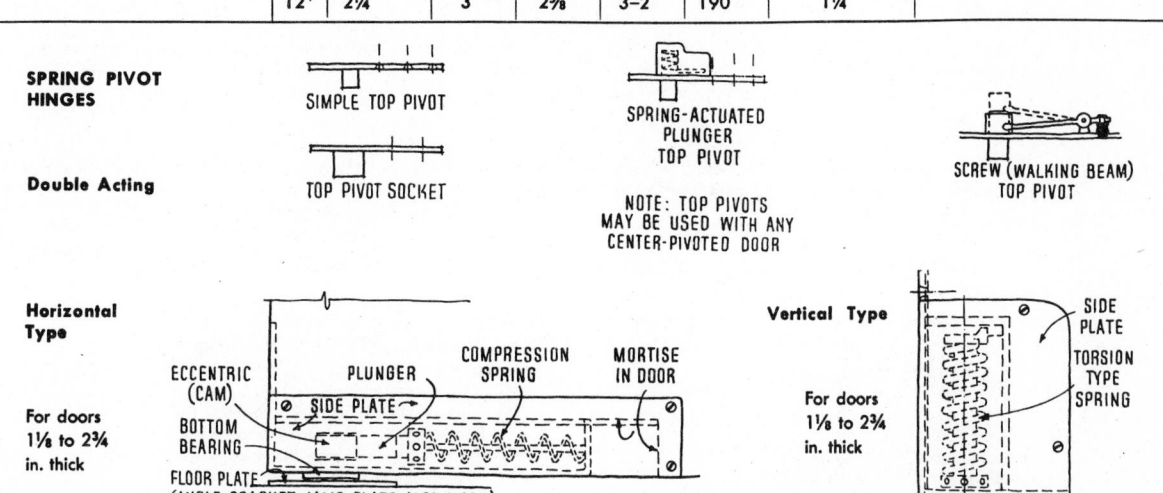

Horizontal Type

For doors 1⅛ to 2¾ in. thick

ECCENTRIC (CAM)
PLUNGER
SIDE PLATE
COMPRESSION SPRING
MORTISE IN DOOR
BOTTOM BEARING
FLOOR PLATE (ANGLE BRACKET JAMB PLATE ALSO MADE)

Vertical Type

For doors 1⅛ to 2¾ in. thick

SIDE PLATE
TORSION TYPE SPRING

DOOR CHECKS (CLOSERS)

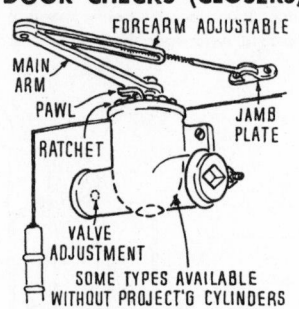

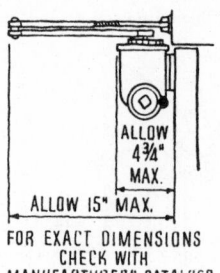

OVERHEAD CLOSERS

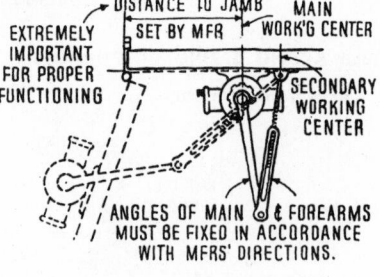

Surface Type

Dimensions approx. Check with mfr. for exact sizes

Angle to which door may be opened is set by:
closer to jamb distance; length of main arm (may be available in different sizes) and fore arm (adjustable); jamb and butt conditions; projection of closer. When specifying, state max opening angle desired.

Mounted on door, hinge side, with regular (exposed) arm.

Door weight carried on hinges or pivots

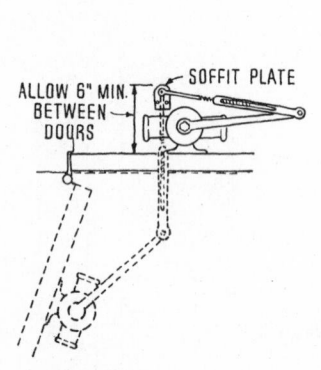

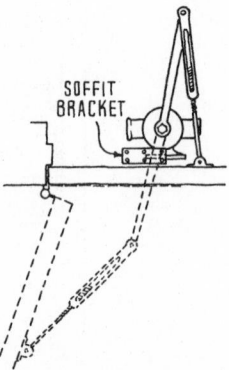

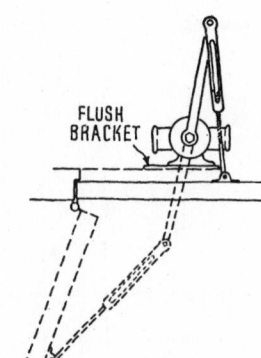

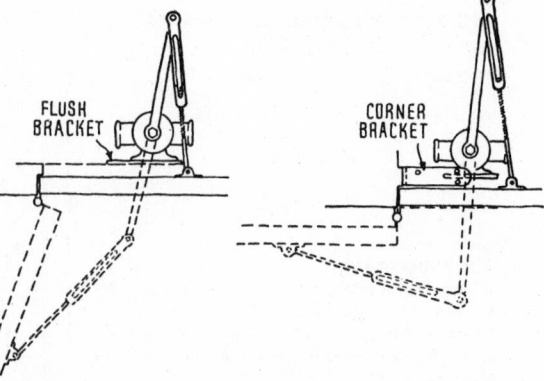

Parallel Arm

Mounted on stop side of door. Used where min clearance is required; e.g. between two doors. Effective power reduced; use next larger size.

Soffit Bracket

Soffit bracket usual type. Distance from jamb to main working center maintained for full effectiveness.

Flush Bracket

Mounted on brackets on stop side to keep closer out of weather, to hide, or when trim interferes.

Flush type mounted on face of opposite side when soffit is narrow. Working center distance maintained.

Corner Bracket

Corner bracket used to obtain 180° opening or for less obstruction. Effective power reduced; use next larger size.

Special Arms Available: Two or three point hold open arms for hospitals (private—about 10° for ventilation; semi-private—about 45°; passage—about 95°); and hold open arms with fusible links for automatic closing in case of fire. Hold open arms cannot always be depended on for exterior doors opening out; use separate holder if necessary.

Semi-Concealed Type

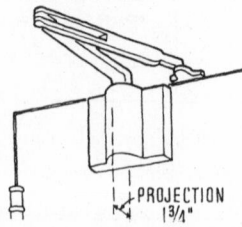

Partly mortised into upper door rail. Usually requires 1¾ in. wood, 1½ in. metal door.

Fully Concealed Type

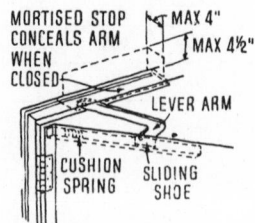

Housed in head above door. For doors on hinges, offset or center pivots.

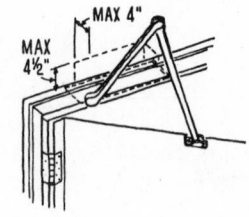

Housed in head above door. Projecting arm gives greater power than concealed arm. Door on hinges or pivots. Arm projects on stop side. Also used on outswinging wood doors when door top is not weather protected.

Sizes of Overhead Door Closers *(From Dept. of Commerce CS22-40)*

Where strong drafts are encountered and as noted above under bracket and parallel arm installations, use next larger size.

Size	Description, Max Door Size (Approx.)
I	Ordinary screen, light interior doors 1⅛ in. by 2 ft-6 in. by 6 ft-6 in.
II	Heavy screen doors, 1⅜ in. by 3 ft by 7 ft Light interior doors, 1⅜ in. by 2 ft-8 in. by 7 ft Closet doors, 1¾ in. by 2 ft-8 in. by 7 ft
III	Light exterior doors, 1¾ in. by 2 ft-6 in. by 7 ft Corridor or office doors, 1¾ in. by 3 ft by 7 ft

Size	Description, Max Door Size (Approx.)
IV	Ordinary exterior doors, 1¾ in. by 3 ft by 7 ft-6 in. Heavy interior doors, 2¼ in. by 4 ft by 7 ft-6 in.
V	Heavy exterior doors, 2¼ in. by 3 ft-6 in. by 7 ft-6 in. Heavy interior doors subject to strong drafts
VI	Extra heavy entrance doors 3 in. thick or over, or doors of unusual height or width, refrig. doors, etc.

Fully Concealed Overhead Door Closers (Continued)

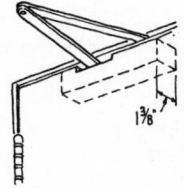

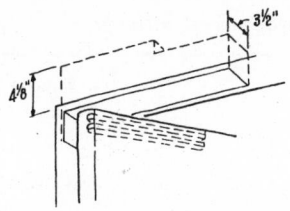

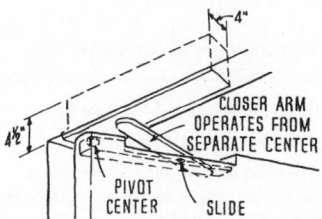

Housed in door. For interior doors only. Also available with concealed arm. Door hung on hinges or pivots.

For double acting interior doors, hung on center pivots. Housed in head above door.

For heavy and exterior double acting doors, hung on center pivots. Housed in head above door.

FLOOR CLOSERS (CHECKING FLOOR HINGES, FLOOR CHECKS)

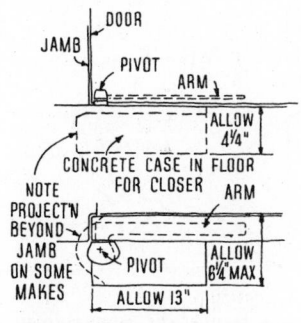

Single Acting On Offset Pivots

Weight carried on closer spindle. Also available with separate closer arm operating from centerline of door.

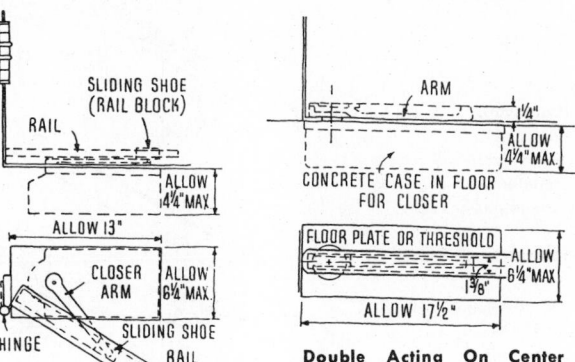

Single Acting on Butt Hinges

Double Acting On Center Pivots

SINGLE-ACTING DOOR RABBETED STYLE

Similar type available for single acting on center pivots (Mechanism is simpler. Only 13 in. length of case needed).

The above type closer is also available with closer arm operating from separate center (weight of door not carried on closer spindle).

See mfr.'s catalogs for sizes required for specific doors and for exact dimensions

PRINCIPLES OF CLOSER MECHANISMS

Designs vary with mfr. and position of closer. Basic operating principle is common to all:

Opening Door:

Energy is stored in spring; shaft, through connecting mechanism, moves a piston, displacing checking fluid through a ball check valve.

Closing Door:

Energy in spring rotates spindle, closing door; at same time piston is moved back. With ball check closed, fluid is forced through ports in cylinder wall into by-pass channel leading to other side of piston. Rate of flow (and rate of closing door) is controlled by valves.

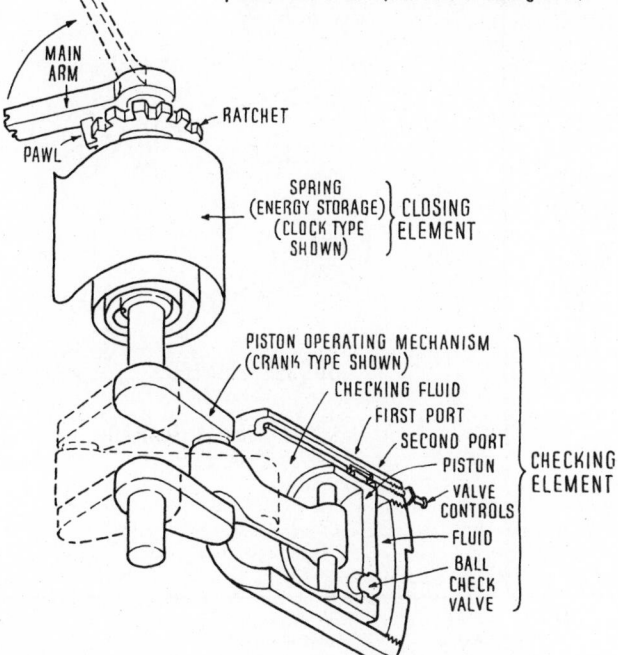

Latching speed may be:

1. Same as general speed
2. Greater than general speed to overcome latch-point resistance (strong draft or latch spring)
3. Less than general speed for silent closing.

Spring May Be:

1. Spiral wound, flat band (clock type)
2. Helical wound, circular, oval or flat wire.

   A. Torison type
   B. Compression type

Piston Operating Mechanism May Be:

1. Crank type (as shown)
2. Cam type (usual in floor closers)
3. Semi Rack and pinion
4. Full rack and pinion
5. Rotary position
6. Diamond block.

3. PISTON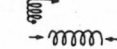

4. PISTON — PISTON

5.

Note: For specific details and sizes, consult manufacturers' catalogs.

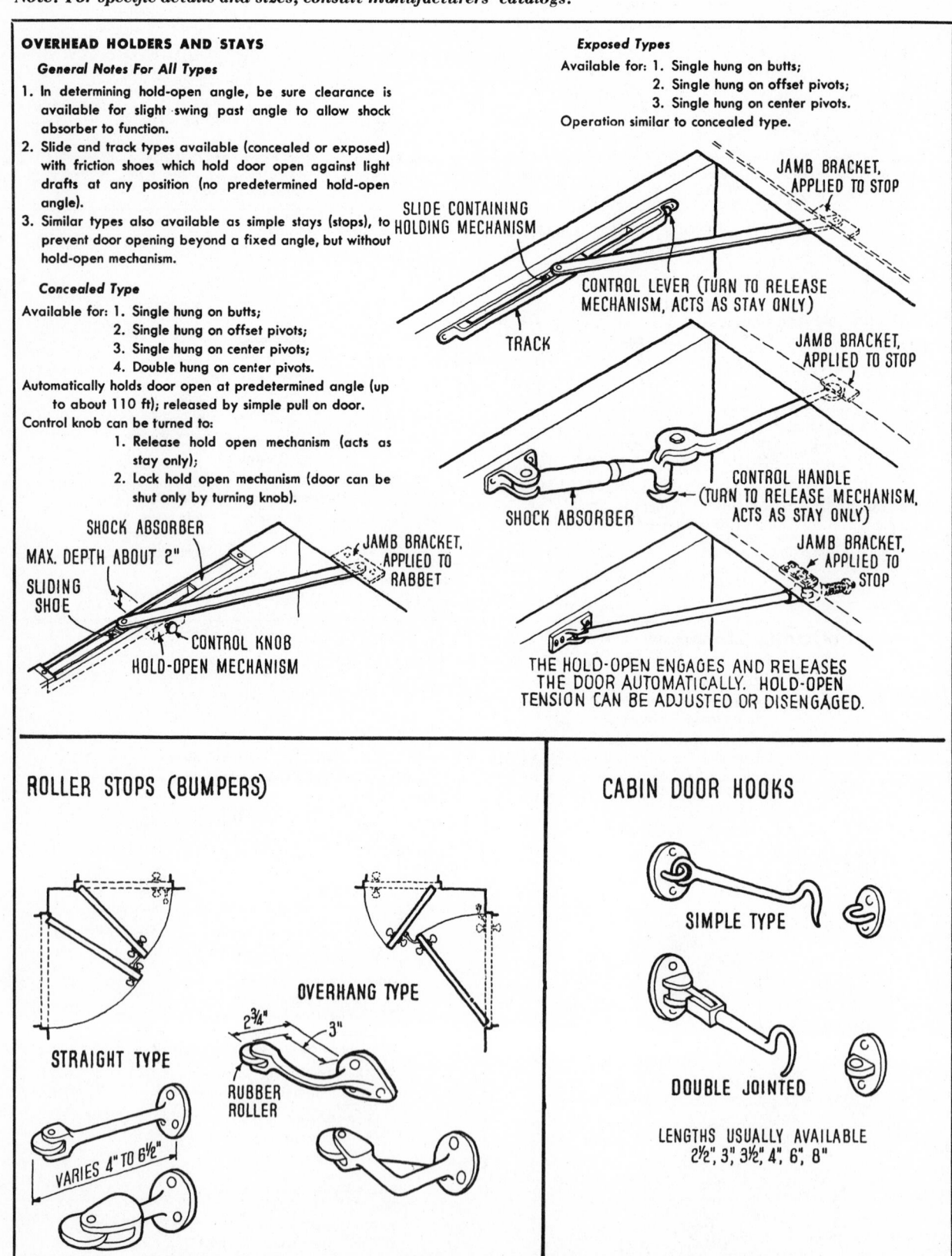

OVERHEAD HOLDERS AND STAYS

General Notes For All Types

1. In determining hold-open angle, be sure clearance is available for slight swing past angle to allow shock absorber to function.
2. Slide and track types available (concealed or exposed) with friction shoes which hold door open against light drafts at any position (no predetermined hold-open angle).
3. Similar types also available as simple stays (stops), to prevent door opening beyond a fixed angle, but without hold-open mechanism.

Concealed Type

Available for: 1. Single hung on butts;
2. Single hung on offset pivots;
3. Single hung on center pivots;
4. Double hung on center pivots.

Automatically holds door open at predetermined angle (up to about 110 ft); released by simple pull on door.
Control knob can be turned to:
1. Release hold open mechanism (acts as stay only);
2. Lock hold open mechanism (door can be shut only by turning knob).

SHOCK ABSORBER
MAX. DEPTH ABOUT 2"
SLIDING SHOE
CONTROL KNOB
HOLD-OPEN MECHANISM
JAMB BRACKET, APPLIED TO RABBET

Exposed Types

Available for: 1. Single hung on butts;
2. Single hung on offset pivots;
3. Single hung on center pivots.

Operation similar to concealed type.

SLIDE CONTAINING HOLDING MECHANISM
JAMB BRACKET, APPLIED TO STOP
CONTROL LEVER (TURN TO RELEASE MECHANISM, ACTS AS STAY ONLY)
TRACK

JAMB BRACKET, APPLIED TO STOP
SHOCK ABSORBER
CONTROL HANDLE (TURN TO RELEASE MECHANISM, ACTS AS STAY ONLY)

JAMB BRACKET, APPLIED TO STOP
THE HOLD-OPEN ENGAGES AND RELEASES THE DOOR AUTOMATICALLY. HOLD-OPEN TENSION CAN BE ADJUSTED OR DISENGAGED.

ROLLER STOPS (BUMPERS)

OVERHANG TYPE
2¾"
3"
RUBBER ROLLER

STRAIGHT TYPE
VARIES 4" TO 6½"

CABIN DOOR HOOKS

SIMPLE TYPE

DOUBLE JOINTED

LENGTHS USUALLY AVAILABLE
2½", 3", 3½", 4", 6", 8"

Note: For specific details and sizes, consult manufacturers' catalogs.

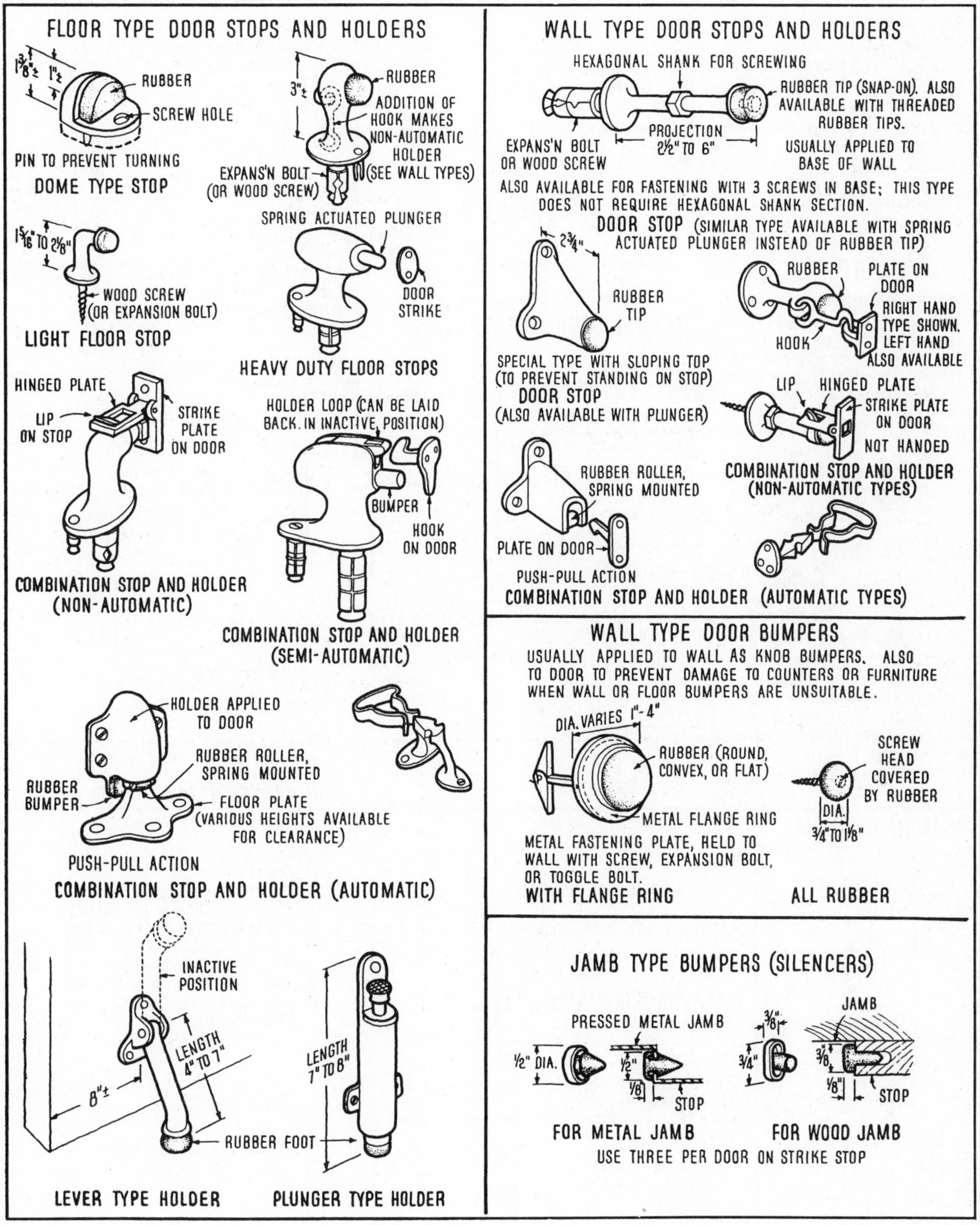

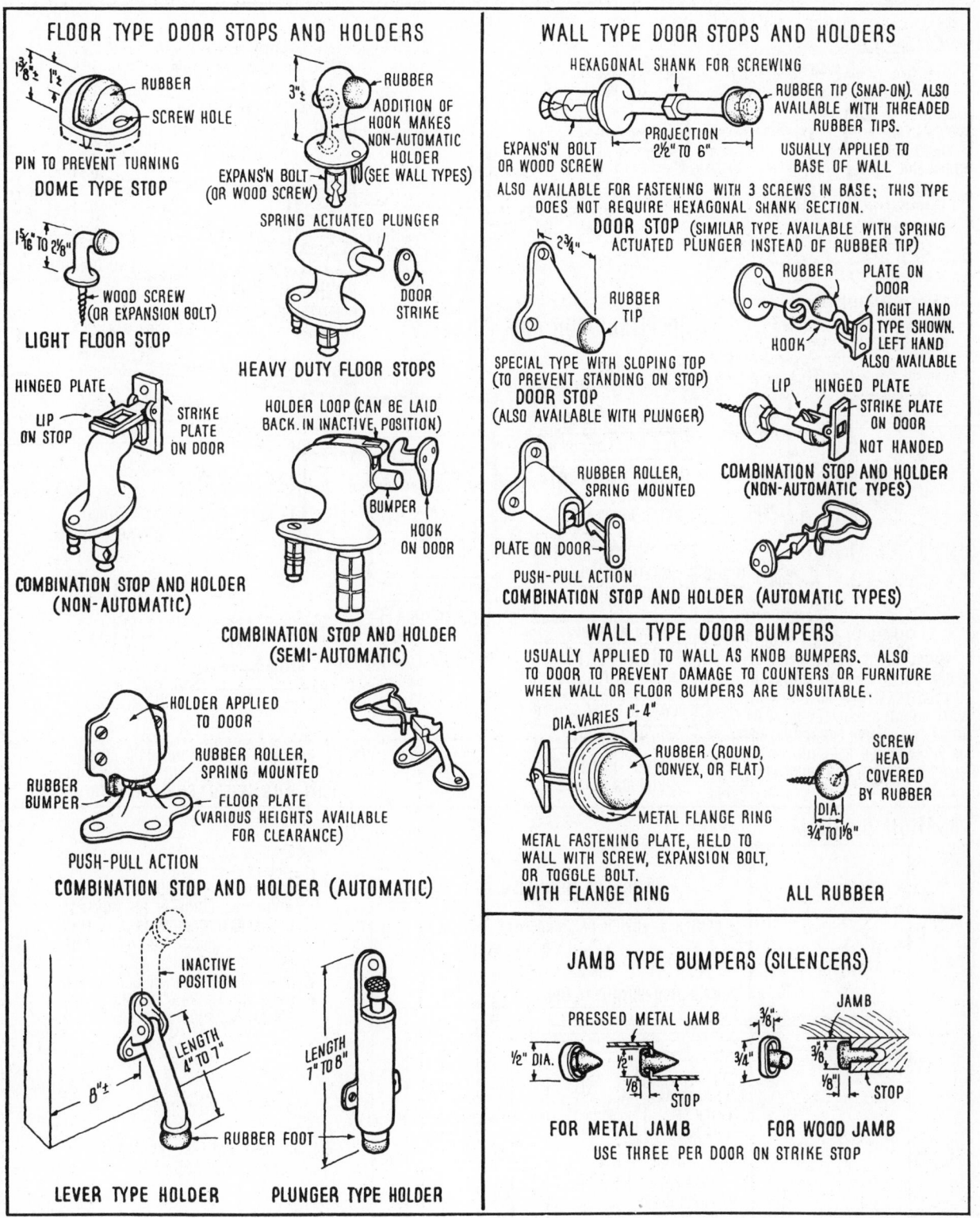

FLOOR TYPE DOOR STOPS AND HOLDERS
1 3/8"± 1"±
RUBBER
SCREW HOLE
PIN TO PREVENT TURNING
DOME TYPE STOP
3"±
RUBBER
ADDITION OF HOOK MAKES NON-AUTOMATIC HOLDER
EXPANS'N BOLT (OR WOOD SCREW)
(SEE WALL TYPES)
1 5/16" TO 2 1/8"
WOOD SCREW (OR EXPANSION BOLT)
LIGHT FLOOR STOP
SPRING ACTUATED PLUNGER
DOOR STRIKE
HEAVY DUTY FLOOR STOPS
HINGED PLATE
LIP ON STOP
STRIKE PLATE ON DOOR
COMBINATION STOP AND HOLDER (NON-AUTOMATIC)
HOLDER LOOP (CAN BE LAID BACK. IN INACTIVE POSITION)
BUMPER
HOOK ON DOOR
COMBINATION STOP AND HOLDER (SEMI-AUTOMATIC)
HOLDER APPLIED TO DOOR
RUBBER ROLLER, SPRING MOUNTED
RUBBER BUMPER
FLOOR PLATE (VARIOUS HEIGHTS AVAILABLE FOR CLEARANCE)
PUSH-PULL ACTION
COMBINATION STOP AND HOLDER (AUTOMATIC)
INACTIVE POSITION
LENGTH 4" TO 7"
8"±
RUBBER FOOT
LENGTH 7" TO 8"
LEVER TYPE HOLDER
PLUNGER TYPE HOLDER
WALL TYPE DOOR STOPS AND HOLDERS
HEXAGONAL SHANK FOR SCREWING
RUBBER TIP (SNAP-ON). ALSO AVAILABLE WITH THREADED RUBBER TIPS.
EXPANS'N BOLT OR WOOD SCREW
PROJECTION 2½" TO 6"
USUALLY APPLIED TO BASE OF WALL
ALSO AVAILABLE FOR FASTENING WITH 3 SCREWS IN BASE; THIS TYPE DOES NOT REQUIRE HEXAGONAL SHANK SECTION.
DOOR STOP (SIMILAR TYPE AVAILABLE WITH SPRING ACTUATED PLUNGER INSTEAD OF RUBBER TIP)
2¾"
RUBBER TIP
SPECIAL TYPE WITH SLOPING TOP (TO PREVENT STANDING ON STOP)
DOOR STOP
(ALSO AVAILABLE WITH PLUNGER)
RUBBER
PLATE ON DOOR
RIGHT HAND TYPE SHOWN. LEFT HAND ALSO AVAILABLE
HOOK
LIP
HINGED PLATE
STRIKE PLATE ON DOOR
NOT HANDED
COMBINATION STOP AND HOLDER (NON-AUTOMATIC TYPES)
RUBBER ROLLER, SPRING MOUNTED
PLATE ON DOOR
PUSH-PULL ACTION
COMBINATION STOP AND HOLDER (AUTOMATIC TYPES)
WALL TYPE DOOR BUMPERS
USUALLY APPLIED TO WALL AS KNOB BUMPERS. ALSO TO DOOR TO PREVENT DAMAGE TO COUNTERS OR FURNITURE WHEN WALL OR FLOOR BUMPERS ARE UNSUITABLE.
DIA. VARIES 1"-4"
RUBBER (ROUND, CONVEX, OR FLAT)
METAL FLANGE RING
METAL FASTENING PLATE, HELD TO WALL WITH SCREW, EXPANSION BOLT, OR TOGGLE BOLT.
WITH FLANGE RING
SCREW HEAD COVERED BY RUBBER
DIA.
3/4" TO 1 1/8"
ALL RUBBER
JAMB TYPE BUMPERS (SILENCERS)
PRESSED METAL JAMB
½" DIA.
½"
1/8"
STOP
3/8"
3/4"
JAMB
3/8"
1/8"
STOP
FOR METAL JAMB
FOR WOOD JAMB
USE THREE PER DOOR ON STRIKE STOP

Note: For specific details and sizes, consult manufacturers' catalogs.

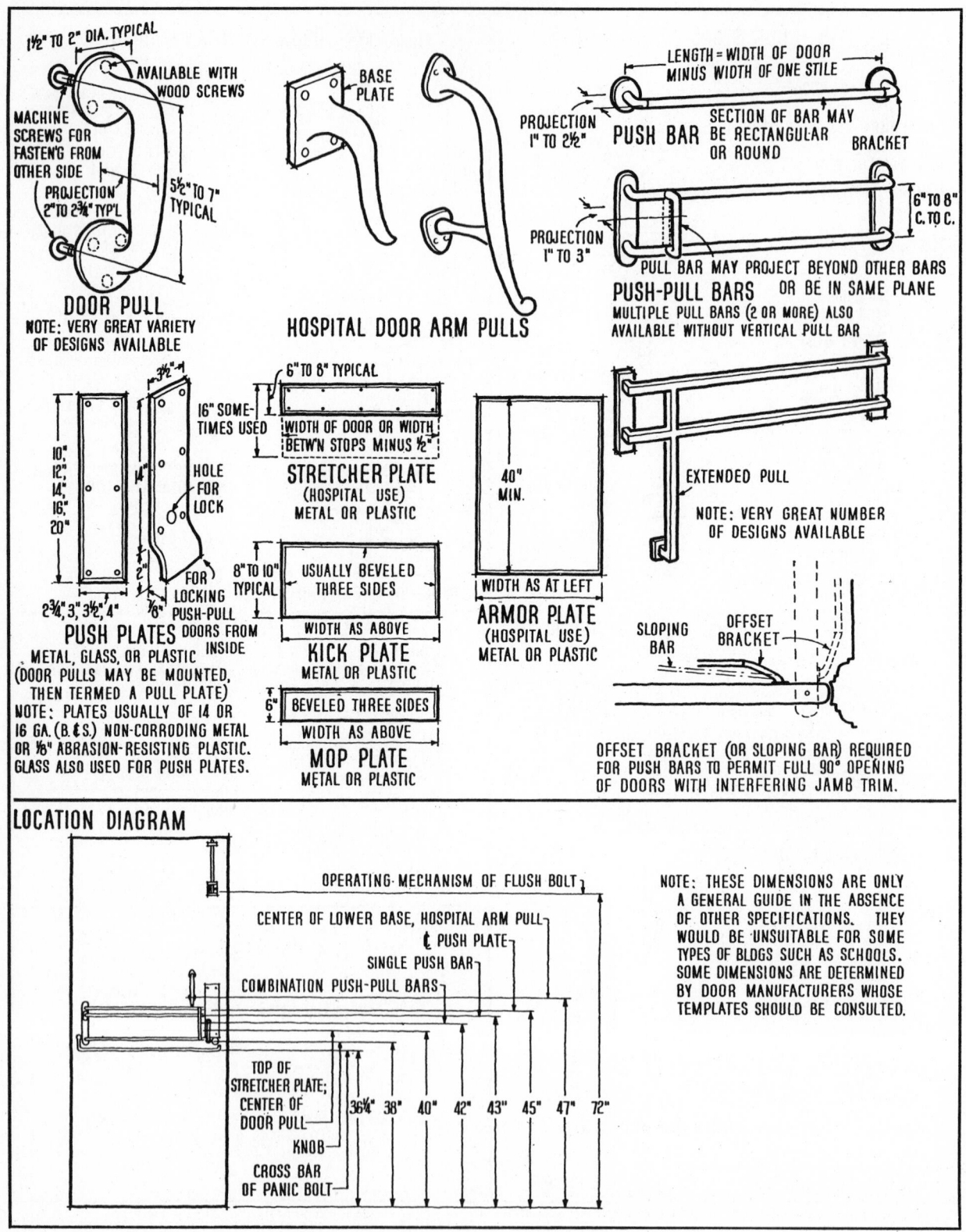

LOCATION DIAGRAM

NOTE: THESE DIMENSIONS ARE ONLY A GENERAL GUIDE IN THE ABSENCE OF OTHER SPECIFICATIONS. THEY WOULD BE UNSUITABLE FOR SOME TYPES OF BLDGS SUCH AS SCHOOLS. SOME DIMENSIONS ARE DETERMINED BY DOOR MANUFACTURERS WHOSE TEMPLATES SHOULD BE CONSULTED.

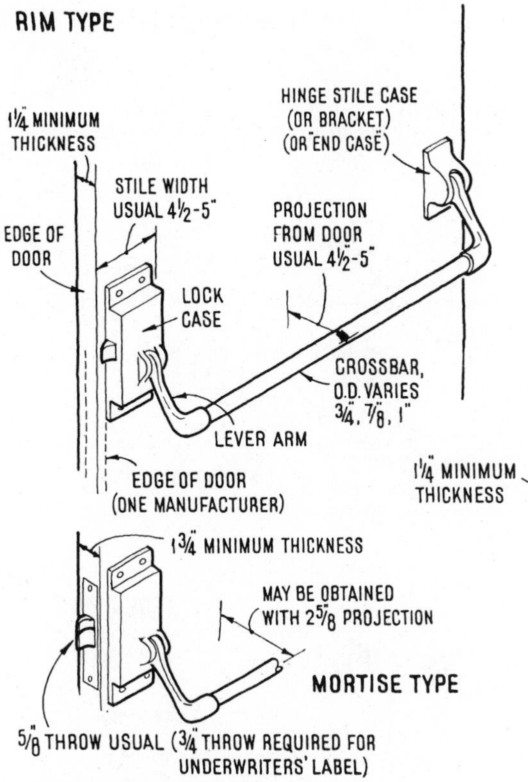

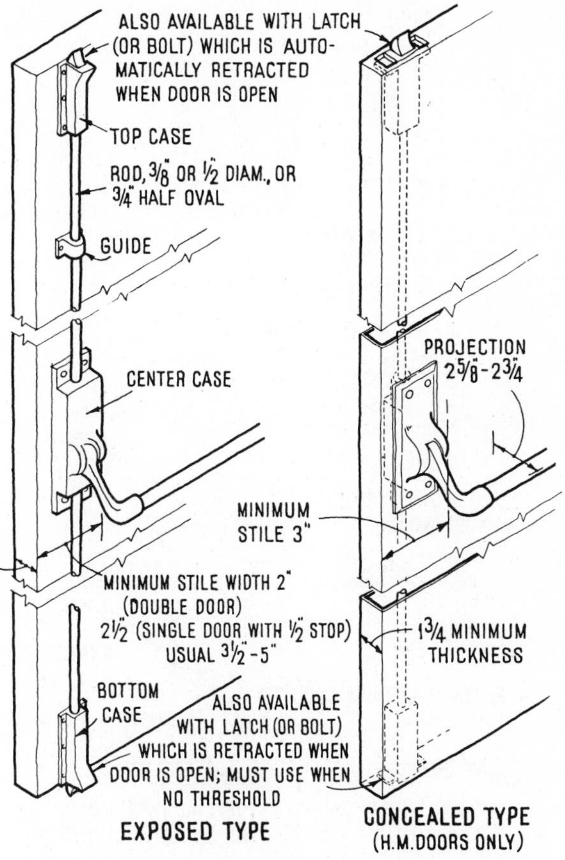

RIM TYPE

1¼ MINIMUM THICKNESS

EDGE OF DOOR

STILE WIDTH USUAL 4½-5"

LOCK CASE

HINGE STILE CASE (OR BRACKET) (OR END CASE)

PROJECTION FROM DOOR USUAL 4½-5"

CROSSBAR, O.D. VARIES ¾, ⅞, 1"

LEVER ARM

EDGE OF DOOR (ONE MANUFACTURER)

1¾ MINIMUM THICKNESS

MAY BE OBTAINED WITH 2⅝ PROJECTION

MORTISE TYPE

⅝ THROW USUAL (¾ THROW REQUIRED FOR UNDERWRITERS' LABEL)

ALSO AVAILABLE WITH LATCH (OR BOLT) WHICH IS AUTOMATICALLY RETRACTED WHEN DOOR IS OPEN

TOP CASE

ROD, ⅜ OR ½ DIAM., OR ¾ HALF OVAL

GUIDE

CENTER CASE

PROJECTION 2⅝-2¾

MINIMUM STILE 3"

1¼ MINIMUM THICKNESS

MINIMUM STILE WIDTH 2" (DOUBLE DOOR) 2½ (SINGLE DOOR WITH ½ STOP) USUAL 3½-5"

BOTTOM CASE

ALSO AVAILABLE WITH LATCH (OR BOLT) WHICH IS RETRACTED WHEN DOOR IS OPEN; MUST USE WHEN NO THRESHOLD

1¾ MINIMUM THICKNESS

EXPOSED TYPE

CONCEALED TYPE (H.M. DOORS ONLY)

CENTER LATCH BOLT TYPES

Used for: (1) single door
(2) active door of a pair (standard for underwriters' labeled fire door)
(3) both doors of a pair with mullion (removable or fixed)

VERTICAL ROD TYPES

Used for: (1) inactive door of a pair (standard for underwriters' labeled fire door)
(2) both doors of a pair
(3) single door (reduces chances of warping or springing)

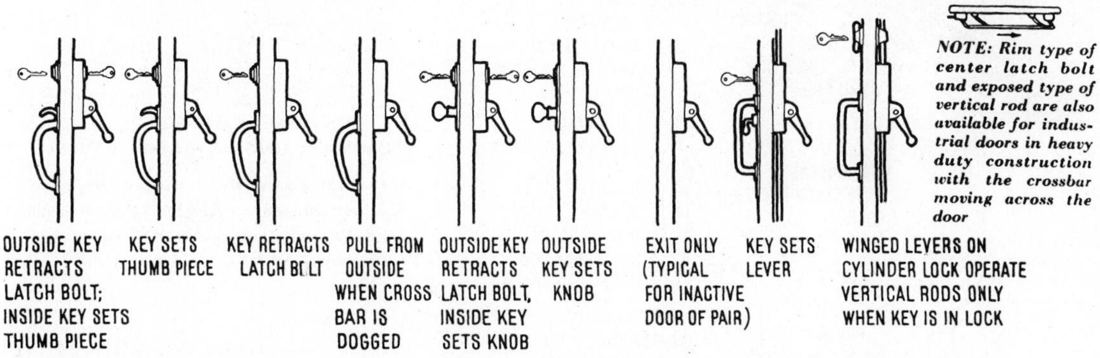

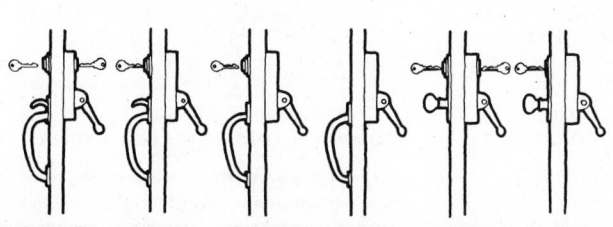

NOTE: Rim type of center latch bolt and exposed type of vertical rod are also available for industrial doors in heavy duty construction with the crossbar moving across the door

OUTSIDE KEY RETRACTS LATCH BOLT; INSIDE KEY SETS THUMB PIECE	KEY SETS THUMB PIECE	KEY RETRACTS LATCH BOLT	PULL FROM OUTSIDE WHEN CROSS BAR IS DOGGED	OUTSIDE KEY RETRACTS LATCH BOLT, INSIDE KEY SETS KNOB	OUTSIDE KEY SETS KNOB	EXIT ONLY (TYPICAL FOR INACTIVE DOOR OF PAIR)	KEY SETS LEVER	WINGED LEVERS ON CYLINDER LOCK OPERATE VERTICAL RODS ONLY WHEN KEY IS IN LOCK
C.L. ONLY	C.L. ONLY	C.L. ONLY	C.L. & V.R.	C.L. ONLY	C.L. & V.R.	C.L. & V.R.	V.R. ONLY	V.R. ONLY

TYPICAL FUNCTION AND TRIM ARRANGEMENTS (ALL TYPES)

Note: Crossbar can be dogged down with latch in retracted position, permitting door to be used push and pull. (Dogging not allowed on underwriters' labeled doors)

MECHANISMS vary with manufacturer and cost. Latches are pivoted type, usually retracted by cam and spring action, though some are made with lever arm acting directly on latch. With vertical rod operation, either pivoted type latch or sliding bolt may be used, actuated by springs, cams and gravity.

METALS: drop forged, extruded and cast brass (or bronze) or malleable iron for formed members; stainless steel or monel for pivots and pins; bars and rods extruded or rolled brass (or bronze) or steel. Tensile, strength, resilience and hardness should be checked against type of use expected.

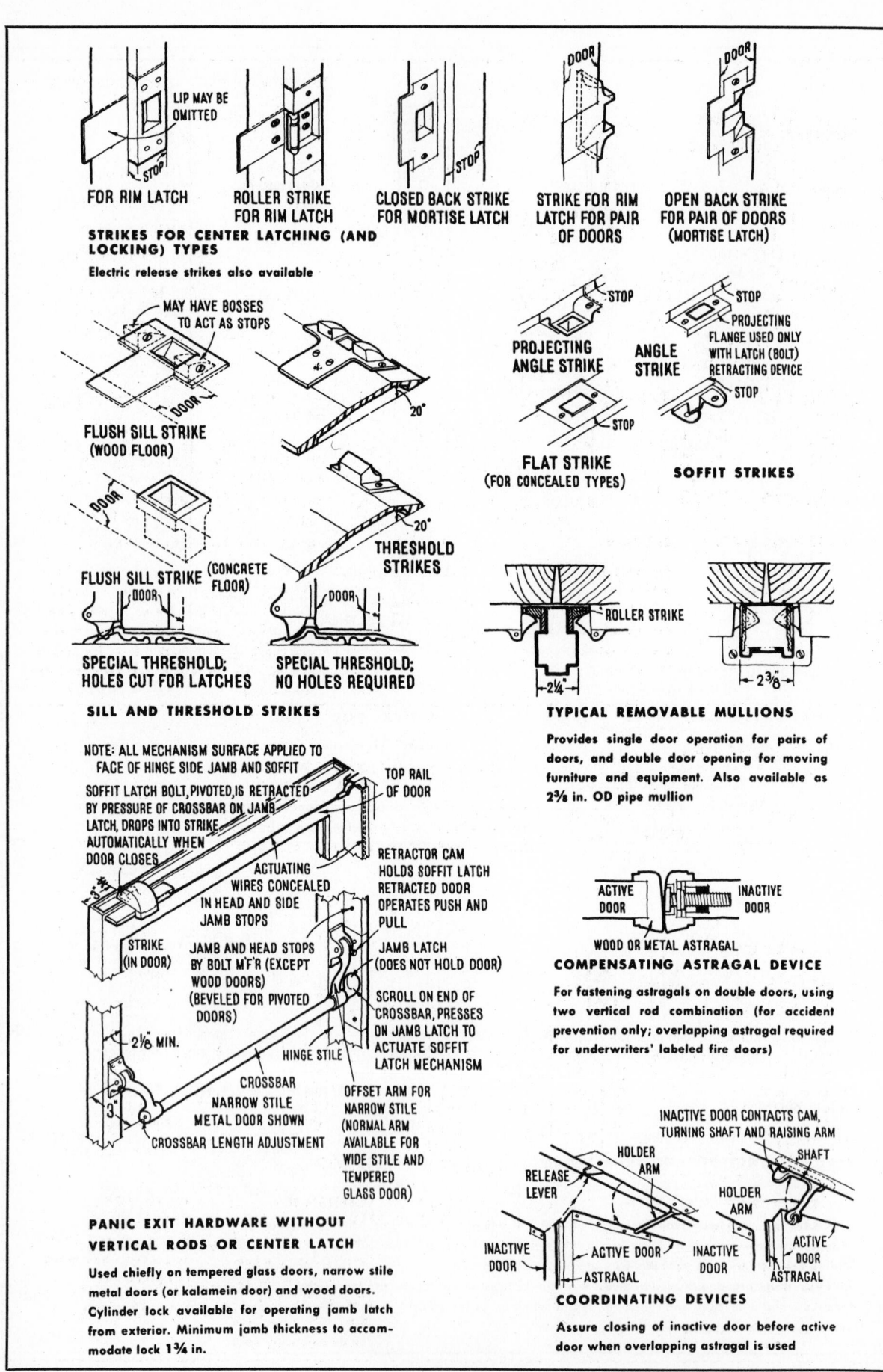

STRIKES FOR CENTER LATCHING (AND LOCKING) TYPES

FOR RIM LATCH

ROLLER STRIKE FOR RIM LATCH

CLOSED BACK STRIKE FOR MORTISE LATCH

STRIKE FOR RIM LATCH FOR PAIR OF DOORS

OPEN BACK STRIKE FOR PAIR OF DOORS (MORTISE LATCH)

LIP MAY BE OMITTED

Electric release strikes also available

MAY HAVE BOSSES TO ACT AS STOPS

FLUSH SILL STRIKE (WOOD FLOOR)

FLUSH SILL STRIKE (CONCRETE FLOOR)

THRESHOLD STRIKES

SPECIAL THRESHOLD; HOLES CUT FOR LATCHES

SPECIAL THRESHOLD; NO HOLES REQUIRED

SILL AND THRESHOLD STRIKES

PROJECTING ANGLE STRIKE

ANGLE STRIKE

PROJECTING FLANGE USED ONLY WITH LATCH (BOLT) RETRACTING DEVICE

FLAT STRIKE (FOR CONCEALED TYPES)

SOFFIT STRIKES

ROLLER STRIKE

2¼

2⅜

TYPICAL REMOVABLE MULLIONS

Provides single door operation for pairs of doors, and double door opening for moving furniture and equipment. Also available as 2⅜ in. OD pipe mullion

NOTE: ALL MECHANISM SURFACE APPLIED TO FACE OF HINGE SIDE JAMB AND SOFFIT

SOFFIT LATCH BOLT, PIVOTED, IS RETRACTED BY PRESSURE OF CROSSBAR ON JAMB LATCH, DROPS INTO STRIKE AUTOMATICALLY WHEN DOOR CLOSES

TOP RAIL OF DOOR

ACTUATING WIRES CONCEALED IN HEAD AND SIDE JAMB STOPS

RETRACTOR CAM HOLDS SOFFIT LATCH RETRACTED DOOR OPERATES PUSH AND PULL

STRIKE (IN DOOR)

JAMB AND HEAD STOPS BY BOLT M'F'R (EXCEPT WOOD DOORS) (BEVELED FOR PIVOTED DOORS)

JAMB LATCH (DOES NOT HOLD DOOR)

SCROLL ON END OF CROSSBAR, PRESSES ON JAMB LATCH TO ACTUATE SOFFIT LATCH MECHANISM

2⅛ MIN.

HINGE STILE

CROSSBAR NARROW STILE METAL DOOR SHOWN

3"

OFFSET ARM FOR NARROW STILE (NORMAL ARM AVAILABLE FOR WIDE STILE AND TEMPERED GLASS DOOR)

CROSSBAR LENGTH ADJUSTMENT

PANIC EXIT HARDWARE WITHOUT VERTICAL RODS OR CENTER LATCH

Used chiefly on tempered glass doors, narrow stile metal doors (or kalamein door) and wood doors. Cylinder lock available for operating jamb latch from exterior. Minimum jamb thickness to accommodate lock 1¾ in.

ACTIVE DOOR

INACTIVE DOOR

WOOD OR METAL ASTRAGAL

COMPENSATING ASTRAGAL DEVICE

For fastening astragals on double doors, using two vertical rod combination (for accident prevention only; overlapping astragal required for underwriters' labeled fire doors)

INACTIVE DOOR CONTACTS CAM, TURNING SHAFT AND RAISING ARM

RELEASE LEVER

HOLDER ARM

SHAFT

HOLDER ARM

INACTIVE DOOR

ACTIVE DOOR

ASTRAGAL

INACTIVE DOOR

ACTIVE DOOR

ASTRAGAL

COORDINATING DEVICES

Assure closing of inactive door before active door when overlapping astragal is used

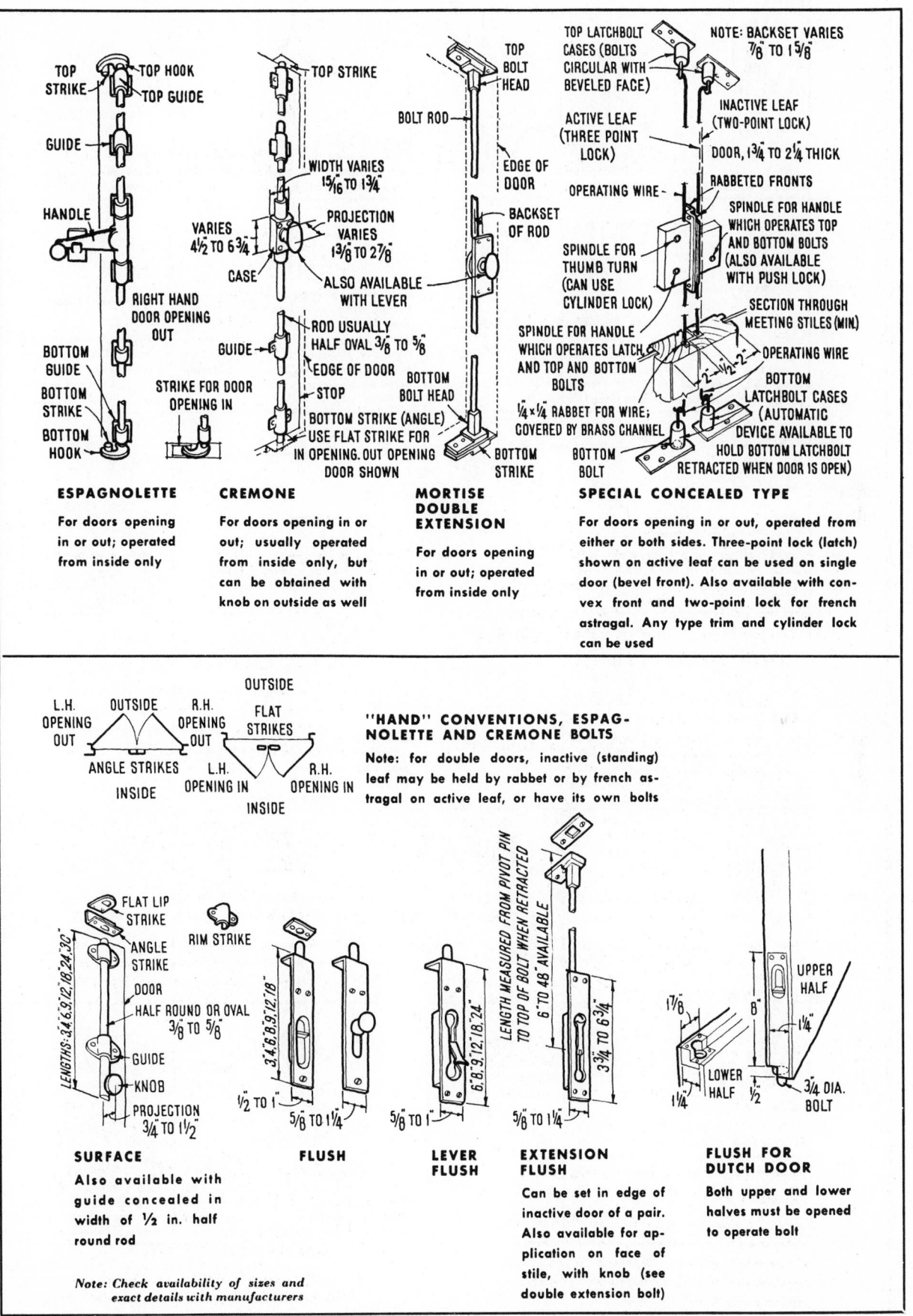

ESPAGNOLETTE

For doors opening in or out; operated from inside only

CREMONE

For doors opening in or out; usually operated from inside only, but can be obtained with knob on outside as well

MORTISE DOUBLE EXTENSION

For doors opening in or out; operated from inside only

SPECIAL CONCEALED TYPE

For doors opening in or out, operated from either or both sides. Three-point lock (latch) shown on active leaf can be used on single door (bevel front). Also available with convex front and two-point lock for french astragal. Any type trim and cylinder lock can be used

"HAND" CONVENTIONS, ESPAG-NOLETTE AND CREMONE BOLTS

Note: for double doors, inactive (standing) leaf may be held by rabbet or by french astragal on active leaf, or have its own bolts

SURFACE

Also available with guide concealed in width of ½ in. half round rod

FLUSH

LEVER FLUSH

EXTENSION FLUSH

Can be set in edge of inactive door of a pair. Also available for application on face of stile, with knob (see double extension bolt)

FLUSH FOR DUTCH DOOR

Both upper and lower halves must be opened to operate bolt

Note: Check availability of sizes and exact details with manufacturers

LINE NO.	MORTISE LOCKS		UNIT LOCKS *Functions same as mortise, unless noted*	CYLINDRICAL LOCKS *Fed. Spec. No. 160 Series & 161 Series*	TUBULAR LOCKS *Functions same as cylindrical*
	CYLINDER	BIT-KEY			
1 KNOB LATCH	**86N, 87N**	**3D, 184, 185**	**90N, 98N** (Fire door)	**160N, 161N**	**150C, 150YC** **2B(2B-9CS** *With turn knob inside*) **2YB (2YB-9CS)**
	Latch bolt by knob from either side. For turn knob on inside, add "CS" to Fed. No., as 3D-CS			Latch bolt by knob from either side. Also available with turn knob on inside; or with outside knob always fixed, bolt dead-locked when door closed	Also available with outside knob fixed, similar to cylindrical
2 PRIVACY	**86L**	**3B; 6B, 6BR**	**90L**	**160L, 161L**	**2A 150B, 150YB**
	Latch bolt by knob from either side. Dead bolt by turn knob from inside. 6B and 6BR (rabbeted front) for French doors with lever handles both sides			Latch bolt by knob from either side, except when outer knob is locked by push button on inside knob. Turning inside knob or shutting door automatically releases push button. Also available with turn button for locking outer knob, which is not automatically released (160Q, 161Q)	Similar function to cylindrical. Also available with knob which is pushed toward door to lock, pulled to unlock
3 BATH ROOM	**86L**	**3B** *Specify emergency key*	**90L, Spec. em. key**	**160L, 161L**	**2A 150B, 150YB**
	Latch bolt by knob from either side. Dead bolt by turn knob from inside and emergency key (screwdriver or pointed tool) from outside			Same functions as above, except emergency access provided. Not dead-locked when door closed	Also available with push button on knob instead of locking device on rose. Also with knob which is pushed toward door to lock
4 COMMUNICATING DOOR	**86M**	**3C**	**90M**	**160M, 161M**	
	Latch bolt by knob from either side. Dead bolt by turn knob from either side, each locking against the other. Also available with cylinder key on each side instead of turn knob			Latch bolt by knob from either side, except when knob on opposite side is locked by turn button on either knob. Also available with keys in both knobs, each locking opposite knob	
5 OFFICE	**85D, 86D**		**90D**	**160B, 161B**	
	Latch bolt by knob from either side; outer knob locked by stop in face; when outer knob is locked, latch bolt by key from outside. Inner knob always free			Latch bolt by knob from either side, except when outer knob is locked by push button on inside knob, then by key from outside. Push button released by turning knob, but not by shutting door	
6 FRONT DOOR	**85A, 86A**		**90A**	**160A, 161A**	**150A, 150YA**
	Latch bolt by knob from either side. Stop in face locks outer knob; with outer knob locked, latch bolt by key from outside; dead bolt by key from outside, turn knob from inside. 121A, 122A: thumb-piece, handle outside, knob inside. 8A, 8AR rabbeted front: French door, lever handles both sides			Latch bolt by knob from either side, except when outer knob is locked by turn button on inside knob, then by key from outside. Latch bolt dead-locked when door closed. Also available with thumb-piece and handle on outside	Functions same as cylindrical. Also available with knob which is pushed in and turned ¼ turn to lock (instead of turn button)

Notes: Numbers shown for locks and latches are U.S. Federal Specification numbers from FF-H-106a, dated 23 November, 1948, and Amendment No. 1, dated 10 December, 1952.

Although lock types are arranged according to similarity of function, all locks in one line are not necessarily suitable for all types of buildings. Choice of lock should be made with consideration to weight, durability, and security appropriate to the specific use.

LINE NO.	MORTISE LOCKS		UNIT LOCKS	CYLINDRICAL LOCKS	TUBULAR LOCKS
	CYLINDER	BIT-KEY	Functions same as mortise, unless noted	Fed. Spec. No. 160 Series & 161 Series	Functions same as cylindrical
7 OFFICE	**85E, 86E, 87E** Latch bolt by knob from either side; by key from outside when outer knob is locked by stop in face. When door is closed, auxiliary bolt shall dead lock latch bolt and stops		**90E, 98E** (Fire door)	Use same lock as shown in line 6	
8 APARTMENT, OFFICE AND PUBLIC TOILET	**86G, 87G** Latch bolt by knob from either side; stop works controlled by inside key; latch bolt by key from outside when outer knob locked; when door is closed, auxiliary bolt deadlocks latch bolt. 123B: same, thumb pieces and handles both sides		**90G, 98G** (Fire door)	**161C** Latch bolt by knob from either side, except when outer knob is locked by inside key, then by key from outside. Inside knob always free	
9 LATCH AND DEAD-LOCK	**85C, 86C** Latch bolt by knob from either side; dead bolt by key from either side. (86CR, rabbeted front) 123A: same, thumb pieces and handles both sides. 6A, 6AR (rabbeted front), same for French doors, lever handles both sides	**3A, 3AA, 6A, 6AR**	**90C**	**161G** Latch bolt by knob from either side except when locked. Key in either knob locks both knobs	**181M 2B**
10 LATCH AND DEAD-LOCK	**85B, 86B** Latch bolt by knob from either side; dead bolt by key from outside, turn knob from inside. (86BR, rabbeted front)		**90B**	**161T** Locked or unlocked by key from outside, locked by push button from inside. Turning inside knob automatically releases push button	
11 WIRE & PIPE SHAFT	**85EW, 86EW** Latch bolt by key from outside, by knob from inside. Outer knob always fixed; inner knob always free. 85DW, 86DW, similar but without auxiliary deadlocking latch		**90DW**, without auxiliary latch **90EW**, auxiliary latch	**160D, 161D** Latch bolt by key from outside, by knob from inside. Outer knob always fixed, inner knob always free. Latch deadlocked when door closed. Also available with fixed thumb-piece and handles outside (for vestibules)	
12 NIGHT LATCH	**183** Latch bolt by turn knob inside and key from outside. When door is closed auxiliary bolt shall automatically deadlock latch bolt. Bolt may be held back by stop in front				**182B** By key one side, turn knob one side. Turn knob or slide stop permits latch to be held in retracted position. Dead-locking guard bolt. 182A same, but no dead-locking

NO.	MORTISE LOCKS		
13 **EXIT** **DOOR**	**CYLINDER** **86F**	Latch bolt by knob inside at all times and by knob outside except when locked by stop in face; by key outside when outer knob locked. Dead bolt by key outside and turn knob inside. When dead bolt thrown, ¼ turn of inside hand knob retracts both latch and dead bolts. 86 F W : no stop works; same operation but outside knob always operates latch	
14 **CLASS-** **ROOM** **DEAD-** **LOCK**	**CYLINDER** **191**	Dead bolt by key from outside and by turn knob from inside. Turn knob shall withdraw but shall not project dead bolt	**BIT-KEY** **188**

LINE NO.	MORTISE LOCKS		UNIT LOCKS *Functions same as mortise, unless noted*	CYLINDRICAL LOCKS *Fed. Spec. No. 160 Series & 161 Series*	TUBULAR LOCKS *Functions same as cylindrical*
	CYLINDER	**BIT-KEY**			
15 **HOTEL**	**86H** Latch bolt by key from outside, by knob from inside. Outside knob rigid. Dead bolt from outside by display and emergency key only; from inside by turn knob. Outside indicator shows when door locked from inside. Emergency key operates dead- and latch-bolts. Note: at least 15 types of hotel locks available with slight variations. Special study required		**90H**	**161H** Latch bolt from outside by guest, display, master, grand-master and emergency key (knob fixed); bolt dead-locked when closed; by knob at all times from inside (except when locked by shut-out key from inside). Push button on inside locks outer knob to all except display and emergency key; indicator button on outside shows when push button operates	
16 **CLASS-** **ROOM**	**86J** Latch bolt by knob from either side except when outside knob locked by key. Cylinder controls stop-works only. Latch bolt dead-locked when door closed. Inside knob always free. Also available with thumb-piece and handle instead of knob	**187**	**90J**	**160R, 161R** Locked or unlocked by key from outside. Inner knob always free. Latch dead-locked when door closed	
17 **DEAD-** **LOCK**	**86T, 190M** Dead bolt by key from either side	**189, 192** **192A, B, C**		**161W** Latch bolt by key in either knob. Both knobs always fixed. Latch bolt dead-locked when door closed	**181M** Same as mortise
18 **DEAD-** **LOCK**	**86P, 190K** Bolt by key from one side and turn knob from other			**MISCELLANEOUS** **193** Hospital Door Roller Latch. By push or pull on door	**181K** Same as cylindrical mortise
19 **DEAD-** **LOCK**	**86S, 190L** Dead bolt by key from one side		Latch bolt by key from outside. Outside knob always rigid. Latch dead-locked when door closed	**194, 195, 196** Rim Night Latch (tubular) Latch by key from outside; turn knob from inside. Slide stop to hold latch retracted	**181L** Bolt by key one side

INDEX TO USES OF LOCK FUNCTIONS

Numbers refer to lines previously published, sheets 18–20.

Door Type	Office, Public and Commercial Buildings	Schools	Hospitals	Hotels	Apartments	Residences
Main Entrance	17, 18, push, pull or panic bolts	panic bolts	17, 18	17, 18	8, 17, 18	6
Store and Shop Entrances	9, 12, 17, 18	—	9, 17, 18	9, 17, 18	9, 17, 18	—
Exterior Doors to roof	1, 14	1, 14	1, 14	1, 14	1, 14	6
French Doors	—	—	—	—	—	2, 9, 16 or 17 or cremone, espagnolette double extension or special mortise bolts
Exterior Fire Stair Doors	panic bolts	panic bolts	panic bolts	panic bolts	panic bolts	—
Other Exterior Doors	5, 6, 8	5, 6, 8	5, 6, 8	5, 6, 8	5, 6, 8	2, 6
Vestibule, Lobby, passage corridor, stair Doors	1, 14, 17, push, pull	1, 14, 17, push, pull	1, 14, 17, push, pull	1, 14, 17, push, pull	1, 14, 17, push, pull	
Public Toilet Locker, Dressing room Doors	8, 11, push, pull	8, 11, push, pull	8, 11, push, pull	8, 11, push, pull	—	—
Fire Exit Doors	panic bolts	panic bolts	panic bolts	panic bolts	panic bolts	—
Auditorium Doors	panic bolts	panic bolts	—	panic bolts	—	
Corridor Doors to offices, apt., teacher's, hotel guest rooms	5, 7, 8, 12	5, 7, 12	—	13	6, 8	
Communicating Doors	4, 17	4	4	4	4	4
Classroom Doors	—	14, 15	—	—	—	—
Ward, Bed, Treatment Doors	—	—	16	—	—	—
Private Toilet, Bathroom Doors	2	2	2	2	—	—
Banquet, Private Dining Room Doors	—	—	—	17	—	—
Bed-pan, Utility, Diet-Kitchen, Dining Kitchen, Operating, Delivery, Anaesthesia Room Doors	—	—	16	—	—	—
Bath, Bedroom Doors	—	—	16	1, 3	3	3
Closet, Locking	7, 11, 16	7, 11, 16	7, 11, 16	7, 11, 16	7, 11, 16	7, 11, 16
Closet, Non-Locking	1	1	1	1	1	1
Other Interior Doors (locking)	7	7	7	10	9	9
Other Interior Doors (non-locking)	1	1	1	1	1	1
Wire-shaft, Pipe Space, slop sink, Janitor's closets (always locked)	11	11	11	11	11	11

* *Note: Although lock types are arranged in the preceding tables according to similarity of function, all locks in one line are not necessarily suitable for all types of buildings. Choice of lock should be made with consideration as to weight, durability and security appropriate to the specific type of building.*

Lock dimensions

Government specification locks (FF-H-106a) *All dimensions are minimum, in inches*

Series No. and Type	Case	Backset	Front *	Bolt	Bolt Throw	Door Thickness	Notes
2 Tubular	¾ to 1 diam. 3¾ long-max	2⅜ to 2½	2 x ⅞	9/16 x ½	7/16	1⅛	*"Designed primarily for housing & residential buildings" (FF-H-106a)*
3 Mortise, Bit-Key	3½ high x 3¼ deep x 9/16 thick	2½ ± 1/32	5½ x ⅞	latch 9/16 x 7/16 dead 13/16 x ⅜	⅜ 7/16	1⅜	
5 Mortise, Bit-Key	4¼ x 3½ x ⅝	2¾ ± 1/32	6 x 1	latch ⅝ x 7/16 dead ⅞ x ⅜	7/16 7/16	1¾	
6 French door, Bit-Key	4 x backset + ¾ x ⅝	1½ ± 1/32 (2″ may be specif.)	5⅞ x ⅞	latch ⅝ x 7/16 dead ⅞ x ⅜	7/16 7/16	1⅜	
8 French door, Cyl. lock	5½ x backset + 1 x ¾	1½ ± 1/32 (2″ may be specif.)	7⅞ x 1 1/16	latch 27/32 x ⅝ dead 1⅛ x 7/16	½ ½	1¾	
85 Mortise, Cyl. lock	5½ x 3½ x ⅝	2½ ± 1/32	7¾ x ⅞	latch 27/32 x ⅝ dead 1⅛ x 7/16	½ ½	1⅜	
86 Mortise, Cyl. lock	5½ x 3¾ x ¾ (6 x 4¼ x 1-max hollow metal doors)	2¾ ± 1/32	8 x 1¼ beveled (8 x 1¼ exact, for h.m. doors)	latch 1 x ⅝ dead 1⅛ x ½	½ ½	1¾	
87 Mortise, Cyl. lock (Fire doors)	same as 86	same as 86	same as 86	latch (plain or antifriction) 1 x ⅝	¾	1¾	*¾″ throw required for underwriters labeled doors*
90 Unit lock	2 high x 2⅞	2¾ ± 1/32	part of case, beveled	latch (hinged) ⅝ x 1¼ dead 5/16 x ⅞	½ ½	1¾ (can be specif. 1⅜ min, 3 max	
98 Same as 90 (Fire doors)	same as 90	same as 90	same as 90	latch (hinged) ⅝ x 1¼ auxil. latch	¾ 5/16	same as 90	*¾″ throw required for underwriters labeled doors*
121 Cyl. entrance door, Mortise, Handle one side	5¼ x 3½ x ⅝	2½ ± 1/32	7⅝ x ⅞	latch 27/32 x ⅝ dead ⅞ x 7/16	½ ½	1¾	
123 Same as 121, Handle both sides	5¼ x 3¾ x ¾ (6 x 4¼ x 1 max hollow metal door)	2¾ ± 1/32	7¾ x 1¼ (8 x 1¼ beveled, for h.m. doors)	latch 1 x ⅝ dead 1⅛ x ½	½ ½	1¾	
140 Mortise, Integral-type (factory assembled)	3 x 2⅜	2¾ ± 1/32	4¼ x 1¼	latch 11/16 x 27/32 auxil. ¼ x 27/32 dead ¼ x 27/32	½ ⅜ ½	1¾ (can be specif. up to 2¼)	
145 Unit, Integral-type	3 x 2⅜	2¾ ± 1/32	2⅞ x thickness of door	same as 140	same as 140	same as 140	
160 Cylindrical (light duty)	2 to 2⅛ diam (concentric with knobs)	2⅜ ± 1/64 (can be specif. 5, 7, 10)	2¼ x 1 (can be specif. bevel)	latch 11/16 x ½ auxil. plunger as needed	⅜	1⅜ to 2-max	
161 Cylindrical (heavy duty)	2 to 2⅛ diam (concentric with knobs)	2¾ ± 1/64 (can be specif. 5, 7, 10)	2¼ x 1⅛ beveled	latch ⅞ x ⅝ auxil. plunger as needed	½ (¾ can be specified)	1⅜ to 2 (can be specif. for thickness)	*¾″ throw required for underwriters labeled doors*
181, 182 Tubular cyl., Dead locks & Night Latches	⅞ to 1 diam (concentric with bolt)	2⅜ to 2½	2 x 1	⅝ x ½	½	1⅜ to 2	
183 Cyl. Mortise, Night Latch	3¼ x 3¼ x ¾	2½ or 2¾	5 x 1⅛	¾ x 9/16	½		
184 Mortise, knob, latch	1⅝ x 3⅛ x 9/16	2½ ± 1/32	3⅜ x 13/16	9/16 x 7/16	⅜	1⅜	
185 Mortise, knob, latch	2¼ x 3½ x ⅝	2¾ ± 1/32	4 x 1	11/16 x 9/16	½	1¾	
187 Classroom, Bit-Key, Mortise	5¼ x 3⅝ x 11/16	2¾ ± 1/32	7 x 1 1/16	⅝ x 7/16	7/16		
188 Classroom, Bit-Key, Dead-lock	3 x 3⅛ x 9/16	2¾ ± 1/32 (2½ can be specif.)	4¾ x 1	⅞ x 7/16	7/16		
189 Mortise, Bit-Key, Dead-lock	2⅛ x 3⅜ x ⅝	2¾ ± 1/32 (2½ can be specif.)	4 x 1	⅞ x 7/16	7/16		
190, 191 Cyl. Mortise, Dead-lock	2⅜ x 3⅝ x ¾	2½ ± 1/32 (1½, 2 or 2¾)	4⅛ x 1 1/16	15/16 x ½	½		
192 Asylum, Bit-Key, Dead-lock (Mortise)	3 x 4 x 13/16	3 ± 1/32	5½ x 1¼	1¾ x ⅝	9/16		

** Flat, unless otherwise indicated*

OVERHEAD SUPPORT

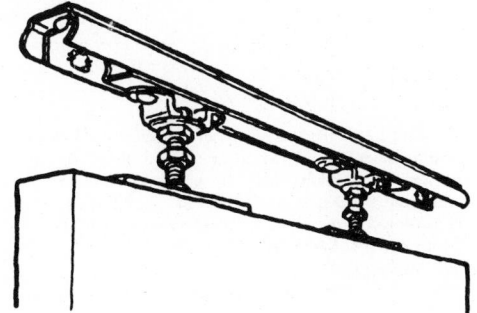

BALL SUPPORTED

(2 rows of ball bearings, in line horizontally)

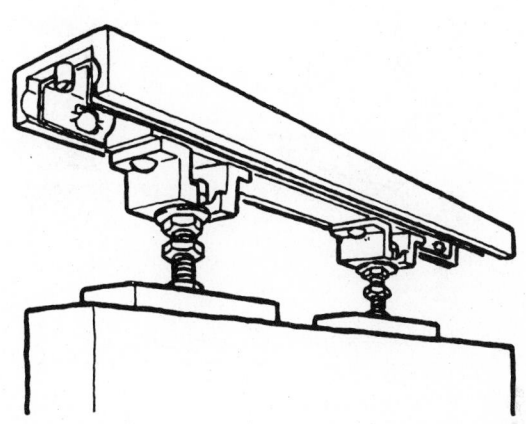

A ball bearing hanger featuring twin rows of ball bearings, accurately hand fitted. Three adjustments compensate for header irregularities. Various hangers are available for loads ranging from 35 to 1,000 lb.

WHEEL SUPPORTED, CHANNEL TRACK

TRACK: rolled steel, formed steel, or extruded aluminum. BEARING: plain, bushed, Oilite bushed, steel balls or steel rollers. WHEELS: steel, brass, fibre, rubber or plastic.

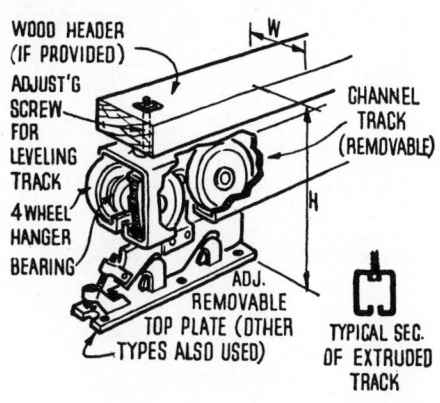

Weight limit (lbs.)	Width "W" (in.)	Clearance "H" (in.)	Notes
125	2¼	6¼	2 wheels only ⎫
175	2¼	6¼	4 wheels only ⎬ as shown
300	3¼	8½	4 wheels only ⎭
100	1⅝	3	With header omitted,
200	1¾	3⅛	non-removable top plate,
300	2⅛	3½	bracket support for track,
50	1	2⅜	and adjustable pendant bolt
50	1	1⅛	Non-adjustable

Also available with special hangers for folding and accordion doors:

Weight (lbs.)	W (in.)	H (in.)
80	3⅝	4⅝ — 4⅞ (higher "H" for folding doors)
110	3⅝	5⅜ — 5⅝
225	5⅝	6⅞ — 7¼

WHEEL SUPPORTED, I-BEAM TRACK, TOP MOUNTED, ADJUSTABLE

WHEELS: nylon, steel ball bearing
TRACK: aluminum

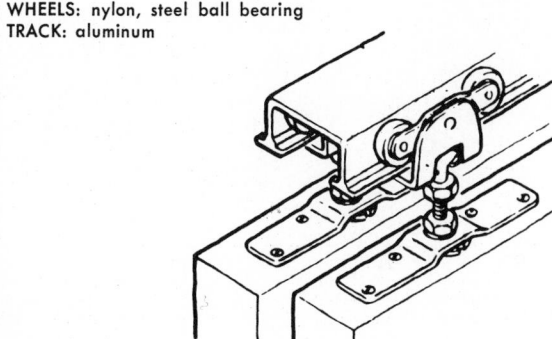

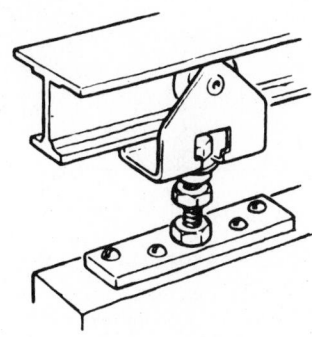

OVERHEAD SUPPORT

WHEEL SUPPORTED

Many variations of track section are available. TRACK: steel or aluminum; double sections are available for by-passing doors. WHEELS: steel, fibre, plastic, rubber or brass. BEARINGS: Oilite, ball bearing or plain. TRACK: may be fastened directly with screws (non-adjustable) or hung from brackets. CARRIER: may be fastened directly or by an intermediary of bracket.

Note: Dimensions, track profiles, hanger styles, vary with manufacturers. Check with catalogs

TYPICAL EXTRUDED SECTION FOR BY-PASSING DOORS

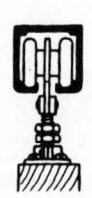 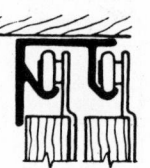 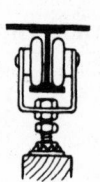

TYPICAL DOOR FASTENING DEVICES

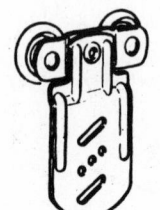 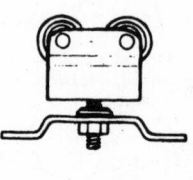 

TYPICAL FLOOR GUIDES & TRACK

CONVERGING DOOR GUIDE

THRESHOLD TYPE

BOT. GUIDE ROLL'R ON D'R — CONTINUOUS METAL TRACK — ANCHORS FOR CONC. FL.

FLUSH TYPE

TRACK FOR FOLDING & ACCORDION DOORS

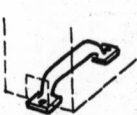

SLOT IN DOOR

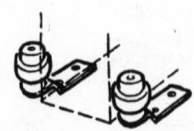

FOR POCKET DOORS ONLY

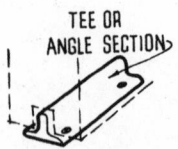

TEE OR ANGLE SECTION

SLOT IN DOOR

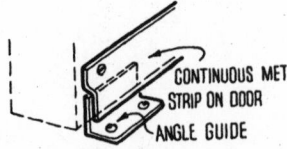

CONTINUOUS MET. STRIP ON DOOR — ANGLE GUIDE

FLOOR SUPPORT

TYPICAL HEAD GUIDES

Note: space "S" must be allowed to permit lifting door up off track.

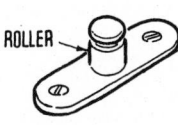

ROLLER

ROLLER GUIDE (1 pair per door). Can run in groove in head, in channel or between hardwood strips

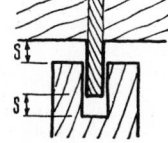

HARDWOOD STRIP IN HEAD, GROOVE IN DOOR.

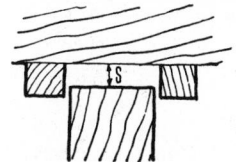

TWO HARDWOOD STRIPS ON HEAD.

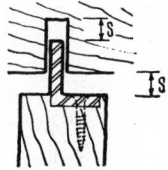

METAL ANGLE ON DOOR, GROOVE IN HEAD.

TYPICAL SHEAVES

Wheels have square edge for channel track, concave edge for T or W shaped track.

HOUSING
WHEEL

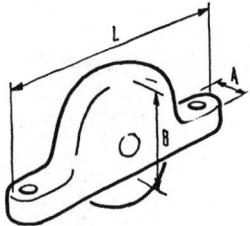

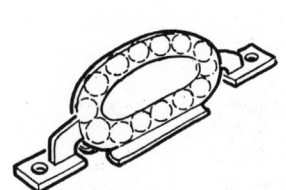

BALL BEARING TYPE
Use with T shaped track.

BEARING: Oilite.
HOUSING: cast iron, brass, bronze, aluminum.
WHEEL: fibre, cast iron, brass, bronze, aluminum; also with rubber tires (square edges only) and all rubber.

TYPICAL TRACK SECTIONS

Special extruded sections are also available with weather-stripping.

Max. Door Weight (1 pr sheaves)	Wheel Dia. (in.)	Housing (in.)		
		A	B	L
50	1 1/16	15/32	7/8	2 15/16
125	1 7/8	1 1/16	1 15/16	4 3/8
200	3	1 3/16	2 7/8	6

TRACK: brass, bronze, aluminum, stainless steel.

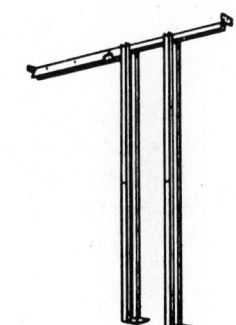

SLIDING DOOR POCKET

All steel pocket frame for vanishing sliding doors. Warp-proof, split jamb and studs consisting of channel sections with wood inserts to which wall panels can be nailed. Designed to take any type of wall material. For 1 3/8 or 1 3/4-in. doors.

TYPICAL PLANS OF SLIDING DOORS
Overhead support shown, but plans are similar for floor support.

For center-folding and edge-folding accordion doors, see section on "Folding Partitions."

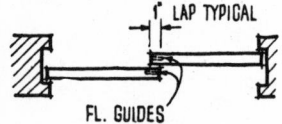

JAMB BOLT (INSTEAD OF LATCH)

FL. GUIDE   LATCH OR LOCK

OPEN SIDE POCKET

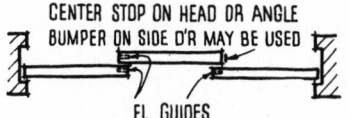

FL. GUIDE

JAMB BOLT   LATCH OR LOCK

WALL POCKET

SINGLE SLIDING DOORS

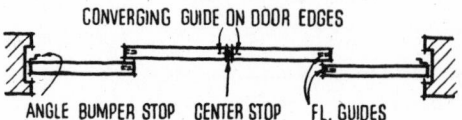

CENTER STOP ON HEAD JAMB   FL. GUIDE

FL. GUIDE   CONVERGING GUIDE ON DOOR EDGES

May be used with open side pockets.

BI-PARTING DOORS—May have jamb bolts on both doors or latch (lock) at center.

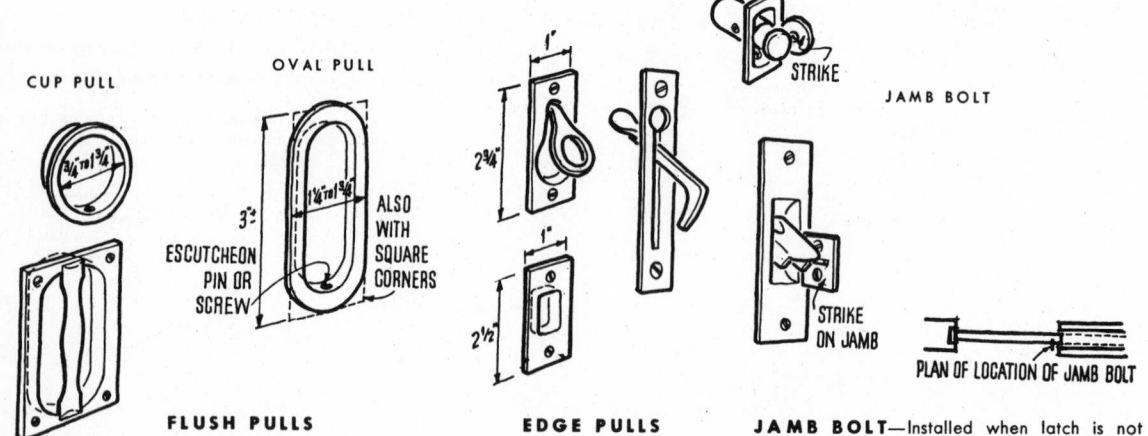

1" LAP TYPICAL

FL. GUIDES

TWO DOORS

CENTER STOP ON HEAD OR ANGLE BUMPER ON SIDE D'R MAY BE USED

FL. GUIDES

Two floor guides required for center door if stop is not used.

THREE DOORS

CONVERGING GUIDE ON DOOR EDGES

ANGLE BUMPER STOP   CENTER STOP   FL. GUIDES

FOUR DOORS

BY-PASSING DOORS (Parallel Doors)

TYPICAL PULLS, JAMB BOLTS, LATCHES & LOCKS (applicable to all types)

CUP PULL

OVAL PULL

3"

ESCUTCHEON PIN OR SCREW

1¼" to 1¾"

ALSO WITH SQUARE CORNERS

FLUSH PULLS

1"

2¾"

1"

2½"

EDGE PULLS

STRIKE

JAMB BOLT

STRIKE ON JAMB

PLAN OF LOCATION OF JAMB BOLT

JAMB BOLT—Installed when latch is not required, on inside face of door near pocket.

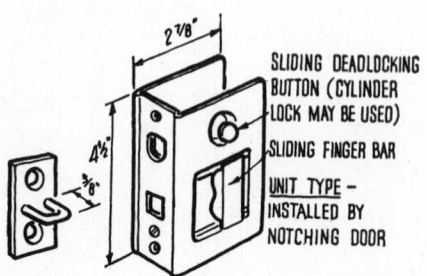

2⅞"

SLIDING DEADLOCKING BUTTON (CYLINDER LOCK MAY BE USED)

SLIDING FINGER BAR

UNIT TYPE— INSTALLED BY NOTCHING DOOR

4½"

⅜"

STRIKE   **LATCH**

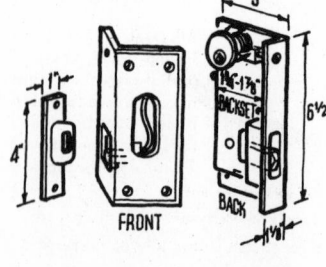

1"

4"

3"

6½"

BACKSET

1⅛"

FRONT   BACK

LOCK, Half Mortise, Latch Type
Fed. Spec. No. 197.

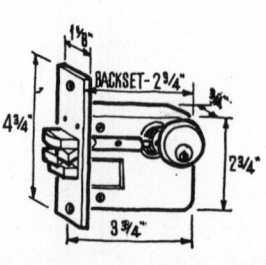

1⅛"

BACKSET - 2¾"

4¾"

2¾"

3¾"

LOCK, Mortise, Deadlock Type
Fed. Spec. No. 198.

HINGES

BUTT HINGES: See Hardware Sheets 6, 7, 8. Use removable pin (except for combination doors). Butts should be galvanized or cadmium plated steel with brass pin, or solid brass, bronze or other non-corroding metal

SPRING HINGES (See also Hardware Sheet 9)

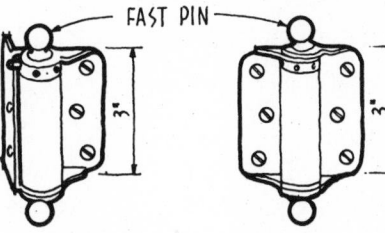

FAST PIN

LOOSE PIN   FAST PIN

ALSO AVAILABLE WITH SPRING ENCLOSED IN BARREL

HALF SURFACE ADJUSTABLE TENSION **FULL SURFACE ADJUSTABLE TENSION** **FULL SURFACE NON ADJUSTABLE**

LATCHES AND CATCHES

HOOK AND EYE
For Cabin Door Hook, see Hardware Sheet 12

PULL

SPRING CATCH

Thumb Latch can be used for these doors; see Hardware Sheet 2

MORTISE STRIKE
RIM STRIKE

RIM LATCH
Typical Backset 1½ in.

TUBULAR LATCH
Also available with rose instead of escutcheon; typical backsets: 1¼, 1⅜ in.

MORTISE LATCH
Also available with slide stop instead of dead bolt; typical backsets: 1¼, 1⅜ in.

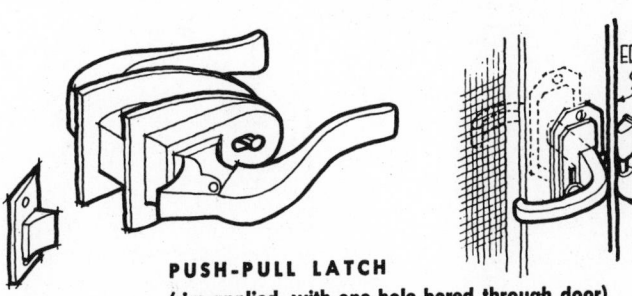

EDGE OF STOP

EDGE OF STOP

PUSH-PULL LATCH
(rim applied, with one hole bored through door)

CLOSING DEVICES

1. **SPRING HINGES** (see top of page)
2. **COIL SPRING** attached to eyes screwed to jamb and to door

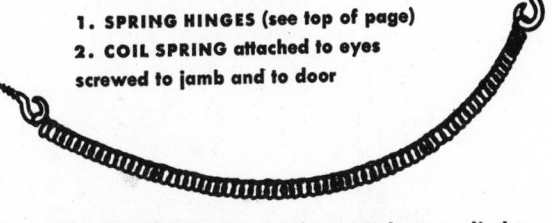

3. **LIQUID CLOSER** (Hardware Sheet 10) best applied to outside of door; parallel arm installation possible between doors if 6 in. clearance provided. This type is used for storm doors and extra heavy screens. Glass in storm doors presents large surface to wind. Strong closing action required and also stay or stop to prevent wind from opening door too far

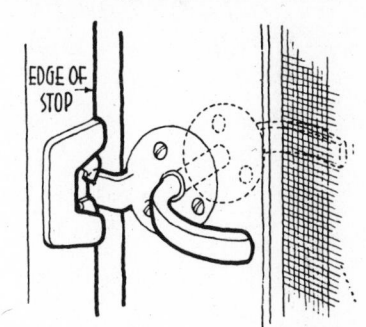

SPRING IN HOUSING

CLOSING SPEED ADJUSTMENT

RATCHET

CYLINDER

PISTON ARM

4. **PNEUMATIC CLOSER** operation similar to liquid closers (see Hardware Sheet 11), but checking element uses air instead of liquid

605

SECTION IV: ENVIRONMENTAL CONTROL

Acoustics:

Introduction 609
Definitions 610
Criteria 614
Sound absorption 616
Sound isolation 625
Auditoriums 636
Sound reinforcing systems 641
FHA requirements 644

Insulation:

Introduction 649
Definitions 649
Theory 649
Estimation of economies 650
U factors for frame walls 653
U factors for masonry walls 656
U factors for frame ceilings 658
U factors for flat roofs 658
U factors for pitched roofs 661
U factors for floors 662
FHA requirements 662
Concrete floor slabs 663

Floor slabs 665
Crawl Spaces 668

Condensation Control:

Causes 671
Design 671
Details 675
Vapor barriers—ceilings 677
Vapor barriers—attics 678
Vapor barriers—roof ventilation 679
FHA requirements 680

Residential Heating and Air Conditioning:

Furnaces 682
Outlets 683
Distribution systems 683
Duct systems 685
Summer air conditioning 688

Heating Systems for Houses:

One-pipe steam systems 691
One-pipe forced hot water systems 694
Forced hot water systems 698
Two-pipe forced hot water systems 700
Hot water baseboard systems 703
Hot water radiant systems 709
Controls for hot water radiant systems 721
Electric radiant systems 725
Use of gypsum plaster with radiant heating 729

Gas Appliances 732

Heating, Ventilating, and Air Conditioning:

Heating loads 739
Cooling loads 743
Solar loads 749
Air distribution 756
Refrigerating plant 767
Heating plant 771
Piping 776
Controls 779
Apartments 781
Hotels and motels 782
Office buildings 782
Stores 783
Eating places 785
Places of assembly 786
Schools 787
Libraries and museums 788
Hospitals 789
Industrial buildings 791
Laboratories 796
Garages 799

Unit Heaters:
    Types 801
    Heat sources 801
    Boiler capacities 801
    Characteristics 802
    Locations 802
    Selection data 802
    Capacities 803
    Controls 804
    Fresh air connections 804
    Piping connections 804
    Louvers, grilles, and deflectors 806
Incinerators:
    Apartment buildings 807
    Municipal and industrial 809
Plumbing:
    Supply and distribution:
        Piping systems 812
        House tanks 814
        Multistory zoning 815
        Domestic hot water 818
        Special distribution systems 821
Drainage systems:
    Sizing and ratings 825
    Cast-iron fittings 831
    Fixtures:
        Public facilities 840
        Industrial facilities 844
    Sewage disposal:
        Design 846
        Septic and siphon tanks 848
        Grease traps 849
        Sludge pits 851
        Distribution boxes 851
        Leaching cesspools 851
        Subsoil disposal beds 853
        Sand filters 854
Daylighting 856
Lighting:
    General 868
    Glossary 873
    Offices 875
    Industrial 885
    Schools 886
    Hospitals 893
    Churches and synagogues 894
    Stores 897
    Cinemas 904
    Hotels 906
    Residential 907
    Other building types 912
    Sports 912
    Parking areas 914
Wiring:
    Loads 915
    Hospitals 919
    Residential 923
Telephones:
    Equipment 929
Sound Systems:
    Sample specifications and definitions 930
    Design considerations 931
    Wiring symbols 932
    Churches 933
Pipe Organs:
    Churches 934
Fire Protection:
    Fire alarm systems 937
    Sprinkler systems 939
Elevators:
    Passenger 941
    Hospital 943
    Freight 944
    Hydraulic 946
Escalators 947

By ROBERT B. NEWMAN and WILLIAM J. CAVANAUGH, *Bolt Beranek and Newman Inc., Consultants in Acoustics*

INTRODUCTION

This section should help the building designer understand the basic principles of architectural acoustics and help him to design buildings in which later "correction" will be unnecessary. The proper acoustics environment for any kind of activity in a building can be determined in advance, and the necessary provisions can be made during the design.

Often acoustics problems are not recognized explicitly by the designer or owner of a building. Everyone knows, for example, that special attention to acoustics is required for an auditorium or a school of music, but too few people realize that every motel and apartment house, every office building and hospital have important acoustical problems. Many of these problems can be handled with little added expense for acoustics itself. Each element of the design and construction of a building has some influence on its acoustical characteristics, and unless all of the factors involved are clearly understood and properly incorporated during the design of the building, satisfactory results will seldom be achieved. The important thing is to understand how much and what kind of influence these various elements have.

As will be shown in this section, acoustics should influence not only the choice of finish materials in rooms, but also the basic disposition of the elements of the building—locating noisy rooms far away from quiet rooms, for example. Much expense for special noise-isolating construction can be avoided simply by using good common sense.

SOURCE, PATH, RECEIVER

Almost every acoustical situation can be described in terms of a source of sound, a path for transmission of sound, and a receiver of the sound. Sometimes the source strength can be increased or reduced, the path can be made less or more effective, and the receiver can be made more attentive by removing distraction, or he can be made more tolerant to disturbance.

If, for example, a noisy air-conditioning unit (source) bothers the occupant of an office (receiver), the problem must be analyzed in terms of what can be done about reducing the noise at the source (selection of the quietest available equipment, proper mountings, etc.), what can

be done about reducing the transmission (path) by way of structure and ducts (resilient separation, absorbent lining, etc.), and what can be done to get the receiver to tolerate a bit of noise. Attack on any single aspect of the problem may result in overdesign or an unsatisfactory solution.

BASIC PROBLEMS AND CRITERIA

Acoustics is one of the many aspects of the environment in which we live. Sounds can distract us; they can make us happy or sad. The quantity of sound we hear and its context determine the over-all effect. The loud noise of an airplane flying overhead may interfere with a telephone conversation or it may bring on a feeling of fear. Laughter in an adjoining classroom may prove quite distracting to students attending a lecture: the knowledge that something funny is going on in the next room will distract the students, although the level of sound transmitted will not interfere with the audibility of speech.

The basic purpose of architectural acoustics is to provide a *satisfactory acoustic environment* for whatever use the space is intended. In the office building the designer may wish to provide freedom from distraction or privacy for conversation. In the concert hall he may wish to provide maximum communication between the performers and the listeners, allowing the room itself to enhance the quality of the musical sounds. In almost any situation one can determine just what the environmental requirements are, and then proceed to design the building to satisfy them.

FACTORS INFLUENCING THE ACOUSTIC ENVIRONMENT

Qualities that characterize the desired acoustic environment vary widely depending on how the space is to be used, how fussy the users may be, and how the space relates to other parts of the building. A library reading room, for example, should certainly be free from distraction. This freedom can be achieved either by having the reading room quiet (forbidding all sorts of disturbing sound) or by allowing the reading room to have a moderate, continuous background sound level of an unobtrusive, unrecognizable character which hides or masks the many minor intrusions that inevitably come along (people entering and leaving, books being delivered

from the stacks, typewriters in operation, etc.). The latter is usually the more realistic approach. In a large business office one might be able to accept even more noise, but here again there are limits beyond which workers would find it difficult to perform their tasks. People usually tolerate a noise conveying no information better than they do one which tells them something about activities in an adjoining space. An expected noise is often more tolerable than an unexpected one of the same magnitude.

In addition to describing the magnitude and dynamic characteristics of the background sound, we should also describe the character of the occupied space. If a room is finished in materials which are highly sound-reflective, then sounds will persist for a long time and will seem to come from all directions; the space will probably be less pleasant than one which has a moderate amount of sound-absorptive finish. Everyone knows the experience of going into an empty house before the furniture has been put in place—how much more pleasant it is after rugs, curtains and upholstered chairs have been moved in. A room can be too "dead," however, and therefore quite oppressive. There are optimum ranges for reverberation time in occupied spaces. All these matters must be thought through carefully when planning a building.

An important aspect of the acoustic environment, often overlooked, is the opportunity to introduce a sequence of sound qualities as one goes from space to space in a building. A uniform acoustic environment throughout a building can be just as monotonous as a uniform lighting environment. It is pleasant to go from a reverberant space where this quality adds a sense of monumentality, to a "dead" space where, perhaps, communication is important, or where one may merely wish to sit down and read, or experience a feeling of enclosure and quiet. Both kinds of space gain by contrast. It is certainly to be hoped that the old specification of "acoustic tile on all ceilings" is now out-of-date!

FACTORS INFLUENCING HEARING CONDITIONS

If the environment is to be favorable to good hearing conditions

1. It must be completely quiet.
2. The desired sounds must be sufficiently loud.

3. The sounds must be well distributed through the room to give a desirable degree of acoustic uniformity, and to avoid disturbing echoes, focusing, or "islands" of low intensity.

4. The reverberation time must be long enough to give proper blending of sounds and yet be short enough so that there is no excessive overlapping and confusion.

These simple criteria, if satisfied, will result in good hearing conditions in any space. Sometimes we can use the natural sounds in the space and, by proper design of the enclosing surfaces, achieve all of the requirements for even the most weak-voiced speakers. In large or noisy spaces it may be necessary to use a carefully designed electronic sound-reinforcing system. But whatever the requirements or whatever the space, good hearing conditions *can* be achieved for any type of use. The important thing, as in all aspects of acoustics, is to recognize the problems in advance and solve them in the design stage of the project, not after it is finished.

BASIC TERMINOLOGY AND DEFINITIONS

To deal effectively with acoustics problems in building design, the architect must be familiar with some of the basic acoustical concepts and terminology. The intelligent evaluation of a product often hinges on simple matters of acoustical terminology. Obviously it is not possible to include here all of the terms and concepts that will be encountered, but it is hoped that those outlined below will cover many practical situations. (For more detailed information, refer to references cited with succeeding sections.)

TERMS DEALING WITH THE CHARACTER OF SOUND

Frequency (f): Frequency is the rate of repetition of a periodic phenomenon. Sound waves are basically periodic phenomena (for example, in air they consist of a series of compressions and rarefactions of air particles moving outward from some vibrating source and this determines the "pitch" of a sound). Frequency is basic to the description of sounds and materials to control sound. The frequency is the reciprocal of the time period, or the time necessary for the phenomenon to repeat. The unit is the cycle per second (cps).

The frequency range for the human ear extends from about 20 to about 16,000 cps for young persons with acute hearing. Some musical instruments encompass almost this entire range, notably the pipe organ.

The range of human speech which is most important for understanding extends from about 600 to about 4,000 cps. On the other hand, if we are concerned with the annoyance of speech sounds, as we might be in an office privacy situation, the lower frequency parts of the speech range may also be important, and this may extend down to about 200 cps.

Pure tone: A pure tone is the simplest kind of sound because it is composed entirely of sound waves of a single frequency. A pure tone can be generated by striking a tuning fork, but very few of the sounds around us are this "pure."

Musical tone: A musical tone is actually a combination of many pure tones. For example, striking a piano key at middle C (256 cps) would give rise to a tone composed of this fundamental frequency plus integral multiples of this frequency, called harmonics. These harmonics are what determine the quality or "timbre" of the musical tone.

Common sounds (speech, music, noise): In real life the sounds that surround us are much more complex than the simple pure tone or musical tone discussed above. These more complex sounds include speech, music, and a much wider range of sounds which we call noise if they are sounds we do not want to hear. Figure 1 shows graphically these various kinds of sounds as well as a pure tone and a musical tone.

Frequency band: For the measurement and specification of matters pertaining to sound it is often convenient to divide the audible frequency range into sections. One common division of the frequency range is into octave bands which divide the frequency range into sections centered at the following frequencies:

Octave Band Center Frequencies, cps

31.5	1,000
63	2,000
125	4,000
250	8,000

Further breakdowns of the frequency range are used for more detailed analyses of sound problems. These include ½ octave bands, ⅓ octave bands, and even smaller divisions of the frequency range.

Velocity of sound (c): A sound wave travels at a velocity that depends primarily on the elasticity and the density of the medium. In air at normal temperature and pressure the sound velocity is approximately 1,100 feet per second (fps). This is extremely slow when compared with the velocity of light, which is 186,000 miles per second.

Wavelength (λ): Knowing the velocity of sound, one can calculate at any frequency the wavelength of the sound (i.e., the dis-

tance that the sound wave travels in one cycle) by the following expression:

$$\lambda = \frac{c}{f}$$

where λ = wavelength, ft
      c = velocity of sound, fps
      f = frequency of sound, cps

A few simple calculations will reveal that high-frequency sounds are characterized by short wavelengths and low-frequency sounds by long wavelengths. For example, at 100 cps the wavelength of sound in air is about 11 ft, while at 1,000 cps the wavelength is only 1 ft.

TERMS DEALING WITH THE MAGNITUDE OF SOUND

Sound power (W): Sound power in watts describes the energy of the sound source. This power may be: (1) the total power radiated by the source over its entire frequency range; (2) the power radiated in a limited frequency range; or (3) the power radiated in each of a series of frequency bands. Obviously the frequency range of sound power (or any of the other quantities dealing with the magnitude of sound discussed below) should be clearly specified.

Sound intensity (I): The sound intensity is the power radiated in a specified direction through unit area normal to this direction; e.g., watts per square foot or watts per square centimeter. This term is analogous to light intensity.

Sound pressure (p): Under certain circumstances the sound pressure of a sound wave is equivalent to the sound intensity. The unit is the microbar (1 dyne/sq cm). Most equipment for measuring sound is pressure-sensitive, and it is usually easier to measure pressure fluctuations than intensities.

Decibels (db): The decibel is a dimensionless unit for expressing the ratio of two numerical values on a logarithmic scale. It is convenient to use decibels in dealing with sound power, sound intensity, or sound pressure because of the tremendous range of values of these quantities that can be perceived by the ear. For example, the range of sound intensities that can be perceived by the normal ear extends all the way from the faint rustle of leaves up to the roar of a jet engine, which encompasses a ratio of sound intensities from one million-million to one. The number of decibels is ten times the logarithm to the base 10 of the numerical ratio of the two quantities. For example, let W_1 and W_2 designate two powers, or I_1 and I_2 designate two sound intensities, and p_1

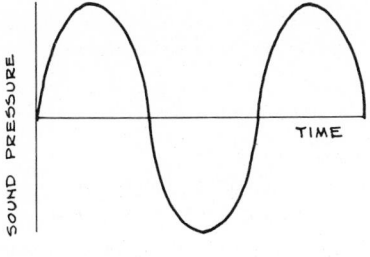

TUNING FORK (PURE TONE)

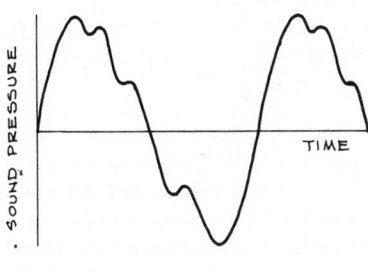

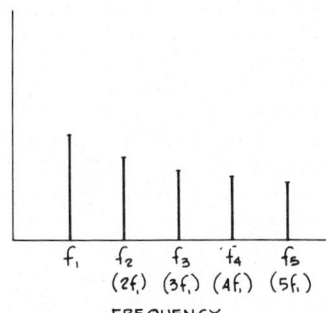

f_1 f_2 f_3 f_4 f_5
$(2f_1)$ $(3f_1)$ $(4f_1)$ $(5f_1)$

FREQUENCY

MUSICAL NOTE (COMBINATION OF SEVERAL PURE TONES)

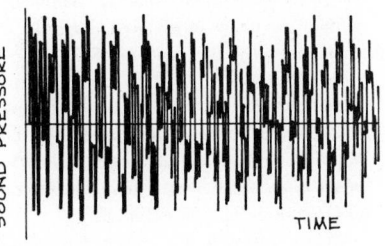

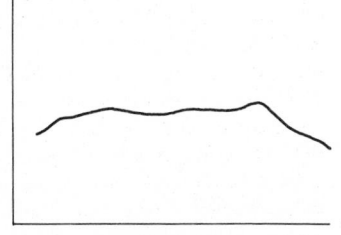

SPEECH, MUSIC, NOISE

Fig. 1. Schematic representations of a pure tone, a musical note, and more complex sounds (speech, music, and noise), showing the variation of sound pressure with time and frequency

and p_2 designate two pressures, then the corresponding number of decibels (M in each case) is

$$M \text{ (sound power)} = 10 \log \frac{W_1}{W_2} \text{ (decibels)}$$

$$M \text{ (sound intensity)} = 10 \log \frac{I_1}{I_2} \text{ (decibels)}$$

$$M \text{ (sound pressure)} =$$
$$10 \log \left(\frac{p_1}{p_2}\right)^2 \text{ (decibels)}$$

A chart converting ratios of any two quantities to the decibel scale is given in Fig. 2.

Addition of decibels: Decibels, since they are logarithmic units and not like ordinary units such as feet and pounds, cannot be added directly. One must convert back to power, intensity, or pressure, add these quantities, and finally convert the total

back to decibels. In other words, 50 db plus 50 db is not 100 db but rather 53 db. A simplified chart for adding quantities in decibels is given in Fig. 3.

Sound-power level (PWL): Sound-power level is the designation in decibels of the ratio of two sound powers. In the English systems the reference power is usually taken to be 10^{-13} watt. Therefore,

$$PWL = 10 \log \left(\frac{W}{10^{-13}}\right) \text{ decibels}$$

Sound-intensity level (IL): Sound-intensity level is the designation in decibels of the ratio of two intensities. The reference intensity is usually taken to be 10^{-16} watt/sq cm. Therefore,

$$IL = 10 \log \left(\frac{I}{10^{-16}}\right) \text{ decibels}$$

Sound-pressure level (SPL): Sound-pres-

sure level is the designation in decibels of the ratio of two pressures squared. The reference value is always taken to be 0.0002 dynes/sq. cm. Therefore,

$$SPL = 10 \log \left(\frac{P}{0.0002}\right)^2 \text{ decibels}$$

As stated above, under some circumstances sound pressure can be taken to be equivalent to sound intensity. For most architectural acoustics problems, then, the sound-pressure level can be considered equivalent to the sound-intensity level. Some typical measured sound-pressure levels are shown in Figs. 4 and 5.

Sound level: Simple sound-measuring devices are available to record the physical magnitude of sound in terms of single numbers. Single-number sound levels are defined as the quantity read on a standard sound-level meter with an appropriate frequency-weighting network. A commonly used system of single numbers are A-scale readings which, for relatively low over-all sound levels, correspond to the way our ear responds to the sound (i.e., they weight or "ignore" the low-frequency end of the sound spectrum). The frequency-weighting network must always be known in order to evaluate single-number readings. Fig. 6 shows the range of some common sounds measured in terms of average levels obtained from sound-level meter readings, using standard A-, B-, and C-scale frequency-weighting networks.

Noise reduction (NR): Noise reduction is the difference in decibels of the sound-pressure levels or the sound-intensity levels at two points along a sound path. Alternatively, it is the difference in decibels of the sound-pressure levels or sound-intensity levels existing at a single point before and after a change of acoustical treatment to a space. Therefore, the following expressions are often used:

$$NR = IL_1 - IL_2 \text{ (decibels)}$$
$$NR = SPL_1 - SPL_2 \text{ (decibels)}$$

Attenuation: Attenuation is often used in the same sense as noise reduction described above.

SOUND UNDER FREE-FIELD CONDITIONS

Inverse square law: Under free-field conditions of sound radiation (i.e., no reflecting surfaces around the sound source) the sound intensity is reduced by ¼ each time the distance from the sound source is doubled. This is expressed as follows:

$$\frac{I_1}{I_2} = \frac{d_2{}^2}{d_1{}^2}$$

where I_1 and I_2 are the sound intensities at distances d_1, and d_2 from the sound source. This phenomenon is analogous to the reduction of light intensity as one moves away from a source of light under free-field conditions. In terms of sound levels (*IL* or *SPL*) the inverse square law means that the level is decreased by 6 db each time the distance from the source is doubled.

SOUND IN ROOMS

Reflection and absorption: When a sound source is placed within an enclosure, reflection of the sound wave traveling outward from the sound source occurs at the boundaries, and the sound waves continue to reflect between the boundaries themselves. If the sound source is continuous, this reflection of sound will establish relatively constant levels within a normal-sized room (except very near the source). These "built-up" or reverberant levels are dependent on the amount of absorption of the sound energy that takes place at each encounter of the sound wave with the enclosing surface. Most hard surfaces (concrete, plaster, glass, etc.) absorb very little sound and are generally classed as sound-reflecting surfaces. Other materials (usually porous, or thin panel materials) absorb appreciable amounts of sound and are termed sound-absorbing material (see section on "Criteria for the Acoustic Environment").

Sound-absorption coefficient (α): The absorption coefficient is the fraction of incident sound energy that is absorbed by a surface. Random incidence of the impinging sound is assumed unless otherwise specified.

Absorption units (*A*): Absorption units are usually expressed in sabins and equal the square foot area of a surface S times its absorption coefficient α. Usually several kinds of surfaces or materials are included in a room, and the total absorption is the sum of the areas times their absorption coefficients.

Noise-reduction coefficient (*NRC*): The noise-reduction coefficient for a sound-absorbing material is the arithmetic average of the absorption coefficients at 250, 500, 1,000, 2,000, and 4,000 cps.

Dead room: A dead room is one characterized by large amounts of absorption.

Live room: A live room is one characterized by very small amounts of absorption.

Room noise reduction (*NR*): The intensity levels or sound-pressure levels in a room built up by repeated reflections of sound from the enclosing surfaces are affected by the amount of absorption present. The difference in levels given by two conditions of total room absorption is as follows:

$$NR = 10 \log \left(\frac{A_2}{A_1} \right) \text{ (decibels);}$$

where A_1 and A_2 are the total absorbing units in sabins in the room before and after treatment.

Reverberation: Reverberation is the persistence of sound after the source of sound has stopped. It is due to the repeated reflections of the sound between the enclosing surfaces even after this source has stopped.

Reverberation time (*T*): The reverberation time of a room is by definition the time required for the sound level to decrease 60 db after the source is stopped. The reverberation time is given approximately by the following expression:

$$T = 0.5 \frac{V}{A} \text{ (sec)}$$

where V = volume of the space, cu ft

A = total room absorption, sabins

Diffusion: Ideally a diffuse sound field is one in which the sound level is everywhere the same. Diffusion is a desirable characteristic for many listening spaces (see section on "Design For Good Hearing").

Echo: An echo is a sound wave reflected or otherwise returned with sufficient magnitude and delay so as to be perceived as a sound distinct from another directly transmitted sound.

Flutter echo: A flutter echo is a rapid succession of reflected sound waves resulting from a single initial sound pulse. This effect often occurs with a sound source between two hard parallel walls.

Creep: Creep is the reflection of sound along a curved surface. It occurs when a

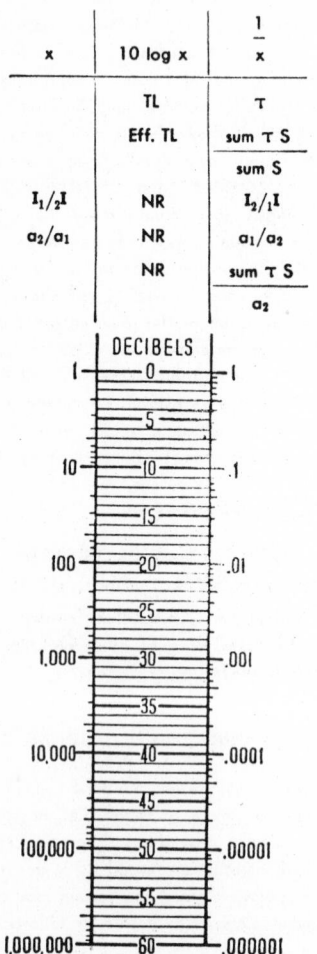

Fig. 2. A decibel calculation chart
With values X or 1/x known, the value of 10 log X can be determined immediately.

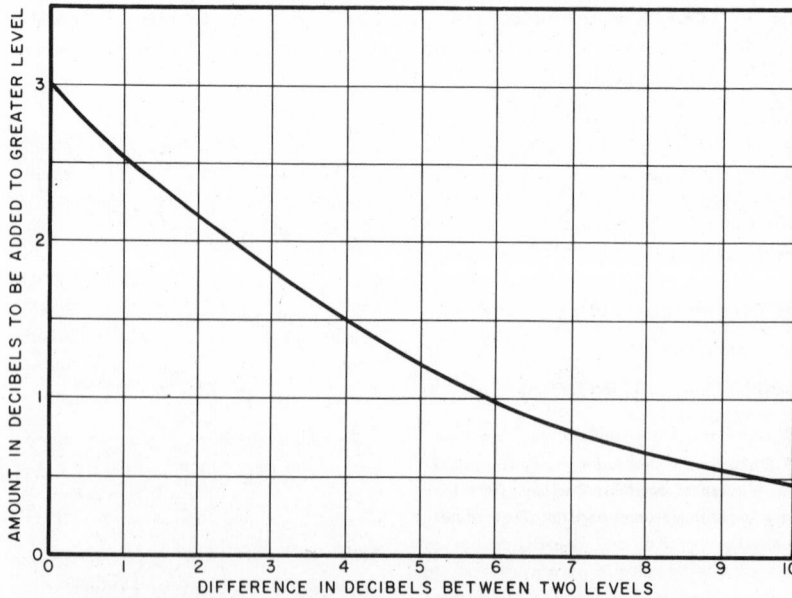

Fig. 3. Chart for adding two sound-pressure levels (*SPL*) or intensity levels (*IL*)

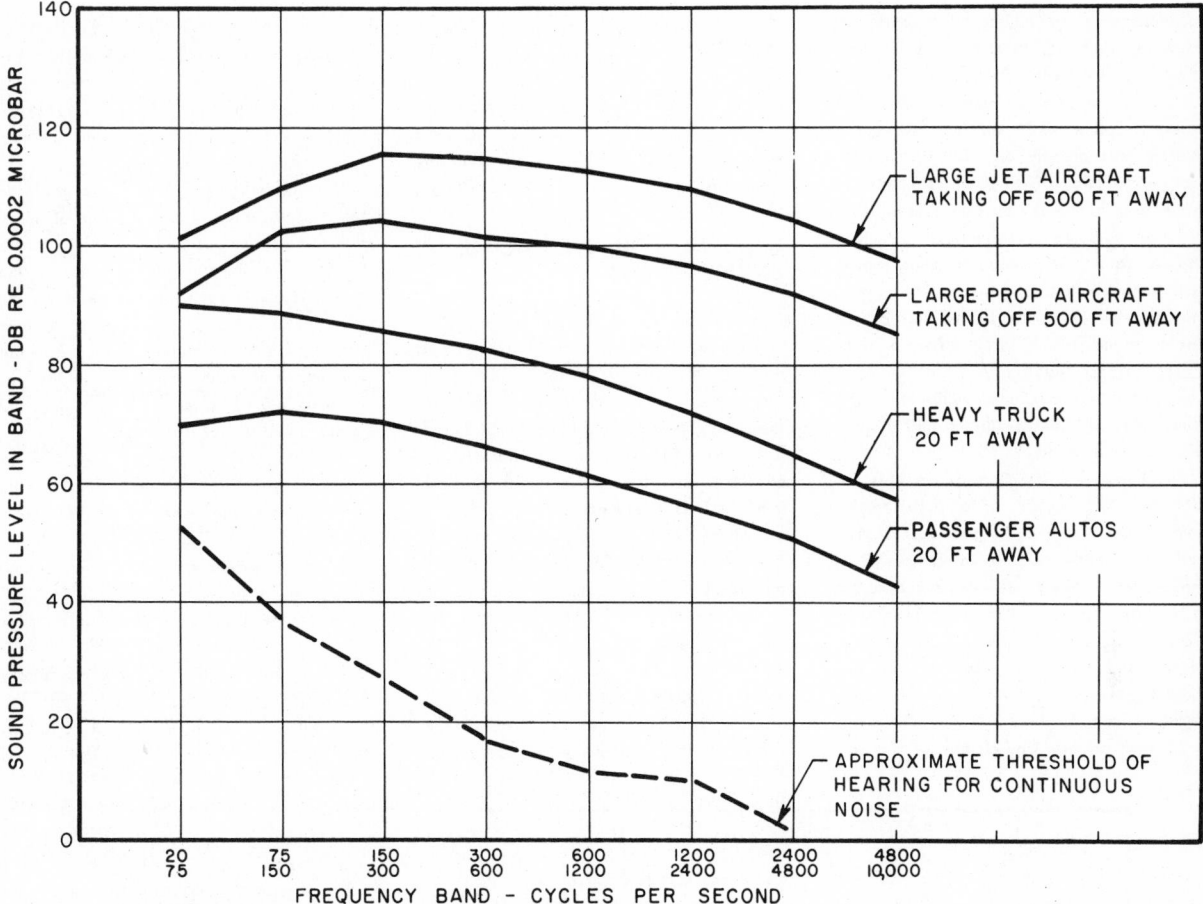

Fig. 4. Sound-pressure levels for some noise sources; measured outdoors

sound source is located close to surfaces such as domes, vaults, etc., so that the reflected sound energy is conserved and can be heard distinctively at some point further along the surface; for example, a "whispering gallery" (see Fig. 37).

Focusing: Focusing occurs when sound waves are reflected from concave surfaces and build up the reflected sound levels at some point or area away from the reflecting surface.

Standing waves: In small rooms, in particular, sound waves can build up nodes and antinodes which are characterized by regions of maximum sound-pressure level and minimum sound-pressure level. Standing-wave effects are usually restricted to the low-frequency range.

SOUND TRANSMISSION BETWEEN ROOMS

Transmission coefficient (τ): The transmission coefficient is the fraction of incident energy that is transmitted through a barrier. Thus

$$\tau = \frac{W_2}{W_1}$$

where W_1 is the sound energy in watts incident on the barrier and W_2 is the sound energy in watts transmitted.

Transmission loss (TL): The transmission loss of a barrier is given by the following expression:

$$TL = 10 \log \frac{1}{\tau} \text{ (decibels)}$$

It is a basic property of a barrier and varies with the frequency of the impinging sound, the surface weight, stiffness, and edge-mounting condition of the barrier.

Effective transmission loss (Eff TL): The effective transmission loss of a barrier consisting of two or more different materials is given by the following expression:

$$Eff\ TL = 10 \log \frac{\Sigma S}{\Sigma \tau S} \text{ (decibels)},$$

where ΣS is the sum of the areas of the parts of the barrier in square feet, and $\Sigma \tau S$ is the areas of materials times their respective transmission coefficients.

Average transmission loss (Ave TL): The arithmetic average of the transmission-loss values measured at several frequencies. This

is an arbitrary rating method not recommended for engineering calculations.

Sound transmission class (STC): A single number rating assigned to a measured transmission-loss curve obtained by comparison to a standard curve in accordance with recommended rules given in ASTM E90-61T (see also discussion in section on "Sound Isolation").

Room-to-room noise reduction (NR): The difference in sound-intensity levels (IL) or sound-pressure levels (SPL) between any two rooms is given approximately by the following expression:

$$NR = TL - 10 \log \frac{S}{A_2} \text{ (decibels)},$$

where TL is the effective transmission loss of the barrier in decibels, S is the total area of the barrier in square feet, and A is the total absorption in the receiving room in sabins.

Attenuation factor: Attenuation factor is sometimes used to describe the room-to-room noise reduction of a particular construction. For example, the noise reduction values through suspended ceiling configurations over two adjacent test rooms are reported in terms of attenuations in decibels (see section on "Sound isolation").

Impact transmission: Impact transmission usually occurs when an impulsive sound source acts directly on the structure and causes radiation of air-borne sound on the other side of the structure in question.

Structure-borne transmission: Structure-borne transmission refers to sound waves transmitted within a structure. These structure-borne waves may be induced by air-borne sound impinging on a barrier or by direct impact sound sources. If the structure-borne waves are of sufficient magnitude, they may be reradiated into a space as air-borne sound.

Background noise: Background noise refers to the ambient or all-encompassing noise associated with a given environment and is usually due to a composite of sounds from many sources near and far.

Masking noise: Masking noise usually refers to the ability of background noise to cover up some other specific intruding sound. This is also referred to as "acoustical perfume."

Speech privacy: Speech privacy is a condition of sound isolation of a room in which the occupant feels he has sufficient freedom from intruding speech sounds, so that he can conduct his work in an undisturbed manner. This is usually achieved when the speech levels transmitted to the space are unintelligible or very nearly so.

CRITERIA FOR THE ACOUSTIC ENVIRONMENT

Before the designer can begin actual engineering work on a building, he must establish his criteria. Basically, a satisfactory acoustic environment is one in which the character and magnitude of all sounds are compatible with the satisfactory use of the space for its intended purpose. While this is a reasonable objective, it is not always easy to express it in quantitative terms. In talking about the thermal environment, for example, one cannot simply say that 70°F is comfortable but must also talk about humidity, air movement, etc. In lighting, one cannot simply say that 100 foot-candles is an ideal light intensity but must also talk about other factors in the luminous environment, such as specular glare, color, continuity, etc. Similarly in acoustics, we cannot just say how much noise we want but rather we must specify what kind of noise, what pitch, whether it is continuous, expected, or contains information, etc.

Human beings are highly adaptable to the various physical phenomena of heat, light, and sound, and their sensitivity varies widely. The human ear can detect the sound-intensity levels of less than 10 db (the gentle rustle of leaves) and yet can survive without permanent hearing damage the powerful roar of a jet engine—as much as 120 db, a million-million times the intensity of the leaf rustle sound.

Psychologists and research workers in acoustics have laid a good deal of the ground work that enables us to understand how much and what kind of noise will affect speech communication, annoyance, and fatigue. Work has also been done on the problem of hearing damage due to high-intensity noise levels, but this is seldom an important problem in ordinary buildings. Although the research results are far from complete, they do lead us to certain generally accepted specifications on

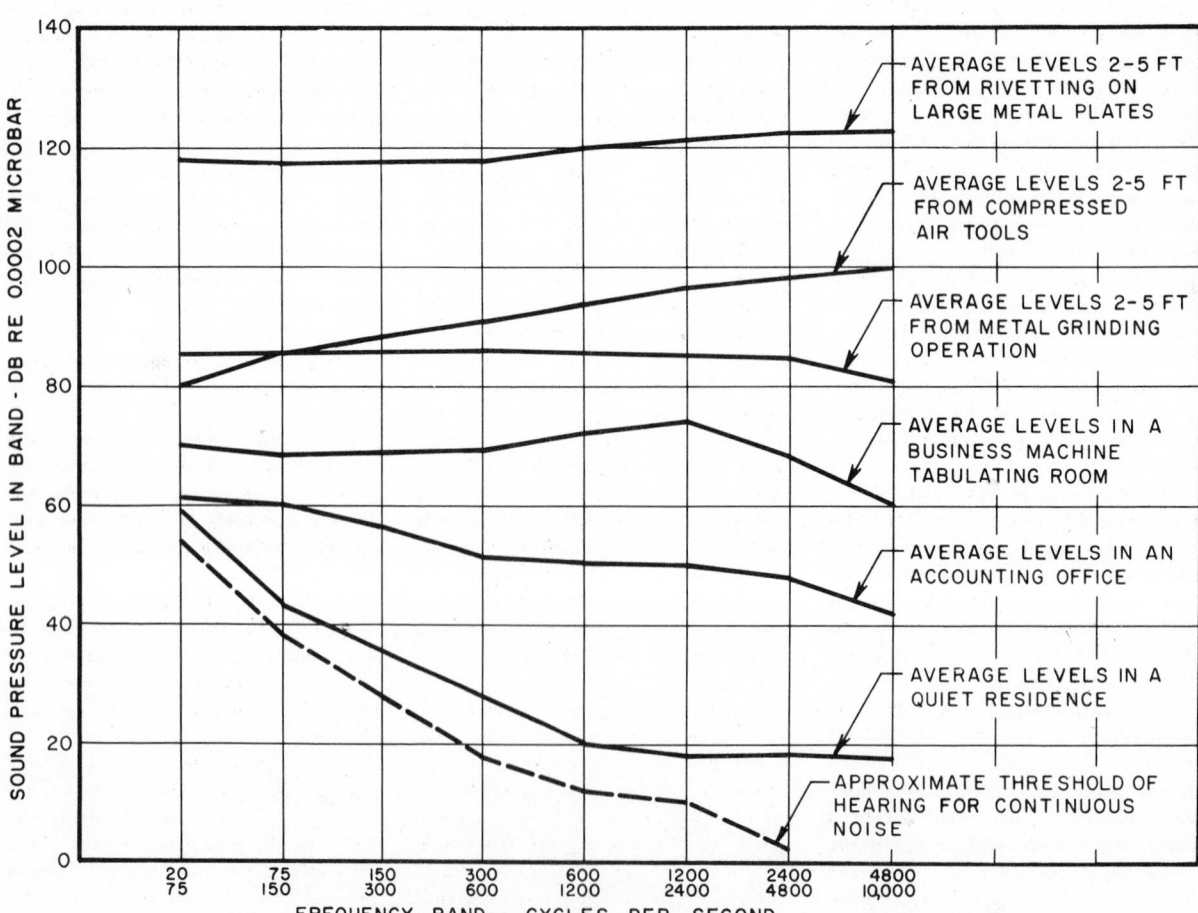

Fig. 5. Sound-pressure levels for some noise sources; measured indoors

the noise environment in many of the kinds of spaces we design.

BACKGROUND NOISE CRITERIA

Although over-all single-number sound-level readings give us some idea of how much noise we have, a much better method of specifying continuous background noise level is the use of the so-called noise criteria (NC) curves (see Fig. 7). This method provides a system of rank-ordering various noise levels in terms of specified sound-pressure levels in each of eight octave frequency bands. Octave bands are convenient for dividing the audible frequency range into sections for purposes of measurement. The NC numbers are the arithmetic average of the sound-pressure levels in the 600 to 1,200 cps, 1,200 to 2,400 cps, and 2,400 to 4,800 cps bands. These frequency bands are very closely related to the important frequencies for speech intelligibility. Thus, the presence of noise in these bands can interfere with speech.

Also shown in Fig. 7 is the subjective evaluation that a listener might give to a particular acoustic environment that has octave band sound levels approximating these curves. Below NC-25, for example, most people would judge a space "very quiet," above NC-55 "very noisy," and between these extremes "quiet," "moderately noisy," and "noisy." In terms of speech communication, a background sound spectrum of NC-30 would permit understanding of speech at normal voice levels at distances up to about 20 ft. An NC-40 spectrum level would require a raised voice to be understood at 20 ft but would only permit normal voice communication at distances up to about 6 ft. With a background spectrum of NC-50 a raised voice would be required to be heard clearly at more than 3 ft between speaker and listener. Even higher spectra than NC-50 would be permissible in a factory where speech communication and annoyance are not too important. However, if the continuous background noise levels exceed NC-70, it is impossible to use the telephone, and with spectrum levels as high as NC-80, there may be a possibility of permanent hearing damage after long exposure.

Some recommended noise criteria for various types of occupancy are indicated in Table 1.

As one might expect, spaces where listening is important require low background levels, and business offices and factories where speech communication is restricted to short distances can have higher background levels.

It should be emphasized that we are

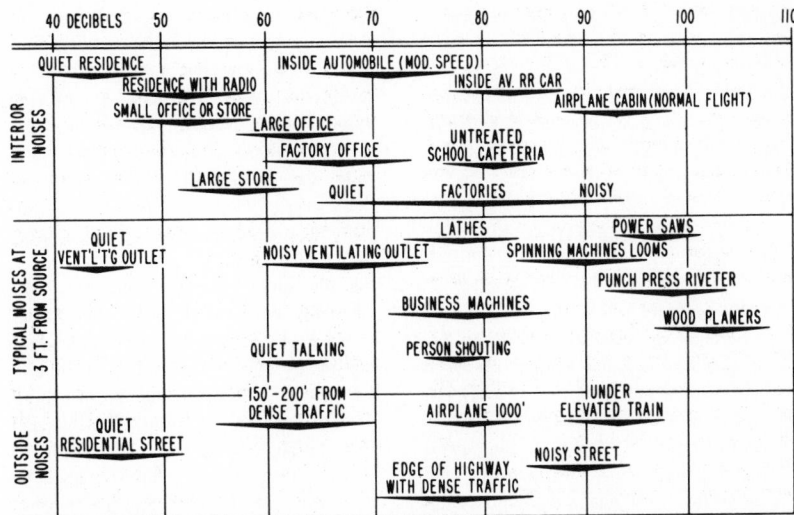

Fig. 6. Average ("single-number") sound levels for typical noises from sound-level meter readings

These values give a measure of the sound level in the frequency range important to the ear. Many of these noise sources cannot be pinned down to specific values; so the tapered lines indicate the range over which they may vary. Single-number sound-level readings must be used with caution when analyzing noise problems.

often just as interested in the minimum as in the maximum permissible levels as described in Table 1. In an office or even in a residence it may be desirable to have a certain amount of "acoustical perfume" to assure adequate acoustical privacy between spaces, and it may well be that our NC curve would be used to specify the bottom limit of background noise levels as well as the maximum. For example, in a small private office the occupant may not object to the noise of a continuous background sound spectrum as high as NC-35 or NC-40. Often, such a background spectrum is provided by the ventilating system in the building. If the ventilating system will not make enough noise, a noisier grille may be selected so that adequate privacy is will, in order to be sure that privacy is achieved with the lightweight, movable wall construction separating one office from another. In other words, while we do not want the background noise to exceed a specified criterion spectrum, at the same time we do not want it to fall much below this spectrum.

In an auditorium, however, where we do not need any "acoustical perfume," we would be quite happy if even lower sound levels than the design goal of NC-20 were met. But there would be no point in spending a lot of money to reach lower background levels because the spectrum NC-20 already represents a very acceptable level and ordinary audience noises will probably exceed it.

The ASHRAE Guide in its chapter on Sound Control describes in detail methods for calculating noise levels due to air-handling equipment and also considers in greater detail the criteria for background level design. With the information provided in the *Guide* and in the manufacturers' literature the architect today is in an excellent position to specify the acoustic environment and then to select the proper materials and equipment to meet the design goals.

CRITERIA FOR SPEECH PRIVACY BETWEEN OFFICES

As will be pointed out below, speech privacy between rooms is determined not only by the transmission loss of the separating partitions, but also by the background noise in the spaces. In the special situation of office privacy, we can give some approximate recommendations for the transmission loss that must be provided by the partitions for particular background noise conditions. These criteria, giving the required transmission loss as a function of frequency in ⅓ octave bands, are shown in Fig. 8. The subjective ratings of background noise correspond with those shown in Fig. 7. It must be carefully noted, however, that Fig. 8 gives approximate criteria values for transmission loss and assumes average levels of speech effort in the adjacent office, and that the office occupant expects average privacy (not complete

By ROBERT B. NEWMAN and WILLIAM J. CAVANAUGH, *Bolt Beranek and Newman Inc., Consultants in Acoustics*

secrecy). More detailed analysis and design procedures are covered in the *Speech Privacy Analyzer* (see "References" in section on "Sound isolation").

CRITERIA FOR REVERBERATION IN ROOMS

Every occupied space has some sort of reverberation characteristic. It may be live or it may be dead but there is always a certain amount of return of energy reflected from distant surfaces to the listener that gives him a "feel" of the space. There are no criteria for exactly what reverberation time one should have in a house or in an office but experience shows that, unless such occupied spaces are furnished or finished with reasonable amounts of sound-absorbing material, they will not be comfortable. The next section contains a discussion of the procedure for calculating reverberation time in a space as well as the effect of the amounts of sound-absorbing treatment in a room on the general sound level in the room. However, the quality of the sound in the space is usually a more important factor than the absolute level, at least within the ordinary range of interest. Sound-absorbing treatment in a space reduces the spreading of sound and localizes the direction of

sources: sounds do not seem to come from everywhere, and the annoyance level from all sorts of noise sources is less. In a restaurant sound-absorbing materials to reduce reverberation time are very important in making an acceptable acoustic environment. With hard surfaces in such spaces the din often becomes unbearable, and corrective measures must be taken later. In the house with an open plan and sparse furnishings some sound-absorbing material on floor or ceiling surfaces can do a great deal to improve the acoustic environment.

In larger rooms where hearing is important, we can put definite numbers on the range of reverberation times which seem to most listeners to be satisfactory. A small conference room or lecture room used primarily for speech needs a relatively low reverberation time in order to achieve high articulation and separation of successive sounds for maximum audibility. At the other end of the scale is the large cathedral church where liturgical music is of major importance and where the audibility of a sermon can be handled with a carefully designed sound-reinforcing system and where maximum blending of the musical sounds must be the criterion for design. Between these extremes lie the whole range of types of performance. In general, the reverberation time of an audi-

torium of any size should lie somewhere between 1 and 2 sec for best results. In general, the larger the hall, the longer the reverberation time must be for satisfactory listening conditions. But for every situation there is considerable latitude in the choice of a design reverberation time that will give satisfaction. In Fig. 9 we show the range of reverberation times generally considered acceptable for various types of use. The preferred range for most uses is shown as a black bar for the given function, and is extended with the dotted sections showing what might be called the extremes of acceptability. An auditorium which must serve many functions must somehow be designed with a compromise reverberation time which perhaps can be altered with changes in surface finish, or room volume to accommodate functions demanding more or less reverberation than the basic design provides. A chart such as this should be considered only a guide for design, and the selection of the criterion for each particular situation should be considered very carefully in the light of the actual proposed uses of the space.

SOUND ABSORPTION

The architect is concerned with the amount of sound absorption in a space for any or all of the following purposes:

1. To reduce noise levels (noise control)
2. To shorten or prolong reverberation (reverberation control)
3. To eliminate echo (echo control), or other undesirable sound reflections (focusing or flutter control)

For example, in a typical school classroom, noise control (i.e., the reduction of activity noise levels built up by repeated reflections of sound from the room surfaces) may be just as important as reverberation control (the avoidance of excessive persistence of reflected sound after the source has stopped). In the latter case, excessive reverberation would result in overlapping of successive syllables and make speech difficult to understand. In a concert hall design, on the other hand, the architect may avoid introducing any sound absorption besides that provided by the audience itself, in order to achieve the longest possible reverberation time. Even the inclusion of sound-absorbing material for echo control may prove undesirable in a concert hall. A preferable solution may be to redesign any offending surfaces so

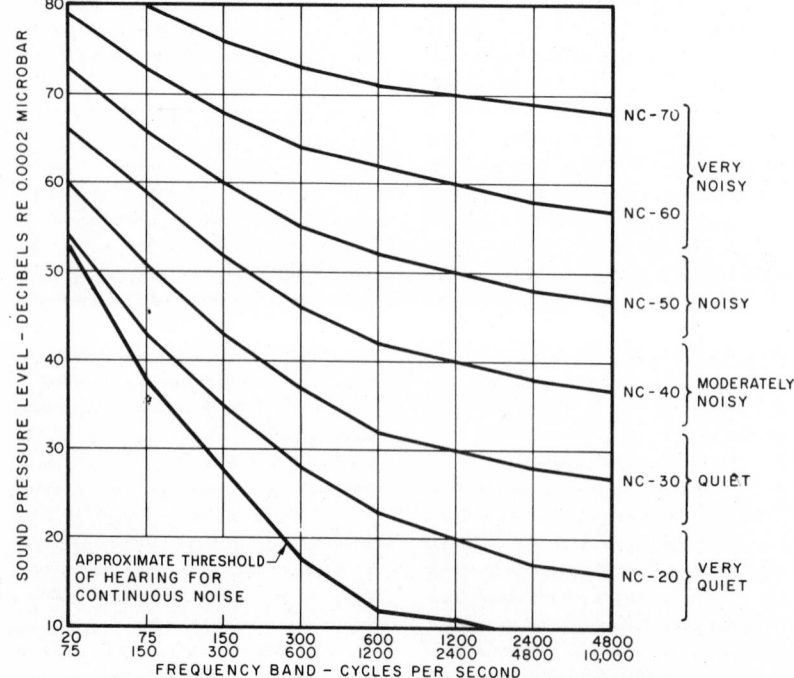

Fig. 7. Noise criteria (NC) curves

that the reflected sound is redirected and no longer heard as a discrete echo.

Thus, the first job of the designer is to determine which of these requirements must be met in the space and to what extent; that is, as in every acoustics problem, the design objective must be clearly defined. The success in meeting these objectives depends largely upon the designer's knowledge and skill in the selection and use of materials.

It should be emphasized that the principal uses of sound-absorbing materials are for the control of sound *within* a space and not for the control of sound transmission between spaces. There is much confusion on this point and much disappointment has resulted from the misapplication of sound "insulating" materials to room surfaces or in the stud space of some partition constructions. Such use of sound-absorbing material often makes no significant difference in the sound transmission between spaces. For the most part, sound-absorbing materials, especially porous lightweight ones, offer little resistance to sound transmission. There are, however, some new specially designed materials (suspended acoustical tile ceilings in particular) which act as both sound absorbers and sound-reducing barriers. (These combination materials will be discussed in the section on Sound Isolation.") However, in general, one should view cautiously any "cure-alls" which promise to solve all acoustics problems with a single homogeneous material of practically no thickness.

THE BASIC MECHANISM OF SOUND ABSORPTION

All materials and objects in a space where a sound field exists absorb some of the sound incident upon their surfaces. Porous, fibrous materials such as carpets, draperies, upholstered furniture, and clothing, and specially designed sound-absorbing materials are capable of appreciable sound absorption (that is, they do not reflect very much of the sound energy which strikes them). Impervious, thin, flexible panels (plywood, etc.) absorb sound also, but their effectiveness is usually limited to the low-frequency range of the audible spectrum. By contrast with these absorbers, most common building materials (brick, concrete, glass, plaster, etc.) are very poor sound absorbers and most often absorb less than 5 per cent of the incident sound energy in the frequency range of interest. In fact, these latter materials may be classified as sound-reflecting materials and can be used effectively in auditorium design to distribute the desired sounds properly.

Table 1. Recommended noise criteria for rooms

Type of space	Recommended noise criterion curve	Computed equivalent sound-level meter readings (A-scale readings in db)
Broadcast studios	NC-15–25	25–35
Concert halls	NC-20	30
Legitimate theaters (no amplification)	NC-20–25	30–35
Music rooms	NC-25	35
School rooms	NC-25	35
Large conference & board rooms (for about 50 or more people)	NC-25	35
Apartments and hotels	NC-25–35	35–45
Assembly halls (with amplification)	NC-25–30	35–40
Homes (sleeping areas)	NC-25–35	35–45
Conference room (for 20 or less)	NC-30	40
Motion picture theaters	NC-30	40
Churches	NC-20–25	30–35
Courtrooms	NC-30	40
Libraries	NC-30–40	40–50
Hospitals	NC-30–40	40–50
Small private offices	NC-30–40	40–50
Restaurants, stores	NC-40–50	50–60
Sports coliseums (amplification)	NC-50	60
General offices (typing & business machines)	NC-40–50	50–60
Factories	NC-40–65	50–75

Sound absorption results when the impinging sound energy is converted to heat energy in the body of the absorber (although the amount of heat is quite small). In the porous type of sound absorber this occurs as the pressure of the air increases and decreases with the arrival of successive sound waves causing the air molecules near the porous surface to migrate into the labyrinth of capillary-like tunnels in rapid to-and-fro motion. Part of the acoustical energy is thus converted to heat by frictional drag. The amount of friction, and hence absorption, provided by the material is, of course, determined by the actual physical properties of the porous layer:

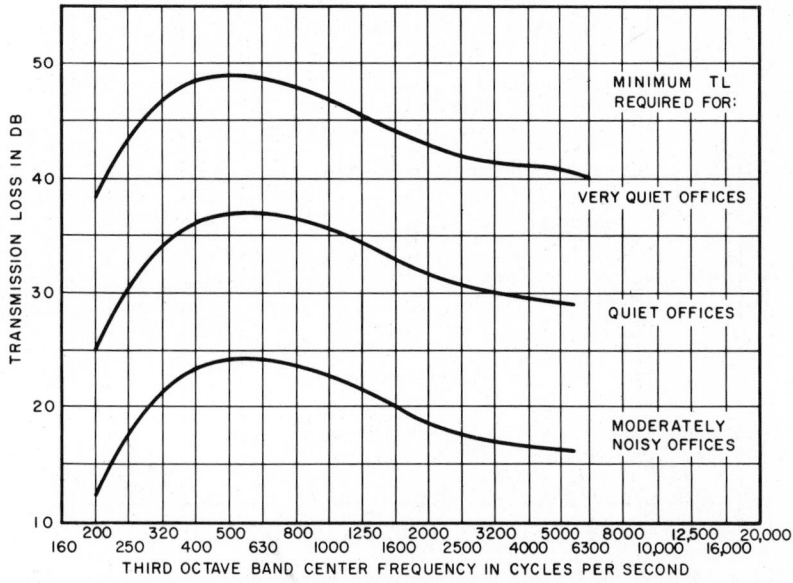

Fig. 8. Approximate transmission-loss criteria for speech privacy between offices

thickness, density, porosity, the orientation of the fibers or passageways, and, of prime importance, the resistance the material offers to the passage of air. The careful design and control of these parameters is the domain of the acoustical researcher and manufacturer. However, it is important for the architect to have some basic understanding of what is involved in absorption by the porous materials that are most commonly used. Only then can he understand why a very thin layer of a so-called "acoustical paint" cannot possibly absorb sound efficiently where, on the other hand, a carefully designed perforated thin sheet material such as that used for sound-absorbing luminous ceiling applications can be an effective sound absorber. But even with these latter materials the ab-

sorption depends on the material in combination with the enclosed air volume behind, and in this context they may actually be thought of as "thick" materials.

With thin, impervious, flexible panels, absorption results when the surface is set in to-and-fro flexural motion by the alternating pressure of the impinging sound wave, and part of the sound energy is converted to heat through internal viscous damping. Few panel absorbers are manufactured and marketed as such, and the architect must rely on the information published in acoustical texts for the effect such materials may have on his room design. Broadly speaking, however, the absorption of thin panels is confined primarily to the low-frequency range.

Another type of absorber called the

volume resonator (or Helmholtz resonator, in honor of its discoverer) uses a restrained volume of air with a small opening or tunnel exposed to the impinging sound wave. This type of absorber has somewhat specialized and limited uses in architectural acoustics but may be carefully designed into a particular room to give effective absorption at particular frequencies. Of course, volume resonators of varying sizes may be distributed throughout the room to give absorption over a wider frequency range. The basic absorption mechanism is, however, the conversion of sound energy to heat by frictional drag of the air molecules in and around the neck leading to the restrained volume of the air behind.

Figure 10 shows the three basic types of sound absorption and their relative characteristics in terms of absorption coefficients.

SOUND-ABSORPTION COEFFICIENT

The effectiveness of any material as a sound absorber is given by its absorption coefficients over the frequency range of interest. The sound-absorption coefficient α describes the fraction of the incident sound energy that the material absorbs. For most architectural materials the coefficients given are those for random incidence of the impinging sound. Theoretically, the coefficient can vary from 0 (no sound absorption) to 1.0 (all the incident sound is absorbed), but practically speaking, all materials lie between these extremes. The most commonly used frequencies for reporting the sound-absorption coefficient are the following: 125, 250, 500 1,000, 2,000, and 4,000 cps. Table 2 lists the absorption coefficients for many common building materials and furnishings as well as for audience and seats. Most of these coefficients have either been derived from laboratory measurements or calculated from measurements in finished rooms. These coefficients are not absolute and may vary in actual practice by as much as 5 or 10 per cent for a given material depending upon different methods of applying the material, amounts of material used or variation sample characteristics and other factors.

A bulletin published annually by the Acoustical Materials Association (AMA) presents the sound-absorption coefficients for a great many products specially designed and manufactured to give efficient absorption. This association, comprising many manufacturers of sound-absorbing products for architectural uses, publishes data obtained only by standard testing procedures to insure that the published coefficients are directly comparable with each other.

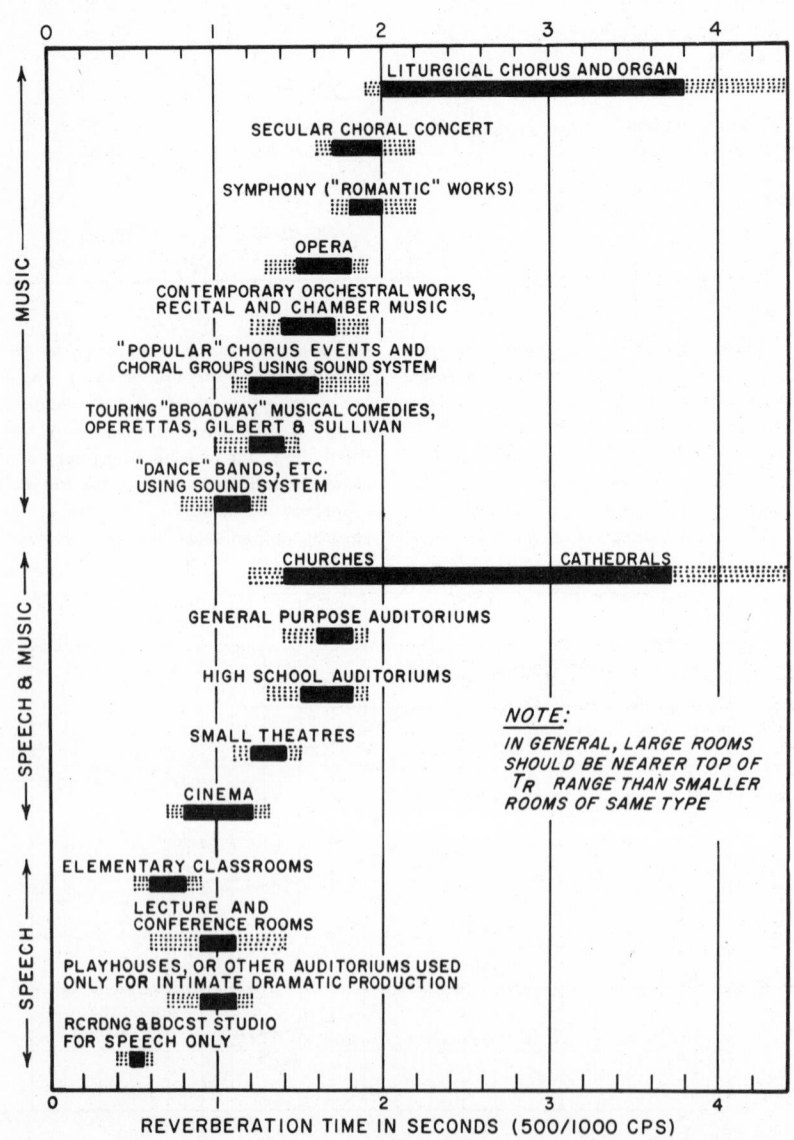

Fig. 9. A guide for determining optimum mid-frequency (500–1,000 cps) reverberation time

Table 2. Coefficients of general building materials and furnishings*

Complete tables of coefficients of the various materials that normally constitute the interior finish of rooms may be found in the various books on architectural acoustics. The following short list will be useful in making simple calculations of the reverberation in rooms.

Materials	Coefficients					
	125 cps	250 cps	500 cps	1,000 cps	2,000 cps	4,000 cps
Brick, unglazed	0.03	0.03	0.03	0.04	0.05	0.07
Brick, unglazed, painted	0.01	0.01	0.02	0.02	0.02	0.03
Carpet, heavy, on concrete	0.02	0.06	0.14	0.37	0.60	0.65
Same, on 40-oz hairfelt or foam rubber	0.08	0.24	0.57	0.69	0.71	0.73
Same, with impermeable latex backing on 40-oz hairfelt or foam rubber	0.08	0.27	0.39	0.34	0.48	0.63
Concrete block, coarse	0.36	0.44	0.31	0.29	0.39	0.25
Concrete block, painted	0.10	0.05	0.06	0.07	0.09	0.08
Fabrics						
Light velour, 10 oz per sq yd, hung straight, in contact with wall	0.03	0.04	0.11	0.17	0.24	0.35
Medium velour, 14 oz per sq yd, draped to half area	0.07	0.31	0.49	0.75	0.70	0.60
Heavy velour, 18 oz per sq yd, draped to half area	0.14	0.35	0.55	0.72	0.70	0.65
Floors						
Concrete or terrazzo	0.01	0.01	0.015	0.02	0.02	0.02
Linoleum, asphalt, rubber or cork tile on concrete	0.02	0.03	0.03	0.03	0.03	0.02
Wood	0.15	0.11	0.10	0.07	0.06	0.07
Wood parquet in asphalt on concrete	0.04	0.04	0.07	0.06	0.06	0.07
Glass						
Large panes of heavy plate glass	0.18	0.06	0.04	0.03	0.02	0.02
Ordinary window glass	0.35	0.25	0.18	0.12	0.07	0.04
Gypsum board, ½ in. nailed to 2 x 4's 16 in. o.c.	0.29	0.10	0.05	0.04	0.07	0.09
Marble or glazed tile	0.01	0.01	0.01	0.01	0.02	0.02
Openings						
Stage, depending on furnishings			0.25—0.75			
Deep balcony, upholstered seats			0.50—1.00			
Grilles, ventilating			0.15—0.50			
Plaster, gypsum or lime, smooth finish on tile or brick	0.13	0.15	0.02	0.03	0.04	0.05
Plaster, gypsum or lime, rough finish on lath	0.02	0.03	0.04	0.05	0.04	0.03
Same, with smooth finish	0.02	0.02	0.03	0.04	0.04	0.03
Plywood panelling, ⅜ in. thick	0.28	0.22	0.17	0.09	0.10	0.11
Water surface, as in a swimming pool	0.008	0.008	0.013	0.015	0.020	0.025
Air, sabins per 1,000 cu ft					2.3	7.2

ABSORPTION OF SEATS AND AUDIENCE

Values given are in sabins per square foot of seating area or per unit

	125 cps	250 cps	500 cps	1,000 cps	2,000 cps	4,000 cps
Audience, seated in upholstered seats, per sq ft of floor area	0.60	0.74	0.88	0.96	0.93	0.85
Unoccupied cloth-covered upholstered seats, per sq ft of floor area	0.49	0.66	0.80	0.88	0.82	0.70
Unoccupied leather-covered upholstered seats, per sq ft of floor area	0.44	0.54	0.60	0.62	0.58	0.50
Wooden pews, occupied, per sq ft of floor area	0.57	0.61	0.75	0.86	0.91	0.86
Chairs, metal or wood seats, each, unoccupied	0.15	0.19	0.22	0.39	0.38	0.30

* SOURCES:

1. *Beranek, L. L. (ed.). Noise Reduction, chap. 13. McGraw-Hill Book Company, Inc., New York (1960).*

2. *Bolt Beranek and Newman Inc., unpublished data.*

† *Number is not a transmission-loss value, but a room-to-room noise reduction value adjusted for a receiving room with a 0.5-sec reverberation time at the listed frequency. The actual transmission-loss value should be within ±2 db of the listed noise reduction value.*

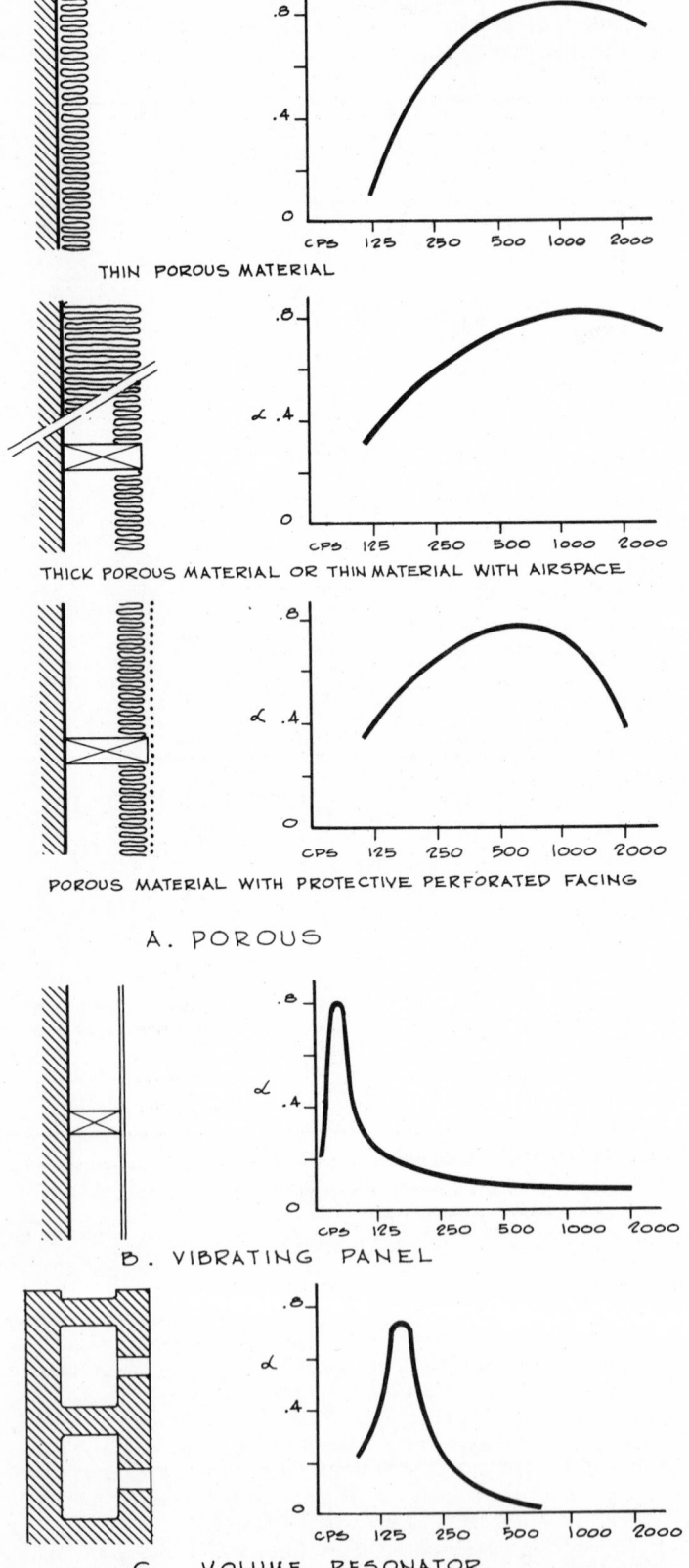

THIN POROUS MATERIAL

THICK POROUS MATERIAL OR THIN MATERIAL WITH AIRSPACE

POROUS MATERIAL WITH PROTECTIVE PERFORATED FACING

A. POROUS

B. VIBRATING PANEL

C. VOLUME RESONATOR

Fig. 10. Basic types and relative efficiencies of sound-absorbing materials

However, not all manufacturers of acoustical materials are members of the AMA. While their products may be appraised by properly qualified laboratories, such as that of the National Bureau of Standards, it must be remembered that the coefficients for these products may not be directly comparable with those obtained by the AMA test procedure (ASTM Test Method C423-60T).

NOISE-REDUCTION COEFFICIENT

A single-number rating that has been used for specifying sound-absorbing products is the noise-reduction coefficient (NRC). This is the arithmetic average of the sound-absorption coefficients at 250, 500, 1,000 and 2,000 cps. Note that this average does not include the coefficients at 125 cps where absorption is often needed but difficult to obtain. Thus, caution should be exercised in the selection of acoustical materials on the basis of NRC. The preferred method for specifying products for use in room acoustics design is to specify minimum sound-absorption coefficients at each of the six test frequencies from 125 to 4,000 cps. The NRC may be adequate, however, where low-frequency absorption is not particularly critical or where the acoustics problem is not serious (for example, lobbies, corridors, general activity spaces, etc.).

SELECTING ACOUSTICAL MATERIALS

The ever-increasing number of building materials specifically designed to meet the demands for effective sound absorption often makes the actual selection difficult. Basically, however, there are four broad categories of acoustical materials. Some of these may be delivered to the job ready for installation; others may require on-site assembly or application:

1. Prefabricated, factory-finished materials
2. Plastic (or "wet") applied materials
3. Special site-assembled materials
4. Suspended baffles or "space" absorbers

Prefabricated materials

This category includes most of the products listed in the AMA bulletin referred to above. Basically, these are factory-finished products or systems. Table 3 gives some idea of the scope of this category of materials.

As discussed previously, the thickness and method of mounting are important in the determination of the absorption coefficient at various frequencies. The AMA test procedure has been standardized to include the various mountings that may be en-

Table 3. Classification of acoustical materials

Courtesy Acoustical Materials Association

Types	Description
I	Regularly perforated cellulose fiber tile
II	Random perforated cellulose fiber tile
III	Slotted cellulose fiber tile
IV	Textured, finely perforated, fissured or simulated fissured cellulose tile
V	Membrane-faced cellulose fiber tile
VI	Cellulose fiber lay-in panels
VII	Perforated mineral fiber tile
VIII	Fissured mineral fiber tile
IX	Textured, finely perforated or smooth mineral fiber tile
X	Membrane-faced mineral fiber tile
XI	Mineral fiber lay-in panels
XII	Perforated metal pans with mineral fiber pads
XIII	Perforated metal lay-in panels with mineral fiber pads
XIV	Mineral fiber tile rated as part of fire resistive assemblies
XV	Perforated asbestos board panels with mineral fiber pads
XVI	Sound-absorbent duct lining
XVII	Special acoustical panels and systems

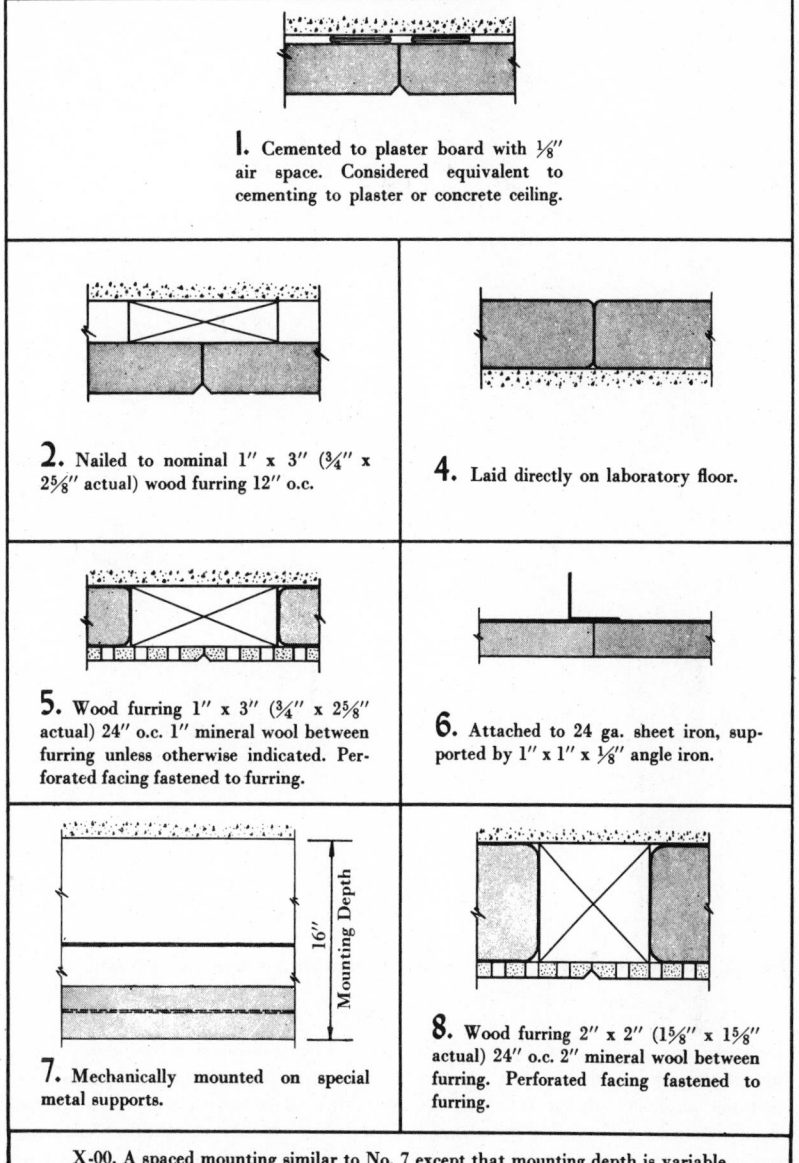

1. Cemented to plaster board with ⅛″ air space. Considered equivalent to cementing to plaster or concrete ceiling.

2. Nailed to nominal 1″ x 3″ (¾″ x 2⅝″ actual) wood furring 12″ o.c.

4. Laid directly on laboratory floor.

5. Wood furring 1″ x 3″ (¾″ x 2⅝″ actual) 24″ o.c. 1″ mineral wool between furring unless otherwise indicated. Perforated facing fastened to furring.

6. Attached to 24 ga. sheet iron, supported by 1″ x 1″ x ⅛″ angle iron.

7. Mechanically mounted on special metal supports.

8. Wood furring 2″ x 2″ (1⅝″ x 1⅝″ actual) 24″ o.c. 2″ mineral wool between furring. Perforated facing fastened to furring.

X-00. A spaced mounting similar to No. 7 except that mounting depth is variable.

Fig. 11. Types of mountings of materials used in laboratory tests to determine sound-absorption coefficients. These are typical of actual installation methods used in the field

Courtesy of the Acoustical Materials Association.

countered in the field (illustrated in Fig. 11). Mountings 1, 2, 3, and 7 are perhaps the most generally used systems for prefabricated products. Mountings 5 and 8 apply to rather specialized applications and 6 applies to sound-absorbing duct linings. When evaluating a product, therefore, on the basis of sound-absorption coefficients, it is important to know what mounting was used.

Plastic-applied materials

This category includes plaster and mineral fiber products to which a binding agent and water are added at the time of application. They are applied in a wet, semiplastic state either by hand troweling or spraying on by machine. Thus, these materials have visual continuity without modular lines or joints. However, the absorption achieved in the field by these products is strongly dependent on careful installation. Coefficients determined from field measurements have been significantly lower than those reported on carefully prepared laboratory samples.

Acoustical plaster uses an aggregate of vermiculite or perlite with a "setting" type of binder, such as gypsum or lime, or a "nonsetting" binder, such as bentonite. These materials must be applied to a hard, back-up surface of scratch or brown-coat plaster or concrete or masonry surfaces, and can rarely be installed in greater than 1 in. total thickness; the more usual application is ½ in. or less. Thus, the low-frequency absorption which can be achieved is quite small and seldom adequate to control sound reflections, especially from curved surfaces that may be causing echo or focusing difficulties in a room. Surface porosity is sometimes improved by wire brush or nail roller stippling, but generally speaking, most acoustical plasters are easily sealed and rendered ineffective by painting. Refinishing and cleaning must follow the manufacturer's instructions very closely to avoid any further reduction of the sound-absorbing properties of the material.

Mineral fiber base products (mostly asbestos fibers) are combined with a binding agent and water in a special spray gun and applied either directly on a hard back-up surface or on an open lath. Greater thicknesses (up to 3 in.) of this

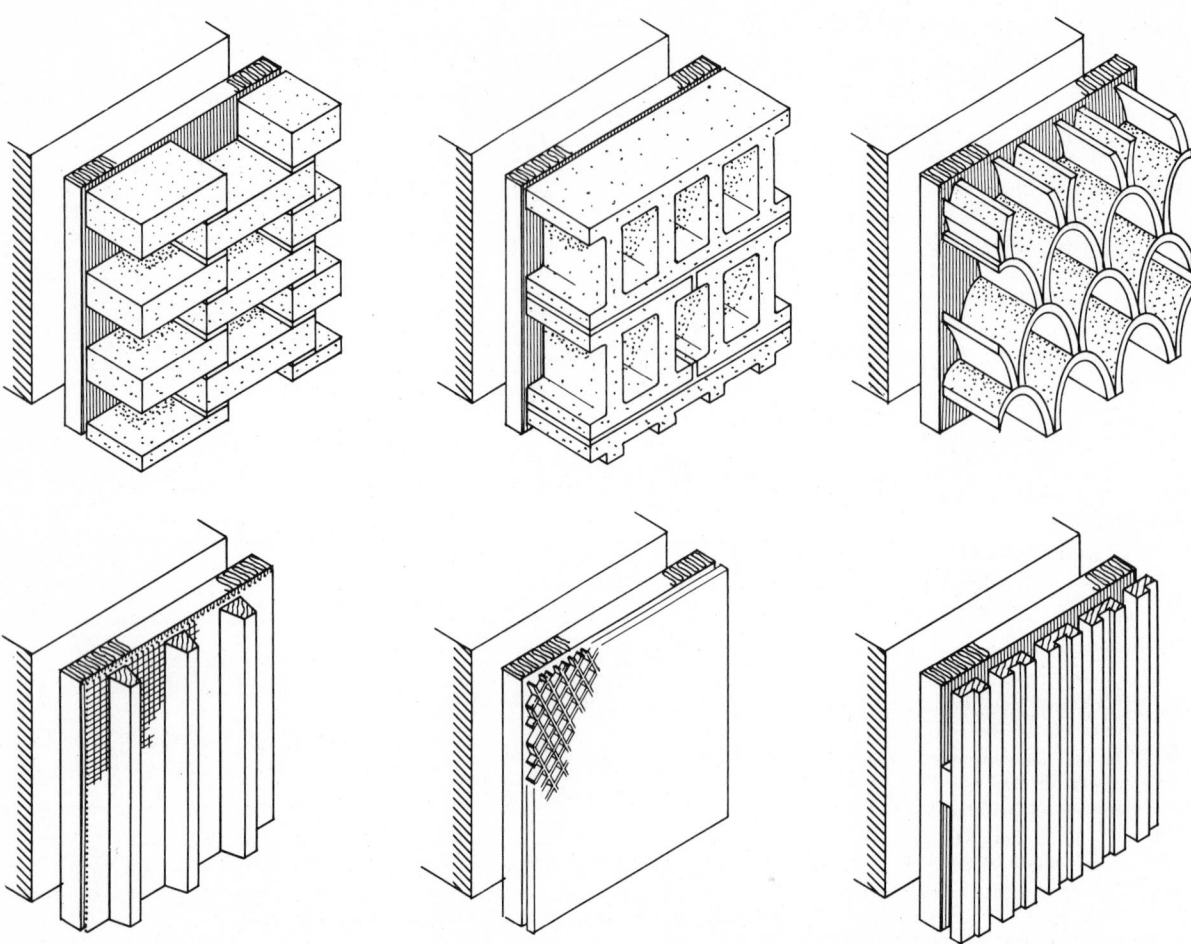

Fig. 12. Examples of some "open" architectural materials that can be used as facings for sound-absorbing treatments

somewhat soft, porous, lightweight material are possible than with acoustical plasters, and the possibility of application on an open lath takes advantage of the airspace behind the surface, thus increasing the low-frequency absorption. Some sprayed asbestos products, because they are relatively soft, may be easily damaged, and matching the color and finish of the remaining area is often difficult in a patching or clean-up process. Despite this disadvantage sprayed mineral fiber products have a certain advantage for the acoustical treatment of domes and other curved shapes, where focusing echoes would seriously interfere with satisfactory hearing conditions.

Special job assembled—composite

In spite of the tremendous variety of "off the shelf" materials, there are occasions when acoustical or visual requirements require a "custom" design. Very often the desired acoustical result can be achieved with a porous sound-absorbing material (1 or 2-in. thick mineral fiber blanket) with

or without an airspace behind to increase the low-frequency absorption. The architectural problem then is in the selection and detailing of an acoustically transparent facing or screening that would have the least effect on the efficiency of the sound-absorbing material. Generally speaking, the effect of a facing is to reduce the high-frequency absorption of the composite construction, or in other words, the facing cuts off the high-frequency absorption above some given frequency. This is because sound energy is reflected from the solid material between the holes or openings in the facing at a frequency where the wavelength of the impinging sound is equal to or less than the dimension of the solid area. For example, spaced wood strips about 3 in. wide would reflect considerable sound at and above the frequency of about 2,000 cps, and would, therefore, not be a suitable treatment for an auditorium rear wall where one might want effective echo control. On the other hand, a flattened expanded metal, having 30 to 40 per cent open area with solid

dimensions less than 3/16 in., would be satisfactory over the entire frequency range. For reverberation or noise control high-frequency absorption may not be critical, especially if other high-frequency absorbing materials are present in the space. Therefore, relatively large-dimensioned grille elements (perforated brickwork, etc.) may be perfectly acceptable. Fig. 12 illustrates a few of the possibilities for imaginative architectural facing treatment of porous sound-absorbing materials. Many of these have been used effectively in contemporary and traditional spaces where no other available treatment adequately solves both acoustical and visual problems.

The procedures for calculating the precise effects of various facings on the sound-absorbing efficiency of a material is a difficult and involved procedure beyond the scope of the present discussion. However, the point to be made here is that the opportunity for satisfying the requirements for sound absorption, even in the most monumental of spaces, is often limited only by the designer's imagination.

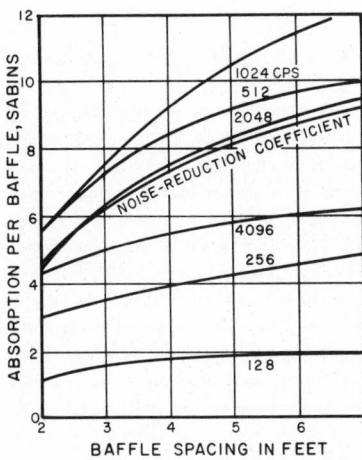

Fig. 13. Absorption per baffle (2 by 4-ft noise stop baffle)
Measured in sabins at several frequencies for spacings of the baffles ranging between 2 and 7 ft. (Courtesy of Owens–Corning Fiberglas Corporation.)

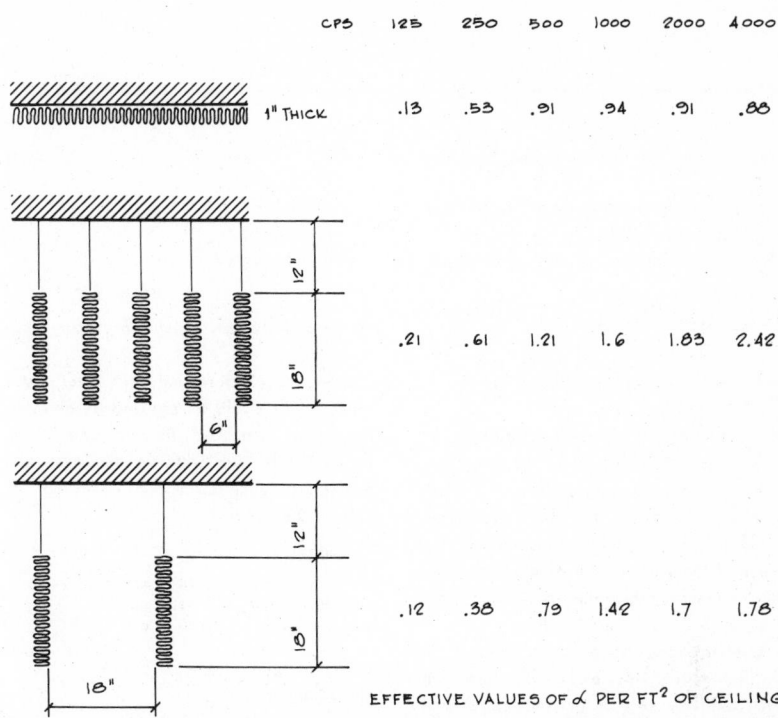

CPS	125	250	500	1000	2000	4000
1" THICK	.13	.53	.91	.94	.91	.88
	.21	.61	1.21	1.6	1.83	2.42
	.12	.38	.79	1.42	1.7	1.78

EFFECTIVE VALUES OF α PER FT² OF CEILING

Fig. 14. Comparative values of the effective sound-absorption coefficient (α per square foot of reflected ceiling area) for a porous material used in a flat ceiling application versus various baffle configurations.

Suspended baffles or space absorbers

Prefabricated special sound-absorbing units (for example, flat baffles, cones, prisms, parallelepipeds, tetrahedrons, etc.) constructed of porous materials with integral or applied facing materials form a class of products which are particularly useful where a continuous application of conventional materials is not feasible. Such baffles or space absorbers have application in industrial plants where the ceiling surfaces are often remote from the source of noise or must be kept free for access to ducts, pipes, etc.

The conventional method of reporting sound-absorption coefficient data on a per unit area basis is not applicable in these instances since the efficiency of the unit depends largely upon the spacing between units. As the spacing between units is increased, the efficiency per unit increases to a maximum at a given spacing which may be determined experimentally for the particular product. The measurements are reported in sabins per unit (1 sabin is equivalent to 1 sq ft of a material having unity sound-absorption coefficient) for given spacings and geometric arrays. The characteristics of one such unit with various on-center spacings are shown in Fig. 13.

Although the efficiency per unit rises with increasing spacing, it may not always be possible to achieve sufficient total absorption in a given room due to the limited number of units that can practically be installed. The optimum design for noise control would be the one which produces

the most absorption (in sabins) with the least number of units. A comparison may be made of the effectiveness of the suspended array by dividing absorption (sabins per unit times the number of units) by the area of the ceiling (sq ft). The result is comparable to the sound-absorption coefficient per unit area of a typical continuous ceiling treatment. Such a comparison is drawn in Fig. 14 for a ceiling finish of 1-in. fibrous material and two configurations of continuous horizontal baffles made of the same material. Note that it is possible to have effective ceiling coefficients greater than unity in these instances. This does not mean, however, that the absorption coefficient per square foot of the material of which the baffle is made exceeds unity.

PRACTICAL CONSIDERATIONS

Since absorption in porous materials requires access by the impinging sound to the interstices of the material, the sound-absorbing efficiency may be seriously affected if the openings are blocked. Common sense dictates that materials having very tiny pores can be easily sealed by repeated painting while large perforations, slots, and fissures are not so easily bridged. Manufacturers usually have specific instructions on their particular products; these

should be strictly adhered to if the original acoustical design of the room is not to be altered in the future.

Light reflection and flame resistance, although of no acoustical concern, are often important considerations in the selection of acoustical materials. The AMA bulletin referred to earlier also gives information of this type for the various products listed. Additional product information is usually available in the manufacturers' literature.

SOME FUNDAMENTAL ROOM ACOUSTICS CALCULATIONS

Room noise reduction

With a steady sound source in a room the sound levels are highest very near the source and fall off as one moves away from the sound source until at some distance (usually within a few feet) the levels become relatively constant throughout the remainder of the room. These constant levels (sometimes called average or reverberant levels) are primarily due to the buildup of reflected sound from the enclosing room surfaces. The reduction of reverberant sound levels is often of interest and is achieved by introduction of absorption on enclosing surfaces. The amount of noise reduction that can be achieved is given by

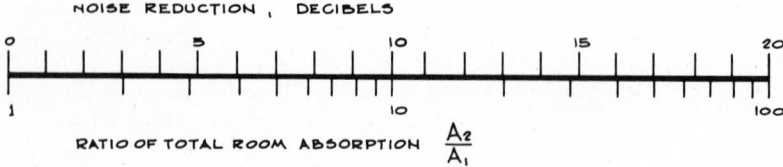

Fig. 15. A chart for determining the reduction of sound levels within a room (NR) due to changing the total room absorption.
(*NOTE: This reduction does not occur near the sound source.*)

the following expression:

$$NR \text{ (in decibels)} = 10 \log \frac{A_2}{A_1}$$

where A_1 and A_2 are the total amounts of sound absorption present in the space before and after the introduction of the additional absorption. The total absorption in both cases is equal to the sum of the areas of the materials in square feet times their respective absorption coefficients (that is, $A = \Sigma S \alpha$).

This equation is solved graphically in Fig. 15. A few calculations will show that it is relatively easy to get between 5 and 10 db of noise reduction by adding absorption to a room. However, it is considerably more difficult to get greater than

10 db of reduction in most practical situations.

Example: What reduction in reverberant sound levels would be realized by finishing the ceiling of a bare concrete room 15 by 20 by 10 ft high with an acoustical tile having a sound-absorption coefficient of 0.80 at 500 cps?:

Condition 1:

concrete floor, 300 sq ft x 0.03 =   9
concrete ceiling, 300 sq ft x 0.03 =   9
concrete walls, 700 sq ft x 0.03 = 21
                                $A_1 = \overline{39}$ sabins

Condition 2:

concrete floor, 300 sq ft x 0.03 =   9
acoustical ceiling, 300 sq ft x 0.80 = 240
concrete walls 700 sq ft x 0.03 =   21
                                $A_2 = \overline{270}$ sabins

therefore,

$$NR = 10 \log \frac{A_2}{A_1} = 10 \log \frac{270}{39} = 9 \text{ db}$$

This means that, if we were to measure a sound level of 50 db in the bare concrete room, the level would be reduced to 41 db by the introduction of this amount of sound-absorbing treatment on the ceiling. Note that the absorption coefficients for most materials vary with frequency and that this calculation should actually be performed at the several representative frequencies for which the coefficients are given. Also, note that the noise reduction discussed above has no effect at all on the noise levels heard very near the source of sound in the room.

Reverberation

The reverberation time of a room is given approximately by the following expression:

$$T = \frac{0.05V}{A}$$

where V = room volume, cu ft
A = total room absorption, sabins

This expression is sufficiently accurate for design purposes in most rooms where the total absorption is not very large (as it may be in broadcast studios, special laboratory test rooms, etc.). A typical calculation for the small lecture auditorium shown in Fig. 16 is given below.

Example: Calculate the reverberation time at 500 cps for the auditorium shown in Fig. 16 (1) with no audience and (2) with an audience of 200 people.

Since the absorption coefficients for most materials vary with frequency, it is usually necessary to perform this calculation for other representative frequencies (e.g., at 125 cps and at 2,000 cps). The optimum values for reverberation time are discussed in the section on "Criteria for the acoustic environment."

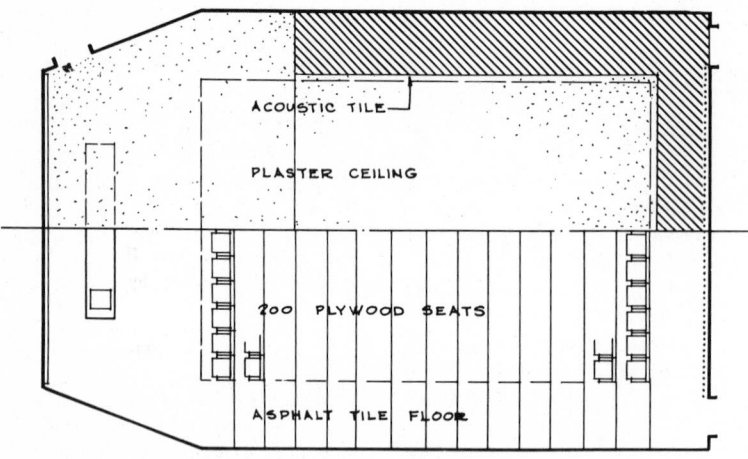

HALF FLOOR PLAN AND REFLECTED CEILING PLAN

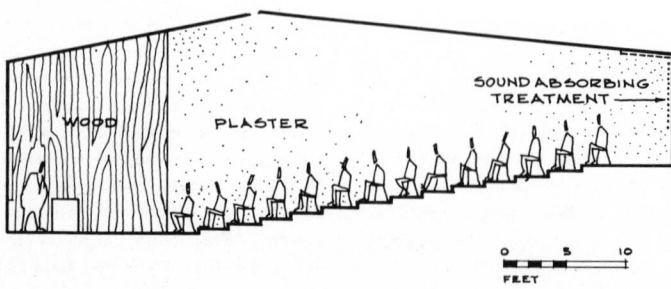

Fig. 16. Lecture room design used in sample reverberation time calculation (see example 2).

REFERENCES

Sound Absorption Coefficients of Architectural Acoustical Materials. Bulletin published annually by Acoustical Materials Association.

Theory and Use of Sound Absorbing Materials. Pamphlet available from Acoustical Materials Association.

Sabine, H. J. *Acoustical Materials,* Chap. 18 in C. M. Harris (ed.), *Handbook of Noise Control.* McGraw-Hill Book Company Inc., New York, (1957).

SOUND ISOLATION

Control of the transmission of unwanted sound into any space within a building is often the major concern of the designer interested in assuring a satisfactory acoustic environment. The undesired sound may be automotive or aircraft noise from the outside, or it may be sound generated in surrounding spaces such as speech in an adjacent classroom, or music or recorded sounds in an adjacent apartment. Or it may be direct impact-induced sound such as footfalls of persons walking on the floor above, rain impact on a lightweight roof construction, or vibrating mechanical equipment.

As far as the designer is concerned, all of these problems can be grouped under the general category of sound isolation but, obviously, the design criterion for the particular intruding sound will vary considerably, depending not only on the use of the space involved but also on the characteristics of the intruding noise source itself. For example, in an auditorium, or any other listening space for that matter, little or no intruding sound of any kind can be tolerated. On the other hand, in a private office, the major concern may be the elimination of intelligible sounds (such as speech from the occupant next door, footfalls from the corridor, etc.), while relatively high levels of continuous bland sounds like the rush of air from an overhead air-conditioning diffuser may be quite acceptable.

Sound-isolation problems in any building can be quite complex from the point of view not only of analyzing the many potential sources of intruding sound, but also of evaluating what levels of intruding sound can be tolerated by the occupants of the space. The designer must not only have some fundamental knowledge of the general aspects of the analysis of a sound-isolation problem, but also some understanding of the important physical characteristics of barriers and how these can best be used to isolate a given space from both air-borne and structure-borne sounds.

The problems of sound isolation are usually considerably more complicated than problems of sound absorption and involve reductions of sound level which are of greater orders of magnitude than can be achieved by either absorption or separation of the noise sources from the listener. These large reductions of sound level from one space to another can be achieved only by continuous, impervious barriers and, if the problem involves structure-borne sound as well, it may be necessary to introduce discontinuities or resilient layers into the barrier also.

The significant point is that sound-absorbing materials and sound-isolating materials are used for entirely different purposes. Just as one does not expect much sound absorption from an 8-in. concrete wall, there is not much reason to expect high sound isolation from a porous, lightweight material that may be applied to the surfaces of the room. As was mentioned previously, some materials have been developed to fill a demand for materials which will perform both tasks simultaneously. However, the basic mechanisms of sound absorption and sound isolation are quite different. This point cannot be emphasized too strongly since much confusion still exists among architects and building designers.

THE SIMPLE CASE OF ROOM-TO-ROOM SOUND TRANSMISSION

In order to illustrate a number of the important variables in any sound-isolation problem, we will try to visualize a simple case of air-borne sound transmission between two rooms separated by a common barrier (Fig. 17). One of the rooms (called the source room) contains a continuously operating noise source, and the other (called the receiving room) has a listener. To keep the situation simple, we will assume that the only way for sound to get to the receiving room is through the common wall which is completely airtight so that all the sound has to go through the material itself. The source room sound which is relatively uniform throughout the room, except very near the source, impinges on the barrier at many angles of incidence. In essence, when the sound impinges, it tries to move the barrier and to the extent that it does move it, sound is reradiated by the barrier to the receiving room. The level of transmitted sound in the receiving room (not very near the wall) is dependent primarily on three factors: (1) the transmission loss (TL) of the wall, (2) the area of the wall, and (3) the amount of absorption in the receiving space. This can be expressed approximately by the following equation:

$$NR = TL - 10 \log \frac{S}{A_2}$$

where NR is noise reduction, db (the difference in reverberant sound levels between the two spaces in question, in this case $SPL_1 - SPL_2$); TL is transmission loss of the wall, db; S is area of the wall, sq ft; A_2 is total sound absorption of the receiving room in sabins (A is the sum of the areas of various materials in the room, sq ft, times their respective sound-absorption coefficients).

The transmission loss accounts for the largest part of the room-to-room noise reduction but, as can be seen, the area of the wall and the amount of sound-absorbing material in the receiving space also have some effect. The larger the wall area is, the more sound energy will be transmitted. The more sound-absorbing material there is in the receiving space, the lower

Material	Area S, sq ft	α 500	S α
1. Empty room condition:			
Ceiling:			
Plaster	1,550	0.04	62
¾-in. acoustical tile	350	0.8	280
Walls:			
Wood	800	0.17	136
Plaster on masonry	1,220	0.02	24
Sound-absorbing treatment	210	0.7	147
Floor:			
Asphalt tile	1,000	0.03	30
Plywood seats	200 seats	0.22	44
Total absorption, A			723 sabins
Reverberation time, empty, $T = \dfrac{0.05(25,200)}{723} = 1.74 \text{ sec}$			
2. Occupied room condition:			
Total absorption in empty room (less absorptive value of seats)			679
Occupied seating area	950	0.88	790
Total absorption, A			1,469 sabins
Reverberation time, full audience, $T = \dfrac{0.05(25,200)}{1,469} = 0.85 \text{ sec}$			

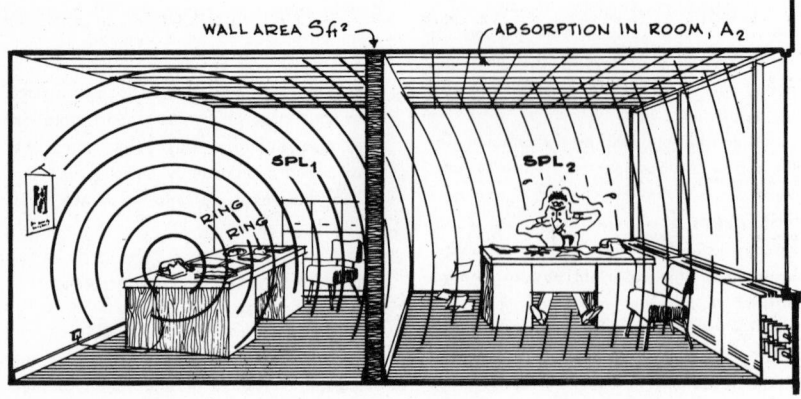

NOISE REDUCTION, NR $= SPL_1 - SPL_2$
$= TL - 10 \log \dfrac{S}{A_2}$

A

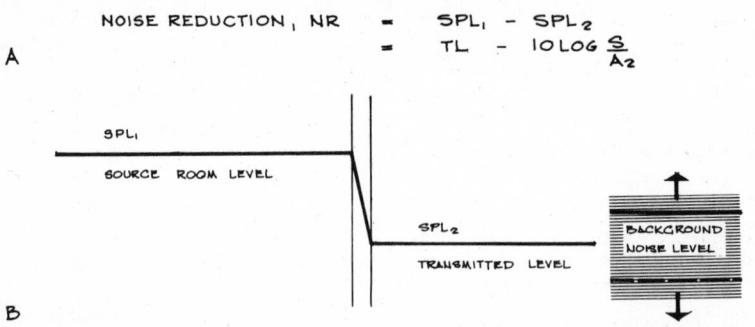

B

Fig. 17. Illustration of the simple case of air-borne sound transmission between adjacent rooms through a common barrier.

With a sound source in one room the transmitted sound level is dependent not only on the transmission loss of the barrier, but also on the area of the barrier and the receiving room absorption. The actual background "masking" noise levels determine whether or not the transmitted sound will be heard.

the reverberant sound level will be. In most practical situations, the correction term which accounts for the area of the wall and the receiving room absorption, usually affects the room-to-room noise reduction by not more than about ±5 db. However, this amount may be quite significant in many sound-isolation designs.

THE ROLE OF MASKING NOISE IN SOUND ISOLATION

Whether or not the transmitted sound will be heard in the receiving room depends on another factor which we have thus far neglected: the level of the background sound in the receiving room. Whether we are aware of it or not, there is always a certain amount of continuous background noise present in any space due to the air-conditioning system, the noise of distant traffic, the noise of activities in other parts of the building, or even crickets or wind noise if we happen to be out in the country. The effect of this masking sound on any sound-isolation problem is perhaps as important as the sound-isolating properties of the barrier itself. This effect

is shown schematically in Fig. 17. With a given construction between two spaces, the level of intruding sound is determined by the level of sound in the source room, the transmission loss and area of the barrier, and the absorption in the receiving space. The background sound, on the other hand, may vary considerably in any building, depending on whether or not the air-conditioning system is on or off; the presence of other activities within the building; or the nature of the exterior noise situation. For example, the background sound in a typical office building may vary by as much as 15 to 20 db, and this variation in background sound level can mean that it will fall either above or below the transmitted sound level. Masking occurs when the background sound either completely covers up the transmitted sound or, at least, the part of it that conveys information. A dripping faucet can be extremely annoying in the deathly silence of the night. However, during the daytime, the same level of noise from this faucet may be completely obscured by the general activity sounds that are present.

In any space whose activities require

extreme quiet, the background sound itself must be very low, and thus the barriers are called upon to provide large amounts of reduction of any intruding sound. This explains why a concert hall, a broadcast studio, or a special laboratory may need very elaborate, double wall construction. On the other hand, in office buildings, considerably higher background sound levels can be tolerated as long as they are continuous and bland in character. This of course places less of a demand on the sound isolation that must be provided by the structure.

Much research is under way to try to arrive at a better understanding of the masking effects of background sound on various kinds of intruding noise. For speech-isolation problems, these effects are well understood, and it is possible to achieve a good balance between partition selection and the background noise to solve speech privacy problems. A design tool for architects, the *Speech Privacy Design Analyzer*, which was published by the Owens-Corning Fiberglas Corporation in 1962, includes not only design procedures for speech privacy problems, but also useful sound-isolation performance and background noise data for a large number of products of many manufacturers (partitions, ceilings, air-conditioning units, diffusers, etc.).

The precise effect of masking on other intermittent, intruding sounds, such as mechanical equipment noise, music, etc., are less well understood and, for the time being, the designer must provide some safety factor in his sound-isolation design so that the transmitted sound will be reduced somewhat below the lowest background noise levels that will actually exist in the space.

TRANSMISSION LOSS

With the understanding that there is more to any sound-isolation problem than the transmission loss of a barrier, we can proceed to discuss intelligently the important variables that affect transmission loss. The transmission loss of a barrier is the ratio expressed in decibels of the acoustical energy transmitted from the barrier to the acoustical energy incident upon it. It can range from 0 db for no barrier to practical limits of 70 db or so at certain frequencies for elaborate-heavy constructions. This represents a range in the ratio of transmitted to incident sound energy of from 1, for a TL of 0 db, to 1/10,000,000 for a TL of 70 db. The measure of this property of a barrier is derived from carefully controlled laboratory or field measurements. Its value

Table 4. Air-borne sound transmission-loss values for some common building constructions derived from field measurements

Building construction	Transmission loss (db) at listed frequencies (cps)						Source*
	125	250	500	1,000	2,000	4,000	
Single walls							
2-in. solid gypsum perlite-aggregate plaster (10 lb/sq ft)	28	30	29	34	40	48	1
2-in. solid gypsum sand-aggregate plaster (18 lb/sq ft)	31	32	33	38	45	53	1
4-in. hollow-core gypsum block, 5/8-in. sand-aggregate plaster both sides (25 lb/sq ft)	30	31	33	39	42	46	1
6-in. hollow-core cinder block, painted both sides (33 lb/sq ft)	29	31	36	40	46	52	1
6-in. hollow-core cinder block, 5/8-in. sand-aggregate plaster both sides (43 lb/sq ft)	36	33	38	45	50	56	1
4½-in. solid brick, plastered both sides (45 lb/sq ft)	34	35	40	51	57	60	1
7-in. stone-aggregate concrete, plastered both sides (90 lb/sq ft)	44	42	52	58	66	70	1
2x4 wood studs, ½-in. gypsum board both sides (6 lb/sq ft)	20	30	36	41	43	42	2
2x4 wood studs, ½-in. sand-aggregate plaster on 3/8-in. gypsum lath both sides (16 lb/sq ft)	27	25	31	44	34	50	1
2½-in. wire studs, 5/8-in. sand-aggregate plaster on metal lath both sides (19 lb/sq ft)	26	24	37	31	37	50	1
2½-in. wire studs, ½-in. sand-aggregate plaster on 3/8-in. gypsum lath both sides (12 lb/sq ft)	26	32	41	45	38	52	1
Double walls							
Two separated rows of ¾-in. furring channels 2¾-in. on center, 5/8-in. sand-aggregate plaster on metal both sides (4¾-in. total thickness) (17 lb/sq ft)	29	35	44	43	46	55	1
2½-in. wire studs, ½-in. sand-aggregate plaster on 3/8-in. gypsum lath on ½-in. resilient metal clips both sides (12 lb/sq ft)	30	37	43	48	43	60	1
Staggered 3¼-in. wire studs, ½-in. sand-aggregate plaster on 3/8-in gypsum lath both sides (5¾-in. total thickness) (13 lb/sq ft)	34	39	44	49	48	60	1
4-in. hollow-core gypsum block, 5/8-in. sand-aggregate plaster one side, ½-in. sand-aggregate plaster on 3/8-in. gypsum lath on 7/8-in. resilient metal clips second side (26 lb/sq ft)	25	33	43	48	49	54	1
Two wythes of plastered 3-in. dense concrete, 3-in. airspace between (bridging in airspace and at edges) (85 lb/sq ft)	38	40	51	54	57	65	1
Two wythes of plastered 4½-in. solid brick, 2-in. airspace between (sound-absorbing material in airspace—bridging at edges only) (90 lb/sq ft)	43	50	52	61	73	78	1
Two wythes of plastered 4½-in. solid brick, 12-in. airspace between (wythes *completely* isolated) (90 lb/sq ft)	57	70	83	93	—	—	1
Floor—Ceilings							
Typical residential floor-ceiling wood finish; and subfloors on wood joists, gypsum lath and plaster below (about 15 lb/sq ft)	24†	32†	40†	48†	51†	54†	1
Concrete floor slab, ½-in. plaster finish coat below (about 45 lb/sq ft)	43†	40†	44†	53†	56†	58†	1
Wood floating floor of finish; and subfloors on 2x2 sleepers on ¾-in. glass fiber blanket on concrete structural slab, ½-in. plaster finish coat below (about 50 lb/sq ft)	38†	48†	55†	61†	59†	55†	1
Doors							
1⅜-in. hollow-core wood door, normally hung	5	11	13	13	13	12	2
1⅜-in. solid wood door, normally hung	10	13	17	18	17	15	2
1⅜-in. solid wood door, fully gasketed	16	18	21	20	24	26	2
Specially constructed 2⅝-in. wood door, full double gasketing	20	23	29	23	31	37	2
Two specially constructed 2⅝-in. wood doors, each with full double gasketing, 12-in. airspace between, each door hung on independent wythe of double wall	31	47	43	48	57	66	2

This table is reprinted through the courtesy of the Acoustical Materials Association. The values reported here are reviewed from time to time as more up-to-date information becomes available from researchers in the field of acoustics. The reader is referred to the annual bulletin of the AMA for future changes.

is dependent on the size of the panel tested, edge-mounting conditions, the weight and stiffness of the panel, and other factors. The transmission loss of a barrier varies with frequency and, as with sound-absorbing materials, test results are usually reported at a number of frequencies in the range between 125 and 4,000 cps. Typical transmission-loss data for some common constructions are given in Table 4. Transmission-loss data are published in bulletin form by laboratories such as the National Bureau of Standards, or they may be found in texts on architectural acoustics and in manufacturers' literature. Some precautions, however, must be observed in evaluating any transmission-loss data because different methods of testing can lead to widely differing results. (For further information see section on "FHA multifamily standards.")

Average transmission loss

The average transmission loss of a barrier (ave. *TL*) is the arithmetic average of the transmission-loss values at several test frequencies (usually 7, 9, or 11 test frequencies in the range 125 to 4,000 cps). The use of average transmission-loss values in evaluating sound-isolating barriers can be quite misleading. For example, relatively high average values can be achieved because of high values at certain frequencies that may not be important to the problem at hand. Likewise, a low value of transmission loss at a particular critical frequency range may be concealed in the over-all average. Average transmission-loss values, if used at all, must be viewed with considerable caution in sound-isolation design problems.

Sound transmission class

To supersede the average transmission-loss rating and to overcome many of the objections to this simple arithmetic average of test results, a single-number rating procedure has been developed in the current ASTM E90-61T *Tentative Recommended Practice for the Laboratory Measurement of Air-borne Sound Transmission Loss of Building Floors and Walls*. This rating procedure yields a single number called the *sound transmission class* (STC) by compar-

By ROBERT B. NEWMAN and WILLIAM J. CAVANAUGH, *Bolt Beranek and Newman Inc., Consultants in Acoustics*

ing the measured sound transmission-loss curves for a construction with a set of hypothetical transmission-loss contours of a given shape. Figure 18 shows the STC contours at 5-db intervals, but there can be intermediate classifications since all the STC contours have exactly the same shape. Each contour is actually composed of three straight-line segments, with the numerical transmission-loss value of the upper flat segment (from 1,400 to 4,000 cps) the portion which designates tthe particular class. The STC for a construction to be rated corresponds to the highest class contour that fits the measured transmission-loss curve according to the following rules:

1. The measured values must lie on or above the middle section of the class contour (350 to 1,400 cps).

2. The measured values can be below the two end sections (125 to 350 cps and 1,400 to 4,000 cps) by as much as 3 db at any one of the three extreme frequencies. However, the average deficiency for the three extreme frequencies must not exceed 1 db.

Figure 18 also shows two measured trans-mission-loss curves, A and B, and how their STC values compare with their average transmission-loss values. The 9-frequency ave. TL value for Curve A is 40.0 db and for Curve B is 40.7 db. In other words, their average transmission-loss values are very close in spite of the very significant dip in the transmission-loss characteristic of the construction represented by Curve B. The STC values, on the other hand, do reflect the significance of deficiencies such as that exhibited by Curve B. The STC value for Curve A is 40 and for Curve B is 30. The STC values in both these cases are set by the middle segment of their respective STC contours, since in rating a particular transmission-loss curve the measured values in this frequency region cannot fall below the STC contour. Other transmission-loss curves being rated can, of course, be such that the values at the extreme lower or upper frequencies determine the highest STC contour fit, in which case the rules given above regarding allowable deficiencies at these frequencies would apply. The STC procedure gives no credit to a construction whose transmission loss is better than it needs to be at certain frequencies.

LABORATORY VERSUS FIELD TRANSMISSION LOSS

Obviously, if laboratory results of sound transmission-loss tests are to be typical of real installations, the laboratory-test samples should duplicate, in so far as possible, the actual field conditions of erection. Laboratory tests on small panel samples generally give higher values of transmission loss than will be achieved in the field. Similarly, tests on unrealistic panel samples (for example, testing only the intermediate panel of a demountable partition system when the field conditions will always consist of an assembly of the panel along with its connecting posts, molding strips, etc.) can give misleading results. Some laboratories are equipped for testing relatively large-size panel samples which duplicate in almost every detail the actual field conditions of erection. Transmission-loss data from different laboratories are not generally comparable, often because of different-sized panel test openings, but also because of the different testing techniques used. ASTM E90-61T mentioned above provides standardization of laboratory testing procedures and requires that the construction being tested include all the essential details as they will occur in field installations, but it does permit relatively small-

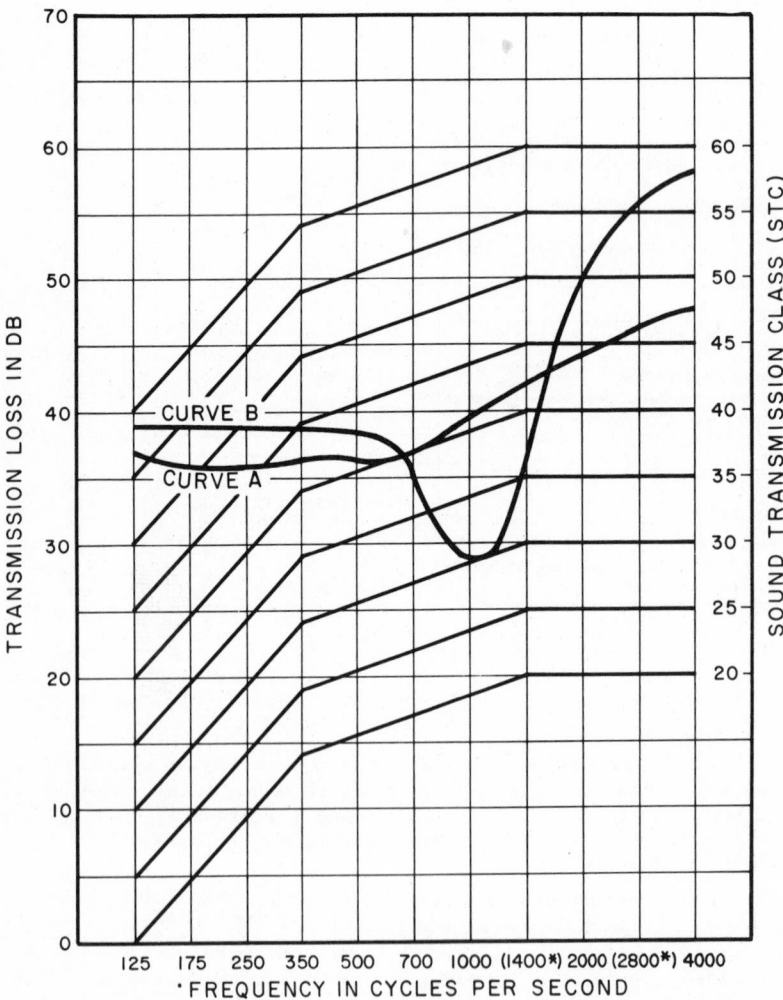

* VALUES NOT USED IN COMPUTING 9 FREQUENCY AVERAGE

Fig. 18. Example of the determination of the STC rating from a partition transmission-loss curve

The STC for Curve A is 40 and for Curve B is 30. See text and ASTM E90 – 61T for further discussion of the use of this transmission-loss rating procedure.

size panel tests (5-ft minimum dimension) which may give misleading results for certain types of construction.

In the absence of realistic laboratory test data on the transmission loss of a barrier, the procedures described below may be used to estimate the transmission loss.

Single homogeneous walls

The traditional method for estimating the transmission loss of single homogeneous barriers has been on the basis of so-called "mass law." Figure 19 shows theoretical transmission-loss curves for what might be called "ideal" panels; that is, the weight or mass of the panel is the controlling factor. Note that there are actually three "mass law." Figure 19 shows theoretical incident sound normal to the barrier surface. The lower curve is for sound impinging on the barrier at all possible angles of incidence from 0 to 90 deg. The middle curve describes the situation that is encountered most often in field conditions of room-to-room sound transmission. Note that the abscissa is given in frequency times surface weight ($f \times w$) so that once the weight of the material is established, we can readily construct a graph or a table of the transmission loss versus frequency for either normal, field, or random incidence of the impinging sound. For example, a manufacturer lists transmission-loss values for his particular product, a solid material weighing 1 lb/sq ft. You could compare the reported data with the theoretical field incidence transmission loss from Fig. 17 as shown in Table 5.

You must conclude from such a comparison that the manufacturer's data are in error, possibly because of an inadequate measuring technique or due to some other reason. The transmission for a single homogeneous partition cannot exceed the theoretical mass law limits. The only way to beat the mass law, as will be discussed below, is to go to a special double or multilayer construction in which case the partition could no longer be considered homogeneous.

Actually very few homogeneous common building materials follow the mass law curve accurately due to the internal stiffness of the materials themselves. Lead and steel sheets, due to their very low stiffness, are among the few materials that follow mass law over a large portion of the frequency range. Most materials—plaster, glass, concrete, etc.—exhibit significant dips in their transmission-loss characteristics at some frequency range depending on the stiffness of the material

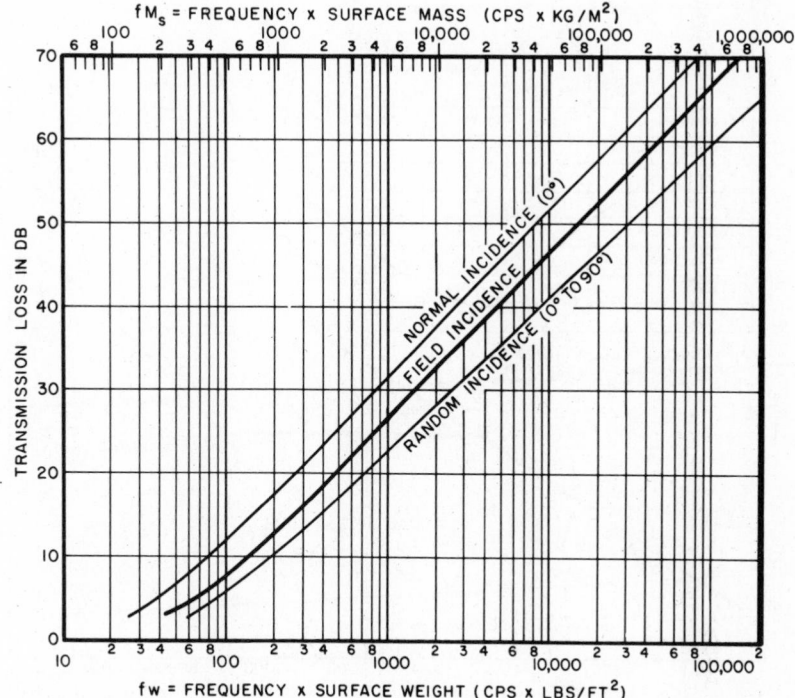

Fig. 19. Theoretical "mass law" curves for estimating transmission loss of single homogeneous panels on the basis of their surface weight alone

involved. A procedure for estimating the transmission loss of common homogeneous materials is given in Fig. 20. The process is outlined as follows:

1. Select a piece of graph paper such as that used to draw Fig. 20. The abscissa should be labeled "frequency in cps" and should be on a logarithmic scale so that each octave (doubling) of frequency has the same extent along the scale. Label the ordinate "TL in db."

2. From data in the table of Fig. 20 and the thickness of the panel, determine the surface weight of the panel. For example, 2-in. sand plaster will weigh 18 lb/sq ft.

3. From the field incidence curve of Fig. 17, select the transmission-loss of the panel from some frequency times surface weight combination (for example,

$f \times w = 125 \times 18 = 2250$. The transmission-loss from Fig. 17 at this $f \times w$ combination = 33 db. Therefore, the transmission loss at 125 cps for the 18 lb/sq ft sand plaster barrier = 33 db). Plot this value on the graph and draw a 6 db per octave slope through it, sloping upwards with rising frequency. This is what the partition transmission-loss would look like if the plaster construction had no internal stiffness.

4. Determine the plateau height from the table in Fig. 21 and draw a horizontal line through it, intersecting the field incidence line at point A (for plaster, this is at 30 db).

5. Determine the plateau breadth from the table and, starting at point A, mark off the number of octaves on the horizontal line. (For plaster, the plateau

Table 5. Comparison of estimated sound transmission-loss values with reported sound-transmission-loss values for 1 lb/sq ft material

Frequency, cps	Field incidence TL from Fig. 18, db	Reported TL, db	Difference, db
125	9	25	11
250	15	26	11
500	21	31	10
1,000	27	37	10
2,000	33	45	12
4,000	39	50	11

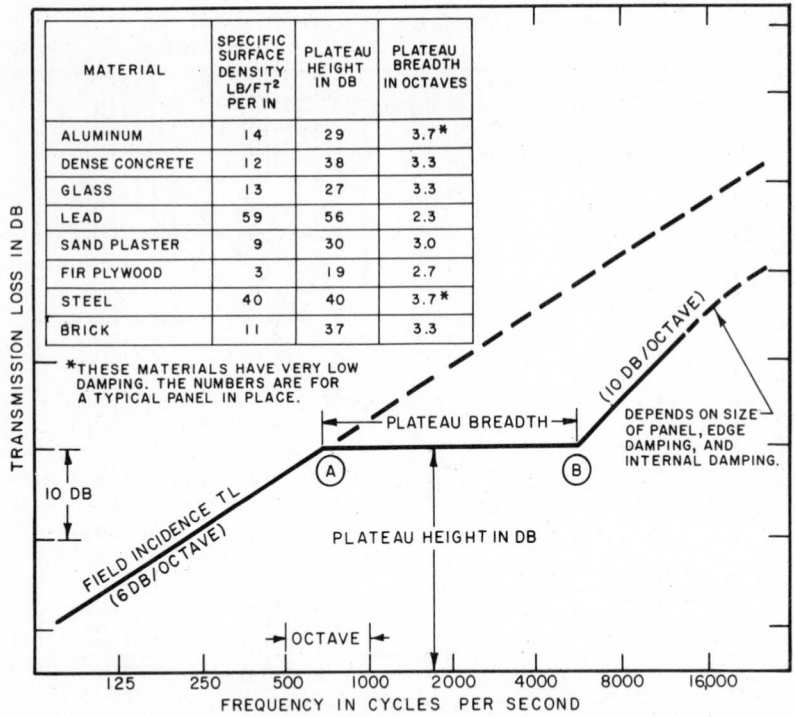

MATERIAL	SPECIFIC SURFACE DENSITY LB/FT² PER IN	PLATEAU HEIGHT IN DB	PLATEAU BREADTH IN OCTAVES
ALUMINUM	14	29	3.7*
DENSE CONCRETE	12	38	3.3
GLASS	13	27	3.3
LEAD	59	56	2.3
SAND PLASTER	9	30	3.0
FIR PLYWOOD	3	19	2.7
STEEL	40	40	3.7*
BRICK	11	37	3.3

*THESE MATERIALS HAVE VERY LOW DAMPING. THE NUMBERS ARE FOR A TYPICAL PANEL IN PLACE.

Fig. 20. Design chart for estimating transmission loss of single homogeneous panels considering both surface weight and stiffness

breadth is 3 octaves; label the end point of the plateau point B.)

6. Above point B, the transmission loss will rise at the rate of about 10 db per octave.

Fig. 21 shows the estimated transmission-loss for a 2-in. plaster barrier calculated using the above procedure and also compares the estimate with an actual field measurement of the transmission loss of a 2-in. standard plaster partition.

Nonhomogeneous single walls

The procedure for estimating the transmission loss of nonhomogeneous single walls is a great deal more complicated. Such walls might include plaster on stud constructions, hollow masonry block walls, metal sandwich panels, etc. Table 6 gives the plateau heights and breadths for a number of masonry block thicknesses, and weights from which the transmission loss can be calculated, using the procedures outlined above for single homogeneous walls.

For other more complex nonhomogeneous single wall constructions the designer is referred to texts on acoustics, or he might attempt to make an estimate, using the procedures discussed above, and assuming plateau heights and breadths for constructions which, on the basis of stiffness, most closely resemble the structure in question.

Double walls

The procedure for estimating the transmission loss of double walls is even more complex. Figure 22 shows schematically the effect on transmission loss of splitting a single wall of a given weight into two separate layers. As can be seen, significant improvement can be achieved except at certain resonant frequencies. With very thin-layered constructions and with very small air spaces such as occur in some thermal glass products (air spaces in the order of ¼ in.), the resonant dips may occur in an important frequency range, and thus, the effective improvement in transmission loss may not be significant. In such cases, it may actually be better to use a single-layer construction of the same total weight. Also, the improvement implies true separation of the layers which can only be approximated in actual practice by careful detailing. Figure 23 provides a simplified approximate method for estimating the transmission loss for double constructions.

Example: Assume that it is required to estimate the improvement in transmission loss at 500 cycles of a wall consisting of two 4-in. thick concrete layers, separated by a 3-in. air space over a single 8-in. thick concrete wall. Assume the density of concrete as 150 lb/cu ft.

Surface weight of 8-in. wall (w) = 100 lb/sq ft

Frequency (f) = 500 cps

$f \times w = 50{,}000$

TL (8-in. concrete) = 60 db (from field incidence curve of Fig. 19)

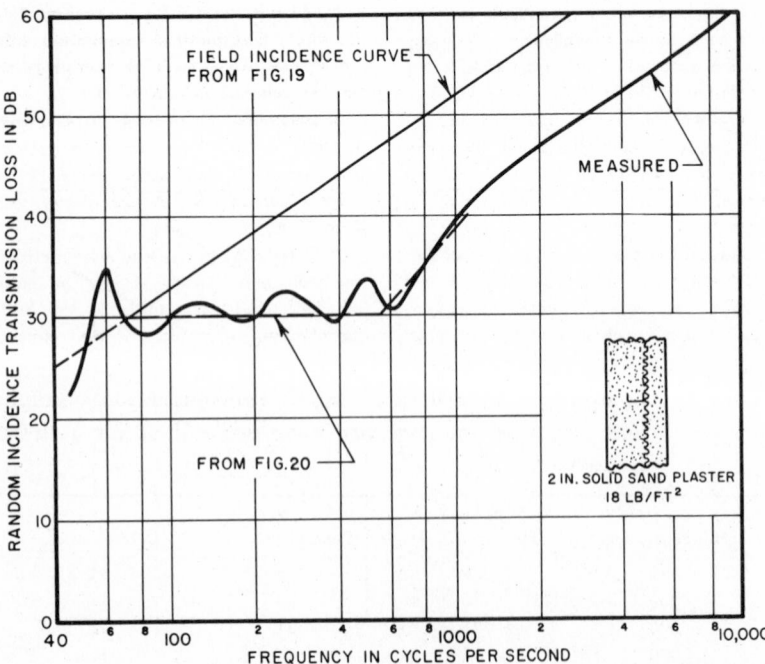

Fig. 21. Comparison of measured versus estimated transmission loss of a panel, from Figs. 19 and 20

Table 6. Approximate plateau heights and breadths for masonry block materials for use in estimating transmission loss*

Aggregate	Thickness, in.	Surface weight, lb/sq ft	Plateau height, db	Plateau breadth, octaves
Cinder	3⅝ hollow	24	29	3.0
Slag	3⅝ hollow	25	28	3.0
Dense	3⅝ hollow	30	29	3.0
Cinder	3⅝ solid	32	33	3.0
Slag	3⅝ solid	33	32	3.0
Dense	3⅝ solid	41	32	3.0
Cinder	5⅝ hollow	30	27	3.0
Slag	5⅝ hollow	32	26	3.0
Dense	5⅝ hollow	39	27	3.0
Cinder	5⅝ hollow with ⅝ plaster each side	41	27	3.0
Cinder	7⅝ hollow	32	33	3.0
Slag	7⅝ hollow	33	32	3.0
Dense	7⅝ hollow	41	32	3.0

* All values for unpainted masonry units unless otherwise noted.

Improvement in $TL = 6$ db (from Fig. 23)

TL (for double concrete) $= 66$ db

In the above example, to get an improvement of 6 db in transmission loss by weight alone rather than by a double construction, it would be necessary to double the weight of the single 8-in. wall (to 16 in.). (See Fig. 19.) Improvement of transmission loss by weight alone very rapidly reaches a point of diminishing return in which the thickness and other practical considerations of the wall become excessive. However, it is extremely important to remember that if the improvement suggested above is really to be achieved in practice, very careful detailing is required to assure that the two layers of the construction are not rigidly bridged by wall ties, conduit or piping, etc.

Composite walls

Most walls contain a number of different constructions. For example, a door or glass transom or a mullion filler panel may occur in the common barrier between two rooms. Figure 24 gives a procedure for calculating the effective transmission loss from the transmission-loss data for the individual elements.

Example: It is required to estimate the effective transmission loss at a particular frequency range for a composite wall containing a door. Assume the following:

$$Wall + Door = 100 \text{ sq ft}$$
$$TL \text{ (Wall)} = 40 \text{ db}$$
$$Door = 20 \text{ sq ft}$$
$$TL \text{ (Door)} = 15 \text{ db}$$

Door occupies 20 per cent of wall surface

Then, TL (Wall) $- TL$ (Door) $= 40$ db $- 15$ db $= 25$ db

Entering the vertical scale of Fig. 24 at 25 db, and reading horizontally to the 20 per cent curve, then vertically to the top horizontal scale, it can be seen that the transmission loss of the composite barrier is 18 db less than the barrier without a door, or an effective transmission-loss of 22 db! (40 db — 18 db.)

Obviously, to achieve a higher degree of transmission loss for the composite structure in the example, it would be necessary to select a door with a higher transmission loss for a greater composite efficiency. On the other hand, if it is assumed that a transmission loss of 22 db is acceptable (presumably, a very marginal requirement for noise or speech isolation), then a wall having a transmission loss of only 25 to 30 db would provide an acoustically balanced design at considerably less cost.

Effect of holes, openings, etc.

A hole has a transmission loss of 0 db, and if one does a few sample calculations with Fig. 24, he will soon discover that it takes very little hole area to reduce the effective transmission loss of a barrier. Cracks around doors, back-to-back light switches, electrical service outlets, pipe penetrations, openings above partitions, etc. are, therefore, extremely important considerations in partition design. Figure 25 illustrates a number of common leaks that are found in building constructions. Obviously, these leaks must be carefully sealed if the full effectiveness of a particular construction is to be achieved. Such leaks can be controlled by inserting solid, impervious barriers in the openings or, at the smaller cracks and holes, by packing with resilient materials and calking

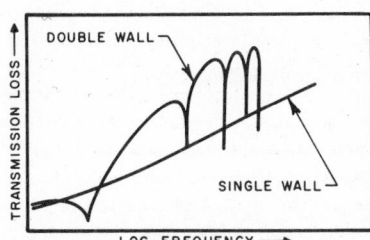

Fig. 22. Curves showing the theoretical transmission-loss improvement of a double wall over a single wall of the same total weight

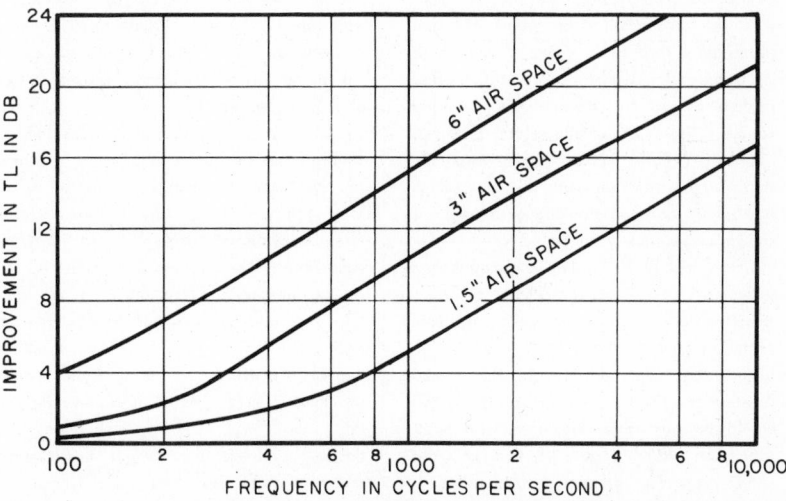

Fig. 23. Curves for estimating the improvement in transmission loss of splitting a wall of a given weight into two separate walls with various spacings

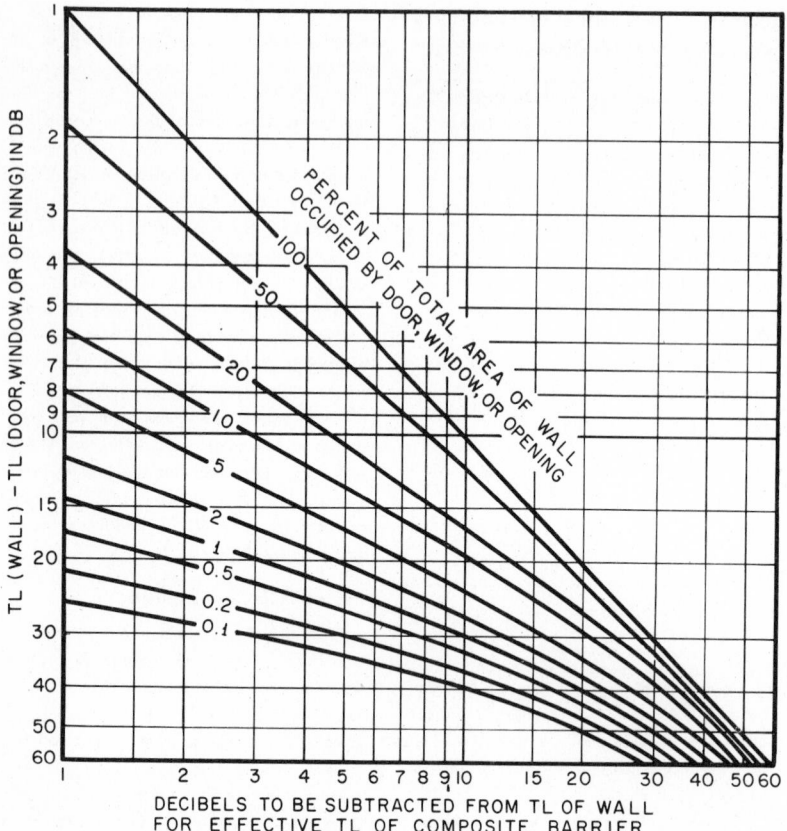

Fig. 24.   Chart for calculating the effective transmission loss of a composite barrier

(Chart axes: vertical axis "TL (WALL) — TL (DOOR, WINDOW, OR OPENING) IN DB"; horizontal axis "DECIBELS TO BE SUBTRACTED FROM TL OF WALL FOR EFFECTIVE TL OF COMPOSITE BARRIER"; curves labeled "PERCENT OF TOTAL AREA OF WALL OCCUPIED BY DOOR, WINDOW, OR OPENING" with values 100, 50, 20, 10, 5, 2, 1, 0.5, 0.2, 0.1)

with mastic. Care and skill on the part of the designer in the drawing stage of a project can do much to eliminate the need for detective work when trying to find the sound leaks once the building has been completed.

FLANKING OF SOUND

Thus far, we have concerned ourselves with the transmission of sound between rooms only through a common barrier. It is usually important to consider other paths for sound transmission between spaces. These may be referred to as "flanking" paths since they bypass the common barrier between the spaces. A number of common flanking problems are shown schematically in Fig. 26.

Doors should be widely separated and gasketed if a high-transmission-loss construction is required between separate rooms. To improve the door problem, illustrated as path 1 in Fig. 26, the revised location for the door in one of the rooms would be advisable. Similarly, with operable sash (flanking path 2), the preferred window opening arrangement is shown.

Flanking of sound through the structure itself is important if high transmission loss

is required between rooms. For example, special "floated" floors or ceilings may be required if high levels of air-borne sound are anticipated in a room which would excite the common lightweight floor or ceiling slab construction and re-radiate into the adjacent space. This degree of concern for air-borne—to—structure flanking of sound is important only if the common barrier between the spaces in question requires high-transmission-loss construction. Such requirements do exist for many broadcast studio spaces, music classroom spaces, etc.

Flanking of sound through suspended ceiling constructions (path 4) is perhaps the most common problem in office buildings today, where large open spaces must be designed for flexible partition arrangement. The obvious solution is, of course, to continue the partition construction beyond the level of the suspended ceiling to the underside of the structure above. However, such a solution is not practical in many situations and really defeats the very flexibility that may be desired. In these instances, it makes more sense to think in terms of a horizontal barrier at the level of the suspended ceiling. The sound-isolation requirement of

the horizontal barrier may not be as great as that which would be required for a vertical barrier, especially if one considers that sound must travel through the barrier in one room, along the plenum space, and thence down through the horizontal barrier into the second space. Reduction of sound energy occurs each time the sound passes through the ceiling, provided the material is reasonably impervious or has an impervious backing. Additional loss of sound energy occurs as the sound proceeds through the plenum space, especially if some sound absorption is provided in the plenum, either on top of the suspended ceiling or on the underside of the floor structure above in the form of sprayed-on porous fireproofing material.

The Acoustical Materials Association (AMA) has sponsored some research on this particular problem, leading toward the development of a test procedure which evaluates the sound-isolation effectiveness of various ceiling products. The procedure is to measure the sound reduction between two test rooms over which the ceiling material is placed in its normal suspension system. To assure that only the sound reduction of the ceiling-plenum-ceiling path is measured, a high-transmission-loss wall is used as the common barrier between the test rooms; this extends up to the level of the suspended ceilings. The result of such tests are reported in terms of "attenuation" in decibels at several frequencies between 125 and 4,000 cps. Note that the term "attenuation" is used here rather than "transmission loss" because the reported sound reduction is not a physical property of the ceiling material but rather a room-to-room reduction of sound energy for a particular suspended ceiling-plenum arrangement. In general, however, in selecting a ceiling system in sound-isolation design, the attenuation of the ceiling configuration should be equal to or slightly greater than the transmission loss of the common barrier between any two spaces in order to assure a balanced acoustical design.

STRUCTURE-BORNE SOUND

Structure-borne sound waves travel quite efficiently (i.e., with little loss of energy) from one part of a rigid structure to another. If the level of sound or vibrational energy which excites these waves is strong enough, they may be reradiated as air-borne sound from the structure. Common structure-borne sound problems in buildings are due to sources which act directly on the structure such as the impact of footballs or vibrations from pianos and from rigidly mounted mechanical equipment. Also, as mentioned previously, high levels of air-borne sound in a space excite structure-borne sound waves which reradiate in adjacent spaces, especially if the common floor or ceiling constructions are relatively lightweight. Some methods for controlling these problems are shown in Figs. 27 and 28. Careful detailing to isolate direct vibration-inducing sources and to avoid bridging of resilient constructions is extremely important where structure-borne sound-transmission problems exist.

Figure 29 shows the relative improvement to be gained in impact sound isolation over a bare concrete floor slab, using various floor finish materials. Note that the carpet and special resilient tiles are effective but their effectiveness is limited to the mid- and upper-frequency range. In other words, by using such materials we may be able to eliminate the annoying "click" of footfall noise, but the low-frequency "thud" may still be heard in the floors below. If it is necessary to achieve high values of impact sound reduction over the entire frequency range (as it may be between apartments or for critical listening spaces above one another), more elab-

orate constructions such as floated floors or special resiliently hung ceilings may be required.

PARTIAL HEIGHT BARRIERS

Very little room-to-room sound isolation can be expected with partial height barriers as can be seen from the previous discussion on composite walls. All one has to do is assume a transmission loss of 0 db for the open space above a partial height wall between two rooms, and a calculation of the effective transmission loss based on the relative areas involved will soon reveal the ineffectiveness of such

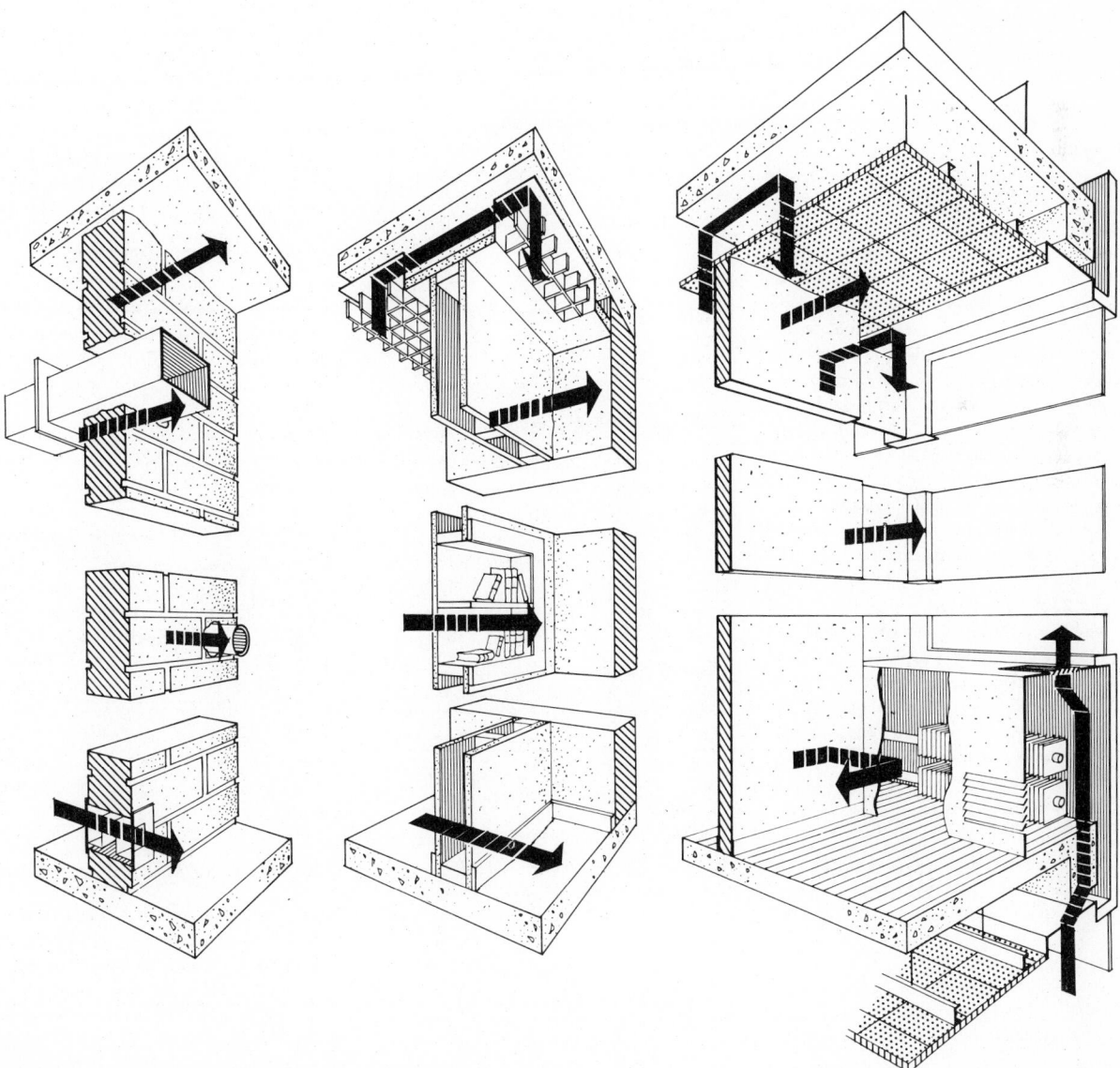

Fig. 25. Some sound-leakage paths commonly found in field constructions
These must be sealed by proper detailing if the full effectiveness of any construction is to be realized.

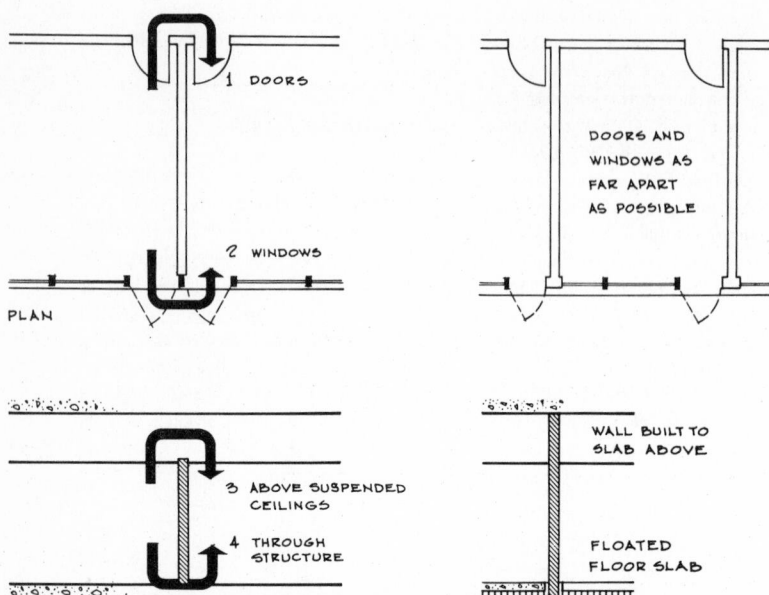

PLAN

SECTION

Fig. 26. Some "flanking" paths for sound between rooms around a common barrier and their remedies

In general, the higher the transmission-loss requirements of the common barrier are, the more serious the flanking problem is.

N (1,000 cps) = 6 ∴ NR = 17 db
N (500 cps) = 3 ∴ NR = 14 db
N (100 cps) = 0.6 ∴ NR = 3 db

From this it can be seen that the acoustical shielding provided by the wall with the assumed conditions produces a significant sound reduction in the middle and higher frequency range (500 and 1,000 cps) where the intruding noises could interfere with speech intelligibility. At the lower frequencies (100 cps), we can expect only a very slight improvement. All this is based on the assumption that the wall is reasonably solid—a row of trees would not suffice.

When the example is viewed in plan, it can be seen that while H remains constant,

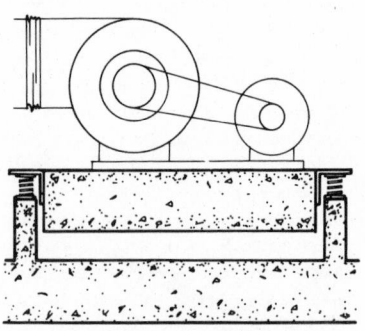

SPECIAL RESILIENTLY MOUNTED INERTIA BLOCK

barriers. In outdoor noise situations, on the other hand, where there are no enclosing surfaces to contain the sound source and build up reverberant levels, walls may have some limited effectiveness under certain conditions. The following example, using the data from Fig. 30 will serve to illustrate the effectiveness and the limitations of this method of sound isolation.

Example: Assume that it is necessary to know the noise reduction due to a vertical wall 15 ft high constructed on a residential property line. The wall is parallel to and 20 ft from the center line of a moving lane of automobile traffic on one side and 100 ft from a patio adjoining a residence on the other side. Since the "line-of-sight" between the listener's ear and the sound source is elevated approximately 5 ft above the ground, we estimate that the effective height of the wall is 10 ft. Therefore,

$$R = 20 \text{ ft}$$
$$H = 10 \text{ ft}$$
$$D = 100 \text{ ft}$$

$$\lambda (1,000 \text{ cps}) = 1 \text{ ft}$$
$$\lambda (500 \text{ cps}) = 2 \text{ ft}$$
$$\lambda (100 \text{ cps}) = 10 \text{ ft}$$

$$N = \frac{2}{\lambda}\left\{ 20\left[\left(1+\frac{100}{400}\right)^{1/2}-1\right] + 100\left[\left(1+\frac{100}{10,000}\right)^{1/2}-1\right]\right\}$$

$$\text{or } N = \frac{2}{\lambda}\left\{2.4+0.5\right\}$$

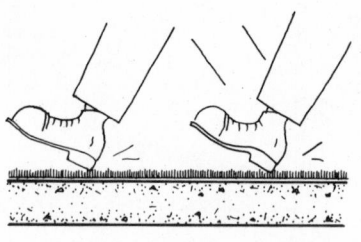

SPECIAL RESILIENT FLOOR COVERING

CONTINUOUS FLOATED FLOOR SLAB ON RESILIENT MATERIAL

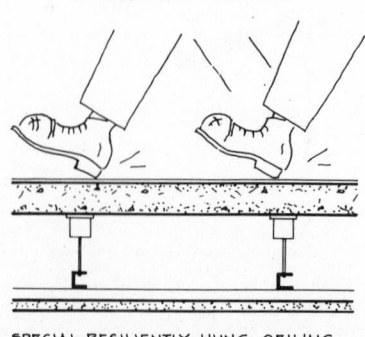

SPECIAL RESILIENTLY HUNG CEILING

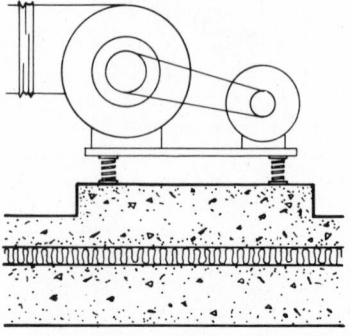

CONTINUOUS FLOATED FLOOR SLAB ON RESILIENT MATERIAL

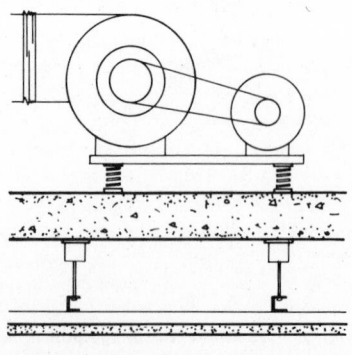

SPECIAL RESILIENTLY HUNG CEILING

Fig. 27. Typical corrective measures for structure-borne sound problems involving (right) vibration-inducing noise sources and (left) direct impact sources

R and D can vary considerably, depending on the location of the sound source along the road with respect to the patio. Therefore, spot-checking several arbitrary positions along the source path is advisable. Obviously, if the wall is not continuous around the property, and flanking will reduce the expected attenuation, depending on the configuration of the wall.

The transmission of sound in out-of-doors situations is actually affected by temperature, humidity, atmospheric turbulence, wind direction, and the nature of the ground cover. However, where distances less than a few hundred feet are involved, these effects may be neglected. In any event, the procedure for calculating noise reduction of outdoor barriers given in Fig. 30 and in the above example should give the designer some general idea of how high a wall must be in order to get any significant relief from an outdoor noise problem. Perhaps the solution may be to find another site for the building. Since there is more emphasis on outdoor living in contemporary architecture, and at the same time, an increase in outdoor noise problems, particularly automotive and truck traffic, the shielding effects provided by walls and terrain features may prove important in sound-isolation design.

SOUND ISOLATION FOR AIR-HANDLING SYSTEMS AND EQUIPMENT

Perhaps one of the most common sources of noise intrusion within buildings is the air-handling system. Not only are there air-borne and structure-borne vibrations associated with the mechanical equipment rooms themselves, but the ducts (*both* supply and return) serving a given space can carry fan noise to the space in question. Finally, the diffusers and induction units within the space at the duct termination generate noise, although we have pointed out earlier in this section under "The Role of Masking Noise" that diffuser noise can be, if controlled properly, a helpful factor in many sound-isolation problems using lightweight partition construction.

The noise control procedures for air-conditioning systems are fully discussed in the chapter on sound control which appears in the ASHRAE Guide (see "References"). Adequate coverage of the problem is not possible in this short discussion. It goes without saying that many of these problems can be greatly minimized in the early planning stages by proper location of the equipment spaces and the provision of adequate duct runs (both supply and return) into which noise control linings and mufflers can be incorporated.

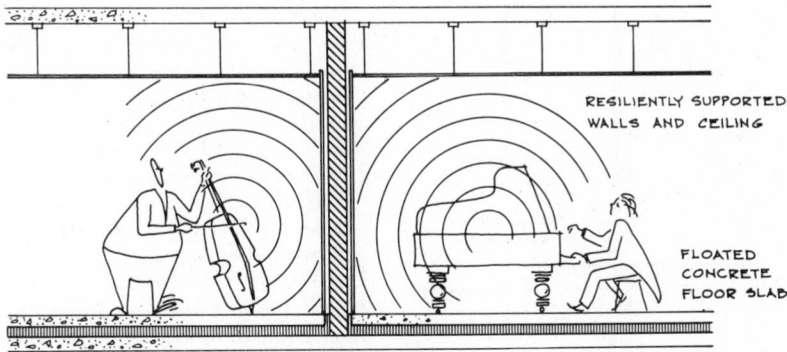

Fig. 28. Schematic representation of constructions required to control the transmission of high levels of air-borne and structure-borne sound

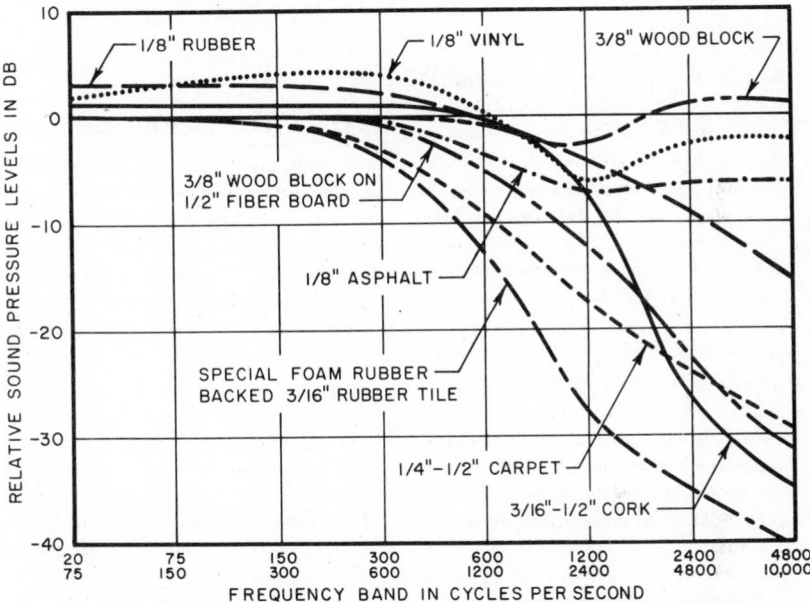

Fig. 29. Curves showing the relative improvement in reducing impact sound transmission of various flooring materials on concrete over a bare concrete slab itself

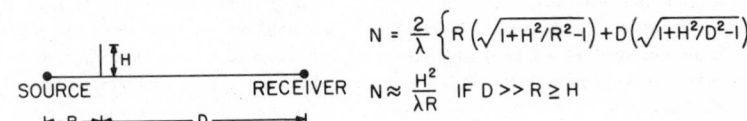

$$N = \frac{2}{\lambda}\left\{ R\left(\sqrt{1+H^2/R^2}-1\right) + D\left(\sqrt{1+H^2/D^2}-1\right)\right\}$$

$$N \approx \frac{H^2}{\lambda R} \quad \text{IF } D \gg R \geq H$$

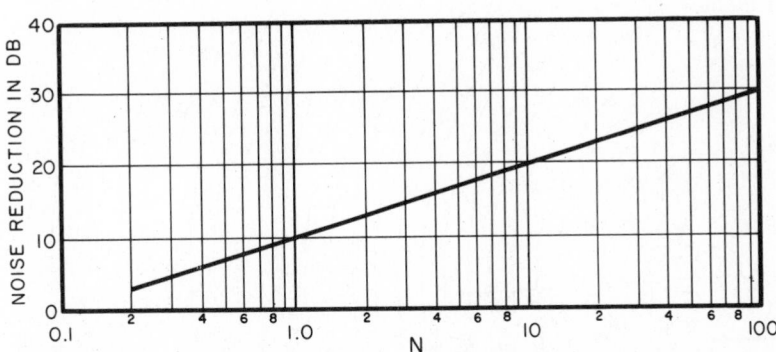

Fig. 30. Chart for estimating the noise reduction between a sound source and observer due to wall of height H

This procedure applies only to outdoor situations (see example).

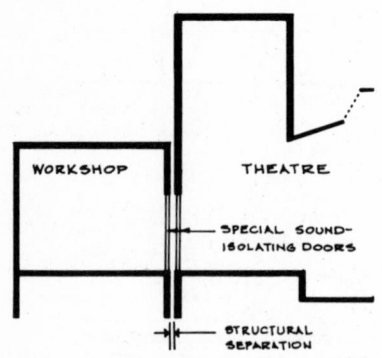

Fig. 31. Stage-scenery workshop isolation

REFERENCES

Beranek, L. L. *Noise Reduction*, chaps. 13 and 23. McGraw-Hill Book Company, Inc., New York (1960).

Cavanaugh, W. J., W. R. Farrell, P. W. Hirtle, and B. G. Watters. Speech Privacy in Buildings, *J. Acous. Soc. Amer.*, vol. 34, April, 1962.

Crede, C. E. *Vibration and Shock Isolation.* John Wiley and Sons, Inc., New York (1951).

Cullum, D. J. W. *The Practical Application of Acoustic Principles.* Spoon Ltd., London (1949).

Parkin, P. H. and H. R. Humphreys. *Acoustics Noise and Buildings.* chaps. 7 and 8. Faber and Faber, Ltd., London, and F. A. Praeger, Inc., New York (1958).

Purcell, J. B. C. Control of Airborne Sound by Barriers, *Noise Control* (July, 1957).

Solution to Noise Control Problems in the Construction of Houses, Apartments, Motels and Hotels. Owens-Corning Fiberglas Corporation, New York.

Noise in Hospitals, U.S. Dept. of Health, Education & Welfare, Public Health Service PHS Pub. No. 930-D-11, U.S. Government Printing Office, Washington, D.C. (1963).

A Guide to Impact Noise Control in Multi Family Dwellings. FHA Report No. 750, Federal Housing Administration, Washington, D.C.

Sound Insulation of Wall, Floor and Door Construction. National Bureau of Standards, Building Materials and Structures, Report No. 144 with supplements, U.S. Government Printing Office, Washington, D.C. (1955).

ASHRAE Guide, Chapter on Sound Control, published periodically by the American Society of Heating, Refrigerating and Air Conditioning Engineers, Inc., New York.

Speech Privacy Design Analyzer. Owens-Corning Fiberglas Corporation, New York (1962).

DESIGN FOR GOOD HEARING

Good hearing conditions in almost any kind of indoor or outdoor auditorium can be assured in advance if the four basic requirements discussed in the Introduction are satisfied: (1) quiet; (2) sufficient loudness; (3) proper distribution; and (4) adequate blending and separation of sounds.

QUIET

Really excellent hearing conditions, either indoors or outdoors, can only be achieved when the listening area is quiet. If we have too much noise, there is no point in worrying about the other factors which make for good hearing conditions. Outdoors, the noise may come from aircraft, from automotive traffic, or even from wind in the trees. Inside buildings, we not only have some of these outdoor noises transmitted through the shell of the building, but we have many noise generators such as air-conditioning systems and adjoining spaces (lobbies, stage work-shops, other auditoriums) that must be kept under control. The techniques of noise control are discussed in the section on "Sound isolation" but unless these are all observed with great care, it is unlikely that an excellent auditorium will result, no matter how carefully the other aspects of room acoustics are considered.

Outdoors, the best noise control technique is to place the audience far away from noise sources. High quality concert music simply cannot be presented outdoors on a noisy site in modern city traffic. Walls and dense woods can help reduce traffic noise; a single row of trees or a low wall is only a visual help.

The indoor auditorium can be made quiet even in a noisy city location. The audience chamber must be treated as an isolated area separated from all other areas by walls, closed doors, lined ducts, and other positive noise control measures. Noises in surrounding areas should be reduced as much as possible at the source. Lobbies, for example, should have heavy sound-absorbing treatment and should always be shut off from the auditorium with closed doors, preferably weather-stripped. If there is a scenery workshop adjoining the stage, it should be separated with a complete structural break (Fig. 31) with double sound-isolating doors to eliminate the noise from hammering and sawing. If one auditorium is located above or next to another, the two must be separated with double construction to permit simultaneous use (see Fig. 27).

The ventilating system for an auditorium should be inaudible. This means that the associated ductwork must be lined with sound-absorbing materials or that special sound traps must be installed. The fans and compressors must either be remotely located or carefully isolated with resilient mountings and heavy housings. Normal "commercial practice" is never good enough for an auditorium.

LOUDNESS AND DISTRIBUTION

It is obvious that the sounds we want to hear should be loud enough, and that all sounds should be uniformly distributed. People in the front of the seating area should not receive great quantities of sound while those in the back barely hear at all. A dead spot or an area of focused high-intensity sound can be just as unsatisfactory as a seat in which a person hears everything twice due to long-delayed echoes. Adequate loudness and good distribution of sound are determined almost entirely by the size, shape, and surface finishes of the room and, in some cases,

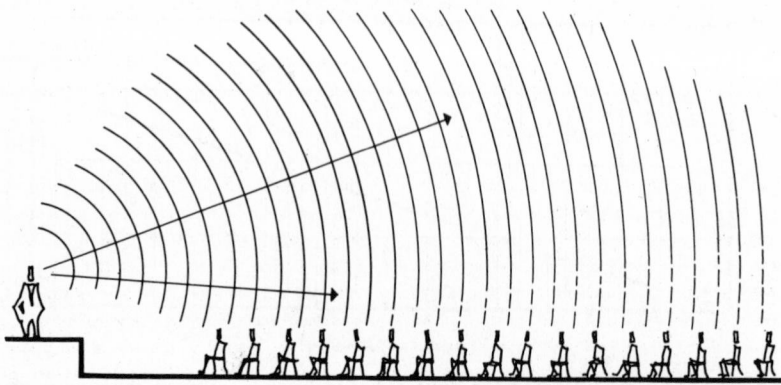

Fig. 32. Sound distribution outdoors over audience

By ROBERT B. NEWMAN and WILLIAM J. CAVANAUGH, *Bolt Beranek and Newman Inc., Consultants in Acoustics*

by the use of carefully designed sound-re-inforcing equipment. In most moderate-sized auditoriums, however, it is not necessary to resort to electronic aid. If the space is designed carefully with well-chosen materials, the enclosure itself provides the needed sound reinforcement and good distribution.

In the small conference room or office there is seldom a problem of adequate loudness, but there can be problems of distribution caused either by concave walls or ceilings, or by flutter echoes between parallel, uninterrupted surfaces. At the other end of the scale, the large sports arena must depend almost entirely on am-plified sound for hearing speech or music, and the enclosure is treated so that it will be as absorptive as possible to reduce troublesome echoes and unwanted con-fusion.

Figure 32 shows the typical distribution of sound to an audience seated on level ground outdoors (or in a large sound-absorbing room). The spherical sound waves radiate outward from the speaker, and the intensity of sound in these waves decreases inversely as the square of the distance. However, as it grazes over the clothing and hair of the sound-absorptive audience, additional losses occur which can amount to as much as 2 db per row. This means that people seated near the back of an audience not only receive less sound energy because they are far away from the sound source, but they are also deprived of sound energy by the people in front of them. Thus, in outdoor, flat audience areas the loudness and distribu-tion requirements are poorly met.

In the ancient Greek and Roman thea-ters this problem was solved by placing the audience on steep hillsides (in quiet locations: no airplanes, trucks, trains or cars). When the audience is placed on a very steep angle (Fig. 33), there is very little energy loss in the freely advancing sound wave, and until the audience is quite far away from the source, there is no great difficulty in hearing. It is always true in any listening situation that the better the sight line for vision, the better will be the hearing.

However, placing the audience on a steep hillside is not the only solution; we can get the same result by raising the sound source position with respect to the audience, or even more simply by using "mirrors." If the sound from the original source is reflected from a hard ceiling sur-face over the audience, it appears to come to the audience from the virtual image

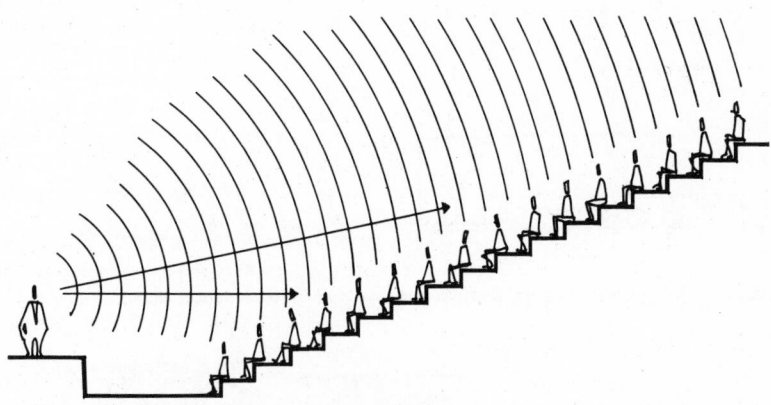

Fig. 33. Steep seating minimizes audience attenuation

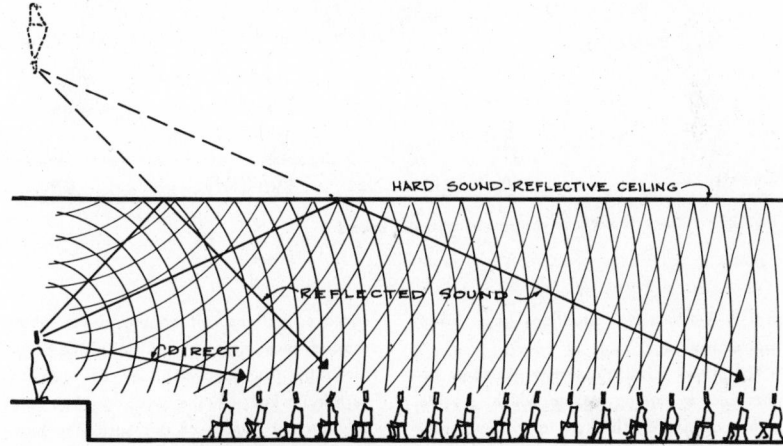

Fig. 34. A sound-reflecting ceiling reinforces the direct sound to the audience

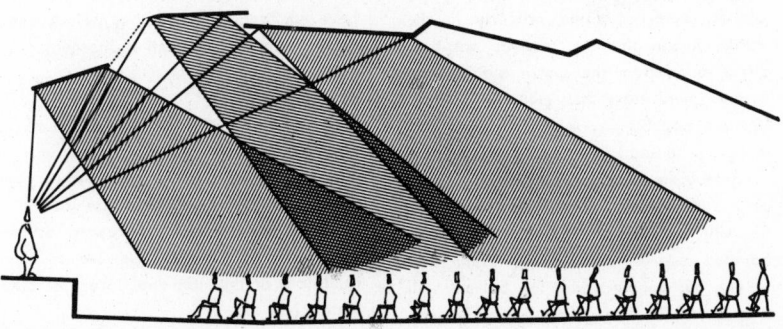

Fig. 35. Uniform distribution of reflected sound can be assured by proper ceiling design

position overhead, and thus, does not ex-perience the grazing incidence losses of the original sound from the source (see Fig. 34). The action of the ceiling as a reflector, bringing sounds down on top of the audience, is extremely important in all auditorium situations. This sound mirror (the ceiling) is probably the most impor-tant surface in the room for determining

good distribution and adequate loudness. The walls are important too, especially where long reverberation time is wanted.

The shape of an auditorium can be varied and refined in many ways but, basically, the ceiling of any room where hearing is important should be hard and sound reflective and should *never* be treated with sound-absorbing materials ex-

Fig. 36. Deep underbalconies deprive some seats of useful reflected sound

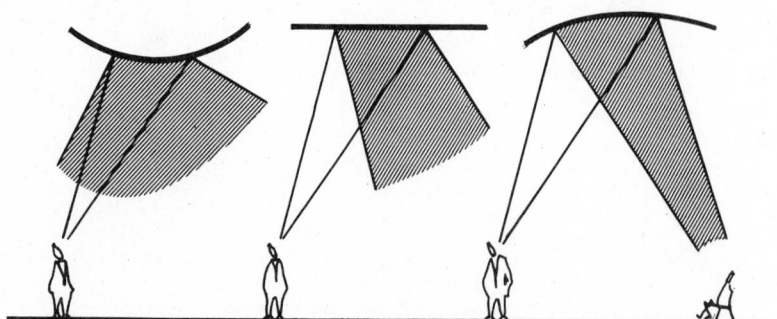

Fig. 37. Effect of surface shape on reflected sound

cept in very special situations (e.g., large sports arena).

Figure 35 illustrates some possible refinements in ceiling design which provide more uniform distribution to an audience. The problems that come from using deep balconies are shown in Fig. 36. For good distribution and adequate loudness a listener must be seated properly in the auditorium so that he receives not only direct sound from the source but also reflected sound from the ceiling and walls. He must be able to "see" the ceiling and if he is seated deep under a balcony (or side aisle in a church) and cannot receive this reflected sound from the ceiling, he will hear poorly. If the balcony is handled as shown in the right-hand side of Fig. 36, people under the balcony will hear well. If the ceiling is made with

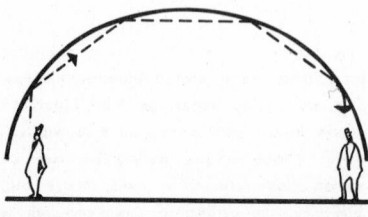

CREEP, OR THE WHISPERING GALLERY

Fig. 38. Sound reflection along curved surfaces often results in strange effects

concave sections, either barrel- or dome-shaped (see Figs. 37 and 38), there will inevitably be concentrations of sound in certain areas of the seating. The only solution for shapes of this sort is to make them highly diffusing (discussed further on in this section) or to make them highly absorptive (in which case, we no longer have an auditorium but a noise control environment or an anti-auditorium).

Plan influence on loudness and distribution

The plan of an auditorium should be determined by many factors including the gross seating capacity; the possible need for short viewing distances; whether the hall is primarily to be a concert hall or primarily an assembly or lecture hall; conditions of the site; and dozens of other factors (see Fig. 39).

Although traditionally the seating is laid out on radial lines, there is no reason why very handsome and adequate arrangements cannot be made with straight sections of seating. Curved plan elements should be avoided whenever possible because they always give rise to troublesome echo problems. The rear wall of an auditorium should never be curved unless it is absolutely necessary and if it is a smooth, concave curve in plan, it must be treated very heavily with sound-absorbing material to reduce the possibility of echo.

A straight or segmented rear wall is always a less troublesome surface. If sound-absorbing treatment must be used to control echo, it usually must be rather deep and the facings must be very open (see section on "Sound absorption"). Balcony fronts generally should be either open railings or tilted so that they do not reflect sound to the front of the room.

There is no "best" plan or section for an auditorium. Every scheme must be considered on its own merits. Certain types of plans are more troublesome than others, especially when the hall becomes quite wide and the time delay between arrival of initial sound and reflected sound becomes great. In general, side wall surfaces near the proscenium should be tilted to direct sounds toward the rear of the hall rather than across the room where long time delays would result (see Fig. 40). A wide fan plan is not as likely to be an excellent auditorium as a somewhat longer, more rectangular scheme.

REFLECTION AND DIFFUSION OF SOUND

We have discussed at some length the reflection of sound from the enclosing surfaces of a room, but it is important to keep in mind that, unless the surfaces or the elements of the surface are large compared with the wavelengths of sound involved, they will not reflect sound in a geometric fashion. The reflecting surfaces should have minimum dimensions of 3 to 6 ft. if they are to act as true sound mirrors. Small objects of a few inches or less will merely allow sound to pass by and will have little effect on the sound field (see Fig. 41). Thus, a pulpit canopy or suspended sound-reflecting panels over an orchestra or in the ceiling of an auditorium, or the elements of a faceted ceiling or side wall, must be sizable to handle sound reflection in a predictable fashion.

On the other hand, it is usually desirable to have a certain amount of random scattering or diffusion in the sound-reflecting property of the enclosure, and we try to introduce a great deal of irregularity in the enclosing sufaces of rooms. Coffers, splayed panels, or offset surfaces of scale ranging from 3 to 10 ft or more with depth of perhaps 1 or 2 ft give good diffusion of sound while at the same time they give good reflection of sound from source to listener. This means that for any of the possible source positions in the room, sound is quite likely to be reflected to all of the listening positions. The analogy can be drawn with a glossy paint surface as compared with a matte surface.

There is a general reflection of light from the latter but without the "hot spots" which are seen in a glossy surface. It is especially important for good balance in a concert hall to have a high degree of diffusion of sound surrounding the performers so that they can all hear each other very clearly. This achievement of good mixing and blending of the sound at the start almost always gives better results than very smooth enclosing surfaces.

REVERBERATION

The reverberation time of an auditorium is probably its most talked-about characteristic. Reverberation time can be measured, and in many cases it can be calculated and predicted in advance. The details for calculating reverberation time are discussed in the section on "Sound absorption."

Reverberation is something quite different from echo, and there is often confusion on this point. Echo is the distinct repetition of a sound reflected from a distant surface (see Fig. 42); it is almost always undesirable. Reverberation, on the other hand, is the smooth decay of sound as it reflects from surface to surface around the room, gradually losing energy on each contact with the absorbing elements in the space. Some reverberation is always desirable in a room to give it life and character. The absence of reverberation indicates an overabundance of sound-absorbing material and energy waste. The designer's problem is to adjust reverberation to an optimum value and to conserve all the sound energy he possibly can for the benefit of listeners.

In general, the reverberation time of an auditorium is largely controlled by the area occupied by the sound-absorbing audience and by the actual cubic volume of the space. These two factors set a limit on how much reverberation one can have, while the sound-absorbing materials added for the control of echo and unwanted reflections have only a minor effect. The shape of the auditorium is very important in determining the reverberation time and smoothness of decay of sound. The sound must have an opportunity to travel around the room and should not all be quickly grounded in the sound-absorbing audience. The more rectangular shapes seem to give the finest reverberation characteristics, especially for musical performances.

In many older concert halls the audiences were more tightly packed than in modern halls with their more luxurious seating. Consequently, for the same vol-

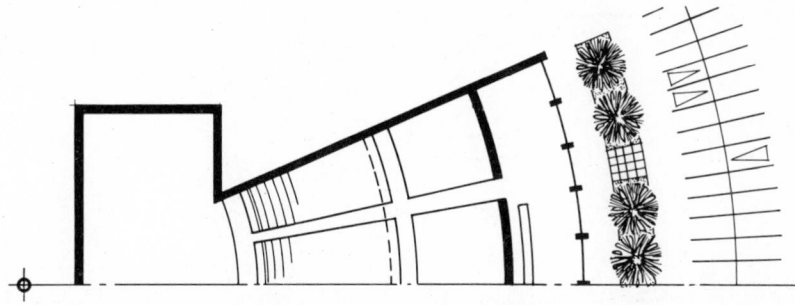

Fig. 39. The beam compass approach to auditorium design does not mean good sound distribution

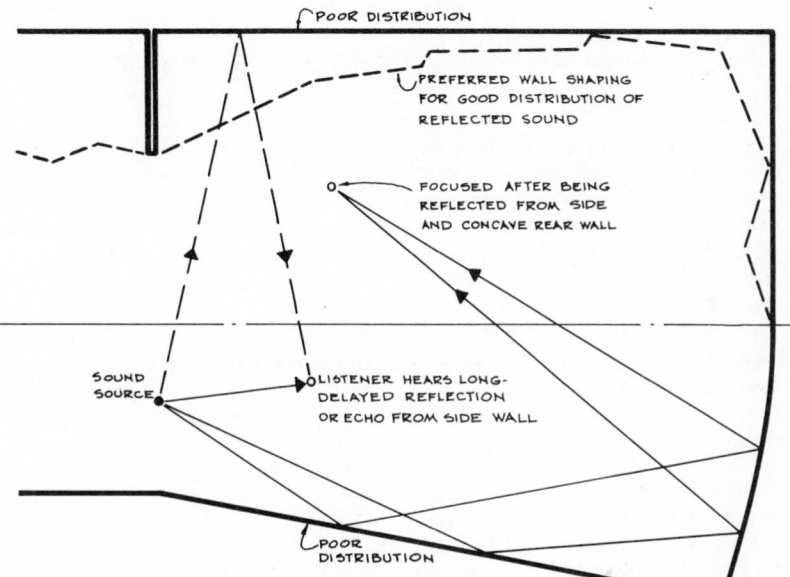

Fig. 40. Effect of wall shaping on sound distribution

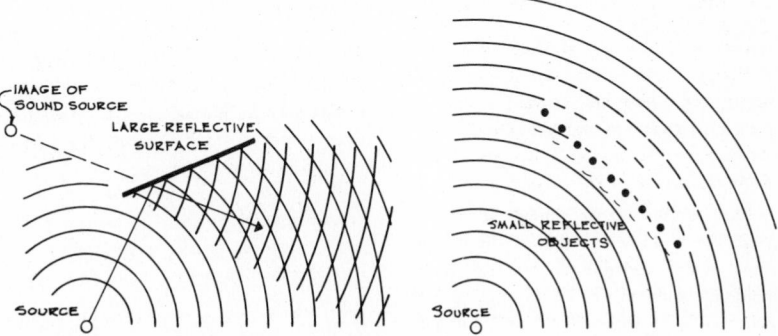

Fig. 41. Effect of size of surface on sound reflection

ume a larger number of people could be accommodated, and therefore, the reverberation time could be higher than in a modern hall with the same seating capacity unless the volume is also increased. But, increasing the volume also reduces the total energy density and if the hall gets too big, the sound tends to lose its "punch."

As we saw in an earlier section, the cri-

teria for reverberation time in auditoriums for various uses show a wide range of acceptable values. These go from less than a second for certain types of speech activity to two or more seconds for liturgical music.

If an auditorium must accommodate a very wide variety of functions, it may be necessary to introduce mechanisms for varying the reverberation characteristics.

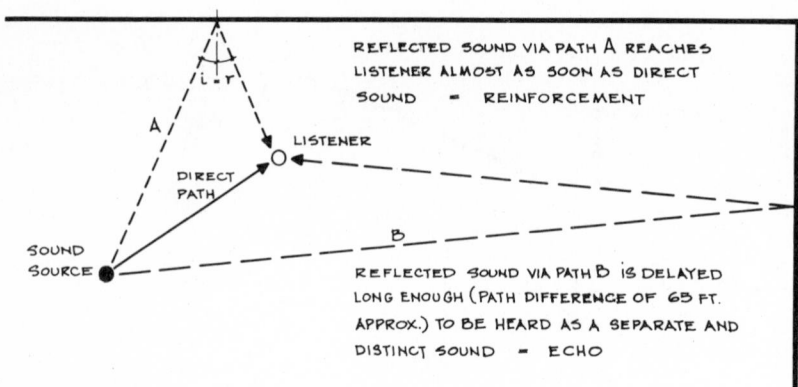

Fig. 42. Long-delayed reflection of sufficient intensity may be heard as echoes

However, if sound-absorbing panels or curtains or other elements are to be introduced to reduce the reverberation time from a high value for music performances to low values for speech, it is necessary to change large areas of the wall surfaces from hard to soft. A significant change cannot be accomplished merely by turning a few panels around or making other minor modifications. Remember that the seating area is a large "flywheel" of absorption, and that, unless one introduces an area of sound absorption almost equal to the seating area, he does not change things very much (see Fig. 43). It should also be evident that the seating area should have a fairly constant sound-absorbing characteristic regardless of audience size. Thus, fabric-upholstered seats are an acoustical necessity in *any* well-designed auditorium.

BUILDINGS WHERE HEARING CONDITIONS ARE IMPORTANT

Schools

Often overlooked in today's quest for flexibility and new structural forms in school design is the basic need for good hearing conditions in all of the spaces, either with or without folding partitions.

In the lower elementary classroom the problem is usually one of noise suppression; thus, an over-all treatment of the

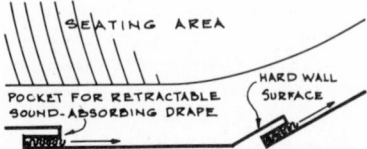

Fig. 43. Example of a method for introducing "variable" sound absorption in room design

ceiling area with a sound-absorbing material is advised. However, in the secondary school classroom where lecture teaching is normal, it is generally better to use the central part of the classroom ceiling as a sound reflector to make the communication between teacher and pupil easier: it is really a small auditorium. A very rough rule-of-thumb says that only about half the ceiling area should be covered with sound-absorbing material in an ordinary thirty-pupil classroom.

Music rehearsal rooms should, in general, have higher ceilings than ordinary classrooms, usually at least 15 ft and preferably 20 ft, and some effort should be made to introduce sound-diffusing elements in the enclosing surfaces. It is almost hopeless to ask a large school band to rehearse comfortably in a room with a 9 ft ceiling covered with acoustical tile! These rooms should be isolated as much as possible from the rest of the building, but if they must be placed close to other classrooms, special double constructions must be used to separate them.

The music department often contains, in addition to the large rehearsal rooms, small practice rooms which must have special attention to isolation details (discussed in section on "Sound isolation"). It is usually a good idea not to open the practice rooms directly into the rehearsal room but rather to have an intervening corridor or sound lock so that the rooms can be used simultaneously.

If the school has an auditorium, its design should follow the basic principles outlined earlier. There should always be a sound-reflecting ceiling in the stage area for the use of musicians when they perform. This can be permanent or removable depending on the program. Also, hopefully, the auditorium will have fabric-upholstered seats so that it will be as satisfactory for rehearsals when empty or for

small groups as it will be for full occupancy. When an auditorium can be used for a variety of functions and audience size it is an achievement of true flexibility.

Often the gymnasium must serve the function of an auditorium, and if it does, a good compromise can be achieved by treating only part of the ceiling with sound-absorbing material for noise and reverberation control leaving the central portion hard for sound-reinforcing reflection. If the stage is at one end of the room, the opposite end can be treated with a sound-absorbing material to reduce echo (see Fig. 44), and sometimes a sound-reflecting panel can be arranged at the platform end of the room to give additional sound-reinforcing reflections. The gymnasium is probably the only space in a school besides the auditorium where a speech reinforcing system may be required and only the highest quality components should be used. These systems should not be merely an extension of the basic paging and announcement system for the school.

Multipurpose auditoriums

Large auditoriums intended for conventions, concerts, plays, ballet, and every other conceivable type of performance are being built in many cities throughout the world. To be really successful, these buildings should not be designed to seat more than 2,500 to 3,000 people, and if concert music is an important part of the program of use, the design should certainly be governed to some extent by good concert hall criteria: i.e., shape, volume, and basic reverberation time. When the auditorium is used for concert purposes, there should *always* be a music enclosure installed on the stage to make the performance area a part of the auditorium and to give the musicians an opportunity to hear each other and achieve good balance. One cannot expect an orchestra or a chorus to perform in the usual stagehouse full of sound-absorbing scenery and draperies. An enclosure for the stage must be made of heavy, sound-reflecting material (plywood, steel, etc.)— it cannot be light painted canvas—and it must be so arranged that it can be put in place and taken down with a minimum of effort (see Fig. 45).

The plan and section for the multipurpose auditorium must of necessity be governed largely by occupancy requirements, but all of the basic rules still hold: no deep underbalconies, no domed ceilings, no curved walls, no over-all sound-absorbing treatment, good doors to the lobbies, well-isolated mechanical equipment and stage scenery shops, and fabric-uphol-

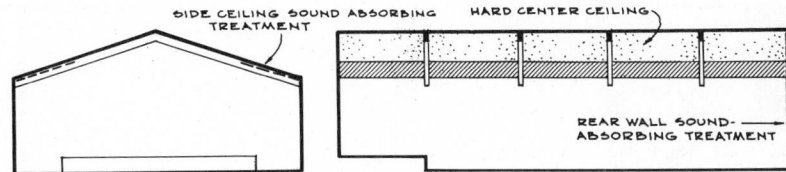

Fig. 44. Example of a simple acoustical treatment for a multipurpose room

stered seats for stable reverberation characteristics. It may be desirable to provide a folding section ceiling to make the auditorium not only visually but acoustically smaller for certain types of use (e.g., theater for 1,200 people in a 2,500-seat hall) (see Fig. 46).

Churches

All of the basic requirements for good hearing must be met in the church, but there are a number of specific matters peculiar to this building type that the designer must take into account. Usually, the form of the church itself will not be governed quite so much by acoustical considerations as would a school auditorium, but basically difficult shapes, such as domes, barrel vaults, ets., should be avoided at all cost. The reverberation time in the church should be designed to be fairly high (upwards of 1.6 sec), and this means special attention must be directed to problems of speech intelligibility. In the larger church (300 seats or more), it will often be necessary to provide either a speech-reinforcing system or a carefully designed pulpit canopy. The latter is often an excellent device to bring direct speech sound to the listeners without the use of electronic reinforcement. The pulpit, of course, does nothing for speech at the altar and in the lectern, but many churches up to 1,000 seats have been designed with good pulpit canopies and no sound amplification with excellent results (see Fig. 47).

An important function of the enclosing surfaces in a church is to give strong, mutually reinforcing reflections to the congregation. This gives every member of the congregation the sense of being part of a group of people singing and praying, and encourages participation in common worship. A church with a sound-absorptive ceiling that does not reflect sound from one part of the room to another leaves each member of the congregation feeling alone and conspicuous, and thus nonparticipating.

Another important acoustics problem in the church is the placement of the choir and the organ and their relation to the congregation. The choir should be out in the open, it should be grouped in as nearly a square array as possible, and it should be immediately in front of the organ (the pipes, not the console) where the singers can hear the organ as the congregation will hear it (see Fig. 48). The choir should *not* be tucked in a low-ceilinged alcove, nor divided across a wide chancel, nor strung out in a long line, nor should the organ pipes be widely distributed. If the organ and choir are

well placed in the church, at either front or rear, if the ceiling and wall surfaces are so arranged that the congregation is in the same space as the musicians, and if all the people in the church receive reinforcing reflections from the enclosing surfaces, almost inevitably good results will be obtained.

REFERENCES

Beranek, L. L. *Music Acoustics and Architecture.* John Wiley and Sons, Inc., New York 1963).

Knudsen, V. O. and C. M. Harris. *Acoustical Designing in Architecture.* John Wiley and Sons Inc., New York, (1950).

Johnson, F. R. Acoustics for Music Performance, *Musical America* (February and March, 1960). Reprinted in abbreviated form in *Architectural Record*, (December, 1960).

Newman, R. B. and R. H. Bolt. Architectural Acoustics, a series of four articles in *Architectural Record* (April, June, September, November, 1950).

Newman, R. B. (ed.) Design for Hearing, *Progressive Architecture* (May, 1959).

SOUND REINFORCING SYSTEMS

In many situations, to obtain adequate loudness and good distribution of sound it is necessary to augment the natural transmission of sound from source to listener by means of a sound-reinforcing system. In large sports arenas, in airport terminal buildings, and in other noisy locations, it is almost always necessary to provide sound reinforcement. Even in rooms where most strong-voiced speakers can be heard clearly, the weaker voices must be amplified, and there is often the need to amplify recorded material or movie sound. In all cases, however, the design of the sound-reinforcing system *must* be carefully integrated with the design of the room and with its acoustical characteristics.

There are two principal types of sound-amplification systems: central and distributed. The preferred type in most situations is the central system in which a loud-speaker (or cluster of loud-speakers) is located directly above the actual source of sound. Only *one* loud-speaker position

is used in a system of this sort, and it is capable of giving maximum realism. The listener with his two ears is readily able to localize the direction of the source of sound, and if the amplified signal comes from the same direction as the original sound, he gets an impression merely of increased loudness or clarity but not of artificial "amplified" sound (Fig. 49).

The other principal type of sound-reinforcing system is the distributed type. In this system one uses a large number of loud-speakers located *overhead*. This type of system operates much like down-lighting. We cover the room with small "pools" of sound, each listener receiving sound from only one loud-speaker. This type of system is used in any situation where the ceiling height is inadequate to use a central system or where all listeners cannot have "line-of-sight" on a central loud-

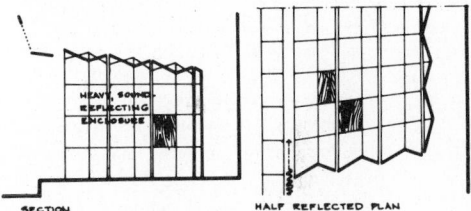

Fig. 45. Example of an orchestral enclosure for a large multipurpose stage

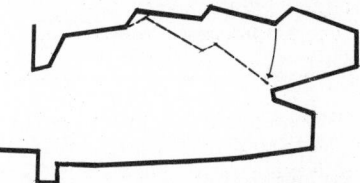

Fig. 46. A large hall can sometimes be converted to a smaller one by using properly designed adjustable elements

Fig. 47. A pulpit canopy may provide effective natural reinforcement of speech in churches

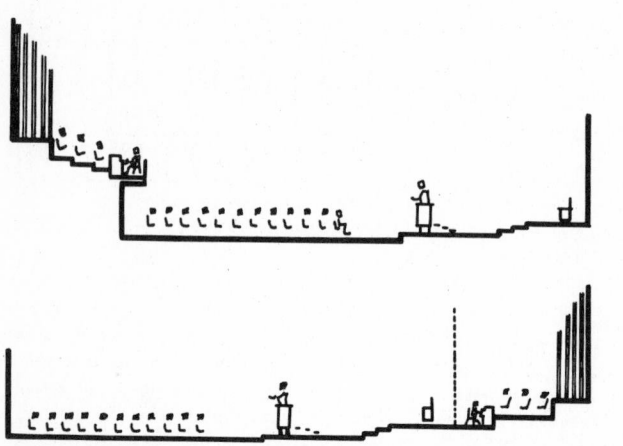

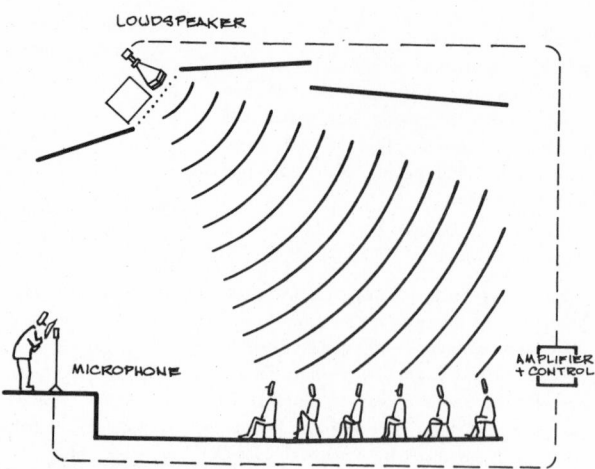

Fig. 48. The organ, choir, and console must be considered a unit of inseparable parts with unobstructed acoustical "line-of-sight" to the congregation. Front or rear gallery locations can be equally effective

Fig. 49. Central loud-speaker system

speaker. It is also used in such spaces as large convention halls, hotel ballrooms, or large conference rooms where there must be a very flexible arrangement of the space for amplifying sources of sound in any position in the hall. It is the logical system for most airport terminal buildings where the amplified signal usually must be somewhat higher in level in order to override the high background noise levels due to aircraft operations. The distributed system is a flexible system, and while it does not give maximum realism, in reinforcing live activities, it can be made to provide high intelligibility in many difficult situations (Fig. 50).

Loud-speakers should not be located at the two sides of the proscenium opening, nor should they be distributed along the

two sides of the room, nor in the four corners of a large reverberant space. These systems never work well, and the hearing conditions in a space can usually be improved by shutting them off! (See Fig. 51.)

CENTRAL SYSTEMS

The loud-speaker for a central system usually consists of a cluster of directional horns, some of which handle the high-frequency end of the audible spectrum, and larger loud-speakers which handle the low-frequency end of the spectrum. The high-frequency horns are usually exponential, multicell, or radial horns and are arranged in clusters to give coverage of specific areas of the seating. It is important that the horns have excellent direc-

tional characteristics, and that the level of operation of the several units be individually adjustable. One *cannot* achieve high-quality sound amplification without loud-speakers with carefully controlled directional characteristics. If a loud-speaker system is to be used only for speech purposes, the system need not have any low-frequency loud-speakers and can be housed in a smaller space than a full frequency range system (used for music). Usually, a speech system is cut off at approximately 300 cps (i.e., these loud-speakers do not amplify sounds below that frequency). This results in no loss in realism and actually improves intelligibility in rooms with "boomy" characteristics.

The designer of an auditorium incorporating a loud-speaker system must realize that the system will take a great deal of space and that it cannot be tucked conveniently into a 1-ft slot. The grille in front of the loud-speaker must be completely transparent to sound and must contain no large-scale elements (see Fig. 52). Every listener in the room must have line-of-sight on the loudspeaker; we do not count on reflection of sound from room surfaces to fill in any areas not covered by direct "line-of-sight."

The operator of the sound system should be located toward the rear of the seating area where he can hear the system as it is heard by the audience. He should not be behind a glass window in a booth receiving sound only on a monitor loudspeaker. The power amplifiers can be in any convenient location but the actual controls must be "in the room."

Microphones must be placed near the sources of sound and if there are to be many sources, as in a play, there must be

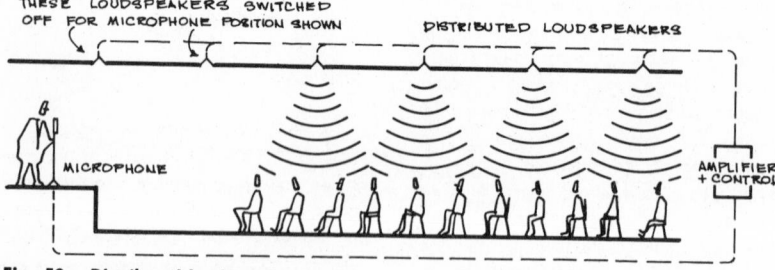

Fig. 50. Distributed loud-speaker system

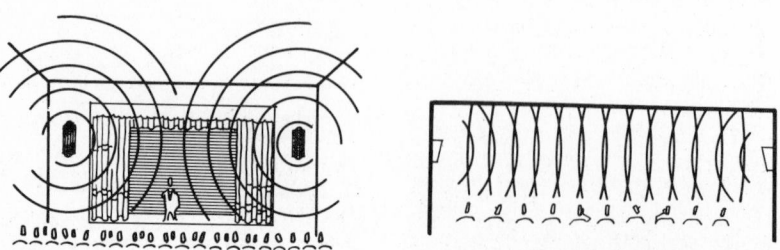

Fig. 51. Poor loud-speaker placement can mean ineffective sound reinforcement

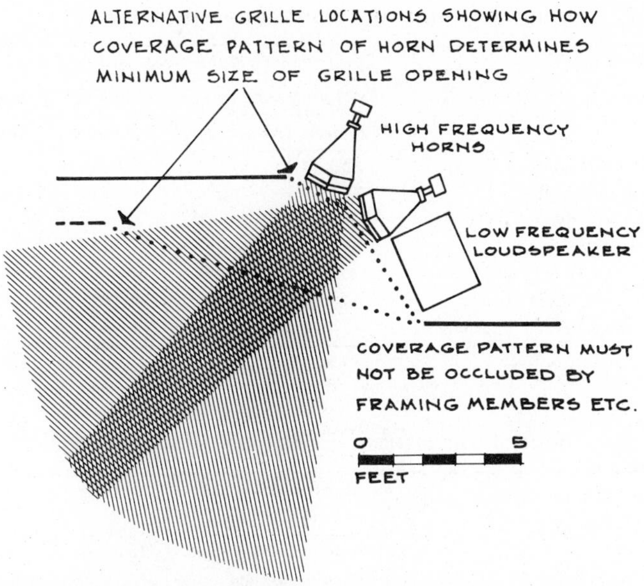

ALTERNATIVE GRILLE LOCATIONS SHOWING HOW
COVERAGE PATTERN OF HORN DETERMINES
MINIMUM SIZE OF GRILLE OPENING

HIGH FREQUENCY HORNS

LOW FREQUENCY LOUDSPEAKER

COVERAGE PATTERN MUST
NOT BE OCCLUDED BY
FRAMING MEMBERS ETC.

0   5
FEET

Fig. 52. Loud-speaker grille sizes are determined by the coverage patterns of the loud-speakers behind them

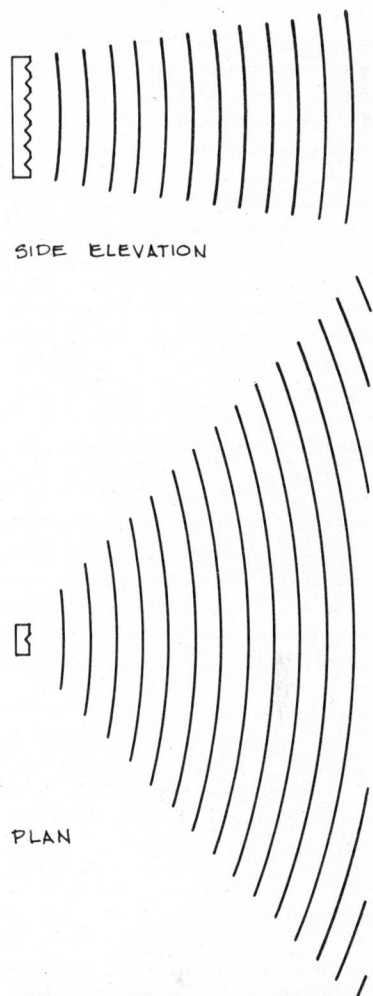

SIDE ELEVATION

PLAN

Fig. 53. A line-source or column loudspeaker and its coverage characteristics

many microphones suspended overhead or concealed in the scenery so that the actors are always relatively close to these pickup devices.

There is also the important problem of feedback of sound energy from loudspeaker to microphone, and the relative locations of microphones to the loudspeakers must be carefully considered to avoid the familiar squealing or howling of a poorly designed and operated system. This is a matter for detailed consideration by the designer of the system, and is not primarily an architectural question except in so far as relative location of loudspeaker to microphone is concerned. In the large arena or sports building, the central cluster of loud-speakers is usually suspended without any attempt at concealment, and some central position can usually be found giving everyone clear "line-of-sight" on the unit.

In some situations, line-source loudspeakers are preferable to radial or multi-cellular horns (see Fig. 53). These units, made up of a series of cone-type loudspeakers, also take space, and this must be carefully considered in the design of the building.

DISTRIBUTED SYSTEMS

In this type of sound-amplifying system it is extremely important to have an adequate number of loudspeaker units. They are generally placed in the ceiling facing down and sounding through appropriate grillage. Each loud-speaker unit is consid-

ered to cover between 60 and 90 deg, depending on the type selected. Even the highest quality units with the most suitable grille do not cover more than 90 deg adequately; when concealed behind fake diffusers, they are far less satisfactory (Fig. 54). Unfortunately, many loudspeakers employed in such systems beam high-frequency energy rather sharply. Uniform, high speech intelligibility is not possible with such systems; also, they must be operated at an uncomfortably high level to permit listeners between loudspeakers to hear properly.

In order to prevent feedback, a flexible system is usually provided with switching arrangements so that certain loudspeakers can be shut off when a source of sound is to be placed immediately under one of the units in a space for flexible use.

As mentioned earlier, loud-speakers should never be placed along the side walls of a room, cross firing. This cross firing always causes the listener to hear from many loud-speakers at the same time, with multiple time delays reducing speech intelligibility. In a church, the loudspeakers might be located in the bottoms of chandeliers over the heads of the worshippers; there are many ways in which loudspeakers can be located properly for such assistance. Sometimes, when a central loud-speaker system is used for an auditorium where people are seated on the platform with the speaker, participating perhaps in a panel or merely serving as background, a few loud-speakers operated at low level can be placed for the

convenience of these listeners so that they hear more than merely the reverberant sound from the hall itself.

TIME DELAY

Artificial echo is often a problem, particularly in distributed systems. Consider a listener at the rear of a long auditorium which may use a distributed loud-speaker system for any of the reasons discussed above. This listener will hear amplified sound almost instantaneously from the

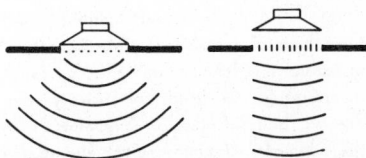

Fig. 54. Poorly chosen loud-speaker grille materials can markedly affect the sound distribution from any loud-speaker

loud-speaker overhead while the natural sound will arrive at some later time, depending on the distance to the platform. This delay in the arrival of the natural sound (due to the fact that sound in air travels at the rate of about 1,120 fps compared with the very much more rapid speed of the electrical signal between the microphone and the loudspeaker) may be sufficient to cause a discrete echo if the delay is in the order of 65 msec or more; or if the delay is somewhat less than this, the echo can appear as simply a muddying effect on the sound heard by the listener. To resolve this problem it is necessary to introduce a delay device in the electrical circuit which, in effect, delays the loudspeaker sound so that it arrives at approximately the same time as the natural sound. For a very long room, two or more delay circuits may be required, serving several zones along the length of the room. These devices have been used most successfully where distributed loud-speaker systems supplement a central system (e.g., under a deep balcony overhang), but of course, they mean additional initial expenditure and maintenance costs. Time delay is usually a last resort and may not ever be required if the sound system design is considered in the early design stages of the space.

REFERENCES

Beranek, L. L. Acoustics. chaps. 6–9, McGraw-Hill Book Company Inc., New York, 1954.

Olson, Harry F. Acoustical Engineering. D. Van Nostrand Company Inc., Princeton, N.J. (1957).

Klepper, D. L. Room Acoustics and Sound System Design, Institute of Radio Engineers Transactions on Audio (May–June, 1960).

Table 7. Sound transmission limitations—partitions

Location of partition	Sound transmission class (STC)[1]			
	Low background noise		High background noise[2]	
	Bedrooms	Other rooms	Bedrooms	Other rooms
Between apartments[3]	50	45	45	40
Apartment to corridor[4]	45	40	45	40
Apartment to public space (average noise)[5]	55	50	50	45
Apartment to public and service areas (high noise)[6]	60	55	55	45
Between rooms within apartment[7]	45		40	

Table 8. Sound transmission limitations—floor/ceilings

Location	Sound transmission class (STC)[1]		Impact noise rating (INR)[7,8]	
	Low background noise	High background noise[2]	Low background noise	High background noise[2]
Between apartments[3]	50	45	0	−2
Corridor floors above apartments	55	50	+5	+2
Apartment floor above public space[9]	50[10]	45[10]	−5	−8
Public space or service areas above apartment[11]	55[10]	50[10]	+5	+5

[1] Determined in accordance with ASTM E90.
[2] For apartments above eighth floor, assume low background noise.
[3] For high-rental apartments, increase all STC values by 5 db.
[4] Corridor floors assumed to be carpeted; if not, increase values by 5 db.
[5] Lobbies, laundries, storage rooms, stairs, etc.
[6] Boiler rooms, mechanical equipment rooms, elevator shafts, incinerator shafts, garages, commercial uses.
[7] Recommended, not mandatory.
[8] Determined by FHA No. 750, "Impact Noise Control in Multifamily Dwellings."
[9] Does not apply to floors over storage rooms, mechanical equipment rooms, or other rooms where noise from above would not be objectionable.
[10] Increase 5 db when over or under boiler rooms, mechanical equipment rooms, or other areas of high noise level.
[11] Not recommended.

FHA REQUIREMENTS

IMPACT NOISE CONTROL DETAILS FOR DWELLINGS

The United States is one of the few highly developed countries of the world which do not have in their building codes some kind of requirement for the control of noise. This has resulted in progressive deterioration of acoustical privacy and comfort and increasing complaints from the occupants of multifamily buildings. By contrast, more and more countries abroad have become concerned over the intrusion of noise and its effect on the health and happiness of their people, and have instituted control measures, based on careful and thorough investigations.

Now for the first time an important American code has established standards in this field. The Federal Housing Administration, in its new Minimum Property Standards for Multifamily Housing (November, 1963), has set minimum requirements for sound transmission which represent a drastic improvement over previous general practice, even in high-rental apartment buildings. The new FHA requirements are given in Tables 7 and 8. For constructions which meet these requirements, see Table 4 in the section on "Sound isolation."

Since data on impact noise were not so plentiful nor so readily accessible as for airborne noise, FHA sponsored a special study[1] of impact noise control by Bolt Beranek and Newman, Inc. A careful examination was made of more than a dozen foreign codes, and of the surveys and technical studies on which they were based. The results were then adapted to the needs of the American people, with consideration being given to significant differences in population density, living habits, noise environment, noise tolerance,

[1] "Impact Noise Control in Multifamily Dwellings," FHA No. 750, 1963.

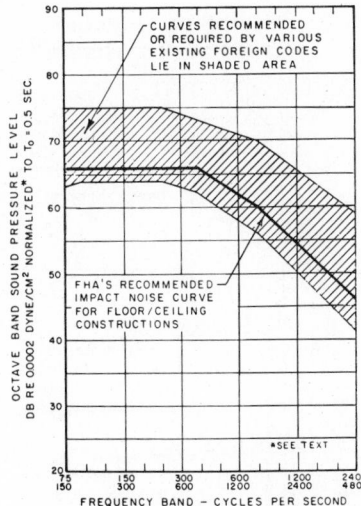

Fig. 55. FHA's curve asks for greater isolation than many foreign codes. The noise transmission is given in decibels.

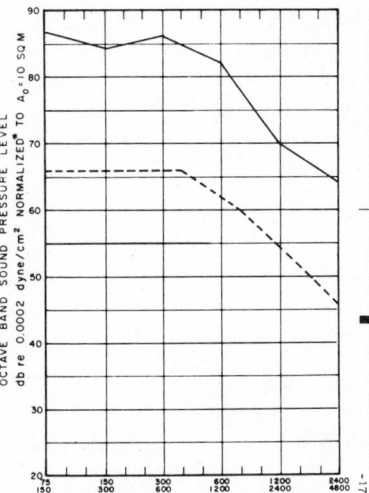

Fig. 56. Solid line is noise through wood joist floor (FHA curve dashed). Impact noise rating (INR) is —17.

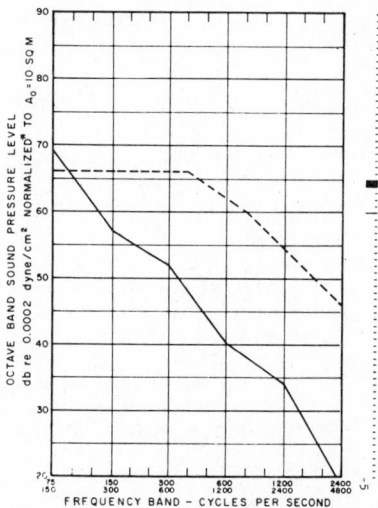

Fig. 57. Solid line is noise through wood joist floor covered by carpet and foam pad. Impact rating is +5.

building costs, etc. An original contribution of the FHA study is recognition of the importance of background noise in setting transmission-loss requirements. Two categories are established, and lower transmission values are permitted when the background noise level is higher (Table 8).

FHA's recommended impact noise curve and its relation to various European code requirements, is shown in Fig. 55. The curve shows for each frequency the maximum acceptable impact sound-pressure level (ISPL) due to thumping a floor overhead with a standard tapping machine. The method of evaluating various constructions is shown in Figs. 56 and 57. The FHA curve is taken as zero and the constructions are rated as plus or minus the number of decibels by which they exceed or fail to meet the standard. The FHA report includes curves and ratings for 47 foreign constructions which are described in detail. Descriptions and ratings for selected constructions which most nearly approximate common American constructions, are given in Table 9.

Selection of a good floor/ceiling construction is not enough. The excellent isolation provided by a floating raft floor can be nullified by careless detailing which permits conduits, ducts, or plumbing to "short-circuit" the isolation, or by poor supervision which permits the raft floor to be attached solidly to the walls at the edges. The FHA report includes a check list of suggestions for avoiding errors of this nature, and a number of sketches of acoustically important details (see the following pages).

Table 9. Impact noise ratings (INR) for various floor/ceiling constructions

Type of construction	INR
Reinforced concrete slab 6½–9½ in. thick; floor ⅝-in. composition, or none; ceiling ½-in. plaster, or none	—17
Reinforced concrete slab 4½ in. thick; floor ¾-in. cement; ceiling suspended gypsum lath and plaster 1 in. thick	—4
Reinforced concrete slab 5 in. thick; floor ⅛-in. linoleum on 2-in. concrete on 1-in. glass fiber blanket; ceiling ½-in. plaster	+1
Reinforced concrete slab 6 in. thick; floor ¾-in. t-and-g boards on 1½ by 2 in. battens on ½-in. pads of fiberboard, asbestos, or cork; ceiling ½-in. plaster	+3
Same except 1-in. glass fiber blanket instead of pads	+7
Reinforced concrete slab 6½ in. thick; floor ¼-in. cork tile; ceiling ½-in. gypsum board on metal clips on furring strips	+4
Wood joists 2 by 8 in., 16 in. on center; floor ¾-in. t-and-g boards; ceiling ⅜ in. gypsum board nailed to joists	—18
Wood joists 2 by 7 in., 16 in. on center; floor ⅞-in. boards on 2 by 2 in. battens on 1-in. glass fiber blanket; ceiling ⅜-in. gypsum board with skim coat of plaster	—8
Same except standard lath and plaster ceiling instead of gypsum board	—4
Wood joists 2 by 8 in., 16 in. on center; floor ¾-in. t-and-g boards; ceiling ⅝-in. gypsum board screwed to resilient metal runners 12 in. on center nailed to joists	—5
Wood joists 2 by 10 in., 16 in. on center; floor ⅜-in. nylon carpet on ¼-in. foam rubber pad, on ½-in. plywood underlay, on ⅝-in. plywood subfloor; ceiling ½-in. gypsum board nailed to joists	+5
Steel bar joists 7 in. deep, 27 in. on center; floor ⅛-in. vinyl-asbestos tile on 2-in. concrete slab on ⅜-in. ribbed lath; ceiling ½-in. plaster on ⅜-in. gypsum lath clipped to furring channels 16 in. on center tied to bottom of joists	—10
Same except floor finish ⅜-in. vinyl carpet on ¼-in. foam rubber pad, instead of ⅛-in. vinyl-asbestos tile	+26

Prepared for FHA by Bolt Beranek and Newman, Inc.

CONCRETE FLOOR STRUCTURE
Floor carpeted; plaster ceiling

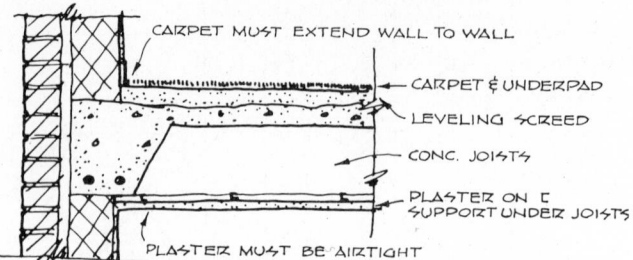

CARPET MUST EXTEND WALL TO WALL
CARPET & UNDERPAD
LEVELING SCREED
CONC. JOISTS
PLASTER ON C SUPPORT UNDER JOISTS
PLASTER MUST BE AIRTIGHT

Plaster must be airtight to get most loss of energy through the structure and to prevent transmission of airborne noise

RESILIENTLY SUSPENDED PLASTER CEILING

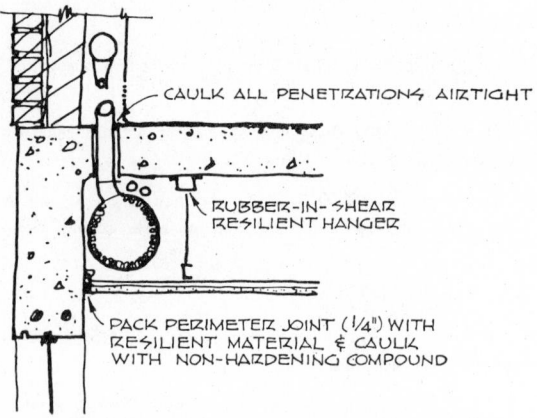

CAULK ALL PENETRATIONS AIRTIGHT
RUBBER-IN-SHEAR RESILIENT HANGER
PACK PERIMETER JOINT (¼") WITH RESILIENT MATERIAL & CAULK WITH NON-HARDENING COMPOUND

All penetrations must be caulked to prevent transmission of impact sound through piping, ductwork; also to stop airborne sound (*above*). Conduit and duct connections must be flexible to maintain impact noise reduction of floor (*below*)

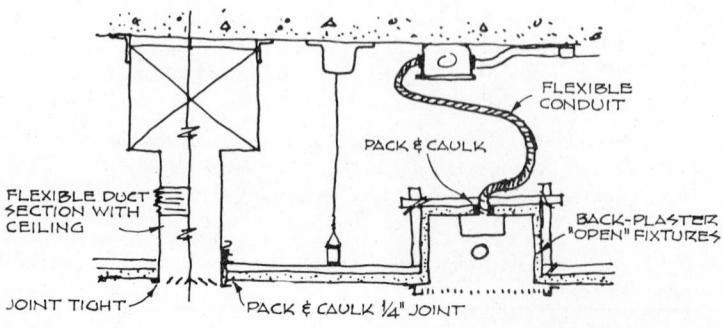

FLEXIBLE CONDUIT
PACK & CAULK
FLEXIBLE DUCT SECTION WITH CEILING
BACK-PLASTER "OPEN" FIXTURES
JOINT TIGHT
PACK & CAULK ¼" JOINT

EXTERIOR OR INTERIOR
WALL-FLOOR INTERSECTION

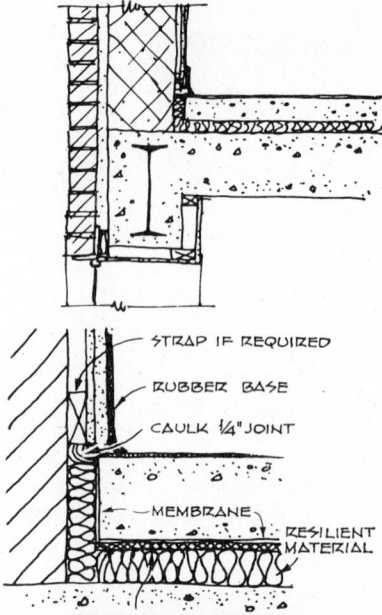

STRAP IF REQUIRED
RUBBER BASE
CAULK ¼" JOINT
MEMBRANE
RESILIENT MATERIAL
PROTECTIVE LAYER FOR MEMBRANE DURING POUR
NOTE: RESILIENT MATERIAL TURNS UP AT ALL EDGES

Bottom sketch shows techniques for isolating concrete topping from the structural slab. Full detail is above

SERVICE PENETRATION AT
EDGE OF FLOATING FLOOR

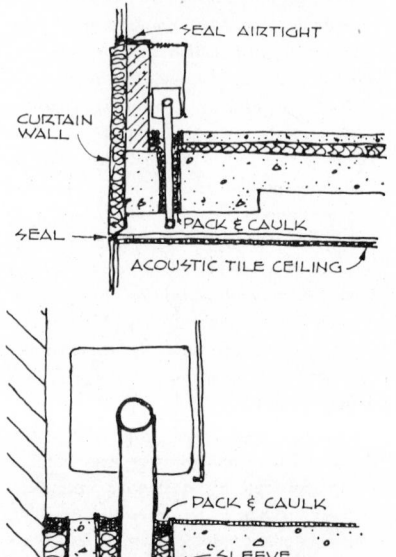

SEAL AIRTIGHT
CURTAIN WALL
PACK & CAULK
SEAL
ACOUSTIC TILE CEILING
PACK & CAULK
SLEEVE
RESILIENT MATERIAL
SLEEVE
PACK & CAULK

Pipe penetrations are sleeved and packed to prevent the impact noise from being carried through the pipe

SHORT-CIRCUITING OF FLOATING RAFT FLOORS

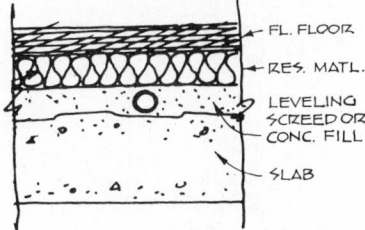

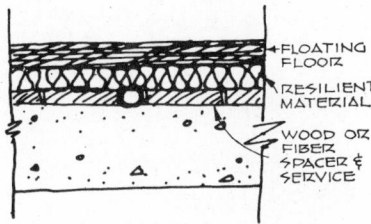

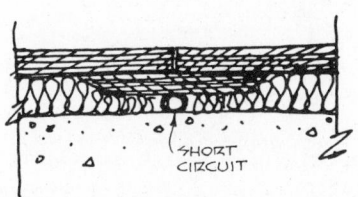

Top two sketches show proper location of services under a floating floor. In bottom sketch, service "shorts out" resilient layer, since it is directly under floor

DETAILS OF WOOD FLOATING RAFT FLOOR

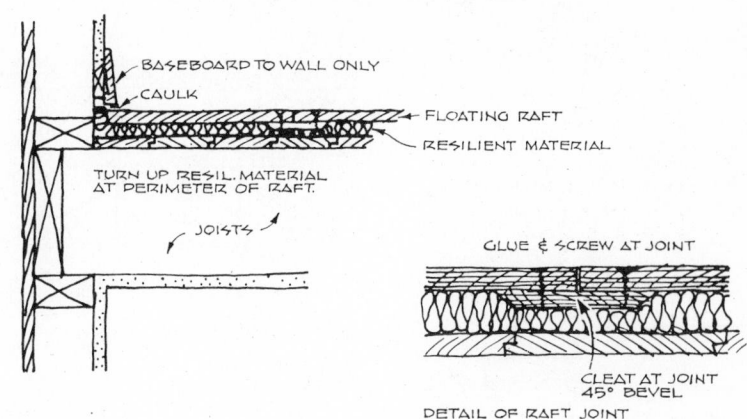

CONSTRUCTION OF A TYPICAL FLOATING RAFT FLOOR

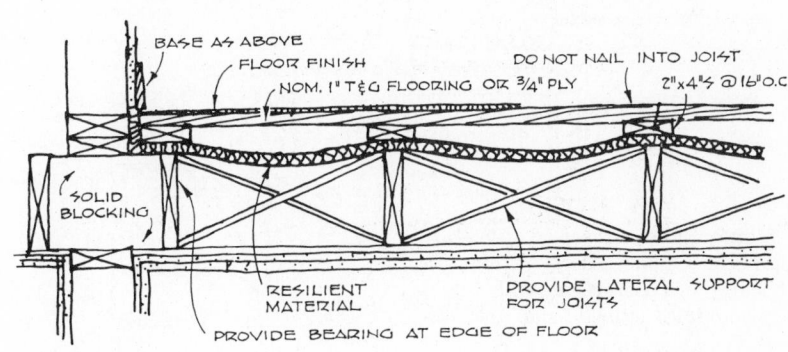

PENETRATION OF CONCRETE FLOATING FLOORS

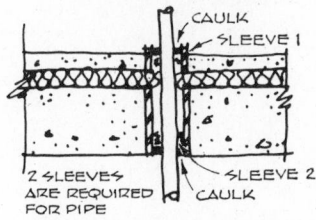

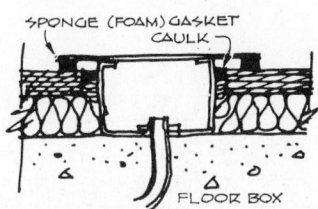

Piping through floors should be sleeved and caulked so that floating floor will not be short-circuited. Electrical boxes should be isolated from the finish floor by a gasket

SERVICE PENETRATION OF FLOATING RAFT FLOOR

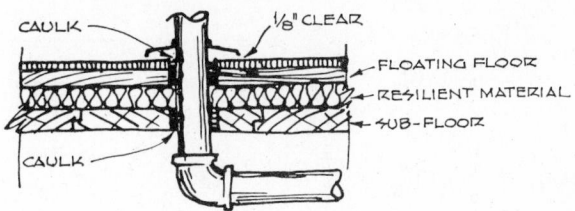

PLASTER CEILING ON RESILIENT CLIPS ATTACHED TO WOOD JOISTS

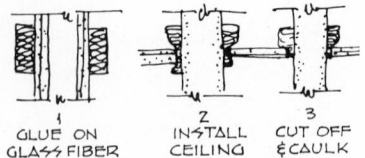

1 GLUE ON GLASS FIBER   2 INSTALL CEILING   3 CUT OFF & CAULK

Packing partition penetration

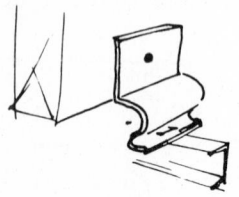

Typical resilient clip

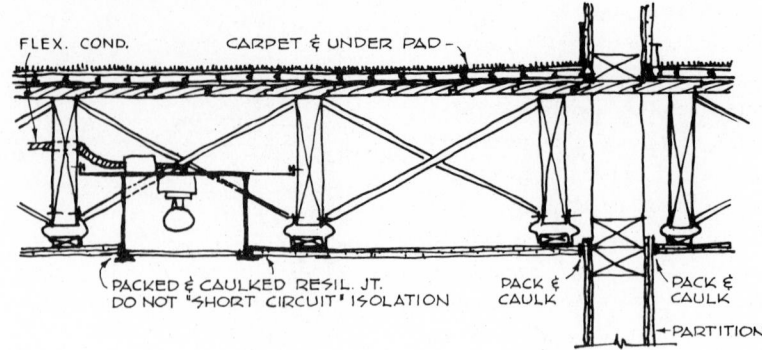

FLEX. COND.   CARPET & UNDER PAD

PACKED & CAULKED RESIL. JT. DO NOT "SHORT CIRCUIT" ISOLATION   PACK & CAULK   PACK & CAULK   PARTITION

"MIXED" CONSTRUCTIONS

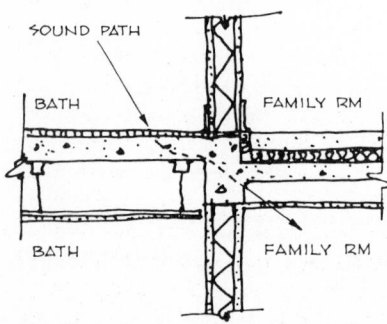

SOUND PATH

BATH   FAMILY RM

BATH   FAMILY RM

If different construction types are flanked, impact noise from the "poorer" construction will travel through structural slab on the floating floor side

IMPROPER PARTITION SUPPORT

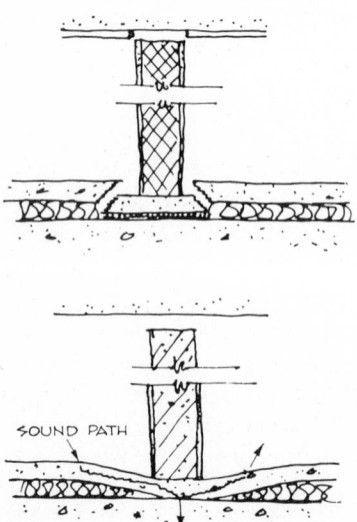

SOUND PATH

If partitions are set atop floating floor, either the topping will shear, or compressed topping and pad will offer direct sound path

CONNECTION DETAILS FOR W.C.

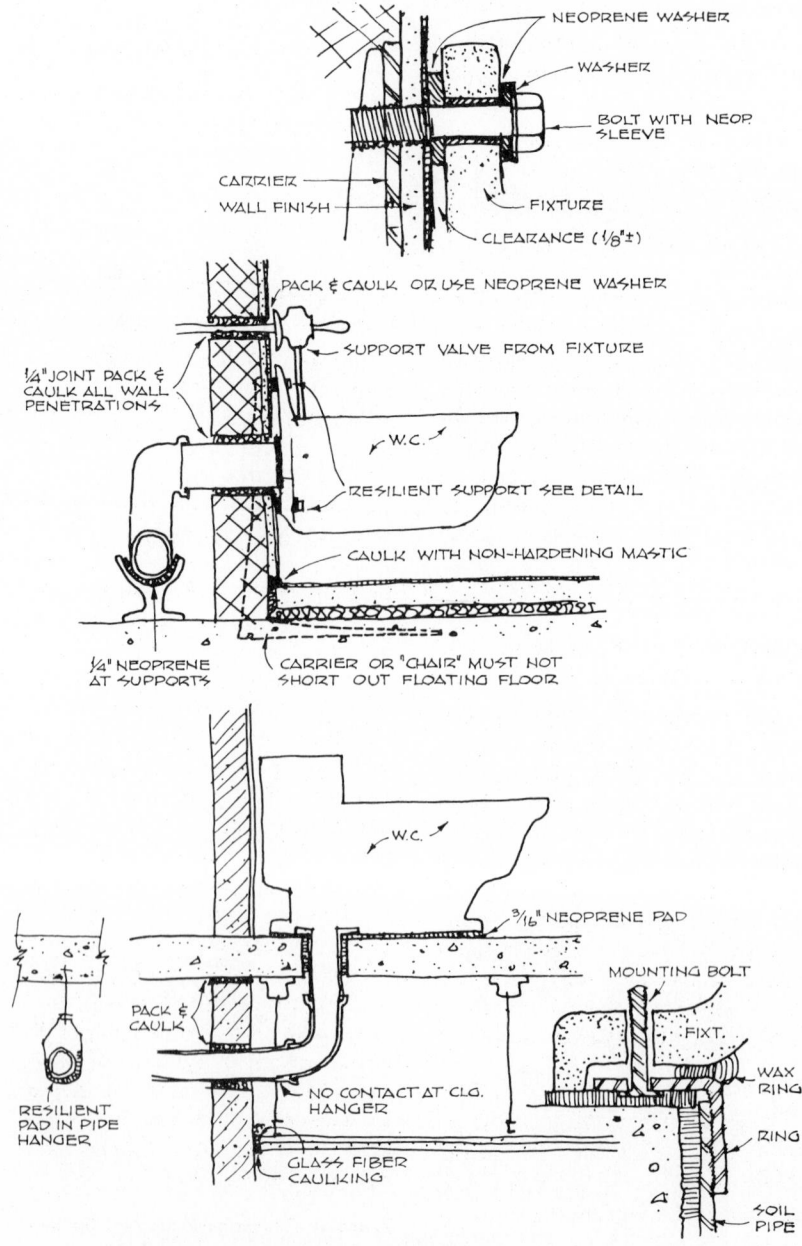

NEOPRENE WASHER

WASHER

BOLT WITH NEOP. SLEEVE

CARRIER

WALL FINISH

FIXTURE

CLEARANCE (1/8"±)

PACK & CAULK OR USE NEOPRENE WASHER

SUPPORT VALVE FROM FIXTURE

1/4" JOINT PACK & CAULK ALL WALL PENETRATIONS

W.C.

RESILIENT SUPPORT SEE DETAIL

CAULK WITH NON-HARDENING MASTIC

1/4" NEOPRENE AT SUPPORTS

CARRIER OR "CHAIR" MUST NOT SHORT OUT FLOATING FLOOR

W.C.

3/16" NEOPRENE PAD

MOUNTING BOLT

FIXT.

WAX RING

RING

SOIL PIPE

RESILIENT PAD IN PIPE HANGER

PACK & CAULK

NO CONTACT AT CLO. HANGER

GLASS FIBER CAULKING

By LAURENCE SHUMAN, *Consulting Engineer*

This section on thermal insulation, based on recent research results, covers: theory of heat transmission (briefly), a method for calculating insulation economies, recommendations on special problems, and tables of heat transmission factors. Advances in this field have been primarily in insulating materials themselves — kinds and numbers, new heat transmission data on building sections insulated with reflective materials, methods for calculating insulation requirements for concrete slabs on grade, and a greater recognition of the problems of condensation. A feature of this section is the comprehensive, easy-to-use set of tables on U factors.

Thermal insulating efficiency is a factor in: (1) temperature of inside surfaces which affect comfort of occupants and aid or deter condensation, and (2) heat transmission through building sections which determines energy requirements for both heating and cooling. Economies in fuel consumption can be calculated with reasonable accuracy (see Sheet 2) and balanced against initial cost of insulation and cost of heating-cooling system.

Coefficient of Heat Transmission, U; Definition

Calculations of heating or cooling loads are usually based on rate of heat flow through building sections, along with ventilation and moisture requirements. The symbol U designates the over-all coefficient of heat transmission for any section of building shell. The units for U are Btu per sq ft of section per hr per deg F temperature difference between inside air and outside air. It is practically always less than one.

Mechanism of Heat Transfer

The heat flow through any structural section is retarded by several elements associated with or incorporated in the section:

1. The outside surface traps a thin film of air which resists heat flow. This film varies with wind velocity and with physical character of the surface.
2. Each layer of material contributes resistance to heat flow. Usually heavy compact materials have less resistance than light ones.
3. Each measurable air space adds to the over-all resistance. Resistances vary with dimensions of the space and character of surfaces facing the space.
4. Inside surface of the section also traps an air film. This film is usually thicker than the outside film due to much lower air velocity.

The sum of these resistances gives the over-all resistance (R), whose reciprocal is U.

Heat absorbed by, or lost from, a building section is a combination of heat transfer by radiation, convection, and conduction. Radiation is controlled by character of the surfaces (emissivity) and temperature difference between surface and opposed objects, buildings, etc. Convection and conduction are functions of the roughness of the surface, air movement, and temperature difference between air and surface.

Thermal Resistance of Materials. When a material is homogeneous, such as insulating board, its ability to transfer heat, thermal conductivity k, is measured as Btu per hr, per sq ft, per degree F, per in. of thickness. The reciprocal $1/k$ is the resistivity. The resistance of any thickness of material is its resistivity per inch times the total thickness. In calculating U values, only the resistances are used.

Non-homogeneous materials, such as hollow building blocks or composite plaster and lath, are laboratory-tested for their actual thicknesses instead of per inch of thickness. The resistance is calculated for the entire thickness. The reciprocal of resistance is conductance. Both are included in Table 2.

Thermal Resistance of Air Spaces. Heat flow across an air space involves the resistance of the air in the space and the materials bounding the space.

Heat passes across the space by conduction from one face to air, then by convection through the space, and finally by conduction to the opposite face. This portion of heat flow is controlled by the dimensions and shape of the air space, the texture of the materials facing the space, the mean temperature of the space, and direction of heat flow.

Heat also crosses the space by radiation from the warm face to the colder face. It is practically unaffected by the depth of the space. It is controlled by the difference in temperature of the two faces and by their relative ability to emit or absorb radiant heat (emissivity). Factors of convection and radiation vary independently in ordinary construction. Emissivities of ordinary building materials are usually high, 0.80 or more, whereas those of metals are low, around 0.05.

When heat flow is upward, the proportion of convective heat to radiant heat is high, and the relative importance of emissivity is low. The reverse is true for heat flow downward. Low emissivity factors are most useful for the latter case, for resistance to solar heat in roofs and ceilings and for reduction of heat losses in floors over unheated areas.

Calculation of U Values

To calculate the U value for any wall, floor, ceiling or roof section, proceed as follows:

1. Select the resistance R or the resistivity $1/k$ of each material, air space or exposed surface of the given section from Table 2.
2. Where resistivity (per in.) is used, multiply by the actual thickness of the material.
3. Total the sum of the various resistances and divide it into 1.00 to get the reciprocal.
4. The result is the coefficient of heat transmission U in Btu per sq ft per hr per degree F.

Intelligent selection can be made from the wide variety of methods for adding thermal protection when the cost factors are known. Economy of operation may be sufficient to offset additional charges for better insulation. Use of insulation beyond that required for structural and comfort conditions should be based on economic analysis, and such insulation methods should be capable of repaying their costs.

A method for evaluating operating economies of insulation treatments is given here. Fuel costs and savings are expressed in terms of fuel units per unit area of building section involved. Where several possible construction assemblies are being considered, it is possible to compare the annual expense of each in terms of fuel requirements through use of their *U* values.

Fuel Requirements Chart

Cost of any building section in terms of fuel units per year can be obtained from curves on the Fuel Requirements Chart and Tables 1 and 2. The curves show the approximate number of therms (1 therm = 100,000 Btu) required by each square foot of section for various heating plant efficiencies and for the appropriate number of degree-days when the *U* factor = 1.00. Multiplying this number of fuel units by the actual *U* values of the sections being studied gives the approximate annual fuel requirement.

The chart curves are derived from formulas published in the *ASHRAE Guide*, with some modifications to indicate the additional fuel requirements in those areas where the heating load is light. Calculations based on the chart are approximately correct to 5 per cent, and take into consideration night cutback to 55 F. Where no cutback is expected, the values should be increased by about 7 per cent, and where longer cutbacks, weekend shutdowns, etc., are contemplated, individual judgment will have to be exercised for adjustments.

Fuel Requirements Chart for *U* = 1.00

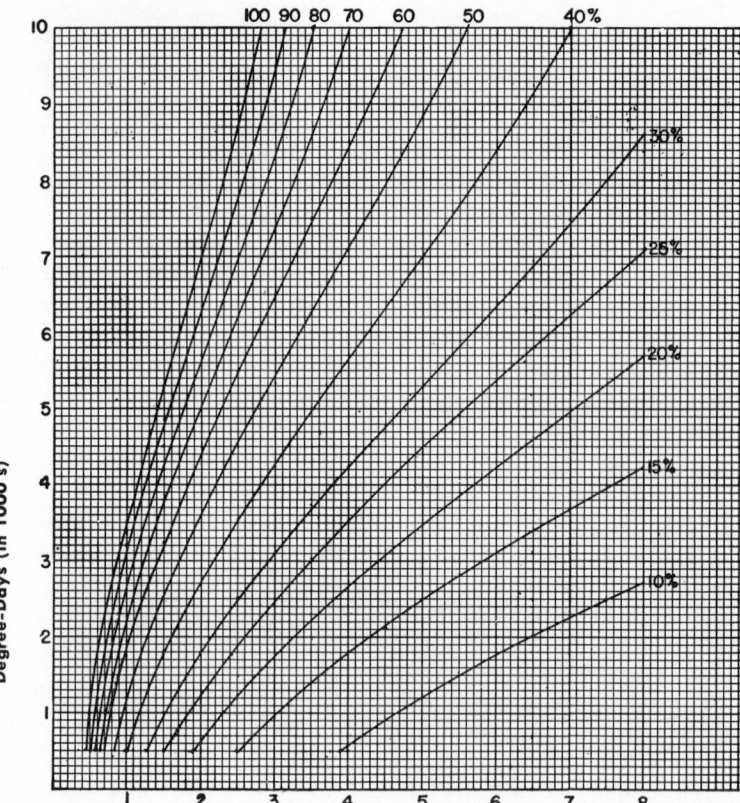

Therms (100,000 Btu's) Per Sq Ft Per Year

Use of Chart

The chart is used as follows:
1. Determine the number of degree-days for the locality of construction from the U. S. Weather Bureau or local sources.
2. Select the appropriate heating efficiency curve. The efficiency will vary with construction quality and design, heating plant design and quality, accuracy of installation, operating control methods and apparatus, and tenant habits. Suggested efficiencies are given in Table 1.
3. Locate degree-days on the vertical scale and proceed horizontally to the appropriate efficiency curve. From this point drop vertically to the horizontal fuel scale, which is in annual number of therms where *U* = 1.00.
4. Multiply this number by the number of square feet of building section and by the *U* factor.
5. Convert the number of therms to the particular type of fuel to be used by Table 2.

Cost Analysis

The annual fuel consumption for each building section allows comparisons of economy to be done as follows:

1. Set up the initial cost of each of the building sections being considered as a yearly charge covering interest and amortization.
2. Add the excess fuel cost for the sections having greater fuel consumption than the one having the least.
3. Totals will show the approximate differences in cost for each type.

For a more refined analysis, such costs as maintenance, repair, etc., should be considered. Also the heating plant may be reduced in size if heating load is cut sufficiently by insulation.

Table 1.   Suggested efficiencies for use with the chart

TYPE OF FUEL	FIRING	Boilers (steam or hot water)	Warm-air furnaces		Overflow heaters (space heaters)
			Forced	Gravity	
Gas	Designed for gas	80	70–80	70	70
	Conversion burners	70	60–70	60	—
Oil	Designed for oil	75	65–75	65	60
	Conversion burners	70	60–70	60	—
Anthracite or coke	Hand-fired:				
	No controls	60	50–60	50	40
	With controls	70	60–70	60	—
	Stoker-fired	75	65–75	65	—
Bituminous coal	Hand-fired:				
	No controls	50	40–50	40	40
	With controls	60	50–60	50	—
	Stoker-fired	65	55–65	55	—

Tables 1 and 2 can be used in conjunction with the Fuel Requirements Chart.

Table 2.   Fuel requirements

Multiply number of therms by factor in left-hand column to find fuel requirements in units at right

Factor	Cu Ft of Gas at
91	1100 Btu/cu ft
100	1000 Btu/cu ft
111	900 Btu/cu ft
125	800 Btu/cu ft
143	700 Btu/cu ft
167	600 Btu/cu ft
200	500 Btu/cu ft

Factor	Lb of Coal at
7.1	14,000 Btu/lb
7.7	13,000 Btu/lb
8.3	12,000 Btu/lb
9.1	11,000 Btu/lb
10.1	10,000 Btu/lb

Factor	Gal of Fuel Oil
0.75	No. 1
0.71	No. 2
0.67	No. 4
0.66	No. 5
0.65	No. 6

Table 3.   Heat transmission coefficients

All values in Btu per hr per sq ft per deg F temperature difference. (Data from ASHRAE Guide and Data Book, 1961.)

CLASS	MATERIAL	DESCRIPTION	CONDUCTIVITY k (for 1″ thickness)	CONDUCTANCE C (for given thickness)	RESISTIVITY $1/k$ or r (for 1″ thickness)	RESISTANCE $1/C$ or R (for given thickness)
Air Films	Inside—or still air	Ordinary materials—				
		heat flow horizontal		1.46		.68
		heat flow up		1.63		.61
		heat flow down		1.08		.92
	Outside—15 mph wind	Ordinary materials		6.0		.17
	Outside—7½ mph wind	Ordinary materials		4.0		.25
Air Spaces	Ordinary material both sides	Vertical—¾″ or more in width		1.08		.92
	Aluminum foil both sides	Vertical—¾″ or more in width		.38		2.64
Insulating Materials	Bats, blankets or fill	Mineral, animal or vegetable fiber	.27		3.70	
	Corkboard	No binder	.30		3.33	
	Insulating board	Wood or vegetable fiber	.33		3.03	
	Mineral or glass wool	Rock, slag or glass fiber	.27		3.70	
	Vermiculite	Expanded	.48		2.08	

(Table 3 continued on next page)

Table 3. Heat transmission coefficients (cont.)

CLASS	MATERIAL	DESCRIPTION	CONDUCTIVITY k (for 1" thickness)	CONDUCTANCE C (for given thickness)	RESISTIVITY $1/k$ or r (for 1" thickness)	RESISTANCE $1/C$ or R (for given thickness)
Exterior Materials	Asbestos shingles			4.76		.21
	Asphalt roll roofing			6.5		.15
	Asphalt shingles			2.27		.44
	Built-up roofing	⅜" thickness		3.00		.33
	Gypsum sheathing	½"		2.25		.45
	Insulating fiberboard	25⁄32"		.49		2.06
	Lap siding, yellow pine			1.28		.78
	Plywood sheathing	5⁄16" thick		2.56		.39
	Slate	½"	10.00	20.00	.10	.05
	Stucco	1" thick	5.00	5.00	.20	.20
	Wood shingles			1.06		.94
	Wood, yellow pine or fir	25⁄32"	.80	1.02	1.25	.98
Interior Materials	Composition wallboard	3⁄16" to ⅜"	.55		1.82	
	Gypsum plaster		5.60		.18	
	Gypsum wallboard	⅜", plain or decorated		3.10		.32
	Gypsum lath and plaster	½" plaster		2.44		.41
	Metal lath and plaster	¾" plaster		7.70		.10
	Plywood	⅜", plain or decorated		2.12		.47
Masonry Materials	Brick, common	4" thick	5.00	1.25	.20	.80
	Brick, face	4" thick	9.00	2.25	.11	.44
	Cement mortar		5.00		.20	
	Clay tile, hollow	3"		1.25		.80
		4"		.90		1.11
		6"		.66		1.52
		8"		.54		1.85
		12"		.40		2.50
	Concrete	Sand and gravel	12.00		.08	
		Cinder	4.9		.22	
		Pumice	2.42		.41	
		Vermiculite	.86		1.16	
	Concrete block, hollow	Cinder, 4"		.90		1.11
		Cinder, 8"		.58		1.72
		Cinder, 12"		.53		1.89
		Gravel, 8"		.90		1.11
		Gravel, 12"		.78		1.28
	Gypsum tile, hollow	4"		.60		1.67
	Gypsum poured	12½% wood chips	1.66		.60	
	Stone		12.50		.08	
	Terrazzo	For flooring	12.50		.08	
Miscellaneous	Aluminum		1416		.0007	
	Glass	Average	6		.167	
	Soil	Average	7		.14	
	Steel		312		.0032	

Legend:

Interior Finishes	Sheathing
A Metal lath and plaster	1 Gypsum ½″
B Gypsum board, ⅜″ decorated	2 Plywood ⁵⁄₁₆″
C Wood lath and plaster	3 Wood and building paper ²⁵⁄₃₂″
D Gypsum lath, ⅜″ and plaster	4 Insulating board ²⁵⁄₃₂″
E Plywood, ⅜″	
F Insulating board, ½″ plain or decorated	
G Insulating board, ½″ and plaster	
H Insulating board, 1″ and plaster	

Wall Type	External Finish	Sheathing	A	B	C	D	E	F	G	H
No insulation of air space	Wood Siding	1	.33	.32	.31	.31	.30	.23	.22	.17
		2	.32	.32	.31	.30	.30	.23	.22	.17
		3	.26	.26	.25	.25	.24	.19	.19	.17
		4	.20	.20	.19	.19	.19	.16	.15	.12
	Wood Shingle	1	.25	.25	.24	.24	.24	.19	.19	.14
		2	.25	.25	.24	.24	.24	.19	.18	.14
		3	.26	.26	.25	.25	.24	.19	.19	.15
		4	.17	.17	.16	.16	.16	.14	.13	.11
	Stucco	1	.43	.42	.40	.39	.39	.27	.26	.19
		2	.42	.41	.39	.39	.38	.27	.26	.19
		3	.32	.31	.30	.30	.29	.22	.22	.16
		4	.23	.23	.22	.22	.22	.18	.17	.14
	Brick Veneer	1	.37	.36	.35	.34	.34	.25	.24	.18
		2	.36	.36	.34	.34	.33	.25	.24	.18
		3	.28	.28	.27	.27	.27	.21	.20	.15
		4	.21	.21	.20	.20	.20	.17	.16	.13

Wall Type	External Finish	Sheathing	A	B	C	D	E	F	G	H
2″ bat or blanket insulation in stud space	Wood Siding	1	.10	.10	.10	.10	.10	.09	.09	.08
		2	.10	.10	.10	.10	.10	.09	.09	.08
		3	.10	.10	.09	.09	.09	.08	.08	.07
		4	.09	.09	.08	.08	.08	.08	.07	.07
	Wood Shingle	1	.09	.09	.09	.09	.09	.08	.08	.07
		2	.09	.09	.09	.09	.09	.08	.08	.07
		3	.10	.10	.09	.09	.09	.08	.08	.07
		4	.08	.08	.08	.08	.08	.07	.07	.06
	Stucco	1	.11	.11	.11	.11	.11	.10	.10	.08
		2	.11	.11	.11	.11	.11	.10	.10	.08
		3	.10	.10	.10	.10	.10	.09	.09	.08
		4	.09	.09	.09	.09	.09	.08	.08	.07
	Brick Veneer	1	.11	.11	.11	.10	.10	.09	.09	.08
		2	.11	.11	.10	.10	.10	.09	.09	.08
		3	.10	.10	.10	.10	.10	.09	.09	.07
		4	.09	.09	.09	.09	.09	.08	.08	.07

Wall Type	External Finish	Sheathing	A	B	C	D	E	F	G	H
1″ bat or blanket insulation in stud space	Wood Siding	1	.15	.15	.14	.14	.14	.12	.12	.10
		2	.15	.15	.14	.14	.14	.12	.12	.10
		3	.13	.13	.13	.13	.12	.11	.11	.10
		4	.12	.12	.11	.11	.11	.10	.10	.08
	Wood Shingle	1	.13	.13	.12	.12	.12	.11	.11	.09
		2	.13	.13	.12	.12	.12	.11	.11	.09
		3	.13	.13	.13	.13	.12	.11	.11	.10
		4	.10	.10	.10	.10	.10	.09	.09	.08
	Stucco	1	.17	.16	.16	.16	.16	.14	.13	.11
		2	.16	.16	.16	.16	.16	.14	.13	.11
		3	.15	.14	.14	.14	.14	.12	.12	.10
		4	.12	.12	.12	.12	.12	.11	.10	.09
	Brick Veneer	1	.16	.15	.15	.15	.15	.13	.12	.11
		2	.15	.15	.15	.15	.15	.13	.12	.11
		3	.14	.14	.14	.14	.14	.12	.12	.10
		4	.12	.12	.12	.12	.12	.10	.10	.09

Wall Type	External Finish	Sheathing	A	B	C	D	E	F	G	H
3″ bat or blanket insulation in stud space	Wood Siding	1	.08	.08	.08	.08	.08	.07	.07	.07
		2	.08	.08	.08	.08	.08	.07	.07	.07
		3	.08	.08	.08	.08	.07	.07	.07	.06
		4	.07	.07	.07	.07	.07	.06	.06	.06
	Wood Shingle	1	.08	.08	.07	.07	.07	.07	.07	.06
		2	.08	.08	.07	.07	.07	.07	.07	.06
		3	.08	.08	.08	.08	.07	.07	.07	.06
		4	.07	.07	.06	.06	.06	.06	.06	.05
	Stucco	1	.09	.09	.09	.09	.09	.08	.08	.07
		2	.09	.09	.09	.09	.09	.08	.08	.07
		3	.08	.08	.08	.08	.08	.07	.07	.06
		4	.07	.07	.07	.07	.07	.07	.07	.06
	Brick Veneer	1	.08	.08	.08	.08	.08	.07	.07	.07
		2	.08	.08	.08	.08	.08	.07	.07	.07
		3	.08	.08	.08	.08	.08	.07	.07	.06
		4	.07	.07	.07	.07	.07	.07	.06	.06

Legend:

Interior Finishes	Sheathing
A Metal lath and plaster	**1** Gypsum ½″
B Gypsum board, ⅜″ decorated	**2** Plywood 5⁄16″
C Wood lath and plaster	**3** Wood and building paper 25⁄32″
D Gypsum lath, ⅜″ and plaster	**4** Insulating board 25⁄32″
E Plywood ⅜″	
F Insulating board, ½″ plain or decorated	
G Insulating board, ½″ and plaster	
H Insulating board, 1″ and plaster	

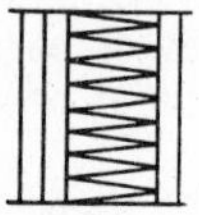

Table 1

Wall Type	External Finish	Sheathing	A	B	C	D	E	F	G	H
Stud space filled with insulation	Wood Siding	1	.08	.08	.08	.08	.07	.07	.07	.06
		2	.08	.08	.08	.07	.07	.07	.07	.06
		3	.07	.07	.07	.07	.07	.06	.06	.06
		4	.07	.07	.06	.06	.06	.06	.06	.05
	Wood Shingle	1	.07	.07	.07	.07	.07	.06	.06	.06
		2	.07	.07	.07	.07	.07	.06	.06	.06
		3	.07	.07	.07	.07	.07	.06	.06	.06
		4	.06	.06	.06	.06	.06	.06	.05	.05
	Stucco	1	.08	.08	.08	.08	.08	.07	.07	.06
		2	.08	.08	.08	.08	.08	.07	.07	.06
		3	.08	.08	.07	.07	.07	.07	.07	.06
		4	.07	.07	.07	.07	.07	.06	.06	.06
	Brick Veneer	1	.08	.08	.08	.08	.08	.07	.07	.06
		2	.08	.08	.08	.08	.08	.07	.07	.06
		3	.07	.07	.07	.07	.07	.07	.07	.06
		4	.07	.07	.07	.07	.07	.06	.06	.05

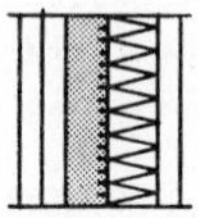

Table 2

Wall Type	External Finish	Sheathing	A	B	C	D	E	F	G	H
2″ bat or blanket insulation in stud space and reflective paper on cold side of insulation 1 air space	Wood Siding	1	.09	.09	.08	.08	.08	.08	.08	.07
		2	.09	.09	.08	.08	.08	.08	.08	.07
		3	.08	.08	.08	.08	.08	.07	.07	.06
		4	.07	.07	.07	.07	.07	.07	.07	.06
	Wood Shingle	1	.08	.08	.08	.08	.08	.07	.07	.06
		2	.08	.08	.08	.08	.08	.07	.07	.06
		3	.08	.08	.08	.08	.08	.07	.07	.06
		4	.07	.07	.07	.07	.07	.06	.06	.06
	Stucco	1	.09	.09	.09	.09	.09	.08	.08	.07
		2	.09	.09	.09	.09	.09	.08	.08	.07
		3	.08	.08	.08	.08	.08	.08	.08	.07
		4	.08	.08	.08	.08	.07	.07	.07	.06
	Brick Veneer	1	.08	.08	.08	.08	.08	.08	.07	.07
		2	.08	.08	.08	.08	.08	.08	.07	.07
		3	.08	.08	.08	.08	.08	.07	.07	.06
		4	.07	.07	.07	.07	.07	.07	.07	.06

Table 3

Wall Type	External Finish	Sheathing	A	B	C	D	E	F	G	H
Aluminum foil backup on cold side of lath. 1 air space	Wood Siding	1	.22	.22	.21	.21	.21	.17	.17	.13
		2	.22	.22	.21	.21	.21	.17	.17	.13
		3	.18	.18	.18	.18	.18	.15	.14	.12
		4	.15	.15	.14	.14	.14	.12	.12	.10
	Wood Shingle	1	.18	.18	.17	.17	.17	.14	.14	.11
		2	.18	.17	.17	.17	.17	.14	.14	.11
		3	.18	.18	.18	.18	.18	.15	.14	.12
		4	.13	.13	.13	.12	.12	.11	.11	.09
	Stucco	1	.27	.27	.26	.26	.25	.20	.19	.14
		2	.27	.26	.25	.25	.25	.20	.19	.14
		3	.21	.21	.21	.21	.20	.17	.16	.13
		4	.17	.17	.16	.16	.16	.14	.13	.11
	Brick Veneer	1	.22	.22	.21	.21	.21	.17	.16	.13
		2	.22	.22	.21	.21	.21	.17	.16	.13
		3	.18	.18	.18	.18	.18	.15	.14	.11
		4	.15	.15	.14	.14	.14	.12	.12	.10

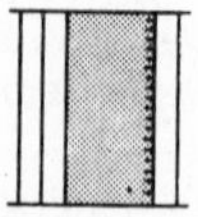

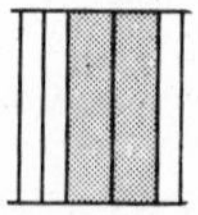

Table 4

Wall Type	External Finish	Sheathing	A	B	C	D	E	F	G	H
1 sheet ordinary building paper placed to form 2 equal air spaces in stud space	Wood Siding	1	.24	.24	.23	.23	.23	.18	.18	.14
		2	.24	.24	.23	.23	.23	.18	.17	.14
		3	.20	.20	.19	.19	.19	.16	.16	.12
		4	.16	.16	.16	.16	.16	.13	.13	.11
	Wood Shingle	1	.19	.19	.19	.19	.19	.15	.15	.12
		2	.19	.19	.19	.19	.18	.15	.15	.12
		3	.20	.20	.19	.19	.19	.16	.16	.12
		4	.14	.14	.14	.14	.13	.12	.11	.10
	Stucco	1	.29	.29	.28	.27	.27	.21	.20	.15
		2	.29	.28	.27	.27	.27	.20	.20	.15
		3	.24	.23	.23	.22	.22	.18	.17	.14
		4	.18	.18	.18	.18	.17	.15	.14	.12
	Brick Veneer	1	.24	.24	.23	.23	.23	.18	.17	.14
		2	.24	.24	.23	.23	.22	.18	.17	.14
		3	.20	.20	.19	.19	.19	.16	.16	.12
		4	.16	.16	.16	.16	.16	.13	.13	.11

Legend:

Interior Finishes	Sheathing
A Metal lath and plaster	1 Gypsum ½"
B Gypsum board, ⅜" decorated	2 Plywood 5/16"
C Wood lath and plaster	3 Wood and building paper 25/32"
D Gypsum lath, ⅜" and plaster	4 Insulating board 25/32"
E Plywood ⅜"	
F Insulating board, ½" plain or decorated	
G Insulating board, ½" and plaster	
H Insulating board, 1" and plaster	

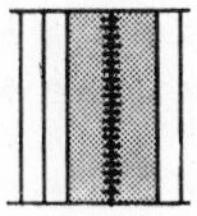

Upper tables

Wall Type	External Finish	Sheathing	A	B	C	D	E	F	G	H
1 sheet reflective paper placed to form 2 equal air spaces in stud space	Wood Siding	1	.16	.16	.16	.16	.16	.13	.13	.11
		2	.16	.16	.16	.16	.16	.13	.13	.11
		3	.14	.14	.14	.14	.14	.12	.12	.10
		4	.12	.12	.12	.12	.12	.10	.10	.09
	Wood Shingle	1	.14	.14	.13	.13	.13	.12	.11	.10
		2	.14	.14	.13	.13	.13	.11	.11	.10
		3	.14	.14	.14	.14	.14	.12	.12	.10
		4	.11	.11	.10	.10	.10	.09	.09	.08
	Stucco	1	.19	.19	.18	.18	.18	.15	.14	.12
		2	.19	.19	.18	.18	.18	.15	.14	.12
		3	.16	.16	.16	.16	.15	.13	.13	.11
		4	.13	.13	.13	.13	.13	.11	.11	.09
	Brick Veneer	1	.16	.16	.16	.16	.16	.13	.13	.11
		2	.16	.16	.16	.16	.16	.13	.13	.11
		3	.14	.14	.14	.14	.14	.12	.12	.10
		4	.12	.12	.12	.12	.12	.10	.10	.09

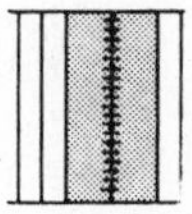

Wall Type	External Finish	Sheathing	A	B	C	D	E	F	G	H
1 sheet aluminum foil placed to form 2 equal air spaces in stud space	Wood Siding	1	.14	.14	.13	.13	.13	.11	.11	.09
		2	.14	.14	.13	.13	.13	.11	.11	.09
		3	.12	.12	.12	.12	.12	.10	.10	.09
		4	.10	.10	.10	.10	.10	.09	.09	.08
	Wood Shingle	1	.12	.12	.11	.11	.11	.10	.10	.08
		2	.12	.12	.11	.11	.11	.10	.10	.08
		3	.12	.12	.12	.12	.12	.10	.10	.09
		4	.09	.09	.09	.09	.09	.08	.08	.07
	Stucco	1	.16	.15	.15	.15	.15	.13	.12	.10
		2	.15	.15	.15	.15	.15	.13	.12	.10
		3	.13	.13	.13	.13	.13	.11	.11	.09
		4	.11	.11	.11	.11	.11	.10	.10	.08
	Brick Veneer	1	.14	.14	.13	.13	.13	.11	.11	.09
		2	.14	.13	.13	.13	.13	.11	.11	.09
		3	.12	.12	.12	.12	.12	.10	.10	.09
		4	.10	.10	.10	.10	.10	.09	.09	.08

Lower tables

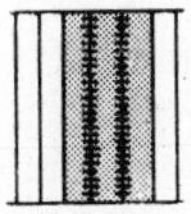

Wall Type	External Finish	Sheathing	A	B	C	D	E	F	G	H
2 sheets aluminum foil placed to form 3 equal air spaces in stud space	Wood Siding	1	.09	.09	.09	.09	.09	.08	.08	.07
		2	.09	.09	.09	.09	.09	.08	.08	.07
		3	.08	.08	.08	.08	.08	.07	.07	.06
		4	.07	.07	.07	.07	.07	.06	.06	.06
	Wood Shingle	1	.08	.08	.08	.08	.08	.07	.07	.06
		2	.08	.08	.08	.08	.08	.07	.07	.06
		3	.08	.08	.08	.08	.08	.07	.07	.06
		4	.06	.06	.06	.06	.06	.06	.06	.05
	Stucco	1	.09	.09	.09	.09	.09	.08	.08	.07
		2	.09	.09	.09	.09	.09	.08	.08	.07
		3	.09	.08	.08	.08	.08	.07	.07	.07
		4	.08	.07	.07	.07	.07	.07	.07	.06
	Brick Veneer	1	.09	.09	.09	.09	.09	.08	.08	.07
		2	.09	.09	.09	.09	.09	.08	.07	.07
		3	.08	.08	.08	.08	.08	.07	.07	.06
		4	.07	.07	.07	.07	.07	.06	.06	.06

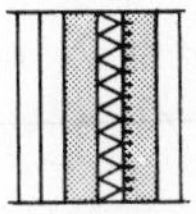

Wall Type	External Finish	Sheathing	A	B	C	D	E	F	G	H
1" blanket insulation placed to form 2 equal air spaces in stud space, and having aluminum foil on warm side of blanket	Wood Siding	1	.10	.10	.10	.10	.10	.09	.09	.08
		2	.10	.10	.10	.10	.10	.09	.09	.08
		3	.09	.09	.09	.09	.09	.08	.08	.07
		4	.08	.08	.08	.08	.08	.07	.07	.07
	Wood Shingle	1	.09	.09	.09	.09	.09	.08	.08	.07
		2	.09	.09	.09	.09	.09	.08	.08	.07
		3	.09	.09	.09	.09	.09	.08	.08	.07
		4	.08	.08	.07	.07	.07	.07	.07	.06
	Stucco	1	.11	.11	.11	.11	.11	.10	.09	.08
		2	.11	.11	.11	.11	.11	.09	.09	.08
		3	.10	.10	.10	.10	.10	.09	.09	.08
		4	.09	.09	.09	.09	.09	.08	.08	.07
	Brick Veneer	1	.10	.10	.10	.10	.10	.09	.09	.08
		2	.10	.10	.10	.10	.10	.09	.09	.08
		3	.09	.09	.09	.09	.09	.08	.08	.07
		4	.08	.08	.08	.08	.08	.07	.07	.06

Legend:

Interior Finishes	Furring Space Treatment
A No finish, plain wall **B** Plaster, ½", direct on masonry **C** Metal lath and plaster **D** Gypsum board, ⅜" decorated **E** Gypsum lath, ⅜", plastered **F** Insulation board, ½", plain or decorated **G** Insulation board, ½", plastered **H** Insulation board, 1", plastered	**1** No furring **2** 1" nominal furring, faced with ordinary materials **3** Same, faced with reflective coated paper 1 side **4** Same, faced with aluminum foil 1 side **5** Same, space filled with flexible insulation

Masonry Material	Masonry Thickness	Furring Space	A	B	C	D	E	F	G	H
Brick	8"	1	.50	.46	..	..	..	..	..	..
		2	..	..	.31	.30	.29	.22	.21	.16
		3	..	..	.24	.23	.23	.18	.17	.13
		4	..	..	.21	.20	.20	.16	.15	.12
		5	..	..	.20	.20	.20	.16	.16	.13
	12"	1	.36	.34	..	..	..	..	..	..
		2	..	..	.25	.24	.23	.19	.18	.14
		3	..	..	.20	.19	.19	.15	.15	.12
		4	..	..	.17	.17	.17	.14	.14	.11
		5	..	..	.18	.17	.17	.14	.14	.12
	16"	1	.28	.27	..	..	..	..	..	..
		2	..	..	.21	.20	.20	.16	.16	.13
		3	..	..	.17	.17	.16	.14	.13	.11
		4	..	..	.15	.15	.15	.12	.12	.10
		5	..	..	.15	.15	.15	.13	.13	.11
Poured concrete	6"	1	.79	.71	..	..	..	..	..	..
		2	..	..	.40	.39	.37	.26	.25	.18
		3	..	..	.29	.29	.28	.20	.20	.15
		4	..	..	.25	.25	.24	.18	.18	.14
		5	..	..	.24	.24	.23	.18	.18	.14
	8"	1	.70	.64	..	..	..	..	..	..
		2	..	..	.38	.37	.35	.25	.24	.17
		3	..	..	.28	.28	.26	.20	.19	.15
		4	..	..	.24	.23	.22	.18	.17	.13
		5	..	..	.23	.23	.22	.18	.17	.14
	10"	1	.63	.58	..	..	..	..	..	..
		2	..	..	.36	.35	.33	.24	.23	.17
		3	..	..	.26	.26	.25	.19	.19	.14
		4	..	..	.23	.23	.22	.17	.17	.13
		5	..	..	.22	.22	.21	.17	.17	.13
	12"	1	.57	.53	..	..	..	..	..	..
		2	..	..	.34	.33	.31	.23	.22	.17
		3	..	..	.25	.25	.24	.19	.18	.14
		4	..	..	.22	.22	.21	.17	.16	.13
		5	..	..	.22	.21	.21	.17	.16	.13
Brick veneer plus poured concrete	4" brick 6" concrete	1	.59	.54	..	..	..	..	..	..
		2	..	B	.34	.34	.32	.23	.22	.17
		3	..	..	.26	.25	.24	.19	.18	.14
		4	..	..	.22	.22	.21	.17	.16	.13
		5	..	..	.22	.22	.21	.17	.17	.13
	4" brick 8" concrete	1	.54	.50	..	..	..	..	..	..
		2	..	..	.32	.32	.30	.23	.22	.16
		3	..	..	.25	.24	.23	.18	.18	.14
		4	..	..	.22	.22	.21	.16	.16	.13
		5	..	..	.21	.21	.20	.17	.16	.13
Brick veneer plus hollow tile	4" brick 6" tile	1	.36	.34	..	..	..	..	..	..
		2	..	..	.25	.24	.23	.19	.18	.14
		3	..	..	.20	.19	.19	.15	.15	.12
		4	..	..	.17	.17	.17	.14	.14	.11
		5	..	..	.18	.18	.17	.14	.14	.12
	4" brick 8" tile	1	.34	.32	..	..	..	..	..	..
		2	..	..	.24	.24	.23	.18	.18	.14
		3	..	..	.19	.19	.19	.15	.15	.12
		4	..	..	.17	.17	.17	.14	.13	.11
		5	..	..	.17	.17	.17	.14	.14	.11
Brick veneer plus hollow block	4" brick 8" gravel	1	.44	.41	..	..	..	..	..	..
		2	..	..	.29	.29	.28	.21	.20	.15
		3	..	..	.22	.22	.21	.17	.17	.13
		4	..	..	.20	.20	.19	.15	.15	.12
		5	..	..	.20	.19	.19	.16	.15	.12
	4" brick 8" cinder block	1	.34	.33	..	..	..	..	..	..
		2	..	..	.24	.24	.23	.18	.18	.14
		3	..	..	.19	.19	.19	.15	.15	.12
		4	..	..	.17	.17	.17	.14	.13	.11
		5	..	..	.17	.17	.17	.14	.14	.11
	4" brick 8" light-weight block	1	.31	.29	..	..	..	..	..	..
		2	..	..	.23	.22	.22	.17	.17	.13
		3	..	..	.18	.18	.17	.14	.14	.12
		4	..	..	.16	.16	.16	.13	.13	.11
		5	..	..	.16	.16	.16	.14	.13	.11
Hollow tile stucco exterior finish	8"	1	.40	.37	..	..	..	..	..	..
		2	..	..	.27	.26	.25	.20	.19	.15
		3	..	..	.21	.21	.20	.16	.16	.13
		4	..	..	.19	.18	.18	.15	.14	.12
		5	..	..	.19	.18	.18	.15	.15	.12
	10"	1	.39	.37	..	..	..	..	..	..
		2	..	..	.26	.25	.24	.19	.19	.14
		3	..	..	.20	.20	.19	.16	.15	.12
		4	..	..	.18	.18	.17	.14	.14	.11
		5	..	..	.18	.18	.17	.15	.14	.12
	12"	1	.30	.28	..	..	..	..	..	..
		2	..	..	.21	.21	.21	.17	.16	.13
		3	..	..	.17	.17	.17	.14	.14	.11
		4	..	..	.15	.15	.15	.13	.12	.10
		5	..	..	.16	.16	.15	.13	.13	.11
	16"	1	.24	.24	..	..	..	..	..	..
		2	..	..	.19	.18	.18	.15	.15	.12
		3	..	..	.15	.15	.15	.13	.12	.10
		4	..	..	.14	.14	.13	.12	.11	.10
		5	..	..	.14	.14	.14	.12	.12	.10

Legend:

Interior Finishes	Furring Space Treatment
A No finish, plain wall **B** Plaster, ½″, direct on masonry **C** Metal lath and plaster **D** Gypsum board, ⅜″, decorated **E** Gypsum lath, ⅜″, plastered **F** Insulation board, ½″, plain or decorated **G** Insulation board, ½″, plastered **H** Insulation board, 1″, plastered	**1** No furring **2** 1″ nominal furring, faced with ordinary materials **3** Same, faced with reflective coated paper 1 side **4** Same, faced with aluminum foil 1 side **5** Same, space filled with flexible insulation

Masonry Material	Masonry Thickness	Furring Space	A	B	C	D	E	F	G	H
Stone	8″	1	.70	.64	..	..	..	..	..	..
		2	..	..	.38	.37	.35	.25	.24	.17
		3	..	..	.28	.28	.26	.20	.19	.15
		4	..	..	.24	.23	.22	.18	.17	.13
		5	..	..	.23	.23	.22	.18	.17	.14
	12″	1	.57	.53	..	..	..	..	..	..
		2	..	..	.34	.33	.31	.23	.22	.17
		3	..	..	.25	.25	.24	.19	.18	.14
		4	..	..	.22	.22	.21	.17	.16	.13
		5	..	..	.22	.21	.21	.17	.16	.13
	16″	1	.49	.45	..	..	..	..	..	..
		2	..	..	.30	.30	.29	.22	.21	.16
		3	..	..	.23	.23	.22	.17	.17	.13
		4	..	..	.20	.20	.20	.16	.15	.12
		5	..	..	.20	.20	.19	.16	.16	.13
	24″	1	.37	.35	..	..	..	..	..	..
		2	..	..	.25	.25	.24	.19	.18	.14
		3	..	..	.20	.20	.19	.16	.15	.12
		4	..	..	.18	.18	.17	.14	.14	.11
		5	..	..	.18	.18	.17	.15	.14	.12
Cut stone veneer plus hollow block	4″ stone 8″ gravel block	1	.47	.44	..	..	..	..	..	..
		2	..	..	.30	.30	.28	.21	.21	.16
		3	..	..	.23	.23	.22	.17	.17	.13
		4	..	..	.20	.20	.19	.16	.15	.12
		5	..	..	.20	.20	.19	.16	.16	.13
	4″ stone 8″ cinder block	1	.36	.34	..	..	..	..	..	..
		2	..	..	.25	.25	.24	.19	.18	.14
		3	..	..	.20	.20	.19	.16	.15	.12
		4	..	..	.18	.17	.17	.14	.14	.11
		5	..	..	.18	.18	.17	.14	.14	.12
	4″ stone 8″ lightweight block	1	.32	.30	..	..	..	..	..	..
		2	..	..	.23	.23	.22	.18	.17	.14
		3	..	..	.18	.18	.18	.15	.14	.12
		4	..	..	.16	.16	.16	.13	.13	.11
		5	..	..	.17	.17	.16	.14	.14	.11
Cut stone veneer plus poured concrete	4″ stone 6″ concrete	1	.63	.58	..	..	..	..	..	..
		2	..	..	.36	35	.33	.24	.23	.17
		3	..	..	.26	.26	.25	.19	.19	.14
		4	..	..	.23	.23	.22	.17	.17	.13
		5	..	..	.22	.22	.21	.17	.17	.13
	4″ stone 8″ concrete	1	.57	.53	..	..	..	..	..	..
		2	..	..	.34	.33	.31	.23	.22	.17
		3	..	..	.25	.25	.24	.19	.18	.14
		4	..	..	.22	.22	.21	.17	.16	.13
		5	..	..	.22	.21	.21	.17	.16	.13

Masonry Material	Masonry Thickness	Furring Space	A	B	C	D	E	F	G	H
Cut stone veneer plus hollow tile	4″ stone 6″ tile	1	.37	.35	..	..	..	..	..	..
		2	..	..	.26	.25	.24	.19	.18	.14
		3	..	..	.20	.20	.19	.16	.15	.12
		4	..	..	.18	.18	.17	.14	.14	.11
		5	..	..	.18	.18	.17	.15	.14	.12
	4″ stone 8″ tile	1	.36	.34	..	..	..	..	..	..
		2	..	..	.25	.24	.24	.19	.18	.14
		3	..	..	.20	.20	.19	.16	.15	.12
		4	..	..	.18	.17	.17	.14	.14	.11
		5	..	..	.18	.18	.17	.14	.14	.12
Hollow concrete blocks, gravel aggregate	8″	1	.56	.52	..	..	..	..	..	..
		2	..	..	.33	.33	.31	.23	.22	.16
		3	..	..	.25	.25	.24	.18	.18	.14
		4	..	..	.22	.22	.21	.17	.16	.13
		5	..	..	.21	.21	.21	.17	.16	.13
	12″	1	.49	.46	..	..	..	..	..	..
		2	..	..	.31	.30	.29	.22	.21	.16
		3	..	..	.23	.23	.22	.18	.17	.13
		4	..	..	.21	.20	.20	.16	.15	.12
		5	..	..	.20	.20	.20	.16	.16	.13
Hollow concrete blocks, cinder aggregate	8″	1	.41	.39	..	..	..	..	..	..
		2	..	..	.27	.27	.26	.20	.19	.15
		3	..	..	.21	.21	.20	.16	.16	.13
		4	..	..	.19	.19	.18	.15	.14	.12
		5	..	..	.19	.19	.18	.15	.15	.12
	12″	1	.39	.37	..	..	..	..	..	..
		2	..	..	.26	.25	.24	.19	.19	.14
		3	..	..	.20	.20	.19	.16	.15	.12
		4	..	..	.18	.18	.17	.14	.14	.11
		5	..	..	.18	.18	.17	.15	.14	.12
Hollow concrete blocks, lightweight aggregate	8″	1	.36	.34	..	..	..	..	..	..
		2	..	..	.25	.24	.23	.19	.18	.14
		3	..	..	.20	.19	.19	.15	.15	.12
		4	..	..	.17	.17	.17	.14	.14	.11
		5	..	..	.18	.18	.17	.14	.14	.12
	12″	1	.34	.33	..	..	..	..	..	..
		2	..	..	.24	.24	.23	.18	.18	.14
		3	..	..	.19	.19	.18	.15	.15	.12
		4	..	..	.17	.17	.16	.14	.13	.11
		5	..	..	.17	.17	.17	.14	.14	.11

U Factors for Frame Ceilings

Legend:

Ceiling Finishes

A Metal lath and plaster
B 3/8" gypsum board, plain or decorated
C 1/4" plywood
D Wood lath and plaster
E 3/8" gypsum lath and plaster
F 1/2" insulation board
G 1/2" insulation board
H 1" insulation board and plaster

Insulation

1 None
2 1" flexible
3 2" flexible
4 3 5/8" flexible
5 Aluminum foil, 1 sheet
6 Aluminum foil, 2 sheets
7 Aluminum foil, 3 sheets
8 1" insulation board

▨ INSULATION
▤ CEILING

Ceiling Type	Insulation	Season	A	B	C	D	E	F	G	H
Open joists. No insulation above	1	Winter	.80	.78	.75	.70	.69	.39	.37	.24
		Summer	.53	.52	.51	.49	.48	.31	.30	.21
	2 (on ceiling)	Winter	.20	.20	.20	.20	.19	.16	.16	.13
		Summer	.18	.18	.18	.17	.17	.15	.14	.12
	3 (on ceiling)	Winter	.12	.12	.11	.11	.11	.10	.10	.09
		Summer	.11	.11	.11	.11	.11	.09	.09	.08
	4 (on ceiling)	Winter	.07	.07	.07	.07	.07	.06	.06	.06
		Summer	.07	.07	.07	.06	.06	.06	.06	.05
Insulation on joists. No insulation on ceiling	5 (at top to form 1 air space)	Winter	.28	.28	.27	.27	.27	.20	.20	.15
		Summer	.08	.08	.08	.08	.08	.08	.07	.07
	6 (to form 2 air spaces)	Winter	.17	.17	.17	.16	.16	.14	.13	.11
		Summer	.05	.05	.05	.05	.05	.05	.05	.04
	7 (to form 3 air spaces)	Winter	.12	.12	.12	.12	.12	.10	.10	.09
		Summer	.04	.04	.04	.04	.04	.04	.04	.04
	8	Winter	.19	.19	.19	.19	.19	.15	.15	.12
		Summer	.17	.17	.17	.16	.16	.14	.14	.11

INSULATION
ALUM. FOIL
INSULATION

Ceiling Type	Insulation	Season	A	B	C	D	E	F	G	H
1" (25/32) subfloor (Yellow Pine) on joists	1	Winter	.32	.32	.31	.30	.30	.22	.22	.16
		Summer	.26	.26	.26	.25	.25	.20	.19	.15
	2 (on ceiling)	Winter	.14	.14	.14	.14	.14	.12	.12	.10
		Summer	.13	.13	.13	.13	.13	.11	.11	.10
	3 (on ceiling)	Winter	.09	.09	.09	.09	.09	.08	.08	.07
		Summer	.09	.09	.09	.09	.09	.08	.08	.07
	4 (on ceiling)	Winter	.06	.06	.06	.06	.06	.05	.05	.05
		Summer	.06	.06	.05	.05	.05	.05	.05	.05
	5 (on top face of ceiling)	Winter	.23	.23	.23	.22	.22	.17	.17	.13
		Summer	.09	.09	.09	.09	.09	.08	.08	.07
	5 (to form 2 air spaces)	Winter	.15	.15	.15	.15	.15	.12	.12	.10
		Summer	.05	.05	.05	.05	.05	.05	.05	.05
	6 (to form 3 air spaces)	Winter	.11	.11	.11	.11	.11	.10	.09	.08
		Summer	.04	.04	.04	.04	.04	.03	.03	.03

FLOOR
INSULATION
FLOOR
ALUM. FOIL

U Factors for Flat Roofs

Legend:

Insulation on Roof Deck

A None
B 1/2" insulation board
C 1" insulation board
D 1 1/2" insulation board
E 2" insulation board
F 1" corkboard
G 1 1/2" corkboard
H 2" corkboard

Ceiling Finishes

1 None
2 3/8" gypsum board or plaster
3 1/2" insulation board
4 3/8" gypsum board and 1" flexible insulation over ceiling
5 3/8" gypsum board and 2" flexible insulation over ceiling
6 3/8" gypsum board and 3 5/8" flexible insulation over ceiling

▪ ROOFING
▨ INSULATION
▤ CEILING

Roof Deck	Ceiling Finish	Season	A	B	C	D	E	F	G	H
Metal roof deck	1	Winter	1.04	.43	.27	.24	.15	.25	.18	.14
		Summer	.78	.37	.25	.22	.15	.23	.17	.13
MET. DECK	2	Winter	.46	.28	.20	.16	.13	.19	.15	.12
		Summer	.41	.26	.19	.15	.12	.18	.14	.11
	3	Winter	.29	.21	.16	.13	.11	.15	.12	.10
		Summer	.28	.20	.15	.13	.11	.15	.12	.10
	4	Winter	.17	.14	.11	.10	.10	.11	.09	.08
		Summer	.16	.13	.11	.10	.09	.11	.09	.08
MET. DECK	5	Winter	.10	.09	.08	.07	.07	.08	.07	.06
		Summer	.10	.09	.08	.07	.07	.08	.07	.06
	6	Winter	.06	.06	.05	.05	.05	.05	.05	.05
		Summer	.06	.06	.05	.05	.05	.05	.05	.05

Roof Deck	Ceiling Finish	Season	A	B	C	D	E	F	G	H
Concrete roof deck 2" thick	1	Winter	.89	.40	.26	.19	.15	.23	.17	.14
		Summer	.70	.35	.23	.18	.14	.22	.16	.13
CONCRETE	2	Winter	.43	.27	.20	.15	.13	.18	.14	.12
		Summer	.39	.25	.18	.15	.12	.17	.14	.11
	3	Winter	.28	.20	.16	.13	.11	.15	.12	.10
		Summer	.26	.19	.15	.12	.11	.14	.12	.10
	4	Winter	.16	.13	.11	.10	.09	.11	.09	.08
		Summer	.16	.13	.11	.10	.08	.11	.09	.08
CONCRETE	5	Winter	.10	.09	.08	.07	.06	.08	.07	.06
		Summer	.10	.09	.08	.07	.06	.08	.07	.06
	6	Winter	.06	.06	.05	.05	.05	.05	.05	.05
		Summer	.06	.06	.05	.05	.05	.05	.05	.05

(Continued on next page)

Legend:

Insulation on Roof Deck	Ceiling Finishes
A None	1 None
B ½" insulation board	2 ⅜" gypsum board or plaster
C 1" insulation board	3 ½" insulation board
D 1½" insulation board	4 ⅜" gypsum board and 1" flexible insulation over ceiling
E 2" insulation board	5 ⅜" gypsum board and 2" flexible insulation over ceiling
F 1" corkboard	6 ⅜" gypsum board and 3⅝" flexible insulation over ceiling
G 1½" corkboard	
H 2" corkboard	

■ ROOFING
▧ INSULATION
▨ CEILING

Left table

Roof Deck	Ceiling Finish	Season	A	B	C	D	E	F	G	H
Concrete roof deck 4" thick	1	Winter	.78	.37	.25	.18	.15	.23	.17	.13
	1	Summer	.63	.33	.23	.17	.14	.21	.16	.13
	2	Winter	.41	.26	.19	.15	.12	.18	.14	.11
	2	Summer	.36	.24	.18	.14	.12	.17	.13	.11
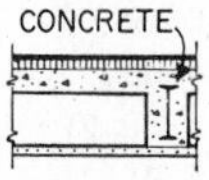	3	Winter	.27	.19	.15	.13	.11	.15	.12	.10
	3	Summer	.25	.19	.15	.12	.10	.14	.11	.10
	4	Winter	.16	.13	.11	.10	.08	.11	.09	.08
	4	Summer	.16	.13	.11	.09	.08	.10	.09	.08
	5	Winter	.10	.09	.08	.07	.06	.08	.07	.06
	5	Summer	.10	.09	.08	.07	.06	.08	.07	.06
	6	Winter	.06	.06	.05	.05	.05	.05	.05	.05
	6	Summer	.06	.06	.05	.05	.05	.05	.05	.05
Concrete roof deck 6" thick	1	Winter	.70	.35	.24	.18	.14	.22	.16	.13
	1	Summer	.57	.32	.22	.17	.13	.17	.16	.12
	2	Winter	.38	.25	.19	.15	.12	.17	.14	.11
	2	Summer	.34	.23	.17	.14	.12	.16	.13	.11
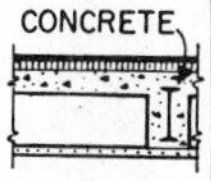	3	Winter	.26	.19	.15	.12	.11	.14	.12	.10
	3	Summer	.24	.18	.14	.12	.10	.14	.11	.10
	4	Winter	.16	.13	.11	.10	.08	.10	.09	.08
	4	Summer	.15	.12	.11	.10	.08	.10	.09	.08
	5	Winter	.10	.09	.08	.07	.06	.07	.07	.06
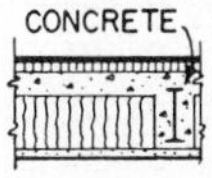	5	Summer	.10	.09	.08	.07	.06	.07	.07	.06
	6	Winter	.06	.06	.05	.05	.05	.05	.05	.04
	6	Summer	.06	.06	.05	.05	.05	.05	.05	.04
Wood roof deck 1" thick	1	Winter	.52	.30	.21	.16	.13	.20	.15	.12
	1	Summer	.44	.27	.20	.16	.13	.19	.14	.12
	2	Winter	.32	.22	.17	.14	.11	.16	.13	.11
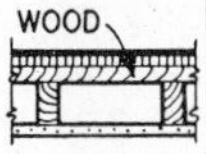	2	Summer	.29	.21	.16	.13	.11	.15	.12	.10
	3	Winter	.23	.17	.14	.12	.10	.13	.11	.09
	3	Summer	.22	.17	.13	.11	.10	.13	.11	.09
	4	Winter	.14	.12	.10	.09	.08	.10	.09	.08
	4	Summer	.14	.12	.10	.09	.08	.10	.09	.08
	5	Winter	.09	.08	.07	.07	.06	.07	.06	.06
	5	Summer	.09	.08	.07	.07	.06	.07	.06	.06
	6	Winter	.06	.06	.05	.05	.04	.05	.05	.04
	6	Summer	.06	.06	.05	.05	.04	.05	.05	.04
Wood roof deck 1½" thick	1	Winter	.41	.26	.19	.15	.13	.18	.14	.12
	1	Summer	.36	.24	.18	.14	.12	.17	.13	.11
	2	Winter	.28	.20	.16	.13	.11	.15	.12	.10
	2	Summer	.25	.19	.15	.12	.10	.14	.12	.10
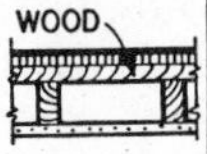	3	Winter	.20	.16	.13	.11	.10	.12	.10	.09
	3	Summer	.19	.15	.13	.11	.09	.12	.10	.09
	4	Winter	.14	.11	.10	.09	.08	.09	.08	.07
	4	Summer	.13	.11	.10	.09	.08	.09	.08	.07
	5	Winter	.09	.08	.07	.07	.06	.07	.06	.06
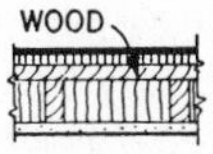	5	Summer	.09	.08	.07	.06	.06	.07	.06	.06
	6	Winter	.06	.05	.05	.05	.04	.05	.05	.04
	6	Summer	.06	.05	.05	.05	.04	.05	.05	.04

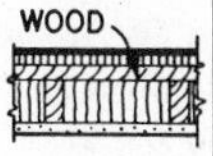

Right table

Roof Deck	Ceiling Finish	Season	A	B	C	D	E	F	G	H
Wood roof deck 2" thick	1	Winter	.34	.23	.18	.14	.12	.17	.13	.11
	1	Summer	.31	.22	.17	.13	.11	.16	.13	.11
	2	Winter	.25	.18	.15	.12	.10	.14	.11	.10
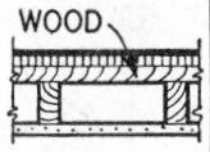	2	Summer	.23	.17	.14	.12	.10	.13	.11	.09
	3	Winter	.19	.15	.12	.11	.09	.12	.10	.09
	3	Summer	.18	.14	.12	.10	.09	.11	.10	.08
	4	Winter	.13	.11	.09	.08	.07	.09	.08	.07
	4	Summer	.12	.11	.09	.08	.07	.09	.08	.07
	5	Winter	.09	.08	.07	.06	.06	.07	.06	.06
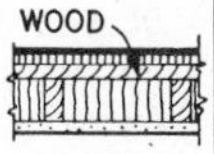	5	Summer	.09	.08	.07	.06	.06	.07	.06	.06
	6	Winter	.06	.05	.05	.05	.04	.05	.04	.04
	6	Summer	.06	.05	.05	.05	.04	.05	.04	.04
Wood roof deck 3" thick	1	Winter	.26	.19	.15	.12	.11	.14	.12	.10
	1	Summer	.24	.18	.14	.12	.10	.14	.11	.10
	2	Winter	.20	.15	.13	.11	.09	.12	.10	.09
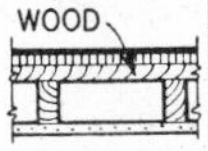	2	Summer	.18	.15	.12	.10	.09	.12	.10	.09
	3	Winter	.16	.13	.11	.10	.08	.11	.09	.08
	3	Summer	.15	.12	.11	.09	.08	.10	.09	.08
	4	Winter	.11	.10	.09	.08	.07	.08	.07	.07
	4	Summer	.11	.10	.09	.08	.07	.08	.07	.07
	5	Winter	.08	.07	.06	.06	.05	.06	.06	.05
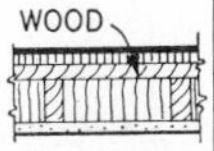	5	Summer	.08	.07	.06	.06	.05	.06	.06	.05
	6	Winter	.05	.05	.05	.04	.04	.05	.04	.04
	6	Summer	.05	.05	.05	.04	.04	.05	.04	.04
Gypsum fiber concrete roof deck 2½" thick	1	Winter	.39	.26	.19	.15	.12	.18	.14	.11
	1	Summer	.35	.24	.18	.14	.12	.17	.13	.11
	2	Winter	.27	.20	.15	.13	.11	.15	.12	.10
	2	Summer	.25	.18	.14	.12	.10	.14	.11	.10
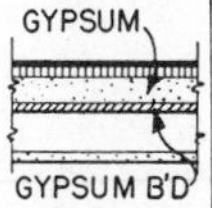	3	Winter	.20	.16	.13	.11	.09	.12	.10	.09
	3	Summer	.19	.15	.12	.11	.09	.12	.10	.09
	4	Winter	.13	.11	.10	.09	.08	.09	.08	.07
	4	Summer	.13	.11	.10	.08	.08	.09	.08	.07
	5	Winter	.09	.08	.07	.06	.06	.07	.06	.06
	5	Summer	.09	.08	.07	.06	.06	.07	.06	.06
	6	Winter	.06	.05	.05	.05	.04	.05	.05	.04
	6	Summer	.06	.05	.05	.05	.04	.05	.05	.04
Gypsum fiber concrete roof deck 3½" thick	1	Winter	.32	.28	.20	.16	.12	.16	.13	.11
	1	Summer	.29	.26	.19	.15	.11	.15	.12	.10
	2	Winter	.23	.17	.14	.12	.10	.13	.11	.09
	2	Summer	.21	.16	.13	.11	.10	.13	.11	.09
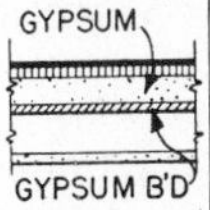	3	Winter	.18	.14	.13	.10	.09	.11	.10	.08
	3	Summer	.17	.14	.12	.09	.09	.11	.09	.08
	4	Winter	.12	.10	.09	.08	.07	.09	.08	.07
	4	Summer	.12	.10	.09	.08	.07	.09	.08	.07
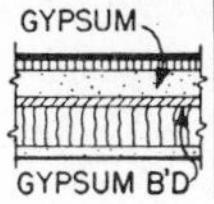	5	Winter	.08	.08	.07	.06	.06	.07	.06	.06
	5	Summer	.08	.08	.07	.06	.06	.07	.06	.06
	6	Winter	.06	.05	.05	.05	.04	.05	.04	.04
	6	Summer	.06	.05	.05	.05	.04	.05	.04	.04

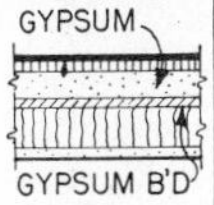

Legend:

Insulation on Roof Deck		Ceiling Finishes	
A None	**E** 2″ insulation board	**7** 1 sheet aluminum under air space at least 7½″, no ceiling	**10** Aluminum foil back-up on lath and 1 sheet foil, two air spaces, plastered
B ½″ insulation board	**F** 1″ corkboard	**8** Aluminum foil back-up on lath, plaster ceiling	**11** 3 sheets aluminum foil, three air spaces, no ceiling
C 1″ insulation board	**G** 1½″ corkboard	**9** 2 sheets aluminum foil, two air spaces, no ceiling	**12** Aluminum foil back-up on lath, 2 sheets foil, three air spaces, plastered
D 1½″ insulation board	**H** 2″ corkboard		

▮ ROOFING
▨ INSULATION
▦ CEILING

Roof Deck	Ceiling Finish	Season	A	B	C	D	E	F	G	H
Metal roof deck	7	Winter	.30	.21	.16	.13	.11	.15	.12	.10
		Summer	.10	.08	.07	.07	.06	.07	.06	.06
	8	Winter	.30	.20	.16	.13	.11	.15	.12	.10
		Summer	.11	.09	.08	.07	.06	.07	.07	.06
	9	Winter	.19	.15	.12	.10	.09	.12	.10	.08
		Summer	.07	.07	.06	.05	.05	.06	.05	.05
	10	Winter	.19	.15	.12	.10	.09	.12	.10	.08
		Summer	.08	.07	.06	.06	.05	.06	.06	.05
	11	Winter	.14	.11	.10	.08	.07	.09	.08	.07
		Summer	.06	.05	.05	.05	.04	.05	.04	.04
	12	Winter	.13	.11	.10	.08	.07	.09	.08	.07
		Summer	.06	.06	.05	.05	.04	.05	.05	.04
Concrete roof deck 2″ thick	7	Winter	.29	.20	.15	.14	.11	.14	.12	.10
		Summer	.10	.08	.07	.07	.06	.07	.06	.06
	8	Winter	.28	.20	.15	.14	.11	.14	.12	.10
		Summer	.11	.09	.08	.07	.06	.07	.07	.06
	9	Winter	.19	.14	.12	.10	.09	.11	.09	.08
		Summer	.07	.06	.06	.05	.05	.06	.05	.05
	10	Winter	.18	.14	.12	.10	.09	.11	.09	.08
		Summer	.08	.07	.06	.06	.05	.06	.06	.05
	11	Winter	.13	.11	.09	.08	.07	.09	.08	.07
		Summer	.06	.05	.05	.05	.04	.05	.04	.04
	12	Winter	.13	.11	.09	.08	.07	.09	.08	.07
		Summer	.06	.06	.05	.05	.04	.05	.05	.04
Concrete roof deck 4″ thick	7	Winter	.27	.19	.15	.14	.10	.14	.11	.10
		Summer	.10	.08	.07	.07	.06	.07	.06	.06
	8	Winter	.27	.19	.15	.14	.10	.14	.11	.10
		Summer	.11	.09	.08	.07	.06	.08	.07	.06
	9	Winter	.18	.14	.12	.10	.08	.11	.09	.08
		Summer	.07	.06	.06	.05	.05	.06	.05	.05
	10	Winter	.18	.14	.11	.10	.08	.11	.09	.08
		Summer	.08	.07	.06	.06	.05	.06	.06	.05
	11	Winter	.13	.11	.09	.08	.07	.1/2	.08	.07
		Summer	.06	.05	.05	.04	.04	.05	.04	.04
	12	Winter	.13	.11	.09	.08	.07	.09	.08	.07
		Summer	.06	.06	.05	.05	.04	.05	.05	.04
Concrete roof deck 6″ thick	7	Winter	.26	.19	.15	.13	.10	.14	.11	.09
		Summer	.09	.08	.07	.06	.06	.07	.06	.06
	8	Winter	.26	.19	.14	.12	.10	.14	.11	.09
		Summer	.10	.09	.08	.07	.06	.08	.07	.06
	9	Winter	.17	.14	.11	.10	.08	.11	.09	.08
		Summer	.07	.06	.06	.05	.05	.06	.05	.05
	10	Winter	.17	.14	.11	.10	.08	.11	.09	.08
		Summer	.08	.07	.06	.06	.05	.06	.05	.05
	11	Winter	.13	.10	.09	.08	.07	.09	.08	.07
		Summer	.06	.05	.05	.04	.04	.05	.04	.04
	12	Winter	.13	.10	.09	.08	.07	.09	.08	.07
		Summer	.06	.05	.05	.05	.04	.05	.05	.04

Roof Deck	Ceiling Finish	Season	A	B	C	D	E	F	G	H
Wood roof deck 1″ thick	7	Winter	.22	.17	.13	.11	.10	.13	.11	.09
		Summer	.09	.08	.07	.07	.06	.07	.06	.06
	8	Winter	.22	.17	.13	.11	.10	.13	.11	.09
		Summer	.10	.09	.08	.07	.06	.07	.07	.06
	9	Winter	.16	.13	.11	.09	.08	.10	.09	.08
		Summer	.07	.06	.06	.05	.05	.05	.05	.05
	10	Winter	.16	.13	.11	.09	.08	.10	.09	.08
		Summer	.07	.07	.06	.05	.05	.06	.05	.05
	11	Winter	.12	.10	.09	.08	.07	.08	.07	.06
		Summer	.05	.05	.05	.04	.04	.05	.04	.04
	12	Winter	.12	.10	.09	.08	.07	.08	.07	.06
		Summer	.06	.05	.05	.04	.04	.05	.04	.04
Wood roof deck 1½″ thick	7	Winter	.21	.16	.13	.11	.09	.12	.10	.09
		Summer	.09	.08	.07	.07	.06	.07	.06	.05
	8	Winter	.21	.16	.13	.11	.09	.12	.10	.09
		Summer	.09	.08	.07	.07	.06	.07	.06	.06
	9	Winter	.15	.12	.10	.09	.08	.10	.08	.07
		Summer	.07	.06	.05	.05	.05	.05	.05	.05
	10	Winter	.15	.12	.10	.09	.08	.10	.08	.07
		Summer	.07	.06	.06	.05	.05	.06	.05	.05
	11	Winter	.11	.10	.08	.07	.07	.08	.07	.06
		Summer	.05	.05	.04	.04	.04	.04	.04	.04
	12	Winter	.11	.10	.08	.07	.07	.08	.07	.06
		Summer	.06	.05	.05	.04	.04	.05	.04	.04
Wood roof deck 2″ thick	7	Winter	.19	.15	.12	.10	.09	.11	.10	.08
		Summer	.08	.07	.06	.06	.05	.06	.06	.05
	8	Winter	.18	.15	.12	.10	.09	.11	.10	.08
		Summer	.09	.08	.07	.06	.06	.07	.06	.06
	9	Winter	.14	.11	.09	.08	.07	.09	.08	.07
		Summer	.07	.06	.05	.05	.05	.05	.05	.04
	10	Winter	.14	.11	.09	.08	.07	.09	.08	.07
		Summer	.07	.06	.06	.05	.05	.06	.05	.05
	11	Winter	.10	.09	.08	.07	.06	.08	.07	.06
		Summer	.05	.05	.04	.04	.04	.04	.04	.04
	12	Winter	.10	.09	.08	.07	.06	.08	.07	.06
		Summer	.06	.05	.05	.04	.04	.05	.04	.04
Wood roof deck 3″ thick	7	Winter	.15	.12	.11	.09	.08	.10	.09	.08
		Summer	.07	.07	.06	.06	.05	.06	.05	.05
	8	Winter	.15	.12	.11	.09	.08	.10	.09	.08
		Summer	.08	.07	.06	.06	.05	.06	.06	.05
	9	Winter	.12	.10	.09	.08	.07	.08	.07	.06
		Summer	.06	.05	.05	.04	.04	.05	.05	.04
	10	Winter	.12	.10	.09	.08	.07	.08	.07	.06
		Summer	.06	.06	.05	.05	.05	.05	.05	.04
	11	Winter	.09	.08	.07	.06	.06	.07	.06	.06
		Summer	.05	.04	.04	.04	.04	.04	.04	.04
	12	Winter	.09	.08	.07	.06	.06	.07	.06	.06
		Summer	.05	.05	.04	.04	.04	.04	.04	.04

U Factors for Flat Roofs

Legend:

Insulation on Roof Deck		Ceiling Finishes	
A None **B** ½″ insulation board **C** 1″ insulation board **D** 1½″ insulation board	**E** 2″ insulation board **F** 1″ corkboard **G** 1½″ corkboard **H** 2″ corkboard	**7** 1 sheet aluminum under air space at least 7½″, no ceiling **8** Aluminum foil back-up on lath, plaster ceiling **9** 2 sheets aluminum foil, two air spaces, no ceiling	**10** Aluminum foil back-up on lath and 1 sheet foil, two air spaces, plastered **11** 3 sheets aluminum foil, three air spaces, no ceiling **12** Aluminum foil back-up on lath, 2 sheets foil, three air spaces, plastered

◼ ROOFING
▨ INSULATION
▦ CEILING

Roof Deck	Ceiling Finish	Season	A	B	C	D	E	F	G	H
Gypsum fiber concrete roof deck 2½″ thick	7	Winter	.20	.15	.12	.10	.09	.12	.10	.08
		Summer	.08	.07	.07	.06	.06	.06	.06	.05
	8	Winter	.20	.15	.12	.10	.09	.12	.10	.08
		Summer	.09	.08	.07	.06	.06	.07	.06	.06
	9	Winter	.14	.12	.10	.09	.08	.10	.08	.07
		Summer	.06	.06	.05	.05	.05	.05	.05	.04
	10	Winter	.14	.12	.10	.09	.08	.09	.08	.07
		Summer	.07	.06	.06	.05	.05	.06	.05	.05
	11	Winter	.11	.10	.08	.07	.06	.08	.07	.06
		Summer	.05	.05	.04	.04	.04	.04	.04	.04
	12	Winter	.11	.10	.08	.07	.06	.08	.07	.06
		Summer	.06	.05	.05	.04	.04	.05	.04	.04

(GYPSUM / GYPSUM B'D / GYPSUM / GYPSUM B'D)

Roof Deck	Ceiling Finish	Season	A	B	C	D	E	F	G	H
Gypsum fiber concrete roof deck 3½″ thick	7	Winter	.17	.14	.11	.10	.08	.11	.09	.08
		Summer	.08	.07	.06	.06	.05	.06	.06	.05
	8	Winter	.17	.14	.11	.10	.08	.11	.09	.08
		Summer	.09	.08	.07	.06	.06	.07	.06	.05
	9	Winter	.13	.11	.08	.08	.07	.09	.08	.07
		Summer	.06	.06	.05	.05	.04	.05	.05	.04
	10	Winter	.13	.11	.08	.08	.07	.09	.08	.07
		Summer	.07	.06	.06	.05	.05	.06	.05	.05
	11	Winter	.10	.09	.08	.07	.06	.07	.07	.06
		Summer	.05	.05	.04	.04	.04	.04	.04	.04
	12	Winter	.10	.09	.08	.07	.06	.07	.07	.06
		Summer	.05	.05	.05	.04	.04	.04	.04	.04

(GYPSUM / GYPSUM B'D)

U Factors for Pitched Roofs

Legend:

Insulation or Ceiling on Underside of Joists			
A Roof only, underside of joists open **B** Metal lath and plaster **C** ⅜″ gypsum board **D** Wood or gypsum lath and plaster **E** ⅜″ plywood **F** ½″ rigid insulation board **G** ½″ rigid insulation board, plastered	**H** 1″ rigid insulation board **I** 1″ rigid insulation board, plastered **J** 1″ flexible insulation **K** 2″ flexible insulation **L** 2″ flexible insulation, and gypsum board, lath and plaster **M** 3⅝″ flexible insulation	**N** 3⅝″ flexible insulation, and gypsum board, lath and plaster **O** 1 sheet reflective aluminum, 1 air space **P** Aluminum foil back-up on lath, and plaster **Q** 2 sheets reflective aluminum, 2 air spaces	**R** 1 sheet reflective aluminum plus aluminum foil back-up on lath and plaster, 2 air spaces **S** 3 sheets reflective aluminum, 3 air spaces **T** 2 sheets reflective aluminum plus aluminum foil back-up on lath and plaster, 3 air spaces

Type of Roofing	Season	A	B	C	D	E	F	G	H	I	J	K	L	M	N	O	P	Q	R	S	T
Slate or tile on wood sheathing	Winter	.56	.34	.34	.32	.31	.23	.23	.17	.17	.17	.10	.09	.06	.06	.22	.23	.14	.15	.10	.11
	Summer	.52	.34	.33	.32	.31	.23	.23	.17	.17	.17	.10	.10	.06	.06	.15	.18	.10	.11	.07	.07
Asphalt shingles or roll roofing on wood sheathing	Winter	.53	.33	.33	.31	.30	.23	.22	.17	.16	.16	.10	.09	.06	.06	.21	.23	.14	.15	.10	.11
	Summer	.49	.33	.32	.31	.30	.23	.22	.17	.17	.17	.10	.10	.06	.06	.15	.18	.10	.11	.07	.07
Wood shingles on wood strips	Winter	.49	.31	.31	.30	.29	.22	.21	.17	.16	.16	.09	.09	.06	.06	.21	.22	.14	.14	.10	.11
	Summer	.46	.31	.31	.29	.29	.22	.21	.17	.16	.16	.10	.09	.06	.06	.15	.17	.09	.10	.07	.07

U Factors for Above-Grade Floors

Legend:

Type of Insulation or Ceiling under Wood Floor, or Ceiling suspended at Least 7½ in. under Concrete Floors

- **A** Floor only, no insulation
- **B** Metal lath and plaster
- **C** ⅜″ gypsum board
- **D** Gypsum or wood lath and ½″ plaster
- **E** ⅜″ plywood
- **F** ½″ rigid insulation board
- **G** ½″ rigid insulation board, plastered
- **H** 1″ rigid insulation board
- **I** 1″ rigid insulation board, plastered
- **J** 2″ flexible insulation
- **K** 3⅝″ flexible insulation
- **L** 1 sheet reflective aluminum, 1 air space
- **M** 2 sheets reflective aluminum, 2 air spaces
- **N** 3 sheets reflective aluminum, 3 air spaces

Type of Floor	A	B	C	D	E	F	G	H	I	J	K	L	M	N
13/16″ hardwood flooring	.39	.24	.24	.23	.23	.19	.18	.15	.14	.09	.06	.08	.06	.05
13/16″ hardwood flooring and 25/32″ yellow pine subflooring	.28	.19	.19	.19	.19	.16	.15	.13	.13	.08	.06	.07	.06	.05
Bare concrete, 3″ thick	.53	.29	.29	.28	.27	.21	.21	.16	.16	.10	.06	.08	.06	.05
6″ thick	.47	.27	.27	.26	.26	.20	.20	.16	.15	.09	.06	.08	.06	.05
10″ thick	.41	.25	.25	.24	.24	.19	.19	.15	.15	.09	.06	.08	.06	.05
Tile or terrazzo on concrete, 3″ thick	.51	.29	.28	.27	.27	.21	.20	.16	.16	.10	.06	.08	.06	.05
6″ thick	.45	.27	.26	.26	.25	.20	.19	.15	.15	.09	.06	.08	.06	.05
10″ thick	.40	.24	.24	.24	.23	.19	.18	.15	.15	.09	.06	.08	.06	.05
Parquet flooring on concrete, 3″ thick	.38	.24	.23	.23	.22	.18	.18	.14	.14	.09	.06	.08	.06	.04
6″ thick	.35	.22	.22	.22	.21	.17	.17	.14	.14	.09	.06	.08	.06	.04
10″ thick	.31	.21	.21	.20	.20	.17	.16	.13	.13	.09	.06	.08	.06	.04
Hardwood flooring, and yellow pine subflooring on sleepers on concrete, 3″ thick	.22	.16	.16	.16	.16	.14	.13	.11	.11	.08	.05	.07	.05	.04
6″ thick	.21	.16	.16	.15	.15	.13	.13	.11	.11	.07	.05	.07	.05	.04
10″ thick	.20	.15	.15	.15	.14	.13	.12	.11	.11	.07	.05	.07	.05	.04

FHA Requirements[1]

Requirements[1] of the Federal Housing Administration for the insulation of single-family houses are as follows:

Total calculated heat loss of the living unit must not exceed 50 Btu per hr per sq ft of floor area of the heated space, measured to outside faces of exterior walls. If electrical heat is used, the total heat loss must not exceed 40 Btu per hr per sq ft of floor.

Ceilings: U-value for heat flow upward through a ceiling to an unheated space above must not exceed 0.15; if ceiling heating panels are used, the *U*-value must not exceed 0.06. Blowing- or pouring-type insulation may not be used if the roof slope is less than 3 in 12.

Walls: Total heat loss through all walls, including doors and windows but excluding infiltration loss, must not exceed 30 Btu per hr per sq ft of floor area of the heated space.

Floors: Heat loss through floors over unheated spaces must not exceed 15 Btu per hr per sq ft of floor area. Heat loss from concrete slab floors on grade must not exceed 5 Btu per hr per sq ft; insulation may be omitted where annual degree-days do not exceed 2,800, or monthly degree-days do not exceed 650.

Crawl space plenums: Perimeter wall must be insulated to provide a maximum heat loss of 35 Btu per hr per lin ft of wall, assuming an air temperature of 70°F for return plenums and 110°F for supply plenums.

Insulation must comply with the following standards:

Structural fiber insulation board
  Commercial Standard CS42
Wood fiber blanket
  Commercial Standard CS160
Mineral wool
  Federal Specification HH-I-521
Vegetable or wood fiber
  Federal Specification HH-I-515
Redwood bark, shredded
  Federal Specification LLL-I-533
Cotton batts
  Federal Specification HH-I-528
Roof insulation, fiberboard
  Federal Specification ASTM C 208, Class C or LLL-F-321
Cellular glass
  Federal Specification HH-I-551a
Corkboard
  Federal Specification HH-I-526a
Vermiculite
  Federal Specification HH-I-585
Perlite, minimum density 8 pcf
  Federal Specification HH-L-526a modified
Perimeter insulation must comply with FHA test procedure.

Other types of insulation will be considered on the basis of tests conducted in accordance with ASTM, CS131, or other recognized methods.

Insulation for cooling[2]

Total calculated heat gain of the living unit must not exceed that obtained when the floor area, measured to the outside of the exterior walls, is multiplied by the Btu per hr per sq ft value derived through use of the chart on next page. For living units of more than 1,500 sq ft, use the value on the chart for 1,500 sq ft.

Ceilings below an uncooled space

[1] *Minimum Property Standards for One and Two Living Units, FHA No. 300, Federal Housing Adminstration, revised 1959.*

[2] *Interim Revision No. 14, effective March 25, 1963.*

shall have a maximum coefficient of heat transfer (*U* value for heat flow down) of 0.08 Btu per hr.

Insulation of On-Grade Concrete Slabs

Heat transfer through concrete floor slabs on the ground is dependent on: (1) the difference in temperature between the air outside the structure and the air within the structure, (2) the floor material and (3) the conductivity of the surrounding earth. While data concerning the conductivity of the ground are not ordinarily available, tests indicate that where the area of the slab floor is on the order of 6 to 12 times its perimeter, the heat loss may be calculated proportionally to the exposed edge of the floor slab. For buildings of greater area, where the ratio of area to perimeter is much over 12 to 1, the heat loss should be determined proportionally to the area.

Tests show that the heat loss from uninsulated concrete floors laid on the ground is about 0.81 Btu per hr per lineal ft of exposed edge per degree temperature difference between air on the warm and on the cold side of the building. Recommendations of the Building Research Advisory Board for insulation of the perimeter of such slab floors give the amount of perimeter insulation deemed necessary to reduce the edge heat loss to satisfactory limits. The Federal Housing Administration lists these limits in the MPR Revision No. 54, August 1955.

When the building area is greater than 12 times the perimeter, the heat loss from slab floors at grade should be calculated at approximately 0.10 Btu per hr, per sq ft of floor, per degree F temperature difference between inside and outside air. Heat loss of basement walls below grade usually is calculated at twice this rate or 0.20 Btu per hr per sq ft per F. However, where specific rooms are located along the outside of the structure, it is recommended that their heat loss be calculated using the perimeter method to find the floor loss of the room.

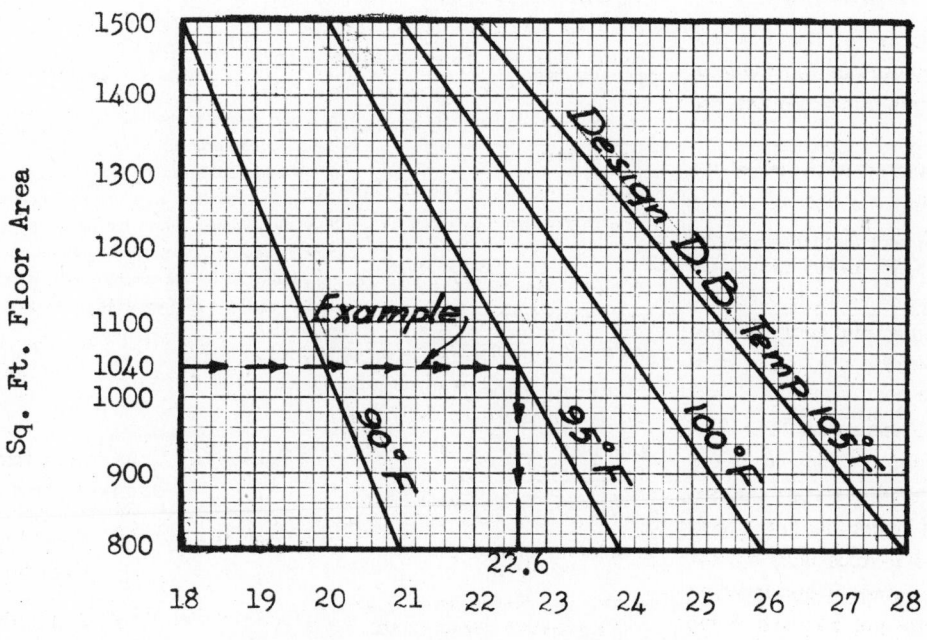

Maximum Calculated Heat Gain — Btuh per sq. ft. of floor area

NOTE: *The Btu per hr per sq ft is obtained by extending a line horizontally from the point on the chart representing the floor area of the living unit to its point of intersection with the appropriate design dry bulb temperature line. From this point extend a vertical line down to the bottom of the chart and find the maximum Btu per sq ft heat gain. The example shown on the chart represents a living unit with a floor area of 1,040 sq ft in a geographic area having a design dry bulb temperature of 95°F. By following the dotted lines in the direction of the arrows, it will be seen that a maximum heat gain of 22.6 Btu per hr per sq ft of floor area is permitted. Thus, the maximum heat gain of the example living unit is 22.6 × 1,040 = 23,504 Btu per hr.*

Table 4. Perimeter insulation for various design temperatures

	Maximum Conductance (C) (Btu/hr/sq ft/deg. F) for Various Widths of Insulation					
Outside Design Temp., F	Total Width of Insulation (see sketches)					
	Unheated Floor Slab			Heated Floor Slab		
	2 ft	1½ ft	1 ft	2 ft	1½ ft	1 ft
— 30 and lower	0.15	—	—	—	0.30	0.20
— 20 to — 29	0.20	—	—	0.40	—	0.30
— 10 to — 19	0.20	—	—	—	—	0.40
0 to — 9	0.30	0.20	0.15	—	—	0.40
+ 1 to + 10	0.40	0.30	0.20	—	—	0.40
11 to 20	—	—	0.40	Vertical edge		only
21 to 30	Vertical edge		only	Vertical edge		only
31 and above	None required			None required		
Summer Air Conditioning	Uncooled slab 0.40			Cooled slab		0.40

Table 5. Perimeter loss of unheated slabs

Total Width of Insulation	HEAT LOSS (Btu/lineal ft/deg. F difference between inside and outside air)					
	Conductance (C) of Insulation					
	0.15	0.20	0.25	0.30	0.35	0.40
1.0 ft	0.29	0.38	0.49	0.58	0.67	0.77
1.5	0.26	0.35	0.44	0.52	0.61	0.70
2.0	0.25	0.33	0.42	0.50	0.59	0.67

Table 6. Perimeter loss of heated slabs

Total Width of Insulation	(Btu/lineal ft/deg. F difference between inside and outside air)					
	Conductance (C) of Insulation					
	0.15	0.20	0.25	0.30	0.35	0.40
1.0 ft	0.32	0.43	0.57	0.70	0.83	1.00
1.5	0.28	0.39	0.50	0.62	0.75	0.88
2.0	0.27	0.37	0.48	0.59	0.71	0.83

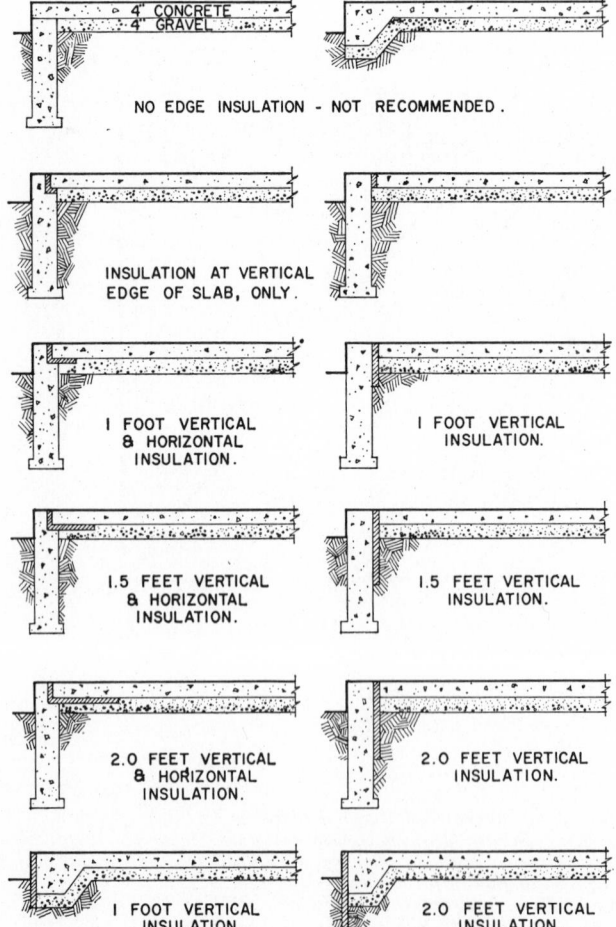

NO EDGE INSULATION - NOT RECOMMENDED.

INSULATION AT VERTICAL EDGE OF SLAB, ONLY.

I FOOT VERTICAL & HORIZONTAL INSULATION.

I FOOT VERTICAL INSULATION.

1.5 FEET VERTICAL & HORIZONTAL INSULATION.

1.5 FEET VERTICAL INSULATION.

2.0 FEET VERTICAL & HORIZONTAL INSULATION.

2.0 FEET VERTICAL INSULATION.

I FOOT VERTICAL INSULATION.

2.0 FEET VERTICAL INSULATION.

When the perimeter method of calculation is followed, the Federal Housing Administration requires the thermal value and width of perimeter insulation to be as given in Table 4, above. The term "heated floor slab" means any installation such as a radiant floor panel, warm air perimeter loop, or warm air perimeter radial system where heating pipes or ducts are installed in or under the concrete slab. The conductivity of the insulation at the slab perimeter must not exceed the figures in the tables.

Table 7. Conversion factors for conductivity and conductance

Conductivity (K)	INSULATION CONDUCTANCE (C)			
	Thickness of insulation, in.			
	2	2½	1	¾
0.2	0.1	0.13	0.2	0.27
0.25	0.13	0.17	0.25	0.33
0.3	0.15	0.20	0.3	0.4
0.35	0.18	0.23	0.35	0.47
0.4	0.2	0.27	0.4	0.53

Adapted from A Study of Slab-on-Ground Construction of Residences, *conducted by the Building Research Advisory Board for FHA*

BASIC DESIGN CONSIDERATIONS

The physical characteristics of the site and the nature of the soil are the controlling factors. The type of soil, its load-bearing and capillary characteristics must be known in order to have an efficient and effective slab-on-ground design. Surface drainage in every direction is essential, and, if necessary, a positive underground drainage system must be provided. Proper elevation of the slab above the finished grade is critical. Many moisture problems will not occur if elevation of the slab and drainage are properly handled. A moisture condition may cause a failure of the flooring surface material, and increase thermal problems.

Moisture control involves controlling the water transfer by capillarity and by vapor phase migration. The capillary rise of water can be broken by using a layer of granular base material under the slab. A vapor barrier separating the slab from the ground will limit vapor transmission and may also serve as a water stop. Under certain conditions, it is desirable to use either one or the other of these slab protections; at other times, both are needed. Likewise, there are sites where neither would be required. The important thing is to know what is required in order to overcome any moisture difficulties that may exist for the specific site.

The major thermal consideration is to provide comfort. A less important consideration is to achieve some economy from heat loss through the slab. Two essentials are required: first, a suitable insulation material, correctly placed around the perimeter of the slab; and second, a properly designed heating system.

SITE PREPARATION AND GRADING

Fills Outside Foundation

(1) Grading fill should be clean soil, from which all roots or foreign material have been removed. Grading fill should be mechanically compacted in not more than 4-in. layers.

(2) Backfill used against the outside of foundation walls or grade beams should be thoroughly compacted by tamping.

Site Grading and Drainage

(1) Finish grades should slope downward away from structures having slab-on-ground construction, a minimum of 12 in. for a distance of 25 ft in all directions (4 per cent slope). Where property lines, retaining walls, etc., limit the distance from the structure to less than 25 ft, no less than 4 per cent slope should be provided.

(2) Wherever less than a 4 per cent slope is used adjacent to the structure, such as for

a terrace, a positive means of drainage should be provided.

(3) In side-hill locations, the site should be so graded that surface water will be diverted around the structure. In addition, a positive system of underground drainage may be required for certain conditions.

Height of Floor Above Finish Grade

(1) For an unheated slab or where heating coils are embedded in the slab, the finish grade at the outside wall should be not less than 8 in. below the top of the concrete slab.

(2) Where warm air ducts are used in or under the slab, the finish grade at the outside wall should be not less than 2 in. below the bottom of ductwork adjacent to the foundation wall.

SLAB BED

Soil Capillarity

The underside of a concrete slab should not be in contact with liquid water. Capillary water rises through soil from the water-level or water-table to various heights depending on the type of soil. (See sketch.) A base

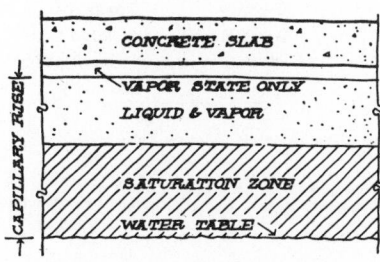

Moisture and vapor in covered soil

material of limited capillarity of sufficient thickness will break the capillary rise of water. Effective drainage will prevent the base from being a reservoir of water.

Limits of Capillary Rise

(1) The capillary rise of liquid water in a material used in a slab bed should not exceed 2 in. under a recognized test for capillarity for the material to be considered of limited capillarity:

Material of Limited Capillarity

Gravel or crushed rock, 1/4 in. and larger in size or other material which will qualify by recognized test. The permeance of limited capillarity is necessary in such a test.

Capillary Material

Clay, silt, sands, bank-run gravel, or other solids unless shown to be otherwise by a recognized test for capillarity. This

classification applies to both undisturbed soil and foundation fill.

Foundation Fill

(1) Areas within foundation walls should have vegetation, topsoil, roots or foreign materials removed. The desired height should be established with clean foundation fill.

(2) Foundation fill and backfill should be thoroughly compacted in not more than 4 in. layers to assure uniform support for the slab. Compaction should be obtained by either mechanical means or by tamping.

Base

(1) A base for a concrete slab-on-ground when required by design conditions must be at least 4 in. in thickness.

(2) To qualify as a base of limited capillarity, the material should be a selected and clean material, 1/4 in. or larger in size, or other material as described above.

(3) The base should be thoroughly compacted by rolling or tamping to assure uniform support for the slab.

Waterproof Membrane

A building site having either hydrostatic pressure in the soil or a liquid water condition, less than 6 in. below the natural surface of the ground, should not be used for a house incorporating slab-on-ground construction. With such condition a waterproof membrane under the slab would be required.

Vapor Barrier

(1) The permeance of vapor barriers should not exceed 0.20 perms when tested by the ASTM methods.

(2) Vapor barrier joints should be lapped a minimum of 6 in. Sealing is not required.

(3) Vapor barriers should be capable of withstanding handling and construction traffic without puncture or displacement.

(4) Vapor barriers should be required under design conditions 1 and 2, as shown in Table 1.

Separator

(1) When a vapor barrier is used it also serves as a structural separator between the concrete and the slab bed.

(2) A separator should withstand handling or construction traffic, but qualities of durability or low permeance are not required.

(3) A separator should be used under the following conditions:
  (a) When a slump test of a concrete mix is more than 4 in. by standard test.
  (b) When water-heating coils or warm-air ducts are embedded in the slab.

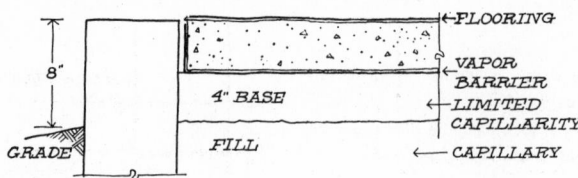

Four slab-on-ground designs are described in Table 1 which covers the conditions which may be created by various combinations of soil, fill, base, vapor barriers and floorings. These four designs apply for both heated and unheated slabs. Slabs are to be a nominal 4 in. in thickness. The design requirements are recommended as a guide for specific cases and for decisions on allowable floorings.

If more than 20 per cent of a slab is planned as a cement finish and not covered by a flooring material, only design conditions No. 1 and No. 2 will be satisfactory.

Table 1. Slab-on-ground design conditions relative to moisture

Design No. 1 (shown above)
Design No. 2 (both base and fill capillary)
Design No. 3 (no vapor barrier)
Design No. 4 (no vapor barrier, base capillary)

Construction Item	Design No. 1	Design No. 2	Design No. 3	Design No. 4
Vapor Barrier	Provide	Provide	No vapor barrier. Separator as noted [1]	No vapor barrier. Separator as noted [1]
Base of Limited Capillarity Material	Provide [2]	None	Provide [2]	None
Fill or Base	Capillary	Capillary	Capillary	Capillary
Flooring Material	Group A or B	Group A Group B only as noted [3]	Group A Group B not allowed	Group A only as noted [4] Group B not allowed

[1] Provide as listed under the subhead, "Separator"
[2] A duct or plenum system should have a 4 in. base material of limited capillarity under the entire system.
[3] To determine if Group B flooring may be used with Design No. 2:
  (a) determine type of soil.
  (b) from table for capillary rise of water in various soils, determine figure which applies to this soil.
  (c) if the water table for the site is at a distance below the ground surface greater than this figure, Group B floorings may be used.
[4] To determine if Group A flooring may be used with Design No. 4:
  (a) and (b) same as in Note 3.
  (c) if the water-table for the site is at a distance below the ground surface greater than this figure, Group A flooring may be used.

Capillarity figures

Capillary water does not rise above the water table more than the following height in these soils

Gravel	0.0 Ft.
Coarse Sand	2.6 Ft.
Fine Sand	7.5 Ft.
Silt	11.5 Ft.
Clay	11.5 Ft.

Flooring types

Group A: Asphalt tile, rubber tile, vinyl-asbestos tile, flexible vinyl tile (un-backed).

Group B: Cork tile, linoleum, felt or fabric backed flooring compositions, wood block.

INSULATION

Properties

(1) Insulation should be required to be non-capillary, not permanently harmed by wetting, or harmed by contact with wet concrete mix, and not subject to damage by termites or fungi.

(2) Insulation must have a compressive strength equal to or more than that required to pass the following test:

(a) Preload insulation to a loading of 50 lb per sq ft. Measure the thickness of the insulation under this preload.

(b) Add an additional loading of 40 lb per sq ft for live load equivalent.

(c) Measure the thickness of the insulation under the second loading. The compression of the insulation under the second loading must be not more than 6 per cent of the thickness measured after the preload specified under (a).

Location

(1) The slab perimeter must be insulated in its entirety.

(2) If the highest known water-table of a site is 2 ft. or more below outside grade, perimeter insulation may be placed in either a vertical or horizontal position. If the highest known water-table is 4 ft or more below the outside grade, it is generally recommended that perimeter insulation be placed in a vertical position.

(3) If the highest known water-table is less than 2 ft below the outside grade, perimeter insulation must be placed in a horizontal or L-shaped position. An exception should be made if a special drainage system is provided to prevent moisture from reaching the insulation.

Thermal Resistances

It is recommended that the method of es-

tablishing thermal resistances for the selection of insulation be determined by using the outdoor design temperatures for the region.

Summer Cooling

(1) The frequent or continuous use of embedded coils for the purpose of cooling the house in summer is not recommended with slabs-on-ground as they are presently designed.

(2) For unheated slabs where summer air conditioning is contemplated, see perimeter insulation recommendation, Table 2.

Comfort

The achieving of comfort should not be dependent upon the provision of carpeting by the home owner. Therefore, the thermal conductivity, density, and specific heat of the flooring surface material or uncovered concrete floor surface should be taken into account in any consideration of comfort.

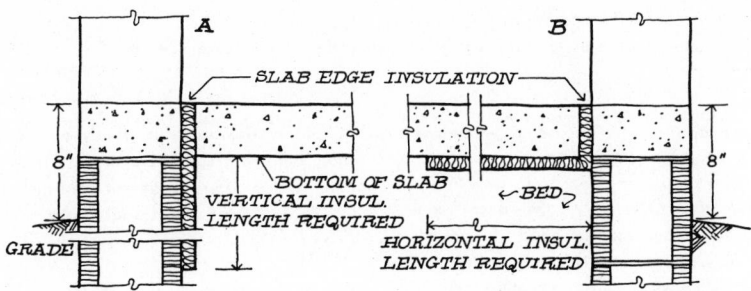

Note: If foundation wall is more than 8 in. above finish grade, vertical insulation should be increased a like amount.

Note: Either A or B for design temperatures below 30 F.

Note: Use for design temp. of 30 F and above. Additional 6 in. if air conditioning is contemplated.

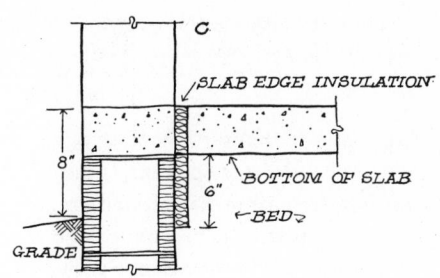

Table 2. Recommended minimum insulation requirements for concrete floor slabs

OUTSIDE DESIGN TEMP.	INSULATION CONDUCTIVITY	INDIRECTLY HEATED	PANEL HEATED	WARM-AIR PERIMETER
	(Nominal) Btu Inch (hr)(sq ft)(F)	VERTICAL 18-in. or L-Type 24-in. length of Insulation [1]	VERTICAL 18-in. or L-Type 24-in. length of Insulation [1]	VERTICAL 18-in. or L-Type 12-in. vertical 12-in. horizontal length of Insulation [2]
F	K	Insulation thickness, in.	Insulation thickness, in.	Insulation thickness, in.
−30	0.2	1½	1	1
−30	0.3	2	1½	1½
−30	0.4	2½	2	2
−20	0.2	1	¾	¾
−20	0.3	1½	1	1
−20	0.4	2	1½	1½
−10	0.2	1	¾	¾
−10	0.3	1½	¾	¾
−10	0.4	2	1	1
			VERTICAL 12-in. or L-Type 18-in.	
0	0.3	1	¾	¾
0	0.4	1½	1	1
		VERTICAL 12-in. or L-Type 18-in.		
10	0.3	1	¾	¾
10	0.4	1½	1	1
20	0.3	¾	¾	¾
20	0.4	1	1	1
30	0.4	1-in. thick VERTICAL 6-in.[3]	1-in. thick VERTICAL 6-in.[3]	1-in. thick VERTICAL 12-in.[3]

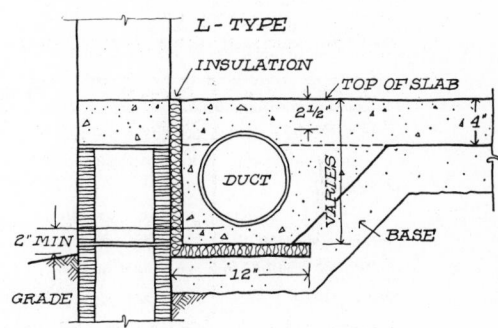

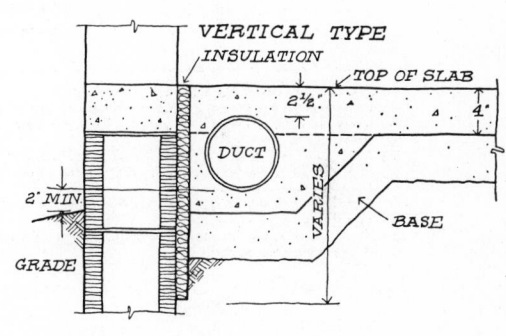

Note: Ducts encased in concrete unless of crush-resistant, non-corrosive non-absorbent materials.

[1] Length measured from bottom of slab, and is in addition to edge insulation which is equal to thickness of slab.
[2] Length measured from top of slab.
[3] For Summer Air Conditioning, where design temperature exceeds 30F (See Fig. C).

By RUDARD A. JONES, AIA; Architectural Consultants: F. M. LESCHER and W. H. KAPPLE
Data used by permission of the University of Illinois Small Homes Council from its copyrighted publication Crawl-Space Houses

Crawl-space houses should, and can, be constructed so that: (1) they are free from problems of moisture, (2) they resist termite attack, and (3) the floor and rooms above crawl space can be kept at comfortable temperatures.

MOISTURE

Excessive moisture within a house can result from dampness in a crawl space due to improper grading of the lot for drainage or due to the omission of moisture control devices, such as ground cover, vapor barrier and ventilation openings. An uncorrected moisture problem can cause decay of wood and eventually structural failure of the house.

The only satisfactory way of avoiding moisture problems is to prevent moisture (vapor and liquid) from entering the crawl space.

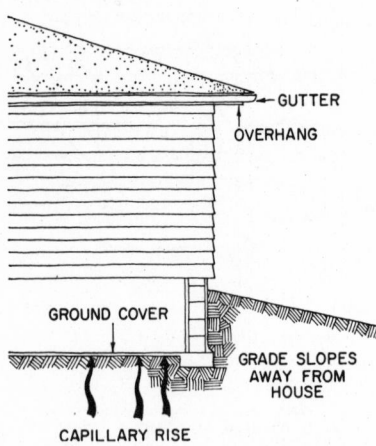

Moisture in the crawl space can be due to:
1. High ground-water level in the area.
2. Surface water.
3. Capillary rise of ground moisture.
4. Moisture from the house.

SOURCE OF MOISTURE

1. GROUND WATER

Sometimes the level of the water in the ground (water table) is raised above the bottom surface of the crawl space due to:
  a. Heavy or prolonged rains.
  b. A spring which appears only in wet seasons and is not discovered when the house is built.

RECOMMENDATIONS: Crawl-space construction is not recommended if ground-water level in an area is so high that it can flood the crawl space periodically.

Where a spring is discovered during or after construction, or where unexpected flooding occurs:
  a. Install drainage collector lines within the crawl space. Grade the bottom of the crawl space so that any water will drain to the tile. Cover the crawl-space area with coarse, washed gravel (fine gravel or sand tends to block the tile).
  b. Costs and installation problems make impractical the use of other methods of control, such as a membrane waterproofing system.

2. SURFACE WATER

Rain water on ground or from roof passes through, or under, the foundation walls.

In some areas, heavy soils may retain surface drainage and cause water pressure against the walls of the crawl space. (See recommendations No. 3 and No. 4.)

RECOMMENDATIONS: Surface drainage problems usually occur because the floor of the crawl space is 2 to 3 ft below finished grade.[1] To avoid such problems:
  a. Grade the lot so that drainage is away from the house and no water is allowed to stand on the site. Minimum grading specifications, listed below, will suffice for most surface drainage conditions:
(1) Slope of the grade should be at least 6 in. in 25 ft.
(2) The ground should fall at least 6 in. on all sides of the house.
(3) Slope should extend at least 10 ft except where side yards are narrower.
  b. Use wide overhangs and/or gutters and downspouts. (Do not connect downspouts to footing drains.)
  c. Install a footing drain of field tile with open joints.
  d. Waterproof the outside of the walls with a bituminous coating. Masonry walls should have a half inch coat of mortar applied first.

3. CAPILLARY RISE OF GROUND MOISTURE

Moisture travels upward from lower layers of certain soils by capillary action (as much as 18 gal. per day have been noted under a 1000 sq ft house) and evaporates within the crawl space.

Capillary rise occurs in nearly all crawl spaces built in areas where the soil is clay or silt. Such moisture is present even though the ground in the crawl space may seem dry and dusty.

RECOMMENDATIONS: Moisture from capillary rise can be kept out of the crawl space:
  a. By using a vapor-barrier type of ground cover which is not susceptible to damage by fungi.
  b. Grade and smooth the ground before installing the ground cover.
  c. Turn up ground cover 4 to 6 in. on the walls of the crawl space.

4. MOISTURE FROM THE HOUSE

Theoretically in a cold open crawl space, excessive moisture from the house may travel downward through the floor into the crawl space. The moisture may condense on walls or floor of the crawl space if they are cold.

RECOMMENDATIONS: To prevent downward flow of moisture into an open crawl space:
1. Install a vapor barrier above the floor insulation—either directly above it, or between the subfloor and the finish flooring.

VENTILATION

Before the effectiveness of ground cover was proven, large ventilation openings were required in the foundation wall to allow moisture to escape from the crawl space. With the use of ground cover which prevents moisture rise from the ground into the crawl space, a minimum amount of ventilation[2] is needed. Provide at least four corrosion-resistant foundation vents which can be closed during the heating season. Four 8-in. by 16-in. units will satisfactorily vent a house up to 1400 sq ft—install an additional vent for each additional 350 sq ft. (Screen the vents with 8-in. by 8-in. corrosion-resistant mesh—64 openings per sq in.—to keep out insects.)

---

[1] No surface drainage problem will occur if the ground level of the crawl space is higher than the ground outside; however, because this design raises the house a number of feet above grade with a resulting awkward appearance, it is not commonly used.

[2] FHA regulation: A minimum of two vents, giving a total free area of ventilation equivalent to 1/1500 of the crawl-space area, is required when ground cover is used. Without ground cover, ten times as much ventilation area is required.

OPEN CRAWL SPACES

To achieve warm floors in a crawl-space house, either (1) insulate the floor above an open crawl space, or (2) insulate the exterior walls of a closed crawl space.

Open crawl spaces are those which are ventilated to such an extent that the temperature within the crawl space approaches that of the outside air. In cold areas, it is necessary to insulate water pipes in such crawl spaces to protect against freezing, heating pipes or ducts to prevent excessive heat loss, and floors to make them comfortable.

RECOMMENDATIONS FOR RESISTANCE [3] OF FLOOR INSULATION

Table 1 shows the minimum amount of insulation required to maintain the surface temperature of a hardwood floor over a plywood subfloor [4] at 65 F. (the minimum temperature recommended for comfort) or higher. These insulation requirements will also limit heat loss through the floor to 5.5 Btu/hr/sq ft (see Table 1).

CLOSED CRAWL SPACES

The moisture control provided by ground cover is so effective that crawl-space ventilators can usually be kept closed during the heating season. This "closed" crawl-space

[3] Resistance equals 1/C where "C" is equivalent to the thermal conductivity of the insulating material (expressed in Btu/hr per sq ft per Fahrenheit degree temperature difference.)
[4] Denser flooring materials, such as asphalt, vinyl and ceramic tile, require slightly more insulation.

construction is recommended except under severe moisture conditions since it provides maximum floor comfort with a minimum expenditure for insulation. Insulation around water pipes and heat ducts and pipes is not needed; furthermore, a closed crawl space can also serve as the plenum for a warm-air heating system.

If the temperature of the crawl space can be maintained at 70 F., the surface temperatures of the floors in the rooms above will also be a comfortable 70 F. Heat from uninsulated warm-air ducts or hot-water heating pipes can often keep a well-insulated, closed crawl space near the 70 F. level. Sometimes, however, additional heat may have to be introduced into the space.

The walls enclosing the crawl space must be insulated to reduce heat loss and to help maintain the temperature of the crawl space at 70 F. (Heat loss to the ground through the earth floor of a crawl space is small.) To accomplish this:

a. The box-sill headers and the end joists of the floor must be insulated, preferably with a flexible-type insulation (batt or blanket) which has a vapor barrier on one side. The vapor barrier should face the interior of the crawl space.

b. For the exterior walls, insulation in sheet or block form is most easily applied. Tempered nails or an adhesive mastic are suggested. Insulation should be of a type not affected by termites or dampness. If it is not vaporproof, a vapor barrier should be installed on the inside face of the insulation since moisture condensation is otherwise likely to occur between the insulation and the wall, or within the wall cavity.

HEATING SYSTEMS

Heating systems which supply heat near the floor along the exterior walls of the house are very effective for a crawl-space house since they eliminate or reduce uncomfortable drafts along the floor. For this reason, perimeter heating or baseboard heating is recommended.

In a warm-air perimeter system, the heat can be distributed (1) through ducts in the crawl space, or (2) by using the crawl space, if it is closed, as a plenum.

When a closed crawl space is used as a plenum the temperature in the space will approach 100 F. See the table below for recommendations for wall insulation. Insulation and ground cover selected for a plenum-type crawl space should be fire-resistant. To reduce dust, a floor in the crawl space is necessary.

FOUNDATION-WALL INSULATION FOR HEATED CRAWL SPACES

The recommended minimum insulation shown in the table will limit the heat loss to 50 Btu/hr per lineal foot of wall around the crawl space. These insulation standards are based on economy since, with a warm crawl space, floor comfort is no problem. The more thoroughly a wall is insulated, the lower is the heat loss and the greater is the fuel saving.

Recommendations are for a crawl space which is 3 ft deep, and which is enclosed with a concrete block wall that is 8 in. thick. The box-sill construction is insulated with a 2-in. corner pack, and the foundation wall with sheet or block insulation 3 ft high. If more than 12 in. of the foundation wall is

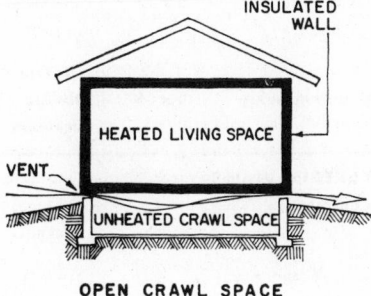

OPEN CRAWL SPACE

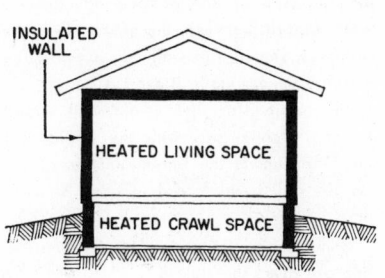

CLOSED CRAWL SPACE

Table 1. Resistance of floor insulation

Outside Design Temperature [5]	Resistance of Insulation
−30°	13.26
−20°	11.42
−10°	9.58
0°	7.74
10°	5.90
20°	4.06
30°	2.22

[5] Approximates the average annual minimum temperature.

exposed above grade, additional insulation is recommended (see Table 2).

CONSTRUCTION DETAILS

The minimum depth of the crawl space should be 2 ft under the floor joists or 18 in. under the girder.

Two types of crawl-space construction for houses are presented on this page: (1) foundation-wall construction for a closed crawl space (illustrated), and (2) pier construction.

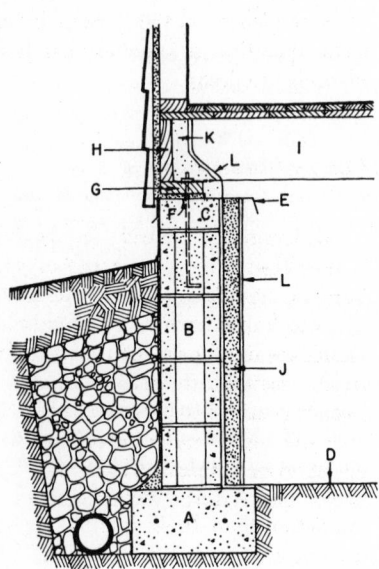

FOUNDATION-WALL CONSTRUCTION
(Key to illustration)

A. *POURED CONCRETE CONTINUOUS WALL FOOTING* either 12 by 16 in. or 12 by 8 in., preferably with two round, ½-in. steel reinforcing rods.

Size of footing depends on bearing value of soil. Footings specified above are suitable for most conditions.

B. *WALLS FOR FRAME HOUSES*, 8-in. masonry or 6-in. poured concrete. (Check local building code.)

Where the exterior walls to be supported by the foundation are thicker (as in an 8-in. solid brick house), the foundation wall must be correspondingly thicker.

Foundation wall should extend at least 8 in. above grade and remain exposed at least 6 in.

C. *HOLLOW-MASONRY FOUNDATION WALL* must be capped with (1) a course of solid masonry, or (2) a 4-in. poured concrete cap reinforced by No. 14 wire mesh 2 by 2 in.

D. *GROUND COVER.*

E. *METAL TERMITE SHIELD.* Use corrosion-resistant metal which is stiff enough to retain the form shown. Where anchor bolts penetrate the shield, the area should be well sealed with coal-tar pitch or tight lead washers.

F. *SEALER FOR THE SILL PLATE.* Use material similar to expansion joint.
G. *SILL PLATE* 2 by 6 in., anchored with ½-in. bolts, 8 ft on center—minimum of two bolts to each piece of sill.

Lumber that is pressure treated with preservative is recommended for sill plate (a) to prevent decay in lumber likely to be caused by condensation, and (b) to discourage termites.

H. *HEADER OF BOX SILL.*

I. *JOISTS.*

J. *FOUNDATION-WALL INSULATION.*

K. *CORNER-PACK INSULATION.*

L. *VAPOR BARRIER.*

PIER CONSTRUCTION

Where the outside walls and the outer edge of the floor of a house rest upon a beam supported by piers, the crawl space is usually enclosed by non-loadbearing (curtain) walls placed between the piers. (In some instances, the curtain wall may support the masonry veneer walls above it.)

The footing for the curtain wall should be poured integrally with the footings of the piers, unless the bottom section of the curtain wall is reinforced to span between piers.

Common size limitations for pier construction are given in Table 3.

Table 2. Resistance [6] of heated crawl space insulation

Outside Design Temperature [7]	For Closed Crawl Space	For Crawl Space As Plenum
—30	5.03	7.61
—20	4.25	6.74
—10	3.45	5.85
0	2.71	5.03
10	1.98	4.25
20	1.27	3.45
30	.59	2.71

[6] Resistance equals 1/C where "C" is equivalent to the thermal conductivity of the insulating material (expressed in Btu/hr per sq ft per Fahrenheit degree temperature difference).

[7] Approximates the average annual minimum temperature.

Table 3. Common limitations for size of piers and curtain walls

	Minimum Dimensions (Inches)	Limit on Height
PIERS		
Concrete	8 dia	10 times the least dimension
Solid Masonry	8 x 12	10 times the least dimension
Hollow Masonry	8 x 16	10 times the least dimension
CURTAIN WALLS		
Concrete	4	14 times thickness [8]
Solid Masonry	4	14 times thickness [8]
Hollow Masonry	4	10 times thickness [8]

[8] Unbalanced fill against a 4-in. curtain wall should not be higher than 2 ft.

Data from Condensation Control in Dwelling Construction by Forest Products Laboratory in collaboration with Housing and Home Finance Agency, 1948.

A FEW years ago little or no attention was given to condensation in dwellings. Either it did not occur or was so minute that it was not a serious problem. Difficulties resulting from lack of condensation control, such as paint peeling and wood decay, have increased recently, and many troubles little understood heretofore are now attributed to lack of sound condensation control practices. Presented here are recommended methods of condensation control by the use of vapor barriers and ventilation based on engineering tests and practical experience, and applicable mainly to small house construction.

Why Condensation Troubles Today?

Condensation troubles are more prevalent now because dwellings have higher relative humidities than before. High prices, the scarcity of building materials, and other economic conditions favor the building of smaller, more compact houses, with resultant higher humidities. Improvements in the machining of wood parts, new materials, and the use of weather strips and storm windows now make both new and old houses tighter than formerly by restricting air leakage or infiltration. Humidifiers, when used indiscriminately, sometimes add greatly to the condensation problem, especially during extremely cold weather.

Today, people make more extensive use of appliances discharging water vapor into the living space than in the past, thus making condensation control more essential. Basements are frequently omitted in low-cost construction, and instead there is substituted an enclosed crawl space below the building. This crawl space may often be damp and thus contribute large quantities of water vapor which may find its way up into walls, attics, and living areas.

Thermal insulation is also used to a greater extent than formerly and as a consequence, outside wall surfacing materials (sheathing and siding) are somewhat colder than those of uninsulated construction. The use of thermal insulation, however, is not, as is often assumed, the only factor contributing to condensation nor does it attract moisture. It must, however, be properly installed with whatever collateral materials or other means that are necessary to prevent condensation trouble.

Common Troubles

One of the most common and widespread types of damage for which condensation is often responsible is in exterior painting. Condensed water vapor often collects behind the siding of a building in the form of free water or ice. This excess moisture may absorb extractives from the wood and result in stains as it runs out over the surface of the siding. In some cases the condensate thoroughly soaks the siding, causing paint blisters and early paint peeling. If moist conditions prevail for a long enough time, decay may also result.

Another type of condensation damage may occur in houses having unventilated flat roofs. Sometimes water vapor passes through the ceiling and condenses on the roof sheathing from which it drips back to the ceiling, causing the plaster to crack.

In basementless houses without crawl space ventilation or soil cover, the outside walls, plate, sills, and adjoining joists exposed in the crawl space of the building are often cooled to temperatures below the dew point in the enclosed space. When this happens water often condenses on the surfaces in sufficient quantity to produce conditions favorable to decay.

Control Methods

Condensation control in dwellings is possible by the proper use of vapor barriers, ventilation or a combination of both. Vapor barriers are membranes, aluminum or oil paint films, rubber base paints, metallic sheets, or other materials or coatings that prevent objectionable amounts of water vapor from being absorbed or transmitted through walls, floors, and ceilings. Vapor barriers are no better than their quality or thoroughness of their installation. They should be selected for quality and should be carefully placed. Ventilation is suitable for reducing water vapor concentration in attics and in unheated crawl spaces below living quarters. In some dwellings it is desirable to provide ventilation for the living quarters in order to lower the relative humidity and thereby reduce condensation hazards.

Added roof protection at the eave line to prevent backing up of melted snow and ice is advisable. Trouble from this source is often erroneously blamed on condensation.

Many materials used as interior surfaces of outside walls, ceilings, and roofs will permit water vapor to pass through them slowly when the relative humidity or vapor pressure is different on opposite sides unless a vapor barrier is provided. When the relative humidity or vapor pressure within the house at the wall surface is greater than that within the wall, water vapor will migrate in the absence of an effective vapor barrier through the plaster or other finish into the wall cavity and will condense if it comes in contact with surfaces below its dew point. This process may continue throughout the heating season at varying rates depending on conditions in and out of the house.

The water vapor generated within a dwelling is first diffused through the space within the building, increasing the relative humidity. Some of it is absorbed by rugs, fabrics, and other house furnishings, and some is condensed on windows. This water may be removed slowly from the living quarters by the opening of outside doors, by diffusion through walls and ceilings into cavities or attic spaces, by leakage around windows and doors, by way of air supplied to burning fuel in heating equipment vented into chimneys, and by air exhausted by kitchen ventilating fans, etc.

Vapor Barriers. Adequate, well-installed vapor barriers are an effective means of preventing troublesome deposits of frost or water in walls and attics of houses exposed to low temperatures.* The vapor barrier should form a tight envelope near the warm side of the building element in which it is installed.

A number of satisfactory materials or combinations of materials are available that restrict the movement of water vapor. These include asphalt impregnated and coated papers having a glossy or bright finish. This feature is important since thin, dull-surfaced papers are not generally so effective as is the glossy finish. Duplex papers composed of two sheets of 30-lb kraft paper with a 60-lb per 3000 sq ft asphalt layer between them; aluminum foil mounted on one or two sides of a paper support, or attached to the plaster base; or aluminum paint, oil paint, or rubber base paint in sufficient coats to give a smooth glossy finish are types of material that may be expected to give satisfactory service.

Papers used to support insulating materials which have narrow strips of

asphalt as an adhesive to join the paper and insulating materials are not usually good vapor barriers and their value for this purpose should be accurately confirmed before purchasing.

Sheathing. In contrast to the vapor-tight properties of the warm side of a wall, those of the cold side should be just the opposite — a construction capable of losing moisture that might gain entrance to the wall is highly desirable. On the other hand, the exterior surface must resist rain and strong winds. Sheathing paper, sometimes called breathing paper, between the sheathing and the finish siding has been customarily used to reduce infiltration of cold air and to prevent the penetration of wind-driven rain. In order that there be as little restriction as possible to the release of moisture, it is recommended that the sheathing paper and the sheathing be of types that will readily transmit water vapor.†

Ventilation. In proper amounts and correctly applied, ventilation is a recognized means of controlling condensation in buildings. By introducing fresh air into living quarters during the winter, some water vapor is forced out of the building, and air containing a low vapor content is introduced. In this way high vapor pressures which are a factor in producing condensation are reduced considerably. Ventilation is effective in preventing condensation in unheated attics, spaces below flat roofs, and crawl spaces in basementless houses. Although much is yet needed in experience and test data to prove the efficiency and effectiveness of ventilation in the cold cavities of walls to prevent condensation, there are some data indicating favorable results with an upward air movement on the cold side of any insulation in the cavity. This air movement should have the intake from the outside and should exhaust to the outside at the top of the wall unless provision is made to disperse the moisture added to other spaces above the wall. The burning of fuels for heating tends to increase the amount of fresh air entering a building and thus provides ventilation in the

occupied spaces. No special provision is ordinarily made for it to enter since it usually gets in through infiltration around doors and windows. Where the construction is weather stripped and has tight exteriors, additional openings may be required.

Attic spaces are sometimes a source of trouble because of condensation on roof boards, shingles, or on long nails extending through the roof into the attic. Where the attic floor is well insulated, adequate ventilation in the attic is a safeguard against such condensation difficulties.

Ventilation in the cold cavities of walls by openings at both top and bottom is considered effective in preventing condensation in the cavity provided they open to the outside. Research to date indicates that 1 in. of opening per running foot of wall at both top and bottom is effective.

During the warmer months of the year a deposit of water or condensation is frequently found on basement walls and floors that are in contact with the soil. This type of water deposit is often confused with or thought to be water seeping through the concrete. In most cases, it does little harm; but where the floor or walls are covered with decorative materials, precautions are necessary to prevent decay or discoloration.

Good Practice Recommendations

Ventilator Size. There has been some confusion in the past on amounts of ventilation area intended when terms such as "area," "free area," "gross area," "net area," and just plain ventilation are used. The effect of air movement restriction such as (1) louvers, (2) fine mesh insect screen, and (3) grilles containing relatively small holes has not been completely understood.

For specification purposes and as used in the following discussion of amounts of ventilation recommended, the values given will be the "net amount of ventilation." The net area is the approximate unobstructed, clear or free opening through which air may move. The "gross area" is the total area of ventilator, louver, or grille and includes the net

---

* A good vapor barrier when installed should not have an average vapor transmission rate greater than 1.25 grains per sq ft, per hr, per in. of mercury differential including joints, fittings around outlet boxes, and the like. It should have sufficient mechanical strength to permit handling during erection without damage. It should also retain its vapor resistance qualities for the life of the building or, if a paint film, until it is renewed.

† A satisfactory sheathing paper or sheathing should be capable of passing 5 or more grains of water vapor per sq ft, per hr, per in. of mercury when tested by a dry method and should be resistant to wetting by free water and have satisfactory strength for handling and service.

Map divides country into three zones so that recommended condensation control practices can be established for different outside design temperatures. Zone I roughly includes temperatures —20 F and colder; Zone II, 0 to —10 F; Zone III warmer than 0 F

area as well as the solid material obstructing the flow of air. The relation between "net" and "gross" area for calculation purposes may be considered to be as set forth below:

Gross Ventilator Area =
Net Area × Factor A

Ventilator Covering	"A"
1. ¼ in. mesh hardware cloth	1
2. screening, 8 mesh to the in.	1¼
3. insect screen, 16 mesh to the in.	2
4. louvers and ¼ in. mesh hardware cloth	2
5. louvers and screening, 8 mesh to the in.	2¼
6. louvers and insect screen, 16 mesh to the in.	3

Crawl Space Ventilation. If there is no other effective condensation control, and if the soil may be a large supplier of moisture to the crawl space, the total net amount of ventilation should be 2 sq ft per 100 lineal ft of building per-

imeter plus one-third of 1 per cent of the crawl space ground area.

Good practice in condensation control in crawl spaces includes the following:

1. At least four ventilating openings, with one near each corner of the building.

2. The openings should be placed as high as possible in the walls of the crawl spaces.

3. When the ventilation is the only means of condensation control, the ventilator should not be closed during any time of the year.

4. When ventilation serves as condensation control, insulation may be required in the floor and around exposed mechanical lines for comfort and to prevent deterioration.

Ground Cover. Where it is not practical to allow a free sweep of cold air below a dwelling floor, condensation in crawl spaces can be controlled by covering the ground with a vapor-resistant, durable material. A good water-proofed concrete slab or heavy roll roofing has been found effective. A roll roofing, either mineral surfaced or plain, weighing at least 55 lb per 100 sq ft, laid with

Recommended good practice — loft and attic ventilation [1]

Type of roof and occupancy	Condensation zone		
	I	II	III
(a) Flat roof — Slope less than 3 inches in 12 inches. No occupancy contemplated.	Total net area of ventilation should be 1/300th [2] distributed uniformly at the eaves *plus* a vapor barrier in the top story ceiling. Free circulation must be provided through all spaces.	Same as for zone I.	Same as for zone I.
(b) Gable roof — Slope over 3 inches in 12 inches. No occupancy contemplated.	Total net area of at least 2 louvers on opposite sides located near the ridge to be 1/300th [2] *plus* a vapor barrier in the top story ceiling.	Same ventilation as for zone I. A vapor barrier is not considered necessary.	Same as for zone II.
(c) Hip roof — No occupancy contemplated.	Total net area of ventilation should be 1/300th [2] with 1/600th [2] distributed uniformly at the eaves *and* 1/600th [2] located at the ridge with all spaces interconnected. A vapor barrier should also be used in the top story ceiling.	Same ventilation as for zone I. A vapor barrier is not considered necessary.	Same as for zone II.
(d) Gable or hip roof — With occupancy contemplated.	Total net area of ventilation should be 1/300th [2] with 1/600th [2] distributed uniformly at the eaves *and* 1/600th [2] located at the ridge with all spaces interconnected. A vapor barrier should also be used on the warm side of the top full story ceiling, the dwarf walls, the sloping part of the roof, and the attic story ceiling.	Same as for zone I.	Same as for zone I except that a vapor barrier is not considered necessary if insulation is omitted.

[1] *It is recognized that in many areas increased ventilation may be desirable for summer comfort.*
[2] *Refers to area enclosed within the building lines at the eave level.*

2-in. lapped joints over a rough-graded surface, should serve satisfactorily for many years. Generally, the lap joints need no cementing material.

Where a good cover is applied over the entire surface of the ground in the crawl space, very little ventilation is needed. However, to be on the safe side, it is recommended that at least 10 per cent of the ventilation indicated by the two plus one-third formula (see section on "Heating, Ventilating, and Air Conditioning") be provided.

Walls. It is recommended that where the walls contain materials adversely affected by moisture or by freezing in the presence of moisture, an effective vapor barrier be provided on the warm side of the wall under the following conditions:
1. When the wall is insulated so that the overall heat transmission coefficient ("U") is numerically lower than 0.25 Btu per hr, per sq ft, per degree Fahrenheit. This applies to dwelling construction erected in any of the three condensation zones shown on the map.

2. When the wall has siding, sheathing, or sheathing paper or any other material on the cold side of the wall which, as applied, has a water vapor permeability of less than 5 grains per hr, per sq ft, per 1 in. of mercury pressure differential, and the dwelling is located in Condensation Zones I or II.

Lofts or Attics. In many instances, ventilation has been counted on in the past for condensation control in lofts, attics, etc. Ventilation will still perform satisfactorily if effectively installed; this requires (1) an adequate amount, (2) proper location, (3) continuous operation, and (4) circulation through all spaces to be ventilated.

The table on this page sets forth recommended good practice for the usual conditions encountered in dwelling construction.

For flat roofs, ventilation at the eave lines only is not effective in itself. Vapor barriers are definitely recommended in addition to ventilation in all zones.

For roof construction where the ventilation is advantageously placed high in the gable ends, vapor barriers are not absolutely necessary except in the severe Condensation Zone I. A vapor barrier

was omitted as a positive recommendation in Condensation Zone II and III because of costs.

Net amounts of ventilation in the table are given in fractions, thus: 1/300 or 1/600. They apply to the area of the building or part thereof at the eave line.

Vapor barriers, combined with ventilation and proper insulation, help prevent moisture accumulations in dwellings and subsequent damage and rot.

Use of Vapor Barriers

Vapor barriers should form a light, carefully installed envelope near the warm side of the building element in which they are placed, to prevent vapor reaching the cool surfaces. The cold side of a wall should be capable of losing moisture yet should be able to resist rain and strong winds.

Vapor barriers should always be used when outside of walls have low permeability, in northern climates, and where walls contain materials adversely affected by moisture or moisture freezing.

Concrete Floors Laid on Ground (Fig. 1)

1. Vapor barrier of durable paper or heavy roll roofing between gravel fill and concrete slab checks water seepage.

2. Thermal insulation (waterproofed) $1\frac{1}{2}$ ft wide around perimeter and over edge of floor slab checks condensation on floors cooled by conduction to walls in winter, by breaking continuity of the concrete. Provide recess in gravel fill and around wall for the insulation.

3. Vermiculite in a low density concrete aggregate or thermal insulation below floor prevents condensation caused by heat conduction to soil cooler than air in summer.

Floors Over Unheated Crawl Spaces (Figs. 2, 3)

1. Ventilate crawl space with min of 4 vents, placed high near corners of building for free air movement. Net ventilation should equal 2 sq ft per 100 lineal ft of building perimeter plus $\frac{1}{3}$ of 1 per cent of crawl space ground area.

2. Ground Cover of roll roofing (55 lb per 100 sq ft or heavier) restricts evaporation and reduces need of ventilation to 10 per cent amount indicated

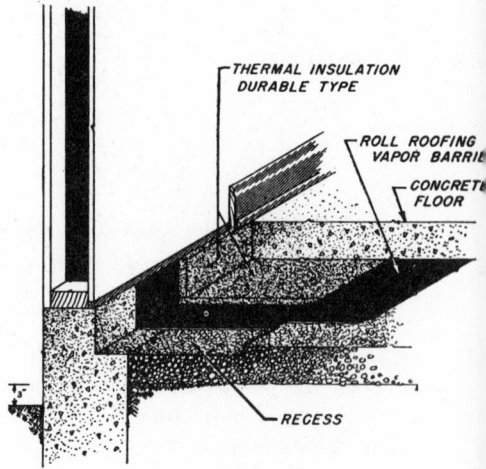

Fig. 1

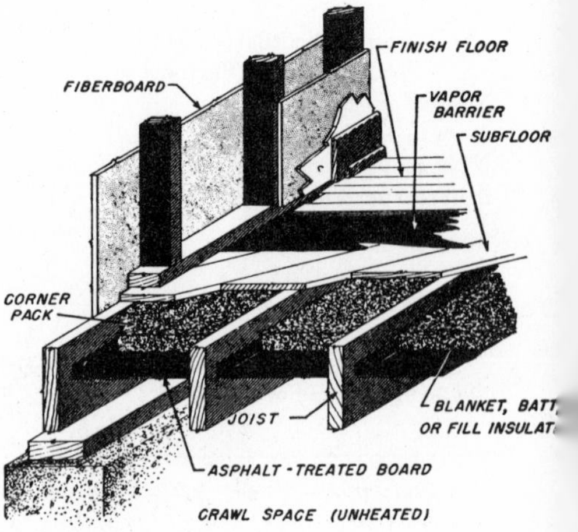

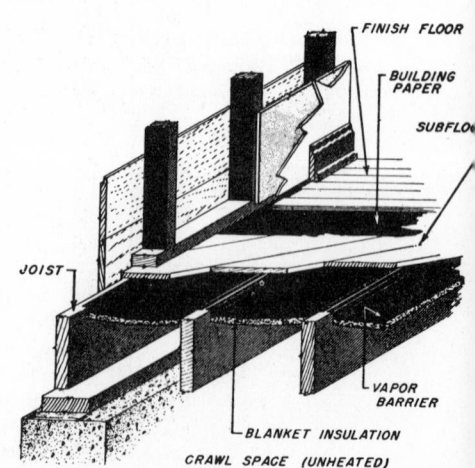

Fig. 2

Fig. 3

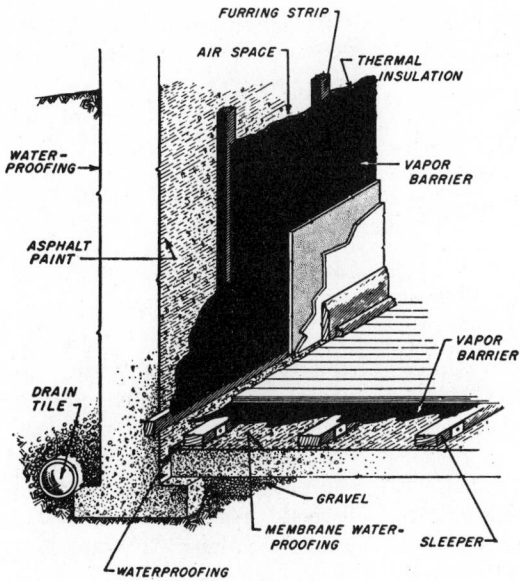

Fig. 4

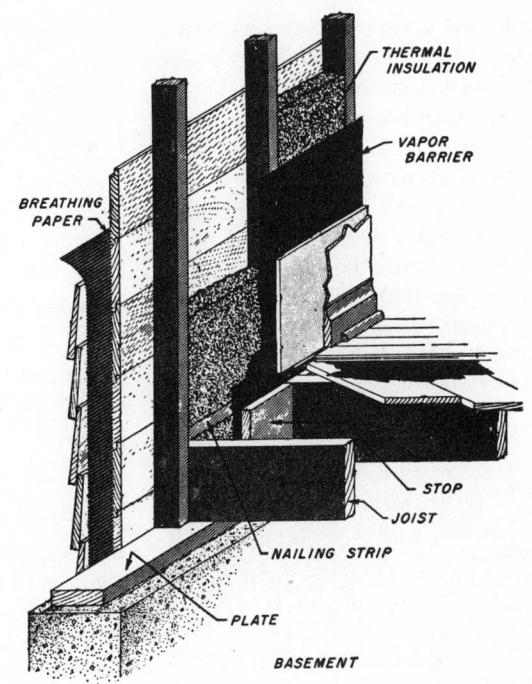

Fig. 6

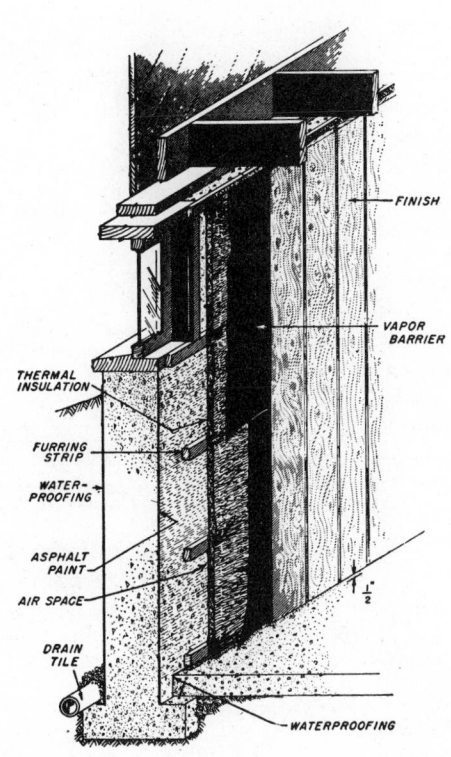

Fig. 5

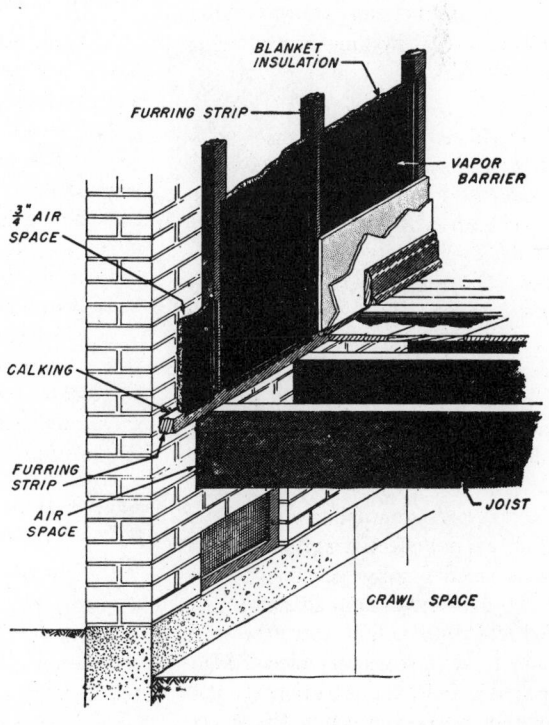

Fig. 7

above. Lap edges at least 2 in. Four in. of gravel may be used but requires more ventilation.

3. Drainage, preferably underground, is necessary on sloping sites. Soil surface below building should be above grade if there is a chance water might get inside foundation wall on level sites.

4. Vapor barrier is not required in floor if lower (cold) side is permeable. It is recommended, however, between finish and sub floors to prevent possible buckling from dampness in crawl space.

5. Insulate floors and pipes so vents can be left open all year, if necessary for condensation control. Some blanket insulations are made with good quality vapor barriers; when used, place building paper (or vapor barriers if desired) between finish and sub floors. Low surface temperature of reflective insulation necessitates use of vapor barrier. Allow min of ¾-in. air space between such insulation and adjacent surfaces. It is not practical to seal joints of asphalt-treated board supports for insulation, therefore use of a vapor barrier is indicated. Where corner packs are used along outside joists, crawl space must be well vented and ground covers used in wet locations.

Basement Floors (*Fig. 4*)

1. Vapor barrier below finish floor prevents entry of water into space between concrete and finish floor.

2. Membrane waterproofing is recommended over concrete sub floors.

3. Gravel should be placed below concrete for drainage.

Basement Walls (*Fig. 5*)

1. Vapor barrier placed behind surface, parallel to furring strips and lapped only over solid supports, prevents accumulation of free water behind finish surface.

2. Insulation is not essential, but will keep finish at a higher temperature, lower moisture content, and keep basement warm in winter. Allow air space between wall and insulation.

3. Drain tiles are recommended near footings in wet soils as well as waterproofing coating on outside of wall.

4. Asphalt paint is recommended on inside of masonry wall.

5. Furring strips should be durable wood or treated with preservative. Strips at top, bottom, and around openings should be continuous to form a good seal. Both wall finish and furring strips

should be kept ½-in. above concrete floor.

Floors Over Basements (*Fig. 6*)

1. Vapor barriers should be placed over insulation above foundation wall.

2. Building paper should be placed between finish and sub floors.

Side Walls (*Figs. 7, 8, 9*)

1. Vapor barriers should be placed over inside (warm) face of studs and run vertically through full story height, lapping only over studs. Fit closely around all openings and partitions.

2. Insulation is best placed on the warm side of wall, as water will be dispersed more readily than if placed against sheathing. Air space should be left on one or both sides of insulation if possible. If blanket insulation with vapor barrier is used, thoroughly close openings at top and bottom of stud spaces or other horizontal obstructions such as fire stops. Reflective insulation requires a separate vapor barrier.

3. Ventilation in cold cavities of walls is effective if opened to the outside. Use 1-in. of opening per running ft of wall, at both top and bottom.

4. Brick walls over crawl spaces, with

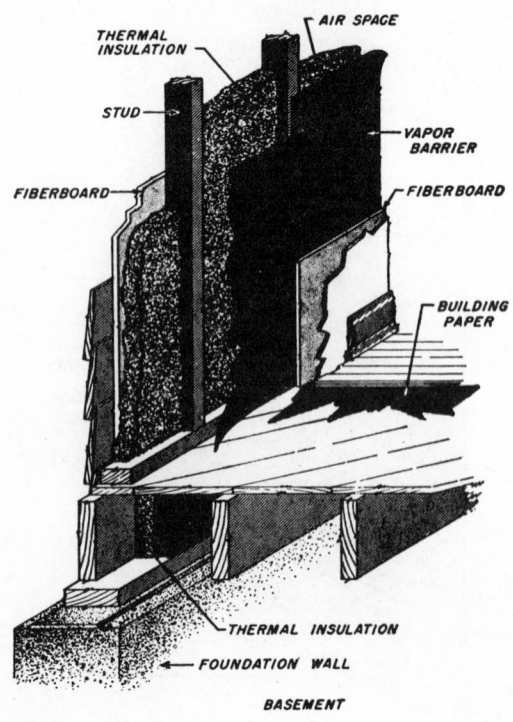

Fig. 8

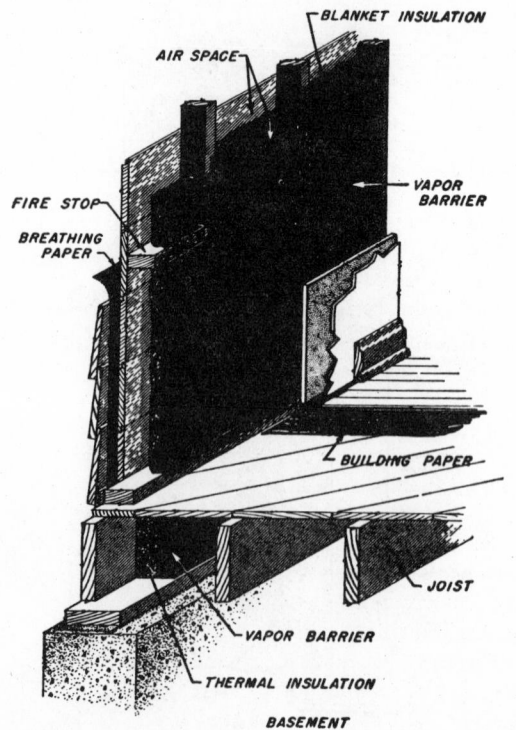

Fig. 9

vapor barriers, require a horizontal furring strip fixed tightly to the brick over joists or above sub floor. Fill any gaps with caulking compound to prevent migration of water vapor from crawl space to attic. Allow air space between insulation and brick.

Junction of Second Floor and Wall (Fig. 10)

1. *Vapor barriers* should be carefully placed over nailing strips at end of spaces between joists and along wall at joist level, to restrict flow of water vapor into outside walls. Floor and ceiling provide large surfaces through which water can penetrate into enclosed area. These can contribute more vapor to end of space than an equal area of outside room walls.

2. *Insulate* wall sections between floor joists and along wall at joist level as carefully as the main wall areas; heat loss will be as great as in other outside wall areas.

3. *Air spaces* should be allowed on both sides of insulation where practical, and always when reflective-type insulation is used.

Ceilings Adjacent to Unheated Attic (Figs. 11, 12)

1. *Vapor barriers* are considered necessary on the warm side of all top story ceilings in areas with temps of −20 F and colder, and with flat roofs in warmer climates. They should be applied below joists and running parallel to them, prior to attachment of ceiling. Lap over side wall plate and fit carefully around openings. Hatches should be closed tightly by catches. In existing buildings, barriers can be applied above ceiling and held in place by wood strips fixed over barrier edges turned up against joists.

2. *Insulation*, when used, should be placed over ceiling after latter has been applied, and on backs of all doors into unheated spaces.

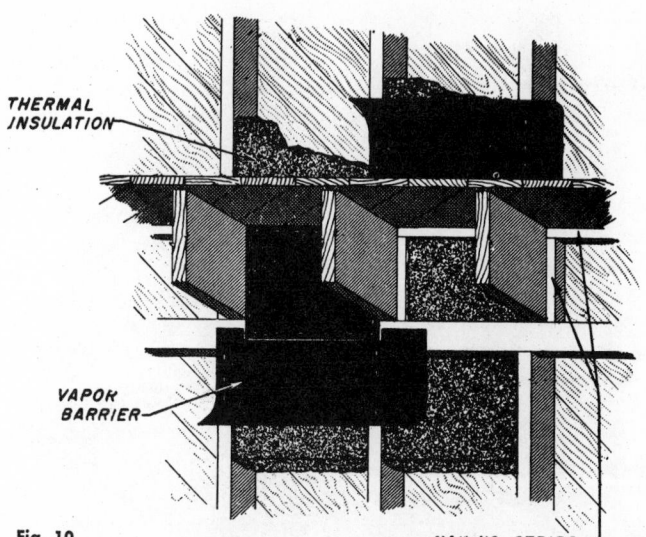

THERMAL INSULATION

VAPOR BARRIER

NAILING STRIPS

Fig. 10

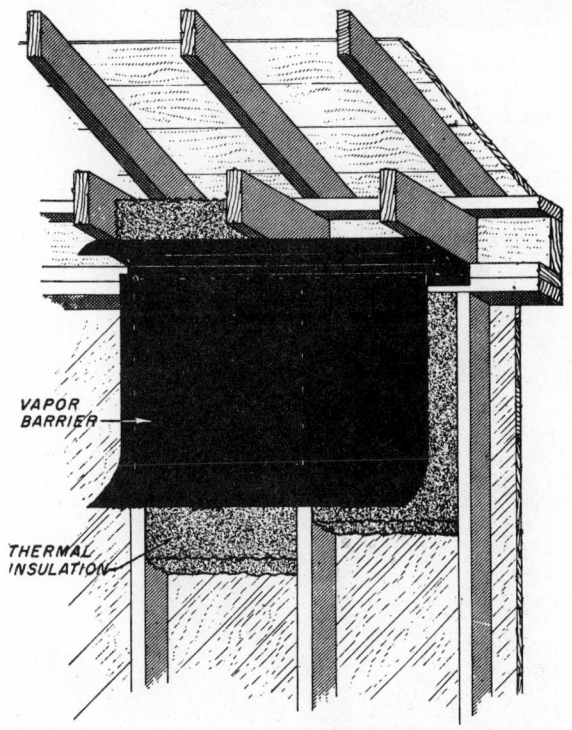

VAPOR BARRIER

THERMAL INSULATION

Fig. 11

UNOCCUPIED ATTIC SPACE

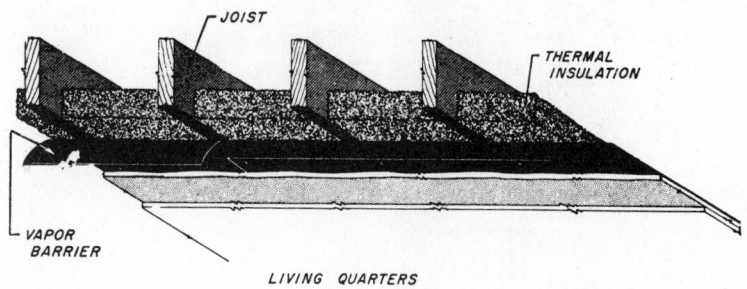

JOIST

THERMAL INSULATION

VAPOR BARRIER

LIVING QUARTERS

Fig. 12

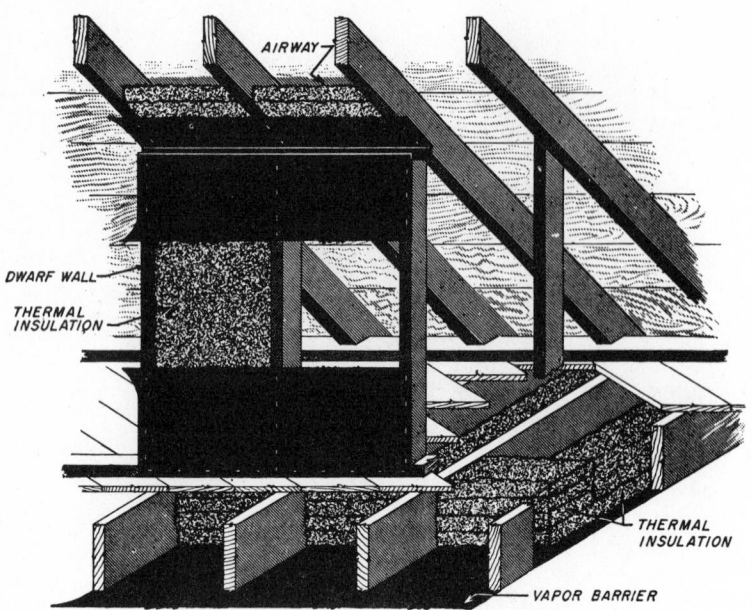

Fig. 13

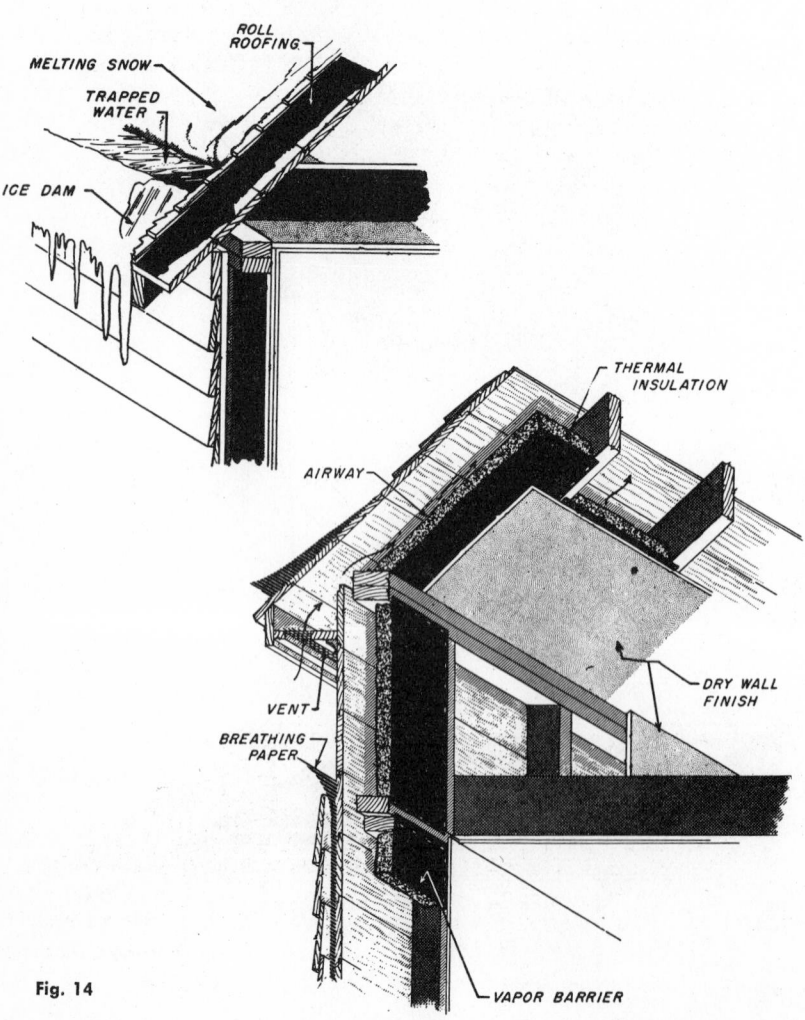

Fig. 14

Partly Finished Attic With Dwarf Walls (Fig. 13)

1. *Vapor barriers* should be installed on ceilings beneath unheated attic spaces as noted before. They may extend from between joists below dwarf walls, back to outside wall, but it would probably be less expensive and better to cover entire ceiling than to fit barriers between joists. Except in the southern states when insulation is omitted, dwarf walls, ceilings and roof over attic living areas should be carefully fitted with barriers. Fit doors to unheated spaces tightly to stops by weather strips or other seals. Thin doors inclined to warp should be held by catches.

2. *Insulation*, if used, should be placed on ceiling below unheated attic, on dwarf wall, roof over heated space and backs of doors to cold spaces.

3. *An airway* should be provided over insulation in roof. Provide for air circulation behind dwarf wall and between rafters.

Finished Attics (Fig. 14)

1. *Vapor barriers* should be placed around heated areas as noted in the previous section. Some form of dry wall finish is best along walls and lower part of roof to prevent damage to barrier. Ice along eaves often causes water to back under shingles and into building. To prevent this, lay single course of heavy roofing felt, roll roofing or sheet metal over eaves, and extend under shingles well above line of wall. Long nails projecting into attic or wall may condense water and collect ice in cold weather. As a safeguard against stained ceilings, etc., resulting from this, clip nails close to wood.

2. *Insulation*, when used, should be on both side wall and between rafters of roof.

3. *An airway* over insulation in roof should be allowed.

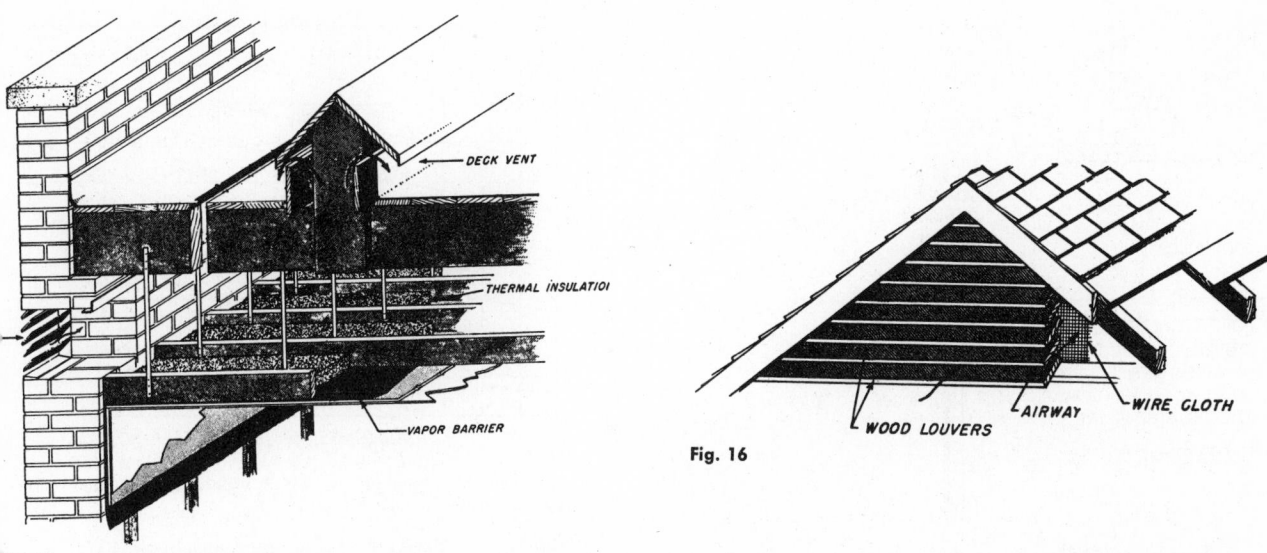

DECK VENT

THERMAL INSULATION

VAPOR BARRIER

ig. 15

WOOD LOUVERS AIRWAY WIRE CLOTH

Fig. 16

Ventilation alone may effectively control condensation in attics if ceiling below is not insulated, provided there is:
(1) an adequate amount,
(2) proper location,
(3) continuous operation,
(4) free circulation.
With insulation added or with very tight roofs, ventilation alone is not as effective, and vapor barriers are recommended.

Net amounts of ventilation should equal 1/300th of area of building or part thereof at eave line. In many areas increased ventilation may be desirable for summer comfort.

Low-pitched roof decks (Fig.15) are best aired by vents along sides of building and deck vent running perpendicular to run of joists. Where ventilation in side walls is effective and in proper amount, center vent may be omitted. Vapor barriers are recommended where condensation is a major problem.

Gable and hip roofs, when finished for occupancy, should have: ½ required vent area in continuous air inlets below eaves (Fig.14); airways, interconnected, through roof; and ½ vent area in outlets (such as Fig. 17) near ridge. Where occupancy is

planned, gable roofs should have at least two louvers (Fig.16)on opposite sides, located near ridge.

Flat roofs (Fig.18) should be provided with vapor barriers, vents uniformly distributed at eaves, and airways clear from one side of building to the other. Place vents as near outside of cornice as possible to minimize amount of snow driven in by wind.

The diagrams (Fig. 19) show the location of vapor barrier, insulation, and ventilation in various common building types.

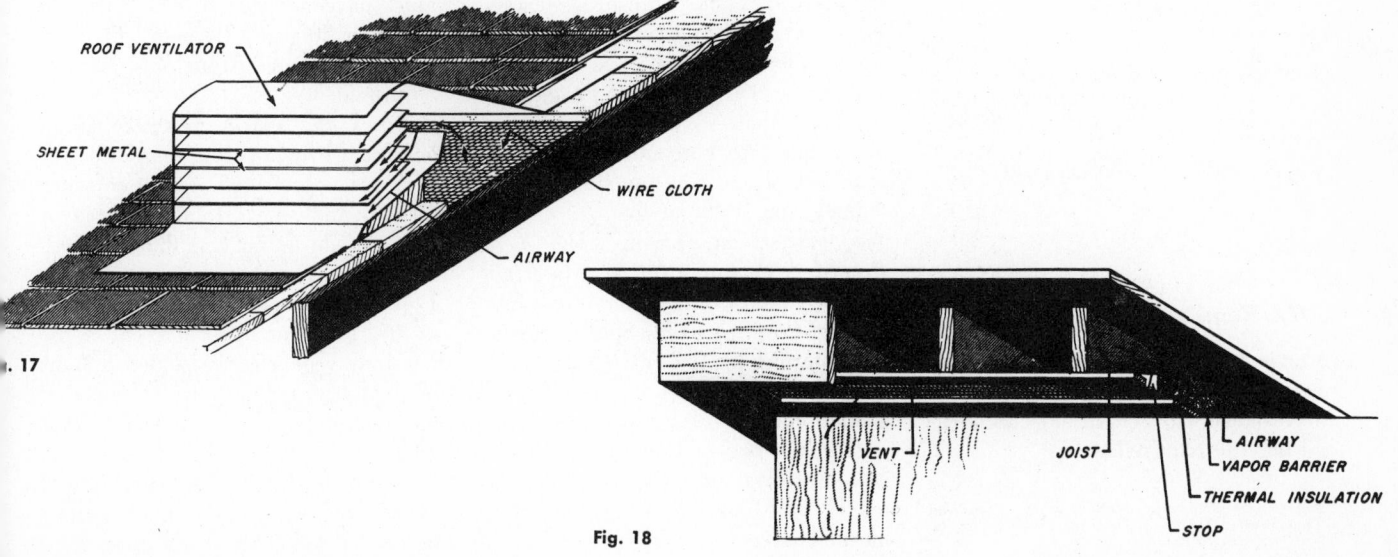

ROOF VENTILATOR

SHEET METAL

WIRE CLOTH

AIRWAY

. 17

VENT   JOIST   AIRWAY
VAPOR BARRIER
THERMAL INSULATION
STOP

Fig. 18

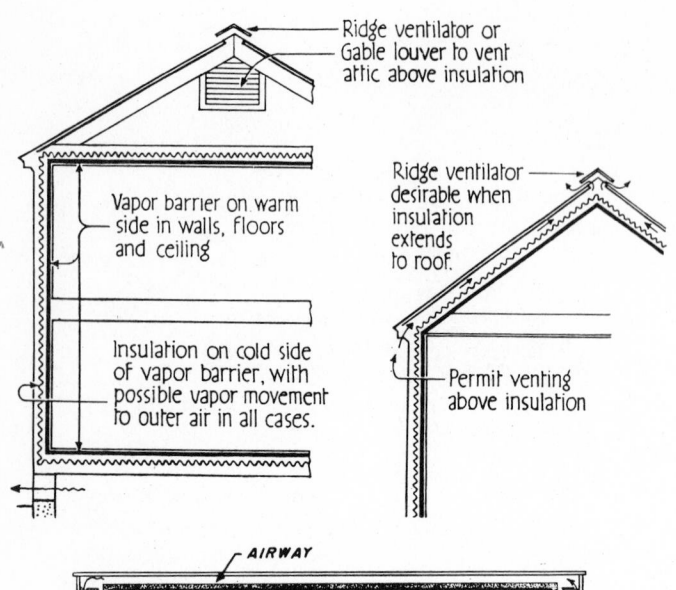

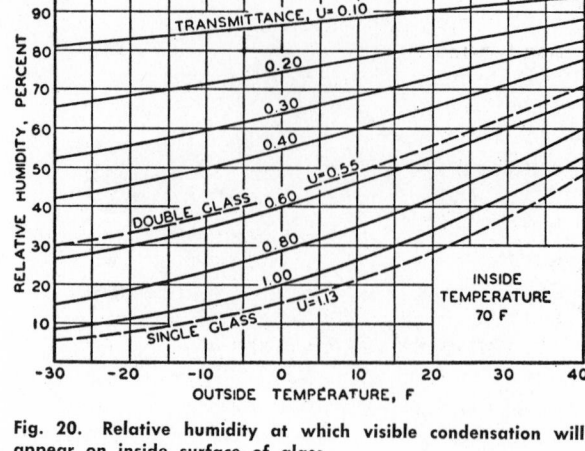

Fig. 20. Relative humidity at which visible condensation will appear on inside surface of glass

Courtesy ASHRAE Guide and Data Book, *1961.*

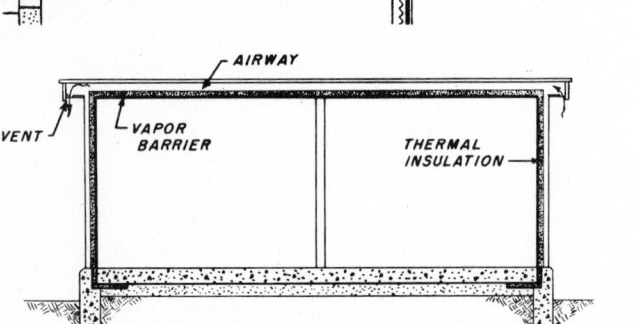

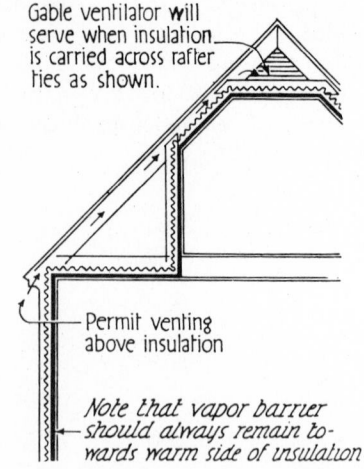

Fig. 19. Methods of ventilating roofs

FHA Requirements‡

Vapor barriers. Test data indicating vapor transmission rate determined in accordance with ASTM dry-cup method may be required.

‡ *Minimum Property Standards for One and Two Living Units, Federal Housing Administration, revised 1959.*

Walls: Vapor transmission rate not exceeding 1 perm; locate near warm side; required when *U*-value of wall is less than 0.25 or when siding, paper, and sheathing, or other materials or combination of materials on the cold side of the wall, have a combined vapor transmission rate of less than 5 perms, and the outside design temperature is 0° or less.

Ceilings: Vapor transmission rate not exceeding 1 perm; locate near warm side.

Roof decks (no ceiling): Permeance not more than ½ perm; locate near warm side; seal at sides and ends; required where the outside design temperature is 10° or less.

Floors: Comply with FHA *Test Procedure for Vapor Barrier Materials for Use Under Concrete Slabs and For Ground Cover in Crawl Spaces*; maximum permeance under concrete slabs ½ perm; maximum permeance for ground cover in crawl spaces 1 perm.

Building paper: Comply with Federal Specification UU-P-147 Class D or HH-F-191 or ASTM D 226; permeance not less than 5 perms.

Ventilation

Crawl spaces: Provide at least 4 vents, one near each corner, having an aggregate net area of not less than 1/250th of the ground area, or install vapor barrier ground cover as specified above and provide 2 vents having an aggregate net area of 1/1,500th of the ground area. When used as a *plenum,* vapor barrier and insulation must have a flame spread rating of less than 200, and 2 vents with tight closures operated from outside must be provided.

Attics and spaces between ceiling and roof: Provide cross ventilation for each space, protected against entrance of rain and snow; total net area of vents should be not less than 1/150th of ceiling area, except that it may be 1/300th if a vapor barrier is provided in the ceiling or if 50 per cent of the required vent area is located 3 ft or more above eave vents which make up the remainder of the required vent area.

Screening: All required vents should be covered with ⅛-in. mesh screen fabric; metallic screening must comply with Commercial Standard CS138; plastic-coated fibrous glass screening must comply with Federal Specification L-S-137.

Data from *ASHRAE Guide and Data Book*, 1961.

Vapor transmission rates can be calculated by methods analogous to those used for the calculation of thermal transmission. The unit of *permeance* is the *perm*, which equals 1 grain per sq ft per hr per in. of mercury vapor pressure difference. The unit of *permeability* is the *perm-inch*. Resistance to vapor flow is the reciprocal of permeance, and the overall resistance of an assembly of materials such as a wall is the sum of the resistances of its parts. Overall permeance (M_t) can be calculated from the individual permeances (M)

of the components by use of the following formula:

$$M_t = \frac{1}{1/M_1 + 1/M_2 + 1/M_3 \cdots + 1/M_n}$$

Permeance and permeability of building materials are given in Table 1.

Visible condensation usually occurs on glass but may occur on any surface whose temperature is below the dew point of the interior air. Conditions under which condensation will occur are shown in Fig. 20. To prevent surface condensation increase the temperature of the surface or reduce the relative humidity of the air, or both. The inside surface temperature of glass may be increased by the use of double glass or by passing a current of warm air across it. The inside sur-

face temperature of other material may be increased by the use of insulation. The relative humidity of the inside air may be lowered by ventilation (exhaust fans in kitchens, baths, laundries, etc.) or by reducing the output of humidifiers, or both.

Condensation in cooled buildings: When the interior of a building is cooled, the vapor barrier should theoretically be located near the outer (warm) side of the structure. In the case of air-conditioned buildings this is not necessary since the interior temperature is very rarely below the dew point of the outside air. In the case of cold storage buildings, however, the conditions are severe and a vapor barrier with a permeance of not more than 0.1 perm should be installed near the outside surface.

Table 1. Permeance and permeability of materials to water vapor

Data from ASHRAE Guide and Data Book, *1961.*

Material	Perme-ance Perm	% RH₁-RH₂	Method†	Material	Perme-ance Perm	% RH₁-RH₂	Method†
AIR (still)	120*	92–73	b	WOOD			
INSULATION				Sugar Pine	0.4–5.4*	various	tv
Cellular glass	0.0*		d	Plywood (Exterior type 3 ply D.F.), ¼ in.	0.72	50–	4
Corkboard	2.1–2.6*	75–0	d	Plywood (Interior type 3 ply D.F.), ¼ in.	1.86	50–	4
Corkboard	9.5*	100–45	w				
Structural Insulating Board (vegetable, uncoated)	20–50*	40–x	t	MASONRY			
Mineral Wool (unprotected)	116*	100–30	w	Concrete (1:2:4 Mix)	3.2*	100–45	w
				Concrete (8 in. cored block wall, limestone agrgt.)	2.4	79–68	t
INTERIOR FINISH				Brick wall—with mortar—4 in.	0.8	50–x	t
Plaster on wood lath	11	100–30	w	Tile wall—with mortar—4 in.	0.12	50–x	t
Plaster on metal lath—¾ in.	15	40–x	t				

Material	Lb per 500 sq ft	Permeance-Perms	
		dry cup	wet cup
**BUILDING PAPERS, FELTS, AND PLASTIC FILMS			
Duplex sheet, asphalt laminae, *aluminum foil* one side	43	0.002	0.176
Saturated and *coated* felt heavy roll roofing	326	0.05	0.24
Kraft and *asphalt laminae*, Reinforced 30-120-30	34	0.3	1.8
Insulation back up, asphalt-sat., one side glossy	31	0.4	0.6–4.2
Asphalt-saturated and coated sheathing paper	43	0.3	0.6
Asphalt-saturated sheathing paper	22	3.3	20.2
15-pound asphalt felt	70	1.0	5.6
15-pound tar felt	70	4.0	18.2
Single sheet Kraft, double infused	16	30.8	41.9
PLASTIC FILMS			
2 mil polyethylene	4.9	0.16	0.14
4 mil polyethylene	10.0	0.08	0.07

Additional Interior Finish and Paint rows:

Material	Perme-ance Perm	% RH₁-RH₂	Method†
Plaster on plain gypsum lath (with studs)	20	40–85	t
Gypsum wall board—plain—⅜ in.	50	50–20	v
Insulating wall board (uncoated)—½ in.	50–90	40–x	t
**PAINT—2 coats			
Asphaltic paint on plywood	0.4	100–30	w
Aluminum in varnish on wood	0.3–0.5	95–0	d
Enamels, brushed on smooth plaster	0.5–1.5	92–0	b
Primers or *Sealers* on insulating wall board	0.9–2.1	40–x	t
Various *Primers* +1 coat flat paint on plaster	1.6–3.	40–x	t
Flat paint (alone) on insulating wall board	4	40–x	t
Water Emulsion on insulat-wall board	30.–85.	40–x	t
**PAINT—Exterior, 3 coats			
White *lead & oil* prepared paint on wood siding	0.3–1.0	50–0	d
White lead-zinc oxide & linseed oil on wood	0.9	95–0	d

* These boldface values are permeability in perm-inches.
** Description is a guide only, and does not insure permeance.
† Methods: d—dry cup; w—wet cup; t—two temperatures; b—special cell; v—air velocity both sides; 4—average of four methods.

RESIDENTIAL HEATING AND AIR CONDITIONING—1
Furnaces

By S. KONZO, *Professor of Mechanical Engineering, University of Illinois*
E. J. BROWN, *Research Associate in Mechanical Engineering, University of Illinois*

Generally a warm-air system is one which circulates warm air; hence, it could include anything from a blast coil heated by steam to a parlor stove. More strictly, however, a warm-air system is defined as one containing a direct-fired furnace over which air is circulated. When the air circulation is by natural gravity the system is referred to as a *gravity warm-air system*, a type which has been superseded by the *forced warm-air system* in which the air circulation is by means of a fan. Positive circulation by the blower (centrifugal fan)

permits the use of relatively small ducts, means for filtering the air, and provisions for supplying tempered outdoor air, if desired. The forced warm-air system is characterized by its adaptability to a wide variety of building types, its rapid response to changing weather demands, and its possible combination with summer cooling.

The forced warm-air system consists of a furnace, a burner with necessary automatic controls, a blower, a supply-air distribution duct system, supply outlets, and a return-air duct system.

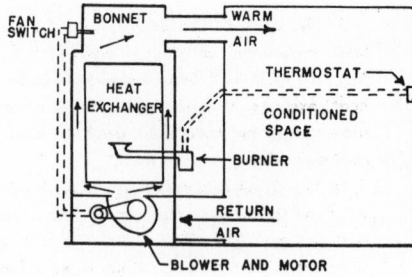

Fig. 1.   Basic furnace arrangement

Furnaces and Basic Control

A number of possible arrangements of control equipment have been tried, but the basic arrangement is that illustrated in Fig. 1. The furnace, which is sold in "packaged" form in smaller sizes, consists of a burner (oil, gas, or electric), a heat exchanger (usually steel), a jacket (or casing), a blower, a filter, and automatic controls. An automatic humidifier is often included.

The sequence of operation is extremely simple, and most effective if the control settings are properly made in accordance with so-called "Comfort Air Circulation" principles, advocated by the National Warm Air Heating and Air Conditioning Association. Essentially the operating sequence

of a warm-air system is as follows:

a) When the room temperature drops, the room thermostat demands heat and closes the burner switch.

b) The generation of heat within the heat exchanger results in a rapid rise in bonnet-air temperature, since the blower is not operating.

c) When the temperature of the bonnet air reaches the setting of the fan switch (such as 110 F) the blower begins operation.

d) The delivery of heated air through the duct system to the room results in a gradual increase in room-air temperature. When the room-air temperature reaches the desired value set on the thermostat the burner is shut down.

e) The blower continues to operate until the bonnet-air temperature is reduced to some low value (such as 80 F), at which time the blower is shut down.

f) The cycle is repeated. The successful operation of the system requires that the fan-switch settings be so arranged that the blower starts operating whenever the bonnet-air temperature reaches a value of the order of 110 F.

Furnaces are classified according to the direction in which air flows through them. For example, in the upflow furnace, generally used in houses with basements, the air flow is upward through the furnace (Figs. 2a and 2b). The upflow furnace may be either of the *low-boy type* (Fig. 2a)

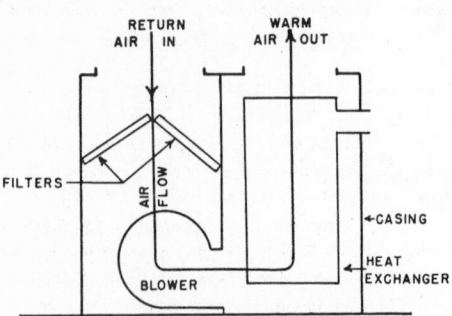

Fig. 2a.   Low-boy furnace with blower adjacent to heat exchanger

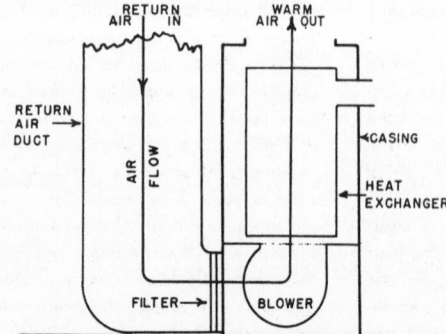

Fig. 2b.   High-boy furnace with blower below heat exchanger

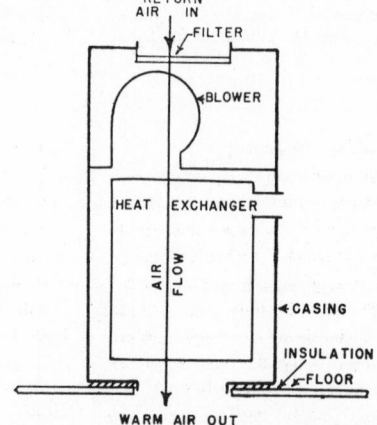

Fig. 3.   Counter-flow furnace used over crawl spaces and concrete slabs

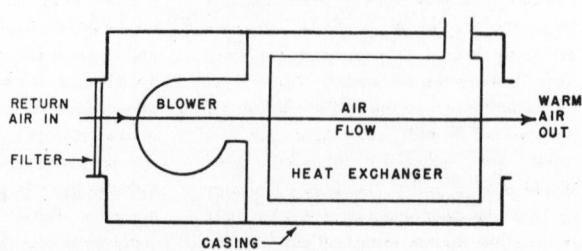

Fig. 4.   Horizontal furnace located in attic or crawl space

with the blower located adjacent to the heat exchanger, or of the *high-boy type* (Fig. 2b) with the blower located below the heat exchanger. Both types require approximately the same floor area when the return-air ducts are included.

In the *counter-flow furnace* (Fig. 3) the air flows downwards opposite to the direction of flow of the flue gases. The blower is mounted above the heat exchanger. This type of furnace is commonly used for houses built over a crawl space or on a concrete slab floor, and the furnace is often located in a closet or utility room.

The *horizontal furnace* (Fig. 4) can be suspended from floor joists in a crawl space or mounted on top of ceiling joists in an attic space. The air flow is horizontal over the heat exchanger.

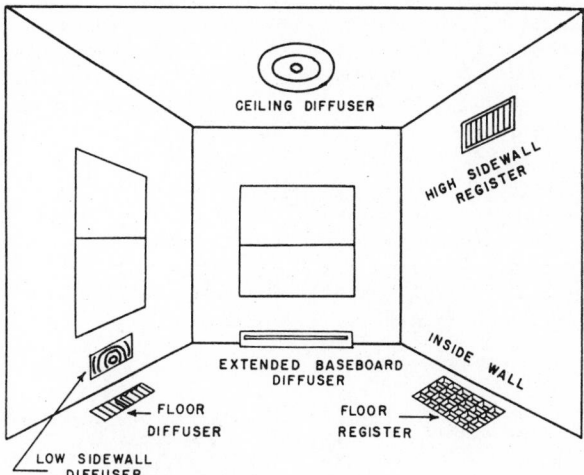

Fig. 5. Various types of supply outlets

Supply Outlets:
Types, Locations, and Applications

A *supply outlet* is an opening through which air is delivered into a conditioned space. Outlets are grouped under the broad classification of *registers* and *diffusers*. Although the difference between registers and diffusers is not sharply defined, a *register* is commonly considered as an outlet which discharges the air in a confined jet. On the other hand, a *diffuser* is an outlet which discharges the air in a spreading jet. Registers and diffusers may be placed at a number of locations (Fig. 5), including the floor, baseboard, low sidewall, high sidewall, and ceiling.

For heating purposes the preferred location of supply outlets is in the floor, at the baseboard, or low sidewall of the *outside* wall and preferably under windows. The next preferred locations are diffusers located low on an inside wall, or registers high on the same wall. The ceiling location is the least desirable from the standpoint of heating.

On the other hand, for cooling purposes, the high sidewall register on an inside wall or the ceiling diffuser provide the best air distribution. There is no one outlet location which will provide the best air distribution both summer and winter, so a compromise location is demanded. The floor, baseboard, and low sidewall locations at the exposed wall provide good conditions for winter and acceptable conditions for summer, if adequate air velocity is maintained at the outlet face and the air is directed upwards towards the ceiling. The ceiling location (and high sidewall outlets) do provide good conditions for summer, but do not compare in winter with diffusers or registers located low in the outside wall.

Air Distribution Systems

One of the most satisfactory air-distribution systems for a residence is designated as the *perimeter* system, in which the conditioned air is introduced vertically into the living space through supply outlets located in or near the outside wall. For a house built over a basement or crawl space, these perimeter outlets may be served by an *extended plenum* duct system (Fig. 6). The same extended plenum can also serve to supply inside wall outlets.

The return-air duct system is usually short and direct; in small homes the return system frequently consists of a single return-air grille, so located that a short duct may serve to carry the air back to the furnace. In larger houses, a return-air inlet should be provided in each room. Rooms not provided with individual return-air inlets should have a grille in or above the door or have the door undercut by ¾ in. to 1 in. to allow for the return of air from the room.

A method for the admission of outdoor air to the duct system is also shown in Fig. 6. The outdoor air is admitted through the return-air duct and tempered before entering the supply-air duct system.

In the summer the forced-air system may be operated without heat, to circulate air within the house. At night, cool outside air may be admitted through the fresh-air intake and circulated throughout the house.

The house built upon a *concrete floor slab* came into prominence after World War II and introduced many difficulties from the standpoint of heating. Extensive research has indicated that this type of house can be effectively heated with warm air if the perimeter duct is embedded in the slab. The heated ducts in the floor serve not only to take care of the heat loss through the edge of the floor slab, but also serve to maintain comfortable temperatures at the floor surface. Heat is introduced indirectly into the room through the warm slab and directly into the living space through the warm air discharged through registers near the perimeter. The *perimeter-loop* duct sys-

tem (Fig. 7) is more effective than the simpler *perimeter-radial* duct system (Fig. 8).

Details of slab construction for the embedded duct systems, as recommended by the National Warm Air Heating and Air Conditioning Association, are given in Fig. 9. The *edge insulation*, which is mandatory, decreases the heat loss from the edge of the slab to the ground and to the outdoor air. The vapor barrier, usually specified below the embedded duct, prevents the migration of moisture from the ground into the duct system. Ducts may be formed of light-gage metal, impregnated paper tubes, or vitrified clay pipe. In any case they should be round and covered on all sides by concrete at least 2 in. thick. Ducts must be tied down or weighted to keep them from floating when the concrete is poured over them. Edge insulation must be of the rigid type and not subject to deterioration in the presence of moisture. Glass fiber, foamed plastic, or foamed glass boards are satisfactory. In northern climates, the in-

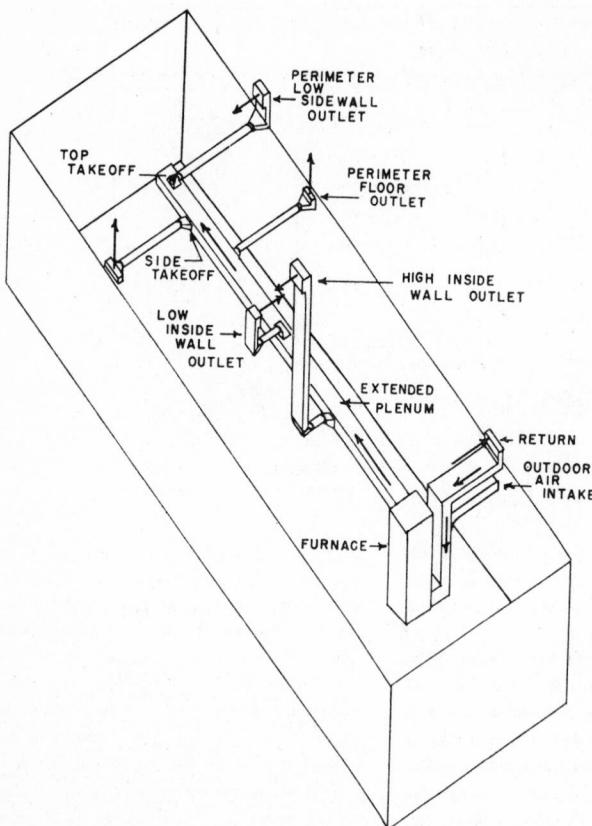

Fig. 6.   Extended plenum distribution system

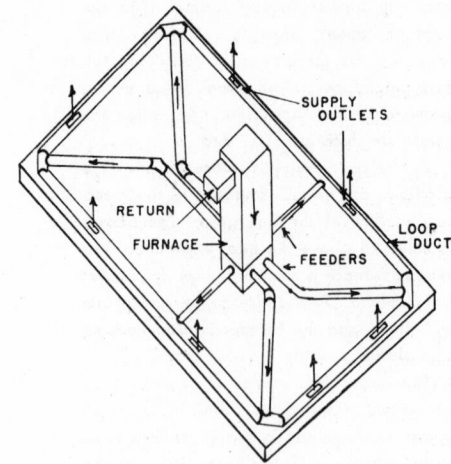

Fig. 7.   Perimeter-loop distribution system

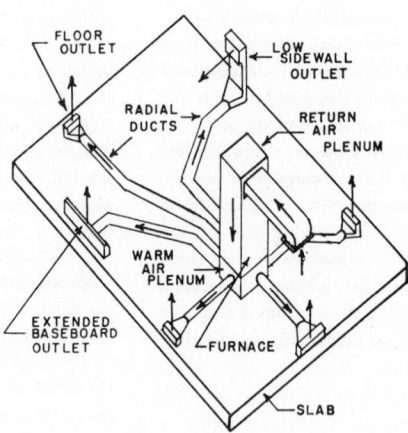

Fig. 8.   Perimeter-radial distribution system

sulation should be at least 2 in. thick.

The house built over a crawl space has also come into common use since World War II. For this type of construction, the *perimeter-radial* system is particularly well adapted, as it is also to a house with full basement. For the house built over a crawl space, in which no basement space is available, the *counter-flow* type of furnace is usually located in a utility (or furnace) room on the first floor, and the warm air is discharged downwards from the furnace into the plenum chamber below the furnace. The radial system may utilize low sidewall and baseboard outlets, as well as floor outlets.

The return-air system shown in Fig. 7 consists of a grille and a short stub duct connected to the side of the return-air plenum. This simple system has the disadvantage of permitting noise from the blower to issue directly into the adjacent room. Quiet blower units must be selected and sound insulating material used on the inside of the return duct and return-air plenum. In Fig. 8 another simple return-air duct system is shown in which the return-air grille is located in the ceiling. This arrangement reduces the transmission of blower noise to the

room and is preferred to the simpler arrangement of Fig. 7.

Any ductwork which is located in a closed crawl space or basement is usually not insulated, since any heat loss from the duct serves to warm the floor of the living space above. However, any supply duct or return-air duct which passes through a ventilated crawl space or an attic space must be heavily insulated, since the space can become cold and any heat loss from the duct is lost and not available for heating the house. Supply ducts require insulation of 2-in. thickness and return-air ducts require 1-in.-thick insulation. If such ducts are to be used for summer cooling, the insulation must be carefully covered with a vapor barrier to prevent the passage of water vapor through the insulation and the formation of condensation on the cool duct surfaces.

Design of Air-Distribution Systems
Flexibility of the forced warm-air system has resulted in dozens of different design methods for special buildings and special

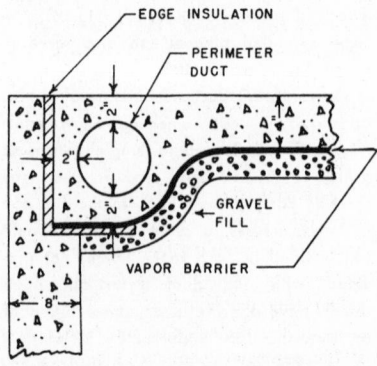

Fig. 9.   Slab construction for embedded duct systems

cases. Detailed information for these is available in the Manuals of the National Warm Air Heating and Air Conditioning Association, 640 Engineers' Building, Cleveland, Ohio. In the following pages we will outline the design steps for two common forced warm-air systems, to indicate design procedures and the extensive tables and data available in the literature. For illustration of these systems see Sheet 3.

The first step in the design of any warm-air heating system is to determine the design heat loss of the individual rooms to be heated. The furnace capacity at the bonnet should be equal to, or slightly greater than, the total design heat loss of the house. Procedures are given in Manual No. 3 of the National Warm Air Heating & Air Conditioning Association.

Perimeter-Loop System
(For Concrete Floor Slab)
Following are the steps to be taken in the design of a perimeter-loop system for small houses in which the design heat loss does not exceed 100,000 Btuh (Btu per hr), where the perimeter of the house is less than 210 ft, and where the maximum length of feeder duct is less than 30 ft. Detailed design procedure is given in Manual No. 4 of the National Warm Air Heating & Air Conditioning Association:

1) Locate the perimeter-loop duct on floor plan, avoiding kitchen cabinets and plumbing.

2) Locate diffusers below or near windows, allowing one diffuser for each 6000 to 8000 Btuh design heat loss. For rooms with two or more exposed walls, place diffusers on each of the exposed walls if possible.

3) Locate the *feeder-ducts* from the sub-floor plenum to the perimeter duct so that the feeders supply the perimeter loop at the areas of greatest heat loss. Allow one feeder duct for each 15,000 Btuh heat loss. In general, no more than 35 ft of perimeter loop duct should exist between any two feeders, and no more than three diffusers between two feeders. The feeders should connect at right angles to the perimeter loop and at least 18 in. from a diffuser. If the distance between diffusers is more than 20 ft, that section of perimeter loop should be served by its own feeder.

4) Determine the diameter of the feeder duct from Table 1. Assume that each diffuser will be supplied by the nearest feeder. The Btuh delivered to the feeder, together with the length of the feeder, determines the diameter of the feeder duct.

5) The perimeter loop duct should be constant in diameter and should be equal to that of the largest feeder duct.

6) Determine the *total free area* of all the

Table 1. Diameter of feeder ducts for perimeter loop system

Btuh Per Feeder	Length of Feeder in Feet	
	0-15 Feet	16-30 Feet
up to 7,999	6"	6"
8,000 to 8,999	6"	7"
9,000 to 10,999	7"	7"
11,000 to 11,999	7"	8"
12,000 to 12,999	7"	8"
13,000 to 17,000	8"	8"

Tables on Sheets 4, 5, and 6 have been adapted from Manual 4, National Warm Air Heating and Air Conditioning Association

diffusers required for each room by means of Tables 2a, 2b, or 2c. The particular table to be used depends upon the "length of the feeder duct under room plus ½ length of perimeter duct under room." Obviously, if this length is great, a large heat input to the room occurs through the floor slab. The *total free area* for the diffusers in the room is divided by the number of diffusers to obtain the average free area of individual diffusers. Actual diffuser sizes can be determined from manufacturers' catalogues.

Perimeter-Radial System
(For Crawl Space or Basement)
Essentially, the procedure is as follows:

1) Locate the diffusers on the floor plan, allowing at least one diffuser for each room. The diffusers should be located under windows if possible and the maximum delivery should be limited to about 7000 Btuh.

2) Make a line drawing of the *perimeter-radial duct system*, in which individual ducts extend from the plenum to the individual registers.

3) Measure the length of each radial duct and note the number of elbows in the duct.

4) With the information at hand, and with the aid of Table 3, the heat delivery to the room through a 6-in. diameter duct can be determined. The table refers to sidewall and floor diffusers only. Additional data are provided in the manuals for other sizes of ducts and for other types of register outlets.

5) If the total Btu which all radial ducts will actually deliver to a room is less than the design heat loss of the room, more ducts and diffusers are required.

6) Use the "cfm values" in the table to determine the size of diffuser required, as listed in the manufacturers' tables.

A complete design procedure for the use of 4-in. diameter pipes, referred to as the

small-pipe perimeter system, is available in Manual No. 10 of the National Warm Air Heating and Air Conditioning Association.

Extended Plenum Systems
(Use with Perimeter Register Systems)
It is possible, of course, to use a trunk duct system in which all the branch ducts extend from a tapered, large central duct, in the same manner that the branches of a tree extend from the trunk. (See Sheet 3.) The *extended plenum duct* differs from the conventional trunk-and-branch arrangement since the main trunk is constant in size from the plenum to the end of the trunk. At first glance the arrangement appears to be a wasteful use of metal. A careful scrutiny will show, however, that savings in cost can be made because of the absence of special transitions for reducing the size of the trunk duct every few feet, and the use of standardized take-off fittings for branch ducts. The pressure characteristics of the extended plenum system have also been found to be most favorable, since the use of a constant sized duct tends to provide for a more nearly constant pressure along the entire duct.

Detailed design procedures for the extended plenum system are presented in Manual No. 4 of the National Warm Air Heating and Air Conditioning Association.

Because of the diversity of systems used in the field, the manual presents several tables for top take-off fittings, side take-off fittings, and various types of register outlets. For the purposes of this article, however, these tables would be confusing and hence have not been included.

Return-Air Duct Systems
The return-air duct system in a house installation is a relatively simple arrangement,

Table 2. Total free area of room diffusers

2a: Length of Feeder—2 to 10 ft

Heat Loss of Room Btuh	Lgt. of feeder duct under rm. plus ½ lgt. of perimeter duct under rm., ft.						
	0-9 Ft.	10-19 Ft.	20-29 Ft.	30-39 Ft.	40-49 Ft.	50-59 Ft.	60-69 Ft.
	Total Diffuser Free Area Required for Room, Square Inches						
0 to 3,999	20						
4,000 to 5,999	32	27	23	18			
6,000 to 7,999	43	39	34	29	25	20	
8,000 to 9,999	55	50	45	41	36	32	27
10,000 to 11,999	66	61	57	52	48	43	38
12,000 to 13,999	77	72	68	63	59	54	50
14,000 to 15,999	88	84	79	75	70	66	61
16,000 to 17,999	100	95	91	86	82	77	72
18,000 to 19,999	111	106	102	97	93	88	84
20,000 to 21,999	122	118	113	109	104	100	95
22,000 to 23,999	134	129	125	120	116	111	106
24,000 to 25,999	145	140	136	131	127	122	118
26,000 to 27,999	156	151	147	142	138	133	129
28,000 to 29,999	168	163	159	154	150	145	141
30,000 to 31,999	179	174	170	165	161	156	152
32,000 to 34,000	190	185	182	176	173	167	164

2b: Length of Feeder—10 to 20 ft

Heat Loss of Room Btuh	Lgt. of feeder duct under rm. plus ½ lgt. of perimeter duct under rm., ft.						
	0-9 Ft.	10-19 Ft.	20-29 Ft.	30-39 Ft.	40-49 Ft.	50-59 Ft.	60-69 Ft.
	Total Diffuser Free Area Required for Room, Square Inches						
0 to 3,999	23	18	18				
4,000 to 5,999	36	31	26	21	16	16	
6,000 to 7,999	49	44	39	34	29	24	19
8,000 to 9,999	61	56	51	46	41	36	31
10,000 to 11,999	73	68	63	58	53	48	43
12,000 to 13,999	86	81	76	71	66	61	56
14,000 to 15,999	99	94	89	84	79	74	69
16,000 to 17,999	111	106	101	96	91	86	81
18,000 to 19,999	123	118	113	108	103	98	93
20,000 to 21,999	135	130	125	120	115	110	105
22,000 to 23,999	148	143	138	133	128	123	118
24,000 to 25,999	161	156	151	146	141	136	131
26,000 to 27,999	174	168	164	158	154	148	144
28,000 to 29,999	186	181	176	171	166	161	156
30,000 to 31,999	198	194	188	184	178	174	168
32,000 to 34,000	211	206	201	196	191	186	181

2c: Length of Feeder—20 to 30 ft

Heat Loss of Room Btuh	Lgt. of feeder duct under rm. plus ½ lgt. of perimeter duct under rm., ft.						
	0-9 Ft.	10-19 Ft.	20-29 Ft.	30-39 Ft.	40-49 Ft.	50-59 Ft.	60-69 Ft.
	Total Diffuser Free Area Required for Room, Square Inches						
0 to 3,999	27	21	21				
4,000 to 5,999	42	36	30	24	18		
6,000 to 7,999	57	51	45	39	33	27	21
8,000 to 9,999	72	66	60	54	48	42	36
10,000 to 11,999	86	80	74	68	62	56	50
12,000 to 13,999	101	95	89	83	77	71	65
14,000 to 15,999	116	110	104	98	92	86	80
16,000 to 17,999	131	125	119	113	107	101	95
18,000 to 19,999	145	139	133	127	121	115	109
20,000 to 21,999	160	154	148	142	136	130	124
22,000 to 23,999	175	169	163	157	151	145	139
24,000 to 25,999	190	184	178	172	166	160	154
26,000 to 27,999	205	199	193	187	181	175	169
28,000 to 29,999	220	214	208	202	196	190	184
30,000 to 31,999	234	228	222	216	210	204	198
32,000 to 34,000	249	243	237	231	225	219	213

consisting of a return plenum at the furnace, a simple duct, and one or more return-air grilles in the rooms. The sizing table for return-air ducts is presented in Table 4, from which it may be observed that the length of a duct, the number of 90-deg turns in it, and the Btuh design heat loss in the rooms to be served by the duct are required. The design procedure can be stated as follows:

1) Locate the return-air grille in the floor plan. The grille can be placed low in the sidewall, high in the sidewall, or in the ceiling.

2) Make a line drawing of the duct system.

3) Determine the Btuh design heat loss served by the return-air grille. For example, a grille in a central hallway may serve a large number of rooms adjacent to the hall.

4) Measure the length of the return-air duct, and determine the number of elbows in the duct. This information, together with Table 4, enables one to determine the free area of the duct. The free area of the grille is shown also in Table 4 (Column 1), and a manufacturer's catalogue will give the required commercial size.

Heat Losses, Insulation, Vapor Barriers Heat losses may be substantially reduced by: (1) the addition of insulation to the walls and ceilings, (2) the use of storm sash and storm doors, (3) the application of weatherstripping to doors and windows, and (4) the caulking of the joint between the sill and the foundation.

In new construction, full-thickness insulation in the sidewalls and as much as 6 in. in the ceiling are recommended. The insulation must have a *vapor barrier* which should be applied on the room side of the insulation.

The best vapor barriers are often punctured by electrical wiring and plumbing, reducing the effectiveness of the barrier. Any water vapor that does pass through the insulation should have an unimpeded path towards a vented attic space. In tightly enclosed attic spaces, especially with flat-deck roofs, any water vapor that passes through the sidewall and ceiling insulation will be trapped in the space and will condense on the cold underside of the roof sheathing. Ventilation of such attic spaces is essential, even when vapor barriers have been specified for the insulation.

Table 3.   Heat delivery through 6-in. diameter duct

No. of Elbows	Capacity	\multicolumn{16}{c}{Actual Length of Pipe in Feet From Bonnet to Diffuser}
		5	10	15	20	25	30	35	40	45	50	55	60	65	70	75	80
0	Btuh										8700	8060	7460	6920	6430	5960	5550
	CFM										127.7	124.8	122.3	119.7	117.4	115.0	113.0
1	Btuh									8620	8000	7430	6900	6400	5930	5500	5100
	CFM									122.8	120.0	117.6	115.3	113.0	111.0	109.0	107.3
2	Btuh								8600	7960	7390	6860	6380	5940	5530	5150	4800
	CFM								118.5	116.2	114.0	112.0	110.0	107.8	106.0	104.5	103.0
3	Btuh							8640	8020	7450	6950	6460	6020	5600	5200	4850	4500
	CFM							114.0	112.0	110.0	108.2	106.5	104.7	103.0	101.4	99.6	98.0
4	Btuh						8760	8160	7580	7050	6540	6080	5640	5250	4880	4550	4250
	CFM						110.2	108.4	106.6	105.0	103.0	101.5	100.2	99.0	97.5	96.0	94.5
5	Btuh					8850	8250	7670	7140	6640	6170	5740	5340	4960	4620	4290	3990
	CFM					106.8	105.0	103.5	102.0	100.5	99.0	97.5	96.0	94.6	93.4	92.0	91.0
6	Btuh				9050	8420	7840	7280	6750	6300	5850	5440	5060	4700	4370	4060	3760
	CFM				104.0	102.5	100.7	99.2	97.8	96.5	95.2	94.0	92.6	91.4	90.0	88.7	87.5

Table 4.   Return air duct and grille sizes

ACTUAL FT.		UP TO 10 FT.						11 TO 20 FT.						21 TO 30 FT.						31 TO 40 FT.					
Grill Free Area sq in.	No. of 90° Turns	1	2	3	4	5	6	1	2	3	4	5	6	1	2	3	4	5	6	1	2	3	4	5	6
	Btuh.											Duct Free Area, sq in.													
16	5,000	14	17	20	23	26	28	15	19	22	25	27	28	17	20	23	25	27	29	18	21	24	27	28	30
32	10,000	27	32	37	42	46	49	29	34	39	43	47	49	31	36	41	45	48	51	33	38	43	47	49	51
47	15,000	37	44	50	55	60	64	40	46	52	57	61	65	43	49	54	58	63	67	45	51	56	61	64	67
63	20,000	46	54	61	66	73	78	49	57	63	69	75	79	53	60	65	71	77	82	55	62	68	74	78	83
79	25,000	54	64	72	79	86	92	58	68	75	82	88	94	62	71	78	84	91	96	66	74	80	87	92	98
95	30,000	62	73	82	89	97	104	67	76	85	93	100	106	71	80	88	95	102	108	75	84	91	99	104	110
111	35,000	69	82	92	101	111	119	74	85	95	106	114	121	79	91	99	108	117	124	84	94	103	113	119	126
126	40,000	77	90	100	110	121	130	82	94	105	116	124	132	87	99	109	118	128	137	92	103	113	123	130	140
158	50,000	89	105	119	132	146	158	95	111	124	138	150	161	102	117	129	142	155	166	108	123	135	148	158	170
190	60,000	100	122	139	154	170	181	111	129	145	161	174	184	119	137	151	165	178	189	126	143	158	172	181	193
221	70,000	117	139	158	174	191	203	127	147	164	182	195	206	135	155	171	186	200	213	144	162	178	193	203	216
252	80,000	128	155	175	191	208	222	140	164	182	198	214	225	151	172	188	203	219	231	160	179	195	211	222	235
284	90,000	141	168	188	205	225	244	153	177	195	213	232	248	164	186	201	218	240	256	173	193	209	229	244	262
316	100,000	154	180	200	221	247	265	166	189	209	233	252	270	176	198	217	239	258	277	185	206	227	250	265	285

Air Distribution for Heating and Cooling

The air-flow rate for cooling is, in general, greater than that required for heating. The ducts required for cooling therefore are necessarily larger than those for heating. If a system is to be used for both heating and cooling, or if the addition of cooling at a later date is contemplated, the duct system should be designed for cooling. A procedure for designing a year-round air-distribution system is included in Manual No. 9 of the National Warm Air Heating and Air Conditioning Association.

A cooling unit should not only maintain a reduced air temperature indoors, as compared with that of outdoors, but should maintain a satisfactory level of indoor relative humidity. The conventional cooling unit accomplishes these ends by the removal of *sensible heat* (as indicated by a reduction in air temperature), and the removal of *latent heat* (as indicated by a reduction in moisture content).

Summer Heat Gains

The heat gains from *external sources* include: (a) transmission heat gain, (b) solar gains, and (c) infiltration heat gains. The transmission heat gains through walls, windows and ceiling surfaces result from the temperature difference between indoor air and outdoor air, and are largely dependent upon the construction of the barrier between indoor air and outdoor air. Solar gains result from sunlight passing through unshaded windows, and from sunlight striking a wall or ceiling surface and increasing the surface temperature. Infiltration gains are caused by the introduction of warm outdoor air through cracks around doors and windows into the conditioned space. Heat gains from *internal sources* arise from lighting fixtures, domestic appliances, cooking and bathing operations and from occupants.

Heat Gains as Affected by Construction

The cost of the original cooling equipment, as well as operating cost, may be minimized by the use of house insulation and by the proper selection of exterior colors of walls and roofs and by shading devices. Adequate insulation should be provided in new construction, not only in the ceilings, but also in the sidewalls. Full-thickness insulation is recommended for sidewalls and more than 4 in. for ceilings. In existing construction, insulation should be added in ceiling and sidewalls if con-struction permits. All sidewall and ceiling insulation should be provided with a vapor barrier on the *room side* of the wall or ceiling in order to reduce the migration of water vapor from outdoor air into the house. The room side is specified primarily for the more serious condensation problem in winter.

Light-colored walls and roof surfaces serve to reflect sunlight and thereby permit smaller heat gains than do dark colored surfaces. Shading devices, such as trees, awnings, exterior Venetian blinds, overhanging roofs are effective not only in reducing the solar gain through windows exposed to sun, but also in preventing an increase in wall temperatures. For new construction, it is possible to consider the benefits to be gained by proper orientation of the house. For example, large windows which face north will be least affected by sunlight. A window on the south wall can be readily protected by a roof overhang from solar heat gain in summertime. Windows located on east and west walls cannot be protected by roof overhangs because the sun is relatively low in the sky during morning and evening hours when it is shining on east and west walls. Hence, special care must be taken to minimize the solar load on these unfavorable exposures. This can be done by omitting windows, by decreasing their size, or by providing shading devices such as awnings, exterior Venetian blinds, shutters, vertical louvers, trellises, trees, or, window screens that are specially designed with louvered strips to exclude the sun.

Weatherstripping around doors and windows will serve to reduce the infiltration of warm outdoor air into the conditioned space. Infiltration of outdoor air is not considered as a major influence in heat gain during the summer because wind velocities are low. Furthermore, some amount of infiltration is considered desirable in order to minimize odors that arise indoors.

Heat Gain Calculations

Heat gain calculations should be made with a reasonable degree of precision. An undersized cooling unit may not provide sufficient cooling capacity to maintain satisfactory indoor air temperatures on a hot day. On the other hand, this does not imply that a greatly oversized unit should be selected. Research findings have demonstrated that a greatly oversized unit may be able to maintain room-air temperatures at a satisfactory level by on-and-off cycling of the compressor, but the resulting wide fluctuations in indoor relative humidity have proven most annoying to the occupants. In general, a cooling unit that can be operated almost continuously during average hot weather is preferred to a greatly oversized unit.

One of the many accepted procedures for determining heat gain of a building is presented in Manual No. 11 of the National Warm Air Heating and Air Conditioning Association. In addition, the Manual gives methods for designing the air-distribution system, as well as a method for the selection of equipment.

Cooling Equipment

The most common air-cooling unit (shown schematically in Fig. 10) consists of the following parts:

a) A *compressor*, in which a refrigerant is pumped to a high pressure and a high

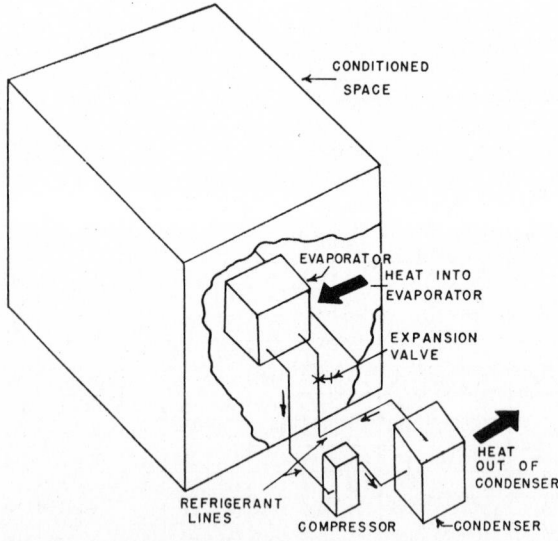

Fig. 10.   Air-cooling system

temperature by means of an electric motor drive.

b) The *refrigerant*.

c) A *condenser* which serves to cool the hot gas that comes from the compressor and changes it to a liquid, but still at high pressure. The condenser can be of *water-cooled* design, in which cool water is pumped through pipes inside of the condenser. Because of the cost of water for this purpose, water-saving devices known as *cooling towers* have been commonly used. In this case, the water that has circulated through the condenser is cooled in the cooling tower and delivered back to the condenser. In other words, the water is used over again except for that which is lost through evaporation. In smaller residential applications, *air-cooled* condensers are most commonly used. A large fan delivers relatively large quantities of air directly from outdoors over the condenser coils where heat is absorbed, and then returns the heated air to the outdoors. In many respects the condenser is the most important part of the cooling unit, since its location will determine the relative complexity of the installation as well as the operating performance.

d) The *expansion valve* or the capillary tube, which is a constriction in the line that reduces the pressure of the liquid from the high pressure existing at the condenser to the low pressure existing downstream of the expansion valve.

e) The *evaporator* which contains the gaseous refrigerant for cooling and drying room air. The moisture which is condensed out of the circulating air is discarded to a drain.

Self-contained units are those which house the compressor, condenser, and evaporator in the same cabinet, as indicated in Fig. 11, which shows a self-contained unit located outside the house. The cabinet also contains a fan which circulates air through the duct system to the conditioned space. The self-contained unit projects through the wall and may be located in the basement, crawl space, or attic. The unit shown in Fig. 12 is installed separate from the heating system, although it could be connected to an existing forced-air duct system.

The *split unit*, as indicated in Fig. 12, provides for two locations of the component parts: the compressor and condenser are located in the cabinet outside of the house, while the evaporator is located inside of the house, usually in the plenum chamber of an existing forced-air furnace. The refrigerant is piped from the remotely located condenser to the evaporator through well-insulated piping. The furnace

blower is utilized for circulating the conditioned air through the duct system.

"Packaged" heating-cooling units for houses are now generally available on the market. The compressor and evaporator are usually included in the "package," and an air-cooled condenser is provided to be located outdoors. A seasonally operated damper directs the air through the cooling coils or the heat exchanger, as required. Heating-cooling units are available in the same types that were described earlier in the discussion of furnaces—low-boy, high-boy, counter-flow, and horizontal.

In the South and other areas where power cost is favorable, the relatively new *heat-pump* may be a practical solution. The heat-pump is simply an air-conditioner so arranged that the flow may be reversed in the winter. During the heating season

the warm air from the condenser is used to heat the house, and the cold air from the evaporator is discharged outdoors. Heat-pumps are now available in "packaged" form in sizes suitable for residential use. Many of them include auxiliary electric heating coils for use in the coldest weather. Heat-pumps occupy relatively little space and eliminate the need for a chimney and for fuel storage, but at present both installation and operational costs are generally higher than for other types of heating and cooling equipment.

Location of Supply Outlets for Cooling

The locations of supply outlets were discussed in the section on Forced Warm Air Heating Systems. For cooling only, either

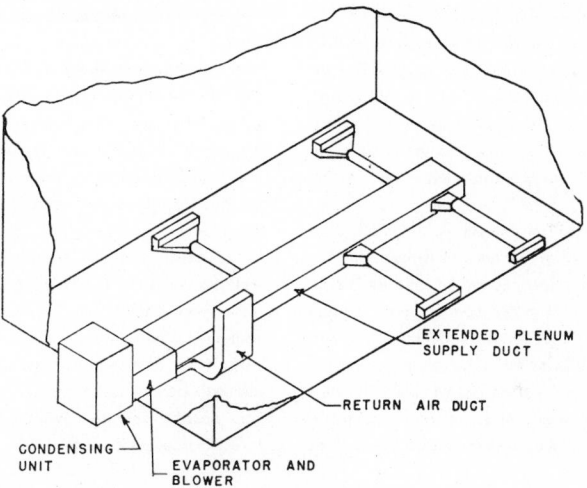

Fig. 11.   Self-contained air-cooling unit

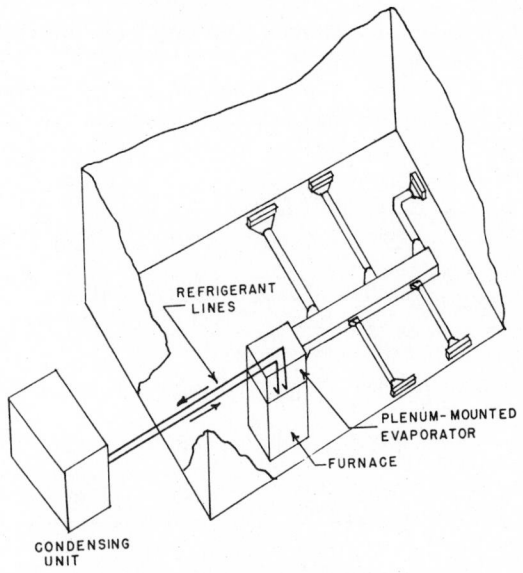

Fig. 12.   Split-location air-cooling unit

high sidewall or ceiling outlets provide satisfactory results in the form of uniform room-air temperature and air motion. Low sidewall and floor outlets located along the exposed wall and discharging vertically will prove acceptable if the recommendations of the National Warm Air Heating and Air Conditioning Association are followed.

Design of Air Distribution System

In Manual No. 11 of the National Warm Air Heating and Air Conditioning Association, step-by-step design procedures are shown in considerable detail for four different types of duct distribution systems, as follows:

a) trunk duct system
b) perimeter-radial system
c) perimeter-loop system
d) small pipe (4-in. round) system

The details of the design procedures should be obtained from the Manuals. However, pertinent information concerning the design of a 4-in. round duct system, with floor diffusers, will be presented here to show the type of information available in the Manuals.

This small-pipe system is similar to the perimeter-radial system described in the warm-air heating section of this article in that individual pipes connect each supply outlet with the furnace plenum. The system is ideally suited to a plenum-mounted evaporator connected to remotely located compressor and condenser. The principal details of the duct system can be itemized as follows:

a) Determine the heat gain for each room to be conditioned.
b) Locate floor diffusers under windows wherever possible.
c) Locate the furnace plenum (in which the evaporator is housed).
d) Show the tentative duct plan connecting the diffusers with the plenum. The length of the individual ducts should be noted on the plan, as well as the number of right-angled elbows in each individual duct.
e) Refer to Table 5 which lists the Btuh capacities of individual 4-in. ducts according to the length and the number of elbows. For example, a duct which is 22 ft long and contains 3 elbows shows a Btuh capacity of 1680 Btuh under summer conditions. (Note that this capacity does not apply to winter heating conditions). If the capacity of a single duct is not sufficient for the room, additional ducts should be used.
f) Locate the return-air duct system, which should be simple and direct. In small homes, a single return-air grille located in a central hallway is usually sufficient. Complete details for the design of the return-air ducts system are given in Manual No. 11.

The total air-flow rate for a given installation is determined by the capacity of the cooling unit that is installed, and manufacturers' catalogues will indicate the magnitude of the flow rate that must be maintained. A deficiency in the air-flow rate passing over the evaporator may lead to difficulties in operation. For this reason,

the duct design should be conservative and the number of ducts ample. If the airflow rate is found to be inadequate in installation, a larger blower may be installed or the speed of the existing blower increased. The latter alternative is not recommended since even a slight increase in speed can result in greatly increased power requirements, frequently beyond the capacity of the existing motor.

Insulation of Ducts for Summer Cooling Installations

It must be realized that cooling effects are obtained at considerable expenditure of electrical energy and with relatively large sized equipment. Any loss of the cooling effect of the circulating air before it reaches the conditioned space is a most expensive one. For this reason, all ducts located in unconditioned spaces must be carefully and thoroughly insulated. On the outside of the insulating blanket must be applied an effective vapor barrier, which serves to reduce the passage of water vapor from the unconditioned space to the cold duct surface. Obviously, any moisture which condenses on the cold duct surface will penetrate the insulation, thereby reducing its efficiency, and may drip on surfaces below the duct. All joints should be effectively sealed with vapor-proof tape to prevent access of water vapor at the weakest link in the armor surrounding the duct. Preferred industry practice calls for 2-in. thick insulation on supply ducts and 1-in. thick insulation on return-air ducts.

Table 5. Summer air conditioning—sizing 4-in. individual pipe system

No. of Elbows	Total cooling Btuh (sensible plus latent)									
	Length of Pipe (feet)									
	0-5	6-10	11-15	16-20	21-25	26-30	31-35	36-40	41-45	46-50
1	2280	2140	2000	1920	1840	1760	1680	1620	1560	1510
2	2140	2000	1920	1840	1760	1680	1620	1560	1510	1460
3	2000	1920	1840	1760	1680	1620	1560	1510	1460	1430
4	1920	1840	1760	1680	1620	1560	1510	1460	1430	1400
5	1840	1760	1680	1620	1560	1510	1460	1430	1400	1370
6	1760	1680	1620	1560	1510	1460	1430	1400	1370	1320

By WILLIAM J. McGUINNESS, M.E., *Professor of Architecture, Pratt Institute*

Characteristics

A one-pipe steam heating system is rugged and easy to operate and maintain. In cost of installation and fuel use it is generally comparable with forced warm air and forced hot water. If well designed and maintained, and if boiler water is kept hot by an aquastat it is prompt to respond to calls for heat. When rooms are at temperature or when outside temperature increases, it shuts off promptly. A disadvantage is that the boiler must be in a basement or deep pit to permit the return flow of condensate.

Design

The first step in design of any heating system is determination of hourly heat losses in Btu from each room or space. Since each square foot of free-standing cast iron steam radiation emits 240 Btu per hour, it is necessary only to divide hourly heat loss by 240 to arrive at the amount of radiation needed. From the accompanying tables the designer may select a radiator of proper size to make up heat loss and to fit space available.

Pipe sizes are fixed by the amount of radiation served. They can be selected from the table given herein, keeping in mind that they fall into three categories: (1) mains; (2) runouts, risers and radiator connections; and (3) returns.

Not of least importance in general design is a space layout of the system to insure proper operation and architectural suitability. Good operation suggests adequate height from boiler to start of main, pitch of all pipes, proximity of radiator to riser, proper location of all air vents, space for servicing boiler, location of radiators below glass areas, and use of two or three radiators in large rooms. Space requirements include recessing of radiators if possible, maintenance of basement headroom and location of piping to permit finishing of basement rooms.

Maintenance

It is difficult and expensive to boil greasy water. New installations should have boiler and piping cleaned and blown out thoroughly after a short period of operation. Water should be drained and refilled, and the stack cleaned, yearly. Radiator control valves must be kept tight to prevent steam leakage into rooms. Air vents on radiators and mains must exhaust air quickly or heating will be slow and fuel consumption excessive. These difficulties or the passing of steam through vents may indicate need for their replacement.

In oil burners, efficiency tests are now quite standardized and easy to make. Taking stack temperature and analyzing flue gases will indicate whether combustion is complete and efficient. A slight adjustment in air intake, draftostat, etc., may result in great savings.

CAPACITIES OF PIPE IN SQ. FT. OF RADIATION

PIPE SIZE (inches)	STEAM MAIN** (Condensate and steam flowing in same direction)	RUNOUTS, RISERS, RADIATOR CONNECTIONS*	WET RETURN
1	––	28	700
1¼	––	62	1200
1½	––	93	1900
2	386	169	4000

Courtesy Institute of Boiler and Radiator Manufacturers

* If runout to radiator exceeds 8 ft. in length increase pipe one size.
** Based on "Equivalent Length" of 200 ft. To determine equivalent length add to actual length (boiler to farthest radiator) 4.3 ft. for each elbow and 8 ft. for each tee. Recommended minimum size for main is 2 in.

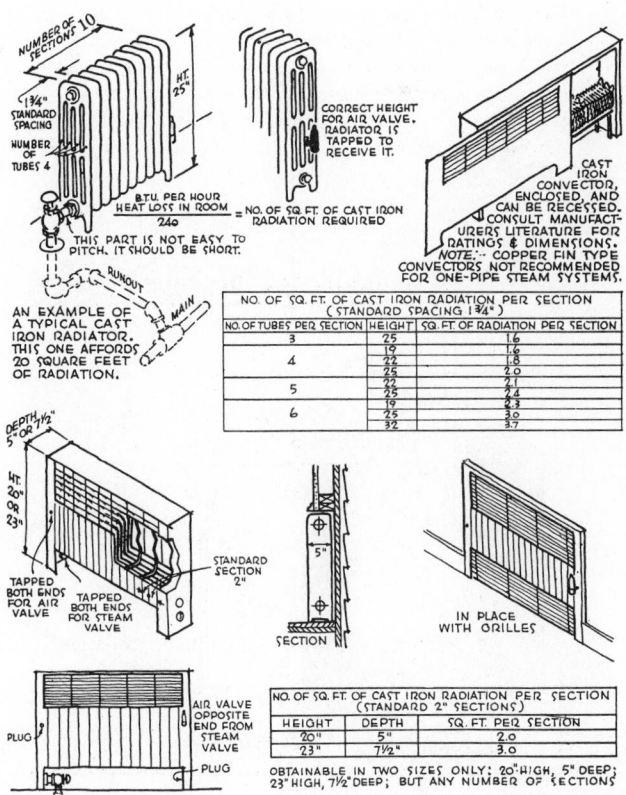

Fig. 1. Types of radiation

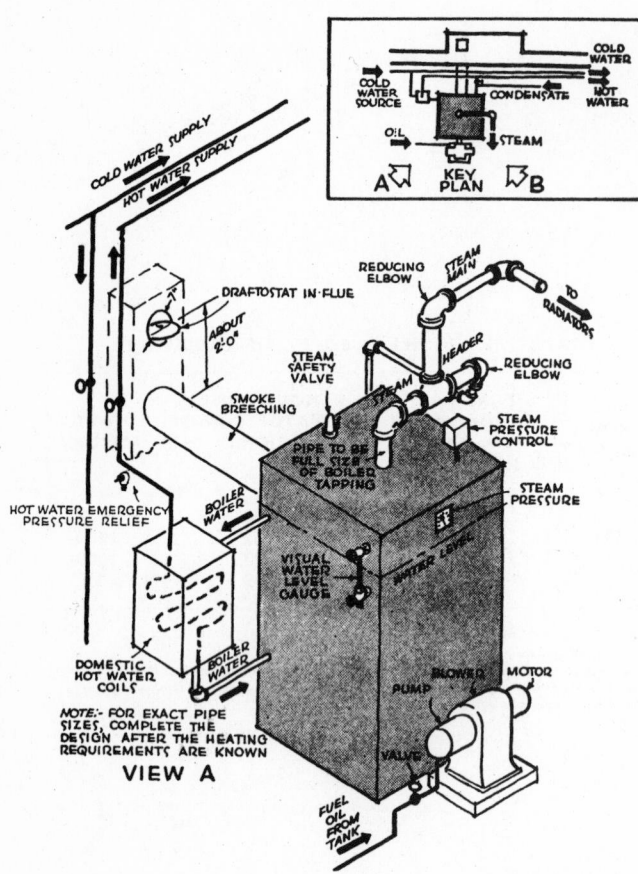

VIEW A

Boiler and Piping

Selection of boiler depends on a number of things besides system capacity, including: whether the boiler is steel or cast iron; kind of fuel (oil, coal or gas); and whether or not generation of domestic hot water is included.

The *net* output of the selected boiler should be equal to or slightly greater than the heat loss from the house in Btu per hr. A boiler so selected usually includes an allowance for domestic hot water for kitchen, laundry, and one or two bathrooms. Black iron pipe is most common and covering should be provided for mains and for runouts and risers in exterior walls. Return lines are not usually covered. The boiler should be well insulated.

Domestic hot water can be produced by coils in a unit adjacent to the boiler as shown here, or by submerged coils within the boiler (both producing continuous flow of hot water); or smaller coils can be used to supply a storage tank

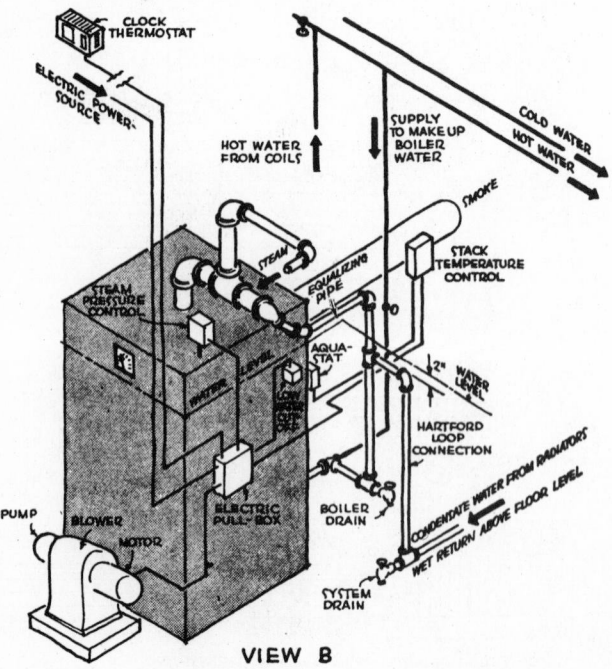

VIEW B

Fig. 2. Typical oil-fired boiler for a one-pipe steam system

Controls

The **valves** at radiators must be either fully open or fully shut. A small opening will cause hammering between steam and condensate. The **pressure control** shuts off the oil burner when steam pressure becomes excessive. High steam pressure will also operate the spring-loaded **safety valve** and afford a mechanical relief. The **aquastat** is adjustable to maintain boiler water at a temperature high enough to produce domestic hot water. It will turn the oil burner on and off to accomplish this. An additional advantage of this control is that when heat is called for the boiler water has a start and need not be heated up from a very low temperature. The **clock thermostat** turns the oil burner on and off to maintain an optimum temperature in the heated space. The clock attachment changes this temperature between day and night. The **low-water cutoff** will stop the fire if the boiler water level drops, saving the boiler from burning out. The **stack temperature control** will stop the oil pump and blower if the burner has failed to ignite within a time limit. The **oil burner switch** at the a remote location will cut off the system in an emergency or when a shut-down is desired.

GENERAL NOTES

Pitch mains, returns, and radiator runouts ½" in 10 ft. Main changes to return pipe size by a reducer, below boiler water level. Quick vent air valves must be at least 15" away from the vertical drop at end of mains. To prevent boiler water backing into return, a Hartford loop connection should join the return with the equalizing pipe 2" below boiler water level. Quick vent valves should be placed as high as possible by extending them above the main. It is preferable to connect the supply end of the main to a horizontal header instead of by a vertical pipe to the boiler. Basement radiators are possible only above boiler water level, if drained to a wet return. It is usually difficult to find space for them at this awkward height.

Fig. 3. Suggested main layouts

For small rectangular houses with center girder

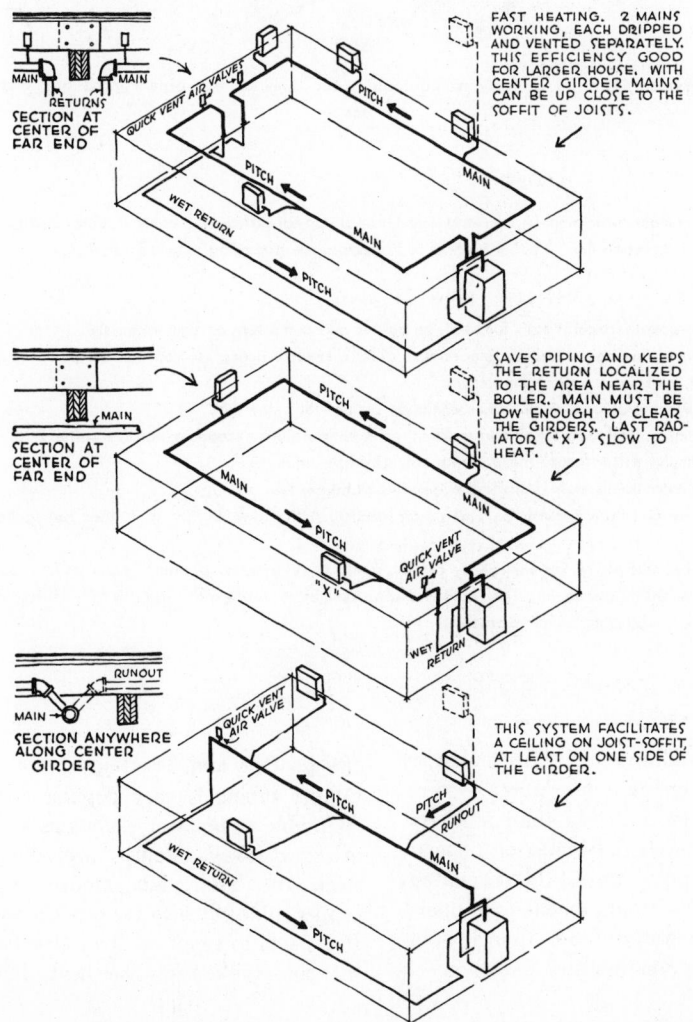

FAST HEATING. 2 MAINS WORKING, EACH DRIPPED AND VENTED SEPARATELY. THIS EFFICIENCY GOOD FOR LARGER HOUSE. WITH CENTER GIRDER MAINS CAN BE UP CLOSE TO THE SOFFIT OF JOISTS.

SAVES PIPING AND KEEPS THE RETURN LOCALIZED TO THE AREA NEAR THE BOILER. MAIN MUST BE LOW ENOUGH TO CLEAR THE GIRDERS. LAST RADIATOR ("X") SLOW TO HEAT.

THIS SYSTEM FACILITATES A CEILING ON JOIST-SOFFIT, AT LEAST ON ONE SIDE OF THE GIRDER.

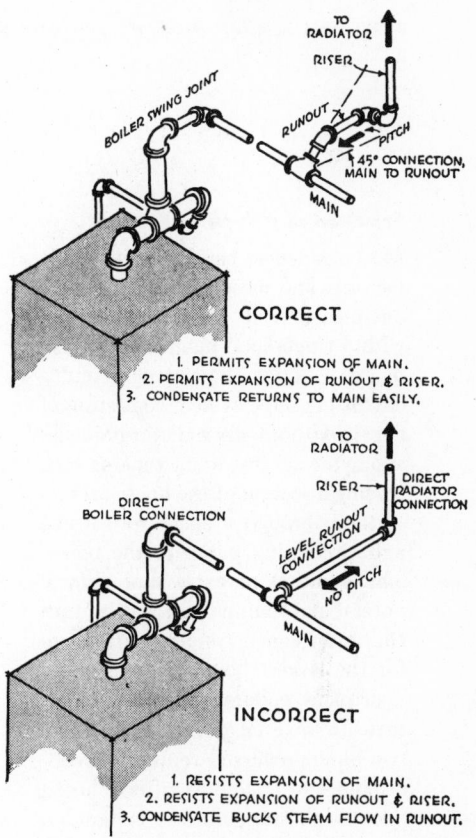

CORRECT
1. PERMITS EXPANSION OF MAIN.
2. PERMITS EXPANSION OF RUNOUT & RISER.
3. CONDENSATE RETURNS TO MAIN EASILY.

INCORRECT
1. RESISTS EXPANSION OF MAIN.
2. RESISTS EXPANSION OF RUNOUT & RISER.
3. CONDENSATE BUCKS STEAM FLOW IN RUNOUT.

Fig. 4. Correct and incorrect boiler and radiator connections

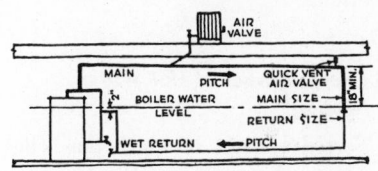

Usual type; can follow cellar wall near floor.

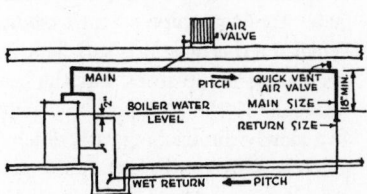

When return must be concealed it may be buried in or below slab; coat outside of return with asphaltic paint; do not put return in water-bearing soil or cinders. Pit is required if system is to be drained.

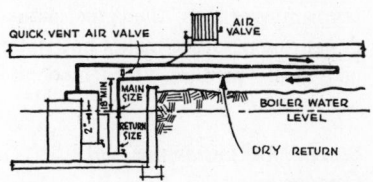

Space limitation may necessitate dry return; do not connect radiator runouts to it. Note position of quick-vent valve and minimum height of return above boiler water level.

Fig. 5. Reasons for three kinds of returns

By WILLIAM J. McGUINNESS, M.E., Professor of Architecture, Pratt Institute

Selection of a Type of System

Most residences can be served satisfactorily and most economically by a one-pipe forced circulation system with a single loop main. Larger residences call for the use of a multi-circuit one-pipe system consisting of a main without any radiator branches supplying several branch mains each serving a section of the house and returning through a single return line and circulating pump to the boiler. The addition of extra flow control valves and pumps can easily turn this into a zoned system good enough for the largest house or for a small apartment building or similar structure. In very large installations the two-pipe, reversed-return, forced-circulation system is often chosen because the return water is handled very positively by a separate return main and will not cool the water flowing to other radiators in the circuit.

Characteristics of Hot Water Heating

Forced systems in which the boiler water is kept hot by water temperature controls are very fast in response to calls for heat. They are much faster than one-pipe steam systems. When the thermostat is satisfied, the circulating pump stops, but the heat emission of the radiators continues at a slowly diminishing rate which is much better than the speedy stopping of a steam system in which all the steam in a radiator has condensed, drawing air into the radiator. The possibility of circulating water at temperatures less than the actual design temperature makes hot water an ideal medium for moderate weather.

Economy of Installation and Operation

The cost of a pump, flow control valves, special return fittings and

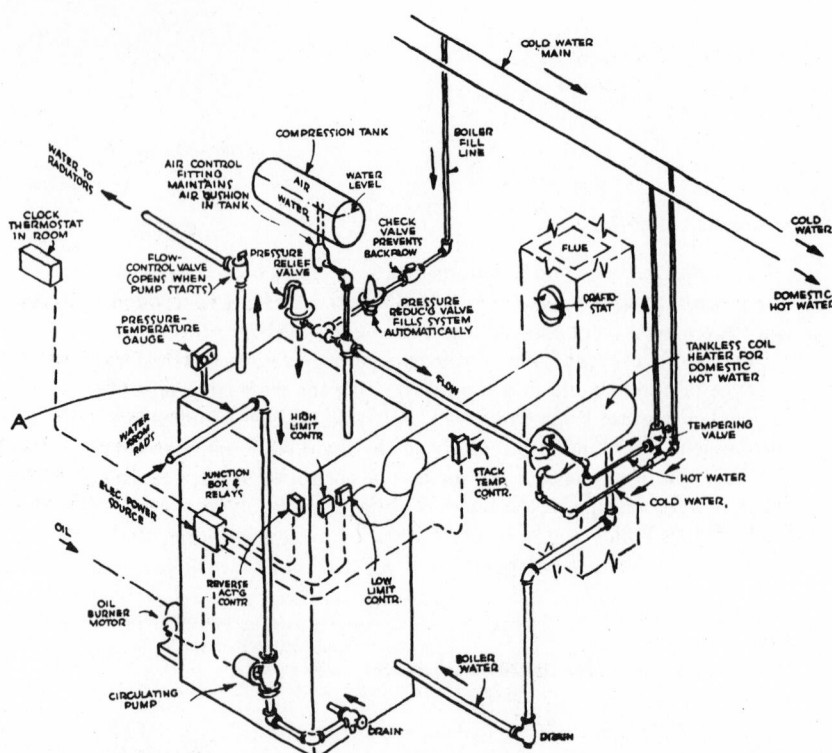

Fig. 6. Typical oil-fired boiler and equipment for one- or two-pipe forced hot water systems

Note direct main connections (A, no swing joints); expansion not sufficient to cause trouble. Circulating pump is in return line, in either vertical or horizontal run according to pump requirements

Operation

1. When room thermostat calls for heat, oil burner and pump turn on simultaneously
2. If water drops below limiting temperature (160°), reverse-acting control turns off pump until oil burner has raised water temperature
3. Low-limit control turns on oil burner whenever water falls below 160°
4. High-limit control turns off oil burner when water temperature exceeds a high limit (often 200°), thus stabilizing water temperature during capacity operation
5. When room thermostat is satisfied, pump and oil burner turn off
6. Stack temperature control, an emergency control, shuts down burner if it does not ignite promptly
7. Pressure relief valve, an emergency control, opens to relieve any pressure in excess of a set value (often 30 lb. per sq. in.). This valve should be set above boiler, otherwise if it failed it would drain boiler, subjecting boiler to cracking

larger radiators sometimes make the installation of a hot water system slightly more costly than a steam one-pipe system. Because of the heat retaining qualities of the circulated water it is usually cheaper to operate a hot water system than it is to operate a one-pipe steam system.

Fittings, Pipe and Covering

Copper tubing is very popular and adaptable to hot water systems and in a great many instances is replacing steel. In these cases bronze and copper solder fittings are often used. It is usual to cover all steel pipe for the conservation of the heat, but

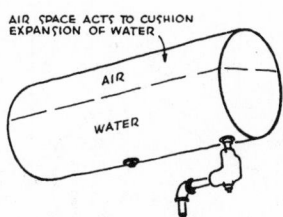

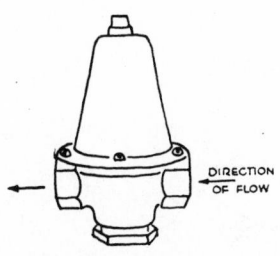

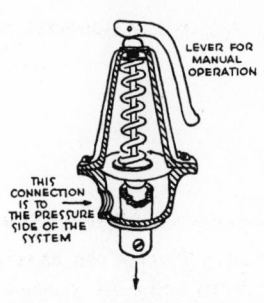

COMPRESSION TANK WITH AIR CONTROL FITTING
SELECT TANK SIZE TO FIT SYSTEM

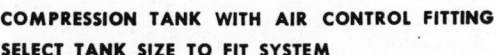

Capacity in sq. ft. of radiation	Tank capacity gallons	Tank dimensions
to 300 sq. ft.	15	12″ x 30″
300 to 500 sq. ft.	18	12″ x 36″
500 to 700 sq. ft.	20	12″ x 42″
700 to 1000 sq. ft.	24	12″ x 48″

PRESSURE REDUCING VALVE

Fill line to boiler; adds water when pressure drops below 12 lb. per sq. in.

Other side connected to city water pressure (40 to 50 lb. per sq. in.; too high for system) Full system is needed; it's easy to forget to add water to boiler. This valve adds it automatically

PRESSURE RELIEF VALVE

Spring-loaded diaphragm raises when system pressure exceeds 30 lb. per sq. in., permitting water flow through center tube

Drip. Valve seldom opens under proper operation, however, drip can empty into dry well or sink, *not sewer*

In systems where compression tank replaces high-gravity tank, pressure-relief valve is needed because system is otherwise closed. If air cushion in compression tank is too small (through improper operation), this valve operates to relieve system and prevent bursting of parts

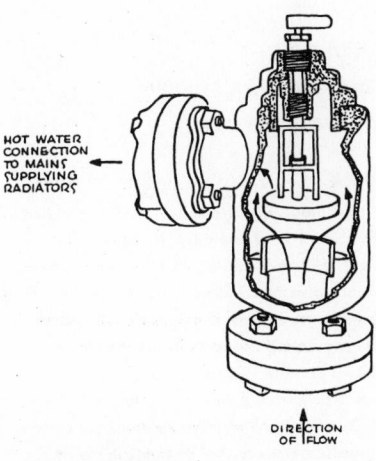

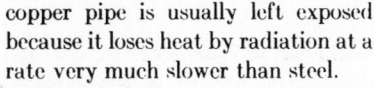

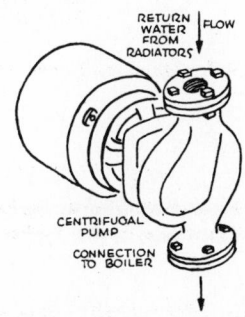

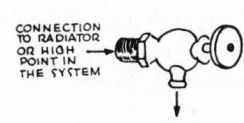

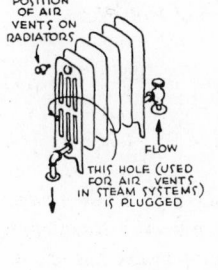

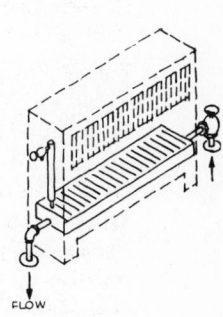

FLOW CONTROL VALVE

When circulating pump starts, water flow raises the valve seat. When the pump is not operating, it closes against circulation. This is important in summer when hot water must be retained in boiler (for domestic hot water) but must not flow through radiators

CIRCULATING PUMP

Electric motor turns on, forcing water through system, when heat is called for and if water is hot enough (160°). Select pump as directed on following pages

AIR VENT

When opened, pressure forces air out. When water starts to flow this vent must be closed. Automatic vents are available at slightly higher cost. Note (lower drawing): air vent must be extended high above cast iron or copper convectors to keep air out of the water passages

The author and editors wish to acknowledge with thanks the assistance of several manufacturers of heating equipment, and of the Institute of Boiler and Radiator Manufacturers.

copper pipe is usually left exposed because it loses heat by radiation at a rate very much slower than steel.

Maintenance.

The elimination of air is one of the most important things in good operation of a hot water installation. If this is manually accomplished at the radiators it should be done several times during the heating season. The water level in the compression tank should be adjusted at the same time if this function is not automatic. It is important to provide proper lubrication for the pump. All equipment such as flow control valves, pressure relief valves etc. should be checked for proper adjustment.

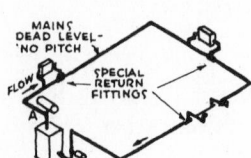

ONE-CIRCUIT ONE-PIPE SYSTEM

For larger installations multicircuit systems are preferred

Fig. 7. One-pipe systems

Radiators receive water from main and discharge back into same main

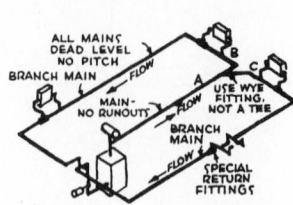

MULTI-CIRCUIT ONE-PIPE SYSTEM

Main A is sized to serve entire system; mains B and C are sized to serve respective circuits; same size held through to boiler. This type of system, with sufficient circuits, can serve the largest residence

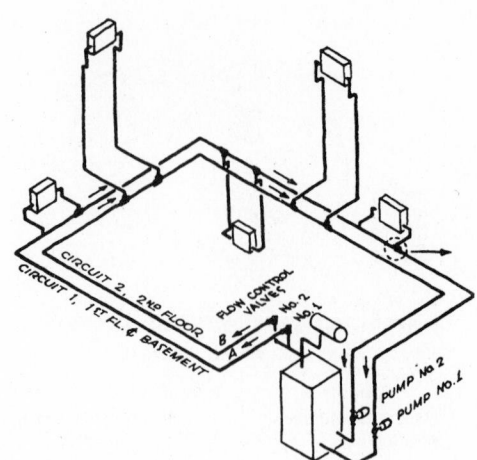

1. Average Water Temperature and Temperature Drop

In the following typical example, an average water temperature of 197 F will be assumed and the temperature drop in the system will be taken as 20 F. Water will leave the boiler at 207 F and return at 187 F.

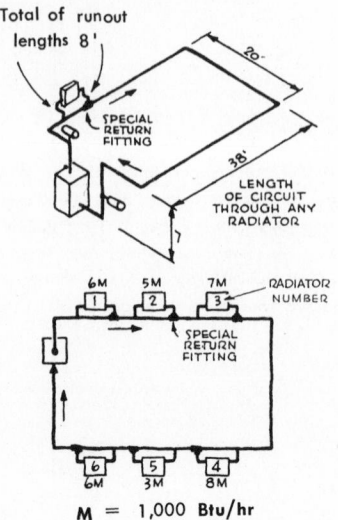

M = 1,000 Btu/hr

2. Water Flow Required to Make up Hourly Heat Loss in the System

The total heat loss is 35,000 Btu per hour. Dividing this by 9600 (see Sheet 10) the answer is 3.63 gal. per minute.

3. Length and Equivalent Total Length of System

The length of the circuit through any radiator is:

Length	38
	38
Width	20
	20
Height	7
	7
Runouts (rad.)	8
	138 ft.

To arrive at the total equivalent length of system including the resistance of fittings, multiply by 1.5 (add 50 per cent). Total equivalent length is 207 ft.

ZONED ONE-PIPE FORCED HOT WATER SYSTEM

Zoning

An advantage of forced-circulation hot water heating is its adaptability to zoning. When Zone 1 calls for heat, pump No. 1 starts; flow control valve No. 1 opens, permitting flow in circuit 1. Flow control valve No. 2 remains shut preventing circulation in circuit 2. If instead, Zone 2 called for heat, pump and valve No. 2 would operate with flow in circuit 2 and not in circuit 1. Simultaneous action is possible. Separate thermostats operate pumps 1 & 2. Joint use is made of one boiler whose water is kept hot by water temperature controls

Basement land Second Floor Heating

Aside from zoning, sketch also illustrates several uses of special return tees

1. For 1st floor radiators, use of one special return fitting is common & riser size is found in Table 2, Section E. Two fittings are possible, in which case riser size is found in Table 2, Section A, and is smaller for same capacity

2. For 2nd & 3rd floor radiators, use of two special return fittings is common & riser is found in Table 2, Sections B & C. If one fitting is used, larger riser is chosen from Table 2, Sections F & G

3. For downfeed risers to basement, use of two special return fittings is necessary; size of riser is shown in Table 2, Section D

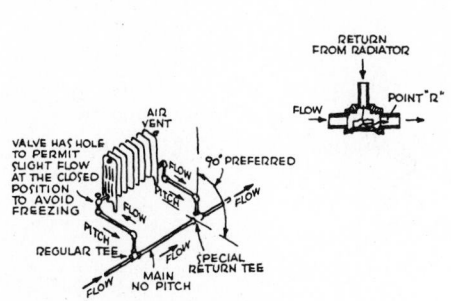

SPECIAL RETURN TEE

For one-pipe systems only; insert constricts flow, diverts some supply water into supply tee. Venturi action at R pulls water out of radiator. Note that colder water flows at bottom of main; hence radiator branches should be 90° to horizontal

Courtesy Bell & Gossett Co.

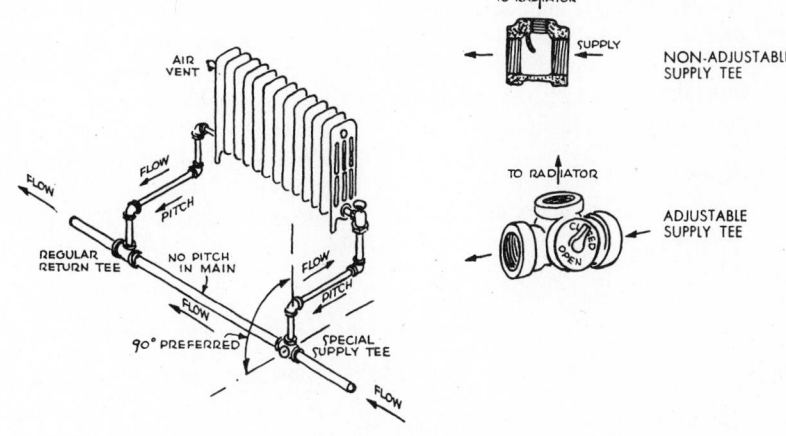

SPECIAL SUPPLY TEES can be used instead of special return tees

Courtesy H. A. Thrush & Co.

4. Select a Pump

Referring to Fig. 8, it is found that the selection of a 1¼-in. pump will result in the need to maintain in the system frictional resistance the equivalent of 6.2 ft. of head.

5. Pressure Drop in the System

Section A of Table 1, on the next page indicates that for 6 ft. of head (the closest to our requirement) and a length of 200 ft. the friction loss will be 350 milinches per foot in the system.

6. Selecting Size of Main

In the 350-milinch column, Table 1, Section B, it will be found that a 1-in. main will carry 59,000 Btu per hour which is adequate. Our loss is 35,000 Btu. It is to be noted that 1 in. is a minimum for mains in one-pipe systems. In one-pipe systems the main size, selected on the basis of the total capacity, is carried at this size through the system and back to the boiler.

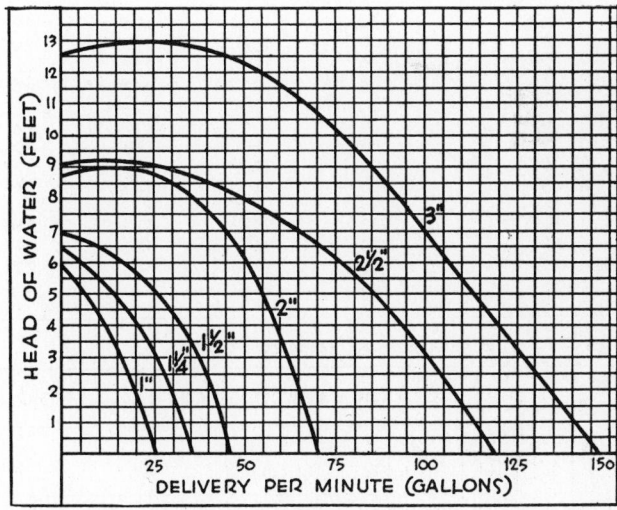

Fig. 8. Typical performance characteristics of circulating pumps (boosters)

For performance of specific equipment, consult manufacturers.

7. Sizing Runouts and Risers

Risers in one-pipe systems must be a little larger than for two-pipe systems. Table 2 lists the sizes needed for various capacities.

The largest radiator in the system carries 8000 Btu per hour and will require ½-in. supply and return. Because this is a minimum it will be used for all the radiators. In larger systems there would be a noticeable difference between the risers in one- and two-pipe systems.

8. Selection of Radiators

An average temperature of 197 F will result in emission of 200 Btu per square foot of cast iron radiation or cast iron convectors (see Table 3). Dividing the hourly heat loss in each room by 200, the number of square feet of radiation can be determined. Radiator No. 1 will have to provide 30 sq. ft. In the entire system there will be 175 sq. ft.

9. Selection of Boiler

For 175 ft. of connected radiation select a hot water boiler, specifying the type of firing. Allowances for pipe loss, pickup and normal domestic hot water requirements are usually included by the manufacturer in his ratings.

Table 1. Pipe sizing table for mains

One- and two-pipe forced circulation hot water systems with special return fittings

SECTION A

BOOSTER HEAD PRESSURES	TOTAL EQUIVALENT LENGTH OF PIPE IN FEET								
2'	40	48	60	68	80	96	120	160	240
2½'	50	60	75	86	100	120	150	200	300
3'	60	72	90	103	120	144	180	240	360
3½'	70	84	105	120	140	168	210	280	420
4'	80	96	120	137	160	192	240	320	480
4½'	90	108	135	154	180	216	270	360	540
5'	100	120	150	171	200	240	300	400	600
5½'	110	132	165	188	220	264	330	440	660
6'	120	144	180	206	240	288	360	480	720
6½'	130	156	195	223	260	312	390	520	780
7'	140	168	210	240	280	336	420	560	840
7½'	150	180	225	257	300	360	450	600	900
8'	160	192	240	274	320	384	480	640	960
8½'	170	204	255	291	340	408	510	680	1020
9'	180	216	270	308	360	432	540	710	1080
9½'	190	228	285	325	380	456	570	760	1140
10'	200	240	300	342	400	480	600	800	1200
10½'	210	252	315	360	420	504	630	840	1260
11'	220	264	330	377	440	528	660	880	1320
11½'	230	276	345	394	460	552	690	920	1380
12'	240	288	360	411	480	576	720	960	1440

SECTION B (Based on 20° Temperature Drop)

PIPE SIZE	MAIN CAPACITIES FOR LAND TWO-PIPE SYSTEMS, AND BRANCHES FOR TWO-PIPE SYSTEMS								
	MILINCHES								
	600	500	400	350	300	250	200	150	100
½"	19.1	18.2	16.3	15.1	13	12.5	10.8	9.2	7
¾"	41	37.7	33	30.5	28	26.7	23.5	20	15
1"	80	71	64	59	53	48	42	37	31
1¼"	170	160	140	130	118	102	90	78	63
1½"	260	240	210	185	175	156	140	121	94
2"	500	450	410	360	322	294	261	227	182
2½"	810	750	670	610	551	523	460	385	310
3"	1600	1400	1300	1150	1000	900	800	680	550
*3½"	2300	2100	1850	1650	1500	1350	1190	1020	825
*4"	3200	2900	2600	2300	2100	1950	1700	1350	1140

* Trunk main capacities only. Fittings are not made larger than 3".

NOTE — The figures shown in these tables apply to both steel pipe and Type L copper tubing, as capacity differences are not sufficient to cause design errors.

Table 2. Pipe sizing table for risers

One-pipe forced circulation hot water systems with special return fittings

(Based on 20° Temperature Drop)

CAPACITY OF RISERS WITH TWO FITTINGS (In Thousands of BTU)

	PIPE SIZE	600	500	400	350	300	250	200	150	100
						MILINCHES				
					Upfeed Risers—First Floor (See Note 1)					
A	½″	23	22	19	18	17	16	14	12	10
	¾″	43	41	37	33	30	28	26	22	20
	1″	80	73	64	60	55	50	45	39	32
	1¼″	180	140	120	110	100	93	80	74	62
					Upfeed Risers—Second Floor (See Note 2)					
B	½″	16	15	14	13	11	10	10	8	7
	¾″	31	28	25	24	22	21	18	15	13
	1″	58	52	45	43	37	33	32	28	25
	1¼″	122	108	92	90	79	72	68	59	50
					Upfeed Risers—Third Floor (See Note 2)					
C	½″	14	12	11	10	9	8	8	7	6
	¾″	26	24	23	21	19	18	16	14	12
	1″	47	43	38	36	34	31	29	28	25
	1¼″	99	91	81	77	70	66	59	56	46
					Downfeed Risers (See Note 3)					
D	½″	16	15	14	12	11	9	8	FOR LESS THAN 200 MILINCH RESISTANCE. BASE CALCULATIONS ON PUMP WITH HIGHER HEAD PRESSURE.	
	¾″	33	30	26	24	20	18	14		
	1″	58	52	43	41	34	29	25		
	1¼″	117	106	86	83	69	59	49		

NOTE — The figures shown in these tables apply to both steel pipe and Type L copper tubing, as capacity differences are not sufficient to cause design errors.

CAPACITY OF RISERS WITH ONE FITTING (In Thousands of BTU)

	PIPE SIZE	600	500	400	350	300	250	200	150	100
						MILINCHES				
					Upfeed Risers—First Floor					
E	½″	16.5	15	13	12	11	10.6	10	9.2	8
	¾″	29	27	25	24	21	19	18	17	15
	1″	50	48	44	41	37	35	33	31	28
	1¼″	95	88	78	76	69	62	55.6	48	40
					Upfeed Risers—Second Floor					
F	½″	11	10	9	8	7	7	6	6	4
	¾″	20	19	17	16	14	13	12	11	11
	1″	34	32	29	28	25	24	22	21	18
	1¼″	70	68	59	57	51	49	45	43	36
					Upfeed Risers—Third Floor					
G	½″	9	8	7	7	6	6	6	5	4
	¾″	18	16	14	14	12	12	11	10	9
	1″	31	29	28	27	24	22	21	20	18
	1¼″	63	60	56	52	48	45	43	41	36

READ THESE NOTES CAREFULLY BEFORE SIZING RISERS

NOTE 1. 1st FLOOR UPFEED RISERS—Capacities shown in the table are based upon horizontal branches not more than 3 feet long, with stubs 18″ long, or a total of 9 feet of pipe. 6 elbows, one valve and one union ell, and one C.I. radiator are added for the equivalent length.
For each additional 10 equivalent feet of pipe, move 2 milinch columns to the right.

NOTE 2. 2nd and 3rd FLOOR UPFEED RISERS—Capacities shown are based upon horizontal branches not more than 3 feet long, with risers 10 feet high and 20 feet high respectively. 8 elbows, one valve and one union ell, and C.I. radiator are added for the equivalent length.

For each additional 10 equivalent feet of pipe, move 2 milinch columns to the right.

NOTE 3. DOWNFEED RISERS—Capacities shown are based on a drop of seven feet to the *center of the radiator*, with not over 3 feet total in horizontal branches, 6 elbows, one valve and one union ell and one C.I. radiator. For every additional 2 feet of vertical drop, move one column to the right in milinch table.
On downfeed jobs the main MUST be pitched up and a vent installed on end of main.

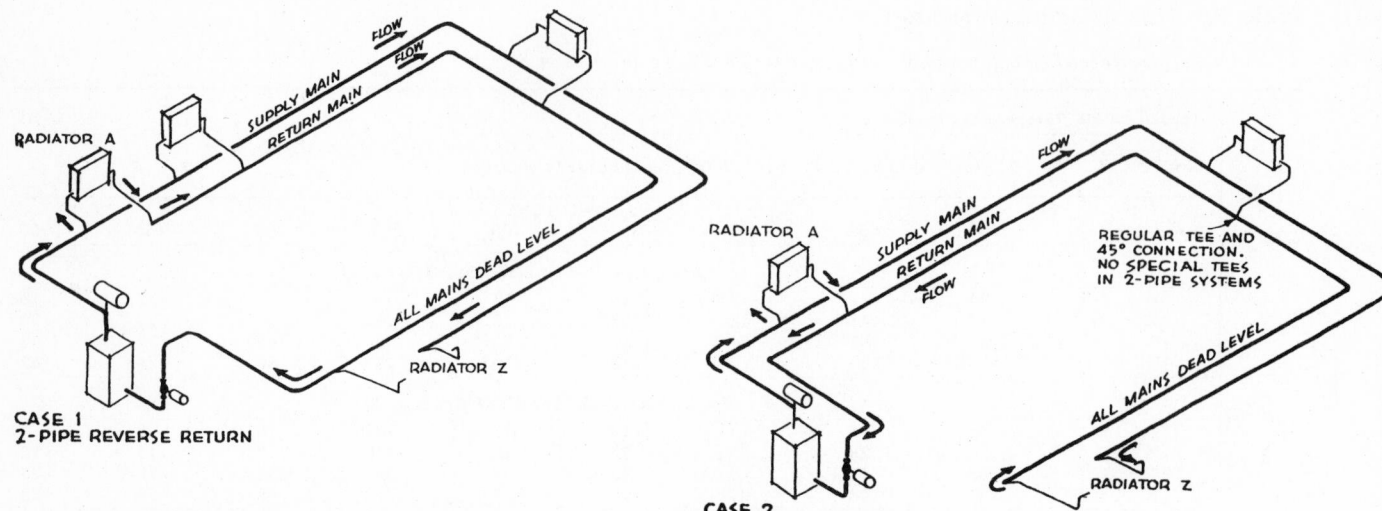

Fig. 9.   Types of two-pipe hot water systems

The two-pipe reverse return is preferable and is usually chosen. Note (Case 1) that the length of circuit supply and return to A is identical with that to Z giving equal heating. In Case 2 note how much radiator A is favored by comparison with the long travel to and from Z. On a straightaway circuit the piping needed for Case 1 is somewhat greater. It is chosen, however, for its equal circuits through every radiator.

1. Average Water Temperature and Temperature Drop in the System

With closed systems under pressure it is possible to circulate water at or above the temperature of the boiling point of water if desired, without generating steam, because the boiling point of water increases with increasing pressure. However, this is not always done. A frequently used used in this design is as follows: the average temperature of water in the system is 197 F. The drop in temperature between the boiler delivery and return water is 20 F. Thus the water will leave the boiler at about 207 F and return at about 187 F.

2. Water Flow Required to Make Up Hourly Heat Loss

This house loses 118,000 Btu. per hour. The specific heat of water is one. This means it takes one Btu. to heat one pound of water one degree F.

In cooling, water will give off one Btu. for each pound losing one degree F. With a fixed heat loss and a fixed water temperature drop, the equation for quantity of water to be circulated becomes — Gallons per minute x 8 pounds per gallon x 1 Btu.

per pound x 20 degrees F equals Btu. per hour heat loss, or

$$\text{GPM} \times 60 \times 8 \times 1 \times 20 = \text{Btu./Hr.}$$

$$\text{or GPM} = \frac{\text{Btu./Hr.}}{9600}$$

which is a standard formula for these conditions. Substituting the actual value of 118,000 Btu. per hour heat loss we arrive at 12.2 gallons per minute to be circulated in order to make up the hourly heat loss.

3. Length and Equivalent Length of Circuit

In a two-pipe reverse return system the length of travel of water from the boiler through the supply main, through a radiator and through the balance of the return main is the same for any radiator. It should be computed accurately from the building layout. This installation has a length of travel of approximately 184 ft. as follows:

width	30 ft.
	30
length	50
	50
height	8
	8
runouts (1 rad.)	8
	184 feet

The "Equivalent Total Length" is a length of imaginary straight pipe equivalent to the run computed above plus an allowance for the resistance of fittings, boiler, valves, etc. On large jobs of unusual design it is customary to compute this accurately. For our purpose it is sufficient to add 50 per cent. The equivalent total length of this installation is thus 184 x 1.50 = 276 ft. This will be used in later calculations.

4. Select a Pump

Besides selecting a pump it is necessary to establish sizes for all pipes. One step depends on the other. The amount of water pumped through per minute must not vary. This is 12.2 gallons per minute. A powerful pump can circulate at this rate through very small pipes while a weak pump can deliver the same quantity per minute only through large pipes. If from Fig. 8 we select a 1½ in. pump, we discover that it will pump our 12.2 gallons per minute against a "head" of 6.4 ft. Now it is necessary to select a piping system that offers resistance of the value of 6.4 ft. to assure flow of 12.2 gallons per minute.

ISOMETRIC WITH DIMENSIONS

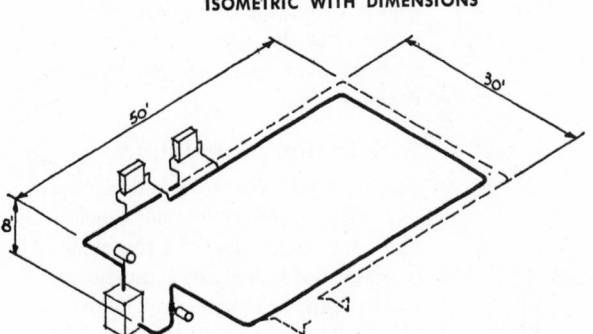

PLAN WITH HEATING REQUIREMENTS

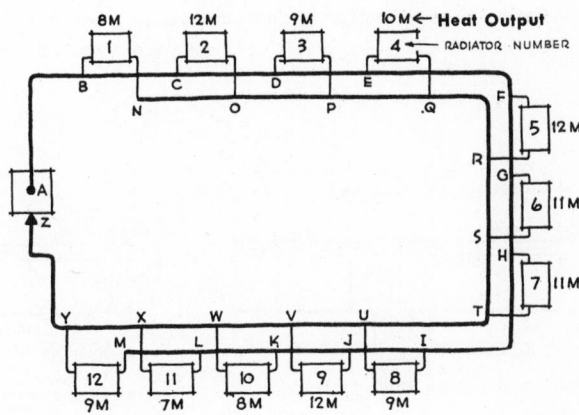

Fig. 10. Typical design of a two-pipe reverse return forced circulation hot water heating system

Left: Sketch showing general dimensions of the system and the length of the circuit through one (any) radiator. Right: General plan layout identifying the mains, numbering each radiator and giving each room heat loss in thousands of Btu./hr. Example: 8M = 8000 Btu./hr.

5. Meaning of Pressure Drop in Milinches Per Foot

"Feet of head" means that the 1½ in. pump will deliver 12.2 gallons per minute if it is raising the water 6.4 ft. in height. Since the heating circuit is closed, the water returns to the same level and the only resistance to pumping is frictional. The difference in the pressure at the pump discharge and the pump suction due to the friction caused by the "equivalent length" of the system is represented by 6.4 ft. of head. Thus the water loses 6.4 ft. of head in 276 ft. of pipe. A milinch is one one-thousandth of an inch. There are thus 12,000 milinches in one foot of height. Lost in the system will be 6.4 × 12,000 milinches or 76,800.

The loss per foot will be $\frac{76,800}{276}$ or 270 milinches per foot. If this loss is maintained the circulation will be correct. It is possible to establish this milinch loss directly from Table 1 which has the results of calculations such as we have completed above. In the left-hand column of

Section A the closest head is 6½ ft. Go to the right until you reach the nearest total equivalent length. This is 260. Directly below in this column in the horizontal line labeled "Milinches" is the value 300 milinches per foot. This is close enough for our purpose to the accurately computed value of 270 arrived at previously. This table is used always instead of the calculation which was made to explain the process. We shall now use the "300 Milinch Column" in selecting all pipe sizes.

This is a good average pressure loss. High pressure drops result in speed and noise and low pressure drops result in slow speed and consequent slow response.

6. Selecting of Mains and Returns

Section B of Table 1 gives the size of mains and returns at the left size of mains and returns at the left for any value of heat per hour to be delivered, the latter being read in the 300 milinch column. The supply mains are thus sized as follows:

Main	Capacity M Btu./Hr.	Size to be used
AB	118	1¼ in.
BC	110	1¼
CD	98	1¼
DE	89	1¼
EF	79	1¼
FG	67	1¼
GH	56	1¼
HI	45	1
IJ	36	1
JK	24	¾
KL	16	¾
LM	9	½

In reverse order the return mains would be sized in similar manner.

Return	Capacity M Btu./Hr.	Pipe Size to be used
NO	8	½ in.
OP	20	¾
PQ	29	1
QR	39	1
RS	51	1
ST	62	1¼
TU	73	1¼
UV	82	1¼
VW	94	1¼
WX	102	1¼
XY	109	1¼
YZ	118	1¼

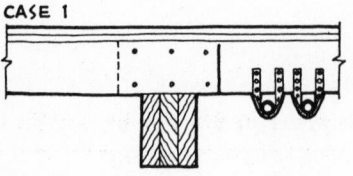
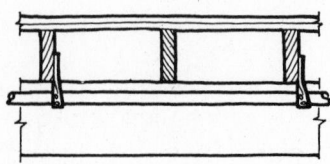

Mains not passing through girders can be supported dead level directly below joists but with slight clearance to prevent noise caused by expansion

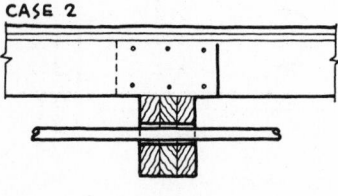
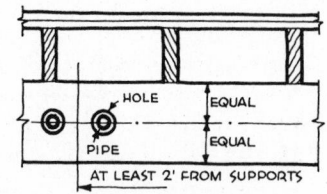

In average installations having mains of about 1" diameter, holes slightly oversize for clearance will provide convenient passage for the pipes without weakening girder, if holes are kept at mid-height and away from supports

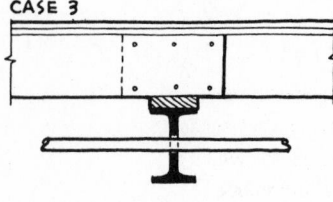
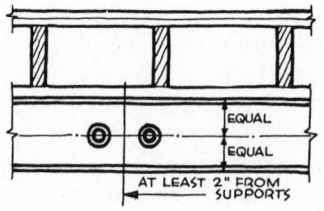

Similar arrangement with steel girder. In Cases 2 and 3 pipes should be supported on hangers, should not rest on bottom of girder-hole, which would result in noise during expansion. All mains and returns in forced systems can be level

Fig. 11. Structural details

Table 3. Heat emission—hot water radiators

EMISSION PER SQ. FT.	AVERAGE RAD. TEMPERATURE	BOILER TEMPERATURE
240 BTU	215°	225°
225 BTU	210°	220°
200 BTU	197°	210°
180 BTU	190°	200°
160 BTU	175°	185°
150 BTU	170°	180°

7. Radiator Branch Size

The size of all radiator branches both supply and return will be ½ in. selected also from Section B of Table 1 on the same basis. There it is seen that a ½ in. pipe carries 13,000 Btu. per hour at this pressure drop which is more than that required by any radiator.

8. Selection of Radiators

The heat emission from one square foot of cast iron radiation depends upon the temperature of the steam or water inside and the temperature on the other, or room, side. The room side is 70 as in most systems, but instead of 212 F temperature as in steam systems the average temperature of the water is 197 F. So instead of 240 Btu. per sq. ft. per hour as in the case of steam radiation the hourly emission is somewhat less At 197 F this is found to be 200 Btu. per hour per sq. ft. of radiation by reference to Table 3. In each case the hourly loss is divided by 200 to arrive at the square feet of radiation required. Radiator No. 1 must have 40 sq. ft., No. 2 60 sq. ft. and so forth. The total radiation for the house is 590 sq. ft. The individual radiators may be selected from the standard sizes given in the table in Fig. 1. Copper convectors are quite popular. They may be sized from information furnished by manufacturers.

9. Selection of a Boiler

If this house has normal requirements for domestic hot water, the figure of 590 sq. ft. of radiation and the kind of firing, oil in this case, are items of information necessary to select a boiler to carry the load.

Most manufacturers rate their boilers at the connected load and make allowance for pipe heat loss and pick up from cold condition as well as an allowance for normal domestic hot water requirements. It is well to read carefully the boiler ratings in the manufacturer's catalogue.

By WILLIAM J. McGUINNESS, M.E., *Professor of Architecture, Pratt Institute*

Comparison With Other Systems

Baseboards distribute heat better than radiators or convectors and are less conspicuous. Properly installed, there is less wall streaking because of the top seal strip and nonconcentrated convection currents. Lower parts of rooms are warmer, as shown in Charts A and B, making them adaptable to basementless construction. Response to starting and shutting off is quicker with baseboards than with radiant heating.

Heating Medium

Hot water forced circulation is the most adaptable heat source for baseboards and may be used in any of the three circuits illustrated here. Operation is like any hot water system using conventional radiation, and operation cost is about the same. If there is a minimum wall space for baseboards, heat losses can be cut by further insulation, double glazing, etc.

Types of Baseboard

There are two general classifications of heating elements for use in baseboard heating. They are the cast iron (RC) and the nonferrous (fin tube). The former is usually valve-regulated and the latter may be valve-regulated or it may have a damper to reduce the output by shutting off the convection currents while hot water continues to flow.

A typical unit of each type was chosen for illustration (Fig. 12) from the many listed in the latest edition of *Baseboard Ratings* by the Institute of Boiler and Radiator Manufacturers. The outputs of these two examples at various water temperatures and at the standard water flow rate of 500 lb per hr are listed in the following table.

Outputs in Btu per hr per lin ft

Average water temp., deg F	Cast iron (RC)	Nonferrous (Fin tube)
150	390	450
160	460	520
170	520	600
180	590	680
190	660	760
200	720	830
210	790	910
220	860	980

Range of Output

The examples selected are fairly typical. A few lower-output cast iron types are manufactured. One of the highest outputs listed is for a nonferrous unit which emits 1080 Btu per hr per lin ft at a water temperature of 220° F.

Cast iron (RC)

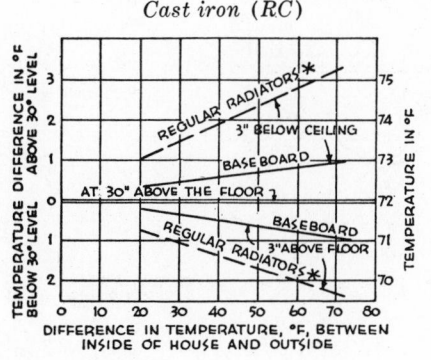

A

Chart A. *Room air temperature at various levels: at 70 deg inside to outside temp., a difference of 2 deg between floor and ceiling is shown for baseboards against almost 6 deg for radiators. *Small tube recessed radiators*

Nonferrous (fin tube)

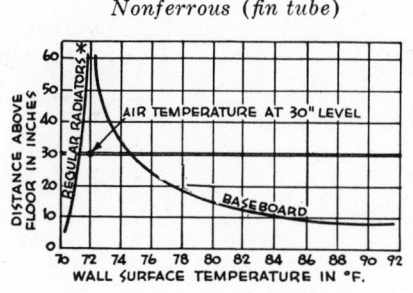

B

Chart B. *Baseboard keeps lower walls warmer, overcomes cold floors. Studies made when temp. indoors at 30 in. level was 72 deg, outdoors 32 deg.*

Fig. 12. Examples of baseboards

Water Flow Rate

The IBR listings of output are for the standard water flow rate of 500 lb of water per hr. An increase in output of about 6 or 7 per cent is achievable with a greatly increased flow rate, usually about 3,000 lb per hr. These higher outputs at the greater flow rates are also included in the published ratings of IBR and may be used if the designer calls for the correctly increased circulation pumping facilities.

Types of Systems

Baseboard heating lends itself to simple piping systems, and the three most common ones are shown here. Since valves cannot be used in the series-loop system, the system is employed most often with non-ferrous baseboards, which can be regulated by dampers. The ductile nature of copper tubing under conditions of expansion also commends this system. When cast iron units are used, the one-pipe system is most often chosen. Its pipe swings accommodate the expansion of the iron, and valves in the branch run-outs control individual baseboard assemblies.

Use in New Construction

Residences of contemporary design are well served by baseboard heating. Glass walls or picture windows call for a more dispersed source of heat than that afforded by radiators or convectors. The lowering of the window sill suggests the use of lower and longer heating elements. Baseboard heating is extensively used not only in houses but also in apartment houses and other large buildings.

Adaptability to Old Buildings

Cast iron baseboards can be used in conversion jobs where gravity hot water systems are in use. Two-pipe steam systems in larger buildings can be used with baseboards, but in one-pipe steam systems, the long run of condensing radiation makes it difficult to get the condensate out the same end that the steam enters.

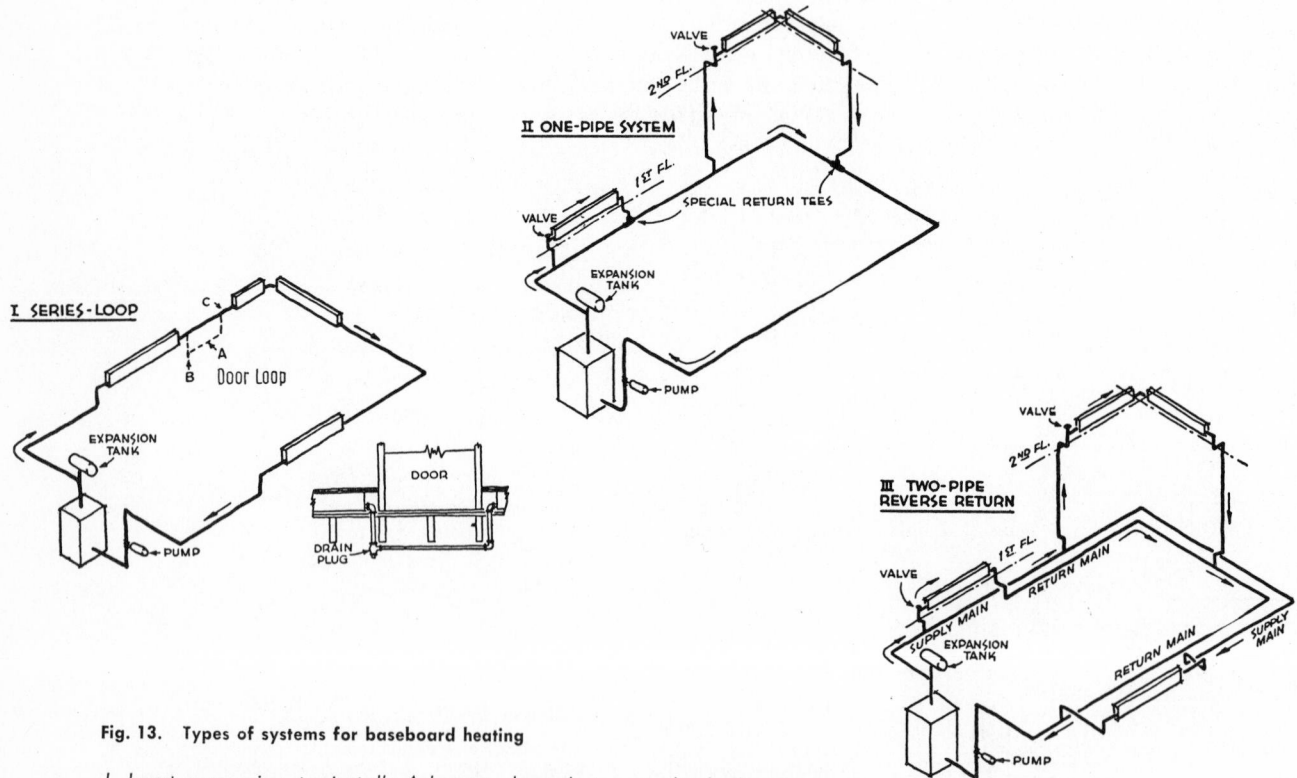

Fig. 13.   Types of systems for baseboard heating

I. Least expensive to install. Adequate heat but no individual valve control of units. If pipes drop to avoid doorways as at point A, drainage must be provided at point B, and vent at point C.

II. Most popular for small and average size installations. Control of individual units by valves.

III. Best for large installations. Each baseboard element controlled separately and receives water at maximum temperature directly from supply main.

In the design of baseboard heating systems reference is made to the following sources of information:

ASHRAE Guide and Data Book, American Society of Heating, Refrigerating, and Air-Conditioning Engineers.

IBR Heat Loss Calculation Guide, No. H-20.

IBR Installation Guide, Forced Circulation Hot Water Heating Systems, No. 500.

IBR Piping Guide, Residential Heating Systems, No. 700, Institute of Boiler and Radiator Manufacturers.

Steps in Design

1. Determine Heat Loss. The usual calculations for hourly heat loss in BTU should be completed and recorded for each room in the sketch.

2. Select Baseboards And/Or Radiators. The order of preference for baseboard location is a) under windows, b) on outside walls, c) on inside walls. As a trial length, outside walls are measured and recorded in each room. Heat loss of the room per ft of baseboard should be computed. The max required output (515 BTU per ft in the living room) sets the water temperature which must be used throughout the system. In this case 200 F is chosen as the average water temperature and results in baseboard lengths which fit the space. Baseboards of the desired height and type may be selected from manufacturers' literature to make up heat losses. Cast iron radiators may be used with cast iron baseboards. The loss in the kitchen and bathroom where there is not room for baseboards can be handled by using radiators. Use Tables 3 and 4. It is necessary in selecting baseboard lengths to leave space for expansion, piping, and end cover boxes for valves.

3. Select Boiler. A boiler with a net rating of 45,000 BTU per hr will be adequate for this system. Boilers are made large enough to supply the pick up, pipe loss and domestic hot water needs, unless these are unusual.

4. Select Air Cushion Tank. To facilitate expansion in the system, allow 1 gal of tank volume for each 30 sq ft of radiation. Dividing 222.9 sq ft by 30, the min volume usable is 7.4 and the next larger stock size tank will be selected.

5. Select Pump Size. Tables used are based on a temperature drop in the system of 20 F. Since this is the drop we have chosen, use Table 5 to select a pump size. Since our heat loss is below 50,000 BTU per hr, a 1 in. standard pump is acceptable. The head developed by the pump in supplying water to make up the heat loss at the given temperature drop may be found from Table 6. For a 1 in. pump and nearly 50,000 BTU per hr, the head will be about 5.25 ft.

6. Determine Main Size. In determining the length of the system it is usual to allow 12 ft for each heating element in addition to the measured length of the main. The total of these

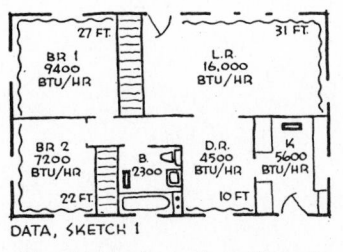

DATA, SKETCH 1

Heat loss and outside wall length

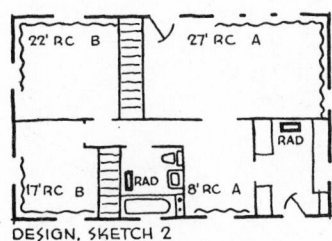

DESIGN, SKETCH 2

Length and type of baseboard

Temp. drop of water in system 20°
Length of System:
   Measured length of main   130
   Radiator allowance
     (6 heating elements x 12)   72
   (Use 200' in Table 7)   202

Fig. 14. Design of cast iron baseboard system

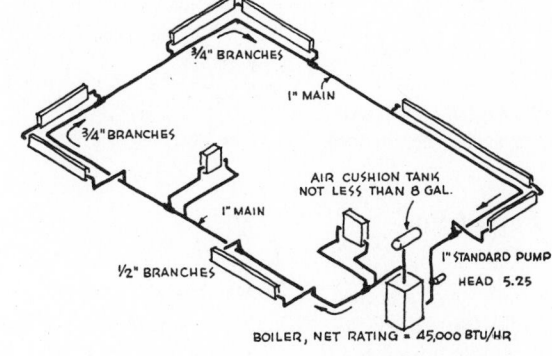

Design of a baseboard heating system using one-pipe forced hot water and cast iron baseboards

	DATA, SKETCH 1			DESIGN, SKETCH 2		
1 SPACE	2 BTU/HR HEAT LOSS	3 LINEAR FT. OF EXTERIOR WALL AVAILABLE	4 BTU/LIN. FT. OF EXTERIOR WALL	5 TYPE * OF BASEB'D SELECTED	6 LENGTH OF BASE TO BE USED	7 SQ. FT. OF RADIATION
L.R.	16,000	31	515	RC A	27'	78.8
D.R.	4,500	10	450	RC A	8'	23.3
K.	5,600	NONE, USE RADIATOR	—	RADIATOR	22"-4T-16SEC	28.8
BR 1	9,400	27	347	RC B	22'	45.8
BR 2	7,200	22	327	RC B	17'	35.4
BATH	2,300	NONE, USE RADIATOR	—	RADIATOR	22"-4T-6SEC	10.8
TOTALS	45,000					222.9

* A—600 Btu/hr/lin ft; B—430 Btu/hr/lin ft.

for the example given is 202 ft. Using this length and the head of 5.25 ft enter Table 7 and find that 1 in. is the right size for a main that will supply the BTU's required.

7. *Determine Branch Sizes.* Using the lengths of the baseboards in each room, it is found from Table 8 that branches are to be ½ and ¾ in. as recorded on the final piping diagram. Size of branches for small-tube cast iron radiation as used in the kitchen and bath is found from Table 2, Section E. At 300 milinches per ft., ½ in. risers will deliver 11,000 BTU/hr, more than enough for either of these radiators. Use ½ in. (The unit pressure loss is computed as follows: $\frac{5.25 \times 12,000}{202} = 310$ milinches per foot.)

Table 4. Small tube cast iron radiators

Number of square feet of cast iron radiation per section (standard spacing 1¾ in.)

NO. OF TUBES PER SECTION	HEIGHT	SQ FT OF RADIATION PER SECTION
3	25	1.6
4	19	1.6
	22	1.8
	25	2.0
5	22	2.1
	25	2.4
6	19	2.3
	25	3.0
	32	3.7

board series loop circuits in quite large buildings.

Pipe Expansion

Straight runs of over 30 ft are not recommended unless expansion is provided for by means of a door loop (if it occurs), an expansion loop placed horizontally in a partition or other available space, or a mechanical expansion coupling designed for this purpose.

Nonferrous Baseboards and the Series Loop

Nonferrous baseboards are most frequently used in connection with series loop circuit and using forced hot water. They can be used successfully in a two pipe forced hot water system or in a conventional one pipe forced hot water system, where they are connected individually like radiators. Another possible use is in two pipe steam systems. They are not adaptable to one pipe steam systems because of the difficulty of steam and condensate passing each other in the small pipes.

Series Loop, Forced Hot Water

The water flows through a series of baseboards and then back to the boiler by the motive power of a pump. If limited to circuits not exceeding 30,000 to 45,000 Btu per hour heat loss, the temperature of the heating water does not drop greatly. Average temperatures up to 240 F are used and the temperature drop in the system is usually designed as 20 F. A number of such circuits are possible, supplied by a single main, picked up by a single return and adjusted by balancing valves. With this arrangement it is possible to use base-

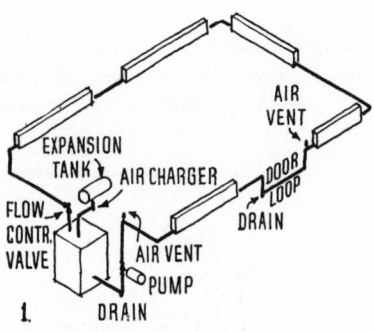

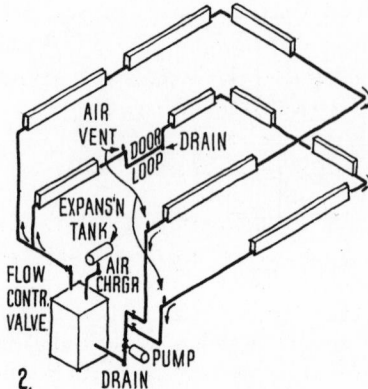

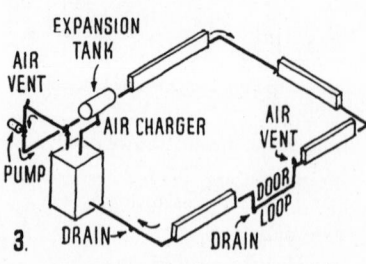

1. Single circuit series loop.
2. Multi-circuit (2 story) series loop. Note balancing valves above pump.
3. Series loop, convectors level with or below boiler. Note recommended position of pump.
Notes: Examples are series loop and forced hot water, the most commonly used type. Drain all low points and vent all high points in each system.

Fig. 15. Typical layouts appropriate for nonferrous baseboards

Table 5. Trial pump size

Total Load on System Btu/Hr.	Standard Pump
Up to 50,000	1"
50,001 to 100,000	1¼"
100,001 to 150,000	1½"
Over 150,001	1½"

Table 6. Pressure head developed by pump

This table is based on conservative averages. Consult manufacturers' data for closer accuracy.

Total Load Btu/Hr.	PRESSURE HEAD IN FT. OF WATER		
	Standard Pump		
	1"	1¼"	1½"
25,000	5.50	6.25	6.75
50,000	5.25	6.00	6.75
75,000	4.75	5.75	6.50
100,000	4.50	5.50	6.50
125,000	4.00	5.25	6.25

Table 8. Branch sizes for baseboards

Based on the use of one-pipe fittings in the main

Location of Baseboard	If Baseboard is 10 ft. or less in Length	If Baseboard is Longer than 10 ft.*
1st Floor Below Main	¾"	¾"
1st Floor Above Main	½"	¾"
2nd Floor Above Main	¾"	¾"

Table 7. Main sizes—iron pipe or type L copper tube

For pressure heads between 4.8 and 6.7 ft of water

Measured Length plus radiator allowance, Ft.	Capacity in Btu/Hr.			
	¾" Pipe	1" Pipe	1¼" Pipe	1½" Pipe
100	34,000	64,000	116,000	176,000
110	33,000	63,000	113,000	172,000
120	32,000	61,000	110,000	168,000
130	31,000	60,000	107,000	164,000
140	30,000	58,000	104,000	160,000
150	30,000	56,000	101,000	156,000
160	29,000	54,000	99,000	153,000
170	28,000	53,000	98,000	150,000
180	27,000	52,000	96,000	147,000
190	27,000	51,000	94,000	144,000
200	26,000	50,000	92,000	141,000
210	25,000	49,000	90,000	139,000
220	25,000	48,000	89,000	136,000
230	24,000	47,000	87,000	134,000
240	24,000	46,000	86,000	132,000
250	24,000	45,000	84,000	130,000
300	21,000	41,000	78,000	120,000
400	19,000	36,000	68,000	105,000
500	16,000	33,000	62,000	95,000
600	15,000	30,000	56,000	88,000

† It is recommended that not more than 40 lin ft. of baseboard be connected to the main with a single supply and return riser.

Design of a Baseboard Heating System Using Forced Hot Water Series Loop and Nonferrous Baseboards

The house used here (Fig. 16) has the same heat loss as the one used in the previous example (Fig. 14).

Room heat loss is computed in the same manner as for other conventional heating systems. The series loop system is very economical of pipe since most of it is in the heated space.

The finned areas of nonferrous baseboards make up heat loss in each room. Length of the unit will depend on its rating. Many designers feel that the lower output units are desirable because they come closer to filling up the length of the entire exterior wall, thus distributing heat better. A similar argument is offered for use of lower water temperatures. Units which discharge at the front cause less

Step 1. Compute hourly heat loss. This computation is the usual one and is not affected by use of baseboard convectors:

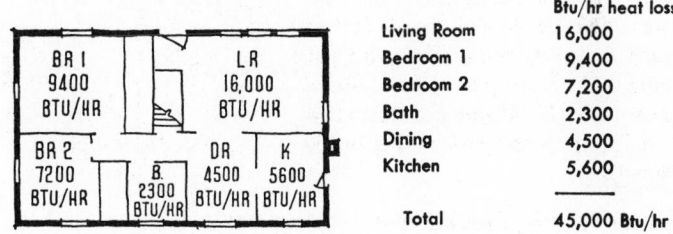

	Btu/hr heat loss
Living Room	16,000
Bedroom 1	9,400
Bedroom 2	7,200
Bath	2,300
Dining	4,500
Kitchen	5,600
Total	45,000 Btu/hr

Step 2. Establish average water temperature and temperature drop in system:

Average temperature	180 deg
Temperature drop	20 deg

Step 3. Compute gallons per minute (GPM) to be circulated at 20 deg drop to make up heat loss:

$$\frac{45{,}000 \text{ Btu/hr}}{9{,}600 \text{ (Factor)}} = 4.7 \text{ GPM}$$

For an explanation of step 3 and of factor 9,600 see Sheets 10–12, "Two-pipe forced hot water systems."

Fig. 16. Design of a series loop, forced hot water system using nonferrous baseboards

Step 4. Make layout and dimensioned pipe drawing to establish measured length and equivalent total length:

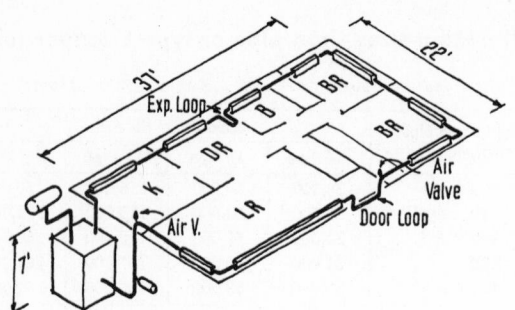

Actual Circuit Length:

Length	37
	37
Width	22
	22
Height	7
	7
	——
	132 ft

Total equivalent length to include resistance of fittings, boiler, etc:

132 x 1.50 (add 50 per cent) = 197 ft
Say 200 ft.

Step 5. Select pump and establish "head" against which it must pump:

See Fig. 8.

A 1-in. pump will deliver 4.7 GPM against 5.5 ft of head.

Step 6. Select size of main:

Consult Table 1 Sec. A, which also applies to this type of circuit. With an equivalent length of 200 ft and a head of 5½ ft, the pressure drop per ft will be 350 milinches per ft.

Section "B" of this table shows that a 1-in. pipe will supply 59,000 Btu/hr at a 20 deg drop. This is adequate and a 1-in. main will be selected. The capacity is found in the 350-milinch column.

Step 7. Select type of baseboard and by its output, compute the length required in each room:

For example, use a baseboard whose output at 180 F is 636 Btu/ft.

$$\frac{\text{Room heat loss}}{\text{Output/ft}} = \text{Length}$$

Space	Heat Loss	Length
L. R.	16,000	25.0 ft
B. R. 1	9,400	15.0
B. R. 2	7,200	11.5
Bath	2,300	3.6
D. R.	4,500	7.1
K.	5,600	8.8

Step 8. Select expansion tank:

Btu Load	Tank Size
80,000/hr	8 Gals
150,000	15
180,000	18

An 8-gal tank is used.

Step 9. Select boiler:

Total heat loss of 45,000 Btu/hr and type of firing will be used in selecting boiler. Manufacturers make allowance for pipe-loss, pick-up and normal domestic hot water demand.

Step 10. Lay out system:

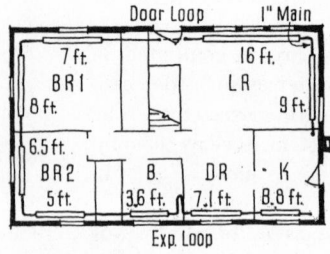

Fig. 16. Design of a series loop, forced hot water system using nonferrous baseboards (*Continued*)

wall streaking but are slightly less efficient. Selection of pump and pipe sizes follows closely the usual procedure in designing radiator-type forced hot water systems. High points must be vented and low points drained. Baseboards and loops are run level. It is advantageous for incidental piping to pitch to drains. Lengths obtainable vary with manufacturers, but usually units come in multiples of 1 ft. The base enclosure or casing which covers the unit can often be cut to exact size on the job. Individual room controls are not possible within a circuit except by dampers in some models. The several circuits in a large system can be balanced with valves or zoned by the use of separate pumps or automatic valves.

By WILLIAM J. McGUINNESS, M.E., *Professor of Architecture, Pratt Institute*

Radiant Systems in General

Radiant or Panel Heating, which consists of making up heat losses by creating warm surfaces within the rooms, can have as its heating medium hot water, electricity or warm air. The response, economy and design differ somewhat. This section is limited to systems which use hot water.

Human Comfort

The function of any heating system as it affects human comfort is to maintain a constant rate of heat loss from the body. The possible adjustments to regulate this loss are temperature of the air and temperatures of surrounding surfaces of spaces, air motion and relative humidity.

The latter two are confined largely to convection systems, but the proper relationship of the first two is the special province of radiant heating. By raising the temperature of the room surfaces, radiant loss from the body is retarded and the convective body loss can be increased by dropping the air temperature.

With a lower room temperature, the hourly heat loss from the room is reduced with a favorable effect on operating economy. The combined effect of warm surrounding surfaces and a lower air temperature is one which most people consider more comfortable and even invigorating.

Other comforts are inherent in this system. Temperature distribution throughout the room is very uniform. This is especially noticeable in the constancy of the air temperature at various heights above the floor. Often the temperatures from floor to ceiling remain within 2 deg, while in other systems they often vary from 10 to 15 deg with cold floors and hot ceilings.

The absence of hot radiators prevents the "baked" sensation in the air and eliminates fast vertical convection air currents which cause dirt streaks on walls and ceilings. The relative humidity is slightly higher in radiant systems because of the lower air temperature.

Relative Economy

The comparative cost of radiant heating and other methods is quite special to the individual installation. In general, it is 15 to 20 per cent more costly to install, although some radiant installations have cost less than conventional ones. Structural savings, like the omission of basements and crawl spaces, can offset the extra cost of radiant heating.

Floor systems are often more economical to install than ceiling systems. Operating costs as already stated are usually less than in other heating systems because of the lower room temperature that can be maintained for equivalent comfort.

While there is a difference in the actual material cost of copper, wrought iron and steel, the total job cost will depend largely upon the facilities available for fabrication. This should be investigated locally.

Panel Location

Floor, ceilings and walls are available as possible panel locations. Walls are seldom used because of the difficulty in finding enough area to provide sufficient heat output. Their use is generally confined to auxiliary panels.

Fig. 17 illustrates the most commonly used ceiling and floor panel constructions. For simplicity, this discussion is confined to use of these types. The floor slab which is more economical is well suited to basementless houses with concrete slabs on the earth. The mass of concrete surrounding the pipes has greater heat retaining qualities than the thinner plaster panels of the ceiling and therefore is appropriate to houses in which the call for heat is steady without fast fluctuations.

Ceiling panels, though more expensive than floor panels, are more truly radiant, have a greater permissable temperature and output, and will heat or cool off more rapidly upon demand. They are suitable for houses with much glass. Ceiling pipes must have at least one-half of their surfaces imbedded in the plaster. Fig. 18 shows three types of houses: two

Panel Details

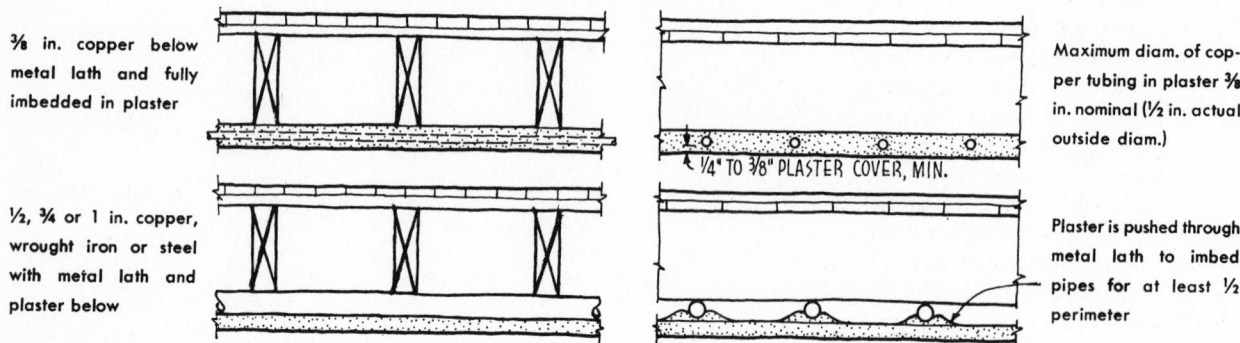

⅜ in. copper below metal lath and fully imbedded in plaster

½, ¾ or 1 in. copper, wrought iron or steel with metal lath and plaster below

¼" TO ⅜" PLASTER COVER, MIN.

Maximum diam. of copper tubing in plaster ⅜ in. nominal (½ in. actual outside diam.)

Plaster is pushed through metal lath to imbed pipes for at least ½ perimeter

Either of the above ceiling types will perform as shown in A, B and C below

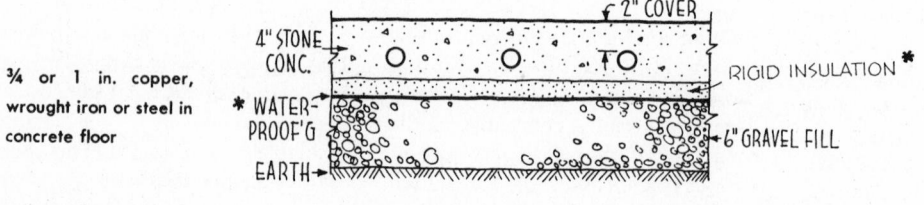

¾ or 1 in. copper, wrought iron or steel in concrete floor

2" COVER
4" STONE CONC.
RIGID INSULATION *
* WATER-PROOF'G
6" GRAVEL FILL
EARTH →

Floor Panel Performance as shown in D and E below

Panel Performance (based on above details)

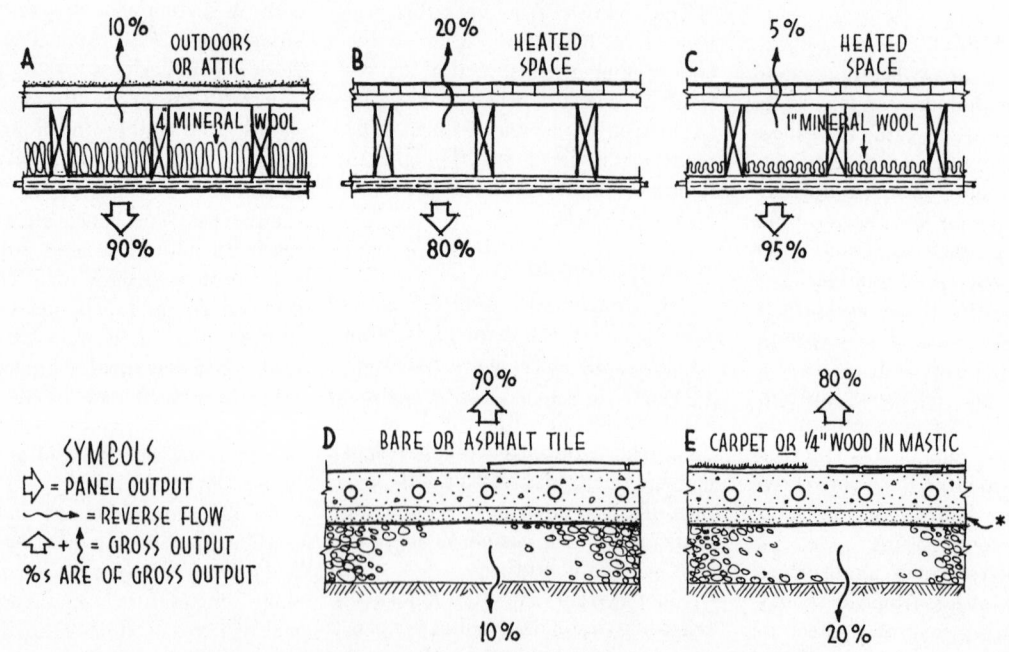

A 10% OUTDOORS OR ATTIC 4" MINERAL WOOL 90%

B 20% HEATED SPACE 80%

C 5% HEATED SPACE 1" MINERAL WOOL 95%

SYMBOLS
⇨ = PANEL OUTPUT
⌢ = REVERSE FLOW
⇧ + ⌇ = GROSS OUTPUT
%s ARE OF GROSS OUTPUT

D BARE OR ASPHALT TILE 90% 10%

E CARPET OR ¼" WOOD IN MASTIC 80% 20%

Necessary only when slab is directly above ground water, heavy clay or rock. Otherwise may be omitted with negligible change in reverse flow.

Fig. 17. Typical ceiling and floor panels

choices for panel locations in each case. Either (a) or (b) is possible for the basementless, one-story house. The one-story house with basement is served by either (c) or (d). The two-story basementless house can use (e) or (f). For concrete slabs directly on the earth, floor coils in the concrete are preferred. If, however, large heat loss or the need for fast response indicates a ceiling panel, the problem of the cold slab-on-ground may ·be solved by carpet or auxiliary perimeter floor coils.

Coils and Grids

Sinuous coils (Fig. 19) offer more resistance to the flow of water than grids but are easier to fabricate. They are almost universally chosen for residential work where coil lengths are not great enough to cause excessive friction. Grids find their largest use in industrial work where friction needs to be minimized in extensive piping.

Ferrous and Nonferrous Piping

The ruggedness of steel and wrought iron pipe recommends them for use in industrial jobs and for floor installation in residences. All connections within the panel must be welded. Copper tube, by its lightness and ease of bending, is well suited to ceiling installations. Solder consisting of 95 per cent tin and 5 per cent antimony should be used in sweat-fitting connections within the panel.

All of the materials mentioned will resist the corrosion commonly encountered. Since water is added in very small quantities, its corrosive action, if any, is quickly spent with little damage, and thereafter it is harmless. Corrosive action on the outside of pipes is a hazard which can be avoided by imbedment of pipes in weather-protected ceilings or in the concrete of slabs on dry, well-drained ground. Floor pipes must be kept out of the acid reaction of cinder fill.

While ⅜ in. copper tube is often set below metal lath and buried in the plaster and larger ferrous piping cast in concrete slabs, the order can be reversed. It is entirely possible to use

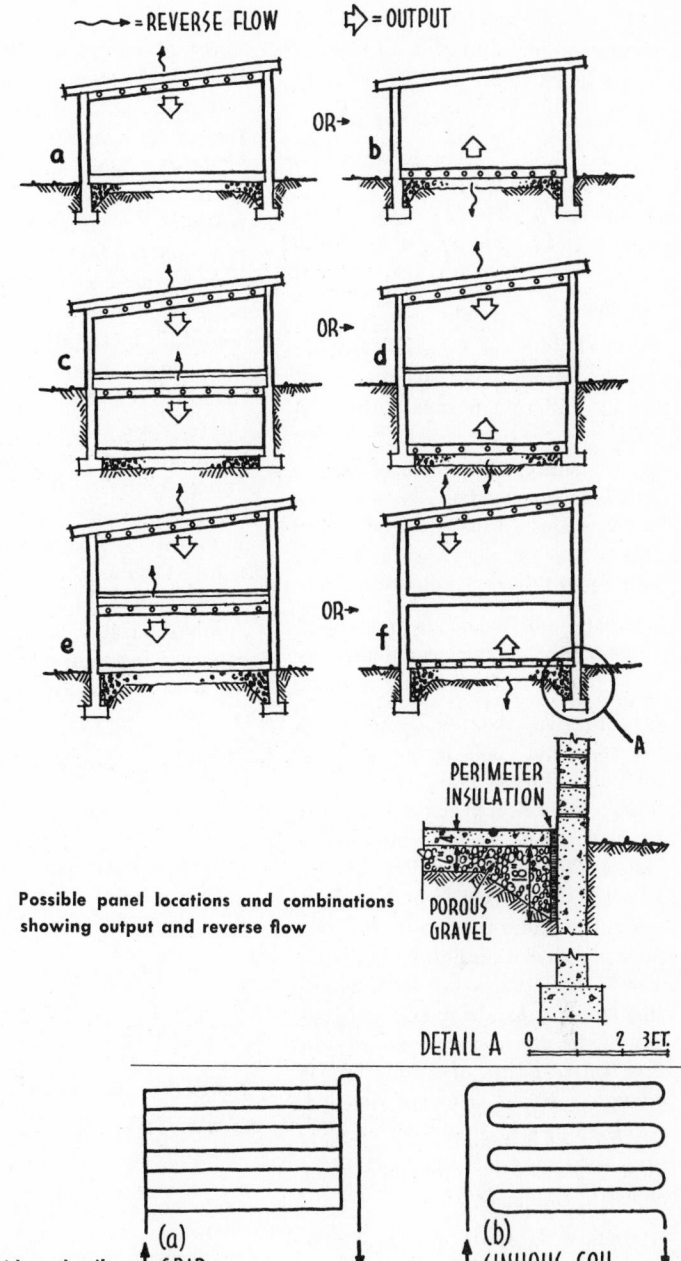

Fig. 18. Possible panel locations and combinations showing output and reverse flow

Fig. 19. Grids and coils

ferrous pipe (usually ½-in. dia or larger) connected to the soffit of joists with metal lath and plaster below, the plaster being forced through to partially imbed the pipes (one-half perimeter is enough). Likewise, copper tube may be used in floors if care is exercised in protecting it until the concrete floor is set. The heat-emitting qualities of the several pipe materials when imbedded in the panel are comparable.

Layout and Circuits

Radiant heating, more than any other system, must conform to the architectural and heating needs of the house. In layout work the following guides may be helpful.

(a) It is recommended that the warm ends of coils where the water starts be placed near glass or the perimeter of the house, and the cool ends toward the interior.

(b) Equalize as much as possible the length of all coils served by the same header. Short bathroom coils may be valved down later to avoid short-circuiting of the water.

(c) Keep the coil lengths within the recommended approximate friction limits listed in the following table:

Nominal Diameter	Coil Length Tube	Pipe
3/8 in.	120 ft	—
1/2 in.	150 ft	250 ft
3/4 in.	250 ft	350 ft
1 in.	500 ft	500 ft

(d) The coils should be in a plane. Pipes should not cross within the panel. Maintain the spacing in all supply and return runs within the panel.

(e) Generally, the entire ceiling or floor is used instead of a small portion of those areas. Pipes may be spaced closely near the glass areas and wider near the interior.

(f) Place all balancing and vent valves in accessible places. They may be at the ends of coils, near headers.

(g) Effective insulation between ceiling coils and roofs is necessary to minimize reverse flow. The reverse flow to other heated space is credited to that space in designing other panels. This condition is illustrated in Fig. 18 (c) and (e). In both of these cases, the under-the-roof panels can have a reduced output. Fig. 17 (c) shows insulation used to diminish this flow if separate zoning and control of the upper story is desired. In this case, 1 in. of insulation is enough; 4 in. are not needed.

(h) Ease of fastening ceiling coils is accomplished if the pipes run at right angles to the joists.

(i) In floor slabs, wire mesh is of some advantage in preventing cracks but is not essential if the earth is properly compacted.

(j) Avoid when possible, placing warm coil supply lines directly adjacent to cool return lines, particularly in plaster. Cracking may result if the temperature difference is large.

Basic Assumptions

1. **Occupancy.** Radiant systems may be used in a variety of structures. The design conditions in such varied occupancy as airplane hangars, gymnasiums, factories and houses differ widely. It is intended to present information for use in houses only. Large residences and 2 or 3 family houses may be included, but not enough data are given to design the heating for apartment houses.

2. **Panel Type and Location.** A great many different panel types are possible. For simplicity, two ceiling types and one floor type are suggested and the data given apply to them only. The ceiling panel output varies according to the insulation and the floor output according to the floor covering. For some additional cost, the response of floor panels may be improved and the reverse flow reduced slightly by the use of an insulating layer under the whole slab.

3. **Perimeter Insulation.** In all floor slab installations, it is assumed that 18 in. deep of 2 in. waterproof insulation separates the slab from the concrete foundation wall and that the 6 in. gravel fill thickens to 18 in. at the perimeter. This, or its equivalent, is mandatory in good practice (see Detail A, Fig. 18).

4. **Panel Surface Temperatures.** Many systems of design establish first a required panel temperature and then select the conditions to assure it. Since there is much difference of opinion about desirable limits of temperature and indeed even about the probable output for any given temperature, *outputs* only are discussed and they are kept within safe limits.

5. **Pipe or Tube Spacing.** For fixed water temperatures and pipe or tube diameters, the output varies depending upon the linear ft of pipe or tube per sq ft of panel. Actual efficiency improves with wider spacings and decreases with closer spacings. Except in refined calculations, this may be neglected.

6. **Units for Expressing Output.** Design tables often read in output per sq ft of panel surface. Others read in output per linear ft of pipe. The latter system is chosen here but it is necessary that an arithmetic check be made on the output per sq ft of panel, so that it is kept within the stated limits.

7. **Effect of Metal Surface Area on Output.** For the same nominal diameter, ferrous pipes have a larger outside perimeter than copper tubing. Theoretically, a different output might be expected. An average output is stated in Table 9 which can apply to either material.

Table 9. Gross output (including reverse flow)

Btu/hr/lin ft of pipe or tubing at average water temperature (135 F). For other temperatures, apply correction factors shown below

Nominal tube or pipe Diam.-in.	PLASTER CEILINGS			CONCRETE FLOORS	
	Coil Location	Output Btu/hr/lin ft	Suggested limits tube or pipe spacing in. o.c.	Output Btu/hr/ft	Suggested limits tube or pipe spacing in. o.c.
3/8	Coils Below Lath	24	4 1/2 to 9*	36	4 1/2 to 12
1/2	Coils	30	4 1/2 to 9	43	6 to 16
3/4	Above	41	6 to 9	57	9 to 20
1	Lath	51	6 to 9	72	9 to 24

Important Note: The NET output, Btu/hr/sq ft of panel surface, must not exceed 75 for ceilings or 55 for floors unless special conditions justify it.
Space in ceilings in excess of 9 in. may cause surface discoloration

CORRECTION FACTORS. For avg. water temps other than 135 F, correct gross outputs as shown

Avg Water Temp (F)	100	105	110	115	120	125	130	135	140	145	150
Multiply gross output by:	.46	.54	.62	.69	.77	.85	.93	no change	1.08	1.16	1.22

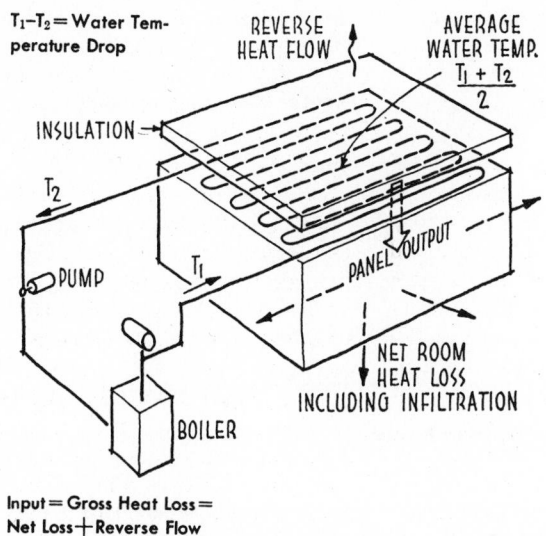

Fig. 20.   Design items and their determining factors

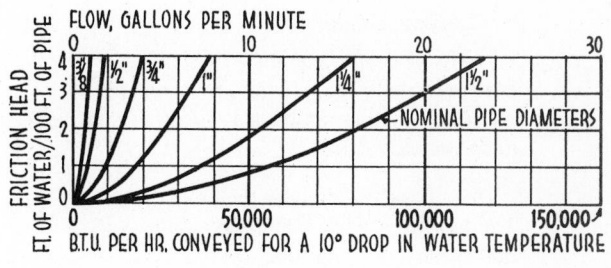

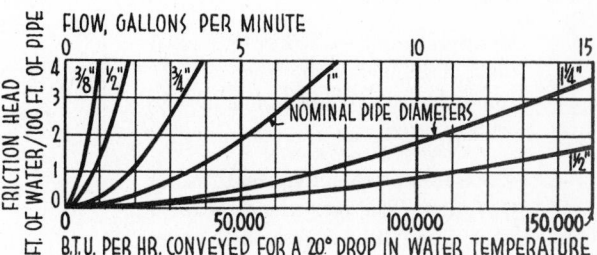

Fig. 21.   Heat capacity, flow, and friction

ITEM	FIXED BY
Required Panel output Btu/sq ft/hr	Net room heat loss ÷ panel area High Limits (Btu/sq ft/hr) Ceilings 75 Floors 55
Actual Panel Output Btu/sq ft/hr	Avg water temp, pipe size, lin ft of pipe per sq ft of panel (Must not exceed above limits)
Reverse Flow	Kind of panel and insulation behind it
Gross Output (Entire Panel)	Net room heat loss (total panel output) plus reverse flow
Choice of Temp Drop	Size of piping (ceilings 20 deg, floors 10 deg)
Water Flow (gallons per minute)	Gross output and temp drop
Pipe Friction	Total equivalent length of pipe, water flow and pipe size
Pump Rating	Water flow (gal per min) and total friction in longest run (ft of head)
Boiler Rating	Gross output
Compression Tank Capacity	Water volume and temperature rise

8. Water Temperatures. Curves and tables are frequently issued for each of the possible average water temperatures with outputs varying accordingly. For brevity, Table 9 is based on 135 deg only. This temperature is chosen quite arbitrarily. The correction factors must be applied for all other temperatures.

9. Limitations on Table 9. It is apparent that the scope of Table 9 is such that conditions of temperature, size and spacing may be selected resulting in sq ft outputs above the ideal limits. It is understood that adjustments must be made to maintain these limits. The spacings are suggested only and can be varied except for the upper limit of 9 in. for ceilings. Greater spacing is inadvisable in plaster.

10. Mean Radiant Temperature. This is an important item in many design manuals intended for use in a wide variety of structures. However, since this article is limited to residential design in which the MRT (average temperature of room surfaces) does not vary greatly, detailed calculations are not necessary. Table 9 is based upon an MRT of 70 deg which is on the safe side and usually results in a slight overdesign.

11. Heat Carrying Capacity of Pipes. The differing surface and inside dimensions of steel, wrought iron and copper affect somewhat their heat carrying capacities for the same nominal size. Fig. 21 is based on the qualities of black iron pipe it can be applied without appreciable error to other materials.

Note. The effect of the above standardizations and short cuts have been well considered and they are in accord with acceptable practice. They may be used with confidence. Slight variations in performance can be adjusted by a change in water temperature or adjustment of flow by balancing valves.

Designing a System

The following procedure is suggested.

1. Layout — Make a tentative layout of the system applying the foregoing principles.

2. Heat Loss — Compute the hourly heat loss from each room, including infiltration but omitting any loss through the surfaces selected to act as panels.

3. Adjustment — Reduce individual room heat losses by the amount gained by reverse flow from panels in ceilings below.

4. Establish the Required Panel Output — The panel in each room must give out enough heat to make up the losses found in steps 2 and 3. Divide this loss by the available panel area to find the required net output in Btu per hr per sq ft. Provide enough panel area to keep this output below 75 for ceilings and 55 for floors, otherwise discomfort or damage may result. If the ceiling is chosen, a portion of the floor may be added or vice-versa.

5. Find the Gross Output for Each Panel—Fig. 17 (A–E): relation of effective (panel) output and the additional reverse heat flow. Together they make up the gross output. Using the percentages for the selected type of panel, establish the gross output in each case.

6. Select a Water-Temperature Drop — When smaller temperature drops are selected, larger pumps are required, for a fixed length of coil and a given tube size. For ceiling installations, with smaller pipes and their greater resistance to flow, a 20 deg drop is suggested, while the larger pipes used in floors work well with 10 deg drops.

7. Select an Average Water Temperature—For a Fixed MRT, assumed to be 70 deg), the panel output depends upon the size of pipes, their spacing and the average temperature of the water. Critically high outputs are achieved only by large pipe, closely spaced and high water

Table 10. Heat carrying capacity of mains

Nominal Diam. of Main (pipe or tube)	Heat Conveyed in Btu Per Hour	
	For a 10 deg drop	For a 20 deg drop
1 in.	up to 35,000	up to 70,000
1¼ in.	35,000 to 70,000	70,000 to 140,000
1½ in.	70,000 to 100,000	140,000 to 200,000

Table 11. Compression tanks

Net Heat Loss From Entire House (Btu per hr)	Capacity of Compression Tank (gallons)
Up to 50,000	15
50,000 to 100,000	18
100,000 to 150,000	24

temperatures. It is best to provide enough panel area to keep the required outputs well within the prescribed high limits. Another conservative choice is to use a little extra pipe and a correspondingly lower average water temperature. A temperature of 130 deg is suggested as a trial temperature for ceilings. Temperatures over 140 deg should be avoided to prevent possible calcining of the plaster. For floors, a trial temperature of 110 deg is suggested.

8. Design the Critical Panel — Using the panel with the maximum required output, select a pipe size and average water temperature and, by means of Table 9, find the length of pipe needed for the panel. Lay out the panel keeping the spacing within the limits suggested. Note that the table is based upon the gross output of the panel. The pipes may be spaced closely at the outside wall and increase in spacing toward the interior. Maintain the length of pipe required for the entire panel.

9. Design the Other Panels — Using the average water temperature of

step 8, which must now remain constant for the entire system, find the length of pipe needed for the other panels, using Table 9. Lay out the panels, indicating the spacing of the pipe. Generally one material — copper, wrought iron or steel — is used throughout one installation. If it is necessary to use two different average water temperatures, special equipment is needed. This should be avoided if possible.

10. Size the Mains — When a number of coils are served by a main it may be selected from Table 10 on the basis of its heat-carrying capacity for the temperature drop selected for the system.

11. Compute the Water Flow — The required flow of water to make up the heat loss in the system is found by dividing the hourly heat loss by a factor dependent upon the water temperature drop. The flow is expressed in "gallons per minute" — GPM.

Flow through any circuit can be found by dividing the heat loss in that circuit by the same factors.

$$\text{For a 20 deg drop, Gpm} = \frac{\text{Btu/hr}}{10,000}$$

$$\text{For a 10 deg drop, Gpm} = \frac{\text{Btu/hr}}{5000}$$

12. Select a Pump — On the basis of the number of gallons per minute of water to be pumped through the system and the frictional resistance of the system expressed in "feet of water," select a pump from Fig. 8. The frictional resistance is called "head" and is established as follows:

Trace the longest circuit through which water passes. Find the lengths of the main, the long coil and the return main. For each of these find the friction in ft per 100 ft of pipe from Fig. 21.

The total friction of each may now be found by multiplying the length by the unit friction. Add these and increase by 50 per cent to allow for the effect of boiler and fittings. With the total head and the total flow, select a pump.

13. Select a Boiler — The net rating of the boiler selected must at least equal the gross output of the system. In the usage of most manufacturers, there is enough capacity in a boiler so chosen to take care of normal domestic hot water needs. For unusual hot water demands, the capacity of the boiler must be increased accordingly.

14. Compression Tank — From Table 11 select a tank of the proper volume to permit expansion in the system.

Design Example 1—Ceiling Panels

This is a modern house, fully insulated and double-glazed. The floor slab rests on the ground, there is no cellar. An air space separates the insulated ceiling from a slightly sloping roof. Either ceiling or floor panels may be used. Example 1 uses ceiling panels. Carpet is used throughout.

1. Layout—Figs. 22 and 23 show the room use, the size and the area available for panels. Even though Fig. 24 is a final drawing summarizing the findings of the design, it is necessary in the preliminary stages to make many sketches like Fig. 24 in order to anticipate the most desirable location for the boiler, headers, adjusting valves etc. and the possible routing and location of coils.

2. Heat Loss — If the ceiling is used for panels, there is no loss from the room through this surface so it is not included in the net room heat loss upon which the panel net output is based. The gross output of the panel coil is later computed to include the reverse loss of the panel. The net loss in this case must include floor or perimeter loss, and of course, in all cases infiltration. Table 12 shows a convenient form for use as a work sheet in designing the system. Column 1 is reserved for the net hourly heat loss.

3. Adjustment — Since no heat flows from the back of a panel into another usable space, there is no adjustment to be made.

4. Net Output — If the net heat loss be divided by the available panel area in each room, the required output is arrived at in each case. This is listed in column 4 of Table 12. Since none of these outputs exceeds 75 Btu per hr per sq ft, it is unnecessary to plan for auxiliary floor coils in this example.

5. Gross Output—Figure 17A represents the condition of reverse flow in this house. The net output represents 90 per cent of the total heat loss from panels. By dividing the net output in each room by .90 the gross output of each panel is determined. This will finally establish the length of pipe or tube needed in each panel when the water temperature is chosen.

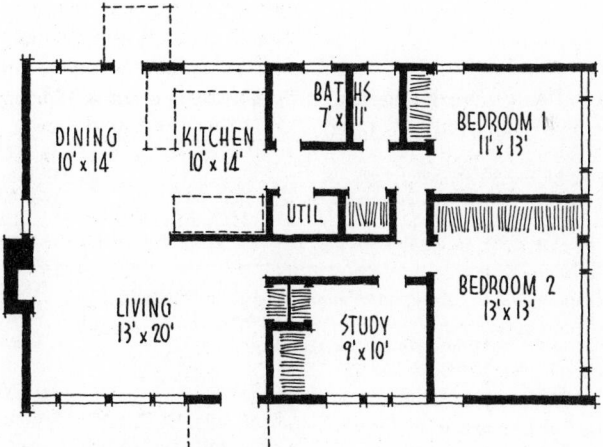

Fig. 22. Plan, example 1

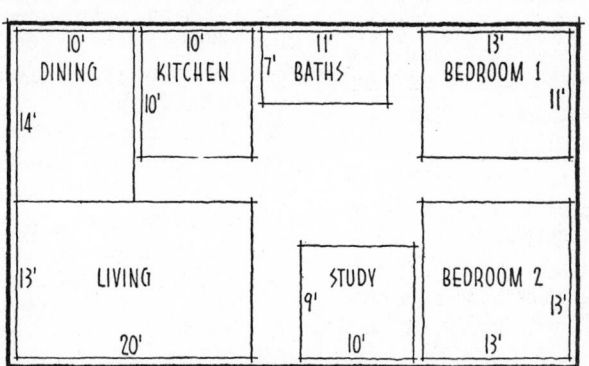

Fig. 23. Panel areas available, example 1

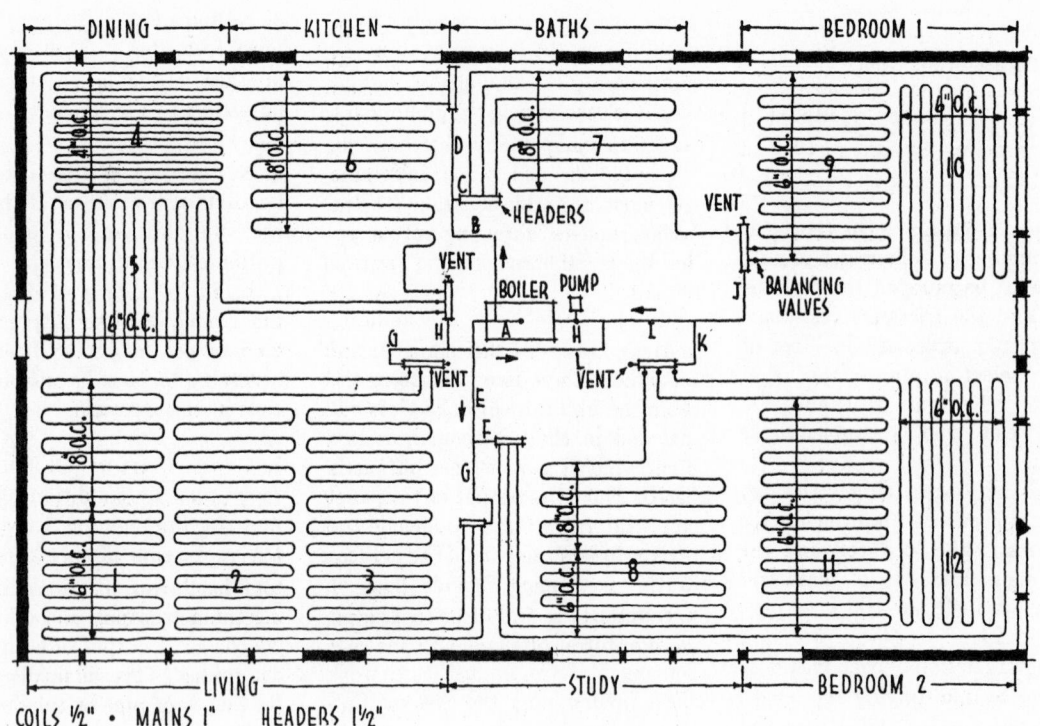

Fig. 24. Coil layout, example 1

Table 12. Design work sheet, example 1 (house shown in Fig. 22)

General Design Data, Coil Location Ceiling   Average Water Temp. 135° F
Tube Size ½ Copper   Gross Unit Output, Btu/hr/ft of Tube 30†   Temp. Drop in System 20° F

Col. Nos.	1	2	3	4	5	6	7	8	9	10	11
	Net Room Heat Loss	Available Panel		Unit Output of Panel	Reverse Flow	Gross Heat Loss	Tube Req'd. Per Room	Sinuous Coils	Identification	Approximate Tube Spacing	
		Dimensions	Area							Trial	Final
	Btu/hr	Feet	Sq. ft.	Btu/hr/s.f.	% of Gross	Btu/hr	Feet	Number Per Room	Coil Numbers	Inches C. to C.	Inches C. to C.
Living	11,320	13 x 20	260	43	10	12,600	420	3	1,2,3	7	6 & 8
Dining	8,060	10 x 14	140	*57	10	9,000	300	2	4,5	5	4 & 6
Kitchen	2,860	10 x 10	100	29	10	3,200	107	1	6	10	8
Baths	2,560	7 x 10	77	34	10	2,900	97	1	7	8	8
Study	3,550	9 x 10	90	39	10	3,900	130	1	8	7	6 & 8
Bedroom 1	6,590	11 x 13	143	46	10	7,300	242	2	9,10	6½	6
Bedroom 2	8,200	13 x 13	169	49	10	9,100	303	2	11,12	6	6
Totals	43,160					48,000	1,599	12			
Notes	Not Incl. Ceiling Loss	See Fig. 23		Col. 1 ÷ Col. 3		Col. 1 ÷ .90	Col. 6 ÷ 30†	No coil to Exceed 150 Feet	See Fig. 24	See explanation in Text	See Layout Fig. 24

Critical Output (Not to exceed 75 for Ceilings)

6. Temperature Drop — The use of relatively small diameter tube in this installation suggests the use of a 20 deg drop in the water temperature. It is recorded as the design drop in Table 12.

7. Average Water Temperature — The critical output of 57 Btu per sq ft per hr in the dining area is quite moderate, therefore it is unnecessary to choose a high water temperature. 135 deg will be used.

8. Critical Panel — In order to avoid the close spacing that might be necessary with ⅜-in. tube at this moderate temperature, ½-in. nominal size tube is used, attached to the joists with metal lath and plaster below it. In Table 9, the ½ in. tube has a gross output of 30 Btu per hr per lin ft of tube at 135 deg. Dividing the gross heat loss from the dining space panel by 30, it is found that 300 ft of tube is required in this panel. Making the assumption that the tube will lie about 6 in. within the available panel limits, it is found that 5-in. spacing will provide the required length. For instance, if a tentative scheme called for 13 ft long tubes in the dining area, there would have to be 300 ÷ 13, or 23 lengths. The distance between the outer and inner tube would be 9 ft or 108 in. 108 ÷ 22 spaces is about 5 in. Of course, two coils are needed because ½-in. tube may not exceed 150 ft in length. Also, closer spacing is indicated near glass. Finally, the job would do well to confine itself to two or three standard spacings. This job is adapted to the use of 4-, 6-, and 8-in. spacing. A little study of the dining area and some more arithmetic result in coils 4 and 5, which together provide the required length of tube. Each designer will improvise his own system. Simplicity of layout, ease of fabrication, plan-readability, uniformity of tube size and spacing are all important. Note that the coils start at the glass and at the perimeter with hot water supplied through header at the termination of main branch "D." Balancing valves and a vent precede the header which feeds return main "H."

9. Other Panels — Having established that the critical panel can operate with the spacing as chosen (4 in. is about the minimum possible spacing) it is possible to lay out the other panels, all of which operate at the average temperature of 135 deg, and in which the spacing of tube will be somewhat greater. The approximate tube spacings arrived at by the method already described can be entered in column 10 of Table 12 and standard spacings worked out and listed in column 11. Coils 9 and 10 use 6-in. spacing instead of 6½ and therefore fill less than the panel area. Coil 6 uses 8-in. spacing instead of 10 and also uses a little less panel area than was planned. In each case the lin ft of tube must be as shown in column 6 of Table 12 and must divide into multiples of 150 ft.

10. Size the Mains—Table 10 shows that a 1-in. main will supply up to 70,000 Btu per hr in a system using a 20 deg drop. Since our total gross heat load is 48,000 Btu, a 1-in. main is satisfactory and is used in that size to supply all the headers.

11. Water Flow — Dividing 48,000 Btu by the factor of 10,000 for a 20 deg drop, the hourly pumping rate is found to be 4.8 gal. per min.

12. Select a Pump — The friction through the longest circuit expressed in feet of head must be determined before the pump may be chosen. The following arrangement of computation is convenient. The flow is that through coil number 12 from the boiler and back. See Table 13 for example worked out.

Adding 50 per cent for the effect of the friction of the fittings, boiler, flow-control valve, the total friction is .921 x 1.50, or 1.38 of head.

With a delivery of 4.8 GPM and a head of 1.38 ft, any of the pumps shown in Fig. 8 will be satisfactory, since the curves of performance for all of them lie above the point of intersection of the two known characteristics. It is well to use a 1-in. pump as a minimum size, and it is chosen.

13. Boiler — The connected load for heating is 48,000 Btu per hr, and a boiler is selected to carry this load together with the demands for domestic hot water.

14. Compression Tank — A tank of 15 gal. capacity will be satisfactory, as shown in Table 11.

General

Figure 25 shows how to trap entrained air at the end of the coils so

Table 13.   Friction in the longest run (coil 12)

Tube Identification	Heat Conveyed	Tube Size	Actual Length	Friction Ft/100 Ft Tube	Friction Head Ft
A	48,000 Btu	1 in.	2 ft	1.8	.036
E	25,600	1	5	.5	.025
F	13,000	1	2	.2	.004
½" to coil	4,550	½	33	.4	.132
Coil No. 12	4,550	½	151	.4	.604
½" to header	4,550	½	12	.4	.048
K	13,000	1	2	.2	.004
I	23,200	1	8	.4	.032
H	48,000	1	2	1.8	.036
					.921

From Fig. 20

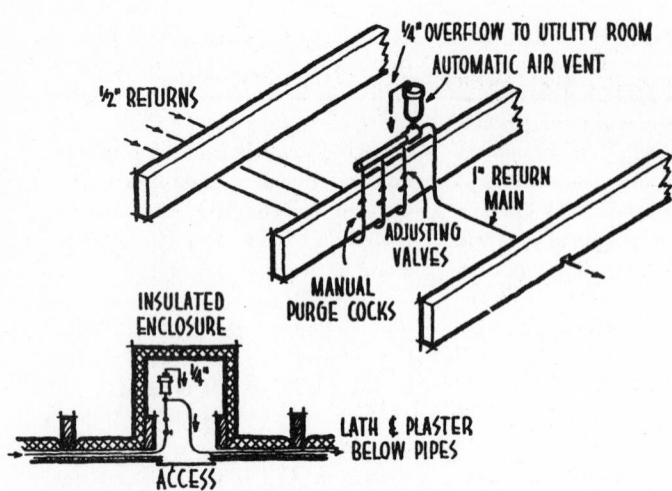

Fig. 25. Return header arranged for venting and adjustment, example 1

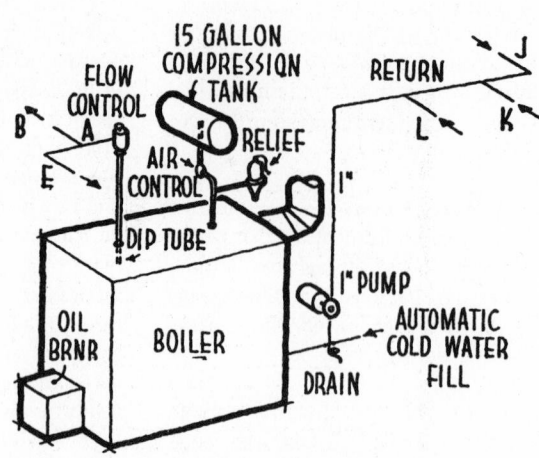

Fig. 26. Boiler connections, example 1

that it may be vented automatically from the header. An overflow protects the plaster. At this point, adjusting (balancing) valves are accessible, together with purge cocks for the purpose of bleeding or blowing out the air at the beginning of operations. The whole must be insulated against freezing and heat loss. Fig. 26 shows the more important of the boiler connections. For simplicity, the domestic hot water facilities have been omitted in the sketch. This and the other boiler controls are very largely as shown previously for hot water heating.

Design Example 2—Floor Panels

Example 2 illustrates the design of a system of floor coils for heating the same house (Fig. 27) as shown in Fig. 22. It is still assumed to be fully insulated and double glazed. Carpets may, in this case, be eliminated with some advantage to the operating economy.

1. Layout

The available panel areas are shown in Fig. 27. Coils should not be run below any fixed equipment such as kitchen floor cabinets. The bathroom panel might have been made smaller to avoid the area of bathtubs, although they are good transmitting surfaces and some piping below them assures comfort while bathing. Fig. 29 is a final summary of the design. Preliminary sketches like Fig. 29 should be made to study the possible location of coils and equipment and the routing of mains.

2. Net Hourly Heat Losses

Column 1, Table 14, lists the heat losses from the several rooms. For the use of floor coils, they include the losses through glass, walls and ceilings as well as infiltration of air. Perimeter floor loss is not included. The reverse flow from the pipes to the ground is later added to establish the gross heat loss (column 7, Table 14) from which the linear feet of pipe is selected for the coils.

3. Adjustment

Because this is a one-story house, there is no gain in any heated space from heat flowing in by reverse loss from a panel in a room above or below. Adjustment is not needed.

4. Net Output

It is well to keep the net output in

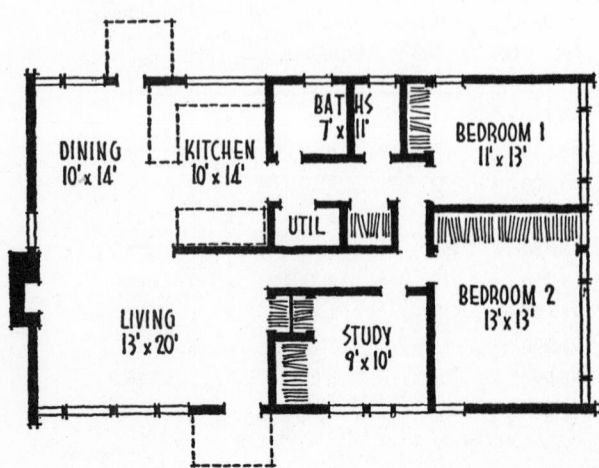

Fig. 27. Plan, example 2

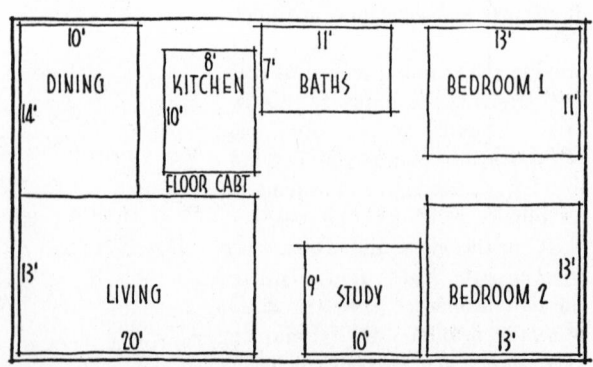

Fig. 28. Panel areas available, example 2

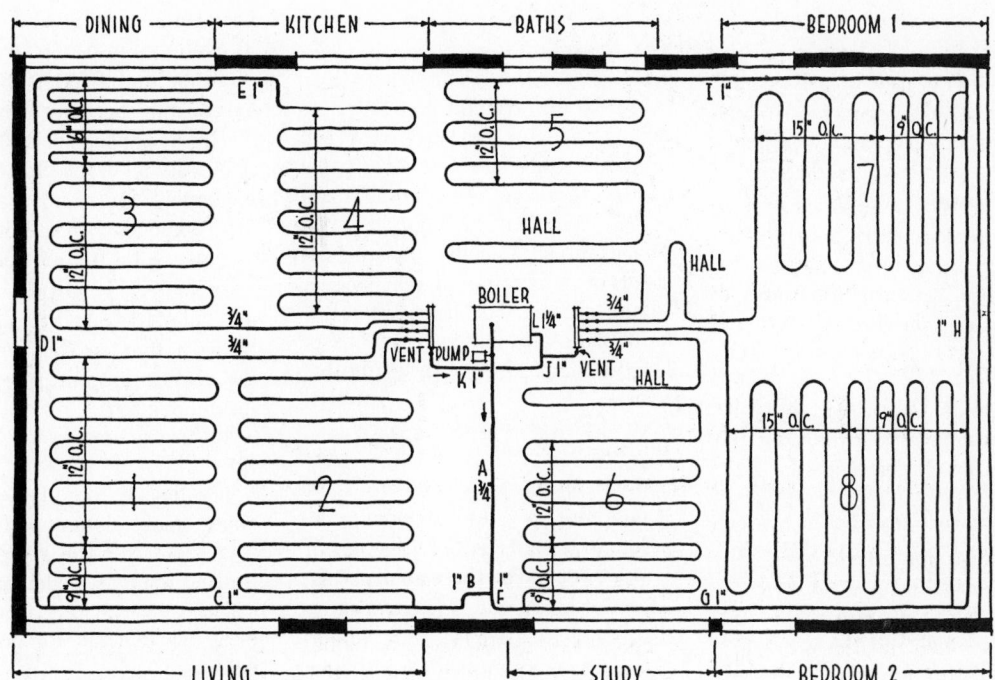

Fig. 29.   Coil layout, example 2

Table 14.   Design work sheet, example 2 (house shown in Fig. 27)

General Design Data			Coil Location—*Floor* Pipe Size ¾ in. wrought iron or steel			Gross Unit Output, *Btu/hr/ft or pipe*—53†† Avg. Water Temp. *130° F* Temp. Drop in System *10° F*					
Col. Nos.	1	2	3	4	5	6	7	8	9	10	11	12
		Available Panel		Unit Output of Panel	Floor Covering	Reverse Flow	Gross Heat Loss	Pipe Req'd. Per Room	Sinuous Coils	Identifi- cation	Approximate Pipe Spacing	
	Net Room Heat Loss	Dimen- sions	Area								Trial	Final
	Btu/hr	Ft	Sq Ft	Btu/hr/ s.f.	Material Selected	% of Gross	Btu/hr	Ft	Number Per Room	Coil Numbers	Inches c. to c.	Inches c. to c.
Living	11,440	13 x 20	260	44	Carpet	20	14,350	270	2 @ 135	1, 2	11	9 & 12
Dining	7,700	10 x 14	140	55†	Asphalt Tile	10	8,550	160	1	3	9	6 & 12
Kitchen	3,250	8 x 10*	80	41	Asphalt Tile	10	3,620	68	1	4	13	12
Baths	2,740	7 x 10	70	39	Ceramic Tile	10	3,050	58	1	5	12	12
Study	3,760	9 x 10	90	42	¼ in. wood in mastic	20	4,700	88	1	6	11	9 & 12
Bedroom 1	6,300	11 x 13	143	44	Asphalt Tile	10	7,000	132	1	7	12	9 & 15
Bedroom 2	8,100	13 x 13	169	48	Asphalt Tile	10	9,000	170	1	8	11	9 & 15
Totals	43,290						50,270	946	8			
Notes	Not incl. floor pe- rimeter loss	*Exclusive of floor cabinets		Col 1 ÷ Col 3		See Fig. 17	Col—by .80 or .90	†† Col 7 ÷ 53	L.R. Divided for equali- zation	See Fig. 29	See Text	See Layout Fig. 29

† *Critical output, (not to exceed 55 for floors)*   †† *From Table 9, 57 × .93 = 53 Btu/hr/ft of pipe*

Btu per hr per sq ft of panel below 55 in floors. Columns 1, 3, and 4 (Table 14) establish output in the case of each room. The dining room is critical at 55 and should be considered first.

5. Gross Output

The water circulated through the pipes must bring in enough heat to make up the net heat loss from the rooms and also the reverse loss to the ground. Fig. 17 shows approximate reverse loss for floor coverings. Columns 5, 6, and 7 of Table 14 show the method of arriving at the gross heat loss for each space.

6. Temperature Drop in the System

Pipes of wrought iron or steel ¾ in. in diameter will be used for the coils. In these relatively large pipes the friction is small and the water can be pumped through them quite rapidly. A small temperature drop can be expected and 10 deg is chosen.

7. Average Water Temperature

A trial computation was made using 110 F as the average water temperature, and it was found that the pipe spacings in the dining area were too small. A temperature of 130 F was then chosen and is used here. Table 9 gives the output per ft of ¾ in. pipe as 57 × .93 = 53 Btu/hr at 130 F.

8. Critical Panel

If the gross heat loss of the dining area be divided by the output per ft of pipe (53 Btu), it is found that 160 ft of pipe are required. This is an average spacing of 9 in. on center, and is in accord with suggested spacings in Table 9. To overcome greater loss near glass, the pipes will be spaced 6 in. on center near the glass and wider as the coil recedes from the glass. 6 in. is greater than the closest possible spacing of ¾ in. pipe as determined by the minimum bend radius. Comments under the item "Critical Panel" in Example 1, may be helpful in layout and study.

9. Other Panels

Columns 8 through 12 in Table 14 are a summary of the trial and final

spacings based upon the required total linear footage for all coils. Coils up to 350 ft in length are permissible using ¾ in. wrought iron or steel pipe. It will be seen that all of the proposed coils are less than this length, resulting in a simpler coil layout than that of Example 1. In that example, 12 coils were used instead of 8 because of the smaller tubing chosen. The living room requirements are met by two coils or lengths comparable to those in other rooms.

10. Size of Mains

Mains A and L convey more than 35,000 Btu per hr. Reference to Table 10. results in the selection of 1¼ in. mains at these two points. All other mains can be 1 in. because their capacities are less than 35,000 Btu. The mains are shown in heavy lines on Fig. 29.

11. Water Flow

Sufficient water must be pumped to make up the gross heat loss. Dividing the gross heat loss of 50,270 Btu by the factor 5000 for a 10 deg drop, 10 gallons per minute is found to be the necessary rate.

12. Selection of a Pump

The pump size will depend upon the rate of pumping and the friction

head through the longest circuit (Coil 3) expressed in ft of water. The path of water and friction of each pipe length may be traced in Table 15. The resulting head of 2.38 ft of water makes no allowance for fittings and equipment for which 50% is commonly added. 2.38 x 1.50 = 3.57 ft of water, total friction head. If these coordinates (10 GPM and 3.57 ft) are plotted on Fig. 8, it will be seen that in this small system the usual minimum pump size of 1 in. is adequate.

13. Boiler

The hourly requirement of this house under design performance is 50,270 Btu for the gross connected heating load. A boiler must be selected to carry this load and also meet the demand for domestic hot water.

14. Compression Tank

A 15 gallon tank will permit the required expansion of the water in this system according to Table 11 since the *net* heat loss is less than 50,000 Btu/hr.

Boiler Connections

The piping arrangements at the boiler are pictured in Fig. 30. For simplicity, some of the boiler controls, valves in the piping and do-

Table 15.   Friction in the longest run (coil 3)

Pipe Identification	Heat Conveyed	Pipe Size	Actual Length	Friction Ft/100 ft Pipe	Friction Head, Ft
A	50,270 Btu	1¼ in.	19 ft	1.8 ft	.34 ft
B	26,520	1	5	2.0	.10
C	19,350	1	18	1.2	.22
D	12,180	1	36	.4	.14
Coil 3	8,550	¾	170*	.8	1.37
K	26,520	1	8	2.0	.16
L	50,270	1¼	3	1.8	.05
Total					2.38 ft
Notes	Fig. 28 & Table 14	Table 10	*160 + 10 ft to header	Fig. 21	

mestic hot water connections have been omitted. The boiler will deliver water through main A at 135 F and it will return through L at 125 F. This is necessary to achieve the 130 deg average water temperature and the 10 deg drop. The bypass from the return line and the temperature regulating valve permit the boiler to operate at 180 deg or more, assuring a temperature high enough for domestic hot water (135 is not enough). The hot water of the boiler is mixed with the cooler return water to produce the supply water at 135. This mixing arrangement is needed in most cases where domestic hot water is generated by the same boiler. It would have to be used if domestic hot water were desired from the boiler in Example 1, Fig. 26. Actual piping might be much more compact than Fig. 30 shows, resulting in the inclusion of the vents and adjusting valves within the utility room. Otherwise, the adjusting valves would have to be in a recess in the floor covered by an access plate. The automatic vents would have to be above the floor in a partition or utility space.

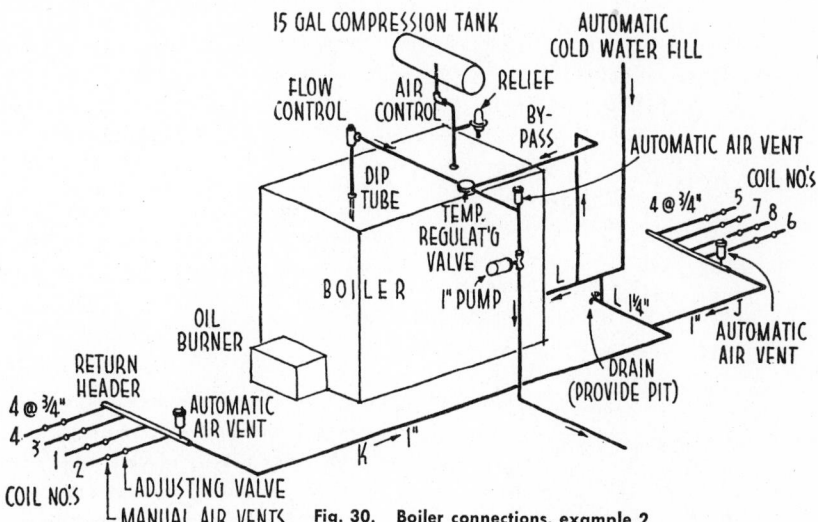

Fig. 30. Boiler connections, example 2

All vents and controls must be accessible.

Venting and Adjustment

The dip tube prevents air from favoring a path through the main. It collects in the air chamber of the compression tank. Entrained air in the supply and return mains is exhausted by the automatic air vents at high points in the supply main and return headers. The manual air vents

are petcocks which can be opened and the air purged from one circuit by closing off the others and pumping through the open circuit only until the air is driven out. This may have to be done at the beginning of operations. The adjusting valves may be used to cut down the flow to coils which are overhot. Care should be taken not to constrict the general flow too much, but only to equalize or balance it.

By WILLIAM J. McGUINNESS, M.E., Professor of Architecture, Pratt Institute

CONTROLS

Basic Assumptions

If domestic hot water need not be generated from the same boiler, the boiler may be used to deliver water at the lower temperature needed for radiant panels. However, since most modern installations produce both water for heating and domestic hot water from the same plant, it will be assumed that the boiler water temperature must be kept at about 180 to 200 F, and that some mixing device is needed to produce water in the usual range of about 100 to 150 deg for use in the radiant panels. The second assumption is that the fuel used is gas or oil, rather than coal. The systems of control described ap-

ply to these two fuels. The third assumption is that high- and low-limit aquastats are used to operate the automatically controlled gas or oil fires to keep the boiler water at a fairly constant temperature for use in the mixing devices.

Water Temperature Control

The common method of delivering water of the temperature required is to mix some of the hot water from the boiler with the cooler return water from the radiant coils. Fig. 31 shows three methods for doing this. The first of these uses gate valves, which may be adjusted manually to deliver water at the correct temperature. An improvement on this scheme is seen

in the second example where a thermostatic mixing valve is used. It can be set to deliver water at any desired temperature provided the boiler water temperature is higher. Either of these is suitable for use with a circulator which operates at intervals to make up the heat losses as required. The third method in Fig. 31 is a blending valve which constantly changes the temperature of the water delivered in accord with the dictates of indoor and outdoor bulbs, as described later. This valve is used with a circulator which operates continually, except that, occasionally, it is turned off for brief intervals when the room temperature exceeds that set for it. The graph in

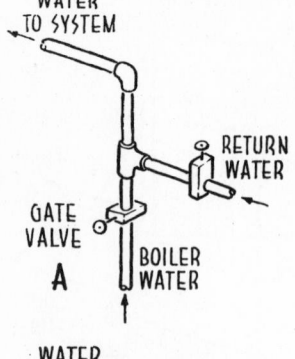

A

Valves on return water and boiler water can be adjusted manually to deliver water to coils at proper design temperature. System works quite satisfactorily with intermittent use of circulator

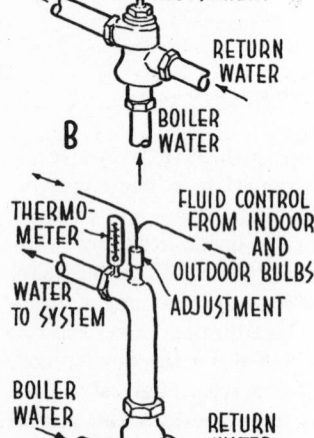

B

Temperature control valve with thermostatic element will assure delivery of water at any predetermined temperature, provided boiler water temperature is higher. It is an improvement over "A" at some additional expense

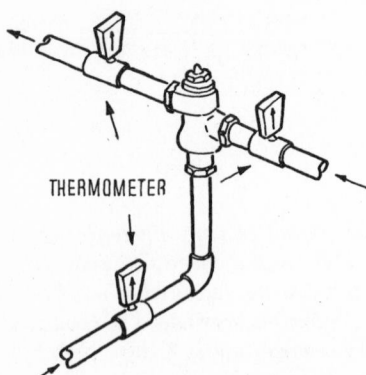

C

When circulator is run continuously, temperature of water delivered to coils can be changed by this automatic blending valve. Control is by indoor and outdoor bulbs

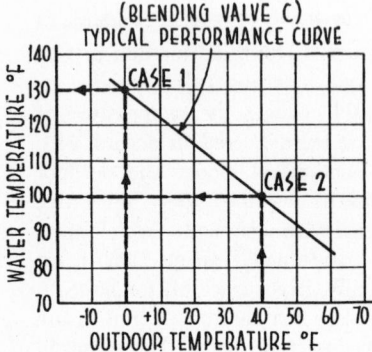

In any system, liberal use of thermometers is recommended as an adjustment aid

(BLENDING VALVE C) TYPICAL PERFORMANCE CURVE

Case 1. Design conditions. Water delivered at design temperature (130° F) when outside temperature is 0° F

Case 2. Mild weather. Water delivered at lower temperature, in this case 100° F, when outside temperature is 40° F

Fig. 31. Three methods of adjusting temperature of water for coils

Fig. 31 shows two typical points on the curve of operations for such a valve. Case 1 occurs when the outside temperature is zero (design temperature in many localities). In this case, the water is delivered at 130 deg, which could be the design temperature called for at this critical condition. At the milder outdoor temperature of 40 deg, the water is delivered at 100 deg, which is sufficient to make up the smaller heat losses which occur at this higher outdoor temperature.

Systems of Control

Two important influences in selecting a control system are the thermal lag of the panel and the amount of glass facing south, which makes solar heating a part of the heating system. For houses having little glass and employing ceiling coils, fixed proportions for water mixing are possible with intermittent use of the circulator, controlled by a simple electric thermostat. (Mixing as shown in Fig. 31, A or B.) Ceiling coils have a fast response. They heat quickly and cool quickly. This house is little influenced by changes in the intensity of sunshine. (Fig. 33 (A) shows arrangement.) Use of floor coils in concrete in this kind of house would preclude the possibility of night set-back because of the thermal lag. Otherwise, the control could be the same. Outdoor control might be of some advantage in this case if budget permits.

In solar houses receiving much heat gain from glass on the south, the use of outdoor controls is recommended in all cases, and they are most necessary with the use of floor coils. It is necessary to anticipate the heat that will come from the sun and to shut off the system before this heat is received. Conversely, when the sun is about to set and outside temperature drops, it is well that the system start in response to an outside sensing device early enough to replace the effect of the sun when it sets. The additional importance of anticipating outside temperature changes by regulating the temperature of coils in concrete slabs is obvious because of their greater thermal lag.

1. Aquastats

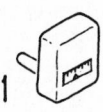

High and low limit immersion aquastats in the boiler water turn fire on and off to maintain water temperature high enough to generate domestic hot water, and for use in radiant coils after mixing

2. Circulating Pump

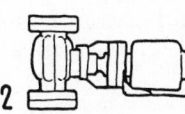

Intermittent use with fixed water temperature or continuous use with varying water temperature are two usual schemes. In both cases, room thermostats or room controls generally stop circulator when room temperature is adequate

3. Thermostat

For intermittent circulator use, thermostat turns circulator on when heat is called for, and off when satisfied. This type with no automatic night set-back is often used when lower temperature is inadvisable at night, as in concrete floor slabs. Heavy slabs recover slowly from low temperatures

4. Clock Thermostat

The temperature of ceiling panels may be lowered at night (morning recovery is fast). For this purpose, clock thermostat may be used

5. Outdoor Thermostat

This device is part of a tandem arrangement. Together with thermostat, it operates circulator. It anticipates cooling off of house by sensing a drop in outdoor temperature and changing the control point of the indoor thermostat. The outdoor thermostat is placed on a north wall

6. Outdoor Bulb

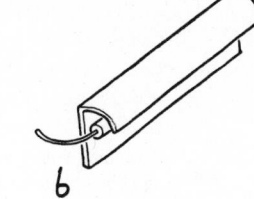

When outdoor temperature drops, outdoor bulb causes a contracting liquid to open valve at boiler water supply, increasing temperature of mixed water. With outside rise, reverse occurs. It is placed on a north wall

7. Indoor Bulb

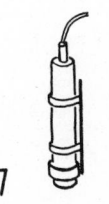

This is operated by the thermostat. When room temperature exceeds setting of room control, it warms indoor bulb electrically. Indoor bulb then delivers an expanding liquid to blending valve. This tends to close boiler water opening in blending valve, reducing temperature of water delivered.

8. Blending Valve

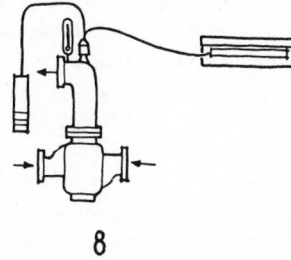

Continuous use of circulator demands varying water temperature. Increased temperatures of either indoor or outdoor bulb cause an expanding liquid to depress mechanically the valve which admits hot boiler water to mixture. This reduces temperature of water delivered to system. With decreasing bulb temperatures, hotter water is delivered

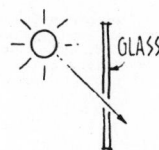

200 ± Btu
Per Sq. Ft.
Per Hour

9. The Sun

In solar houses with much glass on the south, sun is part of heating system and is more than adequate to heat a house. Interior heating system, or at least the south zone, must turn off when sun is operating

Fig. 32.   Control devices (see Fig. 33 for combined uses)

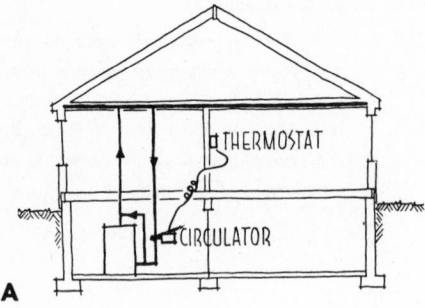

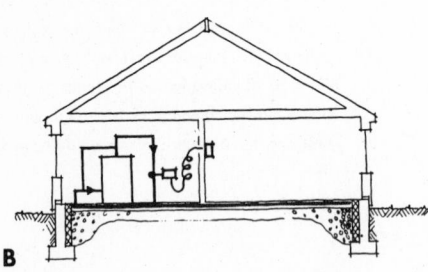

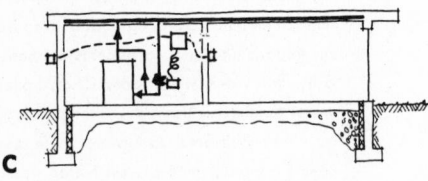

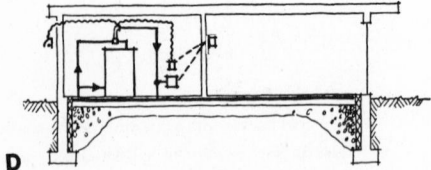

Fig. 33. Recommended control systems for radiant panels

A. Conventional House, Ceiling Panel

Glass represents about 10 to 20 per cent of wall areas, orientation is unimportant. Circulator is operated intermittently by clock thermostat which can serve for night set-back. Outdoor controls not needed

B. Conventional House, Floor Panel in Concrete Slab

Glass and orientation same as case "A" above. Plain thermostat without night set-back operates circulator intermittently. Outdoor controls are of some advantage. If used, they could be as in case D below. Night set-back not recommended because of slow return of slab temperature

C. Solar House, Glass on South, Ceiling Panel, Intermittent Circulation

Circulation of water at constant temperature is begun when either indoor or outdoor thermostat senses a temperature drop. Circulator is shut off when either thermostat senses a suitable increase in temperature

D. Solar House, Glass on South, Floor Panel in Convective Slabs, Blending Valve Control

Outdoor bulb and combination of room thermostat and indoor bulb regulate blending valve. Temperature of water varies to compensate for varying outdoor temperatures. Circulator operation is continuous unless indoor bulb cannot cool slab quickly enough, in which case room control turns off circulator. No night set-back.
Note: System may be used for ceiling panel as in case "C" without change except night set-back may be added

and in larger installations, both situations where, because of great thermal capacity, the panels would not be flexible enough to follow quick changes in heat delivered to coils.

ZONING
Selection of Zones

In planning modern solar houses the first zone to identify is the no-sun zone. In Fig. 34 it is on the north side of the house. It receives no sun during the day, and at low outdoor temperatures the heating panels might operate all day. Under these same conditions and when the sun is shining, all south zones might be turned off. A further split could be between the sleeping and living wings. This is possible only when ceiling systems are used, permitting night set-back. Further zones might be suggested by remote, isolated wings or second stories. In these cases, the north sides of isolated wings or upper stories should still be separately zoned if the south receives much sun during the day.

Piping For Zone Control

The piping which is shown in Figs. 26 and 30 for single zone systems would have to be modified for multi-zone operation. For instance, in a three-zone system such as shown in Fig. 34, a header would be needed to receive the mixed water. The three mains serving the zones would each start through a separate flow-control valve. The piping for each zone would run separately and return as a zone-return-main from each of the zones. A circulating pump would serve each individual zone-return-main before the return water was assembled in a master return header.

Controls for Zoning

A full set of controls is required for each zone. In the house shown in Fig. 34, three sets of controls are needed. A ceiling system is assumed. If the controls were electric, they would comprise three each of: clock thermostat and outdoor thermostat. If continuous operation were selected, the controls would

Selecting A System

In Fig. 33 electric and mechanical systems are shown for the control of radiant panels. In general, the electric systems use a fixed water **temperature adjustment with intermittent circulator operation, while the mechanical systems use a blending valve and continual circulator** operation. Each has its particular merits. The electric system is inexpensive and very sensitive. The **system of continuous circulator operation has the advantage of adjusting closely to the actual heat loss from the house. By some it is thought** that continuous operation is a distinct advantage in floor slab panels

comprise three each of: blending valve, outdoor bulb, indoor bulb, and thermostat. In either case, three pumps and three flow-control valves would be needed. In some designs, the separate zone pumps are replaced by a single pump and motorized valves on the several zone supply pipes, controlled by the equipment described.

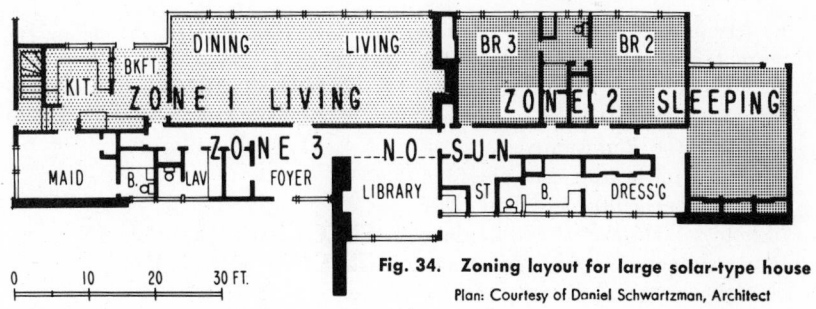

Fig. 34. Zoning layout for large solar-type house
Plan: Courtesy of Daniel Schwartzman, Architect

By WILLIAM J. McGUINNESS, M.E., *Professor of Architecture, Pratt Institute*

PLANNING AND OPERATION

There is little difference in the performance of a good radiant system whether the heating medium is hot water or electricity. There are, however, several good qualities in the planning and operation of electric systems in preference to hot water systems when the relative cost permits the use of electricity. They are:

1. A switch and thermostat in each room makes control much easier and more compact than more bulky and costly controls of hot water. Individual control of rooms is seldom attempted in hot water radiant heating.
2. There is greater freedom of planning due to the elimination of pipes, utility rooms, fuel storage.
3. There is no need for drainage in cold weather when the house is left unoccupied and unheated.
4. Water leaks are eliminated.
5. Flue gas odors and the possibility of carbon monoxide poisoning are eliminated.
6. There is frequently a lower fire risk when low temperature resistance wires replace a fuse.
7. Faster response in the use of glass wall panels and prefabricated panels of thin material for ceiling installations.
8. No responsibility in ordering fuel.

Economy

Electric radiant heating is nearly always cheaper to install than hot water radiant. Sometimes the saving

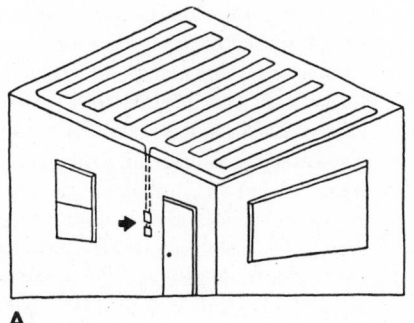

A.

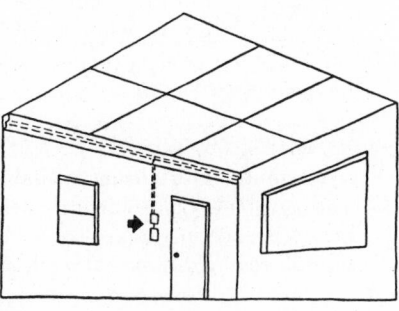

B.

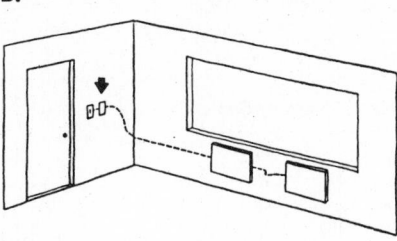

C.

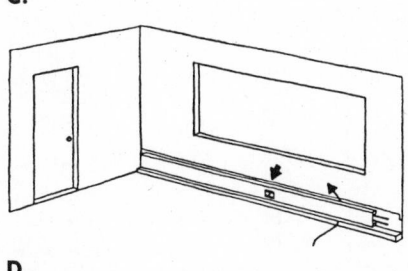

D.

Fig. 35. Methods of electric radiant heating

A. Electric Cables in Ceiling or Floor

Low-temperature, insulated heating wire imbedded in the plaster or in concrete floors and connected to the power source by normal wiring.

    Most invisible system.

    May be used in both ceiling and floor, and concentrated in cold spots.

    Low temperature and even distribution.

B. Prefabricated Ceiling Panels

A layer of rubber containing conductive material set between layers of phenolic resin and backed with asbestos board. Thickness ¼ in. Similar construction in wall-paper thin material and other similar products available.

    Dry construction.

    Thin panel makes for fast response.

    Joints show.

    Low temperature and even distribution.

C. Radiant Glass Panels

Glass panels on the back of which an aluminum grid forms a resistance element for heating.

    Low thermal capacity assures fast response.

    Drapes must not cover.

    Good also as auxiliary panels in other heating systems.

D. Electric Baseboard

A convector type metal baseboard with resistance wires in the protected air space.

    Mostly convective.

    Drapes must not blanket air flow.

    Effective in reversing cold down draft at windows or cold walls.

All four methods suitable to switch and thermostat control in each room.

is very great. The cost of electric current is usually greater than the cost of gas or oil. Depending on the rate per kilowatt-hour in various localities the comparative cost of electricity for heating can vary from the same or slightly less than other fuels to a high level of two or three times as much. A careful comparison of original cost and of yearly expense for fuel, maintenance and amortization of debt must be made for a specific installation in a given location before a choice can be made on the basis of cost. In favor of electricity are the following reductions in items of original cost or the amortization thereof —

1. Elimination of heating equipment such as boilers and burners and the fire-safe construction to house them.
2. Omission of fuel storage equipment and enclosures.
3. Omission of chimney and flue.

Items of periodic expense that may be avoided by the use of electricity are—

A. Yearly cleaning and adjustment of heating plant.
B. Service and replacement of mechanical parts.

Methods of Electric Radiant Heating

These may be grouped into four categories (see Fig. 35):

1. Electric cables in ceiling or floor
2. Prefabricated ceiling panels
3. Radiant glass or ceramic panels
4. Electric baseboard

ELECTRIC CABLES IN CEILING OR FLOOR

The Method

Factory made units consisting of coils of resistance wiring with special insulation and connected to non-heating leads are used (Table 16). In each room, one or more of these units are imbedded in the plaster ceiling or the concrete floor or both. They are connected in parallel through a thermostat to a room switch. Each room is served by wiring connected to a general load center where overload protection is provided. For the larger outputs higher voltage is selected resulting in a smaller current and smaller wires to serve the heating elements. The general electric service for lighting and other non-heating use joins the heating load center and is connected to the main house switch.

Material and Equipment Used

A manufacturer's list of available heating cables is shown in Table 16. They are made in various lengths to suit different conditions. It will be noted that all the cables have an output of precisely 2.75 watts per ft of length. It is necessary only to select the necessary length to make up the room heat loss. Element outputs in Btu per hour may be found by the conversion factor of 1 watt equals 3.41 Btu per hour. The smallest and largest units have outputs as follows —

Unit 1   195 Watts
          665 Btu per hour

Unit 15 2810 Watts
          9600 Btu per hour

Small bathrooms frequently have an hourly heat loss of about 1200 Btu per hour and a large modern living room with much glass often has a loss of 30,000 Btu per hour. Thus small and average rooms will require one unit while large rooms may require as many as three or four, corresponding to the three or four coils of pipe or tubing in a large room heated by hot water radiant coils.

Special thermostats have been developed by manufacturers of equipment for electric radiant heating. Some of these when connected to two coils in parallel will operate one coil in mild weather at low output and connect the second coil under severe conditions for full output. Wiring from room controls to the load center is installed in accord with long-existing rules of the National Electric

Table 16. Typical schedule of heating elements

1 Unit No.	2 Rated Volts	3 Rated Watts	4 Length, Feet
1		195	70
2		421	153
3	120	885	322
4		1120	407
5		1405	510
6		350	128
7		775	281
8	220	1620	590
9		2055	747
10		2570	935
11		390	140
12		840	306
13	240	1770	644
14		2240	814
15		2810	1020

Conversion Factor 1 watt = 3.41 Btu per hour

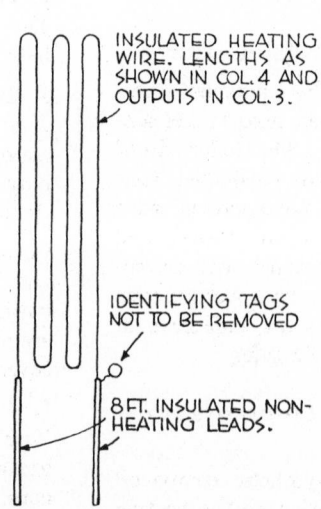

INSULATED HEATING WIRE. LENGTHS AS SHOWN IN COL. 4 AND OUTPUTS IN COL. 3.

IDENTIFYING TAGS NOT TO BE REMOVED

8 FT. INSULATED NON-HEATING LEADS.

Units must be used as received from the manufacturer. Shortening the heating wire or the leads will void the approval by Underwriters Laboratories. Ratings, courtesy of L. N. Roberson Co., Seattle, Washington.

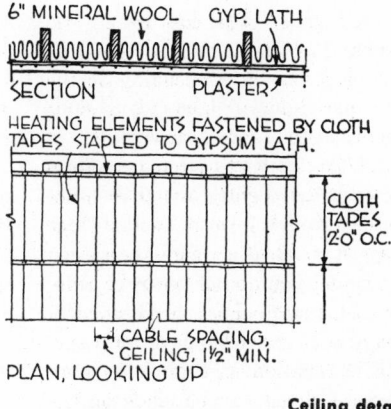

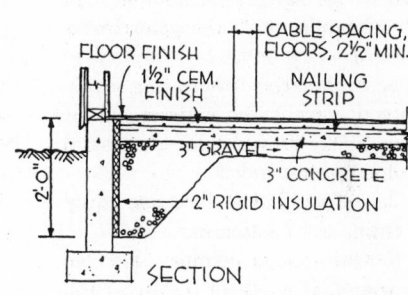

Ceiling details

Floor details

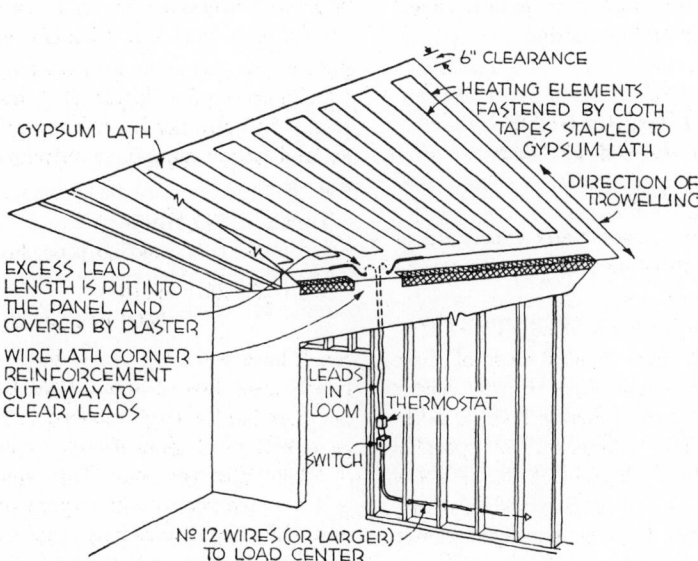

Fig. 36. Installation methods

Code. The only variation from conventional wiring is that at some locations this non-heating supply wiring passes in enclosed joist spaces directly adjacent to the heating elements. Here the wire and insulation must be selected to operate at temperatures higher than the usual house temperature. This higher temperature is assumed to average 50 deg Centigrade (122 F).

Underwriters' Approval

In the use of this equipment architects and engineers need to feel confident of its safety. The Underwriters' Laboratories have conducted tests and have given full approval when labelled products are chosen and installed in accordance with recommended practices. The following tests and their results are indicative of qualities needed for safety:

1. Physical Properties of Insulation

The special synthetic compound used as insulation on the heating element was found to be satisfactory in tensile strength and elongation.

2. Electrical Properties of Insulation

Tests proved these to be acceptable in spite of the wetting processes of plastering and concreting.

3. Factory Splices

The connection of the heating element to the non-heating leads was found strong, well insulated.

4. Input Test

The rated input was checked and found to be as stated.

5. Burnout Test

The heating elements withstood reasonable overloads and will not burnout if properly fused.

6. Mechanical Abuse Test

Considerable care is needed to protect heating wire and insulation during installation. Check tests are recommended during and after covering the wire.

7. Cracks in Concrete

Wire and insulation were not broken by cracking simulating normal settlement of a house. Only violent cracking damaged units.

8. Temperature Test

It was found that wires supplying the heating elements and located in the structure adjacent to the heated surfaces should be selected to operate in temperatures higher than room temperatures.

9. Resistance of Insulation in Place

When insulation was purposely damaged it showed as a bad condition while the plaster and concrete were wet but it improved as these materials dried out.

10. Locating Damaged Insulation

It is possible to locate damaged insulation of wires imbedded in plaster or concrete by a metal probe moving on panel surface.

METHODS OF INSTALLATION

Fig. 36 shows typical methods of installing cables in ceiling or floor panels. In ceilings the ½ in. diameter heating element is held against gypsum lath by cloth tapes 2 ft on centers. Staples through the tape on each side of the wire hold both tape and wire against the lath. Excess

ELECTRIC CABLES IN CEILING OR FLOOR (Cont.)

lead length must not be cut off and may be attached to the ceiling like the heating wire and later imbedded in plaster. Leads run through protective covering known as loom to the thermostat. Heating wires are usually kept about 6 in. clear of side walls and may be spaced evenly throughout the ceiling or concentrated in areas of greatest heat loss. All metal including metal lath corner reinforcement must be kept 2 in. clear of wiring. Plaster is applied in the direction of the heating wires and great care must be exercised to prevent damage to the wire or insulation. For insulation in the roof joist space above panels 6 in. of mineral wool is recommended.

Floor installations are made by fastening the heating wires to a concrete slab by cementing them in place or tacking them through cloth tapes to nailing strips imbedded in the concrete surface. The wires are then surrounded and covered by a 1½ in. dense cement finish. Gravel below the slab and 2 in. of rigid perimeter insulation follow the usual radiant heating requirements for slab insulation. The leads that connect to the floor heating element can be run in rigid conduit. Round-edge bushings of insulating material protect the leads as they enter the metal junction boxes.

Inspection and Tests

When the heating wires are in place and fastened but not covered and when all other wiring is installed and not closed an inspection should be called for. An ohm-meter or megger is used for checking possible damage to insulation. A lamp in series with the heating element will flicker or go out to indicate a severed heating wire. Tests should be made both before and after plastering or concreting. If trouble is found at either time, broken wires can have repair splices applied and damaged insulation can be reinforced by thermoplastic tape.

Design Procedure

1. Compute hourly heat losses in each room without regard to the planned location of the panels. Losses should include heat flow through floors, ceilings, walls, perimeter and glass. Infiltration must be included.
2. Divide the hourly heat loss from each room in Btu per hr by the factor of 3.14 to obtain the required wattage of units to be selected for the room.
3. Select from Table 16 one or more standard heating units for each room. Their total rated wattage must equal the wattage required in the room.
4. Make a layout of the placing of these units, maintaining a minimum spacing of 1½ in. for ceilings and 2½ in. for floors.
5. Select locations for room thermostats where they will not be too directly affected by sunlight, draughts or the action of heating panels.
6. Make a layout of the connections from rooms to the load center and size all wiring.
7. Design the load center and show its connection to other general house wiring for lighting, etc., and to the house switch.

Spacing and Output of Cables

If a coil of heating wire is distributed uniformly over the entire ceiling (or floor) and if one unit is used, the spacing between wires may be established by the formula

$$S = \frac{12 \times (W-1) \times (L-1)}{C}$$

where: S = spacing in inches between turns
W = width of the room in ft
L = length of the room in ft
C = length of the coil in ft

This is based on a space of 6 in. between wire and walls which should be observed. In the case of rooms with great heat loss it is well to consider the maximum possible output of ceiling and floor panels. For ceilings the recommended minimum spacing of 1½ in. between wires gives the following output in Btu per hr per

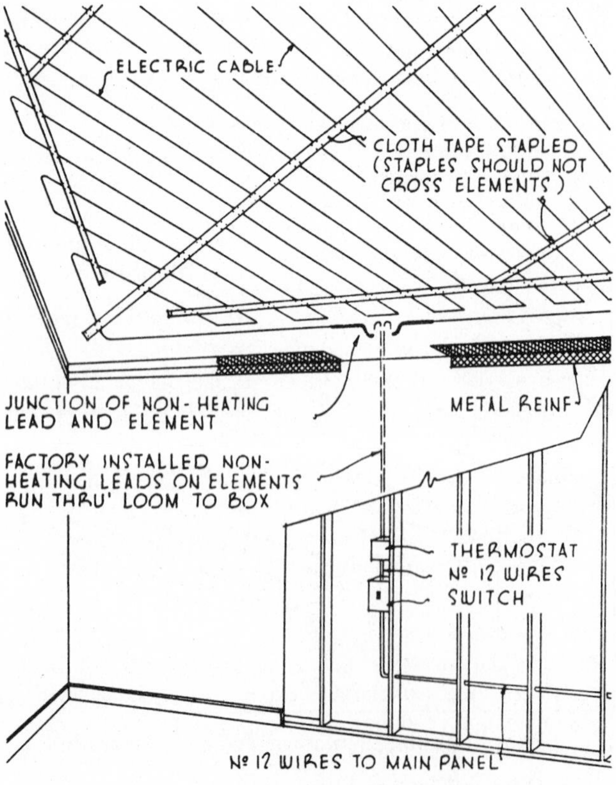

ELECTRIC CABLE

CLOTH TAPE STAPLED (STAPLES SHOULD NOT CROSS ELEMENTS)

JUNCTION OF NON-HEATING LEAD AND ELEMENT

FACTORY INSTALLED NON-HEATING LEADS ON ELEMENTS RUN THRU' LOOM TO BOX

METAL REINF

THERMOSTAT
No 12 WIRES
SWITCH

No 12 WIRES TO MAIN PANEL

Fig. 37. Variation in typical cable layout

sq ft of panel:

$$\frac{12''}{1.5''} \times 2.75 \times 3.14 = 69.5 \text{ Btu per hr-per sq ft}$$

NOTE: 2.75 is the number of watts per ft of length for all cables 3.14 is the number of Btu per hr equal to 1 watt

For floors the recommended minimum spacing is 2½ in. and gives an output of:

$$\frac{12''}{2.5''} \times 2.75 \times 3.14 = 41.5 \text{ Btu per hr-per sq ft}$$

Table 9 will recall the recommended maximum outputs of 75 and 55 Btu per hr per sq ft for ceilings and floors respectively. It will be seen that the maximum outputs that are achieved by the minimum spacing of wires in electrical systems are within these limits.

The heating wires operate at about 165 F and therefore do not subject the plaster to a general average temperature of more than 150 F, which is the practical limit for plaster. If the suggested minimum spacing limits are observed, surface temperature of ceilings will not exceed 115 F and floors 85 F — which are often considered the high limits for comfort.

Use of Gypsum Plaster

The editors wish to express appreciation to the Gypsum Association, and to its general manager, Lloyd H. Yeager, for the data presented in these pages. The association has studied the performance of plaster in ceiling panel radiant heating systems for the past several years and has arrived at the following recommendations for installation and operational procedures.

Types of Systems

The following types of panel heating systems can employ gypsum products:

1. Systems in which small elements for heat conducting mediums, such as pipes up to a maximum of ½ in. o.d., electrical wires or screens, are embedded in plaster.
2. Systems in which larger elements, including pipes exceeding ½ in. o.d., are embedded in plaster.
3. Systems in which the heating elements are located behind the ceiling panel, either directly in contact with the gypsum product or spaced away from it.
4. Convection or plenum systems, where gypsum products form one or more faces of the ducts or plenums.

Plaster Characteristics

Attention to the characteristics of plaster, with reference to the resistance to heat flow through the material, thermal expansion coefficients and densities, is vitally important. Certain precautions must be taken to minimize, for example, cracking due to thermal shock, 'shadowing' under pipes due to unequal drying rates, or unusual calcination which might be caused by overheating.

One of the most important considerations is the type and thickness of plaster specified for the radiant heating job. Heat resistance values vary with the type of plaster and aggregate used. The "k" value (thermal conductance) of gypsum sanded plaster is about 4.25. On the other hand, the "k" value of lightweight aggregate plaster may vary from 1.23 to 1.84, depending on the type of aggregate used and the proportion of plaster to aggregate. The "k" value of some acoustical plasters is as low as .50.

Any proportioning of plaster and aggregate may be specified for the panel heating job, when consideration is taken of the heat losses and the heat flow resistance of the type of plaster specified.

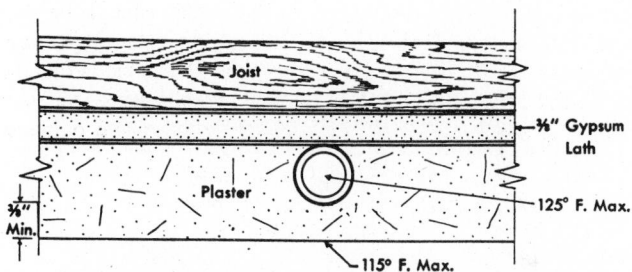

Detail of Recommended Installation Procedure

Where heating elements are embedded in gypsum plaster, a minimum of ⅜ in. plaster thickness must be maintained beneath the heating elements. Ceiling surface temperature should not exceed 115 F, and water temperature in pipes should not exceed 125 F (see footnote on following page)

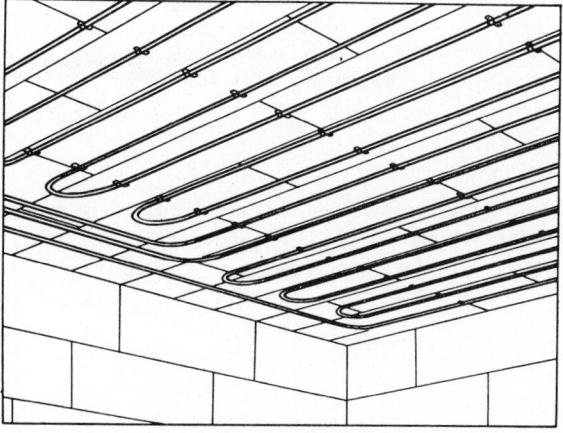

Panel Heating Elements Ready for Plastering

Tubing must be permanently attached to structural framing members, and not to the gypsum lath

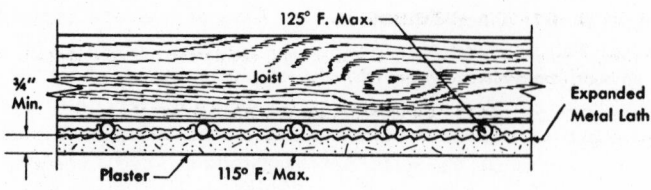

1 In one typical installation of panel heating systems with gypsum plaster, the metal lath is placed below the heating elements. This type of installation requires only the standard plaster thickness of ¾ in., but the plaster keys partially surround the heating elements

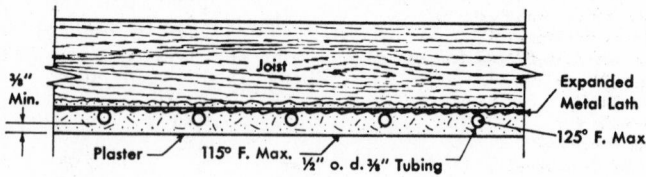

2 In another type of installation which also utilizes metal lath, heating elements, as shown, are completely embedded in plaster and placed below lath. A minimum plaster thickness of ⅜ in. is required beneath the heating elements in this installation

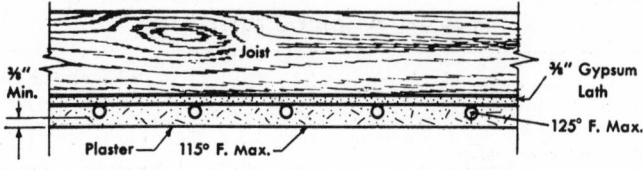

3 A third installation employs gypsum lath, with heating element located directly below plaster base

The heat transmission characteristics of plaster mixes depend on the density of the plaster mix. The densities of set and dry plaster mixes are:

1. Gypsum sanded plaster—105 to 115 lbs per cubic foot
2. Gypsum light-weight-aggregate plaster—40 to 50 lbs per cubic foot

In large unbroken ceiling areas, care should be taken to provide relief for expansion of the panel from the induced heat. Careful attention to the thermal expansion coefficients of plaster mixes is required since plaster will expand and contract to a minute degree. If exposed to abrupt thermal shock, cracking may result.

When gypsum lath and gypsum plaster are used in radiant heating panel systems, they should be used in accordance with the applicable provisions of ASA No. A42.1—1950 "Standard Specifications for Interior Lathing and Furring."

The following points are recommended for the use of gypsum lath and plaster in radiant heat installations:

1. In radiant panel heating systems where gypsum products are employed, the surface temperature should not exceed 115 F.
2. In those systems where pipes are embedded in gypsum plaster, water temperature in the pipes in contact with the plaster must not exceed 125 F.*
3. The temperature of the gypsum plaster should not exceed 90 F or atmospheric temperature (whichever is higher), until the plaster has set and is thoroughly dry. The heating system should not be used to aid in plaster drying.
4. Where heating elements are embedded in gypsum plaster, a minimum of ⅜ in. plaster thickness shall be maintained over the outside of the heating elements.
5. When heating elements are to be embedded in gypsum plaster applied to metal or gypsum lath, the heating elements must be secured to the framing and not to the lath. This does not apply to thin electrical resistance elements embedded in the plaster.
6. When turning the heating system on or off the changes in temperature of the circulating medium should be gradual so that damage from thermal shock will be avoided as much as possible.

*There is some difference of opinion among heating authorities as to the limitation of water temperature to 125 F. Lloyd H. Yeager defends the Gypsum Association's position with the following points: (1) if higher water temperatures are used to permit a wider spacing of pipes or coils (thereby reducing the cost of the system) this would create a less uniform panel surface temperature and, in their opinion, reduce performance quality. (2) According to their laboratory and field tests, a surface temperature of 115 F which required a water temperature of 125 F did not create a hazardous condition within the plaster, but extremely high temperatures may cause plaster failures. This is not to infer that temperatures slightly higher than 125 F are definitely detrimental, but they feel that temperatures of 140 F may be detrimental to the successful performance of a plastered ceiling.

"Check Points and Job Practices"

1. The construction should be inspected closely to make certain that the weight of the heating elements is supported by permanent attachment to the structural framing members.

2. The circulation elements of the system should be checked for leaks and operating efficiency before plastering.

3. Grounds for plaster should be thoroughly checked to insure a minimum plaster coverage of ⅜ in. beneath the heating elements.

4. Care should be exercised that the plaster is mixed and applied according to ASA specifications for the type of plaster specified.

5. The radiant heating system should never be used to heat the building during plastering operations. If the plastering is done in cold weather, it is recommended that heat be furnished by temporary, portable heat circulators, with ventilation. Care must be taken to avoid a concentration of heat on the ceiling, which may result from use of salamanders. The building should be uniformly heated in a range of 55 to 70 F.

6. When the heating system is put in operation the temperature rise should be gradual. It is recommended that the increase in temperature does not exceed 5 degrees F in 24 hours until the maximum temperature within the heating element has been reached.

7. Decoration, including sizing or sealing, should not be started until the heating system has operated at maximum temperature for at least 24 hours. Decorating of the gypsum materials should not be performed while the heating system is in operation.

8. It is also recommended where textures or tinted finishing plasters or decoration begins. The decoration should be allowed to set and dry thoroughly before resumption of heating operations

DESIGN DATA GYPSUM MATERIALS.

The following Conductivities (k) Conductances (c) and Resistances are recommended for use in calculating Heat Transmission Coefficients (U)

HEAT TRANSMISSION CHARACTERISTICS

	C		R	
	k	c	1/k	1/c
Air Spaces				
*Bounded by **ordinary** materials (Horizontal or Vertical)		1.10		0.91
*One air space faced with aluminum foil				
Heat Flow Upward or Horizontally		0.46		2.17
Heat Flow Downward		0.15		6.51
Gypsum lath ⅜″		3.1		0.32
Gypsum lath ½″		2.82		0.35
Gypsum board ⅜″		3.1		0.32
Gypsum board ½″		2.82		0.35
Gypsum lath ⅜″ with Plaster ½″		2.4		0.42
Metal Lath and Plaster ¾″		4.40		0.23
Gypsum Concrete 87½% Gypsum:				
12½% Wood chips	1.66		0.60	
Gypsum Tile 3″		0.61		1.64
Gypsum Tile 4″		0.46		2.18
Gypsum Sheathing ½″		2.82		0.35
Expanded Vermiculite	0.48		2.08	
Perlite	0.48		2.08	
Sand (Ottawa)	10.0		.10	
Plastering Mixes				
Gypsum sand				
100:200 lbs	4.32 to 5.55		0.18 to 0.23	
100:300 lbs	4.24 to 5.77		0.17 to 0.24	
Gypsum Perlite				
100 lb: 2 cu. ft.	1.52 to 1.68		0.60 to 0.65	
100 lb: 3 cu. ft.	1.23 to 1.35		0.74 to 0.81	
Gypsum Vermiculite				
100 lb: 2 cu. ft.	1.78 to 1.84		0.54 to 0.56	
100 lb: 3 cu. ft.	1.44 to 1.63		0.61 to 0.69	

* — ¾″ or more in width

THERMAL EXPANSION COEFFICIENTS

Type of Plaster	Inches per Inch per Degree Fahrenheit
Gypsum Sanded Plaster Gypsum Vermiculite Plaster Gypsum Perlite Plaster	0.000005 to 0.000009
Gypsum Wood Fiber Plaster	0.000009 to 0.000015
Specific Heat of Gypsum ($CaSO_4.2H_2O$)	0.26

DENSITIES

Plaster Mix Set and Dry
(1 part gypsum: 2 parts aggregate to 1 part gypsum to three parts aggregate)

Gypsum—Sanded Plaster	105 to 115 pounds per cu. ft.
Gypsum—Vermiculite Plaster Gypsum—Perlite Plaster	40 to 50 pounds per cu. ft.

through the embedded elements.

9. Be certain the job specifications are being followed. For example, the substitution of one aggregate for another would change the rate of heat flow, which may give results that would make the entire installation unsatisfactory.

The following data are from *American Standard Installation of Gas Appliances and Gas Piping*, ASA Z21.30-1959, sponsored by the American Gas Association, Inc. In applying these standards, reference should also be made to the manufacturer's instructions, serving gas supplier regulations, and local building, heating, plumbing, or other codes in effect in the area in which the installation is made.

PIPING PLAN

It is recommended that before proceeding with the installation of a gas piping system, a piping sketch or plan be prepared showing the proposed location of the piping as well as the size of different branches. Adequate consideration should be given to future demands and provisions made for added gas service.

Gas consumption

The quantity of gas to be provided at each outlet shall be determined, whenever possible, directly from the manufacturer's Btu rating of the appliance which will be installed. In case the ratings of the appliances to be installed are not known, Table 1 is given to show the approximate consumption of average appliances of certain types in Btu per hour.

To obtain the cubic feet per hour of gas required, divide the total Btu input of all appliances by the average Btu heating value per cubic foot of the gas. The average Btu per cubic foot of the gas in the area of the installation may be obtained from the serving gas supplier.

PIPING SIZE

Size of gas piping required can be determined from Tables 2–4 using the length from the meter to the most remote outlet. The tables include an allowance for an average number of fittings. For gas having a specific gravity greater than 0.70, multiply the capacities found in Tables 2 or 3 by the factors listed in Table 5.

Piping material for utility gases

Gas pipe shall be steel or wrought-iron pipe complying with the American Standard for Wrought-Steel and Wrought-Iron Pipe, ASA B36.10-1950. Threaded copper or brass pipe in iron pipe sizes may be used with gases not corrosive to such materials.

Piping material for liquefied petroleum gases

Gas piping for use with undiluted liquefied petroleum gases shall be steel or

Table 1. Approximate gas input for some common appliances

Appliance		Btu per hr Input (approx.)
Range, free standing, domestic		65,000
Built-in oven or broiler unit, domestic		25,000
Built-in top unit, domestic		40,000
Water heater, automatic storage 30- to 40-gal tank		45,000
Water heater, automatic storage 50-gal tank		55,000
Water heater, automatic instantaneous		
Capacity	2 gal per minute	142,800
	4 gal per minute	285,000
	6 gal per minute	428,400
Water heater, domestic, circulating or side-arm		35,000
Refrigerator		3,000
Clothes dryer, domestic		35,000

For specific appliances or appliances not shown above, the input should be determined from the manufacturer's rating.

wrought-iron pipe, brass or copper pipe, or seamless copper, brass, steel, or aluminum tubing. All pipe or tubing shall be suitable for a working pressure of not less than 125 lb per sq in. Copper tubing may be of the standard grade K or L, or equivalent, having a minimum wall thickness of 0.032 in. Aluminum tubing shall not be used in exterior locations or where it is in contact with masonry or plaster walls or insulation.

CONCEALED PIPING

Concealed piping shall not be smaller than ½ in. iron pipe size, and shall not be located in solid partitions. In solid floors such as concrete, piping should be laid in channels in the floor and be suitably covered to permit access. Underground piping should be one size larger than shown in Tables 1 and 2, but not less than 1¼ in. in diameter. Piping must not be laid in contact with cinders. Where piping passes through the foundation it should be protected by a sleeve and sealed tight. Where piping passes under a building it should be run in a watertight, vented conduit.

INSTALLATION OF PIPING

All gas piping shall be pitched not less than ¼ in. in 15 ft. Provide drips at the low points for the collection of condensate and dirt. Piping should not be bent and should be supported by metal hangers spaced not more than shown in Table 6.

Electrical bonding and grounding

A gas piping system within a building

shall be electrically continuous and bonded to any grounding electrode, as defined by the National Electrical Code, ASA C1-1959.

Test methods for piping systems

Before appliances are connected, piping systems shall stand a pressure of at least 6 in. mercury or 3 lb gage for a period of not less than ten minutes without showing any drop in pressure.

Systems for undiluted liquefied petroleum gases shall stand the pressure test in accordance with the above or, when appliances are connected to the piping system, shall stand a pressure of not less than 10 in. water column for a period of not less than ten minutes without showing any drop in pressure.

APPLIANCE INSTALLATION

All gas appliances and accessories installed for domestic or commercial use shall:

1. Be listed by a nationally recognized testing agency, or

2. Comply with applicable American Standard Approval or Listing Requirements covering safe operation, substantial and durable construction and acceptable performance, or

3. Be acceptable to the authority having jurisdiction.

The word "listed" refers to appliances and accessories which are shown in a list published by an approved nationally recognized testing agency such as the American Gas Association, Inc., Laboratories, and Underwriters' Laboratories, Inc.

DRAFT HOODS

Every vented appliance, except incinerators, dual oven-type combination ranges, appliances with sealed combustion chambers and units designed for power burners or for forced venting, shall be installed with a draft hood. The draft hood supplied with or forming a part of listed vented appliances shall be installed without alteration, exactly as furnished and specified by the appliance manufacturer. If a draft hood is not supplied by the appliance manufacturer when one is required, it shall be supplied by the installing agency and be of a listed or approved type, and in the absence of other instructions shall be the same size as the appliance flue collar.

The draft hood shall be in the same room as the combustion air opening of the appliance. In no case shall a draft hood be installed in a false ceiling, in a different room, or in any manner that will permit a difference in pressure between the draft hood relief opening and the combustion air supply.

Accessibility for service

Every gas appliance shall be located with respect to building construction and other equipment so as to permit access to the appliance. Sufficient clearance shall be maintained to permit the cleaning of heating surfaces; the replacement of filters, blowers, motors, burners, controls, and vent connections; the lubrication of moving parts where required; and the adjustment and cleaning of burners and pilots. For attic installation the passageway and servicing area adjacent to the appliance shall be floored.

Permissible temperatures on combustible materials

All gas appliances and their vent connectors shall be installed so that continued or intermittent operation will not create a hazard to persons or property. They shall not, during operation, raise the temperature of unprotected combustible walls, partitions, floors, or ceilings more than 90°F above normal room temperature.

AIR FOR COMBUSTION AND VENTILATION

Appliances shall be installed in a location in which the facilities for ventilation permit satisfactory combustion of gas, proper venting, and the maintenance of ambient temperature at safe limits under normal conditions of use. Appliances shall be located in such a manner as not to interfere with proper circulation of air with-

Table 2. Maximum capacity of pipe in cubic feet of gas per hour

Based upon a pressure drop of 0.3 in. water column and 0.6 specific gravity gas.

Nominal iron pipe size, inches	Length in feet													
	10	20	30	40	50	60	70	80	90	100	125	150	175	200
½	132	92	73	63	56	50	46	43	40	38	34	31	28	26
¾	278	190	152	130	115	105	96	90	84	79	72	64	59	55
1	520	350	285	245	215	195	180	170	160	150	130	120	110	100
1¼	1050	730	590	500	440	400	370	350	320	305	275	250	225	210
1½	1600	1100	890	760	670	610	560	530	490	460	410	380	350	320
2	3050	2100	1650	1450	1270	1150	1050	990	930	870	780	710	650	610
2½	4800	3300	2700	2300	2000	1850	1700	1600	1500	1400	1250	1130	1050	980
3	8500	5900	4700	4100	3600	3250	3000	2800	2600	2500	2200	2000	1850	1700
4	17500	12000	9700	8300	7400	6800	6200	5800	5400	5100	4500	4100	3800	3500

Table 3. Maximum capacity of pipe in cubic feet of gas per hour

Based upon a pressure drop of 0.5 in. water column and 0.6 specific gravity gas.

Nominal iron pipe size, inches	Length in feet													
	10	20	30	40	50	60	70	80	90	100	125	150	175	200
½	175	120	97	82	73	66	61	57	53	50	44	40	37	35
¾	360	250	200	170	151	138	125	118	110	103	93	84	77	72
1	680	465	375	320	285	260	240	220	205	195	175	160	145	135
1¼	1400	950	770	660	580	530	490	460	430	400	360	325	300	280
1½	2100	1460	1180	990	900	810	750	690	650	620	550	500	460	430
2	3950	2750	2200	1900	1680	1520	1400	1300	1220	1150	1020	950	850	800
2½	6300	4350	3520	3000	2650	2400	2250	2050	1950	1850	1650	1500	1370	1280
3	11000	7700	6250	5300	4750	4300	3900	3700	3450	3250	2950	2650	2450	2280
4	23000	15800	12800	10900	9700	8800	8100	7500	7200	6700	6000	5500	5000	4600

in the confined space. In unconfined spaces in buildings of conventional construction, infiltration normally is adequate to provide air for combustion, ventilation, and draft hood dilution. When buildings are so tight that normal infiltration does not meet air requirements, outside air shall be introduced.

Air for combustion, ventilation, and draft hood dilution for gas appliances vented by natural draft normally may be obtained by application of one of the methods covered in Figs. 1–5.

Louvers and grilles

In calculating free area, consideration shall be given to the blocking effect of louvers, grilles or screens protecting openings. Screens used shall not be smaller than ¼ in. mesh. If the free area through a design of louver or grille is known, it should be used in calculating the size opening required to provide the free area specified. If the design and free area are not known, it may be assumed that wood louvers will have 20–25 per cent free area and metal louvers and grilles will have 60–75 per cent free area.

CLEARANCES

Domestic ranges

Clearance from combustible material: Listed domestic ranges when installed on combustible floors shall be set on their own bases or legs and shall be installed with clearances of not less than shown on the marking plate and the manufacturer's instructions. In the absence of clearance information on the marking plate, the range shall be installed with clearances not

Table 4. Capacity of semirigid tubing of different outside diameters and lengths

Measured in thousands of Btu per hour of undiluted liquefied petroleum gases at a pressure drop of 0.50 in. water column.

Outside diameter, inches	Length of tubing, ft									
	10	20	30	40	50	60	70	80	90	100
⅜	39	26	21	19						
½	92	62	50	41	37	35	31	29	27	26
⅝	199	131	107	90	79	72	67	62	59	55
¾	329	216	181	145	131	121	112	104	95	90
⅞	501	346	277	233	198	187	164	155	146	138

Table 5. Multipliers to be used only with Tables 2 and 3 when applying the gravity factor

Specific Gravity	Multiplier	Specific Gravity	Multiplier
.35	1.31	1.00	.78
.40	1.23	1.10	.74
.45	1.16	1.20	.71
.50	1.10	1.30	.68
.55	1.04	1.40	.66
.60	1.00	1.50	.63
.65	.96	1.60	.61
.70	.93	1.70	.59
.75	.90	1.80	.58
.80	.87	1.90	.56
.85	.84	2.00	.55
.90	.82	2.10	.54

Table 6. Minimum spacing of supports for gas piping

Size of Pipe (Inches)	(Feet)	Size of Tubing (Inch O.D.)	(Feet)
½	6	½	4
¾ or 1	8	⅝ or ¾	6
1¼ or larger (horizontal)	10	⅞ or 1	8
1¼ or larger (vertical)	every floor level		

less than shown in Table 6. In no case shall the clearance be such as to interfere with requirements for combustion air, accessibility for operation, and servicing.

Unlisted domestic ranges shall be installed with at least a 6-in. clearance from back and sides. Combustible floors under unlisted appliances shall be protected in an approved manner.[1]

[1] *For details of protection refer to NBFU Code for the Installation of Heat Producing Appliances, available from the National Board of Fire Underwriters, 85 John St., New York, 38, N.Y.*

Vertical clearance above cooking top

Domestic ranges shall have a vertical clearance above the cooking top of not less than 30 in. to combustible material or metal cabinets. When the underside of such combustible material or metal cabinets is protected with asbestos millboard at least ¼ in. thick covered with sheet metal of not less than No. 28 U.S. gage the distance shall be not less than 24 in. The protection shall extend 9 in. beyond the sides of the range.

Built-in domestic cooking units

Listed built-in domestic cooking units shall be installed in accordance with their listing and the manufacturer's instructions. Listed built-in domestic cooking units may be installed in combustible material unless otherwise marked.

The installation shall not interfere with the requirements for combustion air and accessibility for operation and servicing.

Unlisted built-in domestic cooking units shall not be installed in, or adjacent to, combustible material.

Water heaters

Water heaters shall not be installed in bathrooms, bedrooms, or any occupied rooms normally kept closed.

Water heaters shall be located as close as practicable to the chimney or gas vent. They should be located so as to provide short runs of piping to fixtures.

Listed water heaters shall be installed in accordance with their listing and the manufacturer's instructions. In no case shall the clearances be such as to interfere with the requirements for combustion air, draft hood clearance and relief, and accessibility for servicing (see Table 7).

Unlisted water heaters shall be installed with a clearance of 12 in. on all sides and rear. Combustible floors under unlisted water heaters shall be protected in an approved manner.[1]

Room heaters

Room heaters installed in sleeping quarters for use of transients, as in hotels, motels and auto courts, shall be of the vented type and shall be connected to an effective chimney or gas vent and equipped with an automatic pilot.

Listed room heaters shall be installed with clearances not less than specified in Table 8. Unlisted room heaters shall be installed with clearances from combustible material not less than the following: circulating type with outer jacket, 12 in. at sides and rear; radiating type, 18 in. at sides and rear. Combustible floors under

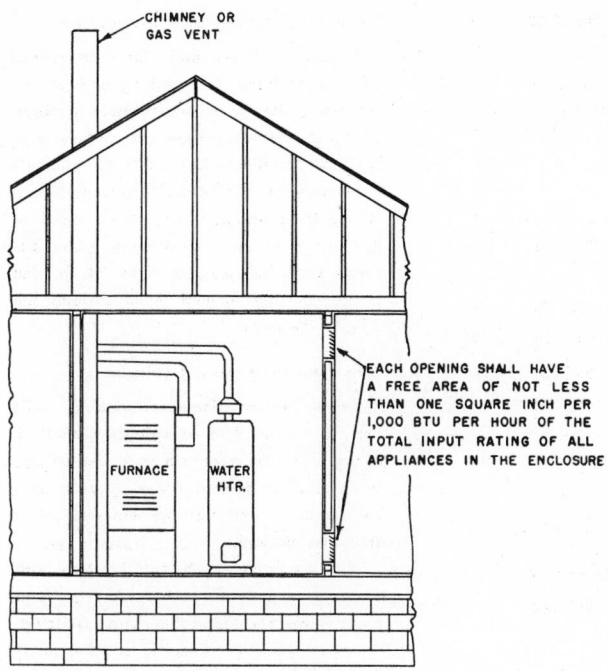

Fig. 1. Appliances located in confined spaces

All air from inside the building.

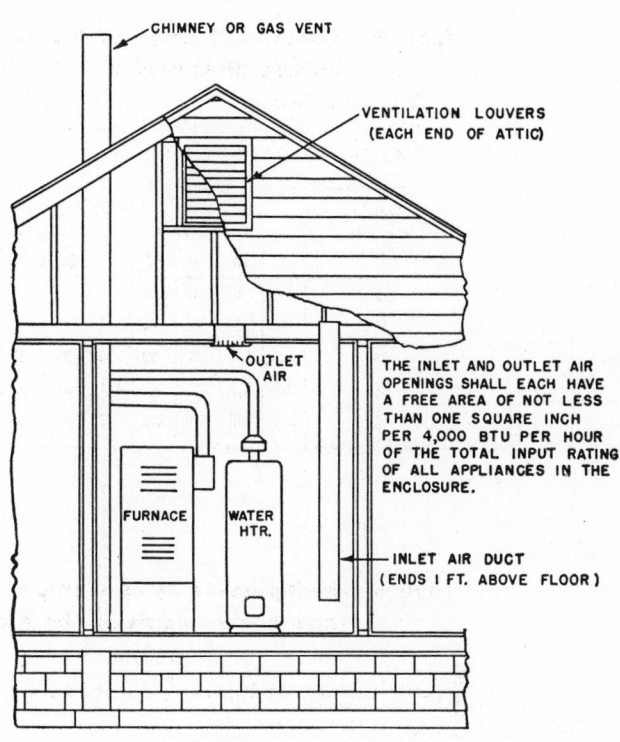

Fig. 3. Appliances located in confined spaces

All air from outdoors through ventilated attic.

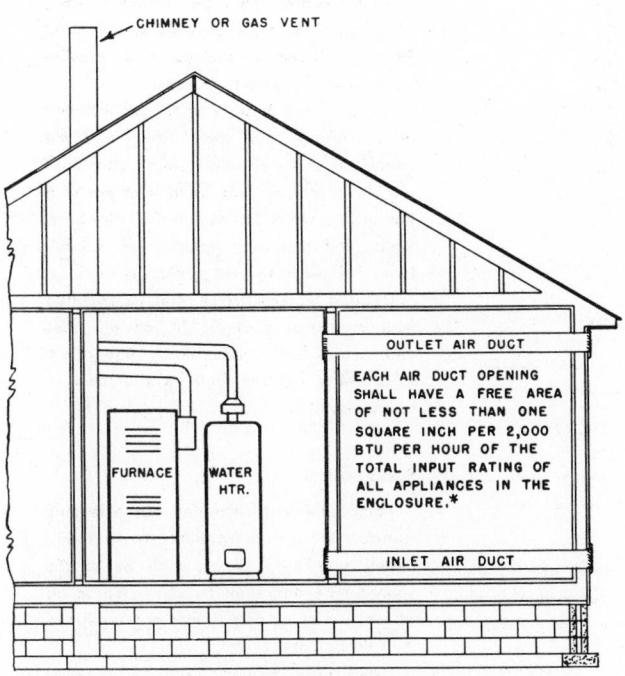

*IF THE APPLIANCE ROOM IS LOCATED AGAINST AN OUTSIDE WALL AND THE AIR OPENINGS COMMUNICATE DIRECTLY WITH THE OUTDOORS, EACH OPENING SHALL HAVE A FREE AREA OF NOT LESS THAN ONE SQUARE INCH PER 4,000 BTU PER HOUR OF THE TOTAL INPUT RATING OF ALL APPLIANCES IN THE ENCLOSURE.

Fig. 2. Appliances located in confined spaces

All air from outdoors.

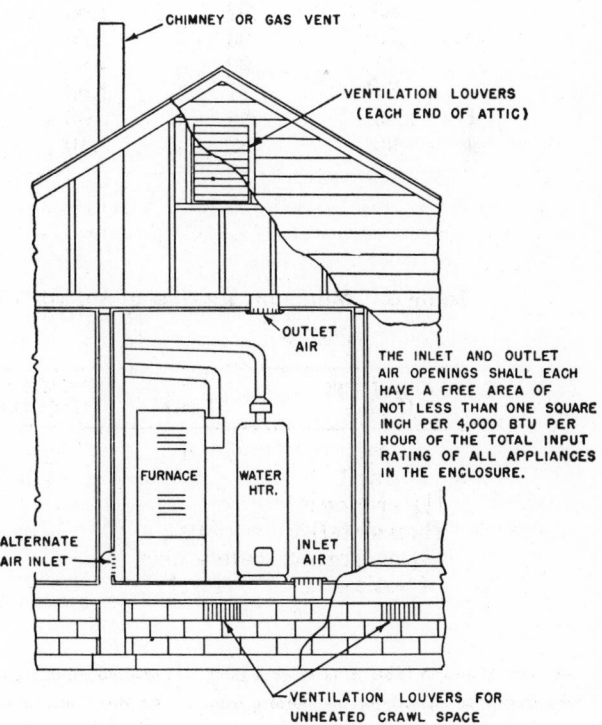

Fig. 4. Appliances located in confined spaces

All air from outdoors—inlet air from ventilated crawl space and outlet air to ventilated attic.

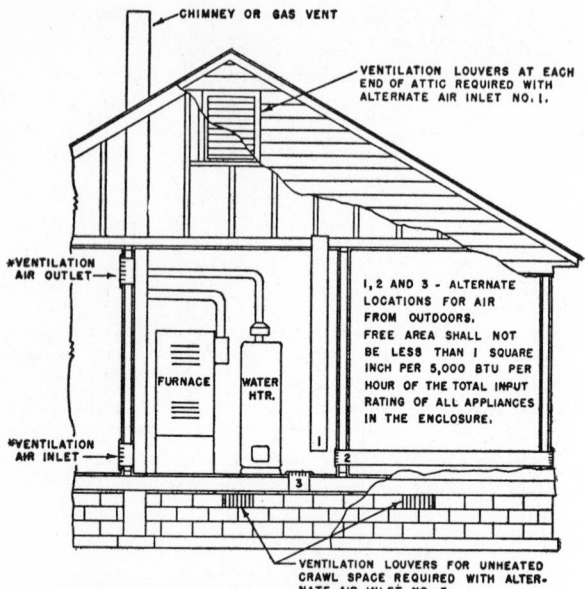

DUCTS USED FOR MAKE-UP AIR MAY BE CONNECTED TO THE COLD AIR RETURN OF THE HEATING SYSTEM ONLY IF THEY CONNECT DIRECTLY TO OUTDOOR AIR.

CHIMNEY OR GAS VENT

VENTILATION LOUVERS AT EACH END OF ATTIC REQUIRED WITH ALTERNATE AIR INLET NO. I.

*VENTILATION AIR OUTLET

1, 2 AND 3 - ALTERNATE LOCATIONS FOR AIR FROM OUTDOORS. FREE AREA SHALL NOT BE LESS THAN I SQUARE INCH PER 5,000 BTU PER HOUR OF THE TOTAL INPUT RATING OF ALL APPLIANCES IN THE ENCLOSURE.

FURNACE   WATER HTR.

*VENTILATION AIR INLET

VENTILATION LOUVERS FOR UNHEATED CRAWL SPACE REQUIRED WITH ALTERNATE AIR INLET NO. 3.

*EACH VENTILATION AIR OPENING FROM INSIDE THE BUILDING SHALL HAVE A FREE AREA OF NOT LESS THAN I SQUARE INCH PER 1,000 BTU PER HOUR OF THE TOTAL INPUT RATING OF ALL APPLIANCES IN THE ENCLOSURE.

Fig. 5. Appliances located in confined spaces

Ventilation air from inside building—combustion and draft hood dilution air from outside, ventilated attic or ventilated crawl space.

Table 7. Minimum clearances for listed water heaters

Type of Heater*	Distance from Combustible Material Inches	
	Nearest Part of Jacket	Flat Side
Type A	6	- - -
Type B	2	- - -
Type C	- - -	Flush
Counter Type Unit	In accordance with manufacturer's instructions.	

* Type A—Miscellaneous (including circulating tank, instantaneous, uninsulated, underfired).
Type B—Underfired, insulated automatic storage heaters.
Type C—Type B units with one or more flat sides and tested for installation flush to wall.
Counter Type—Type B units specifically designed for installation in or beneath a counter.

Table 8. Minimum clearances for listed room heaters

Types of Appliance	Distance from Combustible Material, Inches	
	Jacket, Sides and Rear	Projecting Flue Box or Draft Hood
Warm Air Circulators	6	2
Radiant Heaters	6	2
Wall Heaters	Flush	. . .

unlisted heaters shall be protected in an approved manner.[1]

Furnaces and boilers

Listed central heating boilers and furnaces installed in rooms which are large in comparison with the size of the appliance, shall be installed with clearances not less than specified in Table 9.

Central heating furnaces and boilers may be installed in rooms, but not in confined spaces such as alcoves and closets, with reduced clearances to combustible material provided the combustible material or the appliance is protected as described in Table 10.

Unlisted central heating boilers and furnaces shall be installed with clearances from combustible material of not less than 18 in. above the appliance and at sides, front and rear, and 9 in. from projecting flue box or draft hood.

APPLIANCES REQUIRED TO BE VENTED

Appliances of the following types shall be vent connected or provided with other means for removing the flue gases to the outside atmosphere.

1. Central heating appliances, including steam and hot water boilers, warm air furnaces, floor furnaces, and vented recessed heaters

2. Unit heaters and duct furnaces

3. Incinerators

4. Water heaters with inputs over 5,000 Btu per hour

5. Built-in domestic cooking units listed and marked as vented units only

6. Room heaters listed for vented use only

7. Appliances equipped with gas conversion burners

8. Other listed appliances which have draft hoods supplied by the appliance manufacturer

When unvented appliances are installed so that the aggregate input rating exceeds 30 Btu per hr per cu ft of room or space in which they are installed, one or more of them shall be vent connected or provided with an approved means for removing the vent gases to the outside atmosphere so that the aggregate input rating of the remaining unvented appliances does not exceed the 30 Btu per hr per cu ft figure. When the room or space in which they are installed is directly connected to an-

other room or space by a doorway, archway, or other opening of comparable size, which cannot be closed, the volume of such adjacent room or space may be included in the calculations.

METHODS OF VENTING

Chimneys shall be used for venting the following types of appliances:

1. Incinerators

2. Appliances which may be converted readily to the use of solid or liquid fuels

3. Combination gas-oil burning appliances

4. Appliances listed for use with chimneys only

Chimneys may be listed, factory-built chimneys, or masonry or metal chimneys built and installed in accordance with nationally recognized building codes.[2]

[2] *Article X of the National Building Code of the National Board of Fire Underwriters, 85 John St., New York 38, N. Y., or the Standards on Chimneys, Flues & Vents NFPA No. 211 of the National Fire Protection Association, 60 Batterymarch St., Boston 10, Mass., are such nationally recognized codes and standards.*

Table 9. Clearances to combustible material for furnaces and boilers installed in rooms which are large in comparison with size of appliance

	Minimum Clearance, Inches				
	Above and Sides of Bonnet or Plenum	Jacket Sides and Rear	Front (See Note 1)	Projecting Flue Box or Draft Hood	Vent Connector
I. Listed or unlisted automatically fired, forced air or gravity system, equipped with 250 F temperature limit control installed in accordance with Note 2.	1 (See Note 3)	6	18	9 (See Note 5)	9 (See Note 5)
II. Listed automatically fired, forced air or gravity system, equipped with limit control not conforming to Note 2, but that will limit outlet air temperature to 250 F. See Note 4.	2	6	18	6	6
III. Heating Boilers — Steam boilers operating at not over 15 pounds gage pressure and hot water boilers operating at not in excess of 250 F of the water-wall type or having a jacket or lining of masonry or other satisfactory material.	6	6	18	9 (See Note 5)	9 (See Note 5)

Notes Applicable to Table 9
1 Front clearance shall be sufficient for servicing the burner and furnace.
2 Listed limit control that cannot be set higher than 250 F installed not more than 10 inches above the top surface of heat exchanger in a supply plenum that extends at least 12 inches above the top surface of the heat exchanger.
3 Clearance above supply ducts within 3 feet of the plenum shall be not less than 1 inch.
4 Clearance above supply ducts within 6 feet of the plenum shall be not less than that specified above the bonnet or plenum.
5 This clearance may be reduced to 6 inches for listed gas burning furnaces and boilers. The gas vent clearance does not apply to listed Type B gas vents.

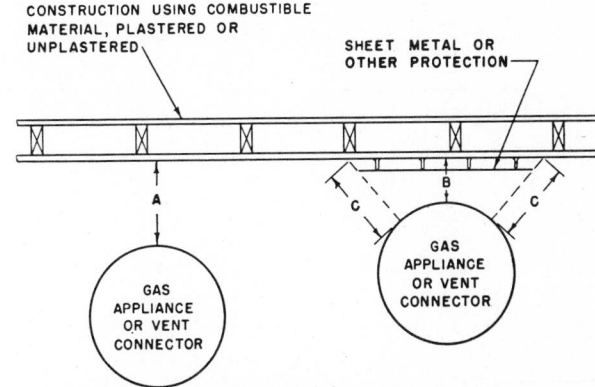

A equals the required clearance with no protection specified in Tables 9 and 11 and in the sections applying to various types of appliances.

B equals the reduced clearance permitted in accordance with Table 10. The protection applied to the construction using combustible material shall extend far enough in each direction to make C equal to A.

Fig. 6. Extent of protection required to reduce clearances from gas appliances or vent connectors

Appliances not required to be connected to chimneys may be vented by gas vents of Type B, B-W, or C. Types B and B-W are listed, factory-made products. Type B-W is for use in combustible walls not more than one story high, for venting listed recessed wall heaters only. Type C gas vent is constructed of sheet copper not less than No. 24 U.S. Standard gage or galvanized iron of not less than No. 20 U.S. Standard gage, or other approved noncombustible corrosion-resistant material.

Type C gas vents shall be used only for runs directly from the space in which the

Table 10. Clearances, in inches, with specified forms of protection*

Type of Protection Applied to the combustible material unless otherwise specified and covering all surfaces within the distance specified as the required clearance with no protection. (See Fig. 11). Thicknesses are minimum.	Where the required Clearance with no protection is:													
	36 inches			18 inches			12 inches		9 inches	6 inches		
	Above	Sides & Rear	Vent Connector	Above	Sides & Rear	Vent Connector	Above	Sides & Rear	Vent Connector	Above	Sides & Rear	Vent Connector
(a) ¼ in. asbestos millboard spaced out 1 in. ▾	30	18	30	15	9	12	9	6	6	3	2	3
(b) 28 gage sheet metal on ¼ in. asbestos millboard	24	18	24	12	9	12	9	6	4	3	2	2
(c) 28 gage sheet metal spaced out 1 in. ▾	18	12	18	9	6	9	6	4	4	2	2	2
(d) 28 gage sheet metal on ⅛ in. asbestos millboard spaced out 1 in. ▾	18	12	18	9	6	9	6	4	4	2	2	2
(e) 1½ in. asbestos cement covering on heating appliance	18	12	36	9	6	18	6	4	9	2	1	6
(f) ¼ in. asbestos millboard on 1 in. mineral fiber bats reinforced with wire mesh or equivalent	18	12	18	6	6	6	4	4	4	2	2	2
(g) 22 gage sheet metal on 1 in. mineral fiber bats reinforced with wire or equivalent	18	12	12	4	3	3	2	2	2	2	2	2
(h) ¼ in. asbestos cement board or ¼ in. asbestos millboard	36	36	36	18	18	18	12	12	9	4	4	4
(i) ¼ in. cellular asbestos	36	36	36	18	18	18	12	12	9	3	3	3

* Except for the protection described in (e), all clearances shall be measured from the outer surface of the appliance to the combustible material disregarding any intervening protection applied to the combustible material.
▾ Spacers shall be of noncombustible material.

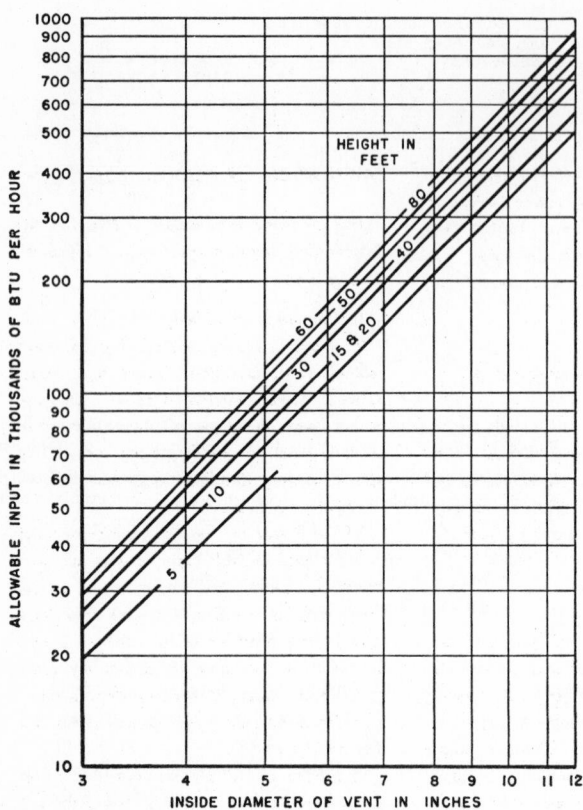

Fig. 7. Sizing chart

Capacity in Btu per hour for gas vents or chimneys serving more than one appliance.

Table 11. Vent connector clearances for gas appliances

Appliance	Minimum Distance from Combustible Material	
	Listed Type B Gas Vent Material	Vent Connectors of Other than Type B Material
Listed Boiler	As Listed	6 inches
Listed Warm Air Furnace	As Listed	6 inches
Listed Water Heater	As Listed	6 inches
Listed Room Heater	As Listed	6 inches
Listed Floor Furnace	As Listed	6 inches
Listed Incinerator	Not Permitted	18 inches
Listed Conversion Burner (with draft hood)	6 inches	9 inches
Unlisted Appliances having draft hoods	6 inches	9 inches
Unlisted Appliances without draft hoods	Not Permitted	18 inches

appliance is located through the roof or exterior wall to the outer air. Such gas vents shall not originate in any unoccupied attic or concealed space, and shall not pass through any attic, inside wall, concealed space, nor through any floor.

When a Type C gas vent passes through an exterior wall or roof constructed of combustible material, it shall be guarded at the point of passage by a noncombustible thimble not less than 4 in. larger in diameter than the vent pipe.

SIZE OF GAS VENT OR CHIMNEY

The gas vent or chimney when connected to a single appliance shall be not less than the size of the draft hood outlet.

When more than one appliance is connected to a gas vent or chimney, the area of the passageway shall be not less than the area of the largest vent connector plus 50 per cent of the areas of additional vent connectors, or as provided in Fig. 7.

Gas vents shall extend at least two feet above the highest point where they pass through a roof of a building and at least two feet higher than any portion of a building within ten feet. Chimneys shall

extend at least three feet above the highest point where they pass through the roof of a building and at least two feet higher than any portion of the building within ten feet.

Gas vents or chimneys shall not terminate less than four feet in vertical height above the highest connected appliance draft hood outlet or flue collar.

Top of vent or chimney shall be of a design to prevent rain and debris from entering.

VENT CONNECTORS

That portion of the vent system which connects the gas appliance to the gas vent or chimney is called a vent connector.

Vent connectors used for gas appliances having draft hoods shall be constructed of materials having resistance to corrosion and heat not less than that of No. 28 U.S. gage galvanized steel, except that Type B vent material may be used as the connector between the draft hood and the chimney.

Vent connectors shall not be smaller than the size of the flue collar or the draft hood outlet.

When two or more vent connectors enter

a common vertical gas vent or chimney, the smaller connector should enter at the highest level consistent with available headroom or clearance to combustible material.

Two or more gas appliances may be vented through a common vent connector or manifold located at the highest level consistent with available headroom or clearance to combustible material.

The manifold, all junction fittings, and the common vent connector shall be of a size adequate for the combined volume of the vent gases.

The horizontal run of the vent connector shall be as short as possible and the appliance shall be located as near the gas vent or chimney as practicable. The maximum length of an uninsulated horizontal run of vent connector shall not exceed 75 per cent of the height of the gas vent or chimney.

Minimum clearances of vent connectors to combustible material shall be in accordance with Table 11. The clearances from vent connectors to combustible materials may be reduced when the combustible material is protected as specified in Table 10.

REFERENCES

American Standard Requirements for Installation of Gas Equipment in Large Boilers. ASA Z21.33.

Proposed American Standard for Installation of Consumer-Owned Gas Piping and Gas Equipment on Industrial and Commercial Premises not covered by ASA Z21.30 or ASA Z21.33. American Gas Association (1958).

American Standard Installation of Domestic Gas Conversion Burners. ASA Z21.8.

Gas Vent Tables; Research Report No. 1319. American Gas Association Laboratories (1960).

By ALFRED GREENBERG, P.E., *Environmental Consultant*

HEATING LOADS

INTRODUCTION

The purpose of this section is to present information that will be helpful to the architect in estimating and evaluating the heating, ventilating, and air-conditioning requirements for any building. Although it may be possible to design some complete, simple systems from the data given here, that is not the primary intent of this section. Except for the simplest buildings, all heating, ventilating, and air-conditioning systems should be designed by a qualified environmental engineer, who should be consulted at the earliest design stage.

The first part of the section deals with the technical aspects of the subject—calculation of loads and design of systems—and in the second part the application to various building types is discussed.

Some of the data on the calculation of heating and cooling loads have been taken, with permission, from the *ASHRAE Guide and Data Book, Fundamentals and Equipment, 1963,* published by the American Society of Heating, Refrigerating, and Air Conditioning Engineers. For further information, that publication (hereafter referred to as ASHRAE Guide) should be consulted.

DEFINITION OF AIR CONDITIONING (from ASHRAE Guide)

"The process of treating air so as to control simultaneously its temperature, humidity, cleanliness and distribution to meet the requirements of the conditioned space."

PURPOSE

The architect should be generally acquainted with the tools and procedures used by engineers in arriving at heating and cooling loads. The methods used and information given in the following pages are based upon sound present-day practices and should produce reasonably accurate results.

CALCULATION OF HEATING LOADS

The following information is required for determining heating and winter air-conditioning loads:

1. *Volume* in cubic feet.
2. *Areas* in square feet of all walls, floor, ceiling, roof, partitions, glass and doors between areas having different temperatures. These measurements may be taken room-by-room or zone-by-zone depending upon whether detailed loads or general information is desired.
3. *Coefficient of thermal transmission (U)* of each type of wall, floor, ceiling or roof, partition, glass and door construction. These may be found in this book and more fully in the ASHRAE Guide. Tables 2 and 3 in this section give *U* factors for glass and wood doors. *U* factors for all other types of construction are given in the section on "Insulation."
4. *Infiltration* of air through the crackage of doors and windows. See Tables 1 and 4.

Table 1. Infiltration through windows

Expressed in cubic feet per foot of crack per hour. (*Reprinted by permission from* ASHRAE Guide and Data Book, *1963.*)

Type of window	Remarks	Wood velocity, miles per hour					
		5	10	15	20	25	30
Double-hung wood sash windows (unlocked)	Around frame in masonry wall—not calked	3	8	14	20	27	35
	Around frame in masonry wall—calked	1	2	3	4	5	6
	Around frame in wood frame construction	2	6	11	17	23	30
	Total for average window, nonweatherstripped, $\frac{1}{16}$-in. crack and 3/64 in. clearance. Includes wood frame leakage	7	21	39	59	80	104
	Ditto, weatherstripped	4	13	24	36	49	63
	Total for poorly fitted window, nonweatherstripped, $\frac{1}{32}$ in. crack and $\frac{3}{32}$ in. clearance. Includes wood frame leakage	27	69	111	154	199	249
	Ditto, weatherstripped	6	19	34	51	71	92
Double-hung metal windows	Nonweatherstripped, locked	20	45	70	96	125	154
	Nonweatherstripped, unlocked	20	47	74	104	137	170
	Weatherstripped, unlocked	6	19	32	46	60	76
Rolled section steel sash windows	Industrial pivoted, $\frac{1}{16}$-in. crack	52	108	176	244	304	372
	Architectural projected, $\frac{1}{32}$-in. crack (best)	15	36	62	86	112	139
	Architectural projected, 3/64-in. crack (average)	20	52	88	116	152	182
	Residential casement, 1/64-in. crack (best)	6	18	33	47	60	74
	Residential casement, $\frac{1}{32}$-in. crack (average)	14	32	52	76	100	128
	Heavy casement section, projected, 1/64-in. crack (best)	3	10	18	26	36	48
	Heavy casement section, projected, $\frac{1}{32}$-in. crack (average)	8	24	38	54	72	92
Hollow metal, vertically pivoted window		30	88	145	186	221	242

The fit of the average double-hung wood window was determined as $\frac{1}{16}$-in. crack and $\frac{3}{64}$-in. clearance by measurements. A $\frac{3}{32}$-in. crack and clearance represent a poorly fitted window.

Table 2. Heat transmission coefficients of solid wood doors

Btu/hr/sq ft/°F difference in temperature inside and outside the door at 15 mph wind velocity outside. (Reprinted by permission from ASHRAE Guide and Data Book, *1961.)*

NOMINAL DOOR THICKNESS	ACTUAL THICKNESS	EXPOSED DOOR	DOOR WITH GLASS STORM DOOR
1	25/32	0.69	0.35
1¼	1 1/16	0.59	0.32
1½	1 5/16	0.52	0.30
1¾	1⅜	0.51	0.30
2	1⅝	0.46	0.28
2½	2⅛	0.38	0.25
3	2⅝	0.33	0.23

A value of 0.85 should be used for single exposed doors containing thin wood panels or single panes of glass, and a value of 0.39 for the same door if protected by glass storm doors.

Table 3. Heat transmission coefficients for windows, skylights and block walls

Btu/hr/sq ft/°F difference in temperature, air to air, inside and outside building. (Reprinted by permission from ASHRAE Guide and Data Book, *1961.)*

Vertical glass sheets

NUMBER OF SHEETS	ONE	TWO			THREE		
Air space, in.	None	¼	½	1	¼	½	1
U	1.13	0.61	0.55	0.53	0.41	0.36	0.34

Horizontal glass sheets

NUMBER OF SHEETS	HEAT FLOW UP			
	ONE	TWO		
Air space, in.	None	¼	½	1
U	1.40	0.70	0.66	0.63

Hollow glass block walls

DESCRIPTION	OUTDOOR EXPOSURE
5¾ x 5¾ x 3⅞ in. thick	0.60
7¾ x 7¾ x 3⅞ in. thick	0.56
11¾ x 11¾ x 3⅞ in. thick	0.52
7¾ x 7¾ x 3⅞ in. thick, with fiber glass screen dividing cavity	0.48

Application factors for windows: multiply flat glass U values by these factors

WINDOW DESCRIPTION	SINGLE GLASS	DOUBLE GLASS	WINDOWS WITH STORM SASH
Sheets	100% glass, 1.00	100% glass, 1.00	
Wood sash	80% glass, 0.90	80% glass, 0.95	80% glass, 0.90
Wood sash	60% glass, 0.80	60% glass, 0.85	60% glass, 0.80
Steel sash	80% glass, 1.00	80% glass, 1.20	80% glass, 1.00
Aluminum sash	80% glass, 1.10	80% glass, 1.30	80% glass, 1.10

5. *Desired indoor temperature and humidity*—see Table 5.

6. *Prevailing winter outside air conditions*—see Table 7.

WORK SHEETS

All calculations should be clearly recorded and properly filed for reference and checking. Many calculations required for determining heating loads are also needed for cooling-load calculations. Any form of record may be used, but Table 6 is recommended as a guide.

In using the work sheet, a separate line should be used for each area having a different *U* value. It is usually advisable to calculate the glass area first. Fill in columns I, II, III, IV, V, VI, VII, VIII. Enter in column XII the product of columns V, VII, and VIII.

If air is used to heat or ventilate the room, and more air is supplied than is exhausted, then the infiltration can usually be neutralized and thus need not be considered in the heat-loss calculations. If infiltration is to be considered, then use the next line on the work sheet and fill in columns VII, IX, X, and XI. In column VII

Table 4. Infiltration through 72-in. revolving door and 36-in. swinging door

Cubic feet per person per passage. (Reprinted by permission from ASHRAE Guide and Data Book, 1963.)

Usage	Freely revolving door	Door equipped with brake
Infrequent	75	60
Average	60	50
Heavy	40	40
36-in. swinging door		20 to 100

NOTE: These figures are based on the assumption that there is no wind pressure and that swinging doors are in use in one wall only. Any swinging doors in other walls should be kept closed to insure air conditioning in accordance with these recommended standards.
From Application Engineering Standards for Air Conditioning for Comfort 1947, Air Conditioning & Refrigeration Institute, Inc., Washington, D.C., and from experimental data of National Bureau of Standards. Used by permission.

enter the factor 1.08.[1] In column XII enter the product of columns VII, VIII, and XI.

If the particular exposure contains windows of different sizes, it might be advantageous to list each size on a different line. When all the glass has been accounted for, on the next line enter the wall. List the over-all dimensions of the wall in column IV and in column V enter the gross area of the wall less the glass area.

On succeeding lines follow the same procedure for other walls, roof, floor, ceiling or partitions. When all heat-loss items

[1] 1.08 is a factor calculated from the specific heat of air, 0.24 Btu/(lb)(hr) (°F), and the density of air, 0.075 lb/per cu ft, and 60 min/per hr at 70°F, 29.92 in. Hg atmosphere pressure.

Table 5. Winter indoor dry-bulb temperatures usually specified

Reprinted by permission from ASHRAE Guide and Data Book, 1963.

Type of building	°F	Type of building	°F	Type of building	°F
Schools:		Private rooms (surgical)	70–80	Dining rooms	72
Classrooms	72–74	Operating rooms	70–95	Kitchens and laundries	66
Assembly rooms	68–72	Wards	72–74	Ballrooms	65–68
Gymnasiums	55–65	Kitchens and laundries	66	Toilets and service rooms	68
Toilets and baths	70	Toilets	68		
Wardrobe and locker rooms	65–68	Bathrooms	70–80	Homes	73–75
Kitchens	66			Stores	65–68
Dining and lunch rooms	65–70	Theaters:		Public buildings	72–74
Playrooms	60–65	Seating space	68–72	Warm air baths	120
Natatoriums	75	Lounge rooms	68–72	Steam baths	110
		Toilets	68	Factories and machine shops	60–65
Hospitals:		Hotels:		Foundries and boiler shops	50–60
Private rooms	72–74	Bedrooms and baths	75	Paint shops	80

NOTE: *The most comfortable dry-bulb temperature to be maintained depends on the relative humidity and air motion. These factors considered together constitute what is termed the* effective *temperature. (See ASHRAE Guide.) When relative humidity is not controlled separately, optimum dry-bulb temperature for comfort will be slightly higher than shown in this table.*

Table 6. Heating calculations

Project No. _____ Designed by _____ Date _____ Checked by _____ Date _____

Project Name _____ Location _____

Outside Design Conditions: DB _____F RH _____% *Inside Design Conditions: DB _____°F RH _____%

Outside Wind Velocity: _____MPH Direction _____

* Except where otherwise indicated.

I	II	III	IV	V	VI	VII	VIII	IX	X	XI	XII	XIII
									Crackage		Btu/hr.	
Room Name or No.	Item	Exp.	Dimensions	Net area sq. ft.	Volume cu. ft.	Temp. diff.	U or factor	Lineal Ft.	CFM/Lin. Ft.	Tot. CFM		Remarks
A ___												
B ___												
C ___												
D ___												
E ___												
F ___												

Table 7. Winter climatic conditions *

Extracted by permission from ASHRAE Guide and Data Books, 1963 and 1964.

State	Station	Design winter temperatures, °F Frequency of Recurrence, Years Minimum Average Daily Temperature			Average Wind speed, Dec., Jan., Feb., mph	Degree-days	State	Station	Design winter temperatures, °F Frequency of Recurrence, Years Minimum Average Daily Temperature			Average Wind speed, Dec., Jan., Feb., mph	Degree-days
		Once in 40	Once in 13	Once in 5					Once in 40	Once in 13	Once in 5		
Ala.	Birmingham	6	12	18	8.0	2780	Neb.	Lincoln	−22	−15	−9	10.6	6104
	Mobile	17	22	27	9.9	1612		Omaha	−24	−17	−10	9.7	6160
	Montgomery	11	18	23	7.5	2137	Nev.	Reno	−4	3	9	6.0	6036
Ariz.	Flagstaff	−12	−4	3	7.7	7525	N. H.	Concord	−17	−11	−5	6.2	7612
	Phoenix	33	36	39	5.4	1698	N. J.	Atlantic City	3	8	12	15.8	4741
Ark.	Fort Smith	0	6	12	8.3	3188		Elizabeth	−4	2	7	11.2	5252, 5252
	Little Rock	2	8	15	8.3	2982		Trenton	−4	2	7	10.9	5068
Calif.	Fresno	29	32	34	5.4	2532	N. M.	Albuquerque	3	8	14	7.3	4389
	Los Angeles	37	41	44	6.4	2105		Roswell	−4	4	11	7.1	3424
	Sacramento	27	30	33	7.2	2822	N. Y.	Albany	−16	9	−4	10.5	6962
	San Diego	41	43	46	6.3	1574		Binghamton	−12	7	−2	6.8	7537
	San Francisco	34	37	40	7.5	3421		Buffalo	−11	5	0	17.1	6838
Colo.	Denver	−19	−12	−5	7.5	6132		New York	1	5	9	16.8	4989
	Grand Junction	−11	−3	4	4.4	5796		Rochester	−9	−4	1	9.6	6863
	Pueblo	−24	−14	−5	7.9	5709		Syracuse	−16	−10	−4	11.2	6520
Conn.	Hartford	−7	−2	3	8.7	6139	N. C.	Asheville	−2	5	11	9.5	4072
	New Haven	−5	0	5	9.4	6026		Charlotte	9	14	19	7.3	3205
D.C.	Washington	5	10	14	7.8	4333		Raleigh	9	14	18	7.9	3369
Fla.	Jacksonville	24	28	33	9.0	1243		Wilmington	16	20	25	9.4	2323
	Key West	50	53	56	10.6	89	N. D.	Bismarck	−38	−31	−24	9.1	9033
	Tampa	32	36	41	8.6	674	Ohio	Cincinnati	−9	−3	3	8.5	5195
Ga.	Atlanta	5	11	17	11.7	2826		Cleveland	−11	−5	1	14.7	6006
	Augusta	15	20	25	6.5	2138		Columbus	−9	−3	2	11.6	5615
	Savannah	19	24	28	9.5	1710		Toledo	−11	−5	0	12.1	6394
Idaho	Boise	−20	−10	0	9.1	5890	Okla.	Oklahoma City	−9	−1	6	11.5	644
	Pocatello	−27	−17	−7	8.9	6976	Ore.	Portland	1	10	18	7.3	4632
Ill.	Chicago	−17	−11	−5	11.7	6310	Pa.	Erie	9	−3	2	13.6	6116
	Peoria	−20	−13	−6	8.3	6087		Harrisburg	0	4	8	7.6	5258
Ind.	Fort Wayne	−13	−7	−2	10.4	6287		Philadelphia	1	6	11	11.0	4866
	Indianapolis	−11	−8	−1	11.3	5611		Pittsburgh	−9	−3	2	11.6	5905
	Terre Haute	−12	−6	0	10.2	5366		Scranton	−8	−2	3	7.6	6047
Iowa	Davenport	−18	−12	−5	10.5	6091	R. I.	Providence	−4	1	5	12.1	6125
	Des Moines	−19	−13	−8	10.1	6446	S. C.	Charleston	17	22	27	10.5	1973
	Dubuque	−22	−15	−9	7.1	7271		Columbia	11	19	24	8.0	2435
	Sioux City	−22	−16	−11	11.5	7012	S. D.	Huron	−17	−21	−17	10.7	7902
Kan.	Dodge City	−16	−9	−2	10.6	5058	Tenn.	Knoxville	−3	5	12	7.2	3590
	Topeka	−15	−8	−2	9.2	4209		Memphis	0	6	13	9.3	3137
	Wichita	−13	−6	0	12.4	4571		Nashville	−4	3	10	9.8	3513
Ky.	Louisville	−9	−2	4	9.8	4439	Tex.	Amarillo	−10	−2	5	12.1	4345
La.	New Orleans	21	26	30	8.6	1317		Corpus Christi	16	23	29	11.0	1011
	Shreveport	8	14	20	8.8	2117		Dallas	1	8	15	10.6	2272
Me.	Eastport	−14	−9	−5	12.6	8246		El Paso	15	20	25	9.0	2641
	Portland	−15	−9	−3	10.4	7681		Fort Worth	0	8	15	10.5	2361
Md.	Baltimore	3	8	13	8.2	4787		Galveston	16	23	29	11.2	1233
Mass.	Boston	−6	0	4	12.4	5791		Houston	13	19	25	10.5	1388
Mich.	Detroit	−10	−4	1	12.0	6469		San Antonio	12	19	25	8.3	1579
	Grand Rapids	−9	−4	1	12.1	7075	Utah	Salt Lake City	−8	1	6	7.8	5866
	Lansing	−14	−8	−3	9.8		Vt.	Burlington	−23	−17	−11	11.6	7865
	Marquette	−22	−16	−10	10.6		Va.	Lynchburg	7	11	15	8.1	4153
Minn.	Duluth	−32	−27	−22	13.4	9937		Norfolk	11	15	20	12.1	3454
	Minneapolis	−28	−23	−18	11.3	7853		Richmond	6	11	16	8.1	3955
Miss.	Meridan	8	14	20	6.3	2333	Wash.	Seattle	9	15	21	9.8	4438
	Vicksburg	9	15	21	8.3	2000		Spokane	−28	−16	−5	6.2	6852
Mo.	Kansas City	−15	−8	−2	10.3	4888		Tacoma	9	15	20	8.0	4866
	St. Louis	−12	−5	1	11.8	4699	W. Va.	Parkersburg	−7	−1	5	7.2	4750
	Springfield	−12	−5	1	11.0	4693	Wis.	Green Bay	−27	−20	−14	10.5	8259
Mont.	Billings	−42	−31	−21	12.4	7106		Madison	−25	−19	−13	10.1	7417
	Helena	−53	−39	−27	7.4	7250		Milwaukee	−24	−17	−10	12.1	7205
							Wyo.	Cheyenne	−26	−19	−12	13.3	7562
								Yellowstone Park	−15	−34	−23	8.8	9605

* *Data compiled from U.S. Weather Bureau records by H. C. S. Thom.*

in a room have been tabulated, a room total may be obtained. Skip a line and proceed to the details of the next room.

Most engineers add a safety factor of about 10 per cent to allow for faulty construction and extreme weather conditions. However, the engineer should also consider the heat given off by lights, people, and appliances and the heat-storage capacity of the room.

COOLING LOADS

Information required for calculating summer cooling loads is as follows:

1. Type, usage, and hours of occupancy of the building
2. Orientation of the building
3. Items I through VI and VIII from heating-load work sheet (Table 6)
4. Indoor design conditions
5. Outdoor design conditions
6. Type of glass and shades to be used
7. Ventilation requirements
8. Number of occupants and type of activity
9. Amount and type of artificial lighting and hours of use
10. Number and type of heat-producing appliances and equipment and extent of use

Work sheet suggested for use in calculating cooling loads is shown in Table 10. Lines 2 and 3 of the work sheet refer to any calculations which may have been done on separate sheets. In line 6 "Cfm/Air Change" is the room volume divided by 60. In line 7 note that sun time, not daylight saving time, should be used. For line 8 see Table 8. For line 10 see Table 11. For line 11 see Table 9.

For lines 14 through 17 see section on Solar loads further on in this section. In lines 18 through 21 enter the appropriate figures from Tables 12 and 3 in the Δt and Factor columns, respectively. In lines 22 through 26 obtain the correct Δt from Tables 14 and 15 and U factors from the section on *insulation*. For line 27 see Tables 12 and 3. For line 28 see Table 2.

In lines 30 and 40 enter the number of people, if known; otherwise use Table 16 as a guide; sensible and latent heat for various degrees of activity may be found in Table 13. In line 31 enter the total lighting wattage, if known; otherwise refer to section on "Lighting" for recommended illumination levels and estimate the wattage on the basis of 1 watt per sq ft for 5 ft-c (foot-candles) of incandescent lighting and 15 ft-c of fluorescent lighting. In lines 32 and 41 enter the total sensible and latent heat, respectively, produced by appliances; if not known, estimate from manufacturers' data on tables in the ASHRAE Guide. On

Table 8. Outdoor air requirements

Columns 1 through 5 reprinted by permission from ASHRAE Guide and Data Book, *1963.*

Application	Smoking	Cfm per person Recommended	Cfm per person Minimum *	Cfm per sq ft of floor Minimum *	No. of air changes per hr * Recommended	No. of air changes per hr * Minimum
Apartment:						
Average	Some	20	10			
DeLuxe	Some	20	10			
Banking space	Occasional	10	7½		8	6
Barber shops	Considerable	15	10		12	8
Beauty parlors	Occasional	10	7½		12	8
Brokers' board rooms	Very heavy	50	20		20	12
Cocktail bars		40	25		20	12
Corridors (supply or exhaust)				0.25	6	4
Department stores	None	7½	5	0.05	10	6
Directors' rooms	Extreme	50	30		20	12
Drug stores	Considerable	10	7½		12	8
Factories †	None	10	7½	0.10		
Five and Ten Cent stores	None	7½	5		8	6
Funeral parlors	None	10	7½		8	6
Garages *				1.0	8	4
Hospitals:						
Operating rooms ‡	None			2.0	20	12
Private rooms	None	30	25	0.33	8	6
Wards	None	20	10		8	6
Hotel rooms	Heavy	30	25	0.33	8	6
Kitchens:						
Restaurant §				4.0	40	25
Residence				2.0	8	6
Laboratories	Some	20	15		20	12
Meeting rooms	Very heavy	50	30	1.25	20	12
Offices:						
General	Some	15	10		8	6
Private	None	25	15	0.25	10	8
Private	Considerable	30	25	0.25	12	10
Restaurants:						
Cafeteria	Considerable	12	10		15	10
Dining room	Considerable	15	12		15	10
Schoolrooms †	None	20				
Shop, retail	None	10	7½		10	6
Theater †	None	7½	5		7	5
Theater †	Some	15	10		8	6
Toilets † (exhaust)				2.0	20	12

* *When minimum is used, take the larger of the three.*
† *See local codes which may govern.*
‡ *All outside air recommended to overcome explosion hazard of anesthetics.* See National Board of Fire Underwriters' Pamphlet No. 56.
§ *Often dependent upon range hood size.*

Table 9. Design room conditions usually specified for summer average peak load in comfort air conditioning

Type of installation	Dry-bulb temp.	Wet-bulb temp.	Relative humidity, %	Grains per lb
Ample capacity	76	63.3	50	67.2
Economy application	78	65	50	72.7
Occupancy up to 40 min maximum	80	67	51	78.5

Table 10. Work sheet for calculating cooling loads

1 PROJECT_____   SHEET NO._____OF_____

2 NOTE: FOR DETERMINATION OF FACTORS USED   CALC. BY_____DATE_____

3   SEE SHEETS NOS._____DATED_____   CHECKED BY_____DATED_____

			AT	FACTOR	AREA OR NO.	BTU/HR	AREA OR NO.	BTU/HR	AREA OR NO.	BTU/HR	AREA OR NO.	BTU/HR
4	ROOM NAME OR NUMBER											
5	DIMENSIONS & AREA											
6	VOLUME | CFM/AIR CHANGE											
7	HRS. OF OCCUPANCY—(SUNTIME)											
8	AIR CHANGES REQUIREMENTS—(PER HR.)											
9	COOLING DATA			DB WB %RH gr/lb	DB WB %RH gr/lb		DB WB %RH gr/lb		DB WB %RH gr/lb			
10	O. A. AT PEAK ROOM LOAD											
11	ROOM DESIGN CONDITIONS											
12	DIFFERENCE			— —	— —		— —		— —			
13	HEAT GAIN ITEM	AT	FACTOR									
14	N, NW GLASS (SOLAR)	—										
15	E, NE " (SOLAR)	—										
16	S, SE " (SOLAR)	—										
17	W, SW " (SOLAR)	—										
18	N, NW GLASS (TRANSMISSION)											
19	E, NE "											
20	S, SE "											
21	W, SW "											
22	N, NW WALL											
23	E, NE "											
24	S, SE "											
25	W, SW "											
26	ROOF											
27	SKYLIGHT											
28	DOORS											
29	TOT. OUTSIDE LOAD	—	—	—		—		—		—		
30	PEOPLE (INT. SENSIBLE)	—										
31	LIGHTS	—	3.41									
32	APPLIANCES	—										
33	MOTORS hp.	—	3000									
34	FLOOR, CLG.											
35	PARTITION											
36	INFILTRATION*		1.08									
37	FAN HORSEPOWER											
38	TOT. ROOM SENS.	—	—	—		—		—		—		
39	(A) = RSH = 1.1***TOT. RM. SENS.	—	—	—		—		—		—		
40	PEOPLE (INT. LAT.)	—										
41	APPLIANCES	—										
42	INFILTRATION*	gr/lb	0.67									
43												
44	TOT. RM. LATENT	—	—	—		—		—		—		
45	(B) = RLH = 1.05***TOT. RM. LAT.	—	—	—		—		—		—		
46	(A+B) = ROOM TOTAL HEAT											
47	(C) = O. A. SENS = 1.08×__Δt×CFM											
48	(D) = O. A. LAT. = 0.67×__gr/lb×CFM											
49	(A+B+C+D) = GRAND TOT. HEAT											
50	SHF = (A) ÷ (A+B)											
51	CFM = (A) ÷ (1.08×__Δt)											
52	AIR CHANGES = 60×CFM ÷ RM. VOL.											

53 REMARKS:
1. * USE WHEN NOT PRESSURIZED
   ** TYPICAL VALUES ONLY
2. COIL BY-PASS FACTORS NOT CONSIDERED

Table 11. Summer climatic conditions

State	Station	Elevation, ft	Design dry-bulb temp. in common use	Design wet-bulb temp. in common use	Average summer wind velocity, mph	State	Station	Elevation, ft	Design dry-bulb temp. in common use	Design wet-bulb temp. in common use	Average summer wind velocity, mph
Ala.	Birmingham	711	95	78	5.4	Nebr.	Lincoln	1,189	95	78	9.7
	Mobile	143	95	80	8.0		Omaha	1,219	95	78	
	Montgomery	293	95	78		Nev.	Las Vegas	1,882	115	75	
Ariz.	Flagstaff	6,957	90	65			Reno	4,588	95	65	7.2
	Phoenix	1,122	106	76	6.0	N. H.	Concord	343	90	73	4.9
Ark.	Fort Smith	545	95	76	6.1	N. J.	Atlantic City	45	95	78	
	Little Rock	451	95	78	6.2		Newark	15	95	75	
Calif.	Fresno	387	105	74	7.9		Trenton	144	95	78	8.8
	Los Angeles	534	90	70	5.8	N. M.	Albuquerque	5,022	95	70	7.8
	Sacramento	116	100	72	7.9		Roswell	3,643	95	70	
	San Diego	90	85	68		N. Y.	Albany	114	93	75	7.5
	San Francisco	164	85	65	10.7		Binghamton	915	95	75	
Colo.	Denver	5,398	95	64	6.9		Buffalo	726	93	73	12.1
	Grand Junction	1,587	95	65	6.3		New York	425	95	75	12.5
	Pueblo	1,770	95	65			Rochester	609	95	75	
Conn.	Hartford	229	93	75			Syracuse	465	93	75	
	New Haven	180	95	75	7.4	N. C.	Asheville	2,280	93	75	5.6
D. C.	Washington	128	95	78	5.9		Charlotte	809	95	78	
Fla.	Jacksonville	104	95	78	8.4		Raleigh	405	95	78	6.3
	Key West	23	98	78			Wilmington	78	95	78	8.4
	Miami	153	91	79	8.7	N. D.	Bismarck	1,675	95	73	9.5
	Tampa	111	95	78	7.4	Ohio	Cincinnati	772	95	78	5.6
Ga.	Atlanta	1,020	95	76	7.9		Cleveland	669	95	75	11.1
	Augusta	195	98	76			Columbus	812	95	76	
	Savannah	115	95	78	8.0		Toledo	668	95	75	
Idaho	Boise	2,818	95	65	5.8	Okla.	Oklahoma City	1,264	101	77	9.8
	Pocatello	4,522	95	65		Ore.	Portland	98	90	68	6.5
Ill.	Chicago	601	95	75	9.5	Pa.	Erie	771	93	75	
	Peoria	660	96	76	8.2		Harrisburg	339	95		
Ind.	Fort Wayne	885	95	75			Philadelphia	200	95	78	9.7
	Indianapolis	816	95	76	8.9		Pittsburgh	929	95	75	8.9
	Terre Haute	1,146	95	78			Scranton	877	95	75	
Iowa	Davenport	648	95	78		R. I.	Providence	77	93	75	9.5
	Des Moines	979	95	78	8.6	S. C.	Charleston	59	95	78	9.8
	Dubuque	740	95	78			Columbia	401	95	75	
	Sioux City	1,093	95	78		S. D.	Huron	1,342	95	75	10.3
Kans.	Dodge City	2,515	95	78		Tenn.	Knoxville	1,024	95	75	5.7
	Topeka	991	100	78			Memphis	348	95	78	7.3
	Wichita	1,497	100	75	11.8		Nashville	714	95	78	
Ky.	ouisville	563	95	78	7.2	Texas	Amarillo	3,686	100	72	11.3
La.	New Orleans	85	95	80	6.9		Corpus Christi	21	95	80	
	Shreveport	179	100	78	7.0		Dallas	732	100	78	9.3
Me.	Eastport	100	90	70			El Paso	3,792	100	69	8.4
	Portland	185	90	73	8.7		Fort Worth	708	100	78	9.5
Md.	Baltimore	114	95	78	7.4		Galveston	128	95	80	9.7
Mass.	Boston	356	92	75	12.5		Houston	198	95	80	8.8
Mich.	Detroit	1.000	95	75	9.5		San Antonio	770	100	78	7.8
	Lansing	861	95	75		Utah	Salt Lake City	4,346	95	65	9.8
	Marquette	721	93	73		Vt.	Burlington	409	90	73	8.5
Minn.	Duluth	1,133	93	73		Va.	Lynchburg	644	95	75	
	Minneapolis	945	95	75	10.2		Norfolk	91	95	78	10.1
Miss.	Meridian	410	95	79	4.6		Richmond	180	95	78	6.4
	Vicksburg	316	95	78	6.4	Wash.	Seattle	104	85	65	7.7
Mo.	Kansas City	780	100	76	9.1		Spokane	2,030	93	65	6.5
	St. Louis	646	95	78	9.5		Tacoma	279	85	64	
	Springfield	1.270	96	78	8.7	W. Va.	Parkersburg	685	95	75	5.2
Mont.	Billings	3,584	90	66		Wisc.	Green Bay	598	95	75	9.2
	Helena	4,175	95	67	8.1		Madison	1,008	95	75	7.9
							Milwaukee	744	95	75	9.8
						Wyo.	Cheyenne	6,144	95	65	9.2

Data compiled from U.S. Weather Bureau Data and various other sources.

Table 12. Solar heat gain factor [a]—Btuh per square foot—for August 21

Reprinted by permission from ASHRAE Guide and Data Book, 1963.

Latitude	Sun Time [b] AM▼➤	N	NE	E	SE	S	SW	W	NW	Horiz	Sun Time
	6 A.M.	7	46	56	31	2	2	2	2	8	6 P.M.
	7	12	130	173	116	9	9	9	9	54	5
24 Deg	8	14	136	203	146	15	14	14	14	124	4
North	9	18	104	185	148	27	18	18	18	188	3
	10	20	55	136	128	43	20	20	20	234	2
	11	22	23	65	89	54	22	22	22	264	1
	12 N	23	23	23	43	59	43	23	23	273	12 N
	6 A.M.	8	60	74	41	3	3	3	3	11	6 P.M.
	7	9	126	173	124	9	9	9	9	55	5
32 Deg	8	14	122	202	158	21	14	14	14	121	4
North	9	18	84	184	166	46	18	18	17	179	3
	10	20	36	133	152	71	20	20	20	223	2
	11	21	21	64	115	91	25	21	21	250	1
	12 N	22	22	22	64	97	64	22	22	259	12 N
	6 A.M.	8	70	88	51	3	3	3	4	13	6 P.M.
	7	9	120	174	127	9	9	9	9	55	5
40 Deg	8	13	108	199	169	32	13	13	13	114	4
North	9	17	65	180	183	69	17	17	17	168	3
	10	19	23	130	172	102	19	19	19	207	2
	11	20	20	62	141	126	37	20	20	231	1
	12 N	21	21	21	89	134	89	21	21	240	12 N
	6 A.M.	8	79	100	59	4	4	4	4	16	6 P.M.
	7	9	113	174	129	11	9	9	9	56	5
48 Deg	8	13	92	193	175	44	13	13	13	105	4
North	9	16	46	175	195	91	16	16	16	152	3
	10	18	18	126	188	131	18	18	18	187	2
	11	19	19	60	155	156	56	19	19	209	1
	12 N	19	19	19	111	165	111	19	19	216	12 N
		N	NW	W	SW	S	SE	E	NE	Horiz	◀ P.M.

[a] *Values in bold face are for hours when sun is striking fenestration.*
[b] *Values for morning hours must be selected by reading down for the proper direction listed at the top of the columns.*
[c] *Values for afternoon hours must be selected by reading up for the proper direction listed at the bottom of the columns.*

Table 13. Rates of heat gain from occupants of conditioned spaces—based on 78°F room temperature

Degree of activity	Typical application	Total heat adjusted, Btu/hr	Sensible heat, Btu/hr	Latent heat, Btu/hr
Seated at rest	Theater—matinee	330	200	130
	Theater—evening	350	215	135
Seated, very light work	Offices, hotels, apartments	400	215	185
Moderately active office work	Offices, hotels, apartments	450	220	230
Standing, light work; or walking slowly	Department store, retail store, dime store	450	220	230
Walking; seated Standing; walking slowly	Drugstore, bank	500	225	275
Sedentary work	Restaurant	550	245	305
Light bench work	Factory	750	250	500
Moderate dancing	Dance hall	850	270	580
Walking 3 mph; moderately heavy work	Factory	1000	330	670
Bowling Heavy work	Bowling alley Factory	1450	510	940

1. Adjusted total heat gain *is based on normal percentage of men, women, and children for the application listed, with the postulate that the gain from an adult female is 85 per cent of that for an adult male, and that the gain from a child is 75 per cent that for an adult male.*

2. Adjusted total heat value for sedentary work. restaurant, *includes 60 Btu/hr for food per individual (30 Btu sensible and Btu latent).*

3. For bowling *figure one person per alley actually bowling, and all others as sitting (500 Btu/hr) or standing (550 Btu/hr).*

Table 14. Total equivalent temperature differentials for calculating heat gain through sunlit and shaded walls

Reprinted by permission from ASHRAE Guide and Data Book, *1963.*

North latitude wall facing	Sun time																	
	A.M.						P.M.											
	8		10		12		2		4		6		8		10		12	
	Exterior color of wall—D = dark, L = light																	
	D	L	D	L	D	L	D	L	D	L	D	L	D	L	D	L	D	L
Frame																		
NE	22	10	24	12	14	10	12	10	14	14	14	14	10	10	6	4	2	2
E	30	14	36	18	32	16	12	12	14	14	14	14	10	10	6	6	2	2
SE	13	6	26	16	28	18	24	16	16	14	14	14	10	10	6	4	2	2
S	−4	−4	4	0	22	12	30	20	26	20	16	14	10	10	6	6	2	2
SW	−4	−4	0	−2	6	4	26	22	40	28	42	28	24	20	6	4	2	2
W	−4	−4	0	0	6	6	20	12	40	28	48	34	22	22	8	8	2	2
NW	−4	−4	0	−2	6	4	12	10	24	20	40	26	34	24	6	4	2	2
N (shade)	−4	−4	−2	−2	4	4	10	10	14	14	12	12	8	8	4	4	0	0
4-in. brick or stone veneer + frame																		
NE	−2	−4	24	12	20	10	10	6	12	10	14	14	12	12	10	10	6	4
E	2	0	30	14	31	17	14	14	12	12	14	14	12	12	10	8	6	6
SE	2	−2	20	10	28	16	26	16	18	14	14	14	12	12	10	8	6	6
S	−4	−4	−2	−2	12	6	24	16	26	18	20	16	12	12	8	8	4	4
SW	0	−2	0	−2	2	2	12	8	32	22	36	26	34	24	10	8	6	6
W	0	−2	0	0	4	2	10	8	26	18	40	28	42	28	16	14	6	6
NW	−4	−4	−2	−2	2	2	8	6	12	12	30	22	34	24	12	10	6	6
N (shade)	−4	−4	−2	−2	0	0	6	6	10	10	12	12	12	12	8	8	4	4
8-in. hollow tile or 8-in. cinder block																		
NE	0	0	0	0	20	10	16	10	10	6	12	10	14	12	12	10	8	8
E	4	2	12	4	24	12	26	14	20	12	12	10	14	12	14	10	10	8
SE	2	0	2	0	16	8	20	12	20	14	14	12	14	12	12	10	8	6
S	0	0	0	0	2	0	12	6	24	14	26	16	20	14	12	10	8	6
SW	2	0	2	0	2	0	6	4	12	10	26	18	30	20	26	18	8	6
W	4	2	4	2	4	2	6	4	10	8	18	14	30	22	32	22	18	14
NW	0	0	0	0	2	0	4	2	8	6	12	10	22	18	30	22	10	8
N (shade)	−2	−2	−2	−2	−2	−2	0	0	6	6	10	10	10	10	10	10	6	6
8-in. brick or 12-in. hollow tile or 12-in. cinder block																		
NE	2	2	2	2	10	2	16	8	14	8	10	6	10	8	10	10	10	8
E	8	6	8	6	14	8	18	10	18	10	14	8	14	10	14	10	12	10
SE	8	4	6	4	6	4	14	10	18	12	16	12	12	10	12	10	12	10
S	4	2	4	2	4	2	4	2	10	6	16	10	16	12	12	10	10	8
SW	8	4	6	4	6	4	8	4	10	6	12	8	20	12	24	16	20	14
W	8	4	6	4	6	6	8	6	10	6	14	8	20	16	24	16	24	16
NW	2	2	2	2	2	2	4	2	6	4	8	6	10	8	16	14	18	14
N (shade)	0	0	0	0	0	0	0	0	2	2	6	6	8	8	8	8	6	6
12-in. brick																		
NE	8	6	8	6	8	4	8	4	10	4	12	6	12	6	10	6	10	6
E	12	8	12	8	12	8	10	6	12	8	14	10	14	10	14	8	14	8
SE	10	6	10	6	10	6	10	6	10	6	12	8	14	10	14	10	12	8
S	8	6	8	6	6	4	6	4	6	4	8	4	10	6	12	8	12	8
SW	10	6	10	6	10	6	10	6	10	6	10	8	10	8	12	8	14	10
W	12	8	12	8	12	8	10	6	10	6	10	6	10	6	12	8	16	10
NW	8	6	8	6	8	4	8	4	8	4	8	4	8	6	10	6	10	6
N (shade)	4	4	2	2	2	2	2	2	2	2	2	2	2	2	4	4	6	6

1. *Notes 1, 2, 5, and 6 for Table 15 apply to this Table.*

2. Color of exterior surface of wall. *Use temperature differentials for light walls only where the permanence of the light wall is established by experience. For cream colors use the values for light walls. For medium colors interpolate half way between the dark and light values. Medium colors are medium blue, medium green, bright red, light brown, unpainted wood, natural color concrete, etc. Dark blue, red, brown, green, etc., are considered dark colors.*

Table 15. Total equivalent temperature differentials for calculating heat gain through sunlit and shaded roofs

Reprinted by permission from ASHRAE Guide and Data Book, 1963.

Description of Roof Construction[a]	Sun Time								
	A.M.			P.M.					
	8	10	12	2	4	6	8	10	12
Light Construction Roofs—Exposed to Sun									
1″ Wood[b] or 1″ Wood[b] + 1″ or 2″ insulation	12	38	54	62	50	26	10	4	0
Medium Construction Roofs—Exposed to Sun									
2″ Concrete or 2″ Concrete + 1″ or 2″ insulation or 2″ Wood[b]	6	30	48	58	50	32	14	6	2
2″ Gypsum or 2″ Gypsum + 1″ insulation 1″ Wood[b] or 2″ Wood[b] or + 4″ rock wool 2″ Concrete or in furred ceiling 2″ Gypsum	0	20	40	52	54	42	20	10	6
4″ Concrete or 4″ Concrete with 2″ insulation	0	20	38	50	52	40	22	12	6
Heavy Construction Roofs—Exposed to Sun									
6″ Concrete	4	6	24	38	46	44	32	18	12
6″ Concrete + 2″ insulation	6	6	20	34	42	44	34	20	14
Roofs Covered with Water—Exposed to Sun									
Light construction roof with 1″ water	0	4	16	22	18	14	10	2	0
Heavy construction roof with 1″ water	−2	−2	−4	10	14	16	14	10	6
Any roof with 6″ water	−2	0	0	6	10	10	8	4	0
Roofs with Roof Sprays—Exposed to Sun									
Light construction	0	4	12	18	16	14	10	2	0
Heavy construction	−2	−2	2	8	12	14	12	10	6
Roofs in Shade									
Light construction	−4	0	6	12	14	12	8	2	0
Medium construction	−4	−2	2	8	12	12	10	6	2
Heavy construction	−2	−2	0	4	8	10	10	8	4

[a] Includes ⅜ in. felt roofing with or without slag. May also be used for shingle roof.

[b] Nominal thickness of the wood.

Notes

Explanation: $\left\{\begin{array}{l}\text{Total heat transmission from solar}\\ \text{radiation and temperature difference}\\ \text{between outdoor and room air. Btu}\\ \text{per (hr) (sq ft) of roof area}\end{array}\right\} = \left\{\begin{array}{l}\text{Equivalent temperature}\\ \text{differential from above}\\ \text{table}\end{array}\right\} \times \left\{\begin{array}{l}\text{Heat transmission}\\ \text{coefficient for sum-}\\ \text{mer Btu per (hr)}\\ \text{(sq ft) (F deg)}\end{array}\right\}$

1. *Source.* Calculated by Mackey and Wright method

2. *Application.* These values may be used for all normal air conditioning estimates; usually without correction, in latitude 0 deg to 50 deg north or south when the load is calculated for the hottest weather. Note 5 explains how to adjust the temperature differential for other room and outdoor temperatures.

3. *Peaked Roofs.* If the roof is peaked and the heat gain is primarily due to solar radiation, use for the area of the roof, the area projected on a horizontal plane.

4. *Attics.* If the ceiling is insulated and if a fan is used in the attic for positive ventilation, the total temperature differential for a roof exposed to the sun may be decreased 25 percent.

5. *Corrections. For temperature difference when outdoor maximum design temperature minus room is different from 15 deg.* If the outdoor design temperature minus room temperature is different from the base of 15 deg, correct as follows: When the difference is greater (or less) than 15 deg add the excess to (or subtract the deficiency from) the above differentials.

For outdoor daily range of temperature other than 20 deg. If the daily range of temperature is less than 20 deg, add 1 deg for every 2 deg lower daily range; if the daily range is greater than 20 deg, subtract 1 deg for every 2 deg higher daily range. For example, the daily range in Miami, Florida is 12 deg or 8 deg less than 20 deg, therefore, the correction is +4 deg at all hours of the day.

Table 16. Average occupancy of various building types

Type of building space	Sq ft/person	Type of building space	Sq ft/person
Apartments	100–325	Libraries—Book stacks	100–200
Department and variety stores—1st & bsmt.	16–44	Reading areas	40–100
Rest	20–73	Museums	40–80
Eating places—quick service	13–17	Office buildings—General offices	80–130
Hotels—public spaces	10–78	Small suites	50–130
Hospitals—patients' rooms	80–100	Banks	40–80
Industrial buildings—general	100–300	Places of assembly	6–10
Laboratories	100–200	Schools	10–20

line 33 list the total horsepower of all motors, including electric typewriters and business machines and apply a diversity factor of 0.50 to 0.75.

In lines 36 and 42 enter in the Area column the product of the linear feet of crack and the appropriate cfm of infiltration as determined from Table 1. In lines 39 and 45 add safety factors of 10 and 5 per cent, respectively. Lines 47 and 48 are used only if through-the-wall cooling units are to be employed; they are calculated in the same manner as for infiltration air.

Building tonnage: The tons of refrigeration required for cooling the room can be found by dividing the total heat (line 49) by 12,000. But the sum of the room tonnages should not be used for the building tonnage because it will be 20 to 50 per cent higher than necessary. To obtain the building tonnage, calculate the total instantaneous heat for the building as a whole, and divide it by 12,000.

Building cfm: Total outside air requirements for the building may be obtained by adding the cfm requirements for each room.

SOLAR LOADS

Solar loads through glass can be extremely high. The incident solar load received by a vertical surface often exceeds 200 Btu/(hr)(sq ft) (see charts on the following page). If the surface is glass, most of this heat is transmitted instantaneously to the building interior. For every 100 sq ft of unshaded, unfavorably oriented glass in air-conditioned buildings in most parts of the country, an additional ton of cooling capacity must be provided at a cost of $600 to $1,800 (see charts on the page after next). The annual operating cost of air conditioning directly attributable to each square foot of glass may be several dollars.

Solar loads vary with latitude, orientation, ratio of glass to solid wall, type of glass, and degree of shading. Except the first, all these factors are normally controllable by the architect.

Orientation: Glass facing north receives the least solar radiation, and glass facing south receives next least. Therefore, if a building can be oriented so that most of its glass faces north and south, it will have a much lower solar load than if the principal glass areas face east and west (see table on page after next).

Glass ratio: Since the solar load is directly proportional to the glass area, it is obvious that the load can be reduced by the use of smaller windows.

Special glass: Various special types of glass may be used to reduce the solar load (Table 17). The extra cost of the glass must be compared with the saving it produces by reduction in the cooling load. Not shown in the table but often used is "glare-reducing" glass, a tinted glass which reduces the transmission of visible light as well as heat (see section on "Glass").

Shading: Large areas of glass may be used without significantly increasing the solar load if they are completely shaded from the direct rays of the sun. The effects of various common types of shading are shown in Table 18. As shown in the table, the most effective type of shading is external, since the reflected and absorbed heat can then be carried off by the ambient air. Although it is comparatively simple to design a moderately effective external shading device, it is far from simple to design one which cuts off all direct sun during the cooling season only, and admits sun at other seasons. To add to the difficulty of the task, the shading device should also be acceptable in architectural appearance, moderate in cost, durable in all kinds of weather, low in maintenance requirements; it should admit as much natural light as possible, and obscure the view outward as little as possible. Examples of various shading devices are shown in the following pages and in the section on "Masonry Construction."

Solar radiation, both light and heat, consists of direct, diffused, and reflected radiation (Fig. 1). Direct radiation usually makes up the largest single component of the peak solar load. In clear weather the diffuse factor is usually about 7 to 15 per cent of the direct radiation. Reflected radiation is the most difficult to calculate because it is determined not only by the location of the sun and the configuration of the shading device but also by the reflective characteristics of the surfaces off which the heat bounces. The reflectivity of various building and landscaping materials is given in the section on "Daylighting." Under ordinary conditions, for preliminary estimates, reflected radiation may be taken at twice the diffused factor at peak solar loads.

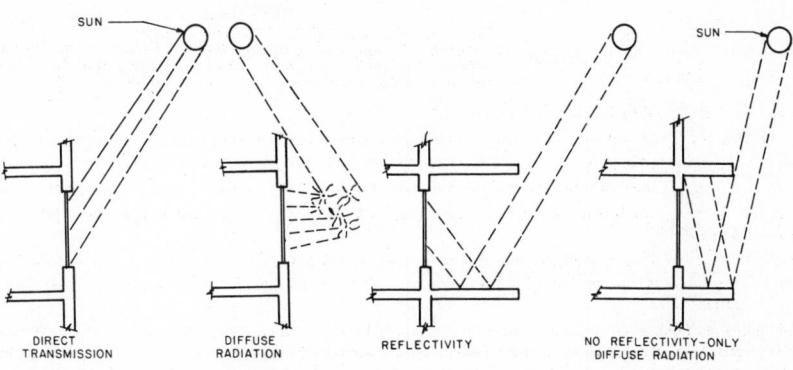

Fig. 1. Types of solar radiation

Table 17.   Types of glass and their effect on solar load

Type	Approximate cost, $/sq ft	Per cent reduction in solar load per sq ft
Single clear plate, ¼ in.	1.25	0
Double clear plate, ½-in. air space	4.50	22
Single heat absorbent	1.75	47*
Double, 1 clear plate, 1 heat absorbent, ½-in. air space	5.50	55
Double clear plate with venetian blind in air space	7.00†	70

*30–35 per cent if inside shades are used.
† Total window cost; others must have cost of shades added.

The solar load through glass is usually the most difficult portion of the cooling load to establish accurately. This is especially true where overhangs or other types of external shading devices are used. The accurate calculation of solar loads through glass is somewhat complicated (see the ASHRAE Guide). However, for estimating purposes, the curves on the following page may be used. The combined effect on the cooling load of glass ratio, type of glass, and degree of shading are shown in the charts on the page after next.

Table 18.   Shading coefficients (a.)—glass in sun

Extracted by permission from ASHRAE Guide and Data Book, *1964.*

Type of glass	Nominal thickness of glass	Solar transmittance (Outer)	(Inner)	No shading	Venetian blinds Light	Venetian blinds Medium	Draperies Light	Draperies Medium	Draperies Dark	Roller shade, opaque Light	Roller shade, opaque Dark	Double glazing Venetian blinds Light	Double glazing Venetian blinds Medium	Louver sun shade
Regular Sheet	3/32 to ¼	.87–.80		1.00	.55	.64	.56	.61	.66	.25	.59			
Regular Plate	¼ to ½	.80–.71		.95–.88										
Regular Pattern	⅛ to 9/32	.87–.79		—										
Heat-Abs Pattern	⅛	—		—										
Gray Sheet	3/16, 7/32, ¼	.74–.67		.86–.78										
Heat-Abs Sheet	7/32	.51		.71	.53	.57	.48	.52	.56	.30	.45			
Heat-Abs Plate	¼	.46		.67										
Heat-Abs Pattern	3/16, ¼	—		—										
Gray Sheet	⅛, 7/32	.59, .45		.78–.66										
Gray Plate	13/64, ¼	.52, .45		.72–.70										
Heat-Abs Sheet, Plate or Pattern	—	.44–.30		—	.52	.54	.44	.48	.52	.28	.40			
Heat-Abs Plate	⅜	.34		.57										
Gray Plate	⅜	.33		.56										
Heat-Abs Sheet, Plate or Pattern	—	.29–.15		—	.50	.50	.51	.42	.46	.50	.28	.36		
Gray Plate	½	.24		.50										
Regular Sheet Out / Regular Sheet In	b. 3/32, ⅛	.86	.86	.90	.51	.57	.54	.59	.64	.25	.60	.33	.36	.43
Regular Plate Out / Regular Plate In	c. ¼	.80	.80	.83								—	—	.49
Heat-Abs Plate Out / Regular Plate In	b. ¼	.46	.80	.56	.36	.39	.41	.43	.45	.22	.40	.28	.30	.37
Gray Plate Out / Regular Plate In	c.	.46	.80	.56								—	—	.41
Gray Plate with Sun Control Film Out, Regular Plate In	¼	.23	.80	.36										

NOTE: a *For any specific type of glass or window, refer to manufacturer's certified data for exact information.*
b *Air space consists of shade in contact with glass or shade separated from glass by air space.*
c *Air space consists of shade in contact with glass-voids filled with plastic.*

From a report by Princeton University School of Architecture for Committee of Stainless Steel Producers, American Iron and Steel Institute

COOLING LOADS DUE TO SOL-AIR

A number of interrelated design factors influence the cooling costs due to heat transfer through walls of buildings having various degrees of glass area:

1. Building orientation

2. Proportion of transparent and opaque wall surfaces

3. Extent of sun control in the transparent areas of the wall, either by use of heat-resistant glass or by shading

4. Insulation of opaque areas

NOTE: In order to deal with cooling loads on a generalized basis, representative of a national average condition, the comparisons in the graphs are based on the "summer design data" temperatures (for peak conditions—July 21) given in the 1956 ASHRAE Guide. The Guide recommends that these may safely be used for design estimating purposes throughout the United States, and that correction for latitude is necessary only when a high degree of accuracy is essential.

The specific heat gains through several types of glass, both shaded and unshaded are shown in the four charts on this page.

Building Orientation

The direction a wall faces makes a considerable difference in the heat impact it receives. To illustrate these differences, a long narrow building with bilateral glazing may be assumed, and comparison is made in the table (on the next page) of the cooling tonnage which will be required for optional east-west or north-south orientation of its length.

These comparisons are based on average sol-air temperature,[2] and would of course involve slightly differing values in each region. The amount of solar heat gain on the east, west and north walls differs little throughout the United States, but the impact on south-facing walls varies considerably.

Data shown for the 100 per cent shaded condition might indicate that orientation has little significance when glass is completely shaded. Provision of total shading on east and west walls, however, is a relatively complex and expensive procedure.

Cooling Tonnage

The required cooling tonnage per square foot of wall surface, to counteract the solar heat impact, depends upon:

a. the cooling loads imposed due to the heat conductivity characteristics of the opaque and transparent materials.

b. the ratio of areas of these opaque and transparent materials.

[2] *Sol-air temperature reduces joint effect of solar radiation and air temperature to a single value.*

HEAT TRANSMISSION THROUGH MATERIALS AT SUMMER PEAK CONDITIONS

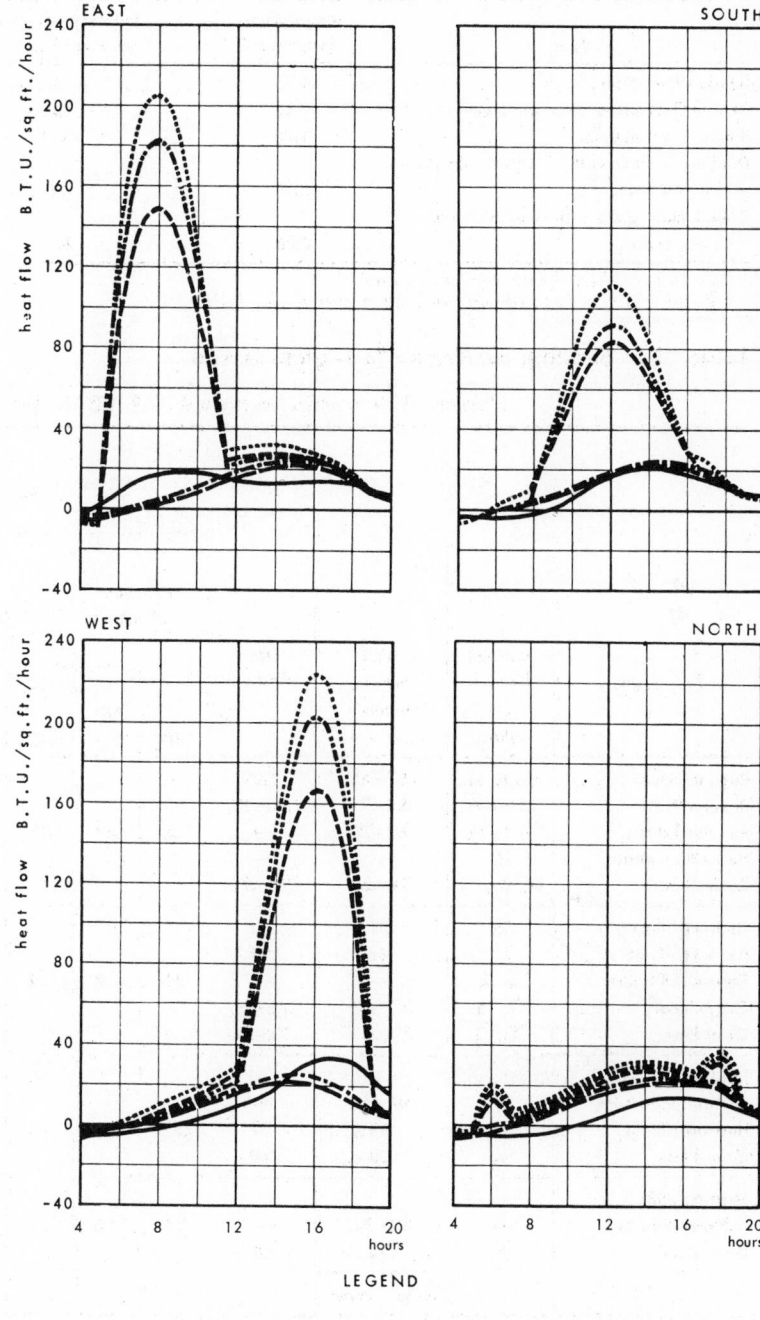

LEGEND

.... single glass, unshaded

—·—·—·— double glass, unshaded

———— heat absorbent glass, unshaded

———— opaque wall, U = 0.13, unshaded

—··—··— single glass, 100% shaded

———— double glass, 100% shaded

Charts that follow indicate the cooling tonnages required to offset the heat gains imposed by the summer sol-air design temperatures on walls facing each of the four orientations. For each wall, values are indicated for a variety of transparent areas and a range of transparency ratios.

The ratio of transparent surface area to total wall area is seen as a highly significant factor in cooling costs, with almost a linear relationship indicated. In general, with any type of unshaded glass, or with shading of any amount up to 50 per cent, a tripling of the transparent area approximately doubles the cooling load.

The cooling load contributed by the opaque surface is shown by the trapezoidal shaded area in each of the charts.

EFFECT OF BUILDING ORIENTATION ON COOLING LOAD
Tons of Refrigeration for 100 sq ft of wall

	North-South Orientation of Long Glazed Walls		East-West Orientation of Long Glazed Walls		Preference Ratio of North-South to East-West Orientation
Clear Glass Unshaded	N .15	S .45	W .87	E .76	2.7 to 1
Heat-Absorbing Glass	N .14	S .37	W .67	E .56	2.4 to 1
Clear Glass 50% Unshaded	N .14	S .30	W .54	E .45	2.3 to 1
Clear Glass 100% Unshaded	N .13	S .17	W .21	E .15	1.2 to 1

Note: Walls with glazing, 50% transparent, 50% opaque. Heat impact on solid end walls neglected

COOLING LOADS ON WALLS AT SUMMER PEAK CONDITIONS
Per 100 sq ft of surface

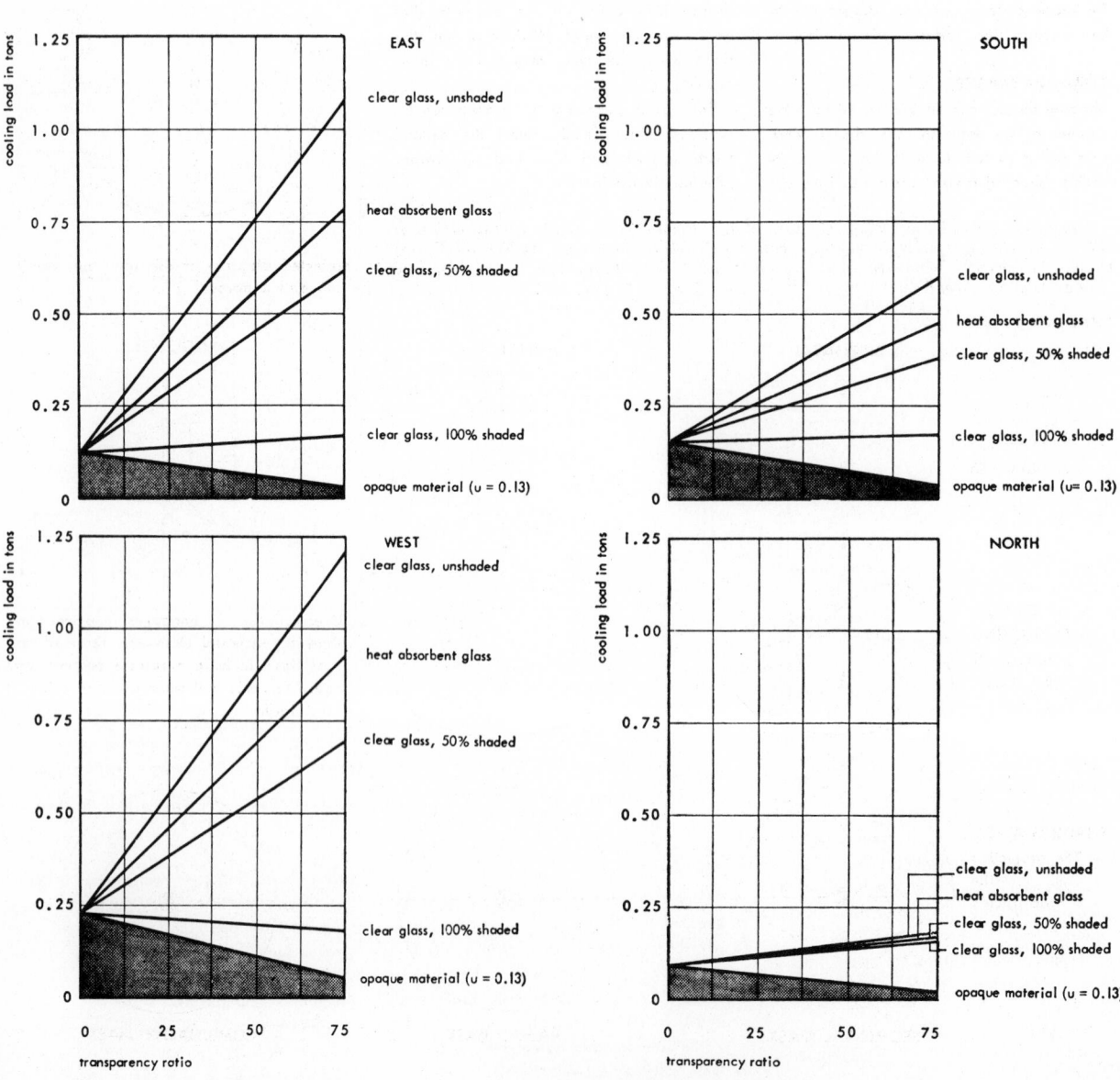

DESIGN OF SOLAR SHADING *

SUN PATHS

Location of the sun for any time of day can be found by use of the "sun path diagram," (right, bottom) which shows the sky-vault (right, top) projected onto the horizon plane. On such a diagram the horizon line appears as a circle at the outside edge, with the sun paths as curved lines. Only paths during the solstices and the equinox are drawn in this case. Connecting lines indicate the hours where the sun is at the given time. Thus the sun's position can be determined at any time by its bearing angle from the south point (on the perimeter of the diagram) and its altitude angle by means of an equally graduated scale measured from the center point.

The sun's paths will change according to the latitude of the location in question. Therefore a series of such diagrams will be required for various latitude ranges.

SHADING MASKS

Shading devices can be plotted in the same manner as sun paths to show during what time sun is excluded (see below). Here so-called "shading masks" are used. They are projections of the surface covered on the sky vault, as seen from an observation point at the center of the diagram. These projections also represent those parts of the sky vault from which no sunlight will come; if the sun passes through such an area, the observation point will be shaded.

Any building element will define a characteristic form in these projection diagrams, which we know as "shading masks." Masks of horizontal shading devices (overhangs) will show a segmental character; those of vertical fins produce a radial pattern; and masks of eggcrate types, are basically a combination of these forms. A shading mask can be drawn for any shading device, even for very complex ones, by simple geometrical methods. Since they are geometrical projections, they are independent of latitude and orientation, and may be used in any location.

By overlaying a shading mask in the proper orientation on the sun-path diagram, one can read off immediately the times when the sun's rays will be intercepted.

For design purposes, the process can be reversed. One can determine the needed shading mask and then find the proper shading device for it.

* *Thermal Behavior of Metal Curtain Walls, Study No. 6 in the investigation of the use of stainless steel in curtain wall construction, based on studies by Victor Olgyay, Research Associate and Associate Professor, Princeton University and Aladar Olgyay, Architect.*

SUN PATHS AND THEIR PROJECTIONS

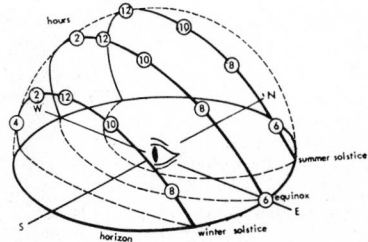

Half-sphere of the imaginary sky vault with sun paths. The projections of the sun paths are shown in dashed lines on the horizontal plane

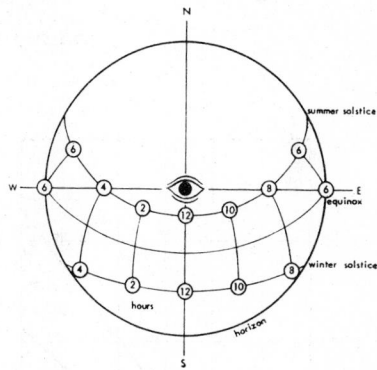

Projected diagram of the sky vault called "sun path diagram"

SHADING MASKS

HORIZONTAL	VERTICAL	EGGCRATE

TYPES OF DEVICES

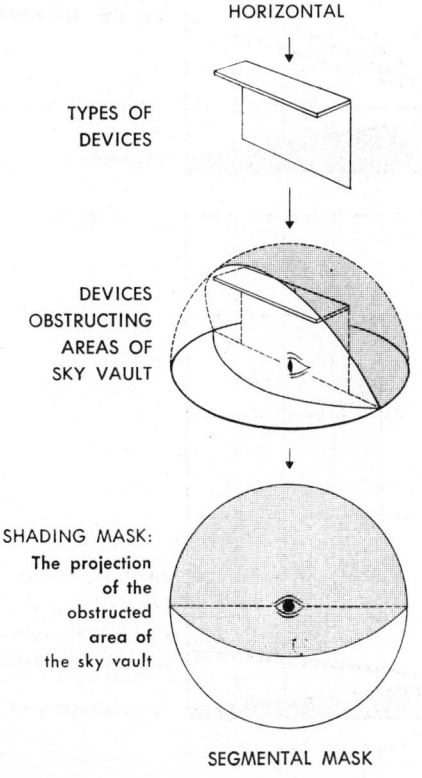
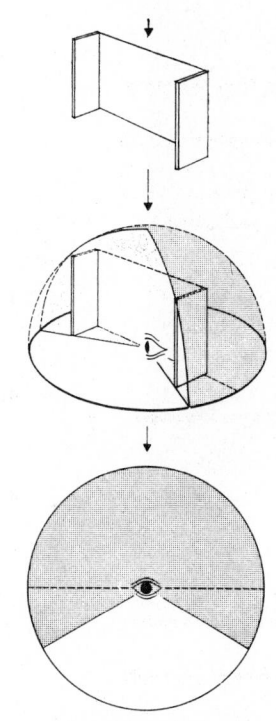
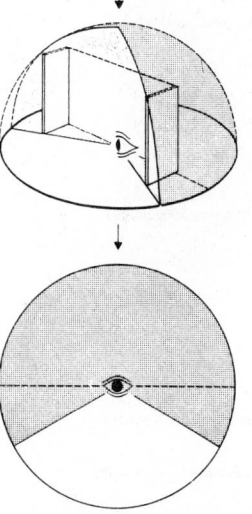
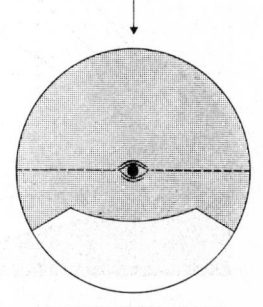

DEVICES OBSTRUCTING AREAS OF SKY VAULT

Obstructions of horizontal devices will show a segmental character; those of vertical fins will have a radical pattern, and eggcrate types will show a combination of these forms

SHADING MASK: The projection of the obstructed area of the sky vault

SEGMENTAL MASK   RADIAL MASK   COMBINATIVE MASK

Types of Devices

HORIZONTAL
TYPES

VIEW: SECTION: MASK.   CHARACTERISTIC:

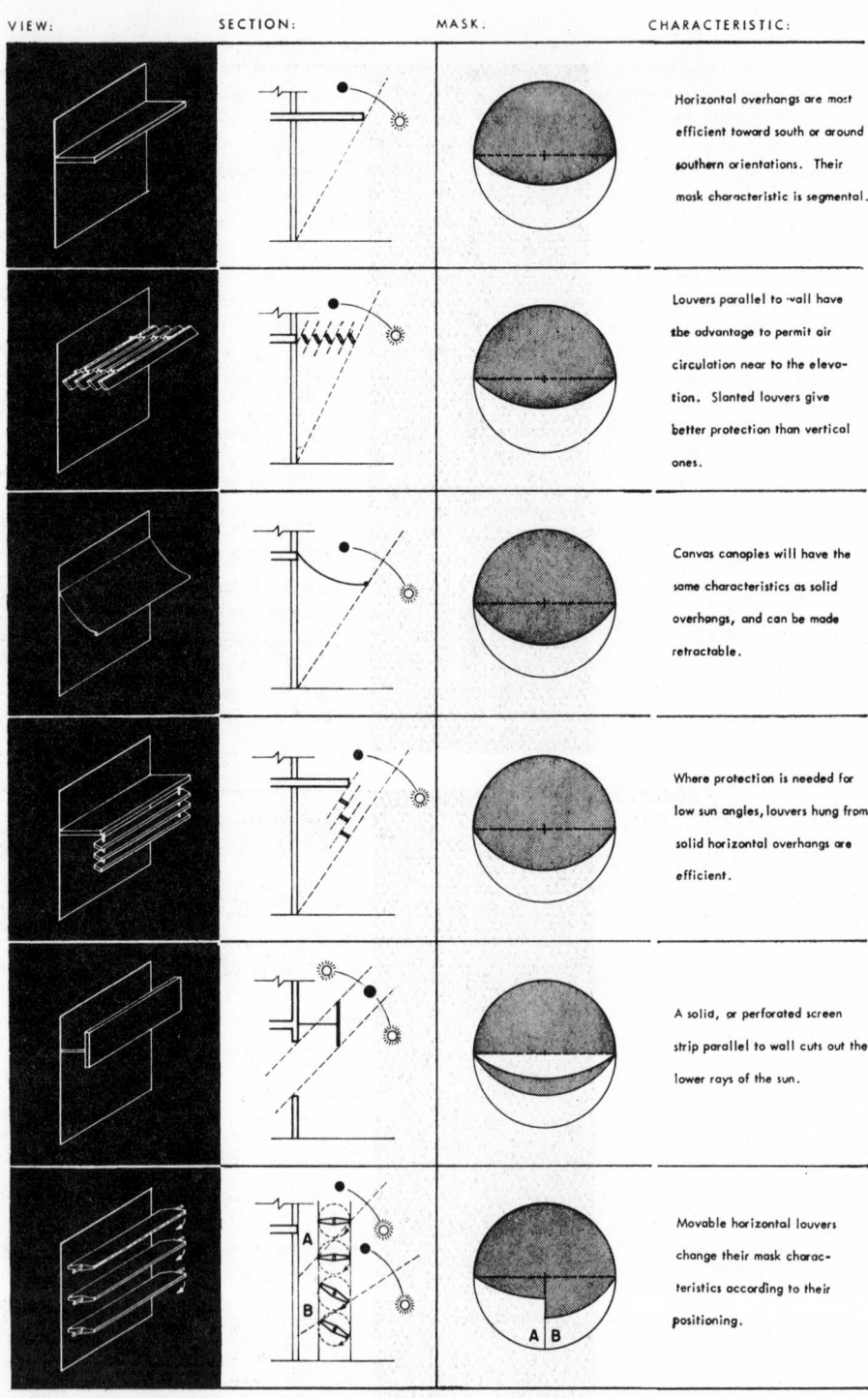

Horizontal overhangs are most efficient toward south or around southern orientations. Their mask characteristic is segmental.

Louvers parallel to wall have the advantage to permit air circulation near to the elevation. Slanted louvers give better protection than vertical ones.

Canvas canopies will have the same characteristics as solid overhangs, and can be made retractable.

Where protection is needed for low sun angles, louvers hung from solid horizontal overhangs are efficient.

A solid, or perforated screen strip parallel to wall cuts out the lower rays of the sun.

Movable horizontal louvers change their mask characteristics according to their positioning.

General rules can be deduced for the types of shading to be used for different orientations. Southerly orientations call for shading devices with segmental mask characteristics, and horizontal devices work in these directions efficiently. For easterly and westerly orientations vertical devices serve well, having radial shading masks. If slanted, they should incline toward the north, to give more protection from the southern positions of the sun. The eggcrate type of shading works well on walls facing southeast, and is particularly effective for southwest orientation. Because of this type's high shading ratio and low winter heat admission, its best use is in hot climate regions. For north walls, fixed vertical devices are recommended but their use is needed only in hot regions. In the very low latitudes (under 23°) horizontal devices work well also for this orientation.

Whether the shading devices be fixed or movable, the same recommendations apply in respect to the different orientations.

The movable types can be most efficiently utilized where the sun's altitude and bearing change rapidly: on the east, south-

Types of Devices *Continued*

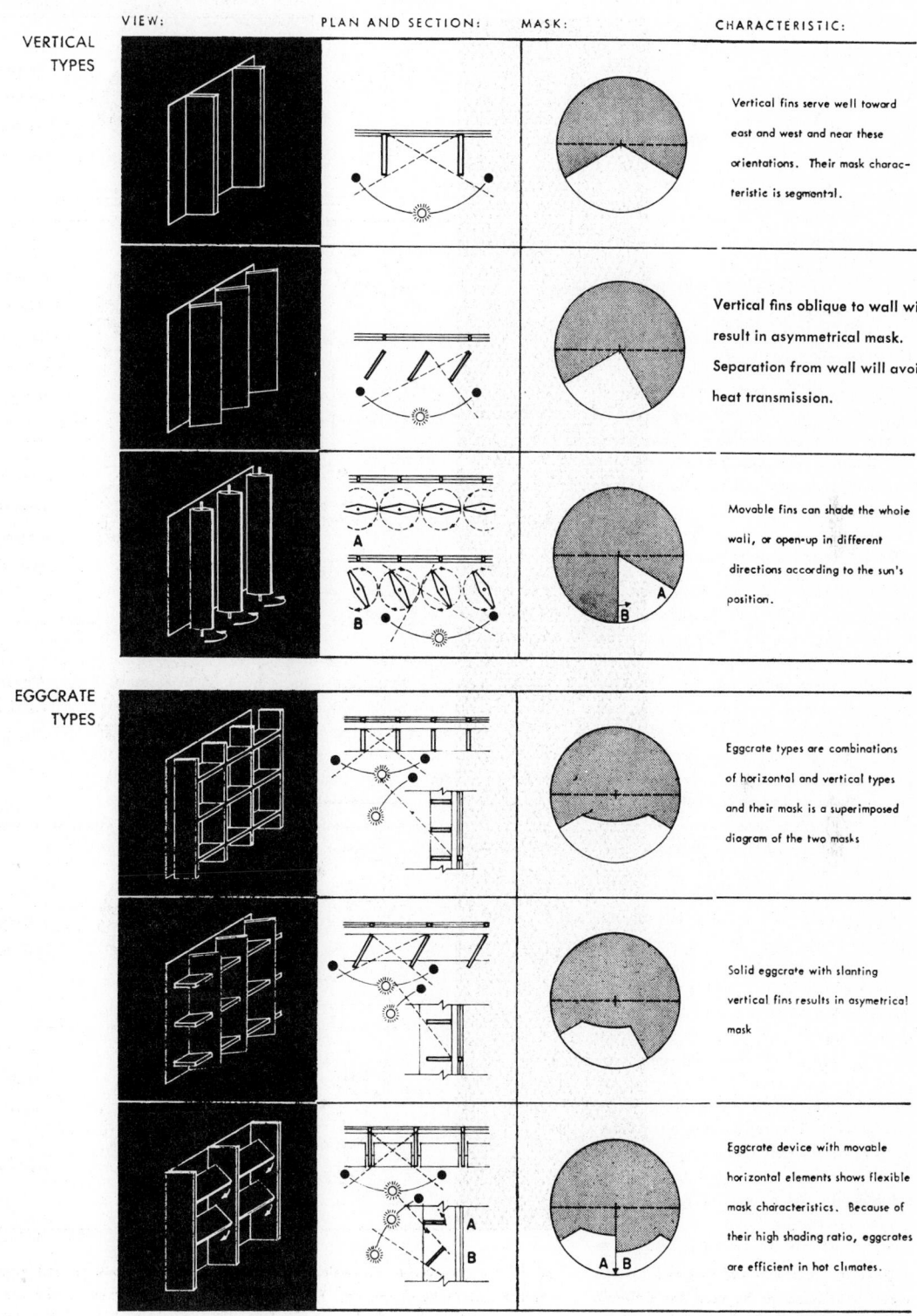

VIEW: PLAN AND SECTION: MASK: CHARACTERISTIC:

VERTICAL TYPES

Vertical fins serve well toward east and west and near these orientations. Their mask characteristic is segmental.

Vertical fins oblique to wall will result in asymmetrical mask. Separation from wall will avoid heat transmission.

Movable fins can shade the whole wall, or open-up in different directions according to the sun's position.

EGGCRATE TYPES

Eggcrate types are combinations of horizontal and vertical types and their mask is a superimposed diagram of the two masks

Solid eggcrate with slanting vertical fins results in asymetrical mask

Eggcrate device with movable horizontal elements shows flexible mask characteristics. Because of their high shading ratio, eggcrates are efficient in hot climates.

east, and especially, because of the afternoon heat, on the southwest and west.

The illustrations on this and the previous page show a number of basic types of devices, classified as horizontal, vertical, and eggcrate types.

The dash lines shown on the section diagram in each case indicate the sun angle at the time of 100 per cent shading.

The shading mask for each device is also shown, the extent of 100 per cent shading being indicated by the gray area.

By ALFRED GREENBERG, *P.E., Environmental Consultant*

AIR DISTRIBUTION

TYPES

Air-distribution systems include the following types:

1. Low velocity, single duct
2. Low velocity with zone control
3. Air-water induction
4. Fan-coil units
5. High velocity, single duct (with and without reheat)
6. High velocity, dual duct
7. Self-contained units

Components for each of the above systems are similar (Fig. 2). Many variations in arrangement and location of components are possible. Below about 20,000 cfm, factory-built units are generally used; above 20,000 cfm, field-built units are preferred by most engineers although factory-built units are available up to about 40,000 cfm.

1. *Low-velocity, single-duct* systems are the most commonly used because of their simplicity and economy. Two special types of low-velocity air-distribution systems are available which utilize the floor or ceiling plenum to provide heating or cooling partially by radiant means. The air eventually enters the room to furnish some thermal effect and satisfy ventilation requirements. The underfloor scheme consists of metal, clay, or concrete forms which, in effect, create a hollow floor through which conditioned air passes before it enters the space through registers at the walls.

2. *Low velocity with zone control.* For areas having widely differing heat loads, at a given time, it may be expedient to zone the low-velocity, single-duct system and place a heating (or cooling) coil in each branch to take care of peak loads (see Fig. 3). Where the building is comparatively small and only a few zones are required, the use of secondary coils is reasonably economical. On the other hand, using recooling coils involves a more costly initial investment with an elaborate automatic control setup. A third type of zone control involves the automatic adjustment of the amount of air entering the zone as the heat load varies.

3. *Air-water induction* system is mostly used for perimeter applications. The air comes from a central source for each zone and furnishes the humidity control and outside air requirements for the room as well as taking care of the room's fixed heat load. This air, called the primary air, goes through nozzles and induces about

4 to 8 times as much room air along with it through the water coil and out into the room (see Fig. 4).

The water flow to each unit or group of units is controlled by an automatic control valve to take care of the variable portions of the room load and all the outside transmission and solar load. Each control valve will serve from 1 to 6 units and each thermostat from 1 to 4 control valves. The air ducts and the water piping are often run vertically at the perimeter of the building. Several common schemes are shown in Fig. 5. The ductwork is generally run at high velocity (2,500 to 4,500 fpm) especially when run at the perimeter, in order to conserve space. Induction units serve a perimeter area which generally extends 14 to 18 ft from the exterior of the building. They find their greatest use in new multistory buildings.

4. *Fan-coil units,* as the name implies, contain a fan and a coil and also filters and a condensate pan, if required. In most

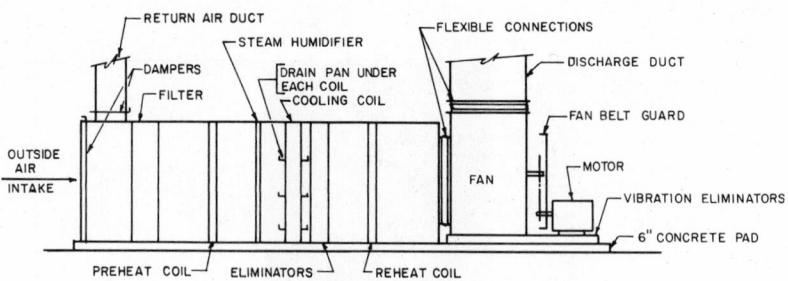

Fig. 2. Components of typical air-distribution system

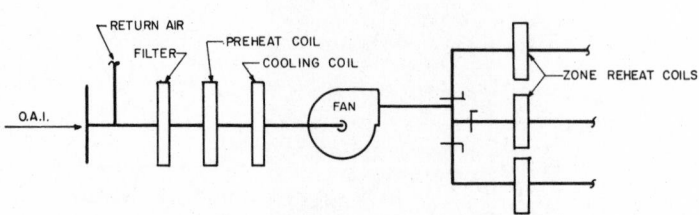

Fig. 3. Single-duct system with zoned reheat

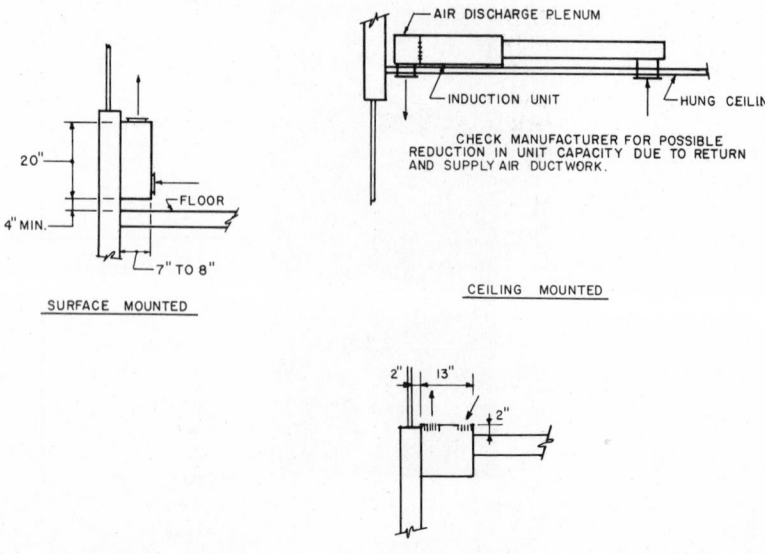

Fig. 4. Air-water induction units

Length of induction units varies from 20 to 64 in.

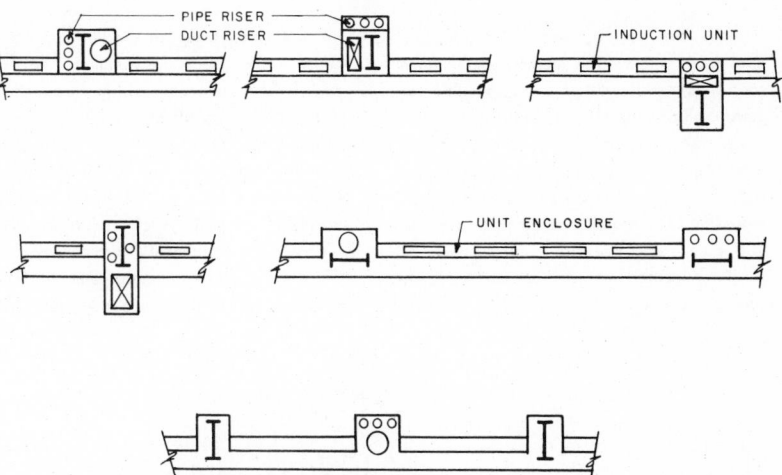

Fig. 5. Various arrangements of perimeter risers

cases, these units are furnished for perimeter wall use and get their air from openings in the outside wall. See Fig. 6a and b. A central outside air supply may be furnished, especially when the fan-coil units are located in the interior of the room, generally at the ceiling, in a closet, or over the door (Fig. 6c). The piping system is centralized, and a control system similar to that used for the induction system can be used for the water cycle. The standard fan-coil unit is not designed to handle outside air quantities in excess of about 40 per cent. However, for greater outside air quantities, the classroom-type unit ventilator (Fig. 7), which is a larger version of the fan-coil unit, can be used.

The fan-coil units serve an area up to 25 ft from the exterior wall. They are slightly noisier than the induction system and do not maintain environmental conditions as closely, but are satisfactory for most applications. The fan-coil system has a lower first cost than the induction system but will probably require more maintenance as the years go by.

Three- or four-pipe systems: A refinement in temperature control of both air-water induction and fan-coil units is provided by furnishing a 3- or 4-pipe water system to each unit. Each has a hot and cold water pipe, and a common or separate return water line. A special valve is used to meter just the proper amount of either hot or cold water to each unit thus maintaining correct room temperature all year round (see Fig. 8). It eliminates the problem of changeover temperature conditions since hot and cold water are always available to take care of all heat-load situations.

Changeover temperature is that outside temperature at which the air-conditioning system is switched from summer to winter use, i.e., from chilled water to hot water. This temperature is a function of many factors such as building construction, system operation, location of building, etc. The changeover temperature is generally different for each exposure. Therefore, on most large buildings, each exposure is zoned so that it can be individually changed from summer to winter operation or vice versa. In the intermediate seasons, it is possible to require changeover several times a week for a given zone.

5. High-velocity, single-duct. Where a single-duct air-distribution system is desired and zone control is sufficient for the areas served but conventionally sized ducts will not fit the space allotted, then a high-velocity single-duct system may be used. The major difference besides the fact that it has smaller ducts is that a terminal box may be required for reducing the velocity

and noise level of the air before discharging it into the room. A variation of this system is to use air-pressure-reducing valves in the ducts and acoustical lining before discharging the air into the space. A single-duct zone system with terminal boxes may be used where each box has a reheat coil (Fig. 9). If loads vary, volume control at each unit plus fan volume control will probably be more economical.

6. High-velocity, dual-duct, all-air systems furnish the greatest degree of individual room flexibility of the systems discussed. They furnish quantities of properly mixed hot and cold air to satisfy all load conditions (Fig. 10). They also require the largest amount of shaft and ceiling space and are generally the most expensive to install. Low-velocity dual-duct systems are seldom used because of space limitations.

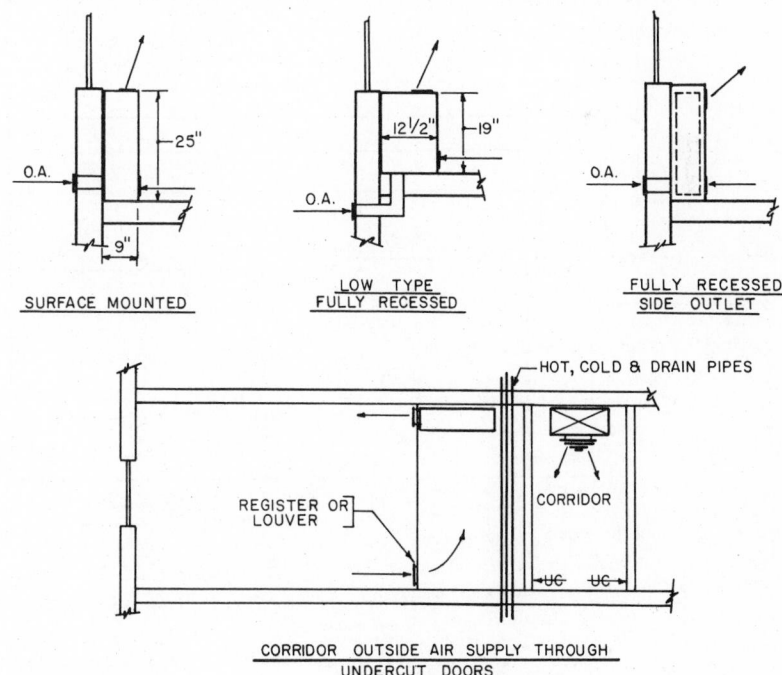

Fig. 6. Fan-coil units

Outside air openings can be any shape. The smaller the opening, the less the problem with stack effect, wind, and rain, but the less outside air can be brought in. Outside air grille can be located remotely by using ductwork to the unit, but this may reduce unit capacity because of higher static pressure.

For maximum coil protection, provide automatic outdoor air damper.

Length of fan-coil units varies from about 16 to 60 in.

There are several ways of controlling dual-duct systems. One method uses volume control for each unit; this is applicable for private offices and other comparatively small areas requiring individual control conditions. Another uses duct static pressure control; this is suitable for open offices, general manufacturing, stock, and other such areas. The duct static pressure controls must be properly located in order for the system to function properly. See Fig. 11.

7. *Self-contained air-conditioning units* furnish relief from the summer heat but most of them have poor air-distribution patterns, are comparatively noisy, and have no humidity control. However, they are the cheapest type of air-conditioning system available, are easy to install, have a high degree of portability, often furnish purge (100 per cent exhaust) air control, and can relieve building management of all operating and maintenance expenses. Operating and maintenance costs for these units are generally higher per ton of refrigeration than for any other system.

DUCT DESIGN

Sizing within the pressure, temperature, and velocity ranges at which most commercial and many industrial air systems operate, reasonably accurate results can be obtained with a minimum of theoretical design considerations. The equation used for calculating air quantities is:

$$cfm = \frac{SH}{1.08 \times t_r - t_a}$$

where cfm = cu ft of air per min at 70°F and 29.92 in. Hg

SH = sensible heat load, Btu/hr of area for which air quantity is desired

t_r = room or area temperature, °F

t_a = temperature of air in duct entering room, °F

The sizing of all ductwork is generally based upon the ASHRAE criteria. Figures 12 and 13 show a convenient method of calculating duct sizes. Table 19 converts round duct sizes to equivalent rectangular ducts.

The duct-sizing charts are based on galvanized iron ducts. Where materials with rougher or smoother surfaces are used, correction factors should be applied as indicated in the ASHRAE Guide. Correction factors for friction loss of ducts internally lined for acoustic attenuation are shown in Table 20.

Regardless of which air-distribution system is used, it is imperative that the balance between supply and return and exhaust air for each area and the building as a whole be reasonably close to avoid drafts and improper system functioning.

In many instances a small percentage of positive or negative air pressure is desirable. Bathrooms and kitchens, for instance, are often kept under a 10 to 15 per cent negative pressure, and typical rooms with operable sash are usually kept under positive pressure, in order to prevent infiltration.

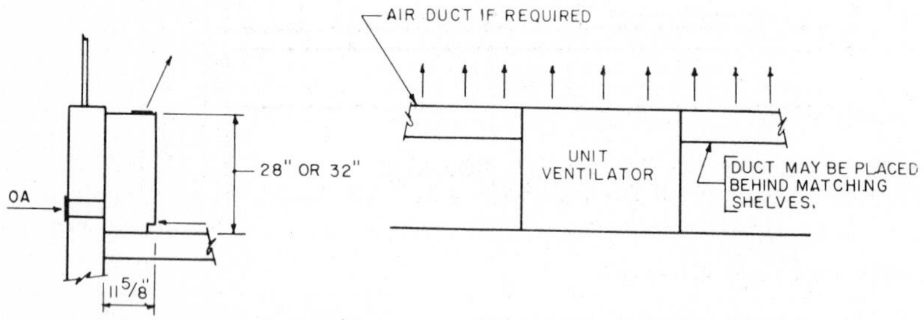

Fig. 7. Classroom-type unit ventilator

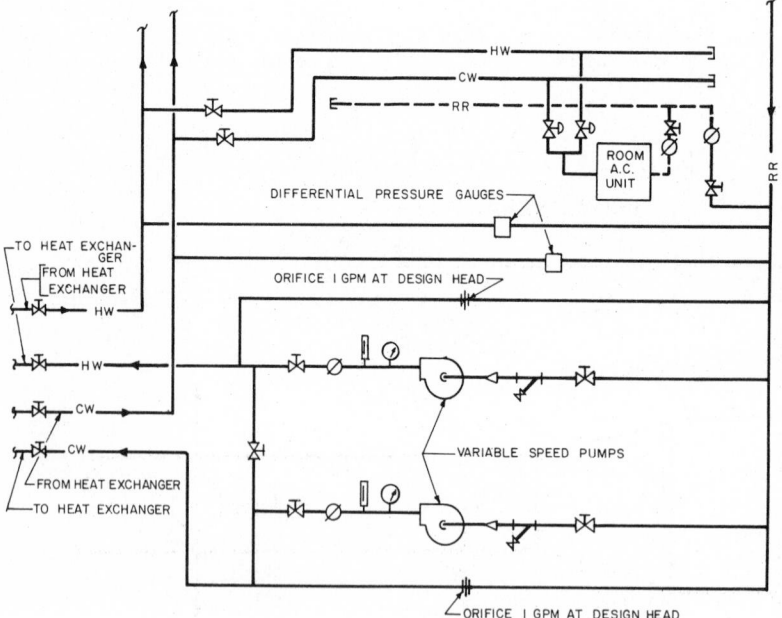

Fig. 8. Unzoned three-pipe system

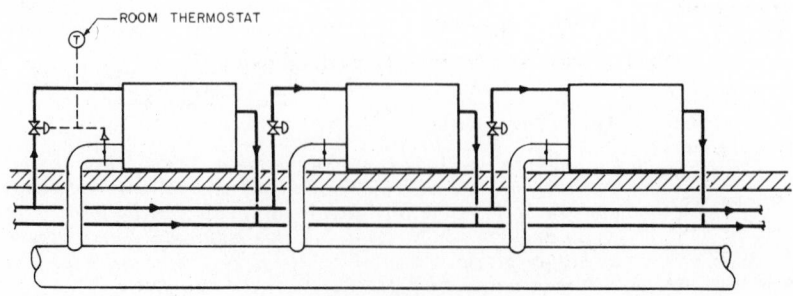

Fig. 9. High-velocity single-duct system with reheat coils

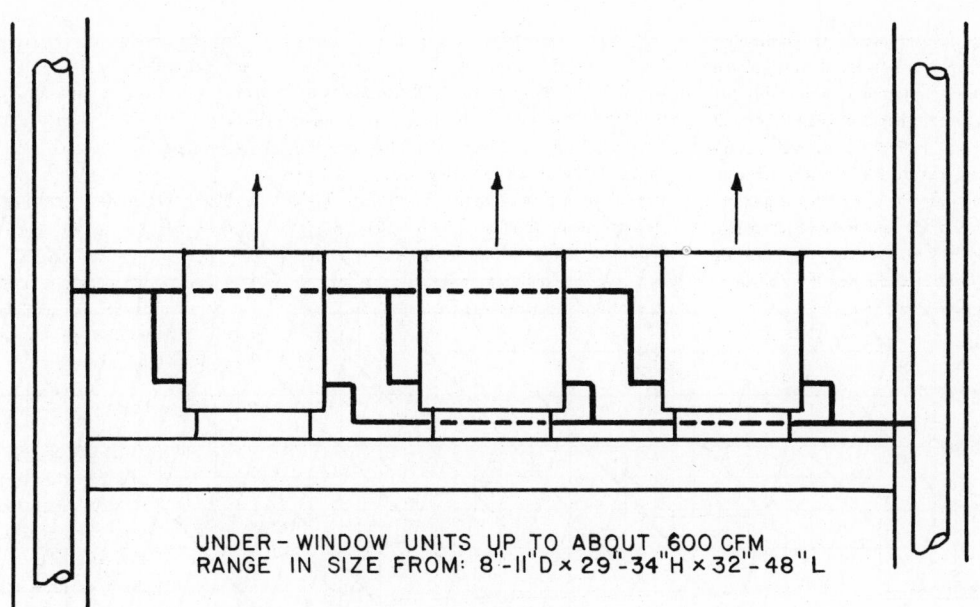

UNDER - WINDOW UNITS UP TO ABOUT 600 CFM
RANGE IN SIZE FROM: 8"-11"D × 29"-34"H × 32"-48"L

Fig 10.   High-velocity dual-duct system

Approximate dual-duct box sizes

Cfm	D	W	L
Up to 300	8	24	30
301 to 600	10	30	36
601 to 1,000	12–14	42	48
1,001 to 4,000	25	30	54

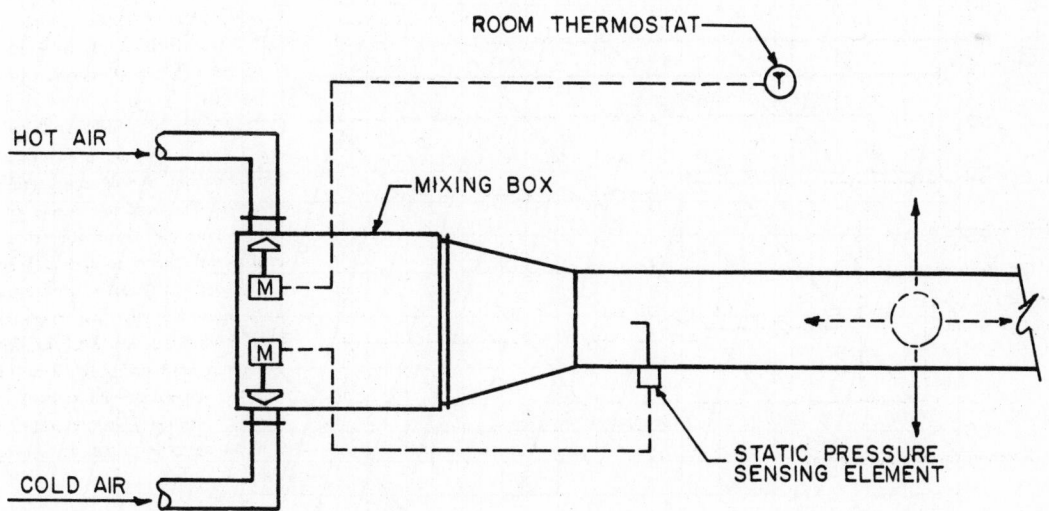

Fig. 11.   Static pressure control for dual-duct system

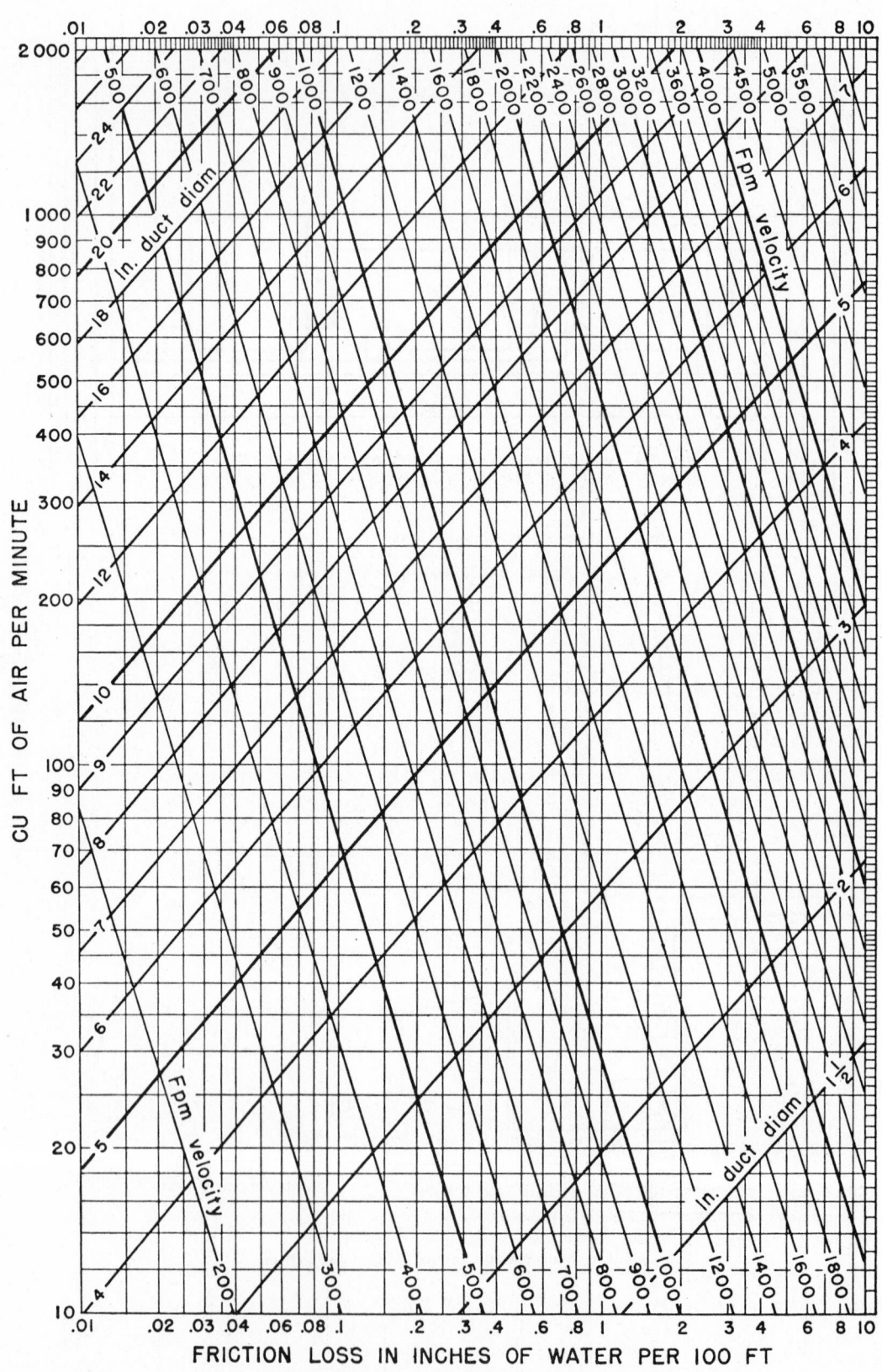

(Based on Standard Air of 0.075 lb per cu ft density flowing through average, clean, round, galvanized metal ducts having approximately 40 joints per 100 ft.) Caution: Do not extrapolate below chart.

Fig. 12.   Friction of air in straight ducts for volumes of 10 to 2,000 cfm

Reprinted by permission from ASHRAE *Guide and Data Book, 1963.*

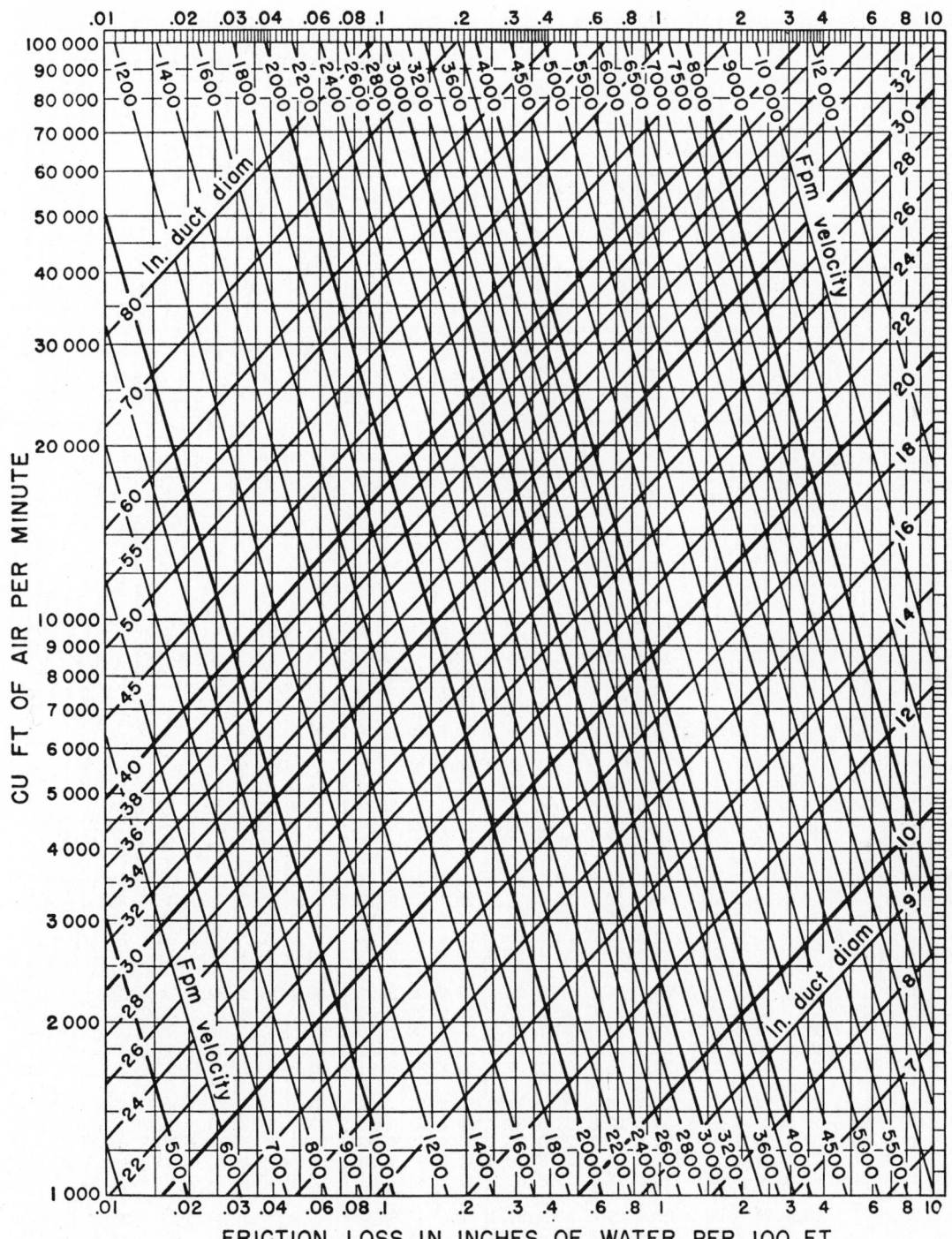

(*Based on Standard Air of 0.075 lb per cu ft density flowing through average, clean, round, galvanized metal ducts having approximately 40 joints per 100 ft.*)

Fig. 13.   Friction of air in straight ducts for volumes of 1,000 to 100,000 cfm

Reprinted by permission from ASHRAE Guide and Data Book, *1963*.

Table 19. Circular equivalents of rectangular ducts for equal friction and capacity

Dimensions in inches. (Reprinted by permission from ASHRAE Guide and Data Book, 1963.)

Side Rectangular Duct	4.0	4.5	5.0	5.5	6.0	6.5	7.0	7.5	8.0	9.0	10.0	11.0	12.0	13.0	14.0	15.0	16.0
3.0	3.8	4.0	4.2	4.4	4.6	4.8	4.9	5.1	5.2	5.5	5.7	6.0	6.2	6.4	6.6	6.8	7.0
3.5	4.1	4.3	4.6	4.8	5.0	5.2	5.3	5.5	5.7	6.0	6.3	6.5	6.8	7.0	7.2	7.4	7.6
4.0	4.4	4.6	4.9	5.1	5.3	5.5	5.7	5.9	6.1	6.4	6.8	7.1	7.3	7.6	7.8	8.1	8.3
4.5	4.6	4.9	5.2	5.4	5.6	5.9	6.1	6.3	6.5	6.9	7.2	7.5	7.8	8.1	8.4	8.6	8.9
5.0	4.9	5.2	5.5	5.7	6.0	6.2	6.4	6.7	6.9	7.3	7.6	8.0	8.3	8.6	8.9	9.1	9.4
5.5	5.1	5.4	5.7	6.0	6.3	6.5	6.8	7.0	7.2	7.6	8.0	8.4	8.7	9.0	9.4	9.6	9.8

Side Rectangular Duct	6	7	8	9	10	11	12	13	14	15	16	17	18	19	20	22	24	26	28	30	Side Rectangular Duct
6	6.6																				6
7	7.1	7.7																			7
8	7.5	8.2	8.8																		8
9	8.0	8.6	9.3	9.9																	9
10	8.4	9.1	9.8	10.4	10.9																10
11	8.8	9.5	10.2	10.8	11.4	12.0															11
12	9.1	9.9	10.7	11.3	11.9	12.5	13.1														12
13	9.5	10.3	11.1	11.8	12.4	13.0	13.6	14.2													13
14	9.8	10.7	11.5	12.2	12.9	13.5	14.2	14.7	15.3												14
15	10.1	11.0	11.8	12.6	13.3	14.0	14.6	15.3	15.8	16.4											15
16	10.4	11.4	12.2	13.0	13.7	14.4	15.1	15.7	16.3	16.9	17.5										16
17	10.7	11.7	12.5	13.4	14.1	14.9	15.5	16.1	16.8	17.4	18.0	18.6									17
18	11.0	11.9	12.9	13.7	14.5	15.3	16.0	16.6	17.3	17.9	18.5	19.1	19.7								18
19	11.2	12.2	13.2	14.1	14.9	15.6	16.4	17.1	17.8	18.4	19.0	19.6	20.2	20.8							19
20	11.5	12.5	13.5	14.4	15.2	15.9	16.8	17.5	18.2	18.8	19.5	20.1	20.7	21.3	21.9						20
22	12.0	13.1	14.1	15.0	15.9	16.7	17.6	18.3	19.1	19.7	20.4	21.0	21.7	22.3	22.9	24.1					22
24	12.4	13.6	14.6	15.6	16.6	17.5	18.3	19.1	19.8	20.6	21.3	21.9	22.6	23.2	23.9	25.1	26.2				24
26	12.8	14.1	15.2	16.2	17.2	18.1	19.0	19.8	20.6	21.4	22.1	22.8	23.5	24.1	24.8	26.1	27.2	28.4			26
28	13.2	14.5	15.6	16.7	17.7	18.7	19.6	20.5	21.3	22.1	22.9	23.6	24.4	25.0	25.7	27.1	28.2	29.5	30.6		28
30	13.6	14.9	16.1	17.2	18.3	19.3	20.2	21.1	22.0	22.9	23.7	24.4	25.2	25.9	26.7	28.0	29.3	30.5	31.6	32.8	30
32	14.0	15.3	16.5	17.7	18.8	19.8	20.8	21.8	22.7	23.6	24.4	25.2	26.0	26.7	27.5	28.9	30.1	31.4	32.6	33.8	32
34	14.4	15.7	17.0	18.2	19.3	20.4	21.4	22.4	23.3	24.2	25.1	25.9	26.7	27.5	28.3	29.7	31.0	32.3	33.6	34.8	34
36	14.7	16.1	17.4	18.6	19.8	20.9	21.9	23.0	23.9	24.8	25.8	26.6	27.4	28.3	29.0	30.5	32.0	33.0	34.6	35.8	36
38	15.0	16.4	17.8	19.0	20.3	21.4	22.5	23.5	24.5	25.4	26.4	27.3	28.1	29.0	29.8	31.4	32.8	34.2	35.5	36.7	38
40	15.3	16.8	18.2	19.4	20.7	21.9	23.0	24.0	25.1	26.0	27.0	27.9	28.8	29.7	30.5	32.1	33.6	35.1	36.4	37.6	40
42	15.6	17.1	18.5	19.8	21.1	22.3	23.4	24.5	25.6	26.6	27.6	28.5	29.4	30.4	31.2	32.8	34.4	35.9	37.3	38.6	42
44	15.9	17.5	18.9	20.2	21.5	22.7	23.9	25.0	26.1	27.2	28.2	29.1	30.0	31.0	31.9	33.5	35.2	36.7	38.1	39.5	44
46	16.2	17.8	19.2	20.6	21.9	23.2	24.3	25.5	26.7	27.7	28.7	29.7	30.6	31.6	32.5	34.2	35.9	37.4	38.9	40.3	46
48	16.5	18.1	19.6	20.9	22.3	23.6	24.8	26.0	27.2	28.2	29.2	30.2	31.2	32.2	33.1	34.9	36.6	38.2	39.7	41.2	48
50	16.8	18.4	19.9	21.3	22.7	24.0	25.2	26.4	27.6	28.7	29.8	30.8	31.8	32.8	33.7	35.5	37.3	38.9	40.4	42.0	50
52	17.0	18.7	20.2	21.6	23.1	24.4	25.6	26.8	28.1	29.2	30.3	31.4	32.4	33.4	34.3	36.2	38.0	39.6	41.2	42.8	52
54	17.3	19.0	20.5	22.0	23.4	24.8	26.1	27.3	28.5	29.7	30.8	31.9	32.9	33.9	34.9	36.8	38.7	40.3	42.0	43.6	54
56	17.6	19.3	20.9	22.4	23.8	25.2	26.5	27.7	28.9	30.1	31.2	32.4	33.4	34.5	35.5	37.4	39.3	41.0	42.7	44.3	56
58	17.8	19.5	21.1	22.7	24.2	25.5	26.9	28.2	29.3	30.5	31.7	32.9	33.9	35.0	36.0	38.0	39.8	41.7	43.4	45.0	58
60	18.1	19.8	21.4	23.0	24.5	25.8	27.3	28.7	29.8	31.0	32.2	33.4	34.5	35.5	36.5	38.6	40.4	42.3	44.0	45.8	60
62	18.3	20.1	21.7	23.3	24.8	26.2	27.6	29.0	30.2	31.4	32.6	33.8	35.0	36.0	37.1	39.2	41.0	42.9	44.7	46.5	62
64	18.6	20.3	22.0	23.6	25.2	26.5	27.9	29.3	30.6	31.8	33.1	34.2	35.5	36.5	37.6	39.7	41.6	43.5	45.4	47.2	64
66	18.8	20.6	22.3	23.9	25.5	26.9	28.3	29.7	31.0	32.2	33.5	34.7	35.9	37.0	38.1	40.2	42.2	44.1	46.0	47.8	66
68	19.0	20.8	22.5	24.2	25.8	27.3	28.7	30.1	31.4	32.6	33.9	35.1	36.3	37.5	38.6	40.7	42.8	44.7	46.6	48.4	68
70	19.2	21.	22.8	24.5	26.1	27.6	29.1	30.4	31.8	33.1	34.3	35.6	36.8	37.9	39.1	41.3	43.3	45.3	47.2	49.0	70
72															39.6	41.8	43.8	45.9	47.8	49.7	72
74															40.0	42.3	44.4	46.4	48.4	50.3	74
76															40.5	42.8	44.9	47.0	49.0	50.8	76
78															40.9	43.3	45.5	47.5	49.5	51.5	78
80															41.3	43.8	46.0	48.0	50.1	52.0	80
82															41.8	44.2	46.4	48.6	50.6	52.6	82
84															42.2	44.6	46.9	49.2	51.1	53.2	84
86															42.6	45.0	47.4	49.6	51.6	53.7	86
88															43.0	45.4	47.9	50.1	52.2	54.3	88
90															43.4	45.9	48.3	50.6	52.8	54.8	90
92															43.8	46.3	48.7	51.1	53.4	55.4	92
96															44.6	47.2	49.5	52.0	54.4	56.3	96

Equation for Circular Equivalent of a Rectangular Duct:[5]

$$d_c = 1.30 \frac{(ab)^{0.625}}{(a+b)^{0.250}} = 1.30 \sqrt[8]{\frac{(ab)^5}{(a+b)^2}}$$

where
a = length of one side of rectangular duct, inches.
b = length of adjacent side of rectangular duct, inches.
d_c = circular equivalent of a rectangular duct for equal friction and capacity, inches.

Table 19. Circular equivalents of rectangular ducts for equal friction and capacity (cont.)

Dimensions in inches. (Reprinted by permission from ASHRAE Guide and Data Book, 1963.)

Side Rectangular Duct	32	34	36	38	40	42	44	46	48	50	52	56	60	64	68	72	76	80	84	88	Side Rectangular Duct
32	35.0																				32
34	36.0	37.2																			34
36	37.0	38.2	39.4																		36
38	38.0	39.2	40.4	41.6																	38
40	39.0	40.2	41.4	42.6	43.8																40
42	39.9	41.1	42.4	43.6	44.8	45.9															42
44	40.8	42.0	43.4	44.6	45.8	46.9	48.1														44
46	41.7	43.0	44.3	45.6	46.8	47.9	49.1	50.3													46
48	42.6	43.9	45.2	46.5	47.8	48.9	50.2	51.3	52.6												48
50	43.5	44.8	46.1	47.4	48.8	49.8	51.2	52.3	53.6	54.7											50
52	44.3	45.7	47.1	48.3	49.7	50.8	52.2	53.3	54.6	55.8	56.9										52
54	45.0	46.5	48.0	49.2	50.6	51.8	53.2	54.3	55.6	56.8	57.9										54
56	45.8	47.3	48.8	50.1	51.5	52.7	54.1	55.3	56.5	57.8	58.9	61.3									56
58	46.6	48.1	49.6	51.0	52.4	53.7	55.0	56.2	57.5	58.8	60.0	62.3									58
60	47.3	48.9	50.4	51.8	53.3	54.6	55.9	57.1	58.5	59.8	61.0	63.3	65.7								60
62	48.0	49.7	51.2	52.6	54.2	55.5	56.8	58.0	59.4	60.7	62.0	64.3	66.7								62
64	48.7	50.4	52.0	53.4	55.0	56.4	57.7	59.0	60.3	61.6	62.9	65.3	67.7	70.0							64
66	49.5	51.1	52.8	54.2	55.8	57.2	58.6	59.9	61.2	62.5	63.9	66.3	68.7	71.1							66
68	50.2	51.8	53.5	55.0	56.6	58.0	59.5	60.8	62.1	63.4	64.8	67.3	69.7	72.1	74.4						68
70	50.9	52.5	54.2	55.8	57.3	58.8	60.3	61.7	63.0	64.3	65.7	68.3	70.7	73.1	75.4						70
72	51.5	53.2	54.9	56.5	58.0	59.6	61.1	62.6	63.9	65.2	66.6	69.2	71.7	74.1	76.4	78.8					72
74	52.1	53.9	55.6	57.2	58.8	60.4	61.9	63.3	64.8	66.1	67.5	70.1	72.7	75.1	77.4	79.9					74
76	52.7	54.6	56.3	57.9	59.5	61.2	62.7	64.1	65.6	67.0	68.4	71.0	73.6	76.1	78.4	80.9	83.2				76
78	53.3	55.2	57.0	58.6	60.3	62.0	63.4	64.9	66.4	67.9	69.3	71.8	74.5	77.1	79.4	81.8	84.2				78
80	53.9	55.8	57.6	59.3	61.0	62.7	64.1	65.7	67.2	68.7	70.1	72.7	75.4	78.1	80.4	82.8	85.2	87.5			80
82	54.5	56.4	58.2	60.0	61.7	63.4	64.9	66.5	68.0	69.5	71.0	73.6	76.3	79.0	81.4	83.8	86.2	88.6			82
84	55.1	57.0	58.9	60.7	62.4	64.1	65.7	67.3	68.8	70.3	71.8	74.5	77.2	79.9	82.4	84.8	87.2	89.6	91.9		84
86	55.7	57.6	59.5	61.3	63.0	64.8	66.4	68.0	69.5	71.1	72.6	75.4	78.1	80.8	83.3	85.8	88.2	90.6	92.9		86
88	56.3	58.2	60.1	62.0	63.7	65.4	67.0	68.7	70.3	71.8	73.4	76.3	79.0	81.6	84.2	86.8	89.2	91.6	93.9	96.3	88
90	56.9	58.8	60.7	62.6	64.4	66.0	67.8	69.4	71.1	72.6	74.2	77.1	79.9	82.5	85.1	87.8	90.2	92.6	94.9	97.3	90
92	57.4	59.4	61.3	63.2	65.0	66.8	68.5	70.1	71.8	73.3	74.9	77.9	80.8	83.4	86.0	88.7	91.2	93.6	95.9	98.3	92
94	57.9	60.0	61.9	63.8	65.6	67.5	69.2	70.8	72.5	74.1	75.6	78.7	81.7	84.3	86.9	89.6	92.1	94.6	96.9	99.3	94
96	58.4	60.5	62.4	64.4	66.2	68.2	69.8	71.5	73.2	74.3	76.3	79.4	82.6	85.2	87.8	90.5	93.0	95.6	97.9	100.3	96

Table 20. Correction factors for friction loss of ducts acoustically lined

Air velocity	Correction factor	Air velocity	Correction factor
500	1.25	1,800	1.41
600	1.28	2,000	1.42
700	1.30	2,500	1.45
800	1.31	3,000	1.47
900	1.32	3,500	1.49
1,000	1.33	4,000	1.50
1,200	1.36	4,500	1.52
1,400	1.38	5,000	1.54
1,600	1.40	5,500	1.55
		6,000	1.56

Static pressure: In commercial applications, the following criteria are widely used for sizing ductwork:

Type	Max static pressure/ 100 equiv. ft	Max vel.
Conventional low velocity	0.10	1,500
Medium velocity	0.50	2,500
High velocity	1.0	3,500

Table 21. Static pressure drop for louver assemblies

Net velocity through free area of louver	Static pressure, in. water
722	0.11
967*	0.198
1,220	0.308
1,360	0.397
1,522	0.501

Normal Design Standard.

It will be noted from the duct-sizing charts that for the larger air quantities, the static pressure will drop off in order not to exceed the maximum velocities. For best results and ease of balancing the systems, terminal unit static pressure should be high compared to duct static pressure.

When system static pressures are calculated to determine fan horsepower requirements, the ASHRAE Guide should be consulted to determine static pressure losses for ductwork fittings. Table 21 gives field-obtained values of static pressure for louver assemblies consisting of fixed architectural louvers, bird screens, and automatic louver dampers.

Air velocities: There are many types of supply and return air outlets and inlets available. Most air-outlet manufacturers give sufficiently reliable data to enable determination of the correct sizes for given applications and their operating characteristics.

Recommended return-intake face velocities are given in Table 22.

Table 23 gives a guide for recommended and maximum duct and system component velocities for conventional systems.

Air-handling equipment: The fan and motor should be set on an integral vibration eliminator base and the inlet and discharge connections should be made with flexible connections to minimize vibration transmission through the ducts.

Figure 2 shows typical air-handling components. Face velocity across components in the casing is generally kept at 500 fpm, although this may vary widely for different components. Air velocities across the cooling coils seldom exceed 500 fpm because of the posibility of water carryover due to condensation on the coil. When heating coils are located on the discharge side of fans, they are often sized at from 800 to

Table 23. Recommended and maximum duct velocities for conventional systems

Reprinted by permission from ASHRAE Guide and Data Book, 1963.

Designation	Recommended velocities, fpm		
	Residences	Schools, theaters, public buildings	Industrial buildings
Outdoor air intakes*	500	500	500
Filters*	250	300	350
Heating Coils*	450	500	600
Air washers	500	500	500
Suction connections	700	800	1,000
Fan outlets	1,000–1,600	1,300–2,000	1,600–2,400
Main ducts	700–900	1,000–1,300	1,200–1,800
Branch ducts	600	600–900	800–1,000
Branch risers	500	600–700	800
	Maximum velocities, fpm		
Outdoor air intakes*	800	900	1200
Filters*	300	350	350
Heating coils*	500	600	700
Air washers	500	500	500
Suction connections	900	1,000	1,400
Fan outlets	1,700	1,500–2,200	1,700–2,800
Main ducts	800–1,200	1,100–1,600	1,300–2,200
Branch ducts	700–1,000	800–1,300	1,000–1,800
Branch risers	650–800	800–1,200	1,000–1,600

These velocities are for total face area, not the net free area; other velocities in table are for net free area.

Table 22. Recommended return intake velocities

Intake location	Velocity over gross area, fpm
Above occupied zone	800 and up, depending on height
Within occupied zone, not near seats	600–800
Within occupied zone, near seats	400–600
Door or wall louvers	200–300
Undercutting of doors, through undercut area	200–300
Under seat mushrooms	100–200
Gravity part of mechanical supply—gravity exhaust or reverse	100–250

Table 24. Static pressure of filters (in inches of water)

Extracted by permission from ASHRAE Guide and Data Book, 1963.

Clean filter	Dirty filter (should be changed)
Up to 0.10	0.40–0.50
0.11–0.25	0.60–1.0
0.26–0.60	1.0–1.5
0.61 up	1.5 up

1,000 fpm face velocity to conserve space. When these higher velocities are used, discharge transitions must be carefully designed to minimize pressure losses (Fig. 14). Filters are generally not sized for face velocities exceeding 550 fpm because the static pressures increase rapidly above that figure. When calculating system static pressure, the value used for the filter should be that at which it should be replaced (Table 24). In systems using more than one filter it is customary to apply a diversity factor of 50 to 70 per cent.

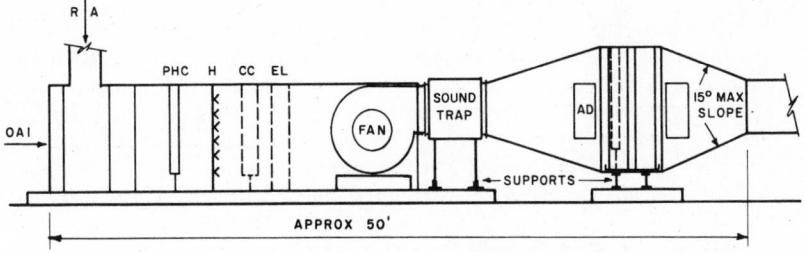

Fig. 14. Air-handling unit with heating coils on discharge side of fan

See Fig. 2 for explanation of terms.

FILTERS

Filtration is necessary to purify the air. Outside air is seldom clean enough to be used directly. Even though it may be satisfactory for breathing, the air deposits particles on equipment and occupied spaces with the result that extensive maintenance is required. Return air also has to be filtered because of the particles and odors which are entrained in it. Filtering of the return air can materially reduce the amount of outside air required, thus permitting reductions in refrigerating plant capacity and operating costs.

Determination of the type of filter to be used for a given application is based upon many factors, among which are the following:

1. Outside air characteristics for the various seasons of the year.
2. Inside air characteristics desired for the various functions of the building.
3. Type of maintenance expected for the building.
4. Space requirements for filters and spares.
5. Cost of filters.
6. Life expectancy of filters.

All of the above except the first and sixth can be ascertained with reasonable accuracy. Air pollution studies now make it possible to determine the first item for certain areas of the country.

There are four standard methods for testing filter efficiency, based on weight, discoloration, count, and radioactivity. Since, on the average, 10 per cent of the particles account for 90 per cent of the weight, the test based on weight is not suitable for use with atmospheric air. Radioactivity tests are too new and too expensive. For most applications, filter efficiency should be based upon the NBS discoloration test using atmospheric air, conducted at the locale where the filters are to be used. For more accurate results, the count test may be used.

Types of filters

All efficiencies are given in terms of the NBS Dust Spot Atmospheric Air Test.

1. *Electrostatic filters* in which ionized plates attract and hold particles. Efficiency 85 to 95 per cent. Prefilters are required only where linty atmospheres are anticipated, but after-filters are usually needed to catch large particles which may flake off from the plates, especially during starting and stopping of the fan. Automatic cleaning of the plates can be provided. First cost and maintenance cost are high. Not recommended for operating rooms, white rooms, and other critical areas unless very high efficiency after-filters are used.

2. *Replaceable cartridge filters:* Efficiency 30 to 99.9 per cent. These come in either rigid frame construction or expandable element type, in which the air flow keeps the filter element extended. Sizes are generally

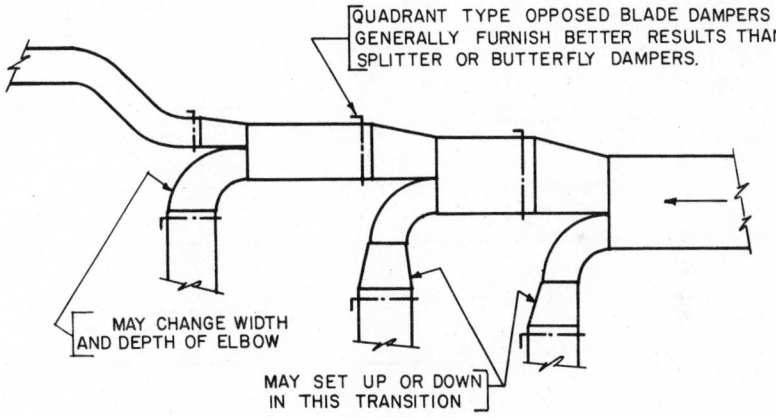

QUADRANT TYPE OPPOSED BLADE DAMPERS GENERALLY FURNISH BETTER RESULTS THAN SPLITTER OR BUTTERFLY DAMPERS.

MAY CHANGE WIDTH AND DEPTH OF ELBOW

MAY SET UP OR DOWN IN THIS TRANSITION

GOOD, BUT REQUIRES MOST CEILING SPACE

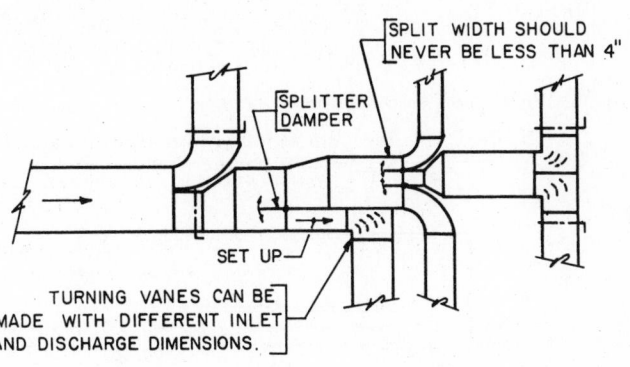

SPLIT WIDTH SHOULD NEVER BE LESS THAN 4"

SPLITTER DAMPER

SET UP

TURNING VANES CAN BE MADE WITH DIFFERENT INLET AND DISCHARGE DIMENSIONS.

SATISFACTORY, MORE ECONOMICAL OF SPACE

Fig. 15. Ductwork details

24 by 24 in., with operating lengths from 12 to 36 in. The high efficiency types compete with electrostatic filters and are often preferred in critical applications because of their positive action. The lower efficiency types are used for prefiltering and for main filters where economy is required and a high degree of cleanliness is not essential.

3. *Cleanable or renewable media filters:* Efficiency 20 to 95 per cent. These types offer certain maintenance economies where a staff is available for cleaning the filters and space exists for the cleaning equipment. The renewable media type is cut to size and wound through a multi-V-shaped frame. These have efficiencies in the higher ranges. The cleanable type consists of metal mesh frames which are cleaned with water and re-oiled.

4. *Roll-type disposable media filters:* Efficiency 20 per cent. This type has generally replaced the traveling curtain oil bath-type filter because of its lower cost and higher efficiency.

5. *Throwaway filters:* Efficiency 3 to 10 per cent. These usually consist of ½ to 4-in. thickness of glass fiber or similar material in a cardboard or light metal frame. Their principal use is for window unit air conditioners. In large systems this type is used only for prefiltering.

DUCTWORK

Ductwork: The layout of the ductwork should be carefully designed to minimize motor power losses, keep fan and system noises to a minimum, and keep space headroom as high as possible. Figures 15 and 16 show some typical details of recommended practices. Flush seam construction is more costly than the other types and should be used only where space conditions make it mandatory. Attempts should be made to keep volume dampers, air valves, and dual duct-mixing boxes out of finished spaces because they require ceiling access. Sometimes, access may be provided through ceiling lights or air outlets. It should be borne in mind that duct sizes given on drawings are almost always clear inside dimensions, and 2 or more inches must be added to these dimensions for total space requirements.

Noise reduction: Transmission of noise through ductwork is not usually a problem in low-velocity, conventional systems. However, in high-velocity systems, fan noise is greater and ductwork, dampers, mixing boxes, induction units, and all other items must be carefully designed and selected to produce maximum attenuation and minimum noise regeneration from air-mixing boxes. In all systems, the outlet devices must be properly selected so that the sound-power level developed is less than the maximum noise criteria for the room. Noise criteria for various occupancies are given in the section on "Acoustics."

Low-velocity systems seldom require sound traps, although for low-sound-level spaces duct lining may be required. Generally, 25 ft of 1-in. duct lining is less expensive to install than an equivalent sound trap, but the trap does a better job, especially at the low frequencies. On high-velocity systems sound traps may be required. Where special precautions are required to prevent noise transmission from one room to another, special care in ductwork design will be less expensive than furnishing individual room sound traps (see Fig. 17).

Space requirements: Where perimeter air-distribution systems are employed, they generally take from 7 to 18 in. of space from the inside of the exterior wall and 11 to 30 in. of vertical height. Interior shaft space is also required to take care of return and exhaust air, interior supply air, chilled and condenser water piping, steam and return piping, electric closets, telephone closets, plumbing piping, and possibly pneumatic tubes. The combined shaft space requirements generally range from 2 to 5 per cent of gross floor area with the heating and air conditioning requiring about 70 per cent of the space requirements and plumbing and electrical each needing 15 per cent. These are rough averages but should be helpful in the development of core areas. In general, with duct shafts having a width-to-length ratio of 2:1 to 4:1, rectangular shapes are easier to develop than large square shafts.

Fan rooms require from 35 to 60 sq ft of floor space per 1,000 cfm of supply air furnished. The lower limit is applicable to simple air-handling systems in rooms with few columns and no interference from elevator machine rooms, electrical rooms, etc.

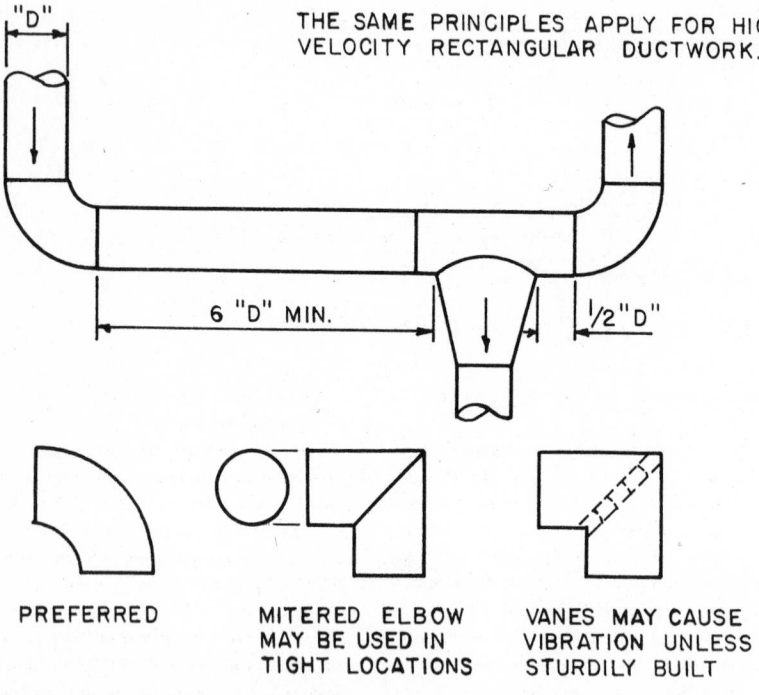

THE SAME PRINCIPLES APPLY FOR HIGH VELOCITY RECTANGULAR DUCTWORK.

"D"

6 "D" MIN.   ½ "D"

PREFERRED

MITERED ELBOW MAY BE USED IN TIGHT LOCATIONS

VANES MAY CAUSE VIBRATION UNLESS STURDILY BUILT

Fig. 16.   High-velocity ductwork details

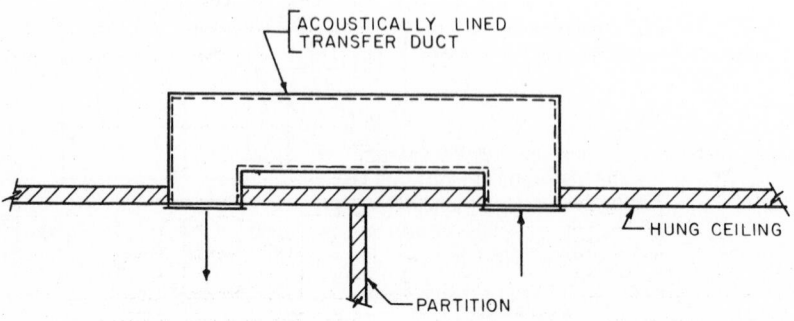

ACOUSTICALLY LINED TRANSFER DUCT

HUNG CEILING

PARTITION

Fig. 17.   Acoustically lined transfer duct

Fan rooms usually require 13 to 18 ft clear height, depending upon the size of the ducts and the amount of crossovers necessary between ductwork, electrical conduits, and piping.

REFRIGERATING PLANT

Refrigeration and boiler-plant equipment space requirements are given later on in this section.

Tons: The unit by which refrigeration capacity is measured is the *ton*, which equals 12,000 Btu/hr. It derives from the fact that it requires 288,000 Btu to melt 1 ton of ice to water at 32°F. If this is assumed to take place in one day, the hourly rate would be 288,000 divided by 24 or 12,000 Btu/hr.

Systems: The most commonly used systems for air conditioning are as follows:

1. Air to refrigerant to air (Fig. 18). In this system, room air is cooled by contact with cool refrigerant, which then becomes warm. The warm refrigerant is then cooled by contact with outside air. This is the manner in which self-contained window units and most other packaged units operate.

2. Air to refrigerant to water to air (Fig. 19). If air-cooled condensers are not feasible and cheap water is not available, then a cooling tower must be used. This will take the water that has removed the heat from the hot refrigerant and allow it to give up its heat to the outdoor air. This type of system is practical for commercial installations up to about 150 tons.

3. Air to water to refrigerant to water to air (Fig. 20). Although five complete heat-transfer operations are required, this cycle has produced the most economical and practicable results for large systems to date.

Compressors: The types of refrigeration compressors are:

1. Reciprocating
2. Centrifugal
3. Absorption

For up to 100 tons of refrigerant capacity, reciprocating (Fig. 21) or absorption units are used because centrifugal compressors are not manufactured in these sizes. In the higher tonnages centrifugal machines, even though they cost more and take up more space, are generally used because they are quieter and have fewer vibration problems, less maintenance, and better operating control (Fig. 22).

All types of compressors are available in open or hermetically sealed models. In general, hermetic units are recommended

Shafts: From the foregoing, general shaft space requirements can be determined. Shafts should be centrally located so that each shaft serves all areas within 50 to 100 ft. Preliminary shaft sizes may be estimated on the basis of preliminary air quantity calculations (cfm) divided by 1,000. Multiply this figure by 1.3 to obtain total shaft requirements for all mechanical trades.

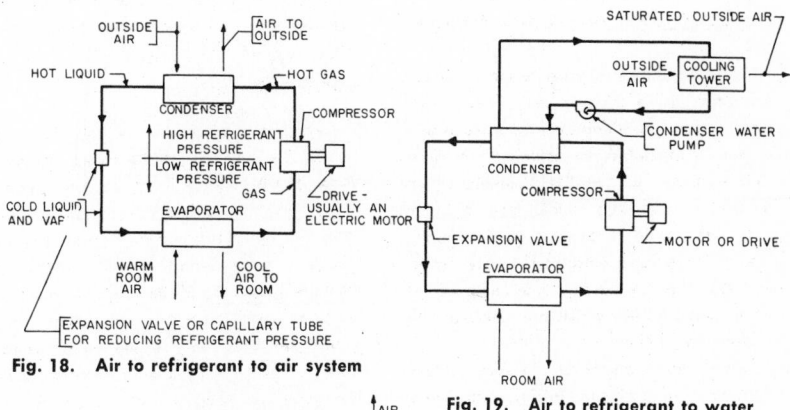

Fig. 18. Air to refrigerant to air system

Fig. 19. Air to refrigerant to water to air system

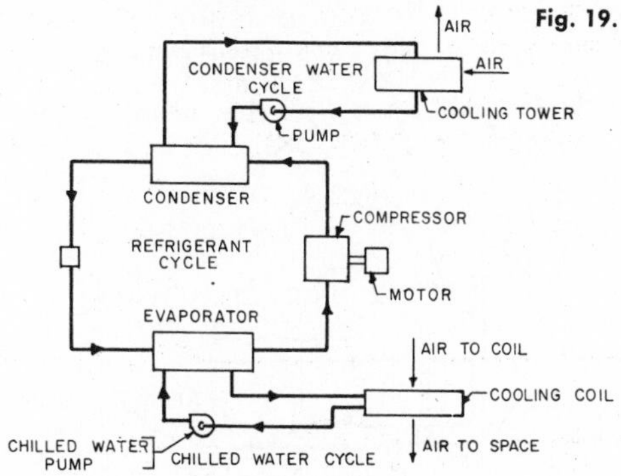

Fig. 20. Air to water to refrigerant to water to air system

because of their reduced maintenance requirements.

Hermetic machines are generally electrically driven, but open-type compressors can be driven by electric motors, steam turbines, gas engines, or any other motor or engine drive. Open-type machines are made in capacities up to about 5,000 tons, whereas hermetics stop at about 1,700 tons.

Starters: Electric motors require starting devices which take up wall and floor space. A reduced-voltage autotransformer starter for a 250-hp machine will require approximately 14 sq ft of floor space and 7½ ft of height. Where a refrigeration plant has a number of motors, they may be combined

in a motor control center, for centralized operation and maintenance.

Steam: With steam turbines, steam condensers are used to cool and condense the exhaust steam from the turbines (Fig. 23). This type of refrigeration plant takes up more floor space than any of the others discussed here, but where economic analysis shows steam to be the most economical fuel, space must be provided. Steam turbines are available for almost all steam pressures. The lower the steam pressure available, the larger will be the turbine for a given tonnage requirement.

Absorption machines (Fig. 24) are simpler to operate than steam turbines and

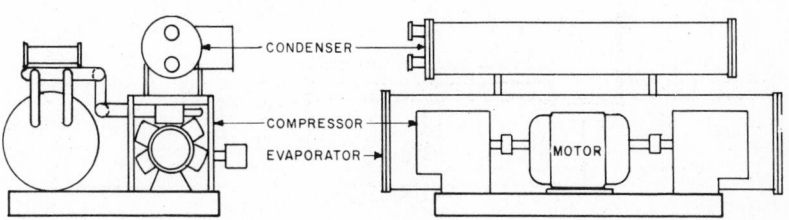

Fig. 21. Reciprocating compressor, 100 to 150 tons

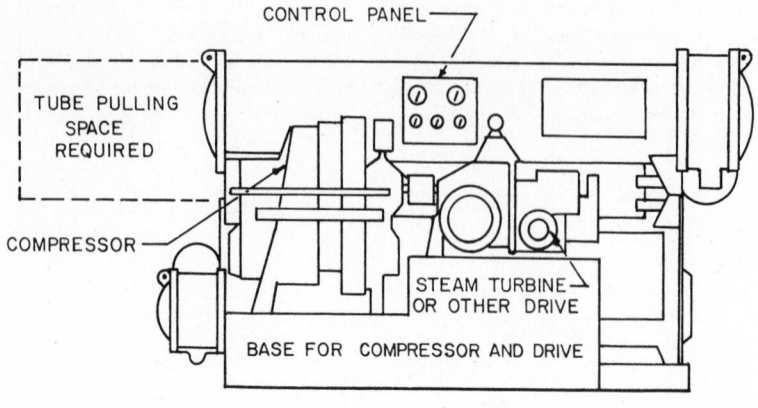

FRONT ELEVATION

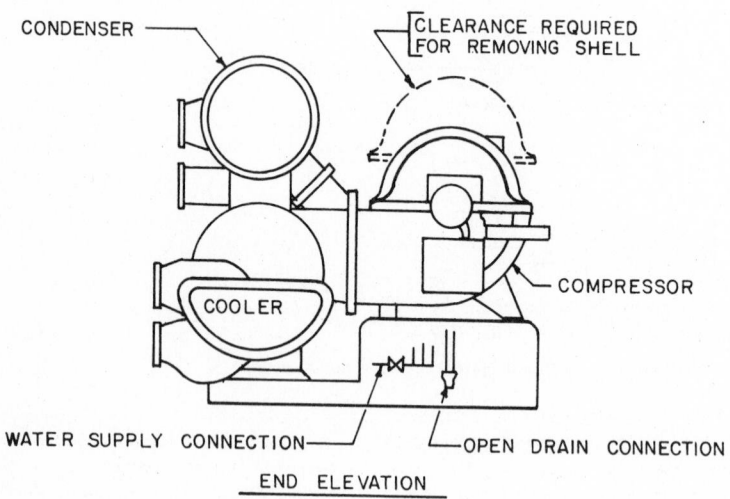

END ELEVATION

Fig. 22.   Open-type centrifugal compressor

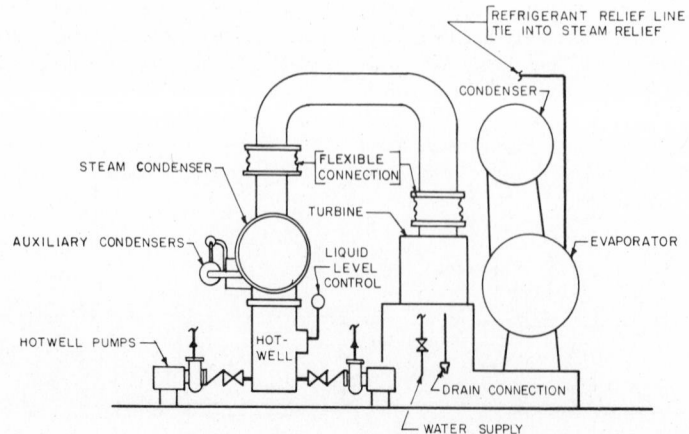

Fig. 23.   Steam turbine compressor with steam condenser

take up less floor space, but they are limited in capacity to about 1,000 tons. They can use high-temperature hot water or steam up to 12 psi. In some areas licensed refrigeration operators are not required for absorption machines, which may give an economic advantage to this type of compressor. They are also quieter than reciprocating compressors and produce less vibration.

Well water: Where an assured, reasonably economical source of well or river water is available for cooling the hot refrigerant, it should be used. The well water, if cold enough, may even be able to furnish part or all of the refrigeration effect (which would eliminate the need for a compressor). Provision must be made for disposing of the well water after it has been heated, in such a manner that it does not mix with the cool well water.

Cooling tower: In most instances a motor-driven induced- or forced-draft cooling tower is the most economical method for cooling and saving the water which removes the heat from the refrigerant (Fig. 25). Since the heat picked up inside the building has to be eliminated somewhere and since the air is the most convenient and cheapest place to get rid of it, cooling towers are the most effective device for transferring this heat to the air. For preliminary design purposes, a cooling tower for an electric-drive refrigeration compressor will require about 0.75 sq ft area per ton; for a steam-drive compressor, 1.0 sq ft per ton. Since cooling towers weigh from 120 to 200 psf when operating, their load must be considered in the design of the building structure. Another item is the noise and vibration from cooling towers. Airborne noise is generally a source of concern to areas within 100 ft of the cooling tower. To eliminate vibration, the fan platform, consisting of fan gearbox and motor, should be set on an isolation base consisting of either rubber-in-shear or springs, and the base of the tower should be set on ribbed neoprene pads.

For reasons of appearance the cooling tower is often enclosed in a louvered wall which must have sufficient free area so that enough air is drawn through the tower to remove the heat of the condenser water. As a general rule, a cooling tower needs about 320 cfm of air per ton of electric-drive refrigeration and 540 cfm per ton of steam-drive refrigeration, and the air velocity through the free area should not exceed 1,000 fpm. Also, in most cases, the cooling tower basin has to be set at least 4 ft above the roof in order to install the discharge piping and for maintenance purposes.

Mechanical equipment room: In the refrigeration plant room there is generally other equipment, such as chilled-water pumps, condenser-water pumps, and an air-ventilation system. In larger buildings a refrigerant receiver tank and a pump-down compressor may be required. In some instances, air-handling, plumbing, and electrical equipment may be installed in the same room. For these reasons it is difficult to give space requirements for refrigeration rooms. A typical layout for a mechanical equipment room is shown in Fig. 26. In larger plants, a monorail system for moving equipment may be advantageous. Provision should be made for replacing equipment without interfering with the operation of the building.

Pumps are of two general classifications, both centrifugal: the close-coupled vertically split-casing type, used for smaller capacities (up to about 300 gal per min); and the horizontally split-casing type, used for larger applications. The two types overlap considerably in their range of operation. The vertically split pumps are generally cheaper, but the horizontally split pumps are more rugged and easier to maintain and service.

Piping losses should be kept to a minimum in order to keep electric operating costs down. Piping should generally be sized to maintain a pressure drop of 3 to 6 ft of water pressure head loss per 100 equivalent lineal feet of pipe. Water velocities should be no more than 4 fps for pipes under 2 in. and less than 10 fps for pipes 6 in. and over to prevent water noise transmission.

Noise and vibration control: The pump should be set on an inertia block equal to one to two times the operating weight of the pump plus all piping to the first hangers. This block will minimize the transfer of vibrations from the pump to the piping. The inertia block should be set on some type of vibration isolation base, depending upon the degree of transmission desired (Fig. 27). Flexible connections may be used between pump and piping, and the latter should be supported by vibration-eliminating-type hangers (Fig. 28).

Vents: All systems except the absorption system require a refrigerant relief-vent pipe to the atmosphere. The steam condensers on the steam turbine system require a steam pressure-relief pipe. The chilled-water system requires an expansion tank, which is usually of the open type.

Heat pump is the name given to any type of refrigeration compressor which is designed so that its evaporator and condenser sections can be interchanged to provide either cooling or heating, as required (Fig. 29). The typical heat pump is the air-to-air system, which gives off excess

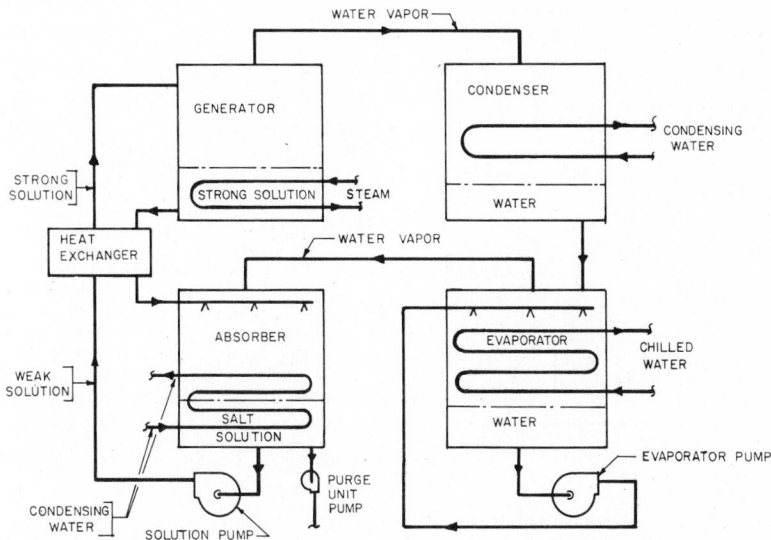

Fig. 24. Absorption refrigeration cycle using lithium bromide

(Reprinted by permission from ASHRAE Guide and Data Book, 1963.)

Approximate sizes of absorption machines

Tons	L	W	H
50	11'6"	4'8"	8'0"
200	18'8"	4'10"	8'6"
500	19'6"	7'7"	12'2"
750	25'6"	7'7"	12'2"
1,000	34'6"	7'7"	14'0"

heat to the outside air in the summer and takes in heat from the air in the winter to heat the building. Well or river water or the ground can be used instead of outside air to carry off excess heat in the summer and to supply heat in the winter. The air-to-air system is the most commonly used, even though its horsepower requirements are greater, because water is usually not available and use of the ground presents operating and maintenance difficulties.

In the warmer climates where the temperatures do not get below 20°F, a single stage of refrigerant gas compression is usually sufficient to provide winter heating requirements. Below 20°F, either supplementary electric resistance heating must be used or two stages of refrigerant compression are required to furnish sufficient heating capacity.

A heat-pump system is generally considerably more costly to design and to

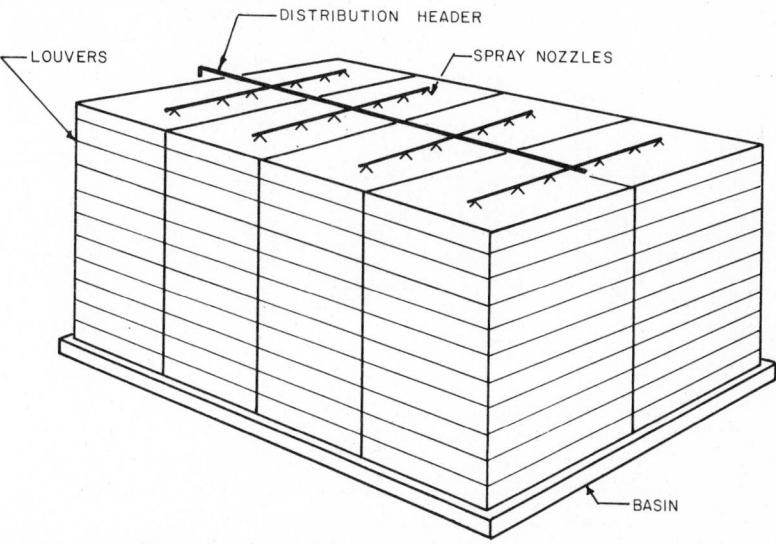

Fig. 25. Spray-filled atmospheric cooling tower

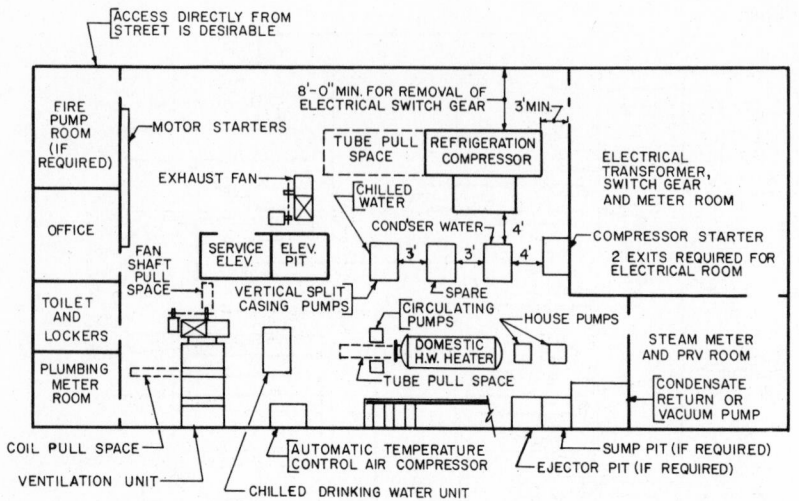

Fig. 26. Typical mechanical equipment room layout showing heating, ventilating, air-conditioning, electrical, and plumbing requirements

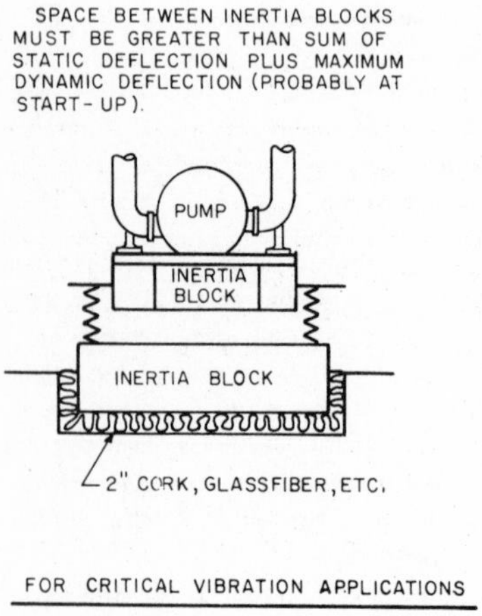

install than an equivalent refrigeration system which performs summer cooling only. Air-to-air heat pumps should have the compressors reasonably close to the evaporative air condensers in order to keep the refrigerant lines as short as possible. Therefore, on taller buildings (over 50 or 60 ft high) the compressors should be located on the roof, and care must be taken to isolate their noise and vibration from the rest of the building.

Only under certain conditions is the heat pump the best choice; careful analysis of each case is required. Conditions that favor the use of the heat pump are:

1. Low electric power rates
2. Large interior area with high lighting load
3. Building with small amount of perimeter glass, with or without large interior area
4. Low outside air requirements
5. Ratio of design heating load to design cooling load of 0.6 or less

Central refrigeration plant: Where a number of air-conditioned buildings are contemplated in a given area, serious consideration should be given to the construction of a centralized refrigeration plant, similar to a central steam plant. Total investment costs will in most instances be less, maintenance and operating costs will be lower, and more space will be available in the buildings for other uses.

SPACE BETWEEN INERTIA BLOCKS MUST BE GREATER THAN SUM OF STATIC DEFLECTION PLUS MAXIMUM DYNAMIC DEFLECTION (PROBABLY AT START-UP).

PUMP

INERTIA BLOCK

INERTIA BLOCK

2" CORK, GLASSFIBER, ETC.

FOR CRITICAL VIBRATION APPLICATIONS

Fig. 27. Vibration isolation of pump

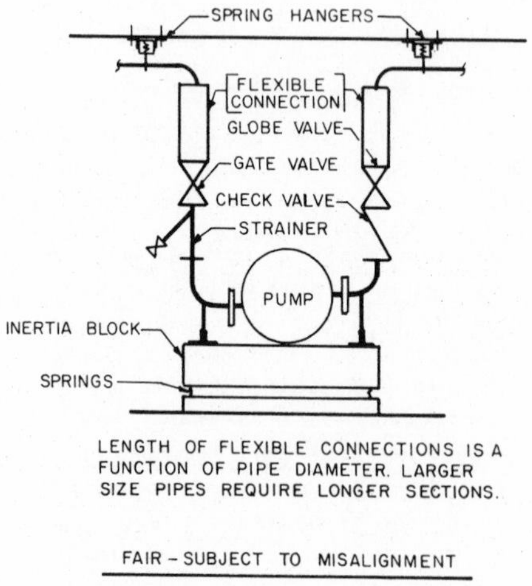

SPRING HANGERS

FLEXIBLE CONNECTION
GLOBE VALVE
GATE VALVE
CHECK VALVE
STRAINER

INERTIA BLOCK

PUMP

SPRINGS

LENGTH OF FLEXIBLE CONNECTIONS IS A FUNCTION OF PIPE DIAMETER. LARGER SIZE PIPES REQUIRE LONGER SECTIONS.

FAIR—SUBJECT TO MISALIGNMENT

Fig. 28. Flexible connections and vibration-reducing pipe hangers

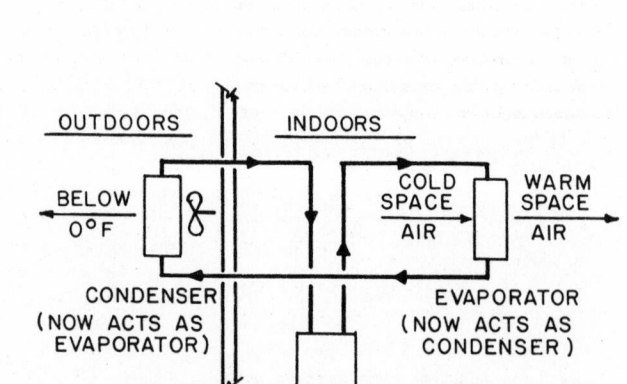

Fig. 29. Basic heat-pump cycle

By ALFRED GREENBERG, P.E., *Environmental Consultant*

HEATING PLANT

Most heating systems, other than residential, are based on the use of steam or hot water. However, a few other types of heating are occasionally used. These are outlined below.

1. *Space heaters* come in many sizes and shapes for floor, wall, or ceiling mounting (Fig. 30). They are often called "unit heaters," and they are discussed under this name in a later section of this book. They are usually gas- or oil-fired and are used in factories, warehouses, garages, markets, etc. Space heaters are relatively inexpensive and simple to operate and maintain; they can be relocated with a minimum of alteration.

2. *Electric* heating requires no maintenance, takes up the least space, provides individual control, and can produce uniform temperature conditions. It comes in a variety of forms: radiant element, infrared lamps, low-temperature radiant panel, fan-coil units, and baseboard convectors. Electric heating requires low electric rates and well-insulated buildings in order to be economical.

3. *Forced-warm-air* systems are often used in stores, small office buildings, etc., especially if summer cooling is to be provided. This is essentially a residential system, as was discussed in an earlier section of this book.

4. *Heat pump,* as discussed previously.

Boiler plants: Most commercial and industrial buildings require boiler plants to furnish their heating and processing requirements. In some of the larger cities, steam is available for purchase from the local utility company. However, in the majority of cases, a boiler plant must be provided as part of the project.

Total heat load: To determine the total heat load on the boiler, consider the following categories:

1. Direct heating-convectors, unit heaters, radiators, etc.
2. Tempering—heating of ventilation air
3. Domestic hot-water requirements
4. Kitchen requirements
5. Process requirements—laboratory hoods, sterilizers, cleaning, manufacturing, laundry, refrigeration plant, etc.

These items should be given in Btu's per hour or pounds of steam per hour. The loads should be tabulated on the basis of separate summer and winter requirements. Steam pressure requirements must also be known.

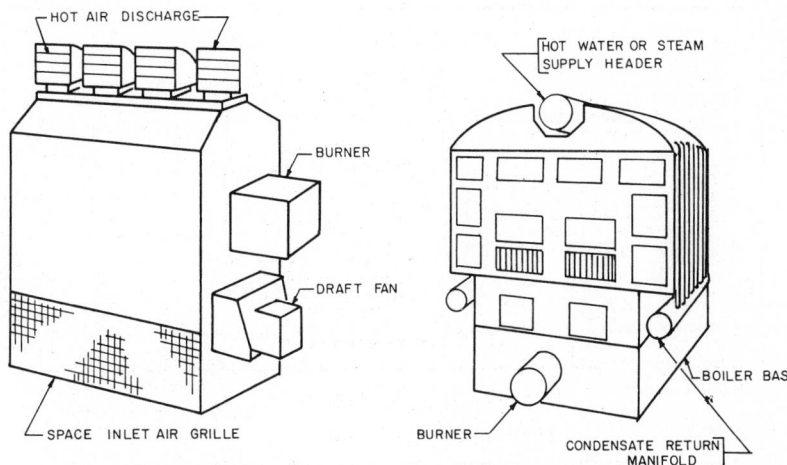

Fig. 30.   Direct-fired space heater

Fig 31.   Cast-iron sectional boiler

Sizes range from approximately 3 to 8 ft wide, 6 to 9 ft high, and 3 to 16 ft long. Larger sizes are also available.

Boilers: The following types of boilers are in common use:

1. *Cast-iron sectional boilers* are used for capacities up to about 8,000 lb of steam per hour. They require less space than fire-tube types, and additional capacity can be obtained by adding more sections. These boilers have long life and low maintenance (see Fig. 31). Special units can be made in sizes up to about 25,000 lb per hour.

2. *Fire-tube boilers* may be furnished as complete packages with burner and controls or as a separate unit for mounting on a firebrick chamber. Capacities range to about 22,000 lb per hour and sizes from 10 to 27 ft long, 4 to 10 ft wide, and 6 to 12 ft high. Space must be provided in front of boiler for tube pulling (see Fig. 32).

3. *Packaged water-tube boilers* can be obtained in capacities from 8,000 to about 100,000 lb of steam per hour. Sizes vary greatly among manufacturers. These boilers are somewhat more costly than fire-tube boilers but are usually more efficient and long-lasting (see Fig. 33).

Where a project requires heating for comfort conditions and domestic hot water only, a hot-water boiler plant may be sufficient for its needs, as long as the water-pumping costs are not too high. The last condition would probably rule out most buildings over six stories high and/or over 200 ft long. On long, low buildings, it may still be advantageous to use a hot-water heating system in order to save on the trenching costs required with a steam distribution system.

In projects consisting of a number of buildings and with heat-load requirements exceeding 75 to 100 million Btu per hour, the high-temperature hot-water distribution system should be investigated. This system uses pressurized water from 220 to about 450°F for furnishing heat and process requirements. For equivalent volumes, it holds considerably more heat than steam, does not require pitched lines, and often

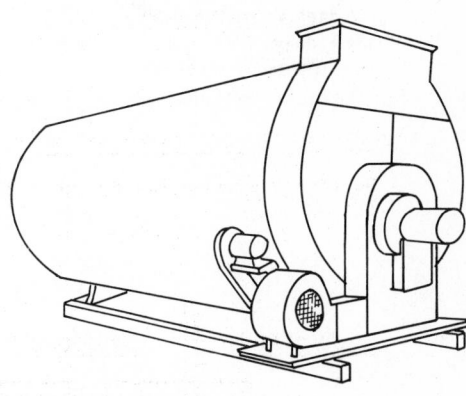

Fig. 32.   Fire-tube boiler

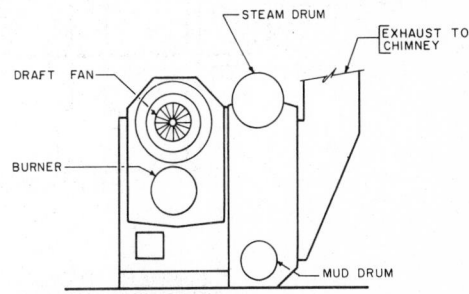

Fig. 33.   Water-tube boiler

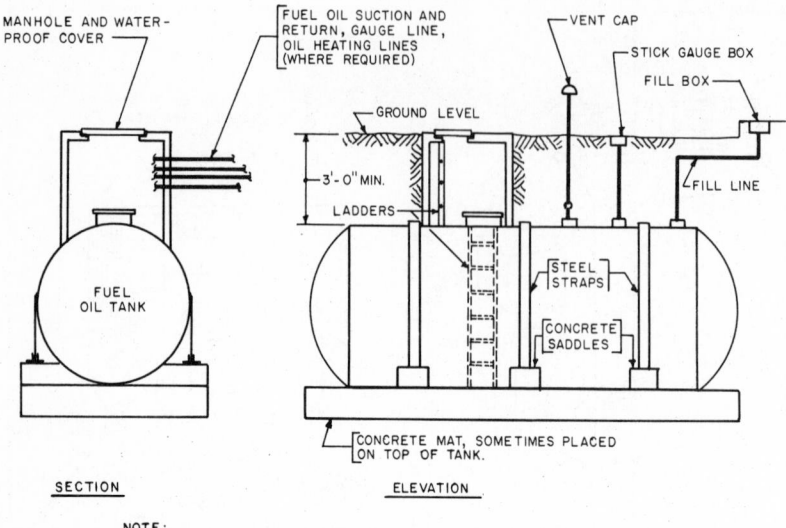

SECTION   ELEVATION

NOTE:
PIPING TO MANHOLE SHOULD GENERALLY BE PROTECTED BY SPLIT-
TILE ENCLOSURE, TRENCH OR OTHER WATER-PROOF PROTECTION

Fig. 34. Oil storage tank

saves on first, maintenance, and operating costs.

Location of boiler plant: In most projects which involve only one building, the boiler plant is generally located in the basement, which produces the least structural load and keeps the plant remote from the building's functional areas. Also, it allows the maximum height for the chimney, which may be sufficient to allow use of natural draft for boiler operation, thus saving on operating costs.

Undesirable rock excavation or soil conditions (high water table) or economic value of basement areas may make it necessary to locate the boiler plant else-

where, such as in a separate structure on the site, or on the roof of the building. Where the plant is remote from the building, a piping distribution system is required. Steam piping must be buried or placed in trenches or tunnels. Hot-water piping may be concealed in covered walkways, thus eliminating excavation problems.

Type of chimney: If the building is tall enough, the chimney need go no higher than 4 to 6 ft beyond the high point of the building. However, for most low buildings where appearance is an important consideration, mechanical-draft fans are used in order to keep the height of the chimney to a minimum, that is, just above

the roof line. In industrial buildings, where low operating costs are more important than appearance, natural-draft chimneys are generally preferred. For many applications, these can be obtained in prefabricated metal sections.

Chimney size may be estimated from the data given in the following discussion.

Type of fuel: Most packaged fire-tube boilers are limited to either gas or oil as fuel. Water-tube boilers are available for use with any type of fuel. (See the ASHRAE Guide for diagrams of typical coal-firing arrangements.)

Where gas is available, all that is usually required is a gas meter and possibly a pressure-reducing and/or pressure-regulating station. These do not take up much space. Where oil is to be used as the fuel, storage tanks are required. The capacity of these tanks usually ranges from 1 to 4 weeks' supply for the coldest month. A 2-week supply is average. Where tank size requirements exceed 20,000 to 30,000 gal (8 to 10 ft diameter by 30 to 40 ft long), multiple tanks are often installed. Most often the tanks are buried in the ground (Fig. 34), although sometimes they are placed in vaults which have to be explosion-proof and ventilated. The tanks are generally secured to concrete foundations to prevent settling and floating. The tanks should have a cover of at least 3 ft and should be as close to the boiler plant as practicable in order to keep oil-pumping costs low (Fig. 35). Fill boxes for the oil tanks should be located so that the fuel trucks have ready access to them. Tank vent lines can usually be located inconspicuously alongside the building.

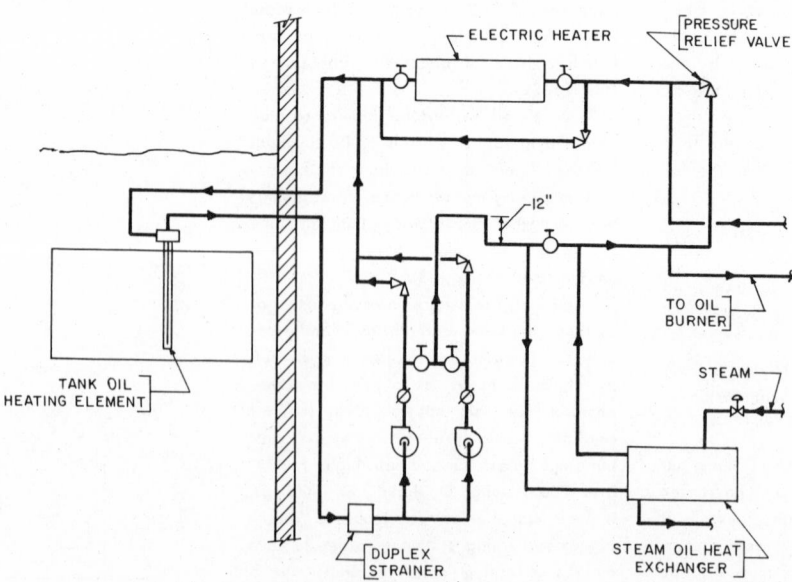

Fig 35. Schematic piping diagram for heavy fuel oil

By ARTHUR L. SPAET, *P.E.*

Consulting Engineer

In the very early stages of hospital planning it is necessary to establish the general architectural outlines and preliminary structural framing for the building. Before any detailed design has been started on the boiler plant, the approximate size of the chimney must be determined. Manufacturers' catalogs usually give a recommended chimney size for a small plant, suitable for a school or modest sized building. For large plants in the power and heavy industrial fields, the design will usually be done by a specialist. The hospital plant falls in between, and information for sizing chimneys has been conspicuously lacking.

The applicable principles have been well established. The problems of draft, chemistry of combustion, the use of draft fans, etc. are available in texts and trade literature. However, the fundamental problem of architect and engineer in the early design stage is that of establishing a chimney size without doing a week's worth of calculation. The table given here can be used for boiler plants other than hospitals provided the conditions below apply. This table will suffice for *preliminary design* under the following conditions and assumptions. Final chimney sizing must be engineered in detail for each application:

1. Elevation of plant—sea level to 500 ft above sea level.
2. The chimney is of masonry or brick construction.
3. Minimum chimney height—90 ft.
4. Average chimney temperature—540 F.
5. Boiler pressure—125 psi.
6. A forced draft fan or induced draft fan will be used to overcome boiler and wind box losses.

Minimum chimney height is that required to clear the flue gases of the highest nearby building or roof; or to clear the highest part of the hospital itself to prevent a health or nuisance hazard. A suggested minimum height is 80 ft above the breeching although a minimum of 90 or 100 ft is preferable.

A round chimney section is preferable to a rectangular section. Where architectural considerations require a rectangular appearance, a circular inside construction is strongly recommended. In addition the fire underwriters express a strong preference for round chimney sections for safety reasons.

Lb stm/hr (Peak load)	Lb stm/hr (Incl. 30% standby)	Boiler hp (Corresponding to previous column)	Oil Pump Rate gal/hr	Flue Gas Cfm Oil—above / Coal—Below		Flue Gas lbs/hr Oil—above / Coal—Below		Chimney Diam. ft.		Velocity ft/min	
				Oil	Coal	Oil	Coal	Oil	Coal	Oil	Coal
20,000	26,000	750	520	17,000	20,400	31,000	47,000	4½	5	1,060	1,050
25,000	32,500	950	650	21,000	25,000	51,000	57,000	5	5½	1,070	1,050
30,000	39,000	1,130	780	25,000	30,000	61,000	70,000	5½	6	1,050	1,060
40,000	52,000	1,500	1,000	34,000	41,000	81,000	94,000	6	7	1,200	1,070
50,000	65,000	1,900	1,200	42,000	50,000	100,000	117,000	7	7½	1,090	1,130

By ALFRED GREENBERG, P.E., Environmental Consultant

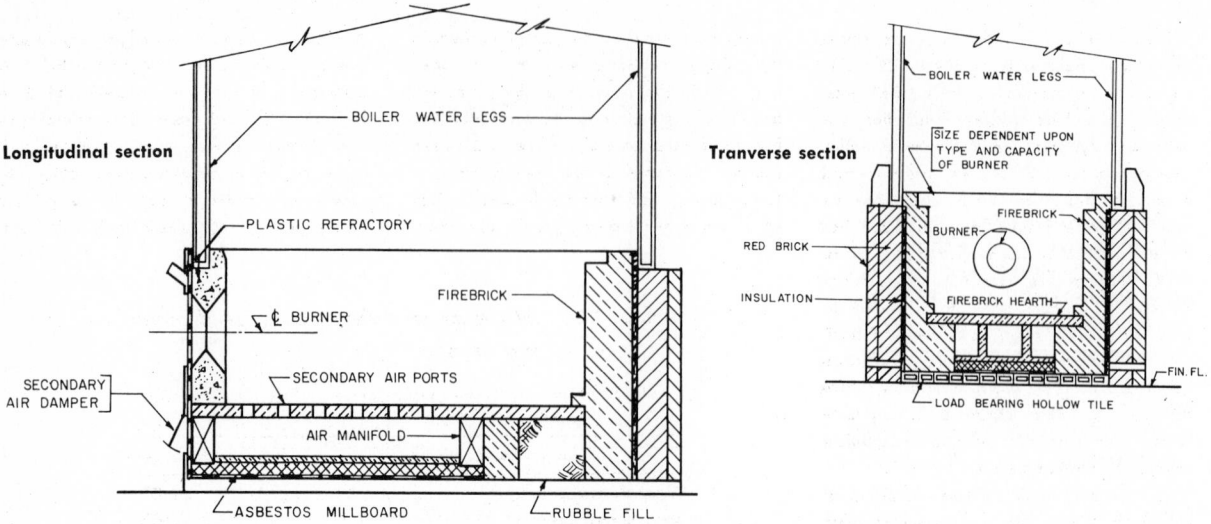

Fig. 36. **Firebrick combustion chamber for boiler** *Size of combustion chamber is dependent upon type and capacity of burner.*

If coal is used for fuel, storage space (indoors, if possible) should be provided for a 45-day supply. One ton of coal requires 40 cu ft of space. In addition, handling equipment must be furnished to get the coal to the boilers and provisions taken for preventing spontaneous combustion.

The plant may be designed so that it can operate on either gas or oil as the fuel, depending on costs and availability.

Firebrick combustion chambers: Boilers set on firebrick combustion chambers (see Fig. 36) have in the past provided the most reliable service and will probably outlast factory-assembled boiler packages and boiler-burner sets. They are somewhat more costly to install due to the brickwork, and if they are not properly installed, operated, and maintained, relining of the brick is an expensive item. For most applications, packages and sets will perform satisfactorily for many years, in most cases at least twenty.

Water treatment: One item of continued maintenance on boilers is the feedwater treatment. A boiler that does not have its water treated will seldom last more than a few years before corrosion and leaks force it out of service. On the smaller installations, the chemicals are intermittently and manually fed to the boilers, whereas on larger systems, pumps and chemical feed systems are employed. Oxygen in the water is the most dangerous element tending to produce corrosion. Larger systems and deluxe smaller ones employ deaerator feedwater heaters to remove the oxygen. This piece of equipment can add many years to the life of a boiler plant and can pay for itself and the extra space required many times over.

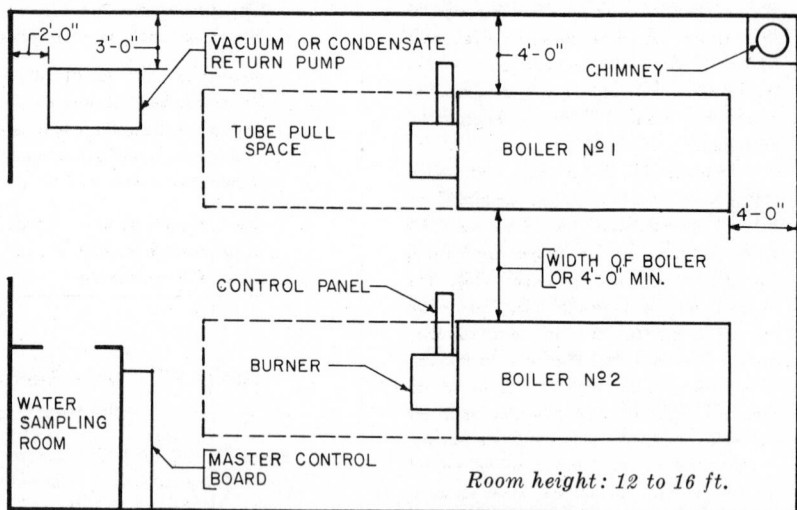

Fig. 36a. **Layout of simple boiler room utilizing packaged fire-tube boiler-burner set**

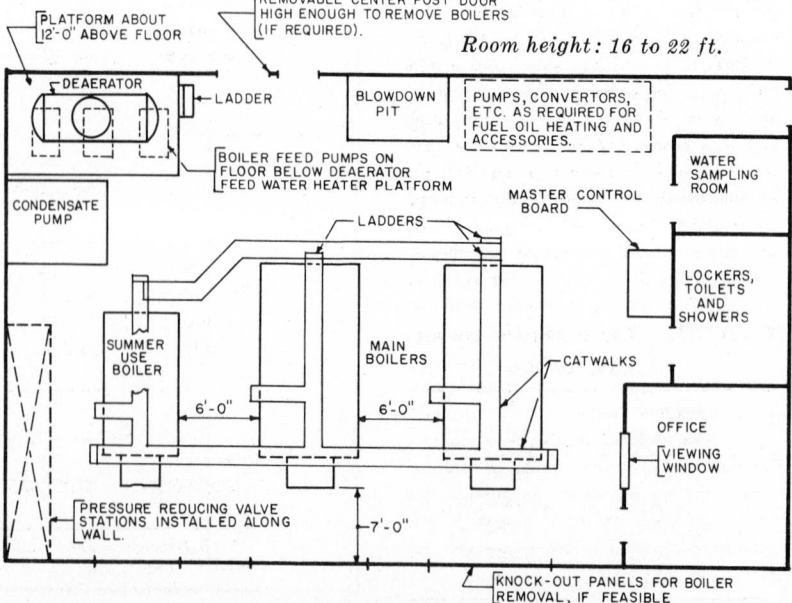

Fig. 36b. **Basic elements of larger-type boiler plant with water-tube boilers**

Pressure-reducing stations: Where steam at various pressures is required, the steam boiler has to operate at the highest pressure. If the high-pressure quantities are comparatively small, then the main boiler may be operated at a lower pressure and a small high-pressure steam boiler can be provided. Where the steam pressure has to be reduced, pressure-reducing valve (PRV) stations are required. A sufficient number of stations must be provided to give the proper steam pressures and flexibility in operation. Because they emit large quantities of heat, pressure-reducing valve stations are often enclosed in separate rooms and provided with a mechanical exhaust ventilation system.

Steam-meter room: Where metering of the steam is required, a steam-meter room should be located as close to the source of the steam service as possible. The size of the service will determine the size room required. Where the building has its own boiler plant, it may be advantageous to record the steam quantity produced by each boiler.

Ventilation: The boiler room and steam-meter room should also be ventilated to prevent heat buildup. The boiler room requires sufficient air for proper combustion. For preliminary size purposes only, the outdoor air requirements may be safely figured as ½ cfm per lb of steam capacity per hr. The boiler room exhaust ventilation system should be carefully designed so that the fan does not pull too much air out of the room and thus starve the boilers.

Safety relief valves are required on all boilers. Provision should be made to have the steam go to an isolated areaway or the roof.

Condensate return systems are of three general types. The high-temperature condensate pump system eliminates the need for flash tanks and has widespread use in the process industries, laundries, hospitals, etc. Low-pressure condensate return pump and vacuum return pump systems are most commonly used in commercial applications. Vacuum pumps are generally used on large direct-heating systems with long pipe runs. The advantages of this system are that it

continuously removes the air entrapped in the piping, thus improving heat transfer, and uses smaller pipe sizes. Since the system operates under a vacuum (pressure less than atmospheric), if the condensate reaches the pump at too high a temperature, flashing into steam will occur, which will adversely affect pump operation.

Where such conditions exist, condensate pumps should be used. When the building uses steam at pressures in excess of 5 to 10 psig, the condensate return should be emptied into a flash tank which will remove the excess heat and then return the condensate to the condensate pump. The excess heat in the flash tank will form

Table 26. Efficiency of utilization over the heating season

Reprinted by permission from ASHRAE Giude and Data Book, *1963.*

Type of fuel-burning unit	Efficiency, %
Gas, designed unit	75–80
Gas, conversion unit	60–80
Oil, designed unit	65–80
Oil, conversion unit	60–80
Bituminous coal, hand-fired with controls	50–65
Bituminous coal, hand-fired without controls	40–60
Bituminous coal, stoker-fired	50–70
Anthracite, hand-fired with controls	60–80
Anthracite, hand-fired without controls	50–65
Anthracite, stoker-fired	60–80
Coke, hand-fired with controls	60–80
Coke, hand-fired without controls	50–65
Direct electric heating	100

Table 27. Unit fuel consumption constants (U) for gas *

Based on 0°F outdoor temperature, 70°F indoor temperature. (Reprinted by permission from ASHRAE Guide and Data Book, *1963.)*

Heating value of gas, Btu/cu ft	Hot water	Steam	Warm air	
	Cu ft gas/degree-day/sq ft EDR	Cu ft gas/degree-day/sq ft EDR	Cu ft gas/degree-day/1,000 Btu hourly design heat loss	
	Over 1,200 sq ft	Over 700 sq ft	Gravity	Fan systems
500	0.134	0.231	0.896	0.861
535	0.216	0.216	0.840	0.805
800	0.085	0.144	0.560	0.538
1,000	0.068	0.116	0.449	0.431

	Gas consumption, therms/degree-day			
1 therm = 100,000 Btu	0.000675	0.00116	0.00450	0.00430

* *Abstracted from* Comfort Heating, American Gas Association *(1938) and 5 per cent added for operation without night reduction of temperature.*

Table 25. Temperature correction factors

Outdoor design temp.	C_f
−20	0.778
−10	0.875
0	1.000
10	1.167
20	1.400

Table 28. Unit fuel consumption * constants (U) for oil †

Based on 0°F outdoor temperature, 70°F indoor temperature. (Reprinted by permission from ASHRAE Guide and Data Book, 1963.)

Unit ‡	Efficiency, %	
	70	80
Gal oil per sq ft steam radiator	0.00105	0.00092
Gal oil per sq ft hot water radiator	0.00066	0.00058
Gal oil per 1000 Btu/hr heat loss	0.00437	0.00383

* Based on a heating value of 141,000 Btu per gal.
† Abstracted by permission from Degree-Day Handbook (2d ed., 1937), by C. Strock and C. H. B. Hotchkiss. Seven per cent added for operation without night reduction of temperature and change to heating value of 141,000 Btu per gal.
‡ Per degree-day.

Table 29. Unit fuel consumption * constants (U) for coal †

Based on 0°F outdoor temperature, 70°F indoor temperature. (Reprinted by permission from ASHRAE Guide and Data Book, 1963.)

Unit‡	Efficiency, %				
	40	50	60	70	80
Lb coal per sq ft steam radiator	0.0216	0.0172	0.0143	0.0123	0.0108
Lb coal per sq ft hot water radiator	0.0135	0.0108	0.0091	0.0078	0.0068
Lb coal per 1000 Btu/hr heat loss	0.0889	0.0717	0.0592	0.0507	0.0444

* Based on a heating value of 12,000 Btu per lb.
† Abstracted by permission from Degree-Day Handbook (2d ed., 1937), by C. Strock and C. H. B. Hotchkiss. Eight per cent added for operation without night reduction of temperature.
‡ Per degree-day.

some low-pressure steam and must be vented to the atmosphere or the low-pressure steam line.

Table 26 gives efficiency of utilization for various types of fuels, Table 25 gives correction factors for various outdoor design temperatures, and Tables 27, 28, and 29 give U values for various types of fuels. Degree days may be found in Table 7 in an earlier part of this section. A period of two to four weeks is selected during the coldest month to determine peak fuel needs and, thus, in the case of oil and coal, the storage capacity required.

Fuel consumption can be estimated by use of the formula

$$F = UNDC_f$$

where F = fuel consumption for the estimate period
U = unit fuel consumption
N = calculated Btu/hr heat loss
D = number of degree days [3] for the estimate period
C_f = temperature correction factor

[3] Degree days are the number of degrees by which each day's mean temperature falls below the base of 65°F

Boiler rooms: Schematic layouts of typical boiler rooms are shown in Figs. 36a and 36b. Boiler, PRV, and meter rooms located within a building must be well insulated thermally from the rest of the building. It may be desirable to set the boiler on a hollow tile base so that the underside of the boiler may be ventilated. There are noise and vibration problems in connection with boiler plants and PRV rooms, and acoustical isolation may be required.

PIPING

Piping is necessary to convey steam, condensate return, hot water, chilled water, condenser water, drain piping, and air (in pneumatic control systems). Problems encountered in the design of piping that require special attention are:

1. Expansion and contraction
2. Methods of supporting larger sizes due to heavy weights involved, especially where liquids are carried
3. Corrosion
4. Leakage
5. Relative inflexibility of piping in maneuvering through tight spaces
6. Pitching

Expansion: The ASHRAE Guide suggests a formula which will satisfactorily solve many expansion problems:

$$L = 6.16 \sqrt{D\Delta}$$

where L = length of pipe, ft
D = outside diameter of pipe, in.

Δ = deformation, in. (based on a fiber stress less than or equal to 16,000 psi)

It is recommended that expansion loops (Fig. 37) be installed wherever practicable since they require almost no maintenance. Where space does not permit, expansion joints as made by various manufacturers may be used. In general, steam, condensate

return, and hot-water systems will require expansion loops about every 150 to 200 lineal ft of straight pipe. To control the movement of the piping system, the piping is rigidly anchored to the structure midway between the loops. Changes in direction of the piping provide some protection against expansion and in some instances may be sufficient to take care of all expansion requirements.

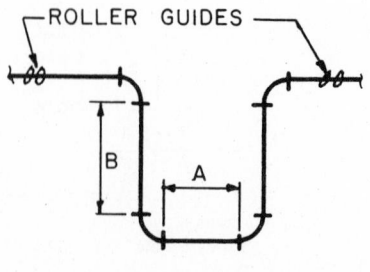

L = A + 2B

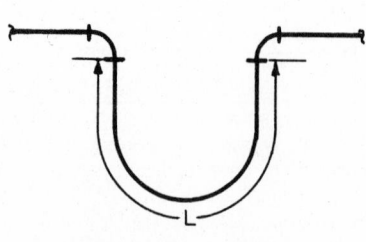

Fig. 37. Expansion loops

Chilled-water systems may require an expansion loop every 300 to 400 ft of continuous linear pipe with an anchor in between. Condenser water pipes seldom need expansion loops; anchoring them is usually sufficient to minimize pipe stresses.

Support: Several methods of supporting vertical piping are shown in Fig. 38. Piping that is run horizontally through a building is generally supported from various types of beam clamps where steel construction is used, or from inserts in concrete construction. There are many types of pipe hangers and supports available (Fig. 39). Spring or rubber-in-shear hangers are sometimes required on piping to minimize transmission of vibration through the structure. These generally require more vertical height for installation than standard hangers.

Corrosion and leakage are problems that are best solved by proper specifications, installation, and maintenance.

Inflexibility: Piping, especially in hung ceilings, must be carefully coordinated with ductwork and recessed lighting as well as with the structure of the building. Where piping has to be diverted around an obstacle, Fig. 40 shows approved methods for doing it. Low-pressure condensate return and drain pipes should never be set up if possible. Where there is insufficient space for a pipe to pass below a beam, it may be possible to run it through the web of the beam (Fig. 41); it may be necessary to increase the size of the beam in order to do this.

Pitch: The difficulties of running piping through tight spaces are complicated by the necessity for pitching the pipes. Steam, drain, and condensate return pipes should pitch downward in the direction of flow, while pipes full of water should pitch upward in the direction of flow.

Reverse return: In the design of all but the simplest piping systems, it is desirable to set up a reverse return system. This simplifies the balancing of the system initially, and changes in flow to units on the system do not tend to upset this balance to any appreciable degree.

Sizing: Table 30 gives the pressure drops in common use for the sizing of steam piping. Low-pressure steam-piping systems (2 to 10 psig) are normally sized for pressure drops from 1/8 to 1/2 psi per 100 equivalent ft of pipe. The sizing must be such as to assure that all parts of the system have sufficient pressure to operate properly. Piping for higher-pressure systems may be sized at larger pressure drops, depending on operating pressures required at equipment. The pipe sizes should not be so small that the steam velocity gets high (6,000 to 10,000 fpm) and creates noise.

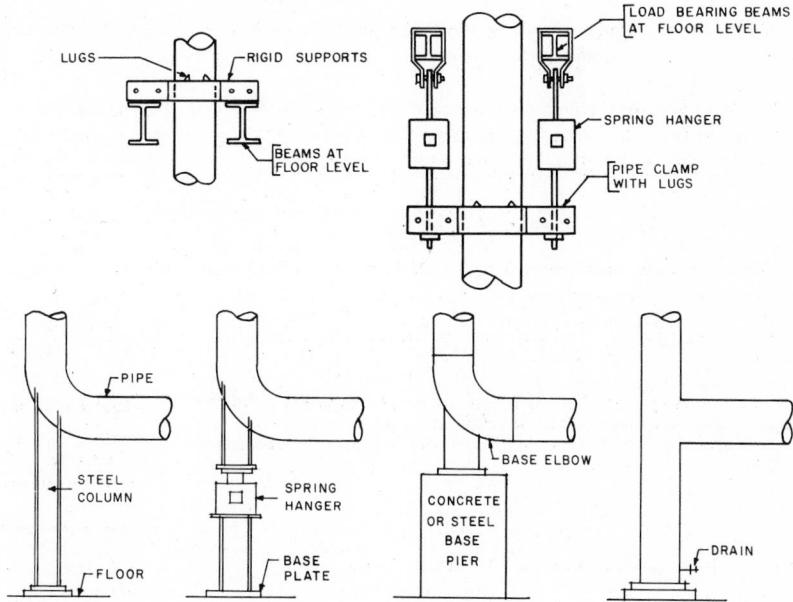

Fig. 38. Methods of supporting vertical piping

Water-distribution systems, as previously noted, are generally sized on the basis of 3 to 6 ft of water head per 100 equivalent ft of pipe with a maximum water flow velocity of 4 fps for pipes under 2 in. and 10 fps for pipes over 6 in.

All piping systems should be carefully designed to minimize the possibility of water hammer and noise.

Radiant panels: Piping systems for radiant heating and/or cooling systems require special consideration since they generally form a part of the ceiling, wall, or floor. Details of typical radiant heating installations are shown in the section on *Residential Heating.* Another type of radiant heating and cooling ceiling panels is shown in Fig. 42. In this system the piping sup-

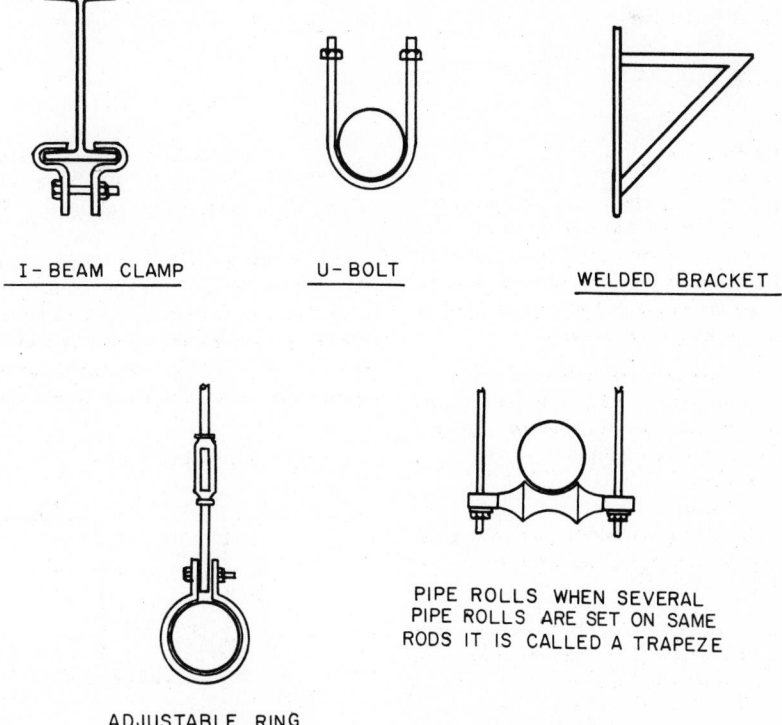

I-BEAM CLAMP   U-BOLT   WELDED BRACKET

ADJUSTABLE RING HANGER

PIPE ROLLS WHEN SEVERAL PIPE ROLLS ARE SET ON SAME RODS IT IS CALLED A TRAPEZE

Fig. 39. Methods of supporting horizontal piping

ports a perforated-metal-pan acoustical ceiling, in which lighting fixtures, air diffusers, and partitions are integrated.

One of the most critical examples of a radiant panel installation is an ice-skating or hockey rink (Fig. 43). The pipe lengths may be up to 200 ft long, and the liquid may have to travel up to 400 ft from supply to return header. Flow has to be uniform through each pipe, and no air

must be trapped or else melted spots may appear on an otherwise solid ice surface. This means that the piping must be properly sized, installed, and pitched. Extreme care must be taken to prevent ground water or water from above from coming in contact with the pipes; this is the major cause of failure in such installations. Wrought-iron pipe is recommended.

Mechanical equipment rooms must be

carefully laid out so that all piping that requires frequent operation or maintenance is easily accessible. It is customary to locate steam, chilled, hot, and condenser piping overhead at the lowest level above 8-ft headroom. Condensate return piping is usually run low along the walls. Above the piping are the various air ducts, and above these the plumbing lines, and at the highest level the electrical conduits.

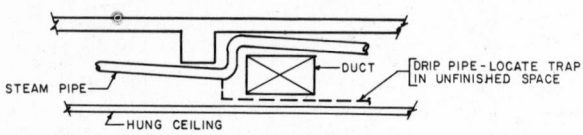

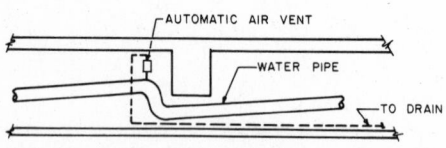
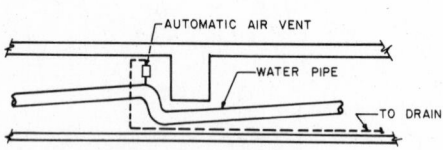

Fig. 40. Piping diverted around obstacles

Table 30. Pressure drops in common use for sizing steam pipe

For corresponding initial steam pressures. (Reprinted by permission from ASHRAE Guide and Data Book, 1964.)

Initial steam pressure, psig	Pressure drop per 100 ft, psi	Total pressure drop in steam supply piping, psi
Subatmos, or vacuum return	2–4 oz	1–2 psi
0	½ oz	1 oz
1	2 oz	1–4 oz
2	2 oz	8 oz
5	4 oz	1½ psi
10	8 oz	3 psi
15	1 psi	4 psi
30	2 psi	5–10 psi
50	2–5 psi	10–15 psi
100	2–5 psi	15–25 psi
150	2–10 psi	25–30 psi

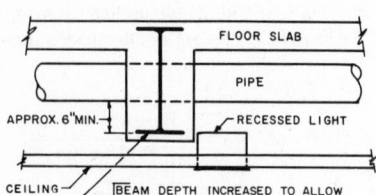

Fig. 41. Piping run through web of beam

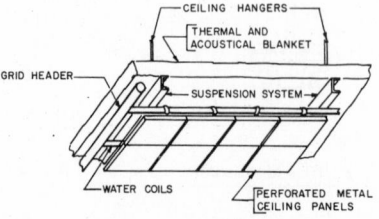

Fig. 42. Integral radiant piping and ceiling

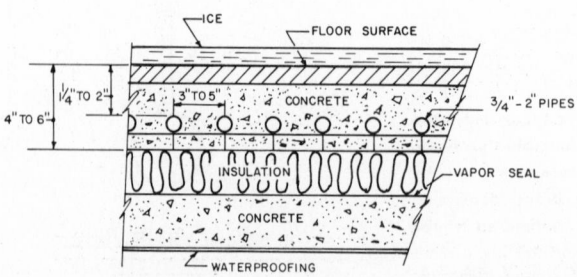

Fig. 43. Section through ice-rink floor

By ALFRED GREENBERG, P.E., *Environmental Consultant*

AUTOMATIC CONTROLS [4]

The automatic control system represents the nervous system of the heating, ventilating, and air-conditioning installation. It transmits environmental information from the outdoors and the controlled areas to central locations where adjustments are made to produce the required results. As buildings have increased in complexity, so have the automatic control requirements.

Many modern buildings feel the effect of weather changes much faster than older buildings because of more glass and less weight in the exterior walls. Further, there is the distinction between varying conditions at the exterior and the relatively stable thermal conditions in the interior of a building—all of which must be sensed and reacted to by the control system.

Because of solar and electrical loads, it is not uncommon for the refrigeration plant to operate throughout the winter months, making necessary another complex set of automatic devices to enable the cooling tower to operate in the heart of winter without the danger of freezing.

Automatic controls can save between 10 and 30 per cent of the annual operating costs for a given system. With controls costing about 3 per cent of the total for the heating and air-conditioning installation, this cost could be amortized in about six years.

Automatic controls contribute to the following ends:

1. Human comfort.
2. Fuel economy.
3. Industrial process conditions. (This is where air conditioning began.)
4. Safety. (For example, shutdown of fans in case of fire, stopping a refrigeration condensing unit if there is no water in the system, or preventing steam coils from freezing.)

DEFINITION OF AUTOMATIC CONTROLS

Automatic controls include three basic types of devices:

1. A sensing or pilot device
2. An actuating or motor device
3. A reading or indicator device

Sensing devices may be responsive to air or water temperature, humidity, steam

[4] *Based on an article by Arthur L. Spaet, P.E., Consulting Engineer, in* Architectural Record, *January, 1960. See also section on "Heating Systems for Houses."*

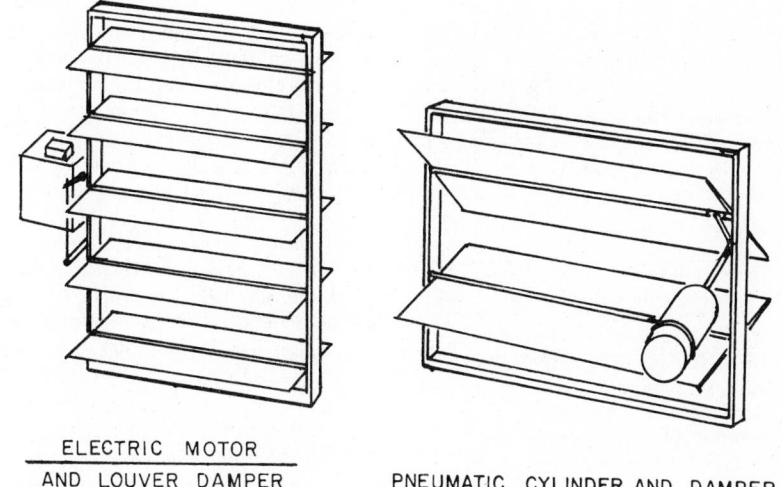

ELECTRIC MOTOR
AND LOUVER DAMPER

PNEUMATIC CYLINDER AND DAMPER

Fig. 44. Motor-operated dampers

pressure, or air velocity, and include such instruments as thermostats, aquastats, static pressure regulators, and similar devices. These are the "eyes and ears" of any control system. The sensing devices for any system may be electric, pneumatic, electronic, or combinations of any two or all three.

The second group, the actuating and operating devices, are essentially motor-controlled dampers or valves, corresponding to the fingers and muscles of the systems (Fig. 44). The "motors" may be hydraulic or pneumatic cylinders, air diaphragms, or electric motors, frequently with reversible and adjustable speeds.

The third type of equipment, the instrumentation of the system, in addition to thermometers and gages, include such refinements as clockwork mechanisms to start

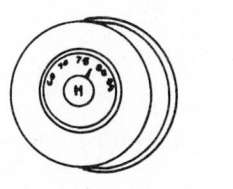

PNEUMATIC ROUND THERMOSTAT

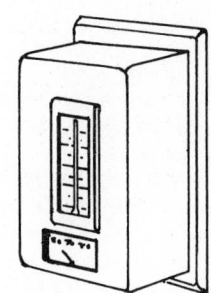

PNEUMATIC ROOM THERMOSTAT

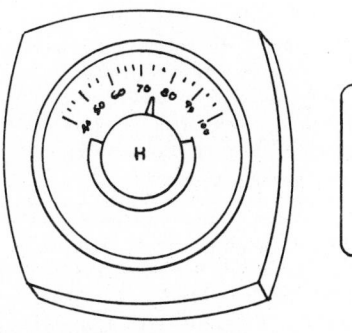

ELECTRIC ROOM THERMOSTAT

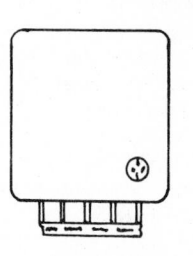

ELECTRIC HEAT-COOL THERMOSTAT
FAN CONTROLLER

Fig. 45. Thermostats

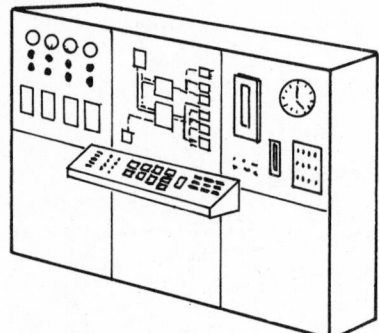

Fig. 46. Data-control center

Typical supervisory data center with visual portrayal of system selected for observation shown on screen. Approximate size of unit shown is 8 ft long by 6 ft 4 in. high by 26 in. wide with desk extending out an additional 10 in. (Courtesy Minneapolis-Honeywell.)

and stop motors, radiant thermometers, hygrostats, draft gages, two- and three-pen recording controllers, etc. (Fig. 45). These are now being made in "miniature" sizes, with dials approximately 3 in. in diameter.

All-electric controls are the usual choice for smaller systems. As the number of control devices and control points increases, a break-even point is reached after which pneumatic controls are less expensive. Packaged air-conditioning equipment up to about 50 tons usually falls within the range where electric controls afford optimum economy. Central systems with several zones, from roughly 30 tons or over, are usually controlled most effectively by pneumatic equipment. Above 50 tons, the economic advantage is generally with pneumatic systems.

More and more frequently, electric and electronic devices are integrated with pneumatic systems. However, if the system has a central air compressor and runs of pneumatic (air) tubing, it is usually classed as pneumatic.

The difference between electric and electronic systems lies in a somewhat esoteric refinement in equipment. In an electric control system, the thermostat sends its signal directly to the damper or valve motor. In an electronic control system, the thermostat sends a minute signal to an electronic relay, where the signal is measured and amplified. The relay in turn affects the control over the damper or valve, or over supplementary control circuits. The electronic control equipment may be used to activate any type of electric or pneumatic device, in any of numerous modes or cycles of operation.

REMOTE MOTOR CONTROLS

In a large plant or office building, centralized starting and stopping of small- and medium-sized motors for the air-conditioning equipment have distinct advantages. This applies to motors up to approximately 50 to 75 hp. Larger motors are preferably started locally, with the motor in full sight of the operator. It is now possible to have remote starting and stopping of electric motors without interconnecting control wiring. This system transmits a high-frequency signal through the house wiring from a central control panel. At some remote point, a crystal receiver acts as a relay to actuate a motor control circuit.

REMOTE READING GAGES

Electrically operated remote-reading temperature devices now offer the additional refinement of remote reset or remote adjustment of temperatures.

Plasticized or semirigid polyvinyl chloride or polyethylene tubing can now be used for pneumatic control piping, instead of steel or copper tubing. The plastic tubing is installed in multiple, with many color-keyed tubes grouped together inside a single protective jacket.

PREWIRED PACKAGED CONTROL ASSEMBLIES

Complete preengineered control assemblies applied to small low-pressure steam boilers and small air-conditioning plants are now generally available. The only wiring required in the field is that between the terminal strip and the actuating and operating devices.

Location of thermostats

The thermostat must be located where it can sense the needs of the space to be controlled. Care must be taken in locating the thermostat so that it is not exposed to conditions which are not representative of the space, such as direct sunlight or proximity to a heating or cooling unit.

If, for esthetic reasons, concealment of the thermostat is necessary, consider the following possibilities:

1. Eliminate the thermostat from the room by locating it in the return duct.
2. Install the thermostat in a recess behind a flush decorative wall plate, which permits convection of room air over the thermostat.
3. Aspirate room air with a small fan through a sampling tube which permits the thermostat to be located remotely, in a

closet, behind a coat rack, or in any convenient location.

4. Use an electric-resistance-type thermostat which consists of wire electrically sensitive to changes in air temperature. The wire may be wrapped inconspicuously around a picture, sculpture, molding, chandelier, etc.

CONTROL CENTERS

A touch of glamor as well as increased utility for heating and air conditioning resulted from the development of data-control centers, where over-all control readings can be taken and adjustments made in the settings of operating devices, thermostats, etc., located at remote points in the building (Fig. 46).

CHECKLIST

1. Plot plan, including utility survey
2. Local code requirements for heating, ventilating, and air-conditioning requirements; addresses where codes can be obtained
3. Availability and rates of oil, gas, coal, electricity, steam, hot water, river or well water, etc., for heating or air-conditioning requirements; addresses of utility and fuel companies
4. Orientation of building to true North
5. Necessity for heating plant and types considered
6. Heating, ventilating, and air-conditioning requirements for the various areas of the proposed building
7. Special heating, ventilating, and air-conditioning requirements
8. Hours of occupancy and usage of the various portions of the building
9. Location and sizes of boiler room and chimney, refrigeration plant, and other mechanical equipment rooms; determination of whether equipment should be located in roof penthouse or basement or elsewhere
10. Perimeter construction details and structural scheme for building
11. Adequacy of space above hung ceiling, including allowances for other trades
12. Location and sizes of duct and pipe shafts
13. Location and sizes of outside air-intake and exhaust-air louvers
14. Manner in which equipment can be brought into or taken from the mechanical equipment rooms
15. Snow melting requirements; details of construction to be thoroughly analyzed and coordinated
16. Location of cooling tower, if required
17. Requirements for incinerators
18. Requirements for kitchen-range hood exhaust, laboratory hoods, etc.

19. Location of fuel-oil tanks or coal bins, and recommended size of same, depending upon availability of fuel

20. Operating weight of all major pieces of equipment

21. Sound and vibration isolation criteria

APARTMENT BUILDINGS

Air conditioning in apartment houses has the following characteristics:

1. 7-days-per-week, 24-hours-per-day requirements.

2. Low loads due to people and lights.

3. Heavy appliance load in kitchen all day.

4. Nonoccupancy of bedrooms during day except for preschool children, children using rooms as playrooms, sick and old people, etc.

5. Possible heavy people load in dining and living rooms during the day.

6. Interior kitchens and toilets must have exhaust ventilation. Exterior kitchens should also have exhaust ventilation.

7. Occasional heavy concentrated loads due to parties or meetings indicate the desirability of providing large amounts of outside air to eliminate odors with means of rapidly exhausting this vitiated air.

The above indicates a variable and shifting load that would require a complex system to maintain accurate conditions at all times in each room. Few systems will accomplish all the above results.

General practice today in non-air-conditioned buildings is to provide central-heating facilities serving all apartments. This is usually provided by gas, oil, or coal-fired boilers. Most of the taller buildings use a steam-distribution system to convectors. Garden-type apartments and smaller tenements may find hot-water systems economical.

Most new apartment houses built with air conditioning included use through-the-wall self-contained units, sometimes with an integral heating coil for winter heating. The popularity of this system is due to its low first cost. Maintenance and operating costs are generally higher than for a central system. This type of system is usually the noisiest and produces the least uniform environmental conditions. One advantage it does have is that many units include an exhaust fan setting for purging the room of odors and smoke.

Of the central air-conditioning systems, the dual-duct and the 3 and 4-pipe induction systems have the potential of providing the most satisfactory results. However, the ductwork required for the first takes up

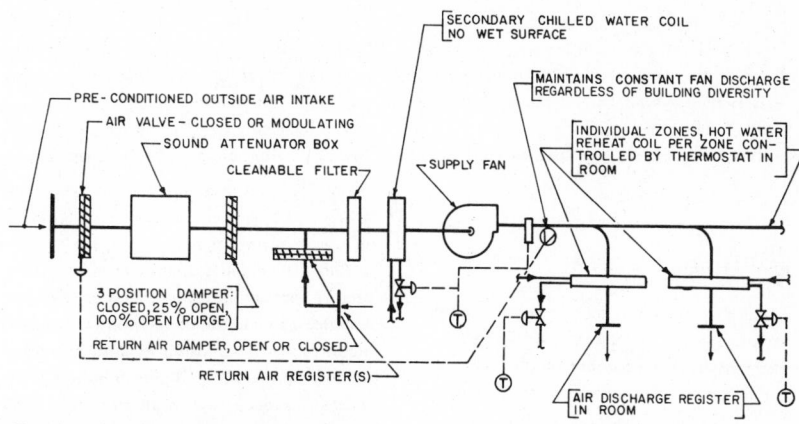

Fig. 47. Apartment air-conditioning unit

more space than any of the other systems, and it is the most expensive to install. With this system, the air is usually fed from the ceilings and/or walls and a separate heating system furnished for perimeter heating.

Induction systems, which use a combination of air and water to furnish both cooling and heating, are becoming more common in central air-conditioning systems for apartment house application, according to a 1961 survey. Next to the dual-duct system, induction systems require the most space and are the most costly to install. They furnish a high degree of temperature and humidity control, are quiet, and therefore are used in most deluxe applications. The 3 or 4-pipe system furnishes a more accurate degree of control, greater economy of operation, and elimination of change-over temperature problems.

Through-the-wall fan-coil units with perimeter vertical-pipe distribution are sometimes used. This system is less costly than the induction system and furnishes a higher degree of control than is available with self-contained units. Fan-coil units are also generally quieter than self-contained units. In most cases, fan-coil motors are connected to the apartment's electric meter, if the apartment is separately metered.

All piping and ductwork is generally run vertically along the perimeter of the building so as not to cut down on interior closet and room space. Horizontal ductwork or piping, except over corridor ceilings, is generally avoided in apartment buildings.

One of the biggest drawbacks of all perimeter air-conditioning systems is that the air flow conflicts with window drapes and curtains and causes undesirable movement; this may affect the air distribution in an adverse manner. Also, the purging of odorous and smoky air is not possible in most cases.

As apartment buildings get taller, above 20 stories, through-the-wall units become increasingly more risky due to the effects of wind, rain, and stack effect. Because of this, through-the-wall units are not recommended for apartment houses over 20 stories high.

Stack effect also manifests itself in the interior toilet and corridor ducts of tall buildings. It is for this reason that the New York City Code requires that no toilet exhaust duct be over 250 ft from the first to the last outlet. This increases the duct-shaft requirements but minimizes the possibility of drafts. The same criteria should apply to supply duct systems.

For the ultimate in flexibility and control of internal environment, as well as freedom from curtain rustle, a perimeter radiation system plus a central air-handling system for each apartment is required (Fig. 47). It is also the most costly. The proportion of outside air can be varied from 0 to 100 per cent and may come from exterior wall louvers or a central outside air shaft (Fig. 48). For tall buildings, care must be taken to guard against stack effect. Chilled water is furnished from a central system. The ductwork should be zoned with central hot-water or electric reheat coils or dampers to maintain temperatures or air flow as desired. Return ductwork to the unit is usually required.

This system requires a separate mechanical equipment room in the apartment, or the equipment may be placed in a furred

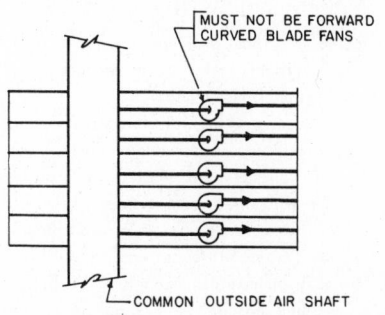

Fig. 48. Outside air from central shaft

soffit or above a hung ceiling over a corridor or closet. Access to the unit should be through the service corridor or entrance. This system is identical to that in a deluxe single-family residence.

Interior corridors and lobbies must have ventilation, preferably designed so as not to draw apartment odors into the corridors.

In individual apartment buildings, heating and air-conditioning equipment is generally located in the basement with the cooling tower on the roof. Special care must be taken to prevent objectionable noise transmission of equipment to the apartments. In multiple-building projects, serious consideration should be given to a centralized air-conditioning and heating system for all the buildings in the project.

HOTELS AND MOTELS

Each guest room must have the ability to provide its own thermal environment as dictated by the occupant at all times. This limits the type of system to the following:

Self-contained units

Single-duct, reheat- or recool-coil per room

Dual-duct

Fan-coil units

Induction system

The first has the lowest initial cost and space requirements, but a separate heating system is required; it is rarely used in new construction.

The single-duct reheat-coil system and the dual-duct system are rarely used because of their high cost and large space requirements.

The dual-duct system is, however, widely used in the dining- and meeting-room areas of hotels where the size of rooms is flexible and the load is highly variable.

The fan-coil-unit system is most commonly used in motels because it requires the least amount of additional equipment and is the least costly to install next to packaged window units. A 3 or 4-pipe fan-coil system should produce even greater operating economy. Fan-coil units have a high ventilation rate for rapidly heating or cooling the room. The unit can be shut off when the room is not occupied. Fan-coil units are fairly quiet in operation and produce reasonably good environmental conditions.

Most new hotels use the induction system; motels can seldom justify the use of this system because of the comparatively small number of rooms served. This system furnishes a closer degree of control than fancoil units, is slightly quieter, and produces better results in intermediate seasons when the outdoor temperature is between 40 and 50°F. The 3 or 4-pipe induction system may offer even greater first- and operating-cost economies.

In tropical climates where humidity control and mildew are serious problems, a single duct system using a recool coil for each room is proving to be economical and effective.

Whichever type of air-conditioning system is used, a source of hot water or steam must be available for heating the building. In motels, it is generally desirable to place the refrigeration and boiler units in a central location to minimize the piping. In milder climates, the central heating plant may be replaced by small gas-fired or electric heaters in each room.

Hotels usually locate the refrigeration and boiler plants in the basement, with some of the air-handling equipment and the cooling tower on the roof. In motels the cooling tower is usually located on the ground far enough away from the rooms so as not to be heard.

In both motels and hotels, the management office area and lobby are generally air conditioned. In most cases, a separate system is used for this area.

OFFICE BUILDINGS

Office buildings can vary from a structure no larger than a single-family residence to huge skyscrapers. This discussion will be limited to the multistory structures since they involve certain problems which are not present in low buildings.

The type of occupancy may have an important bearing on the type of air-distribution system to be used. If there is one owner or lessee for the entire building, his operations may be clearly enough defined so that a high degree of flexibility is not required. Where different tenants may occupy different floors or even parts of the same floor, the degree of complexity increases. This problem is more acute where tenants may have seasonal and varying overtime schedules.

Entrances and lobbies, stores, restaurants, club facilities, observation decks, etc., should generally be treated as separate entities with their own systems. Where a tenant has a large enough organization to warrant a separate medical department, this may be complex enough to be treated as a small hospital, with separate systems and controls.

One of the largest sources of concentrated heat load in an office area is the computing and tabulating machinery which is increasingly used in large company operations. As accurate an appraisal as possible should be attempted of the amount, size, and type of computer equipment anticipated for the life of the building in order to size the refrigeration air-handling equipment and to make provision for the future installation of added equipment.

Most new office buildings use some form of combination heating and cooling unit for the perimeter of the building. Most have combined air and water induction units or fan-coil units; but some use all-air perimeter induction units, and others use wall-type packaged air conditioners with integral heating coils. Ductwork and piping as required for any of these systems may be run either vertically at the perimeter of the building or vertically in the interior of the building with horizontal distribution at the ceiling for each floor. The latter is usually more costly, but the choice is dependent upon the architectural design of the building. The coordination and detailing of the relationship between perimeter unit location, perimeter wall glass, spandrel beams, piping, and ductwork are very often critical and should be carefully examined in the early stages of design in order to establish the most feasible and economical layout.

Interior spaces seldom need heating since they have continuous light and people heat load and possibly heat-producing equipment, too. In fact, these spaces more than 15 to 20 ft from the exterior walls of the building usually require cooling all year around. Since their heat load is relatively constant, a conventional single-duct, low-velocity system, zoned to meet special conditions such as conference rooms, private interior offices, etc., is generally satisfactory. Where maximum flexibility is required for interior areas, such as on executive floors or where there may be multiple tenants on the floor, a dual-duct system is desirable. A common compromise is to provide both hot and cold ducts in the shafts, thus making it possible to provide either single- or dual-duct distribution systems on any floor (Fig. 49). If space conditions are very tight, the air can be run at high velocities and reduced near the outlets by means of air-reducing valves. The only justification for resorting to high-velocity air distribution is lack of space, since first cost and operating cost are almost always greater.

The total mechanical space requirements for heating and air-conditioning equipment for office buildings range from 5 to 10 per cent of the gross area. The clear height required for fan rooms varies from about 13 to 18 ft, depending upon the complexity of the distribution system and the equipment involved. On typical office floors, the perimeter units take up 1 to 3 per cent of the gross floor area, and interior shafts require about 2 per cent more. Therefore, on each floor, ducts, pipes, and equipment require 3 to 5 per cent of the gross floor area. Electrical and plumbing space requirements per floor average up to 1 per cent of gross area.

The shaft space requirements vary, depending upon the number of fan rooms provided. One mechanical equipment room (MER) usually furnishes the air requirements for from eight to twenty floors, with about twelve being the average. The more floors served, the larger the duct shafts and the equipment in the MER's, with resultant higher fan room heights, greater equipment weight, and higher operating costs due to increased motor horsepower. If fewer floors are served by a mechanical equipment room, then more are required to serve the building. This allows equipment to be smaller and lighter, and mechanical equipment rooms can often be the same height as typical floors. However, initial installation costs will probably be higher. In any case, mechanical equipment rooms must be thermally and acoustically isolated from office floors above or below them.

Cooling towers are the largest single piece of equipment required for the air-conditioning systems. Roughly speaking, the cooling tower requires about 1 sq ft of roof area per 400 sq ft of total building area, and is from 13 to 40 ft high. The building structure must be capable of carrying the cooling tower plus its full load of water

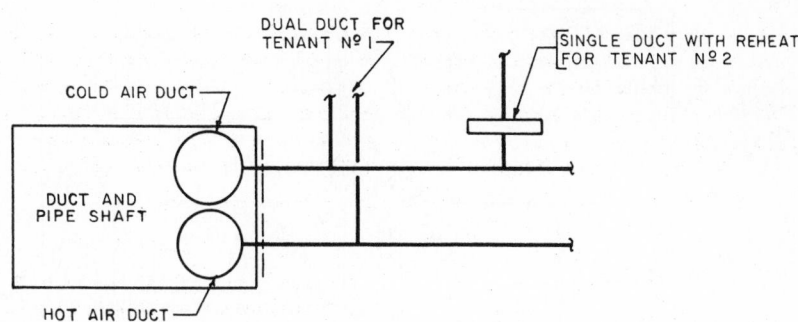

Fig. 49.   Dual-duct risers provide flexibility in distribution systems

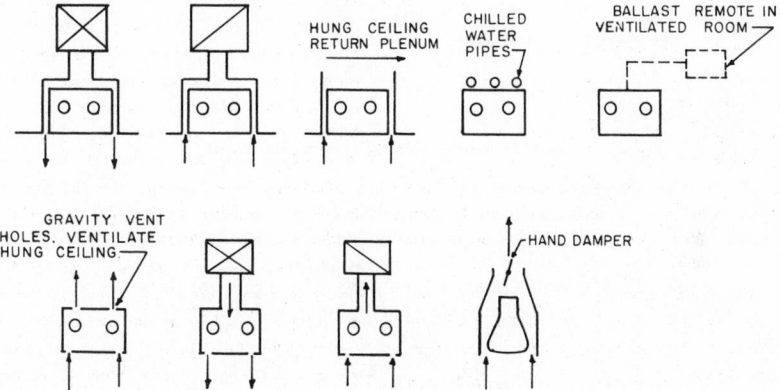

Fig. 50.   Methods of drawing off heat from lighting fixtures

(120 to 200 psf) and must also prevent transmission of vibration from the tower to the structure and wind-load stresses.

Where the building contains kitchens, low-temperature chimneys are usually required for range hoods. They must go up to the roof of the building, at least 100 ft away from any outside air or cooling tower intakes.

Since the lighting load in an office building makes up a large part of the total heat load (25 to 40 per cent), an effort should be made to withdraw the heat at the source by means of supply or exhaust air or water tubing (Fig. 50). By this means, 30 to 60 per cent of the total heat output of the

lights can be withdrawn, and thus it does not enter into the air-conditioning requirements. To connect a duct to each fixture is expensive, so the hung ceiling is often used as a return air plenum and the air drawn into the space above the hung ceiling around the lights.

Areas in office buildings which require special ventilation are elevator machine rooms, electric and telephone closets, electrical switchgear, plumbing rooms, refrigeration rooms, and mechanical equipment rooms. The heat loads in some of these rooms may be so high as to require the installation of air-conditioning units for spot cooling.

DEPARTMENT AND VARIETY STORES

Small stores seldom require more than a packaged air-conditioning unit with no ductwork requirements. Occupancy in the store is for relatively short periods of time, and air distribution, even though uneven, is usually not objectionable.

In department stores the diversity of operations is such that zone control becomes a necessity due to the variation in heat loads and customer location. The

areas requiring the greatest attention are as follows:

Lunch counter—see the following pages.

Live-pet department—air distribution should be even and draftless especially where birds are concerned.

Lighting display counter—this area generally develops a large amount of heat which must be drawn off at the source. Air should be transferred from other areas, where possible, in order to cut down on the air-conditioning load.

Meat, vegetable, and fish counters should have local exhaust to prevent the spread of odors. The same is true for baked goods and candy counters, except that some odor carryover may be desirable to attract customers.

The main floor in multistory stores generally has a higher population density than the other floors. This is usually about 50 sq ft per person, with half as many people on the other floors.

In clothing and carpeting areas it may

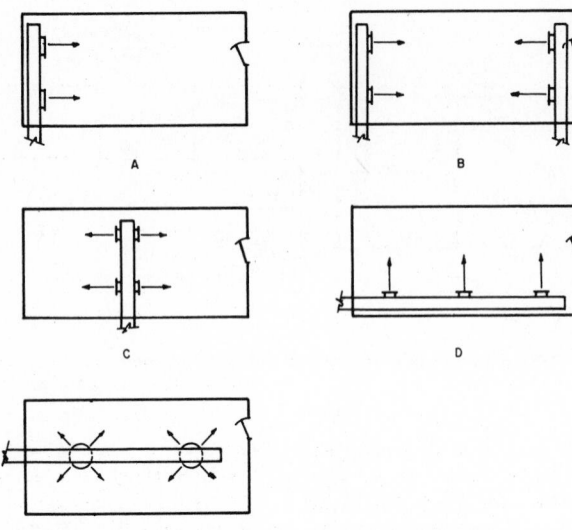

Fig. 51. Air distribution systems for stores

A. High outlet velocity; satisfactory for certain applications, if properly designed. Excessive air motion and drafts may result if outlets are too low or throw is too long.

B. Moderate air movement; air from outlets should not collide so as to cause down drafts in the center.

C. Good air movement; no collision of air streams; good results.

D. Good air movement; blow toward exposed wall; good results.

E. Generally gives best results, especially for low ceiling heights.

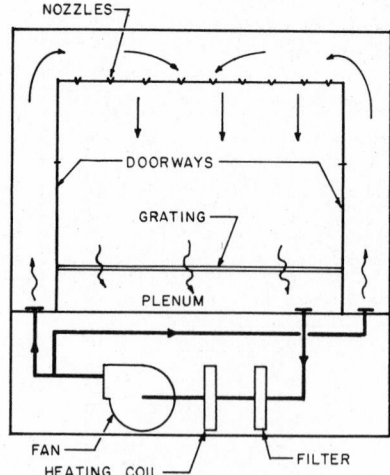

Fig. 52. Air-curtain doorway

Nozzles should be adjustable.

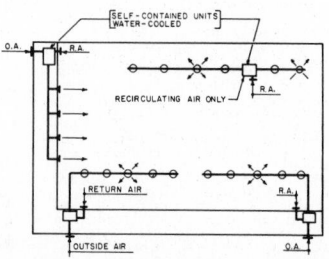

Fig. 53. Air conditioning for an existing store, using self-contained units with water-cooled condensers and central cooling tower.

be desirable to provide humidity control to minimize the effects of static electricity.

Other areas that might require special consideration are beauty parlors and tailor-shop areas. These areas have high-heat-producing equipment which must be properly exhausted. In addition, beauty parlors have odors that should be eliminated.

Dressing-room areas should have draft-less air distribution. The store should be kept slightly pressurized to prevent outside air from coming in through the entrances. If possible, the food areas should be kept at a slightly negative air pressure.

In order to display their wares to advantage, department and variety stores generally have a high lighting intensity concentrated around display groupings. Since displays are frequently changed and moved, and the lighting with it, it is desirable to set up the air-distribution system on a modular basis. This is seldom done because of the added ductwork expense

and return air is generally taken back at only two or three points on a floor. This increases the cost of system operation since the conditioned air has to enter the space at a lower temperature than would be required if the lighting heat were drawn off directly. Commonly used systems of air distribution are shown in Fig. 51.

Perimeter solar load is seldom an important factor in this type of building because most of the wall space is used for storage. Where show windows are used, they must be properly ventilated to prevent heat buildup. Where the store is spread out over a large area, the roof heat load may become an appreciable factor. Several inches of roof insulation or roof sprays will materially reduce this load.

Care should be taken in designing the entrances and exits in order not to create drafts at the sales areas nearby. Revolving doors and/or vestibules will minimize this problem. Consideration should be given to

the use of an air curtain as an entrance and exit. If properly designed, it can keep outside and inside conditions separate and can prevent the wind from breaking through (Fig. 52).

In existing stores it is often convenient to put in a number of large self-contained packaged units and distribute the ductwork as required (Fig. 53). This involves a minimum of capital expenditure and usually space can be allocated without too much difficulty. Outside air must be furnished to the space, so some of the units are generally placed against exterior walls where openings can be cut through. A cooling tower will most likely be required, and provision must be made for running the condenser water piping to the tower. This type of system has a high degree of flexibility but will probably require higher maintenance costs than a central plant. These units can be obtained in sizes up to 50 to 60 tons each.

RESTAURANTS, CAFETERIAS, LUNCHEONETTES, BARS, AND NIGHT CLUBS

Restaurant occupancy may vary from zero to maximum within less than one hour, and this may happen two or three times a day. This results in a great fluctuation in heating and cooling demands. Some form of modulating control is therefore desirable.

Heating and air-conditioning systems should be designed so that all areas, including private rooms, semiprivate accomodations such as booths or alcoves, table locations along windows, behind interior columns, and in general open areas, are equally comfortable. "Cold pockets" or drafts could result in loss of revenue. In restaurants the air conditioning should be neither felt nor heard (Fig. 54).

Cafeterias and luncheonettes generally have some or all of the food preparation in the same room as the diners. These eating places are usually noisier than restaurants, so noise from the air-conditioning equipment is not as critical a factor. Since the diners do not remain as long, they seldom require the degree of comfort that would be mandatory in restaurants. The air-distribution system must be designed so that the spread of food smells from the serving counters to the areas where patrons are eating is minimized (Fig. 55). This will usually necessitate heavy exhaust-air requirements at the serving counters with the air coming from the eating areas. Exhaust air must also remove the heat from hot trays, coffee urns, ovens, etc., in order to minimize discomfort to patrons and employees. These factors will often create greater air-conditioning loads for cafeterias and luncheonettes than for restaurants, with correspondingly greater air quantities required in the eating areas.

Bars serving alcoholic beverages produce pungent vapors that must be drawn off in order not to build up strong odors. Therefore, the area of the bar should have a positive exhaust.

Night clubs where the patrons dine and

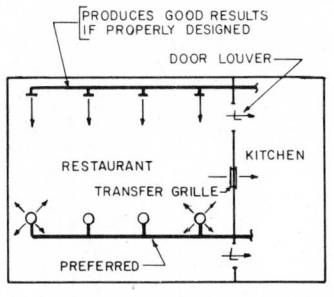

Fig. 54. Air-distribution system for restaurant

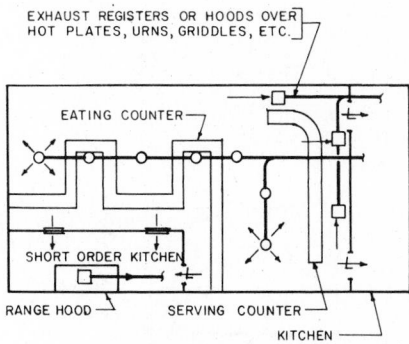

Fig. 55. Air-distribution systems for luncheonette and cafeteria

dance require considerably greater air quantity and larger air-conditioning units than those which have only a floor show. Night clubs and bars generally have heavier smoking loads than other types of dining establishments, and therefore exhaust and outside air requirements are greater. Hence, special care must be taken with the air distribution to prevent discomfort to patrons from drafts.

In any type of dining establishment, the entrances and exits must be completely shielded from the diners so that they are not seated near drafts. Vestibules provide a measure of protection, but in practice both vestibule doors are often open simultaneously. To offset this disadvantage, revolving doors may be used and local means may be provided for heating or cooling the inflowing air.

Employee comfort is difficult to maintain at a uniform level, partly because of the difference in temperature between kitchen and dining room, partly because employees are constantly in motion while patrons are seated. However, maintenance of satisfactory temperature and atmospheric conditions for customers goes far toward alleviating employee discomfort.

The location of outside air-intake and kitchen exhaust louvers must be such that exhaust air is not drawn back into the system, nor should the exhaust air cause discomfort to outside passers-by. Also, louvers

to kitchen must be designed so that kitchen noise is not heard in the eating areas.

Private dining rooms present such varied load conditions that individual control for each unit is generally a necessity. Depending upon the size of the areas to be partitioned, it may be expedient to use a dual-duct, single-duct reheat, or a separate air-conditioning unit for each area (Fig. 56).

The kitchen has the greatest concentration of heat load and odors, and ventilation is the chief means of removing them. The most common method in small restaurants is the ordinary exhaust fan. Another method, applicable to larger establishments, employs a simple kitchen vent and requires the building up of a positive air pressure within dining areas. Under these conditions air flow is always from the dining room to the kitchen in a practically continuous current which carries smoke and odors along with it. In designing a system of this kind it is necessary to provide slightly more exhaust capacity than the supply of recirculated and fresh air. It is of course imperative than no air exhausted from kitchens, locker rooms, toilets, etc., be recirculated. Supplementary ventilation air may be required for the kitchen.

The air quantity required for kitchen ventilation is a function of the equipment in the kitchen. More efficient hoods (Fig. 57) generally cost more, but the resultant ventilation savings justify the extra cost.

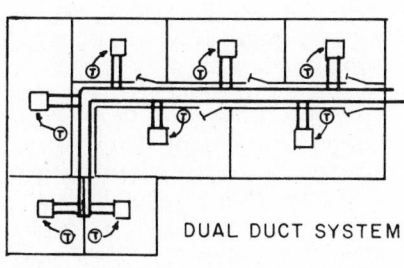

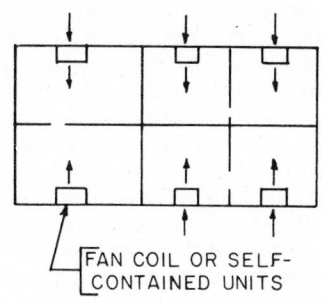

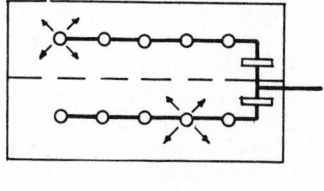

Fig. 56. Air-conditioning systems for private dining rooms

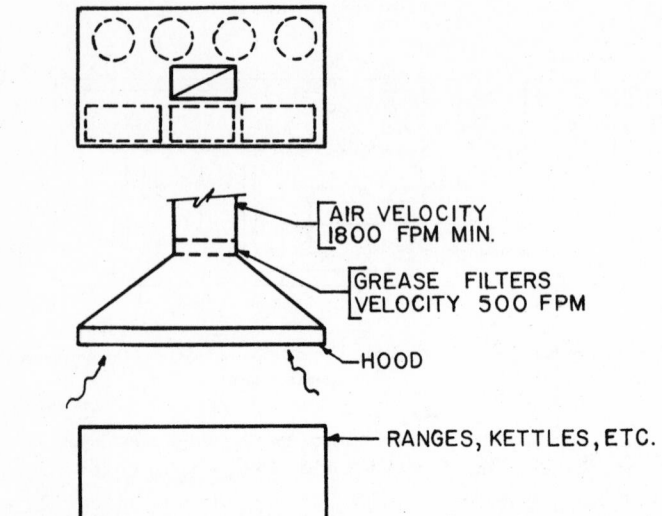

AIR VELOCITY
1800 FPM MIN.

GREASE FILTERS
VELOCITY 500 FPM

HOOD

RANGES, KETTLES, ETC.

AIR VELOCITY ACROSS FACE OF
HOOD: 75 TO 100 FPM

Fig. 57.   Range hood

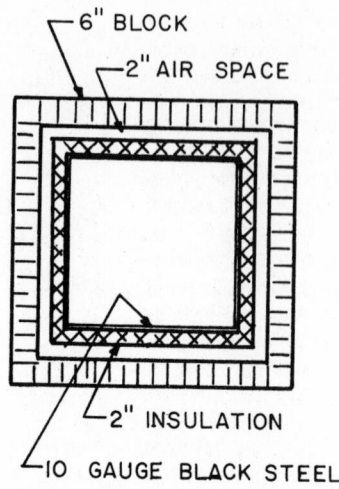

6" BLOCK

2" AIR SPACE

2" INSULATION

10 GAUGE BLACK STEEL

Fig. 58.   Sheet-metal hood duct

For the design of hoods, see pages on "Industrial buildings," farther on in this section. Since fires at hoods over ranges are a serious problem, a steam water or CO_2 quenching system should be installed. The range-hood exhaust duct must be considered as a low-temperature chimney which has to go above the roof (Fig. 58).

THEATERS, AUDITORIUMS, SPORTS ARENAS, HOUSES OF WORSHIP

The common denominator of these buildings is that large numbers of people are assembled in an enclosed space for appreciable periods of time. Although the purposes for congregation may differ, many of the problems and solutions are similar.

The primary problem is to furnish sufficient fresh air and to distribute it properly. Second, heating or cooling is required as environmental conditions dictate.

The seating areas' ventilation requirements are usually set by codes which typically call for 30 cfm of total air flow per person with 15 cfm of outside air. For air conditioning the total cfm requirements per person may be lowered to 15 to 24 cfm with 7½ to 10 cfm of outside air. In most cases this will give from five to eight air changes per hour, which is sufficient for good air circulation. The supply air has to be furnished from the ceiling, the side walls, and in some cases from the edges of balconies (Fig. 59). Uniform air distribution is difficult to attain in the center seating areas unless return air inlets are located there. This is usually done by means of mushrooms under the seats. In small balconies, side-wall supply distribution emptying into the central area is satisfactory, but deeper balconies require some ceiling supply air and possibly under-the-seat returns. Air outlet and inlet velocities must be low enough not to be noticeable. Concert halls have the most critical noise re-

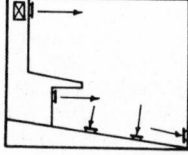 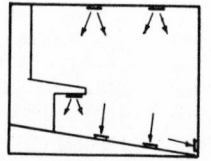 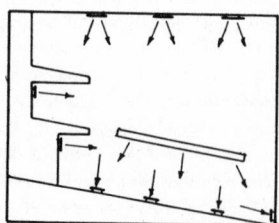

Fig. 59.   Air distribution in typical places of assembly

quirements, with opera houses and theaters next. A small amount of exhaust air should be taken from the ceiling of the seating area in order to prevent formation of pockets of hot air which can produce a radiant effect.

Because of the relatively high latent heat load due to the people, the seating area system should be designed for proper dehumidification as well as humidification control. Thermostat and humidistat location in the seating areas usually is impractical, so they are best located in return air ducts.

The theater stage presents a more complex problem. The lighting load is very heavy, but 40 to 60 per cent of it can be negated by exhausting air around the lights (Fig. 60). Conditioned air should be introduced from the side stage and backstage and returned or exhausted around the lights. The air distribution is complicated by the fact that some pieces of scenery consist of light materials that flutter in the slightest air current. Therefore, low air-movement velocities are required. This demands that the air be distributed over a

wide area with many supply and return registers. Special treatment should be provided for the stage manager and the control board area. Proper air distribution and balancing can minimize the billowing of the curtain when down.

The location of the mechanical and electrical equipment rooms can greatly affect the degree of sound attenuation treatment required to isolate the sound from the seating areas. If possible, mechanical equipment rooms should be located in an area which is separated from the main seating or stage area by a buffer such as lobbies, service areas, etc. Generally, at least one mechanical equipment room should be furnished somewhere on the roof to house the toilet, general exhaust, kitchen, and emergency stage exhaust fans. On the stage, cognizance must be taken of local code requirements for emergency exhaust ductwork requirements which are often sizable and should be incorporated in the earliest designs. See also section on "Skylights."

One of the most flexible of all building types is the combination sports arena and civic auditorium. It can be used for events as diverse as ice hockey, political rallies, rodeos, benefit luncheons, boxing and wrestling matches, basketball, etc. With the stage in the center of the arena for most events and with no possibility of vertical ductwork, flexibility must be obtained through versatility in the design. Multispeed motors or auxiliary air systems are two common means of providing variation in air quantity for different events. Since all air generally originates from the ceiling, the air must come down at velocities sufficient to reach the arena floor area. Return or exhaust is generally from the lower seating areas, either at the side of the aisles or under the seats. The possibility of odors and smoking is greater than in other buildings of mass occupancy. Therefore, positive measures such as activated charcoal filters or electronic ionizers should be used to dissipate odors, whether gaseous or particulate.

When an ice-skating rink is designed into the structure, the problems of ground water conditions, site drainage, structural foundations, insulation, and waterproofing enter into the picture. Ice-melting pits of sufficient size must be furnished. If the

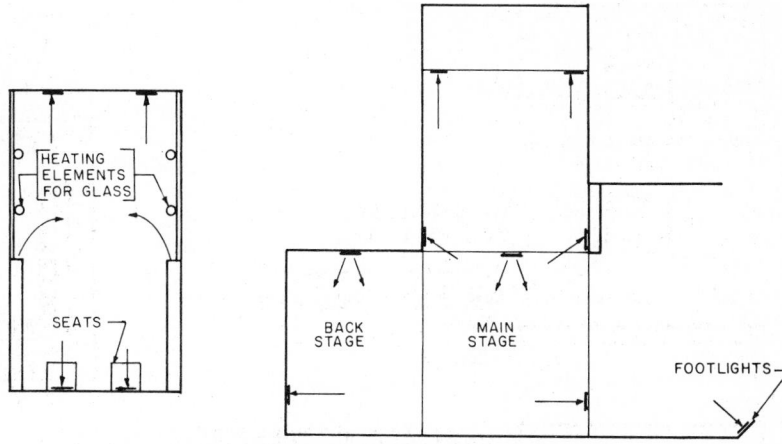

Fig. 60.   Air distribution in theater stage area

Skylight or mechanical exhaust fan in accordance with applicable code requirements.

arena is to be air conditioned, the possibility of combining the air-conditioning system with the ice-rink system should be considered. The radiant effect of the ice on the people and of the roof heat on the ice must be considered in the design and operation of the system.

For these buildings where ceilings are usually quite high, only the lower 12 to 15 ft need be fully cooled because this is where the people are. The ceiling temperature may tend to get high and should be exhausted to minimize convective and radiation effects.

SCHOOLS

The simplest and usually the cheapest type of school heating and ventilating system consists of perimeter radiation (steam, hot water, or electric) with ventilation coming in through the windows. A mechanical exhaust system, with grilles on the interior or corridor wall, draws the air across the room. Gravity exhaust ventilation systems are not recommended for outside design temperatures below 30°F.

If mechanical exhaust systems are used in conjunction with window supply and the windows are closed, then the air will be drawn from corridors. This may produce sufficiently negative pressures in the building to produce poor operating conditions for hooded equipment, boilers, incinerators, etc. Therefore, rooms for such equipment must have adequate air supplies with airtight doors.

A variation of the above system has mechanical supply ventilation, properly filtered and tempered, admitted through registers on the interior wall or through ceiling diffusers.

The perimeter radiation system need be sized to handle only transmission losses if the room is positively pressurized by exhausting less than the supply air quantity. If mechanical supply air is furnished, gravity exhaust may produce satisfactory results.

The mechanical supply air system may be designed to take care of interior heat losses and the radiation operated only when the outside temperature becomes low enough to cause window drafts. This combined system is not very satisfactory in operation since classroom heating requirements are satisfied at relatively low outside temperatures due to the heat load of the students and lights. Therefore, proper ventilation is required to remove this internal heat and allow the radiation to perform satisfactorily.

Panel heating is often used for kindergarten classrooms where students spend much time on the floor. Its biggest drawback is the storage effect which prevents it from following changing load conditions quickly enough. This often results in overheating, an effect which is minimized if a ventilation system is used in conjunction with the panel heating system. Floor-heating panels are relatively ineffective in preventing downdrafts from windows, although wall panels located under the windows have produced satisfactory results.

In general, the most satisfactory environmental conditions can be obtained by means of all-air or combination systems. Any of the air-distribution systems discussed earlier in this section may be adapted for schoolroom use, except the induction system which may not furnish sufficient ventilation to meet local code regulations. If air

is not supplied from under the windows, then in order to counteract downdrafts, return grilles should be located on the window sills. If the returns are below the sills, they will lose most of their effectiveness.

In most instances, if a building is summer air conditioned, it may be possible to reduce the ventilation requirements, which may effect an appreciable saving in first costs. In fact, if a school building is designed for air conditioning, it is possible for total owning and operating costs to be less than for a non-air-conditioned building.

One of the most commonly employed all-air systems in use is the forced-warm-air heating system (see section on "Residential Heating and Air Conditioning"). It is essentially a low-velocity, single-duct, zoned system supplying filtered and heated and, if desired, cooled air.

Unit ventilators also find wide application in schools. They furnish individual room control for heating and provide ventilation usually from through-the-wall openings. They can also be adapted for air conditioning with a minimum amount of alteration and addition of equipment. They should be selected for quiet operation. Unit ventilators may be combined with extended air ducts or finned pipe radiation to combat downdrafts in adjacent windows.

By ALFRED GREENBERG, P.E., *Environmental Consultant*

LIBRARIES AND MUSEUMS

The primary purpose of libraries and museums is to house objects it is desired to exhibit, store, and preserve. For both types of buildings, rapid changes in temperature and humidity are more harmful than the maintenance of reasonable limits at all times. In general, if the atmospheric environment is kept from 70 to 78°F and 40 to 50 per cent relative humidity for most applications, then no harm will be done to the books, works of art, or exhibits. This range of temperature and humidity is the same as required for human comfort, which greatly simplifies the problems of design.

Libraries and museums are difficult to clean, by the very nature of items they contain. Therefore, the efficiency of the air-cleaning apparatus should be at least 85 per cent based on the National Bureau of Standards (NBS) atmospheric air discoloration test.

LIBRARIES

There are various types of libraries, but in general they consist of stack areas, working and office areas, reading rooms, rare-book vaults, and small study rooms.

The stack areas (usually interior spaces) have a relatively low lighting intensity and a low ratio of people to floor area, so the air-conditioning load is not heavy. However, sufficient air must be circulated to maintain uniform temperature conditions throughout the stacks. Generally, four to six air changes per hour are required. If the supply and return pattern is as shown in Fig. 61, then the lower limit may apply; otherwise, six air changes should be used. Where the ceiling is used as a return plenum or has return registers, the air circulation at the lower part of the stacks is not as positive. If the book stacks are adjacent to an exterior wall, then a perimeter air-conditioning system should be designed to act as a buffer, in order to maintain constant stack environmental conditions. Do not use air-conditioning systems that contain steam or water piping in areas where leakage can cause damage.

Office areas are treated in the same manner as those in office buildings. The work areas, however, may use special binding glues and other materials that require a separate exhaust system to eliminate odors.

Reading rooms have a fluctuating people load, which may be high; lighting intensities are high, and these rooms are generally at the perimeter of the building. Therefore, the air-conditioning load is variable, and individual room or zone control is desirable. The reading rooms will generally require from eight to twelve air changes per hour for proper conditioning. Air movement should be below 50 fpm to prevent drafts on people reading at tables for long periods of time. The noise level should be maintained at NC-30 to -35; a level less than NC-30 will tend to accentuate background noises such as page rustling, foot shuffling, chair moving, etc.

Small study rooms (50 to 100 sq ft) are usually located at the exterior walls of the building. The lighting and people loads are relatively low and can be considered constant. When the rooms are located above grade and the exterior wall has glass, the

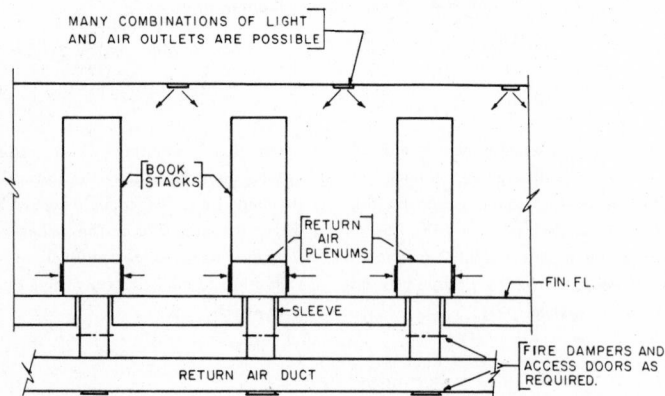

Fig. 61.   Air-distribution system recommended for book stack areas

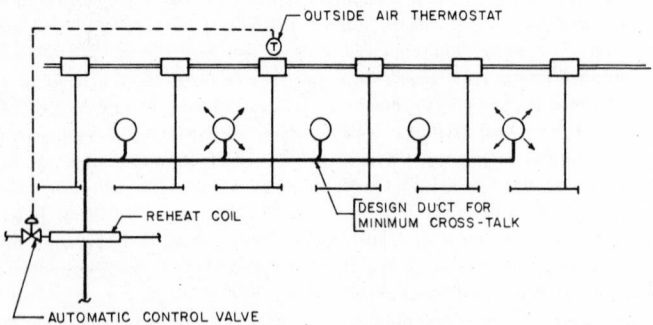

Fig. 62.   Air-conditioning system for outside study rooms

Design ductwork for minimum crosstalk.

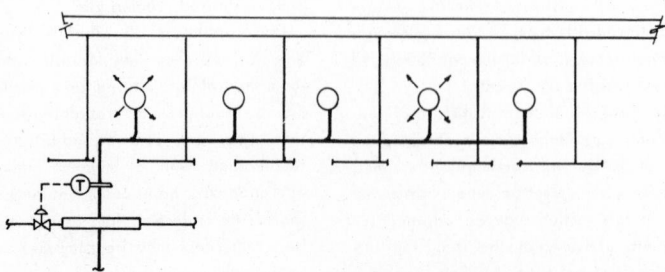

Fig. 63.   Air conditioning for interior study rooms

glass presents the largest load. It is variable but the same for each room on that wall. Therefore, a simple design expedient is to put all the rooms on each facade on one zone and control the air conditions from an outdoor thermostat (Fig. 62). If the rooms are below grade or contain no exterior glass, the air conditions may be controlled from a preset, adjustable thermostat located on the zone discharge duct (Fig. 63).

Many libraries, especially college libraries, operate up to 16 hours a day and may run the air-conditioning equipment about 5,000 hours a year. Such constant usage requires the selection of heavy-duty, long-life equipment needing little maintenance. All book areas and especially the perimeter and roof areas should be on night thermostat and humidistat control to maintain reasonably constant environmental conditions at all times. Library vaults often require closer temperature and humidity control than the general book areas. Hence it is desirable to furnish a separate refrigeration compressor and air-handling system for the vaults. This system should be capable of operating 24 hours a day and should have alarms which indicate any failure to maintain the required environmental conditions.

The location of the mechanical equipment rooms should be as remote as possible from the reading areas in order to minimize noise and vibration.

MUSEUMS

Museums generally have exhibit areas, work areas, offices, and storage areas.

The work areas in art museums consist of restoration rooms, picture framing, sculpture mounting, shipping, and repair rooms, etc. Paints, chemicals, plaster of paris, and other materials are used which may require special temperature, humidity, and air-circulating conditions. A greater variety of functions may be performed in the work areas of natural history museums. Odors and chemicals used may require larger exhaust air quantities. Individual room or area zone control will generally be necessary.

The storage areas in most museums contain large numbers of items for which exhibit space is not available. Most of the time, these storage areas must be kept within fairly close environmental conditions

to preserve the stored items. For example, art storage areas are often maintained at 65 to 72°F ± 1°F and 50 per cent RH ± 2 per cent. Stuffed fur-bearing animals should be stored at about 40 to 50°F and 50 per cent RH for maximum preservation, whereas fossils and old bones will keep better at higher humidities.

The exhibit areas are usually maintained at standard comfort conditions of 70 to 75°F, 50 per cent RH. Lighting loads for art museums are likely to run from 6 to 15 watts per sq ft. At the upper limit, this causes a substantial increase in the size of the air-conditioning equipment. Natural history museums range from 2 to 6 watts per sq ft. People loads vary widely depending on the popularity of the exhibit, the time of day, the weather, etc. All this seems to indicate that individually controlled zones are required to maintain optimum air conditions.

The most difficult problem encountered in designing the air-conditioning system for a museum is that the partitioned areas may be radically changed from one exhibit to another. The air-distribution system, and lighting system as well, must be set up in the most flexible manner possible so as to provide a minimum of obstacles to the setting up of any exhibit.

HOSPITALS

The general criteria for a comfortable atmospheric environment for healthy people are satisfactory for hospital patients, except that more attention must be given to the quietness of the system, the air distribution, relative humidity (RH), and the degree of air filtration and freedom from bacteria. Specific design recommendations for the principal areas of a hospital are as follows:

Area	Summer		Winter	
	°F, D.B.	%RH	°F, D.B.	%RH
Operating suite	68–85	55	68–85	55
Recovery suite	75–80	50–55	75–80	50–55
Patients' areas	74–78	40–50	72	40–50
Peripheral vascular	72–76	40	72–76	40
Maternity suite	74–80	40–50	74–80	40–50
Incubator and nursery	85–90	35–45	85–90	35–45
All other air-conditioned areas	74–78	40–50	72	40–50

D.B. = Dry Bulb Temperature
RH = Relative Humidity

Exercise, physical therapy, X-ray, and locker rooms and bathrooms should be maintained

at 75°F minimum during the heating season. Patients' baths, swimming pools, sitz baths, etc., should be kept at 80°F. Many of the service areas such as kitchens, storage and repair spaces, etc., may be kept at 60°F in the winter.

Patients' bedrooms: The metabolic rate of bed patients is reduced, making them more sensitive to drafts. Hence air distribution should be uniform and air velocity at patients' level no more than 30 to 40 fpm. The air-distribution system must be designed for very quiet operation (NC-30 curve [5]). The exhaust air from rooms of noninfectious patients may be transferred to corridors, toilets, and nurses' working areas. A minimum of 25 per cent outside air is desirable. General patients' quarters and associated nurses' working areas should have their own air-distribution system because they require 24-hr operation.

Areas for patients having infectious diseases or allergies must have 100 per cent outside air, and each room must have a separate exhaust air connection so that none of the air goes into the corridor. If

[5] *Noise criteria curve defining maximum permissible sound level for various frequencies; see ASHRAE Guide and section on "Acoustics."*

room air is transferred into toilets adjacent to the room, it should be carried as a separate toilet exhaust system with its own fan.

Rooms for seriously disturbed mental patients should have heating and air outlets of such design that they are completely tamper-proof so that the patients will not be able to harm themselves or others.

Outpatient clinics and treatment rooms are usually open about 12 hr per day, and should have at least 25 per cent outside air.

Administrative area is treated in much the same manner as an office-building area. Since its operation is usually 10 to 12 hr per day, it can be combined with the outpatient clinic area into one air-distribution system, if it is architecturally or mechanically feasible.

Operating rooms require a wider range of temperature and humidity control than most other areas. The temperature range is to provide optimum comfort conditions for both medical staff and patients and is controlled by the staff. The high level of RH is to minimize the possibility of electrostatic discharges, which may cause explosions. Also, certain types of operations may require a high RH.

The operating room should have 100 per cent outside air, 80 per cent positive room exhaust, and individual room temperature and humidity control. Temperature control can be obtained by means of a reheat coil on a single-duct system or by a dual-duct system. Humidity control by means of steam sprays is recommended rather than pan-type humidifiers because of the possibility of algae formation on the coils and pan (Fig. 64).

Since the heating loads for operating rooms are often substantial, 15 to 24 air changes per hour are normal. This makes good air distribution, preferably by means of perforated ceiling panels, a necessity in order to maintain no more than 50-fpm air velocity around the operating table (Fig. 65). For a good ceiling supply distribution system, low exhaust registers are recommended with a small ceiling outlet to remove operating light heat. A high degree of filtration is required. Much research must still be performed on methods for eliminating bacteria from the air simply and economically.

Maternity and incubator areas require a separate system operating 24 hr a day, with 100 per cent outside and exhaust air. Incubator rooms, delivery rooms, labor rooms, nurseries, and all auxiliary areas require individual temperature and humidity controls. Delivery rooms are treated as operating rooms. Air distribution should maintain about 30-fpm air velocity at infant or mother level.

X-ray and radiology suite operates about 12 hr per day and requires about 25 per cent outside air with standard comfort conditions maintained. Ductwork is often lined with lead to minimize the dangers of the spread of radioactivity.

Laboratory and research areas will generally require 100 per cent exhaust air, depending upon the nature of the work. The requirements for laboratories given farther on in this section generally apply. All hood exhausts should be discharged above the highest roof level. These areas operate about 12 hr per day, but certain experiments may require that the air-conditioning system operate around the clock.

Animal areas require air conditioning 24 hr per day with 100 per cent supply and exhaust. Individual room control of temperature and humidity may be necessary.

Morgue contains a special refrigerated box and an open area for preparation of corpses. It should be served by its own air-handling system, and exhausted above the highest roof level. Exhaust should be 10 to 20 per cent greater than the supply air which should consist of 100 per cent outside air.

Central pharmaceutical and sterilizing area requires 100 per cent exhaust to minimize chemical odors and dissipate the heat from the sterilizers. A large portion of the air to this area may be transferred from other uncontaminated areas if it is feasible to do so. Exhaust registers should be placed over sterilizers, work benches, etc.

Soiled-linen rooms should have, where possible, a separate exhaust system discharging above the highest roof.

Mechanical equipment rooms should be located as far from patients' quarters as practicable in order to minimize noise and

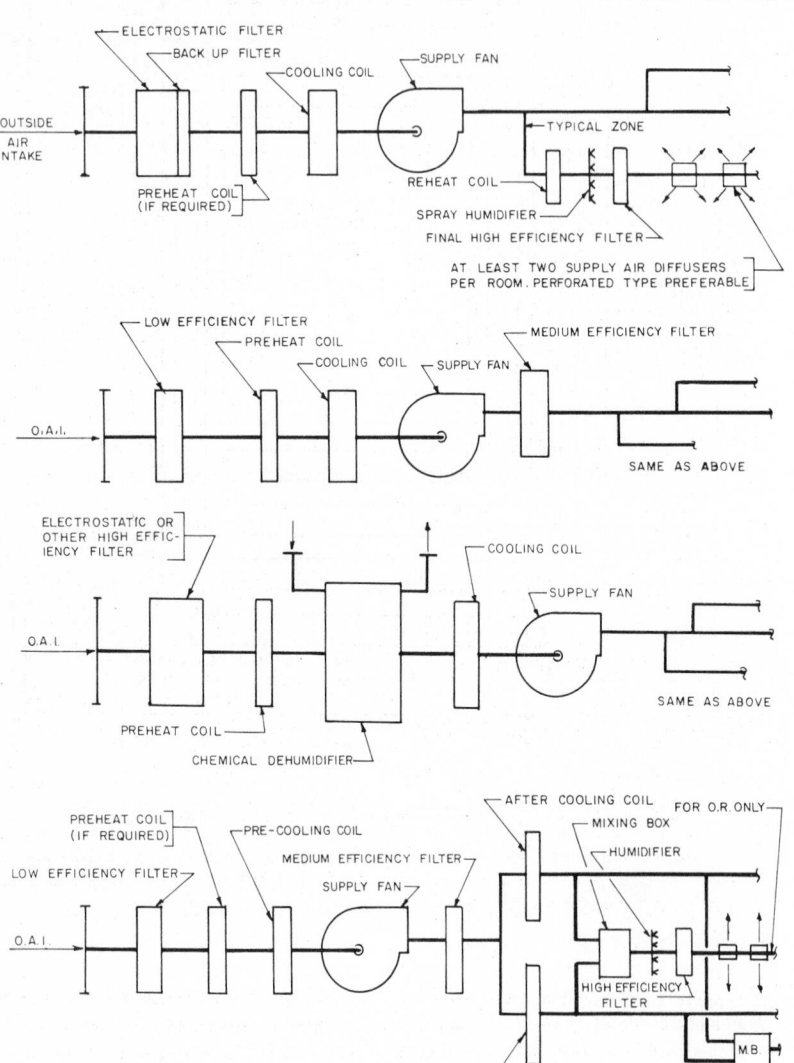

Fig. 64. Air-conditioning systems for operating rooms

Electrostatic filter system: Adequate if maintenance of cooling coils and drain pan is good. Requires least space.

Dry filter system: Less expensive than electrostatic system, but requires more space. Does not eliminate algae growth in cooling coil and drain pan if maintenance is inadequate.

Chemical dehumidification system: High first cost but in some cases may be the most economical. Keeps cooling coil clean since chemical dehumidifier does total dehumidification. Requires more space than previous systems, plus added ducts and louvers. May help to reduce micro-organisms. Relatively high operating costs.

Dual duct system: Excellent control at economical cost. Each room can be custom designed for specific environmental requirements. Largest mechanical room space required. Higher motor fan costs, but best over-all system economy for results obtained.

Note: On any of the systems shown, prehumidifier may be used before cooling unit.

fumes. Similarly, the cooling tower should be located and designed so that it does not transmit noise to patients' areas, or cover the windows with mist.

The refrigeration and boiler plant should have sufficient flexibility so that if any piece of equipment is not able to function, the entire plant capacity will not be affected. Therefore, as a rule, hospitals require more mechanical space than most other types of buildings.

Boiler plants generally operate at 110 to 150 psig in order to provide steam requirements for kitchens (5 to 50 psig), sterilizers and warmers of all types (10 to 70 psig), and laundries (up to 125 psig).

Provision should be made to eliminate the possibility of an electrical service interruption by maintaining an emergency generator to cut in automatically if the electrical power fails. The emergency generator should be located sufficiently far away from patient and critical areas so that noise, vibration, and fumes are not a problem.

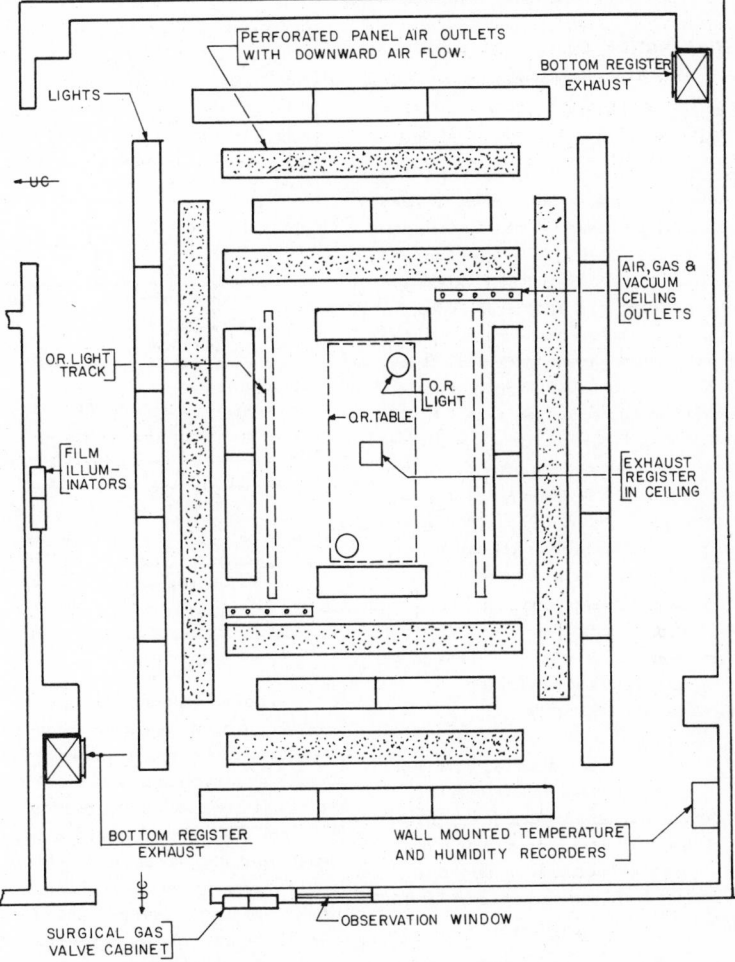

Fig. 65. Reflected ceiling plan of an operating room

Using fluorescent lights, perforated panel air outlets, and 100 per cent outside air; exhaust 80 per cent through bottom register, 15 per cent through doors, 5 per cent through ceiling register.

INDUSTRIAL BUILDINGS

Industrial heating, ventilating, and air conditioning involves several aspects, namely:

1. Product and/or process requirements
2. Personnel comfort requirements
3. Industrial exhaust requirements

Product and process requirements are so varied and numerous that a detailed treatment is not possible here. This section will deal with personnel comfort and industrial exhaust requirements, including some data on the determination of exhaust hood requirements.

In plants where close machining tolerances are required, it is usually not the temperature itself that is critical but the variation in temperature. Therefore, conditions are usually maintained in the comfort range with close limits on the range.

Where static electricity is a problem, it is generally minimized by maintaining the relative humidity of the air at 55 per cent minimum, if it does not harm the product or process.

There are two basic kinds of heat release that will affect the comfort of personnel. One is a hot-dry heat which allows some relief by means of evaporation of body sweat. The other type is warm-moist heat which prevents evaporation of sweat. The latter presents the greater hazard to worker health and comfort. The introduction of outside air with low relative humidities will contribute greatly to personnel comfort in the warm-moist areas.

There are several general methods available for minimizing the effects of heat exposure. One is to control the heat at the source by proper insulation, location of machine or process in cool environment or out of doors, furnishing water or air jacketing for removal of the heat, or enclosing the entire machine or process in a hood and drawing off the heat. The latter is the extreme case of the use of hoods for removing heat from a localized area. Hoods of all types, sizes, shapes, and materials are used in industrial applications to remove heat, dust, fumes, vapors, odors, etc.

Most types of hoods are of an open-construction type and require 100 per cent of their air requirements from the space. For enclosing hoods where it is more expensive or undesirable to obtain the air from the space than from an auxiliary ventilation system, hoods may be designed to take a portion, usually half, of their air requirements from the space and the rest from the auxiliary air system (Fig. 66).

By JACK A. WUNDERLE, *Air Cleaning & Ventilation Engineer, Ohio Department of Health*

DETERMINATION OF EXHAUST HOOD REQUIREMENTS

FREELY SUSPENDED AND SHED TYPE HOODS

There are three basic methods of calculating exhaust requirements for freely suspended and shed type hoods: (1) the face velocity-area method, (2) the ACGIH method and (3) the capture velocity method. Following are an explanation and sample calculation of each. The sample calculations are based on an assumed kitchen which is 30 ft long by 25 ft wide by 10 ft high, in which are located two kitchen ranges, each 4 ft wide by 8 ft long. Two kitchen range hoods, one freely suspended and the other of the shed type, are each 5 ft wide by 10 ft long and located 4 ft above the work surface. The symbols used in these calculations and on the diagrams are as follows:

Q = exhaust volume, cfm

V_f = face velocity, fpm

V_v = average velocity in vertical plane under edges of canopy, fpm

V_c = control velocity, fpm

V_T = transport or duct velocity, fpm

X = perpendicular distance from work surface to hood bottom, ft = 4 ft

W_w = width of work surface, ft = 4 ft

L_w = length of work surface, ft = 8 ft

W_h = width of hood opening, ft = 5 ft

L_h = length of hood opening, ft = 10 ft

A_w = area of work surface, sq ft
  = 4×8 = 32 sq ft

A_h = area of hood opening, sq ft
  = 5×10 = 50 sq ft

P_w = perimeter of work surface, ft
  = $(2 \times 4) + (2 \times 8)$ = 24 ft

P_h = perimeter of hood opening, ft
  = $(2 \times 5) + (2 \times 10)$ = 30 ft

U = volume of kitchen, cu ft
  = $30 \times 25 \times 10$ = 7500 cu ft

D = diameter of ductwork, in.

C = number of air changes per hour

Face Velocity-Area Method

This method is an easily used one for estimation purposes but possesses disadvantages for accurate design work. No provision is made in the calculations for various hood shapes, sizes and designs, nor is there account taken of the variable factor X (distance from hood bottom to work surface).

The volume Q of air to be exhausted is determined by multiplying the area A_h of the hood face (for both the freely suspended and shed type hood) by the face velocity V_f: $Q = A_h \times V_f$. The exhaust volume Q found in this manner is then checked to determine whether it is adequate to provide the

Hood sketches adapted from designs appearing in the ACGIH "Industrial Ventilation Manual," 1954, and ASA Code Z9.1–1951.

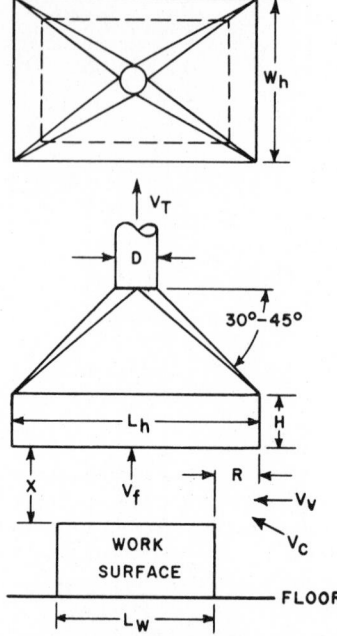

Freely Suspended Hood

minimum general ventilation requirements (e.g., 20 to 25 air changes per hour) figured on the entire kitchen room volume. Should the exhaust fan selected on the basis of the Q value not provide the required minimum air change rate, it should be increased in size to provide necessary air turnover. On the other hand, if the fan provides more than the minimum air change rate, its size would not be decreased, since the exhaust volume it provides has been calculated to be necessary for proper hood operation.

Example

$$Q = V_f \times A_h$$

Using a design face velocity of 55 fpm (recommended by the American Gas Association):

$$Q = 55 \times 50 = 2750 \text{ cfm}$$

For both hoods:

$$Q = 2 \times 2750 = 5500 \text{ cfm}$$

To check this figure against the minimum required rate of 20 to 25 air changes per hour, first change the total exhaust volume of the two hoods to cubic feet per hour:

$$Q = 5500 \text{ cfm} \times 60 = 330,000 \text{ cfh}$$

Divide this figure by the room volume to find the number of air changes per hour:

$$C = Q/U = 330,000/7500 = 44$$

This figure is well over the desired minimum of 20 to 25, and so the fan selected on the basis of $Q = 2750$ cfm for each hood will meet the requirements of the room.

ACGIH Method

The ACGIH (American Conference of Governmental Industrial Hygienists) method has a

distinct advantage over the face velocity-area method in that calculation of exhaust volumes may be suited, by selection of proper design velocity, to the two most common hood types. Actually, it is a modification of the face velocity-area method.

For shed type hoods, it is recommended that a design work face velocity of 100 fpm be used and that the exhaust volume so calculated be checked to ensure that it is not less than:

$$Q = 50 \, P_h \times X$$

For canopy hoods, this formula is suggested:

$$Q = 1.4 \, P_w \times X \times V_v$$

Velocity V_v in this formula ranges from 50 to 250 fpm depending on cross-drafts, condition of contaminant release, etc.

Example

For the shed type hood:

$$V_f = 100 \text{ fpm}$$
$$Q = V_f \times A_h$$
$$= 100 \times 50 = 5000 \text{ cfm}$$

As a check, the exhaust volume must be greater than:

$$Q = 50 \, P_h \times X$$
$$= 50 \times 30 \times 4 = 6000 \text{ cfm}$$

Since the exhaust volume calculated by the first method is less than that determined in the check method, the fan selected on the basis of $Q = 5000$ cfm should be increased in size to meet the requirements of 6000 cfm. For the canopy hood the lower velocity figure of 50 fpm will be used.

$$Q = 1.4 \, P_w \times X \times V_v$$
$$= 1.4 \times 24 \times 4 \times 50 = 6720 \text{ cfm}$$

On this value of Q should be based the selection of a fan for the canopy hood.

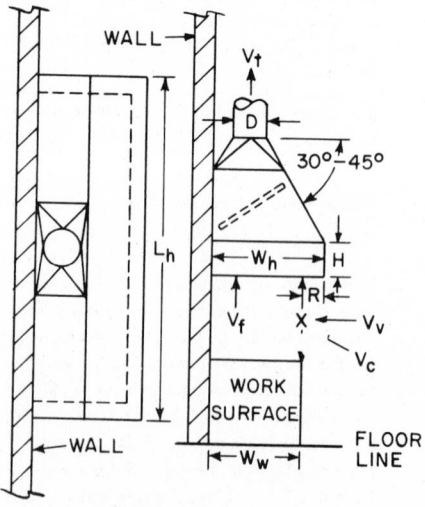

Shed Type Hood

Capture Velocity Method

The third, and most accurate, method of calculating hood exhaust volume requirements is by the use of *capture velocity—velocity contour* principles. It is the preferred method of calculating exhaust hood requirements because it takes into consideration variable hood dimensions, variable hood to work surface distances and control velocities.

Capture velocity may be defined as the velocity at any point in front of a hood necessary to capture the contaminated air at that point and cause it to flow into the hood. This differs from *face velocity*, which is the velocity at the face of the hood. By the proper selection of capture velocity, the designer can ensure the removal of contaminants without outward escapement and with the minimum exhaust volume and power expended. Professor DallaValle of Georgia Tech, who is a respected authority in this field, proposes the use of 30 fpm as the capture velocity to be applied at the outer edge of the working surface of hooded kitchen appliances. This suggested velocity of 30 fpm has merit in that the human body is relatively insensitive to air movements less than 30 fpm, and hence, for worker comfort, it is advisable to keep cross-drafts below this amount.

The *velocity contour* concept states that the velocity distributions (expressed as percentages of the velocity across the hood open area) will be the same for geometrically similar hoods and obstructional arrangements. The importance of this velocity contour relation is realized when one considers that, regardless of the actual dimensions involved, the positions of velocity contours (lines of equal velocity) are the same for similar hood shapes. Thus, when velocities are expressed in terms of face velocity and distances in terms of hood dimensions, a single pattern of contours is representative of all hoods of the same general shape.

These principles are represented by two formulas:

For freely suspended hoods, either square or with side ratios of 1:2:

$$(1) \qquad Q = 14.5 \, V_c \times W_h{}^{0.2} \times X^{1.8}$$

For rectangular shed type hoods:

$$(2) \qquad Q = 8.5 \, V_c \times W_h{}^{0.2} \times X^{1.8}$$

To eliminate laborious mathematical calculations, DallaValle has represented these formulas graphically in the curves reproduced on this page. To further simplify matters, the units of measurement are in terms of hood width W_h. For example, a hood of length $2W_h$ is twice as long as it is wide. Similarly, if the distance from the work surface to hood bottom is $1.5 \, W_h$, then it is one and one-half hood width. It will be noted that there are

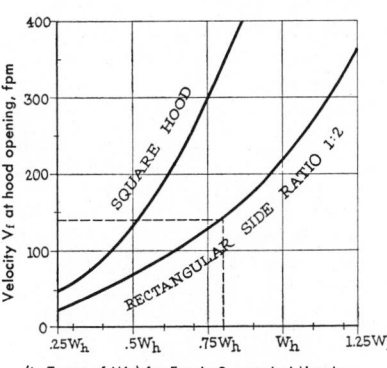

(in Terms of W_h) for Freely Suspended Hoods

several curves on each of the graphs. These curves are labeled for different side ratios (hood width: hood length). A control velocity V_c of 30 fpm was used in calculation of these curves. Knowing the side ratio, hood width and distance X, the face velocity V_f can be found from the curves and the hood exhaust volume calculated using the formula $Q = V_f \times A_h$.

The hood exhaust volume thus calculated will provide a minimum control velocity of 30 fpm at the outer peripheral edge of the work surface. In fact, one may expect more than a 30-fpm velocity, since some contribution will be realized from the chimney effect generated by the hot surfaces. If higher or lower velocities are wanted, the values may be increased or decreased by the ratio of the desired velocity to 30 fpm. Where velocities are reduced, the hood should be lowered to the minimum distance from the work surface and the open areas not in use enclosed with suitable metal shielding.

Example

Using the graphical solutions to formulas (1) and (2), one can determine the hood face velocity which will provide a control velocity of 30 fpm at the edge of the range.

Side ratio = hood width/hood length
= 5/10 = 1:2

X (expressed in terms of hood width)
= 4/5 W_h = 0.8 W_h

For the freely suspended hood:

V_f (from the graph) = 142 fpm
$Q = V_f \times A_h = 142 \times 50 = 7100$ cfm

For the shed type hood:

V_f (from the graph) = 88 fpm
$Q = V_f \times A_h = 88 \times 50 = 4400$ cfm

If a control velocity of 40 fpm is desired instead of the 30 fpm from which the curves were calculated, the values of Q should be increased by the ratio of 40 to 30:

$Q = 7100 \times 4/3 = 9467$ cfm
$Q = 4400 \times 4/3 = 5867$ cfm

DUCTWORK

One may determine the proper duct size (or check a proposed installation for proper duct size) by dividing the exhaust volume through the duct by the recommended transport velocity. As an example, suppose it were required to exhaust 4500 cfm with a transport velocity (V_T) of 1800 fpm:

$$\text{Duct area} = \frac{4500 \text{ cfm}}{1800 \text{ fpm}} = 2.5 \text{ sq ft}$$

Area of a circle = $\pi D^2/4$

$$D = \sqrt{\frac{4 \times A}{\pi}} = \sqrt{\frac{4 \times 2.5}{3.1416}} = 1.787 \text{ ft}$$

1.787 ft $\times$ 12 in./ft = 21.4 in.

Therefore, a 20-in. duct should be used. Where the duct size calculated is an odd size or fraction, the next smaller available duct size should be selected. The smaller size increases rather than decreases the duct velocity (V_T) and thus prevents deposition or settling of entrained contaminants in the system as might be the case if a larger size duct and hence a slower velocity were used. If a 21-in. duct were available, it would be used. However, the usual sheet metal fabricator will have patterns in ½-in. steps for sizes through 5½ in.; 1-in. steps for sizes 6 to 20 in.; and 2-in. steps for sizes 22 in. and larger.

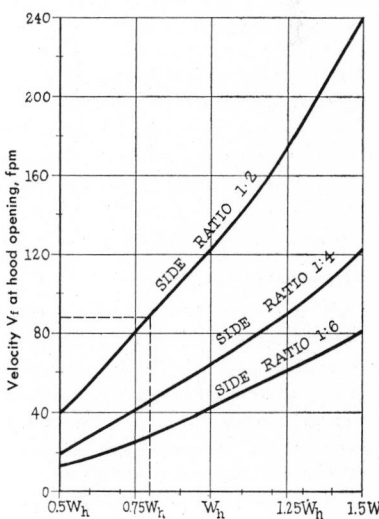

X (in Terms of W_h) for Rectangular Shed Type Hoods

Charts from "Design of Kitchen Range Hoods," by J. M. DallaValle, *Air Conditioning, Heating and Ventilating*, August 1953.

SLOT TYPE EXHAUSTS

For slot type exhausts the methods of calculating exhaust volumes vary depending on the design of the exhaust system. Ducts are usually sized to maintain a duct velocity of 1500 to 2000; slots sized to maintain a slot velocity of 2000 to 2500 fpm.

Lateral Exhaust (Slant Type)

Slots extend along the top and bottom of a plenum face, on which removable metal slats of various widths are adjustable for best control. Two types of construction are common: (1) transition piece tapered down to throat opening E; (2) duct is connected (as shown by dashed line) to top point of slant hood. Design proportions of E, B and C for these two styles are as follows:

	E	$B + C$
Type (1)	$.05\,W_w - .1\,W_w$	$.1\,W_w - .2\,W_w$
Type (2)	$.1\,W_w - .2\,W_w$	$.05\,W_w - .1\,W_w$

The formula used for determining Q is:

$$Q = V_m \times A_w$$

where V_m is the minimum ventilation rate in cfm per sq ft of hot surface, and A_w is the area of the work surface. The recommended values of V_m vary with the ratios between width and length of work surface, as follows:

W_w/L_w	V_m
0 — .09	100
.1 — .24	125
.25 — .49	150
.5 — .99	175
1.0 — 2.0	200

Lateral Exhaust (Rear or Side Draft)

The formula used for determining Q is:

$$Q = V_f \times A_w$$

where the recommended values for V_f are 150 fpm for hot surfaces with end shields and baffles, and 200 fpm without shields and baffles. The slot should be sized to maintain a slot velocity of 2000 to 3000 fpm. The length of the slot is the same as the length of the work surface, and the width can be determined, after Q is calculated, by substituting in the formula $W_s = Q/(V_s \times L_s)$, where V_s is the desired slot velocity and L_s is the slot length.

The exhaust hood should be extended out over the appliance as far as use permits, but not less than $W_w/4$. The maximum width of the appliance should be 4 ft, but ideally it should be only 3 ft. The maximum length of the transition piece should be 4 ft, using multiple take-offs for larger hoods.

Lateral Exhaust (Slot Type)

With the slots on a vertical surface, the formula for determining Q is:

$$Q = 2.8\,V_f \times L_s \times W_w$$

where L_s is the slot length, W_w is the width of the work surface and the recommended values of V_f are 150 to 250 fpm depending on room conditions and degree of work surface enclosure. If the surface is enclosed, the slots can be sized for a slot velocity of 1000 fpm. However, if the surface is not enclosed, they should be sized to maintain a velocity of 2000 fpm or higher.

Lateral Exhaust (Enclosing Hood Type)

This type of enclosing hood, actually not a slot type exhaust but a combination of shed type hood and lateral exhaust, is designed to exhaust laterally across the work surface, giving essentially a horizontal air flow. To provide horizontal flow, air is drawn around and over a distributing or baffle plate. The formula used for determining Q is:

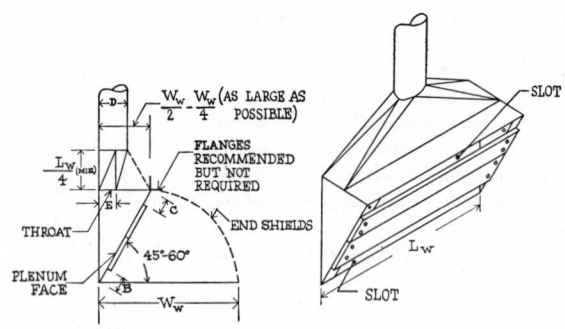

Lateral Exhaust (Slant Type)

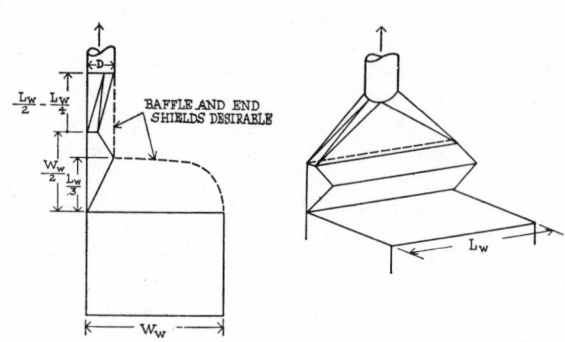

Lateral Exhaust (Rear or Side Draft)

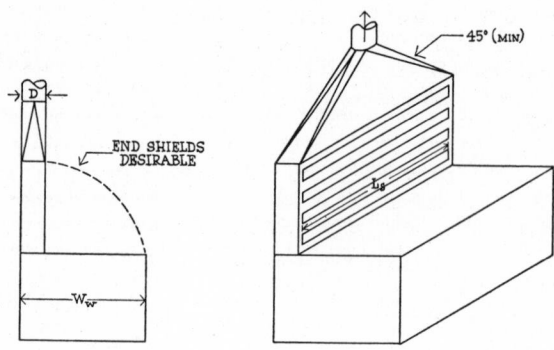

Lateral Exhaust (Slot Type)

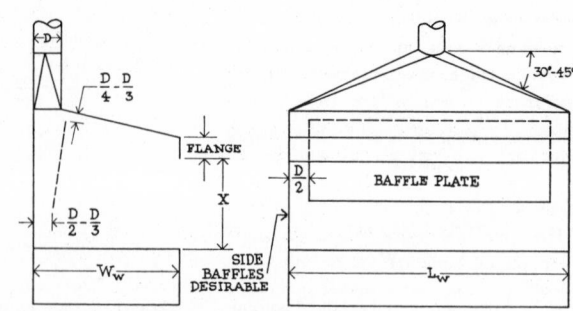

Lateral Exhaust (Enclosing Hood Type)

$$Q = V_c \times A_o$$

where V_c is the control velocity and A_o is the area of all openings into the hood. The recommended values for V_c vary depending on the number of sides which are enclosed:

With only one open side, $V_c = 65$ fpm

With two open sides, $V_c = 90$ fpm

With three open sides, $V_c = 100$ fpm

Hoods are applicable for exhaust of localized areas having comparatively acute heat, fume, vapor, odor, or dust conditions. In many large industrial areas it is unnecessary and impractical to have hoods over each piece of equipment. Furnishing supply air to the whole area (dilution ventilation) in sufficient quantity to remove most of the heat will usually be satisfactory. The determination of the air quantity is obtained from the formula:

$$Cfm = \frac{Btu/hr \ heat \ load}{1.08 \ (t \ space - t \ outside)}$$

The temperature differential varies with the amount of heat to be removed, the type of work being done, the height of the roof (if gravity ventilation is used), and the cost of supplying and exhausting the air. The supply air should be introduced where the personnel are located in order to achieve maximum benefit. Gravity exhaust may produce satisfactory results if the roof is high, the temperature differential is sufficient for a large stack effect, and the wind conditions are favorable. However, for best and most uniform results mechanical exhaust should be used. In some areas, such as warehouses, which have relatively low heat loads spread over large areas, the cost of mechanical exhaust would not be practical unless the nature of the materials stored was such as to require it.

Where ovens, furnaces, foundries, etc., are located, the major portion of the heat load is in the form of radiant heat. Ventilation is ineffective in reducing the effects of radiant heat. Three methods commonly used to minimize the spread of the radiant heat energy are:

1. Insulation
2. Water-cooled surfaces
3. Radiation shields

Insulation reduces the rate at which the heat is emitted from the machine, whereas water cooling reduces the surface temperature. In both cases, since the surface temperature is lower, the radiant heat effect is reduced. Both methods are comparatively efficient.

Where it is not practicable to do either of the above, radiation shields are used. A shield is a sheet of material, opaque to infrared rays, which is placed as close as possible around the equipment emitting the radiant heat, short of touching it. There should be an air space between the equipment and the shield so that the shield is not heated by conduction. Sheets of reflective metal, aluminum foil-faced curtains, transparent shields of heat-reflective tempered glass, reflective garments including asbestos suits with

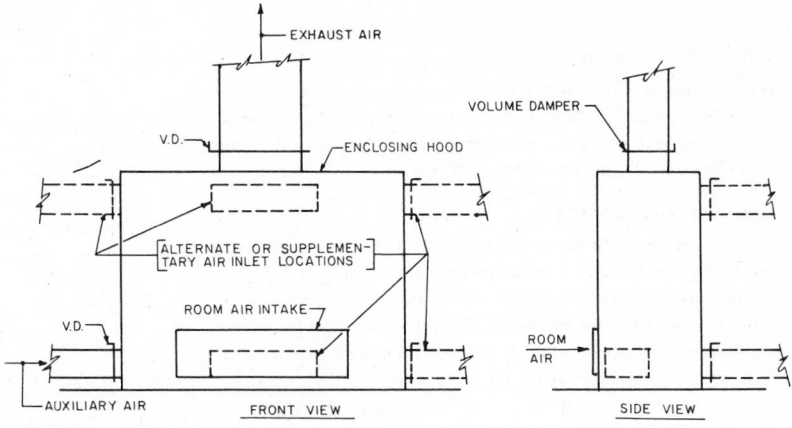

Fig. 66. Completely enclosing hood

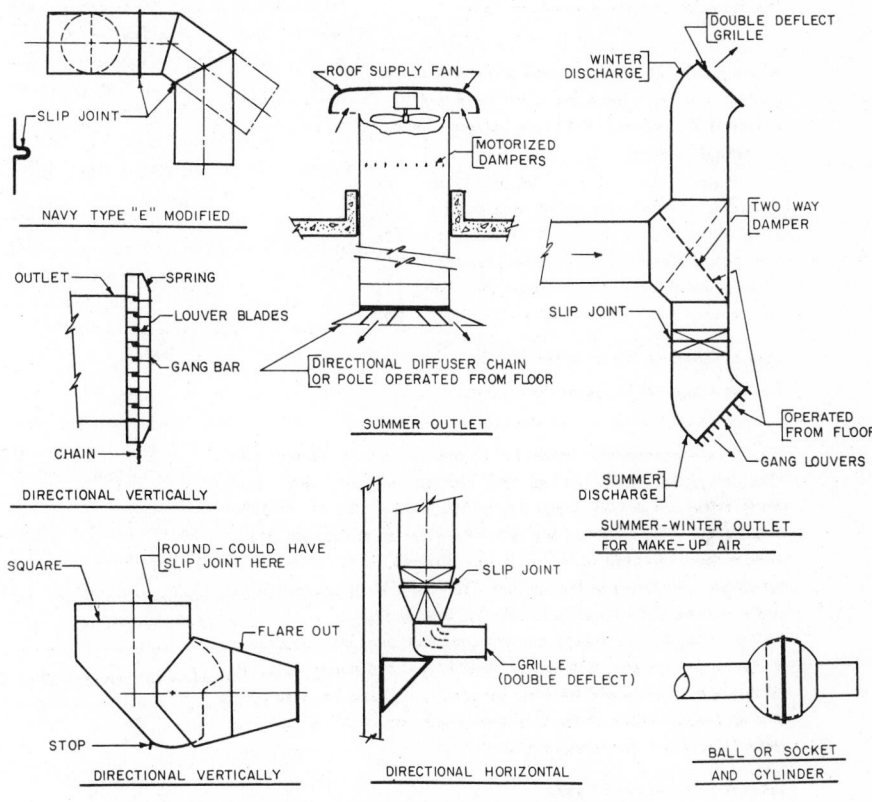

Fig. 67. Directional outlets for spot cooling

Reprinted from ASHRAE Guide and Data Book, *1964.*

atomized aluminum exteriors, gauntlets, and face shields are effective radiation shields. There are many variations, depending upon the particular application involved.

In the design of the local ventilation or spot cooling system, care must be taken that the air velocity at the workers' level does not exceed 200 fpm for continuous exposure. For light-duty work, 50 fpm should be maintained. Air conditioning does increase the first cost but requires less air to do the same job and does it more

effectively. In most instances, worker efficiency has gone up, and this has justified its use economically.

Where spot cooling is used, as stated before, the outlets should be close to the work level (about 7 ft high) to be most effective. Outlet velocities will normally be between 1,000 and 2,000 fpm, or higher if the outlets are located more remotely. Control of air direction is often essential from both the worker's and the product's viewpoint, so directional outlets are necessary. Various types are shown in Fig. 67.

By ALFRED GREENBERG, *P.E., Environmental Consultant*

LABORATORIES

A laboratory is a place devoted to experimental study in any science, or to the testing and analysis of materials. It may be used for education, research, or product control. It may consist of a single room with very limited equipment in a building primarily used for other purposes, or it may be a large building with several floors, designed and constructed to provide a number of rooms with special equipment, or it may be some intermediate arrangement between these extremes.

The one item of equipment that differentiates laboratories from most other types of buildings is the necessity for partial or complete enclosure fume hoods. Even those laboratories that have no hoods often have special exhaust air requirements due to the nature of their operations. They may require large quantities of air which are in excess of room air-conditioning requirements, which means that additional sources of air must be obtained. In most cases, it is generally desirable to exhaust more air than is supplied.

There are several types of laboratory hoods available:

The conventional hood (Fig. 68) is the cheapest and simplest. When the hood door is closed, no air flows through the hood, and auxiliary means for exhausting room air must be furnished. When the hood is in use, auxiliary exhaust must be shut off to ensure hoods getting sufficient air. This involves a damper control arrangement which in a building wtih many hoods could become complex.

The modified hood (Fig. 69) is a simple variation intended to overcome this problem. An open slot is provided above or below the door so that it can never be completely closed and exhaust air goes through the hood at all times.

In air-conditioned laboratories the use of large quantities of conditioned air to satisfy the hood air requirements may be too expensive. Therefore, a third type of system has evolved (Fig. 70) which takes only 50 per cent of its total air requirements from the room, whether the hood door is open or closed. The rest of the air is furnished by an auxiliary air supply system consisting of outside air, tempered and filtered. This requires an additional fan and ductwork system and more expensive hoods, which may offset the savings in reduced room air quantities.

Secondary air hoods: With conventional or modified hoods it is difficult to maintain fixed air conditions in the laboratory room. To meet this objection the secondary air hood was developed. In this type auxiliary air is furnished to the hood at all times and practically no room air is used. It has the further advantage of reducing the minimum air speed across the face of the hood from 50 to 75 fpm to about half that amount.

In general, the following velocities across the face of the hood with a full front opening are considered advisable:

50 to 60 fpm for high schools.
60 to 80 fpm for colleges and hospitals.
80 to 100 fpm for industrial laboratories.
100 to 150 fpm for radioactive and virus laboratories.

Downdraft table-type hoods should have a capacity of about 150 cfm.

Room air-conditioning systems: Most laboratories are designed for dual-duct, single-duct with zone or individual reheat, or unit ventilators adapted for use with high outside air quantities. The first two systems

require large ceiling spaces for distribution and are generally more costly than the unit ventilator system, but provide closer temperature and humidity control. The unit ventilator system generally uses through-the-wall air openings, although this is not essential.

Space requirements: The amount of mechanical equipment room and shaft requirements for some laboratories may be as much as 25 to 50 per cent greater than for office buildings or other types of commercial buildings. This is due to hood and laboratory equipment duct and piping needs as well as the requirement for special systems to handle special functions such as animal quarters or radioactive materials.

Administrative areas should be air conditioned in a manner similar to office buildings. The main difference is that the supply air from these areas will probably have to be transferred to laboratory areas in order to make up the air requirements needed.

Following are general minimum requirements for different types of laboratories.[6]

EDUCATIONAL

High school laboratories generally consist of a few rooms equipped for ele-

[6] *The portion of this section dealing with the general requirements for different types of laboratories has been generally based upon an article published in* Air Conditioning, Heating, and Ventilating, *November, 1953, by J. E. York, Building Service Engineer, Stone & Webster Engineering Corporation, Boston, Mass., entitled* Ventilation and Air Conditioning for Laboratories.

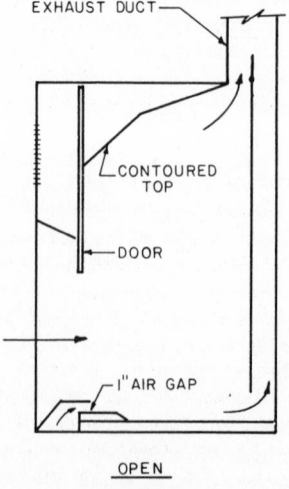

Fig. 68. Conventional hood

Fig. 69. Modified hood

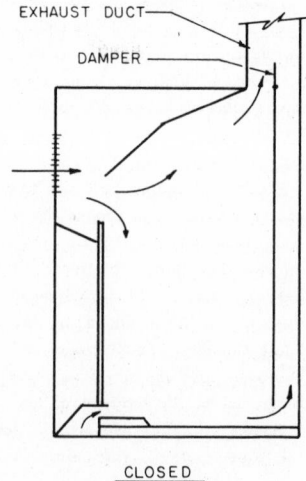

mentary instruction in physics, chemistry, and dietetics. The general ventilation for these rooms should be in accordance with the state code or municipal requirements, and one or two hoods with natural or mechanical ventilation may be installed in the chemistry laboratory for the removal of objectionable odors or fumes.

College, technical, or medical school laboratories usually have at least one large lecture room, several small lecture and demonstration rooms, and rooms for laboratory instruction.

Large lecture rooms may seat from 200 to 500 students. For demonstrations of chemical reactions a special table equipped with the common laboratory services and a downdraft hood may be wheeled into the lecture room from a nearby preparation room.

Large volumes of air must be handled to meet even the minimum ventilation code requirements, and it is advisable to provide supply and exhaust ventilation systems which may be operated independently of the other parts of the building.

Small lecture and demonstration rooms should have general ventilation in accordance with state or local requirements, and exhaust ventilation from a downdraft hood on the lecture table or through a regular hood as in the large lecture room.

General chemistry laboratory is frequently equipped with individual downdraft table-type hoods at each working space to enable students to do all their work at their assigned locations. Ductwork for these hoods should be installed below the table tops at the back of drawer or cabinet space. One or two large hoods may be provided for special experiments.

Analytical chemistry laboratory may use individual downdraft table-type hoods similar to those in the general chemistry laboratory, or a few large hoods may be provided. If large hoods are used, then about a 4 ft length of hood for every ten students will be required.

Organic chemistry laboratory requires one open front hood for every four to eight students. As experiments which release hydrogen chloride gas are frequently made on an open table, it is essential that good general room ventilation be provided, and that there be no dead spots where fumes may collect.

Laboratories for preparations and for research work should have one hood for every two students, and these hoods should be equipped with their own exhaust fans.

Rooms in which combustion furnaces for analytical organic laboratories are located should be well ventilated.

Microanalytical laboratories for organic

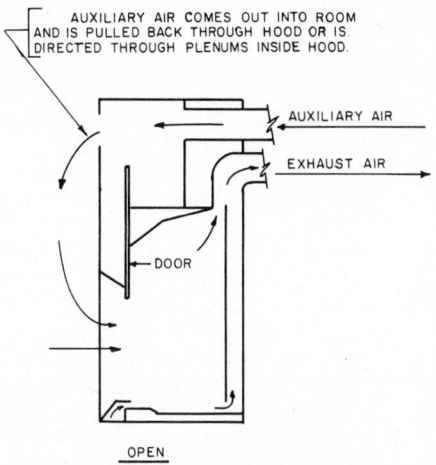
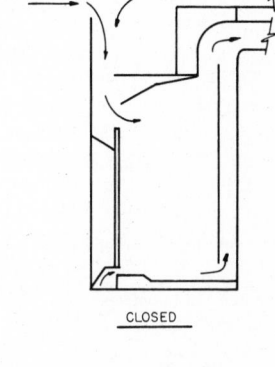

AUXILIARY AIR COMES OUT INTO ROOM AND IS PULLED BACK THROUGH HOOD OR IS DIRECTED THROUGH PLENUMS INSIDE HOOD.

AUXILIARY AIR

EXHAUST AIR

DOOR

OPEN

CLOSED

Fig. 70. Auxiliary-air type laboratory hood

work require a room in which a hood is provided and a separate balance room, both of which should be air conditioned to 75°F and 50 per cent relative humidity. The hood in the laboratory should be of the closed type and should take its air supply from outside this room.

Biological laboratory: In addition to the laboratory which is equipped with chemical exhaust hoods, rooms may be required for housing animals, insects, plants, or bacteria cultures. Hoods should be of the closed type, which take their air supply from outside the air-conditioned area.

Animal rooms, in general, should be kept at about 78°F and 50 per cent relative humidity. Odors in these areas may be controlled by circulating the air through a bed of activated carbon, although 100 per cent supply and exhaust air is recommended. Some insect rooms may require as high as 90 per cent RH.

For the study of microbiology, small dustproof rooms are required in which low air velocities should be maintained.

Biochemical laboratory is often of sufficient size for classes of a hundred or more students. One lineal foot of hood space per student is desirable, and consequently large quantities of air must be exhausted.

Balance rooms require low-velocity air free from dust or corrosive fumes. Ceiling diffuser-type inlets are recommended. If a balance room opens directly off a laboratory, fresh air may be supplied through it to the laboratory to prevent any possibility of corrosive fumes entering the balance room and damaging the balances. Four or more air changes per hour are recommended.

A small room for slow evaporation and concentration of solutions is sometimes provided and should have exhaust ventilation. Glass-blowing rooms should also be well

ventilated. A cold room in which there is a closed hood is sometimes located near the organic laboratory and should be air conditioned to about 40°F.

Physical and electrochemical laboratory: In addition to the laboratory proper, which should be equipped with a large hood, there may be an optical room, a balance room, and a darkroom for elementary work; for advanced or research work, there may be a cold room, a dust-free room, a mass-spectrograph room, and constant-temperature rooms.

Clean, dry air should be supplied to the optical room; exhaust ventilation should be provided for the hood; and air conditioning should be supplied for the spectrograph room, the dust-free room, and constant-temperature rooms.

Chemical engineering laboratories usually have a distillation column which is of greater height than a normal two-story structure. If a pit is provided, an exhaust fan should be installed near the bottom to remove dense vapors. The fan should be of sparkproof construction, with an explosionproof motor, and should discharge the gases to a safe location.

If a crushing and grinding room is provided, it should have exhaust ventilation for the removal of dust.

Furnaces, except small laboratory models, should be housed in a special room with adequate ventilation for removal of excessive heat.

Metallographic laboratories include the following rooms:

Laboratory in which microscopes, furnaces, etching equipment, and a fume hood are located

Shop and grinding room for preparation of samples

Polishing room for finished work on samples

Photomicrographic room and a darkroom

Air conditioning is desirable for all parts of this laboratory except the shop and rough grinding room, which should be well ventilated for dust removal.

Physics and physical and electrical measurements laboratories ordinarily do not require any special ventilation; but where primary gages are stored and used, both temperature and humidity should be maintained within close limits to ensure gage accuracy. Temperatures commonly maintained are between 75 and 78°F with ±10°F tolerance, and relative humidities are between 40 and 50 per cent, ±5 per cent.

Air supplied to these conditioned rooms should be free from dust, and both impingement and electrostatic filters may be required to obtain the desired degree of cleanliness.

INDUSTRIAL

Many industries maintain laboratories for product control or for research in the development of new products or processes. Typical examples are listed in alphabetical order:

Alkali products laboratory includes a number of small analytical laboratories equipped with hoods, each of which is ventilated by its individual exhaust fan located in a penthouse. Purifying equipment is provided to remove noxious odors and fumes from the air before it is released to the atmosphere. Air is supplied to the building through electrostatic filters and tempering coils in sufficient quantity to maintain a slight positive pressure in the building and thus prevent infiltration of dust-laden air.

Cement laboratory has physical and chemical laboratories equipped with hoods and a special room for sample grinding and preparation. The entire laboratory is air conditioned in summer and winter.

Chemical plant laboratory is equipped with a large number of hoods, each of which is provided with a cast-iron exhaust fan of 1,000-cfm capacity. Face velocities from 25 to 40 fpm are generally used through open hoods. The total volume of air exhausted equals approximately six changes per hour. Exhaust ducts should be of acid-resistant metal. Filtered and tempered air is supplied to the building.

A microanalytical laboratory with a fume hood and a balance room are independently air conditioned to approximately 77°F and 55 per cent RH. Dust-free air is supplied to the balance room through air diffusers to reduce air currents to a minimum.

Distilling laboratory requires no fume hoods; mechanical ventilation should be provided for the entire laboratory.

Food products laboratory requires no fume hoods; mechanical ventilation should be provided.

Forest products laboratory should be air conditioned throughout. It may have a number of rooms which must be maintained at different conditions of temperature and relative humidity. Adsorption equipment is used for removal of moisture from the air where very low relative humidities are necessary.

Glass laboratory requires some fume hoods and mechanical ventilation for the entire laboratory.

Metals laboratory (a laboratory for the determination of physical properties of metals) is equipped with exhaust ventilation for removal of heat and fumes.

Laboratory for the analysis of brasses, bronzes, lead, solders, and flux is equipped with fume hoods, a perchloric acid hood, and a hydrogen sulfide hood. Mechanical ventilation must be provided.

Laboratory for the analysis of aluminum alloys requires a large fume hood.

A microscope room should be supplied with filtered air which is exhausted through an adjacent sample preparation room to prevent dust from this room from entering the microscope room.

Spectrographic equipment room should be air conditioned to maintain a temperature of 75°F and 40 per cent relative humidity at all times.

Paper laboratory, should be kept at 75°F and 50 per cent RH.

Petroleum laboratory should be equipped with fume hoods and air conditioned throughout.

Pharmaceutical laboratory should be liberally equipped with fume hoods and should be air conditioned throughout. Spectrographic rooms and small laboratories for the control of finished products are supplied with conditioned air for control of temperature and humidity and for protection against dust and air-borne bacteria.

Physical measurements laboratory: Large amounts of power are used by equipment for making tensile, compression, and impact tests. The equipment is therefore so arranged that the space where the operators have to work is partitioned off from the equipment and is air conditioned.

Electron microscopes and electronic diffraction equipment generate considerable heat and require dust-free air. The laboratory is therefore air conditioned to maintain temperatures around 75°F with 50 per cent RH, and a high efficiency filter is used to remove dust from the air. Special precautions must be taken to prevent the transmission of vibration from the air-conditioning system to the electron microscope.

Mass spectrometer equipment releases approximately 4 kva as heat and must therefore be located in an air-conditioned room. Air conditioning is also required for the laboratory in which X-ray and spectrographic equipment are used. Emission spectrographic equipment releases the heat equivalent of 5 kva and requires dust-free air. High efficiency filters are used for cleaning the air; air conditioning is provided to maintain a temperature of about 75°F and 50 per cent RH. The infrared spectroscopy room is air conditioned to maintain a temperature of 76°F and a relative humidity of 35 ±2 per cent.

In order to prevent destructive condensation on gage surfaces, the electrical measurements and instrument calibration laboratories are air conditioned to maintain 25 per cent RH.

Plastics and rubber testing laboratory should be air conditioned to maintain standard conditions of 77°F ±2°F and 50 ±2 per cent RH.

Rubber laboratory requires several fume hoods and mechanical ventilation.

SCIENTIFIC AND MEDICAL RESEARCH

Laboratory using radioisotopes: Special radiochemical hoods are used in the laboratory with air velocities of 100 fpm across the face of hoods as required by the Atomic Energy Commission regulations. Each hood has its own independent exhaust system; fans and ductwork are of stainless steel except where HCl fumes are present in appreciable quantities.

Air leaving these hoods is passed through filters for removal of small particles of radioactive material before it is discharged to the atmosphere. The filters are located as near the hoods as possible to reduce the amount of surface exposed to contamination.

Counting rooms in the laboratory are air conditioned to maintain temperatures of 75°F ±2°F and relative humidities of 45 ±5 per cent.

Laboratory for study of infectious diseases: All the air exhausted through hoods used in the study of virus infections is passed through a hot gas flame or electric grids before it is released to the atmosphere.

Red Cross blood laboratory: Sealed rooms provide sterile conditions for handling blood during processing. These rooms are air conditioned to provide accurate temperature control, which is neccesary during the processing.

Environmental laboratory: Special rooms, provided for this purpose in a hopsital, may be maintained at widely varying temperatures and relative humidities with permissible temperature variations of less than 1°F and relative humidity variations of less than 4 per cent. Some rooms are equipped to provide rapid changes in temperature and humidity.

AIR FLOW

In order to reduce to a minimum the possibility of any flow of air from rooms where fumes, odors, or excess heat are generated to other parts of the building, such rooms should be maintained under negative pressure while in use, and other rooms should be kept under a positive pressure.

HOOD EXHAUST SYSTEMS

Hoods for Kjeldahl digestion and distillation should each have a separate exhaust fan and duct constructed of high-silicon iron. Exhaust ducts of stoneware or lead are sometimes used for these hoods.

Hoods equipped with water or steam baths must handle an excessive amount of moisture and provision should be made for draining condensation from the ductwork.

Perchloric acid reactions generate perchlorates that are easily detonated in the presence of organic matter. Materials used for the construction of perchloric hoods should be inert, nonabsorbent, and free of any organic impregnation. Separate cast-iron fans and corrosion-resisting welded metal vertical exhaust stacks should be provided for each hood. Water spray nozzles should be installed at the top of the duct and at bends for cleaning. Provision should be made for draining the wash water from the fan and ductwork.

Etching hoods should have separate exhaust fans and ducts to ensure control of the fan operation until the acid bath has cooled sufficiently to stop fuming. Horizontal ducts should be sloped to suitable drain connections.

The exhaust from virus hoods should pass through a hot flame or electric grid and should be heated to at least 600°F before it is discharged to the air.

Canopy hoods over sinks for the disposal of fuming liquids, steam tables, etching tanks, and grinding operations should be larger than the area of the working surface below, and while it is desirable to keep hoods as low as possible, proper headroom for equipment and for access must be provided. As these canopy hoods are frequently open on all sides, cross drafts will carry the fumes and vapors outside the area of the canopy unless high inlet velocities at the hoods are maintained. The use of double hoods with a narrow slot around the periphery makes it possible to maintain high velocities around the perimeter of the hood without exhausting excessive quantities of air.

INDIVIDUAL VS. CENTRAL EXHAUST SYSTEMS

Individual exhaust systems offer these advantages:

1. A hood with a separate exhaust fan may be used if necessary when the full laboratory is not in use.
2. The operation of the fan may be controlled to suit the work being carried on in the hood.
3. Fans and ductwork which must be built of expensive materials to resist the corrosive effect of fumes may be kept small, thus reducing the cost.
4. The possibility of leakage of noxious or hazardous fumes between rooms through ductwork is reduced.
5. Small vertical discharge ducts from individual fans may be concealed in furred spaces and carried up through the roof.

Central exhaust systems have the following advantages:

1. Fans and motors may be easily serviced.
2. None of the ductwork conveying noxious or hazardous fumes will be under a positive pressure, thus reducing the possibility of leakage of fumes.
3. There is less chance that a room which is supposed to be operating under a negative pressure will actually be operating under a positive pressure due to the exhaust fans being shut down.

GARAGES

Of the various types of parking facilities, the only one that presents a serious problem to the health and safety of human beings is the underground or windowless garage. In this category should be included very large garages having interior areas which are more than 50 to 75 ft from the windows.

The problem is threefold. The first and most serious part is the carbon monoxide (CO) gas emitted by automobiles. This is a colorless, odorless gas which, in sufficient concentration, can cause death or serious illness. The second part is the oil and gasoline fumes which can cause nausea in many people. The third involves the lack of movement of the air and the resultant stale atmosphere that develops due to the increase in the carbon dioxide (CO_2) content.

Minimum ventilation requirements, as set up by the National Bureau of Standards, ASHRAE, and New York State Department of Labor, are primarily concerned with preventing the buildup of a noxious concentration of carbon monoxide. These are predicated on the basis that the CO concentration should never be higher than 2 pp (parts per) 10,000 air (1 pp 10,000 = 0.01 per cent concentration) for a continued occupancy of 8 hours or 175,000 cu ft per hr of air per car based on the production of 35 cu ft per hr of CO per car (see Fig. 71). Once it is determined how many cars will be in operation at any one time, it is a relatively easy matter to calculate the cfm requirements. Determining how many cars will probably be in operation at any given time is more difficult. An underground garage serving an apartment house would be expected to have a lower instantaneous traffic rate than one serving a sports stadium, for instance.

The third aspect affecting the buildup of CO is the length of time that the peo-ple are in the garage or that cars in operation will remain in the garage. This is a function of garage design and size. In general, this time will run from 1 to 10 min with 5 min as an average.

However, keeping the CO level within safe limits is no guarantee that patrons or employees in the garage will experience no discomfort. The air furnished will probably be sufficient to eliminate any staleness in the atmosphere, but the greatest discomfort is caused by oil and gasoline fumes. These fumes are especially noticeable in areas having poor air circulation and at poorly ventilated ramps. Present design standards for air circulation range from 4 to 25 air changes per hour. The former is for apartment house garages, the latter for large garages with short, concentrated peak usage periods. For comparison, most underground tunnels are designed for 20 to 30 air changes per hour.

The types of systems applicable to

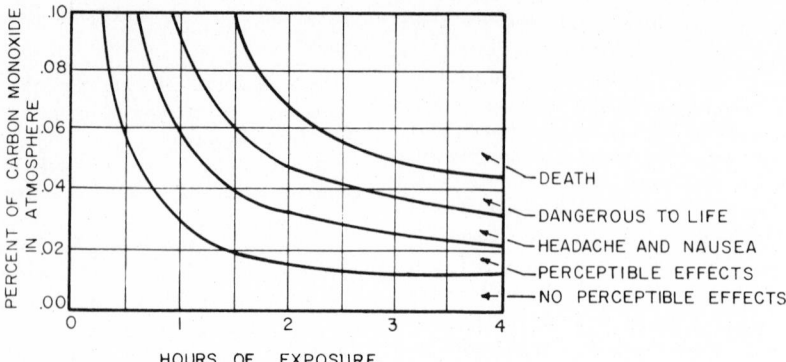

EFFECTS OF CARBON MONOXIDE
FOR A GIVEN TIME ON HUMAN BEINGS

DATA FROM NATIONAL BUREAU OF STANDARDS
TECHNICAL PAPER 212

Fig. 71.   Effect of carbon monoxide on human beings

garage use with their advantages and disadvantages are as follows:

1. *Mechanical supply and exhaust* (Fig. 72)
   a. Most positive means of air movement.
   b. Requires fewer air changes per hour.
   c. Requires less shaft space for ducts.
   d. Requires largest mechanical equipment space.
   e. Highest initial and operating costs.

2. *Gravity supply and mechanical exhaust*
   a. More air changes required.
   b. Larger supply airshafts and larger air intake louvers required.
   c. Less mechanical equipment space required.
   d. Lower initial and operating costs.
   e. Space is positively exhausted, preventing buildup of pockets of contaminated air.

3. *Mechanical supply and gravity exhaust*
   a, b, c, d, are same as No. 2 above except change supply to return.
   e. Since exhaust air is forced out of exhaust air louvers by means of positive pressure within the space, air movement is more sluggish than with the other two schemes, and pockets of contaminated air may form to cause local areas of discomfort.

Under any of the schemes, supply air may be brought in high or low, but air should be exhausted from both high and low levels. At the ramps, low exhaust registers are preferable (Fig. 73).

Ducts or shafts for mechanical systems should be sized for air velocities of from 1,500 to 2,000 fpm, depending on the size of the system. Gravity ducts should be sized for an air velocity no greater than 250 fpm in order to assure adequate free-air motion.

If possible, the supply and exhaust air should be distributed uniformly along opposite walls of the garage so that all areas get uniform air motion.

The areas that generally develop the greatest CO and oil and gas fumes are the ramps to the outside. These should be given from ten to twenty air changes per hour of exhaust ventilation.

Unless local codes require it, underground garages will generally not require any heat. Special areas such as toilets, offices, employee operating booths, and patrons' waiting rooms should have heat provided. Toilets will in most instances require a separate exhaust system.

If the garage has interior gasoline-dispensing pumps, a separate explosion-proof duct, fan, and motor system should be furnished. The exhaust register should be located right at the pumps, and the controls should operate so that when the fan is not running, the pumps cannot dispense gasoline. Furnish a minimum of 2,000 cfm per dispensing pump. If a vault is used to contain the gasoline tanks, it must have a continuously operating explosion-proof exhaust system with a constant source of supply air furnishing from fifteen to thirty air changes per hour.

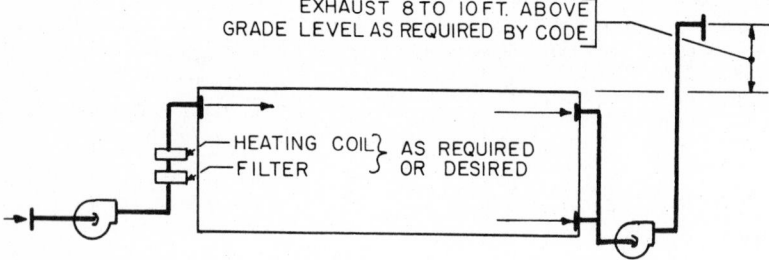

EXHAUST 8 TO 10 FT. ABOVE
GRADE LEVEL AS REQUIRED BY CODE

HEATING COIL } AS REQUIRED
FILTER } OR DESIRED

Fig. 72.   Mechanical supply and exhaust system

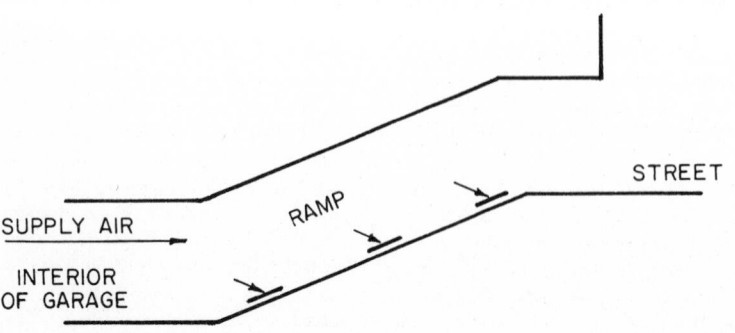

STREET

SUPPLY AIR

RAMP

INTERIOR
OF GARAGE

Fig. 73.   Low exhaust outlets on ramps

DEFINITION

Unit heaters are defined by ASHRAE as consisting of a combination of a heating element and a fan or blower within a common enclosure which is placed within or adjacent to the space to be heated. In general no ducts are employed, although many applications may require equipping the heater with directional outlets, baffles, diffusers, or adjustable louvres.

TYPES

There are two major types of unit heaters: The centrifugal housed fan type, Fig. 1 (commonly called a "Blower"); and the propeller fan type with the fan mounted directly behind the heating element and blowing air through it as in Fig. 2, or with the fan mounted directly in front of the heating element and drawing air through it as in Fig. 3. When arranged in the latter manner the unit is commonly called a projection heater.

Centrifugal fan type heaters deliver heated air at velocities ranging from 1,300 to 3,000 ft. per minute, have rated capacities of 135,000 to 1,300,000 Btu., and may have lengths of throw up to approximately 200 ft.

Propeller fan type heaters have outlet velocities from 400 to 1,200 ft. per minute, rated capacities of 18,000 to 340,000 Btu., and maximum throws of almost 80 ft. The vertical delivery type or projection unit heaters may be mounted up to heights of approximately 50 ft.

SPECIAL TYPES

The electric type, used principally only where electric power is abundant and cheap or where other fuels are scarce and expensive, employs an electrical resistance heating element in place of the steam or hot water convector. These are available in both the horizontal and vertical discharge models, and may be used in conjunction with directional louvers or other air-diffusing equipment.

The direct-fired gas burning unit is another type. These are of the warm air type and use fans to force air over the heating surfaces and direct it to the space to be heated. This type is often

used where the installation of a steam or hot water plant is not justified and for temporary heat during building construction. For permanent installations it is usually advisable to provide an exhaust duct from the unit to remove combustion products from the occupied space.

A type employing a steam turbine to drive the fan is sometimes used where high pressure steam is available. The exhaust steam from the turbine, reduced in pressure, passes through the coil and acts as the heating medium.

HEAT SOURCE

Low or high pressure steam is generally used as the heating medium. Proper venting of air from the coil must be obtained with all steam pressures, and with high pressure steam it is essential that properly constructed traps and some form of thermostatic air by-pass be used as well as adequate condensing legs.

Where low pressure steam is used, it is necessary that proper means be provided for the removal of heavy condensate. The use of vacuum or return pumps and receivers is desirable in all jobs of sufficient size to warrant the use of such equipment. Where gravity systems are employed it is essential that the difference in level between boiler and heater be large enough to compensate for the pressure loss through the convector at its highest condensation rate.

Only a few manufacturers today make unit heaters for sole use with hot water. Most adapt the more popular steam type. If hot water is used as the heating medium it should be mechanically rather than gravity circulated, and at a rate based upon manufacturer's recommendations for the particular type of heater used.

Normally, the heat output of a heater of a given size and type will be somewhat less if hot water is used rather than steam.

BOILER CAPACITY

Boiler capacity should be based on rated capacity of the heaters at the lowest entering air temperature likely to occur, plus allowance for losses in lines. The beginning of the heating

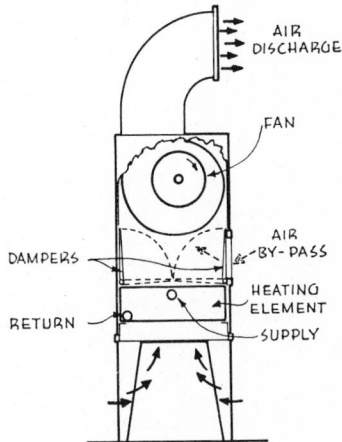

Fig. 1. Floor-mounted centrifugal fan (blower) type

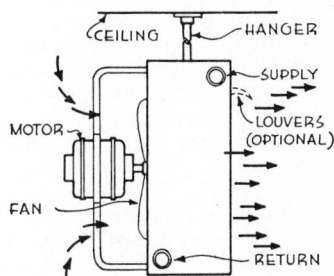

Fig. 2. Suspended propeller type

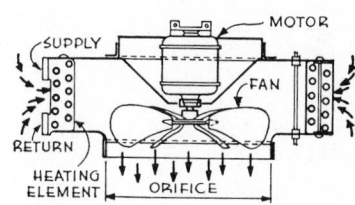

Fig. 3. Suspended projection type

period usually marks the lowest temperature for recirculating heaters and is commonly accepted as 40°F. If outside air is brought in the lowest entering temperature will be the extreme expected in the district. Good practice recommends that at least two heating units be used on any boiler. Sudden fluctuations of load that occur under thermostatically controlled units would require more attention than is normally warranted.

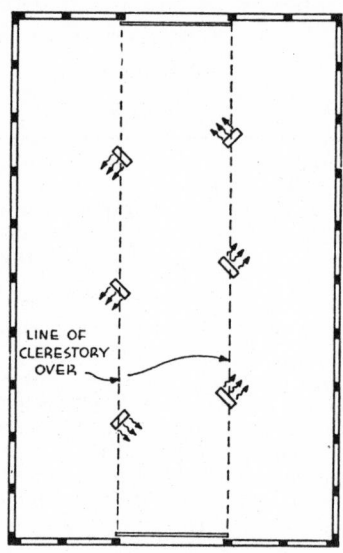

Fig. 4.   Horizontal delivery

Line installation arranged to direct the heated air at an angle to the wall, to blanket doors, and to reinforce general one-way circulation.

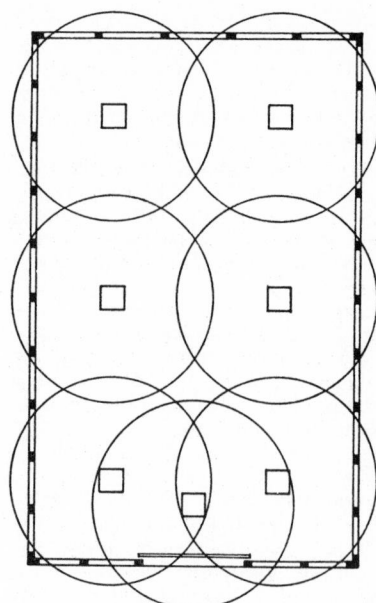

Fig. 5.   Vertical delivery

Projection type unit installation showing approximate floor and wall surface spread.

OPERATING CHARACTERISTICS

In general, centrifugal fan type or blower units discharge heated air at high velocities and are, therefore, indicated where long horizontal distances of throw are necessary or where heat must be concentrated to overcome heavy loads due to infiltration, such as at frequently opened doors. This type is also effective for operation against resistance where duct work is used. Slow speed blower type units are indicated when quiet operation is a prerequisite because of the inherent quietness of the blower type fan.

Horizontal delivery propeller **type** heaters are best used in those applications where blower type units would be eliminated through economic reasons or where a positive directional throw toward or along an exposed surface is necessary to exert a mixing effect with cool air. Vertical delivery or projection type unit heaters are used to advantage in those applications where exceptionally high ceilings are encountered and where ceiling construction is such that reservoirs of waste heat gather at the ceiling. They are to be recommended wherever conditions call for a more directly downward delivery of air than is provided by horizontal delivery units.

Unit heater systems properly installed should:

1. Provide quick heat where it is needed.

2. Reduce temperature differentials between floor and ceiling.

3. Provide rapid circulation of air without objectionable draft.

4. Direct heated air so that uniform temperature distribution will prevail in the space heated.

5. Eliminate cold air stratum usually at floor level.

6. Reduce piping because of fewer heating elements required.

7. Save valuable floor space due to flexibility of mounting on floor, wall or ceiling.

Location with respect to height above the floor and direction and length or spread of throw is an important factor in the application of unit heaters. Most manufacturers give the recommended maximum mounting height and maximum and minimum length of throw for each unit model and for each fan speed. In most cases the distances given, particularly those referring to the length of throw, are approximate only and must be regarded as representative for the average.

Centrifugal fan or blower type units in general may be floor, wall, or ceiling mounted. Floor mounted types draw cold air from the floor and discharge heated air immediately above the head level. They are particularly adapted to closely occupied quarters.

Horizontal delivery propeller fan type heaters are most effective in spaces with ceiling heights of 20 ft. or less. Suspended, they should be located as close to the working zone as possible without directly discharging heated air on room occupants. This and the blower types should be arranged to blow toward or along exposed surfaces, pre-ferably striking the wall at a slight angle so the heated air will mix with cool air along the wall. They should also be arranged so that the resulting air circulation will be rotational, reinforcing one another rather than resisting.

Vertical delivery or projection type units should be installed as close to the ceiling as practical in order to overcome stratification of air at high points. If units are not near exposed walls, they may be placed as evenly as practical to produce only slight overlapping of heat circles based on manufacturers' ratings of heat spread over floor areas.

SELECTION DATA

The performance of unit heaters is greatly affected by the care used in their selection and application. Of first importance is the unit heater capacity in Btu., which must be in all cases at least equivalent to the total heat load. Standard practice is to rate the units in Btu. per hour at a steam pressure of 2 lbs. and entering air temperature of 60°F. Many manufacturers also give the number of cubic feet of air at a given temperature which the unit will deliver when operating at a given speed. Since the capacity of a unit increases as the steam pressure increases, and decreases as the entering air temperature increases, tables of constants[1] have been established for determining the capacity for any condition of steam pressure and entering air temperatures. To determine capacity, multiply constant from table by rated capacity at 60°F entering air and 2 lbs. pressure. Table 1 is used for the blow-through type heaters, and Table 2 for the draw-through type units.

Entering-air temperatures will be higher for suspended type units than for floor mounted units, and this difference should be taken into account in determining the effective capacity of the units. Common practice allows 1½° increase in entering-air temperature per foot of height the unit suspended above the 5-ft. level.

Other factors upon which selection should be based are air quantity and distribution and final temperature. Good practice is to circulate the air at a rate not less than three air changes per hour based on room volume, and to avoid final temperatures in excess of 135°.

[1] ASHRAE

Table 1. Constants for determining the capacity of blow-through type unit heaters for various steam pressures and temperatures of entering air

Based on steam at 2lb gage and 60°F entering air

Steam Pressure Lb. per Sq. In.	Temperature of Entering Air											
	—10°	0°	10°	20°	30°	40°	50°	60°	70°	80°	90°	100°
0	1.538	1.446	1.369	1.273	1.191	1.110	1.034	0.956	0.881	0.809	0.739	0.671
2	1.585	1.495	1.405	1.320	1.237	1.155	1.078	1.000	0.926	0.853	0.782	0.713
5	1.640	1.550	1.456	1.370	1.289	1.206	1.127	1.050	0.974	0.901	0.829	0.760
10	1.730	1.639	1.545	1.460	1.375	1.290	1.211	1.131	1.056	0.982	0.908	0.838
15	1.799	1.708	1.614	1.525	1.441	1.335	1.275	1.194	1.117	1.043	0.970	0.897
20	1.861	1.769	1.675	1.584	1.498	1.416	1.333	1.251	1.174	1.097	1.024	0.952
30	1.966	1.871	1.775	1.684	1.597	1.509	1.429	1.346	1.266	1.190	1.115	1.042
40	2.058	1.959	1.862	1.771	1.683	1.596	1.511	1.430	1.349	1.270	1.194	1.119
50	2.134	2.035	1.936	1.845	1.755	1.666	1.582	1.498	1.416	1.338	1.262	1.187
60	2.196	2.094	1.997	1.902	1.811	1.725	1.640	1.555	1.472	1.393	1.314	1.239
70	2.256	2.157	2.057	1.961	1.872	1.782	1.696	1.610	1.527	1.447	1.368	1.293
75	2.283	2.183	2.085	1.990	1.896	1.808	1.721	1.635	1.552	1.472	1.392	1.316
80	2.312	2.211	2.112	2.015	1.925	1.836	1.748	1.660	1.577	1.497	1.418	1.342
90	2.361	2.258	2.159	2.063	1.968	1.880	1.792	1.705	1.621	1.541	1.461	1.383
100	2.409	2.307	2.204	2.108	2.015	1.927	1.836	1.749	1.663	1.581	1.502	1.424

Table 2. Constants for determining capacity of draw-through type unit heaters for various steam pressures and entering-air temperatures

Based on steam at 2lb gage and 60°F entering air

Steam Pressure Lbs. Per Sq. In. Gauge	Temperature of Entering Air																				
	—10°	0°	10°	20°	30°	40°	45°	50°	55°	60°	65°	70°	75°	80°	85°	90°	100°	120°	150°	175°	200°
0	1.483	1.405	1.329	1.253	1.178	1.105	1.070	1.032	.997	.962	.926	.892	.858	.822	.788	.754	.688	.556	.368	.218	.070
2	1.520	1.442	1.363	1.290	1.215	1.141	1.105	1.069	1.035	1.000	.965	.930	.895	.861	.825	.792	.728	.598	.407	.255	.108
5	1.565	1.485	1.410	1.334	1.260	1.187	1.150	1.114	1.080	1.045	1.010	.975	.940	.906	.872	.838	.771	.641	.452	.302	.155
10	1.637	1.558	1.480	1.403	1.328	1.253	1.219	1.182	1.148	1.112	1.078	1.042	1.008	.973	.938	.903	.838	.708	.518	.368	.223
15	1.688	1.610	1.533	1.458	1.382	1.310	1.274	1.239	1.204	1.168	1.133	1.099	1.063	1.028	.993	.960	.895	.763	.572	.422	.276
20	1.728	1.649	1.572	1.498	1.421	1.350	1.313	1.278	1.243	1.208	1.172	1.138	1.104	1.070	1.035	1.002	.936	.807	.620	.468	.322
30	1.803	1.725	1.648	1.572	1.497	1.423	1.387	1.352	1.318	1.281	1.247	1.212	1.179	1.145	1.112	1.078	1.010	.882	.698	.547	.403
40	1.864	1.787	1.710	1.637	1.563	1.491	1.455	1.420	1.385	1.350	1.318	1.282	1.249	1.215	1.181	1.148	1.081	.952	.767	.615	.470
50	1.927	1.850	1.773	1.700	1.628	1.554	1.520	1.483	1.450	1.416	1.382	1.347	1.312	1.278	1.245	1.211	1.145	1.015	.828	.676	.528
60	1.973	1.897	1.820	1.748	1.673	1.601	1.565	1.531	1.500	1.463	1.430	1.394	1.360	1.325	1.293	1.260	1.194	1.065	.878	.725	.578
70	2.018	1.943	1.869	1.795	1.722	1.651	1.617	1.582	1.548	1.512	1.478	1.443	1.410	1.377	1.343	1.310	1.243	1.113	.925	.772	.625
75	2.043	1.970	1.895	1.822	1.750	1.680	1.645	1.609	1.573	1.540	1.505	1.471	1.438	1.402	1.369	1.333	1.268	1.138	.950	.798	.650
80	2.064	1.988	1.914	1.841	1.770	1.698	1.663	1.629	1.595	1.560	1.525	1.491	1.458	1.442	1.389	1.354	1.288	1.158	.970	.818	.670
90	2.102	2.028	1.951	1.878	1.804	1.732	1.697	1.661	1.625	1.590	1.557	1.523	1.490	1.457	1.421	1.387	1.321	1.189	1.000	.848	.698
100	2.150	2.071	1.994	1.919	1.845	1.770	1.735	1.700	1.665	1.630	1.595	1.560	1.527	1.492	1.460	1.425	1.359	1.227	1.038	.885	.738
125	2.213	2.137	2.061	1.985	1.911	1.840	1.805	1.770	1.734	1.700	1.663	1.629	1.593	1.560	1.528	1.493	1.428	1.297	1.105	.955	.808
150	2.277	2.200	2.125	2.050	1.978	1.906	1.870	1.835	1.801	1.768	1.733	1.698	1.662	1.630	1.599	1.564	1.497	1.364	1.175	1.022	.873
175	2.336	2.259	2.183	2.108	2.037	1.967	1.931	1.805	1.860	1.824	1.790	1.757	1.723	1.690	1.656	1.622	1.555	1.423	1.232	1.082	.932
200	2.389	2.311	2.237	2.163	2.090	2.018	1.981	1.947	1.913	1.880	1.845	1.810	1.775	1.742	1.709	1.675	1.609	1.477	1.287	1.132	.982

USEFUL DATA

$$\frac{Btu}{240} = \text{sq. ft. of Radiation}$$

$$\frac{\text{Sq. ft. of Radiation}}{4} = \text{Lbs. of water per hr.}$$

$$\frac{Btu}{966 \ (\text{Latent Heat})^2} = \text{Lbs. of water per hr.}$$

[2] See Table 3—"Temperature and latent heat of steam at various pressures."

Table 3.   Temperature and latent heat of steam at various pressures

Approx. Gauge Pressure	Temperature Deg. F.	Latent Heat	Approx. Gauge Pressure	Temperature Deg. F.	Latent Heat	Approx. Gauge Pressure	Temperature Deg. F.	Latent Heat
0	212	970.4	25	267	933.5	90	331	885.5
2	219	965.9	30	274	928.6	100	338	879.9
3	222	963.9	35	281	923.5	110	344	875.1
5	227	960.7	40	287	919.1	120	350	870.1
6	230	958.7	45	292	915.4	130	356	865.2
8	235	955.4	50	298	911.0	140	361	861.0
10	239	952.8	60	307	904.2	150	366	856.8
15	250	945.3	70	316	897.3	175	377	847.3
20	259	939.1	80	324	891.0	200	388	837.9

CONTROLS AND WIRING

Most manufacturers supply a range of manual, magnetic, and thermostatic temperature controls to meet any condition. Wiring diagrams are usually furnished with each unit and should be followed carefully to avoid blown fuses or damaged motors. Motors and all controls are of standard manufacture in almost all cases.

FRESH AIR CONNECTIONS

Although unit heaters are designed primarily to handle all recirculated air, they may be installed to handle either partial or total outdoor air. In such cases there will be some reduction in the volume of air handled and in the Btu. capacity of the unit due to resistance of the ductwork. Fig. 6 shows details of outside ventilating connections. The proportion of fresh air to recirculated air can be regulated to suit almost any condition by simple damper control.

Where ventilators admit air at temperatures below freezing, as sometimes occurs in northern climates, a minimum steam pressure of 5 lbs. must be maintained on the heating surfaces to prevent freezing of condensate in the tubes.

PIPING CONNECTIONS

Piping for unit heaters must conform to the system requirements, at the same time allowing the units to serve as intended. Especially during heating-up periods rapid condensation of steam is characteristic of this type of equipment. Piping should be planned to accommodate this sudden condensation; at the same time be ample in supply to carry adequate steam to the surfaces to replace that condensed. Sufficient pipe size is, therefore, essential to all heating surfaces over which air is forced to flow. This is especially important where the fan operates under start-and-stop control and where air handled may consist either wholly or partly of cold air from outside. Condensation rate may vary rapidly in such installations and the need for ample pipe capacity may be acute.

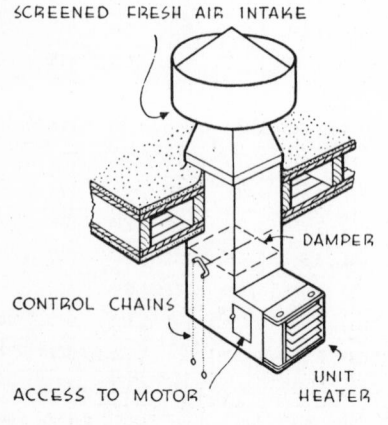
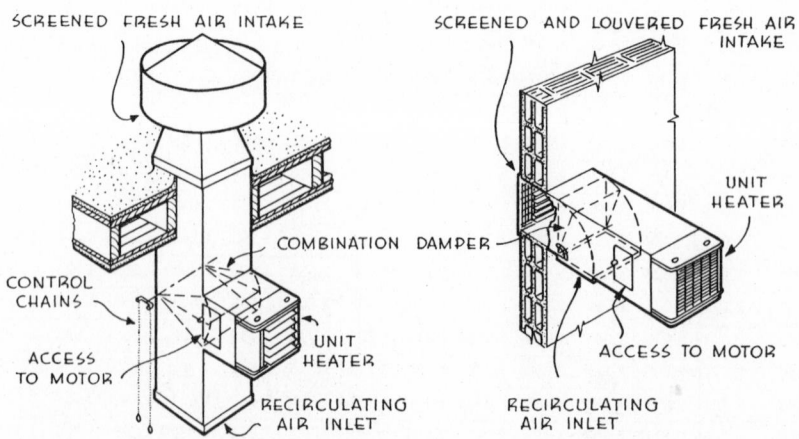

Fig. 6.   Ventilating details; outside connections

PIPING CONNECTIONS FOR UNIT HEATERS

Recommended piping connections for unit heaters are shown in Figs. 7–10 (courtesy ASHRAE Guide and Data Book 1961).

In steam systems the branch from the supply main to the heater should pitch toward the main, and be connected to its top to prevent condensate in the main from draining through the heater where it might reduce capacity and cause noise.

The return piping from steam unit heaters should provide a minimum drop of 10 in. below the heater so that the head of water required to overcome resistances of check valves, traps, and strainers will not cause condensate to remain in the heater.

Rapid condensation of steam, especially during heating-up periods, is characteristic of steam unit heaters. The return piping must be planned to keep the heating coil free of condensate during periods of maximum heat output, and the steam piping must be ample enough to carry a full supply of steam to the unit to take the place of the steam which has been condensed. Adequate sizes of piping are especially important where a unit heater fan is operated under on-off control because the condensate rate fluctuates rapidly.

Dirt pockets at the outlet of unit heaters are essential, and strainers with 1/16 in. perforations to prevent rapid plugging are recommended as an additional means of retaining dirt and scale which might affect operation of check valves and traps. Strainers should always be installed in the steam supply line if the heater is equipped with the steam-distributing type of coils or is valve-controlled.

An adequate air vent is required for low-pressure closed-gravity systems. The vertical pipe connection to the air vent should be at least ¾ in. IPS to permit separation of the water from the air passing to the vent.

Figs. 11–13 illustrate the three standard piping connections for centrifugal fan or blower type unit heaters, and cover the majority of applications. For vacuum systems a pitch of 1 in. in 40 ft. is recommended, but with gravity returns, for either high or low pressure, the pitch should be increased to 1 in. in 20 ft.

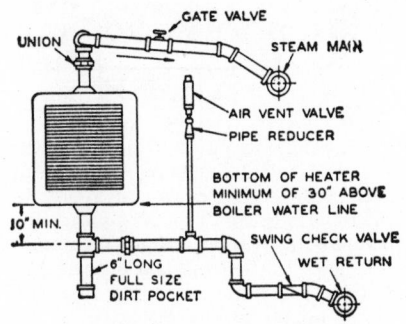

Fig 7. Unit heater connection to low-pressure steam closed gravity system

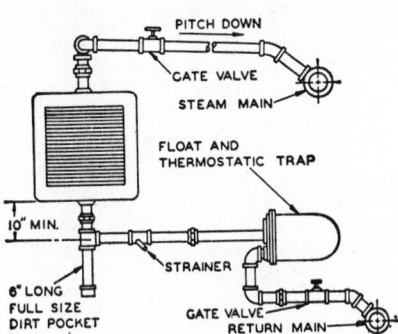

Fig. 8. Unit heater connection for low-pressure steam open gravity or vacuum return system

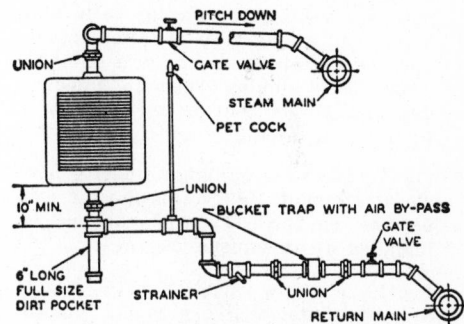

Fig. 9. Unit heater connection to high-pressure steam system

Courtesy ASHRAE Guide and Data Book, *1961.*

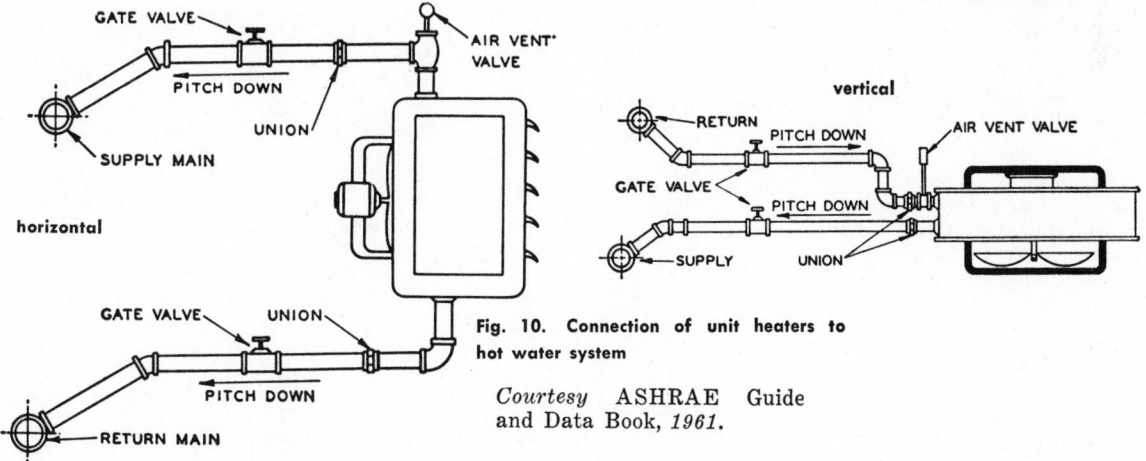

Fig. 10. Connection of unit heaters to hot water system

Courtesy ASHRAE Guide and Data Book, *1961.*

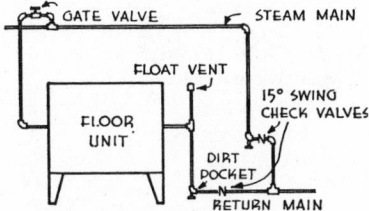

Fig. 11. Low-pressure gravity return

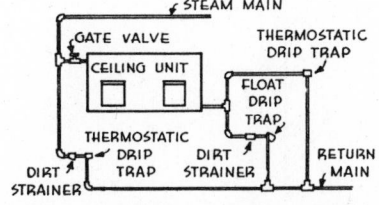

Fig. 12. Low-pressure vacuum or gravity return with condensation pump

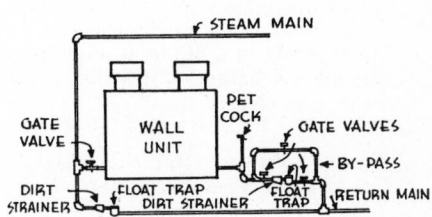

Fig. 13. High pressure

DIRECTIONAL LOUVERS, GRILLES AND DEFLECTORS

Heated air to do an effective job must be directed.

Practically all types of unit heaters employ some means to direct the air as it leaves the unit. These outlet air directional devices range from the simple louver type, Fig. 14, to the three-way multiple deflectors on triple nozzle blower units, in Fig. 24. Between these extremes is found the variety of standard and special purpose outlet controls illustrated here.

Fig. 14 shows standard equipment individually adjustable louvers, designed to direct high-velocity heated air down to the working zones and floor areas.

Fig. 15 illustrates a "splitter duct" attached to the heater outlet. Type "A" divides the air equally between the two outlets, directing it at a 45° horizontal angle, and giving a 10 per cent adjustment of the air by means of a damper. Type "B" is similar except for unequal delivery; 30 per cent on one outlet and 70 per cent on the other.

Fig. 16 shows a 90° high velocity nozzle attachment. With this the air can be directed vertically when the unit is installed at an unusual height.

Fig. 17 shows a variation of the standard horizontal delivery model placed in an inverted position with four-way diffusers.

Fig. 18. A projection type heater equipped with cone diffuser, recommended for applications where low ceiling mounting is encountered.

Fig. 19 shows a louver arrangement suggested in cases where it is desirable to direct the air stream toward one general area.

Fig. 20 illustrates a projection type heater provided with a combination of angle and vertical deflectors. Grille may be swung on track to direct air stream, thus eliminating necessity of turning or relocating unit.

Fig. 21. Vertical type unit deflectors, individually adjustable, making it possible to spread the air stream and increase the area of distribution, or to concentrate it on a given spot.

Fig. 22. Revolving type unit heater with adjustable deflectors at bottom of discharge outlets. Each deflector should be adjusted to a different angle so that the air discharged will scribe two concentric circles.

Fig. 23. Louvers in the nozzle type outlets of a blower model heater.

Fig. 24. Directional, three-way triple nozzle, for blower type units.

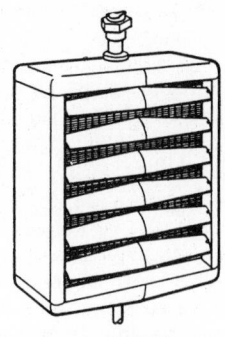

Fig. 14. Fixed louvers

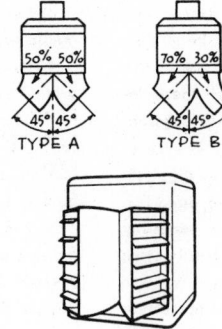

Fig. 15. Splitter duct with louvers

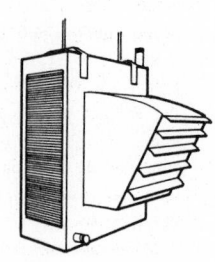

Fig. 16. Cowl deflector with adjustable louvers

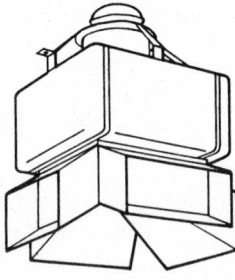

Fig. 17. Four-way diffuser

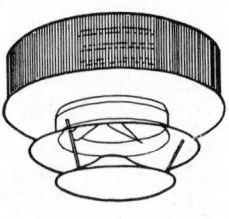

Fig. 18. Cone diffuser

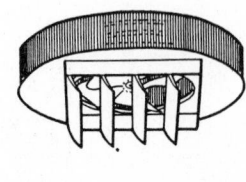

Fig. 19. Adjustable louvers

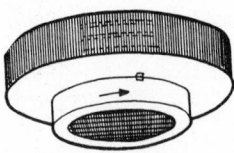

Fig. 20. Adjustable directional flow grille

Turn collar to change direction.

Fig. 21. Variable air deflector

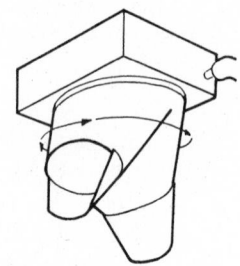

Fig. 22. Revolving discharge

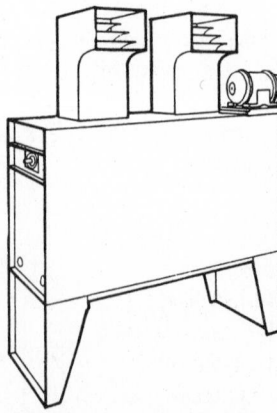

Fig. 23. Directional louver, double nozzle, floor-mounted blower

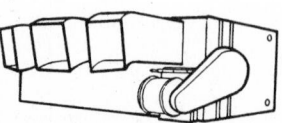

Fig. 24. Three-way, triple nozzle, ceiling-hung blower

Apartment building incinerators are major contributors to the atmospheric pollution which afflicts most of our cities. The proper design and operation of these incinerators so that they will cause substantially less atmospheric pollution has been the subject of many studies by the U.S. Public Health Service and other agencies. However, at present there is no generally accepted standard for their construction or performance.

Measures that can be taken to reduce air pollution from apartment incinerators are of three general types:

1. Prevention of opening of hoppers during firing
2. Improved combustion

3. Treatment of flue gases to remove impurities.

Air pollution from incinerators can be greatly reduced by preventing the hoppers from being opened during firing. This can be done by means of electrically controlled locking devices on the hopper doors. When hopper locks are used, firing must be done on a regular schedule, and the hours when tenants cannot use the incinerator must be posted. A better solution is the use of a double flue or, more correctly, a separate garbage chute and flue (Fig. 1). This arrangement requires no restriction on tenant use of the incinerator and permits firing at any time.

Air pollution from incinerators can also be reduced by improving the combustion.

Various devices can be used for this purpose. Probably the simplest is the introduction of an air-jet manifold above the fire. The use of a gas flame in addition to the air jets effects still further improvement (Fig. 2). Sometimes a secondary combustion chamber is provided.

Flue gases can be treated by various means to remove impurities before they are discharged into the atmosphere. The gases can be conducted through a devious path which reduces their velocity and permits the heavier particles to settle out by gravity (Fig. 4). Or the gases may be sent through a water spray scrubber before being discharged into the air (Fig. 3). Both settlement chamber and scrubber are sometimes used.

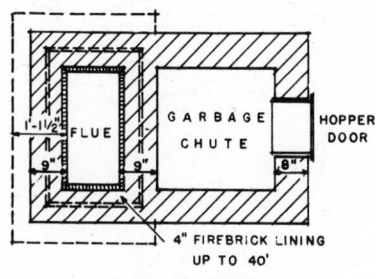

Fig. 1.   Double flue

Scale: ¼ in. = 1 ft

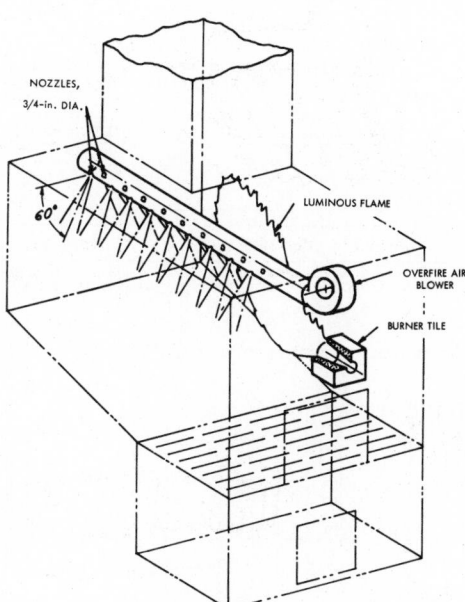

Fig. 2.   Secondary combustion by means of overfire air jets and gas flame

SOURCE: *E. R. Kaiser, et al.,* Modifications to Reduce Emissions from a Flue-fed Incinerator, *New York University Technical Report 552.2, 1959, sponsored by the National Institutes of Health, U.S. Public Health Service, Project S53.*

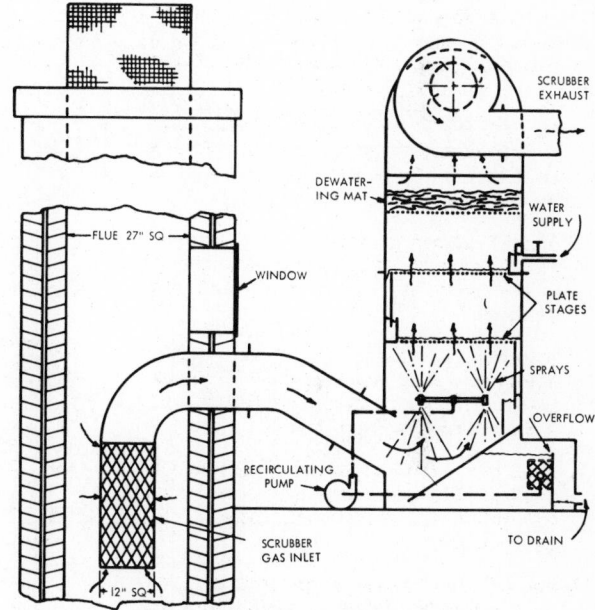

Fig. 3.   Flue gas scrubber on roof

Diagram illustrates test installation in existing flue. Except for the window, the arrangement shown is suitable for new construction since it is necessary to provide for free discharge of flue gases past the scrubber in the event of power failure. Scrubber exhaust may be through the main flue, if desired. (SOURCE: *E. R. Kaiser, et al.,* Modifications to Reduce Emissions from a Flue-fed Incinerator, *New York University Technical Report 552.2, 1959, sponsored by the National Institutes of Health, U.S. Public Health Service, Project S53.*)

INCINERATORS—2
Apartment buildings

Probably no one of the measures described above is sufficient to reduce the air pollution effect of incinerators to an acceptable level. For best results, all of them should be used.

The New York City Housing Authority in collaboration with the Department of Air Pollution Control has developed the details shown in Figs. 4 and 5. This design includes the following antipollution measures: sin-

gle-pipe overfire air-jet manifold with blower and gas burner, settlement chamber, and bypass flue to second-floor level. Dimensions of combustion chambers for buildings of various sizes are given in Table 1.

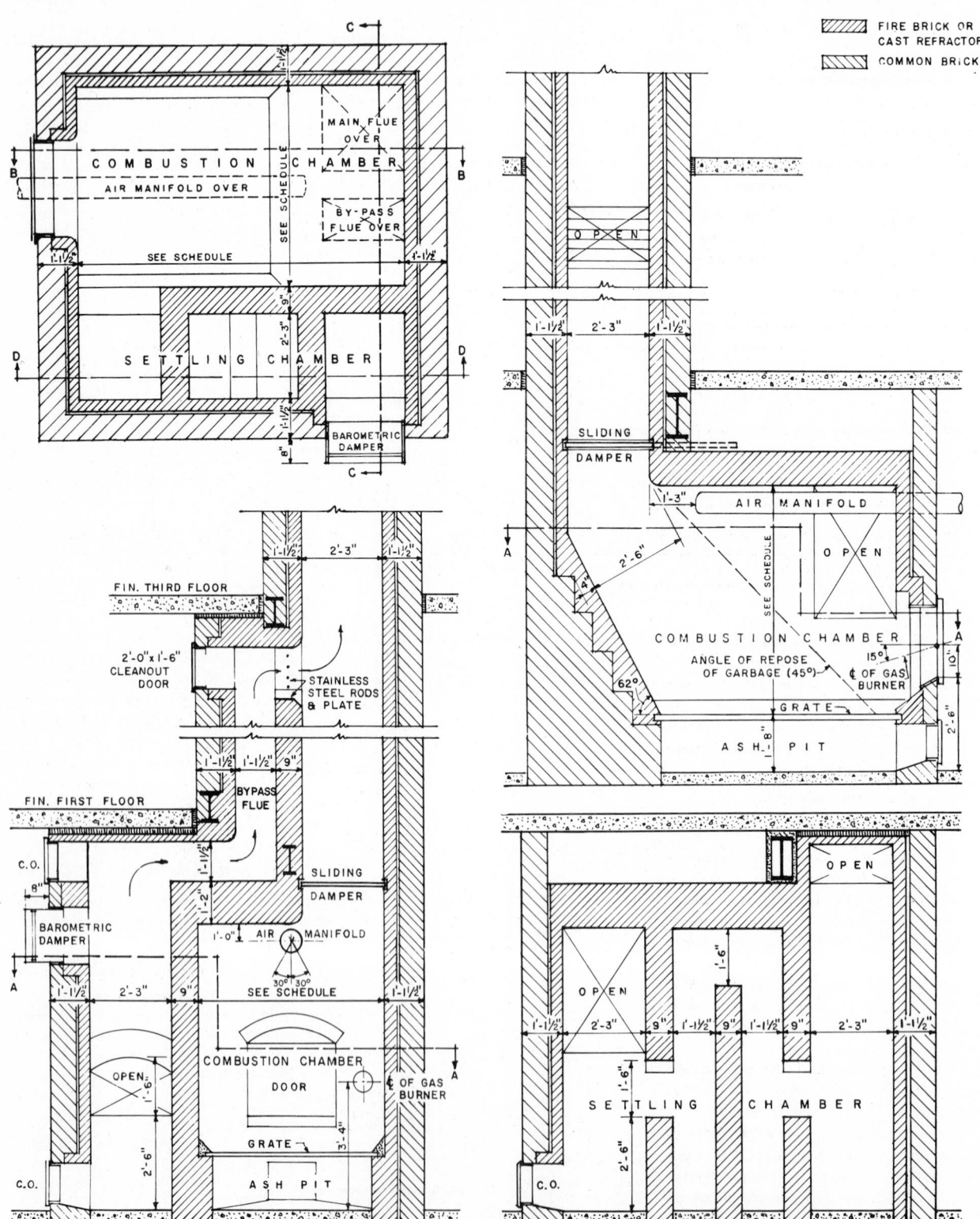

Fig. 4. Incinerator for high-rise apartment building SOURCE: *New York City Housing Authority* (see text).

Scale: ¼ in. = 1 ft

Table 1. Schedule of sizes for flue-fed incinerators

SOURCE: *New York City Housing Authority* (see text).

1. Number of persons or construction rooms		100	200	400	600	800	1,000	1,200
2. Burning area—grate & hearth	sq ft	18.8	18.8	32	48	64	80	96
3. Recommended grate & hearth		2'6" by 7'6"	2'6" by 7'6"	4'0" by 8'0"	5'4" by 9'0"	6'6" by 9'10"	7'6" by 10'9"	8'9" by 11'0"
4. Recommended grate size		2'0" by 4'6"	2'0" by 4'6"	3'0" by 6'0"	4'6" by 6'6"	5'6" by 7'0"	6'0" by 8'0"	7'0" by 8'6"
5. Furnace volume primary furnace	cu ft	80	80	160	240	320	400	480
6. Arch height above grate min.		5'0"	5'6"	6'0"	6'6"	7'0"	7'6"	7'6"
(preferred)		7'6"	7'6"	7'6"	7'6"	8'0"	8'6"	8'6"
7. Overfire air manifold—Pipe diam.	in.	6	6	6	8	8	10	12
No. holes		10	10	20	30	26	26	26
Hole diam.	in.	¾	1	1	1	1¼	1¼	1¼
7a Overfire air fan	cfm	103	206	410	624	1,174	1,415	1,760
8. Undergrate or ash pit door air ports	sq in.	6.5	12.8	25.7	38.5	51.4	64.2	77.0
(preferred)	sq in.	10.7	10.7	21.3	32.0	42.7	53.3	64.0
9. Flame port area	sq ft	1.2	2.4	4.8	7.2	9.6	12	14.4
(preferred)	sq ft	1.32	2.63	5.27	7.9	9.84	12.3	14.76
10. Separation chamber port area—min.	sq ft	1.0	1.0	1.7	2.55	3.4	4.25	5.1
(preferred)	sq ft	1.54	1.54	3.07	4.61	6.15	7.68	9.22
11. Bypass flue—barometric damper min. (fixed ventilation 1.5 times bypass flue area)	sq ft	1.0	1.0	1.4	2.1	2.8	3.5	4.2
12. Auxiliary burner in primary furnace	Btu/hr	155,000	310,000	620,000	930,000	1,250,000	1,550,000	1,860,000

NOTE: Provide adequate aisle space for observation, air port and damper adjustment, burner maintenance and furnace, ash-pit and separation chamber cleaning.

Details and dimensions are still being studied by the two agencies. Present indications are that sizes shown in Table 1 may eventually be considerably reduced. The New York City Housing Authority standard also includes a greatly enlarged spark arrester, as shown in Fig. 5.

MUNICIPAL AND INDUSTRIAL INCINERATORS

Analyses of municipal refuse show an average of 25 per cent moisture, 12½ per cent ash and other incombustible material, and 62½ per cent dry combustible material. In modern practice the latter is considered simply as solid fuel having the heat content shown in Table 2. This averages 8000 Btu per lb for dry combustible material, or 5000 Btu per lb of refuse delivered at the incinerator.

Furnace volume should be great enough to release heat at a rate of not more than 20,000 Btu per hr. Higher rates result in excessive gas velocities with consequent fly ash problems, too much smoke, and costly refractory damage. Similarly, furnace grates must be large enough to release heat at a rate of not more than 300,000 Btu per sq ft per hr, to avoid damage to

the grates. This converts to 60 lb of raw refuse per sq ft per hr, which is considered good furnace practice. By using 100 per cent excess air, the furnace temperature can be held to or below 2000°F.

A guide to the design of large incinerators is given in Table 3. One ton of refuse per day equals 83.4 lb per hr or 0.417

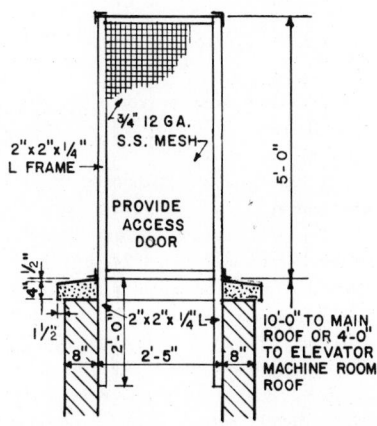

Fig. 5. Spark arrester for incinerator flue

SOURCE: *New York City Housing Authority.*

million Btu per hr. Combustion air required is 524 lb per hr per ton of refuse. The weight of the gas at 100 per cent excess air is 594 lb per hr per ton; at 50 per cent excess air it is 467 lb per hr per ton, or 1,100 lb per hr per million Btu.

All large incinerator plants use some form of automatic stoking which spreads the refuse evenly and permits continuous operation under closely controlled conditions with a minimum of manual labor. The traveling-grate type shown in Fig. 6 is

Table 2. Heating values of main constituents of municipal refuse

Material (Dry and free from ash and inert materials)	Btu per lb
Brush	8600
Wood	8240
Cellulose	8000
Paper	7900
Garbage	7280
AVERAGE	8040

Table 3.   Incinerator design data

Tons per day (24 hr)	50	100	150	200	250	300
Lb per hr	4,160	8,340	12,500	16,600	20,800	25,000
Million Btu per hr	20.8	41.7	62.5	83.4	104.0	125.0
Grate area, sq ft	69.3	139.0	208	277	347	417
Furnace volume, cu ft ...	1,040	2,085	3,125	4,160	5,200	6,250
Forced draft, cfm	5,860	10,450	15,200	20,400	25,150	30,325
Gas weight at furnace outlet, lb per hr	29,650	59,400	89,000	118,500	148,000	178,000
Gas volume at 2000°F, cfm	30,150	60,300	91,000	120,600	150,200	180,900
Flue area at 1,000 fpm, sq ft	30.7	60.3	91.0	120.6	150.2	180.9

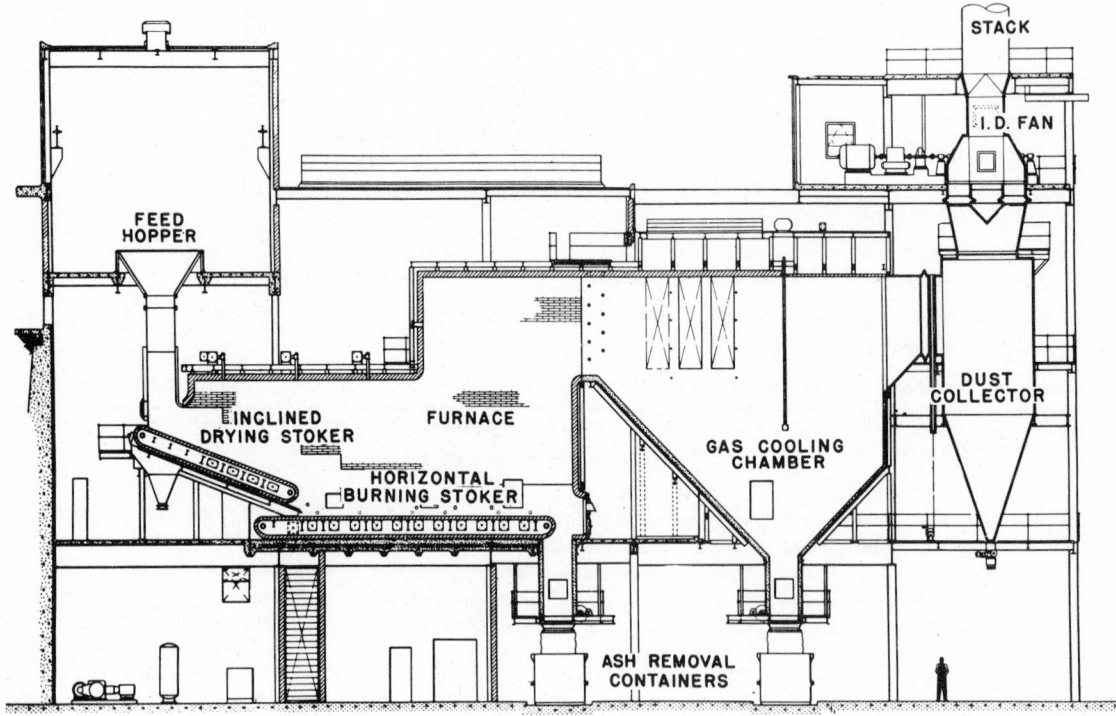

Fig. 6. Section through typical municipal incinerator with traveling grates, drying stoker, and dust collector   SOURCE: *Combustion magazine.*

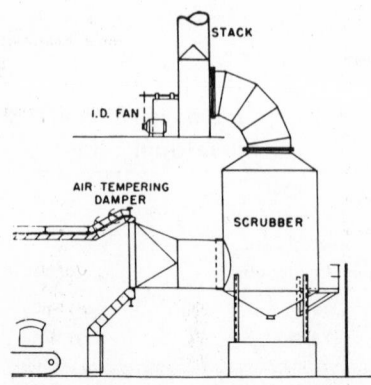

Fig. 7.   Wet-type dust collector or scrubber

SOURCE: *Combustion magazine.*

commonly used. A radial type is also available. Overfire air is provided to promote complete combustion.

The dust loading limitation set by the American Society of Mechanical Engineers is 0.85 lb of fly ash per 1,000 lb of gas at 50 per cent excess air, or 0.943 lb per million Btu. Local air pollution regulations may be more severe than this, and dust collectors (Fig. 6) or scrubbers (Fig. 7) may be required. These devices have the additional advantage of eliminating the 150 to 200-ft chimney which is otherwise required.

The heat generated by an incinerator should be utilized as fully as possible. At the very least the hot gas can be used for the predrying of wet garbage, as shown in Fig. 6. Waste gas can often be used to generate sufficient steam, hot water, and electricity to meet the needs of the plant. Larger plants can often serve a group of buildings. Industries having large and regular quantities of combustible waste can use the incinerator as a major, sometimes the only, source of power. In these cases it is usually more efficient to design the incinerator as a boiler (Fig. 8). Municipal incinerators are sometimes located adjacent to sewage treatment plants so that the waste heat can be used to flash-dry the sludge (Fig. 9).

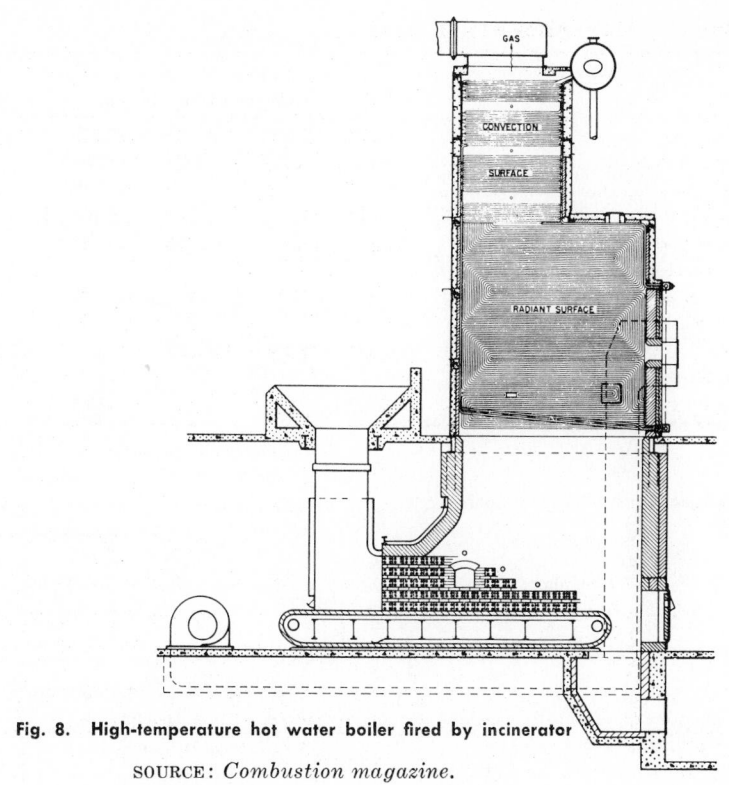

Fig. 8. High-temperature hot water boiler fired by incinerator

SOURCE: *Combustion magazine.*

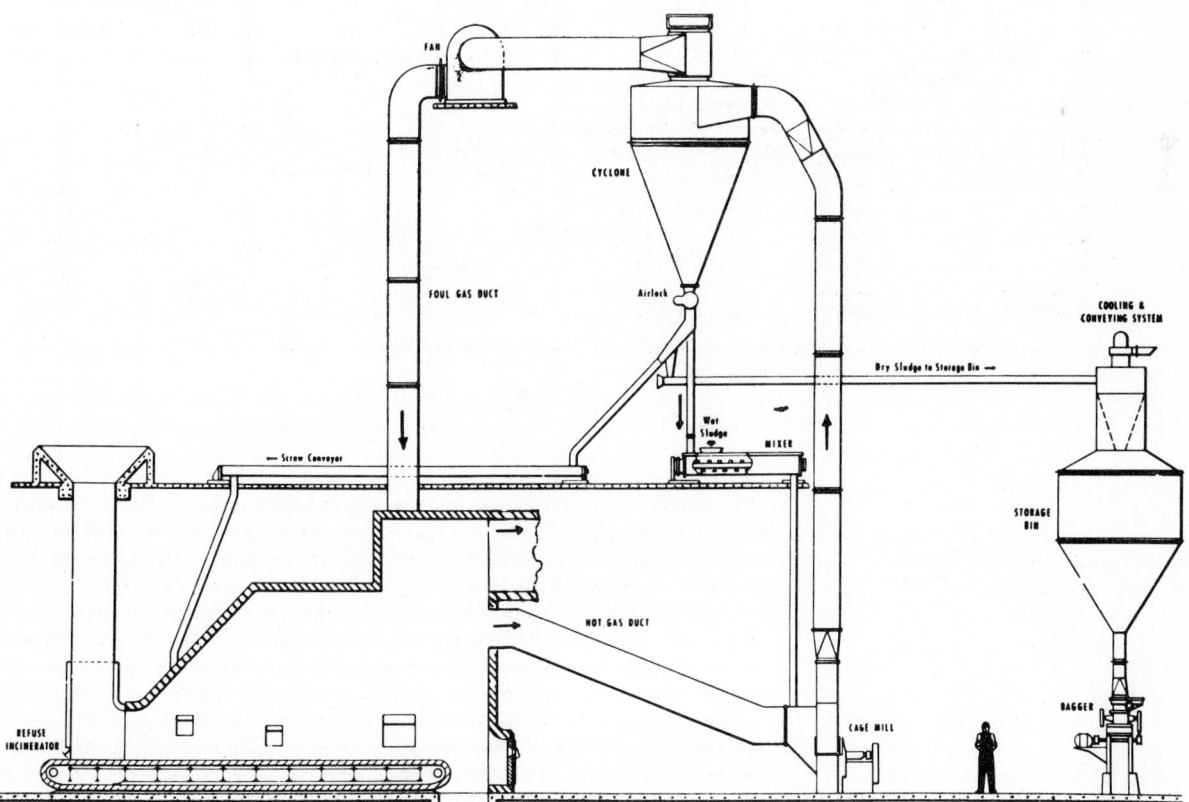

Fig. 9. Incinerator and flash dryer for sewage sludge disposal

SOURCE: *Combustion magazine.*

PLUMBING—SUPPLY AND DISTRIBUTION—1
Piping systems

By GEORGE R. JERUS, P.E.
Associate—Meyer, Strong and Jones, Mechanical and Electrical Engineers

OUTLINE OF PIPING MATERIALS

Hot and cold water piping

   a. Brass pipe with cast-brass fittings.
   b. Copper tubing (Type K, or L) with cast- or wrought-copper fittings and 95–5 tin-antimony solder.
   c. Type TP or B copper tubing with cast-brass fittings and silver solder.
   d. Galvanized pipe with galvanized malleable fittings.
   e. Plastic pipe and fittings.
   f. Cast-iron waterworks pipe and fittings (for underground piping).

Gas

   a. Black steel pipe with galvanized malleable fittings.

Oxygen and nitrous oxide piping

   a. Copper tubing with wrought- or cast-copper fittings with silver solder.

Vacuum piping

   a. Copper tubing with copper fittings and 95–5 tin-antimony solder.

Compressed air

   a. Copper tubing with copper fittings and 95–5 tin-antimony solder.
   b. Black steel pipe with galvanized malleable fittings.

Drainage piping including leaders

   a. Cast-iron pipe and fittings.
   b. Galvanized wrought-iron pipe with recessed black cast-iron fittings.
   c. Galvanized steel pipe with black cast-iron recessed fittings.
   d. Copper drainage tubing (Type K, L, or M) with cast- or wrought-copper fittings.

WATER DISTRIBUTION SYSTEMS

The diagrams in Fig. 1 show typical good practice in the design of hot and cold water distribution systems for residences. These diagrams are based on the essentials of distribution under various sets of practical conditions, but should not be interpreted as a complete solution to any specific residential problem. The pipe sizes and arrangements shown, however, are generally adaptable without substantial change to most small houses, being adequate for dwellings that contain two bathrooms in addition to a first-floor lavatory and toilet and the usual kitchen and laundry fixtures.

Pipes for both hot and cold water are sized for permanently clean bores. It is assumed that the water supply will be comparatively soft, so that no precipitated coating will form on pipe walls, reduce inside diameters, and prevent free flow of water. In localities where the water contains a concentration of hardness (expressed as calcium carbonate) sufficient to cause even a slight precipitation in cold water lines, it may be necessary either to increase pipe sizes in both hot and cold lines or to install a water softener.

COLD WATER LINES

Tap from the street water main can be ⅝ in. for very small houses, and ¾ in. for houses containing a number of fixtures equivalent to three bathrooms in addition to kitchen and laundry fixtures.

Service pipe, or house main, can be ¾ in. for small houses, but must be at least 1 in. for larger houses as defined above.

Pressure-reducing valve is unnecessary if the street pressure is 50 psi or less. Street pressures above 50 psi should be reduced through a valve located in the house main on the street side of the meter.

Drips should be installed in the lower portions of basement lines so that the entire system can be completely drained.

Shut-off valves are necessary in the basement on the street side of fittings in the supply main, adjacent to the air chamber, on the line supplying the hot water heater, and at the bases of all supply risers. Fixtures should be individually valved.

Air chamber will prevent water hammer throughout the piping system, and can be located in any convenient part of the main on the house side of the

Acid drainage

   a. Silicon iron pipe and fittings with cast-iron or tellurium lead trap asbestos and lead caulking.
   b. Glass pipe with glass fittings.
   c. Plastic pipe with plastic fittings. (Type of discharge from fixture must b known in order to select proper plastic.)
   d. Knightware pipe and fittings with poured-mastic joints.

Vent piping

   a. Cast-iron pipe and fittings.
   b. Galvanized-steel or wrought-iron pipe with black cast-iron or malleabl cast-iron fittings.
   c. Copper tubing and fittings.

Sewers (Outside building, more than 5 ft from foundation wall)

   a. Extra-heavy cast-iron pipe with cast-iron fittings.
   b. Vitreous tile pipe and fittings with hot-poured-mastic joints, factory applied slip-seal joints, or cement joints.
   c. Concrete pipe with hot-poured-mastic joints, ribbed neoprene gaske or cement joints.
   d. Asbestos-cement pipe and fittings with ribbed neoprene gaskets.
   e. Asphalt-wrapped pipe (Orangeburg) with tapered joints and fittings.

Subsoil drainage

   a. Agricultural tile with open joints.
   b. Porous-wall cement pipe.
   c. Perforated asbestos-cement pipe.
   d. Perforated asphalt-wrapped pipe.
   e. Corrugated-steel pipe for culverts.

meter. It should be fitted with shut-offs and pet cocks, for it will requi draining when the air within it is absorbed by the water. Instead of an a chamber, a commercially stocked shock absorber may be installed.

Water softeners are available in various sizes and types, all of which r quire a salt tank for regeneration. Regeneration can be accomplished man ally or automatically; automatic regeneration is usually controlled by meter on the softened-water line. A floor drain for disposal of filter was water is essential if a water-softening device is to be used.

Insulation of cold water pipes is desirable throughout the building, prevent damage from condensation drip, to maintain proper water temper tures, and to muffle flow noises. Wrappings of ½-in. glass fiber (or simila material) with vapor-barrier jacket are satisfactory.

HOT WATER LINES

A simple form of circulation can be accomplished by connecting the h water house supply to the hot water return circulation in a simple loop the basement ceiling. Such a loop can be tapped by supply risers to serve fixtures.

The type of circulating hot water distribution shown is adaptable to mo residences. A more elaborate type would require individual supply and retu risers to serve each bathroom or group of superimposed fixtures.

The hot water heating layout indicates an arrangement of pipes that w give unusually quick hot water service from fixtures in a noncirculating syste and nearly instantaneous service in a circulating system. This service is a complished by connecting the hot water supply line (from the heater) direct to the house supply instead of to the tank. When a faucet is opened, wat is drawn first from the supply line from the heater, thus stimulating circula tion in the returns from the tank. Check valves prevent cold water from bein drawn into the house hot water supply pipe.

Insulation of hot water lines throughout the building tends to conserve th hot water supply and ensure quick service at faucets. Coverings of ½-i glass fiber are satisfactory.

Drips should be sufficient in number to drain all hot water pipes, ar should be installed approximately as shown in relation to water heating ar storage equipment.

With Non-circulating Hot Water

With Circulating Hot Water

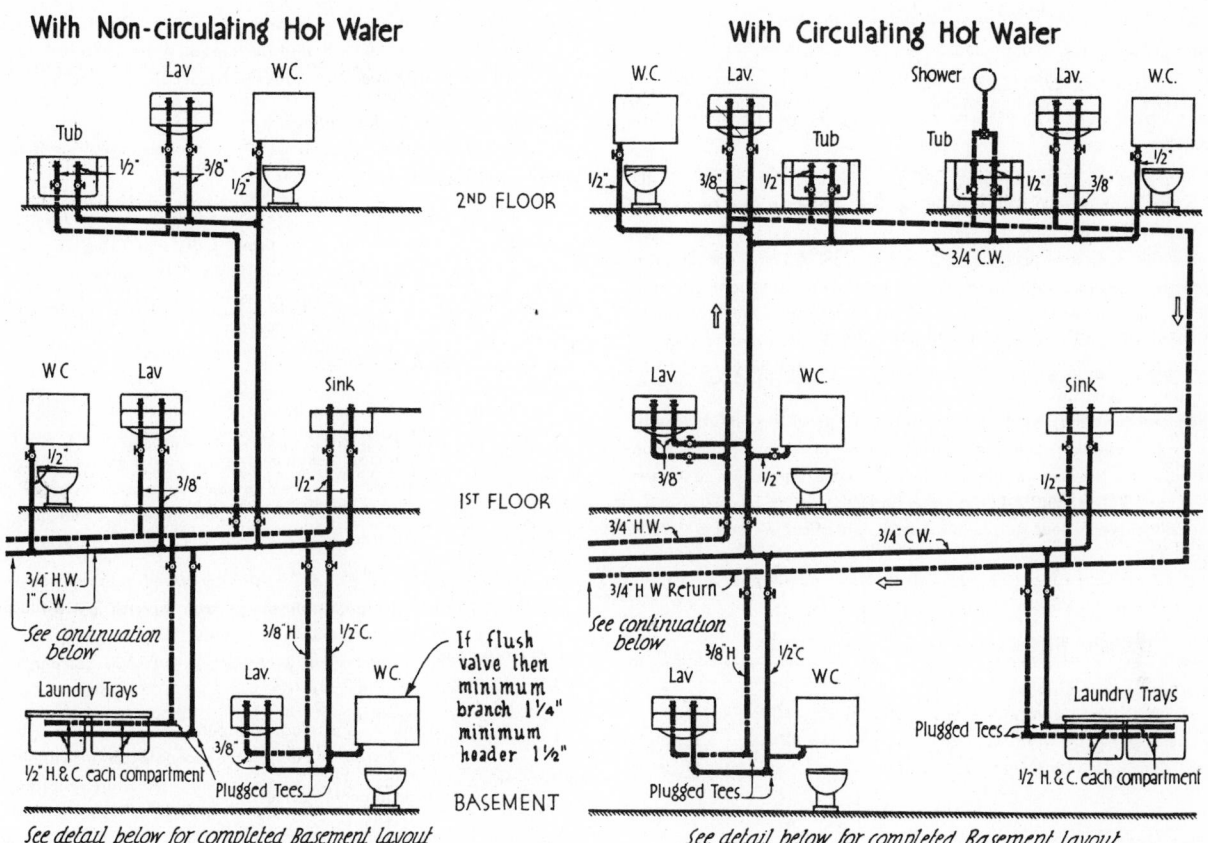

NOTE! *These sections are diagrammatic and drawn to no scale.*

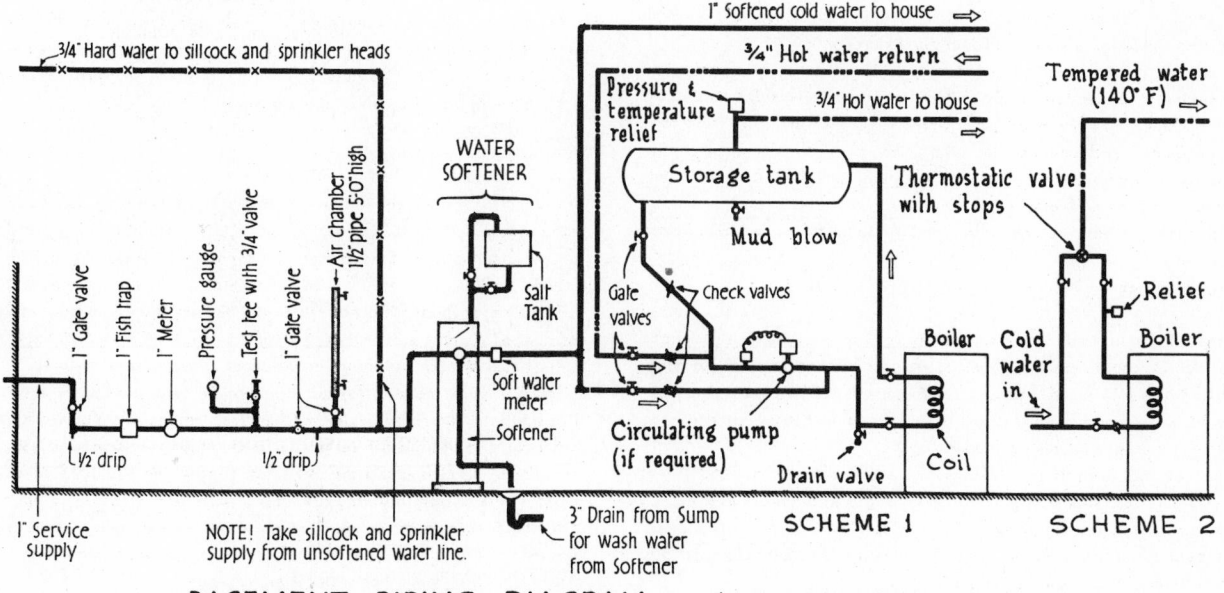

BASEMENT PIPING DIAGRAM *(see Sections above for continuations)*

Fig. 1. Basement piping diagram

House tanks

Basement shut-off valves are necessary to close the hot water return circulation line and to close individual risers in case of repairs or other emergencies. All fixtures should be individually valved.

Check valves should be installed on the heater return from the tank, on the cold water supply to the heater, and on the hot water return circulation li■

Relief valve should be installed on the hot water storage tank. A combin■ tion pressure and temperature relief valve should be used.

HOUSE TANKS

If the height of a building requires water pressure in excess of that in the city mains, a house tank must be provided. A tank would also be required if the peak draw would reduce the pressure on the highest usable floor to less than 10 psi—the minimum pressure required for satisfactory operation of fixtures, particularly those with flush valves. To provide sufficient pressure, the bottom of the tank must be elevated about 31 ft above the highest fixture, an elevation ensuring a static pressure of 13.5 psi. If water is required above the highest fixture (as, for example, in air conditioning), a booster pump or separate pressure tank may be needed.

More than one tank may have to be installed to provide pressure breaks within a very tall building; the supply from a tank in the penthouse might produce excessive pressures at the lower floors, and thus cause excessive wear on washers, valves, and other moving parts.

Tanks usually serve a dual purpose: domestic water supply and a reserve for fire protection.

Materials for house tanks

Tanks may be constructed of either wood or steel. Wood tanks are circu■ and require ample ventilation to prevent dry rot. Table 1 gives the dime■ sions, weight, and capacity of wood tanks. Steel tanks may be built to a■ shape, and may include a dividing partition to permit cleaning of one co■ partment without interrupting water service to the building. Table 2 giv■ the dimensions and capacity of various steel tanks.

Capacities of tanks

The required capacity of a tank varies with the capacity and running ti■ of the house or fill pumps. A half-hour supply of domestic water is general■ sufficient if pump capacity is equal to the hourly load. Table 3 gives wate■ consumption figures that can be used to determine tank and pump capacitie■

For example, assume that a commercial office building has an occupancy ■ 4500 persons:

$$4500 \times 3.8 \text{ gal per hr per person} = 17,100 \text{ gal per hr}$$
$$\text{Tank should have } \tfrac{1}{2}\text{-hr supply} = 8,550 \text{ gal}$$
$$\text{Pump should have 1-hr supply} = 17,100 \text{ gal per hr}$$
$$= 285 \text{ gpm}$$

Two pumps should be installed to provide breakdown service. The pum■ size would have to be modified to accommodate an air-conditioning loa■ which would be divided between the pumps. Make-up requirements for c■ conditioning are dependent upon the method of refrigeration, and therefo■ the design engineer should be consulted.

Table 1. Weight and capacity of wood tanks

Cap. Gal	Weight, Tons	8	9	10	11	12	13	14	15	16	17	18	19	20	Dimensions	Weight, Tons	Cap. Gal.
		1.68	2.12	2.61	3.16	3.75	4.39	5.07	5.81	6.60	7.43	8.32	9.25	10.23	Weight per Ft Depth, Tons		
		376.01	475.89	387.52	710.9	846.03	992.91	1151.5	1321.9	1504.1	1697.9	1903.6	2120.9	2350.1	Gal per Ft Depth		
2,444	11.2	8						14								73.2	16,524
3,093	14.0		8							12						78.7	17,828
3,196	14.5	10			20											81.6	18,369
3,819	17.3			8			16									74.0	16,697
3,948	17.8	12						14								83.0	18,801
4,045	18.3		10				16									85.0	19,168
4,700	21.2	14								12						88.0	19,988
4,994	22.5			10											15'-3½" dia. x 16'-0" H	88.0	20,000
4,997	22.5		12			18										84.1	19,000
5,452	24.5	16						14								93.5	21,224
5,949	26.8		14					16								96.2	21,809
6,043	27.2				10		18									96.4	21,811
6,169	27.8			12							12					98.0	22,269
6,900	31.0		16			20										94.3	21,303
7,191	32.2					10		14								104.6	23,795
7,344	33.0			14			20									108.0	24,455
7,464	33.5				12			16								108.4	24,620
8,440	37.7						10	18								109.4	24,818
8,519	38.2			16											17'-0½" dia. x 16'-0" H	110.3	25,000
8,883	39.7					12				14						116.3	26,511
8,886	39.8				14				16							121.2	27,602
9,788	43.6						10		20							122.6	27,826
10,308	46.1				16			18								123.2	28,015
10,426	46.5					12							14			128.5	29,376
10,575	47.2					14									17'-6½" dia. x 18'-0" H	130.2	30,000
11,236	50.0						10			16						134.8	30,753
11,730	52.4			18					18							137.9	31,409
12,091	54.0					12		20								138.1	31,411
12,267	55.0					16					16					149.0	34,076
12,441	55.2						14			18						154.3	34,995
12,785	56.7								20	10						155.3	35,217
13,152	58.7			20							18					169.6	38,777
13,880	61.5					12			20							171.8	39,237
13,960	63.0				18										19'-1½" dia. x 20'-0" H	175.2	40,000
14,394	64.0							14			20					189.9	43,477
14,397	64.0						16					22				210.5	48,177
15,000	66.5	14'-2½" dia. x 14'-0" H													21'-6½" dia. x 20'-0" H	220.6	50,000
15,652	70.0					20									23'-6½" dia. x 20'-0" H	260.4	60,000
15,793	69.8												12		23'-10½" dia. x 24'-0" H	325.0	75,000
16,383	73.0						18								28'- 6" dia. x 24'-0" H	450.0	100,000

Note: Inside Diameter, Feet shown across top (8–20); values within the grid give Depth of Tank, Feet.

Table 2. Capacity of steel tanks

Tank Area, Sq Ft	Height of Tank, Feet, Allowing 1 Ft for Floats and Overflow						
	4.0	4.5	5.0	5.5	6.0	7.0	8.0
	Capacity of Tanks, Gallons						
60	1350	1580	1800	2030	2250	2700	3150
80	1800	2100	2400	2700	3000	3600	4200
100	2250	2620	3000	3370	3750	4500	5250
120	2700	3150	3600	4050	4500	5400	6300
140	3150	3670	4200	4730	5250	6300	7350
160	3600	4190	4800	5400	6000	7200	8400
180	4050	4720	5400	6080	6750	8100	9450
200	4500	5230	6000	6730	7500	9000	10500
220	4950	5750	6600	7400	8250	9900	11600
240	5400	6300	7200	8100	9000	10800	12600
260	5850	6810	7800	8800	9750	11700	13600
280	6300	7350	8400	9450	10500	12600	14700
300	6750	7890	9000	10500	11250	13500	15800

Table 3. Water consumption in office buildings

Building Type	Consumption Gal per Hr per Person
Commercial, no air conditioning	3.8
Commerical, with air conditioning	7.3–9.2
Owner-occupied, with kitchen and laundry, no air conditioning	7.3
Owner-occupied, with kitchen, laundry, and air conditioning	9.0

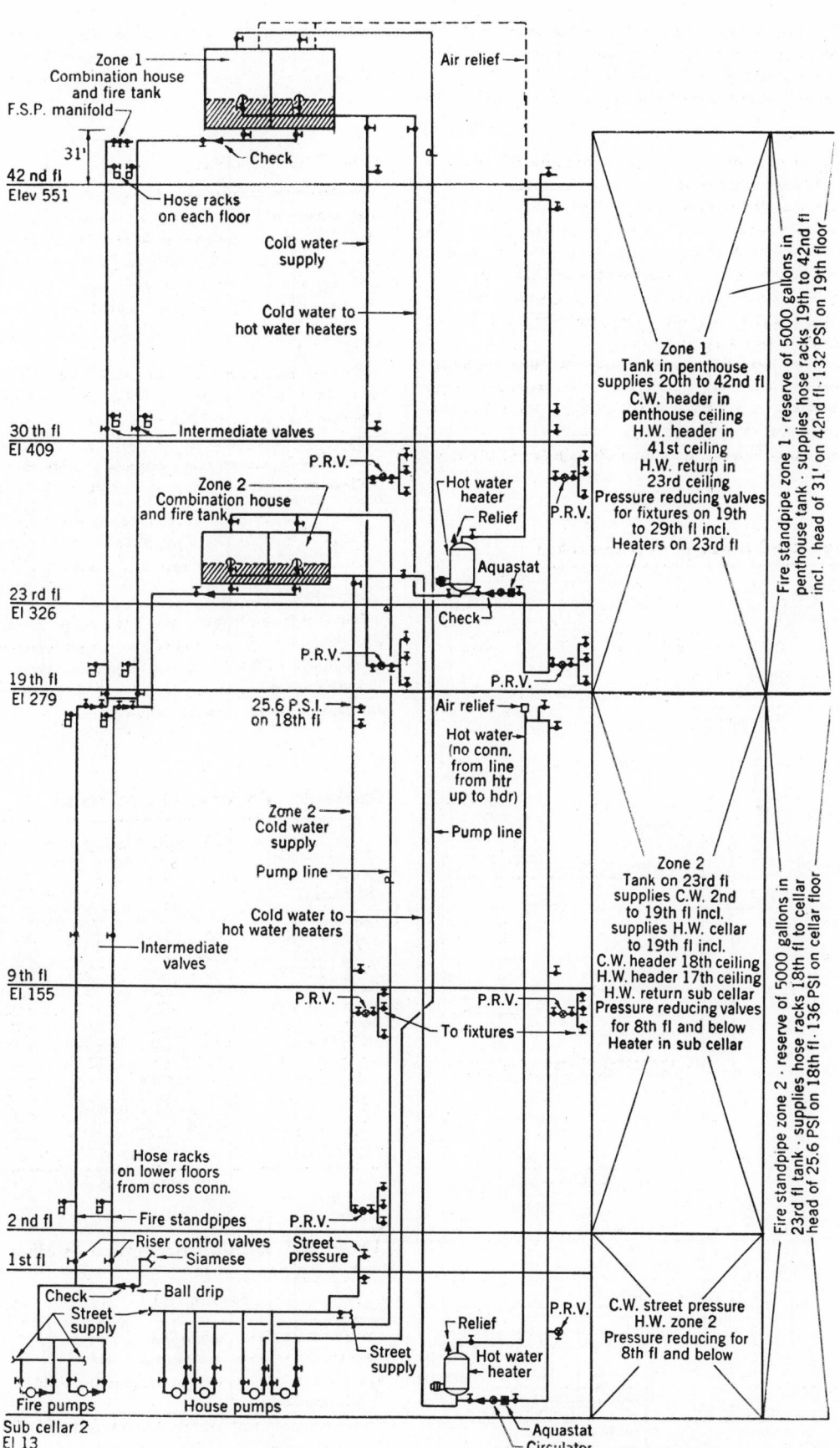

Fig. 2. Gravity water supply system with pressure-reducing valves, serving two zones

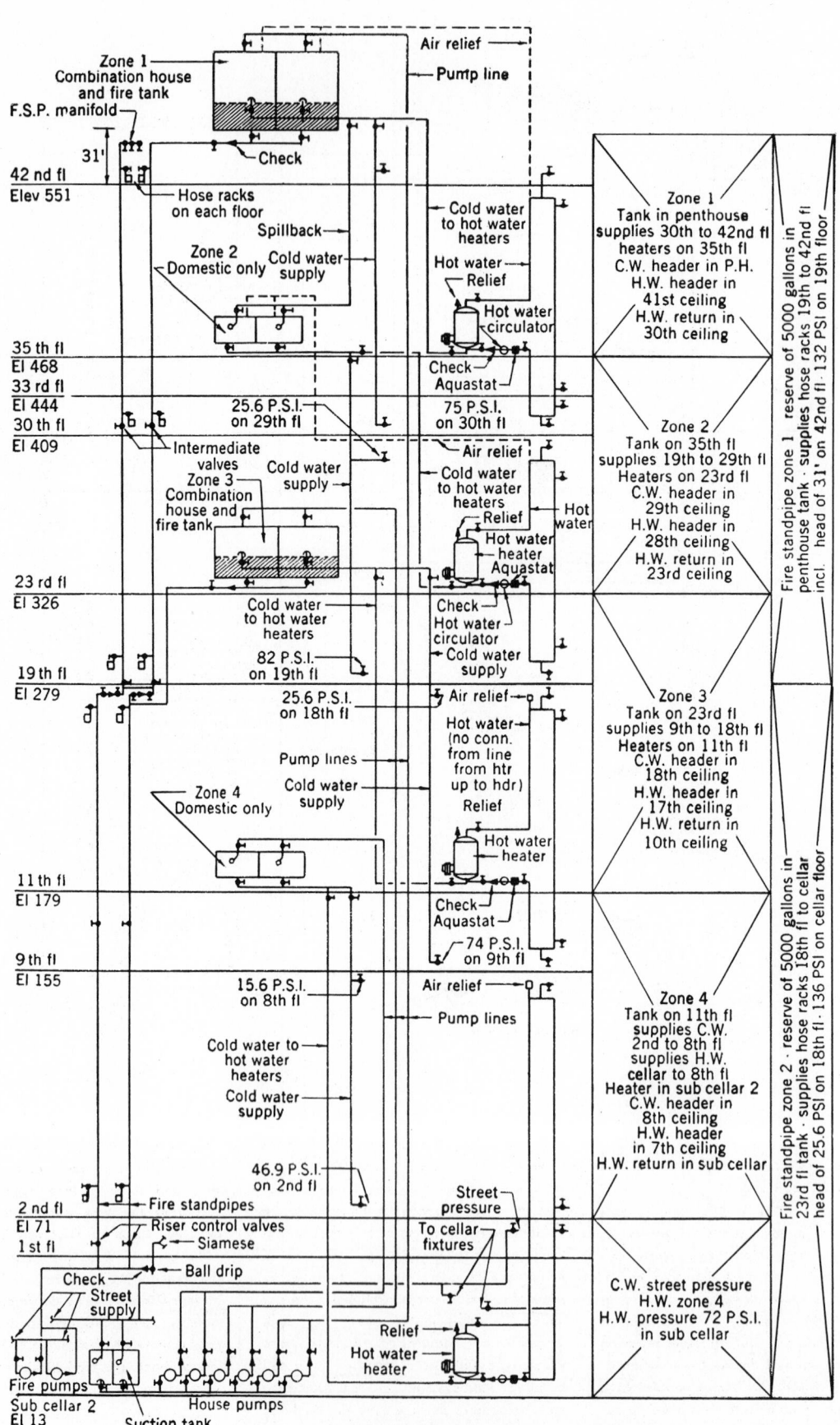

Fig. 3. Gravity water supply system without pressure-reducing valves, serving four zones

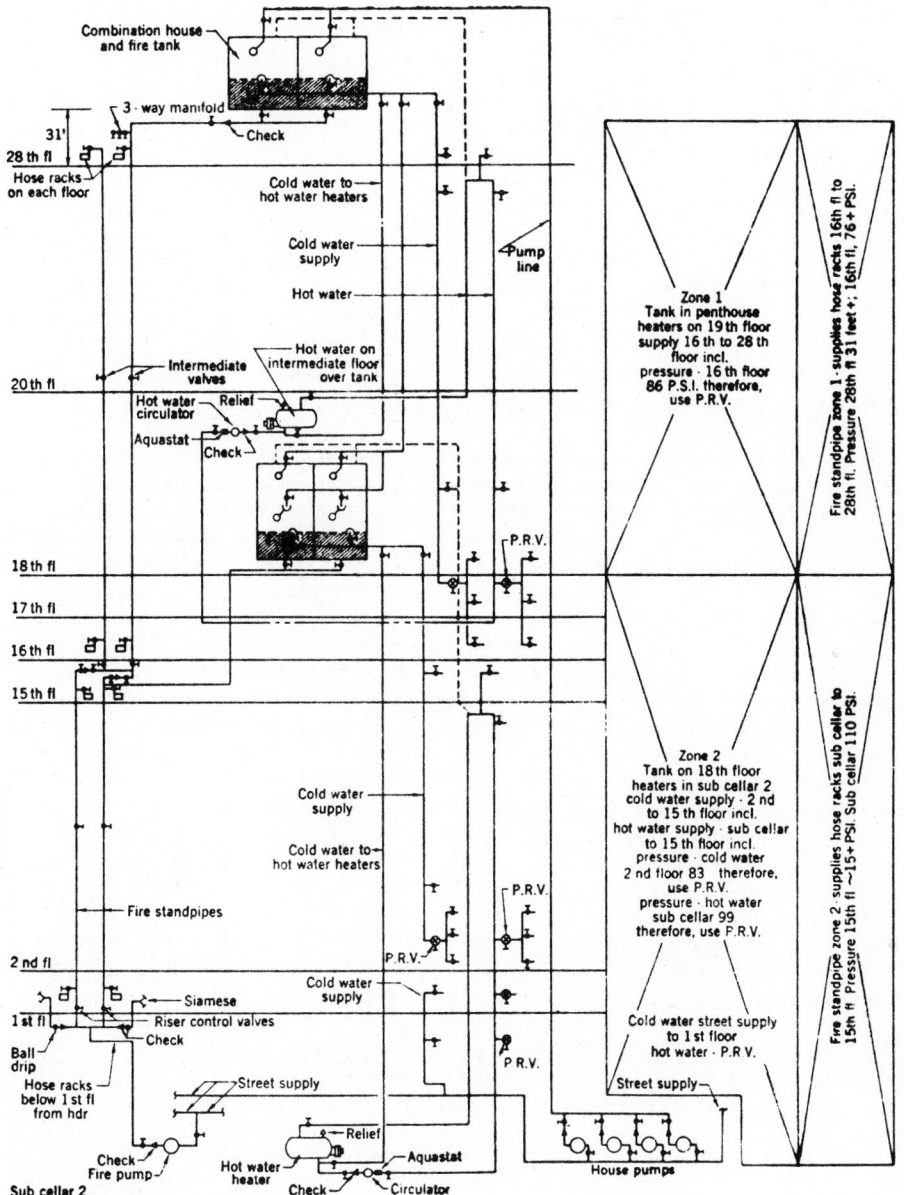

Fig. 4. Gravity tanks—spillback system

The riser diagrams in Fig. 2, 3, and 4 show typical methods of zoning the services for high-rise buildings.

Figure 2 shows a gravity water supply system with pressure-reducing valves. In this system, the pumps take suction from the city mains, and must therefore be selected with a nonoverload characteristic for varying street pressures. The number of zones is reduced, but pressure-reducing valves are required on the lower floors of each zone. These valves may require high maintenance and must be installed in accessible locations.

Figure 3 shows an ideal arrangement for a very tall building, since maintenance problems are cut to a minimum. Installation of a suction tank enables the pump head to be kept constant and a very efficient pump selected. A suction tank is mandatory in many localities in order to prevent excessive pressure drops in the city main. The equipment for supplying each zone, however, requires considerable space, which is usually at a premium in a tall building. Moreover, this system would be more expensive initially than the modified version shown in Fig. 2.

Figure 4 shows a "spillback" system. All of the water is pumped up to the highest tank, and some is then allowed to spill back into the tank supplying the lower zone. A system of this type is employed if the capacity of the high-zone pump is too small for the head required and pump efficiency is very low; the pumping of all water for the building into one tank enables a more efficient pump to be selected. The spillback line must be sized to provide for the peak draw in the lower zone.

A certain amount of calculation is necessary before equipment can be selected for heating, storing, and distributing domestic hot water. The calculation of precise requirements often involves many technicalities that call for specialized engineering knowledge. In any event, the architect's attention is required to solve planning problems that arise prior to the installation of any sort of mechanical equipment.

As a basis for the preliminary selection of domestic hot water equipment, and as an aid in planning its proper installation, rule-of-thumb approximations can be made that will allow the architect to determine with reasonable accuracy the required capacity and dimensions.

Determining domestic hot water requirements involves, first, the capacity of the heating plant and, second, the capacity of one or more hot water storage tanks, unless an instantaneous or tankless hot water heater is to be installed. Heating plant and tank capacities must be mutually adjusted to solve the particular problem at hand. For example, if space for hot water storage is at a premium, the capacity of the heating plant should be increased to deliver the amount of hot water required during periods of greatest demand. If, on the other hand, tanks are to be used, it is good practice to size the heater capacity to deliver hot water sufficient for average hourly demands and provide a storage tank of sufficient capacity to supply additional demands during peak periods.

Domestic hot water requirements depend largely upon the type of building and its use. Since the types, characteristics, and activities of building occupants vary widely, a liberal estimate of water consumption should be made. Thus it is customary to estimate hot water requirements on the basis of cold water consumption per person.

COLD WATER CONSUMPTION

It has been found that the average cold water consumption per person in a house of average size and equipment is close to 50 gal per day. On this basis, consumption allowances have been developed for other types of buildings.

For large residences, allow 100 gal per person per day. This figure includes supply for all normal requirements and wastage.

For low-rent apartments, allow 75 gal per person per day. This figure is a minimum based upon minimum plumbing fixture requirements.

For high-class apartments, allow 100 gal per person per day. A rough estimate of water consumption in apartments can be made by multiplying the number of bedrooms by 200.

For hotels, allow 100 gal per person per day. Approximate total water consumption in hotels is commonly figured on the basis of 60 per cent occupancy. Thus, 60 per cent of the number of bedrooms, multiplied by 100, would give a reasonably safe average figure. That figure, however, would not include requirements for kitchen, laundry, or cold-storage equipment, or any other type of mechanical unit.

For office buildings, allow 25 gal per person per day. To estimate building occupancy, allow 125 sq ft of floor space per person, exclusive of elevator space, corridors, or service areas.

Probable maximum peak loads for cold water are relatively unimportant in apartments, hotels, and office buildings that use cold water storage tanks. Such tanks are required in most high-rise buildings (see House Tanks).

HOT WATER REQUIREMENTS

Consumption of domestic hot water is usually estimated as one-third the amount of the cold water consumption.

Heater capacities and storage tank sizes are based upon the maximum probable hourly demand for hot water—the hourly peak load. Instantaneous heaters, which have no storage tanks, are sized to satisfy a peak gallon-per-minute draw. If, for example, average hourly consumption in actual use was 60 gal per hr, all of which was used in 10 minutes, then the instantaneous heater would have to supply 60 gal within that 10 minutes. Thus, unless an unlimited quantity of heat is available, instantaneous heaters should not be used.

The heating load on a boiler or heater required for a desired supply of domestic hot water is based primarily upon the average hourly demand for hot water.

Rule 1. To determine total daily consumption of cold water, multiply the number of building occupants by the number of gallons per person per day as listed in Table 4.

Rule 2. To determine total daily consumption of hot water, divide the result of Rule 1 by 3.

Rule 3. To determine the maximum probable hourly demand for hot water, divide the total daily hot water consumption (from Rule 2) by 10.

Rule 4. To determine the average hourly demand for hot water, divide the total daily consumption of hot water (from Rule 2) by 24.

In lieu of the above calculations, Table 8 gives hot water consumption figures obtained from surveys of actual buildings.

HEATER CAPACITY

Domestic hot water is commonly considered as cold water whose temperature has been raised 100°F. The average temperature difference is between 40° and 140°F. Heater ratings are based on the number of square feet of steam or hot water radiation required to raise the temperature of 1 gal of water 100°F (see Table 5).

Steam boiler rating: One sq ft of steam radiation is equal to 240 Btu, and 833 Btu are required to raise the temperature of 1 gal of water 100°. Therefore 833/240 (or 3.5) sq ft of equivalent direct steam radiation (EDR) would be required to accomplish that result.

Hot water boiler rating: One sq ft of hot water radiation is equal to 150 Btu (833 Btu are required to raise the temperature of 1 gal of water 100°F). Therefore 833/150 (5.6) sq ft of hot water radiation would be required to accomplish that result.

Table 4.   Cold water consumption

Type of Building	Gals. per person per day
Residence, Average	50
" Large	100
Apartments, Low-rent	75
" High-class	100
Hotels	100
Office Buildings	25

Rule 5. To find required capacity of hot water heater in terms of equivalent direct radiation (EDR) per hour:

For a steam boiler, multiply the average hourly demand for hot water (Rule 4) by 3.5. This gives a one-hour rating. For a two-hour rating, multiply by 1.75.

For a hot water heater, multiply the average hourly demand for hot water (Rule 4) by 5.6. This, also, is a one-hour rating. (For a two-hour rating, multiply by 2.8.)

STORAGE TANK CAPACITY

With the hourly demand for hot water determined, storage requirements can be quickly estimated. To ensure hot water at all faucets, it is customary to assume that only 75 per cent of the tank capacity will be available as hot water. Thus tanks should be oversized by 25 per cent of the calculated storage requirements.

Rule 6. To determine hourly storage requirements for hot water, subtract the average hourly demand (supplied by heater) from the probable maximum hourly demand (Rule 3 minus Rule 4). Then divide by 0.75.

If using hourly consumptions (Table 8), provide 1/3 storage and 2/3 heating.

Summary example

Suppose that an apartment building contains 50 bedrooms and is to be heated with a steam boiler plant. What will be the required size of the hot water storage tank, and what additional capacity must the boiler have to meet requirements for domestic hot water?

Total cold water consumption

$$50 \times 200 = 10,000 \text{ gal}$$
$$\text{For peak} \quad +50\% = 5,000$$
$$\text{Total} \quad = 15,000 \text{ gal}$$

Total hot water consumption

$$15,000 \div 3 = 5,000 \text{ gal}$$

Maximum probable hourly demand

$$5,000 \div 10 = 500 \text{ gal}$$

Average hourly demand

$$5,000 \div 24 = 208 \text{ gal}$$

Required tank capacity on an hourly rating

$$\frac{500 - 208}{0.75} = 389 \text{ gal}$$

Additional boiler capacity required

$$208 \times 3.5 = 728 \text{ sq ft EDR}$$

In selecting a standard-sized tank to meet calculated storage requirements, choose one that slightly exceeds those figures rather than one that falls just short (see Table 7).

Table 5.   Equivalent direct radiation loads for heating domestic hot water

HOT WATER	REQUIRED HEATING CAPACITY	
Max. Probable Hourly Demand in Gallons	Sq. Ft. Radiation Required— Steam	Sq. Ft. Radiation Required— Hot Water
10	35	56
20	70	112
30	105	168
40	140	224
50	175	280
60	210	324
70	245	392
80	280	448
90	315	504
100	350	560
150	525	840
200	700	1120
250	875	1400
300	1050	1680
350	1225	1960
400	1400	2240
450	1575	2520
500	1750	2800
550	1925	3080
600	2100	3240
650	2275	3520
700	2450	3920
750	2625	4200
800	2800	4480
850	2975	4760
900	3150	5040
950	3325	5320
1000	3500	5600

Table 6. Range boilers

Capacity in gals.	Diameter	Length
18	1'-0"	3'-0"
24	1'-0"	4'-0"
30	1'-0"	5'-0"
32	1'-2"	4'-0"
40	1'-0"	5'-0"
42	1'-4"	4'-0"
52	1'-4"	5'-0"
66	1'-6"	5'-0"
82	1'-8"	5'-0"
100	1'-10"	5'-0"
120	2'-0"	5'-0"
144	2'-0"	6'-0"
192	2'-0"	8'-0"

Tanks are vertical.

Standard pressure is 85 lbs. per sq. in.

Extra-heavy pressure is 150 lbs. per sq. in.

Table 8. Hot water consumption in apartment buildings*

	Public housing, gal	Apt.-hotel, gal
Average daily		
per apartment	79	59
per person	28	41
per room	22	36
Maximum daily		
per apartment	92	69
per person	33	48
per room	26	43
Maximum hourly		
per apartment	8.9	7.6
per person	3.2	5.3
per room	2.5	4.9
Average of 4 peak hours		
per apartment	7.1	7.8
per person	2.5	5.0
per room	2.0	3.0

Allow 0.4 gal per hr per person for hot water consumption in office buildings and 1.0 gal per hr per meal in cafeterias.

Table 7. Hot water storage tanks

Average capacity, gal	48	60	72	84	96	108	120	132	144	156	168	180	192	Average weight, lb
89	24													1,514
112		24												1,830
136			24											2,154
159				24										2,470
179	30													2,510
210		30												2,918
252			30											3,442
289				30										3,924
298		36												3,948
326					30									4,362
351			36											4,563
362						30								4,800
402		42												5,037
404				36										5,178
457					36									5,793
474			42											5,834
510						36								6,408
545				42										6,623
562							36							7,023
614			48											7,801
615								36						7,630
617					42									7,421
690						42								8,727
708				48										8,866
762							42							9,025
802					48									9,851
833								42						9,325
889			54											10,175
896						48								10,837
905									42					9,625
977										42				9,925
990							48							11,862
1,005				54										11,325
1,049											42			10,225
1,084								48						12,917
1,120												42		10,525
1,124					54									13,279
1,178									48					13,942
1,234				60										14,500
1,243						54								14,530
1,272										48				14,958
1,362							54							15,755
1,366											48			15,983
1,381					60									16,312
1,460												48		17,018
1,481								54						17,022
1,528						60								17,912
1,600										54				18,280
1,675							60							19,502

Average capacity, gal	120	132	144	156	168	180	192	Average weight, lb
1,720						54		20,780
1,822		60						21,102
1,839							54	21,764
1,958	72							22,000
1,969					60			22,743
2,116						60		24,343
2,170		72						25,000
2,263							60	25,900
2,381			72					26,500
2,593				72				30,000
2,804					72			32,500
3,016						72		35,000
3,203			84					36,500
3,227							72	36,800
3,491				84				37,000
3,778					84			41,900
4,066						84		46,000
4,134			96					48,000
4,354							84	49,500
4,510				96				50,500
4,886					96			51,500
5,262						96		55,900
5,638							96	60,200

The trend in modern hospitals and laboratories is toward central systems to supply oxygen, vacuum, nitrous oxide, and compressed air. With the use of the tables on the following pages, central systems for these special services can be properly designed.

OXYGEN

Oxygen contained in a cylinder is in liquid form; when released to atmospheric pressure, it becomes a gas. Although the gas is nonflammable, it is dangerous to handle because it supports combustion vigorously and can cause the slightest glow to erupt into an inferno. (For methods of installing oxygen systems, consult the National Fire Protection Association, Pamphlet No. 565.)

The oxygen system may be supplied from either a bulk supply or a cylinder manifold. Each should include both a normal service supply and an adequate reserve supply, which would become available automatically when the service supply was exhausted. Gas suppliers should be consulted on the type of storage most economical for a particular installation, considering the volume of gas to be used and the location of the installation. A bulk storage should not be located within 50 ft of any structure.

A low-pressure alarm should be installed where the supply line from the bulk storage or cylinder manifold enters the building. This alarm, signaling a loss of pressure in the supply line (that is, a leak), should be both visual and audible.

From that point, a copper tubing header—Type K, with silver soldered fittings—should supply all oxygen risers and outlets.

Each floor to be equipped for oxygen therapy should be served by more than one riser, so that if the supply to one riser is shut off, the entire floor will not be deprived of oxygen, and the patients can be moved to other rooms on the same floor for continuation of their oxygen therapy.

The size of the piping is usually determined by the length of piping required from the supply to the farthest outlet. It should be noted, however, that the piping for a particular outlet closer to the supply could be sized on the basis of its own length, although generally this would not substantially reduce the over-all cost of the system.

Having determined the over-all distance, and assuming a pressure drop of 2 psi, we can refer to Table 9 for a direct reading of the number of liters of oxygen that a given pipe can deliver per minute.

Operating rooms, recovery rooms, and delivery rooms should all be supplied directly from the main, with a shut-off valve outside each room. The supplies for patients' rooms must be zoned by valves, which should be located in boxes with break-glass fronts, in order to eliminate the possibility of their being shut off by unauthorized persons. Valves can be either the packless diaphragm type or the Neoprene "O" ring cock type. The diaphragm type is preferable because it provides a positive shut-off.

Riser control valves and valves 1 in. or more in diameter must be specially packed for oxygen service and must be free of oil. All piping in the system must be washed with a solution of trisodium phosphate to remove all grease before oxygen is admitted to the system.

NITROUS OXIDE

All the statements made in reference to oxygen apply to a nitrous oxide installation with the exception of the bulk storage. Because of the small quantities of gas involved, the system manifold can be located within the building in a fireproof room. Table 10 can be used for sizing nitrous oxide piping.

COMPRESSED AIR SYSTEMS

Compressed air for use in laboratories must be oil free and cooled. The pumps for this system may be either rotary or reciprocating. If a reciprocating pump is used, an aftercooler is required to reduce the temperature of the compressed gas. The units should be lubricated by carbon rings in order to eliminate oil particles in the compressed gas.

A receiver is also required in a compressed air installaltion, and the supply header from the receiver must be provided with an air filter. (See Table 11 for pipe sizes and capacities.)

VACUUM

A high vacuum is rarely required, since even a 15-in. (mercury column) vacuum can damage skin tissue. It is the quantity, not the pressure, that is most important.

In this system also, sizing is determined by the pressure drop required and the length of the longest run (see Table 12). The vacuum pumps are sized for the peak draw; duplex pumps should be used to ensure a continuous source of supply. If the units required become too large for one pump, then two-thirds of the total capacity should be placed in each of two pumps. The pumps evacuate a receiving tank to which the vacuum header is connected. The exhaust from the pumps should discharge to the outside air, and should be provided with a silencer.

Pumps may be either rotary vane or reciprocating. Care must be taken in the location and installation of reciprocating pumps, however, because they are noisy and require a large foundation to prevent vibration and movement. The receiving tank should be hot-dipped galvanized steel, because condensation will form and collect in it.

Pressure switches for the motor starters should be mounted directly on the receiver, with only a wire running from the pressure switch to the starter, to ensure a continuous vacuum supply.

EXAMPLES

Oxygen: Assume that a line is to supply 60 oxygen outlets, with a developed length of 250 ft from the source to the farthest outlet. The piping being used is Type K copper tubing, and the allowable pressure drop is 2 psi. The required capacity can be expressed as follows: 60 outlets times 10 liters per min per outlet times 40 per cent diversity, or 240 liters per min.

In Table 9 we look opposite 277 ft under the column for ¾-in. K and find 212 liters per min, which is too small; under 1-in. K we find 450, which is ample even after deducting the percentage for fittings. Hence, the line should be 1 in. in size. If screw pipe were to be used, we would select the appropriate column marked "P," and if Type TP copper tubing were to be used, we would select a column marked "B".

Compressed Air: Assume that there is an outlet pressure of 40 psi, 1,000 ft of pipe, and an allowable pressure loss of 22 psi. In Table 11, in the column for 40 psi, we read down to 22, and then across, to find that a 1-in. black steel pipe of this length can supply 59 cfm, a 3-in. pipe can supply 1,020 cfm, and so on. Knowing the quantity required, we can easily select the proper pipe size.

Table 9. Capacity of oxygen piping

Quantities listed are for pressure drops of 1 in. and 55.36 in. (or 2 psi) of water (at specific gravity 1.105). Assume 10 liters per minute per outlet. Deduct 10 per cent from listed quantities for friction loss due to valves and fittings. Diversity factor (percentage of simultaneous use) is 40 to 100 (see Table 11). Key: P = IPS threaded brass pipe; B = Type TP copper tubing; K = Type K copper tubing.

Capacity, liters per minute

Length of pipe, ft	Pressure drop, in. H₂O	3/8 P	3/8 B	3/8 K	1/2 P	1/2 B	1/2 K	3/4 P	3/4 B	3/4 K	1 P	1 B	1 K	1¼ P	1¼ B	1¼ K	1½ P	1½ B	1½ K	2 P	2 B	2 K	2½ P	2½ B	2½ K	3 P	3 B	3 K	4 P	4 B	4 K
55.36	1																														
50	0.9	177	230	105	310	445	205	640	840	505	1210	1580	1050	2300	3120	1750	3350	4200	2800	6400	7820	5700	10500	13000	9800						
55	1.0	165	212	100	290	420	193	610	800	480	1160	1490	980	2150	2850	1650	3200	3950	2650	6000	7400	5400	9800	12500	9100						
111	2.0	118	155	70	210	300	138	435	580	335	820	1050	700	1520	2080	1200	2250	2820	1900	4300	5400	3800	6900	8800	6500	11200	14400	10000			
166	3.0	98	125	58	170	245	112	352	470	276	670	870	580	1250	1700	980	1850	2350	1530	3500	4250	3100	5700	7200	5200	9000	11800	8300			
221	4.0	84	110	50	148	212	98	310	400	240	580	760	500	1100	1480	850	1600	2010	1320	3050	3720	2700	5000	6300	4650	7900	10000	7200			
277	5.0	75	98	45	133	192	89	275	360	212	515	680	450	980	1300	760	1440	1800	1180	2720	3350	2410	4200	5500	4125	7000	9100	6400			
332	6.0	68	89	41	122	172	80	252	330	196	490	620	405	900	1200	700	1320	1650	1100	2500	3050	2200	4050	5050	3750	6400	8100	5900			
388	7.0	63	83	38	112	160	75	235	305	182	440	580	375	840	1110	640	1220	1530	1010	2320	2820	2080	3710	4650	3500	6000	7600	5450			
443	8.0	60	78	35	103	150	70	220	285	170	415	540	350	780	1050	610	1140	1450	960	2150	2650	1920	3500	4400	3250	5500	7100	5100			
498	9.0	56	74	33	98	142	65	205	265	161	382	500	330	730	960	566	1080	1350	900	2030	2500	1850	3300	4080	3050	5200	6700	4800			
554	10	53	69	32	94	135	62	196	255	153	375	480	316	700	930	540	1020	1280	860	1910	2350	1725	3150	3900	2900	5000	6400	4600	9900	11800	9300
1107	20	38	50	28	68	96	44	138	182	108	265	340	225	500	670	380	740	920	605	1360	1650	1210	2220	2800	2100	3520	4500	3200	6950	8300	6500
1661	30	31	40	18	55	77	36	113	148	89	218	280	185	400	550	316	595	730	490	1120	1380	1000	1850	2300	1720	2900	3720	2650	5800	6800	5400

Pipe size, in. — column groups: 3/8, 1/2, 3/4, 1, 1¼, 1½, 2, 2½, 3, 4

Table 10. Capacity of nitrous oxide piping

Quantities listed are for pressure drops of 1 in. and 55.36 in. (or 2 psi) of water (at specific gravity 1.522). Assume 10 liters per minute per outlet. Deduct 10 per cent from listed quantities for friction loss due to valves and fittings. Diversity factor (percentage of simultaneous use) is 100. Key: P = IPS threaded brass pipe; B = Type TP copper tubing; K = Type K copper tubing.

Capacity, liters per minute

Length of pipe, ft	Pressure drop, in. H₂O	3/8 P	3/8 B	3/8 K	1/2 P	1/2 B	1/2 K	3/4 P	3/4 B	3/4 K	1 P	1 B	1 K	1¼ P	1¼ B	1¼ K	1½ P	1½ B	1½ K	2 P	2 B	2 K	2½ P	2½ B	2½ K	3 P	3 B	3 K	4 P	4 B	4 K
55.36	1																														
22	0.4	242	308	145	435	580	285	870	1150	680	1620	2180	1400	3050	4150	2420	4600	5900	3710	8200	10600	7600									
28	0.5	212	275	128	380	520	251	770	1020	600	1480	1920	1250	2720	3720	2120	4080	5300	3340	7400	9500	6700									
33	0.6	197	252	118	355	500	230	700	930	545	1320	1725	1140	2510	3400	1950	3710	4850	3050	6700	8600	6200									
39	0.7	182	230	108	327	445	210	650	860	500	1230	1600	1050	2320	3160	1820	3450	4500	2820	6210	8000	5600	10500	13000	9700						
44	0.8	170	218	100	302	417	200	608	810	470	1150	1520	970	2120	2920	1700	3260	4150	2650	5800	7400	5300	9800	12200	9100						
50	0.9	161	202	96	285	390	188	562	760	442	1090	1420	930	2050	2750	1600	3050	3900	2450	5420	7000	5000	9300	11400	8500						
55	1.0	151	195	91	270	375	176	550	725	420	1020	1350	883	1910	2600	1510	2860	3720	2320	5100	6700	4700	8800	10800	8000						
111	2.0	108	138	64	192	262	123	383	510	298	722	960	620	1350	1820	1060	2050	2600	1630	3620	4800	3320	6200	7800	5600	10100	12500	9100			
166	3.0	87	112	51	158	215	101	312	417	242	590	780	501	1120	1520	870	1630	2110	1350	2950	3800	2700	5000	6300	4650	8300	10200	7300			
221	4.0	75	97	45	135	185	89	271	355	210	510	662	435	960	1290	745	1450	1820	1160	2550	3300	2320	4320	5500	4000	7200	8800	6350			
277	5.0	68	87	40	122	165	79	243	318	188	450	600	388	860	1150	680	1280	1650	1050	2260	2950	2100	3850	4850	3520	6500	7900	5500			
332	6.0	61	79	37	110	151	77	220	290	171	418	510	355	780	1050	620	1160	1520	950	2100	2700	1900	3520	4450	3250	5900	7200	5200	11300	13500	10400
388	7.0	56	72	34	102	140	66	203	270	158	383	462	328	720	950	562	1070	1380	890	1910	2500	1760	3250	4100	3000	5420	6700	4800	10500	12500	9600

Pipe size, in. — column groups: 3/8, 1/2, 3/4, 1, 1¼, 1½, 2, 2½, 3, 4

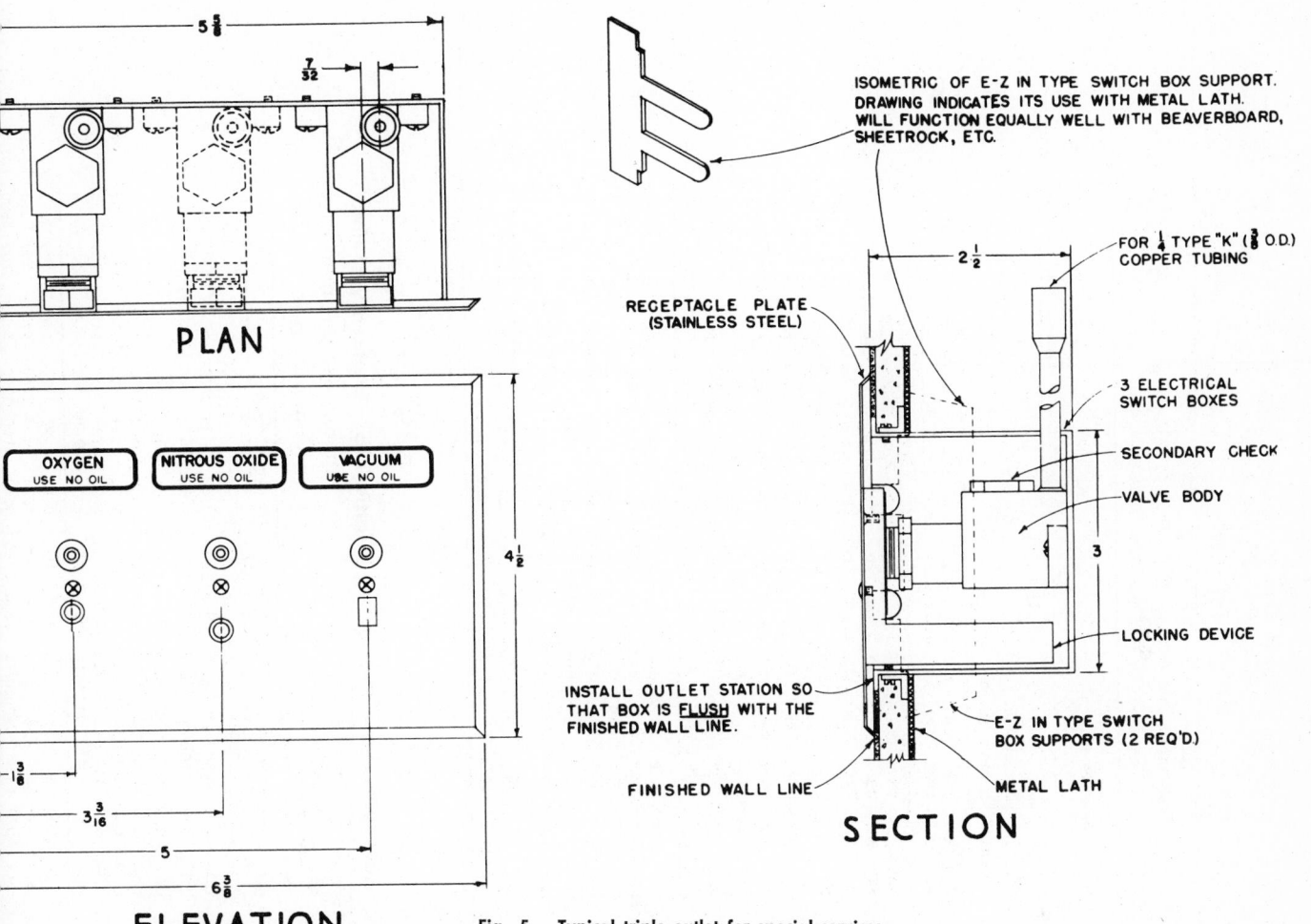

PLAN

ISOMETRIC OF E-Z IN TYPE SWITCH BOX SUPPORT. DRAWING INDICATES ITS USE WITH METAL LATH. WILL FUNCTION EQUALLY WELL WITH BEAVERBOARD, SHEETROCK, ETC.

RECEPTACLE PLATE (STAINLESS STEEL)

FOR $\frac{1}{4}$ TYPE "K" ($\frac{3}{8}$ O.D.) COPPER TUBING

3 ELECTRICAL SWITCH BOXES

SECONDARY CHECK

VALVE BODY

LOCKING DEVICE

INSTALL OUTLET STATION SO THAT BOX IS FLUSH WITH THE FINISHED WALL LINE.

E-Z IN TYPE SWITCH BOX SUPPORTS (2 REQ'D)

FINISHED WALL LINE

METAL LATH

OXYGEN USE NO OIL   NITROUS OXIDE USE NO OIL   VACUUM USE NO OIL

ELEVATION

SECTION

Fig. 5.   Typical triple outlet for special services

Table 11.   Capacity of compressed air piping

Quantities are based on IPS steel pipe.

Outlet gauge pressure, psi														Pipe size, in.											
150	125	100	90	80	70	60	50	40	35	30	25	20	15	3/8	1/2	3/4	1	1¼	1½	2	2½	3	4	5	6
Pressure loss, psi per 1000 ft of pipe														Factor for Type K copper tubing in per cent of IPS steel pipe											
														60	64	76	84	77	81	93	93	89	90	90	90
														Capacity, cfm											
0.5	0.6	0.7	0.7	0.8	0.9	1	1.2	1.4	1.6	1.8	2.2	2.6	3.4	1.8	3.2	8.2	15	32	48	92	150	265	540	980	1600
1.0	1.1	1.4	1.5	1.6	1.8	2	2.4	2.9	3.2	3.6	4.3	5.2	6.7	2.5	4.5	11.5	21.5	45	67	130	210	375	770	1380	2300
1.4	1.7	2.0	2.2	2.4	2.7	3	3.6	4.3	4.8	5.5	6.5	7.8	10	3.1	5.5	14.0	26.5	55	82	160	260	460	940	1700	2800
1.9	2.2	2.7	2.9	3.2	3.5	4	4.8	5.7	6.4	7.3	8.6	10.4	13.4	3.5	6.3	16.0	30.5	64	95	185	300	530	1090	1950	3200
2.3	2.7	3.3	3.6	4.0	4.4	5	5.9	7.2	8	9.1	10.8	13	16.8	3.9	8.0	18.0	34	71	108	208	330	600	1200	2160	3600
4.6	5.4	6.6	7.1	7.9	8.8	10	11.8	14.3	16	18.2	21.5	26	34	5.5	10	25.5	48	100	150	290	470	840	1700	3100	5100
6.9	8.1	10	11	12	14	15	18	22	24	28	33	41	50	6.7	12	31	59	122	185	360	570	1020	2100	3700	6200
9.2	11	14	15	16	18	20	24	29	32	37	43	52	67	7.7	14	36	68	142	215	410	660	1180	2450	4300	7200
12	14	17	18	20	22	25	26	36	40	46	54	65	84	8.6	15.8	40	76	158	240	460	720	1320	2730	4420	8000
14	17	20	22	24	27	30	36	43	48	55	65	78	100	9.4	17.2	44	84	172	262	500	800	1450	3000	5300	8800
17	19	24	25	28	31	35	42	50	56	64	76	91	118	10	18.6	48	90	186	285	545	870	1570	3250	5700	9600
19	22	27	29	32	35	40	48	58	64	73	86	104	134	10.8	20	51	96	200	300	580	940	1700	3400	6100	10200
23	27	33	36	40	44	50	59	72	80	91	108	130	168	12	22	57	108	220	340	650	1050	1880	3850	6800	11500
28	33	40	43	48	53	60	71	86	96	110	129	156	201	13	24	62	118	245	375	720	1150	2050	4200	7500	12600
33	38	47	50	56	62	70	83	100	112	128	151	182	235	14	26	67	128	260	400	770	1230	2200	4500	8000	13600
37	44	53	57	64	71	80	95	115	128	146	175	208	268	15	28	72	137	280	430	820	1320	2350	4900	8600	14500
42	49	60	64	72	80	90	107	128	144	164	194	234	302	16	30	76	145	300	460	870	1400	2500	5200	9100	15500
46	54	66	71	79	88	100	118	144	160	182	215	260	340	17	31	80	150	310	480	910	1480	2600	5400	9600	16200

Table 12. Capacity of vacuum piping

Quantities listed are for pressure drops of 1 and 2 in. of mercury (at specific gravity 1.00). Deduct 10 per cent from listed quantities for friction loss due to valves and fittings. Key: P = IPS threaded brass pipe; B = Type TP copper tubing; K = Type K copper tubing.

Capacity, cfm

Length of pipe, ft — Pressure drop, in. Hg (2)	(1)	3/8 P	3/8 B	3/8 K	1/2 P	1/2 B	1/2 K	3/4 P	3/4 B	3/4 K	1 P	1 B	1 K	1¼ P	1¼ B	1¼ K	1½ P	1½ B	1½ K	2 P	2 B	2 K	2½ P	2½ B	2½ K	3 P	3 B	3 K	4 P	4 B	4 K
40	20	8.6	11.2	5.3	15.8	22.0	10.3	31.6	42.3	24.6	60.8	80.0	51.6	113	153	88.3	166	216	140	308	391	283	516	641	483						
60	30	7.2	9.2	4.3	13.0	18.0	8.3	25.8	34.5	20.0	49.1	65.0	41.6	91.6	125	71.6	138	175	113	250	320	233	416	525	391						
80	40	6.2	7.8	3.7	11.3	15.3	7.2	22.5	30.0	17.5	44.1	55.8	36.3	80.0	108	61.6	118	153	98.3	216	278	200	366	450	338	600	733	533			
100	50	5.6	7.0	3.3	10.0	13.5	6.4	20.0	26.4	15.5	38.3	50.0	32.5	70.0	96.6	55.0	106	136	88.3	191	246	176	323	400	300	533	666	475			
120	60	5.0	6.6	3.0	9.2	12.6	5.8	18.3	24.1	14.1	35.0	45.8	29.1	65.0	88.3	50.8	96.6	123	80.0	176	225	161	291	366	276	491	608	433			
140	70	4.7	5.9	2.8	8.5	11.6	5.4	16.6	22.5	13.0	32.0	42.5	27.1	60.0	81.6	46.6	90.0	115	73.3	165	208	150	273	341	256	450	566	400			
160	80	4.3	5.5	2.6	7.8	10.8	5.1	15.6	21.0	12.1	30.0	39.1	25.3	55.8	76.6	43.3	83.3	108	68.3	153	191	140	255	316	236	425	525	375			
180	90	4.1	5.2	2.5	7.5	10.1	4.7	14.8	19.5	11.5	28.3	36.6	24.1	52.5	71.5	41.1	78.3	101	65.0	143	181	131	241	300	225	396	500	350			
200	100	3.8	4.9	2.3	7.0	9.6	4.5	14.0	18.6	10.8	26.6	35.0	22.8	51.6	68.3	39.1	75.0	95.0	61.6	136	173	125	228	283	213	376	475	333			
250	125	3.4	4.4	2.1	6.3	8.6	4.1	12.6	16.6	9.8	24.1	30.8	20.1	44.1	60.0	35.0	66.6	85.0	55.0	121	153	111	203	253	188	333	425	300			
300	150	3.2	4.0	1.9	5.7	7.9	3.6	11.5	15.1	8.8	21.1	28.3	18.5	40.8	55.0	31.6	60.8	78.3	50.0	111	140	103	186	233	173	308	383	271	608	716	550
350	175	2.9	3.8	1.7	5.3	7.3	3.4	10.6	14.0	8.1	20.1	26.3	17.1	37.5	50.8	29.1	55.8	71.6	46.6	103	130	95.0	171	213	160	285	355	250	558	650	508
400	200	2.7	3.5	1.6	5.0	6.8	3.2	10.0	13.1	7.6	19.0	24.6	16.0	35.0	47.5	27.5	52.5	66.6	43.3	96.6	121	88.3	161	200	150	266	333	233	525	616	475
500	250	2.4	3.2	1.5	4.4	6.1	2.9	8.8	11.8	6.8	17.0	22.0	14.3	31.6	42.5	24.5	46.6	60.0	39.1	85.0	108	78.3	143	180	133	238	300	208	466	550	430
600	300	2.2	2.8	1.3	4.0	5.6	2.6	8.1	10.8	6.2	15.3	20.0	13.0	28.3	38.6	22.5	43.3	55.0	35.1	78.3	98.3	71.6	130	163	121	216	271	191	425	500	390
700	350	2.0	2.6	1.2	3.7	5.1	2.4	7.5	9.9	5.7	14.1	18.5	12.0	26.3	35.8	20.8	40.0	50.8	32.8	73.3	91.6	66.6	120	150	113	200	250	178	391	458	363
800	400	1.9	2.4	1.1	3.5	4.8	2.2	7.0	9.3	5.4	13.3	17.3	11.3	24.6	33.3	19.5	36.5	47.5	30.6	68.3	85.0	61.6	113	140	106	188	233	165	366	433	333
1000	500	1.7	2.2	1.0	3.1	4.3	2.0	6.2	8.3	4.8	11.8	15.5	10.0	22.1	30.0	17.1	33.0	44.1	27.0	60.8	76.6	55.0	100	125	93.3	166	208	148	330	383	300
1200	600	1.6	2.0	0.9	2.8	4.1	1.8	5.7	7.5	4.4	10.8	14.1	9.1	20.0	27.3	15.6	30.0	38.8	25.0	55.0	70.0	50.8	91.6	115	86.6	151	190	135	300	350	273

Table 12a. Required capacity of vacuum piping in hospital rooms

Type of room	Capacity, cfm	Per cent of simultaneous use
Laboratories, cystoscopic, and pharmacies	1.0	40
Dental operating rooms	0.5	40
Major operating rooms	2.0	100
Single rooms and wards	1.0	40
Surgical, acute medical, and single rooms for decompression (Tuberculosis hospital)	2.0	100
Surgical recovery and anesthesia rooms	1.0	40
Eye, ear, nose, and throat operating rooms	0.5	40
Broncography (Tuberculosis hospital)	1.0	100

Table 12b. Frequency of simultaneous use per number of vacuum outlets in hospitals

Number of outlets	Per cent
1–2	100
3	90
4–5	80
6	70
7–8	60
9	50
10 or more	40

by GEORGE R. JERUS, P.E.

Associate—Meyer, Strong and Jones, Mechanical and Electrical Engineers

Necessary data for the design of a plumbing drainage system in any building include discharge ratings of individual fixtures as a basis for estimating the probable load that the system must carry. Equally essential is a knowledge of safe limits for the carrying capacities of stacks and vents, gutters and leaders, house drains and horizontal branches.

The discharge ratings for the most commonly used plumbing fixtures are given in Table 1. On the following page are listed the limiting carrying capacities of soil and waste stacks (Table 2); the sizes and maximum lengths of vents in relation to safe carrying capacities of soil and waste pipes (Table 3); and the sizes of gutters in relation to the areas to be drained (Table 4). Data on the capacities of storm, sanitary, and combined house drains, and also house sewers, are given on subsequent pages. (All tables have been extracted from American Standard National Plumbing Code, ASA A40.8—1955, with the permission of the publisher, The American Society of Mechanical Engineers, 345 East 47th Street, New York 17, N.Y.) The values in the tables do not always agree with all current building codes. Where differences exist, local requirements should of course govern. The data can be safely used, however, to establish limiting requirements applicable generally as a basis for drainage system design.

FIXTURE UNIT RATINGS (TABLE 1)

Carrying capacities of drainage pipes are listed in units of fixture discharge that indicate the rate of flow in cubic feet per minute. The unit of discharge flow is called a "fixture unit," and is equivalent to a flow of 1 cfm—the rate of discharge of an ordinary washbasin having a nominal 1¼-in. outlet, trap, and waste.

STACK CAPACITIES (TABLE 2)

The type of fitting used to connect fixtures or horizontal branches to waste and soil stacks has an important influence on the practical capacity of the stack. A stack will take the capacity discharge of two branches of the same diameter as the stack if the fitting is a double 45° Y or a combination Y-and-⅛ bend. Stack capacities are decreased, however, by "sanitary T" fittings.

Limitations of discharge within an 8-ft section of stack—a branch interval—are rarely significant in residential work, but constitute a desirable margin of safety in more extensive installations. In such installations, the discharge through a 45° Y or combination Y-and-⅛ bend should never exceed, within any branch interval, 2½ times the number of fixture units permissible on any one branch of the same diameter, pitched ¼ in. to the foot. Comparable limits for sanitary T fittings in a branch interval are 1½ times the number of fixture units on a branch of similar size and pitch.

Base fittings that connect the lower ends of soil stacks to the house drain may be a size larger than the stack itself, in order to reduce the possibility of back pressure that exists even in small installations. In larger systems, if the house drain is more than one size larger than the stacks, fittings of intermediate size are advisable. For example: in a small system with a 3-in. stack and 4-in. house drain, a 4-in. fitting should be used; in a larger system with a 3-in. stack and 5-in. house drain, a 4-in. fitting can be used as well.

Table 1. Fixture units per fixture or group

Fixture type	Fixture-unit value	Minimum diam of trap, in.*
1 bathroom group (water closet, lavatory, and bathtub or shower stall)	6, 8†	
Bathtub (with or without overhead shower)‡	2	1½
Bathtub‡	3	2
Bidet	3	1½ (nominal)
Combination sink-and-tray	3	1½
Combination sink-and-tray with food-disposal unit	4	1½ (separate traps)
Dental unit or cuspidor	1	1¼
Dental lavatory	1	1¼
Drinking fountain	½	1
Dishwasher, domestic*	2	1½
Floor drains§	1	2
Kitchen sink, domestic	2	1½
Kitchen sink, domestic, with food-waste grinder	3	1½
Lavatory‖	1	1¼ (small P.O.)
Lavatory‖	2	1½ (large P.O.)
Lavatory, for barber or beauty parlor	2	1½
Lavatory, surgeon's	2	1½
Laundry tray (1 or 2 compartments)	2	1½
Shower stall, domestic	2	2
Showers (group), per head*	3	
Sinks:		
Surgeon's	3	1½
Flushing-rim (with valve)	8	3
Service (trap standard)	3	3
Service (P trap)	2	2
Pot or scullery*	4	1½
Urinal, pedestal, siphon jet, blowout	8	3 (nominal)
Urinal, wall-lip	4	1½
Urinal stall, washout	4	2
Urinal trough (each 2-ft section)*	2	1½
Wash sink, circular or multiple (each set of faucets)*	2	1½ (nominal)
Water closet, tank-operated	4	3 (nominal)
Water closet, valve-operated	8	3

See American Standard National Plumbing Code (1955), Par. 11.4.3 and 11.4.4 for method of computing unit value of fixtures not listed in this table or for rating of devices with intermittent flows.

† Bathroom group with tank water closet has fixture unit value of 6, with flush-valve water closet 8.

‡ A shower head over a bathtub does not increase the fixture value.

§ The size of the floor drain is determined by the area of surface water to be drained.

‖ Lavatories with 1¼ or 1½-in. trap have the same load value; larger P.O. plugs have greater flow rate.

Base fittings may be long-sweep ¼ bends with reducing hubs, two Y fittings, or a combination Y-and-⅛ bend. Sanitary T fittings should not be used as base fittings.

In going from a horizontal to a vertical line, a short-turn fitting may be used; but in going from a vertical flow to a horizontal flow, a long-turn fitting must be used. In buildings of any significant height, fixtures should not be connected to the horizontal piping from the base of the stack within 40 pipe diameters from the stack, to prevent back-up of fixtures on the lower floor from back pressure caused by a hydraulic jump in the stack base.

VENT REQUIREMENTS (TABLE 3)

The size and length of vent pipes are directly dependent upon both the size of soil and waste pipes and the volume of discharge for which the waste pipes were designed. Unless adequate venting is assured, the flow of fixture discharges through soil and waste stacks can produce pressure variations in branches that may damage the seals of fixture traps—"blowing" them because of positive or back pressure in lower parts of the system, and siphoning them because of negative pressure in upper parts.

Table 3 lists permissible sizes and lengths for the vent stacks and branch vents necessary to ensure the proper functioning of a drainage system, based on the stack sizes and capacities set forth in Table 2.

Table 3. Maximum length of vents

Diam of soil or waste stack, in.	No. of fixture units connected	1¼	1½	2	2½	3	4	5	6	8
					Maximum length of vent, ft					
1¼	2	30								
1½	8	50	150							
1½	10	30	100							
2	12	30	75	200						
2	20	26	50	150						
2½	42		30	100	300					
3	10		30	100	200	600				
3	30			60	200	500				
3	60			50	80	400				
4	100			35	100	260	1,000			
4	200			30	90	250	900			
4	500			20	70	180	700			
5	200				35	80	350	1,000		
5	500				30	70	300	900		
5	1,100				20	50	200	700		
6	350				25	50	200	400	1,300	
6	620				15	30	125	300	1,100	
6	960					24	100	250	1,000	
6	1,900					20	70	200	700	
8	600						50	150	500	1,300
8	1,400						40	100	400	1,200
8	2,200						30	80	350	1,100
8	3,600						25	60	250	800
10	1,000							75	125	1,000
10	2,500							50	100	500
10	3,800							30	80	350
10	5,600							25	60	250

Table 2. Maximum number of fixture units for horizontal fixture branches and stacks

Diam of pipe, in.	Any horizontal fixture branch*	One stack of 3 stories in height or 3 intervals	More than 3 stories in height	
			Total for stack	Total at one story or branch interval
1¼	1	2	2	1
1½	3	4	8	2
2	6	10	24	6
2½	12	20	42	9
3	20†	30‡	60‡	16†
4	160	240	500	90
5	360	540	1,100	200
6	620	960	1,900	350
8	1,400	2,200	3,600	600
10	2,500	3,800	5,600	1,000
12	3,900	6,000	8,400	1,500
15	7,000			

Does not include branches of the building drain.
† Not over two water closets.
‡ Not over six water closets.

Table 4. Size of gutters

Diam of gutter,* in.	Maximum projected roof area in sq ft for gutters of various slopes			
	1/16-in. slope	1/8-in. slope	1/4-in. slope	1/2-in. slope
3	170	240	340	480
4	360	510	720	1,020
5	625	880	1,250	1,770
6	960	1,360	1,920	2,770
7	1,380	1,950	2,760	3,900
8	1,990	2,800	3,980	5,600
10	3,600	5,100	7,200	10,000

Gutter sizes are based on semicircular sheet-metal shapes. Other shapes may be used if they have an equivalent cross-sectional area.

Table 5. Maximum number of fixture units for any portion* of building drain or sewer

Diam of pipe, in.	Fall per ft			
	1/16-in.	1/8-in.	1/4-in.	1/2-in.
2			21	26
2½			24	31
3		20†	27†	36†
4		180	216	250
5		390	480	575
6		700	840	1,000
8	1,400	1,600	1,920	2,300
10	2,500	2,900	3,500	4,200
12	3,900	4,600	5,600	6,700
15	7,000	8,300	10,000	12,000

Includes branches of the building drain.
† *Not over two water closets.*

Table 6. Size of vertical leaders

Size of leader or conductor,* in.	Maximum projected roof area, sq ft
2	720
2½	1,300
3	2,200
4	4,600
5	8,650
6	13,500
8	29,000

The equivalent diameter of a square or rectangular leader may be taken as the diameter of the circle that can be inscribed within the cross-sectional area of the leader.

Table 7. Size of horizontal storm drains

Diam of drain, in.	Maximum projected roof area in sq ft for drains of various slopes		
	1/8-in. slope	1/4-in. slope	1/2-in. slope
3	822	1,160	1,644
4	1,880	2,650	3,760
5	3,340	4,720	6,680
6	5,350	7,550	10,700
8	11,500	16,300	23,000
10	20,700	29,200	41,400
12	33,300	47,000	66,600
15	59,500	84,000	119,000

Tabular data on this and the following page list limiting capacities for sanitary house drains, and storm drains, for slopes of 1/8 in., 1/4 in., and 1/2 in. per ft. Figure 1 gives limiting capacities for combined sanitary and storm house drains and house sewers in terms of the sanitary load in fixture units and the drainage area in square feet.

As previously noted, this material may not conform to some detailed provisions of various local building codes. It is generally applicable, however, as a basis for preliminary estimation in establishing safe limitations for drainage system design.

Capacities of house drains

Pipe capacities have been taken into account in determining the allowable maximum drainage loads. These loads have been expressed in fixture units, to allow for the probability of coincident and overlapping discharges of plumbing fixtures, and are based on mathematical calculation applied to documented experience.

SANITARY HOUSE DRAINS

The required size of a sanitary house drain for a given drainage load can be read directly from Table 5.

Rule 1. Determine total drainage requirements in fixture units (total discharge in cubic feet per minute) from values in Table 1.

Rule 2. Establish pitch of drain. Minimum pitch is 1/8 in. per ft, particularly in small installations; a lesser pitch would increase the possibility of fouling. Generally a 1/4-in. pitch is preferred.

Rule 3. Select the required pipe diameter from Table 5. The proper sizes for both a sanitary house sewer and a branch of the sanitary house drain not receiving discharge from fixtures on its own floor or level can be similarly determined from Table 5.

Table 5 is based on gravity flow in drains one-half full, since full practical capacity is reached at approximately that point because of trapped air.

STORM DRAINS

Tables 6 and 7 for leaders and storm drains are based upon gravity flow in a full pipe and a maximum rate of rainfall of 4 in. per hr. Required sizes can be read directly from the tables.

Rule 1. Determine drainage requirements in square feet of the horizontal projection of the area to be drained.

Rule 2. Select size of vertical leaders from Table 6.

Rule 3. Establish pitch of drain.

Rule 4. Determine required pipe diameter from Table 7.

Rule 5. To modify table if necessary to meet local conditions of rainfall, multiply each given drained area by 4/X, with X the prevailing rate of rainfall in inches per hour.

COMBINED HOUSE DRAINS OR HOUSE SEWERS

By reference to the chart (Fig. 1), the required sizes of combined sanitary and storm house drains, house sewers, and their branches can be determined.

Rule 1. Determine the horizontal projection of the drainage area and the number of fixture units to be carried by the drain.

Rule 2. Establish pitch of drain. Preferred minimum is 1/4 in. per ft; absolute minimum is 1/8 in. per ft.

Rule 3. Find the required minimum diameter of the combined drain in Fig. 1, where the selected pitch curves through or closest above the coordinate point of the drainage area and the number of fixture units to be carried by the drain.

Wherever sewage is treated, in either a private disposal system or a central plant, storm water must be excluded; hence, combined sewers cannot be used. In view of the increasing prevalence of sewage treatment, it would probably be wise to provide separate storm drains and house sewers within the building, even though they are to be connected to a combined public sewer. Then, if separate public sewers are installed at some future date, the new connections can be made with a minimum of expense and inconvenience to the occupants of the building.

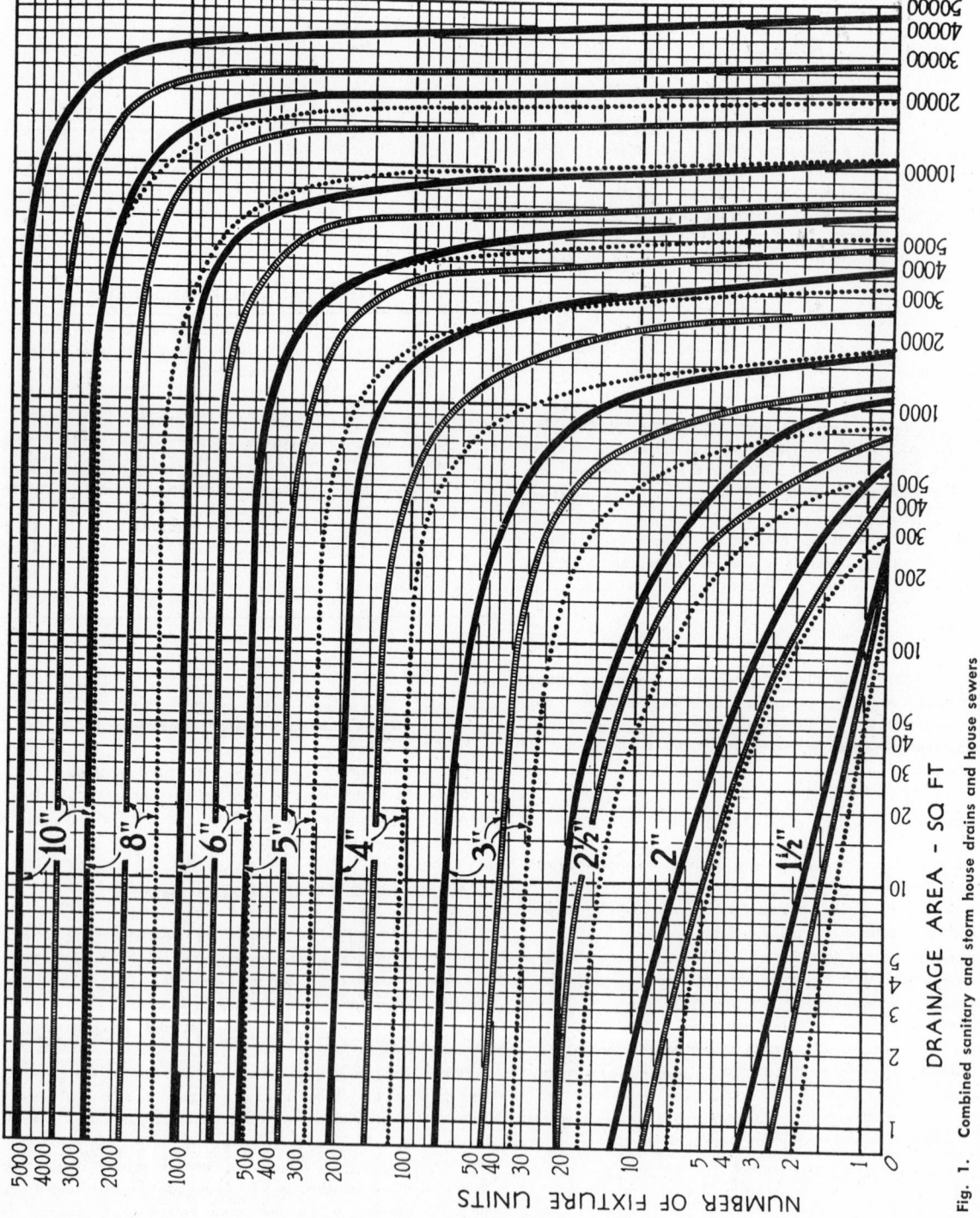

Fig. 1.   Combined sanitary and storm house drains and house sewers

Diagrams on this sheet illustrate various types of plumbing details applicable to both residential and commercial buildings. Because of the wide variance in plumbing regulations throughout the country, some of these diagrammatic details may be prohibited in certain localities; other details may indicate methods far in excess of mandatory requirements in other localities. All of them, however, reflect solutions to typical drainage problems by methods that generally constitute good plumbing practice.

RESIDENTIAL DRAINAGE SYSTEMS

The pipe sizes shown in Fig. 2 will meet every requirement usually encountered in residential work. A 3-in. main soil stack is adequate for residential use in the opinion of many authorities; a 4-in. main soil stack is mandatory, however, in some localities. Main house drains should never be less than 4 in. If house sewers are connected to the septic tank of a private sewage disposal system, no house trap or fresh air inlet is necessary.

COMMERCIAL DRAINAGE SYSTEMS

Figure 3 shows a composite of drainage problems encountered in a wide range of commercial and industrial work; the installations are not typical for any specific kind of building. As in the house sections, soil and waste lines are shown solid; vent lines are broken.

Group A: Bathroom unit is rated at 6 fixture units, individually vented and connected by preferred methods to main soil and vent stacks.

Group B: Bathroom unit is rated at 7 fixture units, individually vented and connected by the preferred method to a horizontal soil branch.

Loop vent, A, and *circuit vent, B,* are both types of venting in which the branch drain is a "double-duty" pipe carrying both air and discharge. The use of this pipe constitutes "wet-venting," prohibited by some codes. It is generally not a desirable method of venting. If used, circuit or loop vents should not be connected to a group of more than 8 fixtures in series. In a loop vent, a continuation of the branch runs up and over the fixtures to connect with the vent stack adjacent to the main soil. In a circuit vent, the connection is to a main vent stack opposite the main soil stack.

Yoke vent, C, connects the main soil and waste stacks, with the soil at the lower end of the yoke. The connection of fixtures as at C adds greatly to the safe capacity of soil stacks. This type of connection can be made to bathroom units in residential as well as commercial work.

Bow vent, D, can be used for light discharge loads to avoid installation of an additional vent stack.

Stacks 1 and *2* indicate the need for separate venting of the sewage ejector and the oil separator from garage drains. The vent from a pneumatic sewage ejector should not be joined to any other pipe; sewage pumps do not require any special considerations.

Stack 3 is the vent from an indirect waste line discharging into a cast-iron sink. Its fixtures must be trapped. If an indirect waste line is over 100 ft in developed length, it should be extended through the roof.

Stacks 4, 5, and *6:* The vents should be connected into these stacks at their lower ends, so that discharge will scour the connection and thus prevent fouling. Such a connection is specifically required for cast iron because of scaling.

Stack 10 applies to a special-purpose type of installation. Corrosive wastes require acid-proof pipe for waste, soil, and vent lines, for fittings, and for the house drain up to the base fitting of the next main soil stack.

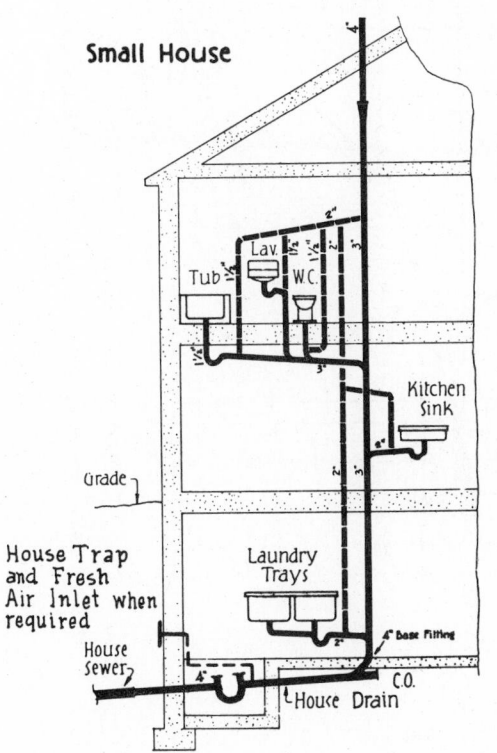

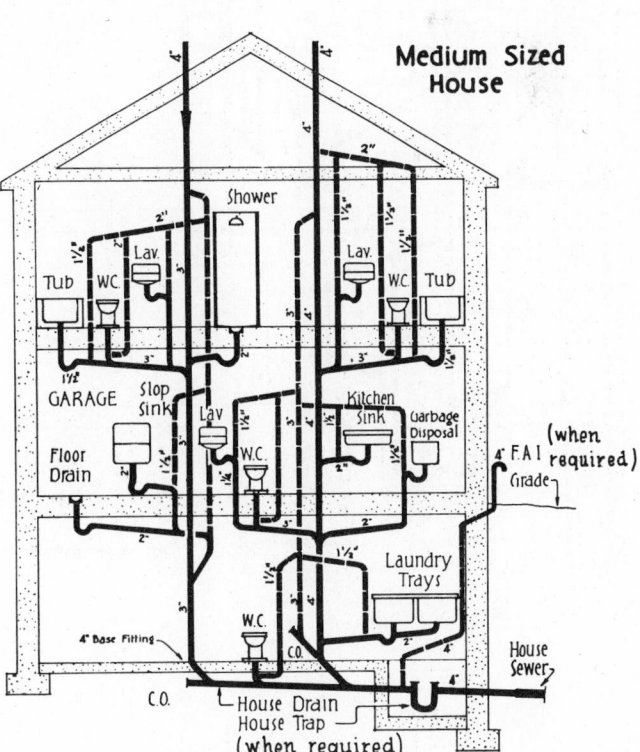

Fig. 2.   Residential drainage systems

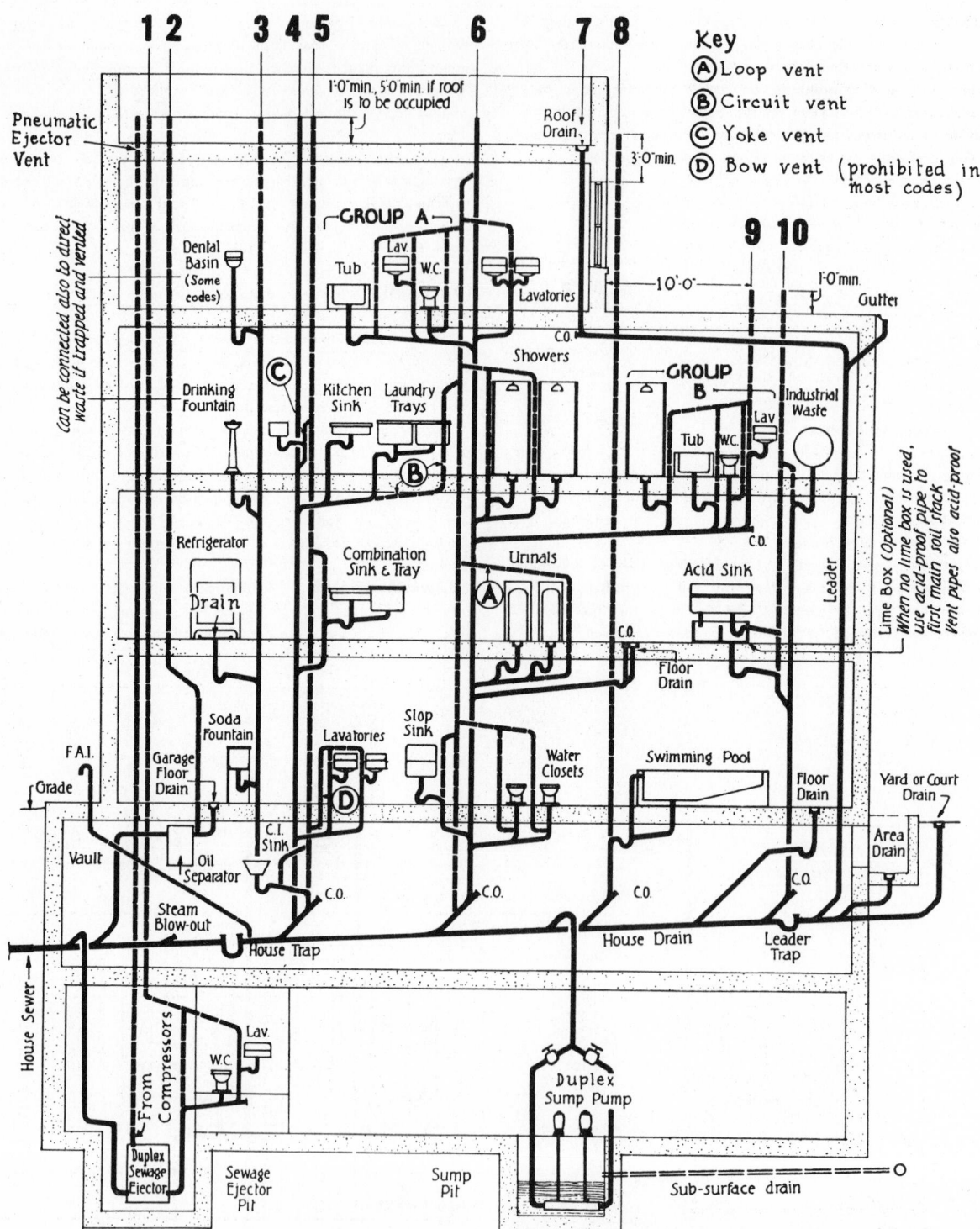

Fig. 3. Drainage systems for commercial buildings

PURPOSE

Data on this and the following pages indicate limiting dimensions of cast-iron or malleable-iron fittings most commonly employed in building drainage systems. Clearances necessary for concealed cast-iron fittings often determine the depth of floors, walls, or furred spaces in which they are housed. Therefore, these dimensions are safe maxima when space for pipe installations is a factor governing design.

Hub and spigot fittings are used with cast-iron or wrought-iron pipe and require a lead-caulked joint. Recessed-threaded fittings should be used preferably with wrought-iron or steel pipe, although threaded cast iron is available for verticle soil and vent lines.

Copper is also available for drainage piping, but, because of the wide variety of fittings, the manufacturers' catalogs should be consulted.

The proper weight classifications are designated in the tables by 'XH' (extra heavy) and 'SV' (service weight). Unless otherwise noted, dimension X in the tables indicates the laying length.

⅛ bend offset (Tables 8–12)

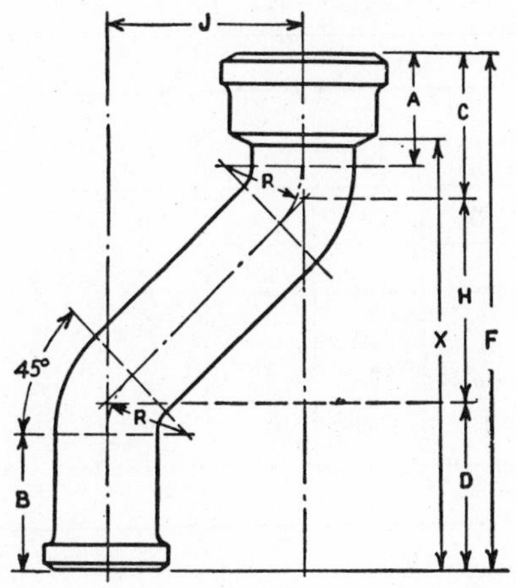

Table 8. ⅛ bend offset, 2-inch

Size (inches)	Dimensions in inches									Weight (pounds)	
	A	B	C	D	F	H	J	R	X	'XH'	'SV'
2 by 2	2¾	3½	3½	4¼	9¾	2	2	2	7¼	5	4½
2 by 4	2¾	3½	3½	4¼	11¾	4	4	2	9¼	6	5
2 by 6	2¾	3½	3½	4¼	13¾	6	6	2	11¼	8	6½
2 by 8	2¾	3½	3½	4¼	15¾	8	8	2	13¼	9	7¼
2 by 10	2¾	3½	3½	4¼	17¾	10	10	2	15¼	10	8
2 by 12	2¾	3½	3½	4¼	19¾	12	12	2	17¼	11	9
2 by 14	2¾	3½	3½	4¼	21¾	14	14	2	19¼	12	9¾
2 by 16	2¾	3½	3½	4¼	23¾	16	16	2	21¼	13	10½
2 by 18	2¾	3½	3½	4¼	25¾	18	18	2	23¼	14	11
2 by 20	2¾	3½	3½	4¼	27¾	20	20	2	25¼	15	12
2 by 22	2¾	3½	3½	4¼	29¾	22	22	2	27¼	16	13
2 by 24	2¾	3½	3½	4¼	31¾	24	24	2	29¼	17	13½

Table 9. ⅛ bend offset, 3-inch

Size (inches)	Dimensions in inches									Weight (pounds)	
	A	B	C	D	F	H	J	R	X	'XH'	'SV'
3 by 2	3¼	4	4¼	5	11¼	2	2	2½	8½	10	7
3 by 4	3¼	4	4¼	5	13¼	4	4	2½	10½	12	8
3 by 6	3¼	4	4¼	5	15¼	6	6	2½	12½	14	9½
3 by 8	3¼	4	4¼	5	17¼	8	8	2½	14½	16	11
3 by 10	3¼	4	4¼	5	19¼	10	10	2½	16½	18	12
3 by 12	3¼	4	4¼	5	21¼	12	12	2½	18½	20	13½
3 by 14	3¼	4	4¼	5	23¼	14	14	2½	20½	22	15
3 by 16	3¼	4	4¼	5	25¼	16	16	2½	22½	24	16
3 by 18	3¼	4	4¼	5	27¼	18	18	2½	24½	26	17½
3 by 20	3¼	4	4¼	5	29¼	20	20	2½	26½	27	18
3 by 22	3¼	4	4¼	5	31¼	22	22	2½	28½	29	19½
3 by 24	3¼	4	4¼	5	33¼	24	24	2½	30½	31	21

Table 10. ⅛ bend offset, 4-inch

Size (inches)	Dimensions in inches									Weight (pounds)	
	A	B	C	D	F	H	J	R	X	'XH'	'SV'
4 by 2	3½	4	4¾	5¼	12	2	2	3	9	14	10
4 by 4	3½	4	4¾	5¼	14	4	4	3	11	16	11
4 by 6	3½	4	4¾	5¼	16	6	6	3	13	19	13
4 by 8	3½	4	4¾	5¼	18	8	8	3	15	21	14
4 by 10	3½	4	4¾	5¼	20	10	10	3	17	24	16
4 by 12	3½	4	4¾	5¼	22	12	12	3	19	26	18
4 by 14	3½	4	4¾	5¼	24	14	14	3	21	29	20
4 by 16	3½	4	4¾	5¼	26	16	16	3	23	31	21
4 by 18	3½	4	4¾	5¼	28	18	18	3	25	34	23
4 by 20	3½	4	4¾	5¼	30	20	20	3	27	36	24
4 by 22	3½	4	4¾	5¼	32	22	22	3	29	39	26
4 by 24	3½	4	4¾	5¼	34	24	24	3	31	41	28

Table 11. ⅛ bend offset, 5-inch

Size (inches)	Dimensions in inches									Weight (pounds)	
	A	B	C	D	F	H	J	R	X	'XH'	'SV'
5 by 2	3½	4⅛	4¹⁵⁄₁₆	5⁹⁄₁₆	12½	2	2	3½	9½	17	12
5 by 4	3½	4⅛	4¹⁵⁄₁₆	5⁹⁄₁₆	14½	4	4	3½	11½	21	15
5 by 6	3½	4⅛	4¹⁵⁄₁₆	5⁹⁄₁₆	16½	6	6	3½	13½	24	17
5 by 8	3½	4⅛	4¹⁵⁄₁₆	5⁹⁄₁₆	18½	8	8	3½	15½	27	19
5 by 10	3½	4⅛	4¹⁵⁄₁₆	5⁹⁄₁₆	20½	10	10	3½	17½	30	21
5 by 12	3½	4⅛	4¹⁵⁄₁₆	5⁹⁄₁₆	22½	12	12	3½	19½	33	23
5 by 14	3½	4⅛	4¹⁵⁄₁₆	5⁹⁄₁₆	24½	14	14	3½	21½	36	25
5 by 16	3½	4⅛	4¹⁵⁄₁₆	5⁹⁄₁₆	26½	16	16	3½	23½	39	27
5 by 18	3½	4⅛	4¹⁵⁄₁₆	5⁹⁄₁₆	28½	18	18	3½	25½	42	29
5 by 20	3½	4⅛	4¹⁵⁄₁₆	5⁹⁄₁₆	30½	20	20	3½	27½	45	31
5 by 22	3½	4⅛	4¹⁵⁄₁₆	5⁹⁄₁₆	32½	22	22	3½	29½	48	33
5 by 24	3½	4⅛	4¹⁵⁄₁₆	5⁹⁄₁₆	34½	24	24	3½	31½	51	35

Table 12. ⅛ bend offset, 6-inch

Size (inches)	Dimensions in inches									Weight (pounds)	
	A	B	C	D	F	H	J	R	X	'XH'	'SV'
6 by 2	3½	4⅛	5	5⅝	13	2⅜	2	4	10	21	15
6 by 4	3½	4⅛	5³⁄₁₆	5¹³⁄₁₆	15	4	4	4	12	25	18
6 by 6	3½	4⅛	5³⁄₁₆	5¹³⁄₁₆	17	6	6	4	14	28	20
6 by 8	3½	4⅛	5³⁄₁₆	5¹³⁄₁₆	19	8	8	4	16	32	22½
6 by 10	3½	4⅛	5³⁄₁₆	5¹³⁄₁₆	21	10	10	4	18	36	25
6 by 12	3½	4⅛	5³⁄₁₆	5¹³⁄₁₆	23	12	12	4	20	39	27
6 by 14	3½	4⅛	5³⁄₁₆	5¹³⁄₁₆	25	14	14	4	22	43	30
6 by 16	3½	4⅛	5³⁄₁₆	5¹³⁄₁₆	27	16	16	4	24	46	32
6 by 18	3½	4⅛	5³⁄₁₆	5¹³⁄₁₆	29	18	18	4	26	50	35
6 by 20	3½	4⅛	5³⁄₁₆	5¹³⁄₁₆	31	20	20	4	28	54	37
6 by 22	3½	4⅛	5³⁄₁₆	5¹³⁄₁₆	33	22	22	4	30	57	40
6 by 24	3½	4⅛	5³⁄₁₆	5¹³⁄₁₆	35	24	24	4	32	61	42

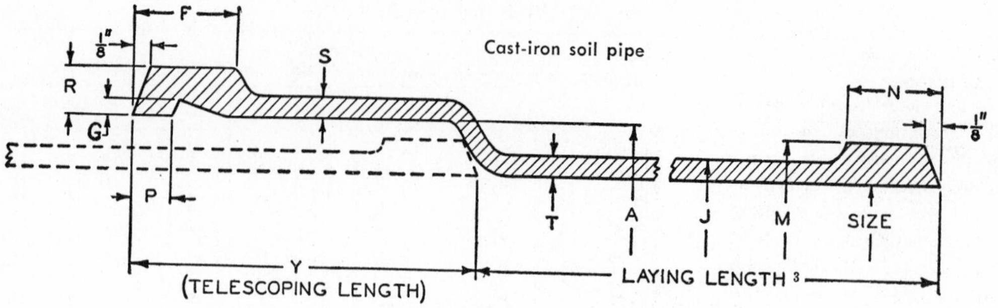
F
1/8"
S
Cast-iron soil pipe
R
G
N
1/8"
P
T
A
J
M
SIZE
Y
(TELESCOPING LENGTH)
LAYING LENGTH 3

Table 13. Hubs and spigots for extra-heavy soil pipe and fittings (dimensions in inches)

Size	Inside diameter of hub	Outside diameter of spigot	Outside diameter of barrel	Telescoping length	Thickness of barrel	
	A	M	J	Y	T (nominal)	T (min.)
inches	*inches*	*inches*	*inches*	*inches*	*inch*	*inch*
2	3.06	2.75	2.38	2.50	0.19	0.12
3	4.19	3.88	3.50	2.75	.25	.18
4	5.19	4.88	4.50	3.00	.25	.18
5	6.19	5.88	5.50	3.00	.25	.18
6	7.19	6.88	6.50	3.00	.25	.18
8	9.50	9.00	8.62	3.50	.31	.25
10	11.62	11.13	10.75	3.50	.37	.31
12	13.75	13.13	12.75	4.25	.37	.31
15	17.00	16.25	15.88	4.25	.44	.37

¼ bend

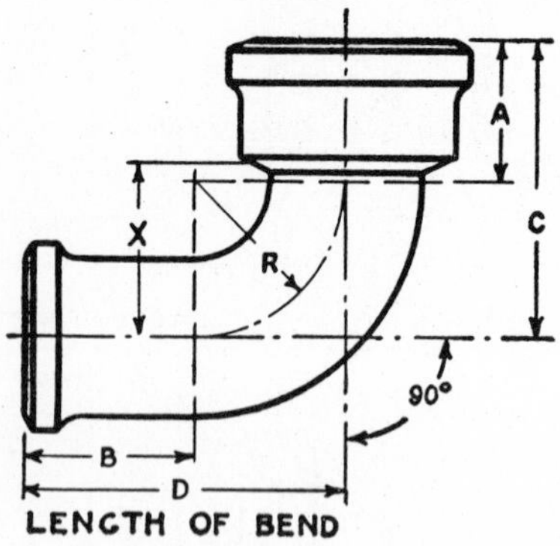
A
C
X
R
90°
B
D
LENGTH OF BEND

Table 14. ¼ bend

Size (inches)	Dimensions in inches						Weight (pounds)	
	A	B	C	D	R	X	'XH'	'SV'
2	2¾	3	5¾	6	3	3¼	5	4
3	3¼	3½	6¾	7	3½	4	10	7
4	3½	4	7½	8	4	4½	15	10½
5	3½	4	8	8½	4½	5	19	13
6	3½	4	8½	9	5	5½	24	17
8	4⅛	5½	10⅛	11½	6	6⅝	51	34
10	4⅛	5½	11⅛	12½	7	7⅝	78	55
12	5	7	13	15	8	8¾	111	80
15	5	7	14½	16½	9½	10¼	169	118

Table 15. Short sweep

Size (inches)	Dimensions in inches						Weight (pounds)	
	A	B	C	D	R	X	'XH'	'SV'
2	2¾	3	7¾	8	5	5¼	6	5
3	3¼	3½	8¾	9	5½	6	13	9
4	3½	4	9½	10	6	6½	18	12½
5	3½	4	10	10½	6½	7	23	16
6	3½	4	10½	11	7	7½	28	20
8	4⅛	5½	12⅛	13½	8	8⅝	57	38
10	4⅛	5½	13⅛	14½	9	9⅝	88	62
12	5	7	15	17	10	10¾	123	89
15	5	7	16½	18½	11½	12¼	187	130

Short and long sweeps
(Tables 15 and 16)

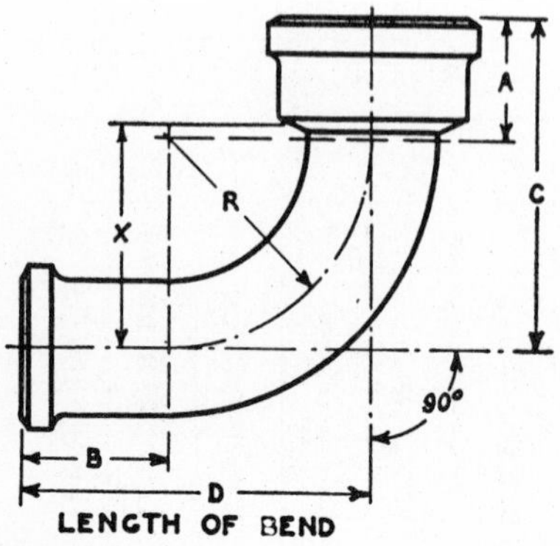
A
C
R
X
90°
B
D
LENGTH OF BEND

Table 16. Long sweep

Size (inches)	Dimensions in inches						Weight (pounds)	
	A	B	C	D	R	X	'XH'	'SV'
2	2¾	3	10¾	11	8	8¼	8	6½
3	3¼	3½	11¾	12	8½	9	16	11
4	3½	4	12½	13	9	9½	22	15
5	3½	4	13	13½	9½	10	28	19½
6	3½	4	13½	14	10	10½	34	24
8	4⅛	5½	15⅛	16½	11	11⅝	67	45
10	4⅛	5½	16⅛	17½	12	12⅝	103	72
12	5	7	18	20	13	13¾	141	101
15	5	7	19½	21½	14½	15¼	212	147

Single and double Y branches

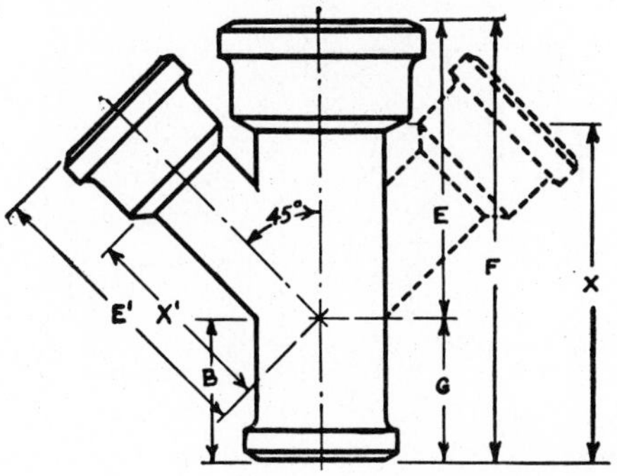

Table 17. Single and double Y branches

Size (inches)	Dimensions in inches							Weight, single (pounds)		Weight, double (pounds)	
	B (min.)	E	E′	F	G	X	X′	'XH'	'SV'	'XH'	'SV'
2	3½	6½	6½	10½	4	8	4	8	6½	11	9
3	4	8¼	8¼	13¼	5	10½	5½	17	12½	23	16
4	4	9¾	9¾	15	5¼	12	6¾	24	17	32	23
5	4	11	11	16½	5½	13½	8	32	22	41	28
6	4	12¼	12¼	18	5¾	15	9¼	40	28	51	36
8	5½	15 5/16	15 5/16	23	7 11/16	19½	11 13/16	82	55	107	73
10	5½	18	18	26	8	22½	14½	133	94	168	120
12	7	21⅛	21⅛	31¼	10⅛	27	16⅞	186	135	236	173
15	7	25	25	35¾	10¾	31½	20¾	290	204	368	262
3 by 2	4	7 9/16	7½	11¾	4 3/16	9	5	14	10	18	13
4 by 2	4	8⅜	8¼	12	3⅝	9	5¾	17	12	21	15
4 by 3	4	9 1/16	9	13½	4 7/16	10½	6¼	20	14	26	19
5 by 2	4	8⅞	9	12	3⅛	9	6½	20	14	24	17
5 by 3	4	9⅝	9¾	13½	3⅞	10½	7	24	16½	30	21
5 by 4	4	10 5/16	10½	15	4 11/16	12	7½	27	19	35	24
6 by 2	4	9 7/16	9¾	12	2 9/16	9	7¼	23	16½	27	20
6 by 3	4	10⅛	10½	13½	3⅜	10½	7¾	27	19	33	23
6 by 4	4	10 13/16	11¼	15	4 3/16	12	8¼	31	22	39	28
6 by 5	4	11 9/16	11¾	16½	4 15/16	13½	8¾	35	24	45	31
8 by 2	5½	10⅞	11	14	3⅛	10½	8½	42	29	46	32
8 by 3	5½	11 9/16	11¾	15½	3 15/16	12	9	47	32	53	37
8 by 4	5½	12¼	12½	17	4¾	13½	9½	52	36	60	42
8 by 5	5½	13	13	18½	5½	15	10	57	39	66	45
8 by 6	5½	13 11/16	13½	20	6 5/16	16½	10½	63	44	73	51
10 by 4	5½	13 7/16	14⅛	17	3 9/16	13½	11⅛	74	53	82	59
10 by 5	5½	14 3/16	14⅝	18½	4 5/16	15	11⅝	80	57	89	63
10 by 6	5½	14⅞	15⅛	20	5⅛	16½	12⅛	86	61	97	70
10 by 8	5½	16½	16 15/16	23	6½	19½	13 7/16	110	77	135	94
12 by 4	7	15⅛	15 7/16	19¼	4⅛	15	12 7/16	97	70	105	76
12 by 5	7	15⅞	15 15/16	20¾	4⅞	16½	12 15/16	104	74	113	81
12 by 6	7	16 9/16	16 7/16	22¼	5 11/16	18	13 7/16	111	80	122	88
12 by 8	7	18 3/16	18¼	25¼	7 1/16	21	14¾	136	96	161	113
12 by 10	7	19 11/16	19 5/16	28¼	8 9/16	24	15 13/16	160	115	195	142
15 by 6	7	18¼	18¾	22¼	4	18	15¾	152	109	163	117
15 by 8	7	19⅞	20 9/16	25¼	5⅜	21	17 1/16	182	127	207	146
15 by 10	7	21⅜	21⅝	28¼	6⅞	24	18⅛	213	152	248	176
15 by 12	7	22 13/16	23 7/16	31¼	8 7/16	27	19 3/16	242	170	292	210

View A showing cleanout plug on main

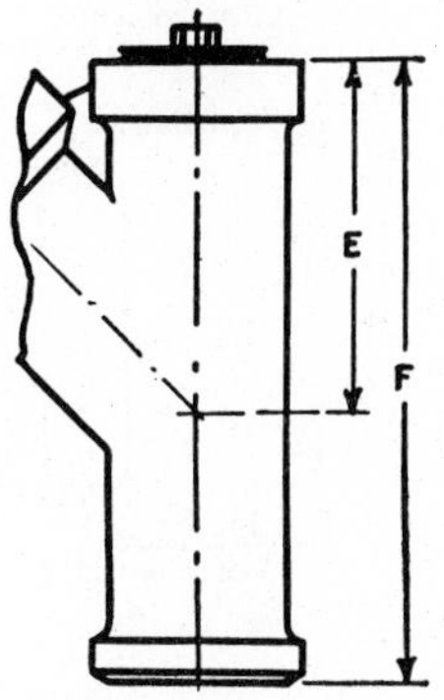

Table 18. Y branch cleanout with screw plug on main

Size (inches)	Dimensions in inches					Minimum I.P.S. tapping		Weight without plug (pounds)	
	E	E′	F	G	X′	'XH'	'SV'	'XH'	'SV'
2	5¼	6½	9¼	4	4	1½	1½	9	7¼
3	6⅝	8¼	11⅝	5	5½	2½	2½	15	10½
4	7⅞	9¾	13⅛	5¼	6¾	3½	3½	21	14½
5	9⅛	11	14⅝	5½	8	4	4	28	19
6	10⅜	12¼	16⅛	5¾	9¼	5	5	37	26

View B showing cleanout plug on branch

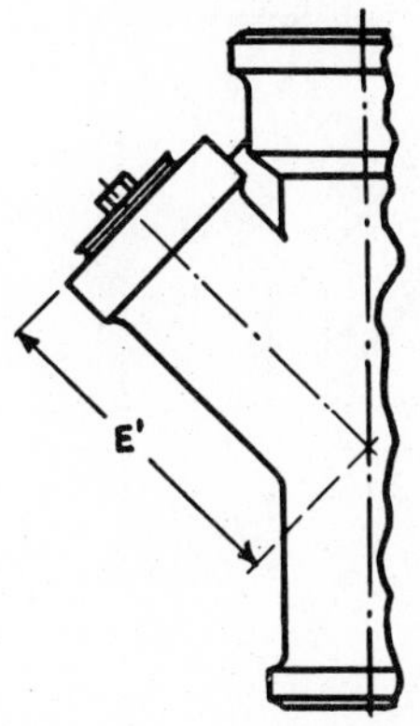

Table 19. Y branch cleanout with screw plug on branch

Size (inches)	Dimensions in inches					Minimum I.P.S. tapping		Weight without plug (pounds)	
	E	E′	F	G	X	'XH'	'SV'	'XH'	'SV'
2	6½	5¼	10½	4	8	1½	1½	9	7¼
3	8¼	6⅝	13¼	5	10½	2½	2½	15	10½
4	9¾	7⅞	15	5¼	12	3½	3½	21	14½
5	11	9⅛	16½	5½	13½	4	4	28	19
6	12¼	10⅜	18	5¾	15	5	5	37	26

Upright Y branch

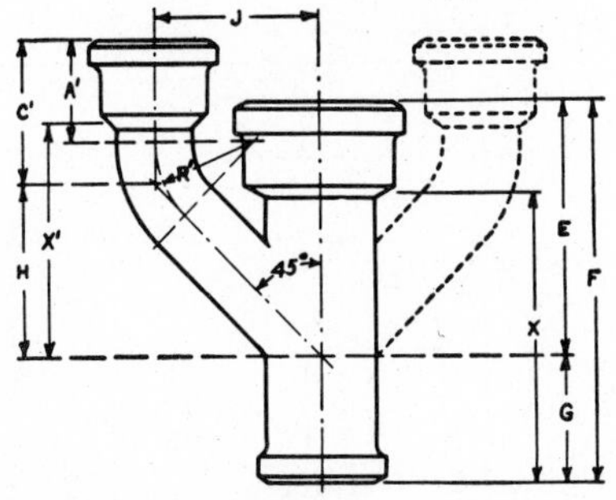

Table 20. Single and double upright Y branches

Size (inches)	Dimensions in inches										Weight, single (pounds)		Weight, double (pounds)	
	A′	C′	E	F	G	H	J	R′	X	X′	'XH'	'SV'	'XH'	'SV'
2	2¾	4	6½	10½	4	4½	4½	3	8	6	10	8	15	12
3	3¼	4 11/16	8¼	13¼	5	5½	5½	3½	10½	7 7/16	20	13½	30	20½
4	3½	5 3/16	9¾	15	5¼	6½	6½	4	12	8 11/16	28	19½	42	29
5	3½	5⅜	11	16½	5½	7½	7½	4½	13½	9⅞	37	25	56	38
6	3½	5 9/16	12¼	18	5¾	8½	8½	5	15	11 1/16	47	33	70	49
3 by 2	3	4¼	7 9/16	11¾	4 3/16	5	5	3	9	6¾	16	11¼	20	14
4 by 2	3	4¼	8 5/16	12	3 11/16	5½	5½	3	9	7¼	19	13½	24	17
4 by 3	3¼	4 11/16	9	13½	4½	6	6	3½	10½	7 15/16	23	16	34	23½
5 by 2	3	4¼	8⅝	12	3⅜	6	6	3	9	7¾	22	15	27	19
5 by 3	3¼	4 11/16	9½	13½	4	6½	6½	3½	10½	8 7/16	27	18½	38	26
5 by 4	3½	5 3/16	10¼	15	4¾	7	7	4	12	9 3/16	32	22	46	31
6 by 2	3	4¼	9 5/16	12	2 11/16	6½	6½	3	9	8¼	25	18	30	21½
6 by 3	3¼	4 11/16	10	13½	3½	7	7	3½	10½	8 15/16	30	21	41	28½
6 by 4	3½	5 3/16	10¾	15	4¼	7½	7½	4	12	9 11/16	35	24½	49	34
6 by 5	3½	5⅜	11 7/16	16½	5 1/16	8	8	4½	13½	10⅜	40	28	60	41

Table 21. Single and double combination Y-and-1/8 bend

Size (inches)	Dimensions in inches											Weight single (pounds)		Weight double (pounds)	
	A′	B min.	C′	E	E′	F	G	H	R′	X	X′	'XH'	'SV'	'XH'	'SV'
2	2 3/4	3 1/2	4	6 1/2	7 3/8	10 1/2	4	3 3/8	3	8	4 7/8	10	8	15	12
3	3 1/4	4	4 11/16	8 1/4	9 3/4	13 1/4	5	5 1/16	3 1/2	10 1/2	7	20	14	29	20
4	3 1/2	4	5 3/16	9 3/4	12	15	5 1/4	6 13/16	4	12	9	29	20	43	30
5	3 1/2	4	5 3/8	11	14	16 1/2	5 1/2	8 5/8	4 1/2	13 1/2	11	38	26	56	38
6	3 1/2	4	5 9/16	12 1/4	15 7/8	18	5 3/4	10 5/16	5	15	12 7/8	50	35	75	53
3 by 2	3	4	4 1/4	7 9/16	8 1/4	11 3/4	4 3/16	4	3	9	5 3/4	15	10 1/2	20	14
4 by 2	3	4	4 1/4	8 5/16	8 3/4	12	3 11/16	4 1/2	3	9	6 1/4	18	13	23	16 1/2
4 by 3	3 1/4	4	4 11/16	9	10 1/4	13 1/2	4 1/2	5 9/16	3 1/2	10 1/2	7 1/2	24	17	33	23
5 by 2	3	4	4 1/4	8 5/8	9 1/4	12	3 3/8	5	3	9	6 3/4	21	14 1/2	26	18
5 by 3	3 1/4	4	4 11/16	9 1/2	10 3/4	13 1/2	4	6 1/16	3 1/2	10 1/2	8	27	18 1/2	36	25
5 by 4	3 1/2	4	5 3/16	10 1/4	12 1/2	15	4 3/4	7 5/16	4	12	9 1/2	33	23	47	32
6 by 2	3	4	4 1/4	9 5/16	9 3/4	12	2 11/16	5 1/2	3	9	7 1/4	24	17	29	21
6 by 3	3 1/4	4	4 11/16	10	11 1/4	13 1/2	3 1/2	6 9/16	3 1/2	10 1/2	8 1/2	30	21	39	27
6 by 4	3 1/2	4	5 3/16	10 3/4	13	15	4 1/4	7 13/16	4	12	10	36	25	50	35
6 by 5	3 1/2	4	5 3/8	11 7/16	14 1/2	16 1/2	5 1/16	9 1/8	4 1/2	13 1/2	11 1/2	42	29	60	41

Combination Y-and-1/8 bend

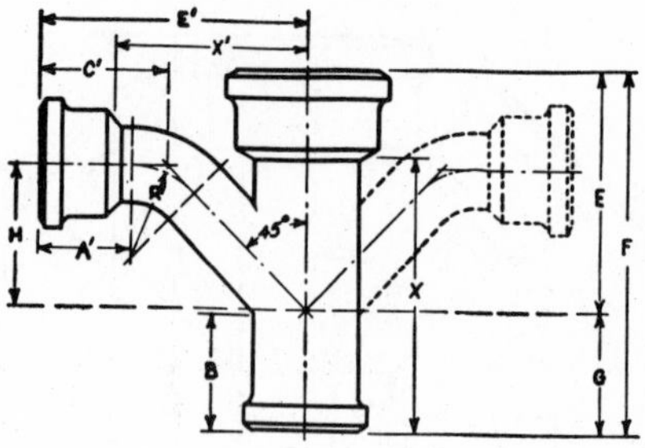

Table 22. Combination Y-and-1/8 bend cleanout with screw plug on main

Size (inches)	Dimensions in inches [1]		Min. I.P.S. tapping [2]	Weight without plug (pounds)		Size (inches)	Dimensions in inches [1]		Min. I.P.S. tapping [2]	Weight without plug (pounds)	
	E	F		'XH'	'SV'		E	F		'XH'	'SV'
2	5 1/4	9 1/4	1 1/2	9	7 1/4	5	9 1/8	14 5/8	4	34	23 1/2
3	6 5/8	11 5/8	2 1/2	17	11 1/2	6	10 3/8	16 1/8	5	47	33
4	7 7/8	13 1/8	3 1/2	26	17 1/2						

View A showing cleanout plug on main

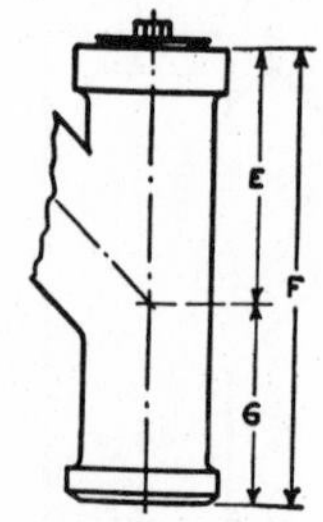

Table 23. Single and double inverted Y branches

Size (inches)	Dimensions in inches						Weight single (pounds)		Weight double (pounds)	
	E	E′	F	G	X	X′	'XH'	'SV'	'XH'	'SV'
2	3 1/4	5 7/8	12	8 3/4	9 1/2	3 3/8	9	7 1/4	12	9 3/4
3	4	7 3/8	15 1/4	11 1/4	12 1/2	4 5/8	18	12 1/2	23	16
4	4 1/2	8 7/8	17	12 1/2	14	5 7/8	25	17 1/2	32	22 1/2
5	4 3/4	10 1/8	18 1/2	13 3/4	15 1/2	7 1/8	33	23	42	29
6	5	11 3/8	20	15	17	8 3/8	41	29	51	37
3 by 2	3 1/4	6 5/8	13 3/4	10 1/2	11	4 1/8	15	11	18	13
4 by 2	3 1/16	7 3/8	14	10 15/16	11	4 7/8	18	13	21	15
4 by 3	3 3/4	8 1/8	15 1/2	11 3/4	12 1/2	5 3/8	22	15 1/2	27	19
5 by 2	2 5/8	8 1/16	14	11 3/8	11	5 9/16	22	15	25	17 1/2
5 by 3	3 5/16	8 13/16	15 1/2	12 3/16	12 1/2	6 1/16	25	17	31	21
5 by 4	4	9 9/16	17	13	14	6 9/16	29	20	37	26
6 by 2	2 3/16	8 3/4	14	11 13/16	11	6 1/4	25	18	29	21
6 by 3	2 7/8	9 1/2	15 1/2	12 5/8	12 1/2	6 3/4	29	20	34	24
6 by 4	3 9/16	10 1/4	17	13 7/16	14	7 1/4	33	23	40	28
6 by 5	4 1/4	10 3/4	18 1/2	14 1/4	15 1/2	7 3/4	37	26	46	32

Inverted Y Branch

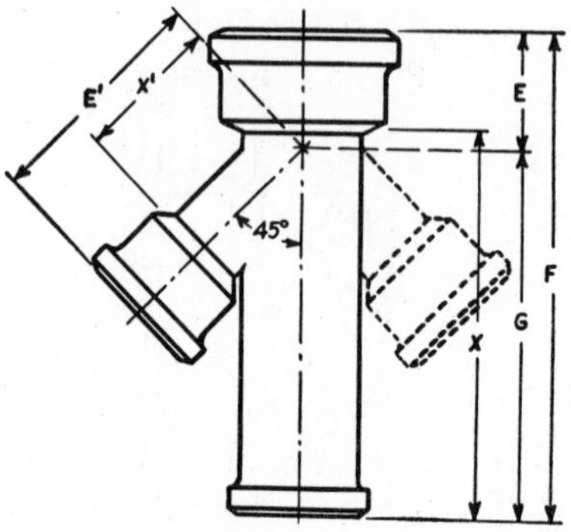

Table 24. Single and double vent branches

Size (inches)	Dimensions in inches							Weight single (pounds)		Weight double (pounds)	
	B	E	F	G	J	R′	X	'XH'	'SV'	'XH'	'SV'
2	3 1/4	4 1/4	10 1/2	6 1/4	4 1/2	3	8	9	7 1/4	12	9 1/2
3	4	5 1/4	12 3/4	7 1/2	5 1/2	3 1/2	10	18	12	23	15 1/2
4	4	6	14	8	6 1/2	4	11	25	17	32	22
5	4	6 1/2	15	8 1/2	7 1/2	4 1/2	12	32	22	41	28
6	4	7	16	9	8 1/2	5	13	41	29	51	35
3 by 2	4	4 3/4	11 3/4	7	5	3	9	14	9 1/2	17	11 1/2
4 by 2	4	5	12	7	5 1/2	3	9	18	12 1/2	21	14 1/2
4 by 3	4	5 1/2	13	7 1/2	6	3 1/2	10	21	14 1/2	26	18
5 by 2	4	5	12	7	6	3	9	21	14	24	16
5 by 3	4	5 1/2	13	7 1/2	6 1/2	3 1/2	10	24	16	29	17
5 by 4	4	6	14	8	7	4	11	28	19	35	24
6 by 2	4	5	12	7	6 1/2	3	9	22	15 1/2	25	17 1/2
6 by 3	4	5 1/2	13	7 1/2	7	3 1/2	10	27	19	32	22
6 by 4	4	6	14	8	7 1/2	4	11	31	22	38	26
6 by 5	4	6 1/2	15	8 1/2	8	4 1/2	12	36	25	45	31

Vent branch

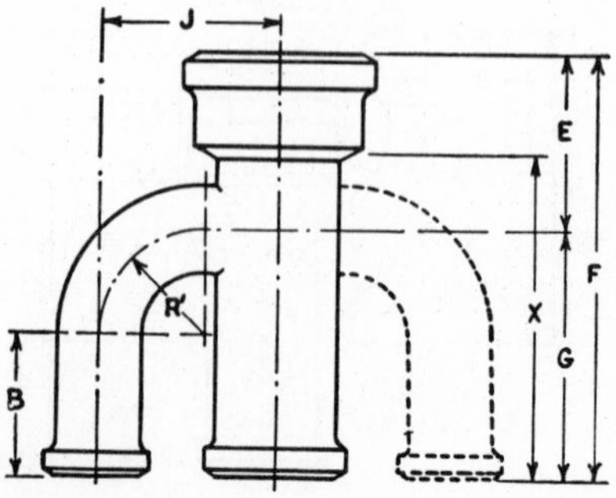

Sanitary T branch

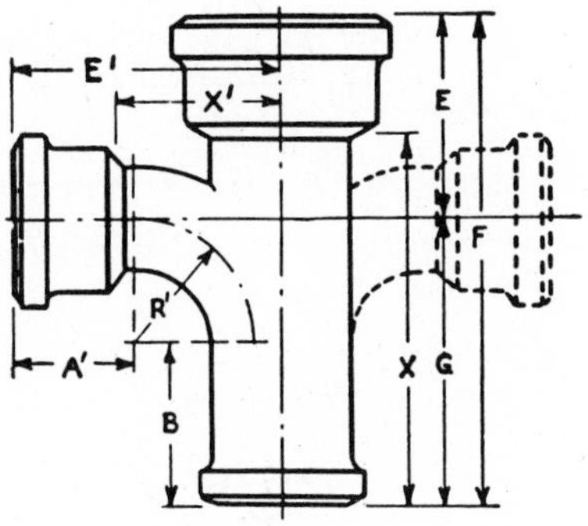

Table 25. Single and double sanitary T branches

Size (inches)	Dimensions in inches									Weight, single (pounds)		Weight, double (pounds)	
	A'	B	E	E'	F	G	R'	X	X'	'XH'	'SV'	'XH'	'SV'
2	2¾	3¾	4¼	5¼	10½	6¼	2½	8	2¾	8	6½	11	8¾
3	3¼	4	5¼	6¾	12¾	7½	3½	10	4	16	12	21	14½
4	3½	4	6	7½	14	8	4	11	4½	22	15½	29	20
5	3½	4	6½	8	15	8½	4½	12	5	28	19	36	25
6	3½	4	7	8½	16	9	5	13	5½	34	24½	44	32
8	4⅛	5¾	8¾	10⅛	20½	11¾	6	17	6⅝	72	49	92	63
10	4⅛	5¾	9¾	11⅛	22½	12¾	7	19	7⅝	108	78	132	97
12	5	7	11¾	13	26¾	15	8	22½	8¾	153	113	187	140
15	5	7	13¼	14½	29¾	16½	9½	25½	10¼	229	164	272	185
3 by 2	3	4	4¾	6½	11¾	7	3	9	4	14	10	18	13
4 by 2	3	4	5	7	12	7	3	9	4½	17	12	21	15
4 by 3	3¼	4	5½	7¼	13	7½	3½	10	4½	20	14	25	17½
5 by 2	3	4	5	7½	12	7	3	9	5	20	14	24	17
5 by 3	3¼	4	5½	7¾	13	7½	3½	10	5	23	16	28	19
5 by 4	3½	4	6	8	14	8	4	11	5	26	18	33	23
6 by 2	3	4	5	8	12	7	3	9	5½	23	16½	27	19
6 by 3	3¼	4	5½	8¼	13	7½	3½	10	5½	26	18½	31	22
6 by 4	3½	4	6	8½	14	8	4	11	5½	29	21	36	26
6 by 5	3½	4	6½	8½	15	8½	4½	12	5½	32	22	40	28
8 by 2	3	5¾	5¾	9	14½	8¾	3	11	6½	43	30	47	33
8 by 3	3¼	5¾	6¼	9¼	15½	9¼	3½	12	6½	47	32	52	36
8 by 4	3½	5¾	6¾	9½	16½	9¾	4	13	6½	51	35	58	40
8 by 5	3½	5¾	7¼	9½	17½	10¼	4½	14	6½	55	38	63	43
8 by 6	3½	5¾	7¾	9½	18½	10¾	5	15	6½	57	40	67	47
10 by 4	3½	5¾	6¾	10½	16½	9¾	4	13	7½	70	50	77	55
10 by 5	3½	5¾	7¼	10½	17½	10¼	4½	14	7½	73	52	81	58
10 by 6	3½	5¾	7¾	10½	18½	10¾	5	15	7½	76	55	85	62
10 by 8	4⅛	5¾	8¾	11⅛	20½	11¾	6	17	7⅝	96	68	115	81
12 by 4	3½	7	7¾	11½	18¾	11	4	14½	8½	95	69	102	74
12 by 5	3½	7	8¼	11½	19¾	11½	4½	15½	8½	99	71	107	76
12 by 6	3½	7	8¾	11½	20¾	12	5	16½	8½	103	74	113	82
12 by 8	4⅛	7	9¾	12⅛	22¾	13	6	18½	8⅝	120	85	140	99
12 by 10	4⅛	7	10¾	12⅛	24¾	14	7	20½	8⅝	134	97	155	114
15 by 6	3½	7	8¾	13	20¾	12	5	16½	10	142	102	150	108
15 by 8	4⅛	7	9¾	13⅝	22¾	13	6	18½	10⅛	162	115	180	128
15 by 10	4⅛	7	10¾	13⅝	24¾	14	7	20½	10⅛	180	130	200	145
15 by 12	5	7	11¾	14½	26¾	15	8	22½	10¼	198	143	230	168

T branch cleanout
with screw plug

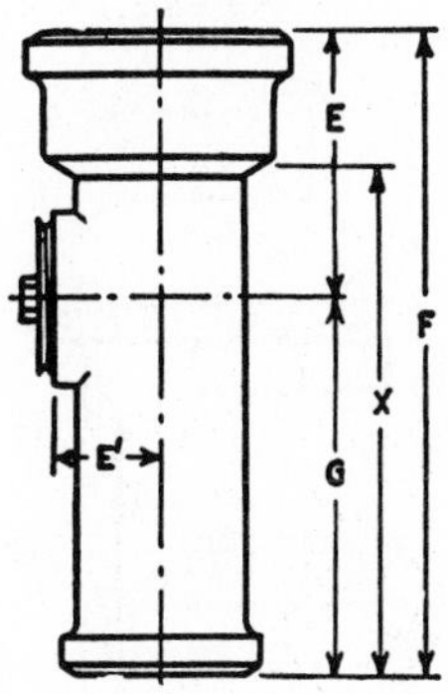

Table 26. T branch cleanout with screw plug

Size (inches)	Dimensions in inches					I.P.S. Tapping	Weight Without Plug (pounds)	
	E	E'	F	G	X		'XH'	'SV'
2	4¼	2	10½	6¼	8	1½	7	5¾
3	5¼	2½	12¾	7½	10	2½	13	8
4	6	3	14	8	11	3½	17	10½
5	6½	3½	15	8½	12	4	22	15
6	7	4	16	9	13	4	28	20

½-S trap with or without
vent and cleanout

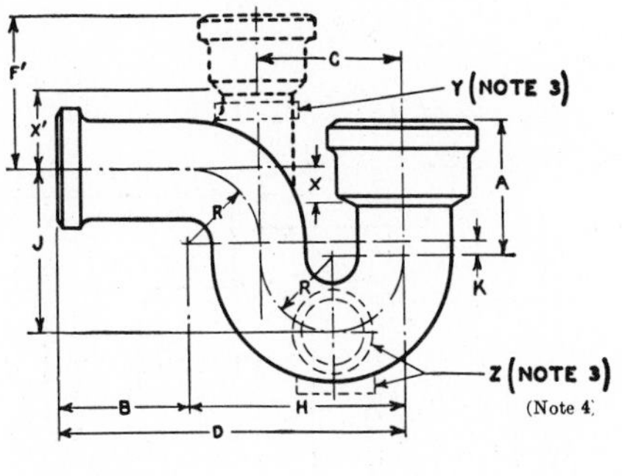

(Note 4)

Table 27. ½-S traps with or without vent and cleanout

Size (inches)	Dimensions in inches (Notes 1 and 2)											Weight without hub vent (pounds)		Weight with hub vent (pounds)	
	A	B	C	D	F'	H	J	K	R	X	X'	'XH'	'SV'	'XH'	'SV'
2 by 2	3	3½	4	9½	4½	6	4	-----	2	1½	2	8	6½	11	9
3 by 2	4½	4½	5	12	5	7½	5½	½	2½	1¼	2½	17	11½	20	14
3 by 3	4½	4½	5	12	5¼	7½	5½	½	2½	1¼	2½	17	11½	21	14½
4 by 2	5½	5	6	14	5½	9	6½	½	3	1	3	25	17	28	19
4 by 3	5½	5	6	14	5¾	9	6½	½	3	1	3	25	17	29	20
4 by 4	5½	5	6	14	6	9	6½	½	3	1	3	25	17	31	21
5 by 4	6½	5	7	15½	6½	10½	7½	½	3½	½	3½	34	23	40	27
5 by 5	6½	5	7	15½	6½	10½	7½	½	3½	½	3½	34	23	41	28
6 by 4	7½	5	8	17	7	12	8½	½	4	-------	4	45	31	51	35
6 by 6	7½	5	8	17	7	12	8½	½	4	-------	4	45	31	54	38
8 by 4	10	7	10	22	8¼	15	11	1	5	½	5¼	97	65	103	70
8 by 6	10	7	10	22	8¼	15	11	1	5	½	5¼	97	65	107	73
10 by 6	12	7	12	25	9¼	18	13	1	6	1½	6¼	166	113	175	121
12 by 6	13½	8	15	30½	10¼	22½	15	-----	7½	1¾	7¼	242	171	251	173
12 by 8	13½	8	15	30½	10¾	22½	15	-----	7½	1¾	7¼	242	171	264	182
15 by 8	16¾	8	18½	35¾	12¼	27¾	18½	-----	9¼	3¼	8¾	398	270	425	292

NOTE 1.—A minimum water seal of 2 inches is provided for the 2-inch size; of 2½ inches for sizes 3 to 6 inches, inclusive; of 3 inches for sizes 8 to 12 inches, inclusive; and of 3½ inches for the 15-inch size.

NOTE 2.—Dimensions D, X, and X' are laying lengths. Dimension X is measured below the horizontal center line on sizes 5 by 5 inches and smaller, and above the horizontal center line on sizes 8 by 4 inches and larger.

NOTE 3.—Traps with tapped vent and cleanout shall have tappings of sizes indicated below.

NOTE 4.—Tape at position Z shall be specified as right side, left side, or bottom.

Table 28. Running traps with or without single or double vents and cleanout

Size (inches)	Dimensions in inches (Notes 1 and 2)											Weight (pounds)					
												W1		W2		W3	
	A	B	C	F	F′	H	J	K	R	X	X′	'XH'	'SV'	'XH'	'SV'	'XH'	'SV'
2 by 2	3	3½	4	14½	4½	8	4	---	2	12	2	9	7¼	12	9½	15	12
3 by 2	3¼	4½	5	17¾	5	10	5½	½	2½	15	2½	19	13	22	15	25	17½
3 by 3	3¼	4½	5	17¾	5¼	10	5½	½	2½	15	2½	19	13	23	16	27	19
4 by 2	3½	5	6	20½	5½	12	6½	½	3	17½	3	28	19	31	22	34	24
4 by 3	3½	5	6	20½	5¾	12	6½	½	3	17½	3	28	19	32	22	36	25
4 by 4	3½	5	6	20½	6	12	6½	½	3	17½	3	28	19	34	23	40	28
5 by 4	3½	5	7	22½	6½	14	7½	½	3½	19½	3½	37	26	43	29	49	34
5 by 5	3½	5	7	22½	6½	14	7½	½	3½	19½	3½	37	26	45	31	51	35
6 by 4	3½	5	8	24½	7	16	8½	½	4	21½	4	48	33	54	37	60	42
6 by 6	3½	5	8	24½	7	16	8½	½	4	21½	4	48	33	57	40	66	47
8 by 4	4⅛	7	10	31⅛	8¼	20	11	1	5	27⅝	5¼	103	70	109	74	115	78
8 by 6	4⅛	7	10	31⅛	8¼	20	11	1	5	27⅝	5¼	103	70	112	76	121	83
10 by 6	4⅛	7	12	35⅛	9¼	24	13	1	6	31⅝	6¼	175	120	184	127	193	134
12 by 6	5	8	15	43	10¼	30	15	---	7½	38¾	7¼	256	176	265	183	274	190
12 by 8	5	8	15	43	10¾	30	15	---	7½	38¾	7¼	256	176	278	191	300	206
15 by 8	5	8	18½	50	12¼	37	18½	---	9¼	45¾	8¾	414	284	436	299	463	317

Weights are given as follows: W_1, without hub vent; W_2, with single hub vent; W_3, with double hub vent.

NOTE 1.—A minimum water seal of 2 inches is provided for the 2-inch size; of 2½ inches for sizes 3 to 6 inches, inclusive; of 3 inches for sizes 8 to 12 inches inclusive; and of 3½ inches for the 15-inch size.
NOTE 2.—Dimensions X and X′ are laying lengths.
NOTE 3.—For traps with tapping at Y and Z, see table 50, note 3.
NOTE 4.—Tap at position Z shall be specified as right side, left side, or bottom.

Running trap with or without single or double vents and cleanout

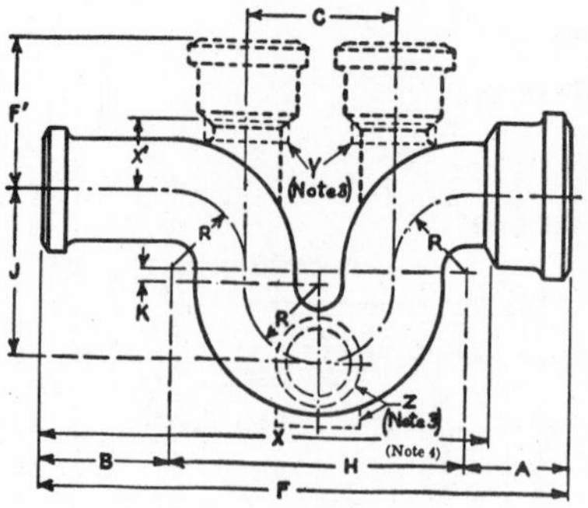

Table 29. Double hub

Size (inches)	F	X	Weight (pounds) 'XH'	Weight (pounds) 'SV'	Size (inches)	F	X	Weight (pounds) 'XH'	Weight (pounds) 'SV'
	Inches	*Inch*				*Inches*	*Inches*		
2	6	1	5	4	8	8¼	1¼	35	24
3	6½	1	8	6	10	8¼	1¼	50	40
4	7	1	11	8	12	10	1½	67	54
5	7	1	13	9	15	10	1½	91	73
6	7	1	15	11					

Double hub

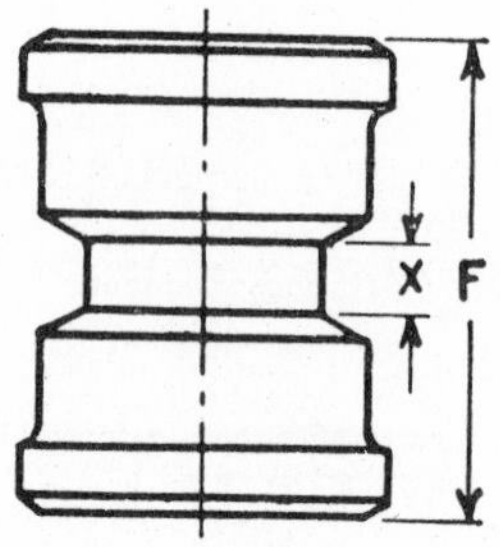

Table 30. Reducers

Size (inches)	B	F	X	Weight (pounds) 'XH'	Weight (pounds) 'SV'	Size[1] (inches)	B	F	X	Weight (pounds) 'XH'	Weight (pounds) 'SV'
	Inches	*Inches*	*Inches*				*Inches*	*Inches*	*Inches*		
3 by 2	3¾	7¼	4¾	6	4½	8 by 6	4½	9	6	21	15
4 by 2	4	7½	5	7	5	10 by 4	4½	9	6	25	17
4 by 3	4	7¾	5	9	6½	10 by 5	4½	9	6	26	17½
5 by 2	4	7½	5	8	6	10 by 6	4½	9	6	27	19
5 by 3	4	7¾	5	10	7	10 by 8	4½	9½	6	35	24
5 by 4	4	8	5	11	8	12 by 4	5¼	9½	6½	33	22
6 by 2	4	7½	5	9	6½	12 by 5	5¼	9½	6½	34	23
6 by 3	4	7¾	5	11	7½	12 by 6	5¼	9½	6½	35	24
6 by 4	4	8	5	12	8½	12 by 8	5¼	10	6½	45	31
6 by 5	4	8	5	13	9	12 by 10	5¼	10	6½	51	37
8 by 2	4½	8½	6	17	12	15 by 6	5¼	9½	6½	44	30
8 by 3	4½	8¾	6	18	12½	15 by 8	5¼	10	6½	55	38
8 by 4	4½	9	6	19	13	15 by 10	5¼	10	6½	60	43
8 by 5	4½	9	6	20	13½	15 by 12	5¼	10¾	6½	67	50

Reducer

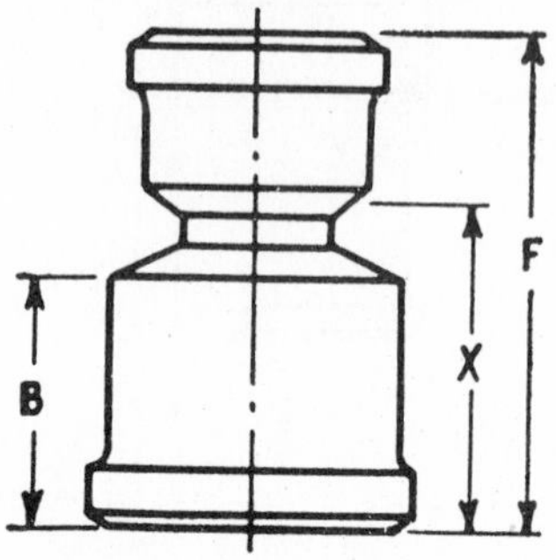

Table 31. Spigot and tapped long increasers

Sizes (inches) (Note 1)	A	B	C (Note 2)	L (Note 3)	D		Weight, spigot (pounds)		Weight, tapped (pounds)	
					'XH'	'SV'	'XH'	'SV'	'XH'	'SV'
	in.	*in.*	*in.*	*in.*	*in.*	*in.*				
2 by 4 by 24	8½	4	4½	24	4½	4¼	19	12½	19	13
2 by 4 by 30	8½	4	4½	30	4½	4¼	23	15½	24	16
2 by 4 by 36	8½	4	4½	36	4½	4¼	27	18	29	19
2 by 4 by 48	8½	4	4½	48	4½	4¼	39	26	40	27
3 by 4 by 24	8½	4	4½	24	4½	4¼	20	13½	20	13½
3 by 4 by 30	8½	4	4½	30	4½	4¼	25	17	26	17½
3 by 4 by 36	8½	4	4½	36	4½	4¼	30	20	31	21
3 by 4 by 48	8½	4	4½	48	4½	4¼	41	27	42	28
4 by 5 by 24	8½	4	4½	24	5½	5¼	25	17	26	17
4 by 5 by 30	8½	4	4½	30	5½	5¼	31	21	33	22
4 by 5 by 36	8½	4	4½	36	5½	5¼	38	25	39	26
4 by 5 by 48	8½	4	4½	48	5½	5¼	51	34	52	35
4 by 6 by 24	8½	4	4½	24	6½	6¼	29	19	30	20
4 by 6 by 30	8½	4	4½	30	6½	6¼	36	24	38	25
4 by 6 by 36	8½	4	4½	36	6½	6¼	44	29	45	30
4 by 6 by 48	8½	4	4½	48	6½	6¼	59	40	61	41

NOTE 1.—First size given for long increasers is spigot size.
First size given for long increasers, tapped, is tapping size.
NOTE 2.—All markings shall be on small end and in space indicated by dimension C.
NOTE 3.—Dimension L is the laying length.

Spigot and tapped long increaser

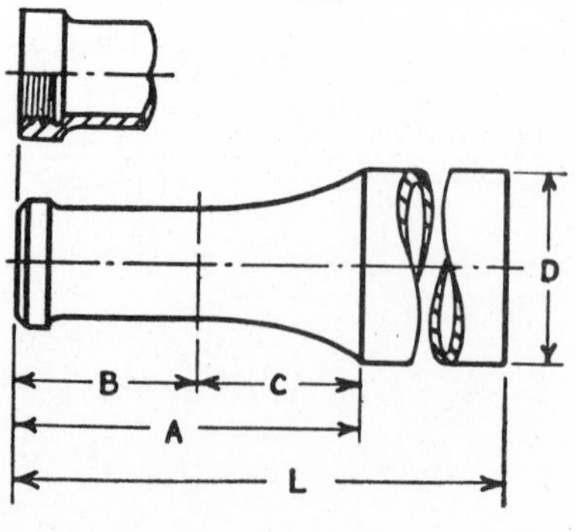

Table 32. Increasers

Size (inches)	B	F	X	Weight (pounds)		Size (inches)	B	F	X	Weight (pounds)	
				'XH'	'SV'					'XH'	'SV'
	Inches	*Inches*	*Inches*				*Inches*	*Inches*	*Inches*		
2 by 3	4	11¾	9	9	6½	5 by 8	4	15½	12	34	24
2 by 4	4	12	9	10	7	5 by 10	4	15½	12	44	33
2 by 5	4	12	9	12	8½	6 by 8	4	15½	12	35	24
2 by 6	4	12	9	13	9½	6 by 10	4	15½	12	45	33
3 by 4	4	12	9	12	9	6 by 12	4	16¼	12	58	44
3 by 5	4	12	9	14	9½	8 by 10	5½	15½	12	55	40
3 by 6	4	12	9	15	11	8 by 12	5½	16¼	12	64	48
4 by 5	4	12	9	15	10½	8 by 15	5½	16¼	12	82	61
4 by 6	4	12	9	16	11½	10 by 12	5½	16¼	12	73	54
4 by 8	4	15½	12	32	22	10 by 15	5½	16¼	12	88	65
5 by 6	4	12	9	18	13	12 by 15	7	16¼	12	97	71

Table 33. Tapped increasers

Size (inches) (note 1)	B	F	X	Weight (pounds)	
				'XH'	'SV'
	Inches	*Inches*	*Inches*		
1½ by 2	4	10½	8	7	5
2 by 3	4	11¾	9	9	6½
2 by 4	4	12	9	11	8
2 by 5	4	12	9	12	8½
2 by 6	4	12	9	14	10

NOTE 1.—Tapping boss may be tapped for 4¼-, 1½-, or 2-inch pipe, except size 1½ by 2 inches, which may be tapped 1¼ or 1½ inches only.

Table 34. Plugs for hub

Size (inches)	F	Weight (pounds)		Size (inches)	F	Weight (pounds)	
		'XH'	'SV'			'XH'	'SV'
	Inches				*Inches*		
2	3½	1¾	1¼	8	4½	15	11¼
3	3¾	3	2¼	10	4½	23	17¼
4	4	4½	3¼	12	5¼	33	24¾
5	4	6	4½	15	5¼	50	37½
6	4	8	6				

Tapped increaser

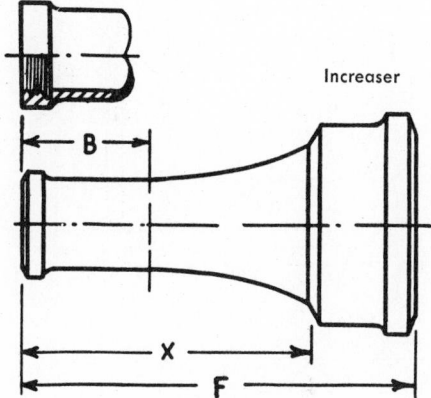

Increaser

Plug for hub

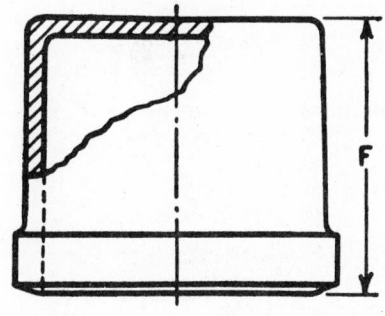

Cast-iron fittings

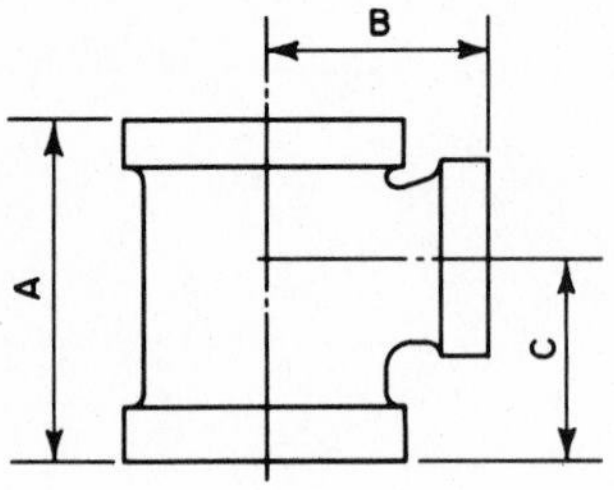

Reducing Y
(short TY)

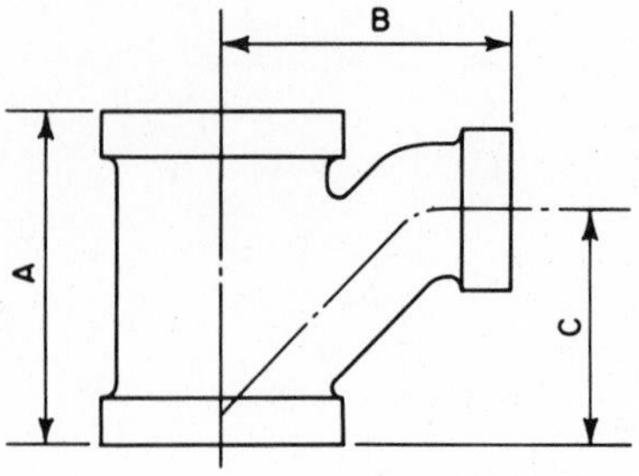

Reducing Y
(long TY)

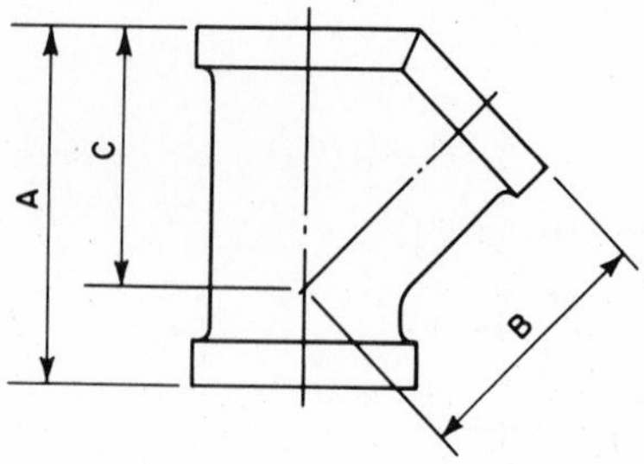

Reducing Y
(45° Y)

Table 35. Reducing Y branches

Size, in.	Dimensions in inches								
	Reducing short TY			Reducing long TY			Reducing 45° Y		
	A	B	C	A	B	C	A	B	C
1 1/2x1 1/4	4 3/8	2 3/4	2 3/4	5 7/16	4 3/16	3 7/8	5 1/4	3 7/16	3 7/16
2x1 1/4x1 1/2							5 1/8	3 5/8	3 5/8
2x1 1/2x1 1/4							5 1/8	3 5/8	3 5/8
2x1 1/2x1 1/2	4 1/2	2 1/2	2 3/4				5 1/8	3 5/8	3 5/8
2x1 1/2x2							5 7/8	3 15/16	4
2 x1 1/4	4 7/16	2 13/16	2 11/16	5 13/16	4 1/2	4 1/2	5 15/16	4 1/4	4 1/4
2 x1 1/2	4 15/16	3	2 7/8	5 13/16	4 1/2	4 1/2	5 15/16	4 1/4	4 1/4
2 1/2x1 1/4	5 1/8	3 1/4	3						
2 1/2x1 1/2	5 1/8	3 1/4	3	5 3/4	4 1/2	4 1/4	6 3/8	4 3/4	4 5/8
2 1/2x2	5 1/2	3 11/16	3 1/8	8 1/4	6 3/16	6 1/16	6 3/8	4 3/4	4 5/8
3 x1 1/2	5 1/16	3 5/16	2 15/16	5 7/8	5 1/4	4 9/16	6 5/8	5 1/16	4 11/16
3 x2	5 3/4	3 5/8	3 1/4	6 5/8	5 1/2	4 1/2	6 3/4	5 1/4	5 1/8
3 x2 1/2							8 3/8	6	6
4 x1 1/2	5 13/16	4 1/16	3 3/8	7	6 3/8	5 1/8	7 5/8	5 5/8	5 7/16
4 x2	5 13/16	4 1/16	3 3/8	7	6 3/8	5 1/8	6 5/8	5 7/8	5 5/8
4 x2 1/2	7 3/8	4 3/4	4 5/16	9 1/4	7 3/4	6 1/2	7 1/4	5 7/8	5 3/4
4 x3	7 3/8	4 3/4	4 5/16	9 1/4	7 3/4	6 1/2	8 1/2	6 5/8	6 3/8
5 x1 1/2	5 9/16	4 3/8	3 3/16	7 3/8	6 11/16	5 5/8			
5 x2	6 1/8	4 1/2	3 11/16	7 3/8	6 11/16	5 5/8	7 1/8	6 3/4	6
5 x3	7 3/4	5 3/16	4 1/2	9 1/2	8 7/16	7	8 3/4	7 1/2	7 1/8
5 x4	9 1/4	5 13/16	5 1/4	11 1/8	9 7/16	7 15/16	10 5/16	8	7 7/8
6 x2	6 5/16	5 3/16	3 11/16	6 1/2	6 3/4	4 7/16	7	7 1/2	6 5/8
6 x3	9 1/4	5 15/16	5 7/16	8 7/8	7 1/4	6 1/4	8 13/16	8 1/4	7 1/2
6 x4	9 1/4	5 15/16	5 7/16	11 1/4	9 13/16	8 1/4	10 1/2	9	8 7/8
6 x5	10 3/8	5 15/16	5 15/16	13	10 11/16	9 7/16	11 1/2	9 1/8	9
7 x4				10 1/4	9 5/8	7	10 1/4	10 1/2	9 5/8
8 x3	11 5/8	7 5/8	7 1/2	8 3/4	9 1/4	5 7/8	10 3/8	10	8 7/8
8 x4	11 5/8	7 5/8	7 1/2	10 5/8	10	7 1/4	10 3/8	10	8 7/8
8 x5	12 3/4	8 1/16	8 3/8	14 1/4	10 3/4	8 3/4	11 3/8	10 5/8	9 3/4
8 x6	12 3/4	8 1/16	8 3/8	14 1/4	10 3/4	8 3/4	14	12	11 1/2
10 x4	13 3/8	9 15/16	8 3/8	16 1/8	14 1/8	11 5/8	11 7/8	12 5/8	11 5/8
10 x5	13 3/8	9 15/16	8 3/8				13 7/8	13 5/8	13
10 x6	13 3/8	9 15/16	8 3/8	16 1/8	14 1/8	11 5/8	13 7/8	13 5/8	13
10 x8	19 1/2	12 1/4	12 1/4	17 3/8	11 1/4	11 1/8	20 1/4	15 1/4	15 1/4
12 x4							15	13 3/8	11 3/8

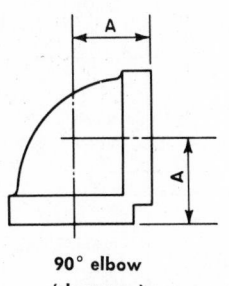

90° elbow
(short turn)

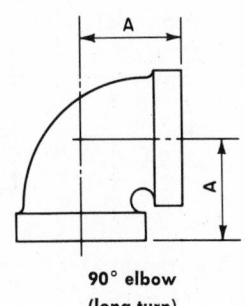

90° elbow
(long turn)

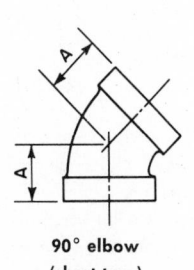

90° elbow
(short turn)

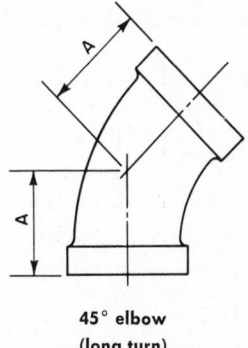

45° elbow
(long turn)

Table 36. Short- and long-turn elbows

| Size, in. | Dimension A, in. | | | |
| | 90° elbow | | 45° elbow | |
	Short turn	Long turn	Short turn	Long turn
1¼	1⅞	2⅜	1⁵⁄₁₆	1¾
1½	2	2½	1½	1⅞
1½x1¼	2			
2	2¼	3¹⁄₁₆	1⅝	2¼
2½x1½	2⅛			
2½	2¹³⁄₁₆	3¹¹⁄₁₆	1¹¹⁄₁₆	3
3	3⅜	5⅞	2⅜	4⅝
4	3¹⁵⁄₁₆	6¾	2⁷⁄₁₆	4⅝
5	4⅝	6⅛	3¹⁄₁₆	5⁷⁄₁₆
6	5¹¹⁄₃₂	7⅛	3	6
7	5¹¹⁄₁₆	9½	3⅜	
8	6½	11⅞	3½	6¾
10	7⅞	12¼	4⁷⁄₁₆	7½
12	9	13	5½	8¼

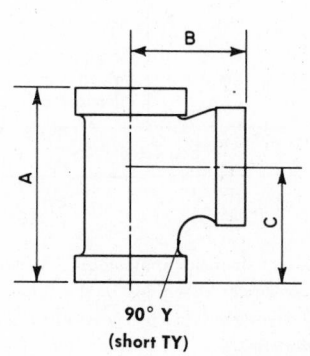

90° Y
(short TY)

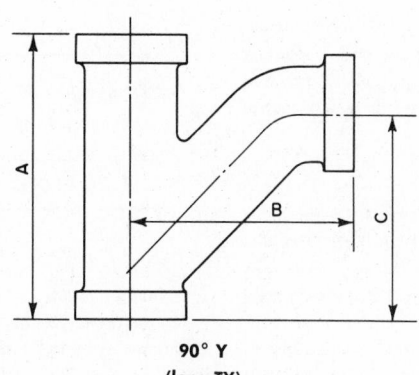

90° Y
(long TY)

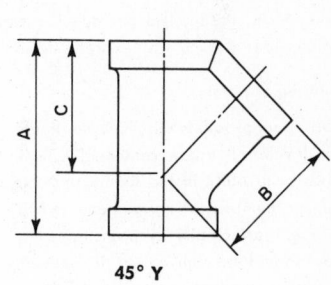

45° Y

Table 37. Y branches

| Size, in. | Dimensions in inches | | | | | | | | |
| | Short TY | | | Long TY | | | 45° Y | | |
	A	B	C	A	B	C	A	B	C
1							4	2¹¹⁄₁₆	2¹¹⁄₁₆
1¼	3¹³⁄₁₆	2³⁄₁₆	2³⁄₁₆	4¾	3⅝	3⁷⁄₁₆	5³⁄₁₆	3⁷⁄₁₆	3⁷⁄₁₆
1½	4⁵⁄₁₆	2½	2⁷⁄₁₆	5⁷⁄₁₆	4³⁄₁₆	3⅞	5¼	3⁷⁄₁₆	3⁷⁄₁₆
2	5¾	3³⁄₁₆	3³⁄₁₆	6½	5⅛	4⅝	6¼	4⅛	4⅛
2½	6⅝	3⅞	3¾	8¼	6³⁄₁₆	6¹⁄₁₆	8	5¼	5¼
3	7¼	4³⁄₁₆	4³⁄₁₆	9	7	6½	8	6	6
4	8¾	5³⁄₁₆	5³⁄₁₆	10¾	8⅜	7⅝	10⅞	7¹¹⁄₁₆	7¹¹⁄₁₆
5	10¼	6³⁄₁₆	6³⁄₁₆	13	10³⁄₁₆	9⁵⁄₁₆	11⅜	8⅜	8⅜
6	12	7⅛	7⅛	14¼	10¾	10¼	13¼	10	10
7	13¾	8⅝	8½	16	12⅛	11¼	15¼	11¼	11¼
8	15¼	9⅛	9⁵⁄₁₆	17⁷⁄₁₆	13¼	11⅝	16½	12⅜	12⅜
10	19½	12¼	12¼	22¾	16⁷⁄₁₆	15⅜	20¼	15¼	15¼
12				26⅝	19	20	24¼	19⅝	19⅝

By GEORGE R. JERUS, P.E.

Associate—Meyer, Strong and Jones, Mechanical and Electrical Engineers

PLANNING

On this and the following pages are presented data useful in the design of public toilets.

Park toilets

Park toilet installations are of two general types: (1) Small parks, small recreation areas, and city squares; (2) Municipal picnic grounds, bathing beaches, and large recreation areas. Both types should be accessible to, but not directly on, routes of main circulation; and should be provided with tamper-proof fixtures, door hinges, paper holders, hooks, and the like. Type 1 is purely utilitarian, with a minimum number of fixtures and space. Type 2 may be expanded to include pay toilets for both men and women or a women's lounge room equipped with settees or easy chairs, or may be planned in conjunction with locker or dressing rooms used in recreational areas.

Control is very important, because of uncertainty as to the type of patronage. Slop sinks and supply lockers (and attendant's office, if provided) should be located near the entrance. *Number of fixtures* is indeterminate, varying from 2 or 3 water closets per toilet for Type 1, to approximately 1 water closet per 1,500 persons for large municipal bathing beaches. *Access corridors* should be provided, with *wall-hung water closets* and *stall urinals* mounted so that plumbing is serviced through the access corridor.

Construction should be of impervious material throughout. Concrete and tile, with slate on the fixture wall, are often used; when cost will permit, however, denser materials (such as terrazzo for floors or flush metal partitions) are preferable.

Artificial ventilation is preferable, with a recommended minimum of 1 air change per 6 minutes (consult local codes). Access corridors may also serve as exhaust plenum chambers. If toilets are underground, exhaust vents should be carried up in sidewalk posts to a point more than 6 ft above the sidewalk.

Subway toilets are similar to park toilets, Type 1. New York City municipal subways employ as a toilet unit: 2 water closets, 2 urinals, and 1 lavatory (for men); 2 water closets and 1 lavatory (for women). One unit is provided per outlying local station; two per outlying express station; three per central local station; four per central express station.

Railroad-terminal toilets

Railroad-terminal toilets are likewise divided into two groups: (1) Terminals in highly developed urban centers; (2) Terminals in city outskirts. The distinction lies principally in the fixture and use ratios (see Table 1). Type 2 is used by large numbers of nonpassengers (ratio to passengers, approximately 5 to 1); Type 1 principally by passengers.

Location should be convenient for passengers but not too accessible to the man on the street. Space assigned to public toilets should be the least valuable. If several toilet rooms are provided, the largest should adjoin waiting rooms. *Size* should be determined by station capacity, which in turn is determined by track capacity; however, plans should permit additions to existing facilities to accommodate future increases.

Facilities should include showers, dressing rooms, men's smoking rooms, and women's restrooms, in addition to free and pay toilets, lavatories, and urinals. The modern tendency is to include as many pay toilets as possible within the required number. These need constant supervision, necessitating provision of a porter's closet, preferably opening off a common corridor serving all pay toilets. Storage space should be provided for towels, soap, combs, and the like, sold or rented by porters.

Plan: A lobby should give access to all parts of each toilet group; it may serve as a men's smoking room or women's lounge, and may also contain bootblack stands and the like. Use of separate corridors for free toilets, pay toilets, urinals, lavatories, showers, and dressing rooms provides an efficient and desirable means of segregating fixtures by types. Artificial ventilation is preferable, with 1 air change per 6 minutes.

Table 1. Fixtures and use ratios

TYPE OF TOILET	FIXTURE RATIO	USE RATIO
PARK (and Subway)	3 men to 2 women; allow 1 urinal & 1 lav. per 2 w.c. for men; 1 lav. per 2 w.c. for women	Indeterminate, depending on location
R. R. TERMINAL (City center)	3 men to 1 woman; allow 1 urinal & 1 lav. per 2 w.c. for men; 1 lav. per 2 w.c. for women	1 water closet per 1500 persons (passengers + transient)
R. R. TERMINAL (Outskirts)	2 men to 1 woman; allow 1 urinal & 1 lav. per 2 w.c. for men; 1 lav. per 2 w.c. for women	1 water closet per 500 persons (passengers + transient)
HOTEL (Restaurant, Bar, Lobby)	1 man to 1 woman; allow 2 urinals & 1 lav. per 2 w.c. for men; 1 lav. per 2 w.c. for women	1 water closet per 15 persons in restaurants; per 50 in public rooms
HOTEL (Ballroom)	2 men to 1 woman; allow 2 urinals & 1 lav. per 1 w.c. for men; 1 lav. per 2 w.c. for women	1 water closet per 50 persons
THEATER (Continuous)	7 men to 3 women	men: 1 w.c. per 75 persons, 1 urinal per 100, 1 lav. per 250; women: 1 w.c. per 75 persons, 1 lav. per 250
THEATER (Legitimate)	7 men to 3 women	Increase no. fixtures given for continuous theaters by 20%
OFFICE BLDG.	See Table II	

Theater toilets

Theater toilets serve two types of houses: "continuous" and "legitimate." In the former, audiences are constantly changing; in the latter, audiences change at stated intervals and consequently must have adequate facilities for peak loads. Continuous-show theaters are divided into three groups: *class A* (large theaters in metropolitan centers) with separate toilets on each floor; *class B* (neighborhood theaters) with only one group of toilets, usually on the mezzanine; and *class C* (intimate theaters, inexpensive theaters) with one group of toilets in the basement. In legitimate theaters, toilets are in the basement or on the mezzanine. Appearance of toilets is important in attracting patronage, especially for women. Fixtures, fittings, and interior finish should be of high quality. Artificial ventilation should be used, with 1 air change per 6 minutes.

Control is not important. In large installations, however, some supervision is generally provided, especially in women's rooms. Slop sinks and lockers should always be provided.

Hotel toilets

Hotel toilets should be convenient to guests, but not easily accessible from the street. They may be divided into two types: (1) Those serving restaurants and public rooms; (2) Those serving ballrooms and banquet floors. The location of both types should be in the least valuable areas—preferably on low-

le 2. Minimum toilet facilities

xtracted from American Standard National Plumbing Code (ASA 40.8—1955) with the permission of the publisher, The American ociety of Mechanical Engineers.

These are minimum requirements. Facilities should be increased f the type of occupancy calls for it and the budget permits.

In applying this schedule of facilities, the designer must consider the ccessibility of the fixtures. Conformity purely on a numerical basis might not result in an installation suited to the needs of the individual establishment. Schools, for example, should be provided with toilet facilities on each classroom floor.

Facilities for temporary workmen: 1 water closet and 1 urinal for each 30 men. A 24-in. urinal trough can be considered equivalent to 1 urinal; a 36-in. trough, 2 urinals; a 48-in. trough, 2 urinals; a 60-in. trough, 3 urinals; a 72-in. trough, 4 urinals.

e of building ccupancy *	Water closets		Urinals	Lavatories		Bathtubs or showers	Drinking fountains †
ing or apart- nt houses ‡	1 per dwelling or apartment unit			1 per dwelling or apartment unit		1 per dwelling or apartment unit	
ols §	Male	Female					
mentary	1 per 100	1 per 35	1 per 30 males	1 per 60 persons			1 per 75 persons
condary	1 per 100	1 per 45	1 per 30 males	1 per 100 persons			1 per 75 persons
e or public ildings	No. of persons	No. of fixtures	Wherever urinals are provided for men, one water closet less than the number specified may be provided for each urinal installed, except that the number of water closets in such cases shall not be reduced to less than ⅔ of the minimum specified	No. of persons	No. of fixtures		1 per 75 persons
	1–15	1		1–15	1		
	16–35	2		16–35	2		
	36–55	3		36–60	3		
	56–80	4		61–90	4		
	81–110	5		91–125	5		
	111–150	6					
	1 fixture per additional 40 persons			1 fixture per additional 45 persons			
facturing, rehouses, rkshops, loft ildings, found- s and similar ablishments	No. of persons	No. of fixtures	Same substitution as above	1–100 persons, 1 fixture per 10 persons.		1 shower per 15 persons exposed to excessive heat or to skin contamination with poisonous, infectious, or irritating material	1 per 75 persons
	1–9	1		Over 100: 1 per 15 persons ‖			
	10–24	2					
	25–49	3					
	50–74	4					
	75–100	5					
	1 fixture per additional 30 employees						
itories #	Male: 1 per 10 persons Female: 1 per 8 persons Over 10 persons: add 1 fixture per additional 25 males and 1 per additional 20 females		1 per 25 men Over 150 persons: add 1 fixture per additional 50 men	1 per 12 persons. (Separate dental lavatories should be provided in community toilet rooms. Ratio of 1 dental lavatory per 50 persons is recommended.) Add 1 lavatory per 20 males, 1 per 15 females		1 per 8 persons. In the case of women's dormitories, additional bathtubs should be installed at the ratio of 1 per 30 females. Over 150 persons: add 1 fixture per 20 persons	1 per 75 persons
ers, ditoriums	No. of persons	No. of fixtures	No. of persons	No. of fixtures	No. of persons	No. of fixtures	1 per 100 persons
		Male Female	1–200	1	1–200	1	
	1–100	1 1	201–400	2	201–400	2	
	101–200	2 2	401–600	3	401–750	3	
	201–400	3 3					
	Over 400: add 1 fixture per additional 500 males and 1 per 300 females		Over 600: 1 per additional 300 males		Over 750: 1 per additional 500 persons		

Building category is not shown on this table. Will be considered separately e administrative authority.

Drinking fountains shall not be installed in toilet rooms.

Laundry trays — one single compartment tray for each dwelling unit or 2 artment trays for each 10 apartments. Kitchen sinks — 1 for each dwelling artment unit.

This schedule has been adopted (1945) by the National Council on School-house Construction.

‖ Where there is exposure to skin contamination with poisonous, infectious, or irritating materials, provide 1 lavatory for each 5 persons. Also, 24 lin in. of wash sink or 18 in. of a circular basin, when provided with water outlets for such space, shall be considered equivalent to 1 lavatory.

Laundry trays — 1 for each 50 persons. Slop sinks — 1 for each 100 persons.

PLUMBING—FIXTURES—3
Public facilities

Table 3. Recommended aisle widths

TYPE OF W.C. DOOR		W.C. Doors Open IN	W.C. Doors (2'-2") Open OUT
CLEARANCE BETWEEN WALL AND FIXTURE ROW	Aisle lengths up to 16'-0"	3'-6" to 4'-0"	4'-6"
	Longer aisles	4'-0" to 6'-0"	4'-6" to 6'-6"
CLEARANCE BETWEEN TWO ROWS OF FIXTURES	Aisle lengths up to 16'-0"	5'-6" to 6'-0"	6'-6"
	Longer aisles	6'-0" to 8'-0"	7'-0" to 9'-0"

ceilinged mezzanines below ballroom floors, convenient to checkrooms. Restaurant and first-floor toilets may be located in the basement.

Type 1: Restaurants and first floors may have common toilet rooms, unless the floor area served is excessively large. In such cases, provide separate toilets for bars and grilles, since these will receive the heaviest use. Other facilities may be distributed as desired, preferably near coatrooms.

Type 2: Women's toilets should have adjoining lounge or powder rooms. Closets and lockers for porters and matrons must also be provided for slop sinks, equipment, and matron's accessories. Dressing rooms should be provided in the ratio of 1 dressing room per 2 water closets, and should contain, in addition to a water closet and lavatory, a pier glass, a small stool or chair, and a dressing table. Men's toilets should contain an attendant's locker and porter's slop sink.

Use and fixture ratios for Type 2 should be carefully followed to accommodate peak loads. Constant control of both types by a matron or attendant is usually provided.

Office-building toilets

Office-building toilets are restricted to the use of tenants; they are often kept locked, and keys distributed to tenants. Location is determined by the value of floor space and the position of plumbing stacks and other services. Rentable space is the building's only commodity; hence toilets should occupy the least valuable space, usually near the center of the building in windowless areas. Control is unnecessary.

The corridor plan is ordinarily used, with a battery of water closets on one side and urinals and lavatories on the other. Ventilation need only comply with minimum code requirements. Doors should open inward. Whenever possible, vestibules should be provided. If that is not possible, toilet doors should open so as to shield the interior. Wall-hung toilets and urinals and ceiling-hung partitions are generally used.

FIXTURES

Lavatories may be leg, counter-set, or wall-hung. Wall-hung types are easiest to clean, but must be supported on suitable chair carriers in order to avoid unsightly cracks between wall and fixture. Color is preferably white or light shades, although other colors are in common use in hotels, theaters,

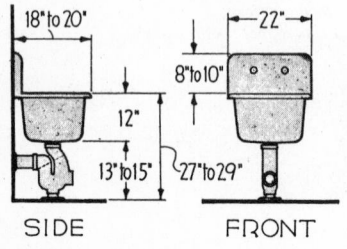

18" to 20"   22"
8" to 10"
12"
13" to 15"   27" to 29"

SIDE   FRONT

Type shown is commonly used in Office Buildings, Hotels, R.R. Stations, etc.

For Parks or Subways, size usually is 22"x24" with cold water only

Sinks may be mounted at or close to floor line if traps can be concealed

Fig. 1. Slop sinks

and office buildings. Typical sizes are given in Fig. 2. Center-to-center spacing is normally between 1 ft 10 in. and 2 ft 2 in., but may be increased for greater comfort in theaters, hotels, and the like.

Urinals are of three types: stall, wall-hung, and pedestal. Wall-hung are recommended. Partitions or fins are usually installed between pedestal wall-hung urinals, rarely between stall types. Many wall-hung urinals, however, have integral shields, which serve as partitions. Color is usually white. Dimensions are shown in the drawings. Center-to-center spacing ordinarily varies from 2 ft to 2 ft 4 in., but may be increased as suggested for lavatories. If the space between stall urinals will be too small for easy cleaning, pockets should be filled flush with materials having an impervious surface. Floor drains are generally not recommended in toilet rooms.

Water closets are of two types: wall-hung and floor (or pedestal). Floor types are most difficult to clean and consequently are recommended only for toilets whose use will be restricted. Wall-hung types are generally recommended. Seats should be unbreakable, with open fronts, and impervious surfaces—preferably white in color. Color recommendations are the same as for lavatories. Flushometers are recommended for all types. Floor treads or seat-operated valves are also used.

Water closet compartments may be of masonry, opaque glass, or metal. Doors are usually metal, and may be single or double. Compartment dimensions vary as shown in the drawings with inswinging or outswinging doors. Larger compartments are preferred where space permits, particularly in hotel or theater toilets.

Preferred compartments are those having flush surfaces. Doors are omitted on some park and subway compartments, and occasionally on other types as well. Partitions should be stopped approximately 1 ft above the floor.

Various kinds of metal partitions are manufactured, including post-and-panel assemblies with or without overhead bracing, and flush panels with integral posts, floor-supported or ceiling-hung.

Fittings, including lavatory, urinal, and water-closet fittings, should be tamper-proof and simple to operate. Clothes hooks should be provided in compartments and dressing rooms. Pay-toilet coinboxes should be easy to operate, and should clearly indicate when the compartment is in use.

Additional equipment may include scales, automatic hand driers, soap and towel dispensers, and mirrors. Smoking rooms or lounges should contain easy chairs, couches, and smoking stands; in railroad terminals, they should include bootblack and hat-cleaning stands as well.

FIXTURE ARRANGEMENT

For convenience, lavatories are usually nearest the door, urinals next, and water closets and dressing rooms farthest. Where space is at a premium (as in office buildings) in the narrow corridor plan commonly used, urinals are placed nearest the door to allow a wider aisle. Aisle dimensions are shown in Table 3.

Fixtures are arranged in batteries. Stall urinals have a trap beneath the floor level; if the floor-slab thickness will not accommodate the indicated average dimension of the trap, urinals may be placed on a platform 4 in. high by approximately 2 ft wide, with its surface pitched to the fixtures.

Dressing rooms are called for in men's and women's railroad-terminal and women's banquet-room or ballroom toilets. Those in terminals in outlying districts are usually of the smallest type shown, and contain only a lavatory and water closet; the largest type, containing showers, lavatories, and toilets, are ordinarily used only in large midcity terminals. Types used in hotel toilets should be generous in size to accommodate women in evening dress, but need not contain showers. Enclosures may be of any impervious material—masonry, opaque glass, tile finish, or metal (either prefabricated or job fitted).

Clearances between fixtures in batteries are covered in the center-to-center spacings given in Fig. 2. For water-closet and prefabricated dressing-room partitions, allow 1 in. per partition. Clearances between rows of fixtures or between fixtures and walls are shown in Table 3.

Slop-sink closets are ordinarily located close to the toilet rooms, generally with separate doors. Typical sinks are shown in Fig. 1.

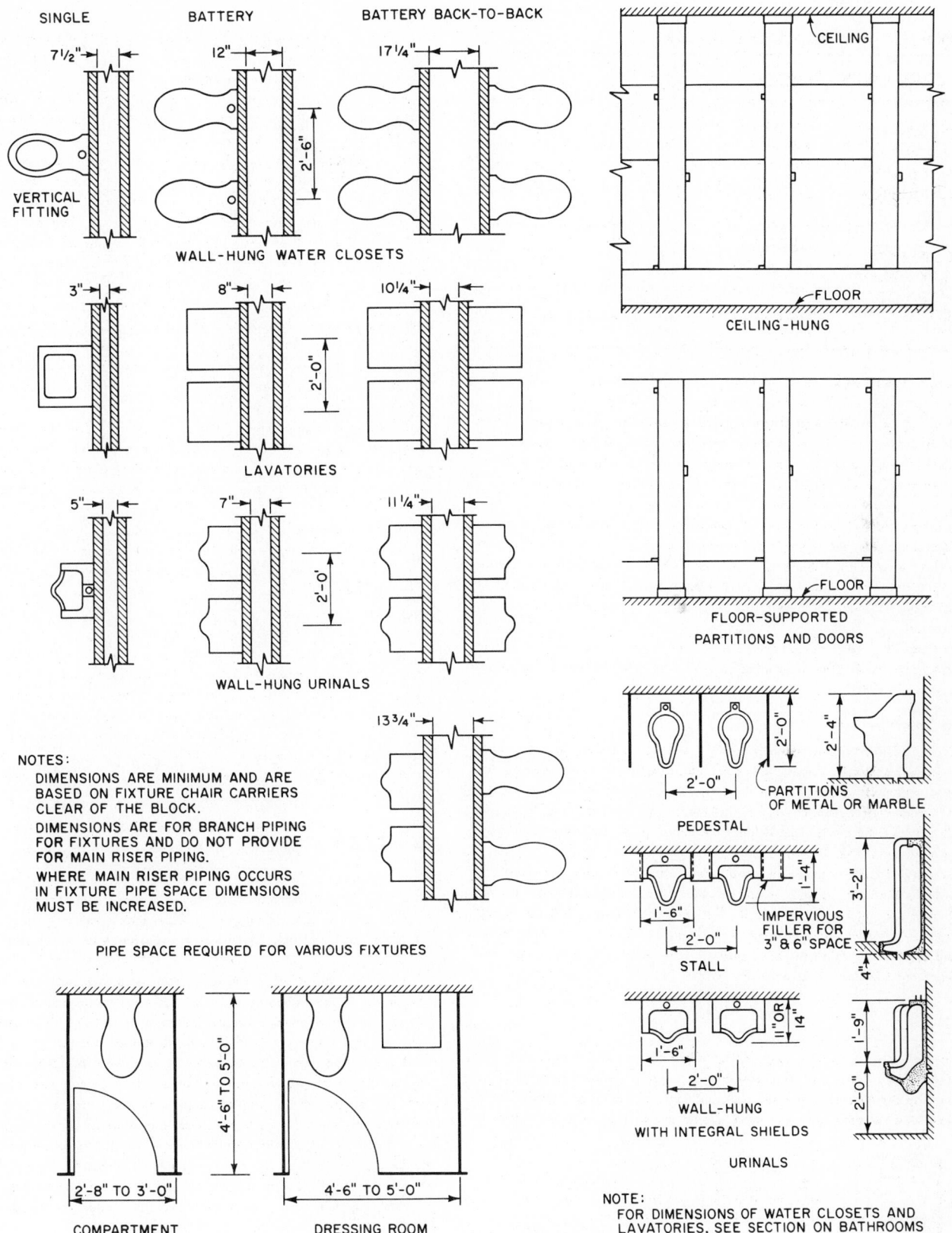

SINGLE

7½"

VERTICAL
FITTING

BATTERY

12"

2'-6"

BATTERY BACK-TO-BACK

17¼"

WALL-HUNG WATER CLOSETS

3"

8"

2'-0"

10¼"

LAVATORIES

5"

7"

2'-0'

11¼"

WALL-HUNG URINALS

13¾"

NOTES:
DIMENSIONS ARE MINIMUM AND ARE
BASED ON FIXTURE CHAIR CARRIERS
CLEAR OF THE BLOCK.
DIMENSIONS ARE FOR BRANCH PIPING
FOR FIXTURES AND DO NOT PROVIDE
FOR MAIN RISER PIPING.
WHERE MAIN RISER PIPING OCCURS
IN FIXTURE PIPE SPACE DIMENSIONS
MUST BE INCREASED.

PIPE SPACE REQUIRED FOR VARIOUS FIXTURES

4'-6" TO 5'-0"

2'-8" TO 3'-0"

COMPARTMENT

4'-6" TO 5'-0"

DRESSING ROOM

CEILING

FLOOR

CEILING-HUNG

FLOOR

FLOOR-SUPPORTED
PARTITIONS AND DOORS

2'-0"

2'-0"

2'-4"

PEDESTAL

PARTITIONS
OF METAL OR MARBLE

1'-6"

2'-0"

1'-4"

STALL

IMPERVIOUS
FILLER FOR
3" & 6" SPACE

3'-2"

4"

1'-6"

2'-0"

11" OR
14"

WALL-HUNG
WITH INTEGRAL SHIELDS

1'-9"

2'-0"

URINALS

NOTE:
FOR DIMENSIONS OF WATER CLOSETS AND
LAVATORIES, SEE SECTION ON BATHROOMS

DETAILS OF FIXTURES AND PARTITIONS FOR PUBLIC TOILETS

SCALE: ¼"=1'-0"

Fig. 2.   Details of fixtures and partitions for public toilets

The following data offer means of determining numbers of fixtures, clearances, and areas for factory toilets and locker rooms. Information was prepared, in part, by Jule Robert von Sternberg, Architect.

Factory sanitary facilities are of several general types. Most important is the "change" room (hereafter called "locker room"). This area may consist of a locker room proper, containing lavatories, lockers, and showers, plus a separate toilet room. Showers are sometimes located in a separate room. Requirements vary, however, from industry to industry and from factory to factory. In a compact, single-building plant, one pair of locker rooms is ordinarily provided close to the employees' entrance. In plants that occupy several buildings, locker rooms are usually provided in each main unit. They are sometimes located in a separate building, or in an adjoining "tower" building, or on a mezzanine above the working floor. Whatever the general location, locker rooms should be as close to the job as possible, yet must not interfere with plant operation.

Architectural finish: Walls, floor, and ceiling have to resist penetration of water and water-borne dirt; ceilings are often acoustically treated; floors have to stand up under heavy traffic, soap and water, acid and alkali; every piece of equipment has to withstand punishment.

Ventilation: Windows are optional. Artificial light and forced ventilation are often substituted—usually to advantage, for they permit close control of light and air. The number of air changes varies from 10 to 20 per hr.

Lighting: Illumination should be bright enough to promote cleanliness and employee comfort. In general, 6 to 8 lumens per sq ft are adequate. Lights are placed to give direct illumination to lockers, lavatories, and occasionally showers. Lighting in toilets is placed to discourage reading.

Size varies with industry requirements. In general, the dirtier and hotter the work, the greater the demand for showers and lavatories.

Least standardized are lockers. The type usually recommended is the individual locker 12 in. wide, 18 in. deep, and 72 in. high, with a built-in lock. Smaller sized lockers are often used, however. Some manufacturers (of jewelry, for example) do not install lockers for fear employees will secrete company property in them. Instead, all clothing is hung in the open where it can be watched.

Arrangement: The locker room should be arranged to facilitate the flow of traffic. Toilets, lockers, showers, and lavatories have to be selected and arranged so that the entire working force can use them in the shortest time. Thus consideration must be given to the relative usefulness of each type of equipment, numbers of shifts and of men per shift, work habits of men, and the relationship of factory work areas and parking areas to the locker room. Because no modern factory is designed to remain fixed in form and function for its lifetime, locker rooms, whenever possible, should have provision for expansion.

Other types of toilets: Secondary toilets, containing water closets, urinals, and lavatories, must be provided at convenient intervals. The average worker should not have to walk farther than 100 to 125 ft to a toilet. In areas where very few men work, that distance may be increased to a maximum of 200 ft.

A separately housed toilet may be provided in the yard if enough men work there. If not, yard workers can use boiler-house or plant toilets.

Toilets are also provided for office workers and visitors in the administration building. Such provisions are similar to those in office buildings.

Women's restrooms adjoin women's toilets. These restrooms must conform to local codes, and usually contain space for a couch and reclining chairs. It is also customary to provide women's showers with private dressing booths.

Table 4. Minimum fixture requirements

Fixture requirements indicated are those specified by New York State Labor Code. Requirements of National Plumbing Code (see Table 2) are somewhat higher, especially for lavatories.

No. of MEN	Water Closets	Urinals	No. of WOMEN	Water Closets	No. MEN or WOMEN	Wash Basins
1–9	1	0	1–15	1	1–20	1
10–15	1	1	16–35	2	21–40	2
16–40	2	1	36–55	3	41–60	3
41–55	2	2	56–80	4	61–80	4
56–80	3	2	81–110	5	81–100	5
81–100	4	2	111–150	6	101–125	6
101–150	4	3	151–190	7	126–150	7
151–160	5	3	191–240	8	151–175	8
161–190	5	4	241–270	9	176–200	9
191–220	6	4	271–300	10	201–225	10
221–270	6	5	301–330	11	226–250	11
271–280	7	5	331–360	12	251–275	12
281–300	7	6	361–390	13	276–300	13
301–340	8	6	391–420	14	301–325	14
341–360	8	7	421–450	15	326–350	15
361–390	9	7	451–480	16	351–375	16
391–400	10	7	481–510	17	376–400	17
401–450	10	8	511–540	18	401–425	18
451–460	11	8	541–570	19	426–450	19
461–480	11	9	571–600	20	451–475	20
481–520	12	9	601–630	21	476–500	21
521–540	12	10	631–660	22	501–525	22
541–570	13	10	661–690	23	526–550	23
571–580	14	10	691–720	24	551–575	24
581–630	14	11	721–750	25	576–600	25
631–640	15	11	751–780	26	601–625	26
641–660	15	12	781–810	27	626–650	27
661–700	16	12	811–840	28	651–675	28
701–720	16	13	841–870	29	676–700	29
721–750	17	13	871–900	30	701–725	30
751–760	18	13	901–930	31	726–750	31
761–810	18	14	931–960	32	751–775	32
811–820	19	14	961–990	33	776–800	33
821–840	19	15	991–1020	34	801–825	34
841–880	20	15			826–850	35
881–900	20	16			851–875	36
901–930	21	16			876–900	37
931–940	22	16			901–925	38
941–990	22	17			926–950	39
991–1000	23	17			951–975	40
					976–1000	41

Table 5. Wash fountains required

Number of Fixtures	Persons Accommodated By:			
	54" CIRCULAR (8 each)	54" SEMI-CIRCULAR (4 each)	36" CIRCULAR (5 each)	36" SEMI-CIRCULAR (3 each)
1	1–175	1–80	1–100	1–60
2	176–375	81–175	101–225	61–125
3	376–575	176–275	226–350	126–200
4	576–775	276–375	351–475	201–275
5	776–975	376–475	476–600	276–350
6	976–1175	476–575	601–725	351–425
7		576–675	726–850	426–500
8		676–775	851–975	501–575
9		776–875	976–1100	576–650
10		876–975		651–725
11		976–1075		726–800
12				801–875
13				876–950
14				951–1025

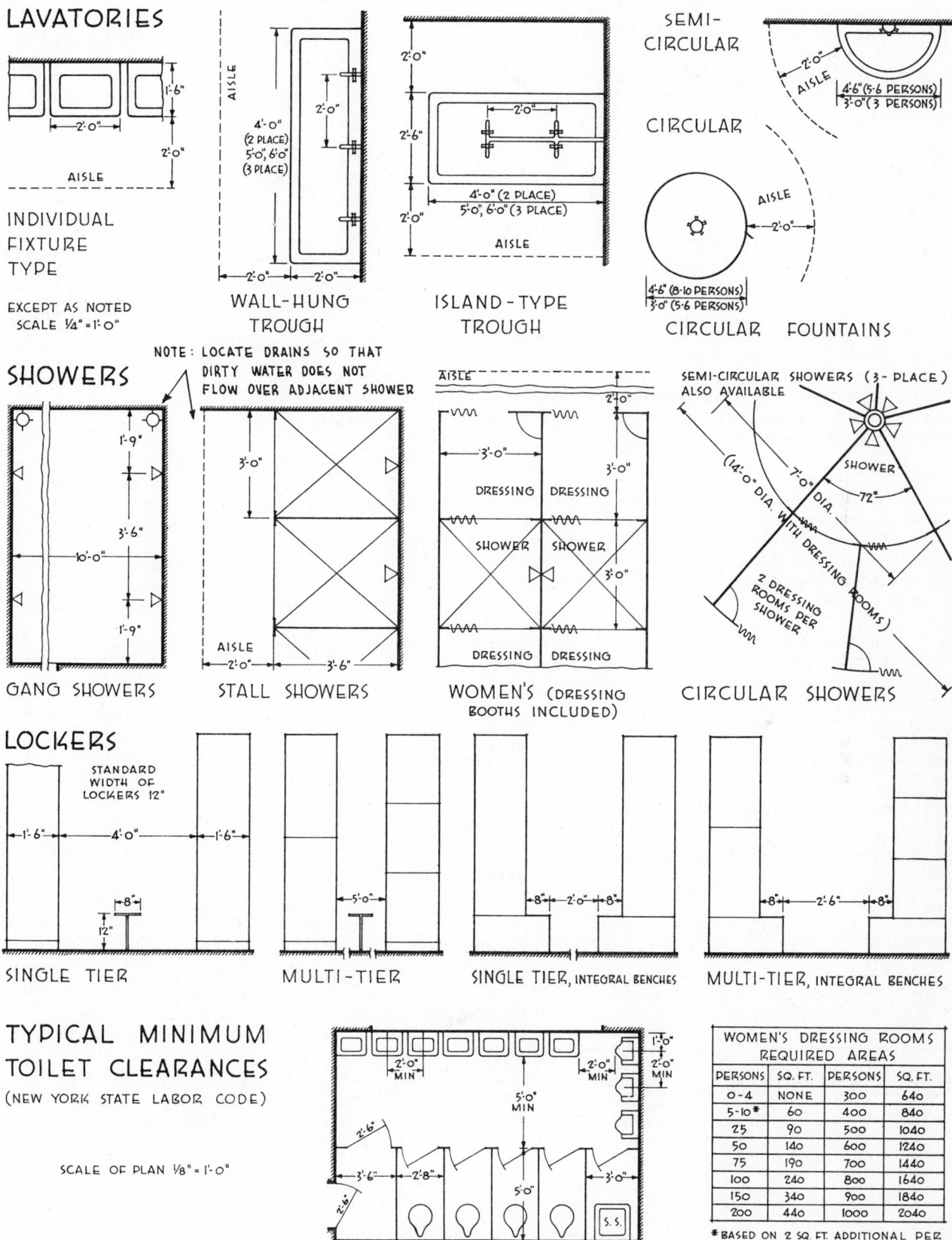

LAVATORIES

INDIVIDUAL FIXTURE TYPE

EXCEPT AS NOTED
SCALE ¼" = 1'-0"

WALL-HUNG TROUGH

ISLAND-TYPE TROUGH

SEMI-CIRCULAR

4'-6" (5-6 PERSONS)
3'-0" (3 PERSONS)

CIRCULAR

4'-6" (8-10 PERSONS)
3'-0" (5-6 PERSONS)

CIRCULAR FOUNTAINS

SHOWERS

NOTE: LOCATE DRAINS SO THAT DIRTY WATER DOES NOT FLOW OVER ADJACENT SHOWER

GANG SHOWERS

STALL SHOWERS

WOMEN'S (DRESSING BOOTHS INCLUDED)

SEMI-CIRCULAR SHOWERS (3-PLACE) ALSO AVAILABLE

(14'-0" DIA. WITH DRESSING ROOMS)
7'-0" DIA.
2 DRESSING ROOMS PER SHOWER

CIRCULAR SHOWERS

LOCKERS

STANDARD WIDTH OF LOCKERS 12"

SINGLE TIER

MULTI-TIER

SINGLE TIER, INTEGRAL BENCHES

MULTI-TIER, INTEGRAL BENCHES

TYPICAL MINIMUM TOILET CLEARANCES
(NEW YORK STATE LABOR CODE)

SCALE OF PLAN ⅛" = 1'-0"

COURTESY LOCKWOOD-GREENE ENGINEERS, INC

WOMEN'S DRESSING ROOMS REQUIRED AREAS			
PERSONS	SQ. FT.	PERSONS	SQ. FT.
0-4	NONE	300	640
5-10*	60	400	840
25	90	500	1040
50	140	600	1240
75	190	700	1440
100	240	800	1640
150	340	900	1840
200	440	1000	2040

*BASED ON 2 SQ. FT. ADDITIONAL PER EACH ADDITIONAL PERSON OVER TEN (NEW YORK STATE LABOR CODE)

Fig. 3.   Typical minimum toilet clearances

Clearances shown are those specified by New York State Labor Code.

PLUMBING—SEWAGE DISPOSAL—1
Design

By GEORGE R. JERUS, P.E.
Associate—Meyer, Strong and Jones, Mechanical and Electrical Engineers

The following data on sewage disposal enable the architect to design private (or self-contained) sewage disposal systems for residences, camps, summer cottages, schools, factories, hospitals, institutions, and the like, for any number of occupants up to the equivalent of fifty persons in residences. For larger systems, a sanitary engineer should be consulted.

Past experience, engineering practice, and bacteriological research have proven that the old-time sewage cesspool is both a menace to health and a nuisance. Sanitary engineers agree that all sewage disposal systems must include a septic tank, in which sewage is decomposed by anaerobic bacteria into gases and an effluent liquid, which is then rendered harmless by earth leaching, in which aerobic bacteria oxidize all obnoxious components. This article has been prepared from data supplied by Ralph Eberlin, C.E., Harold R. Sleeper, AIA, and the U.S. Dept. of Health, Education and Welfare.

DESIGN

A complete sewage disposal system, with all essential and optional elements, is presented on the next page. The final design of a specific installation is influenced by (1) the amount of sewage to be handled, which is based on the "equivalent occupancy," and (2) the character of the soil, as expressed by its "relative absorption." Both of these factors can be determined for any project by the methods described below.

Equivalent occupancy

The amount of sewage that will be handled is related to the type of building and its occupancy. The base is the normal amount of sewage obtained under residential conditions per person per 24 hours (see Table 1). In residential service, 50 gal of sewage per person must be treated each 24 hours; the requirements of other types of buildings are obtained from this base by means of a conversion factor.

Rule 1. To find the equivalent occupancy of any project, multiply the number of persons occupying the building by the conversion factor given for its type in Table 1.

Equivalent occupancy governs the size of the septic tank, and of course also influences the capacity required in the effluent disposal system.

Relative absorption

The porosity or absorption of the soil is a vital factor in design. A simple field method of determining the characteristics of any soil in relation to effluent disposal, consists of digging a pit of fixed dimensions and measuring the outflow rate of water from the pit.

The depth below grade to which the test pit should be dug, varies according to the unit under consideration. The size of the pit is always 12 in. square and 18 in. deep, as illustrated in Fig. 1. The pit should first be filled with water, which is allowed to seep into the ground. Then, while the bottom is still wet, pour in water to a depth of 6 in. (about 3¾ gal). Note the time required for the water to disappear, and take 1/6 of that time as the average time required for the water level to fall 1 in. This average time is the relative absorption factor for the soil; it is commonly expressed as rapid, medium, slow, semi-impervious, or impervious, as indicated in Table 2.

Design procedure

A tentative layout of the proposed sewage disposal system, similar to the diagrammatic plan in Fig. 2, should be made over a topographic plot plan of the property. Test pits should be dug at the sites of any proposed leaching cesspools or other effluent disposal areas, and the relative absorption of the soil determined.

With the tentative layout, relative absorption factor, and equivalent occupancy available, reference can then be made to Tables 3 and 4 to select the type of effluent disposal system best suited to project conditions.

Table 1. Equivalent occupancy

Type of Building	Gallons per Person	Conversion Factor
Residence	50	1
Camp	25	1/2
Summer Cottages	40	4/5
Day Schools Without Showers or Kitchens	15	3/10
Factories Without Showers or Kitchens	15	3/10
Day Schools With Showers and Kitchens	30	3/5
Institutions except Hospitals	100	2
Hospitals	200	4

NOTE: To find Equivalent Occupancy multiply number of persons occupying Type of Building by Conversion Factor.

Table 2. Relative absorption

Time—1" drop in minutes	Relative Absorption
0— 3	Medium
3— 5	Rapid
5—30	Slow
30—60	Semi-impervious
60—up	Impervious

For LEACHING CESSPOOLS see Sheet 4
SUB-SOIL DISPOSAL 5
SAND FILTERS 6

Table 3. Selection of effluent sewage disposal system

CONDITIONS		TYPE OF DISPOSAL SYSTEM		
		Leaching Cesspool	Sub-soil Drainage	Sand Filter
RELATIVE ABSORPTION:	Rapid	YES	YES	NO
	Medium	YES	YES	NO
	Slow	YES	YES	NO
	Semi-impervious	NO	YES	NO
	Impervious	NO	NO	YES
AVAILABLE AREA:	Large	YES	YES	YES
	Moderate	YES	YES	YES
	Small	YES	NO	NO
GROUND WATER: Below Grade		8'0" minimum	2'0" minimum Only required for semi-impervious soils	4'0" minimum
FINAL DISPOSAL OF EFFLUENT		Not Necessary		Always Necessary
RELATIVE INITIAL COST		LOW	MEDIUM	HIGH

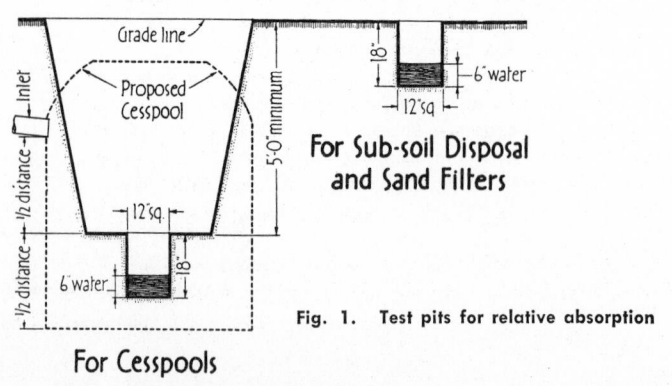

Fig. 1. Test pits for relative absorption

For Sub-soil Disposal and Sand Filters

For Cesspools

Table 4. Absorption-area requirements for private residences

Absorption area is for standard trenches (figured as trench-bottom area) and seepage pits (figured as effective side-wall area beneath the inlet). Absorption area should always be adequate for at least two bedrooms. Figures below include allowance for garbage grinder and automatic-sequence washing machine.

1-in. water drop, in minutes	Absorption area, sq ft per bedroom	1-in water drop, in minutes	Absorption area, sq ft per bedroom
1 or less	70	10	165
2	85	15	190
3	100	30*	250
4	115	45*	300
5	125	60*†	330

* *Unsuitable for seepage pits if over 30.*
† *Unsuitable for leaching systems if over 60.*

ELEMENTS OF SEWAGE DISPOSAL SYSTEMS

House sewer: The house sewer extends from the "house main" to the septic tank. The house main is a continuation of the cast-iron soil line to a minimum of 5 ft beyond the foundation; no trap or fresh-air inlet is required in it.

The house sewer may be vitreous clay tile, cement bell and spigot pipe, or (preferably) cast-iron pipe, laid with poured joints. Always use cast-iron pipe within 100 ft of any potable water supply or near trees. Never connect surface drainage lines to a sewage disposal system.

Requirements: Size: 6 in. preferable; 4 in. minimum. Pitch: 1 in. in 8 ft for 6-in. pipe; 1 in. in 4 ft for 4-in. pipe. Grade: for northern latitudes, 1 ft 6 in. minimum below surface; for southern latitudes, sufficient depth to cover.

Grease-bearing waste and trap are optional elements, used to separate grease and oil from waste. If installed, grease-bearing waste is carried from the building to the trap, and degreased waste on to the house sewer.

Septic tank: The septic tank is the essential element of a sanitary disposal system. It should be located as far to leeward of the building as possible. Its function is to retain the raw sewage out of contact with air until anaerobic bacteria can break down the solids into gases (which escape through vents) and an effluent liquid (which is subsequently purified by oxidation). (In addition, some solids settle as sludge.) Construction and operating details are given on the following page.

A siphon tank is required in large installations or if a sand filter is used; it is desirable but not essential for small septic tanks. It collects effluent from the septic tank and periodically discharges it in the effluent disposal system.

Sludge drain and pit are optional; if used, they draw sludge from the septic tank without interrupting its operation for cleaning. The drain is similar in construction to a house sewer.

Effluent disposal: There are three principal types of effluent disposal systems—leaching cesspool, subsoil drainage, and sand filter—the choice of which is governed by soil conditions and topography. All are designed to permit the effluent to come in contact with air and soil, where it may be oxidized and rendered harmless by aerobic bacteria.

An effluent sewer is an element common to all systems. It is a closed sewerage line, similar in construction and size to the house sewer, which extends from the septic or siphon tank through a distribution box or gate to the chosen type of effluent disposal element. Minimum pitch is 1 in. in 16 ft.

The distribution box or gate is a device that distributes the effluent to one part or another of the disposal system in order to "rest" the part not in use.

The choice of a particular effluent disposal system is governed by factors determined from Tables 1 and 2. Selection may be made from Tables 3 and 4.

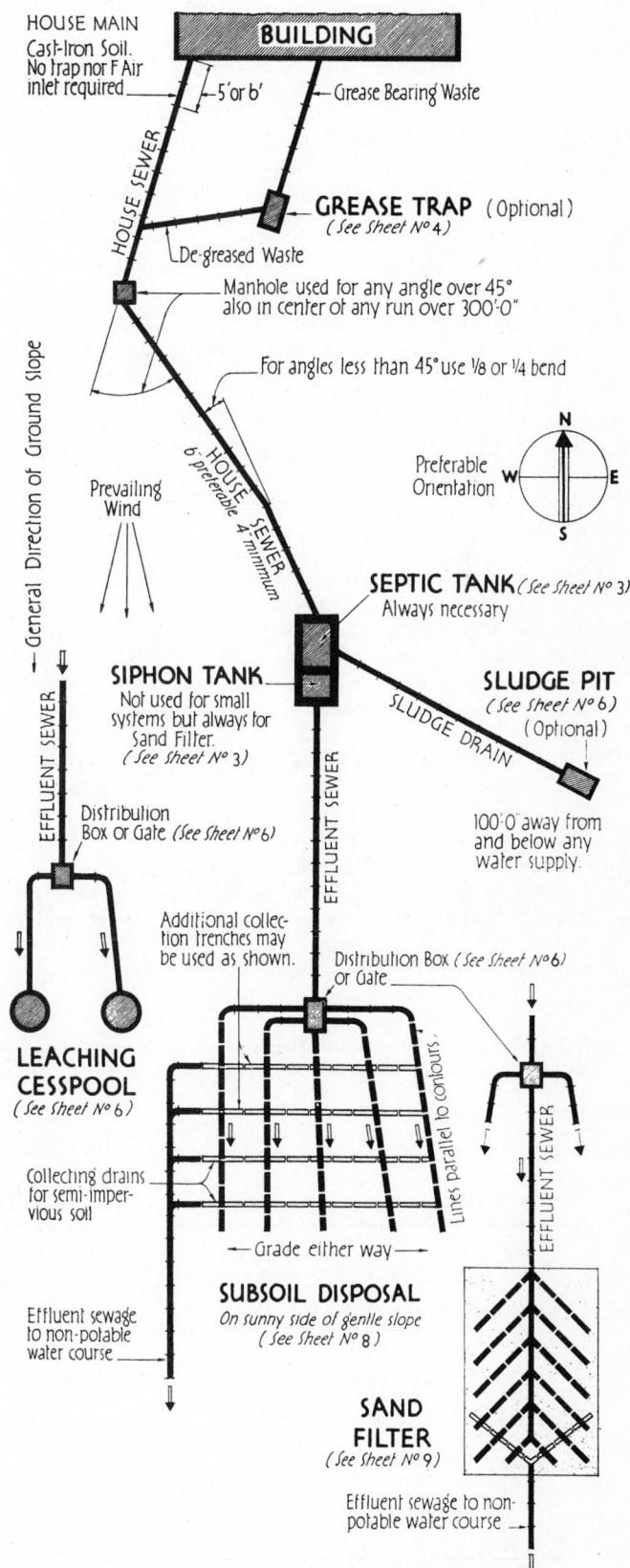

Fig. 2. Key diagram of sewage disposal system

SEPTIC AND SIPHON TANKS

The septic and siphon tanks discussed here are of reinforced concrete construction, and can be constructed by any competent contractor without requiring the use of any patented or manufactured element other than the automatic siphon that is an essential part of every siphon tank. Septic tanks are also made as commercial units, however—of steel, precast concrete, and other materials—and are available in all parts of the country. If commercial septic and siphon tanks are used, the detailed design given here will not be needed; the data given, however, will still aid in the selection of a commercial unit of the proper size.

Operation

Raw sewage from the house sewer enters the septic tank, where, by means of a submerged intake, it reaches the liquid in the tank below the overflow level. The mixture quickly forms three distinct layers or strata: Solid matter or sludge settles to the bottom, effluent sewage forms the main, liquid content in the middle, and the upper stratum is composed of a scum that keeps air out of contact with the effluent sewage and permits anaerobic bacterial action (or septicization) to take place. Most of the suspended solid matter is changed by this action into gases that escape through vents provided for that purpose and effluent sewage that overflows either directly or through the siphon tank into the effluent sewer and then to the effluent disposal system.

The sludge that forms at the bottom of the septic tank must be periodically removed, to avoid filling the tank with solid matter. In large installations, where interruption of septic-tank operation for cleaning is undesirable, a sludge drain and sludge pit should be provided to permit removal of sludge while the tank is in continuous operation. Layout of sludge drain and pit is shown in Fig. 2, and the design of these elements is discussed on the following pages.

If an effluent disposal system of sand-filter type is used, whenever the system is designed for 1000 gal or more daily capacity (and also, preferably, in all residences), the septic tank should be equipped with a small siphon tank. The small tank, however, is not necessarily required in small installations using leaching cesspools or subsoil disposal beds.

The siphon tank collects overflow from the septic tank and discharges it periodically through the action of the automatic siphon into the effluent sewer and the disposal system, thus permitting the disposal units to absorb the effluent intermittently and preventing saturation of the disposal beds.

Design

The size of a septic tank—and thus the size of its companion siphon tank—is governed wholly by the number of gallons of sewage to be treated per 24 hours. This amount can be determined from the data for equivalent occupancy given in Table 1.

Rule 1. To find the equivalent occupancy of any project, multiply the number of persons occupying the building by the conversion factor given for its type in Table 1.

Rule 2. To find the dimensions and construction details for any reinforced concrete septic tank and siphon tank detailed on the accompanying drawings, refer to Table 5. Find in the first column the equivalent occupancy nearest that calculated for the project, and read horizontally for all dimensions not given directly on the drawings.

Rule 3. To find the capacity of any commercial septic tank, find in Table 5 the capacity in gallons (second column) that corresponds to the equivalent occupancy calculated for the project (first column), and select a unit guaranteed by the manufacturer to treat that quantity of sewage per 24 hours. The siphon tank best adapted to the commercial septic tank will be indicated by the manufacturer's own data.

Location

If a septic tank is equipped with a sludge drain and pit, it can be buried and its manhole cover identified merely by the position of the protruding vent or vents. The manhole for access to the sludge-drain gate valve, however, should be carried near enough to the surface so that it can be exposed conveniently in order to operate the valve. If no sludge drain and pit are provided, on the other hand, the septic tank should be so located that the covering earth can be periodically removed without disfiguring the property. The same precautions pertain to the manhole cover for the siphon tank.

Maintenance data

The owner of a septic tank should be provided by the designer with a written memorandum containing the following:

1. A plan indicating the exact location of the septic- and siphon-tank manholes (and sludge-drain gate valve manhole if used).

2. Advised inspection of the septic tank each spring and fall by removing the vent caps and testing the depth of the sludge with a rod or plumb-bob; also, the periodical examination of the vents during severe weather, to see that excess interior flow has not obstructed their operation.

3. Provision that whenever the sludge level appears to reach the low end of the intake or discharge pipes, or there are any signs of flooding, the septic tank should be cleaned out immediately (or the sludge drawn off to the sludge pit).

4. Provision that whenever the septic tank requires cleaning, it will be advisable to remove the manhole cover of the siphon tank as well, and inspect and clean the automatic siphon.

Table 5. Septic and siphon tanks—selection and design

Equivalent Occupancy	SEPTIC TANK					SIPHON TANK			SIPHON		CONCRETE THICKNESS		
	Cap. in Gals.	Length A	Width B	Air Space C	Liquid Depth D	Length E	Width F	Depth G	Size L	Drawing Depth M	Walls J	Top I	Bottom K
1-4	*325	5'-0"	2'-6"	1'-0"	3'-6"	**							
5-9	450	6'-0"	2'-6"	1'-0"	4'-0"	**3'-0"	**2'-6"	**3'-0"	3"	1'-6"	6"	4"	6"
10-14	720	7'-0"	3'-6"	1'-0"	4'-0"	**3'-6"	**3'-6"	**3'-0"	3"	1'-6"	6"	4"	6"
15-20	1000	8'-0"	4'-0"	1'-0"	4'-0"	4'-0"	4'-0"	3'-0"	4"	1'-8"	6"	4"	6"
21-25	1250	9'-0"	4'-6"	1'-0"	4'-3"	4'-6"	4'-6"	3'-0"	4"	1'-8"	7"	5"	6"
26-30	1480	9'-6"	4'-8"	1'-3"	4'-6"	4'-8"	4'-8"	3'-6"	4"	2'-2"	8"	5"	6"
31-35	1720	10'-0"	5'-0"	1'-3"	4'-8"	5'-0"	5'-0"	3'-6"	4"	2'-2"	8"	5"	6"
36-40	1950	10'-6"	5'-3"	1'-3"	4'-9"	5'-3"	5'-3"	3'-6"	4"	2'-2"	9"	5"	6"
41-45	2175	11'-0"	5'-6"	1'-3"	4'-10"	5'-6"	5'-6"	3'-6"	5"	2'-2"	9"	5"	6"
46-50	2400	11'-6"	5'-9"	1'-3"	5'-0"	5'-9"	5'-9"	3'-6"	5"	2'-2"	9"	5"	6"

Capacity of tanks based on 50 gallons per Equivalent Occupancy per 24 hours. *Smallest size recommended.
**Siphon Tank not essential for Septic Tanks under 1000 gallons capacity. Rarely used on smallest size.

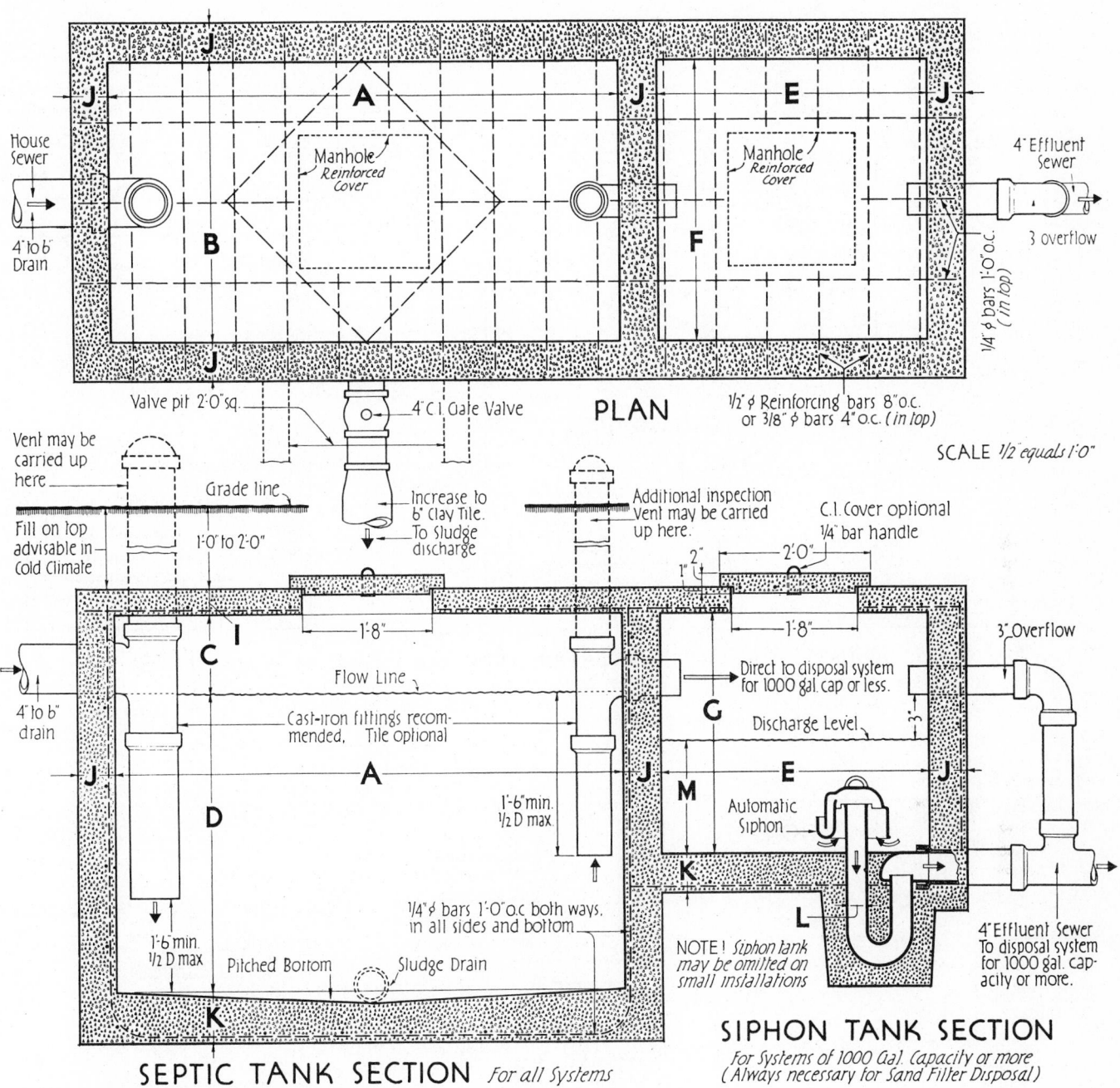

Fig. 3.   Septic tanks and siphon tanks—construction details

GREASE TRAPS

The function of a grease trap is to separate grease and oil from kitchen, laundry, and other specialized wastes, and thus prevent it from entering the sewage disposal system. Grease and oil may interfere with the formation of a proper scum in the septic tank, and may also clog or reduce the porosity of leaching cesspools, subsoil disposal beds, or sand filters. The use of a grease trap is therefore recommended in the majority of installations, but is not a mandatory requirement in small installations where no great quantity of grease or oil occurs.

The grease traps detailed in Fig. 4 are of concrete construction for use outside the house. Such a unit is not required where a metal grease trap is installed indoors in waste lines carrying grease or oil. Indoor traps offer

greater convenience for cleaning, and may be used in small or medium-sized projects, if the odor that arises during their cleaning operation is not a serious objection.

Complete design data are contained in the accompanying drawings. The size of the grease trap does not vary materially with the size of the building it serves; if the quantity of waste causes rapid flow, however, it is advisable to use a rectangular trap with a baffle.

Owners should be advised to clean grease traps frequently; therefore, the trap should be located at a point where the loose earth over the cover may be removed and replaced without impairing the appearance of the property. The grease trap should be located as far as possible (within reason) from the building, and to the leeward, to minimize objections to the odor that always follows a grease-trap cleaning operation.

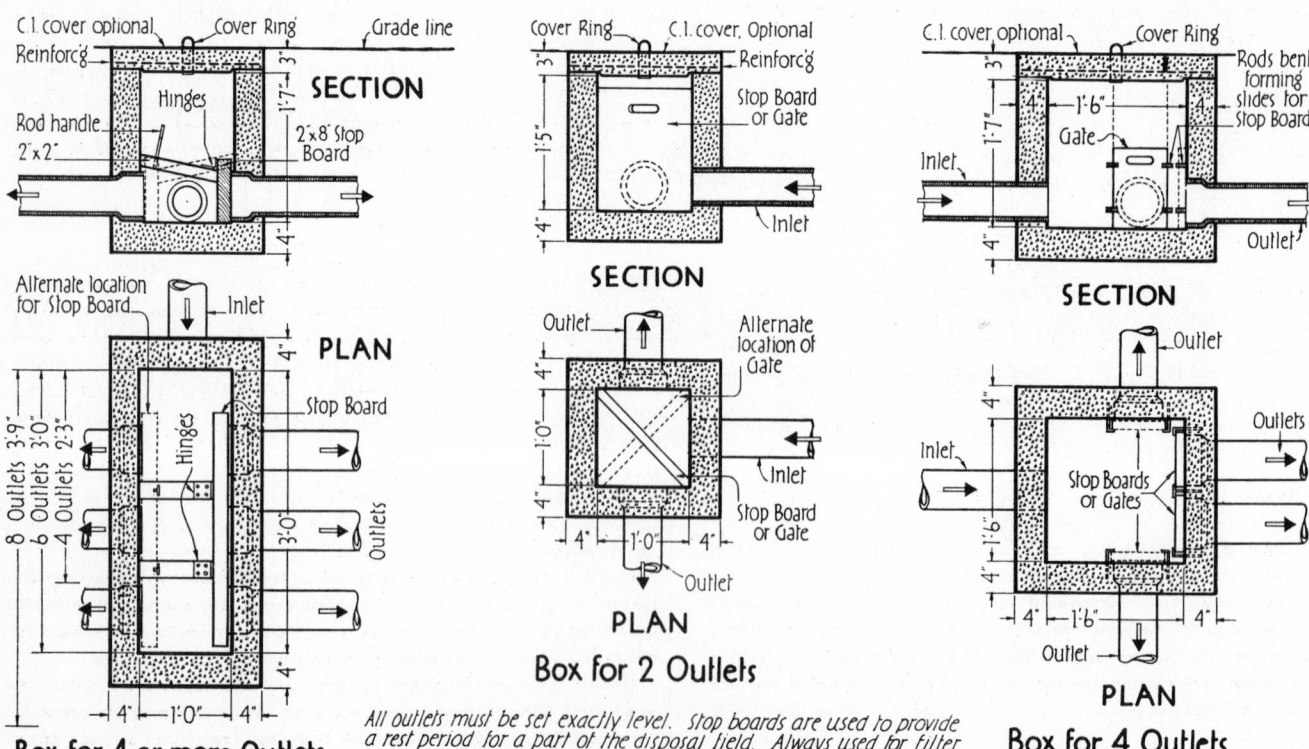

SECTIONS

Grade line — Loose Earth
Cover Ring
1/4" reinforcing bars spaced 8" o.c. both ways, or mesh.
4" clay pipe
Increaser
Outlet
Inlet
Loose Earth
Cover Rings
Increaser
2" cast iron 4" preferable
1'-0"
8" min.
1'-6"
3'-1"
Optional
4" clay pipe
Baffle
6"

PLANS

Outlet
Inlet
2'-8"
2'-6"
2'-0"
2'-0"

Inlet
Outlet
2" planks or 2" rein. conc. baffle plate.
3'-2"
2'-2"
1'-6"
4"   2'-6"   4"
6"

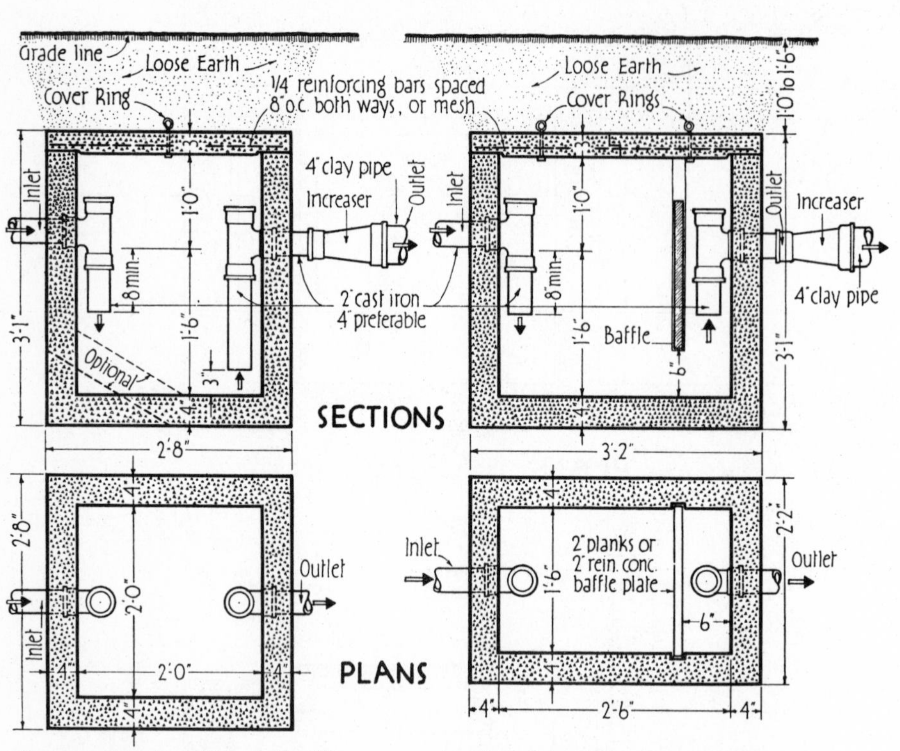

Square Type without Baffle   Rectangular Type with Baffle
Cast Iron Connections shown but these may be Clay Tile for economy.

Fig. 4.   Grease traps   *Scale 1/2"=1'-0"*

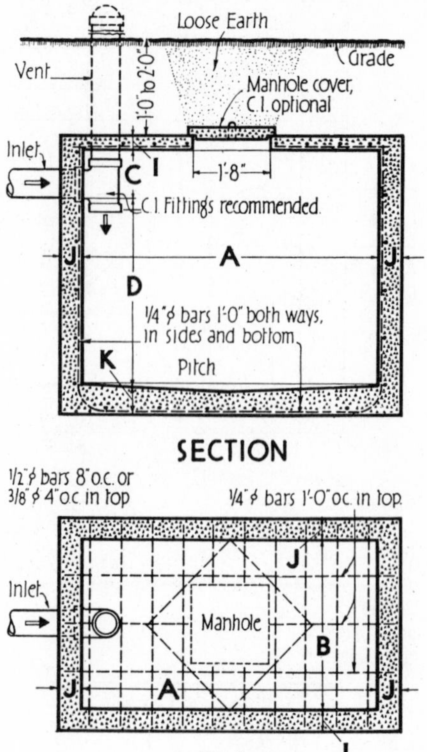

Loose Earth
Vent
Grade
1'-0" to 2'-0"
Manhole cover, C.I. optional
Inlet
1'-8"
C.I. Fittings recommended.
1/4"∅ bars 1'-0" both ways, in sides and bottom.
Pitch
A
C
D
K
J

SECTION

1/2"∅ bars 8" o.c. or 3/8"∅ 4" o.c. in top
1/4"∅ bars 1'-0" o.c. in top
Inlet
Manhole
A
J   J
J
B

PLAN
Scale 1/4"=1'-0"

Fig. 5.   Sludge pit

C.I. cover optional   Cover Ring   Grade line
Reinforc'g
SECTION
Hinges
Rod handle
2"x2"
2"x8" Stop Board
1'-7"   3"   4"

Alternate location for Stop Board
Inlet
PLAN
Stop Board
Hinges
8 Outlets 3'-9"
6 Outlets 3'-0"
4 Outlets 2'-3"
Outlets
3'-0"
4"   1'-0"   4"
4"

Box for 4 or more Outlets

Cover Ring   C.I. cover, Optional
Reinforc'g
Stop Board or Gate
SECTION
3"
1'-5"
4"
Inlet

Outlet
Alternate location of Gate
Inlet
Stop Board or Gate
Outlet
4"
4"
4"
1'-0"
4"   1'-0"   4"

PLAN
Box for 2 Outlets

C.I. cover optional   Cover Ring
Rods bent, forming slides for Stop Board
Inlet
Gate
Outlet
SECTION
3"
1'-7"
1'-6"
4"

Outlet
Inlet
Stop Boards or Gates
Outlets
Outlet
4"   1'-6"   4"
4"
4"
1'-6"

PLAN
Box for 4 Outlets

All outlets must be set exactly level. Stop boards are used to provide a rest period for a part of the disposal field. Always used for filter beds and recommended for all but very small installations of all types

Fig. 6.   Distribution boxes   *Scale 1/2"=1'-0"*

Table 6. Sludge pit dimensions

Equivalent Occupancy	Cap. in Gallons	Length A	Width B	Air Space C	Liquid Depth D
1- 4	325	5'-0''	2'-6''	1'-0''	3'-6''
5- 9	450	6'-0''	2'-6''	1'-0''	4'-0''
10-14	720	7'-0''	3'-6''	1'-0''	4'-0''
15-20	1000	8'-0''	4'-0''	1'-0''	4'-0''
21-25	1250	9'-0''	4'-6''	1'-0''	4'-3''
26-30	1480	9'-6''	4'-8''	1'-3''	4'-6''
31-35	1720	10'-0''	5'-0''	1'-3''	4'-8''
36-40	1950	10'-6''	5'-3''	1'-3''	4'-9''
41-45	2175	11'-0''	5'-6''	1'-3''	4'-10''
46-50	2400	11'-6''	5'-9''	1'-3''	5'-0''

Sludge pits should be of the same capacity
as the septic tanks they serve.

SLUDGE PITS

As previously indicated, the use of a sludge pit depends upon the need for cleaning septic tanks without interrupting their operation. The location of the sludge pit is shown in Fig. 2.

Since a sludge pit must have a capacity equivalent to the septic tank it serves, refer to preceding pages for methods of determining the size required, and to Table 6 for all dimensions not shown directly in Fig. 5.

DISTRIBUTION BOXES

The location and general use of distribution boxes are indicated in the general design (Fig. 2), and also in the following pages concerning effluent disposal methods.

Distribution boxes control and direct the flow of effluent sewage from the effluent sewage main to various parts of the effluent disposal system, permitting part of that system to recover while another part (or parts) is functioning.

The type of distribution box varies according to the number of outlets and the manner in which the flow must be controlled. It should be noted that in every installation the distribution box should be designed to provide one or more outlets in addition to those contemplated in the initial installation, to facilitate the extension, removal, or relocation of effluent disposal units. Complete design data for concrete distribution boxes are contained in Fig. 6.

LEACHING CESSPOOLS

The following page gives complete design data on leaching cesspools, which constitute one of the three types of effluent disposal methods from which the designer may choose. The choice is governed largely by soil conditions and the amount of land area available, as defined in detail on the first page of this series.

Advantages and limitations

Advantages of the leaching cesspool: It requires a minimum of land area, and can be used on a site of any slope. Its initial cost is low, and it seldom requires cleaning at more frequent intervals than two years. It can be used in all reasonably absorptive soils.

Limitations of the leaching cesspool: It can never be used in a soil rated as semi-impervious or impervious. It requires a location where the normal ground water level is at least 8 ft below grade or 2 ft below the bottom of the cesspool. It should never be located within 100 ft of a potable water supply, nor within 15 ft of the building it serves.

Leaching cesspools are limited in capacity; thus several units may be required to handle the effluent from large septic tanks. The spacing (and thus the total land area) required for multiple leaching cesspools is indicated in Fig. 7. It is recommended that if two or more cesspools are used, at least the first pair be connected through a distribution box for alternate operation rather than installed in tandem.

Operation

Leaching cesspools receive the effluent sewage from the septic or siphon tank. The walls of the pool are laid below the inlet with open seepage joints, to allow the liquor to pass through to a surrounding layer of broken stone and thence into the earth. The bottom of the pool, also, is a porous surface. All masonry above the inlet, however, should be laid with tight mortar joints, to minimize the entrance of surface water as well as add structural strength. Precast units are also available. The cesspool should be set on spread footings to minimize settlement.

Design

To determine the size and number of leaching cesspools required by any project, it is first necessary to determine the equivalent occupancy (which governs the amount of effluent to be treated) and the relative absorption of the soil (which influences the capacity of the individual units). Methods of determining these two factors are given on the first page of this series.

To find the dimensions of any cesspool and the number of cesspools required for a given equivalent occupancy and relative absorption, refer to Table 7 and Fig. 7. Note that the table is divided into three parts, according to the type of soil; in each part, the first column indicates the number of cesspools required. Cesspools can be of other dimensions, but must provide the same surface area.

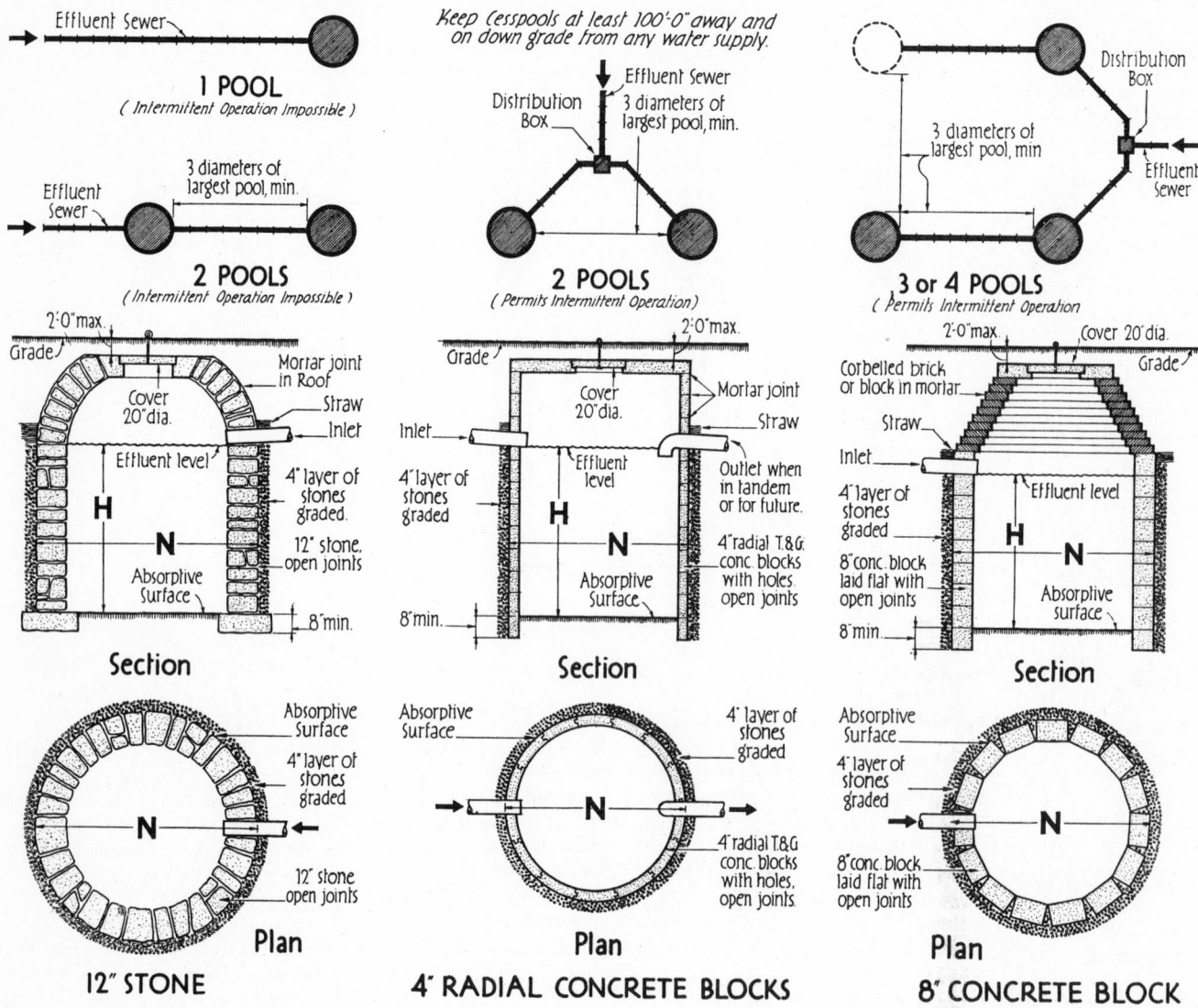

Fig. 7. Leaching cesspools—construction details

Table 7. Leaching cesspools—selection and design

Equivalent Occupancy	RAPID ABSORPTION COARSE SAND OR GRAVEL				MEDIUM ABSORPTION FINE SAND OR SANDY LOAM				SLOW ABSORPTION CLAY WITH SAND OR LOAM			
	No. of Cesspools	Dia. N	Depth H	Absorptive Area per Person (Sq Ft)	No. of Cesspools	Dia. N	Depth H	Absorptive Area per Person (Sq Ft)	No. of Cesspools	Dia. N	Depth H	Absorptive Area per Person (Sq Ft)
1-4	1	5'	5'	24.5	1	6'	6'	35.0	2	5'	5'	49.0
5-9	1	6'	6'	15.7	2	6'	6'	31.3	2	8'	7'	48.0
10-14	1	8'	6'	14.4	2	8'	6'	28.7	2	10'	8'	46.7
15-20	2	6'	6'	14.1	2	9'	7'	26.14	3	10'	8'	49.5
21-25	2	7'	6'	13.6	2	10'	8'	27.1	4	9'	8'	46.4
26-30	2	8'	6'	13.4	3	9'	7'	26.14	4	10'	8'	43.6
31-35	{1 / 1	8' / 9'	7' / 7'}	13.6	{1 / 2	9' / 10'	7' / 8'}	26.1	5	10'	8'	46.7
36-40	{1 / 1	9' / 9'	7' / 8'}	13.7	4	9'	7'	26.1	4	12'	10'	48.9
41-45	3	8'	6'	13.4	4	9'	8'	25.7	5	12'	10'	54.3
46-50	2	10'	8'	13.0	4	10'	8'	26.1	5	12'	10'	48.9

SUBSOIL DISPOSAL BEDS

This page covers the design of subsoil disposal beds—one of three methods for disposing of liquid effluent after it leaves the septic tank or siphon tank.

Advantages and limitations

Advantages of the subsoil disposal bed: It may be used in any soil except that rated as impervious. If used in soils rated as rapid, medium, or slow, distribution drains only are required; if used in soils rated as semi-impervious, however, both distribution and collection drains are needed, and the filtered effluent sewage from the collection drains must be either disposed to more absorptive soil or carried to a nonpotable watercourse. The bed may be located on ground that is level or slightly sloping, or occasionally on relatively steep slopes by proper arrangement of drainage lines. It requires little or no cleaning if the septic tank is kept in good operating condition. If possible, the disposal bed should be placed on a southern slope.

Limitations: Ground water should be more than 2 ft below grade. The initial cost of subsoil disposal beds is usually greater than the cost of leaching cesspools, though less than that of sand filters. The amount of land area required is greater than that required for either cesspools or sand filters.

Operation

Subsoil disposal beds consist of a series of drain lines laid with tight joints where the slopes are relatively steep, with continuations of these lines laid with open joints through which the effluent sewage filters into the surrounding soil. The open-lines are laid at slopes ranging from 1 in. in 24 ft. to 1 in. in 32 ft; thus they usually follow the contour lines. The arrangement of lines shown in the accompanying drawings is purely diagrammatic.

Design

Capacity of a subsoil disposal bed is governed by the number of lineal feet of 4-in. drainage line laid with open joints. The drainage lines laid with tight joints, which provide proper separation of the seepage lines, are not counted in computing the capacity of the bed. Capacity, of course, is related to both the equivalent occupancy upon which the entire system is designed and the relative absorption of the soil. (Methods of determining these factors are covered in the first page of this section.) Porous wall pipe or perforated pipe can be substituted for the open-joint tile.

Table 8. Length of subsoil drainage lines

Equivalent Occupancy	RELATIVE ABSORPTION		
	RAPID Coarse Sand or Gravel	MEDIUM Fine Sand or Sandy Loam	SLOW or SEMI-IMPERVIOUS Clay with Sand or Loam
	Lineal Feet of 4" Open Joint Tile Drain Required		
1- 4	100	150	250
5- 9	200	350	700
10-14	340	500	1000
15-20	475	650	1250
21-25	600	800	1500
26-30	725	1025	1800
31-35	850	1150	2100
36-40	975	1300	2400
41-45	1100	1450	2700
46-50	1200	1600	3000

To find the number of lineal feet of 4-in. open-joint tile drain required for any equivalent occupancy and any relative absorption (up to impervious soil), refer to Table 8. Find in the first column the equivalent occupancy figure nearest that determined for the project, and read to the right for the lineal feet in the proper soil column. Note that the same number of lineal feet of tile is used for soil of slow absorption as for that rated as semi-impervious; the only difference between the systems is the use of collection drains in semi-impervious soil.

Method of laying tile

Complete data on the layout of subsoil disposal drains are contained in Fig. 8 and 9, which also show accepted methods for protecting the open joints between tiles. It is suggested that stakes and boards be used for accurately aligning the slope of drainage lines. The choice of a particular type of drainage line is governed largely by local availability and cost, and ease of laying under project conditions.

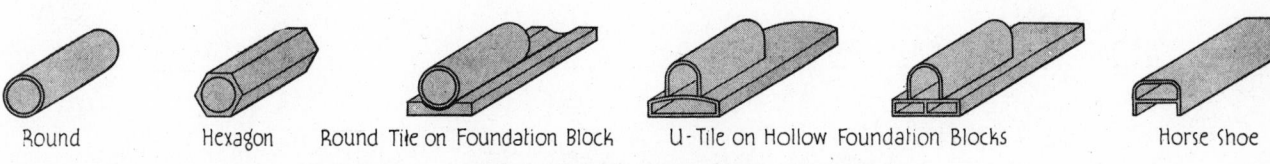

Round   Hexagon   Round Tile on Foundation Block   U-Tile on Hollow Foundation Blocks   Horse Shoe

TYPES OF DRAINAGE TILES

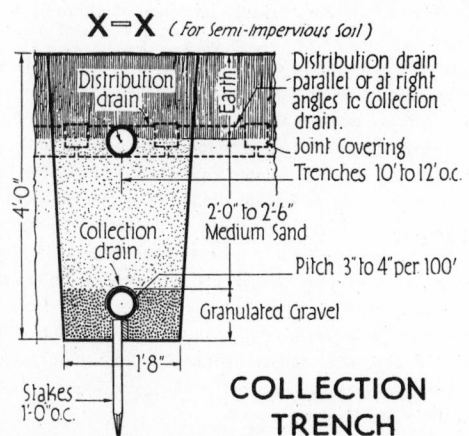

X—X (For Semi-Impervious Soil)

Distribution drain

Earth

Distribution drain parallel or at right angles to Collection drain.
Joint Covering
Trenches 10' to 12' o.c.

4'-0"

Collection drain.

2'-0" to 2'-6" Medium Sand

Pitch 3" to 4" per 100'

Granulated Gravel

1'-8"

Stakes 1'-0" o.c.

COLLECTION TRENCH

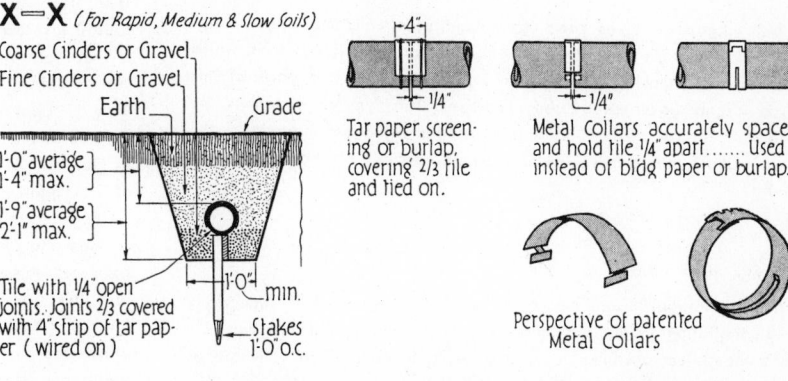

X—X (For Rapid, Medium & Slow Soils)

Coarse Cinders or Gravel
Fine Cinders or Gravel
Earth   Grade

1'-0" average
1'-4" max.

1'-9" average
2'-1" max.

Tile with 1/4" open joints. Joints 2/3 covered with 4" strip of tar paper (wired on)

1'-0" min.

Stakes 1'-0" o.c.

DRAIN TILE TRENCH

4"
1/4"
Tar paper, screening or burlap, covering 2/3 tile and tied on.

1/4"
Metal Collars accurately space and hold tile 1/4" apart....... Used instead of bldg paper or burlap.

Perspective of patented Metal Collars

DRAIN TILE CONNECTORS

Fig. 8.   Subsoil disposal beds—construction details

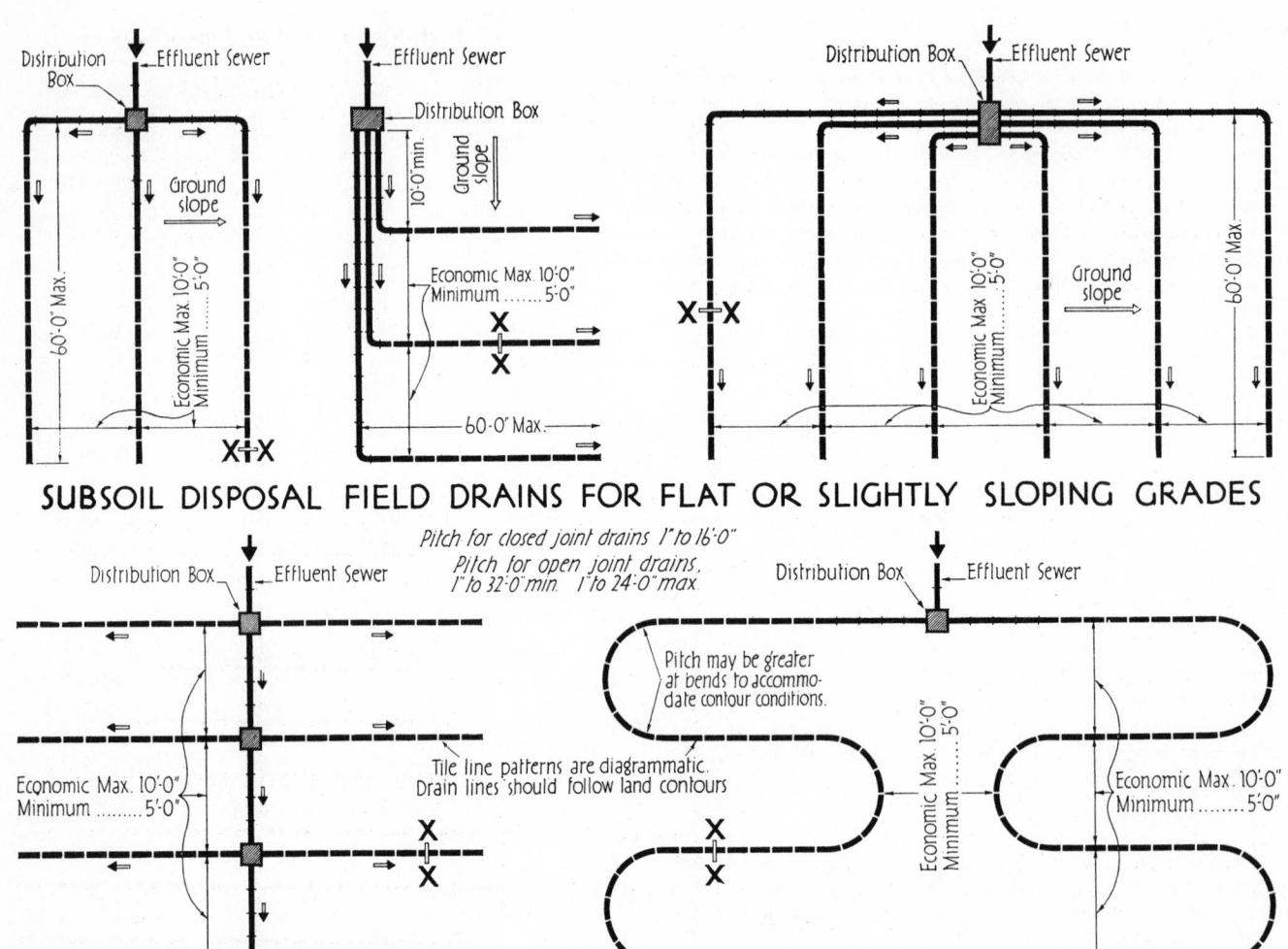

Fig. 9.   Subsoil disposal beds—layout

SAND FILTERS

The following page gives complete design data on sand filters, which constitute the last of the three types of effluent disposal methods from which the designer may choose. The choice, as indicated on the first page of this section, is largely governed by soil conditions. This type of system is the only effluent disposal method adaptable to soils rated as impervious; the other two methods, being less expensive, would normally be chosen for other soil conditions.

Advantages and limitations

The sole advantage of sand filters lies in their adaptability to impervious soils. Their limitations and disadvantages are that collection drains must be used, and the collected effluent carried either to a nonpotable watercourse or to leaching cesspools or subsoil disposal beds in more absorptive soil. The cost is relatively high, because the entire area of the filter bed must be ex-

cavated and refilled with suitable filtering material—usually clean, coarse sand. The total area, however, is considerably less than that required for subsoil disposal beds.

There are two types of sand filters: closed and open. The closed type carries both distribution and collection drains underground in the filter bed, with the upper layer of drains covered with earth. These closed sand filters may be laid out in approximately rectangular or round patterns as indicated in Fig. 10; or, if circumstances of both site and capacity permit, in the form of a long filter bed, having a single pair of distribution and collection drains.

The open type is usually far less desirable, because it exposes the effluent sewage and requires a filter bed free of any covering over the sand. In some instances, however, it is less expensive to construct, and may be adapted to institutions or large estates where the filter bed can be placed far from the building. The effluent sewage is conveyed in closed-joint drainage lines above the surface of the bed, with outlets discharging into wood troughs that serve as splash boards, which are laid out in the same manner as the lateral branches of a drain tile system.

Design

The capacity of a sand filter bed is expressed as its surface area in square feet, and is related, of course, to the equivalent occupancy of the building it serves. This system is normally used only in soil rated as impervious by tests for relative absorption. Methods of determining equivalent occupancy and relative absorption are discussed in the first page of this section.

To find the surface area of sand filter bed required for a project, find in the first column of Table 9 the equivalent occupancy nearest that computed for the project, and read to the right for the area in square feet of earth.

The detailed design for sand filters is shown in Fig. 10.

Table 9.   Area of filter beds

Equivalent Occupancy	AREA IN SQUARE FEET	
	Closed Type	Open Type
1- 4	200	100
5- 9	900	450
10-14	1400	700
15-20	2000	1000
21-25	2500	1250
26-30	3000	1500
31-35	3500	1750
36-40	4000	2000
41-45	4500	2250
46-50	5000	2500

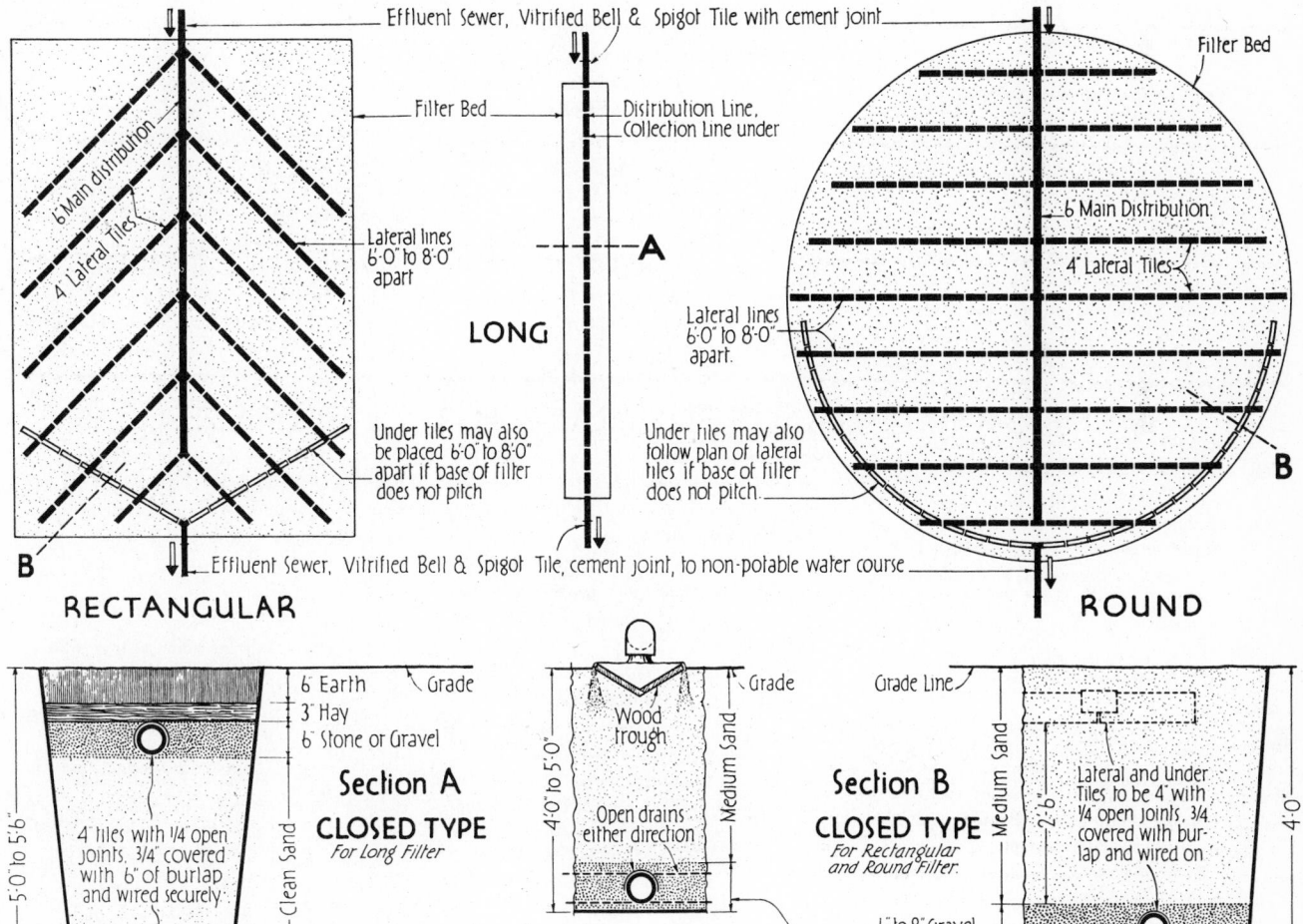

Fig. 10.   Sand filter beds—layout and construction

Data on this and the following pages have been derived from *Recommended Practice of Daylighting* by Illuminating Engineering Society (1962).

DAYLIGHT AND ARCHITECTURE

Daylight is an integral part of the architectural design of the vast majority of modern buildings. It determines, in large part, the utilitarian as well as the esthetic environment provided by the designer. Consequently, it calls for the most careful planning and the highest skill of the architect and his engineers.

The requirements for good lighting design can be achieved by skillful application of daylighting techniques. These differ from the design methods for electric lighting because of the variations in the amount of daylight, the changing position of the sun, and the deep-seated desire of many persons for a view of the outdoors. The window, and/or other means for admitting daylight into an interior, can be treated much like any other light source, and effective correlation can readily be achieved between daylighting and electric lighting. The variations in the amount, the direction and the color of incident daylight, however, add an interest to the daylighted interior which no static lighting system can possibly produce. Daylight, skillfully employed, provides the architect with one of his most effective modes of esthetic architectural expression.

DESIGNING FOR DAYLIGHT

In order to use daylight to advantage, various design factors must be taken into account. These include the following:

1. Variations in the amount and direction of the incident daylight
2. Brightness and brightness distribution of clear, partly cloudy, and overcast skies
3. Variations in sunlight intensity and direction
4. Effect of local terrain, landscaping, and nearby buildings on the available light

The incident daylight which enters and is made available for use inside the lighted space depends upon (1) the architectural design of the fenestration and daylight control systems, and (2) the decoration and furnishings of the interior.

Daylight variability

The amount of daylight available for use is continually variable. The daily and seasonal motions of the sun with respect to a particular building surface, for the latitude at which the building is located, produce a regular and predictable pattern of gradual variation in the amount and direction of the available light. Superimposed, however, is another variable pattern caused by the less regular changes of the weather, particularly the degree of cloudiness. Finally, there are rapid changes often occurring in a matter of seconds, resulting from cloud movements and other local conditions which affect the amount, color, direction and character of the daylight received at the building.

This variability may seem the most difficult factor with which the daylighting designer must cope. However, it is precisely this variation which adds so much interest to the daylighted interior. Moreover, the seasonal variation in day length can be determined readily, and data on the number of clear and cloudy days, and the number of annual and daily sunshine hours have been collected for many years (see Fig. 1). These data, compiled for various points in the continental United States by the U.S. Weather Bureau, have been reviewed by various investigators and found to provide a statistically reliable guide to the daylight which can be anticipated in any area.

Table 1 shows the results of a continuous record for an entire year of the daylight illumination received during the working day on exterior surfaces at Ann Arbor, Michigan. This study, conducted in one of the cloudier regions of the U.S., indicates that the daylight available during normal working hours is an important light source.

The sky as a light source

The primary source of light for daylighting is the sun. Light from the sun is scattered in its passage through the earth's atmosphere by dust and by the gaseous molecules of the air itself. As a result, the sky appears more or less bright during the daylight hours, and is a major source of daylight illumination on exterior surfaces.

As compared with the sun, the sky has a large visual area and a relatively low brightness. The relative amounts of daylight received from the sky and the sun depend on the atmospheric conditions and position of the sun. For design evaluation, one or more of three conditions are usually considered:

1. Incident light from overcast sky
2. Incident light from clear sky only
3. Incident light from clear sky plus direct sunlight

The amount of light received from an overcast sky, and the directions from which this light reaches the windows of a building, depend on the brightness pattern of the sky. The brightness and brightness distribution of an overcast sky vary with the location, time, density, and uniformity of the overcast. A "uniformly" overcast sky is normally 2½ to 3 times as bright overhead as near the horizon. As a simplifying assumption, however, a single value representing equivalent uniform sky brightness may be employed for design purposes (Table 2). The sky brightness on clear days varies with the position of the sun and the amount of atmospheric dust or haze. Except in the immediate vicinity of the sun, the clear sky is normally brighter near the horizon than overhead. The concept of equivalent sky brightness may also be used for clear skies (Table 3).

The sun as a light source

Only about half the solar energy which reaches the earth's surface is visible. When absorbed, virtually all of the radiant energy from the sun, visible and invisible, is converted into heat. Thus sunlight and solar heat are merely different names for radiant solar energy. The proportion of visible light in the solar spectrum varies with the depth of atmosphere the light traverses. It depends upon both the elevation of the sun above the horizon and the variable atmospheric factors such as dust and moisture.

The position of the sun with respect to any reference point on the earth's surface at any instant is usually expressed in terms of two angles. One of these is the solar altitude, which is the vertical angle of the sun above the horizon. The second is the

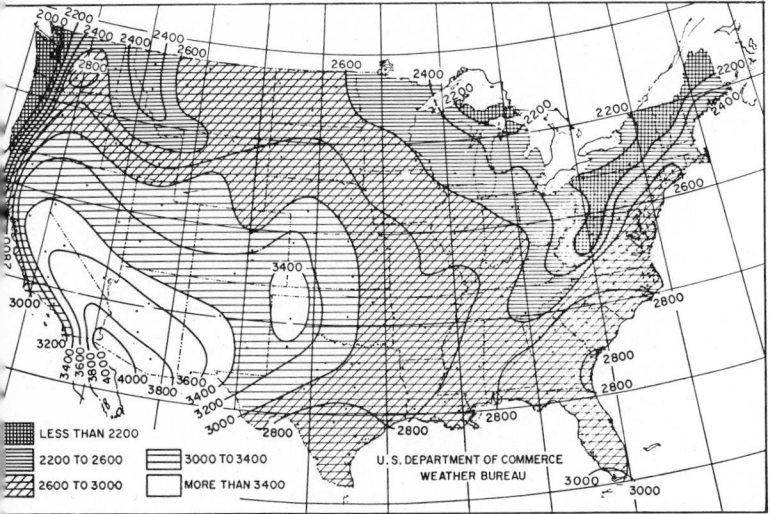

LESS THAN 2200
2200 TO 2600
2600 TO 3000
3000 TO 3400
MORE THAN 3400

U. S. DEPARTMENT OF COMMERCE
WEATHER BUREAU

1. Average annual amount of sunshine in hours

Table 1. Daylight availability, Ann Arbor, Michigan, for hours 8 AM to 5 PM, inclusive, throughout calendar year

Incident Exterior Illumination, footcandles	Percentage of Total Time Incident Illumination Exceeded Value in Left Column				
	North Vertical Surface	East Vertical Surface	South Vertical Surface	West Vertical Surface	Horizontal Surface
500	83%	85%	86%	85%	92%
1000	58%	65%	74%	63%	82%
1500	35%	48%	66%	47%	74%
2000	20%	38%	59%	36%	67%

Table 2. Equivalent sky brightness in foot-lamberts for average overcast day

Latitude	8 A.M. 4 P.M.	9 A.M. 3 P.M.	10 A.M. 2 P.M.	11 A.M. 1 P.M.	Noon
December 21					
30° N	420	740	1020	1210	1270
32	350	700	960	1150	1200
34	320	650	910	1100	1140
36	260	600	840	1020	1070
38	230	550	790	940	1000
40	190	500	740	900	930
42	150	450	660	820	860
44	100	380	600	760	790
46	60	340	550	680	730
48	40	290	470	630	650
50	0	240	420	560	580
March 21 or September 21					
30° N	910	1320	1710	2010	2140
32	880	1290	1650	1940	2070
34	860	1250	1600	1870	1980
36	840	1220	1560	1800	1900
38	800	1200	1500	1740	1840
40	790	1140	1460	1670	1760
42	760	1120	1410	1600	1690
44	740	1080	1340	1540	1620
46	710	1030	1229	1470	1550
48	690	990	1240	1410	1480
50	650	940	1180	1330	1400
June 21					
30° N	1270	1730	2250		
32	1280	1730	2240		
34	1290	1730	2220		
36	1290	1730	2200	2960	
38	1290	1720	2160	2840	
40	1290	1700	2120	2650	3060
42	1300	1690	2080	2540	2860
44	1290	1670	2050	2430	2660
46	1290	1640	2010	2330	2520
48	1290	1620	1960	2250	2400
50	1260	1590	1900	2160	2280

Table 3. Equivalent sky brightness in foot-lamberts for clear days *

Latitude	December 21					March and September 21					June 21				
	8 AM	10 AM	Noon	2 PM	4 PM	8 AM	10 AM	Noon	2 PM	4 PM	8 AM	10 AM	Noon	2 PM	4 PM
North															
30°N	450	600	600	600	450	700	1000	1050	1000	700	1550	1400	1000	1400	1550
34°N	350	550	550	550	350	800	800	900	800	800	1350	1400	950	1400	1350
38°N	300	550	550	550	300	750	800	900	800	750	1350	1300	950	1300	1350
42°N	250	500	500	500	250	700	750	800	750	700	1300	1300	950	1300	1300
46°N	150	450	500	450	150	700	750	750	750	700	1300	1250	950	1250	1300
South															
30°N	1100	1950	2250	1950	1100	1700	2300	2800	2300	1700	1200	1600	2400	1600	1200
34°N	1100	1900	2200	1900	1100	1700	2650	2900	2650	1700	1350	1650	2300	1650	1350
38°N	900	2300	2200	2300	900	1700	2700	2950	2700	1700	1350	1650	2300	1650	1350
42°N	600	2100	2150	2100	600	1700	2700	2450	2700	1700	1350	2000	2500	2000	1350
46°N	400	1900	2100	1900	400	1700	2700	2900	2710	1700	1350	2100	2700	2100	1350
East															
80°N	1550	1500	1000	700	400	2000	2500	1500	900	700	2800	2650	1400	1000	700
34°N	1350	1400	950	700	400	2400	2600	1600	950	650	2800	2700	1450	1000	700
38°N	1200	1300	900	650	350	2500	2600	1500	900	600	2800	2700	1400	1050	700
42°N	750	1200	850	600	250	2400	2400	1450	800	600	2900	2600	1400	1000	700
46°N	500	1100	800	500	150	2300	2100	1400	700	600	2850	2600	1400	100	700
West															
30°N	400	700	1000	1500	1550	700	900	1500	2500	2000	700	1000	1440	2650	2800
34°N	400	700	950	1400	1350	650	900	1600	2600	2400	700	1000	1400	2700	2800
38°N	350	650	900	1300	1200	600	900	1500	2600	2500	700	1050	1400	2700	2800
42°N	250	600	850	1100	750	600	800	1450	2400	2400	700	1000	1400	2600	2900
46°N	150	500	800	1100	500	600	700	1400	2100	2300	700	1000	1400	2600	2850

*Average values, direct sunlight excluded.

Table 4. Average solar illumination as a function of altitude

Latitude		Illumination (Footcandles)								
Date		December 21			March, September 21			June 21		
Hour		8 AM 4 PM	10 AM 2 PM	Noon	8 AM 4 PM	10 AM 2 PM	Noon	8 AM 4 PM	10 AM 2 PM	Noon
	Plane									
30° N	Perp.*	4200	7000	7700	6400	8300	8600	7700	8600	8900
	Horiz.	700	3400	4400	2600	5900	7000	4400	7200	8500
34° N	Perp.*	3100	6500	7100	6300	8100	8400	7600	8600	8900
	Horiz.	400	2700	3700	2400	5600	6700	4700	7100	8400
38° N	Perp.*	2500	6000	6900	6100	8000	8300	7600	8500	8900
	Horiz.	100	2000	3000	2100	5400	6200	4400	7000	8300
42° N	Perp.*	2000	5500	6400	6000	7800	8200	7600	8400	8800
	Horiz.	100	1600	2700	2000	4800	5800	4700	6800	7900
46° N	Perp.*	500	4500	5800	5800	7600	8100	7600	8100	8800
	Horiz.	——	1000	1800	1800	4400	5500	4400	6700	7400

*Perpendicular to sun's rays.

solar azimuth, which is usually taken as the horizontal angle of the sun from the due south line.

The illumination produced on an exterior surface by the sun is influenced by the altitude angle of the sun, the angle between the incident sunlight and the surface on which the sunlight falls, and the amount of dust and haze in the atmosphere. Data on solar azimuth and altitude for various latitudes may be found in the section on "Solar Angles." Solar illumination on exterior surfaces at selected seasons and hours is given in Table 4.

The ground as a light source

Light reflected from the ground, or from other exterior surfaces, is important in daylighting design. As with other light sources, it may require brightness control. The light reflected from the ground on sunny elevations commonly represents 10 to 15 per cent of the total daylight reaching a window area. It frequently exceeds this proportion if reflected from light, sandy soils, light vegetation, or snow cover. On non-sun exposures, the light reflected from the ground may account for more than half the total light reaching the windows.

The direction from which the ground light is received is such that it can be utilized most effectively in the interior of the space, particularly at points well removed from the window area. Furthermore, ground light is under the control of the architect or engineer to a considerable extent. By use of light-colored ground-surfacing materials near the building, the daylight incident on the window areas and reaching the inner portions of the rooms can be increased significantly. Reflectances of various ground-surfacing materials are shown in Table 5.

ARCHITECTURAL DESIGN

Because it influences building structure, daylighting design is a major concern of the architect. It must be incorporated into the building design in such a way that the building and its occupied spaces provide satisfactory visual and thermal environments. Daylight affects the architect's choice of the basic building section, the building arrangement on its site, and the architectural elements to be incorporated into the design for daylight control. Consequently, it affects profoundly the esthetic as well as the utilitarian aspects of the design—the exterior appearance, as well as the interior atmosphere.

Building sections

Most of the "classic" building sections derive directly from daylighting considerations; virtually all are affected by them. From the daylighting standpoint, the items to be considered in selection of a particular building section are that it should admit enough light to all parts of the interior space, and that it should allow for adequate control of brightness to meet the visual requirements of the intended occupants.

Sidelighting: The placement of windows in the sidewall of the daylighted space has both advantages and disadvantages. In addition to admitting the daylight, the window area can provide for natural ventilation and can afford the room occupants a view of the outdoors, which is desirable. However, the distance from window to farthest work area is a design limitation, and the window, which is the light source for the room, is prominent in the field of view. Its brightness may be troublesome unless controlled.

Toplighting: Toplighting arrangements have the advantage that they can be used without limitation on the width of the lighted space. The daylight openings afford only a view of the sky, however, and even this is usually obstructed by diffusing or shielding elements. Consequently, buildings of this design are usually provided with some side-wall fenestration, to provide a view of the outdoors. Toplighting can be effectively controlled, so that illumination can be distributed throughout the lighted space, and brightness can be held within desirable limits. In addition, the electric lighting design can be correlated readily with toplighting designs.

Table 5. Reflectances of building materials and outside surfaces

Material	Reflectance (In Per Cent)	Material	Reflectance (In Per Cent)
Bluestone, sandstone	18	Asphalt (free from dirt)	7
Brick		Earth (moist	
light buff	48	cultivated)	7
dark buff	40	Granolite pavement	17
dark red glazed	30	Grass (dark green)	6
Cement	27	Gravel	13
Concrete	55	Macadam	18
Granite	40	Slate (dark clay)	8
Marble (white)	45	Snow	
Paint (white)		new	74
new	75	old	64
old	55	Vegetation (mean)	25

Unilateral section: The unilateral side-lighting design is shown, in section, in Fig. 2a. It is the simplest of the architectural sections, and the most common. The design lends itself to continuous fenestration and to curtain wall construction. In contemporary design, window heads are usually placed close to the ceiling line. In order to achieve recommended brightness ratios the effective width of the room should be limited to the range 2 to 2½ times the height from floor to window head.

Bilateral section: The bilateral daylighting design doubles the feasible room width. For a given ceiling height, it is possible to design a wider room by adding a window in the wall opposite the main window wall. This second window often occupies only the upper part of its wall, as shown in Fig. 2b. The two sets of windows afford a path for natural cross ventilation if both can be opened. The use of a reflecting roof under the secondary windows contributes materially to the total light entering the room. Since at least one set of windows in the bilateral design faces a sun exposure, sun controls are required with this design. It is also necessary to provide effective brightness controls, since persons in the room will face a window more often than in the unilateral design. Sloping ceilings sometimes employed with this design have little effect on either quantity or distribution of illumination.

Roof monitor section: The building section employing a roof monitor as shown in Fig. 2c is usually an industrial building section. It is particularly advantageous for designs where a center high-bay area is needed between two low-bay areas. The roof monitor usually has windows only on opposite sides, but in some cases is provided with windows in all four sides. Consequently, sun controls are necessary on some of the window areas, and brightness controls are often more important. The roof surfaces below the monitor window should be treated as reflecting surfaces for maximum efficiency of the design.

Clerestory section: A clerestory window facing in the same direction as the main window is sometimes employed to overcome the room width limitations of the simple unilateral section. The clerestory window is used in a roof monitor in some designs, and with a sloping roof in others, as shown in Fig. 2d. Sun controls must be employed on sun exposures, but brightness control is not so prominent a problem as with the bilateral design. The roof under the clerestory window should be treated as a reflector. A more detailed consideration of clerestory lighting may be found in the following pages.

Sawtooth section: The sawtooth section

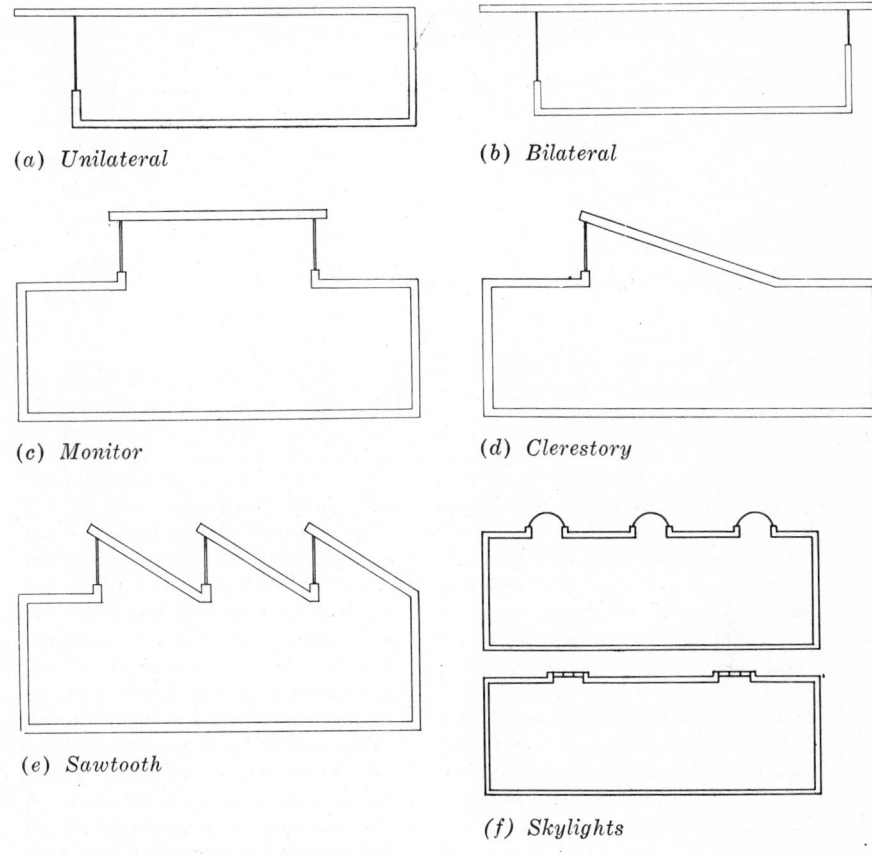

(a) *Unilateral*

(b) *Bilateral*

(c) *Monitor*

(d) *Clerestory*

(e) *Sawtooth*

(f) *Skylights*

Fig. 2. Typical building sections for daylighting

shown in Fig. 2e is used principally for industrial building construction. It is suitable for low-roofed structures extending over a considerable area. The sawtooth windows usually are faced to the north in northern latitudes, so that sun controls are not required. The windows are sometimes slanted, which increases the admission of skylight. However, such slanting results in increased dust collection, adding to the maintenance problem.

Skylight section: Modern skylights assume many forms (Fig. 2f) and are widely used in contemporary architecture. Several recent developments in the field of toplighting design have added to the architect's range of choice. Among these are the plastic "sky dome," the roof panel of glass block with integral sun and brightness control, and the roof panel of glass-fiber reinforced plastic. Toplighting by means of skylights is an efficient method of admitting daylight to an interior.

Building arrangement

Orientation: In northern latitudes of the United States and Canada, consideration should be given to orientation of the windows in a southerly direction. Assuming

suitable sun controls, this orientation affords the maximum daylight, particularly in the winter months, and permits the effective utilization of solar energy as an aid to heating. In southern latitudes of the United States, northerly exposures should be considered to limit the solar heating.

As a general rule, east-west orientations present the most difficult problems of daylight control, and complicate heating and air-conditioning designs.

Single-story construction: This type of construction greatly increases freedom of daylighting design. Almost any version of sidewall lighting or toplighting, or combinations of the two, can be used.

Multiple story construction: In modern multistory buildings with large expanses of glass daylighting designs obviously are the sidewall type.

Where light courts are employed in the design, or tall buildings are located in close proximity, high-reflectance exterior walls and setbacks increase the daylight received at the lower floors.

Materials and control elements

Materials and control elements are se-

Table 6. Transmittance data of glass and plastic materials

Material	Transmittance (In Per Cent)
Polished Plate Window Glass	80-90
Sheet Drawn Window Glass	85-91
Heat-Absorbing Plate Glass	70-80
Heat-Absorbing Drawn Sheet Glass	70-85
Neutral Low Transmission Glass	10-60
Configurated Glass	70-90
Corrugated Glass	80-85
Glass Block	60-80
Clear Plastic Sheet	80-92
Neutral Low Transmission Plastic	9-42
Colorless Patterned Plastic	80-90
White Translucent Plastic	10-80
Glass Fiber Reinforced Plastics	5-80

lected for their ability to transmit, diffuse, refract, absorb, or reflect light.

Transmitting materials: (see Table 6).

Transparent materials: The transparent high-transmittance materials include sheet glass, polished plate and wire glass, acrylic plastic sheet and formed panels, and clear glass block.

Low-transmittance glasses and plastics offer a measure of brightness control which increases as their transmittance is decreased. With such materials, view *out* is not noticeably affected during the day but view *in* is materially reduced. The reverse is true at night. Reduction in radiant solar heat transmittance accompanies the reduction in visible light transmittance. If these materials are neutral in the visible region, color distortion is avoided. The reduction in daylight which accompanies the use of low-transmittance materials must be allowed for in over-all lighting design.

Diffusing materials: Included in this category are the diffusing glasses such as opal and surface-treated glasses, diffusing and patterned plastics and sheet glass, corru-

gated glass and plastics, and diffusing glass block. All are characterized by a predominantly nonselective diffusion of the transmitted light, and by the fact that they prevent clear vision through the medium. As a rule, transmittance and brightness decrease as diffusion increases. Some types may become excessively bright on sun exposures, hence require brightness control.

Directional transmitting materials: These materials produce a definite, controlled change in the direction of the transmitted light by refraction. They include prismatic sheet glass and plastics, but the most widely used types are the light-directing glass blocks. They are also designed to restrict the brightness seen from normal viewing angles.

Selective transmitting materials: There are two types of selective transmitting materials used in daylighting: those which are directionally selective and those which are spectrally selective.

The directionally selective transmitting materials include two types of prismatic glass block; one for sidelighting, the other for toplighting installations. The materials are designed to reject most of the light from the directions along which the strongest sunlight arrives at the panel, admitting a greater proportion of the more diffuse light from the rest of the luminous exterior. Certain louvered materials and toplight closures described in later sections can also be considered as directionally selective transmitting materials.

The spectrally selective transmitting materials include the various colored and heat-absorbing transmitting materials. The heat-absorbing glasses are designed to pass the visible light but absorb the infrared radiations. Considerable research effort has been expended on most daylight-transmitting materials, so that they will not be color-selective in the visible part of the spectrum, both initially and after exposure

to sunlight and the weather. However, in some of the glass and plastic materials employed in daylighting, colors are incorporated deliberately. The esthetic effect of stained glass windows is a major attribute of the daylighting design in some of the finest church architecture.

Shielding elements and materials: The shielding elements and materials employed in daylighting practice include the various opaque structures, shades, and draperies which intercept light. They include building overhangs, vertical fins and similar building elements, as well as opaque and translucent screens, shades or curtains, and landscaping elements including trees. (See section on "Heating, Ventilating, and Air-Conditioning: Design of solar shading.")

Properly designed overhangs shade the windows from direct sunlight, and reduce the brightness of the upper part of the windows. They do this, however, at a sacrifice in the amount of light reaching the window. Overhangs of practical length do not provide complete shading at all times. In multiple-story buildings, a balcony can serve as overhang for the window of the story below.

Vertical elements have been employed effectively on east and west walls as sun controls. Combinations of vertical and horizontal elements have been used in some designs. They have been most common in tropical applications.

Shielding materials also include opaque shades and draperies used when it is desired to exclude daylight from a room.

Landscaping: Trees are effective shading devices when properly located with respect to the building and its fenestration. Deciduous trees and vines provide shade and protect against sky glare during the warm months but allow the sun to reach the building during the winter. The use of vegetation as a seasonal daylight control has not been exploited as imaginatively as it might be.

Louvers: Louvers are widely used as shielding elements in daylighting design. Practical louvers commonly embody slats which are reflecting elements as well as shielding elements. Some use slats which are made of diffuse transmitting materials. Louvers are found in many forms, located inside or outside the lighted space or serving as the weather closure itself. Slat widths range from minute dimensions to major dimensions as great as several feet. Slats can be either horizontal or vertical.

The adjustable horizontal louver is found as the interior venetian blind, the jalousie, and the exterior adjustable blind. It can be adjusted as needed for the varying solar altitude to prevent entry of direct sunlight, while reflecting a high proportion of sun

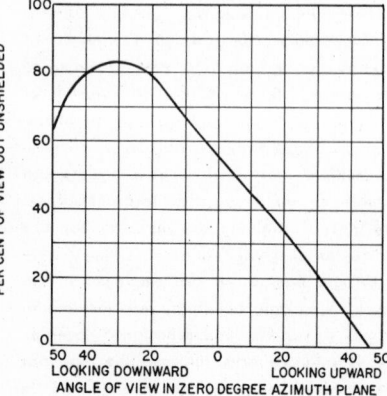

Fig. 3. Shielding of exterior view by use of darkened metal screening with minute horizontal louvers

and sky light into the interior. It permits entry of light reflected from the ground with minor obstruction. It also permits the passage of natural ventilation in warm weather periods.

The fixed horizontal louver is frequently employed as an exterior sun control and as a shield for high sky brightness. It is found with slats of all sizes, and it can be a very effective heat control as well as light control device. It permits the entry of ground light and light reflected from the top of the slats as well as natural ventilation. One type of horizontal louver employs minute louver slats, spaced so closely that they blend unobtrusively into the view, minimizing the psychological barrier presented by many other daylight controls (see Fig. 3).

Overhangs meant primarily for sun control are sometimes made of louver elements, so that more of the sky light can reach the windows than would be the case with a solid overhang (see Fig. 4). Louvers are also employed both above or below the skylight or other toplighting arrangement.

Light-reflecting materials and elements: All materials encountered in lighting practice reflect some light. Those which are employed specifically for their reflecting qualities are largely diffusely reflecting. Shiny surfaces which produce specular or mirror reflections are apt to cause disturbing brightness in the field of view and should be avoided where good visual conditions are desired.

Reflecting elements can often be incorporated effectively into the over-all architectural design. Reflecting pavements and similar treatment of the terrain surrounding the building can be particularly effective at distances from one-half to twice the height from the ground to the top of the windows. Reflecting materials or finishes on roofs and similar projections below window areas and vision strips can also add to the total daylight entering the space.

The interior reflecting surfaces of the building should be controlled by the architect. The use of white or near-white ceilings contribute to the effective utilization of ground light in the room. Wall finishes of 50 to 60 per cent reflectance make for effective daylight utilization and for good brightness control in the surroundings of visual tasks. Light finishes on the floors and on the interior furnishings are also recommended.

DAYLIGHTING COMPUTATIONS

Various computation methods have been developed for the design and evaluation of

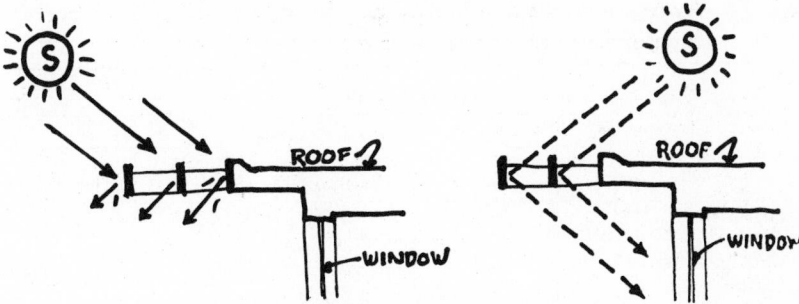

Fig 4. Louvered overhangs may be used to prevent entry of direct sunlight or to provide indirect sunlight

daylighting systems. Such a procedure involves: (1) determination of the daylight available at the windows, (2) the light flux actually entering the lighted space, (3) the distribution of the light flux within the room, and (4) the illumination produced on the surfaces of interest.

Determination of incident daylight

The daylight incident on the fenestration of a building consists of light received directly from the sky, directly from the sun, and by reflection from the ground or other surfaces visible from the windows. The actual amount is influenced by the location, the orientation of the windows, the date and time of day, the weather conditions and the local terrain. Consequently, tabular data for a geographic area should always be modified as necessary in order to account for the local conditions.

Sky light: The daylight received in the plane of the fenestration directly from the sky can be obtained from Tables 2 and 3. For purposes of comparative evaluation, it is sometimes assumed that the sky produces some arbitrary value of illumination at the windows. One such basis is that of a sky having a theoretically uniform brightness of 1,000 ft-l. Such a sky would produce an illumination of 1,000 ft-c on a horizontal skylight and 500 ft-c on a vertical window. Some publications have used as an alternate basis an overcast sky which provides 1,000 ft-c on vertical windows, and 2½ times this value, or 2,500 ft-c, on toplighting panels.

Sunlight: The direct sunlight incident on the fenestration can be obtained from Table 4. Given the exact angle of incidence, the illumination on a plane perpendicular to the sun's rays (Table 4) multiplied by the cosine of the angle of incidence, will give the illumination produced by the direct sunlight on the plane of the fenestration.

Ground light: The illumination produced at the plane of a window by reflection

from the ground is influenced by several factors. These include the illumination produced on the ground by the sky and the sun, the reflectance of the ground (Table 5), and the slope or tilt of the fenestration. There is, of course, no ground light reflected onto a horizontal window or skylight.

A vertical window, however, receives illumination from a uniformly bright ground equal in footcandles to one-half the ground brightness in footlamberts. For example, a uniformly bright sky of 1,000 ft-l, which produced 500 ft-c directly on the window, would also produce 1,000 ft-c on the ground. With a diffuse ground reflectance of 20 per cent, the ground brightness would be 200 ft-l. The illumination produced on a vertical window by this ground brightness would be 100 ft-c, which is one-fifth as much as was directed to the window from the sky alone.

With higher ground reflectance values, as for reflecting roofs under clerestory windows, or for cases where there is sun on the ground but not on the windows, the proportion of ground light to sky light may be much higher.

Determination of light flux entering room

Only a portion of the light flux incident on the fenestration area actually enters the lighted space. The gross fenestration area is reduced by the mechanical supports of the glazing material, such as mullions, window members, or mortar joints. The reduction in transmission area is a matter of simple geometry and can be readily determined.

There is also a transmission loss in the glazing material itself. Data on transmittance of glazing materials are included in Table 6. There is a further loss attributable to dirt collection on the glazing material (Table 7), which should be included in computations as a maintenance factor. Finally, there is absorption or reflection by daylight controls, such as shades, lou-

Table 7. Average window maintenance factors expressed as percentage of clean glass transmission

	Window Position				
	Office*	Factory**			
	Vertical	Vertical	30° from Vertical	60° from Vertical	Horizontal
Avg. value over 6 mo. period	83%	71%	65%	58%	54%
Value end of 3 mo. period	82	69	62	54	50
Value end of 6 mo. period	73	55	45	39	34

*Typical clean location.   **Typical dirty location.

vers, prismatic devices, overhangs, or by the light wells of toplighting arrangements.

It should be emphasized that daylight is generally abundant, and that simple efficiency of transmission into the room can and must often be compromised with other factors such as control of sunlight, heat gain, or glare, in the over-all daylighting design.

Illumination toplighting: For toplighting systems of daylight design, employing lighting elements or areas mounted horizontally or in the plane of a nearly level roof, determination of the average illumination produced in the lighted space can be made by much the same principles as are used for electric lighting practice. The basic relationship is

$$E_{tl} = \frac{E_h \times A_{tl} \times K_u \times K_m}{A_r}$$

where E_{tl} = average illumination produced on the work plane by the toplighting system, lumens per sq ft (ft-c)

E_h = incident illumination on exterior of toplighting element, lumens per sq ft

A_{tl} = gross area of toplighting element, sq ft

K_u = utilization coefficient, dependent on room geometry, reflectances, design of toplighting element (from Tables 8 and 9)

K_m = maintenance factor (from Table 7)

A_r = room area, sq ft.

Toplight transmission: The net transmittance of a toplight can be obtained from the manufacturers of prefabricated units (see Table 10).

Light well effect: A toplight panel is usually located at the roof level, with a light well below it extending down to the ceiling level of the room. This depth may be in a range from a few inches to several feet, depending upon the depth of the roof trusses and other factors. The interflections of the light in this well result

in a decrease in the net transmission of the total assembly.

Uniformity: The formula above permits the calculation of the average illumination produced on the work plane for the assumed exterior lighting conditions but gives no information concerning the uniformity of the lighting distribution over the work area. Uniformity of multiple toplighting will usually be adequate if the spacing between centers of adjacent toplighting elements does not exceed twice the height of the ceiling above the work plane for large area sources and one times the ceiling height for small area sources.

Toplighting example: As an example of the procedure, determine the average illumination for a toplighting design based on the following assumed conditions:

Room 20 x 30 ft, with 12-ft ceiling height
Reflectances: walls, 50 per cent; ceiling, 75 per cent; floor, 30 per cent
Overcast sky, producing 1,500 ft-c horizontal surface illumination
Toplighting panels: six, each 3 x 5 ft, of hammered heat-absorbing wire glass, with shallow light wells and egg-crate louvers
Net transmittance: 40 per cent of incident light
Maintenance Factor: 0.7

Computation:
From Table 5, room ratio = 1.3
From Table 6, K_u = 0.30
Therefore, E_{tl} =

$$\frac{1500 \times (3 \times 5) \times 6 \times 0.30 \times 0.7}{(20 \times 30)}$$
$$= 47 \text{ ft-c average}$$

Illumination sidelighting

The calculation of illumination produced by sidelighting is somewhat more complex than for toplighting. First, the light source is located asymmetrically with respect to the work plane. Second, light reaching the fenestration from above the horizontal is affected differently than light from below the horizontal in most daylighting systems.

The basic approach is the same as for toplighting. A coefficient is applied to the light flux incident on the fenestration, to determine the illumination on the work plane in the room. Since the work-plane illumination varies with the distance from the window, coefficients are determined for three points on the work plane in a line at right angles to the middle of the window. Five feet from the window gives a value E_{max}. The midpoint of the room gives a value E_{mid}. Five feet from the inner wall gives a value E_{min}. For each point, separate computations must be made

Table 8.   Room ratios: toplighting

Room Length in Feet	Room Width in Feet	Ceiling Height Above Floor in Feet					
		8	10	12	15	19	23
12	12	1.1	0.8	0.6	0.5		
	16	1.3	0.9	0.7	0.6		
	20	1.4	1.0	0.8	0.6	0.5	
	24	1.5	1.1	0.8	0.7	0.5	
	30	1.6	1.1	0.9	0.7	0.5	
	40	1.7	1.2	1.0	0.7	0.6	0.5
20	20	1.8	1.3	1.1	0.8	0.6	0.5
	24	2.0	1.5	1.2	0.9	0.7	0.5
	30	2.2	1.6	1.3	1.0	0.7	0.6
	40	2.4	1.8	1.4	1.1	0.8	0.7
	60	2.7	2.0	1.6	1.2	0.9	0.7
	80	2.9	2.1	1.7	1.3	1.0	0.8
30	30	2.7	2.0	1.6	1.2	0.9	0.7
	40	3.1	2.3	1.8	1.4	1.0	0.8
	60	3.6	2.7	2.1	1.6	1.2	1.0
	80	4.0	2.9	2.3	1.7	1.3	1.1
	100	4.2	3.1	2.4	1.9	1.4	1.1
	120	4.4	3.2	2.5	1.9	1.5	1.2
40	40	3.6	2.7	2.1	1.6	1.2	1.0
	60	4.4	3.2	2.5	1.9	1.5	1.2
	80	4.9	3.6	2.8	2.1	1.6	1.3
	100	5+	3.8	3.0	2.3	1.7	1.4
	120	5+	4.0	3.2	2.4	1.8	1.5
	140	5+	4.1	3.3	2.5	1.9	1.5

for sky light and ground light, and the results added to obtain the total work-plane illumination at the point.

The basic relationship for illumination produced by sidelighting is

$$E_p = E_i \times A_w \times K_u \times K_m$$

where E_p = work-plane illumination at point P, lumens per sq ft

E_i = illumination from sky or ground incident on vertical windows, lumens per sq ft

A_w = gross area of fenestration, sq ft

K_m = maintenance coefficient

K_u = utilization coefficient, which includes the effect of fenestration design, daylight controls, interior reflectances, and room geometry

Utilization coefficient tables: Values of the utilization coefficients $K_{u\ max}$, $K_{u\ mid}$, and $K_{u\ min}$ are given for several typical fenestration and control systems in *Recommended Practice of Daylighting,* published by the Illuminating Engineering Society.

Combination designs: Daylighting designs which have side-wall fenestration in more than one wall or combined with toplighting, may be treated by superposition. That is, the values obtained by the several calculations may simply be added.

BRIGHTNESS

The methods for computing brightness in a lighted space are not too well advanced, particularly for daylighting designs. However, certain brightness values can be determined for almost any design.

Task brightness

Task brightness in foot-lamberts can be computed by multiplying the work-plane illumination in foot-candles by the diffuse reflectance of the task. For paper work or printed matter, a diffuse reflectance of 70 per cent is a reasonable average value in common use. If work plane illumination is 100 ft-c, a task of this sort has a brightness of 70 ft-l.

Table 9. Coefficients of utilization for toplighting

Net Toplight Transmittance (Including Light Well Effect, Controls, Etc.)	Room Ratio	Ceiling Reflectance			
		75 Per cent		50 Per cent	
		Wall Reflectance			
		50 Per cent	30 Per cent	50 Per cent	30 Per cent
70%	0.6 (J)	.37	.34	.36	.34
	0.8 (I)	.45	.42	.44	.41
	1.0 (H)	.49	.46	.48	.45
	1.25 (G)	.52	.50	.51	.49
	1.5 (F)	.55	.53	.53	.51
	2.0 (E)	.58	.56	.57	.55
	2.5 (D)	.61	.59	.60	.58
	3.0 (C)	.63	.61	.62	.60
	4.0 (B)	.65	.62	.63	.61
50%	0.6 (J)	.26	.24	.26	.24
	0.8 (I)	.32	.30	.31	.29
	1.0 (H)	.35	.33	.34	.32
	1.25 (G)	.37	.36	.36	.35
	1.5 (F)	.39	.38	.38	.36
	2.0 (E)	.41	.40	.41	.39
	2.5 (D)	.44	.42	.43	.41
	3.0 (C)	.45	.44	.44	.43
	4.0 (B)	.46	.44	.45	.44
30%	0.6 (J)	.16	.15	.16	.15
	0.8 (I)	.19	.18	.19	.18
	1.0 (H)	.21	.20	.21	.19
	1.25 (G)	.22	.21	.22	.21
	1.5 (F)	.24	.23	.23	.22
	2.0 (E)	.25	.24	.24	.24
	2.5 (D)	.26	.25	.26	.25
	3.0 (C)	.27	.26	.27	.26
	4.0 (B)	.28	.27	.27	.26
10%	0.6 (J)	.05	.05	.05	.05
	0.8 (I)	.06	.06	.06	.06
	1.0 (H)	.07	.07	.07	.06
	1.25 (G)	.07	.07	.07	.07
	1.5 (F)	.08	.08	.08	.07
	2.0 (E)	.08	.08	.08	.08
	2.5 (D)	.09	.08	.09	.08
	3.0 (C)	.09	.09	.09	.09
	4.0 (B)	.09	.09	.09	.09

Table 10. Net transmittance of white translucent plastic dome skylights, wells, and ceiling diffusers expressed as fractions of equivalent overcast sky brightness (well walls and axes of domes vertical)

Well Characteristics		Skylight Dome Transmittance											
		.30	.50	.70	.30			.50			.70		
Surface Reflectance	Well Index*				Ceiling Diffuser Transmittance								
					.40	.60	.80	.40	.60	.80	.40	.60	.80
.80	0.1	.28	.47	.65	.16	.22	.25	.24	.33	.40	.30	.44	.55
	0.2	.25	.43	.60	.14	.19	.23	.21	.30	.38	.28	.40	.51
	0.3	.23	.40	.55	.13	.17	.21	.20	.28	.35	.26	.37	.47
	0.4	.22	.37	.51	.12	.16	.19	.18	.26	.32	.24	.34	.44
	0.5	.20	.35	.48	.11	.15	.18	.16	.24	.30	.22	.32	.41
	1.0	.14	.24	.34	....	.10	.12	.11	.17	.21	.15	.22	.29
	1.5	.10	.17	.25	....	....	.09	....	.12	.15	.11	.15	.20
.50	0.1	.26	.44	.63	.14	.21	.24	.22	.31	.38	.28	.41	.52
	0.2	.23	.38	.57	.11	.17	.21	.18	.26	.33	.24	.35	.46
	0.3	.20	.33	.51	.10	.15	.18	.16	.22	.28	.21	.31	.40
	0.4	.17	.30	.46	....	.12	.16	.13	.19	.25	.18	.27	.36
	0.5	.15	.27	.41	....	.10	.14	.12	.17	.22	.16	.24	.32
	1.0	.09	.15	.24	....	....	.08	....	.09	.12	.10	.14	.19
	1.5	....	.09	.14	....	....	....	....	....	.07	....	.08	.11

*Well Index $= \dfrac{\text{depth (length + width)}}{2 \times \text{length} \times \text{width}}$

Surround brightness

The surround brightness is usually somewhat more difficult to determine. Where the immediate surround is in the work plane, such as a desk or table top, its brightness will be the work-plane illumination multiplied by the diffuse reflectance of the desk surface. Reflectance of dark woods, and dark green or gray lineoleums ranges from 10 to 20 per cent. Lighter woods and compositions range from 20 to 40 per cent reflectance. For a work-plane illumination of 100 ft-c, a light gray desk top will have a brightness of 30 ft-l if it has a reflectance of 30 per cent. For the two preceding examples, the brightness ratio of the visual task to its near surround will be 70/30, or 2.33/1, which is considered close to ideal (see section on "Lighting").

Brightnesses of floors, walls, or ceilings are more difficult to compute. However, considerable data showing room brightnesses have been published during recent years, and intelligent approximations can be made by those engineers who are familiar with these investigations.

Source brightness

Brightness of fenestration areas can be approximated in one of several ways. For clear glazing, brightness of the sky visible through the windows can be taken as the sky brightness assumed for the illumination computation, multiplied by the transmittance of the glazing material. Thus a sky brightness of 1,500 ft-l, viewed through a glass having a transmittance of 80 per cent, will have an apparent brightness of 1,200 ft-l. For a low transmittance glass of 30 per cent transmittance, the apparent brightness would be 450 ft-l.

Brightness through minute louvers: The dark-colored, minute-louvered materials produce a reduction in apparent brightness of an exterior view by interposing the unobtrusive dark slats of the louver material into the field of view. The brightness of the exterior viewed through such a material can be closely approximated by multiplying the brightness of the unshielded view by the proportion of the view unimpeded by the louver slats from Fig. 4. A sky having a brightness of 1,500 ft-l viewed at an angle where only 20 per cent of the view is visible through the slats, will have an apparent brightness of only 300 ft-l.

REFERENCES

A bibliography of 277 items is included in *Recommended Practice of Daylighting*, published by the Illuminating Engineering Society.

By BERNARD F. GREENE, *Lighting Consultant, New York*

Designing for Daylight with Clerestory Windows

Natural lighting is an important part of the design of a building. For good lighting the type, area and dimensions of the window openings must be carefully planned to obtain adequate, well distributed illumination which is free from glare. To meet this challenge the science of daylighting is steadily being developed. Daylighting designs based on intuition and fancy are gradually being replaced by products of sound engineering methods.

Designing for daylight can be accomplished today by the same rules used in artificial lighting systems. However, because of the many more factors involved in daylighting design, it is important to follow a systematic approach in which each phase of the problem is considered separately. The purpose of this section is to describe one phase of daylighting—the clerestory window. Other problems such as sunlight control, window spacing, skylight and monitor design, etc., can be discussed separately.

The design of clerestory windows lends itself to engineering analysis; by the application of mathematical methods, clerestory window arrangements can be designed which are applicable to schools, offices, factories or homes.

Approach to Daylighting Design

In the design of a system of lighting utilizing daylight, certain criteria must be established in order to insure that there is enough light at different times and for different locations and weather conditions. One criterion, which is easy to use and which yields accurate results, is the assumption that the sky is a uniform source of light with a known brightness value. This can be taken as equal to that obtained in the late afternoon on an overcast day in December. If we assume this value to be 600 foot lamberts (units of brightness), then the sky would be brighter than this value approximately 85 per cent of the daylight hours in the vicinity of 42° north latitude. Values of twice this brightness would be obtained 50 per cent of the daylight hours and values of three times this brightness 15 per cent of the daylight hours.

The assumed value of 600 foot lamberts is the basis for design. Recommended levels of light throughout a room can be obtained for this condition, and when the sky is brighter the illumination levels are proportionately higher. When the sky brightness is less, however, an artificial lighting system should be used to maintain the desired illumination.

Once the problem of daylighting has been reduced to that of calculating the light distribution from a source of uniform brightness, light distribution from different window arrangements can be obtained by the use of mathematical formulas. Following this procedure, the direct component light distribution from side-wall and clerestory arrangements was calculated, and the results were compiled to yield the recommended design principles for clerestory windows which are described below.

The Clerestory Arrangement

A clerestory arrangement usually consists of a side-wall window and a clerestory window mounted overhead (Fig. 5). The problem is then to find the proper relationship between the side-wall and clerestory window, and to determine the clerestory setback, the height of the clerestory window, the room depth, the window positions, etc., in order to obtain the desired illumination level and nearly uniform light distribution. Once these are obtained,

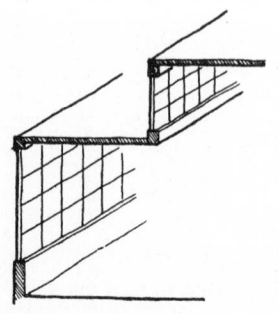

Fig. 5. Clerestory, side-wall window arrangement

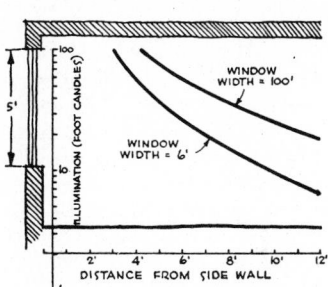
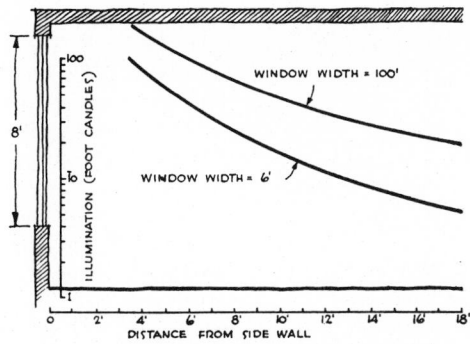

Figs. 6, 7. Daylight from side-wall windows is maximum near the window sill and decreases as the distance increases. Amount and distribution of light varies with window height, width as shown here

Note: curves are based on illumination at working plane; combination curves show total illumination from side-wall and clerestory windows.

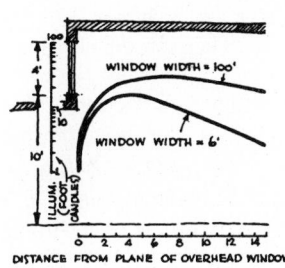
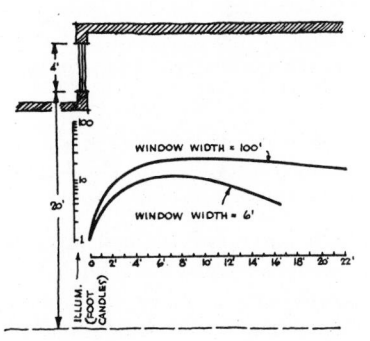
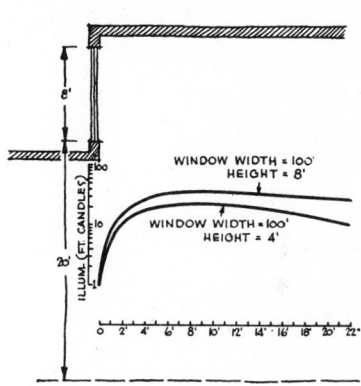

Figs. 8–10. Daylight directly below clerestory window is zero when window is mounted vertically. Both mounting height and window height affect the distribution of daylight

Fig. 11. Improper clerestory arrangement

When clerestory faces opposite direction from side-wall window, illumination is high near wall and very low near clerestory.

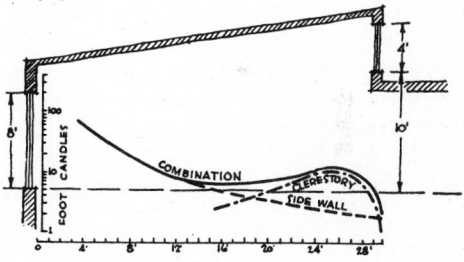

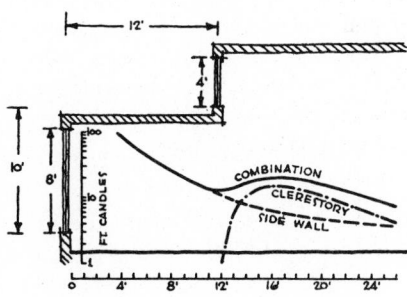

Fig. 12. Correct clerestory arrangement

Light from clerestory complements that from the side-wall window to get more even distribution. Window widths were taken as 6 ft for Figs. 11, 12. Curves for wide windows are similar (see Fig. 14).

it will be found that for the condition of an overcast sky, the brightness contrasts through the room for almost all daylighting designs will be less than those usually encountered in artificial lighting-system designs.

Light Distribution from Side-Wall Windows

First let us consider the case of the side-wall window. The daylight distribution from such a window is at a maximum near the window sill, and drops off as the distance from the window increases (Figs. 6, 7). The amount and distribution of this daylight for any particular time varies with respect to the window height and width and the material in the window opening. The

window widths given are for small windows (where the window width is approximately equal to the height) and for wide windows (where the window width is greater than four times the height).

The type of material in the window opening has little effect on the daylight distribution for overcast sky conditions. The light-distribution curves in Figs. 6 and 7 are based on clear or diffusing flat glass or acrylic plastic in the window opening.

Light Distribution from Overhead Windows

Now let us take the case of overhead or clerestory windows. By the use of the mathematical formulas by which light

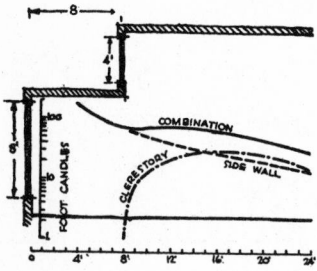

Fig. 13. When clerestory setback equals the side-wall window height, illumination is high near wall and clerestory, but distance to the opposite wall is limited— illumination at 28 ft is about 15 ft-c

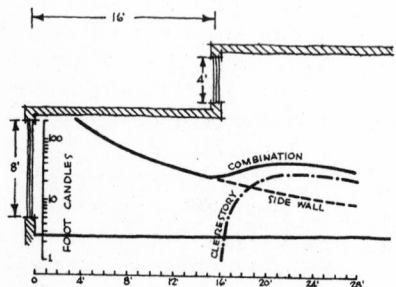

Fig. 14. When setback is twice side-wall window height, illumination is well distributed and wall-to-wall distance can be greater than in Fig. 13. Illumination at 28 ft is about 35 ft-c

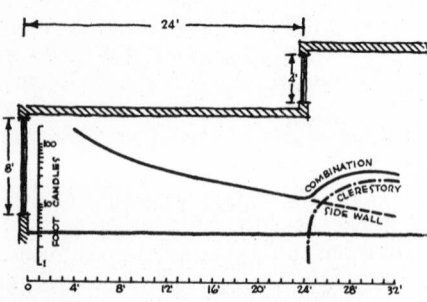

Fig. 15. When setback is too great, illumination is not well distributed. At lowest point, illumination is about 15 ft-c

distribution from side-wall windows was calculated, the illumination from overhead windows can be similarly obtained. The results of these calculations for different arrangements of overhead windows are shown in Figs. 8–10.

From these diagrams it will be noted that the illumination directly below the overhead windows is zero when the window is mounted on a vertical plane, and that it increases to a maximum value before tapering off. The position of the maximum varies with the mounting height of the window sill above the working plane (Figs. 8 and 9). Increasing the height of the window itself (distance from sill to top of window) also has some effect on the distribution of illumination (Fig. 10).

Combination of Side-Wall and Overhead Window Arrangements

The illumination obtained from the combination of a side-wall window and an overhead or clerestory window can be calculated by adding the values of illumination for each window. Following this procedure, let us consider what is the most desirable plane for mounting the two windows. The combination of a side-wall window on one side of a room with the clerestory window mounted on the opposite wall results in an illumination which is at a minimum at the rear of the room and which is nonuniform throughout (Fig. 11). Now by mounting the clerestory window on the opposite wall, or on the same side as the window wall, but set back from it, a more uniform light distribution can be obtained (Fig. 12).

It will be noted from Fig. 12 that the illumination from the clerestory window complements the illumination from the side-wall window so that a more uniform illumination is obtained. For our first rule, therefore, we can say that *for typical clerestory and side-wall window arrangements, the clerestory window should be mounted on the same side as the side-wall window.*

Setback of Clerestory from Side Wall

The next step in clerestory window design is to determine the required

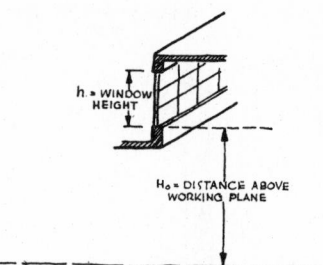

Fig. 16. Mounting height of the clerestory window affects light distribution, while height of the window, for a specific mounting height above the working plane, has greater effect on the amount of daylight

setback between the window wall and the plane of the clerestory. The spacing between the planes of the clerestory and side-wall window wall are related to the window heights and widths. Figs. 12–15 show the effects of different clerestory setbacks and window widths.

From these diagrams it will be noted that there is an optimum relation between the side-wall window height and the setback for near-uniform illumination. *For narrow windows, the recommended setbacks are of the order of one and one-half times the side-wall window height* (Fig. 12). *For wide windows these setbacks should be about twice the window height* (Fig. 14).

Distance to Back Wall

Another factor in the design of clerestory windows is the effective room

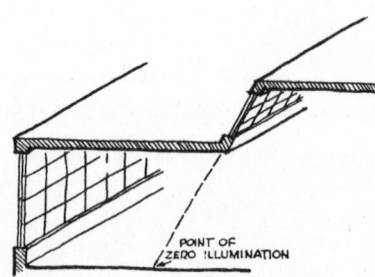

Fig. 17. Light from sloping clerestory window is zero at the point of intersection of the window plane and the working plane

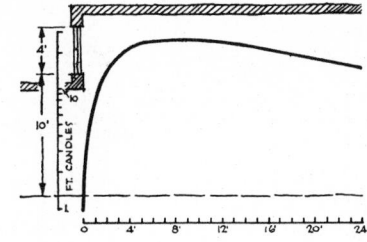

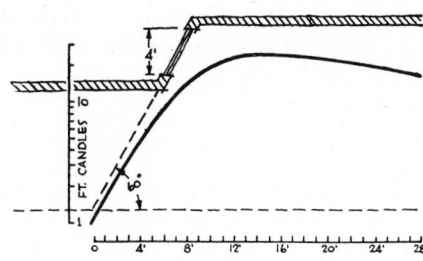

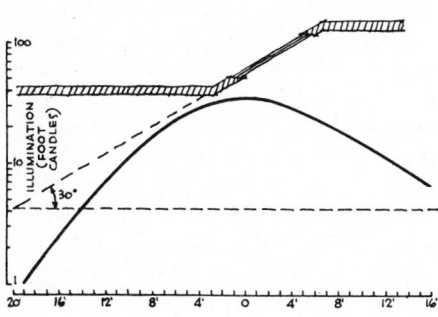

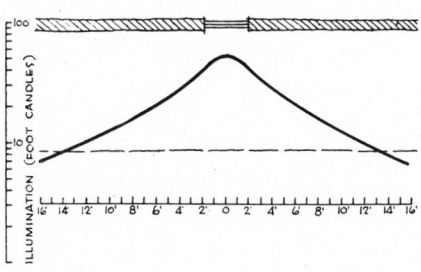

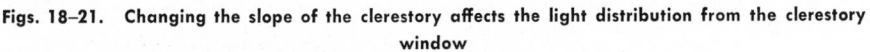

Figs. 18–21. Changing the slope of the clerestory affects the light distribution from the clerestory window

For obtaining the best light distribution from side-wall and clerestory windows combined, a clerestory slope of 30° from the vertical is best. When the clerestory window is vertical, the combined illumination curve has a dip in it (see Fig. 14) because the maximum point of the clerestory curve is almost directly above the minimum point. When the maximum point shifts to the right (this occurs with a 30° slope) the combination curve becomes flatter (see Fig. 22).

width measured from the plane of the overhead window to the opposite wall. From inspection of the light-distribution curves from overhead windows (Figs. 8–10) it will be noted that this effective width (flatter curves give better light distribution) depends upon the clerestory window mounting height. *For typical clerestory arrangements utilizing narrow windows, recommended depth from the plane of a clerestory window to the opposite wall should be approximately equal to the mounting height of the clerestory window above the working plane. For wide clerestory windows, the room depth from the plane of the clerestory window should be approximately one and one-half times the clerestory mounting height. When the area near the back wall is not to be used for critical seeing, these values can be exceeded.*

Height of Overhead Window

It will be noted that the mounting height of the clerestory window has a pronounced effect on the light distribution (Figs. 8 and 9), while the height of the clerestory window for a given mounting height above the working plane has a greater effect on the amount of light (Fig. 10). In order to obtain a uniform and adequate level of light, *the height of the clerestory window should be approximately equal to one-half the side-wall window height, where the sill height of the clerestory window above the working plane is no greater than one and one-half times the side-wall window height. Where the sill height of the clerestory window is of the order of three times the side-wall window height, the clerestory window should be equal in height to the side-wall window.*

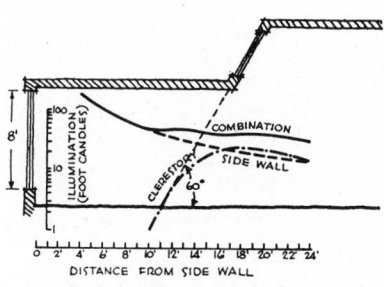

Fig. 22. Best slope for a clerestory window is 30°, giving even light distribution

Sloping Overhead Windows

Changing the slope of the clerestory window also affects the light distribution. In the case of sloping overhead windows, the point of zero illumination is located at the point of intersection of the working plane and the plane of the sloping window (Fig. 17). Changing slope of the window changes the point of zero illumination as well as the light distribution. Distribution from clerestory windows arranged at slopes of 0°, 30°, 60°, and 90° are shown in Figs. 18–21.

The combination of sloping clerestory windows with vertical side-wall windows permits greater variation in room sizes. *By the use of a sloping clerestory window arrangement at an angle of 30° from the vertical, the distance from the side-wall window to the clerestory window can be increased to twice the side-wall window height when narrow windows are used, and two and one-half times the side-wall window height when wide windows are used (Fig. 22).*

Conclusions

The design principles for clerestory lighting described above illustrate how a rigid theoretical approach can be applied to yield simple and useful rules of thumb for daylighting designs. These principles can be applied in the design of clerestory windows for all types of buildings. Engineered daylighting designs make it both practical and economical to achieve buildings well lighted throughout most of the daylight hours.

Data from publications of the Illuminating Engineering Society

VISUAL ENVIRONMENT

Physically, the visual environment is a three-dimensional pattern of brightness and colors, visible to a person within the environment. It also includes emotional and esthetic values, less easily measured, but none the less important to the design.

The visual field

That portion of a person's visual environment which can be detected by his eyes when they are directed along some particular line of sight is referred to as the visual field. Because of the nature and distribution of the photoreceptors in the eye, this visual field divides logically into two concentric regions, the central field and the surround (see Fig. 1).

The central field: The central field is that region of the visual space which extends roughly 1 deg outward from the line of sight, in all directions. Within this region lie the eye's greatest abilities to distinguish fine detail and perceive color. The eyes, the head, and the body of a person attempting to recognize some visual detail are adjusted by both conscious and subconscious adjusting mechanisms to bring the desired visual task into this portion of the visual field.

The surround: The surround is that portion of the visual field which extends outward from the central field to the spatial limits of visual sensation. The abilities to distinguish detail or to perceive color decrease rapidly as the angle with the line of sight increases and are virtually absent beyond 30 deg from the line of sight.

LIGHTING AND VISION

Light is needed for seeing and the amount required for good seeing is greater than that required for mere discernment. The brightness resulting from the amount of light on a task can be controlled more readily and extensively than can the other factors of seeing—contrast, size, and time of viewing. Brightness is therefore used to compensate for deficiencies in the other factors.

FACTORS AFFECTING VISUAL RECOGNITION

Most of the studies of light and vision conducted in the past have dealt with the ability to distinguish detail in the central field on or very near the line of sight. It has been found that the ability to recognize detail in this part of the visual field

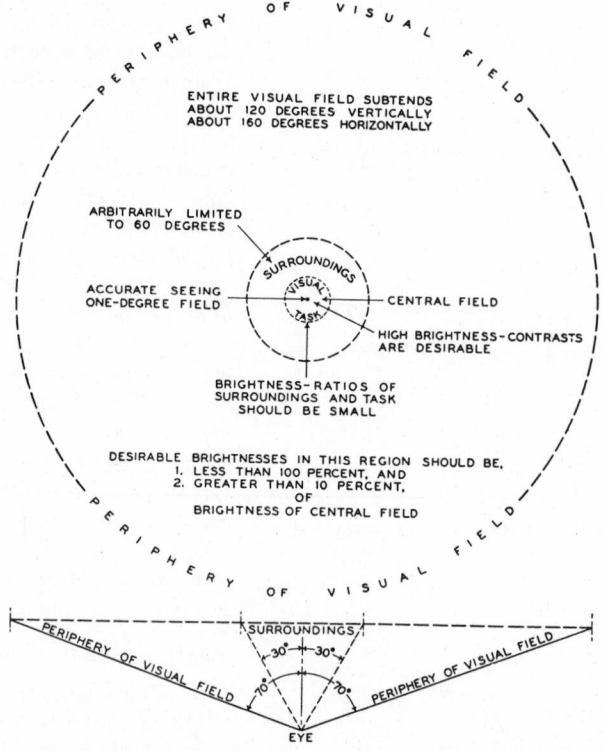

Fig. 1. Diagram of the entire visual field

varies with respect to four physical factors:

1. Contrast between the details of a task and its immediate background
2. Brightness of the task
3. Size of the task
4. Time of viewing

Each factor is sufficiently dependent upon the magnitude of the others that a deficiency in one, within limits, may be compensated by augmenting one or more of the others. Only the factors of contrast, size, and, in certain instances, that of time, are inherent in the task itself.

Contrast: Each critical detail of a seeing task must differ in brightness or color from the surrounding background in order to be seen. Visibility is a maximum when the brightness contrast (and color contrast if present) of details with the background is greatest. Task contrasts vary widely. For instance, examples of tasks with high contrast are: in schools, black type on white paper; in offices, typed originals with good ribbon; in stores, price tags in ink; and in industry, light stitching on blue serge cloth. Examples of tasks of poor contrast in similar locations are: spirit-duplicated materials; typed carbon, 5th copy; price tags in pencil; and gray stitching on gray silk.

Size: Within a given range, the larger the task detail, the more easily or accurately seeing is done. It has been found that up to a certain point if the contrast and time available for seeing are kept constant, the smallest detail which can be detected becomes progressively smaller as the brightness of the visual task is increased.

Time of viewing: Tests have shown that the time required to recognize an object of a given size and background with complete certainty is reduced as the brightness of the background is increased.

VISUAL PERFORMANCE

Recent research has taken all these factors into consideration in developing a system for determining illumination levels on the basis of performance data. The values of equivalent contrast have been divided into five categories representing general levels of task difficulty. The designations arbitrarily selected to describe these levels and the range of corresponding brightness values are shown in Table 1. These general recommendations were then applied to the specific requirements of various common building types to produce the illumination tables included later in this section.

Table 1. Recommended brightnesses for various tasks

Category of Seeing Task	Guide Brightness in Footlamberts
Most difficult	420 up
Very difficult	120-420
Difficult	42-120
Ordinary	18-42
Easy	below 18

NOTE: Footcandles will depend upon the reflectance of the task. Tasks having lower reflectances will require much higher footcandle levels. For example:

	60% Reflectance	6% Reflectance
Most difficult	700 fc	7000 fc
Very difficult	200-700 fc	2000-7000 fc
Difficult	70-200 fc	700-2000 fc
Ordinary	30-70 fc	300-700 fc
Easy	30 fc and below	300 fc and below

Table 2. Recommended brightness ratios *

		Offices	Schools	Industrial Buildings	Homes
1.	Between task and adjacent surroundings	1 to 1/3	1 to 1/3	1 to 1/5	1 to 1/10**
2.	Between task and more remote darker surfaces	1 to 1/10	1 to 1/3	1 to 1/20	1 to 1/10
3.	Between task and more remote lighter surfaces	1 to 10	1 to 10†	....	1 to 10
4.	Between fenestration (or luminaires) and adjacent surfaces	20 to 1	....	40 to 1	....
5.	Anywhere within the normal field of view	40 to 1	....	80 to 1	....

*These ratios are recommended maxima; reductions are generally beneficial.
**For special considerations (tasks of long duration and/or relatively high in brightness) no more than task and not less than 1/3 task.
†At 30 footcandles. The ratio should decrease as the level of illumination increases.

AGE AND SUBNORMAL VISION

The eyes like other organs of the body degenerate with age. Visual acuity, compared to that at age 20, is reduced by age 40 to 90 per cent, by age 60 to 74 per cent, and by age 80 to 47 per cent.

Pupil size: The size of the pupil decreases with age so that higher brightness of object is required to create the same degree of brightness on the retina of older eyes as obtained with younger eyes having larger pupils. It is possible to establish the brightness necessary to compensate for the loss of pupil size of an older person as compared with a 20-year-old "normal" eye (Fig. 2).

Accommodation: Accommodation is the adjustment of the lens of the eye to fix upon objects at different distances. Age tends to flatten the lens permanently. The ability of an eye, old or young, normal or subnormal, to accommodate is improved with increases in illumination, with the greatest improvement shown for the eye with subnormal accommodation.

QUALITY OF ILLUMINATION

Brightness: Brightness relationships of the various surfaces in the visual area must be kept within recommended limits (Table 2). If there is much difference between task brightness and field brightness, visual acuity is reduced and discomfort is experienced. Under optimum conditions for visual comfort and efficiency, the brightness of the task should be equal to or slightly greater than the brightness of the entire visual environment. The brightness of surfaces immediately adjacent to the visual task is more critical than that of more remote surfaces in the visual surround. Surfaces immediately adjacent to the task should not exceed the brightness of the task and should not be less than one-third the brightness of the task. Daylighting and artificial lighting systems should conform to the same brightness principles and should be coordinated in design to assure the effective contribution of both.

Glare: If anywhere within the visual field there are brightness conditions that reduce visibility or cause visual discomfort, they are categorically described as glare. Those which are directly associated with the source of lighting and its immediate surroundings are classified as causing *direct glare*. Those directly associated with the visual tasks and their immediate surroundings are considered as contributing to *reflected glare* (Fig. 3).

Direct glare: Unshaded windows are a frequent cause of *direct glare*. They often permit direct view of the sun, bright portions of the sky, and the brightness of adjacent buildings. These often constitute large areas of very high brightness in the usual fields of view. The condition may be controlled by employing shade, blind, louver or baffle systems on windows. (See section on "Daylighting.")

Luminaires which are too bright for the environment in which they are located produce direct glare. The eyes are quite susceptible to glare in the zone from the line of sight, which seldom is higher than horizontal, to about 45 deg above. The shading of luminaires visible below the 45-deg angle is therefore recommended (Fig. 4).

A criterion has been developed for dealing with luminaire brightness under certain conditions. The "scissors curve" (Fig. 5) may be used to check fluorescent luminaires for direct glare provided that the illumina-

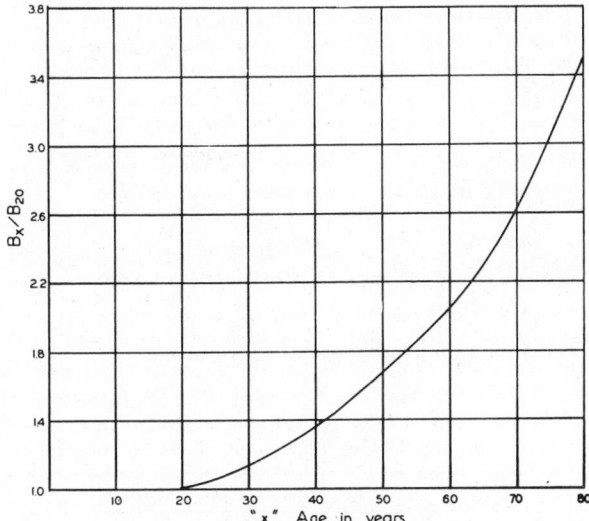

Fig. 2. Increase in brightness necessary to compensate for decrease in pupil size due to advancing age

B_x = *brightness required at x years.* B_{20} = *brightness required at 20 years.*

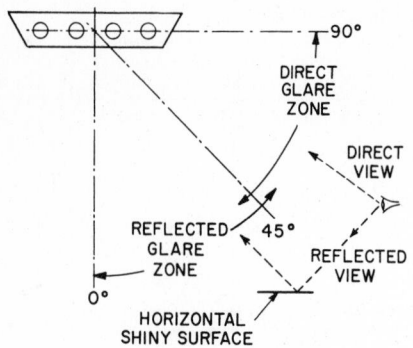

Fig. 3. The direct and reflected glare zones are generally defined as shown by the above diagram

It should be noted that there is no sharp line of demarcation between these zones at 45 deg.

tion is in the 30 to 100-ft-c range, the reflectances fall within the limits shown in Table 3, and the room size is not greater than 100 by 100 ft. Table 4 gives brightness distributions for several typical limiting curves and may be used in place of the scissors curve, if preferred. To prevent distracting nonuniformity in brightness, the ratio of maximum to average luminaire brightnesses should preferably not exceed 3 to 1, and must not exceed 5 to 1. (In no case should the maximum brightness for a given angle be more than 3 times the average brightness value of the sloping solid line.

Because higher brightnesses are permissible for luminaires of smaller area, luminaires which have an area of approximately 1 sq ft projected area at 0 deg, may have double the brightness indicated in Fig. 5. It is recognized that in small offices the brightness at the highest angles may not be significant [1] and the brightness limita-

[1] *The highest significant angle may be determined by making a cross-sectional sketch of the office with an occupant seated (eye level 4 ft above floor) in the least favorable location (at one end of room) viewing the most remotely located luminaire drawn in at its proposed mounting height and location.*

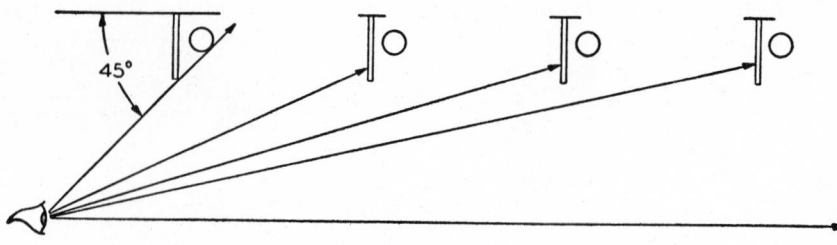

Fig. 4. To protect the eyes in the potential direct glare zone, luminaires should be shielded to about 45 deg, as illustrated

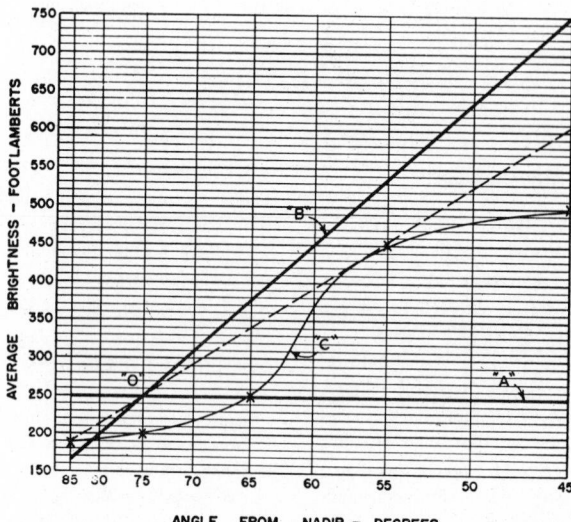

Fig. 5. The "scissors curve" for the limitation of direct glare from luminaires

Direct glare should not be a problem in 30 to 100-ft-c fluorescent installations if ceiling and wall reflectances comply with Table 3 and luminaires have crosswise and endwise brightness distributions falling entirely below any straight line drawn through point 0 between limiting curves A and B. C is the brightness plot of a sample luminaire and its limiting line is shown in dashes.

tions for these angles could, therefore, be disregarded without impairing seeing comfort.

Progress has been made in quantitatively evaluating the comfort or discomfort aspects of direct glare. Glare is reduced and seeing is improved by:

1. *Decreasing the brightness of the light sources and lighting equipment*

Table 4. Limitations on brightness of luminaires

Any luminaire whose average brightness at each of the angles in the table below does not exceed the brightnesses in any single column of the table will comply with the limitations described in Fig. 5.

Angle	Average Brightness (Footlamberts)								
85°	250	240	230	220	210	200	190	180	165
75°	250	250	250	250	250	250	250	250	250
65°	250	265	280	295	310	325	340	355	375
55°	250	285	315	350	385	415	450	480	535
45°	250	310	365	420	480	540	600	660	750

Table 3. Recommended reflectance values in per cent

Ceiling	85	(70–90)
Walls	60	(50–70)
Furniture and equipment	40	(35–50)
Floor	30	(20–50)

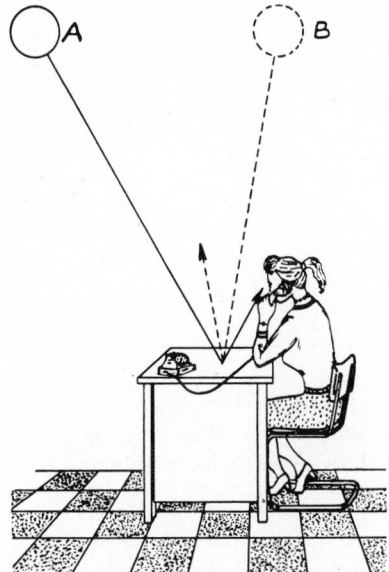

Fig. 6. Reflected glare

A lighting unit positioned at A is an inherent source of reflected glare in the desk top, whereas at B there is little likelihood of its causing this complaint.

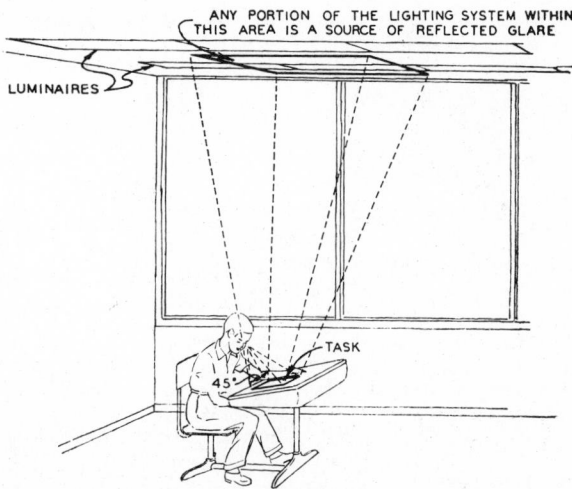

Fig. 7. A method for determining the zone in which potential reflected-glare sources may be located

2. *Diminishing the area* of potentially glaring high brightnesses

3. *Increasing the angle* between the glare source and the line of sight

4. *Brightening the surroundings* against which the glare source is seen, but not increasing the surround brightness excessively to a point where the surround becomes a glare source (e.g., an overly bright ceiling with an indirect lighting installation).

Reflected glare: Reflected glare may occur within the visual task itself or in the area immediately surrounding the task. It occurs when shiny surfaces reflect images of bright sources of illumination toward the eye (Figs. 6 and 7). Such reflections in the task itself veil the detail and reduce visibility. Source reflections in shiny surfaces immediately adjacent to the task can be distracting, uncomfortable, and can reduce the ability to see.

A subtle form of reflected glare is sometimes called "veiling glare"; here the bright area is indistinct but nevertheless interferes with clear vision and causes real discomfort.

The effects of glare on both visual acuity and comfort are cumulative. Slight glare that may not be noticeable at first will result after continuous exposure in a marked reduction in visual acuity and an increase in discomfort.

The main controlling factors related to reflected glare are:

1. Degree of specularity (shininess) of task and surround

2. Reflectances of task and surround

3. Direction of light reflected from the task and adjacent area

4. Amount of illumination contributed by the glare source as compared with the total illumination on the task and adjacent area

5. Brightness and size of light source.

All these factors should be controlled in so far as is practicable to provide the best seeing conditions at the task. To this end the following recommendations should be observed:

1. The task and its surround should be matte (nonglossy).

2. The task and its surround should have high reflectance, but the reflectance of the surround should not exceed that of the task.

3. Locate work surfaces with respect to the fenestration and electric light sources so that the image of the source is reflected away from the observer's eyes.

4. Light sources should be so located that the illumination on the task comes from several different directions.

5. When it is not possible or practicable to observe any of the above recommendations, special precautions as to fenestration and luminaire brightness should be observed. Luminaires and fenestration having *maximum* brightnesses (brightest square inch) in the order of 350 ft-l, and less, have generally proved satisfactory.

UNIFORMITY OF ILLUMINATION

Uniformity of illumination is considered satisfactory if the minimum value (between luminaires) is two-thirds or more of the maximum value (under the luminaires). If the minimum value is half of or less than the maximum, perceptible differences in illumination exist. Most manufacturers publish maximum spacing-to-mounting (or ceiling)-height ratios which should not be exceeded for their luminaires, and data are also available for predicting the daylight distribution from various types of fenestration. In most instances, the distance between luminaires and the wall should not exceed one-half the distance between luminaires; and where desks are along the wall, the distance between luminaires and walls should preferably be 2½ ft and in no case should exceed one-third the spacing between luminaires. The ends of continuous rows of fluorescent luminaires should preferably be within 6 in. to 1 ft of the wall and in no case more than 2 ft from the wall.

Shadows: Shadows cast on *the visual task* reduce the brightness of the task and hence impair effective seeing. When sharply defined at or near the task, shadows are annoying.

Shadows will be softened if the light comes from many directions. High-reflectance matte finishes on room surfaces become effective secondary light sources and materially reduce shadows by reflecting a significant amount of diffused light into shadowed areas.

QUANTITY OF ILLUMINATION

Illumination as a quantity is expressed in foot-candles, and is a measure of the light incident on a surface. The light reflected from the surface (i.e., the brightness), the light by which we actually see, is expressed in foot-lamberts. The brightness in foot-lamberts of common nonglossy tasks is equal to the illumination in foot-candles on the surface multiplied by the reflectance of the surface.

The lighting recommendations in the following pages are based on conservative interpretations of presently available laboratory data. They are graded according to the difficulty of the visual tasks encountered. These recommendations represent levels that are practical from the standpoints of techniques and economics.

The illumination values given are minimum values which should be provided on the visual task, regardless of its location in the room, or other conditions which would reduce the illumination level. An allowance should be made for such conditions as glare (since no lighting system is completely glare-free) and loss in illumination through depreciation of luminaires, lamps, and painted surfaces. Even under conditions of good maintenance an average lighting level of from 25 to 35 per cent less than the initial level may be expected under normal operating conditions. With poor maintenance the lighting level may well average less than 50 per cent of the initial value.

ELECTRIC LIGHTING SYSTEMS

Lighting systems can be divided into five classifications: (1) Indirect; (2) Semi-indirect; (3) General diffuse (or direct-indirect); (4) Semidirect; and (5) Direct. They differ principally in the proportion of the light directed upward or downward, as shown in Table 5.

Indirect lighting systems are characterized by relatively low source brightnesses, good diffusion, freedom from shadows, and low to moderate utilization. On the other hand, utilization is generally good with direct lighting, but the quality of the lighting may be poor unless special precautions are taken. Intermediate systems combine the characteristics of direct and indirect lighting in varying degrees depending upon the predominant component. Indirect lighting systems require matte high-reflectance ceilings that are well maintained. With high levels of illumination the ceiling may become so bright as to be a source of glare. The shadowless light may be unsatisfactory for three-dimensional work. Direct light, on the other hand, may produce disturbing shadows and reflected glare unless the units are of large area or are closely spaced. The use of high-reflectance room and furniture surfaces is essential. Ceiling area lighting, extending essentially from wall to wall, is another form of direct lighting which greatly reduces reflected glare. Light from sources in a large cavity is directed downward, through cellular louvers or translucent diffusing material. Although this system is often used to obtain higher illumination levels, the brightness of the shielding or transmitting medium should be limited to the values of the scissors curve.

No one system can be recommended to the exclusion of all others. Each has qualities which may match the requirements for a given situation. Selection should be based on the performance, architectural, and budget requirements of the particular job.

MAINTENANCE OF ILLUMINATION

In any system the illumination level will fall below the initial value due to depreciation of lamps, luminaires, and other light control elements and room surfaces. In the design stage, one should select, as a minimum level, the lowest value which will be tolerated in the final installation. The initial value should be based on this minimum level and maintenance conditions.

The illumination levels depreciate in two ways: first, through the aging of the lamps themselves, and, second, through the collection of dirt, dust, and foreign matter on the luminaires and the reflecting surfaces of the room. The efficiency of some lighting systems is more affected by dirt than others, but all systems will require regular cleaning to ensure efficiency. The reflecting surfaces in a room will also require regular cleaning, especially when these surfaces are expected to supply a large amount of reflected light.

To help reduce the amount of dirt which collects on reflecting and transmitting surfaces, the ventilation system should be considered. With window ventilation dirt is carried about by convection currents and is deposited on reflecting surfaces and luminaires. If the ventilation system is mechanical, involving filtering or cleaning, less dirt will be present to lower the efficiency of the lighting system.

Some reflecting materials have texture characteristics which make them easy to clean. When designing a building, the architect should consider the type of material chosen with respect to the way in which it will be cleaned. For cleaning electric and daylight sources in special rooms such as gymnasiums and auditoriums, installations of catwalks or the use of luminaires having disconnecting hangers may be considered.

LIGHT SOURCES

The two most commonly used electric light sources are the incandescent bulb and the fluorescent tube.

Incandescent lamps are available in a wide variety of sizes, shapes, and colors. Some of the commoner types are illustrated in Fig. 8. Wattages range from 10 to 1,500. The standard ("medium") base is used for lamps of up to 300 watts, and the large ("mogul") base for those of higher wattages; 300-watt lamps are available in

Table 5.   Types of lighting systems

Data from Recommended Practice for Office Lighting, *Illuminating Engineering Society, 1960*

Classification	Approximate Distribution of Light Emitted by Luminaire	
	Upward	Downward
Indirect	90–100%	10– 0%
Semi-Indirect	60– 90	40–10
General Diffuse	40– 60	60–40
Semi-Direct	10– 40	90–60
Direct	0– 10	100–90

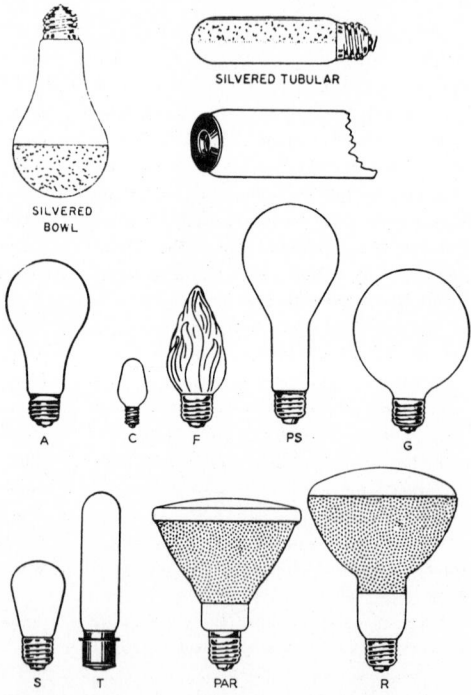

SILVERED TUBULAR

SILVERED BOWL

A C F PS G

S T PAR R

Fig. 8.   Common types of incandescent lamps

both types of base. Incandescent lamps produce from 8 to 22 lumens per watt and have a life of 750 to 1,000 hours. Surface temperatures of the bulbs range from 106 to 510°F. Most incandescent bulbs are now inside-frosted, which makes the surface of the bulb the light source, instead of the much smaller and brighter filament.

Some standard-shape bulbs are available with a partial coating of silver for the purpose of concentrating the light in one direction only. More efficient for this purpose, though, are the special inside-silvered reflector lamps, available in spot (concentrated-beam) and flood (wide-beam) types, in sizes from 30 to 300 watts and in several colors. Projector lamps are similar but are of special construction that permits them to be used outdoors, exposed to the weather; they are available in spot or flood types, in sizes from 75 to 150 watts.

Another special incandescent lamp is the "three-lite" bulb, available in wattages of 30–70–100, 50–100–150, 50–200–250, and 100–200–300 (mogul base). Another special shape is the tubular lamp, known as "lumiline"; it is 1 in. in diameter and has a disk-type base at each end. Lumiline lamps are available in 30, 40, and 60-watt sizes in various colors.

Fluorescent lamps are tubular light sources which are characterized by higher light efficiencies, cooler operating temperatures, and longer life than incandescent lamps giving the same quantity of illumination. They range in size from 4 watts, 6 in. long, ⅝-in. diameter to 100 watts, 96 in. long, 1½-in. diameter.

All fluorescent light sources require a current-limiting and control device called a ballast, which is located in a metal enclosure. For the operation of some fluorescent tubes an automatic switch known as a starter is required in addition to the normal wall switch. The starter is a small metal can inserted into the fixture body or channel and is a replaceable part. The following are several methods of fluorescent-tube operation in common use.

Preheat: These require starters and take several seconds to light.

Rapid-start: No starter required, but rapid-start tubes and ballasts are needed; they light within a fraction of a second.

Preheated-rapid-start: A new universal tube which replaces the former preheat and rapid-start types. This new tube will operate equally well in either preheat or rapid-start fixtures, but with a time delay in fixtures with starters.

Trigger-start: Preheat-type fluorescent tubes (14, 15, and 20-watt) which operate on a trigger-start ballast without starters and light in a fraction of a second.

Slimline: Another type of fluorescent tube which requires no starter and lights instantly. Slimline tubes vary in length from 42 to 96 in., have single-pin bases, and come in three diameters: ¾, 1, and 1½ in. They require bulky sockets and larger and heavier ballasts than do the preheat and rapid-start tubes.

The preheat type of fluorescent tube has a rated life of 7,500 hours, and the rapid-start type has one of 4,000 hours. Both produce 50 to 60 lumens per watt.

Fluorescent tubes are also available in circular shape ("circline") in three sizes: 22 watts, 8¼-in. outside diameter; 32 watts, 12-in. diameter; and 40 watts, 16-in. diameter.

Fluorescent lamps are available in a number of colors and in no less than seven "whites," ranging from a very cool blue-white to a warm pinkish-white. Listed below are the seven "whites" with a description of the color characteristics of each.

Improved-color-rendition warm white:[2] Creates a warm atmosphere and blends well with incandescent bulbs. Enhances complexions, foods, and warm tones in furniture, fabrics, and paint.

Improved-color-rendition cool white:[2] Flatters all colors and creates a cool atmosphere. This type gives the most accurate color rendition of all fluorescent tubes, but its cool light is quite different in appearance from the mellow, yellowish light from incandescent bulbs.

Warm white: Blends well with incandescent lighting but somewhat adversely affects both warm and cool colors.

Cool white: Produces a cool atmosphere, but dulls warm colors and intensifies cool colors.

White: Compromise between warm white and cool white; slightly dulls the appearance of warm colors.

Daylight: Very blue-white light, grays complexions, dulls warm colors, and creates a very cold atmosphere.

Soft white: Pinkish-white light that emphasizes reds and pinks but has a tendency to gray cool colors.

Current passing through a ballast produces a low humming sound. Generally this faint sound is not noticeable with even less than average noise levels. Once in a while there is an exceptional case where the room noise level is very low because of isolated surroundings or more than average insulation. In these unusual cases, if the lighting method requires a number of ballasts, it is recommended that they be

[2] *To produce the improved color rendition achieved, about 25 per cent of the light output is sacrificed. Improved-color-rendition tubes should be used only where color appearance is of importance.*

placed in ventilated metal boxes in a remote location—attic, basement, or closet. Ballasts should be located where they will be easily accessible and where no obstruction of any kind can prevent ventilation or circulation of air around the metal box.

Fluorescent tubes may produce interference (noise) in radio reception, although television reception is not affected. Locating the radio and its aerial at a distance of about 9 ft from fluorescent tubes or installing proper radio interference filters will reduce direct radiation from the tubes.

The principal characteristics of the two commonest types of light source—incandescent and fluorescent—are summarized below.

Incandescent bulbs

1. Provide a point source of light that can be focused or directed over a limited area if desired.

2. Most household bulbs have the same size base, thus lighting from fixtures or lamps can be increased or decreased within certain limits by a change to bulbs of a different wattage.

3. Most types are less expensive to buy than fluorescent tubes. Incandescent lighting fixtures are also generally less expensive; they require no ballast or starter.

Fluorescent tubes

1. Provide a line of light, thus in work areas the light coming from several angles tends to wipe out the shadows. These "lines" of light can also be used over mirrors, kitchen work surfaces, and in window valances, cornices, and coves or other architectural features to provide both useful and decorative illumination.

2. Provide three to four times as much light per watt of electricity as incandescent-filament light bulbs, with less heat produced.

3. Will operate about seven to ten times longer than incandescent bulbs before replacement is required.

GLOSSARY OF TERMS USED IN LIGHTING

For other, or more detailed definitions, see "IES Lighting Handbook" and "IES Nomenclature and Photometric Standards."

Absorptance: Ratio of light absorbed by a material to the light falling upon it.

Absorption: Loss when light strikes or traverses any medium. Dark objects absorb more light.

Accent lighting: Directional lighting to emphasize some area or object.

Ampere (amp): Measure of rate of flow of

electricity. A milliampere (ma) is one-thousandth of an ampere.

Ballast: Electrical device required to operate fluorescent tubes.

Black light: That portion of invisible ultraviolet radiation which causes certain materials to fluoresce or glow visibly.

Brightness or luminance: Intensity of optical sensation caused by viewing a surface from which light comes to the eyes. Everything visible has some brightness. Brightness is measured in foot-lamberts.

Cathode or electrode: That part of a fluorescent tube which conducts electricity into the gas.

Channel or channel strip: Metal enclosure, containing the ballast, starter, lampholder, and wiring for fluorescent tubes.

Clerestory: That part of a building which rises above the roofs and whose walls contain windows.

Coefficient of utilization: Ratio of lumens received on the work plane to lumens emitted by lamps.

Cornice lighting: System where light sources are shielded by a panel parallel to the wall and attached to the ceiling to distribute light over the wall. Direct lighting.

Cove lighting: System where light sources are shielded by a ledge to distribute light over the ceiling and upper wall. Indirect lighting.

Current: Alternating current (a-c). Electric current which reverses its direction of flow, usually at the rate of 120 times a second. This rate of change is 60 cycles. Direct current (d-c). Electricity which flows continuously in one direction.

Cutoff angle: Angle up from the vertical at which the reflector or shield cuts off the view of the light source.

Dado: Lower part of a wall separated from the upper part by a horizontal molding, called a dado rail or chair rail, or simply by paint of another color.

Diffuser: Translucent glass or plastic used to diffuse light.

Diffusion: Scattering of light rays to emit or reflect them over broad angles.

Dimmer: Device to control the amount of light by reducing the voltage or the current. Rheostat.

Direct lighting: A lighting system or luminaire in which over 90 per cent of the light is distributed downward.

Direct-indirect: A lighting system or luminaire in which light is directed almost equally upward and downward, but with little or none directed horizontally.

Downlight: Fixture producing concentrated direct lighting from a single bulb. It may be recessed in, or mounted on, the ceiling.

Efficiency: The efficiency of a lighting fixture is the ratio of the light it emits to the total light produced by the bare bulb or tube. The effectiveness (efficacy) of a light source is the ratio of the light output in lumens to the power input in watts.

Electrode: See Cathode.

Eyeball: Recessed, or semirecessed, lighting unit with a rotating spherical element that may be turned to project light in any direction.

Fenestration: Any opening or arrangement of openings to admit daylight. The term usually includes devices for the control of daylight.

Filter: A device which changes either the amount or color, or both, of the light passing through it.

Fluorescent tube: A light source produced by a fluorescent powder, usually phosphor, coated on the inside of a tube. A mercury-vapor arc between electrodes (sealed into both ends of the tube) generates ultraviolet radiation, which is converted into visible light by the phosphor.

Foot-candle (ft-c): Quantitative unit of measure for evaluating illumination equal to 1 lumen per sq ft. It is approximately the amount of light produced by a plumber's candle at a distance of 1 ft (see Fig. 9).

Foot-lambert (ft-l): A quantitative unit for measuring brightness equal to 1 lumen per sq ft. The foot-candles striking a diffuse reflecting surface multiplied by the reflectance of the surface equals the brightness of the surface in foot-lamberts. If a surface that is perfectly white and diffuse is placed 1 ft from a candle, the brightness of that surface is approximately 1 ft-l.

General diffuse lighting: Lighting system or luminaire in which almost an equal amount of light is produced in all directions.

Glare: The effect of brightness in the field of view which causes annoyance or discomfort or interferes with seeing. It may be direct (from the light source) or reflected (from a glossy surface).

High-hat: Term often applied to "can" type of recessed incandescent downlight.

Illumination: Intensity of luminous flux on a surface. It is the quotient of the flux divided by the area of the surface.

Indirect lighting: Lighting system or luminaire in which over 90 per cent of the light is distributed toward the ceiling.

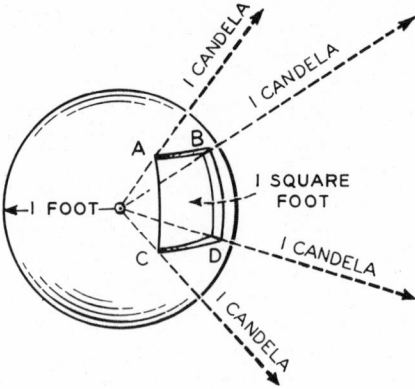

Fig. 9. Lumens

Relationship between candelas, lumens, and foot-candles. A uniform point source (luminous intensity or candlepower = 1 candela) is shown at the center of a sphere of 1-ft radius. It is assumed that the sphere is perfectly transparent (i.e., has 0 reflectance). The illumination at any point on the sphere is 1 ft-c (1 lumen per sq ft). The solid angle subtended by the area A, B, C, D is 1 steradian. The flux density is, therefore, 1 lumen per steradian, which corresponds to a luminous intensity of 1 candela, as originally assumed. The sphere has a total area of 12.57 (4π) sq ft, and there is a luminous flux of 1 lumen falling on each square foot. Thus the source provides a total of 12.57 lumens.

Lampholder: A socket.

Light: Radiant energy evaluated according to its capacity to produce visual sensation.

Light distribution of luminaires: Lighting fixtures are classified as direct, semidirect, general diffuse, semi-indirect, and indirect, depending on how they control or distribute the light.

Louver: Shield used with luminaire to restrict view of the light source.

Lumen: Quantitative unit for measuring light output. Lamps and other light sources are rated in lumens (see Fig. 9).

Lumiline: A tubular incandescent lamp with a disk base at each end.

Luminaire: A complete lighting unit, comprising lamp or lamps, parts designed to distribute the light, to position and protect the lamps and to connect them with the power supply.

Luminous ceiling: False ceiling of diffusing

material with light sources mounted above.

Maintenance factor: Ratio of the illumination on a given area after a period of time to the initial illumination on the same area.

Plenum: In luminous ceilings, the air chamber or cavity between the structural ceiling and the false, or luminous, ceiling.

Preheat: Type of fluorescent-tube operation requiring a starter and resulting in some delay in starting.

Rapid-start: Type of fluorescent-tube operation that does not require a starter.

Reflectance or reflection factor: The ratio of light reflected by a surface to the light falling upon it.

Reflected glare: Glare from reflections of light sources in shiny (specular) surfaces.

Reflection, diffuse: A beam of light is diffusely reflected from a rough or matte surface because the latter breaks up the beam and scatters it in all directions.

Reflection, specular: A beam of light is specularly reflected from a shiny or glossy surface—such as a mirror.

Reflector: Element of luminaire designed to direct light in desired direction.

Refraction: Bending a ray of light as it passes obliquely from one medium to another of different density.

Semidirect: Lighting system or luminaire which directs from 60 to 90 per cent of the light downward. See *Direct lighting.*

Semi-indirect: Lighting system or luminaire which directs from 60 to 90 per cent of the light upward. See *Indirect lighting.*

Shielding: Arrangement of light-controlling material to prevent the direct view of the light source. See *Louver.*

Shielding angle: Angle measured downward from the horizontal at which the shielding medium conceals the light source.

Slimline: Fluorescent tubes which have single-pin bases and instant-start ballasts.

Specular surface: Any shiny or glossy surface that reflects an image of the luminaire or light source.

Starter: Automatic switch which permits preheating of certain types of fluorescent tubes.

Transmission: Passage of light through a medium.

Transmission, diffuse: Passage of light through a material which destroys the shape of the beam and scatters the light in all directions.

Transmittance or transmission factor: The ratio of the light transmitted by a material to the amount of light falling upon it.

Valance lighting: System where light sources are shielded by a panel parallel to the wall, usually across the top of a window. It usually provides light both downward and upward.

Volt: Measure of electrical pressure. Most residential electric circuits in the United States have voltages between 110 and 120.

Watt: Measure of electrical power used to rate the consumption of electricity.

Work plane: Surface on which the visual task is located. Illumination is specified for and measured at this location.

Data from Recommended Practice for Office Lighting, Illuminating Engineering Society, 1960

LIGHTING QUANTITY

Recommended illumination levels for offices are shown in Table 6. These recommended levels are commensurate with the difficulty of the various groups of seeing tasks and the general cost of lighting. Higher values than those given are desirable and with proper lighting quality and environmental conditions will result in more efficient visual performance.

Illumination should not be permitted to fall below values specified in the table. Initial values of illumination will have to be greater by a percentage sufficient to compensate for the depreciation expected.

Some visual tasks are on slanting or vertical surfaces where illumination is only one-half to one-third of that on a horizontal plane. Compensation should be made for such tasks and for work locations at the sides of a room where illumination is usually less than in the center.

LIGHTING QUALITY

Room finishes

Ceilings, walls, and floors are important factors in determining the brightness ratios between the lighting equipment and its surrounding. They act as secondary light sources of large areas and, if finished in accordance with Table 3 in section on "Lighting: General," will increase light utilization and reduce shadows.

However, under certain conditions either higher or lower reflectances may be satisfactory or even desirable. The ceiling finish may, for example, be carried down the walls to the level of luminaires having a high upward component; utilization may be increased as much as 10 per cent by doing this. Conversely, a darker dado is sometimes employed on lower walls to minimize maintenance. Dadoes should have a reflectance of at least 25 per cent, however; darker dadoes are undesirable from the standpoint of visual comfort since the lower wall occupies an important part of the visual field. Small sections of walls may have reflectances higher or lower than the extremes permitted by the range given in Table 3. If these areas are thought of as accents and restricted to about 10 per cent of the total wall area in the room, little harm will be done to the efficiency of the lighting system or to the significant environmental brightness ratios, while the environment can be made to look considerably more pleasant and interesting.

Because it is human nature to desire at least occasional change, architects and lighting designers will be wise to specify the reflectances for all surfaces in an interior and plan the lighting so the colors can be changed without destroying the planned effect. If this information is included in the specifications and marked on all blueprints anyone can not only do the original color for the room but any replacement color plan as long as the lighting system is in use.

When window shielding media act as walls, they should have at least as high a reflectance as that recommended for the walls.

Office equipment finishes

Furniture—No surface in the office is more important visually than the desk top. For a person working at a desk, the top occupies most of the visual field. The task is usually of high reflectance, and desk tops having the reflectance recommended in Table 3 are necessary to prevent the brightness ratio between the task and its surround from exceeding the one to one-third ratio that is considered desirable and practical. Matte finishes are, of course, essential to minimize reflected glare.

All office furniture should have a light finish that harmonizes with the environment and promotes seeing comfort by minimizing brightness ratios between the various surfaces within the visual field. It is particularly important that the vertical surfaces of desks and file cabinets have finishes of the recommended reflectance, for they occupy a significant portion of the visual field. Since these surfaces receive less illumination than adjacent horizontal surfaces, light finishes are necessary to make them even moderately bright.

Machines: Business machines rank with desk tops in visual importance. In use they occupy a central and dominating part of the visual field even when operated by the touch system. Finishes having the recommended reflectances are essential for seeing comfort; shiny surfaces and dial covers should be completely eliminated, for even a small amount of specular trim can be distracting and annoying even though it may not be viewed directly.

LIGHTING AND SEEING IN SPECIFIC AREAS

Private offices

Private offices are usually of moderate or small size. Either direct or indirect lighting can be applied satisfactorily since much of the lighting equipment on the ceiling itself is generally not within the visual field. The arrangement of furniture in the private office is often fixed and permits the placing of direct lighting equipment to minimize both direct and reflected glare.

Not only is it necessary to provide satisfactory illumination for the occupant at the point of work, but sufficient brightness on walls, floors, and other areas is necessary to avoid high brightness ratios with the work. The use of dark-paneled walls, desks, and floor coverings is not conducive to comfortable seeing, and higher-reflectance materials with equal decorative character are now available.

The illumination required in private offices varies from that necessary for casual seeing during interviews to high values for prolonged study of reports, financial statements, plans and specifications. Where possible, the lighting system should be flexible to provide the order of illumination the varying tasks require. The higher values should be employed only when adequate provision is made for reduced brightness ratios between the lighting system and the environment, between the work and the environment, and among the environmental areas themselves.

General offices

Most general offices are moderate- to large-sized areas in which there may be many luminaires located directly in the field of view. In these areas, it is particularly important that the luminaire brightness limitations outlined in Fig. 5 be observed. At the same time, it is in the general office that seeing is most frequently

Table 6.   Recommended illumination levels

Type of Office or Work	Footcandles on Task*
Cartography, designing, detailed drafting	200
Accounting, auditing, tabulating, bookkeeping, business machine operation, reading poor reproductions, rough layout drafting	150
Regular office work, reading good reproductions, reading or transcribing handwriting in hard pencil or on poor paper. Active filing, index references, mail sorting, critical visual tasks in conference rooms	100
Reading or transcribing handwriting in ink or medium pencil on good quality paper, intermittent filing	70
Reading high contrast or well-printed material, tasks and areas not involving critical or prolonged seeing such as conferring, interviewing, inactive files and washrooms	30
Corridors, elevators, escalators, stairways	20**

*Minimum on task at any time.
**Or not less than ⅕ the level in adjacent areas.

difficult and most nearly continuous and, for this reason, quality and seeing comfort should never be compromised. The minimum quantity of light in use should be in keeping with recommendations in Table 6. Finishes, color, and other environmental factors should be selected to assure full benefit from the lighting and to supplement all the advantages that can be realized in the tasks themselves.

Since many office operations require more than one orientation of personnel, lighting and seeing should be comfortable for all directions of view. Changes in routine or personnel frequently require rearrangement of desk locations and partitions. General lighting installations originally designed to be comfortable from all directions need not be modified with changes in office procedure or organization.

Since it is always possible that large offices may be subdivided in the future, every attempt should be made to arrange the pattern of light spacing in such a way as to facilitate subdivision rather than impede it. This requires close cooperation between the architect and the engineer responsible for the lighting layout to ensure that ceiling and lighting modules are compatible and suitable for possible subdivision.

Care should be taken to provide the recommended quantity of illumination on the actual work surfaces. Most are horizontal, but some are vertical or sloping. Extra precautions should also be taken to ensure proper distribution of light along the sides and ends of offices. Desks are frequently placed along walls where the amount of light is inherently less if provisions have not been made to offset this reduction. This is generally accomplished

by spacing luminaires more closely along the walls of an office area as recommended earlier in this section. For desks in such positions, use wall reflectances in the upper part of the range in Table 3.

Drafting rooms

Drafting makes very serious demands upon the eyes and requires a high level of high-quality illumination. Drafting involves accurate discrimination of fine details, frequently over long periods of time. The contrast between the work detail and its background may be very poor, as, for example, when tracing a faint blueprint or worn pencil drawing. Specular drawing surfaces, polished T-squares, plastic triangles, and scales are potential sources of reflected glare. Shadows along the drawing edge of the T-square or a triangle may materially reduce visibility; or strong, multiple shadows from the drawing instruments or the draftsman's hands may prove annoying.

Reflections: On nearly horizontal boards, any ceiling or luminaire brightness may be reflected by the work to the eyes of the draftsman. Such reflections may sometimes be eliminated by proper positioning of the source or control of the direction of light flux with respect to the specular surfaces so that reflections will be directed away from the eye. It is usually more practical to minimize the effect of these reflections by controlling the brightness of the luminous area that is reflected to a low and fairly uniform value. This may be accomplished by employing lighting systems in which the lamps are completely concealed from the work. With the board in a nearly vertical position, specular reflections cause little if any trouble since they will be reflected toward the floor (see

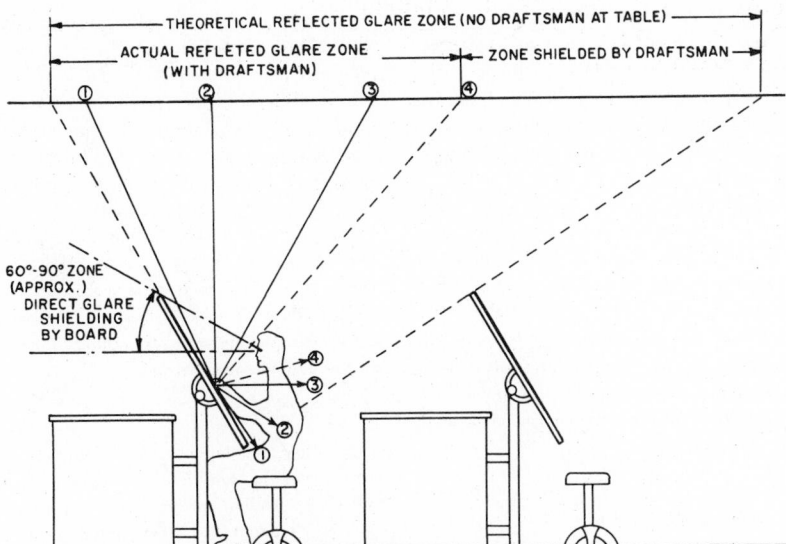

Fig. 10. Specular reflections

With drafting boards tilted in a nearly vertical position, as shown in drawing above, the specular reflections are reflected down toward the floor. The drafting boards may be high enough to shield the draftsmen's eyes from the luminaire brightness which, otherwise, would be in the field of view.

Fig. 10). Furthermore, the nearly vertical board may be high enough to shield the eyes of the draftsman from luminaire brightness otherwise in the field of view.

Shadows: Where boards are near horizontal, edges of T-squares or triangles parallel to line sources having strong direct components may cast sharp line shadows. The use of indirect, semi-indirect, or other forms of over-all ceiling lighting will minimize such shadows. Where this type of lighting is not applicable or feasible, the frequency of occurrence of such shadows may be minimized by orienting either the luminaires or the drafting tables to create an angle of 15 to 20 deg between the long axes of the luminaires and any of the major straight-edge positions. The use of vertical drafting boards also virtually eliminates shadows on the task.

Transillumination: A drafting table with a diffusing surface panel lighted from behind provides an efficient means of improving the visibility of tracing tasks. General room lighting should be used while tracing drawings since it also contributes to visibility and helps visual comfort by raising the surround brightness and reducing brightness ratios in the field of view.

For tracing original drawings which have a relatively high transmittance (40 to 50 per cent) a luminous surface having a brightness of about 200 ft-l provides excellent visibility. For tracing reproductions which are usually on heavier paper of lower transmittance (such as blueprints)

300 to 400 ft-l is desirable. To avoid direct glare, the draftsman should use opaque paper to cover the portion of the glass which is not concealed by the drawing.

The varying requirements for brightness suggest that the lamps be dimmer-controlled to permit selection of the optimum value for a specific task. In addition, it is desirable to keep the temperature of the tracing table as low as possible. Therefore, fluorescent lamps having a high luminous efficacy should be used. Simple ballasts and variable autotransformers are available for dimming 40-watt (48 in. long) and 30-watt (36 in. long) rapid-start fluorescent lamps.

Files

Files present the particular problem of work surfaces that are vertical, inclined and horizontal, and frequently stacked one against the other. In order to provide the recommended values of illumination *on work surfaces other than horizontal,* it is generally true that considerably higher values will need to be developed on horizontal positions. In *active filing* areas, the work is likely to be of protracted nature and the visual task is of more than average severity. Where the room is primarily devoted to files, consideration should be given to luminaires designed and located to provide the recommended illumination level on vertical surfaces.

Cabinet finishes of recommended reflect-

ance will provide comfortable brightness ratios within the environmental areas of file rooms and will improve the seeing conditions at the point of work. Lighter finishes will reflect more light down between filed items which frequently are read without removal from the files.

Mail rooms and stockrooms

Rapid sorting and routing of incoming mail involves rather difficult seeing, requiring the illumination level recommended in Table 6.

Conference and board rooms

Effective coordination of good seeing conditions with the architectural and decorative designs of these rooms will result in comfortable and attractive areas. As in private offices, the use of these rooms varies considerably, but critical and prolonged seeing is encountered at times in most of them and the lighting level should be adequate for the most difficult, commonly occurring task. The illumination should be *designed* to *minimize* shadows on the faces of persons seated around the table. Undesirable reflections should be avoided. Moderately high reflectance matte finishes are recommended. Special attention to lighting of vertical surfaces is important if charts, displays or illustrations are frequently studied. Supplementary lighting is recommended for this purpose. Flexibility in providing light suited to varying use can be provided through suitable switching or dimming.

Reception rooms

Lighting for casual seeing fulfills the requirements of the usual reception room. Glare should be avoided to make the room pleasant in general appearance and to provide comfortable seeing for those visitors who choose to read while waiting. The choice of higher reflectance values for room surfaces and furnishings will assist in making the room comfortable and seemingly more spacious.

If a receptionist occupies the room, this person should be provided with lighting in keeping with the tasks assigned. Frequently, general office work is part of the assignment and the seeing requirements are more exacting than those for the casual occupant. Brightness ratios in the receptionist's visual field should be limited to low values and either a uniform amount of light should be provided throughout the room or more light provided at the work area, commensurate with the severity of the work assignments. The latter requires particular attention to brightness patterns on walls, floors and desk tops.

If a telephone switchboard with signal light indicators is present, it is important that the general lighting not "wash out" the signal lights (particularly if they are located on a horizontal plane). Care should also be taken to prevent reflections of bright light sources in the signal light caps.

Stairways, elevators, and escalators

The need for good lighting at these points is paramount in the interest of safety. Installations should be so designed that failure of one lamp will not leave an area inadequately lighted. Floor, wall and overhead finishes should be of high reflectance to gain the maximum utilization of the light and to reduce shadows.

Stairways: Stairway lighting equipment should be so located and shielded that persons neither cast shadows on the stairs nor encounter glare at eye level. A unit should be located at least on every landing and closer if necessary.

Special treatment may be necessary to call attention to changes in elevation in corridors where one or two steps are necessary. This may be accomplished by placement of small, shielded lighting units recessed near the floor or by distinctive painting of the edges of the steps.

Elevators: Good lighting of the threshold should be provided to call attention to any difference in level between the landing and the car. It is recommended that the car interior be of as light a finish as is consistent with reasonable ease of maintenance.

Escalators: Good lighting should be provided on the tread, using shielded supplementary luminaires in the balustrade if necessary. Finishes should be of a light nonspecular type.

Corridors and hallways

The primary considerations in lighting corridors and hallways are safety, general appearance and brightness difference with adjacent offices. The spacing of lighting equipment from center to center should not exceed one and one-half times the mounting height. It is recommended that the amount of light in hallways be no less than 20 per cent of that in adjacent areas. Hallway illumination levels that are at least one-third of the levels in adjacent offices have been found to be preferable from the standpoint of relieving brightness differences between hallways and offices. The illumination values recommended for hallways should be provided at floor level. Reflectances for ceilings, walls, and floors should equal or exceed those recommended for the offices. If dark finishes must be used from the maintenance standpoint, they should be limited to the dado.

Personal service

Sanitary maintenance of restrooms and washrooms is considerably improved by sufficient illumination throughout the areas.

When lounges are incorporated as part of washrooms, casual reading will require an illumination level in accordance with such tasks (see Table 6). This may be provided by supplementary lighting if desired. Mirror lighting and similar residential treatments improve the appearance and usefulness of these rooms.

By JOHN J. NEIDHART,[3] *IES Committee on Office Lighting*

SELECTION GUIDE TO GENERAL OFFICE LIGHTING

A simplified procedure for selecting lamps and luminaires to control direct glare from illumination in general office space is given here. Factors to be considered in selection of lamps and lighting equipment for offices include the illumination level to be maintained, size and surface finishes of rooms, available mounting height, degree of brightness control required, and esthetic considerations. Selection procedure will be approached here by first considering continuous row spacings for a maintained illumination level of 100 footcandles (fc) using several types of equipment with different lampings and lamp loadings. This basic situation then can be converted to other practical ranges in illumination lev-

[3] *Member since 1949; chairman 1951 to 1956. Mr. Neidhart is manager, Application Engineering, The Miller Co., Meriden, Conn.*

el. It seems logical to assume the use of continuous rows for this demonstration since they are so widely used and have the advantages of acceptable appearance and minimum wiring and installation expense.

A key factor in luminaire selection is comparison of the average brightness distribution of proposed luminaires against the scissors curve (dark lines in Fig. 11) introduced by IES as a guide for selecting luminaires without fear of creating a direct-glare problem. (See the 1960 revision of *Recommended Practice for Office Lighting.*) To use the scissors curve, one needs merely to plot the crosswise and lengthwise average brightnesses of the luminaire using manufacturers' data in footlamberts at 45, 55, 65, 75, and 85 degrees from the vertical (nadir). (These averages are here again averaged to make a single curve for simpler demonstration. In practice, they would be plotted separately.) If the curves so plotted lie entirely

below any straight line drawn through the scissors curve fulcrum and between the heavy lines shown in Fig. 11, the luminaires can be used for 30- to 100-fc installations in any size office without creating a direct-glare problem. Although there are insufficient data to assure accurate extension of the range of the scissors curve beyond a 100-fc level, in the absence of any alternative it seems reasonable to use it as a guide throughout the 50- to 200-fc range. The first type of luminaire to be considered (Fig. 11) is a widely used, suspended, direct-indirect unit with 45 by 45 degree louver. In Table 7, the continuous row spacings that will maintain an average level of 100 fc at desk height with three possible lampings of the luminaire are tabulated for three different room sizes. The spacings given in Table 7 can be converted easily to other lampings or to 50- or 200-fc levels by simple multiplication and division. For example, rows of fixtures with 2-430 ma lamps

Table 7. Suspended direct-indirect units with 45 by 45 deg louver

Continuous row spacings for 100 ft-c.

Room Ratio	Number and Loading of Lamps		
	4 430 ma	2-800 ma	2-1500 ma
	Space Between Rows, ft		
0.8	5	4	7
1.5	9	6	10
3.0	12	8	13

Maximum spacing; 1.1 x mounting height
Reflectances: ceiling, 80%; walls, 30-50%; floor, 10%. These apply to Tables 1 through 5

Table 8. Surface unit with plastic louver using 430-ma lamps

Continuous row spacings for 100 ft-c.

Room Ratio	No. of Lamps & Sizes of Luminaire		
	2-1p, 1'x4'	2-1p, 2'x4'	4-1p, 2'x4'
	Space Between Rows, ft		
0.8	3	3½	7
1.5	4	5	9½
3.0	5	6	11½

Maximum spacing: 0.8 x mounting height

could be 6 ft apart for 100 fc or 12 ft for 50 fc in a room with ratio 3.0.

Maximum permissible spacings are noted in these tables for uniform illumination. Minimum spacing is largely a matter of esthetics, but indirect light from the ceiling would be more or less trapped if there were insufficient open space between rows. A spacing of 5½ to 6 ft would be a practical minimum for the unit in Fig. 11 and Table 7.

Average brightness distributions for this direct-indirect luminaire with different lampings are shown in Fig. 11. All lampings plotted, except for 2–1500 ma lamps, fall below the scissors curve limits. Fig. 11 also includes a summary with the table of row spacings converted into illumination ranges that could be maintained by practical installations for an assumed set of conditions.

Surface-Mounted Luminaires

Lower ceiling heights often preclude the use of suspended luminaires. Furthermore, surface-mounted or recessed units are frequently preferred for esthetic reasons. Although the direct-indirect luminaires discussed above can be surface-mounted, their distribution will change to direct or semi-direct and their brightnesses will be increased since much of the normal upward component will be redirected through the luminaire. Where surface-mounting is required, it is generally preferable to use luminaires specifically designed for the purpose. Fig. 12 illustrates such a luminaire and the scissors curve plot

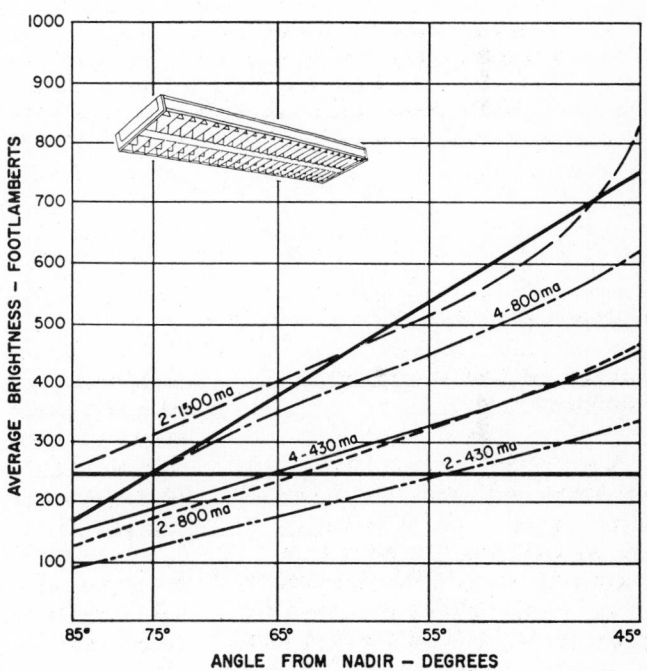

Fig. 11. IES scissors curve brightness comparison for direct-indirect luminaire with 45 by 45 deg louver

35 by 45 deg with 1500-ma lamps.

Summary of practical, maintained illumination ranges:

LAMPING	BRIGHTNESS RATING	ILLUMINATION RANGE, Fc*		
		SMALL ROOMS (Ratio = 0.8)	MEDIUM ROOMS (Ratio = 1.5)	LARGE ROOMS (Ratio = 3.0)
2- 430 ma	Excellent	30- 50	40- 75	50-100
4- 430 ma	Excellent	50- 90	75-150	100-200
2- 800 ma	Excellent	35- 75	50-100	75-130
4- 800 ma	Good	70-150	100-200	150-200+
2-1500 ma	Fair	70-125	90-175	120-200+

*Assuming continuous rows 5½ to 11 ft on centers, 10-ft mounting height

for three lampings and sizes which are typical for this unit.

Row spacings to provide 100 fc are given in Table 8. Close row spacings of this type of equipment can have a good appearance while minimizing shadows and reflected glare. Hence a spacing of 4 ft between row centers would be desirable, and the maximum spacing for uniform illumination would be 8 ft if the mounting height were 10 ft. This range was used for the summary in Fig. 12. Slightly wider spacings can be used with 2-lamp, 2-ft-wide units than with

2-lamp, 1-ft-wide units because lamps operate at lower temperature and there is less trapped light.

Another significant advantage of the 2-lamp, 2-ft-wide luminaire is that it is the only unit having a brightness distribution within the scissors curve limits. These units, therefore, would be first choice in this group, although practical illumination levels are somewhat limited.

A somewhat different form of equipment designed for surface mounting is the plastic wrap-around. Initially, such luminaires had a sim-

ple, diffusing closure or wrap. In more recent years, advancement in technology of plastics has made possible the accurate formation of refracting prisms in clear plastic extrusions with a much higher degree of light control, improved utilization, and lower brightness in the direct-glare zone. The improvement in utilization can be noted in Table 9 where it is apparent that 2-lamp units with a diffusing wrap are not practical for 100 fc installations but a well-designed prismatic closure does permit practical spacings for 100 fc. It can

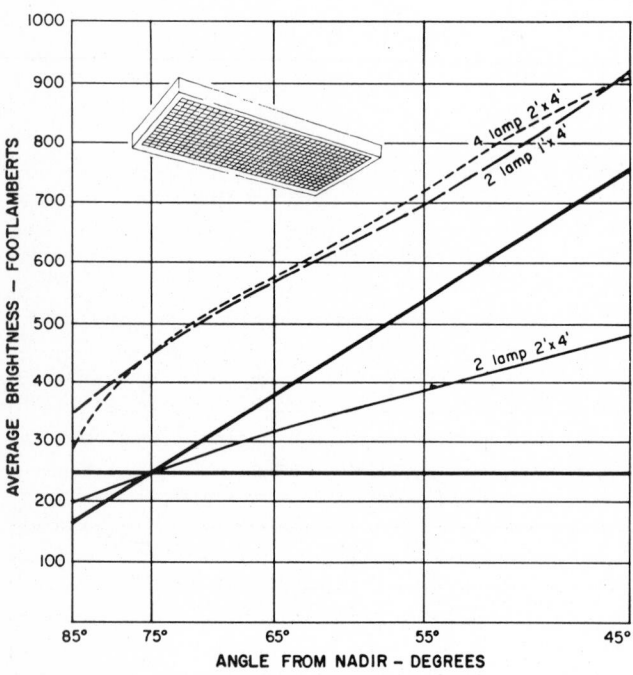

Fig. 12. Brightness comparison for surface-mounted units using 4-ft, 430-ma lamps

Higher lamp loadings lose efficiency through high temperature operation in these units.

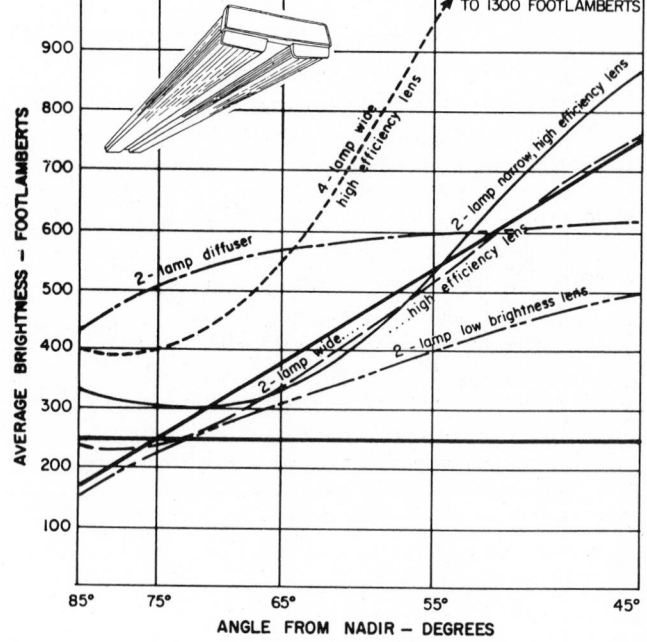

Fig. 13. Brightness comparison for plastic wrap-around surface-mounted units with 430-ma lamps

Various types shown in Table 9.

Summary of practical, maintained illumination ranges:

LAMPING AND SIZE	BRIGHTNESS RATING	ILLUMINATION RANGE, Fc*		
		SMALL ROOMS	MEDIUM ROOMS	LARGE ROOMS
2 Lamp 1'x4'	Fair	40- 75	50-100	60-125
2 Lamp 2'x4'	Excellent	45- 90	65-125	75-150
4 Lamp 2'x4'	Fair	90-175	120-225	150-250

*Assuming continuous rows spaced 4 ft to 8 ft on centers with luminaires at 10-ft mounting height

Summary of practical, maintained illumination ranges:

CLOSURE	NUMBER LAMPS	BRIGHTNESS RATING	ILLUMINATION RANGE, Fc*		
			SMALL ROOMS	MEDIUM ROOMS	LARGE ROOMS
Diffuser	2	Fair	30- 60	35- 85	50-100
Narrow, High Eff. Lens	2	Good	45-100	60-140	75-170
Wide, High Efficiency Lens	2	Very Good	45-100	60-140	75-170
	3	Good	65-150	100-200	115-250
	4	High	85-180	120-270	140-300+
Low Br. Lens	2	Excellent	35- 75	50-100	55-125

*Assuming continuous rows 4 ft to 10 ft (Diffuser) or 9 ft (Lens) on centers with luminaires at 10-ft mounting height

LIGHTING—14
Offices

Table 9.   Plastic wrap-around surface units using 430-ma lamps

Continuous row spacings for 100 ft-c.

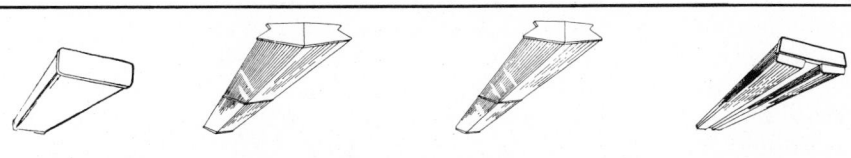

Room Ratio	Diffuser 2-lamp	High Efficiency Lens Narrow—2-lamp	High Efficiency Lens-Wide			Low Brightness Lens, 2-lamp
			2-lp.	3-lp.	4-lp.	
			Space Between Rows, ft			
0.8	2½	4	4	6	7½	3
1.5	3½	5½	6	9	11	4
3.0	4½	7	7	10½	13	5

Maximum spacing: diffuser 1.0, lens 0.9 x mounting height

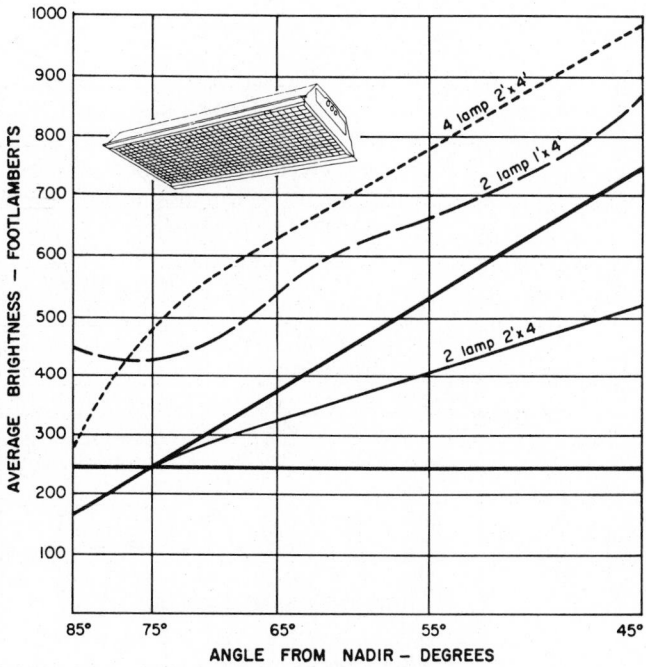

Fig. 14. Brightness comparison for white enameled troffer with 45-deg plastic louver and 430-ma lamps

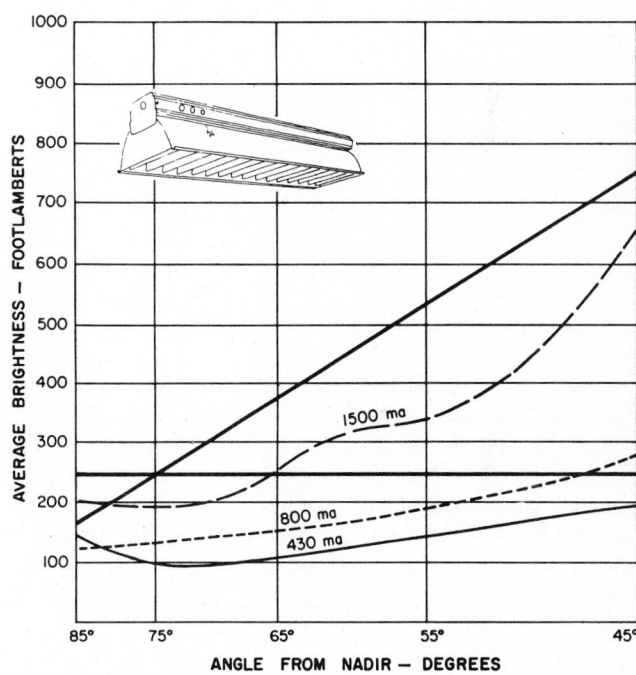

Fig. 15. Brightness comparison for aluminum troffer with 45 by 45 deg louver

Summary of practical, maintained illumination ranges:

LAMPING AND SIZE	BRIGHTNESS RATING	ILLUMINATION RANGE, Fc*		
		SMALL ROOMS	MEDIUM ROOMS	LARGE ROOMS
2 Lamp 1'x4'	Fair	40- 75	50-100	65-130
2 Lamp 2'x4'	Excellent	45- 90	65-130	80-160
4 Lamp 2'x4'	Fair	100-190	125-250	150-300

*Assuming continuous rows spaced 4 ft to 8 ft on centers with luminaires at 10-ft mounting height

Summary of practical, maintained illumination ranges:

LAMPING	TROFFER	BRIGHTNESS RATING	ILLUMINATION RANGE, Fc*		
			SMALL ROOM	MEDIUM ROOM	LARGE ROOM
430 ma	Single	Excellent	30- 50	30- 65	30- 80
	Twin	Excellent	40-100	50-130	60-160
800 ma	Single	Excellent	30- 65	30- 85	35-100
	Twin	Excellent	50-130	60-170	70-200
1500 ma	Single	Very Good	45-115	60-150	65-170
	Twin	Very Good	90-130	120-300	130-340

*Assuming continuous rows spaced on 3- to 8-ft centers with luminaires at 10-ft mounting height

also be seen that even higher levels can be obtained practically with 3-lamp or 4-lamp prismatic units.

The brightness control advantages of properly designed refracting closures are shown in Fig. 13. It can be seen that the uncontrolled diffusing closure has the highest brightness of any of the 2-lamp units. The 2-lamp, high-efficiency, prismatic, wraparound unit has somewhat better brightness control despite its higher efficiency, because the light is directed down to the work plane and away from the direct-glare zone. Only the low-brightness prismatic unit, however, has a brightness distribution entirely below the scissors curve limiting line.

Recessed Troffers
Recessed lighting installations are becoming increasingly popular, and white-enameled troffers similar to the one illustrated in Fig. 14 are often used. The performance of such units is similar to that of the surface unit illustrated in Fig. 12 although there are small differences in the data as shown by Table 10 and Fig. 14. stallation shown in Fig. 6 is typical of results that can be obtained with this type of lighting.

The more highly loaded lamps have been applied thus far in this discussion only in the direct-indirect luminaires. The scissors curve brightness comparisons have also indicated that even if it were possible to use 800 ma or 1500 ma lamps in the surface or recessed units discussed, they would not be at all satisfactory from the brightness standpoint. It is known, however, that considerably better brightness control is possible in troffers having properly contoured

Table 10. White enameled troffer with plastic louver using 430-ma lamps

Continuous row spacings for 100 ft-c.

Room Ratio	2-lamp 1'x4'	2-lamp 2'x4'	4-lamp 2'x4'
	Space Between Rows, ft.		
0.8	3+	4—	7+
1.5	4+	5+	10
3.0	5+	6+	12

Maximum spacing: 0.8 x mounting height

aluminum reflectors for each individual lamp. Furthermore, the size of such units and the fact that they require only one lamp per foot of width results in a much cooler operation of the luminaire.

Continuous-row spacings of such a luminaire with 430 ma, 800 ma, and 1500 ma lamps are shown in Table 11. The high degree of brightness control afforded by such a unit is shown in Fig. 15, and it is evident that comfortable installations can be provided even with the 1500 ma lamp. In fact, it is only with the more highly loaded lamps that this unit is practical, since the row spacings with 430 ma lamps are absurdly close except at relatively low illumination levels. Since a wide range of illumination levels can be satisfactorily provided by the 800 ma and 1500 ma units and since adequate brightness control is provided with these lamps, there is no reason for using 430 ma lamps in this unit. Because the low brightness of this unit makes it tend to blend into the ceiling, it is believed that a somewhat closer row spacing of 3 ft between centers can be used, and this was

Table 11. Single lamp aluminum troffer with 45-deg louver

Continuous row spacings for 100 ft-c.

Room Ratio	430 ma	800 ma	1500 ma
	Space Between Rows, ft.		
0.8	1½	2	3½
1.5	2	2½	4½
3.0	2½	3	5

Maximum spacing: 0.8 x mounting height

used in developing the summary of results for Fig. 15. It should also be noted that either single or twin versions of this unit may be used, with the twin unit consisting of two of the 1-ft-wide reflectors banked together in a structural assembly.

Since the ballasts for the more highly loaded lamps are somewhat noisier, some concern has been expressed regarding the use of these ballasts in office applications. It should be recognized, however, that the overall noise level of a lighting installation is the cumulative effect from all of the ballasts in the area. It can be shown by sound-rating calculations that in offices with good acoustical ceilings the total noise level of an installation of 2-lamp ballasts for 8-ft 1500 ma lamps will be below the normal 40-45 db ambient noise level of an office. In fact, it can be shown that the ballast noise level for such an installation will be only slightly higher than that of an installation of 2-lamp 430-ma units because there would then be four times as many 430-ma ballasts.

The approach to selection described here can be applied to any other luminaires desired.

By K. STEVE RASIEJ, *Syska & Hennessy, Inc., Consulting Engineers*

FLUORESCENT LIGHTING FOR LARGE AREAS

The purpose of these two pages is to present an easy-to-use guide for appraising the relative practical merits of various fluorescent lighting systems as used in office, commercial and institutional buildings. Data given in the tables are predicated on over-all performance and cost. Fixture appearance is not considered. Since the various systems are rated for a particular set of room conditions, the figures serve only as bases of comparison, and not as final designs for many conditions.

The following criteria were selected to indicate the performance of each system:

Average (maintained) foot-candles (ft-c)—Gives the amount of light obtained at the desk level

Watts per square foot—Gives the amount of electrical energy consumed

Foot-candles per watt per square foot—Indicates efficiency of the system in terms of energy used

Installation cost—Indicates relative costs of various systems. Installation cost includes cost of fixtures and wiring beginning with first outlet of the circuits in any particular layout. Installation cost of system A in continuous 9-ft spacing is taken to be 1.00

Visual Comfort Index (VCI)—The percentage of persons who will find the direct view of the lighting system visually comfortable, assuming that observers are in the least favorable position (center rear of space) and are occupied at visual tasks of some severity. Figures are based on data published by Lamp Division of General Electric Company.

EXAMPLE ROOM

Ceiling Height—9 ft
Ceiling/Wall Reflectance—75/50 per cent
Maintenance Factor—70 per cent
Lamps—Warm White
Fixture Spacing—5, 7 and 9 ft, continuous and individual spacing.

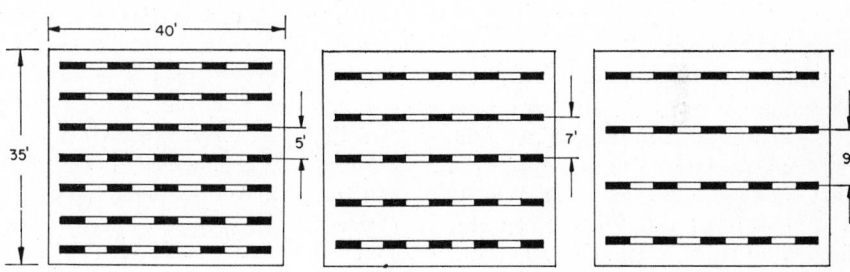

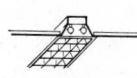 **A**—2-lamp recessed troffer, with egg-crate louver for 40° x 40° shielding

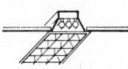 **B**—same as type A except with 3 lamps

 **C**—2-lamp recessed troffer, with Albalite glass diffuser

 **D**—same as type C except with 3 lamps

 **E**—2-lamp recessed troffer, with low brightness glass diffuser

 **F**—same as type E except with 3 lamps

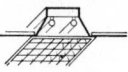 **G**—2-lamp recessed troffer, 2 ft x 4 ft, with egg-crate louver for 35° x 35° shielding

 **H**—same as type G except with 3 lamps

 **I**—two type M fixtures side by side, forming 2 ft x 4 ft, 2-lamp recessed double parabolic troffer

 **J**—suspended, 2-lamp, direct-indirect unit with metal sides and metal louvers for 40° x 40° shielding

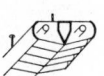 **K**—suspended, 2-lamp, direct-indirect unit with metal sides and metal louvers for 35° x 25° shielding

 **L**—suspended, 2-lamp, direct-indirect unit with ribbed glass sides and metal egg-crate louvers for 40° x 40° shielding

 **M**—1-lamp recessed deep parabolic troffer with aluminum cross louvers 6 in. o-c. This type of fixture is suitable for installation at close spacing only and is so considered in the chart

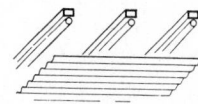 **N**—luminous ceiling of diffusing corrugated plastic

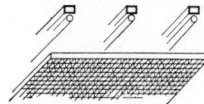 **O**—louvered ceiling with 2 in. x 2 in. x 2 in. cells, white steel louver

NOTES

1. All fixtures are 1 ft x 4 ft except where indicated.
2. For types J, K and L fixtures: assumed ceiling height—9 ft 6 in. fixture mounting height, 8 ft 0 in. For types N and O: assumed ceiling height—9 ft 0 in. Distance lamp to ceiling is 16 in. for 2 ft spacing, 24 in. for 3 ft spacing and 32 in. for 4 ft spacing.

Guide to Fixture Selection

	Fixture Type	5 FT Avg FT-C	Watts/Sq Ft	FT-C/Watts/Sq Ft	Install. Cost	5 FT VCI Lengthwise	Crosswise	7 FT Avg FT-C	Watts/Sq Ft	FT-C/Watts/Sq Ft	Install. Cost	7 FT VCI Lengthwise	Crosswise	9 FT Avg FT-C	Watts/Sq Ft	FT-C/Watts/Sq Ft	Install. Cost	9 FT VCI Lengthwise	Crosswise
INDIVIDUAL FIXTURES RECESSED	A	43	2.5	17.1	1.23	70	68	31	1.8	17.1	.88	78	76	25	1.4	17.1	.63	82	80
	B	62	3.8	16.5	1.60	47	45	44	2.7	16.5	1.09	52	50	35	2.1	16.5	.92	55	53
	C	46	2.5	18.1	1.31	75	75	33	1.8	18.1	.94	81	81	26	1.4	18.1	75	85	85
	D	62	38	16 5	1.64	47	47	44	2.7	16.5	1.17	52	52	35	2.1	16.5	.94	55	55
	E	48	2.5	19.1	1.51	81	83	34	1.8	19.1	1.08	84	86	27	1.4	19.1	.86	86	88
	F	64	3.8	17.1	1.85	64	66	46	2.7	17.1	1.32	70	72	37	2.1	17.1	1.05	72	74
	G	51	2.5	20.2	1.67	80	85	36	1.8	20.7	1.20	84	89	29	1.4	20.2	.95	87	91
	H	72	3.8	19.4	2.00	67	68	52	2.7	19.4	1.42	71	72	41	2.1	19.4	1.14	74	76
	I	50	2.5	19.8	2.64	82	97	35	1.8	19.8	1.86	84	97	28	1.4	19.8	1.51	86	97
SUSPENDED	J	45	2.5	17.8	.92	97	97	32	1.8	17.8	.66	97	97	26	1.4	17.8	.54	97	97
	K	46	2.5	18.2	.88	91	82	33	1.8	18.2	.63	92	83	27	1.4	18.2	.51	93	94
	L	45	2.5	17.8	1.40	94	84	32	1.8	17.8	1.01	96	86	26	1.4	17.8	.82	97	87
CONTINUOUS FIXTURE ROWS RECESSED	A	77	4.5	17.1	1.75	53	51	55	3.2	17.1	1.25	65	63	45	2.6	17.1	1.00	67	65
	B	111	6.7	16.5	2.32	35	33	79	4.8	16.5	1.61	43	41	63	3.9	16.5	1.33	45	43
	C	82	4.5	18.1	1.87	57	57	59	3.2	18.1	1.34	68	68	47	2.6	18.1	1.07	72	72
	D	111	6.7	16.5	2.38	35	35	79	4.8	16.5	1.70	43	43	63	3.9	16.5	1.37	45	45
	E	86	4.5	19.1	2.10	75	77	61	3.2	19.1	1.57	78	81	49	2.6	19.1	1.26	81	83
	F	115	6.7	17.1	2.70	54	55	82	4.8	17.1	1.93	58	60	66	3.9	17.1	1.55	64	66
	G	91	4.5	20.2	2.42	64	69	65	3.2	20.2	1.73	75	80	52	2.6	20.2	1.39	76	81
	H	130	6.7	19.4	2.94	55	58	93	4.8	19.4	2.10	63	65	74	3.9	19.4	1.68	65	67
	I	89	4.5	19.8	3.85	74	96	64	3.2	19.8	2.78	80	97	51	2.6	19.8	2.21	82	97
SUSPENDED	J	80	4.5	17.8	1.44	94	94	57	3.2	17.8	1.03	96	96	46	2.6	17.8	.82	97	97
	K	82	4.5	18.2	1.37	85	76	58	3.2	18.2	.98	88	79	47	2.6	18.2	.78	90	81
	L	80	4.5	17.8	2.20	87	77	57	3.2	17.8	1.57	91	81	46	2.6	17.8	1.25	93	83

		3 FT						4 FT						5 FT					
RECESSED	M	78	3.8	20.4	33.5	89	96	58	2.9	20.4	2.50	90	97	45	2.2	20.4	1.96	91	97

CONTINUOUS LAMPS LUMINOUS CEILINGS		2 FT						3 FT						4 FT					
	N	96	6.1	15.7	3.05	69	69	68	4.3	15.7	2.42	83	83	51	3.2	15.7	2.10	90	90
	O	75	6.1	12.3	4.51	97	97	53	4.3	12.3	3.88	97	97	40	3.2	12.3	3.57	97	97

Data from American Standard Practice for Industrial Lighting (A11.1-1952)

LIGHTING METHODS FOR INDUSTRIAL AREAS

Introduction: A mere abundance of light does not constitute good lighting. To provide satisfactory shop illumination three main conditions must be met:

1. Quantity of illumination must be sufficient for all visual tasks.

2. Quality of lighting must be in accordance with the recommendations given earlier in this section.

3. Lighting systems, painting of interior surfaces, machines, etc., should help provide a proper environment for the working interior.

The proper method of lighting a specific area is also dependent upon the size and proportions of the room.

General lighting

Modern industrial lighting practice requires the establishment of a base or minimum quantity of light throughout the room. This is termed general lighting. The quantity may vary depending upon the purpose for which the space is to be used. If visual tasks are particularly severe, much higher illumination over restricted areas can be added to this base. This additional light, known as supplementary lighting, is usually provided by luminaires placed relatively close to the area being illuminated.[4]

The general lighting system usually consists of luminaires placed ten feet or more above the floor. The purpose of the general lighting system is to provide sufficient light for most seeing tasks and promote safety and plant protection.

Localized general lighting

Many industrial plants have machinery of such a nature and so located that a uniform intensity of illumination is not necessary throughout the area. Luminaires may be mounted above the visual task,

[4] *See* Recommended Practice for Supplementary Lighting *by Illuminating Engineering Society.*

supplying adequate levels of illumination at the particular work points and at the same time providing sufficient illumination for adjacent areas.

Where supplementary lighting is necessary the general lighting should keep the brightness difference between the well-lighted immediate work area and the surroundings within the ranges specified in Table 2 in section on "Lighting: General."

Low-bay areas: In rooms relatively wide and long in proportion to the height, a spread type of direct lighting equipment is usually applicable. (Rooms of this category have a width greater than three times the height.) Here good quality illumination is provided by fluorescent luminaires mounted in continuous rows, spaced to give the proper quantity and distribution of light.

The use of continuous rows of fluorescent units run at right angles, forming a grid or checkerboard pattern, provides higher levels of illumination, reduces shadows, and assures more even brightness of machine dials, regardless of the angle at which these dials may be placed.

High-bay narrow interior: In areas where the width is equal to or less than the height, direct lighting equipment which concentrates the light is usually used in order to provide efficiently the necessary illumination at the working plane. Usually incandescent or mercury vapor sources are used for this application either alone or in combination.

Mercury lamps have the advantage of longer life and higher efficiency. When the two types of sources are used together the filament lamps supply an excess of red light to offset the deficiency in red of the mercury, the result being a synthetic "white" widely employed for industrial areas. Also the use of combination systems alleviates the problem created by temporary power interruptions since the mercury lamps do not restart for several minutes. Percentages of the two usually range from equal quantities of the mercury and filament light to twice as much mercury light as filament.

High-bay wide interior: Some of the newer manufacturing areas, notably air-

plane assembly plants, are enormous in both length and width, while at the same time the ceiling height is 30 or 40 ft or more. Concentrating types of direct lighting equipment can be used, mounted on appropriate spacings to provide the quantity of illumination required.

However, because of the extreme width and length, spread types of direct lighting equipment can be used to good advantage with a large number of luminaires each contributing a small amount of light to any given point. This reduces shadows to a minimum and gives higher vertical surface illumination. With fluorescent units the effect approaches that of indirect lighting. These fluorescent luminaires are preferably mounted in continuous rows, which simplifies installation and wiring.

Nonproductive and service areas: In areas such as warehouses, boiler and pump rooms, freight elevators, washrooms, lockers, corridors, etc., the lighting requirement is usually one of providing reasonable diffusion, comfort, and appearance with a minimum of cost. For these areas the requirements can be met with incandescent lamps in direct (spread) equipment or in semidirect units. Where better appearance is a factor or where a higher level of illumination is necessary, it is desirable to use direct or semidirect fluorescent equipment.

Special requirements: Some types of work require precise color discrimination, and for these areas "improved-color-rendition cool white" fluorescent tubes should be specified. Where third-dimension perception is important, care should be taken to provide sufficient shadow for the modeling of solid forms. A wide variety of special types of lighting is used in connection with inspection processes. Among these are low-angle, silhouette, transillumination, magnification, projection, fluorescence, polarized, and stroboscopic lighting.

QUANTITY OF ILLUMINATION

Recommended illumination levels for many specific industrial tasks are given in "Recommended Levels of Illumination," Illuminating Engineering Society, 1958.

Data from American Standard Practice for School Lighting (A23.1-1962)

CHANGING NEEDS IN SCHOOL LIGHTING

The school building must be designed for future educational programs and community services as well as those in use today. The content, scope, methods and processes of education are constantly changing as society changes, as the need for education changes, as technology advances, and as more is discovered about how learning takes place.

The old concept of 30 or more children seated in five rows in fixed furniture, facing a teacher in a regimented study-recite program no longer prevails. A system of illumination based on such a pattern will not suffice. Children work individually and in groups; they read, write, print, type, discuss, and construct; they work in shops and laboratories; they move about as necessary; they work on problems or projects which have meaning for them and are of interest and are within their comprehension.

The program will continue to change. It will involve increased used of a wide variety of instructional materials, equipment and methods of presentation. Television, films, slides, film strips, teaching machines, radio, and other devices unknown at present will be used. A wide variety of visual tasks will be encountered.

It follows that the design of the building, including the provision for seeing, must be highly flexible. The best results in building design will be achieved when the resources of architects, engineers, and educational planners are coordinated.

The goal in school lighting: The goal in school lighting must be to allow students and instructors to see comfortably and efficiently and without undue distraction. It follows then that an adequate level of illumination for efficient performance of visual tasks is necessary, and the quality of lighting should help to maintain a comfortable and pleasing environment.

Visual tasks in schools: The visual tasks occurring in the various school grades are numerous. Between the simplest and the most complex, there are hundreds varying in size, direction and viewing distance from the eye, brightness difference, and so on.

Within the total visual environment there are small area tasks, such as reading and writing, which commonly require prolonged and close attention. There may be close-to-the-eye tasks or distant tasks; small print or large print; tasks on matte or glossy paper. Pupils may be required to change from reading manuscript writing at the desk to reading cursive writing on the chalkboard; from looking almost straight down, to looking along and above the horizontal; from cutting and pasting, to viewing projected pictures.

Illumination

Recommended illumination levels for various school tasks are listed in Table 12. To ensure the quality of the illumination, brightness ratios should not exceed those shown in Fig. 16, and reflectances should not be less than those recommended in Fig. 17. Particular care should be taken to prevent glare, both direct and indirect, as discussed in detail in the section on "Lighting: General."

Special tasks require special lighting

It would be impractical to light a classroom by providing only the amount needed for one given task. In a classroom, individual students may be performing different tasks at the same time. Also, the whole working area, as potential teaching space, must be provided with a satisfactory minimum level of illumination. The general lighting level will be designed for a commonly found, most difficult task.

Certain classrooms are used for special purposes. In these it is desirable, indeed necessary, to light for the specific task. Where physical disabilities play a part, special levels of illumination will be required. In school shops, sewing rooms and art classrooms, lighting should be planned on a specific visual task basis. In some cases, supplementary lighting may be used to provide sufficient illumination for specific areas (i.e., the lighting of a chalkboard, Fig. 18).

Chalkboards should meet two brightness standards. They should be light enough to blend well with the background, and dark enough to provide sufficient contrast to chalk writing. A chalkboard should be measured for reflectance under "in use" conditions, with a typical amount of chalk film on its surface. Colored boards should not exceed 20 per cent reflectance under these conditions. Black chalkboards in use are not usually black, but dark gray, with 5 to 10 per cent reflectance.

For viewing motion picture and slide projector screens or TV in the classroom the comfortable visual environment should be much the same as for any other visual work. The area immediately surrounding these screens should be slightly less bright than the screen itself, and the entire visual surroundings should be kept as light as possible without causing the image on the screen to lose contrast.

SPECIAL APPLICATIONS

Illumination levels recommended for various specific areas in schools are listed in Table 13. Some of these areas are discussed in the following paragraphs.

Art rooms: As the appearance of colors in an art room is a paramount consideration, the light source used should render the colors as accurately as possible. While the standard cool white fluorescent lamp is satisfactory for most school applications, the improved-color-rendition cool white fluorescent provides a more natural appearance of colors even though it is lower in efficacy, by about 25 per cent, as compared to the standard cool white.

Supplementary lighting from spot lamps is useful on displays and models for improved visibility at a distance and for

Table 12. Recommended illumination levels for various school tasks

	Footcandles
Reading printed material	30
Reading pencil writing	70
Spirit duplicated material	
Good	30
Poor	100
Drafting, benchwork	100**
Lip reading, chalkboards, sewing	150**

*Minimum on the task at any time.
**Obtained with a combination of general lighting plus specialized supplementary lighting. Care should be taken to keep within the recommended brightness ratios. These seeing tasks generally involve the discrimination of fine detail for long periods of time under conditions of poor contrast. To provide the required illumination, a combination of the general lighting indicated plus specialized supplementary lighting is necessary. The design and installation of the combination system must provide not only a sufficient amount of light but also the proper direction of light, diffusion and eye protection. As far as possible it should eliminate direct and reflected glare as well as objectionable shadows.

modeling purposes. Such lighting creates the desired highlights and shadows on art arrangements being painted or drawn. Supplementary lighting, such as that from adjustable desk lamps which can provide a definite directional light, is frequently desirable when students work on or study surfaces involving glaze or texture.

Drafting rooms: See section on "Lighting: Offices."

Auditoriums: The auditorium is made up of a seating area (house), and a stage area. It may serve as an assembly and lecture hall, study room, theater, concert hall, audio-visual aid room (including television), and for many other activities. Many schools today are developing speech and drama programs, not only among students, but also among adult groups. The auditorium serves so many purposes it must be well planned and properly equipped to satisfy them all.

For general auditorium use, there is need for atmosphere lighting which can be incorporated into the architecture as ceiling or wall coves, luminous ceiling treatments or decorative suspended indirect luminaires. Facilities to provide more than one level of illumination are desirable since this area may serve several purposes.

The basic lighting for the seating area should be planned for audience assembly purposes, and at dramatic presentations for such intermission tasks as reading programs. It should be dimmer-controlled, preferably from several stations (stage lighting board, stage manager's station, rear of main floor seating area, projection booth) which will allow for gradual transitions and for lower levels to be used in showing slides and motion pictures. If windows are used, means should be provided to darken them during projection.

Supplementary illumination is required if the seating area is used for study or testing purposes. Several circuits of this supplementary system, well distributed over the seating area and providing additional illumination for penciled handwriting and reading, can be set up for independent switching. Special care should be taken to avoid specular reflection from any direct downlighting.

Aisle and exit lights, with a low level of nondistracting illumination, should be provided. The aisle lights should not be visible to any of the seated audience. Because of the high brightness ratios in a semidarkened room, they may prove irritating despite low surface brightness. If there are steps in the aisles, small and well-shielded step lights offer a safety aid. These should be located in the side of the step, not in the riser, to prevent

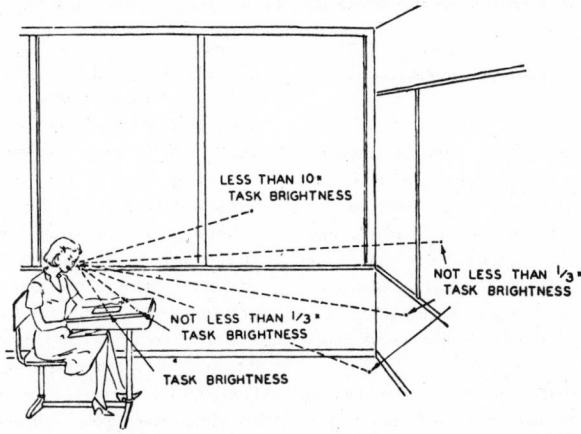

Fig. 16. Recommended maximum brightness ratios for school classrooms

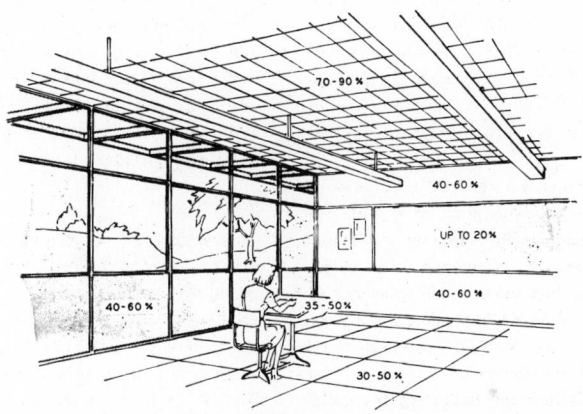

Fig. 17. Recommended reflectances for surfaces and furnishings in the classroom

Note: control media are used at windows to reduce exterior brightnesses so that they are in balance with interior brightnesses.

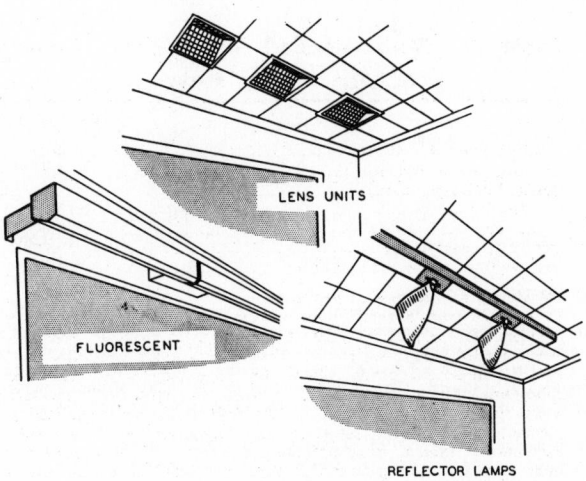

Fig. 18. Chalkboard lighting units

Table 13. Levels of illumination currently recommended for specific areas of schools

Data from Illuminating Engineering Society Lighting Handbook, *3d ed., 1959.*

AREA	FOOTCANDLES ON TASKS*	AREA	FOOTCANDLES ON TASKS*
Auditoriums (See also Theatres)		Basketball	
Assembly only	15	College and professional	50
Exhibitions	30	College intramural and high school with spectators	30
Social Activities	5	College intramural and high school without spectators	20
Cafeterias		Volleyball	
Dining area†	30	Tournament	20
Cashier	50	Recreational	10
Food displays	70	Library	
Kitchen		Reading room	
Inspection, checking, pricing	70	Study and notes	70
Other areas	30	Ordinary reading	30
Classrooms		Stacks	30
Art rooms	70	Book repair and binding	50
Drafting rooms	100**	Cataloging	70
Home economics rooms		Card files	70
Sewing	150**	Check-in and check-out desks	70
Cooking	50	Lounges	
Ironing	50	General	10
Sink activities	70	Reading books, magazines, newspapers	30
Notetaking areas	70	Offices	
Laboratories	100	Accounting, auditing, tabulating bookkeeping, business machine operation and reading poor reproduction	150
Lecture rooms		Regular office work, reading good reproductions, reading or transcribing handwriting in hard pencil or on poor paper, active filing, index references, mail sorting	100
Audience area	70		
Demonstration area	150**		
Music rooms		Reading or transcribing handwriting in ink or medium pencil on good quality paper, intermittent filing	70
Simple scores	30		
Advanced scores	70‡	Reading high contrast or well-printed material, tasks and areas not involving critical or prolonged seeing such as conferring, interviewing and inactive files	30
Shops	100**		
Sight-saving rooms	150**		
Study halls	70	Parking areas	1
Typing	70	Storerooms	
Corridors and stairways	20	Inactive	5
Dormitories		Active	
General	10	Rough bulky	10
Reading books, magazines, newspapers	30	Medium	20
Study desk	70	Fine	50
First aid rooms		Swimming pools	
General	50	General and overhead	10
Examining table	100	Underwater	#
Gymnasiums		Theaters	
Exhibitions, matches	30	During intermission	5
General exercising and recreation	20	During motion picture	0.1
Dances	5	Toilets and washrooms	30
Lockers and shower rooms	20		
Badminton			
Tournament	30		
Club	20		
Recreational	10		

*Minimum on the task at any time.
**In some cases it is necessary to use local lighting to supplement the general illumination. These cases are generally found where it is economically unfeasible to produce the recommended footcandle levels from a general lighting system. Quite frequently seeing tasks are on oblique rather than horizontal surfaces. This results in a reduction in illumination and a consequent loss in task brightness. Also, some of the seeing tasks are more difficult because the contrast between the paper and the printing may be very low. In both of the foregoing cases, supplementary illumination is sometimes required or indicated. Care should be used in the choice of supplementary lighting units, so that they will not direct objectionable glare into the eyes of any student. The distribution of the light across the working surface should be as uniform as is possible. (Page 11-21, IES Lighting Handbook.)
†If used also as a study hall a level of 70 footcandles is recommended.
‡When score is substandard size and notations are printed on the lines a level of 150 footcandles or more is needed.
#100 lamp lumens per square foot of pool surface.

light spilling on the stage or into eyes of people going up the steps.

Particular attention should be given to local building codes regarding exit lights, panic controls, and so on. It is desirable that an emergency lighting system be installed which would be automatically operated and connected to a separate power supply from that of the main lighting system.

Proper lighting facilities for the stage must include more than sufficient illumination. Stage lighting is an art embracing a knowledge of color, shading and three-dimensional composition. During a production all these factors are brought into account and may be changed continually from one scene to the next. The layout of lighting equipment and a lighting control system may range from a simple plan with a minimum of equipment to a complex plan with elaborate equipment, as might be required in a school with a strong dramatics program. The layout will be affected by the amount the stage may be used, the budget, and future plans for the auditorium. Detailed layout for a small school stage will be found at the end of this section.

Adequate provision must be made in the house area for spotlights to cover the downstage (close to the audience) area. These lights should be located at a sufficiently low angle with the horizontal to avoid unpleasant shadows from a strong downward beam of light. These spotlights should be mounted so that they may be adjusted vertically and horizontally and the focus changed by a person having a full view of the stage. In choosing a spotlight, first consideration should be given to the ease with which the shape and definition of the light beam can be controlled, since this is of prime importance in preventing light spill on the curtains and walls around the stage.

Spotlights are also required over the whole stage to light the various acting areas. Borderlights and footlights of the individual reflector or compartment type provide a convenient source of general lighting and add an over-all blending to the lighting picture. Auxiliary striplights, floodlights and spotlights may be required to light various areas and backings. The upstage (away from the audience) area will require as much attention as the downstage area, if the general effect of the whole stage lighting is to be uniform. In addition to circuits necessary for overhead lighting, groups of stage-type receptacles are required on or near the stage floor around the acting area for additional lighting units which may be plugged in from

time to time. Separate worklights are also necessary for the stage.

With the possible exception of borderlights and footlights, no lighting unit should be permanently wired to a branch lighting circuit. All other special lighting units should be wired to make them readily portable.

It is desirable that all stage lighting branch circuits be brought into a central interconnecting panel. The panel provides a switching or interplugging system whereby any stage branch circuit can be connected to any dimming circuit.

The dimming components may be either of the manually operated or remotely operated type. Manually operated systems are less expensive; remotely operated systems offer ease of control and added versatility. Dimmer systems may be of the electronic tube, magnetic amplifier, saturable reactor, or autotransformer types.

The operator of the equipment should be able to see and hear the stage action and be readily accessible. The interconnecting panel is usually placed in a convenient backstage location.

Cafeterias and kitchens: In eating areas the lighting should create a cheerful, comfortable area. Good lighting promotes cleanliness. Dining areas are frequently used as supplementary study halls and when so used the lighting should provide the levels of illumination recommended for the task. Where the appearance of food is a prime consideration, as in the cafeteria, improved-color-rendition fluorescent lamps should be used. Additional incandescent lighting may also be used over the serving counter to give the food eye appeal and to speed up the selection of food at the serving counter. Good general diffuse lighting, either incandescent or fluorescent, is needed in the kitchen, especially at ranges, work tables and sinks, to assure cleanliness, safety and good housekeeping.

Corridors: Corridors are the transition areas from the high brightnesses of the outdoors to the lower brightnesses of the classrooms. They should be well lighted to promote traffic safety and discipline and to assure good housekeeping in the lockers which frequently line the corridors. Continuous fluorescent luminaires with crosswise shielding are commonly used. Care should be taken that the lamps are not exposed to unshielded view from within classrooms, through windows common to the corridor and classroom. Where students, as monitors, are stationed in corridors, supplementary lighting should be provided at their stations. Incandescent corridor lighting units which are designed

for good lengthwise visual comfort and which deliver good lighting to the ceiling, walls and lockers are available.

Dormitory rooms: Dormitory rooms are commonly provided with two systems of illumination, one of relatively low level for general illumination, the other of higher value for study purposes. Such an installation is particularly desirable where a room is shared by two or more students in order that one may retire with comfort if the other wishes to continue studying. See section on "Lighting: Residential."

Every dormitory room should be provided with sufficient convenience outlets to afford a variety of furniture arrangement. Outlets should be provided for such supplementary lighting units as dressing table lamps and bed lamps.

Suitably illuminated mirrors and handy convenience outlets in dormitory rooms will avoid congestion in washroom lavatories. Such mirrors should be lighted by means of two two-tube brackets, one at each side of the mirror, mounted approximately 5 ft 3 in. from the floor to the center of the bracket, higher level lighting being delivered on each side of the face.

Gymnasiums: The modern school gymnasium is a multipurpose as well as a multisport area which can serve a variety of needs of the student body during the daytime, and in many instances, the community at night. In addition to its varied athletic uses, the school gymnasium is often used for such activities as assemblies, dances, concerts, lectures, and community meetings. Because of the wide divergence of seeing tasks that can be encountered, a choice of lighting levels may be desirable. Such variations in the general illumination are most often achieved by circuiting. The lighting system is designed for the highest illumination level required. Then, by placing portions of the total system on separate circuits which can be operated independently or in combination with other circuits, a range of illumination levels can be obtained.

For special activities, such as dances, where the creation of a mood or an atmosphere is the primary lighting objective, and low illumination levels are desired, the most satisfactory results can often be achieved through the use of portable or temporary supplementary lighting equipment, such as small floodlights, reflectorized lamps, and colored filters.

Caution must be exercised in positioning luminaires relative to critical surfaces, such as glass backboards, to avoid blinding reflections. Windows in a gymnasium are unsatisfactory in the amount of illumination they provide, and can produce undesirable reflections or blinding glare if improperly located. Gymnasium floors should be finished with a nonglossy finish to avoid undesirable reflections and possible veiling glare.

To prevent breakage, it may be necessary to cover otherwise unprotected luminaires with a protective cover or wire grid. This will reduce their efficiency and should be compensated for in the initial system design by multiplying the luminaire efficiency by the average transmittance of the cover or grid.

Laboratories: These involve special laboratory tables or benches at which very detailed work is carried out in dissection, inspection of reactions, instrumentation and measurement. Good diffusion with some directional component and appropriate color quality is required.

Many times fluorescent lighting equipment is run continuously along the benches or tables just above head height. This gives localized general lighting with maximum illumination where the work is being carried out. An upward component for lighting the ceiling is essential, as is adequate shielding to meet the "scissors curve." Where color reactions are to be observed, improved-color-rendition cool white fluorescent lamps should be used.

Laboratories commonly require special electrical provisions such as portable table reflectors to assist in microscope work and in reading precision instruments and meters. Numerous convenience outlets should be provided at work tables and at the sides of rooms to permit connection to electrical apparatus and to portable lighting equipment for experiments. For zoology and anatomy lecture rooms, and laboratories where dissection by the instructor is part of the class work, a large mirror at an angle of about 45 deg, suitably located and combined with higher level concentrated illumination over the lecture table, will permit students to visualize experimental work in both the top horizontal as well as the vertical plane (see Fig. 19).

Lecture rooms: The typical lecture room should be provided with a comfortable general lighting system which is flexible enough to provide a moderately high level for general use and a subdued level for use during projection or special demonstrations. Many times downlighting is used to avoid spilling light on the screen. However, all downlighting should be carefully designed to avoid loss of visibility due to specular reflection in handwriting and printed materials. If a demonstration table is used, directional downlights should be aimed down on this table and the lecturer. These spotlights should be located within a 45 to 60-deg angle above horizontal as measured from the probable location of a speaker's head when he stands behind the table. This arrangement assures minimum glare and provides good lighting on the speaker's face. Special chalkboard lighting such as illustrated in Fig. 18 significantly improves visibility and attention power.

Libraries and reading rooms: The lighting should be of the same quality as for classrooms. All surfaces should be well lighted to give the desired brightness ratios. Luminaires should meet the "scissors curve." If reference material is being studied, and penciled notes made, the level of illumination should be in keeping with the pencil writing. If only reading is occurring, the illumination should meet that for reading printed material. In either case pencil marks or printed illustrative matter involves glossy reflections of overhead lighting. Therefore, special care should be taken to use lighting equipment that will minimize the concentration of the light directly downward which causes reduction of contrast. Many times the ceilings of library rooms are high and the tendency to use concentrated downlights, for better utilization, is natural. However, without the precaution to reduce light in the 0 to 45-deg zone, the resulting visibility may be greatly reduced.

Stacks and wall cases should be lighted with a concentration of downward lumens to adequately light the lower shelves, as well as the upper shelves. This may be from continuous fluorescent luminaires or from individual incandescent units designed for shelf lighting. Shielding from the lengthwise direction should prevent glare toward the eyes of the people using the stacks.

Locker rooms: The lighting of locker rooms and dressing room areas is principally a matter of arranging the lighting equipment so that the interior of the lockers is illuminated and general lighting is supplied for safe movement about the room. This usually can be accomplished by means of continuous fluorescent luminaires located between rows of lockers. The equipment used may be the same type of fluorescent unit as used in corridors. Incandescent corridor lighting units may also be used.

Medical examination rooms: These rooms should be painted in light pastel colors for maximum reflection and diffusion. The lighting should provide general illumination with additional spotlighting for the examination table from overhead or a floor stand. The eye examination chart on the wall should have 15 ft-c of vertical illumination (not more).

In case dental work is done, the room should have 70 ft-c general and a spotlighting in the mouth of 500 to 1,000 ft-c.

Offices: These should be treated the same as classrooms but with higher illumination to be commensurate with the greater difficulty of the tasks and longer time duration (see section on "Lighting: Offices").

Safety: Provisions for general emergency lighting of stairways and corridors should be made to permit classrooms, auditoriums, and dormitories to be vacated in safety in case of any interruptions or failure of the regular lighting. Exit lights should be located over all auditorium and building exits and along any intervening stairs or corridors. Low-level lighting in the auditorium should also be served by the emergency system. Attention is directed to the hazard of panic, particularly in an auditorium occupied at night or one without daylighting.

An automatic "throw-over" switch should be installed to connect the safety lighting to the emergency system if power fails on the regular lighting system. The fusing for such circuits should be independent of the main fuses and if an entirely independent source of supply can be made available, the exit lights should be supplied from such a source. All city, state, or local regu-

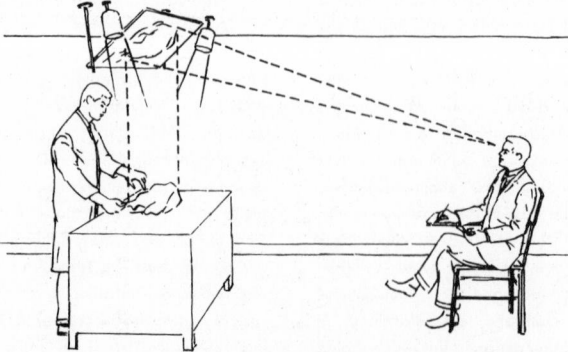

Fig. 19. Lighting and mirror arrangement for viewing laboratory lecture experiments

lations should be consulted and followed.

Care should be taken to provide sufficient lighting units as part of an exit system so that a lighted pathway, even though of low level, will be provided from any area of concentration within the building to the exterior.

Sewing rooms: In the high school the most difficult seeing tasks generally encountered by the girls are those involved in sewing. The process of seeing the fine stitching on cloth which matches the thread in color is inherently difficult and fatiguing. The stitching on a piece of fabric is seen in part by the reflected glint from the thread and by the variations in shades and shadows produced by the thread as it weaves in and out of the cloth. For this reason, equipment which provides a slight directional component to the lighting is desired. Supplementary lighting by spotlights, portable floor lamps and sewing machine attachment lamps is desirable for the same reason and is especially useful when the sewing is being done on dark cloth where the brightness level is inherently low. Upward light from the general lighting is required for ceiling and upper wall brightness.

Shops: Students working with power tools are generally novices, inexperienced with the dangers of machine operation. The lighting of a school shop should follow the best industrial lighting practice for the types of industrial activities practiced in the shop, with special emphasis to assist accuracy (see section on "Lighting: Industrial").

Either incandescent or fluorescent luminaires, similar to those used in the rest of the school, may be used. Consideration may also be given to the use of low-bay improved-color mercury lighting units. In addition to general lighting the use of localized lighting on high speed tool points and saws is desirable to further improve seeing and safety.

For printing shops parabolic specular metal reflectors, which spread the brightness of the lamps out over the width of the reflector, or prismatic closure plates which do likewise, should be used over the make-up racks and composing stone. For multiple presses light should be directed from the side into the machine, preferably from continuous fluorescent luminaires. For color work improved-color-rendition cool white fluorescent lamps should be used for the general area.

Swimming pools: Underwater pool lighting is an important safety provision and furnishes maximum satisfaction to the swimmers. The structural surfaces of the pool should always be finished in a light color.

Overhead general lighting luminaires installed in swimming pool areas should be of a type which can withstand the high humidity which prevails in such areas. Continuously moist conditions are detrimental to the life of the units unless the internal portions are protected by sealing.

Care should be taken to avoid placing lighting units above the water where accessibility is difficult and breakage serious. Well-diffused illumination is desirable to avoid the reflection of light sources from the surface of the water.

By STANLEY McCANDLESS, *Professor of Lighting, Yale University; Research and Development, Century Lighting, Inc.*

LIGHTING THE SMALL SCHOOL STAGE

These pages show a suggested layout and equipment for a small stage. Anything less should be considered a speaking platform and be treated as such. Equipment listed in the tables is a conservative minimum. A discussion of the lighting equipment and some special portable units follows:

Spotlights: generally there should be acting area lights directed so that the actor is lighted from the front diagonals with a warm and a cool color. Ellipsoidal spotlights are used in front of the proscenium because they will not spill light on the audience; fresnel lens spots behind the proscenium blend the lighting of adjacent areas easily.

Border and Background Lights: There should be a borderlight behind each masking border to light the next cloth border or back curtain. Background lights are for lighting the back-drop or cyclorama (plastered back wall in this case), window backings, ground rows, and all parts of the scene visible to the audience but outside the acting area. These instruments are used primarily for exterior scenes. The

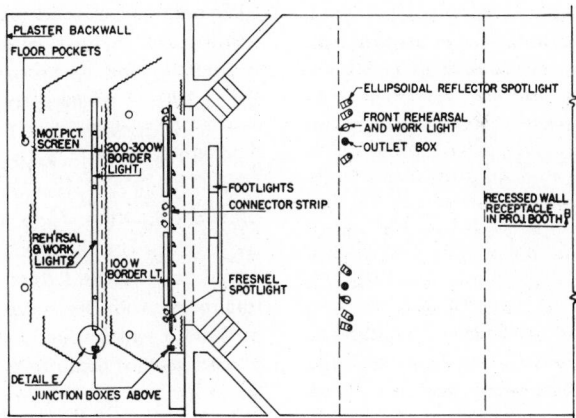

Lighting Layout

Switchboard Diagram

LIGHTS

UNIT	FUNCTION	QUANTITY
6-in. Ellipsoidal Reflector Spotlight, 250–750-w	Lighting front acting areas	6
Disappearing Footlight, 100-w, nine lamps	Toning of faces and set	3
6-in. Fresnel Spotlight, 250–750-w	Lighting rear acting areas	6
Borderlight, 100-w, 8-ft long, 16 lamps, four colors, one work light	Blending of acting areas	2
Borderlight, 200–300-w, 25 ft, 4 in., 36 lamps, three colors, four work lamps	Lighting background	1
Front Rehearsal and Work Lights, 500-w, R-40 lamps, adjustable sockets	As indicated by name	2

OUTLETS

UNIT	QUANTITY
Connector Strip, 24-ft long	1
Surface Mounted Outlet Box	2
Floor Pockets, 4-way	4
Recessed Wall Mounted Receptacle, 2-way, 50 amp	1

back-drop or plastered back wall not over 75 ft away from the stage. As a measure of safety and reliability, all portable connections should be made by 20-amp twistlocks.

Dimmers: lighting equipment is useless without a certain number of dimmers to permit (1) color mixing and intensity balancing, (2) individual or group dimming or brightening at some course of action in the play. In theory each circuit should be dimmed separately, but cost will probably necessitate a compromise. calls for considerable wattage. Strips placed close to the base at the foot of the back-drop can give effects of sunset, etc.

Special Lights: (1) instruments used for emphasizing doorways and special pieces of furniture (generally spotlights); (2) high-powered units to simulate sunlight and moonlight (3) "effect machine" to project patterns or Linnebach Lantern for shadow patterns; (4) a 2000-w ellipsoidal reflector follow spot for musicals, which should be mounted on a stand

A practical way for grouping several circuits is through use of an interplugging panel. With this panel any one or group of load circuits can be connected to any dimmer control. Auto-transformer type dimmers are used because they will dim any load proportionally up to their rated capacity; this is not true of resistance dimmers. Note on the drawing of the switchboard that house light dimmers are separate. Large dimmers can serve as proportional masters over the six smaller dimmers, or be used as individual large dimmers for controlling background lighting. In the patch panel, the 1000-w dimmer controls have two jack pockets and the 6000-w units have four jack pockets. Each load circuit representing outlets placed about the stage is protected by a circuit breaker, and the whole panel has a locked door to prevent tampering with the setup. As far as possible, switchboards should be placed so that the operator can see the stage.

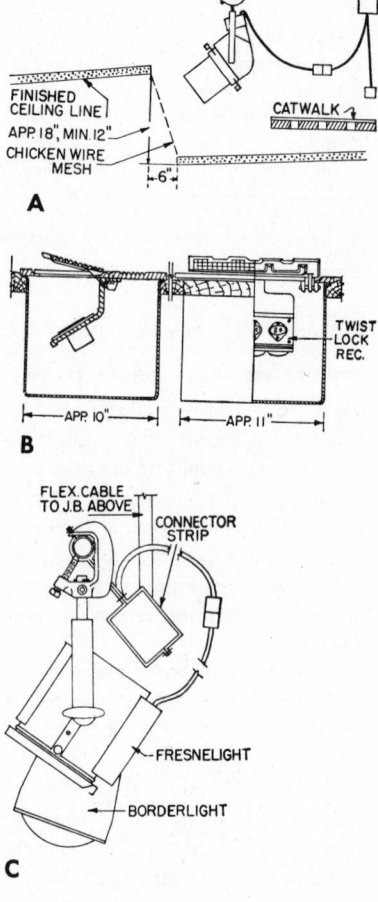

A

B

C

E

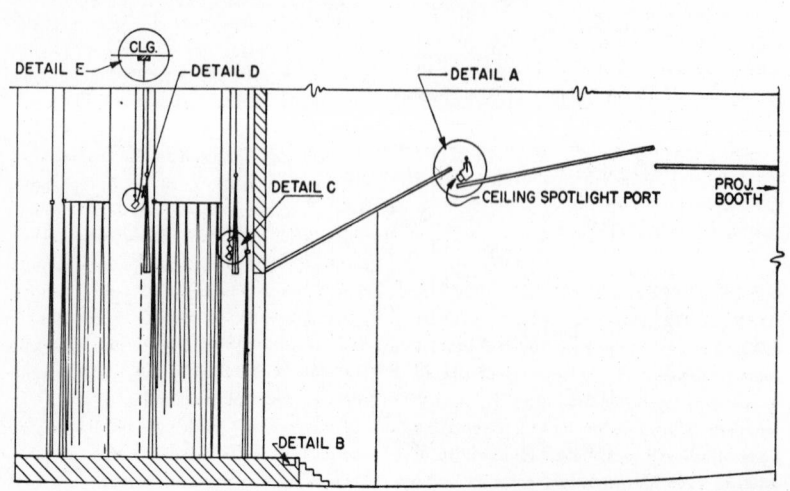

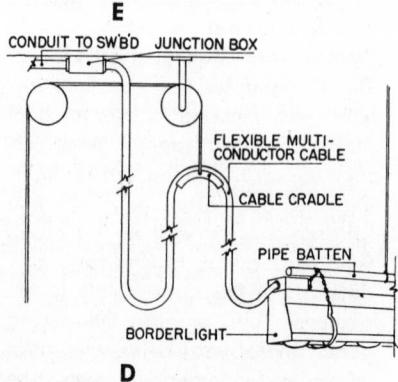

D

By NOYCE L. GRIFFIN, *Electrical Engineer, Architectural and Engineering Branch, Division of Hospital and Medical Facilities*

Lighting in all areas of the hospital should be designed for comfortable seeing. Luminaires should be durable, a standard type, neat, attractively designed, easily cleaned and relamped.

WORK SPACES should be relatively free from shadows and have sufficient illumination on work areas to eliminate the need for portable units with extension cords on floor or work area.

GENERAL AREAS. The lighting of offices, corridors, assembly halls, shops, boiler and machine rooms, kitchens, and storage spaces can be treated as in other types of buildings. *The Illuminating Engineering Society Handbook*, 3rd ed., 1959, should be consulted.

PATIENTS' ROOMS should have installed lighting for three distinct services: (1) general illumination for the room, (2) a reading light for each patient, and (3) a night light in the room. A fourth service, a doctor's examining light, may be an installed unit or a feature incorporated into the patient's reading light, or the light may be supplied by a portable lamp with an extension cord. This examining light should produce approximately 100 foot-candles over a limited area. A fixed ceiling-mounted examining light arranged to illuminate the entire bed area might be uncomfortably glaring for the patient, but it need not be left on longer than required for the examination. Such an arrangement is preferred to hand-held or portable examining lights.

NIGHT LIGHTS can be included as an added feature to the reading light or other units, but the flush wall-mounted type is generally preferred. Wall-mounted night lights should be about 18 in. above the floor, located so that they are not likely to be covered by furniture or drapes. Night lights should be switched at the door.

RECOVERY ROOMS and intensive care rooms of Progressive Patient Care units should have about 30 foot-candles of general illumination.

Patients frequently complain about the radiation of heat from a nearby reading light. A unit with an output intensity sufficient to permit adequate lighting when the unit is located a greater distance from the patient will reduce the objectionable heat. Where two or more beds are located in one room, the reading lights should be of a type that can be installed or adjusted so as not to shine in other patients' eyes. Each reading light should have a switch control accessible to the patient.

OPERATING AND DELIVERY ROOMS should have general illumination of about 100 foot-candles for the room area and special, separately controlled lights for the tables.

The major operating light should provide a multibeam of larger area for directing a minimum of 2500 foot-candles in the center of a 10-in. diameter circular area on the operating table, and tapering to not less than 500 foot-candles at the edge of that circle.

DELIVERY ROOMS require about the same general illumination as operating rooms. If the room is used for all deliveries, including Caesarean section and others which require extensive surgery, lighting at the table should be equal to that recommended for operating rooms. Where it is contemplated that the room will be used only for normal deliveries and for those which require only minor surgery, the light at the table may be somewhat less than that required for operating rooms.

MINOR SURGERY, EMERGENCY ROOMS, CYSTOSCOPIC ROOMS, AND AUTOPSY ROOMS should have about 100 foot-candles general illumination. These rooms should have supplemental lighting either by ceiling-mounted adjustable luminaires or portable units which will provide spot intensities of 2000 to 2500 foot-candles.

FRACTURE ROOMS need about 90 foot-candles general illumination with supplemental lighting for the table of about 200 ft-c.

LABORATORIES require about 50 to 100 foot-candles, depending upon the seeing task. Currently recommended foot-candles listed in the *IES Lighting Handbook*, should be consulted.

Where critical observation of color is required, as in surgery, laboratories, and autopsy rooms, color correction of the light may be necessary to provide a color effect as nearly as possible to that by which tests or specimens are ordinarily viewed. Daylight and incandescent filament lamp lighting have in the past been the most commonly accepted sources of illumination for critical seeing involving color determination.

EMERGENCY LIGHTING should be provided for safety of patients, staff, and protection of plant. As a minimum in any case, emergency lighting should be provided for operating and delivery rooms, exits, stairs, corridors, switchboard, and boiler rooms. Additional emergency lighting will be needed where hospitals may be without the normal service for days or weeks due to disasters and where care is to be provided for a large number of casualties.

Exit, stair, and corridor lighting should conform to local and State codes, or if such codes are not in effect, the *Building Exits Code* of the National Fire Protection Association.

Illuminated signs may be required in areas where there is much visitor traffic, such as at the information desk, cashier's office, and outpatient department. Where such lighting is likely to be required, plug-in receptacles should be conveniently located.

An X-ray film illuminator is required in each operating room. It is also desirable that one be installed in the doctors' locker room of the obstetrical suite.

Recommended levels of illumination for specific areas of hospitals are listed in Table 14.

Table 14. Currently recommended illumination foot-candles for hospital lighting

(Minimum on the task at all times)

Anesthetising and preparation
room 30
Auditorium
  Assembly 15
  Exhibition 30
Autopsy and morgue
  Autopsy room 100
  Autopsy table 2500
  Morgue, general 20
Central sterile supply
  General 30
  Needle sharpening 150
Corridor
  General 10
  Operating and delivery
  suites and laboratories. . 20
Cystoscopic room
  General 100
  Cystoscopic table 2500
Dental suite
  Waiting room
    General 15
    Reading 30
  Operatory, general 70
  Instrument cabinet 70
  Dental chair 1000
  Laboratory, bench 100
  Recovery room 5
Dining areas 20
Encephalographic suite
  Office 100
  Workroom 30
  Patients' room 30
Emergency room
  General 100
  Local 2000
EKG, BMR and Specimen room
  General 20
  Specimen table (supplementary) 50

Examination and treatment room
  General 50
  Examining table 100
Eye, ear, nose and throat suite
  Dark room 10
  Eye examination and
    treatment room 50
  Ear, nose and throat room . . . 50
Exits, at floor 5
Flower room 10
Formula room 30

Fracture room
  General 50
  Fracture table 200
Kitchen
  Central 70
  Floor, kitchen and pantry . . . 70
  Dishwashing 30
Laboratories
  Assay rooms 30
  Work tables 50
  Close work 100
Laundry
  General 30
  Pressers and ironers 70
  Sorting 70
Libraries 70
Linen closet 10
Locker rooms 20
Lobby 30
Lounge rooms 30
Maintenance shop
  General 30
  Work benches 100
  Paint storage 10
Medical records room 100
Nurses' station
  General 20
  Desk and charts 50
  Medicine room counter 100

Nurses' workroom 30
Nurseries
  General 10
  Examination table 70
  Play room, pediatric . . . 30
Obstetrical
  Cleanup room 30
  Scrubup room 30
  Labor room 20
  Delivery room, general . . 100
  Delivery table 2500
Offices
  General 100
  Bookkeeping and fine work. 150
  Conference and
    consultation room 30
  Information and switchboard 30
  Retiring room 10
  Waiting room 20
Parking lot. 5
Power plant. . . . .
  Boiler room 10

Machine room 20
Switchboard room 30
Transformer room 10
Pharmacy
  General 30
  Work table 100
  Active storage 30
  Alcohol vault 10
Private rooms and wards
  General 10
  Reading 30
Psychiatric disturbed
  patients' areas 10
Radioisotope facilities
  Radiochemical laboratory 30
  Uptake measuring room 20
  Examination table 50
Retiring room 10
Sewing room
  General 20
  Work area 100
Solariums 20
Stairways 20
Storage, central
  General 15
  Office 70
Surgery
  Instrument and sterile
    supply room 30
  Cleanup room (instruments) . . . 100
  Scrubup room 30
  Operating room, general 100
  Operating table 2500
  Recovery room 30
Therapy
  Physical 20
  Occupational 30
Toilets 10
Utility room 20
Waiting room
  General 15
  Reading 30
X-ray room and facilities
  Radiography and fluoroscopy. . . 10
  Deep and superficial therapy . . 10
  Dark room 10
  Waiting room, general. 15
  Waiting room, reading. 30
  Viewing room 30
  Filing room, developed films . . 30
  Storage, undeveloped films . . . 10

Data from Church Lighting, Illuminating Engineering Society, 1962

Lighting in architecture usually has a dual purpose. In addition to its utilitarian function of facilitating vision, it is also an important part of the architectural design. The spaces created by the architect can be seen, in the absence of daylight, only by means of the lighting he designs for them, and the lighting itself profoundly affects the appearance of the spaces. In no type of building is lighting so important a part of architectural expression as in the church or temple. Religious concepts vary widely from one religion to another, even from one congregation to another. But whatever concept the architect seeks to express, lighting is one of the tools he must use for this purpose.

In many cases church lighting is also designed to play an active part in the church service, creating different moods for the various parts of the service. It can also have a different character for different services or occasions—weddings and funerals, for example, or Easter and Christmas.

Illumination levels currently recommended for churches and synagogues are shown in Table 15.

LIGHTING FOR THE MAIN WORSHIP AREA

Pastor, Priest or Rabbi: In speaking to his congregation, a preacher wants his face to be seen. Part of the force of what he says comes from the earnestness of his facial expression. On the other hand, he does not wish to be annoyed by glare, nor should his face be distorted by lighting that creates black shadows around his eyes and harsh lines on his face. Many ministers prefer that general lighting in the pew area be decreased during the sermon so that the congregation may more easily keep its attention on the speaker.

The Congregation: People in the pews should not have to sit facing glaring light of any kind. Glare from the sky as well as from excessively bright panels of diffusing glass and exposed bulbs and fluorescent tubes are distressing.

Those in the congregation who are elderly must have ample light to be able to read fine print.

Lighting for the main body of the church usually consists of a combination of systems. For a high-ceilinged church where a feeling of mystery is sought, concealed downlights may furnish all the illumination. But in most cases downlights should be supplemented by cove lighting or luminaires which will light the walls and ceiling. Cove lighting or luminaires can supply up to 50 or 60 per cent of the total illumination, but the remainder should be downlighting. In most cases it is impossible to light a church satisfactorily by means of suspended luminaires only.

One lighting method is to cover the ceiling with light from a cove on each wall, and to provide downlights recessed in the ceiling. Each cove should have fluorescent tubes mounted end-to-end as follows:

For a meditation chapel 10 to 12 ft wide—one line of 20- or 25-mm, 120-ma cold cathode tubing or equivalent low brightness hot cathode tubing.

For a church 12 to 18 ft wide—one line of 40-watt T12 tubes.

For a church 25 to 35 ft wide—two lines of 40-watt T12 tubes.

For a church 35 to 50 ft wide—two lines of 800-ma [5] T12 tubes or one line of 1500-ma [5] tubes.

Better light distribution on the ceiling is obtained from 75-watt louvered reflector spot lamps a foot apart in cove Fig. 21. Also needed are 2 to 3 watts per sq ft of downlights or swiveled units behind beams. Where it is felt that the bright ceiling may offer psychological competition with the speaker, cove wattage may be cut in half, downlight wattage increased.

Another method for use in larger rooms, where some prefer the added interest of decorative lighting equipment, is the installation of appropriate luminaires (from 1 to 3 watts per sq ft) and recessed downlights (2 watts per sq ft), the latter for use on cloudy days and after dark.

The following specifications are for "lantern" (suspended luminaire) wattages used with the downlights: for light to be diffused out through the lantern sides—¼ to ½ watt per sq ft, depending on lantern size; for light directed down and up—1 watt per sq ft to supplement the ceiling downlights.

The manufacturer's limits of spacing as related to mounting height should not be exceeded. Shielding should be greater than 45 deg.

Many authorities prefer a church lantern whose side panels or other means of control result in more light being directed toward the altar than toward the eyes of the congregation. These are called unsymmetric units.

Example of the use of swiveled units concealed behind beams or trusses: for a church 42 ft wide with beams 16 ft apart, use twelve 150-watt units behind each beam except the one nearest to the chancel, which should have 24 units; total wattage, 2.7 per sq ft, plus fluorescent cove lighting of 1.1 watts per sq ft.

Stations of the cross should not be as bright as the main or side altars; a brightness one-third that of the main altar is suggested. Shielded light sources can be concealed in the ceiling or, in the case of churches with aisles, can be placed high on nearby columns.

Baptismal services should be lighted from several concealed sources so that sharp shadows are avoided. Lights should be shielded from the view of the audience.

Multipurpose auditoriums must provide lighting for a wide variety of functions. These are discussed further on in the section about parish halls.

Chancel lighting

In each form of worship, the relative importance of different features of the chancel's design and furnishing should be expressed in the relative brightness provided by the lighting. For example, in Roman Catholic churches, the high altar is brightest. In Ukrainian Catholic churches, the icon screen in front of the altar is brightest. In Quaker meeting houses, no part of the interior should be brighter than any other.

Light in the chancel should be largely directional, aimed from the front to the back. If the lighting comes from many sources, shadows will be softer. Multiplicity of sources also provides flexibility of control. Most chancel lights, whether incandescent or fluorescent, can be of the spot-flood type. Sometimes a controlled-beam spot, like a single pencil of light, is used for the cross or ark; an enclosed theatrical "box-spot" type of fixture is used for this purpose.

Light should arrive at the ark or altar from a direction that does not result in undesirable shadows. If the chancel is shallow, it may be necessary to have some of the spotlights out in the nave, partly or wholly concealed. When the priest or curate is reading with his back to the congregation, shadows should not prevent him from seeing his reading matter.

Both the ark and the Torah are a focus of interest and must have proper illumination. The lighting within the ark is usually automatically turned on by the opening of the ark doors. The background behind the scrolls should have a lower reflectance than the scroll covers.

In general, the ark receives the most attention, the face of the speaker at the rostrum the next greatest amount of light, the cantor slightly less, and the whole chancel area a little less, but more than the seating space of the auditorium. Separately controlled floodlighting for bar

	Footcandles
Altar, ark, reredos	100**
Choir*** and chancel	30**
Classrooms	30
Pulpit, rostrum (supplementary illumination)	50**
Main worship area***	
Light and medium interior finishes	15**
For churches with special zeal	30***
Art glass windows (test recommended)	
Light color	50
Medium color	100
Dark color	500
Especially dense windows	1000

*Minimum on the task at any time.

**Two-thirds this value if interior finishes are dark (less than 10 per cent reflectance) to avoid high brightness ratios, such as between hymnbook pages and the surround. Careful brightness planning is essential for good design.

***Reduced or dimmed during sermon, prelude or meditation.

[5] *Remote location of ballasts is suggested. A single line of 1500-ma tubes could replace the 800-ma tubes.*

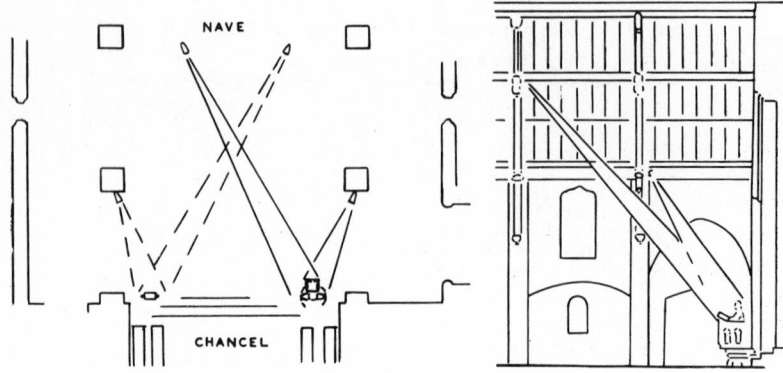

Fig. 20. Accent lighting should come from two or more locations well above the speaker's face

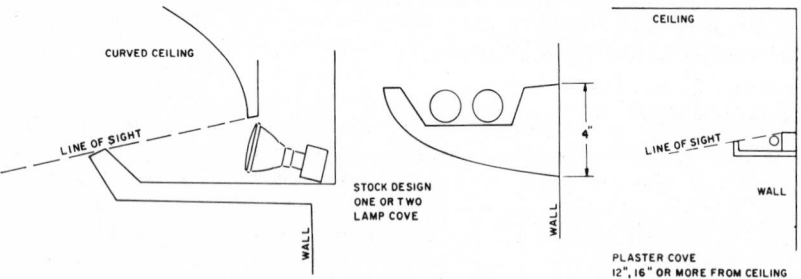

Fig. 21. Sections through several types of coves

mitzvah services in front of the ark has many advocates.

Wiring should be provided for the Eternal Light and the Menorahs. While the ordinary incandescent lamp is designed to operate efficiently for 750 or 1,000 hr, the life of any lamp can be extended indefinitely by reducing the voltage from the normal 115 or 120 volts to a lower figure. As a general guide, each time the voltage is reduced by 5 per cent, light output drops 15 per cent but life is doubled. Low-cost wall-box dimmers are available. Some

congregations use a "fishtail" jet gas flame for the Eternal Light. The faint flicker is thought pleasant.

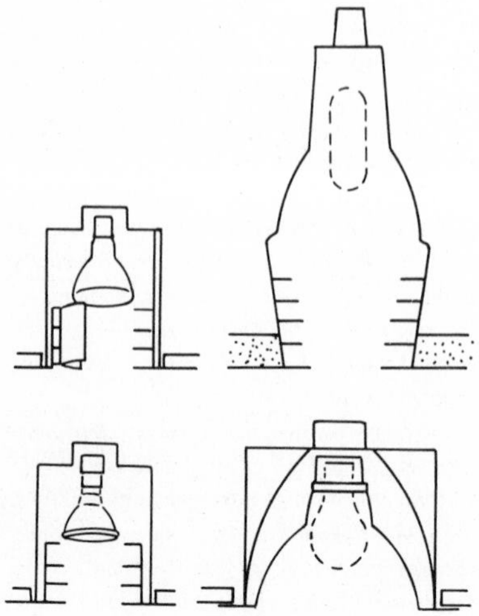

The choir is generally provided with more light than the pews but considerably less than the altar or ark. Supplementary lighting is often used for the organist and the choir to permit the reading of musical scores; it must be carefully shielded from the view of the worshippers, of course. Choir lighting should be reduced or dimmed during the sermon, prayer, and other nonmusical portions of the service.

Lighting on the face of the preacher in the pulpit or the reader at the lectern should come from well above the speaker's face and from several directions, in order to soften the shadows (Fig. 20). During the sermon, reading, or prayer, brightnesses in the chancel and nave should be reduced so that attention is focused on the speaker.

Lighting equipment

The following types of luminaires are used in church lighting: (1) Lanterns; (2) Wall brackets; (3) Wall urns; (4) Suspended bowls (indirect); (5) Coves; and (6) Downlights (several types, including recessed and swivel). Several of these are illustrated in Figs. 21–23. For additional data on the design of cove lighting, see the section on "Lighting: Residential;" for downlighting, see the section on "Lighting: Stores." Downlight shielding, however, should be greater than the 45 deg which is the usual

standard in commercial lighting; 50 to 60 deg is recommended.

Controls can vary from simple load centers or panelboards with letter or color coding to complete theatrical-type switchboards with dimming and presetting features. Lighting plans of intermediate complexity can often achieve flexibility at low cost by the use of low-voltage controls. Motor-operated dimmer controls are preferred when funds are available. Even more convenient is the newer compact reactance or autotransformer. The slow lighting changes are scarcely noticed as one effect follows another without distracting from the service.

Lighting maintenance is likely to be poorer in churches than in other types of buildings. Instead of the usual maintenance factor of 60 or 70 per cent, it is advisable to use a lower factor, in the order of 40 or 50 per cent.

Stained glass windows, which play such an important role in many types of church architecture, may be lighted from the outside for the benefit of worshippers attending evening services. If the church is surrounded by trees or other buildings, the outside lighting can be installed without injury to the exterior appearance of the building. The amount of light required may vary from more than 100 watts per sq ft for thick glass in dark colors to 1 watt per sq ft for thin glass in light colors. An experimental installation is advisable to determine the exact amount of light required and the best location of the sources. Relative brightness of the window and the interior wall must be considered; to be fully effective the window must be considerably brighter than the interior wall. Windows may also be lighted from the inside on nonservice evenings, for the benefit of passers-by. Such installations are often clock-controlled.

Outdoor lighting

Floodlighting of the church may require as much as 1 watt per sq ft of wall surface to be lighted for a red brick church on a lighted city street, or as little as one-tenth that amount for a white-painted church on a dark country road. Light sources may be concealed in trees or behind planting, and for lighting the steeple they may, in some cases, be placed on the roof. In choosing locations for the lighting units, consideration must be given not only to the lighting effect created but also to the appearance of the units during the daytime and their accessibility for cleaning and relamping. An experimental installation, using portable units, is recommended. If only the front facade is to be lighted, some light should be allowed to fall on the sides in

Fig. 22. Some types of fixed recessed downlights

order to avoid the one-dimensional effect of a lighted billboard.

Outdoor services are best lighted, where conditions permit, by reflection from the leaves of trees overhead. For this purpose floodlights should be placed above eye level and aimed straight up. A light-colored wall of a building or a cliff may also be used as a source of reflected light, if the audience faces away from it. Otherwise, direct lighting must be used mounted on poles, preferably 20 ft high, around the sides and rear of the seating area.

Lighting for other parts of the church

Narthex or vestibule should have sufficient light so that people can see each other's faces, read announcements, and make notes. Lighting should be sufficiently diffuse so that faces appear pleasantly lighted, without harsh shadows.

Many churches have a *parish hall* or *multipurpose room* used for various purposes other than worship. Each of these activities has its own lighting requirements. Recommended illumination levels are as follows:

STORES

These charts make recommendations for 34 types of stores, giving preferences of the Committee as to the color of light — the K value in degrees — the method of lighting, and the level in footcandles.

The report stresses the fact that footcandle measurements are but a convenient device, footcandle values being "merely a step in getting the end-product brightness." The actual brightness of an object is a function of the amount of light and the reflection coefficient of the object itself. The amount of light, expressed in footcandles, multiplied by the reflection factor, which is the percentage of light reflected, equals the brightness, measured in *footlamberts*.

Brightness in either footlamberts or candles per square inch are as readily measured as footcandles. There are several types of meters usable for this purpose: the simplest is the indicating type that employs a light-sensitive cell calibrated to read footcandles. By employing a suitable correction factor, which compensates for the light lost through striking the glass cell cover at a grazing angle, these meters will measure the footlamberts of brightness of diffuse reflecting or transmitting surfaces.

Other types of instruments measure brightness by direct comparison of two fields of brightness, a calibrated known brightness against the

	Foot-candles
Fairs and exhibitions; study hall	30
Lectures; church dinners	15
Concerts	5
Plays, movies, slides	1/10
Plays, movies, slides, at intermission	5
Dances	1

In most cases supplementary lighting is also required, on the lecturer or orchestra, for example, and also for color and sparkle at dances. For stage lighting, see section on "Lighting: Schools." If the room is sometimes used for athletic activities, rugged equipment, suitably protected, should be specified. In such cases, spotlighting can be provided by the use of portable fixtures plugged into "fan receptacles" [6] on the walls or ceiling beams.

[6] *The fan receptacle has a single receptacle and a screw post below it, so that a fan can be fastened by the post and plugged into the outlet. Thus a spotlight can be attached for a single performance.*

unknown. With a suitable system of filters usable over either the test or comparison brightness fields, these meters make possible a very wide range of brightness values that can be measured.

Although brightness is the actual end product desired, it is not simple at the present stage of lighting science to completely specify store lighting in terms of brightness and, by calculation, arrive at those values.

Many designers who are experienced in using footcandles as a criterion of lighting values, will still use them as a basis for store lighting design. If they are to take advantage of newest practices in lighting design, then calculations should include the brightness that will occur on major room surfaces, an estimate of the resulting brightness pattern in producing a pleasing interior, and an analysis of the relative brightnesses of kinds of merchandise sold in those areas.

Illumination levels currently recommended for stores by the Illuminating Engineering Society are shown in Table 16, from *Recommended Levels of Illumination*, August, 1958. Detailed recommendations by the Store Lighting Committee of IES are given on the following three pages. These recommendations were issued in 1948; although they have long been under

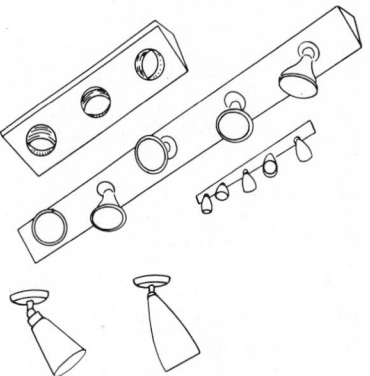

Fig. 23. Some types of swiveled accent units

For information on *classroom* lighting, see section on "Lighting: Schools."

Clergyman's study is basically a workroom and should provide good seeing conditions for long hours of work. Most clergymen prefer a homelike atmosphere for the study, which may also be used for counseling. If the study is also used for board and committee meetings, appropriate lighting must be supplied.

study by the Committee, revised recommendations have not yet been released.

Table 16. Recommended illumination levels for stores

SHOW WINDOWS	Footcandles
Daytime lighting	
General	200
Feature	1000
Nighttime lighting	
Main business districts—highly competitive	
General	200
Feature	1000
Secondary business districts or small towns	
General	100
Feature	500
Open-front stores (see display lighting under Store Interiors)	
STORE INTERIORS	
Circulation areas	30
Merchandising areas	
Service	100
Self-service	200
Showcases and wall cases	
Service	200
Self-service	500
Feature displays	
Service	500
Self-service	1000
Stockrooms	30

1. Above values are illumination on the merchandise on display or being appraised. The plane in which lighting is important may vary from horizontal to vertical.
2. Specific appraisal areas involving difficult seeing may be lighted to substantially higher levels.
3. Color rendition of fluorescent lamps is important. Incandescent and fluorescent usually are combined for best appearance of merchandise.
4. Illumination may often be made nonuniform to tie in with merchandising layout.
* Minimum on the task at all times.

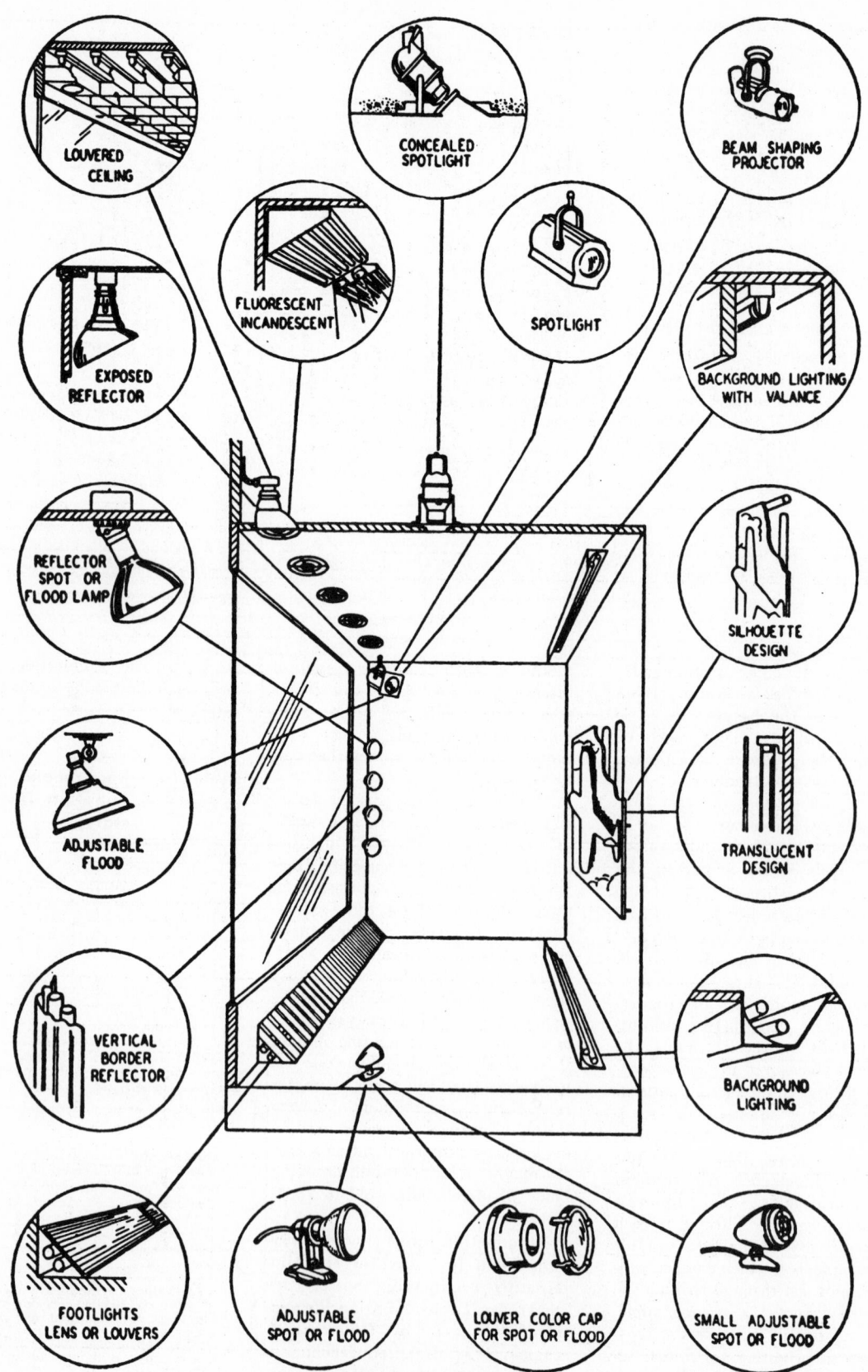

Fig. 24.   Show window lighting

Table — Recommended Lighting for Stores (by classification of merchandise)

Column structure (rotated table):

- Classification Number
- Classification of Merchandise
- **Selling or Appraisal Lighting** — Light Source Degrees K (2800, 3500, 4500, 6500); Method (Direct, Semi-Direct**, General Diffuse, Direct-Indirect, Semi-Indirect, Indirect); Level in Foot-candles (10, 25, 50, 75)
- **General Environmental Lighting** — Light Source Degrees K (2800, 3500, 4500, 6500); Method (Direct, Semi-Direct**, General Diffuse, Direct-Indirect, Semi-Indirect, Indirect); Level in Foot-candles (10, 25, 50, 75)
- **Displayed Stock Lighting** — Light Source Degrees K (2800, 3500, 4500, 6500); Method (Direct); Level in Foot-candles (25, 50, 100, 150)
- Remarks

No.	Classification of Merchandise	Remarks
1	Jewelry	Combination of 4500° or 6500° fluorescent environmental lighting and concentrated filament downlighting maintain brilliant reflections in jewelry and the refractive effect of the faceted gems. Color of backgrounds important. Caution should be observed in lighting watch display cases to avoid drying the oil.
2	Silverware, Flat & Hollowware, Clocks	Silverware and similar Merchandise depends to a large degree upon reflections of large area low brightness surfaces. When direct lighting is used this effect is obtained from large area, luminous panels, coffers or similar architectural treatment. The environmental lighting can be reflected on the merchandise to produce the effect desired. Reflected colors should be cool to prevent tarnished look.
3-a	Handbags, Gloves, Hosiery	
3-b	Handkerchiefs, Neckwear, Ornamental Flowers, Umbrellas	Mirror lighting is important in connection with neckwear and ornamental flowers.
4	Drugs, Cosmetics, Toilet Articles, Stationery, Books, Photographic Supplies, Candy, Nuts	Mirror lighting often required for cosmetic section. Appraisal zone of up to 50-60 footcandles is needed for color matching. High level of illumination desirable over prescription counter. Vertical illumination necessary on shelves and counter displays for attention and appraisal. Small details of photographic equipment often important. Surface often specular. Required high value of diffuse appraisal lighting. Bright attractive atmosphere required for candy and nuts. Unusual brightness patterns possible. Fluorescent lamps often preferred for unpackaged confections. Soft White lamps often preferred for case lighting important in reducing heating effects detrimental to confections, perfumes, tobacco, etc. May sometimes be located outside of case.
5	Men's Clothing, Hats, Sportswear	High levels of illumination are necessary on dark material to see color, texture and workmanship.
6	Shoes	Shoes stores require good horizontal illumination at the floor level to facilitate fitting and appraisal. It is best not to have a multiplicity of light sources reflected in the shoes. Combination of filament (conc. sources) and fluorescent often employed for general lighting.
7	Notions	Where color matching is important equipment should be provided for this purpose.
8	Underwear, Negligees & Corsets	See text on mirror lighting.
9	Millinery	Fitting room sales and environment important. See text on mirror lighting. At the mirror it is important to illuminate both the hat and the face. Use warm tones on face with more nearly daylight colors on the hat. It is desirable to have light reflected from the table top to eliminate shadows on the face.
10	Coats, Women's and Misses'	
11	Furs	In the fur department the General Lighting should be psychologically cool since most furs are sold in summer months. Combination fluorescent and incandescent lighting is desirable to bring out sheen, texture and color. To emphasize browns and yellows, 2800° sources are suitable. Mirror lighting very important; darker furs require levels of 300 to 400 footcandles from concentrated sources.
*	Women's & Girls' Dresses, Sportswear, Uniforms	
12	Infants' Wear & Infants' Furniture	
13		See text on Mirror Lighting. Where sportswear is displayed it may be desirable to use 6500° light sources.

Legend:
- o Satisfactory method
- O Preferred method
- ——— Satisfactory range
- ▬▬▬ Preferred range
- ** Semi-Direct

(Note: "Selling or Appraisal System may provide environmental lighting" is noted across classification 4 and classification 7.)

No.	Classification of Merchandise	Remarks
14	Yard Goods & Trimmings	High values of illumination make it possible to see texture of material quality, and pattern. For appraisal of texture, directional lighting is most effective. Suitable provision should be made for color matching. Attraction lighting is essential for showcases. Absolute... displays... 35,000 to 50,000 foot-candles are desirable for dark fabrics, particularly woolens.
15	Art Needlework	Selling or Appraisal System may provide environmental lighting
16	Linens, Blankets	
17	China, Glassware & Gifts	Selling light should be from large area low brightness sources. China... special directional lighting discloses form and texture. Glassware has a beautiful appearance when displayed against a dark background and resting on a glass shelf lighted from beneath by daylight or 4500K fluorescent lamps. Other interesting effects can be secured through the use of back lighting, silhouette lighting, edge lighting and similar special applications.
18	Miscellaneous, Housewares & Toys, Sporting Goods, Auto Accessories, Small Appliances	Usually open displayed stock using general lighting for display. Attraction lighting of shelf displays of small housewares, tools, guns, toys... and adds to store brightness. Vertical lighting is important. With specular surfaces such as in small electrical appliances, it is important to avoid the use of only concentrated sources such as spotlights as their brightness highlights are valuable and can be produced as reflections of environmental brightnesses.
19	Radio & Phonographs	Wall displays of radios and phonographs can have local overhead valance lighting. Concentrated sources should be avoided. Special attention should be paid to accent lighting for record albums.
20	Major Appliances	Majority of this merchandise is white with metallic trim. High levels of attraction lighting necessary. Spotlighting is effective.
21	Garden Supplies, Building Supplies	Garden supplies often sold in open in spring and summer only. Can use floodlighting techniques. Wall displays used for building supplies.
22	Paint, Wallpaper	Displayed stock often uses general lighting. Good vertical surface lighting required for shelves and wall displays. Illuminated shelf niches can be used to advantage for specialty items. Floor and table displays of paints and impulse items should be spotlighted to attract attention. It is often desirable to furnish a stand and lamp so that samples under the same color quality of white light as well as to illuminate them as in actual use.
23	Pictures, Frames, Mirrors, Lampshades	Individual pictures may be featured by spotlighting. Majority of pictures and mirrors displayed on walls. Can use valance type lighting. Reflection of light sources in mirrors to be avoided as they are usually distracting. Lamps may provide their own illumination. Display much more effective if lamps are lighted.
24	Draperies and Curtains	Draperies and curtains are both displayed and appraised when hung vertically in most cases. Vertical surface Perimeter lighting should be used with special features particularly when food or spotlights. Glass curtains are very attractive when displayed against lighted backgrounds or artificially lighted windows.

Legend: ● Satisfactory method   ○ Preferred method   — Satisfactory range   — Preferred range

Table column groups: Selling or Appraisal Lighting (Light Source Degrees K: 2800, 3600, 4500, 6500; Method: Direct, Semi-Direct, General Diffuse, Direct-Indirect, Semi-Indirect, Indirect; Level in Foot-candles: 10, 25, 50, 75); General Environmental Lighting (Light Source Degrees K: 2800, 3600, 4500, 6500; Method: Direct, Semi-Direct, General Diffuse, Direct-Indirect, Semi-Indirect, Indirect; Level in Foot-candles: 10, 25, 50, 75); Displayed Stock Lighting (Light Source Degrees K: 2900, 3600, 4500, 6500; Method: Direct; Level in Foot-candles: 25, 50, 100, 150)

Selling or Appraisal Lighting

Classification Number	Classification of Merchandise	Light Source Degrees K: 2800	3500	4500	6500	Method: Direct*	Semi-Direct**	General Diffuse	General Diffuse Direct-Indirect	Semi-Indirect	Indirect	Level in Foot-candles: 10	25	50	75
25	Floor Coverings	━	━	━	—		O	O	O	o			━		
26	Furniture & Pianos	━	━	━					O	O	O	━	━		
27	Musical Instruments	━	━			O	O						━		
28	Luggage	━	━	━		O	O	o	O				━		
29	Baked Goods, Pantry Shops Novelty Package Goods	━	━			O	O	o	o	o			━		
30	Groceries Meat & Fish	━	━	━	—	o	o	O	O				━	━	
31	Package Liquors Bottled Goods		━	━			o	O	O				━		
32	Tobacco, Cigars Smokers' Supplies	—	━	━			o	O	O				━	━	
33	Florist Shop Cut Flowers	—		━	━	o	o	O	O				━	━	
34	Barber Shops & Beauty Parlors	━	━					O	O				━		

General Environmental Lighting

Classification Number	Light Source Degrees K: 2800	3500	4500	6500	Method: Direct	Semi-Direct**	General Diffuse	General Diffuse Direct-Indirect	Semi-Indirect	Indirect	Level in Foot-candles: 10	25	50	75
25		━	━	—			o	o	O	O	━			
26	━	━	━							O	━			
27		━	━				o	o	O	O	━			
28			━	━	o	o	o	o	O	O	━			
29		━	━				o	o	O	O	━			
30	Selling or Appraisal System may provide environmental lighting													
31	Selling or Appraisal System may provide environmental lighting													
32	Selling or Appraisal System may provide environmental lighting													
33		━	━				o	o	o	O	━			
34	━	━					o	o	O	O	━			

Displayed Stock Lighting

Classification Number	Light Source Degrees K: 2800	3500	4500	6500	Method: Direct	Level in Foot-candles: 25	50	100	150
25	━	—	━		O		━		
26	━				O		━		
27		━	━		O		━		
28	━	━	━		O		━		
29	━	━	━		O		━		
30	—	━	━	—	O		━		
31	—	━	━	—	O		━		
32		━			O		━	━	
33	—		━	━	O		━	━	
34		━	━		O		━		

Remarks

Classification Number	Remarks
25	Carpets and rugs are usually displayed on horizontal platforms which require high levels of horizontal illumination for appraisal of the dark materials, patterns, and textures. To show colors correctly dual quality lighting systems, using daylight fluorescent and filament lamps are advisable. When hung vertically, fluorescent perimeter lighting combined with incandescent reflectors may be used.
26	To avoid specular reflections in polished wood and metal surfaces of furniture the lighting should be from diffused, large area, low brightness ceiling fixtures or from indirect sources. Highlights from concentrated sources are objectionable. Adequate illumination is required for rapid appraisal of details of fabrics and upholstery, style, color and design. A combination of cool fluorescent and diffused incandescent has proved satisfactory in most cases.
27	Usually openly displayed stock, using selling light for display.
28	Usually openly displayed stock. Featured spot lighted displays important.
29	High brightness from general lighting gives the impression of sanitation and encourages good housekeeping. Incandescent selling lighting should be located over counters and display cases. With baked goods warm incandescent downlighting should mix with cool fluorescent case lighting to give good color value on goods.
30	Atmosphere of brightness and cleanliness important. Shelves and gondolas in self-service food stores require good vertical illumination. Spot lighting of impulse items important. High intensity near cashier's counter helps toward checking out and making correct change. Filament and Soft White fluorescent lighting preferred for meats and cheese display and sales areas.
31	Goods displayed on shelves. Cornice shelf lighting may be used. Fixtures with strong vertical component desirable, arranged fairly close to walls.
32	Tobacco stock kept in showcases and wall cases. Humidifiers are used in cases. Heat and color important. Wall cases may be lighted by vertical component from ceiling fixtures or valence lighting may be used.
33	Lighting of daylight color quality is recommended for flowers in the natural setting. Fluorescent lamps suitable for refrigerated cases. Baskets, vases of flowers, urns, and table displays should be spot lighted.
34	Both horizontal and vertical components of lighting are essential in hair cutting. An attempt should be made in the barber shop to prevent reflections of bright sources in mirrors by proper location of luminaires with respect to chairs. In a beauty parlor mirror lighting should be given special consideration to furnish shadowless illumination of complementary color on the face.

NOTES:

Abbreviations and symbols denote the following:

Direct:	Luminaire with 90% to 100% downward component	
Semi Direct:	" " 60% to 90% " "	
General Diffuse	" " 40% to 60% " "	Distributes light nearly uniformly in all directions.
General Diffuse Direct-Indirect	" " 40% to 60% " "	Produces very little light in a horizontal direction.
Semi Indirect	" " 10% to 40% " "	
Indirect	" " 0% to 10% " "	

* Where direct method is shown for Selling and Appraisal it is assumed that some environmental lighting is also used and floors, cases and other appointments are light in color.
** The use of semi-direct equipment with large component near the horizontal should be avoided in large rooms.

━ Preferred range of values under "Level in ft-c." and range of color temperature under "Light Source Degrees K" that would be satisfactory depending on the competitive situation as to illumination values and individual choice as to color.
— Satisfactory range of values.
O Preferred method of installation.
o Satisfactory method of installation.
Symbols of equal weight indicate a choice of method.

Values given under color temperature and footcandle levels for General Lighting, Selling Lighting and Displayed Stock Lighting are for each of these individual elements of the system. The footcandle values are accumulative in the final result. For example, with 15 foot-candles of General Lighting and 40 foot-candles of Selling Lighting, the level of illumination in the selling area would be 55. Again in this store with Displayed Stock lighting of 100 foot-candles the resulting illumination in a glass showcase may amount to about 130 foot-candles or more depending on the amount of light transmitted through the glass.

When feature displays are used, the foot-candle values should be about double those recommended for Displayed Stock Lighting.

By DANIEL SCHWARTZMAN, FAIA, Architect

GENERAL LIGHTING

1. *Luminous Ceilings:*
A. Overall suspended metal or plastic louvers with incandescent or fluorescent lamps mounted above.
B. Overall white plastic panel ceiling in suspended metal frames with fluorescent lamps above.
2. *Evenly Distributed lighting Fixtures.* Light source brightness reduced by use of recessed surfaces, louvers, lenses, diffusing glass or plastic.

4- by 4-ft fixture recessed, surface mounted or suspended with six or eight fluorescent lamps, shielded by metal or plastic eggcrate louvers on 12- to 14-ft centers. These may be supplemented by incandescent spotlights, floodlights or downlights to fill odd spaces in an irregularly shaped area.

WALL LIGHTING

1. Continuous fluorescent strip light coves or cornices, or closely spaced incandescent floodlights supplement the general store lighting, while also lighting the merchandise in the wall cases.
2. Glass enclosed wall cases (and show cases) require additional fluorescent light. Strip lighting may be used over open shelves in self selection fixtures.
3. Certain types of merchandise (jewelry, silverware) require additional direct, incandescent light from continuous rows of reflector lamps in the ceiling.

ORNAMENTAL LIGHTING

Chandeliers and other pendant lighting fixtures can be used in key locations and high style departments, but should be limited in number and relied on only for supplementary lighting.

DISPLAY LIGHTING

At least two lights are required on each subject of a feature display to avoid deep shadows and to bring out the soft reflected light which emphasizes the form and texture of the merchandise on display.

SPECIAL REQUIREMENTS

The following selling departments have special electrical requirements:
1. Restaurant and Kitchen
2. Beauty Salon
3. Lamp department and Home Lighting
4. Radio, T.V. and Records (Master Antenna systems)
5. Appliances
6. Snack Bar
7. Refrigerated cases at delicacies, candy and bakery.

Fig. 25(a)

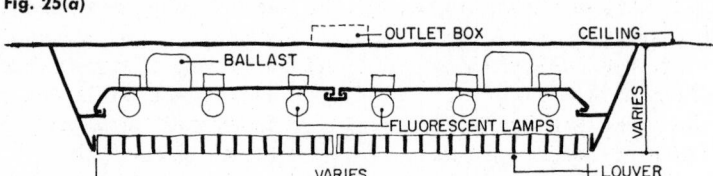

Surface Mounted Fluorescent with Metal or Plastic Louver

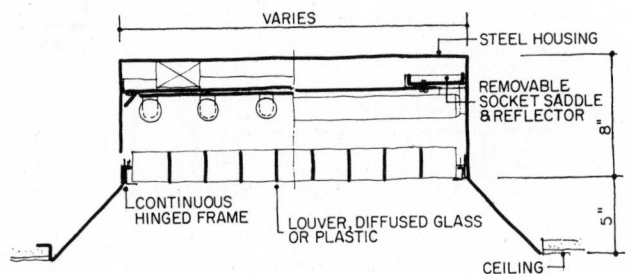

Recessed Fluorescent

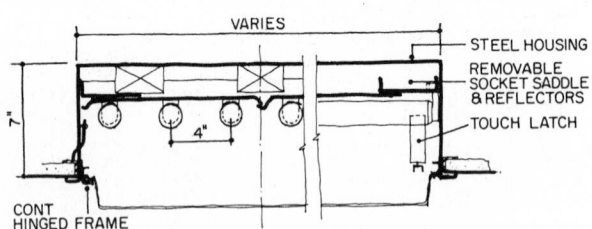

Flush Recessed Fluorescent with Plastic Shield

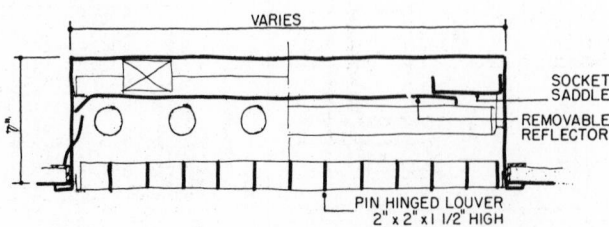

Flush Recessed Fluorescent with Metal Louver

OUTLETS

All interior columns should have one duplex convenience outlet about 14 in. above the floor; one duplex convenience outlet about 12 in. below ceiling; and one telephone receptacle. All exterior columns should have one duplex outlet about 14 in. above floor.

Outlet Locations:

1. Cashier's Room for Calculating and adding machines
2. Cloth winder measurograph machines
3. Pilot lights for all machines, executive office equipment
4. Luggage stamping machines
5. Alteration Room for: Steam irons, sewing machines, steam generating unit boiler, pants pressing machine
6. Stationery department pen stamping machine
7. Drinking fountains and dispensing machines
8. Hospital sterilizer and stove
9. Pharmacy sterilizer and stove
10. Carpentry shop power equipment
11. Ticketing machines in marking areas
12. Store time-card clocks
13. Burglar protection
14. Sprinkler wiring system
15. Local fire alarm system
16. Store clock system and dismissal bell
17. High and low water alarm
18. Automatic time control system of exterior signs
19. Ventilating smoke and heat detection
20. Annunciator System
21. Automatic time control for show window lighting
22. Telephone system
23. Pneumatic tube blower system
24. Service bell at receiving platform
25. Night bell at store entrance
26. Cash register outlets on electric circuit separate from lighting circuits.

Fig. 25(b)

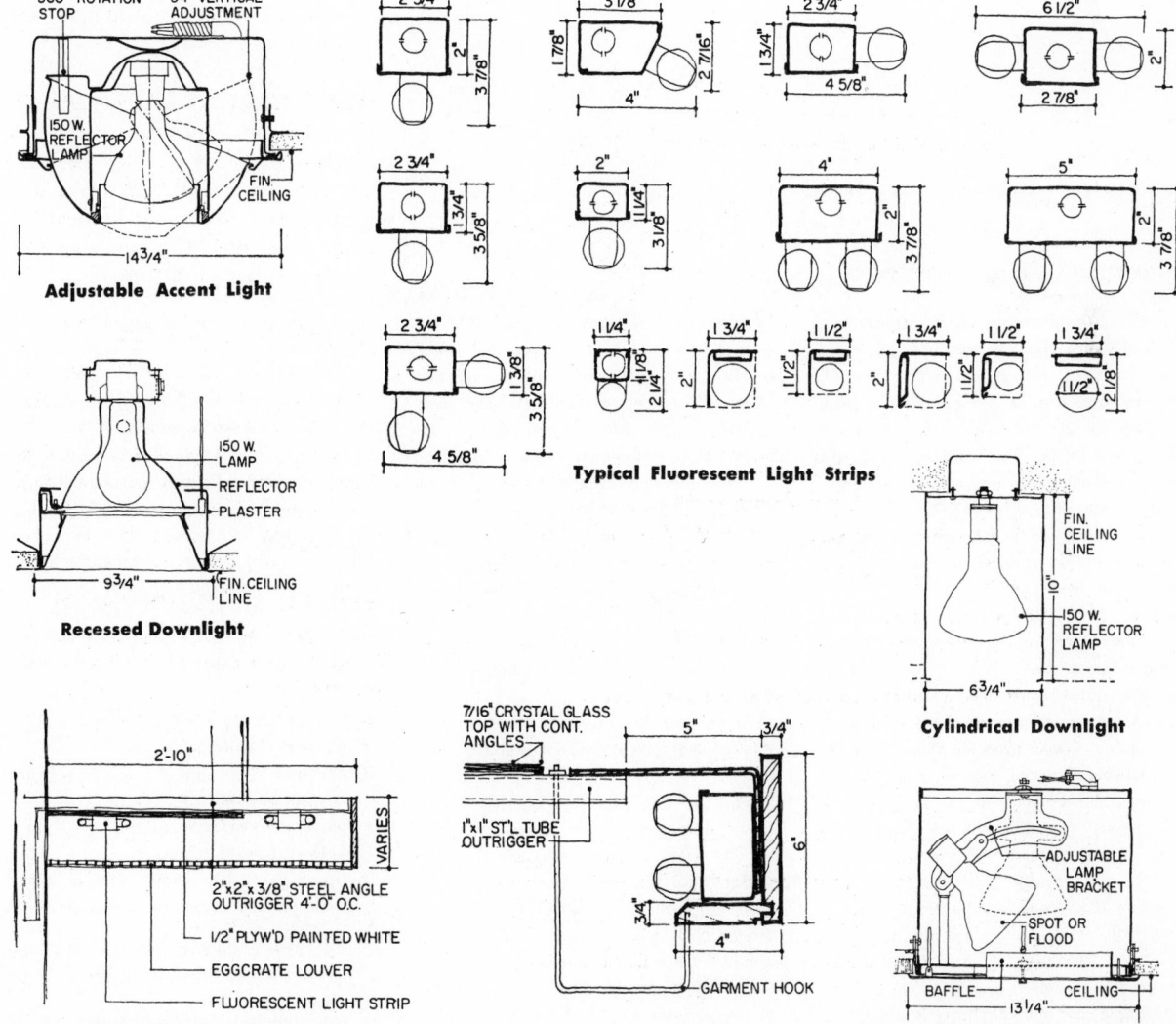

Adjustable Accent Light

Recessed Downlight

Typical Fluorescent Light Strips

Cylindrical Downlight

Lighted Soffit at Back Wall

Typical Light Cornice

Recessed Adjustable Accent Light

By Henry L. Logan, Vice President in charge of Research, Holophane Company, Inc.

ESTIMATING LIGHTING REQUIREMENTS

Screen brightnesses have increased in recent years from a minimum of 9 ft-l (foot-lamberts) and a maximum of 14 ft-l, at the center of a blank lighted screen, to 10 to 20 ft-l. The average screen brightness with film running, and the proper illumination of the theater interior, can be related to these values.

Black and white film averages 8 per cent of blank screen brightness, and colored film averages 15 per cent, or from 0.8 to 3 ft-l. The general brightness of the auditorium from the viewpoint of spectators facing the screen can therefore be in this range while film is running, provided that the brightness of the same auditorium as viewed from the stage is as low as possible. Thus the auditorium must be designed and illuminated so that it has a brightness compatible with the screen brightness, as seen from the seats, but looks dark when viewed from the stage. One method is to construct the walls and ceiling with V-shaped ridges, as shown in Fig. 26. The surface of each ridge that faces the spectators should be set at such an angle that no light from it can diffuse back towards the screen. This surface can be of any color consistent with a reflection factor of about 50 per cent. The surface of each ridge that faces the screen should be a dark grey, with a reflection factor of no more than 10 per cent.

These ridges can be as small, or as large, as the designer wishes; they can be small on one area and large on another—an infinite variety of combinations can be worked out to produce original and pleasing architectural patterns. Most important is the accuracy of the angles of the surfaces in relation to the screen; that is, the high light-reflecting surfaces should be so angled as to be louvered from the screen.

A lighting layout that would give a total of 5 ft-c (foot-candles) over the auditorium floor area is shown in plan and section in Fig. 26. The lighting system should be connected to dimmers so that the low level of light necessary during a performance can be determined by experiment and then pre-set. For the best reception of screen images, the surround should have about the same brightness as the screen itself with film running. Because of the variable brightness of film subjects, however, this is not practical, although it could be accomplished by a quick-acting photo-cell circuit set to respond to screen brightnesses. Generally the most satisfactory compromise will be to pre-set the lighting at the level that is satisfactory for black and white subjects.

In a typical individual component of the most economical lighting system, the lights should be recessed above ceiling level to prevent stray light from reaching the screen. The two rows of lights nearest the screen would be out during a performance.

The reflection factors of auditorium surfaces, compatible with continuous film running, are as follows:

	Per cent
Floor	10
Seat coverings, except backs	20
Seat backs	40
Side walls and ceiling:	
Surface toward screen	10
Surface toward spectators	50
Surfaces parallel to screen, such as front balcony face and rear wall	20

The foyer brightness should be about the same as the auditorium with all house lights on full, or 5 ft-c.

For additional information, see section on "Cinemas: General lighting."

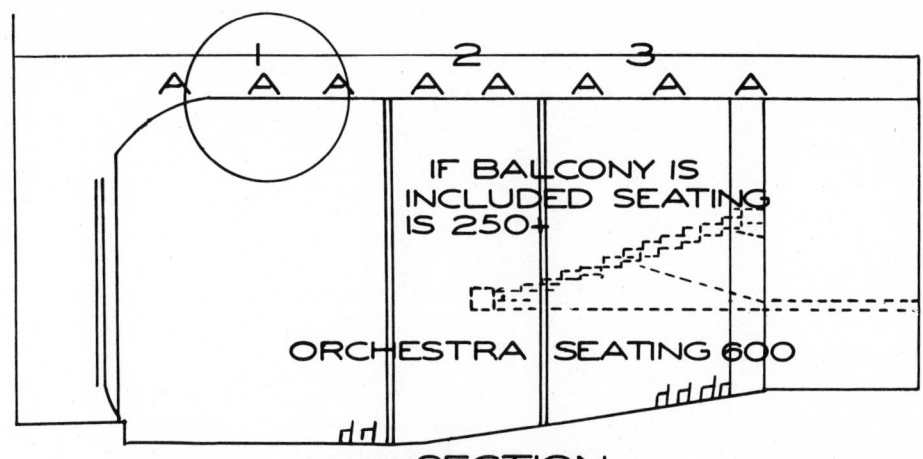

SECTION

DETAIL OF SECTION OF WALL OR CEILING SHOWING
CRITICAL ANGLE OF SURFACE OF WALL OR CEILING
THAT FACES TOWARD AUDIENCE.

10° FOR WALL AND CEILING PANEL NO.1
25° FOR WALL AND CEILING PANEL NO.2
35° FOR WALL AND CEILING PANEL NO.3

○ LOCATIONS OF LIGHTING UNITS IN MAIN CEILING
AND IN SOFFIT OF BALCONY WHEN BALCONY IS
INCLUDED.

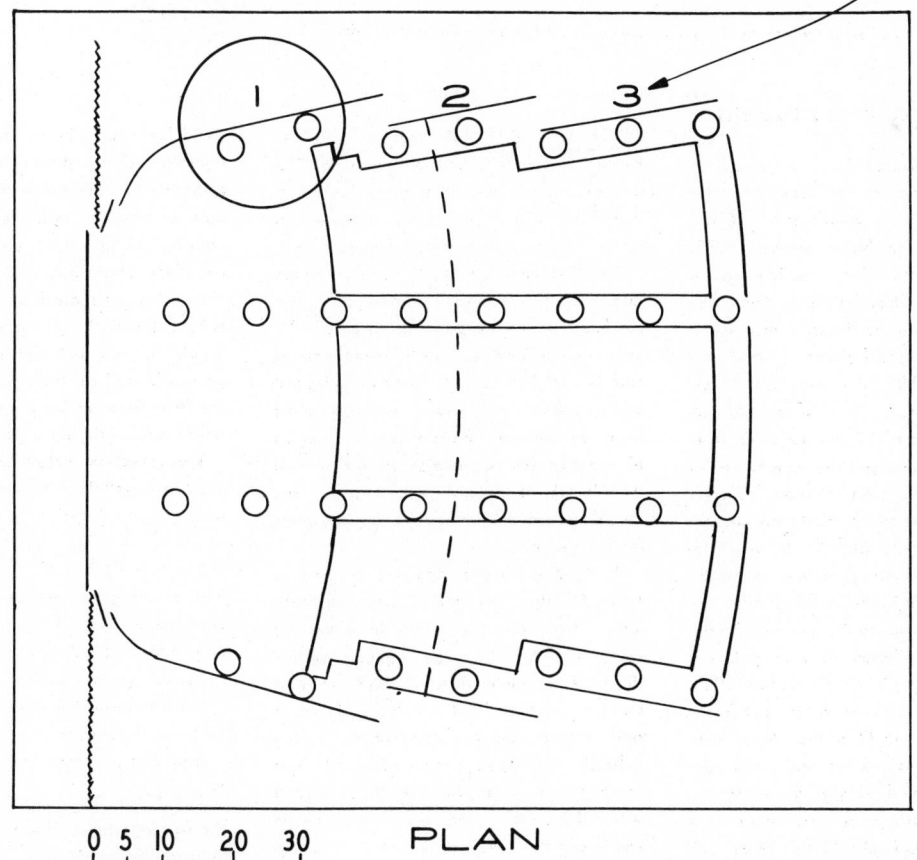

PLAN

Fig. 26

Data from Lighting for Hotels, *Illuminating Engineering Society, 1958*

Illumination levels currently recommended for hotels are shown in Table 17. Additional comments on certain areas are given below.

Entrance foyer should have a high level of illumination in order to create a smooth and comfortable transition between the brightly lighted marquee or bright daylight and the lobby.

Lobby should have a pleasant level of general illumination with higher-level lighting in special locations such as the desk, newsstand, telephones, bulletin boards, displays, shops, etc. Lighting methods usually combine direct and indirect lighting. Totally indirect lighting may result in overly bright ceilings and insufficient shadows for perception of the third dimension; downlighting used exclusively may produce sharp shadows and unpleasantly dark ceilings. Luminous ceilings combine the best features of direct and indirect lighting.

Lounge lighting calls for a softer treatment, and the general illumination level can be somewhat lower. Local lighting, often in the form of portable lamps, should be provided for reading. Properly located outlets are required if portable lamps are to be used.

Corridors: Adequate corridor lighting creates a pleasant atmosphere and makes it easier to read room numbers and find door keyholes. Well-designed ceiling fixtures spaced at intervals of twice the ceiling height usually give adequately uniform illumination. If possible, corridor switches should be placed near guest room doors. Building codes require emergency lighting for hotel corridors which will operate in the event of failure of the normal source of electricity.

Guest room lighting should provide for the following:

General room illumination
Writing at a desk
Reading in bed
Reading in an easy chair
Grooming at the dresser or dressing table
Illumination in clothes closets.

General illumination should be controlled by a wall switch at the door, as a safety factor. Both general and local illumination may be supplied by ceiling or wall fixtures

Table 17. Current recommended illumination levels for hotels

	Footcandles		Footcandles
Auditoriums		Laundry	
Assembly only	15	Washing	30
Exhibitions	30	Flat work ironing	50
Dancing	5	Machine and press finishing	70
Bars and Cocktail Lounges*		Linen Room — Sewing	100
Bathrooms		Lobby	
Mirror	30	General lighting	10
General	10	Reading and working areas	30
Bedrooms		Machine Shop	
Reading (books, magazines, newspapers)	30	Rough Bench and machine work	50
Inkwriting**	30	Medium Bench and machine work	100
Make-up†	30	Fine Bench and machine work	500
General	10	Marquee	
Corridors and Stairs	20	Dark surroundings	30
Dining Areas		Bright surroundings	50
Cashier	50	Offices	
Intimate type —		Accounting	150
Light environment	10	General	100
Subdued environment	3	Reception	30
For cleaning	20	Power Plants	
Leisure type		Boiler rooms	10
Light environment	30	Equipment rooms	20
Subdued environment	15	Store Interiors	
Quick service type		Circulation areas	30
Bright surroundings‡	100	General merchandise	100
Normal surroundings‡	50	Showcases	200
Entrance Foyer	30	Feature displays	500
Front Office	50	Stock rooms	30
Kitchens		Storerooms	10
Inspecting, checking, pricing	70		
Other areas	30		

*See Dining Areas — Intimate.
**Pencil handwriting, reading of reproductions and poor copies require 70 footcandles according to latest studies. Hotels catering to such business needs may wish to provide this illumination at the desk area.
†This may be done in the bathroom, but if a dressing table is provided, local lighting should provide the level recommended.
‡Including street and nearby establishments.

or by portable lamps, or by a combination of the two see (section on "Lighting: Residential").

Guest bathrooms: see section on "Lighting: Residential."

Dining rooms and bar may be dimly lighted for effect, but the illumination should be sufficient so that guests can read the menu without straining. Small dining rooms and cocktail lounges can often be effectively illuminated by means of brightly lighted mural decorations. If fluorescent lighting is used, care must be taken to specify colors that are flattering to food as well as to complexions (see section on "Lighting: General").

Kitchens: In the application of light to modern kitchens there is one very serious problem which probably cannot be completely overcome, i.e., the problem of reflections from highly polished surfaces such as stainless steel. Large lighting units with low brightness should be used; for example, fluorescent or large-area incandescent sources.

If fluorescent lamps are used, they should be of the improved-color-rendition type. Several areas in the kitchen require special lighting: at the bandsaw used in the meat department, at food choppers and mixers, in the hoods over the ranges, at the tables where clean silver and glassware are inspected, and at the checker's stand. Attention should be given to the form of the lighting unit, avoiding horizontal surfaces on which dust and dirt may collect. For more detailed information see *Lighting for Commercial Kitchens*, by the Illuminating Engineering Society, 1956.

Service areas should be lighted in accordance with the visual tasks. In areas where the seeing task is not critical, sufficient illumination should be provided for safety and easy maintenance. Stairs, elevators, and moving machinery should be well lighted for safety. Pilot lights are recommended for rooms that are rarely entered. Telephone switchboard rooms should be lighted to not more than 15 ft-c so that switchboard signal lights will be readily visible.

Data from Lighting Keyed to Today's Homes, Illuminating Engineering Society, 1960

Architectural lighting, planned as an integral part of the structural design of an interior, may be purely decorative or may be designed to provide functional lighting in a decorative manner. It may be applied to any type of architecture and to almost any room in the house.

Window and wall lighting

Window areas, the daytime source of light, may also be utilized to provide functional and decorative illumination after the sun sets. In contemporary architecture particularly, with its large areas of glass, it seems appropriate to retain the concept of light emanating from those areas. The only other suitable treatment is to leave the glass uncovered and provide lighting outside in the garden or patio.

The simplest form of window or wall lighting is to conceal tubular light sources behind a valance or cornice board. In modern lighting parlance, a *valance* is a horizontal strip mounted on the wall across the top of the drapery treatment (see Fig. 27). A valance usually directs light up to the ceiling as well as down over the drapery. A cornice is a horizontal member similar to a valance but attached to the ceiling; thus all of the light is directed downward (see Figs. 32 and 33).

The faceboard of a valance may be tilted outward at the top to send more light across the ceiling, or it may be double tilted for added interest. In either case, the degree of tilt from vertical may be 15 to 20 deg. If the board is tilted outward at the bottom some form of shielding (diffusing glass, plastic or louvers) may be necessary to prevent a direct view of the light sources (see Fig.

28). Other variations of valance lighting are shown in Figs. 29–31.

For effective window or wall lighting the fabric or wall surface should be light in color. Nonglossy wall finishes of medium reflectance, generally between 35 and 55 per cent, are desirable.

Valance faceboard depth should be a minimum of 6 in. for a length of not more than 8 ft. For longer lengths and/or greater ceiling heights the depth should be increased to 8 or 10 in. In general, the depth of the valance or cornice faceboard in inches should be about the same as the height of the valance above the floor in feet.

Light leaks between the cornice faceboard and the ceiling can be prevented by the application of a molding or by attaching a piece of white felt to the top of the faceboard before it is installed.

Valance-type fixtures may also be used for local lighting. They should be installed at the correct height for their intended use and shielded when necessary (Fig. 34).

Dimensions of standard wiring channels and tubular light sources are shown in Fig. 35. In all cases of valance or cornice lighting there must be sufficient illumination from other sources so that the faceboards do not appear as silhouetted forms.

Incandescent lamps may also be used for wall or window lighting. Units may be of the reflector or lens type and may be suspended, surface-mounted, or recessed in the ceiling. They may be installed to give a uniform wash of light on the wall or, if preferred, a scalloped effect.

Tall, narrow windows with deep reveals, usually found in old houses, may often be effectively lighted by means of tubular

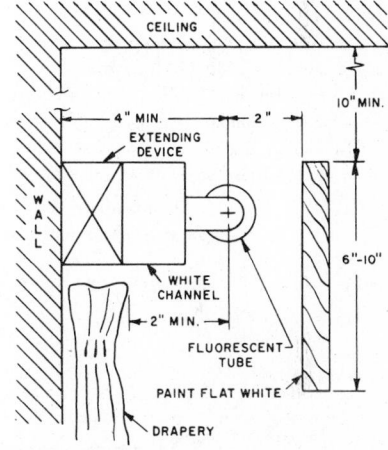

Fig. 27. Minimum dimensions for valance lighting installation

If draperies are bulky or heavily lined or if both glass curtains and overdrapes are used, distance of lamp from wall should be increased to 6 in. If ceiling reflectance is less than 65 per cent, distance to top of faceboard should be increased to 12 in.

sources at each side behind the draperies but in front of the shades (Fig. 36).

Cove lighting

Cove lighting is a fully indirect system in which the ceiling is lighted from continuous sources concealed in a cove on one or more walls somewhat below the ceiling. It produces a feeling of height and spaciousness, but, if used alone, tends to be flat and monotonous. Direct lighting from downlights or portable lamps

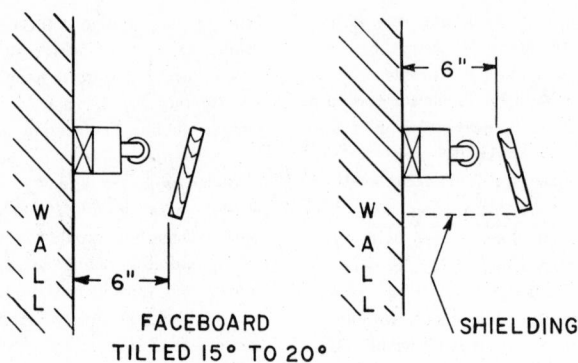

FACEBOARD
TILTED 15° TO 20°

SHIELDING

Fig. 28. Valance faceboard may be tilted

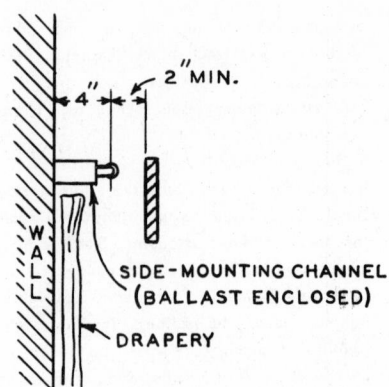

SIDE-MOUNTING CHANNEL
(BALLAST ENCLOSED)

DRAPERY

Fig. 29. With side-mounting channels, no extender is necessary

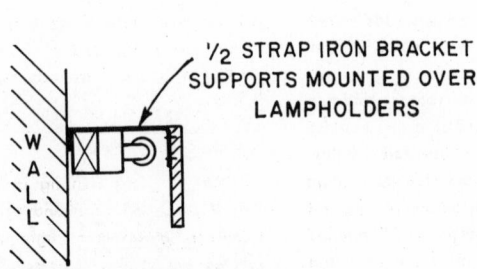

½ STRAP IRON BRACKET SUPPORTS MOUNTED OVER LAMPHOLDERS

Fig. 30. Intermediate brackets are required to support long faceboards

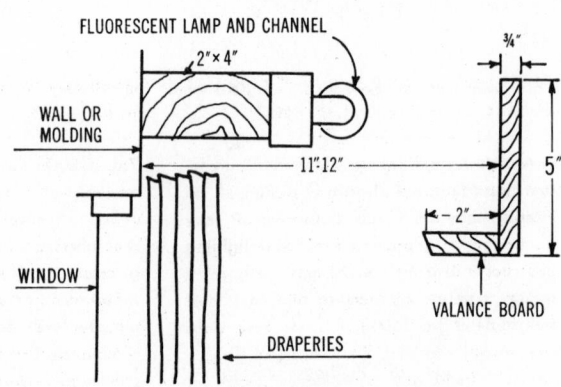

FLUORESCENT LAMP AND CHANNEL

WALL OR MOLDING

WINDOW

DRAPERIES

VALANCE BOARD

Fig. 31. Variation of valance lighting

If distance between wall and lamp is increased, light will be distributed more evenly, but shielding may be required at the bottom of the faceboard.

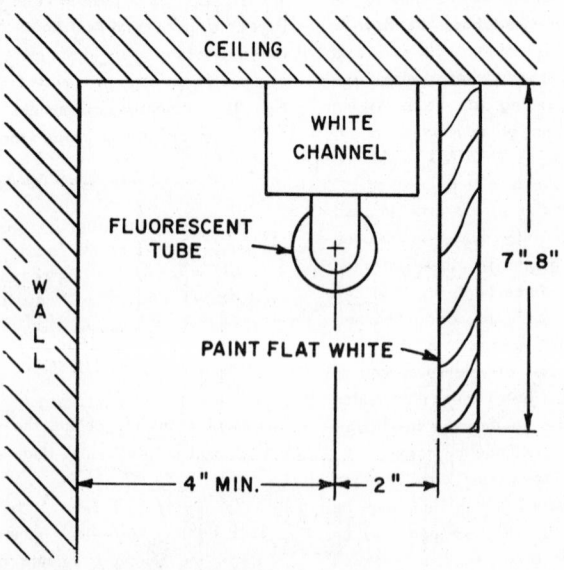

CEILING

WHITE CHANNEL

FLUORESCENT TUBE

PAINT FLAT WHITE

7"-8"

4" MIN.

2"

Fig. 32. Minimum dimensions for cornice lighting installation

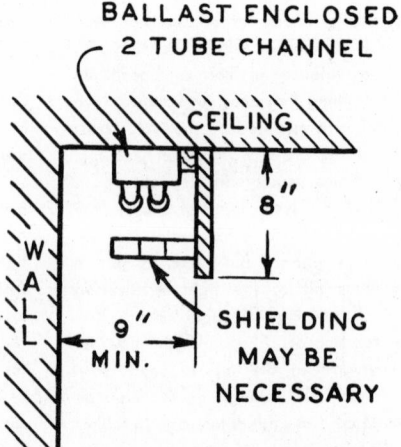

BALLAST ENCLOSED 2 TUBE CHANNEL

CEILING

8"

9" MIN.

SHIELDING MAY BE NECESSARY

Fig. 33. Cornice lighting with two tubes may require shielding

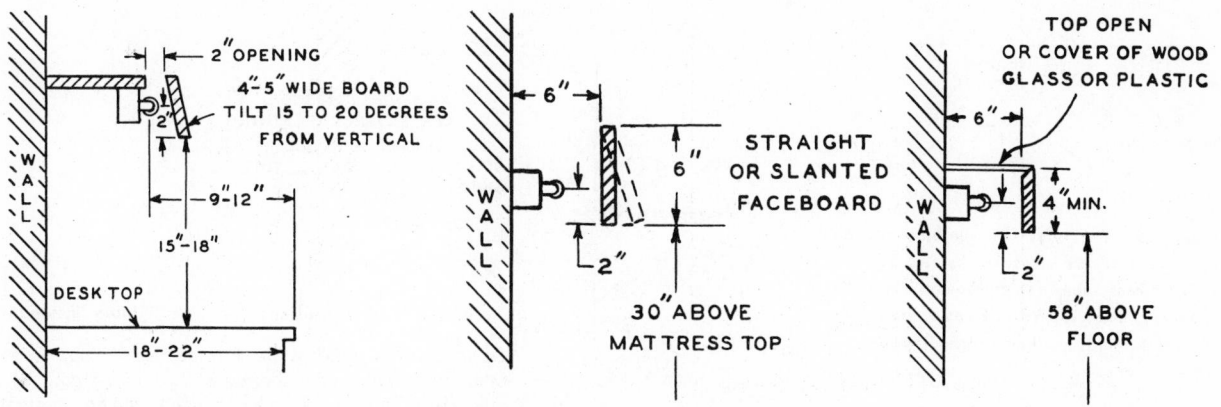

Fig. 34. Valance-type wall units for local lighting

(a) Desk, (b) bed, (c) range. Type b, installed 65 in. above the floor, can be used for lighting lounge furniture, dining tables, etc.

should be used with cove lighting to add shadows, highlights, and sparkle.

Critical dimensions for the design of cove lighting are shown in Figs. 37 and 38 and must be carefully observed for a successful installation. Combinations of cove lighting and valance-type or downlighting are shown in Figs. 39 and 40.

The principle of cove lighting can also be used on walls (Fig. 41). Because walls are directly in the line of sight, brightnesses should be kept lower than for ceilings.

Downlighting

The term downlighting usually refers to relatively small units using incandescent lamps as light sources. They may be suspended or surface-mounted, but more often they are recessed in the ceiling. The recessed type consists of a square or round metal box with shielding of metal fins or louvers, or diffusing glass or a glass lens (Fig. 42). The box may contain a reflector for use with regular bulbs, or it may be designed for the use of reflector bulbs. Where more accurate control of the beam is required, special-purpose units may be specified. One of these is the "pinhole" spot (Fig. 43). Some of these are equipped with an optical system of light control and adjustable shutters, making it possible to shape the beam precisely—square, round, or rectangular—to the object to be lighted. Another useful fixture is the "eyeball" (Fig. 44). This semirecessed unit can be rotated and swiveled within its housing in order to direct the light where desired.

Downlighting is often called accent lighting because that is its principal use.

It is not well suited to general lighting and should always be used with other types of lighting which will throw some light on the ceiling.

Luminous panel lighting

Luminous panel lighting is downlighting that is larger in area and often lower in brightness than accent lighting. The light sources are usually fluorescent tubes, and the shielding may be metal or plastic eggcrates but is more often a diffusing plastic sheet. In the smaller sizes (2 to 12 sq ft) luminous panels may be used as local lighting (Fig. 45) and in the larger sizes they may serve as general lighting. In either case, other types of lighting should be employed to light the ceiling. If fluorescent and incandescent lamps are to be used in the same room, care must be exercised

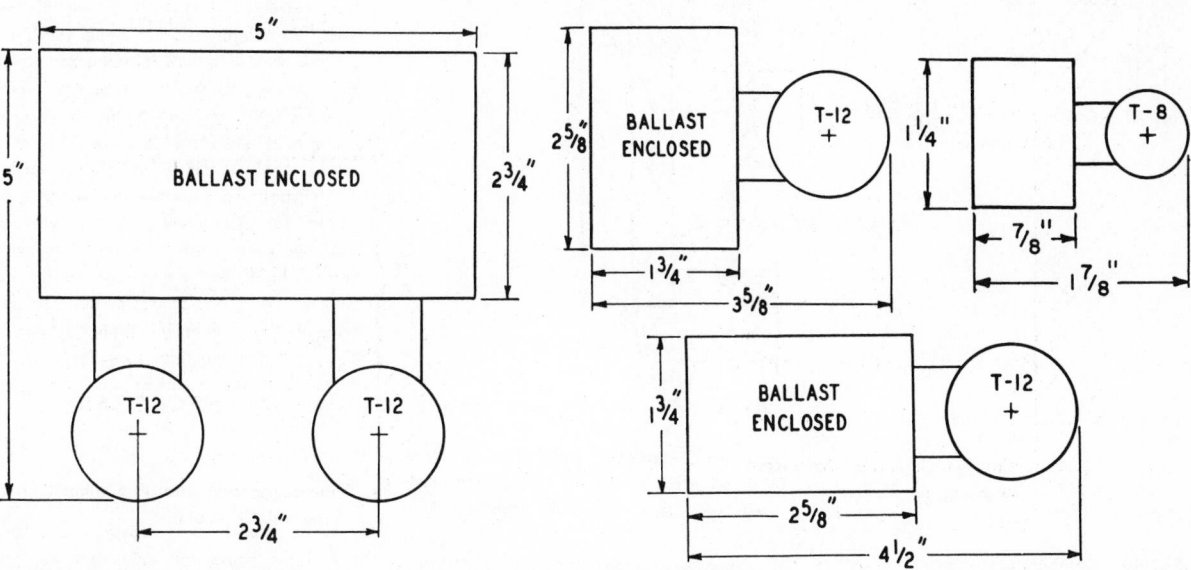

Fig. 35. Dimensions of standard metal wiring channels for fluorescent and lumiline tubes

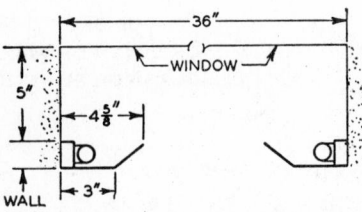

Fig. 36. The effect of sunshine coming in the windows is created by two 30-watt fluorescent tubes set end-to-end vertically behind metal shields in front of the venetian blinds but behind the draperies

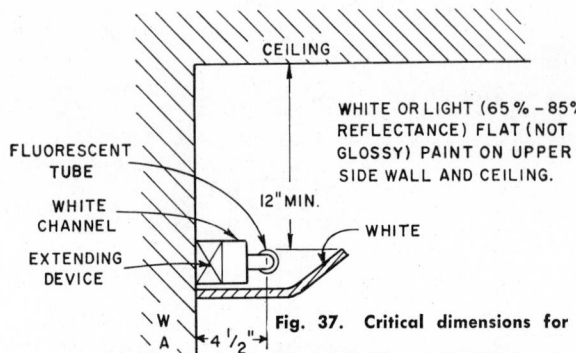

Fig. 37. Critical dimensions for cove lighting installation

Lampholders should be butted back-to-back or overlapped, if space permits, to assure continuous light on walls and ceiling without dark spaces between tubes.

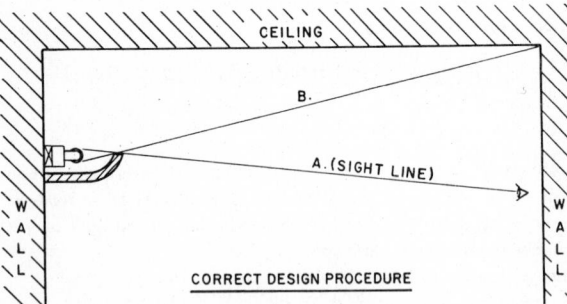

Fig. 38. Method of determining location of upper edge of cove so that light source is not visible and entire ceiling is lighted

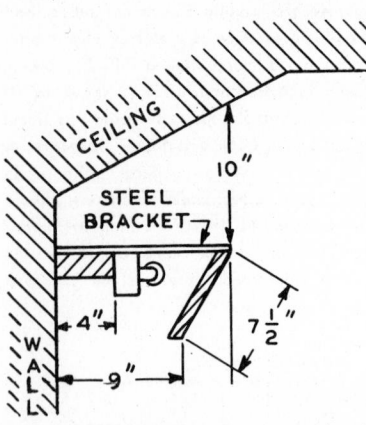

Fig. 39. Combination of cove and valance lighting

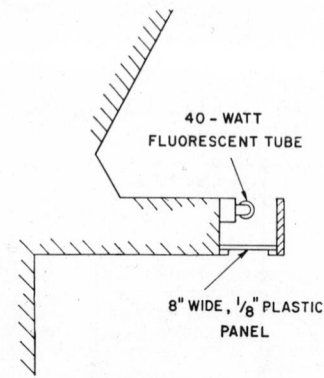

Fig. 40. Combination of cove and luminous panel downlighting

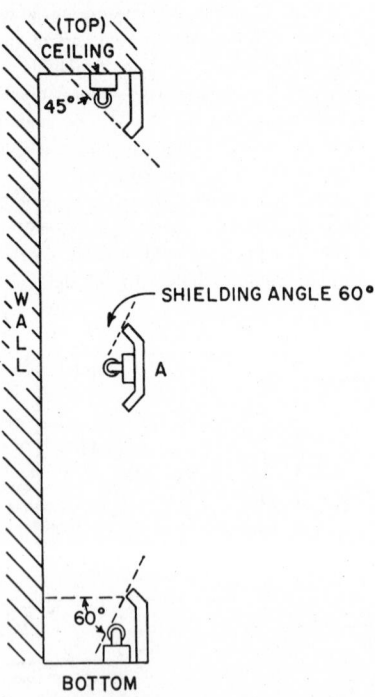

Fig. 41. Cove lighting used for walls

to select a fluorescent color which combines well with the yellowish light of incandescent lamps (see section on "Lighting: General").

When a luminous panel fills the entire ceiling, it is known as a luminous ceiling.

This gives an entirely different architectural character to the room, and of course eliminates the problem of the dark ceiling. When unlighted, the luminous ceiling has the appearance of a structural ceiling; when lighted, it has much the effect of a skylight. Luminous ceilings may be designed for high or low levels of illumination; dimmer control is advantageous for use in living and dining rooms.

The basic relationship for the design of luminous panels is shown in Fig. 46. An example of a luminous ceiling design is shown in Fig. 47.

Luminous walls may be designed in the same manner as luminous ceilings. When lighted, a luminous wall can give the effect of a sheer-curtained window wall.

Dimmers

Moderately priced and compact dimmers of sizes suitable for residential use are now available for both incandescent and fluorescent lamps. They are of two types: the autotransformer type which reduces power consumption proportionally to illumination, and the resistance type which consumes an appreciable amount of electricity even when the illumination is at a low level. Fluorescent lights require special dimmer ballasts. Separate dimmers are required for fluorescent and incandescent lights. A compromise "dimmer" for incandescent lights is the high-low switch; the low setting gives approximately 30 per cent of the full light output. It should be noted that the light from incandescent bulbs becomes yellower as they are dimmed.

Outdoor lighting

There are four types of outdoor lighting:

1. To provide safe passage into and out of the house and between house and garage, patio, and garden

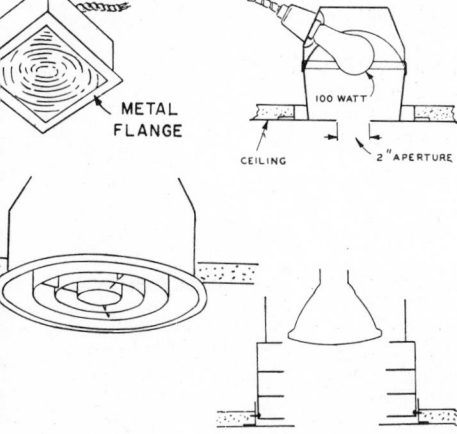

Fig. 42. Common types of downlights

For other types see Store Lighting and Church Lighting.

2. To discourage trespassers and disclose prowlers

3. To provide comfortable seeing for outdoor family activities

4. To enhance the beauty of garden and grounds. See section on "Landscaping."

A great variety of weatherproof lighting

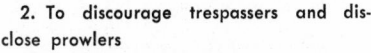
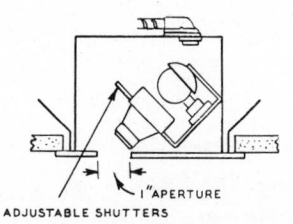

Fig. 43. "Pinhole" spot, a recessed downlight with adjustable shutters to shape beam pattern

units is available for these applications. Light sources should always be concealed.

Illumination levels

Illumination levels currently recommended for residences are shown in Table 18.

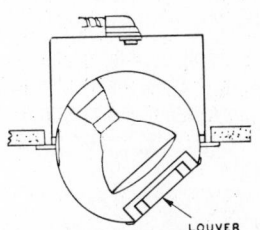

Fig. 44. "Eyeball" semirecessed fully adjustable downlight

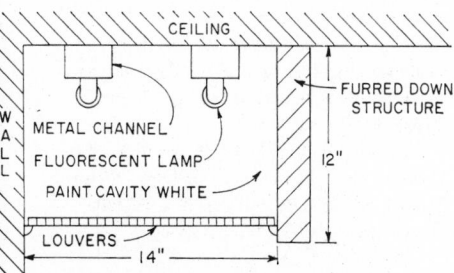

Fig. 45. Luminous panel or soffit lighting, used over a kitchen or bathroom counter

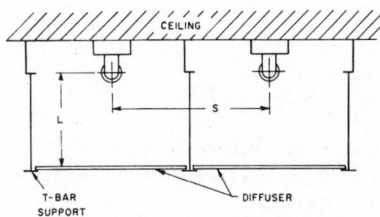

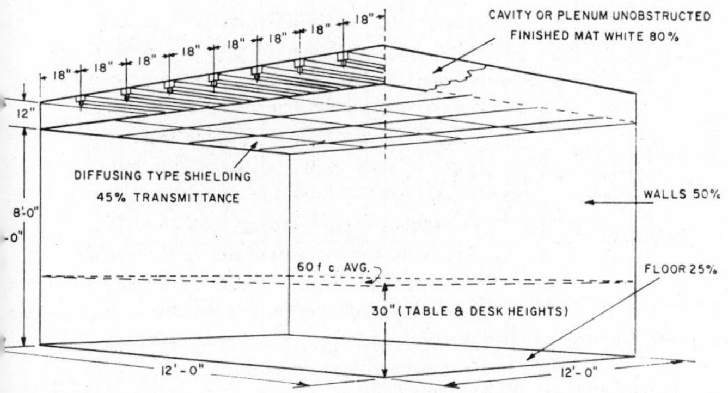

Fig. 46. Critical dimensions for luminous panel and luminous ceiling lighting

S should not exceed 1½ to 2 times L.

Table 18. Recommended illumination levels for residences

	Footcandles
SPECIFIC VISUAL TASKS*	
Table games	30
Kitchen activities	
Sink	70
Range and work surfaces	50
Laundry, trays, ironing board, ironer	50
Reading and writing, including studying	
Books, magazines, newspapers	30
Handwriting, reproduction and poor copies	70
Desks, study	70
Reading music scores	
Simple scores	30
Advanced scores	70
(When score is substandard size, and notations are printed on the lines, 150 footcandles or more are needed.)	
Sewing	
Dark fabrics (fine detail, low contrast)	200
Prolonged periods (light to medium fabrics)	100
Occasional periods (light fabrics)	50
Occasional periods (coarse thread, large stitches, high contrast thread to fabric)	30
Shaving, make-up, grooming; on the face at mirror locations	50
Work shop, bench work	70
GENERAL LIGHTING	
Entrances, hallways, stairways, stair landings	10†
Living room, dining room, bedroom, family room, sun room, library, game or recreation room	10†
Kitchen, laundry, bathroom	30

*Minimum on the task at all times.
**Brightness of visual task must be related to background brightness.
†General lighting for these areas need not be uniform in character.

Fig. 47. Basic relationship for the design of luminous panels

A light level of 60 ft-c is produced by seven rows of three 40-watt fluorescent tubes on 81-in. centers. Light distribution and surface brightness are approximately uniform.

Data from Recommended Levels of Illumination, Illuminating Engineering Society, 1959

	Foot-candles *
Art Galleries	
General	30
On paintings (supplementary)	30
On statuary and other displays	100

(1) Dark paintings with fine detail should have 2 to 3 times higher illumination.
(2) In some cases, much more than 100 ft-c is necessary to bring out the beauty of statuary.

Banks	
Lobby	
General	50
Writing areas	70
Tellers' stations	150
Posting and keypunch	150
Regular office work	100

* Minimum on the task at all times.

Depots, Terminals, and Stations	
Waiting room	30
Ticket offices	
General	100
Ticket rack and counters	100
Rest room and smoking room	30
Baggage checking	50
Storage	20
Concourse	10
Platforms	20
Toilets and washrooms	30

Drafting Rooms (See "Lighting: Offices")

Municipal Buildings (Fire and Police)	
Office work, corridors, elevators, stairways, washrooms (see "Lighting: Offices")	
Police	
Identification records	150
Jail cells and interrogation rooms	30
Fire Hall	
Dormitory	20

Recreation room	30
Wagon room	30

Museums (See Art Galleries)

Post Offices	
Lobby, on tables	30
Sorting, mailing, etc.	100
Storage	20
Files (see Offices)	
Corridors and stairways	20

Professional Offices (See "Lighting: Hospitals")

Restaurants (See "Lighting: Hotels")

Service Stations (at grade)

	Dark surround-ings	Light surround-ings
Approach	1.5	3
Driveway	1.5	5
Pump island area	20	30
Building faces (exclusive of glass)	10	30
Service areas	3	7

Data from Current Recommended Practice for Sports Lighting, Illuminating Engineering Society, 1961

The goal of sports lighting is to enable the players to perform their visual task and the spectators to follow the course of the play. The illumination levels recommended in Table 19 are currently considered minimum values of good practice, taking into account both players and spectators. Unless otherwise noted, the values in this table are foot-candles on the horizontal playing surface or, for "aerial" sports, on a horizontal plane 36 in. above the ground or floor.

As important as the quantity of light is the quality of the light. The principal factors affecting the quality of the lighting are glare, uniformity, and direction.

Glare control: A floodlight is inherently a glare source; therefore, one of the pri-

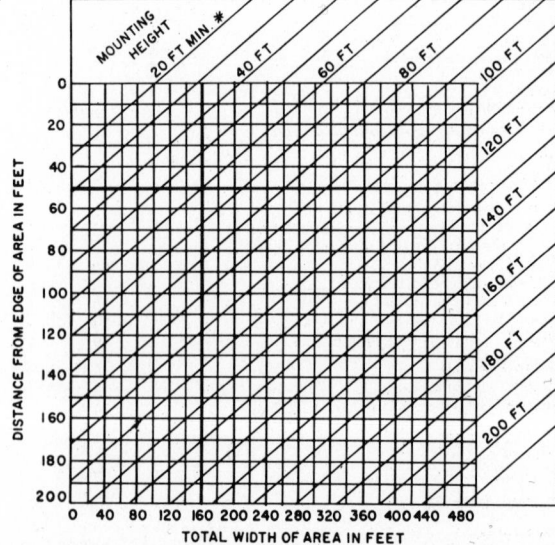

*FOR GROUND AREA SPORTS. 30 FEET IS MINIMUM FOR AERIAL SPORTS.

Fig. 49. Mounting height chart for all sports areas—minimum height to bottom floodlight crossarm

Read mounting height along diagonal at intersection of appropriate horizontal and vertical lines. For example, where area width = 160 ft and pole setback = 50 ft, minimum height of 60 ft is indicated by diagonal at intersection of 50 and 160 ft.

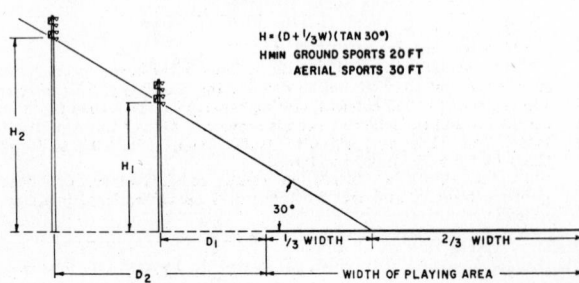

H = (D + 1/3 W)(TAN 30°)
HMIN GROUND SPORTS 20 FT
AERIAL SPORTS 30 FT

Fig. 48. Formula for determination of minimum mounting height

Table 19. Current illumination recommendations

	Average Horizontal Footcandles in Service*	
	Target	*Shooting Line*
Archery		
Tournament	10**	10
Recreational	5**	5
Badminton		
Tournament		30
Club		20
Recreational		10
Baseball	*Infield*	*Outfield*
Major League	150	100
AA and AAA League	70	50
A and B League	50	30
C and D League	30	20
Semi-Pro and Municipal League	20	15
Recreational	15	10
Class I and Class II Junior League	40	30
On seats during game		2
On seats before and after game		5
Basketball		
College and Professional		50
College Intramural and High School with Spectators		30
College Intramural and High School without Spectators		20
Recreational (outdoor)		10
	On Land	*150 feet from shore*
Bathing Beaches	1	3**
Billiards		*On Table*
Tournament		50
Recreational		30
General Area		10

Bowling‡	*Approaches*	*Lanes*	*Pins*
Tournament	10	20	50**
Recreational	10	10	30**

Bowling on the Green	
Tournament	10
Recreational	5
Boxing or Wrestling	
Championship Ring	500
Professional Ring	200
Amateur Ring	100
Seats during bout	2
Seats before and after bout	5

Casting	*Pier or Dock*	*Target*
Bait	10	5**
Dry Fly	10	5**
Wet Fly	10	5**

Croquet	
Tournament	10
Recreational	5

Curling	*Tees*	*Rink*
Indoor	20	10

Football (Regulation and Rugby)	
Index: Distance from nearest sideline to the farthest row of spectators†	
Class I: over 100 feet	100
Class II: 50 feet to 100 feet	50
Class III: 30 feet to 50 feet	30
Class IV: Under 30 feet	20
Class V: No fixed seating facilities	10
Six-Man Football	
High School or College	20
Jr. High School or Recreational	10
Golf Driving Range	
General on the Tees	10
At 200 Yards	5**
Golf Putting Greens	10
Gymnasiums	
Exhibitions, Matches	30
General Exercising and Recreation	20
Assemblies	15
Dances	5
Locker and Shower Rooms	20
Handball	
Tournament	30
Club	20
Recreational	10
Hockey	
Field	20
Ice	
College or Professional	50
Amateur	20
Recreational	10

	Average Horizontal Footcandles in Service*
Horseshoes	
Tournament	10
Recreational	5
Lacrosse	
High School or College	20
Quoits	5
Playgrounds	5
Racing	
Bicycle	20
Dog	30
Horse	20
Motor (Midget Auto or Motorcycle)	20
Rifle and Pistol Range	
On Target	50**
Firing Point	10
Range	5
Roque	
Tournament	20
Recreational	10
Shuffleboard	
Tournament	10
Recreational	5
Skating	
Roller Rink	5
Ice Rink	5
Lagoon, Pond or Flooded Area	1
Skeet Shoot	
Target, Surface at 60 feet	30**
Firing Point, General	10
Ski Slope Practice	3
Soccer	
Professional and College	30
High School	20
Recreational	10

Softball	*Infield*	*Outfield*
Professional and Championship	50	30
Semi-Pro	30	20
Industrial League	20	15
Recreational	10	7

Squash	
Tournament	30
Club	20
Recreational	10
Swimming Pool	
General—Overhead	10
Underwater	
Outdoors, 60 lamp lumens per square foot of surface	
Indoors, 100 lamp lumens per square foot of surface	

Tennis	*Lawn*	*Table*
Tournament	30	50
Club	20	30
Recreational	10	20

Trap Shoot	
Target at 150 feet	3**
Firing Point—General	1
Volleyball	
Tournament	20
Recreational	10

* On playing surface.
** Vertical surface.
† It is generally conceded that the distance between the spectators and the play is the first consideration in determining the class and lighting requirements. However, the potential seating capacity of the stands should also be considered and the following ratio is suggested: Class I for over 30,000 spectators; Class II for over 10,000 to 30,000; Class III for 5,000 to 10,000; and Class IV for under 5,000 spectators.
‡ Levels shown are based on visual considerations. Otherwise for public attraction and increased business considerations, practice is as follows:

Class	Approaches	Lanes	Pins
Tournament	70	100	200 Vertical
Recreation	50	70	150 Vertical

mary tasks of the illumination designer should be to reduce the objectionable effects of glare to a minimum. The basic means by which the designer may accomplish this task are proper beam spread, adequate mounting heights, proper luminaire locations, and proper floodlight aiming.

Beam spread: As the distance from the floodlight to the area to be lighted increases, the beam spread of the floodlight used should be decreased. Beam spreads vary from a minimum of 10 to more than 100 deg.

Mounting height: Recommended minimum mounting heights are shown in Figs. 48 and 49.

Luminaire location: Every effort should be made to locate light sources so that they are not in the normal line of sight of either players or spectators. Glare shields and special louvers can be designed to reduce the brightness of spill light which may cause discomfort to spectators or sometimes even to the inhabitants of the surrounding area.

Uniformity: Acceptable uniformity occurs when the ratio of maximum to minimum illumination does not exceed 3 to 1.

Direction of light: Except for unidirectional sports such as archery, bowling, and golf driving, lighting should come from several directions in order to avoid excessive shadow contrast.

Floodlights: These are classified as heavy duty, general purpose, and open type. *Standards Publication for Floodlights* by the National Electrical Manufacturers Association specifies the minimum beam efficiency that each type should provide. Recommended maintenance factors are 75 per cent for the covered type and 65 per cent for the open type.

Layouts and *tables* showing the number, type, and location of the floodlights for 56 specific sports are given in *Current Recommended Practice for Sports Lighting* by the Illuminating Engineering Society.

Data from Recommended Practice for Outdoor Parking Area Lighting, *Illuminating Engineering Society, 1960.*

The basic requirement in lighting an outdoor parking area is to provide good visibility with a minimum of glare. The most severe problem in such applications is to provide a measure of illumination in the many small, narrow "corridors" formed by adjacent parked cars. In order to get some light into these "corridors" it is recommended that any point in the entire parking area be provided with illumination from at least two, and preferably

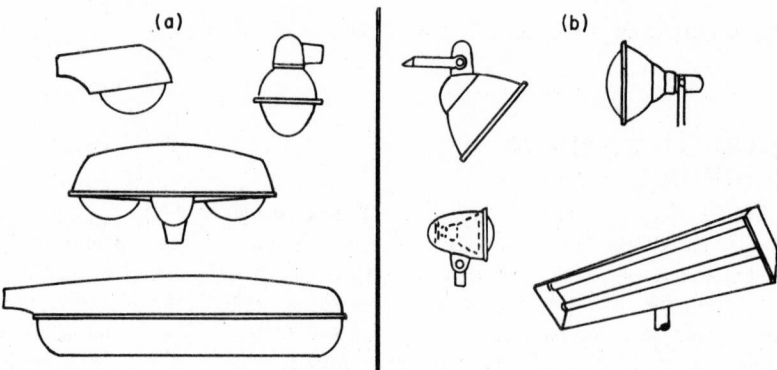

Fig. 50. Typical outdoor area lighting luminaires

(a) Street lights; (b) floodlights.

four, lighting (pole) locations with equipment mounted as high as possible, at a minimum of 20 ft.

Basic illumination requirements: The minimum recommended illumination levels for the barest seeing essentials on the parking lot proper are as follows:

Type of parking area	Average maintained horizontal foot-candles
Self-parking area	1.0
Attendant parking area	2.0 *

* Higher illumination values are required for attendant parking lots than for self-parking lots because, with the former, closer parking, greater movement, and speed and accuracy of handling vehicles are important for greater monetary returns and avoidance of damage claims.

Where additional lighting is desired for business attraction or customer convenience, values of 5 ft-c and upward are often used.

Uniform illumination is desirable, and the lowest foot-candle value at any point on the pavement should not be less than one-fourth the recommended average.

Entrances and exits: The illumination levels at entrances, exits, loading zones, and collector lanes of parking areas should not be less than twice the illumination of the adjacent parking area or the adjoining street, whichever is greater.

Light sources: Light sources used for the illumination of outdoor parking areas can be incandescent, mercury, fluorescent or any combination of the three.

Types of lighting equipment: A number of different types of luminaires are available for parking area lighting although floodlights or street lighting units are most commonly employed.

Street lighting luminaires are available to accommodate incandescent, fluorescent, and mercury lamps (Fig. 50a), and are designed to produce both symmetric and asymmetric light control. Narrow and wide patterns of light are available.

Floodlights are available in a wide range of light distributions from concentrating (for lighting areas at a distance) to wide spread (for lighting close-up areas), in symmetric, asymmetric, and rectangular beam patterns to fit a large number of different requirements. Floodlights are available for use with many sizes of incandescent, mercury, fluorescent, and reflectorized lamps (Fig. 50b).

Isolux charts: As a design aid in determining illumination levels and coverage, isolux diagrams, curves showing illumination at various distances from the source, are often used. They may be obtained from manufacturers of lighting equipment. By superimposing these diagrams on a proposed layout of a parking area drawn to the same scale, the approximate illumination level at a specific point may be determined. This is useful also in studying the uniformity of illumination that a particular lighting unit will provide in a particular arrangement.

Luminaire spacing: The ratio of the luminaire (or pole, in the event of multiple-mounted luminaires) spacing to the mounting height should be kept to a minimum. For both floodlights and street lights a maximum spacing-to-mounting height ratio of 4 to 1 represents current good practice.

Pole locations: Lighting poles should be located generally along the parking barriers and outside boundaries. Where poles are located near automobiles, the use of wheel barriers will save both cars and poles.

Aiming: Special care should be taken to avoid objectionable spill light and glare on adjacent property.

By LOUIS A. BELLO, *Syska & Hennessy, Inc., Consulting Engineers*

ELECTRICAL LOADS IN LARGE BUILDINGS

In the last decade, typical electrical loads in office buildings have doubled because of air conditioning, higher lighting intensities, more business machines, more appliances and the impact of automation.

A clear understanding of the types and magnitudes of electrical loads in office buildings, hospitals, schools and laboratories is essential in anticipating their growth. One way of accomplishing this is through a listing of commonly encountered loads, a brief description of each and a tabulation of their capacities in typical buildings.

TYPES OF ELECTRICAL LOADS

1. Lighting
2. Convenience outlets
3. Heating, ventilating and air conditioning (HVAC)
4. Sanitary equipment
5. Elevators, moving stairways and material handling equipment
6. Cooking appliances
7. Business machines
8. Laboratory equipment
9. Shop equipment
10. X ray equipment
11. Miscellaneous equipment

Lighting

Lighting is one of the largest loads, and its requirements must be well established before an accurate total load can be computed. However, for preliminary design, estimating and checking purposes watts per square foot (w/sq ft) is a common and useful means for determining such loads, based on a particular foot-candle level and type of lighting system.

The finally selected fixture types should be checked to verify these loads. Also, electrical codes have mandatory minimum requirements regarding lighting loads to be used in determining minimum feeder sizes. See Article 220 in the National Electrical Code.

Convenience Outlets

Outlets usually are a minor load, but they are closely related to and associated with lighting. An allowance of between ½ to 1½ w/sq ft is quite common; the actual figure is determined by the density of receptacle application. Underfloor duct and cellular floor systems will usually require 1 to 1½ w/sq ft.

The National Electrical Code (Article 210) has a minimum requirement of 1½ amperes (180 watts) per convenience outlet.

Heating, Ventilating and Air Conditioning

These power requirements will, of course, be determined by the amount of ventilation and the amount of heat to be supplied or removed from a building.

For heating and ventilating purposes only, equipment such as the following may be encountered:

1. Fuel combustion motors and controls
2. Pumps (vacuum, condensate, circulating)
3. Heaters (unit, space, fuel and induct)
4. Unit ventilators
5. Fans (supply and exhaust)
6. Heating cable
7. Snow melting equipment

Air conditioning equipment usually consists of:

1. Refrigeration compressors
2. Pumps (chilled water, condensate, condenser and circulating)
3. Fans (supply, return, exhaust and cooling tower)

Unlike lighting and convenience outlet loads, which are more or less equally distributed throughout a building, HVAC loads are usually concentrated in basements, penthouses and fan or machine rooms.

Sanitary (or Plumbing) Loads

These are relatively modest in comparison to HVAC; however, where fire pumps, house water pumps and well pumps are encountered, they can comprise a sizable load. Some commonly encountered equipment includes:

1. Sump pumps
2. Sewage ejectors
3. Circulating pumps
4. Vacuum pumps
5. Fire pumps
6. Well pumps
8. Compressors
9. Chilled water pumps (for drinking fountains)

Most of these loads are located in basement areas and/or penthouse machine rooms.

Elevators, moving stairways and material handling equipment are formidable loads in tall buildings and hospitals and may consist of:

1. Elevators
2. Moving stairways
3. Dumbwaiters
4. Conveyors
5. Pneumatic tubes
6. Various hoists and lifts

Major factors affecting the capacities of such equipment are speed of travel and weight being handled.

Cooking appliances can generally be classified into two categories:

1. All-electric
2. Gas and/or steam with or without electric auxiliaries

The number of persons to be served, the type of service and equipment used determine actual electrical load. The tables indicate kitchen loads of actual installations. The commercial-type dishwasher may require electric booster heaters to raise the temperature of the normal building hot water supply. Loads up to 50 kw for such purposes are not uncommon.

Business Machines

A large portion of loads falling under this heading are supplied from convenience outlets, underfloor ducts and cellular floor systems. Major exceptions are data processing ma-

AVERAGE ELECTRICAL LOADS FOR VARIOUS BUILDING TYPES PER 1,000 SQ FT OF FLOOR AREA

		Floor area, sq ft	Level of illumi-nation, ft-c	Light and recep-tacles, kva	HVAC, hp	Plumb-ing, hp	Elevator, kva	Kitchen, kva	Com-puter, kva	Fire pump, hp	Miscel-laneous, kva
Office buildings	Av.	852,900	56	5.1	3.7	0.21	0.93	0.40	0.25	0.20	0.56
(10 buildings in eastern	High	1,900,000	80	9.7	7.0	0.44	2.1	0.97	0.64	0.30	1.1
half of U.S.)	Low	125,000	35	3.7	2.0	0.08	0.19	0.06	0.05	0.11	0.23
									Labora-tory, kva	X ray, kva	Emer-gency, kw
Hospitals	Av.	347,400		5.3	4.5	0.32	0.95	0.96	0.63	0.64	3.5
(4 general hospitals and	High	789,800		8.4	7.6	0.53	1.7	2.8	1.7	1.2	5.8
3 additions)	Low	43,000		3.0	2.7	0.02	0.41	0.16	0.19	0.25	1.9
Schools	Av.	136,589	33	4.2	1.2	0.08	0.12	0.66			
(9 schools in New York	High	270,000	45	5.2	1.8	0.13	0.18	2.0			
area)	Low	20,300	30	3.6	0.72	0.03	0.05	0.36			
Laboratories	Av	89,500	47	3.5	5.6	1.5	1.1	1.1	6.9		
(6 laboratories, all different	High	175,000	50	5.6	7.5	2.4	2.0	1.9	14.6		
types)	Low	33,000	40	1.2	1.4	0.43	0.63	0.34	1.4		

chines, electric typewriters, card punch equipment, etc., which are scattered throughout office spaces and are taken care of by the load allowances of convenience receptacles.

Data processing machines are confined to specially designed spaces with a high degree of temperature control and flexible wiring provisions in the form of raised floors or floor troughs.

Laboratory Equipment
It is difficult to determine laboratory loads because of the diversity of equipment usage and the flexibility required. Individual laboratory loads may vary between 20 to 40 w/sq ft, exclusive of special equipment. These may in some cases be diversified to

50 per cent for individual feeders supplying groups of laboratories. Further diversifications for service to the laboratory building or suite may reduce this load to as low as 15 per cent of the original 20 to 40 w/sq ft. The actual initial loads and diversifications depend on the type of laboratory and its use.

Shop Equipment
This is usually a minor load for the commercial building, however, it may be heavy for concentrated areas in high schools.

X ray Equipment
Although usually associated with hospitals, such equipment may also be found in office buildings and lab-

oratories on a smaller scale. It is important to note that these loads tax a distribution system for only a few seconds, and they are usually well diversified with other X ray equipment.

Miscellaneous Equipment
Where large quantities of individual equipment are present, it may be necessary to have accurate individual load capacities for over-all load determination.

SUMMARY
The tables indicate the range of loads that have actually been installed in a number of buildings. Tabulations such as these can be useful for both preliminary estimates and final checking.

ELECTRICAL CAPACITIES OF BUILDING EQUIPMENT

Cooking Appliances

Appliance	Elec. Capacity, KVA
1. Range (4 burner)	12
2. All purpose oven (1 section—60 lb of beef per hour)	6
3. Bake ovens (1 section—40 lb of bread)	7.5
(1 section—60 lb of bread)	11
4. Broiler (1 section—100 lb per hour)	12
5. Fry kettles (40 lb potatoes per hour)	12
(90 lb potatoes per hour)	18
6. Griddles (16 hamburgers)	3
(32 hamburgers)	6
(48 hamburgers)	12
7. Hotplate (2 plates)	2.5
8. Roll warmers (48 buns)	1.65
9. Food warmer	1.65
10. Steam tables (8 wells)	12.
11. Warming cabinets (dishes, utensils, etc. 300 to 400 w per ft of length)	.5 to 10
12. Coffee urns (500 w per gal)	1.5 to 10
13. Compression steam cooker	12
14. Dishwashers	.6 to 50
15. Glass washers	.5
16. Food choppers	1/4 to 10 hp
17. Food cutters	1/3 to 3/4 hp
18. Food mixers	1/6 to 1/3 hp
19. Slicers	1/8 to 1/3 hp
20. Tenderizer	1/3 hp
21. Peelers	1/3 to 1/2 hp
22. Waste Disposer	1 1/2 hp

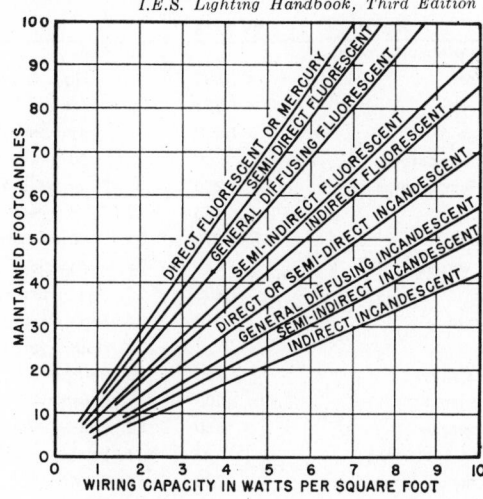

I.E.S. Lighting Handbook, Third Edition

Lighting Loads

Approximate wiring capacity in watts/square foot to maintain a given illumination level in a room of average size (Room Index E; see I.E.S. Lighting Handbook) by means of various types of lighting installations

Shop Equipment

Item	Elec. Capacity	Size
1. Drill press	½ hp	15-in. dia stock
2. Grinder	⅓ hp	6-in. dia wheel
3. Grinder	½ hp	7-in. dia wheel
4. Grinder	¾ hp	8-in. dia wheel
5. Grinder	1 hp	10-in. dia wheel
6. Jointer	¾ hp	6-in. table width
7. Jointer	1½ hp	8-in. table width
8. Kiln	4.5 kva	14- by 14- by 14-in. cabinet 2000 deg F
9. Kiln	6.0 kva	16- by 17- by 18-in. cabinet 2,000 deg F
10. Lathe (variable speed)	1 hp	12-in. dia
11. Milling machine	⅓ hp	9-in. travel
12. Milling machine	1 hp	14-in. travel
13. Milling machine	2 hp	17-in. travel
14. Mortiser	¾ hp	6- by 30-in. table
15. Oven	1 kva	28- by 24- by 20-in. cabinet
16. Oven	2 kva	cabinet 325 deg F
17. Planer	2 hp	4- by 12-in.
18. Potters wheel	¼ hp	19- by 30-in. table
19. Router	1¼ hp	
20. Sander, belt & disc (floor mtd)	½ hp	10-in. dia, 6-in. belt
21. Sander, comb. belt & disc	½ hp	4-in. dia, 10-in. belt
22. Sander, spindle (floor mtd)	1 hp	20- by 24-in. table
23. Saw, arbor	2 hp	10-in. dia
24. Saw, band	½ hp	14-in. dia
25. Saw, band	1½ hp	20-in. dia
26. Saw, circular	3 hp	10-in. dia
27. Saw, jig	⅓ hp	24-in. throat
28. Saw, radial	¾ hp	9-in. dia
29. Saw, scroll	⅓ hp	26-in. throat
30. Surfacer	5 hp	6- by 18-in.
31. Surfacer	7½ hp	8- by 24-in.
32. Surfacer	10 hp	8- by 30-in.
33. Welder, arc	7.5 kva	
34. Welder, spot	1.5 kva	1/8-in. thickness
35. Welder, spot	2.5 kva	3/16-in. metal thickness

Residential Appliances

Item	Watts	Item	Watts
1. Air conditioners (room)		30. Fans	
½ ton	880	Floor circulator	120
¾ ton	1,225	Attic	345
1 ton	1,540	Kitchen exhaust	75
2. Aquarium aerator	50	Portable	50
3. Aquarium aerator	250	31. Floor polisher	475
4. Blanket	175	32. Food freezer	up to 460
5. Blender	275	33. Food warmer	310
6. Bottle warmer	440	34. Fry kettle	1,300
7. Broiler	1,400	35. Frying pan	1,085
8. Casserole	510	36. Food mixer	130
9. Clock	2	37. Hair dryer	415
10. Clothes dryer	4,760	38. Refrigerator	230
11. Coffee maker	up to 1,000	39. Roaster	1,320
12. Corn popper	440	40. Sandwich grill	960
13. Heating equipment		41. Sewing machine	75
Warm air furnace fan	320	42. Serving tray	600
Oil burner	230	43. Shaver	11
Humidifier	185	44. Steam iron	1,040
14. Ice cream freezer	115	45. Sun lamp	275
15. Ironer	1,455	46. Tea kettle	550
16. Knife sharpener	50	47. Toaster	1,130
17. Odorizer	11	48. Trivet	50
18. Pressure cooker	1,400	49. T. V. receiver	275
19. Power tools	up to 1,000	50. Vacuum cleaners	
20. Projector	300	Bag type	340
21. Radio	30	Canister type	725
22. Range	up to 23,000	Tank type	555
23. Recorder	95	Hand type	310
24. Record player	50	51. Heat lamp	250
25. Dehumidifier	185	52. Heating pad	60
26. Door chime	15	53. Heater	up to 1,650
27. Dishwasher	1,325	54. Vaporizer	385
28. Dry iron	1,025	55. Waffle baker	960
29. Egg cooker	440	56. Washers	
		Automatic	400
		Nonautomatic	380

X-Ray Equipment

Use	KVA
1. Simple radiography and fluoroscopy	15
2. Advanced radiography and fluoroscopy	25
3. Operating room radiography	25
4. Cystoscopic room radiography	15
5. Emergency (and/or admission) room radiography	15
6. Special procedures radiography and fluoroscopy	37½
7. Cardiology radiology and fluoroscopy	25

Large Data Processing Equipment

Use	Elec Capacity, KVA (not including ventilation or air conditioning requirements)
1. Automatic production recording, continuous accounting and typewriter tabulating control	15
2. Similar to above except greater storing capacity and remote station operating features	20
3. Engineering and scientific computations	5
4. Banking, billing, inventory, insurance and accounting	10
5. Similar to above except faster and greater storage capacity	25
6. Engineering, aircraft and heavy industry computations	32
7. Payrolls, management reports, accounting at very high speeds. (300,000 plus decisions per second)	45
8. Design of missiles, rockets, jet engines, nuclear reactors, etc.	35

By NOYCE L. GRIFFIN, *Electrical Engineer, Architectural and Engineering Branch Division of Hospital and Medical Facilities, U.S. Public Health Service*

A REFERENCE GUIDE TO HOSPITAL ELECTRICAL FACILITIES

It is essential that the electrical supply for hospitals be adequate and dependable. Blood banks, refrigerators, respirators, surgical lighting, as well as other vital equipment, cannot be without electrical power for even short periods.

The demand on electrical energy is usually higher than for most building types. For this reason, the quality of materials and equipment must be high and future maintenance must be considered during the course of the design.

ELECTRICAL SERVICE
MAIN ELECTRIC SERVICE

The electric service brought into the building may be primary or secondary depending upon the load demands and other local conditions. An underground service usually costs four to eight times that of a conventional overhead service but is generally preferred for hospitals because of landscaping and reduction of the probability of service interruption due to storms, ice loads, or other overhead disturbances.

TRANSFORMERS. If the service brought into the hospital is primary or high voltage, several types of step-down transformers may be used. A nonflammable, nonsludging, insulating, liquid-filled transformer offers high impulse strength and low maintenance. However, air-cooled and gas-cooled transformers of high quality are available.

The open dry-type transformer has less impulse strength than the liquid-filled type. Frequent cleaning is required and it is suitable for indoor use only. The sealed dry-type transformer has many advantages of the liquid and the open dry types, and it has the same impulse strength limitations as the open dry-type transformer; but in addition it is dust-tight and weatherproof. It can be installed at lower cost and requires less space than the liquid type.

CIRCUIT BREAKERS for switching of main secondary circuits are usually the drawout type in larger hospitals, or the molded case type in smaller hospitals. The drawout type is more expensive to install but provides a higher degree of protection, reliability, and ease of maintenance.

DISTRIBUTION. Three-phase, 4-wire 208y/120 volt distribution systems are generally preferred for small hospitals because of economy and convenience in providing for both 3-phase and single phase connections at the distribution panels. A higher voltage system such as the 3-phase, 4-wire 480y/277 volt system, using dry-type transformers for 120-volt service may be more economical for large hospitals which operate several large motors. The nominal voltage of any distribution system should be that of an industry standard conforming to American Standards Association Publication 84.1, "Preferred Voltage Ratings for A-C Systems and Equipment."

The simplest and cheapest scheme of distribution is the "simple radial system." Improvement in flexibility and dependability

may be obtained at additional cost by one of several variations of this system. Many schemes of distribution are workable, and general information may be obtained from handbooks on electrical facilities for hospitals.

EMERGENCY POWER

A reliable source of emergency power for lighting and for operation of essential equipment is necessary. The three sources of power which have been used are storage battery, second utility line, and generator. A generator on the hospital site is preferable to either a storage battery or a second utility line for the following reasons: (a) storage batteries have a limited capacity and the direct current for services such as operation of motorized equipment or fluorescent lighting; (b) a second utility line is usually subjected to the same factors contributing to power interruption as those of the main utility service.

When a second utility line is used as the only source of emergency power, it should be from a generating plant separate from the source of main power and should be routed and connected so that any fault on the main feeder would not be transmitted to, or likely to cause an outage of the emergency feeder.

Generators on the hospital site may be driven by any suitable prime mover such as gasoline, gas, or diesel oil internal combustion engines or steam turbines. The selection of the type of generating unit is usually influenced by the dependability of fuel supply or whether the emergency power will be used frequently to carry a part of the load during normal operation. Generally, the internal combustion engine generating units are intended as a standby service only, while the steam turbine units are sometimes operated during periods of maximum demands daily, and where such operation may result in a more favorable power rate from the utility company.

A switch-over gas and gasoline fuel supply for small and medium sized internal combustion engines offers greater flexibility of operation in case of scarcity or depletion of either fuel. Starting gasoline engines on bottled gas and then switching to gasoline has been suggested as a more positive assurance of avoiding failure of automatic starting.

An arrangement of feeders so that a planned selection of loads may be connected or dropped from the emergency service is desirable, to more fully utilize the available capacity of the emergency service and also to prevent overloading to the point of trip-out of the entire service. Such a design is a particularly important convenience when adding fixed or mobile emergency capacity to an existing system and also for minimizing a trip-out of service to a highly important area. The switching of emergency power for critical areas should be automatic. Pickup or dropout of other circuits should be selective and may be either manual or automatic. In some hospitals designed for treatment of poliomyelitis patients, circuit feeders are divided into three groups designated as "critical," "semicritical," and "noncritical."

TELEPHONE SERVICE should be brought into the building underground, where practicable, and should be kept well separated from electric power service. Telephone cables should be routed to avoid locations where they would be subject to mechanical injury, excessive heat, or chemical erosion.

PANELBOARDS AND SWITCHBOARDS

All panelboards and switchboards should be of the dead front type, enclosed in metal cabinets with hinged doors and latches, and with the connection schedule under a transparent protective material. Where locked cabinets are provided, all locks should be keyed alike.

Suitable working space at panelboards and switchboards should be provided and maintained as required by the National Electrical Code, Section 1116.

Switchboards which have thermal trip overload devices should be located in a well ventilated space to prevent trip-out at less than the preset current rating due to excessive ambient temperature.

Distribution panelboards should be lo-

cated in corridors rather than in confined spaces such as linen or janitor's closets. Panelboards serving lighting circuits should be located on the same floor as the respective lighting outlets and should be spaced so that the length of the branch circuits will not exceed approximately 100 ft.

SWITCHES

Automatic circuit breakers for power and light feeders and for the lighting and receptacle branch circuits, while more expensive than fused switches for the initial installation, are preferred.

The general types of automatic circuit breakers usually employed are thermal or magnetic, or a combination of both. The thermal type will permit a long delay before tripping on light overloads or a short delay on heavy overloads. The magnetic type will permit instantaneous tripping on heavy overloads or short circuits. A combination thermal and magnetic tripping action for the circuit breaker has wide applications and is preferred for protection of small wires and flexible cords used on lighting and appliance branch circuits.

Local and wall switches of the silent type are recommended in all patient areas to reduce noise. Wall-mounted switches are preferred to pull switches to reduce maintenance. Where lights are installed in small closets, door-operated switches are recommended. Switches installed or operated within a location defined as hazardous because of use or storage of combustible anesthetic agents should be approved for use in Class 1, Group C hazardous atmospheres. Switches controlling the ungrounded circuits in anesthetizing locations such as operating and delivery rooms must have a disconnecting pole in each conductor.

Switching of lighting circuits by means of a low voltage control system is applicable to hospitals, particularly in large areas such as auditoriums, assembly halls, or laboratories.

WIRE

All feeders and branch circuits should have high grade insulation as required or permitted by the National Electrical Code to assure optimum life and dependability of the electrical system. High temperature wire is required at range hoods, boilers, etc. Lead sheath or waterproof wire should be used underground and where condensation may form, as in outdoor conduits, refrigerator boxes, roof slabs, and connections to outside lights. The Code should be consulted for special conditions.

CONDUIT

All hospital wiring should be in conduit to facilitate alterations and repairs. Wiring for the patient-nurse call system should be in conduit of ample size to permit a reasonable amount of change in the system with a minimum amount of labor and structural changes.

Where only one set of service conductors is brought into the building underground, spare conduit facilities should be provided to expedite restoration of service in case of a failure in the service conductors between the building and the street or main service connection.

Underground conduit should be nonmetallic and encased in concrete. Explosion-proof wiring must be in rigid conduit. Spare conduits or conduit sleeves through walls or floors are advisable where future service is planned or contemplated.

RECEPTACLES

Convenience outlets should be installed in all places where plug-in service is likely to be required. Duplex receptacles are generally preferred, except for heavy duty service or other specific requirements. Grounding type receptacles should be installed in kitchens, pantries, utility rooms, laundries, laboratories, boiler rooms, and other work areas likely to have wet floors.

Each operating and delivery room should be provided with not less than three receptacles of the lock-in type suitable for interchangeable type plugs as described in NFPA No. 56 of The National Fire Protection Association.

Patients' bedrooms should have at least three duplex outlets for single-patient rooms, with two outlets near the head of the bed. Rooms for more than one patient should have a similar arrangement of outlets. Preferably, there should be two duplex outlets at the head of each bed, or at least three outlets on the head wall for each two beds side-by-side.

Each bed in recovery rooms and in intensive care nursing rooms should have two duplex receptacles near the head of the bed. Intensive care nursing rooms should, in addition, have two 3-phase, 4-pole outlets, 30 amperes or larger, as required, for motorized equipment and mobile X-ray. The recently introduced 30 ma mobile X-ray requires 60-ampere, 230-volt receptacles.

Corridors should have grounding type outlets, rated at 20 or 30 amperes, as required for use of mobile X-ray and cleaning machines. In corridors of patient areas, outlets should be spaced on 40-ft.

HAZARDOUS LOCATIONS

Anesthetic storage rooms within the surgical suites are considered hazardous throughout. Rooms for bulk storage of unopened containers of anesthetic agents in a relatively remote area are generally not considered hazardous locations.

The extent of the hazardous location of an anesthetizing space for administering flammable anesthetics or disinfectants is considered to include the entire floor area of the room, and to a height of 5 ft above the floor. All hazardous locations require special attention to construction, equipment, and operation as precautions against ignition of these agents which cause fires and explosions. All equipment used in these areas should be approved for use in Class 1, Group C hazardous atmospheres. For specific requirements, see NFPA No. 56.

All hazardous locations require conductive floors for electrically intercoupling all people and equipment in the room to prevent electro-static sparks which might ignite flammable gasses or vapors.

Operating and delivery rooms require ungrounded electrical distribution systems for all wiring, except for fixed nonadjustable lighting fixtures located more than 8 ft above the floor for the purpose of minimizing the hazard of electric shock and sparks from the electric system.

A ground detector system is required for the purpose of warning of accidental or fault ground on the ungrounded system. Wiring and equipment installed above hazardous location, more than 5 ft above the floor, should be enclosed or guarded to prevent sparks or hot particles from falling into the hazardous location. All furniture and mobile equipment should be conductive and in electrical contact with the conductive floor.

Controlled humidity of at least 50 per cent is considered an important factor in the control of static electricity.

COMMUNICATION SYSTEMS

NURSES' CALL SYSTEMS

Call systems for nursing service vary from the simplest type of a signal system to two-way voice communication. An important feature common to all systems is that the switch provided for patients' use will register the call at the nurses' station. This feature may be varied to fit any practicable situation by the various types of switches for actuating calls and the various points and means of registering calls. Cord operated switches are preferable for isolation or contagious areas because these cords are inexpensive

and may be removed and incinerated. A new cord can then be installed for each new patient.

Registration of calls should include a signal light in the corridor over the door of the room where the call originates. A selection of lights, buzzers, bells, chimes, and annunciators are available for registering calls at the nurses' station, floor pantries, utility rooms, or other duty stations.

Emergency calls, actuating distinctive signals, are usually installed in patients' toilets and sometimes incorporated into the regular call station at the patient's bed for use by the nurse when she needs assistance. Call stations should be provided for nurses' use in nurseries, children's wards, operating, and delivery rooms.

Two-way voice communication is a feature which may be added to the signal system described. Where it is planned for economy reasons to first install a signal system and later add the voice feature, conduits large enough to accommodate the wiring of the final installation should be included in the original installation.

PAGING SYSTEMS

Paging systems for doctors and staff may be the wired or radio type. The wired paging system usually includes a microphone and/or a sending station for calling or signaling to one or a combination of the following: loud speakers, coded chimes, illuminated numerals, bell taps, or annunciator drops.

DOCTOR'S IN-AND-OUT REGISTER

Usually these registers include boards containing staff doctors' names at all entrances normally used by doctors and at the telephone switchboard. All boards are electrically connected to register the same signal simultaneously. A recall feature may be included which consists of a flasher unit having a motor driven interrupter which actuates a flashing light at the doctor's name on all register boards. The control for this unit is located at the telephone switchboard. The recall feature assures the doctor's attention upon entering or leaving the hospital.

CALL-BACK SYSTEM

Call-back systems provide a relatively inexpensive means of "wake-up" or calling service for interns and nurses. Calls originating in the office or at the switchboard actuate a bell or buzzer in the quarters. An answer switch is provided for acknowledgement that the call has been received. Wiring

may be arranged for individual calls or, if desired, it can be connected so that one button may call several rooms or stations simultaneously.

TELEPHONES

Interconnecting telephones should be provided for all department heads, assistants, operation and delivery suites, nurses' stations, offices, housekeeper, maintenance supervisor, doctors' rooms, record rooms, and diet kitchens. These may be connected on a dial system which will permit interior communication through the hospital switchboard without the assistance of an operator. At all private and semi-private beds, telephone jacks should be installed so that a telephone can be plugged in at any time, with a minimum rental charge to the hospital. This arrangement is efficient and satisfactory.

Conduit should be provided for all telephone wiring. Installation and connection of wiring is usually done by the telephone company. Provision should be made for public telephones at convenient locations for visitors and others requiring the use of pay stations.

INTERCOMMUNICATION SYSTEMS

Telautograph transcribers which transmit written messages from one department to another are being used successfully in some hospitals. These systems leave a written record of the mesage at the sending and receiving stations. Where installation of this equipment is contemplated, conduit should be installed for the necessary wiring. This equipment may be obtained on a rental or purchase agreement.

Audible speaker systems are frequently used for communication between departments and within specific branches. These systems may be arranged for individual as well as collective announcements.

Loud speaker systems which include microphone, amplifier, and loud speakers are often required for extending the voice range, as in auditoriums, outdoor assembly, parking lot, or to issue general instructions as in the case of fire or any other type of disaster.

CARRIER TUBE SYSTEMS

Pneumatic tube systems are extremely useful to carry records, prescriptions, or orders from one department to another. The carriers of these systems are propelled by electrically operated vacuum systems or vacuum-pressure combinations.

Nonpowered gravity drops with hand-operated lifts are sometimes useful between one floor and another directly above or below.

ELEVATORS

Size and shape of the elevator car and its door opening are related to the needs of vehicle traffic. The length and width of patients' beds are determining factors in car depth and door width.

Hospital elevators are usually limited to three sizes, as standardized by the industry and the National Elevator Manufacturers' Institute. These sizes comply with the requirements of the American Standard Safety Code for Elevators, A17.1-1955 and in respect to rated load capacity in pounds and the outside dimensions of the car platform the sizes are as follows: 3500 lb, 5 ft 4 in. by 8 ft; 4000 lb, 5 ft by 8 ft 4 in.; and 5000 lb, 7 ft by 8 ft 4 in.

Small and medium size hospitals, where comparatively few elevators are needed, use these hospital-size cars almost exclusively because of the economic advantage of their "all-purpose" characteristics. Automatic operation without an attendant, except during peak service demands, visiting periods, and vehicle transportation, is common practice in most of the small and medium size hospitals. Larger hospitals sometimes employ a few "office building-size" cars for passenger service only. Automatically operated elevators should be provided with a keyed switch which permits an attendant to bypass any calls and travel directly to any station. This feature is needed for hospital-type elevators as it is not desirable to combine passenger traffic with vehicle traffic such as bed or stretcher patients or food carts.

It is desirable that the electric service to elevators be arranged so that at least one of the hospital-type elevators may be operated on the emergency system. Switching should be arranged to permit connection of the emergency power to bring any elevator to a landing in case it has been trapped between floors by interruption of the normal power.

FIRE ALARMS

Fire alarms are required in every hospital. Alarms as required by the "Building Exits Code" apply except where they may be modified by additional requirements of local or state codes.

Devices used in the alarm system should be listed by Underwriters Laboratories, Inc., or Factory Mutual Laboratories, or certified to comply with the requirements of the listed devices. In all cases the system should be electrically supervised, preferably the code signal type and should comply with NFPA No. 72, "Proprietary Signaling Systems." To minimize panic among patients when a fire alarm is sounded, a pre-signal feature is generally recommended, designed so that the initial signals will sound only in department offices, engine rooms, fire brigade stations, nurses' stations, and other central locations. Chimes or lighted signal gongs are recommended in nursing areas.

CLOCKS

An electric clock system, rather than individual clocks, should be provided with clocks in all offices, nurses' stations, main lobby, waiting rooms, telephone switchboard, kitchen, dining room, laundry, boiler room, operating and delivery rooms. The clocks should be of the recessed type, preferably with a narrow frame. Clocks in operating and delivery rooms should have sweep second hands. The need for elapsed time indicators in operating and delivery rooms is controversial.

Two types of clock systems are available: the wired and the electronic. The wired system requires wiring from the individual clocks to the master control clock. The electronic system requires no wiring connection between the individual clocks and the master clock. Control is by means of electrical impulses sent out by the master control clock and picked up by a radio-type receiver in each clock which is operated from any convenience outlet.

X-RAY

Voltage supplied to the X-ray unit should be nearly constant so that images and pictures will be uniform. An independent feeder with capacity sufficient to prevent a voltage drop greater than 3 per cent is recommended. A separate transformer for the X-ray feeder is desirable and is a requirement for most installations.

REFERENCES

1. U. S. Department of Commerce, National Bureau of Standards, *National Electrical Safety Code*, Handbook H30, U. S. Government Printing Office, Washington 25, D. C., 1949, 408 pp.
2. National Fire Protection Association, *National Electrical Code*, NFPA No. 70, National Fire Protection Association, Boston, Mass., 1956, 491 pp.
3. Illuminating Engineering Society, *Lighting Handbook, 3rd Edition,* Illuminating Engineering Society, New York, N. Y., 1959, 1100 pp.
4. National Fire Protection Association, *Building Exits Code, 15th Edition*, NFPA No. 101, National Fire Protection Association, Boston, Mass., 1958, 256 pp.
5. National Fire Protection Association, *Recommended Safe Practice for Hospital Operating Rooms*, NFPA No. 56, National Fire Protection Association, Boston, Mass., 1956, 48 pp.
6. American Society of Mechanical Engineers, *Safety Code for Elevators, Dumbwaiters and Escalators, A17.1-1955,* The American Society of Mechanical Engineers, New York, N. Y., 1955, 290 pp.
7. Underwriters Laboratories, Inc., 207 East Ohio Street, Chicago 11, Ill.
8. Factory Mutual Laboratories, 1151 Boston-Providence Turnpike, Norwood, Mass.
9. National Fire Protection Association, *Proprietary, Auxiliary, Remote Station and Local Protective Signaling Systems*, NFPA No. 72, National Fire Protection Association, Boston, Mass., 1958, 29 pp.
10. American Standards Association, *Preferred Voltage Ratings for A-C Systems and Equipment. ASA 84.1* (EEI R-6; NEMA 117), American Standards Association, 1954.
11. General Electric Company, *Hospital Handbook for Architects and Engineers,* General Electric Company, Schenectady, N. Y., 1949.
12. Westinghouse Electric Corporation, *Hospital Electrical Planning for Architects and Engineers,* Westinghouse Electric Corporation, East Pittsburgh, Penna., 1951, 238 pp.
13. Griffin, N. L., *Emergency Power for Hospitals,* (AIEE Conference Paper No. Cp 56-278), American Institute of Electrical Engineers, New York, N. Y., Jan. 30-Feb. 3, 1956.
14. Griffin, N. L., "Telephone Systems for Hospitals," *Architectural Record,* Vol. III, No. 6, pp. 221-225, June 1952.
15. Griffin, N. L., "Recomended Lighting Practices—Put the Hospital in its Best Light," *Modern Hospital,* Vol. 84, No. 3, pp. 84-87, March 1955.
16. Griffin, N. L. "Electrical Safety in Hospital Operating Rooms," (AIEE Conference Paper No. 58-579), American Institute of Electrical Engineers, New York, N. Y., April 30, 1958. Published in *Power Apparatus and Systems,* No. 38, pp. 698-702, Oct. 1958.
17. Kusters, N. L., "The Ground Detector Problem in Hospital Operating Rooms," *Transactions,* Vol. 2, No. 1, Engineering Institute of Canada, Ottawa, Canada, 1958.
18. McKinley, D. W. R., "An Electronic Ground Detector," *Transactions,* Vol. 2, No. 1, Engineering Institute of Canada, Ottawa, Canada, 1958, 44 pp.

LOAD AND CIRCUIT CHART

	Typical Connected Watts	Preferred Circuit	Volts	Wires	Circuit Breaker or Fuse	Outlets on Circuit	Type of Outlet	Notes
Kitchen								
Range	12000	10 kw	120/240	3 #6	50A	1	Special Purpose	Use of more than one outlet is not recommended.
Oven (built-in)	4500	6 kw	120/240	3 #10	30A	1	Special Purpose	
Range Top	6000	6 kw	120/240	3 #10	30A	1	Special Purpose	May be direct-connected.
Range Top	3300	4 kw	120/240	3 #12	20A	1	Special Purpose	
Dishwasher	1200	2 kw	120	2 #12	20A	1	Parallel Grounding	These appliances may be direct-connected on a single circuit. Grounded receptacles required, otherwise.
Waste Disposer	300	2 kw	120	2 #12	20A	1	Parallel Grounding	
Broiler	1500	2 kw	120	2 #12	20A	1 or more	Parallel Grounding or Parallel	Heavy-duty appliances regularly used at one location should have a separate circuit. Only one such unit should be attached to a single circuit at one time.
Fryer	1300	2 kw	120	2 #12	20A	1 or more	Parallel Grounding or Parallel	
Coffeemaker	1000	2 kw	120	2 #12	20A	1 or more	Parallel Grounding or Parallel	
Refrigerator	300	2 kw	120	2 #12	20A	1 or more	Parallel Grounding or Parallel	Separate circuit serving only refrigerator and freezer is recommended.
Freezer	350	2 kw	120	2 #12	20A	1 or more	Parallel Grounding or Parallel	
Laundry								
Washing Machine	1200	2 kw	120	2 #12	20A	1 or more	Parallel Grounding	Grounding type receptacle required. Separate circuit is recommended.
Dryer	5000	6 kw	120/240	3 #10	30A	1	Special Purpose	Appliance may be direct-connected —must be grounded.
Ironer	1650	2 kw	120	2 #12	20A	1 or more	Parallel Grounding	
Hand Iron	1000	2 kw	120	2 #12	20A	1 or more	Parallel	Consider possible use in other locations.
Water Heater	3000						Special Purpose	Consult utility company for load requirements.
Living Areas								
Workshop	1500	2 kw	120	2 #12	20A	1 or more	Parallel Grounding	Separate circuit recommended.
Portable Heater	1300	2 kw	120	2 #12	20A	1	Parallel	Should not be connected to circuit serving other heavy duty loads.
Television	300	2 kw	120	2 #12	20A	1 or more	Parallel	Should not be connected to circuit serving appliances.
Portable Lighting	1200	2 kw	120	2 #12	20A	1 or more	Parallel	Provide one circuit for each 500 sq ft. Divided receptable may be switch-controlled.
Fixed Utilities								
Fixed Lighting	1200	2 kw	120	2 #12	20A	1 or more		Provide at least one circuit for each 1200 watts of fixed lighting.
Air Conditioner (¾ hp)	1200	2 kw	120	2 #12	20A	1	Parallel Grounding	Consider 4-kw 3-wire circuits to all window or console type air conditioners. Outlets may then be adapted to individual 120- or 240-volt machines. Connection to general purpose or appliance circuits is not recommended.
Air Conditioner (1½ hp)	2400	4 kw	120/240	3 #12	20A	1	Tandem Grounding	
Central Air Conditioner	5000	6 kw	120/240				Special Purpose	Consult manufacturer for recommended connections.
Sump Pump	300	2 kw	120	2 #12	20A	1 or more	Parallel Grounding	May be direct-connected.
Heating Plant	600	2 kw	120	2 #12	20A	1		Direct-connected. Individual circuit is recommended.
Fixed Bathroom Heater	1500	2 kw	120	2 #12	20A	1		Direct-connected.
Attic Fan	300	2 kw	120	2 #12	20A	1 or more	Parallel Grounding	May be direct-connected. Individual circuit is recommended.

From *Electrical Construction and Maintenance,* Copyright 1955.

Service Entrances

Calculation of a service entrance which has adequate capacity to supply the load requirements of a house is a straightforward procedure. A sample calculation is shown below based on the ratings given in the load and circuit table.

First the loads are figured for the branch circuits, which are divided into three categories:

1. *General purpose circuits:* They serve lights throughout the house and convenience outlets everywhere except in kitchen, laundry, dining area, and utility room. Generally, circuit capacity can be figured on the basis of 3 or 4 watts per sq ft (w/sq ft). Using the higher value of 4:

$$4 \text{ w/sq ft} \times 1500 \text{ sq ft} = 6000 \text{ watts}$$

2. *Small appliance circuits:* They serve convenience outlets in the kitchen, laundry, dining area, and utility room. The load on each circuit can be assumed to be 1500 or 2000 watts. Using the higher figure of 2000, the two circuits shown in the diagram will have a capacity of

$$2 \text{ circuits} \times 2000 \text{ watts} = 4000 \text{ watts}$$

However, it can be assumed that not all of the load on these two types of branch circuits will be used at any one time. So, in order to determine the service requirements for them, it can be assumed arbitrarily that the first 3000 watts will be operated at 100 per cent capacity and the remainder at only 35 per cent.

$$3000 \text{ watts} \times 100 \text{ per cent} = 3000 \text{ watts}$$
$$7000 \text{ watts} \times 35 \text{ per cent} = 2450 \text{ watts}$$

Total service requirements of general purpose and small appliance circuits = 5450 watts

3. *Fixed appliance circuits:* They serve the heavy-duty appliances, each of which requires a separate circuit. Capacities taken from the load and circuit table are listed above right. The typical household range is calculated at only two-thirds of its rated capacity, since it is assumed that not all of its elements will be operating at full load at any one time.

Range ....8000 watts

The other fixed appliances except for the heating and cooling system, are calculated at an assumed 75 per cent demand factor:

Refrigerator
    freezer .... 650 watts
Dishwasher and
    disposer ....1500 watts
Clothes washer ...1200 watts
Clothes dryer .....5000 watts
Water heater .....3000 watts
Workshop ....1500 watts
              ———————
              12,850 watts

$$12{,}850 \text{ watts} \times 75 \text{ per cent} = 9637.5 \text{ watts}$$

In calculating the heating-cooling load, the higher value of the two systems is used, since it is assumed that they will not be operating at the same time. It is recommended that the architect consult the local utility for information about central air-conditioning systems. However, for purposes of this calculation a value of 5000 watts is assumed. Since this is higher than the total of 600 watts for the heating plant and 1500 watts for the bathroom heater, this will be the value used.

Central air
    conditioning ....5000 watts
Total capacity of fixed appliance
      circuits = 22,637.5 watts
Total watts of service capacity =
5450 + 22,637.5 = 28,087.5 watts

Thus, the required current-carrying capacity of the service entrance conductors for a 120/240-volt, 3-wire, single-phase service is

$$I = \frac{P}{V} = \frac{28{,}087.5}{240} = 115 \text{ amp}$$

Knowing the current requirements for the service entrance, the proper combination of switches, control center units and wire sizes can be determined easily, as in the typical service entrance schedule shown below.

TYPICAL SERVICE ENTRANCE SCHEDULES FOR VARIOUS LEVELS OF UTILIZATION (120/240 VOLTS, 3-WIRE, SINGLE-PHASE)

Nominal Rating, Amperes	Maximum Capacity, Watts	Main Switch	Main Control Center Units	Size of Service Wire	Size of Conduit	Utilization Circuits
100	24,000	100A Sw. or 100A Cir. Bkr.	2-50A 1-20A (Water heater)	2 #2 1 #4	1¼"	General Purpose Electric Cooking Electric Laundry Water Heater Air Conditioning
150	36,000	200A Sw. (150A Fuses) or 150A Cir. Bkr.	3-50A 1-20A (Water heater)	2 #2/0 2 #2	2"	Same as for 100 amp plus electric heating for small homes
200	48,000	200A Sw. (200A Fuses) or 200A Cir. Bkr.	4-50A 1-20A (Water heater)	2 #4/0 1 #2/0	2"	Same as for 150 amp in temperate climates

From "Live Better . . . Electrically."

WIRES AND CABLES

Type	Description	Applications
R	Single conductor with rubber insulation and braided cotton covering.	General wiring where moisture is not present. Temperature rating 60 C.
RH	Similar to Type R except rubber insulation has higher resistivity to heat.	General wiring where moisture is not present; has higher current carrying capacity than Type R. Temperature rating 75 C.
RW	Similar to Type R except with moisture-resistant rubber insulation.	In all areas including damp conditions. Temperature rating and current-carrying capacity same as Type R.
RH-RW	Rubber insulation has heat- and moisture-resistant properties of Types RH and RW.	For damp locations, the temperature rating and current-carrying capacity of Type RW are used; otherwise the higher ratings of Type RH apply.
RHW	Similar to Type RH-RW.	Similar to Type RH-RW except ratings of Type RH apply for all installations.
TW	Polyvinyl chloride insulation is highly resistant to moisture, heat and corrosion. Rated at 60 C. Current capacity of Type R.	General use and use in damp areas. While allowable conduit occupancy is the same as Type R in new installations, the smaller dimensions of Type TW are used in calculating the number of conductors allowed in existing conduit or rewiring; this permits substantially higher capacities than other types of wire.
NM (non-metallic sheathed cable)	Rubber or thermoplastic-insulated conductors, with or without separate grounding conductor, covered by heavy paper wrapping and a strong braid.	Interior wiring—exposed or concealed in dry locations. Not allowed where exposed to corrosive fumes or vapors, nor embedded in masonry, concrete, fill or plaster. Use non-metallic boxes or surface devices unless grounding wire is in NM cable.
NMC (moisture- and corrosion-resistant)	Same as NM except with corrosion-resistant outer covering of impregnated braid or other material.	Same as NM except may be embedded in plaster or run in chase provided protection is afforded from nails by 1/16-in. steel plate. Neither NM or NMC may be embedded in concrete or used for service entrances.
UF (underground feeder)	Thermoplastic-insulated and jacketed conductors in single or multiple conductor styles.	Single conductor for direct burial feeders (all legs in one trench). Multi-conductor UF may be used as NMC.
AC and ACT (called armored cable)	Rubber (AC)- or thermoplastic (ACT)-insulated conductors enclosed in wound and interlocked steel armor; bonding strip under armor.	All interior wiring except in moist areas embedded in masonry, or in block walls below grade.
ACL	Same as Type AC except with lead sheath.	Moist areas, underground and embedded in concrete.
SE Style U (un-armored)	2 rubber-insulated conductors and bare neutral strands (usually spiraled around insulated conductors) covered by protective layers of rubber tape and impregnated braid. Also available with insulated neutral.	For service entrances; interior wiring of range, dryer or water heater providing heater is not fed by uninsulated conductor. With insulated neutral, use is governed by code provisions on NMC.
SE Style A (armored)	Same as Style U except with bonded steel tape under outer layer of rubber tape. Interlocked armor (not bonded) sometimes used in place of steel tape.	Same as Style U except interior applications governed by code provisions on armored cable. For interior use, tape or armor must be grounded.
SD (service drop)	Similar to SE Style U.	Primarily for drop from pole to service mast.
USE Style RR	Rubber-insulated conductors encased in neoprene jacket single or multiple conductor. (All RR conductors are not UL-approved for USE applications.)	Underground service entrances and runs in conduit or direct burial. Also used for aerial runs.
MI (mineral insulated—metal sheathed)	Conductors insulated by highly compressed refractory mineral material and enclosed in a liquid- and gas-tight flexible metallic tube.	All normal residential applications including underground, embedded in concrete and service entrance. Approved connectors required.

From "Live Better . . . Electrically."

Data from *Aspects of Electrical Conduit Installations in Houses* by Jefferson D. Brooks, Technical Bulletin No. 12, Housing and Home Finance Agency (January, 1950).

CONDUITS

Types and Uses

1. *Rigid conduit* is an older, heavier type, softer than water pipe for easy bending, but sized for same tools. Internal diameter is a bit larger than nominal size. Galvanized or other rust-resistant finish is required if ex-posed to dampness. Enameled iron conduits may be used only indoors, with no severe corrosive influences. Materials especially suited to such conditions must be used; avoid dissimilar materials. Place conduit at least 18 in. under cinder fill subject to permanent moisture, or encase in 2 in. of non-cinder concrete. In wet locations, system must be water tight; leave at least 1/4 in. air space between conduit or boxes and wall.

2. *Thin wall conduit* or *EMT* (electrical metallic tubing) is a lighter type, usually galvanized or similarly finished. It is used for exposed or concealed work where not subject to severe mechanical injury. Use is restricted in hazardous locations. Otherwise it is used as rigid conduit.

3. *Flexible conduit* is strong flexible tubing of spirally wound, interlocked steel strip, usually galvanized. Use in dry locations unless lead-covered or type RW (moisture resistant) wiring is employed. Do not use in hazardous locations. Conduits less than 1/2 in. size are used only for under-plaster extensions, fixtures, motor leads. Occasionally 3/8 in. size is permitted up to 48 in. (or longer) where larger size is not practicable.

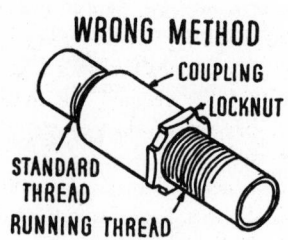

Fig. 1. Conduit connections

Fittings

1. *Running threads must not be used on rigid conduit for connections at couplings; unions must be used. Threads are finer than for standard pipe; threadless connectors are often used. The latter must be watertight if buried in masonry, concrete, fill, or used in wet places*

2. *Bushings must be used on ends of conduit unless box or fitting affords equal protection. A bushing may re-place box where more than 4 conductors leave conduit at control apparatus, if wires are bunched, taped and painted; bushings must be of insu-lated type, except for lead-covered wires*

3. *All ends of conduit must be reamed to remove rough edges*

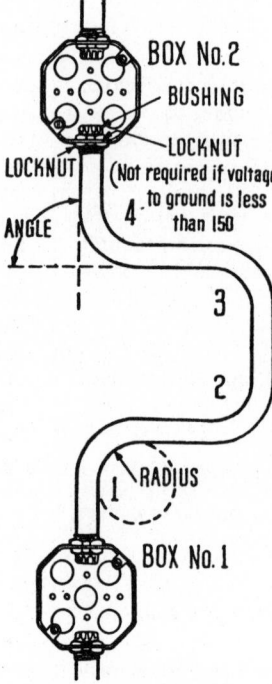

Fig. 2. Bends in circuit

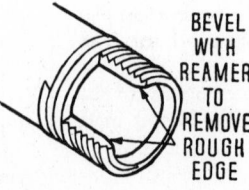

Fig. 3. Reamed end of conduit

TABLE 1	Radius of bends in inches	
Conduit (trade size) (inches)	Ordinary conductors	Lead-covered conductors
1/2	3.7	6.2
3/4	4.9	8.3
1	6.3	10.5
1 1/4	8.3	13.8
1 1/2	9.6	16.1
2	12.4	20.6
2 1/2	14.8	24.6
3	18.4	30.6
3 1/2	21.3	35.5
4	24.1	40.2
4 1/2	27.0	45.0
5	30.3	50.4
6	36.4	60.6

Bends must not injure conduit or ef-fectively reduce internal diameter. Radius of the inner edge of any bend not made by manufacturer must not be less than shown in Table 1. Conduit between 2 outlets, fittings, or combi-nation, must not have more than equiv-alent of 4 quarter bends (Fig. 2)

TABLE 2. Max Support Intervals For Con-ductors in Vertical Conduits

	Feet
No. 0 and smaller...................	100
No. 00 to No. 000.................	80
250 to 350 MCM...................	60
400 to 500 MCM...................	50
600 to 750 MCM...................	40
800 MCM and larger...............	35

Supports: conductors in vertical con-duits must be supported by clamps, wedges or insulators at intervals not greater than shown in Table 2. All conduits must be securely fastened in place. Runs must be continuous from box to box with no splices

Miscellaneous Requirements

Wires must not be inserted in conduits until rough mechanical work on house is completed. Pull wires are inserted after making up conduit connections. Graphite, talc or approved compound are used as wire lubricant; cleaning agents must not be used.

Conductors of signal or radio systems must not occupy same conduit with those of light or power systems, except for elevators, sound recording and remote control. Conduits must not pass through dust or vapor removal ducts. Rigid conduit, or flexible conduit with lead covered conductors, may pass through air-conditioning ducts only where necessary, and must not obstruct fire dampers. Switch enclosures must not be used as junction boxes to make taps or feed through.

Secondary wiring to cold cathode lamps of 1000 volts or less may occupy same conduit as branch circuit conductors. Light and power circuits of 600 volts or less may occupy same conduit, whether a-c or d-c. Circuits over 600 volts must be separated from those under 600 volts. Prevent air circulation from warmer to colder areas through conduit.

Vertical conductors No. 1 or larger require the following gutter widths if deflected where they leave cabinet:

No. 1......................3 in.
No. 0 to 200 MCM..........4 in.
250 to 900 MCM............6 in.

Where ungrounded conductors of No. 4 or larger are deflected more than 30 deg at ends of conduit run, an insulating bushing is required.

Conductors in Multiple

Where circuit capacity makes it impracticable to run all conductors in one conduit, additional conduits may be used if conductors in any one conduit are balanced in size and include one from each phase. Current in one direction must substantially equal current in the opposite direction (Fig. 4). In the case of circuits supplying cold cathode tubes, x-ray apparatus, and underplaster extensions, currents are so small that a single con-

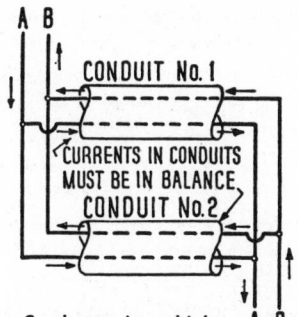

Fig. 4. Conductors in multiple

ductor may be placed in a conduit without trouble from induction. Conductors in sizes No. 0 to 500 MCM may be run in multiple if they are same length and have same area and type of insulation. Terminate both ends in manner to insure equal division of current. Except by special permission, not more than number of wires shown in Table 3 may be installed in multiple.

TABLE 3. Max No. of Wires To Be Installed in Multiple

No. of wires:	Size
3	No. 0
4	No. 00
5	No. 000 to 500 MCM

Wire Carrying Capacity

Standard tabulated carrying capacities of wires are based upon 3 or less wires in a conduit, and a surrounding temperature of not more than 86 F. Capacity must be reduced to 80 per cent of that listed for 4, 5 or 6 wires in a conduit; to 70 per cent for 7, 8 or 9 wires. A neutral conductor used with balanced circuits is not counted in applying percentages. If

TABLE 4. Temp Reduction Factors (percentages)

Max Temp (°F)	Type of insulation			
	R, RW, RU, T, and TW	RH	V and AVB	AVA and AVL
104	82	88	90	94
113	71	82	85	90
122	58	75	80	87
131	41	67	74	83
140		58	67	79
158		35	52	71
167			43	66
176			30	61
194				50

one of the system wires is missing from circuit (as in a 3-wire circuit from a 4-wire system) the neutral conductor must be counted, for it carries the unbalanced current which would have been carried by the missing wire. All current-carrying capacity must be separately reduced for high surrounding temperatures by percentages given in Table 4. If room temp is within 18 deg of a maximum allowable temp, use insulation with next higher maximum.

Conduit Size Selection

Due to bunching effect of wires in conduit, all space inside conduit cannot be filled with wire (Fig. 5). Percentages of allowable fill are calculated in sq in. of net cross-sectional area for standard size conduits, for various numbers of wires, in Table 5; Section A is for non-lead-covered wires, Section B is for lead-covered.

Where conduits cannot be replaced without damage to house, it is satisfactory to rewire conduits, for increased capacity, with more or larger wires which occupy more space than permitted for original installations. These increased values in sq in. are given in Table 5, Section C.

Cross-sectional areas of the various types of wires, in sq in., are given in Table 6. Values are added together for any combination of wires to be installed in a single conduit. This total permits ready selection of a conduit size, filled to a given percentage, from Table 5. Portion of conduit available for wires must be not less than shown for number and kinds of wires involved.

Where all wires are of one size, non-lead-covered, and for new installations, use Table 7 to select conduit size.

In general, one conduit must not contain more than 9 wires. Table 8 shows conduit capacity for a greater no. of wires, where specially permitted.

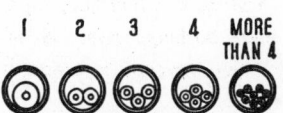

Fig. 5. Cross-sectional area of conduit which conductors may occupy

TABLE 5.—*Net cross-sectional areas in square inches of conduit and tubing available for wires and cables for general use*

Conduit (trade size) (in.)	Diameter (in.)	Area (sq. in.) (100 percent)	A. Conductors not lead-covered				B. Lead-covered conductors					C. Rewiring		
			1 conductor (53 percent)	2 conductor (31 percent)	3 conductors (43 percent)	Over 3 conductors (40 percent)	1 conductor (55 percent)	2 conductors (30 percent)	3 conductors (40 percent)	4 conductors (38 percent)	Over 4 conductors (35 percent)	1 conductor (60 percent)	2 conductors (40 percent)	Over 2 conductors (50 percent)
½	0.622	0.30	0.16	0.09	0.13	0.12	0.17	0.09	0.12	0.11	0.11	0.18	0.12	0.15
¾	.824	.53	.28	.16	.23	.21	.29	.16	.21	.20	.19	.32	.21	.27
1	1.049	.86	.46	.27	.37	.34	.47	.26	.34	.33	.30	.52	.34	.43
1¼	1.380	1.50	.80	.47	.65	.60	.83	.45	.60	.57	.53	.90	.60	.75
1½	1.610	2.04	1.08	.63	.88	.82	1.12	.61	.82	.78	.71	1.22	.82	1.02
2	2.067	3.36	1.78	1.04	1.44	1.34	1.85	1.01	1.34	1.28	1.18	2.02	1.34	1.68
2½	2.469	4.79	2.54	1.48	2.06	1.92	2.63	1.44	1.92	1.82	1.68	2.87	1.92	2.39
3	3.068	7.38	3.91	2.29	3.17	2.95	4.06	2.21	2.95	2.80	2.58	4.43	2.95	3.69
3½	3.548	9.90	5.25	3.07	4.26	3.96	5.44	2.97	3.96	3.76	3.47	5.94	3.96	4.95
4	4.026	12.72	6.74	3.94	5.47	5.09	7.00	3.82	5.09	4.83	4.45	7.63	5.09	6.36
4½	4.506	15.95	8.45	4.94	6.86	6.38	8.77	4.78	6.38	6.06	5.57	9.57	6.38	7.97
5	5.047	20.00	10.60	6.20	8.60	8.00	11.00	6.00	8.00	7.60	7.00	12.00	8.00	10.00
6	6.065	28.89	15.31	8.96	12.42	11.56	15.89	8.67	11.56	10.98	10.11	17.33	11.55	14.44

TABLE 6.—*Areas of conductors to be used in determining the number of wires of various sizes and combination that may be installed in a conduit*

Wires—approximate area in sq in.

Wire size	RF-32;[1] R;[1] RH;[1] RW[1]	TF;[2] T;[2] TW;[2] RU[2]	Lead-covered RL and RHL—individual cables			AVA	AVB	AVL	Bare
			1 conductor	2 conductors	3 conductors				
18	0.0167	0.0088	...	...	...	...	...	...	0.0013
16	.0196	.0109	...	...	...	...	...	...	.0020
14	.0327	.0135	0.062	0.115	0.273	0.047	0.033	0.080	.0032
12	.0384	.0172	.066	.146	.301	.055	.040	.091	.0051
10	.0460	.0224	.096	.180	.363	.064	.047	.102	.0081
8	.0760	.0408	.132	.255	.528	.075	.057	.119	.0130
6	.1238	.0819	.188	.369	.738	.122	.094	.145	.027
4	.1605	.1087	.237	.457	.916	.155	.123	.181	.042
3	.1817	.1263	...	...	...	...	...	...	.053
2	.2067	.1473	.283	.578	1.146	.200	.166	.255	.067
1	.2715	.2027	.352	.756	1.49	.268	.229	.300	.087
0	.3107	.2367	.396	.859	1.70	.307	.264	.341	.109
00	.3578	.2781	.454	.980	1.94	.353	.307	.390	.137
000	.4151	.3288	.515	1.123	2.24	.406	.358	.447	.173
0000	.4840	.3904	.593	1.302	2.68	.478	.425	.521	.219
250	.5917	.4877	.754	...	3.20	.616	.572	.715	.260
300	.6837	.5581	.850	...	3.62	.692	.649	.800	.312
350	.7620	.6291	.950	...	4.02	.778	.731	.885	.364
400	.8365	.6969	1.02	...	4.52	.850	.800	.960	.416
500	.9834	.8316	1.18	...	5.28	.995	.945	1.118	.520

[1] For general use. [2] For rewiring existing conduits.

TABLE 7.—*Number of conductors in conduit or tubing—for general use in new installations*

Wire types RF-32, R, RH, RW, RU, TF, T, and TW

Wire size	Maximum number of wires in conduit or tube								
	1	2	3	4	5	6	7	8	9
18	½	½	½	½	½	½	½	¾	¾
16	½	½	½	½	½	½	¾	¾	¾
14	½	½	½	½	¾	¾	1	1	1
12	½	½	½	¾	¾	1	1	1	1¼
10	½	¾	¾	¾	1	1	1	1¼	1¼
8	½	¾	¾	1	1¼	1¼	1¼	1½	1½
6	½	1	1	1¼	1½	1½	2	2	2
4	½	1¼	[1] 1¼	1½	1½	2	2	2	2½
3	¾	1¼	1¼	1½	2	2	2	2½	2½
2	¾	1¼	1¼	2	2	2	2½	2½	2½
1	¾	1½	1½	2	2½	2½	2½	3	3
0	1	1½	2	2	2½	2½	3	3	3
00	1	2	2	2½	2½	3	3	3	3½
000	1	2	2	2½	3	3	3	3½	3½
0000	1¼	2	2½	3	3	3	3½	3½	4
250	1¼	2½	2½	3	3	3½	4	4	4½
300	1¼	2½	2½	3	3½	4	4	4½	4½
350	1¼	3	3	3½	3½	4	4½	4½	5
400	1½	3	3	3½	4	4	4½	5	5
500	1½	3	3	3½	4	4½	5	5	6

[1] 1 in. for services not over 50 ft long, with not more than 2 quarter bends, and using bare neutral.

TABLE 8—*More than 9 conductors in conduit (between motor and controller, stage pockets, border circuits, sign flashers, and elevator control wires)*

Wire types RF-32, R, RH, RW, RU, TF, T, and TW

Wire size	Maximum number of wires in conduit or tube						
	¾ in.	1 in.	1¼ in.	1½ in.	2 in.	2½ in.	3 in.
18	12	20	35	49	80	115	176
16	10	17	30	41	68	97	150
14	....	10	18	25	40	59	90
12	....	....	15	21	35	50	77
10	....	....	13	17	29	41	64
8	....	....	....	10	17	25	38
6	....	....	....	....	....	15	23

EXAMPLE—

Problem: what size conduit is required for 3 No. 14, 3 No. 10 and 2 No. 6 type RW wires for a new installation.

Solution: from Table 6 select:

No. 14—0.0327 × 3—0.0981
No. 10— .0460 × 3—0.1380
No. 6— .1238 × 2—0.2476
Total 0.4837 sq in.

From Table 5, for more than 3 conductors, 0.60 sq in. represents the smallest conduit, 1¼ in. size, which will receive the wires and be filled to not more than 40 per cent of its total cross-sectional area. However, a 1-in. conduit would receive the 6 smaller wires.

Data from the Bell Telephone System

Recent improvements and expansion of telephone service, such as direct in and out dialing, teletypewriters, telephone-connected data-processing machines, cordless switchboards, loud-speaker telephones, automatic answering telephones, etc., require more wiring and switching equipment than the earlier and simpler systems. Adequate space must be provided for this purpose.

In recent years, major advances have been made in determining the most effective and economical allowances for telephone equipment installation. These average allowances are presented here with a word of caution. With telephone technology ever changing, these equipment-to-floor area ratios should be used only as a guide or starting point for planning. The local telephone company consultant should be called in to review the specific requirements for any building.

Underfloor layouts

For the two general types of underfloor distribution systems—duct-type and cellular steel—minimum telephone requirements for the modern building are as follows.

Duct-type underflooring: Parallel runs should be spaced approximately every 4½ ft. Cross runs and junction boxes should be located every 40 ft or less, depending on floor layout.

Cellular steel: The system must have sufficient header ducts connecting to telephone equipment closets. These headers should be connected to the cell area at intervals of not more than 50 ft.

It is desirable to have telephone raceways separate from electrical conduit systems. The standard space allocation: one desk per 100 sq ft floor space. Allow one telephone per desk.

Raceway capacity should be provided accordingly: 1 sq in. of raceway for every 100 sq ft of floor area served.

Zones

Large floor areas should be divided into smaller areas called "zones" with an equipment closet for each. Maximum zone size, limited by the resistance of the cable, is 10,000 sq ft. Recommended zone size for economy is 4,000 to 6,000 sq ft.

Zone equipment closets

Preferred practice is to locate switching equipment for all telephones in one zone in a special closet provided for that purpose. This eliminates noise, improves overall office appearance, and permits telephone personnel to work without seriously disturbing the tenants. The total effect is more efficient use of building space than if separate equipment were mounted near each of the telephone set locations.

Planning data for the zone equipment closet are shown in the following table:

	Walk-in closet	Shallow closet
Depth (feet)		
Minimum	3	1½
Maximum	None	2½
Width (feet)		
Minimum	5	3 ft
Maximum	None	None
Floor area (sq ft/ 1,000 sq ft floor)	6	None
Length of walls (ft/ 1,000 sq ft floor)	2½	2½
Minimum height doors	6 ft 8 in.	6 ft 8 in.*
Minimum width doors	3 ft	3 ft †

When shallow closets are used, the center post between double doors should be eliminated, where possible.

†*Minimum for single door: 2½ ft for double doors.*

In addition, all closets should have the following:

Walls lined with ¾-in. thick 8-ft high plyboard

At least one ceiling light controlled by a wall switch

One separately fused 20-ampere 3-wire circuit run to at least two 110-volt duplex receptacles or an electrical plug-in strip

Terminal rooms and equipment rooms

Main terminal rooms and equipment rooms (where needed) should be centrally located and adequately sized. They must be properly lighted, well ventilated, provided with power outlets, as dustproof as possible, and located in areas not subject to dampness or flooding. They must be readily accessible to telephone service personnel at all times. Equipment loads may be heavy and special structural provisions may be required. It is imperative that the telephone company be consulted in the design of these rooms.

Separate equipment rooms are required in most large installations, especially where switchboards or PBX systems are used. Where direct in and out dialing is used, equipment rooms may not be required.

Risers: Riser cables from the main terminal room to the various floors of the building may be brought up through conduits or shafts, depending upon the type and size of the building. For maximum efficiency they should be centrally located. Large buildings may require more than one riser shaft.

Entrance: Telephone service is brought to the building by the telephone company by either underground or aerial cable, depending upon the type of service available in the area. Where the local service is overhead, the entrance to the building may be by underground cable through a conduit provided by the owner according to the specifications of the telephone company.

By J. F. McPARTLAND, *Engineering Editor, Electrical Construction and Maintenance*

A. "A jack panel 2 in. wide, 19 in. long with 24 pairs of jack inputs shall be mounted on front of amplifier cabinet. Nine pairs of jacks shall terminate microphone lines through seven pairs of jacks on second row which shall connect seven preamplifiers. Four additional pairs of jacks shall terminate telephone wire and input lines from rooms as indicated in drawings."

B. "The amplifier cabinet shall house a selenium rectifier designed to supply 110 volts dc for field excitation of three auditorium electrodynamic speakers."

C. "Power amplifier shall furnish all voltage for its own requirements and for the pre-amplifiers. Output shall be 50 watts with less than 5% harmonic distortion, or 40 watts with less than 2% harmonic distortion. Tube complement shall provide push-pull driver stage and push-pull parallel output stage. Overall gain of voltage and power amplifier is to be 105 db at 1000 cycles. Frequency response shall be flat from 50 to 10,000 cycles within plus or minus 2 db. Output transformer shall have tapped secondary providing a 4 to 250 ohm impedance range."

D. "A high-quality balance line transformer coupling output of power amplifier to telephone wire line input shall be furnished. Frequency response shall be 30 to 15,000 cycles within plus or minus 1 db."

E. "Voltage amplification shall be accomplished by seven preamplifiers and the master mixer. Each preamplifier shall have a separately controlled 250-ohm input impedance and shall use a 1612-type tube, the filament and plate voltages of which are supplied by the associated power amplifier.
  "The master mixer unit shall be furnished having a high-impedance input and master gain control. Control of gain to be accom-

SOUND SYSTEM LAYOUT FOR LARGE SCHOOL

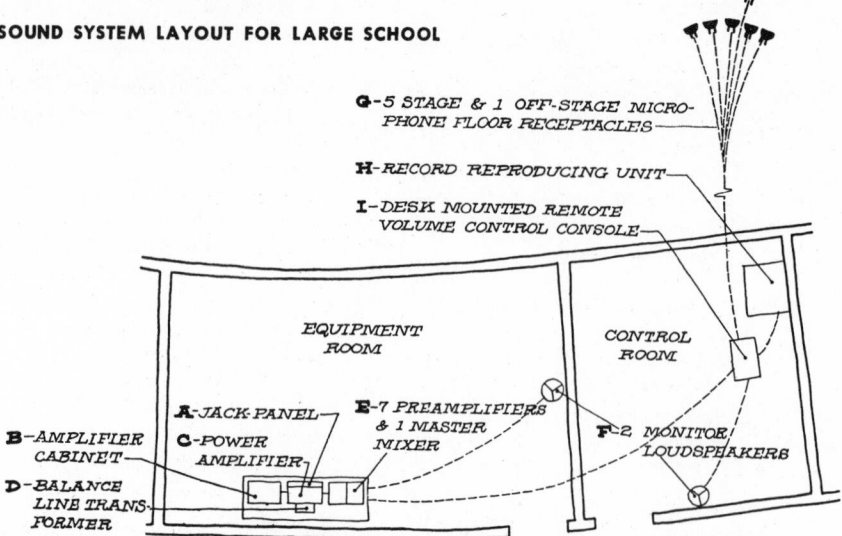

G—5 STAGE & 1 OFF-STAGE MICRO-PHONE FLOOR RECEPTACLES

H—RECORD REPRODUCING UNIT

I—DESK MOUNTED REMOTE VOLUME CONTROL CONSOLE

EQUIPMENT ROOM

CONTROL ROOM

B—AMPLIFIER CABINET

C—POWER AMPLIFIER

D—BALANCE LINE TRANSFORMER

A—JACK PANEL

E—7 PREAMPLIFIERS & 1 MASTER MIXER

F—2 MONITOR LOUDSPEAKERS

plished in same manner as preamplifiers."

F. "There shall be provided two monitor loudspeakers, one each in equipment room and control room; surface type; 3-watt; 7 in. diameter; 4-in deep cones; voice coils 6 ohms; impedance actuated by Alnico permanent magnets equipped with multi-tap speaker-matching transformers. The cones shall have a frequency range from 70 to 8000 cycles with a distribution angle of 165 degrees at 1000 cycles. Speakers shall be mounted behind metallic grille cloth in a sloping front surface-type wall housing, sloped to blend with wall at bottom."

G. "Five stage and one off-stage microphone floor receptacles are to be equipped with one each varacoustic microphone having a frequency response of 80 to 8000 cycles; adjustable characteristics so as to permit

its use in non-directional, bi-directional, or uni-directional pickup. Impedance 250 ohms, output 58 db."

H. "Reproduction of recorded programs shall be by means of high-quality record reproducing unit having a cushion-mounted motorboard and a felt-covered balanced 16-in. turntable disc, driven by a high-torque motor, through rollers which will permit operation at either 78 or 33⅓ RPM. Frequency response of turntable shall be 70 to 8500 cycles."

I. "A desk-mounted remote volume control console, to be located in control room, shall be provided for monitoring of reproduction from a remote point. Controls are to be connected in parallel to the controls on voltage amplifiers. A volume control shall be provided for the monitor speaker."

SOME TERMS USED IN SOUND WORK

Acoustic Feedback — The transfer of sound from the loudspeaker back into the microphone in such a manner as to create an annoying squeal or howl.

Amplifier — A device of electronic components used to strengthen the originating signal from a microphone or record player to the point where it will operate loudspeakers

Baffle — Most commonly used synonymously with loudspeaker housing and may be a suspended, or surface or recessed, ceiling or wall mounting device made of wood, plastic or metal, in which a loudspeaker is housed.

Booster Amplifier — An amplifier designed to boost the level of a signal from a pre-amplifier to provide power for driving loudspeakers.

Decibel — A unit used to measure the relative loudness of sound. Engineers employ the term also to designate power or voltage ratios.

Gain — Usually expressed in decibels, this

term is applied to indicate the increase in voltage or power output over the voltage or power input.

Impedance — Literally the opposition that a circuit offers to the flow of alternating current. Primarily used in the sound field as an important characteristic of amplifiers, microphones and accessories.

Loss — A term usually expressed in decibels to indicate the decrease of voltage or power output from voltage or power input.

Mixer — Usually a pre-amplifier which permits several microphones, record player and/or radio tuner to be combined through volume controls. The suitably mixed signal is then usually fed to the input of a booster amplifier.

Monitor Loudspeaker — A small loudspeaker mounted in a console or cabinet rack (or adjacent to these) which provides an audible indication of the sound level of the system and which permits preliminary adjust-

ment of the amplifier output before distribution to remote loudspeakers.

Pre-Amplifier — Frequently used synonymously with mixer, although it may be designed to provide for increasing the level of only one input signal.

Radio-Tuner — Permits reception of AM or FM programs. Differs from receiver in that it does not incorporate audio amplifier and loudspeaker.

Reproducer — The cartridge mounted in the tone arm which tracks the record grooves by means of a stylus (needle), picking up the electrical signal equivalent of the music or sound which was recorded.

Turntable Pickup — Includes the tone arm, cartridge and stylus (needle) which follows the record grooves and provides an electrical signal suitable for feeding into a pre-amplifier, mixer or amplifier.

Volume Level Indicator — A device (meter, neon bulb, etc.) which permits the operator of a sound system to determine visually the sound level output.

1. LOUDSPEAKERS
   A. Number of speakers (depends upon size, shape and type of area)
      1. One or a few, each operating at high output (high-level speaker system)
      2. Relatively large number, each operating at low output (low level speaker system)
   B. Types of speakers
      1. Cone speakers in wall-mounted, ceiling-mounted, or suspended-baffle enclosure
      2. Horn speaker (trumpet, projector horn, re-entrant horn, etc.)
   C. Amplifier connection
      1. Direct connection to amplifier output taps corresponding in impedance value (ohms) to impedance value (ohms) of a single speaker or of a number of speakers in series, parallel, or series-parallel
      2. Connection to amplifier constant-voltage output taps (70, 100, 140 volts, etc.) through constant-voltage line-matching transformers
      3. Connection to amplifier high-impedance output taps (250 or 500 ohms) through constant-impedance line-matching transformers.
   D. Placement of speakers
      1. Assure uniform loudness (eliminate dead or hot spots)
      2. In churches, theatres and auditoriums, place speakers well forward of microphones to prevent feedback (squealing)
      3. Minimize reverberation

2. AMPLIFIERS
   A. Power output
      1. Typical ratings: 6, 10, 15, 30, 50, 70, 100, 125, 250 watts
      2. Output required depends upon size and type of area to be covered in sound system (see accompanying table)
   B. Number and types of inputs (terminals for connecting high- and/or low-impedance microphones, record player or radio tuner)
   C. Output taps (impedance values)
      1. Direct connection: 4-, 8- and 16-ohm taps
      2. Constant-voltage line transformer connection: 70-, 100-, or 140-volt taps
      3. Constant-impedance line transformer connection: 250- and/or 500-ohm taps

   D. Special functions
      1. Record player built into amplifier housing
      2. Amplifier, microphone and speakers in carrying case (portable system)
   E. Controls
      1. Tone
      2. Anti-feedback
   F. Remote volume controller (plug-in unit for use at distance from amplifier)
   G. Power source
      1. 110–125 v ac, 60 cycles
      2. 115 v ac, 25 cycles
      3. 115 v dc
      4. 6 or 12 v dc
   H. Amplifier mounting
      1. Portable, with protective cage
      2. Panel-mounted, for installation on rack
   I. Cost (increases with power rating and fidelity of reproduction)

   J. Separate preamp unit (for one or more remotely located power or booster amplifier)
   K. Custom assemblies (amplifier, preamp, ratio tuner, record player, or other input devices mounted in vertical cabinet rack or console cabinet)

3. INPUT DEVICES
   A. Microphones
      1. Crystal, dynamic or velocity
      2. Omni-directional, bi-directional, or uni-directional (cardioid)
   B. Record player (automatic or manual)
   C. Tape player
   D. FM-AM radio tuner
   E. Tone generator
      1. To produce tone signal for factory work shifts, lunch periods, etc.
      2. Electronic siren for alarm applications
      3. To simulate sound of large bell in church belfry

AMPLIFIERS AND SPEAKERS FOR VARIOUS APPLICATIONS

Application	Sq. Ft. Area	Amplifier Rating (Watts)	Number of Speakers	Type of Speakers
Auditoriums	2,000	15	2	12″ Cone in Wall Baffles
	5,000	30	2	12″ Cone in Wall Baffles or
	15,000	50	4	12″ Projector Horns
Ballrooms	2,000	15	4	
	4,000	30	4	12″ Cone in Wall Baffles
	10,000	50	6	
Churches	1,000	10	2	10″ Cone in Wall Baffles
	4,000	15	2	12″ Cone in Wall Baffles
	15,000	30	4	
Classrooms, Offices and Stores	500	10	1	8″ Cone in Wall Baffles
	2,000	15	2	10″ Cone in Wall Baffles
	8,000	30	4	
Factories	1,000	15	2	12″ Projector Horns
	4,000	30	4	
	8,000	50	4	Re-Entrant Horns
	40,000	100	10	
Funeral Parlors	1,000	10	1	12″ Cone in Wall Baffles
	4,000	15	4	
	10,000	30	8	
Restaurants and Night Clubs	1,000	15	2	12″ Projector Horns
	5,000	30	6	
	10,000	50	12	
Stadiums and Gymnasiums	3,000	15	2	12″ Cone in Wall Baffles
	10,000	30	4	Re-Entrant Horns
	50,000	100	8	

NOTE: Values given in table are averages — not minimums or maximums.

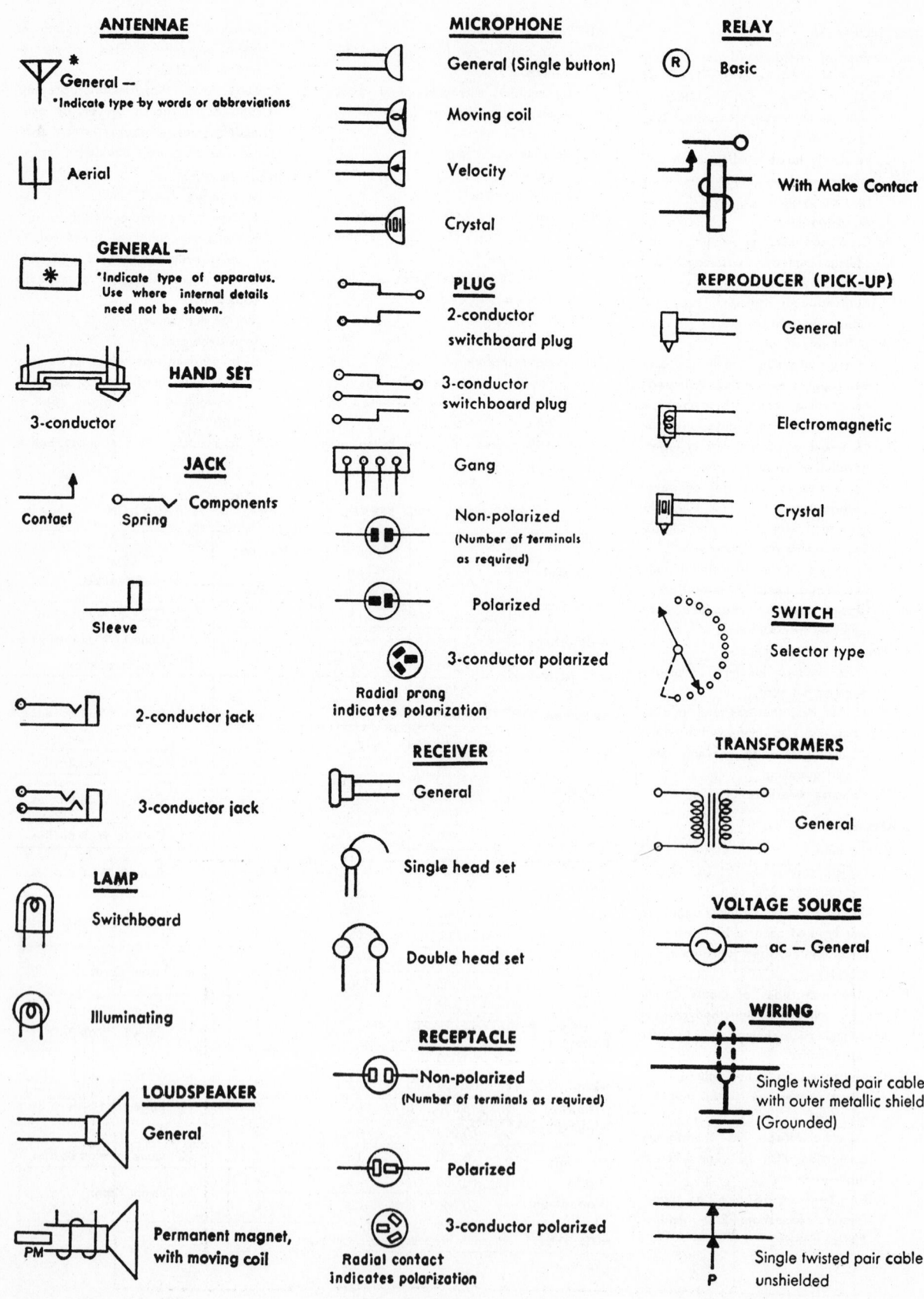

ANTENNAE

General — *
*Indicate type by words or abbreviations

Aerial

GENERAL —
*Indicate type of apparatus. Use where internal details need not be shown.

HAND SET

3-conductor

JACK

Contact   Spring   Components

Sleeve

2-conductor jack

3-conductor jack

LAMP

Switchboard

Illuminating

LOUDSPEAKER

General

Permanent magnet, with moving coil

MICROPHONE

General (Single button)

Moving coil

Velocity

Crystal

PLUG

2-conductor switchboard plug

3-conductor switchboard plug

Gang

Non-polarized
(Number of terminals as required)

Polarized

3-conductor polarized
Radial prong indicates polarization

RECEIVER

General

Single head set

Double head set

RECEPTACLE

Non-polarized
(Number of terminals as required)

Polarized

3-conductor polarized
Radial contact indicates polarization

RELAY

R   Basic

With Make Contact

REPRODUCER (PICK-UP)

General

Electromagnetic

Crystal

SWITCH

Selector type

TRANSFORMERS

General

VOLTAGE SOURCE

ac — General

WIRING

Single twisted pair cable with outer metallic shield (Grounded)

Single twisted pair cable unshielded
P

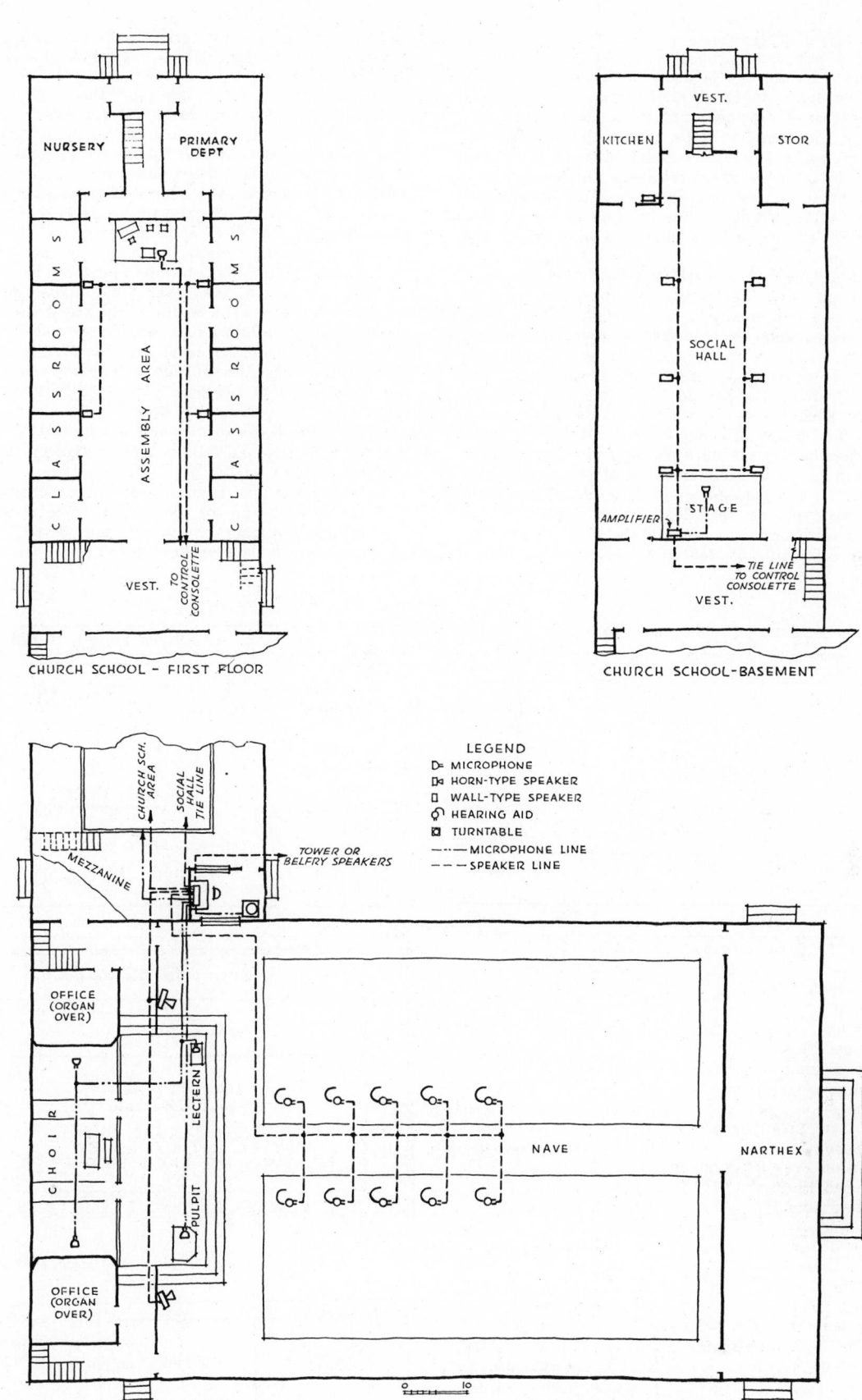

CHURCH SCHOOL - FIRST FLOOR

CHURCH SCHOOL - BASEMENT

LEGEND

D= MICROPHONE
Dロ HORN-TYPE SPEAKER
ロ WALL-TYPE SPEAKER
♪ HEARING AID
⊠ TURNTABLE
—·—·— MICROPHONE LINE
— — — SPEAKER LINE

SINGLE CHANNEL SOUND SYSTEM FOR CHURCH, CHURCH SCHOOL AND SOCIAL HALL

This section presents essential data for preliminary planning of proper space for a pipe organ. Any organ, because it is a wind-driven instrument, **must have space to breathe.** Its musical value may easily be lost if crowded into inadequate space.

Usually the smallest pipe organ that should be considered for any church should have at least five stops (a "stop" being one complete set of pipes). Such an organ could be used in a church seating up to three hundred people, but its limited variety of tone would be more in keeping with a chapel seating up to one hundred people.

In Table 1, below, church auditoriums have been listed by size together with what normally can be accepted as a minimum and fair size pipe organ. This table is based upon no scientific or musical law and will therefore be a rough guide in early stages of planning. It provides an indication of the minimum number of stops that should be included in the pipe organ for a church of known seating capacity.

Table 2 is a specification for a typical pipe organ installation having eleven stops and one independent pedal stop (a large, deep-toned set of pipes played by foot pedals), and perhaps a set of chimes. The names of the stops in the specifications are given in the picturesque technical nomenclature of the art. The architect will naturally confer with a qualified organist and organ manufacturers and the budget committee before final decisions regarding the specifications are made.

The recommended height for the organ loft is sixteen feet which includes space for pipes and wind chest. However, it is possible to "squeeze" the organ into a twelve-foot height by mitering some of the pipes. The wind chest will determine the length and width of the organ loft. The average length of each chest is 8 ft. 6 in. There will probably be three or more chests, one for each division of the organ ("great," "swell," "choir," etc.). The chest width varies with the number of stops that must be mounted on it, allowing not less than nine inches for each stop. In addition to the width of the chest itself there should run parallel to it a walkboard not less than fifteen inches wide, for servicing. See Fig. 1. On three sides of the chest it would be well to add one foot for the installation of the bass pipes, which may not be installed on the wind chest because of their large size.

The required space for each division of the organ can be estimated as follows: (See Fig. 1)
1. Height=12' to 16'
2. Length=8'-16" (Length of wind chest)+2'-0" (1' on each end for bass pipes), a total of 10'-6".
3. Width=(number of stops) times 9"+15" (walkboard) +1' 0" (for base pipes).

TABLE 1
Number of Manual Stops

No. of Seats	Min.	Fair	No. of Manuals
100 or less	5	8 to 10	2
250	6	12 to 15	2
400	8	15 to 20	2-3
600	10	20 to 30	2-3
800	12	25 to 35	2-3-4
1000	15	35 to 40	2-3-4
1500	20	40 to 45	3-4
2000	30	50 to 75	3-4

TABLE 2

Stop Name	No. of Pipes
Great Organ	
8' Diapason	73 Pipes
8' Clarabella	73 Pipes
4' Octave	73 Pipes
8' Tromba	73 Pipes
8' Stopped Flute	From
4' Flute d'Amour	Swell
8' Aeoline	
Chimes	20 Tubes
Swell Organ	
8' Diapason	73 Pipes
16' Bourdon	
8' Stopped Flute	97 Pipes
4' Flute d'Amour	Unit Stop
2' Flageolet	
8' Viole d'Orchestre	73 Pipes
8' Viole Celeste	73 Pipes
8' Aeoline	73 Pipes
8' Oboe	73 Pipes
8' Vox Humana	73 Pipes
Pedal Organ	
16' Bourdon	44 Pipes
8' Flute	From Bourdon
16' Gedeckt	From
8' Stopped Flute	Swell

TABLE 3

	Pipes	Length	Width	Height
1. Bourbon	16'	44	13'6"	3'6"	10'6"
2. Open Diapason	16'	44	12'0"	2'6"	19'0"
3. Trombone	16'	44	10'4"	1'4"	12'0"*
4. Violone	16'	44	10'4"	1'5"	19'4½"
5. Diapason	32'	12	18'9"	3'8"	34'9"
6. Bombarde	32'	12	10'3"	2'4"	23'0"*
7. Second Bourdon	16'	44	Same as No. 1 approx.		
8. Metal Diapason	16'	44	8'9"	2'9"	21'0"
9. Bourdon	32'	12	15'3"	2'0"	18'0"

*—Average mitered length.

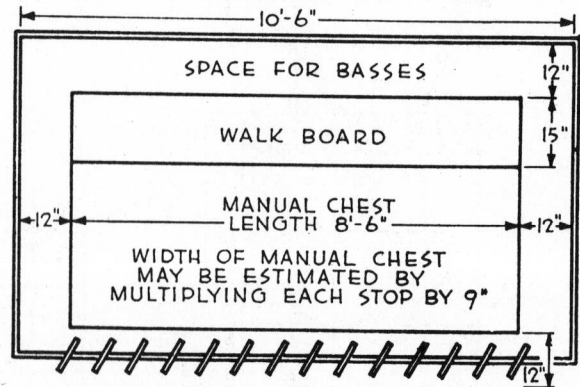

Fig. 1. Above plan is one section of total organ shown below

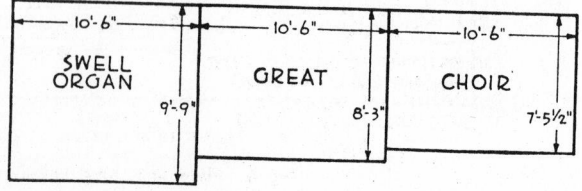

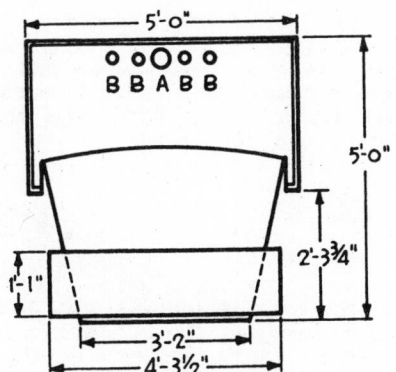

Fig. 2. Plan of organ console

The average organ console is about 4 ft 3 in. high. An organ having more than three manuals requires 3 in. additional height for each manual added.

A 2"-3" CONDUIT, LOW VOLTAGE, CONSOLE TO ORGAN MECHANISM.

B ONE EACH OF FOLLOWING:
1"-1½" CONDUIT TO LOW VOLTAGE FEED LINES AT GENERATOR.
¾"-1" CONDUIT, MOTOR STARTING LINES FROM CONSOLE TO BLOWER MOTOR.
CONDUIT, LIGHTS TO CONSOLE.
CONDUIT TO CHIME OR CARILLON.

These figures would hold good for a pipe organ having up to twelve stops; over that it would be well to allow two feet on three sides of the chest for bass and other large parts that may require extra room.

There still remains for consideration the space that will be required by the pedal organ. Recalling that there should be at least one pedal stop for every six or seven manual stops, it will be necessary to know which stops are most likely to be installed first. Table 3 gives the name and size of the pedal stops in the usual order. To determine which will be used and the size of the pipes, determine how many pedal stops the manual stops require on the basis of one to six or seven, and then take the required number of pedal stops in order, starting at the top of the list.

In order to supply air to the organ an electrically driven blower, similar to that shown in Fig. 3, will probably be used. From the chart and this diagram it is possible to determine the size of the room re-

quired for housing the blower, the weight of the equipment, and the size of the air duct. The horsepower required for the blower will have to be determined by the organ manufacturer. The room housing the blower, usually located below the organ, should allow standing height and a clearance of at least 15 in. on all sides.

Electronic organs are being increasingly used, especially in the smaller churches. They cost considerably less than pipe organs and require much less space. The console is usually somewhat smaller than for a pipe organ, and the only additional space required is for one or more speakers. Electronic organs may also provide carillon effects.

Carillons require an average space of 11 ft. square by 7 ft. high. They are usually electrically operated from a small keyboard about 18 in. long by 12 in. deep. The carillon speaker is usually located in the tower.

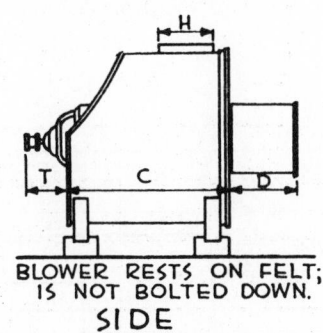

BLOWER RESTS ON FELT; IS NOT BOLTED DOWN.

SIDE

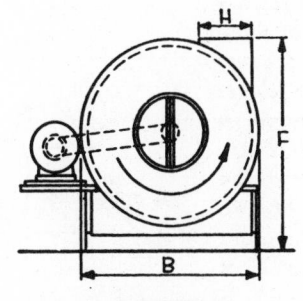

FRONT

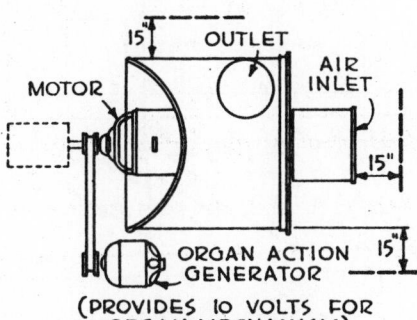

(PROVIDES 10 VOLTS FOR ORGAN MECHANISM)
(MAY BE IN DOTTED POSITION AT LEFT)

PLAN

DIMENSIONS IN INCHES

HORSE POWER	½ *	¾	1	2	3	5	7½
B	27	33½	33½	40	40	46	46
C	22	25	28½	31	36	38	38
D	12	15	15	15	15	15	15
F	34	40	40	46	46	53	53
H	8	10	12	12	15	15	15
T	5	5	7	7	9	10	10

WEIGHT IN POUNDS

WEIGHT (LBS)	400	650	700	950	1025	1150	1300

* SPEED: 1750 R.P.M.   ALL OTHER MOTORS: 1150 R.P.M.

Fig. 3. Plans and chart below may be used to determine the space required for blower room

By ALBERT R. RIENSTRA

Church Design for Music

Reverberation Times

Figure 4 gives reverberation times for church auditoriums from 10,000 to 1,000,000 cu ft in size. These values are higher than generally used for other types of auditoriums because with them organ music is enchanced a great deal and choral music somewhat. While the reverberation times for churches may fall within the range indicated by the gray band, it is recommended that the upper limit be used if possible.

The values in Fig. 4 are absolute reverberation times for the frequency range from 300 to 5,000 cps. Fig. 5, then, gives correction factors to be applied to Fig. 4 for frequencies outside this range.

Organ Space Requirements

Fig. 6 can be used as a guide for the allotment of pipe organ space. Fig. 6A gives dimensions of the pipe space required for organs installed in one section. Solid lines apply when pedal pipes are at the sides and dotted lines when they are in the rear of this section. In large churches it becomes necessary to install the pipes in two or three sections and these situations are covered in Fig. 6B. The depth curves here have a saw-tooth shape, a tooth occurring at every place where the width increases a step. The height of organ space has only two values; 13 ft and 20 ft. If there are no 16-ft open pipes, at least 13 ft height is required for the open, 8-ft pipes. For 16-ft open pipes, at least 20-ft height is required. The height then remains constant until 32 ft pipes come into the picture. For this size, it is not possible to give estimates of space as this falls into the four manual (keyboard) and cathedral classes, and each installation becomes a special one. In the region just below this, after the depth has increased to the second maximum (Fig. 6B) three-keyboard organs are specified. For this size, a third section of width may be added, the choir-pipe division, which is placed on one side of the chancel with the swell division on the other.

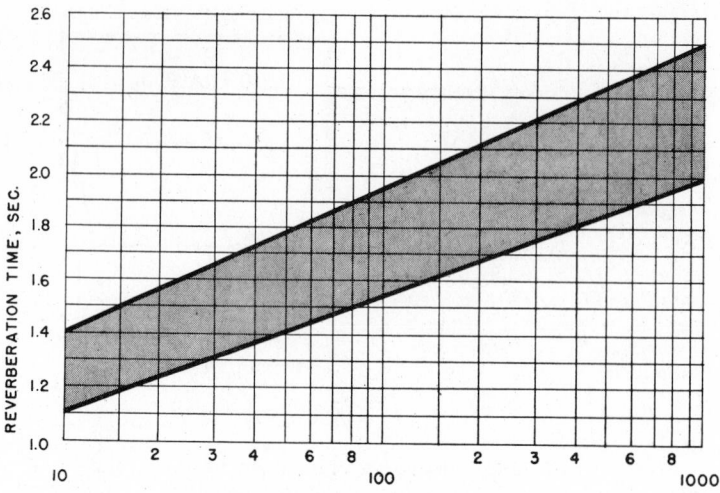

Fig. 4 — ROOM VOLUME - THOUSANDS OF CUBIC FEET

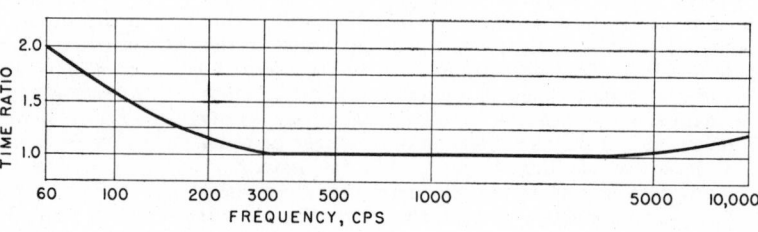

Fig. 5 — FREQUENCY, CPS

Modified from Beranek

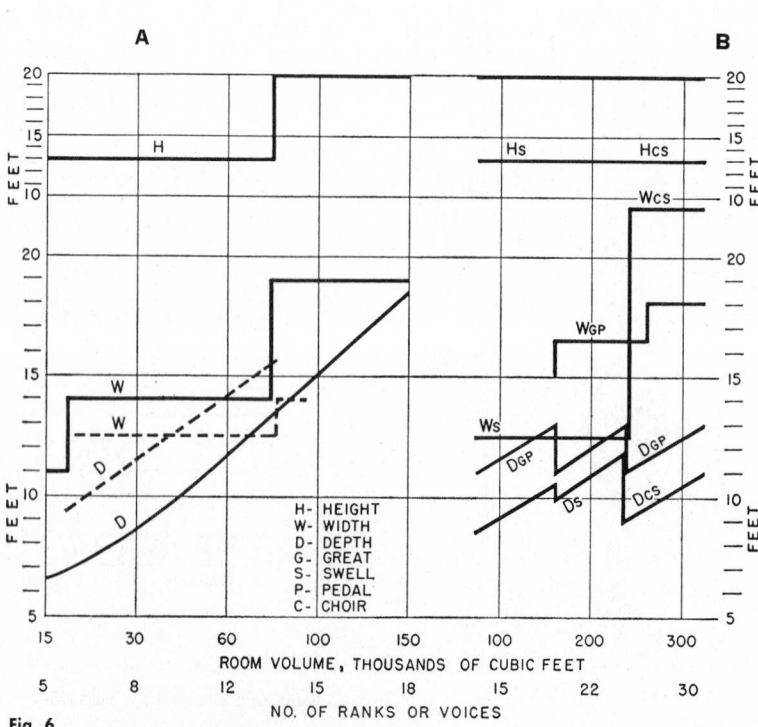

Fig. 6 — ROOM VOLUME, THOUSANDS OF CUBIC FEET / NO. OF RANKS OR VOICES

H- HEIGHT
W- WIDTH
D- DEPTH
G- GREAT
S- SWELL
P- PEDAL
C- CHOIR

By L. T. CHANDLER

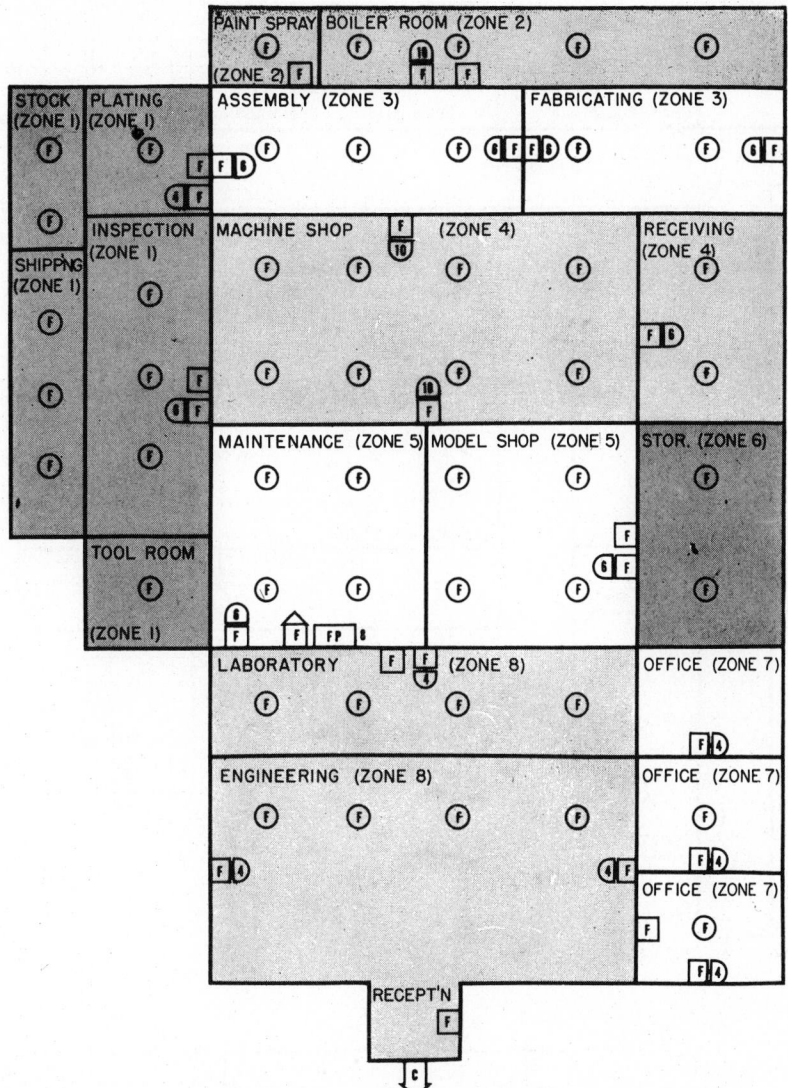

TYPICAL ALARM SYSTEM FOR AN INDUSTRIAL BUILDING

LEGEND

F MANUAL STATION. IN CASE OF CODED SYSTEM, THESE
STATIONS ARE CODED

F FIRE DETECTOR

B/F BELL. NUMERAL INDICATES DIAMETER OF BELL
IN INCHES

F HORN

FP CONTROL PANEL. NUMERAL, IF INCLUDED, INDICATES
NUMBER OF ZONES

F PRESIGNAL CHIME

F TROUBLE SIGNAL

T EXTENSION TROUBLE SIGNAL

FA ANNUNCIATOR

R PUNCH REGISTER AND TIME STAMP

C CITY FIRE ALARM BOX ON PREMISES

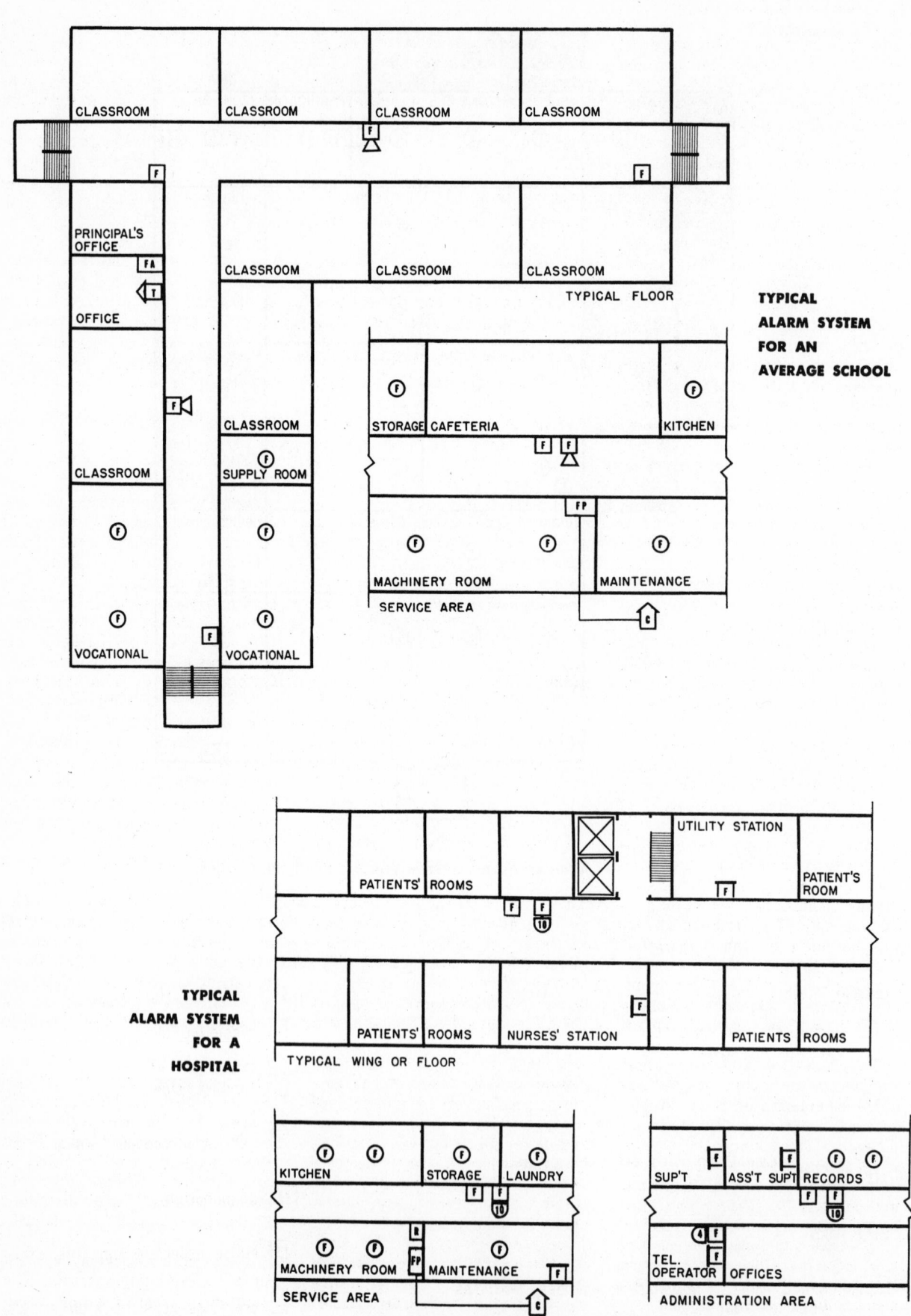

TYPICAL FLOOR

TYPICAL
ALARM SYSTEM
FOR AN
AVERAGE SCHOOL

TYPICAL
ALARM SYSTEM
FOR A
HOSPITAL

TYPICAL WING OR FLOOR

SERVICE AREA

ADMINISTRATION AREA

By HOWARD P. VERMILYA, AIA

The design of sprinkler systems requires the services of an engineer with a specialized knowledge of such systems for several reasons. First, a system must be developed which will meet the requirements of local authorities and the insurance companies. Second, there is the tricky problem of integrating the sprinkler system with the structure, the mechanical and electrical services and the lighting equipment. While a complete design procedure is much beyond the scope of this article, it does give an orientation to the major features and design criteria of sprinkler systems so that their needs can be anticipated in the early planning of a building.

Sprinklers are recommended for all occupancies having combustible contents or flammable liquids. In non-combustible buildings the installations may be limited to specific areas, but in structures with combustible floors or roofs, it is advisable that sprinklers be provided throughout. Sprinklers are recommended also for all concealed spaces involving combustible construction which are not otherwise protected from fire.

A sprinkler system consists of (1) an adequate water supply, (2) a distribution system consisting of pumps, gages, valves, main, riser, feed and branch line piping, (3) sprinkler heads automatically activated by heat and (4) an alarm system. All equipment used must be listed as "approved." Both the Engineering Division of the Associated Factory Mutual Fire Insurance Companies and the Underwriters Laboratories, Inc. maintain testing facilities for the listing of "approved" equipment.

The building authorities and the insurance companies will require complete working drawings of the system for their approval. Sprinkler drawings should show the building construction, equipment, lighting, and storage facilities. The submission of preliminary sketches of proposed systems also is usually required. The system must be thoroughly tested and inspected before acceptance.

In multi-story buildings of fire-resistant construction, it is advisable, where possible, to locate the storage areas in the lower stories, preferably the basement, to facilitate the sprinkler installation and cost.

WATER SUPPLY

Small Properties (good construction):
Single source of water with adequate volume and pressure is required. Public water works connections to two streets is preferable.
Large or Valuable Properties:
Two independent sources are required—primary, which is instantly available, and secondary, which may or may not be automatic.

Primary supply should generally exceed 500 gal/min at a pressure of 15 psi at highest main roof level where cross mains connect to risers or feed mains. Additional volume and pressure are often required depending upon the hazard of occupancy or construction.

Sources

Public Water—one or more connections to reliable public water system of good pressure and capacity are preferable as a primary source.
Elevated Gravity Tanks—Acceptable as a primary source when public water is not available. Capacity is dependent upon height, construction and occupancy of building or buildings and the need to supply hose connections in addition to sprinklers. Tanks may supply secondary source for small property with a limited public supply.
Fire Pumps—A well located fire pump with ample suction supply, capable of maintaining high pressures over long periods is a most satisfactory secondary supply. (Suction supply may consist of tanks, reservoirs or public water mains of low pressure.)
Pressure Tanks—Ordinarily located on or above roof; sometimes an adequate single source.
Fire Department Pumper Connections—An auxiliary supply which utilizes a low pressure source for sprinklers and standpipes.

YARD SYSTEM

This is the portion of the sprinkler system which distributes water from the water supply source to the automatic sprinkler risers. For larger fire protection systems it also distributes water to standpipes and hose connections. All piping is underground (protected from freezing) and outside the building area. Valves are accessible in pits and by use of indicator posts. Manufacturing or domestic water service connections should be separated from fire service systems.

TYPES OF SYSTEMS

1. *Wet Pipe Automatic Systems.* Piping contains water under pressure for immediate release when valve of sprinkler head is activated. Most general type, used in heated areas or areas not subject to freezing.
2. *Dry Pipe Automatic Systems.* Piping contains air under pressure which, when released by activated sprinkler head, permits water to enter pipes automatically by action of dry pipe valve and flow through sprinklers. Generally used when not feasible to heat area which is subject to freezing weather. Small dry pipe systems may be used in conjunction with wet pipe systems for special areas.
3. *Deluge Systems.* A system of open sprinklers, or a combination of open and closed sprinklers controlled by a quick opening mechanical or hydraulic valve (deluge valve), the latter operating either by automatic heat-responsive devices, or by manual control or otherwise. A deluge system is designed to wet down an entire area in which fire may originate. It is designed for special hazards involving possible flash fires and for structures with high ceilings where heat may be dissipated in early stages of fire before it reaches ceiling. Water demands of deluge systems are usually great.
4. *Pre-Action Systems.* A normally closed, automatic dry sprinkler system in which water is admitted by deluge or hy-

draulic valve operated by a heat-responsive device before sprinklers operate. Designed to protect properties where there is danger of serious water damage.

5. *Limited Water Supply Pressure Tank System.* Uses water in tank usually located in basement, under air pressure of 100-110 psi, for light-hazard occupancies involving small areas where not more than 5 to 10 sprinklers will operate in any one fire. Designed for conditions where adequate water supply is not available for occupancies such as schools, small hotels, country clubs etc.

6. *"Junior Systems."* A wet pipe system with small orifice sprinkler heads, usually ⅜ in., which uses copper tubing and is connected to the service water supply where there is sufficient pressure and volume. Designed for basements of dwellings and similar occupancies where not more than 3 or 4 sprinklers are liable to operate.

7. *Special Systems.* Sprinkler systems employing limited water supplies, reduced pipe sizes and other departures from the requirements for standard systems are not classified by the National Board of Fire Underwriters as standard sprinkler systems. Systems of this type may include those pressurized with air or nitrogen. The authority having

jurisdiction may recognize the degree of protection afforded by special types of sprinkler systems.

Sprinkler installations are also classified by hazard of occupancy:

a. "Light-hazard"—residential, business, school, institutional.

b. "Ordinary-hazard"—storage, industrial, theatres, restaurants.

c. "Extra-hazard"—storage and processing of cotton and flammable liquids, dusty areas of woodworking plants.

PIPE SIZES

The number of sprinklers on any one floor undivided by a fire wall and supplied through given sizes of pipe should not exceed that given in Table 1 below, for ordinary hazard occupancy.

Where the piping arrangement provides long risers or feed mains an increase in pipe sizes may be needed to offset friction losses.

Risers

Each system riser should be of sufficient size to supply all sprinklers on the riser of any one floor of one fire section as determined by the schedule of pipe sizes. There should be one or more risers in each building and in each section of building divided by fire walls. Where conditions warrant, the sprinklers in ad-

joining buildings or sections cut off by fire walls may be fed from a system riser in another section or building.

Riser Location

"Center-central" or "side-central" feed to sprinklers is recommended. (See Fig. 1.)

Cross Main and Branch Line Sizes

Branch lines should ordinarily be limited to 8 sprinklers. Not more than 14 branch lines should be allowed on either side of cross main, riser or feed main.

Hangers

Only "approved" pipe hangers installed according to the standards are acceptable.

SPRINKLERS

Automatic Sprinkler Heads

Only "approved" and tested makes and types are acceptable. A ½ in. discharge orifice is standard for all systems other than the "Junior." Automatic sprinklers are designed to discharge water in spray form upon release of valve held on its seat by a mechanism employing some heat-responsive element. Older type deflectors discharged the spray in all directions, wetting the ceiling. The standard spray type deflector directs the spray downward. Side wall sprinkler head deflector directs the water in one direction.

Table 1. Pipe size vs. number of sprinklers

(a) When both the distance between sprinklers on branch lines and the distance between branch lines is 12 ft or less.				(b) When either the distance between sprinklers on branch lines or the distance between branch lines exceeds 12 ft.			
Size Pipe, In.	Max. No. Spklrs	Size Pipe, In.	Max. No. Spklrs	Size Pipe, In.	Max. No. Spklrs	Size Pipe, In.	Max. No. Spklrs
1	2	3	40	1	2	3	30
1¼	3	3½	65	1¼	3	3½	60
1½	5	4	100	1½	5	4	100
2	10	5	160	2	10	5	160
2½	20	6	275	2½	15	6	275
		8	400			8	400

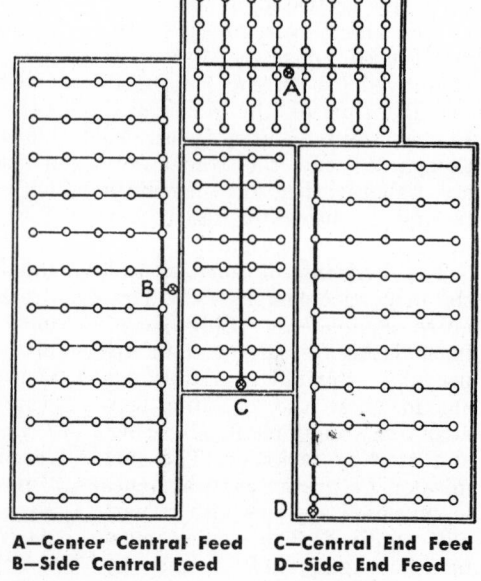

A—Center Central Feed C—Central End Feed
B—Side Central Feed D—Side End Feed

Fig. 1. Location of cross mains and risers

By G. B. GUSRAE, P.E.

Data courtesy of Westinghouse Electric Corporation, Shepard Elevator Company, and Armor Elevator Company, Inc.

Electric traction elevator
General purpose passenger service
Gearless machine
Capacity: 2,500 to 4,000 lbs
Speed: 600 to 1,000 fpm

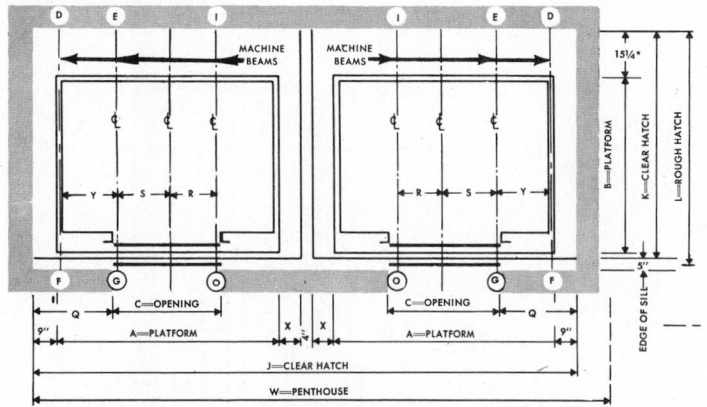

* 17½" REQUIRED WHEN COUNTERWEIGHT SAFETY IS USED AND WHEN SHORT RUNBY CONDITIONS REQUIRE WIDER COUNTERWEIGHT.

NATIONAL ELEVATOR MANUFACTURERS INDUSTRY STANDARD PIT DEPTH AND PENTHOUSE CLEARANCE SHOWN ON THIS AND THE FOLLOWING PAGES. INCREASE IF REQUIRED BY LOCAL CODE.

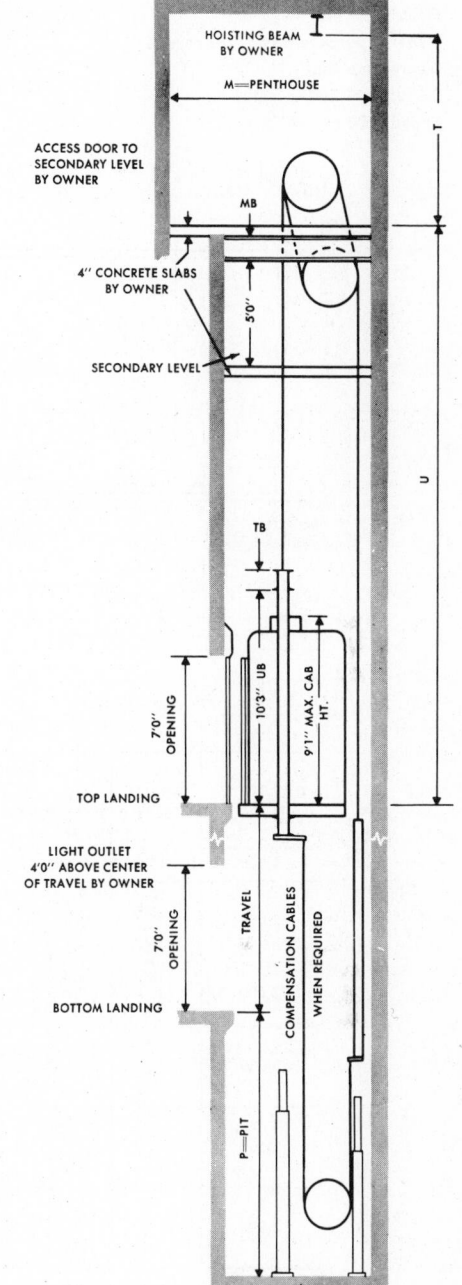

CAPACITY IN LBS.	SPEED FPM	OVERHEAD LOAD IN LBS. (Including Allowance for Impact)					
		D	E	F	G	I	O
2,500	700	0	13,500	0	8,800	17,000	11,200
	800		13,700		9,000	17,400	16,300
3,000	700	0	14,600	0	9,000	18,300	11,200
	800	8,200	10,300	5,000	6,200	21,300	13,000
	1,000	8,600	10,800	5,600	7,000	23,300	15,000
3,500	700	8,800	11,300	5,200	6,400	23,800	14,100
	800	9,100	11,500	5,300	6,700	24,800	14,500
	1,000	9,200	11,550	5,300	6,700	25,950	14,550
4,000	700	8,800	11,000	5,800	7,350	24,600	15,900
	800	8,900	11,250	5,900	7,400	24,700	16,100
	1,000	11,600	13,100	8,000	9,000	28,900	19,850

CAPACITY IN LBS.	SPEED FPM	DIMENSIONS																
		A	B	C	J	K	L	M	P	Q	R	S	T	U	W	X	Y	TB	MB
2,500	700	7'0"	5'0"	3'6"	17'2"	6'4½"	6'5½"	23'0"	12'6"	2'6"	1'1⅞"	2'0⅛"	9'6"	27'6"	21'6"	8"	0	10"	15"
	800												10'6"	29'10"					
3,000	700	7'0"	5'6"	3'6"	17'2"	6'10½"	6'11½"	23'0"	12'6"	2'6"	1'1⅞"	2'0⅛"	9'6"	27'6"	21'6"	8"	2'4½"	10"	15"
	800				17'4"				12'6"		1'3⅛"	1'4⅝"	10'6"	29'10"		9"			14"
	1000				17'4"				13'0"		1'3⅛"	1'4⅝"	10'6"	30'9"		9"			14"
3,500	700	7'0"	6'2"	3'6"	17'4"	7'6½"	7'7½"	23'0"	12'6"	2'6"	1'3⅛"	1'4⅝"	10'6"	27'6"	22'3"	9"	2'4½"	10"	14"
	800							24'0"	13'0"					29'10"					
	1000							24'0"	13'0"					30'9"					
4,000	700	8'0"	6'2"	3'10"	19'4"	7'6½"	7'7½"	23'0"	12'6"	2'8"	1'9¼"	1'7¾"	10'6"	27'6"	24'0"	9"	2'0½"	10"	14"
	800							24'0"	13'0"					29'10"					
	1000							24'0"	13'0"					30'9"					

Variable voltage control. Speed 600 fpm also available in all capacities.

Electric traction elevator
General purpose passenger service
Geared machine
Capacity: 1,200 to 4,000 lbs
Speed: 100 to 350 fpm

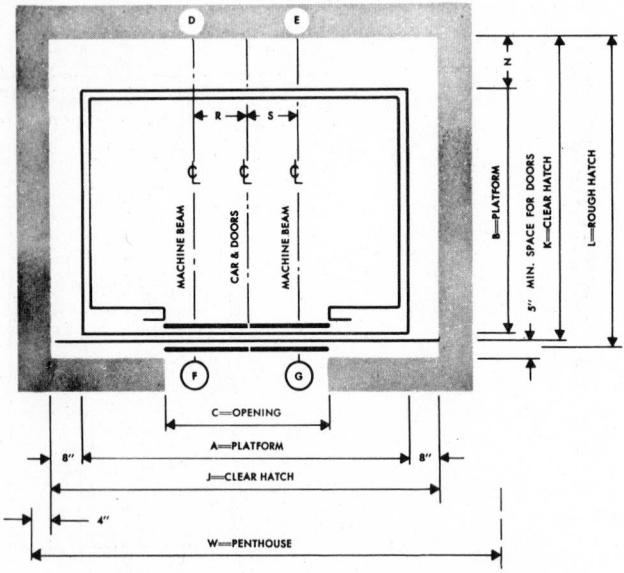

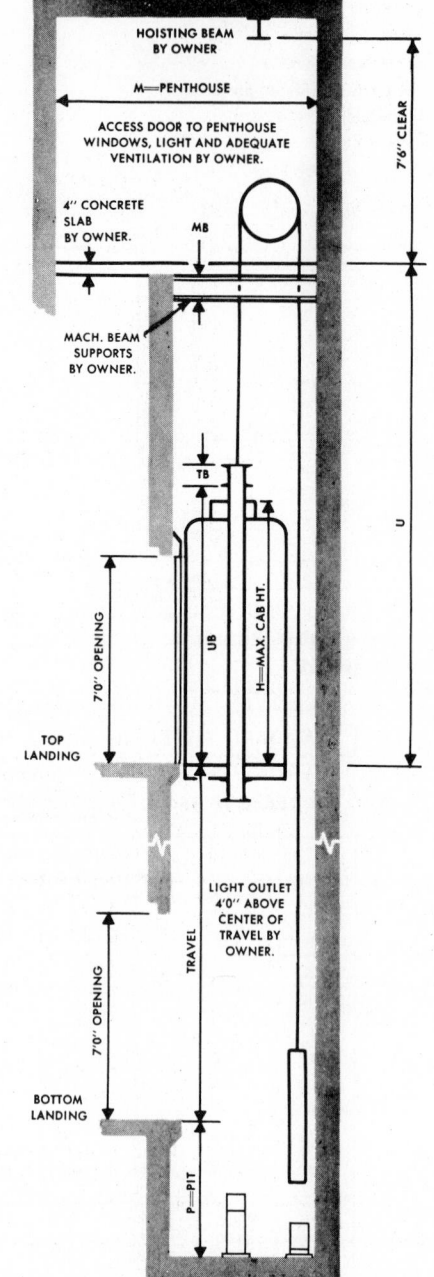

CAPACITY IN LBS.	SPEED FPM	OVERHEAD LOAD IN LBS.* (Including Allowance for Impact)			
		D	E	F	G
1,200	100	6,200	5,800	3,200	3,100
2,000	100	7,500	7,000	3,800	3,600
	200	8,700	7,900	4,500	4,200
	250	9,000	8,200	4,600	4,300
	300	9,200	8,500	4,800	4,400
2,500	100	8,000	7,300	5,500	5,000
	200	9,000	8,200	6,200	5,700
	350	10,700	9,800	6,500	5,800
3,000	100	8,700	7,900	6,000	5,600
	200	10,400	9,500	6,600	6,000
	300	11,100	10,100	7,000	6,300
	350	11,300	10,300	7,100	6,400
3,500	100	9,500	8,800	6,900	6,400
	250	11,700	10,700	7,600	7,000
	300	12,300	10,900	8,100	7,200
	350	13,300	12,600	7,600	7,200
4,000	100	11,900	11,100	7,900	7,400
	200	12,600	11,600	8,400	7,700
	250	13,000	11,900	8,700	8,000
	350	15,000	14,000	8,900	8,200

Including allowance for impact.

CAPACITY IN LBS.	SPEED FPM	DIMENSIONS															
		A	B	C	H	J	K	L	M	N	P	R	S	U	W	MB	TB	UB
1,200	†100	5'0"	4'0"	2'8"	9'0"	6'5"	5'2¼"	5'3¾"	10'6"	13"	5'0"	8"	8"	16'9"	7'0"	8"	7⅞"	9'3"
2,000	†100	6'4"	4'5"	3'0"	9'0"	7'8"	5'7¼"	5'8¼"	11'6"	13"	5'0"	8"	8"	16'9"	11'0"	10"	7⅞"	9'3"
	200								12'0"		5'0"			17'0"			8"	
	250								12'0"		6'8"			17'6"			8"	
	300								12'0"		6'8"			17'6"			8"	
2,500	†100	7'0"	5'0"	3'6"	9'0"	8'4"	6'2¼"	6'3¼"	12'6"	13"	5'0"	8"	8"	16'9"	11'0"	10"	8"	9'3"
	200										5'2"			17'0"		12"		
	350										7'8"			18'3"		12"		
3,000	†100	7'0"	5'6"	3'6"	9'0"	8'4"	6'8¼"	6'9¼"	12'6"	13"	5'0"	8"	8"	16'9"	11'0"	12"	8"	9'3"
	200										5'2"			17'0"			8"	
	300										6'8"			17'6"			10"	
	350										7'8"			18'3"			10"	
3,500	†100	7'0"	6'2"	3'6"	9'0"	8'4"	7'4¼"	7'5¼"	12'6"	13"	5'0"	8"	8"	16'9"	12'0"	12"	10"	10'3"
	250				9'1"				12'6"		6'9"	8"	8"	17'6"		12"		
	300				9'1"				13'6"		6'9"	8"	8"	17'6"		12"		
	350				9'1"				13'6"		7'8"	17"	13"	18'3"		15"		
4,000	†100	8'0"	6'2"	4'0"	9'1"	9'4"	7'5"	7'6"	12'6"	13¾"	5'0"	8"	8"	17'3"	12'0"	12"	10"	10'3"
	200								12'6"		5'4"	8"	8"	17'6"		12"		
	250								12'6"		6'9"	8"	8"	17'6"		12"		
	350								14'0"		7'8"	17"	13"	19'6"		15"		

†*A-C control or d-c resistance; all others variable voltage.*

Electric traction elevator
Hospital service
Geared machine
Capacity: 3,500 to 5,000 lbs
Speed: 75 to 350 fpm

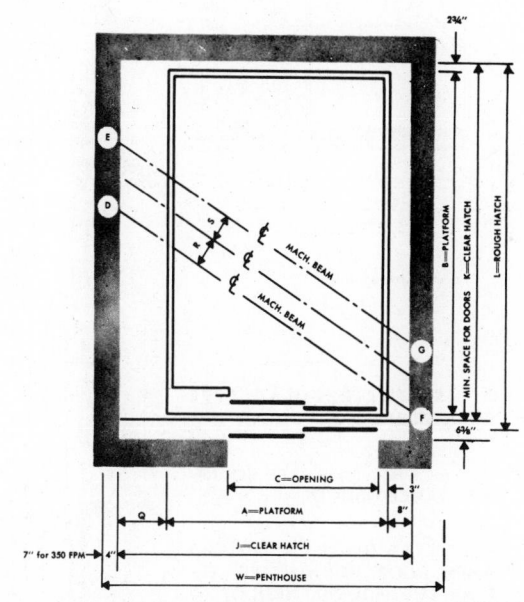

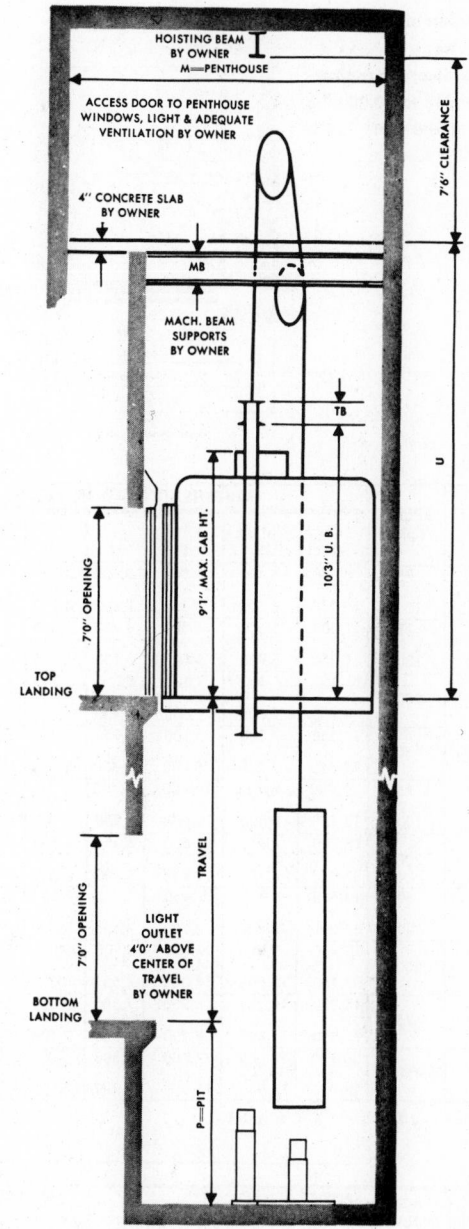

CAPACITY IN LBS.	SPEED FPM	OVERHEAD LOAD IN LBS. (Including Allowance for Impact)			
		D	E	F	G
3,500	† 75	10,500	8,800	6,000	7,700
	†100	10,500	8,800	6,000	7,700
	100	10,600	8,900	6,200	7,800
	300	13,600	9,900	6,600	8,700
	350	15,400	12,000	6,300	9,700
4,000	† 75	12,000	9,300	6,900	8,400
	†100	12,000	9,300	7,000	8,500
	100	12,400	9,700	7,100	8,700
	300	14,300	11,000	7,400	9,100
	350	16,400	12,400	7,100	10,500

CAPACITY IN LBS.	SPEED FPM	DIMENSIONS														
		A	B	C※	J	K	L	M	P	Q	R	S	U	W	MB	TB
3,500	† 75							13'6"	5'0"		8"	8"	16'9"	11'6"		8"
	†100							13'6"	5'0"		8"	8"	16'9"	11'6"		8"
	100	5'4"	8'4"	3'8"	7'3"	8'8"	8'9"	13'6"	5'0"	16"	8"	8"	16'9"	11'6"	12"	8"
	300							13'6"	6'9"		8"	8"	17'6"	11'6"		8"
	350							13'8"	7'8"		17"	13"	18'3"	11'6"		10"
4,000	† 75							13'6"	5'0"		8"	8"	16'2"			8"
	†100							13'6"	5'0"		8"	8"	16'9"			8"
	100	5'8"	8'8"	4'0"	7'8"	9'0"	9'1"	13'6"	5'0"	16"	8"	8"	16'9"	11'6"	12"	8"
	250							13'6"	6'9"		8"	8"	17'0"			8"
	350							13'8"	7'8"		17"	13"	18'3"			10"
5,000	100	5'8"	9'4"	4'0"	7'10"	9'8"	9'9"	13'0"	4'9"				16'9"			
	250							13'6"	6'8"				17'6"			
	350							13'8"	7'8"				18'3"			

※ *Two-speed doors only.*
† *A-C control or d-c resistance; all others variable voltage.*

Electric traction elevator
Freight service
Geared machine; 2:1 roping
Capacity: 4,000 to 10,000 lbs
Speed: 50 to 200 fpm

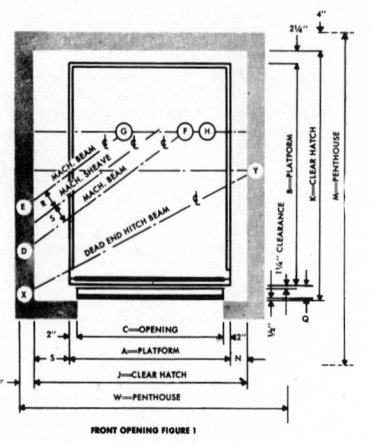

FRONT OPENING FIGURE 1

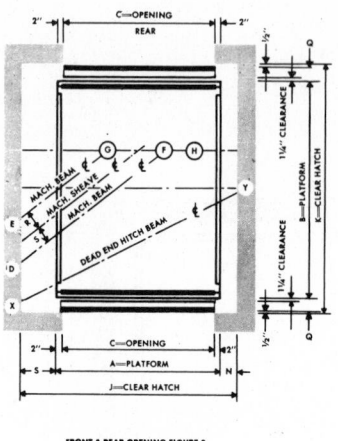

FRONT & REAR OPENING FIGURE 2

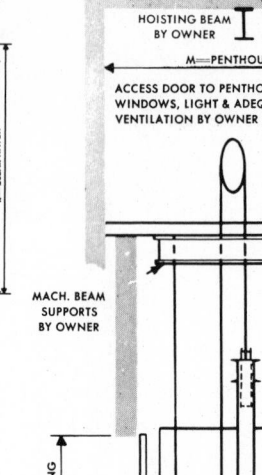

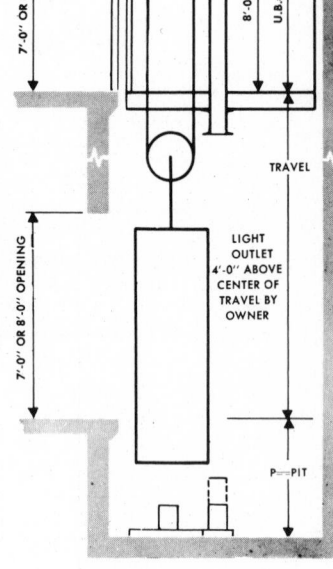

CAPACITY IN LBS.	SPEED FPM	OVERHEAD LOAD IN LBS.*						
		D	E	F	G	H	X	Y
4,000	75	8,650	5,400	4,500	3,900	3,150	5,500	6,200
	100	10,250	6,500	4,050	3,900	4,300	6,100	6,150
5,000	75	11,000	6,600	4,800	4,900	4,850	6,700	7,050
	100	11,350	6,900	5,500	5,100	5,050	6,950	7,550
5,000	200	14,250	7,400	5,300	6,250	5,250	7,300	8,000
		14,400	7,700	11,500	6,400	0	7,300	9,100
6,000	50	11,550	7,000	5,100	5,150	5,250	7,100	7,500
		11,650	7,250	5,700	5,400	5,400	7,150	7,600
6,000	75	12,900	6,750	10,400	5,700	0	6,650	7,300
	100	13,150	7,050	10,600	5,900	0	6,700	8,300
6,000	200	14,700	7,850	5,650	6,450	5,600	7,850	8,350
		15,050	8,100	11,950	6,700	0	7,800	9,400
8,000	50	14,650	8,050	7,450	7,250	7,300	7,300	8,650
	100	15,200	8,350	7,700	7,500	7,500	7,500	9,000
8,000	200	19,450	9,900	16,400	8,200	0	8,400	7,750
		20,150	10,200	17,000	8,500	0	8,700	8,000
10,000	75	15,310	10,200	8,900	7,800	8,350	9,760	11,000
		17,350	11,400	9,200	8,000	9,400	10,850	11,200
10,000	150	20,950	10,600	17,700	8,800	0	9,050	8,300
		21,000	12,500	11,900	11,050	11,500	12,400	12,500

* *Including allowance for impact.*

Q = 5″ FOR REGULAR TYPE COUNTER-BALANCED DOORS.

Q = 6¾″ FOR PASS TYPE COUNTER-BALANCED DOORS.

PASS TYPE DOORS REQUIRED WHEN DOOR HEIGHTS ARE LESS THAN 11'0″ FOR 7'0″ HIGH OPENING AND LESS THAN 12'6″ FOR 8'0″ HIGH OPENING.

UB = 11'0″ FOR 8,000 AND 10,000 LB. CAPACITY.

CAPACITY IN LBS.	SPEED FPM	A	B	C*	J	K—FIG. 1 Q=5″	K—FIG. 1 Q=6¾″	K—FIG. 2 Q=5″	K—FIG. 2 Q=6¾″	K—FIG. 2 Q=φ	S	N	P	R	S	U	M	W	MB	TB
4,000	75	6'4″	8'0″	6'0″	8'5″	8'7¾″	8'9½″	8'11″	9'2½″	9'0¾″	17″	8″	5'0″	8″	8″	15'8″	13'9″	11'1″	10″	9″
	100	8'4″	10'0″	8'0″	10'5″	10'7¾″	10'9½″	10'11″	11'2½″	11'0¾″							12'6″	12'3″		
5,000	75	8'4″	10'0″	8'0″	10'6″	10'7¾″	10'9½″	10'11″	11'2½″	11'0¾″	18″	8″	5'0″	8″	8″	16'1″	13'9″	11'1″	12″	10″
	100		12'0″			12'7¾″	12'9½″	12'11″	13'2½″	13'0¾″										
5,000	200	8'4″	10'0″	8'0″	10'6″	10'7¾″	10'9½″	10'11″	11'2½″	11'0¾″	18″	8″	5'3″	17″	13″	16'4″	15'4″	14'0″	12″	12″
			12'0″			12'7¾″	12'9½″	12'11″	13'2½″	13'0¾″										
6,000	50	8'4″	10'0″	8'0″	10'6″	10'7¾″	10'9½″	10'11″	11'2½″	11'0¾″	18″	8″	5'0″	8″	8″	15'10″	13'9″	11'1″	12″	10″
			12'0″			12'7¾″	12'9½″	12'11″	13'2½″	13'0¾″										
6,000	75	8'4″	10'0″	8'0″	10'6″	10'7¾″	10'9½″	10'11″	11'2½″	11'0¾″	18″	8″	5'0″	8″	8″	16'1″	13'9″	11'1″	12″	10″
	100		12'0″			12'7¾″	12'9½″	12'11″	13'2½″	13'0¾″						16'3″				
6,000	200	8'4″	10'0″	8'0″	10'6″	10'7¾″	10'9½″	10'11″	11'2½″	11'0¾″	18″	8″	5'3″	17″	13″	16'4″	15'4″	14'0″	12″	12″
			12'0″			12'7¾″	12'9½″	12'11″	13'2½″	13'0¾″										
8,000	50	8'4″	10'0″	8'0″	10'10″	10'7¾″	10'9½″	10'11″	11'2½″	11'0¾″	20″	10″	5'6″	8″	8″	16'6″	13'9″	11'4″	15″	12″
	100		12'0″			12'7¾″	12'9½″	12'11″	13'2½″	13'0¾″										
8,000	200	8'4″	10'0″	8'0″	10'10″	10'7¾″	10'9½″	10'11″	11'2½″	11'0¾″	20″	10″	5'6″	17″	13″	16'8″	15'4″	14'0″	15″	12″
			12'0″			12'7¾″	12'9½″	12'11″	13'2½″	13'0¾″										
10,000	75	8'4″	12'0″	8'0″	10'11″	12'7¾″	12'9½″	12'11″	13'2½″	13'0¾″	21″	10″	5'6″	8″	8″	16'10″	15'4″	14'3″	15″	12″
		10'4″	14'0″	10'0″	12'11″	14'7¾″	14'9½″	14'11″	15'2½″	15'0¾″										
10,000	150	8'4″	12'0″	8'0″	10'11″	12'7¾″	12'9½″	12'11″	13'2½″	13'0¾″	21″	10″	6'0″	17″	13″	17'1″	15'4″	14'3″	15″	15″
		10'4″	14'0″	10'0″	12'11″	14'7¾″	14'9½″	14'11″	15'2½″	15'0¾″										

* Vertical rising biparting counterbalanced hoistway doors; vertical rising car gate.

Electric traction elevator
Freight service
Geared machine; 1:1 roping
Capacity: 3,000 to 4,000 lbs
Speed: 50 to 200 fpm

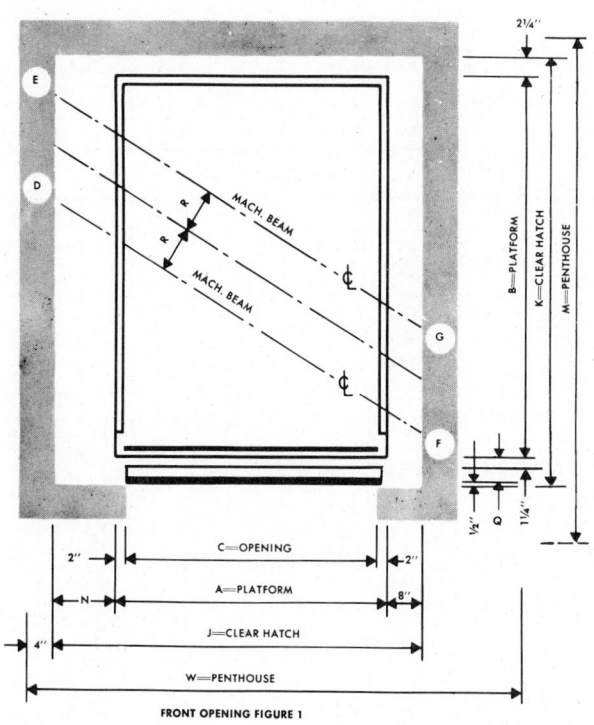

FRONT OPENING FIGURE 1

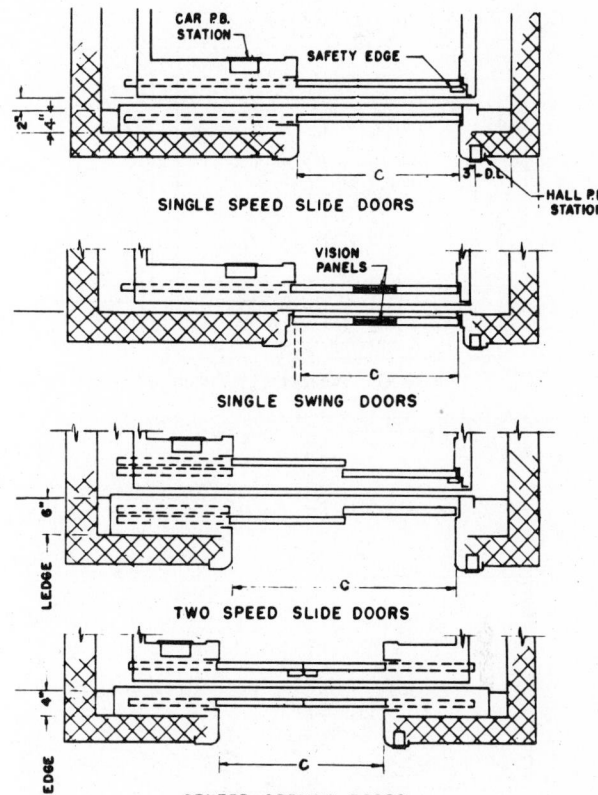

Elevator doors—passenger

| | | SINGLE SPEED SLIDE DOORS |
| SINGLE SWING DOORS |
| TWO SPEED SLIDE DOORS |
| CENTER OPENING DOORS |

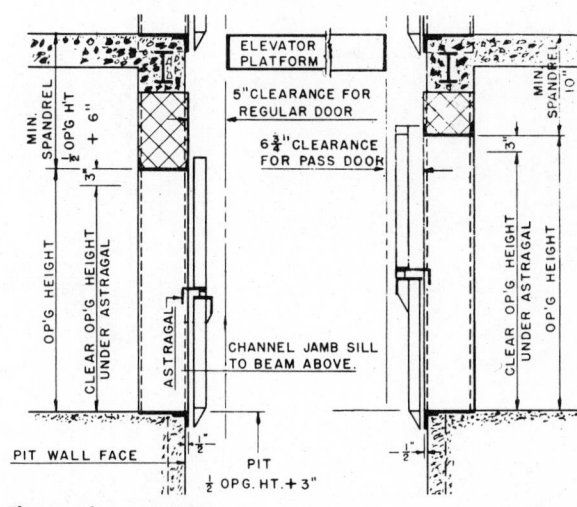

Elevator doors—freight

CAPACITY IN LBS.	SPEED FPM	OVERHEAD LOAD IN LBS. (Including Allowance for Impact)			
		D	E	F	G
3,000	50	8,900	6,650	4,900	5,900
	100	9,200	7,300	5,450	6,100
4,000	200	14,150	10,850	7,800	9,450
		15,150	12,500	9,300	10,350

CAPACITY IN LBS.	SPEED FPM	DIMENSIONS															
						K—FIG. 1		K—FIG. 2									
		A	B	C	J	Q=5"	Q=6¾"	Q=5"	Q=6¾"	Q=φ	N	P	R	U	M	W	MB	TB
3,000	50	5'4"	7'0"	5'0"	7'3"	7'7¾"	7'9½"	7'11"	8'2½"	8'0¾"	15"	5'0"	8"	15'6"	9'9"	10'2"	12"	9"
	100	6'4"	8'0"	6'0"	8'3"	8'7¾"	8'9½"	8'11"	9'2½"	9'0¾"				16'0"	12'6"	11'0"		
4,000	200	6'4"	8'0"	6'0"	8'5"	8'7¾"	8'9½"	8'11"	9'2½"	9'0¾"	17"	5'3"	8"	16'4"	12'6"	13'0"	15"	9"
		8'4"	10'0"	8'0"	10'5"	10'7¾"	10'9½"	10'11"	11'2½"	11'0¾"								12"

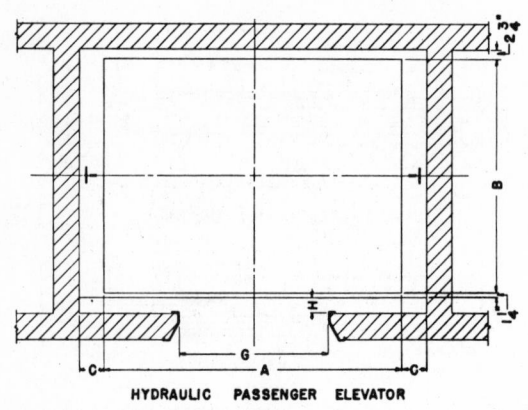

HYDRAULIC PASSENGER ELEVATOR

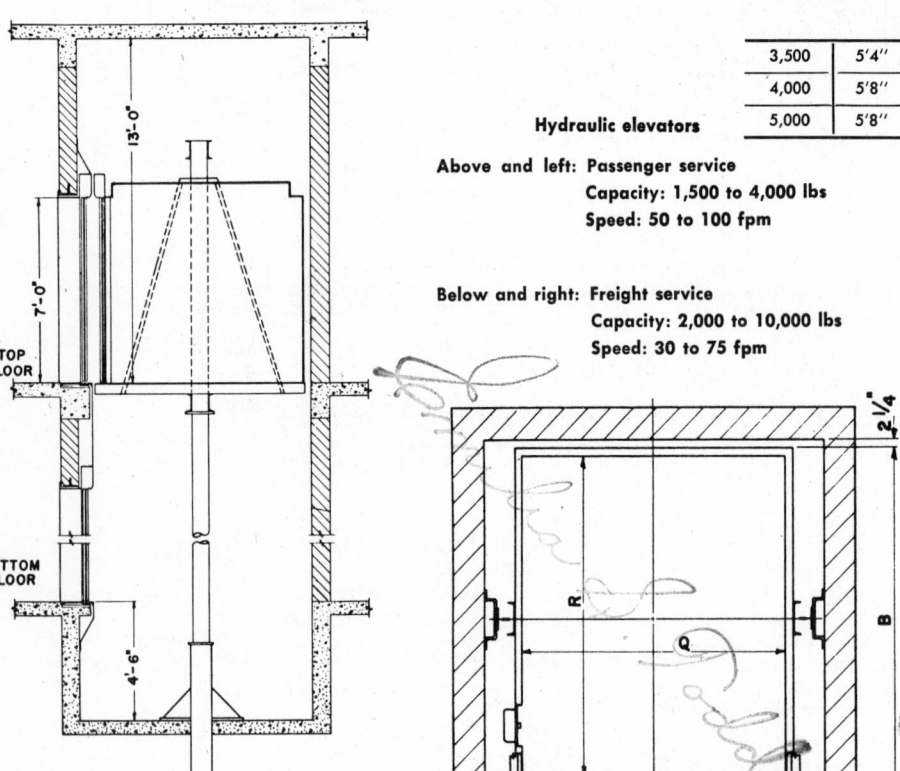

SECTION

PLAN OF SINGLE OPENING

Hydraulic elevators

Above and left: Passenger service
Capacity: 1,500 to 4,000 lbs
Speed: 50 to 100 fpm

Below and right: Freight service
Capacity: 2,000 to 10,000 lbs
Speed: 30 to 75 fpm

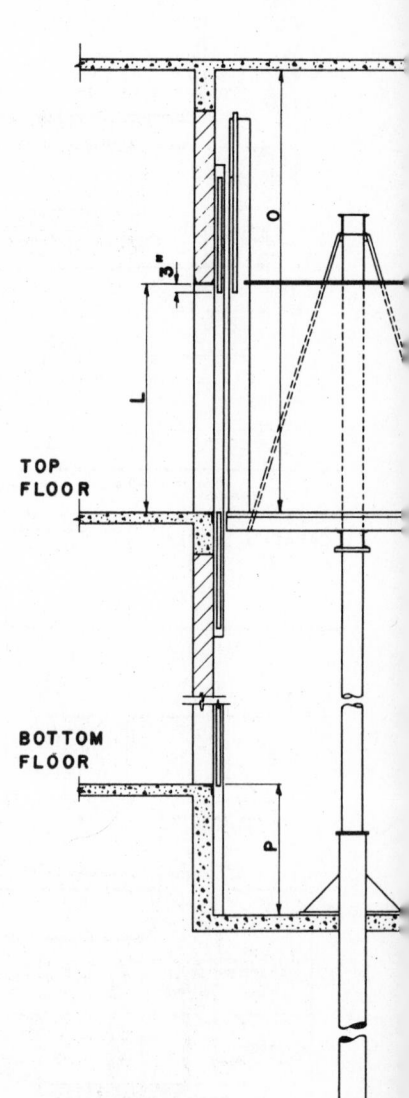

TOP FLOOR

BOTTOM FLOOR

LOAD	DIMENSIONS				ENTRANCE	
	A	B	C	G	TYPE	H Appr
1,500	5'9''	4'0''	7''	2'10''	Single Slide	4½
2,000	6'4''	4'5''	7''	3'0''	Single Slide or Center Opening	4½
2,500	7'0''	5'0''	7''	3'6''	Center Opening	4¾
3,000	7'0''	5'6''	7''	3'6''	Center Opening	4¾
3,500	8'0''	5'6''	8''	4'0''	Center Opening	4¾
4,000	8'0''	6'0''	8''	4'0''	Center Opening	4¾

OFFICE BUILDINGS, BANKS, HOTELS, APARTMENT HOUSES, STORES

HOSPITALS (Single Entrance)

3,500	5'4''	8'0''	8''	3'8''	Two Speed	6⅜
4,000	5'8''	8'4''	10''	4'0''	Two Speed	6⅜
5,000	5'8''	9'4''	10''	4'0''	Two Speed	6⅜

Capacity Lbs.	DIMENSIONS									
	A	B	D	Q	R	G	H	L	O	P
2,000	5'-0''	6'-0''	7''	4'-9''	5'-6''	4'-6''	10''	7'-3''	13'-0''	4'-6''
3,000	5'-6''	7'-0''	7''	5'-3''	6'-6''	5'-0''	10''	7'-3''	13'-0''	4'-6''
4,000	6'-6''	8'-0''	8''	6'-3''	7'-6''	6'-0''	11''	7'-3''	13'-0''	4'-6''
5,000	8'-6''	10'-0''	8''	8'-3''	9'-6''	8'-0''	11''	7'-3''	13'-0''	4'-6''
6,000	8'-6''	12'-0''	8''	8'-3''	11'-6''	8'-0''	11''	7'-3''	13'-0''	4'-6''
7,500	8'-6''	12'-0''	9''	8'-3''	11'-6''	8'-0''	12''	9'-3''	15'-0''	5'-0''
10,000	10'-6''	14'-0''	9''	10'-3''	13'-6''	10'-0''	12''	9'-3''	15'-0''	5'-0''

Dimension N = 5" for Regular Type Counter Balanced Hoistway Doors.
Dimension N = 6¾" for Pass Type Counter Balanced Hoistway Doors.
Pass Type Hoistway Doors required when floor heights are less than 11'6" for 7'3" high opening and less than 14'6" for 9'3" high opening.

Data courtesy Westinghouse Electric Corporation.

Electric stairway (escalator)
Angle of incline: 30 deg
Rise to 25 ft*
Speed: 90 or 120 fpm
Width: 32 in.*
Capacity: 5,000 passengers per hour at 90 fpm
　　　　　5,750 passengers per hour at 120 fpm
Machine: 5 to 10 hp*
Also available in 4-ft width and for rises up to 40 ft; horsepower to 15.

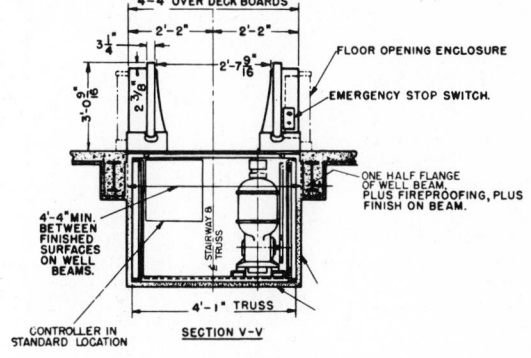

4'-4" OVER DECK BOARDS
FLOOR OPENING ENCLOSURE
EMERGENCY STOP SWITCH.
ONE HALF FLANGE OF WELL BEAM PLUS FIREPROOFING, PLUS FINISH ON BEAM.
STAIRWAY & TRUSS
4'-4" MIN. BETWEEN FINISHED SURFACES ON WELL BEAMS
4'-1" TRUSS
CONTROLLER IN STANDARD LOCATION
SECTION V-V

REACTIONS		
NO INTERMEDIATE SUPPORT	WITH INTERMEDIATE SUPPORT WHEN "B" IS LESS THAN "C"	WITH INTERMEDIATE SUPPORT WHEN "B" IS GREATER THAN "C"
$R_1 = 324A + 2000$	$R_1 = [324A + 2000]\frac{A}{A+C}$	$R_1 = [648A + 4000]\frac{B}{A+B}$
$R_2 = 324A + 4000$	$R_2 = [648A + 8000]\frac{C}{A+C}$	$R_2 = [324A + 4000]\frac{A}{A+B}$
	$R_3 = [324A + 4000]\frac{A}{A+C}$	$R_3 = [324A + 4000]\frac{A}{A+B}$

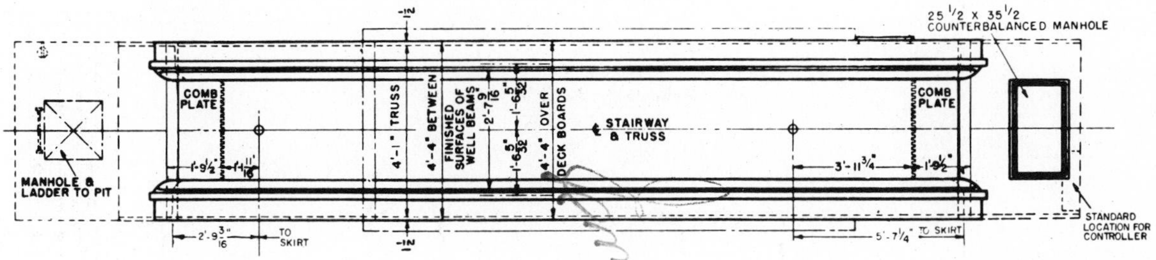

COMB PLATE

25 1/2 X 35 1/2 COUNTERBALANCED MANHOLE

COMB PLATE

MANHOLE & LADDER TO PIT

4'-1" TRUSS
4'-4" BETWEEN FINISHED SURFACES OF WELL BEAMS
4'-4" OVER DECK BOARDS
STAIRWAY & TRUSS

3'-11 3/4"　1'-9 1/2"

STANDARD LOCATION FOR CONTROLLER

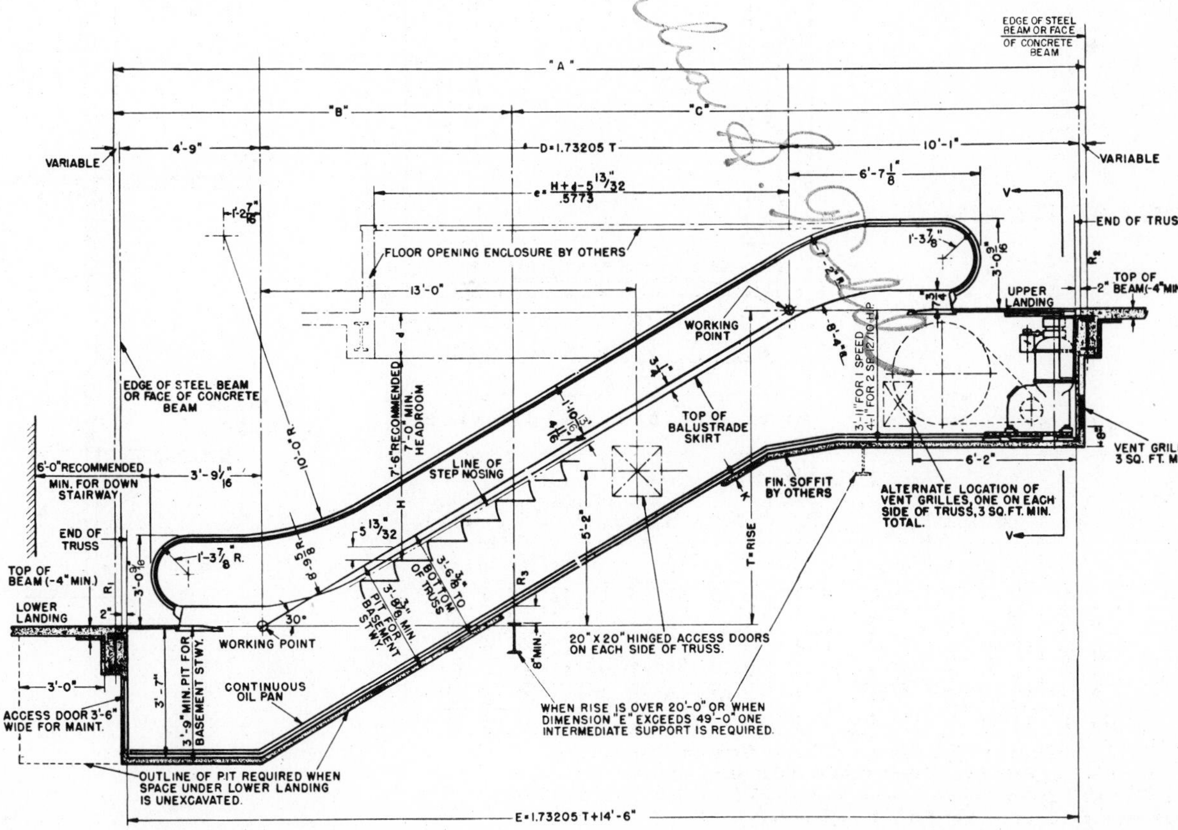

2'-9 3/16" TO SKIRT
5'-7 1/4" TO SKIRT

EDGE OF STEEL BEAM OR FACE OF CONCRETE BEAM

"A"
"B"
"C"

VARIABLE
4'-9"
$D = 1.73205\,T$
10'-1"
VARIABLE

$e = \dfrac{H + 4 - 5\frac{13}{32}}{.5773}$

6'-7 1/8"

FLOOR OPENING ENCLOSURE BY OTHERS

END OF TRUSS

TOP OF 2" BEAM (-4" MIN)

13'-0"

WORKING POINT

TOP OF BALUSTRADE SKIRT

UPPER LANDING

EDGE OF STEEL BEAM OR FACE OF CONCRETE BEAM

LINE OF STEP NOSING

3'-11" FOR 1 SPEED 4'-1" FOR 2 SPEED/10 HP

VENT GRILLE 3 SQ. FT. MIN.

6'-0" RECOMMENDED MIN. FOR DOWN STAIRWAY

3'-9 1/2"

FIN. SOFFIT BY OTHERS

ALTERNATE LOCATION OF VENT GRILLES, ONE ON EACH SIDE OF TRUSS, 3 SQ. FT. MIN. TOTAL.

6'-2"

END OF TRUSS

1'-3 7/8" R.

30°

5-2"

T = RISE

TOP OF BEAM (-4" MIN.)

LOWER LANDING

WORKING POINT

20" X 20" HINGED ACCESS DOORS ON EACH SIDE OF TRUSS.

8" MIN.

CONTINUOUS OIL PAN

3'-0"

ACCESS DOOR 3'-6" WIDE FOR MAINT.

3'-9" MIN PIT FOR BASEMENT STWY.

WHEN RISE IS OVER 20'-0" OR WHEN DIMENSION "E" EXCEEDS 49'-0" ONE INTERMEDIATE SUPPORT IS REQUIRED.

OUTLINE OF PIT REQUIRED WHEN SPACE UNDER LOWER LANDING IS UNEXCAVATED.

$E = 1.73205\,T + 14'-6"$

SECTION V: DESIGN ELEMENTS—RESIDENTIAL

Furniture:
  General 951
  Living room 951
  Dining room 960
  Bedroom 963
Kitchens:
  Planning considerations 967
  Critical dimensions 968
  Storage 970
  Plan types 973
  Appliances 976
  Cabinets 984
Laundries:
  Planning considerations 988
  Space requirements 988
  Kitchen-laundry plans 991
  Separate laundry room plans 992
  Multi-use laundry rooms 994
Bathrooms:
  Planning considerations 995
  Dimensions at lavatory 998
  Dimensions at bathtub and shower 999
  Two-fixture plans 1000
  Three-fixture plans 1001
  Compartmented plans 1002
  Fixtures 1003
Storage:
  Planning considerations 1007
  Bedroom closets for men 1009
  Bedroom closets for women 1011
  Bedroom closets for children 1013
  Coat closets 1014
  Miscellaneous closets 1015
  Closet fixtures 1019
Home Workshops 1021
Darkrooms:
  Design 1024
  Small 1025
  Advanced 1026
  Community 1027
Housing for the Aged 1028
Apartments:
  Building types 1032
  Plan types 1033
  FHA and PHA requirements—sites 1034
  FHA and PHA requirements—exits 1037
  Planning considerations 1038
  Room count and minimum room sizes 1040
  Minimum storage space 1041
Dormitories 1042
Hotels:
  Planning considerations 1045
  Types of guest rooms 1046
  Bathrooms 1048
  Plans 1049
  Space allotments—general 1054
  Space allotments—public areas 1056
  Space allotments—concession and rental areas 1056
  Space allotments—food and beverage services 1058
  Space allotments—general service areas 1060
  Schedule of space allotments 1062
Motels:
  General 1064
  Site location 1064
  Site plan 1068
  Room groups and parking 1068
  Space allotments 1071
Hotel Laundries:
  Advantages and disadvantages 1075
  Utility requirements 1076
  Equipment requirements 1077

GENERAL

Living, dining, and sleeping spaces are as much subject to the requirements of utility as kitchens or bathrooms. Activities which take place in living areas may be less definitely routine than those found in service areas; but the furniture with which living activities are associated has to be adapted so that normal activities result naturally and easily from its use.

Typical furniture-group units

While the typical furniture arrangements presented in the following pages by no means cover the entire range of possibilities, they do cover the fundamental uses to which living, dining, and sleeping spaces are put. From the suggested schemes furniture arrangements can be developed to suit any particular problem or set of problems with which a designer may be confronted.

Furniture sizes may vary slightly; those indicated are the averages commonly met with in upper middle-class homes, and are little affected by changes in style or similar matters of individual preference.

Specific space allowances

In studying furniture groupings, it becomes obvious that certain clearances are required. Spaces, lanes, or paths of different types develop naturally between furniture-group units. Minimum distances for comfort have been established by numerous planners. These, and in some cases, maximum distances based upon requirements for human intercourse, have been incorporated in the diagrams. A listing of those generally applicable to all rooms follows:

1. *Single passage* (not a traffic lane) between low objects, such as a sofa and coffee table: 18 in. is the minimum.
2. *Single passage* (not a traffic lane) between tall objects, hip height or over: 2 ft to 2 ft 6 in. is the minimum.
3. *General traffic lane:* 3 ft 4 in. is the practical minimum. As rooms increase in size, this minimum increases, in order to preserve the space scale of the room. The traffic lane between an entrance door and a major group unit is preferably generous in width. It is desirable to place doors so that the central portions of rooms do not become major traffic ways between different parts of the house.
4. *Seating areas, confined* (for instance, between a desk and a wall): 3 ft is a minimum tolerance, which permits one person to pass back of an occupied chair. This minimum does not constitute a major traffic lane.

LIVING ROOM

Typical furniture groups in the living room are as follows:

1. *Primary conversation group:* chairs and sofa normally grouped around the fireplace
2. *Secondary conversation group:* chairs and love seat at end of room or in corner
3. *Reading group or groups:* chair, ottoman, lamp, table
4. *Writing or study group:* desk, lamp, one or two chairs, bookcases
5. *Music group:* piano, bench, storage space
6. *Game group:* game table and four chairs
7. *Television group:* television set and seating for several people

According to the price of a house and the cubage allotted to the living room, two or three or all of the furniture-group units may be included. The fireplace is so closely associated with living room furniture that it has been included in all schemes.

Clearances

Traffic tolerances in living rooms are important, since numbers of people use the room, and narrow lanes between furniture-group units are uncomfortable. An adequate traffic lane between the main entrance and the major seating group is 3 ft 4 in. wide; 4 ft 6 in. is preferred. The minimum clearance between facing pieces of furniture in a fireplace group is 4 ft 8 in. for a fireplace 3 ft wide. For every inch added to the size of the fireplace, 1 in. is added to the minimum clearance space.

If a wide sofa is placed directly opposite the fireplace, this group is often spread. A 6-ft tolerance is usually considered the maximum because it is difficult to carry on a conversation over a greater distance.

A considerable flexibility in location of doors and windows is possible, and all wall pieces can be shifted. Doors flanking a fireplace are to be avoided in order that the furniture group may be concentrated around the fireplace opening.

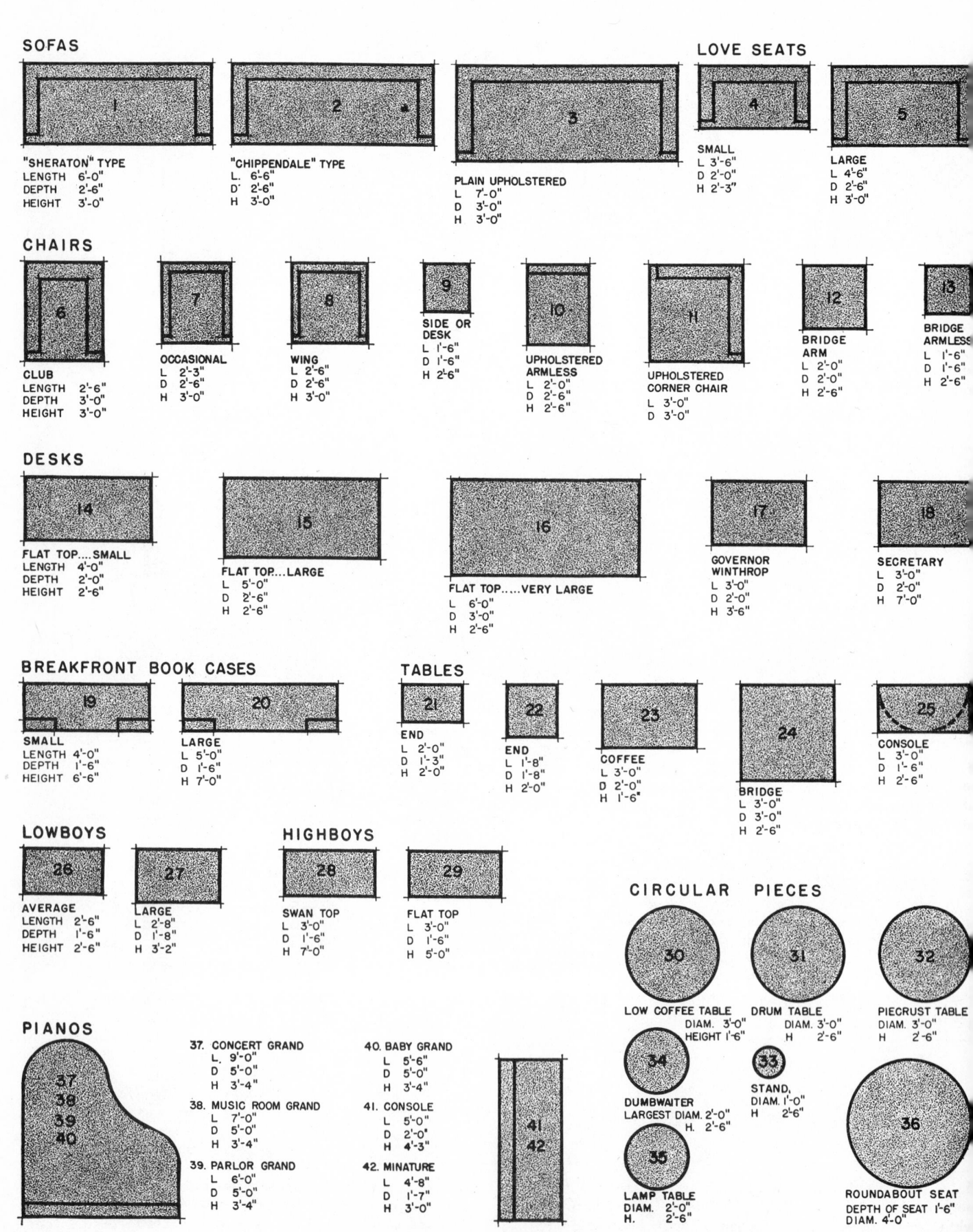

SOFAS

1 "SHERATON" TYPE
LENGTH 6'-0"
DEPTH 2'-6"
HEIGHT 3'-0"

2 "CHIPPENDALE" TYPE
L. 6'-6"
D. 2'-6"
H. 3'-0"

3 PLAIN UPHOLSTERED
L 7'-0"
D 3'-0"
H 3'-0"

LOVE SEATS

4 SMALL
L 3'-6"
D 2'-0"
H 2'-3"

5 LARGE
L 4'-6"
D 2'-6"
H 3'-0"

CHAIRS

6 CLUB
LENGTH 2'-6"
DEPTH 3'-0"
HEIGHT 3'-0"

7 OCCASIONAL
L 2'-3"
D 2'-6"
H 3'-0"

8 WING
L 2'-6"
D 2'-6"
H 3'-0"

9 SIDE OR DESK
L 1'-6"
D 1'-6"
H 2'-6"

10 UPHOLSTERED ARMLESS
L 2'-0"
D 2'-6"
H 2'-6"

11 UPHOLSTERED CORNER CHAIR
L 3'-0"
D 3'-0"

12 BRIDGE ARM
L 2'-0"
D 2'-0"
H 2'-6"

13 BRIDGE ARMLESS
L 1'-6"
D 1'-6"
H 2'-6"

DESKS

14 FLAT TOP....SMALL
LENGTH 4'-0"
DEPTH 2'-0"
HEIGHT 2'-6"

15 FLAT TOP...LARGE
L 5'-0"
D 2'-6"
H 2'-6"

16 FLAT TOP.....VERY LARGE
L 6'-0"
D 3'-0"
H 2'-6"

17 GOVERNOR WINTHROP
L 3'-0"
D 2'-0"
H 3'-6"

18 SECRETARY
L 3'-0"
D 2'-0"
H 7'-0"

BREAKFRONT BOOK CASES

19 SMALL
LENGTH 4'-0"
DEPTH 1'-6"
HEIGHT 6'-6"

20 LARGE
L 5'-0"
D 1'-6"
H 7'-0"

TABLES

21 END
L 2'-0"
D 1'-3"
H 2'-0"

22 END
L 1'-8"
D 1'-8"
H 2'-0"

23 COFFEE
L 3'-0"
D 2'-0"
H 1'-6"

24 BRIDGE
L 3'-0"
D 3'-0"
H 2'-6"

25 CONSOLE
L 3'-0"
D 1'-6"
H 2'-6"

LOWBOYS

26 AVERAGE
LENGTH 2'-6"
DEPTH 1'-6"
HEIGHT 2'-6"

27 LARGE
L 2'-8"
D 1'-8"
H 3'-2"

HIGHBOYS

28 SWAN TOP
L 3'-0"
D 1'-6"
H 7'-0"

29 FLAT TOP
L 3'-0"
D 1'-6"
H 5'-0"

CIRCULAR PIECES

30 LOW COFFEE TABLE
DIAM. 3'-0"
HEIGHT 1'-6"

31 DRUM TABLE
DIAM. 3'-0"
H 2'-6"

32 PIECRUST TABLE
DIAM. 3'-0"
H 2'-6"

33 STAND
DIAM. 1'-0"
H 2'-6"

34 DUMBWAITER
LARGEST DIAM. 2'-0"
H 2'-6"

35 LAMP TABLE
DIAM. 2'-0"
H 2'-6"

36 ROUNDABOUT SEAT
DEPTH OF SEAT 1'-6"
DIAM. 4'-0"

PIANOS

37, 38, 39, 40

37. CONCERT GRAND
L. 9'-0"
D 5'-0"
H 3'-4"

38. MUSIC ROOM GRAND
L 7'-0"
D 5'-0"
H 3'-4"

39. PARLOR GRAND
L 6'-0"
D 5'-0"
H 3'-4"

40. BABY GRAND
L 5'-6"
D 5'-0"
H 3'-4"

41. CONSOLE
L 5'-0"
D 2'-0"
H 4'-3"

42. MINATURE
L 4'-8"
D 1'-7"
H 3'-0"

41, 42

All drawings at scale: 1/4" = 1'-0"

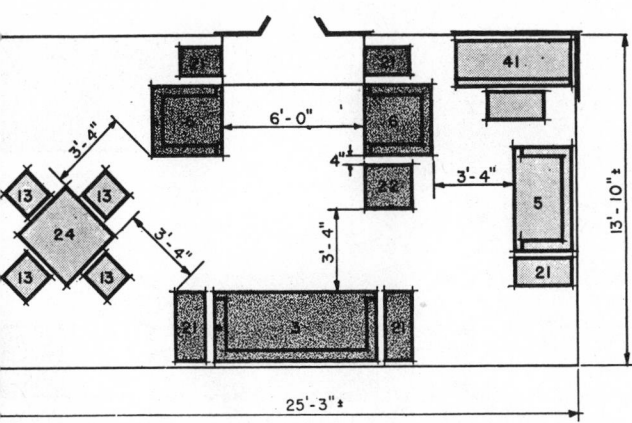

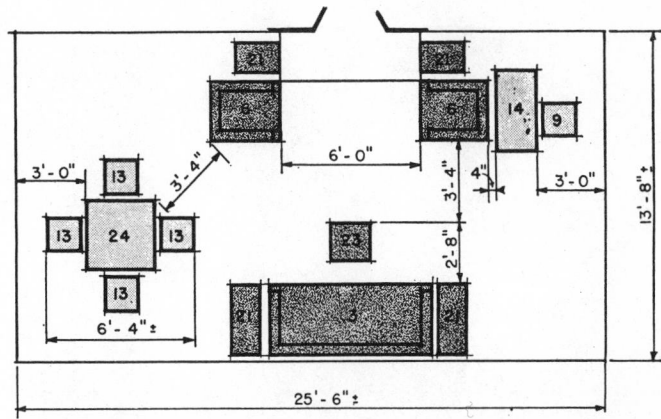

. In all living rooms shown, main conversation group entered about fireplace is dark gray. Bay or picture windows may be used as focal points, instead of fireplaces.

2. Clearance between low coffee table (23) and easy chairs (6) ought to be maintained at 3'-4" even though table is low, because the aisle here constitutes a major traffic way.

All drawings at scale: 1/8" = 1'-0"

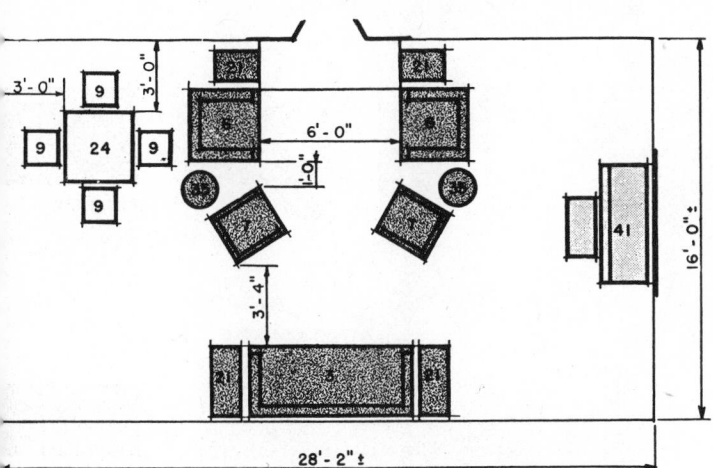

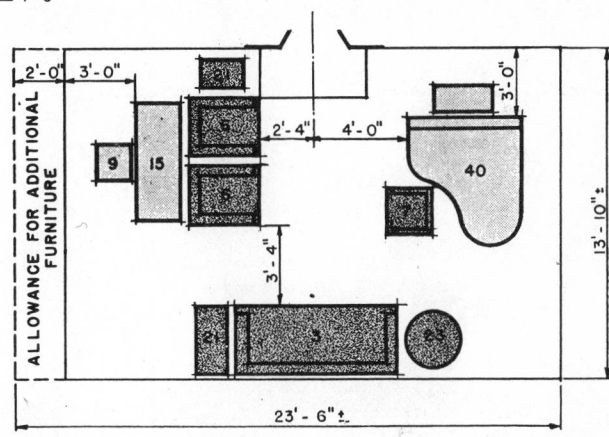

. For larger families, or for those who entertain often, eating for 7 to 8 persons in the primary group is a reason-ble design limitation. Off-center location of game group rovides for a corner entrance door.

4. Minimum length for a room which must contain a baby grand piano is approximately 20'. If minimum clearances of 1' between piano and wall, and 3' between desk (15) and wall, are to be maintained, room length must be increased.

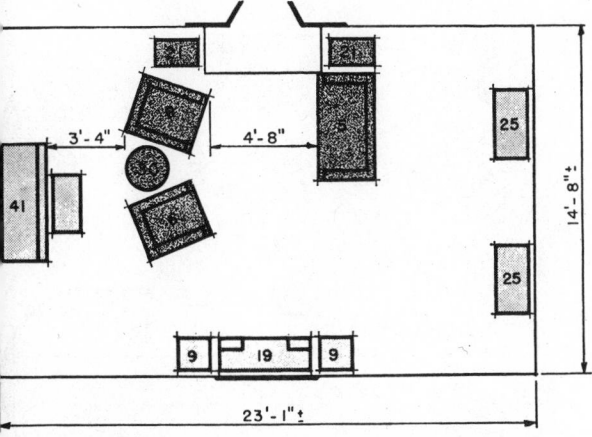

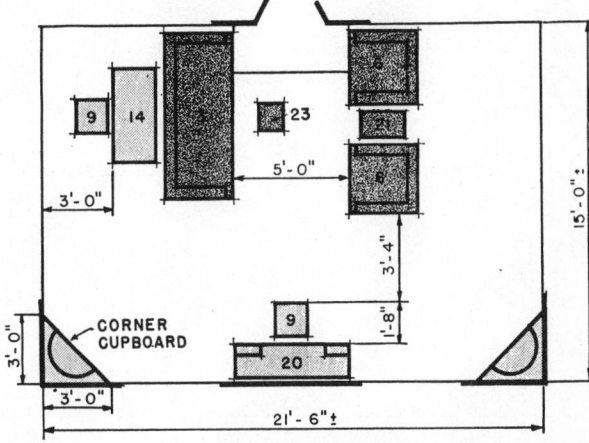

5. If sofa opposite fireplace is omitted, primary group can be brought closer together. In schemes 1 to 4, note that wide groups permit conversation without twisting to see speakers seated on sofa; here this restriction is removed.

6. Here, presumably, doors at ends of room indicate use of one side of room as a traffic route. Primary furniture is grouped closely about fireplace; wall pieces are all that can be used on opposite side.

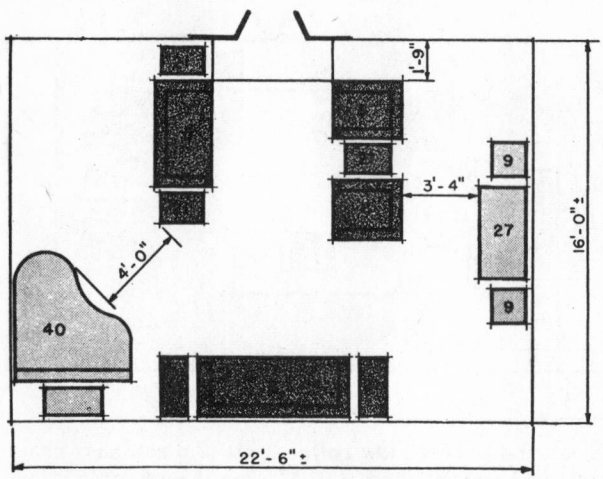

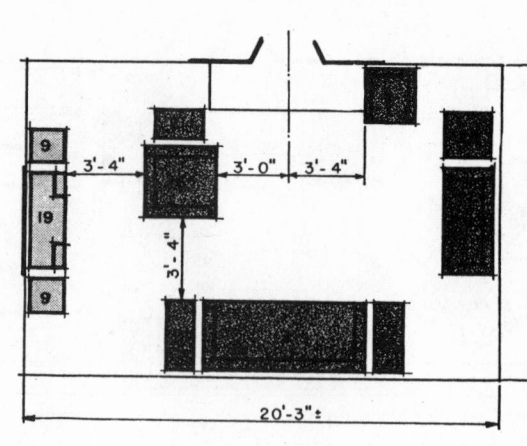

7. Grouping for door locations at both ends of room; ideally, 1-ft clearance is desirable between piano and wall. Chairs (6) are smaller than those previously listed, 2'-6" x 3'-0".

8. If living room has a "dead end" (no doors), primary un[it] may be spread to include entire end of room. Inclusion [of] music or game group would demand more area.

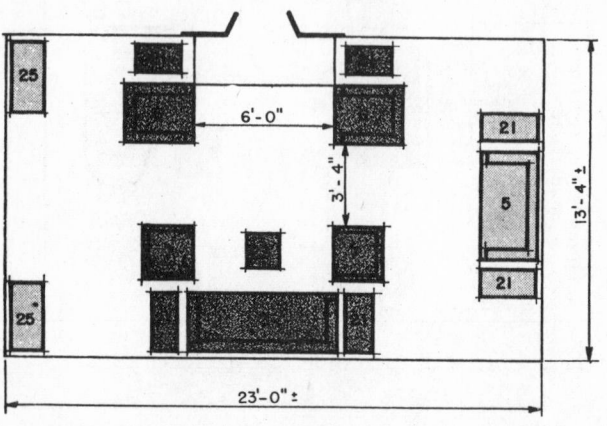

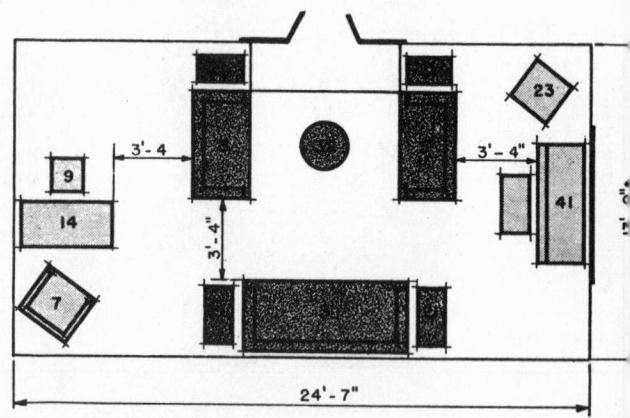

9. Primary group shown is one of most popular arrangements. Unit placing suggests entrance at left end. Secondary conversation unit often becomes music or game group.

10. Writing or study group at left, music or game grou[p] at right, and center primary group, need minimum passage[way] only when room is narrow.

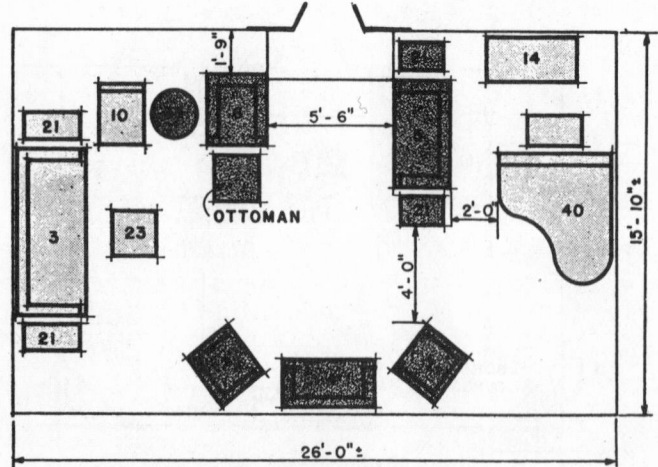

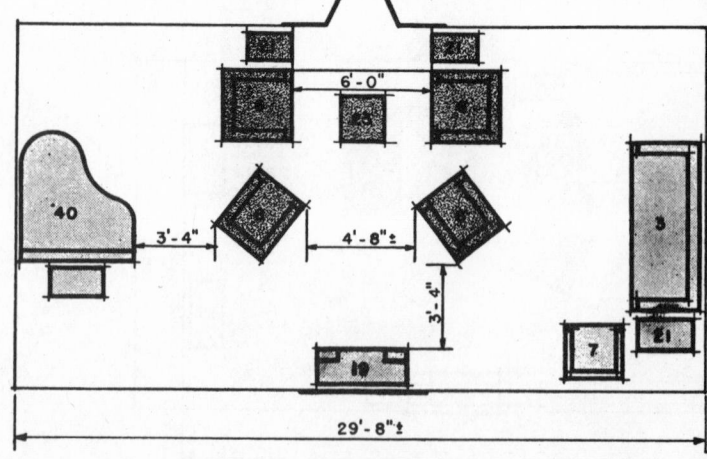

All drawings at scale: 1/8" = 1'-0"

11. Ten persons can be comfortably seated in this type of arrangement, in which primary and secondary conversation groupings almost merge into one.

12. Arrangement designed to permit door locations on side walls rather than ends. Angled chairs (6) are small size[s] noted in Fig. 7, and often used in other arrangements[.]

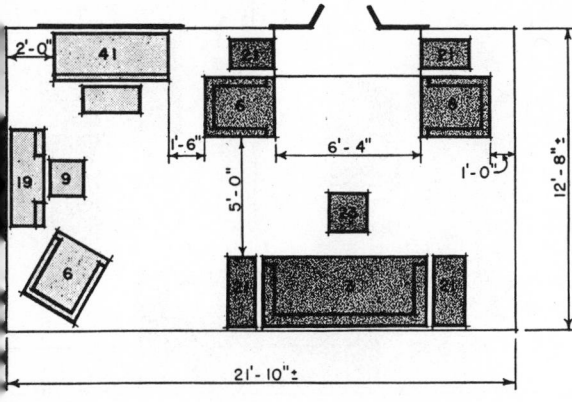

13. Previous diagrams have shown schemes arranged symmetrically about centered fireplaces; on this and the following page are schemes for cases when foci cannot be centered.

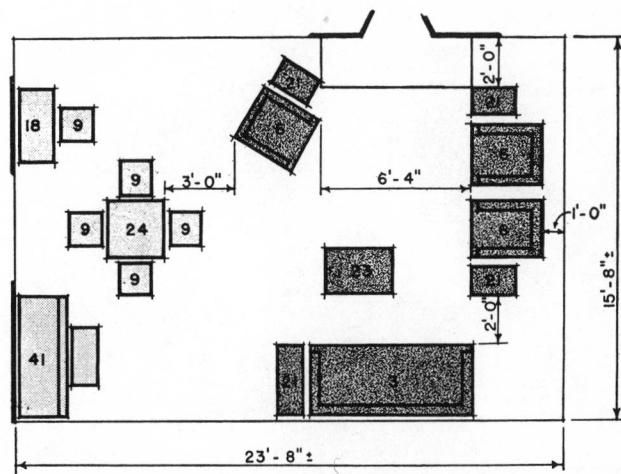

14. Off-center rooms often divide naturally into two parts: primary group, and other groups combined. Clearance no greater than 2' will not accommodate a major traffic lane.

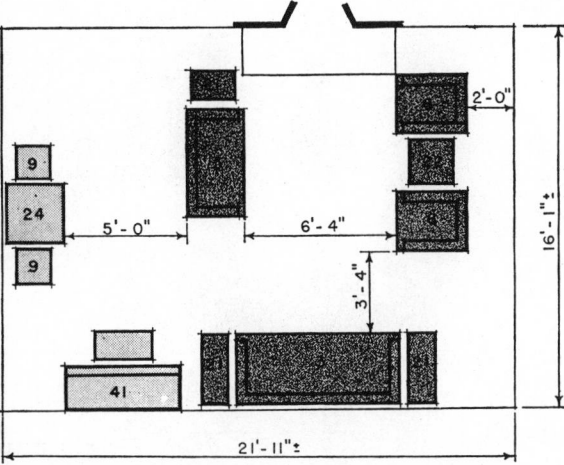

15. If primary, music, and game groups are all to be contained in a small area, one must be curtailed. Here game group consists of table and only two chairs.

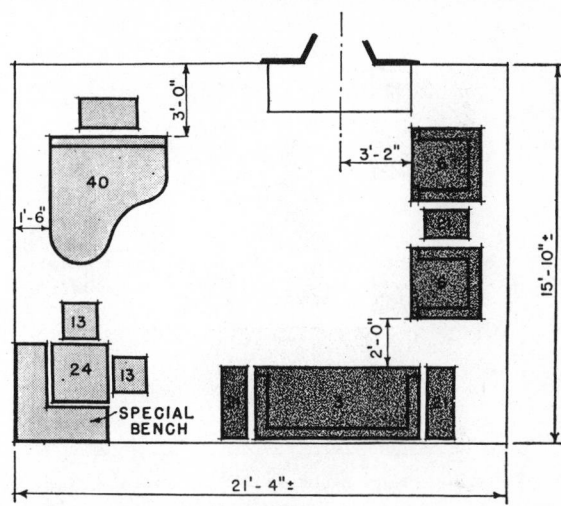

16. In this case the primary conversation group is curtailed to permit inclusion of a grand piano; use of corner bench for game group may result in some loss of comfort.

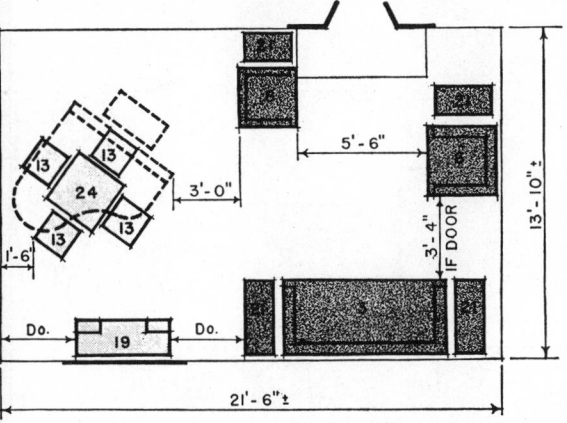

17. Two smaller upholstered chairs (6), each 2'-6" x 3'-0", might be accommodated at the right of the fireplace in this room with only a slight increase in room width.

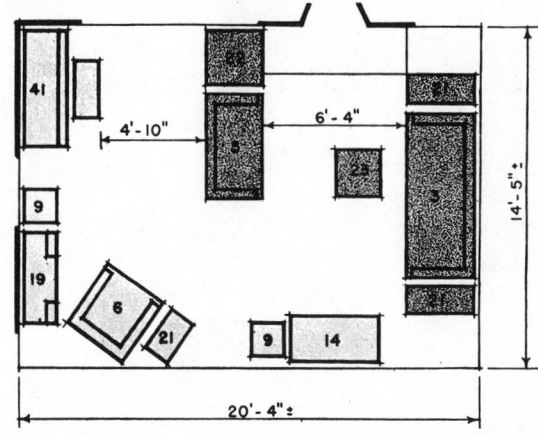

All drawings at scale: ⅛" = 1'-0"

18. In a room with only one door the minimum traffic lane of 3'-4" needs to be increased to at least 4'-10", which will accommodate two persons side by side, without crowding.

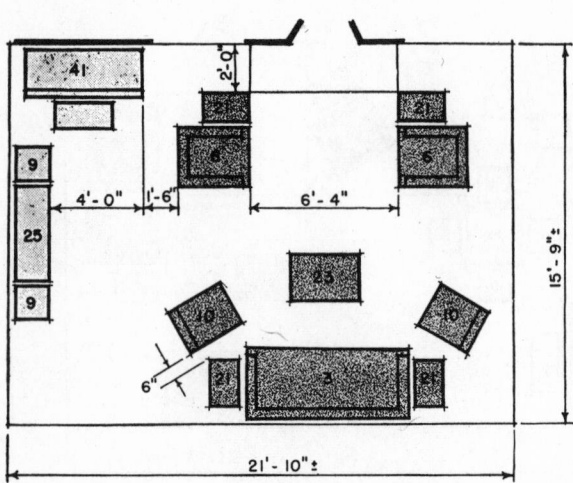

19. Another example of wide entrance lanes. Placement of doors so that at least 10″ is allowed between room corners and door trim will permit installation of "built-in" bookcases.

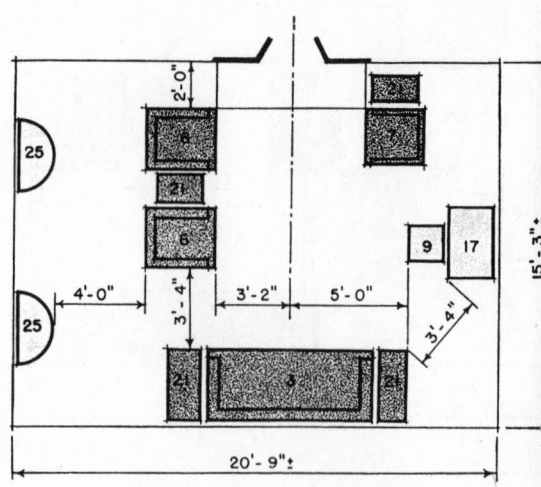

20. Several doors may be accommodated with this type of furniture-group unit arrangement. A traffic lane is assumed to exist at the left end of the room.

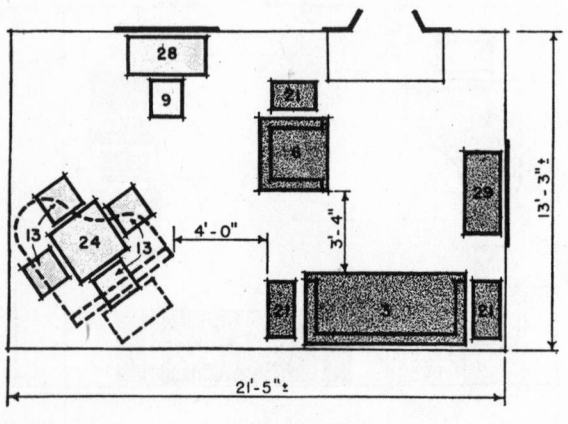

21. Notice that a game-table group occupies almost the same floor area as a baby grand piano. Placement at an angle is intended for informal rooms.

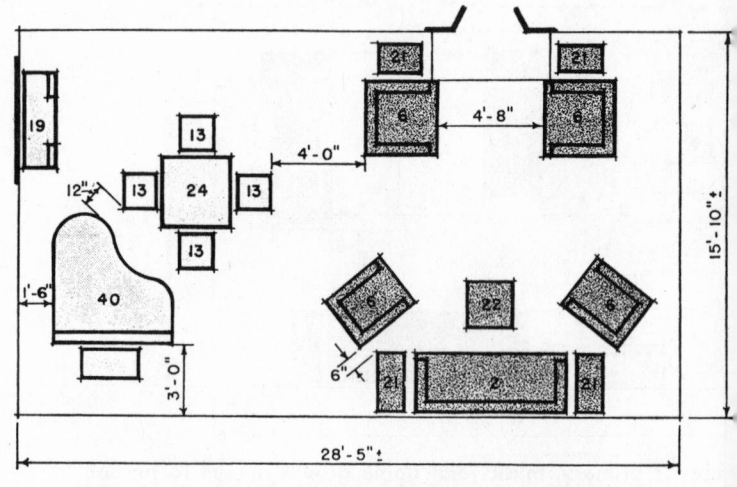

22. Larger rooms may contain four or more furniture-group units; it may be desirable to increase clearances. Use of chairs set at angles requires increased areas.

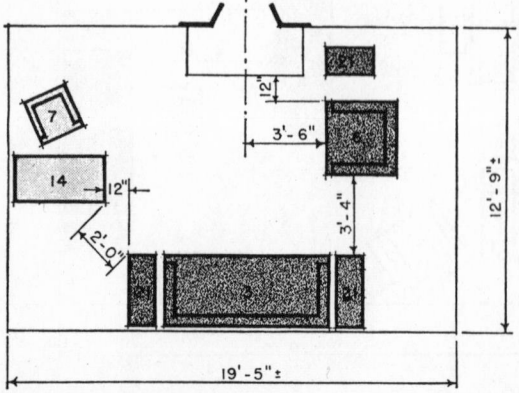

All drawings at scale: ⅛″ = 1′-0″

23. Fireplace chairs set 3′-6″ back from center line of fireplace permit occupants to gaze at the fire comfortably. General traffic cannot be accommodated in a 2-ft lane.

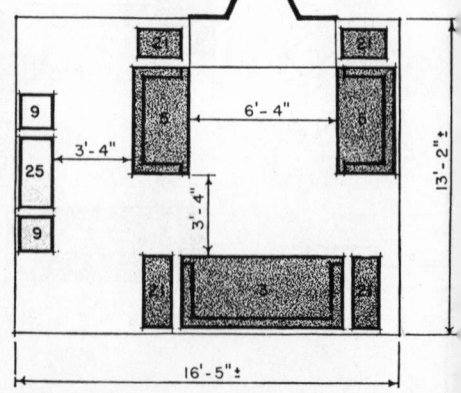

24. By using love seats instead of pairs of chairs at sides of fireplace, considerable space can be saved even though seats are not placed the minimum distance apart.

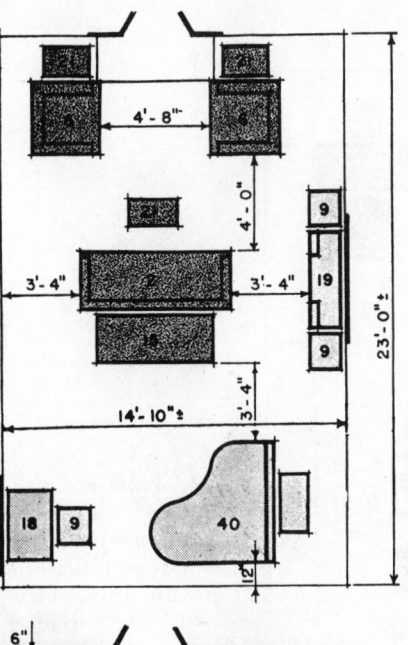

25. In rooms with fireplaces in end walls, as in the schemes immediately preceding, furniture arrangements often fall naturally into two distinct groups.

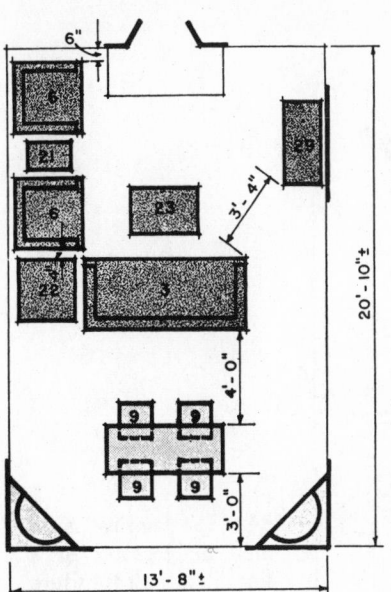

26. One of the two groups may be adapted for dining, eliminating need for a separate dining room. Minimum clearance around dining table should be 3'-0".

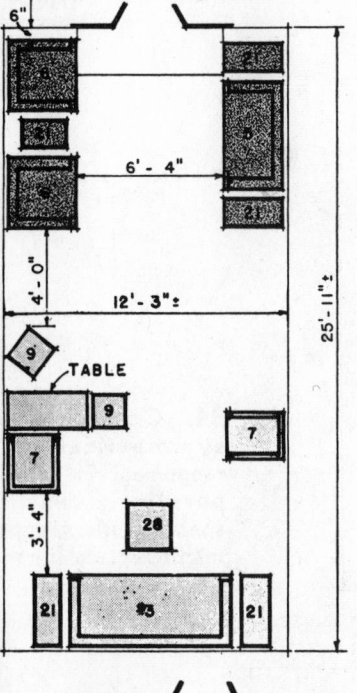

27. In this scheme, by placing the sofa on the long axis opposite the fireplace, furniture is held together as a single unit. There are two obvious positions for an entrance door. It is possible to back the sofa against a group of windows.

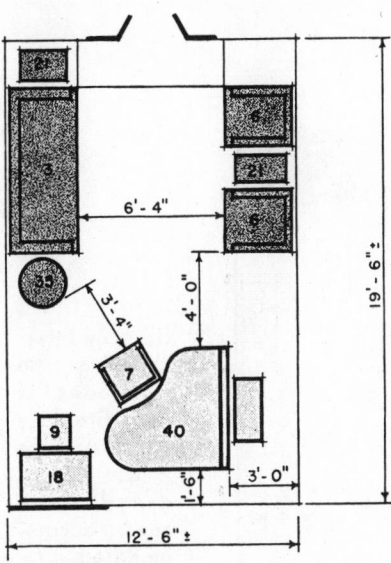

All drawings at scale:
$\frac{1}{8}'' = 1'-0''$

28. Backing the primary-group furniture against walls eliminates passage behind them and reduces room width to a minimum.

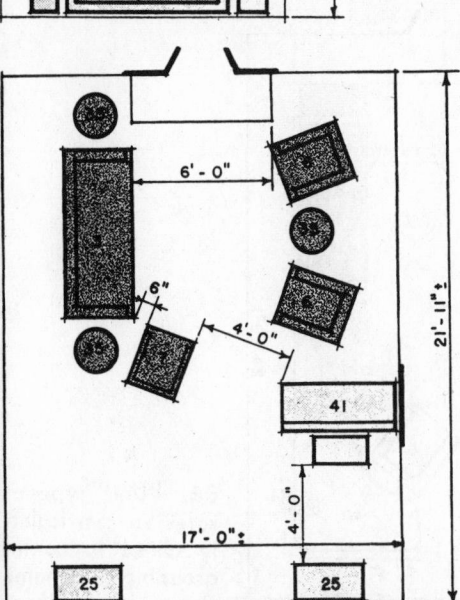

29. Here the left side and end opposite the fireplace are available for doors. Piano should, if possible, be placed against an inside wall.

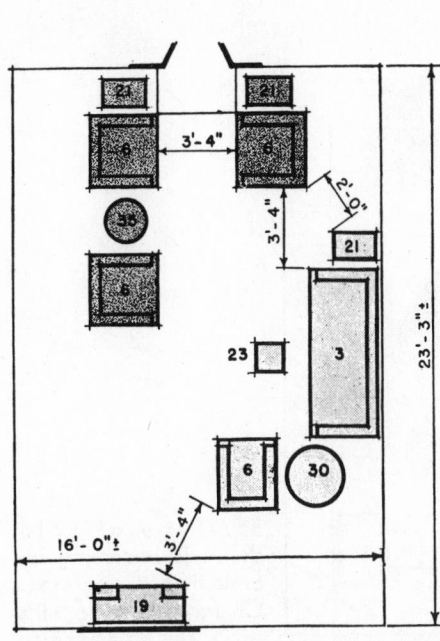

30. Placing the sofa against one side of the room tends to open up the primary group—in effect, to merge with it the secondary conversation-group furniture.

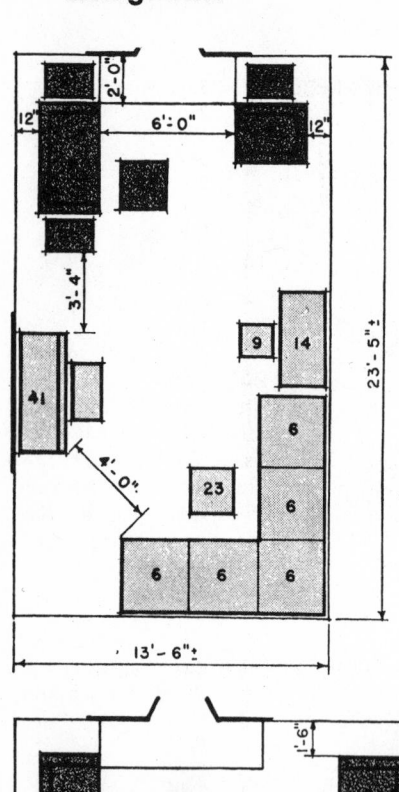

31. The entire area may be treated as a single unit, all furniture being brought into the principal group.

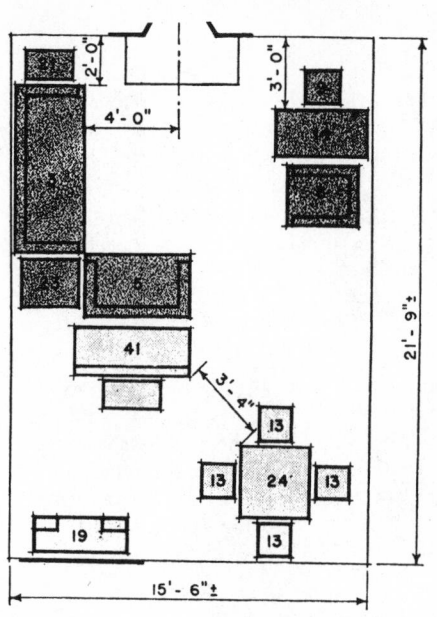

32. Here the placing of the desk group (14) allies it closely with the fireplace unit. Four units are included.

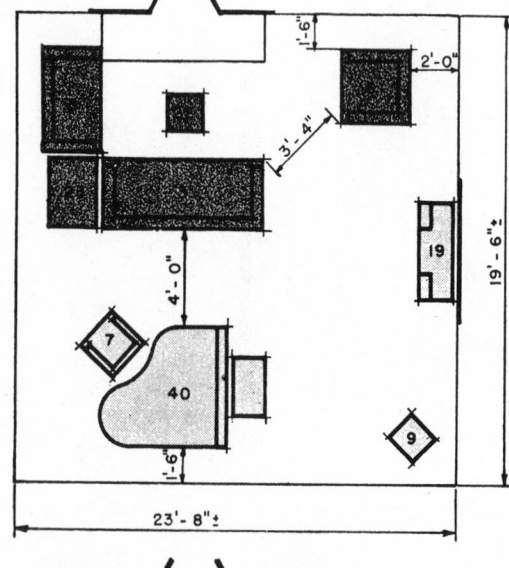

33. By interchanging the positions of the fireplace furniture in Fig. 32, a grand piano can be accommodated.

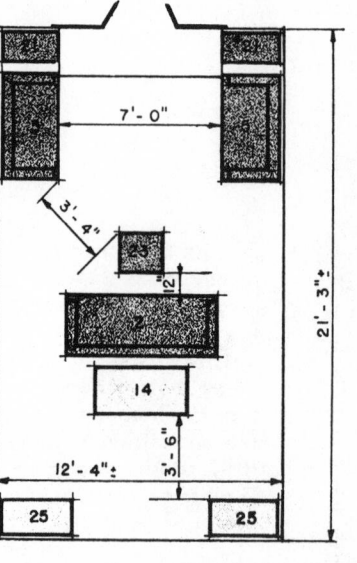

All drawings at scale: $\frac{1}{8}'' = 1'\text{-}0''$

34. Completely symmetrical arrangement in comparatively small space; music group might replace items 14 and 25.

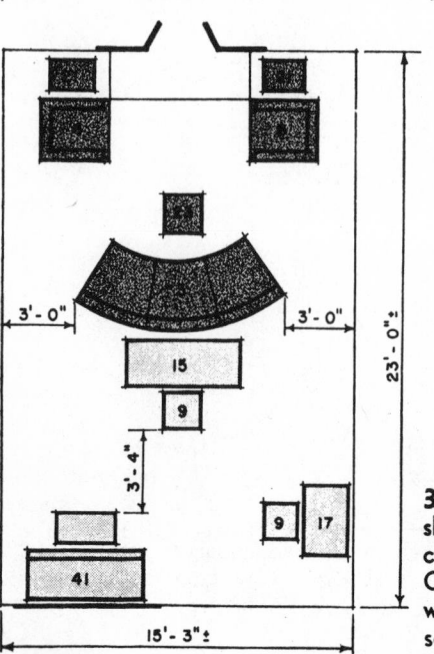

35. Type of sofa shown is becoming increasingly popular. Chairs (6) may be units which can be added to sofa, if desired.

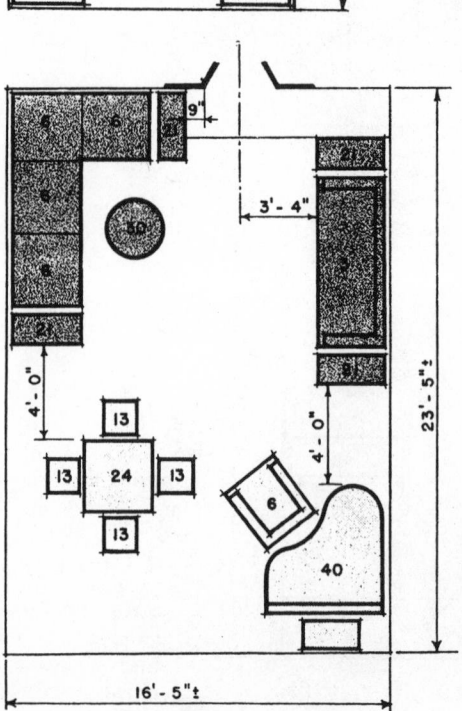

36. "Unit" types of sofas are particularly suited to corner groupings. Scheme shown contains three group units.

SPACE IN the small house for general living activities must often serve a wide variety of functions. Thus, furniture can add greatly to the usefulness of living area if it is adaptable in type and size to a number of different purposes.

Accompanying data give a working basis for providing sufficient space for general living activities. Dimensional information includes only a few of many available sizes and types of furniture. Dimensions of groups refer to clearances necessary for comfortable and convenient use.

Necessary planning considerations include: provision of adequate floor and wall space for furniture groupings; segregation of trafficways from centers of activities; ease of access; and a maximum of flexibility.

Doors in constant use should be placed so that traffic between them will not interfere with furniture groups.

Flexibility implies the varying uses to which space may be put. The lounging group at the right, for instance, requires approximately the same floor space as the card-playing group; the sofa, below, may be a convertible bed. Thus, functions of other areas—such as recreation, sleeping, dining and even storage—may be applicable equally to living rooms.

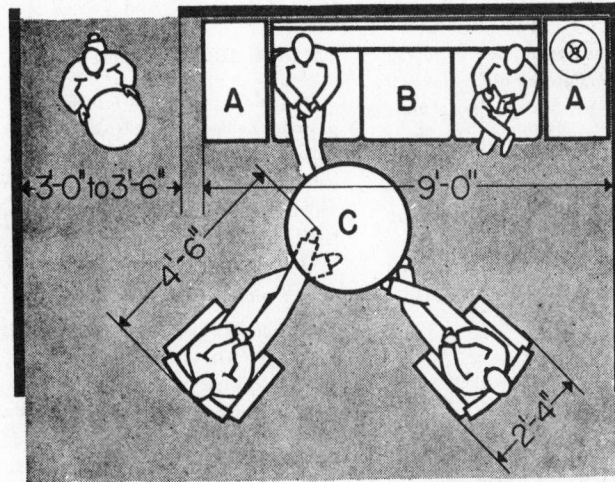

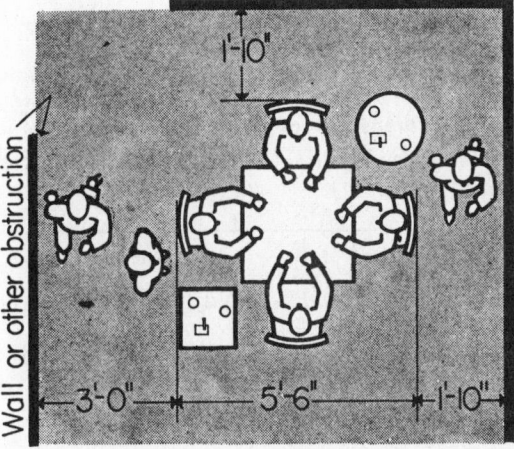

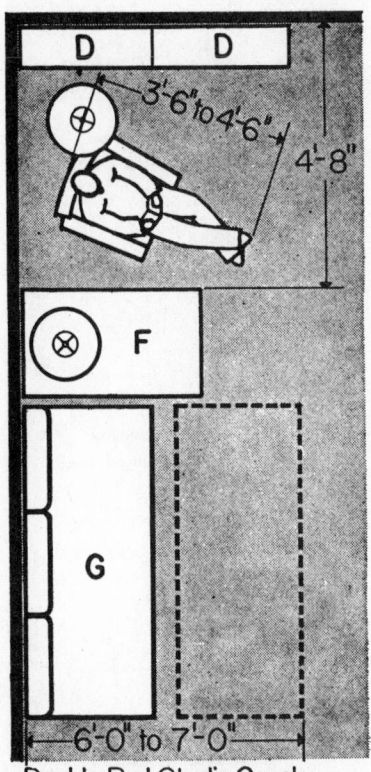

Double Bed Studio Couch

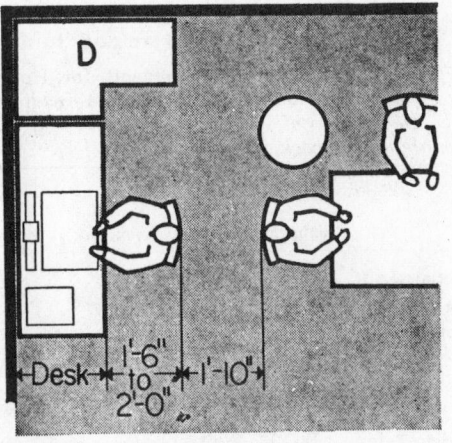

Sofa Sizes (B):
2'-8" to 3'-6" deep
6'-0" to 7'-2" long
Love Seats:
2'-0" to 2'-10" deep
3'-6" to 4'-6" long
End Tables (A):
10" to 1'-2" wide
1'-6" to 3'-0" long
Occasional
Tables (C):
2'-0" to 2'-4" square,
round, oval, draw-top, etc.

Card Tables:
2'-6" to 3'-0" square;
folding type 1½"
thick folded (average)
Side Chairs:
1'-6" to 2'-0" wide
1'-6" to 1'-10" deep

Desks, Sloping Top:
3'-0" to 3'-8" wide
1'-6" to 2'-0" deep
Writing Desks:
2'-8" to 3'-6" wide
1'-6" to 2'-6" deep
Secretaries:
3'-0" to 5'-0" wide
1'-6" to 2'-8" deep

Convertible Sofa-Beds (G): 2'-9" to 3'-3" deep, 6'-2" to 6'-8" long
Living Room Tables (F): 1'-8" to 3'-0" wide, 3'-6" to 10'-0" long
Easy Chairs: Wing, 2'-4" to 2'-10" square; Club, 2'-4" to 3'-3", 3'-9" square
Book Cases (D): 2'-6" to 3'-0" wide, 10" to 12" deep

Sizes of furniture listed on this page are those most commonly in use. Portable units are available in a wide variety of stock sizes. One type is designed so that pieces may be combined in sets to save space and provide utility comparable to completely fitted, built-in units.

FURNITURE—10
Dining room

By GLENN H. BEYER AND ALEXANDER KIRA, *Housing Research Center, Cornell University*

The principal factors to be considered in planning the dining area are as follows: (1) Number of persons to be seated; (2) Space used at the table; (3) Space for chairs and for passage behind them; (4) Seating arrangement; (5) Size and type of furniture; and (6) Storage space for china, glassware, silver, and linen.

Recommended space dimensions, based on recent research, are provided below.

SIZE OF PLACE SETTING

The minimum width needed for each place setting is 21 in.; however, a width of up to 29 in. is desirable for greater freedom of movement. A 25-in. width is usually adequate; this permits chairs 19 in. wide to be placed 6 in. apart. The minimum depth for a place setting is 14½ in. These dimensions allow space for china, glassware, silver, and elbow extension (See Fig. 1).

PASSAGE BEHIND CHAIRS

The minimum space recommended for passage behind chairs is 22 in.; a satisfactory range is 22 to 25 in. If passage behind the chairs is not required, a minimum of 5 in. plus the depth of the chair must be provided for pushing back the chair when leaving the table (See Fig. 3).

Size of table

The minimum width recommended is 36 in.; a satisfactory width is 36 to 44 in.

If 25-in.-wide place settings are provided and if one person is seated at each end of the table, then minimum and recommended table lengths are as follows:

Persons	Minimum, in.	Recommended, in.
4	54	60
6	79	84
8	104	108
10	129	132
12	154	156

If no one is seated at either end of the table, the length may be reduced by approximately 4 in.

Space for total dining area

With the same conditions noted above and with an ample 42-in. space for passage on all sides of a 42-in.-wide table, required sizes are as follows:

Persons	W × L ft	= Area sq ft
4	10½x12	= 126
6	10½x14	= 147
8	10½x16	= 168
10	10½x18	= 189
12	10½x20	= 210

If no one is to be seated at either end of the table, the length may be reduced by 2 ft (21 sq ft).

Storage space

Linear feet of shelf space required for medium-income families, for both moderate and liberal supplies of dishes and glassware, for everyday and guest use, is as follows:

	12-in. shelves, ft–in.	20-in. shelves, ft
Moderate	21–0	2
Liberal	36–9	2

Drawer space for storage of silver is shown in Table 1. Space for storage of table linens is shown in Table 2.

Table 1. Inside dimensions of drawers for storage of silverware

Adapted from Indoor Dining Areas for Rural Homes in the Western Region, Report 118, University of Arizona Agricultural Experiment Station, Tucson (June 1955).

Item	Width, in.	Depth, in.	Height, in.
8 each forks, knives, soupspoons; 12 teaspoons; 6 tablespoons, 4 serving pieces	11	18½	2¾
12 each forks, knives, salad forks or others, butter spreaders, soupspoons; 18 teaspoons, 6 tablespoons, 3-piece carving set, 3 serving pieces	14½	20	3
12 each forks, knives, soupspoons, salad forks or butter spreaders; 24 teaspoons, 6 tablespoons, 6 serving pieces	17	19¾	2¼

Table 2. Dimensions of stacks of folded table linens

Adapted from Storage Space Requirements for Household Textiles, A. Woolrich, M. M. White, and M. A. Richards, Agricultural Research Bulletin 62–2, U.S. Department of Agriculture, Washington, D.C. (1955). Dimensions given are front-to-back, side-to-side, and height.

Item	Space 16 in. deep Minimum, in.	Maximum, in.	Space 20 in. deep Minimum, in.	Maximum, in.
2 large tablecloths, guest use	14x19x3	14x36x2	19x14x3	19x28x2
2 medium tablecloths, everyday use	15x19x1	13x28x1	19x10x1	18x28x1
4 small tablecloths, everyday use	14x10x3	14x28x1	10x14x3	15x14x2
3 small tablecloths, guest use	14x10x2	14x28x1	10x14x2	15x14x2
12 small napkins (2 stacks of 6)	7x10x3	7x10x3	10x 5x3	10x 9x2
12 large napkins (2 stacks of 6)	8x10x2	8x10x2	10x 6x2	10x10x1
6 place mats, everyday use	13x19x1	13x19x1	19x13x1	19x13x1
1 table pad	13x21x3	13x21x3	13x21x3	13x21x3

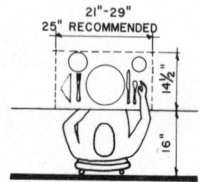

Fig. 1. Size of place setting

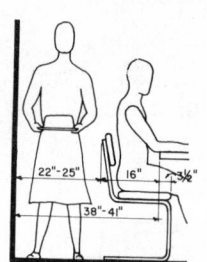

Fig. 2. Passage behind chairs

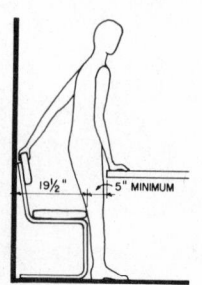

Fig. 3. Leaving the table

DINING AREAS must accommodate furniture—either portable or built-in —for eating, sitting, serving and possible storage. Equipment for these dining functions may also be adapted to meet other possible requirements for this space—as studying, game-playing, etc.

Table space requirements per person are as follows: for crowded seating, 1'-10" on the table's perimeter; for comfort, 2'-0". Adequate clearances for use are indicated on diagrams.

Furniture Sizes:

Portable Tables, round (A):
2'-7" to 5'-10" diam.

Portable Tables, rectangular (C):
2'-6" to 4'-0" by 3'-6" to 8'-0"; or 2'-0" to 4'-0" square

Dining Chairs, portable:
1'-6" to 2'-0" by 1'-6" to 1'-10"

Serving Table (B):
2'-6" to 3'-6" by 1'-2" to 1'-9"

Sideboard or Buffet (B):
4'-0" to 6'-6" by 1'-5" to 2'-1"

China Cabinet (B):
2'-8" to 3'-8" by 1'-2" to 1'-9"

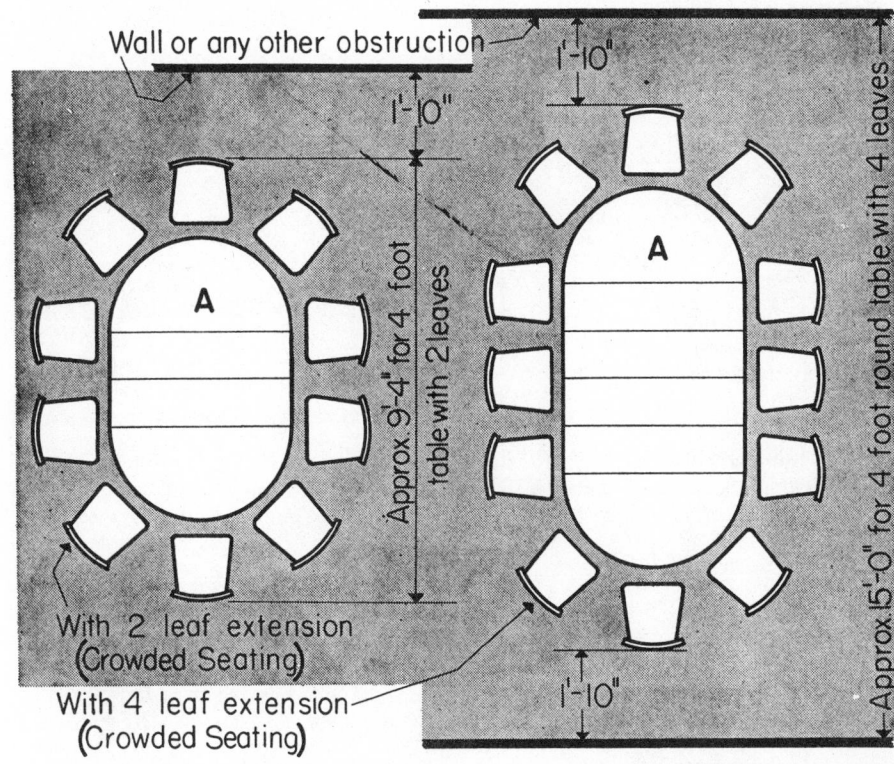

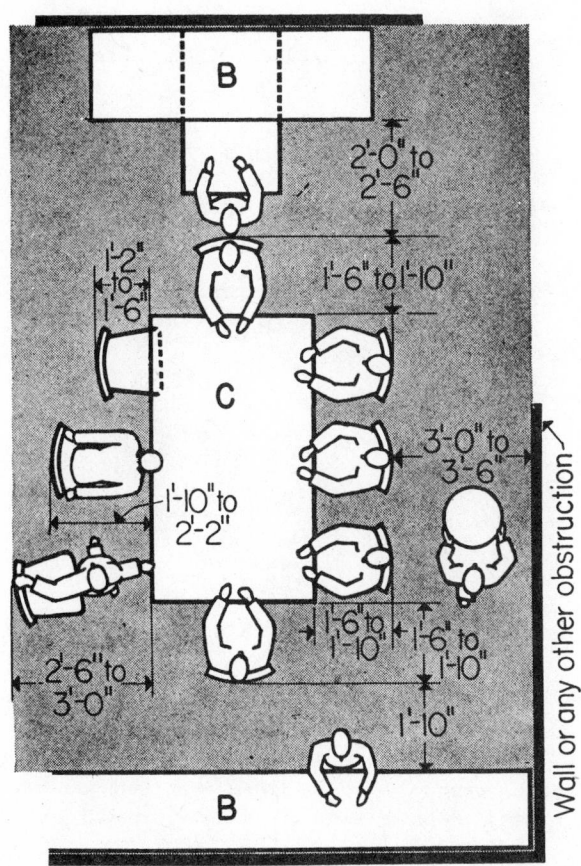

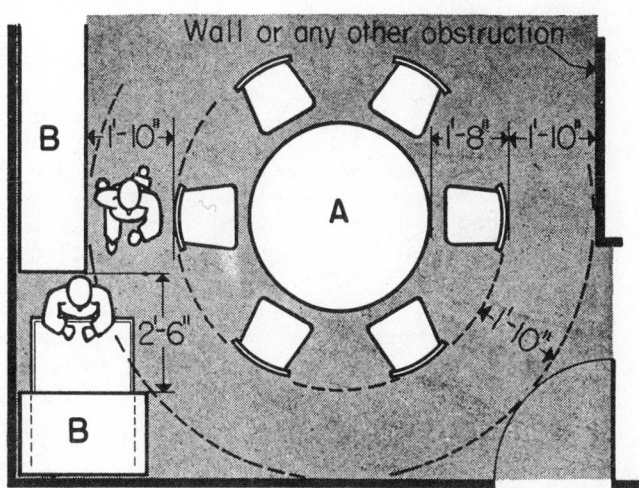

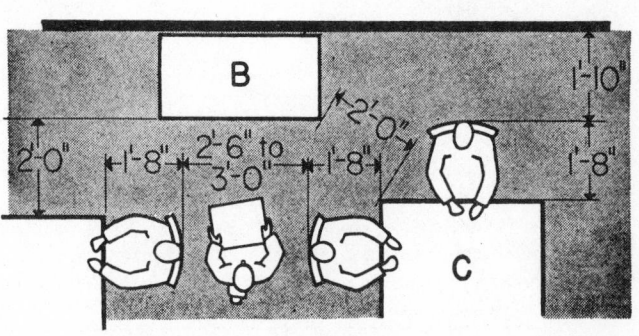

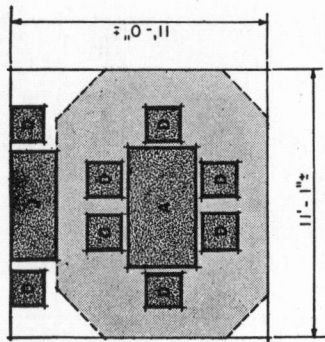

1. Minimum requires 2-ft buffet space on one side only; 3' more length is needed for extension table.

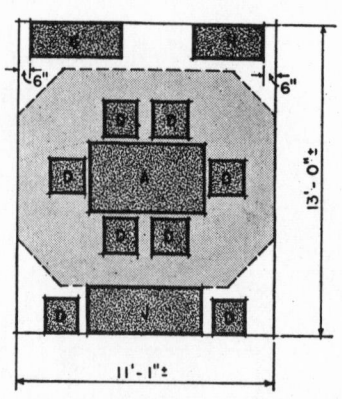

2. Typical dining-room suite, as used in East and on West Coast, requires furniture space on two sides of room.

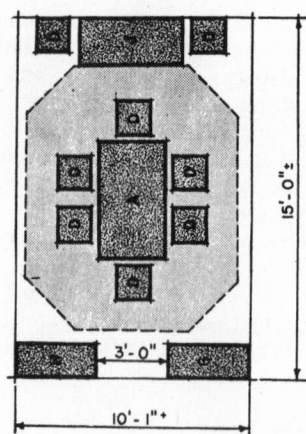

3. Long narrow area with some waste space results when wall pieces are at ends, and end entrance is needed.

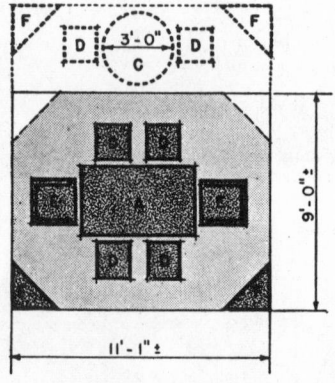

4. Solid lines indicate minimum room with corner cupboards, no wall furniture. Dotted lines indicate added space for 3' breakfast table.

All drawings at scale: 1/8" = 1'-0"

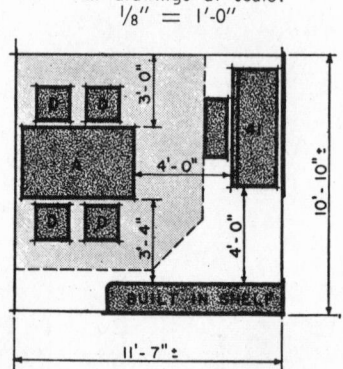

5. Table-and-passage unit in one corner permits use of minimum space for multiple activities; piano may be replaced by desk, love seat, etc.

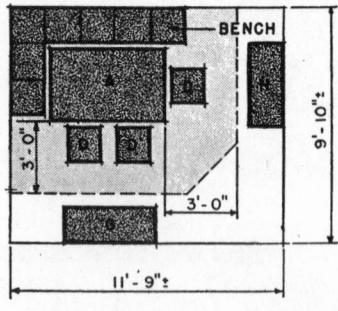

6. Spaces smaller than the usual minimum can be utilized if built-in seats are included; seating and table-service comfort are sacrificed.

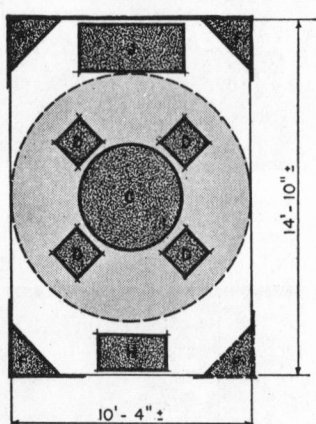

7. The same set of clearances applies to the seldom used round table as to the more popular oblong table.

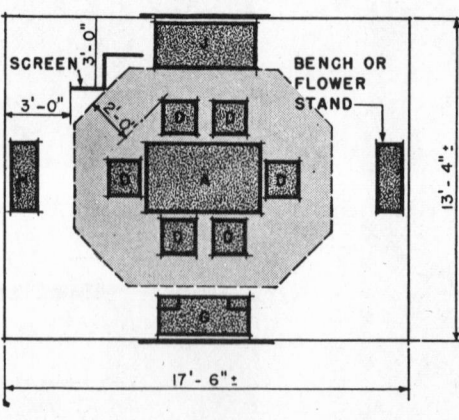

8. Arrangement of typical suite in larger-than-minimum space, when a screen is used at serving door.

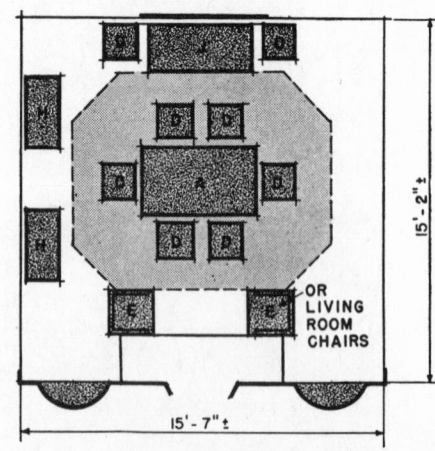

9. Dining rooms with fireplaces have to be larger than minimum for the comfort of those seated at table.

DINING ROOM FURNITURE

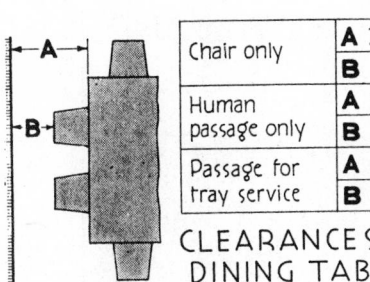

Chair only	A	2'-0"±
	B	4"
Human passage only	A	3'-4"
	B	1'-8"
Passage for tray service	A	4'-10"
	B	3'-2"

CLEARANCES for DINING TABLES

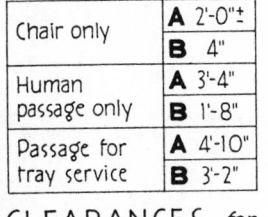

Min. Dimensions for Tray Service

4'-10"
3'-2"
4'-10"

DINING ROOM TABLES

Allow 2 lineal feet per person

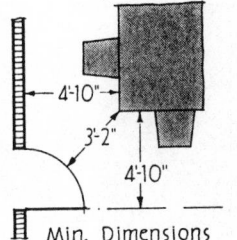

| | | W | 2'-6" to 4'-0" |
| 2, 2½, 3, 4 Feet square | Varies 2'-7" to 5'-10" | L | 3'-6" to 8'-0" |

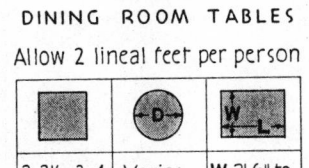

2'-1"
2'-6"

MINIMUM KNEE CLEARANCE DINING TABLES

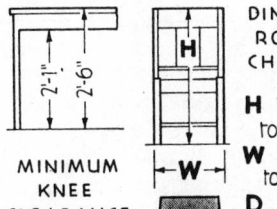

DINING ROOM CHAIRS

H 2'-10" to 3'-3"
W 1'-6" to 2'-0"
D 1'-6" to 1'-10"

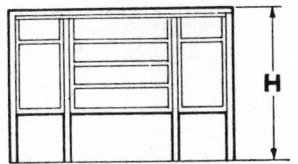

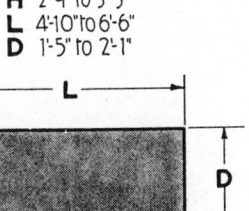

BUFFET
H 2'-9" to 3'-3"
L 4'-10" to 6'-6"
D 1'-5" to 2'-1"

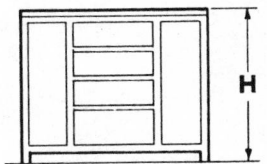

SIDEBOARD
H 2'-9" to 3'-2"
L 4'-0" to 5'-0"
D 1'-8" or 1'-9"

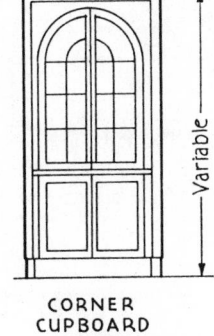

Variable

CORNER CUPBOARD
2'-0" to 3'-0"

Scale 0 1' 2' 3' 4' 5' 6'

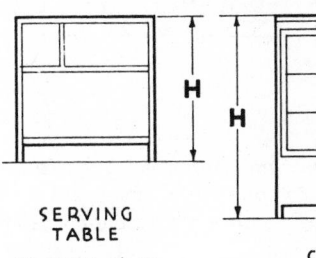

SERVING TABLE
H 2'-6" to 3'-0"
L 2'-6" to 3'-6"
D 1'-2" to 1'-9"

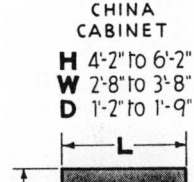

CHINA CABINET
H 4'-2" to 6'-2"
W 2'-8" to 3'-8"
D 1'-2" to 1'-9"

BEDROOM FURNITURE

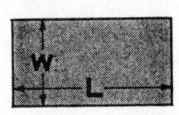

DIMENSIONS OF BEDS

SIZE	MATERIAL	L	W
SINGLE	Metal	6'-10"	3'-0"
	Wood	6'-10"	3'-4"±
TWIN SINGLE	Metal	6'-10"	3'-3"
	Wood	6'-10"	3'-8"±
SMALL 3/4	Metal	6'-10"	3'-6"
	Wood	6'-10"	3'-10"±
LARGE 3/4	Metal	6'-10"	4'-0"
	Wood	6'-10"	4'-4"±
FULL SIZE	Metal	6'-10"	4'-6"
	Wood	6'-10"	4'-10"±

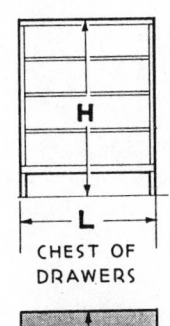
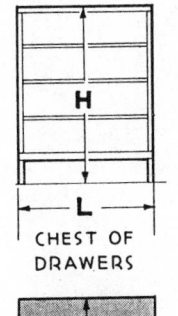

CHEST OF DRAWERS
H 3'-5" to 4'-8"
L 2'-8" to 3'-4"
D 1'-6" to 1'-10"

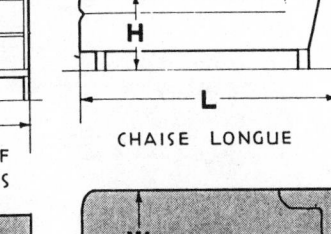
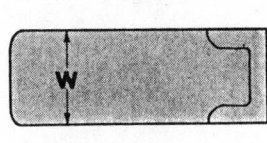
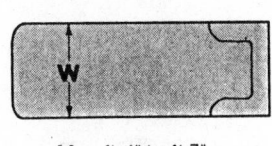

CHAISE LONGUE
H 1'-4" to 1'-7"
L 4'-0" to 5'-6"
D 2'-0" to 2'-4"

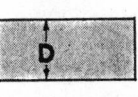

DRESSING TABLE
H 2'-2" to 2'-6"
L 3'-0" to 4'-2"
D 1'-3" to 1'-10"

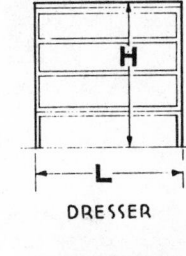
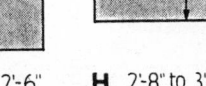

DRESSER
H 2'-8" to 3'-1"
L 3'-0" to 4'-0"
D 1'-6" to 1'-10"

CLEARANCE DIAGRAM - BEDROOM

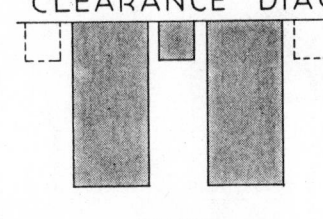

Clearance Diagrams - Scale 1/8"=1'-0"

WIDTH (wall space)		W
Twin Beds	No Night Table	7'-0" to 8'-0"
Twin Beds	1 Night Table	7'-10" to 9'-8"
Twin Beds	2 Night Tables	9'-4" to 12'-2"
Double Bed	1 Night Table	5'-8" to 7'-0"
Double Bed	2 Night Tables	6'-10" to 9'-2"
Single Bed	1 Night Table	4'-2" to 5'-6"

LENGTH DIMENSIONS	L
Bed plus passage	8'-10"
Bed plus passage & dresser	10'-8" to 11'-4"

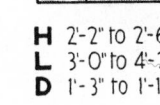

NIGHT TABLE
H 1'-9" to 2'-6"
W 1'-2" to 2'-0"
D 1'-0" to 2'-0"

BOUDOIR CHAIR
H 2'-8" to 3'-4"
W 2'-6" to 2'-10"
D 2'-8" to 3'-2"

DIAGRAMS indicate minimum clearances that should be provided for use of the bedroom furniture shown, dimensions for which are listed below. Many types and sizes of furniture are available; but those listed are most common and can serve as a basis for bedroom design. At least 2″ should be allowed as clearance between walls and furniture; 3″ between furniture units.

Beds:
Single (C), metal: 3′-0″ to 3′-3″ wide; 6′-10″ long. Wood: 3′-2″ to 3′-6″ wide; 6′-10″ long.
Twin (F), metal: 3′-3″ wide; 6′-10″ long. Wood: 3′-6″ to 3′-9″ wide; 6′-10″ long
Three-quarter (E), small, metal: 3′-6″ wide; 6′-10″ long. Wood: 3′-3″ to 4′-0″ wide; 6′-10″ long
Three-quarter (B), large, metal: 4′-0″ wide; 6′-10″ long. Wood: 4′-2″ to 4′-6″ wide; 6′-10″ long
Double, metal: 4′-6″ wide, 6′-10″ long. Wood: 4′-10″ wide; 6′-10″ long
Roll-away beds, (A): 2′-0″ by 5′-0″ on edge, 3″ clearance on all sides

Bed Tables (G):
1′-2″ to 2′-0″ by 1′-0″ to 2′-0″

Bedroom Chairs (H):
Small, 1′-8″ by 1′-8″; larger, 2′-6″ to 2′-10″ by 2′-8″ to 3′-2″

Dressers (3-drawer) (D):
3′-0″ to 4′-0″ by 1′-6″ to 1′-10″

Chest of Drawers (4-drawer) (D):
2′-8″ to 3′-4″ by 1′-6″ to 1′-10″

Chaise Lounge:
2′-0″ to 2′-4″ by 4′-0″ to 5′-6″

Day Bed:
2′-9″ to 3′-3″ by 6′-2″ to 6′-8″

Dressing Table:
1′-3″ to 1′-10″ by 3′-0″ to 4′-2″

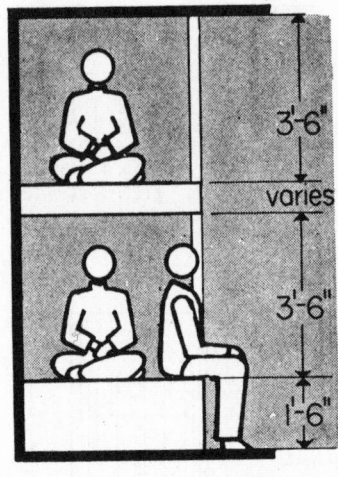

Double-deck bed

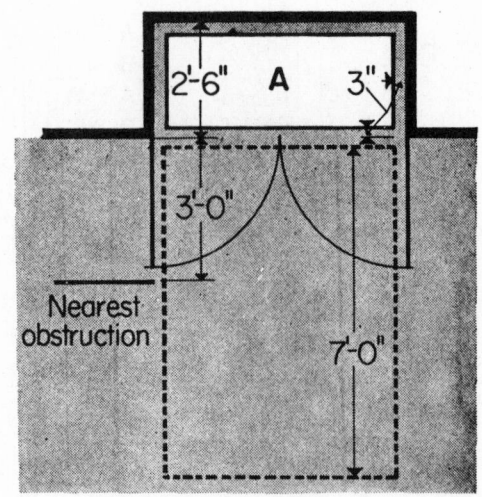

Roll-away bed

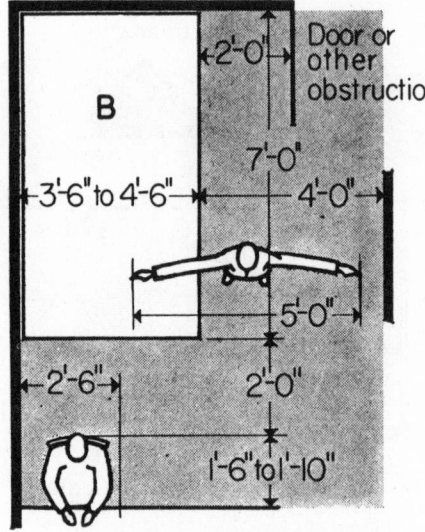

Large three-quarter bed

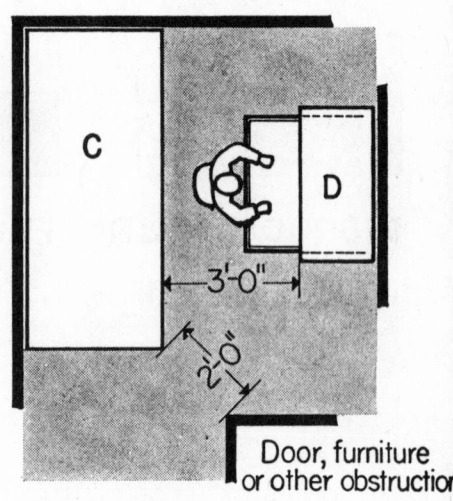

Clearance for dresser

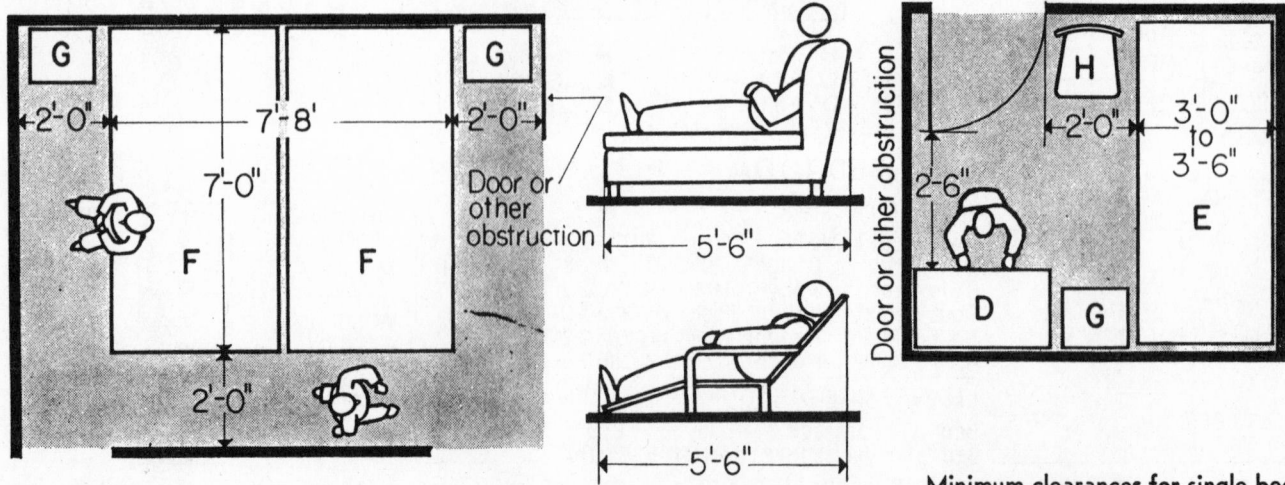

Minimum clearances for twin-bed group

Minimum clearances for single bed and dresser group

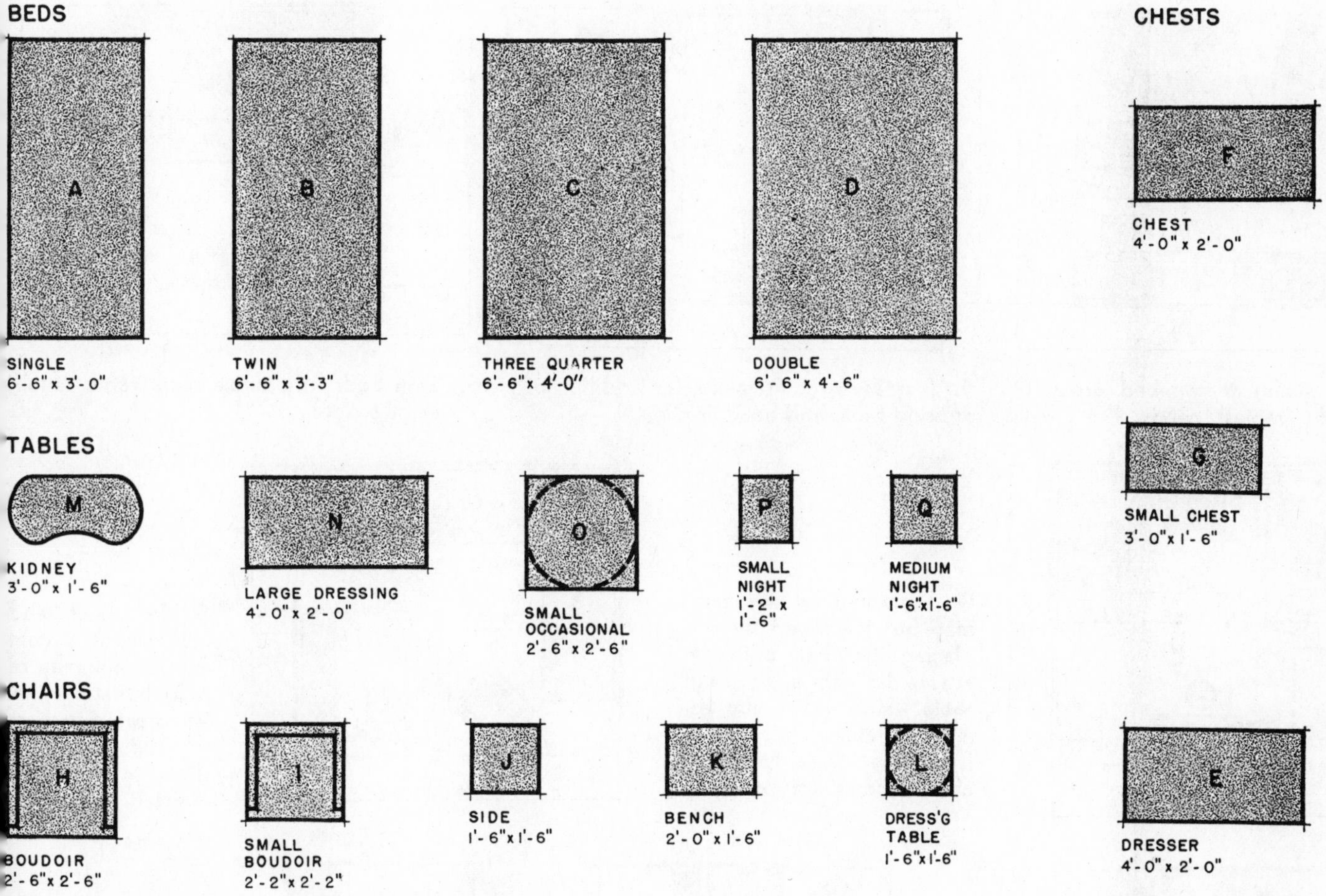

BEDS

A — SINGLE 6'-6" x 3'-0"

B — TWIN 6'-6" x 3'-3"

C — THREE QUARTER 6'-6" x 4'-0"

D — DOUBLE 6'-6" x 4'-6"

CHESTS

F — CHEST 4'-0" x 2'-0"

G — SMALL CHEST 3'-0" x 1'-6"

TABLES

M — KIDNEY 3'-0" x 1'-6"

N — LARGE DRESSING 4'-0" x 2'-0"

O — SMALL OCCASIONAL 2'-6" x 2'-6"

P — SMALL NIGHT 1'-2" x 1'-6"

Q — MEDIUM NIGHT 1'-6" x 1'-6"

CHAIRS

H — BOUDOIR 2'-6" x 2'-6"

I — SMALL BOUDOIR 2'-2" x 2'-2"

J — SIDE 1'-6" x 1'-6"

K — BENCH 2'-0" x 1'-6"

L — DRESS'G TABLE 1'-6" x 1'-6"

E — DRESSER 4'-0" x 2'-0"

TYPICAL AVERAGE FURNITURE SIZES

Scale 1/4" = 1'-0"

TYPICAL UNIT ARRANGEMENTS

Scale 1/8" = 1'-0"

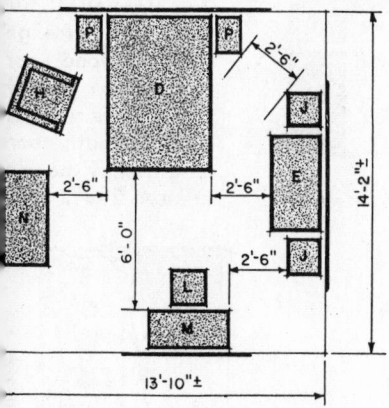

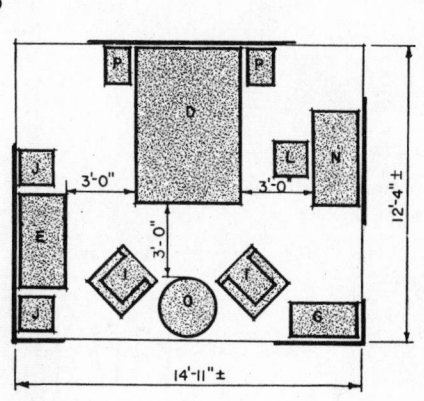

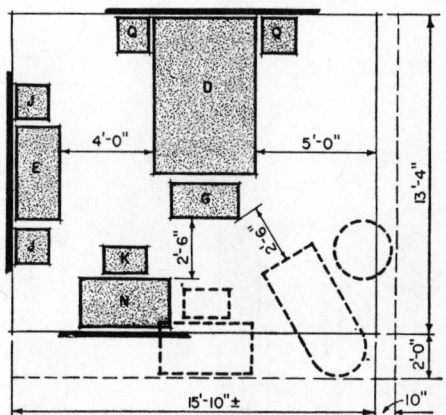

1. For comfort, 2 night tables are desirable with a double bed. A minimum double-bed unit arrangement may be achieved by omitting arm chair and one side chair, and reducing to 3'-6" the traffic lane at foot of bed.

2. Use of small chairs and chest makes possible the addition of conversation or lounging furniture (2 chairs and table) to a typical suite, without increasing square footage. Use of 3-ft passages eliminates crowding.

3. Other types of arrangements beyond the minimum include addition of a chaise longue (shown dotted above), which is usually placed at an angle to walls, requires a table, and necessitates ample passages.

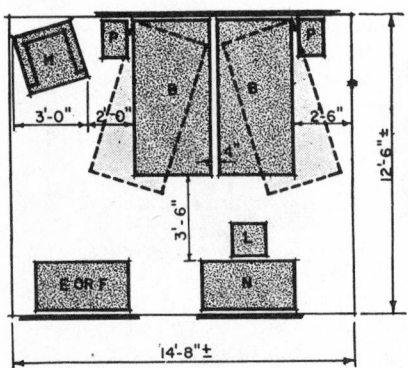

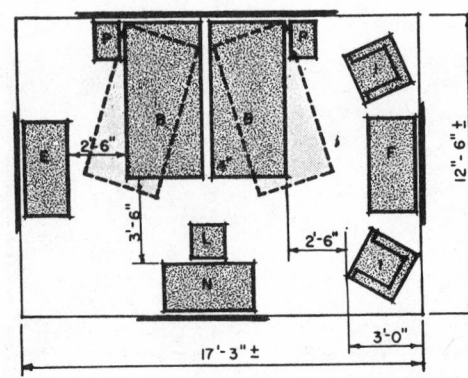

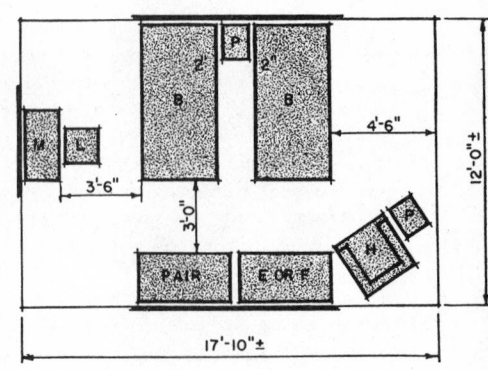

4. Minimum twin-bed group (2 night tables) needs 9'-6" wall.

5. Increased requirements for addition of dressing table and boudoir chair.

6. Twin beds with single night table require 8' of wall space.

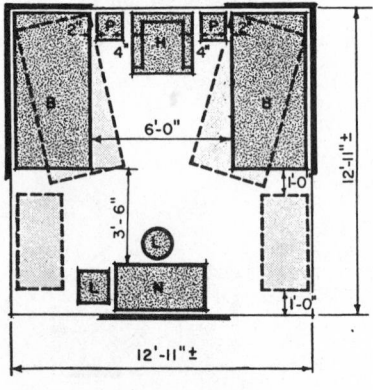

7. Variations on this plan may be developed by replacing the chair between the beds with a dressing table which serves also as a night table. This would free other walls for twin chests, shown dotted.

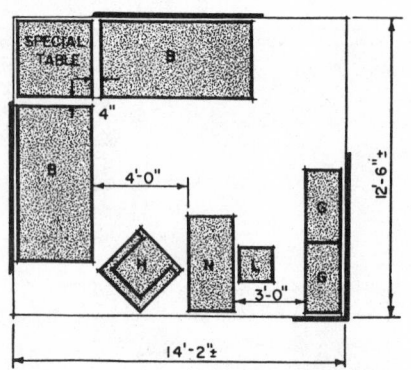

8. Twin beds heading toward a common corner may require less space than is indicated if dressing table and boudoir chair are omitted.

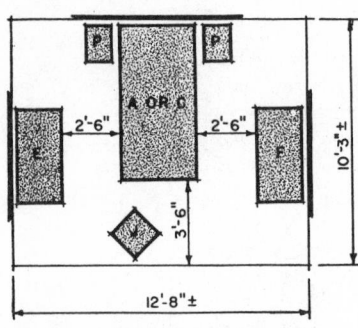

9. Single-bed unit with two night tables requires 6'-6" wall.

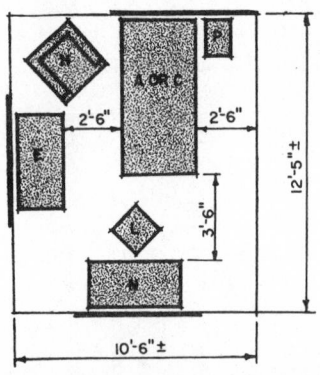

10. Minimum dimensions for passage both sides of bed.

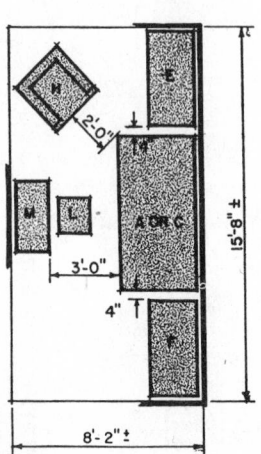

11. Unusual but satisfactory arrangement or long, narrow space; if units E and F are reduced 2'-0" in length, room length may be decreased 2'-0".

SHELF AND LIGHT

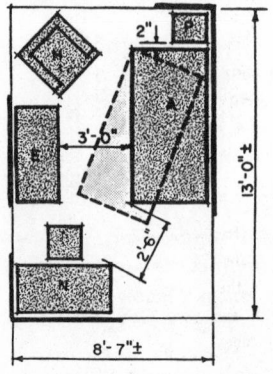

12. Minimum for couch or single bed placed sideways to wall.

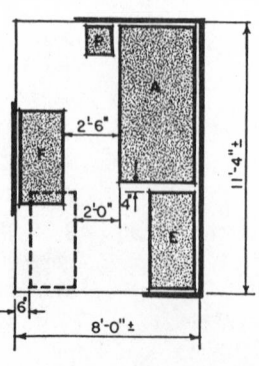

13. If position of chest is changed room width may be reduced 6".

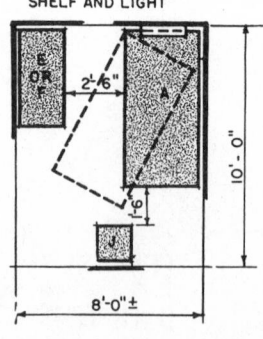

14. Door-swings may require increased clearance at foot of bed.

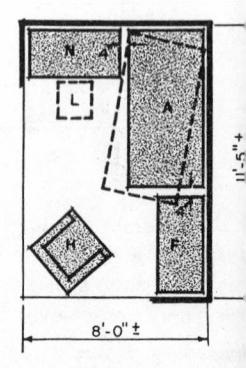

15. Slightly more comfortable than Fig. 14, but bed making is difficult.

By GLENN H. BEYER AND ALEXANDER KIRA, *Housing Research Center, Cornell University*

The kitchen is not a specialized workroom, for it has many uses. It is used for preparation of meals, food preservation, storage of food and utensils, and also, in many cases, for eating, laundering, entertaining, and child care. In it a woman uses her own labor and also makes full use of electric power, tap water, and manufactured or bottled gas; she uses refrigerators, stoves, dishwashers, mixers, toasters, and garbage-disposal units, as well as various kinds of storage compartments and work surfaces.

Since more time and effort are frequently spent in the kitchen than in any other area of the house, careful planning is especially important. This requires careful selection of appliances and storage units and convenient arrangement of the area. Some general planning guides are as follows:

FOOD PREPARATION

Arrangement

It is important to keep the basic work area compact, even if the kitchen is of the large "living" type. Consideration should be given, however, to the possibility of more than one person working there. The arrangement will vary according to the size and shape of space available, but we should always keep in mind relationships among functions in different areas of the kitchen.

Traffic lanes

Traffic lanes through work areas should be avoided. Arrange the service entrance and access to the basement so that traffic not essential to food preparation, service, or storage can by-pass the area.

Storage

Kitchen design should be functional in the sense of minimizing reaching and stooping. Storage facilities should be no higher than a woman can reach with both feet flat on the floor. There should be sufficient space to store items so that they may be easily seen, reached, grasped, and taken down and put back without excessive strain. With proper planning, stored items can be located close to where they are first used, and unattractive items can be kept out of sight. Storage space should be sufficiently flexible to permit its adjustment to varying amounts, sizes, and kinds of food, supplies, and utensils. Shelving should be adjustable.

Counters and working surfaces

The height of counters and working surfaces should permit a comfortable working posture. The worker should be able to sit, if she wishes, while doing certain kitchen tasks, such as working at the sink. Continuous lines and surfaces permit ease of movement, and are easier to keep clean.

Servicing and replacement of appliances

Consideration should be given to ease of servicing and replacement of major appliances, especially built-in units.

Materials

Materials and finishes that minimize maintenance and cleaning should be used, and they should be sufficiently light in color to create a pleasant work atmosphere.

Lighting

Good lighting helps to prevent fatigue, as well as promoting safety and a pleasant atmosphere. Comfortable levels of light, with a minimum of shadows, should be planned throughout the kitchen. Adequate daylight or artificial lighting makes the room more agreeable and attractive than a dark or poorly lighted room.

Ventilation

The kitchen should be well ventilated, with an exhaust fan to remove objectionable kitchen odors.

Safety

Burns, scalds, falls, and explosions should be "designed out" of the kitchen. Sharp corners, exposed handles, and control knobs on kitchen equipment should be avoided, and there should be safety catches on doors and drawers to limit the exploratory activities of young children.

Accessibility

There should be easy access to front and back doors, laundry area, telephone, and bathroom.

Decoration

Color, texture, and decoration should be used to create an atmosphere that is attractive, cheerful, and restful.

OTHER KITCHEN ACTIVITIES

Nonworking areas

Nonworking areas should be segregated from working areas. Avoid interruption of work areas by breakfast nooks, general storage closets, rest areas, and other areas not essential to normal food preparation activities.

Eating facilities

Most families want to eat some meals in the kitchen. Provision should be made for this, if possible, even if a separate dining room is also provided.

Child's play

In younger families, especially, there is likely to be one or more children who want to be near their mother. Provision should be made for a play area out from underfoot, but where adequate supervision is possible. Storage space should be provided for toys and games.

Infant care

It is a well-known fact that many kitchens are used for care of infants. If provision is not made in the bathroom for infant care and related supplies, then it should be made in the kitchen.

Grooming

Washing hands and some personal grooming frequently take place in the

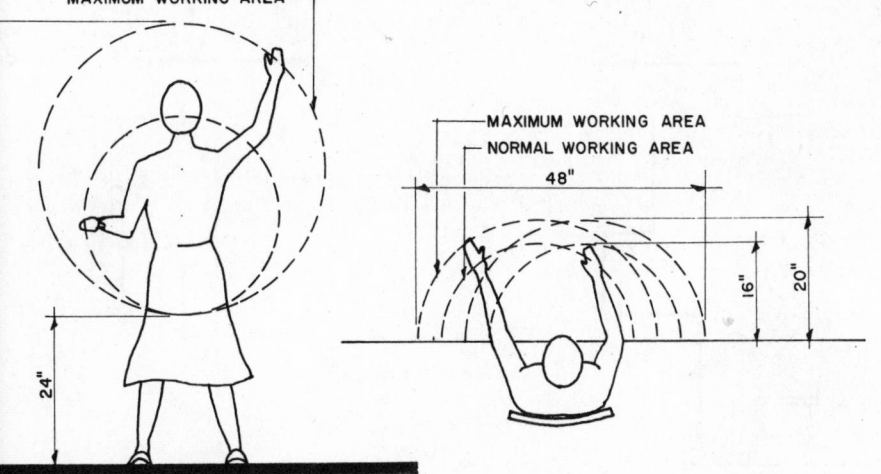

MAXIMUM WORKING AREA

MAXIMUM WORKING AREA
NORMAL WORKING AREA
48"

24"   16"   20"

1. Vertical and horizontal limits of reach   Scale: ⅜ in. = 1 ft

kitchen, especially if there is not ready access to the bathroom. A mirror is desirable.

CRITICAL DIMENSIONS

The "critical dimensions" for working space are illustrated in Fig. 1-4. These dimensions are recommended on the basis of research and do not necessarily coincide with either current practice or currently available cabinets and equipment. Width requirements for counter space, in particular, are based on research covering operations at individual work centers. Overlapping is permissible if work at adjacent centers is not being carried on simultaneously.

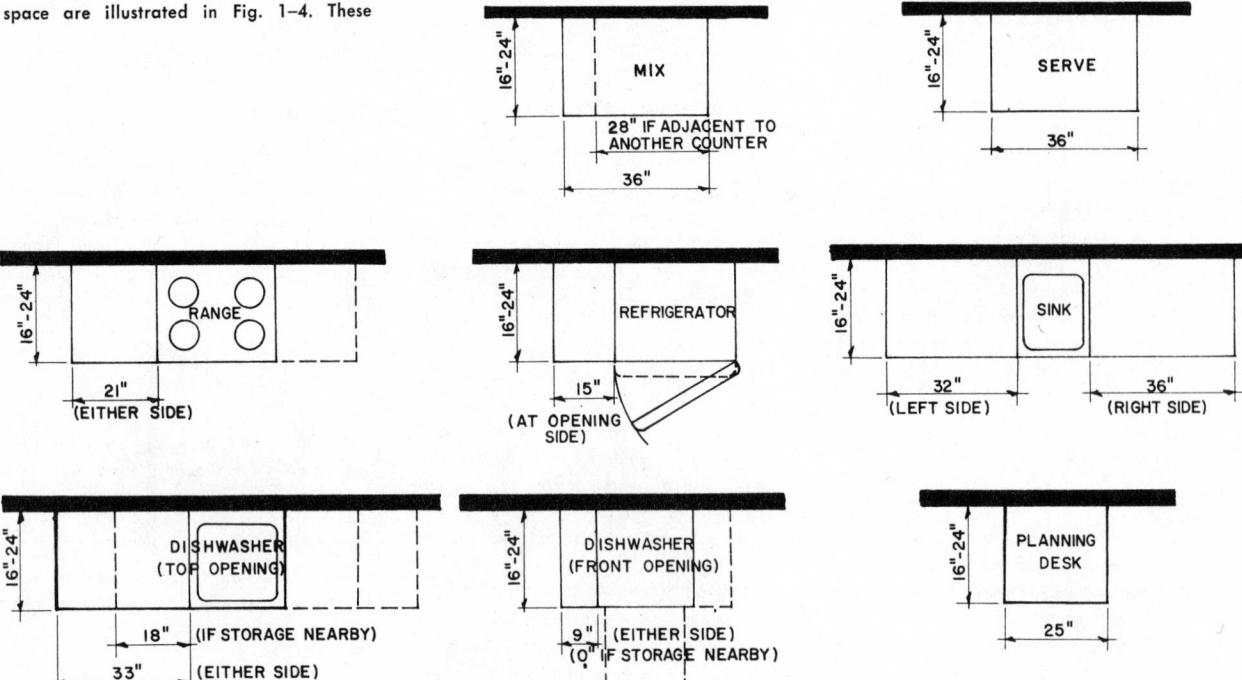

Fig. 2. Minimum counter-width dimensions   Scale: ¼ in. = 1 ft

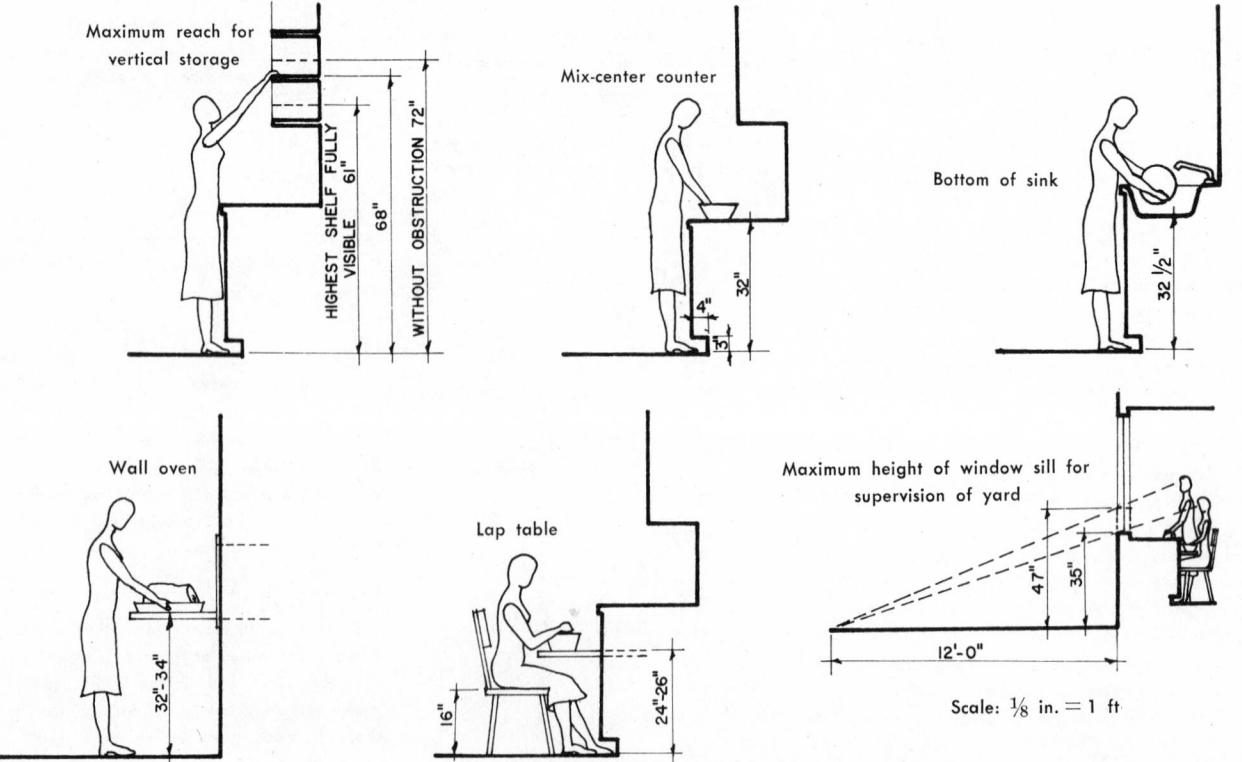

Fig. 3. Comfortable working heights   Scale: ¼ in. = 1 ft

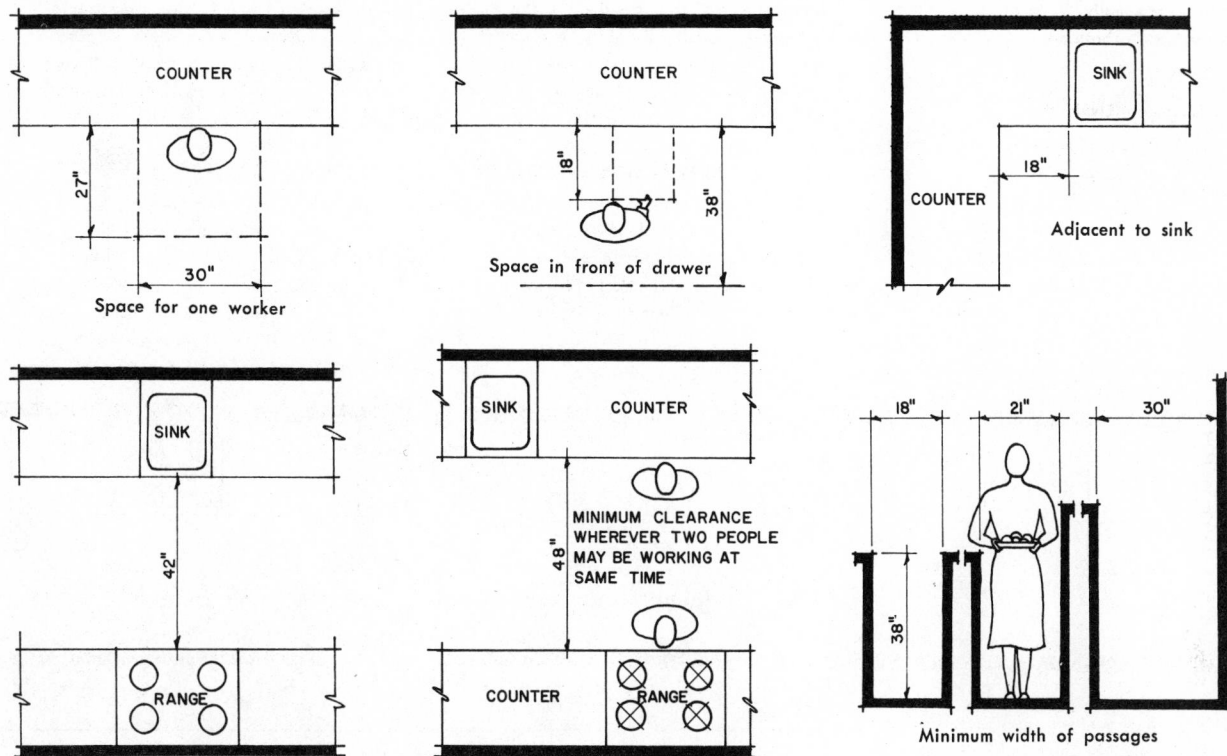

Fig. 4. Minimum clearances—horizontal and vertical Scale: ¼ in. = 1 ft

BASIC WORK AREAS

The work center concept, favorably supported by a great deal of research data from many sources, emphasizes the planning of the kitchen in terms of its major centers of activity. These work centers, in turn, are planned in terms of their constituent parts, their proper functions, and their ideal relationships, one to another. The actual design of the work centers will vary with the size and shape of space available in each project. Four work centers must be considered: sink, range, mix, and serve. In addition, there is the refrigerator (which functions as a closely related *storage* center) and the oven, if it is not an integral part of the range.

Each work center should have three components: (1) Adequate storage space for the various items used there; (2) Adequate counter space for the work to be accomplished; and (3) Necessary utilities and facilities, such as water at the sink, heat at the range, outlet and space for the mixer at the mix center, and adequate lighting at each center.

Equip each work center for the storage of utensils, supplies, and dishes according to their frequency and order of use.

Tables 1–4 list the number of items and the space dimensions required for equipment and food supplies commonly stored

Table 1. Equipment and food supplies stored at range center

| Item | Number stored | | Storage space per item, in.* | | |
	Limited	Liberal	Side to side	Front to back	Height
Equipment					
Potato masher	1	1	3½	13	4½
Knives, forks, spoons	3	3	3½	13	3
Frying pan, 10½-in.	1	1	11	17½	5½
Frying pan, 9-in.	1	2	9½	16	5
Frying pan, 6-in.	0	1	6	12	5
Pot lids	2	4	10½	10½	1
Potholders	4	8	7	7	2†
Food supplies					
Rice, 1-lb pkg.	1	1	2½	4	6½
Spaghetti, 1-lb pkg.	1	1	2½	11½	6
Coffee, 1-lb can	1	1	5½	5½	4
Oatmeal, 3-lb box	1	1	6	6	11
Macaroni, 1-lb pkg.	1	1	2	5½	9
Tea, 8-oz pkg.	1	1	2½	4½	7

*Dimension of the item (including lid, if any) plus clearance for handling.
†Provides for stack of 6 potholders.

at each of the four centers. These lists represent the storage space requirements for the average family, but they may be adapted to the needs of particular families. The storage space dimensions are based on the most recent information available.

KITCHEN ARRANGEMENT

The relative location of work centers should permit a continuity of kitchen activities as follows: (1) Storage (gathering materials needed for the performance of the task); (2) Cleaning and mixing (or initial preparation); (3) Cooking; (4) Serving, or storing for future use; and (5) Cleaning up. (See Fig. 5.)

In principle, any plan that interrupts this continuity with doors, or with nonworking areas or facilities, is faulty because extra steps are required every time the gap is crossed, and, consequently, convenience and working efficiency are reduced.

The actual plan may be U-shaped or L-shaped, or it may be of the corridor type.

The "U" arrangement affords the most compact work area. Frequently, however, this arrangement is impossible to achieve because of the necessity of having a door on one of the three walls. The resulting "Broken U" arrangement still permits compactness, but traffic is allowed through the area. Therefore, special consideration should be given to the arrangement of the work centers in order to minimize the effect of through traffic.

The "L" arrangement is ideally suited where space along two walls is sufficient to accommodate all of the necessary work areas. This arrangement has the advantage of concentrating the work area in one corner, thus minimizing travel, but it has the disadvantage of necessitating longer trips to the extremities of the "L."

The "Corridor" arrangement is satisfactory where doors are necessary at each end of the space. This arrangement frequently has the advantage of the parallel walls being closer together than in the typical "U," but the disadvantage of a greater distance along the corridor.

An important factor in determining the location of specific work areas within any of these over-all arrangements is frequency of use, which in Fig. 6 is expressed as the percentage of trips to and from each area.

Figures 7–9 provide floor plans illustrating some possible arrangements of the basic work centers within each of the plan types. If the space for the kitchen is already established, the number of possible satisfactory arrangements obviously will be limited. If the space is being planned,

however, greater choice of arrangements is possible. In either event, the advantage of a shorter distance between some related areas must be balanced against the resulting increase in distance between other related areas. An end-to-end alignment or a right-angle arrangement between areas of close relationship can eliminate trips and reduce the over-all travel distances. Functional relationships between key work centers are, of course, accommodated more ideally in some of the plans than others.

FHA REQUIREMENTS FOR KITCHEN STORAGE [1]

Total shelf area: 50 sq ft minimum; not less than 20 sq ft in either wall or base cabinets.

Total countertop area: 11 sq ft minimum.

Total drawer area: 11 sq ft minimum. (If a 39-in. range is provided, it may be counted as 4 sq ft of base cabinet shelf area and 2 sq ft of countertop area.)

Wall shelving: 74 in. maximum height.

Countertop: 38 in. maximum height, 30 in. minimum height.

Height between wall cabinets and countertop: 24 in. minimum over range and sink, 15 in. minimum elsewhere. (Shelving may be closer if it does not project beyond a line drawn from the front edge of the wall cabinet at an angle of 60 deg to the bottom of the cabinet.)

Depth of shelving: wall shelving—4 in. minimum, 18 in. maximum; base shelving—

[1]*From* Minimum Property Standards for One and Two Living Units, *Federal Housing Administration, Washington, D.C. (Revised, July 1959).*

Table 2. Equipment and food supplies stored at sink center

In addition to the items listed below, allow space for hand tools (such as can opener, small vegetable brush, paring knives, rubber plate scraper), cleaning supplies (such as soap, soap powder, cleanser, paper towels), garbage and trash containers, and possibly a stool for sitting.

Item	Number stored		Storage space per item, in.*		
	Limited	Liberal	Side to side	Front to back	Height
Equipment					
Dishpans, nested	2	2	16½	18½	8
Dishdrainer	1	2	14½	18½	6
Double boiler	1	1	7½	12	10½
Pressure saucepan	0	1	9	17	7½
Saucepan, 6-qt	0	2	10½	10½	9
Saucepan, 4-qt	1	1	9	11	7½
Saucepan, 3-qt	2	2	8½	15	8
Saucepan, 2-qt	1	1	7½	14	7
Saucepan, 1-qt	1	1	6½	13	6
Colander	1	1	11½	13	6
Coffee pot, 6-cup	1	1	6½	9	10
Dishtowels	8	12	12	11	5(8)
Handtowels	8	12	12	10	5(8)
Aprons	4	6	11	10	5(4)
Dishcloths	6	12	8	8	4(6)
Food supplies					
Potatoes, lb	10	10	9	11	8
Onions, lb	3	3	9	7	8
Fruit, lb	3	3	9	7½	5
Lentils and peas, 2-lb pkg.	1	1	3½	5	9½
Dry beans, 2-lb pkg.	1	1	3½	5	8½
Prunes, 1-lb pkg.	1	1	3	5	8
Canned food, No. 2 can	6	8	4	4	5½

*Dimensions include clearance for handling.

†Number in parentheses refers to number of items in stack for which storage space dimension is given.

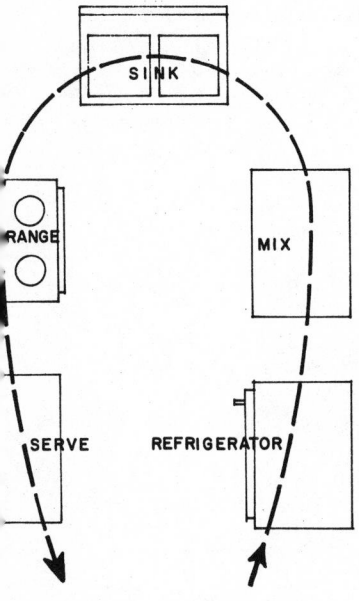

6. Flow of work in food preparation

2 in. minimum, 24 in. maximum; countertop—15 in. minimum, 24 in. maximum.

Spacing of shelving: if depth of shelf is
4–6 in., allow 5 in. minimum spacing, if
6–10 in. allow 6 in., if 10–15 in. allow
8 in., if 15–24 in. allow 10 in.

Backsplash (required where countertop
abuts walls): 4 in. minimum height.

Steel cabinets: minimum gages—case and
drawer slides, 16; gussets and cross rails,
18; bottoms, door and drawer fronts and
sides, 20; elsewhere, 22.

Exhaust fan (required in ceiling or wall
near range, or in hood over range):
minimum capacity—15 air changes per
hour.

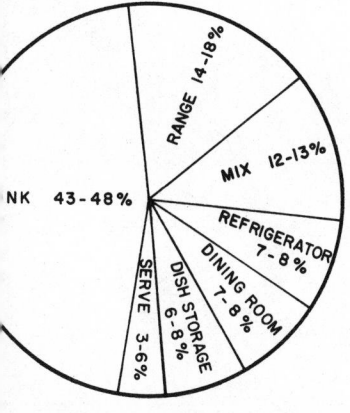

6. Percentage distribution of trips in food preparation

Table 3. Equipment and food supplies stored at mix center

In addition to equipment and supplies listed below, allow space for such miscellaneous items as cookbooks, wax paper, and certain essential hand tools (hammer, pliers, screw driver, and knife sharpener).

Item	Number stored		Storage space per item, in.*		
	Limited	Liberal	Side to side	Front to back	Height
Equipment					
Electric mixer	1	1	7½–12	10–14	10–17
Flour sifter	1	1	6½	9	7
Mixing bowl, 3½-qt	1	1	12½	12½	6
Mixing bowl, 2-qt	1	2	9½	9½	5½
Mixing bowl, 1-qt	1	1	7½	7½	5
Pint measure	1	1	4½	6½	5½
Cup measure, set	1	1	4	5	5
Baking dish, 10½-in. diam	0	1	11	12½	4½
Baking dish, 9½-in. diam	1	1	10	11½	4½
Loaf pan	1	2	6	10½	3½
Biscuit pan	1	1	10	13½	3
Pie pans	1	3	10	10	2½
Cake pans	2	2	12	12	2½
Muffin pan	1	2	11	14	2½
Cookie (baking) sheet	1	2	12½	16	2
Egg beater	1	1	4	12½	4
Cookie cutter	1	1	3	3	3½
Rolling pin	1	1	3	19	3½
Mixing and blending forks	2	6	3	12½	2½
Measuring spoons, 4 sets	1	2	3	6	2½
Egg whisk	0	1	4	12½	2½
Knives and spatulas	2	6	3	14	2
Food supplies					
Cornmeal, 5 lb	1	1	8	8	9
Flour, 5 lb	1	1	8	8	9
Sugar, 5 lb	1	1	8	8	9
Pancake flour, 2-lb pkg.	0	1	2½	6½	10½
Cake flour, 2¾-lb pkg.	1	1	3	7	10½
Vinegar, 1-qt bottle	1	1	4	4	10
Powdered sugar, 1-lb pkg.	1	1	2½	4	8½
Brown sugar, 1-lb pkg.	1	1	2	4	8
Cocoanut, 7-oz pkg.	1	1	2	4	8
Shortening, 3-lb can	1	1	5½	5½	8
Cornstarch, 1-lb pkg.	1	1	2½	4	7½
Cocoa, 1-lb pkg.	1	1	3	4	7½
Raisins, 15-oz pkg.	1	1	2½	4½	7½
Flavorings, 6-in.-tall bottle	3	5	1½	2½	7
Salt, 1-lb 10-oz pkg.	1	2	4	4	7
Baking powder, 1-lb pkg.	1	1	3½	3½	6½
Baking soda, 1-lb pkg.	1	1	2½	4	6½
Package desserts, 3⅝-oz pkg.	1	3	2	4	5½
Spices, 4½-in.-tall can	2	3	2½	3½	5½
Spices, 3-in.-tall can	4	6	1½	2½	4

Dimension of the item (including lid, if any) plus clearance for handling.

BIBLIOGRAPHY

Beyer, Glenn H. *The Cornell Kitchen: Product Design Through Research.* Cornell University Agricultural Experiment Station, Ithaca (1952).

Handbook of Kitchen Design. Small Homes Council, University of Illinois, Urbana (1950).

Heiner, Mary Koll, and McCullough, Helen E. *Functional Kitchen Storage.* Bulletin 846, Cornell University Agricultural Experiment Station, Ithaca (June 1948).

Heiner, Mary Koll, and Steidl, Rose E. *Guides for Arrangement of Urban Family Kitchens.* Bulletin 878, Cornell University Agricultural Experiment Station, Ithaca (1951).

Minimum Property Standards for One and Two Living Units. Federal Housing Administration, Washington, D. C. (Revised, July 1959).

Planning Guides for Southern Rural Homes. Prepared by Southern Regional Housing Research Technical Committee. Southern Cooperative Series Bulletin 58, Georgia Agricultural Experiment Station, Athens (June 1958).

Roberts, Evelyn H., Wilson, Maud, and Thayer, Ruth. *Standards for Working-Surface Heights and Other Space Units of the Dwelling.* State Bulletin 348, Oregon Agricultural Experiment Station, Corvallis (June 1937). Published also as Washington Agricultural Experiment Station Bulletin 345, Pullman.

Space Standards for Home Planners. Western Cooperative Series Research Report 2, Western Region Agricultural Experiment Stations (n.d.). (Publication may be obtained from Institute of Home Economics, Agricultural Research Service, U.S. Dept. of Agriculture, Washington, D.C.)

Wilson, Maud. *Considerations in Planning Kitchen Cabinets.* State Bulletin 445, Oregon Agricultural Experiment Station, Corvallis (November 1947).

———. *A Guide for the Kitchen Planner.* State Bulletin 482, Oregon Agricultural Experiment Station, Corvallis (September 1950).

Wood, Anna L., Ribelin, Shirley, and Lange, Fay. *Location and Counter Area Requirements of a Mechanical Dishwasher.* Bulletin 526, Washington State College, Pullman (1951).

Table 4. Equipment and food supplies stored at serve center

In addition to the items listed below, provide a drawer for silverware and space for such miscellaneous items as lunch boxes, serving tray, and hot-plate pads.

Item	Number stored*		Storage space per item, in.†		
	Limited	Liberal	Side to side	Front to back	Height
Equipment					
Paper napkins, box	1	2	8	8	3
Tablecloth, luncheon	0	1	10	14	3
Tablecloth, dinner	1	2	10	19	2
Cups	8(4)	12(6)	4½	5½	6
Cereal dishes	6(2)	8(2)	7½	7½	5
Dinner plates	8(1)	12(1)	11	11	4
Salad or pie plates	8(1)	12(1)	9	9	4
Fruit dishes	6(1)	12(1)	5½	5½	6
Saucers	8(1)	12(1)	7½	7½	4
Juice glasses‡	6	8	3	3	5
Pitchers, large	1	2	7½	10½	10
Pitchers, medium	1	1	7	8	10
Water glasses‡	8	12	3½	3½	6
Bowls, oval	2(1)	3(2)	13½	9½	9
Bowls, round	2(1)	4(2)	9½	9½	7
Creamer	1(1)	1(1)	5	7	5
Gravy boat	0	1(1)	6	10½	5
Jelly-relish dishes	2(1)	2(1)	7½	7½	2
Platter, large	1(1)	1(1)	16½	13	2
Platter, medium	1(1)	2(1 or 2)	14	11	2
Platter, small	0	1(1)	12	9	2
Serving plates	0	2(1 or 2)	11	11	4
Sugar	1(1)	1(1)	5½	6½	5
Tray, medium	0	1(1)	15½	11½	3
Refrigerator dishes, set of 4	1(1)	1(1)	8	8½	7
Toaster	1	1	6–7	9–12	7–8
Waffle iron	0	1	10–14	8–14	3–5
Food supplies					
Prepared cereals, 11-in.-tall box	2	4	3	8	14
Cookies, 1-lb pkg.	1	2	3	6½	11
Crackers, 1-lb pkg.	1	2	4½	10½	6
Peanut butter, 1-lb 4-oz jar	1	1	3	3	6
Mayonnaise, 1-pt jar	1	1	3½	3½	6
Jam and pickles, 1-pt jar	1	3	3½	3½	2
Bread	1	2	5½	12	6
Cake	1	1	9½	9½	2

*Number in parentheses refers to number of stacks.

†One-half in. added to side-to-side and front-to-back measurement of item or stack and ½ to ¾ in. to height to permit safe handling. For stacked items, clearance is sufficient to remove single item from stack.

‡Glasses placed three rows to a shelf instead of stacking.

§Provides space for two tablecloths.

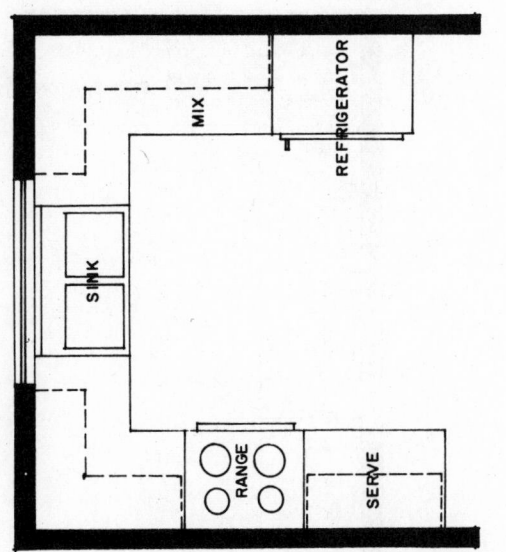

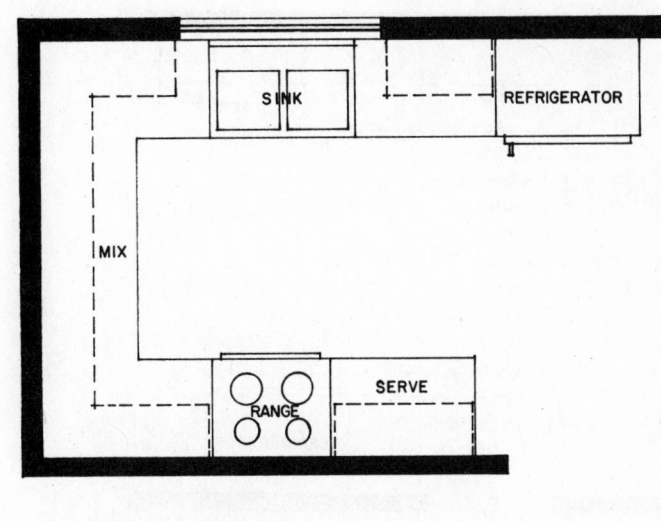

If a dishwasher is desired, it should be located at the sink center.

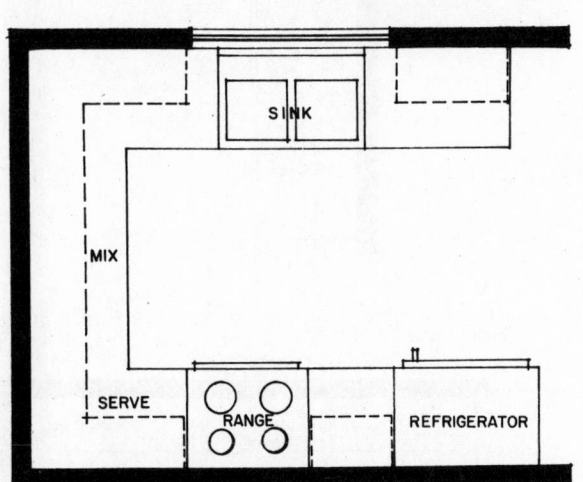

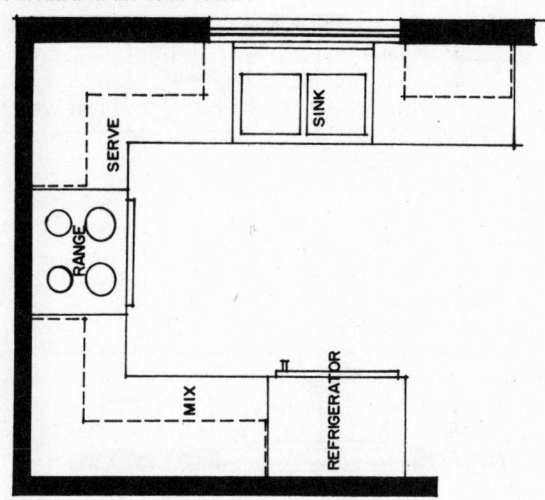

Fig. 7. U-shaped plans Scale: $\frac{1}{4}$ in. = 1 ft

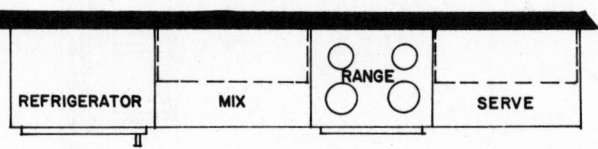

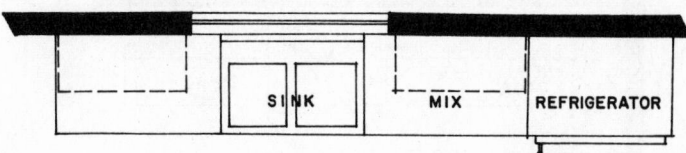

If a dishwasher is desired, it should be located at the sink center.

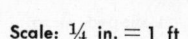

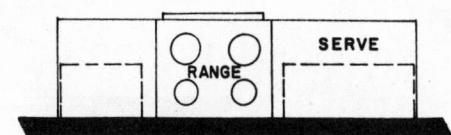

Fig. 8. "Corridor" plans Scale: $\frac{1}{4}$ in. = 1 ft

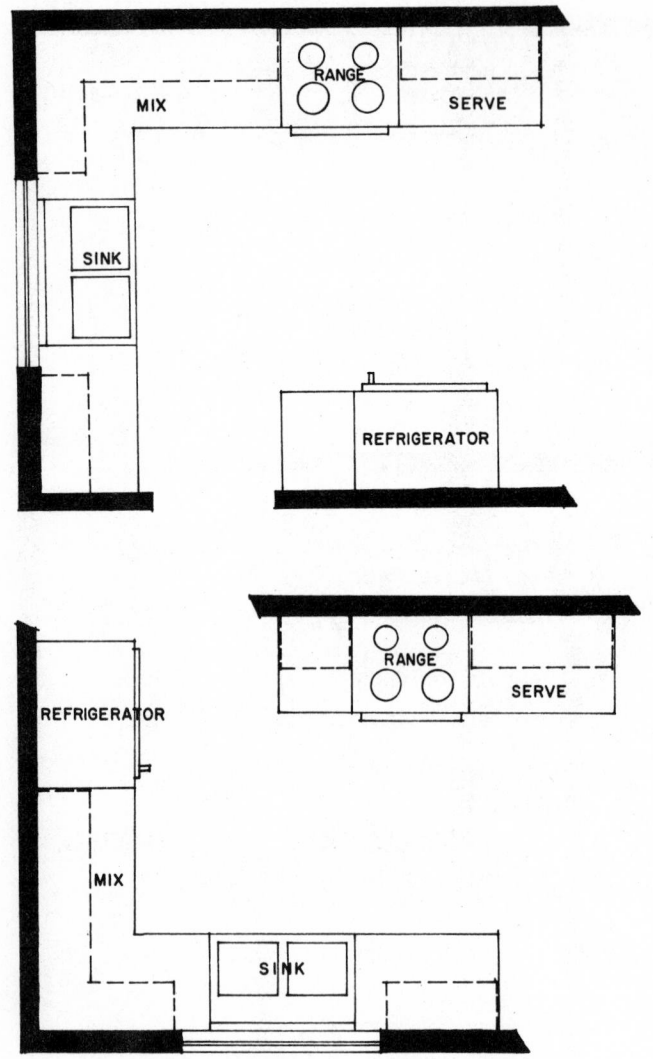

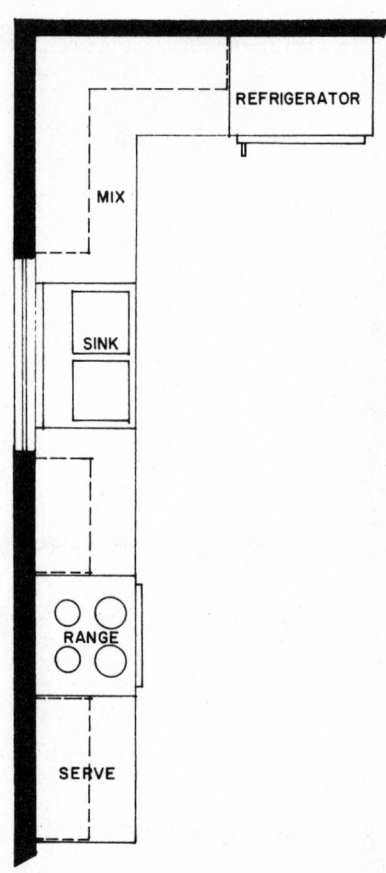

If a dishwasher is desired, it should be located at the sink center.

If a dishwasher is desired, it should be located at the sink center.

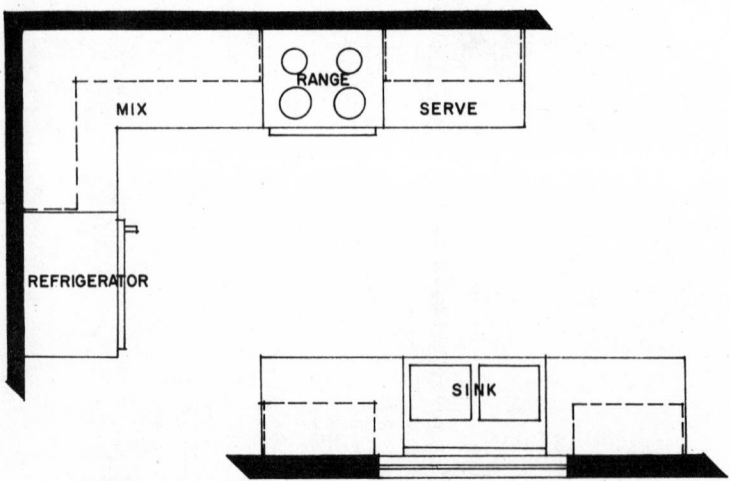

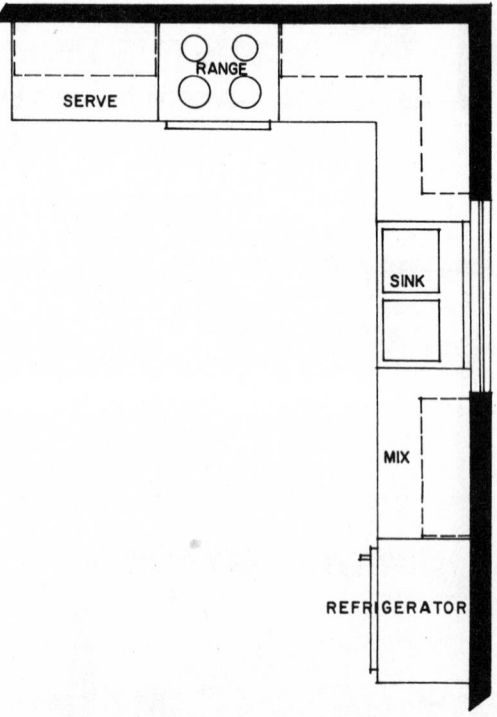

Fig. 9 "Broken-U" plans   Scale: ¼ in. = 1 ft

Fig. 10. L-shaped plans   Scale: ¼ in. = 1 ft

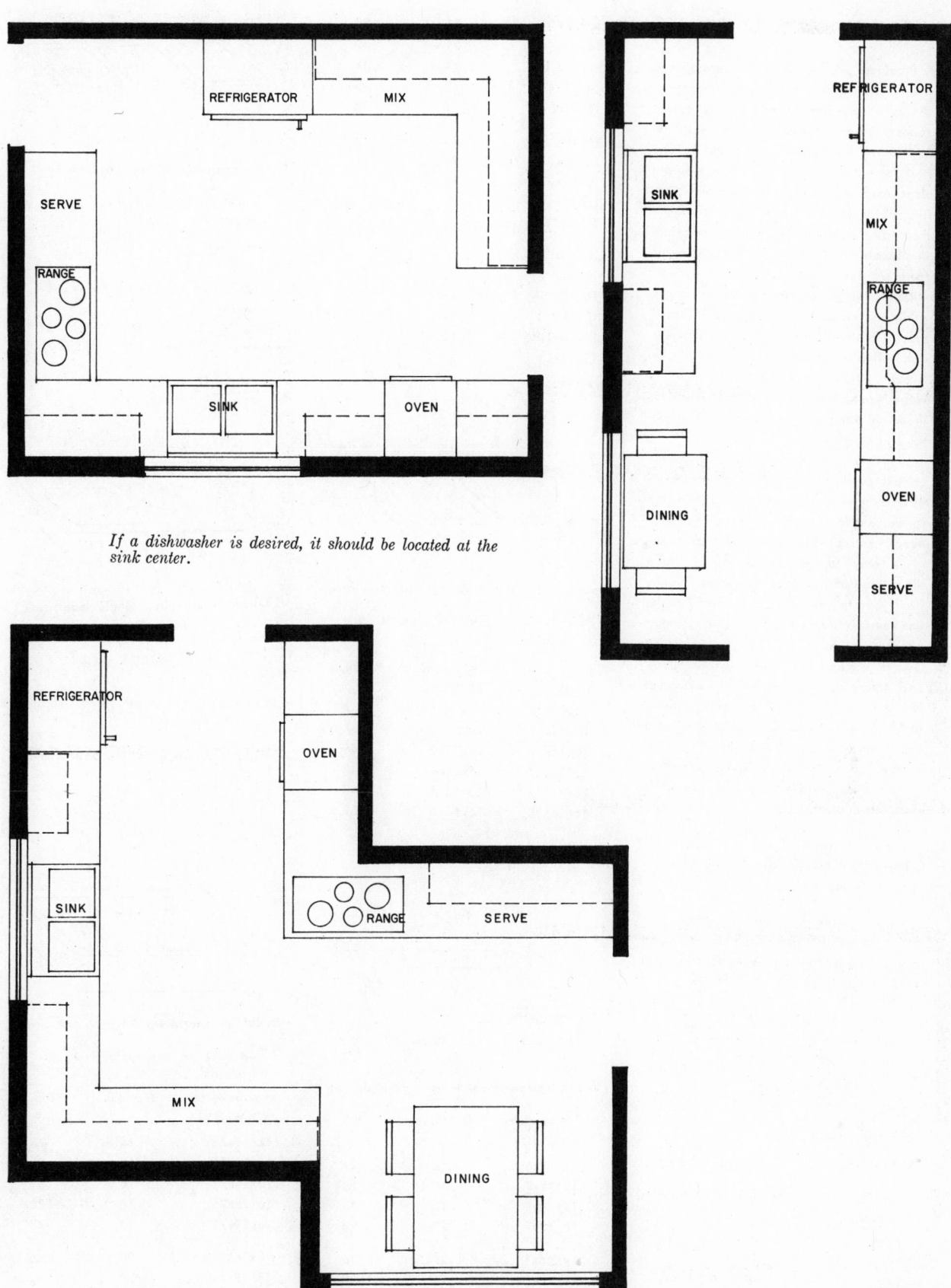

If a dishwasher is desired, it should be located at the sink center.

Fig. 11. Kitchen plans with wall oven Scale: $\frac{1}{4}$ in. = 1 ft

APPLIANCES

Provided on the following pages are illustrations and approximate dimensions of various types of sinks, dishwashers, ranges, ovens, surface cooking units, refrigerators, freezers, and combination and package kitchen units. These dimensions may be used for preliminary planning purposes, but final selection of equipment and detailing of working drawings should always be based on specific manufacturers' data.

Door swings on refrigerators, ranges, cabinet sinks, and cabinet-type dishwashers should be checked against manufacturers' data after units have been tentatively selected. Side-hinged doors designed to swing from the left or right (such as those on refrigerators) can usually be obtained on order.

Dimensions have been drawn from the current catalogs of leading manufacturers of each type of equipment. Odd sizes and special and nonresidential equipment have been omitted. Dimensions are generally given only to the nearest ½ in. since dimensions of new models change slightly from year to year. The method of tabulation varies, depending on what is most appropriate to each type of equipment. Over-all dimensions given for depth, width, and, where appropriate, height correspond to "D," "W," and "H" on the drawings. Inside dimensions of sink bowls are listed under the heading "Size of bowl" for the sections on stainless-steel sinks, porcelain-enamel sinks, stainless-steel sink tops, and porcelain-enamel sink tops.

STAINLESS-STEEL SINKS
(for recessing into countertops)

Custom sizes and custom punching of fitting openings are available for most models. Some ledge-type sinks are available with fittings.

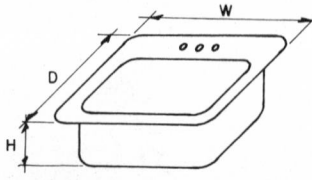

Single-compartment ledge-type sink bowl

Size of bowl, in. (DxWxH)	Depth, in.	Width, in.
16x14x 3½	21	16
15x18x 3½	21	21
16x20x 3½	21	24
16x14x 4	21	16
16x18x 4	21	21

16x22x 4	21	21
16x28x 4	21	30
9x12x 6	14	14
14x16x 7	19	18
16x14x 7	21	16
16x18x 7	21	21
16x20x 7	21	24
12x12x 7½	17	14
16x12x 7½	21	14
12x16x 7½	16	21
16x16x 7½	21	18
16x22x 7½	21	24
16x28x 7½	21	30
10x14x 8	12	18
16x14x10½	12	16
15x18x11	21	21

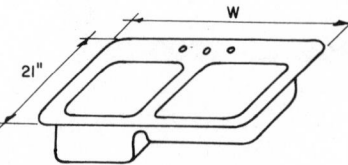

Double-compartment ledge-type sink bowl

Right- or left-hand models are available.

Deep bowl, in. (DxWxH)	Shallow bowl, in. (DxWxH)	Width, in.
16x14x 7	16x14x3½	32
16x14x 7	16x20x3½	37
16x14x 7	16x28x4	46
16x16x 7	16x22x4	42
16x22x 7	16x22x4	48
16x14x10½	16x14x7	32

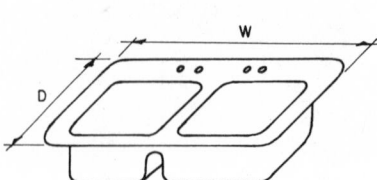

Double-compartment ledge-type sink bowl

Size of bowl, in. (DxWxH)	Depth, in.	Width, in.
12x 9x6	16	21
12x12x7	12	28
12x16x7	17	36
16x12x7	21	28
14x16x7	21	36
16x14x7	21	32
16x16x7	21	36
16x18x7	21	42

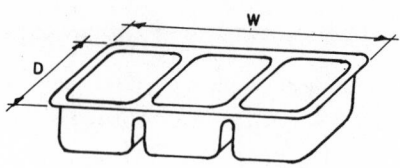

Triple-compartment flat-rim sink bowl

Size of bowl, in. (DxWxH)	Depth, in.	Width, in.
12x 9x7½	14	34
12x12x7½	14	42
16x12x7½	18	40
16x14x7½	18	46
16x16x7½	18	54
16x18x7½	18	60

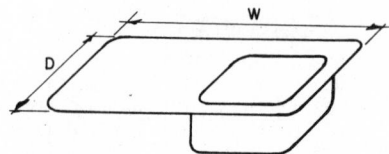

Offset combination single ledge-sink and drainboard

Right- or left-hand models are available.

Size of bowl, in. (DxWxH)	Depth, in.	Width, in.
16x14x7½	21	42
16x18x7½	21	42

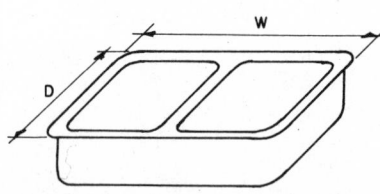

Double-compartment flat-rim sink bowl

The rim is generally 1–1½ in. on all sides.

Size of bowl, in. (DxWxH)	Depth, in.	Width, in.
12x12x7½	14	28
16x12x7½	18	28
16x14x7½	18	31
16x16x7½	18	36
16x22x7½	18	48
18x16x7½	20	36
18x18x7½	20	40
18x20x7½	20	44
18x25x7½	20	54

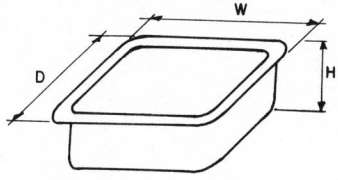

Single-compartment flat-rim sink bowl

*The rim is generally 1–1½ in.
on all sides.*

Depth, in.	Width, in.	Height, in.
9	12	4
9	12	6
18	15	7
12	20	5
12	20	7
20	16	7
12	12	7½
12	16	7½
14	16	7½
16	16	7½
12	18	7½
16	18	7½
16	20	7½
16	22	7½
18	20	7½
18	25	7½
16	28	7½
18	18	7½
18	30	7½

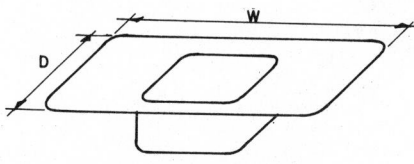

**Combination single ledge-sink
and drainboard**

Size of bowl, in. (DxWxH)	Depth, in.	Width, in.
16x14x7½	21	54
16x14x7½	21	60
16x18x7½	21	54
16x18x7½	21	60

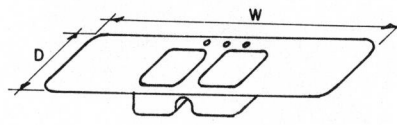

**Combination double ledge-sink
and drainboard**

Size of bowl, in. (DxWxH)	Depth, in.	Width, in.
16x14x7½	21	60
16x14x7½	21	72
16x18x7½	21	60
16x18x7½	21	72

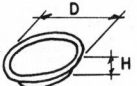

Round sink bowls

The rim is generally 1 in.

Inside diameter, in.	Height, in.
11	4
14	5½

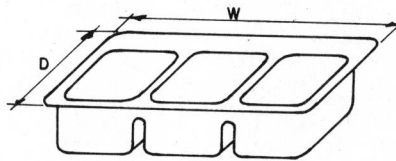

Triple-compartment ledge-type sink bowl

Size of bowl, in. (DxWxH)	Depth, in.	Width, in.
9x12x7½	14	42
12x 9x7½	17	34
12x12x7½	17	42
16x12x7½	21	40
16x14x7½	21	46
16x16x7½	21	54
16x18x7½	21	60

PORCELAIN–ENAMEL SINKS
**(on steel or cast-iron bodies for recessing
into countertops)**

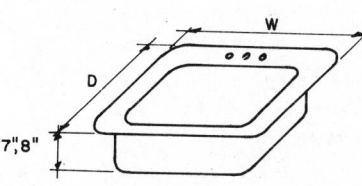

Single-compartment ledge-type sink bowl

*Some models are available in
color.*

Size of bowl, in. (DxW)	Depth, in.	Width, in.
16x22	21	24
16x28	21	30

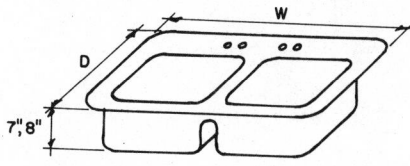

Double-compartment ledge-type sink bowl

Size of bowl, in. (DxW)	Depth, in.	Width, in.
15x13	20	30
16x14	21	32
16x19	21	42

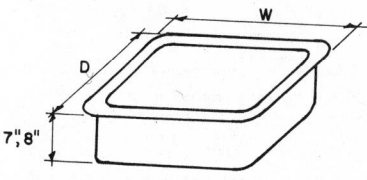

Single-compartment flat-rim sink bowl

*The rim is generally 1–1½ in.
on all sides.*

Depth, in.	Width, in.
12	12
16	20
16	24
18	24
18	30
20	24
20	30

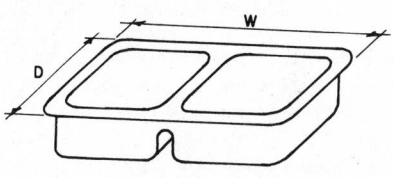

Double-compartment flat-rim sink bowl

Size of bowl, in. (DxWxH)	Depth, in.	Width, in.
18x14x8	20	30
18x14x8	20	32
18x19x8	20	42

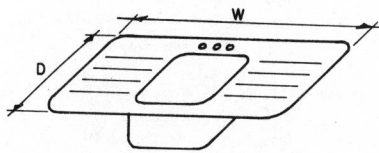

**Combination single ledge-sink
and drainboard**

Size of bowl, in. (DxWxH)	Depth, in.	Width, in.
16x19x8	21	54

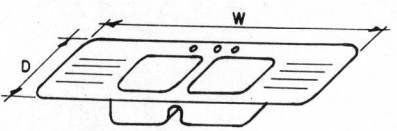

**Combination double ledge-sink
and drainboard**

Size of bowl, in. (DxWxH)	Depth, in.	Width, in.
16x14x8	21	60

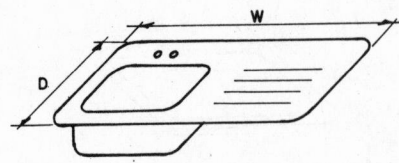

Offset combination single ledge-sink and drainboard

Right- or left-hand models are available.

Size of bowl, in. (DxWxH)	Depth, in.	Width, in.
16x19x8	21	42

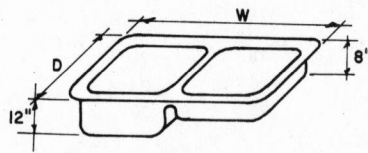

Combination double-bowl flat-rim sink

Size of bowl, in. (DxW)	Depth, in.	Width, in.
18x18	21	42

STAINLESS–STEEL SINK TOPS

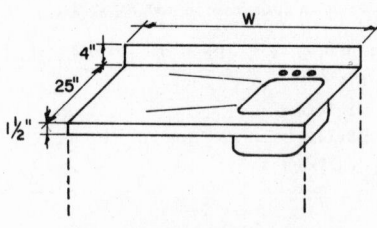

Offset single-compartment sink top with drainboard

Right- or left-hand models are available.

Size of bowl, in. (DxWxH)	Width, in.
16x12x7	39
16x16x7	42
16x18x7	48

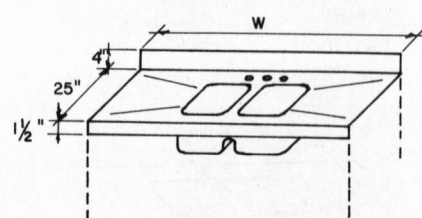

Double-compartment sink top with drainboard

Size of bowl, in. (DxWxH)	Width, in.
16x14x7	60, 66, 72
16x16x7	66, 72, 84, 96

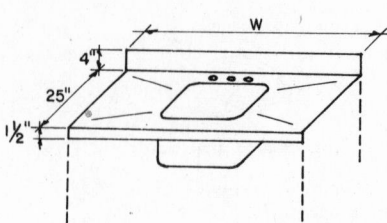

Single-compartment sink top with drainboard

Size of bowl, in. (DxWxH)	Width, in.
16x18x7	54
16x20x7	54
16x20x7	60
16x20x7	66
16x20x7	72
16x20x7	84
16x20x7	96
16x25x7	72

PORCELAIN–ENAMEL SINK TOPS
(on steel or cast-iron bodies)

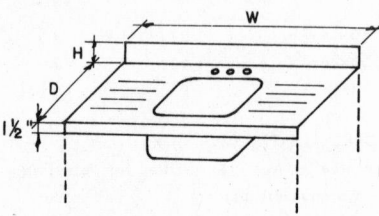

Single-compartment sink top with drainboard

Size of bowl (DxWxH), in.	Depth, in.	Width, in.	Height, in.
15x18x8	22	54	4
15x20x8	22	60	4
18x20x8	25	54	4
18x20x8	25	60	4
18x22x6	22	60	8
20x16x6	25	54	3

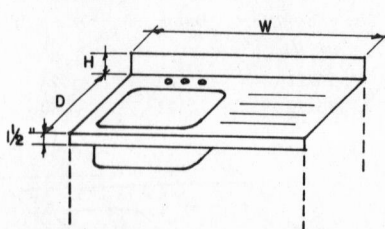

Offset single-compartment sink top with drainboard

Size of bowl (DxWxH), in.	Depth, in.	Width, in.	Height, in.
15x19x8	22	42	4
16x19x8	20	42	4
16x20x6	20	42	8
16x20x6	25	42	3
18x19x8	25	42	4

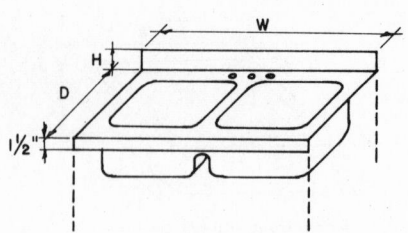

Double-compartment sink top

Size of bowl (DxWxH), in.	Depth, in.	Width, in.	Height, in.
15x18x8	22	42	4
18x18x8	25	42	4

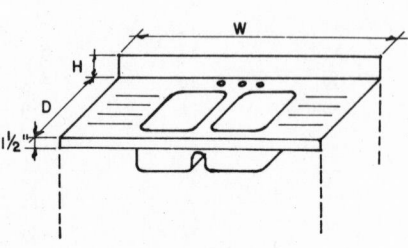

Double-compartment sink top with drainboard

Size of bowl (DxWxH), in.	Depth, in.	Width, in.	Height, in.
18x14x8	25	60	4
18x16x8	25	72	4

CABINET SINKS
(porcelain enamel on steel bodies)

All sinks are 36 in. high; the backsplash varies from 3 to 4 in.

Some models are available with stainless-steel tops, plastic tops, or porcelain-enamel tops on cast-iron bodies. A variety of base cabinet arrangements is generally available.

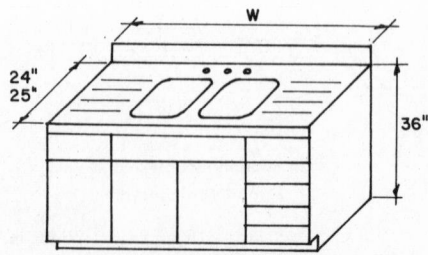

Double-compartment sink with drainboard

This model is available in 60-, 66-, and 72-in. widths.

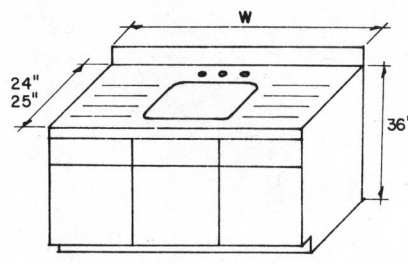

Single-compartment sink with drainboard

This model is available in 54- and 60-in. widths.

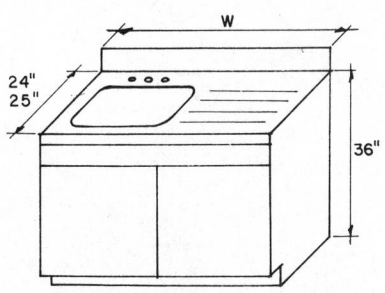

Offset single-compartment sink with drainboard

Right- or left-hand models are available in 42-in. widths.

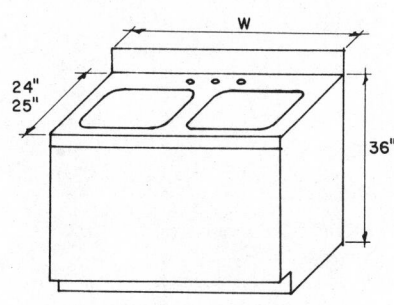

Double-compartment sink

Some models have sliding drainboard; available in 36-, 42-, and 45-in. widths.

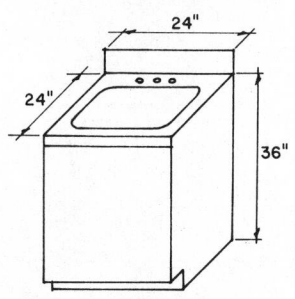

Single-compartment sink

GARBAGE DISPOSERS

Garbage disposers

The height of some models varies up to 12 in. (h).

Depth, in.	Height, in.	Height (h), in.
7–9	13–16	6–8

DISHWASHERS

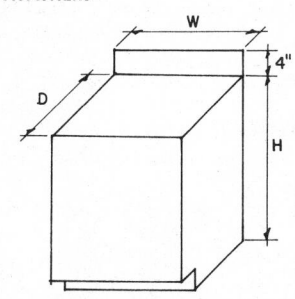

Freestanding dishwashers

This model is 26 in. deep, 24 in. wide, 36 in. high, and may be 42 or 46 in. deep with the doors open. It fits standard base cabinets and is available with drop-down door or pull-out drawer for either front or top loading. Fronts are also available in a variety of materials, finishes, and colors to match standard kitchen cabinets.

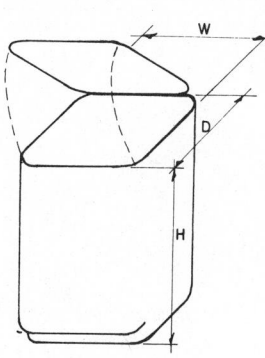

Portable dishwasher

This model is generally the lift-top, top-loading type.

Depth, in.	Width, in.	Height, in.
25	22	33
25	22	35

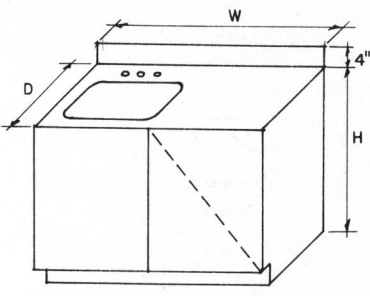

Combination dishwasher and sink

This model is 25 in. deep, 48 in. wide, 36 in. high, and 48 in. deep with the doors open.

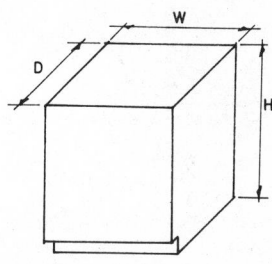

Under-counter, built-in dishwasher

This model is 24 in. deep, 24 or 30 in. wide, 34 in. high, and 45 in. deep with the doors open. It is available with drop-down door or pull-out drawer for either front or top loading.

SURFACE COOKING UNITS—ELECTRIC AND GAS (for built-in installations)

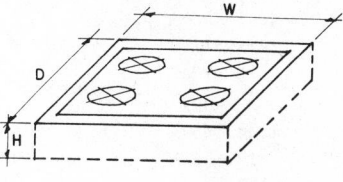

Electric surface burners

If controls are remote, that is, in front of base cabinet or on the backsplash, or alongside, additional space must be allowed. Some models are also available with a deep-well cooker in place of one surface element.

No. of elements	Depth, in.	Width, in.	Height, in.	Controls
2	21	14	5	Front
2	22	15	7	Front
2	21	14	8	Remote
2	22	14	5	Remote
2	22	17	6	Remote

Appliances

4	19	31	5	Top, integral
4	21	27	5	Front
4	21	28	5	Top, integral
4	22	31	10	Remote
4	20	30	5	Top, integral
4	22	20	7	Remote
4	22	32	7	Top, integral
4	22	22	7	Remote
4	21	34	8	Top, integral

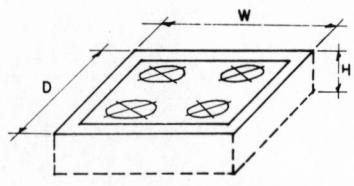

Gas surface burners

No. of burners	Depth, in.	Width, in.	Height, in.	Controls
2	21	15	8	Front
2	22	15	8	Front
4	21	24	8	Front
4	22	24	8	Front

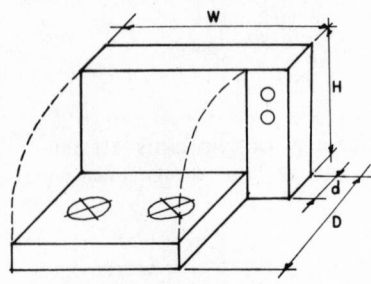

Fold-back surface burners

Some models include griddles.

No. of elements	Depth, in.	Depth (d), in.	Width, in.	Height, in.
2	18	6	24	14

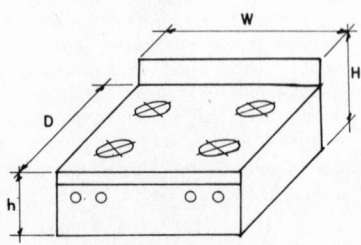

Stack-on surface burners

No. of burners	Depth, in.	Width, in.	Height, in.	Height (h), in.
4	25	24	12	8

WALL OVENS

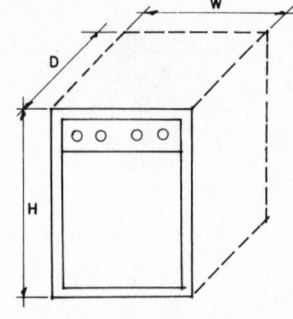

Electric and gas wall oven

Microwave ovens are available in the same sizes, and also as "combinations" with regular electric ovens. Some models are equipped with integral rotisseries; others have integral or separate broiler compartments. Some have single or double doors that open horizontally or vertically. Some doors have view panels.

Depth, in.	Width, in.	Height, in.
22	22	30
22	32	26
24	22	28
24	22	30
24	22	32
24	22	48
24	24	32
24	24	38
24	24	42
24	26	32

RANGES

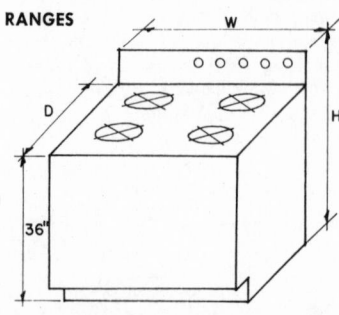

Electric range

Some models have automatic controls and may include surface griddles, rotisseries, and single or double ovens. Twenty- and 30-in. ranges generally require 10–14 kilowatts, 30- and 40-in. ranges 10–18 kilowatts. Forty-in. ranges generally have two ovens, 20- and 30-in. ranges one oven.

No. of elements	Depth, in.	Width, in.	Height, in.
4	24	20	45
4	24	42	48
4	25	20	40
4	25	30	44
4	25	30	45

4	25	36	45–49
4	25	40	48
4	26	21	40
4	26	30	44–47
4	26	30	48
4	26	39	43–50
4	26	40	48
4	27	21	42
4	27	30	45–49
4	28	30	48
4	28	40	44–48
4	29	40	48

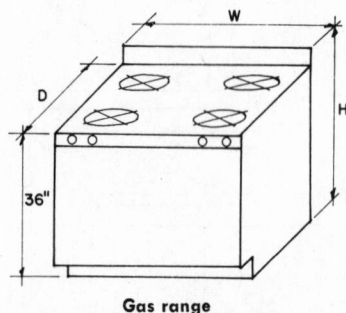

Gas range

Forty-in. ranges generally have two ovens, 20- and 30-in. ranges one oven.

No. of burners	Depth, in.	Width, in.	Height, in.
4	24	20	45
4	25	30	45–49
4	25	36	45–49
4	25	42	47
4	26	30	43–45
4	28	31	44–49
4	28	41	44–49

REFRIGERATORS

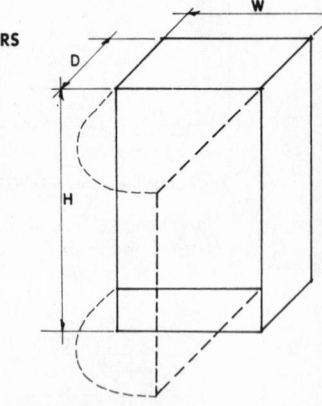

Built-in refrigerator

This model may be installed under the counter, stacked, or side by side.

Capacity, cu ft	Depth, in.	Width, in.	Height, in.
8	24	32*	33*
8	24	35	62*
12	24	35	56*

*Allowance must be made at the top or sides for an air grille.

Freestanding refrigerator

Some models can also be built-in. Many of them include small freezing compartments.

Approximate capacity, cu ft	Depth, in.	Width, in.	Height, in.	Door clearance (C), in.
4	27	24	34	50
8	28	24	58	49
8	28	24	56	48
8	31	24	56	—
10	30	24	59	50
10	30	31	60	56
10	31	28	59	—
11	28	28	64	53
12	25	36	50	—
12	30	30	64	56
12	31	31	61	—
13	28	32	64	57

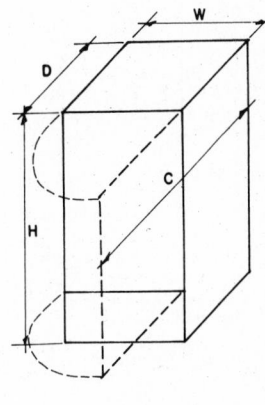

HOME FREEZERS

Freestanding upright freezer

Some models can also be built-in.

Capacity, cu ft	Depth, in.	Width, in.	Height, in.	Door clearance (C), in.
7	25	36	35	—
9	29	28	57	52
11	25	36	50	—
11	29	31	60	—
12	30	32	59	57
12	31	31	62	—
12	33	31	59	—
13	26	30	64	—
14	28	32	70	57
14	32	32	63	—
14	30	32	65	57
16	33	34	65	—
18	30	30	71	—
18	34	32	68	—
20	32	36	69	63
20	35	34	65	—

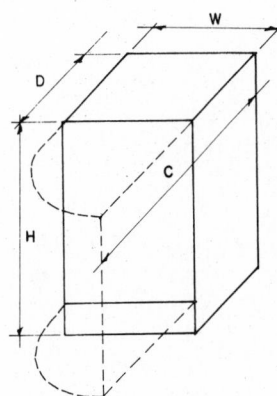

Chest-type freezer

Capacity, cu ft	Depth, in.	Width, in.	Height, in.	Door clearance (C), in.
4	24	33	36	—
10	33	42	37	62
10	33	42	38	—
12	30	54	36	59
15	33	55	38	62
15	33	55	38	—
17	30	71	36	59
17	32	60	37	63
17	33	60	37	—
20	33	71	38	62
20	33	60	37	—
20	33	71	38	—
21	32	71	37	63
26	33	84	37	—

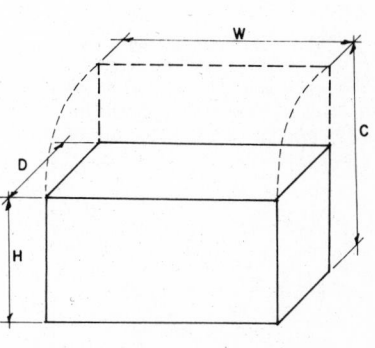

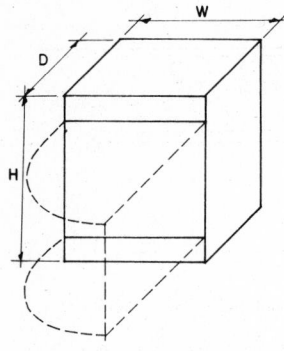

Built-in freezer

This model can be built-in under the counter, stacked with the refrigerator, or wall-hung.

Capacity, cu ft	Depth, in.	Width, in.	Height, in.
6	24	36	42

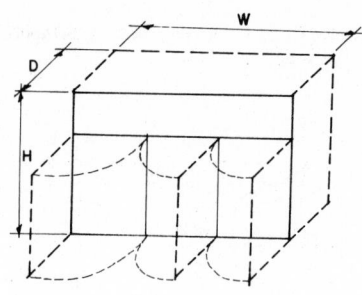

Wall-hung or built-in refrigerator-freezer

Approximate total capacity, cu ft	Depth, in.	Width, in.	Height, in.	No. of doors
11	18	64	40	3
13	24	60	38	2

COMBINATION REFRIGERATOR-FREEZER UNITS

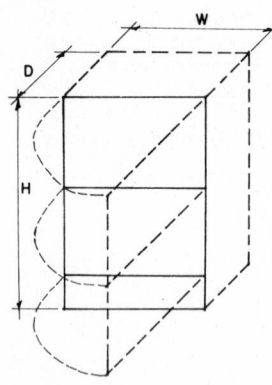

Built-in refrigerator-freezer

This model is 24 in. deep, 36 in. wide, 74 in. high, and has an approximate total capacity of 13 cu ft.

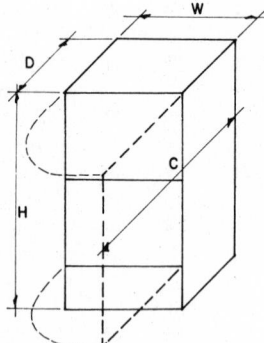

Freestanding refrigerator-freezer

The freezer compartment may be above or below and may vary in size. Some models can also be built-in.

Approximate total capacity, cu ft	Depth, in.	Width, in.	Height, in.	Door clearance (C), in.
7	29	24	54	—
8	32	24	56	50
10	29	28	64	53
10	29	32	59	—
11	26	30	61	54
12	29	32	64	—
12	29	30	64	55
12	32	30	59	56
12½	29	32	64	57
13	26	30	64	54
13	31	31	64	56
14	29	32	70	57
14	29	33	66	57
14	32	32	68	—
15	26	30	71	54
16	32	32	66	—
16	32	33	66	60

COMBINATION UNITS AND APPLIANCE CENTERS

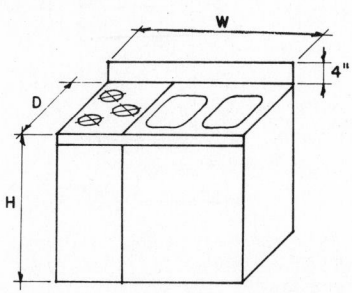

Combination unit

This model is available with electric or gas range.

Depth, in.	Width, in.	Height, in.	Features
25	24	36	2-burner range, refrigerator, single sink
25	24	36	4-burner range, refrigerator
25	29	36	Single sink, refrigerator
25	39	36	Single sink, refrigerator
25	48	36	Single sink, refrigerator
25	48	38	4-burner range, oven, broiler, refrigerator, single sink
28	28	36	3-burner range, refrigerator
28	28	36	3-burner range, refrigerator, single sink
28	42	36	3-burner range, oven, broiler, re-refrigerator, double sink

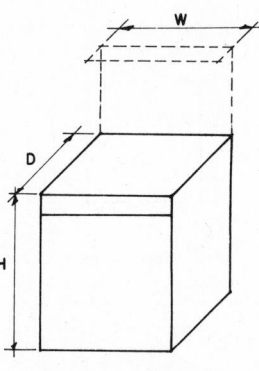

Executive-type unit

This model is available in various metal and wood finishes, as a freestanding unit, and with furniture styling.

Depth, in.	Width, in.	Height, in.	Features
28	29	39	3-burner range, single sink, refrigerator
28	48	39	3-burner range, single sink, refrigerator, storage space

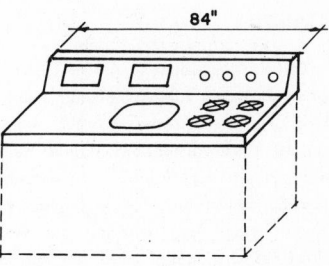

Special utility package unit

This model fits over standard base cabinets and is available in a variety of counter materials. Its features include surface cooking units, griddles, appliance center, and sink. It can also be ordered in combination with under-counter ovens and dishwasher.

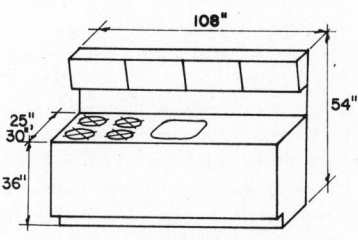

Special utility package unit

Various combinations of equipment are available: surface cooking units, ovens, sink, appliance center, dishwasher, combination washer-dryer, garbage disposer, and storage units. This model may be freestanding or built-in.

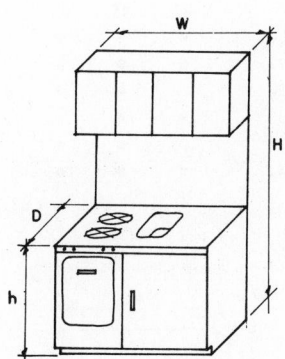

Pullman-type unit

This model is available with either gas or electric range and as a freestanding or built-in unit. Garbage disposers are generally available.

Depth, in.	Width, in.	Height, in.	Height (h), in.	Features
25	39	81	39	2-burner range, refrigerator, single sink
25	48	81, 87	39	2-burner range, oven, broiler, refrigerator, single sink
25	60	87	36	3- to 4-burner range, oven, broiler, refrigerator, single sink
25	69	87	36	3- to 4-burner range, oven, broiler, refrigerator, single sink
25	72	87	36	4-burner range, oven, broiler, refrigerator, single sink
25	63	87	36	
25	48	87	36	3-burner range, oven, refrigerator, single sink
25	51	87	36	

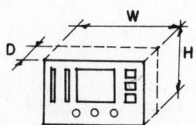

Automatic appliance center

This model may be built into walls or cabinets. Some models are equipped with receptacles, retractable cords, circuit breakers, clocks and timers.

Depth, in.	Width, in.	Height, in.
3	14	6
4	14	8
9½	12	12

CABINETS

Critical dimensions of the principal types of stock kitchen cabinets, of both metal and wood, are illustrated on the following pages. These dimensions should be used only for preliminary planning purposes and specific manufacturers' data should be consulted before final selections and working drawings are made, since not all manufacturers make every cabinet in every size indicated.

The dimensions have been drawn from the current catalogs of the leading manufacturers of stock metal and wood cabinets. Special sizes, features, materials, and finishes are not individually discussed. Such items should always be investigated with the specific manufacturer.

WOOD CABINETS

All base cabinets are $34\frac{1}{2}$ in. high without tops, 36 in. high with tops, and 24 in. deep. Wall cabinets are 13 in. deep and vary in height.

A wide assortment of filler moldings and panels and side or end finishing panels are available for all cabinet sizes and types. Numerous special-purpose base cabinets are also available, such as mixer storage, tray storage, vegetable bins, breadbox drawers, linen storage, pull-out tables, and towel racks. In addition to such specially designed and equipped cabinets, many accessory items are available for installation in stock units.

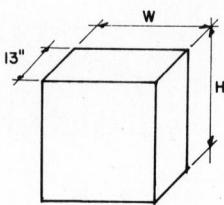

Wall cabinet

Height, in.	Width, in.				
	12	15	18	21	24
24				●	●
30	●	●	●	●	●
32	●	●	●	●	●
33	●	●	●	●	●
45	●	●	●	●	

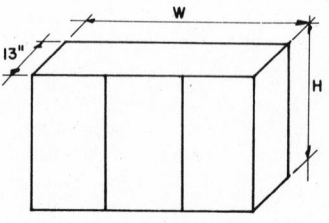

Wall cabinet

Height, in.	Width, in.		
	42	45	48
16	●	●	●
22	●	●	●
24		●	●
32	●	●	●
33		●	●
45	●	●	●

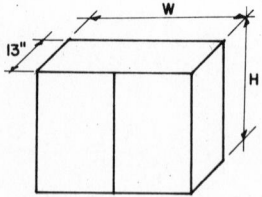

Wall cabinet

Height, in.	Width, in.							
	24	27	30	33	36	39	42	48
15			●	●	●	●		
16	●	●	●	●	●	●	●	
18			●	●	●	●	●	
22	●	●	●	●	●	●	●	
24			●	●	●	●	●	●
30			●	●	●	●	●	
32	●	●	●	●	●	●	●	
33	●	●	●	●	●	●	●	
45	●	●	●	●	●	●	●	

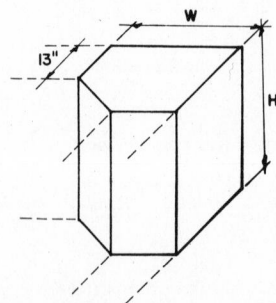

Wall cabinet (single-door corner unit)

Height, in.	Width, in.	
	24	27
24	●	●
32	●	●
33	●	●
45	●	●

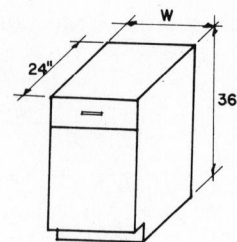

Base cabinet

This model is available in the following widths: 12, 15, 18, 21, and 24 in.

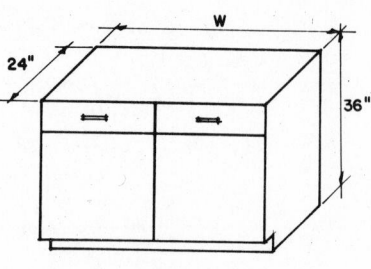

Base cabinet

This model is available in the following widths: 24, 27, 30, 33, 36, 39, 42, and 48 in.

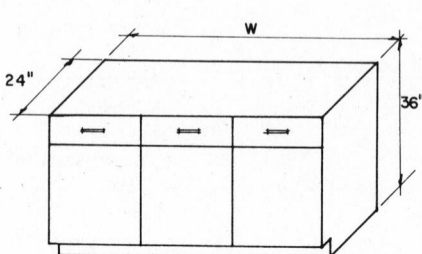

Base cabinet

This model is available in 42-, 45-, and 48-in. widths.

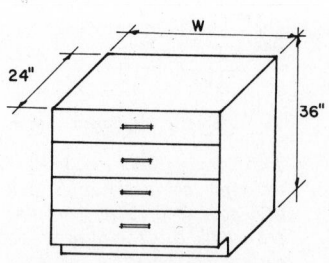

Base cabinet with drawers

This model is available in 15-, 18-, 24-, and 30-in. widths.

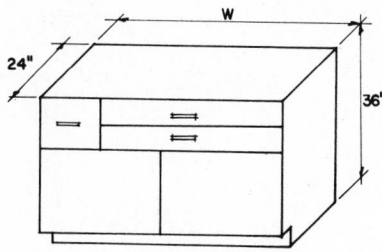

Base cabinet with drawers

No. of drawers	Width, in.
2	15, 18, 21, 24
3	27, 30, 33, 36, 39
4	42, 45, 48

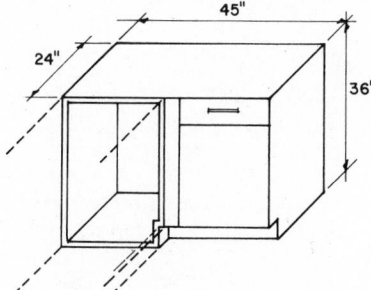

Base cabinet (blind-corner unit)

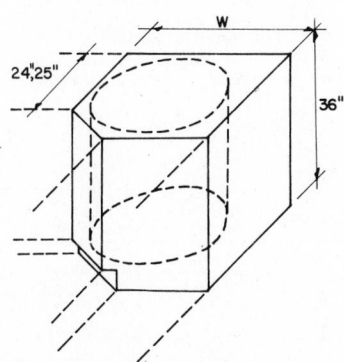

Base cabinet (rotating corner unit)

This model is available in 34- to 36-in. widths.

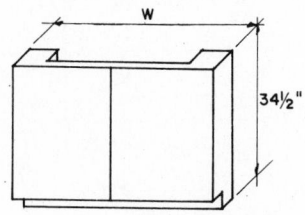

Sink-front cabinet

The base is generally furnished, but not the cabinet floor. Some models are also available in a 28½-in. height for low counters.

Width, in.

18, 21, 24, 27, 30, 33, 36
39, 42, 45, 48, 54

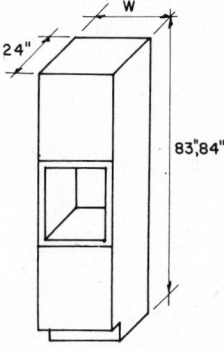

Oven cabinet (for built-in wall ovens)

This model is available in the following widths: 24, 27, 33, and 48 in.

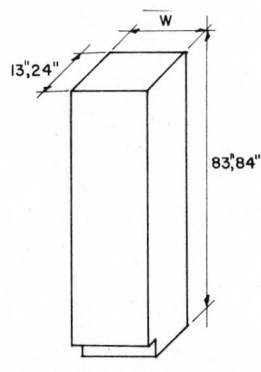

Utility-storage cabinet

This model is available in the following widths: 15, 18, 21, 24, and 36 in.

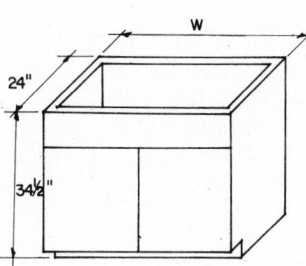

Range cabinet (for built-in surface cooking units)

Some models are 28 in. high for use with "stack-on" cooking units.

Width, in.

18, 24, 27, 30, 36, 42, 48

METAL CABINETS

All base cabinets are 34½ in. high without tops, and 36 in. with tops. The total depth to the edge of the countertop is generally 25 in. The depth of the cabinet itself is generally 24 in. plus or minus ½ in. Wall cabinets are 13 in. deep and vary in height. Doors may be either right or left hand.

All manufacturers offer a wide variety of optional, special-purpose accessories that can be fitted into any of the basic cabinets. A wide assortment of filler moldings and panels and side or end finishing panels are available for all cabinet sizes and types. Most manufacturers offer cabinets in several stock colors, and special colors can usually be matched on special order. Some models have wood doors. Base cabinets are available with or without tops.

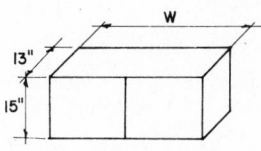

Wall cabinet

Width, in.	No. of doors
36	2

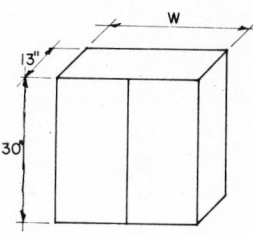

Wall cabinet

Width, in.	No. of doors
12	1
15	1
18	1–2
21	2
24	2
27	2
30	2
36	2
42	2
48	2
54	4

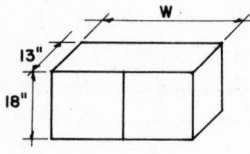

Wall cabinet

Width, in.	No. of doors
18	1
21	2
24	2
30	2
36	2
42	2–4

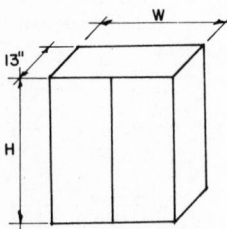

Wall cabinet (island)

This model has two doors and opens on two sides.

Height, in.	Width, in.
18	21
18	24
18	30
18	36
24	24
30	12
30	15
30	18
30	21
30	24
30	27
30	30
30	36

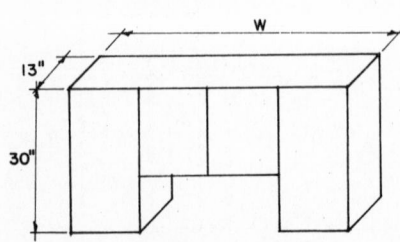

Over-sink cabinet

Width, in.	No. of doors
54	4
60	4

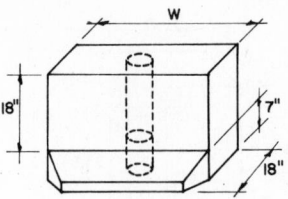

Range-ventilator cabinet

Hoods are available in a variety of metals and finishes; however, some models have no projecting hood.

Width, in.	No. of doors
24	2
30	2
36	2
42	2–4

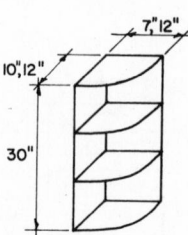

Wall cabinet with open display shelves

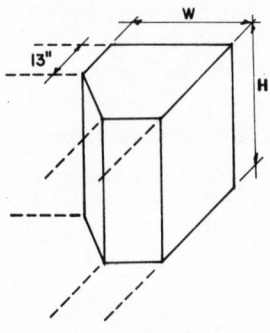

Wall cabinet (single-door, corner-type)

Some models are available with revolving shelves.

Width, in.	Height, in.
21, 25, 26, 27	18, 30

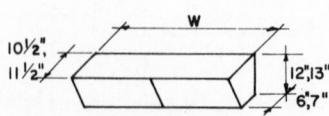

Wall cabinet

This model has by-passing, sliding doors and is available in the following widths: 21, 24, 30, 36, and 48 in.

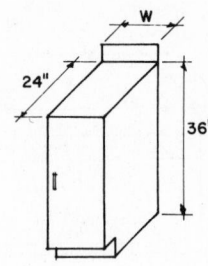

Base cabinet

Width, in.	No. of doors
9	1
12	1
24	2

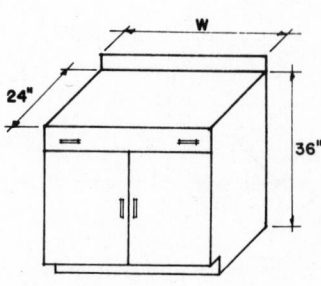

Base cabinet

Width, in.	No. of doors	No. of drawers
12	1	1
15	1	1–2
18	1	1
21	2	1–2
24	2	1–2
27	2	1–2
30	2	1–2
36	2	2
42	4	2

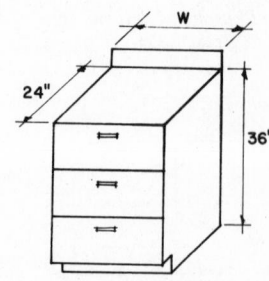

Base cabinet with drawers

Width, in.	No. of drawers
15	3–4
18	3–4
21	4
24	3–4
27	4

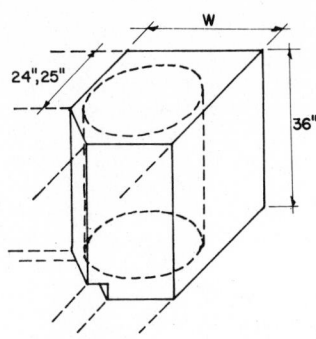

Base cabinet (single-door, corner-unit)

Most models have revolving shelves; available in 31-, 32-, and 33-in. widths.

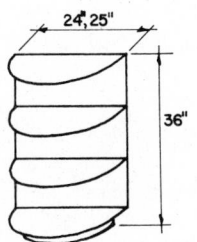

Base cabinet (half-round, open-type)

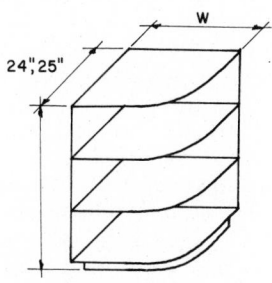

Base cabinet (quarter-round, open-type)

This model is available in 18- and 24½-in. widths.

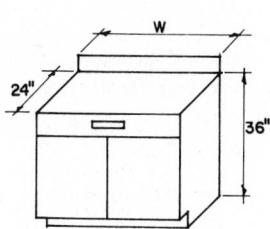

Range base cabinet (for drop-in, surface cooking units)

This model is available in 18-, 24-, 30-, and 36-in. widths.

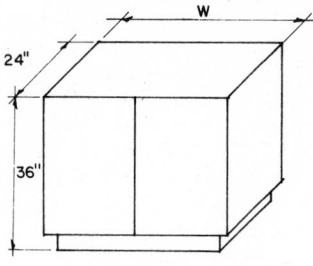

Base cabinet (island)

This model is available with single or double doors accessible on 2 sides.

Width, in.
12, 15, 18, 21, 24,
27, 30, 36, 45

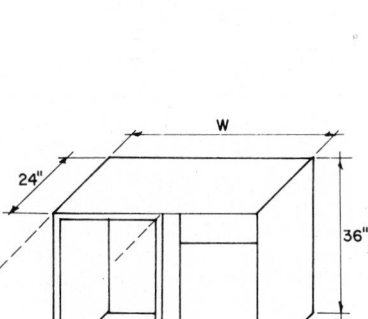
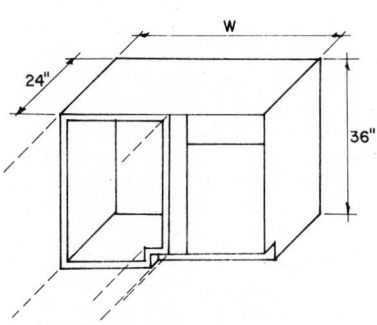

Base cabinet (blind-corner unit)

Right- or left-hand models are available; comes in 42- and 44-in. widths.

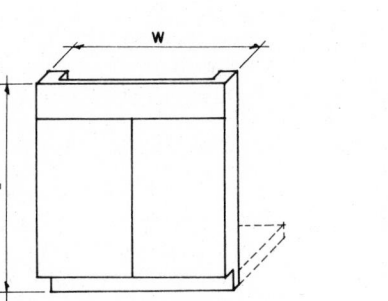

Sink-front cabinet

This model is available in the following widths: 21, 24, 30, 36, and 42 in.

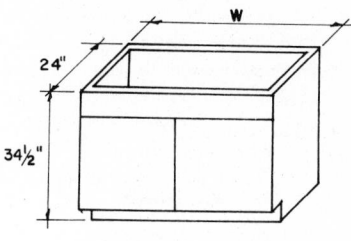

Under-sink cabinet

Width, in.
24, 30, 36, 42, 48,
54, 60, 66, 72

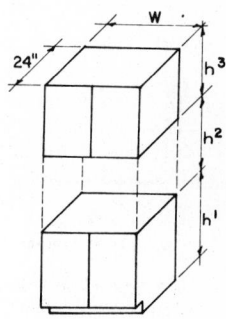

Oven cabinet (for built-in wall oven)

Width, in.	Height (h^1), in.	Height (h^2), in.	Height (h^3), in.
24, 27	18, 22, 28	26, 34, 36 40, 42	18, 24

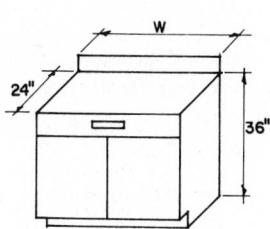

Utility-storage cabinet

Depth, in.	Width, in.	Height, in.
13	21	80
24	24	84

LAUNDRIES—1
Planning considerations

By GLENN H. BEYER AND ALEXANDER KIRA, *Housing Research Center, Cornell University*
(including material adapted from previously published article by Larch C. Renshaw in 3rd ed. of Time-Saver Standards)

Laundering includes a host of tasks—collecting and sorting dirty clothes, pretreating, washing, drying, sprinkling and ironing—all of which are tiring, for they require a great deal of stooping, lifting, and carrying. To reduce the amount of effort required, a laundry center (either separate or combined with another area) should be carefully planned. Some basic planning considerations are as follows:

Arrangement

The sequence of laundering operations should determine the planning of space and facilities and the placing of equipment.

Traffic lanes

With automatic equipment, many families now wash clothes three or four days a week. Therefore, laundering should not be done in any of the congested areas of the house. Passageways should be at least 4 ft wide. If the laundry area adjoins the kitchen, there should be a barrier of some type, at least a counter, between the two areas.

Equipment and facilities

To reduce the amount of effort required, a laundry center should have a sorting table, a heating surface (such as a hot plate), and storage facilities for soiled clothes, washing supplies, and baskets, as well as a washing machine, dryer, and ironing board; some may also have ironers. A laundry tray (usually a 14-in.-deep porcelain enamel sink) is desirable for prewashing, soaking, or starching some items.

Space

The space should be dry, heated, and well lighted, with sufficient electrical outlets, properly located. The space should be ventilated to remove moisture and odors.

Accessibility

Laundry centers today can be more conveniently located because of the compactness of automatic washers and dryers and the elimination of much of the dampness and disorder formerly associated with household washing. Although many locations are possible (such as the kitchen, bath, separate laundry room, or utility room), the laundry center should be accessible both to the work areas of the house (since frequent trips to and from them may be required during any of the laundering processes) and to outdoor summer drying areas.

FLOW OF WORK

Convenience and efficiency are achieved by placing the equipment in their natural order of use: (1) Clothes chute (with or without bins or hampers), (2) Sorting and pretreating table or counter, (3) Washing machine, (4) Laundry tray (if available), (5) Dryer, (6) Ironing board (and ironer, if available), and (7) Standing or hanging bar and counter for ironed items. In addition, a storage closet or cabinet is necessary for cleaning supplies. In some instances, a hot plate is also needed. Some of these facilities and equipment are described in more detail below.

Clothes chute: In two-story houses, the chute is a handy device for delivering clothes from upstairs. It should empty on or near the sorting table so that the clothes will not have to be carried or handled more than necessary. It should be vertical, because curved sections are likely to cause clothes to clog the chute.

Sorting and pretreating table: Ample space should be allowed on a table or counter for sorting and dampening the clothes, and for a clothes basket, as well as space for the worker using the table. The table size required will depend upon the size of the average wash load. Research at Pennsylvania State University indicates that a table 6x2½ ft is required for a 32-lb, 4-load laundry. For pretreating, an area 20x36 in. is adequate for work and equipment (pan, brush, soap, and kettle).

Washing machine: Automatic washers and dryers permit much more convenient and compact arrangements than were possible with nonautomatic equipment. The total floor area needed is determined by the type of washer, the other equipment needed, and the space for the worker. The old-fashioned, galvanized tubs are not required with automatic equipment, but, as indicated earlier, a laundry tray is desirable. To ensure that a laundry area is both economical in use of space and convenient to work in, the dimensions shown in Fig. 4 should be followed.

Drying: The research at Pennsylvania State University revealed that 124 lin ft of line is required to hang a 4-load laundry of 32 lb.

The space requirements for different styles of dryers, and for operating them, are shown in Fig. 5. The combination washer-dryer or the stacked arrangement of washer and dryer requires less floor area than other arrangements. These dimensions are shown in Fig. 6.

Since some garments must be hung to drip-dry, a pull-out drying rod or similar arrangement should be provided, preferably above a laundry tray (or a floor drain, if the laundry is in the basement).

Ironing: An ironing board adjustable from a height of 23 to 37 in. accommodates most women when sitting or standing to iron. The choice of either a built-in or a freestanding board depends upon personal preference. Freestanding boards should be stored where they are readily accessible. The space needed to use a hand iron at a board is shown in Fig. 2. The space needed to use an ironer, with auxiliary equipment, is shown in Fig. 3.

The *storage closet* should be large enough to accommodate soaps, spoons, sieves, bleaches, bluing, stain remover, starch, clothespins, and the like. If a storage cupboard 8 in. in depth is placed over an automatic washer, it should be at least 20 in. above the washer; and if 12 in. in depth, it should be 24 in. above the washer. This clearance allows for head room when using the water faucets.

SPACE ARRANGEMENTS

Laundering may be done in a room designed especially for this purpose, or in a multiuse room, designed also for food preparation, sewing, child play, and the like.

The best location, of course, is convenient to other work centers, such as the kitchen, and to the drying yard so that there will be a minimum of carrying necessary. Generally, basements are not considered desirable locations because of their inconvenience, dampness, and lack of adequate light.

Figures 7–13 provide floor plans illustrating various arrangements of basic work areas needed for the laundering process. In some of the plans shown, the space needed for laundering is treated as a separate area; in others, possible combinations with other areas are indicated.

EQUIPMENT

Figure 1 and Tables 1 and 2 provide basic dimensions of a typical automatic washer, dryer, combination washer-dryer, and ironer. These dimensions may be used for preliminary planning purposes, but final selection of equipment and detailing of working drawings should always be based on specific manufacturer's data.

Dimensions have been drawn from the current catalogs of leading manufacturers of each type of equipment. Special and nonresidential equipment are not included. Dimensions are generally given only to the nearest half inch since dimensions of new models vary slightly from year to year.

Door swings, location of vents, and the specific requirements for power, waste, and water supply should be checked against the manufacturer's data after units have been tentatively selected.

988

Table 1. Dimensions for matched automatic washer and dryer

Washer and dryer may be free-standing or built into adjoining base cabinets. Some models are available without tops and splash-boards for undercounter installa-tion (the height is then 34½ in.), with both doors front-opening. Some models have sloped fronts; others may be stacked vertically, built-in.

Depth, in.	Width (W^1), in.	Width (W^2), in.	Height, in.
24	25	25	36
26	24	24	36
26	25	27	36
26	25	30	36
26	29	29	36
27	27	27	36
28	26	31	36
28	31	31	37

Table 2. Dimensions for combination automatic washer-dryer

Some models are available for undercounter installation (the height is then 34½ in.). Some models are also available with sloped fronts.

Depth, in.	Width, in.	Height, in.
25	30	34½
26	34	45
28	31	36
28	32	37

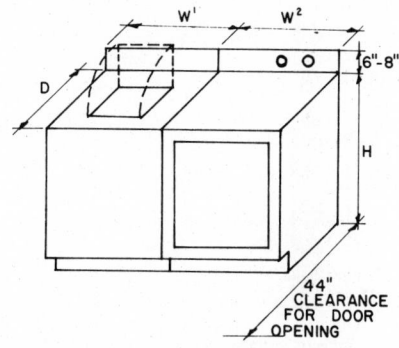

a. Matched automatic washer and dryer

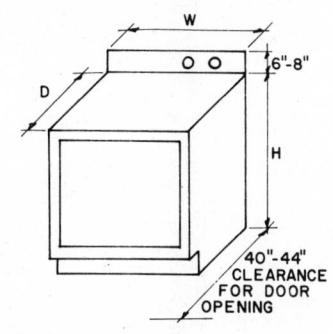

b. Combination automatic washer-dryer

c. Ironer

Fig. 1. Dimensions of household laundry equipment

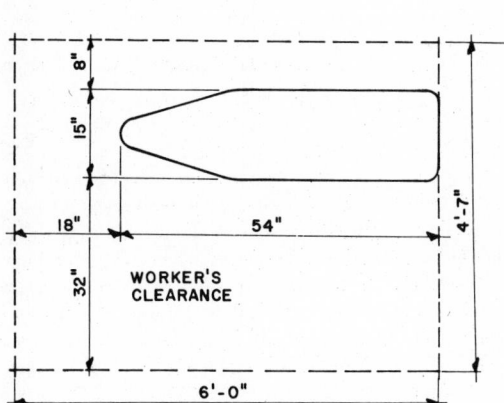

Fig. 2. Space requirements for ironing board

Scale: ⅜ in. = 1 ft

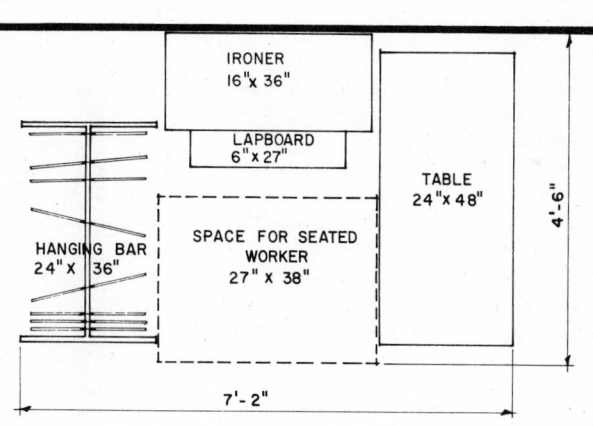

Fig. 3. Space requirements for ironer

Scale: ⅜ in. = 1 ft

Source (Fig. 2 and 3): Cecile P. Sinden and Kathleen A. Johnston, Space for Home Laundering, *Bulletin 658, Pennsylvania State University Agricultural Experiment Station, University Park (July 1959).*

Space requirements

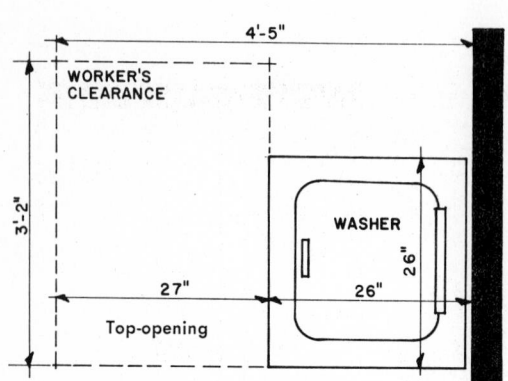

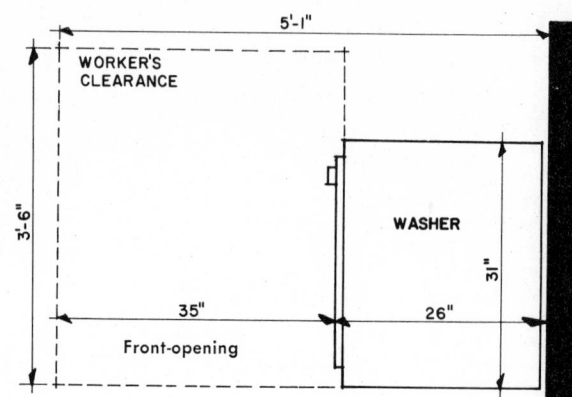

Fig. 4. Space requirements for two types of automatic washers   Scale: ½ in. = 1 ft

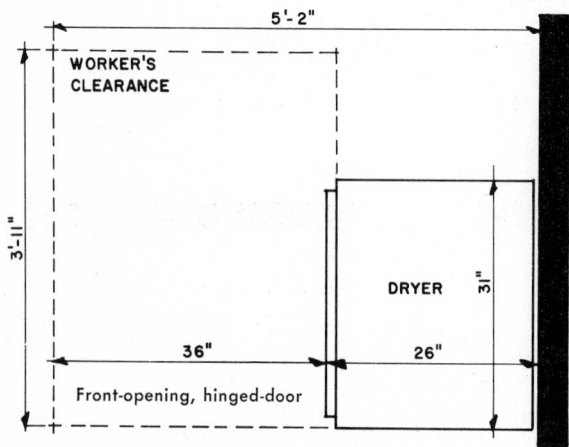

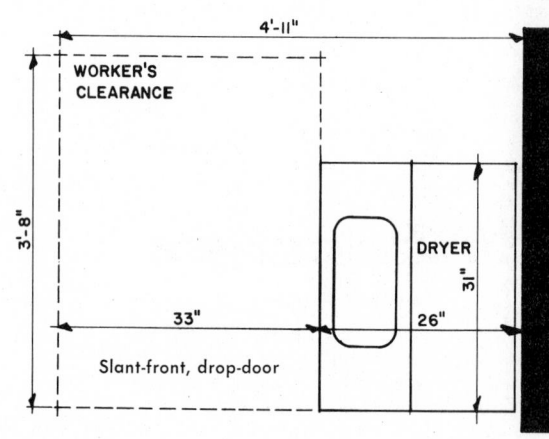

Fig. 5. Space requirements for two types of automatic dryers   Scale: ½ in. = 1 ft

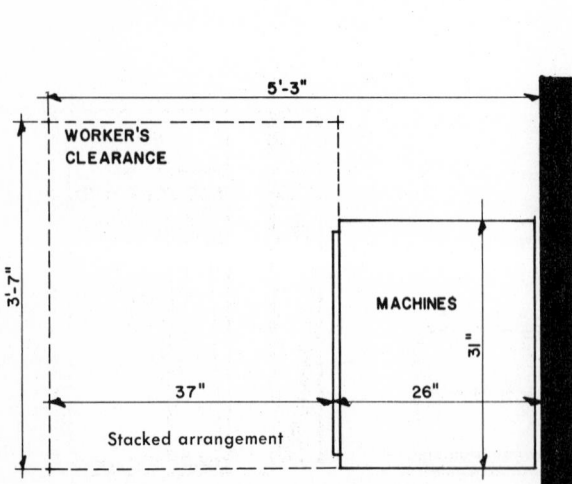

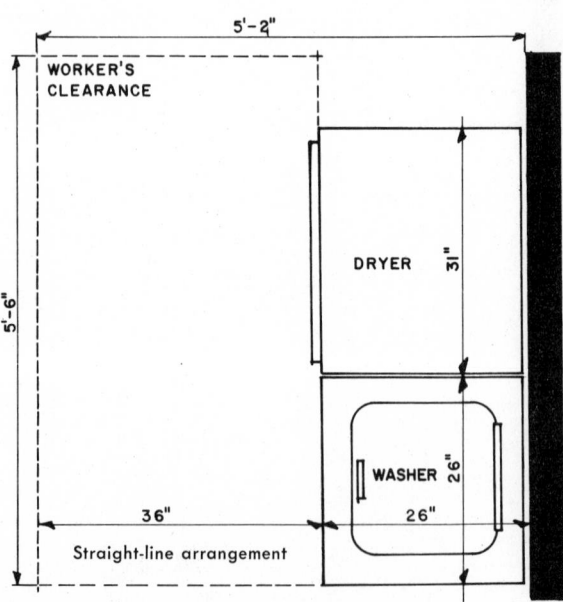

Fig. 6. Space requirements for combination washer-dryer   Scale: ½ in. = 1 ft

Worker's clearance (Fig. 4, 5, and 6) can overlap to either left or right of machines. Source (Fig. 4, 5, and 6): Cecile P. Sinden and Kathleen A. Johnston, Space for Home Laundering, *Bulletin 658, Pennsylvania State University Agricultural Experiment Station, University Park (July 1959).*

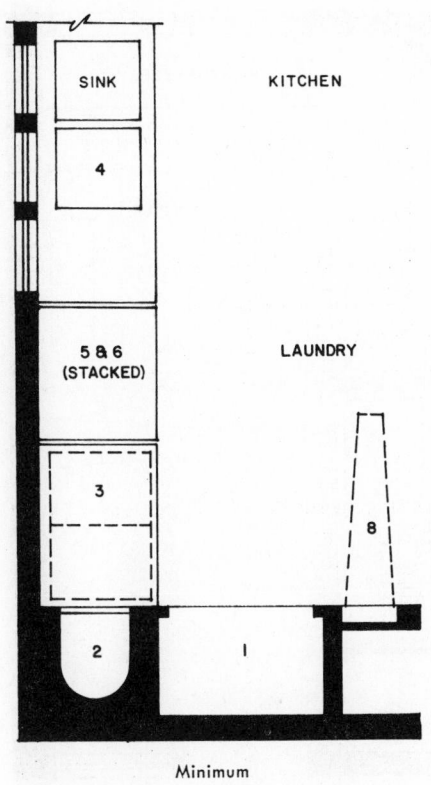

Minimum

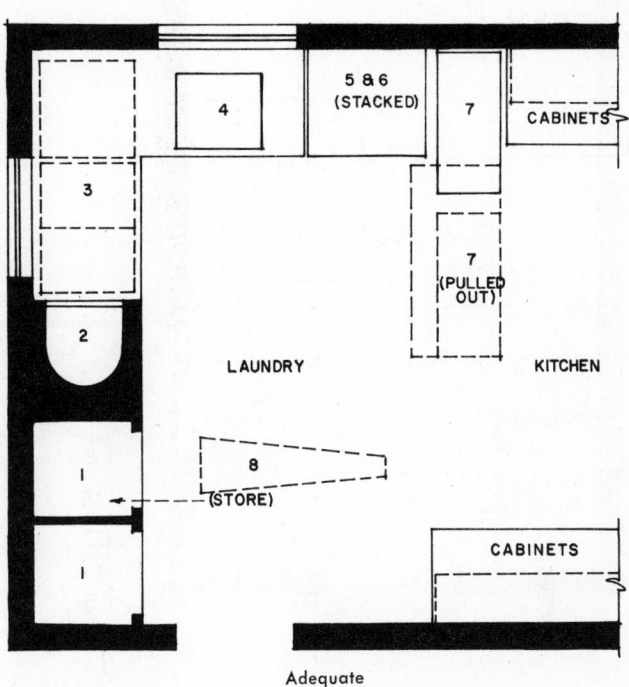

Adequate

Key

1. Storage closet
2. Laundry chute (ventilated)
3. Sorting shelf (ventilated bins below)
4. Laundry tray with mixing faucet and cover
5. Washer
6. Dryer (should be ventilated)
7. Ironer
8. Ironing board

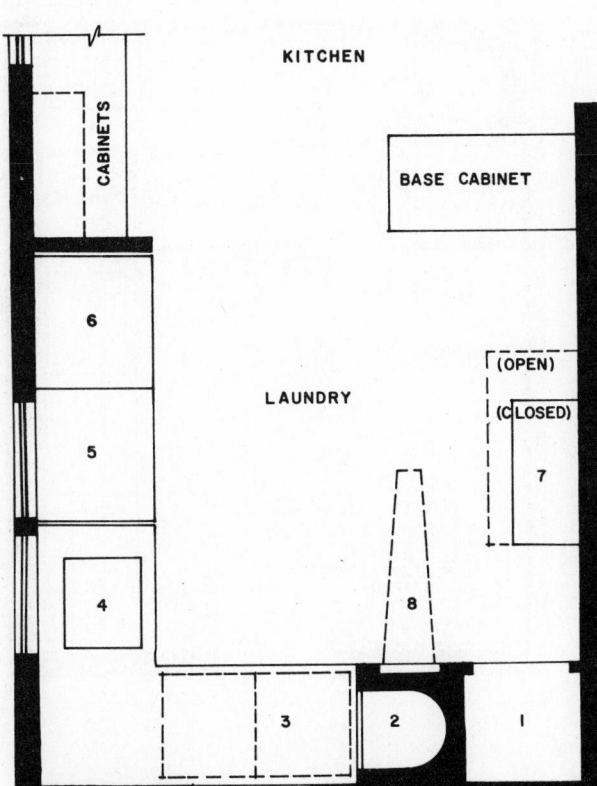

Desirable

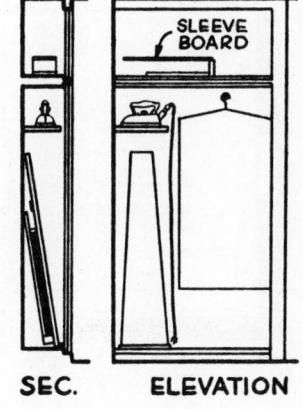

LAUNDRY CART   SEC.   ELEVATION

Fig. 7. Kitchen-laundry plans   Scale: $\frac{1}{4}$ in. = 1 ft

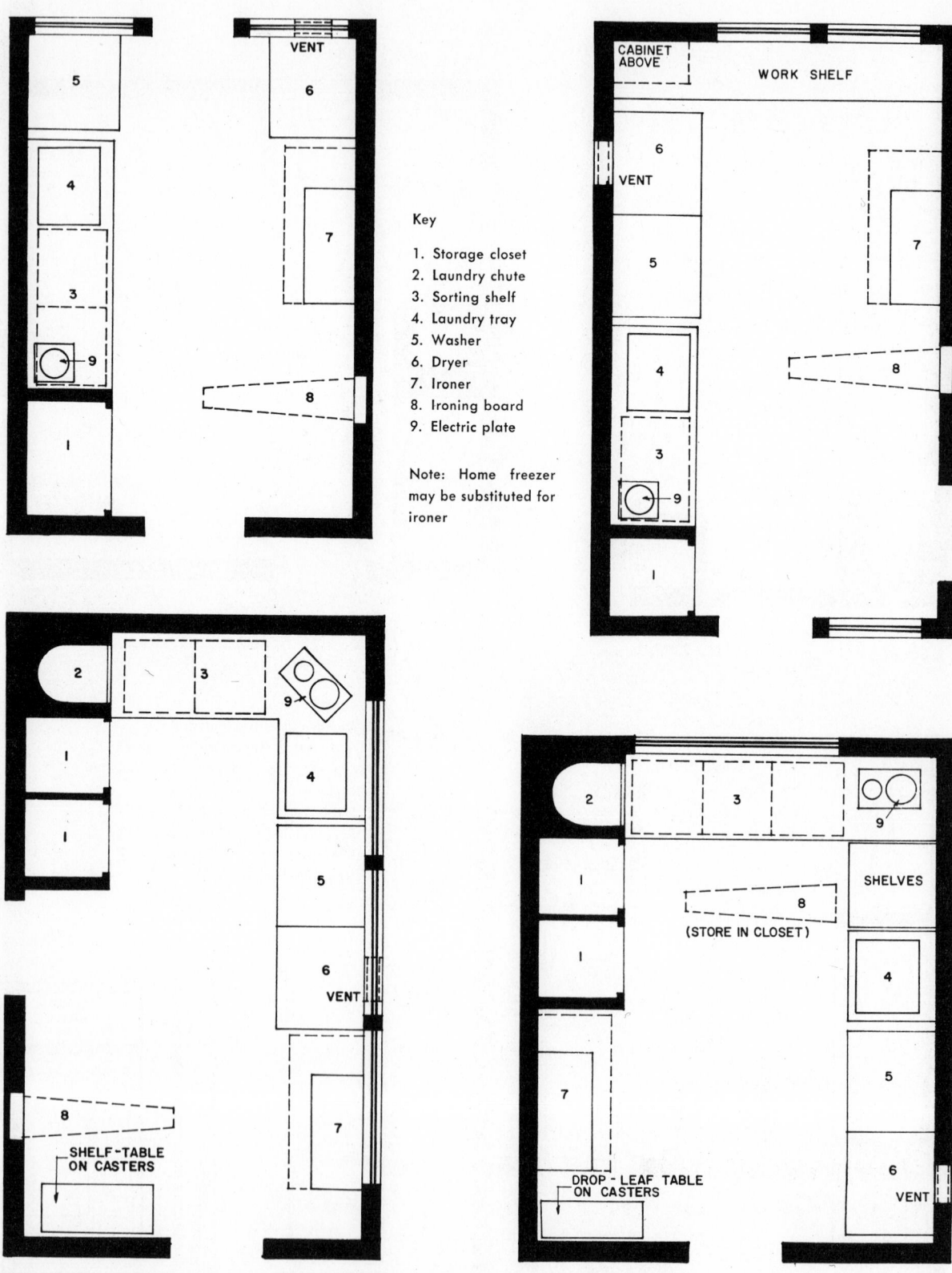

Key

1. Storage closet
2. Laundry chute
3. Sorting shelf
4. Laundry tray
5. Washer
6. Dryer
7. Ironer
8. Ironing board
9. Electric plate

Note: Home freezer may be substituted for ironer

Fig. 8. Separate laundry rooms Scale: ¼ in. = 1 ft

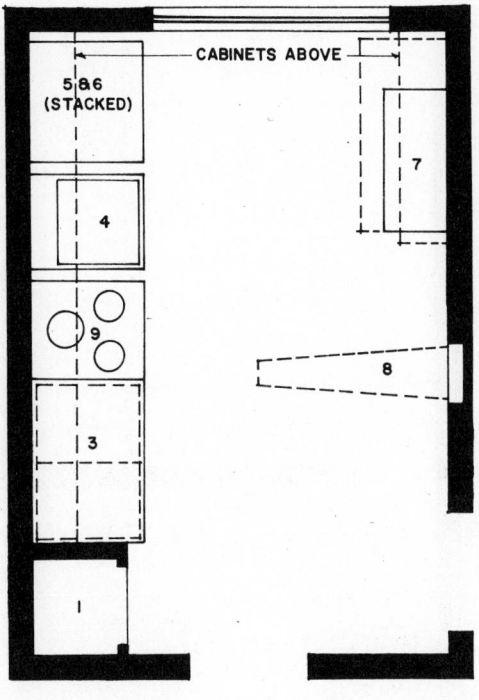

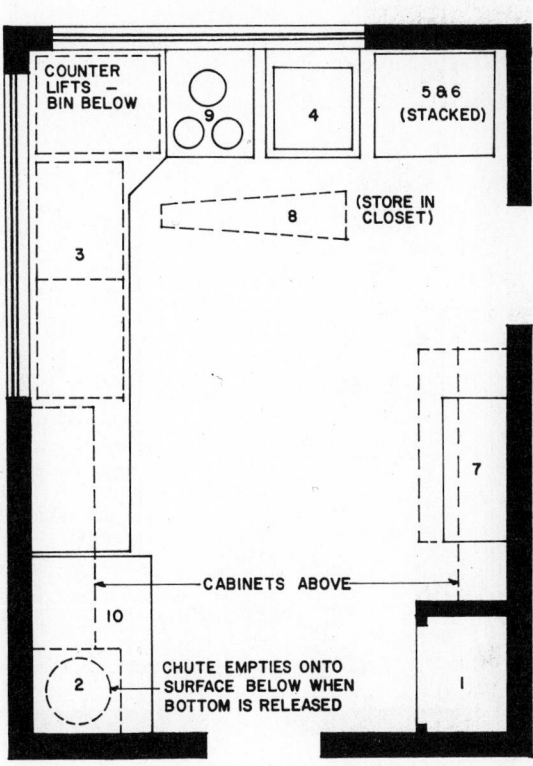

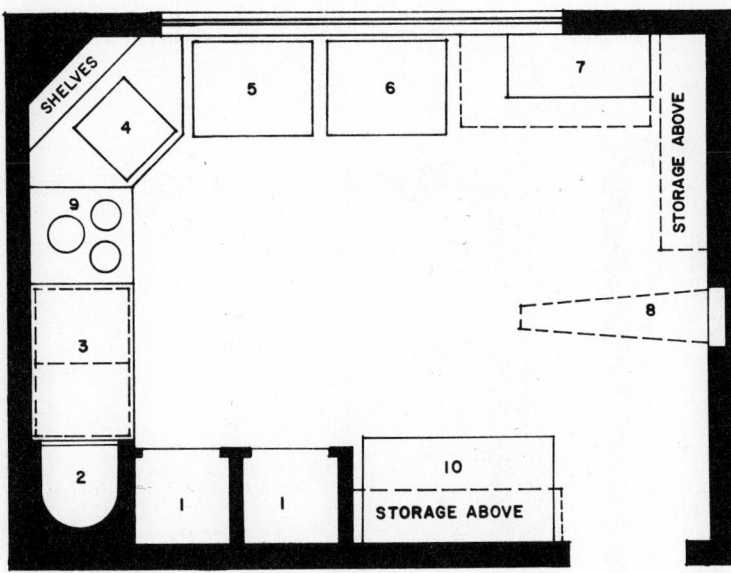

Fig. 9. Separate laundry rooms   Scale: ¼ in. = 1 ft

Key

1. Storage closet
2. Laundry chute
3. Sorting shelf
4. Laundry tray
5. Washer
6. Dryer
7. Ironer
8. Ironing board
9. Electric plate
10. Home freezer

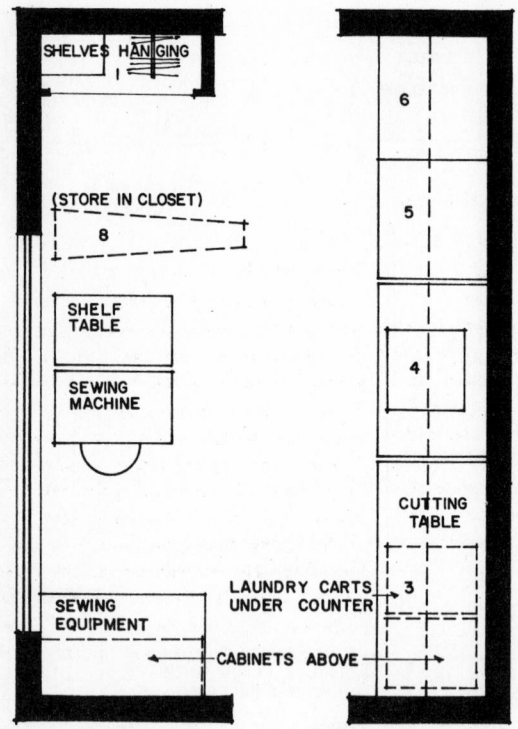

Fig. 10. Combination laundry-sewing room with storage area
Scale: $\frac{1}{4}$ in. = 1 ft

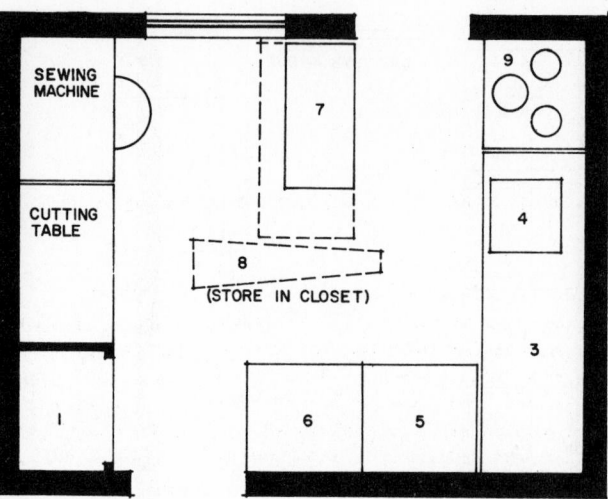

Fig. 11. Combination laundry-sewing room Scale: $\frac{1}{4}$ in. = 1 ft

Key

1. Storage closet
2. Laundry chute
3. Sorting shelf
4. Laundry tray
5. Washer
6. Dryer
7. Ironer
8. Ironing board
9. Electric plate

Note: Home freezer may be substituted for ironer

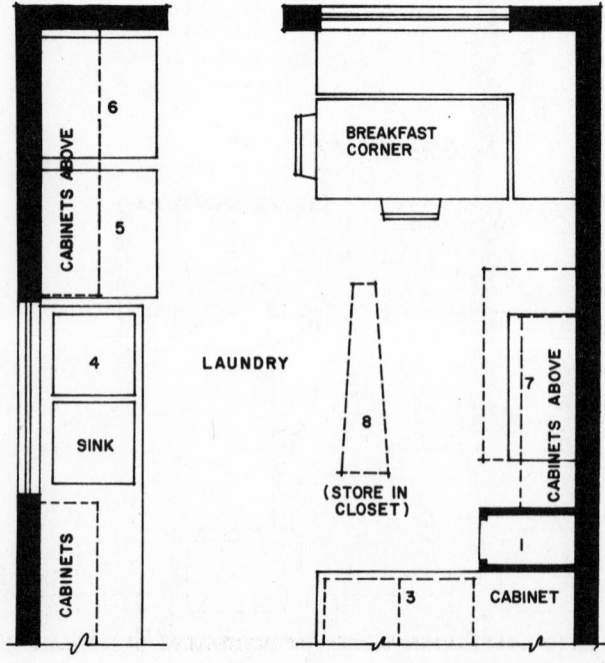

Fig. 12. Combination laundry-breakfast room Scale: $\frac{1}{4}$ in. = 1 ft

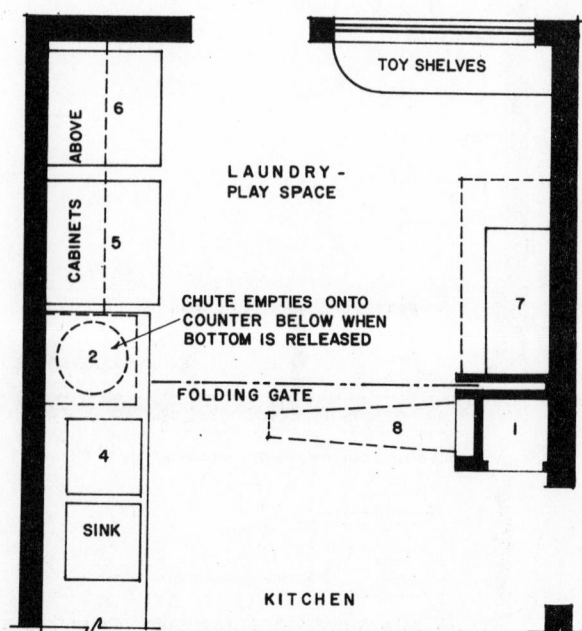

Fig. 13. Combination laundry-playroom Scale: $\frac{1}{4}$ in. = 1 ft

By GLENN H. BEYER AND ALEXANDER KIRA, *Housing Research Center, Cornell University*

Activities commonly performed in the bathroom include washing of hands, face, and hair, bathing, elimination, and grooming, and also such activities as hand laundering and infant care. Often it is also used as a dressing room. Major problems in bathroom design include planning for optimum convenience and privacy of all bathroom functions for all members of the household, adequate provision for storage of supplies and equipment, and ease of cleaning.

Some general planning guides are as follows[1]:

Arrangement

Facilities should be conveniently arranged, with special attention given to clearances. The room arrangement should permit more than one family member to use its facilities at the same time.

[1] *Many of these suggestions are by courtesy of the American Radiator and Standard Sanitary Corporation.*

Illumination

Lighting should be adequate for all of the activities performed. For grooming, direct sources of light are essential in order to illuminate the face from all angles. High strip windows, clerestory windows, and skylights provide excellent over-all illumination in the daytime, while still affording privacy. Luminous ceilings are also effective, particularly in interior bathrooms.

Ventilation

Good ventilation is essential in bathrooms, both to reduce humidity and to dispel odors. If a window is relied upon as the sole means of ventilation, care should be taken in its selection and placement to minimize drafts and to permit easy access. Exhaust fans in the wall or ceiling are often used to supplement natural ventilation. In interior bathroom spaces, a mechanical exhaust is, of course, essential.

Sound control

Lack of acoustical privacy is one of the most common complaints with regard to bathrooms. Noise can be reduced by proper placement of the bathroom in relation to other spaces, by the use of closets and storage walls as sound barriers between it and adjacent spaces, as well as by the use of soundproof partitions and tightly fitted doors. Acoustical treatment of the ceiling makes the room more comfortable to use and reduces somewhat the amount of sound transmitted through the walls. Acoustical tiles for use in the bathroom should be moisture resistant and easily cleaned.

Auxiliary heat

A heat lamp or a radiant wall panel can be used to provide quick warmth in the bathroom.

Materials

It is essential that all surface materials used in the bathroom have moisture-resistant finishes.

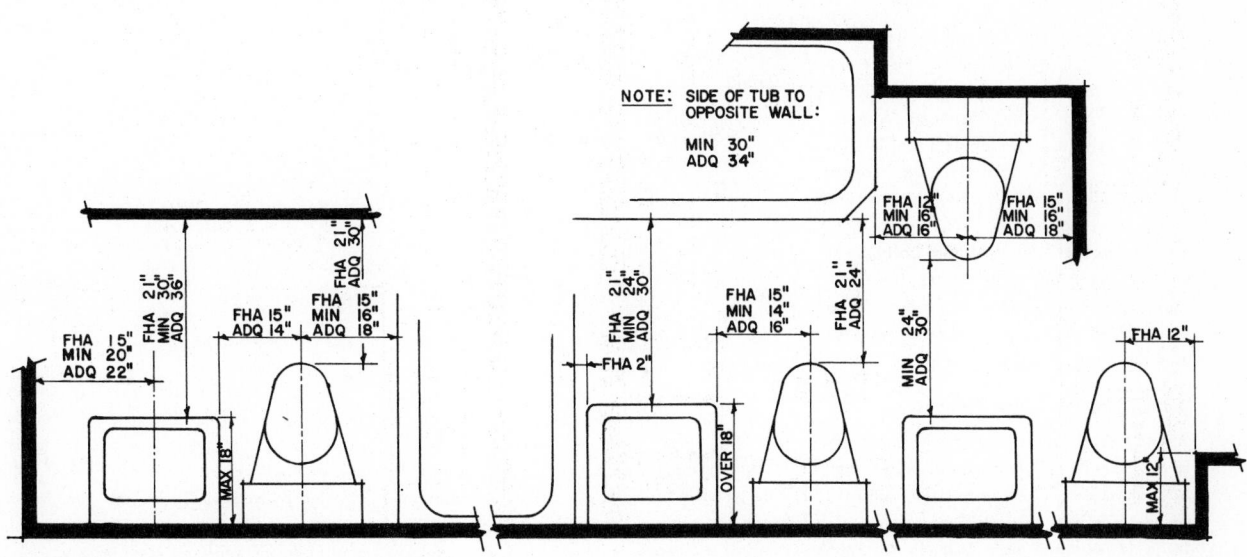

Fig. 1.   Fixture clearances (dimensions in inches)

Planning considerations

Storage

Adequate storage should be provided for current and reserve supplies. Articles in current use should be located near their place of first use. A closet opening from the bathroom and hallway or laundry is convenient for such items as bathroom linen and cleaning supplies. Medicine cabinets should be as large as possible since increasing numbers of toiletries and medicines are being used by American families. Hamper space is desirable for soiled linen and clothes. Install a cabinet with a self-contained hamper, or, in two-story houses, install a chute from the second floor to the laundry. The minimum requirements for storage of bathroom linens, based on recent research, are shown in Table 3.

Increased countertop space

Larger lavatories and increased countertop surfaces provide excellent facilities for light laundry, hair washing, and bathing and dressing the baby.

Children's convenience

Children's height should be considered in the placement of accessory equipment. A dental lavatory can double as a child's lavatory. If a combination lavatory-dressing table is installed, a step-up retractable stool should be provided for children's use.

Mirrors

An atmosphere of luxury and spaciousness is created by mirrors. A full-length mirror is always desirable. Also recommended is a medicine cabinet with a three-way combination of mirrored doors on either side and a mirror in the center.

Safety features

Grab bars should be used vertically for bathtub and shower and should be located for convenient use. They should be of adequate size and securely fastened to sturdy backing or studs. Use nonskid finishes for flooring. Install a door lock that opens automatically from the inside, and from the outside in case of emergency. Locate light switches out of reach of the bathtub or shower—preferably just outside the bathroom. Electric or radiant heaters should be recessed or protected. Provide a lock for medicine compartments.

Drying facilities and accessories

Add extra racks for drying women's hose and other light laundry. Racks may be concealed in well-ventilated cabinets, which, if desired, may include a receptacle for a low-wattage light bulb to facilitate drying. Sufficient robe hooks, bag hooks, and toothbrush holders should also be provided.

Accessibility

A bathroom should generally be accessible to each bedroom without requiring passage through another room. A bathroom is desirable near principal indoor living, work, and play areas, and for guest use.

Table 1. Space required at the lavatory and bathtub

See Fig. 1 and 2 for illustration of dimensions.

Dimension	Space required, in.		
	Adequate	Minimum	FHA minimum
Lavatory			
Width:			
Center axis to adjacent wall	22	20	15
Side edge to side of adjacent tub	—	—	2
Depth:			
Front edge to opposite wall	36	34	21
—If not a traffic lane	—	30	—
Front edge to opposite tub	30	24	21
Horizontal clearance from front edge of lavatory to front edge of shelf 9–15 in. above lavatory	17½	—	—
Mirror:			
Height above floor—top	74	69	—
—bottom (5-ft adult)	48	54 (max.)	—
(3½-ft child)	—	36 (max.)	—
Bathtub			
Side of tub to opposite wall	34	30	—

Table 2. Space required at the toilet

Adapted from Bathroom Working Spaces, *Monroe, Randall, and Bartlett, Report 82, Maine Agricultural Experiment Station (1959); Minimum Property Standards, Federal Housing Administration, Washington, D.C. (revised, July 1959). See Fig. 1 for illustration of dimensions.*

Dimension	Space required, in.			
	Adequate		Minimum	FHA minimum
	1 Person	2 Persons*		
Width:				
Center axis to adjacent wall	18	22	16	15
—If wall projects not more than 12 in.	—	—	—	12
Center axis to side of lavatory 18 in. deep, or less	14	16	—	15
—Lavatory over 18 in. deep	16	18	14	15
Center axis to side of tub	18	18	16	15
Center axis to end of tub	16	18	16	12
Depth:				
Front edge to opposite wall	30	34	—	21
Front edge to opposite tub	24	—	—	21
Front edge to opposite lavatory	30	30	24	—

Space required for one person to assist another at the toilet (dimensions not shown in Fig. 1).

BASIC DIMENSIONS

Space is required not only for the use of particular fixtures but also between fixtures for cleaning purposes and for assisting another person (such as a small child or elderly adult). These last two factors are often completely overlooked. For economy of space, required clearances for each fixture may sometimes overlap.

Recent research has provided some recommendations for the space required around the three basic fixtures: lavatory, toilet, and bathtub and shower. The basic clearances are given in Tables 1-2 and Fig. 1.

Miscellaneous activities

In planning the bathroom, the designer should remember that families with infants usually prefer to bathe them in the bathroom. The lack of adequate space has, in the past, caused many families to use the kitchen, which obviously is less appropriate for this activity than the bath. The minimum space needed to bathe and dress an infant is 1 ft 6½ in. deep by 4 ft 11 in. wide by 3 ft high.

In addition, other important activities are often performed in the bathroom. Most women, at least occasionally, launder small items in the bathroom, and provision for this should be made. Many adults, and children, like to use the bathroom for dressing. Since this requires a considerable amount of space, it should be provided only when requested.

ARRANGEMENT

Bathrooms can be classified into four categories: (1) The conventional three-fixture bath; (2) The larger, compartmented bath; (3) The lavatory or "guest" bath; and (4) The "utility" bath.

Three-fixture bath: The conventional three-fixture bath without separate compartments has traditionally been designed for the occupancy and use of one individual at a time. This type of bath, with combination tub-shower, averages about 40 sq ft of floor space.

Compartmented bath: To avoid the excessive humidity common in the usual three-fixture bath, tub and shower may be located in a separate compartment, with or without an additional lavatory. This plan also affords greater privacy for use of the toilet. Separate doors, possibly with a small entry, are desirable. Connecting doors between compartments are also possible but are not recommended as the only means of access.

Another variation is to make the toilet a separate compartment, affording complete privacy. In even the minimum-sized bath of this type there is generally room for an additional lavatory, and the bath proper is often enlarged into a combination bath-dressing room. Dressing tables may be a combination of lavatory and table or individual fixtures. In the latter case, tables should be sufficiently far from lavatories to prevent damage from splashing water.

Table 3. Minimum dimensions for storage of bathroom linens, including allowance for handling

Adapted from Storage Requirements for Household Textiles, *A. Woolrich, M. M. White, and M. A. Richards, Agricultural Research Bulletin 62–2, U.S. Department of Agriculture, Washington, D.C. (1955).*

Item	Number	Minimum dimensions, in.			
		Width	Depth	Height	
				A*	B†
Bath towels:					
Everyday use	12	24	10	12	10
Guest use	6	12	10	12	10
Hand towels:					
Everyday use	10	7	14	12	10
Guest use	8	10	14	7	5
Wash cloths:					
Everyday use	12	16	8	6	4
Guest use	6	8	7	6	4

*For storage on fixed shelves.
†For storage in drawers or on movable shelves.

Table 4. Sizes of accessories for tiling*

Item	Dimensions, in.						
	12x6	9x6	6x6	3x6	3x3	8½x4¼	4¼x4¼
Toilet-paper holders			•	•		•	
Combination holders for soap, toothbrush, and tumbler	•	•	•	•		•	•
Separate holders for soap, toothbrush, and tumbler			•	•	•	•	•
Bases for towel bars, shelf brackets, door stops, and hooks				•	•		•
Grab bars and soap or sponge holders	•	•					

*Some toilet-paper holders are 6×10 in. Radiant heaters are 15×15 in. or larger.

A still greater expansion of this plan provides a separate dressing room and connecting bath, with a compartment for the toilet. The required floor space ranges from 110 to 140 sq ft.

In all plans for baths, showers should be included, either as stalls or over tubs.

Guest bath: The lavatory, or two-fixture "guest" bath, for living portions of residences may vary in size and appointments from a minimum area of about 14 sq ft to rooms of 22 to 25 sq ft or larger when a dressing table is included.

Utility bath: The "utility" bath provides an area larger than the minimum size required for the three basic fixtures, for other functions, such as laundering.

DOORS AND WINDOWS

Bathroom doors can be as small as 2 ft wide, except for utility bathrooms, for which doors should be not less than 2 ft

4 in. wide to permit passage of equipment as required. In general, bathrooms should contain only one door.

Door swings should be arranged so that: (1) The door cannot strike any person using any fixture; (2) The door will shield or conceal the toilet; and (3) The door may be left fully open for ventilation in warm weather.

Customarily, doors swing into the bathroom. If hall areas are sufficiently large, doors to small bathrooms can sometimes be designed to swing out. In-swinging doors should be set to clear towel-bars or radiators. Sliding doors are frequently desirable, as space savers, between various compartments within the bathroom.

The shape and position of *bathroom windows* is important from the standpoint of light, ventilation, and privacy. Generally, the higher the window, the better. Preferred locations include: clear wall space reserved for portable equipment, space

At lavatory

A. Mirror and medicine cabinet. Size is governed by use of shelf or shelf-topped lavatory; mirror should swing 7 in. over any shelf. (A.1) Fixed mirror is desirable immediately above lavatory for children 7 to 14 years.

B. Shelf. Preferably recessed flush with wall. May be part of medicine cabinet or part of lavatory.

C, D, and E. Soap, toothbrush, and tumbler holders. May be separate units or combined; flush or projecting type.

F. Receptacle for electric razor and hair dryer. Should be above and to right of lavatory; dead front type.

G. Razor blade disposal slot.

H. Towel bars. May be at level of shelf or lavatory top. In congested space provide upper bar for face cloths, lower bar for towels.

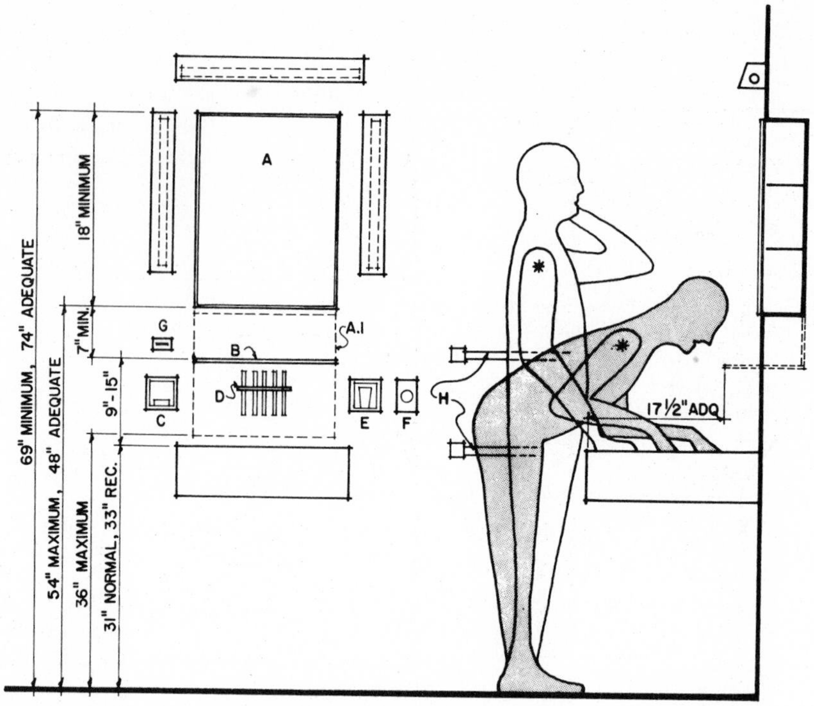

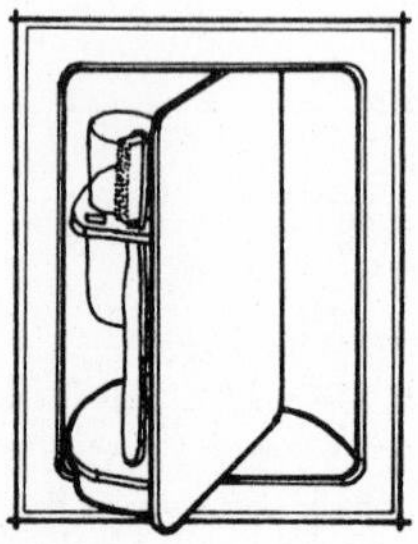

Recessed revolving lavatory unit—holds glass, toothbrush, and soap

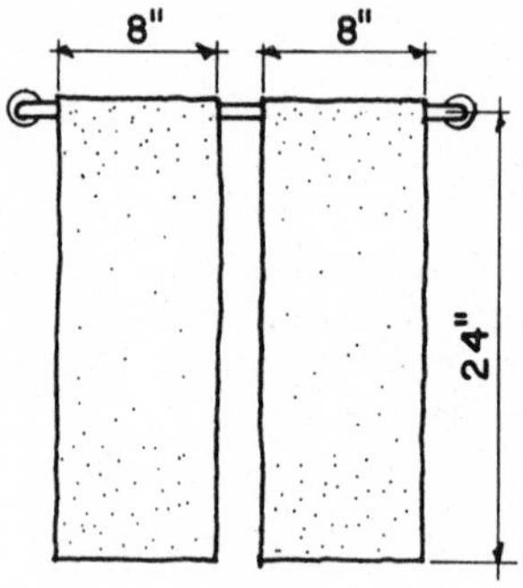

Bath

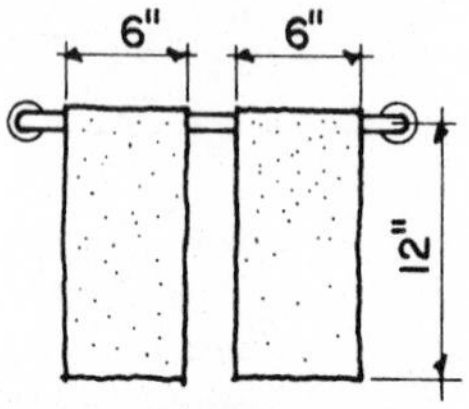

Small face

Towel bars
Stock sizes of bars:
1 ft 6 in., 2 ft, 2 ft 6 in., 3 ft, 3 ft 6 in., 4 ft

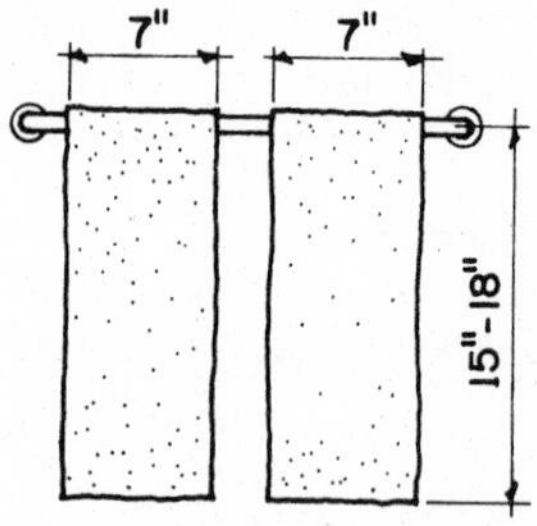

Small bath or large face

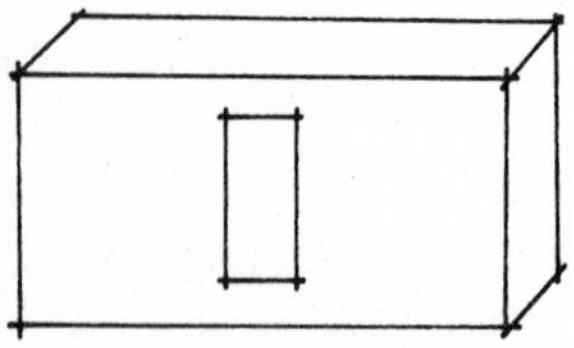

Tissue holder—available surface-mounted or recessed

Towel ring

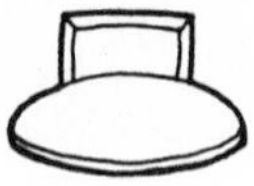

Soap dish

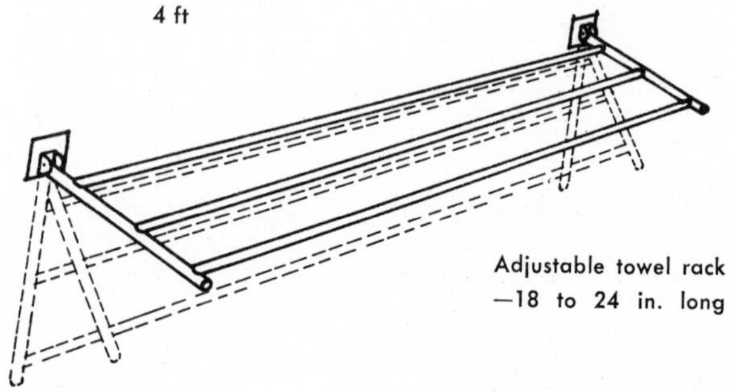

Adjustable towel rack —18 to 24 in. long

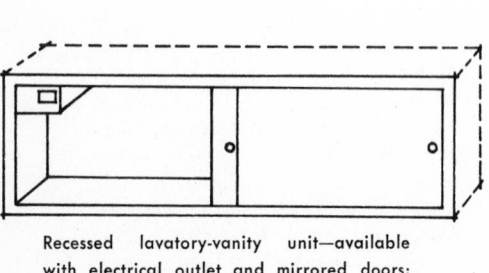
Recessed lavatory-vanity unit—available with electrical outlet and mirrored doors; 30x9x4 in. (nominal)

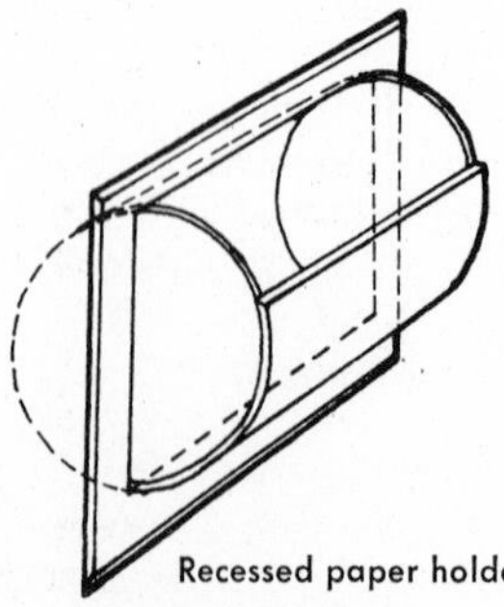

Recessed paper holder

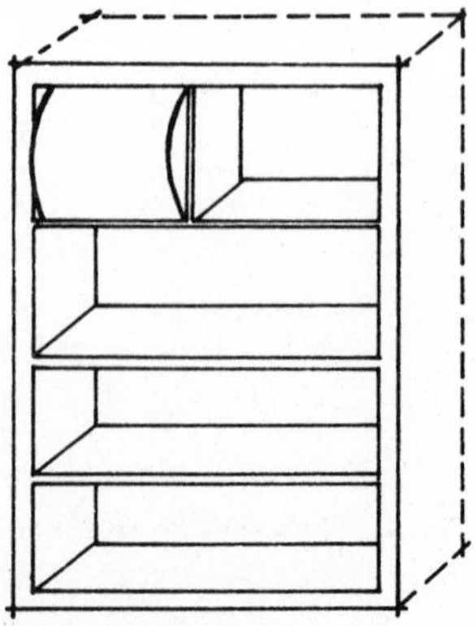

Combination magazine rack, paper holder, and shelf—available surface-mounted or recessed; 12x18x4 in. (nominal)

Fig. 2. Dimensions at lavatory, bathtub and shower
Scale: ½ in. = 1 ft

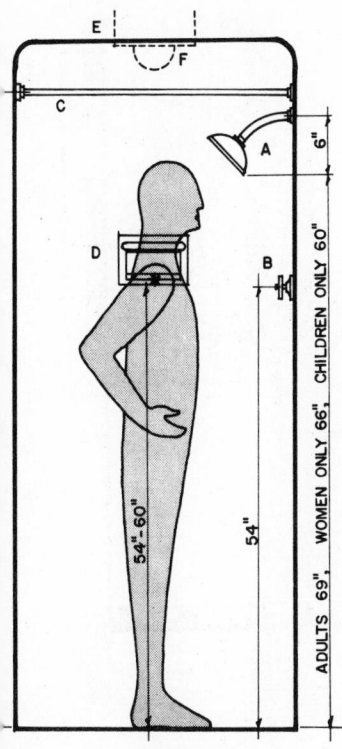

At shower

Shower head. Height is governed by client's preferences; may be overhead for men only.

Shower valves or mixing valves. Always place near entrance to shower.

Shower curtain rod. (C.1) Optional; glass shower enclosure door; place hinges on edge opposite shower control valves.

Combination soap and sponge holder and grab bar. Use draining-lip type. May be on rear wall or on side wall opposite shower head.

Shower ventilator. Desirable to remove steam; may function as vent for bathroom.

Shower stall light. Optional; must be vapor-proof fixture.

At bathtub

A, B, and C. Shower head, shower controls, bath valves and spout. Location is optional with client but must be accessible from outside of tub. See shower stall for recommended heights.

D. Combination soap and sponge holder and grab bar. Draining-lip type preferred.

E. Vertical grab bars. Optional but recommended.

F. Towel bar. Do not use over tub equipped with shower.

G. Curtain rod. Keep within inside face of tub. (G.1) Alternate; glass shower enclosure in place of curtain. Various types, with and without doors, are available.

Not illustrated

Full-length mirror. Usually on door.

Bathroom scale. May be built-in or portable.

Linen hamper. Optional; may be part of cabinet-type lavatory, built-in or portable.

Auxiliary heater. Built-in radiant type desirable; should radiate toward open floor space.

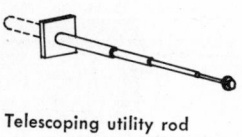

Telescoping utility rod —4 to 14 in.

Robe hook

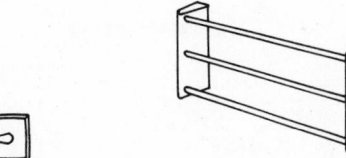

Electric towel rack— 26x13x3 in. (nominal)

Grab bars

Straight bars—9, 12, 15, 18, 24, and 30 in.

Angle bars—16x32 in.

Fig. 3. Bathroom accessories   Scale: ½ in. = 1 ft

The accessories shown are typical. Many other types and styles are available.

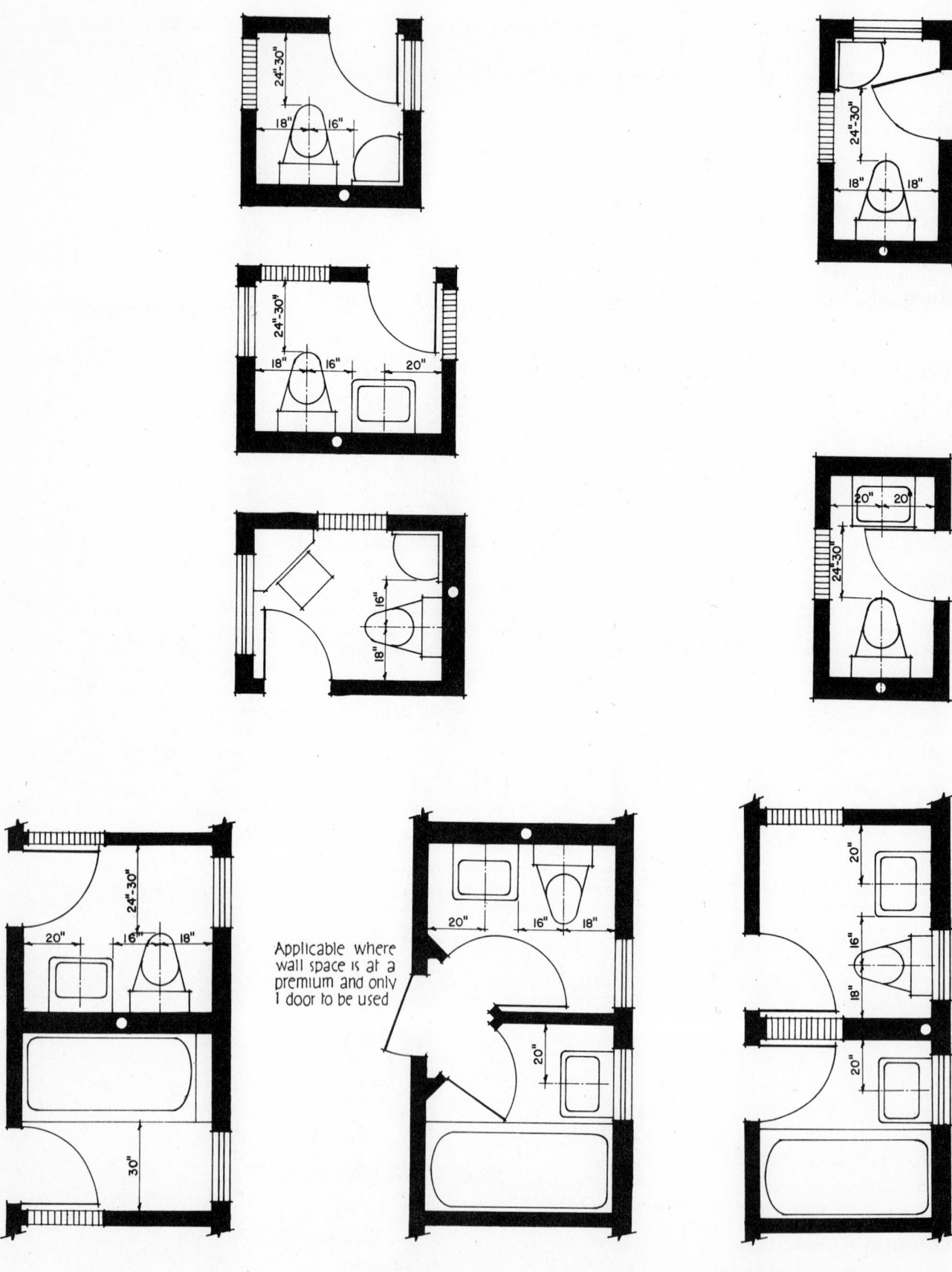

Fig. 4. Two-fixture plans (dimensions in inches)   Scale: ¼ in. = 1 ft

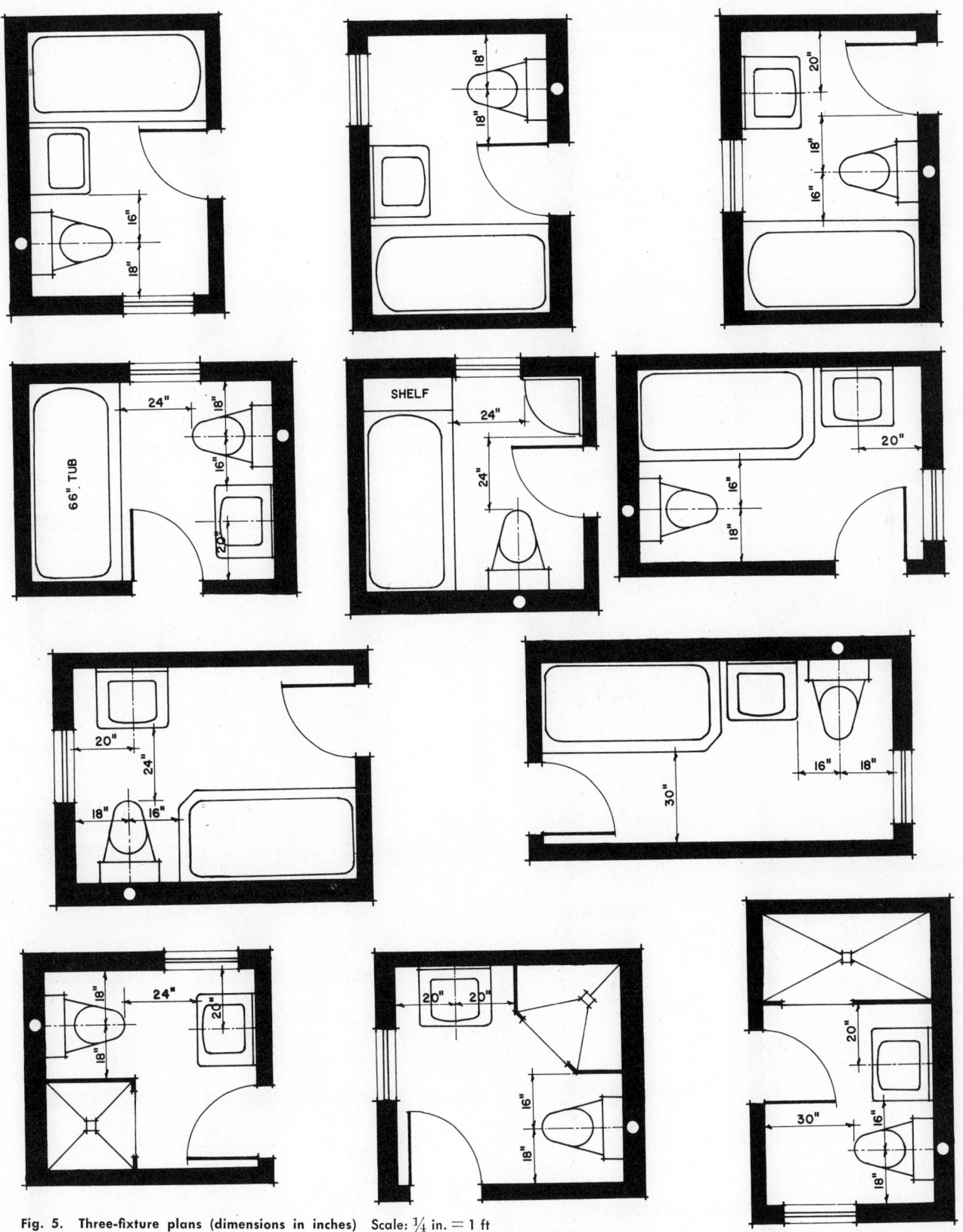

Fig. 5.   Three-fixture plans (dimensions in inches)   Scale: $\frac{1}{4}$ in. = 1 ft

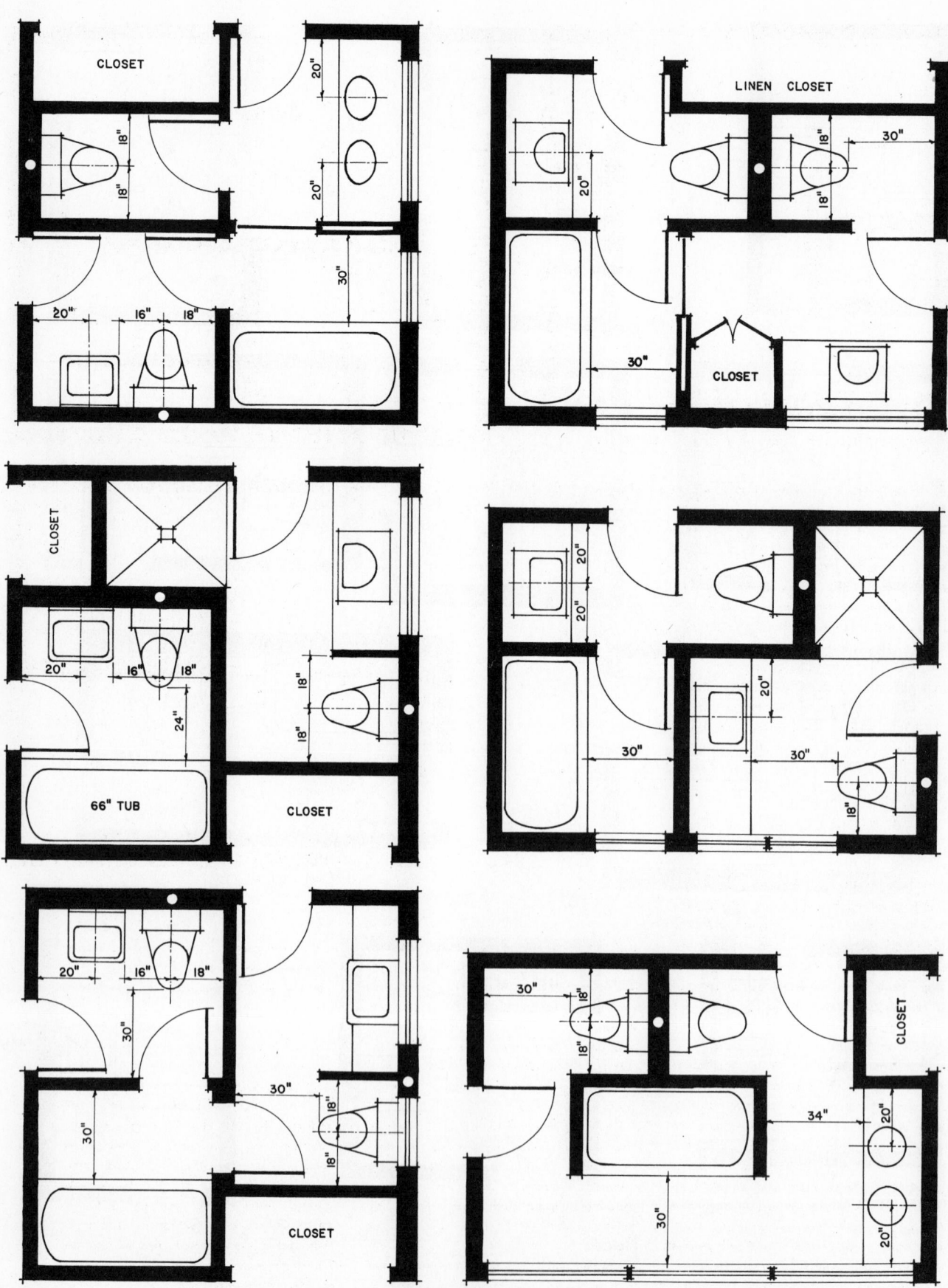

Fig. 6. Compartmented plans (dimensions in inches)   Scale: ¼ in. = 1 ft

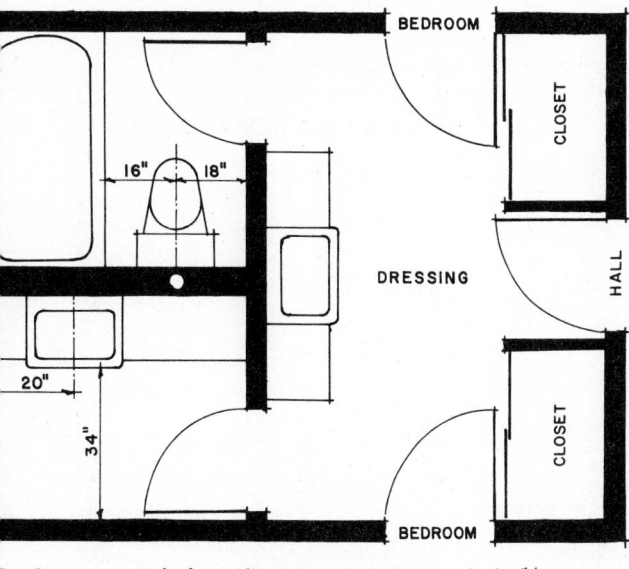

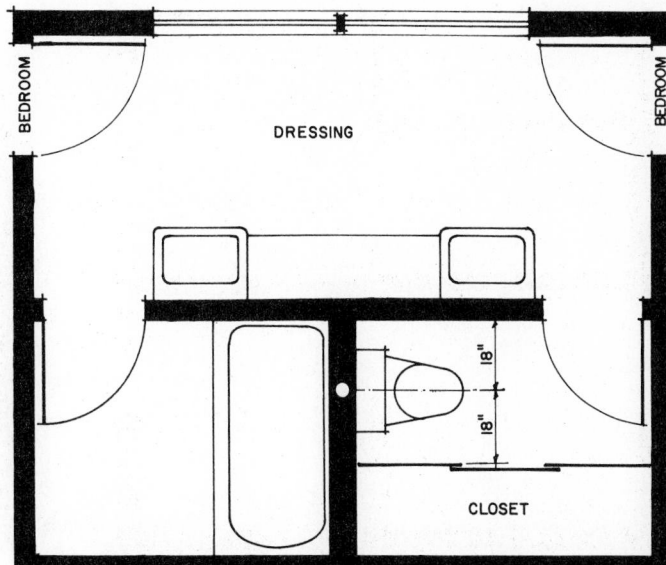

7. Compartmented plans (dimensions in inches)   Scale: ¼ in. = 1 ft

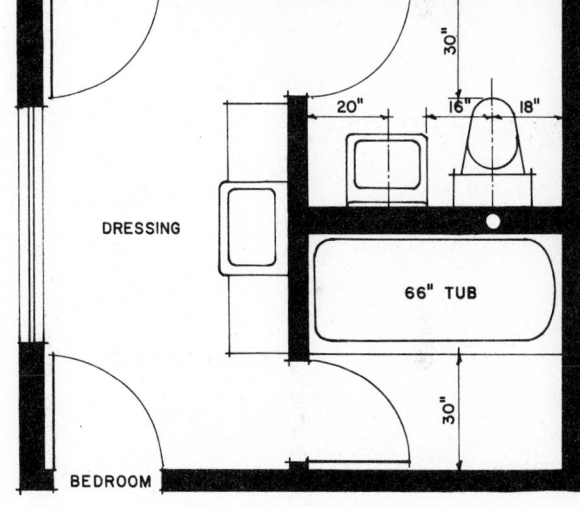

over a dressing table, and space above or on either side of the lavatory. Windows should not be placed over the bathtub unless they are of the casement or awning type opened by a crank. A window behind the toilet is seldom desirable. Skylights may be used to serve top-floor bathrooms if they are large enough to provide adequate light and ventilation. Inside bathrooms without exterior windows are sometimes used but require a dependable system of exhaust ventilation by natural or mechanical means, and greater artificial lighting in lieu of natural light.

ACCESSORIES

The medicine cabinet should be related in size to the type of bathroom or toilet. For guest baths or toilets, space is needed only for dentifrices, shaving accessories, toilet preparations, and a few simple remedies. A bath serving several bedrooms may require a complete supply of medicines in addition to the items mentioned above. Every bathroom should have a storage closet for cleaning utensils and supplies and for reserve stocks of toilet paper, towels, and sundries.

Floor space should be left in every bathroom for portable accessories desired by the owner or needed on occasion for the care of infants or invalids. Also consider allowing space for such items as scales, stool or seat, infant's bath and dressing table (portable type requires about 3 by 4 ft of floor space in use), soiled-linen hamper, exercise devices, dressing table or vanity with bench, and ultra-violet radiation equipment.

Towel bars should be ample in number

and length to serve the needs of each member of the family regularly using the bathroom, or of guests likely to use its facilities, before supplies can be replenished. For each person regularly using the bathroom, there should be separate bar space for bath towel, face towel, and face cloth, as well as an additional rack for guest towels.

Linen storage may consist of towel cabinets recessed in the thickness of plumbing walls (either over fixtures or as full height cabinets) or may be expanded into complete linen closets. Dressing-room baths may include completely fitted wardrobes. (See Table 3.)

Minimum-sized bathrooms and toilets require special planning to ensure ade-

quate wall space for essential accessories (Table 4).

FIXTURES

Information presented here is intended for use only in preliminary planning. Fixture sizes may vary with different manufacturers and with new models and designs. Sizes of built-in units, such as bathtubs, may vary enough within each nominal size classification to affect the spacing of studs or the location of enclosing walls. Hence, working drawings should be checked against the actual dimensions of the selected fixtures and no substitutions should be made without rechecking these dimensions.

LAVATORIES

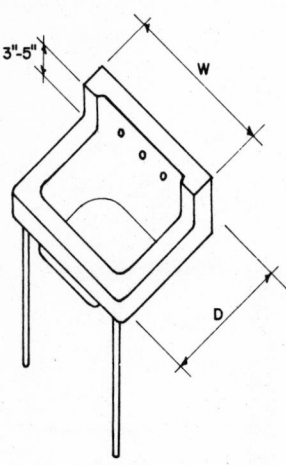

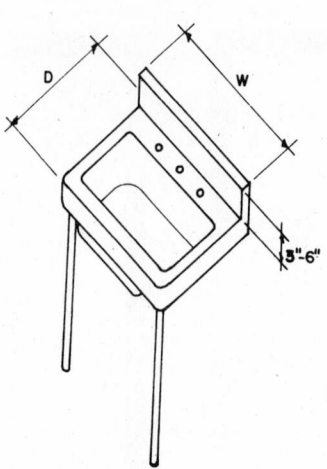

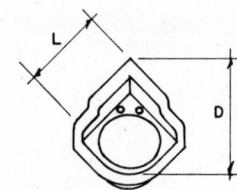

Corner lavatory

Depth, in.	Length, in.	Material
15	12	Vitreous china
16	14	Vitreous china
21	17	Vitreous china, cast iron

Shelf-back lavatory

Width, in.	Depth, in.	Material
18	14	Vitreous china
18	15	Vitreous china
19	17	Vitreous china, steel, cast iron
20	14	Vitreous china
20	18	Vitreous china, steel
22	14	Vitreous china
22	18	Vitreous china, steel, cast iron
24	20	Vitreous china
26	14	Vitreous china
26	22	Vitreous china

Plain-back lavatory

Width, in.	Depth, in.	Material
18	14	Vitreous china
19	17	Cast iron
20	14	Vitreous china
20	18	Vitreous china, cast iron
22	19	Cast iron
24	18	Cast iron
24	20	Vitreous china
26	14	Vitreous china

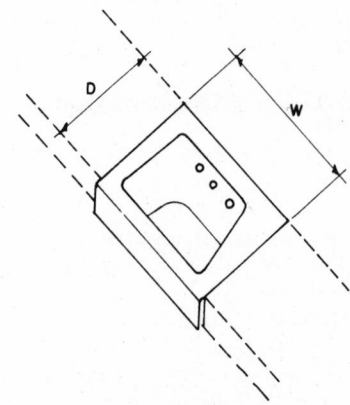

Open-front built-in lavatory

Width, in.	Depth, in.	Material
20	18	Vitreous china
22	18	Vitreous china
24	20	Vitreous china
26	22	Vitreous china
27	21	Vitreous china
30	22	Vitreous china

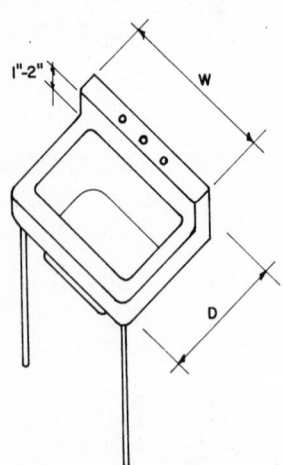

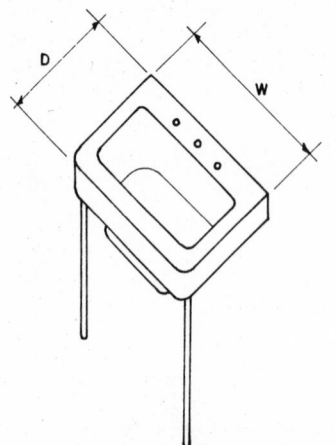

Ledge-back lavatory

Width, in.	Depth, in.	Material
18	15	Vitreous china
19	17	Viterous china, steel
20	18	Viterous china, steel
22	18	Viterous china, steel
24	20	Vitreous china
27	21	Vitreous china

Flat-slab lavatory

Width, in.	Depth, in.	Material
20	18	Vitreous china
24	18	Vitreous china
24	20	Vitreous china, steel, cast iron
27	22	Vitreous china
28	20	Vitreous china
32	18	Vitreous china
32	24	Vitreous china
36	18	Vitreous china
36	22	Vitreous china
42	18	Vitreous china

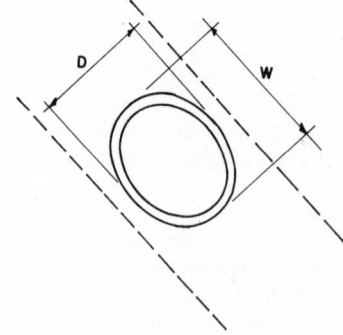

Round or oval built-in lavatory

Width, in.	Depth, in.	Material
19	16	Vitreous china
14	14	Vitreous china
15	15	Vitreous china

TOILETS

BIDET

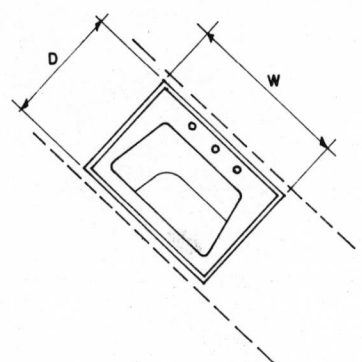

Flat-rim built-in lavatory

Width, in.	Depth, in.	Material
16	14	Vitreous china
19	18	Steel
20	17	Cast iron
20	18	Vitreous china, steel, cast iron
20	19	Vitreous china
21	17	Vitreous china, steel
22	18	Vitreous china
24	18	Vitreous china
24	21	Vitreous china
28	20	Vitreous china

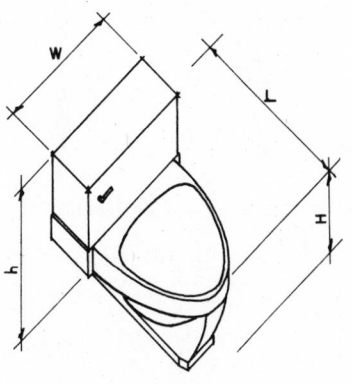

One-piece or close-coupled toilet

The styles available are whirlpool jet, reverse trap, or washdown siphon. This model is available only in vitreous china.

Width, in.	Length, in.	Height, in.	Height (h), in.
21	28	14	19
23	30	14	29
23	28	14	29
24	26	14½	30
23	29	14	24
22	27	14	24
20	29	14½	30

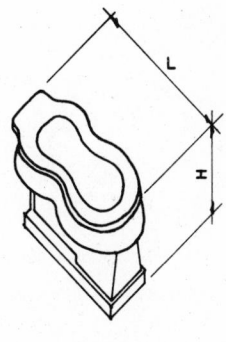

Bidet

This model is available only in vitreous china.

Length, in.	Height, in.
26	14½
25	15
24	15

SHOWERS

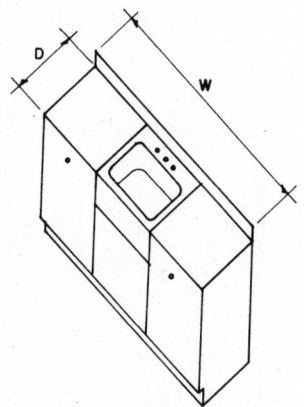

Lavatory-dressing tables

Some models are available with two bowls. Bowls are available in vitreous china, steel, and cast iron. Cabinets are generally available in steel.

Width, in.	Depth, in.	Size of bowl, in. (WxD)
24	22	20x18
30	18	16x13
36	22	20x18
43	18	20x18
43	22	20x18
47	18	24x18
59	18	20x18
63	18	24x18

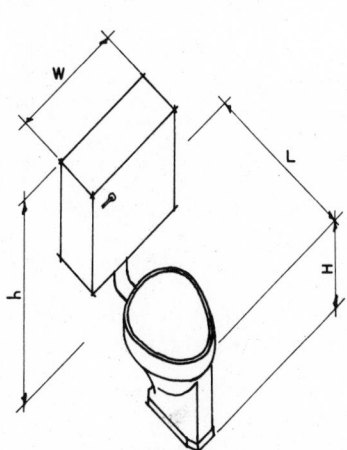

Flush-tank toilet

The styles available are washdown or reverse trap. This model is available only in vitreous china.

Width, in.	Length, in.	Height, in.	Height (h), in.
22	27	14¾	36
20	27	15	36

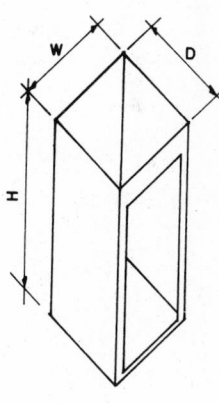

Shower stalls

Prefabricated metal shower stalls are available with or without integral receptor base. Corner and built-in models are also available. All glass enclosures are available in approximately the same stock sizes. Special sizes are generally available on order.

Width, in.	Depth, in.	Height, in.
32	32	81
36	36	81
40	40	81

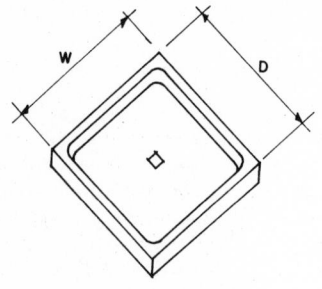

Shower receptors

Preformed and precast shower receptors are available in steel and terrazzo and, on special order, in marble and slate. Special sizes and shapes can generally be obtained on special order.

Width, in.	Depth, in.
32	32
36	36
36	42
40	40
42	44

BATHTUBS

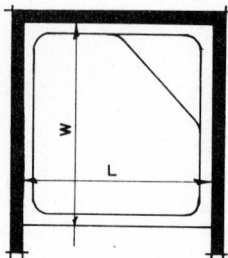

Square recessed bathtub

Width, in.	Length, in.	Height, in.	Material
38	39	12	Cast iron
51	48	16	Cast iron

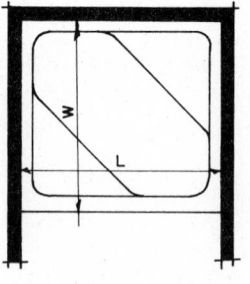

Square recessed bathtub

Width, in.	Length, in.	Height, in.	Material
48	50	16	Cast iron

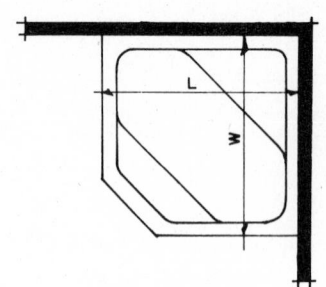

Square corner bathtub

Width, in.	Length, in.	Height, in.	Material
50	50	16	Cast iron

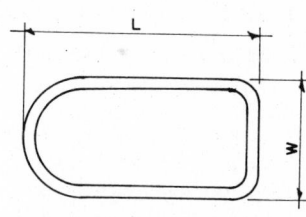

Free-standing bathtub

Width, in.	Length, in.	Height, in.	Material
30	54, 60	23	Cast iron
30	60	20	Cast iron

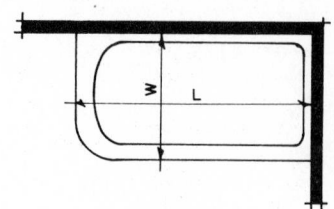

Corner bathtub

Width, in.	Length, in.	Height, in.	Material
31	54, 60,	16	Cast iron
32	60	16	Steel
30	60, 66	16	Cast iron
31	60	16	Steel
31	60	15	Steel

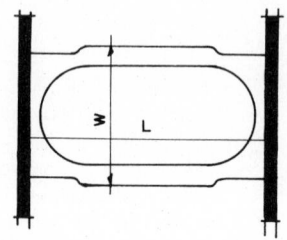

Recessed 2-way bathtub

Width, in.	Length, in.	Height, in.	Material
35	60	15	Steel

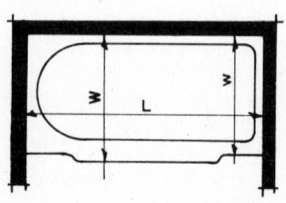

Recessed bathtub

Width, in.	Length, in.	Height, in.	Material
30	60	16	Cast iron
28½	60	14	Cast iron
29	54, 60	16	Steel
32	60	16	Steel
31	54, 60	16	Steel

Recessed wide-ledge bathtub

Stock glass enclosures are available.

Width, in.	Width (w), in.	Length, in.	Height, in.	Material
33	31	54, 60, 66	16	Cast iron
30	25	60	16	Cast iron
32	29	60	16	Steel
33	30	64	17	Cast iron
32	30	48, 54, 60, 66, 72	16	Cast iron
29	28	60	14	Cast iron
31	29	54, 60	16	Steel
30	28	60	14	Cast iron
33	31	54, 60, 66	16	Cast iron
32	31	60	14	Cast iron

By GLENN H. BEYER, and ALEXANDER KIRA, *Housing Research Center, Cornell University*

Drawings by LARCH RENSHAW, *AIA*

"A place for everything and everything in its place" is the slogan for closet designers as well as housewives. Modern closets should be planned for the storage of the particular clothing or objects of the individual or the group using the space. An accurate list of the objects to be stored is necessary for the scientific allotment and arrangement of space and facilities. A "margin of safety" of some 25 per cent increased capacity should be allowed for the usual accumulation of additional belongings. It is better to have too much space than not enough. Much can be stored in little space if sufficient thought is given to the arrangement of the space and the equipment. Too many closets have unused and unusable space due to poor planning.

Good closet design requires planning, arrangement, and fixtures contributing to:

1. Convenience
   a. Ease of access
   b. Maximum visibility
   c. Orderliness
   d. Maximum accessibility
   e. Maximum of used space
2. Preservation
   a. Of pressed condition
   b. Of freshness (ventilation)
   c. From moths
   d. From dust
   e. From pilfering

The above are not all simultaneously obtainable, and some are mutually exclusive; for instance, eliminating doors gives maximum availability but minimum security from dust, moths, and pilfering; adhering to the principle of maximum accessibility would result in unused space at top and bottom of closet.

Modern closets, by the efficient arrangement of space and fixtures, accommodate much more clothing and material than the inconvenient, space-wasting closets of a few decades ago. The modern closet often replaces pieces of furniture and thus provides a greater amount of free, uncluttered space in the room.

Doors should open the full width of the closet whenever possible. In most cases the most efficient and economical doors are the usual hinged type. Two doors for a 5-ft closet will eliminate dark, inaccessible, hard-to-clean corners. Hooks, racks, and accessories on the backs of swinging doors increase efficiency by using otherwise unoccupied space in the closet.

Alternate closet closing methods may involve more complicated or more expensive construction, though they may obviate the objection that swinging doors form an obstruction in the room. Sliding doors can expose the entire interior of the closet to view and make it immediately accessible. Such doors do not block traffic. Sliding doors, however, do not permit the use of special door fixtures such as tie racks, shoe racks or bags, hat hangers, or mirrors, which are handy and easily reached when attached to a hinged closet door. Banks of wardrobe-type closets with sliding doors are becoming more and more popular. Fitted with drawers or trays, they take the place of bureaus, chests, and chiffoniers and make for more spacious, uncluttered rooms.

Doors which expose the full width of the closet are preferable for both visibility and accessibility. "Walk-in" or "walk-through" closets naturally use more area than others with no "circulation." In some rooms, however, a single door to a large "walk-in" closet may be justified by the need for maximum wall space for furniture.

Some of the various closing methods are shown in Fig. 1.

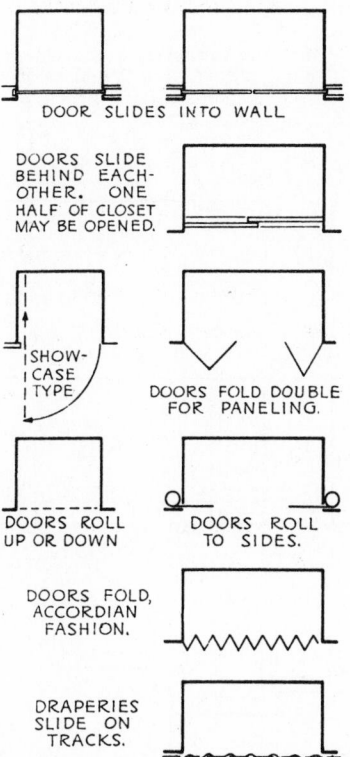

Fig. 1. Closet closing methods
Scale: ³⁄₁₆ in. = 1 ft

Lighting is considered essential and standard in the modern closet unless room lights are located to illuminate fully all portions of the closet. A single tubular or bulb light with a diffusing reflector placed just above the door inside the front of the closet is usually sufficient. Automatic door switches are convenient.

Ventilation is often desirable, particularly in hall closets where damp outer garments or work clothes might be stored. It can be accomplished readily by providing louvers in the closet door or by using louver doors.

Types of closets

Closets are required for various purposes, in different parts of the house. Some have already been mentioned in other sections of this volume: kitchen supplies; dinnerware, glassware, and table linens (discussed under "Kitchens"); and bathroom supplies (discussed under "Bathrooms"). Closets must also be provided for the storage of clothing, bedding, cleaning equipment, book, magazines and phonograph records, toys and other children's and adults' recreation equipment, and certain items such as luggage that are used only seasonally or infrequently. The discussion here relates only to "active" storage space, and not to space needed only infrequently.

Clothes closet: For clothes closets in bedrooms or dressing rooms, 2 ft is standard depth (2 ft 6 in. if a hook strip is to be used). This permits clothing to be on hangers on poles, with sufficient clearance. Clothes closet width, parallel to the doors, should be from 3 to 6 ft per person, depending on amounts of clothing and

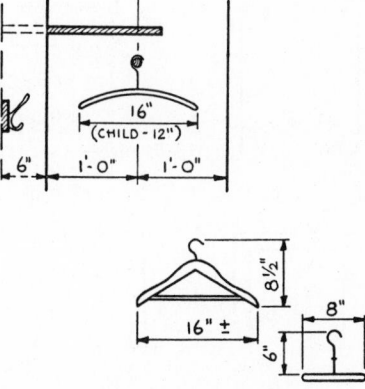

Fig. 2. Closet depth and hanger sizes
Scale: ½ in. = 1 ft

whether drawers or trays are to be provided in the closet or wardrobe for such items as have in the past been kept in bureaus or other pieces of furniture. Some typical closet plans are illustrated in Fig. 4; suggested layouts for bedroom closets for men, women, and children are shown in Figs. 5–9.

Coat closets, located near the entrance doors, are sometimes made 2 or 3 in. deeper than bedroom closets, to allow for the bulkiness of some overcoats, and to permit better air circulation around the garments which are often damp when hung in the closet. Several designs for coat closets are shown in Figs. 10 and 14.

Closet for cleaning equipment: The dimensions of the storage space needed for cleaning equipment will depend in large part upon the type of vacuum cleaner used: horizontal, upright, or canister; recommended dimensions for each type are shown in Fig. 11. Since families may change from one type of vacuum cleaner to another, the cleaning closet should be made large enough for any type. The closet should be located as near the center of the house as possible, and should be provided with a convenience receptacle so that the vacuum cleaner can be left connected and can reach most areas of the house. A suggested design for a cleaning equipment closet is shown in Fig. 12.

Storage for bedroom linens and bedding: Limited and liberal lists of articles of bedding that require storage, and the minimum dimensions of the space required, are shown in Table 1.

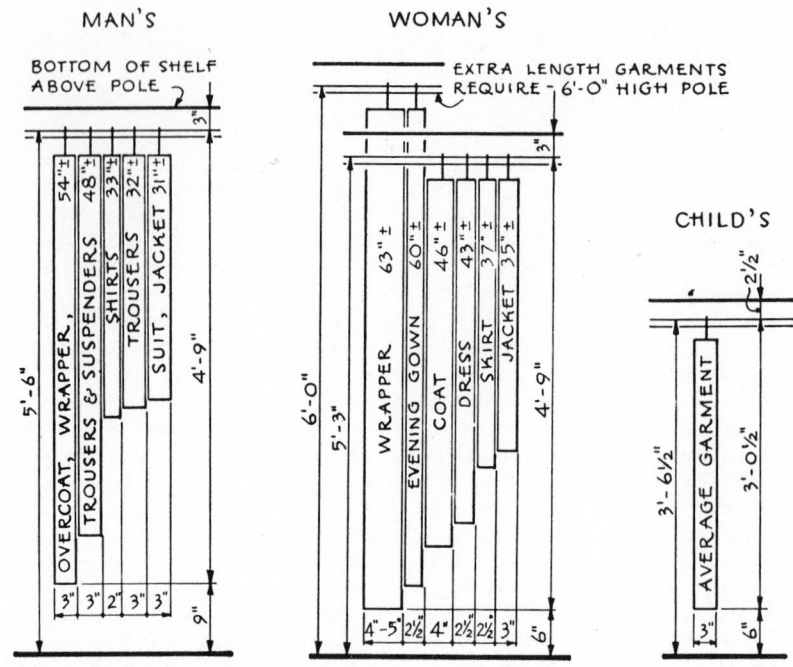

Fig. 3. Sizes of clothes hung in closet
Scale: ½ in. = 1 ft

FHA[1] requirements for linen closets are as follows: minimum interior dimensions, 18 in. wide by 14 in. deep (24 in. maximum); shelves spaced approximately 12 in. on center vertically; highest shelf, 74 in. above the floor; minimum total shelf area for one- and two-bedroom house, 9 sq ft, for three- and four-bedroom house, 12 sq ft; drawers may replace 50 per cent of the shelves. These are minimum dimensions, and about twice this amount is recommended, especially if both bedroom and bathroom linen are to be stored. A suggested layout for such a combined linen closet is shown in Fig. 12.

[1] Minimum Property Standards for One and Two Living Units, *Federal Housing Administration, Washington, D.C., revised July, 1959.*

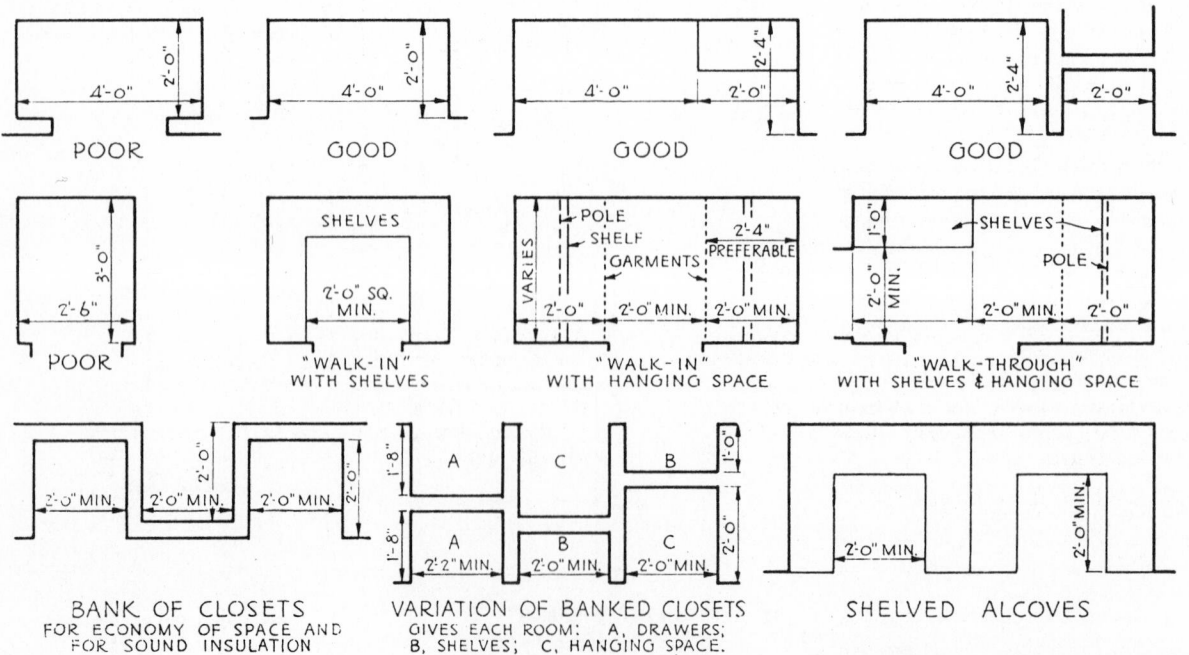

Fig. 4. Typical closet plans   *Scale: ¼ in. = 1 ft*

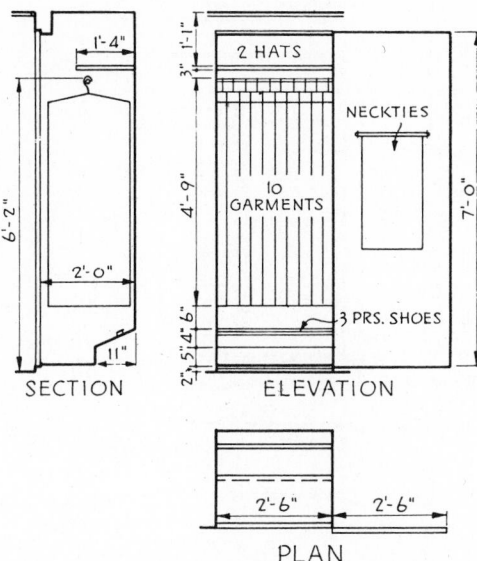

SECTION ELEVATION

PLAN

A minimum size closet of a usual type. Shoes can be stored on the raised shelf-rack and three additional pair on the floor in front of the rack. Door could be arranged for hats as shown below, leaving shelf for other storage.

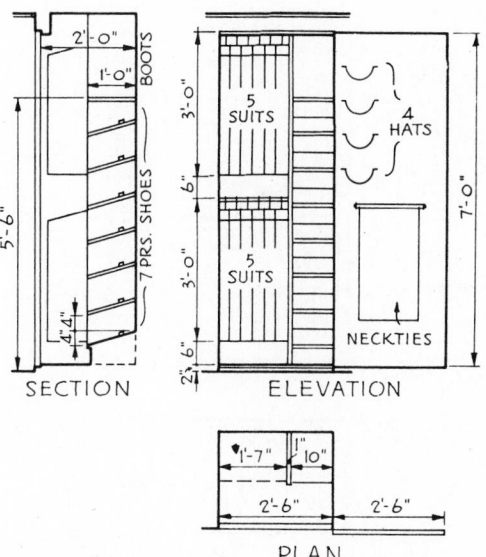

SECTION ELEVATION

PLAN

Minimal closet arranged to make shoes more visible and reachable. There is space for hats without crushing or for night clothes hooks if hats are normally stored in a hall closet. Neckties might be in two tiers.

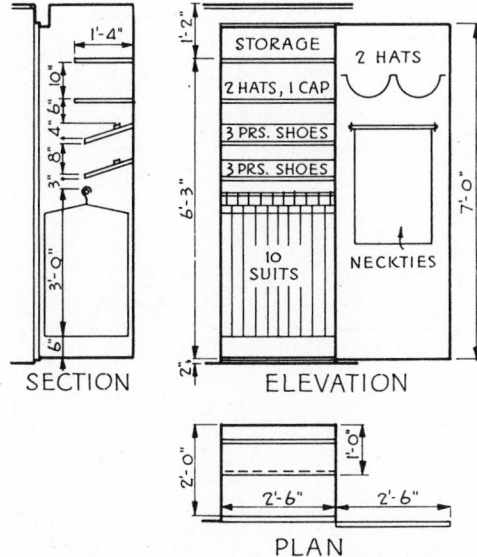

SECTION ELEVATION

PLAN

An alternate to the scheme above giving maximum view of shoes and an additional shelf. Trousers would have to be folded over the crossbar of the suit hanger rather than being hung separately from the pole with trouser-hangers.

Fig. 5. Bedroom closets for men
  Scale: ¼ in. = 1 ft

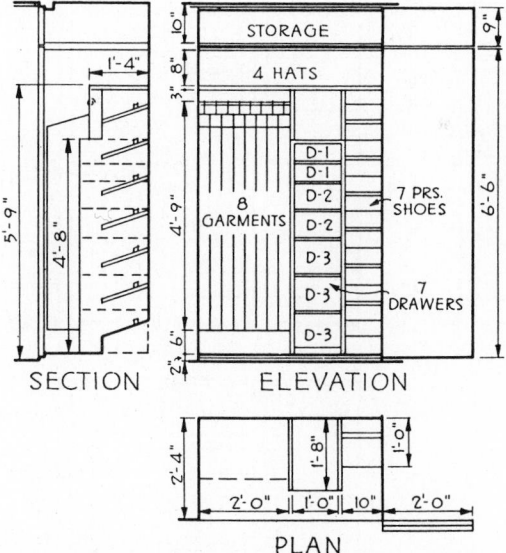

SECTION ELEVATION

PLAN

A four-foot closet with seven drawers for shirts, socks, underwear, etc., and a vertical-tier of shoe racks (as above). Night clothes and bathrobe hooks are best on the right hand door, necktie racks flat against the left hand door.

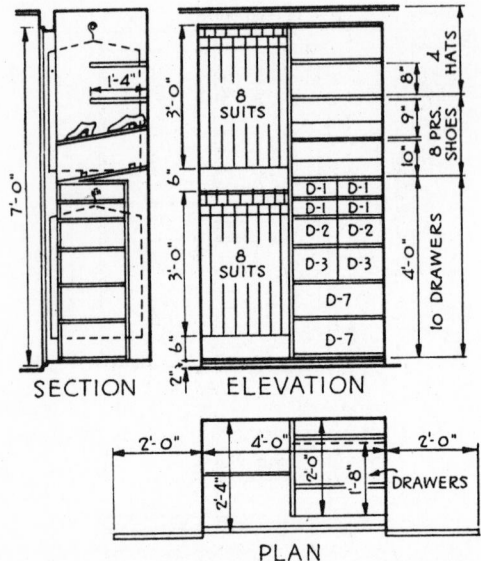

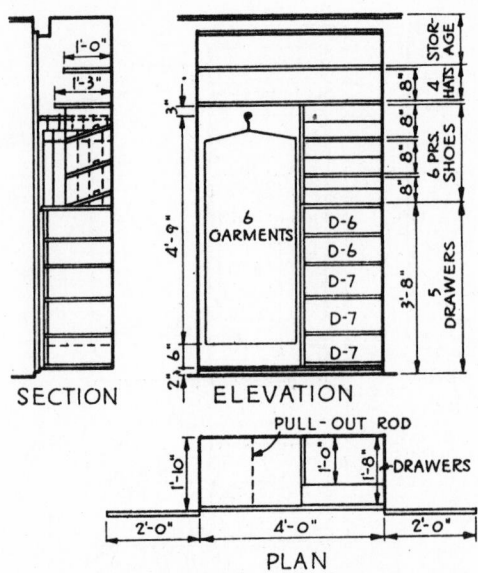

Another four-foot closet with ten standard drawers conveniently arranged. Shoes are placed tandem above the drawers for visibility and reachability. Poles are one above the other, requiring reaching.

A solution to the shallow closet problem. A pull-out rod takes care of the suit, coat and trouser hanging. Five drawers take the place of a small bureau or chest. Shoes are at "no stoop, no squat, no squint" levels.

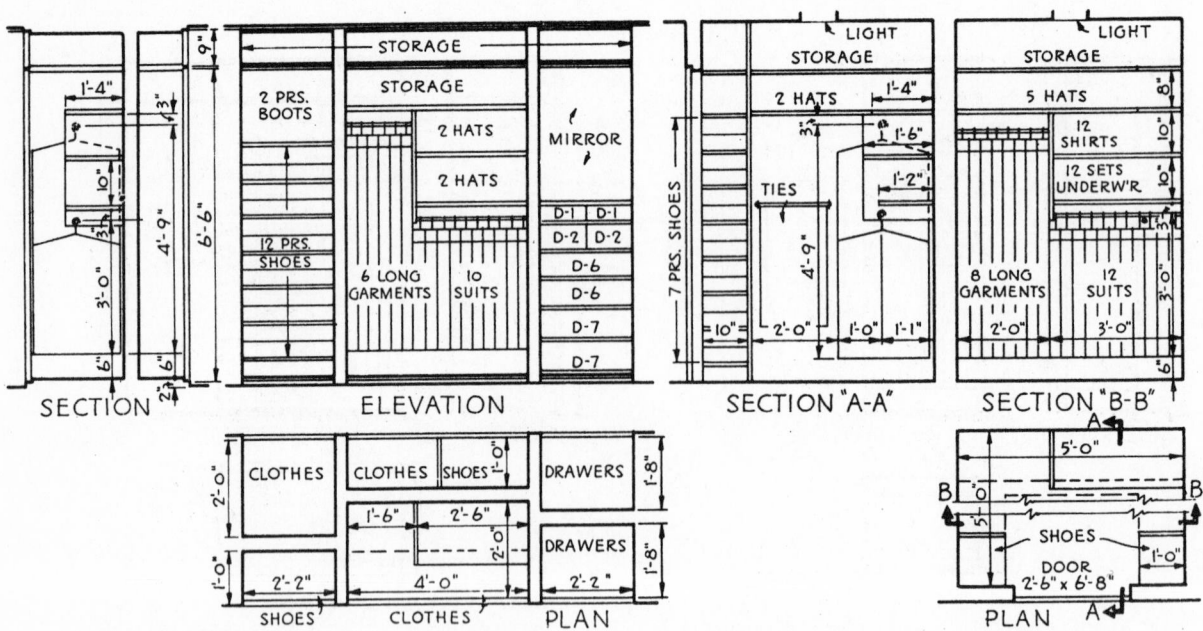

Wide wardrobe closets of more luxurious size planned as part of walls separating two rooms. Four doors, sliding or swinging, can be used. Lower portion of shoe-tiers could be replaced with mothproof "dead-storage" drawers.

A deep walk-in closet. High tiers of shoe racks flank the door jambs. Shelves for live and dead storage on three sides, upper levels. Suit poles range the back wall. Ties are on the left wall, night clothes hooks on right wall.

Fig. 6. Bedroom closets for men
Scale: ¼ in. = 1 ft

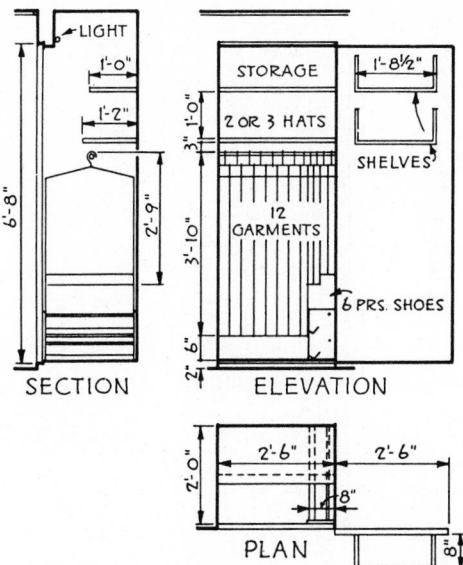

A small closet with shoe racks at the side under short hanging garments. Additional shoe pockets might be placed on the door under the hanging shelves. These handy shelves fold into the space in front of the hat and storage shelves.

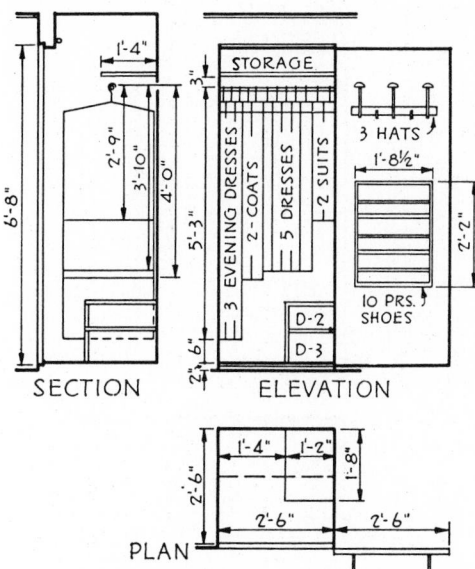

An alternate minimum closet arrangement with a high pole for long dresses. Two drawers below the shorter hanging garments. Depth of closet permits a door type shoe rack and a hat rack. Wide hats can go on upper shelf.

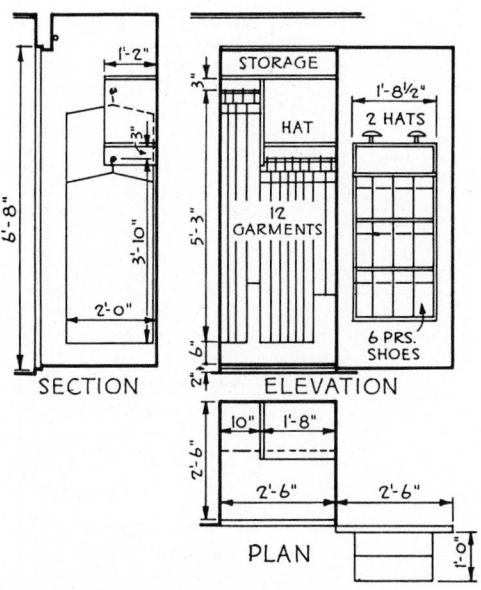

Alternate to closet above. It provides a high pole for hanging evening dresses and a lower pole for other dresses and suits. A large hat shelf is provided above the low pole as well as a hat rack and shoe pockets on the door.

Fig. 7. Bedroom closets for women
  Scale: ¼ in. = 1 ft

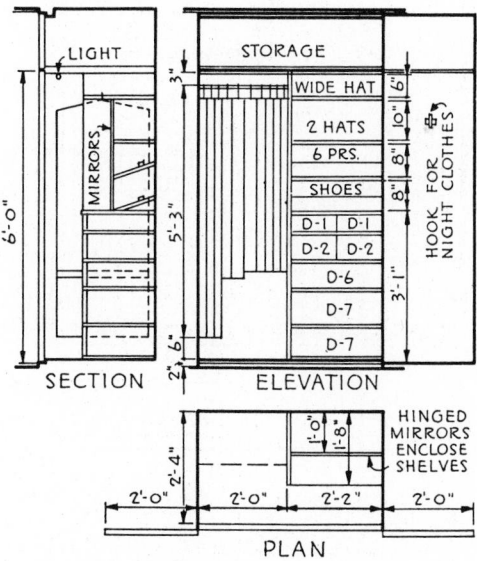

A four-foot closet combining hanging and shelf space with drawers for stockings, underthings, and what-not. Shoes are easily seen and chosen from the almost eye-level cleat rack above the drawers. Hat storage on the shelves.

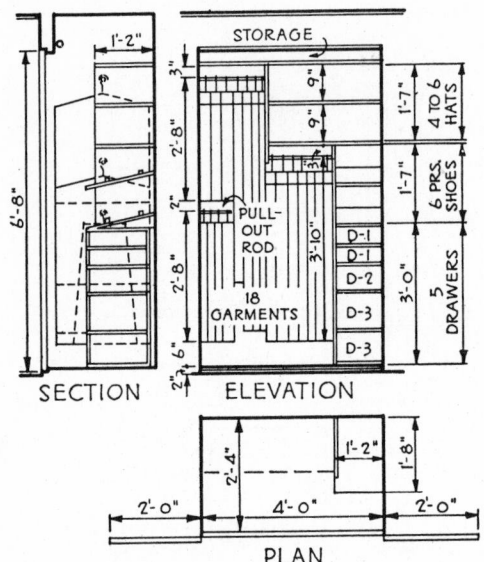

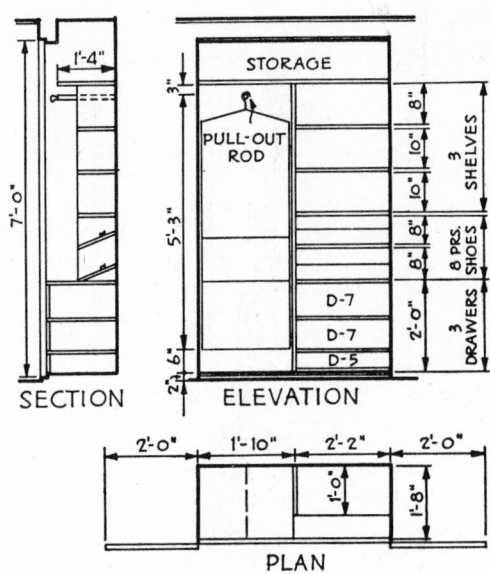

Another four-foot closet with a short canti-lever pole at the left allowing two-decker hanging. Closet drawer space would naturally be supplemented by a bureau or other furniture. A shoe rack on the door would increase capacity.

The shallow closet problem solved by the use of a pull-out rod firmly anchored to the back wall. Drawers again at lower right with cleated shoe shelves above, and hat shelves above them. Drawers may have to be shorter than standard.

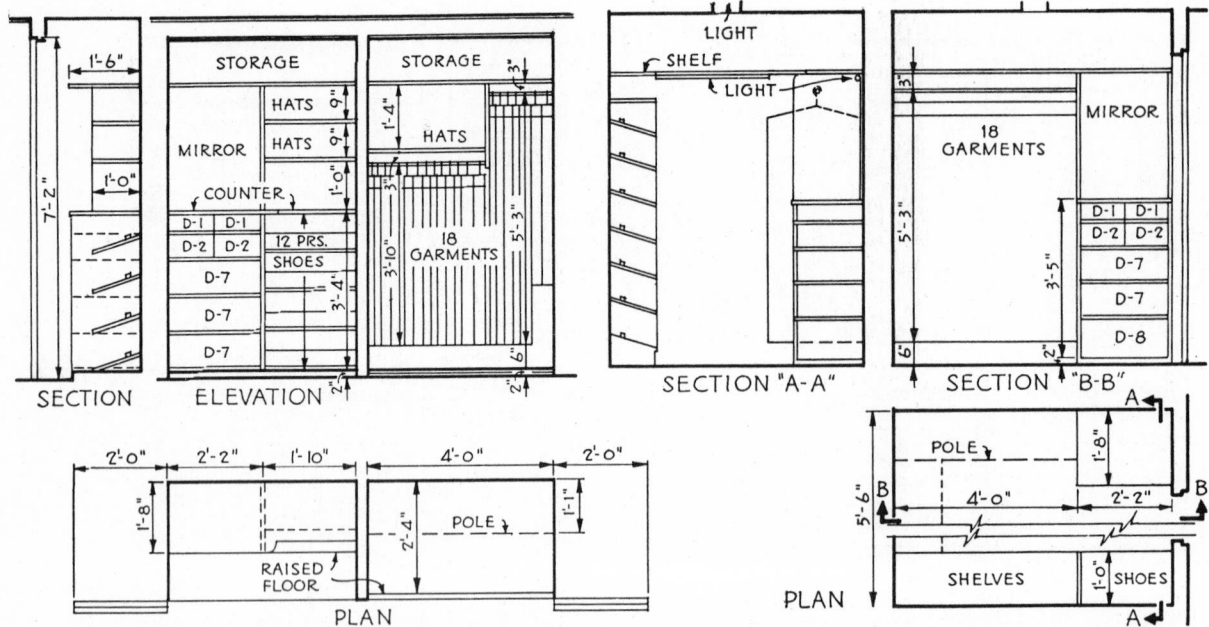

Large double wardrobe type closet, almost half devoted to hanging space. Left half fitted with large and small drawers and wide shelf-counter with mirror above. Sliding doors may be preferred and center partition minimized.

A walk-in closet, shoe racks and shallow shelves at one side drawers and hanging pole at the other. Drawers next to door are convenient but hazardous if left open. They could be placed at the back with hanging space near door.

Fig. 8. Bedroom closets for women
  Scale: ¼ in. = 1 ft

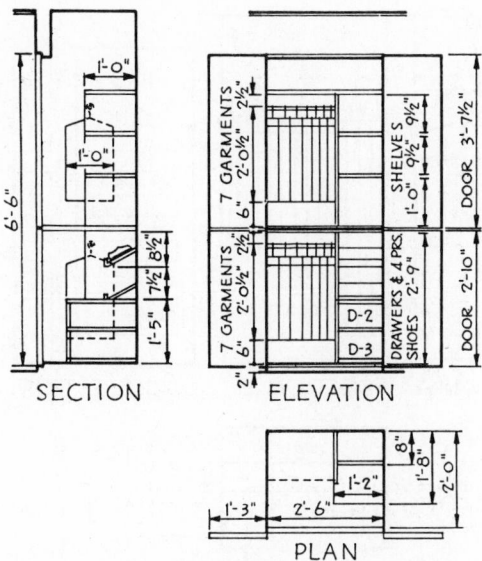

SECTION   ELEVATION

PLAN

Closet for infants up to about 5 years old
Low hanging pole shelves and drawers permit habits of care and orderliness to be developed at an early age. Upper part would
be used by adults. Note two sets of doors.

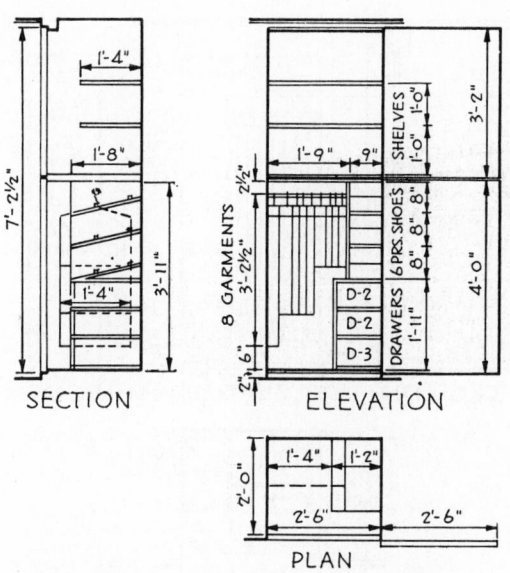

SECTION   ELEVATION

PLAN

Small closet designed for a child of from 6
to 10 years. Pole at higher but easily
reached level. Drawers and shoe racks at
convenient heights. Ample shelf room provided above for the storage of possessions.

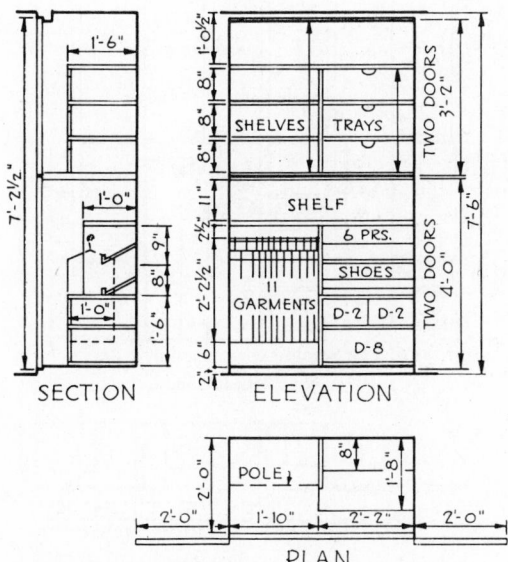

SECTION   ELEVATION

PLAN

Alternate, and larger, closet for an infant
up to 5 years of age. Trays or drawers for
folded garments at an upper level for adult
use. Hanging space, drawers and shelf
available to child using the lower doors.

Fig. 9. Bedroom closets for children
    Scale: ¼ in. = 1 ft

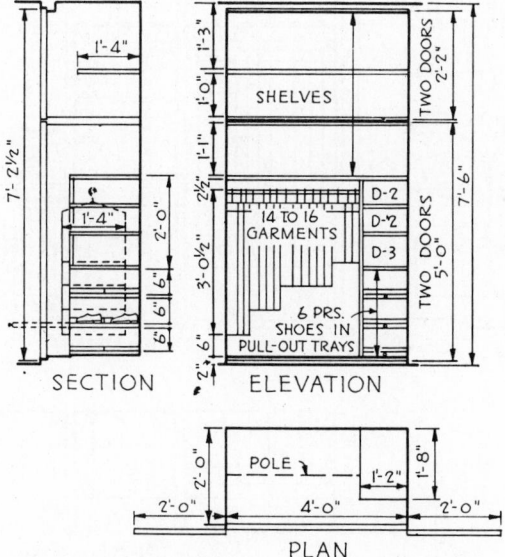

SECTION   ELEVATION

PLAN

Closet for youngster up to 10 years old,
providing greater length of hanging pole
and different shoe arrangement, trays instead of cleat racks. A large shelf for hats,
toys, or "collections" available to child.

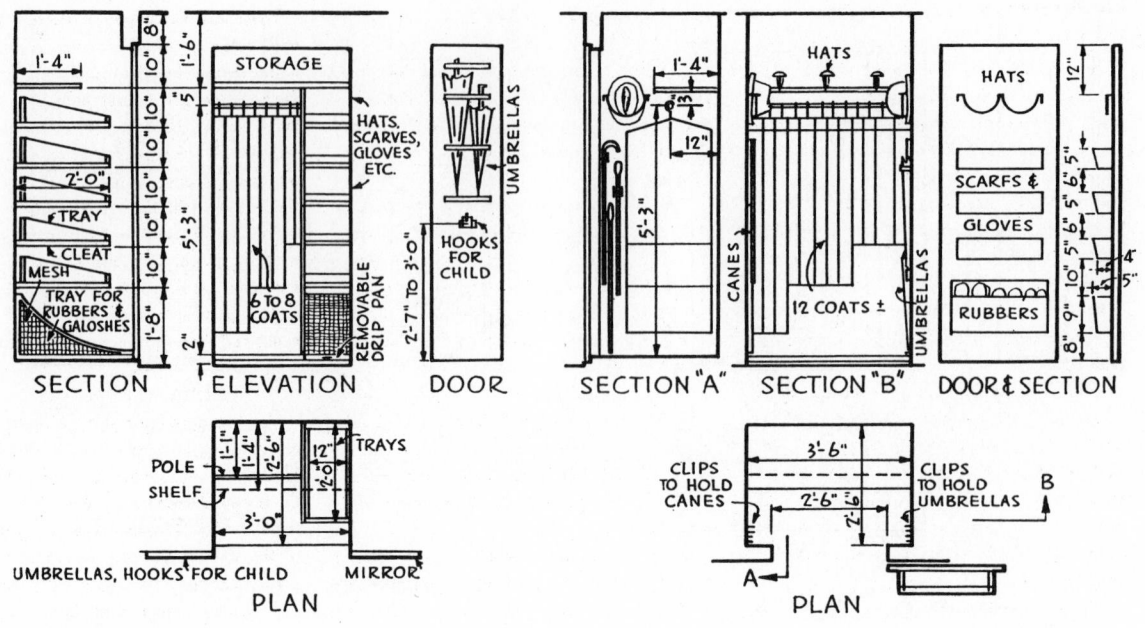

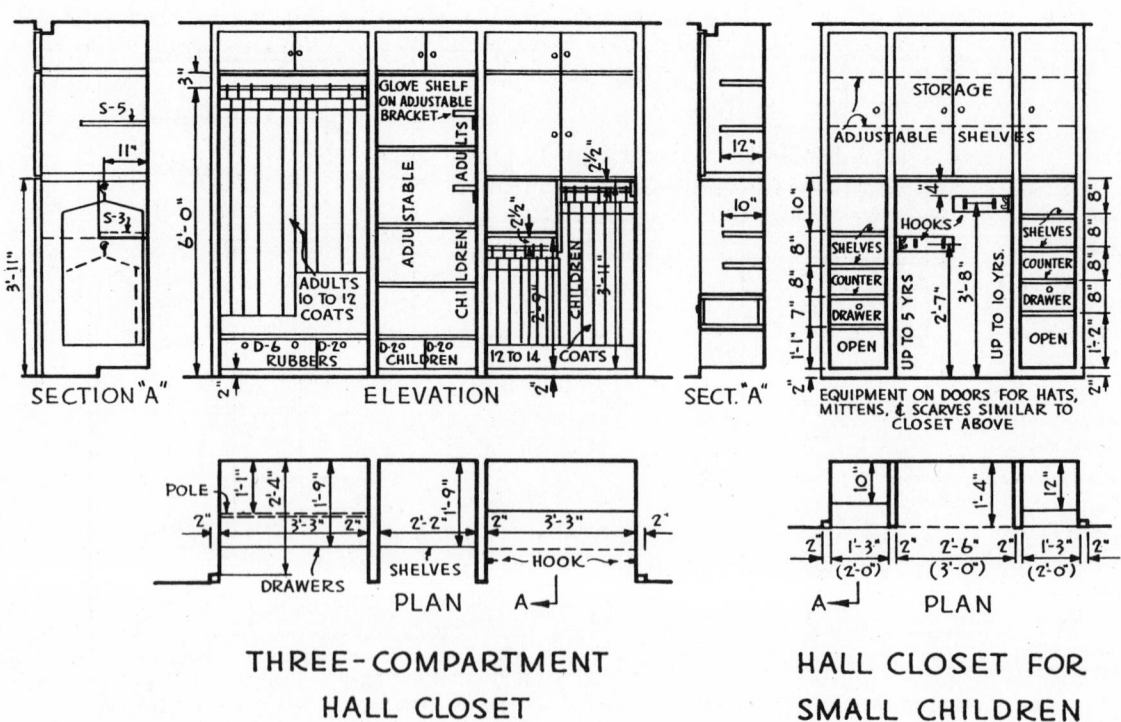

THREE-COMPARTMENT
HALL CLOSET

HALL CLOSET FOR
SMALL CHILDREN

Fig. 10. Coat closets
  Scale: ¼ in. = 1 ft

Miscellaneous storage

A large variety of other articles that are in regular use must be stored somewhere. Included in this category are books, magazines, phonograph records, card tables and chairs, games, movie and slide projectors, screens and film, toys, sports equipment, and tools. If adequate and conveniently located built-in storage is not provided, then portable units (furniture) will have to be used for this purpose.

Book storage is usually required in the living room, study, and each bedroom. Most books (85 per cent) can fit comfortably on shelves 8 in. deep (front to back); some books (10 per cent) need 10-in. shelves, and a few (5 per cent) require 12-in. shelves. Vertical spacing between shelves varies from 8 to 16 in., with the greatest use in the 10 to 12-in. range. Horizontally, books average 7 to 8 volumes per linear foot of shelf.

Phonograph records (12 in.) in albums require shelves with a clear height of 14 in. and a depth of 15 in. (14 in. for long-playing records in cardboard folders).

Card tables are usually 30 in. square but may be as large as 36 in., and are 2 to 3 in. thick when folded. Folded chairs vary widely in dimension, but a fair average is 30 by 16 by 3 in. Space should also be provided for cards, score cards, rule books, poker chips, chess, etc. (see Fig. 13).

Toy and game storage should be provided in children's bedrooms and wherever the toys are regularly used. Toy storage should be designed for future conversion to other use.

Sports equipment, especially golf bags, skis, and camping equipment, may present a serious storage problem. For some families, a separate closet for this purpose may be justified; a suggested design is shown in Fig. 13. Such a closet should be located near the outside entrance which is most used by the family.

Tools and associated items should, of course, be stored in the workshop, which every house must have. Paints, because of odor and fire hazard, are best stored outside the house.

General storage is required for bulky, seldom-used items, such as trunks, boxes, and extra furniture.

Outdoor storage (i.e., directly accessible from outdoors) is required for lawnmowers, wheelbarrows, sprays, rakes, and other garden tools and equipment; for snow shovels and sleds, ladders, screens, and storm windows; for outdoor furniture, barbecues, hammocks, croquet sets; for bicycles, tricycles, scooters, and perambulators (see Fig. 14).

These last two types of storage (general and outdoor) were provided in the traditional house by the basement, attic, and garage. Modern houses may have none of these spaces, and, in such cases, the architect should take particular care to provide adequate general and outdoor storage space. FHA minimum requirements are 200 cu ft plus 75 cu ft per bedroom, of which at least 25 per cent and not more than 50 per cent should be indoors. Again, it should be emphasized that this is a minimum requirement; more is recommended.

Basic elements

The standard elements of closet storage are shelves, drawers, poles, hooks, and special fixtures. Practically any object can be stored efficiently by one or another of these means. The choice and arrangement of the fixtures depend on the amount and nature of the materials to be stored.

Shelves: Shelves are simple and inexpensive to install, require a minimum of effort to use, and are adaptable to the storage of many types of things, especially those of odd or bulky shape, folded articles, and, of course, books, magazines, etc. However, if open, they are exposed to dust. Also small objects become hidden behind one another if the shelves are deep. A 12-in. shelf is usually adequate for most

Table 1. Storage requirements for bedroom linens and bedding, including allowance for handling

Article	Median number		Minimum dimensions, in.		
	Limited	Liberal	Depth	Width	Height*
Sheets, double bed					
Everyday use	6	6	12	14	12
Guest use	—	4	12	14	9
Pillow cases (pairs)					
Everyday use	5	5	12	8	8
Guest use	3	3	12	8	6
Blankets, comforters, quilts	4†	4†			
Pile of 4			23	19	26
2 piles of 2			23	38	14
Bedspreads, double bed					
Cotton damask	2	2	16	15	9
Chenille	1	1	18	16	8
Pillows		3	18	26	17

* *For storage on fixed shelves. For storage on sliding shelves or in drawers, deduct 1 to 2 in.*

† *Number of warm bed coverings owned is normally larger than this, but balance can be stored in less accessible location than linen closet.*

Source: Avis Woolrich, Mary M. White and Margaret A. Richards, Storage Space Requirements for Household Textiles, *U.S.D.A. Agricultural Research Bulletin 62–2, Washington, 1955.*

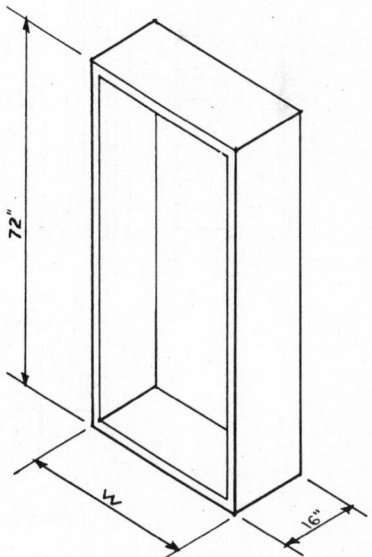

Fig. 11. Cleaning closet sizes for various types of vacuum cleaners

Scale: ¼ in. = 1 ft
Upright type   W = 28 in.
Cannister type W = 35 in.
Horizontal type W = 41 in.
Source: H. C. Potter, The Storage of Cleaning Equipment, *Journal of Home Economics, March, 1953.*

things. Articles of larger dimensions or greater depth should have their special places; linens, for instance, are frequently folded for a 16-in. shelf. Some useful shelf-support methods are illustrated in Fig. 15.

Drawers: Drawers are growing in popularity in closet design because they accommodate numerous articles with a minimum of space and a maximum of convenience. They provide practically dust-free storage and present a neat appearance even when carelessly used. Drawers of different widths and depths make possible classified "filing" of different items, thus providing a great saving in time and an incentive to orderliness. A cabinet made up of a battery of standard drawers, selected for the storage of the known possessions of the user, can easily be made from a comprehensive list, with allowance made for the accumulation of additional items.

Drawer construction is cabinetwork requiring both skillful craftsmanship and the best materials. They must operate freely under all seasonal and climatic conditions.

A recent logical outcome of this situation has been the development of molded plastic drawers in a variety of stock sizes. Fronts of various materials can be attached. All that is required of the builder is the construction of the supporting enclosure.

Poles: Hanging pole length can be estimated roughly at 3 in. per hanger for men's suits (4 in. for heavy coats) and 2 in. per hanger for women's clothing. Height of pole above floor should average 64 in., but should be adjusted to the individual. Clearance between pole and shelf above should be 3 in. Hardwood poles 1 in. in diameter should have intermediate supports if over 4 ft in length. Consult manufacturers for special-purpose hanging rods, extension poles, brackets, etc.

Hooks: A variety of hooks is available. Some of the types are illustrated in Fig. 16.

Special features: Such special features as shoe and hat racks and miscellaneous racks are on the market and greatly increase convenience in storage (see Fig. 16).

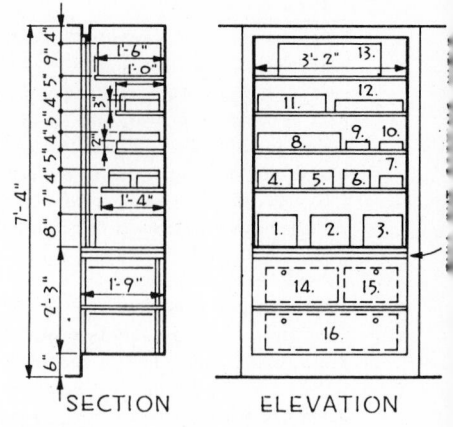

SECTION   ELEVATION

1. 8 SHEETS   (10" x 18" x 8" high)
2. "
3. 8 REG. TURKISH TOWELS (10" x 16" x 8" high)
4. 8 REG. PILLOW CASES (9½" x 14" x 4" high)
5. "
6. 12 REG. HAND TOWELS (7" x 14" x 4" high)
7. 12 REG. WASH CLOTHS (2 PILES) (6" x 6" x 3" h.)
8. 4 REG. BATH MATS (22" x 10" x 4" high)
9. 12 SMALL HAND TOWELS (6" x 12" x 2" high)
10. "
11. 4 BLANKET COVERS   (18" x 10" x 4" high)
12. 2 SHOWER CURTAINS (18" x 9" x 3" high)
13. 2 PILLOWS   (26" x 17" x 9" high)
14. 4 SUMMER BLANKETS (20" x 18" x 8" high)
15. 2 MATTRESS COVERS (14" x 18" x 8" high)
16. 3 WINTER BLANKETS (34" x 18" x 9" high)

BED & BATH LINEN

PLAN

BATHROOM & MEDICINE

SECTION   ELEVATION

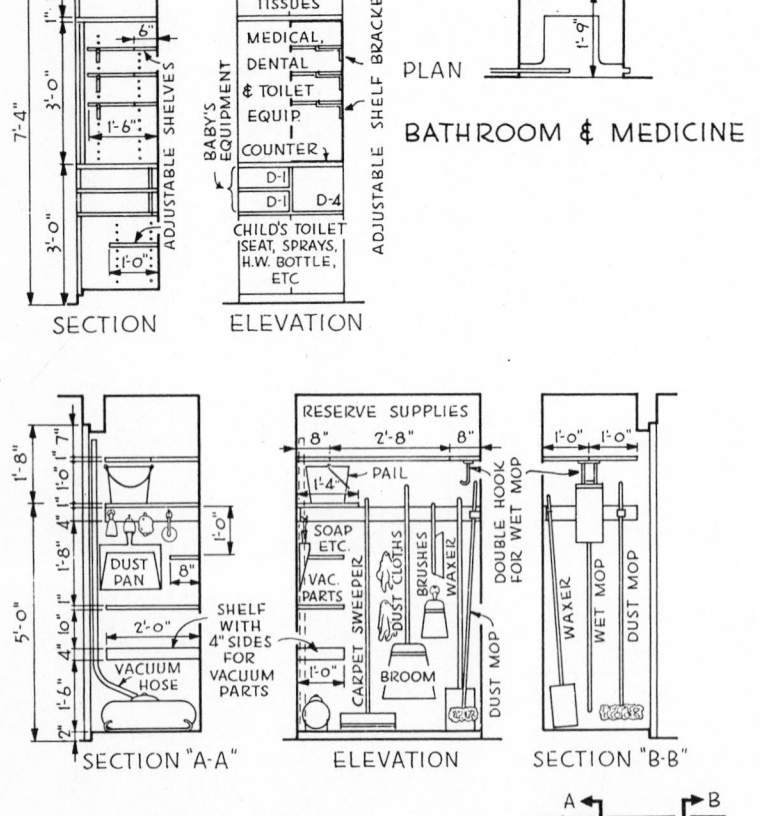

SECTION "A-A"   ELEVATION   SECTION "B-B"

CLEANING CLOSET

PLAN

Fig. 12. Miscellaneous Storage
Scale: ¼ in. = 1 ft

1016

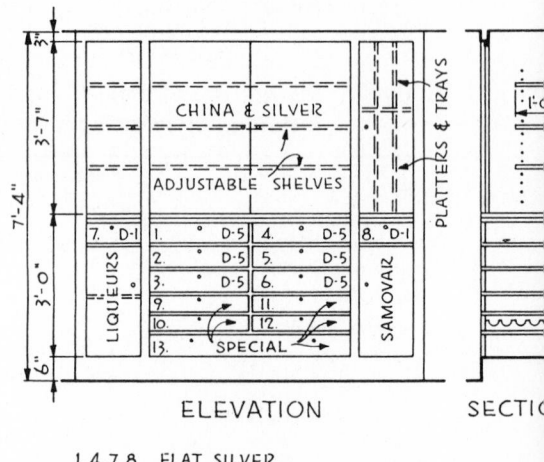

ELEVATION   SECTION

1, 4, 7, 8.   FLAT SILVER
2, 3, 5, 6.   NAPKINS, TABLE CLOTHS, DOILIES, ETC.
9, 11.   PLACE MATS (SHALLOW)
10, 12.   SPECIAL LINEN ROLLERS
13.   EXTENSION LEAVES.

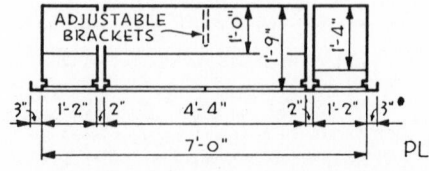

PLAN

DINING ROOM STORAGE

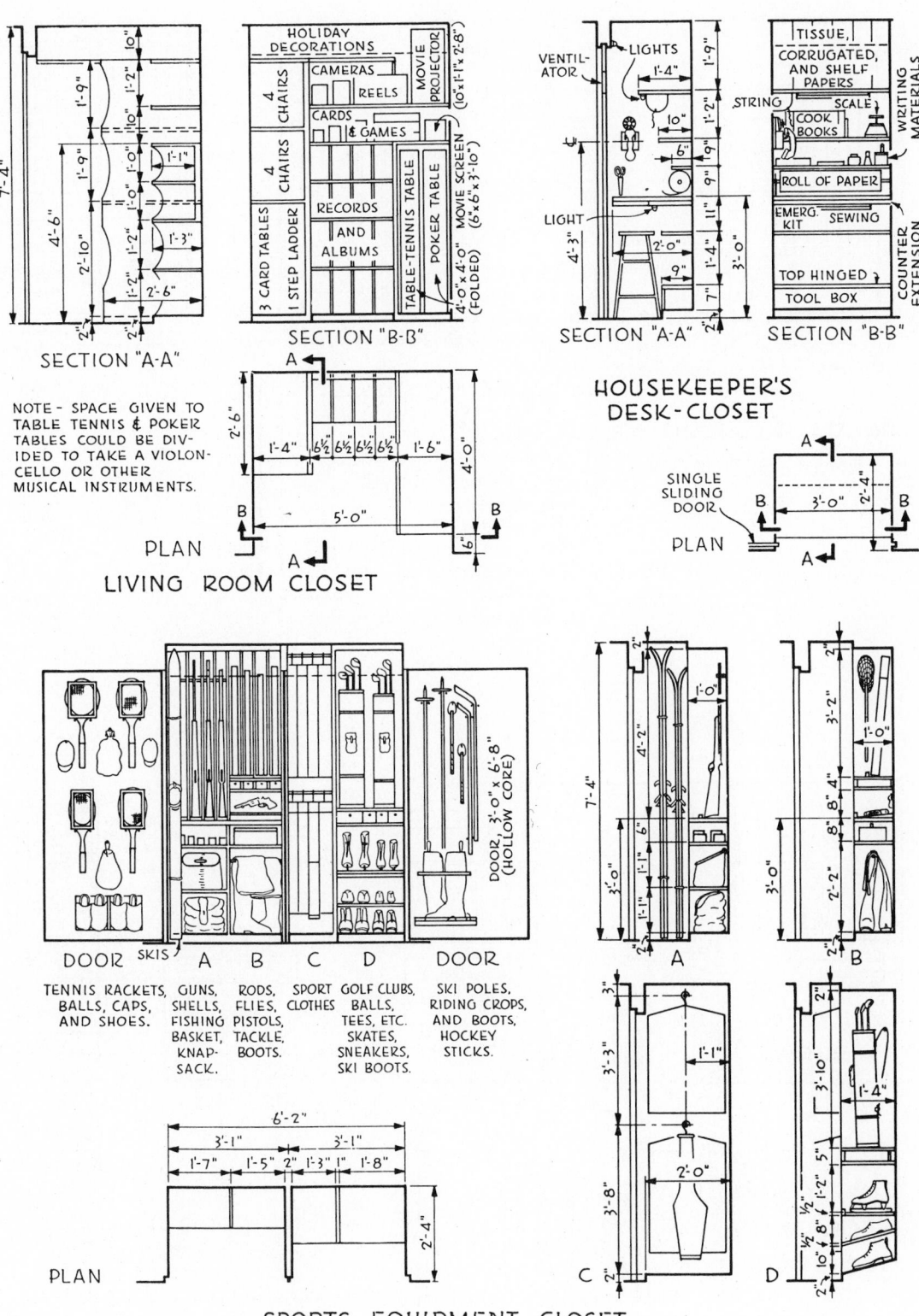

SECTION "A-A"

SECTION "B-B"

SECTION "A-A"

SECTION "B-B"

HOUSEKEEPER'S
DESK-CLOSET

NOTE - SPACE GIVEN TO
TABLE TENNIS & POKER
TABLES COULD BE DIV-
IDED TO TAKE A VIOLON-
CELLO OR OTHER
MUSICAL INSTRUMENTS.

PLAN
LIVING ROOM CLOSET

SINGLE
SLIDING
DOOR

PLAN

DOOR   SKIS   A   B   C   D   DOOR

TENNIS RACKETS, GUNS,   RODS,   SPORT GOLF CLUBS,   SKI POLES,
BALLS, CAPS,   SHELLS, FLIES, CLOTHES BALLS,   RIDING CROPS,
AND SHOES.   PISTOLS, TACKLE,   TEES, ETC.   AND BOOTS,
    FISHING   BOOTS.   SKATES,   HOCKEY
    BASKET,   SNEAKERS,   STICKS.
    KNAP-   SKI BOOTS.
    SACK.

PLAN

SPORTS EQUIPMENT CLOSET

Fig. 13. Miscellaneous closets
Scale: ¼ in. = 1 ft

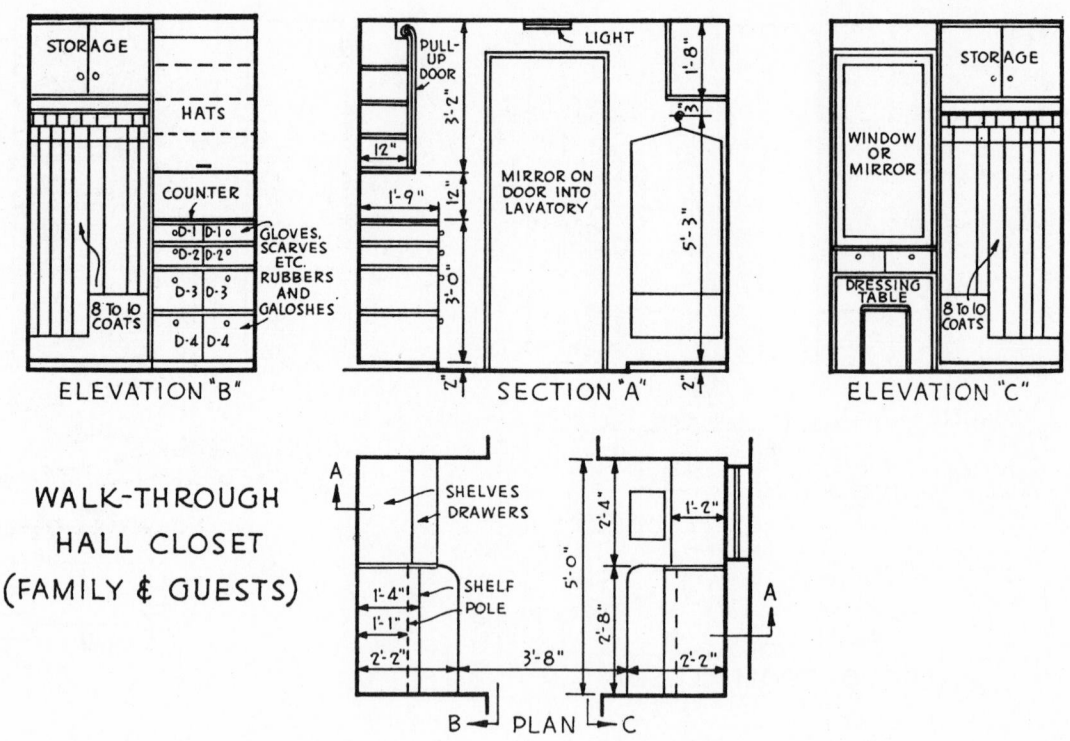

WALK-THROUGH
HALL CLOSET
(FAMILY & GUESTS)

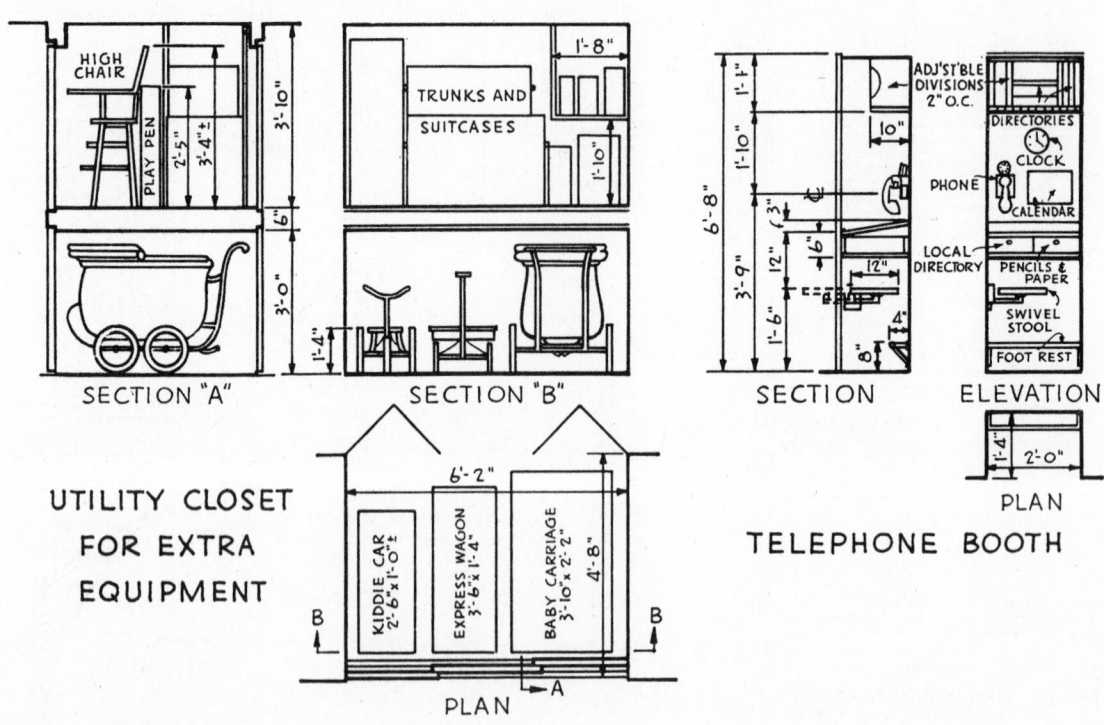

UTILITY CLOSET
FOR EXTRA
EQUIPMENT

TELEPHONE BOOTH

Fig. 14.   Miscellaneous closets
Scale: ¼ in. = 1 ft

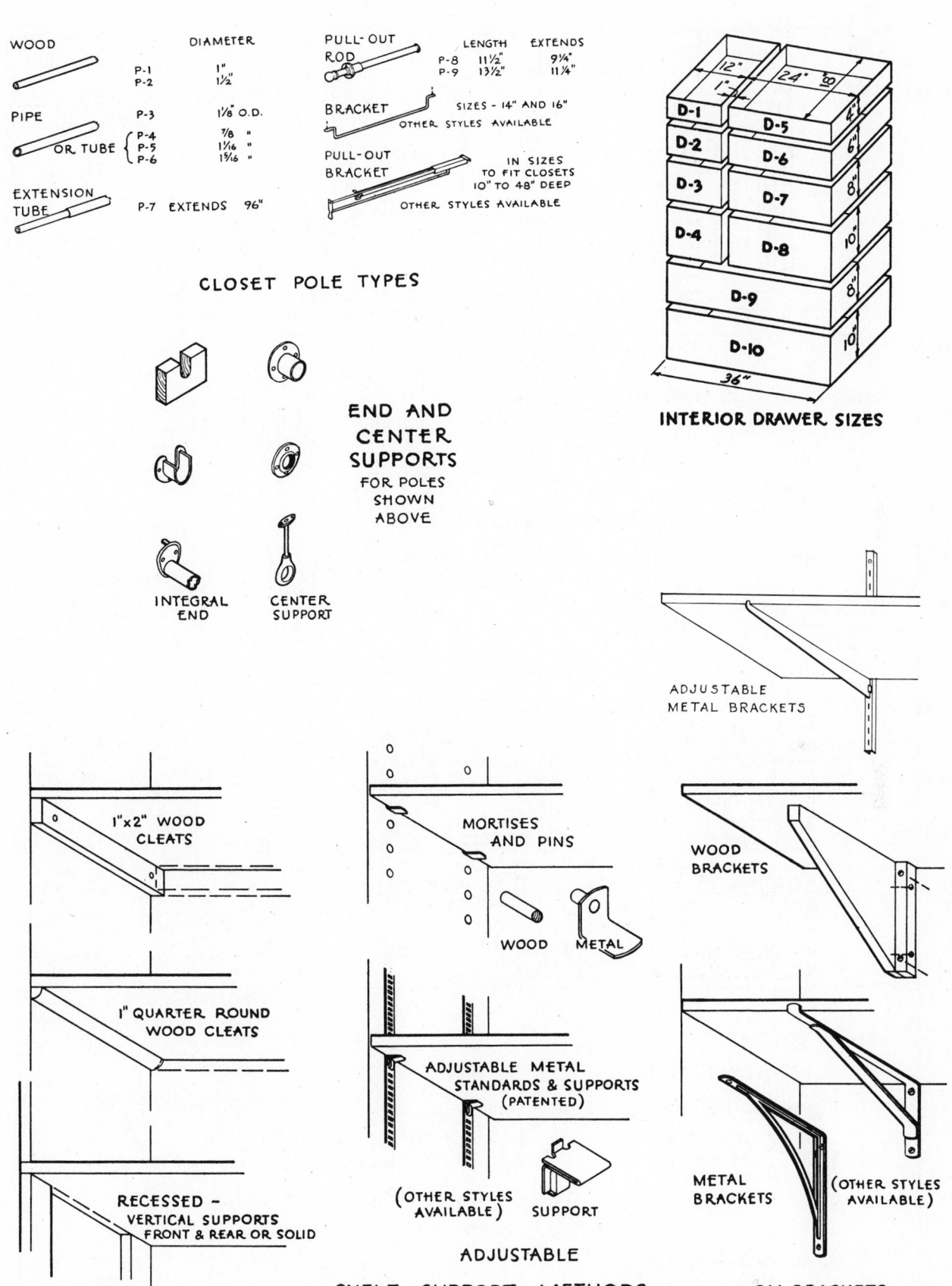

CLOSET POLE TYPES

END AND CENTER SUPPORTS FOR POLES SHOWN ABOVE

INTERIOR DRAWER SIZES

ADJUSTABLE METAL BRACKETS

WOOD BRACKETS

METAL BRACKETS (OTHER STYLES AVAILABLE)

FIXED

SHELF SUPPORT - METHODS

ON BRACKETS

Fig. 15. Closet fixtures—shelves, rods, and drawers

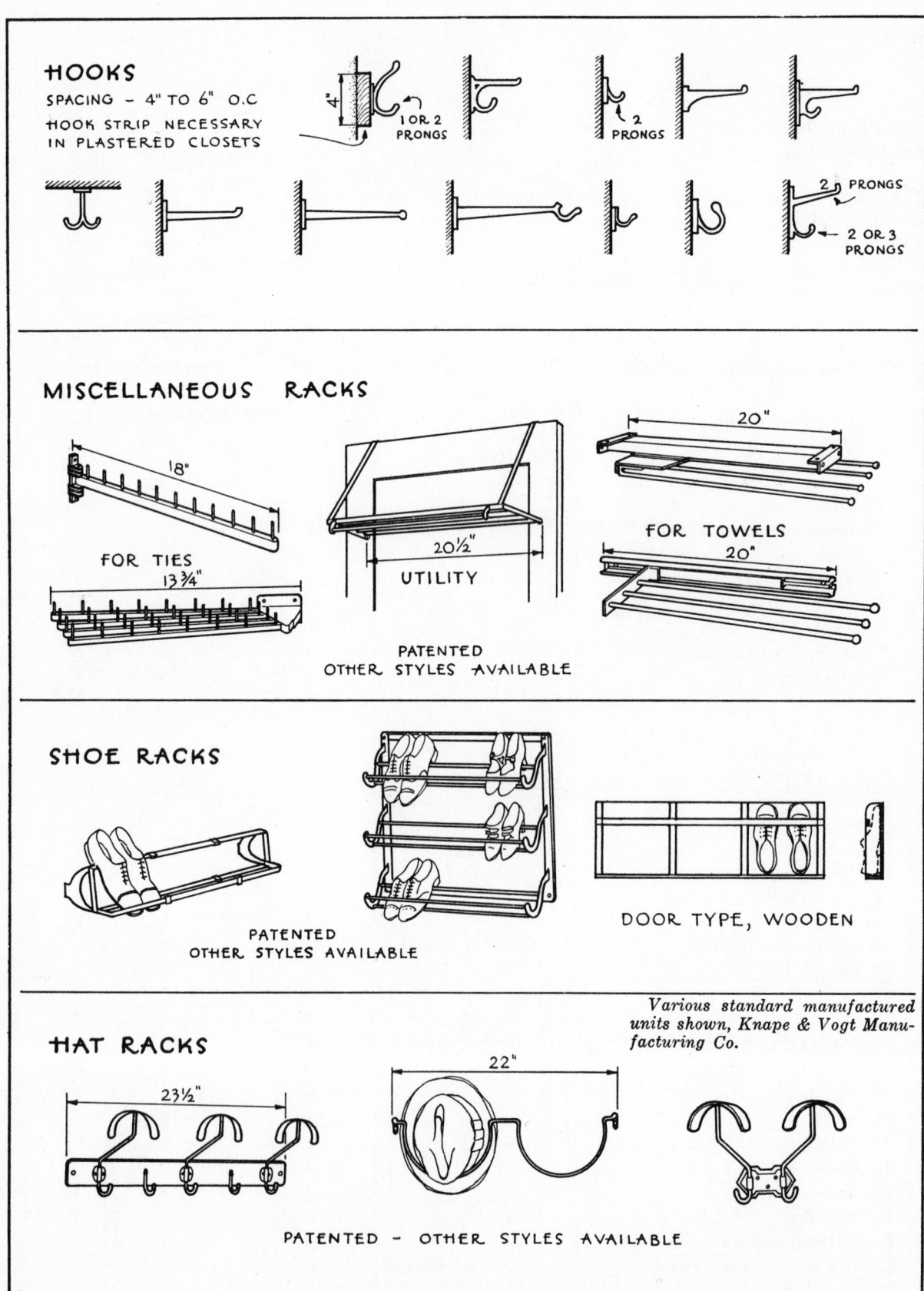

HOOKS
SPACING — 4" TO 6" O.C.
HOOK STRIP NECESSARY
IN PLASTERED CLOSETS

1 OR 2 PRONGS
2 PRONGS
2 PRONGS
2 OR 3 PRONGS

MISCELLANEOUS RACKS

18"
FOR TIES
13¾"

20½"
UTILITY

PATENTED
OTHER STYLES AVAILABLE

20"
FOR TOWELS
20"

SHOE RACKS

PATENTED
OTHER STYLES AVAILABLE

DOOR TYPE, WOODEN

Various standard manufactured units shown, Knape & Vogt Manufacturing Co.

HAT RACKS

23½"

22"

PATENTED — OTHER STYLES AVAILABLE

Fig. 16. Closet fixtures—hooks and racks

By WALTER E. SCHUTZ

Space Requirements for Machines and Equipment

The table below shows the area of the most popular machines and the equipment used in the home workshop.

These are the minimum dimensions of machines and the minimum distances allowable between machines and surrounding units.

There is quite a bit of variation in the size of storage shelves, tool accessory panels, bench extensions, nail and screw cabinets and similar built-in units. Usually these are built to fit the space available and special individual requirements.

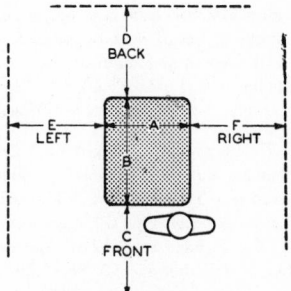

Machine or Unit	Area In Inches		Spacing Requirements In Feet			
	A Width	B Depth	C Front	D Back	E Left	F Right
1. Circular Saw	48	27	12	12	6	6
2. Jointer	18	42	12	12	2	1
3. Band Saw	34	15	4	4	1	6
4. Scroll Saw	16	38	3	0	2	2
5. Woodworking Lathe	56	12	3	0	2	0
6. Drill Press	14	28	3	0	2	2
7. Comb. Belt and Disc Sander	30	20	3	2	2	3
8. Wood Shaper	21	15	4	0	4	4
9. Planer	30	16	12	12	3	1
10. Radial Arm Saw	22	25	4	0	10	10
11. Comb. Sander-Buffer-Grinder	16	16	3	3	2	2
12. 10-in. Metalworking Lathe	58	26	3	0	2	2
13. Tool Grinder	22	12	3	0	1	1
14. Milling Machine	34	26	3	0	3	3
15. Metal Shaper	18	36	4	0	2	2
16. Power Hack Saw	14	24	2	0	6	6
17. Arc Welder	14	28	6	0	4	4
18. Punch Press	12	16	3	0	2	2
19. Sheet Metal Brake	24	10	4	4	1	1
20. Shear	24	24	4	4	1	1
21. Slip Roll	20	12	3	3	1	1
22. Nibbler	18	24	2	0	3	3
23. Shear Clamp Head	12	18	4	0	3	3
24. Metal Cutting Band Saw	20	26	4	4	2	4
25. Heat-treating Furnace	30	30	4	0	0	0
26. Forge	36	36	4	0	0	0
27. Heating Oven for Plastics	24	18	2	0	0	0
28. Kiln	36	48	3	0	0	0
29. Potter's Wheel	24	30	3	0	2	2
30. Woodworking Bench	72	30	6	0	3	2
31. Metalworking Bench	60	28	4	0	2	2
32. Tool and Accessory Panel	60	48 high				
33. Storage Shelves (open)	48	12				
34. Storage Cabinets	48	18				
35. Counters	48	18	33 in. high			

WOODWORKING SHOP

Circular saw and jointer must be in center with adequate room front and rear, since the entire length of board must be passed over them; door opening gives extra space. Finishing room (1) has swinging door, normally closed to keep dust out. Vent finishing room with exhaust fan.

1. Finishing room 2. Exhaust fan 3. Cabinets for finishing materials 4. Panel for drill press accessories 5. High speed drill press 6. Panel for lathe accessories 7. Woodworking lathe, 12-in. 8. Band saw, 12-in. 9. Storage cupboard and shelves 10. Panel for scroll saw accessories 11. Scroll saw, 24-in. 12. Combination disc and belt sander 13. Storage shelves and drawers 14. Bench with woodworking vise 15. Panel for hand tools 16. Tilting arbor circular saw, 10-in. 17. Jointer, 6-in. 18. Overhead lumber storage rack

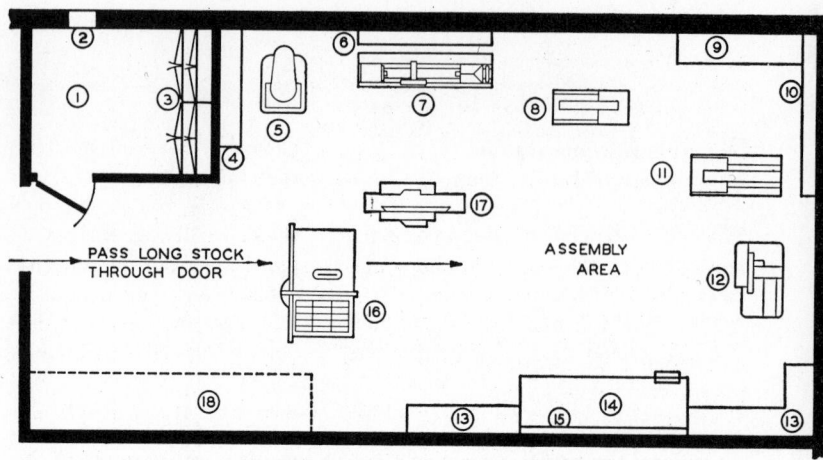

PLASTICS SHOP

This same layout, less oven, is adaptable to a small jewelry shop, or even a small woodworking shop

1. Storage shelves with drawers 2. Bench with woodworking vise 3. Panel for hand tools 4. Electric oven for plastics molding 5. Storage cabinet with shelves below for sheet plastics 6. Storage shelves to ceiling for small items 7. Scroll saw, 16-in. 8. Panel for scroll saw accessories 9. Combination disc sander-buffer-grinder-drill 10. Panel for storing combination accessories

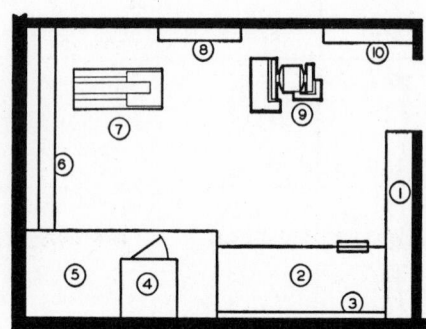

CERAMICS SHOP

If kiln is gas-fired a flue must be provided. Water supply and drain are necessary. Only "machine" is a potter's wheel

1. Sink with hot and cold water 2. Sink counter 3. Storage shelves to ceiling 4. Table 5. Kiln 6. Flue (if kiln is gas-fired) 7. Storage shelves to ceiling 8. Slip barrel 9. Wedging table 10. Potter's wheel 11. Storage shelves and drawers

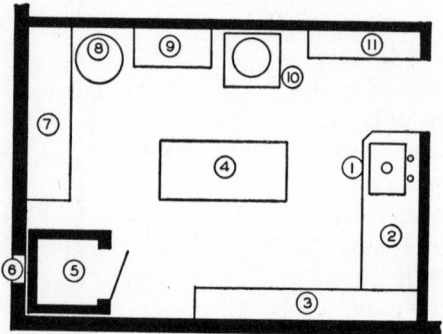

MODEL-BUILDING SHOP

This identical layout can be used also as a home repair center. As a model-building shop it has plenty of storage shelves and all the machines usually used.

1. Combination sander-grinder-buffer-drill mounted on stand 2. Scroll saw, 16-in. (both combination unit and scroll saw are run from same motor, as shown) 3. Stool 4. Bench with woodworking vise 5. Storage shelves to ceiling, some drawers for small items 6. Storage shelves to ceiling 7. Panel for hand tools

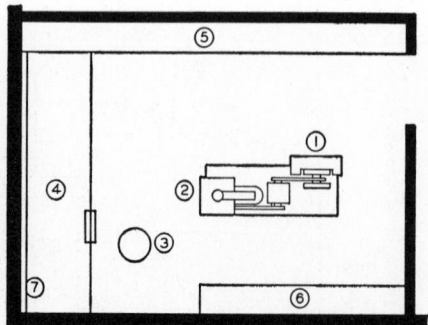

CABINET SHOP

Cabinets take considerable space for gluing and assembly, so more shop area and benches, (4) and (6), should be provided than for wood working. Lumber racks (14) should easily take 12-in. boards. Circular saw (16) jointer (15) and planer (17) must have plenty of room for passing through full-length stock. Cut-off saw (18) is built into lumber rack for simple handling of stock. Provide bench-high counters on both sides to support boards

1. Storage shelves, to ceiling 2. Table-high layout and gluing board on movable horses. 3. Hardware storage shelves, drawers below bench for nails, screws 4. Bench with woodworking vise 5. Panel for hand tools 6. Bench-high storage cabinet, some drawers 7. Storage shelves to ceiling 8. Bench tool grinder 9. Band saw, 12-in. 10. Floor-type, high-speed drill press, 15-in. 11. Spindle shaper 12. Panel for drill press accessories 13. Panel and drawers for shaper accessories 14. Lumber racks 15. Jointer, 6-in. 16. Tilting arbor circular saw, 10-in. 17. Planer, 12-in. 18. Radial arm saw, 10-in.

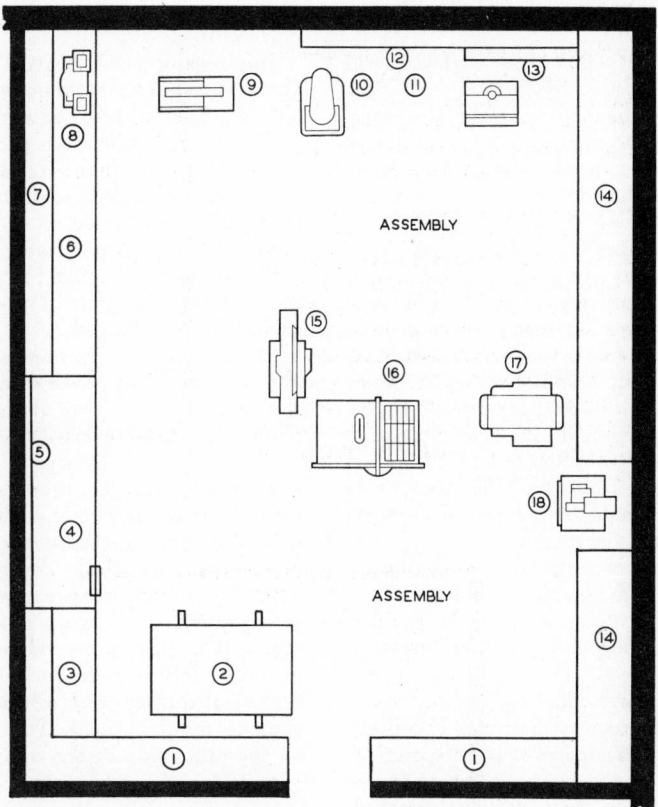

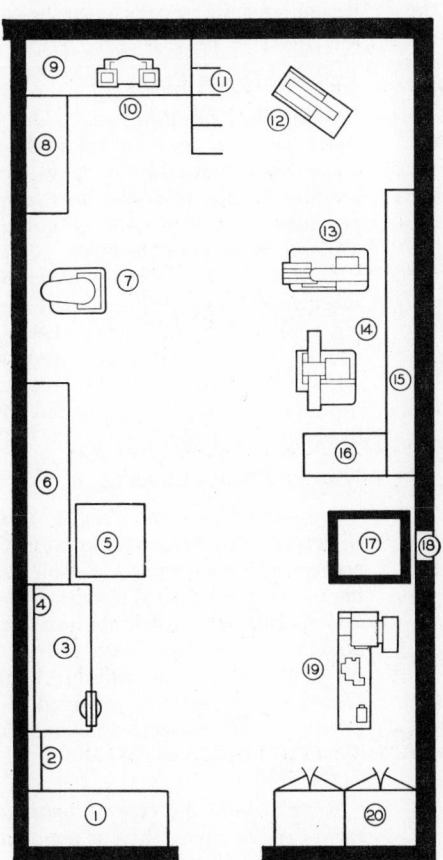

MACHINE SHOP

1. Storage cabinet with shelves 2. Small parts storage, drawers 3. Bench with metalworking vise 4. Panel for hand tools 5. Movable table on casters 6. Storage shelves 7. Slow speed drill press, 15-in. 8. Storage cabinet 9. Bench-high drawer cabinet 10. Tool grinder 11. Vertical "stand-up" rack for storing metal 12. Metal-cutting band saw, 20-in. 13. Metal shaper 14. Milling machine 15. Storage cabinet, shelves, drawers 16. Bench-high counter 17. Heat-treating furnace 18. Flue 19. Metalworking lathe, 29-in. 20. Storage cabinet

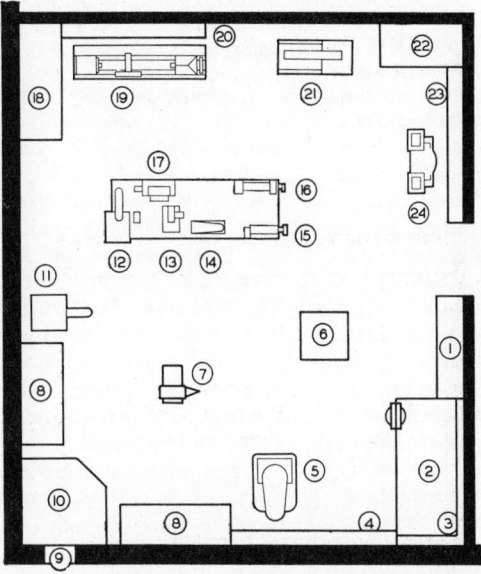

ART METAL SHOP FOR WROUGHT IRON

1. Storage shelves for small parts 2. Bench with metalworking vise 3. Panel for hand tools 4. Panel for drill press accessories 5. Slow-speed drill press, 15-in. 6. Movable table on casters 7. Anvil on block 8. Storage cabinet 9. Flue for forge 10. Forge 11. Arc welder 12. Nibbler 13. Punch press 14. Shear clamping head 15. Shear 16. Slip roll 17. Metal brake, 12-in. 18. Storage shelves 19. Woodworking lathe for metal spinning 20. Panel for lathe accessories 21. Metal-cutting band saw, 20-in. 22, 23. Storage shelves 24. Tool grinder

DARKROOMS—1
Design

By N. C. FERGUSON, *Eastman Kodak Company*

THE construction of the darkroom will be influenced by these factors: How often will the room be used? How many people are to work in it simultaneously? And, what type of work is to be done there — film development, contact printing, enlarging, or the "works"?

A room that is to be used frequently, even by only one person, should naturally be larger and better fitted for convenient operation than one which is to be used only on occasion. Likewise, two workers will definitely require more space than one. And since photography is a companionable art, and most photographers enjoy having another work with them from time to time, two workers should be considered the rule rather than the exception.

As for processing operations, contact printing and film development require relatively little space, but enlarging is a bit more demanding. Many amateur photographers today either own enlargers or have definite plans for acquiring one as soon as possible. Therefore, from any standpoint it is not practical to think of the home darkroom exclusively in terms of an additional closet. A darkroom may be located in a large closet, but for photographic efficiency and for added home appeal, it is advisable to approach the proposed darkroom as a room — complete in itself, and yet an integral part of the house.

Location Fundamentals

The location of the darkroom will, of course, be determined by what space is available, yet consideration must be given to convenience in relation to plumbing and electrical facilities, uniformity of temperature, and dryness.

An attic is seldom satisfactory for a darkroom, because unless well insulated it is likely to be too hot in summer and too cold in winter. The installation of plumbing in the attic is often difficult and usually expensive. Spillage and overflows can cause extensive damage. A *damp* cellar, on the other hand, is just about as poor a location as an attic. Dampness causes deterioration of films and papers, and results in weak, mottled pictures. A first or second floor room is likely to work out nicely if space can be allotted there, but the *ideal* location for the darkroom is a dry basement — particularly if uniform temperatures are maintained there — since plumbing and electrical connections are usually nearby.

But regardless of location and size, the first requirement is obviously that the room be capable of excluding all light. The sensitivity of modern photographic materials is such that total darkness is an absolute necessity. No white light can be permitted to leak in around the door or through any other opening.

The second requirement is that space for necessary equipment and apparatus should be so arranged as to allow the work to progress in the most convenient and efficient manner with a minimum of lost motion. The general flow of all photographic processing is from dry work to wet, and, finally, to drying or dry work again. In printing, this is exemplified by dry work at the contact printer or enlarger, then wet work as the print moves through the developer, stop bath, fixing bath, and wash water, and dry work once more as the print is dried again. It is therefore good practice to plan the darkroom in such a manner that all of the dry work can be done on one side, or at one end, and the wet work on the other side or the opposite end.

A darkroom of the type shown in Plan A is very well adapted to all amateur work, and provides all necessary facilities for processing and print making, so that the home photographic unit is complete. Notice that the number of electrical outlets in the room provides for two safelights on the "wet" side, a safelight and outlets for the printer and enlarger on the "dry" side, and a central overhead indirect lighting box. An indirect lighting box can be used, incidentally, for a white light, or if preferred, for a general over-all safelight.

Home Darkroom Sinks

Since the majority of the operations on the "wet" side of the darkroom will center about the sink, and since several operations may be carried on in the sink itself, it is important that the sink be large and properly placed.

A good standard size for the sink is 36 to 48 in. long and 18 to 20 in. wide. The best sinks for darkroom work are those made of stainless steel, but they are also the most expensive. Enameled iron sinks are also very satisfactory, but if a metal sink is not obtainable, wooden sinks can be utilized.

Waterproofed plywood has made good sinks, but cypress is more or less the standard wood for such construction. Tongue and groove joints should be used and the sides of the sink should be held

in position by steel tierods. A rubber-based paint, when obtainable, gives a good binding for wooden sinks. Wooden sinks are, by and large, not as good for amateur use as metal, for the main trouble with wooden sinks is that when used only intermittently, they may dry out with resulting opening of the seams.

Whatever type of sink is used, however, it is best to overlap the linoleum or other shelf covering about the edges of the sink, so that spillage or drippings may be easily wiped off the shelf surface and into the sink. Note in the sketches of Plan A how the linoleum shelf covering, on both the wet and dry sides, rounds the corner and runs in an unbroken sheet up the wall to a height of 6 or 8 in. Such design prevents seepage down the corner and protects the wall from splashings.

Tray and Drying Racks

Note also, on the "wet" side, that space has been provided below the sink for a tray rack. If the tray rack is built as a unit, to slide into the space provided, it may be easily removed for cleaning as occasion demands.

On the "dry" side of the darkroom a most important inclusion is that of drying racks for prints. These racks are simple wooden frames covered with cheese-cloth — on which the prints may be laid — designed to slide in and out on fixed wooden supports.

Floor and Bench Covering

A sheet of linoleum which is given a slight turn-up at the sides to protect the corners, is recommended for floor covering in a darkroom of this type. Benches and shelves are all mounted on 2 by 4 studding and covered with at least $\frac{1}{4}$-in. plywood or other suitable lumber. Note that toe space is provided at the bottom of all cabinets and structures.

Ventilation

Regardless of the type of home darkroom decided upon, there is one further factor that should be taken into consideration in planning and construction — that is, the matter of proper ventilation. Small darkrooms which are not ventilated properly will show a decided rise in temperature, as the result of enlarger and body heat, in a short period of time. The best solution to this problem is the use of an automatic darkroom fan for forced draft ventilation, but if this is not possible, light-trapped ventilators should be installed near the floor and ceiling.

Plan A (by Eastman)   Approx. scale: ⅜" = 1'

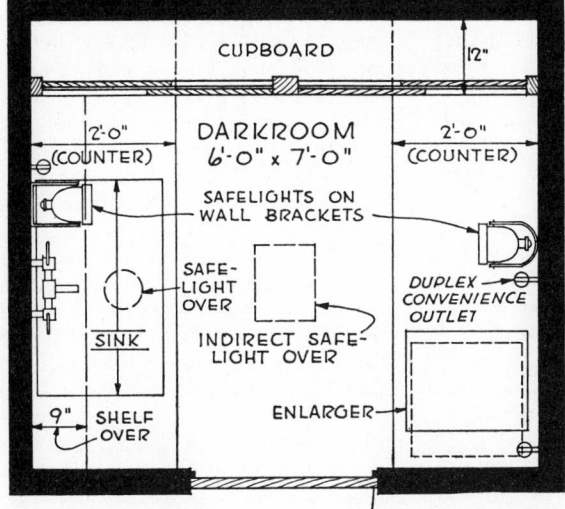

CUPBOARD

DARKROOM
6'-0" x 7'-0"

2'-0" (COUNTER)

2'-0" (COUNTER)

12"

SAFELIGHTS ON WALL BRACKETS

SAFE- LIGHT OVER

DUPLEX CONVENIENCE OUTLET

INDIRECT SAFE- LIGHT OVER

SINK

9" SHELF OVER

ENLARGER

Plan B (by Lee Parsons Davis)   Approx. scale: ⅜" = 1'

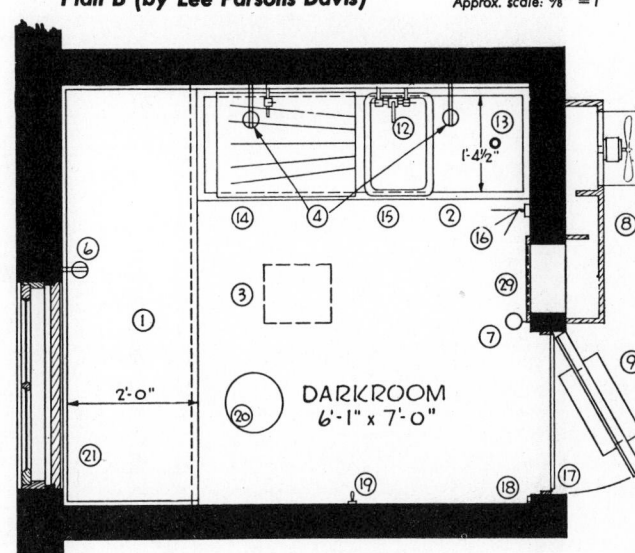

1'-4½"

DARKROOM
6'-1" x 7'-0"

2'-0"

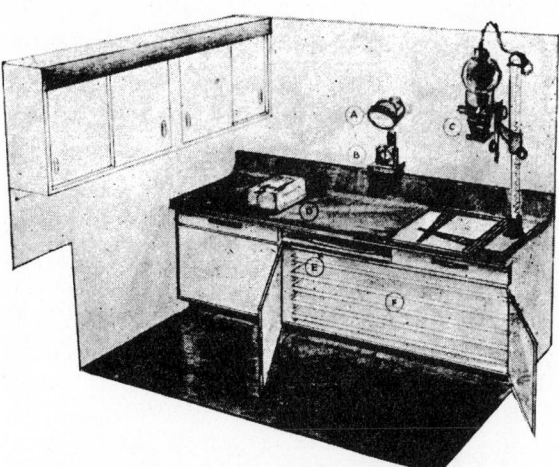

A — Adjustable safe- light
B — Timer
C — Precision enlarger
D — Printer
E — Trimming board
F — Print drying racks

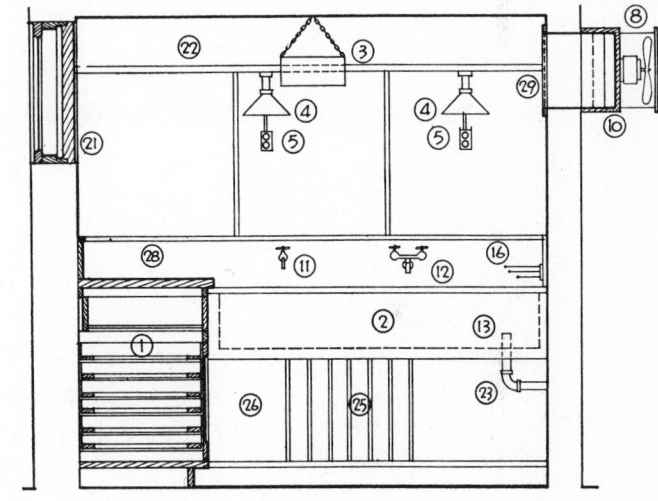

A — Darkroom lamp
B — Adjustable safe- light
C — Graduates
D — Tray rack
E — Negative drying line

1. Print drying racks
2. Lead lined sink
3. Indirect safelight
4. Adjustable safe- lights
5. Convenience outlets
6. Enlarger outlet
7. Bright light
8. Exhaust fan
9. Light-trapped air inlet
10. Foul air outlet
11. Cold water faucet
12. Hot and cold water
13. Variable drain pipe
14. Removable drain board
15. Sliding trays
16. Towel rack
17. Door gasket
18. Air thermometer
19. Coat hook
20. Stool
21. Window blind
22. Storage shelf
23. Storage space
24. Trimming board
25. Tray rack

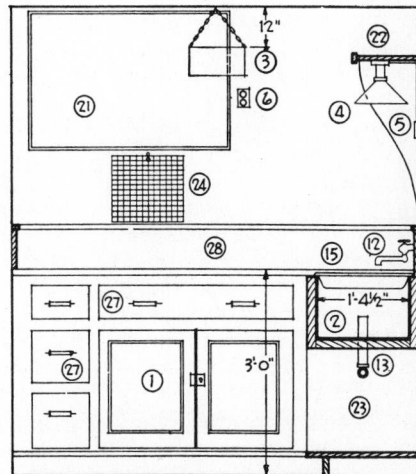

1'-2"

3'-0"

1'-4½"

26. Storage space
27. Full depth drawers
28. Micarta back board
29. Air outlet grille

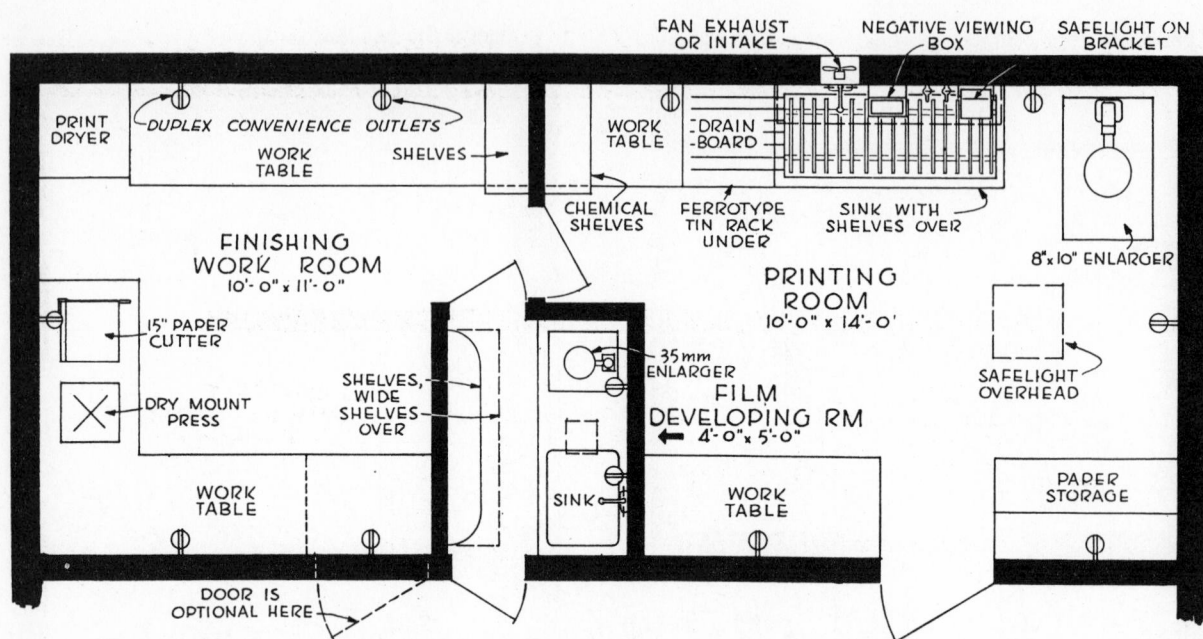

FAN EXHAUST OR INTAKE

NEGATIVE VIEWING BOX

SAFELIGHT ON BRACKET

PRINT DRYER

DUPLEX CONVENIENCE OUTLETS

WORK TABLE

SHELVES

WORK TABLE

DRAIN BOARD

8"x 10" ENLARGER

FINISHING WORK ROOM
10'-0" x 11'-0"

CHEMICAL SHELVES

FERROTYPE TIN RACK UNDER

SINK WITH SHELVES OVER

15" PAPER CUTTER

PRINTING ROOM
10'-0" x 14'-0"

DRY MOUNT PRESS

SHELVES, WIDE SHELVES OVER

35mm ENLARGER

FILM DEVELOPING RM
← 4'-0"x 5'-0"

SAFELIGHT OVERHEAD

WORK TABLE

SINK

WORK TABLE

PAPER STORAGE

DOOR IS OPTIONAL HERE

Advanced Amateur — Small Professional Workshop. Planned by Willard D. Morgan

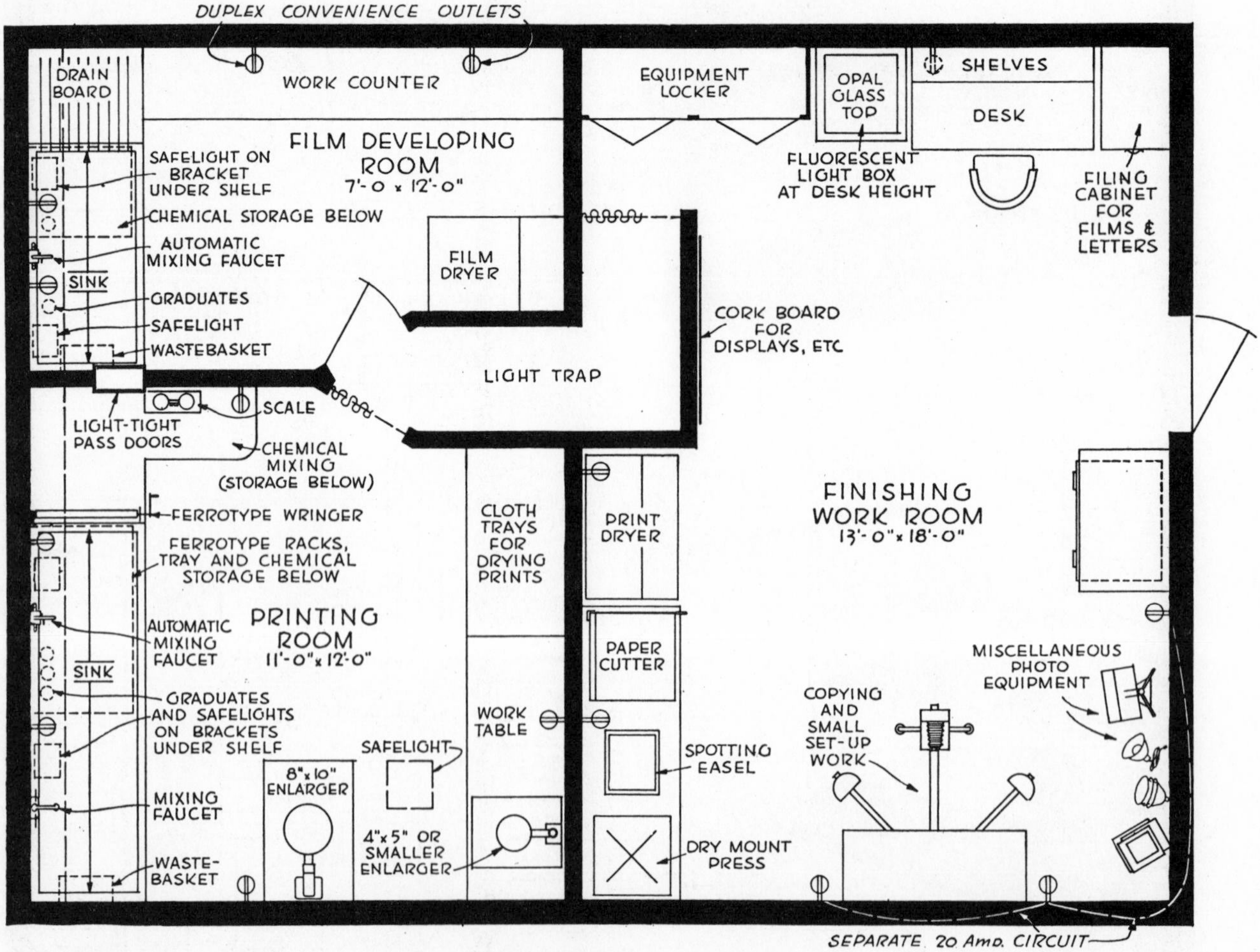

DUPLEX CONVENIENCE OUTLETS

DRAIN BOARD

WORK COUNTER

EQUIPMENT LOCKER

OPAL GLASS TOP

SHELVES

DESK

FILM DEVELOPING ROOM
7'-0 x 12'-0"

SAFELIGHT ON BRACKET UNDER SHELF

CHEMICAL STORAGE BELOW

AUTOMATIC MIXING FAUCET

FILM DRYER

FLUORESCENT LIGHT BOX AT DESK HEIGHT

FILING CABINET FOR FILMS & LETTERS

GRADUATES

SAFELIGHT

SINK

WASTEBASKET

CORK BOARD FOR DISPLAYS, ETC

LIGHT TRAP

SCALE

LIGHT-TIGHT PASS DOORS

CHEMICAL MIXING (STORAGE BELOW)

FERROTYPE WRINGER

FERROTYPE RACKS, TRAY AND CHEMICAL STORAGE BELOW

CLOTH TRAYS FOR DRYING PRINTS

PRINT DRYER

FINISHING WORK ROOM
13'-0"x 18'-0"

AUTOMATIC MIXING FAUCET

PRINTING ROOM
11'-0"x 12'-0"

PAPER CUTTER

SINK

GRADUATES AND SAFELIGHTS ON BRACKETS UNDER SHELF

MIXING FAUCET

8"x 10" ENLARGER

SAFELIGHT

WORK TABLE

SPOTTING EASEL

MISCELLANEOUS PHOTO EQUIPMENT

COPYING AND SMALL SET-UP WORK

4"x 5" OR SMALLER ENLARGER

DRY MOUNT PRESS

WASTE-BASKET

SEPARATE 20 Amp. CIRCUIT

Professional Workshop. Planned by Willard D. Morgan

Approx. scale: ¼" =1'

Community Center Photo Workshop. Planned for groups of 12–15 by Willard D. Morgan

Approx. scale: ¼" = 1'

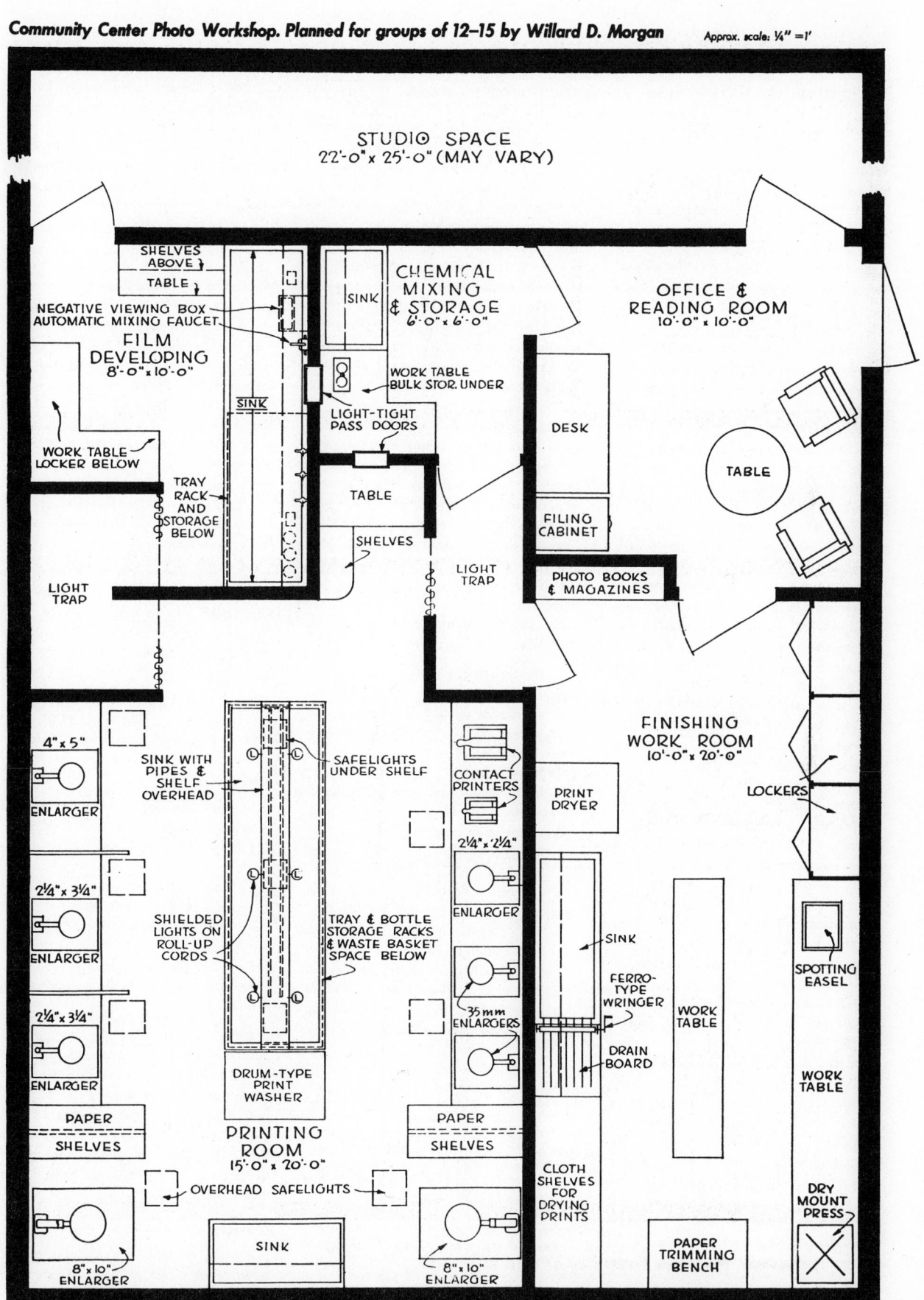

STUDIO SPACE
22'-0" x 25'-0" (MAY VARY)

SHELVES ABOVE
TABLE

NEGATIVE VIEWING BOX
AUTOMATIC MIXING FAUCET

CHEMICAL MIXING & STORAGE
6'-0" x 6'-0"

SINK

OFFICE & READING ROOM
10'-0" x 10'-0"

FILM DEVELOPING
8'-0" x 10'-0"

SINK

WORK TABLE BULK STOR. UNDER

LIGHT-TIGHT PASS DOORS

DESK

TABLE

WORK TABLE
LOCKER BELOW

TRAY RACK AND STORAGE BELOW

TABLE

SHELVES

FILING CABINET

LIGHT TRAP

LIGHT TRAP

PHOTO BOOKS & MAGAZINES

LIGHT TRAP

4" x 5"
ENLARGER

SINK WITH PIPES & SHELF OVERHEAD

SAFELIGHTS UNDER SHELF

CONTACT PRINTERS

FINISHING WORK ROOM
10'-0" x 20'-0"

LOCKERS

2¼" x 2¼"
ENLARGER

PRINT DRYER

2¼" x 3¼"
ENLARGER

SHIELDED LIGHTS ON ROLL-UP CORDS

TRAY & BOTTLE STORAGE RACKS & WASTE BASKET SPACE BELOW

SINK

FERRO-TYPE WRINGER

SPOTTING EASEL

2¼" x 3¼"
ENLARGER

35 mm
ENLARGERS

DRAIN BOARD

WORK TABLE

WORK TABLE

PAPER SHELVES

DRUM-TYPE PRINT WASHER

PRINTING ROOM
15'-0" x 20'-0"

PAPER SHELVES

CLOTH SHELVES FOR DRYING PRINTS

OVERHEAD SAFELIGHTS

DRY MOUNT PRESS

8" x 10"
ENLARGER

SINK

8" x 10"
ENLARGER

PAPER TRIMMING BENCH

NOTE - STRIP-TYPE CONVENIENCE OUTLETS, 1'-0" ABOVE TABLE LEVEL, CONTINUOUS AROUND ALL ROOMS.
SEPARATE FUSES FOR 8" x 10" ENLARGERS, PRINT DRYER AND DRY MOUNT PRESS.

HOUSING FOR THE AGED—1

By GLENN H. BEYER and ALEXANDER KIRA, *Housing Research Center, Cornell University*

BACKGROUND

In the next ten years, a greater proportion of houses, apartments, and institutional accommodations will be built for elderly persons than at any previous time in our history. There are several reasons for this. First is the well-known fact that the lifespan of mankind has increased through advances in medical science; thus the proportion of older people in the population has increased. Second, with the passing of the three-generation household, more elderly persons are living by themselves and therefore require separate housing accommodations. Third, increased social security benefits and private pension payments have enabled more aged people to pay for suitable accommodations. Finally, many nonprofit groups such as church, labor, and fraternal organizations, charitably supported groups, and tax-supported bodies are, and will continue to be, engaged in the provision of housing specifically for the elderly.

In 1959 there were approximately 15½ million persons in the United States over the age of 65; by 1975 it is expected that this number will increase to 20 million. Contrary to popular opinion, these people are not concentrated in a few states with year-round mild climates; the New England and Middle Western States have a higher percentage of aged than Florida and California.

Ordinary design criteria do not always apply to housing for the aged. One of the most striking differences is the high concentration of one- and two-person families as a result of children leaving home or the death of one spouse. Also important are the needs caused by physical deterioration in old age, which requires special design treatments and facilities.

In addition, certain basic psychological and sociological principles should be observed in planning for the elderly. People in this age group usually do not want to break their ties with family and neighborhood and be placed in a new and foreign environment. They need activities, not merely hobbies, and they want to participate in community functions. The objectives, programs, and physical facilities for the housing of the aged should encourage and support the continuance of earlier patterns of living, daily routines, personal care habits, social contacts, and recreational activities. An important objective is to maintain independent living as long as possible.

NEIGHBORHOOD AND SITE

A desirable neighborhood for the elderly should have many of the characteristics of any good neighborhood. It should be basically residential, possess the normal range of community facilities, have convenient public transportation, and be removed from particularly objectionable land uses. In terms of the individual aged person, the ideal neighborhood is often the one in which he has lived most of his life. The development of a broad program and the selection of a particular site should give consideration to old established neighborhoods where many of the aged are likely to be living and to have their roots.

From the point of view of the community itself, there are also many advantages in housing the aged in well-established neighborhoods, where there are more existing facilities and generally better public transportation. Another advantage, which is frequently overlooked, is the sympathy and help that are extended to the aged by friends and neighbors, young and old alike.

The selection of an actual site involves the following considerations:

1. The topography should be as level as possible to minimize the need for steep walks, ramps, or stairs. Relatively level sites encourage walking—a highly desirable exercise for the aged.

2. The site should not be bounded on all sides by major traffic arteries. It should be possible to go shopping or to the park without having to cross a major street.

3. Essential commercial facilities should be close at hand and easily accessible—supermarkets, cleaners, laundries, shoe repair shops, drug stores, and the like.

4. Basic community facilities such as churches, libraries, health services, and recreation facilities should also be close at hand. In this connection it should be noted that a half-mile is the maximum walking radius of many aged persons.[1]

---

[1] *Most aged persons place great emphasis on the proximity of essential services and facilities such as shops. In one study (Scottish Housing Advisory Committee, Housing of Special Groups, Edinburgh: H.M.S.O. 1952), approximately 90 per cent of the aged persons surveyed considered proximity to shops essential. The other facilities desired were, in order: churches, 65 per cent; parks, 50 per cent; social centers, 37 per cent; movies, 30 per cent; and active recreation areas, 25 per cent.*

5. Public transportation should be immediately available at the site, since many of the services that the aged require, such as specialized medical attention, will in all likelihood be located elsewhere. Transportation is also important for obtaining part-time work, for visiting distant relatives or friends, and generally for maintaining a spirit of self-sufficiency.

6. The site should not be immediately adjacent to a school building or a children's playground, or an active recreation area used by teenagers or adults.

7. The site should be large enough to permit the development of adequate outdoor areas for both active and passive recreation. Ideally, these areas would be in addition to, and out of the way of, those areas used by other residents, particularly children.

8. Consideration should also be given to possible changes in the over-all land use pattern, in terms of probable trends and projected plans.

These considerations must be taken into account whether the site is to accommodate solely aged persons or whether the aged represent only a portion of a larger "project" population.

DESIGN AND PLANNING PRINCIPLES

In very general terms the criteria for planning housing accommodations for the aged are:

1. Small size and compactness for convenience and economy

2. Fireproof construction planned for maximum safety

3. Minimizing of the problems and effort of housekeeping and daily activities

4. "Livability," pleasantness, and the effect of spaciousness

5. A high degree of privacy

6. Careful avoidance of an institutional look.

Other criteria affecting the different functional areas of the dwelling are discussed briefly in the following paragraphs. Many states have established official standards dealing with minimum areas, design features, etc., for housing for the aged (see Table 1). Before proceeding with specific designs, such local standards, if any, should be consulted.

Leisure areas

Because the aged are generally retired, a comfortable and pleasant living area is highly important. Particular pains should be taken in the design of these spaces because they are not only intensively used but also tend to be quite small. Some suggested state standards, for example, call for living areas of 80 to 90 sq ft for single-person occupancy. Interesting views and southern exposure should be provided if possible. Extra-wide window stools for plants, and built-in shelves and storage spaces are desirable. Privacy from the front door should be provided. If a dining area is included as a part of the living area it should permit location of the table by a window. A light and/or a convenience outlet should be easily accessible to the table.

Sleeping areas

A separate bedroom is necessary for two-person occupancy, but a sleeping alcove or a combined living-sleeping arrangement is often satisfactory for single persons. The separate bedroom should always be large enough to accommodate twin beds, and it is often desirable to be able to divide the room in two with a screen.

A combined living-sleeping arrangement is the most economical in terms of space but has the disadvantages of lack of privacy and a tendency to be untidy. The sleeping alcove is a generally satisfactory compromise, since it offers almost the same economy as the combined arrangement but without its drawbacks. The alcove should be large enough to accommodate all the essential items of any sleeping area—bed, night table, storage chest, closet, and chair—and it should be possible to close off this area from the living area if desired. There should always be an operable window in the alcove for light and ventilation.

Regardless of which arrangement is used, certain details should receive attention:

1. The space should permit placement of the bed with a minimum clearance of 18 in. on three sides, to facilitate bed-making and nursing. In the case of two-person occupancy, 3 ft is often recommended as the clear distance between beds. Some agencies recommend an allowance of at least 5 ft at one side of the bed for a wheelchair.

2. There should be space for an oversize bedside table to hold medicines, water, tissues, and the like, in large quantities.

3. The plan should permit placement of the bed so that a bedridden person can see out the window.

4. It is often desirable to provide a bell or buzzer near the bed so that a person can summon assistance.

5. In close proximity to the bed there should be a convenience outlet which is hooked up with a switch at the door or the entrance to the space. Thus a bed lamp could serve as the essential "night-light." Because of the two-way switching possible, this arrangement is preferable to the use of a single-switch ceiling or wall fixture.

6. There must be a short and direct access from the bed to the bathroom.

Bathrooms

For safety and convenience the proper location and arrangement of the bathroom is of utmost importance. Many of the difficulties and accidents which the aged experience occur in, or on the way to, the bathroom, particularly since the occasion of its use is often of an emergency nature, the person being either in a hurry, or dizzy and weak, or both.

Interior bathrooms are acceptable and may even be preferable from the point of view of privacy and absence of drafts. Of course ventilation must be provided. A minimum area of 35 to 40 sq ft is acceptable but, because of the possibility that crutches or wheelchairs may need to be accommodated, 50 to 60 sq ft is often recommended. It should be possible to unlock the door from the outside in an emergency. Since they are often used for support, all towel rods should be of metal or wood, securely mounted, and grab bars should be provided at the toilet and tub or shower. The toilet should be placed next to the tub (if a tub is used) so it can be used as a seat when filling the tub or simply for resting. Showers should have mixing controls, preferably thermostatic. A seat, either built-in or removable, is desirable for both tub and shower. Medicine cabinets should be extra large and preferably recessed. Projecting accessories near the lavatory should be avoided whenever possible.

Kitchen

Because kitchens are potentially as dangerous as bathrooms, equal care should be given to their layout and design. Although compactness is generally desired in accommodations for the aged, pullman-type kitchens are not recommended. Their extreme compactness results in awkwardness of use and dangerous reaches and stoops. A complete minimum kitchen of approximately 40 to 60 sq ft is preferable. An additional 20 to 40 sq ft are necessary if space for eating is to be provided. Interior locations are acceptable if mechanical ventilation is provided.

Equipment should be electric for greatest safety and should be arranged for maximum efficiency (see section on "Kitchens"). Ranges should be provided with front rather than back controls. Heating elements should visibly glow when hot. A wall oven set at waist height is desirable. Although refrigerators need not be larger than a 6 or 7-cu ft capacity, they should have a large freezing compartment and should be self-defrosting.

Storage spaces should be arranged as nearly as possible so that the bulk of the regular-use items can be stored between 27 and 63 in. from the floor. Ideally, stored items should be visible as well as physically accessible. Storage spaces over ranges and refrigerators should be avoided. Sliding cabinet doors are preferable to swinging doors.

Double sinks or sink-and-tray combinations should be provided to facilitate hand laundering. Consideration should be given to the provision of complete laundry facilities, particularly in projects. If full laundry facilities are not possible, at least drying racks should be provided.

General storage

Ample, lighted closets should be provided for clothes, linens, and miscellaneous

Table 1. Room areas for various types of housing accommodations

Data in this table have been compiled from various state regulations and recommendations.

No. of persons	No. of rooms	Types of rooms	Bedroom (B)	Living room (L)	Dining (D)	Kitchen (K)	Bath	Total Area
1	4	B,L,D,K	100	80–90	40	50	50	320–330
1	3	B,L–D,K	100–120	120–160		50	35–50	305–380
1	2	B–L,D–K	180			90	50	320
1	2	B–L,D–K		175–200		45–50	35–40	255–290
2	3	B,L,D–K	130–140	150	75–90		40–50	355–430
2	3	B,L–D,K	125–130	155–190		50	40–50	370–420

HOUSING FOR THE AGED

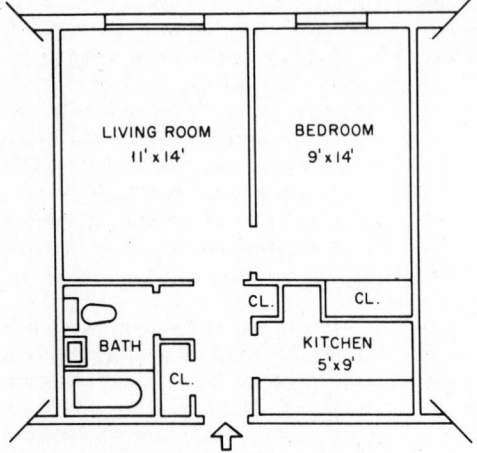

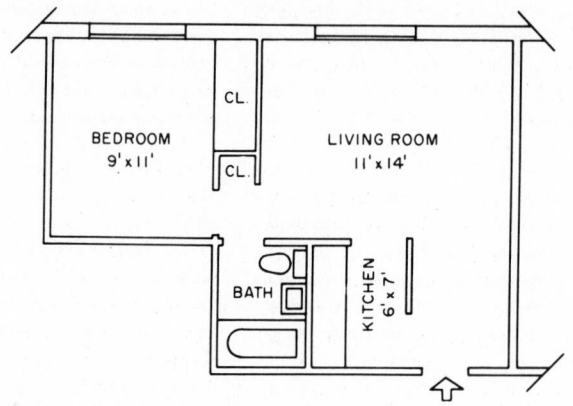

Fig. 1.   Typical plans   Scale: ⅛ in. = 1 ft

household items. Closets should either have sliding doors or be arranged for the use of curtains or screens. Provision must also be made for general storage of bulky items, such as trunks and furniture.

CONSTRUCTION, EQUIPMENT, AND FURNISHINGS

In designing housing for the aged special consideration must also be given

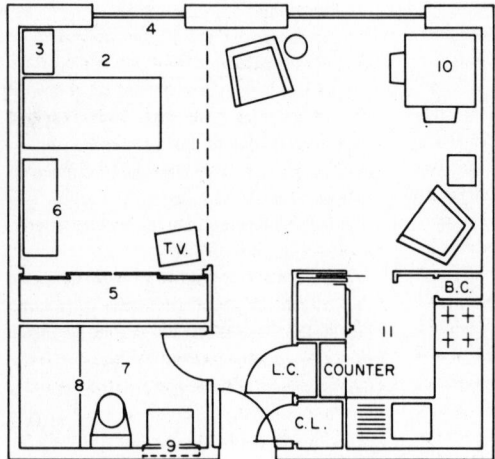

Fig. 2.   Living-sleeping arrangement (with sleeping alcove) for single-person occupancy   Scale: ⅛ in. = 1 ft

Key

1. Allowance should be made for a partition between sleeping alcove and living area.
2. A minimum clearance of 18 in. is necessary on three sides of bed.
3. An oversize bedside table is desirable.
4. A window in alcove is necessary for light, ventilation, and view from bed.
5. A closet with sliding doors is desirable.
6. Dresser.
7. An area of 50 to 60 sq ft is necessary if crutches or wheelchair are to be accommodated.
8. A toilet adjacent to tub is desirable to serve as seat.
9. Extra-large medicine cabinets.
10. The desirable location of dining table is at window; it also serves as desk and work table.
11. The kitchen should have an area of 40 to 60 sq ft; the pullman type is not recommended because of the dangerous reaches and stoops required.

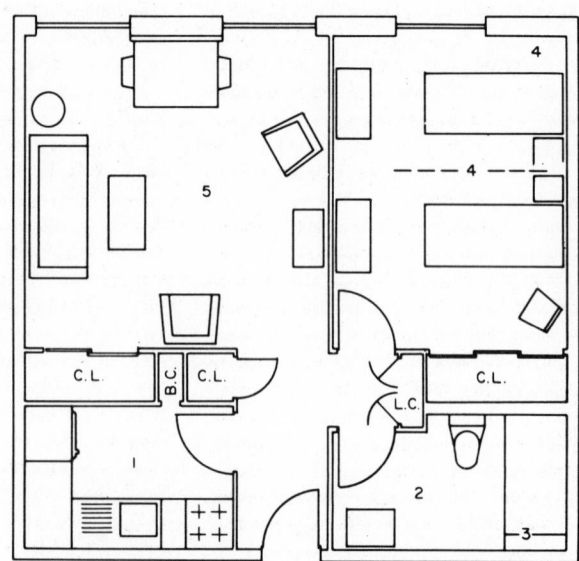

Fig. 3.   Separate bedroom arrangement for two-person occupancy

Scale: ⅛ in. = 1 ft

Key

1. A kitchen 40 to 60 sq ft is recommended. An additional 20 to 40 sq ft is necessary if eating space is to be provided here.
2. The bathroom requires a minimum of 40 sq ft; 50 to 60 sq ft is necessary if crutches or wheelchair are to be accommodated.
3. A built-in seat is desirable for use with tub.
4. A minimum clearance of 18 in. is necessary on three sides of bed (5 ft is necessary at one side if wheelchair is to be accommodated). Three feet between beds is recommended so that room can be divided by a screen.
5. Combined living and dining area of 155 to 190 sq ft is recommended.

to the selection of materials, hardware, and equipment. Just as a particular space arrangement can contribute materially to the comfort and safety of an elderly person, so can a particular material or item of equipment. Some criteria that should govern the selection of these items are presented below.

Floors

All floor surfaces should be nonslip, outside as well as inside the basic dwelling unit. In this connection, apparent slipperiness is as important, because of the psychological danger, as actual slipperiness. This is particularly pertinent to the design of lobbies and other public spaces which often have large expanses of glossy, although perhaps nonslip, surface. Suitable flooring materials include unglazed tile, cork, vinyl or vinyl-asbestos tile, unwaxed wood, and wall-to-wall carpeting. Throw rugs or deep-pile rugs are generally unsatisfactory because of the danger of tripping. Unwaxed wood floors are particularly satisfactory for the wheelchair user. Floors should be smooth and level, and particular care should be taken with highly jointed materials such as ceramic tile or brick or stone. Door thresholds and minor changes in floor level should be avoided whenever possible.

Doors and hardware

Door openings should be 3 ft wide to permit easy passage of wheelchairs, stretchers, and persons using crutches. Precautions should be taken to see that doors fit properly and do not stick. Large, easy-to-grasp door knobs or lever-type handles should be used. Revolving and double-acting doors and automatic door closers are particularly dangerous and should be avoided. In projects, outside doors should be master-keyed and all devices prohibited which cannot be operated from the outside. It is also desirable to provide peepholes or vision panels. Sliding doors conserve valuable space in small units and eliminate the danger of walking into half-open doors.

Windows

Whenever possible, windows should look out on an interesting view. Sill heights should be no more than 30 in. from the floor, to permit seeing out while comfortably seated. If lower sill heights are used, a guard rail must be provided at approximately chest height (42 to 48 in. from the floor). Window arrangements that produce a uniform distribution of light are preferable to a spotty placement of openings. All operable sash should be easy to reach and operate. Insect screens, weatherstripping, and storm sash should be pro-

vided for all windows, depending upon the location and climate.

A southerly orientation is most desirable, but provision should be made for shading devices. Roller shades should be avoided because of the danger involved in retrieving a released shade. Venetian blinds or draw-type draperies are preferable.

Lighting

Illumination levels should be approximately double those generally used in residential practice. Light sources should always be shielded. Ceiling-mounted fixtures are not recommended because of the dangers inherent in cleaning the fixtures and changing the bulbs. As indicated earlier, it is highly desirable to plan lighting layouts so that lights can always be switched on from a doorway. Switched outlets are particularly important in bedrooms or sleeping alcoves so that the elderly person need not stumble around in the dark when looking for the switch or after turning off the light. A night-light in a central location is often useful, as are luminous switch plates. Convenience outlets should never be located less than 18 in. above the floor (30 to 40 in. above the floor is preferable).

Heating

The aged generally require a higher temperature level than the standard; approximately 80°F. The heating system should be quick-acting and arranged to provide a uniform distribution of heat. If the aged are to be housed in structures with younger occupants, consideration should be given to the provision of separate temperature controls or supplementary heat sources. If steam or hot water systems are used, exposed radiators and risers should be avoided. Exposed radiators under operable windows are particularly hazardous. Although cold floors are to be avoided, radiant panel floors seem to be undesirable because they aggravate conditions of impaired blood circulation in the legs.

Sound control

While a certain degree of acoustical privacy is necessary in any building, it is perhaps more important in housing for the aged than in other residential work. There is a strong desire on the part of the aged to protect their privacy and to be assured of quiet during their rest periods and in the event of illness. Elderly occupants tend to be especially sensitive to the noise of children.

Communications and alarm systems

In any building devoted exclusively to housing the aged, an automatic fire alarm

system should be provided. Because of the difficulties many elderly persons experience in bedrooms and bathrooms, particularly at night, it is desirable to provide some form of signaling device whereby they can summon help. Usually the device sounds in a neighboring apartment or in a resident manager's or superintendent's suite. In buildings or projects devoted exclusively to the aged, it may also be desirable to provide a conveniently located public telephone booth, since many aged cannot afford a private telephone.

Vertical circulation

Whenever possible, accommodations for the aged should be on one level and located on the ground floor, unless elevators are used. In the case of low buildings where elevators are uneconomical, the aged should not be expected to climb more than one flight. For small unavoidable changes in level, ramps are preferable to stairs. Where stairs must be used, the following precautions should be observed:

1. Risers should not be more than 7 in. high.
2. The proper proportion of run to rise should be scrupulously observed.
3. Fewer than two risers should be avoided.
4. Winders or curved treads should never be used.
5. Nonslip nosings should be used and should be of a contrasting color.
6. Continuous handrails should be provided on both sides of the stairs.
7. Handrails should be of the proper height, of a cross section which is easily grasped, and sturdy in appearance as well as in fact.
8. Stairs should not be less than 3 ft 3 in. in clear width.
9. No doors should open directly onto the stairs.
10. Traffic should not cross the top or bottom of the stairs.
11. The stairs should be well lighted with shielded sources.

Some special considerations should also be observed with respect to elevators:

1. Self-operated elevators should be equipped with automatic doors.
2. A signaling device should be provided to summon assistance.
3. Continuous handrails should be provided, and if the car is sufficiently large, a small bench should be considered.
4. An automatic leveling device is necessary and should be inspected frequently.
5. If there is a possibility of use by a disabled person in a wheelchair, the control panel should be mounted low enough to be reached from a sitting position.

APARTMENTS—1
Building types

By HOWARD P. VERMILYA, AIA, and JOHN HANCOCK CALLENDER, *Professor of Architecture, Pratt Institute*

"Apartment," a term familiar to everyone, is surprisingly difficult to define. A "multiple dwelling," as defined by most building codes, is a building containing three or more dwelling units. But row houses, which are really attached single-family houses, are often used in garden-apartment developments. Even the dwelling units in a two-family house are often called apartments, especially if they are rented. The most workable definition of an apartment appears to be: any family dwelling unit other than a free-standing single-family house.

Apartments, like houses, are built to serve the needs of all kinds of people—rich and poor, old and young, small families and large families. Apartment units range in size from one to fifteen or more rooms. Apartment buildings may contain from two to a thousand or more units and may range in height from one to sixty stories. They may be built in the heart of the city, in outlying sections, or in the suburbs.

Apartments for low-income families are built by government agencies (public housing authorities), usually in large multi-building developments known as housing projects. Apartments for middle-income families are often built by private developers with some public assistance; these are also often referred to as housing projects. Apartments built without governmental assistance are never called "housing."

OWNERSHIP

Apartments are usually rented but they may be, and are with increasing frequency today, owned by the occupants. Under the *cooperative* system of ownership, the occupant of an apartment owns a share in the entire building or project. The share may be sold or the unit may be rented, but subject to certain limitations established to protect the value of the property. If there is a mortgage, it is a single one covering the entire property, which is subject to foreclosure in the event of default. Under the newer *condominium* system of ownership, the occupant of an apartment owns a share of the common facilities such as land, walls, and stairs, but owns his own apartment outright, with a separate deed or title in fee simple. The owner is free to sell or mortgage his apartment; if he defaults on the mortgage the foreclosure on his apartment does not involve the other owners.

UNIT TYPES

Apartment units are most often on one level (hence the term "flats") but may be on more than one. Two-story apartments (duplexes) are not uncommon and offer certain advantages. Three-story and split-level apartments are occasionally encountered.

BUILDING TYPES

There are three distinct apartment building types: row houses, walk-up apartments, and elevator apartments. Each has its advantages and limitations, but the determining factor in the use of any one type is likely to be density. Where land cost requires greater density than is practical for single family house development, for which the maximum is about six families per acre, the row house, whether built for sale or rental, is the logical choice. Where densities of more than 16 families per acre are required, walk-up apartments can be used, and for densities greater than 40, elevator apartments must be used.

Row houses or "town houses" give the apartment dweller the same intimate relationship to the ground which the house dweller enjoys. He can indulge in gardening and outdoor living, but he may also have to cut the grass and shovel snow off the walk. From the owner's point of view, row houses, having no public space indoors and little or none outdoors, have the great advantage of requiring a minimum of operating expense. Row houses vary in height from one to three stories and in width from 45 ft to 25 ft, depending upon the density required; widths of less than 25 ft are not recommended. When built for sale row houses usually include a garage or carport, and therefore must front on a street. Rental row-house developments usually provide separate garage or parking compounds and the houses front on landscaped courts (Fig. 1).

Walk-up apartments are generally limited to three stories in height except where a hillside site permits entering above the first floor. The typical plan has only two apartments per floor and each apartment has privacy and through ventilation. There are no public corridors since the only public space is the stair hall (Fig. 2). These six-family units may be joined end-to-end or in various offset arrangements (Fig. 3).

"Garden apartments" are popular in suburban areas. They consist of row houses or walk-up apartments, or often both, occupying less than 25 per cent of the site. Building design, site planning, and landscaping are usually informal and small in scale, in keeping with surrounding areas dominated by single-family houses.

Elevator apartments: Although six- and seven-story walk-up buildings were formerly built in this country and are still being built abroad, it is now generally agreed that in any apartment building of four

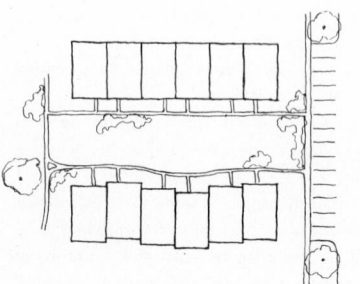

Fig. 1. Row-house-type apartments

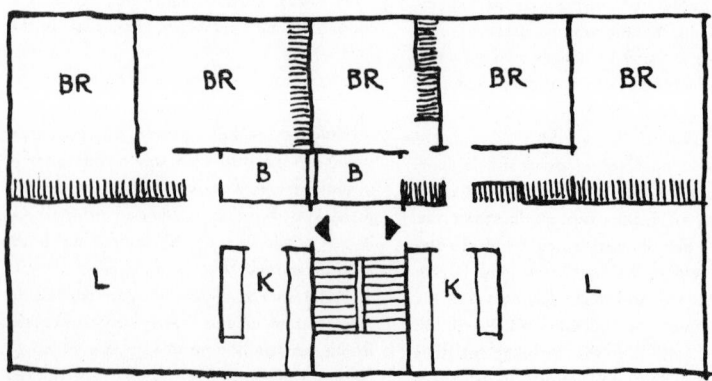

Fig. 2. Typical plan of walk-up apartment

2 apartments, 9 rooms per floor

stories or more an elevator is required. Buildings of seven or more stories require two elevators. An elevator is a very expensive piece of equipment and its use drastically affects the building plan. The elevator building can not afford to have only two apartments (8 to 10 rooms) per floor, as in walk-up buildings, but must spread the high cost of the elevators over many more units. Some buildings, where maximum economy was sought, have as many as 16 apartment (64 to 80 rooms) per floor. The practical minimum for elevator buildings is four apartments (16 to 20 rooms) per floor.

PLAN TYPES

Four apartments per floor results in a generally square plan, approximately 60 to 75 ft on a side, with a minimum of service space and perimeter wall (Fig. 4). Economies resulting from the compactness and high efficiency ratio of this scheme partially offset the high unit cost of the elevators and make the square plan practical for middle- and upper-income apartment buildings. Each apartment occupies one corner of the building and thus has cross ventilation, but not through ventilation.

More than four apartments per floor requires interior corridors, which prevent the through ventilation of apartments. Cross-shaped plans (Fig. 5) permit the maximum number of apartments per elevator and were therefore characteristic of early public housing projects. Plans of T and Y shape (Fig. 6) are compromises between the cross plan and the straight line or "slab" plan. The latter (Fig. 7) is the most commonly used plan today for both public and private developments. It usually has eight apartments (32 to 40 rooms) per floor but may have more.

Exterior corridors: Long interior corridors are disliked by tenants because of noise, depressing appearance, and the lack of through ventilation. They are disliked by the building owner because they are expensive to build and maintain. One solution to this problem is to put the corridor outdoors in the form of a balcony or gallery. This makes the corridor a pleasant place and permits every apartment to have through ventilation, but at the cost of some loss of privacy. Exterior corridors cost less to build than interior corridors and they do not have to be heated, although provision must be made for snow removal. Exterior corridors are single-loaded, of course, with the result that the building tends to become very long and narrow (Fig. 8); in high-rise buildings special wind bracing may be necessary.

Skip-stop: Since people will walk up two

floors in a walk-up apartment building, it is not unreasonable to expect them to do the same in an elevator building. This would permit the use of the standard walk-up plan (Fig. 2) with its advantages of privacy and through ventilation. In the scheme shown in Fig. 9 no one would have to walk up more than one floor or down two floors. The scheme shown in Fig. 10 eliminates the public stair hall by putting the stairs within the apartments; this also eliminates the need for fireproof stair construction. Although the skip-stop scheme results in certain economies, its principal advantage is the better planning made possible on the intermediate floors. Skip-stop may be combined with exterior corridor, thereby providing full privacy and unimpeded view to the apartments on the intermediate floors, as well as through ventilation for all apartments (Figs. 9 and 10).

"Maisonettes": Ground-floor apartments in elevator buildings are sometimes provided with direct entrances from the outside. These apartments are often rented as professional offices, but they are also popular as dwelling units. For the latter purpose duplex units are usually employed and they are sometimes called "maisonettes."

Balconies and terraces, long popular in European apartment buildings, are now generally provided, even in low-rent buildings. Many new buildings have a balcony or terrace for every apartment.

Air conditioning is now generally provided in most parts of the country in all but the lowest-priced apartments. Self-contained through-the-wall units are the usual method, but high-quality buildings often provide air-conditioning from a central plant (see section on "Heating, Ventilating, and Air Conditioning"). The introduction of air conditioning greatly reduces the disadvantage of the interior corridor plan with its lack of through ventilation.

Parking: Provision for on-site parking is now required by most building and/or zoning codes. In urban areas one parking space for each two to four apartments may be required; this is usually by necessity located in the basement of the apartment building. In suburban areas one parking space for each apartment is usually required and more is often provided; suburban parking space is usually on grade and uncovered.

Subsidiary facilities: Even a small apartment development ordinarily provides walks, drives, landscaping, parking space, tenant storage, laundry room, superintendent's office and shop, and space for mechanical equipment. Large projects may also provide playgrounds, wading pools,

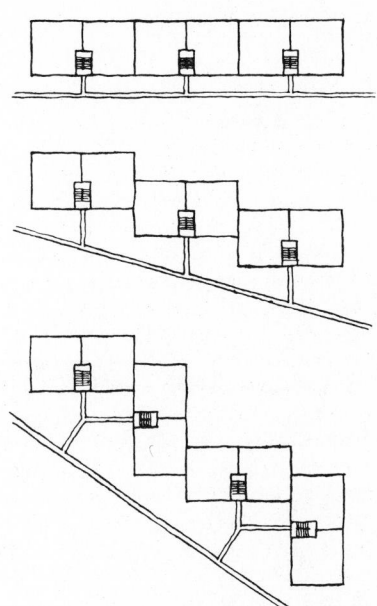

Fig. 3. Walk-up apartment buildings combined in various ways

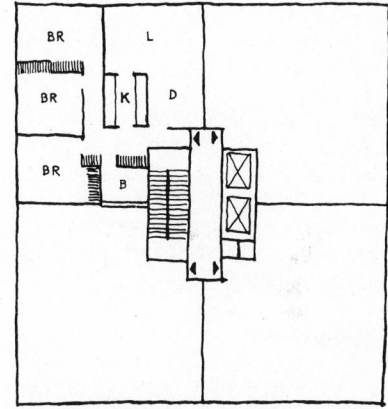

Fig. 4. Square- or tower-type elevator apartment building
4 apartments, 22 rooms per floor

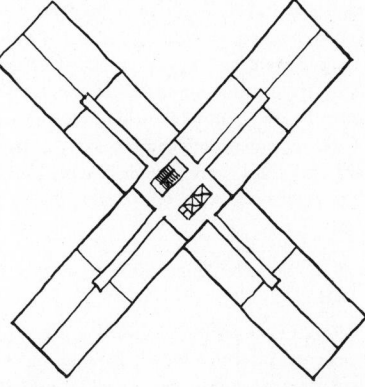

Fig. 5. Cross-type elevator apartment building
16 apartments, 76 rooms per floor

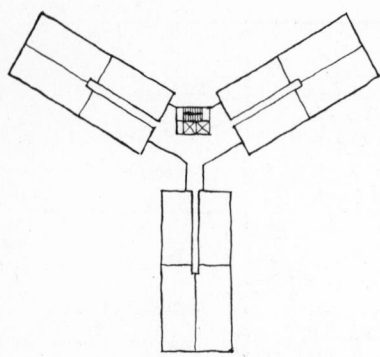

Fig. 6. Y-type elevator apartment building
12 apartments, 56 rooms per floor

Fig. 7. Straight-line or slab-type elevator apartment building
9 apartments, 43 rooms per floor

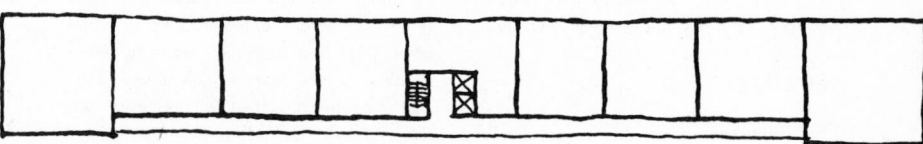

Fig. 8. Exterior corridor type elevator apartment building
9 apartments, 43 rooms per floor

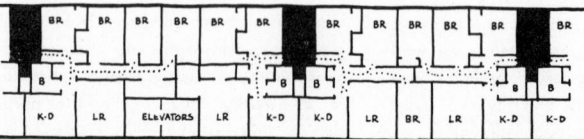

Non-corridor floor (2, 3, 4, 6, 7, 8, 10)

Corridor floor (5, 9)

Fig. 9. Skip-stop scheme with public stairs

Section

tennis courts, swimming pools, parking for bicycles and perambulators, community rooms, hobby shops, day nurseries, canteens, management offices, maintenance shops, and boiler room. Diagrammatic layout for the maintenance space for a large project is shown in Fig. 11.

REGULATIONS

The design of apartment buildings is beset with more than its share of regulations. Besides the local zoning laws and building code there are often special laws covering multiple dwellings. If FHA (Federal Housing Administration) financing is sought, the design must conform to FHA regulations. For public housing or publicly assisted private housing there are regulations issued by the PHA (Public Housing Administration) and often by state and local housing authorities. These regulations affect site coverage, density, height, setbacks, yards, courts, parking, room sizes, room counts, window sizes, etc.

Site development requirements by FHA and PHA

FHA requirements on coverage, density, yards, courts, and distance between buildings are given in Table 1. PHA requirements for building spacing are given in Table 2. PHA has no specific requirements on coverage or density.

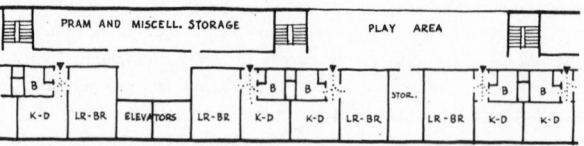

Intermediate floor   **Corridor floor**

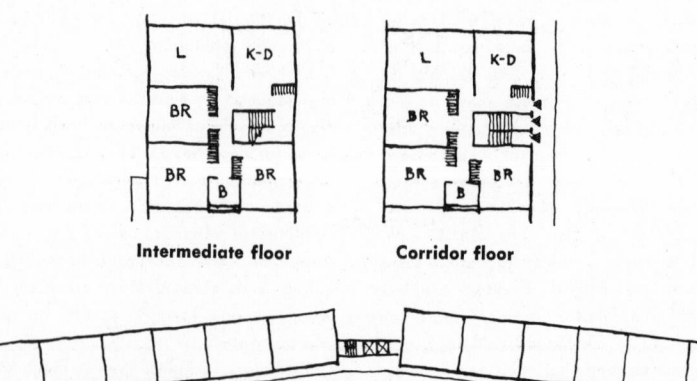

Fig. 10. Skip-stop scheme with private stairs

12 apartments, 62 rooms per floor

**Borgia Butler Houses, New York City
Joseph and Vladeck, Architects**

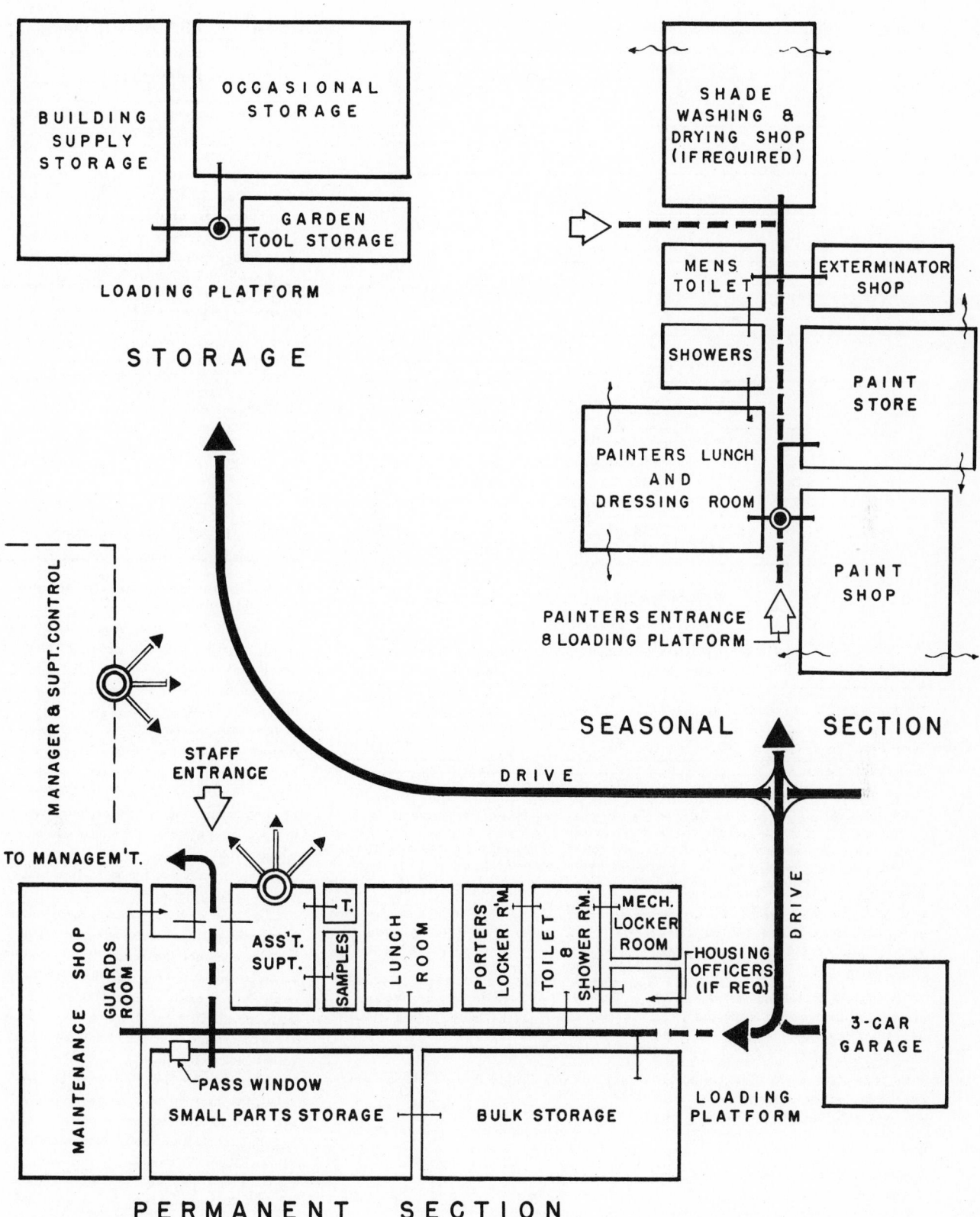

Fig. 11.   Maintenance facilities for a large housing project

*Courtesy New York City Housing
Authority*

Table 1. FHA site requirements[1]

Area[2]	Maximum coverage[3]		Maximum density[3]	
	Per cent of plot area		No. DU's per acre	
	interior	corner[4]	interior	corner[4]
Type A	35	45	40	50
Type B	25	25	25	25

Minimum yard requirements

Area	Front, ft[5]	Rear, ft	Other	No. openings	Side yards, ft[6]				Other
					More 25%		Less 25%		
					LR	BR	LR	BR	
Type A[7]	70	20	15	0	18	9	9	6	6
Type B[8]	70	20	15	0	20	12	12	9	9

Outer courts[9]

Area	Minimum width[10], ft					Maximum depth[11], ft
	When required ventilation from windows in opposing walls is				Other	
	LR	BR	LR	BR		
	25% or more		Less than 25%			
Type A[12]	36	18	18	12	12	1½ x width
Type B[13]	40	24	24	18	18	1½ x width

Distance between buildings[14]

Area	Minimum distance, ft			
	When required ventilation from windows facing open space is			
	25% or more		Less than 25%	
	LR	BR	LR	Other conditions
Type A[15]	36	18	18	12
Type B[16]	40	24	24	18

[1] *Minimum Property Requirements for Three or More Living Units, March, 1961.*
[2] *Type A Area—general land use is high-density residential in excess of 25 units per acre. Type B area—residential land use suitable for medium or low density use such as one and two family detached or row houses or two-story apartments.*
[3] *Applies only to structures three stories or under in height. In Type A areas where existing use warrants, coverage or density may be increased subject to administrative approval.*
[4] *Corner plot is that portion of plot not exceeding 22,500 sq ft in area for each corner adjacent to two intersecting streets; balance of plot is interior. Land area is entire plot including private streets, drives, parking and play areas but excluding public areas and areas to be dedicated to public use.*
[5] *Distance from building face to building line on opposite side of street. For buildings facing one or more streets, each such face shall be considered as front and the others as side yards except that where a building faces one street only the face opposite the street frontage shall be the rear.*
[6] *Where windows in wall provide required ventilation or percentage of required ventilation.*
[7] *Increase widths to provide adequate light and ventilation when opposing structure exceeds three stories.*
[8] *Does not apply to structures over three stories in height.*
[9] *When windows occur only in the wall facing open end, the depth requirement only, applies.*
[10] *Outer court is formed by three walls or two walls and property line. In latter case minimum required width is reduced by one half.*
[11] *Depth shall not exceed three times the width when one side is a property line.*
[12] *Increase widths to provide adequate light and ventilation when structures exceed three stories in height. Inner courts—minimum width 50 ft.*
[13] *Inner courts are not permitted in Type B Areas. Widths shown do not apply to structures exceeding three stories in height.*
[14] *When overlap does not exceed 15 ft*
　(a) *no windows overlapping walls—not less than 9 ft*
　(b) *windows of habitable rooms in one wall only—two-thirds distance established above but not less than 12 ft.*
[15] *Increase distances to assure adequate light and ventilation when structures exceed three stories in height.*
[16] *Does not apply to structures exceeding three stories or more in height.*

Table 2. PHA requirements on distances between buildings

1. Distance between parallel walls—one story 50 ft plus 5 ft for each additional story.
2. Distance between end walls—one and two story 25 ft plus 5 ft for each additional story above two stories.
3. Distance between walls of dwelling buildings only and property lines (not street rights of way) ½ distance in 1 and 2.

* Standards for planning and design of PHA-aided low-rent housing, January, 1961. The regulations cited above are not complete and exceptions are permitted under special conditions. They are given as an indication of minimum acceptable practice and of some of the factors to be given consideration when siting structures.

Additional regulations pertaining to site development are summarized below:

Walking distance to dwelling entrance from street or driveway or parking area—less than 100 ft desirable, maximum 250 ft (FHA); maximum 200 ft measured along paved walk (PHA).

Walks—width 6 ft for main walks, 4 ft for secondary walks and 3 ft for minor service walks (FHA). Single riser grade changes not permitted (PHA). Grades may be as steep as 10 per cent with handrail (PHA); maximum 5 per cent (FHA). Stepped ramps designed for ordinary walking habits with maximum 6-in. risers permitted (FHA).

Driveway width—minimum 18 ft in addition to parking space (FHA).

Closed-end driveways must provide turning space—80 ft diameter minimum (FHA).

Garage or parking spaces (FHA)—Type A areas minimum—one car for each two units; Type B areas minimum—one car for each unit.

Parking areas must be 25 ft minimum from buildings (PHA).

Access to each building must be provided for fire fighting, refuse collection, and snow removal equipment (PHA).

Children's (pre-school) playgrounds—FHA—2,500 sq ft equipped areas per 100 dwelling units. PHA—10 sq ft per bedroom in minimum areas of 1,000 sq ft each dispersed within site area unless related to a community building with nursery or day-care facilities.

Laundry drying areas, when provided—2,500 sq ft per 100 units for rotated use (FHA).

Exit requirements by FHA and NFPA

One- and two-story row structures: These usually provide a front and rear entrance (exit) at grade to each family living unit, although only one exit is required. The private stair in the two-story row structure is not considered a stair under the exit requirement, but it is considered when measuring the travel distance within living units from any room to the exit. This distance is limited to 50 ft by the Building Exits Code of the NFPA (National Fire Protection Association). The FHA limits the number of units between fire walls (2-hr fire resistance) to not more than eight.

Multistory apartments four or more stories in height, are usually served by elevators which are not considered exits, however, by fire protection authorities. Two enclosed exit stairways are usually a minimum requirement, arranged so as to be remote from each other. According to NFPA requirements, one exit must be not more than 100 ft (150 ft if sprinklered) from the entrance to an apartment, with not more than 20 ft of corridor (dead-end) travel distance being common to the travel to either exit. FHA permits a dead-end corridor to be 30 ft long.

The Building Exits Code of NFPA will permit one exit only in buildings of fire-resistive construction of any height with not more than two living units per floor, with a smokeproof tower or an outside stairway as the exit, immediately accessible to all apartments served thereby.

Public stairway widths are usually established at a minimum of 3 ft which must be increased in width when the floor next above accommodates more than a given number of persons. Widths are based on an aggregate width of 22 in. for each 30 persons or fraction thereof occupying the floor next above. FHA measures the occupants on the basis of 1¾ persons per bedroom while NFPA measures on the basis of one person for each 125 sq ft.

Elevators are essentially a service facility and should be designed to meet the requirements of the apartment. These will vary with the height, the number of apartments per floor and the income level of the occupants. Different travel speeds (feet per minute) may be selected and several cab sizes (usually expressed in weight) are available (see section on "Elevators").

The PHA has established guides to aid in the selection of elevators for low-rent projects (Bulletin No. LR-10, 1956). These are confined to two cab sizes: 1,200 lb capacity with a speed of 100 ft per min and 2,000 lb capacity with speeds of 100, 200, or 300 ft per min (Table 3).

Walk-up apartments—two story:

	One exit	
	FHA	NFPA
Stairway	¾-hr fire resistance	Enclosed—1-hr fire resistance
Travel to stairway		20 ft
Corridors	¾-hr fire resistance	Fire-resistant construction
No. of units total both floors	10 units	16 families / 12 families if combustible
Maximum floor area	4,500 sq ft per floor if combustible	4,000 sq ft per floor if combustible
First floor construction over basement	2 hr	2-hr fire resistance not over 8 ft 6 in. above grade

NOTE: NFPA also permits one exit direct to street or yard at grade by outside stair, or 1-hr fire-resistant enclosed stair serving that unit only and not communicating with basement.

Walk-up apartments—three story:

	FHA	
	1 exit	2 exits
Stairway } flame spread, 0–25 Corridors }	Enclosed	2 hr incombustible ¾ hr[1]
Travel to stair		2
No. of units total	12	12
Construction		2-hr fire resistance (exterior walls)
First floor construction		1 hr (incombustible)[3]

	NFPA	
	1 exit	2 exits (enclosed)
Stairway	Smokeproof tower or outside stair	1-hr fire resistance
Corridors	No limitation	Finish—flame spread less than 75[4]
Travel to stair	No limitation	100 ft[5] (150 ft sprinklered)
No. of units total	2 per floor	No limitation
Construction	Fire resistant	No limitation
First floor construction	Fire resistant	No limitation

[1] *When separated from stairway by Class C (Underwriters Laboratories) door; otherwise considered as part of stairway, requiring 2-hr fire resistance (incombustible) with Class C self-closing doors for each family unit entrance.*

[2] *Limitations of the number of units serves as an effective limitation on length of corridors or public hallways.*

[3] *Penetration of first floor construction permitted for 1 stairway where 2 exits are provided for access to basement units, laundry rooms or storage rooms only when their openings are protected by Underwriters Class C doors.*

[4] *Method of Test Surface Burning Characteristics of Building Materials (tunnel test), NFPA No. 255.*

[5] *Not over 20 ft of travel distance may be in dead-end corridor.*

The speed selection will be influenced by, among other factors, the number of stories:

Building height	Satisfactory speed
Stories	Feet per minute
5 or 6	100
7 or 8	100 or 200
9 or 10	100, 200, or 300
11 to 14	200 or 300
15 to 18	300

Other factors would be the capacity of the cab, 40 per cent more for the 2,000 lb than the 1,200 lb, as well as the door size, 2 ft 8 in., of the smaller cab which limits furniture sizes that can be carried.

The passenger-carrying capacity of an elevator system is expressed as that percentage of the building population which can be carried one way in a given period —usually 5 minutes. For low-rent projects, PHA considers 5 per cent adequate.

Table 3. Comparative elevator data[1]

Item	1,200-lb Capacity 100 fpm[2]	2,000-lb Capacity 100 fpm[2]	2,000-lb Capacity 200 fpm	2,000-lb Capacity 300 fpm
Clear shaft opening[3]	6'4" x 5'3"	7'8" x 5'8"		
Platform size[3]	5'0" x 4'0"	6'4" x 4'5"		
Shaft door—clear opening[3]	2'8" x 7'0"	3'0" x 7'0"[3]		
Number of local floors to be served [4], [5]	10[2]	10[2]	14	18
Maximum persons who can be carried each trip	8	13	13	13
Persons carried per trip (normal peak)[6]	6	10	10	10

[1] *This is a compilation of data contained in a "Buyers Guide" booklet prepared by an elevator manufacturer.*

[2] *While the table indicates that a 100-fpm elevator can serve up to ten floors, most elevator manufacturers do not usually recommend the installation of a single elevator for a building greater than eight stories high, regardless of the number of persons to be served; therefore, two elevators will normally be required for a building more than eight stories high if 100-fpm elevators are selected.*

[3] *These dimensions are standard with the elevator industry. The shaft door clear openings assume swing-type doors for 1,200-lb capacity elevators and sliding-type doors for 2,000-lb capacity elevators; when swing doors are desired for 2,000-lb capacity elevators the shaft door clear opening can be reduced to 2'10" by 7'0".*

[4] *Maximum adjustments, based on information furnished by an elevator manufacturer with respect to 2,000-lb 100-fpm elevator. Similar adjustments made for other elevators by PHA engineer.*

[5] *When elevators are designed to stop at the basement level, the basement should be included as a local floor to be served.*

[6] *Assumes 80 per cent of maximum number of persons who can be carried.*

(Where better service is required, a higher percentage may be necessary.) To determine the number of elevators required, the PHA has developed a table (Table 4) showing the number of persons who can be served adequately by a single elevator of given capacity and speed in buildings of various heights.

Room count

A convention used to describe the number of rooms in a living unit has, because of room-cost limitations contained in legislation affecting the PHA and FHA programs, become highly significant in planning apartments. The use of combination rooms that combine several functions such as cooking and eating, living and eating, or living and sleeping, and the introduction of features such as foyers, balconies, or second baths, has required a modification of the traditional room count (See Tables 5–7).

Room sizes

The room sizes shown in the tables of FHA and PHA, are minimum sizes. Size alone is not a criterion of the adequacy of the room for its function, however. FHA specifies minimum widths of rooms and, in the case of bathrooms, minimum fixtures, and PHA specifies minimum furniture size requirements and equipment

where pertinent. The amount of wall space, the location of windows and doors, the shape and the circulation within the room, all tend to influence the effectiveness of the room area and much more so when approaching these minimum sizes, which are applicable only in low-income projects. For other types of projects, one architect with considerable experience in this field uses the following average room sizes:

	Room sizes (sq ft)	
	Medium income	High income
Living room	222	294
Dining room	90	132
Dining alcove	80	110
Kitchen	67.5	88
Bedroom (master)	130	195
Other bedrooms	100–110	132–168
Balcony	72	90

PLANNING

Corridors and other public areas should be kept to a minimum because they increase costs of construction and maintenance. Large public lobbies may be justified in high-rise luxury apartments. Long interior corridors eliminate the possibility

of through ventilation. Exterior corridors should have only service areas opening on them and windows should be high for privacy. PHA specifies a maximum width of 5 ft for these galleries and will not permit required bedroom windows to open on them. PHA also requires that buildings served by exterior corridors must be not less than 34 ft thick.

Entrances to apartments should be located so as to avoid the use of the living room as a passage to other rooms. Entrance foyers, giving access to all rooms, are recommended. When passage through the living room is unavoidable, it should be designed so as not to interfere with good furniture groupings.

Kitchens in apartments tend to be too compact. Adequate counter-top workspace is essential. FHA requires a minimum of 8 sq ft of counter-top and 48 sq ft of wall shelf space for one- and two-bedroom apartments and 54 sq ft for three-bedroom or larger apartments. Dishwashers and laundry washing and drying equipment, the latter permitting the omission of central laundries and drying areas, are becoming standard items in many apartments. Open planning of kitchens is often employed to give a greater sense of space; with adequate mechanical ventilation open, as well as inside, kitchens are practical and permit more attractive living areas with larger expanses of outside wall.

Storage is essential both within the unit and in centralized areas. Clothes closets with full width and ceiling high openings provide greater utilization but should be supplemented by other general storage closets. PHA requirements for closet and storage space are given in Table 8. Space should also be provided at grade level for baby carriages, bicycles, and wheel toys. PHA requires from 10 to 15 sq ft per apartment for this purpose. Often storage is combined with individual garages, in which case storage area should be enclosed and lockable.

Baths are often used as dressing rooms, in which case they should be larger than the minimum. At least one bath should be accessible from the living area without passing through another room. With adequate mechanical ventilation they may be placed on the inside of the building, which is generally to the advantage of the over-all plan and the economy of the plumbing installation.

Through ventilation of the entire apartment is desirable. Cross (corner) ventilation of individual rooms is satisfactory, but cross ventilation of entire apartments is not very successful. Air conditioning may ameliorate inadequate ventilation. Mechani-

Table 4. Total number of persons who can be served by one elevator of a given capacity and speed[1]

No. of stories		Total number of persons[2]								
		Floor-to-floor stops[3]				Alternate-floor stops[4]				
		1,200 lb	2,000 lb				1,200 lb	2,000 lb		
	No. of stops	100 fpm	100 fpm	200 fpm	300 fpm	No. of stops	100 fpm	100 fpm	200 fpm	300 fpm
5	5	461	618	—	—	3	—	—	—	—
						3	480	715	—	—
6	6	391	521	—	—	3	—	—	—	—
						4	420	595	—	—
7	7	336	465	500	—	4	—	—	—	—
						4	375	550	566	—
8	8	313	431	465	—	4	375	550	566	—
						5	339	495	535	—
9	9	295	408	431	465	5	339	495	535	—
						5	302	434	504	545
10	10	281	387	408	431	5	302	434	504	545
						6	274	397	468	521
11	11	—	—	387	419	6	—	—	468	521
						6	—	—	444	483
12	12	—	—	368	402	6	—	—	444	483
						7	—	—	419	468
13	13	—	—	350	387	7	—	—	419	468
						7	—	—	400	447
14	14	—	—	335	375	7	—	—	400	447
						8	—	—	379	428
15	15	—	—	—	363	8	—	—	—	428
						8	—	—	—	413
16	16	—	—	—	350	8	—	—	—	413
						9	—	—	—	397

[1] *In using this table to determine the number of elevators required, the local authority should exclude persons occupying the bottom terminal-stop floor from its count of building occupants who will require service.*
[2] *Where a dash, instead of a number, appears in any box it means that installation of an elevator of that capacity or speed is not recommended for the particular number of stories.*
[3] *"Floor-to-Floor Stops" assumes a single elevator stopping at every floor.*
[4] *"Alternate-Floor Stops" assumes two elevators, each stopping at alternate floors, except that one elevator is assumed for five-, six-, and seven-story buildings. The top number in each box relates to the alternate-stop elevator whose top terminal stop is the floor below the top floor; the bottom number in each box relates to the alternate-stop elevator which includes the top floor among its stops.*

cal ventilation of inside kitchens and baths is required and is desirable even for outside kitchens.

Noise is a troublesome problem. Street noises should be screened by planting or set-backs. Partitions between units should reduce sound transmission to the degree necessary for comfort; PHA requires a reduction of 45 decibels; FHA requires 50 or more. Floors should be constructed to reduce both air-borne and impact sounds. Noise sources in mechanical equipment, elevators, and heating, ventilating, and plumbing systems require isolation. (See section on "Acoustics.")

Adequate wiring particularly in kitchens to care for portable equipment is essential. Both capacity and number of outlets need study. An intercommunication system between each apartment and the building entrance is required in all but the smallest buildings. This is often combined with a buzzer-type door release for buildings which do not have a doorman on duty at all times. Telephone conduit and master television antenna systems are usually advisable.

Laundry: Common laundry facilities within the apartment building are required by PHA and are commonly provided in large apartment buildings of all rental classes. PHA requires one double laundry tray per 10 families in a space of 20 sq ft per family for clothesline drying. Generally coin-operated automatic washers and dryers are installed and in that case PHA requires a minimum of one machine per 17 families in a space of 2 to 3 sq ft per family.

Recreational facilities: The Play School Association recommends the following for middle-income cooperative projects:

Indoor—minimum facilities: community room, 1,000 sq ft on ground floor, with soundproof folding partition and 3 closets, lavatories and toilets for men and women, complete kitchen, and office of 250 sq ft. For projects of 100 to 300 families, add a recreation room of 450 sq ft, with sink and storage. For projects of 300 to 500 families, add to the minimum facilities a recreation room of 750 sq ft, with sink and storage. For projects of 500 to 1,000 families, add to the minimum facilities 2 recreation rooms of 450 sq ft each, with sinks and storage. (PHA requires a *maximum* of 4.5 sq ft per family for indoor community facilities.)

Outdoor—separate areas for nursery, school-age, and adult groups, preferably adjacent to and extensions of the indoor recreational space, minimum size 3,000 sq ft plus 30 sq ft per family over 100 families. (PHA requires for school-age and

Table 5. Allowable room count and minimum room sizes for separate rooms (FHA)

Name of space[1]	Room count	LU with 0-BR[1] Minimum area, sq ft	LU with 1-BR Minimum area, sq ft	LU with 2-BR Minimum area, sq ft	LU with 3-BR Minimum area, sq ft	LU with 4-BR Minimum area, sq ft	Least dimension
LR	1	—	160	160	170	180	12'0"
DR or DA[2]	1	—	100	100	110	120	8'4"
K[3]	1	—	60	60	70	80	5'4"
K'ette[4]	½	40	40	—	—	—	3'6"
BR, primary[5]	1	—	120	120	120	120	9'4"[5]
Total area, BR's	1	—	120	200	280	380	—
OHR	1	—	80	80	80	80	8'0"
Bathroom[6]	½	—	—	—	—	—	—
Half-bathroom[6]	¼	—	—	—	—	—	—
Foyer[7]	¼	25	25	25	25	25	4'0"
Balcony or porch[8]	¼	70	70	70	70	70	6'0"
Terrace[8, 9]	¼	120	120	120	120	120	8'0"

[1] Abbreviations used in this table:

LU—Living Unit   DA—Dining Area   BR—Bedroom
LR—Living Room   K—Kitchen   OHR—Other Habitable Room
DR—Dining Room   K'ette—Kitchenette   O-BR—LU with no separate Bedroom

[2] Room count for Dining Area shall be counted in only one location of a living unit.

[3] O-BR Units having a full-size Kitchen, a maximum of ½ room count will be given.

[4] Kitchenettes less than 40 sq ft are acceptable in O-BR living units, but receive no room count. Minimum length of kitchen equipment and cabinets to receive ½ room count is 7½ linear ft.

[5] Primary bedrooms shall have at least one uninterrupted wall space at least 10 ft 0 in.

[6] Room count credit for additional Bathrooms or Half-bathrooms is permissible only in Living Units of 1-BR and larger in size, but not for Units having no separate Bedroom. A Half-bathroom is defined as a room containing a water closet and lavatory but not including bathing facilities.

[7] A Foyer is defined as an entrance space to a living unit, enclosed by at least two floor-to-ceiling partitions in addition to that containing the entrance doorway, and having a coat closet opening directly on the space. An entrance space not complying with these criteria is permitted but shall receive no room count.

[8] Room count credit will be given for only one Balcony, Porch or Terrace for each living unit. A Balcony, Porch or Terrace not complying with criteria in this Schedule although permitted, shall receive no room count.

[9] For room count credit, a ground level terrace shall have a paved area of at least 120 sq ft, adjoin the living unit, and shall be visually screened from adjacent living units by permanent materials.

Table 6. Allowable room count and minimum room sizes for combined spaces (FHA)

Combined space[1,2]	Combined room count	LU with 0-BR Minimum area, sq ft	LU with 1-BR Minimum area, sq ft	LU with 2-BR Minimum area, sq ft	LU with 3-BR Minimum area, sq ft	LU with 4-BR Minimum area, sq ft
LR-DA[3]	1½	—	200	200	220	230
LR-DA (DR size)[3, 4]	2	—	240	240	260	270
LR-DA-BR[3, 4]	2	240	—	—	—	—
LR-DA-K[3]	2½	—	260	270	290	310
LR-BR[5]	1	190	—	—	—	—
K-DA[2]	1½	100	110	110	120	140
K-DA (DR size)[2]	2	—	150	150	160	180
K'ette-DA	1	80	80	—	—	—

[1] See Note ([1]) Table 5 for abbreviations of Rooms and Combined Spaces.

[2] For two adjacent spaces to be considered a combined space, the clear horizontal opening between spaces shall be at least 8 ft wide, except for least dimension of K-DA. For 1½ room count of K-DA, least dimension 6 ft, clear opening 4 ft minimum; for 2 room count—least dimension 10 ft, clear opening 10 ft minimum, and shall meet natural light and ventilation requirements.

[3] A combined LR-DA shall provide for undisturbed use of both living and dining furniture and shall meet light and ventilation requirements.

[4] For a room count credit of 2, a combined LR-DA or LR-DA-BR shall have a clear dimension of not less than 16 ft, measured parallel to the exterior wall. Otherwise, the credit will be 1½ count.

[5] O-BR Unit shall include (a) Entrance through Foyer from public space to living room; (b) Dressing Room having space for chest of drawers and its use, adequate circulation for simple storage with closet including clothes rod and shelf space of 6 linear ft; (c) access to Bathroom from either Dressing Room or Foyer.

Table 7. Minimum room and other space sizes (PHA)

No. bedrooms	Room count[1]	Living room	Kitchen and dining space sq ft	1st BR sq ft	2nd BR sq ft	3rd BR sq ft	4th BR sq ft	5th BR sq ft
Alcove	3							
1	3½	145	70*	125				
2	4½	155	90*	125	100			
3	5½	160	110*	125	100	90		
4	6½	165	130*	125	100	100	90	
5	7½	170	150*	125	100	100	90	90

Plus 6 sq ft when space for washing machine is planned in kitchen.

[1] *Room count for living, dining and kitchen is 2½, each bedroom is 1, bed alcove is ½.*

NOTES: The minimum size for a three-fixture bathroom shall be 35 sq ft.

If living room instead of kitchen is planned for dining, use this table for minimum sizes of living room and kitchen:

No. Bedrooms	LR and DA combined	Kitchen
1	170	50*
2	185	60*
3	205	75*
4	220	90*
5	230	100*

Plus 6 sq ft when space for washing machine is planned in kitchen.

The room areas given above are net areas inside room walls, exclusive of closets or offset entrances.

Where room heaters are used in living rooms, add 15 sq ft for the space occupied by the heater.

Minimum width of living room 10'6"; of first bedroom 8'6".

Table 8. Minimum closet and storage space sizes (PHA)

Bedroom closets: for first bedroom, 10 sq ft; other bedrooms, 8 sq ft

Coat closets: for one-bedroom units 4 sq ft and 2 sq ft additional per bedroom for larger units

Linen closets: for one-bedroom units 4 sq ft and 1 sq ft additional per bedroom for larger units

NOTE: The closets shall be proportioned and designed to obtain maximum efficiency in use of the space.

General storage space: for one-bedroom units 25 sq ft plus 5 sq ft additional per bedroom for larger units. In any case not less than one-fifth of the required area shall be adjacent to the kitchen. When laundry work is planned to be in the kitchen the general storage area adjacent to the kitchen shall be not less than one-fifth of the required general storage area plus 6 sq ft for storage of the washing machine or the minimum kitchen area increased 6 sq ft.

Table 9

Building type	Area, sq ft				
	1-BR	2-BR	3-BR	4-BR	5-BR
One-story houses; rows; detached; semidetached	565	740	920	1,140	1,335
Two-story houses; rows; detached; semidetached. two-story flats	585	805	1,015	1,195	1,400
Three-story apartments	545	750	905	1,150	1,320
Multistory apartments	620	805	985	1,210	1,425

adult recreation a *maximum* of 200 sq ft per bedroom plus 50 sq ft per bedroom over 100 bedrooms. For PHA and FHA requirements for preschool playgrounds, see Site Development Requirements on a previous page.)

Maximum unit sizes (PHA)

(1) The room, storage, closet and other areas given above are minimum required sizes. Any or all such areas may be increased by any amount consistent with the use of the space, provided that the total floor area of the unit, measured between the inner finish of enclosing exterior walls and between partitions separating units, does not exceed the applicable area determined from Table 9.

(2) For apartment or flat buildings the areas given include the proration of public space[1] on typical floors. The apartment areas include only the portion of general storage space required to be in-

[1] *Public space includes public corridors, public halls, elevators and stairways measured between the inner faces of dividing walls, and ½ area of public gallery. Total public space for typical floor is divided by the total number of room count (on that floor), then assigned to each unit by multiplying by the room count for each unit on that floor.*

side the dwelling units; if more of the *total* required space is located inside the unit, the above total gross areas may be increased accordingly.

(3) The above gross areas assume that room heaters will be used in row houses and flats. If central heat is used, deduct 15 sq ft from the areas given for row houses and flats. If warm air or hot water heat is used and a heater room is required, the gross areas given for row houses and flats may be increased by 15 sq ft if the fuel is gas and 30 sq ft if the fuel is coal or oil.

By JOHN HANCOCK CALLENDER, *Professor of Architecture, Pratt Institute*

CHARACTER

The most important consideration in the design of college dormitories, according to leading specialists in this field, is the avoidance of institutional or hotel character. Scale should be kept small and emphasis should be placed on the individual and on small groups. A variety of accommodations should be provided—single rooms, double rooms, and suites.

PLAN

There are two basic dormitory plans: the entry type and the corridor type. In the former, all rooms open off the stair hall and there are no corridors. The entry scheme, traditional at the older eastern colleges (Fig. 1) has many advantages: small scale, noninstitutional appearance, variety, adaptability to irregular sites, quiet and privacy for the occupants. It is more expensive than the corridor plan because of the large number of stairs and bathrooms required.

A reasonable compromise is the use of the entry plan with short corridors, thereby reducing the number of stairs by half (Fig. 2). Another compromise is the use of large suites consisting of four or more bedrooms with a common living room entered from the stair hall (Fig. 3).

The less expensive corridor plan is the type most often used and here the avoidance of hotel character is difficult. Successful examples are shown in Figs. 4 and 5. A small study—lounge should be provided on each upper floor, in addition to the main social rooms on the ground floor.

Rooms: The suites characteristic of the traditional entry plan have generally given way to the more economical double rooms. Some of the benefits of the suite can be provided in the double room by the proper placement of furniture and storage units (Figs. 6 and 7).

Married students' housing, unknown before World War II, is now a prominent part of most college housing facilities. This is family housing, differing in no respect from standard apartments. Married students housing is usually of the garden-apartment type, although in some urban colleges elevator buildings are used.

CHECK LIST OF UNITS AND RECOMMENDED PRACTICE

This section was prepared with the assistance of Elizabeth C. Gibbs, Manager of Residence Halls, Teachers' College, Columbia University. Acknowledgments are made to Moore & Hutchins, Shreve, Lamb & Harmon, Hornbostel & Bennett, Jens Larson, architects.

Student bed and study rooms

Single room: Approximately 40 sq ft of space is required for mere placement of furniture, based on the following usual dimensions: *bed,* 3 by 6½ ft; *dresser,* 1½ by 3 ft; *desk,* 2 by 3 ft (minimum); *bookcase,* ¾ by 3 ft; *chair (desk),* 1½ by 1½ ft; *chair (easy),* 2 by 2 ft. Provision for arrangement and use of these articles requires a total space allowance of at least 80 sq ft. Additional provision for marginal and "living" space sets a total single room standard of 108 sq ft of clear space, *minimum,* with 120 to 140 sq ft desirable. Width of single room should never be less than 8 ft; 9 or 10 ft, is preferable.

Double room: Two hundred sq ft of clear space, minimum; more where possible. Twelve-foot minimum width is desirable to provide each student with his own bed, dresser, desk, study and easy chairs, and at least part of a bookcase, suitably arranged in relation to convenience, comfort and light.

Bookshelves: Twelve feet of bookshelf space is required for graduate students; 6 ft for undergraduates. Built-in shelves are recommended.

Closets: Space should not be taken off room area. Closets should be for *individual* use, with 32 by 40 in. the absolute minimum allowance; more is particularly

desirable for women, and in moist climates. All closets should be ventilated (louvered), and should provide shelves for hats, racks for shoes, rods high enough for long evening dresses. Towel racks should not be installed in closets.

Electrical outlets: Provision should be made for desk, reading, and bedside lighting and a light over the lavatory. At the desk, within student's field of view (at least 150 deg), brightness ratios over large areas should ideally approach unity, with ratios of 3 still being considered good. If light on the desk is 25 ft-c and the reflection factor of tasks is between 45 and 80 per cent, then footlamberts of brightness should be not less than 5 ft-l, minimum, or 15 ft-l, desirable. In practical terms, even a strong down light on the desk will not achieve this standard by itself, and in some form (indirect or direct—indirect), additional light must be thrown on surfaces in this area.

Locks: It is desirable to have the same key open room door, closet door and post office box.

Bath and toilet facilities

Lavatories should be included in individual rooms, especially women's, wherever possible. Medicine cabinets, glass shelf, towel rack and good light should complete the installation.

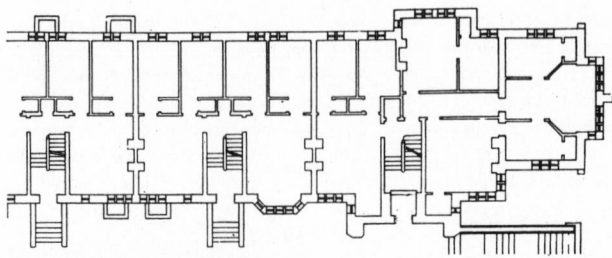

Fig. 1. Traditional entry plan
Princeton; 1920's

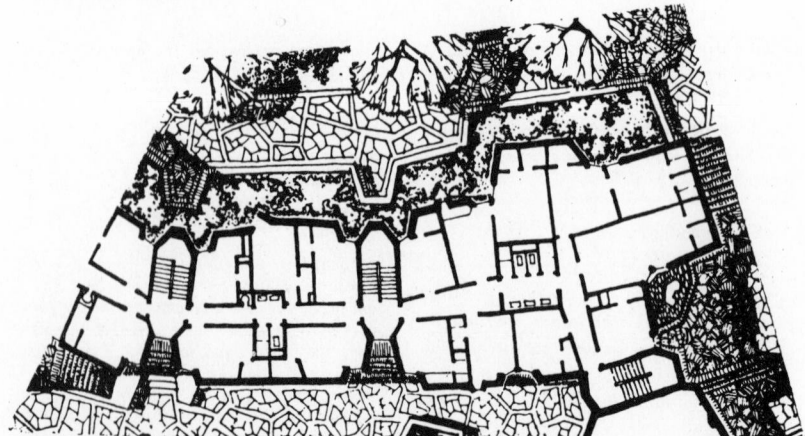

Fig. 2. Entry plan with short corridors
Yale; Eero Saarinen and Associates, Architects

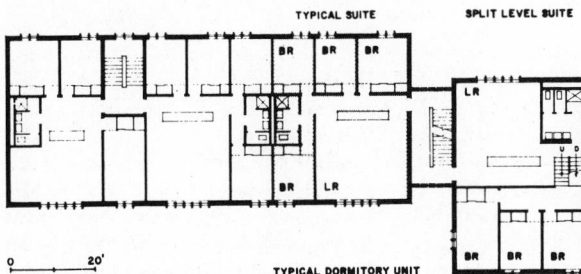

Fig. 3. Entry plan with large suites
Princeton; Sherwood, Mills and Smith, Architects

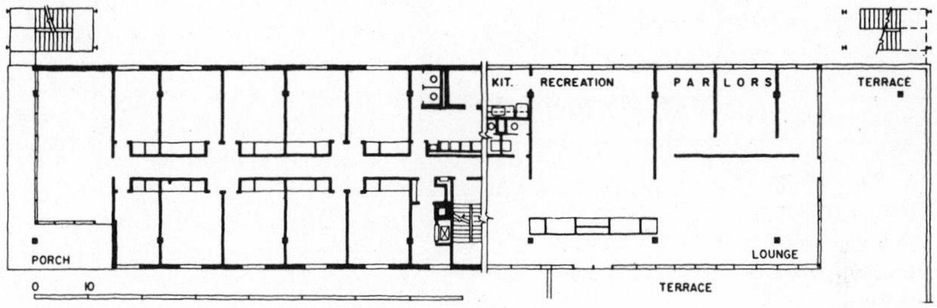

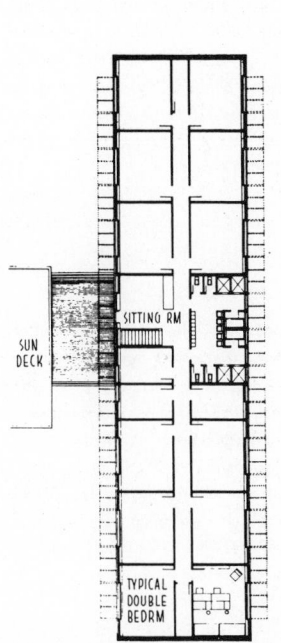

Fig. 5. Corridor plan, women's dormitory
Vassar, Marcel Breuer, Architect

Fig. 4. Corridor plan, men's dormitory
Antioch; Skidmore, Owings and Merrill, Architects

Common bath and toilet rooms: Separate but adjoining rooms, one for toilets and basins and one for showers is the preferred arrangement. Currently acceptable ratios of fixtures to users are as follows: 1 toilet to 5–6; 1 shower to 6–7; 1 basin to 3–4 (where lavatories are included in individual rooms, 1 or 2 basins in the common area are considered sufficient). In women's dormitories, tubs, in addition to showers, must be provided at a ratio of 1 to 15–20. Minimum space allowances are as follows: 3 by 4 ft for each toilet compartment; 5½ by 6 ft for each tub; 3 by 4 ft for each shower compartment; 3 by 4 ft towelling space for each shower; 3 by 4 ft for each lavatory compartment. Additional space must be provided for access.

Social and recreational rooms

Such rooms are usually more elaborate in women's dormitories than in men's. Some possible provisions are given below.

Large main living room easily accessible from the main building entrance and large enough to accommodate comfortably all the members of the unit. Plan for removal and temporary storage of furniture during dances. Adjoining kitchenette and service facilities are usually provided. Supplementary rooms or alcoves are often provided for entertaining small groups (parents, etc.).

Smaller lounges or smoking rooms, preferably one on each floor, equipped with easy chairs, radio, card tables, etc. Kitchenette may be provided in conjunction with 1 or 2-burner electric stove, sink, work counter, refrigerator, closets and cupboards.

Recreation or game room providing for ping-pong, radio, phonograph, etc. An adjoining kitchenette is also desirable. Plan for removal of furniture for dancing. Avoid locating rooms in basement.

Library, preferably on an upper floor so that dormitory occupants may use it in informal dress.

The elements listed above may be combined in various ways, but total space allotment for social and recreational rooms should be not less than 20 sq ft per student housed.

Guest facilities should include coat room, connecting toilet and lavatory, adja-

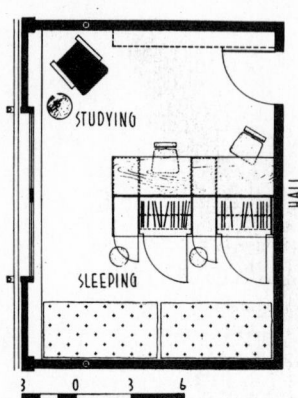

Fig. 6. Double room layout
Vassar, Marcel Breuer, Architect

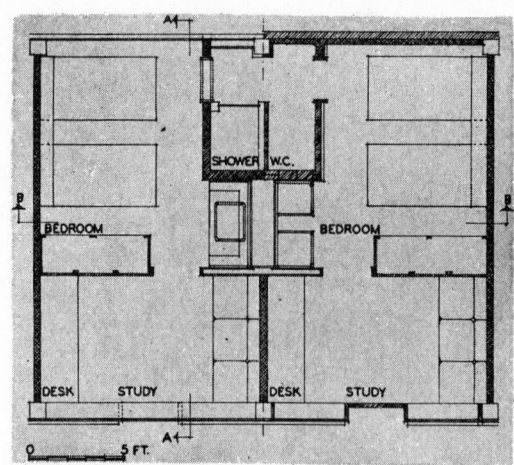

Fig. 7. Double room layout
*Arizona State College; Guirey and
Jones, Architects*

cent to main entrance. Overnight accommodations should include bedrooms, baths; living rooms, if possible.

Administrative utility elements

Administrative office, near the main entrance, usually provides for student mail, messages, packages, etc.; telephone service; record keeping in connection with student life and house management. Customary space allowance is 15 sq ft for each desk and its chair; 5 ft in front of each filing cabinet; aisles between tables and desks, 3–4 ft.

Corridors should be at least 5½ wide to permit passage of maid's truck, furniture and trunks.

Sink and utility closets, large enough to hold maid's truck, vacuum cleaner, brooms, mops, etc.; at least one on each floor; ventilated to the outer air.

Linen closets should be provided on each floor, with white enameled shelves and counter space.

Incinerator with hopper doors, and *linen chute* with openings on each floor.

Trunk storage space, allowing at least 45 cu ft per trunk; if racks are used, additional space must be allowed for handling and movement; *hand luggage store rooms* on each floor.

Freight elevator is required—even in a two or three story building. Should be automatic and large enough for trunks, furniture, stretchers.

Passenger elevator is required in all halls with more than three living floors. Need exists for street level entrance for students in wheel chairs or on crutches.

Housekeeper's office and linen room, preferably on ground floor near employee's and delivery entrance; with storage and counter space for linens and supplies. Provisions for sewing and mending, and for cleaning furniture, rugs, etc.

Locker, lunch, and rest rooms for employees should be adjacent to housekeeper's office.

Laundry: In dormitories with over a hundred beds, with assured steady patronage from this number, house laundries are frequently operated on a self-supporting basis.

Living space for staff and employees: Suites for directors and members of the house staff should be segregated from student areas. Employees such as cooks, maids, etc. should have separate entrances to their living area and well-lighted single bedrooms of 100 sq ft, minimum; double rooms not less than 160 sq ft. Staff members usually eat with students; employees should have own dining room.

Student utility elements

Laundries and pressing rooms are for the most part provided only in women's dormitories. Except where students do all their own clothing and room laundry, 1 tub for 25 occupants is usually adequate, with each tub requiring a minimum of 2 by 6 ft. Pressing boards require 4 by 6 ft; a fair proportion of irons and boards is usually 1 to 20–25 students. Drying rooms or cabinets are essential. Although laundry elements are frequently centralized, smaller units on each floor are preferred, possibly in combination with kitchenettes.

Sewing rooms are considered essential in women's dormitories, and should include 1 or 2 electric sewing machines, long mirror, long work table, ironing facilities unless element is combined with pressing room. Ratio of equipment: 1 to 20–25 users.

Shampoo rooms with shampoo bowls, rinsing sprays, electric dryers, etc., are sometimes provided.

Typing and music practice rooms which are isolated or soundproofed are often provided.

Sports equipment storage and maintenance space is particularly desirable in cold climates.

Telephones: The most satisfactory arrangement is a switchboard in the administrative office, a corridor telephone for each 20–30 residents and a two-way buzzer system to each room.

Infirmaries, if appended, should be isolated at ends of wings nearest kitchen and should have separate entrances.

By FRANK HARRISON RANDOLPH, P.E.
Hotel Planning Consultant and Professor of Hotel Engineering, Cornell University

The basic requirements for a successful hotel were set forth some years ago by H. L. Stevens & Company of Chicago, creators of many profitable commercial hotels. The logic behind these requirements is sound, and they are equally applicable today.

Proper design and construction: Attractive appearance, an efficient plan, suitable materials, and good workmanship are all vital to the proper design and construction of a hotel.

Good location: A good location is the dominant factor in attracting business. Location is permanent, and no hotel can afford a poor one. The most expensive site is usually warranted.

Sound financing: High-cost financing is just as much of a burden as paying premium prices for construction materials and labor. The cost of financing is continued throughout the life of the building.

Competent management: The great diversity of requirements in this highly competitive business requires specific experience in successful hotel operation. The average good business executive does not make a satisfactory hotel manager.

Among the most important criteria for design, as formulated by the eminent architect William B. Tabler, are those concerned with economic ratios of cost and space. Some of these criteria are of direct concern in designing the building; others may have an indirect but powerful influence in determining the principles on which the design is based.

Unlike most businesses, hotel operation makes its money directly from the building it occupies. It operates on a small over-all profit margin, which, in turn, makes the allowable margin for error in the design of the building especially small. Most of the profit will come from the daily rental of guest rooms to the traveling public on a retail basis. Hence, the design of the guest rooms and the typical guest-room floor are of extreme importance. A retail store may sell tomorrow the goods it did not sell today. But revenue lost today through unsold guest rooms cannot be recovered tomorrow.

The designer should remember that the hotel must combine the functions of housing, feeding, entertainment, rentals, services, maintenance, and light manufacturing. These are not isolated activities; they must all be integrated for smooth operation of this complex and diversified business. In short, the business must be planned before the hotel can be designed properly.

The following "rules of thumb" may serve as a guide in planning commercial hotels. Although derived from extensive hotel study by Tabler, the rules should not be applied rigidly; they serve only as a check to determine whether a project is feasible. Also bear in mind that the rules are interrelated and that a modification of one may alter the others.

1. *Construction cost must not exceed $1,000 per $1 of average room rate.* The market and the competition determine the room rate. If the average room rate is $10, then $10,000 per guest room is the maximum construction cost for the finished but unfurnished shell including public space and service areas.

2. *The total area of bedroom floors should be at least as much as the total public space and service areas.* Thus, only the larger hotels can feasibly include extensive public rooms and service areas, which absorb 60 to 65 per cent of construction costs. The burden of nonprofit public space tends to become excessive for the smaller hotels.

3. *The total allowance for all facilities should not exceed 6,000 cu ft per guest room.*

4. *Not over one employee per room.* The requisite number of staff is determined by the basic design, which involves the number of kitchens, methods of food handling, the routing of guests, and "built-in" maintenance shops. Salaries and wages constitute the largest single item of expense in hotel operation. The average hourly wages of hotel employees have increased 243 per cent in the past 20 years. During the same period, average room rates rose only 180 per cent. Wage rates have thus increased much faster than room rates, and it is more important than ever before that payrolls be kept to the minimum.

5. *Land cost should not exceed 10 per cent of the cost of the building.* Nevertheless, the best place for the commercial hotel is usually the high-cost, prime retail location where the largest number of potential customers are available. The resulting increase in revenue is worth more than the premium cost of the land.

6. *Profit ratios.* Profits within individual departments average 70 per cent on rooms, 50 per cent on beverages, 15 per cent on rentals, and nothing on food. Nearly half of the hotel's total revenue normally comes from room sales. Frequently a small profit is shown on food, but often this item does not include space rental value, cost of kitchen equipment, utility services, repairs, and maintenance. Many of the larger areas, such as the ballroom, the main kitchen, and the night club, often simply do not pay their way.

7. *Break-even point at 65 per cent occupancy.* This is a highly controversial figure. The design should permit operating costs to be reduced, proportionately if possible, when business declines by shutting down guest floors and using only segments of the total kitchen facilities. An average occupancy of 70 per cent usually means that the transient commercial hotel is crowded Monday through Thursday but half empty over weekends and holidays. December occupancy usually drops 15 per cent below average. Efficient operation is difficult in the face of such wide fluctuations within the week and throughout the year.

8. *Miscellaneous guest-room "rules."*

a. The net bedroom area, excluding bath, foyer, and closet, should be at least 50 per cent of the gross area of the typical guest floor.

b. If rooms are desired in different price categories, as is usually the case, increments of at least 20 sq ft of floor area are advisable (since the average guest cannot notice any less) to justify the difference in price.

c. The minimum feasible net bedroom areas are 90 to 110 sq ft for a room with a single bed, 130 to 150 sq ft for a room with a double bed, and 160 to 180 sq ft for a room with twin beds.

These figures apply to the sleeping-living area only, exclusive of bath, foyer, and closet.

In designing a hotel, the first step is to write a detailed program. "Rules of thumb" are useful, but there are many possible solutions. Other problems must also be considered, such as climate, environment, site, orientation, approach and traffic patterns, esthetics, soil investigations, structural design, and building codes. The criteria for design must thus be adapted to meet the requirements of the particular hotel.

Guest rooms are the principal reason for having a hotel. They warrant the most careful attention since they are the source of the hotel's greatest profit. Other areas in the hotel serve mainly to attract patrons so that more guest rooms will be sold. Certainly these other areas should be inviting, and the guest room itself should fulfill the patron's expectations.

GUEST PREFERENCES

Retail sales are most successful when the customer gets what he wants rather than something he accepts as the best available substitute. The demand will be for rooms for single, double, triple, and occasionally quadruple occupancy. Some persons traveling alone prefer a single bed; probably about half of them would rather have a double bed, especially if they are tall. Most parties of two persons want twin beds, with only a minority preferring a double bed. The studio-type room, with a couch that is converted into a bed at night, is preferred by a minority of guests in most localities. Some experienced hotel operators in certain large cities, however, want over 50 per cent of the rooms to be of the studio type. Ideally, the design should provide every guest with the exact sleeping accommodations that he prefers. The correct assortment of types to meet this requirement is, of course, difficult to forecast.

A guest generally does not voice a complaint because his room is too large or has an extra bed, but he may feel that he is paying for something he is not using. The management, of course, realizes that a vacant bed in an occupied room means loss in potential revenue, and wishes that rooms sold out might mean beds sold out as well. Some designers simply provide half the rooms with a double bed and half with twin beds. This arrangement simplifies the planning and provides a workable solution, but certainly the design is not tailored to fit the demand. If, for example, 75 per cent of the rooms are each occupied by one person, then at least 25 per cent of the rooms have unused sleeping accommodations that are producing no revenue.

OCCUPANCY FIGURES

The typical transient commercial hotel, which caters predominantly to business travelers, normally has 75 to 80 per cent single occupancy and 20 to 25 per cent double occupancy. When this type of hotel is very busy and is filled to capacity, the figures can be expected to approach 45 per cent single occupancy, 50 per cent double occupancy, and 5 per cent triple occupancy. If this hotel holds a convention, the double- and triple-occupancy figures will be higher. Resort hotels tend to have a low single-occupancy figure, about 25 per cent. Some locations that cater almost exclusively to tourists will have only 5 per cent single occupancy.

Table 1. Distribution of guest rooms for transient commercial hotel

The net room areas listed below do not include the bath, foyer, and closet, which total about 100 sq ft additional. The minimum areas are the smallest advisable; the maximum areas are seldom exceeded in luxury-type rooms.

Per cent	Type of room	Net room area, sq ft		
		Minimum	Usual	Maximum
15	Conventional single	90	130	170
30	Conventional double	130	160	200
5	Combination; double with couch	160	200	240
20	Conventional twin	160	190	230
10	Studio twin	140	170	210
13	Combination twin	150	180	220
5	Conventional double-double	200	230	260
2	Sample room (merchandise display)	230	360	500
100				

The best planning guide is to obtain occupancy figures of other hotels in the locality that operate under similar conditions. Such information is often confidential or difficult to obtain, however. The expected normal, full-load conditions should be estimated with care because they determine the assortment of accommodations to be provided in the design. It is not advisable to design for an overload condition that would be realized for only a minor portion of the year, say 5 per cent or less. Rigid adherence to the assortment actually desired, however, is inadvisable, since the clerks will need some leeway in making room reservations and assignments.

TYPES OF GUEST ROOMS

Guest rooms are best classified by the number and type of beds provided. For example, a single room has one single bed, a double room has one double bed, a twin room has two single beds, and a double-double room has two double beds. The necessary floor space increases in the order just listed. Rooms with conventional beds should have an aisle on each side of each bed and therefore require more floor space than rooms with studio beds, which have one side against the wall. Extra maid service is customarily furnished to make up the studio bed at night; consequently, studio rooms might be omitted or limited to a minor fraction of the total. Most hotels, however, desire some studio rooms.

The variety of room types from which to select are as follows:

Conventional single
Studio single
Conventional double
Studio double
Conventional twin
Studio twin
Combination twin
Conventional double-double
Combination with one conventional double bed and one studio single bed.

The room with a conventional double bed and a studio single bed is suitable for three persons. Its appearance is better than one having three conventional single beds (a type that is possible although not listed). The combination twin has one conventional single bed and one studio single bed. Its advantages seem to have been generally overlooked.

Although the height of Americans has increased during the last several generations, the length of beds has not. The percentage of persons over 6 ft tall is, indeed, much greater than it used to be, and these people want to be able to stretch out in comfort. Most tall people prefer a single bed of ample length to a double bed in which they must sleep diagonally. If king-length beds (6 in. longer than standard) are provided, fewer double beds will be needed. It is advisable to plan in advance for king-length beds. After the room layouts have been made for standard-length beds, it is sometimes impossible to substitute the king length because clearances and aisle spaces are too restricted.

Early in the planning stage a decision should be made on the approximate distribution of guest rooms. For the transient commercial hotel, the distribution shown in Table 1 can serve as a basis for planning, subject to modification. Table 1 allots 28 per cent for single occupancy if conventional singles and combination twins are included, and 58 per cent if conventional doubles are added. Should a convention demand double occupancy, 83 per cent of the rooms would be suitably equipped. Moreover, 10 per cent of the rooms are arranged for three persons, and half of these rooms can accommodate four persons.

Table 2. Guest-room furniture — a suggested list

Item	Dimensions, ft-in. * (over-all)	Conventional room				Studio room			Sample room
		Single	Double	Twin	Double-double	Single	Twin	Parlor	
Bed, single:									
Regular †	3-3x6-7								
Long †	3-3x7-1	1		2					
Studio	6-4x2-10					1	2	2	1
Bed, double:									
Regular †	4-6x6-7								
Long †	4-6x7-1		1		2				
Studio ‡	6-4x2-10								
Combination dresser-desk:									
Short	3-0x1-6	1				1			
Regular	4-0x1-7		1	1			1	1	1
Long	5-0x1-8				1				
Dresser and luggage rack	4-8x1-7								
Dresser	2-0x1-9								
Desk	3-0x1-6								
Chair, desk	1-6x1-6	1	1	1	1	1	1	1	1
Chair, wood arms	2-2x2-4	1	1	2	2	1	1	2	2
Chair, upholstered	2-8x2-8								
Table, triangular	2-¼ (each side)	1	1	1	1	1	1	1	
Table, coffee	1-6x3-0			1	1				
Night stand	1-2x1-2	1	1	1	1				
Night table	2-6x1-2					1	1	1	
Grip stand:									
Regular	2-6x1-7	1	1	2	2	1	1	1	1
Folding	2-1x1-8		1		1		1		1
Floor lamp	1-5 (shade diam)	1	1	2	2	1	2	2	2
Television set	1-10x1-8	1	1	1	1	1	1	1	1
Waste basket	9x1-1	1	1	1	1	1	1	1	1

* *The first dimension is the "frontage," parallel to the wall.*
† *Add 2 in. if a footboard is used.*
‡ *The dimension 2 ft 10 in. increases to 6 ft 10 in. when the bed is opened.*

Although Table 1 lists eight room types, this does not mean that eight room sizes are required. Carefully planned layouts will show that a given size may be used for several room types without undesirable crowding or wasted space.

Guest-room layouts provide for the patrons' needs and conveniences, which are about the same in any location. Relatively compact arrangements are favored in commercial hotels and other places where the rental value per square foot of floor space is high. More spacious rooms with about the same complement of furniture are found in motels, luxury hotels, and higher priced residential hotels. Sometimes a low rental value per square foot or low building costs may permit an increase in space.

The logical steps in the design of a typical guest room are as follows:

1. Decide on the number of persons to occupy the room.

2. Determine the type of room: conventional, studio, or combination.

3. Make a preliminary list of the furniture items definitely needed. (See Table 2.)

4. Select the size of each furniture item carefully. Avoid oversize furniture.

5. Determine the furniture arrangement by using scale models or templates, keeping open spaces to a reasonable minimum.

6. Surround the arrangement with walls and locate windows, doors, bathroom, foyer, and closet.

7. Compare the result with generally accepted good practice as to over-all dimensions, furniture provided, and convenient grouping. Revise the layout if necessary.

The same procedure should be followed for each type of guest room. Remember that after the minimum dimensions have been established they may be increased, but not decreased, to fit in with later developments. The following dimensions for guest-room areas are recommended: Clothes closet, minimum inside dimensions—1 ft 11 in. by 4 ft 2 in.; three-fixture bathroom, inside dimensions—5 ft by 6 ft 9 in.; vestibule, minimum width between closet and bath—3 ft 3 in.; door to guest room—2 ft 10 in.; bathroom door—2 ft 2 in.; standard carpet widths—2 ft 3 in.,

9 ft, 12 ft, 15 ft, and occasionally 13 ft 6 in.; ceiling height, finished floor to finished ceiling—8 ft 4 in.

In general, the guest room is planned with the "living area" along the outside wall and extending down one side of the room. The opposite side serves as the "sleeping area." The space adjacent to the corridor is used for an entry foyer, bathroom, clothes closet, luggage rack, and dresser, and is designated the "dressing and unpacking area," for want of a better name. The adjacent areas overlap to some extent and may thus serve a double purpose, as well as adding a sense of spaciousness to the room (Fig. 1).

A dozen examples of guest-room layouts are presented in Fig. 2 and 3 in order to show recent practice. They are representative of various kinds of hotels and illustrate the basic principles of room arrangement. The following types are shown in Fig. 2:

Conventional single: The layout is spacious, as is frequent in motels. For a commercial hotel, the net room area could be reduced to 10 by 13 ft, or 130 sq ft, to conform to the usual figure. Modifying the bathroom would readily provide an entrance from the guest-floor corridor.

Conventional double: With the bed parallel to the outside wall, a generally satisfactory arrangement is developed within the desired area. Guest convenience is emphasized by placing the luggage rack between the desk-dresser and the closet.

Conventional double: In this layout, the bed faces the window—an arrangement sometimes used. A generous room area is provided. The location of the bath and clothes closet is unusual but has some merit.

Combination: For a motel type of installation, the double bed plus the studio couch provides suitable accommodations for two or three persons. The room is both attractive and convenient for guests.

Conventional twin: This layout shows a frequently preferred arrangement that has been developed with care. An additional foot in the depth of the room would, however, improve the layout by providing more space between the chair and the bed. The folding grip stand can be put in the closet if the connecting door is in use.

Conventional double-double: This "family room" combines good design with economy of space. An increase of at least 1 ft in each direction would permit greater aisle space. An extra lavatory is provided near the bathroom.

The following types are shown in Fig. 3:

Combination: A single conventional bed plus a studio couch makes the room attractive and suitable for one or two persons. The furniture is not crowded and yet the room area indicates that economy of space was attained.

Pair of studio- and conventional-twin rooms: An interesting example is shown of a shallow and a deep room of approximately equal areas, which have been effectively paired by offsetting the bathrooms. If king-length beds are used, the room width should be increased.

Studio single: This layout closely approaches the minimum advisable size; it has all the essentials and yet the furniture is not crowded. A large mirror over the desk-dresser makes the room appear larger.

Two studio-twin rooms: Skillful placing of the studio couches has resulted in unusual, attractive, and serviceable layouts. Both rooms depart from the customary arrangements.

These twelve examples provide a suitable basis on which to develop any proj-

ect. They have been carefully selected from the work of experienced designers to show the variety of typical guest-room layouts.

Commercial hotels customarily have a central corridor flanked by guest rooms on both sides, which is known as a "double-loaded" guest-corridor. The highway inn may have the same basic arrangement, except that each guest room would also have an outside entrance. The outside entrance may open on a patio for rooms on the first floor and on a balcony for rooms on the second floor. Some motels have only an outside entrance and no interior corridor. This arrangement is frequently used when the construction is two rooms deep with the bathrooms back-to-back. A typical guest-room layout is generally easy to adapt if its basic arrangement is right.

BATHROOMS

Bathrooms customarily have three fixtures: water closet, lavatory, and tub with shower. The inside dimensions of the bathrooms are usually about 5 by 7 ft. A slight saving in space is possible in lower priced rooms by installing a shower stall instead of a tub. Occasionally a very low-priced room may have only a water closet and lavatory. It has become virtually impossible, however, to rent a room without private toilet facilities. Formerly, the lavatory was sometimes installed outside the bathroom—in the dressing or sleeping area—but the damage to water-splashed walls and carpet make this location inadvisable.

Plumbing and ventilation

Plumbing fixtures should be backed up to the pipe shaft so that they can be served by short, horizontal pipe connections. This arrangement saves piping and eliminates the need for many lines buried in the floor or partitions, where leakage is costly to repair. Each pipe shaft should serve two bathrooms on each floor. The continuous vertical pipe shafts should be large enough to contain the soil and vent stack, hot and cold water lines, circulating ice water lines, steam and condensate return lines for bathroom radiators, and possibly other piped or wired services. The pipe shafts also provide for mechanical ventilation, which is required for inside bathrooms. A wall register near the top of the wall and over the tub permits air removal by an exhaust fan at the top of the shaft. Sound transmission through the exhaust grilles of adjoining bathrooms is very objectionable and warrants giving

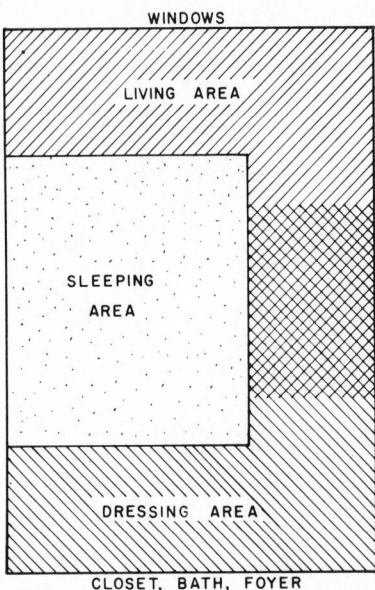

Fig. 1. Functional plan of hotel guest room

careful attention to acoustics. This problem can be remedied by connecting each register to an upturned elbow of sound-absorbing material. The bottom of the bathroom door should clear the sill by about 1 in. to permit ventilation at all times.

An access door to the pipe shaft should be provided on each floor; otherwise, access must be gained through the bathroom wall cabinet over the lavatory.

For additional information on mechanical equipment and services in hotels, see "Heating, Ventilating, and Air Conditioning: Hotels and motels," and "Plumbing—Fixtures: Public facilities."

Electrical

General illumination is often furnished by a flat ceiling dome of translucent glass, centrally mounted, and controlled by a switch at the entrance to the room. Supplementary local lighting is provided where needed, requiring two or three convenience outlets on each side wall. One circuit should serve some of the lights in each of several guest rooms. It is preferable to have each guest room served by two circuits so that a blown fuse will not put out all of a guest's lights. A second switch at the room entrance controls the small light in the foyer. The foyer light, if properly located, may be adequate for the closet. A separate light in the closet may be mounted on the top of the door casing and operated by a pull cord or a door switch. A wall switch controls the bathroom lighting, which is often a single bulb over the mirror, although a pair of shaded lights at the 5-ft level is much better and makes it easy to provide the

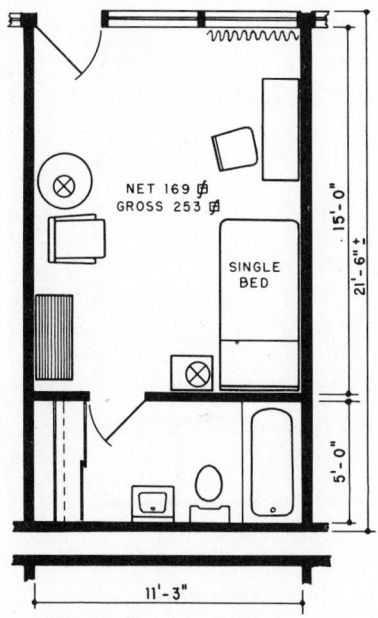

CONVENTIONAL SINGLE
BASED ON THE MOTEL DE VILLE
C. R. COLBERT & ASSOCIATES, ARCH.

NET 169 ☐
GROSS 253 ☐

SINGLE BED

15'-0"
21'-6"±
5'-0"
11'-3"

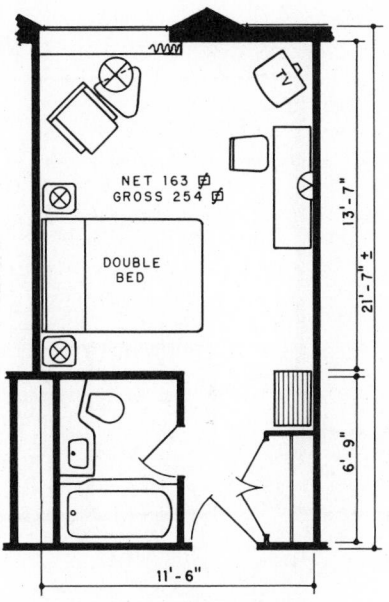

CONVENTIONAL DOUBLE
BASED ON THE PITTSBURGH HILTON
WILLIAM B. TABLER, ARCH.

NET 163 ☐
GROSS 254 ☐

DOUBLE BED

13'-7"
21'-7"±
6'-9"
11'-6"

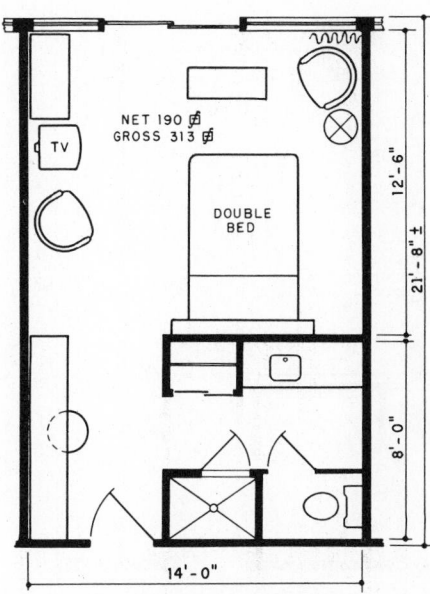

CONVENTIONAL DOUBLE
BASED ON THE CHARTERHOUSE MOTOR HOTELS
VICTOR GRUEN ASSOCIATES, ARCH.

NET 190 ☐
GROSS 313 ☐

TV

DOUBLE BED

12'-6"
21'-8"±
8'-0"
14'-0"

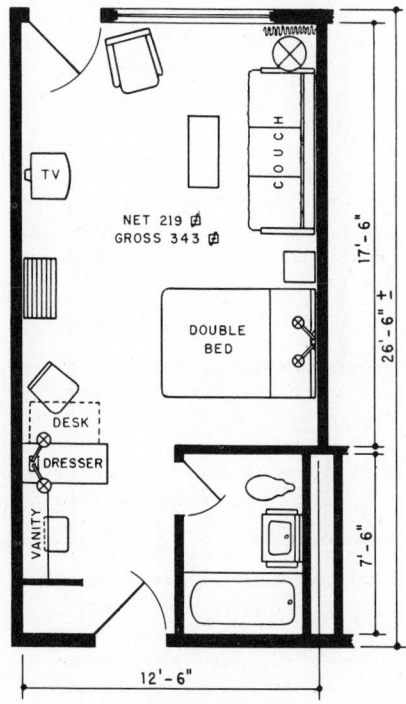

COMBINATION
BASED ON THE SHREVEPORTER
WILLIAM B. WIENER & ASSOCIATES, ARCH.

TV

COUCH

NET 219 ☐
GROSS 343 ☐

DOUBLE BED

DESK
DRESSER
VANITY

17'-6"
26'-6"±
7'-6"
12'-6"

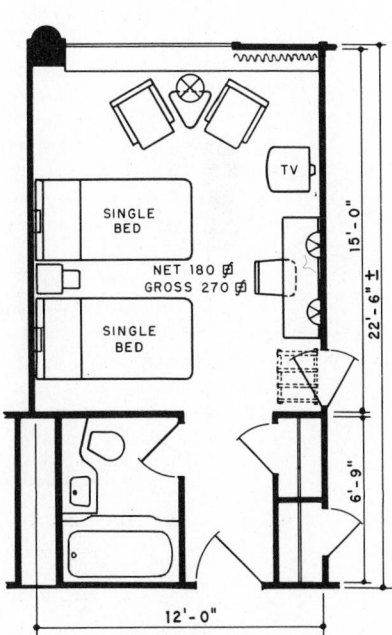

CONVENTIONAL TWIN
BASED ON THE DALLAS STATLER
WILLIAM B. TABLER, ARCH.

TV

SINGLE BED

NET 180 ☐
GROSS 270 ☐

SINGLE BED

15'-0"
22'-6"±
6'-9"
12'-0"

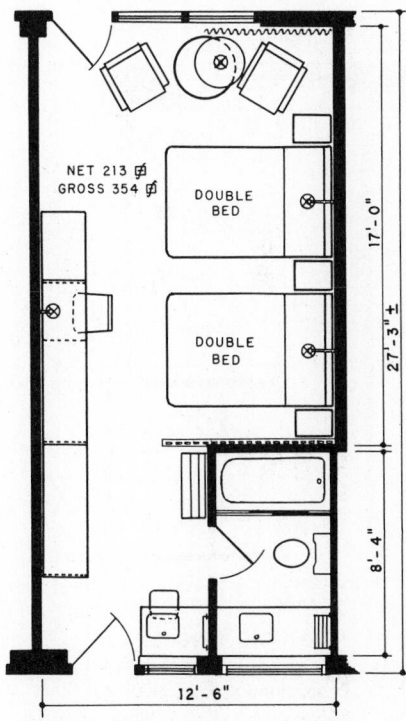

CONVENTIONAL DOUBLE-DOUBLE
BASED ON HOWARD JOHNSON'S MOTOR LODGES
CARL KOCH & ASSOCIATES, ARCH.

NET 213 ☐
GROSS 354 ☐

DOUBLE BED

DOUBLE BED

17'-0"
27'-3"±
8'-4"
12'-6"

Fig. 2. Typical hotel guest room—conventional type

Scale: ⅛ in. = 1 ft

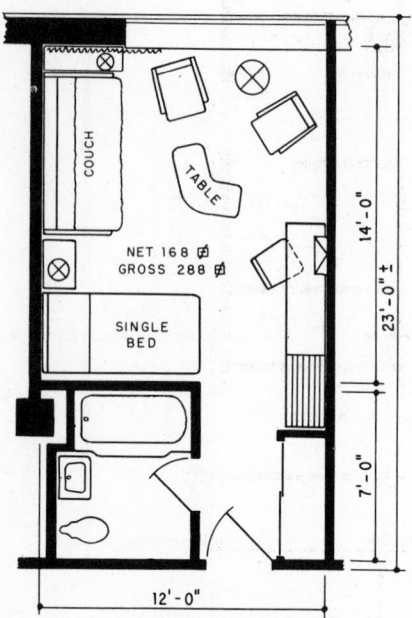

COMBINATION
BASED ON THE INTERCONTINENTAL HOTELS
HOLABIRD & ROOT & BURGEE, ARCH.

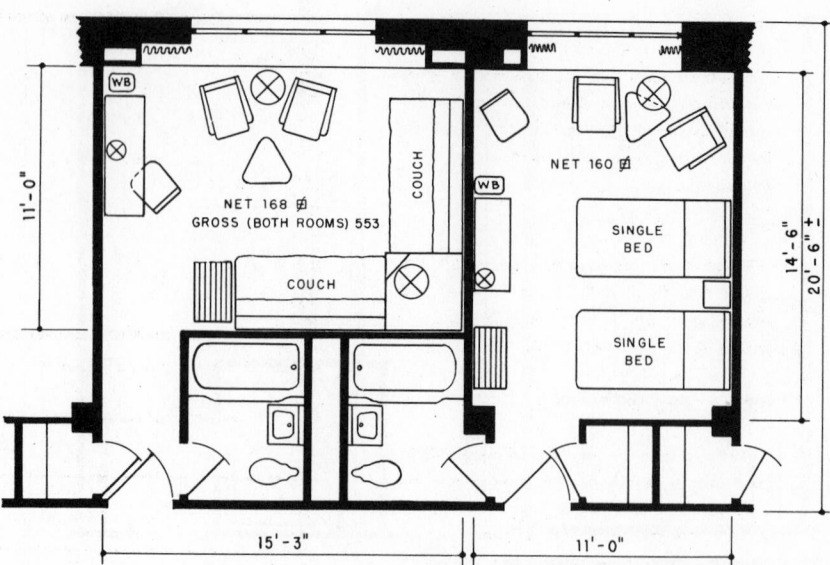

PAIR OF STUDIO & CONVENTIONAL TWIN ROOMS
BASED ON THE WASHINGTON STATLER
HOLABIRD & ROOT, ARCH.

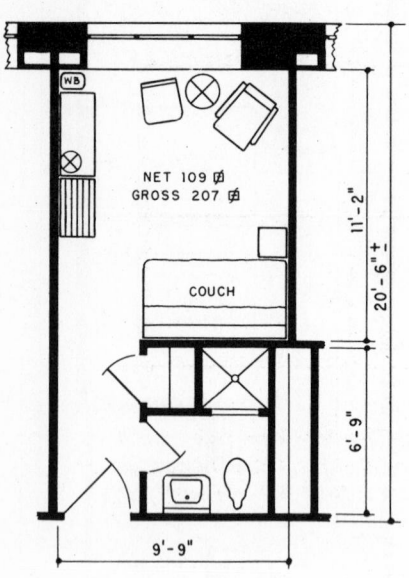

STUDIO SINGLE
BASED ON THE WASHINGTON STATLER
HOLABIRD & ROOT, ARCH.

Fig. 3. Typical hotel guest room—studio type

Scale: $\frac{1}{8}$ in. = 1 ft

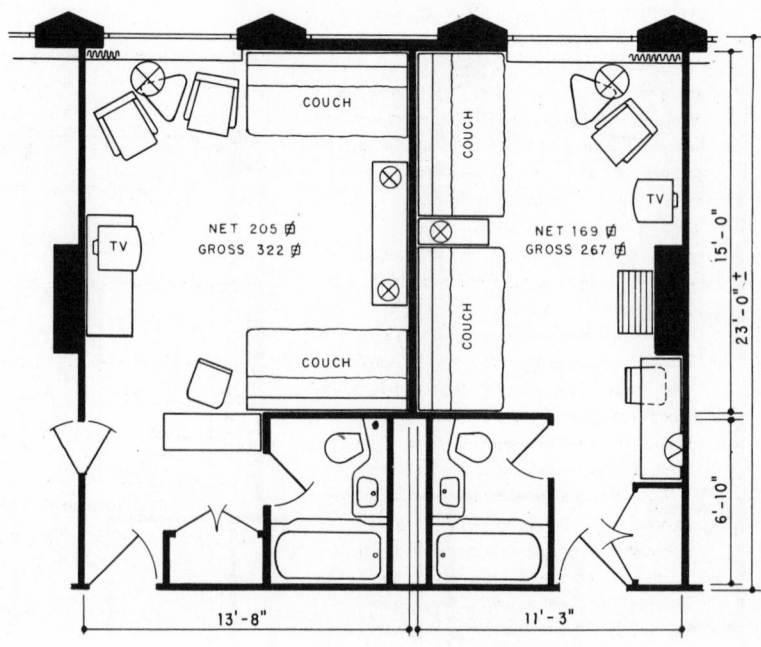

TWO STUDIO TWIN ROOMS
BASED ON THE PITTSBURGH HILTON
WILLIAM B. TABLER, ARCH.

desired convenience outlet for an electric razor. The location of the television and telephone outlets must be determined from the furniture layout. The telephone outlet should be near the bed if the furniture layout provides a bedside table or the equivalent.

Structural frame

Guest-room plans can generally be adapted without difficulty to simple and economical structural framing layouts, as shown in Fig. 4 and 5.

FLOOR PLAN

The portion of the typical guest-floor plan shown in Fig. 6 illustrates a method for obtaining a flexible variety of guest-room sizes together with a good assortment of room types. Each bay, which is usually 23 to 26 ft wide, contains two rooms. The 26-ft bay shown starts with a room width of 10 ft and increases this figure by increments of 1 ft 6 in. This method provides five room widths, not including the full bay taken by the sample room, which may serve for exhibits, meetings, dormitory sleeping, or possibly as a private dining room. The location of the sample room should be convenient to elevator and stairs. The 5 by 7-ft area shown at the right is designated as a closet. If it should later be found desirable to convert the sample room into two guest rooms, the closet could readily be fitted as a bathroom, and a partition with clothes closet constructed.

If deep rooms and shallow rooms are located on opposite sides of the corridor, ten room sizes result without seriously complicating the simple framing pattern. If a 23-ft-wide bay is used, fewer feasible room sizes are possible. An increment of at least 20 sq ft in net room area is necessary to make it apparent to the guest that a higher room rate is warranted.

Appropriate furnishings have been indicated for each room. A complete scale layout should be developed, nevertheless, for all the furniture in each room—even to such small details as the location of the waste basket—before plans are considered complete and satisfactory.

Connecting doors between rooms may be planned in conjunction with the furniture layouts. Relatively few connecting rooms are advisable, for they tend to diminish a guest's feeling of security. In general, for every two connecting rooms there should be about ten separate rooms.

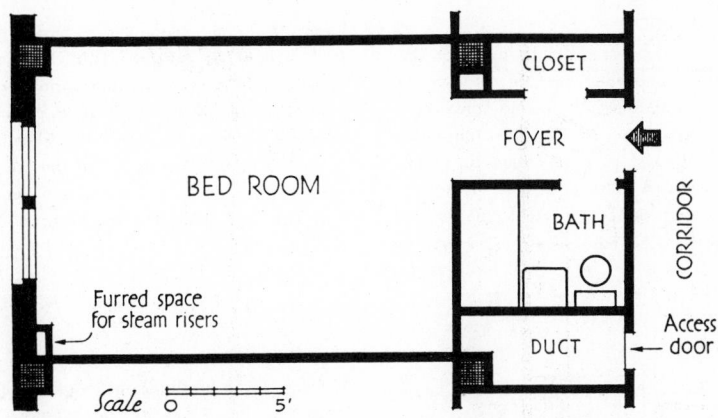

Fig. 4. Guest-room plan in relation to building structure Scale: ⅛ in. = 1 ft

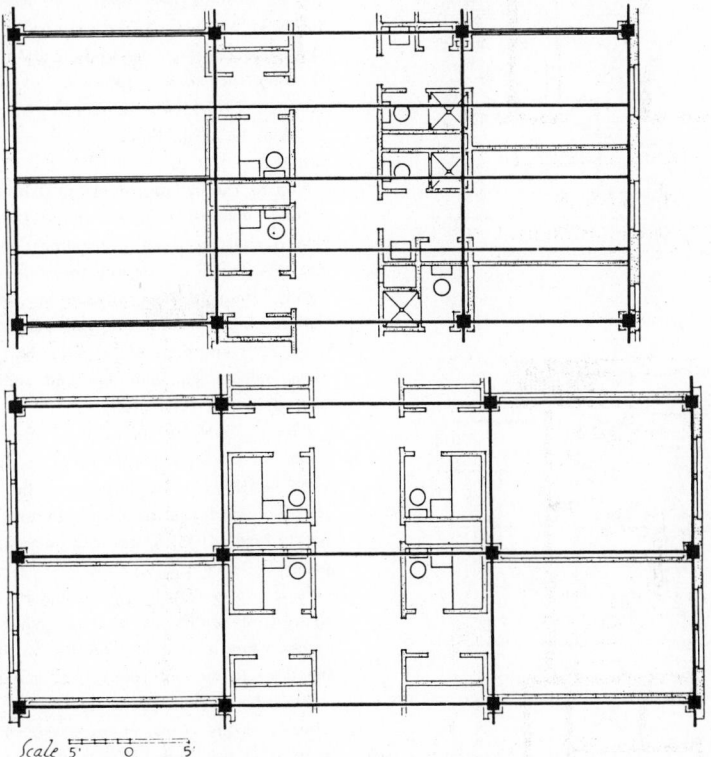

Scale 5' 0 5'

Fig. 5. Methods of adjusting units to typical steel framing Scale: ¹⁄₁₆ in. = 1 ft

Framing members should not block shafts or bathtub traps. Column spacing of 12 ft 6 in. permits variation of room widths from 11 to 13 ft in adjacent bays.

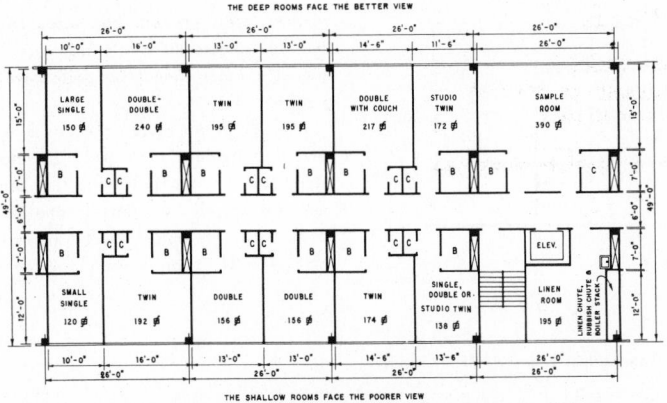

Fig. 6. Typical hotel guest-room floor plan Scale: ¹⁄₁₆ in. = 1 ft

CORNER ROOM

The corner room should open on the guest-floor corridor so that it may be rented separately. It should also have doors connecting to the room on either side so that it may be rented as a two- or three-room suite if desired. This room on the outside corner should be one of the best in the house, but not excessively large. It usually resembles a parlor and is furnished as a studio-twin bedroom; consequently it needs a clothes closet and bathroom. The foregoing factors combine to make the layout a difficult problem, for it must fit in with the design of the typical floor and become an integral part of it. Five floor plans for the corner room are shown in Fig. 7.

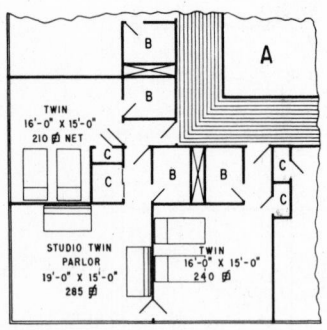

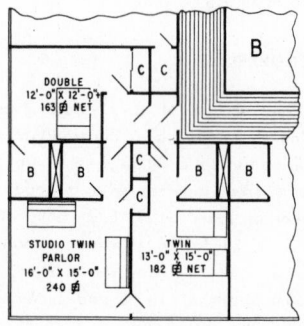

Plan A: The arrangement is quite simple and has the following advantages: (1) Relatively few extra partitions are required; (2) No outside wall space is used for closets or baths; (3) Bathrooms are paired; (4) All closets are conveniently located; and (5) Only the normal space is taken for entrance foyers. The corner room may, however, be a bit difficult for a new guest to find.

Plan B: The arriving guest must follow a slightly longer L-shaped route than in Plan A, but the suite connections are almost the same. The double room does not use its area to best advantage and its bath and closet are not well placed for guest convenience. Moreover, the bath takes outside wall frontage and space is wasted in the vestibule.

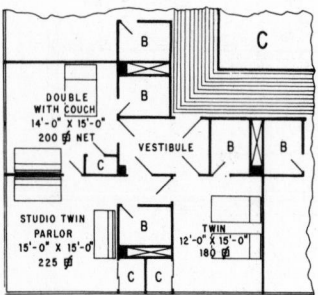

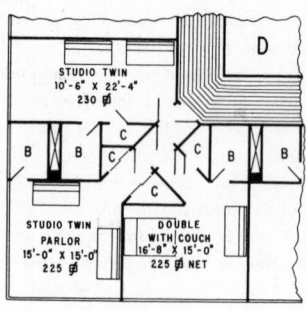

Plan C: Entry to any one of the three rooms is possible only through a large-sized vestibule. The closets on the outside wall and the isolated bath are both poorly located. The suite arrangements are generally satisfactory, although the vestibule becomes private only when all three rooms are rented as a suite. When the corner room is entered from the vestibule, the door to the bathroom is prominent.

Plan D: The diagonal corridor leading directly to the corner room is the striking feature of this layout. The guest does not encounter a confusing maze of corridors, and, despite the diagonal pattern, there are no awkward angles in the rooms to handicap furniture placement. The angles in the closets present little inconvenience. Suite arrangements are good, except that the twin room cannot be paired with the parlor.

Plan E: If the building wing is narrow and the standard room is 12 ft deep (instead of the usual 15 ft), the problem may be solved by bringing one pair of baths up to the outside wall. This arrangement results in an unusually large room (13 ft 6 in. by 19 ft 4 in.), which is best utilized as a double-double. The double-double has a door to the main corridor but cannot be paired as a suite without losing the use of the twin room.

The problem of designing the outside corner room would be simplified by omitting the clothes closets, the usual 3-fixture bath, and the separate entrance. No departure from recognized good design should be permitted, however, because the corner room must be planned to sell readily and at a top price.

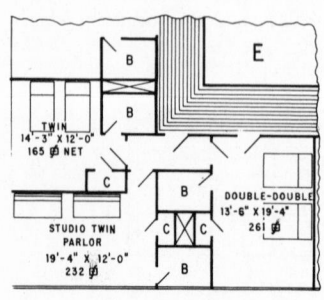

Fig. 7.   Hotel guest rooms—corner rooms
Scale: 1/16 in. = 1 ft

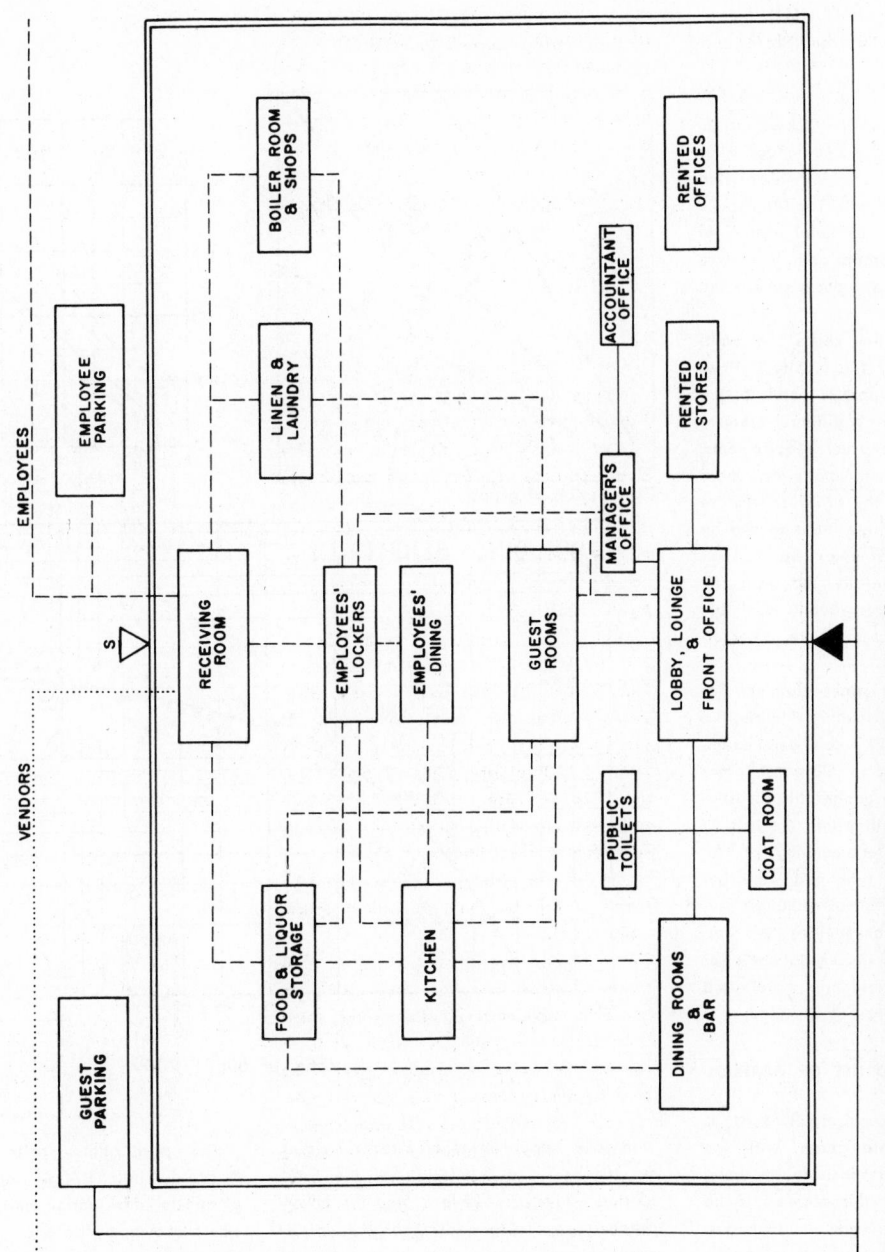

Fig. 8. Functional plan of typical commercial hotel, showing main traffic routes

Space allotments—general

By FRANK HARRISON RANDOLPH, P.E.
Hotel Planning Consultant and Professor of Hotel Engineering, Cornell University

In designing hotels, architects are frequently handicapped by the lack of factual data on space requirements. Too much space results in excessive investment and building-maintenance costs. Too little space makes it difficult for the hotel owners to realize satisfactory profits and, in service areas, causes crowding, reduces speed, and increases payroll.

Information on a few hotels can probably be obtained by the architect. However, the data may apply to hotels of the wrong size, possibly of a different type, or designed to meet unusual requirements. Even with a set of complete plans, there is no assurance that the areas shown are the right size or that the building will be well suited to the complex business of hotel operation. Generally, the data collected from the sources usually available are incomplete, unrepresentative, or otherwise inadequate.

In order to obtain space-allotment figures that would be reasonably reliable, the plans of more than 40 hotels were examined. These ranged up to 500 guest rooms in size, were of wide geographic distribution, and all were built within the last 25 years. They were predominantly of the transient, commercial type and were believed to be representative. Although several were in resort communities, this had little influence on the space allotments for the working areas. Residential hotels and apartment houses were not included.

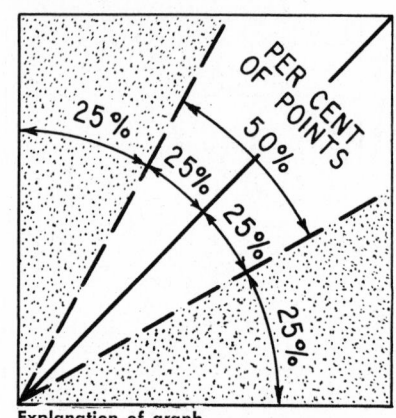

Explanation of graph

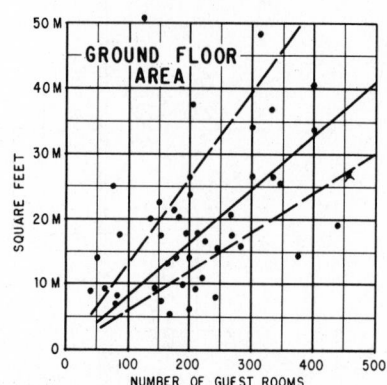

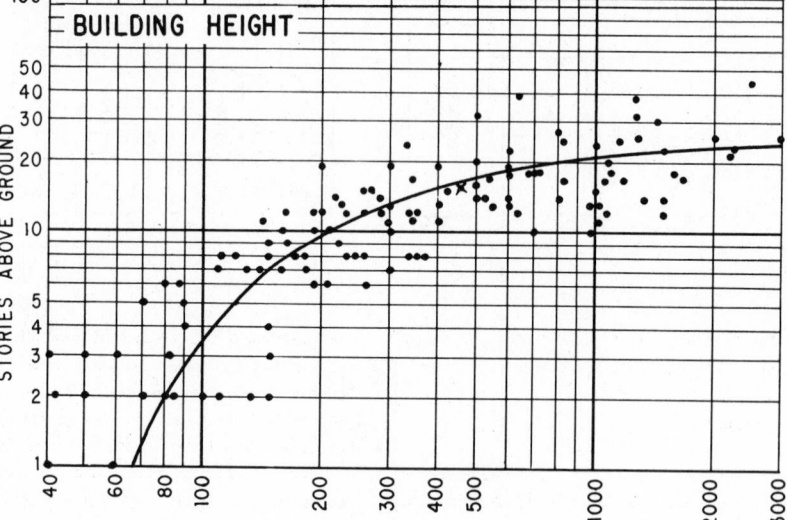

ORGANIZATION AND USE OF GRAPHS

In general, each space allotment is plotted on a separate graph, with the total number of guest rooms in the hotel as the base line, for this appears to be the most feasible common denominator. The plotted points (each representing one hotel) often pepper the graph in a widely scattered manner without suggesting a good location for a trend line running through the field of points. The plotted points for the lobby, main kitchen, and boiler room, however, indicate that the size of these areas varies directly with the number of guest rooms. This is a reasonable expectation for other areas.

To arrange the information in a clear and usable form, a solid diagonal line is started at "zero-zero" in the lower left corner of the graph and located by trial to show the median trend running up through the field of the points so that half the points are above the line and half below it. On most of the graphs, two broken diagonal lines are drawn in addi-

tion. The upper diagonal line is located by trial so that one-fourth of the total plotted points are above it, and the lower diagonal so that one-fourth of the points are below it. As a result, the fan-shaped area between the two broken diagonal lines contains 50 per cent of the points plotted and may be considered as the usual range of practice.

This method of presentation enables the designer to grasp at a glance the relative number of data points, their location, distribution, and trend. He may then determine what deviations from the median value are required for his hotel. The occasional points plotted above the range of the grid are not located to vertical scale.

The generalization that the usual space allotment for the front office is 1 sq ft per guest room is true. By glancing at the graph, however, the designer can estimate the reasonable tolerance above and below this value.

The space allotments for the 455-room Hartford Statler-Hilton Hotel are worthy of special designation and are indicated, where shown, by an X on the data point. The designers, already thoroughly versed in hotel planning and accustomed to attaining high standards of guest comfort and operating efficiency, spent several years of research in planning this structure. The data points that vary appreciably from the median values were for the most part the results of a reevaluation of hotel space requirements, and not due to circumstances peculiar to this hotel.

The method of presentation is such that one or two unusual instances have little influence on the trend line. In contrast, taking an average value might be influenced considerably by one or two abnormally high or low values.

This information is not presented as the final word on space allotments. But it should serve as a reliable guide in

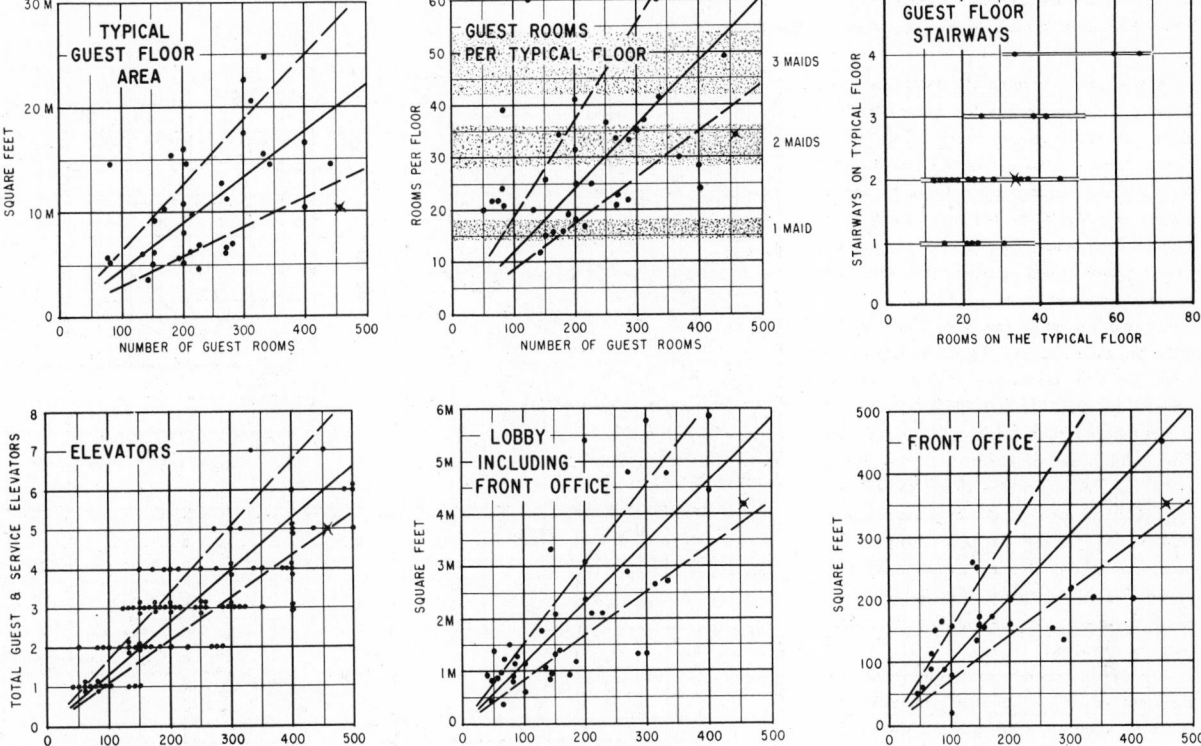

future planning, subject to modifications to meet individual requirements.

GENERAL DATA

Certain general data warrant consideration to give an approximate over-all idea of the typical hotel with any given number of guest rooms.

Building height is indicated by the number of stories above ground. The results of a survey of 125 hotels are shown on the graph, plotted with logarithmic coordinates. The curve rises rapidly, showing the typical 200-room hotel to be 10 stories high, and then tends to level off, showing the typical hotel of 2,000 to 3,000 rooms to be about 25 stories high.

Ground-floor area is shown with the plotted points widely scattered on the graph. The available ground area and the number of guest rooms to be placed on it account for the wide dispersion. In general, the more guest rooms, the greater the ground-floor area. ("M" is the abbreviation for 1,000.)

Typical guest-floor area usually covers about 55 per cent of the ground-floor area, according to the data presented. The guest-floor area may vary greatly, however, depending upon individual circumstances.

Guest rooms per typical floor are shown with a wide dispersion of the plotted points. If there were a standard average-size guest room and a standard percentage addition for corridors, stairways, and the like, then the points on this graph would follow a pattern similar to the graph for the typical guest-floor area, because the area for each data point would be divided by a constant value representing each guest room plus allowances. No such standards exist, however, and therefore the two patterns show no marked resemblance.

Usually each maid is assigned to about 16 rooms, which should all be on the same floor. If feasible, the number of guest rooms on the typical floor should be a multiple of 16 or quite close to it. On the graph, the horizontal bands indicate that one maid would handle from 14 to 18 rooms, two maids twice this number or from 28 to 36 rooms, and three maids three times the number or from 42 to 54 rooms. In more than half the hotels studied, the housekeeper apparently has some difficulty in arranging maid assignments.

Guest-floor stairways tend to increase in number with the number of guest rooms on the typical floor. Regulations limiting the distance from the guest-room door to the nearest stairway entrance usually require a minimum of two stairways on the typical floor. The graph shows that two stairways are usually enough if there are no more than 40 guest rooms per floor. In general, there are about 15 to 20 rooms per stairway.

Elevators are provided according to the number of guest rooms. The number of elevators is of course also influenced by other factors such as the height of the building, the speed of the elevators, and the desired average frequency of service. The total number of guest and service elevators is presented on the graph.

A special study of elevators in 100 hotels showed the distribution between guest elevators and service cars (including short-lift cars) to be as follows:

Number of rooms in hotel	Guest cars per 100 rooms	Service cars per 100 rooms
50–150	1.3	1.0
150–550	0.7	0.5

Expressed another way, about 60 per cent of the elevators are guest cars and about 40 per cent are service cars.

The typical hotel has six main space divisions, classified according to function: (1) Public space, (2) Concession space, (3) Subrental space, (4) Food and beverage service space, (5) Guest-room space, and (6) General-service space. Each division will be considered separately. The percentage of the total area that is productive (revenue producing) space is of special significance. Preferably, at least 50 per cent of the total area should be productive space.

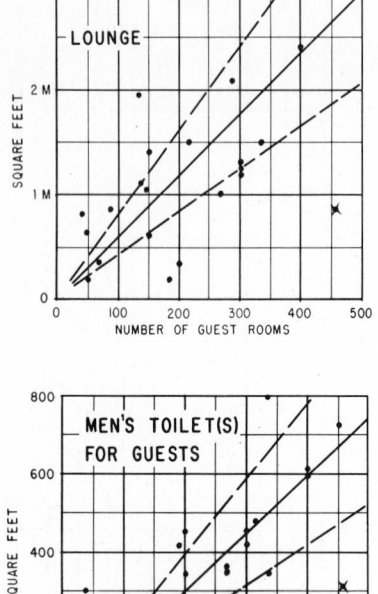

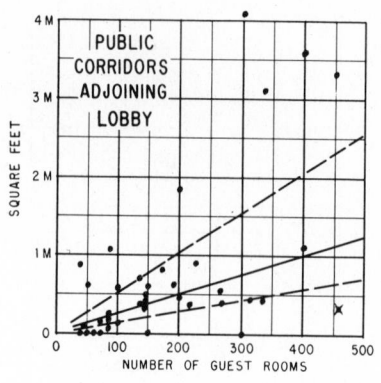

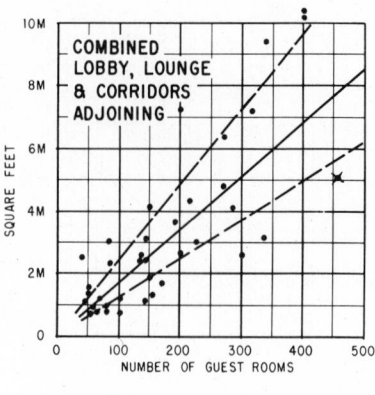

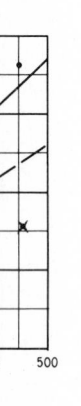

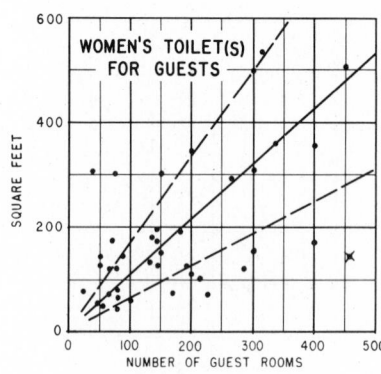

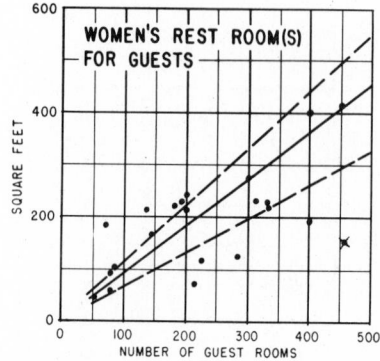

PUBLIC SPACE

Public space comprises those areas that are open to the public as necessary auxiliaries but that generally do not yield a direct profit. Typical inclusions in these areas promoting guest convenience are the lobby, lounge, public toilets, and entertainment rooms.

The lobby including front office is usually assigned about 11 sq ft per guest room. The tendency in recent years has been to reduce the size of this nonproductive area. Formerly, 14 sq ft was not uncommon, but now 9 sq ft is often considered ample. About 40 per cent of the points on the graph do not exceed 9 sq ft per guest room.

The front office is the nerve center or control point for many of the activities of the hotel. The front office, or front desk, has guest-contact stations for the registry, cashier, information, and mail. The average allotment is 1 sq ft per guest room. The specialist in front-office operation and equipment may recommend the dimensions desired for best results. A straight-line counter is generally preferred, with a length of 10 ft for a 50-room hotel, 15 ft for 100 rooms, 20 ft for 200 rooms, and 26 ft for 400 rooms.

The lounge is usually allotted about 6 sq ft per guest room. The graph shows, however, that half the hotels studied use only 4 sq ft and a few even cut this area to 2 sq ft per guest room.

The lounge usually adjoins the lobby so that guests waiting in the lobby can overflow into the lounge. Some designers simply designate the area "Lobby-Lounge" with no demarcation between them.

Public corridors adjoining the lobby are often designed so that the lobby is set back from the street entrance and is reached by one or more corridors flanked by stores, restaurants, or other areas. This nonproductive area is justified if it permits a high return from street-frontage areas. Some layouts require no such corridors. The space allotment is dependent more on design than on the number of guest rooms.

The combined lobby, lounge, and adjoining corridors are quite flexible in the allotment of space. To bring these three nonproductive areas into proper perspective, the sum of the areas is given on the graph. The combined areas show a close correlation with the size of the hotel, with an average allotment of about 16 sq ft per guest room. Some hotels, however, have reduced this nonproductive area to 12 sq ft per guest room.

The men's toilet(s) for guests should be adequate in number, but not excessive. The required space may be divided into two widely separated rooms or simply provided in one location. The convenience of guests and·of restaurant and bar patrons should

be the chief consideration in planning the location. This facility should not be too accessible to the man on the street.

The women's toilet(s) for guests should be provided on the same basis as the men's toilet facilities. In addition, the entrance should be inconspicuous.

The women's restroom(s) for guests frequently precedes the women's toilet. It is an appreciated convenience. The restroom is generally of about the same area as the adjoining women's toilet. The combined allotment for the women's toilet and restroom is typically 1 sq ft per guest room. Some recently planned hotels have cut this figure in half to reduce the nonprofit area.

Entertainment quarters and game rooms are properly classified as public space because they seldom yield an annual profit. Thus, if a ballroom were used only for dances and other entertainment, it would be included under public space. However, since a ballroom is also used for banquets, it is more suitably included under food and beverage service space and will therefore be considered later.

CONCESSION AND SUBRENTAL SPACES

Concession space is for guest-paid hotel services that might be run by the management or sublet on a percentage basis. It may well include a barber shop, beauty

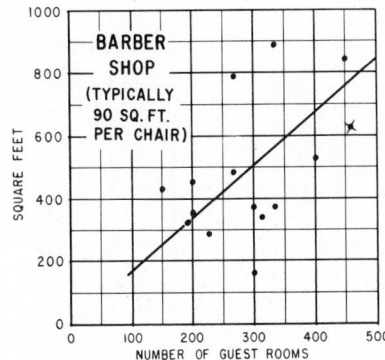

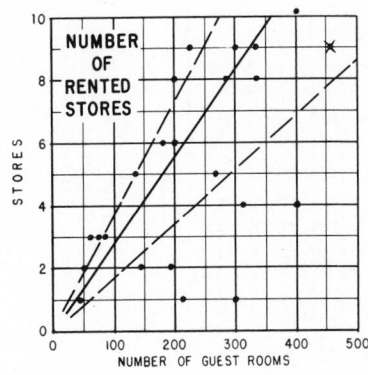

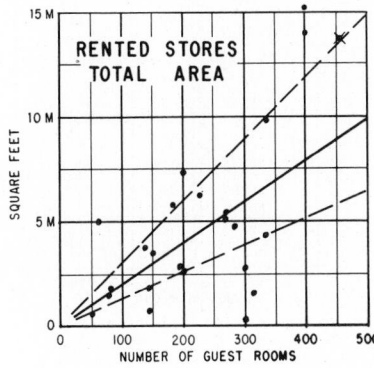

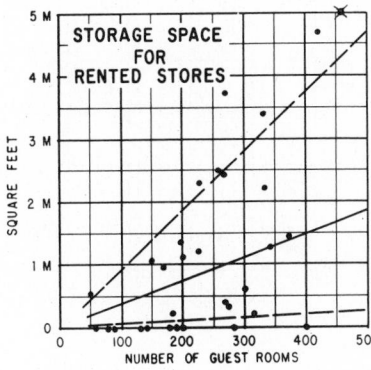

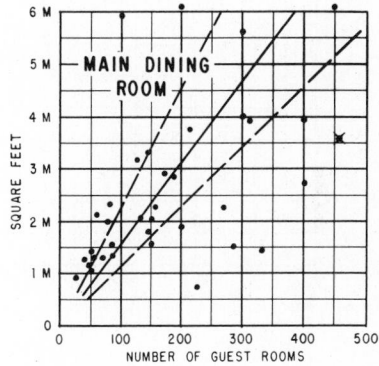

parlor, cigar and news stand, and valet shop.

Subrental space is for services that are not normally provided under hotel operation, such as stores, permanent exhibits, travel agencies, offices, and club quarters. The rental is usually a fixed monthly amount.

These two income-producing divisions are treated together for the purpose of space allotments.

The barber shop is in considerably less demand than formerly. Less than half of the recently constructed hotels have this facility. If provided, the allotment is about 1.5 sq ft per guest room. Typically, the barber shop requires 90 sq ft per chair and a minimum of 4 chairs.

There were insufficient data on the *beauty parlor* to warrant a graph. The beauty parlor, if provided, usually has about half as many chairs as the barber shop in the same hotel. The required area, including space for manicure tables and lockers and toilet for employees, is about 200 sq ft per chair.

The cigar and news stand is customarily operated by the front desk in the smaller hotels. Medium-size hotels often place this area adjacent to the front desk so that it can be operated by a separate clerk during busy hours and by the front-office person-

nel during slack periods. In some hotels, this area is operated by the drugstore concession. The largest hotels may place the cigar and news stand across the lobby from the front desk.

The valet shop handles the pressing and cleaning of the guests' garments. Usually the service is provided for the guest through the bellman. The valet shop is generally located adjacent to the laundry in the larger hotels and is allotted about 1 sq ft per guest room. Many hotels, finding that guests expect this service, have had to improvise because it was not included in the plans. Sometimes the area has no pressing equipment but merely serves as the pick-up and delivery station for a local concern in the business.

A telegraph office, requiring 40 to 60 sq ft, may be desirable in the larger hotels to relieve the front desk of the work of processing guest telegrams.

The extremely high cost of land and the heavy tax assessment in the choice retail district of a city generally make it necessary to count on store rentals to carry the premium cost of the land, regardless of whether the owners prefer the inclusion of stores.

The number of rented stores, as indicated by the wide dispersion of the data

points on the graph, depends more upon circumstances than upon the number of guest rooms. The graph does not indicate the percentage of hotels without stores. If stores are included, however, there is generally about one store for every 35 guest rooms.

The total area of rented stores increases with the size of the hotel. Rented stores are well advised to have a direct entrance from the street; however, an additional entrance from the lobby increases the rental value. If stores are provided, 20 sq ft of store area per guest room is the average allotment. Some designers increase the income potential by raising this figure to 30 sq ft of store area per guest room.

Storage space for rented stores enhances the rental value of the store. Most hotels provide a separate area, often in the basement (where space is far less valuable), to serve as a receiving room, a place to open boxes and to store a moderate amount of merchandise. A comparison of the typical values shows that the storage space is frequently about one-fifth of the store area, and in some instances at least one-third of the store area.

Other subrental areas are sometimes provided for travel agencies, offices, and club quarters. No definite conclusions can

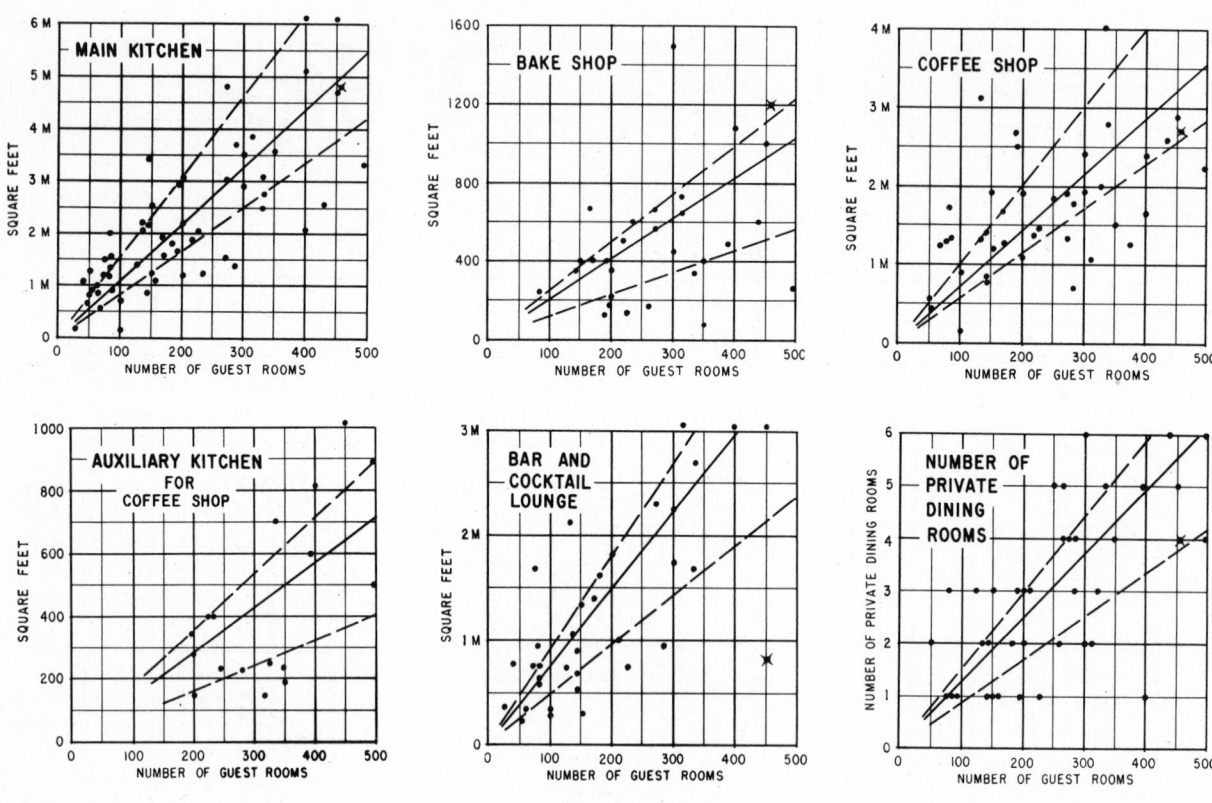

be drawn, however, because of fragmentary data on the scattered uses of these areas.

FOOD AND BEVERAGE SERVICE SPACE

This division includes all areas used for the receiving, storage, preparation, and service of food and beverages for guests, the general public, and employees. It includes the receiving area, storerooms for food and beverage supplies, china, glassware, and silver, and also the kitchen, restaurants, banquet hall, private dining rooms, employees' dining area, food service pantries, bar, cocktail lounge, and garbage room (sometimes with an incinerator).

The main dining room area should not be determined merely on the basis of average data. The probable demand for a main dining room should be estimated with care, for, at best, profitable operation is especially difficult. The difficulty is due to the necessity of long hours of operation at slack load together with competition from other restaurants. About 16 sq ft per seat is required for the dining room. The allotment varies from 18 sq ft for de luxe dining rooms to 14 sq ft for popular priced places. The typical allotment of 16 sq ft of main dining-room area *per guest room* is not especially helpful in planning.

The main kitchen should be sized for the work load. In addition to the main dining room, the main kitchen may also have to service the coffee shop, the banquet hall, private dining rooms, employees' meals, and room service to guests. Such conditions apply to the Hartford Statler, for example, where the kitchen is 33 per cent *larger* than the main dining room. If the kitchen is to service only the main dining room, however, its area is customarily 40 to 45 per cent of the dining room area. In two of the hotels studied the kitchen serviced only the coffee shop; in two other hotels, it serviced the coffee shop, private dining rooms, and, presumably, employee meals.

It was not feasible in analyzing and presenting the data to separate the kitchen work load into its several types of components and their sizes or the number of persons served.

A bake shop, of one type or another, is usually provided. In many of the smaller hotels, the baker occupies a corner of the kitchen. If a separate bake-shop area is provided, the typical allotment is 2 sq ft per guest room. However, it is preferable to size it for the work load. If a separate bake shop is provided, its area is usually equal to 20 per cent of the kitchen area.

The coffee shop provides quick food service at moderate prices. Of the 46 hotels analyzed, 63 per cent had a coffee shop.

About 7 sq ft per guest room is the usual allotment.

The area required per seat in coffee shops is about 18 sq ft per seat for counter service only, (this area includes the counter), 16 sq ft per seat for both counter and table service, and 14 sq ft per seat for table service only. Frequently about one-third of the seats are at the counter.

An auxiliary kitchen for the coffee shop is customarily provided if the coffee shop is remote from the main kitchen. Under these circumstances, the auxiliary kitchen may be "backed-up" by the main kitchen, which prepares such heavy-duty items as roast meats, or it may have complete facilities for cooking almost everything on its menu. The auxiliary kitchen is generally from 20 to 25 per cent of the area of the coffee shop. However, the extra kitchen payroll and equipment required make it desirable to plan so that an auxiliary kitchen is not needed.

The bar and cocktail lounge may be separated, adjoining, or combined. Sometimes one area is shown without the other. For each hotel analyzed, the data point shows the total area. No data point is shown for any of the several hotels that had neither bar nor cocktail lounge.

If the area is provided, 7.5 sq ft per guest room is the typical allotment. However, it is well to estimate the amount of

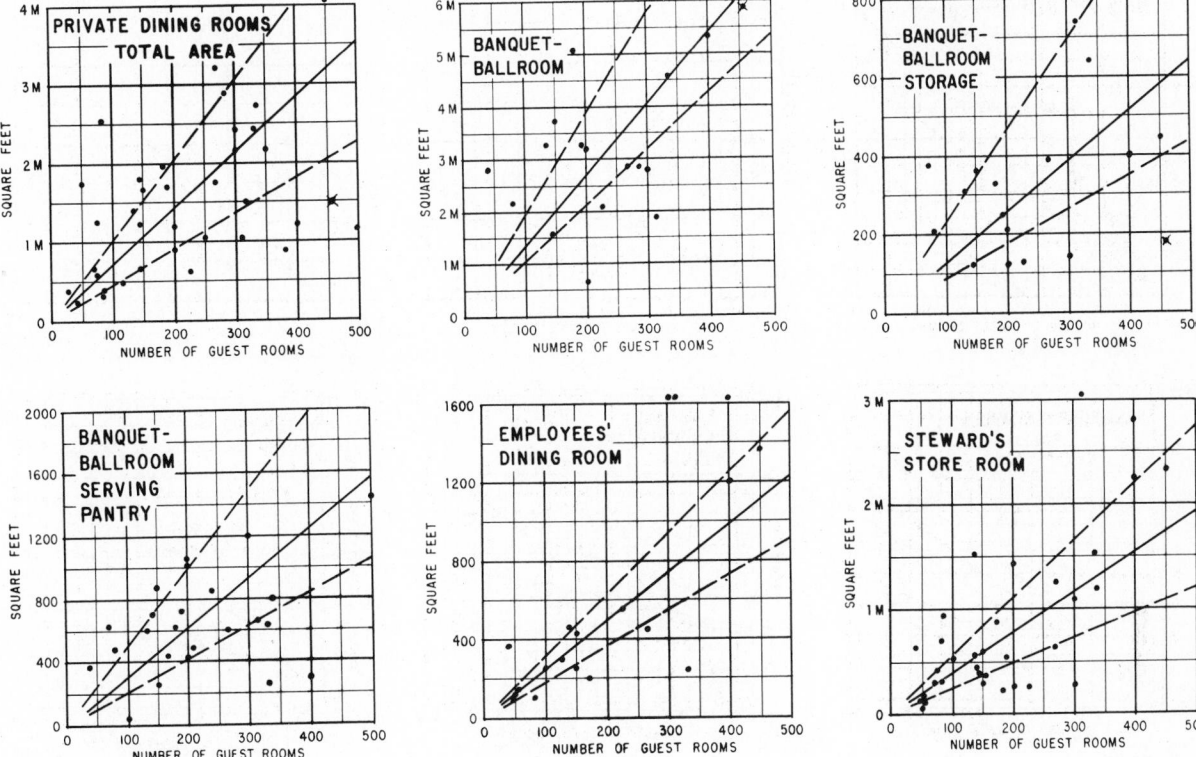

business that the bar and cocktail lounge will handle in view of the characteristics of the community and the type of patronage likely to be attracted. The space allotment should then be altered proportionately.

The number of private dining rooms indicated on the graph does not include instances in which the banquet hall is divided into smaller dining areas by folding walls or sliding partitions. Most hotels that serve food have private dining rooms, with an average of one room for 80 guest rooms. The use of private dining rooms depends more upon the demand in the particular community than upon the number of guest rooms.

The total area of private dining rooms is typically 7 sq ft per guest room, but variations are extremely wide. The seating capacity is often estimated at 10 or 11 sq ft per seat. However, much depends upon the right dimensions to accommodate the desired layout of tables, chairs, and aisle spaces, which have certain minimum sizes. If the room is large and its dimensions are right, 9 sq ft per seat is a possibility. Small rooms with random dimensions may require nearly twice as much area per seat.

The typical private dining room has an area of 600 sq ft, for the graphs show that 6 of them have a total of 3600 sq ft. If several private dining rooms are provided,

it is usual to have the sizes increased progressively to care for various size groups. For example, capacities of 15, 25, 40, and 70 seats would provide a good variety. There is a decided advantage in having private dining rooms adjoining and separated by folding, sound-absorbing partitions.

The banquet-ballroom was provided in half of the hotels studied. It is generally used more frequently for banquets than for dances. The probability of its operation being financially successful is often a serious question. If provided, the allotment is usually from 10 to 20 sq ft per guest room.

A banquet-ballroom foyer is recommended. The size is usually one-sixth to one-third of the banquet-ballroom area.

Banquet-ballroom storage, preferably adjoining the banquet hall, is required for chairs and tables. This storage area is typically about one-tenth of the size of the banquet hall, as may be determined from the two graphs.

The banquet-ballroom serving pantry is often simply a food-assembly and pick-up area. Pantry space is sometimes provided within the main kitchen if adjacent to the banquet hall. In other instances, a separate room is provided adjacent to the banquet hall, with plate warmers, hot-top serving tables, refrigerators, serving counters, coffee urns, and sometimes dishwashing facili-

ties. Occasionally, cooking equipment, such as broilers, is included and the area is then known as the banquet kitchen. Obviously, the requisite space allotment per 100 banquet seats varies with the function of the pantry. The typical ratio assigns to the pantry an area equal to 23 per cent of the banquet-hall area, but in a dozen separate investigations the ratio was from 12 to 38 per cent.

An employees' dining room is provided for the bellmen, maids, elevator operators, and the like. (Other employees such as the staff from the front office and the accounting department usually eat in the coffee shop.) Seats are usually provided for half of those on hand for the noon meal, since all do not eat at one time. Food service is often cafeteria style with a simple menu. The necessary space including the serving counter should be determined on the basis of 18 sq ft per seat and the number of employees to be seated at one time. If this is not feasible, the graph shows that 1.4 sq ft of employees' dining room is the typical allotment per guest room, a value that is generally satisfactory.

The steward's storeroom provides the storage space for dry foodstuffs, canned goods, vegetables, dairy products, and meat. Platforms, shelves, refrigerators, and freezers are needed. Deliveries are usually made at least three times a week, although

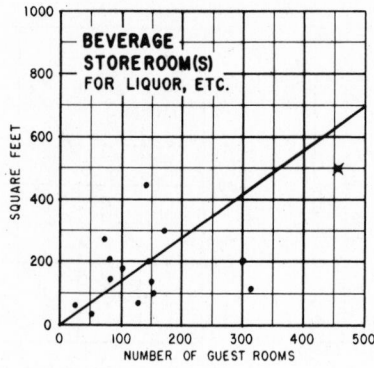

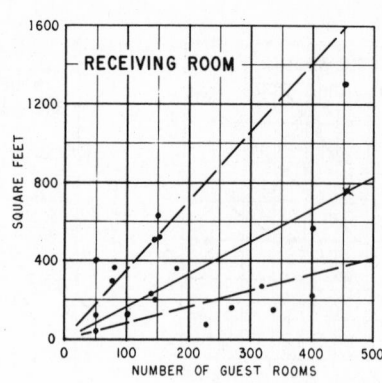

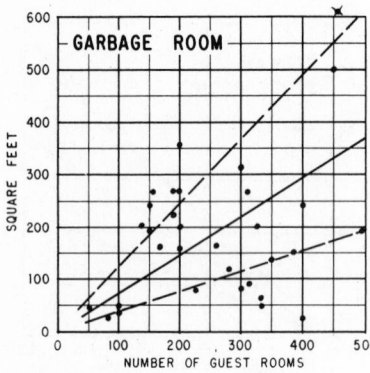

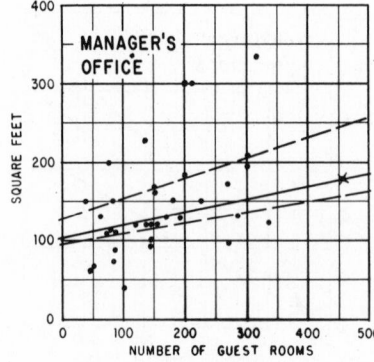

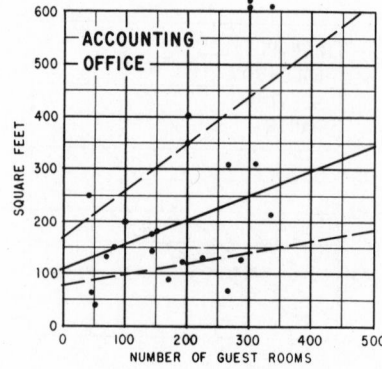

the service is less frequent in larger storage facilities. Typically, 4 sq ft is allowed per guest room for hotels having the average ratio of food and beverage sales to room sales.

Beverage storeroom(s) should be provided separately from general food storerooms in order to ensure adequate control. Sometimes beverage storage space is provided in the steward's storeroom, generally in a fenced-off area. Wine and liquor are of such value as to definitely warrant separate storage under lock and key. Beer and soft drinks are desirably, but not necessarily, stored in separate rooms. The areas on the plans studied are not always marked specifically; the designation may be beverage storage, or wine and liquor storage, or four separate rooms for wine, liquor, beer, and soft drinks. Whatever the designation on the plans, this area was considered as the beverage storage space in the analysis.

The typical allotment is 1.4 sq ft of beverage storage area per guest room, although often this figure was only for wine and liquor. Probably 2 sq ft of total beverage storage should normally be allotted per guest room.

The receiving room is provided for food, beverages, linen, and other supplies which, upon arrival, are customarily checked against delivery slips, weighed, counted, and inspected. These supplies remain in

the receiving room until time and manpower are available to take them to appropriate stock rooms. The typical allotment for the receiving room is 1.6 sq ft per guest room, although the graph shows wide variations.

A garbage room is required for quantities of garbage, bottles, cans, and cartons, which accumulate between daily removals or longer intervals over the weekends. Such refuse should not clutter the receiving room or be placed outside the back door. Health authorities object to garbage cans being kept in the kitchen.

Nearly half of the plans studied in the basic survey had no area designated as the garbage room. Plans of additional hotels were consequently studied to give more data points on the graph. The typical allotment for the garbage room of 0.75 sq ft per guest room is generally satisfactory. The use of garbage- and trash-disposal equipment will also influence the size of the room.

GUEST-ROOM SPACE

This division includes the guest rooms together with guest bathrooms, clothes closets, and entrance vestibules, the sum of which is the area that the guest rents. Also included are the necessary auxiliary areas found on the typical floor, such as guest corridors, stair wells, elevator shafts, and

maid's closets. Any parlors (usually part of a suite) are included. If provided, sample rooms for the display of merchandise are also considered guest-room space, regardless of their location.

A schedule is customarily prepared stating the approximate total number of guest rooms. This is subdivided to give the number and approximate size of each type of room desired, such as single, double, and twin beds, and any sample rooms. Decision must be reached on what proportion of the rooms of each type is to be of the conventional and of the studio styles. King-length beds versus those of standard length must also be considered. Unless stated otherwise, each guest room has a three-fixture bath and a clothes closet.

These problems of guest-room space must not be considered trivial; indeed, the main reason for building a hotel is to rent guest rooms, which are the unquestioned source of greatest profits. Every mistake, every omission, and every point of excellence is multiplied by the number of rooms constructed. Extremely careful planning is warranted for it pays big dividends.

GENERAL SERVICE SPACE

This division, classed as nonproductive space, includes those areas for general administration, operation, maintenance, and storage that are not otherwise classified.

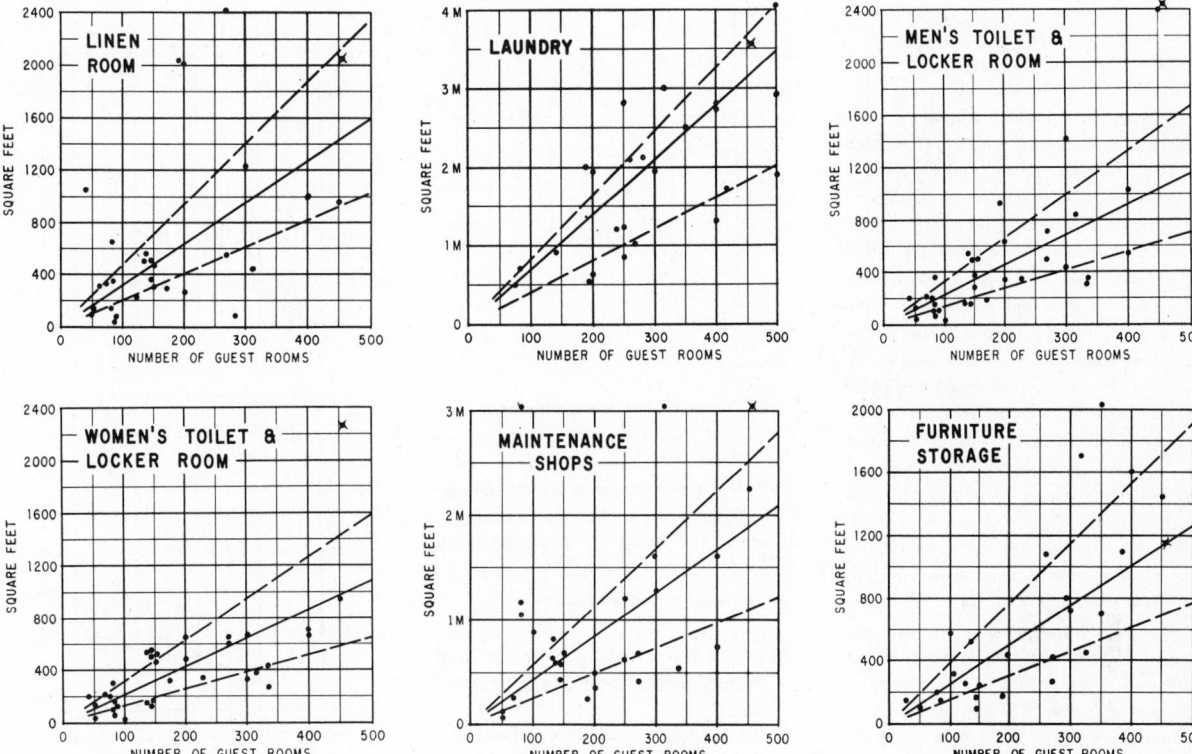

They include executive and administrative offices; areas devoted to the handling and storage of linen; help's quarters; maintenance shops; rooms for housing the mechanical equipment for heat, light, power, ventilation, and refrigeration; and also certain storerooms. Areas related to food and beverage are not included because they have been classified separately.

The manager's office requires a minimum area of about 100 sq ft. (Note that the trend lines on the graph are not drawn through the "zero-zero" point.) This area may well increase slightly with the size of the hotel, but the activities in this office seldom justify more than 200 sq ft. About 140 sq ft is the most common space allotment, regardless of the size of the hotel.

The accounting office should have a minimum area of about 100 sq ft to accommodate one person at a desk with appropriate record-keeping and filing equipment. (On this graph also, the trend lines are not drawn through the "zero-zero" point.) As the size of the hotel increases, more accounting personnel are needed requiring more space. The typical area of the accounting office for a 200-room hotel is shown on the graph as 200 sq ft, whereas for a 400-room hotel it is 300 sq ft.

Quite often the plans do not provide for the accounting office. Since the hotel operator cannot get along without this facility, he is generally forced to adapt one or two guest rooms (along with bathroom, clothes closet, and vestibule) for the purpose. The investment in the bathroom area and plumbing equipment is lost, the potential profit of five dollars per day on the room is wiped out, and the location of the improvised accounting office is often inconvenient. If an effort to economize caused the accounting office to be omitted from the plans, it was certainly misdirected and proved to be very costly.

A linen room is necessary to accommodate the housekeeper's office and the shelves of neatly stacked linens, together with the counter over which the maids receive their supplies. Often the lost-and-found cabinets for articles left in guest rooms are located here. Frequently a sewing machine and mending table are provided. Various employee uniforms are stocked and distributed here. The space allotment for the main linen room is usually from 2 to 4.5 sq ft per guest room, according to the graph, with many hotels favoring the larger value.

A laundry is sometimes operated by the hotel, although frequently the hotel laundry services only flat work and uniforms, and sends out guest laundry. To determine whether the hotel should operate its laundry requires an analysis of the costs of complete linen service, costs of commercial laundering, local wage rates, relative life of linen, availability and costs of space, necessary linen inventory, responsibility of running another department, and other factors. In general, the larger the hotel, the more likely it is to run its own laundry. (For a more detailed discussion of this subject, see section on Hotel and Motel Laundries.)

The graph shows that if a laundry is installed, it is usually allotted 7 sq ft per guest room. In a few cases, the allotment is only 4 sq ft per guest room.

The men's toilet and locker room in the employees' quarters is generally allotted 2.4 sq ft per guest room. Thoughtful planning justifies at least half again as much space, or 3.6 sq ft per guest room. The Hartford Statler with 455 guest rooms allotted 2,550 sq ft, with the ratio being 5.6 sq ft per guest room. There is reason to believe that the average figure results in crowded and unsatisfactory conditions.

Two separate but adjoining rooms are generally but not always provided. In general, about 35 per cent of the area is allotted for the toilet facilities and 65 per cent for the locker room. The requisite number of toilet fixtures for the size of the staff is the logical but more detailed way to arrive at the solution.

The women's toilet and locker room is usually allotted about the same space as the men's, and should be increased by the same amount.

In providing equal space for men and

women, we of course assume that they will be employed in approximately equal numbers. If the operating policy favors waiters instead of waitresses, then the space allotment should be adjusted accordingly.

Maintenance shops are necessary to keep the hotel running. There should generally be a minimum of three separate rooms: (1) Plumbing-and-electric shop, (2) Carpentry-and-upholstering shop, and (3) Paint-and-varnish room. The work in each shop is such that it does not mix well with the others. The plumbing shop is sometimes in the boiler room although not marked on the plans. The typical allotment for maintenance shops is 4 sq ft per guest room.

Some hotels have cut this allotment in half. General maintenance suffers as a result. When the means for repair are lacking, things that could be fixed have to be replaced by buying new ones. The reduction in initial cost is more than offset by increased operating expense.

Furniture storage is required for extra items of furniture and broken pieces awaiting repair. They should not be placed in basement corridors. The typical allotment for furniture storage is 2.5 sq ft per guest room, apparently a reasonable and satisfactory amount.

The boiler room space allotment is determined by many factors, such as the climate, the various uses of steam, the type of boilers, and the capacity of the standby boiler. Water heaters for the usual hot water supply are often placed in the boiler room although not noted specifically on the plans.

The graph shows the angle between the two broken lines to be relatively narrow. The middle 50 per cent of the points do not "fan out" over a wide angle. Consequently, the typical allotment for the boiler room of 6 sq ft per guest room may be used as a preliminary figure subject to possible revision after details have been developed.

Fuel storage is not required if gas or district steam is used exclusively. If coal or oil is the only fuel or reserve fuel used, however, then storage space is needed. The amount of storage, of course, depends on such factors as maximum rate of use, frequency of delivery, and cost of providing storage space. It is not surprising that some of the data points are far from the average line. The typical value for fuel storage is about 2.2 sq ft per guest room. This value may well be revised to suit the specific conditions that apply.

A transformer vault is a necessary part of the hotel's electrical system. The electric energy used goes through a bank of transformers, which are sometimes located out-

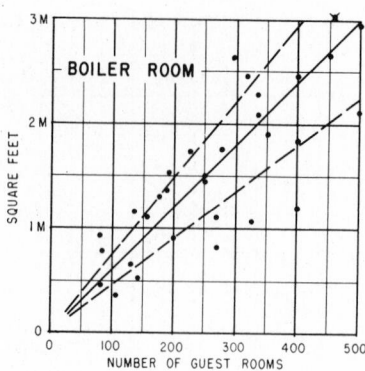

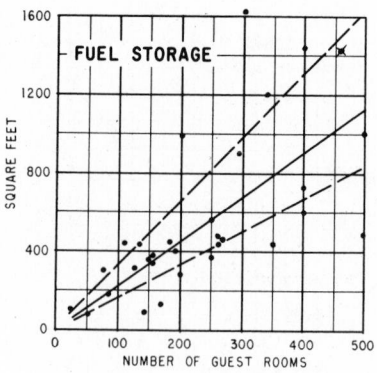

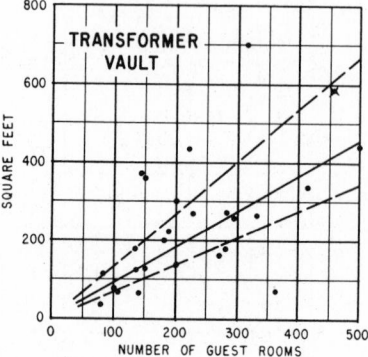

side the hotel but more frequently in the basement in a specially constructed vault. An allotment for the transformer vault of 1 sq ft per guest room is usually adequate. If very extensive use of electricity is planned, the allowance should be checked with the electric service company as a precautionary measure.

PRELIMINARY SCHEDULE OF SPACE ALLOTMENTS AND FLOOR ASSIGNMENTS

The following example of applying the statistics to a proposed typical commercial hotel of 100 rooms is presented as a guide. First the general data indicate the over-all characteristics of the hotel. These data are followed by more specific space allotments, which adhere closely to the typical values shown on the graphs. Items marked with an asterisk have been added to furnish desired areas for which no graph was given; items designated by a question mark may be omitted if the size of the hotel or other considerations do not warrant the area. In addition, the floor assignments are designated as follows: basement (B), ground floor (G), and typical guest floor (T).

Since many of the hotels in this survey were planned without certain desired areas,

SPACE ALLOTMENTS AND FLOOR ASSIGNMENTS FOR TYPICAL HOTEL OF 100 ROOMS

General data and approximations

Height of building above ground (ground floor plus 6 typical guest floors)	7 stories
Ground-floor area	10,000 sq ft
Typical guest-floor area	6,000 sq ft
Guest rooms per typical floor,	17 rooms
Stairways on the typical floor,	2 stairways
Elevators (1 guest and 1 service car)	2 elevators

The first four factors listed above are of course all interrelated and must be organized as a compatible group.

Public space	Productive area, sq ft	Nonproductive area, sq ft
Lobby and front office		1,100(G)
Lounge		600(G)
Corridors adjoining		200(G)
(total of above, 1,900 sq ft)		
Men's toilet for guests		150(G)
Women's toilet for guests		100(G)
Women's restroom for guests		100(G)
*Coat checkroom		120(G)
*Bellman's checkroom		40(G)

	Productive area, sq ft	Nonproductive area, sq ft
Concession space		
Barber shop	180(B)	
*Valet shop	100(B)	
Subrental space		
3 rented stores, (each 800 sq ft)	2,400(G)	
3 storage rooms (each 200 sq ft)	600(B)	
Food and beverage service space		
Main dining room (90 seats)	1,500(G)	
Main kitchen		1,100(G)
Bake shop		200(G)
?Coffee shop (50 seats)	800(G)	
Bar and cocktail lounge	750(G)	
Private dining rooms (250 + 500 sq ft)	750(G)	
?Banquet-ballroom	1,400(B)	
?Banquet-ballroom foyer		450(B)
?Banquet-ballroom storage		140(B)
?Banquet serving pantry		350(B)
Employees' dining room		220(B)
Steward's storeroom		400(G)
Beverage storerooms		180(B)
*China, glass, and silver storage		300(B)
Receiving room		180(G)
Garbage room		80(G)

	Productive area sq ft	Nonproductive area sq ft
Guest-room space		
102 rooms (each 250 sq ft; including bath, closet and vestibule)	25,500(T)	
Auxiliary space (add 40 per cent of above for corridors, stairs, elevators, maid's closets, walls, and partitions)		10,200(T)
General service space		
Manager's office		140(G)
*Secretary's office		100(G)
Accounting office		150(G)
?*Sales and reservations office		140(G)
*Mimeograph room		40(G)
Linen room		350(B)
?Laundry (700 sq ft; omitted)		
Men's toilet and locker room		360(B)
Women's toilet and locker room		360(B)
Maintenance shops		400(B)
Furniture storage		250(B)
*Records storeroom		250(B)
*General storeroom		200(B)
Boiler room		600(B)
*Water-heater tank space		150(B)
Fuel storage		200(B)
Transformer vault		100(B)
*Refrigeration compressor room		400(B)
*Fan rooms, ventilation equipment		400(B)
Total productive area	33,980 sq ft	
Listed nonproductive area		20,800 sq ft
Add for basement corridors, walls, stairways, and elevators		2,500 sq ft
Add for ground-floor stairways and elevators		500 sq ft
Total nonproductive area		23,800 sq ft
Grand total of areas	57,780 sq ft	

it is well to make a liberal estimate of the total ground-floor area.

The above schedule shows a preliminary estimate of 59 per cent productive area and 41 per cent nonproductive area, which is a more favorable ratio than is generally realized in practice.

During the preliminary planning stage, it may be decided to allocate the 1,500 sq ft area to the coffee shop, thus eliminating the main dining room and reducing the size of the main kitchen by about 250 sq ft. The banquet-ballroom, together with its three auxiliary rooms, might be omitted or, if demand for these facilities is assured, placed in the basement. The laundry would probably be omitted, although it was placed in the schedule as a possibility.

From the standpoint of efficiency, it might be convenient to have almost all areas on the ground floor. However, to make the ground-floor and basement area approximately equal, those areas designated (B) have been consigned to the basement.

Thus the area of the ground floor including 500 sq ft for stairways and elevators, but omitting the 800 sq ft coffee shop and deducting 250 sq ft from the main kitchen, amounts to 10,590 sq ft. This figure compares satisfactorily with the preliminary over-all estimate of 10,000 sq ft for the ground floor.

The area of the basement including the banquet-ballroom facilities, but omitting the laundry, and allowing 2,500 sq ft for corridors and the like, amounts to 10,440 sq ft. This figure is about the same as the ground-floor area.

The typical floor has 17 guest rooms. Two stairways, the elevator shaft, and maid's closet increase the floor area by an equivalent of 3 guest rooms, making a total area equivalent to 20 rooms per floor. Ten rooms on each side of the corridor and each room with an assumed average frontage of 12 ft gives 120 ft as the approximate length of the typical guest floor. The width is usually about 50 ft. Thus the area of the typical guest floor (120 ft by 50 ft) is 6,000 sq ft, which checks with the estimate previously made under "general data."

The summary of areas is as follows:

6 typical guest floors, each 6,000 sq ft	36,000 sq ft
Ground floor, figured at 10,590 sq ft	10,500 sq ft
Basement, figured at 10,440 sq ft	10,500 sq ft
Total approximate floor area	57,000 sq ft

MOTELS—1
General

By FRANK HARRISON RANDOLPH, P.E.

Hotel Planning Consultant and Professor of Hotel Engineering, Cornell University

A motel can be defined as any type of sleeping accommodation designed and operated especially for the traveler who travels by car. It may be the most primitive structure, or a virtual palace. It may be called a cabin, a court, a lodge, an inn—or simply a motel.

Growth of the motel business

Since their crude beginning in the 1920's, motels have had a phenomenal growth, paralleling that of the automobile and the highway. Long characterized by small units located on the open highway, motels are now growing larger and moving into the fringes—and even the downtown areas—of large cities. The average size, which was only 15 rooms in 1952, had by 1959 increased to 35 rooms; motels with 100 or more rooms are not uncommon since large corporations have entered the field. Motels are now considered part of the hotel business. Many of the larger motels provide the same services as hotels, and it has become increasingly difficult to draw a sharp line of demarcation between them.

Essentials for success

The success of every motel is influenced by three factors, all of immediate concern to the designer: (1) Good location, (2) Attractive appearance, and (3) Quick, pleasant, and economical service.

TYPE OF PATRONAGE

There are two main types of motel patronage: transient and terminal. The transient motorist, whether traveling on business or for pleasure, generally has certain predictable preferences. Primarily, he wants ready access to his car and quick service. The terminal guest (who may have been a transient yesterday at another motel) has different preferences because he has reached his destination. He wants pleasing surroundings and recreational facilities.

Some motels are designed primarily for transients; others cater only to the terminal guest. Still others must be planned for both types.

Commercial hotels normally derive at least 85 per cent of their room sales from persons traveling on business. The city motel, in the absence of conflicting data, should expect about the same. As a typical example, a 40-room motor court, although 2 miles from the center of a good-sized city, found that business men supplied 85 per cent of its annual business.

And it was a popular motel—its average of 80 per cent room occupancy for the year was nearly 10 per cent above the national average.

Business travel is much greater in volume than vacation or pleasure travel. The volume of business travel is, moreover, fairly constant throughout the year: only 25 per cent more business travel takes place in summer and fall than in winter and spring.

Vacation travel, however, is two to three times greater in summer than in winter. This extreme fluctuation in the volume of business makes it extremely difficult to operate profitably a motel catering solely to vacationers. Most motels of over 50 rooms need almost 50 per cent occupancy to break even. Thus some motels find it necessary to shut down during the off-season to reduce the loss. Real estate taxes and building depreciation, of course, continue nevertheless.

Vacation trips are taken by over 75 per cent of our adult population, but about 60 per cent of these people do not always go to the same place. The most popular vacation destinations in the United States are Florida, California, New York, and Michigan (in that order). Roughly two-thirds of all vacation travel takes place during the summer, and the average vacation travel period is two weeks.

There is a definite need for more acceptable motels for people in the middle- and low-income groups. A new motel should guard against pricing itself out of the market. The designer should be especially careful that construction costs do not result in prohibitively high rental rates.

FEASIBILITY

Determining the probability of financial success for a project is recommended as the first step in planning. A dependable business forecast, based on local controlling conditions, should be made by a competent concern. This forecast should determine whether there is adequate need for a new motel and should give a general indication of the number of guest rooms and the type and extent of services to be provided. The forecast should be followed by selection of the site, working out of the financial plan, and finally, determination of the functional scheme: the number, types, and sizes of guest rooms, public spaces, and food and beverage facilities, the type of building construction, and the extent of mechanical services. Only after these preliminary steps have been completed is the

project ready to be started on the drawing boards. Otherwise, much time, money, and effort may be lost in developing specific ideas that are impractical and yet difficult to discard.

Basic economic survey

Many factors will require careful study by a qualified financial advisor, such as a firm experienced in hotel and motel accounting. Ever-increasing costs of construction and operation are vital considerations. The rapidly expanding and shifting pattern of major highways should be evaluated for its effect on the site. The possibility of an overabundance of motels in the area must not be overlooked. The soundness of the title to the land may be questionable. The decision of whether to purchase the land, build on leased land, or select a sale-and-lease-back arrangement may well have a considerable effect on taxes.

It will aid greatly in planning to have in advance an idea of the type of traveler expected, the probable length of his stay, and the seasonal fluctuations expected in the volume of business. Such a survey is unquestionably a help in determining the financial feasibility of a project. Seasonal variations may require a break-even point at close to 50 per cent occupancy.

Horwath & Horwath, Hotel Accountants and Consultants, stress the importance of determining (1) the rate of economic growth of the area, (2) the probable future development of the community, and (3) the status of existing or contemplated transient housing and feeding accommodations.

LOCATION

Site location is of paramount importance. Geographically, it should be at the end of a day's run for the motorist in order to attract transient business. The average motorist is not interested in stopping for the night except at the end of his day's run, so the site should be a day's run (or a multiple of this) from one or more reservoirs of potential transient business. The typical motorist covers about 300 miles in a day, plus or minus up to 100 miles, depending upon personal preferences and highway conditions, which need individual analysis for a given area. Obviously the motorist will travel considerably farther in a day on limited-access express highways than on the usual improved routes.

Traffic surveys showing the daily volume are of value only if they indicate the number of potential customers passing the site during the critical few hours at the end of the day. The total 24-hour volume of trucks, local passenger traffic, and whatever else comes along means very little. A tally of all passenger-car license plates that passed in each direction during the end-of-the-day period, disregarding, if possible, those issued within a radius of about 200 miles, would give the most helpful indication of potential business for the day or days on which the count was taken. It would give no guarantee of volume, however, for another season or for future years.

Major highway routes are constantly changing, both in pattern and in condition. An excellent location today can become almost worthless next year because a new highway has bypassed it, taking virtually all of its long-distance passenger traffic. Or the condition of a long major route might be so greatly improved that, although the motel was formerly a normal day's drive from a potential reservoir of transient business, it would now be reached by most potential customers by midafternoon—at least two hours before their stopping time. Future highway conditions are difficult to forecast, since highway plans are often changed for unpredictable reasons with disastrous consequences for the motel, which may become virtually stranded. Careful checking with all the various planning agencies, especially the State highway department, is a precaution that must not be overlooked. Indeed, selection of the proper site requires the combined judgment of persons in many fields. The State highway department can forecast traffic characteristics. The chamber of commerce is familiar with recent civic development and building and population trends. The real estate broker knows land values. The construction engineer can report on soil conditions, excavation, and drainage, and indicate probable difficulties in building. The architect experienced in motel design will have a wealth of practical advice. The accounting firm that made the economic survey should be satisfied that the site is properly qualified. The finance company or bank that is to loan the necessary funds must be convinced of the apparent soundness of the venture. If a particular site is vetoed by any one of these qualified parties, the success of the enterprise must be considered open to serious question. There is no satisfactory substitute for an excellent location that meets these various criteria.

When the typical motorist, thinking he has travelled long enough for the day, realizes there is some difficult driving a short distance ahead, and then encounters an attractive motel, he will be nicely conditioned to decide to stop for the night. The

difficulty may be the heavy traffic of a large city, a winding road over a mountain, or a tedious long stretch of road through barren country—something he would rather postpone until morning. Situating the motel suitably in advance of such an obstacle can be definitely rewarding (Fig. 1).

Some motels successfully intercept the traveler just outside a city where he had thought to find lodging (Fig. 2). If several motels are already grouped along the highway leading into a city, a new motel can be expected to be more successful if it joins the group than if it selects an isolated location. Prospective guests tend to be favorably impressed by a large group of motels, which by its very magnitude suggests abundant hospitality and a popular motel area. Once he stops, the traveler is almost certain to stay at one or another of these places (Fig. 3).

If possible, the motel should be on the right-hand side of the road, especially if traffic is at all heavy, since drivers would rather not make a left turn (Fig. 4). If the highway curves, place the motel on the right of a left-hand curve, so that it will be directly in line with the driver's vision (Fig. 5). If the site selected slopes upward from the highway, the hillside location of the motel will add to its prominence (Fig. 6).

The best motel site is the one with the greatest appeal to the largest number of potential customers. The site should of course be plainly visible from a distance. Highway intersections are often excellent places for motels. Approaching motorists will already have reduced speed and be prepared to stop, and can readily size up the situation before reaching the intersection. The order of preference of several possible site locations at an intersection may be influenced by such factors as the slope of the land and the presence of existing or future buildings (Fig. 7, 8, 9).

If travel is about equal in both directions, the motel should aim for those who are going rather than those returning, because of the opportunity for repeat business. Twenty-five per cent of the guests of some motels are repeat customers.

If a town is bypassed by the main traffic route, the motel may be placed on the right-hand side of the road leading to the town, but should be plainly visible from the main highway (Fig. 10). If two towns are not far apart on the highway, the motel should be placed to intercept the major volume of traffic before it reaches either of them. Putting the motel between the towns generally proves unsatisfactory, since most motorists would not be in the mood for stopping on such an in-between stretch (Fig. 11).

It is important to determine well in advance whether the highway department will permit the desired location. Encroachments, set-back regulations, deceleration lanes, and access drives must all be considered. The highway department may not permit direct access from deceleration or acceleration lanes. Definite approval of specific plans should be obtained from the authorities at a very early stage in the planning.

Advance signs advertising the motel and directing the motorist are essential. Often the authorities have very severe restrictions on the placement of such signs; therefore, sign locations must be assured and permissions obtained before the site may be said to be satisfactory.

TYPE OF MOTEL

Motels can be differentiated by their location and purpose. The most common types are as follows:

1. The *city motel* is built in town or on the edge of town. It is intended primarily for commercial travelers with business in the downtown area. It generally involves expensive land, a restricted site, and a structure at least three stories high. Nearly the entire site is used for buildings and parking.

2. The *motor annex*, a relatively new development, adjoins an existing hotel in the city. Whether the motel emphasizes its connection as an annex will depend on the reputation of the hotel and its advertising, location, services, utilities, supervision, and maintenance staff.

3. The *highway motor hotel* furnishes roomside parking for the traveler en route. This type of motel is usually one or two stories high, with a site of at least three acres. If space permits, not more than 15 per cent of the site area is used for buildings and parking.

4. The *resort motel* is intended primarily for guests who have reached their destination, and usually requires ample facilities for recreation. Closing during the off-season may also be necessary. The site, ideally spacious, can be small if necessary.

5. The *airport inn* is built at a major, usually intercontinental, airport. A relatively large and high-class operation, this type of motel often has 150 to 300 rooms, two-story guest-room buildings, and a site of at least 10 acres. Business is supplied by airline patrons, motorists, and guests from the metropolitan area served by the airport. The size of such a motel permits full-scale food and beverage facilities, function rooms, and often as extensive recreational facilities as are found in resort motels. The location usually borders on the outlying in-

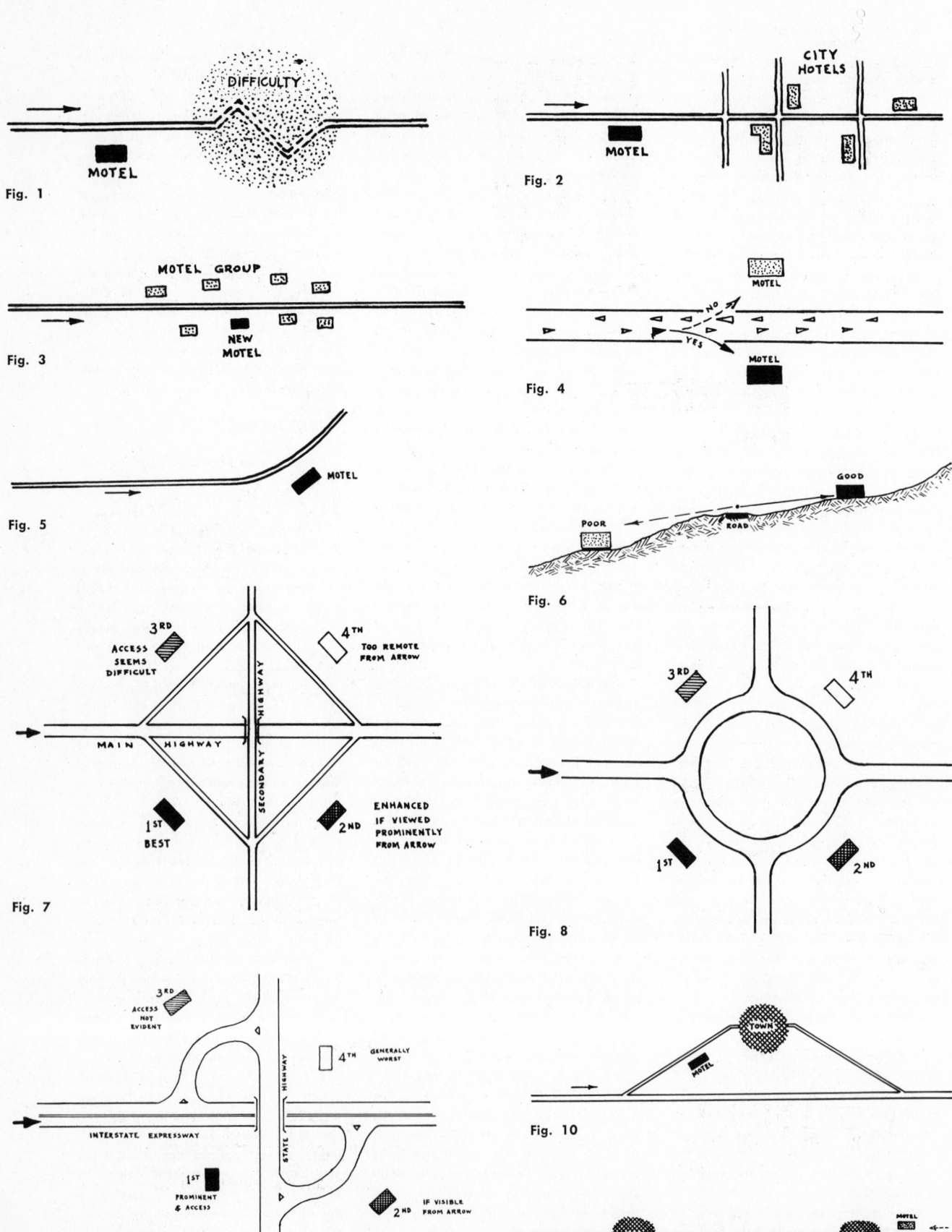

Fig. 1

Fig. 2

Fig. 3

Fig. 4

Fig. 5

Fig. 6

Fig. 7

Fig. 8

Fig. 9

Fig. 10

Fig. 11

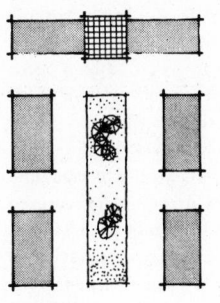

Fig. 12

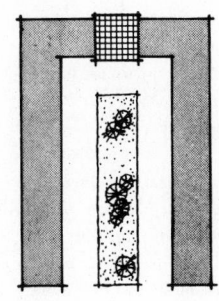

Fig. 13

Fig. 16

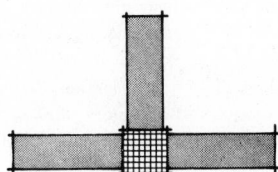

Fig. 17

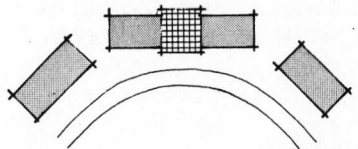

Fig. 14

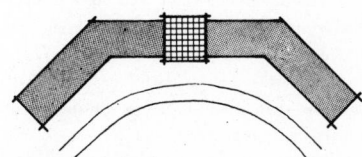

Fig. 15

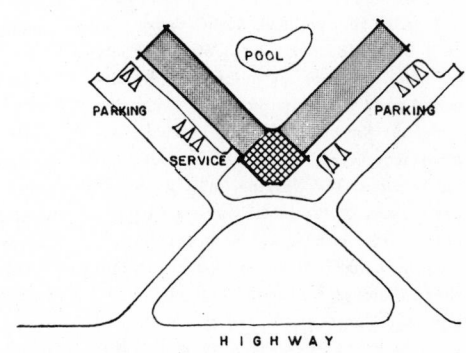

Fig. 18

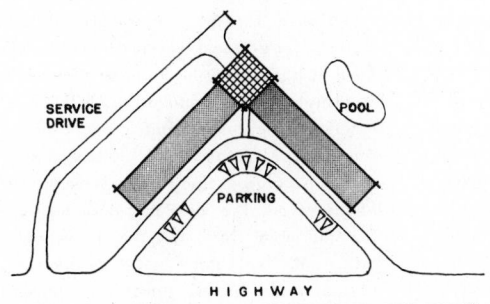

Fig. 19

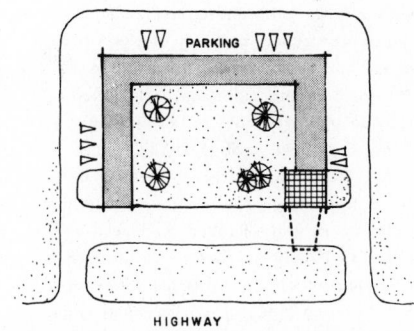

Fig. 20

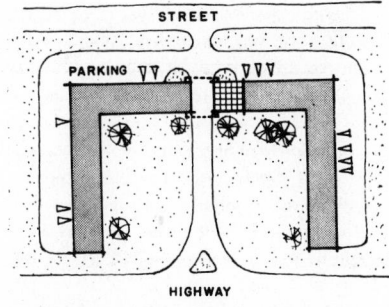

Fig. 21

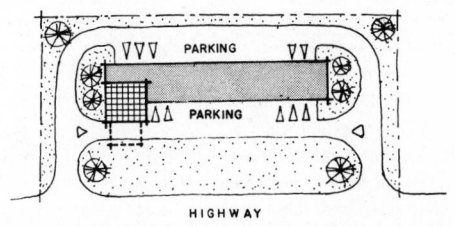

Fig. 22

dustrial area, within easy driving distance of both the suburban residential area and the city.

SITE PLAN

Pertinent factors include the size of the buildings, the area for parking, size of the site, contour of the land, and the extremely important traffic patterns for guests, employees, supplies, and refuse. The ideal arrangement should combine "pull" with privacy—two items that are difficult to attain simultaneously in any site plan. The "pull" or drawing power of an attractive appearance from the highway should be converted to privacy for the guest after arrival. Drawing power is linked with proximity to the highway; privacy is associated with quiet surroundings. Some compromise must be made on the basis of the variety of motel, the type of guest, and the site conditions. One operator may want the motel set far back from the highway; another may want the swimming pool right out in front. The designer must know the preferences of the motel owner and operator in order to produce the results desired.

If the motel is to be located on a high-speed thoroughfare, it should have a frontage of at least 500 ft. The motorist going 60 miles an hour will need about that distance to slow down comfortably in order to turn off the highway.

For a small installation, the guest units may be arranged in a U-shaped pattern, with a lawn area in the center and the guest registration building at the middle of the horizontal portion of the U (Fig. 12). The same arrangement can be modified to provide unbroken construction, with everything under one roof (Fig. 13).

A crescent-shaped arrangement is often quite appealing. The central registration building may be flanked by guest units (Fig. 14). If built as a simple structure, this arrangement usually takes the shape of a half-hexagon (Fig. 15). Or the motel might be designed as a long, straight building, with equal wings extending from the registration office (Fig. 16).

For some sites, a T-shaped structure might be most suitable. With that design, however, the service entrance can be difficult to locate (Fig. 17). The L-shaped layout is deservedly popular. Placing the registration office toward the highway extends an obvious welcome to the motorist. The sight of other cars in the parking area will also be an inducement to the prospective guest. In addition, the garden and pool area will be secluded, so that the guest can escape the noise and confusion of the highway (Fig. 18). Or the position of the L might be reversed, and the ground

areas adjoining the building attractively arranged. The swimming pool, for example, could be placed out in front as an inducement to the traveler (Fig. 19).

If the site is approximately square, and located near or in town, the registration office may best be placed at the tip of one side of a U. This familiar solution is both well-ordered and attractive (Fig. 20). If the site is longer and has access to a rear street parallel to the highway, the U may advantageously be broken by a driveway connecting the streets. The driveway could then be covered at the registration office and access to the parking areas so arranged that control could be exercised by the office over all arrivals and departures (Fig. 21).

A relatively long, narrow site on the edge of town might be developed advantageously by setting the building back from the highway and providing good visibility, roomside parking, and efficient traffic patterns (Fig. 22). If the site were somewhat deeper, the building might be designed as a half-hexagon, with a garden court and recreation area. Whether guests would prefer roomside parking or an adjacent garden court and recreation area depends on such circumstances as the purpose of their visit, length of stay, climatic conditions, and the view from windows not facing the court (Fig. 23).

A large motel in the downtown area may take the form of a hollow rectangle. The example shown in Fig. 24 provides a wide scope of services, including a restaurant, ballroom, shops, room service, year-round swimming pool, and an attractive central garden area. Street-level parking is provided under the guest rooms. A similar pattern is followed in the 68-unit motel shown in Fig. 25. The registration office, gift shop, coffee shop, cocktail lounge, and restaurant are located in the portions of the building nearest the highway. The inner court provides parking space around an island lawn with trees. This arrangement permits good control of cars entering and leaving, brings the cars near the guest rooms, and may thus seem the obvious solution to parking problems. The noise of cars arriving and departing, however, often late at night or early in the morning, will affect all guest rooms facing the court, where the noise is accentuated by reverberation. Also, the headlights of arriving cars will rake the windows facing the court. In northern climates, snow removal can be a difficult problem as well, with the hollow-rectangle arrangement.

The 150-room airport motel shown in Fig. 26 uses the inside of the enclosure for the garden, recreation, and swimming-pool area, with parking facilities around the outside. Business comes from both airline

and motor travelers. Service is comparable to that of large hotels in the city. The circular building contains a dining room and cocktail lounge on the ground floor, and a second floor meeting room.

Individuality is an asset to the motel illustrated in Fig. 27. On a site of moderate area, this motel has a convenient, covered entrance for the motorist and an adjoining circular restaurant building, backed up by an L-shaped, two-story guest section. The outside dining terrace overlooking the lawn and pool is especially inviting with its open, yet secluded atmosphere. Separate parking areas are provided for restaurant patrons and for guests.

A motel may be built on a narrow strip of valuable land between the highway and the ocean, as is frequently done in Florida. The example in Fig. 28 concentrates the three stories of guest rooms (with a double-loaded corridor) perpendicular to the shore line, providing an ocean view from every room. All guest rooms have private balconies. A garage in the semibasement accommodates self-service parking. The single-story lobby, bar, and coffee-shop portion includes a dining terrace that overlooks the circular outdoor dance floor, the pool, and the ocean. The arrangement is open, uncluttered, and inviting.

ROOM GROUPS AND PARKING

Designed for the convenience of the motorist, each room of the motel should have, if possible, at least one window with a desirable view or private outlook on a quiet area (for which landscaping may be required). Bathrooms and clothes closets should be placed along the driveway side of the rooms. The room layout should follow the usual hotel guest-room arrangement, with the central guest corridor replaced by an access driveway. Convenience, privacy, and rooms that are both quiet and cheerful are the objectives. The shape, orientation, dimensions, and topography of the individual site, of course, may necessitate some deviation from the ideal layout.

Ideally, one side of a row of guest units would take full advantage of the view, with the access drive on the opposite side of the row. Bathrooms on the entrance side would have small, high windows to increase privacy and reduce noise, whereas the guest rooms might have large picture windows to capitalize on the view. An extra doorway on the side with the view might be desirable. (See Fig. 29, 31, 32, 34, 36, 40.)

If the strip of land available for guest units is narrow, either because of dimensions or topography, the best solution is generally to set the units well back from

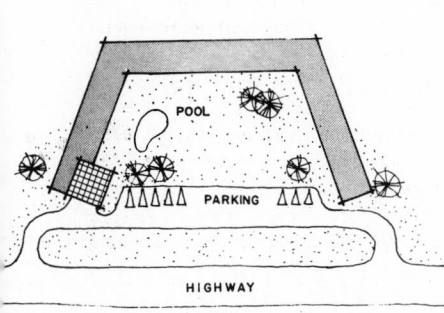

23

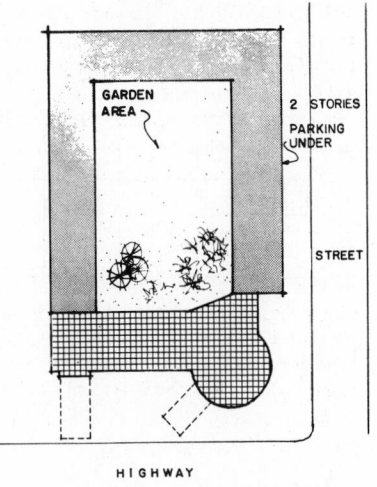

Fig. 24.   Manger Motor Inn, Charlotte, N. C.;
Finn-Jenter, Architect

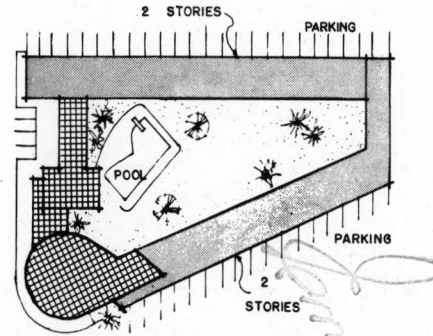

Fig. 25.   Travelers Inn, Fairbanks, Alaska;
Edwin Crittenden, Architect

Fig. 26.   Avis Motel, Midway Airport, Chicago;
Design, Inc., Architect

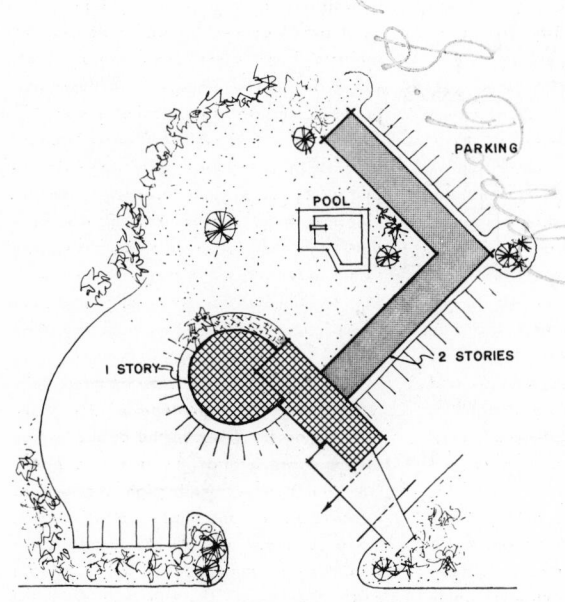

Fig. 27.   O'Hare-Chicago Motor Hotel, Chicago Inter-
national Airport; A. P. Swanson Associates, Architect

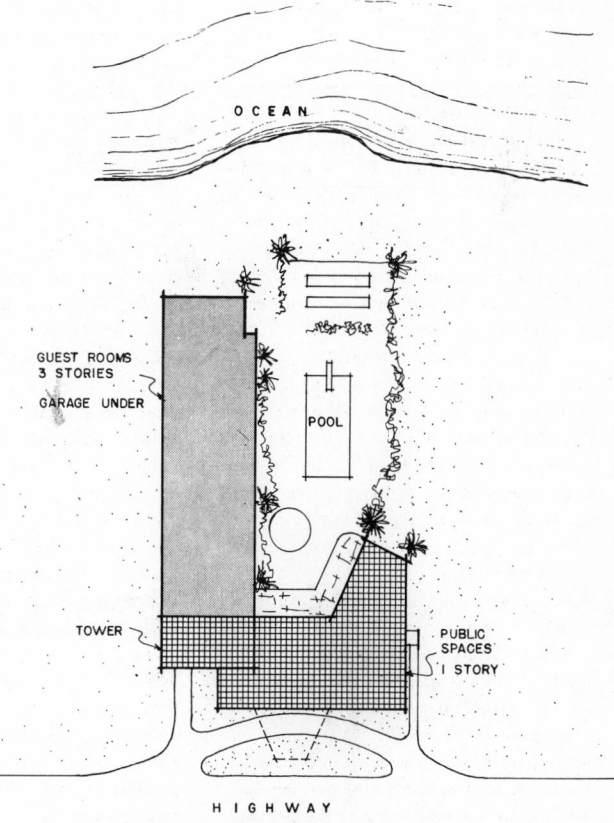

Fig. 28.   Pan American Motel, Miami Beach, Fla.;
Carlos B. Schoeppl & Associates, Architect

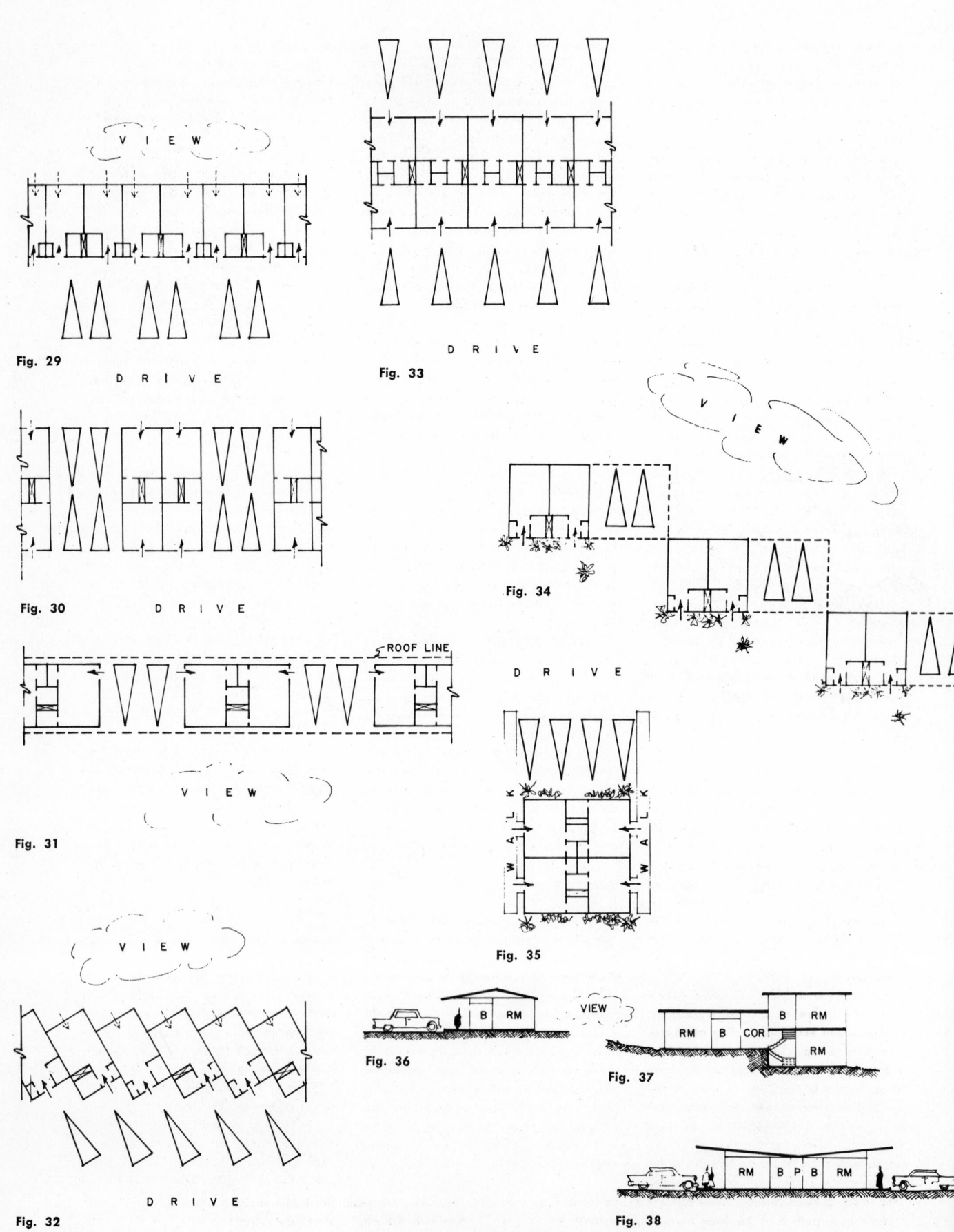

Fig. 29

Fig. 30

Fig. 31

Fig. 32

Fig. 33

Fig. 34

Fig. 35

Fig. 36

Fig. 37

Fig. 38

the road. The effect from the road will be impressive (Fig. 40). If the strip were about 25 ft wider, better results would be obtained by setting the guest units 25 ft back from the parking area, and landscaping the area between.

A level strip on a hillside, even as narrow as 43 ft, can readily accommodate both a drive and a single row of parked cars. Placing each guest room over its parked car solves the problem nicely: The cars are protected from the weather, and each guest is provided with a private balcony (Fig. 41). If the site continues downhill, it may be desirable to sink a guest room into the bank and park its car on the roof (Fig. 42). This arrangement provides privacy and a good view of the valley.

If there is no desirable view and the patronage will be mostly transient, the more economical back-to-back arrangement may be justified, despite its lack of privacy and cross-ventilation. (See Fig. 30, 33, 35, 38, 46, 48.) Two- or four-room units are often arranged with parking space between them, serving to break the monotony and add visual interest (Fig. 30, 31, 34). Another alternative is a four-room unit with all four cars parked in a row (Fig. 35).

Rooms on different levels may be advantageous, depending upon the topography and dimensions of the site, and the number of units required. Guests handling their own luggage generally do not welcome climbing a full story height, but seldom object to half that amount (Fig. 37, 45).

Corridors

An interior corridor will protect the guest in bad weather and be a great help to maid service. With protected inside corridors, a maid is customarily assigned 14 to 16 rooms; if only an outside entrance is provided, one maid would probably handle only 10 to 12 rooms. Moreover, a single interior corridor will make it easier for the management to exercise desired control; the guests, also, will probably feel more secure.

On the other hand, if the only entrance to a room is through an outside doorway, the guest can enjoy the feeling of having a private cottage. That feeling, however, will be appreciably reduced if the open corridor or public walkway is close to the building and protected by an overhanging roof, despite high windows, venetian blinds, or similar remedial devices. Privacy would be greatly improved by placing the public walkway 15 ft or more away from the building, with suitable planting between.

Compare the arrangement of two-story guest-room buildings with open corridors in Fig. 46, with the one with interior corridors in Fig. 47. Note that the construction requires floor slabs of the same width for each. An advantage of the open-corridor plan is that a quarter of the rooms have direct access to parking. The corridors, however, extend along the only windows, and thus reduce the privacy of all the guest rooms. The plan with the inside corridor offers greater privacy, better insulation from outside noise, and full protection from the weather for guests and maids. Moreover, half its guest rooms have either a private balcony or terrace.

A narrow site requiring two guest floors to secure the necessary number of rooms, may necessitate putting the building on stilts, with parking below the guest rooms. (Such an arrangement, however, increases the building height, and adds unwelcome stair climbing—or elevator problems.) With two stories, two access drives are preferable, one on each side of the building. If two drives are not feasible, however, it is possible to use a central driveway, a solution often employed in garages (Fig. 48). Both guest floors can be served by an interior double-loaded corridor, or by open corridors (one on each side) with a pipe-and-vent shaft between the guest bathrooms.

Standard motels have not yet been built. They have appeared, at times, on drawing boards, but individual circumstances—site conditions, food-service demands, and geographic location—invariably have required adjustments. Before beginning the design, the designer should thoroughly discuss with the owner and operator such matters as the choice between interior or exterior corridors, single or double loading, long guest buildings or two- and four-room units, and one- or two-story structures.

GUEST ROOMS

The motel guest wants much the same things in his room as he would want in a hotel. Reference should be made to previous pages concerning typical hotel rooms: types, sizes, design principles, and representative layouts. A motel will often increase the length and width of a similar room by a foot or two, however, to provide a greater spaciousness than would be feasible in a commercial hotel in the city. Some experienced motel operators say that 13 by 16 ft of net bedroom area is the best minimum size for a room to accommodate two persons.

Kitchenettes

Motel guests who have arrived at their destination often want cooking facilities on a modest scale. If the motel will cater primarily to overnight guests, however, the probable demand for kitchenettes should be determined by a careful study, involving a check of other motels in the neighborhood. Representative layouts including kitchenettes are shown in Fig. 49.

Complete factory-assembled kitchenettes are available in 30 to 72-in. lengths. Features included are a range top with 2, 3, or 4 burners (either gas or electric), with an oven underneath; a sink, with a utensil storage cabinet underneath; and a worktable area, with a refrigerator underneath. A storage cabinet for china and nonrefrigerated foodstuffs is usually provided on the wall above the unit.

The kitchenette unit may be placed in an alcove sized to fit it, with louvered doors or an equivalent device to screen it off or even lock it up when not desired by the guests. Or a separate room might be provided.

Wall partitions

Partitions between guest rooms should be of any construction that will reduce sound transmission by at least 45 decibels, a reduction that is usually adequate. In wood frame construction, 2 by 4's are often staggered on 8-in. centers, with a sound-insulating blanket between them. In selecting the method of construction, the designer should consider materials, labor, suitability, fire hazards, transmission loss, and cost.

Number of guest rooms

Several motel chain organizations have made careful studies to determine the minimum number of guest rooms that would be economical to operate. Their conclusions run from 64 rooms for the less elaborate forms of operation to 100 rooms for those organizations that intend all guest conveniences and services to be distinctly superior.

SPACE ALLOTMENTS

Space allotments in motels follow, in general, the pattern for allotments in hotels. Data taken from over a dozen motel plans were used to establish the space allotments listed below. Consideration was also given to the typical values for hotels, as listed on previous pages. Space allotments are directly proportional to the number of guest rooms; the figures provided below for a typical 100-room motel can be adjusted to suit any other size. (For a 60-room motel, multiply by 0.60; for 130 rooms, by 1.30.) Other modifications may be necessary to meet individual requirements. No adjustment should

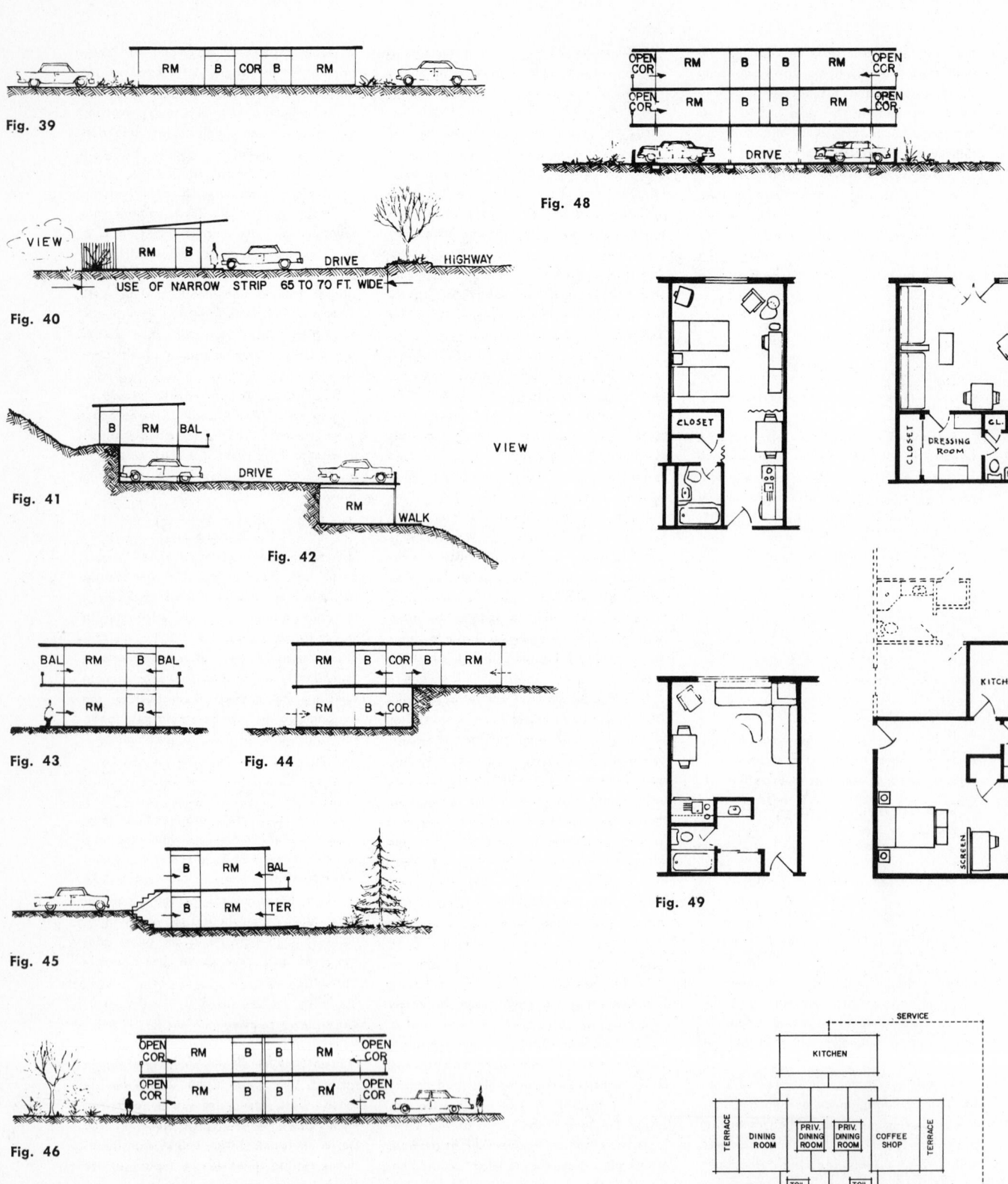

Fig. 39

Fig. 40

USE OF NARROW STRIP 65 TO 70 FT. WIDE

Fig. 41

Fig. 42

Fig. 43

Fig. 44

Fig. 45

Fig. 46

Fig. 47

Fig. 48

Fig. 49

Fig. 50. Schematic layout for motel with full dining service

be made, however, for the manager's office and the secretary's office, as each would still need about the same area.

SPACE ALLOTMENTS FOR TYPICAL 100-ROOM MOTEL

Public space

	Area, sq ft
Lobby	1,100
Front office	100
Lounge	500
Corridors adjoining	300
Men's toilet for guests	140
Women's toilet for guests	120
Women's restroom	100
Coat checkroom	100

Concessions and subrentals

Rented stores	2,000

Food and beverage service space

Dining room (110 seats)	1,700
Coffee shop (70 seats)	1,100
Bar and cocktail lounge (50 seats)	800
Private dining rooms (75 seats)	900
Employees' dining room (20 seats)	260
Kitchen	1,300
Steward's storeroom	300
Walk-in refrigerators	150
Beverage storage	180
China, glass and silver storage	200
Receiving room	200
Garbage room	100

General service space

Manager's office	130
Secretary's office	90
Accounting office	130
Linen room	350
Laundry	600
Men's toilet for employees	100
Men's locker room	150
Women's toilet for employees	120
Women's locker room	170
Maintenance shops	600
Furniture storage	250
General storage	600
Boiler room	750
Transformer and switchboard room	150

Extra items (if needed)

Garage for motorized lawn mowers and snow plows

Swimming pool filters, chlorinator, pump, and heater

Storage for lawn furniture and recreation equipment

Food service is not a lucrative part of the motel business; money invested in rooms would pay better dividends. The motorist, however, will want food service handy; if not actually on the premises, then only a step away. He generally dislikes to go more than a few hundred yards to find a restaurant. Therefore, unless adequate food service is already adjacent, it is advisable to provide it.

For the motel requiring strictly minimum facilities, a good solution is the factory-assembled roadside "diner" with a dozen or more seats, which can be handled by a single employee during slack hours. For the more ambitious but still rather small motel with little outside patronage, the best solution may well be a coffee shop, possibly supplemented by a bar. Such an arrangement helps to keep investment and labor costs within bounds. For the larger motel, a dining room, coffee shop, and bar with cocktail lounge may all be needed. If the motel is near a city, private dining rooms are usually added as well. Outside patronage is necessary to make extensive restaurant operations pay. The larger, more spectacular motel restaurants may derive as much as 75 per cent of their business from persons who are not overnight guests (Fig. 50).

Motel restaurant facilities average about two seats per guest room. The ratio varies, however, from one-half to three or more dining-room seats per guest room.

Care should be taken in applying the schedule of space allotments to ensure that, if any food-service area is modified, the effect on auxiliary facilities is considered.

The lobby should be designed to impress the prospective guest favorably and bid him welcome. The entrance must be easily recognizable and accessible. If feasible, the prospective guest should be sheltered from the weather, from his car to the entrance doors. Within the lobby, the registration desk should have a relatively central location, for it is the main control point of motel operation. If the guest, standing at the registration desk, can look through a large plate-glass window and see the swimming pool, attractive landscaping, or a scenic view, room sales will be greatly aided.

For a discussion of laundry requirements, see the section of this book on "Hotel and Motel Laundries."

Parking

Parking spaces, preferably in separate areas, are generally required as follows: (1) 1 parking space for each guest room (may sometimes be reduced to 0.8 per guest room); (2) 1 parking space for every 5 restaurant seats; (3) 1 parking space for every 3 employees; (4) 2 parking spaces for delivery and service trucks (in addition to space for a truck at the service entrance).

These allotments, of course, should be modified if circumstances warrant it. A motel that is filled to capacity, with a good restaurant, bar, and banquet business from nonguests, may need 2 parking spaces per guest room. On the other hand, a downtown motel, with parking available nearby and many guests arriving by taxi, might get along with parking space equal to two-thirds the number of guest rooms.

For the design of parking areas in general, see the section of this book on "Parking." Special requirements for motel parking are discussed in the following paragraph.

Parking stalls should be adequate for the largest cars commonly used; 19 ft is the recommended minimum length. Planning for only medium and small-size cars invites trouble. Parking stalls 10 ft wide are recommended; where space is limited 9-ft stalls may be used, but this width should be considered the absolute minimum. Double stripes, 1½ ft apart, between the stalls will result in better centering of the cars within the allotted space. Since almost all motel guests unload baggage from their cars, and reload it upon leaving, adequate and safe space should be provided for this activity. Motel parking lots planned for maximum guest convenience provide parking stalls 11 ft wide by 23 ft long, allowing 4 ft behind a 19-ft car for loading and unloading. Parking spaces under buildings should be 11 ft wide and have a clear height of 7 ft. In the design of sidewalks adjacent to parking areas, consideration must be given to the overhang of the car beyond the curb or wheel buffer; this overhang may be as much as 2½ ft in front or 4½ ft in the rear of the car.

Entrance drive

The turnoff from the highway to the motel should be at an angle of 30 to 45 deg; sharper turnoff angles are inadvisable. The driveway should be 20 to 25 ft wide, and the radius of the curb on the driver's right should be at least 50 ft. If a restricted site frontage should require a right-angle turnoff, then the driveway should be 25 ft wide and the curb have a 30-ft radius. A curb radius of less than 30 ft is inadvisable under any circumstances.

A slope of 6 per cent is the usual maximum for turnoffs from state highways. A slope of 12 per cent is customary for ramps, but can be as much as 15 per cent. The parking lot should be nearly level. The central driveway may be crowned, with a 1 per cent slope to the edges, so that persons on foot will find it relatively free from water after rain or from ice in winter.

Gas station

Motels sometimes include a service station where the motorist can conveniently obtain gasoline and oil, and possibly tire, battery, lubrication, and car-washing service. The decision of whether to include a gas station, however, should depend upon its being profitable in itself.

Swimming pool

About 50 per cent of the motels built in 1959 included swimming pools. The trend is to provide pools, even in motels in the downtown area of the city. Although the pool may be actually used by only a minority of the overnight guests, many more will enjoy watching the activities. Thus the pool should be surrounded by a suitable terrace at least 10 ft wide; if a diving board is provided, the terrace should be 20 ft wide in back of the board. Grass areas beyond the terrace are also recommended.

The motel pool should generally be of the recreation type. A free-form pattern, either kidney-shaped or oval, is usually suitable, but of course is subject to topography and the designer's judgment. The minimum size recommended for the pool is 20 by 40 ft, which is large enough for about 15 people in the water and 20 to 30 bathers around the edge. One motel chain prefers a 24 by 48-ft pool. Another chain, operating motels of 150 rooms and more, considers 35 by 75 ft to be the minimum.

A separate wading pool is often provided—sometimes with spray fittings or a small fountain to enhance its appearance. A fairly wide terrace should surround the pool, with benches on the terrace for parents.

Toilet facilities for men and women bathers should be accessible from the pool area. Such facilities are required by law in many states. Provision should also be made, within 40 ft of the deep end of the pool, for housing the necessary water filters, pumps, purification equipment, and heater. A water heater can extend the use of the pool over a longer season.

Other planning considerations concerning the pool and surrounding area include food and beverage service and adequate illumination for evening activities.

The inclusion of a cabana club may be considered, if there is sufficient local demand. In addition to membership fees, the cabana club may bring other profitable business to the motel. Since cabana club members are not overnight guests, however, provision must be made for dressing rooms, lockers, showers, and toilets. The

attracting the attention of prospective customers. Most people stop at a motel because they like its sign.

Signs should be neat, bold, brief, and members will also expect an ample poolside terrace area with tables and chairs, umbrellas, and reclining lawn chairs, in addition to the cabanas. The cabanas themselves, though, may serve as a windbreak, and thus help to prolong the pool season.

Recreation areas

Although the pool will probably be the most popular recreation area, a children's play yard, and areas for adult games may also be desirable. Some such games are listed below; the dimensions indicate the area for the game, including the usual surrounding border.

Game	Width x length, ft
Shuffleboard	10 x 60
Clock golf	40 x 40
Croquet	50 x 95
Horseshoes	12 x 60
Table tennis	12 x 20
Tennis	60 x 120
Handball	30 x 45

Barbecue facilities may also be desirable. An area of about 15 by 20 ft is generally ample. The play yard for small children should be enclosed by a fence. Suitable modern equipment should be selected and installed.

Indoor recreation facilities may include a television room, one or more card rooms, reading room and library, table tennis, movies, piano, and electric organ. These facilities should be discussed and decided upon in the early planning stages, because it is often impossible to fit them into a completed plan at the last minute.

Landscaping

Landscaping is important—it is one of the things the guest sees first. Well-kept, neatly defined lawns and drives will make a favorable impression; the parking arrangement should be logical and practical. Hard-surfaced walks should be so arranged that lawns may be preserved; retaining walls should be installed to prevent erosion and enhance appearance. The right varieties of trees will provide attractive shade. Undesirable views should be screened by dense plantings, trimmed hedges, stone walls, or louvered fences.

Outdoor advertising

Signs are the most effective means of

distinctive. Their message must be grasped at a glance. The entrance sign should be plainly visible a good hundred yards from the turnoff, with letters at least 18 in. high. Copy should be reduced to a bare minimum, and only unusual services advertised.

A distinguishing emblem, trade mark, or coat of arms should be unique and easily remembered. Select one that can be used at the motel entrance, in the lobby, and on stationery, menus, and souvenir match books. Avoid using too many colors in a sign. Simplicity is effective.

Signs should be durable and suited to the climate of the location. Night illumination is essential, at least for the sign in front of the motel, but care should be taken that guests will not be annoyed by beams of light, glare, flashing off and on, or other features that might bother a person wanting to sleep. The sign at the motel customarily has a "Vacancy—No Vacancy" indication.

Heating and air conditioning

Guest rooms are best served by a central plant, with individual room temperature controls provided. A system favored by some of the more experienced organizations circulates water through convectors concealed beneath the guest-room windows. The circulating water is heated in winter and chilled in summer, the water temperature being varied in accordance with weather conditions. Each guest-room conditioning cabinet has a multispeed, manually controlled, motor-driven fan to blow air over the coils. The guest can regulate the fan speed to vary the rate of heat transfer.

Other parts of the building—such as the lobby, restaurant, kitchen, and employees' quarters—should be divided into "zones," according to their hours of use and type of air treatment needed. Each zone will have its own separately controlled equipment to supply heat or air conditioning. Air conditioning is supplied in the summer for public spaces, restaurant, and bar facilities frequented by guests. Ample exhaust ventilation will be needed for the kitchen and the employees' locker rooms and toilets. Care should be taken to avoid having to operate an entire zone of rooms with short hours of use just to accommodate one or two that will be used many hours a day.

For additional information, see "Heating, Ventilating, and Air Conditioning: Hotels and motels."

By FRANK HARRISON RANDOLPH

Hotel Planning Consultant and Professor of Hotel Engineering, Cornell University

There are three ways of supplying and laundering hotel linen:

1. Linen supply service: The hotel contracts with a supplier to furnish and launder the linen.

2. Commercial laundry: The hotel owns the linen and sends it to a commercial laundry.

3. Hotel laundry: The hotel owns the linen and launders it on the premises.

The selection of the method to be adopted should be based on total costs, quality of the work, and satisfaction with the service. The decision in each case will depend on the particular needs and circumstances of the hotel.

Linen supply service, which has made recent gains in acceptance, is the simplest solution. No investment is required. Costs, quality, and general satisfaction vary. The linen supply company is not necessarily local; some companies operate within a radius of a hundred miles.

Commercial laundries service hotel-owned linen at special wholesale rates. Competition generally requires them to give attention to quality and service.

Some hotels have discontinued the operation of their laundries, whereas others, initially without laundries, have installed them and been pleased with the results.

DISADVANTAGES OF THE HOTEL LAUNDRY

If available space and funds are limited, management should consider the following disadvantages of the hotel laundry:

1. Responsibility of another department to supervise and maintain the laundry.

2. Increased size of building to contain the laundry.

3. Increased plant investment in machinery, often at a cost of $100 or more per guest room.

4. Additional space required for laundry supplies and extra employees.

5. Provision must be made for adequate supply of hot and cold water, sewer capacity, high-pressure steam or gas, electric service, exhaust fans, and ventilation ducts.

6. Capacity of plant, which is necessarily limited, may be inadequate for an unusual peak load.

7. Possible annoyance because of vibration, noise, heat, and odor.

8. Hazards of fire and water leakage.

9. May be prohibited by community zoning and building regulations.

ADVANTAGES OF THE HOTEL LAUNDRY

If space and investment capital are both available, the management should consider the following advantages of the hotel laundry:

1. Cost per pound of laundered goods may be from 20 to 40 per cent less than if sent out.

2. Linen life is usually lengthened; sheets receive an average of 50 per cent more launderings, and other items about 25 per cent.

3. The increased speed in returning the laundry may reduce the linen inventory required.

4. Quality of work may be better for it is subject to control.

5. Record keeping and checking quantities and claims for loss or damage are less troublesome because the laundered goods do not leave the hotel.

The prevalence of laundries in commercial hotels was determined several years ago by a nationwide survey of over 7,000 hotels by the American Hotel Association. This survey showed that in hotels of 50 to 99 rooms, 18 per cent operated a laundry; 100 to 199 rooms, 22 per cent; 200 to 299 rooms, 45 per cent; and over 500 rooms, 94 per cent.

The smaller and medium-size hotels customarily launder only the flat work. Many of these hotels installed one or two ironing boards and a garment press for employees' uniforms. If immediate installation of such equipment is not contemplated, it may nevertheless be advisable to provide extra space for possible future installation. Some of the medium-size hotels, and most of the larger ones, handle guests' work. This service requires considerably more space, equipment, and employees, but is very profitable if there is sufficient volume.

The typical hotel laundry, excluding such areas as the clean-linen storeroom, supply room, and toilet facilities, has 7 sq ft of floor space per guest room. Manufacturers of laundry machinery recommend, in general, 8 sq ft per guest room. Relatively few hotels exceed this last figure. An attempt to economize by allotting insufficient space often results in congestion, slow operation, high labor costs, and general dissatisfaction. The space requirement for a given production capacity in pounds per hour will be considerably smaller if only hotel flat work is laundered than if additional equipment is installed for employees' uniforms and guests' work.

The quantity of goods laundered is usually 8–9 lb per occupied room per day. However, if linen is used sparingly and low occupancy is expected, the figure may be as low as $6\frac{1}{2}$ lb per available room per day. Restaurant service imposes an additional load frequently estimated at $1\frac{1}{2}$ lb per room per day. This figure can well be decreased slightly or increased considerably, depending on the number of meals served per day by the restaurant and the elaborateness of its linen service. Ten lb per room per day is a good average for first-class hotels with the usual amount of restaurant and banquet business. Some high-class hotels average 12 lb, and a few go up to 14 lb.

Although hotels operate 7 days a week, the laundry usually operates only 5 days a week and consequently must be able to handle about 50 per cent more laundry per day than the daily linen requirement of the hotel. However, the average weekly occupancy of guest rooms cannot be expected to be 100 per cent. For design purposes, a figure of 90 per cent may be used, although the national average is almost always less than 80 per cent. Laundered goods may ordinarily average from 8 to 10 lb per occupied room per day. Laundry operation is usually planned for 40 hours per week, although some motel laundries operate about 30 hours per week and some of the large hotels about 44 hours per week. The size of the laundry and its equipment and hourly capacity cannot be determined satisfactorily solely from the number of rooms. The following computations on desired capacity will illustrate this fact.

Thus the hotel with twice the number of rooms may require less hourly production because of different circumstances.

LAUNDRY REQUIREMENTS FOR WATER, STEAM, GAS, AND ELECTRICITY

Service demands for water, steam, gas, and electricity vary widely during each hour. However, the average hourly demand is quite constant during the working day. An allowance of up to 50 per cent above the average hourly figure is sometimes made to sustain the short-duration peak loads.

Water requirements for washing are theoretically about 3 gal per pound of linen. In actual practice, according to the American Institute of Laundering, the total water consumption in the average plant is about 4½ gal per pound of linen (3 gal of hot water at 180°F, plus 1½ gal of cold water). The maximum rate of water flow is typically 50 per cent more than the average rate of flow when the plant is operating.

Water treatment, using a zeolite softener, is generally advisable. Water hardness is expressed in grains per gallon, or in parts per million, of equivalent calcium carbonate (1 grain per gallon = 17 parts per million). If the hardness is less than 2 grains per gallon, a softener is rarely installed. But at 10 grains or more per gallon, very few laundries try to get along without a softener. Hard water wastes soap, results in harsh linens, causes a gray color and shortens linen life. The cost of a softener installation, when the hardness is 10 grains per gallon, is generally repaid within two years by the saving in soap alone.

Steam consumption, including water heating, is about 2–2½ lb of steam per pound of linen. Water heating ordinarily creates about two-thirds of the demand; the remaining one-third is required for steam-heated equipment such as flat-work ironers, drying tumblers, and presses. The amount of steam that must be available for heating water should be based on the maximum hourly rate of hot water consumption.

The water heater is customarily selected with an hourly heating capacity in gallons of from 2 to 3 times the pounds per hour of linen capacity of the plant. The volume of the hot water storage tank in gallons is about one-half the hourly capacity of the heater. The minimum hourly hot water demand is generally 60 per cent of the maximum hourly hot water demand.

High-pressure boiler operation is required for a steam-heated flat-work ironer with steam delivered to the ironer at 100-psi gage pressure or slightly higher. This requirement often influences the smaller plants to install gas-fired ironers, tumblers, and water heaters. The maximum expected steam demand for laundry equipment is approximately 80 per cent of the total connected steam load. The installed boiler capacity, based on statistics, ranges from 15 to 25 boiler horsepower per 100 hotel rooms.

Electricity consumption ranges from 0.05

$$\frac{50 \text{ rooms} \times 100\% \text{ occupancy} \times 10 \text{ lb/rm./day (with restaurant)} \times 7 \text{ days/wk.}}{30 \text{ hr wk. of laundry operation}} = 117 \text{ lb/hr}$$

$$\frac{100 \text{ rooms} \times 80\% \text{ occupancy} \times 8 \text{ lb/rm./day (no restaurant)} \times 7 \text{ days/wk.}}{44 \text{ hr wk. of laundry operation}} = 102 \text{ lb/hr}$$

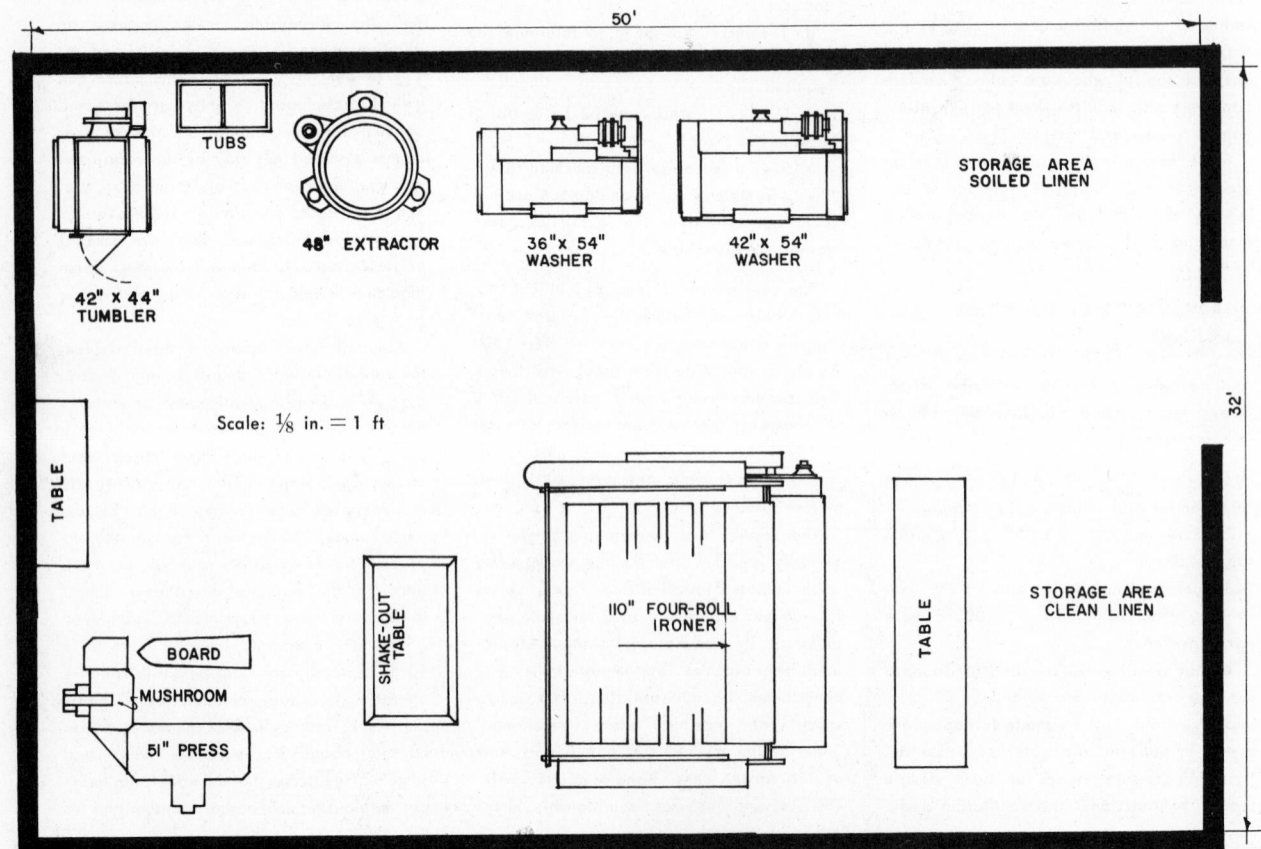

Fig. 1. Laundry plan for typical 200-room hotel or motel

Table 1. Equipment requirements for typical hotel laundries

The data in this table (courtesy Troy Laundry Machinery) is based on a 40-hr work week, 100 per cent occupancy, and a linen use of 10 lb per room per day. Estimated laundry production includes guest work (70 per cent ironed, 25 per cent tumbled, and 5 per cent pressed).

Equipment	Number of rooms in hotel					
	50	100	150	200	300	400
	Production, lb per hr					
	88	175	263	350	525	700
...shers	one 42x28 in.	one 36x21 in. one 42x28 in.	one 36x21 in. one 42x54 in.	one 28x20 in. one 42x28 in. one 42x54 in.	one 28x20 in. one 42x54 in. one 42x84 in.	one 28x20 in. one 42x28 in. one 42x54 in. one 42x96 in.
...ractors	one 30 in.	one 30 in.	one 20 in. one 40 in.	one 30 in. one 40 in.	one 30 in. one 48 in.	one 30 in. one 54 in.
...mblers	one 37x30 in.	one 37x30 in.	one 42x42 in.	one 42x42 in.	two 42x42 in.	two 42x42 in.
...ner	one S16x100 in.	one 100 in. (2-roll)	one 120 in. (4-roll)	one 120 in. (4-roll)	one 120 in. (6-roll)	one 120 in. (8-roll)
...der						one 2-lane
...nditioning tumbler				one 48 in.	one 48 in.	one 72 in.
...parel press unit	one 451	one 451 one 222	one 451 two 222	one 451 two 222	one 451 two 222	one 451 two 222 one 554 two 222
...rt presses	1-Unit 1-Girl	1-Unit 1-Girl	1-Unit 1-Girl	1-Unit 2-Girl	1-Unit 2-Girl	1-Unit 2-Girl
...p tank (optional)		one 60 gal	one 60 gal	one 60 gal	one 100 gal	one 100 gal
...rch cooker	one 15 gal	one 15 gal	one 15 gal	one 15 gal	one 15 gal	one 25 gal
...ning board	1	1	1	1	1	1
...compressor capacity (cfm of 70 lb air)	1.11	1.85	2.5	2.5	2.5	3.8
...ndry tub (2 components)	1	1	1	1	1	1
...ndkerchief press						1
...sell master sock form						1
...ommended capacity of hot water storage ...ank (gal)	200	300	400	550	775	1,050
...prox. total sq ft required for soiled and ...ean linen, equipment, toilets, and supply ...torage	1,175	1,500	2,900	3,150	4,000	4,700
...ommended capacity of hot water heater ...gal per hr)	400	625	800	1,100	1,550	2,100
...er hp (all equipment operating)	20	30	40	50	75	100

to 0.08 kwhr per pound of linen. The maximum demand is estimated at 80 per cent of the total connected electrical load. The average load during plant operation is estimated at 60 per cent of the total connected load, according to the American Institute of Laundering. In addition to the demand for laundry equipment, the total connected load for lighting and for ventilating fans must be considered.

Gas consumption for operating the tumbler and flat-work ironer will vary considerably with conditions. For a laundry serving a hotel of 100 rooms and handling 175 lb of linen per hour, a gas consumption of from 300,000 to 600,000 Btuh (Btu per hr) can be expected for the tumbler and flat-work ironer. If a gas-fired water heater is also used, average gas-consumption figures are as follows: water heater, 550,000 Btuh; tumbler, 170,000 Btuh; ironer, 230,000 Btuh; or a total of 950,000 Btuh.

SUMMARY

Laundry planning consists essentially of three logical steps:

1. Decide upon the scope; in addition to flat work, determine whether to include uniforms and guests' work.
2. Compute the laundry production rate in pounds per hour.

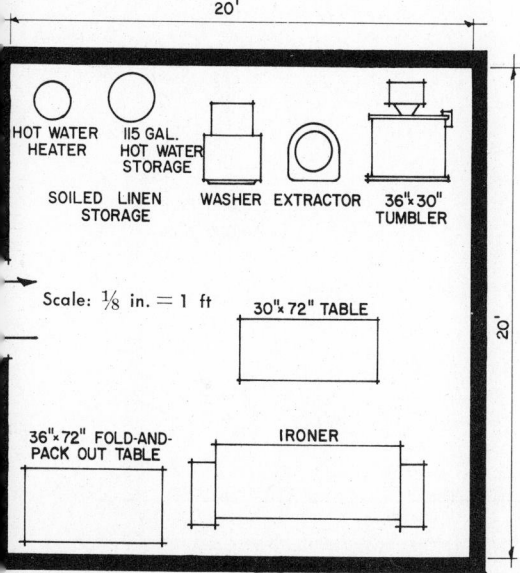

Scale: ⅛ in. = 1 ft

2. Laundry plan for typical 50-room motel

Table 2. Laundering loads per occupied room per day

Courtesy American Laundry Machinery Co. Allowance is included for the average percentage of double occupancy.

Item	No. of pieces	Unit weight, lb	Total weight, lb
Sheets	3.3	1.59	5.25
Pillow cases	2.2	0.35	0.77
Face towels	2.0	0.19	0.38
Bath towels	1.8	0.60	1.09
Bath mats	0.87	1.25	1.09
Wash cloths	1.87	0.10	0.20
	12.04		8.78

3. Develop an appropriate layout considering separation of wet and dry floor areas, routing of linens, and location of soiled- and clean-linen sorting and assembly areas. Be guided by plans of laundries having both the same scope and the same production rate.

All corridors through which quantities of linen must pass to and from guest rooms and restaurants should be free from steps, because transportation should be by wheeled trucks, each carrying a load of 50 lb or more. A hotel of 100 rooms moves about 1,000 lb of clean linen and 1,000 lb of soiled linen per day.

Gravity linen chutes, conveniently located, can save enough labor to warrant careful study when developing the preliminary plans of the building. As afterthoughts, linen chutes can seldom be placed to best advantage.

The larger the laundry, the greater the desirability of working with a qualified consultant or with manufacturers of laundry machinery. The manufacturers, interested in having satisfied customers, have developed standard plans for hotel and motel laundries. They will develop specific plans for a job and provide detailed drawings for gutters, foundations, and service connections. The manufacturer's recommendations should be followed for sizing utility services and foundations.

Table 3. Average load requirements and service connections for laundry equipment

Courtesy American Laundry Machinery Co. Steam supplied to ironers, presses, and tumblers should have at least 100 lb of pressure at the equipment.

Item	Capacity		Motor hp	Water		Steam			Drain, in.
	lb per load	Loads per hr		Hot	Cold	Inlet	Outlet	lb per hr	
				in.-diam		in.-diam			
Washer:									
36x18 in.	50	1	1	1¼	1¼	½		105*	3
36x54 in.	165	1	3	2½	2½	¾		347*	6
42x24 in.	100	1	2	1¼	1¼	½		210*	3
42x54 in.	225	1	3	2½	2½	¾		472*	8
Extractor:									
30 in.	80	3	3						3
40 in.	150	2.5	5						4
48 in.	250	2.5	5						4
Tumbler (gas):									
37x30 in.	50	2	0.25 (fan) 0.5 (cyl.)			¾ (gas)		(127,000 Btuh)	
Tumbler (steam):									
37x30 in.	50	2	0.25 (fan) 0.5 (cyl.)			2¾	2¾	168	
44x42 in.	100	2	1 (fan) 0.5 (cyl.)			2¾	2¾	312	
Ironer (gas):									
Single roll, 110–111-in. diam	(80–130 lb per hr)		0.5			1 (gas)		(230,000 Btuh)	
Single roll, 110–116-in. diam	(100–160 lb per hr)		0.75			1 (gas)		(450,000 Btuh)	
Ironer (steam):									
Four rolls, 100 in.	(260–290 lb per hr)		3			1½	1½	309	
Four rolls, 100 in.	(310–340 lb per hr)		3			1½	1½	309	
Other equipment:									
Press (51 in.)						½	½	50	
Mushroom press						½	½		
Ironing board			(1000 w)						
Air compressor (2½x3½ in.)			1.5						

Pounds of steam per hour for washers assumes that 70 per cent of the total water is hot and that 3 gal of the total water is used per pound of washer capacity. One lb of steam will raise one gal of water from tapwater temperature to 180° F.

SECTION VI: DESIGN ELEMENTS—NONRESIDENTIAL

Shopping Centers 1081
Retail Stores:
    Merchandise list 1090
    Fixtures 1091
    Store fronts 1095
Restaurants and Bars 1096
Motion Picture Theaters:
    General requirements 1101
    Projection booths 1104
Auditoriums:
    Basic seating data 1107
    Seating dimensions 1109
Offices:
    Furniture 1111
    Clearances 1113
    Layout 1115
Schools:
    Site planning 1116
    Site selection 1117
    Playgrounds 1117
    Circulation 1121
    Working heights 1123
    Pupil capacity 1124
    Lockers 1125
    Classrooms 1128
    Classroom facilities 1130
    Multipurpose rooms 1132
    Gymnasiums 1133
    Auditoriums 1137
    Libraries 1138
    Cafeterias 1140
    Science 1144
    Fine arts 1146
    Music 1147
    Homemaking 1148
    Shops 1149
    Language laboratory 1150
    Ventilation 1151
Libraries:
    School libraries 1152
    Bookstack data 1153
    Carrels 1155
Hospitals:
    Introduction and flow charts 1157
    Bedrooms 1158
    Nursing units 1161
    Surgical suite 1162
    Nursery 1166
    Pediatric department 1170
    Diagnostic x-ray suite 1173
    Teletherapy unit 1180
    Cobalt-60 1182
    Electroencephalographic suite 1185
    Laboratory 1187
    Physical therapy department 1188
    Occupational therapy department 1193
    Checklist for mental health center 1197

Design for the Handicapped 1198
Service Stations 1202
Truck Terminals:
    Docking facilities 1203
    Terminal plan 1205
Bus Terminals:
    General requirements 1207
    Loading docks and concourse 1209
Railroad Terminals:
    Details 1211
Hangar Doors:
    Balanced canopy doors 1213
    Accordion and canopy doors 1214
    Sliding doors 1215
Firehouses:
    Design 1216
    Construction details 1217
Jails:
    Cell design 1218
    Cell construction 1219

By VICTOR GRUEN, AIA*

The shopping center is one of the few new building types created in our time. Because shopping centers represent groupings of structures and because of the underlying cooperative spirit involved, the need for environmental planning for this building type is obvious. Where this need has been fully understood, shopping centers have taken on the characteristics of urban organisms serving a multitude of human needs and activities.

SELECTING THE SITE

Location

For the purposes of this discussion, the term "location" indicates the general area in which to select a shopping center site. The merits of location, whether the land has already been acquired or is being sought, must always be subjected to careful economic analysis. If the site has already been acquired, the economist directs his study toward the economic characteristics of the location in an effort to decide whether the particular property should be developed as a shopping center project, and if so, what its size and character should be. If the site has not yet been acquired, the economist must make a study of the general area within which the most suitable location can be pinpointed. This over-all study may involve as large an area as the metropolitan area of a large city.

First, an analysis is made of the total available economic potential of the general area. The search is gradually narrowed down through analysis of various segments of the larger area; a specific area within the chosen segment that seems to offer the most advantageous potential is then examined, and finally, a defined location within this specific area is chosen. If properly undertaken, this procedure will usually establish the most suitable location for a shopping center.

Inherent in any economic analysis is a study of the following factors:

Population
Income
Purchasing power

* The illustrations and certain other material in this section have been reprinted, with permission, from Shopping Towns USA by Victor Gruen and Larry Smith, published by Reinhold Publishing Corp., New York (1960).

Competitive facilities
Accessibility
Other related considerations.

Attention must be paid not only to the existing population but also to prospects for future growth, which may be forecast by reference to past growth rates, the trend of population shifts, and the availability of remaining suitable land for residential development.

Population

In forecasting the population trend for ten or fifteen years, consideration must be given to such factors as existing population density, zoning restrictions, physical or man-made barriers to the development of new residential areas (mountains, waterways, industrial areas, public parks, cemeteries, airports), and other land uses that would forestall residential development.

The composition of the population in the trade area, as far as racial or economic characteristics are concerned, is important in various regions of the country.

In areas where strong traditions or prejudices exist, it may be unreasonable to expect that various ethnic groups will shop together. Also, it is unreasonable to expect that persons of low- or middle-income groups will patronize a high-quality type of shopping center or, conversely, that persons in the highest income groups will shop generally in centers that feature medium- or low-priced merchandise.

Trade area

The term "trade area" is normally defined as "that area from which is obtained the major portion of the continuing patronage necessary for the steady support of the shopping center."

The defining factors used in delineating a trade area vary from center to center. They include, but are not limited to, the size and influence of the proposed retail facilities, planning and design characteristics, travel time to and from the location, the existence of natural or man-made barriers—such as railroads and rivers—that

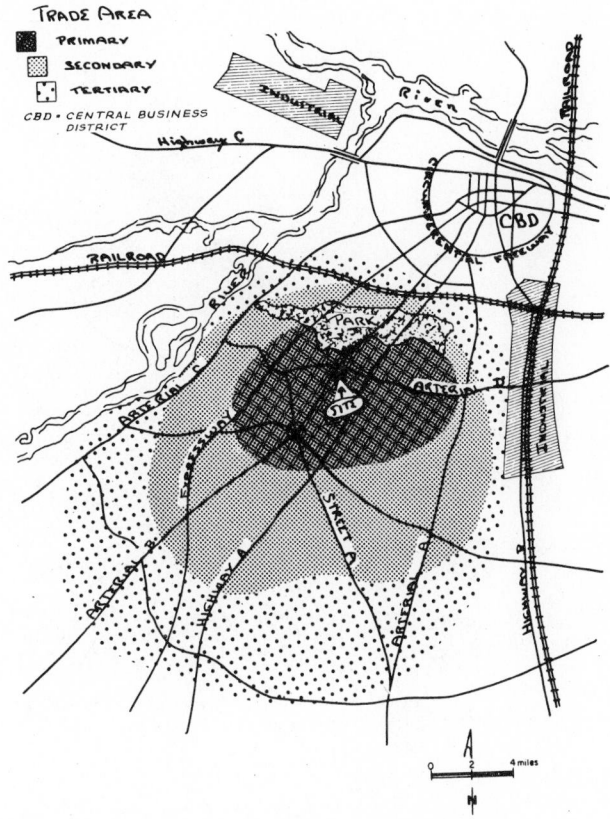

Fig. 1. Schematic plan of a shopping center location

Shown in the plan are trade areas, means of access, and various barriers to accessibility.

would limit accessibility either in fact or psychologically, and the existence of competitive facilities. Thus the trade areas for various locations will not necessarily assume similar sizes or shapes (Fig. 1).

Site qualifications

It is important that the land to be used possess, to the greatest degree possible, the following qualifications:

1. The site must be located in the most desirable general area as established by the economic survey.

2. The site must be owned or controlled by the developer, or offer the possibility of acquisition.

3. Land cost must be in keeping with over-all economic considerations.

4. Existing zoning must permit shopping center development, or a reasonable likelihood of rezoning must exist.

5. The site must contain sufficient land to permit construction of facilities to meet the sales potential.

6. The land must be in one piece, free of intervening roadways, rights-of-way, easements, major waterways, or other obstacles that would force development in separated portions.

7. The topography and shape of the site must permit advantageous planning and reasonably economical construction.

8. The surrounding road pattern and accessibility must allow full utilization of the business potential.

9. The structure must be visible from major thoroughfares.

14. Surrounding land uses should be free of competitive developments, and, if possible, should be of a nature that enhances the operation of the shopping center.

Rarely will a site completely fulfill all the above requirements, and advantages will have to be weighed and balanced against shortcomings. If the site already exists, it is sometimes difficult to separate the affection an owner may have for it (because of family sentiment or other reasons) from the hard facts of suitability, but it is well to remember that most poorly operating centers in the United States are located on just such "accidental" sites. It is, of course, possible that an existing site

may also fulfill the standard requirements, but determination should be made only after the same thorough scrutiny and analysis that would be given to a site to be purchased.

The following list indicates the relative importance of various considerations in site selection:

Location (value of 50)	*Value*
Population within 1 mile—quantity	5
Population within 1 mile—quality	3
Population within 5 miles—quantity	7
Population within 5 miles—quality	4
Population from rural area—quantity	2
Population from rural area—quality	1
Pedestrian traffic shopping at adjacent stores	4
Pedestrian traffic nearby for other purposes	3
Public transportation	5
Automobile traffic—quantity	4
Automobile traffic—availability	4
Direction of population growth	7
Area (value of 15)	
Size of plot	15

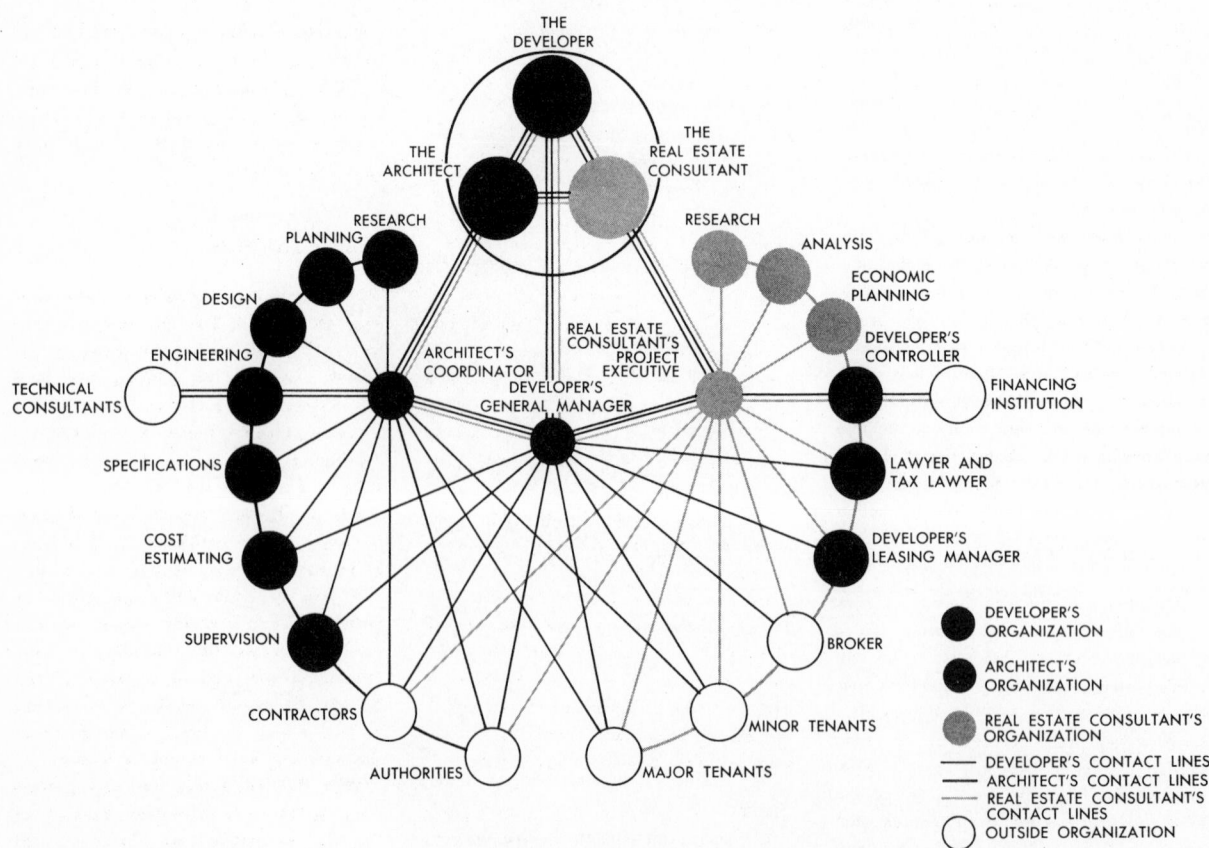

Fig. 2. The planning team

Physical characteristics (value of 25)

Shape of plot for design	4
Plot not divided by traffic lanes	8
Location on arterials for ease of traffic control	4
Cost of clearing and grading	2
Cost of utilities and drainage	2
Visibility	3
Surrounding areas	2

Availability (value of 10)

Ease of acquisition and time	6
Cost	4
	100%

ZONING

Contrary to nineteenth-century precepts of strict separation of industrial and residential land, brought about by rapid industrialization, most progressive planners and zoning boards today recognize that not all types of nonresidential activities are necessarily undesirable in predominantly residential areas.

The modern shopping center that integrates commercial, business, entertainment, and cultural facilities within a carefully planned framework, separates various modes of traffic from one another, and provides for the protection of surrounding residential areas from any objectionable uses, has made a significant contribution in this direction.

The developer may encounter any of the following zoning conditions:

1. The site is commercially zoned, or zoned for a "lower" use, in which case there is no problem.

2. The community has not yet adopted a zoning master plan, and the local planning board is willing to grant suitable zoning.

3. The entire site area is zoned residentially, or only a small portion, usually a narrow strip along the highways, is zoned for commercial use. The owner will then have to apply for rezoning of all or part of the site.

THE PLANNING TEAM

Depending on the size and complexity of the project, the planning team might, in neighborhood and intermediate centers, consist of the developer, the architect, and in some instances, a leasing consultant or lease broker. In projects of greater complexity and size, such as regional shopping centers, it may be well to add to the team an experienced consultant in real estate matters, well versed in shopping center economics (Fig. 2).

THE PLANNING SCHEDULE

Shopping center planning is a lengthy process in which each step must logically follow from the previous one. Impatient or snap decisions may result in catastrophe. First, a tentative planning and construction schedule is outlined which may be divided into five phases:

Exploratory phase
Preliminary phase
Final planning phase
Construction phase
Opening phase.

For regional centers, each of these phases is likely to be clearly defined and even subdivided into various stages; for smaller centers the activity may be consolidated into fewer stages.

1. *Exploratory phase:* All pertinent circumstances and conditions are thoroughly probed, and the conceptual image of the shopping center is established.

2. *Preliminary phase:* Negotiations with major tenants and financing institutions are undertaken, and necessary adjustments are made. Preliminary drawings indicating all architectural and engineering aspects are completed. Preliminary specifications are written, and a reliable preliminary cost estimate is arrived at.

3. *Final planning phase:* Working drawings and specifications are completed, establishing a reliable basis for competitive bidding and for construction. Building permits are obtained. Invitations to bid are written.

4. *Construction phase:* Contracts are awarded. The architect is engaged in general supervision, supported by clerks-of-the-works who are usually retained by the developer. The architect chooses materials, selects colors, and integrates landscaping and art work. The developer and the economist are active in completing leasing, getting the center on an operational basis, and preparing for the opening.

5. *Opening phase:* The opening is an important event that calls for imagination as well as careful planning. In recent years, shopping centers of varying size throughout the country have been opened with ceremonies ranging from the quiet, unobtrusive opening of a few stores at a time, to mass opening ceremonies lasting for several days and featuring various kinds of attention-getting promotions.

Timing

It is difficult to estimate the time periods necessary for each phase of the planning

schedule, because of fluctuations in size and complexity of the project, availability of major tenants and of financing, climatic conditions, and the like. The following tabulation gives time ranges for regional projects proceeding under normal conditions:

	Time span, weeks
Exploratory phase (26 to 56 weeks)	
Feasibility study	8 to 12
Conceptual planning stage	4 to 6
Presentation stage	4 to 8
Development stage	10 to 30
Preliminary phase (10 to 22 weeks)	
Adjustment stage	4 to 10
Consolidation stage	6 to 12
Final planning phase	20 to 30
Construction phase (62 to 114 weeks)	
Bidding	4 to 6
General building construction	52 to 100
Tenants' building—interior construction	6 to 8
Total for planning and construction	118 to 222
	(27 to 51 months)

For intermediate centers (100,000 to 300,000 sq ft), a reasonable time span is 18 to 40 months; for neighborhood centers the span, depending largely on tenant availability, is likely to range from 12 to 24 months.

SPACE ALLOTMENTS

The architect's work starts with the planning of the site. For this task he must have at his disposal the findings of the economic analysis establishing the total rental area that can be supported by the shopping potential, broken down into main merchandising categories. He must have some idea of other uses to which the land should be devoted, and an idea of other probable zoning problems. On the basis of feasibility studies, he now has a general idea of traffic and accessibility, as well as full information about physical conditions of the site (including a topographic survey) and, as a result of test borings, about soil conditions. Sometimes he also knows the basic requirements of the potential major tenant or tenants.

With this information, he begins planning by carefully allocating portions of the land to specific uses. These uses fall into seven basic categories:

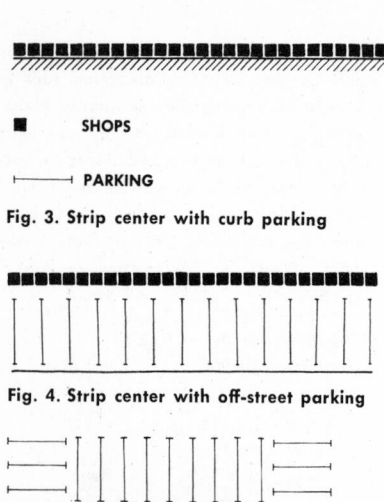

■ SHOPS

⊢——┤ PARKING

Fig. 3. Strip center with curb parking

Fig. 4. Strip center with off-street parking

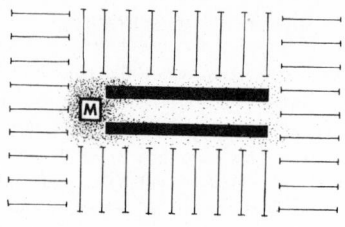

**Fig. 6. Mall center with only
one magnet**

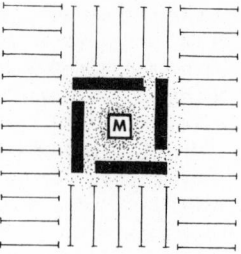

Fig. 8. Cluster-type center

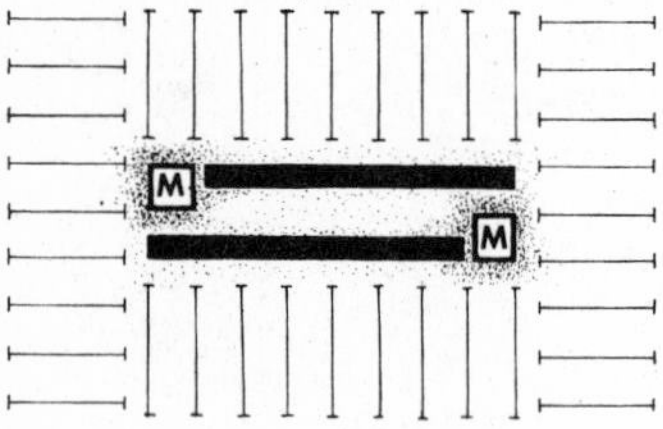

**Fig. 5. Double-strip center with
off-street parking**

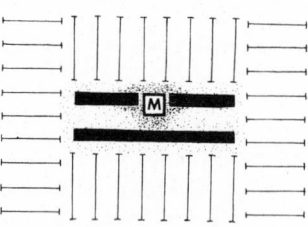

**Fig. 7. Mall center with magnet
centrally placed**

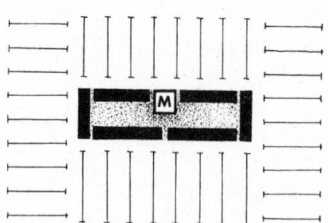

Fig. 9. "Introverted" center

1. *Structures*
   a. For retail purposes (retail areas)
   b. For service purposes (heating and air-conditioning plants, electric substations, maintenance shops, truck roads, loading docks, and equipment storage)
   c. For other commercial uses (offices and recreational facilities)
   d. For public use such as civic and social facilities (community center, auditorium, exhibition space, and children's play areas)
2. *Car storage areas*
   a. Surface parking lots
   b. Double-deck or multiple-deck garages
3. *Pedestrian areas*
   a. Malls, courts, lanes, and plazas
   b. Covered pedestrian areas, such as public corridors and covered malls or courts
4. *Automobile movement areas*
   Distribution road system on site
5. *Public transportation areas*
   Bus roads, bus terminals, and taxi stands
6. *Buffer areas*
   Landscaped areas separating car storage areas or service areas from the public road system, or areas separating parking areas from one another or parking areas from service areas
7. *Reserve areas*
   Portions of site to be held in reserve

for the planned growth of the shopping center.

SITE PLANNING PRINCIPLES

The allocation of space for these and possibly other uses should be guided by certain planning principles in order to attain the highest feasible productivity of the land over an extended period of time: (1) Safeguard surrounding areas against blight; (2) Expose retail facilities to maximum foot traffic; (3) Separate various mechanized traffic types from one another and from foot traffic; (4) Create a maximum of comfort and convenience for shoppers and merchants; and (5) Achieve orderliness, unity, and beauty.

Foot traffic

Exposure of all individual stores in a shopping center to the maximum amount of foot traffic is the best assurance of high sales volume. Suburban business real estate often has been evaluated on the basis of passing automobile traffic—an evaluation which overlooks the fact that automobiles do not buy merchandise. It is only after the driver of even the most expensive car leaves it and becomes a pedestrian that he can become a buyer. Therefore, if shopping centers are to prosper, dense foot traffic must be created. "Shopping traffic," the act of walking from store to store, creates the lifeblood of a

shopping center; and proper circulation of this shopping traffic ensures business success.

Bearing in mind the relative importance in each instance of the size of the center, the shape of the site, the character of the tenancy, and other related circumstances, it is possible to weigh the advantages and drawbacks of various types of site planning to achieve the desired foot traffic. The manner in which site planning can influence the quantity of shopping traffic is illustrated in the schematic plans (Figs. 3 through 9) discussed below.

The degree of completeness of the separation between transportation and pedestrian areas depends on the size of the shopping center. In a single commercial building, this separation becomes effective only after the customer has entered the store. If there are two buildings, it might be possible to arrange a separated pedestrian area between them. The chances to create separated pedestrian areas are slightly higher in an intermediate center. In a regional center, complete separation is almost always possible and should be effected. Even in the smallest grouping of stores, such as a neighborhood center, it is possible to achieve a certain amount of separation by means of broad sidewalks with landscaping, low garden walls, and the like.

Strip center with curb parking (Fig. 3): In this plan, the shopping center is comprised of a row of stores extending 2,000 ft along the highway. The shopper parks at the curb in front of the store, transacts his business, and then is likely to enter his car and drive off. Shopping or foot traffic is limited.

Strip center with off-street parking (Fig. 4): This shopping center consists of a 2,000-ft-long row of stores set back from the highway sufficiently to permit parking in front. The sidewalk, or covered walkway, encourages foot traffic along the store fronts. This plan generates a certain amount of shopping traffic and thus is clearly superior to the type shown in Fig. 3. Shopping traffic is nevertheless limited, chiefly because of the 2,000-ft distance between the extreme ends of the strip. The shopper may return to his car after each transaction and drive to the next store on his list, ignoring intervening merchants.

Double-strip center with off-street parking (Fig. 5): Here, the strip is divided into two rows of stores, facing each other along a pedestrian mall, with parking on four sides. A "magnet" (department store, junior department store, or other major tenant store) is placed at each end. The 2,000-ft strip of stores is now divided into two 1,000-ft-long strips. With the distance between the two magnets now only half as great, foot traffic will be greater and the intervening stores will profit accordingly. Also, the creation of a highly desirable pedestrian area shielded from the noise, smells, confusion, and hazards of automobile traffic will contribute to greater shopping traffic.

Mall center with only one magnet (Fig. 6): In this plan, the existence of only one magnet, located at the extreme end of the pedestrian mall, reduces shopping traffic because of lack of interchange. The stores farthest from the magnet will participate very little in the traffic it generates.

Mall center with magnet centrally placed (Fig. 7): The arrangement of the pedestrian mall is the same as that shown in Fig. 6, except that the magnet is moved to a center position on one side of the mall. This modification represents a considerable improvement over the previous example.

Cluster-type center (Fig. 8): The major tenant is placed in the center of a cluster arrangement. Nearly all stores thus become neighbors of the most powerful shopping-traffic puller.

"Introverted" center (Fig. 9): This type exemplifies what might be called the "introverted" center, in which all store fronts are turned toward the inside of the building cluster. Entry into individual stores directly from the parking lot is diminished

or completely excluded. Shopping traffic is funneled through a limited number of entrance arcades into pedestrian areas—a plan that markedly increases the density of shopping traffic and controls its direction.

Separation of traffic types

1. *Pedestrian from transportation:* The separation of pedestrian areas from transportation areas is one of the cornerstones of good planning. The constant movement of vehicles within transportation areas inevitably creates a certain amount of danger, noise, fumes, and confusion, which distract the shopper and diminish shopping enjoyment.

2. *Service from customer traffic:* Service traffic in shopping centers represents a considerable portion of mechanized traffic. Even in the smallest shopping center, service vehicles for deliveries, pick-ups, garbage and trash collection, repair crews, construction and fixture contractors, and utility companies create a significant portion of the over-all traffic. Separation of service traffic from customer traffic is essential and may be accomplished on one or two levels.

Service areas on the merchandising or ground level in the form of truck roads, service courts, and other types of loading facilities, are practical in the neighborhood and intermediate centers. Good planning principles demand that such areas be properly shielded by screen walls or landscaping and that service vehicles be able to enter or leave without interference from automobiles or pedestrians.

Service areas on nonmerchandising levels permit the most productive space to be totally freed from service functions. Only the large center can achieve this separation, for which there are a number of possible arrangements. The truck tunnel under the shopping center mall is an expensive solution that is more talked about than used. Service roads located at the basement level provide a less expensive solution and are widely used. Where subsurface or topographical conditions make the construction of basements impractical, service and storage areas may be placed above the merchandising level and connected to it by ramps.

3. *Public transportation from customer traffic:* Separation of public transportation from customer traffic is essential. The designer must also consider the space needs for public transportation. Generous arrangements for public carriers with well-located and well-protected waiting areas will encourage transportation companies to

use them. Space requirements for existing and future public transportation facilities should be discussed at the outset of site planning work, and if possible, provisions should exceed the required minimum. Storage space for buses should be provided on or near the site so the transportation company can make extra facilities available for peak periods, especially at closing hours.

Orderliness, unity, and beauty

The concept of orderliness, unity, and beauty is a major planning principle; it must be applied to every major and minor aspect of the project, and must permeate all architectural expressions. Landscaping, signs, the architecture of structures, architectural treatment of spaces between structures, composition of structures in relation to one another, colors, and materials—all must adhere to this vital principle.

PLANNING THE SURROUNDING AREA

The term "surrounding area" can be understood either in its narrowest sense, that is, strips of land on the opposite side of the public roads adjoining the shopping center, or in its widest sense: the entire community within which a shopping center is located.

A reciprocal relationship exists between a shopping center and its surrounding area. A well-planned center can exert a highly invigorating influence on the area surrounding it, while a well-planned surrounding area can add in large measure to the prosperity of the center. Conversely, a poorly planned or unplanned commercial grouping of stores can have a deteriorating effect on its surrounding area, while the success of even the best-planned center can be endangered by a poorly planned or blighted surrounding area. The degree to which effective planning can be applied depends on the general location of the center, the size of the center, the investment policy of the developer, and existing zoning and economic conditions.

In general, if the site for a shopping center is the one remaining piece of land within a completely built-up area, there will obviously be meager possibilities for influencing the character of the surrounding area. Shopping centers in such areas usually operate under the handicap of having to be fitted into existing area and traffic conditions. On the other hand, one should consider the undoubted advantage of being provided with a fully developed buying potential.

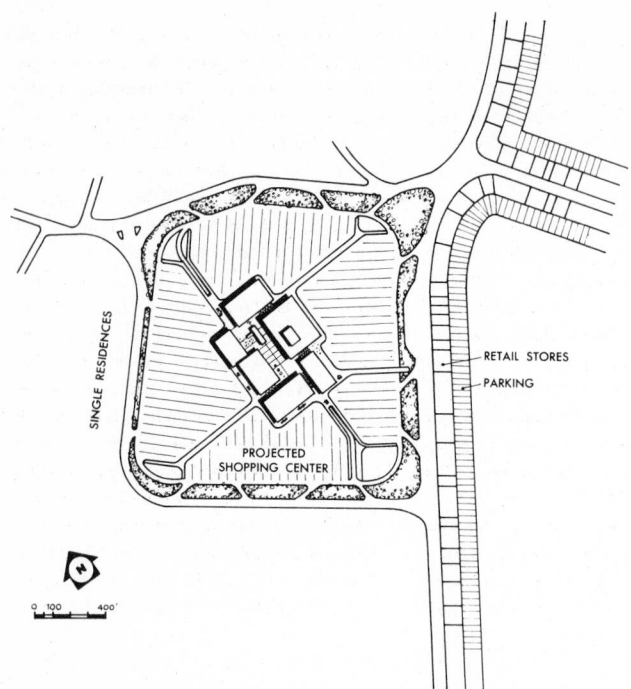

Fig. 10. Original zoning plan

*The plan shows zoning conditions as they existed
when the original shopping center was projected.*

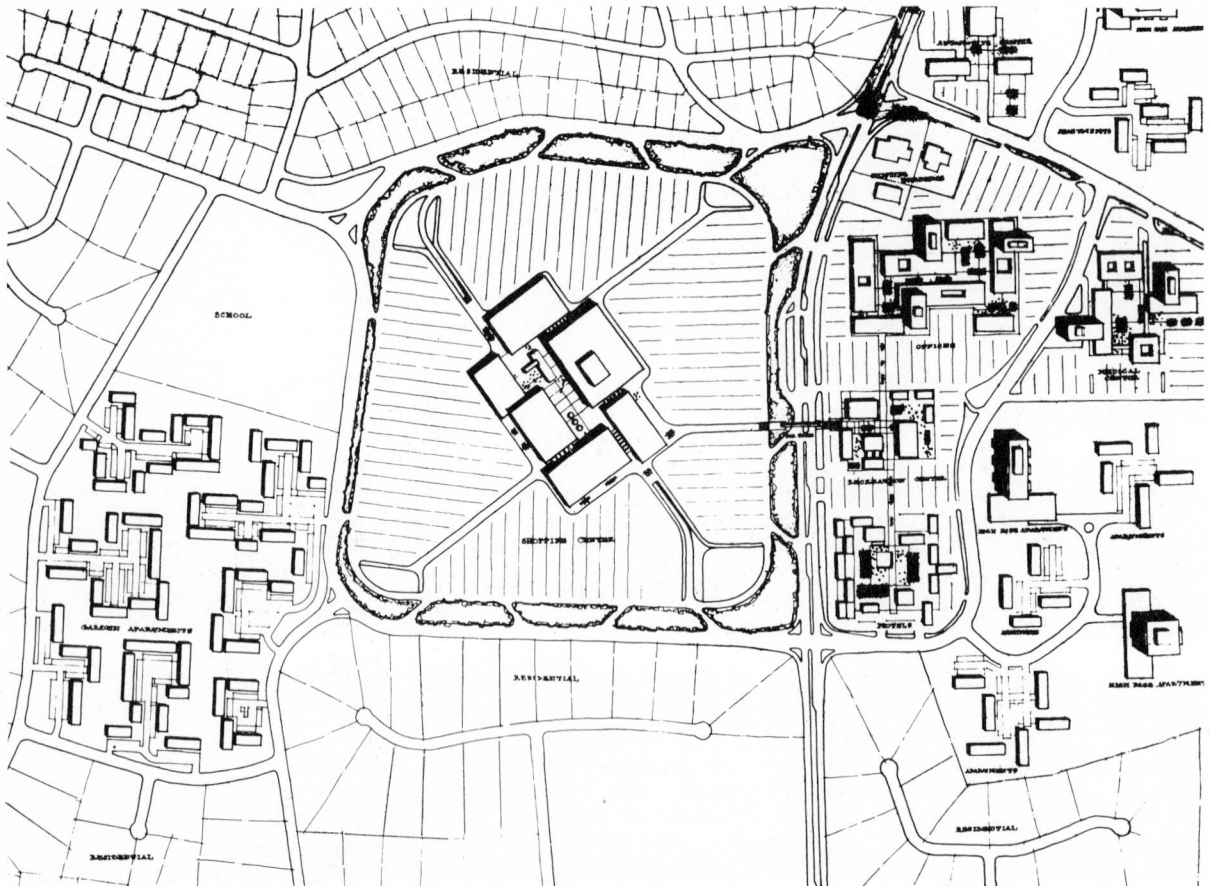

Fig. 11. Revised zoning plan

*The plan represents the architect's suggestions for the surrounding land
use for the same shopping center shown in Fig. 10. The revisions ensure
control of the surrounding land by the developer.*

SHOPPING CENTERS—7

Most shopping centers do not fall into this category since it would be rare to find a sufficiently large site for such construction within a fully built-up area. Large tracts of land can usually be found only on the fringe of suburban developments or in comparatively empty areas between suburban growth. This fact applies especially to the large regional shopping center and, to a lesser degree, to the intermediate one. With some planning, however, both types can create sufficient pulling power to reduce the disadvantage of being at some distance from densely populated areas.

The greatest opportunity for effective planning of surrounding areas in relation to the shopping center is afforded when new communities are projected. Then it is often possible to set aside, in the master plan, sites of ideal size.

Whether the shopping center developer

acquires surrounding land with the intention of developing it himself, or intends to negotiate with the owners of such land in order to persuade them to develop along the lines of best common interest, it is important to make a comprehensive plan for the land use of the surrounding area (Figs. 10 and 11).

PLANNING FOR EXPANSION

Planning for expansion should be considered if the shopping center is located in a steadily growing area. In such a situation the department store and other major stores will often express the desire to enlarge when their sales volume reaches a stated figure.

In order to make planning for expansion feasible, certain prerequisites must exist. The carrying potential of surrounding public roads must be sufficient to absorb

additional traffic loads. The site must be large enough to permit the developer to hold space in reserve for additional building, parking, and traffic areas; alternatively, additionally created income must be such as to justify capital investment for double-deck or multiple-deck parking structures at the time of enlargement. Most important, the developer must be reasonably certain that the growing buying potential of the area will not be more efficiently served by existing or future competition. For example, if suitable shopping center sites exist within the trade area, the likelihood of such future competition is great. These and other related factors must be carefully considered before making a decision to plan for expansion.

If it is decided to plan with a view to expansion, certain measures must be taken. Since the desire of department stores and other major tenant stores for growth is

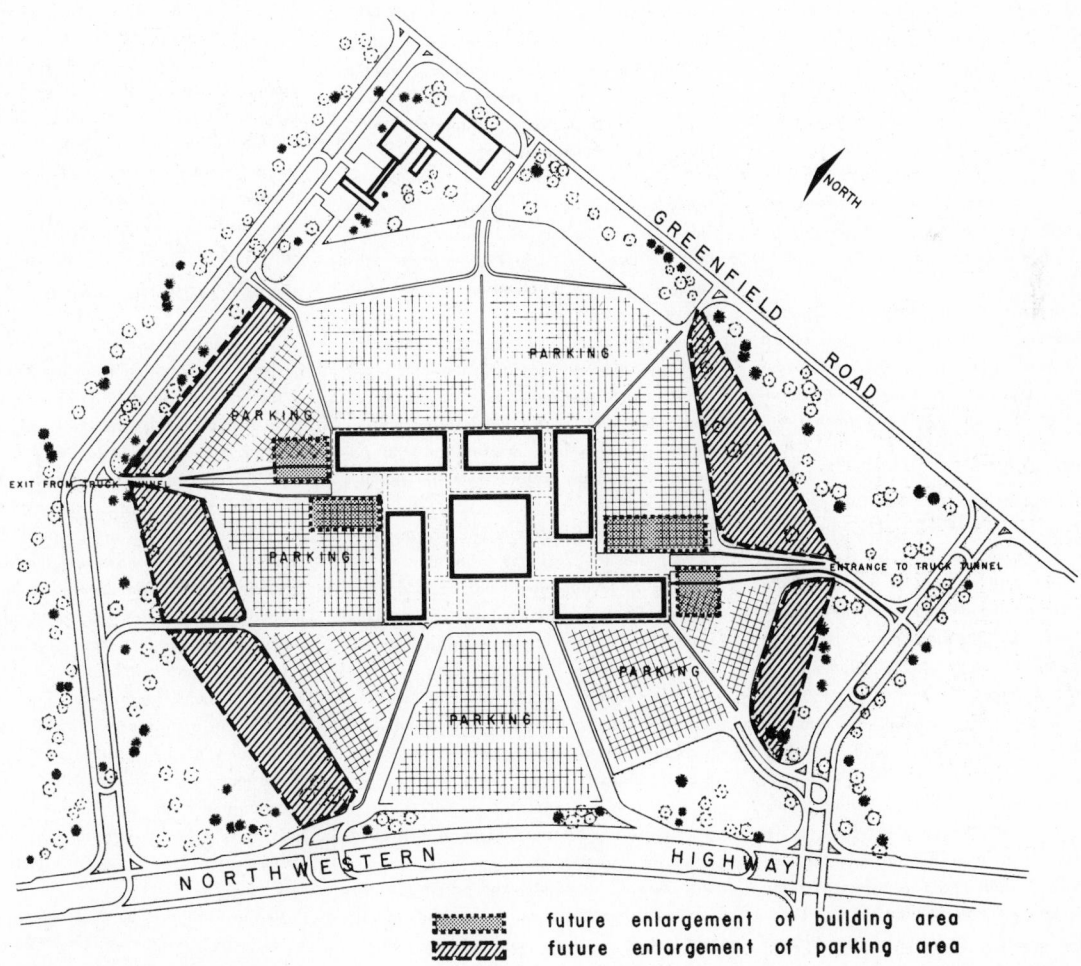

future enlargement of building area
future enlargement of parking area

Fig. 12. Plan for expansion

Northland Center, Detroit; Victor Gruen Associates, Architects.

usually best met by provisions for vertical additions, the construction of larger foundations and heavier columns as well as roof slabs strong enough to carry future floor loads are required. Horizontal growth is difficult to accomplish without destroying the relationship between shopping center buildings and other elements. Land must be held in reserve for the enlarged parking needs that will be created by expanded shopping facilities. When the original construction is completed, these reserve areas will have to be properly landscaped in order not to mar the over-all appearance of the center. Central air-conditioning and heating-plant structures must be dimensioned to provide space for additional equipment, and all underground utility lines should be of sufficient size to meet ultimate needs. The general plan shown in Fig. 12 indicates existing structures and provisions for expansion.

PLANNING FOR DEVELOPMENT IN STAGES

Planning for development in stages should be considered if the shopping center site is located in an area that has not reached its ultimate population potential and if a quick acceleration of population growth may be expected. Another motivation for development in stages may be the desire of a land owner to make some immediate use of his land even though full utilization will be practical only in future years.

Planning for development in stages can be successfully accomplished only if a total master site-use plan is completed before construction or even detailed planning of the first stage is undertaken.

TRAFFIC

Traffic planning, an integral part of planning the site and the surrounding area, plays an important role in the proper functioning and success of the shopping center. It should be borne in mind, however, that the shopping center is not to be planned to serve traffic; rather, traffic is to be planned to serve the shopping center. Basic traffic planning concerns the planning team as a whole and the architect in particular.

Before the site is finally decided upon, serious consideration must be given to its accessibility. It is essential to gather all information about existing roads and the traffic-carrying capacities of the surrounding road system, as well as to establish the expected additional traffic load generated by the new shopping center.

Although the architect will avail himself of the assistance of a traffic engineer, the specialist should not be expected to furnish basic concepts but should assist the architect in finding solutions within the framework of general and specified planning aims. Traffic planning is the responsibility of the architect since it is part of the general planning of the center.

Aims of traffic planning

1. *Easy traffic flow on surrounding road system.* The existence of enterprises that would result in a constant entering and exiting of cars along the roads opposite the shopping center would disrupt the flow of traffic and is therefore highly undesirable. (This is one reason why proper planning of the surrounding area is so important.) The existence of many side roads opposite the shopping center would also interfere with good traffic flow. The planner's main task is to see to it that automobiles can enter the site without slowdowns.

2. *Effective transfer of road traffic onto the site.* If automobiles were driven directly from an adjoining highway onto parking-lot lanes, chaos would result. The circulatory road that functions as a turn-off lane from the highway, making possible a gradual change of speed from fast-moving traffic to slower parking-lot traffic, plays an extremely important role.

3. *Even and effective distribution of traffic on the site.* The customer should be free to drive to any of the parking areas that surround the center so that he may come as close as possible to the store where he will make his first purchase. Secondary traffic movements within the parking area must be facilitated. In larger centers, arrangements must be made to guarantee the easy flow of circulatory traffic, avoiding any interference with pedestrians walking to and from the center's structures.

4. *Convenient and efficient arrangement of car storage facilities.* The aim of the parking-lot layout should not be to achieve the greatest possible number of parking stalls, but rather to ensure the greatest possible turnover of cars during a given period. Parking capacity is a valid measuring stick only if it denotes the number of conveniently arranged and dimensioned parking stalls.

Walkways for pedestrians will result in greater safety for shoppers and will eliminate the slowing down of vehicles, but will reduce the number of parking spaces in any area. Surfacing of good quality will speed parking and reduce maintenance costs. Lanes should be clearly numbered with signs visible to the motorists when entering the lot as well as when returning from shopping. Proper illumina-

tion is essential for safety and speed of parking operations.

No formula for proportioning parking area to sales area is recommended. Existing successful shopping centers provide from 3 to 9 car spaces per 1,000 sq ft of rentable area; however, each project must be decided on its own merits. An allowance of 400 sq ft per stall, including drives, walks, and landscaping, is recommended. Wide stalls arranged at a 45-deg angle permit the fastest and most comfortable parking. The maximum size recommended for a single parking lot is 800 cars.

5. *Separation of service vehicles from customer car traffic.* For service vehicles (trucks, trailers, and garbage- and trash-collecting vehicles), separate roads, branching off from the general road system at points removed as far as possible from the shopping area, should be provided. Ideally—and this can be accomplished in large regional shopping centers—separate entrances and exits to the public road system should be planned. If this arrangement is not feasible, the service roads should branch off from the perimeter circulatory road or, in smaller centers, from general entrance and exit roads before such roads take on the characteristics of parking lanes. Under no circumstances should service vehicles cross roads that directly serve parking operations. Public transportation vehicles should be similarly separated from customer car traffic.

CHARACTER OF THE BUILDINGS

The shopping center establishes a new environment resulting from the banding together of individual businesses in cooperative fashion with the aim of creating greater commercial effectiveness through unified endeavor. It is important that the individual characteristics of the participants not be suppressed, but encouraged. It is equally important, however, that a strong common denominator be created to tie the individual enterprises into a homogeneous unit. These dual aims can be achieved by skillful planning and design. Buildings for single tenancy, for example, are planned not only in accordance with the specific requirements of the specific tenant, but also in harmony with the character of the over-all shopping center architecture. Such buildings thus offer a variation of the main theme rather than the introduction of a new one (Fig. 13).

Regimentation is as much to be shunned as anarchy. Complete control of store-front design results in monotony and dullness, and diminishes the enjoyment of window shopping, which thrives on excitement created by ever-changing designs and colors.

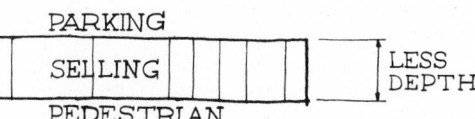

PARKING

SELLING — LESS DEPTH

PEDESTRIAN

ll depth is needed if service facilities are in basements and
estrian traffic moves only on one side of structure

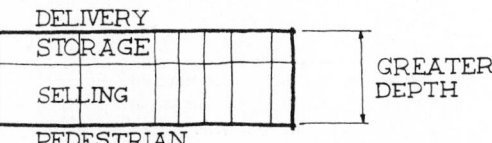

DELIVERY

STORAGE

SELLING — GREATER DEPTH

PEDESTRIAN

ater depth is needed if delivery is at back of store on
nd level and storage facilities have to be provided on
nd level for each tenant

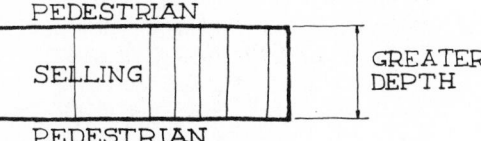

PEDESTRIAN

SELLING — GREATER DEPTH

PEDESTRIAN

ater depth is needed if shopping traffic moves on both sides
ndividual stores

13. Depth requirements for tenant stores

The cooperative spirit is best expressed if individual design of tenant stores is encouraged within established limits; around these individual design areas there must be a framework of architecturally controlled areas large enough and treated with sufficient forcefulness to hold the varying expressions firmly together (Fig. 14).

PEDESTRIAN AREAS

Open spaces must be more than narrow lanes between long rows of stores. They must be busy and colorful, exciting and stimulating, must make walking enjoyable,

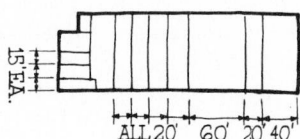

Stores of varying depth and width can be arranged between multiple-tenant structures by skillful division and orientation of stores

and provide places for rest and relaxation. All the senses should be rewarded. Trees, flowers, fountains, sculpture, and murals, as well as the architecture of freestanding structures, are vital parts of the over-all scheme. Public events such as fashion shows, holiday celebrations, and exhibitions are all parts of the life in these open spaces, as are snack bars, outdoor cafes, and restaurants.

Shopping must thus be understood as more than a utilitarian activity. The environment should be so attractive that customers will enjoy these trips, will stay longer, and return more often. This will result in cash registers ringing more often and recording higher sales.

Anarchy in store-front design

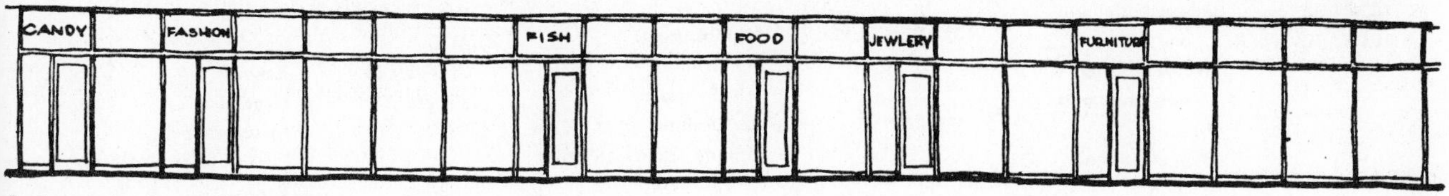

Regimentation in store-front design

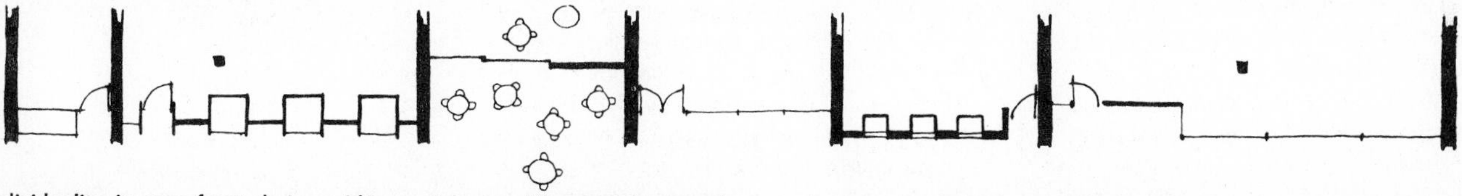

Individuality in store-front design within a strong architectural framework

Fig. 14. Store-front design

By DANIEL SCHWARTZMAN, *FAIA, Architect*

Merchandise category list

1. PIECE GOODS	Dress fabrics
	Patterns
	Sewing machines
			Womens sportswear
			  including blouses
			Budget sportswear
				12. DRAPERY	Curtains and
					  draperies
					Upholstery

2. DRY GOODS	Linens and towels
	Domestics
	Blankets
			Street floor
			  sportswear
			Junior sportswear
					Blinds and awnings
					Bedspreads and
					  boudoir

3. SMALLWARES	Notions, including
	  sewing
	  accessories and
	  closet shop
			Junior suits and
			  coats
			Junior dresses
				13. FASHION
				HOME
				FURNISHINGS
					Silverware
					China and glass
					Giftware

	Drugs
	Cosmetics
	Stationery and
	  greeting cards
	Books
		7. CHILDRENS
		WEAR
			Infants wear,
			  includes layette
			Infants furniture
			Boys 3–6x and
			  7–14
					Pictures and mirrors
					Lamps

4. WOMENS
FASHION
ACCESSORIES
	Umbrellas, neck-
	  wear and
	  handkerchiefs
			Girls 3–6x and
			  7–14
			Hosiery
				14. HOUSEWARES	Bath shop
					Laundry and
					  cleaning
					Oilcloth and paper

	Handbags Small leather goods Costume and better jewelry		Millinery Accessories Shoes Girl and boy scouts		Kitchen gadgets Cutlery Pots and pans Pantryware

	Hosiery
	Gloves
	Belts
	Millinery, including
	  hat bar
			Sub-teens wear
			Sub-teens
			  accessories
			Teens wear
			Teens accessories
					Kitchen and
					  unpainted
					  furniture cabinets
					Hardware and
					  paints

	Shoes, including
	  casual and
	  slipper bar
		8. MENS WEAR	Clothing
			Sportswear
			Furnishings
			Hats
					Small electrics

5. INTIMATE WEAR	Underwear Corsets and bras Robes and negligees		Shoes	15. MAJOR APPLIANCES	Refrigerators Ranges Dishwashers Washing machines Air conditioners Vacuum cleaners
		9. MISCELLANEOUS	Cameras Luggage Sporting goods Toys	16. MUSIC	Radios, T.V., Hi-Fi Records Musical instruments

6. WOMENS
READY TO WEAR
	Misses better suits
	  and coats
	Womens better
	  suits and coats
		10. FURNITURE	Upholstered
			  furniture
			Living room
			  furniture
				17. MISCELLANEOUS
				AND
				CUSTOMER
				SERVICES
					Pet shop
					Candy
					Bakery
					Groceries

	Furs
	Budget suits and
	  coats
	Misses better
	  dresses
			Dining room
			  furniture
			Terrace furniture
			Occasional
			  furniture
					Liquor shop
					Beauty salon
					Photo studio
					Optical

	Womens better
	  dresses
	Formal and bridal
	Budget dresses
	Maternity
			Outdoor furniture
			Bedding
					Smoke shop
					Garden shop
					Restaurant, coffee
					  shop
					Auto shop

	Aprons and
	  uniforms
	Cotton dresses
	Misses sportswear
	  including blouses
		11. FLOOR
		COVERINGS
			Broadloom
			Carpets
			Summer rugs
			Orientals
			Resilient flooring
			Small rugs and
			  mats
					Fur repair and
					  storage
					Shoe repair
					Jewelry repair
					Appliance repair
					Gift wrap

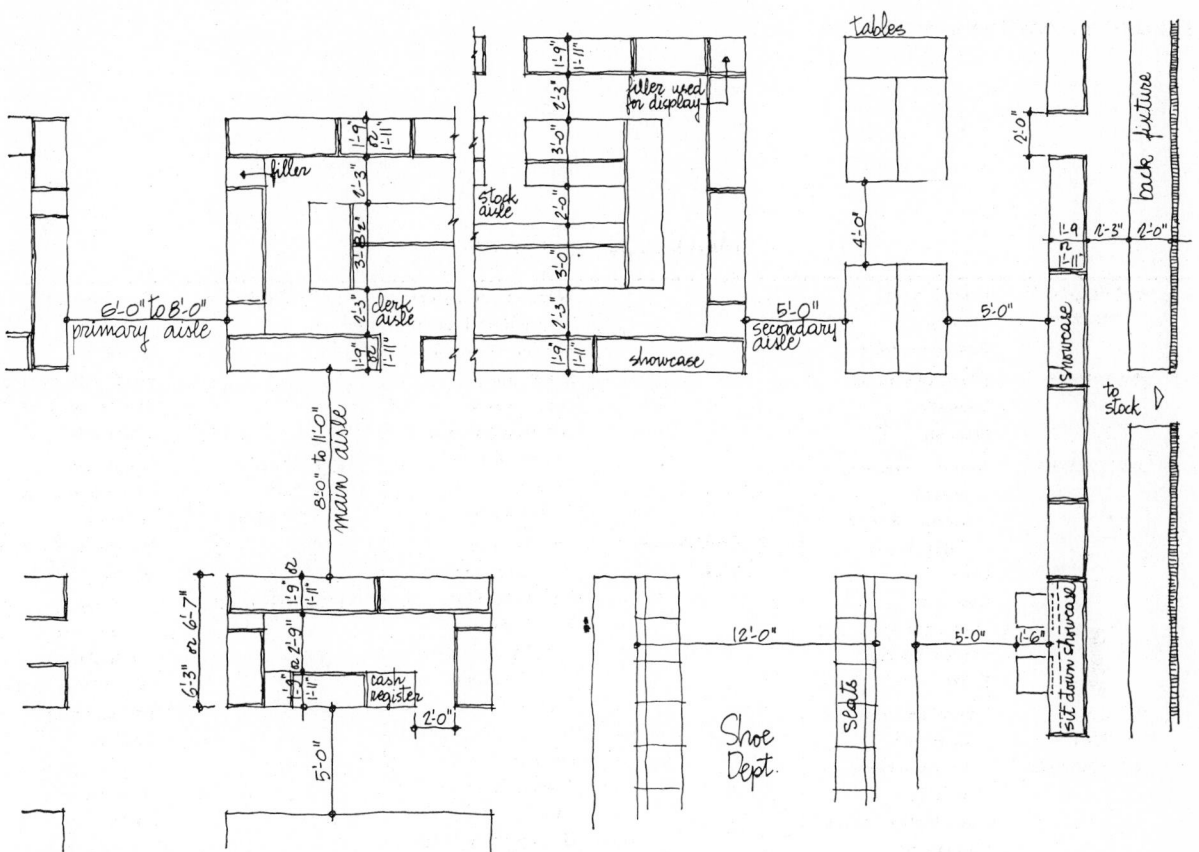

TYPICAL FIXTURE LAYOUT AND STANDARD AISLE WIDTHS. Scale: ⅛ in. = 1 ft

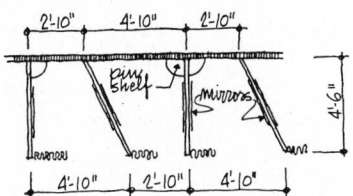

TYPICAL FITTING ROOM

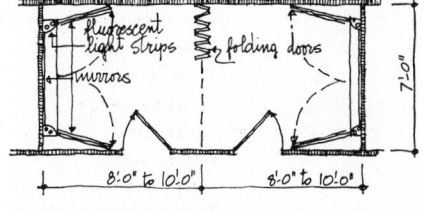

BRIDAL FITTING ROOMS

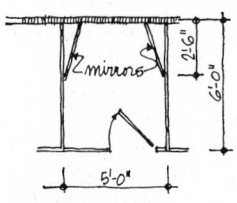

**BETTER DRESSES
FITTING ROOM**

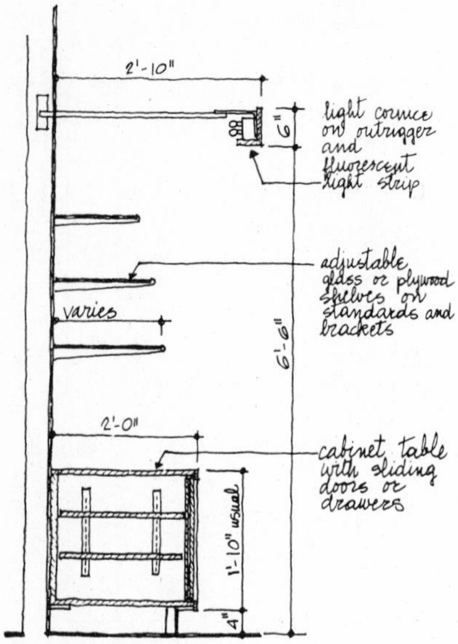

2'-10"
light cornice on outrigger and fluorescent light strip
6"
adjustable glass or plywood shelves on standards and brackets
varies
6'-6"
2'-0"
cabinet table with sliding doors or drawers
1'-10" usual
4"

BACK FIXTURE WITH SHELVES AND CABINET UNIT BELOW

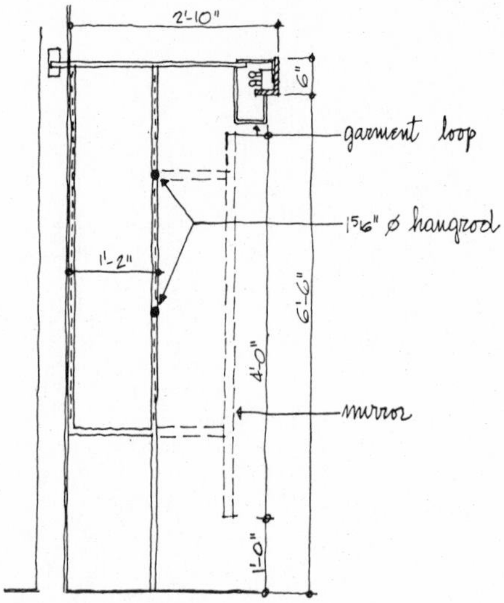

2'-10"
6"
garment loop
1⁵⁄₁₆" ø hangrod
1'-2"
6'-6"
4'-0"
mirror
1'-0"

BACK FIXTURE WITH SINGLE OR DOUBLE HANGING; CAN BE CONVERTED TO SHELVING

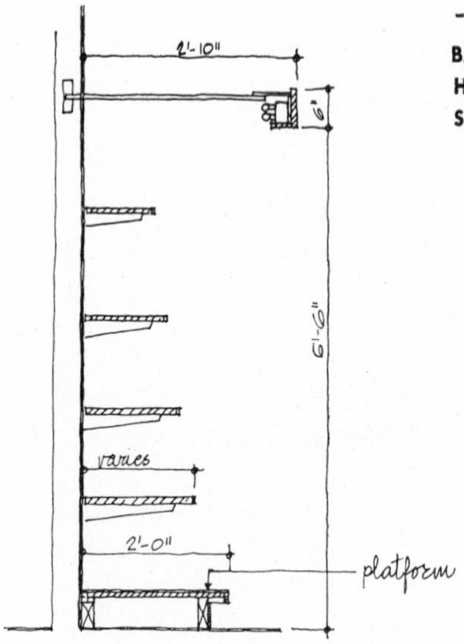

2'-10"
6"
6'-6"
varies
2'-0"
platform

BACK FIXTURE WITH SHELVES ONLY

2'-6⅜"
2'-4½"
glass
¾" clear
1⁵⁄₁₆" hangrod
2'-0"
steel tube end frame and stretcher
4'-1"
5'-7"
1'-6"
adjustable every 4"

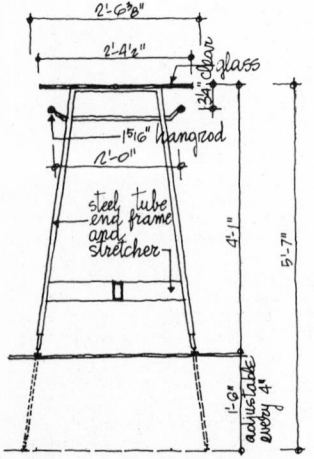

FREE STANDING HANGING RACK

1. length of hanging rack: 5 ft

BACK
FRONT
1'-9" or 1'-11"
glass
glass shelf
sliding doors
standard
varies
drawer insert
varies
4" base
3'-2" or 3'-4"
2'-6" for sit down stools
3'-4" for s.d. high stools
8"
6"

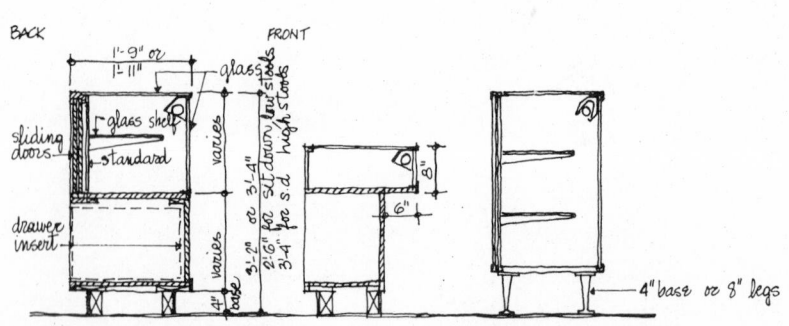

SHOWCASE—WOOD FRAME

1. depth of glass front varies from 1 ft to full height
2. length of showcase is determined by lamp size and is 3 ft 9 in., 5 ft 7 in.
3. showcase ends, either glass or plywood

4" base or 8" legs

SHOWCASE—METAL FRAME

1. frame can be stainless steel or extruded nickel silver or bronze

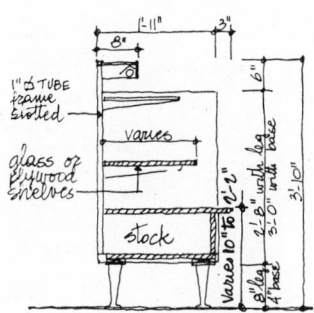

SELF SELECTION UNIT
1. length varies
2. special merchandise requires special inserts

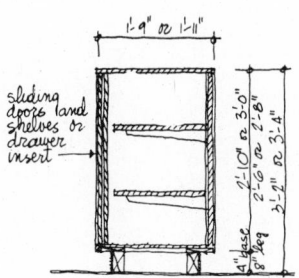

PLAIN COUNTER
Length varies 3 ft-9 in., 5 ft-7 in. or 7 ft-4 in.

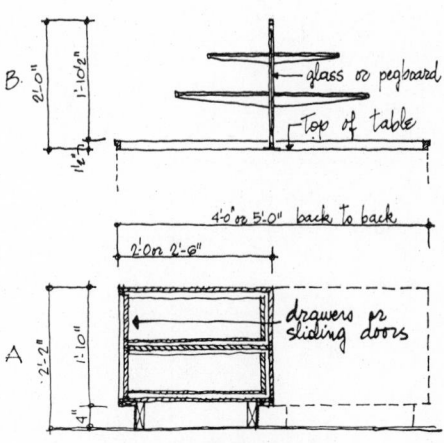

CABINET TABLE
A—without superstructure
B—with superstructure
1. with drawers or sliding doors and shelves
2. length varies 4 ft, 5 ft
3. no. of drawers varies 4, 6, 9

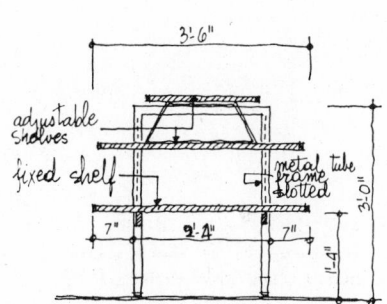

PIECE GOODS TABLE
1. length varies: 4 ft to 8 ft
2. shelves are formica covered

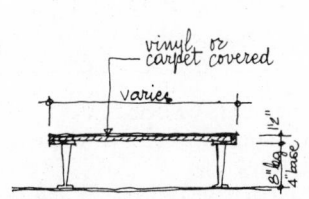

PLATFORM with LEGS or BASE
1. length varies
2. corners rounded, 2 in. radius

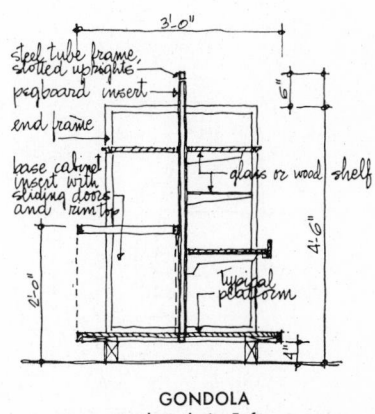

GONDOLA
length is 5 ft

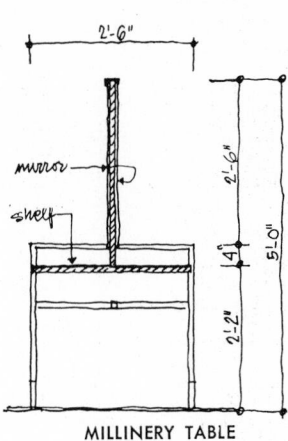

MILLINERY TABLE

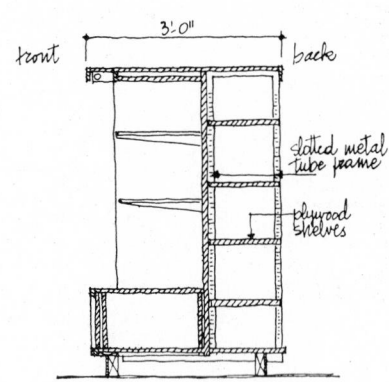

ISLAND BACK FIXTURE
with CABINET and STOCK SHELVING

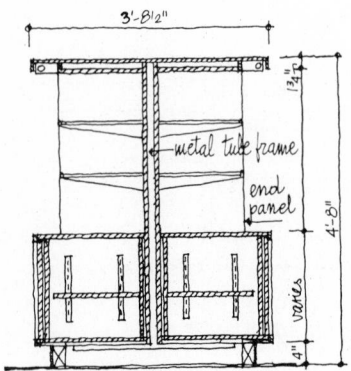

ISLAND BACK FIXTURES
BACK to BACK, with CABINETS
Number of shelves and base cabinet inserts
vary according to type of merchandise

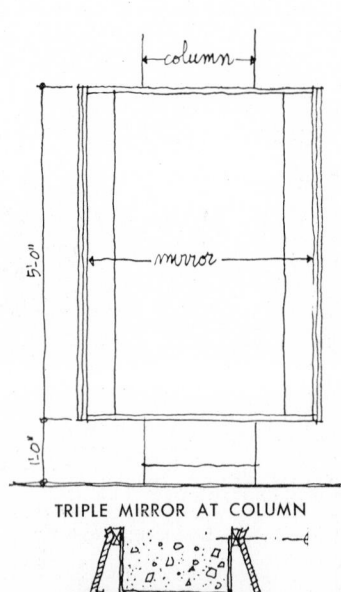

TRIPLE MIRROR AT COLUMN

for 1'-9" x 1'-9" column

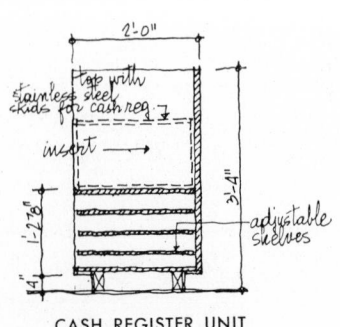

CASH REGISTER UNIT
1 ft-9 in. or 1 ft-11 in. wide when at
showcase line

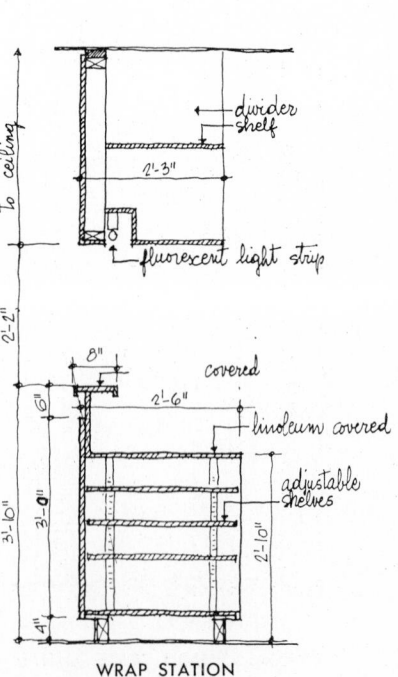

WRAP STATION

STORE FRONTS

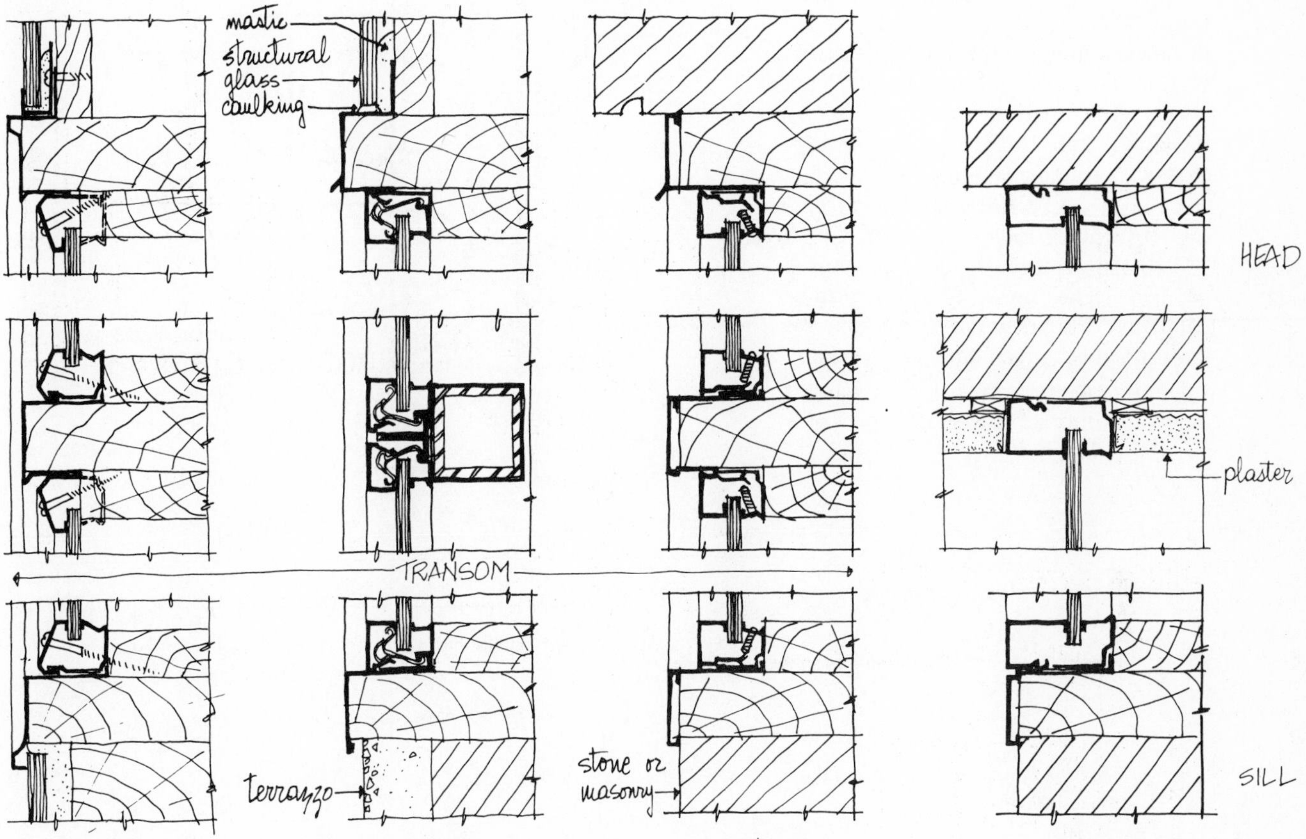

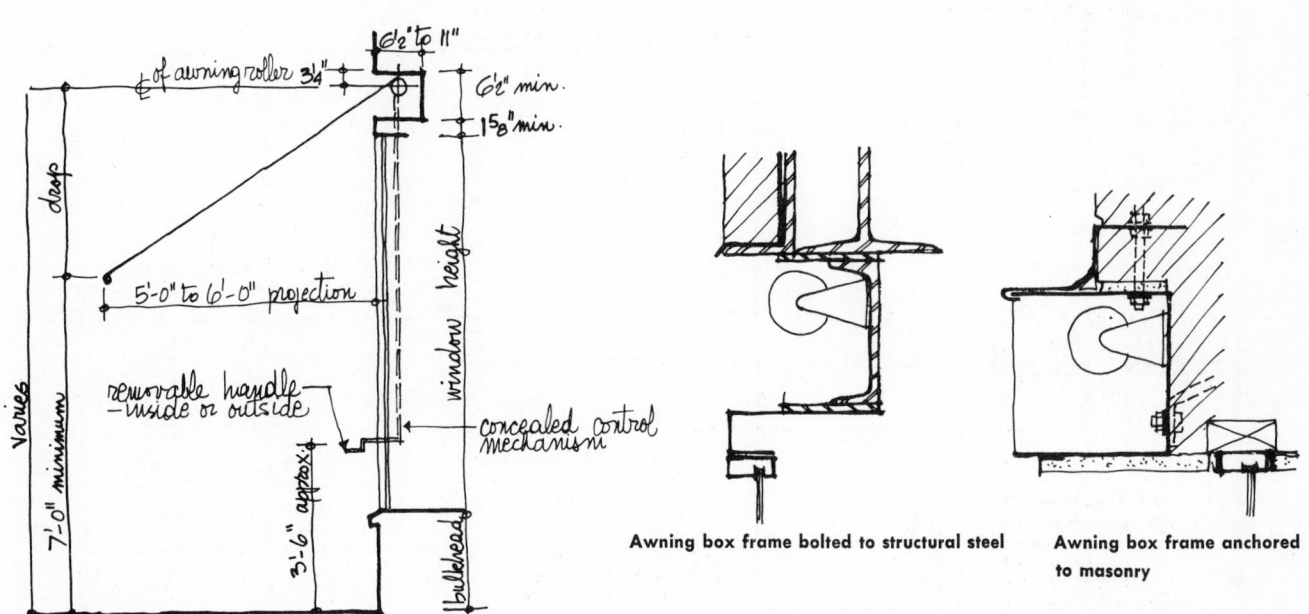

mastic
structural
glass
caulking

HEAD

plaster

TRANSOM

SILL

terrazzo

stone or masonry

Outside set

Snap-on

Inside set

Flush type

TYPICAL SETTING DETAILS. SCALE: 3 IN. = 1 FT

℄ of awning roller 3¼"

6½" to 11"

6½" min.

1⅝" min.

5'-0" to 6'-0" projection

drop

window height

removable handle
—inside or outside

concealed control
mechanism

Varies

7'-0" minimum

3'-6" approx.

bulkhead

Awning box frame bolted to structural steel

Awning box frame anchored to masonry

TYPICAL SECTION. SCALE: ¼ IN. = 1 FT

AWNING CONSTRUCTION DETAILS. SCALE: ½ IN. = 1 FT

Data on space allocations and clearance contained on this and the following four pages is presented as an aid in determining capacities, desirable seating layouts, and necessary clearances. Information was furnished by the John Van Range Co. and Albert Pick Co., restaurant equipment specialists; Louis A. Brown, architect; and the Brunswick-Balke-Collender Co.

Tabulations are divided into three groups. The most luxurious establishments ordinarily use as minima the largest figures given, and vice-versa.

Dining room area per seat ranges from a minimum 9.5 sq ft to a comfortable 12.5 sq ft.

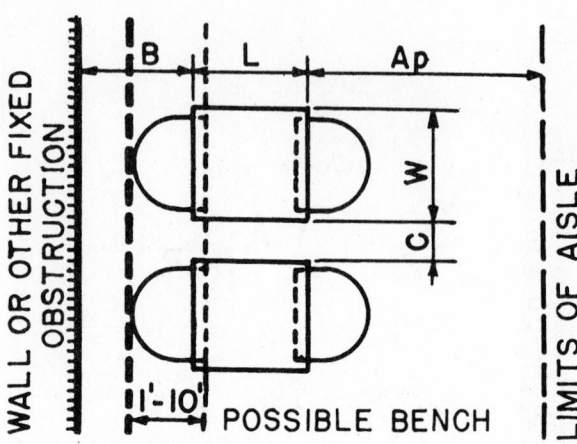

POSSIBLE BENCH

Scale: 1/4 in. = 1 ft; dimensions in feet and inches

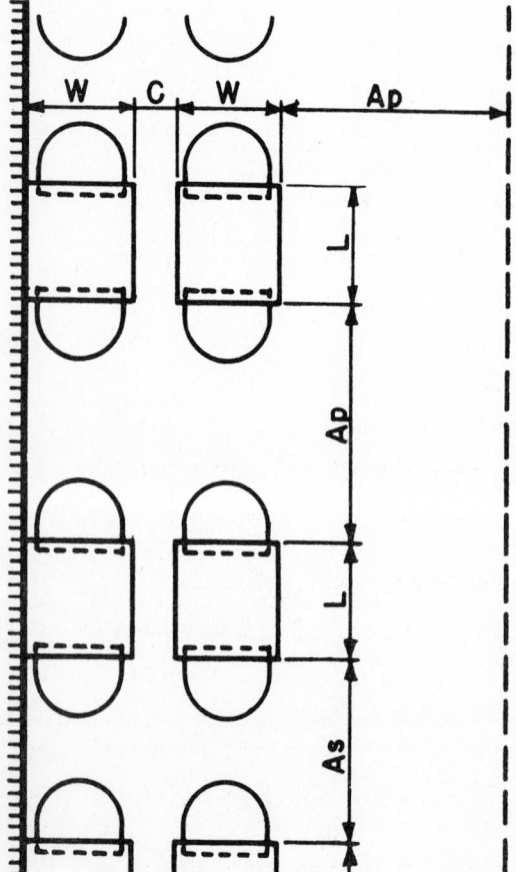

		Abs. Min.	Des. Min.	Comfort-able
Ap	Public circ'n	3–0 to 4–6	3–6 to 5–0	3–9 to 5–0
As	Service aisle	3–6 to 4–6	4–0 to 5–0	4–0 to 5–6
B	To wall	1–8 to 2–0	2–0 to 2–6	2–0 to 3–0
C	Between units	0 to 8	6 to 1–0	1–0
	Length	1–8 to 2–0	2–3 to 2–4	2–4 to 2–6
	Width	1–8 to 2–0	2–2 to 2–3	2–4 to 2–6

		Abs. Min.	Des. Min.	Comfort-able
Ap	Public circ'n	*1–10 to 4–6	2–3 to 5–0	3–0 to 5–0
As	Service aisle	3–0 to 3–6	3–6 to 4–0	3–9 to 4–0
C	Between units	0 to 3	4 to 6	6
Length		1–8 to 2–0	2–3 to 2–4	2–4 to 2–6
Width		1–8 to 2–0	2–2 to 2–3	2–4 to 2–6

*Lower range only if chairs, etc., do not project into aisle

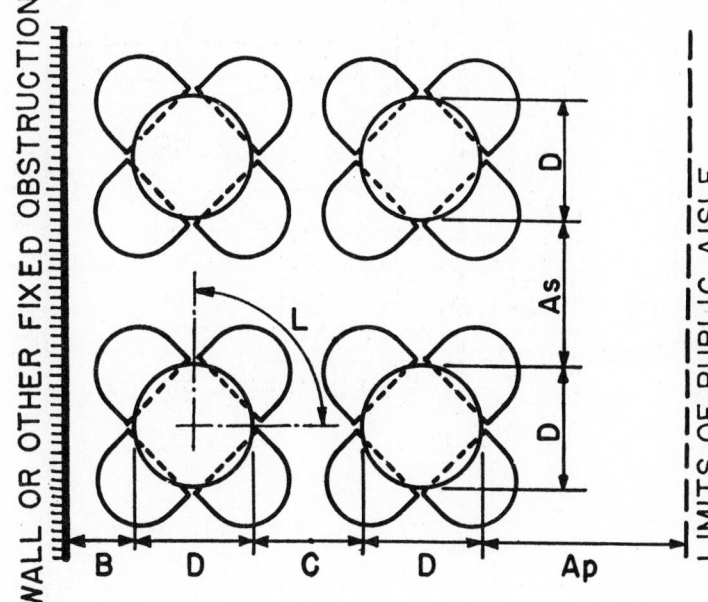

WALL OR OTHER FIXED OBSTRUCTION

LIMITS OF PUBLIC AISLE

		Abs. Min.	Des. Min.	Comfort-able
Ap	Public circ'n	3-0 to 3-6	3-6 to 4-6	3-6 to 4-6
As	Service only	2-0	2-6	3-0
B	To wall	6 to 1-0	10 to 1-0	1-0 to 1-3
C	Between units	1-6	1-10	2-0
	Diameter	2-8	2-10	2-10
*L	Perimeter per seat	1-10	2-0	2-2

*For seating units for more than 4 persons, round tables are usually recommended; diameter depending on perimeter necessary to seat required number.

Scale: 1/4 in. = 1 ft; dimensions in feet and inches

WALL OR OTHER FIXED OBSTRUCTION

LIMITS OF PUBLIC AISLE

WALL OR OTHER FIXED OBSTRUCTION

1'-10"

→ POSSIBLE BENCH

LIMITS OF PUBLIC AISLE

		Abs. Min.	Des. Min.	Comfort-able
A	Service or pub. circ'n	2-0 to 3-6	2-6 to 4-6	3-0 to 5-0
C	Between units	3-0 to 3-6	3-6 to 4-0	3-9 to 4-0
	Length	3-6	3-10 to 4-0	4-0
	Width	1-8 to 2-0	2-0 to 2-3	2-4 to 2-6

		Abs. Min.	Des. Min.	Comfort-able
A	Service or pub. circ'n	3-6 to 4-6	4-6 to 5-0	5-0 to 5-6
B	To Wall	2-0	2-0 to 2-6	2-0 to 3-0
C	Between units	0 to 1-0	1-0	1-6
	Length	3-6	3-10 to 4-0	4-0
	Width	1-8 to 2-0	2-0 to 2-3	2-4 to 2-6

THERE ARE, in some localities, code and other restrictions on booth furniture dimensions. Authorities having local jurisdiction should be consulted. One designer consulted regarded the 2-person booth (side-by side) as a waste of space; others recognize that conditions may arise when no other type of furniture will suffice. Booths for more than four persons are not commonly encountered.

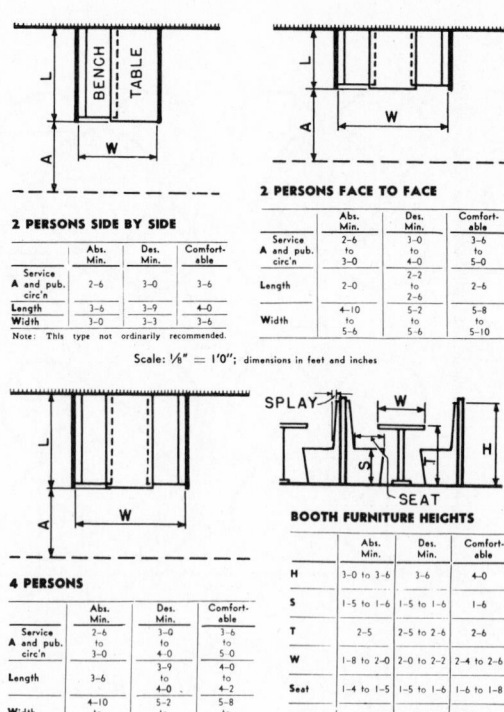

2 PERSONS SIDE BY SIDE

	Abs. Min.	Des. Min.	Comfort-able
Service A and pub. circ'n	2-6	3-0	3-6
Length	3-6	3-9	4-0
Width	3-0	3-3	3-6

2 PERSONS FACE TO FACE

	Abs. Min.	Des. Min.	Comfort-able
Service A and pub. circ'n	2-6 to 3-0	3-0 to 4-0	3-6 to 5-0
Length	2-0	2-2 to 2-6	2-6
Width	4-10 to 5-6	5-2 to 5-6	5-8 to 5-10

Note: This type not ordinarily recommended.

Scale: 1/8" = 1'0"; dimensions in feet and inches

4 PERSONS

	Abs. Min.	Des. Min.	Comfort-able
Service A and pub. circ'n	2-6 to 3-0	3-0 to 4-0	3-6 to 5-0
Length	3-6	3-9 to 4-0	4-0 to 4-2
Width	4-10 to 5-6	5-2 to 5-6	5-8 to 5-10

BOOTH FURNITURE HEIGHTS

	Abs. Min.	Des. Min.	Comfort-able
H	3-0 to 3-6	3-6	4-0
S	1-5 to 1-6	1-5 to 1-6	1-6
T	2-5	2-5 to 2-6	2-6
W	1-8 to 2-0	2-0 to 2-2	2-4 to 2-6
Seat	1-4 to 1-5	1-5 to 1-6	1-6 to 1-8
Splay	0 to 0-3	0-2 to 0-3	0-3½ to 0-4

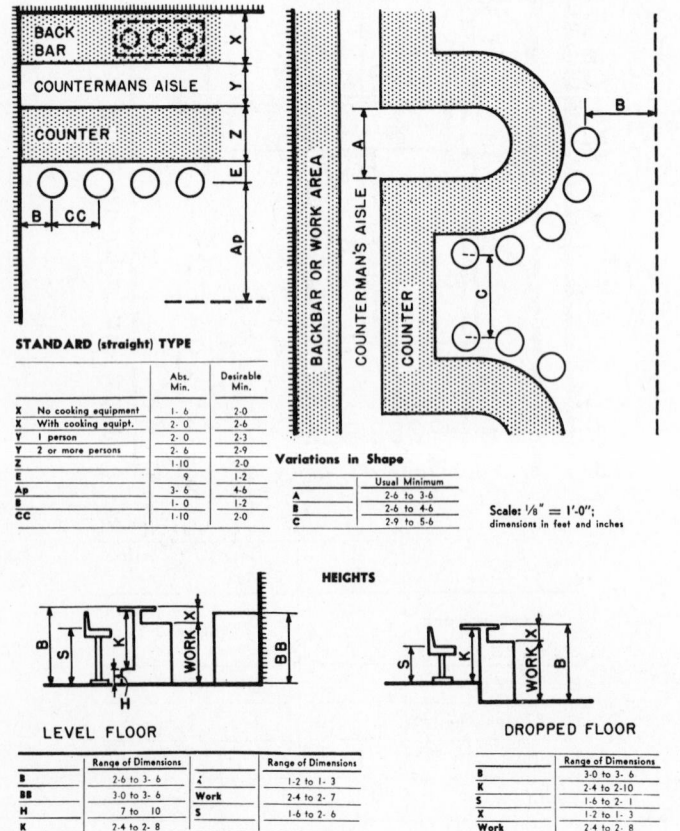

STANDARD (straight) TYPE

		Abs. Min.	Desirable Min.
X	No cooking equipment	1- 6	2-0
X	With cooking equipt.	2- 0	2-6
Y	1 person	2- 0	2-3
Y	2 or more persons	2- 6	2-9
Z		1-10	2-0
E		9	1-2
Ap		3- 6	4-6
B		1- 0	1-2
CC		1-10	2-0

Variations in Shape

	Usual Minimum
A	2-6 to 3-6
B	2-6 to 4-6
C	2-9 to 5-6

Scale: 1/8" = 1'-0"; dimensions in feet and inches

HEIGHTS

LEVEL FLOOR

	Range of Dimensions		Range of Dimensions
B	2-6 to 3- 6	K	1-2 to 1- 3
BB	3-0 to 3- 6	Work	2-4 to 2- 7
H	7 to 10	S	1-6 to 2- 6
K	2-4 to 2- 8		

DROPPED FLOOR

	Range of Dimensions
B	3-0 to 3- 6
K	2-4 to 2-10
S	1-6 to 2- 1
X	1-2 to 1- 3
Work	2-4 to 2- 8

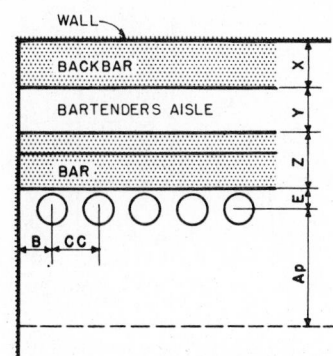

STRAIGHT TYPE—with or without stools

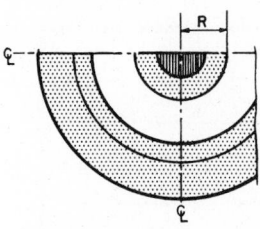

CURVED TYPES: Radius R should be at least 2 ft.; other dimensions as for straight types.

		Abs. Min.	Des. Min.	Comfort-able
Ap	Public aisle	3-6 to 4-6	4-0 to 5-0	4-6 to 6-0
B	Stool to wall	1-0 to 1-6	1-2 to 1-6	1-4 to 1-6
CC	Stool, cent. to cent.	1-9 to 2-0	2-0	2-2 to 2-6
E	Stool to bar	9 to 1-0	1-0	1-1 to 1-2
X	Back bar	1-6 to 1-8	1-8 to 2-0	2-0 to 2-3
Y	Bartender's aisle	2-0 to 2-2	2-6	3-0
Z	Bar	2-3 to 2-6	2-5 to 2-6	2-8 to 2-9

Bar length: Allow from 1 ft. 8 in. to 1 ft. 10 in. per person for standup bars; 2 ft. for each stool.

Bar depth: No increase in depth is needed for more than 1 bartender, as each man should be provided with his own "set-up" space in the work counter and back-bar.

Service bars: These are usually from 6 to 8 ft. long, for 1-man service; from 10 to 12 ft. long if 2 bartenders are needed for peak service periods. No footrail, counter overhang, or stools are required. Location is often adjacent to kitchen and concealed from patrons; however, advertising values sometimes cause it to be set in public view. In the latter case, a rope rail or similar device, to discourage patrons from standing at the bar, is often advisable.

Scale: $\frac{1}{8}$" = 1'-0" unless otherwise noted; dimensions in feet and inches

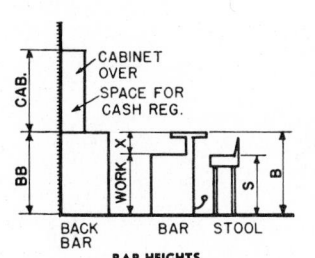

BAR HEIGHTS

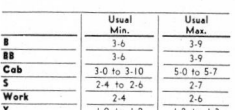

RAIL OR STEP
Scale $\frac{1}{4}$" = 1' 0"
P = 7 to 10
H = 7 to 10

	Usual Min.	Usual Max.
B	3-6	3-9
BB	3-6	3-9
Cab	3-0 to 3-10	5-0 to 5-7
S	2-4 to 2-6	2-7
Work	2-4	2-6
X	1-0 to 1-2	1-2 to 1-3

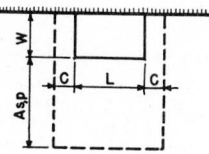

SERVING TABLE (& sideboard)

		Abs. Min.	Des. Min.	Comfort-able
As	Service only	2-6	3-0	3-6
Ap	Public circ'n	2-0	2-6	3-0
C	Clearance to adjacent units	2-0	2-3	2-6
Length				
Width	30" x 20" x 42" is average.			

Display tables (hors d'oeuvres, etc.) usually 5' 0" x 2' 0"; (wines), 3' 0" round

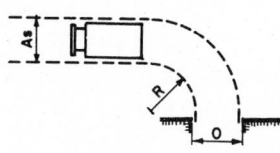

SERVING CART

		Abs. Min.	Des. Min.
As	Service only	2-0	2-6
R	Turn radius	3-0	3-6
O	Door, opening width	2-0	2-6

Approx. area when stored: 38" x 21½" x 35"

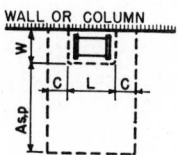

TRAY STAND

		Abs. Min.	Des. Min.	Comfort-able
As	Service only	2-6	3-0	3-6
Ap	Public circ'n	2-0	2-6	3-0
C	Clearance to adjacent units	2-0	2-3	2-6
Length (tray)				
Width (tray)	Depends on type of restaurant.			

Approx. area of stand, stored: 5" x 20" x 34"

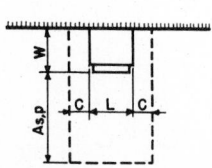

WATER COOLER

		Abs. Min.	Des. Min.	Comfort-able
As	Service circ'n	2-6	3-0	3-6
Ap	Public circ'n	2-0	2-6	3-0
C	Clearance to adjacent units	Can arrange on top or front		
Length				
Width	Depends on capacity and if glass storage included.			

Scale: $\frac{1}{8}$" = 1' 0"; dimensions in feet and inches

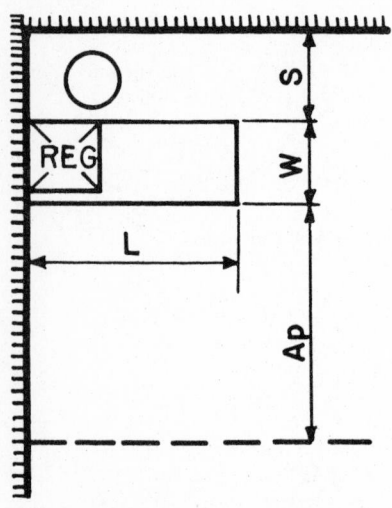

CASHIER'S DESK and COUNTER

		Usual Minimum
S	Cashier's Aisle	2–0 to 2–6
Ap	Public Aisle	3–6 to 5–0
Length		4–0 to 8–0
Width		2–0 to 2–4

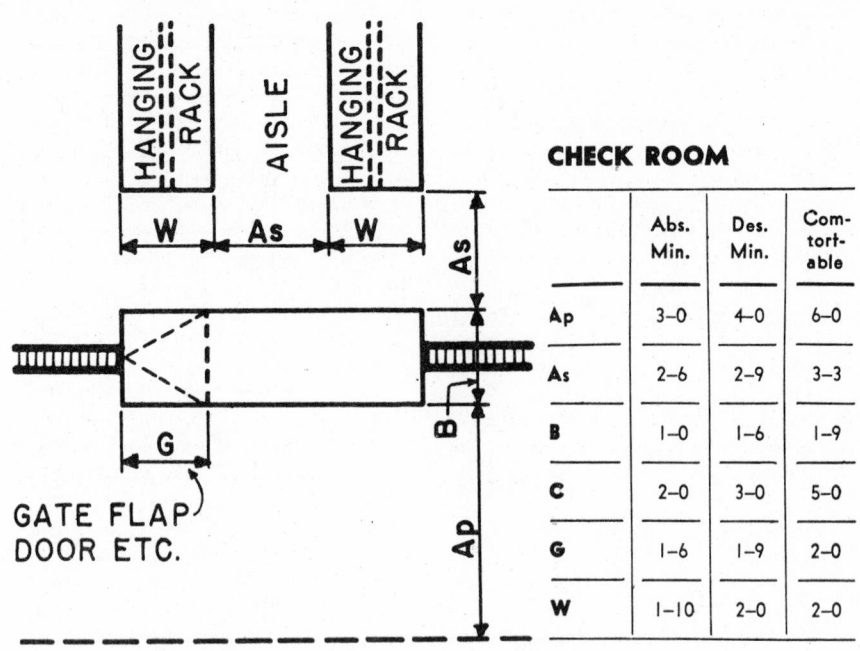

GATE FLAP DOOR ETC.

Scale: 1/4 in. = 1 ft; dimensions in feet and inches

CHECK ROOM

	Abs. Min.	Des. Min.	Comfortable
Ap	3–0	4–0	6–0
As	2–6	2–9	3–3
B	1–0	1–6	1–9
C	2–0	3–0	5–0
G	1–6	1–9	2–0
W	1–10	2–0	2–0

DIAGRAMS, TABLES and other data given on this page illustrate only a few of the many types of non-dining spaces and clearances required. Data included here may, however, suggest methods of solving most problems.

Cashier

Preferred location for the cashier's desk or counter, according to the Albert Pick Co., is on the right hand side of the door when leaving, in order to avoid cross-traffic and resulting congestion. Dimensions vary from those given in the table according to what merchandise is sold by the cashier and can best be determined in conjunction with each job. If quantities of tobacco, etc., are sold, a back wall case may be necessary.

Coat checking

The diagram illustrates only one type of check room layout; selection of type and size depends on the job under consideration. It is generally considered uneconomical, except in the most luxurious restaurants, to provide check rooms capable of accommodating garments for the peak load of patrons, for the following reasons: (1) Women usually do not check coats; (2) not all male patrons check coats; (3) space required can usually be used otherwise to greater advantage. The Albert Pick Co. estimates that approximately 5 garments can be hung per linear foot on each side of the type of racks diagrammed.

Use of coat trees in dining areas is termed "necessary but never desirable." These occupy approximately 20 by 20 in., are 72 in. high, and can accommodate 8 garments per customer. Overshoe racks are considered undesirable; umbrella racks, desirable in check rooms.

Telephone facilities

Booths are usually preferred to telephone jacks, probably because of costs of installation and of relocating wiring when redecorating or replanning. Booths should be out of direct vision yet convenient to dining and lounge areas. One booth per 125 seats is the usual recommendation, or one phone jack per dining booth.

By BEN SCHLANGER, *Architect*
Theater Consultant

Design requirements for cinemas, including auditory and visual considerations combined with showmanship and economy of structure, call for a type of building entirely distinct from stage theaters. The success of a commercial cinema depends on its ability to present good films in an effective manner, affording the maximum volume of patronage at admission prices that will insure an adequate profit. All patrons expect proper vision of the screen image, true reproduction of sound effects, and such comforts as will enable them to give undivided attention to the presentation.

LOCATION

The location of the cinema site is determined by its accessibility, land costs, parking facilities, and potential patronage. Big shopping centers have large parking areas that are generally unused in the evening, and may therefore be desirable locations for motion picture theaters.

SIZE

Home television and new systems of motion picture projection have brought about new criteria for determining optimum seating capacities for motion picture theaters. Home television has greatly reduced the need for the large-capacity (over 1,500 seats) "movie palaces" in urban locations, and also for the small motion picture theater in rural communities. These changes in circumstances place the cinema in somewhat the same category as the other dramatic arts of the living stage theater, where

the success of any one production depends on its quality or unusual character. The new systems of picture projection add a new dimension or an unusual character to a film, but they cannot be depended upon alone to draw the large patronage enjoyed in the era prior to home television.

Technically, the larger screens, wider films (70 mm), and new optical systems (such as Cinemascope) make possible an increase in the size of the audience that can see the film at one time. The increasing competition of home television, however, has made it almost impossible to profit from the potentially larger audience. Reduced patronage and high film-production costs have resulted in higher admission prices, which, in turn, tend to reduce further the size of the audience.

It has only recently been realized that there is a distinct advantage in having a relatively small audience with a maximum-size projected picture. The psychological effect that is thus created is that of "picture dominance," or an "at-the-scene feeling" for the viewer. Under these conditions, the picture practically fills the viewer's central range of vision (approximately 60 deg), and the distraction of the auditorium shell is greatly minimized.

Two distinct types of motion picture theaters have now developed. First is the general type of theater, catering to the more popular taste in films and requiring capacities of from 600 to 1,500 seats. The larger units must have a choice location with an adequate population to draw from and adequate parking facilities.

The second type has acquired the label "art theater." These small theaters are found mostly in the larger cities and in the university towns where there is a more sophisticated audience. Foreign films and

the better U.S. films are shown in these theaters. They usually prove profitable at capacities of from 400 to 900 seats, and often command the highest admission prices.

SHAPE AND SIZE OF PROJECTED PICTURE

Picture shape and viewing patterns are determined by fixing visual standards that enable each viewer to see the picture satisfactorily. The picture must appear undistorted, its view must be unobstructed, and its details discernible.

The average width of the projected picture, which was about 18 ft in 1938, has now approximately doubled for the 35 mm Cinemascope and 70 mm film systems, introduced in 1953. The quality of the projected picture affects the size and shape of the seating pattern. The quality of the projected picture varies with the size of the film used, however, and unfortunately most theaters still use more than one film size and projection system. Although picture widths have increased, the width of standard 35 mm film has not; consequently, when 35 mm film is used, the seats nearest the screen are less acceptable because film graininess becomes visible from these locations. When 70 mm film is used, the seats nearest the screen become desirable since film graininess is greatly reduced and these seats enable the viewers to experience the dramatic impact of "picture dominance."

A more nearly ideal motion picture theater could be designed if only one type of projection system and film width were used. For the best compromise design, to provide for all of the current systems and film widths, the following general guide may be used:

1. The first row of seats should be no closer to the screen than a position determined as follows: The angle formed with the horizontal by a line from the top of

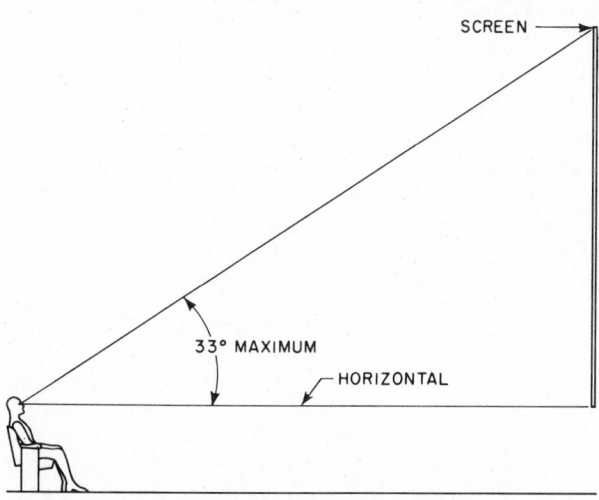

Fig. 1. Method of determining minimum distance from screen to first row of seats

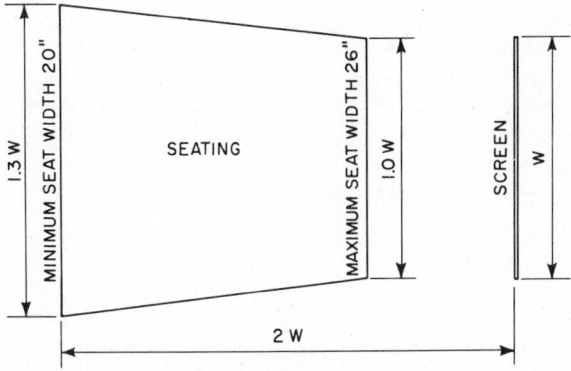

Fig. 2. Maximum viewing distance and maximum width of seating pattern

the projected picture to the eye of the viewer in a front-row seat, should not exceed 33 deg. (The top level of the projected picture should be the same for all systems of projection in a given auditorium.) See Fig. 1.

2. The maximum viewing distance should be no greater than twice the width of the widest picture to be projected (Fig. 2).

3. The width of the seating pattern should vary from 1 times the widest projected picture at the first row to 1.3 times at the row farthest from the screen (Fig. 2).

The resultant shape will be less rectangular than the long narrow theaters of the past, which are more economical to build but are unfortunately not well suited for the new systems of projection.

The seats nearest the screen will remain acceptable for use if the following general rule is followed: Projected picture widths should not exceed 35 ft for standard 35 mm film, 45 ft for Cinemascope 35 mm film, and 65 ft for 70 mm film. (See later notes regarding modification of these widths in connection with picture masking.)

In some instances in which a large seating capacity is desired, it is necessary to resort to a balcony in order to avoid the excessive viewing distance that would otherwise develop.

SCREENS AND PROJECTION OPTICS

Projection angle is the angle formed with the horizontal by a line from the projection lens to the midheight of the projected picture. Because of the increased picture width and screen curvatures recently introduced, it becomes increasingly important to have a minimum projection angle (0 deg is ideal but usually impossible). The angle should not exceed 10 deg and should be kept as low as possible in order to have a minimum distortion of picture detail.

A slight curvature in the width of the screen and semimatte screen surfaces are used to increase screen light reflection and to provide better dispersed screen illumination. This extra light is necessary for the larger screen sizes. The curvature should have a radius equal to about 1¼ times the projection distance.

PROJECTION LENSES

When a new theater is proposed it is important to determine at the outset the lens requirement for the various film systems to be projected. This information will determine the location of the projection room. The better lenses have greater focal lengths and require longer projection distances.

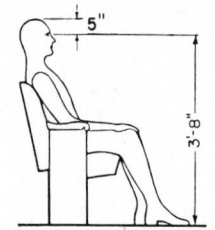

Fig. 3. Human-figure dimensions used in determining sight-line clearances

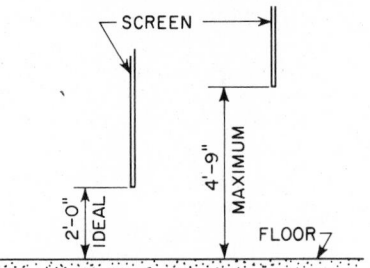

Fig. 4. Height of screen above floor at first row of seats

PICTURE MASKING

The most common method for masking the projected picture is to use a matte black surround. This is the simplest and least expensive way to absorb the fuzzy edges of the projected picture. These maskings may be in the form of a curtain that can be adjusted to mask various picture widths.

Another method is to use specially designed walls and ceiling that meet the picture edges. Instead of black trim, the masking is luminous from light reflected from the screen and blends with the projected picture. The author has designed several of these installations that have proved most satisfactory. Eye fatigue is reduced and greater dramatic impact is obtained.

If Cinemascope and 70 mm film are to be used in one theater, the luminous masking frame must be the same size for both systems, in which case a compromise is made by accepting a somewhat larger Cinemascope picture and a somewhat smaller 70 mm picture.

A compromise in the aspect ratio of the screen shape must also be made. The aspect ratio for 70 mm screen is 1 to 2.22 (height to width). For Cinemascope, the aspect ratio is 1 to 2.34. The Cinemascope frame can be cropped in the projector aperture to conform to the 1 to 2.22 aspect ratio without any meaningful loss of Cinemascope picture material.

The shape of the architectural light box in front of the screen requires special study for each seating, projection, and screen pattern.

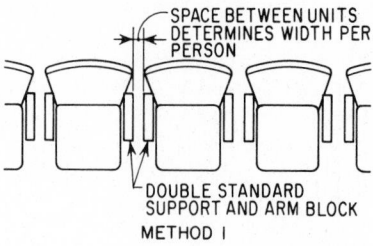

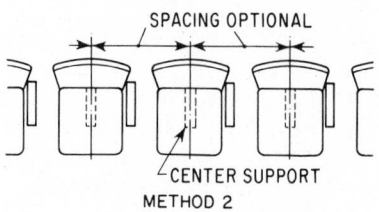

Fig. 5. Methods of obtaining wider spacing for chairs nearest screen

Maximum spacing for first row is 26 in.

FLOOR SLOPES AND SEATING

In the design of floor slopes and upper level steppings for cinema seating, it is necessary to establish the physical dimensions of the seated patron (Fig. 3) and standards for vision of the screen image. Most important is elimination of objectionable screen obstruction caused by persons seated in front of the viewer. For best dramatic impact, the bottom of the projected picture should be as close as possible to the floor under the first row of seats (Fig. 4). This in turn will require a more steeply pitched floor slope under the seats, and will eliminate the possibility of an upper tier of seats, which would have to be too steep in pitch.

The slope of the main-floor seating would also be increased for one-row vision. One-row vision provides unobstructed vision over the heads of persons in the row immediately ahead. Two-row vision is not ideal, but it is acceptable and permits milder slopes and the inclusion of an upper level of seats. Two-row vision is made more acceptable by staggering the seats to permit a view between the heads of the persons in the row immediately in front. With two-row vision the heads of all persons two or more rows in front will not obstruct any view of the screen. Two-row vision is further improved by using the widest chairs (and therefore the widest space between heads) in the rows nearest the screen. (See Fig. 5.) The view between heads is usually too narrow in the front rows where two-row vision is used. Minimum seat widths should be 20 in. for the rows farthest from screen.

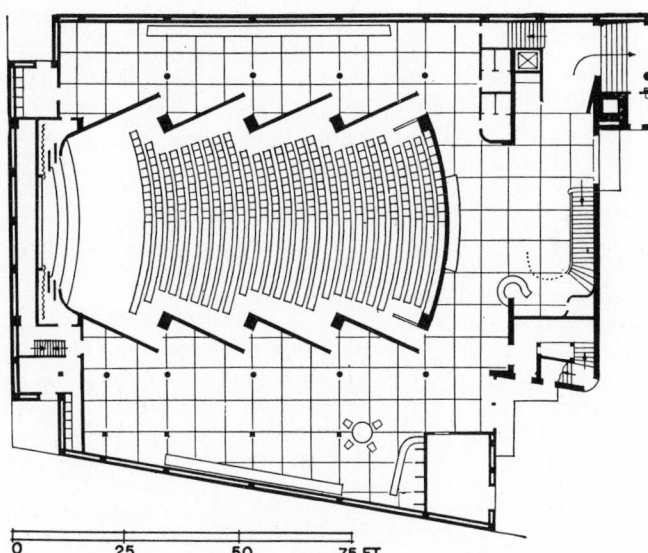

0   25   50   75 FT.

Fig. 6.   Example of "continental seating"

Cinema at Turku, Finland; Erik Bryggman, architect. Minimum row spacing of 40 in. is required. More seats can be used in width to conform to larger screen requirements.

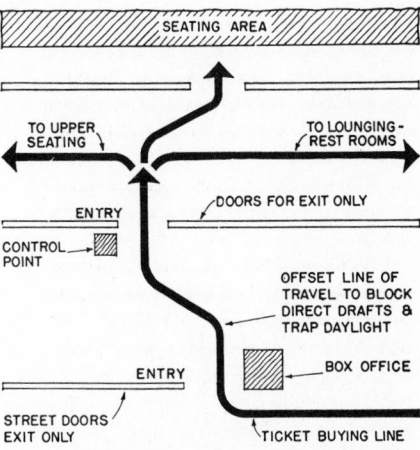

Fig. 7.   Circulation diagram, showing relation of street lobby, foyer, and auditorium doors

ROW SPACING AND AISLES

Minimum spacing between rows should be 34 in., with 1-in.-thick chair backs. Greater chair-back thickness is wasteful and unnecessary. Where 40 to 42 in. can be used for row spacing, many building-code authorities permit the elimination of all longitudinal aisles other than the aisles against the side walls. These codes, however, require frequent exit doors along the wall aisles for this type of seating. The capacity is about the same for the 34- and 40-in. spacing because of the different aisle arrangement.

The 40-in. seating scheme is sometimes termed "continental seating" because of its popularity in Europe. The extra comfort and safer egress afforded by this arrangement account for its increasing use. (See Fig. 6.)

SCREENS

All screens are perforated to allow for sound transmission from speakers placed behind the screen. (A depth of 5 ft should be provided behind the screen for the speakers.) All screens are vinyl plastic with a diffusive surface or a coated surface to increase light reflection. Lenticulated screens are also available. The screen material must be selected in accordance with the shape of the seating pattern and the strength of the projector light source.

GENERAL LIGHTING

The lighting of a cinema auditorium serves three separate functions: (1) Emergency exit and mood lighting, used during screen presentation; (2) Lighting needed during intermissions; and (3) Lighting of sufficient intensity for making announcements, clearing the house, or other rare occasions.

Types and sources of light for these needs are as follows: (1) Light reflected from the screen, of varying intensity dependent on film density; (2) Wall and ceiling surface illumination by standard lamps or tubes installed on the surface to be illuminated; and (3) Light projected on walls, ceiling, or audience from remote or concealed positions. All lighting normally required during the presentation is supplied in the front half of the auditorium by screen-reflected light. The rear portion must be illuminated by other light sources, placed so that the source is not within the spectators' normal range of vision. Placement choices are: first, at the junction of ceiling and side walls; second, on the ceiling; and third, on the side walls. The side walls rarely offer an acceptable location because, here, even low intensities are often objectionable.

Lighting during a performance should consist of a low-intensity, evenly diffused bath of light completely covering all surfaces in view, rather than either complete darkness or spotty lighting.

In considering the utilization of screen-reflected light, it is important that areas immediately surrounding the screen should not cause a lack of clarity in the projected image. Surfaces closest to the screen can be shaped, finished, and related to the screen surface so as to enhance the picture.

Emergency lighting generally must be provided separately. Where separate service lines are available, one may be used with an emergency motor generator. Alternative means of providing energy are battery systems kept charged automatically, gasoline, Diesel or gas engine generators, water turbines, and the like.

Exit signs are connected to the general emergency lighting circuit and should be legible from any point viewed. Lettering is usually a minimum of 8 in. high. All circulation areas, including foyers, lounges, and lobbies should likewise be on the emergency circuit.

TICKET BOOTHS

The *location* of the ticket booth depends on the space available, the character and direction of street and pedestrian traffic, and the volume and habits of patronage. The ticket booth may be isolated (as an island), centered, or included in the corner of the entrance. It should, of course, be readily identified with its function. In metropolitan areas, ticket booths are almost universally placed as close to sidewalks as building codes permit in order to attract casual passers-by. In suburban and other centers where patrons leave their homes with the express purpose of attending the cinema, ticket booths may be removed from sidewalk lobbies and placed either within secondary lobbies or in foyers. It is possible to adopt a continental custom—use of an open counter located conveniently to the manager's office—in an effort to achieve an "intimate" atmosphere. When operated by only one person an area approximately 4 by 4 by 8 ft is adequate; for larger theaters, where there are generally two ticket sellers, clearances are required.

Heating is often provided from the theater heating system if the theater cellar extends under the ticket-booth space. Although electric heaters are sometimes used, they are not always satisfactory because they concentrate great amounts of heat in single spots without providing general heating. Natural ventilation is usually provided by ventilators in roofs and louvers in doors. Occasionally air-conditioning ducts are run to booths from theater systems. Space is required for change makers and electrically or manually operated ticket dispensers. It is almost universal practice to install an outside telephone for the attendant's convenience in answering calls about the program. This telephone is usually connected to another in the manager's office, with a two-way signal.

LOUNGES AND TOILETS

Lounge areas, on either level, serve to separate the toilets from the theater seating. For capacities of over 600 seats, at least two lounge areas should be provided and arranged so as to be partially or wholly visible from the lobby, foyer, or circulating areas. It is also desirable to have some part of the lounge command a view of both seating and screen in order that waiting patrons may follow seat availability as well as performance progress.

Recommended minimum toilet fixture requirements are as follows:

Theater capacity	Men	Women
Up to 400 seats	1 basin	1 basin
	1 toilet	2 toilets
	1 urinal	
400–600 seats	2 basins	2 basins
	2 toilets	3 toilets
	2 urinals	
600–1,000 seats	2 basins	2 basins
	2 toilets	4 toilets
	3 urinals	

Local codes, of course, will govern. (See also "Plumbing — Fixtures: Public facilities.")

PROJECTION ROOMS

The usual code requirements are 48 sq ft for the first projection machine and 24 sq ft for each additional projector. Dimensions based on necessary clearances around projectors are given in Fig. 8.

Rewinding: Although at least one state law requires that film rewinding be done in the projection room, a separate rewind room adjacent to the projection room is usually considered advisable. Rewinding is done on a small table; observation ports opening to both the projection room and the auditorium permit a single operator to supervise a presentation easily while rewinding used film.

Film storage: Up to 12,000 ft of film is usually permitted to be stored in metal containers. Film safes are required for greater amounts, 24,000 ft being the usual maximum. The location should be convenient to the rewind table.

Toilet, containing water closet and basin,

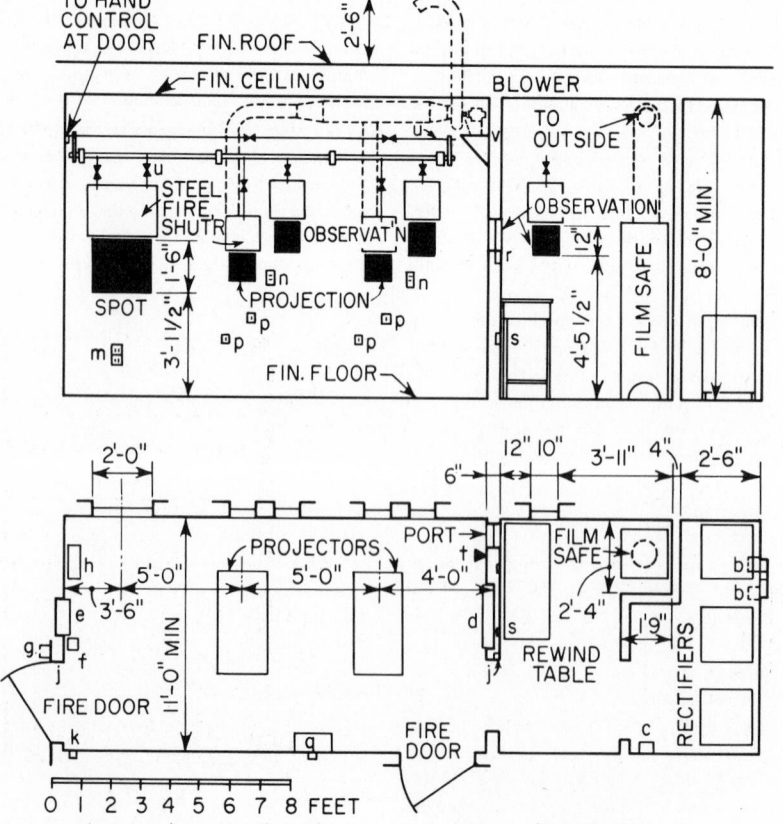

Key

a. Line fuses
b. Line switch
c. Line switch
d. Panel box (d-c)
e. Panel box (a-c)
f. Motor starter
g. Booth exhaust blower control and pilot
h. Dimmer
j. Light switch
k. Arc blower switch
m. 15A Duplex receptacle (twist lock)
n. Signal buttons
p. Sound control
q. Amplifier
r. Vaporproof fixture
s. T-L receptacle
t. Interphone
u. Fuse link support for steel fire shutter
v. Blower receptacle

Fig. 8. Plan of projection room and elevation of wall toward auditorium

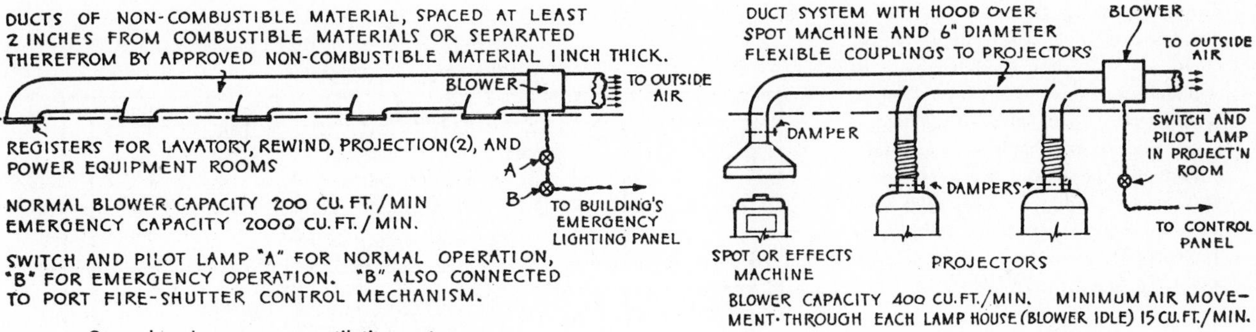

DUCTS OF NON-COMBUSTIBLE MATERIAL, SPACED AT LEAST 2 INCHES FROM COMBUSTIBLE MATERIALS OR SEPARATED THEREFROM BY APPROVED NON-COMBUSTIBLE MATERIAL 1 INCH THICK.

BLOWER
TO OUTSIDE AIR

REGISTERS FOR LAVATORY, REWIND, PROJECTION (2), AND POWER EQUIPMENT ROOMS

NORMAL BLOWER CAPACITY 200 CU. FT./MIN
EMERGENCY CAPACITY 2000 CU. FT./MIN.

A
B
TO BUILDING'S EMERGENCY LIGHTING PANEL

SWITCH AND PILOT LAMP "A" FOR NORMAL OPERATION, "B" FOR EMERGENCY OPERATION. "B" ALSO CONNECTED TO PORT FIRE-SHUTTER CONTROL MECHANISM.

General and emergency ventilation system

DUCT SYSTEM WITH HOOD OVER SPOT MACHINE AND 6" DIAMETER FLEXIBLE COUPLINGS TO PROJECTORS
BLOWER
TO OUTSIDE AIR
SWITCH AND PILOT LAMP IN PROJECT'N ROOM

DAMPER
DAMPERS
TO CONTROL PANEL

SPOT OR EFFECTS MACHINE
PROJECTORS

BLOWER CAPACITY 400 CU.FT./MIN. MINIMUM AIR MOVEMENT·THROUGH EACH LAMP HOUSE (BLOWER IDLE) 15 CU.FT./MIN.

Equipment ventilation system

Fig. 9. Separate ventilation systems required in projection rooms

is for convenience as close as possible to the projection room but, to reduce fire hazard, usually opens on a passageway rather than directly from the projection room.

Power equipment is housed in a generator room or closet, opening on the projection room proper, with space for rheostats.

VENTILATION

Ventilation provisions are made for the general area and, independently, for each projection machine, for the film safe, and for the motor-generator room. For general areas, 6 to 10 air changes per minute form the usual minimum desirable, 4 per minute the absolute minimum. Ducts are not cross-connected to auditorium supplies in any way that will permit entry of smoke or flame from possible projection room fires.

Ventilation for machines consists of 6-in. round metal ducts to convey fumes and heat arising from action of arc lamps on film. Ducts exhaust directly to the outer air and are equipped with exhaust fans. Maximum desirable fan capacity is usually

50 cfm per arc. Types of fans in which motors are not mounted in duct space are preferred, because carbon and dust blowing across motors soon cause motor failure. A minimum of 4 air changes per minute is recommended for the motor-generator room. Film-safe ducts are 8 in. round or 8 by 10 in. and exhaust directly to the outside air.

For additional information, see "Heating, Ventilating, and Air Conditioning: Theaters."

FIRE PROTECTION

Fire-protection measures include materials and methods of construction and finish, which are usually prescribed by codes. Legal and insurance requirements for fire doors, dimensions, and other regulations, are generally outdated; reasonable modern provisions usually far exceed minimum legal provisions. Automatic sprinklers are sometimes required in projection and rewind rooms, although the value of water in combating film fires is debatable. More valuable are portable chemical extinguish-

ers, one per machine, and sand, one bucket per machine. The latter also serve as safe depositories for used carbon stubs from arc lamps.

Fire doors, usually Kalamein, are required; those which isolate projection room areas (including generator, rewind, and projection rooms) are self-closing, open outward, and are equipped with fusible link releases. One such door, 2 ft 6 in. by 6 ft 8 in., is commonly provided; two doors, at opposite ends of the hazardous area, are preferable. All ports opening to other than projection areas have vertical sliding shutters whether the ports are glazed or not. Typical shutter releases are shown in the drawings.

Floors must have at least a "4-hr" rating as prescribed by insurance codes. The floor material is usually reinforced concrete, with an average slab thickness of 4 in. One inch of cement finish is ordinarily applied but almost always necessitates cutting the slab to accommodate conduits. Two inches of finish accommodate most conduits without cutting.

Walls and *ceilings* are subject to the

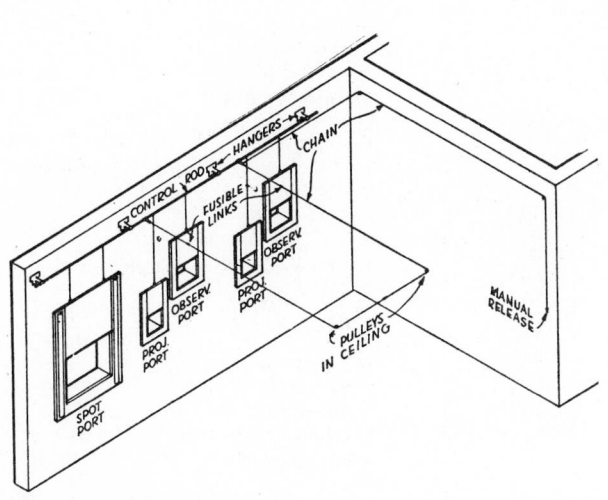

Fig. 10. Porthole shutter system

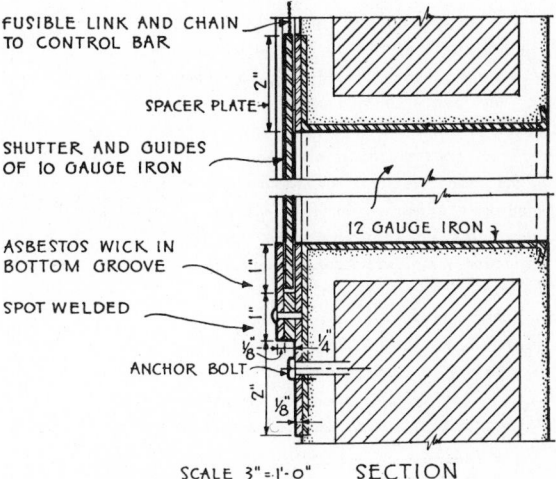

Fig. 11. Shutter construction

same conditions as floors. Four-inch hollow tile, terra cotta, and the like are used for walls; 4-in. reinforced concrete or precast materials are used for ceilings. Cement, 1 in. thick on both sides of walls and ¾ in. thick on ceilings, is the usual finish.

Ports may be glazed to prevent sound from entering auditoriums, with plate glass used in observation ports and optical glass in projection ports. Frames must be fireproof.

EQUIPMENT

Operating equipment consists of projectors, spots, effect machines, and possible stereopticon dissolvers. Minimum equipment is two projectors; the usual average is two projectors and one spot; the usual maximum, two projectors, one spot, and one effect machine. More equipment will be needed if special features are expected.

Power equipment for common modern types of arc-lamp projectors and the like consists of 45-v d-c motor generators. Since all types of operating equipment are now available for use with the same voltage, varying voltages are no longer required. Rectifiers may be used on a-c supply lines.

Control of operating equipment requires a d-c panel board—usually wall-mounted at convenient operating height—and a rheostat for each projector, spot, and effect machine. Sound equipment volume controls and monitor, wall-mounted, are usually close to projector sound heads. Sound amplifier and power units may be mounted on any clear wall space. Ventilator fan motors and lighting require a separate panel, a-c or d-c depending on the type of current supplied. Auditorium light controls are so located that operators can conveniently manipulate them while attending projection machines. Emergency controls for ventilating systems and lights (not always required by law) are placed outside fire exits, with pilot light indicators. Ventilation emergency controls may be powered by independent emergency wiring.

Signal system consists of a house telephone from the projection room to the manager's office or the ticket booth. If operation is not controlled solely from the projection room, a buzzer or annunciator or both are required.

Lighting and convenience outlets are indicated as to type and location in Fig. 12. Fixtures are vaporproof; those not mounted in locations giving automatic protection against lamp breakage are protected with wire guards.

Additional information on theaters can be found under "Acoustics: Theaters."

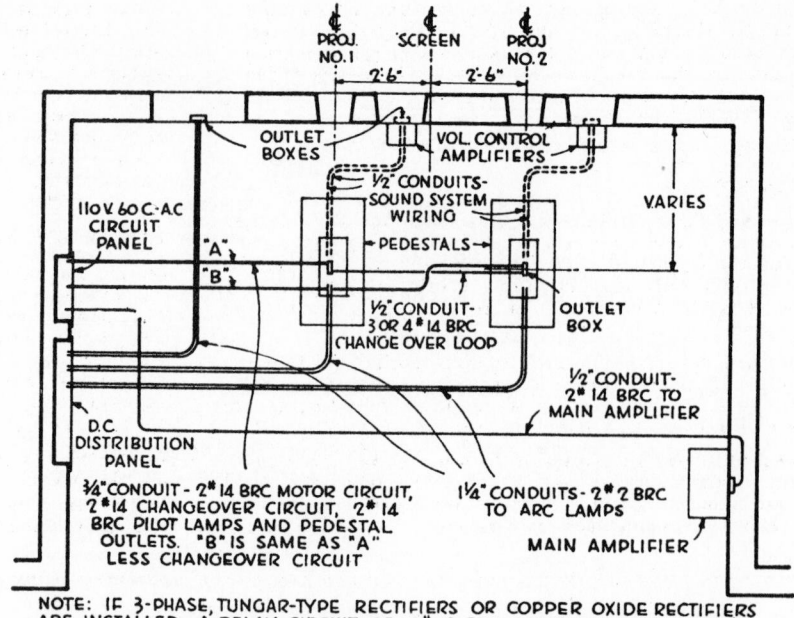

NOTE: IF 3-PHASE, TUNGAR-TYPE RECTIFIERS OR COPPER OXIDE RECTIFIERS ARE INSTALLED; A RELAY CIRCUIT OF 2 # 12 BRC MUST BE RUN DIRECT FROM EACH RECTIFIER TO EACH PEDESTAL   THIS CIRCUIT NOT SHOWN.

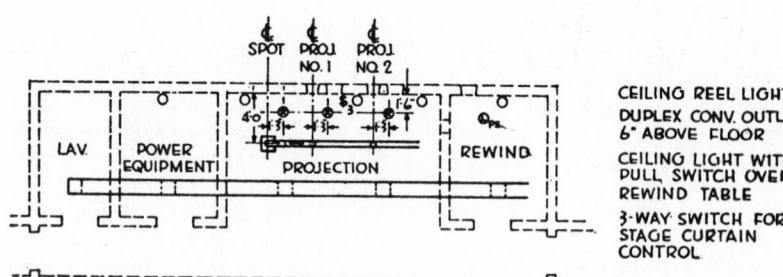

Fig. 12.   Electrical layout for projection room

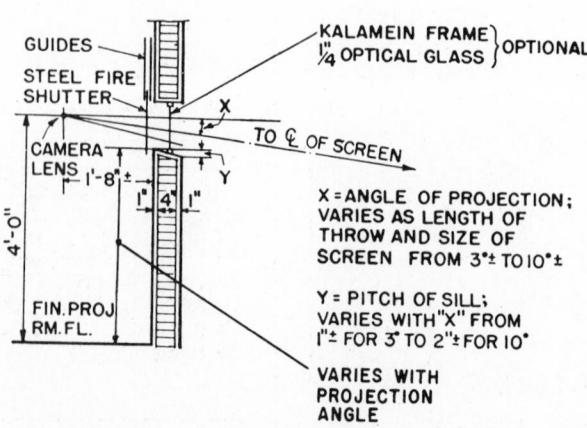

Fig. 13.   Location of projection port and pitch of sill

Seating standards for use in theaters, auditoriums and similar buildings are developed on this and the following three pages, which give tabular data and methods for laying out seating plans. Material is the result of research by Frederic Arden Pawley. Sources include architectural offices specializing in theaters, and seating manufacturers.

TYPES OF SEATS

Construction and finish. Upholstery variations include *spring-edge* seats (most luxurious, more expensive); *box-spring* (nearly as comfortable); *spring-back* and *padded-back*. Veneer-back seating is suitable only for conditions subject to hard usage, as schools. Acoustical control is more satisfactory with upholstered types.

Sizes. Seats are designated by width, the depth front-to-back varying only slightly. Common sizes and recommended uses are shown below. In pew seating without individual arms, as in churches or arenas, a "sitting" is usually 18" wide.

Pitch of back will vary according to the vertical angle of vision to the center of interest. In general, greater pitches are used for front portions of orchestra floors and more nearly vertical backs for elevated banks such as balconies.

Clearances. In addition to those noted diagrammatically below, the following points should be considered: *Coves* at intersection of floor and walls (or risers) should be kept small (1½" radius) to permit close fitting and leveling of seat standards. *Balcony risers* cause cramped knee-room when 12" high, unless back-to-back seat spacing is increased. End clearances in balconies should be increased to 2½". *Pitch of back* greater than average (see drawing below) also requires increased back-to-back spacing.

TYPES OF LAYOUTS

Rows may be straight across entire theater, side banks may be canted, or entire rows may be curved. Advantages of each type are shown in the accompanying diagrams. Min. radius for curved rows, due to seat construction, is 20'-0". Center for radii of rows and center of screen or stage need not coincide, although this is the ideal case. When rows are curved, a sloping auditorium floor should be a compound curve or amphitheater type to prevent tilted side seats.

Aisles may be straight or curved, parallel or radial. Aisles should run at right angles to rows to eliminate "pockets."

Combinations of row and aisle types commonly used are shown in the diagrams. For layouts see T-S.S. Serial No. 85

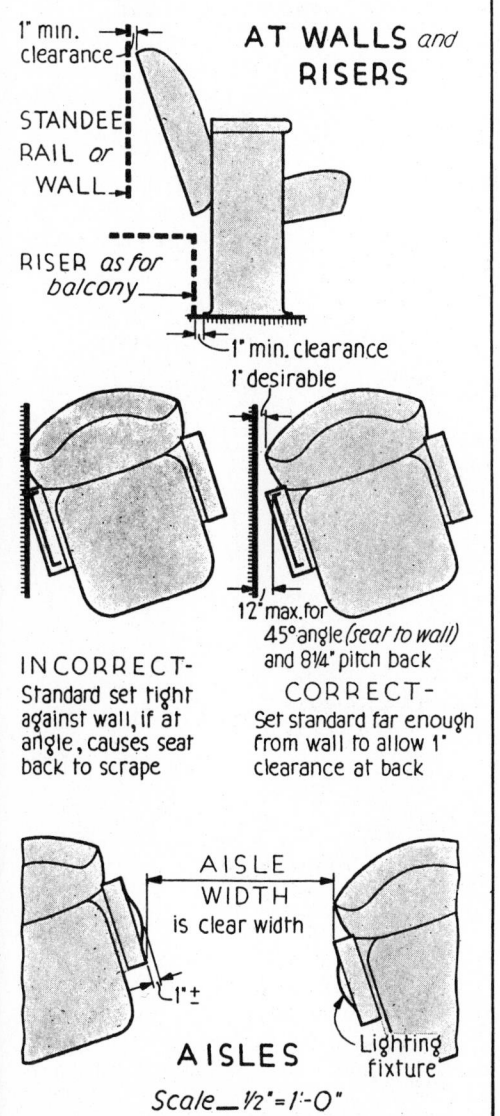

INCORRECT—
Standard set tight against wall, if at angle, causes seat back to scrape

CORRECT—
Set standard far enough from wall to allow 1" clearance at back

AISLE WIDTH is clear width

AISLES
Scale ½"=1'-0"

CLEARANCES

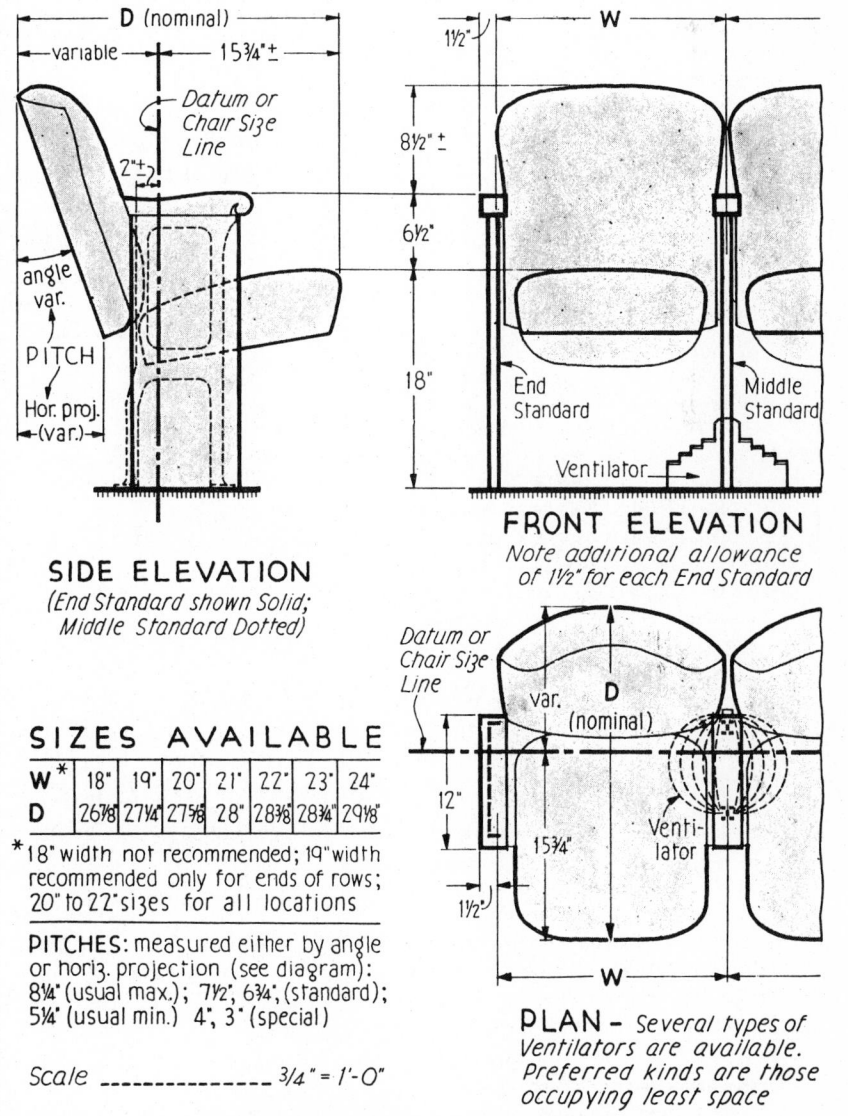

SIDE ELEVATION
(End Standard shown Solid; Middle Standard Dotted)

FRONT ELEVATION
Note additional allowance of 1½" for each End Standard

SIZES AVAILABLE

W*	18"	19"	20"	21"	22"	23"	24"
D	26⅞	27¼	27⅝	28"	28⅜	28¾"	29⅛

*18" width not recommended; 19" width recommended only for ends of rows; 20" to 22" sizes for all locations

PITCHES: measured either by angle or horiz. projection (see diagram): 8¼" (usual max.); 7½", 6¾", (standard); 5¼" (usual min.) 4", 3" (special)

Scale — — — — — — — — ¾" = 1'-0"

PLAN — *Several types of Ventilators are available. Preferred kinds are those occupying least space*

TYPICAL SEATS

Continental seating, most commonly used abroad, involves use of rows with unlimited number of seats. Local codes in this country often either prohibit its use or impose many restrictions. However, existing examples have proved safe and comfortable due to increased back-to-back seat spacing (up to 42″) which is essential to scheme. Larger than usual side aisles or foyers and many side exits are required.

Code requirements govern (1) maximum number of seats in a bank, (2) aisle width, (3) cross-overs (not uniform). Usual requirements are: (1) no seat more than 7 seats from an aisle; (2) min. aisle width of 3′-0″, increasing by varying factors in relation to length of aisles. (3) Requirements for cross-overs not uniformly subject to codes, vary. Consult local authorities.

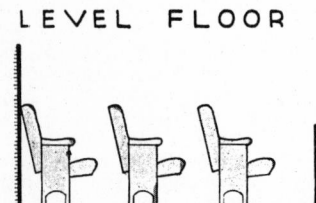

LEVEL FLOOR

Dimensions to chair-size line

9″ — 31″ — 31″ — 31″

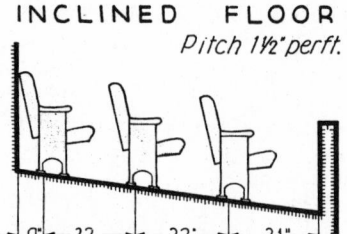

INCLINED FLOOR
Pitch 1½″ perft.

9″ — 32 — 32″ — 31″

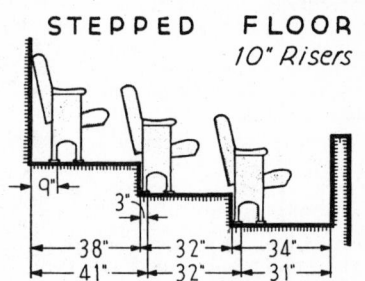

STEPPED FLOOR
10″ Risers

9″ 3″
38″ — 32″ — 34″
41″ — 32″ — 31″

MINIMUM SPACINGS FOR VARYING FLOOR CONDITIONS
Based on stock sizes with 5¼″ pitch back

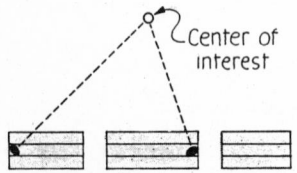

Center of interest

STRAIGHT ROWS
Uncomfortable for spectators at side, unequal stress on seats and backs

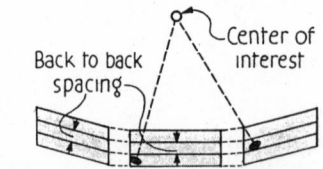

Back to back spacing

Center of interest

STRAIGHT, CANTED SIDE-BANKS
Same defects as straight rows though to less degree. Note that rows do not line up. Steps if required in aisles will be unsafe

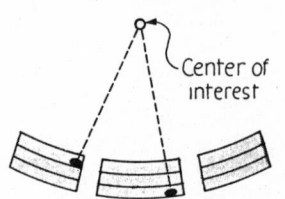

Center of interest

CURVED ROWS
Recommended for comfort, ease of vision and safety

TYPES OF ROWS

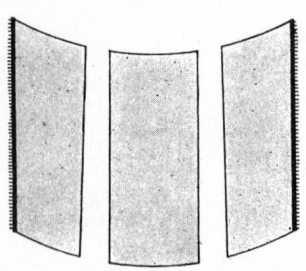

STRAIGHT
(poorest type)

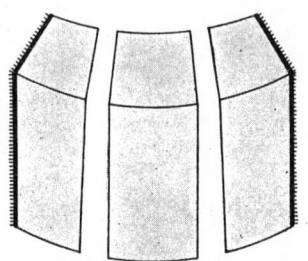

COMPOUND

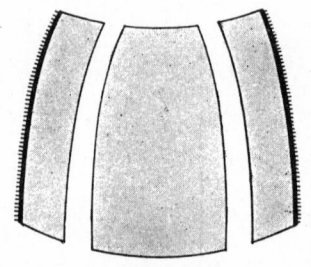

CURVED

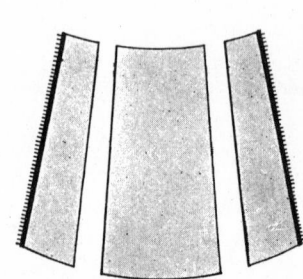

FAN
(ideally best)

COMMON THREE-BANK LAYOUTS
see also "Continental Seating" in text

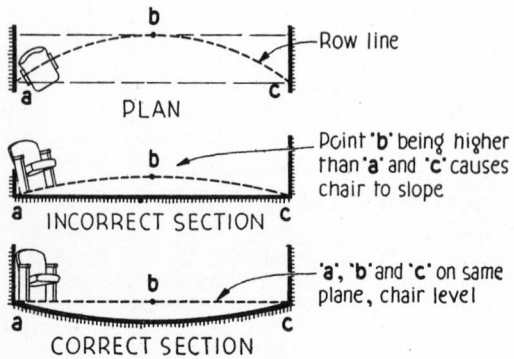

b
Row line
PLAN
a c

Point "b" being higher than "a" and "c" causes chair to slope
b
a INCORRECT SECTION c

"a", "b" and "c" on same plane, chair level
b
a CORRECT SECTION c

SIDE RAKE *(Curved Rows)*

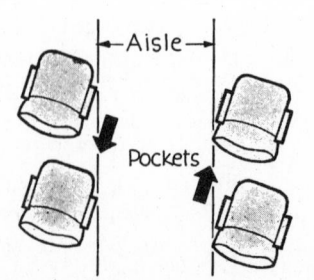

Aisle
Pockets

Aisles cutting diagonally across rows produce dangerous "pockets" and waste space

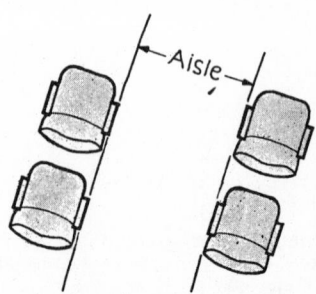

Aisle

Curved or straight radial aisles reduce number and size of "pockets"

DIRECTION OF AISLES

AUDITORIUM DIMENSIONS

Preliminary estimates may be based upon the "Rule of Thumb" which is sufficiently accurate for rough sketches.

Tables. For such purposes as financing, working drawings, etc., follow method outlined in Examples A, B, C and D. Variations between the two methods are to be expected.

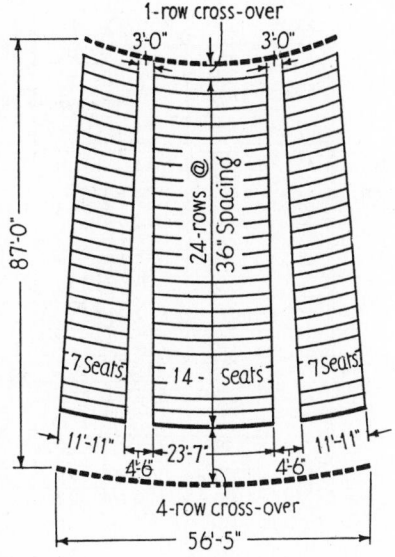

EXAMPLE A: Given auditorium area = 87'-0" x 56'-5" or 4900 + sq. ft., how many 20" seats, 36" back-to-back?

1. Rows: In Table I, 36" col., at 87'-0" depth, No. rows = 29
   less cross-overs (1 row at front, 4 at rear) = — 5
   Rows available for seats = 24

2. Aisles: Table II, increase in aisle width per row = 0.75"; 0.75 x 24 =
   Total increase = 1'–6"
   Min. aisle = 3'–0"
   Max. aisle = 4'–6"

3. Seating Scheme: Select tentative scheme; 2 aisles, 2 dead-end seat banks, 1 center bank. From typical code, dead-end rows may be 7 seats long, center rows 14 seats. In Table IV 14—20" seats = 23'– 7"
   7—20" seats = 11'–11"
   7—20" seats = 11'–11"
   From (2) above, 2 aisles = 9'– 0"
   Total width = 56'– 5"
   Seats per row = 28

4. Total No. of Seats: (Table III)
   or 28 x 24 = { 672 seats }

EXAMPLE B: Given capacity of 672 seats, what are auditorium dimensions?
This problem is the converse of "A".

EXAMPLE C: What is radius of any row?
To radius of back of first-row seats add desired value from Table I.

EXAMPLE D: How many and what sizes of seats can be used in rows shortened by curved or radial aisles? See Table IV.

RULE of THUMB for SEATING AREA:

Allow 7½ sq. ft per Seat, including Aisles and Cross-overs.

This is sufficiently accurate for preliminary planning.

Table I - Depth Dimensions (Ft.-In.) for Various Spacings

No. Rows	overall										
	32"	**33"**	**34"**	**35"**	**36"**	**37"**	**38"**	**39"**	**40"**	**41"**	**42"**
1	2-8	2-9	2-10	2-11	3-0	3-1	3-2	3-3	3-4	3-5	3-6
2	5-4	5-6	5-8	5-10	6-0	6-2	6-4	6-6	6-8	6-10	7-0
3	8-0	8-3	8-6	8-9	9-0	9-3	9-6	9-9	10-0	10-3	10-6
4	10-8	11-0	11-4	11-8	12-0	12-4	12-8	13-0	13-4	13-8	14-0
5	13-4	13-9	14-2	14-7	15-0	15-5	15-10	16-3	16-8	17-1	17-6
6	16-0	16-6	17-0	17-6	18-0	18-6	19-0	19-6	20-0	20-6	21-0
7	18-8	19-3	19-10	20-5	21-0	21-7	22-2	22-9	23-4	23-11	24-6
8	21-4	22-0	22-8	23-4	24-0	24-8	25-4	26-0	26-8	27-4	28-0
9	24-0	24-9	25-6	26-3	27-0	27-9	28-6	29-3	30-0	30-9	31-6
10	26-8	27-6	28-4	29-2	30-0	30-10	31-8	32-6	33-4	34-2	35-0
11	29-4	30-3	31-2	32-1	33-0	33-11	34-10	35-9	36-8	37-7	38-6
12	32-0	33-0	34-0	35-0	36-0	37-0	38-0	39-0	40-0	41-0	42-0
13	34-8	35-9	36-10	37-11	39-0	40-1	41-2	42-3	43-4	44-5	45-6
14	37-4	38-6	39-8	40-10	42-0	43-2	44-4	45-6	46-8	47-10	49-0
15	40-0	41-3	42-6	43-9	45-0	46-3	47-6	48-9	50-0	51-3	52-6
16	42-8	44-0	45-4	46-8	48-0	49-4	50-8	52-0	53-4	54-8	56-0
17	45-4	46-9	48-2	49-7	51-0	52-5	53-10	55-3	56-8	58-1	59-6
18	48-0	49-6	51-0	52-6	54-0	55-6	57-0	58-6	60-0	61-6	63-0
19	50-8	52-3	53-10	55-5	57-0	58-7	60-2	61-9	63-4	64-11	66-6
20	53-4	55-0	56-8	58-4	60-0	61-8	63-4	65-0	66-8	68-4	70-0
21	56-0	57-9	59-6	61-3	63-0	64-9	66-6	68-3	70-0	71-9	73-6
22	58-8	60-6	62-4	64-2	66-0	67-10	69-8	71-6	73-4	75-2	77-0
23	61-4	63-3	65-2	67-1	69-0	70-11	72-10	74-9	76-8	78-7	80-6
24	64-0	66-0	68-0	70-0	72-0	74-0	76-0	78-0	80-0	82-0	84-0
25	66-8	68-9	70-10	72-11	75-0	77-1	79-2	81-3	83-4	85-5	87-6
26	69-4	71-6	73-8	75-10	78-0	80-2	82-4	84-6	86-8	88-10	91-0
27	72-0	74-3	76-6	78-9	81-0	83-3	85-6	87-9	90-0	92-3	94-6
28	74-8	77-0	79-4	81-8	84-0	86-4	88-8	91-0	93-4	95-8	98-0
29	77-4	79-9	82-2	84-7	87-0	89-5	91-10	94-3	96-8	99-1	101-6
30	80-0	82-6	85-0	87-6	90-0	92-6	95-0	97-6	100-0	102-6	105-0
31	82-8	85-3	87-10	90-5	93-0	95-7	98-2	100-9	103-4	105-11	108-6
32	85-4	88-0	90-8	93-4	96-0	98-8	101-4	104-0	106-8	109-4	112-0

Overall Depth for Seat Spacing (Back-to-back) of:

Table II - Aisle Width Increase (in inches) Per Row of Length

Seat Spacing Back-to-Back	Fire Underwriters Code: 3'-0" plus ¼" per 1'-0"	N.Y. City Code: 3'-0" plus 1½" per 5'-0"
32"	0.67	0.80
33"	0.69	0.83
34"	0.71	0.86
35"	0.73	0.88
36"	0.75	0.90
37"	0.77	0.93
38"	0.79	0.95
39"	0.81	0.98
40"	0.83	1.00
41"	0.85	1.03
42"	0.88	1.05

Proper factor x no. of rows = total increase in inches,
Add to 3'-0" minimum aisle width

Table III - Seating Capacities, 1-32 Rows

No. of Rows	7 Seats	14 Seats	28 Seats	No. of Rows	7 Seats	14 Seats	28 Seats
1	7	14	28	17	119	238	476
2	14	28	56	18	126	252	504
3	21	42	84	19	133	266	532
4	28	56	112	20	140	280	560
5	35	70	140	21	147	294	588
6	42	84	168	22	154	308	616
7	49	98	196	23	161	322	644
8	56	112	224	24	168	336	672
9	63	126	252	25	175	350	700
10	70	140	280	26	182	364	728
11	77	154	308	27	189	378	756
12	84	168	336	28	196	392	784
13	91	182	364	29	203	406	812
14	98	196	392	30	210	420	840
15	105	210	420	31	217	434	868
16	112	224	448	32	224	448	896

Table IV - Numbers of Seats (Stock Sizes) for Any Row Length

Row Length Ft.-In.	In.	19"	20"	21"	22"
5- 0	60	3			
5- 1	61	2	1		
5- 2	62	1	2		
5- 3	63		3		
5- 4	64		2	1	
5- 5	65		1	2	
5- 6	66			3	
5- 7	67			2	1
5- 8	68			1	2
5- 9	69				3
6- 7	79	4			
6- 8	80	3	1		
6- 9	81	2	2		
6-10	82	1	3		
6-11	83		4		
7- 0	84		3	1	
7- 1	85		2	2	
7- 2	86		1	3	
7- 3	87			4	
7- 4	88			3	1
7- 5	89			2	2
7- 6	90			1	3
7- 8	91				4
8- 2	98	5			
8- 3	99	4	1		
8- 4	100	3	2		
8- 5	101	2	3		
8- 6	102	1	4		
8- 7	103		5		
8- 8	104		4	1	
8- 9	105		3	2	
8-10	106		2	3	
8-11	107		1	4	
9- 0	108			5	
9- 1	109			4	1
9- 2	110			3	2
9- 3	111			2	3
9- 4	112			1	4
9- 5	113				5
9- 9	117	6			
9-10	118	5	1		
9-11	119	4	2		
10- 0	120	3	3		
10- 1	121	2	4		
10- 2	122	1	5		
10- 3	123		6		
10- 4	124		5	1	
10- 5	125		4	2	
10- 6	126		3	3	
10- 7	127		2	4	
10- 8	128		1	5	
10- 9	129			6	
10-10	130			5	1
10-11	131			4	2
11- 0	132			3	3
11- 1	133			2	4
11- 2	134			1	5
11- 3	135				6
11- 4	136	7			
11- 5	137	6	1		
11- 6	138	5	2		
11- 7	139	4	3		
11- 8	140	3	4		
11- 9	141	2	5		
11-10	142	1	6		
11-11	143		7		
12- 0	144		6	1	
12- 1	145		5	2	
12- 2	146		4	3	
12- 3	147		3	4	
12- 4	148		2	5	
12- 5	149		1	6	
12- 6	150			7	
12- 7	151			6	1
12- 8	152			5	2
12- 9	153			4	3
12-10	154			3	4
12-11	155	8		2	5
13- 0	156	7	1	1	6
13- 1	157	6	2		7
13- 2	158	5	3		
13- 3	159	4	4		
13- 4	160	3	5		
13- 5	161	2	6		
13- 6	162	1	7		
13- 7	163		8		
13- 8	164		7	1	
13- 9	165		6	2	
13-10	166		5	3	
13-11	167		4	4	
14- 0	168		3	5	
14- 1	169		2	6	
14- 2	170		1	7	
14- 3	171			8	
14- 4	172			7	1
14- 5	173			6	2
14- 6	174	9		5	3
14- 7	175	8	1	4	4
14- 8	176	7	2	3	5
14- 9	177	6	3	2	6
14-10	178	5	4	1	7
14-11	179	4	5		8
15- 0	180	3	6		
15- 1	181	2	7		
15- 2	182	1	8		
15- 3	183		9		
15- 4	184		8	1	
15- 5	185		7	2	
15- 6	186		6	3	
15- 7	187		5	4	
15- 8	188		4	5	
15- 9	189		3	6	
15-10	190		2	7	
15-11	191		1	8	
16- 0	192			9	
16- 1	193	10		8	1
16- 2	194	9	1	7	2
16- 3	195	8	2	6	3
16- 4	196	7	3	5	4
16- 5	197	6	4	4	5
16- 6	198	5	5	3	6
16- 7	199	4	6	2	7
16- 8	200	3	7	1	8
16- 9	201	2	8		9
16-10	202	1	9		
16-11	203		10		
17- 0	204		9	1	
17- 1	205		8	2	
17- 2	206		7	3	
17- 3	207		6	4	
17- 4	208		5	5	
17- 5	209		4	6	
17- 6	210		3	7	
17- 7	211		2	8	
17- 8	212	11	1	9	
17- 9	213	10	1	10	
17-10	214	9	2	9	1
17-11	215	8	3	8	2
18- 0	216	7	4	7	3
18- 1	217	6	5	6	4
18- 2	218	5	6	5	5
18- 3	219	4	7	4	6
18- 4	220	3	8	3	7
18- 5	221	2	9	2	8
18- 6	222	1	10	1	9
18- 7	223		11		10
18- 8	224		10	1	
18- 9	225		9	2	
18-10	226		8	3	
18-11	227		7	4	
19- 0	228		6	5	
19- 1	229		5	6	
19- 2	230		4	7	
19- 3	231	12	3	8	
19- 4	232	11	1 2	9	
19- 5	233	10	2 1	10	
19- 6	234	9	3	11	
19- 7	235	8	4	10	1
19- 8	236	7	5	9	2
19- 9	237	6	6	8	3
19-10	238	5	7	7	4
19-11	239	4	8	6	5
20- 0	240	3	9	5	6
20- 1	241	2	10	4	7
20- 2	242	1	11	3	8
20- 3	243		12	2	9
20- 4	244		11	1 1	10
20- 5	245		10	2	11
20- 6	246		9	3	
20- 7	247		8	4	
20- 8	248		7	5	
20- 9	249		6	6	
20-10	250	13	5	7	
20-11	251	12	1 4	8	
21- 0	252	11	2 3	9	
21- 1	253	10	3 2	10	
21- 2	254	9	4 1	11	
21- 3	255	8	5	12	
21- 4	256	7	6	11	1
21- 5	257	6	7	10	2
21- 6	258	5	8	9	3
21- 7	259	4	9	8	4
21- 8	260	3	10	7	5
21- 9	261	2	11	6	6
21-10	262	1	12	5	7
21-11	263		13	4	8
22- 0	264		12	1 3	9
22- 1	265		11	2 2	10
22- 2	266		10	3 1	11
22- 3	267		9	4	12
22- 4	268		8	5	
22- 5	269	14	7	6	
22- 6	270	13	1 6	7	
22- 7	271	12	2 5	8	
22- 8	272	11	3 4	9	
22- 9	273	10	4 3	10	
22-10	274	9	5 2	11	
22-11	275	8	6 1	12	
23- 0	276	7	7	13	
23- 1	277	6	8	12	1
23- 2	278	5	9	11	2
23- 3	279	4	10	10	3
23- 4	280	3	11	9	4
23- 5	281	2	12	8	5
23- 6	282	1	13	7	6
23- 7	283		14	6	7
23- 8	284		13	1 5	8
23- 9	285		12	2 4	9
23-10	286		11	3 3	10
23-11	287		10	4 2	11
24- 0	288		9	5 1	12
24- 1	289		8	6	13
24- 2	290		7	7	
24- 3	291		6	8	
24- 4	292		5	9	
24- 5	293		4	10	
24- 6	294		3	11	
24- 7	295		2	12	
24- 8	296		1	13	
24- 9	297			14	
24-10	298			13	1
24-11	299			12	2
25- 0	300			11	3
25- 1	301			10	4
25- 2	302			9	5
25- 3	303			8	6
25- 4	304			7	7
25- 5	305			6	8
25- 6	306			5	9
25- 7	307			4	10
25- 8	308			3	11
25- 9	309			2	12
25-10	310			1	13
25-11	311				14

End Allowances: Normal 3" allowance to accommodate 2 end standards per row is included above. For balconies with steps in aisles allow 2" additional.

Seat Sizes: Common sizes shown. Seats are also available 18", 23" & 24" wide. 18" size not recommended. Limit use of 19" seats to ends of rows for comfort.

Choice of Seats: Note that for longer rows two choices of seat sizes are available. Example: Row length = 14'- 9"; six 19" seats and three 20" may be used; or, two 21" and six 22". Dotted lines separate choices. Dimensions not fitted by stock sizes are omitted.

Basic elements of office furniture and equipment are illustrated on this and the following page, as a guide to the planning of office space. Specialized types of equipment, such as bookkeeping and accounting machines, punching machines, reproducing machines, etc., are not included. Consult manufacturers' literature for data required for detailed planning of spaces which include these special types.

Dimensions given cover the ordinary range of sizes found in equipment currently on the market. Slight variations in size exist between wood and steel equipment, and among manufacturers. Sizes given are adequate for planning purposes.

Clearances are given for desk and chair arrangements in both executive's and stenographer's offices. These are minima only, based on requirements for circulation, chair rotation, and clearance for open drawers. See the following pages for further data on clearances.

Files. Fractional variations in height and depth dimensions for each type occur among the various makes of files within a maximum range of 2 to 3 in.

Counter-height files may be employed as space planning elements to form secondary partitions within large working areas. Special units such as gates, cupboards, knee space sections, etc., are available for this purpose.

EXECUTIVE OFFICE

Double pedestal desk
Depth 24 to 40 in.

Single pedestal desk
Depth 24 to 32 in.

Wing or return units
Plan

Flush
Height 29 to 30 in.

Dropped
Height 25½ to 26½ in.

Swivel armchair

Rigid armchair

Upholstered armchair

Sofa

WORK TABLE
2'-10" x 5'-6"

3'-0" for passage

2'-6" Min. using swivel chair

DESK
2'-10" x 5'-6"

Clearance diagram

Conference table
D = 30 to 42 in.
W = 60 to 120 in.

Scale
0 1' 2' 3' 4' 5' 6'

Freestanding partitions
Panel widths 12 to 60 in.,
in increments of 6 in.

GLASS OR PLASTIC – CLEAR OR DIFFUSING

DOOR   DOOR

METAL PANELS

OPEN   BASE

GENERAL OFFICE

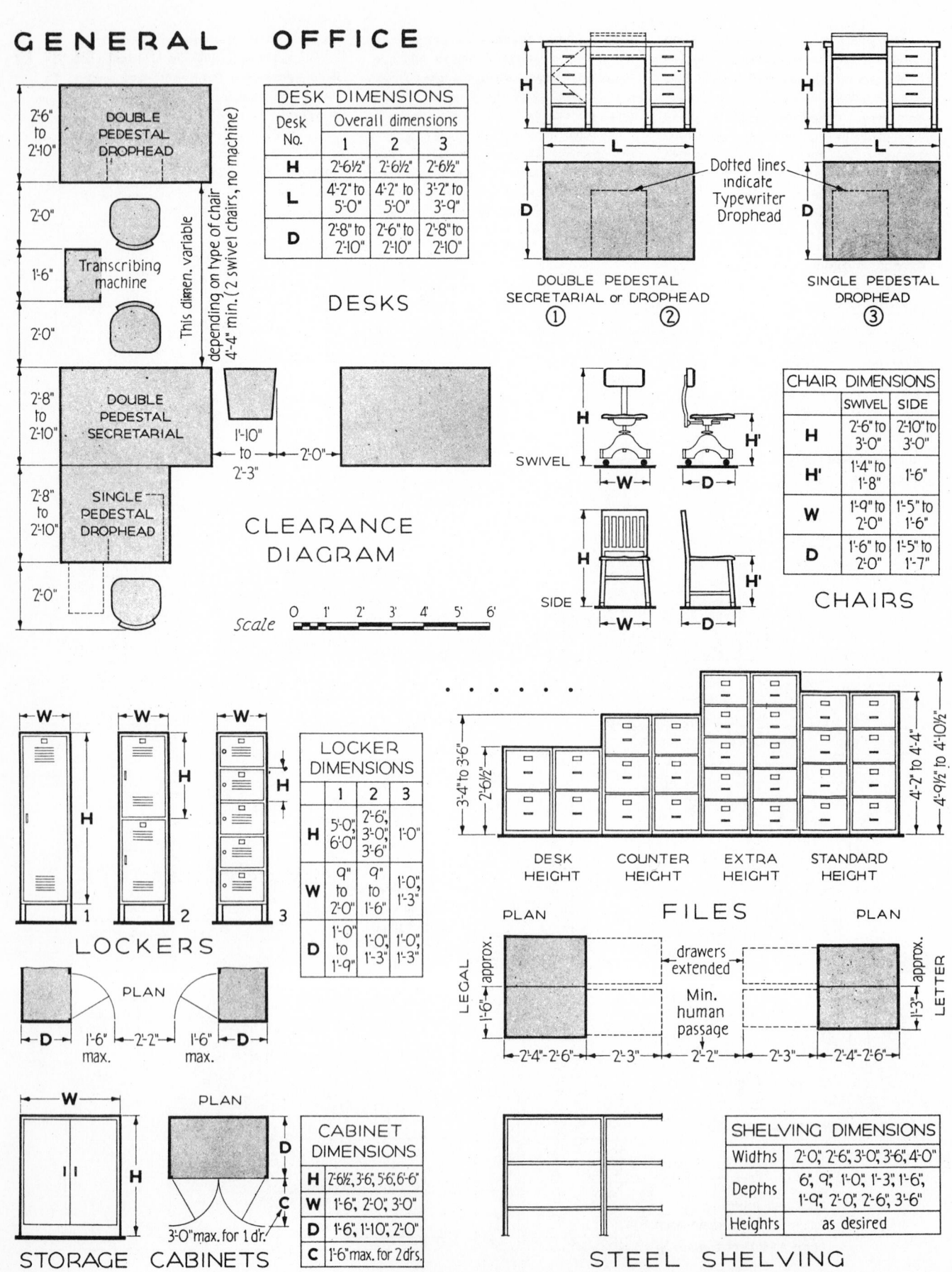

DESK DIMENSIONS

Desk No.	Overall dimensions		
	1	2	3
H	2'-6½"	2'-6½"	2'-6½"
L	4'-2" to 5'-0"	4'-2" to 5'-0"	3'-2" to 3'-9"
D	2'-8" to 2'-10"	2'-6" to 2'-10"	2'-8" to 2'-10"

DESKS

2'-6" to 2'-10" — DOUBLE PEDESTAL DROPHEAD

2'-0"

1'-6" — Transcribing machine

2'-0"

This dimen. variable depending on type of chair 4'-4" min. (2 swivel chairs, no machine)

2'-8" to 2'-10" — DOUBLE PEDESTAL SECRETARIAL

2'-8" to 2'-10" — SINGLE PEDESTAL DROPHEAD

2'-0"

1'-10" to 2'-3" — 2'-0"

CLEARANCE DIAGRAM

Scale 0 1' 2' 3' 4' 5' 6'

Dotted lines indicate Typewriter Drophead

DOUBLE PEDESTAL SECRETARIAL or DROPHEAD ① ②

SINGLE PEDESTAL DROPHEAD ③

CHAIR DIMENSIONS

	SWIVEL	SIDE
H	2'-6" to 3'-0"	2'-10" to 3'-0"
H'	1'-4" to 1'-8"	1'-6"
W	1'-9" to 2'-0"	1'-5" to 1'-6"
D	1'-6" to 2'-0"	1'-5" to 1'-7"

SWIVEL

SIDE

CHAIRS

LOCKER DIMENSIONS

	1	2	3
H	5'-0", 6'-0"	2'-6", 3'-0", 3'-6"	1'-0"
W	9" to 2'-0"	9" to 1'-6"	1'-0", 1'-3"
D	1'-0" to 1'-9"	1'-0", 1'-3"	1'-0", 1'-3"

LOCKERS

PLAN

1'-6" max. — 2'-2" — 1'-6" max.

3'-4" to 3'-6"
2'-6½"

DESK HEIGHT

COUNTER HEIGHT

EXTRA HEIGHT

STANDARD HEIGHT

4'-2" to 4'-4"
4'-9½" to 4'-10½"

FILES

PLAN

LEGAL 1'-6" approx.

2'-4"-2'-6" — 2'-3" — drawers extended — Min. human passage — 2'-2" — 2'-3" — 2'-4"-2'-6"

PLAN

LETTER 1'-3" approx.

CABINET DIMENSIONS

H	2'-6½", 3'-6", 5'-6", 6'-6"
W	1'-6", 2'-0", 3'-0"
D	1'-6", 1'-10", 2'-0"
C	1'-6" max. for 2 drs.

PLAN

3'-0" max. for 1 dr.

STORAGE CABINETS

SHELVING DIMENSIONS

Widths	2'-0", 2'-6", 3'-0", 3'-6", 4'-0"
Depths	6", 9", 1'-0", 1'-3", 1'-6", 1'-9", 2'-0", 2'-6", 3'-6"
Heights	as desired

STEEL SHELVING

Necessary clearances between typical items of office furniture and equipment are shown on this and the following page. Minima for reasonably comfortable use are shown, rather than absolute minima. The generally high cost per square foot of office space has been considered in the development of these data. The three drawings immediately below are the result of recent research and should be considered more authoritative than the other drawings. It should be noted, however, that the 36-in. dimension marked "space to use desk" is based on full access to the center drawer without moving from the chair. If this is not considered to be a requirement then this dimension can be reduced to 30 in.

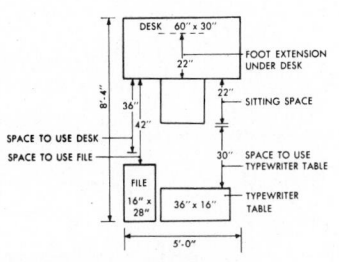

(a) Parallel arrangement

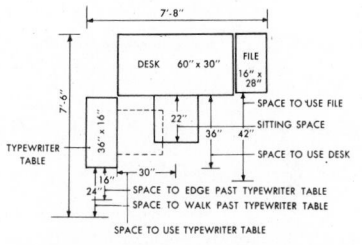

(b) Right angle arrangement

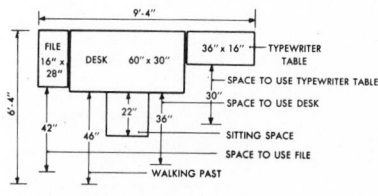

(c) One-wall arrangement

Clearances required in a secretarial office

From Bulletin 686, University of Illinois Agricultural Experiment Station, 1962.

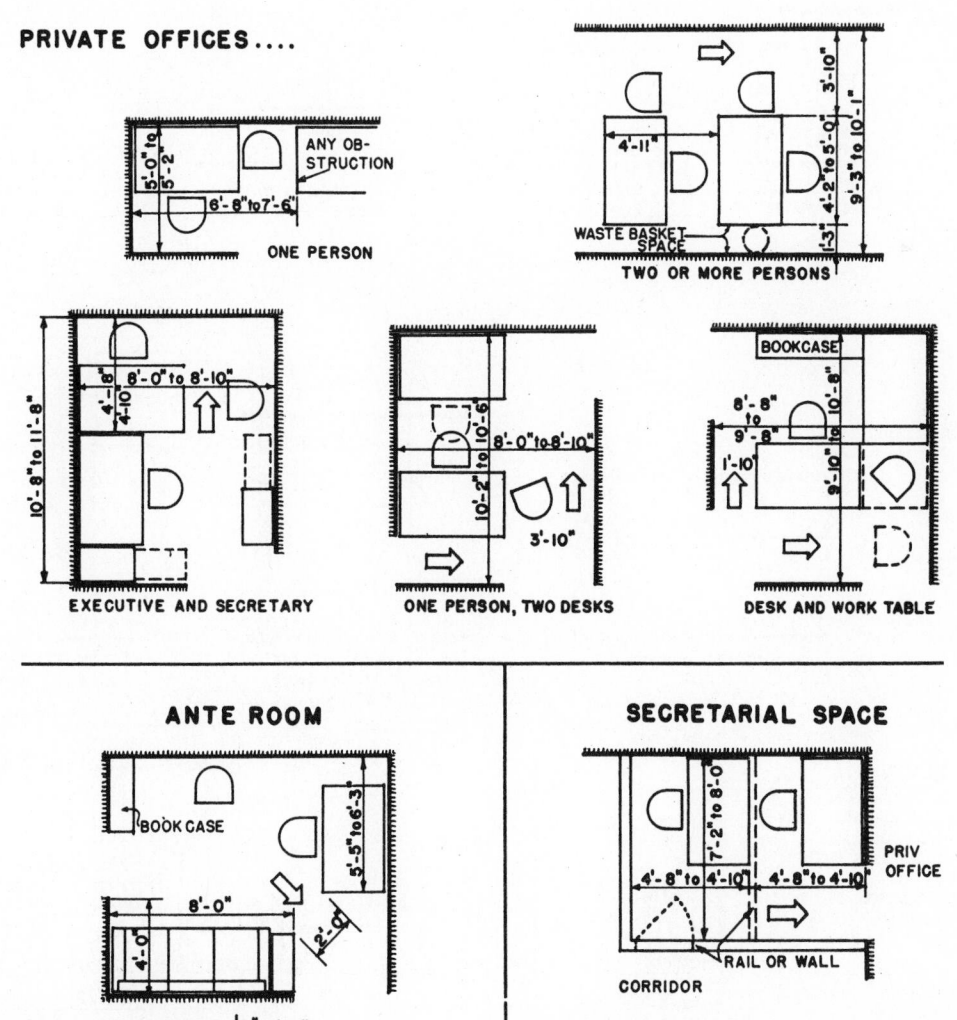

PRIVATE OFFICES....

ONE PERSON

TWO OR MORE PERSONS

EXECUTIVE AND SECRETARY

ONE PERSON, TWO DESKS

DESK AND WORK TABLE

ANTE ROOM

SECRETARIAL SPACE

SCALE, ALL DRAWINGS: 1/8" = 1'-0"

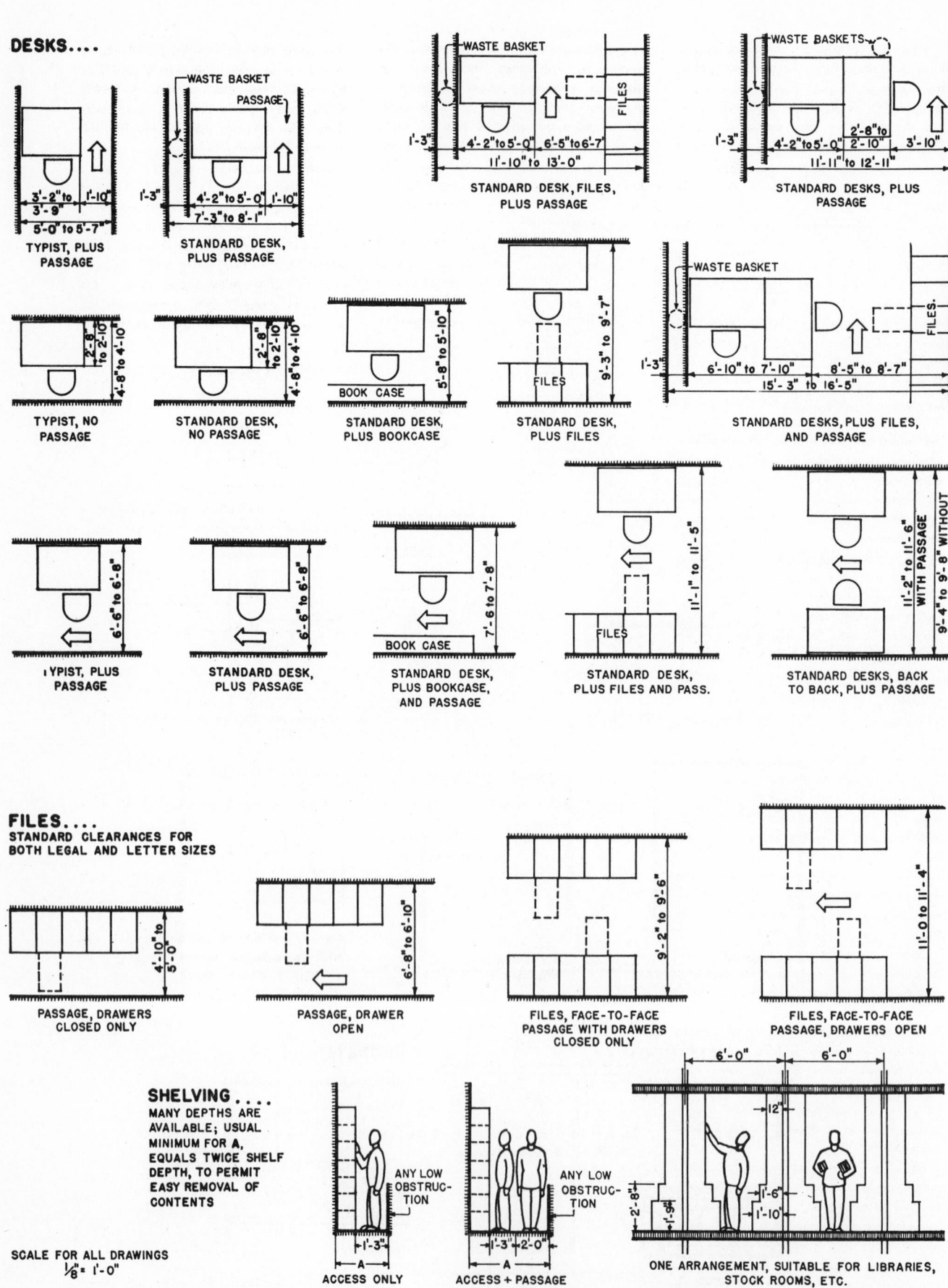

DESKS....

TYPIST, PLUS PASSAGE

STANDARD DESK, PLUS PASSAGE

STANDARD DESK, FILES, PLUS PASSAGE

STANDARD DESKS, PLUS PASSAGE

TYPIST, NO PASSAGE

STANDARD DESK, NO PASSAGE

STANDARD DESK, PLUS BOOKCASE

STANDARD DESK, PLUS FILES

STANDARD DESKS, PLUS FILES, AND PASSAGE

TYPIST, PLUS PASSAGE

STANDARD DESK, PLUS PASSAGE

STANDARD DESK, PLUS BOOKCASE, AND PASSAGE

STANDARD DESK, PLUS FILES AND PASS.

STANDARD DESKS, BACK TO BACK, PLUS PASSAGE

FILES....
STANDARD CLEARANCES FOR BOTH LEGAL AND LETTER SIZES

PASSAGE, DRAWERS CLOSED ONLY

PASSAGE, DRAWER OPEN

FILES, FACE-TO-FACE PASSAGE WITH DRAWERS CLOSED ONLY

FILES, FACE-TO-FACE PASSAGE, DRAWERS OPEN

SHELVING....
MANY DEPTHS ARE AVAILABLE; USUAL MINIMUM FOR A, EQUALS TWICE SHELF DEPTH, TO PERMIT EASY REMOVAL OF CONTENTS

SCALE FOR ALL DRAWINGS
⅛" = 1'-0"

ACCESS ONLY

ACCESS + PASSAGE

ONE ARRANGEMENT, SUITABLE FOR LIBRARIES, STOCK ROOMS, ETC.

Office layout is generally based upon a module derived from standard furniture and equipment and the necessary clearances. For large general offices, the planning unit or module is based upon one desk and chair and is thus about 5 by 5 ft. Since this dimension is also satisfactory for aisles between rows of desks the module can be used to form a regular grid for the planning of large office areas (Fig. 1).

In the layout of private offices the controlling factors are the minimum practical office layout with the wall and window design. A planning module of 4 to 5 ft works reasonably well for this purpose. With this module the smallest office (2 modules) would be 8 to 10 ft wide, and a convenient range of office sizes is provided in increments of one module (Fig. 2). If the exterior wall consists of continuous windows, one module in width, then the office widths are limited to even modules. If windows alternate with solid walls, then office widths do not have to be in even modules but may vary widely (Fig. 3). This type of wall design permits greater flexibility in office layout, at the expense of less natural light in the offices.

The planning module and the exterior wall module must be reconciled with the structural module or column bay. If all of these modules coincide, then the wall or window units adjacent to the column must be smaller than the intermediate units (Fig. 4a). If the wall units are kept uniform in size, then the planning module is interrupted by the column width (Fig. 4b). If the columns are set inside the walls, they do not interfere with the wall module but they create a serious limitation on the layout of private offices (Fig. 4c). If the columns are set outside the walls, then the planning module and the wall module are not affected by them (Fig. 4d).

Column spacing most frequently used in multi-story steel-framed office buildings is around 25 ft, center to center. Recent trend is toward larger spacing; 30 to 35 ft is not uncommon. Flexibility of interior space is so important in office building design that the extra cost of clear span framing with the elimination of all interior columns, is sometimes considered worthwhile; clear spans of 60 to 70 ft have been used.

Efficiency of an office building design is measured by the ratio of rentable space to total space. Average efficiency is about 70 per cent; maximum possible is about 85 per cent. The nonrentable space consists of the elevators, stairs, and toilets and their associated lobbies, corridors, pipe and duct shafts, and janitor's closets. These facilities are usually planned in a

compact unit called the service core. For preliminary assumptions, the number of elevators required may be estimated on the basis of one elevator per 25,000 sq ft of rentable area. Elevator lobbies should be 6 to 9 ft wide if elevators are on one side only; 10 to 12 ft if elevators are on both sides. Corridors are usually 5 to 6 ft wide (Fig. 5), wider if very long, narrower if very short.

Since the floor space within 25 to 30 ft from the exterior wall brings premium rentals, office buildings tend to assume a slab-like shape, 60 to 70 ft wide by 150 ft or more long, with the service core in

the center (Fig. 6). For greater flexibility in the rental space, the service core may be moved completely outside the office space. When this scheme is combined with clear span framing, the ultimate in flexibility is achieved (Fig. 7).

Floor-to-floor heights are usually about 12 ft, ranging from 11 to 14 ft. Finished ceiling heights are generally about 10 ft, ranging from 9 to 11 ft. The space above the ceiling is required for ducts and recessed lighting. In order to avoid excessive depths in this utility space, girders are sometimes designed with openings in the web to permit the passage of ducts.

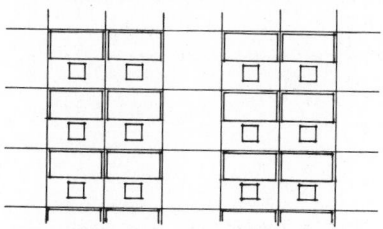

Fig. 1. Planning module for layout of general office space

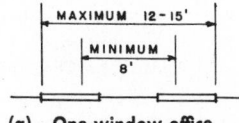

(a) One-window office

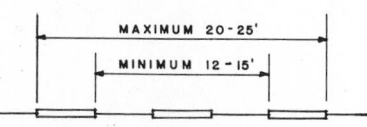

(b) Two-window office

Fig. 3. Private office widths using a module of 4 to 5 ft with windows alternating with solid wall

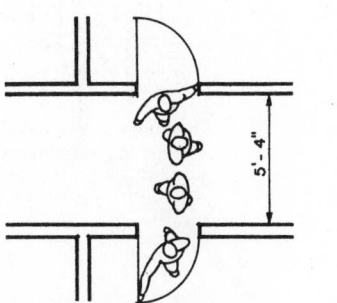

Fig. 5. Corridor width based on requirements of human figure

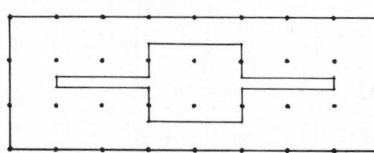

Fig. 6. Typical slab plan with service core at center

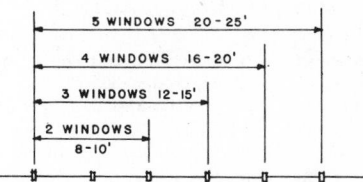

Fig. 2. Private office widths using a module of 4 to 5 ft with continuous windows

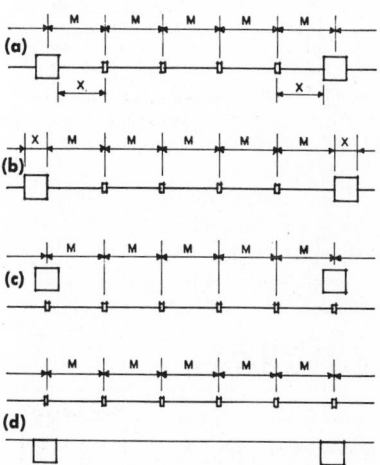

Fig. 4. Relation of planning module and wall module to column spacing and location

Note: all plans drawn with outside at bottom

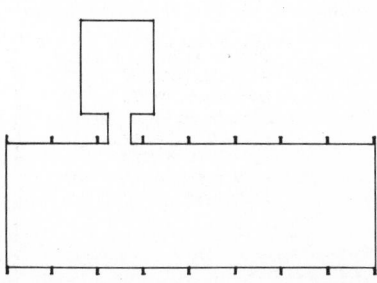

Fig. 7. Maximum flexibility of rental area achieved by use of clear-span framing and separate service tower

By Dr. N. L. ENGELHARDT, Jr.,

Engelhardt, Engelhardt and Leggett, Educational Consultants

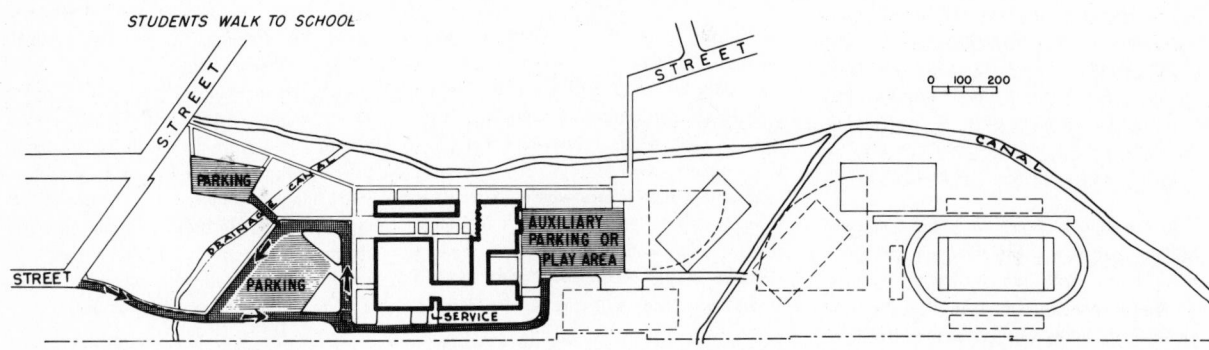

Fig. 1 *Warren H. Ashley, Architect*

SCHOOL SITE PLANNING

One of the first and most important aspects of school plant planning is site selection and development. Many small sites, which prevailed during the early part of this century, have proved inadequate for the modern educational program. Modern school buildings are usually one-story structures for reasons of safety and economy and thus require a much greater area. For example, a building planned for 3,000 students may cover as much as five acres of land.

Other land needed for educational purposes may include playfields for physical education and outdoor areas for art groups, music, and dramatics; space for experimental projects in science studies, such as growing plants, cages for animals, nursery developments, and developed nature trails; and space where students may develop competence in driver-training education before training on public roads.

Traffic safety should be built into the site plan with consideration for pedestrians, and buses, automobiles, service vehicles, and bicycles. A determined portion of the site should be reserved for the movement and parking of vehicular traffic. Driveways should be planned to give traffic a simple and direct access to parking areas, auditorium, gymnasium, service entrance, and pupil-unloading platforms. Equally important is the movement of this traffic off the site in a simple and direct manner, avoiding student activity areas and pedestrian walkways. Care should be taken not to bisect or parallel play areas with driveways.

The Cresskill (N.J.) Junior-Senior High School (Fig. 1) is located on a long, narrow site with only one vehicular access point. Two access points would be more desirable, and a second point may be developed in the future. However, there is no bus traffic since students walk to school. A few students may drive cars and, of course, the usual suburban parent pick-up is expected. The overflow parking area provides an outdoor play area during the day and a public parking area during the evening or for special activities.

The majority of students in the Concord-Carlisle (Mass.) Regional High School are transported by car and bus (Fig. 2). This plan provides an easy vehicular flow with a minimum of cross-traffic. Students can be transported to the main centers of the school, and parking facilities are located to service the day and evening programs. Direct access to play areas is possible without walking across driveways or parking areas. Provision for delivery service removes trucks from the main traffic flow.

The main parking areas are located away from student activity; the large auxiliary parking area near the gymnasium is mainly used as a hard-surface play area, with parking only at special times.

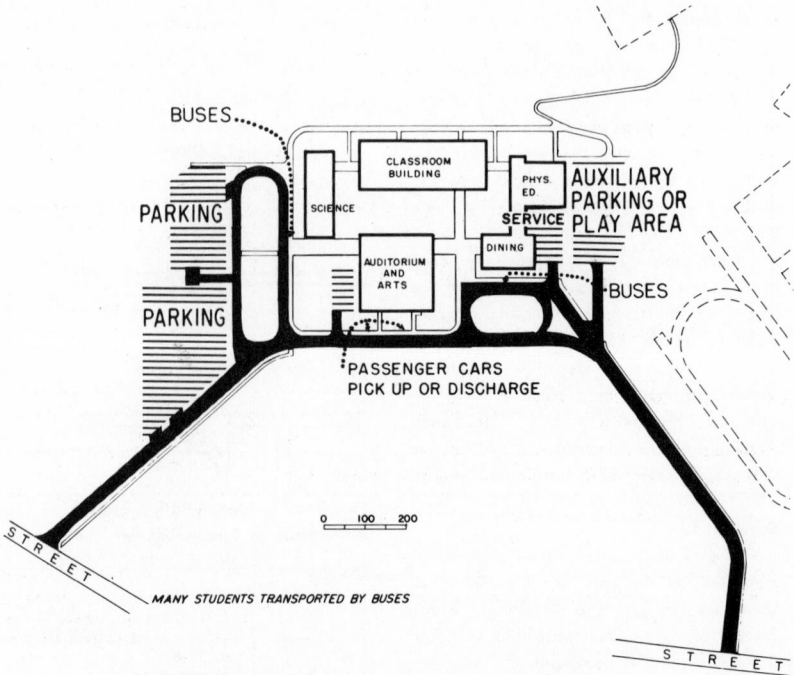

Fig. 2 *Warren H. Ashley, Architect*

The plan of this school in Scarsdale, N.Y. (Fig. 3), provides an easy and rapid vehicular traffic flow, assisted in part by the location of the different building units. Students are transported in close proximity to their activity areas, and all general areas used by students and public have easy access to the roadway. The off-street stopping area to the right helps to accommodate the large number of parents who transport their own children.

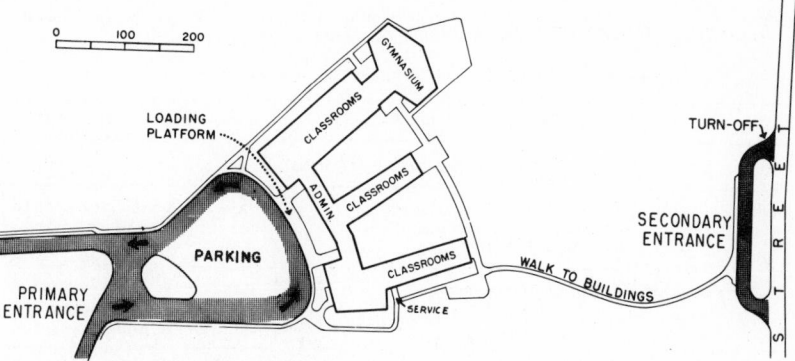

Fig. 3   *Moore and Hutchins, Architects*

SELECTING THE SITE

Future educational needs of the community will play a major role in the selection of a school site. These needs should be determined as the first step and some weight or measure placed on each. These values can be used for the final assay.

A score card should be developed for placing the various site characteristics in their proper perspective. The card will provide a factual and realistic basis on which to make an unbiased, unemotional, and nonpolitical decision.

This card should represent a complete site analysis and include such items as detailed studies of present and future en-

vironment, community planning, an over-all comprehenive school building plan, size of required site, accessibility, site characteristics, utility services, cost of site development, and land costs. The score card in Table 1 has been effectively used as an aid for site selection.

OUTDOOR PLAY AREAS

The design of play areas should be determined by the activities of different age levels of school groups: kindergarten,

primary, intermediate, junior high school, and senior high school.

Some aspects of well-designed play areas, however, are common to all types. There should be a minimum of crossing between play areas and between buildings. Different play areas used by various age groups should be isolated. Hedges, fences, or even the building itself can serve as a screen.

Play areas should not be adjacent to roadways, driveways, railroads, or open water. If conditions demand close prox-

Location of Site Under Consideration _____

	ITEM	DESCRIPTION	1	2	
I.	PRESENT AND FUTURE ENVIRONMENT			75	
A.	Nature of present surroundings				
	1. Character of nearby residential housing	General locality should offer only the most favorable social influences			
	2. Freedom from business distractions	Not near commercial centers or shops which take on undesirable characteristics			
	3. Freedom from noise, odors, dust, and traffic of industry	Set distinctly apart from industry and its inconveniences. Prevailing winds fully considered	50		
	4. Remoteness from railroads, landing fields, docks	Without impact of disturbing conditions from these traffic centers			
	5. Remoteness from heavily-traveled highways	Sufficiently protected from highway noises and hazards			
B.	Protection from present and possible future air travel routes	Location approved after careful study of take-off and landing practices and low-flying of airplanes	10		
C.	Future prospect for surroundings	Conservation of an attractive community setting seems assured	15		
II.	INTEGRATION WITH COMMUNITY PLANNING			75	
A.	Acceptability in complete community plan	The site satisfies the requirements of the comprehensive community plan and contributes its share of values	50		
B.	Non-interference with other community projects	Sufficiently remote from hospital, church, and other community zones so that they will suffer no disturbance from large groups of children	15		
C.	Value for extensive community use	Accessible and readily adjusted to adult use	10		

(cont.)

Use the second half of Column 1 for the scores on the lettered subdivisions when a specific site is being rated. The second half of Column 2 permits summation of these scores.

	ITEM	DESCRIPTION	1		2	
III.	ROLE IN COMPREHENSIVE SCHOOL BUILDING PLAN				100	
A.	Scientific determination of location with respect to present and future population	Objective techniques used to measure population in all aspects contributing to best choice	25			
B.	Integration with existing schools	Serves a territory without overlapping or duplication with existing schools which have the promise of permanence	25			
C.	Place in ultimate school program	Permanent dedication to education as far as foreseeable	25			
D.	Official approval of general location	Satisfactory to Board of Education and approved by current faculty	25			
IV.	SIZE OF SITE				300	
A.	Conformity to present and future educational programs	Makes for satisfactory educational use and for educational expansion	50			
B.	Compliance with following suggestions as the minimum in each case	The minimum should be met. Characteristics of locality and costs affect the final decision				
	1. Ten acres for an elementary school	Fifteen acres may not be found excessive				
	2. Thirty acres for a junior high school	Present and future junior high school programs make this a defensible minimum	150			
	3. Forty acres for a senior high school	Acreage in excess of this minimum usually makes a good purchase				
C.	Safeguarding of future educational extensions	The vision in selection encompasses all foreseeable extension needs	50			
D.	Provision for present and future play areas for all groups	Character of land and orientation ensure play and recreational facilities for all	50			
V.	ACCESSIBILITY				100	
A.	Accessibility for general public	Free from approach and exit hazards. No dangerous gradients	25			
B.	Optimum travel distances for children					
	1. 1-1/2 to 2 miles for senior high school	Based upon national practices and not in conflict with local traditions. Distances measured as the crow flies. Travel routes protected by traffic lights and with police cooperation. These distances usually make possible schools of acceptable enrollments				
	2. 1 to 2 miles for junior high school		25			
	3. 1/2 mile for elementary school					
	4. 1/4 to 1/2 mile for home-school units					
C.	Feasibility of approaches	Pedestrian and vehicular approaches possible without congestion				
	1. Pedestrian	Attractive and readily traversable				
	2. Bicycle	Possible planning without cross conflicts	25			
	3. Automobile	Without cross currents and excessive grades				
	4. School bus	Easy access to loading center possible				
D.	Safety of approaches	Safety is first consideration				
	1. Freedom from hazardous cross roads	Entrance and exit routes unhampered by conflicting traffic				
	2. Provision of sidewalks and good roads	Assurance of sidewalks and preferred road approaches	25			
	3. Elimination of conflicting travel currents	Freedom from heavy travel at school opening and closing hours				
	4. Provision of underpasses, pedestrian bridges	Man-made protection from crossing heavy or through traffic lines				

(cont.)

	ITEM	DESCRIPTION	1	2
VI.	SITE CHARACTERISTICS			200
A.	Shape of site	Square or rectangular is preferred over very irregular or "shoestring" sites	50	
B.	Present utilization	Site should be free of structures involving high costs for removal	25	
C.	Aesthetic value of site	Maximum capitalization of views at a distance and at close range	25	
D.	Influence of site on building design	Stimulation of community-acceptable design through characteristics of site	10	
E.	Possibility of preferred orientation for all rooms and all game areas	Dimensions of site offer no restriction to freedom of planning	25	
F.	Prevalence of characteristics usable to educational advantage	Abundance of natural resources such as trees, water, and elevations	15	
G.	Ease of surface adaptation for buildings, play areas, and parking	Surface and near-surface conditions offer no known handicap to planning	25	
H.	Subsoil conditions	No excessive fill, rock, quicksand, or subsurface water conditions known	25	
VII.	UTILITY SERVICES			50
A.	Proximity of utility connections	Ready access to utilities should be possible		
1.	Water connections	Excessive trenching not required		
2.	Sewage connections	Reasonably near connections are possible	25	
3.	Gas	Distance for gas connections reasonably short		
B.	Feasibility of making serviceable utility connections	Freedom from undesirable subsurface conditions	25	
VIII.	COSTS			100
A.	Cost of land	Favorable comparison with other nearby land costs per acre	50	
B.	Cost of site preparation	No unusual site features necessitate excessive costs		
1.	General adjustment of land contours for building and play areas	Site characteristics lend themselves to complete and distinctive planning		
2.	Sufficient elevation for safeguarding drainage at reasonable cost	Sufficiently commanding location for buildings and reasonable adjustment for play areas		
3.	Freedom from drainage from contiguous land	Proposed site, rather than adjoining land, controls the drainage problem	25	
4.	Ease of preparation of parking areas, entrances, and service raods	Parking areas feasible for teachers, visitors, and students. Ready creation of roads possible		
5.	Additional charges for piling, rock excavation, tree removal, and the like	Site conditions make for no serious costs for these items		
6.	Removal or razing of existing buildings	Salvage value of existing structures establishes low cost		
C.	Cost of utility connections	Reasonably low		
1.	Length of trenchwork necessary	Not excessive	15	
2.	Extent of pumping needs	Not beyond average expectation		
D.	Cost of new improvements adjoining and approaching site	Much of this cost not chargeable to the school		
1.	New street paving required	Payment follows local practice	10	
2.	New sidewalk installations	This requirement will entail costs chargeable to the school building budget		
		MAXIMUM POSSIBLE SCORE	1000	1000

imity to these potential hazards, a high chainlink fence should be installed for the pupils' safety.

Ground coverings for play areas may vary according to their use. For safety, a tough sod is desirable for most outdoor activities, but play is then limited to clear weather. Hard bitumen surfaces and covered play areas provide a solution to the weather problem; they also cost less to maintain.

A combination of bitumen and sod play areas on the school site is recommended for the modern program. An analysis of play area ground covers is given in Table 2.

Table 2. Analysis of playground surfacing

From School Sites, *No. 7, U.S. Dept. of Health, Education, and Welfare.*

Type of surface	Year-round utility use	Multiple use	Dustless	Fine-grained, nonabsorbent	Durable	Resilient	All-weather footing	Reasonable cost	Low maintenance	Pleasing appearance
Earth		•		•	•			•		•
Turf		•	•	•		•		•		•
Aggregate	•				•		•	•		
Bitumen	•	•	•	•	•		•	•	•	•
Concrete	•				•		•	•	•	
Masonry	•	•			•		•		•	
Miscellaneous*	•	•				•		•	•	

* *Tanbark, sawdust, cottonmeal, rubber, plastics and vinyls, asbestos-cement boards, wood.*

In the site plan of the North Shore Junior High School, Glen Head, N.Y. (Fig. 4). skillful use has been made of an irregular-shaped site. Roadways and parking areas are located away from the classrooms. Several hard-surface play areas are situated near the gymnasium to give flexibility in scheduling activities and more outdoor play time. The size of the site is adequate for future expansion of activities.

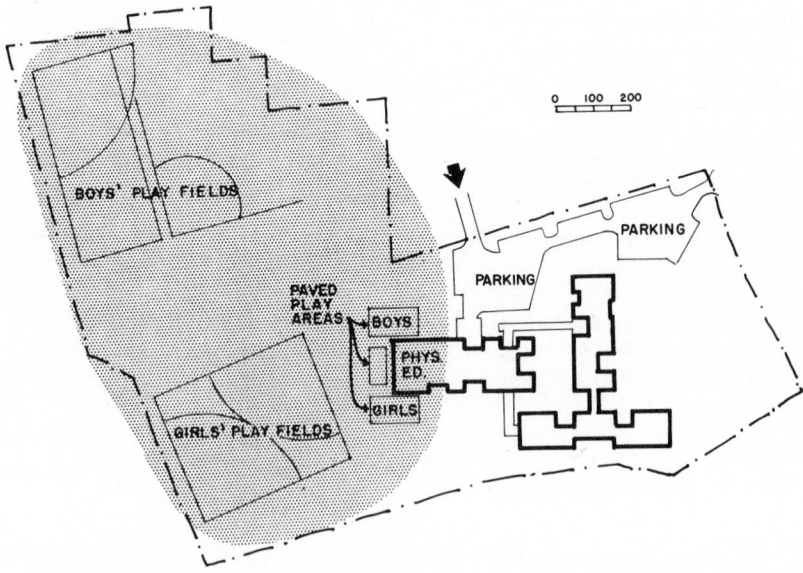

Fig. 4 *Perkins and Will, Architects*

The plan of the Ulloa Elementary School in San Francisco, Calif. (Fig. 5), indicates a possible solution when the land available for play areas is very limited. Traffic hazards have been reduced by placing the building along two of the surrounding streets and providing walls, fences, and shrubbery along the other streets to separate traffic from children. Safety is provided inside the play areas by placing a serpentine wall between primary and intermediate children. The building is used as another barrier for kindergarten play. The areas used by younger children are furnished with technical play equipment, which permits more physical activity and student participation per square foot of space.

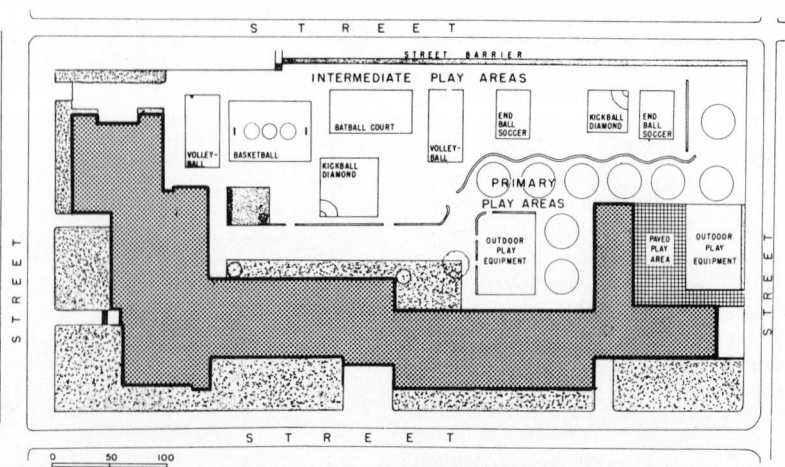

Fig. 5 *A. F. Roller, Architect*

The architects have utilized a high percentage of the total land area at the White Plains (N.Y.) High School (Fig. 6). The gymnasium location provides for spectator parking, direct access to playfields, and noise control between the high and low noise levels of the plant. Walkways to the different playfields permit students to move from field to field, or field to gym, without interrupting other activities. The number and variety of play areas give the physical education program balance, flexibility, and completeness, and also provide better facilities for community activity.

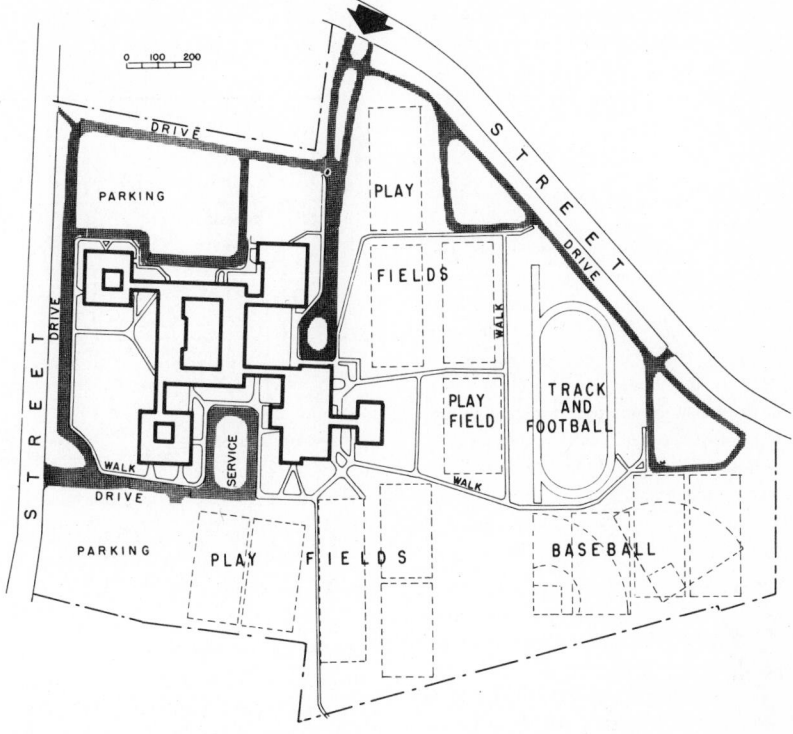

Fig. 6   *Perkins and Will, Architects*

TRAFFIC FLOW WITHIN A BUILDING

Traffic flow in a school is of utmost concern. Congestion may disrupt class schedules and cause discipline problems.

Consideration should be given to the traffic flow between periods, public use of the building, the level of the school group, and administrative organization. The proper placement of large group activity areas such as cafeteria, gymnasium, auditorium, library, and student centers can assist in the over-all distribution of traffic.

Standards have been established by the National Board of Fire Underwriters for building exits. These recommended dimensions and designs are minimum and are not necessarily adequate for the proper flow of student traffic. For example, stairways that meet code requirements may

not be adequate for two passing students with books under their arms.

When it is necessary for a community to provide only one building to house students of different age levels, every effort should be made to separate the several levels. Traffic patterns have a major role in this separation. For example, a well-planned junior-senior high school will have areas with a separate identity for each of these two student groups. The areas common to both age levels, such as

The campus-type plan of the Ashley Park School, Charlotte, N.C. (Fig. 7), shows that it was designed with the idea in mind of a "little school within a school." This design requires considerable outdoor traffic flow, which reduces the amount of corridor and stair area in the buildings. The economical covered walkways between the buildings permit free and comfortable student traffic flow during inclement weather. Notice how the future "little school" traffic can blend into the existing pattern. Traffic congestion in this plant is reduced by the proper distribution of large group areas such as auditorium, gymnasium, and cafeteria.

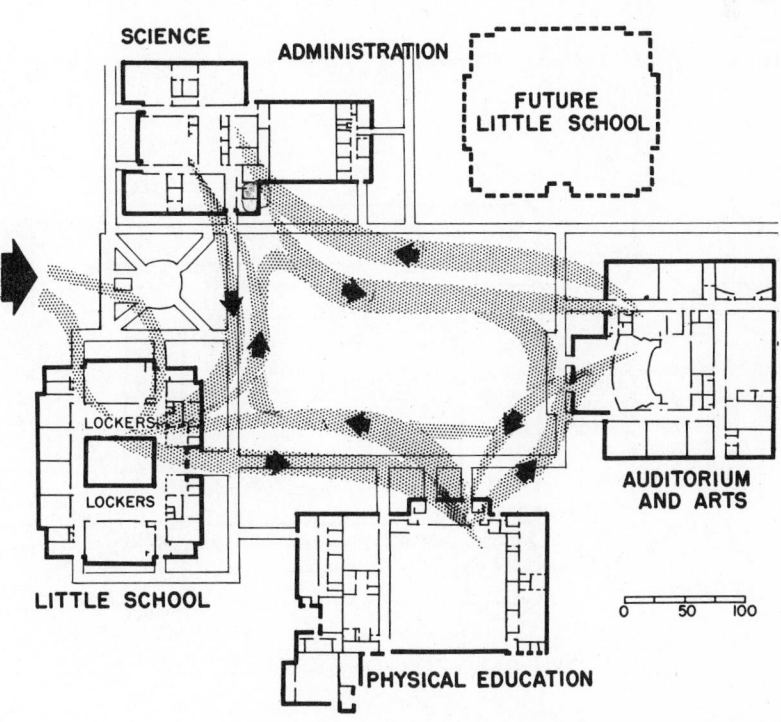

Fig. 7   *M. McDowell Brackett, Architect*

the gymnasium, auditorium, cafeteria, special subject areas, and over-all administration, should be given direct access to each group, with a minimum of cross traffic.

Certain conditions in the community of Cresskill, N.J., led to the decision of including 7th and 8th grades on the senior high school campus (Fig. 8). The design gives each of these two group areas a separate identity. The regular classrooms for each group are located on opposite sides of the school plant. Special subject and assembly areas used by students from both divisions are centrally located. This pattern of traffic flow eliminates cross traffic and congestion.

School exits

Exits and emergency exits should be clearly marked so that at no time is there any doubt or hesitation as to their purpose. A sign indicating the nearest exit should be visible from every point in the corridor. Two or more exits should be provided from any area within the school. Some states require two exits from each classroom.

It should be possible to open every door from the inside at all times, even after school is closed for the day.

A well-defined exit will include a lighted red exit sign and a white security light connected to an emergency power supply in the event of main power failure.

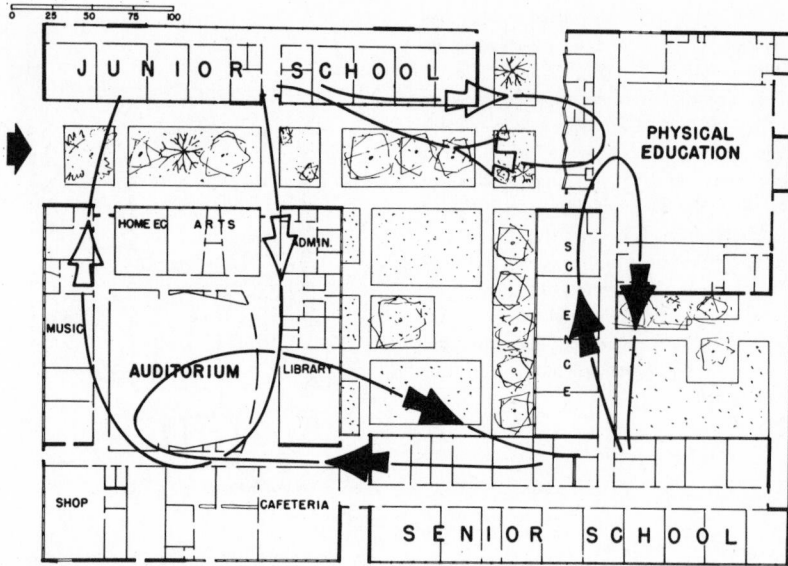

Fig. 8   *Warren H. Ashley, Architect*

Stairways

One of the most critical parts of school traffic design is the stairway, which should be located in relation to the over-all traffic pattern, keeping in mind load distribution, safety, destination of students between periods, and elimination of cross traffic. The stairways should be designed for easy, fast, and safe movement of boys and girls.

The plan (Fig. 9) shows good vertical and horizontal traffic patterns found at the Woodbridge (N.J.) Senior High School.

Stairways not only provide egress to and from various floor levels, but they are used every period for the vertical circulation of students changing classes. It is important that stairways be designed so that boys and girls with books under their arms may walk side by side to avoid congestion; a width of 4 ft 8 in. to 5 ft between handrails is recommended. Stairways should be of fireproof construction, leading directly to the outdoors. They should be provided with smoke-control facilities, separating the stairwells from the corridors which they serve.

Fig. 9   *Frederic P. Wiedersum, Architect*

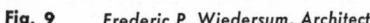
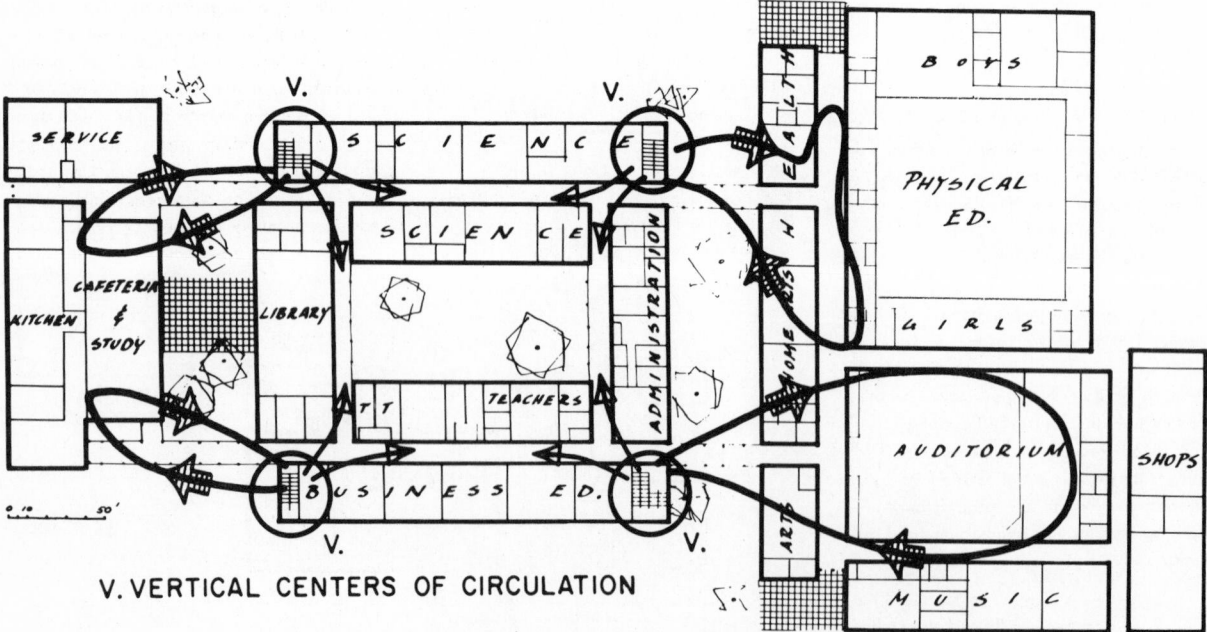

V. VERTICAL CENTERS OF CIRCULATION

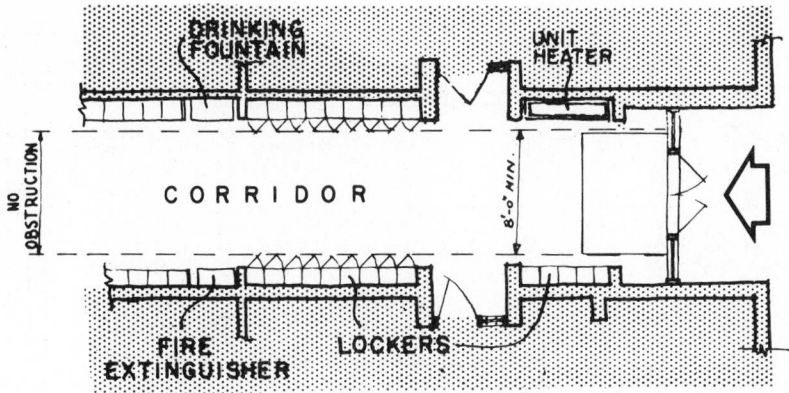

Fig. 10

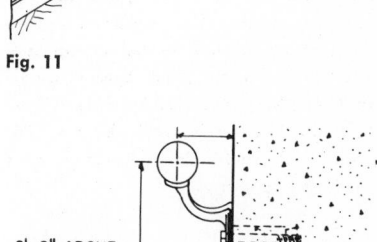

Fig. 11

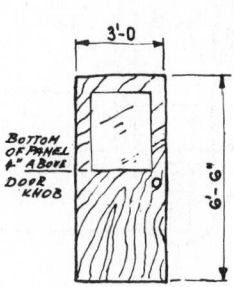

Fig. 12

Corridors

A well-designed school has corridors that accommodate the free and informal movement of students. The narrow corridor usually requires formal, regimented, and supervised traffic flow.

The walls of corridors should be free of all projections. Heat units, drinking fountains, fire extinguishers, lockers, doors, and display cases should be recessed in the interest of student safety (Fig. 10).

Acoustical properties are desirable to reduce hall noise. Corridors should be well lighted, with emergency provision in the event of main power failure. Floor covering should be durable, nonskid, and easy to maintain.

The maximum length of unbroken corridors should not exceed 150 to 200 ft. Longer sections give an undesirable perspective.

Stair treads

Standard dimensions of stair treads and risers should be used in schools. Odd dimensions increase the stair hazards for children as well as adults. Wax used on classroom and corridor floors may be deposited on stair treads by students' shoes. One way to reduce this hazard is to de-

sign a tread that will give traction regardless of wax application. Inserted carborundum treads have proved adequate (Fig. 11). Surface-mounted strips are unsatisfactory.

Handrails

Handrails are necessary on both sides of stairways in accordance with the National Building Code. They should be installed with attachment brackets permanently anchored in the masonry wall (Fig. 12). Brackets anchored with lead, wood, or leather expansion bolts often result in unsafe support and considerable maintenance.

Doors

Boys and girls are not expected to use caution in opening and closing doors. The hazard of striking students with doors can be reduced by including a vision panel in the door (Fig. 13) and by recessing the door. The location of this panel should be in proportion to the varying heights of children. Use of tempered or wire glass will provide safety.

Vision panels placed next to doors allow students to see someone approaching the door from the opposite direction. These

panels should be designed with opaque sections near the floor and mullions at suitable intervals to clearly identify them as windows, not passageways.

Covered walkways to accommodate interbuilding traffic should be designed to protect students and not for appearance alone. The roof deck should be wide and low. Provision should be made to carry off roof water. Proper outside lighting will be necessary under the roof deck.

WORKING HEIGHTS FOR STUDENTS

Table 3 can be used as a general guide to acceptable working heights for elementary and junior and senior high school children. There is a large variation in the size of children within a particular classroom group and in various geographical sections of the country. The architect should obtain the median child height in the particular community and select minimum, optimum, or maximum heights as indicated.

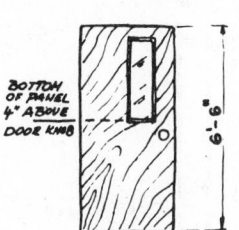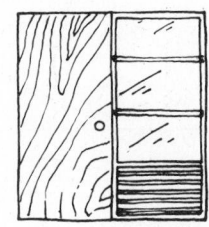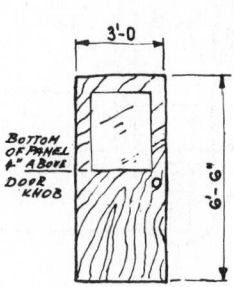

Fig. 13

Table 3. Working heights in inches for elementary and secondary school children

Item	Elementary									Junior high			Senior high		
	Kindergarten			Grades 1–3			Grades 4–6			Grades 7–9			Grades 10–12		
	Min.	Optimum	Max.	Min.	Optimum	Max.	Min.	Optimum	Max.	Min.	Optimum	Max.	Min.	Optimum	Max.
Cabinet, display (top)		54			56			66			74			77	
Cabinet, display (bottom)		26			29			34			38			39	
Cabinet, pupil use (top)			50			56			65			74			79
Chairs and bench	10	11	11	10	12	13	12	14	16	13	15	17	14	16	18
Chalkboard (top)	68	70	73	72	73	74	76	77	78	79	80	82	80	82	84
Chalkboard (bottom and chalkrail)	20	22	25	24	25	26	28	29	30	31	32	34	32	34	36
Counter, cafeteria	21	27	32	25	31	34	29	36	39	32	40	45	33	42	48
Counter, classroom work (standing)	20	24	26	24	26	29	28	30	34	31	34	38	32	36	39
Counter, general office	20	27	32	24	31	34	28	36	39	31	40	45	32	42	49
Desk and table, classroom	17	18	19	18	20	22	21	23	25	23	26	28	24	27	29
Desk, typing											26			26	
Door knob	19	27	32	24	31	35	28	36	40	30	40	46	31	42	49
Drinking fountain	20	24	27	24	27	29	28	32	34	32	36	40	32	40	44
Fire extinguisher (tank)*															
Hook, coat	32	36	48	38	41	51	47	48	58	53	54	64	54	55	68
Lavatory and sink	20	23	25	24	26	27	28	29	31	32	33	35	32	35	38
Light switch	27	27	46	31	35	49	36	40	56	40	46	64	42	50	68
Mirror, lower edge		35				38			43			48			52
Mirror, upper edge	46			56			65			71			71		
Panic bar	21	27	32	25	31	34	29	36	39	32	40	45	33	42	48
Pencil sharpener	20	27	33	25	31	35	28	36	40	32	40	46	32	42	49
Rail, hand and directional	20	21	32	24	24	34	28	29	39	31	32	45	32	33	48
Shelf, hat and books		41	48		46	51		54	58		60	64		62	68
Soap dispenser	20	27	33	25	31	35	28	36	40	32	40	46	32	42	49
Stool, drawing		19			21			26			28			29	
Table, drawing		26			29			34			38			39	
Table and bench, work (standing)	25	26	28	26	29	32	30	34	38	36	38	41	37	39	42
Tackboard (top)	72	84		72	84		72	84		72	84		72	84	
Tackboard (bottom)	20	22	25	24	25	26	28	29	30	31	32	34	32	34	36
Telephone, wall mounted			35			37			43			48			52
Toilet stall, top of partition	44	44		52	52		61	61		67	67		69	69	
Towel dispenser	23	27	46	28	31	49	33	36	56	37	40	64	37	42	68
Urinal (bottom)				3	3–15	17	3	3–17	20	4	4–18	22	4	4–19	24
Wainscotting	54	54	54	54	54	54	54	54	54	60	60	60	60	60	60
Water closet (seat)	10	10½	12	11	11½	12	13	13½	14	14	14½	15	14½	15	15
Window ledge		29			30			34			38			41	

Recessed at baseboard height.

PUPIL CAPACITY

Elementary schools

Before any calculation of school capacity can be made, the school system must have an educational policy establishing the optimum capacity of classrooms. In many schools this figure is set at 27 pupils, which, when used as an average class size, may mean that some rooms will exceed this number. Kindergartens may be set at 20 pupils in each of the morning and afternoon sessions.

Some schools do not like to exceed 25 pupils per class. It is frequently recommended that when a class goes to 32 pupils it be divided into two sections with two teachers. It is also advisable in determining the capacity of an elementary school to consider each grade separately so that there will be no single classroom housing more than one grade.

High schools

Determining capacity on the secondary school level is considerably more complex than on the elementary school level. Capacity in a good secondary school reflects the kind of educational program and the educational goals of the community.

The character of the classroom and the subject are determinants of the classroom

Table 4. Classroom capacity for high schools

Type of space	No. of units	Capacity of units	Total capacity
Classroom	19	x 27	513
Science laboratory	3	x 25	75
Commercial education	4	x 25	100
Home economics	2	x 25	50
Art	1	x 25	25
Shop	3	x 20	60
Band or chorus	2	x 35	70
Gymnasium, playroom	1	x 35	35
Gymnasium with partition	1	x 70	70
General education laboratory or study hall		x 35	
		Maximum capacity:	998
	Optimum capacity at 80 per cent utilization:		798

size. Physical education classes may run to 35 or 40 students; shop classes should not exceed 20 students. Many other areas should not exceed 25 students and might, more likely, hold 20 pupils, including science rooms, homemaking, and fine arts. These class sizes may be adjusted from community to community, but for comparative purposes it would be helpful to maintain a standard formula for determining capacity (Table 4 and Schedule 1).

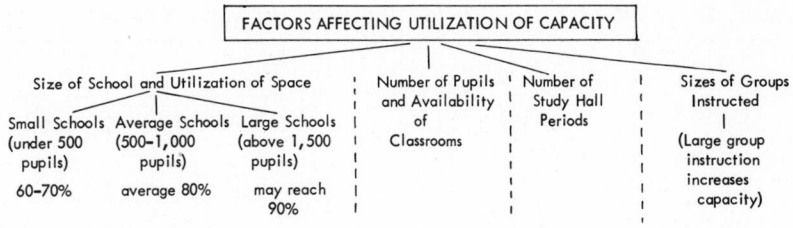

FACTORS AFFECTING UTILIZATION OF CAPACITY			
Size of School and Utilization of Space	Number of Pupils and Availability of Classrooms	Number of Study Hall Periods	Sizes of Groups Instructed

Small Schools (under 500 pupils)	Average Schools (500–1,000 pupils)	Large Schools (above 1,500 pupils)
60–70%	average 80%	may reach 90%

(Large group instruction increases capacity)

STUDENT LOCKERS

Many different solutions have been developed to solve the problem of storing coats and personal belongings of students. In the elementary school, proximity to the homeroom for ease of teacher supervision is important. Lockers in the high school should be located for easy access between periods. Circulation in the locker areas should be sufficiently adequate to prevent congestion. It is generally necessary to provide arrangements whereby students may lock up personal belongings and books. Most high schools also provide lockers with locks for coats. However, others have been successful in providing small security lockers and open coat racks.

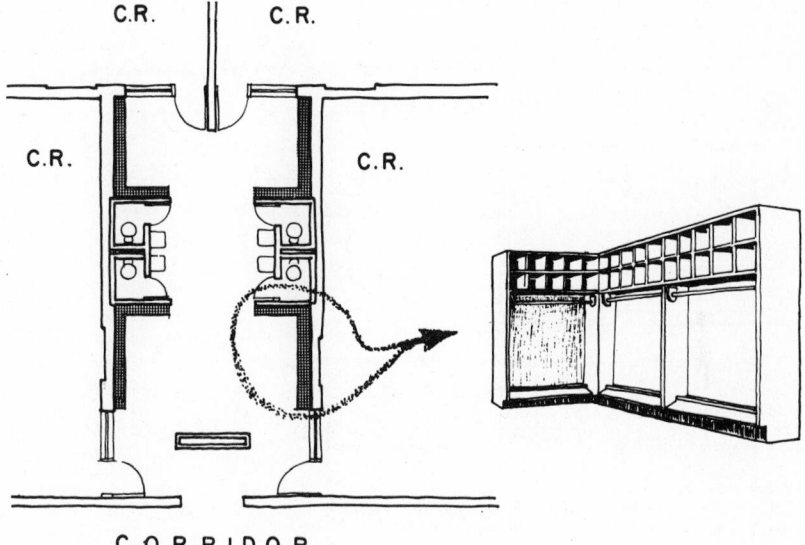

C.R. C.R.

C.R. C.R.

CORRIDOR

Fig. 14

Figure 14 shows one way of storing coats, boots, and small personal articles in a four-classroom unit of an elementary school. Ventilation can be provided economically. This type of open cubicle should have permanently attached coat hangers. The boot rack should be constructed of materials resistant to water and dirt.

Another way of storing coats is within a classroom (Fig. 15), where the storage area serves also for passage of pupils. The area is convenient for teacher supervision. The coat and toilet areas for all four classrooms are located together, permitting economical utilities.

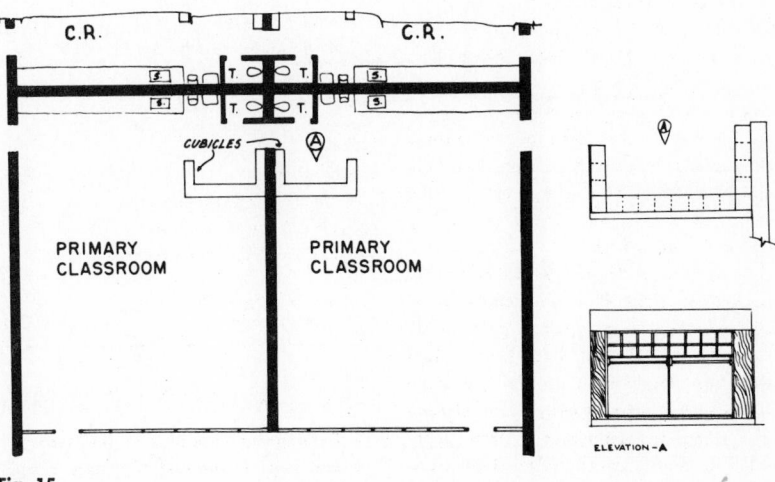

C.R. C.R.

CUBICLES

PRIMARY CLASSROOM

PRIMARY CLASSROOM

ELEVATION-A

Fig. 15

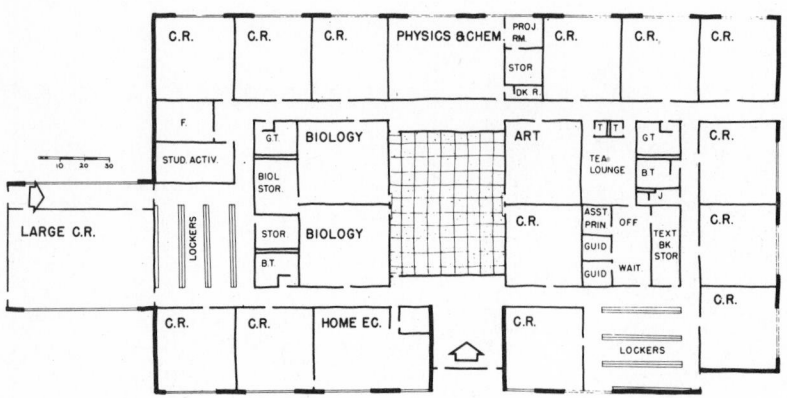

Fig. 16 A. G. Odell, Jr. and Associates, Architects

Lockers may be concentrated in several conveniently located areas (Fig. 16). These areas are completely open and the wide spaces between rows provide comfortable circulation. This type of locker arrangement eliminates congestion in corridors and frees corridor walls for display and vision panels. As locker alcoves are difficult to supervise, it is essential to provide complete circulation around the entire space.

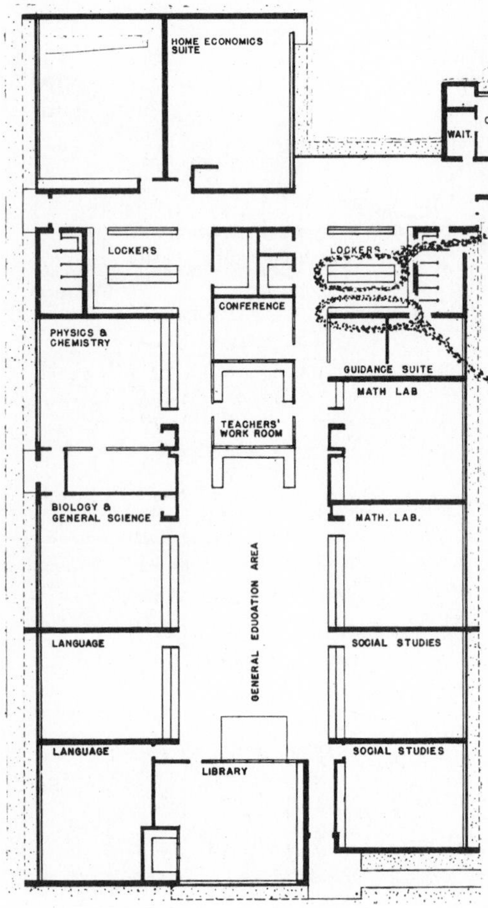

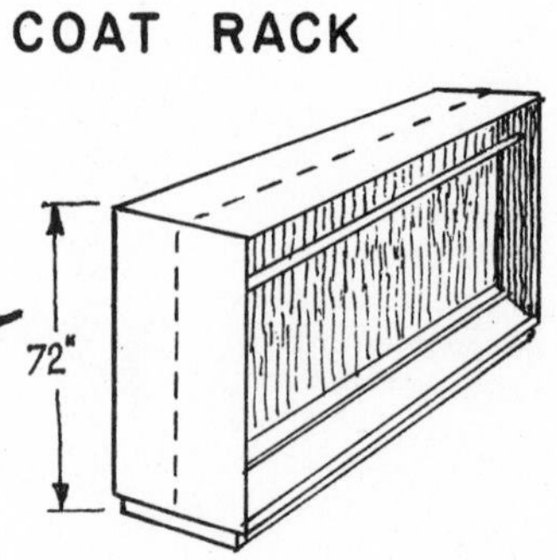

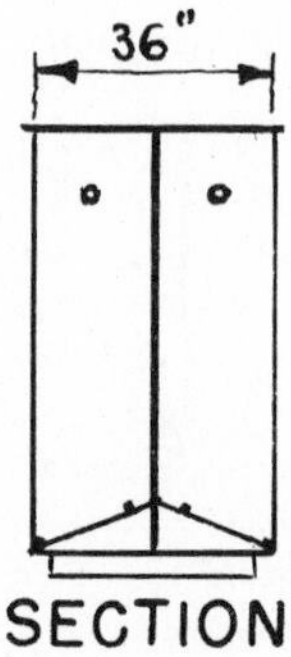

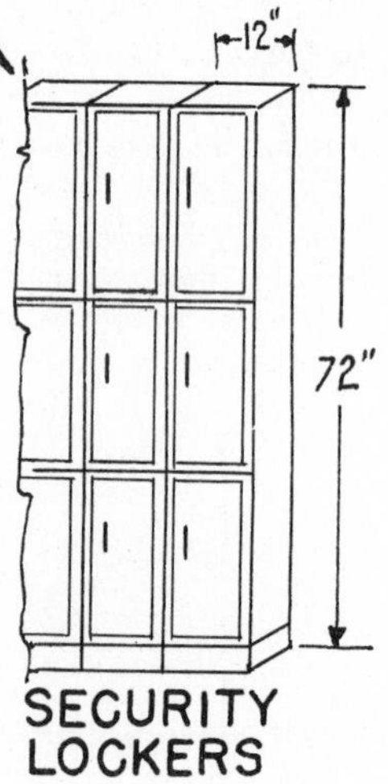

COAT RACK

72"

36"

SECTION

Fig. 17 Chapman and Leffler, Architects

Another way of treating locker installation in a high school is shown in Fig. 17. The lockers have been concentrated in two areas near the entrance and student center. The areas have been left open with ample space for comfortable circulation. Restrooms are adjacent to the locker area, which may reduce corridor traffic and save student time. Each student is assigned a security locker for books and personal items. Coats and boots are stored in open coat racks.

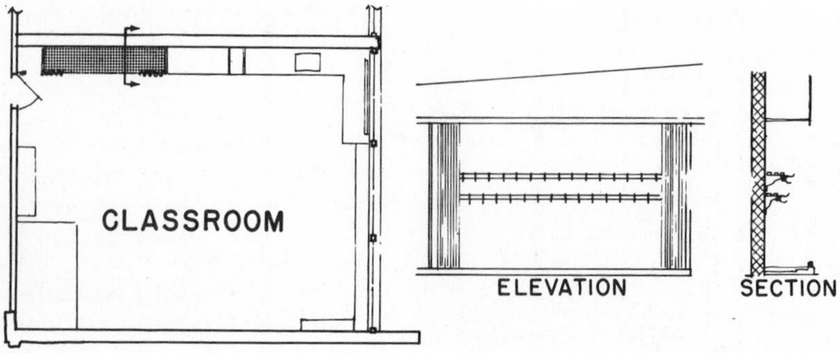

12"

72"

SECURITY LOCKERS

CLASSROOM

ELEVATION

SECTION

Fig. 18

Coat storage (Fig. 18) in a classroom can be closed off by means of a folding partition. This arrangement gives students easy access to wraps. The area is convenient to supervise and the classroom area provides space for dressing and circulation. Mechanical ventilation is needed to dry wet clothing and avoid odors. However, this plan uses up wall space that might better be used for educational purposes.

Fig. 19

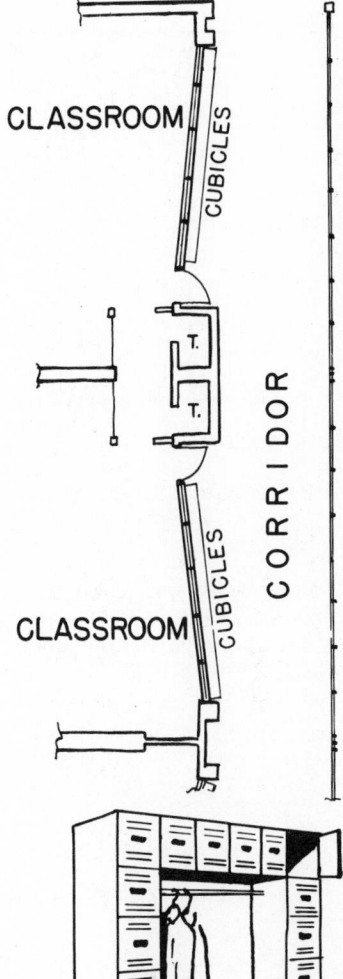

CLASSROOM

CUBICLES

CLASSROOM

CUBICLES

CORRIDOR

Fig. 21

The type of storage shown in Fig. 19 is usually found in elementary schools where open cubicles are desirable. These units are located on the classroom side of a single-loaded corridor for convenient supervision. The walls have been splayed to relieve corridor congestion during the arrival and dismissal of children. The splayed wall also provides a recess for the classroom door.

The locker unit (Fig. 21) is used as a space saver. These units give an economical approach to coat storage. Each student may be assigned a personal locker for books and small personal belongings. The coats are hung on permanently attached hangers. This unit permits natural air circulation for drying coats and is convenient to supervise.

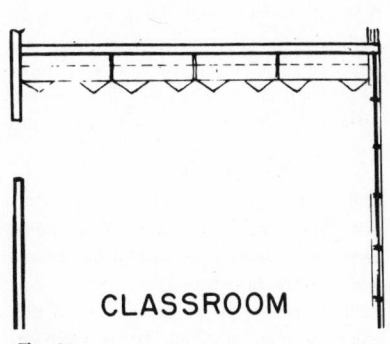

CLASSROOM

Fig. 20

In Fig. 20, panels fold to provide the doors on the wardrobe. Mechanical ventilation is essential. The large amount of wall area used by this system may introduce serious handicaps in the use of the room for teaching purposes.

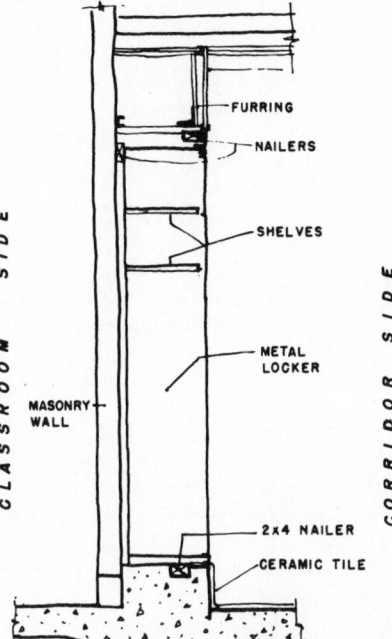

FURRING
NAILERS
SHELVES
METAL LOCKER
MASONRY WALL
CLASSROOM SIDE
CORRIDOR SIDE
2x4 NAILER
CERAMIC TILE

FRONT ELEVATION OF RECESSED LOCKERS

Fig. 22

The detail to the left shows the recessed corridor lockers, which are seen above in elevation (Fig. 22). The ceramic tile base is used to simplify floor maintenance. The ceiling is furred down to eliminate the accumulation of dust and trash on top of the lockers. These units can be ventilated by pulling air through lower front vents and into the plenum above.

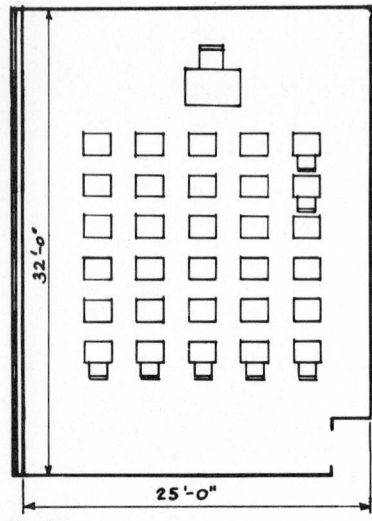

Fig. 23

The classroom layout in Fig. 23 represents a standard size room with a recessed corridor door and a standard seating arrangement.

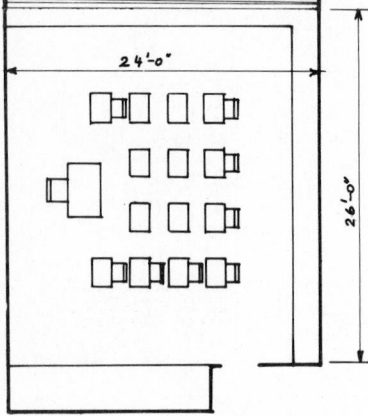

Fig. 24

Figure 24 shows a room designed for ten to fifteen pupils. Rooms of this size can be used for a variety of purposes, such as conference room, student council room, or for small class groups.

CLASSROOMS

The development of the teaching process, extension of classroom activities, and use of group techniques within the classroom have led to new classroom design in recent years. Square classrooms have been proving more satisfactory than rectangular ones. The area of the classroom is increasing with the realization that small classrooms of the past have been the greatest handicap to the improvement of the educational program.

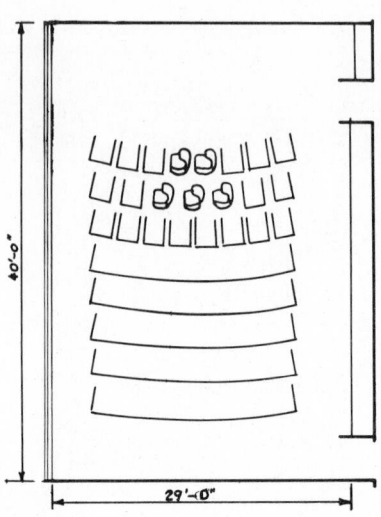

Fig. 25

The large group lecture and demonstration room in Fig. 25 is provided with 64 tablet-armed chairs. Proximity to the demonstration table is important for all students. Seats should be tiered for better visibility. In the case of science demonstration, the demonstration table should be immediately adjacent to the preparation room. Natural lighting is generally undesirable but, if required, provision should be made for automatic operation of blinds. The light switch should be near the demonstration table.[1]

[1] *Scale of all plans on this page is* 1/16 *in. equals 1 ft; layouts are by American Seating Co.*

Recommended classroom sizes for elementary schools range from 850 to 1,150 sq ft. High school classrooms may range from 750 to 900 sq ft. In some instances where large group teaching or team teaching is taking place, double classrooms may be desirable. In other instances, regular classrooms may be divided by the use of a folding partition which has a satisfactory acoustical separation.

GENERAL REQUIREMENTS FOR ALL CLASSROOMS

Design

1. Sufficient space is needed near the front of the room for setting up audio-visual equipment, such as projection screens and charts.

2. Ceilings should be a maximum of 9½ ft high.

3. Light from windows should, if possible, come over a pupil's left shoulder. No teacher should be required to face the windows when addressing the class from the normal teaching position.

4. Ceilings and/or walls should be acoustically treated.

5. Floors should have a cushioning material.

Location

The classroom should have as quiet a location as possible, away from noisy outdoor areas. Ease of access to specialized facilities outside the academic unit should be ensured.

Light control

Color films, television, and slides are becoming more and more widely used. Darkening curtains or light-tight blinds should be provided for light control in all teaching areas. The architect should give careful consideration to the problem of darkening clerestories, skylights, and other sources of light. Consideration might be given to the type of venetian blinds that ride in side channels and are easier to operate and to clean than other blinds.

Electrical services

1. A double electric outlet should be located on each of the three interior walls, and above all counters for use with equipment such as projectors and phonographs. Locations near sinks should be avoided.

2. Eight-inch clocks should be placed in all educational rooms.

3. A fire-alarm system is required.

4. Light switches should be located at the door. It is suggested that switches for corridor lighting be located so that pupils do not have access to them.

5. In planning the building, consideration should be given to ease of wiring a coaxial cable for television, if it will be needed later. Conduit is not recommended, but access to furred ceilings above corridors for this purpose would be desirable. Television reception from broadcast stations may be desirable in large group classrooms. Antennas might be provided here and at other selected points in the building.

6. Telephone service will be required to administrative offices and to other critical points in the school.

Doors

1. Doors should be placed at the front of the classroom and should be recessed so that they do not protrude into the corridor.

2. Thresholds should be avoided so that equipment on wheeled tables, such as mounted movie projectors, can be rolled in and out easily.

3. All doors should have a vision panel of tempered or wire glass.

4. Door hardware should be such that doors cannot be locked from inside the classroom.

Two large classrooms separated by a movable partition are shown in Fig. 26. When the folding door is open these rooms become an assembly room or an area for large group instruction. Caution should be exercised when selecting a folding door. It should be easy to operate and it should provide suitable acoustical properties. Rooms of this type should have two exits, one for each area.

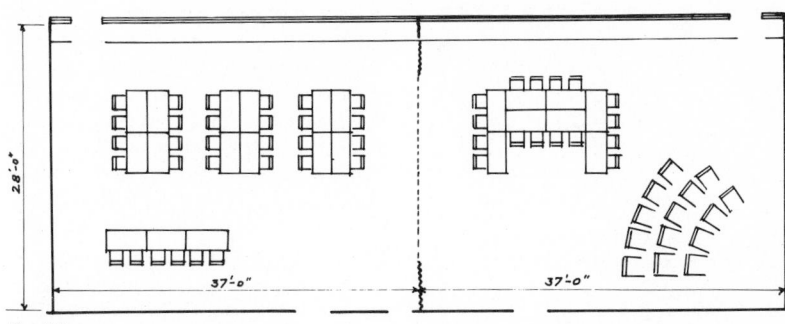

Fig. 26

The split-level plan of the Dundee Elementary School in Greenwich, Conn. (Fig. 27), shows classroom space needed for a team-teaching program. Team teaching, a relatively new technique, is being used in both the elementary and the high school level. The principal requirement for building facilities in team-teaching programs is flexibility—the ability to have space for small, average, and large-size classes, and to be able to shift these spaces from hour to hour. In this type of school the rooms may be constant or variable in size, and in both categories there are small, average, and large-size groups. The illustration indicates how this has been done by the installation of electrically operated folding partitions in many of the rooms. Under this program the movement of pupils is generally much greater than under the homeroom type of elementary program.

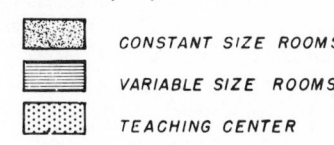

Ample corridors and stairs are essential. This program also indicates the need for compact design to avoid excessive travel time between rooms. The lower portion of the plan is at ground level; the upper portion is one half story higher. Below the upper level are additional classrooms and the administrative offices.

CONSTANT SIZE ROOMS

VARIABLE SIZE ROOMS

TEACHING CENTER

Fig. 27   Perkins and Will, Architects

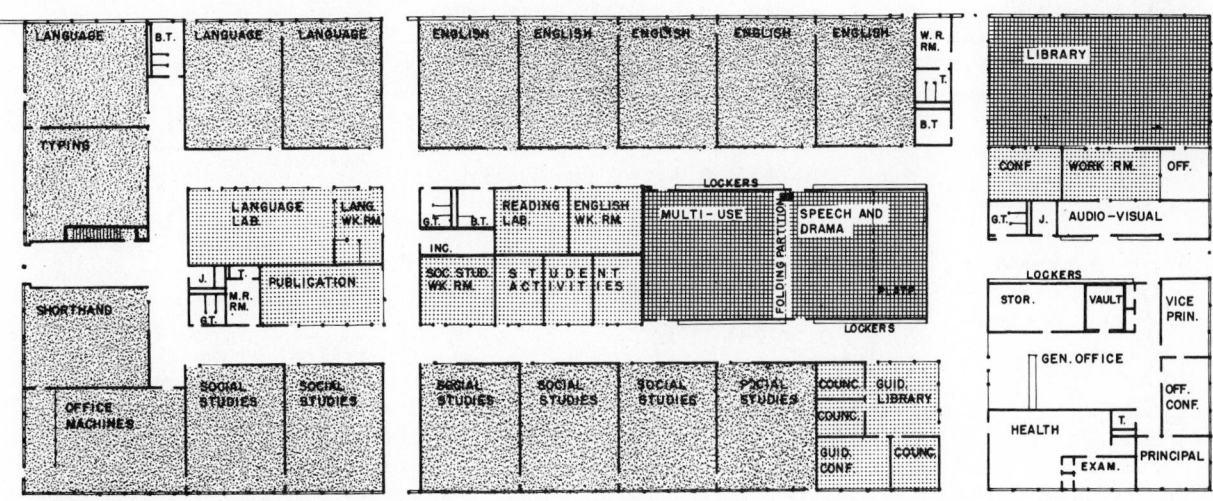

SCALE |⊢⊢⊢⊢⊢|⊢⊢⊢⊢⊢⊢⊢⊢⊢⊢⊢| FEET
       10 5 0 10   20   30 40

LEGEND

INDIVIDUAL AND SMALL GROUP FACILITIES

MEDIUM SIZE GROUP FACILITIES

LARGE GROUP FACILITIES

Fig. 28   Warren H. Ashley, Architect

This plan of the Concord-Carlisle Regional High School, Concord, Mass. (Fig. 28), gives an indication of the variation in sizes of rooms needed to support a modern comprehensive program. Adaptation of room sizes to the needs of the class ensures maximum use of space.

Grouping of students within classes is quite common and calls for the availability of small spaces where small groups from classes may meet informally. Likewise, there are many occasions when it is desirable to join two or more classes for a large group experience.

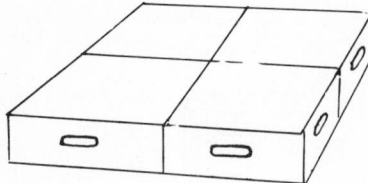

TYPICAL ASSEMBLY: 4 - PIECE PLATFORM

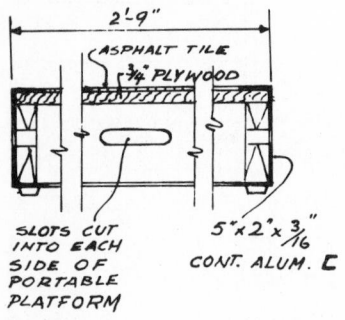

2'-9"

ASPHALT TILE

¾ PLYWOOD

SLOTS CUT INTO EACH SIDE OF PORTABLE PLATFORM

5"x 2"x 3/16" CONT. ALUM. ⊏

Fig. 29

A small platform unit (Fig. 29) is recommended for elementary classrooms. It is portable and designed in four sections. The sections may be used together or separately for a variety of educational activities. This portable unit keeps the floor area flexible, whereas a permanent built-in platform limits the use of a section of the classroom.

CLASSROOM FACILITIES

Modern teaching procedures require more complex classroom facilities than were considered necessary in the past. Provision should be made for books, audio-visual equipment, recorders, television, tack space, and writing surfaces.

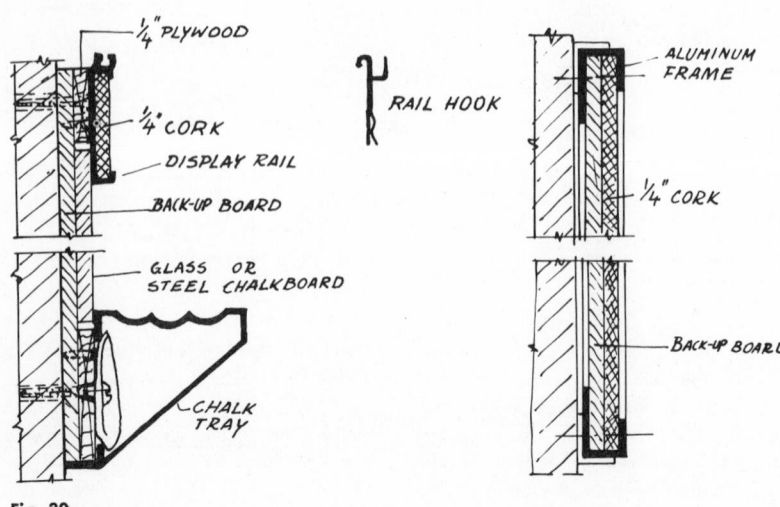

¼" PLYWOOD

¼" CORK

DISPLAY RAIL

BACK-UP BOARD

GLASS OR STEEL CHALKBOARD

CHALK TRAY

RAIL HOOK

ALUMINUM FRAME

¼" CORK

BACK-UP BOARD

Fig. 30

Many communities are building a self-contained classroom in elementary schools. This room requires facilities for teaching various subjects, such as English, mathematics, reading, arts and crafts, music, social studies, and science. This area is used exclusively by one group of pupils. Other schools provide certain facilities in special areas for use by numerous classroom groups. This design, however, may limit the program because it becomes necessary for groups to conform to a time schedule.

The elementary classroom will require storage for such items as science projects and equipment, reference books, paints, paper, posters, maps, globes, coats, boots, audio-visual equipment, records, lunches, and small playground equipment. For kindergarten and primary grades, toilets and coat storage areas located in or adjacent to the classroom are convenient for the teacher to assist the smaller children. Central toilet facilities should be provided for the intermediate grades and above. Drinking fountains in or adjacent to classrooms are desirable.

Several educational activities require such facilities as sink, counter work area, portable stage, hot and cold water, earth bed, and special furniture. Provision should be made for such items in accordance with the educational program when the building is planned.

Storage needs in high school

1. Storage space for each group using the classroom should be provided with locks.

2. Storage is needed for the following items: Supplies, such as paper and pencils; books and magazines; special equipment for the subject taught in the room (such as blueprints for mechanical drawing, globes and paper-back reprints for social studies, and compasses and protractors for mathematics); teacher's coat and personal belongings, if not provided for elsewhere.

3. A standard storage closet, either of metal or wood, is recommended for all classrooms.

Chalkboard and tackboard

1. The demands for chalkboard and tackboard will vary from subject to subject in the high school. Generally, English and mathematics require more chalkboard than do the social studies, which in turn require more tackboard. The minimum amount of chalkboard in any classroom should be 16 lin ft, and up to 48 lin ft could be used to advantage in many mathematics rooms. Approximately 16 to 32 lin ft. of tackboard should be provided.

2. A display rail extending the entire length of the chalkboard is an essential teaching aid. Such a display rail should have hooks with clip fasteners. Provision might also be made for hanging pictures, maps, and charts on other walls of the room. Embedded picture molding should be installed on three walls at a suitable height.

3. Consider installing display cabinets to serve as classroom showcases.

Chalkboard installation is of great importance. For each room, consideration should be given to the type, amount, height, and necessary attachments. The recommended mounting heights can be determined by reviewing the "working heights" chart (Table 3).

Chalkboard may be purchased in several different materials. Glass, slate, and porcelain-enameled steel have proved satisfactory; however, asbestos-cement may be more economical. Avoid hardboard types. If the steel type is used, a three-coat finish will give more lasting results. The chalk tray should be designed for easy cleaning. A map rail is needed, complete with hooks and cork strip (Figs. 30 and 31).

Corkboard should be distributed throughout the school. Display of educational materials will support the educational program. Sixteen-foot sections are recommended for most classrooms and placed for easy viewing by students. The cork should be at least ¼ in. thick if staples or thumbtacks are used for mounting displays (Fig. 31).

A pegboard may be used to display three-dimensional objects on brackets, hooks, or shelves. The thickness of the board should be no less than ¼ in.; the tempered grade will give better service.

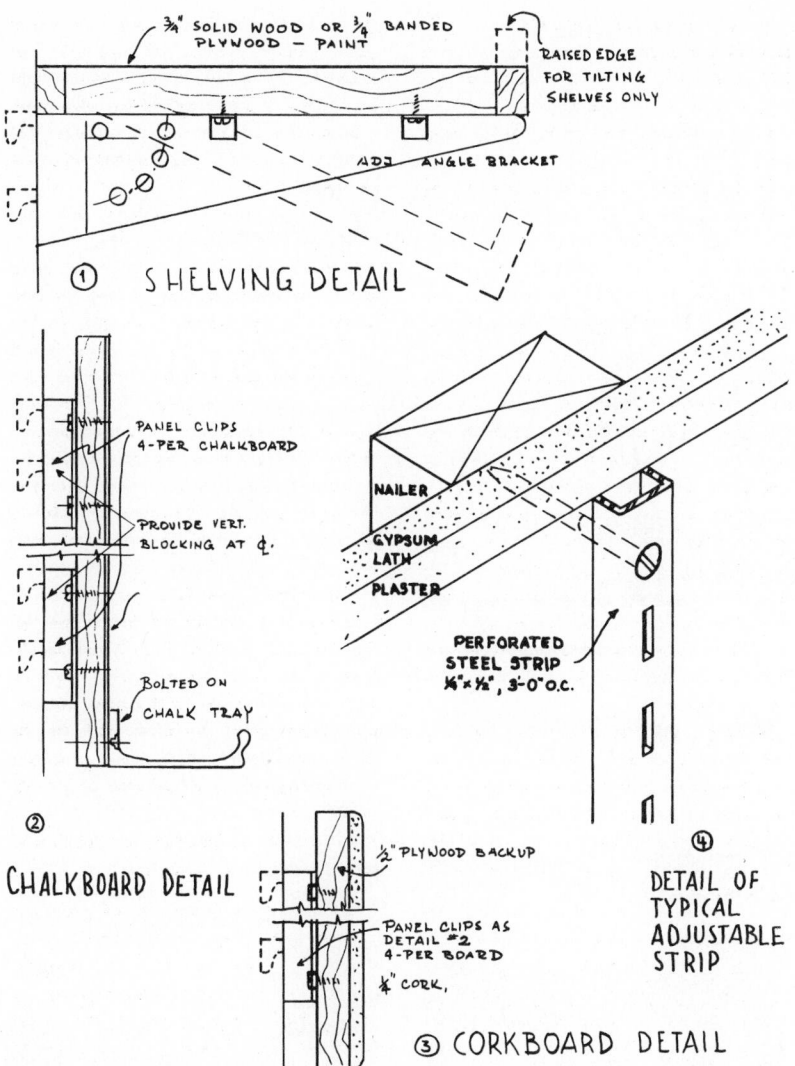

¾" SOLID WOOD OR ¾" BANDED PLYWOOD — PAINT

RAISED EDGE FOR TILTING SHELVES ONLY

ADJ. ANGLE BRACKET

① SHELVING DETAIL

PANEL CLIPS 4-PER CHALKBOARD

PROVIDE VERT. BLOCKING AT ₵.

BOLTED ON CHALK TRAY

NAILER

GYPSUM LATH

PLASTER

PERFORATED STEEL STRIP ¼"×½", 3'-0" O.C.

② CHALKBOARD DETAIL

½" PLYWOOD BACKUP

PANEL CLIPS AS DETAIL #2 4-PER BOARD

¼" CORK

④ DETAIL OF TYPICAL ADJUSTABLE STRIP

③ CORKBOARD DETAIL

Fig. 31

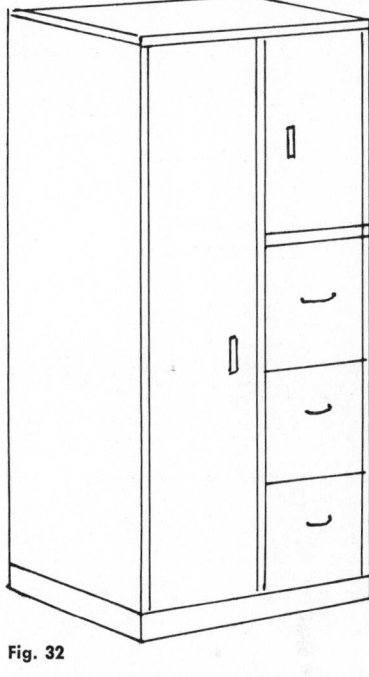

Fig. 32

A high degree of flexibility in the use of wall area can be obtained by building in adjustable hanging strips (Fig. 31).

Steel cabinet (Fig. 32) is a combination of teacher's wardrobe, file drawers, and a small cabinet for personal belongings. This unit should be equipped with a locking device. It can be built into a wall, set in a recess or corner of the classroom. A coat hanger rod and mirror should be included on the wardrobe side.

The unit in Fig. 33 may be used for storing large charts (24 by 48 in.), maps, graphs, large paper, paintings, projects, and audio-visual equipment. The lower half includes long, deep drawers and the top section provides a very flexible space with adjustable shelving. This unit will have its greatest use in elementary schools.

The storage unit in Fig. 34 serves also as a work counter and sink. The height is determined by the size of students. The sliding doors are safer and need less maintenance than swinging doors. The top and splashboard should be a durable plastic.

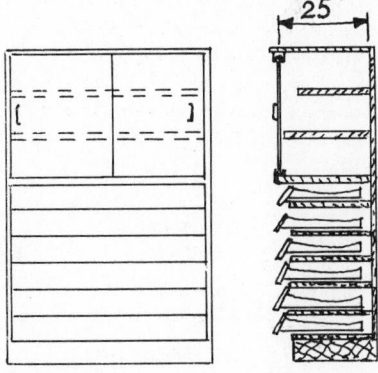

25"

Fig. 33

Figure 35 shows shelving or base cabinets along a window wall. The storage unit makes good use of this area and provides counter space for plants and displays. The units may be prefabricated or custom built.

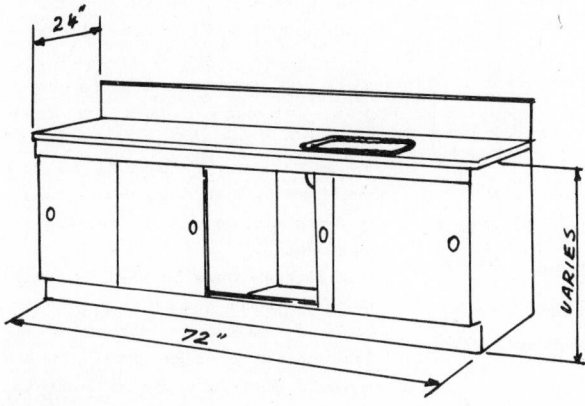

24"

72"

VARIES

Fig. 34

SHELVING   UNIVENT   SHELVING

CLASSROOM

Fig. 35

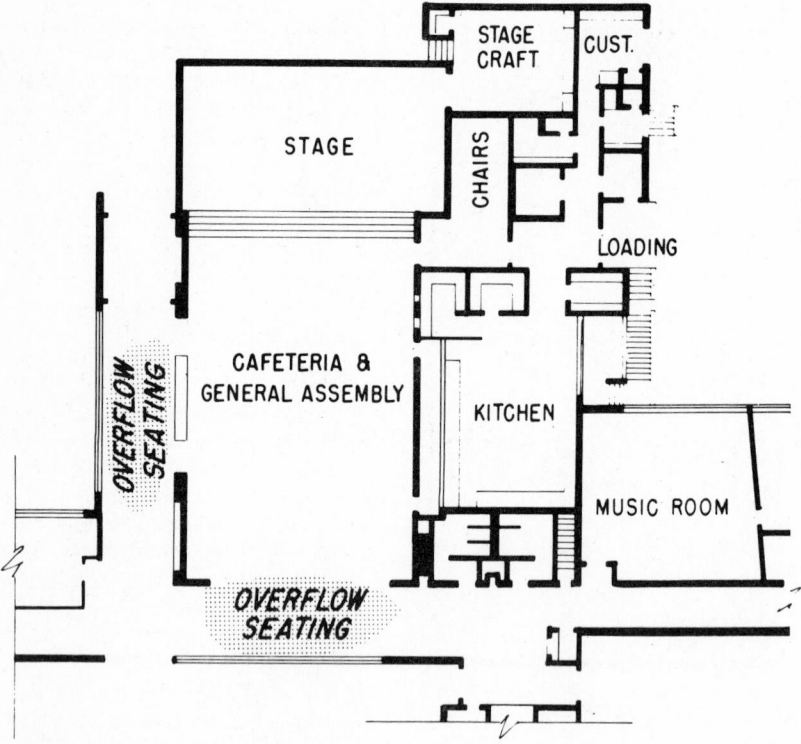

Fig. 36 *Chapman and Leffler, Architects*

MULTIPURPOSE ROOM

The following information and drawings are primarily concerned with large areas in school buildings which are designed and equipped for two or more group activities. The most frequently used room combinations include assembly-cafeteria, assembly-cafeteria-gymnasium, assembly-gymnasium, and a student activity area where many small learning centers may operate at one time.

Assembly-cafeteria

The assembly-cafeteria combination is popular because the room can be designed with a pleasing environment for both eating and assembly. This type of room is also more adaptable to scheduling without limiting other phases of the educational program.

The room should be furnished with tables that can be quickly moved into a nearby storage area. A large portable folding unit containing table and benches has proved satisfactory for elementary schools. Tables that fold into the wall are also available. Many high schools prefer the smaller folding table and stacking chairs, which permit a more informal and flexible arrangement.

This type of room should have a stage, stage curtain, backdrops, and adequate lighting for dramatic presentations.

Student traffic flow in this area should be planned. Minimum cross traffic is essential during the lunch period when children are carrying food. During student assembly periods good circulation may reduce discipline problems.

Assembly-cafeteria-gymnasium

The assembly-cafeteria-gymnasium combination can be found in schools where limited funds are available. This arrangement may seriously curtail the educational program. The time necessary to set up the cafeteria furniture, feed the children, clean the room, and remove the cafeteria furniture will consume a large portion of the school day. The remaining time available for physical and assembly activities may be insufficient for a good program. It is also difficult for the architect to design a room in which the atmosphere is conducive to dining, physical education, and assembly productions.

Assembly-gymnasium

The assembly-gymnasium combination is a possible solution to seating the total student enrollment when a small or no auditorium is available. This area should

The layout in Fig. 36 was designed for a small high school. As the student enrollments increase and additional classrooms are built, the stage will be removed and this area converted to dining. The room is located at the main entrance to the building, with a combined corridor and lounge. The chair and table storage is well placed with direct access to the service entrance. The room is opened up to the two wide corridors—an arrangement that permits overflow seating during special assemblies or public performances. The openings can be closed with drapes when desired. The openness reduces traffic congestion and discipline problems.

This cafeteria-assembly room (Fig. 37) is opened up on two sides, with the kitchen at one end. Overflow seating is available on the corridor side. The plan provides space for an adequate program within a limited budget.

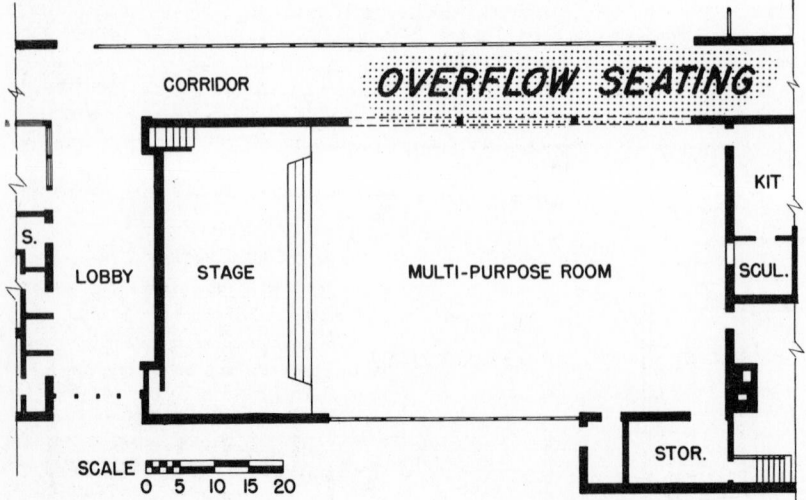

Fig. 37 *Chapman and Leffler, Architects*

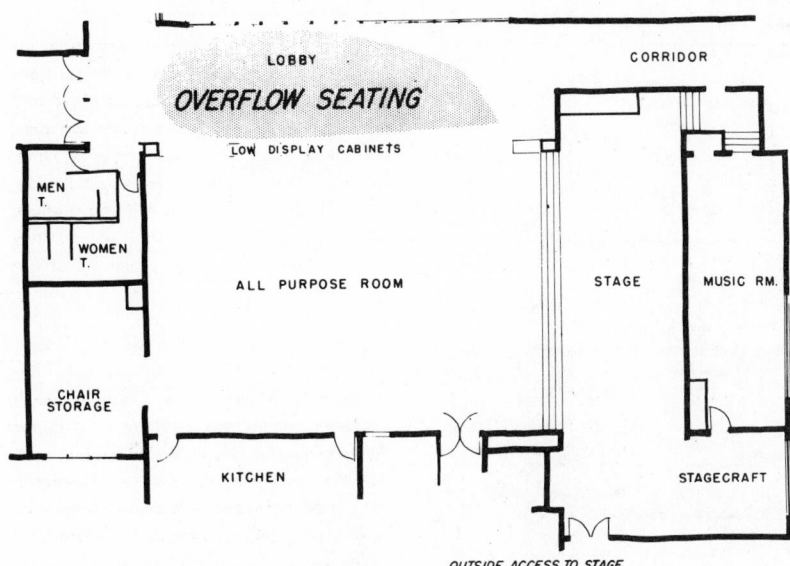

Fig. 38 *Chapman and Leffler, Architects*

Adequate chair storage is provided in this cafeteria-assembly combination (Fig. 38) for an elementary school. The low display can be moved and overflow seating is available in the lobby corridor. Public toilets are well placed. The stage has outside and inside access independent of the main room. The music room and the stagecraft area provide adequate space for school or public performance preparation.

PHYSICAL EDUCATION

The need for a well-developed physical education program is becoming increasingly apparent. Space should be provided for development of individual skills, team play, collective work, and community recreation programs. Elementary schools generally require one small gymnasium; secondary schools need a larger gymnasium, usually supplied with folding partitions, to enable boys and girls to use the facilities simultaneously. Two double gymnasiums are often needed for schools of 800 or more students. Schools with enrollments of 1,500 or more students may need a total of six teaching stations.

be designed with a stage that can also be used for physical activity. Storage space will be needed for chairs, gymnasium equipment, and stage equipment. Acoustics, lighting, ventilation, and traffic flow should be adequate for assembly and physical education. This arrangement is not considered as satisfactory as the assembly-cafeteria combination.

The gymnasium in Fig. 40 includes separate facilities for boys and girls. The larger boys' gymnasium is also used for competitive sports with public spectators. The auxiliary spaces and utilities are combined in the area between the two gymnasiums and offer maximum coordination and supervision.

The gymnasium-assembly combination shown in Fig. 39 provides chair storage, gymnasium storage, stage, and exercise rooms. The large gymnasium has a large folding door which provides two teacher stations. The stage can be divided with a folding door to provide two more stations. Access to shower rooms is on either side of the stage, and the stage can be entered from the corridor on either side. Folding bleachers close the proscenium opening when the stage is used as exercise rooms.

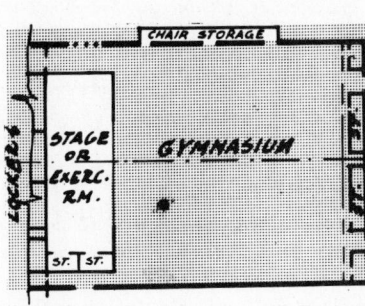

Fig. 39

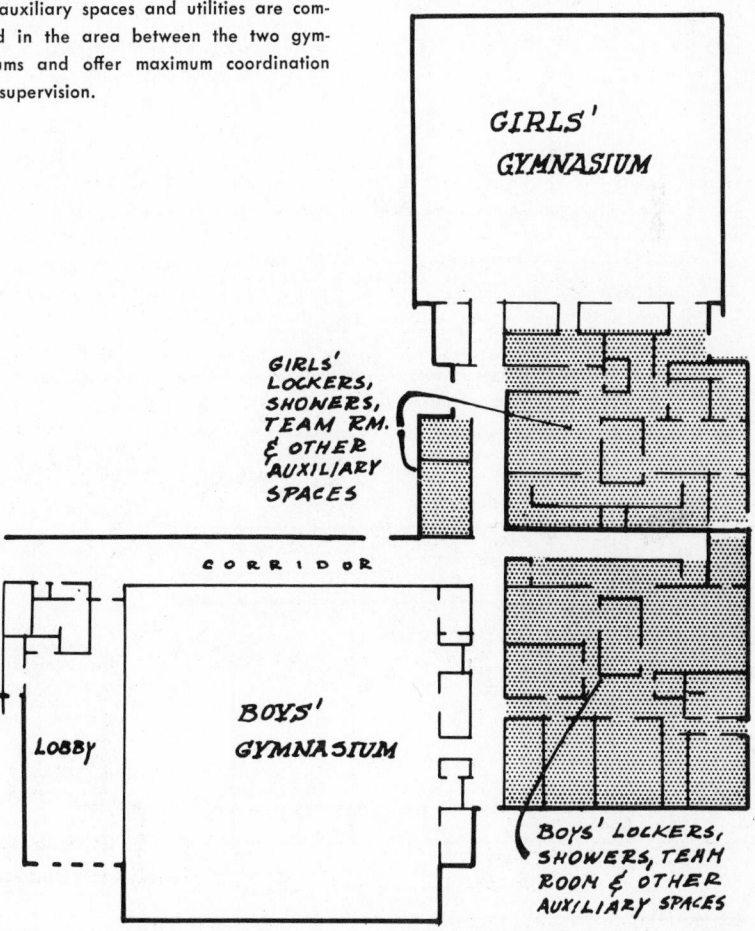

Fig. 40 *David Ludlow, Architect*

Table 5. Recommended dimensions in feet for gymnasiums

School	W	L	W₁*	L₁*	Seats
Small elementary	36	52			
Large elementary	52	72			
Junior high school*	65	86	42	74	400
Small senior high school†	79	96	50	84	700
Large senior high school†	100	104	50	84	1,500

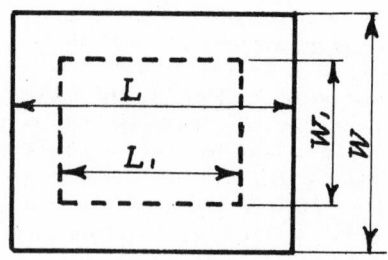

* W_1 and L_1 are dimensions of basketball court.
† Use folding partition.

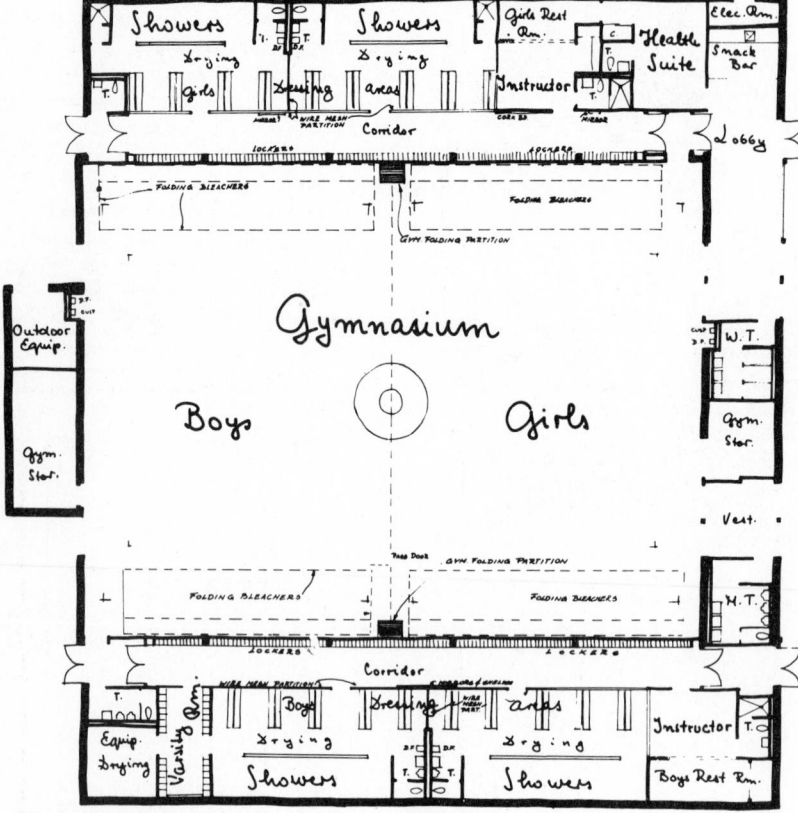

Fig. 41   McLeod and Ferrara, Architects

The gymnasium in Fig. 41 is planned for a high school of 1,200 students. The large area is divided by a folding door, making two group stations. Adequate equipment storage is provided for both stations, and storage space is available for outdoor physical education equipment. Natural lighting is provided on the side walls between the roof of the shower rooms and the roof of the main room.

The lobby area includes public toilets, display board and case, and snack bar for use during off-school hours. The toilets are accessible to boys and girls on the playgrounds.

The gymnasium in Fig. 42 offers good facilities for a varsity or intramural sports program. The small gymnasium can be divided for use by small groups or individuals. It is possible to have three intramural games being played at one time. The team room, locker rooms, and storage rooms are ample to care for an extensive competitive sports program.

The playroom in Fig. 43 was designed for an elementary school that is used extensively by community groups, such as Boy Scouts, Girl Scouts, Cub Scouts, boys' and girls' clubs, junior league competitive sports, garden club, and service organizations. The room can be completely shut off from the rest of the building and used during off-school hours and vacation periods. Access to the toilet is provided from the gymnasium or the playfields.

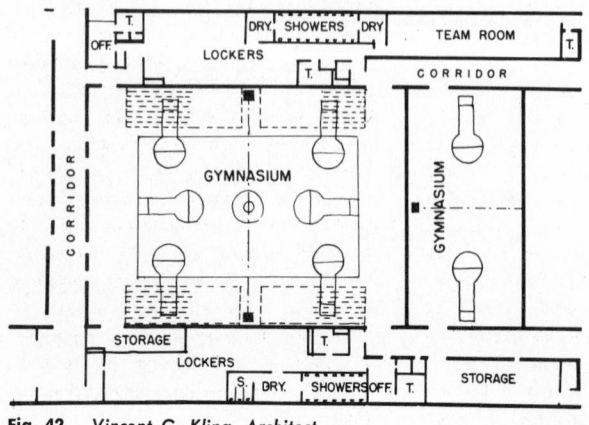

Fig. 42   Vincent G. Kling, Architect

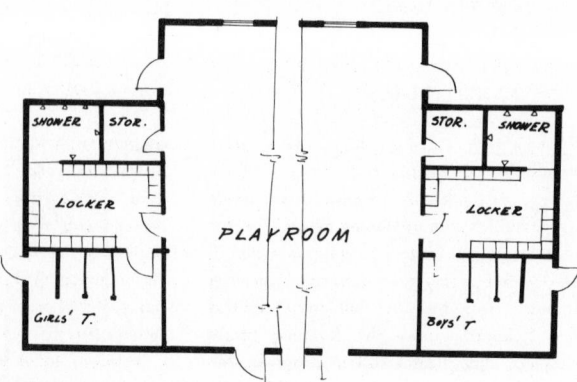

Fig. 43

A few schools have taken advantage of the low cost per cubic foot usually characteristic of fieldhouse construction. The fieldhouse makes available a large unobstructed floor area, easily adaptable to a variety of uses. The floors are often a mixture of clay, sand, and sawdust. Portable wooden floors are needed for tennis and basketball; if space is available, permanent flooring may be used.

The gymnasium should include an 8-ft run-off on either end of the basketball court, with a minimum of 6 ft between the court and side walls. Recommended dimensions for basketball courts and gymnasiums are given in Table 5. See also section on *Recreation Areas*. Floors may be of 1⅛-in. hard maple. The lower section of the walls should be smooth to avoid injury. The upper walls may be of simple materials, such as painted cinder blocks. Ceilings should be acoustically treated. Good lighting and air circulation are essential. Provision must be made to protect students from glass breakage. Windows should be easy to operate by hand or by mechanical means.

The artificial light should be glareless and evenly distributed, providing at least 30 foot-candles of illumination at floor level. Lighting fixtures, heating units, clocks, drinking fountains, and soundspeaker units should be recessed and protected from damage by flying balls and moving gymnasium equipment.

The traffic flow is well organized in the plan in Fig. 44 with a minimum of cross traffic. The exercise gymnasium doubles as spectator area. Public toilets are located in the balcony area, which reduces congestion on the main floor during intermissions. The emergency exit from the balcony level leads directly outdoors.

This gymnasium contains ample space for a good physical education program, with an auxiliary health classroom and first-aid room. Storage space has been planned for both levels.

DRESSING ROOMS, SHOWERS, AND GYMNASIUM STORAGE

Gymnasium dressing rooms and showers should provide ample space and facilities for the maximum size of class. These areas are used for visiting teams as well as for regular classes. Lockers for team use should be located in an area separate from the regular class lockers. Full-length lockers are generally used for hanging street clothing while classes are in progress. Another method is to provide a small security

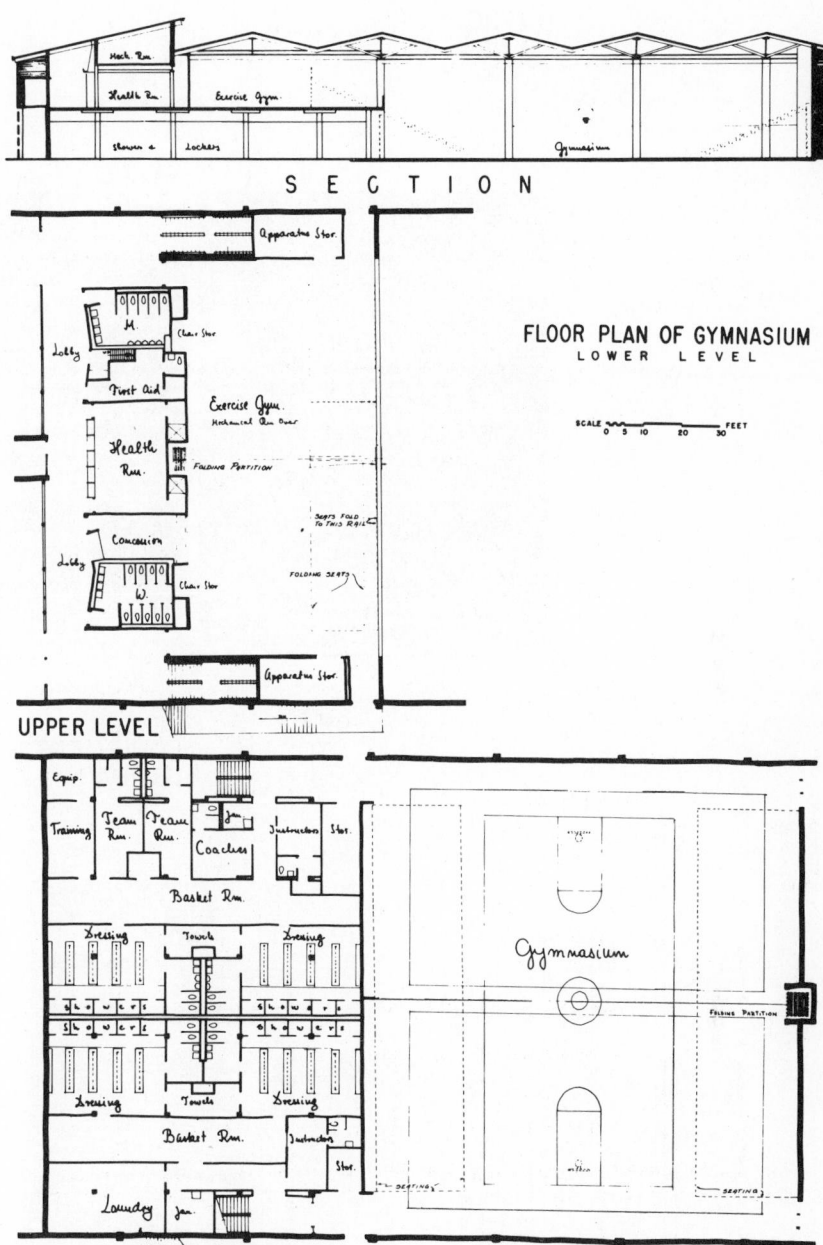

Fig. 44   *Perkins and Will, Architects*

locker 9 by 12 by 20 in. for personal belongings and an open rack for street clothes. The small locker is also used to store physical education uniforms between classes. See section on *Recreation Areas*.

Group showers are satisfactory for boys whereas individual showers and dressing booths are generally required for girls. In some schools both group and individual showers are available to girls and have proved to be a satisfactory arrangement. The number of these facilities should be sufficient to accommodate the largest enrolled class in physical education.

Adjacent toilet facilities should be provided for all dressing and shower rooms.

Full-length mirrors, drinking fountains, and towel service should also be provided.

The instructor's office, which is centrally located, is convenient for distribution of supplies and supervision of the entire area. Locker rooms should be planned to give access to outside play areas without traversing the gymnasium. Shower rooms should be warm, well-ventilated, and supplied with natural light. All hot water should be controlled with master regulating valves. The walls and floors should be constructed of a material that reduces accumulation of bacteria and, in the case of floors, reduces the possibility of students slipping.

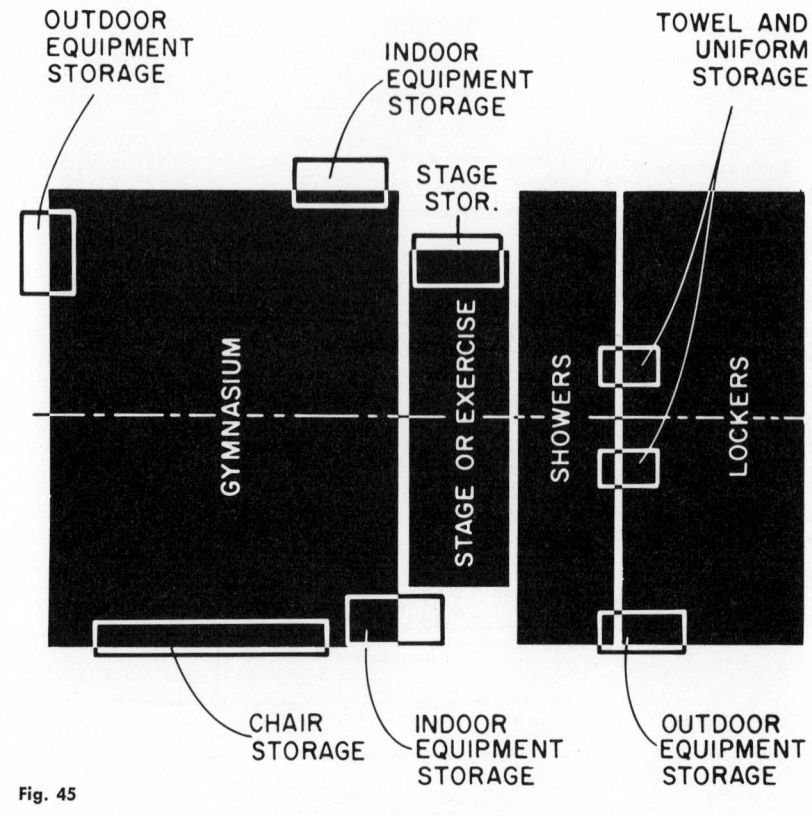

OUTDOOR EQUIPMENT STORAGE

INDOOR EQUIPMENT STORAGE

STAGE STOR.

TOWEL AND UNIFORM STORAGE

GYMNASIUM

STAGE OR EXERCISE

SHOWERS

LOCKERS

CHAIR STORAGE

INDOOR EQUIPMENT STORAGE

OUTDOOR EQUIPMENT STORAGE

Fig. 45

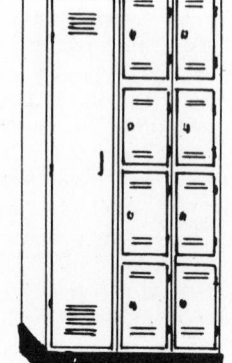

Fig. 46

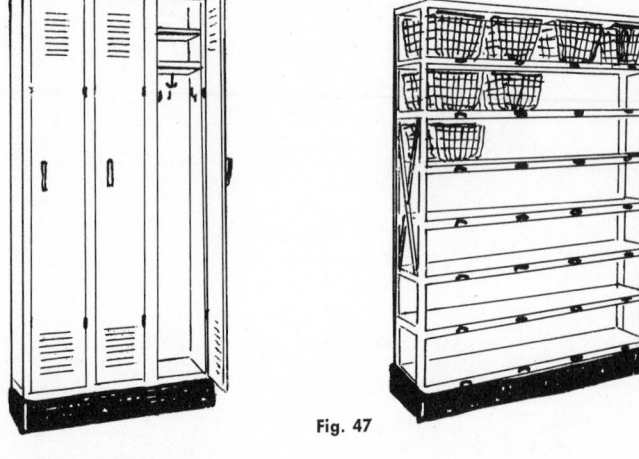

Fig. 47

Figure 45 indicates locations of storage areas for physical education equipment and supplies.

The standard type of full-length locker (Fig. 46) should be set on a masonry base to facilitate cleaning. The unit should be complete with two top shelves, ventilating grilles, and four hooks for hanging clothes. Some type of locking device should be furnished.

Wire baskets may be used (Fig. 47) in place of the small lockers for the storage of gym clothes. Although in some cases the baskets have been mounted in a fixed position, it is more desirable to place them on trucks which can be locked in a well-ventilated storage space. The basket system is generally more difficult to manage than the locker system.

A common arrangement is to provide one large dressing locker, together with six storage lockers (Fig. 48). This permits the student to have a large locker in which to hang his street clothes and also provides him with a small locker for the storage of gym clothes.

The dressing bench shown in Fig. 49 is used in conjunction with a security locker. Seats are provided with a basket in between for street shoes. Hooks or pipe hangers may be used for hanging street clothes during gym periods.

Fig. 48

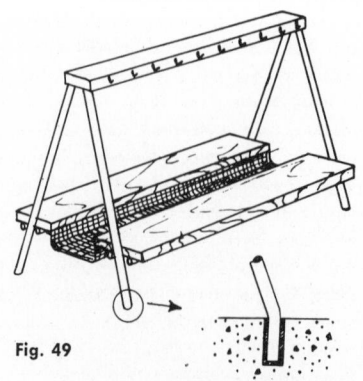

Fig. 49

The supervision of students in this dressing room (Fig. 50) can be very efficient. The vision panel in the office and the locker arrangement permit the instructor to view most of the area at one time. Special individual showers give some degree of privacy. Regular individual shower and dressing booths have also been provided for complete privacy. This room contains a laundry equipped with a washer and dryer for laundering towels and gymnasium uniforms.

AUDITORIUMS

The school auditorium is frequently used as a center for community affairs. It should be so designed and equipped that it may be used effectively by all groups —amateurs, professionals, youth and adult alike. The use of this facility will extend over a wide range, including concerts, plays, motion pictures, forums, and other forms of presentation.

The stage is the essential educational facility, for it is on the stage that young people have the opportunity to learn to present themselves before large groups. It should be designed for ease of movement of performers and stage sets. Areas that support production, such as stagecraft, band room, choral room, storage, dressing rooms, and restrooms, should be located to give rapid and convenient access to the stage.

Many school officials have expressed a preference for auditoriums without any natural lighting. Absolute light control is essential for a good performance. In some schools, windows can be darkened by automatic controls operated from a central point. Stage lighting should be flexible and simple enough to permit amateurs to operate the equipment effectively. See section on *Lighting*.

The seating of the auditorium is not as important from an educational point of view as it may be from the community use standpoint. There is no need for the school auditorium to seat the entire student body. It is best designed when the audience is small enough to make participation possible in group discussions and to ensure a reasonably full assembly area under most types of usage. A capacity of 300 to 800 would normally meet all school requirements. Additional capacity would be dictated largely by community use.

The school auditorium in Figs. 51 and 52 will comfortably seat about 850 students. A ticket booth is located in the foyer of the auditorium lobby. This lobby provides ample circulation space immediately outside the seating area. The placement of

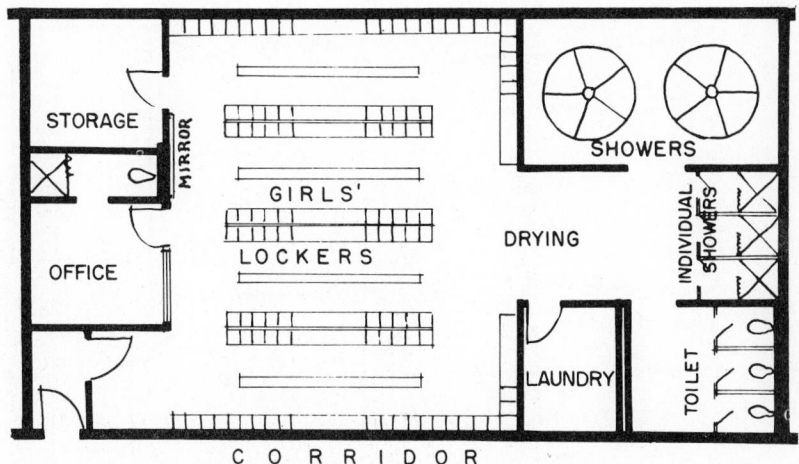

Fig. 50   *M. McDowell Brackett, Architect*

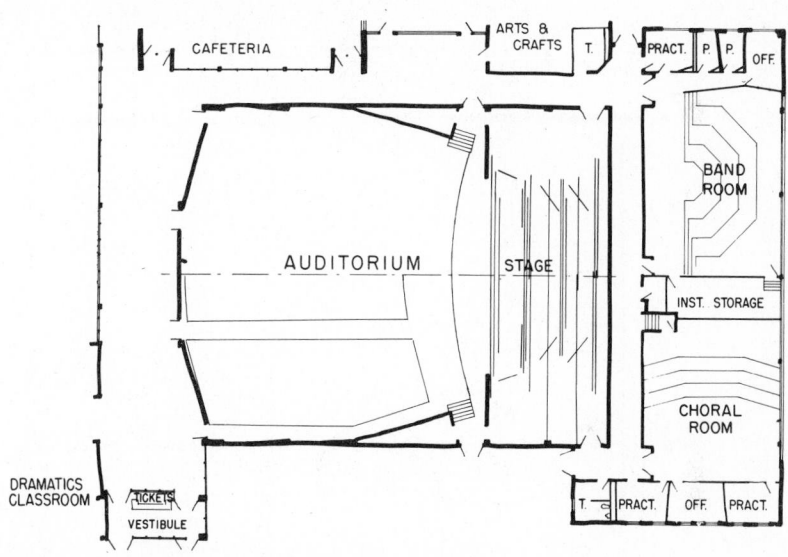

Fig. 51   *F. O. Wolfenbarger and Associates, Architects*

seats and aisles gives good traffic circulation. The entire seating area has adequate sight lines giving good view of the stage from all seats. The front of the stage platform extends beyond the main curtain, providing area for a speaker or discussion panel while the main stage is being set up for a following performance. The stage curtains, teasers, borders, and cyclorama shown on the drawing are adequate to support the various stage activities. The ample corridor space and doors back stage provide rapid circulation of performers, stage crews, and properties. The band and choral rooms are conveniently located with direct access to the stage. Music practice rooms are also used as dressing rooms for performers. This auditorium has direct access to a delivery area, which is convenient when delivering or removing stage properties.

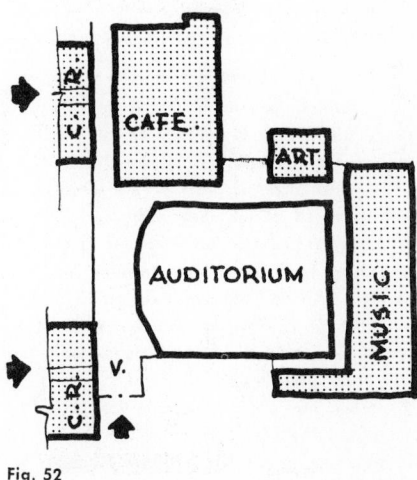

Fig. 52

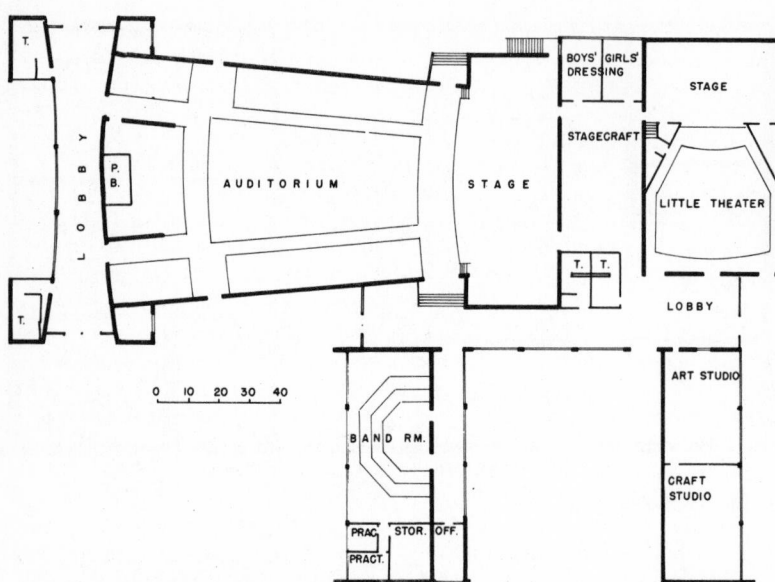

Fig. 53   *W. B. Ittner, Architect*

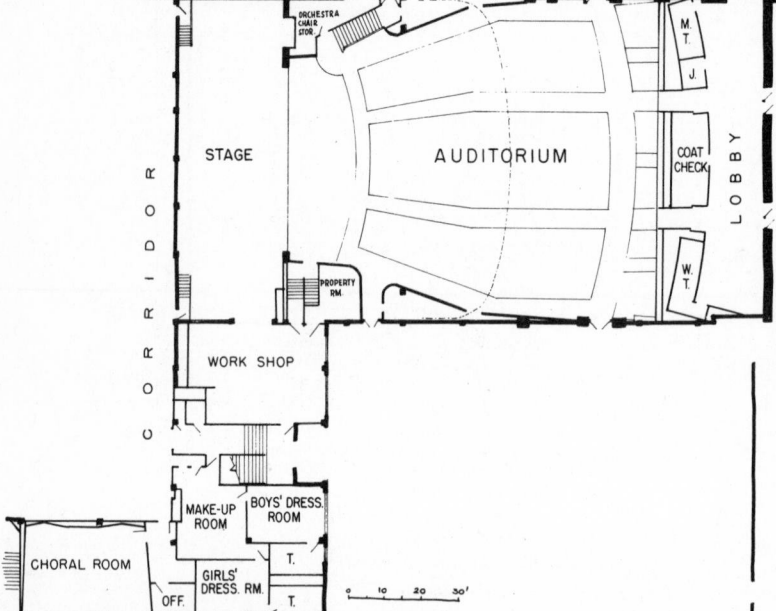

Fig. 54   *LaPierre, Litchfield and Partners, Architects*

This auditorium unit (Fig. 53) is a community art center. Integration of all the arts with the auditorium is highly desirable.

The educational program of the school and the needs of the community resulted in this extensive auditorium center (Fig. 54). Over 1,400 seats are provided on the main floor and balcony area. Adjacent to the stage is a workshop room where scenery and properties may be designed, built, and moved directly to the stage. This room also provides storage for flats and props. The area in front of the stage is large enough to seat a band or orchestra with adjacent storage for music

chairs and stands. Student and adult performers are provided with dressing rooms, make-up room, and toilets.

Figures 55 and 56 illustrate an auditorium unit where considerable emphasis is placed on teaching and preparation for theater, television, and radio productions. This design may be considered more advantageous for student use than for use by community groups. Note the relation in area of the stage and seating space.

LIBRARIES

The modern school library service is the information and resource center for the entire school. It is used extensively by teachers and students to obtain knowledge from all types of media. Books, magazines, newspapers, pamphlets, film strips, microfilm, motion pictures, recordings, still pictures, art work—all have their place in the school library. Libraries are needed in both elementary and secondary schools. The atmosphere should be pleasant and quiet. The library should be centrally located, preferably near the English and social studies classrooms and remote from such areas as music and shop, which might cause noise interference.

Libraries should seat 10 to 15 per cent of the student enrollment. An allowance of 30 sq ft per pupil is desirable. The number of volumes to be housed in bookcases or stacks should approximate 10 books per pupil enrolled in the school.

Fig. 55

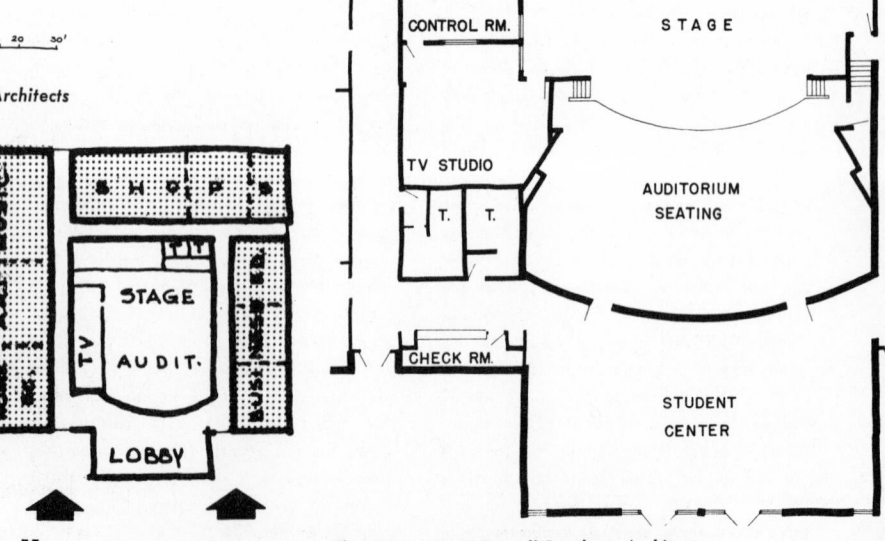

Fig. 56   *M. McDowell Brackett, Architect*

Elementary school libraries would generally include from 3,000 to 6,000 volumes; high school libraries from 6,000 to 20,000 volumes. See following section on *Libraries.*

Frequently in high school libraries a room may be divided by low bookcases in such a way as to provide a reference and study area and an informal browsing section for casual reading.

Supporting facilities should include a library classroom, which a librarian might use for instruction in the use of the library without interfering with those study-ing in the reading room, a librarian's workroom, a magazine storage room, a conference room, a librarian's office, carrels for individual study, a listening room with record player, and an audio-visual room for previewing films and storing and repairing equipment. In addition, it is frequently necessary to provide open stacks apart from the bookcases in the reading room.

Natural lighting, if used, should be so designed as to avoid direct sunlight and sky glare. In northern latitudes where there is snow, windows should not come down to the floor. Snow glare is particularly objectionable in reading rooms.

Particular care is necessary in planning exits from the library. The main entrance should lead past the checkout desk; other doors should be available for emergency exit but not for free entrance. A door directly to the outside may prove helpful.

The small related rooms in the library (Fig. 57) separate the reading areas from the noise of corridors and other school areas. The L-shaped room makes it convenient to separate the study area from the browsing section. Individual student booths are provided for recordings adjacent to the audio-visual room. The location of the librarian's office is convenient to workroom, storage room, library, corridor, and audio-visual area.

Figure 58 shows an elementary school library. Libraries for younger children do not require the many supporting areas that are usually found in high school libraries. The workroom should be adequate for parent participation and the audio-visual room should be adequate to store most of the school's audio-visual equipment.

The library (Fig. 59) offers a circular conference room for discussion groups or for students working on group research. The librarian's office is combined with the workroom, and stacks are adjacent and easily supervised. Bookshelves are placed throughout the room to provide more open shelving than would otherwise be possible.

In Fig. 60, the unusual shape of the building lends itself very well to the requirements of a modern library. The arrangement of stacks on the outer periphery provides alcoves for study and yet assures adequate supervision. The circular traffic pattern tends to reduce traffic movement.

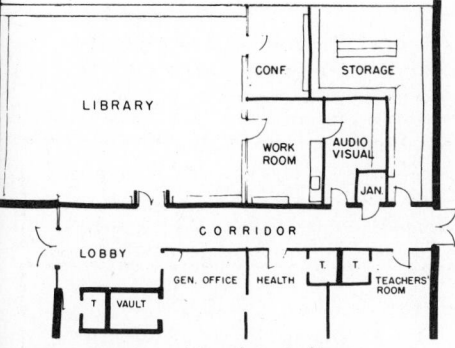

Fig. 57   *J. N. Pease, Architect*

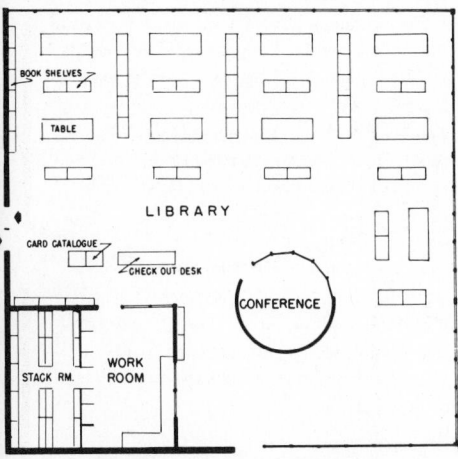

Fig. 58   *Higgins and Ferrebee, Architects*

Fig. 59   *Van Keuren, Davis and Co., Architects*

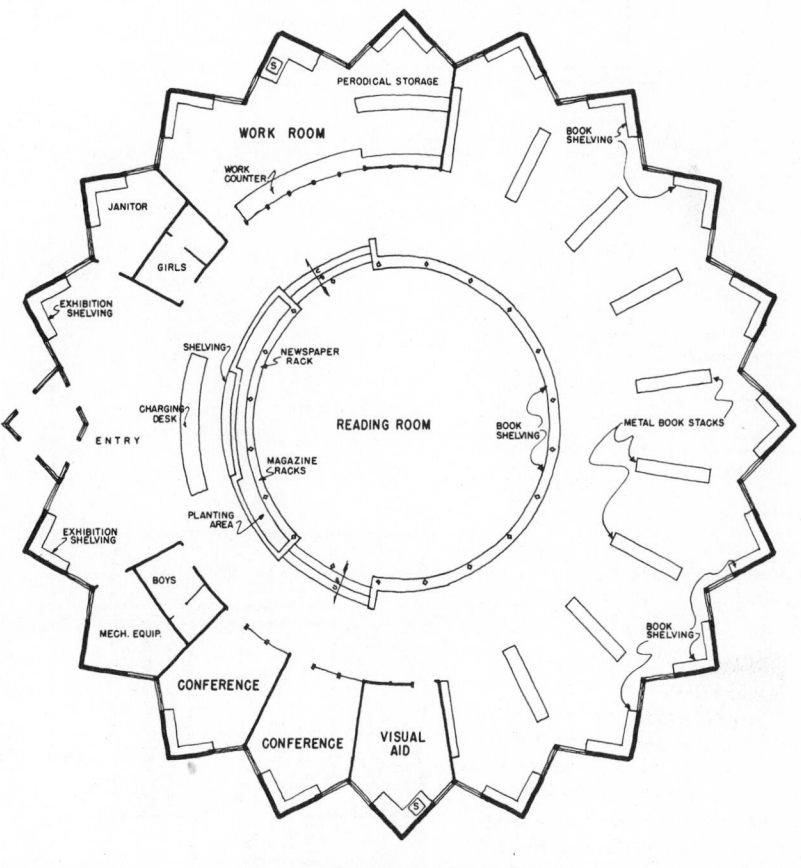

LIBRARY UNIT

Fig. 60   *A. G. Odell, Jr. and Associates, Architects*

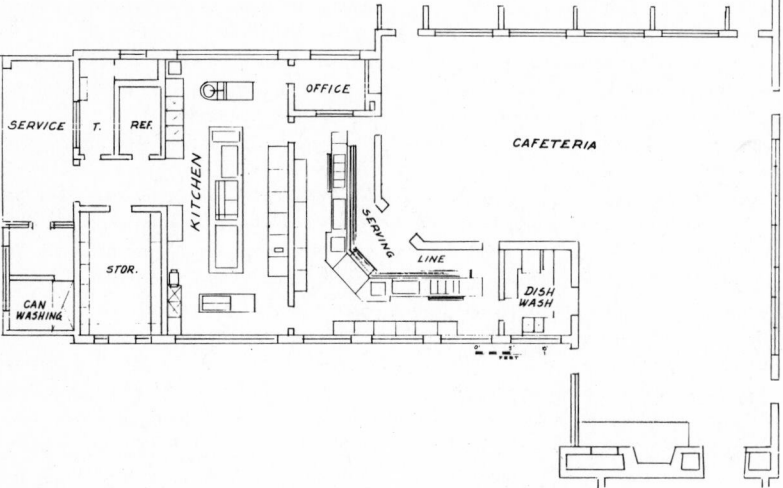

Fig. 61 *Malone and Williams, Architects*

The cafeteria (Fig. 61) provides two serving lines for students. Can washing is done outside the kitchen area and near the service area. Storage and refrigeration are conveniently located for deliveries and for kitchen use. The traffic flow in the kitchen is well designed with double aisles in both directions. The location of the office permits supervision of both kitchen and serving areas. The location of the pass-through window in the dishwashing room reduces cafeteria cross-traffic.

Figure 62 illustrates a central kitchen. Food is prepared, put in specially designed food carts, and moved to separate dining areas in the same building. The food carts are electrically heated to keep the food at the correct temperatures during transportation. These food carts usually serve as serving counters when they reach their destination.

CAFETERIA AND FOOD SERVICE

Lunch service in schools may be provided in several different ways, the most common of which is the central cafeteria and kitchen. This room would normally seat one-half or one-third of the student body and would be provided with one service line for each 125 students being served at one time.

In some schools the lunchrooms have been planned as multipurpose rooms and are located in several sections throughout the building. Food is then served in these areas by means of hot carts from a central kitchen. This plan has the great advantage of making it possible to reduce the size of the cafeteria in terms of the number of students eating in each room, and also to make maximum use of these rooms outside the lunch hour. Service lines, one for each 125 students to be served, are located in the satellite multipurpose rooms and are usually formed by the hot carts themselves.

Informal seating arrangements are desirable, utilizing small rather than large tables, and chairs rather than benches, especially at the secondary school level. Acoustical treatment is essential to reduce the noise level and to permit complete freedom of conversation. Kitchen and service areas should be completely isolated from the eating space by solid soundproof walls and doors.

Traffic patterns to and from cafeteria areas should be carefully studied to ensure the elimination of congestion during the lunch hour. It is desirable to provide a separate dining room for teachers which may be part of the teachers' restroom.

Kitchen

The kitchen should have a rectangular shape and be located near the receiving area, stock rooms, and serving area.

The cooking equipment should consist of the following: gas ranges with heat-controlled insulated roasting ovens, each oven equipped with two oven racks; combination steam cooker and steam kettle or 40-gal tilted steam kettles; electric bake ovens with four compartments complete with thermostatic controls; 30-qt mixer with 20-qt adaptor, equipped with bowls of each size, plus beater and whip; 12-qt mixer equipped with bowls, beater, and whip; electric potato peeler (if instant potatoes are not used); vegetable-slicing machine; electric meat-slicing machine; hamburger grill (optional).

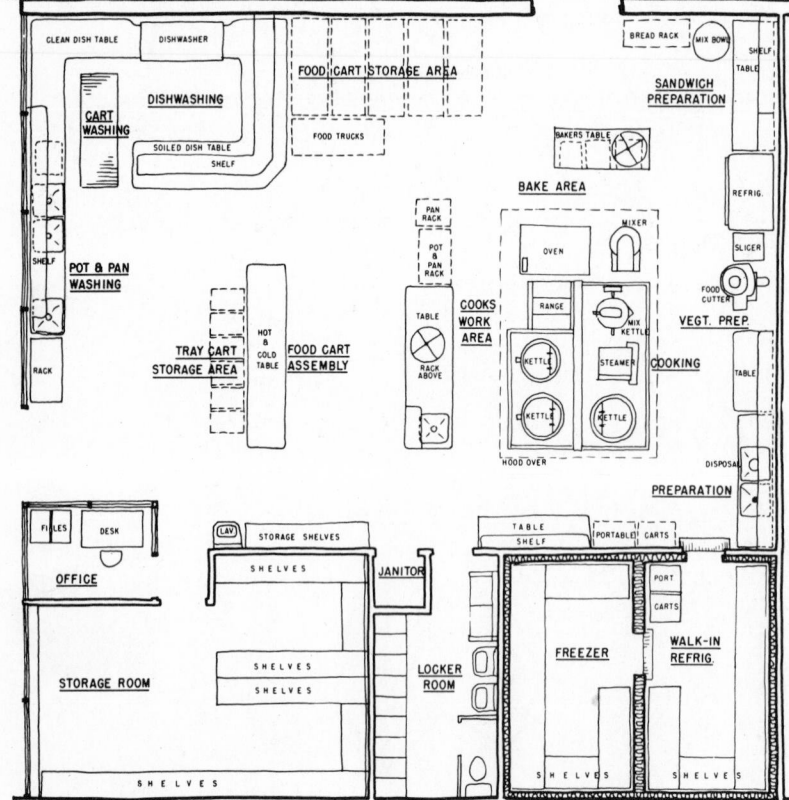

Fig. 62 *Flambert and Flambert, Food Service Consultants*

Other pieces of equipment include two-compartment stainless-steel vegetable sink with garbage disposal; extra-wide drain-pipe and drainboards; two-compartment stainless-steel pot sink with drainboard on each side; preparation counter with sink (under the counter, a tier of three or four drawers and center shelves, equipped with stainless-steel sliding doors, to be used for storage); cook's stainless-steel table with sink; utensil rack over table; baker's table with wooden top and stainless-steel body; scales; table to hold vegetable slicer; stainless-steel table (near walk-in refrigerator); pot-and-pan rack; hand sink; utility trucks; janitor's closet with sink next to kitchen; baker's cabinet; wide walk-in refrigerator containing shelves; one electric chopper or cutter; one reach-in, pass-through refrigerator; one fire blanket; portable cooling racks; utensil racks.

If there is natural ventilation, there should be a cross current. There should be hoods over all cooking equipment. Six air changes per hour with two-speed fans are recommended. Mechanical ventilation should be separate from that of the school system.

Natural lighting, in addition to artificial, is desirable. All working areas should be well lighted. Drainage and waste lines should be easily accessible. There should be a separate drain for each piece of equipment requiring one.

The kitchen should have the same automatic heating system as the rest of the school, but should have separate temperature control. Special wiring facilities for heavy-duty equipment are required.

The ceiling should be light in color, easy to keep clean, and acoustically treated; the walls light in color, smooth, and easily cleaned (glazed tile is good). Washable tile should be used near work areas and sinks. Floors should be nonresilient and of a slip-resistant type, such as quarry tile. Floors should be pitched ⅛ in. per ft toward the drain. Baseboards should be coved. Windows should have a 48-in. sill height and be screened.

Dishwashing

Dishwashing facilities should be adjacent to the dining area. The space should be rectangular. An 8-ft-wide window provided with a lock should serve as the receiving station for soiled dishes.

The equipment should include automatic, stainless-steel dishwasher containing scraping and garbage-disposal machine, two tanks for dishwashing, and also rinse in-

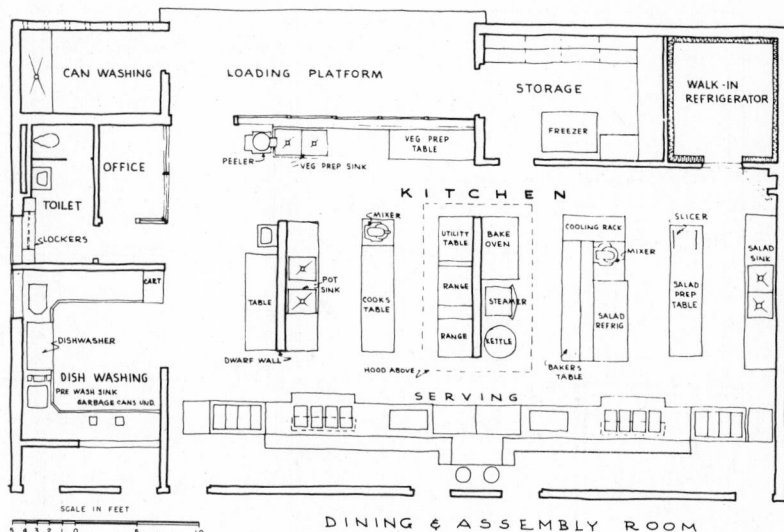

Fig. 63 Flambert and Flambert, Food Service Consultants

The kitchen design in Fig. 63 provides immediate service from the food preparation area to the counters. The over-all traffic circulation is controlled by locating equipment for the various preparation centers together. The office is properly located for deliveries and for kitchen supervision. Natural lighting is provided by windows along the loading platform. The storage area can be serviced directly from the loading dock, thus eliminating possible congestion in the kitchen area.

The "scramble system" (Fig. 64) of serving student lunches is becoming more popular. A service area has replaced the serving line. Students are free to secure their food at several counters. This arrangement tends to split up the service, since it is unlikely that anyone needs to wait in line while another student is making a decision.

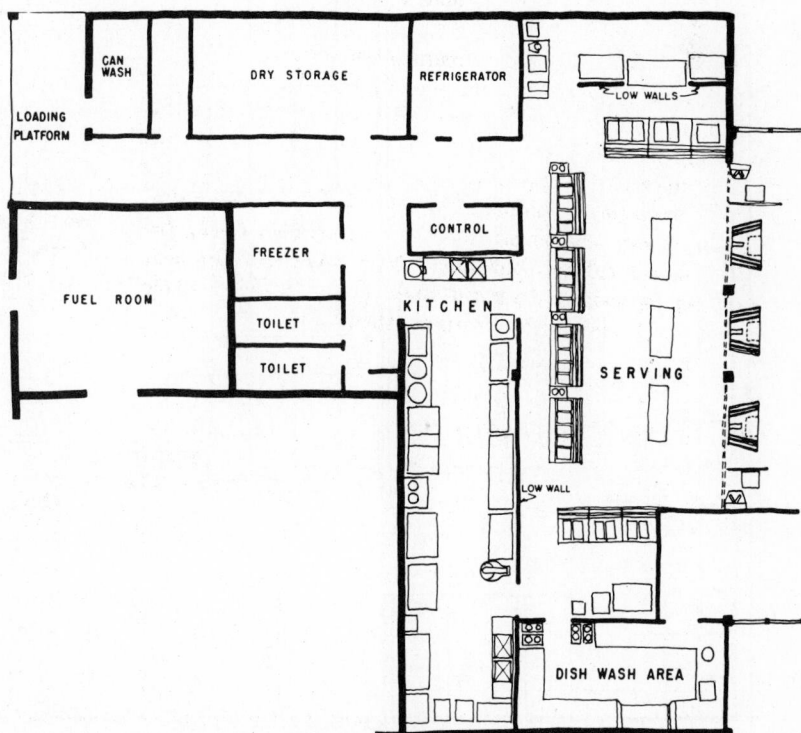

Fig. 64 A. G. Odell, Jr. and Associates, Architects

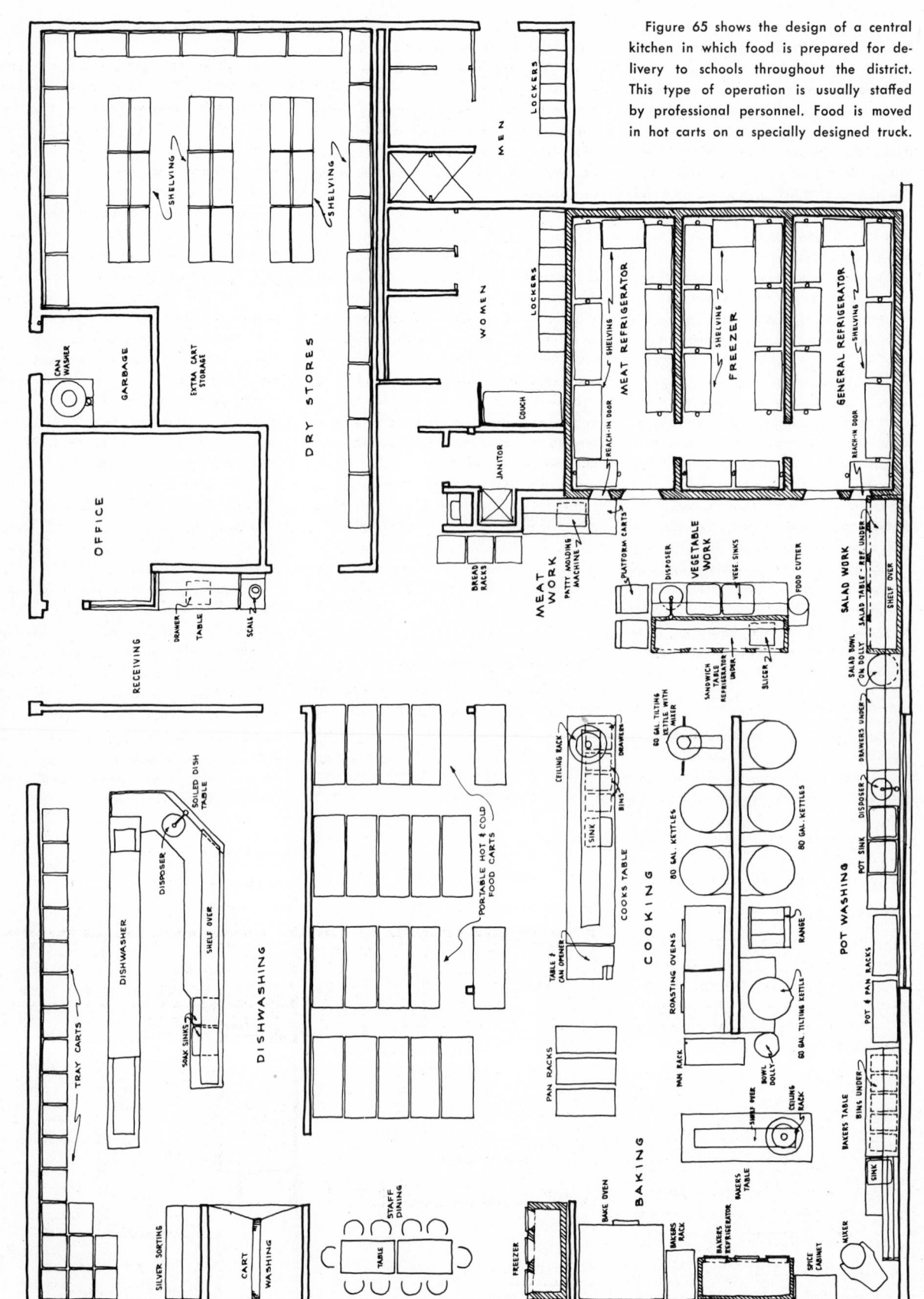

Figure 65 shows the design of a central kitchen in which food is prepared for delivery to schools throughout the district. This type of operation is usually staffed by professional personnel. Food is moved in hot carts on a specially designed truck.

Fig. 65 *Flambert and Flambert, Food Service Consultants*

jector or stainless-steel automatic-conveyor dishwashing machine. If a conveyor machine is used, it should be housed in a dish room where pupils can go to unload their trays. This arrangement eliminates the need for the large window, two dish trucks, and the scraping of dishes in the dish room, and saves on labor. Dishwasher should be connected to stainless-steel dish table with shelves underneath. One two-compartment sink and stainless-steel three-decker dish trucks are needed.

Good ventilation and proper plumbing and electrical outlets are necessary, as are acoustical ceiling, glazed tile walls for easy daily cleaning, and slip-resistant floor.

Office

The office is used for planning menus, conducting conferences with employees, interviewing, and clerical work. It should provide vision into kitchen and serving area, if possible, with glass on at least two sides. It is best placed near the receiving area and lavatory facilities. Privacy should be ensured so that planning and clerical work may be done efficiently. An outside telephone line is helpful for use when the school office is closed. Desk, telephone, chairs, clock, bookcase, filing cabinets, and adding machine are necessary equipment.

Vegetable storage

Vegetable storage should be next to dry food storage and, if possible, near an outside door for ease of delivery. The space should be free of uninsulated pipes, water heaters, and refrigeration condensing units; the floor slip-resistant; walls and ceiling light in color, impervious to moisture, easy to keep clean, and vermin-proof.

Dry food storage

Dry food storage should be convenient to receiving area and kitchen and located so that it is not a passageway to areas having no relationship to the cafeteria. The space should be the same as that for vegetable storage.

Receiving area

The receiving area should be near storeroom and kitchen but away from pupil traffic; screened from public view; convenient to service driveways. Trash and garbage area should be adjacent to loading platform and accessible from outside the building for garbage collection after hours.

Its function is receiving supplies, picking up garbage, and washing and storing cans. It is best to have a hard floor, a wainscot surface that can be washed readily, and a basket trap in floor of garbage area.

Provision should be made for storing and washing four garbage cans, for non-freezing plumbing, and for hot-water spray for cleaning cans. Outside doors should have self-closing devices and locks, metal frames, and fly screens. All interior doors near this area should have locks so that garbage and trash pickups may be made at off-hours.

Locker-toilet area for employees

The locker-toilet area should be near the employees' entrance to the kitchen. Furniture and equipment should include venetian blind on window, toilet, and lavatory (hot- and cold-water mixing faucets), large lockers or large closet with rod to hold coats with shelf above, individual small lockers recessed in wall for pocketbooks and personal items, couch, comfortable chairs, small table, wastebasket, and mirror, 15 by 20 in.—avoid placing over sink to keep hair from clogging drains.

Natural and artificial light is desirable. If there is no window, there should be a fan for mechanical ventilation. Walls and ceiling should be light in color and easy to keep clean. Asphalt tile is preferred for floor.

Freezer and refrigerator area

A walk-in refrigerator unit is suggested, large enough to accommodate perishable supplies. The freezing unit should be located in the same area, but not necessarily inside the walk-in unit, to eliminate loss of valuable wall space.

SPECIAL ROOM DESIGNS

The following figures illustrate special room designs that have been successfully used in modern school systems—rooms that have been specifically designed for arts and crafts, chemistry, physics, biology, general science, home arts, industrial arts, music, and language laboratory.

The development of special rooms in a school depends in large part upon local philosophy, industry, enrollment, standard of living, allocated class time, and economy. The main aim of high school science courses, at one time, was to prepare a few students to become science specialists. Today, however, the science program must satisfy two goals: (1) It must identify scientifically gifted students and teach them as much as they can learn, and (2) It must give all other students the essential background that they need to make them scientifically literate.

If scientifically talented students are to be encouraged to advance in the field, space for individual experimentation and research must be provided.

All laboratory furniture should be acid-resistant and easy to clean. Floor or wall utilities should be planned for movable laboratory tables. Safety precautions should be taken to render these spaces as nearly accident-proof as possible. Fire extinguishers and emergency first-aid kits should be installed and plainly marked. All state and local codes governing laboratories and the use of poisons and flammable material should be observed.

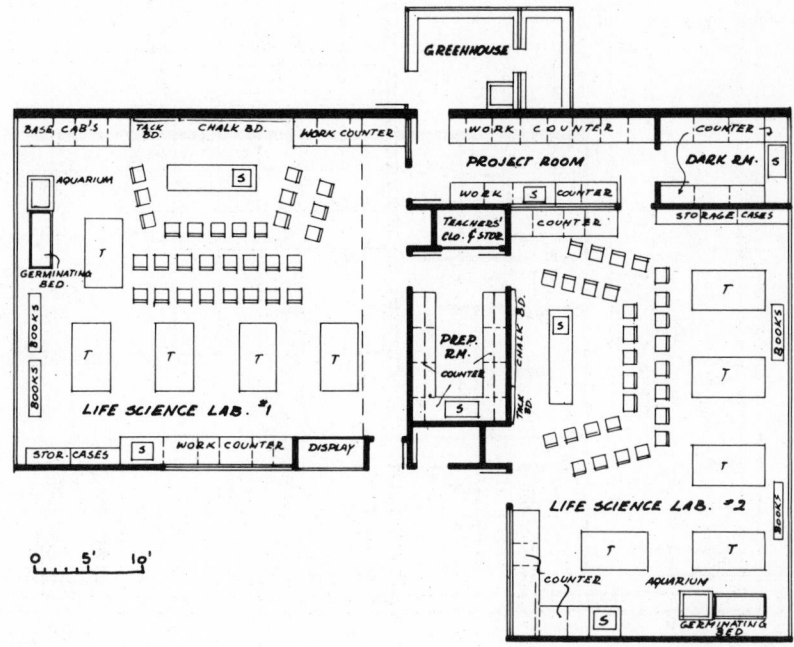

Fig. 66

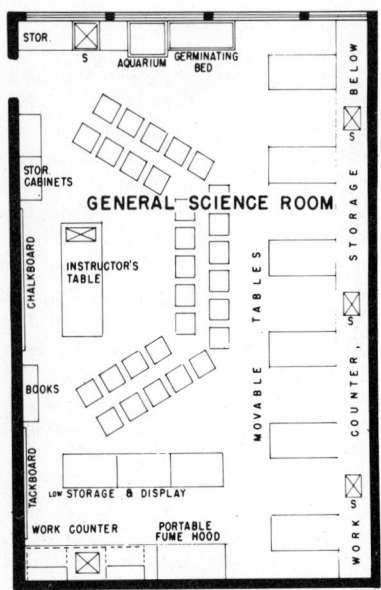

Fig. 67

SCIENCE

General science rooms and biology laboratories

General science rooms and biology laboratories should be located on the first floor, with windows facing south or southwest, a door opening into preparation room, and a door opening to the campus so that classes may study outdoors without passing through the building.

Activities include lectures, demonstrations, viewing projected materials, individual and group study, writing, and experimentation with animals and plants.

The front wall should be equipped along its entire length with chalkboard, the center section of which should be

raisable. There should be a display rail over everything except the raisable section of board. Provision should be made for a projection screen at the front of the room. Corkboard 4-ft wide should cover the entire width of the back wall above the wainscoting. It is suggested that counters be installed along two sides of the room, one being the window side. Such counters should include several sinks and outlets for gas and electricity.

All laboratory furniture should be acid-resistant and easy to wash and clean. Equipment includes a display case for biological specimens that opens to corridor from within the room; teacher's combination wardrobe and closet; legal-size file with lock; storage areas for notebooks, aprons, microscopes, instruments, specimens, biologicals, pupil projects, micro-projector, and books. A storage cabinet at counter height might be installed along window wall. Locked sliding door extending the entire length of the storage cabinet and metal shelves are desirable. Instructor's demonstration desk should be equipped with hot and cold water, duplex a-c receptacle, soapstone sink, upright rods with clamps and wood cross bar, and double gas cock. Also needed are two-student biology desks with one cupboard and two book compartments; chairs, mock-up table; herbarium, aquariums; projection screen; microscopes; models, charts; dissecting trays; specimens; portable germinating bed; terrarium; micro-projectors; three sinks with towels and soap dispensers; experiment sheet filing cabinet near tackboard; first-aid cabinet; fire extinguisher.

Electric outlets should be located on each of the walls. If the entire class uses electrically lighted microscopes, tables will

need electric outlets. Sinks and outlets for gas and electricity are needed in counters.

Storage and preparation rooms

Storage and preparation rooms should be adjacent to general science and biology. These rooms are used for teacher preparation, storage of bulk supplies, conferences and offices.

This area should be lined with storage spaces for materials and equipment of various sizes. There should be provision for teachers' records and professional books. Room should be outfitted with a sink and gas and electric outlets. Access windows should open into the laboratories.

Storage provision should be made for equipment used in general science and biology. A storage bin, made up of many small drawers, each measuring approximately 4 by 4 in., should be included for efficient storage of small items of equipment. Also needed are desks and chairs; preparation table on wheels; preparation table with drawers; standing storage cabinet for charts; cabinet for slides; bookcase; shelving to ceiling; sink with hot and cold water; gas and electric outlets.

Plant and animal room

The plant and animal room should be located adjacent to the biology laboratory, possibly adjacent to a biology storeroom. Easy access to the outdoors is desirable.

Southern exposure is desirable. This area should be arranged like a greenhouse, with sanitary finishes and a concrete floor with drain so that the room can be hosed down. In addition to sunlight, the plant room will require special ventilation and heating so that it does not get cold overnight. Special heating,

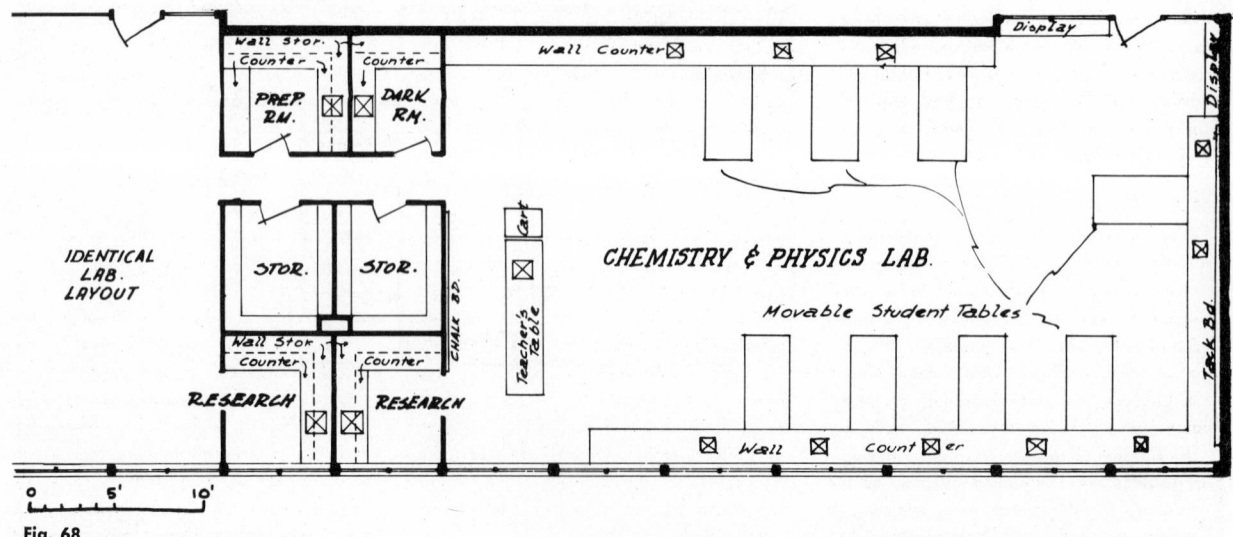

Fig. 68

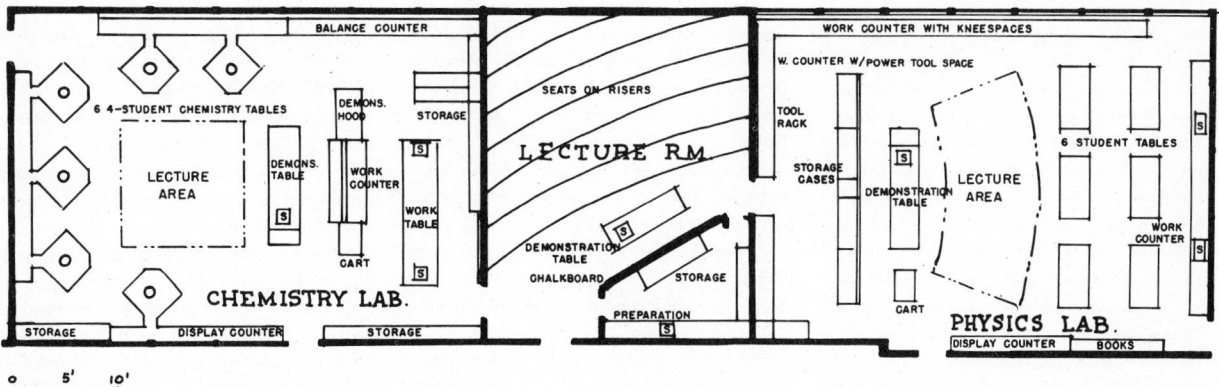

Fig. 69

thermostatically controlled and separate from other parts of the building, should ensure even heating during weekends and holiday periods.

Equipment includes table and racks for plants; growing beds on wheeled tables; animal cages; feeding trays; storage for food, tools, equipment; sink with hot and cold water; hose; pails; hand garden tools; bins for loam, sand, and peat moss.

Chemistry laboratories

Chemistry laboratories should be readily accessible from individual research and preparation rooms. Laboratory activities include demonstrations, individual and group study and experimentation, writing, viewing projected materials, and lectures.

At a comfortable height there should be student stations for 24 students, consisting of tables with large free working area and all services available: a-c and d-c variable voltage should be provided. The front wall should be equipped for its entire length with a chalkboard, the center section of which should be raisable. There should be a display rail over all but the raisable section of board. On the back wall above the wainscoting level, there should be some corkboard and pegboard with hardware. A fume hood, accessible from three sides, should be provided.

One end of the room should contain the teacher's desk and a demonstration area with a 5-in.-high dais for demonstration. Demonstration table should have a stone top, spotlight lighting, and a roll-away extension. All services should be provided for the demonstration, including variable a-c and d-c voltage. Sound cable should be installed in the floor for projection purposes. Provision should be made for darkening the room.

Special attention should be given to the furniture for this space. As a minimum, it should be acid- and base-resistant and

easy to wash and to clean. It should include tablet armchairs; teacher's combination wardrobe and closet; acid-proof sinks with dilution tank; storage for chemical supplies; storage space in laboratory tables; normal chemistry laboratory equipment for semi-micro techniques; salt and solution cabinets; three rolling tables to service tables; standard reagent storage area; locked cupboards for delicate instruments and dangerous chemicals; fire extinguishers and first-aid kits; storage for notebooks and aprons; experiment-sheet filing cabinet; charts and models; projection screen.

Physics laboratories

Physics laboratories are used for lectures, demonstrations, viewing projected material, individual and group study, writing, individual and group experimentation.

Around the room on three sides at a comfortable height (higher than the ordinary table) should be a work station for each student, consisting of a table with a large free working area and all services available; a-c and d-c variable voltage should be provided to all stations; voltage should be supplied by several portable voltage regulating units. Sinks should be available. Some attention should be given to permanent or semipermanent laboratory stands for rigging equipment.

One end of the room should contain the teacher's desk and a demonstration area with a 5-in.-high dais for the demonstration table. The demonstration table should have a stone top, spotlight lighting, and a roll-away extension. All services should be available. Down-draft ventilator is suggested, but it should be positioned so as to give as much unobstructed broad area on table surface as possible. It should not be centrally placed. Tablet armchairs should be placed in front of the demonstration desk.

The room should have as much chalkboard space as possible, since chalkboard work with problems constitutes a considerable part of class time. Ample corkboard space and some pegboard with hardware are needed.

Attention should be given to darkening the room properly. This is important for the projection of movies and slides, as well as for demonstrations that require a darkened room, and for some laboratory work such as photometry. Sound cable should be installed for projection purposes and antenna facilities for television and radio reception. There should be central control of lighting.

Doors should open into the front of the laboratory. An open-joist ceiling has the advantage of permitting hanging of apparatus. A ceiling hook capable of holding a ½-ton load should be provided.

One of the main problems for the physics area will be provision of adequate storage space for a vast amount of demonstration equipment and specialized scientific apparatus. Storage space with glass doors for visibility, bookshelves for reference library, and a cabinet for notebooks should be provided.

Preparation and storage rooms for chemistry and physics laboratories

Preparation and storage rooms should be adjacent to laboratories, with a door leading to corridor and laboratory.

They are used for teacher preparation, storage of bulk supplies, and conferences.

The area should be lined with storage spaces for materials and equipment of various sizes (in chemistry, glass tubing, long items, tall items). All shelves should have lips to prevent slippage, and should be built so that the floor supports the weight, unless the storage area is small and specifically designated for light items.

Chemistry: Open shelving of cabinets is favored for storage of bulk chemicals. Special transite-lined volatile closets vented to the outside for volatile reagents, acids, and alkalies should be provided, along with provisions for the teacher's records and professional books. The room should be outfitted with sink and gas and electricity outlets. It should also have storage provision for all equipment, a preparation table large enough for six analytical balances, adequate work space for preparation, special storage for charts so that they are kept flat, not rolled, desks and chairs, preparation table on wheels, ladders with rail, bookcase.

Physics: A storage bin made up of many small drawers measuring approximately 4 by 4 in. for efficient storage of small items of equipment is suggested. Electric outlets similar to those provided in demonstration table, as well as plentiful 110-volt a-c outlets, and adequate lighting should be provided, as well as ladders with rail to reach stored items, and a workbench and sink with drainboard along one side, to repair and set up equipment. The bench should be rugged enough to take considerable hammering.

Individual research and project rooms for chemistry and physics

Research and project rooms should be adjacent to chemistry and physics laboratories and separated from them by half-glass partitions. They are used for individual and small-group study and experimentation, instruction, and research.

Science shop

The science shop and the darkroom may be built as a unit and placed back to back between the corridor and the window side. The project room should be located on the window side and have a door opening into a laboratory. A glass wall will enable the teacher to keep the area under observation.

The science shop is used for individual work in making and repairing instruments and equipment.

It should have a workbench and sink along one side of room. The bench, for repair and setting up of equipment, should be rugged enough for metalworking.

The furniture and equipment should include equipment drawers, work counter, drill press, small metalworking lathe, some storage shelves for reference books, tool storage, sink, and ample space for electrical equipment. Electric outlets similar to those provided in the demonstration desk should be available, as well as 110-volt a-c outlets.

Darkroom

The darkroom could be placed back to back with the science shop and located on the corridor side with the door opening into the corridor.

It is used for developing film and the storage of darkroom materials and reagents, mounting equipment, and the like.

A vestibule and two-door entrance will prevent light from entering. The area could be divided into a small room near the entrance for weighing and mixing chemicals and a larger room toward the rear for developing and printing.

A counter should be constructed along three sides of the room, 34 to 36 in. high and 24 in. wide. There should be a large chemical-resistant open sink, 24 by 30 in. and 18 in. deep; and a wet bench, at-

tached at either end, draining into the sink. The sink must have both hot and cold water. Stainless-steel surfaces are recommended; finishes must be easily cleaned and stain-resistant. See section on *Darkrooms.*

Shelves 12 in. apart and 10 in. deep should be constructed above the counter. Storage in standard darkroom style should provide tray and chemical storage as well as shelves for dry stock. Since the room will be used for dry work, such as spectroscopy, provision should be made for sit-down as well as stand-up dry work. Walls should be finished a flat green for eye ease. Serious attention must be given to ensure adequate ventilation of this room.

Furniture and equipment will include retouching table; developing, enlarging, and printing equipment; dryer; print washer; trays; paper cutter; hot plate; safe lights; timer; fire extinguisher; clock.

At least four double electrical outlets are needed at the counter. There must be sufficient plugs for all appliances, conveniently placed near all work positions.

FINE ARTS

Arts and crafts rooms

Arts and crafts rooms should be located near auditorium stage, stagecraft area, homemaking, industrial arts, dramatic, and music rooms. Location should facilitate delivery of supplies. They should have an outside door, for use when holding classes outdoors, and good natural lighting.

The space should be arranged with sufficient imagination so that it is flexible and allows the teacher to vary the curriculum from year to year. The program involves the use of a number of media. Rooms,

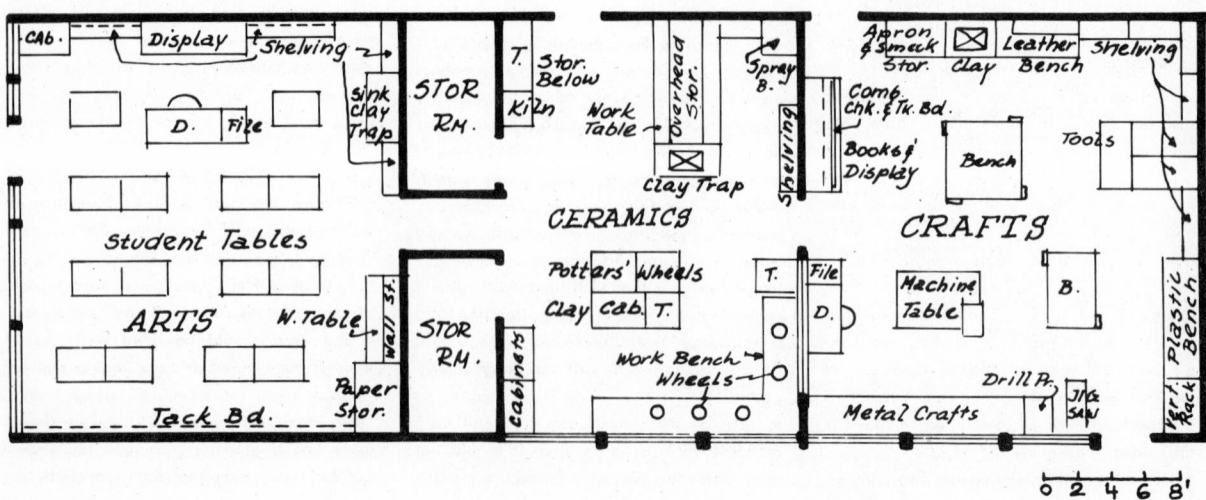

Fig. 70

therefore, should be conceived of as a series of work centers in which activities with different kinds of materials can be carried forward. There is much need for display space for finished work. Walls should be of soft pine or other material that will receive thumbtacks, to eliminate the need for broken-up wall panels and bulletin board. Avoid breaking up wall spaces uneconomically; keep display areas large and simple. Phones, light switches, thermostats, and other necessary electric outlets should be placed where they are accessible but do not interfere with otherwise usable display spaces. Windows should provide adequate light and be high enough for storage and counter space underneath.

Ceilings and/or walls should be acoustically treated. It is preferable to have a vinyl asbestos floor in the general art area; in the ceramics area terrazzo or hardened concrete floor is suggested. Finishes should be easily washed and maintained, and resistant to oils and heat. A chalkboard should be placed where it can easily be seen but where it will not produce reflections or shine. It could be incorporated in a cabinet of vertical sliding balanced sections to include two chalkboards, one corkboard, and one projection screen. A bulletin board, if soft pine walls are not provided, and opaque drapes or light-tight venetian blinds for darkening the room are also necessary.

Suitable lighting is needed to ensure effective color rendering on dark days and in the evening. Semi-indirect lighting with daylight bulbs is recommended. If the room is located on the ground floor, it will need protection against ground glare in lower sash of windows. Double sinks with hot and cold water; drinking fountain outlet; gas outlets; enough electric outlets around room for projectors and spotlights; and heating by ceiling or floor radiation to save floor and wall space, or at least a minimum allocation of space to this utility, are also recommended.

Room for bulk storage and storage of papers, illustrative materials, models, cardboard, finished and unfinished projects will have to be supplied. The area will require much protection against fire. Shelving, suspension facilities, and bins should be arranged for great flexibility.

MUSIC

The music program is usually divided into four parts: instrumental activities; choral activities; classes in music theory, music appreciation, and voice; and corre-

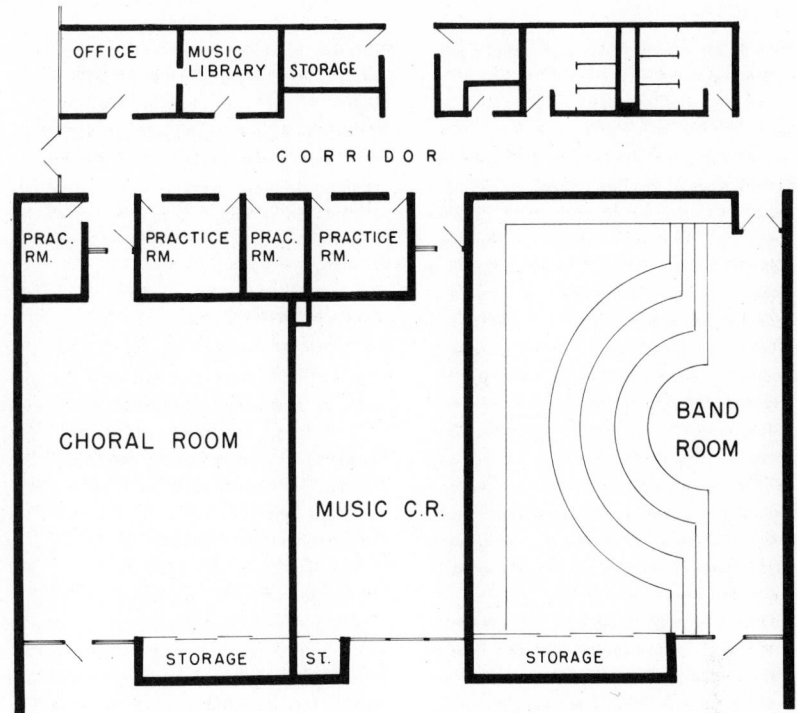

Fig. 71

lated activities, such as drama and opera projects. Good traffic circulation is essential. Instrument storage area should be planned so that students can circulate easily to collect their instruments, attend class, and return instruments for storage. It should be convenient to move large instruments to buses, stage, and playing field.

The size, shape, and construction material are important factors to consider in planning and designing music facilities for the best sound control possible. The architect should aim for rooms that have optimum reverberation time, even distribution of sound, and freedom from undesirable absorption at certain pitches. Nevertheless, the reverberation period must not be reduced below the point mandatory for correct brilliance of tone. Nonparallel walls or splayed walls and ceilings should be considered; soundproof walls and doors are desirable. Acoustic ceilings and walls should be carefully designed to ensure satisfactory conditions within each room. Storage areas should serve as sound-transmission buffer areas to keep interference between music rooms at a minimum. It is recommended that a competent sound engineer be consulted in preliminary planning stages.

Music classroom

The music classroom should be part of the music suite and readily accessible to corridor and office.

It is used for class instruction, choral work, and as a dressing room for large groups.

It should have sound-tight doors, natural lighting, lavatory, and a dressing table.

A chalkboard ruled for music, bulletin board, piano, and tablet armchairs will be needed.

Provision should be made for projection, television, and a high-fidelity sound system.

Choral room

The choral room should be near the rear of the auditorium stage so that choral groups can move easily onto stage for performances.

It is used for boys' and girls' glee clubs and mixed chorus.

The room should have a flat floor and 6-ft-wide doors so that a piano can be moved in and out. It may be rounded at rear. A chalkboard with music ruling on part of it, a pull-type screen over the chalkboard, and a bulletin board are recommended.

Furniture and equipment include movable seats of the drop-arm type, conductor's platform, record player, tape recorder, storage for records and sheet music, piano, television set, portable risers, and clock.

Room should have natural lighting, ventilation, soundproofing, provisions for music recording and reproduction, two built-in 12-in. speakers with proper connection for either record player or microphone plug-in to serve for broadcasting over school public-address system.

Instrumental music room

The instrumental music room should be near the rear of the auditorium so that the band can move instruments easily onto the stage, near an outdoor entrance so that the band can have access to the field without going through the building, and near practice rooms.

It is used for band, orchestra, brass and woodwind ensemble, chamber music groups, and sectional rehearsals.

The space should have a flat floor and doors 6 ft wide to move piano in and out. Doors should be soundproofed. Storage space in back and sides of room, chalkboard with music ruling on part of it, pull-type screen over chalkboard, and bulletin board are suggested.

Furniture and equipment include movable seats, conductor's platform, record player, tape recorder, piano, television set, music stands, small sink, counters for books with music slots below counters, storage for records and musical scores of various size, portable risers, and clock.

The room should have special sound-proofing; natural lighting and ventilation, if possible; provision for music recording and reproduction; two built-in 12-in. speakers with proper connection for either record player or microphone plug-in to serve for broadcasting over school public-address system; outlets for 16 mm sound motion picture projector. Reproduction in music rooms requires high-fidelity equipment.

Practice rooms

Practice rooms should be near band and orchestra room. They are used for practicing and individual instruction.

They may serve as music listening rooms. Soundproof doors, and soundproof windows into corridor, are necessary for supervision.

Equipment includes music rack, small table, music lamp, chairs, clock, and counter for instruments and books. It may have a piano and phonograph.

Electric outlets and artificial lighting are needed. Special acoustical treatment is necessary to prevent interference between rooms and with other areas and to deaden reverberation. Special attention should be paid to mechanical ventilation.

Music office and library

The music office and library should be between the choral and instrumental rooms. It should provide good supervision of spaces in music area.

It is used as an office—for teacher con-ference, teacher preparation, and keeping records—and a library—for research, reading, studying, and storage of music.

Furniture and equipment include teachers' desks and chairs; wardrobe space; conference table; work counter; adjustable shelves on walls; bookcase; cabinet for records; typewriter and stand; phonograph; radio; and playback machines.

Music storage room

The music storage room should provide safe, sanitary protection against robe and uniform destruction. Cabinets, 3 ft deep, 30 ft long, equipped with racks and hangers and space above for hats and lockers, for special band equipment such as flags and batons, and with lockable sliding doors, are desirable.

Instruments need maximum care and preservation from damage. Adjustable shelving must vary according to instrument sizes. Roll-away racks for bulky instruments are needed. Smaller instruments are best cared for in cabinets. Other provisions include lockers with master-keyed padlocks, student benches, record cabinet, music filing cabinet, piano dolly, and music stands. If possible, a small area for instrument maintenance should be provided: sink with hot and cold water, floor drain, shelves, workbench, gas outlet for Bunsen burner, and counter for instrument repair.

HOMEMAKING

Boys as well as girls should have family-life education. Location of this department along a much-traveled route, with inviting vistas into the laboratories, would promote this objective. Proper design and placement will assist in promoting greater understanding of the role of homemaking in the secondary school curriculum. The department should be reasonably accessible from classrooms and near an outdoor garden area.

Food laboratories

The food laboratories may be divided into cooking area, freezing area, laundry, wall storage (for tote drawers, staples, cleaning supplies, and books), and classroom area large enough to accommodate movable desk chairs for students. Grease-resistant asphalt tile or linoleum flooring is necessary. Folding doors or screens could be used to separate areas.

Unit kitchens should contain equipment for about four students and include stoves, double sinks, counter space, and storage cupboards above and below the counters. Enameled-steel upper and lower cabinets with back splashes which are molded into a curved surface rather than joined together with stainless-steel strips are suggested. Movable supply wagons made of materials similar to those of other kitchen equipment can be built to fit into recessed space under the counter surface. Allowance must be made on the window wall for access to windows. Counters should be made of a durable material with two areas large enough to place two boards 16 by 20 in. next to each other so that two students can work side by side at each area. These should not be located at a corner since this does not allow space for two pupils to stand and work together. Minimum desirable length of counter per pupil is 30 in. If counter width is 24 in., minimum desirable size of one unit kitchen should be 11 by 9 ft, or 99 sq ft. Counter heights should be about 33 to 34 in. To accommodate four students at work, space between counters should be 6 to 8 ft. Just outside each kitchen should be space for a kitchen table and four chairs for serving and eating.

Allowance should be made for adequate ventilation to carry away food odors. Exhaust fan for entire room is suggested. Two duplex electric outlets should be provided in each cooking area. In laundry area, provision should be made for 110/220-volt outlet for clothes dryer.

Clothing laboratory

The clothing laboratory should be equivalent in size to a large classroom. It should include a sewing area (preferably along window wall); grooming area; dressing room area (about 8 feet square), walled off by cabinets on at least one side; storage areas (preferably along walls); and fitting area. Folding doors or screens could be used to separate areas.

Storage should be provided for portable machines, notions, tote boxes (5 in. deep by 14 in. wide by 19 in. long), roll of 36-in. wrapping paper, small articles, textbooks, large fashion magazines, patterns, and teacher's wardrobe, four-drawer, legal-size file with lock. Space is needed for hanging student projects.

Provide adequately keyed electric outlets for machines—suggest one double outlet for each machine—electric outlets for irons and visual-aid machines, one fluorescent light over grooming unit, and adequate light at working surfaces.

Family living laboratory

The family living laboratory is used for advanced courses in homemaking: table service, housekeeping, home decoration, selection and arrangement of furniture, entertainment, bed making, home care of sick, leisure time activities, family living, money management, child care, and consumer education.

This is the central core of homemaking facilities. Furniture and equipment should represent advanced solutions of home problems. Space should provide for dining room, living room, and flexible area for home nursing, child care, home furnishing, family living, group discussion, and film viewing. There should be at least one plastered wall for experimentation with wallpapers. Hardwood floors are preferred. Folding doors or screens could be used to separate areas.

Furniture and equipment include upholstered sofa and chairs; side tables and coffee table; lamps and vases; sideboard or hutch; drapes (to be made by class); dining room table and chairs to seat eight; card table and chairs; framed pictures (art project); roll-away bed; built-in storage cabinets for magazines and linens; cleaning supplies; vacuum cleaner; electric drill and attachments for waxing and buffing; samples of home furnishing materials; dishes; silver; table linen; curtain and drapery fixtures; full-length mirrors; home-nursing equipment; child-care supplies. Supplies should be stored near area where they will be used.

There should be artificial lighting and switches adapted to house situations; combination outlet for electric iron, pilot light, switch and outlet; electric clock; special lighting on machines; electric duplex outlet spaced at least every 12 ft of available wall space; sink with hot and cold water.

INDUSTRIAL ARTS

The industrial arts department should be isolated from quieter areas of building, with a service road provided nearby. There should be an outdoor shop area, if possible. Access to shower and locker facilities will be needed. All machines and equipment should be arranged so that a sequence of operations can be carried out with the greatest possible efficiency.

Woodworking shop, finishing, and storage room

The woodworking shop is used for information, experience, and skilled training in woodworking. Materials and processes of manufacturing, as well as vocational opportunities, will be studied. Projects will be constructed.

It should be on the first floor, accessible to the outside.

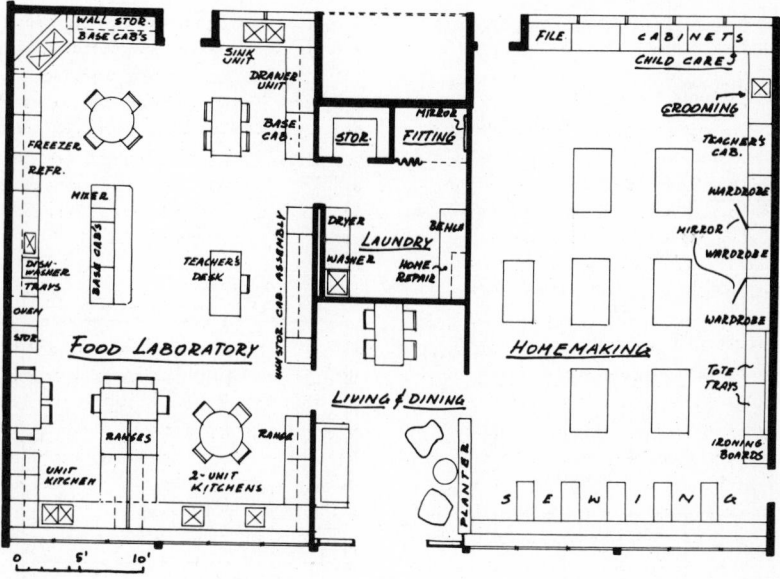

Fig. 72

It should have a large work area, office and planning area, finishing room, and project storage space, hardwood floors. Provide adequate aisles of traffic between individual parts of shop and areas all pupils will use, such as tool and storage rooms.

Office and planning center should have a desk and chair, bookcase, corridor display, group planning area for six to eight students with large planning board which may be demountable, bulletin board, 6 ft of chalkboard, black-out provision for motion pictures, lockers, first-aid kit.

Work area should have wood lathes, grinder, drill press, jigsaw, miter saw, planer, jointer, band saw, mortiser, circular saw, workbenches with four student stations each, glue and assembly bench with clamp rack, sander, safety mats around machines, metal wastebaskets.

Project storage area should contain lumber rack for horizontal storage, plywood storage rack, storage cabinets, open-storage area, drawers, cupboards.

Finishing room should have metal storage cabinets, benches, adjustable drying shelves, ventilating hood for limited bench service (approximately 300 sq ft), safety-type exhaust fan, explosion-proof lights, approved volatile liquid storage, wash sink and spray booth (hooded), worktables. The shop should have gas, water, and electrical provisions; drinking fountain; wash sink; soap and towel dispensers; fluorescent lighting (natural lighting must eliminate glare at working surface, bilateral lighting satisfactory); dust collecting system.

Shop for metals, electricity, and power mechanics

The above shop gives training in metal work (machine skills, wrought-iron, art and sheet metal), electricity, and automobile mechanics.

It should be on the first floor, accessible to the outside.

It should have a large general work area and office and planning area; provide adequate aisles of traffic between individual parts of shops and areas all pupils will use: Monorail, trolley, and chain fall; exhaust ducts; two overhead doors for moving equipment in and out easily.

General work area should have arc welding booths with front asbestos curtain, machine lathes, spinning lathe, layout benches, milling machines, surface grinder, sheet metal benches, grinder, drill press, shaper, welding and casting grinder, squaring shears, box and pan brake, band saw, portable hacksaw, buffer, spot welder, single-face vertical bar rack, wall bench for metal work, soldering bench, molder's bench, heat-treating gas furnace, furnace and anvil, movable test equipment, tune-up equipment, air compressor, battery charger, battery and starter tester, volt and amp tester, transformer, motor generators, starters, switchboard, panel board, cord racks, instrument tables, clock, lockable tool cabinets for smaller items of equipment, and safety mats around machines.

It should have a drinking fountain, wash sink with soap dispensers (grease-

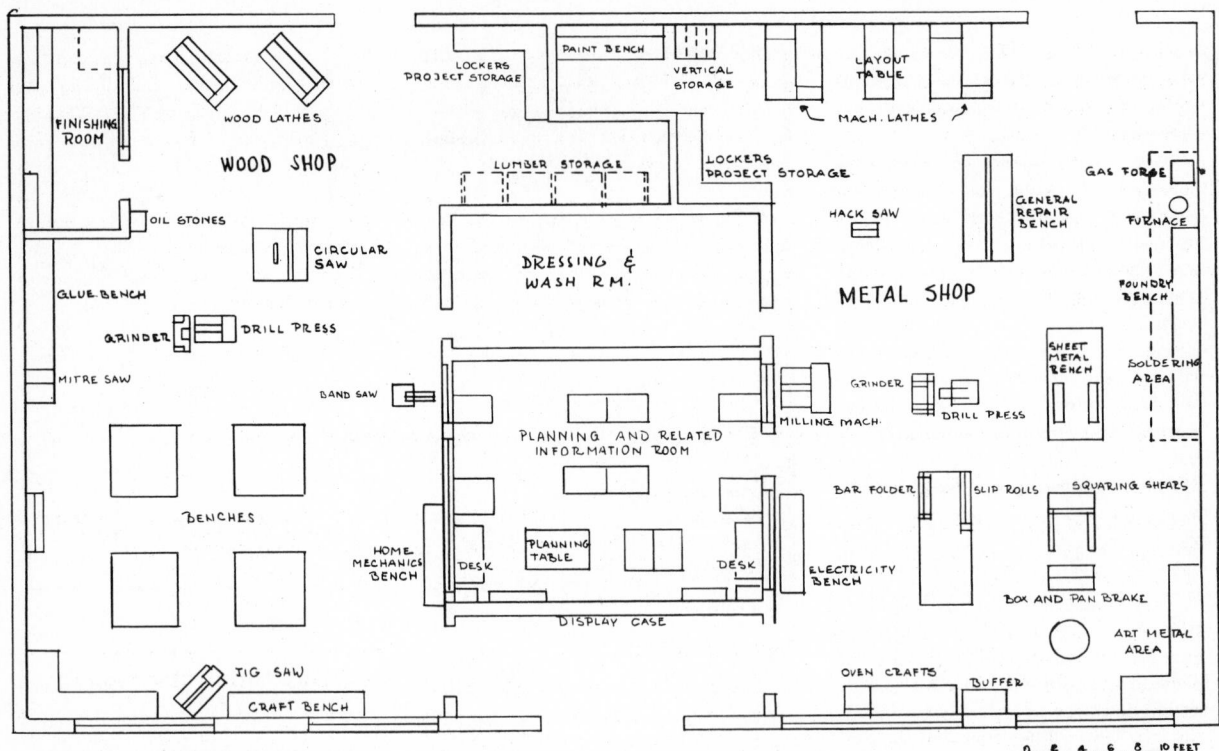

Fig. 73

solvent type), towel dispensers, gas, water, electricity, fluorescent lighting (natural lighting must eliminate glare at work surfaces; bilateral lighting satisfactory). Special attention should be paid to ventilation.

General shop

The general shop should be on the first floor, accessible to the outside.

There should be overhead doors to outside for delivery of materials; space for assembling, lumber storage, and instruction. The shop could be broken down into a discussion and planning area, woodworking area, metal-working area, and locker-washup area. Storage for supplies should be provided.

The discussion and planning area should have shelving, bulletin board, chalkboard, library table, chairs, files, bookcases, storage cabinet, teacher's desk and chair, wash sink with hot and cold water, planning or drawing tables.

The woodworking area should have space for cabinet work, carpentry, model building, pattern making, milling, upholstery; worktables; metal storage cabinets; adjustable drying shelves; vertical pipe lumber racks; safety-type exhaust fan; explosion-proof lights; approved volatile liquid storage; wash sink and spray booth (hooded); soap dispensers; lathes; planer; saws; work-benches; glue pot; paint cabinet.

The metal-working area should have a simple foundry; hand forging and welding facilities; sheet metal wastebaskets; corkboard; chalkboard; rubber safety mats around machines; black-out provisions for motion pictures and slides; two-way vision exhibit case in corridor walls; clock.

There should be lockers and a sink with hot and cold water.

Also needed are drinking fountain outlet; gas, water, and electrical provisions; fluorescent lighting (natural lighting must eliminate glare at working surfaces, bilateral lighting satisfactory); ceiling radiation heating; three remote control master switches.

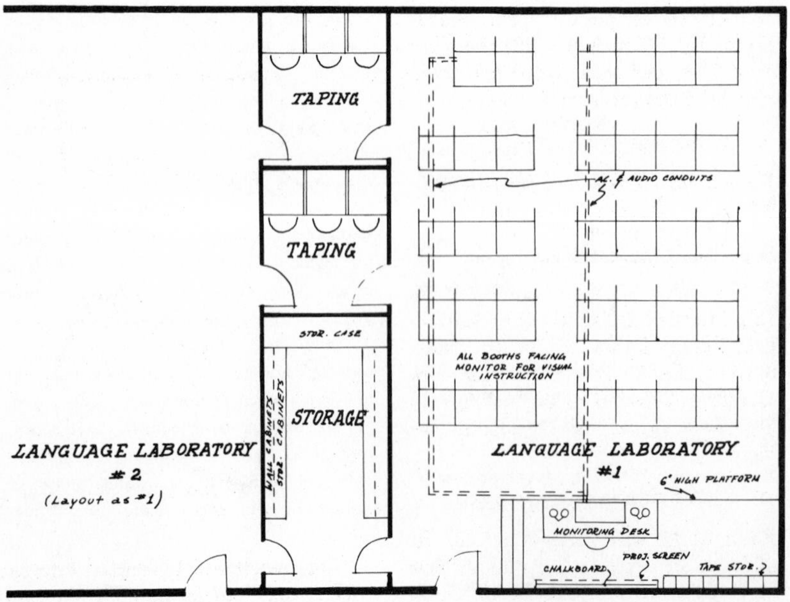

LANGUAGE LABORATORY

The language laboratory provides a place where pupils can listen to recordings in a foreign language, make their own recordings, practice speaking a foreign language in private, and carry out drill exercises.

It should have students' booths constructed of sound-absorbent material, ap-

Fig. 74

proximately 30 or 36 in. wide, 36 in. deep, 54 in. high. These should face the teacher. The top front half should have a see-through glass panel so that the student can see the teacher, and so that the laboratory can easily be adapted for audio-visual aids. The back wall and ceiling should be treated with acoustical or sound-absorbent materials.

Booths should be equipped with head-

phones, microphones attached to a flexible gooseneck stand, magnetic disc or tape recorder, and a control panel with switches for selecting balance and volume. There should be a monitor jack on the same panel.

At the front of the room, the teacher's area should have a platform at least 6 in. high in order to raise the level of vision into the student booths. The master unit

should accommodate three channels for simultaneous programs and should also contain two dual-track tape recorders and two phonographs, four-speed. A small soundproof booth will be necessary to enable the teacher to make master tape recordings. A typewriter with international keyboard is needed.

Storage and small recording rooms should be separate.

Adapted from Space for Teaching, *by William W. Caudill, Bulletin of Agricultural and Mechanical College of Texas*

Air movement around the building

Air movements inside any building depend on the velocity and direction of air movement outdoors.

Every locality has its own characteristic "wind rose" showing the average velocity and direction of prevailing breezes month by month throughout the year. In some localities the prevailing direction as well as the velocity varies with the season; in others the direction may be relatively constant. For most localities data are obtainable from the Weather Bureau.

Site factors qualify these general averages. Trees, tall buildings and other major obstructions must be studied at each site.

Pressure and suction effects

Only a small fraction of the air blowing against the face of a building effects an entry; the remainder is forced around and over the structure and creates a suction area above the building and on the emergent side. The air is pushed in on the windward side or sides and pulled out on the other sides and at the top.

Air movement within the building

To obtain efficient natural ventilation within a building it is necessary that inlet openings and outlet openings have approximately the same area. Rooms having windows on two exposures (preferably opposed sides) will have far better ventilation than those having windows on a single exposure. Again, if prevailing breezes blow at right angles to building walls ventilation will be better than in buildings having their long walls placed at an acute angle to prevailing winds.

The fresh air supply per minute per student, measured in cubic feet, may be computed as follows:

$$\left\{\begin{array}{l}\text{Fresh air supply}\\\text{per minute}\\\text{per student}\\\text{(in cubic feet)}\end{array}\right\} = \frac{\text{Area of inlet (sq. ft.) x Wind velocity (ft. per min.)}}{\text{Correction factor (K) x Volume (per child)}}$$

Typical problem

Assume two classrooms, each having sufficient volume to allow 250 cu. ft. per child. *Classroom "A"* faces south and has 100 sq. ft. of screened inlet opening and 35 sq. ft. of outlet opening. *Classroom "B"* faces southeast and has an outlet opening equal to the inlet opening of 100 sq. ft. What is the air supply per pupil per minute in each classroom if there is a 5-mile per hour wind from the southeast?

Supply in Classroom "A"

The inlet in Classroom "A" is approximately 3 times the area of the outlet. From the Correction Factor Table above we find the value of K to be 18. Wind velocity in m.p.h. may be changed to feet per minute by multiplying by 88; thus (5 x 88) the wind is 440 ft. per min. Applying these values to the formula we have:

$$\text{Air supply} = \frac{100 \times 440}{15 \times 250}$$

Each child will receive approximately 9.8 cu. ft. of fresh air per min.

Supply in Classroom "B"

The inlet in Classroom "B" is equal to the outlet. From the Correction Factor Table we find the value of K to be 4. Other conditions are similar to those in room "A." Applying these values to the formula we have:

$$\text{Air supply} = \frac{100 \times 440}{4 \times 250}$$

Each child will receive 44 cu. ft. of fresh air per min., or *roughly four times as much fresh air as in Classroom "A."*

NATURAL VENTILATION CORRECTION FACTORS

VALUE FOR K		
Ratio of Openings A is area of inlets A' is area of outlets	Perpendicular to wind	Diagonal to wind
A equals A'	2	3
A equals 2A'	4	6
A equals 3A'	6	9
A equals 4A'	8	12
A equals 5A'	10	15

If screens or louvers are used over inlets, multiply the value of K by 2; if both screens and louvers are used, multiply the value of K by 4.

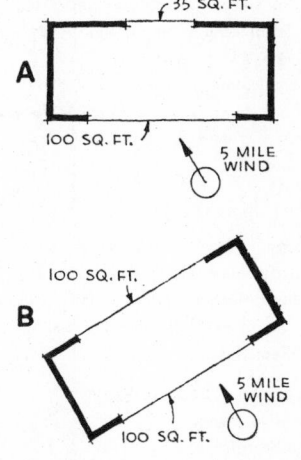

For mechanical ventilation, see "Heating, Ventilating, and Air Conditioning: Schools."

By CHARLES R. McCURDY, *Art Reference Librarian, Pratt Institute*

Since there are several types of libraries, i.e., public, academic (including school, college, and university), and special libraries, only the salient features are noted here. The following design recommendations have been adapted from the sources listed under *References* which specifically deal with the programs and planning of different types of libraries.

In large public and university libraries where the number of books exceeds 200,000, it is generally necessary to concentrate book storage in a multilevel stack area. In such areas the book stacks are usually designed to be self-supporting and the floors (called "decks") are supported by them, as shown in the isometric drawing following. The data on the following pages pertain to this type of installation.

In smaller libraries, however, most librarians prefer to have the normal floor construction of the building designed to carry bookshelves in any location on the floor. This scheme permits complete flexibility in the arrangement of bookshelves and reading space, and facilitates future alterations and expansion.

NOTE: See further discussion and illustrations in section on "Schools."

Reading rooms for academic libraries

Space should be provided to accommodate at least one-tenth of the student body. An allowance of 30 to 35 sq ft per reader is recommended; this provides space for bookshelves, tables, chairs, charge desk, and comfortable circulation.

Shelving should be provided in the reading room for a suitable portion of the book collection. Detailed recommendations for shelving are given elsewhere in this section.

Vertical filing cabinets (legal size) are used for storing miscellaneous material, such as clippings, pictures, and pamphlets. Each cabinet occupies a floor area 18 in. wide by 29 in. deep.

Card catalog: Each unit of 15 drawers provides filing space for cards for 3,000 volumes; a unit is 33 in. wide by 17 in. deep.

Special reading rooms

Large school libraries often provide separate rooms for one or more of the functions listed below. Smaller libraries may use alcoves off the main reading room for these functions.

Reference books
Reserve books
Periodicals
Faculty reading room

Conference rooms

One conference room (120 sq ft minimum) is recommended for every 1,000 students. It should be located adjacent to the main reading room and separated from it by glass partitions, so that it can be supervised from the circulation desk. Conference rooms should be acoustically treated and provided with shelving for books and records.

Audio-visual center

If the audio-visual center is located in the library it should provide the following facilities:

Equipment room (300 to 400 sq ft) provided with locked cupboards for storing the following equipment:

16-mm sound movie projector
2 by 2-in. slide projector
3¼ by 4-in. slide projector
Opaque projector
Overhead projector
Projection screens
Record player
Tape recorder
Radio receiver
Television receiver
Spare parts and supplies; portable stands

It should also provide workbenches or tables for servicing the equipment.

Materials room (300 to 400 sq ft) provided with storage facilities for slides, filmstrips, movie film, tapes, records; also card catalog, workbenches, tables, desks, and chairs.

Viewing and auditioning room (800 to 1,000 sq ft).

Office (150 to 200 sq ft).

Offices and workrooms

Librarian's office—private, receptionist or secretary located in outer office.

Cataloging office—accessible to the public catalog; area of at least 125 sq ft per staff member is required.

Preparation room—adjacent to cataloging office, with connecting door; shelving, storage for supplies, and washbasins should be provided; minimum area, 125 sq ft per staff member.

Other areas

Checkroom and security area in lobby near entrance; turnstiles and guard.
Student toilets; staff toilets.
Student lounge; staff lounge (optional).
Exhibition gallery; small auditorium (optional).

Public libraries contain many features of an academic library. However, they also provide special departments for work with children and young adults, music rooms, and browsing areas. They frequently must provide space for administrative work with bookmobiles and branch and extension centers.

Shelving

All shelving should be freestanding and all shelves should be adjustable in height. Dimensions of shelving are as follows:

Width of section: 3 ft
Height of section: Elementary school—5 to 6 ft
Junior high school—6 ft
Senior high school, college, and public libraries—6 to 7 ft
Height of parts: Base—4 to 6 in.
Cornice, if used—2 in.
Shelf thickness—13/16 in.
Usual distance between shelves—10 to 10½ in.
Depth of shelves: Standard—8 to 10 in.
Oversize—10 to 12 in.
For bound periodicals—12 to 15 in.
For phonograph records and picture books—16 in.
For mounted art reproductions—30 in., with many vertical dividers
For current periodicals—sloping display shelves—16 in. measured along the slope, 12 in. measured from front straight back

Miscellaneous equipment

The following equipment is standard in most types of libraries and space should be provided for it:

Bulletin boards and display cases
Book trucks
Step ladders and stools
Microfilm reader and storage cabinets
Dictionary stands
Index tables for periodical indexes
World globe for reference section
Rapid photocopying equipment

REFERENCES

Standards for School Library Programs. American Library Association, Chicago (1960).

Planning School Library Quarters: A Functional Approach. American Library Association, Chicago (1950). 53 pp.

Ellsworth, Ralph E. *Planning the College*

nd University Library Building: A Book
r Campus Planners and Architects. University of Colorado, Boulder (1960). 102
pp.

vin, Hoyt R., and Van Buren, Martin.

The Small Public Library Building.
UNESCO, Paris (1959). 133 pp.
Hilligan, Margaret P. (ed.). *Libraries for Research and Industry.* Special Libraries Association, New York (1955). 58 pp.

Diagrammatic section of a multi-tier bookstack. The columns of successive rs are joined to form a continuous column which supports both the deck and e shelving

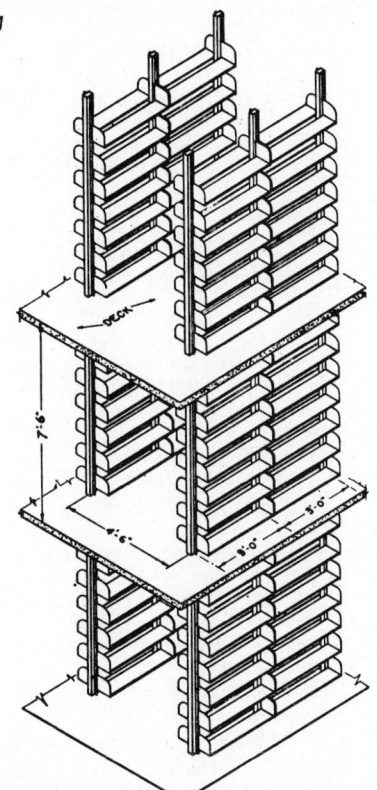

Plan of a bookstack, showing typical components and average spacing

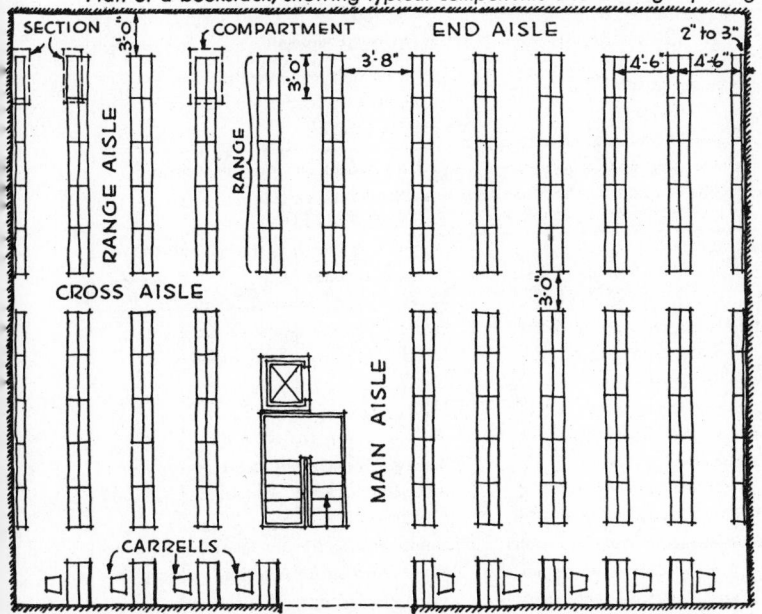

Data courtesy of W. R. Ames Co.; Breeze Corps., Inc.; and Snead & Co.

GLOSSARY OF TRADE TERMS

Section — Shelving between two shelf supports

Compartment — Two sections back to back

Stack Columns — Members which act as shelf supports and vertical uprights, dividing compartments and carrying stack loads

Range — A group of sections (single-faced range) or compartments (double-faced range) with shelf supports common to adjacent sections

Tier — One level in a bookstack

Deck — A stack room floor — usually one of the intermediate floors of a multi-tier stack

Carrell — A space or cubicle provided in a stack for individual study — usually equipped with desk and shelves

Aisles

Main Aisle — The "Main Street" of a bookstack

Cross Aisle — Secondary aisle branching off main aisle

End Aisle — Aisle along the wall of a bookstack

Range Aisle — Aisle between two ranges

Booklift — Dumbwaiter adapted to library use

Book Conveyor — Power-operated device for mechanical delivery of books from stacks to users in a multi-tier installation

SHELF AND STACK DATA

Height of Bookstack — Generally 7 ft. 6 in. measuring from top surface of deck floor to top surface of deck floor above, in multi-tier installations; 7 ft. 2½ in. overall for one-tier stacks

Shelf Sections — Normally 3 ft. long between shelf supports; 8, 9, 10, or 12 in. wide for books, and 18, 20, or 22 in. wide for bound newspapers

Ranges — Length, as required, preferably not over 30 ft., in even multiples of shelf length. Parallel ranges generally spaced on centers 4 ft. 6 in. apart

Aisles — Main, 3 to 4 ft. wide; range, 2 ft. 6 in. to 3 ft.

Stairs — Straight runs: well length, 8 to 9 ft., 12 risers; width, 2 ft. 6 in. or slightly more. Return runs: well length, 6 ft. 8 in., 12 risers; width, 5 ft. or slightly more

Deck Floor — Three general types: (1) reinforced concrete, usually 3½ in. thick; (2) flanged or formed steel plates, ⅛ in. to ³⁄₁₆ in. thick (to bottom of flanges — about 2¾ in.); and (3) steel framework with 1¼-in. marble, slate, or stone (4⅝ in. from top of slab to bottom of supporting steel frame). Resilient floor covering adds only approximately ¼ in. thickness to slabs or plates

UNIT STACK WEIGHTS

BOOKS
25 to 30 lb. per cu. ft. of ranges

STACK CONSTRUCTION
Quoted as 5, 8, and 8 to 10 lb. per cu. ft., depending upon the manufacturer

DECK FRAMING
2 to 4 lb. per sq. ft. of gross deck area

DECK FLOORING
3-in. reinforced concrete slab, 38 lb. per sq. ft.; 3½-in. reinforced concrete slab, 44 lb. per sq. ft. gross area, with ⅛ in. tile or linoleum covering, 45 lb.; flanged steel plate floor, 12 lb. per sq. ft. of gross area; 1¼-in. marble or slate, 18 lb. per sq. ft., aisle area

LIVE LOADS
Building codes vary, but in general, for column loads, assume 40 lb. per sq. ft. of aisle area for live load and reduce this figure 5 per cent for each deck below the top deck

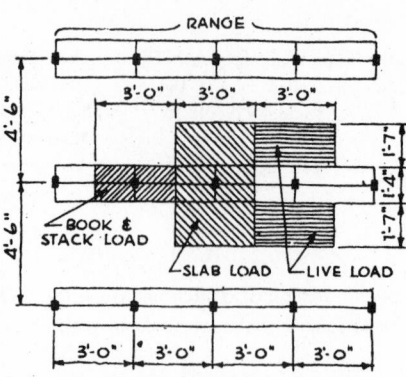

TYPICAL STACK LOADING DIAGRAM

STACK LOADS. The following tables illustrate the general variation of stack loads for from one to twelve tiers.

8″ SHELVING							Including stacks, books, live load, and 3½-in. concrete deck floor (A = typical aisle end support; B = typical intermediate support; C = typical wall end support).						10″ SHELVING	

TIERS	1	2	3	4	5	6	7	8	9	10	11	12	TIERS	1	2	3	4	5	6	7	8	9	10	11	12
A	495	2,320	4,120	5,890	7,630	9,340	11,020	12,670	14,290	15,880	17,440	18,970	A	620	2,570	4,490	6,380	8,240	10,070	11,870	13,640	15,380	17,090	18,770	20,420
B	990	3,000	4,990	6,960	8,910	10,840	12,750	14,640	16,510	18,360	20,190	22,000	B	1,240	4,000	6,240	8,460	10,660	12,840	15,000	17,140	19,260	21,360	23,440	25,500
C	495	1,500	2,600	3,590	4,570	5,540	6,500	7,450	8,390	9,320	10,240	11,150	C	620	1,750	2,870	3,980	5,080	6,170	7,250	8,320	9,480	10,530	11,570	12,600

BOOKSTACK CAPACITIES

Among formulas suggested for use in computing the size of stacks necessary to house a given number of books is the "Cubook" method, devised by R. W. Henderson of the New York Public Library.* The "cubook" is a measurement of stack capacity, defined as the "volume of space required to shelve the average book in the typical library." According to this formula, a single-faced section of stack, 3 ft. long and 7 ft. 6 in. high, has the following capacities:

100 "cubooks" (85 per cent octavos, 13 per cent quartos, and 2 per cent folios) †
117 volumes (87 per cent octavos and 13 per cent quartos)
132 volumes (octavos only)
67 volumes (quartos only)
12 volumes (folios only)

The "cubook" method makes provision for 10 per cent of each shelf to remain unoccupied since it often is impractical to load shelves to their full visible capacity.

To determine the number of sections required when the number of volumes to be shelved is known, the following formulas are used:

Let N = number of single-faced sections required (1 section = 100 "cubooks")

(1) For a typical library, when the "cubook" is considered directly applicable: N = Vols. ÷ 100

(2) For a library made up of octavos and quartos only:
N = Vols. ÷ 117

(3) For a library made up of octavos only: N = Vols. ÷ 132.3

(4) For a library made up of quartos only: N = Vols. ÷ 67.5

(5) For a library made up of folios only: N = Vols. ÷ 11.7

(6) For a library made up of various size groups when the ratios are known:
N = [Octavos + (quartos × 1.96) + (folios × 11.3)] ÷ 132.3

Shelf Size

The foregoing formulas indicate the number of sections required but do not cover the number of shelves or the proportion of shelves of each width (8 in., 10 in., or 12 in.). In general, the following shelf data applies:

For folios — 13 12-in. shelves per section

For octavos and quartos — usually 7 shelves per section, divided as follows:

85 per cent 8-in. shelves
10 per cent 10-in. shelves
5 per cent 12-in. shelves

Area and Volume Requirements

The "cubook" can be reduced to approximate terms of area and volume requirements for bookstacks, as follows:

11.08 "cubooks" require 1 sq. ft. of stack floor area
1.48 "cubooks" require 1 cu. ft. of space in a stack

These values can be used as follows:
Required stack floor area = No. "cubooks" × .090
Required space (cu. ft.) = No. "cubooks" × .676

* Library Journal, Nov. 15, 1934, and Jan. 15, 1936.
† According to American Library Association, an octavo is about 8 to 10 in. high; a quarto, 10 to 12 in.; and a folio, over 12 in.

SHELVING DATA FOR SPECIAL COLLECTIONS (To be consistent with "Cubook" method, figures shown should be reduced by 10 per cent, to avoid overcrowding shelves.)						
TYPE OF BOOK	Vols. per Foot of Shelf	Vols. per Foot of Single-Faced Range	Vols. per Shelf	Maximum Vols. per Single-Faced Section	Shelf Depth	Shelves per Section
Circulating (Non-Fiction)	8	56	24	168	8″	7
Fiction	8	56	24	168	8″	7
Economics	8	56	24	168	8″	7
General Literature	7	49	21	147	8″	7
Reference	7	49	21	147	8″ & 10″	6–7
History	7	49	21	147	8″	7
Technical and Scientific	6	42	18	126	8″, 10″ & 12″	7
Medical	5	35	15	105	8″ & 10″	6–7
Law	4	28	12	84	8″	7
Public Documents	5	35	15	105	8″	7
Bound Periodicals	5	35	15	105	10″ & 12″	5–7
U. S. Patent Specifications	2	14	6	42	8″	7
Art	7	42	21	126	10″ & 12″	5–6
Braille	4	24	12	72	15″	5–6

INDIVIDUAL STUDY CARRELS

From an Educational Facilities Laboratories report*

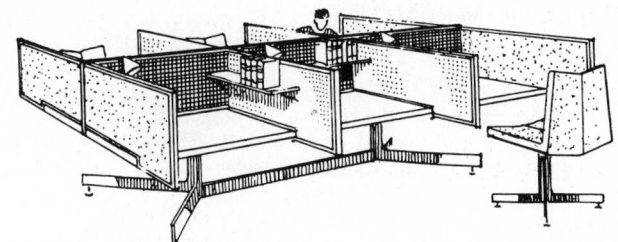

Conventional library table subdivided by panels

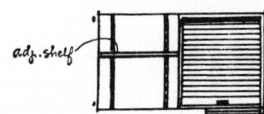

Typical storage units: (*top*) exposed adjustable shelf, (*left*) tambour door, (*right*) sliding doors

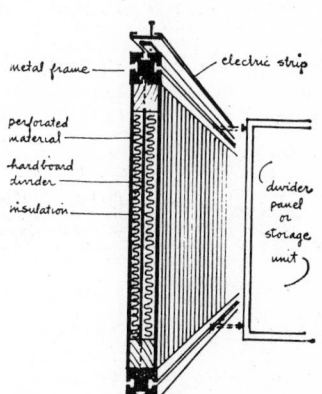

Divider panel and center divider. Side panels or storage units can be slid along tracks of center divider to change carrel size

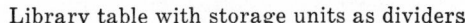

Library table with storage units as dividers

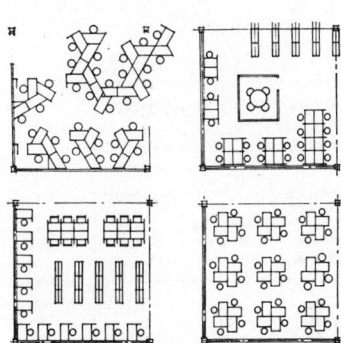

Possible carrel arrangements

*"The School Library, Facilities for Independent Study in the Secondary School," by Ralph E. Ellsworth, Ph.D and Hobart D. Wagener, A.I.A., edited by Ruth Weinstock

Carrels for four student places using octagonal table

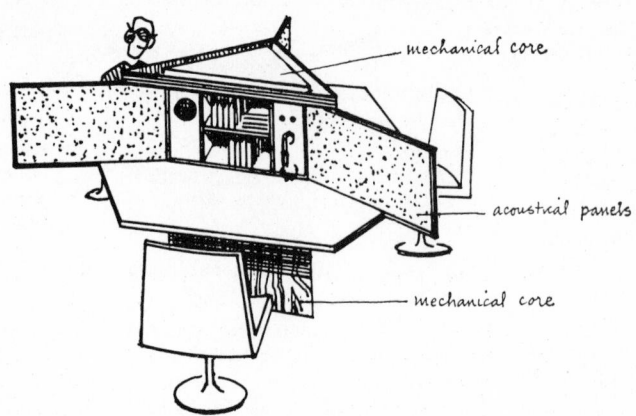

Hexagon-based carrel with mechanical core

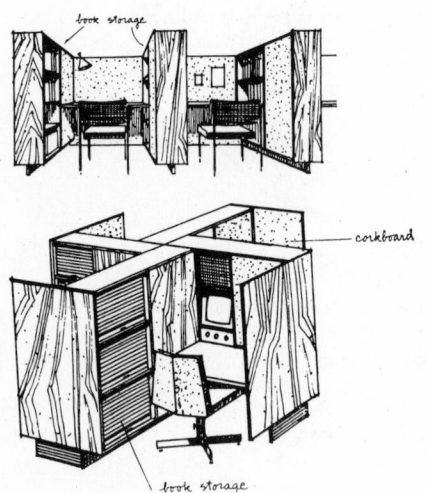

Carrel arrangements using standard bookcases and tables

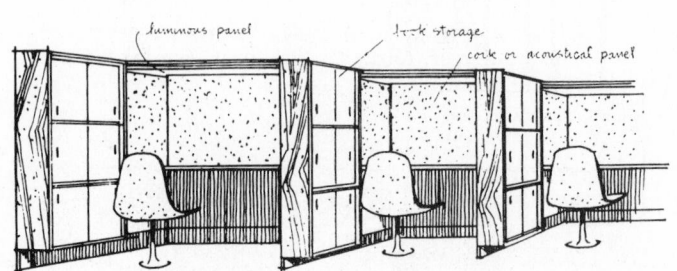

Carrels with storage lockers for books

Carrel provided with typing unit

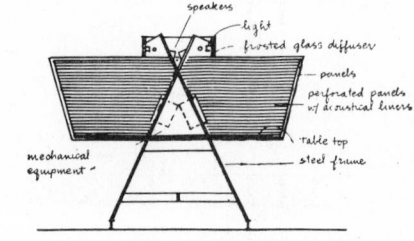

Carrels with audio-visual equipment built in

By AUGUST HOENACK, *Chief, Architectural and Engineering Branch, Division of Hospital and Medical Facilities, Public Health Service, U.S. Department of Health, Education and Welfare*

The hospital as a building type is composed of complex components, each of which could well tax the talents of architects, mechanical engineers, and the other professions and skills involved in their design and construction. Material relating to *all* these components would fill a book. Therefore, the following have been selected for discussion in this section:

Bedrooms
Nursing units
Surgical suite
Nursery
Pediatric unit
Diagnostic X-ray suite

Teletherapy unit
Electroencephalographic suite
Laboratory
Physical therapy department
Occupational therapy department

The material presented here has been selected, not necessarily as a guide from a functional standpoint or to indicate what the hospital may need, but rather as examples of critical space organization involving specialized equipment and facilities which are peculiar to a hospital. The extent of services, kind of equipment, space requirements, etc., will vary with each hospital and must be related to the services the hospital is to perform. Consequently, the information presented here must, of course, be adapted in each case.

Much has been written on the subject of the design and construction of hospitals. An adequate bibliography of this material is beyond the scope of this section. The architect who is not acquainted with hospital design should obtain additional information and bibliographies from such sources as the Bacon Library of the American Hospital Association in Chicago and the U.S. Public Health Service in Washington, D.C.

On this page are shown generalized flow charts for the hospital as a whole and for various departments which are not discussed in the following pages.

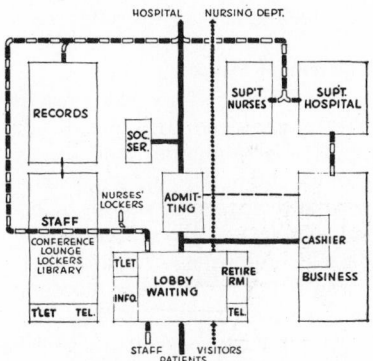

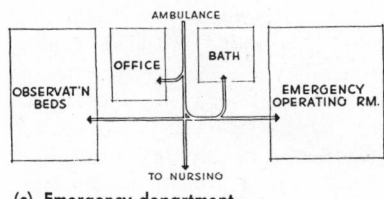

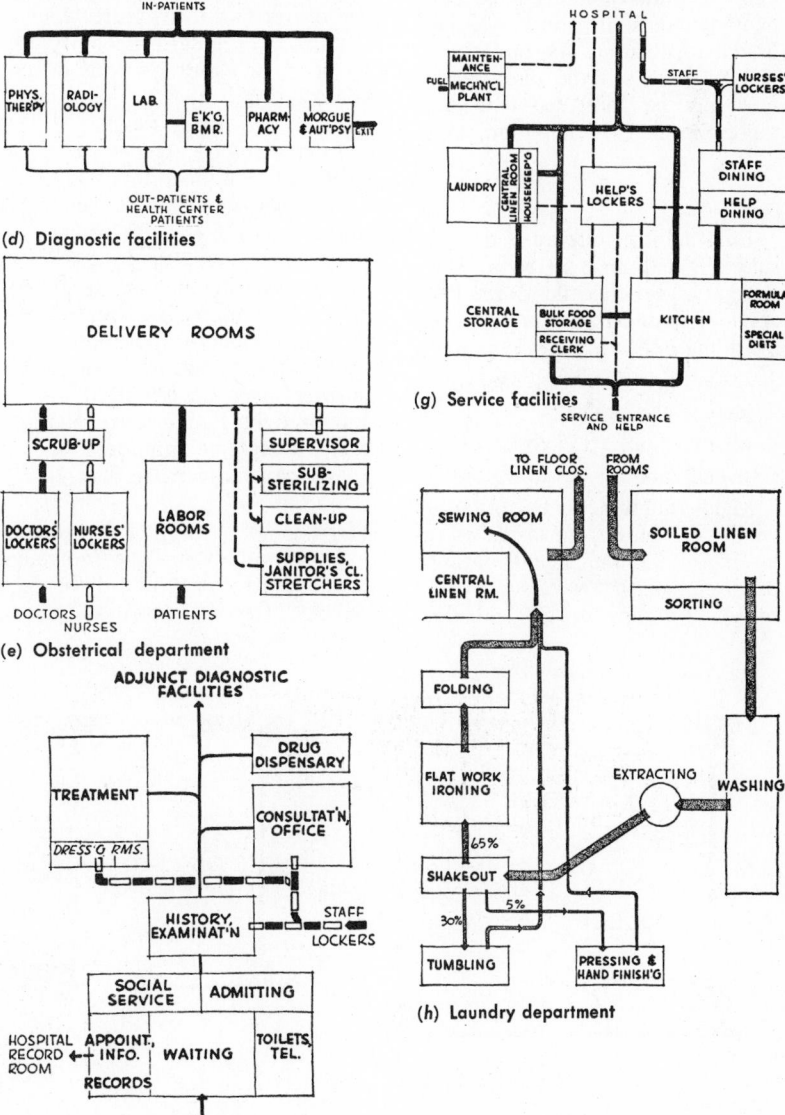

Fig. 1. Flow charts

From Design and Construction of General Hospitals by Public Health Service, U.S. Department of Health, Education and Welfare (1953).

Report by the AIA Committee on Hospitals & Health

It was not the committee's purpose to include an analysis of the number of beds per nursing unit, or the proportions of single, double and four-bed rooms within given units. This study is limited to the individual room *per se,* to a review of numerous small but often vital details that make either a good room or an unsatisfactory one. These details are fine points that an administrator or architect should be familiar with before departing to something more original, if that should be his wish.

In general, the many room plans reviewed have basic similarities but many variations in detail. Accompanying plans have been specially drawn to illustrate the majority of features that will be discussed. It must not be construed that these represent ideal or minimum standards.

Size

First point of interest is the considerable variation in room sizes. Ranges of net clear floor area from corridor door to window stool, not including built-in wardrobes, are:

single rooms: 117 to 172 sf
   (deluxe are larger)

double rooms: 157 to 210 sf

four-bed rooms: 308 to 401 sf

Major differences are found in depth of rooms from inside of exterior wall to room side of corridor partition, all the way from 14'-6" for single rooms or 15'-0" for dou-

* AIA Journal, *September, 1960.*

ble and four-bed rooms to 21'-8" for all types. These differences are caused principally by varied space requirements of one or two beds in combination with various plumbing facilities — they reflect the endless search for a common denominator which will have flexibility to accommodate several combinations of room and toilet requirements within a uniform building dimension and fenestration without waste of expensive space.

In the two and four-bed rooms a clear distance of 14'-0" for two beds and two bedside tables is "snug," but it should be noted that the majority of rooms studied measure nearer to 15'-0" clear, which is the USPHS standard. Lavatory, toilet door, or wardrobe door do not encroach into these clear dimensions in the better rooms.

In the other dimension, comments of administrators evoke no complaints about single rooms as narrow as 10'-0" to centers of partitions—rooms up to 12'-0" on centers draw comments from "excellent" to "more than ample." Majority of double bedrooms are 12'-0" on centers and are well regarded—smaller ones are criticized for being too tight. Four-bed rooms range from acceptable minimum of 20'-0" on centers to more than 24'-0".

Closets

In almost every case individual hanging space is provided for each patient, often in the form of built-in

metal wardrobes—sometimes these are in combination with dressers, with mirrors over. One caution was offered that mirrors should not be so placed as to reflect light into patient's eyes.

Furniture

There is uniformity in every plan reviewed in the way beds are set parallel to exterior wall, so that patients can look out window without facing directly into the bright sky. Motor-operated high-low beds are also uniformly popular—it should be noted that they may be a full 7'-3" in overall length.

There is no uniformity in position of bedside table. It may be placed on near side of bed as one enters room, or on far side, or sometimes on patient's right or left, whichever way the bed faces. No preponderant preference can be detected. The typical bedside table measures about 16" x 20".

Plans reviewed did not concern themselves with other furniture. In single rooms, especially, the presence of a bureau, side chair, arm chair, ottoman, or television set is partly dependent on economic status of patient being served. These items take space and deserve attention in the planning stage—they may well affect overall room size.

Plumbing Fixtures

Next to room size the most important architectural problem is disposition of plumbing facilities. Although minimum budget hospitals are still being built without a toilet connecting to every bedroom, a private toilet is now regarded as a basic feature with each bedroom. It is perhaps axiomatic that in almost every case a bedpan cleansing device is incorporated. 2'-10" to 3'-2" by 3'-10" to 4'-10" are the dimensions noted for individual toilet rooms, usually with grab-bars on one or both side walls. Locating water closet slightly off-center in the room allows a little more space on wider side for manipulating cleanser—the latter needs only cold water and is usually on the right as you face back wall. Some plans indicate bedpan rack or cabinet within toilet room—otherwise bedpan is stored in bedside table.

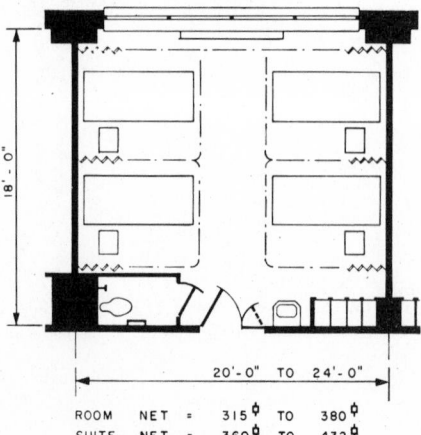

ROOM   NET = 315# TO 380#
SUITE NET = 360# TO 432#

Fig. 2   Four-bed room

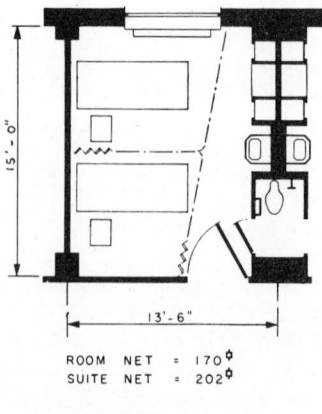

ROOM NET = 170#
SUITE NET = 202#

Fig. 3. Double bedroom, small, shared toilet

Several plans were reviewed which showed shared toilets between two single or double rooms. While this arrangement may save some space and expense, it presents its own problems such as added disturbance to patients, special door hardware, and lack of flexibility in room assignment to patients of opposite sex. It is interesting that the administrators with this type of accommodation offered no comment on these points. The committee infers that the shared toilet is valid only in large hospitals, in which separation of sexes is a lesser problem.

Location of lavatory reveals about an even choice between placing it in bedroom proper, where it invites more frequent use by attending nurses and physicians, or in toilet rooms, where it is less institutional-looking to patient and visitors. It is known that some thoughtful hospitals purposely set lavatories at 3'-0" above floor—in other plans studied, the lower, conventional residential height is observed.

Not many toilet rooms have tubs, which make them complete bathrooms off bedrooms. This choice is undoubtedly a matter of economics of the particular hospital. The fact that almost no shower stalls appear leads the committee to conjecture that most hospitals are content to have shower heads in tubs, relying on suction-cup rubber mats and strong grab bars to avoid injury to patients from slipping.

Doors and Windows

Standard bedroom door width is 3'-10" or 4'-0". This can be reduced by 2" with offset hinges. A slight majority of doors to single and double rooms is hinged on side toward beds, so that door ajar serves as screen to patient. Toilet room door widths are 2'-0" to 2'-4" swinging out into bedroom, except where surface-bolted or pivoted hinges are used, so that doors can be removed in the event a patient in toilet room faints and falls against door.

The wide variety of window treatment suggests that climate, orientation, esthetics, economics and other considerations do more to govern this architectural feature than any predetermined optimum standard. It is interesting that administrators'

comments in this general area say little about psychological or therapeutic values of wide vs narrow or high vs low windows, but do offer practical complaints about windows that are drafty or difficult to clean and wood stools that spot too easily. Preferences are expressed for marble and laminated plastic stools. A definite division of opinion is found between those who prefer nothing but drapes and those who favor only Venetian blinds at windows. The committee notes that low window stools offer patient an opportunity to see out when his motorized bed is in its low position.

Room Finishes

There is no strong preference for one type of flooring material over another. Inquiries made about oversize sloping bases to keep furniture away from walls reveal that those few who have them seem satisfied, whereas only one administrator without them expressed a wish that he might have had them. Wall behind bed is the only location within a bedroom where a sloping base appears to have merit. Plaster walls are most common. Acoustical ceilings are not considered essential, even in multi-bed rooms—use of a suspended acoustical system is more valuable for access to mechanical work than for its acoustical properties.

Built-in Equipment

Built - in wardrobe - dresser - recessed-mirror combinations have been discussed above. Some emphasis is also found for separate 9" wide flower shelves bracketed on wall beside or opposite bed, about 4'-6" above floor. There are a variety of cubicle curtain arrangements in multi-bed rooms, from the simplest cross-room tracks to complete enclosures around each bed.

Lighting

A study of the rooms shows that no single, a few double, and most four-bed rooms have ceiling fixtures for general illumination. In almost all rooms there is a wall fixture over head of bed, mounted from 5'-2" to 6'-6" above floor. There are numerous fixtures on the market today for this purpose, providing varying combinations of direct and indirect light. The one

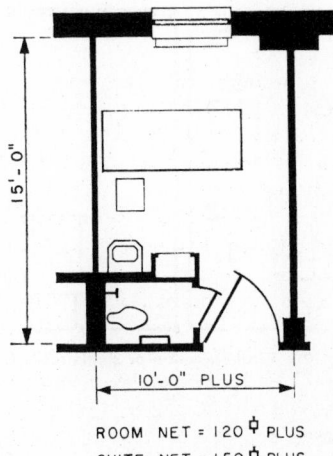

ROOM NET = 120 ☐ PLUS
SUITE NET = 150 ☐ PLUS

Fig. 4. Single room, small

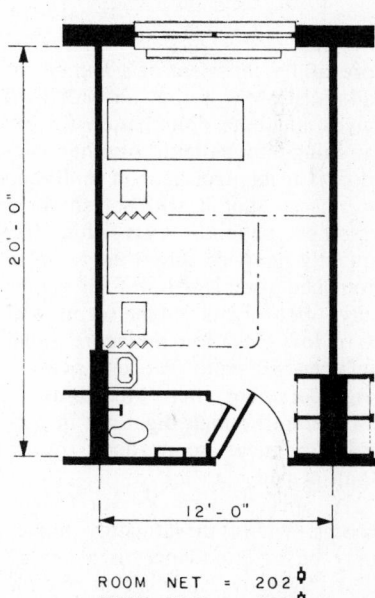

ROOM NET = 202 ☐
SUITE NET = 240 ☐

Fig. 5. Double room, medium size

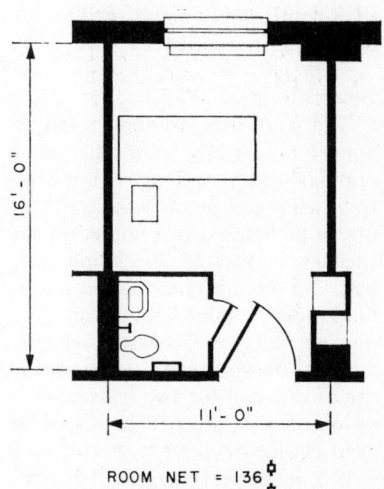

ROOM NET = 136 ☐
SUITE NET = 176 ☐

Fig. 6. Single room, medium size

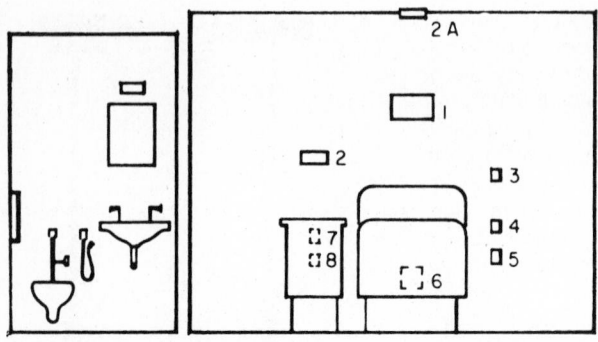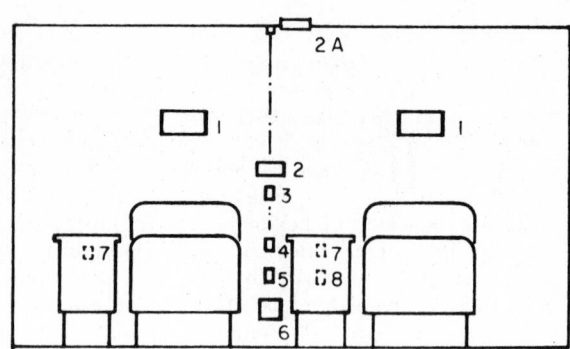

Fig. 7. Wall elevation of single room (left) and double room (right)

Legend

1. Overbed light
2. Nurses' call
2A. Micro speaker in ceiling

3. Oxygen outlet
4. Suction outlet
5. Suction bottle bracket

6. Night light—switch outside room door
7. Double duplex outlet
8. Telephone, radio, TV jacks

prevailing comment of a number of administrators is that no wall light gives adequate illumination for examining the patient. Another caution is to control light in multi-bed rooms so that it will not shine in another patient's eyes—this frequently happens across the room in four-bed rooms. Almost all rooms have night-lights, either set in wall at a low elevation or incorporated in over-bed light. The one prevailing comment here recommends switching the night-light out in corridor or near room door, rather than at bedside.

A special wrinkle for single rooms, where private duty nurses may be in attendance, is a ceiling down-light over a chair near door into the room, at which location the nurse can guard patient from unwanted visitors and at same time read comfortably day or night without bothering patient.

Other Electrical Work

The audio-visual nurse's call is almost universally used and gets a popular rating among administrators who commented—except for use in pediatrics. In some cases the speaker is located in ceiling over bed. In one instance a request is made for the pilot light also in ceiling, as being more easily seen by patient. On walls with two beds the use of one call for two beds or provision of separate calls is about an even choice.

In a small percentage of hospitals several radio channels are piped in at head of bed. In fewer instances

the same is true of TV; most TV sets are portable and provided through a rental agency.

Oxygen and Suction

Oxygen is piped in from a central source in most rooms studied. Outlets are 4'-0" to 5'-6" above floors—5'-0" minimum is the *NFPA Bulletin #565* standard if outlet is not recessed. There is an even division of opinion concerning location of oxygen outlets, either on near side of bed, as one enters room, or on far side. Suction is provided in all rooms in approximately one-third of the hospitals, in some rooms in one-third, and in no rooms in one-third. Outlets are either grouped in same plate with oxygen or they are separate, beside or below oxygen. Piped compressed air in bedrooms is noted only occasionally.

Airconditioning

The incidence of airconditioning is still something that depends on climate and economics. Individual room units present no problems of cross-contamination of air from one room to another. Central systems do create problems if recirculation is desired. A check across the country indicates that opinion is divided on extent to which central recirculation should be permitted.

Organization of Wall Outlets

An over-all glance at the numerous room layouts studied by the committee emphasizes the clutter of wall outlets and paraphernalia of many kinds at head of each bed. In

general they detract from appearance of room. A check-list for a well-equipped bed in a single room will include some 24 different facilities! In order to minimize the scatter effect at normal eye level, the committee suggests that half of these facilities could be consolidated in a low-wall outlet through a single flexible cable to bedside table, where many items would be within reach of patient. Only two items might then occur on wall at eye-level—oxygen outlet (code requirement) and over-bed light (if used). Following check-list gives an indication of the thinking of some of the committee on this point:

Portable Bedside Panel
(Patient's Control)

- nurses' call switch, pilot light, monitor light
- general room illumination switch, dimmer control
- reading light switch
- room thermostat remote control
- electric blanket control
- electric clock
- duplex convenience receptacle
- radio station selector (central radio system)
- jack for pillow speaker (ceiling speaker in private rooms)
- provision for TV remote control to be clipped onto panel
- provision for telephone instrument (bracket type)

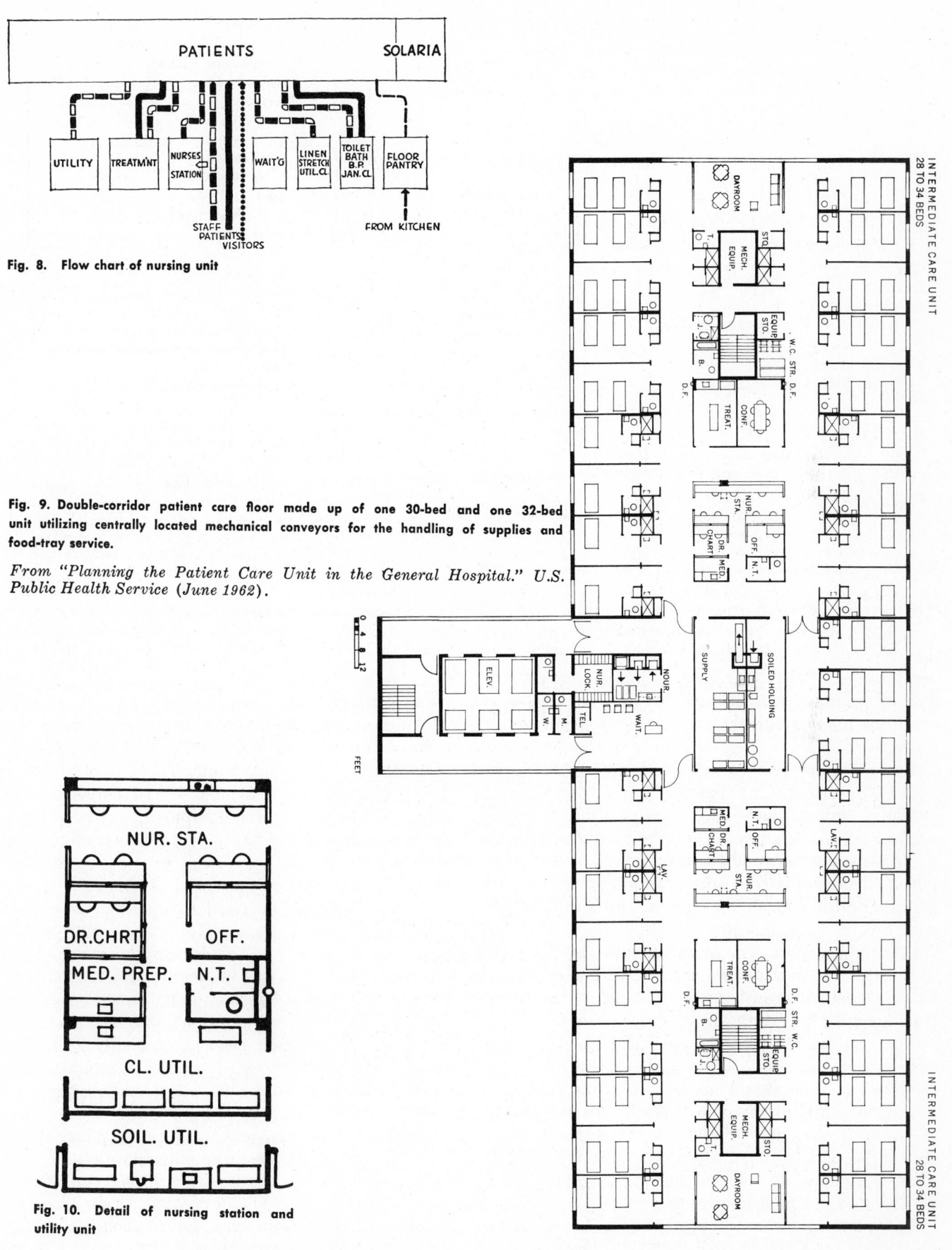

Fig. 8. Flow chart of nursing unit

Fig. 9. Double-corridor patient care floor made up of one 30-bed and one 32-bed unit utilizing centrally located mechanical conveyors for the handling of supplies and food-tray service.

From "Planning the Patient Care Unit in the General Hospital." U.S. Public Health Service (June 1962).

Fig. 10. Detail of nursing station and utility unit

Integral with bed
- bed control (within patient's reach, but with nurse-controlled cut-off feature)

Ceiling
- nurses' call micro-speaker
- radio speaker (private rooms only)

High on Wall (60″ or higher)
- over-bed light fixture (direct and indirect)
- oxygen outlet

Low on Wall (approximately 24″)
- receptacle for portable bedside panel
- night light (switched from corridor)
- telephone jack
- double duplex receptacle (bed, oxygen tent, portable X-ray, heating pad, etc)
- remote recording instrument re-

ceptacles (temp, pulse, respiratory)
- suction outlet
- bracket for suction bottle

DOUBLE CORRIDOR NURSING FLOOR

The plan shows a typical double-corridor nursing unit which is often utilized in hospital planning. It has the following advantages:

1. It permits a closer relationship between the patient bedrooms and the nursing station and other service areas.

2. It permits greater flexibility in segregation of patients for various medical reasons.

3. Much of the staff activity and particularly conversation can be carried on within the service unit complex, thus cutting down noise in the patient corridor.

The detail indicates more clearly the nursing station and utility room arrangement. The clean utility is designed to ac-

commodate carts for storing linens, utensils, and other supplies, which would be brought from a central supply and sterilizing unit. Elevators are located outside the nursing unit to cut down on the amount of noise. This would also permit a future nursing unit to be located on the other side of the elevators.

The success of this plan depends, to a great extent, on well-designed air conditioning and lighting, particularly for the center unit. While this nursing floor consists of two 25-bed nursing units, many authorities believe that greater efficiencies are obtained in having a larger ratio of beds per nursing station. This particular nursing floor might easily be extended one or two bays, increasing the capacity to 62 or 70 beds.

This plan also demonstrates how an intensive nursing service can be integrated into the same module or bay which accommodates the typical patient room. One 6-bed intensive ward is shown, and the adjacent typical double rooms can accommodate intensive-care patients when the need arises.

By AARON N. KIFF and MARY WORTHEN,, *Kiff, Colean, Souder & Voss* (Office of York and Sawyer)

The surgical suite of the general hospital is a very complex workshop. It is one of the most important departments of any hospital, and its planning is complicated by the diversities of opinion and experience of the many persons involved in policy decisions essential to development of a good program of requirements.

We say a "program of requirements" rather than "plan." Before any intelligent planning can be done by the architect, there must be a meeting of minds on the size of department; i.e., the number and type of operating rooms and the work methods to be followed in the supportive areas. Administrators, surgeons, anesthetists, surgical nurses, all must participate in the pre-planning analysis of needs and functional methods. The architect must have a wide understanding of various management procedures to be sure that all are discussed in reaching any conclusions with the particular group involved.

The number and type of operating rooms is the first major decision. In the general hospital, the tendency is to have all major operating rooms as nearly identical as possible to facilitate scheduling of various surgical procedures. Free floor space should be 18 ft by 20 ft, or approximately 350 sq ft. Many surgeons and surgical supervisors recommend 20 ft by 20 ft free floor space.

The planning and equipping of each operating

room is based on a series of questions, such as: (a) size, (b) usage, (c) environmental control*, (d) lighting—surgical and general illumination*, (e) intercommunications and signal systems*, (f) electronic equipment and monitoring system*, (g) service lines, such as suction, oxygen, nitrous oxide, compressed air, (h) provision for X-ray, not only X-ray tube stand but control, transformer, and necessary lead protection, (i) provision for TV camera, movie cameras, other recording equipment, (j) safety precaution in hazardous areas, (k) cabinet work, supply cabinets and storage for operating table appliances, (l) need for clocks, film illuminators.

The rapid development of cardiac and neuro-surgery is creating a demand for one or more extra-large operating rooms. This type of surgery calls for a larger team of surgeons, nurses and technicians, plus a great deal of extra equipment, such as heart-lung machines, hypothermia equipment, etc.; also electronic devices for measuring bodily functions, i.e., electro-cardiograph, electro-encephalograph, blood pressure, respiration, body temperature, etc. Today many architects are providing an "instrumentation" room adjacent to or between two extra-large operating rooms to accommodate such equipment, which is frequently not explosion-proof. The

---

* These subjects have so many ramifications they are only mentioned here.

floor of any such room is usually elevated approximately three ft above the operating room floor. Plate glass panels permit vision into operating rooms, and through-wall conduits accommodate wires and other leads of various appliances in the instrumentation room to the surgical field. Such an area can also house the TV control and monitor (if used), X-ray controls, etc.

In the hospital as a whole, the actual patient area is only a very small per cent of the total. The same is true within the surgical suite. The operating rooms themselves will account for only about one-fourth of the total area required for the suite with its supportive functions such as—

Offices and administration areas, scrub areas, work and supply rooms, laboratory, dark room, post-anesthesia recovery, holding or induction areas, lounge, locker and toilet rooms for various personnel groups, conference or teaching rooms, and circulation within the department.

The analysis of various suites illustrating this article show a spread from 1115 sq ft to 1585 sq ft total gross area per operating or cystoscopic room (if included)—and every suite could use more gross floor area for storage, according to comments. Thus, a suite of eight operating rooms averaging 350 sq ft each = 2800 sq ft $\times$ 4 = 11,200 sq ft estimated total area required—or 1400 sq ft per operating room.

Within the surgical suite we have three basic zones predicated on three types of activity and circulation involved, and the degree of sterility to be maintained. The pre-planning analysis of these areas is just as important as the determination of the number and type of operating rooms.

Outer zone—Administrative elements and basic control where personnel enter the department, patients are received and held or sent to proper holding areas of inner zone; conference, classroom areas, locker spaces, any outpatient reception, etc.

Intermediate zone—Predominantly work and storage areas; outside personnel will deliver to this area but should not penetrate the inner zone. The recovery suite, if completely integrated with the surgical suite, is an intermediate or outer zone activity.

Inner zone—The actual operating rooms, the scrub areas, the patient holding or induction areas. All alien traffic should be eliminated. Here we want to maintain the highest level of cleanliness and aseptic conditions.

Outer zone administrative areas have increased in importance. Offices are needed for the surgical supervisor, the clerks who manage scheduling and paper work, the clinical instructor (particularly if

there is a school of nursing), possibly the chief of staff. There must be provision for surgeons to dictate medical records.

And don't forget the patient. After all, he is the primary concern. Who is responsible for his transportation to the surgical suite, and on whose bed or stretcher? How is he checked in and where does he wait if the room for which he is scheduled is not ready? Who has not seen surgical corridors lined with occupied stretchers for want of adequate holding, preparation or induction areas? Another factor is added if any ambulant outpatient work is to be done. There must be provision for receiving, controlled waiting, dressing rooms and toilets.

A variety of persons must be provided with lounge, locker and toilet space—surgeons (male and female), nurses, technicians, aides, orderlies. Coffee and cola seem to lubricate the entire department; some systematic provision for their supply is warranted.

A conference or classroom for departmental meetings and in-service training programs is easily justified.

The access to all these areas should be removed from strictly surgical areas, as people are entering and leaving in street clothes and should not penetrate into other zones until after changing shoes and clothing.

The planning and equipping of the intermediate zone is based on the method of processing and storing of the thousands of items involved. It is fairly common practice for the central sterile supply department, elsewhere in the hospital, to be responsible for the preparation and autoclaving of all surgical linen packs, gloves, syringes, needles, and external fluids. The storage of these items to be used in surgery becomes the responsibility of the surgical department and adequate space must be provided for a predetermined level of inventory.

The method of processing surgical instruments has been the subject of various research projects, notably at the University of Pittsburgh (see *The Modern Hospital*, November 1955). The new ultrasonic cleaning equipment is eliminating a time-consuming, laborious process. The cost of the equipment discourages duplication and encourages the consolidation of work areas where lay personnel can be trained under close supervision to carry out approved processing techniques.**

The method of packing and sterilizing instruments and utensils will determine the size, type and location of autoclaves needed. Consideration must be given to inclusion of an ethylene oxide sterilizer for cystoscopes, bronchoscopes and delicate surgical instruments which cannot be sterilized by steam or high temperatures. How and where instruments will be stored is another decision to be made.

Suitable storage space must be provided for: (a) clean surgical supplies such as extra linen, tape, bandage materials, etc.; (b) parenteral solutions, external fluids or sterile water; (c) essential drugs and narcotics; (d) blood supplies, bone bank, tissue bank, eye bank, etc.; (e) radium and isotopes used in surgery.

It seems impossible to provide adequate centralized garage-type spaces for bulky equipment not in constant use. Dr. Carl Walter has estimated that an average of 80 sq ft per operating room is needed.

The intermediate zone also houses the facilities for handling waste, soiled linen, etc., and janitorial equipment for routine housekeeping.

The anesthesia service cannot be shortchanged. It may spread over all zones of the surgical suite. Office space is required, work and storage space for equipment. And most important is the decision on where induction of the patient is to take place: centrally to all rooms, locally in induction areas (sometimes referred to as preparation or holding rooms) or in the operating room proper. There are acknowledged hazards in moving anesthetized patients and equipment. Induction areas should permit quicker turn-over in operating room usage, but they also require more anesthetists and nurses to administer.*

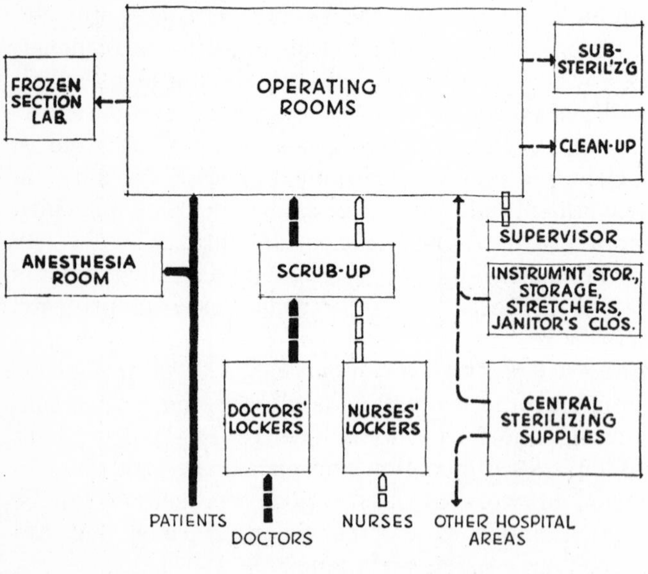

The post-anesthesia recovery room has become an integral part of the surgical suite in most cases. The size will vary from one-and-a-half to two beds per operating room. There is a close relationship between the anesthesia department and the recovery room.

Any frozen section laboratory should be located near the entrance of the surgical suite so that laboratory personnel need not penetrate the inner zone.

Any dark room facilities should be located to serve those rooms generating greatest load of film, normally the cystoscopic, urological and orthopedic services. It should be accessible from a corridor to prevent alien traffic through any operating room.

Inner zone planning includes the operating rooms and their essential supportive elements. Decisions must be made on the type of scrub-up sinks or troughs and their location providing minimum travel to the operating room to eliminate chance of contamination after scrub procedure.

The need for local "sub-sterilizing" rooms is being questioned by many authorities. The trend toward centralization of work areas and sterilizing equipment, and the changing techniques of instrument packaging are reducing the importance of the sub-sterilizing area. Circulation travel distance and work patterns are factors determining the need for decentralized work areas. When such areas are provided there should be staff access for servicing and stocking them without going through an operating room.

The program of need dictates the gross area required for the surgical suite. Recent developments indicate that more efficient departments with minimum travel distances can be planned in bulk, squarish areas. This tendency has affected the location of the surgical suite in relationship to the hospital as a whole. The suite has come downstairs to a lower floor where it is more possible to spread out and achieve the desired shape, divorced from the usually narrow structural pattern of a nursing unit. Planning within the squarish areas has been made possible with the parallel development of air conditioning and artificial lighting. Dependence upon windows for ventilation and light is a thing of the past. The optimum conditions of temperature, humidity, and light level can be controlled by mechanical means far better than by nature.

The surgical suite location must mesh with the

Fig. 11. Flow chart
From Design and Construction of General Hospitals by U.S. Public Health Service, U.S. Department of Health, Education and Welfare (1953).

* Experience with various suites indicates that what was planned for induction frequently is converted to other causes.

total circulation pattern so that patients can be moved to and from surgery with a minimum of travel through other hospital services. Its location is also affected by its close relationship to three other major hospital services—the X-ray department, the clinical laboratories, and the central sterile supply.

One other important factor in the location of the surgical suite is future expansion. Anticipate ways and means to permit growth in an orderly fashion without upsetting the basic relationship of internal organization—or without extending lines of travel to unacceptable or uneconomical lengths.

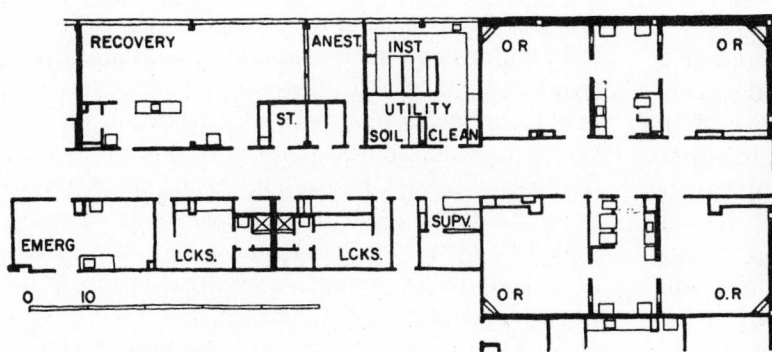

(a) *Sherlock, Smith and Adams, Architects.*

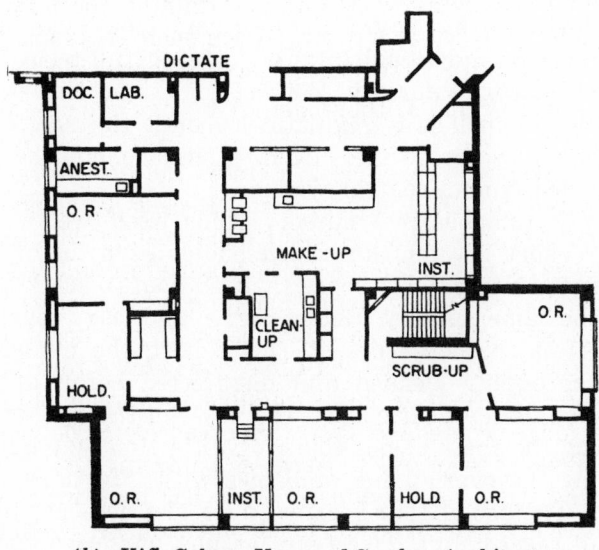

(b) *Kiff, Colean, Voss and Souder, Architects.*

Fig. 12. Typical plans of operating suites

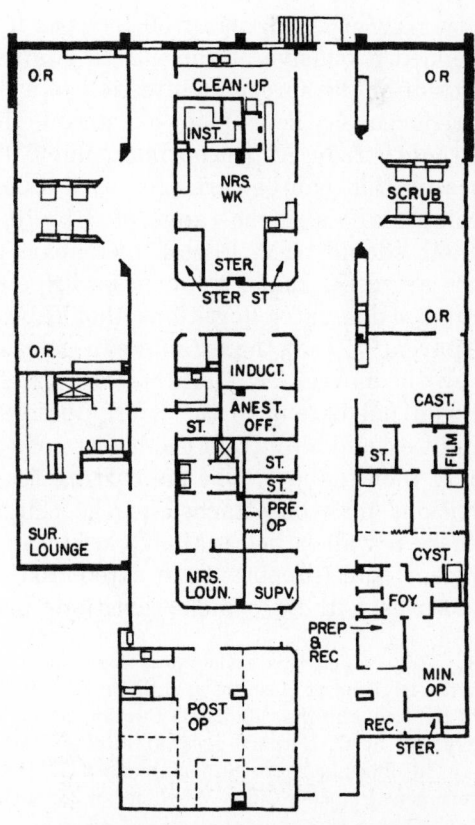

(c) *Louis Allen Abramson, Architect.*

As one of the areas in the hospital where patients are most vulnerable to infection, the nursery should be planned to provide the best means for the care, safety and welfare of the infants. Although the plans and diagrams, shown here, have been developed for hospitals of specified sizes, the principles set forth apply to all hospitals, large or small, new or old.

Basic recommendations for planning nurseries that have been developed, based on clinical experience and study, include: limiting the number of infants in each nursery; wide spacing of bassinets within each nursery; separation of bassinets by cubicle partitions; promoting the use of aseptic techniques and individual care by providing, among other things, ample space and handwashing facilities; limiting the number of bassinets served by one nurses' station; separating facilities for premature infants and for observing infants suspected of having infectious conditions; and providing optimum conditions of temperature, relative humidity and ventilation.

Full-term nurseries should be located in the maternity nursing unit as close to the mothers as possible and away from the line of traffic of other than maternity services. An area of 30 feet per infant is recommended, exclusive of the nurses' station.

The extent of the spread of infection in a nursery can be reduced as the number of infants in each nursery room is reduced. The optimum number of full term infants that can be cared for by a member of the nursing staff is in the range of 8 to 10.

Bassinets should be at least 2 feet apart and, if partitions are used, cubicles should be large enough to permit bedside care. Partitions should be glazed or transparent so that the infants can be easily observed by the nurse. To facilitate cleaning, partitions should not extend to the floor. Cubicle partitions might extend only from the bottom of the bassinet to 24 inches above. The supporting frames of the partitions may be attached to the ceiling and wall. Where a wall is not available, as in an island arrangement, some supports must extend to the floor.

In nurseries without cubicle partitions bassinets

The study, from which this article was condensed, was prepared for the Division of Hospital and Medical Facilities, Public Health Service, and the Children's Bureau, Social Security Administration, by O. Bernard Ives, architect. Copies of the study may be obtained from Superintendent of Documents, U.S. Government Printing Office, Washington 25, D.C.

are often crowded together side by side. Although cubicle partitions may be objectionable from the standpoint of cleaning (and are often unsightly), they help to ensure that bassinets are properly spaced.

Fixed-view windows between the nursery and the corridor permit visitors to view the infants from the corridor. These windows must be wire glass set in steel frames and must conform to National Fire Code requirements. Fixed view windows in partitions between nurseries and the nurses' station or between two nurseries facilitate observation of all infants in the area. These windows may be of clear plate glass or lucite and should be as large as practicable.

A door direct from each nursery to the corridor is recommended to permit faster evacuation in case of fire and easier movement of bassinets from the nursery to the mothers at feeding time and to avoid traffic through the nurses' station. This door, hung in a steel frame, should have a wire glass panel and must conform to National Fire Code requirements.

Furnishings and equipment for each full-term nursery should include, in addition to the items shown in the plans, a suction bulb or a mechanical device with a soft rubber tip and individual catheters for individual infants for each full-term (and premature) nursery. Controls of the suction device should include a regulator to limit the suction to avoid injury to the infant. Suction should be provided from a central system.

A four-bassinet nursery lends itself well to the "cohort" system, in which babies born during the same interval (no more than 48 hours) are kept in the same nursery. Babies arrive and leave together. After the departure of each cohort, the nursery is thoroughly cleaned and disinfected before admission of the next cohort, thereby—in theory—breaking the chain of possible cross-infection by eliminating the overlapping of babies with infections.

The use of four-bassinet nurseries does not imply increased staff. Two four-bassinet nurseries may be under the care of one nursing person if she wears a scrub gown and scrubs properly between visits to each nursery. Two such nurseries may be considered the equivalent of one eight-bassinet nursery in assigning nurses' station and work space. Furnishings and equipment will be the same as those for full-term nurseries.

Since premature infants require more specialized care than full-term infants, a reasonable ratio of staff to premature infants is set at one to five. Thus, a premature nursery room should accommodate no more than five infants and should have a minimum area of 30 square feet per infant. A separate nursery is usually not indicated if less than five infants are to be cared for at one time. In such cases, space for them can often be provided in the full-term nursery. One nurses' station may serve two premature nurseries, or a premature nursery and a full-term nursery if the nurseries are paired.

In a premature nursery where suitable environmental temperature and humidity are maintained, only 50 to 75 per cent of the premature infants may require incubators. Furnishings for premature nurseries will be similar to those in full-term nurseries, aside from the incubators.

An observation nursery should be provided for infants suspected of infection. When positive diagnosis is made, the infant is transferred elsewhere in the hospital and placed on isolation precautions. However, if diagnosis is not positive the infant may be returned to the regular nursery provided he has not been exposed to an infected infant in the observation nursery.

The observation nursery should be a completely separate unit, but it should be located adjacent to a full-term nursery with a glazed partition between to permit observation by the nursery staff. A minimum of 40 square feet per bassinet is recommended to provide adequate space for bedside care and treatment of the infant.

Observation bassinets should be provided at the rate of 10 per cent of the full-term bassinets. A minimum of two—and a maximum of three—bassinets are recommended for each observation nursery. These nurseries may be repeated as many times as necessary to provide the required complement of observation bassinets. Furnishings and equipment will be similar to those in full-term nurseries.

An anteroom should be provided between the nursery and the corridor. This area should contain the same facilities as the work and treatment areas for full-term nurseries.

The nurses' station serves as a control point and also provides workspace for the nurse and an area for treating infants. The nurse's desk should be placed so that the entrances from the corridor and from the station to the nurseries can be supervised. The nurseries should be visible through observation windows in the partitions.

A station between two nurseries will require a double desk for two nurses. No more than two full-term nurseries, each housing 8 to 10 bassinets, should be served by one nurses' station. In the cohort system, four nurseries, of four bassinets each, may be so served.

The nurse's workspace should occupy a separate area at one end of the nurses' station. This arrangement affords the nurse full view of the infants while attending to most activities. The treatment area should be located near the entrance to the nurses' station so the physician need not walk through the workspace. Routine examinations and treatments should be carried out at the bassinets in the nursery. A physicians' scrub area should be located at the entrance of the nurses' station. The description of the full-term nurses' station also applies to premature nurseries, except that the treatment table is omitted. Other necessary areas, not shown in the plans, include formula rooms, nurses' locker rooms, demonstration rooms and storage.

Air conditioning will be required for nurseries to ensure the constant temperature and humidity conditions so beneficial to care of the newborn. In addition, the air-conditioning system, through the ventilating features, will remove odor and will materially reduce the bacterial contamination of the environment.

NURSERY FOR 440 LIVE BIRTHS PER YEAR IN HOSPITAL OF APPROXIMATELY 50 BEDS. The number of bassinets and maternity beds required is based on number of live births expected in hospital per year, rather than a rule-of-thumb relationship to the over-all bed complement. Six to 8 per cent (up to 12 per cent in poor economic areas) of the total live births will be premature (low birth weight of 5 pounds 8 ounces)

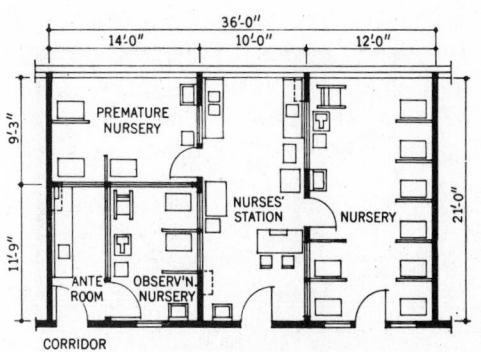

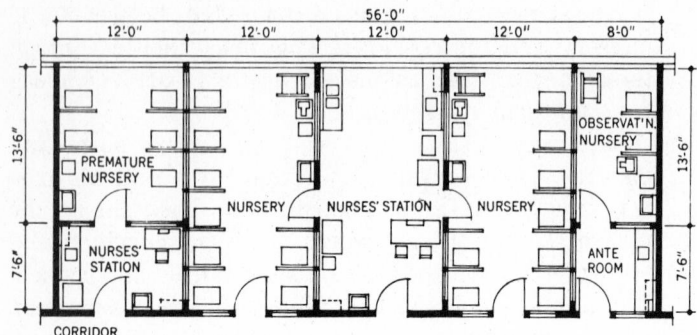

NURSERY FOR 880 LIVE BIRTHS PER YEAR IN HOSPITAL OF APPROXIMATELY 100 BEDS. The estimated number of premature births divided by 18 (number of 20-day average stay periods in a year) will equal the average number of premature bassinets or incubators required. This figure must be adjusted for 100 per cent occupancy (often assumed at 70 per cent). A premature center nearby would eliminate need for such facilities in the hospital

COHORT SYSTEM NURSERY FOR 880 LIVE BIRTHS PER YEAR IN HOSPITAL OF APPROXIMATELY 100 BEDS. In hospitals using the cohort system, babies born within 48 hours of each other are kept in the same nursery, arriving and leaving together, in theory reducing cross-infection through the elimination of over-lapping of babies with infections. Cohort nurseries are thoroughly cleaned and disinfected between discharge of one cohort and admission of the next

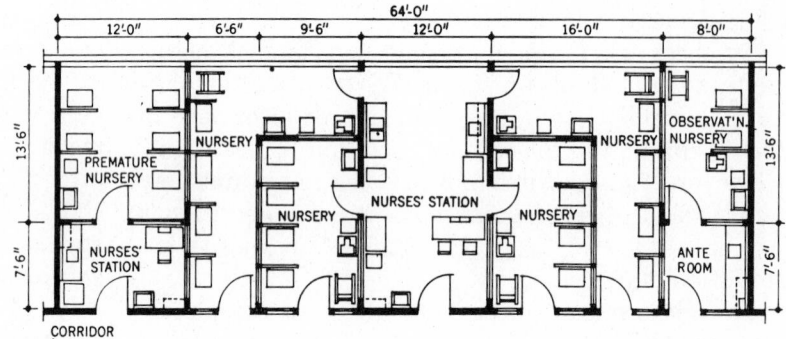

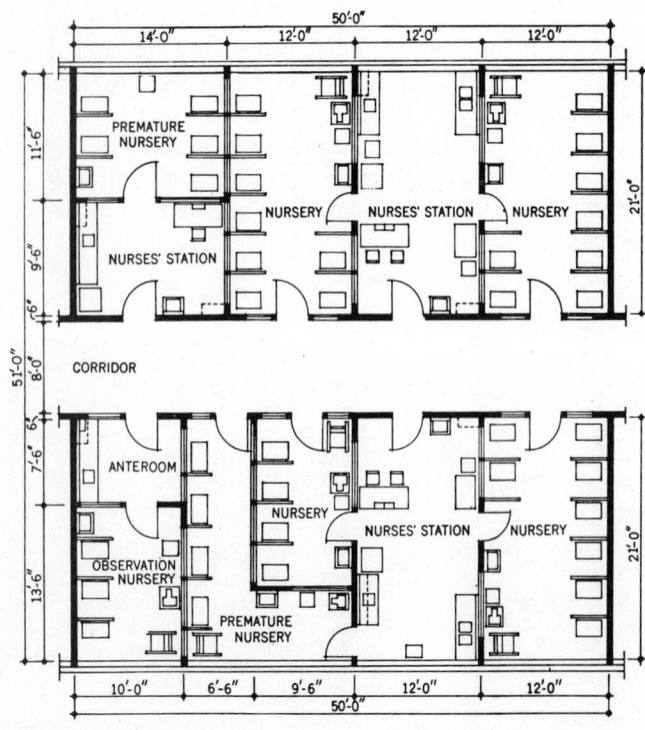

NURSERY FOR 1,500 LIVE BIRTHS PER YEAR IN HOSPITAL OF APPROXIMATELY 200 BEDS. Size of full-term portion of this nursery, as well as the others shown, is based on estimated number of live births per year less the premature births. This figure is then divided by 73 (the number of five-day average stay periods in a year) and adjusted from this 70 per cent occupancy total to a 100 per cent occupancy figure. Observation bassinets are provided at rate of 10 per cent of full-term bassinets, in nurseries with capacity of 20 or more. In smaller nurseries a minimum of two observation bassinets are provided

DETAIL PLAN, TWO EIGHT-BASSINET FULL-TERM NURSERIES AND NURSES' STATION. Typical arrangement of a pair of full-term nurseries with nurses' station between allowing two nurses to tend 16 bassinets (or a maximum of 20) from one position. Recommended items of furnishings and equipment are shown located in what is considered their proper relationship to each other and to the complete nursery-nurses' station layout

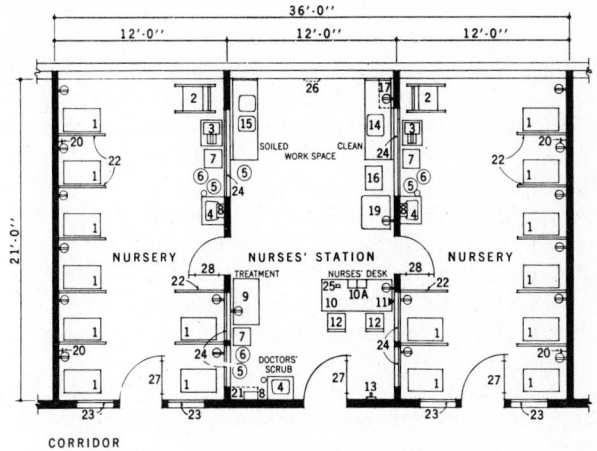

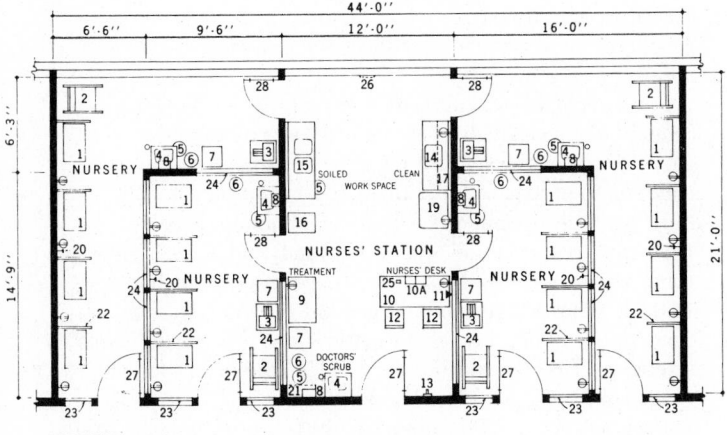

DETAIL PLAN, TWO PAIRS FOUR-BASSINET COHORT SYSTEM NURSERIES AND NURSES' STATION. A cohort system arrangement similar to the layout above, and of the same size. As in the conventional plan (above), the four cohort nurseries may be tended by two nurses working together from a single centrally-located nurses' station. Workspace required will be approximately the same in both types

LEFT: **DETAIL PLAN, FIVE-INCUBATOR NURSERY WITH NURSES' STATION.** *MIDDLE AND RIGHT:* **MAXIMUM (THREE-BASSINET) AND MINIMUM (TWO-BASSINET) OBSERVATION NURSERIES.** The minimum and maximum size observation nurseries have anterooms between nurseries and corridors, provided with approximately the same facilities as work and treatment areas of full-term nurseries

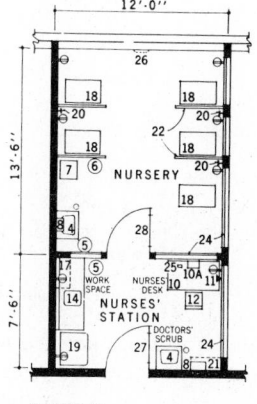 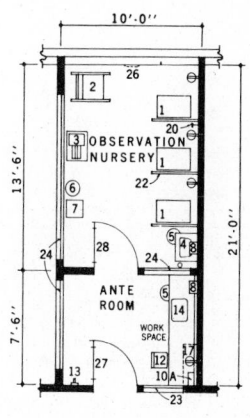 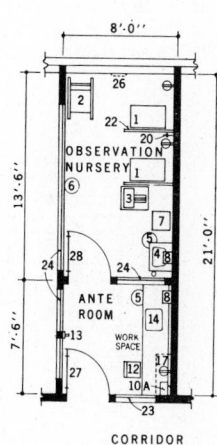

LEGEND

1. Bassinet with cabinet, pull-out shelf below, on 3-inch ball-bearing casters, with wheel lock
2. Rocking chair with armrests, washable finish
3. Utility table, 16 by 20 inches, with top drawer to hold infant scales
4. Lavatory, 18 by 22 inches, with gooseneck spout, knee or foot controls, shelf over
5. Waste receptacle, foot-controlled cover, removable waxed liner
6. Soiled diaper receptacle, foot-controlled cover, removable waxed liner
7. Soiled linen hamper on 3-inch ball-bearing casters, removable waxed liner, foot-controlled cover

8. Paper towel dispenser, enclosed type
9. Treatment table, 24 by 36 by 36 inches high, on 3-inch ball-bearing casters, with wheel lock
10. Nurse's desk, 30 inches high
10A. Chart rack
11. Telephone outlet
12. Office chair, swivel, without arms
13. Hookstrip
14. Sink with gooseneck spout, knee or foot controls, in counter 36 inches high, open below
15. Double compartment sink with gooseneck spout, knee or foot controls, in counter 36 inches high
16. Bottle warmer on portable carriage
17. Wall cabinet
18. Incubator, on 3-inch ball-bearing casters, with wheel lock

19. Refrigerator, with built-in thermometer
20. Double oxygen outlet, one for each four full-term—or each two premature—bassinets
21. Shelves (three), starting 42 inches above floor, for clean gowns, supplies
22. Cubicle partition, starting 30 inches above floor, with 2-foot-high clear glass or lucite panel, wall- and ceiling-hung metal frame
23. Clear wire-glass view panel in steel frame, 1,296 square inches maximum, bottom 42 inches above floor
24. Clear plate-glass or lucite view panel, bottom 42 inches above floor
25. Hand-wind clock, desk type
26. Electric clock
27. Door with upper panel of wire glass
28. Door with upper panel of clear glass

THIS SCHEME for a pediatrics nursing unit, the Public Health Service architects make clear, might have been done in many other dispositions. It is intended, like all similar schemes issued by the Service's architectural department, merely to illustrate a possible arrangement of rooms and facilities considered desirable. This one, for example, is drawn for a fairly typical hospital wing, on the assumption that it would be part of a conventional hospital; but for that imposition the facilities might be still more conveniently arranged. It does, nevertheless, illustrate desirable planning as well as facilities and equipment needed.

Flexibility is the first important objective. The four rooms at the left of the plan, with their own toilets, are intended to be part of the pediatrics nursing unit, or part of an adjoining adult medical or surgical nursing unit, as occasion demands. Double doors are positioned so that the corridor can be arranged as desired. In use presumably older children would be assigned to these rooms, and nurses would not have to exercise close supervision here.

This material was abstracted from "Planning the Pediatric Nursing Unit," in the manual "The Care of Children in Hospitals" of the American Academy of Pediatrics. The chapter is the work of the Committee on Hospital Care for the American Academy of Pediatrics under the chairmanship of Dr. Lendon Snedeker, Assistant Administrator of the Children's Medical Center, Boston. The architectural consultant to the committee was Walter E. Campbell, AIA, of the firm of Campbell and Aldrich of Boston, Mass.

Planning is by O. B. Ives, Hospital Architect of the Architectural and Engineering Branch, Division of Hospital and Medical Facilities, Public Health Service.

Notice that nurses' station and utility rooms are centered for the shorter corridor, without these four rooms.

The smaller unit, with 16 beds, is close to a minimum, incidentally, for a special pediatrics wing, the number 14 being cited in the manual of which this plan is a part. A pediatrics nursing unit could be larger, but should not be as large as an adult unit, since children need more care.

Bed Rooms

The one-bed rooms are required for critically ill patients, those who need quiet or those who are disturbing to other patients. When appropriately equipped, they may be used as isolation rooms for patients with known or suspected infection. They are useful also for very short-stay patients and for new admissions.

Preferably all, but at least some of the one-bed rooms, should be large enough to accommodate two beds, to provide over-night accommodations for parents. Infants and younger children, in particular, need their mothers during an illness.

It has been recommended that the minimum floor area for a one-bed room be 100 square feet and that for a two-bed room 160 square feet. It has been found in practice, however, that these areas are minimal and do not provide sufficient space for working around the patient and moving beds and stretchers. Recommended areas are 125 square feet for single rooms and 190 square feet for two-bed rooms.

Each room should be equipped with an adjustable hospital bed and an over-bed table for trays or toys. The hospital bed can be replaced by a crib or bassinet as required, but such flexibility is predicated on really adequate storage space. Two

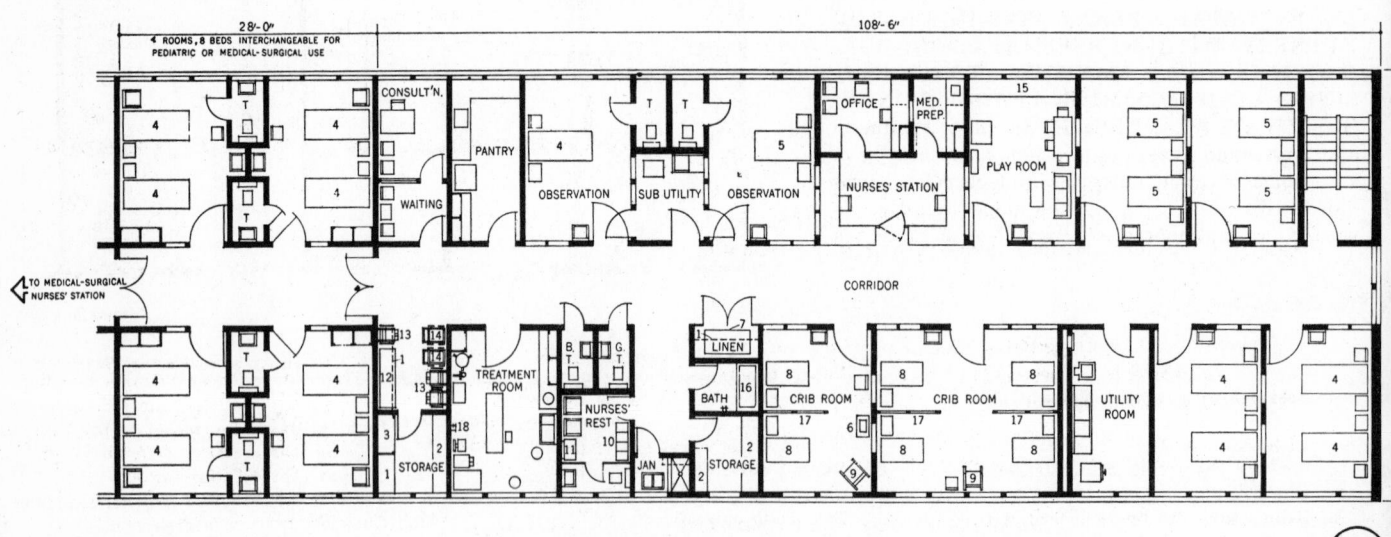

PEDIATRIC NURSING UNIT

NURSING UNIT
1. Shelf, 5 ft. 3 in. above floor
2. Shelving
3. Storage Cabinet
4. Adjustable Hospital Bed
5. Adjustable Youth Bed
6. Infant Scale
7. Linen Cart
8. Crib
9. Rocking Chair
10. Lockers, 12 x 15 x 60 in.
11. Table with Mirror over
12. Stretcher
13. Wheel Chair
14. Stroller
15. Toy Storage
16. Raised Bath Tub, with controls on wall
17. Cubicle Partition, 7 ft. high with bottom of clear glass 36 in. above floor
18. Oxygen and Suction Outlets, 5 ft. 3 in. above floor

nurses' call panels should be installed for use when the room is occupied by two children. The call panel should be placed where it is not within too easy reach in rooms which will be used for pre-school children. There should be a bedside cabinet for articles needed in the nursing care of the patient on one side of the bed, possibly a cabinet for favorite toys or other familiar articles on the other side of the bed. This plan shows only the former. Clothing can be stored, to some extent, in this limited space, but it will be preferable in most instances to provide closet space or lockers for such articles.

Every room should have running water. An adult-sized lavatory with gooseneck spout, with either knee or elbow control, should be installed near the entrance. It is desirable that there be a toilet with bedpan flushing attachment and also a clothes closet for one-bed rooms. Cubicle curtains should be available when the room is occupied by two patients. Every one-bed room should have a comfortable chair and a waste paper receptacle.

Cubicles and Partitions

The use of partitions and cubicles in multiple-bed rooms is quite common but, if they are installed, those in charge of the pediatric unit should be aware of the reasons for their use.

Cubicles are undesirable in that they separate children who otherwise would be able to fraternize and have a happier hospital experience. At the same time it should be recognized that not all children benefit from this social approach.

Cubicles demarcate areas of potential infection, and facilitate the maintenance of precautionary technique, but they cannot be said to decrease airborne infection significantly. The practice of throwing toys from one area to another is discouraged, and visitors are encouraged to confine their attentions to one patient but cubicles increase the difficulty of moving patients. They are relatively expensive to install and keep clean, and in hot weather they greatly reduce air circulation and contribute to discomfort.

If cubicles or partitions are to be used they should permit visibility of patients by nurses and by patients in the same room. They should be made of shatterproof glass above the height of the mattress (36 in.). It is recommended that they be seven feet high and that they extend seven feet from the wall.

Isolation Rooms

It is essential that each pediatric unit be provided with one or more isolation rooms. These should be equipped in the same way as ordinary single rooms, except that they require facilities for maintaining isolation technique. When not utilized for this purpose they serve as part of the regular unit, for severely ill children, for patients who need quiet, or for new admissions. It is desirable that they be remote from rooms for non-infectious cases but convenient to the nurse's station.

Each isolation room should have an adult-sized lavatory with knee action control, a hook strip for gowns near the corridor door and an individual toilet with bedpan-flushing attachments. It should be connected with a sub-utility room equipped with a sink and utensil sterilizer. The isolation room should be large enough to permit the use of an additional full-sized bed for a second patient with the same infection or for a mother to stay with her child.

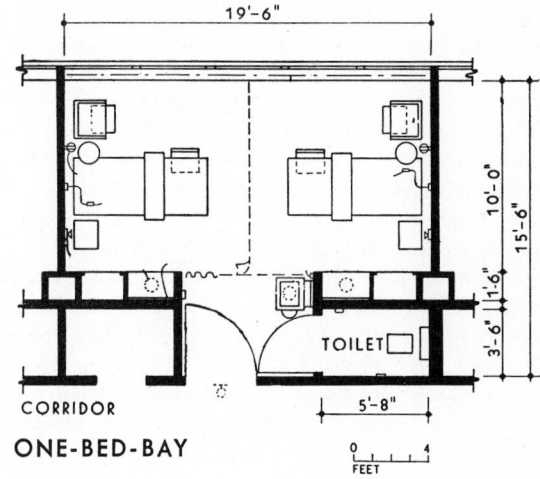

ONE-BED-BAY

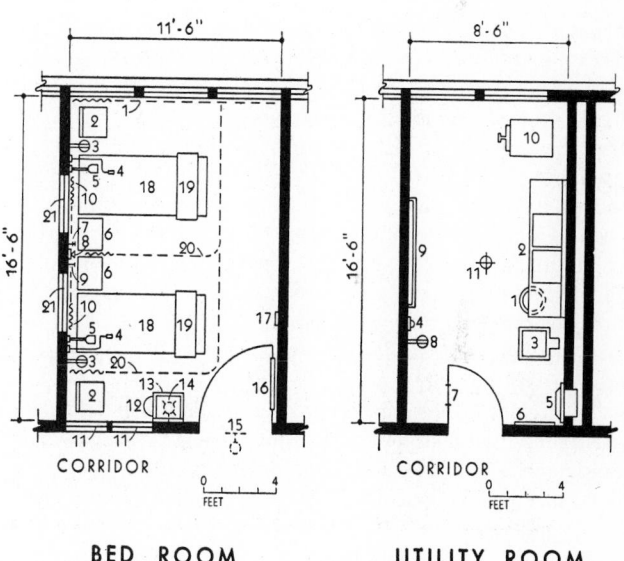

BED ROOM   **UTILITY ROOM**

BED ROOM
1. Sliding Window Curtain
2. Straight Chair
3. Duplex Convenience Outlet
4. Nurses' Calling Station
5. Wall Light
6. Bedside Cabinet
7. Oxygen Outlet, 5 ft. 3 in. above floor
8. Telephone Outlet
9. Suction Outlet, 5 ft. 3 in. above floor
10. Curtain
11. Clear Wire Glass in Steel Frame (1296 sq. in. max.) bottom of glass 36 in. above floor
12. Waste Paper Receptacle
13. Lavatory, Gooseneck spout, Knee or Elbow Control
14. Wall-bracket light, switch controlled
15. Corridor Dome Light
16. Door, upper panel clear wire glass
17. Night Light, switch controlled
18. Adjustable Hospital Bed (Youth beds and cribs may be substituted as required)
19. Overbed Table
20. Cubicle Curtain
21. Clear Glass, bottom 36 in. above floor

UTILITY ROOM
1. Sanitary Waste Receptacle
2. Double Compartment Deep Sink in Counter
3. Clinical Sink
4. Dome Light and Buzzer, 5 ft. 3 in. above floor
5. Bedpan Washer and Disinfector
6. Bulletin Board, 26 x 24 in.
7. Clear Wire Glass Vision Panel
8. Duplex Convenience Outlet
9. Drying Rod
10. Cabinet Pressure Sterilizer 16 x 16 x 24 in.
11. Ceiling Light

Nurses' Station

Every pediatric unit will have its own nurses' station, preferably situated centrally within the unit. As a general rule, rooms designed for the use of the sickest patients and for young infants should be nearest the nurses' station. The location of the nurses' station may also be determined by the hospital's general plan for controlling visitors.

The requirements for the nurses' station in the pediatric unit are much like those in other parts of the hospital. A chart desk and rack, clock and bulletin board should be provided. The nurses' call system will need to be one which can be used by younger children. A television monitoring system for each room would be even more desirable if finances permit. This will, of course, allow visual as well as auditory control of the situation in each room. A medicine preparation room should be provided directly off the nurses' station. It should contain a counter with an acid-resisting sink, cabinets with a locked narcotics compartment above the counter and refrigerator and cabinets below.

A small private office for the supervising nurse should be provided off the nurses' station.

Examination and Treatment Room

Separate examination and treatment rooms but, more often, a combination of both, should be provided. A more satisfactory examination can be done in a quiet room with a good light, where the necessary equipment is easily available, and there are fewer distractions for both the child and the examiner.

It is important that all treatments, dressing or other procedures which are painful or disturbing be done where other children cannot watch. For this reason, the treatment room should be located away from patient rooms. If it is also to be used for doing admitting examinations, as will often be the case in the smaller pediatric unit, it should also be near the entrance to the unit.

Two requisites for a good treatment room are an adequate examining-treatment table and ample lighting fixtures. Pediatric diagnosis and treatment procedures are often difficult at best and next to impossible if these requirements are not met. Sound-proofing is another requisite.

Necessary equipment should include supply cupboard, instrument cabinet, bulletin board, nurses' call, clock, dispenser for soap or detergent, and a combination instrument and scrub sink with gooseneck spout and knee or elbow control.

Waiting and Consultation Room

A waiting room for the pediatric unit is desirable. It should be located close to stairs and elevators and its entrance should be visible from the nurses' station. Comfortable furnishings, soundproofing, and reading matter all should be provided. If possible toilet facilities should be nearby.

Wherever possible, there should be a consultation room for privacy in dealing with parents or children. This may be located near the waiting room and can serve as an office for resident or staff physicians.

The consultation room will often be the only place where nurses can demonstrate the care which the child will need when he goes home. Parent teaching is a very important function of the professional staff, and space must be provided for it. The visitor's room and the consultation and treatment rooms are usually grouped together for convenience in the admission and discharge of patients, but should be shielded from each other.

Playroom Space

Every pediatric unit should have a playroom. It should not be looked upon as a luxury or as a space where more beds may be placed in an emergency, but as a therapeutic adjunct for patients who are convalescent or ambulatory.

The present plan puts the playroom next to the nurses' station for control. If the hospital is able to provide adequate supervision, possibly by volunteers, the playroom might better be a porch at the outer end of the unit.

The playroom can be used for group activities and recreation — as a playroom for younger children, for games, occupational therapy and school work for older children, and a social room and library for adolescents. At meal time it is an ideal place for group feeding. There should be tables and chairs suitable both for food service and play activities. Storage closets and shelves for toys and other materials should also be provided.

Utility Room

The utility room should be centrally located in each nursing unit. This room requires ample cupboard and counter space, sterilizer, utensil cabinet, sink with drainboard, hot and cold water supply with elbow or knee control. Space will be required for a hot plate and a container for crushed ice for non-drinking purposes.

A bedpan washer and disinfector and a clinical sink should also be provided with a recessed cabinet for specimens near at hand. Since individual bedpans and urinals are provided at each bedside, no rack is necessary.

Storage Rooms

Each nursing unit should have separate storage space for linen, supplies, cleaning equipment and such articles as stretchers and wheel chairs.

If the central linen room is large enough, that on the unit need only be large enough to accommodate one day's supply of linen. In the case of infants, a day's linen supply can often be kept in the bedside cabinet.

The stretcher closet should be adequate for the transportation needs of the unit. In a small hospital this area might even be used for the storage of beds of different sizes. A cupboard with shelving may be provided above the level of the stretchers and wheel chairs for additional storage space.

Oxygen Supply

In spite of additional expense in construction, some hospitals, even small ones, are providing an oxygen and suction outlet for each patient room because of the obvious advantage of having them where they are needed without having to move patients to an oxygen outlet. If only certain rooms can be so provided, those to be given high priority are isolation rooms and one-bed rooms where the sickest children are apt to be placed.

By WILBUR R. TAYLOR, CLIFFORD E. NELSON, M.D., and WILLIAM W. McMASTER*

In a recent study it was found that many hospitals allotted inadequate space to the x-ray department, and expansion was often impractical. Adequate space for waiting, toilets, and dressing rooms helps insure continuous routines in handling patients. The lack of adequate space results in needless waste of effort and time in efficiently scheduling examinations. An unsatisfactory layout is a handicap to both the hospital and the radiologist since the hospital loses potential revenue, and the radiologist's time, as well as that of the staff, is needlessly wasted. This is particularly important to a small hospital which has a visiting radiologist, for it is to the advantage of the hospital and radiologist to schedule as many examinations as possible during his visit.

LOCATION

The diagnostic x-ray department should be located on the first floor, conveniently accessible both to outpatients and inpatients. It is also desirable to locate the department close to the elevators and adjoining the outpatient department and near other diagnostic and treatment facilities.

The functional requirements of the department are usually best satisfied by locating the x-ray rooms at the end of a wing. In this location, the activity within the department will not be disturbed by through traffic to other parts of the hospital, and less shielding will be required because of the exterior walls.

PLAN A

Plan A illustrates an x-ray suite that will provide an efficiently operating service for about 8400 patient examinations yearly, or an average of about 35 examinations daily. This average workload is typical in a hospital of approximately 100 beds (or somewhat more) with an outpatient x-ray service. Unforeseen scheduling problems, of course, will occasionally cause the average of 35 examinations per day to be exceeded.

The staff needed for this volume of work usually includes: 1 radiologist, 2 or 3 technicians, 1 secretary-receptionist, 1 secretary-file clerk, 1 orderly (as needed).

This plan will permit the workload to be augmented at least 50 per cent by increasing the staff, if no more than 20 per cent of the x-ray work is fluoroscopic.

Among the desirable characteristics that this plan attempts to provide for is the need for correlating the functions of the working group to obtain maximum efficiency. The arrangement of patient areas and examination rooms around the perimeter, with the administrative staff in the center, makes it possible for these units to operate more efficiently. The technicians' corridor in the rear of the department provides for easy access to the x-ray rooms, film processing rooms, and distribution areas without interference from patients' cross traffic.

ADMINISTRATION SPACES

Every radiologist has specific ideas on the most suitable ways for arranging and operating the administrative functions of the x-ray department. Some of the variables involved are assignment of personnel and functions, reception of patients, sequence of patient examinations, film distribution, and staff viewing facilities. This plan provides for flexibility of space arrangements by allowing for variation of several of the operations within the administrative unit.

Waiting room. General waiting space for about ten patients is located at the entrance to the department. From here the patient is directed to an assigned dressing room. A separate area, to the left of the entrance and in sight of the secretary-receptionist, is provided for wheelchair and stretcher patients. This section is partitioned off by a curtain which may be partially drawn to provide privacy, yet afford the necessary surveillance of unattended patients from the secretary-receptionist's desk. Additional chairs in this area can be used to accommodate the attendants of these patients or for an overflow of waiting patients when needed.

Secretary-receptionist. The administrative functions and business records of the department, scheduling of appointments, receiving of patients, typing of the necessary identification forms and requisitions for examinations, and assigning of patients to dressing rooms are handled by the secretary-receptionist. If time permits, the secretary-receptionist assists in typing the radiologist's reports. The desk is centrally located, directly in front of the entrance between the waiting room and administrative area, so that the secretary-receptionist may supervise waiting patients and have access to correspondence and report files.

Secretary-file clerk. The secretary-file clerk assembles, sorts and files all films and reports, assists the secretary-receptionist when needed, and transcribes and types the radiologist's reports. These functions are not rigidly fixed and can be interchanged, if desired. For example, a technician may be assigned to assist the file clerk with film assembling and sorting, or the file clerk may be given other functions as needed. The desk is located near a counter-partition in the film collection and distribution area. The low counter and the gate (No. 79) are designed so the entrance to the department can be observed and patients directed when required.

* The authors are all engaged in work for Public Health Service, Mr. Taylor and Mr. McMaster as architects in the Architectural and Engineering Branch, Division of Hospital and Medical Facilities, Bureau of Medical Services; Dr. Nelson as a radiologist, Division of Radiological Health, Bureau of State Services.

Doctors' viewing room. The doctors' viewing room is located near the office of the radiologist so that he may be immediately available for consultation. The room is near the film files, convenient to the secretary and file clerk, and situated so as not to intrude upon the functional flow of the work. Its location within the administrative unit provides privacy so that diagnostic comments and discussions will not be overheard by patients.

Radiologist's office. This office is conveniently situated near the x-ray rooms, the secretary-receptionist's desk and the filing distribution area, and is not too easily accessible to the public; it is also provided with a door which opens directly to the technicians' corridor. The fire exit which is located off the technicians' corridor provides a second exit from the department for the radiologist.

Film files. The film files are located in the collection and distribution area and convenient to the radiologist's office. Since it is desirable to keep active films for at least five years, approximately 125 linear feet of filing space is provided. After that time, additional storage space elsewhere will be needed for the less active files. Closed front metal x-ray files are recommended (see Fire Safety). Teaching files may not be needed in a hospital of this size, but if desired, a section of the active files may be allotted for this use.

GENERAL FACILITIES
Dressing rooms. Three dressing rooms for each x-ray machine should be provided so that the equipment and staff can function without delay. Each dressing room should be equipped with a straight-back chair, clothes hook, mirror, and a shelf below the mirror. For the protection of patients' valuables, the doors may be equipped with locks, or centrally located lockers may be provided. Where doors are installed, they should swing outward to avoid the possibility of being blocked by a patient and should be at least 12 inches from the floor.

For the convenience of patients in wheelchairs, an outsized dressing room is provided. Instead of a door, it is equipped with a curtain so that the patient can maneuver easily.

Patients' toilet rooms. Toilets should be immediately available for patients undergoing fluoroscopy, and similar facilities should be conveniently available for waiting patients. A minimum of two toilets should be provided for each x-ray room. All toilets should be located near the x-ray rooms.

At least one toilet room should be directly accessible to each x-ray room and have an opening into the corridor. To prevent the patients from accidentally opening the door between the toilet and x-ray room, this door should be equipped with hardware which is operable only from the x-ray room. The doors of the toilet rooms which

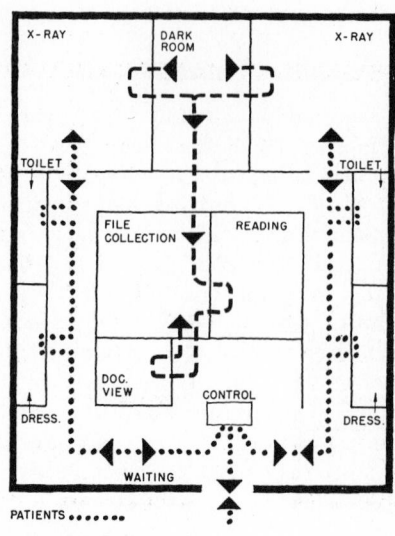

PATIENTS ......

FILMS ━ ━━ ━

LEGEND

1. Paper towel dispenser
2. Waste paper receptacle
3. Lavatory
4. Wall-hung water closet
5. Continuous grab bar
6. Emergency calling station (push button)
7. Hook strip
8. Mirror and shelf below
9. Straight chair
10. Cassette pass box
11. Film loading counter
12. Film storage bin
13. Film hanger racks under counter
14. Safelight
15. Ceiling light, white and red
16. Timer
17. Counter with storage cabinets below
18. Cassette storage bins
19. Trash deposit cabinet
20. Cassette cover retainer and wall guard
21. Door with light-proof louver in upper panel
22. Access panel
23. Door with light-proof louver in lower panel
24. Utility sink with drainboard
25. Refrigerating unit under drainboard
26. Developing tank with thermostatic mixing valve
27. Through-the-wall fixing tank
28. Light-proof panel
29. Washing tank
30. X-ray film illuminator (wet viewing)
31. Film dryer
32. Film dryer exhaust to outside
33. Film corner cutter
34. Film pass slot
35. Flush-mounted counter illuminator
36. Film sorting bins above counter
37. Film sorting counter
38. Counter with cabinets below
39. On-wall or mobile film illuminators
40. Temporary film file cart
41. Stereoscope
42. Executive type desk
43. Executive type chair
44. Telephone outlet
45. Intercommunication system outlet
46. Bookshelves, 42 in. by 14 in.
47. Typist chair
48. Typist desk
49. Filing cabinet, letter size

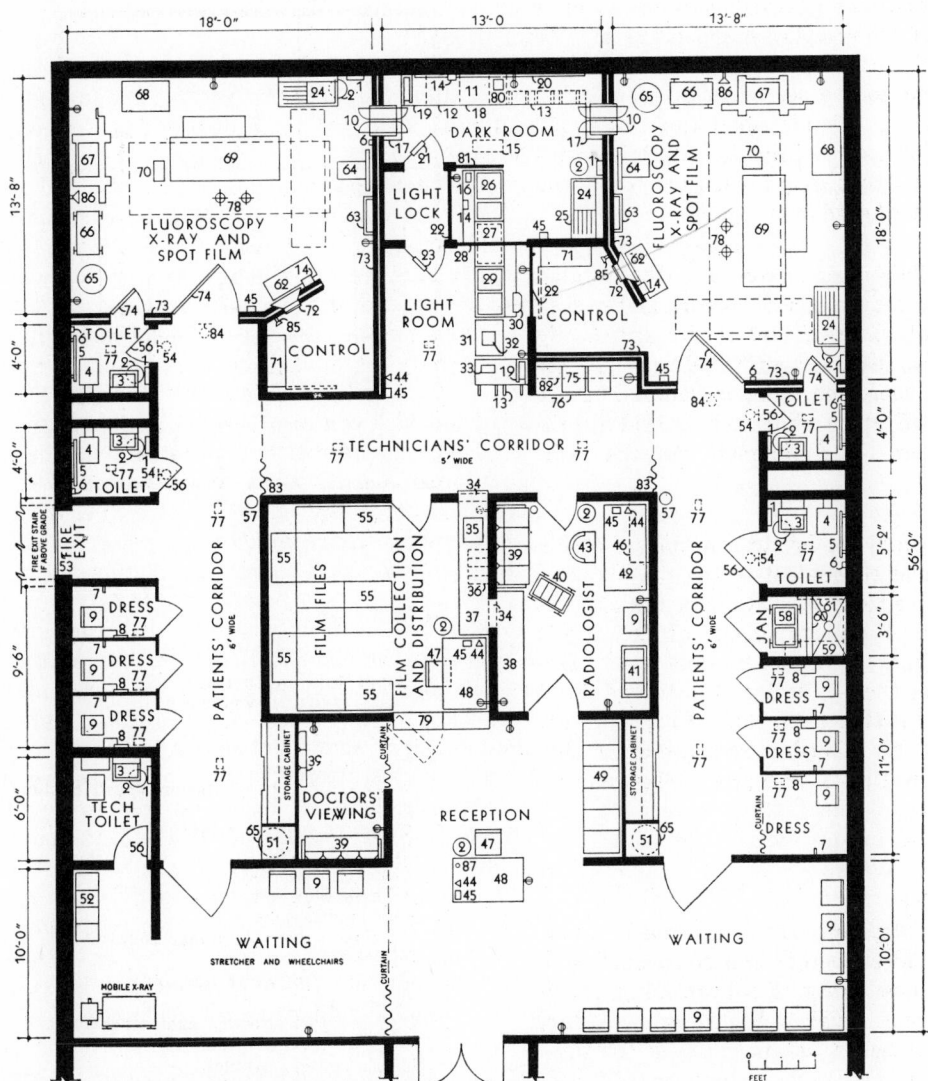

Diagnostic Radiographic Suite—Plan A

50. Gown storage, open shelves, storage cabinet above
51. Gown storage, open shelving with laundry hamper below
52. Technicians' lockers
53. Fire door
54. Dome light, buzzer and annunciator at receptionist's desk
55. Closed metal film files, 5 shelves high
56. Hook on toilet side of door
57. Fire extinguisher
58. Mop truck
59. Shelf
60. Curb and receptor on janitor's sink
61. Mop hanging strip
62. Storage cabinet and writing counter
63. Fluoroscopic apron and glove holder
64. Fluoroscopic chair
65. Laundry hamper
66. Clean linen cart
67. Cassette changer
68. Transformer

69. Radiographic fluoroscopic unit with spot film device
70. Foot stool
71. Control unit
72. Leaded glass view window
73. Lead lining (or other shielding material) as required
74. Lead-lined door, light proofed
75. Barium sink
76. Barium storage (below counter)
77. Red light for dark adaptation
78. Fluoroscopic ceiling light
79. Counter with gate
80. Film identifier, cabinet below
81. Anti-splash panel
82. Wall cabinet over sink
83. Curtain, floor to ceiling
84. Warning light
85. Microphone
86. Loudspeaker
87. Annunciator (for emergency calling station)

open into the patients' corridor should be equipped with bathroom locks, which are operated by knob latch bolts and dead bolts from both sides.

One of the patients' toilet rooms is designed to accommodate a patient in a wheelchair. The room is larger than the others, for easy maneuvering, and has a 3 ft door. The lavatory is set on wall brackets 6 in. out from the wall and 2 ft 10 in. from the floor.

One toilet should be provided with a bedpan flushing attachment. Water closets should be suspended from the wall to simplify cleaning. Each toilet room should be equipped with a grab bar for use by elderly or weak patients. A dome light and buzzer system with an emergency call station in each toilet room and an annunciator at the secretary-receptionist's desk is recommended.

Technicians' toilets and lockers. During busy periods it is essential that the staff be available at all times. Separate toilet and locker facilities are provided for technicians. This reduces the time technicians must be absent from the area and contributes to the efficiency of the department.

STORAGE FACILITIES
General storage. For bulk supplies, a storage cabinet equipped with sliding doors and adjustable shelves is located inside each patients' corridor near the entrance. Materials such as films, opaque solutions, developing solutions, and office supplies are stored here.

Daily linen supplies (x-ray rooms). Clean linen, requisitioned from the hospital central supply, is stored on a cart (No. 66) in each x-ray room; soiled linen is placed in a hamper (No. 65).

Gown storage. Open adjustable shelves for gown storage are placed next to each general bulk supply cabinet, just inside the corridor entrance. The shelving for clean gowns starts about 4 ft from the floor, leaving space beneath for a linen hamper (No. 65) for soiled gowns.

Janitor's closet. The janitor's closet must be readily available for emergency cleaning and it should be convenient to the x-ray rooms and toilets. The closet should contain a floor receptor with a curb or a janitor's service sink, a mop-hanging strip and a shelf, and provide space for parking the mop truck.

DIAGNOSTIC X-RAY ROOMS
X-ray equipment. Both rooms are equipped with combination x-ray and fluoroscopic machines with spot film devices. An overhead type tube support is indicated in the plan, as this facilitates x-raying a patient in bed or on a stretcher. For reasons of economy, however, it may be desirable to equip one room with a floor-ceiling track. If an overhead mounted track is used, it may be supported from the floor by columns or may be bracketed from the

wall, although a ceiling suspension makes a neater installation.

The optimum size of the x-ray room is about 14 by 18 ft. Ceiling height requirements vary for different x-ray machines, but a minimum of 9 ft 6 in. is recommended. The machine and transformer should be placed so as to allow adequate space for admittance of a bed or stretcher in the room. Mounting the transformer on the wall is recommended to save floor space. However, sufficient clearances (at least 2 ft above the transformer) for servicing the transformer should be provided.

The sink and drainboard, for handwashing and rinsing utensils and barium equipment, is equipped with a gooseneck spout. It is located near the foot of the x-ray table. The drainboard can also be used as a barium counter.

It is recommended that the control panel be wired to a signal outside each x-ray room to indicate when the machine is on, to prevent other personnel from inadvertently entering the room. A red light bulb will be satisfactory as a signal for most installations.

Control booth. It is essential that the control booth be located to the right of the machine so that the patient may be observed when the table is inclined, since machines with end-pivoted tables tilt to the right. In the plan, no door is shown on the control booth as the radiation will have scattered at least twice before it reaches the control booth area. This is in accordance with Handbook 60, as amended, issued by the National Bureau of Standards. The arrangement of the control booth to the right and the cassette changer to the extreme left, as shown in the plan, fully meets this requirement. In addition, since the beam is directed toward the outside wall, radiation exposure to other personnel is lessened, and the amount of shielding required is decreased.

If the cassette changers are placed to the right of the machine (on the wall opposite to that indicated on the plan), a door on the control booth or a baffle placed in the room is required to protect the technician in the booth. Furthermore, additional shielding is required to protect films and personnel in the department because the primary beam would not be directed toward the outside wall. In the present scheme, the shielding necessary in the interior walls is principally to safeguard against the scatter radiation.

Storage cabinet and writing counter. A storage cabinet (No. 62), with a safety light above, serves also as a writing counter for the radiologist and technicians. Shelves in the cabinet provide space for storage of accessory items such as sandbags, measuring devices used with x-ray machine, and disposable items needed for patients' examinations.

FILM PROCESSING AND DISTRIBUTION AREAS
Darkroom. This room is located between the two x-ray rooms to facilitate handling of films. Cassettes are loaded

and unloaded on the counter (No. 11). Space is provided for loading and stacking cassettes at both ends of the counter.

A utility sink with a drainboard (No. 24), located opposite the processing tank, is provided for mixing chemical solutions and handwashing. A refrigerating unit (No. 25) for the tank is located in the space beneath the drainboard.

X-ray films are processed in an area separated from the loading counter by a partition (No. 81) at the end of the developing tank which helps to avoid accidental splashing and damage to the screens and films on the loading counter. A through-wall processing unit tank permits the radiologist or staff doctors to read the wet films in the lightroom area without interrupting darkroom procedures.

A lightlock between the darkroom and the lightroom, equipped with interlocking doors, is necessary to allow entrance into the darkroom of other personnel during film processing. Although a maze has some advantages over the lightlock, the additional space needed is not justifiable in a facility of this size. Access panels (No. 22), located in the lightlock and in the control space, are provided to simplify installation and servicing of the processing tanks.

Film processing area. To reduce unnecessary traffic, the film processing rooms are located near the collection and distribution area. This layout allows the technician to work without interruption during the processing routine. Processing of films begins at the developing tank (No. 26) in the darkroom, and continues to the final rinsing tank (No. 29) in the lightroom where the films may be wet-viewed at an illuminator, if desired, and then dried. After the films are dried, they are brought to the counter (33) in the technicians' corridor for final trimming, and passed through to the film collection and distribution area.

Collection and distribution area. Film sorting bins (No. 36) are provided above the counter in the collection and distribution area for temporary filing. After all films have been assembled, they are passed through the film pass slot (No. 34) to the radiologist for interpretation. He returns the films in a file cart or through a slot which leads into a box under the distribution counter. The films may then be temporarily filed for viewing by staff doctors or placed in the active files.

BARIUM MIXING FACILITIES

A two-compartment sink (No. 75) in a counter, located in the technicians' corridor and accessible to both x-ray rooms, is provided for mixing barium. A duplex outlet for plugging in an electric mixer or a heating element is located above the counter unit. Barium supplies for daily use are stored in cabinets under the counter; the bulk supplies can be stocked in one of the general storage cabinets located in the patients' corridors.

DARK ADAPTATION

Patients must be allowed to become accustomed to the low lighting level in the x-ray rooms and the staff must retain their dark adaptation despite the opening of the doors of the fluoroscopic rooms between patients' examinations.

To facilitate dark adaptation, curtains are shown at the intersections of the technicians' and the patients' corridors. In addition to the illumination normally provided in the corridors, patients' toilet rooms, and dressing rooms, it is recommended that these areas be equipped with an independently controlled dim lighting system of red bulbs for dark adaptation.

MISCELLANEOUS SERVICES

It is assumed that the central sterile supply department of the hospital will provide all such services required by the x-ray department.

The mobile x-ray unit should be stored in the radiology department where it will be under the supervision and control of the department and available when needed.

OPTIONAL FACILITIES

Intercommunication system. Provision of a system within the department increases the efficiency of the staff and speeds up service. Outlets are shown at the desk of the secretary-receptionist, in the x-ray rooms and the darkroom, and in the technicians' corridor. It is recommended that a one-way intercommunication system, with a microphone in the control booth and a loudspeaker at the cassette changer, be installed so that the technician need not leave the control booth to give instructions to the patient at the far end of the x-ray room.

Refrigerator. Some items used in the x-ray department, such as barium suspensions for fluoroscopic examinations of the upper gastrointestinal tract, cream for a gall bladder series, and carbonated beverages for carbon dioxide distention of the stomach, require refrigeration. The space under one end of the barium counter at the sink (No. 75) in the technicians' corridor may be used for an under-counter type refrigerator.

High-speed film dryer. The plan provides sufficient space for an anhydrator, if desired, in lieu of the dryer shown (No. 31).

FINISH MATERIALS

Materials used in this department are generally similar to those usually provided in hospitals. However, special attention should be given to some of the areas in the x-ray suite.

Darkroom. The cassette loading counter surface should be of a material which is static-free; wood or linoleum is often preferred. Vinyl or vinyl-asbestos tile, ⅛ in. thick, appears to be a satisfactory material for floors in this size department. Experience indicates, however, that asphalt tile and linoleum floors do not stand up well under the effects of spilled solutions. A pattern of alternating dark and light tiles improves visibility when working under a safe light.

X-ray rooms. No special finishes are required for the x-ray rooms. Asphalt tile floors are satisfactory and a pattern of alternating dark and light tiles is also desirable here. Plaster walls and ceilings are acceptable, but acoustical tile ceilings are preferred since they aid in reducing reverberation.

Toilets. Tile floors and wainscot are highly desirable for easy cleaning.

Doctors' viewing room. Acoustical treatment is recommended to lessen the possibility of doctors' conversations being overheard by nearby waiting patients.

ELECTRICAL INSTALLATIONS
Voltage supplied to the x-ray unit should be constant so that fluoroscopic images and radiographs will be uniform. An independent feeder with sufficient capacity to prevent a voltage drop greater than 3 per cent is recommended. To minimize voltage fluctuations, a separate transformer for the x-ray feeder is required for most installations.

ILLUMINATION
Illumination intensities in the various areas of the suite should comply with recommendations given in the Lighting Handbook, 3rd Edition (1959), published by the Illuminating Engineering Society. Briefly, the general illumination should be not less than 10 footcandles in corridors and in rooms where reading is not required. The waiting room should have 15 footcandles, with supplemental lighting for reading. Offices and areas where clerical work is performed should have at least 50 footcandles, preferably 70 footcandles.

Indirect or cove lighting fixtures are recommended for the x-ray rooms so that patients need not be inconvenienced by glare when lying face upward during radiographic examinations.

Primary barriers should be provided on all surfaces of the x-ray rooms which are exposed, or which may be exposed, to the useful beam between the x-ray tube and occupied areas. Secondary barriers should be provided on all other room surfaces where protection is needed. In determining secondary barriers, consideration should be given to direct or leakage radiation which passes through the tube housing, and also to the secondary or scattered radiation emitted from objects being irradiated by either the useful beam, leakage radiation, or other scattered radiation.

AIR CONDITIONING
Air conditioning with positive ventilation and a well-defined pattern of air movement within the department is

necessary to provide an acceptable environment. In order to prevent the spread of odors from the radiographic and fluoroscopic rooms, darkroom, toilets, and janitor' closets, the ventilation system should be designed so that a negative air pressure relative to the adjoining corridor will be maintained in these rooms. This can be done by exhausting more air from these rooms than is supplied to them, and by reversing this procedure in the corridors. Doors to the toilets and the janitor's closet should be undercut or louvered so that air from the corridor may flow into these areas and be exhausted without recirculation.

Because of the odor problem, the air from the fluoroscopic and x-ray rooms should not be recirculated during the time these rooms are in use, unless adequate odor removal equipment is incorporated in the ventilation system. For economical operation, where odor control equipment is not used, the exhaust system should be provided with motor-operated dampers, switched from within the room, which will direct the air to the outdoors when the rooms are being used, or recirculate the air during idle periods.

As the darkroom will be used for longer periods than the x-ray rooms, an independent system to exhaust the air to the outdoors should be provided. The exhaust from the darkroom should be controlled from a switch in the room and the system should be dampered to regulate the amount of air handled. The exhaust from the film dryer in the lightroom should be connected into the darkroom exhaust system.

The following conditions are recommended for the comfort of patients and personnel:

Administration and waiting areas. A temperature of 72 deg F with a relative humidity of 50 per cent and a ventilation rate of 1-1½ air changes per hour.

Patients' and technicians' corridors. A temperature of 75 deg F to 80 deg F with relative humidity of 50 per cent and a ventilation rate of 2 air changes per hour.

Fluoroscopic and x-ray rooms. A temperature of 75 deg F to 80 deg F with relative humidity of 50 per cent and a ventilation rate of 6 air changes per hour.

Darkroom. A temperature of 72 deg F with relative humidity of 50 per cent and a ventilation rate of 10 air changes per hour.

FIRE SAFETY
To provide an adequate measure of fire safety for the patients and the staff in this department, consideration must be given to factors of design and construction relating to fire prevention and fire protection. The basic structure should be built with fire resistive materials and incombustible finishes and provided with approved equipment.

Closed metal files are recommended for storage of x-ray

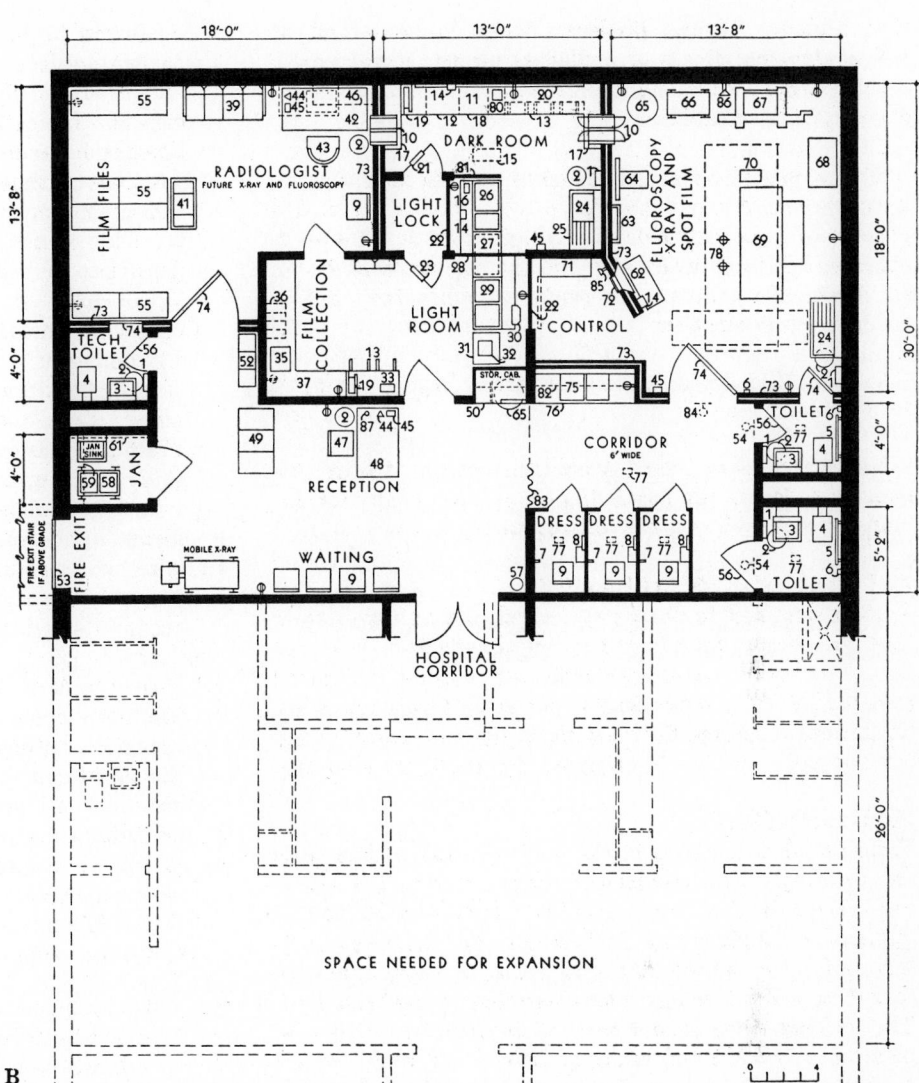

Diagnostic Radiographic Suite—Plan B

SPACE NEEDED FOR EXPANSION

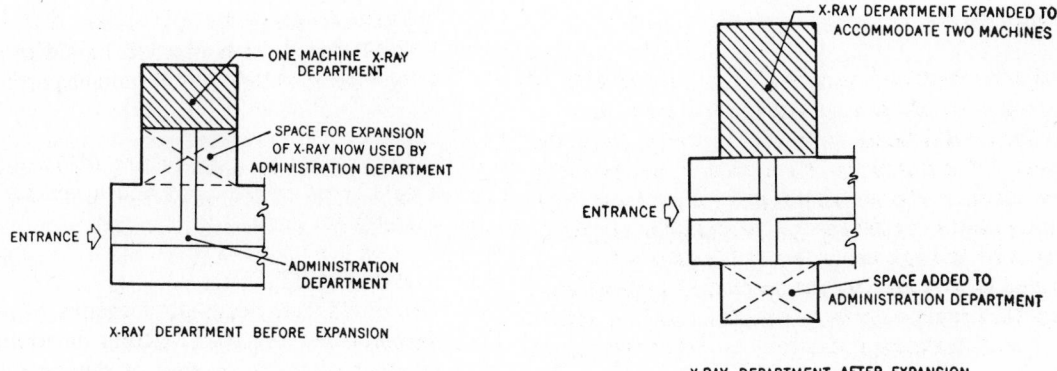

X-RAY DEPARTMENT BEFORE EXPANSION

ONE MACHINE X-RAY DEPARTMENT

SPACE FOR EXPANSION OF X-RAY NOW USED BY ADMINISTRATION DEPARTMENT

ENTRANCE ▷

ADMINISTRATION DEPARTMENT

X-RAY DEPARTMENT EXPANDED TO ACCOMMODATE TWO MACHINES

ENTRANCE ▷

SPACE ADDED TO ADMINISTRATION DEPARTMENT

X-RAY DEPARTMENT AFTER EXPANSION

films. If open shelves are used instead, an automatic sprinkler system should be installed over this storage area to neutralize the hazard of the large volume of combustible materials which would be exposed to possible fire.

Fire extinguishers (carbon dioxide type preferred) should be provided, as located on the plans, to assist in controlling fire.

In accordance with good fire safety practice, two means of egress are provided in the plan: one at the entrance to the department and an emergency exit located off the patient's corridor (door No. 53). The emergency fire exit should lead directly to the ground level outside the building, through an appropriate exit stairway.

PLAN B—DESIGN FOR EXPANSION

This one-machine department, designed to handle a daily average of about 20 patient examinations, could satisfactorily serve a hospital of 50 to 100 beds, depending upon the extent of outpatient services provided. As in Plan A, its volume of examinations can be increased, depending on the staffing pattern and other factors, discussed previously.

The staff usually required for this workload includes: 1 part-time radiologist, 1 technician, 1 secretary-receptionist-technician, 1 orderly (as needed).

This plan will result in a functional unit. It has another important advantage in that it may be expanded to include all the features of Plan A. Such expansion is usually indicated when the hospital is served by a full-time radiologist, when the average daily load approaches 30 examinations per day, and when the proportion of time-consuming examinations becomes high.

By WILBUR R. TAYLOR, WILLIAM A. MILLS, and JAMES G. TERRILL, JR.*

DESIGN OF TELETHERAPY UNITS

Radiation and Architectural Considerations for Cobalt 60 Units

By the term teletherapy, we are restricting ourselves to the use of radiation at a distance; that is, the subject and source are separated by a distance of 50 centimeters or more. In particular, we are concerned with the use of the radioactive isotopes cobalt–60 and cesium–137 as sources of radiation in teletherapy units.

We have restricted our discussion to Co^{60} and Cs^{137}, primarily because they are the more familiar of the isotopes suggested for use in teletherapy units. We are not including the use of radium and high energy X-rays, since some of the problems associated with these are quite different in their solution and nature.

The primary purposes of this article are to furnish

*Wilbur R. Taylor is a Hospital Architect in the Division of Hospital and Medical Facilities, Bureau of Medical Service, Public Health Service, Department of Health, Education, and Welfare; and William A. Mills and James G. Terrill, Jr. are respectively Radiation Physicist and Chief of Radiological Health Program, Division of Sanitary Engineering Services, Bureau of State Services, Public Health Service.

Expansion problems frequently occur in a hospital of 100 beds or less, where there is only one x-ray machine and a part-time radiologist. As the volume of work increases, the radiologist spends more time at the hospital, and a second machine is installed. Unfortunately, in most of these cases, the lack of planning for a future expansion program and expansion area results in an inefficient layout. This limits the usefulness of the equipment and the efficiency of the staff. Examples of such limitations are: poor location of the darkroom in relation to the new x-ray room, inadequate size of the darkroom, insufficient number of toilet facilities and dressing rooms, lack of office and waiting areas, and limited film filing space.

Remodeling an x-ray department is more expensive than remodeling other areas of a hospital because of the shielding, wiring, and plumbing. Expansion of the x-ray department should be incorporated in the original plan. Roughing in the plumbing and building in the shielding and electrical conduits in the expansion space will result in future savings and an efficient x-ray suite.

Minimum alterations to Plan B necessary to duplicate the facilities of Plan A would be the remodeling of the film collection area to accommodate a new control booth, the elimination of the partition between the lightroom and reception space, the elimination of the dressing rooms and the partition behind them.

Until the need for remodeling becomes apparent, part of the administration offices of the hospital may temporarily be situated in the expansion space. When enlarging the x-ray department, other space may then be added to the administration department. The dotted lines on Plan B and on the figures illustrate how this expansion may be designed.

architects who are anticipating a teletherapy unit with information on basic radiation protection ideas and techniques, and to serve as a guide in the solutions of certain architectural problems. We are by no means attempting to evaluate the advantages and disadvantages of Co^{60} and Cs^{137} units against other types of units.

For a discussion of the fundamentals of radiation shielding and a glossary of radiation terminology, see *Architectural Record*, November, 1957, pages 218–220.

IN PLANNING A COBALT INSTALLATION, it should be understood that each type of machine and its location within the building will present a different problem which will require an individual solution. Consequently, no one type plan can be designed which will take care of the various shielding requirements presented by the different machines and installations. The architect is dependent upon other professionals for specific technical information he needs before he can intelligently design a building containing a cobalt teletherapy unit. The problems incurred may materially affect the orientation, location, and structural and functional design of the building. Therefore, during preliminary design stages, close cooperation between architect, radiologist and radiation physicist is necessary to develop an efficient and economical layout.

It should be noted that the Atomic Energy Commission places responsibility upon the applicant for conditions of installation and use of the facility. Since the use of a facility is largely dependent upon the conditions of installation, it is to the applicant's advantage to secure the services of a radiation physicist at the inception of a project. His function is to advise the applicant and architect on radiation requirements, assume responsibility for the final design as to shielding provided and furnish the supporting information required in Application Form AEC-313 relative to exposure rates in areas surrounding the teletherapy room and occupancy factors assigned.

Fundamental decisions as to: (1) the type of machine, (2) strength of the source, (3) desired location, and (4) the shielding required for floor, walls and ceiling must be made before the building's structural system can be designed. During the early design, it may be determined that the structural system cannot support the weight of the shielding, or perhaps soil conditions will not permit sufficient excavation for a subgrade installation. It may then be necessary to change or alter one or more of the following: the machine or its operation, the source strength or the location of the room.

To those not familiar with such shielding problems, the included plans have been developed to illustrate the shielding necessary for three types of machines in specific locations. However, before considering the detailed plans, it may be desirable to discuss some of the general requirements of such facilities.

Location

The cobalt suite should adjoin the X-ray therapy department. This location permits the joint use of waiting, dressing, toilet, examination, work and consultation rooms. In addition, it offers the important advantage of having the staff concentrated in one area, thereby eliminating the considerable loss of time involved in traveling to a remote location. This is an important consideration and justifies the cost of any additional shielding that may be necessary to achieve it.

A location below grade, unoccupied above and below, will require less shielding. However, if such a location separates the cobalt and the X-ray therapy department, it may be more costly in both loss of staff time and efficiency than the cost of concrete shielding amortized over several years. If, for example, twenty-five minutes per day are lost in traveling to a remote location, one additional patient could be treated in this time each day — or 240 patients per year. Assuming a staff salary of $20,000 per year, this loss of twenty-five minutes per day results in an indirect salary loss of $1032 per year, which would soon equal the cost of shielding in a new facility.

A corner location for the cobalt room is usually desirable since through traffic is eliminated, only two interior walls require shielding, distance to the property line utilizes the inverse square law to reduce shielding and the structural requirements are more easily solved.

Teletherapy Room Details

Size. The room size may vary to suit different manufacturers' equipment. A room approximately 15 ft by 18 ft by 9 ft–6 in.

plus the necessary entrance maze, will accommodate most of the machines commercially available with the exception of the largest rotating models. For reasons of cost, the room should be as compact as possible after allowing space to install the equipment and to position the treatment table.

Shielding. The shielding necessary for a room must not only be considered in terms of floor, ceiling and wall shielding, but also such things as doors, windows, ventilation and heating ducts, and safety locks. Radiation that might escape through such possibilities could result in overexposure to personnel, if proper precautions are not taken.

Entrance. The primary purpose of specific entrance construction is to protect personnel. It should also provide sufficient space to admit a stretcher and the largest crated piece of equipment. In some cases, a considerable savings in cost of assembling equipment may be had by making the door and maze large enough to admit the crated assembled machine. For this purpose, some manufacturers specify a door opening of 4 by 7 ft and a minimum distance of 6 ft at the end of the maze.

Rather than add large amounts of lead to doors, the shielding problem may be solved to some degree by having the door to the teletherapy room open into a maze. This maze should be built so that no primary radiation could fall directly on the door. In designing doors for such a room, a good practice is to have a door of wood with a layer of lead. This lead can either be on the inside surface, or between layers of wood. Commercially available x-ray doors serve well for this purpose. The space between the door and floor can usually be shielded by using a lead strip under the door or by making a slight rise in the floor containing lead, on the outer side of the door. Lead shielding at the jamb and head between the frame and buck may be eliminated by the use of a combination frame and buck set in concrete.

For safety precautions, the door lock should be such that the door can be readily opened from inside the cobalt room.

Control View Window. It is standard practice to locate this window at a height which will permit the operator to be seated during the treatment period, 4 ft-0 in. from the floor to the center of the window being an optimum distance. In plan, the window should be located in the area of minimum radiation and for convenient observation of the patient. This position, for a rotational machine, would be along the axis of rotation, and for a fixed beam unit, 90° to the plane of tilt. (See plans on following pages.)

From the control view window the entire room should be in full view, using mirrors when necessary. The glass should contain lead or other materials in amounts which would provide shielding equivalent to the surrounding concrete. The frame is usually packed with lead wool and should be designed to offset the shielding loss of the reduced concrete thickness at beveled areas. The cost of such special glass and frame increases rapidly with size and an 8 by 8 in. window is considered an optimum size.

ROOM FOR COBALT-60 FACILITIES

By U.S. Public Health Service

Fixed beam unit *

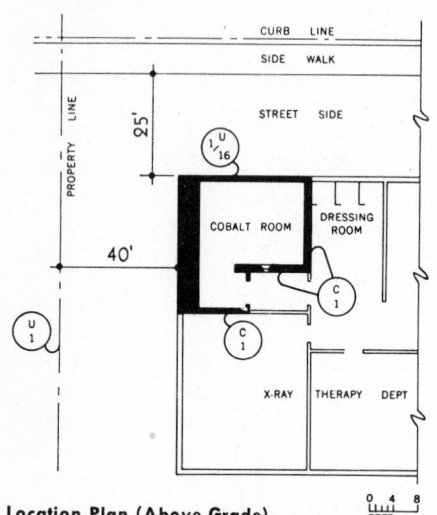

Location Plan (Above Grade)

SYMBOLS

- $\binom{C}{1}$ Full Occupancy Controlled
- $\binom{U}{1}$ Full Occupancy Uncontrolled
- $\binom{U}{1/4}$ Partial Occupancy Uncontrolled
- $\binom{U}{1/16}$ Occasional Occupancy Uncontrolled

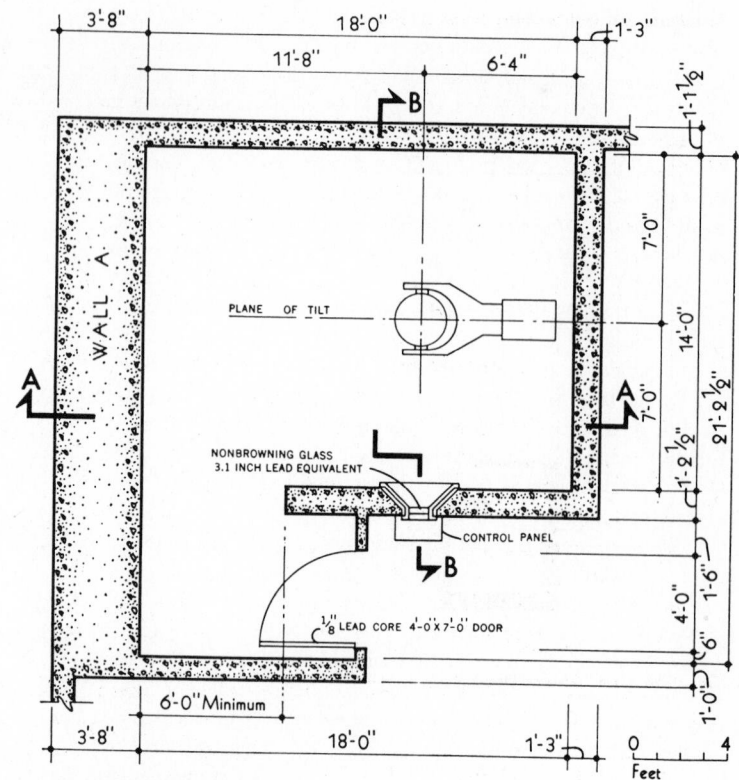

Plan of Cobalt 60 Room

For Design Requirements see next page.

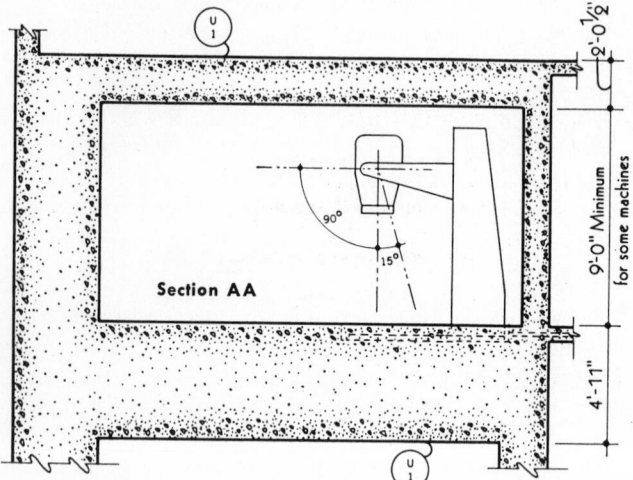

Section AA

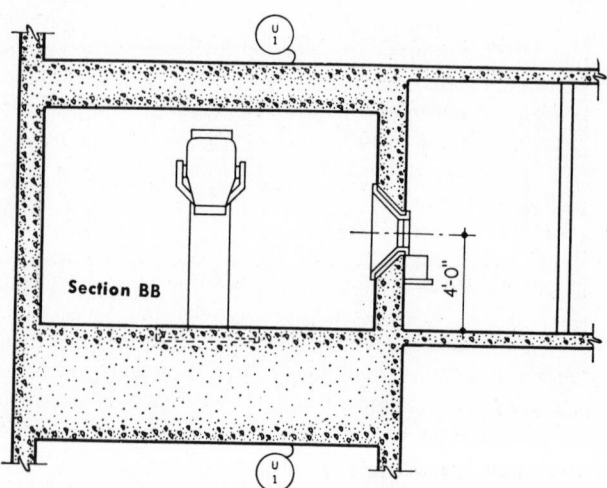

Section BB

The shielding indicated on the accompanying plans was computed on a basis of a 5,000 curie source. Because of its high cost, it is not now commonly used. Reduction of the source, however, does not decrease the shielding requirements significantly. For example, in the plan, use of a 2,000 curie source would result in a reduction of the thickness of wall A by 3 in.; for a 500 curie source, a reduction of 5 in. more. Since greatest cost is in forming, such savings are relatively small.

In new construction, the cost of concrete shielding will, in most cases, be a small part of the total cost of the installation.

To illustrate the maximum required shielding for floor and ceiling, the thicknesses shown have been computed for locations with full-time uncontrolled occupancy above and below. With controlled occupancy less shielding would be necessary and with no occupancy, these slabs could be reduced to the minimum structural requirements. An underground location is the only way, short of limiting the machine, of reducing the thickness of exterior walls.

*With Primary Beam Restricted to Floor and One Wall

Rotational unit with primary beam absorber

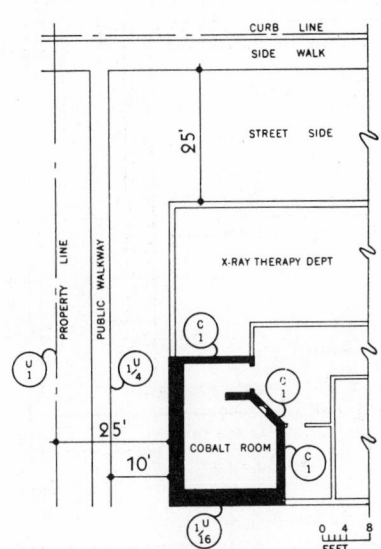

Location Plan (Above Grade)

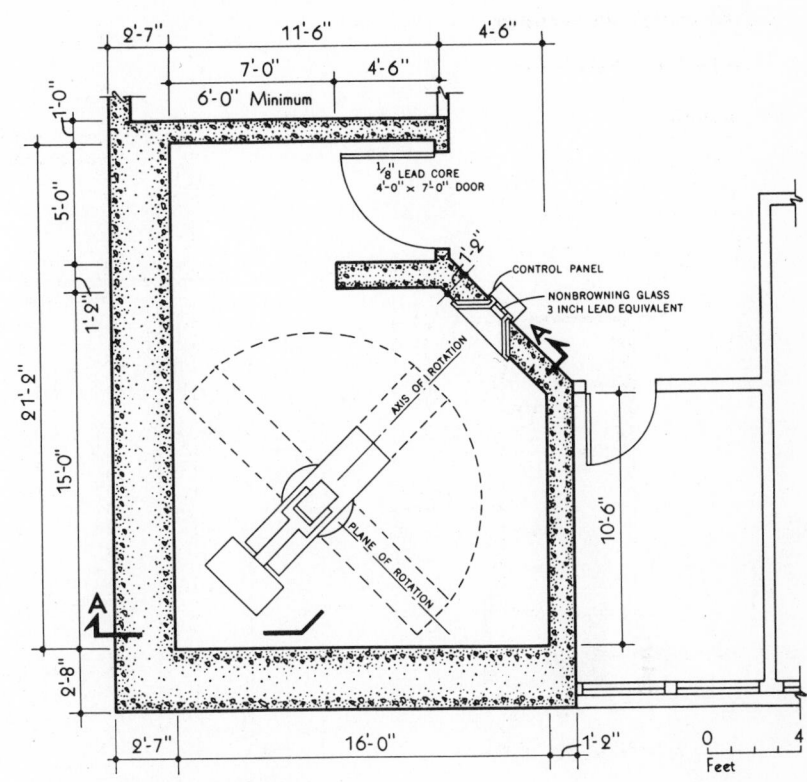

Plan of Cobalt 60 Room

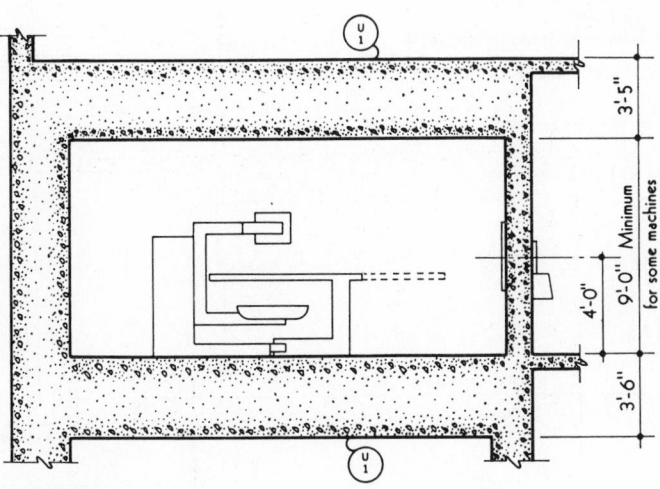

Section AA

SYMBOLS

- ⓒ₁ Full Occupancy Controlled
- Ⓤ₁ Full Occupancy Uncontrolled
- Ⓤ¼ Partial Occupancy Uncontrolled
- Ⓤ¹⁄₁₆ Occasional Occupancy Uncontrolled

DESIGN REQUIREMENTS

Controlled Area $MPD = \dfrac{5.0 \text{ Rem}}{Yr} = \dfrac{5.0 \text{ Rem}}{60 \text{ Wk}} = \dfrac{100 \text{ MRem}}{Wk}$

Uncontrolled Area $MPD = \dfrac{0.5 \text{ Rem}}{Yr} = \dfrac{0.5 \text{ Rem}}{52 \text{ Wk}} = \dfrac{9.6 \text{ MRem}}{Wk}$

Full Occupancy $T = 1$

Control space, residences, play areas, wards, office work rooms, darkrooms, corridors and waiting space large enough to hold desks and rest rooms used by radiologic staff and others routinely exposed to radiation.

Partial Occupancy $T = \frac{1}{4}$

Corridors in X-ray departments too narrow for future desk space, rest rooms not used by radiologic personnel, parking lots, utility rooms.

Occasional Occupancy $T = \frac{1}{16}$

Stairways, automatic elevators, streets, closets too small for future workrooms, toilets not used by radiologic personnel.

Source 5000 Curies

Rotational unit without primary beam absorber

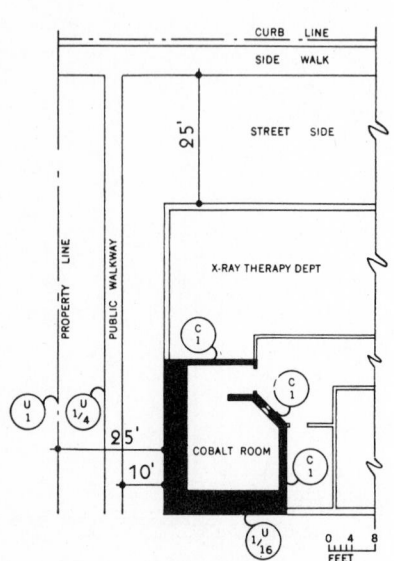

Location Plan (Above Grade)

SYMBOLS

- $\binom{C}{1}$ Full Occupancy Controlled
- $\binom{U}{1}$ Full Occupancy Uncontrolled
- $\binom{U}{1/4}$ Partial Occupancy Uncontrolled
- $\binom{U}{1/16}$ Occasional Occupancy Uncontrolled

For Design Requirements see previous page.

A primary beam absorber on a machine reduces the shielding requirements considerably. However, some radiologists prefer to use a machine without the absorber, because of its greater flexibility, and for this reason some machines are designed to be used with or without the absorber. Under these conditions the room shielding should be designed for use either way. The plan and section shown here illustrate the necessary shielding.

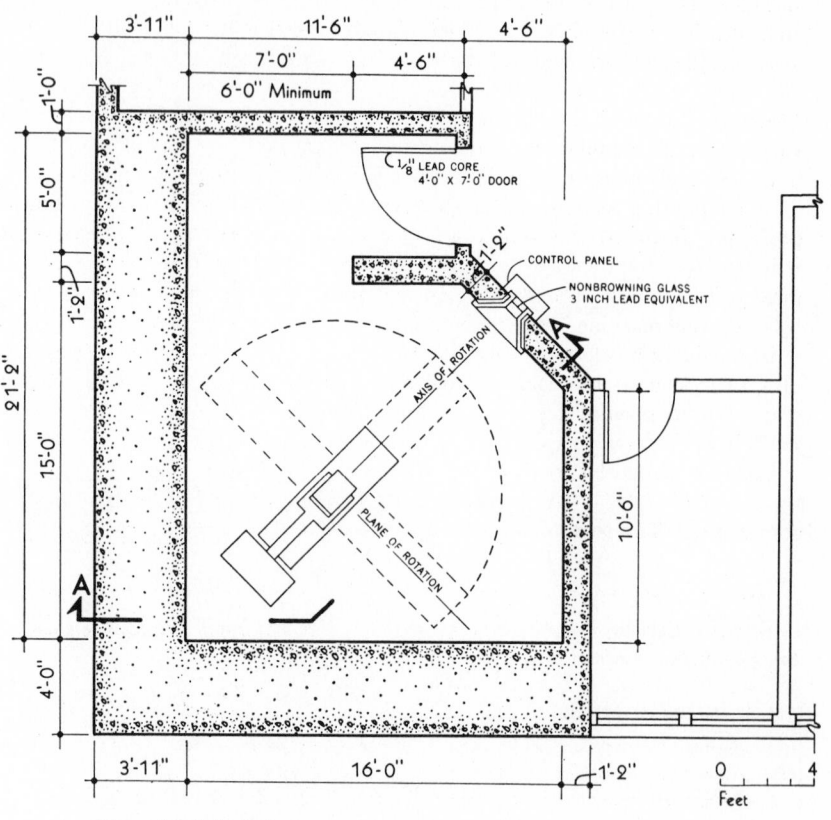

Plan of Cobalt 60 Room

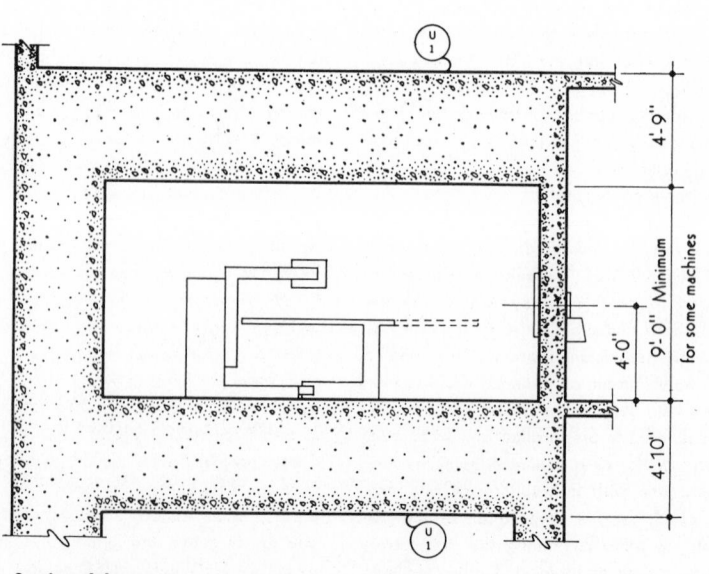

Section AA

Heating and Air Conditioning. The only problem in relation to heating and air conditioning not encountered in other buildings is that of providing shielding where walls are pierced with supply and return ducts. The usual solution is to locate ducts and openings in walls which are least subject to radiation and offset the path of ducts through the wall, lead or other high density material being added, where necessary, to maintain the shielding value of the wall displaced by ducts.

Electrical. Electrical service required for the machine, will vary with each manufacturer's equipment. Voltage will vary from 110-single phase to 220-three phase for large machines.

Room lighting should assure good over-all illumination, preferably from cove lighting or an indirect type of fixture. It is essential that the operator be able to observe any movement of the patient during treatment and shadows produced by a rotating machine interfere with observation.

In providing a safety lock for the door, it has been found of great value to interlock the machine control with the door, so that opening the door automatically shuts off the machine.

Conduits should be provided for power and control wiring.

Environment. The general effect to be created in this department should be one of cheerfulness and restfulness. Use of color and even murals have been used effectively on the walls of the cobalt room.

The usual hospital finishes such as acoustical ceiling tile and resilient flooring are desirable in this area.

Remodeling. Unless previously designed for super voltage X-ray, remodeling an existing building can be expensive. It is often impossible to build in sufficient shielding which makes it necessary to control nearby occupancy and restrict direction of the beam, thereby handicapping the usefulness of the machine. Other problems such as relocating plumbing, heating, electrical services and disturbing the normal operation of the building during remodeling must be considered.

In new construction, concrete shielding is relatively cheap, but in remodeling the cost is high. For this reason the use of masonry units may be preferable since no form work is necessary and the work can be performed intermittently. Good workmanship, of course, is necessary to prevent voids in mortar joints.

In some cases it might be better to add to the building, rather than to remodel an existing portion. Normal hospital operation would not be interfered with, costs may be lower and a more efficient layout would probably result.

By NOYCE L. GRIFFIN, *Electrical Engineer, Architectural and Engineering Branch, Division of Hospital and Medical Facilities, Public Health Service, U.S. Department of Health, Education and Welfare*

ELECTROENCEPHALOGRAPHIC SUITE

Introduction: An electroencephalographic (EEG) examination consists of the measurement of electrical potentials of the brain as measurable at the scalp. It requires an extremely sensitive instrument located so as to be as free as possible from outside electrical disturbances. The examination requires careful preparation of the patient and involves securing several pairs of electrodes to the patient's scalp, connecting the conductors from the electrodes to the EEG unit, operating the EEG unit to obtain recordings under definite physical conditions of the patient, removing the electrodes and any adhesive, if used in attaching the electrodes.

Suitable space must be provided for the neurologist and his staff to examine patients, read the recordings, prepare reports, and keep records. The suite should be arranged to provide office facilities for the neurologist and typist or secretary, a workroom for technician, space for preparation and examination of patients, and storage space for supplies and voluminous EEG recordings. The preparation and examining space should, as a minimum, comprise two rooms: one with a hospital-type bed and equipment for the preparation of the patient; the other containing the EEG instruments, a desk or table, and other facilities needed by the technician (Fig. 13). A more efficient layout may be had by dividing the preparation and examining space into separate rooms. This would increase the patient-handling capacity of the unit, as one patient could be prepared while another is examined (Fig. 14). Toilet facilities should be conveniently available for patients' use.

Although shielding of the patient's room against electrical disturbances is not always required, it is usually desirable. Where such disturbances are excessive for the quality of work required, a completely shielded room may be necessary. The most common electrical disturbances are caused by high-frequency equipment such as diathermy and radio, static electricity, high-voltage transmission lines, large transformer banks, large motors, nearby powerful FM broadcast stations, and conductors carrying heavy currents. To minimize disturbances from power systems, all power conductors in the vicinity of the EEG machine should be metal armored or installed in metal raceway. Large or main electrical conductors should be routed as far away from the EEG examining locations as practicable, both horizontally and vertically, and use of fluorescent lighting in the vicinity of the EEG unit should be avoided.

A reasonable amount of soundproofing of the examining room is desirable.

EEG recordings and case records are bulky and require considerable space for filing. Open shelving of the large pigeon-hole type is reasonably satisfactory for filing the large folders of active case records. This filing space should be located in the office or preferably in an adjacent room convenient to the neurologist.

Workroom: The workroom facilities and equipment normally consist of the EEG unit, preferably the console type, photostimulator panel, a supply cabinet for recording paper, preparation materials, an electric clock with sweep second hand, a workbench with wood top and cabinet below for EEG maintenance and general use, and a general office-type desk or table. Switches for control of lights in workroom and examining room should be located in the workroom. Shelving for EEG recordings and case records may be located in this room unless other suitable space is provided, and should be approximately 12 in. deep.

Examining room: Doors through which patients must pass to enter the examining room should be 3 ft 10 in. wide to permit easy passage of stretcher or wheelchair. The size of the examining room should be

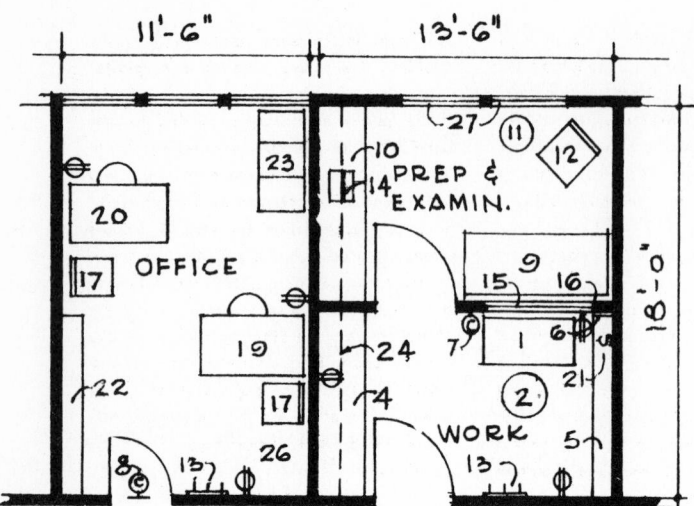

Fig. 13. Minimum EEG suite

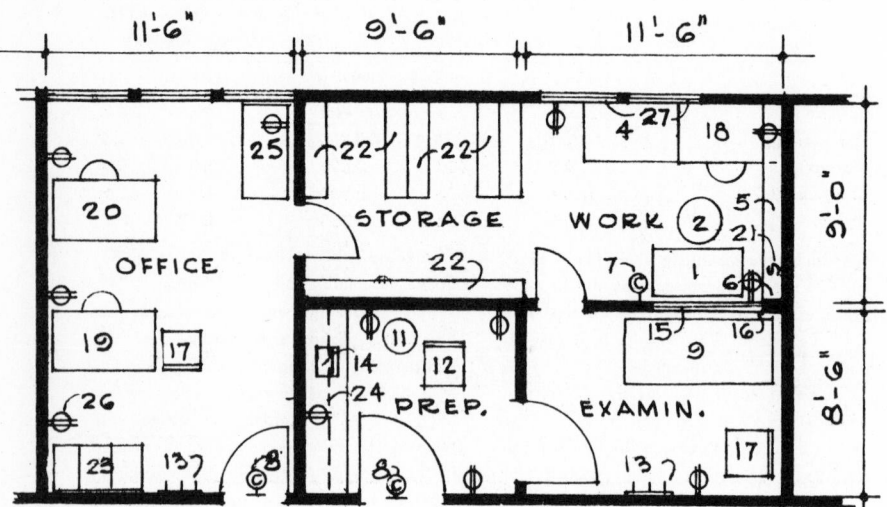

Fig. 14. Recommended suite with separate preparation and examining rooms

Equipment list

1. Electroencephalograph, console type
2. Stool
3. Steel cabinet with shelving and door
4. Work bench, cabinet below
5. Shelf
6. Photostimulator panel (if used)
7. Clock with sweep second hand above glass panel
8. Clock outlet
9. Adjustable hospital bed
10. Sink in counter, cabinets below
11. Sanitary waste receptacle
12. Chair for patient preparation
13. Hook strip
14. Mirror above sink
15. Glass window
16. Two holes through wall, 3 in., 20 in. from floor
17. Armchair
18. General office-type desk and chair
19. Typist's desk and chair
20. Executive-type desk and chair
21. Two-pole switch for light in patient's room
22. Filing compartments for EEG recordings
23. File cabinets, legal size
24. Cabinet above for electrodes, etc.
25. Work table
26. Duplex outlets
27. Venetian blind

sufficient to accommodate a hospital bed and allow enough additional space to permit the technician to work efficiently. For sleep inducement, exterior windows should be equipped with shades to partially darken the room. As it is desirable that the patient be in full view of the operator, the examining room should have sufficient width to permit the bed to be placed parallel to the wall nearest the workroom. This wall should have two 3-in. openings, 20 in. above the floor, one for passing the EEG electrode cable with plug attached, the other for passing the photostimulator conductors.

The partition between the workroom and

the patient's room should be provided with a glass window not less than 24 in. high and 36 in. wide, mounted with the lower edge 43 in. from the floor. This window should be located to provide good vision of the patient. In the preparation area, floor and sink are subjected to staining and eroding effects of chemicals such as acetone and collodion used for setting and removing electrodes to and from patient's scalp. The sink should be vitreous china set in a countertop resistant to acid and alkali, with cabinets below.

A masonry-type floor such as tile or terrazzo is recommended in the preparation area. Solvents such as acetone used for

removal of electrode adhesive, when spilled or dropped on the floor, are injurious to the resilient type of flooring materials such as vinyl, asphalt, rubber, or linoleum.

When air-drying paste is used in setting electrodes, means should be provided for quick drying. Hand-held hair dryers are sometimes used, but a low-pressure compressed-air outlet is preferred. Some technicians use a self-supporting conducting paste for electrode attachment that requires no drying; others use pin-type electrodes, which do not require paste or adhesive, for insertion into the scalp.

Shielding: Shielding may be required, depending upon the equipment used and its location with respect to sources of disturbances and the quality of recordings required. It is recommended that in new construction shielding be provided in all examining rooms, and that omission of shielding be considered only when converting existing rooms.

Properly installed shielding of the examining rooms will eliminate or minimize outside disturbances caused by static electrical discharges and high-frequency equipment. It has little effect on magnetic disturbances such as those produced by power transformers, high-voltage equipment, and current-carrying conductors. For minimizing disturbances due to magnetic forces, the most effective means is distance.

Where shielding is required, panels and equipment for completely shielding the room may be obtained from several manufacturers, or as an alternate, satisfactory shielding may be constructed with copper insect screening. The strips of shielding material should be bonded and soldered at intervals of about 2 ft or less and should entirely cover all walls, floors, ceiling, doors, and windows. The screening should pass on the room side of any lighting fixture or electrical device without making contact with it. Wall and ceiling finish materials and the floor covering may be applied over the shielding if desired. In this case, the shielding material should be copper sheeting to preclude the possibility of interferences developing in the shielding due to the installation of plaster or mastic materials.

The shield should be grounded at one point only. The ground connection should be brought out to a terminal arrangement convenient for connection to the EEG unit and for disconnection for testing. Double screening produces a more effective shield than single screening. Shielding efficiency is further increased by insulating one layer of screen from the other except at the one ground point. If a screened room is provided, all electric conductors entering the screened area should be equipped with filters to prevent disturbances by these conductors.

by U.S. Public Health Service

LABORATORY

The size of the hospital laboratory depends upon how many and what type of tests are performed, rather than upon the number of beds. The number of tests varies widely from one hospital to another, but average figures for two sizes of hospitals are given in Tables 1 and 2. It should be noted that the larger hospitals, averaging only 40 per cent more beds, often perform 100 per cent more tests than the smaller hospitals. A suggested plan for the laboratory of a hospital of 100 to 150 beds is shown in Fig. 17. The laboratory for a hospital of 150 to 200 beds would be similar but slightly larger (50 ft long instead of 40 ft), providing another laboratory bay for biochemistry (see Fig. 16) and additional space for waiting, files, lockers, and storage.

Table 1. Tests performed annually in each laboratory unit
General hospitals—100–149 beds

Unit	Low	High	Median	Technologists required Median	High
Urinalysis	3,000	9,000	4,800	0.2	0.3
Hematology	9,000	37,000	20,200	1.4	2.5
Serology	220	5,600	3,500	0.3	0.4
Biochemistry	1,300	5,300	2,800	0.3	0.6
Bacteriology	85	3,800	700	0.09	0.5
Histology	700	3,100	1,500	0.4	0.8
Parasitology	200	250	200	0.02	0.02
Basal metabolism	20	300	60		
Electrocardiograms	500	3,300	650		
Blood bank tests	20	9,200	2,800	0.5	1.0
Transfusions	400	1,300	700		
Other	80	7,300	400		
Total				3.21	6.12

Table 2. Tests performed annually in each laboratory unit
General hospitals—150–200 beds

Unit	Low	High	Median	Technologists required Median	High
Urinalysis	6,200	20,000	11,300	0.4	0.7
Hematology	29,800	81,200	35,800	2.5	5.6
Serology	3,600	13,500	6,800	0.6	1.1
Biochemistry	2,300	19,600	6,600	0.7	2.0
Parasitology*					
Bacteriology	400	4,700	1,800	0.2	0.6
Histology	700	5,100	1,800	0.5	1.3
Basal metabolism	30	700	400		
Electrocardiogram	800	4,200	1,300		
Blood bank tests	130	23,200	4,500	1.0	2.0
Transfusions	800	2,000	1,000		
Other	500	9,600	1,700		
Total				5.9	13.3

* Included with urinalysis.

Fig. 15. Perspective view of laboratory for general hospital of 150 to 200 beds

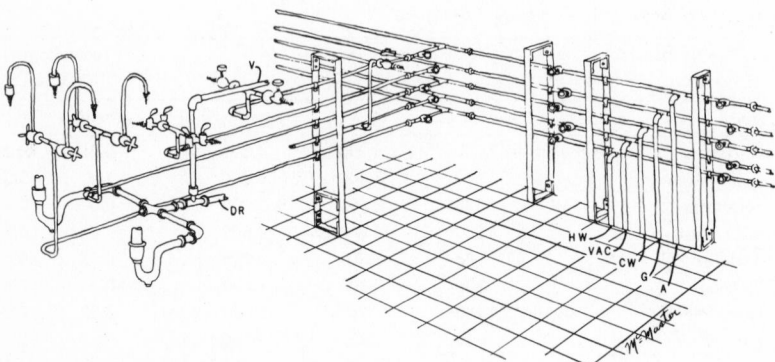

Fig. 16. Diagram of piping behind laboratory workbenches

1. Desk 30 by 40 in., single pedestal
2. Filing cabinet, letter size
3. Counter, 30 in. high
4. Staining sink
5. Cup sink
6. Analytical balance
7. Counter, 36 in. high
8. Cabinets with adjustable shelves, below counter
9. Electric strip outlets, continuous
10. Bookcase
11. Utility sink
12. Gas outlet
13. Table for magazines
14. Suction outlet
15. Compressed-air outlet
16. Table for instruments
17. Straight chair
18. Stool
19. Two-compartment sink, 8 in. deep with drainboards of noncorrosive metal, pegboards located above drainboards
20. Cabinet with trash receptacle mounted on inside of door
21. Utility cart
22. Laboratory pressure sterilizer
23. Hot-air oven
24. Incubator
25. Shelf or table for analytical balance
26. Centrifuge
27. Table for Harvard trip balance
28. Wastepaper receptacle
29. Refrigerator, 8 cu ft
30. Refrigerator, 6 cu ft, blood bank
31. Worktable
32. Microhematocrit centrifuge
33. Examination table
34. Lavatory

This material is condensed from the chapter "Suitable Environment" in the manual Physical Therapy Essentials of a Hospital Department *prepared by the Joint Committee of the American Hospital Association and the American Physical Therapy Association.*

Planning is by Thomas P. Galbraith and Peter N. Jensen, Hospital Architects of the Architectural and Engineering Branch, Division of Hospital and Medical Facilities, Public Health Service.

PHYSICAL THERAPY DEPARTMENT

OF THE MANY environmental factors which condition the effectiveness of physical therapy service to patients, the most important are space, location and work areas. Ventilation, lighting, interior finish and related considerations also contribute toward providing a suitable environment. The keynote is function.

Location

Location is closely related to function. The area selected for physical therapy should be centrally located to minimize problems of transporting patients and to facilitate giving bedside treatment when necessary. At least half of the patients treated in a general hospital physical therapy department are likely to be out-patients. With this in mind, special attention should be given to accessibility, and to having as few steps as possible to climb, as few long corridors and heavy doors to negotiate. A ground floor location, convenient for both in- and out-patients and for access to an outdoor exercise area, is recommended.

Availability of daylight and fresh air should also be considered in selecting a location.

In new hospitals, physical therapy is frequently placed in an area which includes other out-patient services, social service, occupational therapy, recreation. It is particularly important that physical and occupational therapy be in close proximity.

Amount of Space

The amount of space needed depends on the number of patients treated, the kinds of disabilities and the treatments required. Also to be considered is the fact that some space-consuming equipment — such as a whirlpool bath, treatment tables, parallel bars, etc. — are minimum essentials for even a one therapist department. These pieces of equipment will not be multiplied in direct proportion to increases in staff and patient load.

Efforts to correlate bed capacity and physical therapy space requirements are not satisfactory. Hospitals with 50–100

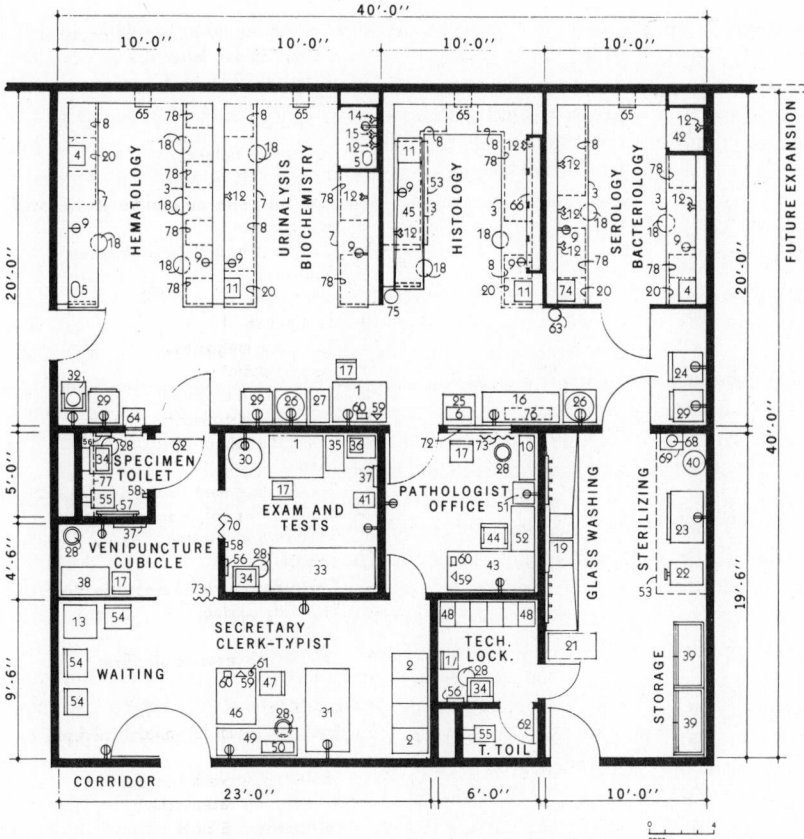

Fig. 17.   Plan of laboratory of general hospital of 100 to 149 beds

35.	Basal metabolism apparatus	
36.	Electrocardiograph	
37.	Hook strip	
38.	Table, 24 by 36 in.	
39.	Storage cabinets	
40.	Water still, 2 to 5 gal per hr	
41.	Adult scale	
42.	Fume hood	
43.	Double-pedestal office desk	
44.	Office chair, swivel, with arms	

45. Noncorrosive metal work surface, slight pitch to sink
46. Typewriter desk
47. Posture chair
48. Technicians' lockers
49. Specimen-receiving table
50. Request file with pigeonholes
51. Slide file cabinet
52. Microscope table
53. Exhaust hood
54. Easy chair
55. Wall-hung water closet
56. Paper-towel dispenser
57. Grab bar, continuous
58. Emergency calling station (push-button) connected to buzzer at secretary's desk
59. Telephone outlet
60. Intercommunication system outlet
61. Buzzer at receptionist's desk from emergency calling stations
62. Hook on toilet side of door
63. Fire extinguisher
64. Pass-through between toilet and laboratory
65. Exhaust air grilles near floor
66. Wall cabinet
67. Refrigerator, 11 cu ft
68. Pipette washer
69. Shelf, for pipette washer, 10 in. from floor
70. Folding door
71. Table for electrocardiograph
72. Window
73. Curtain
74. Sink with electric waste disposal
75. Carbon dioxide cylinder
76. Gas cylinders under table
77. Shelf for urine bottles
78. Drawers with adjustable shelves, below counter
79. Sink with electric waste disposal

beds may serve large numbers of out-patients. The amount of space given over to physical therapy in a small hospital is, justifiably, out of proportion to the bed capacity.

No absolute standard can be recommended as the amount of space needed for physical therapy in a general hospital. The most that can be said is that, if possible, it is desirable to plan for at least a thousand square feet of floor space, free of structural obstructions. About half of that should be exercise area.

This does not mean that a hospital cannot begin an effective physical therapy service in smaller quarters. Many have done so successfully, using to full advantage whatever space resources they had. But crowded quarters do subject the staff to strain and call for more than ordinary ingenuity and good humor in order to make it possible for patients to obtain maximum benefit from treatment.

Work Space Components

Whatever the eventual size of a physical therapy department, from the very beginning plans must be made to provide certain kinds of work space. These essential components can be expanded, multiplied or refined as the physical therapy department grows but the fundamental requirements are the same for a small or large department. They include: (1) reception area, (2) staff space, (3) examining room, (4) treatment areas, (5) toilet facilities, (6) storage.

Experienced physical therapists have many suggestions for increasing the efficiency of physical therapy departments by giving attention to details of planning and arranging these component work areas. For example:

Reception area — accommodations for in-patients and out-patients, if possible. Adequate space for stretcher and wheelchair patients.

Staff space — private. Office space suitable for interviewing patients, attending to administrative and clerical duties, housing files, etc. Writing facilities for the staff adequate for dictation, record keeping. There should be space for staff lockers and dressing rooms separate from the patient area, either within the department or near to it.

Examining room — floor to ceiling partitions for privacy. Arranged so that necessary examining equipment can remain in the room permanently. Possible to use this space for special tests and measurements or for treatment when privacy is desirable.

Treatment area — there are three types of treatment areas: cubicle (dry), underwater exercise (wet) and exercise (open). Each is designed to meet the particular requirements of the special equipment used for different kinds of treatment.

Cubicle — each unit large enough for the physical therapist to work on either side of the table without having to move equipment belonging in the cubicle. Preferably cubicles divided by curtains for easier access for wheelchair and stretcher cases, for expansion of useable floor area for gait analysis, group activity or teaching purposes.

Curtain tracks should be flush with the ceiling and curtains should have open panels at the top for ventilation when drawn. Both curtains and tracks should be sturdy. In or near the cubicles, out-patients need a place or locker for their outer clothing.

Underwater exercise area — all equipment requiring special plumbing and water supply concentrated in one section of the department but accessible and adjacent to other treatment areas. Should include a treatment table, especially in the room with a tank or exercise pool. Fixed overhead lifts are absolutely essential for the efficient use of tanks and failure to provide lifts severely limits the usefulness of this valuable equipment. Plumbing and other installation requirements, humidity and noise from motors call for special care and attention. Electrical and metal equipment in other treatment areas may suffer damage unless the underwater exercise area is carefully planned.

Exercise area — very flexible open space planned to accommodate patients engaged in diverse individual or group exercise activities. Used extensively by people in wheelchairs, on crutches or canes, or with other disabilities which limit their motion and agility. At least one wall should be reinforced for the installation of stall bars and similar equipment.

Toilet facilities — separate toilet facilities for patients and staff, if possible. Patient facilities should be designed to accommodate wheelchair patients. If the department serves small children, seat adaptors with foot rests should be provided.

Storage — designed to meet special needs in and near work areas. Should also be storage space on the wards for equipment and supplies usually needed for bedside treatments. For wheelchairs, stretchers, etc., it is best to plan "carport" space, not closets. All storage space should be accessible, simple, well lighted.

Special Considerations

Ventilation. Adequate, controlled ventilation is of extreme importance in a physical therapy department. Many of the treatment procedures require the use of dry or moist heat, or active exercise, which raise body temperatures. A continuous, reliable flow of fresh air is essential to the comfort of patients and staff. This includes protection from drafts.

Air conditioning, desirable for the entire department, will be a necessity for certain areas of the physical therapy department, in most sections of the country. The reduction of humidity for comfort, protection of equipment and reduction of the hazard of slippery floors makes air conditioning vital in the underwater exercise area. It has been demonstrated as desirable in the exercise area and in treatment cubicles, especially where heat producing equipment is used. Air conditioning engineers should be consulted before ventilation equipment is installed.

Sinks. Hospital hand washing lavatories with hot and cold water mixing outlets, preferably foot operated, should be located at the proper height in convenient places. At least one sink should be of sufficient width and depth to accommodate the care of wet packs and other special washing needs.

Interior finishes. The activity of patients in wheelchairs, on stretchers and crutches subject floors and walls to heavy wear. Materials which will stand up under such rough usage, remain attractive and require a minimum of maintenance should be specified despite higher costs.

All interior wall surfaces of the department should have a durable and attractive wainscot to protect them against

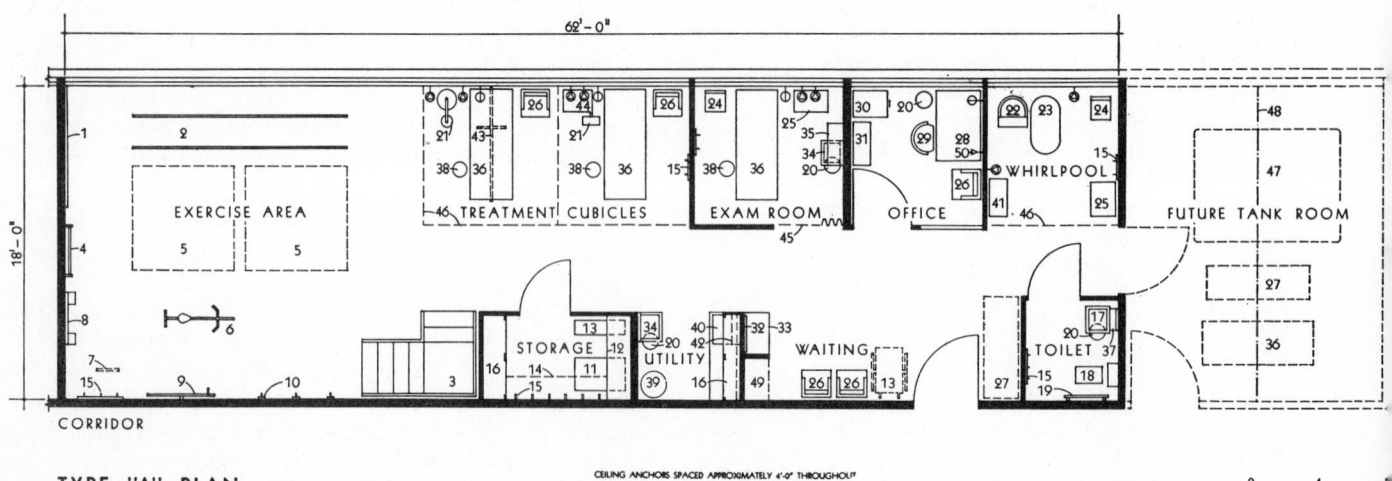

CORRIDOR

TYPE "A" PLAN   AREA 1116 SQUARE FEET

CEILING ANCHORS SPACED APPROXIMATELY 4'-0" THROUGHOUT
ENTIRE TREATMENT AREA DESIGN TO CARRY 500 LBS.

GRAPHIC SCALE

NOTE: MAJOR PIECES OF EQUIPMENT RECOMMENDED FOR ONE
PHYSICAL THERAPIST AND AID INDICATED ON TYPE PLANS

1. Posture Mirror
2. Parallel Bars
3. Steps
4. Stall Bars
5. Gym Mat
6. Stationary Bicycle
7. Sayer Head Sling Attached to Ceiling
8. Pulley Weights
9. Shoulder Wheel
10. Gym Mat Hooks
11. Cart with Open Shelves
12. Open Shelves
13. Wheel Chair
14. Shelf
15. Wall Hooks
16. Wall Cabinet
17. Lavatory, Gooseneck Spout
18. Water Closet
19. Hand Rail
20. Waste Paper Receptacle
21. Portable Equipment
22. Adjustable Chair
23. Whirlpool
24. Chair
25. Table
26. Chair, preferable with arms
27. Wheel Stretcher
28. Desk
29. Swivel Chair
30. File Cabinet
31. Bookcase
32. Bulletin Board
33. Wall Desk (counter, shelf below)
34. Lavatory, Gooseneck Spout and Foot Control
35. Wall Cabinet with Lock
36. Treatment Table, Storage below
37. Mirror and Glass Shelf over Lavatory
38. Adjustable Stool
39. Laundry Hamper
40. Sink with Drainboard
41. Paraffin Bath
42. Glass Shelf over Sink
43. Overbed Trapeze
44. Three Single Outlets on separate branch circuits. 1 outlet 2-pole, 2 outlets 3-pole
45. Folding Door
46. Cubicle Curtain
47. Under Water Exercise Equipment
48. Overhead Lift
49. Coat Rack
50. Telephone Outlet

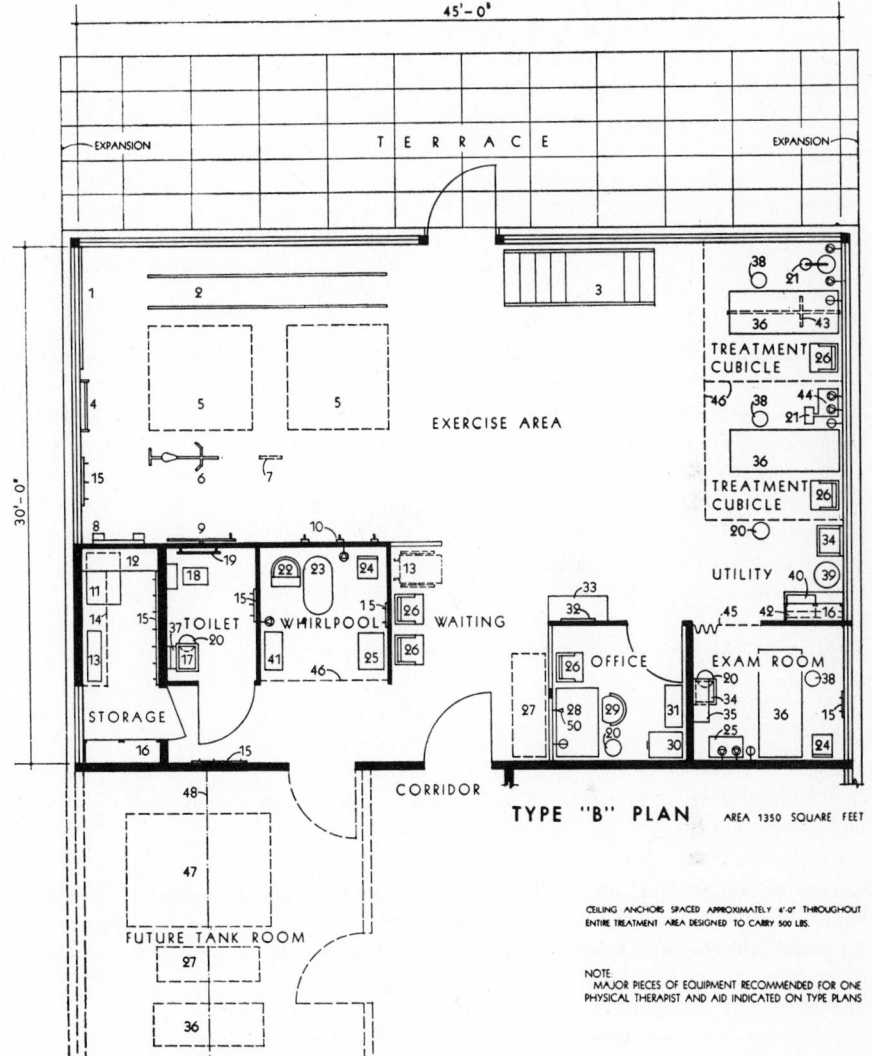

TYPE "B" PLAN   AREA 1350 SQUARE FEET

CEILING ANCHORS SPACED APPROXIMATELY 4'-0" THROUGHOUT ENTIRE TREATMENT AREA DESIGNED TO CARRY 500 LBS.

NOTE:
MAJOR PIECES OF EQUIPMENT RECOMMENDED FOR ONE PHYSICAL THERAPIST AND AID INDICATED ON TYPE PLANS

GRAPHIC SCALE   0   4   8 FT

Perspective sketches by William McMaster

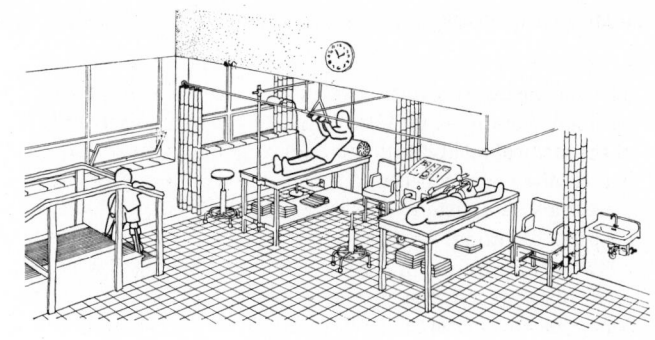

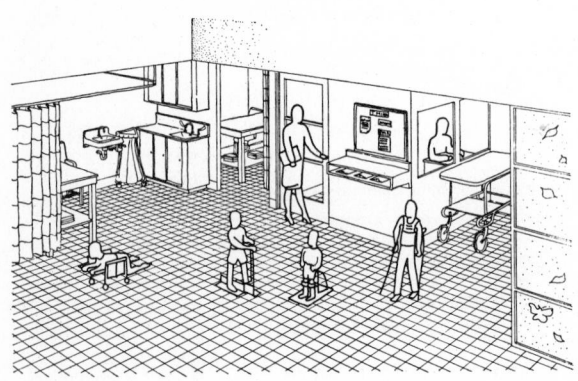

damage by wheelchairs, stretchers and carts. Ceramic wall tile or glazed structural units will serve the purpose but they emphasize the institutional character of the hospital. In patient areas this should be minimized as much as possible. In the last several years vinyl wall covering has gained in popularity as a wainscoting material, and to some extent for the entire wall. Two weights of the material are available; the heavier weight for areas subjected to severe abuse, the lighter weight for other parts of the wall.

The use of decorative colors for interior finishes and equipment is, of course, highly desirable in this department as it is in other parts of the hospital. Research in "color therapy" for hospitals adds to decorators' ideas the therapeutic value of combinations of pastel colors. "Cool" pastels — green, blue, violet and their many derivatives — are considered mildly restful. Some light colors in general are stimulating and may be of advantage in the exercise area.

Doors. For accommodation of stretcher and wheelchair traffic, doors within the department should be at least 40 inches wide. Raised thresholds should be eliminated.

Ceiling moorings. These moorings, strategically located in the ceiling in treatment areas, have been found useful for attaching overhead equipment such as hoists, pulleys, bars,

counter balancing equipment, etc. They should be constructed and attached to joists in such a manner that each supports at least 500 pounds.

Layout

It is impossible to anticipate all of the practical problems of layout in a particular building or to say in advance that one plan or another is the right one. A few guidelines, however, may be useful in making decisions about layout.

Expect to expand and plan for it from the beginning. It is impossible to overestimate the value of the exercise area. Give it as many square feet of appropriate space as possible.

Note the need to have the underwater exercise equipment grouped in one area, separate but adjacent and accessible to the other treatment areas.

When deciding which units to place next to each other or group together, consider how they are used by patients, especially the flow of traffic from one unit to another. Try to avoid needless traffic. Try to conserve the energies of staff.

Visit other physical therapy departments and find out what the physical therapists like or would like to change in the layouts of their own departments.

By ALONZO W. CLARK, AIA, with the collaboration of the American Occupational Therapy Association

The increasing recognition of occupational therapy as an integral part of the medical rehabilitation program has resulted in its becoming an increasingly important element of hospital planning.

These four pages present a summary of the recommendations of the American Occupational Therapy Association on the planning of typical occupational therapy departments. These basic plans and discussions were developed to serve only as guides for designing similar units, and will not be universally applicable without some modification. This material was presented at length in the October, 1950, issue of *HOSPITALS, Journal of the American Hospital Association*. Reprints of this article, which contains extensive equipment and supply lists for planning storage are available from the American Occupational Therapy Association, 250 W. 57th St., New York 19, N. Y.

BASIC SOLUTIONS for occupational therapy departments are largely dependent on the following factors:

1. Number of patients to be treated. On the basis of hospital surveys and committee recommendations, it was agreed that 30 per cent of hospital patients should normally be referred for occupational therapy. About 40 per cent of these would be treated in the clinic, and 60 per cent treated in their beds or on the wards. One occupational therapist in the clinic can generally accommodate about 15 patients in each of two daily sessions, one in the morning, one in the afternoon. This number will vary according to the type of patient — more psychiatric patients, fewer physically disabled patients.

2. Floor space required by patients. Approximately 54 to 61 sq ft per patient is recommended for the entire department, including clinic, office and storage. For the clinic alone, 42 to 47 sq ft per patient is suggested to allow for easy circulation and use of equipment. These figures are based on a study of the needs of a typical department.

3. Types of treatment media to be used. Some 70-odd activities are used in occupational therapy departments throughout the country. Basic requirements for small units are as follows; these should be expanded for larger units:
1. *Bench work* — carpentry, plastics, metal work including painting and finishing of completed projects.
2. *Table work* — leather, blockprinting, fly-tying, sewing and art work.
3. *Loom work* — weaving, braiding.
4. *"Functional equipment"* (not an active classification)—bicycle, jig saws and other adapted equipment for treatment of physical disabilities.

Storage facilities should provide for at least 3 months' supply, as many institutions order on a quarterly basis. All the above items must, of course, be adapted to suit a particular type and size of hospital.

4. Location of the department in a hospital. Daylighted space as close to patient areas as possible and readily accessible to toilet facilities is recommended. Proximity to the physical therapy department is advisable. Necessary facilities include running water, gas, and electric outlets; dust collectors for power woodworking tools are recommended.

THE SMALLER UNIT

For hospitals up to a 250-bed capacity, a basic plan was evolved (see next page). At the rate of referral cited, up to 30 patients should be accommodated. These could be cared for by one therapist, with a possible second therapist for ward service. On the basis of 15 patients per session at 54 sq ft per patient, the entire unit was allotted 813.75 sq ft. (17½ by 46½ ft). The clinic area, planned at 42 sq ft per patient, totals 638.75 sq ft (17½ by 36½ ft). The minimum basic activities were provided for with 20 work stations for flexibility in selection. Activities requiring bulky equipment such as printing and advanced ceramics were omitted. It was assumed that preparation and finishing could be done in the clinic or on a counter top in the storeroom. The following considerations were made for the three specific areas within the department:

1. Clinic area: The first obvious requirement is space for free circulation around the required equipment (see general list following). Space for parking at least 3 wheel chairs is also necessary. Double doors at shop entrance simplify moving equipment and supplies. Sliding doors for upper cabinets avoid interference with patients working at counter tops. No display case for finished articles was included as it was felt that this emphasized the product rather than therapeutic objectives.

2. Storage area: Space was provided for a mobile cart for servicing ward patients. A cabinet with work top was included for preparation and finishing work. It was assumed that only 8-ft lengths of lumber and plywood would be stored in this basic unit, and that other closets, rooms, etc. in various parts of the hospital could be used for "dead storage."

3. Office area: Space was provided for the usual office furnishings. A large glass panel in front of the desk facilitates control and supervision of the unit.

VARIATIONS FOR HOSPITAL TYPES

The basic plan is directly applicable to *psychiatric* and *general medical and surgical hospitals*. In the latter case, a bicycle jig saw is recommended in place of a drill press stand (a table model drill press could be used).

Tuberculosis hospitals require two minor changes: replacement of one floor loom and the braid-weaving frame with two industrial sewing machines.

Pediatric hospitals need the following changes: a plan adaptable to division into two parts — one for small children, one for adolescents. For equipment changes, see plan. Tables should adjust in height.

Physical disability hospitals can use the basic plan with a few variations in equipment. Although fewer patients can be treated per therapist, fewer will be able to come to the clinic for treatment; a second therapist will be needed for treatment in the wards.

Floor Plans For Typical Occupational Therapy Department in Hospitals Up To 250 Bed Capacity

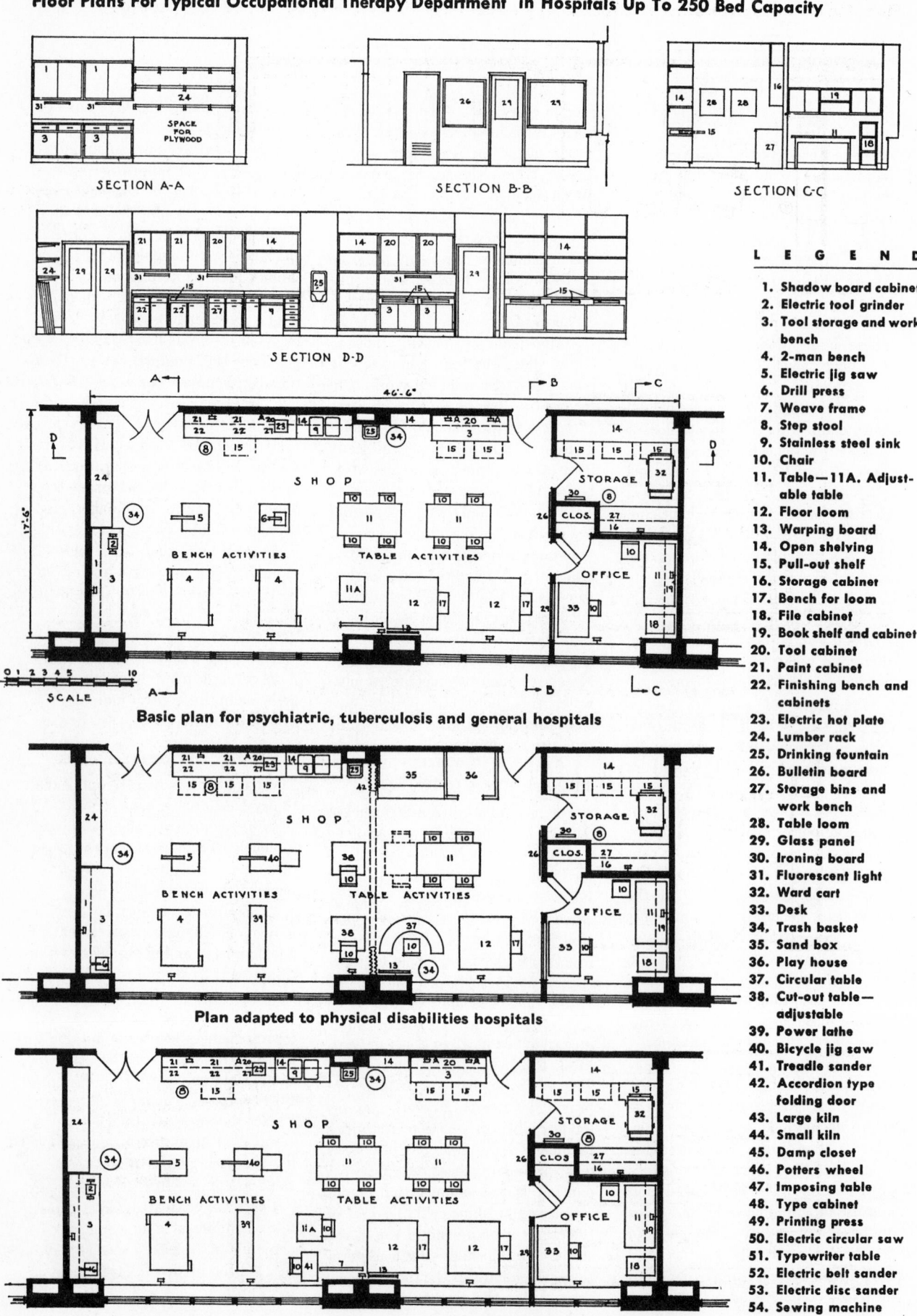

SECTION A-A

SECTION B-B

SECTION C-C

SECTION D-D

A

B

C

D

SCALE

0 1 2 3 4 5   10

Basic plan for psychiatric, tuberculosis and general hospitals

Plan adapted to physical disabilities hospitals

Plan adapted to pediatric hospitals

SHOP

BENCH ACTIVITIES

TABLE ACTIVITIES

STORAGE

CLOS.

OFFICE

L E G E N D

1. Shadow board cabinet
2. Electric tool grinder
3. Tool storage and work bench
4. 2-man bench
5. Electric jig saw
6. Drill press
7. Weave frame
8. Step stool
9. Stainless steel sink
10. Chair
11. Table—11A. Adjustable table
12. Floor loom
13. Warping board
14. Open shelving
15. Pull-out shelf
16. Storage cabinet
17. Bench for loom
18. File cabinet
19. Book shelf and cabinet
20. Tool cabinet
21. Paint cabinet
22. Finishing bench and cabinets
23. Electric hot plate
24. Lumber rack
25. Drinking fountain
26. Bulletin board
27. Storage bins and work bench
28. Table loom
29. Glass panel
30. Ironing board
31. Fluorescent light
32. Ward cart
33. Desk
34. Trash basket
35. Sand box
36. Play house
37. Circular table
38. Cut-out table—adjustable
39. Power lathe
40. Bicycle jig saw
41. Treadle sander
42. Accordion type folding door
43. Large kiln
44. Small kiln
45. Damp closet
46. Potters wheel
47. Imposing table
48. Type cabinet
49. Printing press
50. Electric circular saw
51. Typewriter table
52. Electric belt sander
53. Electric disc sander
54. Sewing machine

Floor Plans For Typical Occupational Therapy Department   in Hospitals Up To 500 Bed Capacity

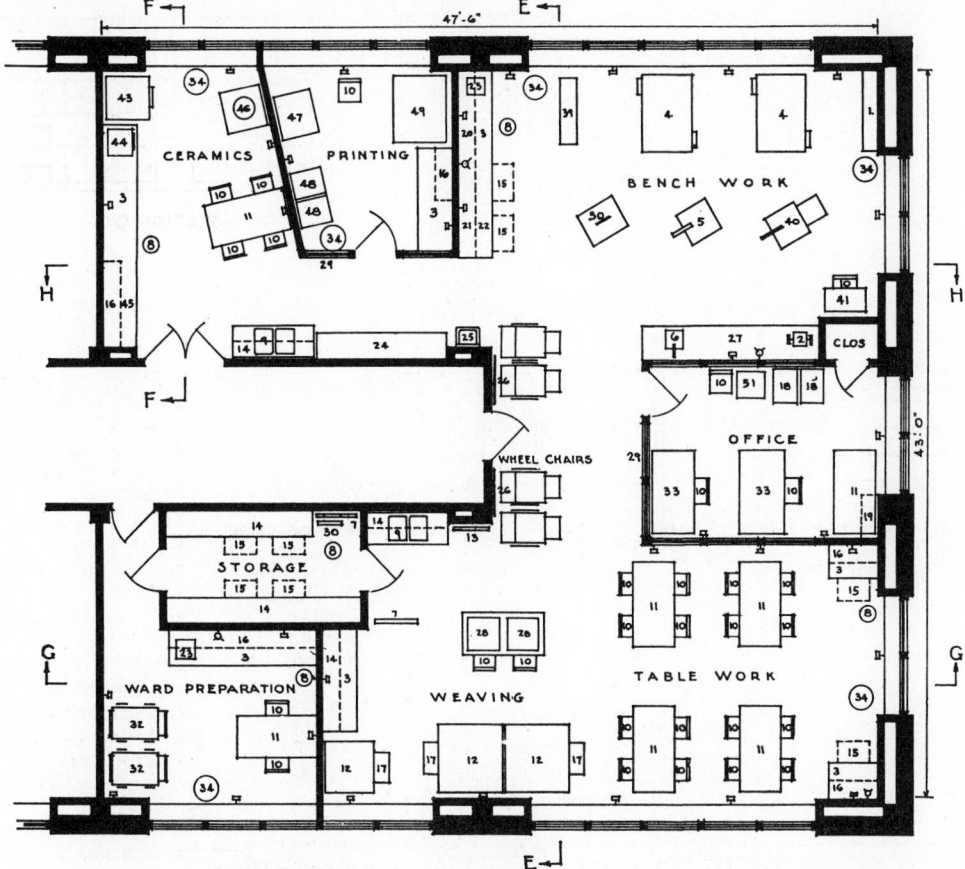

Plan for psychiatric, physical disability and general hospitals

LEGEND

1. Shadow board cabinet
2. Electric tool grinder
3. Tool storage and work bench
4. 2-man bench
5. Electric jig saw
6. Drill press
7. Weave frame
8. Step stool
9. Stainless steel sink
10. Chair
11. Table—11A. Adjustable table
12. Floor loom
13. Warping board
14. Open shelving
15. Pull-out shelf
16. Storage cabinet
17. Bench for loom
18. File cabinet
19. Book shelf and cabinet
20. Tool cabinet
21. Paint cabinet
22. Finishing bench and cabinets
23. Electric hot plate
24. Lumber rack
25. Drinking fountain
26. Bulletin board
27. Storage bins and work bench
28. Table loom
29. Glass panel
30. Ironing board
31. Fluorescent light
32. Ward cart
33. Desk
34. Trash basket
35. Sand box
36. Play house
37. Circular table
38. Cut-out table—adjustable
39. Power lathe
40. Bicycle jig saw
41. Treadle sander
42. Accordion type folding door
43. Large kiln
44. Small kiln
45. Damp closet
46. Potters wheel
47. Imposing table
48. Type cabinet
49. Printing press
50. Electric circular saw
51. Typewriter table
52. Electric belt sander
53. Electric disc sander
54. Sewing machine

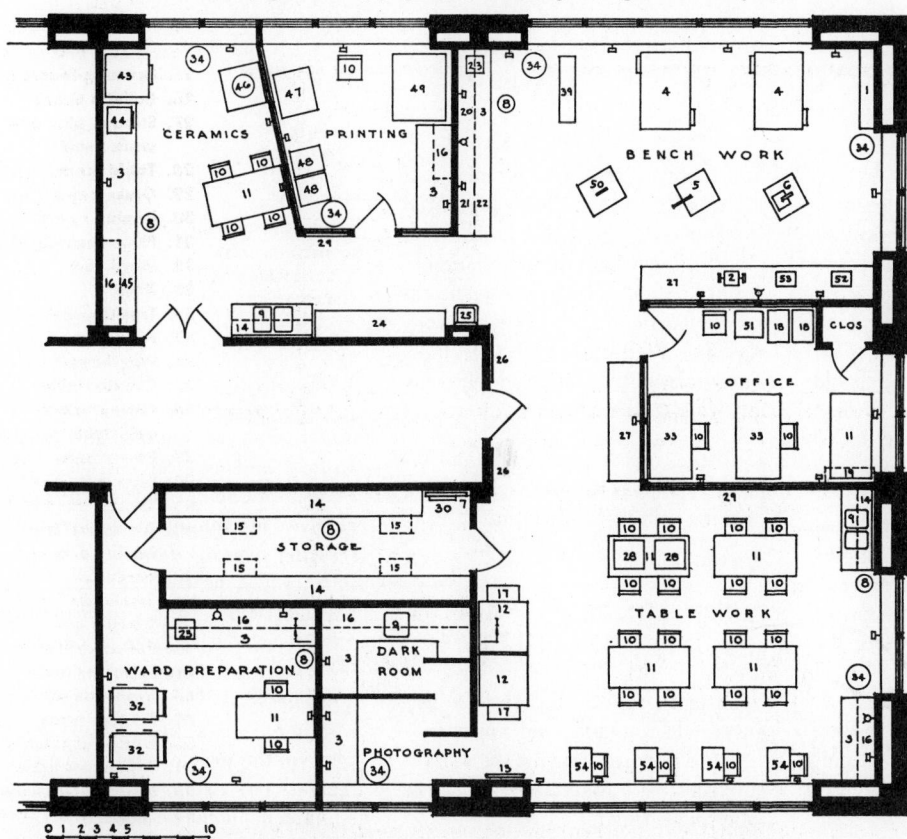

Plan adapted to tuberculosis hospitals 300 to 500 bed capacity

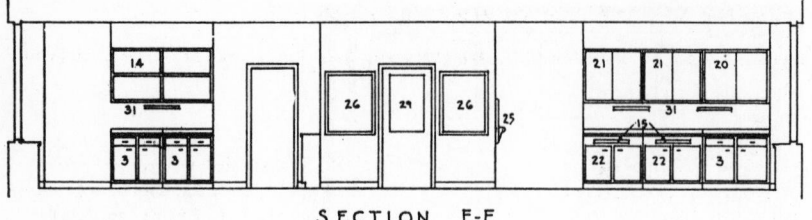

SECTION E-E

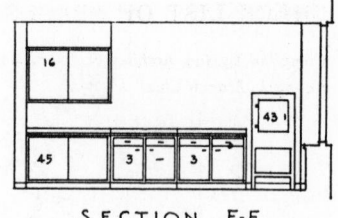

SECTION F-F

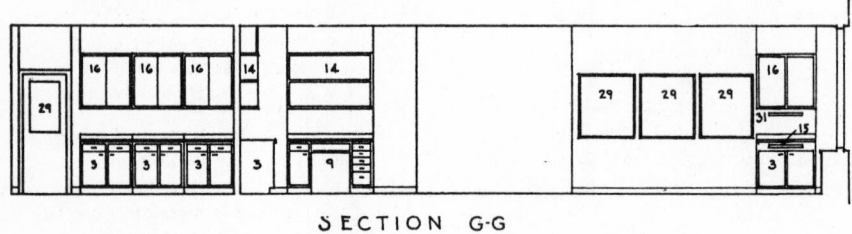

SECTION G-G

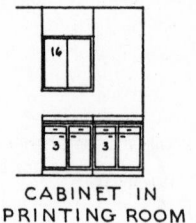

CABINET IN
PRINTING ROOM

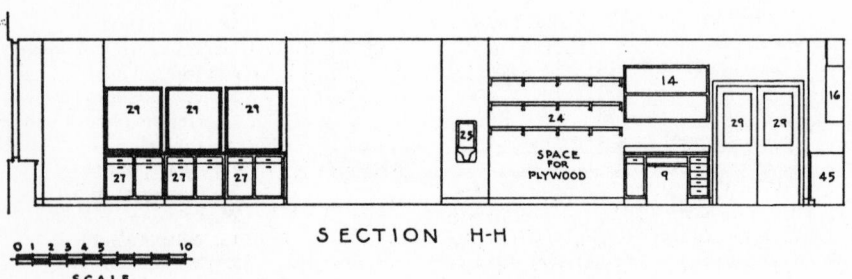

SECTION H-H

SCALE

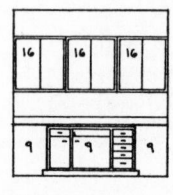

SECTION I-I

Room sections for typical occupational therapy department in hospitals up to 500-bed capacity (see previous page for legend)

THE LARGER UNIT

A basic plan for a typical occupational therapy unit for large hospitals of approximately 500 beds was shown previously. Again using the same basis for rate of patient referrals to the department (30 per cent of rated bed capacity), the large unit should accommodate 150 patients a day. The actual clinic load would be 60 patients (40 per cent of 150), or about 30 in each of two sessions.

The unit as presented was planned on the basis of 31 patients. Using 61 sq ft per person, the gross area allotted the entire unit is approximately 1,880 sq ft. Net area of the clinic is about 1,450 sq ft, or 47 sq ft per person.

This increased space per person over that allowed in the smaller unit is the result of adding two activities requiring bulky equipment and separate rooms. These are ceramics and printing. It was also deemed essential to have a separate ward preparation room to serve the increased number of ward patients. To allow for a necessary dispersion factor, 10 extra work stations are provided in the clinic. The larger unit therefore contains the following sections:

1. Clinic, including weaving and table activities area, bench activities, printing unit, ceramics unit.

2. Office.

3. Storage.

4. Ward preparation area.

Three therapists plus three assistants could run clinic and wards.

Space requirements for the various activities were determined from the following estimate:

Activity	% of Patients	No. of Patients
Wood, plastics, metal	22	7
General crafts (table activities)	64	19
Ceramics	9	3
Printing	5	2
	100	31

Variations for hospital types: the larger plan is suitable for *general medical and surgical hospitals, psychiatric hospitals* and, with minor changes in equipment, for hospitals treating *physical disabilities.* Several units might be used for very large psychiatric hospitals. *Pediatric hospitals* are seldom as large as 500 beds; if so more personnel are needed.

Tuberculosis hospitals require a number of variations as shown on the plan on the previous page. Separate recreational rooms and sterilization equipment might be needed.

CHECK LIST OF SPACES FOR A COMMUNITY MENTAL HEALTH CENTER

Compiled by the Architectural and Engineering Branch, Division of Hospital and Medical Facilities, U.S. Public Health Service; August Hoenack, Branch Chief

Facilities listed are those that may be required in the over-all programs of mental health centers. They can be in one or several buildings on one or several sites, even under one or several cooperating ownerships. The list is for review by architects and administrators whenever new facilities are planned.

ADMINISTRATION

Office space for:
1. Director
2. Assistant director
3. Nursing director
4. Secretaries and typists
5. Business office

Ancillary spaces:
1. Record room
2. Staff lounge
3. Library
4. Conference room
5. Lobby and waiting
6. Toilets: public, personnel

DIAGNOSTIC & TREATMENT

Laboratory:
1. Office
2. Clinical
3. Pathology
4. Bacteriology
5. Washing and sterilizing

Suites:
1. Basal metabolism and electrocardiology
2. Morgue and autopsy
3. Dental
4. Eye, ear, nose and throat
5. Electro-encephalography
6. Radiology

Physical therapy:
1. Electro-therapy
2. Hydro-therapy with exercise
3. Small gymnasium

Pharmacy department

Occupational therapy:
1. Space for small woodworking tools and benches for carpentry, metal work, leather work, printing, weaving, rug making, etc.
2. Office
3. Storage room

OUTPATIENT EXAMINATION AND TREATMENT

Office space for:
1. Psychiatrists
2. Psychologists
3. Social workers
4. Nurses
5. Health educators
6. Occupational therapists
7. Rehabilitation counselors
8. Recreation therapists
9. Clerical operators
10. Aides
11. Research analyst
12. Group therapy and conference

(*Lobby, waiting space, and toilets may be combined with those in the administrative area.*)

INPATIENT FACILITIES

Facilities may be required for the following types of patients grouped in accordance with the local program. (Separate spaces for male and female. Treatment and diagnosis spaces for each category.)

Patients' categories:
1. New admissions
2. Quiet ambulant
3. Disturbed
4. Alcoholic
5. Criminalistic
6. Day care
7. Night care
8. Children
   a. Emotionally disturbed
   b. Retarded

Each patient care unit:
1. Waiting space for visitors
2. Doctors' offices and examination rooms
3. Offices for psychologists, social workers, therapist or others as required
4. Nurses' station and toilet
5. Conference room
6. Therapy space
7. Day room(s)
8. Utility room
9. Pantry or nourishment preparation
10. Dining room

11. Washroom and toilets
12. Patients' lockers
13. Showers and bathrooms
14. Storage (for recreational and occupational therapy equipment)
15. Supply and linen storage
16. Janitors' closet
17. Stretcher alcove

Minimum room areas:
1. 80 sq ft per bed in alcoves and four-bed rooms
2. 100 sq ft in single rooms
3. 40 to 50 sq ft per patient in day rooms, preferably divided into one large and one small room

STERILIZING AND SUPPLY FACILITIES
(*Sufficient to serve both outpatients and inpatients.*)

SERVICE DEPARTMENT

Dietary facilities:
1. Main kitchen and bakery
2. Dietitians' office
3. Dishwashing room
4. Refrigerators
5. Garbage collecting and disposal facilities
6. Can washing room
7. Day storage room
8. Staff dining room

Housekeeping facilities:
1. Laundry
2. Separate sorting room
3. Separate clean linen and sewing room
4. Housekeeper's office and storage (near linen storage)

Mechanical facilities:
1. Boiler room and pump room
2. Engineer's office
3. Shower and locker room

Maintenance shops:
Carpentry, painting, mechanical, repair rooms

Employes' facilities:
Locker, rest, toilet and shower rooms for various categories

Storage:
1. Medical records
2. General storage (a minimum 20 sq ft per bed to be concentrated in one area)

By HOWARD P. VERMILYA, AIA

Building and Facility Standards for Physically Handicapped

If the physically handicapped are to be rehabilitated, they must be able to move about as freely, and with as little assistance as possible. Further, since useful and gainful employment is an essential part of rehabilitation programs, the buildings in which the handicapped may work should be designed to permit use by them. Recreational and educational buildings as well as other buildings used by the public should have similar provisions.

The problems of design of buildings are largely concerned with movement or circulation and the use of facilities with ease and safety. The American Standards Association has recently issued ASA Standard A117.1–1961, *Making Buildings and Facilities Accessible to, and Usable By, the Physically Handicapped,* sponsored by the National Society for Crippled Children and Adults and the President's Committee on Employment of the Physically Handicapped. This standard is comprehensive and includes much of the essential data required by architects to meet the basic needs of the physically handicapped. The following text is based primarily on ASA Standard A117.1–1961. The drawings are taken from Building Standards of the University of Illinois Rehabilitation Center, Timothy J. Nugent, director.

Definition of Handicapped

The physically handicapped represent one out of seven persons, and where capable of movement may be classified as:
1. Confined to wheel chairs
2. Walk with difficulty (require braces or crutches)
3. Blind or see with difficulty
4. Deaf or hear poorly
5. Badly coordinated or subject to palsy or
6. Infirm from age.

Wheel Chair Dimensions

The wheel chair is the basic vehicle for the non-ambulatory person and establishes the fundamental access and use design requirements. Crutch- or brace-supported semi-ambulatory persons are capable of maneuvering within the limitations demanded by the wheel chair. The most commonly used type is collapsible, made of tubular metals with upholstered back and seat.

1. WHEEL CHAIR LIMITS (*standard model, collapsible*)
a. *Length*: 42 in.
b. *Width*: open 25 in.; collapsed 11 in.
c. *Height*: seat 19½ in.; armrest 29 in.; pusher handles 36 in.
2. FIXED TURNING RADIUS, *wheel to wheel* (i.e., tracking of caster wheels and large wheels when pivoting on a spot): 18 in.
3. FIXED TURNING RADIUS, *front structure to rear structure,* measured diagonally from one end of foot platform to opposite rear wheel, when pivoted on a spot: 31.5 in.
4. TURNING AND PASSING SPACE
a. *Area required for 180 degree and 360 degree turns*: average 60 in. by 60 in. Rectangular area 63 in. by 56 in. often preferred to square area.
b. *Minimum corridor width for turning 360 degrees*: 54 in. Minimum corridor width for passing of two wheel chairs: 60 in.
c. *The distance between crutch tips at normal gait is*: average 5 ft 6 in. person—31 in.; average 6 ft 0 in. person—32.5 in.

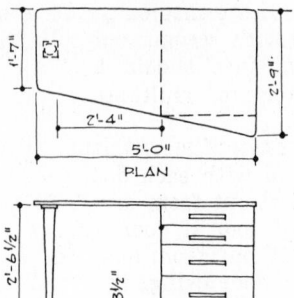

FURNITURE

PLAN

ELEVATION
STUDY DESK

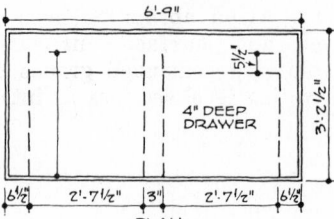

4" DEEP DRAWER

PLAN

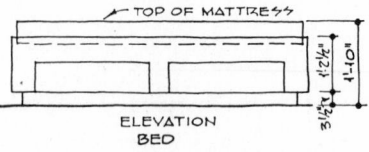

TOP OF MATTRESS

ELEVATION
BED

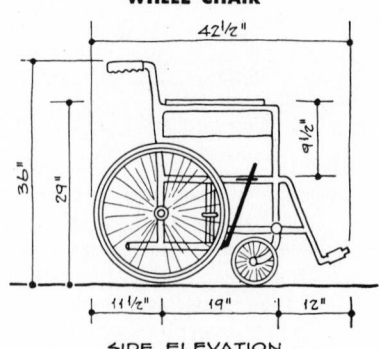

WHEEL CHAIR

SIDE ELEVATION

INDIVIDUAL FUNCTIONING IN WHEEL CHAIR		
	Average	Range
Unilateral vertical reach	60 in.	54-78 in.
Horizontal working reach (table)	30.8 in.	28-33.2 in.
Bilateral horizonal reach (both arms extended to each side, shoulder high)	64.5 in.	54-71 in.
Diagonal reach to object on wall (height on wall)	48 in.	

Design Guides to Permit Use of Wheel Chairs (Exterior)

1. ENTRANCES

a. Service either on grade or by ramp with recommended incline.

b. Entrance should lead to an elevator in multi-story structures.

2. ENTRANCE PLATFORMS. Should be used with each door, extending 5 ft out from and 1 ft each side of door if door swings out, or 3 ft out from door and 5 ft wide if door swings in.

3. WALKS

a. *Minimum width*: 48 in.

b. *Maximum grade*: 5 per cent

Note: Level walks at intersections. Avoid abrupt changes in level and surface materials. Avoid long continued grades by providing level sections at intervals. Bring walk gradually to level of driveways and parking lots. Provide means for blind to recognize intersection of walk with driveway or street (may be done with raised strips in concrete walks).

4. PARKING SPACES (*special and identified*). Should be 12 ft wide to permit room at side of car for wheel chair access to or from spaces. Should avoid need to pass behind parked cars.

5. RAMPS

a. *Surface*: non-slip.

b. *Grade*: maximum slope 1 in 12, or 8.33 per cent.

c. *Length*: not over 30 ft of continuous slope between level platforms.

d. *Platforms* (*level*): should be provided at top, bottom and at locations where changes in direction occur. Size where doors occur, same as for entrance platforms. In other locations, **minimum length 3 ft** except at bottom straight clearance shall be 6 ft.

e. *Guard rails or walls*: both sides if ramp is free standing.

f. *Handrails*: minimum, 1 side; preferably on 2 sides.

Height: 32 in. (Provide additional rails at lower heights where children will use the facility.)

Extend 1 ft beyond top and bottom of ramp on side of continuing wall or guard rails.

g. *Width*: same as walk or corridor. Where serving as required exit, shall comply with current Building Exits Code of National Fire Protection Association.

RAMPS

2"x4" SLATS 3/8" APART OR BROOMED CONCRETE

2"x4" CURBS

1/8" MET. PLATFORM

PLAN

2" O.D. MET. RAILINGS

ELEVATION

SINGLE RUN RAMP

2"x4" CURB

ELEVATION

6'-0"   12'-0"   6'-0"

PLAN

DOUBLE RUN RAMP

TOILET COMPARTMENT

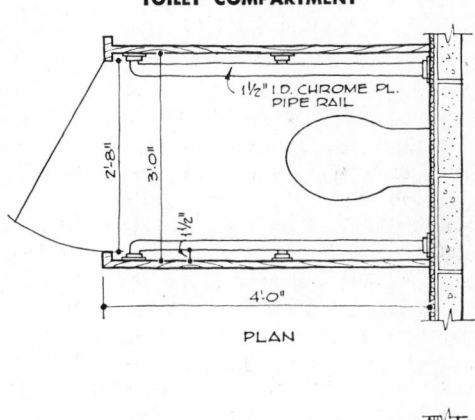

1½" I.D. CHROME PL. PIPE RAIL

2'-8"   3'-0"

1½"

4'-0"

PLAN

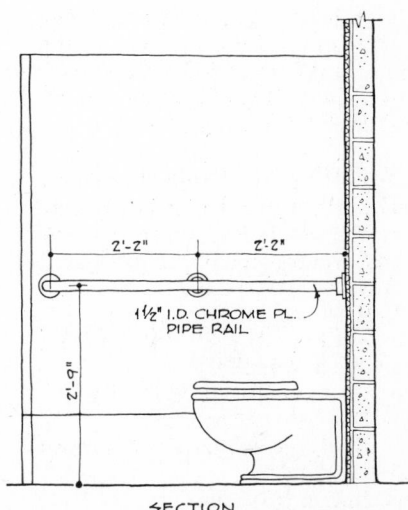

2'-2"   2'-2"

1½" I.D. CHROME PL. PIPE RAIL

2'-9"

SECTION

Interior

1. DOORS

a. *Width*: minimum 32 in. opening when door is open.

b. *Operation*: single-effort, (two leaf doors are inoperable by non-ambulatory and semi-ambulatory persons unless they open with single effort or each leaf provides minimum opening.)

c. *Door closers*: locate so as not to prevent use by disabled. Time-delay type desirable.

d. *Threshholds*: flush or very low.

e. *Platforms (level)*: on each side of every door (same dimensions as for entrance platforms). Recess doors equal to width of door when they swing into halls.

2. RAMPS: see exterior.

3. STAIRS for use of semi-ambulatory persons.

a. *Risers*: 7 in. maximum height.

b. *Nosing*: avoid projecting nosings (see illustrations).

c. *Handrail*: at least one, 32 in. high, extending 18 in. beyond top and bottom risers.

d. *Width*: minimum 36 in. between handrails; when stairs serve as a required exit, comply with Building Exits Code of National Fire Protection Assoc. Note: Open stairs should provide means of warning blind of their existence. One device is the insertion of slightly raised abrasive strips in floor at approach to stair.

4. ELEVATORS. *Essential for multi-story building.* Accessible at entrance level and each floor.

a. *Doors*: minimum 32-in.-wide opening desirable (see wheel chair dimensions if this is not feasible).

b. *Cab area*: minimum 5-ft square or 63 in. by 56 in. Automatic control panel not over 48 in. high.

5. CORRIDORS

a. *Width*: should be minimum 60 in.

b. *Doors opening into corridors*: should be recessed where the traffic is likely to be heavy or where corridor is used by blind people.

Toilet Rooms, Showers Water Fountains

1. TOILET COMPARTMENT

a. *Width*: 3 ft 0 in. *Depth*: 4 ft 8 in. minimum, preferably 5 ft 0 in.

SHOWER SEAT

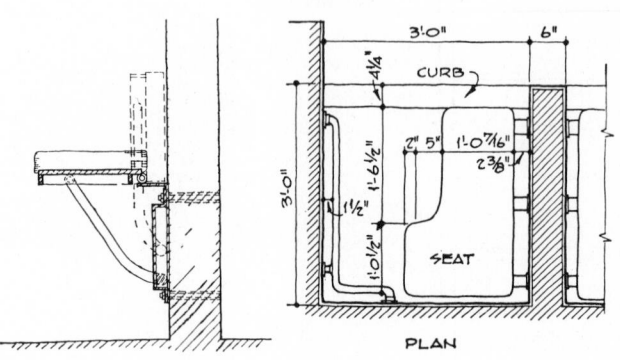

PLAN

SHOWER EQUIPMENT

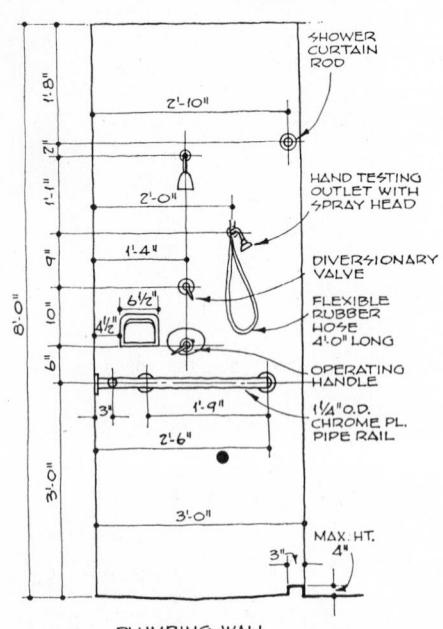

PLUMBING WALL

LAVATORY

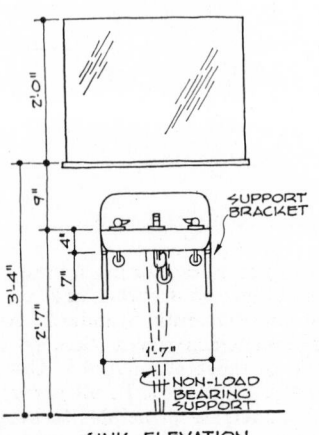

SINK ELEVATION

b. *Door*: 32 in. wide, opening out.

c. *Handrails*: each side, 33 in. high, parallel with floor; strong and well-supported.

2. WATER CLOSET

Seat 20 in. high. Wall-hung type most desirable. If floor supported, under-structure should not interfere with close approach of chair.

3. LAVATORIES

Aprons narrow to permit close approach. Place hot water pipes (or insulate them) so they cannot burn wheel chair occupant, particularly those without sensation.

4. URINALS

Wall hung, opening 19 in. above floor; floor mounted, at same level as floor.

5. SHOWERS

a. *Size*: 3 ft by 3 ft.

b. *Opening*: full width.

c. *Curb*: maximum height, 4 in., preferably lower.

d. *Seat*: folding, along one side, height 1 ft 9 in.

e. *Handrail*; along one side and part of rear wall. Height 3 ft 0 in.

f. *Testing spray*: desirable (using hose attachment).

6. MIRRORS

Over lavatories as low as possible, not over 40 in. above floor.

7. TOWEL RACKS, DISPENSERS, SHELVES

Not over 40 in. from floor.

8. WATER FOUNTAINS

Height (hand operated or hand and foot operated): floor-mounted side fountain, 30 in.; wall-hung basin, 36 in. Recessed not recommended. Alcoves should be wider than wheel chair.

Public Telephones

Public telephone booths are not usable by most disabled persons. Dial and handset should be within reach of person in wheel chair (see illustrations). Confer with local telephone company. Some phones may be especially equipped for those with hearing disabilities (these may be used by all).

Identification for Blind

1. RAISED LETTERS OR NUMBERS *for room identification*:
place 4 ft 6 in. to 5 ft 6 in. high, to side of door.

2. HAZARDOUS OPENINGS
Knurled hardware for door.

3. AUDIBLE SIGNALS
To provide warning.

4. FLOORING MATERIALS
Can aid in directing and locating blind occupants of buildings.

Identification for Deaf

1. Visible signals as warnings.

TELEPHONE BOOTH

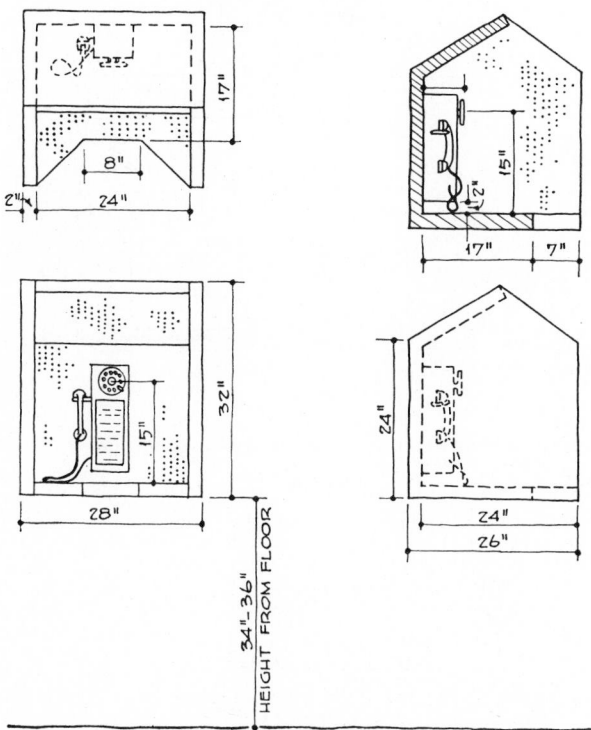

STEP RISERS

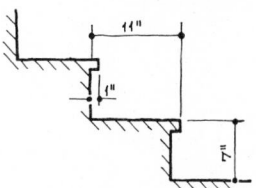

HARDWARE IDENTIFICATION

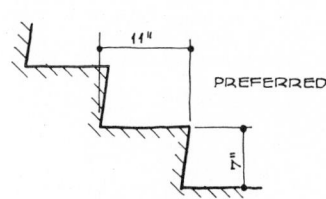

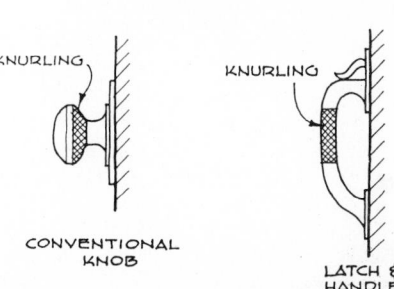

The drawings were prepared for use by the University of Illinois Rehabilitation Center, and to facilitate development of an American Standards Association Standard. The dimensions shown thus do not in all cases correspond to those stipulated in the published A.S.A. Standard A 117.1-1961. In all cases, however, the drawings demonstrate principles to keep in mind in designing facilities for the handicapped

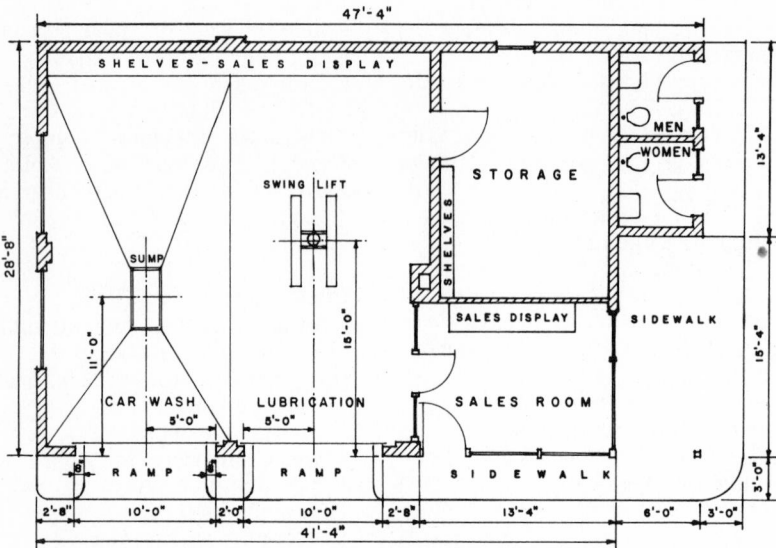

Fig. 1. Plan of typical two-bay service station building

Drawings show the standard plan of a major oil company for a two-bay service station. Additional bays may be added for larger installations.

Minimum recommended dimensions for bay door opening is 10 by 10 ft. Overhead type doors are the most effective. Servicing pits have become obsolete, the mechanical lift being considered more practical.

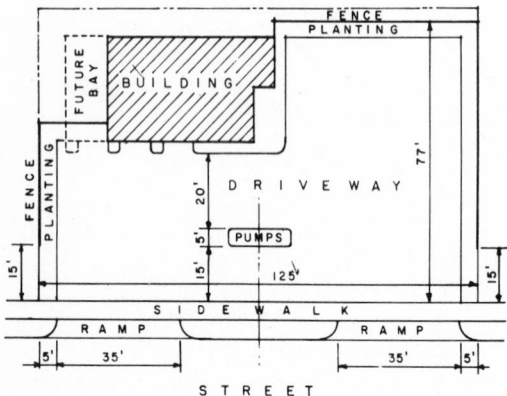

Fig. 2. Plan of service station with one pump island, midblock location

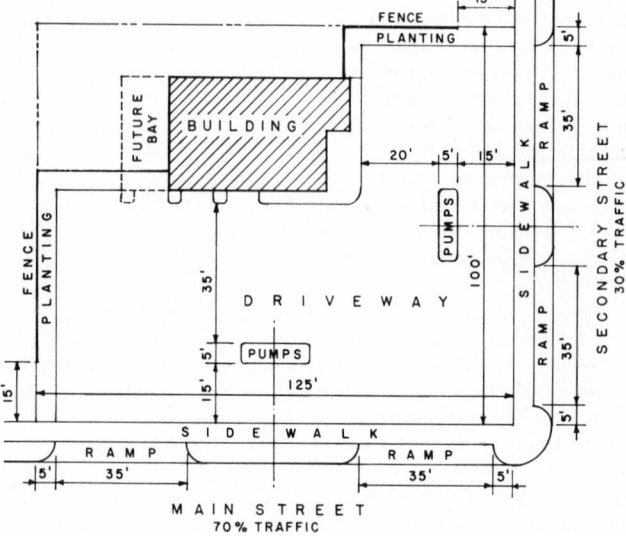

Fig. 4. Plan of service station with two pump islands, corner location

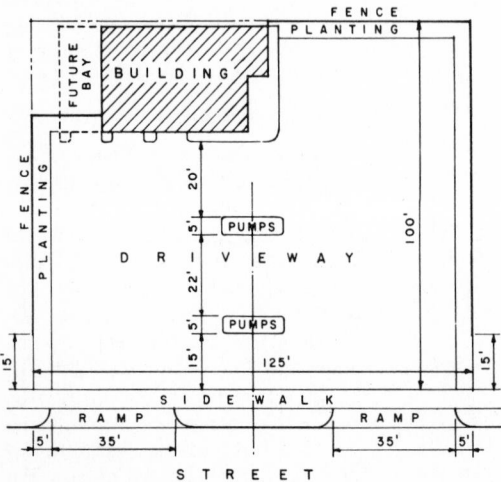

Fig. 3. Plan of service station with two pump islands, midblock location

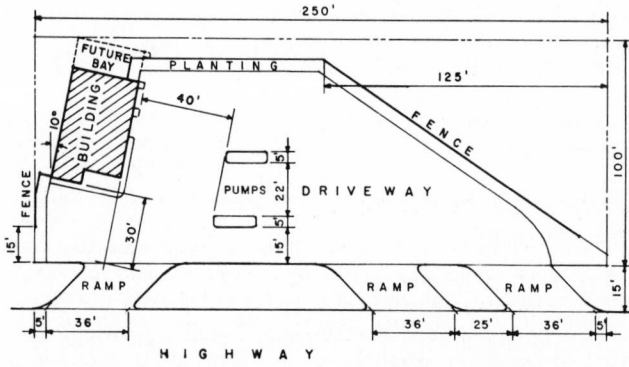

Fig. 5. Plan of service station with two pump islands, highway location

Data supplied by American Trucking Associations, Inc.

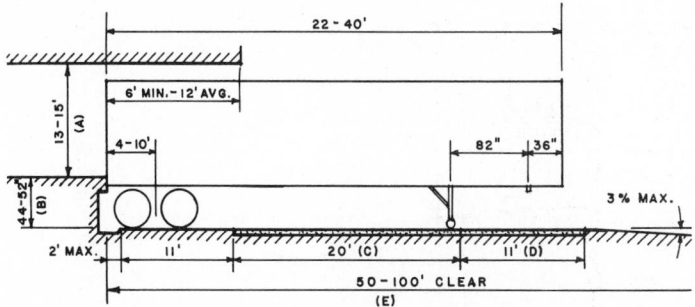

Fig. 1. Recommended dimensions and clearances for truck loading docks

NOTES: (A) *Should be at least 6 in. over legal height for level area, more for slope.*
(B) *Dock height, 48 to 52 in. for road trailers, 44 in. for city trucks.*
(C) *Concrete apron of the dimensions shown will accommodate trailers from 22 to 40 ft long.*
(D) *Additional slab length recommended to support tractor wheels.*

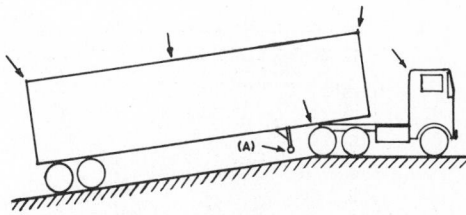

Fig. 2. Critical points for clearance
When designing for ramps, dips, or crowns in the terminal area, special care must be taken to provide clearance at the points indicated in the diagram. Actual dimensions must be obtained. Cab clearances are more critical when the combination is jackknifed. Landing gear height (A) may be as low as 10 in.

(E) *General rule for distance required: total length of tractor-trailer times 2.*
Trailer width—8 ft
Trailer stall width—10 ft minimum, 12 ft recommended.

The primary consideration in planning modern loading and unloading facilities for motor transport equipment is to provide adequate space for efficient maneuvering into and out of loading position at properly constructed docks. No one plan will fit all requirements, but careful study of present needs and future possibilities will determine the type and size of facilities essential to efficient operation.

There is, of course, no set of standard dimensions covering the space required for maneuvering the many possible combinations of tractor-trucks and semi-trailers into and out of loading position at docks or in stalls and driveways. However, the maneuvering space required is largely dependent on three factors: (1) overall length of the tractor-trailer unit; (2) the width of the position in which the vehicle must be placed; and (3) the turning radius of the tractor-truck which pulls the unit. Inasmuch as a tractor-trailer uses slightly more space to pull out than to back in, all reference to maneuvering apron space is based on the requirements for pulling out.

LENGTH OF TRACTOR-TRAILER UNIT

The length of tractor-trailer units to be accommodated will vary in accordance with state laws and differing types of operation. Analysis of the specific problem will determine the largest vehicle to be considered.

For the purposes of this discussion tractor-trailer units of 35, 40 and 45 ft. are considered to be the most prevalent overall lengths. If an appreciable volume of traffic is handled by "for hire" motor transport, it may be expected that the unit length to be accommodated will approximate the legal limit in the state concerned, usually between 45 and 50 ft. It is obvious that commercial haulers will use the maximum size tractor-trailer practical for efficient operation within state limitations. In general, it may be assumed that straight trucks can be accommodated in the space required for tractor-trailer units inasmuch as it has been impractical to build trucks even approaching the length and cubic capacity of modern trailers. In some states trains of more than one trailer are permitted. Such equipment is not being considered as it is assumed that each trailer in a train would be spotted separately.

WIDTH OF POSITION

The maximum allowable width of a truck or trailer is 8 ft. and it may be assumed that virtually all units (other than those for light city delivery) are built to take full advantage of this dimension.

The consensus among transport and traffic men interviewed is that 12 ft. is a very desirable width for stalls or truck positions. Slightly narrower position widths can be utilized when necessary but should be avoided in order to reduce the

possibility of damage to equipment and loss of time for jockeying into position. Also, as position width increases, the apron space required for maneuvering will decrease.

TRAILER DIMENSIONS

Average dimensions of large trailers are shown in Fig. 1, along with recommended dimensions and clearances for dock structures.

TURNING RADII OF TRACTOR-TRUCKS

The turning radii of tractor-trucks have a definite bearing on the apron space required for maneuvering equipment. However, because of the variation in this dimension among trucks of different types, capacities and makes, a high average turning radius has been used in arriving at recommendations regarding space requirements (see Table 1, next page).

The requirements of heavy-duty units with extremely long turning radii have been omitted from the table. If such equipment is a factor in any operation, a special study should be made to determine the space required. Units utilizing cab-over-engine truck-tractors have somewhat shorter turning radii for the same lengths, and consequently, require less apron space than units with conventional tractors. Many of these tractor-trucks are in use, but few shippers can count on their exclusive use.

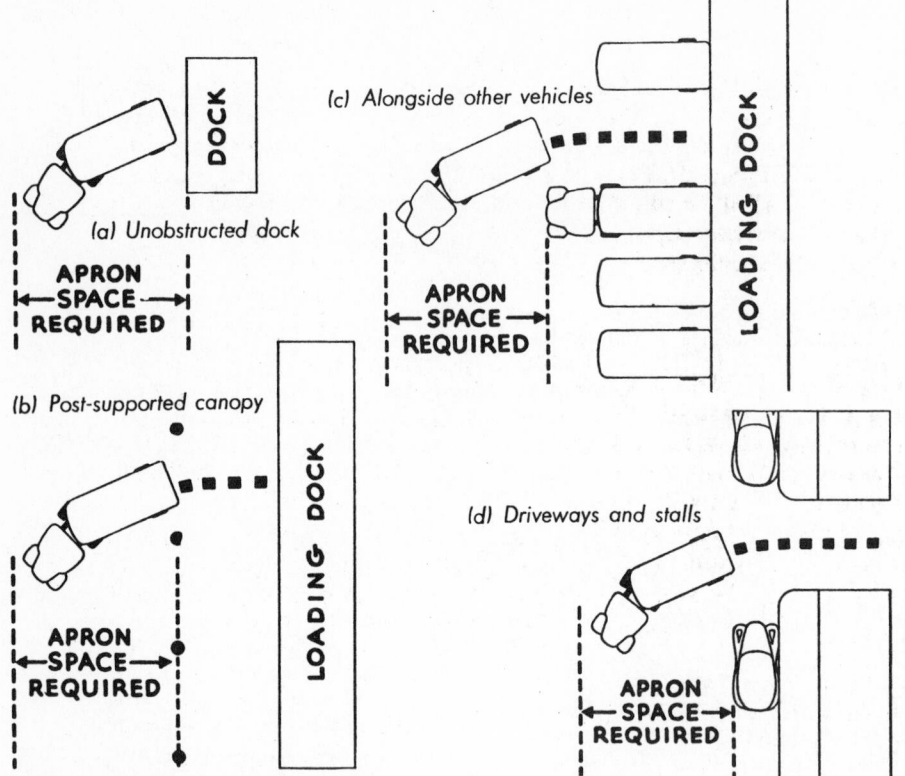

Fig. 3. Apron space required for various conditions

(a) Unobstructed dock

(b) Post-supported canopy

(c) Alongside other vehicles

(d) Driveways and stalls

TABLE I	APRON SPACE REQUIRED FOR ONE MANEUVER INTO OR OUT OF POSITION	
Length of Tractor-Trailer	Width of Position	"Apron" Space
35'	10'	46'
	12'	43'
	14'	39'
40'	10'	48'
	12'	44'
	14'	42'
45'	10'	57'
	12'	49'
	14'	48'

APRON SPACE REQUIRED

The apron space required to maneuver tractor-trailer units into or out of loading position in one maneuver has been worked out in practical tests with standard equipment handled by experienced drivers. Inasmuch as a high average turning radius has been arbitrarily used to provide a margin for differences in equipment, the variable factors were overall length and position width. *The apron space required is measured out from the outermost part of any vehicle or other possible obstruction in the area of the maneuver (Fig. 2).*

In the case of a single-position unobstructed dock (Fig. 3a), the distance would be measured straight out from the dock. However, if a canopy or roof, supported by posts (Fig. 3b) should be present to protect the loading area, the distance would be measured out from the posts. If it is necessary to spot a trailer alongside another vehicle (Fig. 3c), the distance would be measured from the outermost point of the vehicle obstructing the maneuver. When a stall or driveway is involved (Fig. 3d), the distance would be measured from the outermost obstruction, such as

a curb, pole, or vehicle, etc. To facilitate planning, a table of dimensions (Table 1) has been prepared as a guide on space requirements for the most efficient maneuvering of motor transports into and out of loading position, in *one* maneuver.

The figures in Table 1 do not include margin for driver error or any provision for congestion, storage or parking of equipment. It is highly recommended that at least the minimum apron space be allowed and that it be kept clear for the approach and maneuvering of transport units.

In locations where the proper space is not available for parking in one maneuver, trailers can be jockeyed into position. This, however, is a time-wasting, costly, and unsatisfactory process for both commercial and private transport operators.

OVERHEAD CLEARANCE

Standard trailers vary in height up to 12½ ft. Consequently, it is recommended that 14-ft. clearance be provided at docks or in yards, driveways, doors, stalls and interior roadways. Special transportation conditions such as delivery of large machinery may require greater clearance.

DRAINAGE

Roofs or canopies over loading docks should be constructed so as to avoid drainage into the loading area. This precaution will reduce the hazards of mud and ice and the resulting loss of traction. It is particularly important to prevent ice formation on the pavement where tractor and trailer are coupled.

SHUTTLE OPERATION

In many instances, consideration should be given to space requirements at docks, or in yards or buildings, for parking trailers used in shuttle operation, a system utilized in many industries to take advantage of its inherent savings in equipment and labor. Basically, shuttle operation consists in handling two or more trailers with one truck and driver. While one trailer is in transit, another may be at a dock unloading, while a third is being loaded.

TRAFFIC CONGESTION

So far as possible, loading areas and approaches should be free from general traffic and obstructions. Railroad crossings, automobile traffic, parked vehicles, and material carelessly stored outside all contribute to delays in pick-up and delivery.

PITS AND RAMPS

When the use of loading pits and ramps is unavoidable, several factors deserve careful attention. Types of transports, and their loads, should be studied to determine the maximum practical grade which can be negotiated. It may be easy to back into a pit — but can the load be pulled out? Furthermore, such installations should be protected against ice and mud so that power will not be lost through poor traction.

BUILT-IN TRANSPORTATION

More and more interest is being evidenced in the possibilities offered by the use of "built-in" or "run-through" facilities. In many cases, spot delivery inside the plant will facilitate handling of heavy material, or direct delivery to an assembly line or other point may eliminate costly re-handling. A straight one-way "run-through" need be only 10 ft. wide to provide minimum clearance for the 8-ft. maximum width of a transport unit. However, other traffic, unloading problems, or special considerations such as delivery of special equipment on flat-bed carryalls might require extra width, and possibly greater overhead clearance than the 14 ft. previously mentioned. If a right-angle turn must be negotiated in a narrow driveway, extra clear space should be provided on the inside of the turn to eliminate maneuvering.

For instance, in a driveway 12 to 14 ft. wide, the triangular area, formed by the inside corner of the turn and the two points 24 ft. on each side of the corner, should be left clear. This will allow proper clearance for the turning radius of the tractor-truck and the cut-in of trailer wheels.

LOADING LEVEL

A troublesome factor in loading and unloading at docks or loading platforms is the inherent variation in loading level (distance from pavement to floor level) of motor transport equipment. This distance averages 51 in. for heavy equipment but varies within a 6-in. range depending on model, tire size, and load. Due to spring compression, a heavily loaded trailer may be 3 in. lower than when empty. Also, one model trailer may be equipped with any one of a number of tire sizes, depending on the load it is required to carry. This factor can cause a variation of as much as 3 in. in loading level. Dock heights of from 44 to 50 in. are in general use, but only an analysis of the specific operation can determine the proper answer to the loading level problem. In general, 48 to 52 in. is most satisfactory for heavy-duty units, while slightly lower (44 to 46 in.) docks are more convenient for lighter equipment.

If the dock and trailer-bed levels are not equal, it is usually more satisfactory to have the dock level lower than the trailer bed. This will permit opening and closing of trailer doors while in loading position. Except in rare cases, a slight difference in level between trailer and dock is of no great concern, although a large difference is often a handicap. Many ingenious methods have been devised to overcome such a difference and a large percentage of these have succeeded in solving the specific or general problems involved. Some of these methods are illustrated below. Others are adjustable dock platforms and portable steel plates.

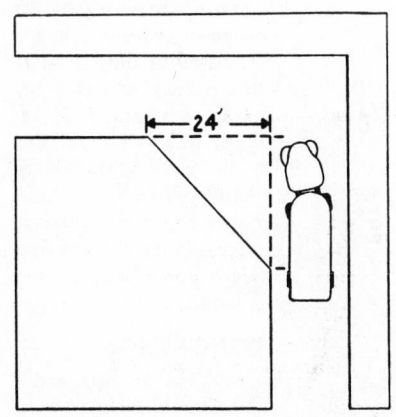

Fig. 4. Turning clearance for driveway

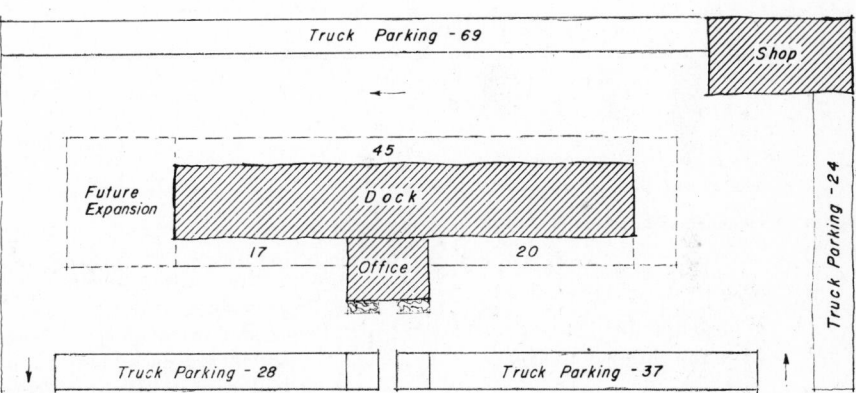

Fig. 5. Typical truck terminal plan

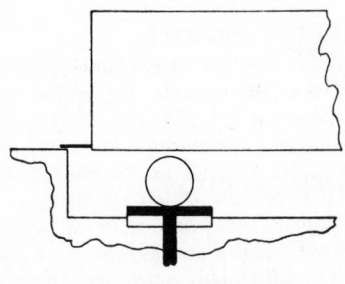

Plunger-type elevator

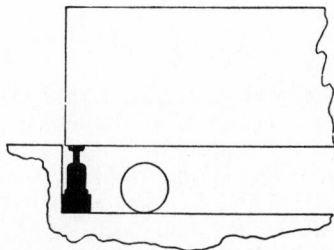

Manual or power-operated jack

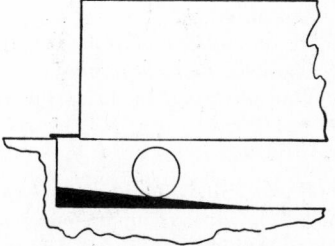

Permanent or movable incline

Fig. 6. Methods used to overcome differences in loading levels

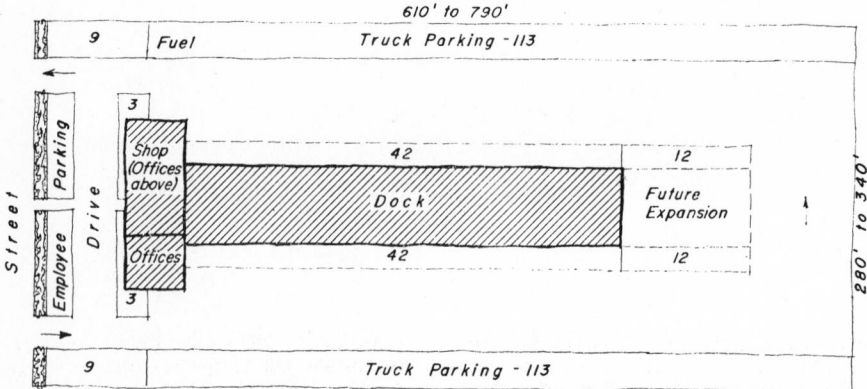

Fig. 7. Truck terminal with short side to street

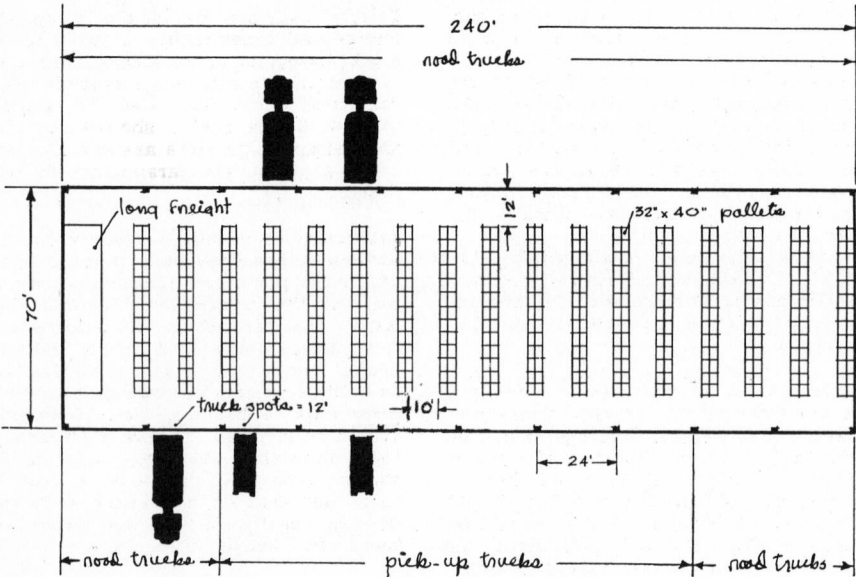

Fig. 8. Truck terminal dock plan for fork-lift truck and pallet storage

SITE

Location: In selecting a site, consider the following factors:

Proximity to pickups, deliveries, and connecting carriers

Accessibility to main traffic arteries

Obstructions such as bridges, underpasses, and railroad crossings

Zoning

Urban and regional plans; future growth pattern of city

Transportation facilities for employees

Utilities

Grade: Site should be approximately level; maximum slope 3 per cent; minimum slope for drainage, 1 per cent. Storm drains recommended 60 to 75 ft on centers, 100 ft maximum.

Pavement: 6-in. concrete slab reinforced with 6 by 6 in. No. 8 gage welded wire mesh; expansion joints 30 ft on centers.

Fence: 2-in. wire mesh No. 9 gage, 7 ft high including several strands of barbed wire at the top. Protect the fence from damage by trucks by placing bumpers or 2-ft-high earth curbs 5 to 15 ft from the fence, depending upon the type of truck using the yard. In car parking areas place bumpers at least 3 ft from the fence.

DOCK BUILDING

Orientation: If possible, place the long dimension of the building parallel to the prevailing storm winds.

Column spacing depends upon stall width. Recommended stall width 12 ft, column spacing 24 ft.

Width of building varies from 45 to 70 ft, depending upon the type of operation; usual figure is 60 ft.

Height: Minimum clear interior height, 12 ft.

Roof overhang or canopy projection—6 ft minimum, no maximum (the longer the better); usual figure, 12 ft.

End walls may be extended a similar distance for better weather protection.

Doors—overhead type, 8 to 10 ft wide by 8 to 9 ft 4 in. high; the larger sizes are more usual.

Floor—reinforced concrete designed for a live load of 150 to 250 psf; nonslip finish (float or abrasive).

Bumpers: Wood usual; steel or rubber may be used.

Steps—iron bar rungs set in concrete dock front are less expensive than stairs; provide one set of steps per four stalls.

Light—15 ft-c (foot-candles) recommended; skylights optional. Floodlights arranged to shine into truck or trailer bodies are required, also floodlights for the general yard area.

Heat required in northern areas; suspended unit heaters or radiant heat in floor slab may be used.

Ventilation: Mechanical ventilation required if fork-lift trucks are used.

Sprinklers recommended for entire dock area.

OFFICES

The office facilities may include any or all of the following:

General office
Message center
Billing office
Cashier
Telephone room
Foreman's office
Office manager
Terminal manager
Operations manager
Salesmen's room
Record room
Heater room
Central checking
Drivers' locker room
Transportation department
Dormitory
Cafeteria
Drivers' ready room

OTHER FACILITIES

Maintenance shop
Fueling area (near shop)
Weighing area
Truck and trailer parking area (two parking spaces per dock stall recommended)
Employee and visitor parking area

Information in this section was prepared by Ronald Allwork from data furnished principally by W. S. Arrasmith of Wischmeyer, Arrasmith and Elswick, Architects. Harry S. Pack, Industrial Designer; Greyhound Bus Lines; and *Bus Transportation* also furnished data.

Plot layout. Plan and arrangement are governed by placement of bus lanes and loading platform. A square lot (most desirable) permits efficient and economical concourse layout, provides for loading busses on two or three sides of waiting room, makes approach to all busses approximately the same. An alternate scheme provides loading on two opposite sides only. Both plans are known as "islands." Narrow, deep lots necessitate stretching elements into a "parallel" plan, in which busses are loaded from one side of the building only. Increased distance between elements makes this type less efficient.

Bus facilities. Except where bus traffic parallels both sides of a building that extends through from street to street, one bus entrance and one exit are normally sufficient. Their width depends on width of street and bus turning radius; 14 ft. is minimum, 16 to 18 ft. preferred. Bus movement should be clockwise, since passenger loading door is on right side of bus.

PASSENGER REQUIREMENTS

Street entrances should be 2 to 6 doors wide. Entrances should be centrally located; from them the elements of the terminal radiate.

Waiting room should be directly accessible from street. Access to concourse should be through multiple doorways or "gates," so located as to distribute passenger traffic uniformly, without congestion even during peak load periods. Seating may be based on approximately 1/3 passenger capacity of loading docks, assuming 35 to 37 persons per bus. Space allowances range from 15 to 35 sq. ft. per person; 20 to 24 sq. ft. is considered satisfactory. Total area averages 20 to 35 per cent of total building area; the smaller the building the larger the percentage. Eight-place settees, with or without separation arms, are commonly used. Drinking fountains, trash baskets and ash receptacles are also needed.

Baggage room should be accessible from both waiting room and concourse. Outside freight has to be delivered without interfering with concourse traffic. Baggage is usually checked over counter from waiting room and trucked to busses, and vice versa. Area of baggage room should be 10 per cent of total building area or contain 50 sq. ft. for each bus loading dock—whichever is the higher. Large storage space (usually in basement) is desirable for holdover and unclaimed baggage. Standard metal racks, one or two units deep and four to five shelves high, are suitable for baggage storage.

Check lockers are desirable in addition to the above facilities and are generally paying concessions. Number of lockers is based on potential earning capacity.

Toilets must be convenient to waiting room. Cement or terrazzo floors and bases are preferred. Wainscot should be 4½ to 5 ft. high. Number of fixtures depends on size of terminal, but as many as economically possible should be provided. Women's lounge should be large enough for a couch, vanity or dressing table, and several chairs. Men's lounge is not desirable.

Ticket office should be prominent in waiting room. In small stations proximity to concourse is desirable but is not essential in large terminals. 50 sq. ft. should be provided per selling position. One position may be provided for each 25 or 30 waiting room seats; but number of positions is usually based on personnel normally required and on anticipated extras for peak periods. It is not necessary for the ticket office to be connected to other offices. Counters should be 42 in. high; cages or windows are not desirable.

ADMINISTRATION AND CONCESSIONS

Dispatcher's office controls bus movement and should be on concourse at a point from which all loading docks can be supervised. It need not be related in plan to waiting room or ticket office, but is usually connected by telephone and telautograph to ticket office, manager's office and bus garage. Public address system is used to announce arrivals and departures of busses.

Offices for terminal manager, passenger agent and switchboard are usually sufficient. These need not contain more than 100 to 200 sq. ft. each. In larger terminals, offices for regional manager, clerical force, meeting rooms, etc., may be required.

Drivers' quarters are usualy limited to lounge and toilet facilities (with shower) in basement or on second floor, and require private entrance accessible from concourse. Space is needed for reading table, lounging chairs, shelves for tool kits. Sleeping quarters are usually provided at local bus garage, not in terminals.

Restaurant is usually necessary for all terminals, has floor area ranging from 15 to 25 per cent of building area; usually, the larger the terminal, the larger the percentage. Larger restaurants have counter and tables. Patrons prefer booths, tables are more flexible, so both are used. Counters generally receive bulk of business. Soda fountains should be included. In larger terminals, soda fountains may be installed in waiting rooms. Kitchen area is from 15 to 35 per cent of restaurant area, depending partly on storage facilities; these are often in basement.

News stand should be adjacent to waiting room and restaurant.

Telephone and telegraph booth is mandatory. In larger terminals a telephone operator is sometimes desirable.

Barber shop and stores are often included. Space economically available, anticipated demand, size of terminal, etc., have to be considered in allocating space or this type of concession. In small terminals some means of increasing revenue is essential; concessions may be the answer. Drug stores are sometimes included. Beauty parlors are seldom included at present.

Travel bureau is important, particularly in large terminals. It should be on or near street, adjacent to waiting room. A show window may be provided on street front.

SERVICES AND CONSTRUCTION

Air conditioning is widely used, especially in large terminals. In northern localities this is often supplemented by steam or hot water radiation.

Lighting in public spaces is often fluorescent, either direct or indirect, with a three-stage control to permit adjustment of light level to variable passenger traffic.

Intercommunicating system includes telephones and telautograph connecting dispatcher, ticket office, manager's office and bus garage. Cut-in on public address system is usually provided so switchboard operator can page individuals.

Construction should be "fireproof," and is ordinarily steel frame or reinforced concrete, depending on building design, availability of material, costs, etc. Partitions are usually tile or gypsum block, and should be planned for economical changes if required for expansion.

Interior finish, where subjected to public use, must be rugged and easy to maintain. Terrazzo or tile floors are usually employed; smaller buildings often use cement. Wainscoting in main areas should be able to take abuse. Ceilings in restaurants, waiting room and telephone office should be acoustically treated.

Exterior finish is often cut stone. Glass block is extensively used. Brick, terra cotta, stucco, and concrete are also used; and glazed brick is commonly employed for concourse wall and rear of building.

Concourse, bus lanes and yards are constructed of 7 or 8 in. thick concrete slabs, of 2,500 lb. concrete, reinforced top and bottom with No. 40 mesh. A surface hardener should be employed.

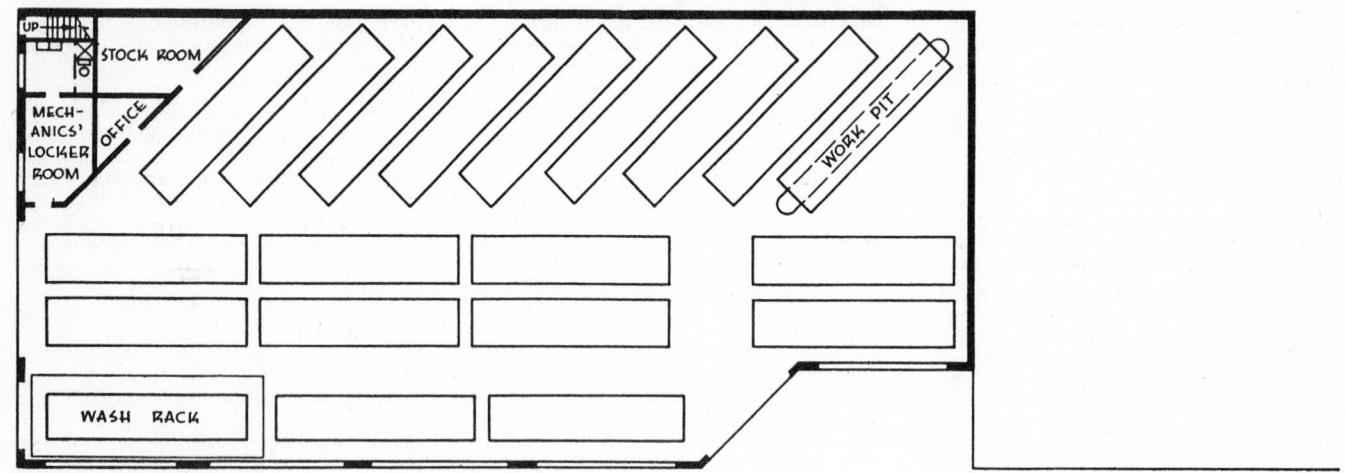

SCALE 1/32" = 1'-0"

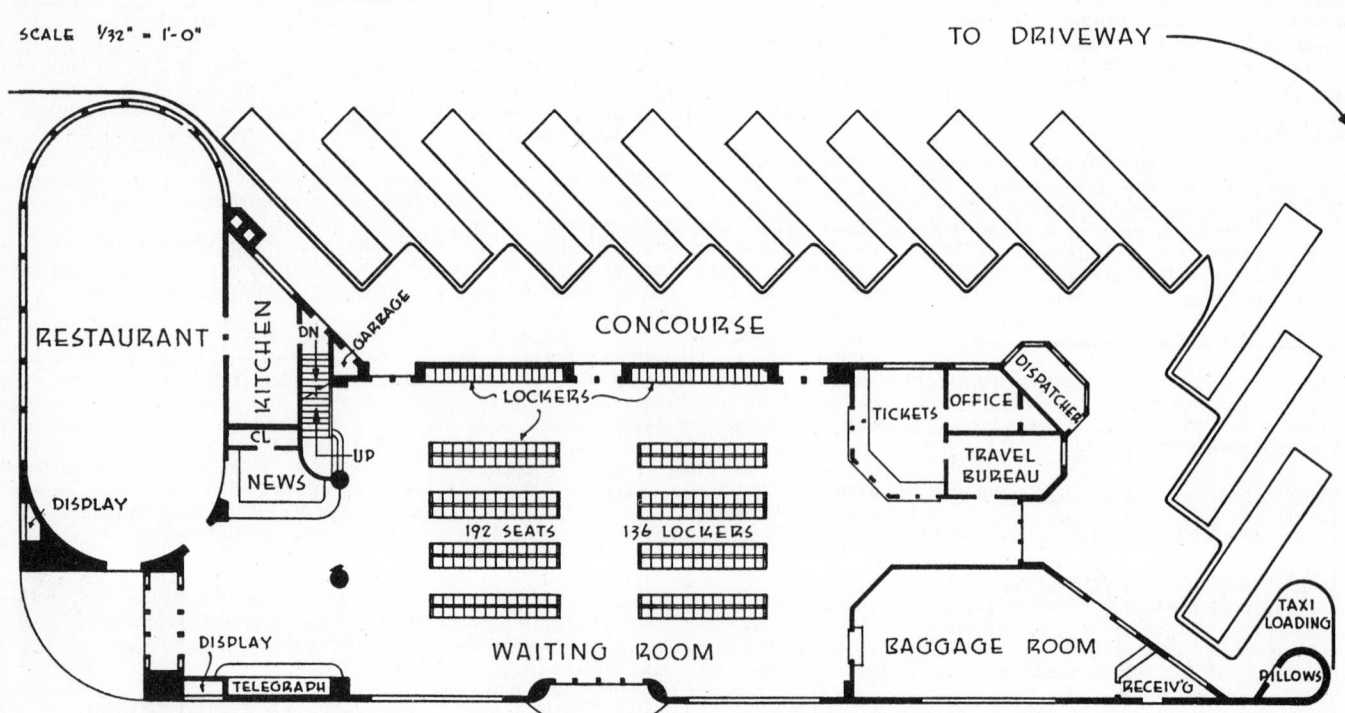

PLAN, typical bus station, fairly large size. Wischmeyer, Arrasmith & Elswick, Architects.   Note bus garage in rear

Data on this and the following page were checked by the Port of New York Authority.

LOADING DOCKS

Parallel loading requires an excessive amount of space per bus. Usually busses in rear cannot move out until first bus exits. In a large terminal several lanes would be required, and overhead or underground passage would be necessary to several island loading platforms. Otherwise passengers would cross bus lanes, an extremely dangerous practice which creates a liability on the bus company.

Right-angle, or head-on, loading is acceptable, but disadvantages include the outswinging bus door which forms a barrier around which passengers must go, and difficulty of maneuvering each bus into its berth. This type of loading is useful when the bus yard is deep, but concourse is limited in extent.

Straight sawtooth loading is efficient, and is employed where lot is comparatively narrow and deep. Passenger has direct approach to loading door, baggage truck can operate between parked busses for loading into side baggage doors.

Radial sawtooth loading is most efficient. Busses may swing into position along a natural driving arc. A minimum of concourse frontage, per bus, is required. In this system each bus space is narrow at front and wide at rear, making maneuvering easy and conserving space.

Number of loading docks is based on average peak loading conditions, size of lot, and size of structure. Abnormal peak conditions such as occur on holidays can be taken care of by "doubles"; that is, by parking additional busses in the lot and immediately running them into loading docks as scheduled busses depart. Limited dock space is not a serious drawback if ample parking space can be provided for "double" busses.

Passenger concourse is protected from weather by overhead canopy which cantilevers over passenger doors of busses in loading docks. This protects passenger getting on and off busses as well as front baggage doors on sides of each bus. Holiday crowds can be controlled by using airplane cord barriers as indicated in diagrams.

BUS YARD

Area depends on type of loading used and number of busses to be parked. Parallel loading requires approximately 12 ft. (width) per driveway; right-angle loading requires approximately 40 ft. from rear of bus to property line; sawtooth loading (straight or radial) requires about 50 ft. from front right wheel of bus to property line (assuming busses parked at 45°, berths 12 ft. 6 in. wide).

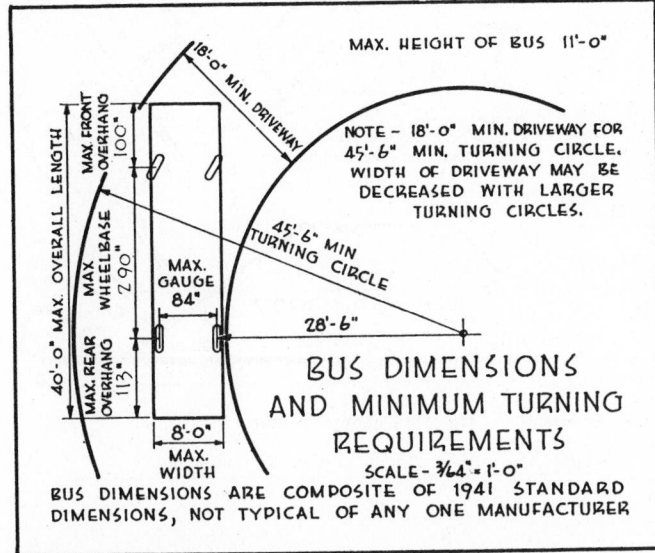

MAX. HEIGHT OF BUS 11'-0"

18'-0" MIN. DRIVEWAY

NOTE – 18'-0" MIN. DRIVEWAY FOR 45'-6" MIN. TURNING CIRCLE. WIDTH OF DRIVEWAY MAY BE DECREASED WITH LARGER TURNING CIRCLES.

45'-6" MIN TURNING CIRCLE

28'-6"

MAX. OVERALL LENGTH 40'-0"
MAX. FRONT OVERHANG 100"
MAX. WHEELBASE 290"
MAX. REAR OVERHANG 113"
MAX. GAUGE 84"
MAX. WIDTH 8'-0"

BUS DIMENSIONS AND MINIMUM TURNING REQUIREMENTS
SCALE - 3/64" = 1'-0"

BUS DIMENSIONS ARE COMPOSITE OF 1941 STANDARD DIMENSIONS, NOT TYPICAL OF ANY ONE MANUFACTURER

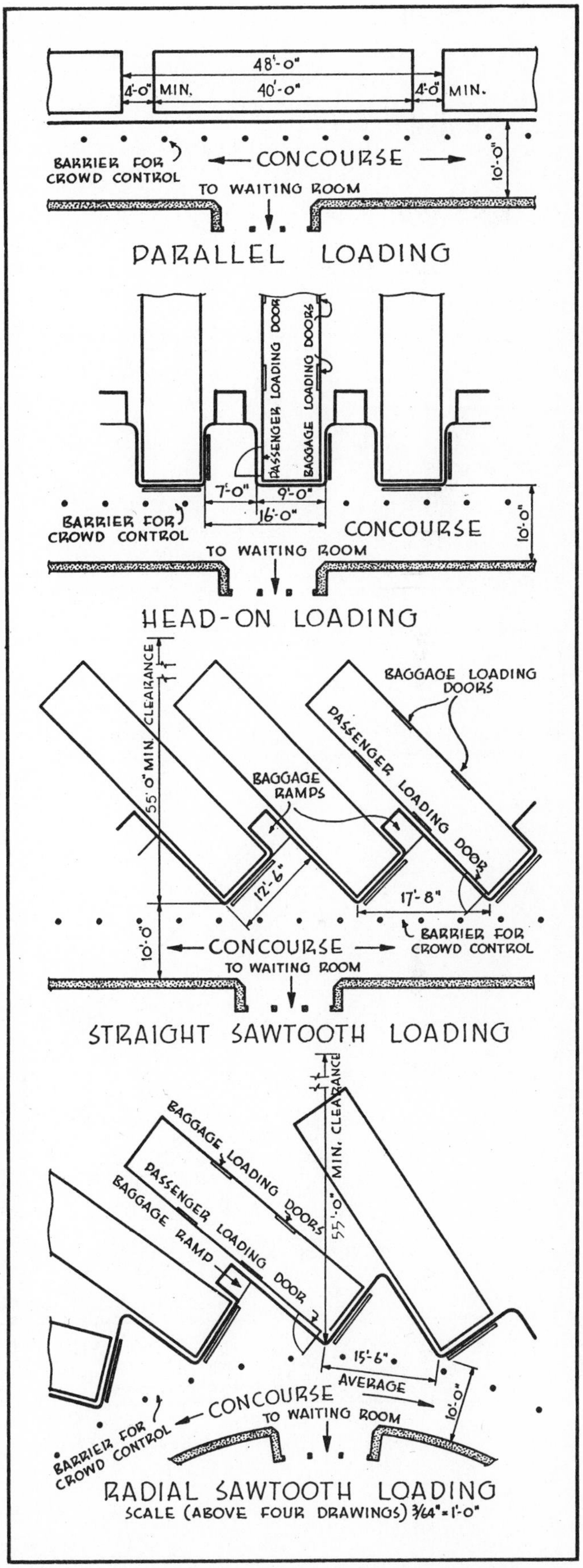

48'-0"
4'-0" MIN. 40'-0" 4'-0" MIN.

BARRIER FOR CROWD CONTROL

←CONCOURSE→

TO WAITING ROOM

10'-0"

PARALLEL LOADING

PASSENGER LOADING DOOR
BAGGAGE LOADING DOORS

BARRIER FOR CROWD CONTROL

7'-0" 9'-0"
16'-0"

CONCOURSE

TO WAITING ROOM

10'-0"

HEAD-ON LOADING

55'-0" MIN. CLEARANCE

BAGGAGE LOADING DOORS
PASSENGER LOADING DOOR
BAGGAGE RAMPS

12'-6" 17'-8"

←CONCOURSE→

TO WAITING ROOM

BARRIER FOR CROWD CONTROL

10'-0"

STRAIGHT SAWTOOTH LOADING

55'-0" MIN. CLEARANCE

BAGGAGE LOADING DOORS
PASSENGER LOADING DOOR
BAGGAGE RAMP

15'-6" AVERAGE

←CONCOURSE→

TO WAITING ROOM

BARRIER FOR CROWD CONTROL

10'-0"

RADIAL SAWTOOTH LOADING
SCALE (ABOVE FOUR DRAWINGS) 3/64" = 1'-0"

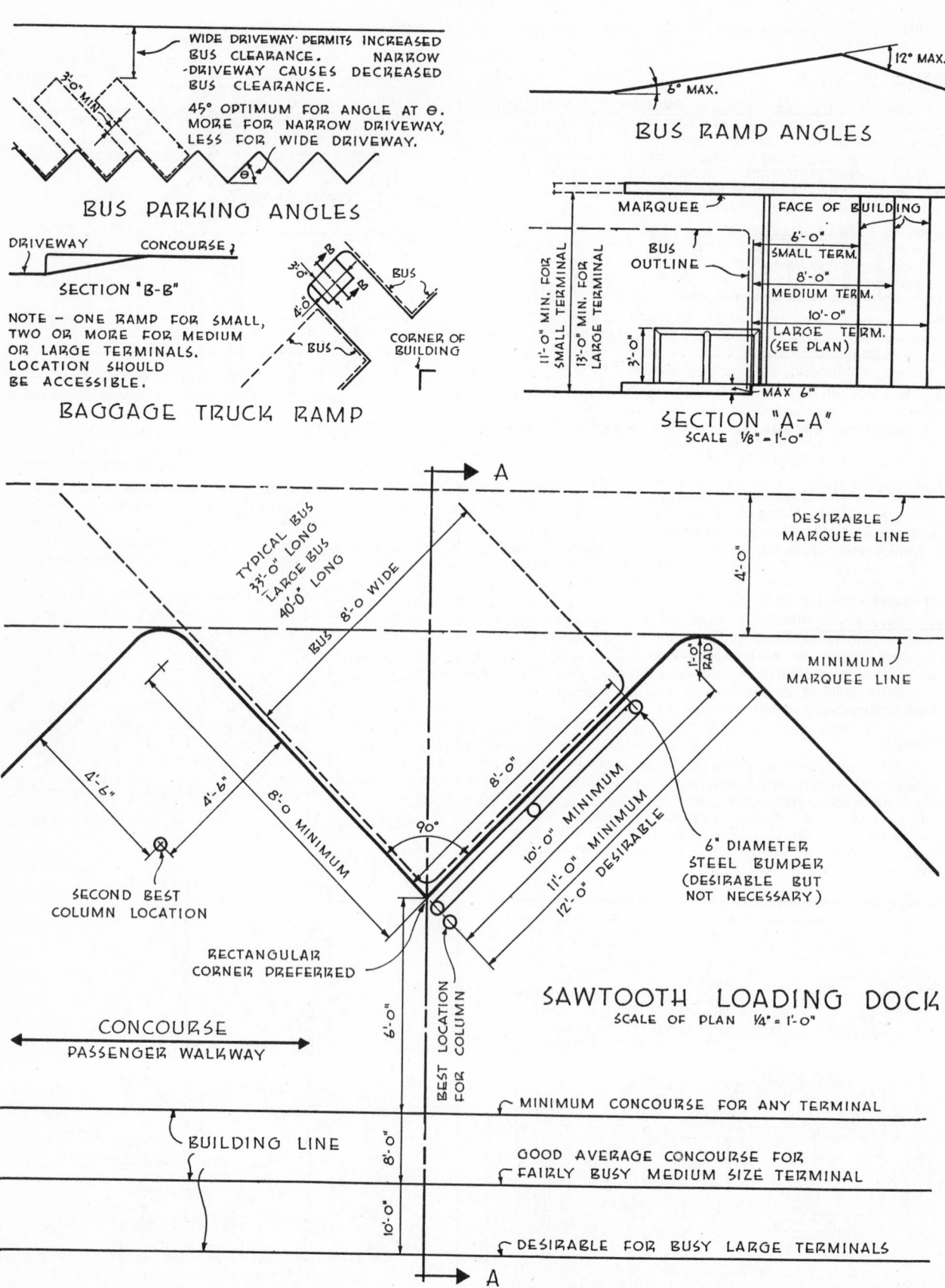

WIDE DRIVEWAY· PERMITS INCREASED BUS CLEARANCE. NARROW-DRIVEWAY CAUSES DECREASED BUS CLEARANCE.

45° OPTIMUM FOR ANGLE AT θ. MORE FOR NARROW DRIVEWAY, LESS FOR WIDE DRIVEWAY.

3'-0" MIN.

BUS PARKING ANGLES

DRIVEWAY   CONCOURSE
SECTION "B-B"

NOTE — ONE RAMP FOR SMALL, TWO OR MORE FOR MEDIUM OR LARGE TERMINALS. LOCATION SHOULD BE ACCESSIBLE.

BAGGAGE TRUCK RAMP

BUS
CORNER OF BUILDING

6° MAX.   12° MAX.

BUS RAMP ANGLES

MARQUEE   FACE OF BUILDING
BUS OUTLINE
11'-0" MIN. FOR SMALL TERMINAL
13'-0" MIN. FOR LARGE TERMINAL
6'-0" SMALL TERM.
8'-0" MEDIUM TERM.
10'-0" LARGE TERM. (SEE PLAN)
3'-0"
MAX 6"

SECTION "A-A"
SCALE 1/8" = 1'-0"

A

DESIRABLE MARQUEE LINE
TYPICAL BUS 33'-0" LONG
LARGE BUS 40'-0" LONG
BUS 8'-0" WIDE
4'-0"
MINIMUM MARQUEE LINE

1'-0" RAD

4'-6"   4'-6"   8'-0 MINIMUM
90°
8'-0"
10'-0" MINIMUM
11'-0" MINIMUM
12'-0" DESIRABLE
6" DIAMETER STEEL BUMPER (DESIRABLE BUT NOT NECESSARY)

SECOND BEST COLUMN LOCATION

RECTANGULAR CORNER PREFERRED

BEST LOCATION FOR COLUMN

SAWTOOTH LOADING DOCK
SCALE OF PLAN 1/4" = 1'-0"

CONCOURSE
PASSENGER WALKWAY

6'-0"

MINIMUM CONCOURSE FOR ANY TERMINAL

BUILDING LINE
8'-0"
GOOD AVERAGE CONCOURSE FOR FAIRLY BUSY MEDIUM SIZE TERMINAL

10'-0"
DESIRABLE FOR BUSY LARGE TERMINALS

A

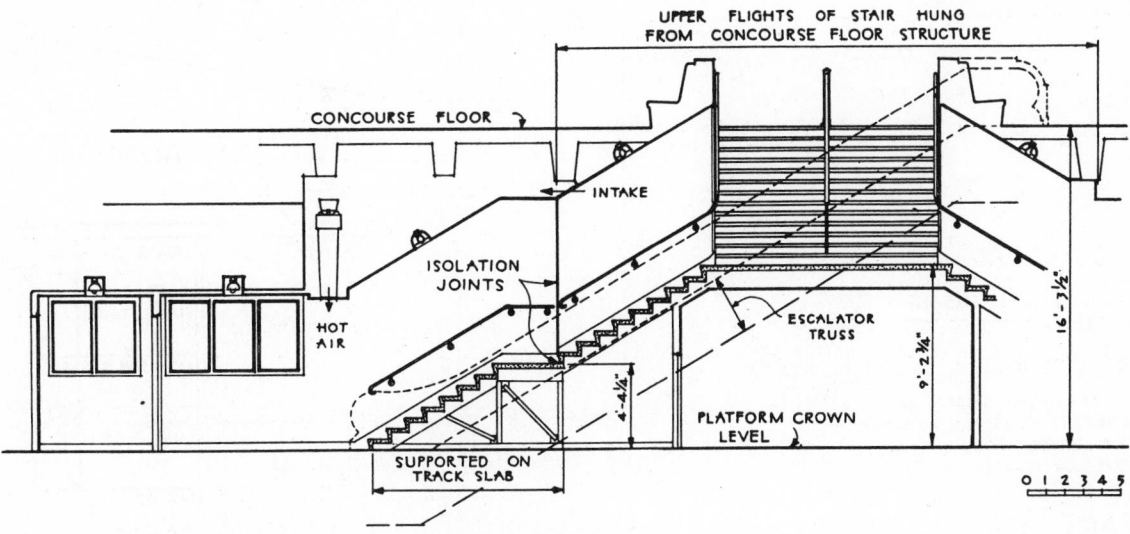

Fig. 1. Stair and escalator for minimal rise from high track platform

Details on this page are all taken from Canadian National Railways' Central Station at Montreal, by CNR architects and engineers.

Stair and escalator section reproduced above is intended to achieve minimal climbing distance for passengers from a high (car-floor level) train platform to an exit centrally located in the concourse above. Escalator is carried entirely on track slab and isolated from building.

Stair is carried one-third its length on track, two-thirds hung from floor above. Incoming and outgoing traffic are separated in the concourse by this plan.

"Inverted" track slab is shown in Fig. 2. Smooth ceiling at sub-track level is obtained by placing supporting beams on top of the slab they carry. Reinforcements for slab and beam are placed before pouring; slab poured first, then beam; cleavage plane filled with waterproofing.

Clearance of high platform at track. Drawing gives distance from track base to approx. top of platform edge as 4 ft. 6 in. Exact measurements are actually taken from top of track; vary with track gauge and equipment used. Distance of platform edge from center of track also varies with equipment, from 5 ft. 2 in. min. to 5 ft. 6 in. max.

Vibration Isolation between track structure and building structure involves use of vibration pad under bldg. column footing. Pad is 2 layers transite 3/8 in. thick separated by steel plate 1/16 in. thick, all enclosed in lead envelope. Two-in. cork column wrapping at intersections is held by toothpicks until concrete is poured. A single accidental fin of concrete breaking the isolation would destroy effect.

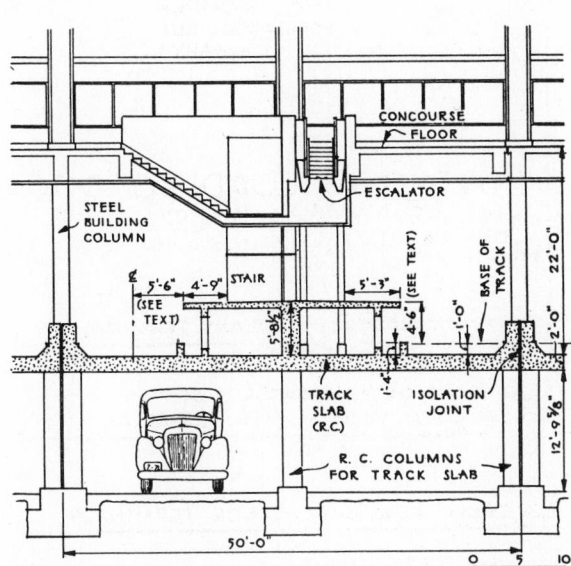

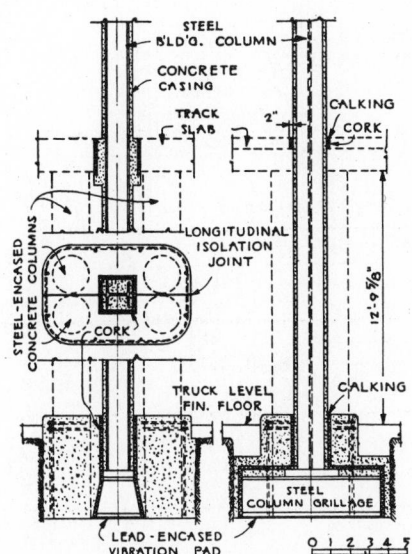

Fig. 2. (a) Platform clearances   (b) Inverted track slab

Fig. 3. Vibration isolation

Canadian National details, continued.

Tail-gate parking clearances for express trucks at sub-track level are shown at right. Column spacing across tracks was unchangeable at 25 ft. center to center. Longitudinal spacing was obtained from full-scale experiments. Drivers of reasonable skill were able to clear columns spaced 1 ft. closer than the spacing finally used.

Diagram shows approximate path followed by two trucks sharing the same parking bay. Car to the left in the drawing must back up once on its way out.

Isolation joint is advisable all around each pair of drop doors at tail-gate, to minimize collision damage. Vertical rails set 1 ft. deep in concrete floor serve as adequate bumpers.

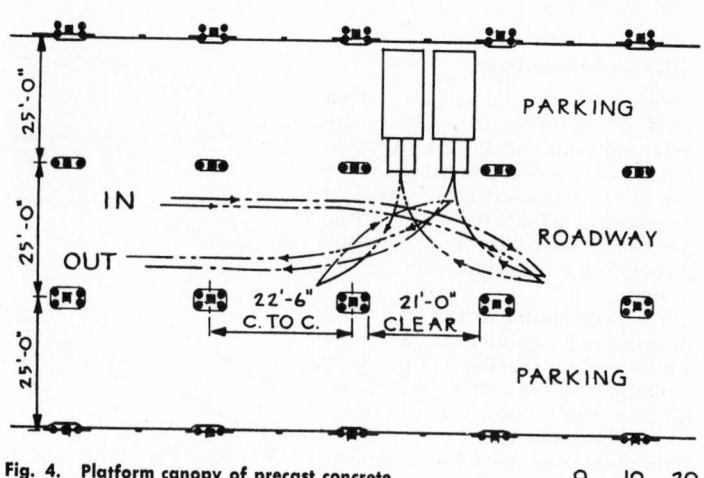

Fig. 4. Platform canopy of precast concrete

Details below are from the station of the Burlington Route at Burlington, Iowa, Holabird & Root, arch's.

Canopy section shown below uses reinforced concrete (pre-cast). The weight of typical roof panel in light silica-aggregate concrete is 32,650 lb., of end-panel with rounded end, 33,200 lb.; of column, 2,700 lb. Specify 3,000 lb. per sq. in. ultimate strength. At track crossings a special dropped section of platform is used. Due to topography, drainage is one-way.

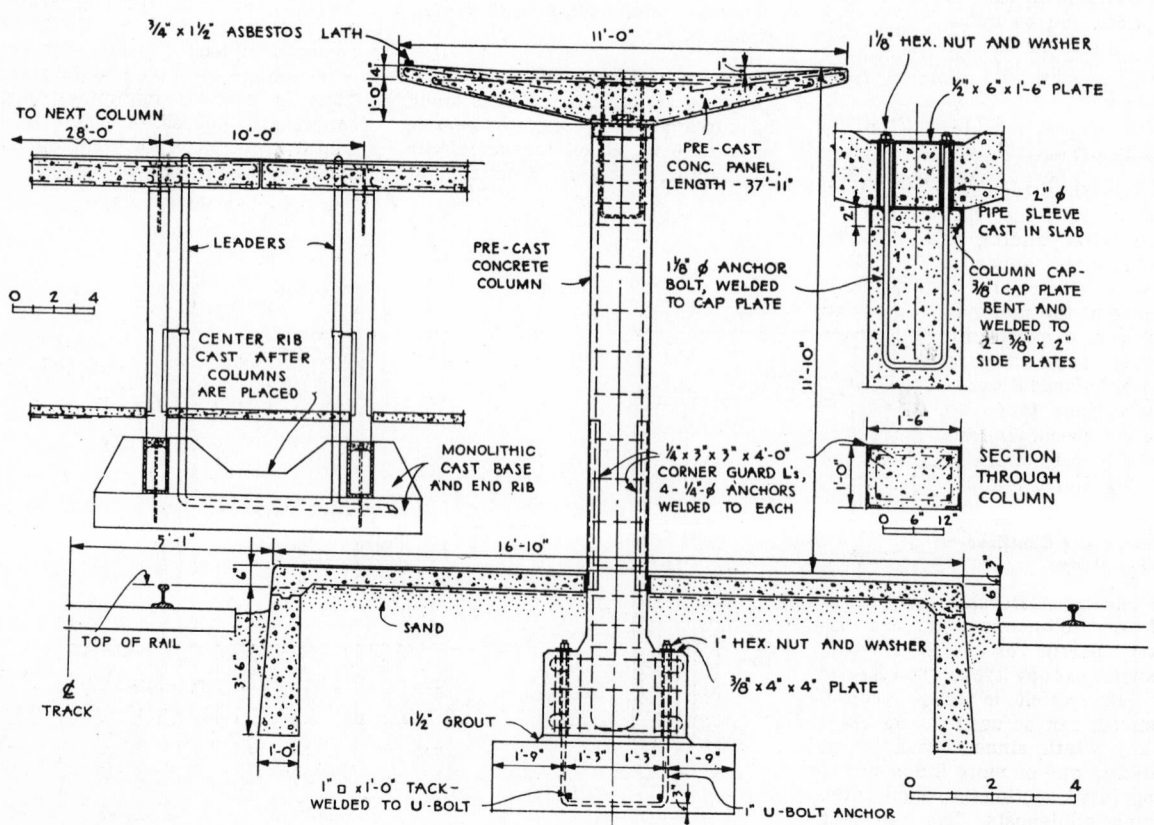

Fig. 5. Tail gate platform

By W. J. WARD, Jr.

Balanced Canopy Doors

There are two types of doors which form a canopy when opened: the balanced type and the cantilevered type. The two doors in this drawing are of the balanced type, so called because, in effect, the door is suspended at its center and balanced throughout its operation by counterweights.

The door shown at the top of the drawing has a guide linkage system which makes possible openings of unlimited width since no intermediate obstructing support is required between the door sections. This guide linkage folds within or above the thickness of the door leaf when open; thus it does not obstruct the opening. The door is designed for heights up to 55 ft. Sections can be operated simultaneously or independently.

The other door, designed for openings up to 120 ft. wide and 30 ft. high, is of single leaf construction and is guided by rollers at the top which run in a curved track and by a roller at the center of the door's height which runs in a straight track at the jambs.

Both these doors are designed for motor operation but can be operated by hand in case of motor failure. Both can be opened or closed in a minute or less. Details were adopted from data furnished by Byrne Doors, Inc.

Accordion Doors

The accordion type door, so called because it folds like accordion pleats after sliding into pockets, is illustrated opposite. The door shown is electrically operated and, because of the method of operation employed, it exerts no shock loads on the supporting steel as do counter-balanced door types. Door construction may be structural steel or wood. Details at top of following page were adapted from data by Horn Manufacturing Co.

Balanced and Cantilevered Canopy Doors

The canopy doors shown on lower half of following page are all either partly or fully counterbalanced canopy types. The one at the left, which is fully counterbalanced, can be used for openings of any width since it can be installed in one or more independently operated sections without interrupting guideposts. The top leaf, hinged both at the lintel and the

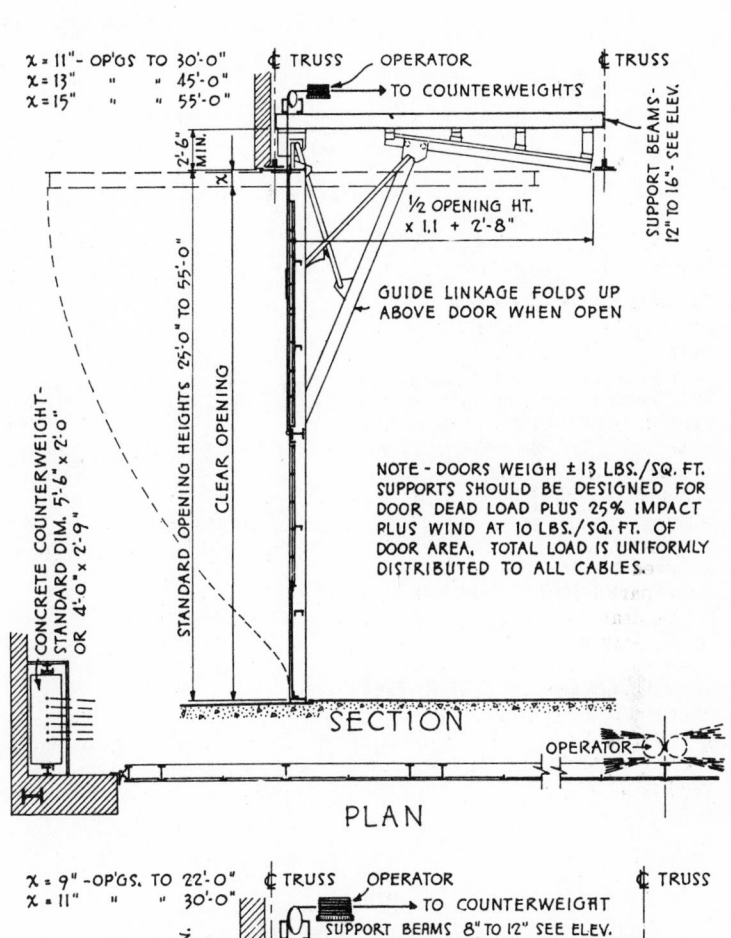

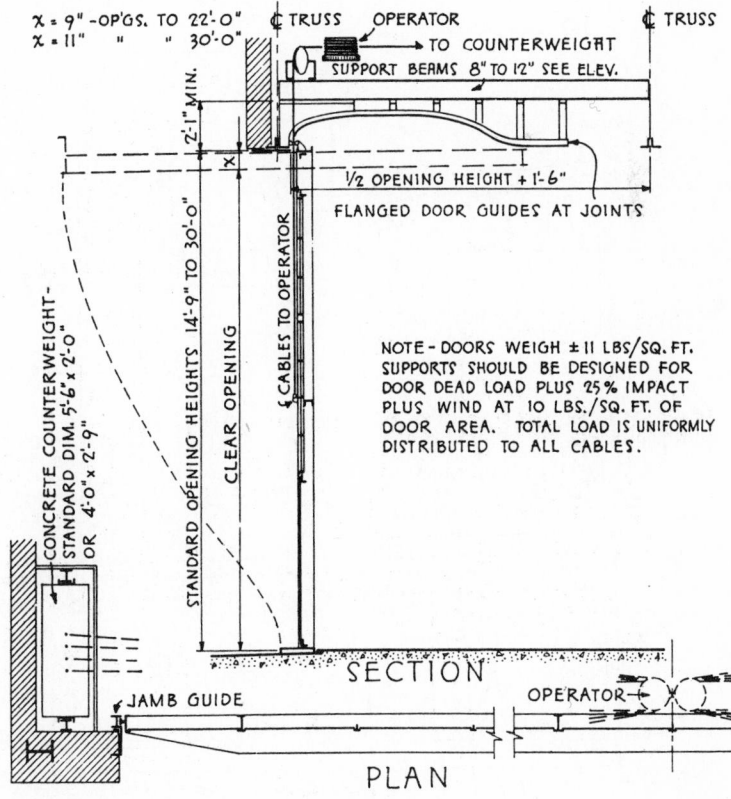

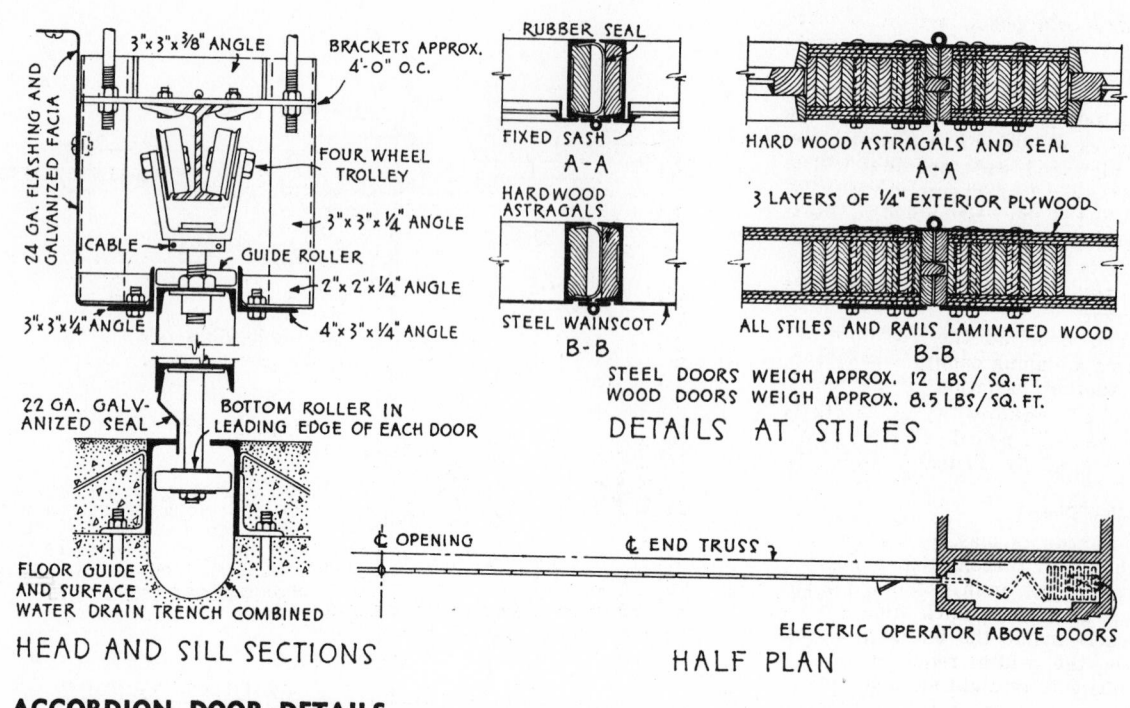

3"x3"x3/8" ANGLE

BRACKETS APPROX. 4'-0" O.C.

24 GA. FLASHING AND GALVANIZED FACIA

FOUR WHEEL TROLLEY

3"x3"x1/4" ANGLE

CABLE

GUIDE ROLLER

2"x2"x1/4" ANGLE

3"x3"x1/4" ANGLE

4"x3"x1/4" ANGLE

22 GA. GALVANIZED SEAL

BOTTOM ROLLER IN LEADING EDGE OF EACH DOOR

FLOOR GUIDE AND SURFACE WATER DRAIN TRENCH COMBINED

HEAD AND SILL SECTIONS

ACCORDION DOOR DETAILS

RUBBER SEAL

FIXED SASH
A-A

HARDWOOD ASTRAGALS

STEEL WAINSCOT
B-B

HARD WOOD ASTRAGALS AND SEAL
A-A

3 LAYERS OF 1/4" EXTERIOR PLYWOOD

ALL STILES AND RAILS LAMINATED WOOD
B-B

STEEL DOORS WEIGH APPROX. 12 LBS/SQ.FT.
WOOD DOORS WEIGH APPROX. 8.5 LBS/SQ.FT.

DETAILS AT STILES

₵ OPENING

₵ END TRUSS

ELECTRIC OPERATOR ABOVE DOORS

HALF PLAN

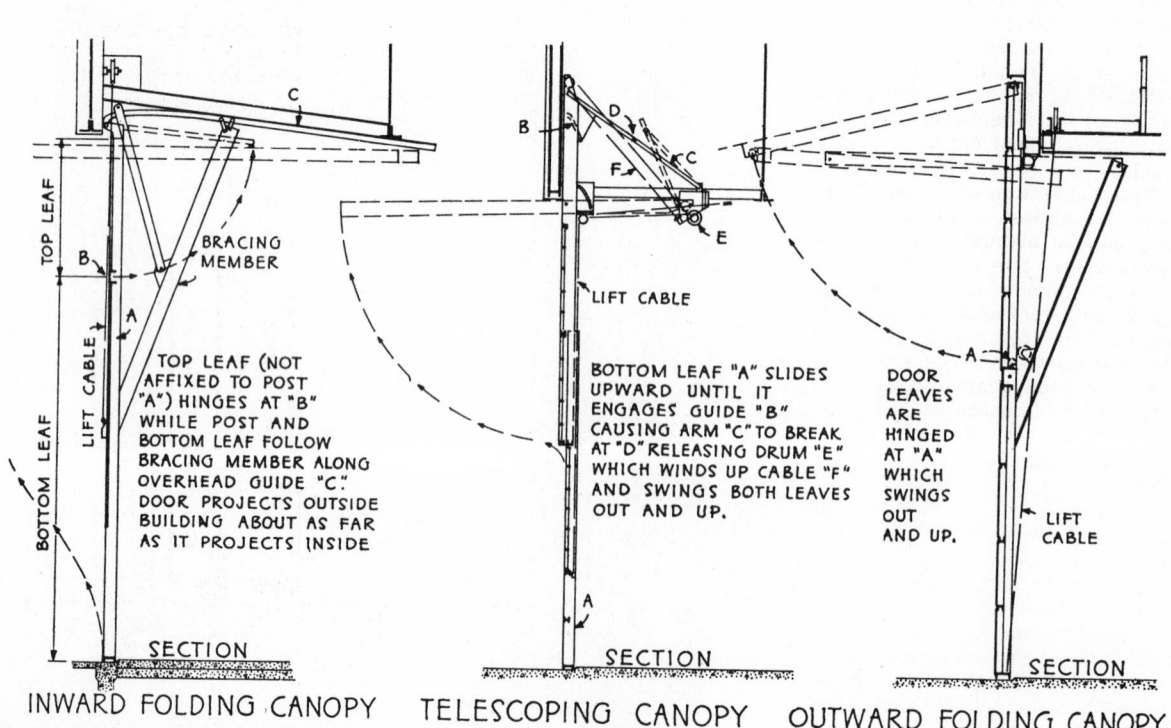

TOP LEAF

B

A

LIFT CABLE

BOTTOM LEAF

C

BRACING MEMBER

TOP LEAF (NOT AFFIXED TO POST "A") HINGES AT "B" WHILE POST AND BOTTOM LEAF FOLLOW BRACING MEMBER ALONG OVERHEAD GUIDE "C". DOOR PROJECTS OUTSIDE BUILDING ABOUT AS FAR AS IT PROJECTS INSIDE

SECTION
INWARD FOLDING CANOPY

B

D

F

C

E

LIFT CABLE

BOTTOM LEAF "A" SLIDES UPWARD UNTIL IT ENGAGES GUIDE "B" CAUSING ARM "C" TO BREAK AT "D" RELEASING DRUM "E" WHICH WINDS UP CABLE "F" AND SWINGS BOTH LEAVES OUT AND UP.

A

SECTION
TELESCOPING CANOPY

A

DOOR LEAVES ARE HINGED AT "A" WHICH SWINGS OUT AND UP.

LIFT CABLE

SECTION
OUTWARD FOLDING CANOPY

BALANCED AND CANTILEVERED CANOPY DOORS

door's own posts, acts as a heat baffle when the door is only partly open.

The door at the center of the drawing is a cantilevered canopy type especially adapted to extremely high and wide openings. Since the lower leaf operates vertically upward in the first half of its opening movement, a minimum of clearance is required for planes located on the apron or just inside the hangar.

The door at the right, which forms a sloping canopy when open, is another variation of the cantilevered canopy type. Details were adapted from data furnished by Truscon Steel Co.

Sliding Doors

Sliding doors may be divided into two types: those which slide in a straight line or in parallel straight lines and those which slide around corners inside the building. To reduce the width required at the jambs with straight sliding doors, a number of parallel tracks may be used so that the doors stand one behind another when in the open position. For very wide openings, more than one door may be mounted on a single track. The same statements apply to around-the-corner sliding doors except that a hinged door is provided at the jambs. Both types of sliding doors may be supported by industrial rails tied together and embedded in the concrete floor or by an overhead track mounted inside the lintel. Of course, in the latter case, the lintel must be designed to support the full load of the door and tracks.

Motor operation of large, sliding doors is almost a necessity but they can be manually operated in emergencies. Ice and snow may make operation of any sliding door installation very difficult, but such installations cost less at the start than canopy types. Details at lower left have been adapted from data furnished by Truscon Steel Co.; at lower right, by Richards-Wilcox Manufacturing Co.

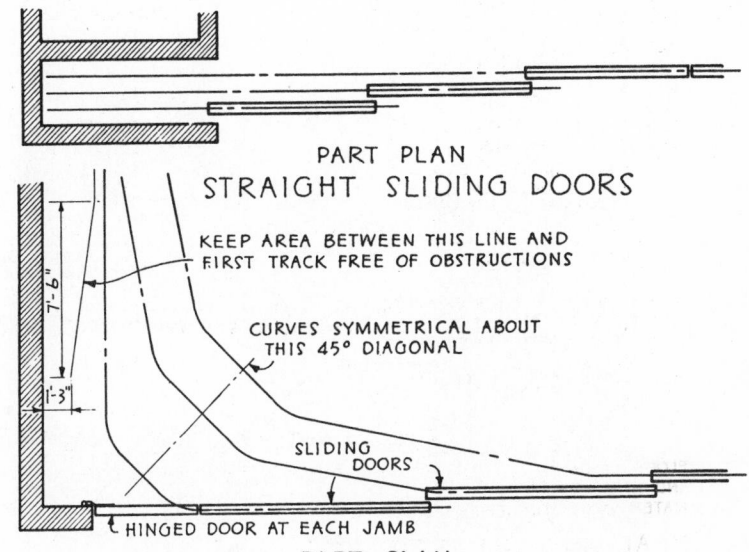

PART PLAN
STRAIGHT SLIDING DOORS

KEEP AREA BETWEEN THIS LINE AND FIRST TRACK FREE OF OBSTRUCTIONS

CURVES SYMMETRICAL ABOUT THIS 45° DIAGONAL

SLIDING DOORS

HINGED DOOR AT EACH JAMB

PART PLAN
AROUND-THE-CORNER SLIDING DOORS

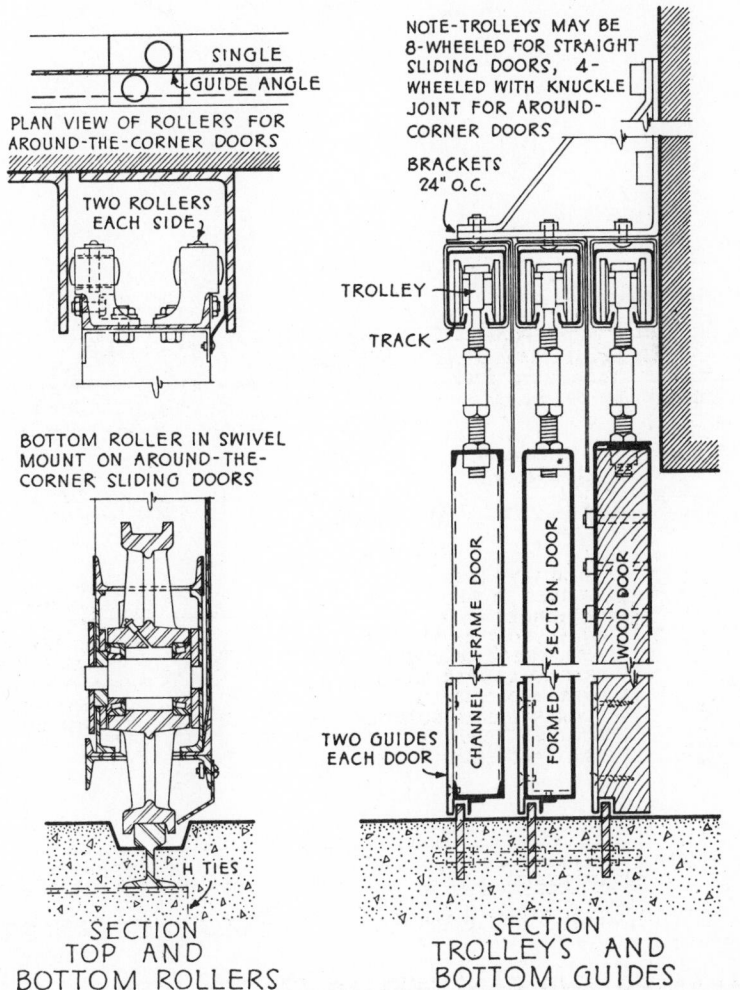

SINGLE GUIDE ANGLE

PLAN VIEW OF ROLLERS FOR AROUND-THE-CORNER DOORS

TWO ROLLERS EACH SIDE

BOTTOM ROLLER IN SWIVEL MOUNT ON AROUND-THE-CORNER SLIDING DOORS

H TIES

SECTION
TOP AND BOTTOM ROLLERS

NOTE-TROLLEYS MAY BE 8-WHEELED FOR STRAIGHT SLIDING DOORS, 4-WHEELED WITH KNUCKLE JOINT FOR AROUND-CORNER DOORS

BRACKETS 24" O.C.

TROLLEY

TRACK

CHANNEL FRAME DOOR

FORMED SECTION DOOR

WOOD DOOR

TWO GUIDES EACH DOOR

SECTION
TROLLEYS AND BOTTOM GUIDES

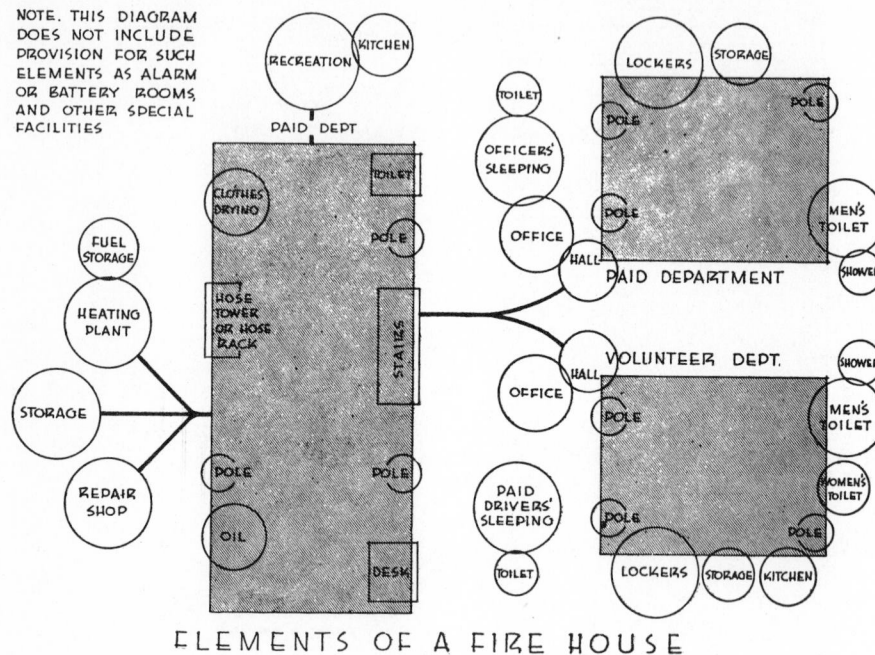

NOTE. THIS DIAGRAM DOES NOT INCLUDE PROVISION FOR SUCH ELEMENTS AS ALARM OR BATTERY ROOMS, AND OTHER SPECIAL FACILITIES

ELEMENTS OF A FIRE HOUSE

Information on this sheet was collected and prepared by Ronald Allwork. Sources included: "The Fire Chief's Handbook"*; The American City; and various manufacturers of fire apparatus.

General. There are two types of fire houses: one is operated by a paid fire department, the other by volunteers. Equipment for both is essentially the same. Differences occur in facilities provided for personnel.

The tendency in fire house design is toward providing for a two-company building. Generally a lot 50 by 100 ft. in extent is ample.

Elements of fire house design are shown in the diagram at the right. All facilities indicated are desirable but not mandatory. In paid departments, one company generally consists of 14 men; in a volunteer department quarters are provided for paid drivers only.

Apparatus room for two trucks should be approximately 25 by 75 ft., with ceiling height of 13 ft. (minimum). Floor should be of concrete, designed to carry a load of 125 lb. per sq. ft. Doors for apparatus should be 12 ft. high, and may be designed to permit passage of both trucks through a single opening; or through two separate openings. A wicket (or access door) should be provided in one panel. Extra heavy hardware and equipment are required. Consider the desirability of motor-operated doors.

Wall surfaces should be of an easily cleaned material, and floor should have sufficient drains to permit flushing with hose. Hot and cold water connections are needed at center of side walls. Desk should be on platform raised 6 in. above apparatus room floor to allow man on duty to remain during cleaning. Floors of closets, toilets, oil room, stair landings, etc., should also be raised for same reason.

If apparatus room is to be used for repairs, provide a repair pit. Also, carbon monoxide gases have to be exhausted to outside, usually by means of underfloor piping, to which motor exhaust may be connected with flexible tubing. (Recreation room on first floor should be raised at least 6 in. for protection against gas.)

Hose-drying tower should accommodate approximately 2,000 ft. of hose in 50-ft. lengths. Area of shaft required for this amount is approximately 4 by 8½ ft.; height, 60 ft. Hose is raised by pulley arrangement to top of tower. See overleaf for detail. Another method of drying hose is by means of inclined hose racks installed on side wall of apparatus room.

Sliding-pole shafts, details of which are shown overleaf, should be provided with doors or self-closing device, in order to prevent drafts and heat losses through the openings.

*"The Fire Chief's Handbook," by Fred Shepperd; Case-Shepperd-Mann Pub. Corp., New York City.

Table 1. Fire apparatus sizes

Note: Turning radius varies from 26 to 48 ft, according to type and make. "Cab-over-engine" type of apparatus is slightly shorter over all.

Village-Size Pumping Engine, 500 g.p.m.	
Length over all	24'–0"
Width over all	7'–6"
Height over all	6'–5"
Triple Combination Pumping Engine, 750 g.p.m. (most used)	
Length over all	28'–0"
Width over all	8'–0"
Height over all	6'–11"
Hook-and-Ladder Truck (removable hand-raised ladders)	
Length over all	41'–3"
Width over all	8'–0"
Height over all	7'–3"
Hook-and-Ladder Aerial Truck (4-wheel type)	
Length over all	58'–9"
Width over all	8'–0"
Height over all	8'–7"
Hook-and-Ladder Aerial Truck (tractor-drawn type, 6-wheel)	
Length over all	63'–6"
Width over all	8'–0"
Height over all	8'–7"
Clearance required	12'–0"

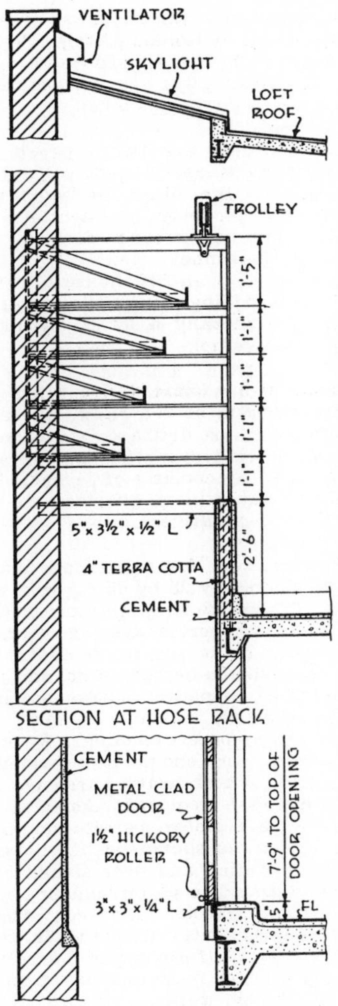

VENTILATOR

SKYLIGHT

LOFT ROOF

NOTE: HOSE IS RAISED TO TOP OF SHAFT BY HAND. SPECIAL HOOKS, WHICH FIT OVER LUG OF HOSE COUPLING, ARE AVAILABLE.

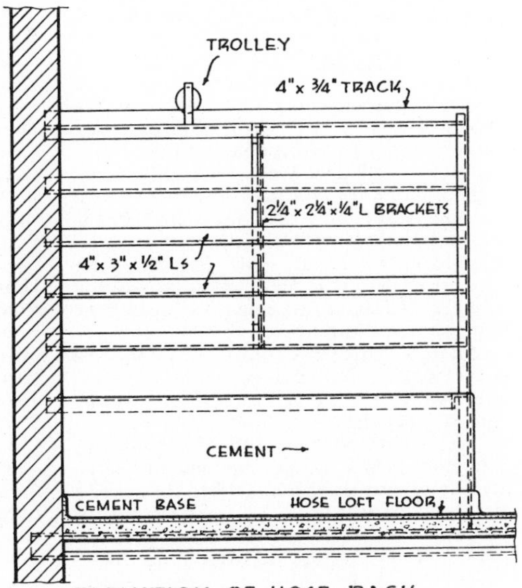

TROLLEY

TROLLEY

4" x ¾" TRACK

2¼" x 2¼" x ¼" L BRACKETS

4" x 3" x ½" Ls

1'-5"
1'-1"
1'-1"
1'-1"
1'-1"

5" x 3½" x ½" L

4" TERRA COTTA

CEMENT

2'-6"

CEMENT

CEMENT BASE

HOSE LOFT FLOOR

SECTION AT HOSE RACK

ELEVATION OF HOSE RACK

CEMENT

METAL CLAD DOOR

1½" HICKORY ROLLER

3" x 3" x ¼" L

7'-9" TO TOP OF DOOR OPENING

5"   FL

CEMENT

LEAD WEIGHT

METAL CLAD WOOD DOORS, TO SLIDE UP

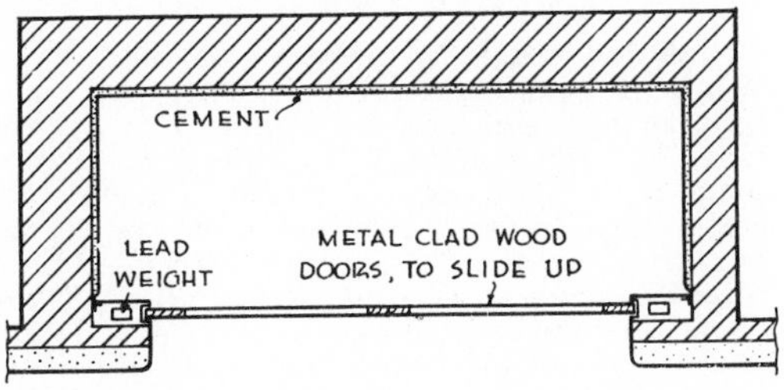

SECTION THROUGH SHAFT

PLAN OF HOSE SHAFT

SCALE ¼" = 1'-0"

DETAIL OF DRYING TOWER

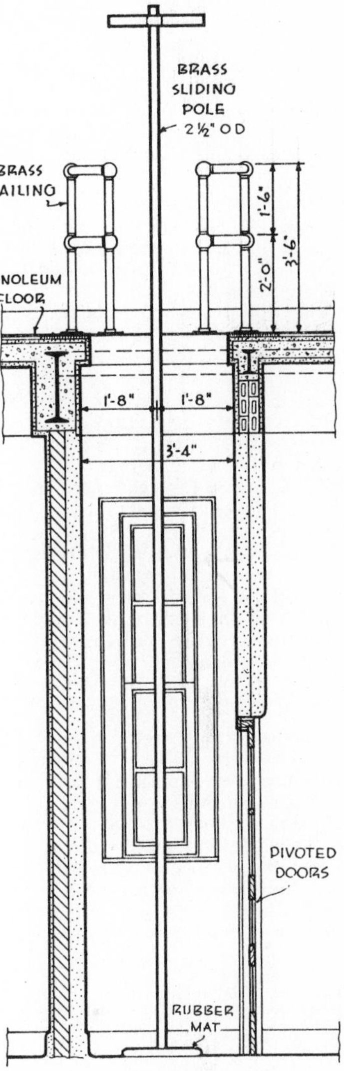

BRASS SLIDING POLE 2½" OD

BRASS RAILING

LINOLEUM FLOOR

1'-6"
2'-0"
3'-6"

1'-8"   1'-8"

3'-4"

PIVOTED DOORS

RUBBER MAT

SECTION

NOTE: SLIDING POLE SHOULD EITHER BE ENCLOSED AS SHOWN IN DETAIL, OR THE OPENING SHOULD BE PROVIDED WITH A CLOSING DEVICE TO PREVENT DRAFTS AND FUMES FROM PASSING THROUGH TO SECOND FLOOR. OPEN POLE SHAFTS RESULT IN HEAT LOSS.

SLIDING POLE EQUIPMENT AND SPECIAL CLOSING DEVICES ARE AVAILABLE FROM THE SEVERAL MANUFACTURERS

FOR VOLUNTEER FIRE DEPARTMENTS, POLE SHAFTS SHOULD BE DESIGNED WITH VIEW TO SAFETY FACTOR

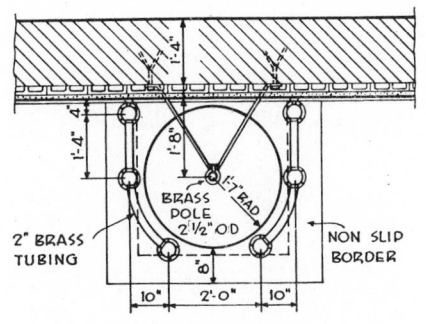

BRASS POLE 2½" OD

2" BRASS TUBING

NON SLIP BORDER

1'-4"
1'-8"
4"

10"   2'-0"   10"

PLAN AT SECOND FLOOR

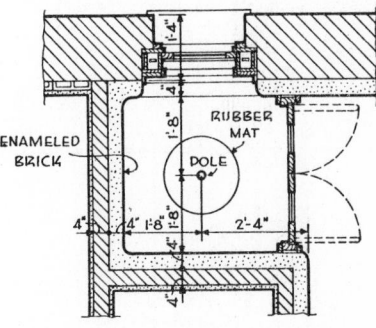

ENAMELED BRICK

RUBBER MAT

POLE

4"   1'-8"   2'-4"

1'-8"

4"

PLAN AT FIRST FLOOR

SCALE ¼" = 1'-0"

DETAIL OF SLIDING POLE SHAFT

Information on this sheet was collected and prepared by Ronald Allwork. Sources include: American Prison Association; Edward R. Cass, Commissioner, New York State Commission of Correction; A. H. MacCormick*; Harvey Wiley Corbett and Charles B. Meyers, Associated Architects.

General. Prime considerations for all jails are: **1,** Fireproof construction; **2,** Security; **3,** Heating; **4,** Lighting; **5,** Ventilation; **6,** Sanitation; and **7,** Low maintenance costs.

Types and sizes of jails vary from those which consist of but a few cells with no other facilities to large jails with many cells and complete facilities. In any case, each jail (or "lock-up") should maintain separate departments for males and females. Cells should not be located in the basement.

Cells are usually grouped in units called *cell blocks,* which may be one to four tiers in height. Single-tier cell blocks are preferred. Multiple tiers reduce the personnel needed for supervision and for guarding quarters. A two-tier cell block has many advantages and few disadvantages; but in small jails, proper classification of prisoners is made easier by using one-tier units.

Cell planning. Cells should accommodate one person only. If, due to unusual circumstances, provision must be made for more than one inmate per cell, each cell should accommodate three or four persons. Two persons should never be put together except in emergencies. Double-decked bunks are permissible.

Cells are of three types: Inside, Semi-outside, or Outside.

*Articles in "Prison World," official organ, American Prison and Nat'l. Jail Associations.

Inside cells are built back-to-back, with space between back walls for a utility corridor for plumbing, electrical conduits, and ventilating ducts. Fronts of cells are separated from outside walls and windows by a corridor, preferably 10 to 15 ft. wide, not less than 4½ ft. wide. A guards' corridor often is included along the outer wall; this may be separated from the day room (see drawing below) by a grille if cells are in single tiers. The guards' corridor may be elevated and equipped with an open rail for multi-tiered cells.

Semi-outside cells are built along the outside wall, but are separated from wall and windows by a narrow guards' corridor. Fronts of cells face a wide central corridor. Both front and back of cell are usually full-grilled for light and ventilation. Note utility shafts below.

Outside cells are built against the outer wall. Each cell contains its own window. Front of cell faces on a wide central corridor.

Day rooms are usually provided for prisoners who are not required to spend all their time in cells. Often the space in front of the cells is used for this purpose. In this case, corridors are approximately 10 ft. wide, and have fixed seats and tables. This prisoners' corridor should be separated from guards' corridor by tool-proof steel grilles.

Cell design. New York State Commissioner of Correction recommends that cells be not less than 5 ft. wide, 7 ft. long, 7 ft. high. Cells 6 ft. wide, 8 ft. long, 8 ft. high are preferred. Other states have similar regulations. Cells are sometimes constructed entirely of reinforced concrete (except for grilles, doors, and locking devices), but walls and ceilings of plate steel, and floors of concrete, are most common. Cell fronts are usually of ⅞-in. steel bars (round or

hexagonal) spaced approximately 5 in. on centers. Certain types, such as isolation cells, have closed fronts. Full-grilled cell fronts permit better supervision; and, in the case of outside and semi-outside types, improve lighting and ventilation of central corridors. Solid cell fronts provide greater privacy and do not permit prisoners to converse across the corridor, but are more difficult to supervise. When this type of front is used, a small glass viewing panel, and ventilating louvers, are needed.

Cell doors are preferably of the sliding type. A "food-pass" should be provided in either the cell front or the door. Cell fronts and doors do not need to be of tool-proof steel. Many jails have tool-proof steel on windows and at exits from prisoners' living quarters, and ordinary steel elsewhere. Detention-type steel sash are now commonly used in place of window-bars.

Locking devices, of a type which will lock or unlock a single cell, any number or combination of cells, or all cells, from a single control point, are desirable. If this type is too expensive, a bar-and-lever type, designed to hold or release all doors in a unit simultaneously, is quite acceptable. This latter type should be supplemented by individual locks on doors.

Furniture and equipment. Each cell requires a vitreous integral-seat water closet, placed directly on the cell wall and operated by a flushometer (if possible) with push button or other simple, not easily broken, device. A lavatory, metal mirror, bunk, seat, table, book shelf, clothes bar, and adequate lighting equipment are also required. All furnishings should be of metal to reduce fire hazard and danger of vermin. All should be firmly and permanently attached to cell walls.

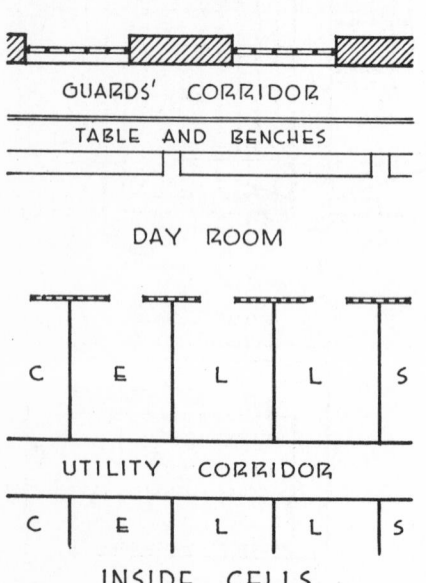

INSIDE CELLS

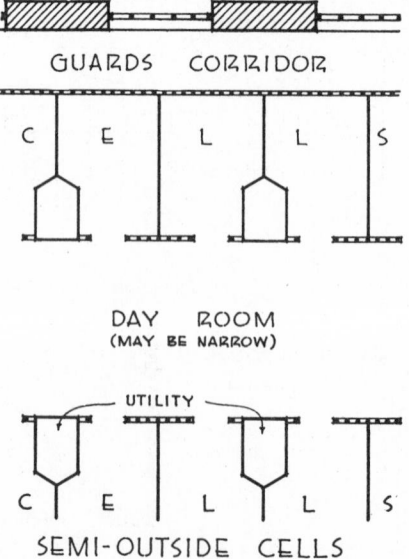

SEMI-OUTSIDE CELLS

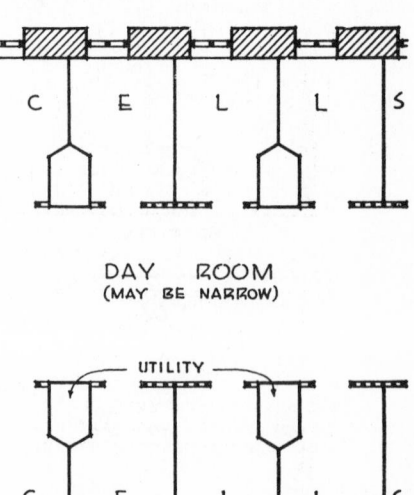

OUTSIDE CELLS

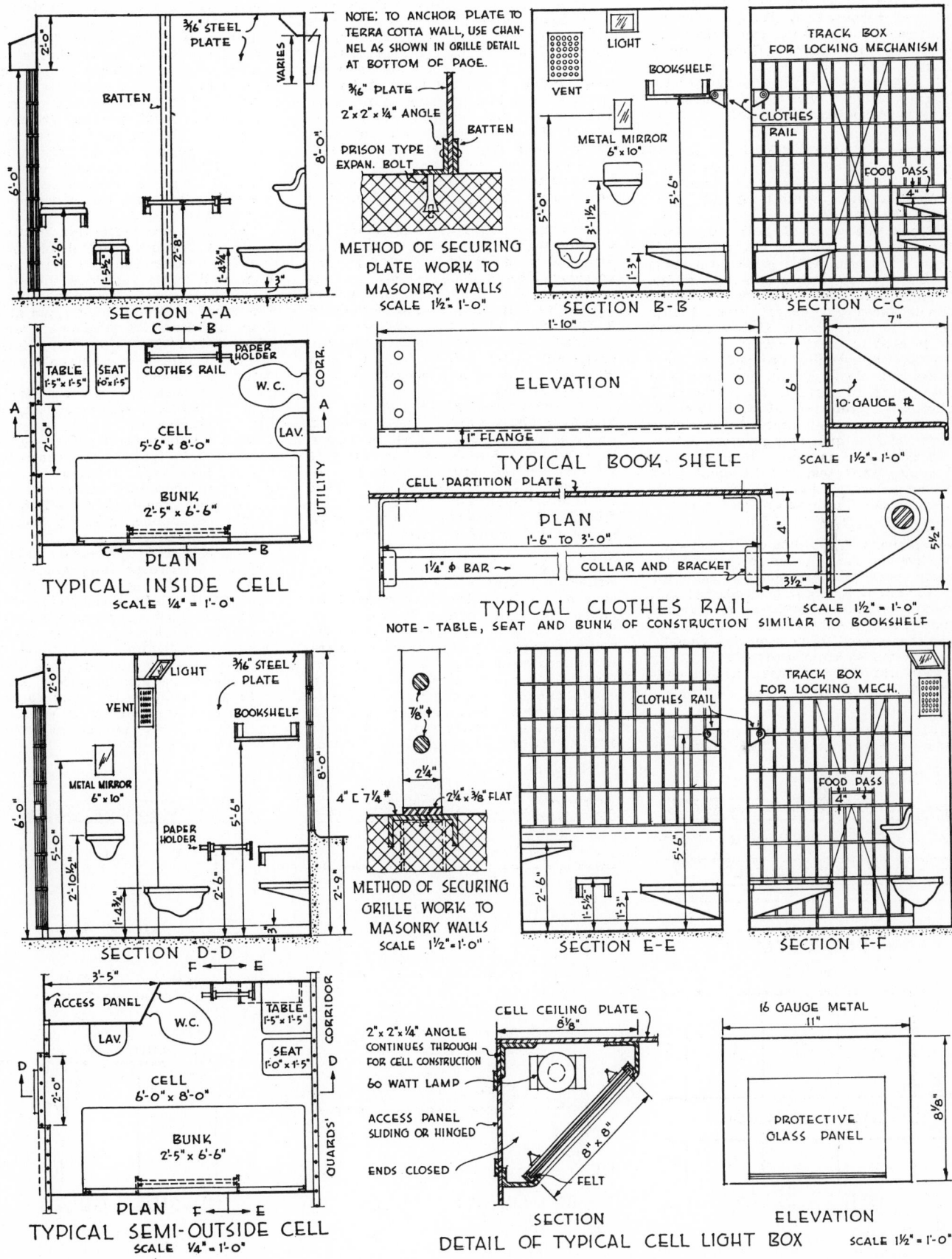

SECTION A-A

3/16" STEEL PLATE

BATTEN

NOTE: TO ANCHOR PLATE TO TERRA COTTA WALL, USE CHANNEL AS SHOWN IN GRILLE DETAIL AT BOTTOM OF PAGE.

3/16" PLATE
2" x 2" x 1/4" ANGLE
BATTEN
PRISON TYPE EXPAN. BOLT

METHOD OF SECURING PLATE WORK TO MASONRY WALLS
SCALE 1½" = 1'-0"

LIGHT
VENT
BOOKSHELF
METAL MIRROR 6" x 10"

SECTION B-B

TRACK BOX FOR LOCKING MECHANISM
CLOTHES RAIL
FOOD PASS

SECTION C-C

TABLE 1'-5" x 1'-5"
SEAT 1'-0" x 1'-5"
CLOTHES RAIL
PAPER HOLDER
W.C.
LAV.
CORR.
UTILITY
CELL 5'-6" x 8'-0"
BUNK 2'-5" x 6'-6"

PLAN
TYPICAL INSIDE CELL
SCALE 1/4" = 1'-0"

ELEVATION
1'-10"
1" FLANGE
7"
6"
10 GAUGE R

TYPICAL BOOK SHELF
SCALE 1½" = 1'-0"

CELL PARTITION PLATE
PLAN
1'-6" TO 3'-0"
1¼" Φ BAR
COLLAR AND BRACKET
4"
5½"
3½"

TYPICAL CLOTHES RAIL
SCALE 1½" = 1'-0"
NOTE - TABLE, SEAT AND BUNK OF CONSTRUCTION SIMILAR TO BOOKSHELF

SECTION D-D

LIGHT
VENT
3/16" STEEL PLATE
BOOKSHELF
METAL MIRROR 6" x 10"
PAPER HOLDER

7/8" Φ
2¼"
4" [7¼ #
2¼" x 3/8" FLAT

METHOD OF SECURING GRILLE WORK TO MASONRY WALLS
SCALE 1½" = 1'-0"

CLOTHES RAIL

SECTION E-E

TRACK BOX FOR LOCKING MECH.
FOOD PASS 4"

SECTION F-F

ACCESS PANEL
LAV.
W.C.
TABLE 1'-5" x 1'-5"
SEAT 1'-0" x 1'-5"
CORRIDOR
GUARDS'
CELL 6'-0" x 8'-0"
BUNK 2'-5" x 6'-6"
3'-5"

PLAN
TYPICAL SEMI-OUTSIDE CELL
SCALE 1/4" = 1'-0"

CELL CEILING PLATE
8⅛"
2" x 2" x 1/4" ANGLE CONTINUES THROUGH FOR CELL CONSTRUCTION
60 WATT LAMP
ACCESS PANEL SLIDING OR HINGED
ENDS CLOSED
8" x 8"
FELT

SECTION

16 GAUGE METAL
11"
PROTECTIVE GLASS PANEL
8⅛"

ELEVATION

DETAIL OF TYPICAL CELL LIGHT BOX
SCALE 1½" = 1'-0"

SECTION VII: SITE PLANNING AND RECREATION

Site Planning 1223
Automobiles:
  Dimensions 1238
  Garages, residential 1239
  Garages, parking 1240
  Parking lots 1243
  Driveways 1245
Landscaping:
  Driveways 1248
  Gutters and curbs 1249
  Drainage 1250
  Walks and terraces 1251
  Steps 1253
  Furniture 1254
  Banks 1254
  Walls 1255
  Trees 1256
  Lighting 1256
  Pools 1257
  Fountains 1258
Recreation:
  Children 1260
  Adults 1263
  Tennis courts 1268
  Squash courts 1270
  Locker rooms 1272
  Bath houses 1274
  Public swimming pools 1276
  Diving pools 1282
  Residential swimming pools 1284
  Stadia: seating design 1287
  Stadia: exit design 1288
  Community buildings: planning 1291
  Community buildings: details 1292

Index 1293

By HOWARD P. VERMILYA, AIA

SITE PLANNING AND SUBDIVISION LAYOUT

Site planning in its narrow sense involves the disposition of space for appropriate uses; the positioning of structures to provide effective relationships (well-proportioned masses with attractive outlooks and good orientation); the provision of access to structures in an expeditious, attractive, and safe manner; the design of the services, walks, streets, parking facilities, drainage, and utilities; the preservation of the natural advantage of the site, and its enhancement by landscaping.

In its larger sense, site planning involves consideration of the site in relation to the physical pattern and economic growth trends of the larger area of which it is a part. An analysis of the area should be made based on population growth, family formations, family size, housing inventory, income levels, schools, taxes and assessments, transportation and traffic patterns, and directions of growth. An analysis of site development costs should be made in terms of densities, housing types, construction types, topography and grading, and local requirements with regard to zoning, subdivision regulations, and utility services. This analysis may be made as a basis for site selection or as a basis for determining the most appropriate use of a particular site. For large sites involving several types of housing, commercial or industrial uses, schools, and churches, more extensive analyses may be necessary. For small sites forming parts of neighborhoods already established, the analysis need not be as comprehensive.

A subdivision site plan can be made for a complete community, involving all types of land use found in a typical town or village, or for a neighborhood, usually considered to be a homogeneous area large enough to support an elementary school, or for a segment of a neighborhood. The

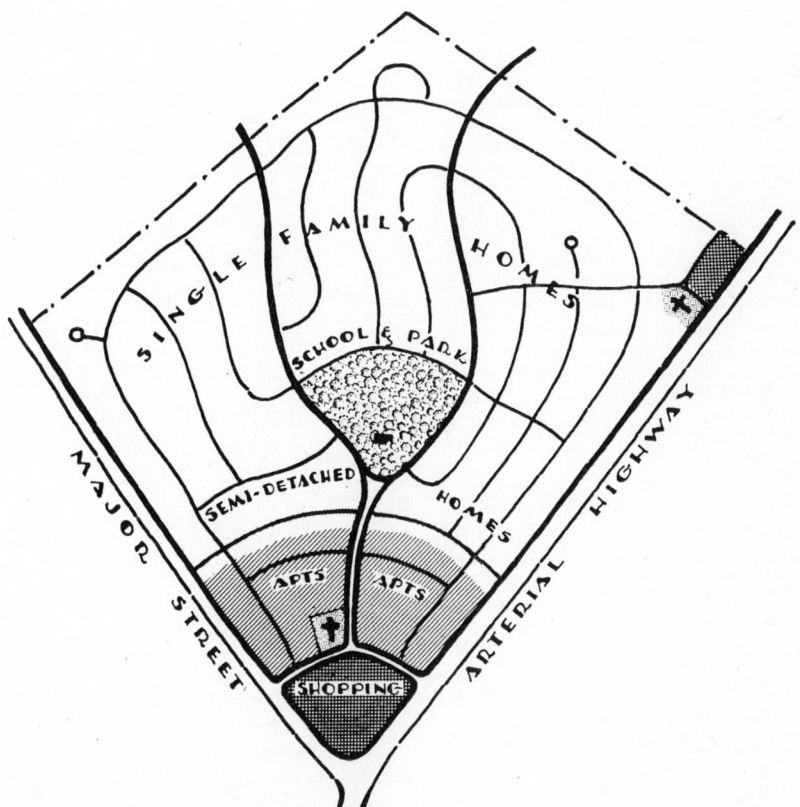

Fig. 1. Principles of neighborhood planning
Courtesy Urban Land Institute

1. *Size.* A residential unit development should provide housing for that population for which one elementary school is ordinarily required, its actual area depending upon its population density.

2. *Boundaries.* The unit should be bounded by arterial streets sufficiently wide to facilitate traffic by-passing the neighborhood instead of passing through it.

3. *Open Spaces.* Small park and recreation space, planned to meet the needs of the particular neighborhood should be provided.

4. *Institution Sites.* Sites for the school and other institutions having service spheres coinciding with the limits of the unit should be suitably grouped about a central point or common, and combined with the neighborhood recreation area, usually.

5. *Local Shopping Center.* If warranted by the population to be served the local convenience shopping facility should be located at the edge preferably at an arterial traffic junction and adjacent to similar commercial districts, if any, of adjoining neighborhoods.

6. *Internal Street System.* The unit should be provided with a special street system, each highway being proportioned to its probable traffic load, and the street net as a whole being designed to facilitate circulation within the unit with good access to main arteries, and to discourage its use by through traffic.

Sites are provided for parks, playing fields and recreational areas.

Church sites are provided in convenient locations.

There is a central shopping area, with off-street parking.

Two school sites are provided, reasonably accessible from all parts of the neighborhood. The Catholic school is off-centre because it also serves adjacent neighborhoods.

"Through" arterial highways, of adequate width, are separated from local service roads by limited access planted strips. Thus both "local" and "through" traffic are safeguarded. There are feeder roads for bus routes. Local residential streets are designed in such a way as to discourage "through" driving, yet remain adequate for local purposes.

At the corners of the area, there are intersections designed to keep "through" traffic moving.

One-family housing is created in an aesthetic as well as a functional setting. Set-backs are arranged to allow for a "rhythmic variation". A buffer strip separates housing from an adjacent industrial zone.

There are also apartments and row housing in a variety of types.

A neighborhood "focus" of larger buildings and open space is included as an essential ingredient of a well-designed residential area.

KEY

☐ Parks, Playing Fields, Recreational Areas

▨ Shopping Centre with off street parking

▨ Apartment and row housing sites

▨ Church

Fig. 2. Example of well-planned neighborhood
Courtesy Urban Land Institute

principles of neighborhood planning are illustrated in Fig. 1; an example of a well-planned neighborhood is shown in Fig. 2.

Housing types

It is no longer considered good practice to limit housing within a subdivision to one type and price range. For sites of fewer than 100 houses the range of types should be restricted but the range in price should permit some variation, the degree of difference being reduced as the size of the site diminishes. For larger sites not only may the types of single-family houses be varied, but rental housing of either high-rise or garden types may be included where zoning permits. Apartments and town houses (row houses in small groups) often provide a very satisfactory transition between the commercial (shopping) areas and the less dense residential areas.

Single-family housing: Lot sizes for the single-family detached house are wider now than they were 30 years ago; 60 ft is considered the minimum width and 70 to 80 ft is more usual. This has come about because of the popularity of the one-story house

with large glass areas and provisions for outdoor living with a reasonable degree of privacy. Devices such as patios and courts and fenced-in areas are used to provide privacy when lot sizes are small. An example of a typical one-story subdivision house of better than average design is shown in Fig. 3. The split-level house is also popular in subdivision work because it provides the economy of the two-story house but requires less stair climbing.

Row houses or, as they are now called, town houses are finding many advocates because of their economical use of land and low site-development costs. When developed with not more than 8 or 10 units (preferably fewer) in one group and located around a court, cul-de-sac, or loop street, the monotonous appearance usually associated with such housing disappears. Lots should be 20 to 25 ft wide; wider lots with side yards should be provided at the ends of the groups. Garages should be provided either within the house structure itself or as a one-story attached structure, often a carport, at the front of the house. An example of the variety possible within this

housing type is shown in Fig. 4; see also Fig. 16.

Rental housing, for more attractive appearance, is now built at lower densities and with more emphasis on open space; it often includes such club-like features as swimming pools and tennis courts. Densities of 15 to 25 families per acre and coverages of 15 to 25 per cent are standard in well-designed garden apartment developments. Garden apartments are usually two stories high and should not be higher than three stories (Fig. 5). High-rise elevator apartments should restrict land coverage to 10 to 15 per cent. The trend in apartment design is toward larger rooms, more storage, and other facilities in keeping with those of single-family housing (see section on "Apartments").

Lot sizes and development costs

The cost of raw land and the cost of installing streets and utilities has greatly increased in recent years. At the same time, as previously noted, lot widths have markedly increased. In order to keep the cost of the developed lot from rising to prohibi-

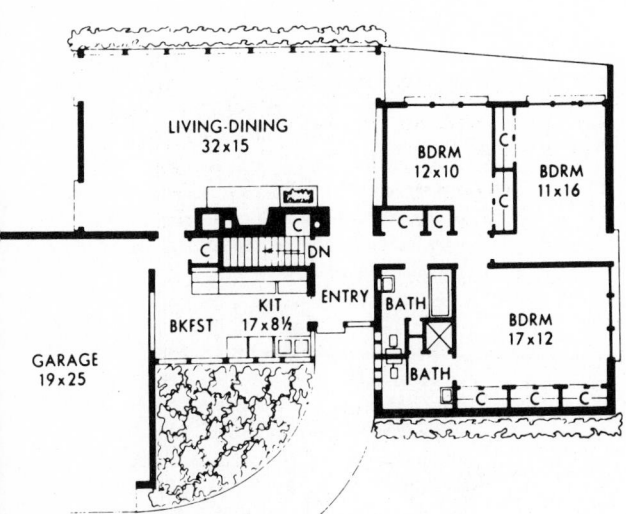

3. One-story house plan
Courtesy National Association of Home Builders

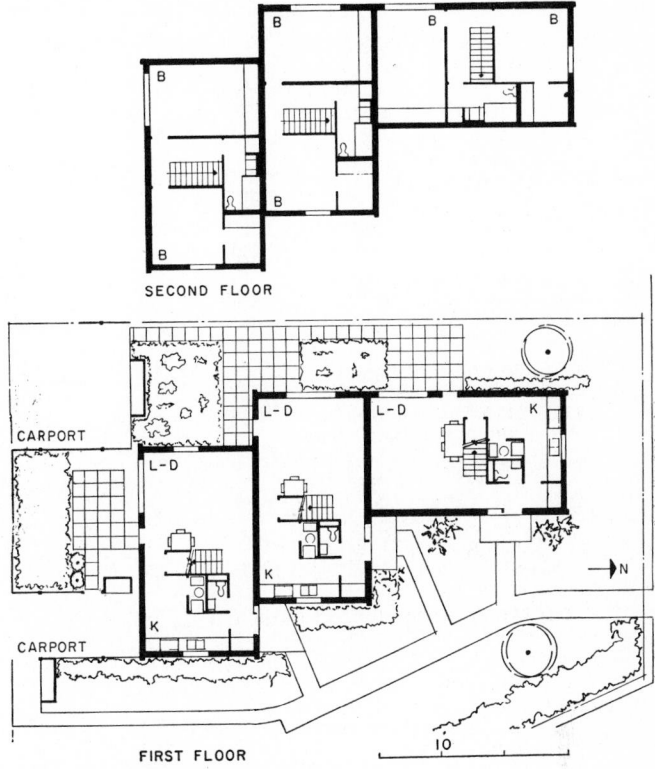

SECOND FLOOR

FIRST FLOOR

Fig. 4. Row house scheme for irregular site
Yost and Taylor, Architects
George E. Treichel, Landscape Architect

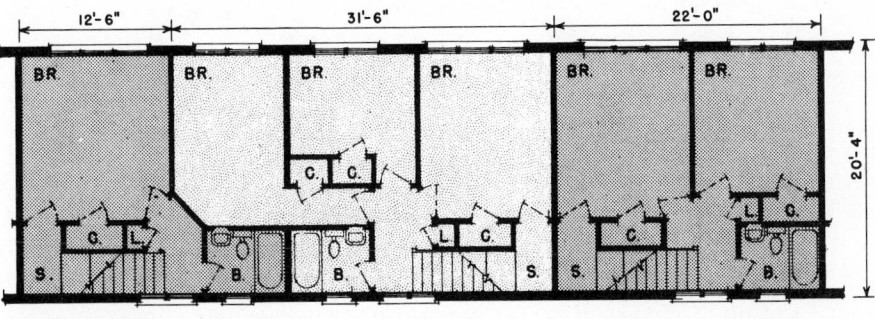

SECOND FLOOR

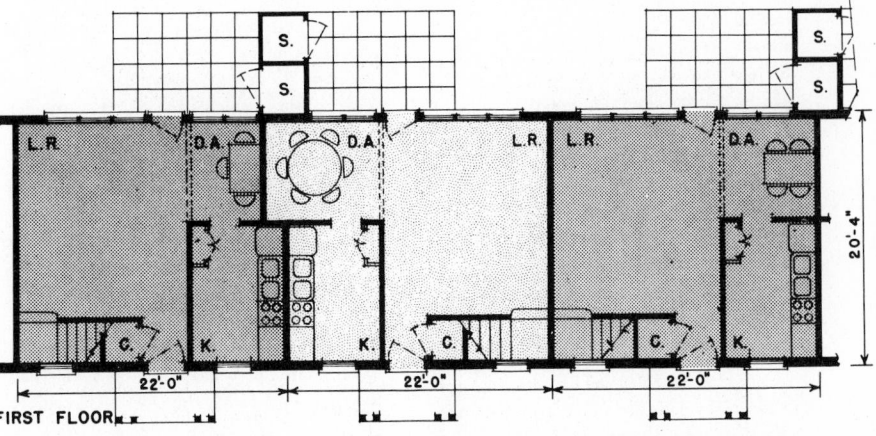

FIRST FLOOR

ONE—BEDROOM UNIT
Total Floor Area 753 Sq. Ft.

THREE—BEDROOM UNIT
Total Floor Area 1036 Sq. Ft.

TWO—BEDROOM UNIT
Total Floor Area 896 Sq. Ft.

Fig. 5. Two-story garden apartment plan
Courtesy Federal Housing Administration

tive levels, site planners have resorted to the "superblock." This is typically a long, shallow block (600–800 ft by 200–250 ft) which reduces the number of cross streets and eliminates the need for utilities in them. Typical lot depths are thus likely to be 1½ to 2 times their width. Deep superblocks, penetrated by culs-de-sac or loop streets, are also used. Further economies in development costs result from the use of a functional street system, as described later on, which permits most of the streets to be built to the most economical specifications (see also Fig. 15 and the discussion of the *cluster* plan).

Basic data for estimating lot costs are given in Tables 1 and 2 and Fig. 6.

Streets

Conformance with the master street plan for the city is usually a requisite for any subdivision plan. As a rule, however, this requirement applies only to major streets. It is a factor which should be given consideration in the initial analysis of the site since it is undesirable to have major streets traverse a residential area. At the boundaries, however, major streets may be an asset if they provide good access to other areas in the community.

Fire protection should be considered in determining the street pattern. Some of the problems to consider are hydrant location, culs-de-sac turn-arounds, access to buildings in multifamily projects and commercial areas, radius of curvature of curbs at intersections, and similar problems.

Streets are necessary evils in a neighborhood or smaller subdivision; they are intended primarily to provide access to and circulation within the area. Streets serving other purposes (arterial streets) should

Table 1.   Lot sizes and dwelling densities

From Community Builders Handbook, *Urban Land Institute.*

Dwelling Unit Type	Lot Dimensions Per Dwelling Unit in Feet	Net Density* Dwelling Units/Acre
Single Family		
Detached houses	100 x 200	2.0
	80 x 160	3.5
	70 x 140	3.3
	60 x 125	4.3
	50 x 100	6.5
Semi-Detached houses	30 x 125	8.7
	26 x 125	10.0
Row houses, two-story	20 x 100	16.3
	16 x 100	20.4
Garden Apartments, two-story		15 – 25
Garden Apartments, three-story		25 – 35
Apartments, multiple story to 12 stories		50 – 85

* Net density represents the number of dwelling units per acre of land within the site, after deducting 25 per cent of the site for allocation to streets, park and recreation areas.

Gross density is computed on the basis of net land area plus area devoted to streets and other nonresidential uses and one-half of bounding streets and one-quarter of bounding street intersections.

Table 2.   Lot areas and dwelling densities

Dwelling Unit Type	D.U.'s per Net Acre	Assumed Average Sq. Ft. of Lot per D.U.
Single-family	1	40,000
" "	2	20,000
" "	3	12,500
" "	4	10,000
Two-family	6	6,000
Row house	15	2,600
Garden apartment*	25	1,600
Multi-story apartments*	50	800

* The more intensive the use of land, the greater need there is for recreation space, wider streets and sidewalks, shorter blocks and off-street parking. In multi-family development careful consideration must be given to land coverage and open space needs. High density, multi-family intrusions into single family residential development must be avoided. Apartment buildings must be spaced and located within the project so as to provide transition between residential land uses. The developer of multi-family areas has a responsibility in making such sections of his city fitting, appropriate and serviceable to his community.

bound rather than penetrate the area. The street pattern within the area should be designed to discourage through traffic. The widths of the interior streets should be consistent with their function and the density of housing they serve and should be no greater than necessary, in the interest of safety and economy of installation and maintenance. Subdivision street types are illustrated in Fig. 7. Collector streets, those carrying traffic from minor streets to arterial streets should have a paved width of 36 ft, consisting of two moving lanes and two parking lanes. Minor streets, depending on the off-street parking provisions and the density of the area they serve, should be 26 ft wide for single-family detached houses and 32 ft wide for row houses and apartments. Short access streets, such as culs-de-sac or loop streets, may have mini-mum paved widths of 20 ft. Culs-de-sac should terminate in a turning circle not less than 80 ft in diameter between curbs. Rights-of-way should be 60 ft wide for collector streets, 50 ft for minor streets, and 40 ft for culs-de-sac and minor access streets. A cul-de-sac should not be in excess of 500 ft in length (see Fig. 8 and Table 3).

The use of the "T" intersection of minor streets and of minor with collector streets, with at least a 125-ft separation between opposing intersections, offers a device to reduce through traffic within a subdivision area and improve the safety conditions (Fig. 9). Slight jogs in the alignment of streets are not desirable.

Where the subdivision borders on arterial highways or streets bearing heavy traffic, houses should not be entered directly from such streets. Instead, the lots should be backed up to the highway and heavy planting should be provided along the rear-lot lines. Or a local access road should be provided parallel to the highway and screened from it by planting (Fig. 10). Either method serves to reduce the number of street intersections with main traffic ways to a minimum and to keep driveways off the main highway.

Sidewalks

The design of sidewalks is often governed by local regulations. Sometimes they may be omitted in low-density areas of single-family detached homes. Some jurisdictions permit installation on one side of the street only, others require sidewalks within certain distances of schools, usually inside the zones beyond which school busses operate. Higher-density areas (more than 5 families per acre) and streets carrying other than local traffic usually require sidewalks on both sides of the street.

Four feet is the customary design width for sidewalks. When combined with the curb they may sometimes be as narrow as 3 ft 6 in.; in commercial areas they should be much wider. When sidewalks are separated from the curb by a planting strip, the strip should be at least 3 ft wide to provide for snow removal; if trees are included it should be at least 7 ft wide (see Fig. 8 and Table 3).

Curbs

The rolled curb is more economical than the straight curb and does not require cutting at driveways. It is not recommended however on steep grades or in hillside developments. When used, rolled curbs should be molded into straight curbs at intersections to discourage corner cutting. The suggested radius of 15 ft for curbs at right-angle intersections discourages speeding and is intended for intersections of minor streets. Cuts in straight curbs for driveways should provide for 3 to 5 ft radiuses and a 9 or 10-ft wide driveway.

Lot layout

The layout of the lots in a subdivision can make the difference between an attractive and an unattractive development, also the difference between an economical and an uneconomical project. Good and poor lotting practices are illustrated in Fig. 11 and methods of lotting around culs-de-sac are shown in Fig. 12.

Topography

Topography can influence the character of a subdivision. Hilly land, with grades steeper than 10 per cent, may be developed for low-density, higher-priced homes,

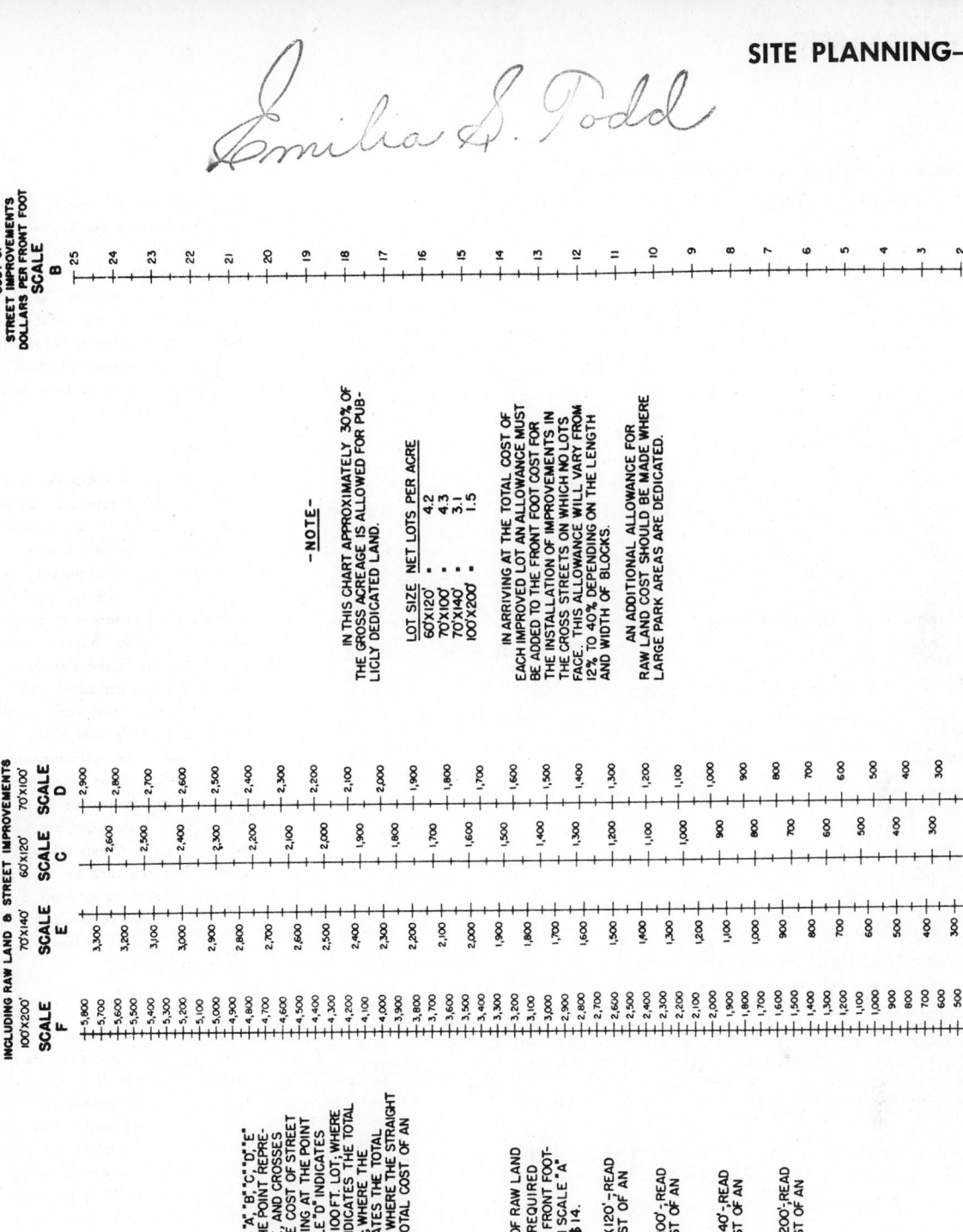

Fig. 6. Computing chart to find the total cost of an improved lot (raw land and street improvements)
Courtesy Federal Housing Administration

or for multifamily projects of relatively low density, but it is rarely adaptable to small lots and lower-cost homes. Flat land, because of the difficulty of obtaining good drainage for sewers and storm drains, may also not be suitable for low-priced homes. Gently sloping land without drainage pockets or swampy areas or underlying rock is best for low-cost development. Where public sewerage is not available the character of the soil is an important factor and may even determine the lot sizes. Soil seepage tests are usually required by health departments where septic tanks and disposal fields are installed. If public water service is not available and individual wells must be used, this too may affect lot sizes. Community water and sewerage systems should be provided wherever possible in these cases; wells and septic tanks should be used only as a last resort.

The nature of the topography will affect the street pattern. Streets should be laid out so as to avoid steep grades, excessive cut and fill, and to provide buildable sites with good surface drainage. In general, streets should follow natural drainage lines or ridge locations. On side hill locations, they should cut across the contour lines, in order to avoid cut and fill operations.

Steep grades can be reduced on hilly land by running streets diagonally across the contours.

Surface drainage: Not only must the entire site be graded for proper drainage, but each individual lot and block must be separately and carefully considered. Examples of proper grading for surface drainage of lots and blocks are shown in Figs. 13 and 14.

Off-street parking: For single-family detached houses parking is usually provided in an attached garage or carport. The setback from the street is normally sufficient to permit overflow parking in the driveway. Apartments are usually provided with parking bays or courts located reasonably near the building entrances. Suggested designs for such parking areas are shown in Fig. 15 (see also sections on "Apartments" and "Automobiles: Parking").

For parking areas at neighborhood shopping centers see sections on "Shopping Centers" and "Automobiles: Parking."

Recreation areas are essential and should represent at least 5 per cent of the residential area and more where the lots are small (see sections on "Apartments" and "Recreation.") Playgrounds for small children ("tot lots") may be quite small but they must be widely dispersed throughout the site. Playgrounds for older children are best provided by enlarging the school site and its playground. This provides an adequate recreation area in one place and simplifies supervision and maintenance. Wherever possible, recreation areas should be maintained by the local government. When recreation areas provided by the developer are not taken over by the local government, they must be maintained cooperatively by the residents through a neighborhood association, as discussed farther on.

Table 3. Design of local residential streets

From Traffic Engineering Handbook *of Institute of Traffic Engineers and* Home Builders Manual for Land Development *of National Association of Home Builders.*

Speed: Based on maximum of 25 m.p.h. in accord with Uniform Vehicle Code recommendation. Recommendations will be reasonably satisfactory if some speeds exceed 25 m.p.h. a little.

	Single-family Units	*Multi-family Units*
Street Width:	50 feet	60 feet
Pavement Width:	26 feet	32 feet
Curbs:	Straight curb recommended	Same
Sidewalks		
Width:	4 feet minimum	Same
Set-Back:	3 feet minimum if no trees, 7 feet minimum with trees	Same
Horizontal Alignment:	200 feet minimum sight distance	Same
Vertical Alignment:	6-8 per cent maximum grade desirable 3-4 per cent per 100 feet maximum rate of change	Same
Cul-de-sac:	400-500 feet maximum length	Same
Turn-arounds:	40 feet minimum curb radius without parking	Same
	50 feet minimum curb radius with parking	Same
Pavement Surface:	Non-skid with strength to carry traffic load	Same

SUBDIVISION REGULATIONS

Subdivision of the land is a permanent change which determines the use of the land for at least a generation and profoundly affects the surrounding area. The public interest is thus directly concerned and local governments now generally exercize strict controls over this important function. Most municipalities, many counties, and some states now have subdivision regulations. These generally require conformance with established standards of design and construction such as:

Streets: location, types, rights-of-way widths, pavement widths and specifications, grades, intersections, curvatures, alignments, curbs, gutters, sidewalks

Blocks: length, width, crosswalks, utility easements
Lots: size, shape, minimum dimensions
Open spaces: size, type
Utilities: storm and sanitary sewers, culverts, bridges, water service; monuments
Names: of area and streets; street numbers

PROTECTIVE COVENANTS

Covenants, sometimes called deed restrictions and sometimes protective covenants, are usually drafted by the subdivider of an area to provide land use regulations for the entire area, either supplementing those of the zoning ordinance or in lieu of it. They are, or should be, recorded and made superior to the lien of any mortgage and are intended to preserve the physical, economic, and esthetic qualities of the subdivision in the interests of the subdivider in aiding his development program and of the purchasers in protecting their investment. Enforcement should be delegated to a home owners or neighborhood association.

Protective covenants, being a contract or agreement between private parties, may include provisions which go well beyond the public health, safety and welfare provisions to which zoning regulations are limited. These may include any or all of the following:

Architectural control—Usually provides procedure for the review of designs for new construction and alterations for approval by a designated individual architect, or committee of the neighborhood

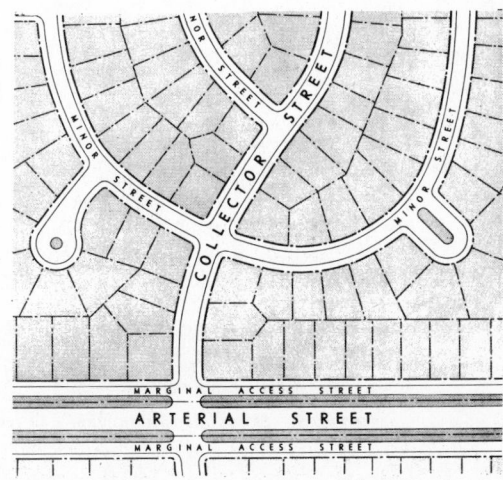

Fig. 7. Subdivision street types
Courtesy Housing and Home Finance Agency

Cross-section A. Provides two-way traffic with parallel parking on both sides. For collector streets in developments of one-family detached houses and for minor streets in apartment developments.

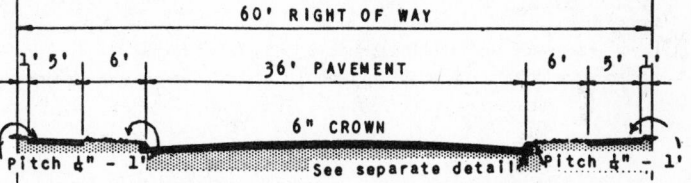

Cross-section B. Provides two-way traffic and one continuous lane of parallel parking on one side or parallel parking alternated on either side of the street. For minor streets in developments of one-family detached houses.

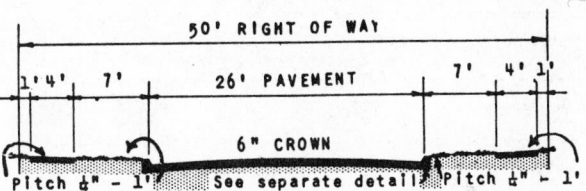

Cross-section C. Provides two-way traffic and drainage with all parking on individual driveways. For streets in country home developments.

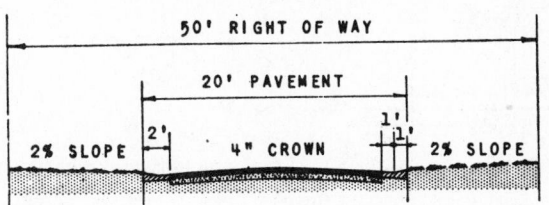

Cross-section D. Marginal access street paralleling an arterial highway. Provides two-way traffic, one lane of parallel parking, safe access to properties and protection from through traffic.

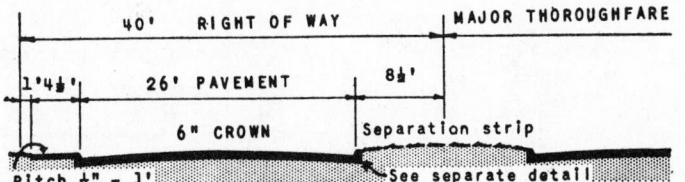

Cross-section E. Provides separated two-way traffic with parallel parking on both sides. For use as collector streets of the boulevard and development entranceway types.

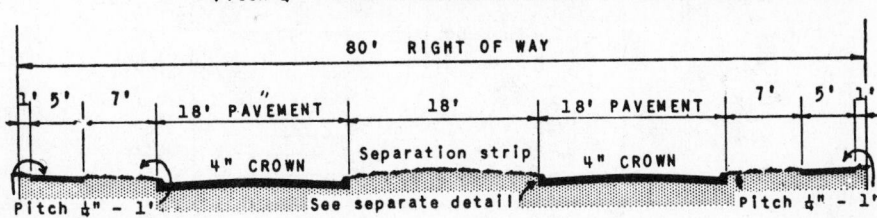

Fig. 8. Typical street cross sections
Courtesy Federal Housing Administration

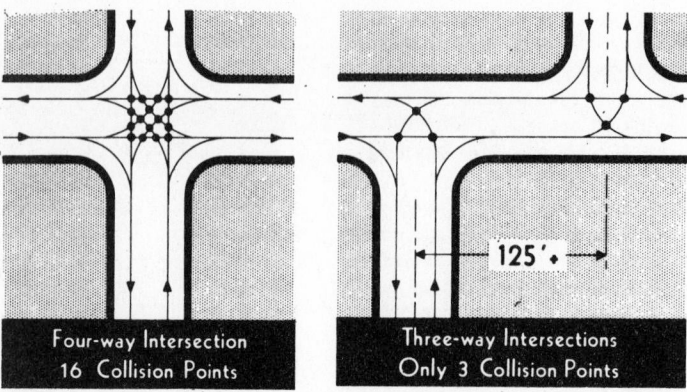

Fig. 9. Street intersection types and resulting traffic patterns
Courtesy Housing and Home Finance Agency

association, as to conformity with the esthetic character of the area.

Use and size of the structure may be limited more severely than required by the zoning ordinance. In particular, minimum sizes may be established. Size limitations may refer to height, number of stories, area, volume, or cost; the latter is not an effective device because of fluctuation of building costs.

Lot sizes and setbacks greater than required by the zoning ordinance may be called for.

Landscaping and fences may be controlled as to placement and height. This may be desirable for various reasons: to ensure visibility at street intersections, to prevent interference with surface drainage, or to preserve a desired esthetic character for the subdivision as a whole.

Nuisances: Various undesirable usages may be prohibited such as business, farming, mining, signs, outdoor garbage or refuse incineration, tents, trailers, etc.

Covenants usually run with the land for a definite term of years, with provision for renewal unless terminated or modified by agreement of the property owners affected. Restrictive covenants based on race or religion have been declared unconstitutional by the Supreme Court of the United States.

HOME OWNERS ASSOCIATIONS

Home owners associations or neighborhood associations, as they are sometimes called, are usually established by the subdivider to provide a means for carrying out certain community functions, such as the maintenance of recreation areas and the enforcement of protective covenants. The management of the association is usually turned over to the owners of the subdivided land when sales progress to a predetermined ratio. The association is usually established as a corporation with a charter from the state and reference to it is made in the protective covenants or deed restrictions. To be effective it should have the power to assess the property owners to obtain the funds necessary to carry out its functions. It should provide for representation of the owners in the selection of the management in an orderly manner through well-drafted bylaws. The functions of the Association can be any of the following:

Action to enforce the protective covenants in case of violation by any property owner, or where continuing action

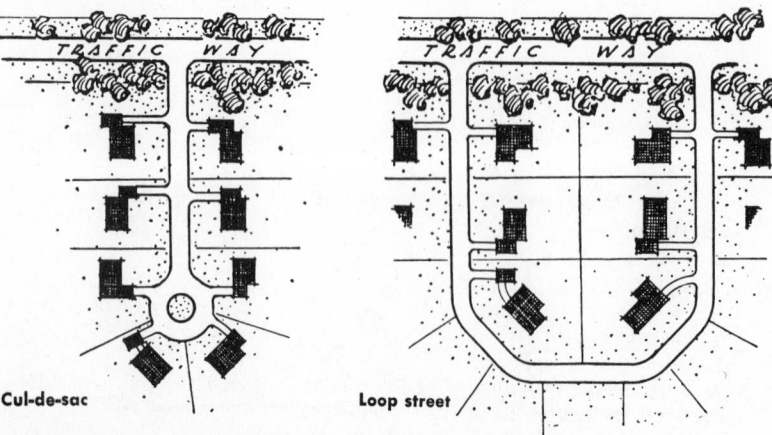

Backing on traffic way   Facing traffic way with access street

Cul-de-sac   Loop street

Fig. 10. Methods of subdividing along heavy traffic ways
Courtesy Urban Land Institute

is required as in the operation of an architectural control of design.

Operation of community facilities, such as club house or community center and recreational facilities such as playgrounds, swimming pools, tennis courts, or golf courses.

Maintenance of common land such as cul-de-sac turn-arounds and planting strips and unimproved property in absentee ownership (see *cluster* plans).

Maintenance and operation of community sewerage and water systems.

Performance of services such as street repair, snow removal, and garbage collection until taken over by the municipality.

Representation of the owners' needs or opinions to the public authorities.

Development of community programs—social, cultural, or recreational.

NEW APPROACHES

Although the standard subdivision technique of today is a vast improvement over the monotonous grid-iron plots of the past, many planners feel that it still leaves much to be desired. They believe that it is possible to preserve the beauty of the natural land, to relate the houses better to each other and to the site and provide more open space, all at less cost than in today's practice.

An early example of this type of thinking is the Radburn plan (1929) in which the houses are grouped on small lots around culs-de-sac which penetrate the periphery

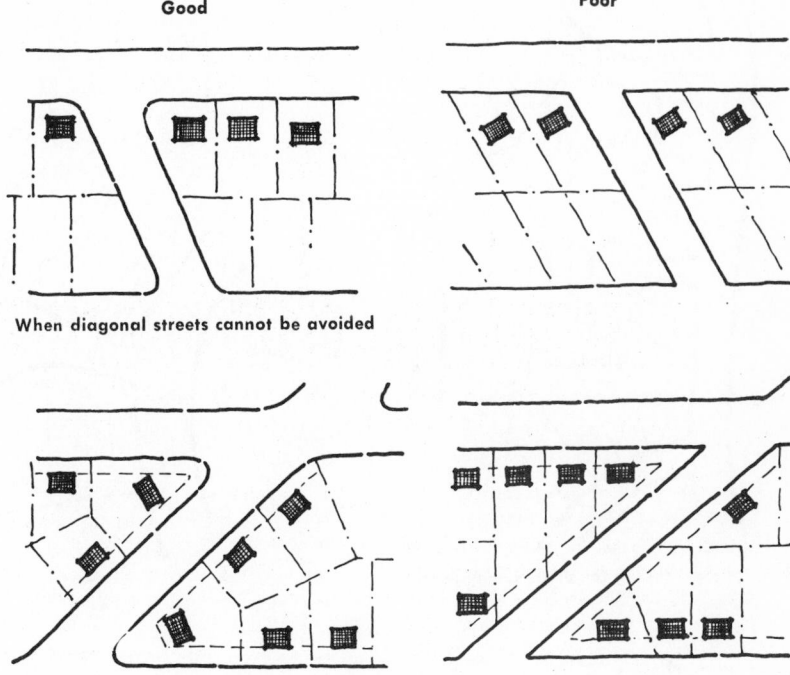

Existing street patterns

Good   Poor

When diagonal streets cannot be avoided

When existing streets form acute-angled intersections

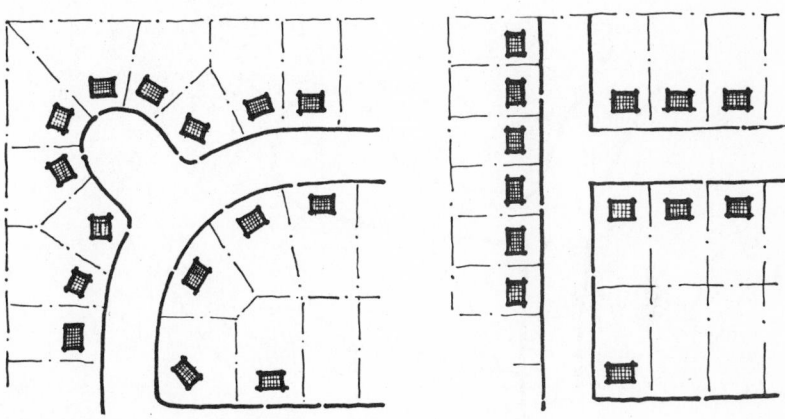

When future street extensions are not required in corners of the property

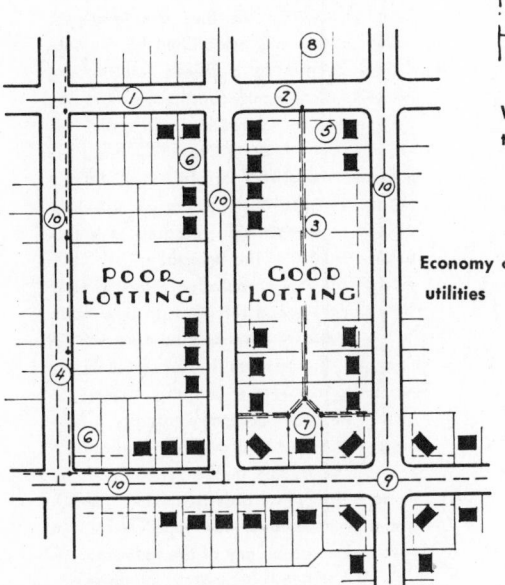

Fig. 11. Good and poor lotting practices
Courtesy Urban Land Institute

Economy of utilities

EXPLANATION

1. Excess underground utilities at end of block required.
2. No underground utilities at end of block.
3. Rear overhead utility easement.
4. Street overhead utilities.
5. Increased corner lot width.
6. Corner lots too narrow.
7. Good use of butt lot.
8. Butt lots require extra utilities with bad view down rear lot line.
9. Good lotting at street intersection.
10. Required underground utilities.

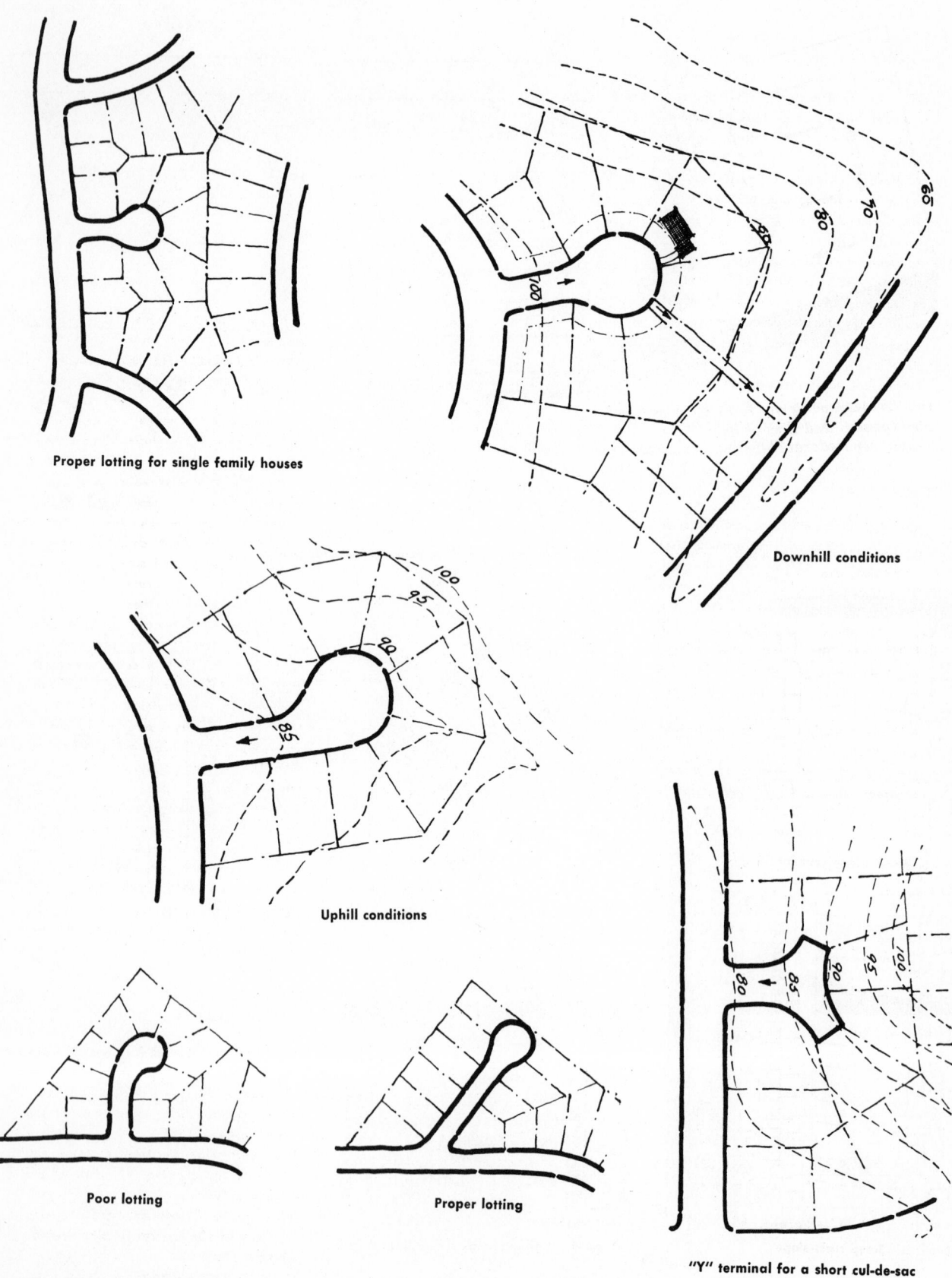

Proper lotting for single family houses

Downhill conditions

Uphill conditions

Poor lotting

Proper lotting

"Y" terminal for a short cul-de-sac

Fig. 12. Lotting around culs-de-sac
Courtesy Urban Land Institute

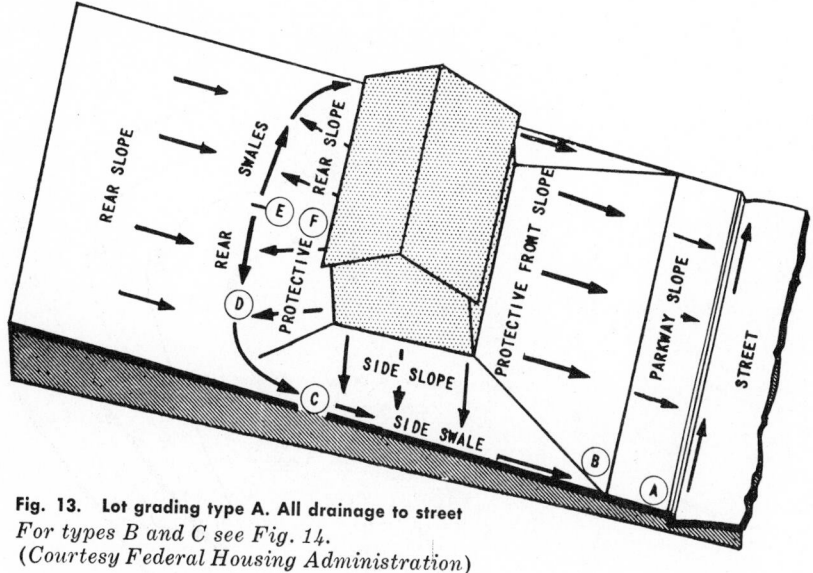

Fig. 13. Lot grading type A. All drainage to street
For types B and C see Fig. 14.
(Courtesy Federal Housing Administration)

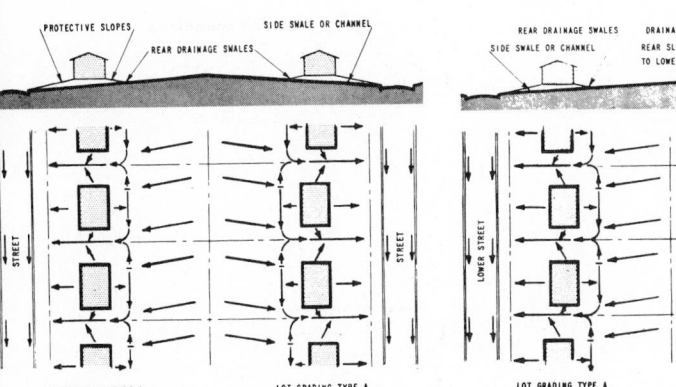

Type 1: Ridge along rear lot lines

Type 2: Gentle cross-slope

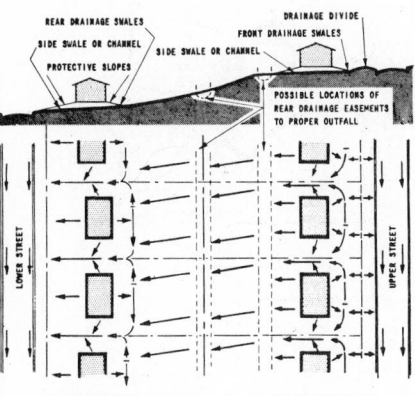

Type 3: Steep cross-slope

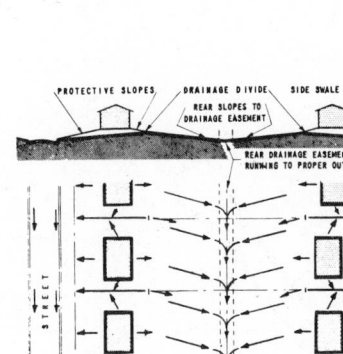

Type 4: Valley along rear lot lines

Fig. 14. Types of block grading
Courtesy Federal Housing Administration

of huge superblocks. The center of each superblock is a park on which all houses face. Pedestrian walks lead through the parks to schools, shopping, and transportation.

A more recent example of the same general approach is the *cluster* scheme shown in comparison with more conventional plans in Fig. 16. This plan reduces the cost of streets and utilities by half and leaves approximately half the total site for recreation. Every house abuts on a park or open land. Although normal suburban densities are maintained, the rural character of the land is preserved, there is less monotony in the appearance of the development, and better living qualities are provided, all at less cost than in conventional subdivisions. The common land must be maintained by a neighborhood association; it could be treated as a park or playground or it could be left in its natural state, especially if wooded, rocky, or otherwise attractive in appearance.

Unfortunately, neither the Radburn plan nor the cluster plan are permitted under most existing zoning ordinances and subdivision regulations. The rigidity of these regulations has been a serious handicap to any significant improvement in subdivision site planning. Further examples of this are illustrated in Fig. 17.

REFERENCES
(all Washington, D.C.)

Home Builder's Manual for Land Development, National Association of Home Builders, 1958.
Community Builder's Handbook, Urban Land Institute, 1956.
New Approaches to Land Development, Technical Bulletin No. 40, Urban Land Institute, 1960.
Neighborhood Standards, Land Planning Bulletin No. 3, Federal Housing Administration, 1956.
Suggested Land Subdivision Regulations, Housing and Home Finance Agency, 1962.

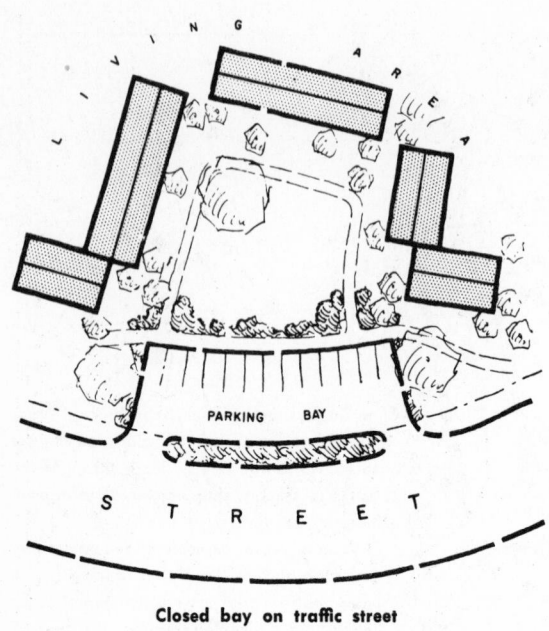

Closed bay on traffic street

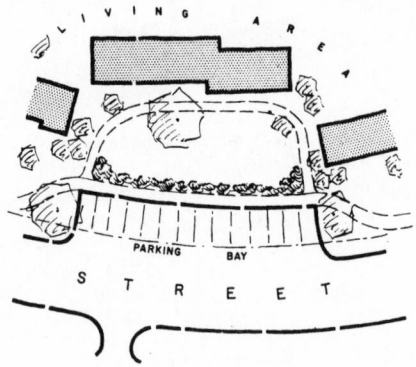

Open bay on minor street

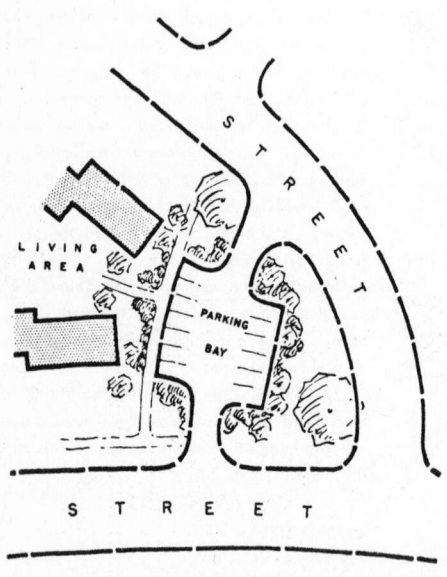

**Drive-through parking at acute-angle
street intersection**

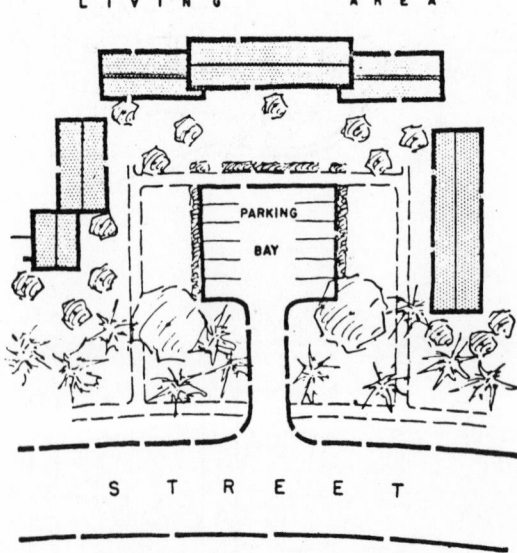

**Parking court used to preserve street trees
and bring parking closer to buildings**

Fig. 15. Parking areas for rental housing
Courtesy National Association of Home Builders

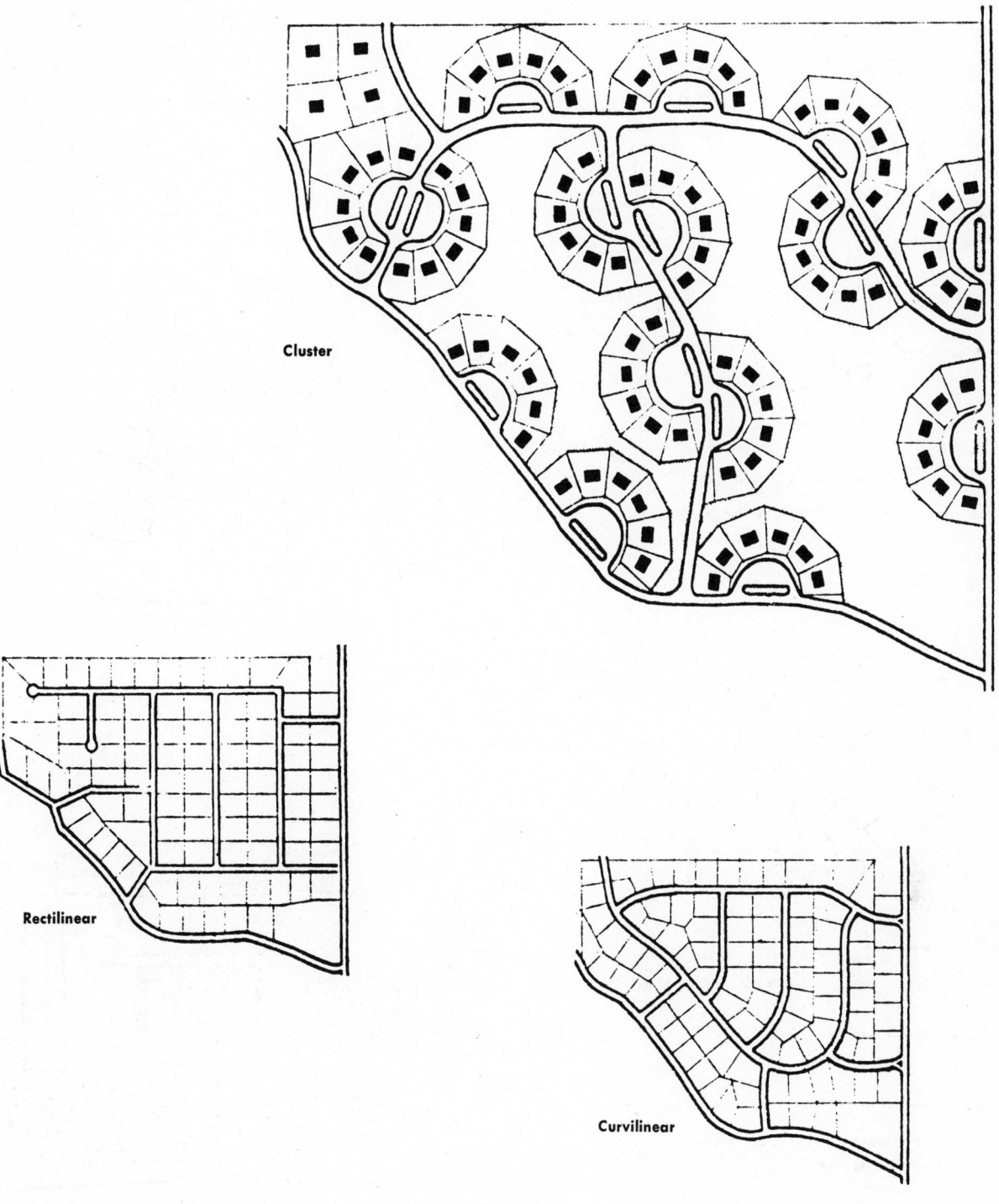

Fig. 16. Cluster scheme compared with conventional subdivision plans for the same site
All schemes have 94 lots. Lot size in cluster scheme is ⅓ smaller than in conventional plans. Linear feet of streets and utilities in cluster plan is half that of the other plans. Cluster plan leaves approximately half of total site as open space. All houses abut on open space. (Stephen Sussna Associates, Designer. Courtesy Urban Land Institute.)

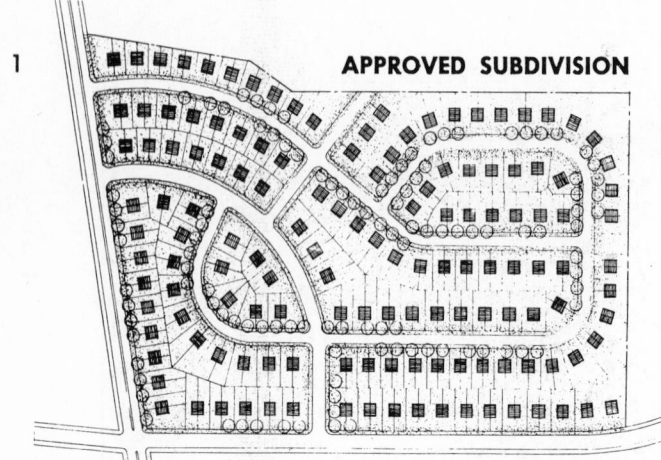

APPROVED SUBDIVISION

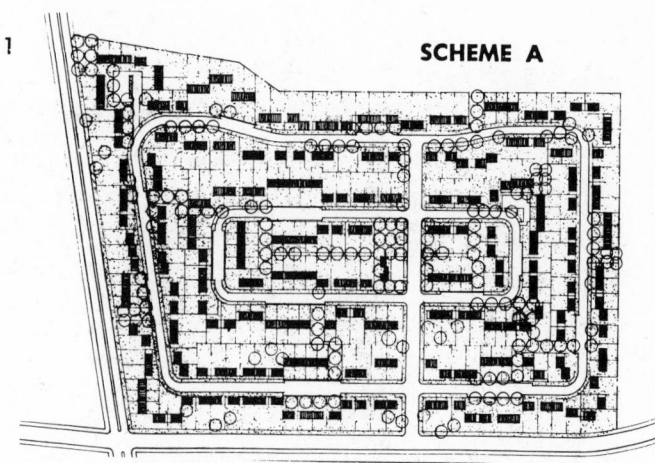

SCHEME A

The approved subdivision represents current development practice fully conforming to most zoning and subdivision ordinances. The subdivision plan (1) provides for 280 families (9.3 families per acre) in twin houses with basement garages. Curving streets are an improvement over the traditional gridiron pattern, but their repetition in numerous subdivisions has created a new monotony. The curving streets only partially obscure another monotony: the uniformly spaced houses. Access from both boundary highways invites through traffic. The similarity of lots, and lack of integrated communal areas, is only too apparent in detail (2). Plan of the typical house, three stories above street level, basement garage, is shown in (3).

Scheme A houses the same 280 families. The new street pattern excludes through traffic. The twin house is replaced by groups of houses of varying lengths and varying setbacks. No houses face on the busy boundary highways. With garages out of the basements, the houses need be only two stories above street level, thus eliminating artificial terraces and giving direct access to private gardens which are supplemented by totlots, sitting areas, a small common, and parklike walks.

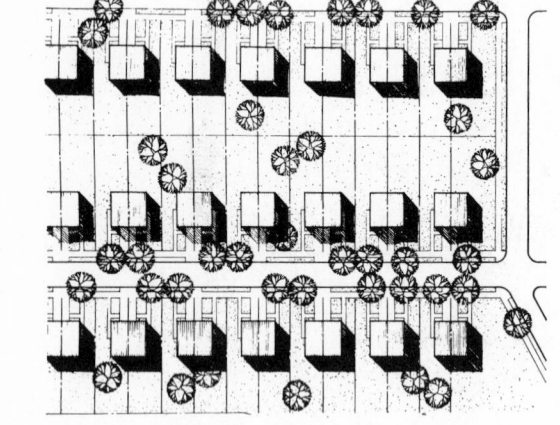

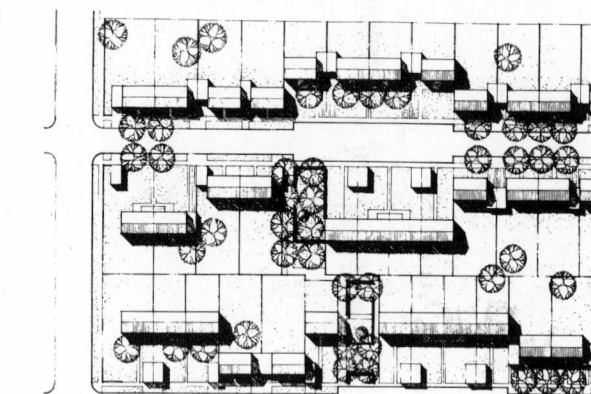

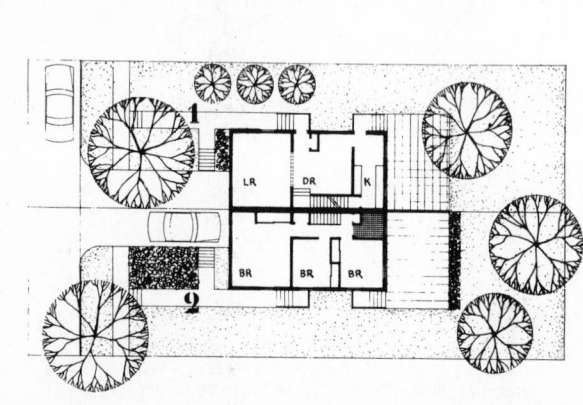

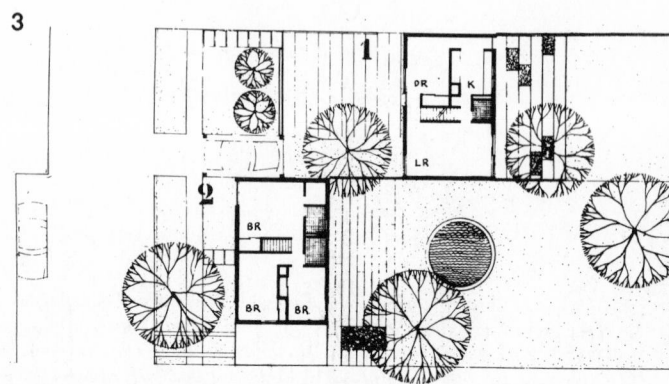

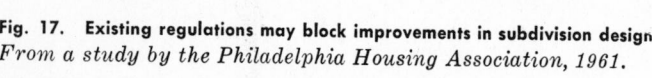

Fig. 17. Existing regulations may block improvements in subdivision design
From a study by the Philadelphia Housing Association, 1961.

SCHEME B

1

SCHEME C

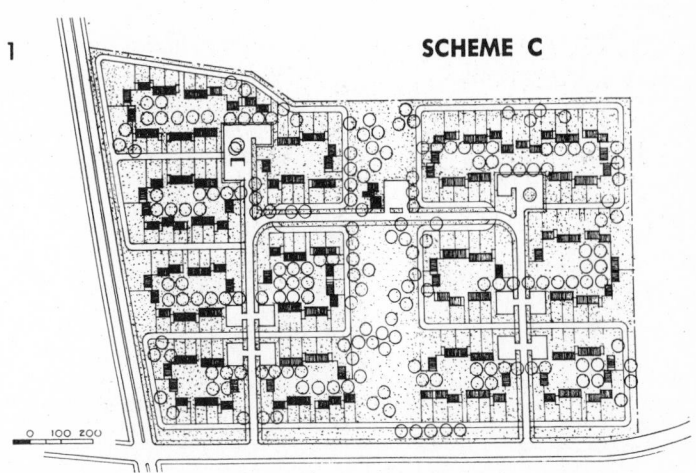

Scheme B also provides for 280 families. Groups of houses face on courts instead of streets. Parking compounds in each court justify elimination of individual garages. As in Scheme A, totlots, sitting areas, common areas and interior walks are provided in addition to private yards and gardens.

Scheme C shows the number of families reduced from 280 to 165 (5.7 per acre). Groups of twelve houses front on pedestrian courts. Access for cars and service vehicles is by looping driveways behind the houses. Visitors park in the compounds at the entrances to the courts. The low density results in even more generous open space than in Schemes A and B. Through traffic is excluded from the subdivision and, again, the boundary streets are not used for lot frontages.

Schemes A, B, and C fulfill the basic objectives of zoning: promotion of health and general welfare, provision of adequate light and air, and prevention of overcrowding of the land, of undue congestion. Yet, under most existing zoning ordinances Schemes A, B, and C cannot be built.

2

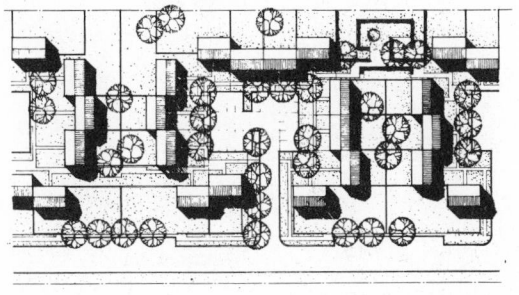

2

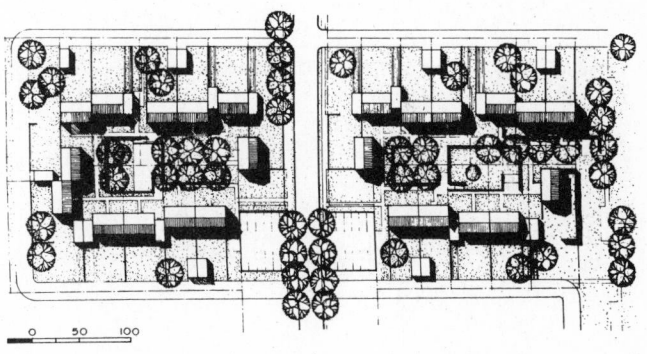

3

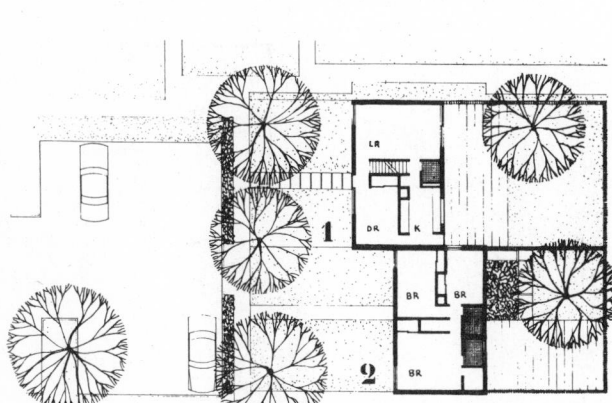

3

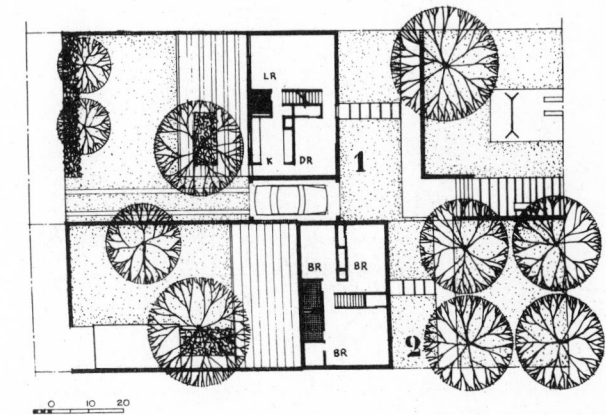

Average and maximum U.S. 1964 automobile dimensions, inches

Symbol	Dimension	Small	Medium	Large	Maximum
L	Over-all length, bumper to bumper	179.4	210.5	223.4	242.3
W	Over-all width	71.0	77.7	80.0	81.7
WD	Width, one door open	104.4	111.9	120.0	125.9
W2D	Width, two doors open	137.8	146.2	160.0	170.1
WB	Wheelbase	105.8	112.8	125.8	149.8
OHF	Overhang front	28.3	32.5	40.3	40.6
OHR	Overhang, rear	43.6	49.9	58.4	60.8
H	Over-all height	53.8	57.5	58.7	64.8
T	Tread	56.2	60.5	62.2	62.7

Turning radii (outside front), feet and inches

	Small	Medium	Large	Maximum
Curb to curb	18–11½	21–1¾	23–4¼	24–4½
Wall to wall	19–5 ¾	21–4¾	23–9¾	25–8½

Critical Angles, in degrees		Minimum	Average	Maximum
AA	Angle of approach	14.4	22.4	29.7
AD	Angle of departure	9.6	13.5	21.2
AR	Angle of ramp breakover	7.3	12.5	16.2
RC	Road clearance, inches	4.7	6.1	6.5

*NOTE: Data from Automotive Industries,
All dimensions are for four-door sedans.*

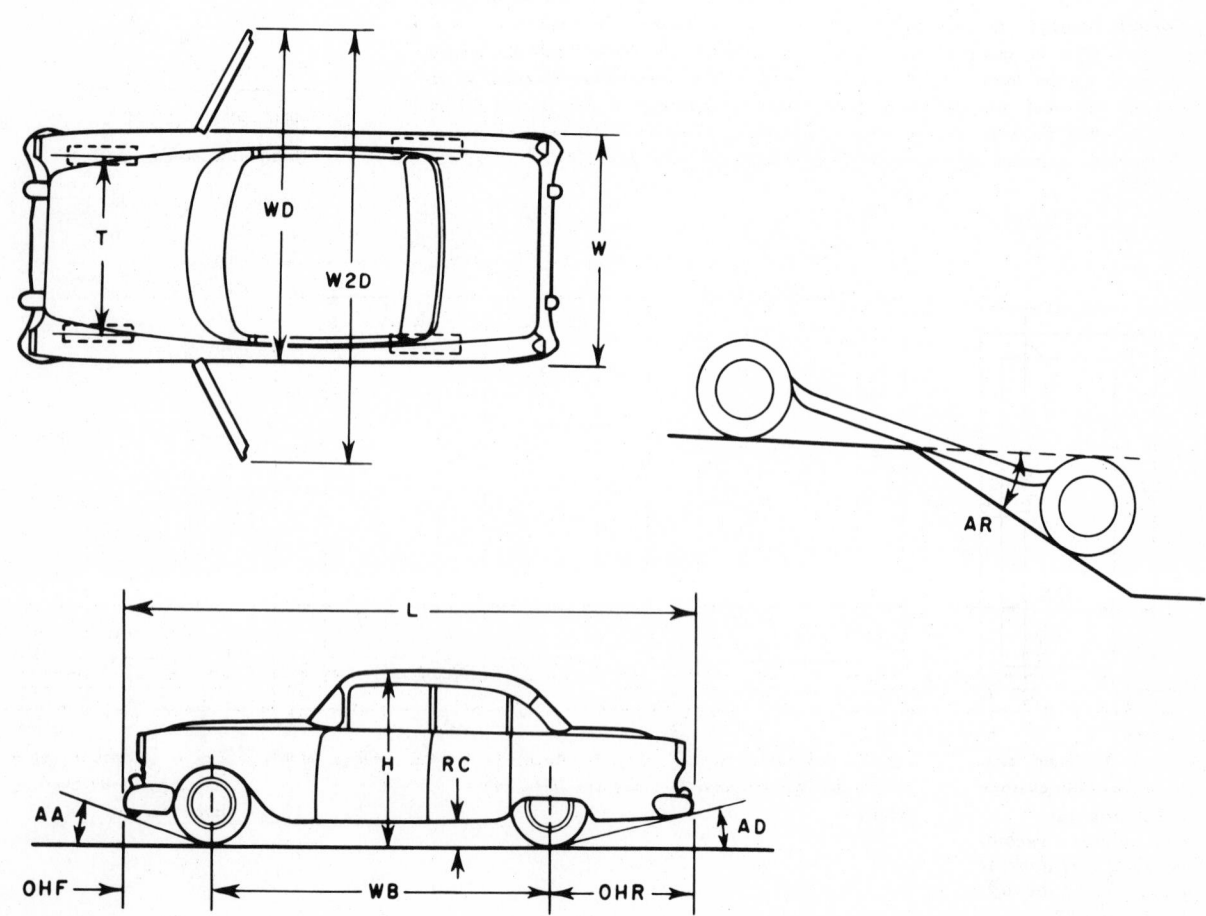

Codes

Garages for one- and two-family houses are usually attached directly to the house or connected to it by a covered passage. If attached, most building codes require 1-hr fire resistance for the wall between house and garage. The one opening permitted in this wall must be protected by a self-closing door having a 1-hr fire rating and a sill 6 in. above the garage floor. If the house extends above the garage the ceiling must also have a 1-hr fire rating.

Size

The minimum size for a one-car garage is 10 by 20 ft, inside dimensions (Fig. 1). This permits access to one side of the car only. The addition of 2 ft in both directions, or 12 by 22 ft, is recommended for comfortable access to both sides of a large car (Fig. 2). For two cars, inside dimensions of 22 by 22 ft are recommended (Fig. 3). These dimensions are for garage use only; if work or storage space is to be included, the dimensions must be increased accordingly. Generally speaking, the garage is not the best location for these spaces.

Carports

Carports require approximately the same roof area as garages. Supporting posts need not be located at the outer edges of the roof provided they are spaced so that there is no interference with car door openings (Fig. 4).

Doors

Garage doors should be of the upward-acting type: either the sectional roll-up type or the one-piece swing-up type (Fig. 5). Hinged, bi-folding, or sliding doors should be used only where special conditions prevent the use of the overhead type. Stock sizes commonly available are: 6 ft 6 in. and 7 ft high by 8, 9, 15, and 16 ft wide. Semicustom sizes range up to 8 ft in height and 20 ft in width. Two-car garages are often provided with a single large door, but the use of two separate doors will result in more accurate placement of the cars and more space between them. The 15-ft width is inadequate for two medium or large cars, and even the 16-ft width does not give comfortable clearances (10 in. at each jamb and between cars). For the spacing shown in Fig. 3, an 18-ft door or two 9-ft doors are required. Designers should take note of the clearances required at jambs, head, and ceiling. Electrical operators are available for most types and sizes of overhead doors.

Floors

Garage floors are usually concrete slabs on grade, 4 in. thick, on a base of coarse gravel or broken stone; reinforcing mesh is recommended. Finish should be integral and floated, rather than troweled, to reduce slipperiness. If the garage is unheated, insulation is not required, but an expansion joint should be provided be-

tween the floor slab and the foundation walls. Floor should be pitched for drainage ⅛ in. per ft toward the door or toward a floor drain.

Utilities

Locate the ceiling lights over the aisle spaces, not over the cars. Provide a minimum of one duplex convenience receptacle on each wall. A sink with hot and cold

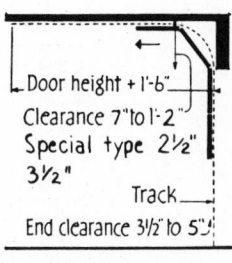

Door height + 1'-6"
Clearance 7" to 1'-2"
Special type 2½"
3½"
Track
End clearance 3½" to 5'-..."

SECTIONAL DOORS

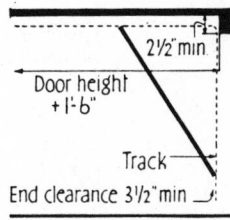

2½" min
Door height + 1'-6"
Track
End clearance 3½" min

ONE-PIECE DOORS

Fig. 5. Garage door types

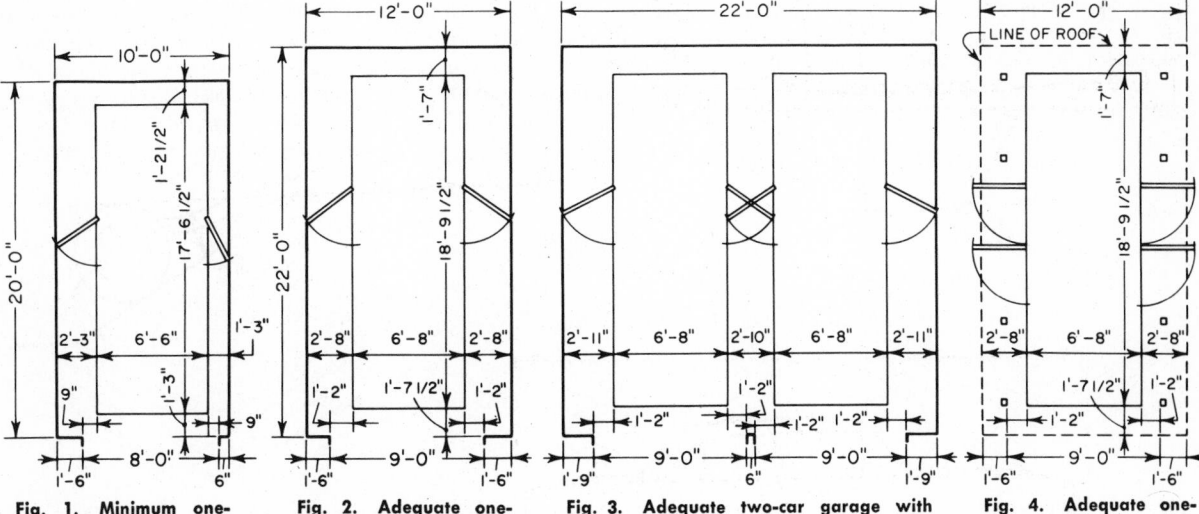

Fig. 1. Minimum one-car garage with average medium-size car
9-ft door recommended; 8-ft door, if used, should be offset as shown.

Fig. 2. Adequate one-car garage with average large car

Fig. 3. Adequate two-car garage with average large cars

Fig. 4. Adequate one-car carport with average large car

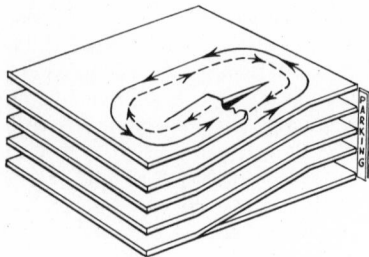

Fig. 6. Straight run, two-way ramp

Simplest arrangement structurally. Inclined plane between floors is wide enough for two cars. Structure is simple to frame. Compares poorly with others because of many friction points, including two-way ramp.

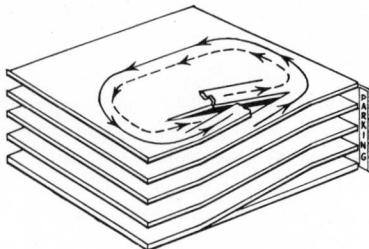

Fig. 7. Straight run, one-way opposed ramp

A logical development from Fig. 6. It is a little harder to frame, but most traffic friction is relieved by same-way circulation and one-way ramps.

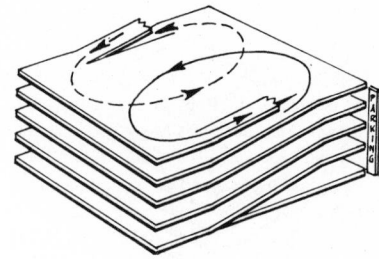

Fig. 8. Straight separated, short circle ramp

New circulation schemes are possible when ramps are separated. This has opposing circulation and two points per floor where paths must cross.

water is desirable, but a hose bibb located near the door is an adequate water supply in most cases. Attached garages may easily be heated, if desired, by extension of the house heating system. In this case, insulation of exposed walls and ceiling and weatherstripping of doors and windows are recommended.

Parking garages

The information in this section was derived from *Commercial Parking Garages*, based on data supplied by the National Parking Association, published in the *Architectural Record*, September, 1958.

Making a profit from parking depends more upon proper planning and design than do many other building projects. A bad guess in the planning stages can be expensive if not disastrous.

New ideas in design come to light each year in planning and building parking facilities. A few firms of consultants specialize in this type of work and are usually better informed than the more general designer.

The available location, with its typical customer, tends to decide the type of operation that will be profitable and, to a degree, the type of structure that should be built on that particular site.

If, for example, the predominant customer is the commuter or the all-day parker, circulation will be important. The garage will have to load up quickly between 8:45 and 9 A.M. and empty in a hurry at 5 P.M.

On the other hand, if most of the prospective customers will be shoppers, emphasis must be put on the accessibility of the cars, rather than on peak-hour speed. Short-term parking usually means that arrival and departure times will be unpredictable.

If there are theaters in the neighborhood the evening activity will tend to be something of a scramble at curtain time. Add evening shopping to this, and the operator will have a heavy exit-demand. Closing time at stores and theaters produce the fastest-growing, impatient group of customers in parking.

A third location may be an area largely occupied by hotels. Here there will normally be no very high peaks of activity beyond a noticeable increase of inbound traffic in the evenings and outbound in the mornings. Here patrons will park for longer periods than at other locations, but they do not all leave or arrive at the same time.

The distribution of shops, offices, theaters and hotels is as important as the traffic pattern of any given area. Some authorities envision no through traffic in downtown areas in the foreseeable future. They believe that the streets serving these parts of a city will serve only as access routes to off-street parking facilities and as delivery routes for trucks and public transit vehicles. The trend is evident. However, the traffic characteristics of any area where a parking garage is contemplated will help to determine the practical size of the structure.

Traffic authorities say that the average street will deliver from 400 to 500 cars per hour per lane. Interlane friction, or

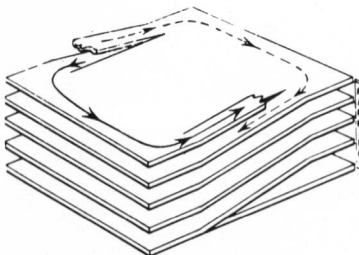

Fig. 9. Straight separated, clear way ramp

Circulation is more logical. It is the most straightforward ramp system.

Fig. 10. Staggered floor, divided, two-way ramp

Simplest of staggered floor system has fault of opposed circulation. In all these staggered floor schemes one floor may be narrowed to mezzanine size.

Fig. 11. Staggered floor, divided, one-way ramp

One-way ramps solve ramp friction problem. Floor circulation is also smoother.

Fig. 12. Staggered floor, two-circle, one-way ramp
Circulation is completely separated. This is most straightforward of the staggered floor systems.

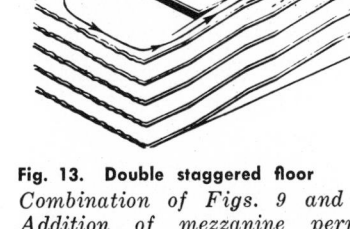

Fig. 13. Double staggered floor
Combination of Figs. 9 and 12. Addition of mezzanine permits smooth circulation but sometimes attendant must drive up to the mezzanine to drive down again.

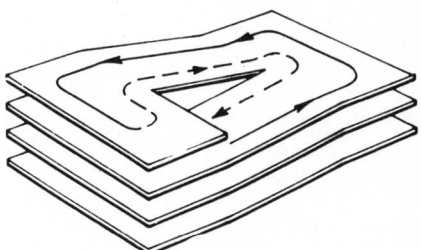

Fig. 14. Single spiral sloping floor
The simplest of this type calls for two-way circulation, a turn-around at the top.

traffic confusion, prevents two lanes from delivering twice this number. Under normal conditions it is felt that the garage should be limited in size by the number of cars that can be delivered to it in an hour. Another practice based on experience is tied in with maximum waiting time for delivery of a car. This is based on the theory that the garage should be able to fill and empty in an hour.

A more obvious size-determining factor is the size of the lot itself. It is possible to erect a building on a lot with a dimension less than 80 ft, but it is impractical. A mechanically operated garage has been built on less, but the "reservoir" space at ground level needed to absorb peak input loads was found to be too small in one of the country's first mechanical parking garages.

An uncramped minimum dimension for ramp garages is 100 ft. The lot should be about 100 by 200 ft, or 120 by 130 ft for building the most economical unit. These dimensions are for designs with present-day techniques and materials, resulting in the least ramp-dilution of space, among other things. New techniques could appear tomorrow, of course.

Today, multilevel structures must rise at least three floors in order to make the per-car cost reasonable. Usually the cost of construction of a single floor for parking above the essentially costless ground floor raises the per-space cost to uneconomic levels. The upper limit in floors is set by the capacity desired, and is based on the theory that people dislike going around a ramp for much more than six levels.

Another rule of thumb, that land should cost no more than the building, may have to be set aside. It may be necessary to allocate part of the ground-floor area to rental space for shops and stores. As an example of first-floor rentals, a garage in Cincinnati takes in more than $150,000 in annual rentals from ground-floor tenants. On a 210 by 100-ft lot, 160 by 100 ft is available on the first floor for parking and circulation.

There are three operating methods today:

1. The traditional operation uses attendants who drive the cars to appointed storage spots and reverse the process when the customer leaves. Many garages are designed so that they cannot be used

any other way. The short, steep ramps, confined spaces and high-density parking necessary for profitable operation requires more driver skill than the average motorist has.

However, attendant parking requires a staff, and the high cost of wages and of training is increasing. If day-and-night parking is provided, the garage must maintain several shifts of attendants.

2. The self-operated or driver-parked system has long been used in open parking lots and is becoming popular for indoor parking. A staff of one or two people is all that is required.

However, the lack of skill of the average car owner makes it necessary to reduce the parking density by about one-third (see Fig. 18), and the circulation pattern of the garage must be planned with this in mind.

The driver-parked garage can take advantage of new machinery developed for this operation. Ticket-delivery machines obviate attendant control of entrances. By using a system of treadles and crossing-type gates, the units assure that the entering driver takes a ticket stamped with his entry time. He surrenders this

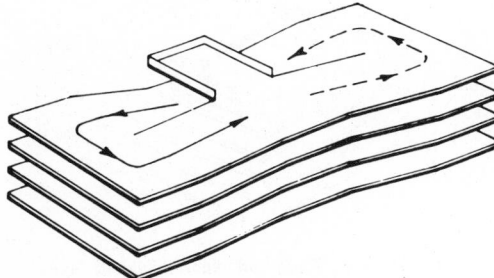

Fig. 15. Double spiral one-way ramp
Two of Fig. 14 schemes are put end-to-end or folded together. Simple circulation and less friction.

Fig. 16. Double thread, one-way ramp
Ramps are steeper because they have only 180 deg to get between floors. Popular design with separated flow.

Fig. 17. Concentric opposed, one-way ramp
Separate ramp movement, but bad crossings at each floor.

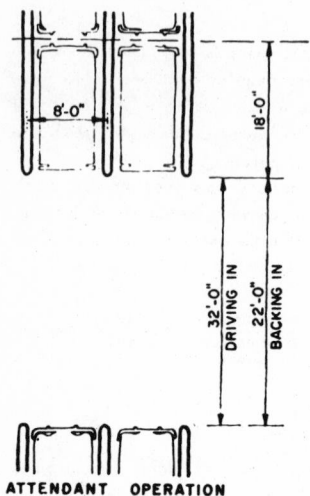

ATTENDANT OPERATION

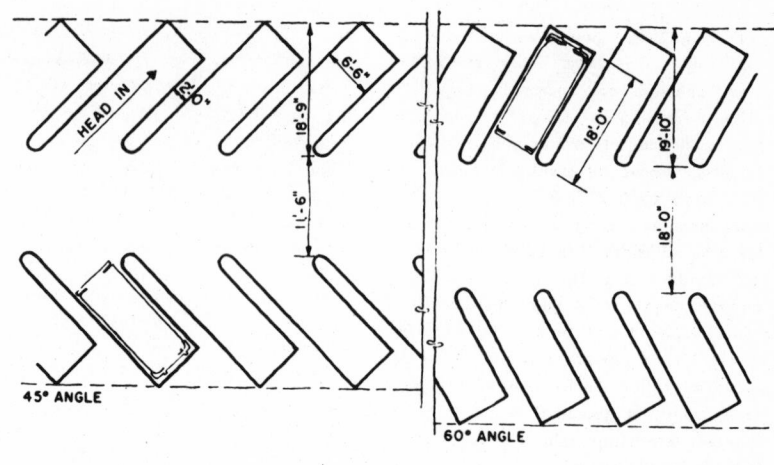

HEAD IN

45° ANGLE

60° ANGLE

DRIVER OPERATION

Fig. 18. Best individual car space arrangements
For attendant parking: 90 deg, narrow spaces and double pileups where necessary. For driver parking: between 45 and 60 deg with aisles to fit and wide space markings.

ticket when leaving. The same treadle system can be modified to keep count of the vehicles in and out, and show the number of vehicles in the building at any time. Simple barriers enforce one-way car movements.

3. Mechanical parking is fairly new, but two such garages built in the 1920's are still in operation. Most mechanical parking systems employ some form of two-dimensional elevators and generally require essentially the same type of structure. There must be an open central slot about 20 ft wide cutting the building in two. On each side of the slot are rows of shelves, either one or two cars deep.

Many floor layouts have been designed to meet specific needs and conditions, such as shape and size of the lot, the slope of the land, type of clientele, etc. Some are shown in the schematics, Figs. 6–17.

There are four main divisions in ramp layout:

Straight run
Staggered floor
Sloping floor
Semicircular

Ramps may be placed at any point on the floor, or outside the floors if the plan permits. Schematic plans 6, 7, 9, 15, and 16 are more suitable for driver-parking operation, with the inclusion of Figs. 8, 11, and 13 as secondary considerations. All are used in attendant operation with the exception of the sloping floor schemes, Figs. 15 and 16, which only come into their own as driver-parking structures.

Opportunities to use the shape of the terrain as part of the garage structure and circulation plan should not be overlooked. Many garages have been built with entrances on all levels directly from the street. This layout makes for more profitable use as driver-parked systems with one of the previously mentioned mechanical ticket dispensers at each entrance, and a single exit manned by the cashier.

Many commercial enterprises have found noncommercial garages profitable. They should be as carefully designed as their commercial counterparts. Department stores, hotels and hospitals have built such garages. Because of the specific needs in each case, no general rule of thumb can be applied to these specialized structures.

REFERENCES

Parking by Baker and Funaro, Reinhold Publishing Corporation, New York, 1958.
Parking Facilities, AIA Building Type Reference Guide No. 7. Includes an excellent bibliography. American Institute of Architects.
Traffic Design of Parking Garages, Eno Foundation for Highway Traffic Control, Saugatuck, Conn.
Parking, National Parking Association, 711 14th St. NW, Washington 5, D.C.
Parking Progress, Applied Parking Techniques, Inc., 824 Transportation Building, Washington 6, D.C.

Manufacturers of mechanical parking systems

Bowser Engineering Co., 112 SW Second Ave., Des Moines 9, Iowa.
Pigeon Hole Parking, Inc., Peyton Building, Spokane 1, Wash.
Speed-Park, Inc., 342 Madison Ave., New York 17, N.Y.

By FRANK HARRISON RANDOLPH, P.E., Professor of Hotel Engineering, Cornell University

Parking stalls should be built to accommodate the larger cars frequently used, although not necessarily the very largest. Planning in hopes of just medium and small size cars invites difficulties. The larger cars have an over-all length of 19 ft, over-all width 6 ft 8 in., with a wide open door projecting 3 ft 4 in. beyond the over-all width. The ramp angle must not exceed 7 deg. The limit of the front approach angle is 14 deg, while the corresponding angle at the rear is limited to 9 deg. When parked at right angles to a curb or buffer, the front overhang[1] generally does not exceed 2 ft 10 in., and the rear overhang[1] seldom exceeds 4 ft 6 in. These dimensions need consideration when planning widths of sidewalks affected by the overhang. A 5-ft sidewalk would have its usable width reduced almost to zero by the rear overhang. The front overhang may be taken at 1 ft 6 in. when figuring closely the minimum feasible spacing between buffers for a minimum width parking lot. When a central driveway is used with 90 deg parking on both sides, the space required is 62 ft wide, but the space between buffers need be only 59 ft because of the overhang.

A single stripe, 4 to 6 in. wide, may be used to mark the parking stalls. Better results in centering the car are obtained by using two 5-in. stripes, separated by 1 ft 6 in., to mark the stalls. The stripes, about 18 ft long, are joined by a semi-

[1] Overhang beyond curb or buffer is about 6 in. less than overhang dimensions (see section on "Dimensions") which are measured from the center of the wheel.

circular arc at the incoming end to form an elongated U (Fig. 21). Experience has shown this method to be very satisfactory and fully worth the extra painting.

Parking stalls should be at least 9 ft wide, 10 ft wide if space is not too restricted. Parking stalls 8 ft 6 in. wide are unsatisfactory because with the car 6 ft 8 in. wide, there is only 1 ft 10 in. between cars. If an adjacent car is only 6 in. off center and the car door is 4 in. thick, only 1 ft remains through which to squeeze, if possible.

Motel parking lots planned for maximum guest convenience, mark off parking stalls 11 ft wide and 23 ft long, allowing

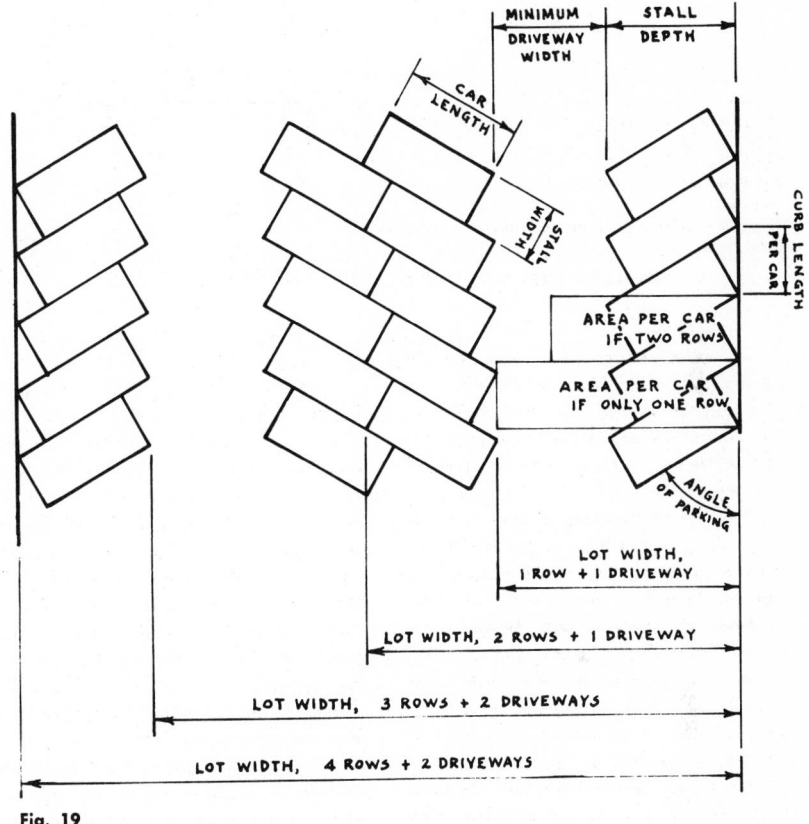

Fig. 19

Table 1. Parking lot dimensions
(Refer to Fig. 19.)

Angle of Parking	Stall width	Curb length per car	Stall depth	Minimum driveway width	Lot width 1 row + 1 driveway	Sq ft per car	Lot width 2 rows + 1 driveway	Sq ft per car	Lot width 3 rows + 2 driveways	Sq ft per car	Lot width 4 rows + 2 driveways	Sq ft per car
Along curb = 0°	9'	23'	9'	12'	21'	483	30'	345	51'	391	60'	345
	10'	23'	10'	12'	22'	506	32'	368	54'	414	64'	368
30°	9'	18'	17'4''	11'	28'4''	510	45'8''	411	66'2''	397	83'6''	376
	10'	20'	18'3''	11'	29'3''	585	47'6''	475	68'0''	453	86'2''	431
45°	9'	12'9''	19'10''	13'	32'10''	420	52'8''	336	79'0''	376	98'10''	315
	10'	14'2''	20'6''	13'	33'6''	490	54'0''	383	80'4''	379	100'10''	358
60°	9'	10'5''	21'0''	18'	39'0''	407	60'	313	95'0''	330	116'0''	305
	10'	11'6''	21'6''	18'	39'6''	455	61'	351	95'6''	366	116'6''	335
90°	9'	9'	19'	24'	43'	387	62'	279	105'	315	124'	279
	10'	10'	19'	24'	43'	430	62'	310	105'	350	124'	310

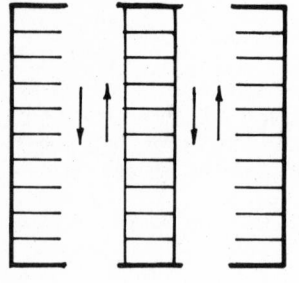 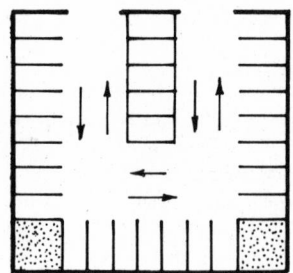 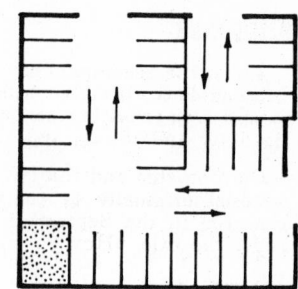

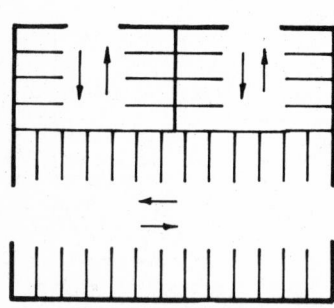 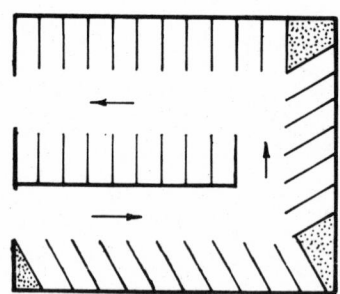 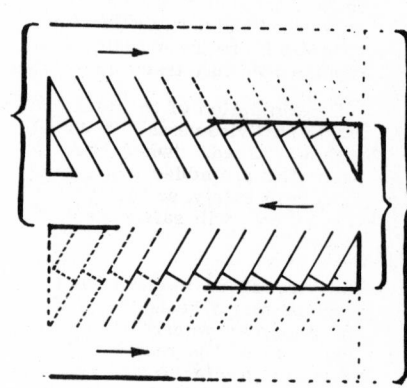

Fig. 20

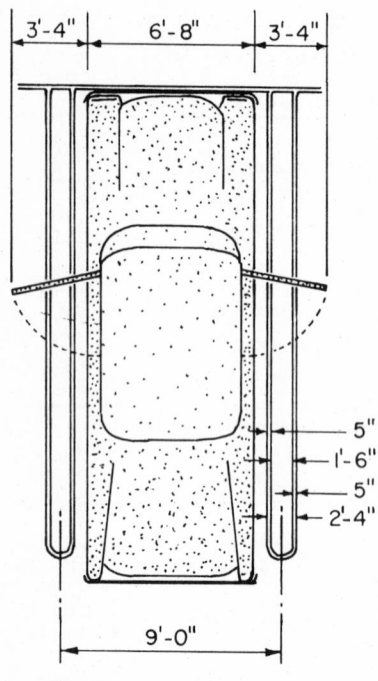

Fig. 21

4 ft behind the 19-ft car for unloading space which is advisably clear of the driveway.

Parking lots, exclusive of drives for entering them, require 350 sq ft per car as a very rough, preliminary figure. The width of the available space and the desired angle of parking are determining factors in economy. The area per car varies from 279 to 585 sq ft under conditions covered in the tabulation of parking lot dimensions. A central driveway with two rows of cars and 90 deg parking gives the best economy. Diagonal parking is easier for the driver, reduces the necessary driveway width, but requires more total space (Fig. 19).

In designing parking spaces, end stalls should be about 1 ft wider than usual, especially if bounded by a building or other obstruction or a driveway. Parking spaces under buildings should be 11 ft wide, watching out for columns, and should have 7 ft height in the clear.

The parking pattern that will be most satisfactory fully warrants careful thought. It depends upon many factors including the possible locations of access drives. These should be 20 ft wide for two-way traffic or 12 ft wide for one-way traffic (Fig. 20). If a restricted site frontage requires a right-angle turnoff, the driveway should be 25 ft wide and the curb should have a 30 ft radius. A curb radius of less than 18 ft is inadvisable.

A slope of 6 per cent is the usual maximum for state highways. A slope of 12 per cent is customary for ramps, but may be as much as 15 per cent. The parking lot should be nearly level. The central driveway may be crowned, with a 1 per cent slope draining to the edges so that persons on foot will find the driveway relatively free from water after rain or from ice in winter weather.

PURPOSE

Use of the accompanying diagrams, dimensions, and formulae will enable the designer to lay out straight or curved driveways to suit any condition between extremes of (1) minimum practicability and safety, and (2) maximum ease of driving.

Data on this and the following two pages were adapted from material originally developed by Ernest Irving Freese which appeared in the September, 1933, issue of American Architect under the title, "How to Design Practical Curved Driveways."[2]

GENERAL

Unless an automobile is driven in a straight line, rear wheels do not follow exactly in the tracks of front wheels, because front wheels only are controlled by the steering gear. Hence, on curved driveways, the inner rear wheel may track off a roadway if the inner radius of the drive is too great. The outer front wheel may track off if the outer radius is too small.

Determination of the minimum width of driveway for various radii (and vice-versa) depends on three properties of an automobile: "tread," "wheel-base," and "turning radius." To these properties are added inside and outside clearances to provide a margin of safety, so that both front and rear bumpers, fenders, trunks, etc., will safely clear shrubbery or walls bordering the drive.

The "tread" of a car is the distance center-to-center of the front or rear wheels. The tread varies both between the front and the rear wheels and with the make or year of the car. The tread of the rear wheels, being a constant on curves and normally greater than that of the front wheels, is used in driveway calculations.

The "wheelbase" is the distance center-to-center between front and rear axles. It also varies.

The "turning radius" is the radius of the circular track of the outer front wheel. It is variable not only with the car, but also with other factors discussed below.

Inside and outside clearances, as used herein, are fixed dimensions which have been calculated to meet necessities of all types of cars. Lesser clearances are not advisable, as their use requires more caution than the average driver habitually employs.

CALCULATIONS

Use of the values of T, B, and X given in Table 2 will result in driveways adequate for any passenger car.

Straight driveways: The minimum width of straight driveways can be calculated from the formula, W = T + 2E, or 7'8", but should not be less than 8'0". A width of 9'0" is recommended for comfortable driving.

Landings: Straight portions of driveway interposed between two curved quadrants will permit a car to be brought nearly alongside a curb or step at an entrance. Theoretically a car cannot be brought exactly parallel to the curb without backing and moving forward again at least once. Actually, a landing 22'0" in length will permit driving close enough to the curb to prevent discomfort in alighting, without "jockeying" (see Fig. 24).

[2] *Editor's note: In spite of the antiquity of these pages, they are less obsolete than one might imagine. The three dimensions in Table 2 on which these designs are based have changed surprisingly little for the largest cars (see "Automobiles: Dimensions"). Tread has not changed at all and wheelbase only slightly. The turning radius, however, of even the largest 1964 cars is considerably less than the 27 ft used in these designs, which therefore can no longer be considered minimal as shown. Using the formulae given here, the designer may readily develop minimum designs if he wishes.*

It should be noted that driveway widths have increased by about a foot since these pages were prepared. Recommended widths are now 9 ft for straight drives and 12 ft for curved drives.

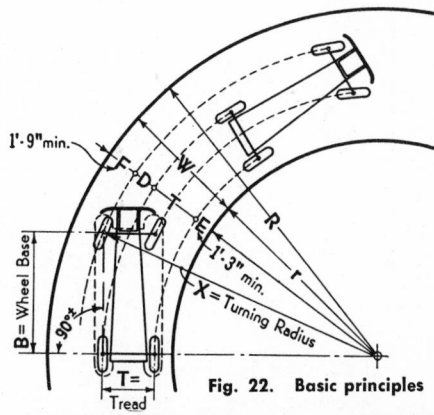

Fig. 22. Basic principles

Basic principles of driveway design may be applied geometrically by following the diagram above or by use of the formulae below. In either case, the turning radius, "X", may be any dimension not less than the minimum.

Table 2. Minimum dimensions and formulae

T, B, and X vary with the make of car; the requirements of all makes for the past six years (1931-36) are met by the values given below.

DIMENSIONS	FORMULAE
T = tread = 5'-2"	R = outside radius of drive = X + F
B = wheelbase = 12'-0"	D = divergence between front and rear wheels = $X - \sqrt{X^2 - B^2}$
*X = turning radius = 27'-0"	W = width of drive for a given radius = T + D + E + F
E = inside radius = 1'-3"	
F = outside clearance = 1'-9"	r = inside radius of drive = R − W
Minimum landing = 22'-0"	

*Note: X may be any desired radius not less than the minimum

Table 3. Minimum standard dimensions for curved driveways

R Outer Radius		W Minimum Width	r Inner Radius	
29'-0"	to 30'-0"	11'-0"	18'-0"	to 19'-0"
30'-0"	to 31'-0"	10'-11"	19'-1"	to 20'-1"
31'-0"	to 32'-0"	10'-10"	20'-2"	to 21'-2"
32'-0"	to 33'-0"	10'-9"	21'-3"	to 22'-3"
33'-0"	to 34'-0"	10'-8"	22'-4"	to 23'-4"
34'-0"	to 35'-0"	10'-7"	23'-5"	to 24'-5"
35'-0"	to 36'-0"	10'-6"	24'-6"	to 25'-6"
36'-0"	to 37'-0"	10'-5"	25'-7"	to 26'-7"
37'-0"	to 38'-0"	10'-4"	26'-8"	to 27'-8"
38'-0"	to 39'-0"	10'-3"	27'-9"	to 28'-9"
39'-0"	to 41'-0"	10'-2"	28'-10"	to 30'-10"
41'-0"	to 43'-0"	10'-1"	30'-11"	to 32'-11"
43'-0"	to 45'-0"	10'-0"	33'-0"	to 35'-0"
45'-0"	to 47'-0"	9'-11"	35'-1"	to 37'-1"
47'-0"	to 49'-0"	9'-10"	37'-2"	to 39'-2"
49'-0"	to 51'-0"	9'-9"	39'-3"	to 41'-3"
51'-0"	to 54'-0"	9'-8"	41'-4"	to 44'-4"
54'-0"	to 57'-0"	9'-7"	44'-5"	to 47'-5"
57'-0"	to 61'-0"	9'-6"	47'-6"	to 51'-6"
61'-0"	to 65'-0"	9'-5"	51'-7"	to 55'-7"
65'-0"	to 70'-0"	9'-4"	55'-8"	to 60'-8"
70'-0"	to 75'-0"	9'-3"	60'-9"	to 65'-9"
75'-0"	to 82'-0"	9'-2"	65'-10"	to 72'-10"
82'-0"	to 89'-0"	9'-1"	72'-11"	to 79'-11"
89'-0"	to 99'-0"	9'-0"	80'-0"	to 90'-0"
99'-0"	to 111'-0"	8'-11"	90'-1"	to 102'-1"
111'-0"	to 126'-0"	8'-10"	102'-2"	to 117'-2"
126'-0"	to 147'-0"	8'-9"	117'-3"	to 138'-3"
147'-0"	to 176'-0"	8'-8"	138'-4"	to 167'-4"
176'-0"	to 219'-0"	8'-7"	167'-5"	to 210'-5"
219'-0"	to 300'-0"	8'-6"	210'-6"	to 291'-6"

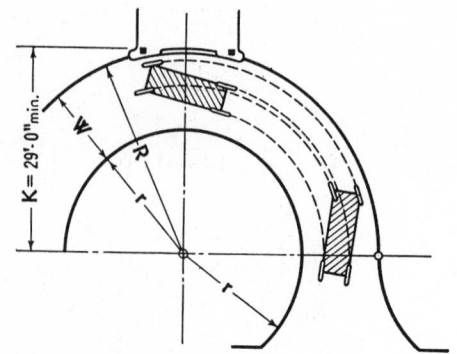

Fig. 23. Circular curves

MINIMUM VALUES: R = 29'·0", W = 11'·0", r = 18'·0"

On a minimum circular curve, automobiles stop in a raking position. Radius of the flare from property line to curb should be the same as the inner radius of curve.

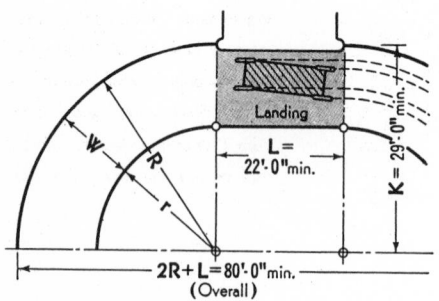

Fig. 24. Landings

MINIMUM VALUES: R = 29'·0", W = 11'·0", r = 18'·0"

A straight portion, or "landing", at the entrance step will lessen the rake of the car. As the tangent in advance of the entrance is lengthened the angle of rake is lessened.

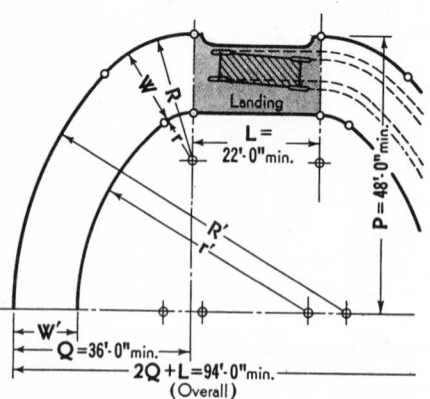

Fig. 25. Compound curves

MINIMUM VALUES

P = 48'·0"
Q = 36'·0"
R = 30'·0"
R' = 60'·0"
W' = 9'·6"
W = 11'·0"
r = 19'·0"
r' = 44'·4"

Compound curves of this type, with the short radius nearest landing, permit greater speed upon entering the drive, but require more manipulation of the steering wheel, and consequently a slower speed near the landing.

Curved Driveways: By substituting the values in Table 2, col. 1, in the formulae in Table 2, col. 2, the least practical outside radius for a curved drive is found to be 27'0" plus 1'9" or 28'9". Similarly, the least practical width of a drive of 29'0" outer radius is 11'0"; the minimum inner radius, 18'0".

The larger the "turning-radius," X, the more may riding comfort and speed be increased. Therefore, it is advisable to use curves having radii as large as practical considerations of site and economy permit. Data in Table 3 constitute a tabulation of the results of substituting varying values of X in the basic formulae. Any one of the three factors, R, W, or r, may govern. For instance: R (outer radius) may be determined by lot lines; W (width of drive) may be prescribed by the distance between two obstructions; r (inner radius) may be the radius of a circular flower bed.

Compound curves: Since ease of driving is dependent primarily on uniformity of curvature, and speed, on radius, a drive formed of circular curves of large radius is theoretically most nearly perfect. Practical considerations of site and expense, however, normally limit the radius. Hence, compound curves approach the maximum of riding ease compatible with practicality. Portions of the drive may be laid out at great radius and other portions at small radius. Relationships of these portions should be carefully studied. Shorter radii may be placed near the landings, where speed is reduced, or greater radii may be so placed when it is desirable to minimize the raking position of the car when stopped. Circumstances of each problem will determine its solution. Figure 25 shows the development and minimum dimensions of compound curves. Basic formulae are the same as for circular curves. Radii and widths of drive for quadrants of varying sizes are given in Table 4.

Double driveways: Minimum safe clearance between two moving cars is 2'0". To determine the total width of a double drive: (1) Establish the inner or outer radius of either lane; (2) determine the minimum width of that lane from Table 3; (3) add the necessary clearance and obtain the inner or outer radius of the other lane; (4) from Table 3 determine the width of the second lane; and (5) add this to the width-plus-clearance already obtained. The result is the total width.

Circular and **elliptical driveways,** and **turn-arounds,** are discussed in T-SS "Circular Driveways, Back-arounds, Junctions".

Table 4. Dimensions of compound driveway quadrants

See Figs. 25 and 28 for applications and reference letters. Dimensions are taken to the nearest inch.

Rectangular Dimensions		Outer Radii		Widths of Driveway (From TABLE I)		Inner Radii	
P	Q	R	R'	W	W'	r	r'
48'·0"	36'·0"	30'·0"	60'·0"	11'·0"	9'·6"	19'·0"	44'·4"
50'·0"	37'·6"	31'·3"	62'·6"	10'·10"	9'·5"	20'·5"	47'·2"
52'·0"	39'·0"	32'·6"	65'·0"	10'·9"	9'·4"	21'·9"	49'·9"
54'·0"	40'·6"	33'·9"	67'·6"	10'·8"	9'·4"	23'·1"	52'·6"
56'·0"	42'·0"	35'·0"	70'·0"	10'·6"	9'·3"	24'·6"	55'·4"
58'·0"	43'·6"	36'·3"	72'·6"	10'·5"	9'·3"	25'·10"	58'·2"
60'·0"	45'·0"	37'·6"	75'·0"	10'·4"	9'·2"	27'·2"	60'·9"
62'·0"	46'·6"	38'·9"	77'·6"	10'·3"	9'·2"	28'·6"	63'·6"
64'·0"	48'·0"	40'·0"	80'·0"	10'·2"	9'·2"	29'·10"	66'·4"
66'·0"	49'·6"	41'·3"	82'·6"	10'·1"	9'·1"	31'·2"	68'·11"
68'·0"	51'·0"	42'·6"	85'·0"	10'·1"	9'·1"	32'·5"	71'·5"
70'·0"	52'·6"	43'·9"	87'·6"	10'·0"	9'·1"	33'·9"	74'·3"
72'·0"	54'·0"	45'·0"	90'·0"	9'·11"	9'·0"	35'·1"	76'·10"
74'·0"	55'·6"	46'·3"	92'·6"	9'·11"	9'·0"	36'·4"	79'·3"
76'·0"	57'·0"	47'·6"	95'·0"	9'·10"	9'·0"	37'·8"	82'·2"
78'·0"	58'·6"	48'·9"	97'·6"	9'·10"	9'·0"	38'·11"	84'·8"
80'·0"	60'·0"	50'·0"	100'·0"	9'·8"	8'·11"	40'·3"	87'·3"

NOTE: The values of r' in this table were computed by means of the following general formula:

$$r' = \frac{(P-W)^2-(Q-W')^2-2r\left[(P-W)-(Q-W')\right]}{2\left[(Q-W')-r\right]} + (Q-W')$$

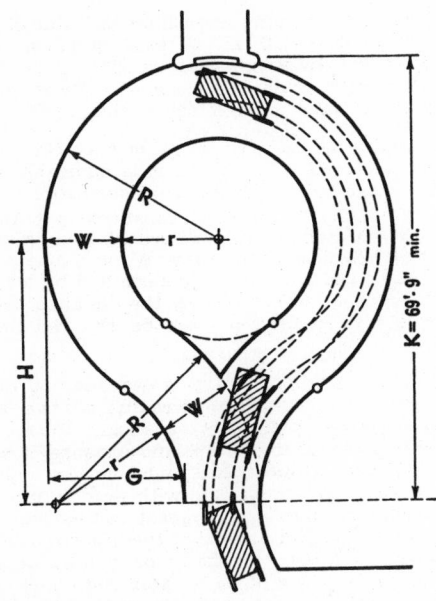

Fig. 26.   Circular driveways

MINIMUM VALUES: R = 29'-0",   W = 11'-0",   r = 18'-0"
FORMULAE: $H = \sqrt{G\ (2R + 2r - G)}$, in which $G = R - \frac{1}{2}W$

The minimum circular turn-around requires great manipulation of the steering wheel where curves are reversed. Nevertheless, uniform width is permissible even at this point. Cars stop in a raking position.

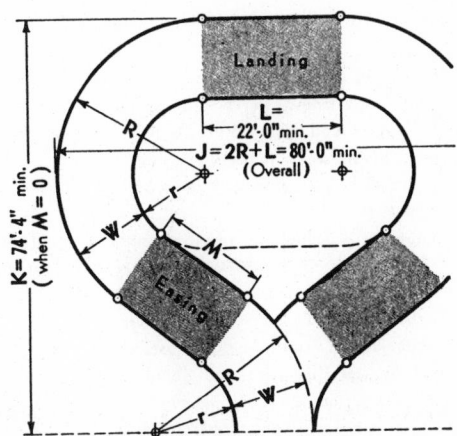

Fig. 27.   Landings and easings

MINIMUM VALUES

R = 29'-0"
r = 18'-0"
W = 11'-0"

K	M
74'-4"	0
75'-0"	.8'-0"
76'-0"	12'-1"
77'-0"	15'-10"
78'-0"	18'-8"
79'-0"	21'-2"
80'-0"	23'-5"

Easings, or tangents at points of reversal of curvature, make driving easier. Note that a great increase in length of the tangent requires only a small increase in overall distance from entrance to curb. Use of a landing lessens the rake of the car upon stopping.

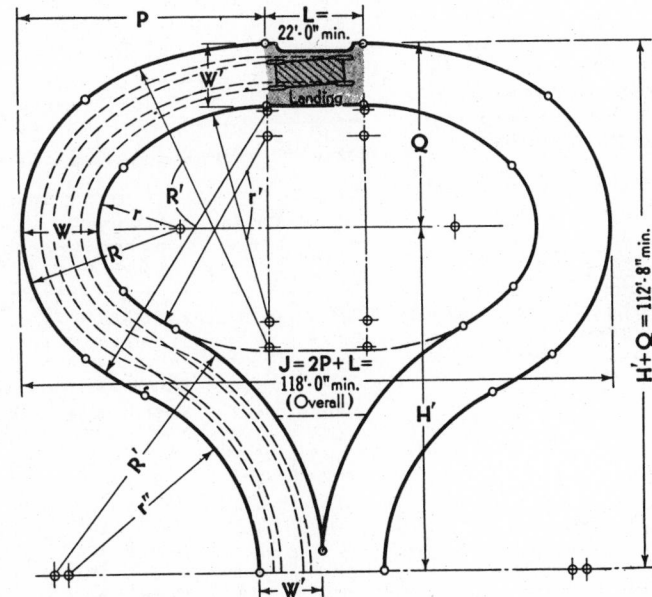

Fig. 28.   Elliptical driveways

FORMULAE:
$$H' = \sqrt{G\ (2R' + 2r' - G)} - (W' + r' - Q)\ \text{in which}\ G = r' + \frac{1}{2}(L + W')$$
$$r'' = \frac{g^2 + h^2}{2g} - R'\ \text{in which}\ g = R' + \frac{1}{2}(L - W'),\ h = H' + R' - Q$$

MINIMUM VALUES:

P = 48'-0"	R' = 60'-0"	r = 19'-0"
Q = 36'-0"	W' = 9'-6"	r' = 44'-4"
R = 30'-0"	W = 11'-0"	r'' = 49'-7"

Ellipses formed of compound curves permit the maximum of speed compatible with both riding and driving ease. In the type shown the shorter radii occur away from the landing, which still further reduces the rake of the car upon stopping.

By CHARLES MIDDELEER, *Landscape Architect*

Widths range from 9 to 12 ft for single lane driveways and from 15 to 18 ft for double lane driveways. If the 9 ft width is used it should be increased to at least 10 ft on curves.

Drainage is essential. Minimum longitudinal pitch for proper drainage is 1 per cent. If gutters are used, runoffs or catch basins should be provided at suitable intervals. Underground drains should be used if required by soil conditions; see detail of typical drain further on in this section.

Bases must be well compacted and well drained. Soft clay soil or heavy truck traffic necessitates a heavier base. Typical bases for driveways are as follows:

A. For dry construction: bank-run gravel or sandy gravel, no air pockets

B. For concrete surfaces: sandy gravel, cinders, crushed stone, slag, or other inorganic porous material

C. Crushed stone, 1½ to 2½ in. in size, rolled with 6 to 10-ton roller

Definition of *bank-run gravel*: stones, sand, some clay for binder; *fine bank-run gravel*: stones up to 1 in. in size; *coarse bank-run gravel*: stones up to 4 in. in size.

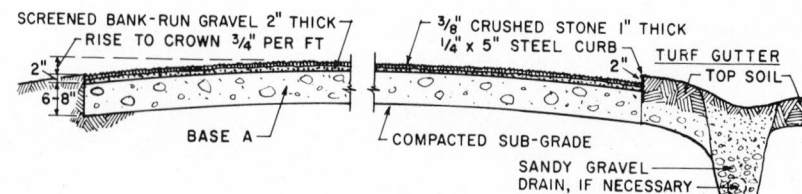

Gravel

Use calcium chloride or two coats of oil on bank-run gravel to keep from dusting. For heavy traffic use two 6-in. courses for base.

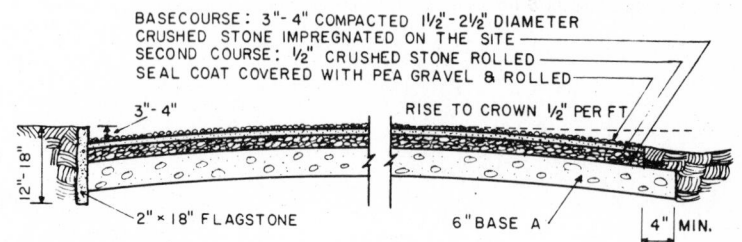

Penetration asphalt

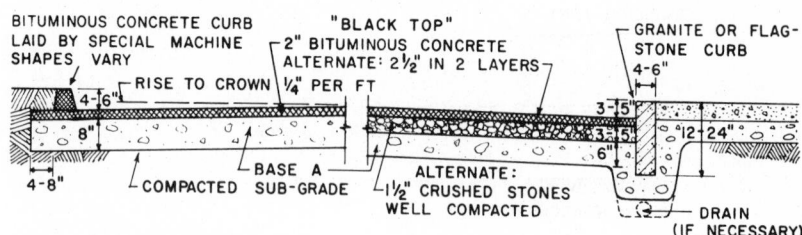

Bituminous concrete ("black top")

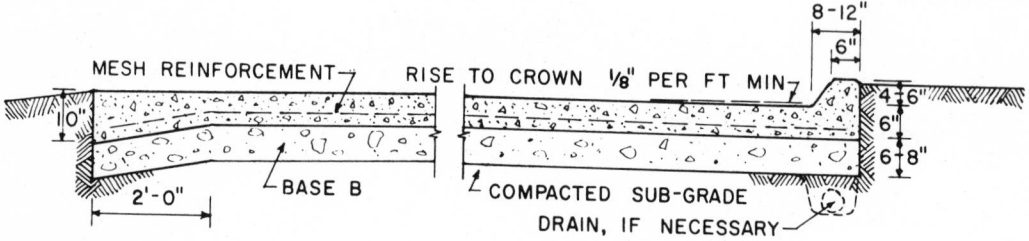

Concrete

Provide asphalt expansion joint every 30 ft. Concrete may be covered with black top 1 to 2 in. thick.

DRIVEWAY CONSTRUCTION
Scale: ¼ in. equals 1· ft

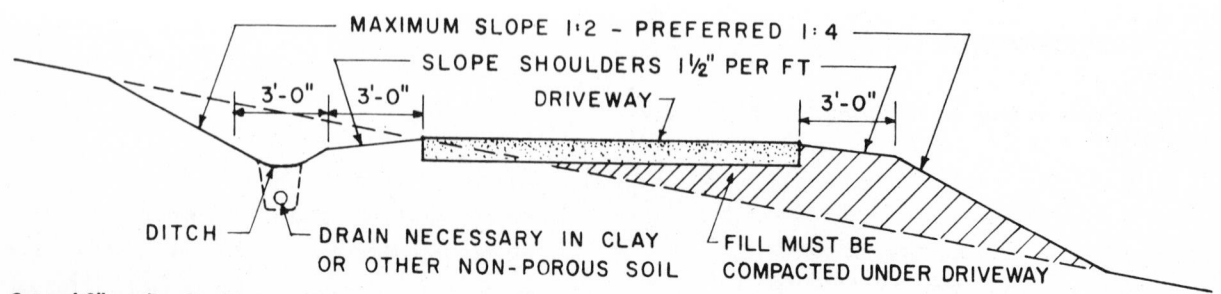

Cut and fill grading for driveway construction
Scale: ⅛ in. equals 1 ft

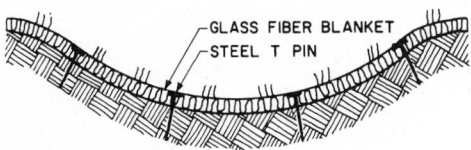

Turf gutter or drainage ditch

Over base of sandy gravel install top soil and grade to smooth contour; apply seed and cover with glass fiber blanket held in place by steel T-pins; grass will come up through the blanket. Blanket available in 1 in. thickness in rolls 6 by 150 ft, weighing 56 lb.

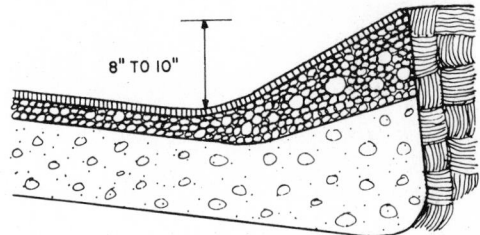

Oiled gutter for oiled gravel driveway

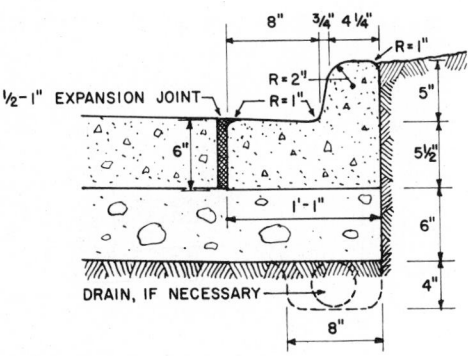

Precast concrete gutter and curb

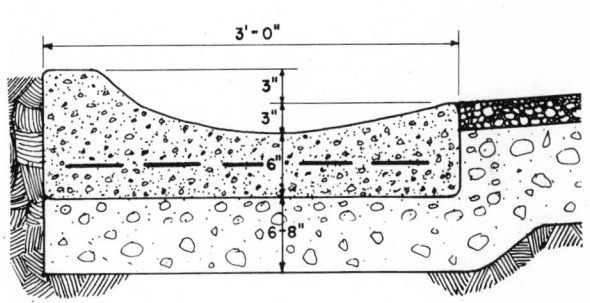

Precast concrete gutter

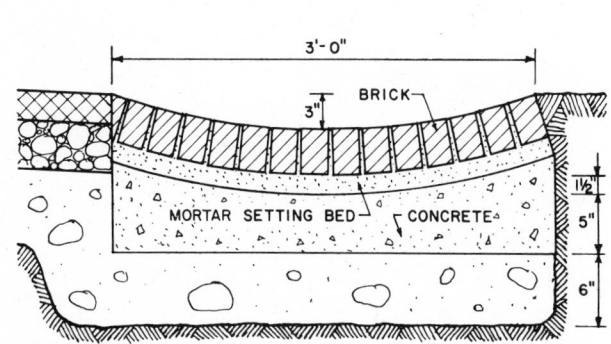

Brick gutter

Cobblestones or Belgian block may be used with similar detail.

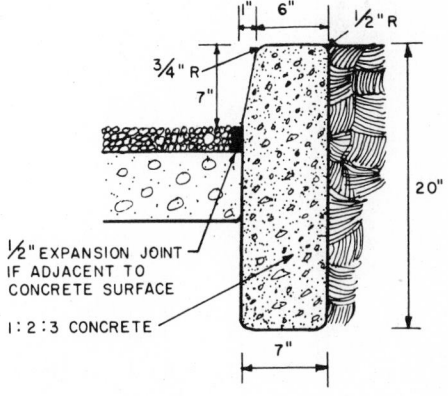

Precast concrete curb

GUTTERS AND CURBS

Scale: ¾ in. equals 1 ft

For turf gutter, bituminous concrete curb, granite or flagstone curb, and integral concrete curb, see previous page.

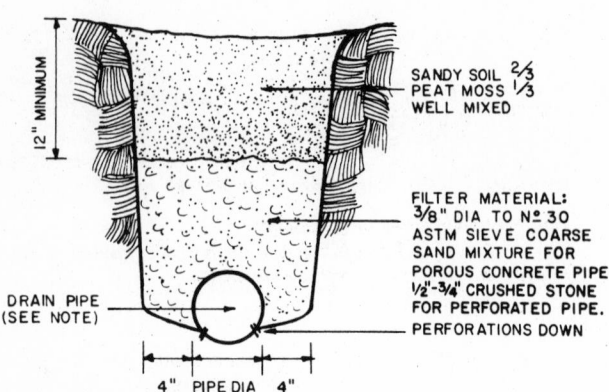

SANDY SOIL 2/3
PEAT MOSS 1/3
WELL MIXED

FILTER MATERIAL:
3/8" DIA TO Nº 30
ASTM SIEVE COARSE
SAND MIXTURE FOR
POROUS CONCRETE PIPE;
1/2"-3/4" CRUSHED STONE
FOR PERFORATED PIPE.

PERFORATIONS DOWN

DRAIN PIPE
(SEE NOTE)

12" MINIMUM

4" PIPE DIA 4"

Detail of typical drain
Scale: ¾ in. equals 1 ft
*Drain pipe may be perforated asphalt, perforated or
porous concrete, or perforated galvanized steel pipe.
Under driveways use pipe strong enough to support
heavy trucks. Minimum pitch for drain pipe is 0.5 per
cent.*

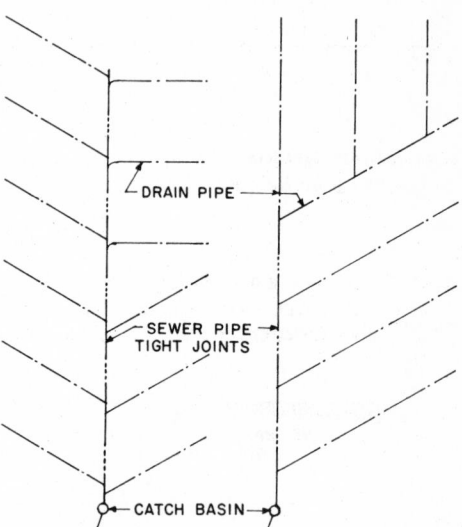

DRAIN PIPE

SEWER PIPE
TIGHT JOINTS

CATCH BASIN

Typical drainage field layout
Not drawn to scale

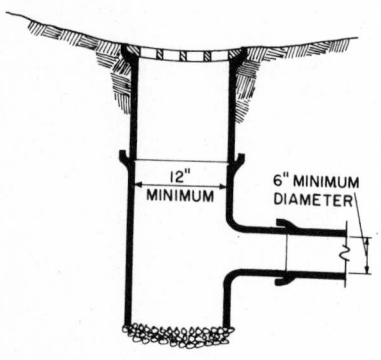

12"
MINIMUM

6" MINIMUM
DIAMETER

Lawn drain
Scale: ⅜ in. equals 1 ft
*Concrete or vitrified clay pipe; standard round cast
iron grate.*

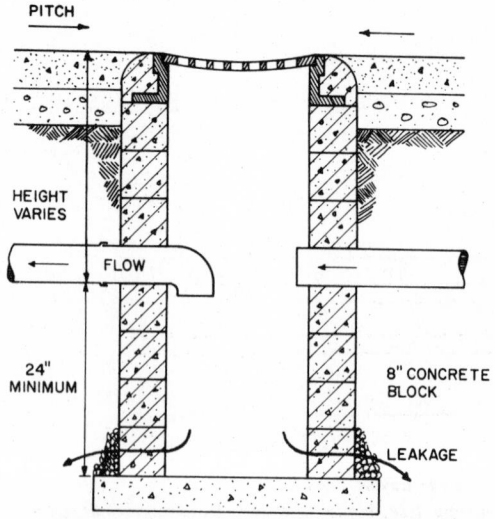

PITCH

HEIGHT
VARIES

FLOW

24"
MINIMUM

8" CONCRETE
BLOCK

LEAKAGE

Catch basin
Scale: ⅜ in. equals 1 ft
*Inside dimensions 12, 18, 24, or 32½ in.; square or
rectangular. Standard cast iron grate, light or heavy
duty, or sidewalk grate.*

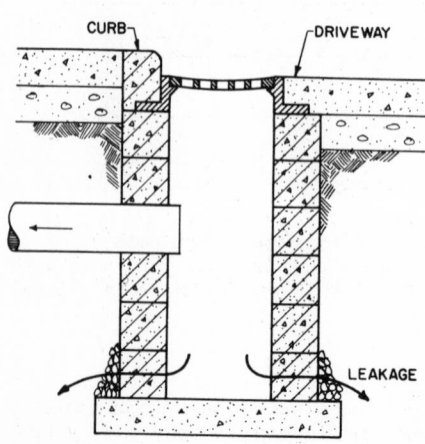

CURB

DRIVEWAY

LEAKAGE

Curb inlet
Scale: ⅜ in. equals 1 ft
Standard cast iron grate 22¾ by 72½ in.

DRAINAGE DETAILS

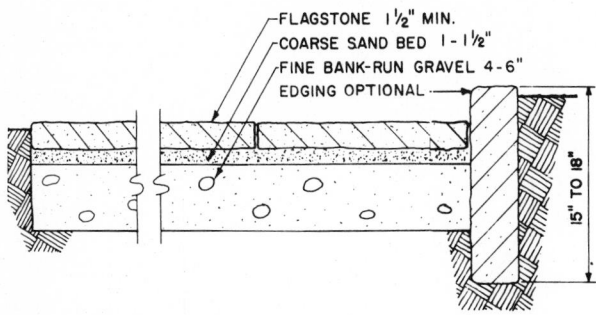

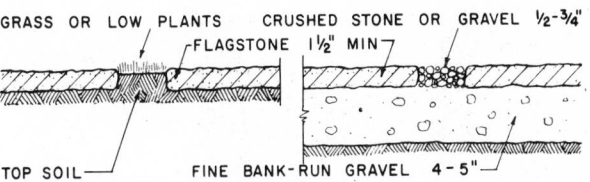

Flagstone with gravel or grass joints
Type shown on left will heave with frost; grass or low plants in joints are hard to maintain.

Flagstone with tight joints
Edging may be Belgian block, granite, or flagstone.

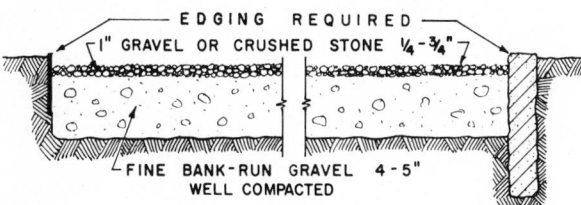

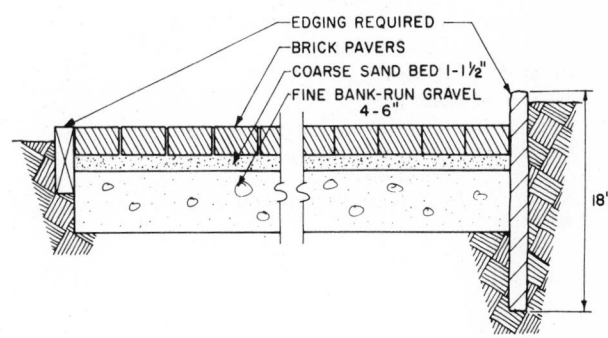

Gravel
Edging may be 1 in. or thicker flagstone 18 in. deep or 3/16 by 5 in. metal; or Belgian block, granite, or pre-cast concrete curb may be used. In frost-free zones, brick on edge, 1/8 by 4 in. metal, or 1 by 6 redwood with 1 by 3 by 18 in. stakes 4 ft on center, may be used. For curved walks use metal edging.

Brick with tight joints
Edging may be 1 by 8 in. redwood, 1½ by 18 in. flagstone, or ¼ by 5 in. metal.

DRY CONSTRUCTION

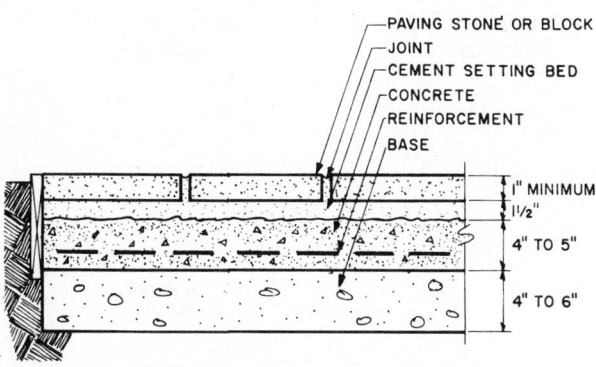

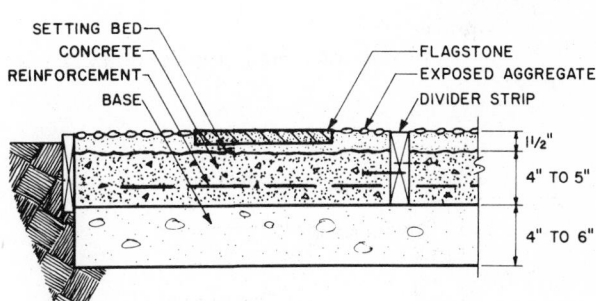

Flagstone or other paving units
Brick, quarry tile, slate, marble, Belgian block, or asphalt block may be set to this same detail. Contact between paving stone and cement setting bed must be total, with no air pockets.

Exposed aggregate concrete
Exposed aggregate 3/8 to 1 in. size, set in natural or colored cement, with or without flagstones. Dividers of 2 by 6 in. redwood may be used, if desired, with 4-in. galvanized spikes 12 in. on center to prevent heaving.

FROST-RESISTING CONSTRUCTION
Base should be coarse bank-run gravel or slag, or 1 to 3 in. crushed stone; must be well drained. Concrete should have asphaltic expansion joints every 20 ft. Top surface should be rough for bond to setting bed. Reinforcement should be 6 by 6 in. welded wire mesh.

Joints should be ¾ in. or less in width and grouted; care must be taken to keep grout from face of paving at all times. Edgings are not required except during construction. In frost-free zones, base and reinforcement may be omitted.

Scale of all drawings: ¾ in. equals 1 ft

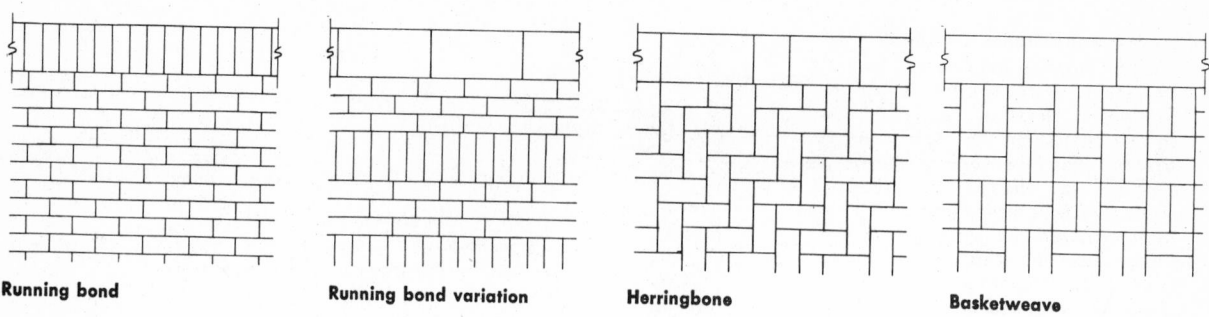

Running bond   **Running bond variation**   **Herringbone**   **Basketweave**

Brick pavement patterns—Scale: ⅜ in. equals 1 ft
Borders may be brick or stone. Edging required with dry construction.

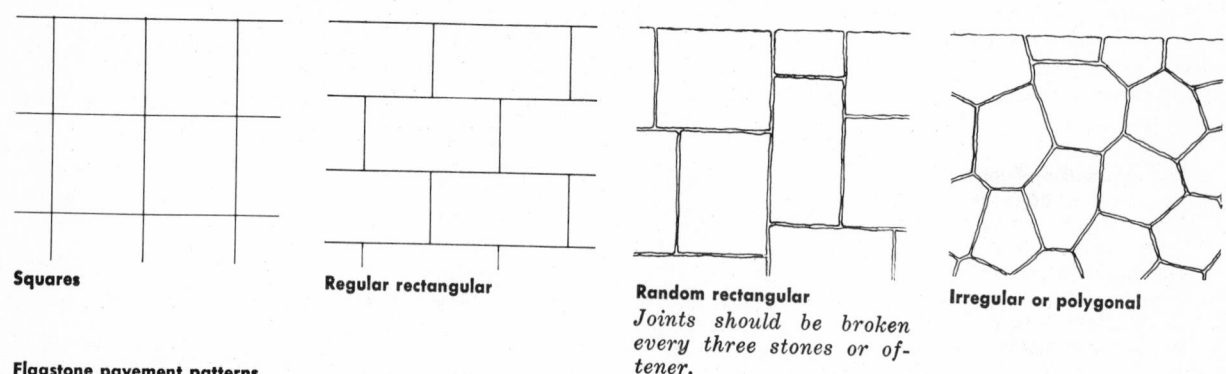

Squares   **Regular rectangular**   **Random rectangular**
Joints should be broken every three stones or oftener.
    Irregular or polygonal

Flagstone pavement patterns
All joints should be tight. Some standard patterns are available in random rectangular. Square and rectangular shapes are also available in precast concrete.

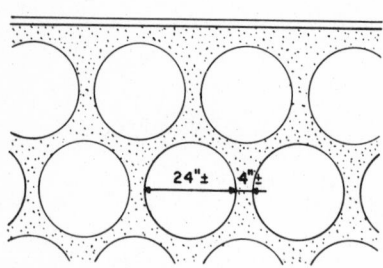

Precast concrete in gravel or exposed aggregate concrete

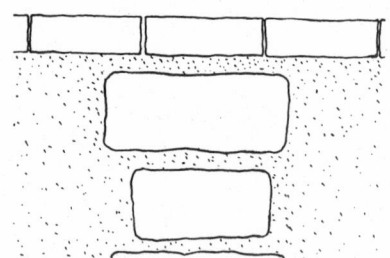

Flagstone or other paving block in exposed aggregate concrete

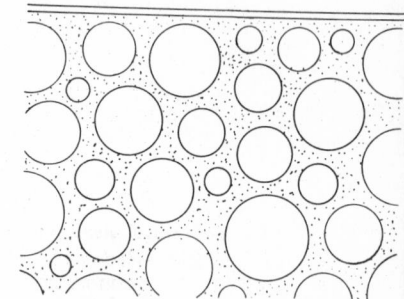

Log sections in gravel
Use cypress, redwood, chestnut, locust, or other durable wood, 6 in. thick, spacing optional. Tan bark or low plants may be used instead of gravel.

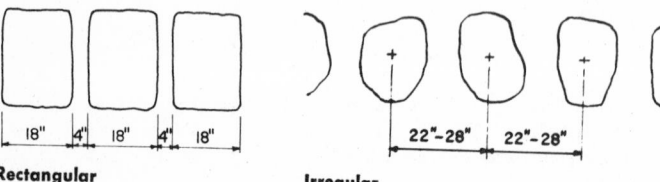

Rectangular   **Irregular**

Stepping stones
Stones should not be less than 1½ in. thick. Common rectangular sizes are 12 by 15, 15 by 20, 18 by 24, 20 by 30, 24 by 36 in.

WALKS AND TERRACES
Scale: ¼ in. equals 1 ft (except brick).

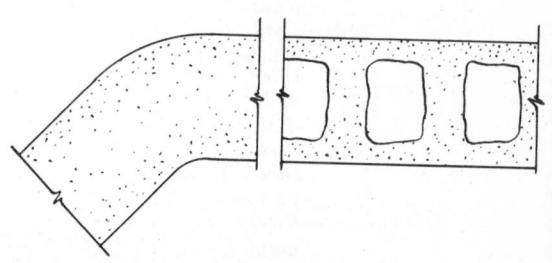

Gravel path with or without stepping stones
Width: single, 1 ft 6 in. to 3 ft; double, 3 ft 6 in. to 5 ft. Edging required.

Bonded frost-resistant construction

Treads may be brick, flagstone, or cut stone. Brick joints should not be wider than ⅜ in. Flagstone treads should be 1½ to 2 in. thick. Risers may be brick, flagstone strips 4 in. wide or selected flat stones with recessed joints. Visible joints should be rodded concave. Care must be taken not to get mortar on masonry faces. Risers must be returned at the sides if cheek wall is not used. Cut stone treads should have some overlap for support. Concrete slab should be 5 to 6 in. thick with suitable reinforcement; top surface roughened for good bond with setting bed. Foundations must extend below frost line.

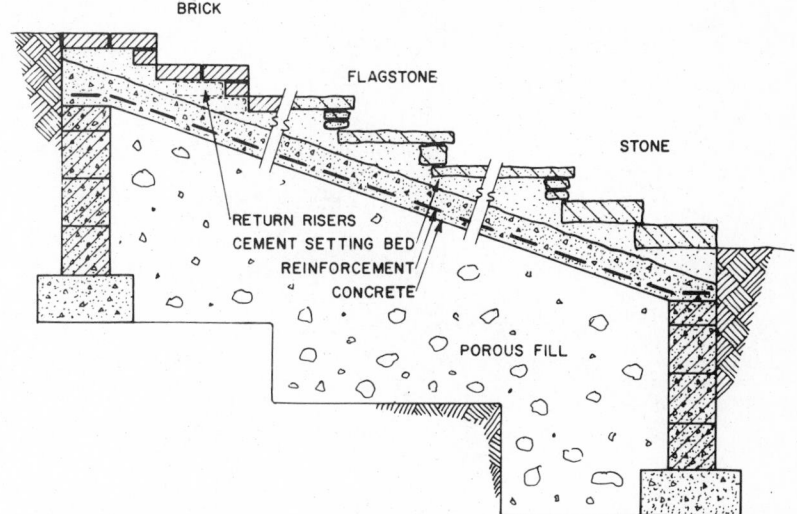

BRICK
FLAGSTONE
STONE
RETURN RISERS
CEMENT SETTING BED
REINFORCEMENT
CONCRETE
POROUS FILL

Dry construction—flagstone treads

Treads 16 to 20 in. long, 1½ to 2 in. thick. Risers may be brick, flagstone strips 4 to 5 in. wide, stone, or concrete block, set dry on treads. Cheek wall is recommended; it may be flagstone 2 to 3 in. thick by 18 in. deep. Set dry on soil fill, no sand.

CHEEK WALL

Dry construction—cut stone

Treads should overlap 4 in. for support. Set dry on soil fill, no sand.

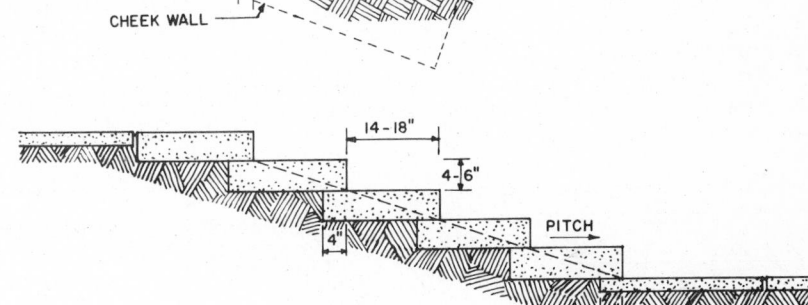

14 - 18"
4-6"
4"
PITCH
4"

Wood and gravel steps—variations

Risers—Redwood 2 by 6 in. minimum; cheek walls 2 by 8 in.; use aluminum or stainless steel nails.

    —Logs, 6 in. or more in diameter, of cypress, juniper, arborvitae, black locust, or other decay-resistant wood.

    —Railroad ties.

Treads—Tanbark or ⅜ in. crushed stone 1 in. thick, over 4 in. base of bank-run gravel.

    —Railroad ties may be used as treads and cheek walls, as well as risers.

Dimensions—Risers: 4 in. maximum. Treads: 16, 40, or 64 in.

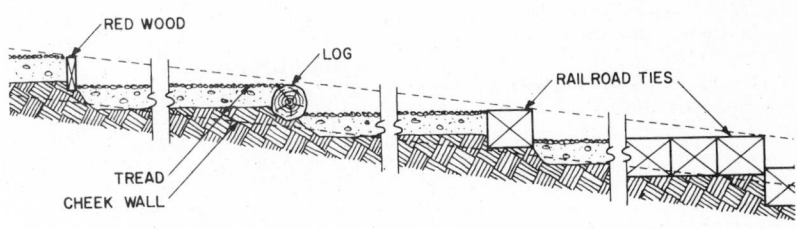

RED WOOD
LOG
RAILROAD TIES
TREAD
CHEEK WALL

STEPS

Scale: ⅜ in. equals 1 ft

Riser-tread ratios should be as follows:

    riser 4 in.—tread 16 to 18 in.
    riser 5 in.—tread 14 to 16 in.
    riser 6 in.—tread 12 to 14 in.

All treads should be pitched slightly for drainage.

NOTE: If ramps are used their slope should not exceed 10 per cent and must not exceed 12 per cent.

12
6

4" x 4"

2" x 4"

2'-6"—2'-8"

1" x 6"
1" x 4"

4" x 4"

STEEL DOWEL

2" x 12" STRING

FLAGSTONE
OR CONCRETE

BOLTS

SEE DETAIL

STEEL DOWEL

BELOW FROST

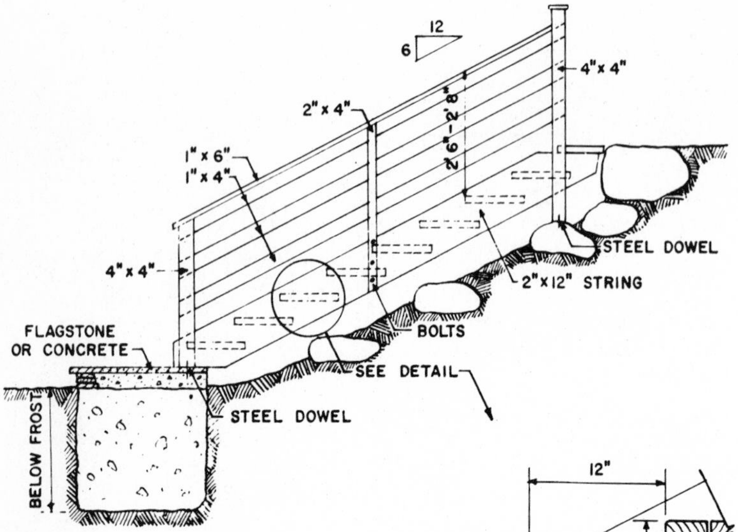

Wood steps
If steps are more than 30 in. wide add center carriage member.

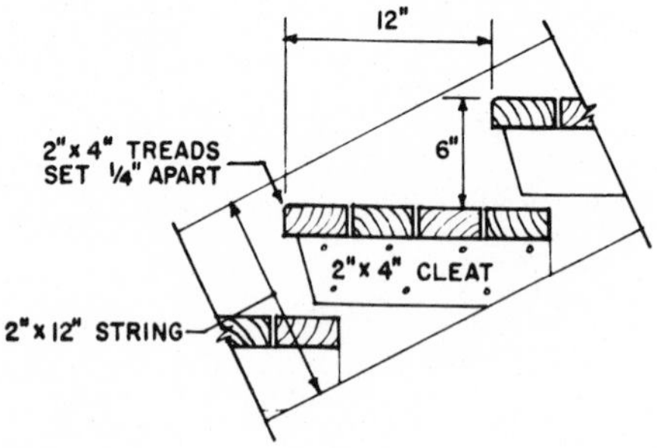

12"

2" x 4" TREADS
SET ¼" APART

6"

2" x 4" CLEAT

2" x 12" STRING

Detail of stair treads
Scale: ¾ in. equals 1 ft

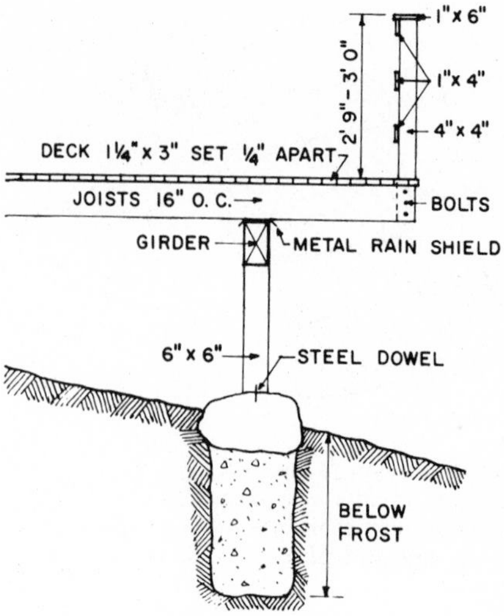

1" x 6"

2'-9"—3'-0"

1" x 4"

4" x 4"

DECK 1¼" x 3" SET ¼" APART

JOISTS 16" O. C.

BOLTS

GIRDER

METAL RAIN SHIELD

6" x 6"

STEEL DOWEL

BELOW FROST

Elevated wood deck

WOOD DECKS AND STEPS
Scale: ¼ in. equals 1 ft
For all exterior wood construction use redwood or cypress with fastenings of aluminum or stainless steel.

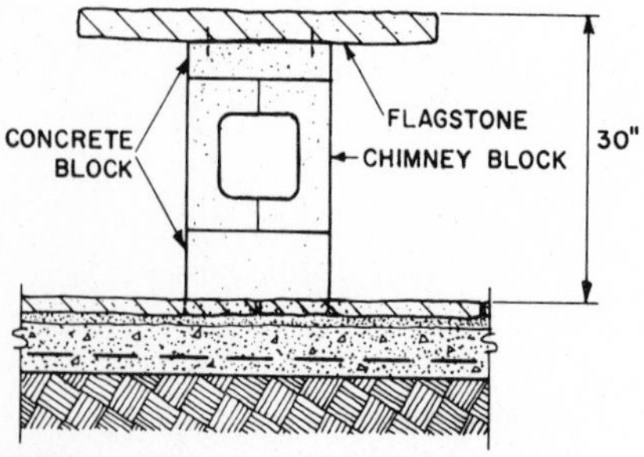

CONCRETE BLOCK

FLAGSTONE
CHIMNEY BLOCK

30"

Table
Top may be flagstone, slate, or concrete, 1½ to 3 in. thick. Supports are a combination of 4 by 8 by 16 in. and 8 by 8 by 16 in. concrete blocks and 8 by 16 by 16 in. chimney block to obtain height of 29 to 30 in.

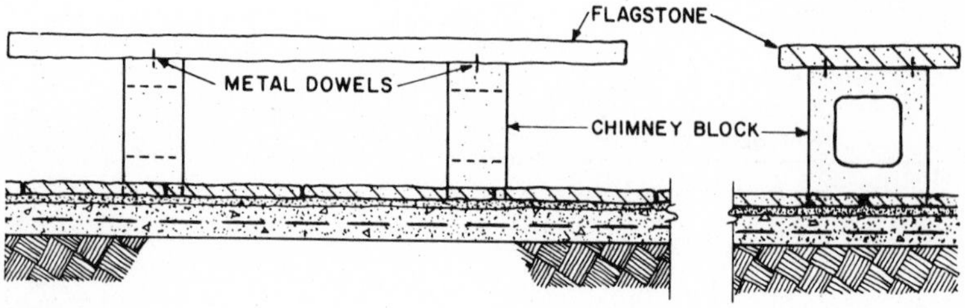

FLAGSTONE

METAL DOWELS

CHIMNEY BLOCK

Bench
Seat may be flagstone or concrete, 2 to 3 in. thick, 18 to 24 in. wide; height 14 to 18 in. Supports are concrete chimney block, 8 by 16 by 16 in.

GARDEN FURNITURE
Scale: ⅜ in. equals 1 ft

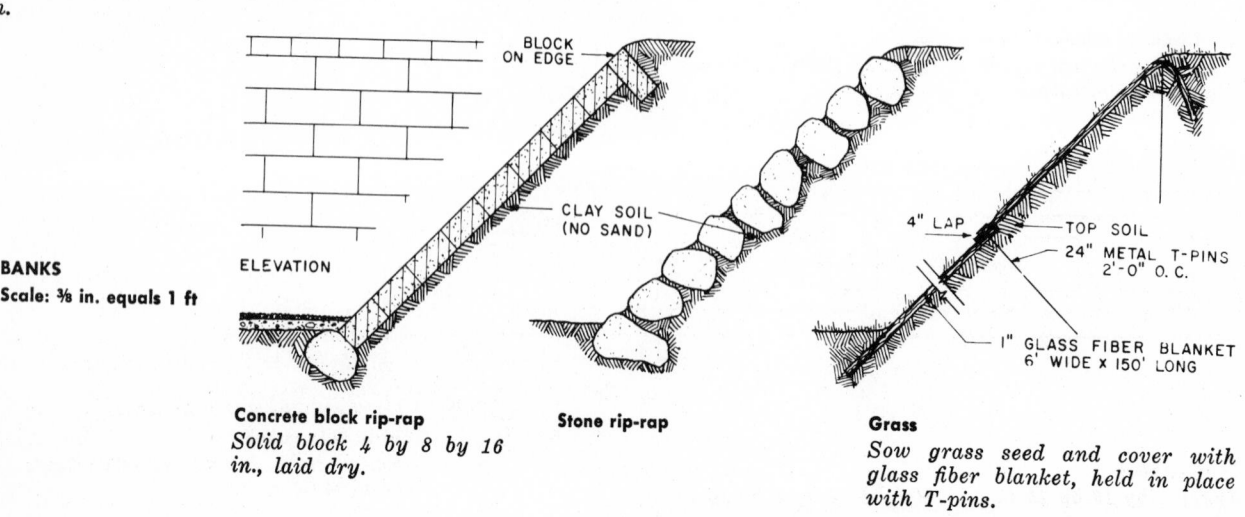

BLOCK ON EDGE

CLAY SOIL (NO SAND)

ELEVATION

BANKS
Scale: ⅜ in. equals 1 ft

4" LAP

TOP SOIL

24" METAL T-PINS 2'-0" O.C.

1" GLASS FIBER BLANKET 6' WIDE x 150' LONG

Concrete block rip-rap
Solid block 4 by 8 by 16 in., laid dry.

Stone rip-rap

Grass
Sow grass seed and cover with glass fiber blanket, held in place with T-pins.

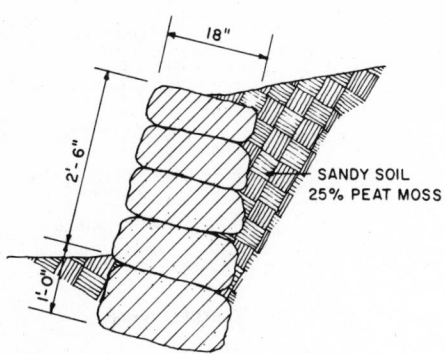

Stone
Batter 3 in. per ft in cold regions, 1½ in. per ft in frost-free regions. Spaces between stones may be filled with top soil and plants, if desired.

DRY RETAINING WALLS
Scale: ⅜ in. equals 1 ft
For masonry retaining walls see section on "Structural Design—Masonry."

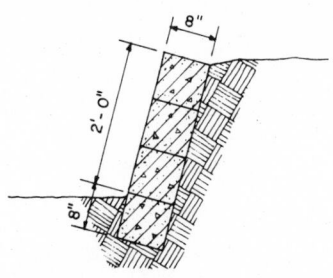

Concrete block
Solid block 8 by 8 by 16 in. Batter 2½ in. per ft. Will be slowly displaced by frost.

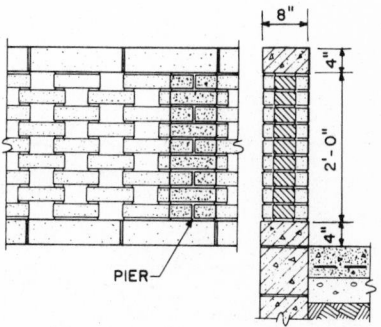

Open wall of brick
Minimum overlap of brick 1½ in. Provide 8 by 8 in. piers 6 to 8 ft on center. Coping and base may be precast concrete or cut stone.

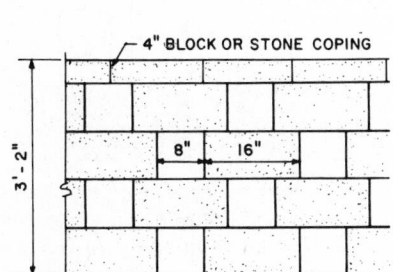

Solid block
8 by 8 by 16 in.

Open walls of standard concrete blocks
Special blocks are available in many patterns for use in building open walls and sun screens.

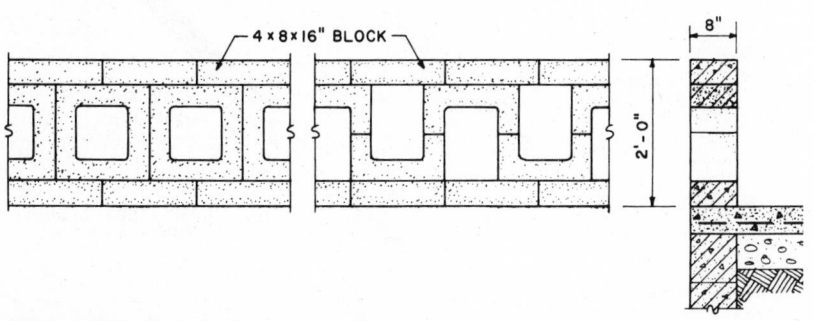

Chimney block
(left) 8 by 16 by 16 in.   (right) 8 by 8 by 16 in.

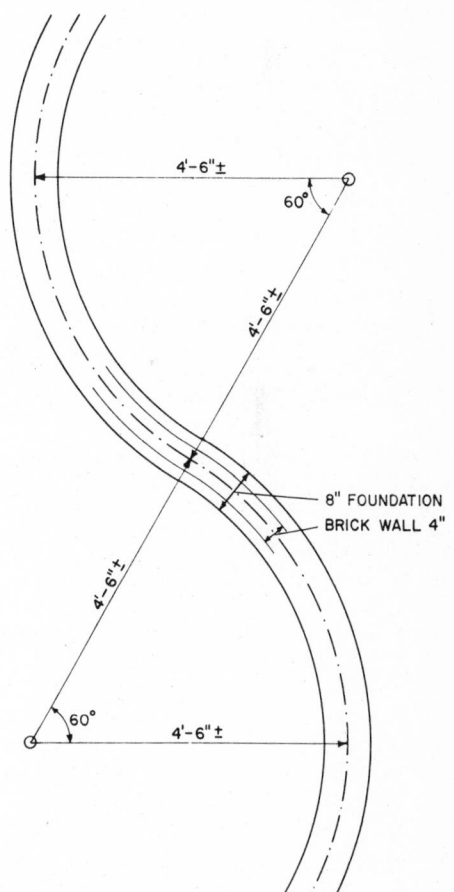

Serpentine brick wall
Attributed to Thomas Jefferson.

FREESTANDING MASONRY WALLS
Scale: ⅜ in. equals 1 ft
Foundations must extend below frost line.

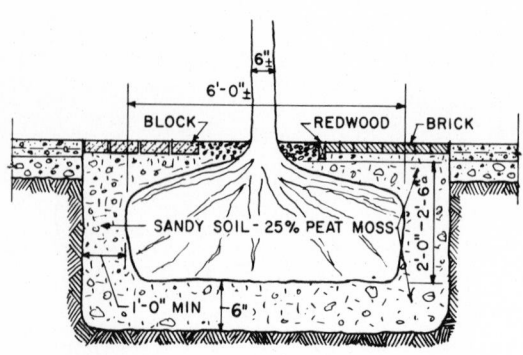

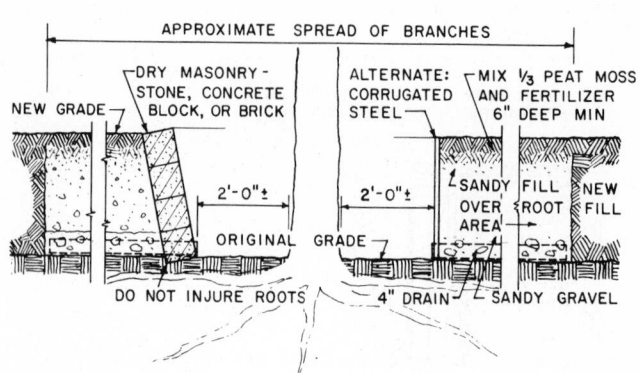

Tree in pavement

Over porous backfill of sandy soil with 25 to 30 per cent peat moss, lay dry paving units with tight joints. Belgian block, granite block, asphalt block, concrete block, brick, or crushed stone may be used. If brick is used, install inner edging of 2 by 4 in. redwood.

Tree in filled ground

Install 8 to 10 drain lines, placed radially around the tree. Drains may be porous or perforated pipe, as previously described, or agricultural tile with open joints covered by 1-in. fiber blanket.

TREE PLANTING DETAILS

Scale: ¼ in. equals 1 ft

Tree roots need air. Sandy soil is porous to air; it should be mixed with peat moss to retain moisture. Do not compress the soil around trees with bulldozers or other heavy equipment. Disturb the roots as little as possible.

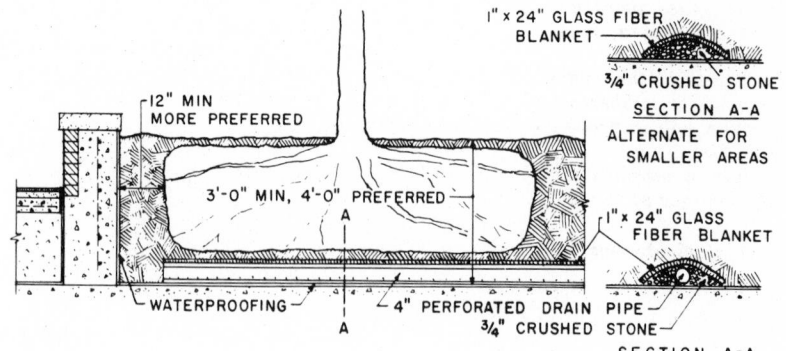

Tree on roof

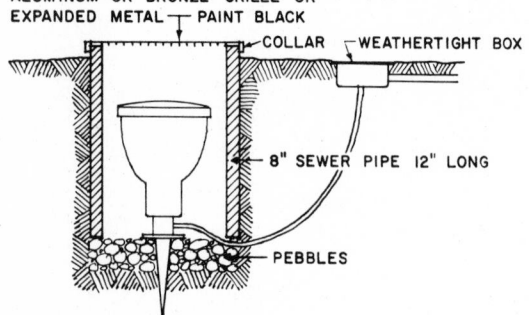

Underground floodlight
To light trees. 75 to 150 watts.

Small spotlight or floodlight
To light statuary. 30 watts.

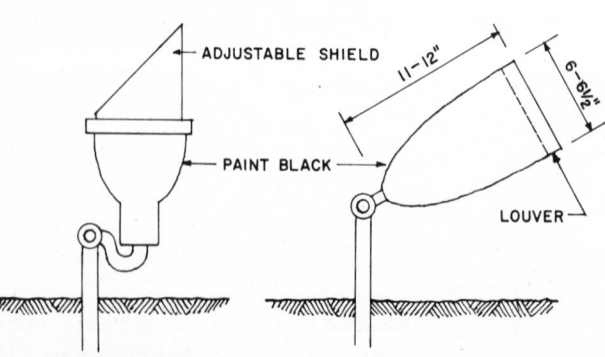

Above ground floodlights
Hidden by stones or bushes. To light trees or house. 75 to 150 watts.

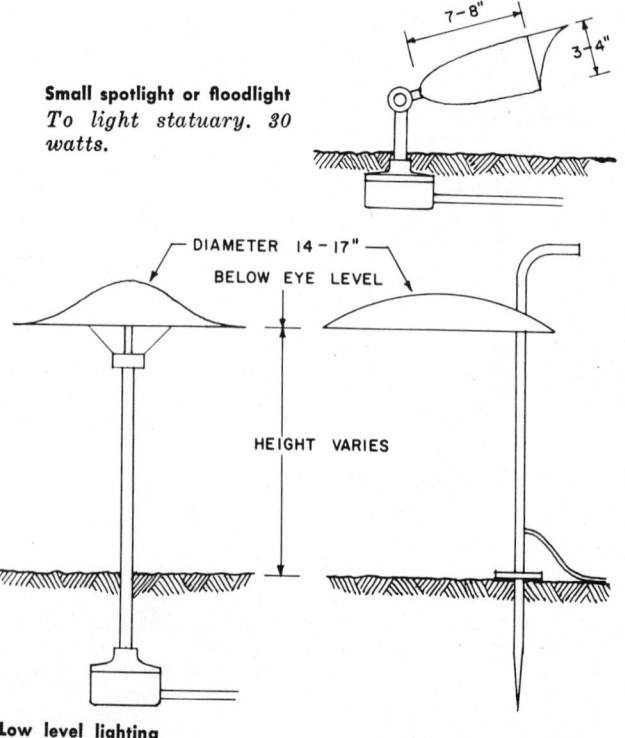

Low level lighting
To light walks or flowers. 75 watts. Permanent or portable.

OUTDOOR LIGHTING
Scale: ¾ in. equals 1 ft

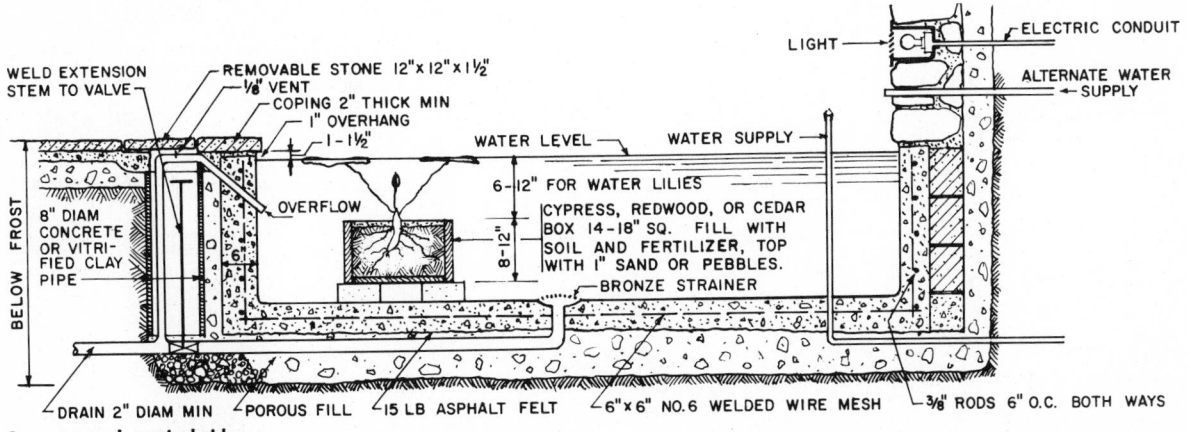

Concrete pool, vertical sides

Labels: WELD EXTENSION STEM TO VALVE; REMOVABLE STONE 12"x 12"x 1½"; ⅛" VENT; COPING 2" THICK MIN; 1" OVERHANG; 1–1½"; WATER LEVEL; WATER SUPPLY; LIGHT; ELECTRIC CONDUIT; ALTERNATE WATER SUPPLY; 6–12" FOR WATER LILIES; CYPRESS, REDWOOD, OR CEDAR BOX 14-18" SQ. FILL WITH SOIL AND FERTILIZER, TOP WITH 1" SAND OR PEBBLES.; 8-12"; OVERFLOW; 8" DIAM CONCRETE OR VITRIFIED CLAY PIPE; BELOW FROST; 6"; BRONZE STRAINER; DRAIN 2" DIAM MIN; POROUS FILL; 15 LB ASPHALT FELT; 6"x 6" NO.6 WELDED WIRE MESH; ⅜" RODS 6" O.C. BOTH WAYS

All concrete pools must be poured or sprayed in one continuous operation without joints. Inside forms, where required, must be supported from the outside and suspended.

Painting the inside of the pool very dark with cement- or rubber-based paint will make the pool look deeper, will improve surface reflections, and will show less dirt.

Water supply outlet must be 6 in. minimum above the surface of the water.

Scale of all drawings: ⅜ in. equals 1 ft

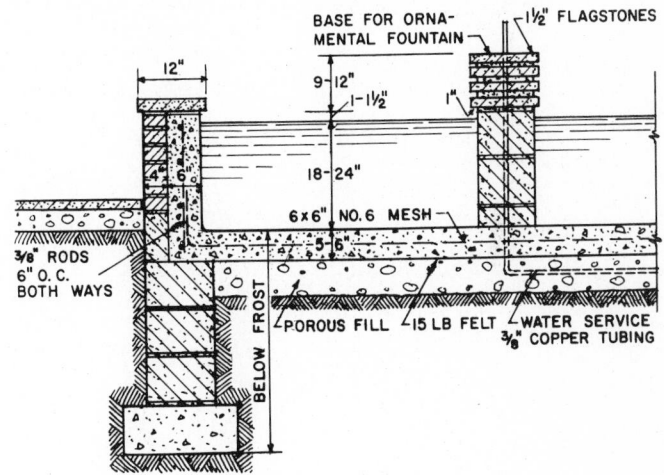

Labels: BASE FOR ORNAMENTAL FOUNTAIN; 1½" FLAGSTONES; 12"; 9-12"; 1-1½"; 1"; 18-24"; 6"; 6 x 6" NO. 6 MESH; 6"; ⅜" RODS 6" O.C. BOTH WAYS; BELOW FROST; POROUS FILL; 15 LB FELT; WATER SERVICE ⅜" COPPER TUBING

Concrete pool above grade
Overflow and drain similar to above figures. Submersible recirculating pumps are available for fountains.

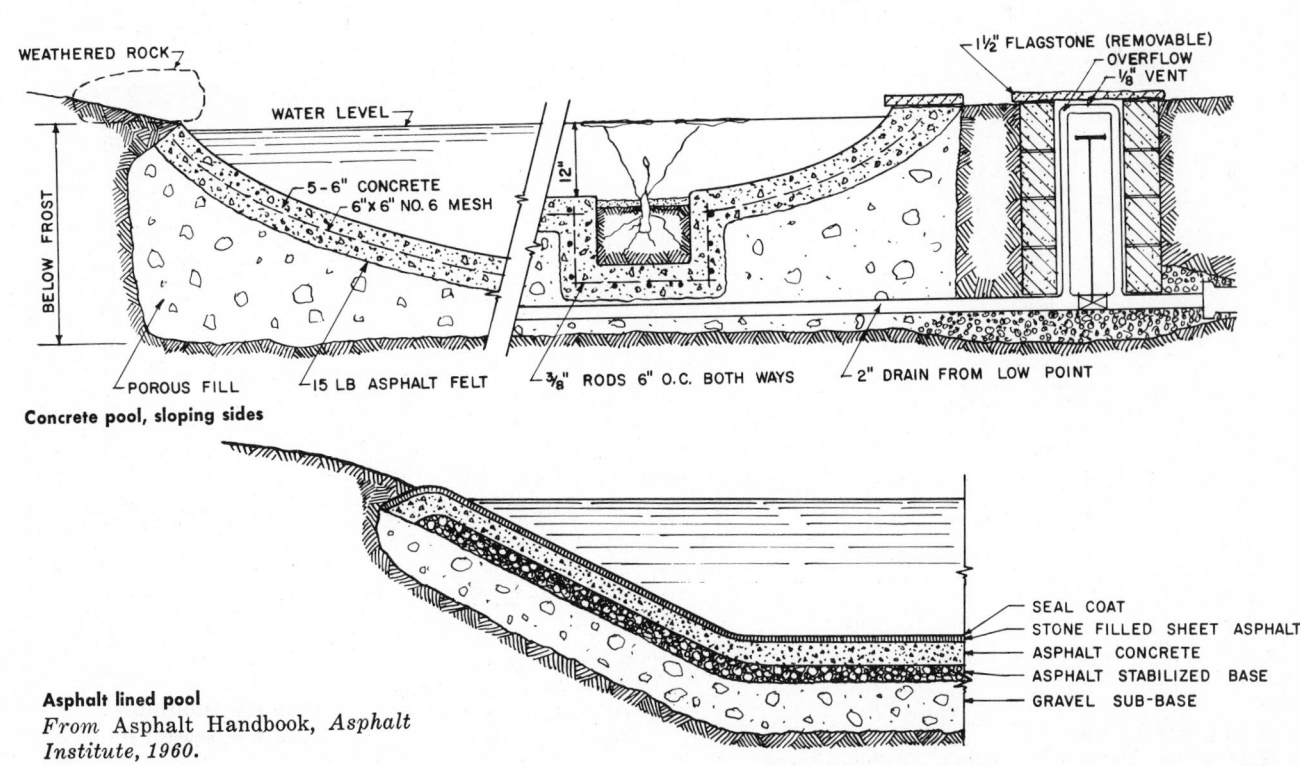

Concrete pool, sloping sides

Labels: WEATHERED ROCK; WATER LEVEL; 1½" FLAGSTONE (REMOVABLE); OVERFLOW; ⅛" VENT; 5-6" CONCRETE; 6"x 6" NO.6 MESH; 12"; BELOW FROST; POROUS FILL; 15 LB ASPHALT FELT; ⅜" RODS 6" O.C. BOTH WAYS; 2" DRAIN FROM LOW POINT

Asphalt lined pool
From Asphalt Handbook, Asphalt Institute, 1960.

Labels: SEAL COAT; STONE FILLED SHEET ASPHALT; ASPHALT CONCRETE; ASPHALT STABILIZED BASE; GRAVEL SUB-BASE

By ROBERT E. FAUCETT, *Outdoor Lighting Department, General Electric Company*

VERTICAL PROJECTION HEIGHT FROM DIFFERENT ORIFICE SIZES OF SMOOTH NOZZLES VS PRESSURE AT NOZZLE

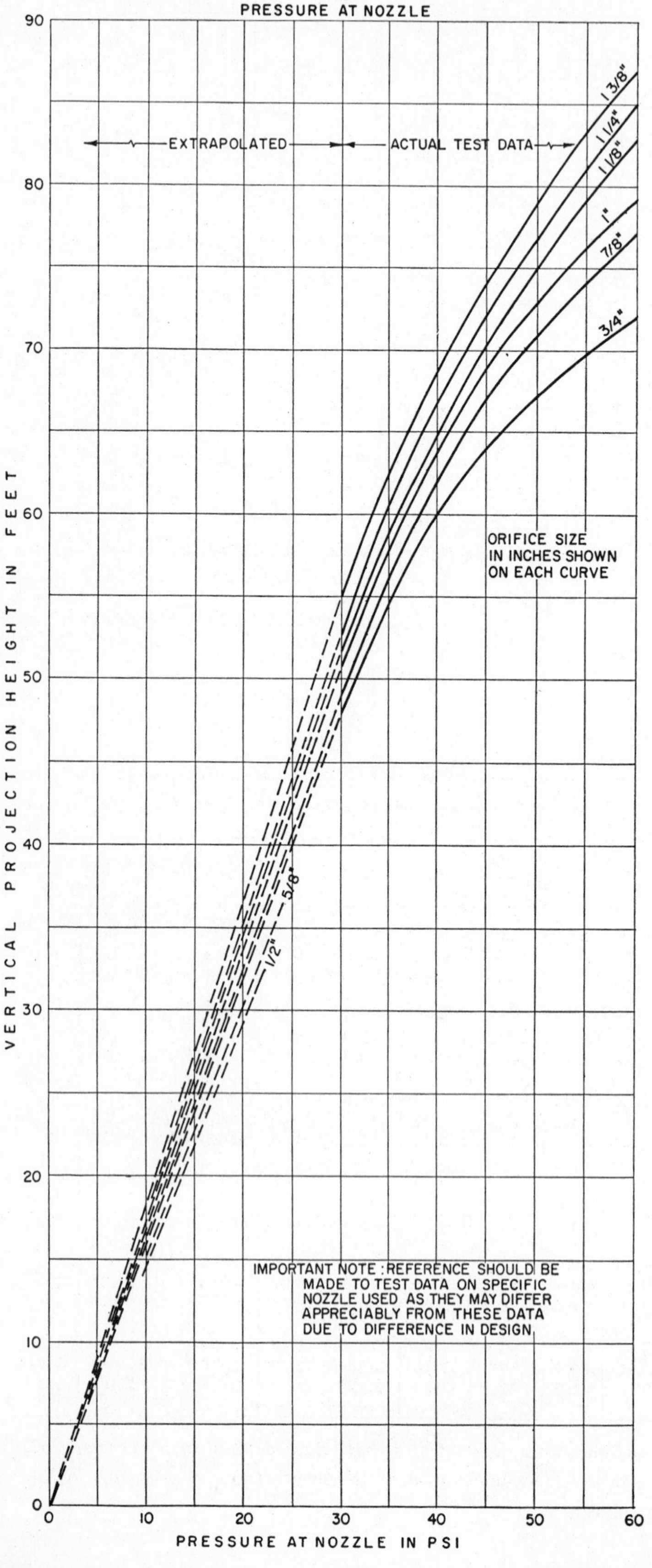

ORIFICE SIZE IN INCHES SHOWN ON EACH CURVE

IMPORTANT NOTE: REFERENCE SHOULD BE MADE TO TEST DATA ON SPECIFIC NOZZLE USED AS THEY MAY DIFFER APPRECIABLY FROM THESE DATA DUE TO DIFFERENCE IN DESIGN.

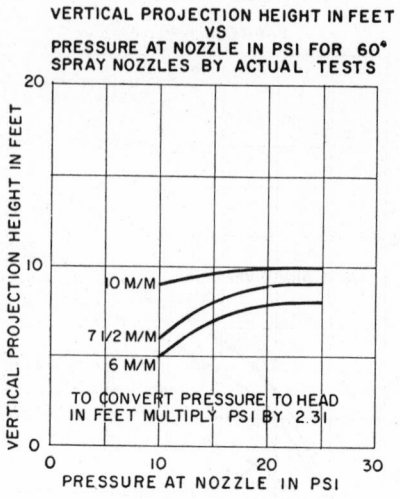

VERTICAL PROJECTION HEIGHT IN FEET VS PRESSURE AT NOZZLE IN PSI FOR 60° SPRAY NOZZLES BY ACTUAL TESTS

TO CONVERT PRESSURE TO HEAD IN FEET MULTIPLY PSI BY 2.31

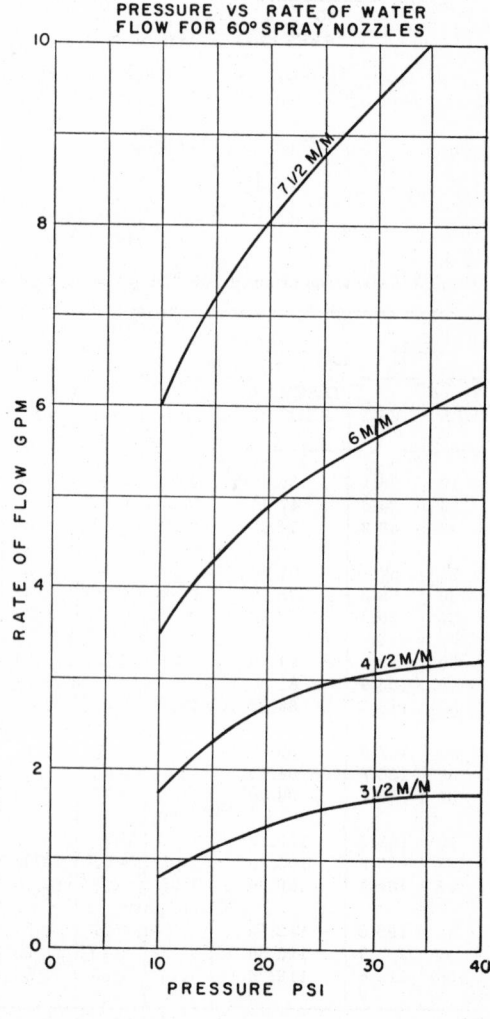

PRESSURE VS RATE OF WATER FLOW FOR 60° SPRAY NOZZLES

NOTE 1—Graph *(left)* plotted from *Table of Effective Fire Streams* by Goulds Pumps, Inc.

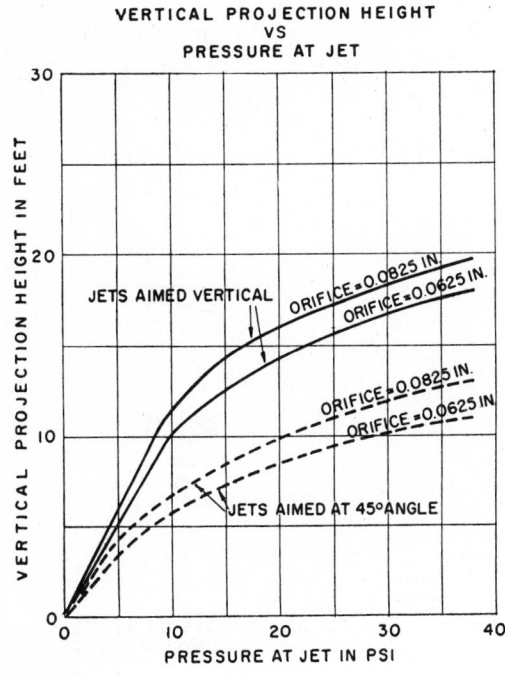

VERTICAL PROJECTION HEIGHT
VS
PRESSURE AT JET

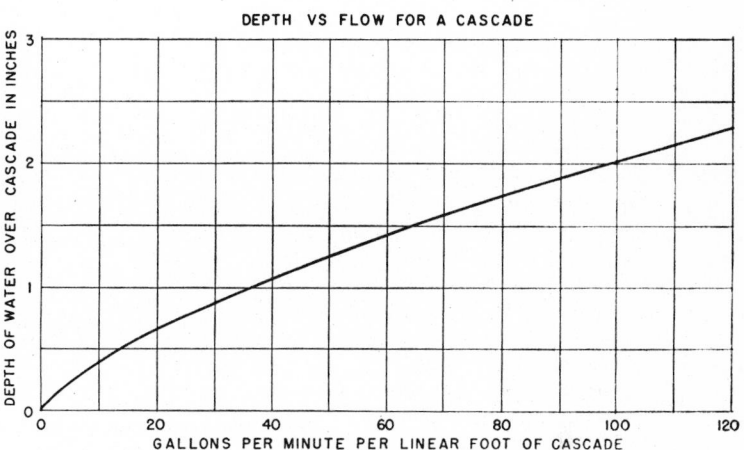

DEPTH VS FLOW FOR A CASCADE

Theoretical discharge of nozzles in U.S. gallons per minute

HEAD		VELOC'Y OF DISCHARGE FEET/SEC	DIAMETER OF NOZZLE IN INCHES												
LBS.	FEET		1/16	1/8	3/16	1/4	3/8	1/2	5/8	3/4	7/8	1	1 1/8	1 1/4	1 3/8
10	23.1	38.60	0.37	1.48	3.32	5.91	13.3	23.6	36.9	53.1	72.4	94.5	120	148	179
15	34.6	47.25	0.45	1.81	4.06	7.24	16.3	28.9	45.2	65.0	88.5	116.0	147	181	219
20	46.2	54.55	0.52	2.09	4.69	8.35	18.8	33.4	52.2	75.1	102.0	134.0	169	209	253
25	57.7	61.00	0.58	2.34	5.25	9.34	21.0	37.3	58.3	84.0	114.0	149.0	189	234	283
30	69.3	66.85	0.64	2.56	5.75	10.20	23.0	40.9	63.9	92.0	125.0	164.0	207	256	309
35	80.8	72.20	0.69	2.77	6.21	11.10	24.8	44.2	69.0	99.5	135.0	177.0	224	277	334
40	92.4	77.20	0.74	2.96	6.64	11.80	26.6	47.3	73.8	106.0	145.0	189.0	239	269	357
45	103.9	81.80	0.78	3.13	7.03	12.50	28.2	50.1	78.2	113.0	153.0	200.0	253	313	379
50	115.5	86.25	0.83	3.30	7.41	13.20	29.7	52.8	82.5	119.0	162.0	211.0	267	330	399
55	127.0	90.40	0.87	3.46	7.77	13.80	31.1	55.3	86.4	125.0	169.0	221.0	280	346	418
60	138.6	94.50	0.90	3.62	8.12	14.50	32.5	57.8	90.4	130.0	177.0	231.0	293	362	438
65	150.1	98.30	0.94	3.77	8.45	15.10	33.8	60.2	94.0	136.0	184.0	241.0	305	376	455
70	161.7	102.10	0.98	3.91	8.78	15.70	35.2	62.5	97.7	141.0	191.0	250.0	317	391	473
75	173.2	105.70	1.01	4.05	9.08	16.20	36.4	64.7	101.0	146.0	198.0	259.0	327	404	489
80	184.8	109.00	1.05	4.18	9.39	16.70	37.6	66.8	104.0	150.0	205.0	267.0	338	418	505
85	196.3	112.50	1.08	4.31	9.67	17.30	38.8	68.9	108.0	155.0	211.0	276.0	349	431	521
90	207.9	115.80	1.11	4.43	9.95	17.70	39.9	70.8	111.0	160.0	217.0	284.0	359	443	536
95	219.4	119.00	1.14	4.56	10.20	18.20	41.0	72.8	114.0	164.0	223.0	292.0	369	456	551

NOTE: The actual quantities will vary from these figures, the amount of variation depending upon the shape of the nozzle and size of pipe at the point where the pressure is determined. With smooth taper nozzles the actual discharge is about 94% of the figures given in the tables.

Desirable standards for recreation facilities have been set up by the National Recreation Association and are generally recognized. Absolute standardization is impossible because of variable factors: climatic conditions; population or institutional needs, habits or preferences; and available land or money. Information on these pages may be used in planning and space allocation.

Basic general standard for public areas is 1 acre of open space per 100 total population; of which 40 to 50 per cent should be devoted to games or other active recreation. (See also recommendations in section on "Apartments.") No set formula has been established for institutions such as churches, schools, colleges. Local conditions, such as extent of participation in organized athletics, available money, etc., should govern the choice; however, playfields for elementary and grammar schools may follow schemes outlined below.

Game areas and layouts contained in the drawings are based on practice of the New York City Department of Parks. Where games are subject to official rules, consult publications of athletic organizations or other governing bodies.

Types of public recreational areas have been set up by the National Recreation Association, based on age groups and urban or suburban needs.

Surfacing of play areas influences utility, extent and cost of upkeep, and extent of playing season. Local materials, climate, soil, intensity of use and tradition influence choice of surfacing. In general all areas require effective surface or subsurface drainage or both.

THE PLAYLOT

Playlots are intended for children of preschool age and are commonly provided in densely populated areas as a substitute for backyard play. They are also provided in interiors of large blocks in neighborhood or housing developments, often for nursery schools.

Size may vary from 6,000 to 10,000 sq ft for each 100 preschool children.

Location should be centered among population served, and accessible without crossing traffic arteries. Interior of a block is ideal if one block only is served. If available space is limited, a corner of children's playground may be used.

Plan elements include: (1) central grass plot; (2) areas with shade trees, in which apparatus and benches are set; (3) hard-surfaced walkway for wheel toys, velocipedes, etc.; (4) surrounding low fence or

AREAS & EQUIPMENT

Table 1. Playlots

Type of Equipment or Area	Area per Unit (Sq. Ft.)	Capacity in Children	Suggested Number Included
Apparatus			
Junglegym, Jr.	180	10	1
Low Slide	170	6	1-2
Low Swing	150	1	4-8
Low See-saw	100	2	4-8
Miscellaneous			
Open Space	48-50 per child	Varies with pop. to be served	
Block Bldg. Platform	20 per child / 150 per platform	7-8 per platform	1
Sand Box *	18-20 per child / 300 per box	15	1-2
Benches & Tables	Optional	Varies	
Shelter for Baby Buggies	Optional	Varies	1
Flag Pole	In open area		1
Bird Bath			1
Drinking Fountain			1

*Sand boxes should be located so as to receive direct sunlight part of each day for reasons of sanitation.

hedge. Distribution of area may vary with topography, apparatus included and child population served. Minimum recommendations of National Recreation Association are given in Table 1.

CHILDREN'S PLAYGROUNDS

These are intended for children 5 to 15 years old. A subdivision of this type, characterized by smaller area and fewer facilities, is called the *Junior* or *Primary Playground*, and is intended for children up to 10 or 11 years.

Size of children's playgrounds ranges from 3 acres (minimum) to 7 acres. General recommendation is 1 acre per 1,000 total population. Two small playgrounds are usually more satisfactory than one of excessive size when population served requires a large acreage.

Location is usually in an area developed for this particular use, adjoining a grade school, in a neighborhood or large park, or a portion of a neighborhood playfield. Maximum radius of area to be served should preferably not exceed one-half mile; in areas of dense population or subject to heavy traffic, one-quarter mile.

Plan elements may be subdivided into apparatus section, specialized sports area, landscaping, and miscellaneous activities. Areas required are given in Table 2. Selection and distribution of areas and equip-

Table 2. Children's playgrounds

Type of Equipment or Area	Area per Unit (Sq. Ft.)	Capacity in Children	Suggested Number Included
Apparatus			
Slide	450	6	1[b]
Horizontal Bars	180	4	3[b]
Horizontal Ladders	375	8	2[b]
Traveling Rings	625	6	1
Giant Stride	1,225	6	1
Small Junglegym	180	10	1
Low Swing	150	1	4[a]
High Swing	250	1	6[a]
Balance Beam	100	4	1
See-saw	100	2	4
Medium Junglegym	500	20	1
Misc. Equip't & Areas			
Open Space for Games (Ages 6-10)	10,000	80	1[a]
Wading Pool	3,000	40	1[a]
Handcraft, Quiet Games	1,600	30	1[a]
Outdoor Theater	2,000	30	1
Sand Box	300	15	2
Shelter House	2,500	30	1[c]
Special Sports Areas			
Soccer Field	36,000	22	1
Playground Baseball	20,000	20	2
Volley Ball Court	2,800	20	1
Basketball Court	3,750	16	1
Jumping Pits	1,200	12	1
Paddle Tennis Courts	1,800	4	2[d]
Handball Courts	1,050	4	2
Tether Tennis Courts	400	2	2[d]
Horseshoe Courts	600	4	2
Tennis Courts	7,200	4	2[d]
Straightaway Track	7,200	10	1[d]
Landscaping	[a]6,000		
Paths, Circulation, etc.	[a]7,000		

(a) Minimum desirable.

(b) One or all of these units may be omitted if playground is not used in conjunction with a school.

(c) May be omitted if sanitary facilities are supplied elsewhere.

(d) May be omitted if space is limited.

ment should be based on local preference, space and money available, and topography. Guides to selection of individual game areas or equipment are included in the footnotes to Table 2 where practicable.

In addition to the usual playground equipment listed on this page, some special equipment intended to stimulate imaginative play is now widely used. The examples (opposite) were pioneering efforts in this field, developed by the New York City Housing Authority in the late 1940's. A play boat and a play airplane, included in the original line of equipment, proved to be too expensive and too hazardous and are no longer used. A wide variety of imaginative playground equipment has been developed in recent years and is available from several commercial sources.

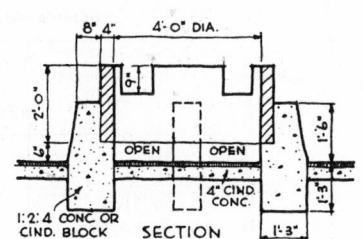
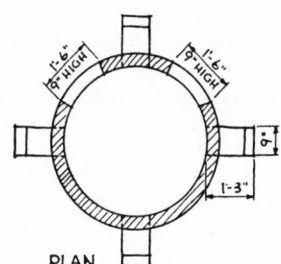

FOX HOLE

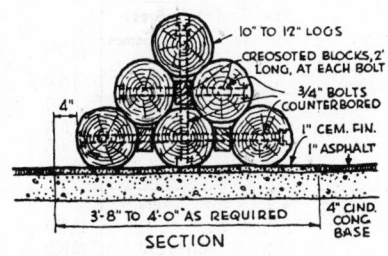
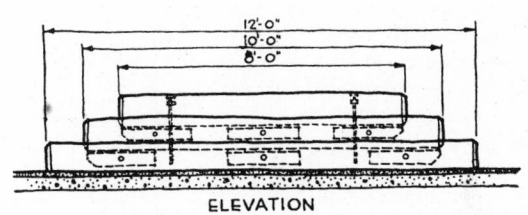

LOG PILE

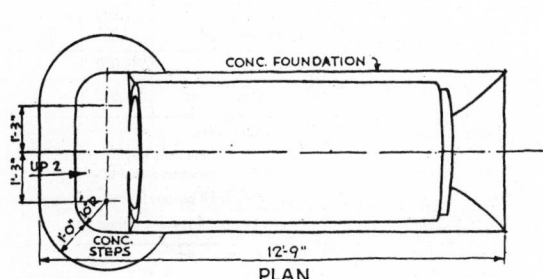
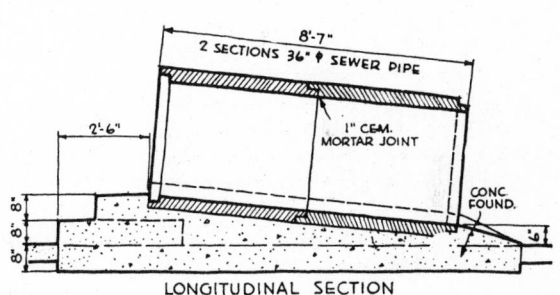

TUNNEL SLIDE

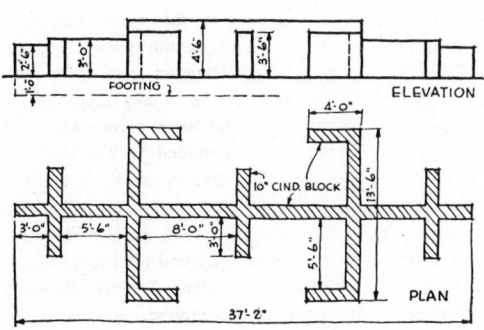
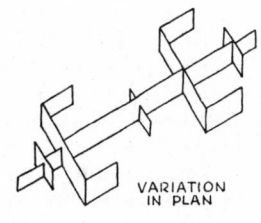

NOTE: PROVIDE OPENINGS FOR SURFACE DRAINAGE AT FINISHED GRADE LEVEL.

DODGER

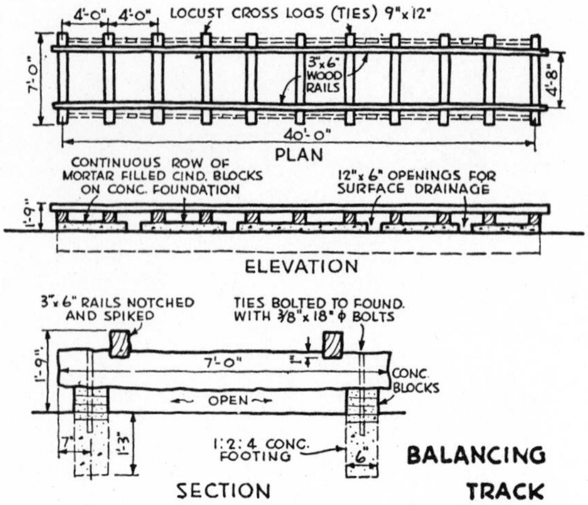

BALANCING TRACK

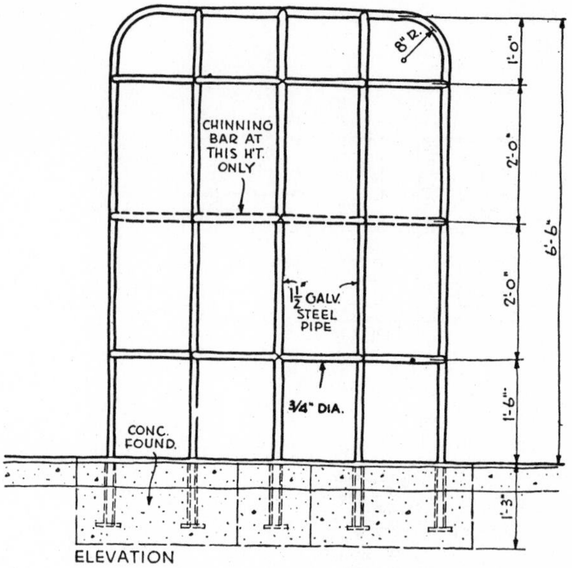

PLAN: 4'-0", 4'-0", LOCUST CROSS LOGS (TIES) 9"x12", 7'-0", 3"x6" WOOD RAILS, 4'-8", 40'-0"

ELEVATION: CONTINUOUS ROW OF MORTAR FILLED CIND. BLOCKS ON CONC. FOUNDATION — 12"x6" OPENINGS FOR SURFACE DRAINAGE — 1'-9"

SECTION: 3"x6" RAILS NOTCHED AND SPIKED — TIES BOLTED TO FOUND. WITH 3/8"x18" φ BOLTS — 1'-9" — 7'-0" — OPEN — CONC. BLOCKS — 7" — 1'-3" — 1:2:4 CONC. FOOTING — 6"

CHINNING BAR AT THIS H'T. ONLY — 8" R — 1'-0" — 2'-0" — 6'-6" — 1½" GALV. STEEL PIPE — 3/4" DIA. — 2'-0" — 1'-6" — CONC. FOUND. — 1'-3" — ELEVATION

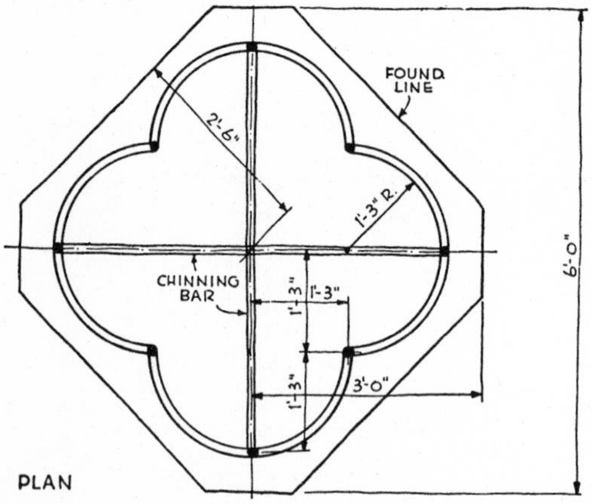

CIRCULAR PLAY UNIT

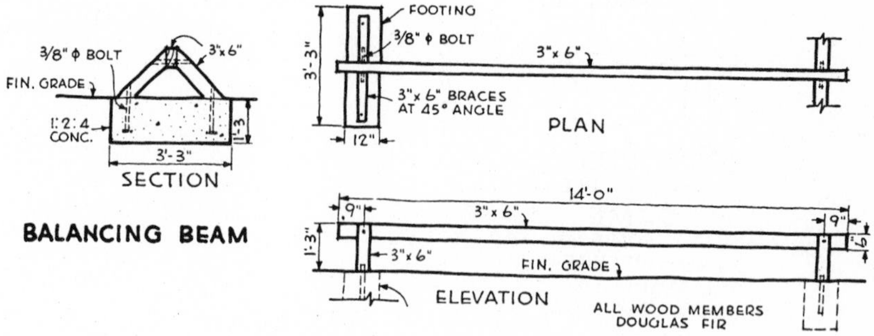

PLAN: FOUND. LINE — 2'-6" — 1'-3" R — CHINNING BAR — 1'-3" — 1'-3" — 1'-3" — 3'-0" — 6'-0"

BALANCING BEAM

SECTION: 3/8" φ BOLT — 3"x6" — FIN. GRADE — 1:2:4 CONC. — 3'-3" — 3'-3"

PLAN: FOOTING — 3/8" φ BOLT — 3"x6" — 3'-3" — 3"x6" BRACES AT 45° ANGLE — 12"

ELEVATION: 9" — 14'-0" — 3"x6" — 1'-3" — 3"x6" — FIN. GRADE — 9" — ALL WOOD MEMBERS DOUGLAS FIR

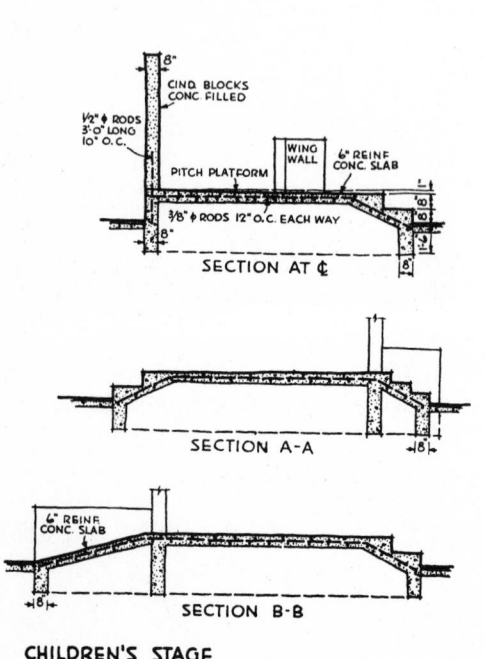

CHILDREN'S STAGE

SECTION AT ₵: 8" — CIND. BLOCKS CONC. FILLED — ½" φ RODS 3'-0" LONG 10" O.C. — PITCH PLATFORM — WING WALL — 6" REINF. CONC. SLAB — 3/8" φ RODS 12" O.C. EACH WAY — 8"

SECTION A-A

SECTION B-B: 6" REINF. CONC. SLAB — 8"

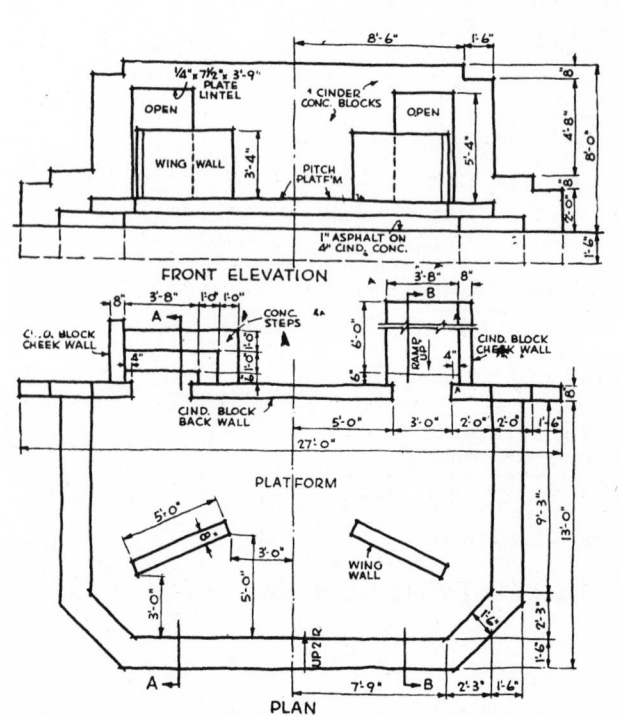

FRONT ELEVATION: 8'-6" — 1'-6" — ¼"x7½"x3'-9" PLATE LINTEL — OPEN — CINDER CONC. BLOCKS — OPEN — WING WALL — 3'-4" — PITCH PLAT'M — 4'-8" — 5'-4" — 8'-0" — 1" ASPHALT ON 4" CIND. CONC.

PLAN: CIND. BLOCK CHEEK WALL — CONC. STEPS — 3'-8" — CIND. BLOCK CHEEK WALL — CIND. BLOCK BACK WALL — RAMP UP — PLATFORM — 27'-0" — 5'-0" — 3'-0" — 2'-0" — 2'-6" — WING WALL — 5'-0" — 3'-0" — 5'-0" — 3'-0" — 9'-3" — 13'-0" — UP 2R — 7'-9" — 2'-3"

Data in this section were selected by Ronald Allwork from standard details prepared by the Department of Parks, New York, N.Y.

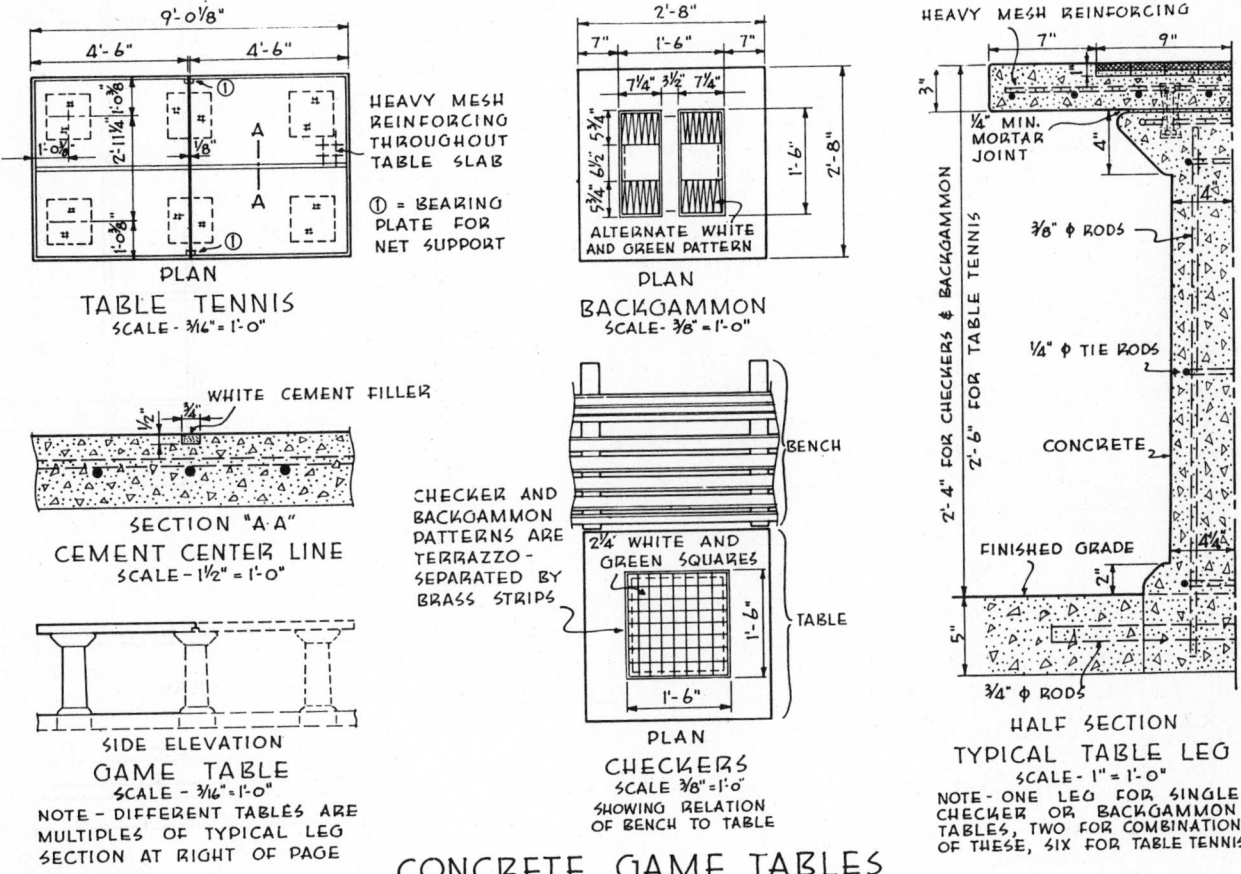

CONCRETE GAME TABLES

PLAN
TABLE TENNIS
SCALE - 3/16" = 1'-0"

HEAVY MESH REINFORCING THROUGHOUT TABLE SLAB

① = BEARING PLATE FOR NET SUPPORT

WHITE CEMENT FILLER

SECTION "A-A"
CEMENT CENTER LINE
SCALE - 1½" = 1'-0"

SIDE ELEVATION
GAME TABLE
SCALE - 3/16" = 1'-0"
NOTE - DIFFERENT TABLES ARE MULTIPLES OF TYPICAL LEG SECTION AT RIGHT OF PAGE

PLAN
BACKGAMMON
SCALE - 3/8" = 1'-0"

ALTERNATE WHITE AND GREEN PATTERN

CHECKER AND BACKGAMMON PATTERNS ARE TERRAZZO - SEPARATED BY BRASS STRIPS

2¼" WHITE AND GREEN SQUARES

BENCH

TABLE

PLAN
CHECKERS
SCALE 3/8" = 1'-0"
SHOWING RELATION OF BENCH TO TABLE

HEAVY MESH REINFORCING

¼" MIN. MORTAR JOINT

3/8" φ RODS

¼" φ TIE RODS

CONCRETE

FINISHED GRADE

¾" φ RODS

HALF SECTION
TYPICAL TABLE LEG
SCALE - 1" = 1'-0"
NOTE- ONE LEG FOR SINGLE CHECKER OR BACKGAMMON TABLES, TWO FOR COMBINATION OF THESE, SIX FOR TABLE TENNIS

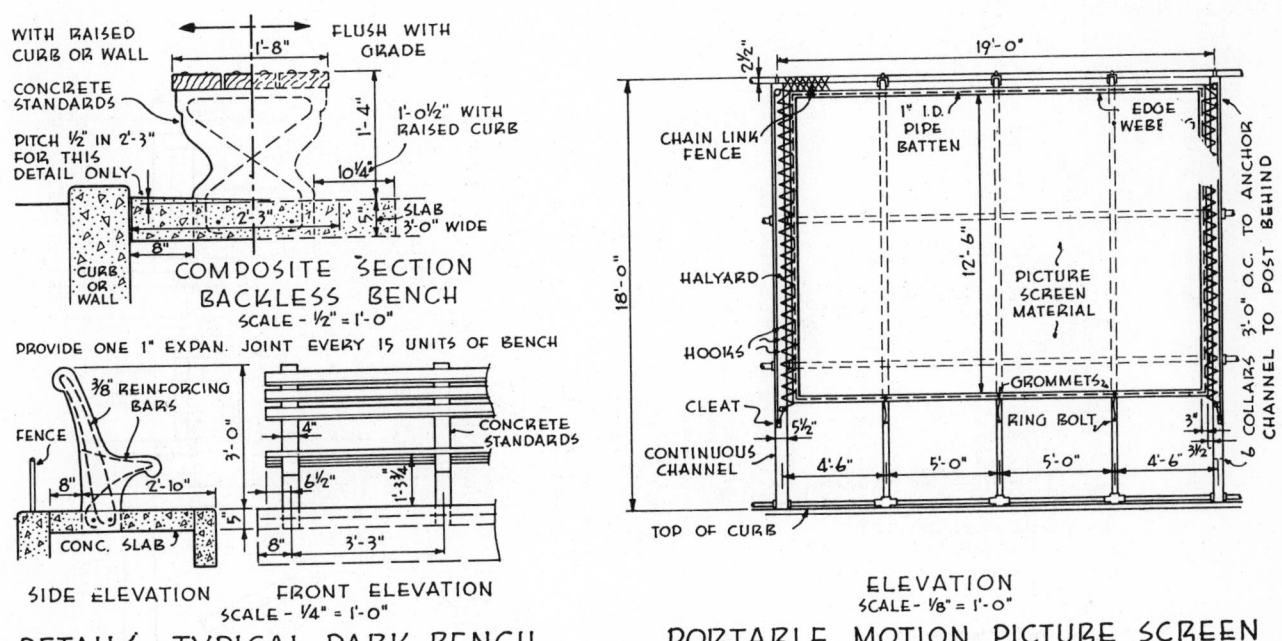

WITH RAISED CURB OR WALL

CONCRETE STANDARDS

PITCH ½" IN 2'-3" FOR THIS DETAIL ONLY

FLUSH WITH GRADE

1'-0½" WITH RAISED CURB

SLAB 3'-0" WIDE

CURB OR WALL

COMPOSITE SECTION
BACKLESS BENCH
SCALE - ½" = 1'-0"

PROVIDE ONE 1" EXPAN. JOINT EVERY 15 UNITS OF BENCH

3/8" REINFORCING BARS

FENCE

CONCRETE STANDARDS

CONC. SLAB

SIDE ELEVATION   FRONT ELEVATION
SCALE - ¼" = 1'-0"
DETAILS - TYPICAL PARK BENCH

CHAIN LINK FENCE

1" I.D. PIPE BATTEN

EDGE WEBB

HALYARD

PICTURE SCREEN MATERIAL

HOOKS

GROMMETS

CLEAT

RING BOLT

CONTINUOUS CHANNEL

6 COLLARS 3'-0" O.C. TO ANCHOR CHANNEL TO POST BEHIND

TOP OF CURB

ELEVATION
SCALE - 1/8" = 1'-0"
PORTABLE MOTION PICTURE SCREEN

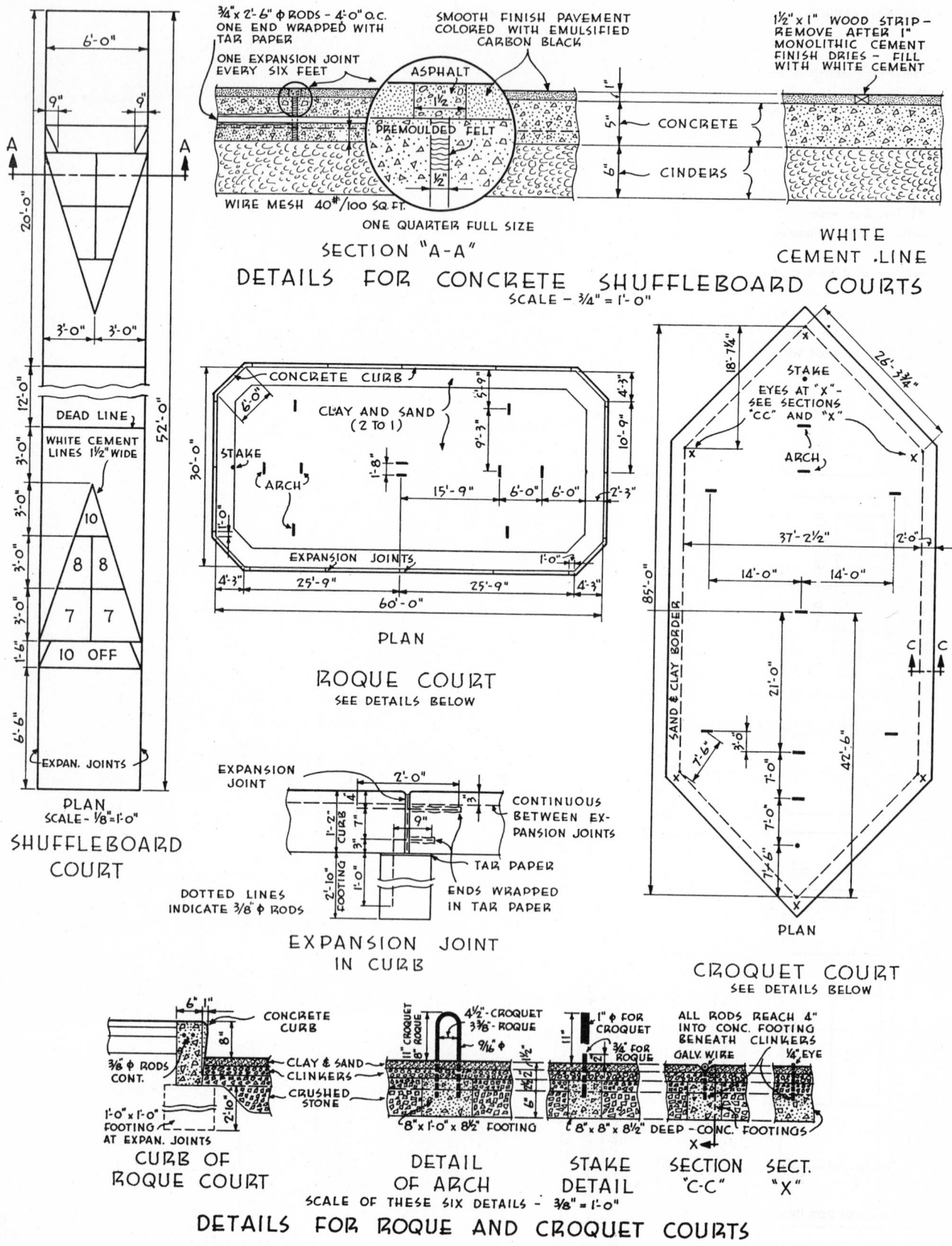

¾" x 2'-6" φ RODS - 4'-0" O.C.
ONE END WRAPPED WITH
TAR PAPER

ONE EXPANSION JOINT
EVERY SIX FEET

SMOOTH FINISH PAVEMENT
COLORED WITH EMULSIFIED
CARBON BLACK

ASPHALT

PREMOULDED FELT

WIRE MESH 40#/100 SQ. FT.

ONE QUARTER FULL SIZE

1½" x 1" WOOD STRIP-
REMOVE AFTER 1"
MONOLITHIC CEMENT
FINISH DRIES - FILL
WITH WHITE CEMENT

CONCRETE

CINDERS

WHITE
CEMENT LINE

SECTION "A-A"

DETAILS FOR CONCRETE SHUFFLEBOARD COURTS
SCALE - ¾" = 1'-0"

PLAN
SCALE - ⅛" = 1'-0"

**SHUFFLEBOARD
COURT**

6'-0"
9" 9"
20'-0"
3'-0" 3'-0"
52'-0"
12'-0"
DEAD LINE
WHITE CEMENT
LINES 1½" WIDE
3'-0"
3'-0"
10
3'-0"
8 8
3'-0"
7 7
1'-6"
10 OFF
6'-6"
EXPAN. JOINTS

CONCRETE CURB
CLAY AND SAND
(2 TO 1)
STAKE
ARCH
EXPANSION JOINTS
30'-0"
6'-0"
5'-9"
9'-3"
1'-8"
15'-9"
6'-0" 6'-0"
2'-3"
4'-3"
25'-9"
25'-9"
4'-3"
60'-0"
4'-3"
10'-9"
1'-0"
1'-0"

PLAN

ROQUE COURT
SEE DETAILS BELOW

EXPANSION
JOINT
2'-0"
1'-2" CURB
7"
9"
2'-0" FOOTING
1'-0"
2'-10"
CONTINUOUS
BETWEEN EX-
PANSION JOINTS
TAR PAPER
ENDS WRAPPED
IN TAR PAPER
DOTTED LINES
INDICATE ⅜" φ RODS

**EXPANSION JOINT
IN CURB**

STAKE
EYES AT "X" -
SEE SECTIONS
"CC" AND "X"
ARCH
18'-7¼"
26'-3¾"
37'-2½"
2'-0"
14'-0" 14'-0"
21'-0"
7'-6" 3'-0"
7'-0"
7'-0"
1'-6"
42'-6"
85'-0"
SAND & CLAY BORDER
X X
X
X
C C

PLAN

CROQUET COURT
SEE DETAILS BELOW

CONCRETE
CURB
6" 1"
8"
CLAY & SAND
CLINKERS
CRUSHED
STONE
⅜" φ RODS
CONT.
1'-0" x 1'-0"
FOOTING
AT EXPAN. JOINTS
2'-0"

4½"- CROQUET
3⅜"- ROQUE
9/16" φ
11" CROQUET
8" ROQUE
8" x 1'-0" x 8½" FOOTING

1" φ FOR
CROQUET
¾" FOR
ROQUE
11"
8" x 8" x 8½" DEEP- CONC. FOOTINGS

ALL RODS REACH 4"
INTO CONC. FOOTING
BENEATH CLINKERS
GALV. WIRE
¼" EYE
X

**CURB OF
ROQUE COURT**

**DETAIL
OF ARCH**

**STAKE
DETAIL**

**SECTION
"C-C"**

**SECT.
"X"**

SCALE OF THESE SIX DETAILS - ⅜" = 1'-0"

DETAILS FOR ROQUE AND CROQUET COURTS

BASKETBALL COURTS

Sizes:

Junior high school: 42 by 74 ft

High school; YMCA: 50 by 84 ft

College; AAU: 50 by 94 ft

Height: minimum 20 ft, more preferred

Width of unobstructed space outside boundaries: minimum 3 ft, 10 ft preferred

All lines 2 in. wide

Basket: 18-in. diameter, 10 ft above floor

Backboard: 4 by 6 ft rectangular, lower edge 9 ft above floor. Optional for high school and AAU: 35 by 54 in., fan shape, top edge curved on 29-in. radius, mounted with top edge 12 ft 8 in. above floor.

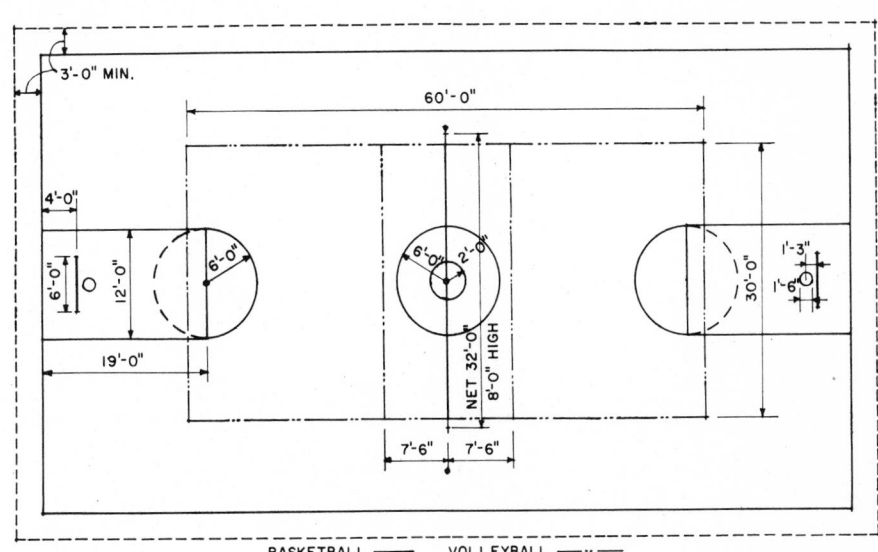

BASKETBALL ——— VOLLEYBALL —·—·——

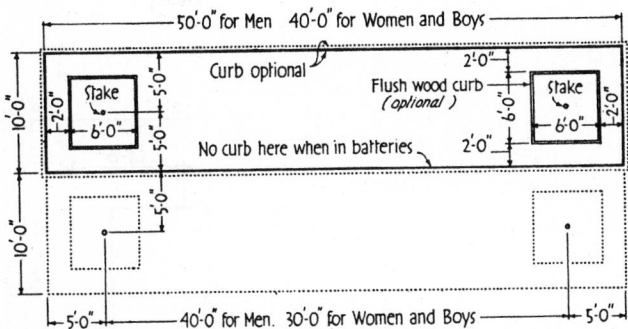

HORSESHOE PITCHING

SCALE 1/16" = 1'-0"

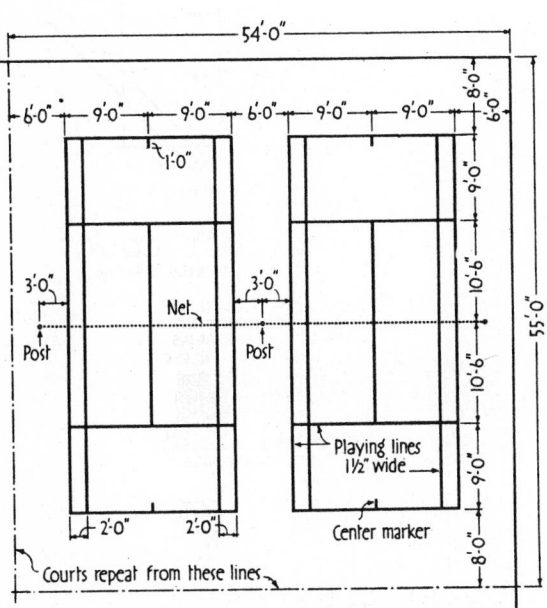

PADDLE TENNIS

SCALE 1" = 20'-0"

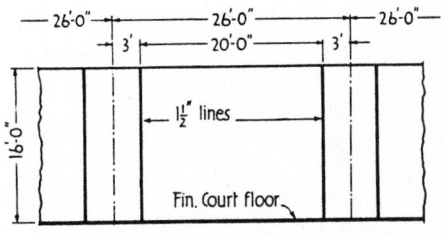

ELEVATION OF BACKSTOP

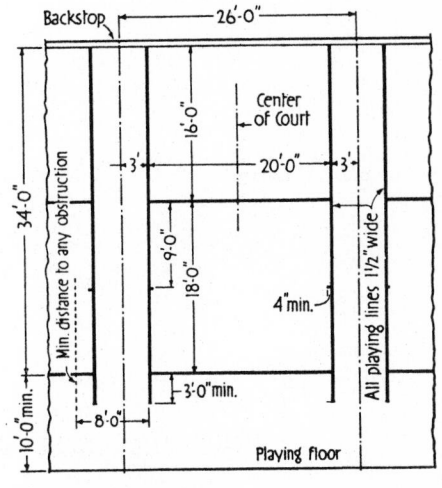

HANDBALL

SCALE 1" = 20'-0"

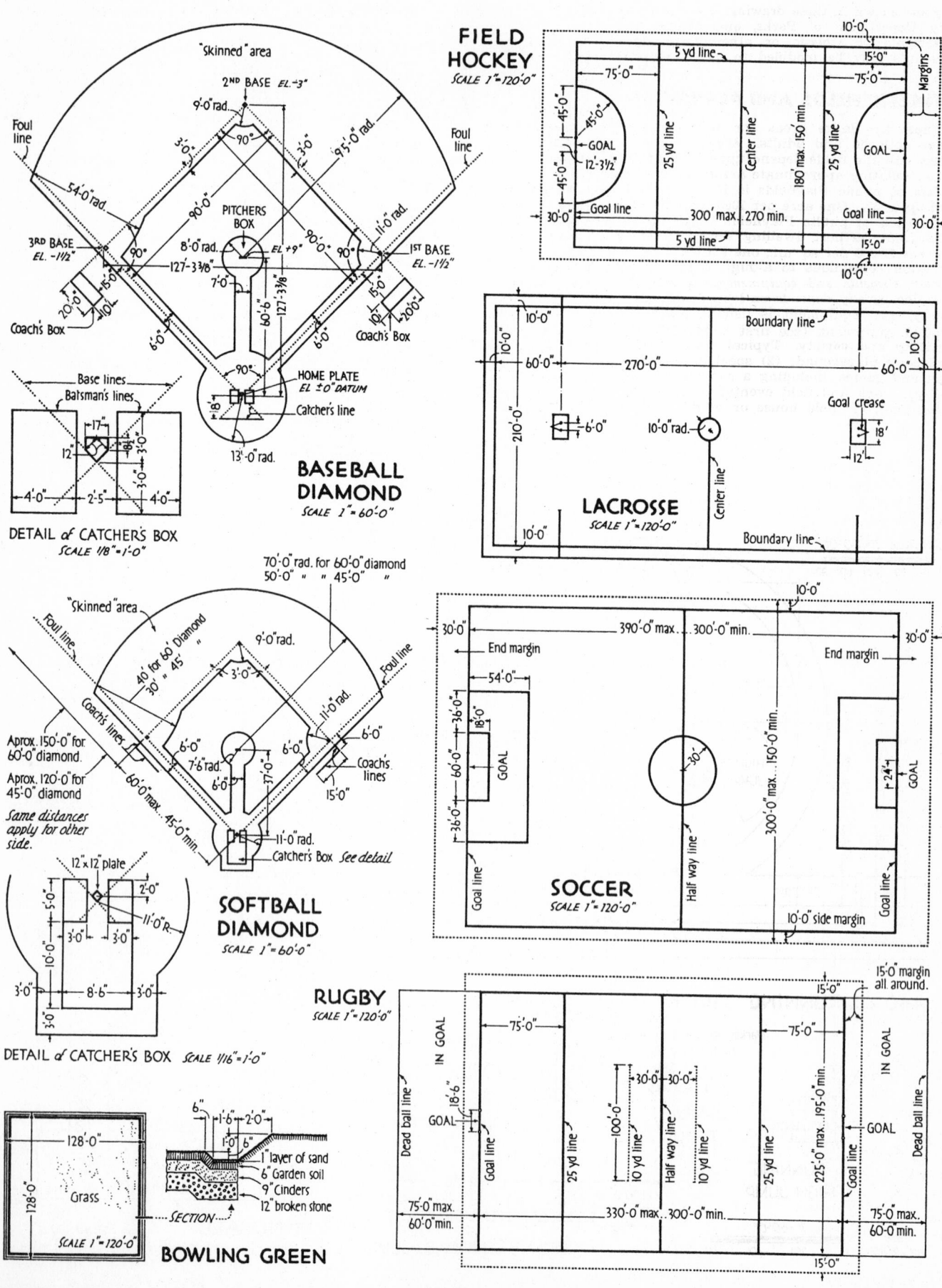

BASEBALL DIAMOND
SCALE 1"=60'-0"

DETAIL of CATCHER'S BOX
SCALE 1/8"=1'-0"

SOFTBALL DIAMOND
SCALE 1"=60'-0"

DETAIL of CATCHER'S BOX SCALE 1/16"=1'-0"

BOWLING GREEN
SCALE 1"=120'-0"

FIELD HOCKEY
SCALE 1"=120'-0"

LACROSSE
SCALE 1"=120'-0"

SOCCER
SCALE 1"=120'-0"

RUGBY
SCALE 1"=120'-0"

Layouts shown in these drawings are standards of the New York City Department of Parks, and should be checked with requirements of athletic or other governing bodies. Suggested standards may be modified to meet institutional requirements.

ATHLETIC FIELDS AND PLAYFIELDS

These are large areas for active recreation, intended for older children and adults. Areas of school or other institutional athletic fields depend upon type of sports included; data for calculating approximate areas are given in the table.

Size of public Playfields is 10 acres minimum, 20 desirable, and up to 50. One acre per 1000 total population is general.

Location of public Playfields is preferably not more than 1 mile from farthest dwelling served; when population density exceeds 20,000 per sq. mi., one Playfield per sq. mi. is desirable. Location contiguous to a high school is also favored.

Plan elements and *equipment* of public Playfields are given. Selection usually depends on local conditions, preferences, topography, etc. Equipment is usually similar to children's playground equipment (see first page of section) but in greater quantity and variety. Typical plans include areas for: (1) a children's playground; (2) specialized sports fields; (3) recreation and games, including a section for girls and women; (4) 440 yd. track and field events; (5) picnic grounds; (6) swimming pool; (7) field house or "club" house; (8) landscaping.

AREAS & EQUIPMENT - Athletic Fields

Type of Sports or Area	Area per Unit (Sq. Ft.)	Capacity in Players	Type of Sports or Area	Area per Unit (Sq. Ft.)	Capacity in Players
Baseball Diamond	97,500	18	Handball	2,000	2-4
Basketball Court	6,000	10	Hand Tennis	1,250	2-4
Basketball Court (women's)	5,000	12-18	Horseshoe Pitching	500	2-4
			Lacrosse	125,000	24
Boccie	2,100	2-4	Paddle Tennis	1,800	2-4
Bowling Alley	2,400	4-8	Playground Ball	22,500	20
			Polo	576,000	8
Clock Golf	706	Any No.	Quoits	2,000	2-4
Cricket	138,545	22	Roque	1,800	4
Croquet	1,800	Any No	Shuffleboard	750	2-4
			Soccer	75,600	22
Field Hockey	59,400	22	Tennis	7,200	4
Football	75,600	22	Tether Tennis	400	2
			Volley Ball	4,000	12-16

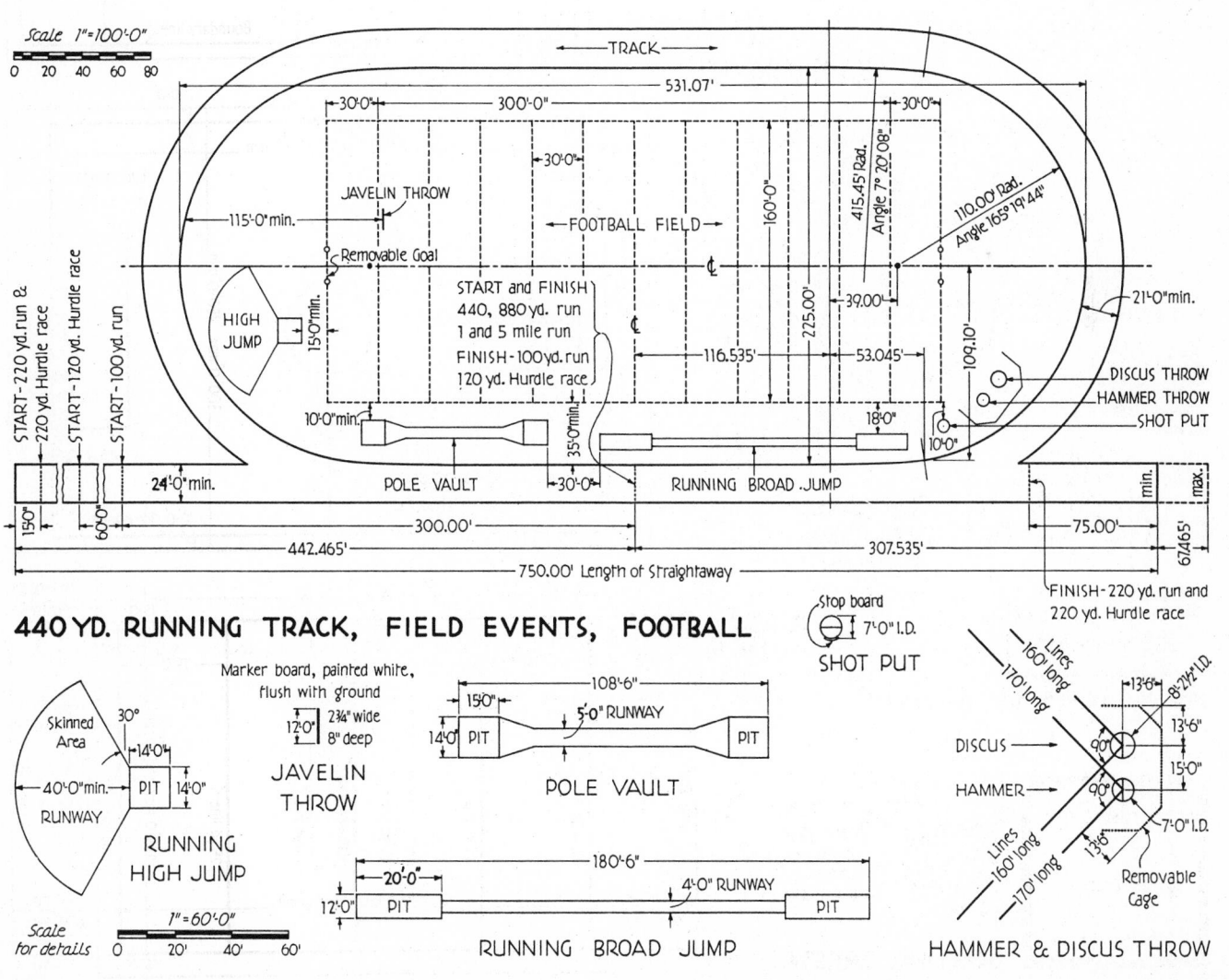

440 YD. RUNNING TRACK, FIELD EVENTS, FOOTBALL

PURPOSE

Details and diagrams on this sheet illustrate approved layouts, construction types and utility arrangements for outdoor tennis courts. The text outlines recommended technical procedure relating directly to the subjects covered by the drawings. While some points are open to varying interpretations, present data have been adapted from the Official Code of the International Lawn Tennis Federation, of which the U. S. Lawn Tennis Association is a member, and the published experience of recognized experts.

GENERAL

Most desirable location of the court is an open, unshaded area with good natural drainage. Orientation should protect players from directly facing the sun. For greatest use in Northern states the long axis should run east of north and west of south. For morning play the axis should run northeast and southwest; for afternoon play, northwest and southeast.

Minimum dimensions, for the court area within backnets of wire or wood lattice, may be as low as 108' x 48', but recommended dimensions are 120' x 60'. Championship court dimensions are 130' x 66', at least one of which should be included in every battery of two or more courts on which tournament play is to be conducted. Usual height for backnets is 10'. Those enclosing ends of championship courts should be at least 12' high, preferably 14'.

DRAINAGE

Natural seepage through porous finishing materials and grading the playing area as indicated on the drawing, together with border drainage trenches, will provide a good playing surface at all times. Subsurface drainage is necessary, particularly under impervious court surfaces, to prevent excessive damage by freezing and thawing weather.

Subsurface drainage lines should be spaced no less than 10 ft. in heavy clay subsoil and 15 ft. in light clay or sandy loam. Tiles can be 4 in. laid with open joints at a pitch of at least ⅛ in. and preferably ¼ in. to the foot. Depth should be at least 1 ft. below court construction for heavy soils and about half that for light, porous soils. Collection lines from lateral tiles can be 6 in. vitrified sewer pipe laid with cement joints at a pitch of ¼ in. to the foot. Surrounding drainage trenches should be partially filled with cinders tamped in layers about 4 in. thick.

CONSTRUCTION

Courts can be surfaced with grass, dirt, clay, wood, concrete, or special types of quick-draining materials.

Dirt. When firm, well-drained subsoil exists, stone or slag foundations are not necessary for inexpensive dirt courts. Remove topsoil and level subsoil by rolling and filling. Surface with at least a 2 in. covering of clay, sand and salt as noted below for clay courts. Subsoil should be raked prior to surfacing to bond the clay mixture to the dirt foundation.

Clay. Remove topsoil and soft earth a foot below grade of finished court. Grade to drain, roll (preferably with a 4-ton roller) and install drain tile as indicated. Necessary filling should be installed in layers of 4 in., thoroughly wetted and rolled. On prepared subgrade spread cinders or good gravel, then wet and thoroughly roll to a finished thickness of 5 in. Next, spread a layer of 1½ in. slag, crushed stone or coarse gravel to a rolled and finished depth of 3 in. Fill voids of the gravel surface with a layer of washed gravel or slag of about ¾ in. screen, well wetted and rolled. Set net posts of wood (cypress, locust or chestnut, creosoted below ground) or pipe in 8 in. vitrified sewer tile sunk to a depth of 3 ft. and filled

with concrete to secure posts. Posts can be installed for removal by setting a sleeve within the tile.

Next, apply clay foundation course. Use stiff clay, of ¾ or 1 in. screen to a 3 in. depth. Before rolling spread a 1 in. surface course consisting of stiff clay pulverized through ¼ in. mesh, clean sharp sand of ⅛ in. mesh, and common farmer's salt. Proportions recommended are: clay, 50 per cent, sand 50 per cent *by weight,* to which should be added one part of salt *by weight* to 40 or 50 parts clay. Before mixing with sand natural clay should contain from 25 to 35 per cent silt and from 75 to 65 per cent pure clay with no sand or organic matter.

When surface course is spread, compact carefully with a 400-500 lb. lawn roller. Allowance should be made for about 25 per cent shrinkage from rolling when spreading clay courses. After rolling check grades with a long straight-edge and level. Then spray until a film of water covers the court. Roll again until all water disappears.

Wood. The detail indicates a high grade construction for wood courts. A less elaborate, but less permanent, construction is satisfactory for ordinary courts. Level the playing area and cover with cinders to about a 5 in. depth. Roll thoroughly and lay cypress mud sills lengthwise of the court to support cross beams. These beams should also be cypress, 4 x 4 in., 20 in. o.c. Over these nail 1 x 3 in. cypress flooring set with a ¼ in. space between each board. Net posts should be set in cement as described for clay courts.

Such courts can be used with no additional treatment or can be covered with painted canvas. Canvas should be stretched by ropes through pulleys at each corner of the court.

Concrete. Structural requirements are indicated in the detail. A 1 in. expansion joint the full depth of slab should be provided at the net line. This can be filled with tar, prepared felt or other elastic material. Troweling of the court surface should be minimized. Slabs should be cured by covering with damp sand or earth sprinkled at intervals with water for at least ten days.

Quick-drying and special surfaces. Solid construction with layers of stone or slag, cinders, gravel and fine stone dust produces a very porous and quick-drying, but firm surface. Other quick-drying surfaces are available as proprietary compounds. Special surfaces include asphalt, macadam, marl dust all of which are satisfactory.

MISCELLANEOUS

Lighting. The multiple-court diagram indicates minimum requirements for lighting—two 2,000 or 1,500 watt projectors on 40-foot poles on each side of court. Recommended lighting for single court includes five 1,500 watt lamps on each side spaced so that one pole is at the net, one at each service line and one slightly behind base line, or 26 ft. from service line. Lights are carried on bracket arms extending over court, 30 ft. above playing surface. For lighting of multiple courts for championship play, advice of a qualified lighting engineer should be sought.

Water. Essential water outlets are indicated in the multiple court diagram. Faucets with hose connection and outlets of ¾ or ⅝ in. are preferable. Each should be well outside playing area and can best be placed below grade in a small concrete box with a hinged cover flush with turf. Each outlet should be supplied with a drain.

Lines should be white and may be of several types. For clay or grass courts lines may be marked with air-slaked lime. Wood or concrete courts should have lines painted with at least 2 coats of white lead and oil. Canvas tapes are obtainable but are likely to rot or stretch and form a playing hazard. Lead tapes for all types of courts are permanent, straight and eliminate playing hazards.

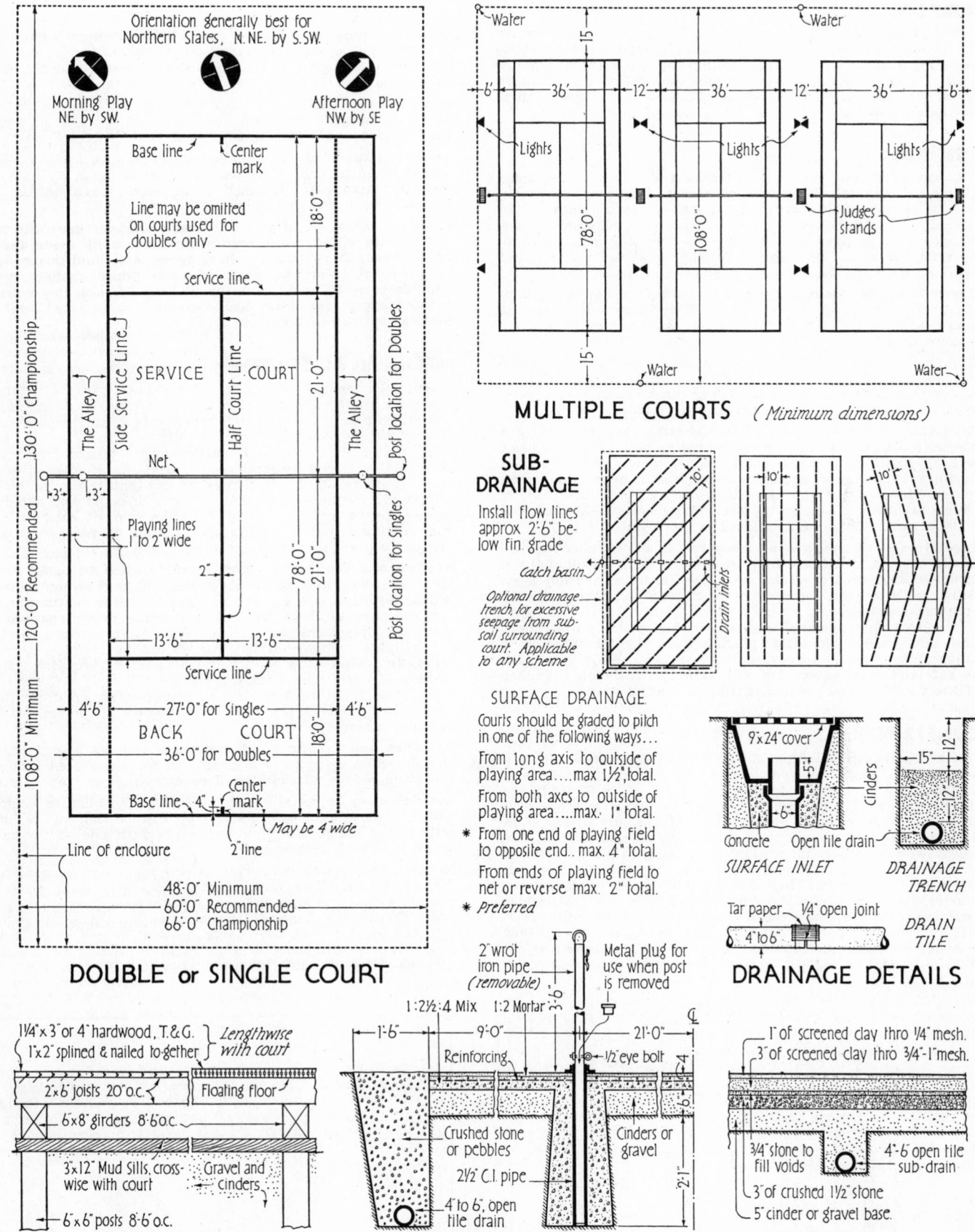

Orientation generally best for Northern States, N. NE. by S. SW.

Morning Play
NE. by SW.

Afternoon Play
NW. by SE.

Base line
Center mark
Line may be omitted on courts used for doubles only
Service line
18'-0"
Side Service Line
SERVICE
COURT
Half Court Line
21'-0"
The Alley
The Alley
Post location for Doubles
130'-0" Championship
120'-0" Recommended
108'-0" Minimum
Net
Post location for Singles
3'
3'
Playing lines 1" to 2" wide
2"
78'-0"
21'-0"
13'-6"
13'-6"
Service line
4'-6"
27'-0" for Singles
4'-6"
BACK
COURT
36'-0" for Doubles
18'-0"
Base line
4"
Center mark
May be 4" wide
2" line
Line of enclosure
48'-0" Minimum
60'-0" Recommended
66'-0" Championship

DOUBLE or SINGLE COURT

Water
Water
15
6'
36'
12'
36'
12'
36'
6'
Lights
Lights
Lights
78'-0"
108'-0"
Judges stands
15
Water
Water

MULTIPLE COURTS (Minimum dimensions)

SUB-DRAINAGE
Install flow lines approx 2'-6" below fin. grade

Catch basin

Optional drainage trench, for excessive seepage from sub-soil surrounding court. Applicable to any scheme

10'
Drain inlets
10'
10'

SURFACE DRAINAGE.
Courts should be graded to pitch in one of the following ways...
From long axis to outside of playing area....max 1½" total.
From both axes to outside of playing area....max. 1" total.
* From one end of playing field to opposite end.. max. 4" total.
From ends of playing field to net or reverse max. 2" total.
* Preferred

9" x 24" cover
5"
6"
Concrete
Open tile drain
SURFACE INLET
15"
12"
12"
Cinders
DRAINAGE TRENCH

Tar paper
¼" open joint
4" to 6"
DRAIN TILE

DRAINAGE DETAILS

1¼" x 3" or 4" hardwood, T.& G.
1" x 2" splined & nailed together
Lengthwise with court
2" x 6" joists 20" o.c.
Floating floor
6" x 8" girders 8'-6" o.c.
3" x 12" Mud Sills, crosswise with court
Gravel and cinders
6" x 6" posts 8'-6" o.c.

WOOD COURT

2" wrot iron pipe (removable)
Metal plug for use when post is removed
3'-6"
1:2½:4 Mix
1:2 Mortar
1'-6"
9'-0"
21'-0"
Reinforcing
½ eye bolt
4"
6"
Crushed stone or pebbles
2½" C.I. pipe
4" to 6", open tile drain
Cinders or gravel
2'-1"

CONCRETE COURT

1" of screened clay thro ¼" mesh.
3" of screened clay thro ¾"-1" mesh.
¾" stone to fill voids
4'-6" open tile sub-drain
3" of crushed 1½" stone
5" cinder or gravel base.

CLAY COURT

PURPOSE

This sheet presents information on the construction of courts for squash racquets and squash tennis including recommendations for heating, ventilating, lighting, soundproofing and painting. Data have been obtained from the Metropolitan Squash Racquets Association, Inc. of N. Y., and from leading professionals and builders.

GENERAL

Squash racquets and squash tennis are played on enclosed courts of identical dimensions with such differences of marking as appear on the drawings. Both games are most often played as singles but can be played less strenuously as doubles. Singles and doubles courts vary in size; one court cannot be used for both. Dimensions of playing surfaces (floor and four walls) must be exactly as shown on drawings.

Courts may be located anywhere within multi-story buildings or in independent structures. The room containing the court may be of any height greater than the minimum enclosure noted.

Construction and finish of playing surfaces should follow specifications outlined below, to assure a uniform rapid game. Above playing limits, wall and ceiling construction may be any type which will provide a light-reflecting finish.

Access to courts (in order of preference) may be (1) by a specially constructed flush door located as near center of back wall as possible, (2) by a sliding ladder which may be raised during play, (3) by as narrow a trapdoor as is practical, located in the floor parallel and close to front wall on center line of court, (4) by a flush door placed anywhere in side or rear walls. Door must never be placed in front wall.

Spectators' galleries are of necessity small. While requirements vary, at least one of a group of courts should have a large gallery, with several rows of seats, for exhibition play. Other galleries may provide a single row of seats or only standing room.

Best location is behind and above back playing wall; next best, outside and above side playing walls. Dressing rooms, if adjacent to court and above playing surfaces, may have plate or safety-glass windows for observation. Continuous benches of the stadium type provide maximum seating space.

CONSTRUCTION

Playing surfaces, including portions of all four walls as well as floor, should be constructed over an extremely rigid base, preferably masonry. For frame construction, 3″ x 6″ studs are recommended. If well braced, 3″ x 4″ studs may prove stiff enough. Wood surfaces should be of maple, air dried. Kiln dried lumber will absorb too much moisture and may buckle when swollen. Floors must always be wood, as masonry floors quickly tire players. Plaster walls may be used for low-cost, non-regulation courts. Their finish should be Portland Cement Plaster, with finish coat of White Portland mixed with white sand; or three coats of Keene's Cement made with white sand. Masonry backing is required for plaster walls as lath will not provide sufficient reinforcement over frame construction. Wire lath may be stapled to masonry to provide a good bond.

Finish of playing surfaces must be absolutely smooth and true. Wood should be planed, traversed, scraped and sandpapered. Plaster should be smoothly troweled and tool marks should be entirely eliminated.

Door must be finished similarly to playing surface on court side, and may be built up on a solid-panel flush door or on any desired base. Hardware should be invisible or flush.

Telltale is made of sheet metal and must give forth a ringing sound when struck. (See details in drawings.) Telltale may be made removable if court is to serve for handball, as a gymnasium, or similar purposes.

Painting. All wood playing surfaces should be sized and given three coats of flat white paint. Lines are all 1″ wide and are painted red. After painting lines, wood walls and floors should be given at least two coats of clear white shellac, rubbed smooth between coats. Plaster playing surfaces need not be painted except for lines. Telltale should be painted white on vertical surface and red on bevel.

MECHANICAL EQUIPMENT

Illumination should be uniform, without glare, and should provide a minimum intensity of 30 foot candles at floor. Indirect reflectors, placed as indicated in drawings, are recommended. Cove lighting, recessed or diffused direct fixtures or any other adequate artificial source is satisfactory. Natural lighting by skylights or clerestories produces variations of intensities and is not recommended Windows or skylights must be outside all playing surfaces, preferably at rear of court and should be double glazed with diffusing glass to prevent heat transfer and eliminate glare. All fixtures should be fitted with wire guards to prevent loss of the ball in play.

Heating and Ventilating. Low temperatures—40 to 50 F—are ideal for play and in most courts heating is unnecessary. When needed it can best be combined with a ventilating system designed to clean air and to provide 10 air changes per hour in courts without galleries. Ventilation through windows or skylights is undesirable. Air should be supplied through grilles in telltale (see detail) and exhausted through registers at rear of court above playing walls.

Air should not be humidified. Summer air conditioning is rarely used, but is practical if extension of playing season justifies expense.

Insulation and furring of all walls and ceilings placed against outside walls or roofs is desirable to maintain even temperatures and reduce possibilities of condensation on playing areas.

Soundproofing is usually not necessary if court is enclosed with masonry walls. Noise of play can be muffled by lining ceiling and areas above playing walls with one of the many sound-absorbing materials.

Miscellaneous. Call and emergency bells are recommended for all courts. The first, located outside playing surfaces, announces playing periods through automatic or manual operation. Emergency signal buttons may be located in the telltale.

In conjunction with the courts, dressing rooms, showers and locker rooms with usual storage facilities should be provided. (See also "Spectators' Galleries" above.)

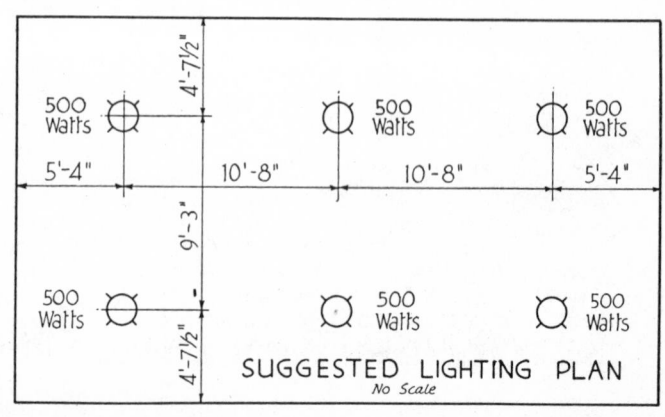

GALLERY DETAIL
Scale ¾″=1′-0″

Pipe Railing — Back Wall Playing Surface — Knee Space — 1′-9½″ — 1′-0″ — 1′-8″ — 3′-0″ — 3½″ — 1′-7½″ — 6′-0″ to Finish Court Floor

SUGGESTED LIGHTING PLAN
No Scale

500 Watts — 4′-7½″ — 5′-4″ — 10′-8″ — 10′-8″ — 5′-4″ — 9′-3″ — 4′-7½″

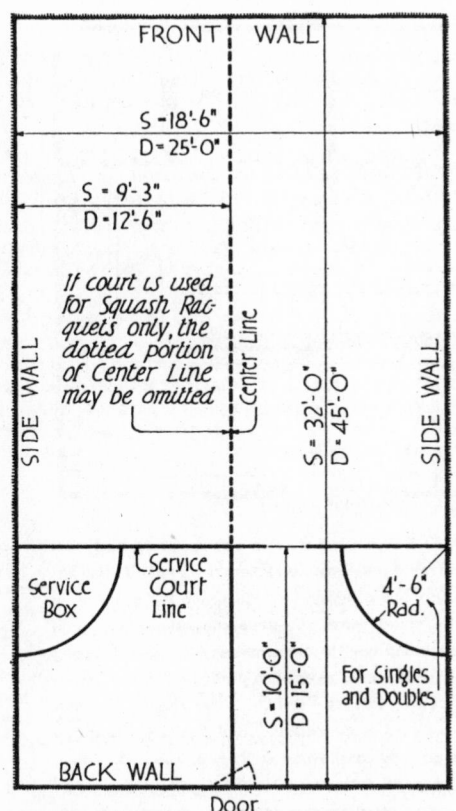

If court is used for Squash Racquets only, the dotted portion of Center Line may be omitted

S - Singles Court   D - Doubles Court
SINGLE OR DOUBLE COURT
Scale ⅛" - 1'-0"

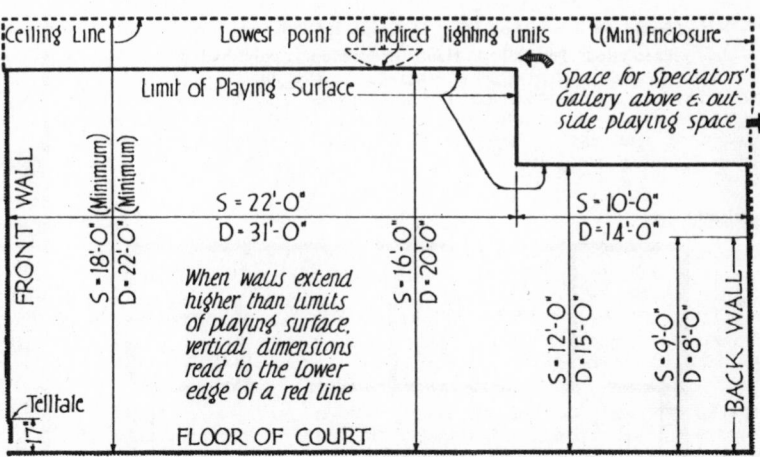

ELEVATION OF SIDE WALLS
Scale ⅛" - 1'-0"

NOTES
All dimensions shown are to Finish Walls & Floor (Playing Surface) and to bottoms of lines unless otherwise noted

Walls & Floor painted white; lines 1" wide painted red

Scale for Details ⅜" - 1'-0" unless otherwise noted

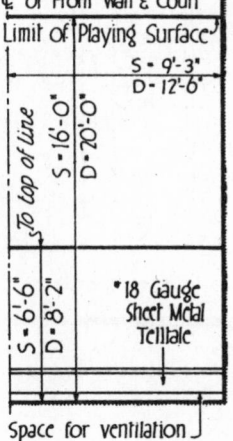

FRONT WALL
(ONE-HALF ELEVATION)
Scale ⅛" - 1'-0"

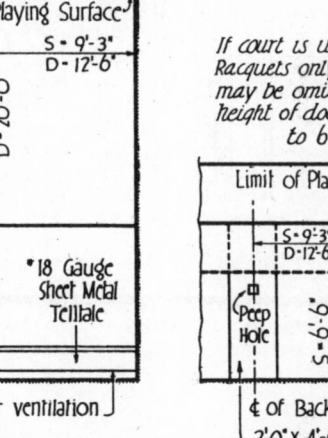

If court is used for Squash Racquets only, the 4'-6" line may be omitted & the height of door increased to 6'-6"

BACK WALL
(PART ELEVATION)

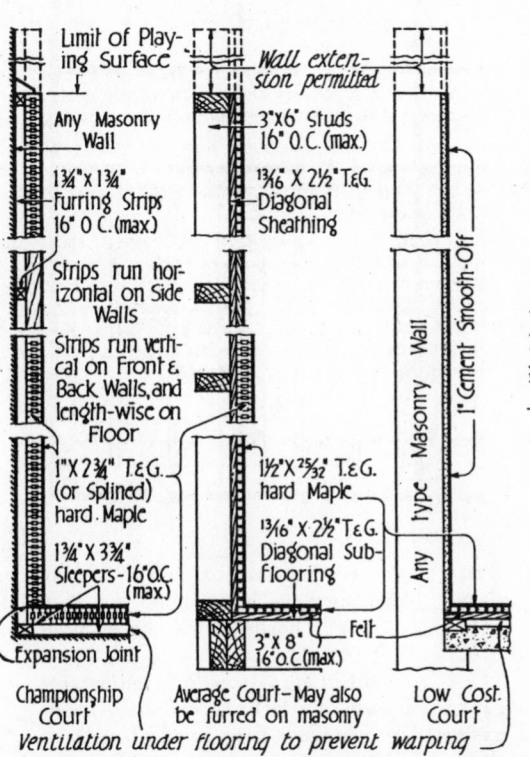

Ventilation under flooring to prevent warping
SECTIONS THRU FLOOR & WALLS

Scale 1½ - 1'-0"
PEEP HOLE DETAILS   ELEVATION

Court face of door must be flush with and finished same as Back Wall. Use invisible or flush hardware.

DOOR DETAILS

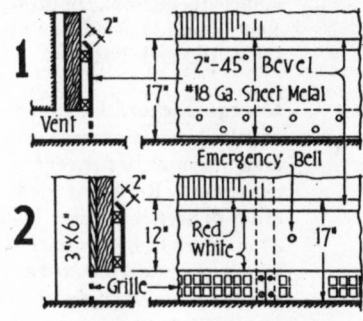

TWO TYPES OF VENT GRILLES
1 Holes in plate   2 Separate grille

SECTIONS   ELEVATIONS

2" wide - 45° Bevel is to be painted red; rest of telltale, white. Telltale shall give forth a ringing sound when struck by ball

DETAILS OF TELLTALE

Based on information from "A Guide for Planning Facilities for Recreation, Physical & Health Education," published by The Athletic Institute, Inc., for the National Facilities Conference.

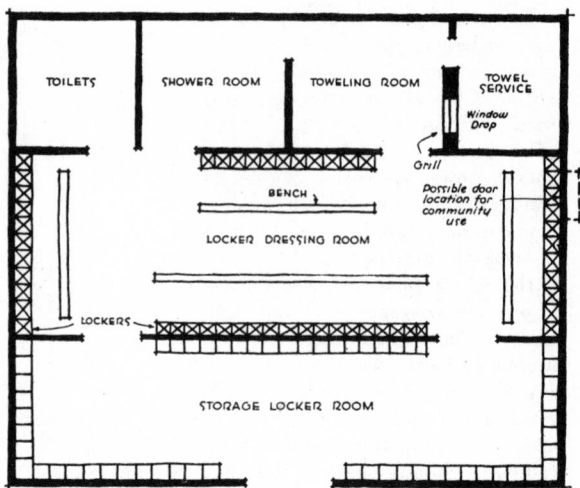

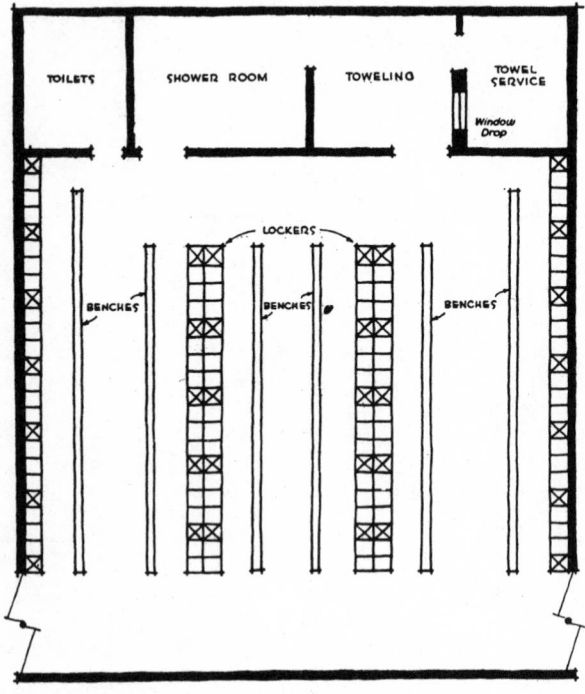

These plans show three dressing-locker room arrangements, each with its own particular advantages. Dressing lockers are marked with X's. Plan 1: storage lockers are grouped in small space for economy in drying uniforms with forced warm air; some congestion may result from dressing lockers being next to one another. Plan 2: distributing dressing lockers over entire area gives each participant ample dressing space. Plan 3: dressing lockers distributed over entire suite; units can be installed in any number desired and lend themselves to group dressing method for girls. By constructing walls A, B, C and D, putting a grille to ceiling above locker tiers and installing grille sliding doors at E, each unit becomes a complete dressing room for community use. Walls A, B, C and D can be omitted and gates F added to get same use and permit towel service and toilet units to be installed at points A and D

DESIGN NOTES

Dressing-Locker Room. An average of 14 sq. ft. per pupil in the designed peak load should be provided exclusive of the locker space so there will be adequate dressing area. Check list: sufficient mirrors, built-in drinking fountain and cuspidor in boys' dressing room, tack board.

Storage Lockers. Each pupil enrolled should have a storage locker, with an additional 10 per cent to allow for expansion. Recommended sizes, in order of preference are: 7½ by 12 by 24 in., 6 by 12 by 36 in., 7½ by 12 by 8 in. These were selected as being the minimum size lockers to store ordinary gym costumes and allow free hanging for ventilation.

Dressing Lockers. Lockers large enough to accommodate street clothes should be provided. The number should equal the peak load plus 10

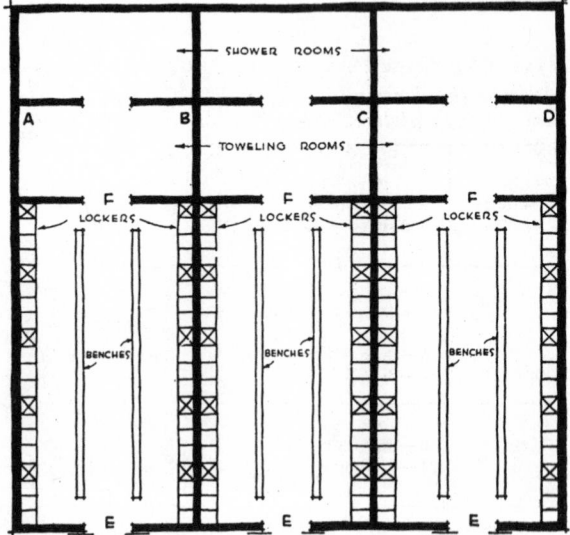

per cent. Lockers 12 by 12 by 72 in. are recommended for secondary schools and 12 by 12 by 54 in. or 12 by 12 by 48 in. for elementary schools.

Shower Room. In the group or gang type shower, the girls should have a number of shower heads equal to

40 per cent of the designed peak load; for boys 30 per cent.

Shower heads should be at least 4 ft. apart, of a non-clogging type; height of spray should be adjustable by use of a lock. If stationary heads are installed, they should be placed so that the top of the spray will be shoulder height (usually 4½ to 5 ft.).

One to three individual shower booths, 3 by 3½ ft., should be provided additionally for girls.

For boys, if walk-way or walk-around shower system is desired, the number of shower heads in the shower room can be reduced by one-third. In the walk-way, spray outlets attached to the water pipe must be focused to provide coverage from shoulder height to feet. There must be a continuous spray the length of the walk-way arranged so that there will be warm, tepid and cool water as one progresses along the walk-way. The walk-way should be arranged in U shape with a total length at least 35 ft. and from 3 to 4 ft. in width. An entrance from the group shower soaping space and egress to the toweling room and swimming pool should be provided.

Both individual and master control should be provided for all groups or gang showers. The booth showers should have individual control; the walk-way only master control.

Toweling Room.
The toweling room should have the same total area as the shower room and be immediately accessible to both showers and dressing room.

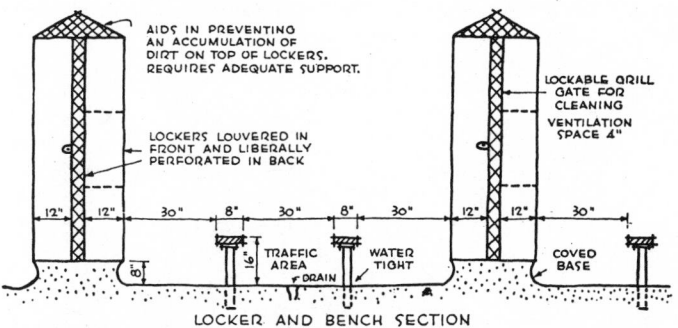

Suggested locker and bench installation
When locker height is kept down to 54 in., entire room can be supervised. Sloping locker top cannot be used, but 4 in. ventilating space should be louvered.

A ledge 18 in. high and 8 in. wide coved at wall and base, with bull nose edge, as foot drying aid is desirable.

If towel distribution is such that hanging of towels in drying room is necessary, a 1-in., non-corrosive towel bar 4 ft. from the floor and 1 to 1½ in. from the wall is recommended.

A non-shatterable, transparent panel for supervision of toweling between the toweling and dressing room may be desired.

Towel Service and Storage Room.
Adjustable shelves in sufficient number to accommodate the load are required. A check-out window should open into or be immediately adjacent to the toweling room. If uniforms are distributed from here, a dutch door or check-out window, with counter, should open into the dressing room.

Toilet Room.
Facilities should be provided in proportion to the peak load on the following basis:

Toilets	Girls	1–30	Min.	3
Toilets	Boys	1–50	Min.	2
Urinals	Boys	1–25	Min.	2
Lavatories	Girls and Boys	1–20	Min.	3

Typical combined storage-dressing locker arrangements

Area of the dressing-locker room suite required for different types of storage and dressing lockers in a typical unit for 240 girls or boys. Proportionate adjustments to be made for varying school enrollments.

Class Periods Per Day	Size of lockers and Battery Arrangement	Typical Installation	Overall height with base	Number students per day	Peak load per period	Area Required, sq. ft.	Recommendation *
six	6—storage 7½ x 12 x 24″ 1—dressing 12 x 12 x 48″ or 6—storage 7½ x 12 x 24″ 1—dressing 12 x 12 x 72″		54″ or 80″	240	40	114.80 or 90.0	1 a. grades 1–12 b. grades 9–12
six	6—storage 6 x 12 x 36″ 1—dressing 12 x 12 x 72″		80″	240	40	100.0	3 grades 10–12 only
six	6—storage 7½ x 12 x 18″ 1—dressing 12 x 12 x 54″		62″	240	40	90.0	2 grades 1–12
eight	8—storage 7½ x 12 x 18″ 1—dressing 12 x 12 x 72″		80″	240	30	67.50	2 grades 9–12
eight	8—storage 7½ x 12 x 24″ 1—dressing 12 x 12 x 48″		54″	240	30	105.0	1 grades 1–12

* Numbered in order of Preference

Information in this section was prepared by Ronald Allwork from data assembled by the Portland Cement Association; Joint Committee on Bathing Places, American Public Health Ass'n.; Conference of State Sanitary Engineers.

General. Capacity and operation of the bathhouse must be such as to avoid overcrowding at times of maximum demand; however, it is better to have an overcrowded condition a few times a year rather than to have facilities so large as to be uneconomical.

Location of bathhouse depends partly on size of pool and space available. When possible, bathhouse should be placed so as to protect pool from prevailing winds. A location at one side of the pool, or better still, at the shallow end, will reduce the danger of poor swimmers and children falling or jumping into deep water.

Size of bathhouse and selection of equipment, in relation to pool size depend on such factors as the need for: lockers, or central checking system; individual dressing rooms, or the "dormitory" system; private or group showers; and extra facilities. If patrons are permitted to use their own suits, some will come ready to swim, and dressing and check rooms may be small. But since all bathers should be required to take a cleansing shower, the number of showers needed will remain the same.

Area of bathhouse is usually 1/3 of pool area; area of dressing room approximates 1/5 pool area. It is recommended that bathhouse facilities, based on the number of bathers present at any one time (2/3 of whom may be assumed to be men), be provided as follows:

1 shower for each 40 bathers
1 lavatory for each 60 bathers
1 toilet for each 40 women
1 toilet for each 60 men
1 urinal for each 60 men

For rough estimate of maximum number of persons within a pool enclosure (pool and walks) assume one person for every 12 sq. ft. of pool area. Hence for a pool 30 x 75 ft., assume 190 persons.

Elements of a bathhouse vary with local requirements, but usually include: entrance lobby, ticket or cashier's booth, concessions, manager's office, public telephones, checking room, suit and towel room, dressing rooms, toilets, showers, first aid room, guard's or attendant's room, mechanical equipment, storage space, etc.

Dressing rooms. Method of checking clothes must be decided before the layout can be determined, as the method chosen affects the entire arrangement. Both individual lockers and central check rooms have been used successfully. Choice depends mainly on local conditions. A combination of the two systems may become the most desirable, since obviously requirements for a well-dressed adult and for a boy in play clothes are not the same. Lockers should be placed on a raised platform to keep them dry and to simplify floor cleaning. Lockers require most space, but tend to keep clothes in better condition. Individual dressing rooms must usually be provided for women and girls, whereas men and boys ordinarily dress in aisles between rows of lockers. A few individual dressing rooms are sometimes provided in men's dressing rooms.

Regardless of the system adopted, dressing and locker rooms should be arranged to admit a maximum of sunlight and air in order to maintain clean, sanitary conditions. Satisfactory results have been obtained from the "open-court" type, in which the roof is omitted over part of the dressing room area.

Toilets of the wall-hung type are recommended.

Showers may be either individual or group-controlled; some type of control, which eliminates any possibility of bathers being scalded, is essential.

There are many types of bathhouse equipment on the market which add to the convenience of the patrons and increase the popularity of the pool. Hair driers, comb-vending machines, exercisers and scales are frequently installed.

Planning of bathhouse elements should be such as to permit operation with minimum of personnel, particularly during slack periods.

Circulation. Arrange all facilities so patrons can pass through quickly, without confusion. The only route from dressing room to pool should be past toilets and shower rooms. Each bather should be required to take a thorough cleansing shower with soap before putting on bathing suit. By requiring each bather to pass through a group of showers before entering the pool a superficial bath will be obtained, but this must not be considered as replacing the required shower in the nude.

Toilets should be accessible directly from both dressing room and pool. Separate ones for "wet" and "dry" bathers are desirable. Disinfecting foot baths should be placed between pool and toilet.

Bathers returning from the pool should preferably pass through a separate drying room to the dressing room, and the "wet" and "dry" bathers should be separated as much as practical. Exit from bathhouse to street should be so arranged that an attendant may collect all keys, checks, suits or other supplies belonging to the establishment.

Construction. Resistance to deterioration and fire is especially important. The constant dampness which usually prevails is harmful to many materials and causes rapid deterioration. Therefore materials which are entirely satisfactory in ordinary buildings may not be desirable for bathhouses. Fire hazard must also be considered in selection of materials, particularly since the building is generally in an isolated location and without attendants a good portion of the year.

Bathhouses must be kept scrupulously clean by frequent washing. Construction should be such that washing with high pressure hose will not damage the building. Floors of bathhouses should be pitched 1/4" per ft. to frequent outlets to assure rapid drainage. Provide an ample number of hose connections to make cleaning easy. Connection should be not less than 1 in. to insure adequate water volume and pressure.

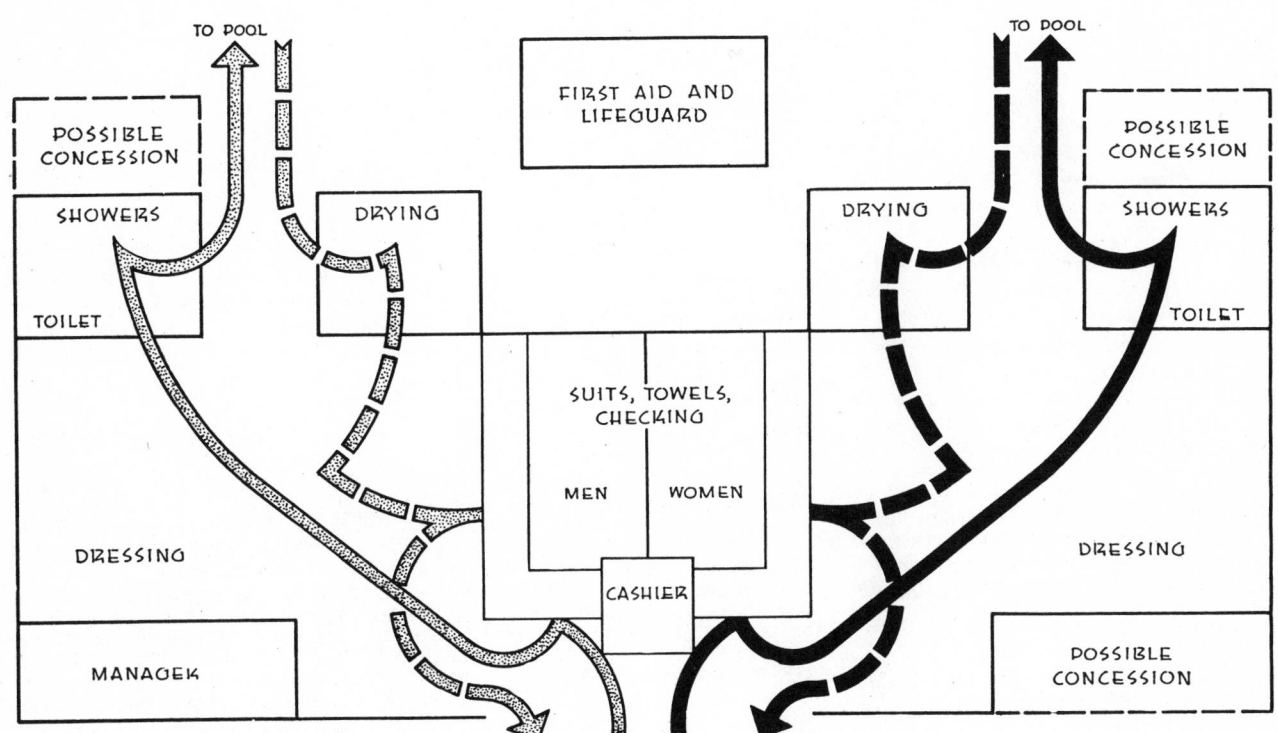

BATHHOUSE CIRCULATION

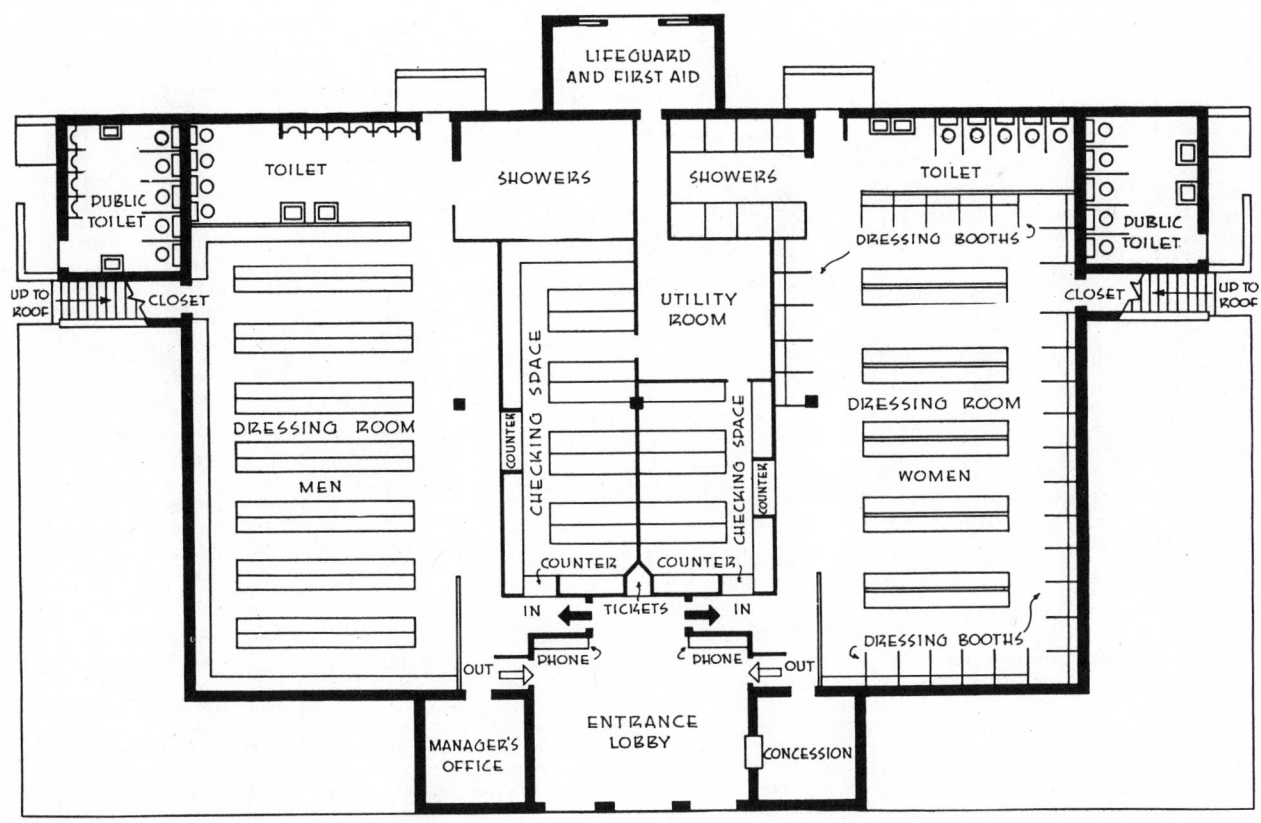

PLAN OF TYPICAL BATHHOUSE   FOR 750 PERSON POOL

SCALE 1⁄16"=1'-0"

Minimum standards prepared by the National Swimming Pool Institute

DEFINITION AND POOL TYPES

1. All artificially constructed swimming pools other than residential pools shall be deemed to be public swimming pools. This shall not be applicable to residential pools as defined or wading or spray pools, which shall be covered under separate sections.

(a) Private pools which are excepted herein shall be defined as follows: "Residential swimming pools include all constructed pools which are used or intended to be used as a swimming pool in connection with a single-family residence and available only to the family of the householder and private guests."

(b) Classifications of Pools: For purposes of minimum standards, public swimming pools shall be defined as listed in the following categories, based upon specific characteristics of size, usage and other factors:

Type "A"—Any municipal pool, community pool, public school pool, athletic or swimming club pool.
Type "B"—Institutional pool (such as Girl Scout, Boy Scout, YMCA & YWCA, Campfire Girls and Boys' and Girls' Camps).
Type "C"—Country Club, large hotels of more than 100 units, with pools having a water surface area in excess of 1600 sq ft.
Type "D"—Motels and apartments, multiple housing units, small hotels of less than 100 units, not open to the general public and with pools having a water surface area not larger than 1600 sq ft.
Type "E"—Treatment pools, therapeutic pools and special pools for water therapy.
Type "F"—Indoor pools.
Exceptions: The above categories shall be the basis for certain specific variations from the Minimum Standards for public swimming pools as a whole.

NOTE: plans and specifications with supporting data, prepared by a professional engineer or architect holding registration in the state where pool is to be constructed, shall be, as a prerequisite, submitted to and approval obtained from said state regulator agency prior to award of any contract for equipment purchase or construction.

STRUCTURAL FEATURES, MATERIALS, MARKINGS

2. Structural Stability: All public pools shall be constructed of an inert and enduring material, designed to withstand all anticipated loading for both pool empty and pool full conditions. Working stresses shall be based upon predetermined ultimate strengths of materials used, with a factor of safety of not less than 2½.

Provision shall be made for the relief of pressures which might occur as a result of unbalanced exterior hydrostatic pressures, or means shall be provided for positive and continuous drainage from under the pool floor or around the pool walls, whether ground water is present, or might occur at some future time.

Special provisions shall be made to protect the pool structures from both internal and external stresses which may develop due to freezing in cold climates.

3. Obstructions: There shall be no obstruction extending from the wall or the floor, extending into the clear area of the diving portion of the pool. There shall be a completely unobstructed clear distance of 13 ft above the diving board.

4. Wall & Floor Finish: Wall and floor finish shall be of masonry, tile or other inert and impervious material and shall be reasonably enduring. Finish shall be moderately smooth and of a white or light color.

5. Depth Markers: Depth of water shall be plainly marked at or above the water surface on the vertical pool wall and on the edge of the deck or walk next to the pool, at maximum and minimum points

The technical data presented here gives basic requirements for public and semi-public pool design, systems and equipment. It is intended by the NSPI to serve as recommended minimum standards, and not as a model code.

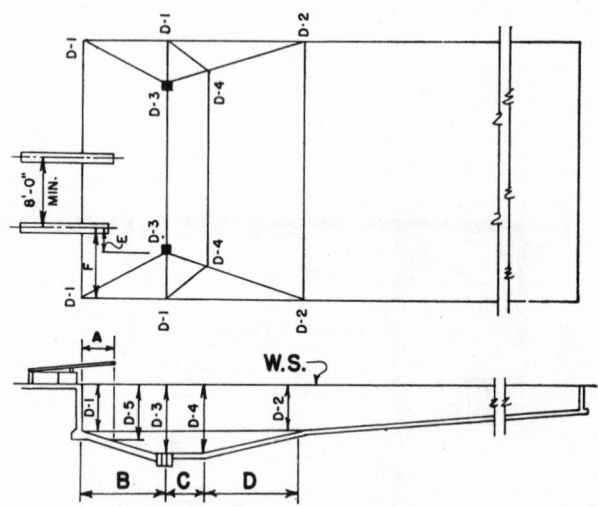

STANDS & BOARDS		Depth—Feet & Inches					Length of Section—Feet & Inches					
		D-1	D-2	D-3	D-4	D-5	A	B	C	D	E	F
3-Meter Board	Min.	5-0	4-6	10-0	9-9	8-6	5-0	*6-0	*9-0	20-0	1-0	8-0
	Max.		5-6				6-0	10-0				
1-Meter Board	Min.	5-0	4-6	8-6	8-3	7-6	5-0	*6-0	*9-0	15-0	1-0	8-0
	Max.		5-6				6-0	10-0				
Deck Level Board	Min.	5-0	4-6	8-0	7-6		2-6	†6-0	†6-0	12-0	1-0	8-0
	Max.		5-6				4-0	10-0				

As D-2 varies between min. and max., D may vary, but slope of D may not exceed 1 ft vert. to 4 ft horiz. D-1 shall be at end wall of diving area, or not more than 12 in. from it

* B & C May vary to attain 15'—0" Min.
† B & C May vary to attain total 12'—0" Min.

and at the points of break between the deep and shallow portions and at intermediate increments of depth, spaced at not more than 25 ft intervals. Depth markers shall be in numerals of 4 in. min. height and of a color contrasting with background. Markers shall be on both sides and ends of the pool.

6. Lifeguard Chairs: Each public swimming pool shall have at least one elevated lifeguard chair. This shall be presumed to be adequate for 2,000 sq ft of pool surface area and one additional lifeguard chair shall be provided for each additional area of 2,000 sq ft or fraction thereof. Where a pool is provided with more than one lifeguard chair and the width is 40 ft. or more, they shall be located on each side of the pool. In Types D & E pools, lifeguard chairs need not be provided.

7. Life Line: A life line shall be provided at or near the break in grade between the shallow and deep portions of a public swimming pool, with its position marked with colored floats at not greater than 5 ft spacing. Life line shall not be less than ¾ in. min. dia. its terminals shall be securely anchored and of corrosion-resistant material and of type which will be recessed or have no projection which will constitute a hazard.

8. Ladders: A minimum of one ladder shall be provided for each 75 ft of perimeter and not less than two ladders shall be provided at any pool. Where stairs are provided in a pool, one ladder may be deleted for each set of stairs provided. A side handrail extending up above and returning to the horizontal surface of the pool deck, curb or coping shall be provided at each side of each ladder.

All stairs entering a public pool shall be recessed. An exception to this may permit the construction of steps directly entering the pool and not recessed into the pool walls, in Types C, D, & E.

POOL DIMENSIONS, WALKS, FENCES

9. Shallow Minimum Depth: Every public swimming pool shall have a minimum depth in the shallow area of the main swimming area of not less than 3 ft, nor more than 3 ft 6 in. from the overflow level to the floor. Exceptions may be made for Types B, C, D & E pools, or in pools built principally for instruction, or in a recessed area of the main swimming pool where pool is of an irregular shape such as the leg of a T, L or Z.

10. Shallow Area: In a swimming pool with a diving area, the shallow portion of the pool shall be defined as the portion between the shallow end and the break point between the shallow area and the diving area. The slope of the floor shall be uniform from the break between the diving area and the shallow portion to the outside edge of the shallow portion and shall not be greater than 1 ft of slope in 12 ft, except in small Type B pools where the pool is less than 42 ft in overall length, in which case the rate of slope shall not exceed 1 ft in 8 ft.

11. Diving Area: The area of a public swimming pool where diving is permitted shall be, in the case of a rectangular pool, at one end, or may be in a recessed area forming one of the legs of a T, L or Z shaped pool, divorced from the main swimming area by a life line, or may be a wholly separate pool structure. Exceptions to this may be made in special-purpose type pools intended for training and instruction.

Pools of the types wherein diving is permitted shall have adequate area and depth of water for safe diving and the minimum depth and area characteristics for this area shall be as indicated in the accompanying chart.

12. Diving Towers: Diving towers in excess of 3-meters in height shall not be considered as acceptable in a public pool without special provisions, controls and definite limitations on their use.

13. Vertical Wall Depth: As a minimum, the pool walls shall be vertical at all points for a depth of not less than 2 ft 6 in.

14. Walks: Walks shall be continuous around the pool with a minimum width of 8 ft of unobstructed clear distance including a curb at the pool edge, if such a curb is used. Exceptions may be made in Types B, C, D, E, & F as follows: B—4 ft; C—4 ft; D—4 ft; E—No minimum; F—4 ft.

A minimum of a 3 ft walk width shall be provided on the sides and rear of any piece of diving equipment.

All walks, decks and terraces shall have a minimum slope of ¼ in. per foot to drains or points at which the water will have a free unobstructed flow to points of disposal at all times.

The finish texture of walks must be non-slip and such that there will be no discomfort to bare feet.

Hose bibbs shall be provided around the perimeter of the deck area at intervals such that all parts of the swimming pool deck area may be reached with a 50 ft hose.

15. Fence: A wall or other enclosure of 4 ft minimum height and with maximum 2 in. mesh, 2 in. wide vertical openings, or otherwise so constructed as to be difficult to climb, shall be provided completely enclosing the pool area, all of which shall be paved.

Exceptions may be made for Types C & D

In Types C & D where the fence is dispensed with, a hedge or other clear demarcation shall be provided, with instructions and posting clearly defining the pool area as for bathers only and from which spectators and others in street clothes are rigidly excluded.

Access to the pool by bathers shall be provided only through the bathhouse or dressing room facilities, and any other fence opening shall be for service operations only.

GUTTERS AND SKIMMERS

16. Overflow Gutters: An overflow gutter shall be installed continuous around all public swimming pools, with the exception that it may be eliminated in Types B, C, D & E. The overflow gutter may be eliminated across the top tread where steps occur.

Overflow gutter shape, wherein the outer edge of the lip is flush with the pool wall above and below and the gutter entirely recessed, shall not be permitted.

The overflow gutter depth below the overflow lip shall be a minimum of 2 in. at the high points between drains. The drains shall be spaced at a maximum of 15 ft on centers and a slope provided in the bottom of not less than 2½ in. in 10 ft. In no sense is this intended to preclude the use of roll-out or deck level type pools where other conditions are met and satisfactory design is provided. In an installation where the overflow gutter is not carried to waste but is a part of the recirculation system, the provisions of spacing of drains and slope at bottom of gutter may be modified but shall conform to good hydraulic design.

The branch piping to each overflow gutter drain shall be not less than 2 in.

Where overflow gutter drains discharge into sanitary sewers, a trap shall be provided in each main before discharge into the sewer.

The overflow gutter mains shall have a sufficient minimum size and be increased as necessary to carry the overflow water freely with a maximum of 2 ft pressure head or surcharge, at all times.

Where overflow gutters discharge into a sanitary sewer or storm sewer, an air-gap of not less than 1 ft shall be provided between the point of discharge of the gutter and the drains into the sewer, or a relief manhole shall be provided where surcharge or back pressure will overflow at a point not less than 12 in. below the elevation of the overflow gutter fittings in the gutter.

Disposal of water from the overflow gutters may be either to waste or may enter the circulation system and be filtered and returned to the pool.

17. Surface Skimmers: Skimmers may be permitted in lieu of overflow gutters on swimming pools of Type B, C, D & E, providing acceptable handhold is installed. At least one skimming device shall be provided for each 800 sq ft of surface area or fraction thereof. The handhold must be no more than 9 in. above the normal water line. Skimming devices shall be built into the pool wall, shall adequately remove floating oils and waste and shall meet the following general specifications:

(a) Each skimmer shall be designed for a flow-through rate of at least 30 gallons per minute and the total capacity of all skimmers in any pool shall be approximately 50% of the required filter flow of the recirculation system.

(b) They shall be automatically adjustable to variations in water level over a range of at least 3 in.

(c) An easily removable and cleanable basket or screen through which all overflow water must pass shall be provided to trap large solids.

(d) The skimmer shall be provided with a device to prevent airlock in the suction line. If an equalizer pipe is used, it shall provide an adequate amount of makeup water for pump suction, should the water of the pool drop below the weir level. This pipe shall be at least 2 in. in diameter and shall be located at least 1 ft below the lowest overflow level of the skimmer.

(e) An equalizer line shall be provided with a valve that will remain tightly closed under normal operating conditions, but will automatically open at a differential of not more than 4 in. between the pool level and the level of the overflow tank.

(f) The overflow weir shall be of sufficient length to maintain a rate of flow of at least 20 gallons per minute per lineal foot of weir lip.

(g) Skimmer shall be of substantial, enduring and reasonably corrosion-resistant material.

One skimmer will be placed at a point in the pool opposite the direction of prevailing summer winds.

FILTRATION

18. Recirculation and Filtrations: All public swimming pools shall have recirculation and filtration equipment provided for water purification in accordance with criteria in this report.

19. Filters, Sand: These minimum standards shall apply, where applicable, to either gravity or pressure sand filters.

Filter tanks shall be designed with a factor of safety of 4 in relation of working pressure to ultimate strength.

The filter bed shall consist of suitable grades of filter sand and a supporting bed of graded gravel or other porous material which shall serve to support the filter bed and distribute both filtered and backwash water uniformly. The supporting bed consisting of graded gravel or other material shall support not less than 20 in. of filter media consisting of silica sand or other durable, inert material with an effective size between 0.4 and 0.55 mm, and a uniformity coefficient not exceeding 1.75.

The minimum freeboard to the draw-off point shall be not less than 12 in. above the normal level of the top of the filter bed. The minimum backwash rate shall be not less than 12 gallons per square foot of filter bed per minute.

Where anthracite coal or other filter media is employed, the freeboard shall be adequate to prevent the media being carried off to waste when the filter bed is backwashed at a rate adequate to carry off foreign material filtered from the water. The freeboard and the rate of backwash

shall be the subject of individual design, based upon specific gravity of the media.

Under-drain system shall be such that uniform distribution of backwash water shall be provided over the entire bed area.

Ratio of total under-drain orifice area to total area of bed shall be not less than 0.25 per cent.

Orifices in the under-drain system shall be spaced at approximately 6 in. on centers both ways throughout the area of filter bed. The total orifice area may be provided by means of porosity of the material over the total under-drain area.

Under-drain system shall be provided of material which is corrosion-resistant and enduring, wherein the orifices shall be so designed and of such material that they will maintain approximately constant area.

Where the under-drain system is of manifold and lateral type, the total area of the manifold shall be equal to not less than the total area of the laterals. The total area of the laterals shall be not less than 1¼ times the total area of the orifices.

Design rate for sand filters shall be 3 gallons per minute, per square foot of bed area, as a minimum standard.

The filter plant shall be provided with influent and effluent pressure gauges, backwash sight glass and air-relief valves.

The filter plant shall be provided with face piping and valving to permit the functions of filtering to pool or backwashing to waste with the battery as a whole or any unit operated singly.

The filter plant shall be provided with means for draining all filter units and piping, so that all parts of the system may be completely drained to prevent damage from freezing.

Each filter unit shall be provided with an access opening of not less than a standard 11 in. by 15 in. manhole and cover.

Pressure filter tanks shall be supported by jack legs or other supports to give a free movement of air under each tank and to permit access for painting.

Filter turn-over cycle shall be of capacity to completely filter the entire pool body in not more than 8 hours.

20. Filters, Diatomite: Where diatomite filters are used, they may be of either pressure or vacuum type. The filter rate shall not exceed 2.5 gpm per square foot of filter surface area.

The cycle of operation between cleaning of the diatomite filters shall be not less than a 24 hr period of continuous operation and this shall not be deemed to apply to initial operation of a pool, but only after operation for a period of 3 days or such period as is necessary to initially clear the pool.

Provisions shall be made to introduce a pre-coat to completely cover the filter elements, upon placing the equipment in initial operation and/or after each cleaning. The equipment shall be so arranged that during pre-coating, the effluent will be re-filtered or disposed to waste without passing into the pool until the effluent is clear of suspended matter.

Equipment shall be provided for the continuous feed of filter aid to the filter influent and the equipment shall have a capacity to feed not less than 0.1 lb of this material per square foot of filter area over a 24 hour period.

Exceptions to the above may be made in Types B, C, D, E & F pools, in cases where this equipment need not be provided.

The tank containing the diatomite filter elements shall be constructed of intermediate carbon steel, plastic or other suitable material which will satisfactorily provide resistance to corrosion, with or without coating, and shall be of adequate strength to resist all stresses resulting from loading with a factor of safety of 4, in relation to the ultimate strength.

The septum or elements which support the filter aid shall be of corrosion-resistant material and shall be provided with openings, the minimum dimension of which shall be not greater than 0.005 in.

The septa shall be constructed to be adequately resistant against crushing or deformation, with the maximum differential pressure between influent and effluent of not less than the maximum pressure which can be developed by the circulating pump and of adequate strength to resist the stresses developed by the cleaning operation, with the impact developed from an accelerated washing operation.

In the complete filter installation, where dissimilar metals are used which may set up galvanic electric currents, the metals shall be insulated with a suitable dielectric which will satisfactorily prevent corrosion from electrolysis.

The filters shall be designed and installed in such a manner that they can be readily disassembled and elements removed and they shall not be installed where inadequate working space above or around is available for such disassembling.

The filter plant shall be provided with pressure differential gages and air-relief outlets where necessary.

21. Filters, Other: In the absence of complete information on operating characteristics, durability, etc., of cartridge and other type filters, no minimum standards can be established at this time and their installation on public pools may only be made on a trial basis.

22. Compound Gauge: The pump suction header shall be provided with a compound gauge between the pump strainer and the pump, which will indicate both positive and negative head.

23. Strainers: At all pressure type filter plants or where the circulating pump is used for vacuum cleaning the pool, a suitable strainer or screen shall be provided to remove solids, debris, hair, lint, etc. Where a wet well is provided, the strainer shall consist of a removable screen through which all water entering the pump shall pass. Where no wet well is provided or where the suction cleaner or any other suction line is piped directly from the pool to the pumps, a pot-type strainer with removable strainer basket shall be provided. The strainer basket shall be of rigid construction sufficiently strong to prevent collapsing when clogged. One extra strainer basket shall be provided.

Any type of screen or strainer basket shall be fabricated of a corrosion-resistant material or shall have a protective coating of such material.

Screen or strainer basket shall have maximum openings no greater than ¾ the size of the solids which will pass through the pump impeller without clogging and the total clear area of all openings shall be not less than 4 times the area of the largest sized pipe from the pool to the strainer influent.

24. Rate-of-Flow Indicator: Every swimming pool provided with recirculation and refiltration system shall be provided with a rate-of-flow indicator on the pump discharge line leading to the filters and shall be calibrated for measuring both water for filtration and backwash and the activating element creating the pressure differential for indication of flow shall be installed with adequate clear distance upstream and downstream to obtain a reasonable degree of accuracy.

The rate indicator shall be calibrated for and provided with a scale reading in gallons per minute and shall have a range of 10% below the established filtration rate and 10% above the backwash rate established.

Where diatomite filters are used, the activating element of the flow indicator shall be installed in the filter effluent line.

POOL POPULATION, SANITARY FACILITIES

25. Capacity of Pool in Bathers: The maximum number of persons in bathing attire within the pool enclosure or the bathing area shall be limited to one person per 20 sq ft of pool and deck area combined.

26. Bathhouse: Adequate dressing and sanitary plumbing facilities shall be provided for every public swimming pool. An exception to this may be made in Types B, C, D, E & F pools where available facilities are provided in connection with the general development for other purposes, etc., of adequate capacity and number, in close proximity to the pool.

Every bathhouse shall be provided with separate facilities for each sex with no inter-connection between the provisions for male and female. The rooms shall be well-lighted, drained, ventilated and of good construction, with impervious materials employed in general, finished in light colors and so developed and planned that good sanitation can be maintained throughout the building at all times.

(a) Minimum sanitary plumbing facilities shall be provided as follows:

Males: One water closet combination, one lavatory and one urinal shall be presumed to be adequate for the first 100 bathers.

One water closet and one urinal shall be provided for each additional 150 bathers or major fraction thereof. One lavatory shall be provided for each 200 additional bathers.

A minimum of three shower heads shall be provided which shall be presumed to be adequate for the first 150 males and one shower outlet shall be provided for each additional 50 male bathers.

Females: A minimum of two water closet combinations shall be provided in each bathhouse building and this shall be presumed to be adequate for the first 100 females.

One additional water closet combination shall be provided for each additional 75 females or fraction thereof.

A minimum of two shower heads shall be provided, which shall be presumed to be adequate for the first 100 females and one shower shall be added for each 50 additional females.

One lavatory shall be provided as a minimum, which shall be considered adequate for the first 75 females. One additional lavatory shall be provided for each additional 75 females in attendance, or major fraction thereof.

These minimum criteria for bathhouse plumbing facilities shall be based upon the anticipated maximum attendance in bathers. Facilities for either sex shall be based upon a ratio of 60% of the total number of bathers being male and 40% being female.

Shower and dressing booths shall be provided in female dressing space and dressing booths shall be provided with curtains or other means of seclusion. This condition may be subject to variation for schools and other institutional use where a pool may be open only to one sex at a time.

(b) *Drinking Fountain:* Not less than one drinking fountain shall be provided available to bathers both at the pool and in the bathhouse.

(c) *Hose Bibbs:* Hose bibbs shall be provided for flushing down the dressing rooms and bathhouse interior.

The floors of the bathhouse shall be concrete, free of joints or openings and shall be continuous throughout the area with a very slight texture to minimize slipping but which shall be relatively smooth to ensure complete cleaning. Floor drains shall be provided to ensure positive drainage of all parts of the building with a slope in the floor of not less than ¼ in. per foot, toward drains.

(d) *Hot Water:* Heated water will be provided at all shower heads. Water heater and thermostatic mixing valve shall be inaccessible to bathers and will be capable of providing 2 gpm of 90 F. water to each shower head, and no other water shall be supplied.

No differences in elevation, requiring steps, shall be provided in the interior of male and female dressing areas. No steps shall be permitted between the bathhouse and the pool deck areas adjoining and should it be necessary that the bathhouse floor be at a different elevation from the pool decks, ramps shall be provided at the access doors. Where ramps are used between the bathhouse and pool decks, the slope shall not exceed 3 in. per ft and shall be positively non-slip.

All partitions between portions of the dressing room areas, screen partitions, shower, toilet and dressing room booths shall be of durable material not subject to damage by water and shall be so designed that a water way is provided between the partitions and floor to permit thorough cleaning of the floor area with hoses and brooms.

(e) *Soap dispensers:* Soap dispensers for providing either liquid or powdered soap shall be provided at each lavatory and between each pair of shower heads and dispensers must be of all-metal or plastic type and no glass permitted in these units.

(f) *Mirrors:* Mirrors shall be provided over each lavatory and toilet paper holders shall be provided at each water closet combination.

(g) *Water:* All water provided for drinking fountains, lavatories and showers shall be potable and meet the requirements and conform with the standards of the U. S. Public Health Service.

27. Food Service: Where provision is made for serving food and/or beverages at the pool, no containers of glass or other material which might be a hazard to bathers' feet, when broken, shall be used. The area shall be so arranged and posted to prohibit the consumption of food and beverages on the pool decks proper.

ELECTRICAL REQUIREMENTS

28. Lighting and Wiring
(a) *Submarine Lighting:* Where submarine lighting is used, not less than 0.5 watts shall be employed per square foot of pool area.

(b) *Area Lighting:* Where submarine lighting is employed, area lighting shall be provided for the deck areas and directed toward the deck areas and away from the pool surface insofar as practical in a total capacity of not less than 0.6 watts per square foot of deck area. Where submarine lighting is not employed and night swimming is permitted, area and pool lighting combined shall be provided in an amount of not less than 2 watts per square foot of total area.

(c) All wiring in connection with requirements for a swimming pool for lighting or power shall conform with the codes of the National Underwriters' Laboratories (National Electric Code).

(d) In addition to any other grounding, each submarine light unit shall be individually grounded by means of a screwed or bolted connection to the metal junction box from which the branch circuit to the individual light proceeds.

(e) *Overhead Wiring:* No electrical wiring for lighting or power shall be permitted to pass overhead within 20 ft of the pool enclosure.

DRAINAGE PIPING

29. Mechanical Pool Fittings: Where overflow gutters are installed, outlet spacing shall not be greater than 15 ft on centers.

Overflow gutter branch lines from each drain fitting shall be not less than 2 in. I.P.S.

Pool inlets and outlets shall be provided and arranged to produce a uniform circulation of water and the maintenance of uniform chlorine residual throughout the pool; there shall be at least four inlets for the smallest pool.

Provisions shall be made to adjust the flow through all inlets.

Maximum flow rates (in gpm) through various sized inlet branches shall be not more than as follows: Size & gpm; 1 in. = 10; 1¼ in. = 20; 1½ in. = 30; 2 in. = 50.

In pools with surface area greater than 1500 sq ft or length in excess of 60 ft, inlets shall be placed around the entire perimeter. In any case, an adequate number of inlets shall be provided, properly spaced and located to accomplish complete recirculation and the maintenance of a uniform and adequate sterilizing medium at all times.

30. Main Drain Spacing: When the outlets to pool pump suction are installed near the end of a pool, the spacing shall be not greater than 20 ft on centers. An outlet shall be provided not more than 15 ft from side wall.

The outlet grate clear area shall be such that when the maximum flow of water is being pumped through the floor outlet, the velocity through the clear area of the grate shall not be greater than 1½ ft per second. Outlet grates shall be anchored and openings in grates shall be slotted and the minimum dimension of slots shall be not more than ½ in.

Where outlet fittings consist of parallel plates, of so-called anti-vortex type where the water enters the fittings from the sides rather than through a grating facing upward, entrance velocities may be increased to 6 ft per second.

All pool fittings shall be of non-corrosive material.

31. Piping: The determination of sizes of pipe, fittings and valves on the complete main pump suction line from the swimming pool shall be based upon a rate of friction losses for piping of not more than 6 ft per 100 ft of pipe, based upon Hazen-Williams formulas for 15-year old piping.

All piping on the discharge side of the pump for filtration and to the point for discharge of backwash water from the filter plant shall have pipe sizes determined on a basis of friction losses which shall be not more than 12 ft per 100 ft and the velocity in any pipe shall not exceed 10 ft per second and pipe selection shall be made based upon Hazen-Williams formulas for 15-year old pipe. In the determination of pipe sizes required, the criterion which would call for the largest pipe size shall govern.

All pool piping shall be supported by piers or otherwise to preclude against possible settlement which will either provide dirt traps or air pockets and a condition which would result in rupture of the lines.

All pressure and suction lines shall have a uniform slope in one direction of not less than 3 in. per 100 ft. Gravity waste lines around the pool 6 in. or smaller shall have a minimum slope of ⅛ in. per ft. Lines larger than 6 in. and all outfall waste mains shall be designed with a size of pipe

and slope to freely carry the maximum flows required with no surcharge or back pressure in the lines. All piping and equipment shall be provided with positive means of completely draining all water to prevent damage from freezing.

32. Direct Connections to Utilities: No direct mechanical connection between a source of domestic water supply shall be made to a swimming pool or to its piping, thereby eliminating a cross connection to what may become a source of contamination.

The water supply for filling the pool, when derived from a potable supply, shall be by means of an over-fall fillspout to the pool, or an over-fall supply to a surge tank, wherein the water will freely overflow at deck level or the top of the surge tank, before coming into contact with the water supply outlet.

The disposition of sanitary sewage from the bathhouse shall be into a sanitary sewer, a septic tank or other waste line which meets with the approval of local health authorities.

Whenever any waste from the swimming pool is connected to a sanitary sewer or a storm sewer, an air-gap or a relief manhole shall be provided which will positively preclude against surge or backflow introducing contaminated water into the swimming pool or the water treatment plant as covered elsewhere.

33. Pump and Motor: Pump and motor unit shall be provided for recirculation of the pool water which has been selected for performance and will meet the conditions of quantity required for filtering and cleaning the filters with the total dynamic head developed by the complete system. The requirements for filtration shall be based upon the maximum head loss developed immediately prior to washing the filters. The motor shall be non-overloading in continuous operation for filtration under all conditions but may be overloaded within the service factor for conditions of backwash and for emptying the pool.

Pump performance curve for the unit to be installed shall be provided and submitted to proper authorities.

34. Vacuum Cleaner: Where facilities are installed integrally in the pool piping system for the operation of a vacuum cleaner, the piping shall be required to produce not more than 15 ft total head loss at the pump,

while moving four gallons per minute per lineal inch of cleaner head.

35. Sterilizing Agent: Some means of sterilizing the pool water shall be used which provides a residual of sterilizing agent in the pool water. Either chlorine or bromine may be used for this purpose. In either case, adequate feeding equipment and equipment for testing residuals must be employed. Inasmuch as chlorine is almost universally used, minimum standards for the use of chlorine are given below.

In all public pools, chlorine shall be supplied by means of a gas chlorinator which controls and introduces the chlorine gas into water solution and introduces it into the pool water. Exceptions to this may be made in Types B, C, D, E & F swimming pools, where chlorine may be applied in the form of hypochlorites fed by a positive feed pump suitable for use with hypochlorite in solution.

Equipment for supplying chlorine or compounds of chlorine shall be of capacity to feed 1 lb of available chlorine per 3000 gallons of pool volume per 24-hour period. This may be reduced by 50% for Type E pools.

36. Instructions: All valves shall be permanently tagged and valve operating schedule shall be provided for every operation. Instructions shall be supplied in not less than two copies.

POOL WATER AND TREATMENT

37. Chlorine Compartment: Where gaseous chlorine equipment is provided below grade in a filter room or in any part of a building which provides housing, the mechanical proportioning device and cylinders of chlorine shall be housed in a reasonably gas-tight corrosion-resistant and mechanically vented enclosure. Air-tight duct from the bottom of the enclosure to atmosphere in an unrestricted area and a motor-driven exhaust fan capable of producing at least one air change per minute shall be provided. Automatic louvers of good design near the top of the enclosure for admitting fresh air are required. An opening at least 18 in. square, glazed with clear glass, and artificial illumination shall be provided in an amount such that the essential performance of the equipment may be observed, at all times, without opening the enclosure. Electrical switches for the control of artificial lighting and ventilation shall be on the outside of the enclosure adjacent to the door. The floor area of the enclosure shall be of adequate size to house the chlorinator, fan, scales and one extra chlorine cylinder. Gas mask approved by the Bureau of Mines for protection against chlorine gas shall be provided, mounted outside the chlorine compartment.

33. Coagulant Feeder: Coagulant feeder of cast-iron pot type with piping arranged to provide a restriction in the flow or other means of creating a pressure differential which will circulate a portion of the filter influent on a ratio proportionate to the rate of flow shall be provided. Pot shall be of good grade gray cast iron with quick-removable, tight-gasketed cover and will be piped with IPS brass pipe to circulate through the feeder with a tapping at the bottom of the feeder for entering water and a tapping at the top for supplying coagulant solution to the filter influent. Control valves, one of which shall be needlepoint type, and a drain cock for draining the equipment when the plant is out of operation shall be provided. The capacity of the pot shall be not less than 2 oz of lump or nut potassium alum per square foot of filter bed area.

39. Testing Equipment: A test set shall be provided for the determination of free chlorine residual and the pH hydrogen-ion content in the pool water of colorimetric type with test tubes and supply of phenol red solution and orthotoluidine agents.

Color standards shall be as follows and the carrying case and test tubes shall be provided of plastic or other material which is permanent and unbreakable:

Chlorine color standards—0.1, 0.3, 0.6, 0.8 ppm; pH color standards—6.8, 7.2, 7.6, 8.0

40. Quality of Water: The equipment when operated in accordance with the manufacturer's instructions, shall provide water meeting the following standards:

(1) Shall meet U.S. Public Health Service requirements for bacteriologically potable water.

(2) Shall have a degree of clarity such that a disc 2 in. in diameter which is divided into quadrants in alternate colors of red and black shall be clearly discernible through 15 ft of water and the different colors readily distinguishable.

(3) Shall have a minimum free available chlorine residual at any point in the pool of not less than 0.25 ppm and not more than 1.0 ppm at any time.

(4) The pH or measure of hydrogen-ion content at no time shall be below 7.0 and shall be maintained between this limit and 8.0 on the hydrogen-ion scale.

41. Pool Temperature: Temperature of indoor pools shall be maintained between 75 and 85 F., with exceptions made in Type E pools.

WADING POOLS

By definition, a wading pool shall normally be a small pool for non-swimming children, only, used only for wading and shall have a maximum depth at the deepest point not greater than 24 in.

Owing to the high degree of pollution likely to be present, a wading pool shall have a maximum turn-over cycle of 4 hours. The supply to the wading pool shall consist of filtered and chlorinated water from the large pool filtration and recirculation system. The circulating outlets from the wading pool may be wasted or may be returned to the circulation system of the large pool at the suction side of the pump for re-filtration. Also a waste outlet shall be provided at the deepest point of the wading pool, by means of which it shall be completely emptied to waste.

In general, standards of sanitation in circulation, surface skimming and all other details shall be equal or superior to those for swimming pools. It is considered to be very desirable to install a spray pool in lieu of a wading pool, wherein no water stands at any time but is drained away freely as it sprays over the area.

By R. JACKSON SMITH, AIA, Eggers and Higgins, Architects

Separation of swimming and diving pools has long been common practice abroad and is an increasing trend in the United States. Diving does not require a very large pool, but it must be deep—at least 14 ft below a 10-meter platform. A swimming pool must be large in area, but it need be no more than 4 or 5 ft deep and can have a flat bottom.

Olympic requirements for diving pools are shown in the accompanying diagram and table. Minimum requirements can be met with a pool 35 by 45 ft, but a somewhat larger size, e.g., 60 by 60 ft, is usually advisable. A water-curling arrangement should be provided so that the diver can see exactly where the surface of the water is. If outdoors, the pool should be oriented so that the sun is not in the diver's eyes. Underwater observation ports are desirable.

Diving pool and platform dimensions for competitive swimming

| | Board size | | Ht. above water level | Distances* | | | | | | | |
	Length	Width		A From edge of pool to end of board		B From center of board to side of pool		C From center of board to center of board		D From end of board to wall ahead	
1-meter springboard	16'	20"	3'- 3"	A-1 7'	5'	B-1 10'	8'	C-1 8'	6'	D-1 28'	25'
3-meter springboard	16'	20"	9'-11"	A-3 7'	5'	B-3 15'	12'	C-3 10'	8'	D-3 33'	30'
5-meter platform	18'	7'	16'- 5"	A-5 7'	5'	B-5 15'	12'	C-5 10'	8'	D-5 43'	35'
10-meter platform	20' 20'	8' 10'	32'-10"	A-10 8'	5'	B-10 20'	15'	C-10 10'	8'	D-10 52'	45'

Preferred dimensions appear in left-hand columns; minimum safe dimensions

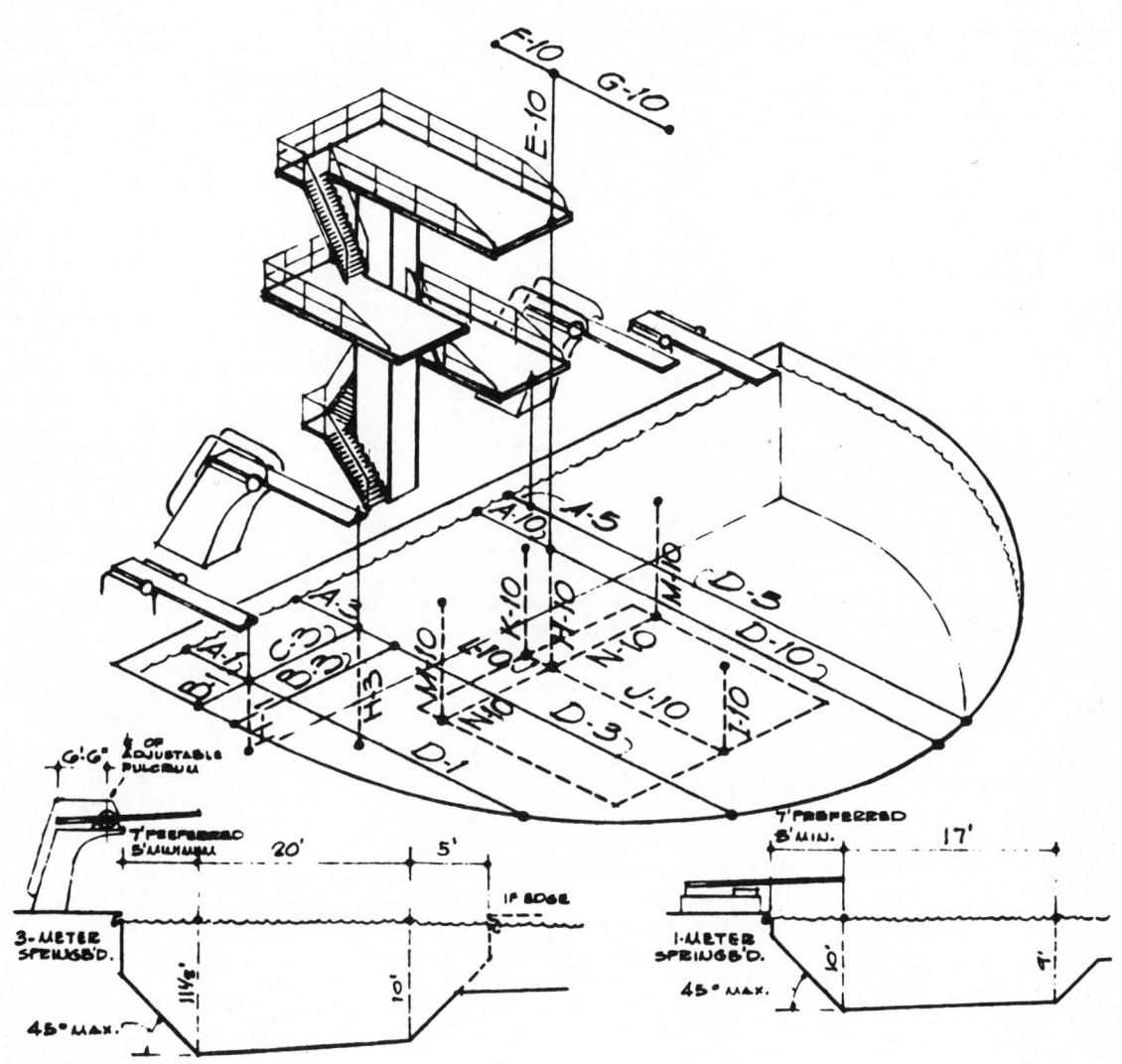

(in accordance with Olympic requirements)

Distances*					Depths						
						In area measured from point below end of board					
E From board to beam or ceiling above	F Clear overhead behind board	G Clear overhead ahead of board	H Preferred	Min. depth	I Depth	J Dist. in front	K Depth	L Dist. in back	M Depth	N Dist. ba. side
E-1	F-1	G-1	H-1		I-1	J-1	K-1	L-1	M-1	N-1
15'	5'	12'	11'	10'	9'	17'	9'	3'	9'	8'
	6'	15'								
E-3	F-3	G-3	H-3		I-3	J-3	K-3	L-3	M-3	N-3
15'	5'	12'	12'	11½'	10'	20'	9'	3'	10'	10'
	6'	15'								
E-5	F-5	G-5	H-5		I-5	J-5	K-5	L-5	M-5	N-5
15'	6'	12'	14'	12½'	11'	25'	9'	3'	11'	10'
15'	8'	15'								
E-10	F-10	G-10	H-10		I-10	J-10	K-10	L-10	M-10	N-10
21'	6'	12'	16'	15'	14'	35'	10'	3'	14'	10'
15'	8'	15'								

appear in right-hand columns.

Minimum standards prepared by the National Swimming Pool Institute

The technical data presented here give basic requirements for residential swimming pool design, systems and equipment. It is intended by the NSPI to serve as recommended minimum standards and not as a model code.

DEFINITIONS AND NOMENCLATURE

1. Swimming Pool—Any constructed pool, used for swimming or bathing over 24 in. in depth, or with a surface area exceeding 250 sq ft.

2. Residential Swimming Pool—Any constructed pool which is used, or intended to be used, as a swimming pool in connection with a single family residence.

3. Main Outlet—The outlet(s) at the deep portion of the pool through which the main flow of water leaves the pool.

4. Main Suction—The line connecting the main outlet to the pump suction.

5. Vacuum Fitting—The fitting in the wall of the pool which is used as an outlet for connecting the underwater suction cleaning equipment.

6. Vacuum Piping—The piping which connects the vacuum fitting to the pump suction.

7. Return Piping—The piping which carries the filtered water from the filter to the pool.

8. Inlet—The fitting or opening through which water enters the pool.

9. Face Piping—The piping with all valves and fittings which is used to connect the filter system together as a unit.

10. Recirculating Piping—The piping from the pool to the filter and return to the pool, through which the water circulates.

11. Backwash Piping—The piping which extends from the backwash outlet of the filters to its terminus at the point of disposal.

12. Receptor—An approved fixture or device of such material, shape and capacity as to adequately receive the discharge from indirect waste piping, so constructed and located as to be readily cleaned.

13. Filter—Any material or apparatus by which water is clarified.

14. Underdrain—An appurtenance at the bottom of the filter to assure equal distribution of water through the filter media.

15. Filter Element—that part of a filter device which retains the filter media.

16. Recirculating Skimmer—A device connected with the pump suction used to skim the pool over a self-adjusting weir and return the water to the pool through the filter.

17. Overflow Gutter—A trough in the wall of the pool which may be used for overflow and to skim the pool surface.

18. Filter Media—The fine material which entraps the suspended particles.

19. Filter Sand—A type of filter media.

20. Filter Rock—Graded rock and gravel used to support filter sand.

21. Pool Depths—The distance between the floor of the pool and the maximum operating level when pool is in use.

22. Pool Decks—The paved area around the pool.

23. Width and Length—Shall be determined by actual water dimensions.

24. Lifeline Anchors—Rings in wall of pool at transition point between shallow and deep area.

CONSTRUCTION

The design and construction, as well as all equipment and materials, shall comply with the following requirements:

1. Structural Design—The pool structure shall be engineered and designed to withstand the expected forces to which it will be subjected.

2. Wall Slopes—To a depth of 5 ft from the top, the wall slope shall not be more than 1 ft horizontal in 5 ft vertical.

3. Floor Slopes—The slope of the floor in the shallow end shall not exceed 1 ft vertical to 7 ft horizontal. The transition point between shallow and deep water shall not be less than 4½ or more than 5 ft deep.

4. Lifeline Anchors—Provide recessed lifeline anchor in wall of pool at transition point between shallow and deep area.

5. Diving Area—Minimum depths and distances shall be as shown in table below.

DIVING AREA—MINIMUM DEPTHS AND DISTANCES

Diving Boards	Maximum Distance Above Water, in.	Minimum Depth, ft	Distance from Diving Wall, ft	Distance from Deep Point to Transition Point, ft	Minimum Overhang, ft	Minimum Width to Center of Board, ft
Deck Level	18	8	10	10	2½	7
Residential	30	8	11	11	2½	7½
1 meter	39.37	8½	12	12	3	8

MECHANICAL

1. Filters—Every pool shall be equipped with a recirculating system capable of filtering the entire contents of the pool in 18 hr*, or less, when the flow is calculated at a maximum of 5 gallons per minute, per square foot of filter area.

a. Filters shall be capable of maintaining the clarity of the water to permit the ready identification, through an 8 ft depth of water, of a disc 2 in. in diameter, which is divided into four quadrants in alternate colors of red and white.

b. Filter capacity shall be such that it need not be cleaned more frequently than once every four days under normal operation.

c. All filters shall be equipped with influent and offluent pressure gauges, to determine the pressure differential and frequency of cleaning.

d. All filter systems shall be equipped with an air release at the high point in the system. Each filter shall be provided with a visual means of determining when the filter has been restored to original cleanliness.

e. Operating instructions shall be posted on every filter system and all valves shall be properly designated with metal tags, indicating purpose.

2. Sand Pressure Filters—Sand filter systems shall be designed and installed to operate at a rate not to exceed 5 gallons per minute, per sq ft of filter area and to backwash at a minimum rate of 10 gallons per minute, per sq ft of surface area.

a. Filter tanks shall be fabricated to 1956 ASME Specifications for noncode pressure vessels, with the exception that standard type dished and flanged heads may be used. Tanks shall be built for a minimum of 50 pounds working pressure and tested at 150 psi. The filter underdrain shall have an effective distribution of at least 25 per cent of the cross-sectional area of the tank. Tanks placed underground shall be steel plate at least $\frac{3}{16}$ in. in thickness, with an approved non-corrosive exterior coating.

b. Filter tanks shall be supported in a manner to prevent tipping or settling.

3. Filter Media Specifications*

a. Filter sand shall be a hard uniformly graded, silica material with effective particle sizes, between 0.45 and 0.55 millimeters in diameter, with uniformity coefficient of 1.45 to 1.69. There shall be no limestone or clay present.

b. Filter sand shall be no less than 19 in.

*Note: Standards for diatomaceous earth filters are presently being prepared by a National Committee of diatomaceous earth filter manufacturers.

in depth with a freeboard of no less than 9 in. or more than 12 in.

c. There shall be no less than four grades of rock, which shall be clean, non-crushed, rounded, non-calcareous material.

d. The total depth of the rock supporting bed shall be no less than 15 in. and each grade shall be 2 in. or greater in depth. Each layer of rock shall be leveled to prevent intermixing of adjacent grades.

e. The top layer shall vary in size between ⅛ and ¼ in. The next layer shall vary in size between ¼ and ½ in. The next layer shall vary in size between ½ and ¾ in. The bottom layer shall vary in size between 1 and 1½ in.

4. Recirculating Pumps—The recirculating pump shall have sufficient capacity to provide the rated flows of the filter system, without exceeding the head loss at which the pump will deliver such flows. The pump motor shall not be operated at an overload which exceeds the service factor.

a. Pool pump shall be equipped on the inlet side with an approved type hair and lint strainer. The basket of the strainer shall be non-corrosive and have an open screen surface of at least four times the cross sectional area of the inlet pipe.

5. Pool Piping—Shall be sized to permit the rated flows for filtering and cleaning without exceeding the maximum head, at which the pump will provide such flows. In general, the water velocity in the pool piping should not exceed 10 ft per second. Where velocity exceeds 10 ft per second, summary calculations should be provided to show that rated flows are possible with the pump and piping provided. The recirculating piping and fittings shall meet the following requirements:

a. The vacuum fitting(s) shall be in an accessible position(s) below water line.

b. A main outlet shall be placed at the deepest point in every pool for recirculating and emptying the pool.

c. Pool recirculation piping, passing through the pool structure, shall be copper tubing (with a minimum wall thickness of Type "L") brass or an approved equal.

d. Filtered water inlets shall be provided in sufficient quantity and shall be properly spaced to provide a maximum circulation of the main body and surface of water.

6. Valves—Fullway valves shall be installed throughout, to insure proper functioning of the filtration and piping system.

a. A valve shall be installed on the main suction line located in an accessible place outside the walls of the pool.

b. Valves up to, and including 2 in. in size

shall be brass. Sizes over 2 in. may have cast-iron or brass bodies. All working parts of valves shall be non-corrosive material.

c. Combination valves may be installed if the materials and design comply with the intent of these standards.

7. Tests—All pool piping shall be in compliance with these standards and the installation and construction of the pool piping system in accordance with the approved plans. The entire pool piping system shall be tested with a water test of 50 psi and proved tight before covering or concealing.

WATER SUPPLY AND TREATMENT

The potable water supply to any swimming pool shall be installed as required in AWWA Standards.

a. Unless an approved type of filling system is installed, such as is required by AWWA, any source of water which may be used to fill the pool shall be equipped with backflow protection.

b. No over the rim fill spout will be accepted unless located under a diving board or installed in a manner approved by local authorities so as to remove any hazard.

GENERAL

Wherever building regulations are established, generally the requirements are similar to those listed below.

a. Before commencing the installation of any swimming pool, a permit authorizing such work shall be obtained from the building department.

b. Application for permits shall be accompanied by plans and calculations in duplicate or triplicate and in sufficient detail showing the following:

1. Plot plan, elevations with dimensions all drawn to scale.

2. Pool dimensions, depths and volume in gallons.

3. Type and size of filter systems, filtration and backwash capacities.

4. Pool piping layout, with all pipe sizes and valves shown, and types of materials to be used.

5. The rated capacity and head at filtration and backwash flows of the pool pump in gpm with the size and type of motor.

6. Location and type of waste disposal system.

7. Structural, calculations and details prepared and signed by a registered engineer.

c. Set Back—Swimming pools shall be classified as accessory structures and conform to setbacks as required for such structures in local building codes.

MINIMUM FILTER AND PIPE SIZES

FOR RESIDENTIAL POOLS WITH CONVENTIONAL SAND PRESSURE FILTERS Based on: Maximum filter rate—5 gpm per sq ft of filter area. Minimum backwash rate—10 gpm per sq ft of filter area. Complete turnover of pool capacity in 18 hours.

POOL CAPACITY	FILTER SIZE		FILTER AND BACKWASH RATES	
Maximum Pool Capacity	Filter Diameter	Filter Area	Filter Rate	Backwash Rate
9,550, gal	18 in	1.77 ft	9 gpm	18 gpm
11,750 gal	20 in	2.18 ft	11 gpm	22 gpm
17,000 gal	24 in	3.14 ft	16 gpm	32 gpm
26,400 gal	30 in	4.90 ft	25 gpm	50 gpm
38,200 gal	36 in	7.07 ft	35 gpm	71 gpm
51,900 gal	42 in	9.62 ft	48 gpm	96 gpm
67,800 gal	48 in	12.57 ft	63 gpm	126 gpm

PIPE VELOCITIES IN FEET PER SECOND (Based on Standard Steel Pipe)

Flow Rate	Pipe Size		Flow Rate	Pipe Size			
	¾ in	1 in		1¼ in	1½ in	2 in	2½ in
9 gpm	5.4		32 gpm	6.6			
10 gpm	6.0		35 gpm	7.5			
11 gpm	6.6		48 gpm	10.2*	7.6		
16 gpm	9.6		50 gpm		7.9		
18 gpm	10.8*	6.7	63 gpm		9.9		
22 gpm		8.2	71 gpm		11.1*	6.9	
25 gpm		9.3	96 gpm			9.2	6.4
32 gpm		11.9*	126 gpm			12.1*	8.4

Do not select suction or backwash line sizes where velocity exceeds 10 ft per second without engineering calculations.

MINIMUM PIPE SIZES*

Diameter of Filter	Maximum Length Suction Line	Main Suction Line	Vacuum Line	Filter Return Line	Backwash Line	Approx. Total Backwash Head
18 in	20 ft	1 in	1 in	¾ in	1 in	32 ft
	30 ft	1 in	1 in	¾ in	1 in	35 ft
	40 ft	1¼ in	1¼ in	¾ in	1¼ in	22 ft
	50 ft	1¼ in	1¼ in	¾ in	1¼ in	24 ft
20 in	20 ft	1 in	1 in	¾ in	1¼ in	29 ft
	30 ft	1¼ in	1¼ in	¾ in	1¼ in	24 ft
	40 ft	1¼ in	1¼ in	¾ in	1¼ in	25 ft
	50 ft	1¼ in	1¼ in	¾ in	1¼ in	26 ft
24 in	20 ft	1¼ in	1¼ in	1 in	1¼ in	28 ft
	30 ft	1¼ in	1¼ in	1 in	1¼ in	31 ft
	40 ft	1¼ in	1¼ in	1 in	1¼ in	34 ft
	50 ft	1½ in	1¼ in	1 in	1¼ in	29 ft
30 in	20 ft	1½ in	1½ in	1¼ in	1½ in	29 ft
	30 ft	1½ in	1½ in	1¼ in	1½ in	32 ft
	40 ft	1½ in	1½ in	1¼ in	1½ in	35 ft
	50 ft	2 in	1½ in	1¼ in	1½ in	28 ft
36 in	20 ft	2 in	1½ in	1½ in	2 in	25 ft
	30 ft	2 in	1½ in	1½ in	2 in	27 ft
	40 ft	2 in	1½ in	1½ in	2 in	29 ft
	50 ft	2 in	1½ in	1½ in	2 in	31 ft
42 in	20 ft	2 in	1½ in	1½ in	2 in	31 ft
	30 ft	2½ in	1½ in	1½ in	2½ in	22 ft
	40 ft	2½ in	1½ in	1½ in	2½ in	24 ft
	50 ft	2½ in	1½ in	1½ in	2½ in	26 ft
48 in	20 ft	2½ in	1½ in	1½ in	2½ in	25 ft
	30 ft	2½ in	2 in**	1½ in	2½ in	27 ft
	40 ft	2½ in	2 in**	1½ in	2½ in	28 ft
	50 ft	2½ in	2 in**	1½ in	2½ in	33 ft

Assumes filter at deck level with backwash outlet plus or minus 2 ft of deck level—not over 30 ft long. Allowable loss due to friction through filter and face piping—15 ft. Five 90° bends in each line is maximum considered.

**1½ in lines acceptable, but not recommended.*

Information in this section was prepared by Ronald Allwork from data assembled by the Portland Cement Ass'n.; Gavin Hadden; A. B. Randall; E. S. Crawley. It is intended to furnish a basis for designing outdoor seating for grandstands, arenas, bowls, theatres, bleachers, etc.

General. The purpose of a grandstand is to provide an audience with a good view of a performance under comfortable circumstances. The view is affected by both the distance to the action and obstructions in the line of sight. Shape and relation of grandstand to action is generally determined by type of performance.

Sight lines. Best view is obtained when the sight line to any part of the field of action clears the heads of the spectators in front. Since this is not always practicable, only sight lines normal to the grandstand are ordinarily considered; oblique lines to different parts of the field are neglected. However, compensation is sometimes made (particularly in bowls) by curving the stands so normal lines approach the center of action.

The focal point—intersection of sight line with playing field—varies according to the type of action. For football, it may be the nearest line of the playing field; for track, at about chest height of the runner in the nearest lane; for baseball, the catcher.

The approximate eye level of a seated spectator is assumed to be 4 ft. above the floor and 6 in. below the top of his hat. Referring to diagrams below, it will be observed that, with focal point and elevation for first row of seats established, required elevation for higher seats is materially affected by the assumed value of c. With a value of 6 in. given to c, an unobstructed view may be assumed, but except for small grandstands, this dimension often results in excessively high rear seats. It is therefore common practice to assign a smaller value to c, especially in large grandstands. It is assumed that spectators will have a satisfactory view if they can see over the heads of those in the second row ahead of them. This requires a value of 3 in. for c.

Diagrams below illustrate two types of sections; the second shows a curved seat section with a common focal point, and the first, a straight seat section with a different focal point for each seat. In the straight section, lower seats have better visibility, and upper seats poorer visibility, than in the curved section, but the average is the same.

STRAIGHT SEAT SECTION
PROVIDES A DIFFERENT FOCAL POINT FOR EACH SEAT

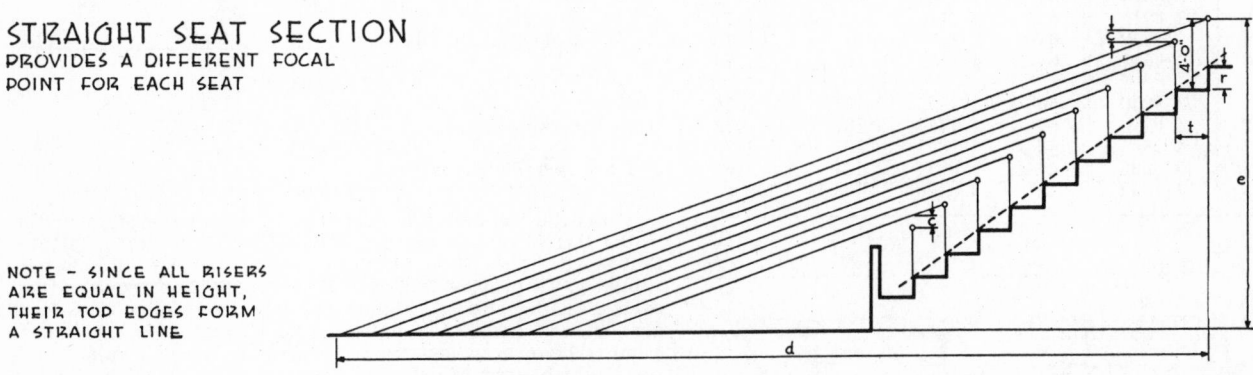

NOTE – SINCE ALL RISERS ARE EQUAL IN HEIGHT, THEIR TOP EDGES FORM A STRAIGHT LINE

NOTE – THE ELEVATION OF FRONT AND REAR SEATS, AND THE SIGHT LINE CLEARANCE, ARE THE SAME FOR BOTH DIAGRAMS. NEITHER DIAGRAM IS DRAWN TO SCALE.

CURVED SEAT SECTION
PROVIDES A COMMON FOCAL POINT FOR EACH SEAT.

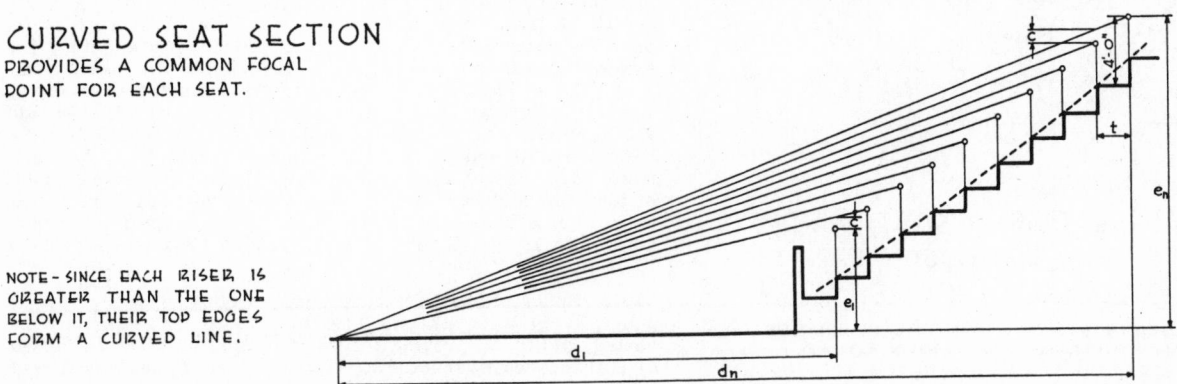

NOTE – SINCE EACH RISER IS GREATER THAN THE ONE BELOW IT, THEIR TOP EDGES FORM A CURVED LINE.

$\frac{d}{t}$	S	$\frac{d}{t}$	S	$\frac{d}{t}$	S
1	0.0000	36	4.1468	71	4.8328
2	1.0000	37	4.1746	72	4.8469
3	1.5000	38	4.2016	73	4.8608
4	1.8333	39	4.2279	74	4.8745
5	2.0833	40	4.2535	75	4.8880
6	2.2833	41	4.2785	76	4.9014
7	2.4500	42	4.3029	77	4.9145
8	2.5929	43	4.3267	78	4.9275
9	2.7179	44	4.3500	79	4.9403
10	2.8290	45	4.3727	80	4.9530
11	2.9290	46	4.3949	81	4.9655
12	3.0199	47	4.4167	82	4.9778
13	3.1032	48	4.4380	83	4.9900
14	3.1801	49	4.4588	84	5.0021
15	3.2516	50	4.4792	85	5.0140
16	3.3182	51	4.4992	86	5.0257
17	3.3807	52	4.5188	87	5.0374
18	3.4396	53	4.5380	88	5.0489
19	3.4951	54	4.5569	89	5.0602
20	3.5477	55	4.5754	90	5.0715
21	3.5977	56	4.5936	91	5.0826
22	3.6454	57	4.6115	92	5.0936
23	3.6908	58	4.6290	93	5.1044
24	3.7343	59	4.6463	94	5.1152
25	3.7760	60	4.6632	95	5.1258
26	3.8160	61	4.6799	96	5.1363
27	3.8544	62	4.6963	97	5.1468
28	3.8915	63	4.7124	98	5.1571
29	3.9272	64	4.7283	99	5.1673
30	3.9617	65	4.7439	100	5.1774
31	3.9950	66	4.7593	101	5.1874
32	4.0272	67	4.7744	102	5.1973
33	4.0585	68	4.7894	103	5.2071
34	4.0888	69	4.8041	104	5.2168
35	4.1182	70	4.8186	105	5.2264

Straight section need be checked for sight lines from top seats only, as these have the poorest view. In this case, the relation between horizontal distance from seat to focal point d, height of eye above focal point e, width of tread t, height of riser r, and clearance c is represented by the formula:

$$\frac{d}{c} = \frac{t}{r-c}$$

Curved section. Relation of the various factors is represented by the formula:

$$e_n = d_n \left[\frac{e_1}{d_1} + \frac{c}{t}(S_n - S_1) \right]$$

in which c_n = *elevation above focal point of eye of spectator in row n.*
e_1 = *elevation above focal point of eye of spectator in row 1.*
d_n = *distance from focal point to row n.*
c = *clearance between successive sight lines.*
t = *width of tread.*

S_1 and S_n = *values from table corresponding to* $\frac{d_1}{t}$ *and* $\frac{d_n}{t}$.

For simplicity the value of d_1 should be an exact multiple of t. As an example of the use of this formula, assume that it is desired to design a grandstand with a common focal point. Assume the factors:

$$e_1 = 6 \ ft., \ d_1 = 32 \ ft., \ c = 0.25 \ ft., \ t = 2 \ ft.$$

Then the formula becomes

$$e_n = d_n \left[\frac{6}{32} + \frac{0.25}{2}(S_n - 3.3182) \right]$$

which can be simplified to
$$e_n = d_n (0.125 S_n - 0.2273)$$
for these specific conditions. For the last row
$$d_n = 78; \ \frac{d_n}{t} = 39;$$

from the table,
$$S_n = 4.2279;$$
and the formula gives
$$e_n = 23.494$$

which is the distance above the focal point of eye of spectator in the last row. Elevation of tread for this spectator is thus $23.49 - 4.0 = 19.49$ ft. The elevation of each row is obtained similarly. To provide this curved seating section requires that each riser be slightly higher than the preceding one. Few grandstands have been built to the theoretical curve but a number have been constructed with a series of straight sections which approximate the theoretical curve. This is obtained by increasing the height of riser for succeeding groups of 5 to 10 rows rather than for each row. This greatly reduces the construction difficulties involved in the use of variable riser heights. Such a plan is recommended for structures containing more than about 25 rows of seats and may be used in smaller structures.

Treads and risers for grandstand seats should be as small as possible for economy but sufficient for comfort and good view. Width of treads may be from 24 to 30 in. Width of 26 in. provides reasonable comfort and is probably satisfactory for average cases. When seats with fixed backs are used, tread should be at least 30 in. Where there is much movement of spectators during the program, as at race tracks, wider treads are required than when spectators remain in their seats. First tread should be wide enough to provide 18 in. between front edge of seat and wall or rail. Distance between back of last seat and rear wall need not be more than 6 in. unless a transverse aisle is provided here. Riser heights may vary from 6 to 18 in. Risers in small stands usually are from 9 to 14 in.

Seats. Space allowed for each seat, lengthwise in the row, is generally between 17 and 18½ in. Width of seats may be varied slightly to provide for varying lengths of rows caused by entrance-ways, aisles, etc. Height of seat from floor should be approximately 18 in.

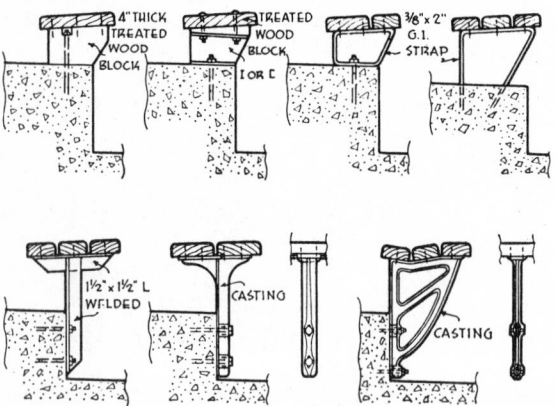

TYPICAL SEATS AND SEAT SUPPORTS

SCALE ½" = 1'-0"

NOTE — DETAILS SHOWN ABOVE ARE IN COMMON USE BUT MANY OTHER DESIGNS ARE EQUALLY AS ACCEPTABLE. THE FIRST TWO UPPER LEFT DETAILS ARE APPLICABLE ONLY TO RELATIVELY HIGH RISERS

Aisles. Stadia are generally divided into sections by transverse aisles. The width of these sections, in terms of number of seats, varies from 24 to 32 seats per row. Most common are sections 26 or 28 seats wide.

Aisles adjacent to end walls of grandstand are advantageous if connected directly to an entrance, but they are not essential. By placing one half section against the wall at each end of the stand, one less aisle will be required.

Aisle widths vary, but 3 ft. is most widely accepted. This width permits a single file in one direction and an usher going in the opposite direction. Aisle 4 ft. wide will permit two lanes of traffic in the same or in opposite directions. If there are aisles on both sides of an entranceway they need be only 2 ft. wide. This width is the minimum advisable to insure sufficient clearance against the hazards of clothing catching in the seats or disturbing the occupants of the end seats.

Seat risers more than 9 in. high will require an extra step in the aisle. In this case make each step riser one-half the height of the seat riser, and the step tread one-half the width of the seat tread. Steps should be full width of the aisle.

Longitudinal aisles, either in front of the first row of seats or part way up the stand should be avoided since their use obstructs the view of spectators seated in back of them. However, where seats are not reserved, an aisle at the entrance level is a considerable convenience to spectators in choosing their seats, although it does interfere with the view of those already seated. When such an aisle is employed part way up the stand, sight lines for several rows above it should be checked to determine the effect of the extra tread width.

Entrances and Exits. In the small stands which do not have entrance through vomitories, it is preferable to have entrances from the field level at each transverse aisle rather than provide entrances at each end only and a longitudinal aisle leading to the transverse aisles. When the small grandstand is built on an embankment, entrance to the transverse aisles can be made from the rear, either directly, or by means of a longitudinal aisle connected with them.

In larger stadia, entrance is usually through vomitories whose widths may vary from 4 to 8 feet. A 6-ft. width is most common. Standard requirements for exits are based on traffic lanes of 22-in. width. Widths of vomitories and passageways should therefore be determined with this minimum in mind. Handrails extending not more than 3½ in. from the walls are not considered as reducing the effective width.

Width of exits is specified by most building codes in terms of number of seats to be handled. For example, if 8 in. is required for each 100 seats, a single vomitory or exit serving a section of 800 seats would require a width of 64 in. This should be increased to 66 in. to provide for three 22-in. traffic lanes, the rule being to increase the width rather than to reduce it.

When seats are not provided with back rests, many spectators approach the exits by walking over the seats rather than in the aisles. In such cases, therefore, it is not necessary to have the width of the aisles equal to the width of the exits, and some codes take this into consideration. The code which required the width of exits to be 8 in. per 100 seats, for instance, permits the aisles to be 6 in. per 100 seats.

The location of vomitories will depend upon the contour of the site and the size of the particular section to be served. Where the section is relatively small, the vomitory can be at the same level as the entrance, thus avoiding ramps or stairs. For larger sections it is advisable to place the vomitory part way up the stand so that it will be served by an aisle below as well as the aisle above. In large stadia, a second row of vomitories is often provided.

Stairways and Ramps. The rate of egress from stairways and ramps is not constant, but some authorities consider 30 persons per minute per 22-in. traffic lane about average for stairways, and 37 persons per minute per 22-in. lane in ramps. Other authorities give higher rates, in some cases assuming a rate of egress of 45 persons per minute per traffic lane for both stairways and ramps. On this basis, if it were desired to exit an entire audience of 10,000 persons in 5 minutes, a total of 45 lane widths would be required for ramps, vomitories, stairways or gates. This total width should be maintained to the outside of stadium and enclosure.

In designing grandstand stairways, common rules are widely used. These require that the sum of riser heights and tread width, in inches, shall not be less than 17½ nor more than 18; that the sum of 2 risers and 1 tread, in inches, shall not be less than 24 nor more than 25; that the product of riser and tread, in inches, shall fall between 70 and 75. Risers of 6½ to 7½ in. with treads of 11 to 10 in. are most commonly used.

The capacity of ramps may be considered as being between that of stairways and level passageways. They are recommended primarily for greater safety rather than for greater capacity. Requirements for building exits often limit ramp slopes to not more than 1 in 10 because of the danger of possible panic from fire or other cause, but since this danger is less in grandstands than in buildings, somewhat steeper slopes are permissible. Ramps with an incline of 1 in 4 have been used, but slopes of 1 in 6 to 8 are safer and more often used. Ramps are longer than stairways of the same height. They are particularly suitable for grandstands where it is not necessary to make maximum use of the space under the deck, and in large stadia.

Walls and Railings. Passage-ways, entrances, back and sides of grandstand must have walls or railings for protection of spectators. These may consist of concrete walls or of pipe sections anchored to concrete or steel, etc., as the case may be. Solid walls in front of the first row should not be more than 3 ft. high above the lower tread. Handrails on enclosed stairways are often placed 32 in. above the lip of the step. Rails and walls at ends of stand and around entrances are usually 3 to 3½ ft. above the front edge of the tread. Solid back walls give spectators protection against strong winds and are frequently made higher for this reason.

Gates and Fences. Entrance gates should be so arranged that a single file of persons entering passes each ticket collector, but should also provide quick, unobstructed passage for exit of the crowd. Swinging gates are commonly employed; sliding gates are also used. Size of gate is determined by same method employed for determining sizes of vomitories, stairs and passages.

If admission is charged, a fence must enclose the entire field. Wire fences are used in a number of instances, but they do not shut off view to people on the outside; hence solid walls of concrete or other material are often employed.

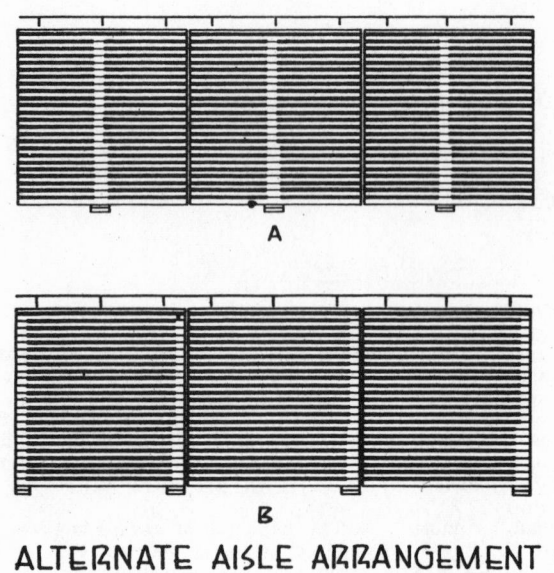

ALTERNATE AISLE ARRANGEMENT FOR SMALL GRANDSTAND
(NOT TO SCALE)

HALF SECTIONS AT EACH END IN SCHEME A REQUIRE ONE LESS AISLE THAN SCHEME B. BOTH ARRANGEMENTS PERMIT CONSTRUCTION OF ADDITIONAL SECTIONS

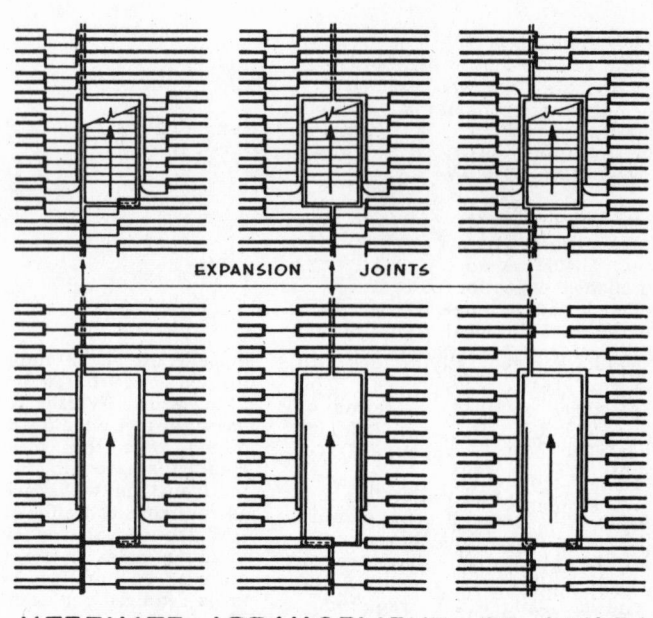

EXPANSION JOINTS

ALTERNATE ARRANGEMENT OF AISLES AT VOMITORIES AND STAIRS
(NOT TO SCALE)

NOTE THE LOCATION OF EXPANSION JOINTS. THIS PERMITS THE WALLS AROUND THE VOMITORIES TO BE CARRIED ON THE DECK WHILE RAMPS AND STAIRS ARE SELF-SUPPORTING AND FREE FROM THE REMAINDER OF THE STRUCTURE

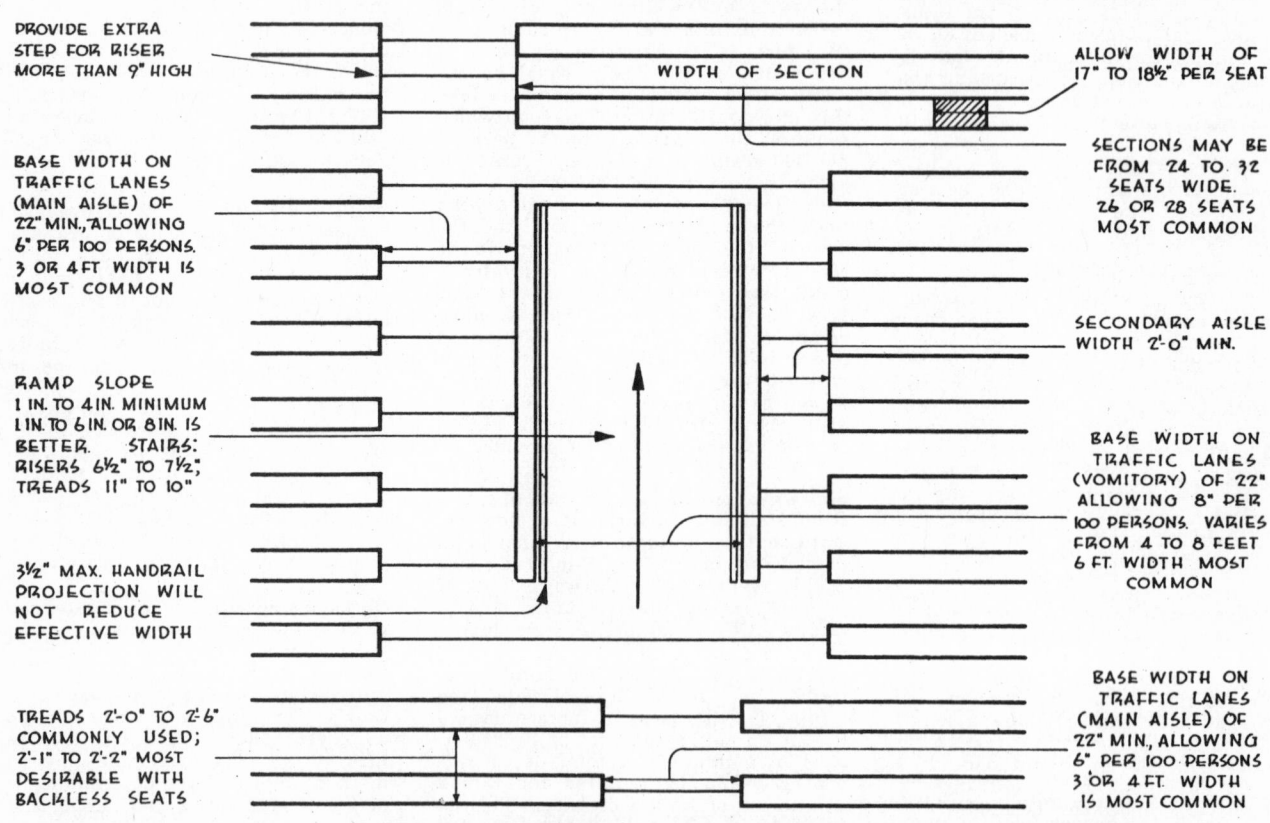

PROVIDE EXTRA STEP FOR RISER MORE THAN 9" HIGH

WIDTH OF SECTION

ALLOW WIDTH OF 17" TO 18½" PER SEAT

BASE WIDTH ON TRAFFIC LANES (MAIN AISLE) OF 22" MIN., ALLOWING 6" PER 100 PERSONS. 3 OR 4 FT WIDTH IS MOST COMMON

SECTIONS MAY BE FROM 24 TO 32 SEATS WIDE. 26 OR 28 SEATS MOST COMMON

RAMP SLOPE 1 IN. TO 4 IN. MINIMUM 1 IN. TO 6 IN. OR 8 IN. IS BETTER. STAIRS: RISERS 6½" TO 7½"; TREADS 11" TO 10"

SECONDARY AISLE WIDTH 2'-0" MIN.

BASE WIDTH ON TRAFFIC LANES (VOMITORY) OF 22" ALLOWING 8" PER 100 PERSONS. VARIES FROM 4 TO 8 FEET 6 FT. WIDTH MOST COMMON

3½" MAX. HANDRAIL PROJECTION WILL NOT REDUCE EFFECTIVE WIDTH

TREADS 2'-0" TO 2'-6" COMMONLY USED; 2'-1" TO 2'-2" MOST DESIRABLE WITH BACKLESS SEATS

BASE WIDTH ON TRAFFIC LANES (MAIN AISLE) OF 22" MIN., ALLOWING 6" PER 100 PERSONS 3 OR 4 FT. WIDTH IS MOST COMMON

DIAGRAMMATIC SKETCH SHOWING MOST COMMON DIMENSIONS
SCALE 3/16" = 1'-0"

Information in this section was prepared from data collected by Ronald Allwork. Sources include F. Elwood Allen, community building consultant, National Recreation Association; John Matthews Hatton, Architect; E. B. Van Keuren, AIA; New York City Park Dept.

General. A community building must fit into the life of those for whom it is designed. Therefore no set pattern can be established. Selection of facilities to be included and arrangement of units has to conform to local conditions. A site in a residential neighborhood, on a secondary street if possible, is usually desirable. Trends of community growth, and traffic have to be considered.

The building may be intended for indoor use only, or as a "field house" for outdoor play, or as a combination of both. Elements shown in diagram at right are those most commonly incorporated, in the experience of the National Recreation Association. Local habits, availability of funds, etc., dictate requirements for specific cases.

Since funds are always limited, low costs, both initial and upkeep, are a prime consideration. In planning, this premise demands that rooms be designed for multiple use, that circulation be simple and direct. In construction and equipment, durability, permanence and easy maintenance are important factors. This may require that fairly expensive materials be used—a practice which, though it may increase first cost, can result in maintenance economies.

TYPES OF SPACES

Gymnasium and auditorium: The Nat'l. Rec. Ass'n. recommends that these be separate rooms to avoid pre-emption of space by one activity at another's expense. In practice, combination of the two is often the only practicable solution, financially. Gymnasium should be large enough for the game requiring the greatest area, usually basketball. For organized teams, a floor 50 by 90 ft., and a 20-ft. ceiling, are desirable. Since the object is to interest members of the community in active participation, a smaller space, still ample for "amateur" groups, is often provided. A room 75 by 60 ft. will accommodate a satisfactory amateur basketball court or two or more smaller game courts, sufficient for 30 or 40 active participants at a time, and will seat 400 to 425 people comfortably when used as an auditorium. The Nat'l. Rec. Ass'n. recommends a minimum of 6 sq. ft. per person.

Stage should have sufficient area for amateur productions, even if these do not seem of great importance at first. If space is available, initiative of those who use it can overcome deficiencies in equipment. Absolute minimum depth is 18 ft.; 20 ft. is a preferable minimum, 30 ft. better. Satisfactory proscenium width is 24 ft., with 12 ft. of wing space at either side. The optimum is wing space at least double the proscenium width, half on each side. Stage ceiling should be at least 3 ft. higher than

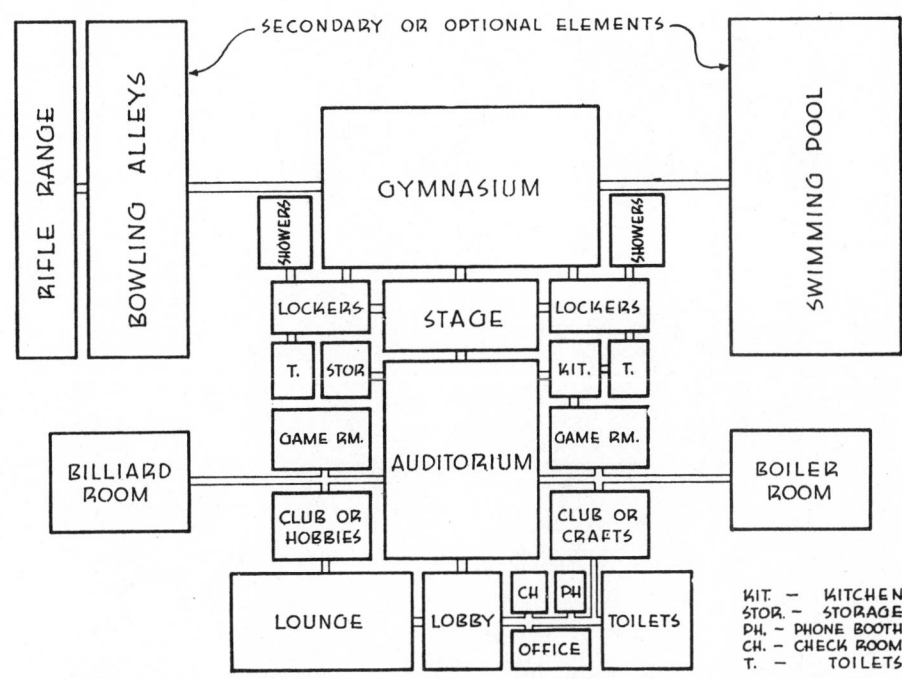

ORGANIZATION OF ELEMENTS, based on recommendations of the National Recreation Ass'n.

proscenium opening; as much more as the budget permits will facilitate use of stage lights, drops, etc.

Two small dressing rooms, with lavatories, are sufficient if other adjacent rooms can be used when needed. Chair storage space is needed (see drawing on next page).

Other types of stages than the permanent one outlined may be considered. Occasionally a series of portable units which can be locked together to form runways, exhibit tables, even outdoor counters, prove practical.

Locker rooms need not accommodate full capacity of gymnasium. E. B. Van Keuren finds in Birmingham, Ala., that 30 lockers for girls, 30 for boys, is reasonable; in most cases, he installs only 20 each. He allows 8 sq. ft per locker. He plans showers in the ratio of 1 to each 5 persons, water closets 1 to 10, for 20-player locker room occupancy.

Game, club and craft rooms are included according to local demands. Most of these can be designed for several purposes. Craft rooms 18 to 20 by 20 to 30 ft., with storage space or lockers for raw materials and work in progress, are ample. Club rooms of about 600 sq. ft. can be used for formal discussion groups seating 50 to 60 persons plus a leader, or by more active groups of 15 to 25 people.

Kitchen may vary from a kitchenette to a well-equipped small kitchen, about 15 by 25 ft. It should be connected to a club room, convenient to the auditorium, and may have its own toilet.

Other recreation units, such as swim-

ming pool, rifle range, etc., are ordinarily eliminated because they are not subject to multiple uses, or are too expensive initially. Local needs govern.

Public toilets should be easily accessible. For the average neighborhood building, 3 or 4 women's water closets, 2 men's closets and 3 urinals are usually sufficient.

Coat room of 100 sq. ft. is usually sufficient; less may be needed.

Public spaces, including lobbies, lounge (if used) and corridors, are best designed for easy circulation. In warm climates, lobbies can be restricted, lounges omitted, and inexpensive outdoor terraces or porches provided for people to congregate and talk. In cooler climates, indoor "visiting" space has to be provided. Trophy case, bulletin board, telephone, cashier's window or table, etc., are included.

Office is preferably unobtrusive. A room of 80 sq. ft., with space for desk, the, chair and possibly a telephone switch board, is ample. There should be a store room of 64 sq. ft. adjacent.

CONSTRUCTION AND FINISH

Gymnasium-auditorium in particular, and also other activity rooms, should be arranged and constructed so noise from one does not interfere with another group, or disturb nearby residences. For this and other reasons, Mr. Van Keuren has found impervious washable masonry desirable for gymnasium, auditorium, locker room, stage and toilet walls. Rubbed concrete, salt-glazed tile or brick, etc., are deemed

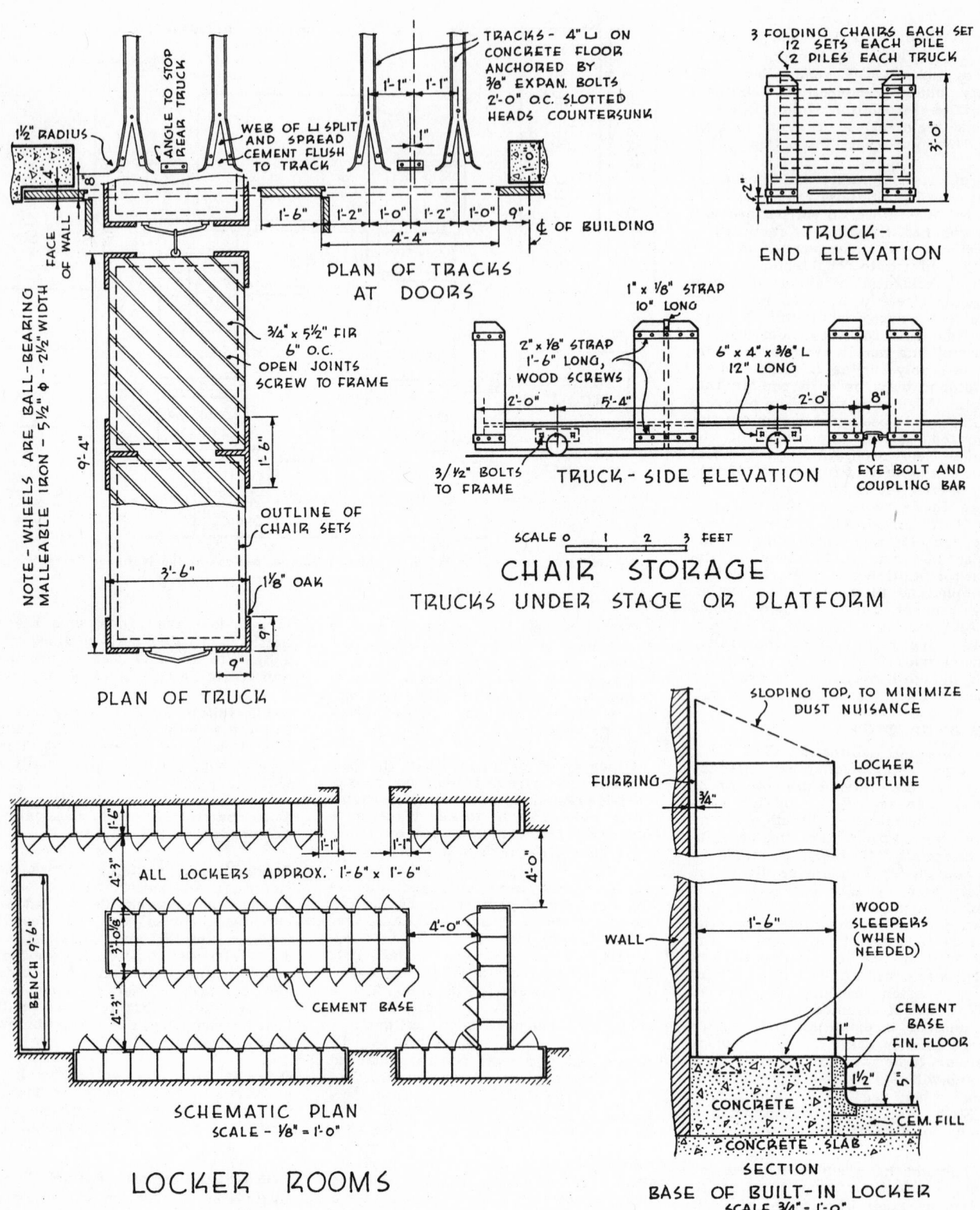

TRACKS - 4" ⊔ ON CONCRETE FLOOR ANCHORED BY ⅜" EXPAN. BOLTS 2'-0" O.C. SLOTTED HEADS COUNTERSUNK

3 FOLDING CHAIRS EACH SET 12 SETS EACH PILE 2 PILES EACH TRUCK

1½" RADIUS

ANGLE TO STOP REAR TRUCK

WEB OF ⊔ SPLIT AND SPREAD CEMENT FLUSH TO TRACK

¢ OF BUILDING

TRUCK - END ELEVATION

PLAN OF TRACKS AT DOORS

FACE OF WALL

NOTE - WHEELS ARE BALL-BEARING MALLEABLE IRON - 5½" Φ - 2½" WIDTH

¾" x 5½" FIR 6" O.C. OPEN JOINTS SCREW TO FRAME

OUTLINE OF CHAIR SETS

1⅛" OAK

PLAN OF TRUCK

1" x ⅛" STRAP 10" LONG

2" x ⅛" STRAP 1'-6" LONG, WOOD SCREWS

6" x 4" x ⅜" L 12" LONG

3½" BOLTS TO FRAME

TRUCK - SIDE ELEVATION

EYE BOLT AND COUPLING BAR

SCALE 0 1 2 3 FEET

CHAIR STORAGE
TRUCKS UNDER STAGE OR PLATFORM

SLOPING TOP, TO MINIMIZE DUST NUISANCE

FURRING

LOCKER OUTLINE

ALL LOCKERS APPROX. 1'-6" x 1'-6"

BENCH 9'-6"

CEMENT BASE

WALL

WOOD SLEEPERS (WHEN NEEDED)

CEMENT BASE

FIN. FLOOR

CONCRETE

CEM. FILL

CONCRETE SLAB

SCHEMATIC PLAN
SCALE - ⅛" = 1'-0"

SECTION
BASE OF BUILT-IN LOCKER
SCALE ¾" = 1'-0"

LOCKER ROOMS

best for toilets, showers, etc., in order to minimize upkeep. Painted (enameled) brick is also used. Floor finishes, doors, hardware, gates, etc. have to be selected for durability and low maintenance.

Door frames are metal, heavily anchored; doors, flush panel with cast hardware. Window stools are glazed tile or brick; base is metal. Floors of auditorium and gymnasium are hard-

wood. Floor of stage should be soft wood to facilitate scene setting. Elsewhere, non-slip, easily cleaned materials (such as asphalt tile) are satisfactory finishes. Acoustic ceilings are needed.

Abbreviations, 11–13
Absorption, sound, 616–624
Accent lights, 897, 903, 911
Accordion doors, hangar, 1213–1214
Acoustical tile ceilings as fireproofing, 445, 450, 461
Acoustics, 609–648
  auditoriums, 636–641
  churches, 641
  criteria, 614–616
  definitions, 610–613
  FHA requirements, 644–648
  introduction, 609
  schools, 640–641
  sound absorption, 616–624
  sound isolation, 625–635
  sound reinforcing systems, 641–644
Adhesives for resilient flooring, 551
Adult recreation, 1263–1292
Adults, dimensions of, 14–15
Aged, housing for, 1028–1031
Air, compressed, distribution system for, 821–823
Air conditioning, of houses, 688–690
  of other buildings, 739–800
  (See also Heating, ventilating, and air conditioning)
Air distribution, in houses, 683–690
  in other buildings, 756–767
Air heating, warm, 682–687
Airport hangar doors, 1213–1215
Allowable stresses, concrete, 185
  masonry, 215, 219, 236
  metals, 389
  steel, 169
  wood, 136–137
Alloys, aluminum, 391–393
  copper, 402
  stainless steel, 394
  steel, 168–169
Altitude of sun, 79–84
Aluminum, alloys, 391–393
  finishes, 390–393
  gravel stops and copings, 306
  hardware, 582–583
  sliding glass doors, 354–357
  windows, 346–353
Amplification, sound, 641–644
Anchorage, flexible, 269–270
  of steel door frames, 576–578
Anchoring, to foundations, 89, 94, 99, 156, 166–167
  to masonry walls, 276–277
Anchors, masonry, 216–277, 399, 435–439
  wood framing, 156–159
Angles, solar, 79–84
Anodized aluminum, 390–393
Anticlastic shells, 123–125
Apartments, 1032–1041
  for the aged, 1028–1031
  air conditioning of, 781–782
  building types, 1032
  elevators, 1037–1039
  exit requirements, 1037
  incinerators, 807–809
  maintenance facilities, 1035
  plan types, 1033
  planning considerations, 1038–1039
  room count and room sizes, 1040–1041
  site planning, FHA and PHA requirements, 1034–1037
Apparatus, fire-fighting, 1216
Appliances, electrical, 917–918, 923–924
  gas, 732–738
  kitchen, 976–983
Arches, masonry, 217–219
  steel, 96–99
  wood, 92–93
Architectural metals (see Metals, architectural)
Architectural symbols (see Graphic symbols)
Architectural woodwork (see Windows, wood; Wood as finish material)
Area-perimeter ratios, 69–71
Areas, surfaces, and volumes, 20–21
Arts and crafts rooms in schools, 1146–1147
Ashlar, 427
Asphalt strip shingles, 307–309
Asphalt tile, 548–551
Athletic fields, 1265–1269
Attenuation, sound, 613, 632
Attic floor joists, 140
Attics, ventilation of, 672–673, 679–681

Auditoriums, acoustics of, 636–641
  air conditioning of, 786–787
  community, 1291–1292
  school, 1137–1138
  seating, 1107–1110
  toilets in, 841–843
Automobile service stations, 1202
Automobiles, 1238–1247
  dimensions of, 1238
  driveways, 1245–1247
  garages, parking, 1240–1242
    residential, 1239
  parking lots, 1243–1244
Awning detail, store front, 1095
Azimuth, 79–84

Background noise, 614–615, 644
Backup, concrete masonry for, 263
Balloon-frame construction, 155
Ballrooms, hotel, 1059–1060
Barrel shells, 111–113
Bars, 1096–1100
  air conditioning of, 785–786
  in hotels, 1058–1060
Baseball diamond, 1266
Baseboard diffusers, 683–684
Baseboard hot water heating systems, 703–708
Basecoat plasters, 467–468
Basement walls, concrete masonry, 258–259
Basement waterproofing, 281–288
Basketball courts, indoor, 1134–1135
  outdoor, 1265
Bath houses, 1274–1275
Bathrooms, 995–1006
  clearances in, 995–996
  dimensions of, 998–999
  in dormitories, 1043
  fixtures, 1004–1006
  in hotels, 1048
  planning considerations, 995–997
  plans, 1000–1003
  storage in, 997
Bathtubs, clearances at, 999
  fixture sizes, 1006
Batten seam roofing, 310–311
Beam formulae, 134–135
Beams, concrete, 187–188
  plywood, 149–150
  steel, 168–171
    fire protection of, 449–450
  wood, 144–145
Bedroom closets, 1009–1013, 1041
Bedroom furniture, 963–966
Bedrooms, hospital, 1158–1160
  hotel, 1046–1052
Benches, garden, 1254
  park, 1263
Bicycle-wheel roof, 109
Bilateral lighting, 859
Bituminous joints, 258–259
Bituminous waterproofing, 284–286, 290
Block, concrete (see Masonry, concrete)
  glass, 363–364, 740
Boilers, 691, 698, 702, 771, 774
Bolted connections, wood, 148
Bond, masonry, pattern, 234
  structural, 216
Bookstacks, 1153–1154
Bowling greens, 1266
Box beams, plywood, 95, 149–150
Braces, corner, wood frame construction, 154–155
  cabinet work, 526
  hurricane, 159
Brass, alloys, 402
  hardware, 582–583
Brick, 214–250
  allowable stresses, 215
  arches, 217–219
  and block walls, 238, 263
  bonds, 216, 234
  cavity walls, 235–238
  courses, 232–233
  lintels, 223–227
  materials, 214
  modular, 228–231
  mortar, 214
  quantities, 228–233
  reinforced, 219–222

Brick, retaining walls, 222
  SCR, 239–241
  (See also Masonry, brick and tile; Structural design, masonry)
Brightness, of luminaires, 869–871
  ratios, 869
  sky, 857
  task, 863, 869
Bronze, alloys, 402
  hardware, 582–583
Broom closets, 1016
Buildings, community, 1291–1292
Built-in gutters, 315–318
Bumpers, door, 590–591
Bus terminals, 1207–1210
Butt hinges, 583–587
Butterfly shells, 114
Butyl sealants, 378–381, 413–415

Cabinet work, 520–528
  finishes for, 558–561
Cabinets, filing, 1112
  kitchen, 984–987
Cafeterias, school, 1140–1143
Capillarity, of concrete, 285
  of soil, 284
Capillary breaks in curtain wall design, 371
Carports, 1239
Cast-iron pipe and fittings, 831–839
Catch basins, 284, 1250
Catenaries, 32–34
Caulking, 378–380
Cavity walls, 235–238, 262
Ceiling diffusers, 683
Ceiling joists, 140
Ceilings, acoustical, 445, 450, 461, 620–624
  gypsum board, 479
  insulation of, 658
  luminous, 883–884, 911
  plaster, 473–475
  radiant heat in, 709–731
Cells, jail, 1218–1219
Cement-base waterproof coatings, 287
Cement plaster, 465, 473
Ceramic veneer, 243–244
Cesspools, leaching, 851–852
Chair storage, 1292
Checkers tables, 1263
Checklist, of building stones, 429–431
  for heating, ventilating, and air conditioning, 780
  for mental health centers, 1197
  for piping materials, 812
Checks, door, 587–589
Chemical-resistant brick and tile, 249–250
Chemical-resistant epoxy flooring, 542
Children, dimensions of, 14
  playgrounds for, 1260–1262
Chimney flashing, 304–305
Chimneys, concrete masonry, 265
  for fireplaces, 572–573
  for gas appliances, 737–738
  general, 772
  for hospitals, 773
Chlorination for swimming pools, 1281–1282
Churches, acoustics of, 641
  air conditioning of, 786–787
  lighting of, 894–897
  pipe organs for, 934–936
  sound systems for, 933–936
Chutes, laundry, 988–994
Cinemas (see Motion picture theaters)
Circle, properties of, 16–17
Circular sections, 18–19
Classrooms, school, 1128–1131
Clearances, bathroom, 995–1002
  bus terminals, 1209–1210
  furniture, 951–966
  for gas appliances, 733–738
  kitchen, 968–969
  ladders, 571
  laundry, 989–990
  offices, 1112–1114
  ramps, 570
  stair, 563–565
  truck loading docks, 1203–1206
Cleats, roofing, 310–313
Clerestory lighting, 859–867

Closers, door, 587–589
Closets, 1007–1020
    in apartments, 1041
    bedroom, 1009–1013
    broom, 1016
    clothes, 1009–1014, 1041
    coat, 1014
    FHA requirements, 1008
    fixtures for, 1019–1020
    linen, 1015–1016
    miscellaneous, 1015–1018
Cluster plan, subdivision layout, 1235
Coat closets, 1014, 1041
Coatings, metal, 390–393
Cobalt-60 suite, hospital, 1182–1184
Cocktail lounge, hotel, 1058–1060
Cocoon wall coating, 553
Coefficients, of heat transmission (U), 649–663, 740
    of linear expansion, 267–268, 389
        of plaster, 467
        of plastics, 418–420
Coffee shops, 1096–1100
    in hotels, 1058–1060
Cold-glazed wall coatings, 553
College dormitories, 1042–1044
Columns, concrete, 189
    Lally, 180–181
    steel, 177–178
        fire protection of, 446–448
    wood, 146
Combustibility of plastics, 418, 423–425
Combustion air, 733–736
Community buildings, 1291–1292
Composite floor slab, 211
Compressed air, distribution system for, 821–823
Compressive strength, of concrete, 185
    of masonry, 215–219
    of mortar, 214
    of plaster, 467
    of wood, 136–137
Compressors, 767–768
Concrete, 185–208
    allowable stresses, 185
    beams, 185–188
    block (see Masonry, concrete)
    columns, 189
    construction details, 190
    design criteria, 186
    fire resistance of, 458, 462–463
    fireproofing, 444–457
    floor systems, 211–213
    forms, plywood, 498
    joists, 191–194
    lift slabs, 194–197
    masonry (see Masonry, concrete)
    materials and mixes, 185, 285
    permeability of, 285
    precast, 194–208
    prestressed, 200–208
    slabs, 191–192
    stairs, 569
    structural design (see Structural design, concrete)
    structural forms (see Structural forms, concrete)
    thin shell, 111–126
    tilt-up, 197–199
Condensation, in curtain walls, 374–375
    on glass, 680
    on skylights, 358–359, 363
Condensation control, 671–681
    causes, 671
    design, 671–674
    details, 674–676
    FHA requirements, 680–681
    roof ventilation, 679–680
    vapor barriers, 677–680
Conditioning, air (see Air conditioning)
Conductivity, thermal, of brick and tile cavity walls, 235, 237
    of facing tile walls, 246–247
    of gypsum board, 477
    of plaster, 467
    of plastics, 418, 420
    of various materials, 652–664
Conduits for residential wiring, 926–928
Cones, 44–46
Conical shells, tilted, 115–117
Conics, 65–67
Connection details, precast concrete, 197–199, 205–208
    steel, 179
    wood, 150, 152, 156–159, 164–167
Conoid shells, 124–125
Control joints, in masonry, 263–264
    in plaster, 473, 475
Controls for heating and cooling systems, in houses, 692–695, 721–724
    in other buildings, 779–780
Cooling, in houses, 688–690
    in other buildings, 743–800
Cooling loads, 688, 743–749
Cooling towers, 768–769

Coordination, modular, 72–78
Copings, 298, 306, 438
Copper, alloys, 402
    flashing, 295–305
    roof drainage, 314–319
    roofing, 310–313
    termite shields, 291–294
Cork tile flooring, 548–551
Corner braces, wood frame construction, 154–155
    cabinet work, 526
Corrosion, electrolytic, 389
Corrugated plastic skylights, 359–361
Corrugated shells, 117, 123
Corrugated steel deck form, 211
Cost, of land improvement, 1224–1227
    of insulation, 650–652
Courses, brick, 232–233
    concrete masonry, 256–257
Cove lighting, 896, 910
Cracking of masonry walls, 273–275
Crawl spaces, 668–670
    ventilation of, 672–673, 680
Creep, of plastics, 418, 423
    of sound, 612–613, 638
Criteria, acoustic, 614–617
Croquet courts, 1264
Cul-de-sac streets, 1225–1232
Curbs, 1248–1249
Curtain walls, 365–387
    condensation, 374–375
    general, 365–366
    infiltration, 370–371
    insulation, 371–373
    joints, 376–377
    movement, provision for, 368–369
    panels, 382–384
    precast concrete, 385–387
    sealants, 378–381
    specification, 384–385
    stone, 436–437
    structural design, 366–367
Curves, and curved surfaces, 26–64
    drawing accurate, 65–68
Cycloids, 35
Cylinders, 42
Cylindrical shells, tilted, 115

Darkrooms, 1024–1027
Daylighting, 856–867
Decibel, 610–612
Decking, steel, 210–211
    wood, 140, 209
Definitions, acoustical, 610–613
    insulation, 649
    lighting, 873–875
    plastics, 418–420
    sound systems, 930
Degree-days, winter, 742
Density, housing types, 1032–1226
Department stores, 1090–1095
    air conditioning, 783–784
    (See also Shopping centers)
Design criteria, concrete, 186
Design for handicapped, 1198–1201
Design loads, 127–133
    dead loads, 127–129
        building materials and constructions, weights of, 128–129
        miscellaneous materials, weights of, 127
    live loads, 129–133
        floor loads, 129–130
        snow loads, 130–131
        for storage warehouses, 133
        wind loads, 130–133
Design temperatures, indoor, summer, 743
    winter, 741
    outdoor, summer, 745
    winter, 742
Desks, office, 1111–1112
Detailing, modular, 72–78
Development costs, subdivision, 1224–1227
Diagnostic X-ray suite, hospital, 1173–1180
Diffusers, air supply, 683
Diffusion, sound, 612, 638–639
Dimensioning, modular, 72–78
Dimensions of human figure, 14–15
Dining room furniture, 960–963
Dining rooms, hotel, 1058–1060
Disposal beds, 853–854
Disposal systems, sewage, 846–855
Distribution boxes, sewage disposal, 850–851
Distribution systems, air, 683–690, 756–767
    gas, 732–734
    gases and vacuum, 821–824
    water, 812–820
        domestic hot water, 818–820
        house tanks, 814
        multistory zoning, 815–817
        piping systems, 812–813
Diving boards, 1276–1277, 1282–1284

Dock, truck loading, 1203–1206
Dome slabs, concrete, 192–194, 213
Domes, concrete, polygonal, 122
    spherical, 119–121
    steel, geodesic, 53–55, 104–106
        lamella, 103–104
        Schwedler, 103
Door frames, steel, 574–578
Door hand, 579
Door hardware, 579–605
Doors, glass in, 412
    hangar, 1213–1215
    heat transmission through, 740
    infiltration through, 741
    sliding glass, 354–357
    steel, 574–575
Dormitories, 1042–1044
    toilets in, 841–843
Double cantilever shell, 114
Downlighting, 896, 902–903, 911
Drafting, lighting for, 877
    modular, 72–78
Drainage, lot and block, 1233
    surface, 1248–1249
    underground, 1250
Drainage systems, 825–839
    cast-iron fittings, 831–839
    sizing and ratings, 825–830
Drains, foundation, 281–284
    house, 827–830
    storm, 827–830
Drawing accurate curves, 65–68
Drips, 298, 370–371
Driveways, 1245–1248
Dry wells, 283
Drywall (see Wallboards)
Duct systems, in houses, 685–687
    in other buildings, 756–767
Durability of plastics, 423

Earth pressure on foundation walls, 281
Echo, 612, 639–640
Economics of insulation, 650–652
Efficiency of heaters, 775
Elastic joint filler, 290, 378–381
Elastomeric sealants, 378–381, 413–415
Electric radiant heating systems, 725–728
Electric shop equipment, 917
Electric unit heaters, 801
Electric wiring, 915–928
    symbols for, 10
Electrical appliances, 917–918, 923–924
Electroencephalographic suite, hospital, 1185–1187
Electrolytic corrosion, 389
Elevators, 941–946
    in apartment buildings, 1037–1039
    in hotels, 1055
Ellipses, 29–30, 45, 65
Ellipsoid, 59–60
Emissivity, 649
Enamel, porcelain, 390–393, 403–408
Epoxy flooring, 542
Equipment, bathroom, 1004–1006
    closet, 1019–1020
    hospital, 1157–1197
    hotel laundry, 1076–1078
    kitchen, 976–987
    laundry, 989–990
    office, 1112
    school classroom, 1130–1131
Escalators, 947
Exit requirements for apartment buildings, 1037
Exits, stadium, 1289–1290
Expansion, coefficients of linear, 267, 389
    of masonry, 266–268
    of plaster, 467
    of plastics, 418, 420
Expansion joints, in masonry, 267–268
    in wood flooring, 547

Fabric flashing, 290, 295
Facing tile partitions, structural clay, 245–248
Factories (see Industrial buildings)
Fan-coil units, 757
Felt, impregnated wool, sealant, 378–381
FHA requirements, acoustical, 644–648
    for apartments, 1034–1037, 1040–1041
    for bathrooms, 995–996
    for closets, 1008
    condensation control, 680–681
    for glass in doors, 412
    for kitchen storage, 970–971
    thermal insulation, 662–664
Fiberboard (see Hardboard; Insulation board)
Filing cabinets, 1112
Filters, air, 764–766
    sand, 854–855
Filtration for swimming pools, 1278–1279, 1285–1286

Finish-coat plaster, 468–469
Finishes, for brick masonry, 242–243
    for cabinet work, 558–561
    for concrete masonry, 264–265
    for floors, 556
    for hardware, 582–583
    for metals, 390
    paints, 554–557
    for plywood, 501
    for stone, 428
    wall coatings, 553
    wall coverings, 552
Fire alarm systems, 937–938
Fire-fighting apparatus, 1216
Fire protection, 937–940
    fire alarm systems, 937–938
    sprinkler systems, 939–940
Fire resistance, of concrete masonry, 255
    of facing tile partitions, 245
    of gypsum board, 477
    of plastics, 418, 420–425
    of reinforced concrete, 458, 462–463
    of various assemblies, 446–464
Fire test, standard ASTM, 444
Firehouses, 1216–1217
Fireplaces, 572–573
    wood framing around, 157
Fireproofing, 444–464
    acoustical ceilings, 445, 450, 461
    beams and girders, 449–450
    columns, 446–448
    floor and roof systems, 451–458
    lightweight, 445
    materials and methods, 444–445
    membrane, 445
    partitions, 464
    reinforced concrete, 462–463
Firestopping in wood frame construction, 154–
    155
Fittings, cast-iron pipe, 831–839
Fixture units, plumbing, 825–828
Fixtures, bathroom, 1004–1006
    closet, 1019–1020
    kitchen, 976–983
    plumbing, 840–845
        industrial facilities, 844–845
        public facilities, 840–843
    retail stores, 1091–1094
Flagging (see Flagstone)
Flagstone, flooring, 441–443
    sizes and types, 426–427
    walks and terraces, 1251–1252
Flammability of plastics, 418, 423–425
Flanking sound, 632–634
Flashing, 290, 295–306
    chimney, 304–305
    copings, 298, 306
    doors, 302
    drips, 298
    eaves, 309
    edge strips, 298
    gravel stops, 302–306
    roofs at walls, 299
    types of, 295
    valleys, 303, 308
    vents, 304
    walls and parapets, 290, 295–302
    windows, 300–302
Flat plate, concrete, 191, 213
Flat seam roofing, 310, 313
Flat slab, concrete, 191, 213
Flexible anchorage of masonry walls, 269–270
Floating raft floors, 646–648
Floodlights, 1256
Floor finishes, 556
Floor framing systems, 209–213
    concrete, 211–213
    steel, 210–211
    wood, 209
Floor joists, 140
Floor loads, 128–133
Floor and roof systems, fire ratings of, 451–458
Floor slabs on grade, 663–667
    radiant heating in, 709–728
    vapor barriers for, 674
Flooring, 538–551
    epoxy, 542
    resilient, 548–551
    stone, 441–443
    terrazzo, 538–541
    wood, 543–547
Floors, floating raft, 646–648
    insulation of, 662–670
Flues, fireplace, 572–573
    incinerator, 807–809
Folded plate, concrete, 126
Football field, 1267
Footing drains, 281–284
Forced hot water heating, 694–724
Forced warm air heating, 682–687
Form board, 486

Forms, concrete, plywood for, 498
    structural (see Structural forms)
Foundation drains, 281–284
Foundations, termite shields, 291–294
Fountains, 1258–1259
Framing, wood, light, 154–159
Framing anchors, wood construction, 156–159
Framing systems, floor, 209–213
Freight elevators, 944–945
Freight terminals, truck, 1203–1206
Fuel consumption, 775–776
Furnaces, 682
Furniture, bedroom, 963–966
    dining room, 960–963
    garden, 1254
    hospital, 1158–1160
    hotel guest room, 1047
    living room, 951–959
    office, 1111–1115
    residential, 951–966
    stair clearances for, 565
Furring, ceiling, 473–475, 479
    wall, 239, 241, 276–277, 482

Gages, metal, 388
Games, outdoor, 1260–1269
Garages, parking, 1240–1242
    ventilation of, 799–800
    residential, 1239
Garden apartments, 1032–1033, 1224–1225
Gardens (see Landscaping)
Gas appliances, residential, 732–738
Gas-fired unit heaters, 801–806
Gas piping, 732–734
Gas vents, 733–737
Gaskets, 378–381
Geodesic domes, 50–55, 104–106
Geometrical mean (golden section), 37
Girders, fire protection of, 449–450
Glare, 869–871
Glare-reducing glass, 410–411
Glass, 409–417
    condensation on, 680
    effect on solar heat loads, 750–752
    FHA requirements, 412
    glazing, 413–415
    sizes, 411–412
    structural glass veneer, 416–417
    types, 409–410
    U values, 740
Glass-block skylights, 363–364
    U values, 740
Glazed wall coatings, 553
Glazing, 413–415
    of aluminum sash, 348–351
    of skylights, 362
    of sliding glass doors, 357
    of steel sash, 340
    of wood sash, 327, 332
Glazing bars, skylight, 362
Glazing compound, 378–379, 413–415
Glossary of terms (see Definitions)
Glued laminated wood, 88–93
    properties of sections, 139
Golden section, 37
Grandstands, 1287–1290
Granite, 430–431, 438–439
Graphic symbols, 3–10
    electrical, 10
        fire alarm systems, 937
        sound systems, 932
    heating, ventilating, and air conditioning, 6–7
    materials, building, 3–4
    piping, 5
    plumbing, 8–9
Gravel stops, 302–306
Grease traps, 849–850
Groundwater, 281–284
Grouted masonry, reinforced, 219–222
Gutters, driveway, 1248–1249
    roof, 315–319
    swimming pool, 1277
Gymnasiums, community, 1291–1292
    school, 1133–1137
Gypsum board, 476–482
Gypsum as fireproofing material, 444–464
Gypsum lath, 468
Gypsum plaster, 465–475
    with radiant heating, 729–731

Hand of doors, 579
Handball courts, 1265
Handicapped, design for, 1198–1201
Handrails, ladders, 571
    ramps, 570
    stairs, 563–564, 568–569
Hangar doors, 1213–1215
Hangers, ceiling, 473–475
Hardboard, 488–490

Hardware, 579–605
    door bolts, 595
    door closing devices, 587–589
    door holders and stops, 590–591
    door pulls, push plates, kick plates, 592
    finishes, 582–583
    hand of doors, 579
    hinges, 583–587
    lock dimensions, 600
    lock functions, 596–599
    panic exit devices, 593–594
    plastic, 422
    screen and storm doors, 605
    types of locks and latches, 580–581
Hardwood plywood, 499–501
Hardwoods, 505–519, 543–547
Headroom, ladder, 571
    ramp, 570
    stairs, 563–567
Hearths, fireplace, 572–573
Heat-absorbing glass, 410–411
Heat gain, 688, 743–755
Heat pump, 769–771
Heat transmission coefficients, 649–663, 740
Heaters, furnaces, 682
    for hot water, 818–820
    space, 771
    unit, 801–806
Heating loads, 739–742
Heating plants, 771–776
Heating systems for houses, 682–731
    electric radiant, 725–728
    hot water, 694–724
        baseboard, 703–708
        one-pipe, 694–699
        radiant panel, 709–724
            controls for, 721, 724
            gypsum plaster with, 729, 731
        two-pipe, 698–702
    steam, one-pipe, 691–693
    warm air, 682–687
Heating, ventilating, and air conditioning, 739–800
    air distribution, 756–767
    of apartments, 781
    checklist, 780
    controls, 779–780
    cooling loads, 743–749
    of eating places, 785–786
    of garages, 799–800
    heating loads, 739–742
    heating plant, 771–776
    of hospitals, 789–791
    of hotels and motels, 782
    of houses, 682–731
    of industrial buildings, 791–795
    of laboratories, 796–799
    of libraries and museums, 788–789
    of office buildings, 782–783
    piping, 776–778
    of places of assembly, 786–787
    refrigerating plant, 767–770
    of schools, 787
    solar loads, 749–755
    of stores, 783–784
    symbols for, 6–7
Heavy timber construction, 166–167
High-pressure plastic laminates, 492
High velocity ducts, 758–759
Hinge connection, 99, 167
Hinges, 583–587
Hockey field, 1266
Home owners' associations, 1230
Home workshops, 1021–1023
Homemaking rooms in schools, 1148–1149
Horseshoe pitching, 1265
Hospitals, 1157–1197
    air conditioning of, 789–791
    bedrooms, 1158–1160
    cobalt-60 suite, 1182–1184
    diagnostic X-ray suite, 1173–1180
    electrical facilities for, 919–922
    electroencephalographic suite, 1185–1187
    elevators for, 943
    fire alarm systems for, 938
    flow chart, 1157
    laboratory, 1187–1188
    lighting, 893–894
    mental health center checklist, 1197
    nursery, 1166–1169
    nursing units, 1161–1162
    occupational therapy department, 1193–1196
    pediatric department, 1170–1172
    physical therapy department, 1188–1192
    surgical suite, 1162–1165
    teletherapy unit, 1180–1185
Hot water, domestic, 812–820
Hot water heating systems, 694–724
    baseboard, 703–708
    one-pipe, 694–699
    radiant, 709–724, 729–731
    two-pipe, 698–702

Hotels, 1045–1063
  air conditioning of, 782
  functional plan, 1053
  guest rooms, 1046–1052
    bathrooms, 1048
    furniture for, 1047
    plans, 1049–1052
    types of, 1046–1047
  laundries, 1075–1078
    advantages and disadvantages, 1075
    equipment requirements, 1076–1078
    utility requirements, 1076
  lighting of, 906–907
  planning considerations, 1045–1046
  schedule of space allotments, 1062–1063
  space allotments, general, 1054–1055
    concession and rental areas, 1057
    food and beverage services, 1058–1060
    general services areas, 1061–1062
    public areas, 1056
  toilets, 840–843
  (See also Motels)
House drains and sewers, 827–830
House tanks, 814
Houses air conditioning for, 688–690
  bathrooms, 995–1006
  closets, 1007–1020
  driveways, 1245–1248
  furniture, 951–966
  garages, 1239
  heating, 682–687, 691–731
  kitchens, 967–987
  laundries, 988–994
  lighting, 907–912
  plumbing, 813, 829, 847
  wiring, 923–928
Housing, 1032–1041
  for the aged, 1028–1031
  types, subdivision, 1224–1225
  (See also Apartments)
Human figure, dimensions of, 14–15
Hung ceilings, 473–475
Hurricane braces, 159
Hydraulic elevators, 946
Hydraulic head, 281–286
Hydrolithic waterproofing, 287–288
Hydrostatic pressure, 281–284
Hypalon wall coating, 553
Hyperbola, 31, 65–67
Hyperbolic paraboloid, 56–58
  thin shell concrete, 123–124
Hyperboloid, 61–63

Illumination, artificial (see Lighting)
  natural (see Daylighting)
Impact noise, 614, 633–635
  FHA requirements, 644–648
Improvement costs, subdivision, 1224–1227
Incinerators, 807–811
  in apartment buildings, 807–809
  municipal and industrial, 809–811
Induction units, 756
Industrial arts in schools, 1149–1150
Industrial buildings, daylighting of, 864–867
  fire alarm system for, 937
  heating, ventilating, and air conditioning of, 791–795
  lighting, 885
  toilets in, 841–843
Infiltration, of air, through doors, 741
    through windows, 739
  of groundwater, 281–284
  of water and air through curtain walls, 370–371
Insulating glass, 410–411
Insulation, thermal, 649–670
  concrete slabs on grade, 663–667
  cooling ducts, 690
  crawl spaces, 668–670
  curtain walls, 371–373
  definitions, 649
  estimation of economies, 650–652
  FHA requirements, 662–664
  introduction, 649
  perimeter heating ducts, 684
  theory, 649
  U values, ceilings, 658
    floors, 662
    roofs, 659–661
    walls, frame, 653–655
      masonry, 656–657
  (See also Condensation control)
Insulation board, 483–487
Integral waterproofing of concrete, 286, 290
Inverted shells, 117
Iron coat waterproofing, 287–288
Isolation, sound, 625–635

J-series joists, steel, 172–173
Jails, 1218–1219

Jalousie windows, 320, 322–323
Joint treatment, gypsum board, 477–480
  hardboard, 489
  insulation board, 483, 486
  particle board, 491
  plastic laminate, 492
  plywood, 500
Joints, bituminous, 258–259
  in cabinet work, 520–528
  control, in masonry, 260–264
    in plaster, 473–475
  in curtain walls, 367–370, 376–381
  expansion, in masonry, 267–268
  in wood flooring, 547
Joists, concrete, 191–194, 212–213
  steel, open web, 172–176, 210
  wood, 140–145, 209

Kitchens, hotel, 1058–1060
  residential, 967–987
    in apartments, 1038–1041
    appliances, 976–983
    cabinets, 984–987
    critical dimensions, 968–969
    in motels, 1071
    plan types, 973–975
    planning consideration, 967
    storage, 969–972
      FHA requirements, 970–971
  school, 1140–1143

LA-series joists, steel, 174–175
Laboratories, air conditioning of, 796–799
  hospital, 1187–1188
  school, 1143–1151
Lacquer, 558–560
Lacrosse field, 1266
Ladders, 570–571
Lally columns, 180–181
Lamella domes, steel, 103–104
Lamella vaults, wood, 94
Laminated gypsum board partitions, 481
Laminated wood (see Glued laminated wood)
Laminates, high-pressure plastic, 492
Landscaping, 1248–1259
  banks, 1254
  curbs, 1248–1249
  drainage, 1250
  driveways, 1248
  fountains, 1258–1259
  furniture, 1254
  gutters, 1248–1249
  lighting, 1256
  pools, 1257
  steps, 1253–1254
  terraces, 1251–1252
  trees, 1256
  walks, 1251–1252
  walls, 1254
Language laboratories, 1150–1151
Latches, door, 580–581
Lath, 467–468
Laundries, in apartment buildings, 1039
  in dormitories, 1044
  in hospitals, 1157
  in hotels and motels, 1075–1078
    space allotments for, 1061
  residential, 988–994
    kitchen-laundry plans, 991
    laundry room plans, 992–993
    multi-use laundry rooms, 994
    planning considerations, 988
    space requirements, 989–990
Lavatories, 995–1006
Layout, subdivision (see Site planning, subdivision layout)
Leaching cesspools, 851–852
Leaders, 314, 319, 827
Leaky walls, 289–290
Libraries, air conditioning of, 788–789
  bookstack data, 1153–1154
  school, 1138–1139, 1152
    carrels, 1155–1156
Lift slab construction, 194–197
Light wood frame construction, 154–159
Lighting, 868–914
  of churches and synagogues, 894–897
  of cinemas, 904–905
  general, 868–875
  glossary of terms, 873–875
  of hospitals, 893–894
  of hotels, 906–907
  of industrial buildings, 885
  landscape, 1256
  loads, 915–917
  natural (see Daylighting)
  of offices, 875–884
  of other building types, 912

Lighting, of parking areas, 914
  residential, 907–912
  of schools, 886–892
  sources, 872–873
  of sports areas, 912–914
  of stores, 897–903
  systems, 972
Lime, in mortar, 214
  in plaster, 465
Limestone, 426–430, 436–437
Linear expansion, coefficients of, 267–268, 389
  of plaster, 467
  of plastics, 418–420
Linen closets, 1008, 1015–1016, 1041
Linoleum, 548–551
Lintels, reinforced brick, 224–225
  reinforced concrete, 227
  reinforced tile, 226
  steel, 223
Living room furniture, 951–959
Loading dock, bus, 1209–1210
  truck, 1203–1206
Loads, cooling, 743–749
  design (see Design loads)
  electrical, 915–924
  heating, 739–742
Locker rooms, 1135–1137, 1272–1273, 1291–1292
Lockers, gymnasium, 1135–1137
  office, 1112
  school, 1125–1127
Locks, door, 580–581, 596–600
Longspan steel joists, 174–176
Lot layout, subdivision, 1226–1232
Lot size, subdivision, 1226–1227
Loud-speakers, 641–644, 931
Louvers, 750–755, 860–861
Lumber-core plywood, 500
Lumber grades for architectural woodwork, 503
Luminaires (see Lighting)
Luminous ceilings, 883–884, 911

Maintenance facilities, hotel, 1061–1062
  housing project, 1035
Marble, 430–434, 436–439, 441–443
Marble chips, 539
Masking noise, 614–626
Masonry, brick and tile, 228–252
  bonds, pattern, 234
  cavity walls, 235–238
  ceramic veneer, 243–244
  chemical-resistant brick and tile, 249–250
  metal-tied walls, 238
  modular sizes and quantities, 228–231
  nonmodular quantities and courses, 232–233
  pattern bonds, 234
  SCR brick, 239–241
  solar screens, 251–252
  solid metal-tied walls, 238
  structural clay facing tile partitions, 245–248
  structural clay tile partitions, 244–246
  surface treatments, 242–243
  terra cotta, 243
  concrete, 253–265
    courses and quantities, 256–257
    properties, 254–255
    types and sizes of units, 253
    wall construction, 258–265
      backup for other materials, 263
      basement walls, 258–259
      cavity walls, 262
      chimneys, 265
      details, 259–262
      finishes, 264–265
      reinforced, 262–263
Masonry construction, 266–277
  anchoring to masonry walls, 276–277
  cracking of masonry walls, 273–275
  flexible anchorage of masonry walls, 269–270
  parapet walls, 271–272
  thermal expansion, 266–268
  (See also Structural design, masonry)
Masonry fireproofing, 445, 447–448, 463–464
Masonry walls, flashing of, 290, 295–300
  U factors for, 656–657
Mat foundations, waterproofing of, 288
Mathematics, 16–25
  areas, 20
  circles, properties of, 16–17
  circular sections, 18–19
  surfaces and volumes, 21
  trigonometric functions, 22–23
  units of measurement, 24–25
Measurements, units of, 24–25
Membrane fireproofing, 445
Membrane flashing, 290, 295
Membrane waterproofing, 286–289
Mental health centers, 1197
Metal coatings, 390–393
Metal lath, 467
Metal roofing, 310–313

Metal-tied masonry walls, 238
Metals, architectural, 388–408
    aluminum, 391–393
    copper, brass, and bronze, 402
    finishes, 390
    gages, coefficients, stresses, 388–389
    porcelain enamel, 403–408
    stainless steel, 394–401
Metric conversion factors, 25
Millwork (*see* Windows, wood; Wood as finish material)
Mineral fiber fireproofing, 444, 449–450, 452–454
Mixes, concrete, 185, 285
    mortar, 214
    plaster, 467–469
Modular brick and tile, 228–231
Modular coordination, 72–78
Modular window sizes, 324, 331, 352–353
Modulus of elasticity, of concrete, 185
    of masonry, 219
    of plaster, 467
    of plastics, 419
    of wood, 136–137
Molded gutters, 315–319
Monitor windows, 341–342
    illumination from, 859
Mortar mixes, 214
Motels, 1064–1074
    air conditioning of, 782
    general, 1064
    parking and room groups, 1070–1072
    site location, 1065–1067
    site plan, 1068–1069
    space allotments, 1073–1074
    (*See also* Hotels)
Motion picture theaters, 1101–1106
    air conditioning of, 786–787
    general requirements, 1101–1103
    lighting, 904–905
    projection booths, 1104–1106
    toilets, 840–843
Movement in curtain walls, provision for, 367–369
Multipurpose rooms in schools, 1132–1133
Museums, air conditioning of, 789
Music rooms in schools, 1147–1148

Nailing, gypsum board, 478–479
    hardboard, 490
    insulation board, 485
    light wood framing, 156, 158–163
    particle board, 491
    plywood, 497
    wood flooring, 545–546
Nails, common, 156
    threaded, 160–163
Neighborhood associations, 1230
Neighborhood planning, 1223–1224
Neoprene gaskets, 378–381, 412–415
NFPA requirements, for apartment exits, 1037
    for conductive flooring, 539
Nitrous oxide, distribution system for, 821–823
Noise, background, 614–615, 644
    impact, 614, 633–635, 644–648
Noise criteria (*NC*), 615–617
Noise-reduction coefficient (*NRC*), 612, 620
Nonmodular brick and tile, 232–233
Nursery, hospital, 1166–1169
Nursing units, hospital, 1161–1162

Occupational therapy department, hospital, 1193–1196
Office buildings, air conditioning of, 782–783
    toilets in, 841–843
Offices, 1111–1115
    clearances, 1112–1114
    furniture and equipment, 1111–1112
    layout, 1115
    lighting, 875–884
Open-joint pipe for drains, 283, 853
Open-web steel joists, 172–176, 210
Organic coatings on metal, 390–393
Organs, pipe, 934–936
Orientation, effect on cooling load, 752
Outdoor air requirements, 743
Outfall of foundation drains, 281, 283, 288
Outlets, air distribution, 683
Oxygen, distribution system for, 821–823

Paddle tennis courts, 1265
Paints, 554–557
Paneling, wood, 527
Panels, in curtain walls, 382–384
    sandwich, 383, 385–387, 487
    stressed-skin plywood, 151–153
Panic exit devices, 593–594
Parabolas, 27–28, 65–67
Parapet walls, 271–272
    flashing of, 290, 295–297

Parking, motels, 1069–1073
    rental housing, 1234
    schools, 1116–1117
    shopping centers, 1084–1088
    truck terminals, 1205–1206, 1212
Parking garages, 1240–1242
    ventilation of, 799–800
Parking lots, 1243–1244
    lighting of, 914
Parks (*see* Landscaping; Recreation)
    toilets in, 840–843
Parquet flooring, 546–547
Particle board, 491
Partitions, comparison of types, 471, 482
    fire resistance of, 464, 482
    masonry, 471
    office, 1111
    solid laminated gypsum board, 481
    solid plaster, 470–472
    steel stud, 464, 470–471
    structural clay facing tile, 245–248
    structural clay tile, 244–246
    toilet, 843
Pattern bond in brick masonry, 234
Paving, driveways, 1248
    walks and terraces, 1251–1252
Pediatric department, hospital, 1170–1172
Peg-board, 489
Perforated hardboard, 489
Perforated pipe, for drains, 283
Perimeter, ratio of area to, 69–71
Perimeter heating system, 683–685
Perimeter insulation, 663–667
Perimeter risers, 757
Perlite aggregate, 444–464, 466–468
Permeance and permeability of materials, 681
PHA requirements for apartments, 1034–1037, 1040–1041
Photographic darkrooms, 1024–1027
Physical therapy department, hospital, 1188–1192
Pipe and fittings, cast-iron, 831–839
Pipe organs, 934–936
Piping, drainage, in buildings, 825–839
    underground, 282–283
    gas, 732–734
    gases and vacuum, 821–824
    hot water and steam, houses, 692–721
        other buildings, 776–778
    plastic, 422
    sewage disposal, 846–855
    sprinkler, 940
    symbols for, 5
    for unit heaters, 804–805
    water, 812–820
Piping materials, 812
Pitch of stairs, ramps, ladders, 570
Plank-and-beam construction, 166, 209
Planning, site (*see* Site planning)
Plants, heating, 682, 692–694, 771–776
    refrigerating, 688–689, 767–770
Plaster, 465–475
    bases, 466
    ceilings, 473–475
    materials, 465
    mixes and coats, 467–469
    properties, 467
    stucco, 473
    walls and partitions, 470–472
Plaster board (gypsum board), 476–482
Plastic-cement wall coatings, 553
Plastic-coat waterproofing, 287–288
Plastic design, steel, 182–183
Plastic laminates, 492
Plastic skylights, 358–361
Plastics, 418–425
    applications, 421–422
    characteristics, 418
    design recommendations, 423
    fire resistance requirements, 424–425
    terminology, 418–420
Platform-frame construction, 154
Playgrounds, for adults, 1263–1267
    for children, 1260–1292
    school, 1117–1120
Plenum, heating, 684–685
Plumbing, 812–855
    drainage systems, 825–839
    fixtures, 840–845
    sewage disposal, 846–855
    supply and distribution systems, 812–824
    symbols, 8–9
Plywood, hardwood, 499–501
    softwood, 493–498
Plywood box beams, 95, 149–150
Plywood stressed-skin panels, 151–153
Pole gutter, 314
Polygons, 43
Polyhedra, 50–52
Polysulfide sealant, 378–381, 413–415
Pools, diving, 1282–1283
    garden, 1257

Pools, swimming, public, 1276–1281
    residential, 1284–1286
    wading, 1282
Porcelain enamel, 390–393, 403–408
Porous pipe for drains, 283
Post-tensioning, 201
Precast concrete, 194–208
    floor systems, 194–197, 201–208, 211–213
    sandwich panels, 385–387
    wall systems, 197–199
Pressure on foundations, earth, 281
    hydrostatic, 281–286
Prestressed concrete, 200–208, 213
Prismatic shells, 126
Prisms, 42
Prisons, 1218–1219
Properties, brick and tile cavity walls, 235
    concrete masonry, 254–255
    facing tile partitions, 246–247
    plaster, 467
    wood sections, 138–139
Protective covenants, subdivision, 1229–1230
Public address systems, 930–933
Public swimming pools, 1276–1283
Public toilets, 840–843
Pulls, door, 592
Pupil capacity of schools, 1124
Putty (*see* Glazing compound)
Pyramids, 46

Quantities, brick and tile, 230–233
    concrete masonry, 256–257

Racquets, squash, 1270–1271
Radiant heating systems, electric, 725–728
    hot water, 709–724
    gypsum plaster with, 729–731
Radiators, cast iron, 691, 698, 702
    baseboard, 703–706
    fin-tube, 703, 706–708
Raft floors, floating, 646–648
Raft foundations, waterproofing of, 288
Rafters, wood, 142–143
    trussed, 162, 164–165
Railroad terminals, 1211–1212
    toilets in, 840–843
Ramps, 570, 1289–1290
Recessed lighting, 882–884, 896, 902–903, 911
Recreation, 1260–1292
    adults, 1263–1267
    bath houses, 1274–1275
    children, 1260–1262
    community buildings, 1291–1292
    diving pools, 1282–1283
    lighting for, 912–914
    locker rooms, 1272–1273
    squash courts, 1270–1271
    stadia, 1287–1290
    swimming pools, public, 1276–1281
        residential, 1284–1286
    tennis courts, 1268–1269
Reflectances of surfaces, 858, 870
Reflection, sound, 612, 637–640
Refrigerating plant, 767–770
Registers, air supply, 683
Reinforced concrete (*see* Structural design, concrete)
Reinforced masonry, 219–222
Residential air conditioning, 688–690
Residential heating (*see* Heating systems for houses)
Residential lighting, 907–912
Residential wiring, 923–928
Resilient flooring, 548–551
Resilient furring, 479
Resistance, thermal, 649–652, 669–670
Restaurants and bars, 1096–1100
    air conditioning of, 785–786
    in hotels, 1058–1060
Retail stores (*see* Stores, retail)
Retaining walls, reinforced masonry, 222
Reverberation, 612, 689
Reverberation time, 612, 624
Rigid frames, steel, 96–99
    wood, 91
Rip-rap, 1254
Risers and treads, stair, 562–563
Roof construction, fire resistance of, 451–458
Roof drainage, 314–319
Roof flashing (*see* Flashing)
Roofing, 307–313
    asphalt strip shingles, 307–309
    copper, 310–313
Roofs, gutters 315–319
    U factors for, 659–661
    ventilation of, 672–673, 679–681
Room count, apartments, 1040
Room sizes, apartments, 1038–1041
    hospitals, 1158–1160
    hotels, 1046–1052

Room sizes, housing for aged, 1029
  motels, 1071
Roque courts, 1264
Rubber-base sealants, 378–381, 413–415
Rubber flooring, 548–551
Rubble, 427
Rugby field, 1266
Running track, 1267

Saddle-shaped shells, 123–125
Sand filters, 854–855
Sandwich panels, 383, 385–387, 487
Schools, 1116–1151
  acoustics of, 640–641
  air conditioning of, 787
  arts and crafts rooms, 1146–1147
  auditoriums, 1137–1138
  cafeterias, 1140–1143
  circulation, 1121–1123
  classroom facilities, 1130–1131
  classrooms, 1128–1129
  fire alarm systems, 938
  gymnasiums, 1133–1137
  homemaking rooms, 1148–1149
  language laboratories, 1150–1151
  libraries, 1138–1139
  lighting, 886–892
  lockers, 1125–1127
  multipurpose rooms, 1132–1133
  music rooms, 1147–1148
  playgrounds, 1117–1120
  pupil capacity, 1124
  science rooms, 1143–1146
  shops, 1149–1150
  site planning, 1116
  site selection, 1117–1119
  toilets, 841–843
  ventilation, 1151
  working heights, 1124
Schwedler domes, 103
Science rooms in schools, 1143–1146
Scissors curve in lighting, 869–870, 879
Scissors stair, 569
SCR brick, 239–241
Screeds for wood flooring, 545–546
Screen door hardware, 605
Screens, motion picture, 1102–1103
  solar, 251–252
Sealants for joints, 378–381
Seating, auditoriums, 1107–1110
  motion picture theaters, 1101–1103
  offices, 1111–1115
  residential, 951–953
  restaurants and bars, 1096–1099
  stadia, 1287–1290
Septic tanks, 848
Service stations, 1202
Sewage disposal systems, 846–855
  design, 846–847
  distribution boxes, 850–851
  grease traps, 849–850
  leachng cesspools, 851–852
  sand filters, 854–855
  septic and siphon tanks, 848
  sludge pits, 850–851
  subsoil disposal beds, 853–854
Sewing room-laundry room, 994
Shading devices, 750–755, 860–861
  masonry, 251–252
Sheathing, gypsum board, 476
  insulation board, 483
  plywood, 159, 497
  wood boards, 154–155, 158
Shells (see Structural forms, concrete, thin shell)
Shields, sun, 251–252, 750–755, 860–861
  termite, 291–294
Shingles, asphalt strip, 307–309
Shop equipment, electrical capacity of, 917
Shopping centers, 1081–1089
  character of buildings, 1088–1089
  planning principles, 1084–1087
  site selection, 1081–1083
  space allotments, 1083–1084
  (See also Stores, retail)
Shops in schools, 1149–1150
Show-window lighting, 897–898
Shower receptor, terrazzo, 541
Showers, 999, 1005
Shuffleboard courts, 1264
Siding, wood, 159
Silicone rubber sealant, 378–381
Sine curve, 37
Siphon tanks, 848
Site planning, apartments, 1034–1037
  motels, 1065–1069
  schools, 1116–1121
  shopping centers, 1081–1089
  subdivision layout, 1223–1237
    cluster plan, 1235
    cul-de-sacs, 1225–1232

Site planning, subdivision layout, densities, 1226
  development costs, 1224–1227
  drainage, lot and block, 1233
  home owners' associations, 1230
  housing types, 1224–1225
  lot layout, 1226, 1230–1232
  lot sizes, 1226–1227
  neighborhood planning, 1223–1224
  new approaches, 1231–1237
  parking areas for rental housing, 1234
  protective covenants, 1229–1230
  street types, 1225–1230
  subdivision regulations, 1228–1229
Size of rooms (see Room sizes)
Skew curves, 39–41
Skip-stop apartment schemes, 1034
Sky brightness, 857
Skylights, 358–364
  glass-block, 363–364
  heat transmission through, 740
  illumination from, 858–864
  metal and glass, 360–364
  plastic, 358–361
Slab band, concrete floor system, 212
Slabs, concrete, 191–197, 210–213
  on grade, 663–667
Slate, 431, 441, 443
Sliding door hardware, 601–604
Sliding glass doors, 354–357, 412
Sludge pits, 850–851
Snow loads, 130–131
Soccer field, 1266
Softball diamond, 1266
Softwood flooring, 543–544
Softwood plywood, 493–498
Soil and waste stacks, plumbing, 825–830
Solar angles, 79–84
Solar heat loads, 749–755
Solar screens, 251–252, 750–755, 860–861
Solid laminated gypsum board partition, 481
Solid plaster partitions, 470–472
Sound, absorption, 616–624
  amplification, 641–644
  attenuation, 613, 632
  diffusion, 612, 638–639
  distribution, 637–643
  isolation, 625–635
  reflection, 612, 637–640
  reinforcing systems, 641–644, 930–933
  structure-borne, 632–634, 646–648
  transmission class (STC), 613, 627–628, 644
  transmission loss, through clay tile partitions, 245
    through concrete masonry partitions, 256
Space allotments, hotels, 1054–1062
  motels, 1073–1074
  shopping centers, 1083–1084
Space frames, 101–102
Space structures, 100
Spandrel flashing, 290, 295–297, 300
Speakers, loud, 641–644, 931
Specifications, for curtain walls, 384–385
  for sound systems, 930
Spheres, 47–50
Spherical trigonometry, 64
Spiral curves, 38
Sports (see Recreation)
Sprinkler systems, 939–940
Squash courts, 1270–1271
Stacks, book, 1153–1154
  soil, waste, and vent, 825–830
Stage lighting, school, 891–892
Stain, 557–560
Stainless steel, types and finishes, 394–401
Stainless steel hardware, 582–583
Stairs, 562–571
  concrete, 569
  critical dimensions, 564–565
  electric, 947
  outdoor, 1253–1254
  ramps and ladders, 570–571
  steel, 568
  terrazzo, 541
  tread and riser data, 562–563
  unit planning data, 566–567
  wood framing for, 157
Standing seam roofing, 310, 312–313
Stations, bus, 1207–1210
  fire, 1216–1217
  railroad, 1211–1212
  service, 1202
Steam heating systems, one-pipe, 691–693
  unit heaters, 801–806
Steel, beams, 168–171, 210–211
  columns, 177–178
  connection details, 179
  deck, 210–211
  domes, 103–106
  doors and frames, 574–578
  floor framing systems, 210–211
  joists, 172–176, 210
  Lally columns, 180–181

Steel, lintels, 223
  plastic design, 182–183
  rigid frames, 96–99
  space frames, 100–102
  stainless, 394–401
  stairs, 568
  suspension structures, 107–110
  types of, 168–169
  welding of, 183–184
  windows, 336–345
Steps, outdoor, 1253–1254
Stone, 426–443
  characteristics, 425
  checklist of building stones, 429–431
  classifications, 427
  finishes, 428
  interior, 441–443
  marble, 432–434
  veneer, 435–440
Stops, door, 590–591
Storage, residential, apartments, 1041
  bathroom, 997
  bedroom, 1009–1013
  for children, 1013
  closet fixtures, 1019–1020
  clothing, 1009–1014
  coats, 1014
  dining room, 960
  kitchen, 969–972
  laundry, 991–994
  miscellaneous, 1015–1018
  planning considerations, 1007–1008
Storage warehouse loads, 133
Store front details, 1095
Stores, retail, 1090–1095
  air conditioning of, 783–784
  fixtures, 1091–1094
  in hotels, 1056–1057
  lighting, 897–903
  merchandising categories, 1090
  (See also Shopping centers)
Storm door hardware, 605
Storm drains, 827–830
Street types, subdivision, 1225–1230
Stressed-skin panels, plywood, 151–153
Stresses, allowable (see Allowable stresses)
Structural clay facing tile partitions, 245–248
Structural clay tile partitions, 244–246
Structural design, 134–227
  beam formulae, 134–135
  concrete, 185–208
    allowable stresses, 185
    beams, 187–188
    columns, 189
    construction details, 190
    design criteria, 186
    dome slabs, 192–194
    joists, 191–194
    lift slabs, 194–197
    materials, 185
    prestressed, 200–208
    slabs, 191–197
    tilt-up construction, 197–199
  curtain walls, 366–367
  floor framing systems, 209–213
  masonry, 214–227
    allowable stresses, 215
    arches, 217–219
    ASA code requirements, 214–216, 219–220
    bond, 216
    lintels, 223–227
    materials, 214
    mortar mixes, 214
    reinforced grouted masonry, 219–222
    retaining walls, 222
  steel, 168–184
    allowable stresses, 169
    beams, 168–171
    columns, 177–178
    connection details, 179
    joists, 172–176
    Lally columns, 180–181
    plastic design, 182–183
    types of steel, 168–169
    welding, 183–184
  wood, 136–153
    allowable stresses, 136–137
    beams and joists, 144–145
    bolted connections, 148
    columns, 146
    decking, 140
    glued laminated wood, 139
    joists, 140–143
    plywood box beams, 149–150
    properties of sections, 138–139
    rafters and roof joists, 142–143
    stressed-skin panels, 151–153
    trusses, 147
Structural forms, concrete, thin shell, 111–126
    anticlastic or saddle-shaped, 123–125
    barrel shells, 111–113

Structural forms, concrete, thin shell, butterfly shells, 114
  conoids, 124–125
  corrugated shells, 117, 123
  curved in one direction, 111–117
  curved in two directions, 118–125
  domes, 119–122
  double cantilever, 114
  hyperbolic paraboloids, 123–124
  inverted shells, 117
  north light shells, 114
  polygonal domes, 122
  prismatic shells, 126
  spherical domes, 119–121
  synclastic or dome-shaped, 118–122
  tilted cylindrical and conical shells, 115
  steel, 96–110
    domes, 103–106
    rigid frames, 96–99
    space frames, 101–102
    space structures, 100
    suspension structures, 107–110
  wood, 87–95
    arches, 92–93
    glued laminated wood, 88–93
    lamella roof construction, 94
    long span construction, 87
    plywood box beams, 95
    rigid frames, 91
Structural glass veneer, 416–417
Structure-borne sound, 632–634, 646–648
Stucco, 473
Stud partitions, 464, 470–471, 480–482
Studios in schools, 1146–1148
Subdivision layout (see Site planning, subdivision layout)
Subdivision regulations, 1228–1229
Summer heat gain, 688, 743–749
Sump, 283–284
Sun, altitude of, 79–84
Sun shields, 251–252, 750–755, 860–861
Sunlight, 856–861
Supply, air, 683–690
  water, 812–824
Surface areas and volumes, 21
Surface treatment, brick, 242–243
  concrete masonry, 264–265
Surfaces and skew curves, 39–41
Surgical suite, hospital, 1162–1165
Suspended ceilings, 473–475
Suspension structures, 107–110
Swimming pools, in motels, 1074
  public, 1276–1283
  residential, 1284–1286
Symbols, graphic (see Graphic symbols)
Synclastic or dome-shaped shells, 118–122

Table tennis, 1263
Tangents, 65–67
Tanks, septic and siphon, 848
  water, 813–817
Tee-sections, precast prestressed concrete, 202–208
Telephones, 929
Teletherapy suite, hospital, 1180–1185
Temperature limits for plastics, 418, 420
Temperatures (see Design temperatures)
Tennis, paddle, 1265
  squash, 1270–1271
  table, 1264
Tennis courts, 1268–1269
Tensile strength, of concrete, 185
  of plaster, 467
  of plastics, 419
  of steel, 169
  of wood, 136–137
Terminals, bus, 1207–1210
  railroad, 1211–1212
  truck, 1203–1206
Termite shields, 291–294
Terra cotta, 243
Terraces, 1251–1252
Terrazzo, 538–541
Theaters, air conditioning of, 786–787
  motion picture (see Motion picture theaters)
  toilets in, 840–843
Therapy, occupational, 1193–1196
  physical, 1188–1192
Thermal conductivity (see Conductivity, thermal)
Thermal expansion (see Expansion, coefficients of)
Thermal insulation (see Insulation, thermal)
Thermoplastics, 418, 420–421
Thermosetting plastics, 418, 421
Thin shell concrete, structural forms, 111–126
Thiokol sealant, 378–381, 413–415
Threaded nails, 160–163
Through-metal conductivity, 372–373
Tile board, 488–489
Tile drains, 283–284

Tile partitions, structural clay, 244–248
Tilt-up construction, concrete, 197–199
Tilted cylindrical and conical shells, 115
Timber construction, 166–167
Time-temperature curve, ASTM, 444
Toilets, in auditoriums, 841–843
  in dormitories, 841–843
  in dwellings, 995–1005
  in factories, 841–845
  in hospitals, 1158–1160
  in hotels, 840–843, 1048
  in motion picture theaters, 840–843, 1104
  in office buildings, 841–843
  in parks, 840–843
  in public swimming pools, 840–843, 1279–1280
  in railroad stations, 840–843
  in schools, 841–843
  in theaters, 841–843
Toplighting, 858–864
Topography in subdivision layout, 1228
Tractor-trailers, truck, 1203–1206
Trailers, truck, 1203–1206
Transmission, heat, coefficient of, 649–663, 740
Transmission loss, sound, 613, 626–635
Transmittance values, of glass, 410
  of glass and plastic, 860–863
Treads and risers, stair, 562–563
Trees, 1256
Trigonometric functions, 22–23
Trigonometry, spherical, 64
Trochoid, 36
Troffers, recessed, 882–884
Truck terminals, 1203–1206
Trussed rafters, 162, 164–165
Trusses, wood, 147
Turning radii, automobiles, 1238
  buses, 1209
  trucks, 1203–1206

U values, 649–663, 740
Underfloor drains, 281–284
Underground drainage, 1250
Underlayments, floor, 547, 550
Unit heaters, 801–806
Unit ventilators, 758
Useful curves and curved surfaces, 26–64
  catenary, 32–34
  cones, 44–46
  cycloid, 35
  cylinders, 42
  domes, 50, 53–55
  ellipse, 29–30
  ellipsoid, 59–60
  geodesic domes, 50, 53–55
  geometrical mean (golden section), 37
  hyperbola, 31
  hyperbolic paraboloid, 56–58
  hyperboloid, 61–63
  parabola, 27–28
  polygon patterns, 43
  polyhedra, 50–52
  prisms, 42
  pyramids, 46
  sine curve, 37
  skew curve, 39–41
  sphere, 47–50
  spherical trigonometry, 64
  spirals, 38
  surfaces and skew curves, 39–41
  trochoid, 36

Vacuum, distribution system for, 821–824
Valance lighting, 907–910
Valley flashing, 303, 308
Vapor barrier, ceilings and roofs, 677–681
  crawl spaces, 668
  slabs on grade, 665
Vapor seals, in curtain walls, 374–375
  in foundation waterproofing, 288–289
Varnish, 556–557
Veneer, stone, 435–440
  structural glass, 416–417
  wood, wall covering, 552
Vent flashing, 304
Ventilation, in schools, 1151
  (See also Heating, ventilating, and air conditioning)
Ventilators, unit, 758
Venting, of attics and roofs, 672–673, 679–681
  of crawl spaces, 672–673, 680
  of curtain wall panels, 375, 384
  of gas appliances, 733–738
  of plumbing systems, 826–830
Vermiculite aggregate, 444–464, 466–469
Vibration control, mechanical equipment, 633–634, 770

Vinyl flooring, 548–551
Vinyl gaskets, 378–381, 415
Vinyl wall coating, 553
Vinyl wall covering, 552
Visual field, 868
Vitreous glazed wall coatings, 553
Volleyball courts, 1265
Volumes of solids, 21
Vomitories, stadium, 1289–1290

Waffle slabs, concrete, 192–194, 213
Walk-up apartments, 1032–1033, 1037
Walks, 1251–1252
Wall coatings, 553
Wall coverings, 552
Wallboards, 476–501
  gypsum board, 476–482
  hardboard, 488–490
  insulation board, 483–487
  particle board, 491
  plastic laminates, 492
  plywood, 493–501
Walls, cooling loads, 747, 750–752
  curtain, 365–387
  flashing of, 290, 295–302
  garden, 1254
  insulation of, 656–658
  plaster for, 470–472
  retaining, 222, 1255
Warehouse loads, 133
Warm air heating, 682–687
Water heaters, 818–820
Water supply and distribution systems, 812–820
Water table, 281–284
Waterproofing, 281–290
  foundation drains, 281–284
  integral and membrane, 286
  of paved roofs, 289
  permeability of concrete, 285
  plastic and iron coatings, 287–288
  vapor seals, 288–289
  of walls and parapets, 289–290
Weep holes, in curtain wall panels, 370–371
  in masonry walls, 235–238, 290
Weights, of building materials and construction, 128–129
  of miscellaneous materials, 127
Welding, 183–184
Wheelchairs, design for use of, 1198–1201
Wind loads, 130–133
  on curtain walls, 367
Wind pressures, 130–133, 367
Windows, 320–353
  aluminum, 346–353
  general, 320–323
  heat transmission, 740
  infiltration, 739
  steel, 336–345
  types and uses, 321–323
  wood, 324–335
Wiring, 915–928
  fire alarm systems, 937–938
  hospitals, 919–922
  loads, large buildings, 915–918
  residential, 923–928
  symbols, 10
Wood, structural design (see Structural design, wood)
  structural forms (see Structural forms, wood)
Wood construction, 154–167
  balloon-frame construction, 155
  heavy timber construction, 166–167
  light wood frame construction, 154–159
  nailing, 156, 158–159
  plank-and-beam construction, 166
  platform-frame construction, 154
  threaded nails, 160–163
  trussed rafters, 162, 164–165
Wood decking, allowable loads for, 140
Wood as finish material, 502–528
  cabinet work, 520–528
    finishes for, 554–561
  flooring, 543–547
  grades and dimensions, 502–503
  hardwoods, 505–519
  softwoods, 504
  veneer wall covering, 552
  windows, 324–335
Wood floor framing systems, 154–155, 166–167, 209
Wood windows, 324–335
Workshops, home, 1021–1023

X-ray suite, hospital, 1173–1180

Zoning of plumbing in multistory buildings, 815–817

Emilia S. Todd

Amelia S. Todd

Emilia S. Todd